ATLA BIBLIOGRAPHY SERIES
Edited by Dr. Kenneth E. Rowe

International Mission Bibliography

1960–2000

Edited by
Norman E. Thomas

ATLA Bibliographies, No. 48

The Scarecrow Press, Inc.
Lanham, Maryland, and Oxford
2003

SCARECROW PRESS, INC.

Published in the United States of America
by Scarecrow Press, Inc.
A wholly owned subsidiary of
The Rowman & Littlefield Publishing Group, Inc.
4501 Forbes Boulevard, Suite 200, Lanham, MD 20706
www.scarecrowpress.com

PO Box 317
Oxford
OX2 9RU, UK

British Library Cataloguing-in-Publication Information Available

Library of Congress Cataloging-in-Publication Data
International mission bibliography, 1960–2000 / edited by Norman E.
    Thomas.
        p. cm. — (ATLA bibliography series ; no. 48)
    Includes bibliographical references and index.
    ISBN 0-8108-4785-X (alk. paper)
        1. Missions–Bibliography. I. Thomas, Norman E. II. Series.
Z7817.I58 2003 [BV2061]
016.266–dc21   2003045638

♾™ The paper used in this publication meets the minimum
requirements of
American National Standard for Information Sciences—Permanence of
Paper for Printed Library Materials, ANSI/NISO Z39.48-1992.
Manufactured in the United States of America.

Contents

Acronyms and Abbreviations

AACC	All Africa Conference of Churches		BR	Burma
AAPSC	African Association for Pastoral Studies and Counseling		BS	Botswana
			CAFOD	Catholic Fund for Overseas Development
ABCFM	American Board of Commissioners for Foreign Missions		CAU	California, USA
			CAV	Centro Antonio Valdivieso
ABS	American Bible Society		CAW	Committee for Asian Women
ACMC	Advancing Churches in Mission Commitment		CBCI	Catholic Bishops' Conference of India
AEAM	Association of Evangelicals of Africa and Madagascar		CBCP	Catholic Bishops' Conference of the Philippines
			CBE	Commander of the Order of the British Empire
AFJN	Africa Faith and Justice Network		CBMS	Conference of British Missionary Societies
AG	Argentina		CCA	Christian Conference of Asia
AICA	African Independent Churches Association		CCBI	Council of Churches for Britain and Ireland
AICs	African Initiated/Indigenous/Independent Churches		CCIA	Commission of the Churches on International Affairs (WCC)
AIDS	acquired immune deficiency syndrome		CCLA	Committee on Cooperation in Latin America
AKU	Alaska, USA		CCPD	Commission on the Churches' Participation in Development (WCC)
ALU	Alabama, USA			
AME	African Methodist Episcopal Church		CD	compact disc
AMECEA	Association of Member Episcopal Conferences in Eastern Africa		*CDCWM*	*Concise Dictionary of the Christian World Mission*
			CE	Sri Lanka
AO	Angola		C.E.	Common Era
ARU	Arkansas, USA		CEBes	communidades de base [BECs]
ASAO	Association for Social Anthropology in Oceania		CEC	Conference of European Churches
AT	Australia		CEHILA	Commission for Latin American Church History
ATESEA	Association for Theological Education in South East Asia		CELA	Conferencia Evangélica Latinamericana
			CELAM	Consejo Episcopal Latinoamericano
ATLA	American Theological Library Association		CELEP	Centro Evangelico Latin Americano de Estudios Pastorales
AU	Austria			
AWCCT	Asian Women's Resource Centre for Culture and Theology		CEP	Centre d'Étude Pastorale
			CETA	Conférence des Églises de Toute d'Afrique (AACC)
AZU	Arizona, USA			
BBC	British Broadcasting Corporation		CF	Congo (Brazzaville)
B.C.	before Christ		CG	Congo (Kinshasa)
BCC	British Council of Churches		CH	China (Republic of)
BCC	British Columbia, Canada		CHIEA	Catholic Higher-Institute of Eastern Africa
BCCs/BECs	Basic Christian/Ecclesial Communities		CICARWS	Commission on Inter-Church Aid, Refugee, and World Service (WCC)
B.C.E.	before Common Era			
BCGA	British Church Growth Association		CICOP	Catholic Interamerican Cooperation Program
BE	Belgium		CIDOC	Inter-Cultural Center for Documentation
BGC	Billy Graham Center		CCIA	Commission of the Churches on International Affairs (WCC)
BL	Brazil			
BO	Bolivia		CIIR	Catholic Institute for International Relations

CIM	China Inland Mission		FI	Finland
CIMS	Consociatio Internationalis Musicae Sacrae		FJ	Fiji
CISR	Christian Institute for the Study of Religion and Society [India — also CISRS]		FLU	Florida, USA
			FR	France
CK	Colombia		FTESA	Foundation for Theological Education in Southeast Asia
CL	Chile			
CLADE	Congreso Latinamericano de Evangelización		GAU	Georgia, USA
CLAI	Concilio Latinamericano de Iglesias		GH	Ghana
CLAIM	Christian Literature Association in Malawi		GR	Greece
CLAR	Confederación Latino Americana de Religiosos		GT	Guatemala
CLC	Christian Literature Crusade		GW	Germany
CLS	Christian Literature Society [India]		GZB	Reformed Mission League, Netherlands Reformed Church
CM	Cameroon			
CMA	Christian and Missionary Alliance		HIU	Hawaii, USA
CMS	Church Missionary Society		HIV	human immunodeficiency virus
CNN	Cable News Network		HKC	Hong Kong, China
COEMAR	Commission on Ecumenical Mission and Relations (UPUSA)		HO	Honduras
			HU	Hungary
COU	Colorado, USA		IAU	Iowa, USA
CR	Costa Rica		ICA	Inter-Church Aid
CROMIA	Churches' Research on Marriage in Africa		ICC	Irish Council of Churches
CSS	Centre for Social Studies [India]		IDC	Inter Documentation Company
CTU	Connecticut, USA		IDOC	International Documentation on the Contemporary Church
CU	Cuba			
CUPSA	Centro de Communicacion Cultural		IDU	Idaho, USA
CWME	Commission on World Mission and Evangelism (WCC)		IE	Ireland
			IFES	International Fellowship of Evangelical Students
CWS	Church World Service (NCCUSA)		II	India
CY	Cyprus		IIMO	Interuniversitair Instituut voor Missiologie en Oecumenica
DCU	District of Columbia, USA			
DD	Doctor of Divinity		ILU	Illinois, USA
DDR	Deutsche Demokatische Republik/German Democratic Republic		IMBISA	Interterritorial Meeting of Bishops in Southern Africa
			IMC	International Missionary Council
DEI	Departamento Ecuménico de Investigaciones		INDEF	Instituto de Evangelizacion a Fundo
DEU	Delaware, USA		INU	Indiana, USA
DK	Denmark		IO	Indonesia
DMS	Danske Missionsselskab/Danish Missionary Society		*IRM*	*International Review of Missions/Mission*
			IS	Israel
DNA	deoxyribonucleic acid		ISBN	International Standard Book Number
DOM	*Dictionary of Mission*		ISEDET	Instituto Superior Evangelico de Estudios Teologicos [Argentina]
EACC	East Asia Christian Conference			
EATWOT	Ecumenical Association of Third World Theologians		ISPCK	India Society for the Promotion of Christian Knowledge
EC	Ecuador		IT	Italy
ECRJ	Evangelical Christians for Racial Justice [UK]		IV	Côte d'Ivoire
EDWM	*Evangelical Dictionary of World Missions*		IVCF	Inter-Varsity Christian Fellowship
EECMY	Ethiopian Evangelical Church Mekane Yesus		JA	Japan
EFS	Evangeliska Fosterlandsstiftelsen/Swedish Evangelical Mission		JBCE	Joint Board of Christian Education [Australia]
			JM	Jamaica
ELCA	Evangelical Lutheran Church in America		JRS	Jesuit Refugee Service
EMS	Evangelical Missionary Society		KDC	Katholiek Documentatie Centrum
EMW	Evangelische Missionswerk		KE	Kenya
ENK	England, UK		KEEP	Kiyosato Education Experiment Project [Japan]
ET	Ethiopia		KGB	Komitét gosudárstvennoi bezopásnosti/ Committee for State Security [USSR]
FECIC	Fundacion para la Educacion, la Ciencia y la Cultura			
FERES	Féderation Internationale des Instituts de Recherches Socio-Religieuses		KO	Korea (South)

KSU	Kansas, USA	*NZM*	*Neue Zeitschrift für Missionswissenschaft*
KYU	Kentucky, USA	OAS	Organization of American States
LAB	Latin American Bureau [UK]	OBSUR	Observatorio del Sur
LAEC	Latin American Evangelization Campaign	OCSHA	Obra de Cooperacón Apostólica Seglar Hispano-americana
LAU	Louisiana, USA		
LCWE	Lausanne Committee for World Evangelization	OFM	Order of Friars Minor (Franciscans)
LE	Lebanon	OHU	Ohio, USA
LO	Lesotho	OKU	Oklahoma, USA
LTC	Lutheran Theological College [SA]	OM	Operation Mobilization
LWF	Lutheran World Federation	OMF	Overseas Missionary Fellowship (formerly China Inland Mission)
LX	Luxembourg		
MARC	Missions Advanced Research and Communication Center	OMSC	Overseas Ministries Study Center [USA]
		ONC	Ontario, Canada
MAU	Massachusetts, USA	OP	Order of Preachers (Dominicans)
MDU	Maryland, USA	ORISI	Pontifical Oriental Institute of Religious Studies
MEU	Maine, USA	ORU	Oregon, USA
MG	Madagascar	PAU	Pennsylvania, USA
MIU	Michigan, USA	PCR	Programme to Combat Racism, WCC
MNU	Minnesota, USA	PCUSA	Presbyterian Church in the USA
MOU	Missouri, USA	PE	Peru
MRL	Missionary Research Library, New York	PEEI	Philippine Evangelical Enterprises, Inc.
MSC	Missionaries of the Sacred Heart	PH	Philippines
MSTM	Movimento de Sacerdotes para el Tercer Mundo	Ph.D.	Doctor of Philosophy
MSU	Mississippi, USA	PIME	Pontifical Institute for Foreign Missions
MTU	Montana, USA	PK	Pakistan
MW	Malawi	PL	Poland
MX	Mexico	PMV	Pro Mundi Vita
MY	Malaysia	PN	Panama
MZ	Mozambique	PO	Portugal
NBCLC	National Biblical Catechetical and Liturgical Center [India]	PP	Papua New Guinea
		PR	Puerto Rico
NCCB	National Conference of Catholic Bishops	*PSTM*	*Philosophy, Science and Theology of Mission in the 19th and 20th Centuries, Parts I and II*
NCCI	National Christian Council of India		
NCCJ	National Conference of Christians and Jews	RCC	Roman Catholic Church
NCCK	National Christian Council of Kenya	RH	Zimbabwe
NCCP	National Council of Churches in the Philippines	RIU	Rhode Island, USA
NCCUSA	National Council of Churches of Christ in the USA	RM	Romania
		RU	Russia
NCSU	Nederlandsche Christen Studenten Vereeniging	SA	South Africa
NCU	North Carolina, USA	SACC	South African Council of Churches
NDU	North Dakota, USA	SAIRR	South Africa Institute of Race Relations
NE	Netherlands	SBC	Southern Baptist Convention
NEU	Nebraska, USA	SCCs	Small Christian Communities (BCCs/BECs)
NGO	non-governmental organization	SCU	South Carolina, USA
NHU	New Hampshire, USA	SCUPE	Seminary Consortium for Urban Pastoral Education (Chicago, USA)
NIE	Nationwide Initiative in Evangelism [UK]		
NIK	Northern Ireland, UK	SDA	Seventh-day Adventist
NIR	National Initiative for Reconciliation [SA]	SDU	South Dakota, USA
NJU	New Jersey, USA	SEDOS	Servizio di Documentazione e Studi
NMU	New Mexico, USA	SFT	Standing for the Truth
NO	Norway	SIL	Summer Institute of Linguistics
NPI	Nairobi Peace Initiative	SI	Singapore
NQ	Nicaragua	SJ	Sudan
NR	Nigeria	SL	Sierra Leone
NVU	Nevada, USA	SMB	Swiss Bethlehem Fathers (Missionary Society of Bethlehem in Switzerland)
NYU	New York, USA		
NZ	New Zealand		

SODEPAX	Committee on Society, Development and Peace (WCC/Vatican)	UK	United Kingdom
SP	Spain	UMC	United Methodist Church
SPCK	Society for Promoting Christian Knowledge	UMCA	Universities' Mission to Central Africa
SPROCAS	Study Project on Christianity in Apartheid Society	UMI	University Microfilms
SQ	Swaziland	UNESCO	United Nations Educational, Scientific, and Cultural Organization
SSSR	Society for the Scientific Study of Religion	UNISA	University of South Africa
STK	Scotland, UK	UPCUSA	United Presbyterian Church in the USA
SUNY	State University of New York	URM	Urban/Rural Mission (WCC)
SVD	Verbites, Missionaries of Steyl (Society of the Divine Word)	US	United States of America
		USCC	United States Catholic Conference
SVM	Student Volunteer Movement for Foreign Missions	USCL	United Society for Christian Literature
		UTU	Utah, USA
SW	Sweden	UY	Uruguay
SX	Namibia	VAU	Virginia, USA
SY	Syria	VC	Vatican City
SZ	Switzerland	VE	Venezuela
TEAM	The Evangelical Alliance Mission	VEM	Vereinigte Evangelische Mission
TEF	Theological Education Fund	VTU	Vermont, USA
TH	Thailand	WACC	World Association for Christian Communications
Th.D.	Doctor of Theology	WARC	World Alliance of Reformed Churches
TMP	The Pentecostal Mission	WAU	Washington, USA
TNU	Tennessee, USA	WCC	World Council of Churches
TO	Tonga	WCCE	World Council of Christian Education and Sunday School Association
TR	Trinidad and Tobago		
TRACI	Theological Research and Communication Institute [India]	*WCE*	*World Christian Encyclopedia* (2nd ed., 2001)
		WEF	World Evangelical Fellowship
TU	Turkey	WIU	Wisconsin, USA
TXU	Texas, USA	WLK	Wales, UK
TZ	Tanzania	WSCF	World Student Christian Federation
UA	Egypt	WVU	West Virginia, USA
UBLA	Baptist Union of Latin America	WYU	Wyoming, USA
UBS	United Bible Societies	YWAM	Youth with a Mission
UCCan	United Church of Canada	ZA	Zambia
UFM	Unevangelized Fields Mission (UFM International)	ZAG	Zuid-Afrikaanische Genootschap
UG	Uganda	ZI	Zimbabwe

Series Editor's Foreword

The American Theological Library Association has been publishing this bibliography series with Scarecrow Press since 1974. Guidelines for projects and selections for publication are made by the ATLA Publications Section in consultation with the editor.

Our goal is to stimulate and encourage the preparation and publication of reliable bibliographies and guides to the literature of religious studies in all of its scope and variety. Compilers are free to define their field, to make their own selections, and to work out internal organization according to the unique demands of the subject.

We are pleased to publish the *International Mission Bibliography* edited by Norman E. Thomas and sponsored by the American Society of Missiology.

The editor studied at Yale University (A.B., M.Div.) and Boston University (Ph.D.). He has authored thirteen books, including *Classic Texts in Mission and World Christianity* (Orbis, 1995), and has edited and co-edited works on development, urban mission, and church and politics in Africa.

As a bibliographer he has authored basic bibliographies on "Missions" and "Evangelism" for the ATLA. From 1985 to 1990 he served as book editor of *Missiology: An International Review* for which he developed its quarterly sections of "Books and Media Received" and "Essential and Important Books." An international leader in develop-

ment of mission bibliographies, he served as chairperson of the Documentation, Archives, and Bibliography Working Group of the International Association for Mission Studies from 1988 to 1992.

Dr. Thomas was born in New Hampshire, grew up in New Jersey, pastored in Portland, Oregon, and served for fifteen years with his wife, Winnie, as United Methodist missionaries in Zimbabwe and Zambia. He has taught at Boston and Yale universities, the Pacific School of Religion, and the Virginia Polytechnic Institute and State University. For twelve years he was the Vera B. Blinn Professor of World Christianity at United Theological Seminary in Dayton, Ohio, and for four years was Heisel Professor of Evangelization and Church Renewal. In 2000 he was named the Vera B. Blinn Professor Emeritus of World Christianity at United.

He is a member of the Academy for Evangelism in Theological Education, the American Society of Missiology, the Association of Professors of Missions, the International Association for Mission Studies, the North American Academy of Ecumenists, the Society of Christian Ethics, and the Society for the Scientific Study of Religion.

Kenneth Rowe
Series Editor

Drew University Library
Madison, NJ 07940 USA

Preface

How does a student of missiology learn about contemporary scholarship in the field? How does a scholar or librarian on a limited budget select books for purchase?

Publishers in their catalogues tout only their own books with descriptions provided only for new titles. Journals publish book reviews but only of selected titles after some delay. They may print lists of books received but without information on their contents or usefulness (with the exception of the "Essential and Important Books" feature of *Missiology* quarterly as part of this project). Bibliographies are the primary resource.

Development

In 1985 I was appointed book editor of *Missiology: An International Review* by the ASM Board of Publications. In addition to the regular "Book Reviews" feature of the journal, I proposed the addition of an annotated list of "Books Received" each quarter. It was agreed that the ASM would sponsor a project to produce an annotated bibliography of contemporary books on missiology. A database would be developed including the quarterly listings as well as other submissions. The initial goal was to produce an annotated bibliography of the most important books published in English from 1960 to 1990. During 1986, subeditors were recruited from among ASM members to cover the proposed twenty subject areas of the bibliography.

The next year the project expanded to become an international bibliography. In January 1987 the International Association for Mission Studies (IAMS) sponsored a workshop in Paris, France, on missiological bibliographies. Participants strongly recommended to the ASM that its project be increased in scope to include a selection of important missiological books in each major European language. This suggestion was accepted. The team of subeditors was enlarged to include language editors, thereby expanding to thirty-seven the international team of bibliographers assisting in the project.

In 1989, the ASM Board of Publications invited IAMS officially to co-sponsor the project. In that same year I became the chairperson of IAMS' Documentation, Archives and Bibliography (DAB) project. In subsequent IAMS workshops steps were taken to agree on a common international format for mission bibliography entries, and beginnings made on a common multi-lingual thesaurus.

Initially subeditors contributed selected annotated bibliographies of the best thirty books in their areas. These were published one each quarter in *Missiology* from 1986 to 1998. A supplemental list of thirty titles in each area is being published in *Missiology* beginning in 2000. Subeditors next submitted additional entries for inclusion in the *International Mission Bibliography*. Each has edited the entries in their subject areas.

Scope

How should the scope of an international bibliography on missiology be defined? Livinus Vriens, a Dutch missiologist, in his *Critical Bibliography of Missiology* (1960) provided the prototype for this project. He defined missiology as "the study of the spread of the Church and of all the problems connected with the realisation of her universality" (5). To this Andrew Walls (and others) would add a second focus— "the whole saving activity of God in the world" (1991:689). It is this second focus that caused the *International Review of Missions* to change its last word to *Mission* in 1969. The church is in mission, responding to the *missio dei*, in all places and all continents.

Content analysis of the major mission bibliographies confirms that these two foci have provided the parameters for the scope of missiology as a discipline. *Bibliotheca Missionum* and the *Dictionary Catalog of Missionary*

Research Library provided Catholic and Protestant sources for the earlier literature. Bibliographies in six serials provided criteria for inclusion of the contemporary literature: *Bibliografia Missionaria, Bibliografia Teologia Comentada del Area Iberoamericana, International Review of Missions/Mission, Missionalia, Neue Zeitschrift für Missionswissenschaft,* and the *Survey of Literature on the Christian Mission and Christianity in the Non-Western World.*

Jan A. B. Jongeneel, in his two-volume study of *Philosophy, Science and Theology of Mission in the 19th and 20th Centuries* (1995, 1997) has provided us with "a comprehensive view of the philosophical, empirical and theological study of mission(s)." Unfortunately his work was not available in the formative stage of this project. References to his material will be made in the introduction to each chapter. While the organization may differ, there is general agreement upon the scope of the field of missiology.

First, mission theory includes the study of the "principles of the mission-apostolate and of its special character in comparison with other Church activities" (Vriens 1960:37). Study of mission theology and history requires familiarity with key literature in cognate disciplines (philosophy, theology, biblical studies, church history, etc.).

Second, mission in practice includes not only cross-cultural missions, but also the growth and renewal of the churches in six continents, and their mission in service and justice ministries in their communities, nations, and continents. It also includes the relation of Christianity to persons of other faiths. Study of mission amidst varied cultures requires awareness of related writings in the social sciences (anthropology, sociology, psychology, political science, economics, communication theory, etc.) and in world religions.

The cognate literature poses a major challenge to mission bibliographers. From its beginning in 1912 the bibliographies in the *International Review of Mission(s)*, included literature on ethnography, economics, politics, and world religions. Missionaries were thus encouraged to read works that contained no specific reference to the church in mission.

A second *gray area* for inclusion is multi-author works containing just one or a few chapters of missiological significance. While acknowledging that God's salvific activity impacts all disciplines of human inquiry, the scope of this bibliography is limited to works intentionally relating the Gospel and/or the church to culture.

Organization

The next step, in the absence of an internationally agreed thesaurus, was to analyze current indexing related to missiology. The general editor began by surveying the subject headings of the Library of Congress (USA) and of *Religion One Index* [of periodical literature]. Later, he examined those of the missiological institutes of IIMO (Leiden) and CEDIM (Paris). From these sources, as well as the major mission bibliographies, the initial subject headings were developed.

An inductive process followed in which content analysis of new works led to new or reorganized categories. This is a continuing process aided by the international team of subeditors. The attempt by IAMS-DAB in 1989-1991 to develop a multi-lingual thesaurus, although abortive, contributed important insights.

In much contemporary literature the term *mission* has replaced *missions*. However, many existing bibliographies use the older term. In this bibliography both terms are used.

Evangelism, church renewal, and *ecumenics* are closely related to missiology. For the purpose of this bibliography *evangelism* and *evangelization* shall be considered synonyms, and as a subsection of missiology concerned with witness, church growth, and church planting. *Church renewal* is related to missiology whenever it involves the outreach of the congregation in witness and service beyond its own membership. Some church renewal literature, therefore, is relevant to the bibliography. *Ecumenics*, as the study of relations between persons of different religious confessions, is relevant wherever it is affected by the church's mission efforts.

Affirmation of the *missio dei* broadens the scope both of mission theology and of practice. Much new theological reflection in Africa, Asia, Latin America, and Oceania is missional in intent and thus included in this bibliography. Similarly, Christian action in service and justice ministries in the world beyond the institutional church is part of the church's mission. Cross-cultural missions within and across national borders falls within the scope of this bibliography.

An eighteen-year project has come to fruition with the publication of this bibliography. It will complete a quartet of major reference works on missiology published in English at the turn of the century. The others are the *Biographical Dictionary of Christian Missions* (1998), the *Evangelical Dictionary of World Missions* (2000), and the *World Christian Encyclopedia,* 2nd edition (2001). Originally planned to cover the 1960-1990 period, this bibliography has been extended to include books published through the year 2000.

Acknowledgments

Since 1985 this project has been a team effort. The American Society of Missiology has been its official sponsor. I am grateful for the support of its Publication Committee, officers, and Publisher Ken Gill. The International Association for Mission Studies provided encouragement enabling me to develop an international team of thirty-seven subeditors covering both subject areas and languages. I am indebted to them for providing many entries not available in Dayton, Ohio. All worked without compensation other than the hope now realized that the data would have wide availability. They are the contributors to this volume.

Financial support has been provided by the American Society of Missiology, United Theological Seminary, the Trinity Grants Program, and by private donors including Dorothy Williams and Mildred Thomas.

I am indebted to Darrel Whiteman, Editor of *Missiology: An International Review*, and to Anne Zahniser, his Editorial Assistant. They helped me to develop confidence and competence as a bibliographer, as quarterly I submitted an annotated listing of "Books Received" for publication. James Nelson, Paul Schrodt, Vanessa Ward, and the late Julie Overton assisted with annotations of non-English entries. Lidice Lima, Sidney Rooy, and Larry Welborn edited the foreign language entries. Lisa Elison and the late Harriet Miller both wrote annotations and edited entries in Spanish and Italian, respectively.

For eighteen years I have labored on this project at United Theological Seminary. Its library has been my second home, and its staff my essential support network on this large project. They have included Elmer O'Brien, Albert Hurd, and Sarah Blair as Directors, and Richard Berg, Paul Schrodt, and Barry Hamilton as Assistant Directors. Books for inclusion have been acquired by Nicole Eby, Kriza Jennings, Patricia Hosey, Suzanne Smailes, Lesia Harvey, and Brillie Scott. Janet McDermott has been a constant help in classification. I am indebted to my work-study students who built the database to its present 15,850 annotated entries: Nancy Ratz, Sharon Carr, John Hughes, Randa D'Aoust, and Tina Anderson. Technical assistants included Farai and Rutendo Rukunda and Kinsey Oleman.

Without technical support this project could not have been completed. Jim Ernst developed the software used for the database. Kenneth Bedell wrote specialized software and provided constant technical support. Cris Decker did copy-editing, and Larry Ramey prepared camera-ready pages in required formats and layout. Finally, I want to thank my wife Winnie for her constant encouragement and partnership with me to perfect the final copy.

MISSIONS: GENERAL WORKS

Stephen Peterson, Subeditor

Following Vriens (1960:9), this section includes all the books that, because of their contents, cannot be listed topically. First are to be found general bibliographies on mission studies.

The next section, entitled "Serials/Periodicals," contains serials or journals that touch on missiology as a whole. Others, more specific in content, have been placed in corresponding sections in the subsequent chapters.

Each chapter also contains a subsection on reference works (handbooks, dictionaries, and atlases). General sources, however, are found here, including many classified by Jongeneel (1995:258-272) under the geography and statistics of Christian mission.

The next subsection on "Documentation and Archives" will be repeated in subsequent chapters. Sources that fall naturally under topics will be placed there, with "see also" cross-references to the documentation and archives section of the chapter. Sourcebooks useful in the study of missiology have been placed in this subsection.

The "Conferences and Congresses" subsection of this chapter includes reports of many general mission conferences. However, those of world ecumenical organizations (WCC, LCWE, etc.) will be found in the "Missions: Ecumenical Aspects" chapter.

General works in mission studies provide the largest number of entries in this chapter. First appear works of a more scholarly nature, including textbooks on missions. They are followed by a subsection containing general works of a more popular nature.

The chapter closes with titles on the study and teaching of missiology. These relate more to the academic study of missions. Study materials for the general education of children, youth, and adults, concerning the church's mission, are to be found in the chapter on "Missions: Methods."

Norman E. Thomas

Bibliographies

See also GW96, CR7, and AF6.

GW1 American Theological Library Association
Missions and Evangelism: A Bibliography Selected from the ATLA Religion Database, January 1985. Edited by Albert E. Hurd and Paul D. Petersen. Chicago, ILU: ATLA, 1985. 788 pp. No ISBN.

Detailed subject, author and editor, and book review indexes compiled from 1949 to 1984 data in *Religion Index I* (periodicals) and *Religion Index II* (multi-author works).

GW2 *Bibliografia Missiólogica*
São Paulo, BL: Associação de Professores de Missões no Brasil, 1993. 28 pp. Paper. No ISBN.

An extensive bibliography of books and articles in Portuguese on Christian mission, with special reference to Brazil.

GW3 Geyer, Douglas W.
International Christian Literature Documentation Project (ICLDP): A Subject, Author, and Corporate Name Index to Non-Western Christian Literature. Evanston, ILU: ATLA, 1993. 2 vols. 0960496076.

An extensive index of printed materials (monographs, pamphlets, and multi-author works) representing the Christian life and thought of peoples of the Two-Thirds World, based on holdings in nine large North American collections [vol. 1: 819 pp.; vol. 2: 896 pp.].

GW4 Hartley, R. W., comp.
Bibliography on the History and Theology of Missions from the Collection in Leigh College Library, Enfield, NSW, Australia. Enfield, AT: Leigh College Library, 1969. 29 pp. Paper. No ISBN.

A bibliography of holdings in one of Australia's major universities.

GW5 Jeppesen, Mogens
Litteratur om dansk mission, 1945-1981. (Special issue of *Mission*). Copenhagen, DK: Dansk Missionsråd, 1981. 101 pp. Paper. No ISBN.

This bibliography of Danish missionary literature was made on behalf of the Danish Missionary Council.

GW6 Kraus, Johann
Missionswissenschaftliche Themen in Festschriften aus den Jahren, 1960-1971. (Schriftenreihe der *NZM*, 25). Immensee, SZ: Neue Zeitschrift für Missionswissenschaft, 1974. v, 85 pp. Paper. No ISBN.

An analysis of missiological themes in eighty-six *festschrift* publications of the previous twelve years, with bibliographical references; originally published in *NZM*, 1973-1974.

GW7 *Missio Nordica: Vol. 1 (1989) - Vol. 6 (1994). Annual*
Uppsala, SW: Nordisk Institut för Missionsforskning och Ekumenisk Forskning, 1989-, 1989-1994. ISSN 11014784.

An annual bibliography of Nordic mission literature, arranged by country of repository, indexed by subject, and published by the Nordic Institute for Missionary and Ecumenical Research.

GW8 Missionary Research Library (New York)
Dictionary Catalog of the Missionary Research Library, New York. Boston, MAU: G K Hall, 1968. 17 vols. No ISBN.

A complete catalog with entries under author, title, and subject, for one of the world's largest collections on Christian missions and related topics, now located at Union Theological Seminary; with photocopies of 273,000 cards for approximately 100,000 individual items.

GW9 Moritzen, Niels Peter, and Friedrich Huber, comps.
Literaturschau zu Fragen der Weltmission, Nr. 19 (Für das Jahr 1992). Stuttgart, GW: Christliches Verlagshaus, 1993. 107 pp. Paper. No ISBN.

A bibliography of 1,287 articles, books, and dissertations on Christian mission, mostly in German, organized by continent and subject, and published as a supplement in *Zeitschrift für Mission* (2/1993).

GW10 Person, Laura, comp.
Cumulative List of Doctoral Dissertations and Masters' Theses in Foreign Missions and Related Subjects as Reported by the Missionary Research Library in the Occasional Bulletin, 1950 to 1960. New York, NYU: MRL, 1961. 46 pp. Paper. No ISBN.

A list of 482 titles indexed by subject and degree-granting institution.

GW11 Rommerskirchen, Johannes, ed.
Bibliotheca Missionum. Freiburg, GW: Herder, 1916-1970. 30 vols. No ISBN.

A comprehensive bibliography of Catholic missiological publications, begun in 1916 and now comprising 30 volumes, nine of which have been published since 1960; listing literature dealing with basic and general questions (1910-1960), mission in America (1910-1960), India/South Asia (1910-1968), South East Asia (1910-1970), Japan and Korea (1910-1970).

GW12 Santos Hernández, Angel
Bibliografía Misional. (Misionologia, 3). Santander, SP: Editorial Sal Terrae, 1965. 2 vols. Paper. No ISBN.

Annotated bibliography of international and ecumenical books and journal articles, published through 1964, on the history of missions throughout the world, and on biblical, theological, and methodological themes [vol. 1: *Parte Doctrinal* (944 pp.); vol. 2: *Parte Histórica* (1300 pp.)].

GW13 Vriens, Livinius, Anastasius Disch, and J. Wils
Critical Bibliography of Missiology. (Bibliographia ad usum seminariorum, E2). Nijmegen, NE: Verlag Bestel Centrale der V.S.K.B, 1960. 127 pp. Paper. No ISBN.

English translation from the Dutch of a brief annotated bibliography on Roman Catholic missions; containing 206 entries arranged by subject; with introductions to each type of literature and an author index.

Serials and Periodicals

See also GW5, EA11, and SO7.

GW14 Baumgartner, Jakob
Missionswissenschaft im Dienste der Weltkirche. (Schriftenreihe, 22). Schöneck/Beckenried, SZ: NZM, 1970. 55 pp. Paper. No ISBN.

A twenty-five-year assessment of the origins and development of the missiological review *NZM*, with an examination of the place of missiology in the formation of students of theology, particularly in the Foreign Mission Society of Bethlehem.

GW15 *Bibliographia Missionaria: Vol. 1 (1937). Annual*
(Annual). Vatican City, IT: Pontificia Università Urbaniana, 1937-. ISSN 03949869.

Initially published as part of *Guida della Missione Cattoliche,* and since 1937 as a separate title, this extensive annual bibliography of books and journal articles on all aspects of missiology is arranged by geographic region, with brief abstracts of more important entries plus subject and author indexes.

GW16 *Bulletin of the Scottish Institute of Missionary Studies.* New Series 1 (1982)-. Annual
Aberdeen, STK: Scottish Institute of Missionary Studies, 1982-. ISSN 00489778.

An annotated and critical survey, arranged both by subject and geographical region, of current books on world mission in most European languages, including both Protestant and Roman Catholic missions.

GW17 Byrnes, Paul A., comp.
Current Periodicals in the Missionary Research Library: A Subject List. New York, NYU: MRL, 1972. ii, 40 pp. Paper. No ISBN.

A subject listing of periodicals in the largest mission library of the time in North America.

GW18 Draper, Edythe, ed.
The Almanac of the Christian World: 1991-1994. Annual. Wheaton, ILU: Tyndale Paper. ISSN 10532670.

A yearly resource book on the history, contemporary status, and future of evangelical Christianity, with country profiles and special sections on mission history, agencies, and future prospects.

GW19 *Evangelical Missions Quarterly.* Vol. 1, no. 1 (Fall 1964) -. Quarterly
Wheaton, ILU: Evangelism and Missions Information Service, 1964-. ISSN 00143359.

A journal devoted to understanding evangelical Protestant missionary thought and practice.

GW20 *Frontier.* Vol. 1, no. 1 (Jan. 1958) - Vol. 18, no. 4 (Winter 1975/76) -. Quarterly
London, ENK: World Dominion Press, 1958-1976. No ISSN.

This "international review of Christian progress" for laity superceded *World Dominion* (1923-1957), the *Christian Newsletter* of the Christian Frontier Council, and the *Reunion Record* of the Friends of Reunion and contained short articles on theological issues, ecumenical and mission concerns, and country updates.

GW21 Girardin, Benoit

Periodiques missionnaires Protestants Romands, 1819-1981: répertoire bibliographique. (Communications from the *Basel Africa Bibliography*, 25). Basel, SZ: Basel Mission, 1982. 29 pp. Paper. No ISBN.

A comprehensive bibliography of twenty-four mission periodicals published in French-speaking Switzerland.

GW22 Hallencreutz, Carl F., and Sigbert Axelson, eds.

Annual Report of Uppsala Studies of Mission: Vol. 1 (1988). Annual. Uppsala, SW: University of Uppsala, Faculty of Theology, 1988-. ISSN 11014474.

An annual publication of papers and articles on mission by scholars of the University of Uppsala's Faculty of Theology.

GW23 *IAMS News Letter.* No. 1 (May 1973) - (1983). Irregular

Leiden, NE: International Association for Mission Studies, 1973-1983. No ISSN.

News of the work of the association and its triennial conferences, plus notes on periodicals in mission studies, and an annotated listing of books and articles by IAMS members.

GW24 *International Bulletin of Missionary Research:* Vol. 5, no.1 (Jan. 1979) -. Quarterly

New Haven, CTU: OMSC, 1979-. ISSN 02726122.

Scholarly articles, documentation, reviews, and book evaluations concerning the church's global mission; superseded *Occasional Bulletin of Missionary Research* and *Gospel in Context.*

GW25 *International Review of Missions.* Vol. 1 (1912) -. Quarterly

London, ENK: IMC, 1912-1961; Geneva, SZ: WCC-CWME, 1962-, 1962-1969. No ISSN.

The premier Protestant and ecumenical journal on global missions, with extensive bibliography on books and articles concerning world missions and related topics of interest to persons in cross-cultural mission; published from 1912 to 1961 by the IMC; continued by the WCC and from 1969 as the *International Review of Mission.*

GW26 *Jahrbuch Mission.* Vol. 1 (1969) -. Annual

Hamburg, GW: Missionshilfe Verlag, 1969-. Paper. 3921620562.

This annual sponsored by the Evangelischer Missionskonferenzen (German Missions Conference) contains short essays on a mission theme or region; supersedes *Evangelische Mission Jahrbuch* (ISSN 05314798).

GW27 Jeroense, P. J. G.

Tijdschrift voor Zendingswetenschap "Mededeelingen": Jaargang 64-85, 1920-1942. Utrecht, NE: Rijksuniversitreit te Utrecht, 1989. 55 pp. Paper. No ISBN.

An index in Dutch by author, subject, and volume for nos. 64-85 (1920-1942) of *Tijdschrift voor Zendingswetenschap*, a leading Dutch missiological journal of the period.

GW28 Jongeneel, J. A. B.

Protestantse zendingsperiodieken uit de negentiende en twintigste eeuw in Nederland, Nederlands-Indië Suriname en de Nederlandse Antillen: een bibliografische catalogue met inleiding. (IIMO Research Pamphlet, 30). Leiden, NE: IIMO, 1990. v, 140 pp. Paper. 9064952329.

An inventory of Dutch Protestant mission journals in the 19th and 20th centuries.

GW29 *Misjon og teologi: Årsskrift for Misjonshøgskolen.* Vol 1, no. 1 (1994) -. Annual

Stavanger, NO: Misjonshøgskolens forlag, 1994-. ISSN 08048193.

Edited by Ove Conrad Hanssen and Anne B. Samuelson, the journal of the School of Mission and Theology in Stavanger, Norway, contains short articles in Norwegian on missions plus a short bibliography of writings by scholars connected with the school.

GW30 *Missiology: An International Review.* Vol. 1, no.1 (Jan. 1973) -. Quarterly

Scottdale, PAU: American Society of Missiology, 1973-. ISSN 00918296.

Superseding *Practical Anthropology*, this official journal of the American Society of Missiology contains refereed articles on missiological issues, extensive book reviews, an annotated listing of books and media received, and evaluation of essential and important books in the field.

GW31 *Mission Studies: Journal of the International Association for Mission Studies.* No. 1 (1984) -. Semiannual

Hamburg, GW: International Association for Mission Studies, 1984-. ISSN 01689789.

This official journal of IAMS contains papers from its triennial conferences, general articles on missiological issues, communications, and book reviews.

GW32 *Missionalia.* Vol. 1, no. 1 (April 1973) -. Three issues yearly

Pretoria, SA: Southern African Missiological Society, 1973-. ISSN 02569507.

Articles mainly on missiological issues in Southern Africa, papers presented at the society's annual conference, book reviews, and abstracts of articles published in major missiological journals.

GW33 *Missionary Research Library Occasional Bulletin.* Vol. 1 (1950) - vol. 26 (1976). Variable

New York, NYU: MRL, 1950-1976. ISSN 0026606X.

Research notes and bibliography from the premier missionary research library in North America; superseded by the *Occasional Bulletin of Missionary Research.*

GW34 Missionary Research Library

Current Periodicals in the Missionary Research Library: Alphabetical List and Indexes. Compiled by John T. Ma. New York, NYU: MRL, 1961. 38 pp. No ISBN.

Second revised edition of a union list for the largest collection on missions in North America.

GW35 *Neue Zeitschrift für Missionswissenschaft.* Vol. 1 (1945) -. Quarterly

Immensee, SZ: Verein zur Foerderung der Missionswissenschaft, 1945-. ISSN 00283495.

Also titled *Nouvelle Revue de science missionaire*, this scholarly journal contains articles, book reviews, and occasional supplements in German, French, English, and Italian.

GW36 *Occasional Bulletin of Missionary Research.* Vol. 1, no. 1 (Jan. 1977) - vol. 4, no. 4 (Oct. 1980). Quarterly

Ventnor, NJU: OMSC, 1977-1980. ISSN 03642178.

Scholarly articles, documentation, bibliographies, and book reviews on the church's mission in, and to, six continents; superseded the *Missionary Research Library Occasional Bulletin*; continued as the *International Bulletin of Missionary Research.*

GW37 *Selly Oak Periodicals*
Birmingham, ENK: Selly Oak Colleges and Newman College, 1991. iv, 92 pp. Paper. No ISBN.

A union list of periodicals in area studies, education, theology, and studies of mission, peace, development, and society in the libraries of the Selly Oak Colleges, Birmingham, England.

GW38 *World Mission*. Vol. 1, no. 1 (Jan. 1950) - vol. 32, no. 4 (Winter 1981/82). Quarterly
New York, NYU: Society for the Propagation of the Faith, 1950-1982. No ISSN.

Short articles on mission concerns of Catholic missionary-sending societies in the United States.

GW39 *Zeitschrift für Missionswissenschaft und Religionswissenschaft*. Vol. 1 (1911) -. Quarterly
Münster, GW: Internationalen Instituts für missionswissenschaftliche, 1911-. ISSN 00443123.

Articles and book reviews, primarily in German, but also in English and French, on various issues in missiology (theology, history, anthropology, etc.) and on Christianity and other world faiths.

Reference Works

See also HI507, ME193, CR37, MI3, SP4, and AF38.

GW40 Anderson, Gerald H., ed.
Biographical Dictionary of Christian Missions. New York, NYU: Macmillan Reference USA/Simon & Schuster Macmillan, 1998. xxvi, 845 pp. 0028646045.

A comprehensive and authoritative record of leaders in the church's mission from Pentecost to the present; contains 2,400 original signed biographies by 350 authors from 45 countries, with extensive indexing and bibliographies.

GW41 Barrett, David B., George T. Kurian, and Todd M. Johnson
World Christian Encyclopedia: A Comparative Survey of Churches and Religions in the Modern World. New York, NYU: Oxford University Press, 2001. 2 vols. 0195103181 (vol. 1), 019510319X (vol. 2), 0195079639 (set).

Second edition of a massive, two-volume study describing empirical Christianity through summaries of survey data, produced by a vast decentralized investigation conducted by churches and religious workers across the world; originally published in 1982 [I, "The World by Countries," xii, 876 pp.; II, "The World by Segments: Religions, Peoples, Languages, Cities, Topics," vi, 823 pp.].

GW42 Brierley, Peter, and David Longley, eds.
UK Christian Handbook: 1980-. Biennial. London, ENK: Christian Research; London, ENK: HarperCollins, 1980-. Paper. 1853211338 (C), 0551032359 (H).

A directory of Christian organizations in the United Kingdom, published initially by MARC Europe and the Evangelical Alliance, and later by Paternoster (1998) and Marshall Pickering (1999).

GW43 Brierley, Peter, and Heather Wraight
Atlas of World Christianity: A Complete Visual Reference to Christianity Worldwide, Including Growth Trends into the New Millennium. Nashville, TNU: Nelson, 1998. 144 pp. 0785209913.

Extensive maps and graphs on the demographic, political, and economic characteristics of nations and on Christian distribution, growth, and ministries around the world.

GW44 Brierley, Peter, comp.
Act on the Facts: Information to Steer By. London, ENK: MARC Europe, 1992. 256 pp. Paper. 0947697993.

An alphabetical listing of facts concerning countries, cities, and subjects from around the world drawing out implications for Christian mission.

GW45 Coxill, H. Wakelin, and Kenneth Grubb, eds.
World Christian Handbook 1968. Nashville, TNU: Abingdon, 1967. xvii, 378 pp. No ISBN.

The fifth edition of this standard reference work, with nine interpretive articles, statistics on Protestant and Anglican missions, and a directory of ecumenical and Protestant mission agencies and of African independent churches; previously published in 1949, 1952, 1957, and 1962 by the World Dominion Trust, and distributed in the USA by Friendship Press.

GW46 Degrijse, Omer
De " Derde Kerk" wordt missionair. Bruges, BE: Tabor Publishing, 1983. 118 pp. 9065972617.

A survey of Catholic mission work in Africa, Asia, and Latin America.

GW47 Deiros, Pablo Alberto
Diccionario Hispanoamericano de la Misión. Miami, FLU: Editorial Unilit/COMIBAM Internacional, 1997. 450 pp. Paper. 0789904446.

This reference work contains more than 1,700 entries of words, phrases, and expressions, followed by information regarding their etymology, function, applications, meanings, and use in Latin America.

GW48 *Descriptio Geographica et Statistica Ecclesiae Catholicae tum Occidentis tum Orientis*
Gabriel, AU: Modling, 1968. 76 pp. No ISBN.

A cartographic work covering all the mission areas of the Catholic Church, including 1968 statistics on membership, and, in five languages, giving the history of the growth of the Church in each country.

GW49 *Dizionario di missiologia*
Bologna, IT: Edizioni Dehoniane; Bologna, IT: Urbaniana University Press, 1993. xiv, 545 pp. 8840110402 (U), 8810205642 (E).

A comprehensive Roman Catholic dictionary of missiology in Italian, with a short bibliography for each entry.

GW50 Dwyer, Judith A., ed.
The New Dictionary of Catholic Social Thought. Collegeville, MNU: Liturgical Press, 1994. xxxi, 1019 pp. 0814655262.

Short entries by 170 Catholic scholars on various subjects related to the social mission and ministries of the RCC.

GW51 Emmerich, Heinrich
Atlas Hierarchicus: Descriptio Geographica et Statistica Ecclesiae Catholicae tum occidentis tum orientis. Modling bei Wien, AU: St. Gabriel-Verlag; Aachen, GW: Missionswissenschaftliche Institut, Mission e.V., 1976. [126], 107 pp. No ISBN.

A standard work of cartography covering all the mission areas of the Catholic Church, giving the history of the growth of the churches in each country, with the latest statistics (1973) related to each map, and the text in English, French, German, Italian, and Spanish.

GW52 Freitag, Anton

The Twentieth Century Atlas of the Christian World: The Expansion of Christianity through the Centuries. New York, NYU: Hawthorn Books, 1963. xi, 199 pp. No ISBN.

A tracing of the expansion of Christianity from a Catholic perspective with numerous photographs and colored maps; translated from the French edition of 1959.

GW53 Goddard, Burton L., ed.

The Encyclopedia of Modern Christian Missions: The Agencies. Camden, NJU: Nelson, 1967. xix, 743 pp. No ISBN.

A comprehensive directory which gives a picture of the extent and variety of the operations of Protestant missions and mission agencies in the mid-1960s.

GW54 Jansen, Frank Kaleb, ed.

Target Earth: The Necessity of Diversity in a Holistic Perspective on World Mission. Kailua-Kona, HIU: University of the Nations; Pasadena, CAU: Global Mapping International, 1989. 175 pp. Paper. 0927545012.

An overview of 159 topics and 219 countries, presenting briefly in maps, charts, tables, and graphs, the factors of human need and environmental threat that contribute to a unified, holistic perspective on world mission; with stories of God's redemptive activity in various places.

GW55 Keeley, Robin, ed.

Christianity in Today's World. (An Eerdmans Handbook). Grand Rapids, MIU: Eerdmans, 1985. 384 pp. 0802836186.

A popular illustrated reference work on the kaleidoscope of Christian faith and life today on six continents, with short contributions by sixty-three specialists.

GW56 Müller, Karl et al., eds.

Dictionary of Mission: Theology, History, Perspectives. (American Society of Missiology Series, 24). Maryknoll, NYU: Orbis Books, 1997. xxvi, 518 pp. 157075148X.

An expansion and update for English readers of an important dictionary of missiology originally published in 1987 in German under the title *Lexikon Missionstheologischer Grundbegriffe.*

GW57 Müller, Karl, and Theo Sundermeier, eds.

Lexikon Missionstheologischer Grundbegriffe. Berlin, GW: Dietrich Reimer Verlag, 1987. xi, 546 pp. Paper. 349600911X.

An ecumenical presentation of the most burning issues in missiology today, in 110 articles by Catholic, Protestant, and Orthodox authors; with detailed bibliographies.

GW58 Myers, Bryant L.

The Changing Shape of World Mission. Monrovia, CAU: MARC, 1993. 49 pp. Paper. 0912552832.

Statistics and graphs describing the state of the world from the perspective of evangelism and Christian mission; originally published in *Mission Handbook, 1993-95* (1993).

GW59 Neill, Stephen Charles et al., eds.

Lexikon zur Weltmission. Wuppertal, GW: Theologischer Verlag Brockhaus; Erlangen, GW: Ev.-Luth. Mission, 1975. xix, 620 pp. 3797400543 (B), 3872140523 (E).

German translation and revised edition of *Concise Dictionary of the Christian World Mission* (1971).

GW60 Neill, Stephen Charles, Gerald H. Anderson, and John Goodwin, eds.

Concise Dictionary of the Christian World Mission. (World Christian Books). Nashville, TNU: Abingdon, 1971. xxi, 682 pp. 0687093716.

Alphabetized descriptions of the status of the church, in countries and areas of the world, with biographies of church leaders, past and present, and a listing of major Christian organizations.

GW61 Rzepkowski, Horst

Lexikon der Mission: Geschichte, Theologie, Ethnologie. Graz, AU: Verlag Styria, 1992. 470 pp. 3222120528.

Reflecting Vatican Council II's concept of mission as an intercultural progressive humanization of the world, this dictionary features brief articles written from historical, theological, and ethnological perspectives.

GW62 Siewert, John A., and Dotsey Welliver, eds.

Directory of Schools and Professors of Mission and Evangelism in the USA and Canada, 1999-2001. Wheaton, ILU: BGC, 1999. xii, 218 pp. Paper. 0912552913.

Latest edition of a directory of over 200 educational institutions and 1,000 individuals, with details of academic programs and courses offered; 1995 edition by MARC in Monrovia, California.

GW63 Thiessen, John Caldwell

A Survey of World Missions. Chicago, ILU: Moody, 1961. xii, 504 pp. No ISBN.

Revised third edition of a global missionary survey by geographical regions, from a conservative evangelical standpoint, reflecting political, religious, economic, and social changes.

Documentation and Archives

See also HI20.

GW64 Bellagamba, Anthony

The Mission of the Church: A New Look. Nairobi, KE: St. Paul Publications-Africa, 1993. 96 pp. Paper. 996621092X.

A study guide with commentary and study questions on the encyclical *Redemptoris Missio* (1990), by Pope John Paul II.

GW65 Burrows, William R., ed.

Redemption and Dialogue:Reading Redemptoris Missio *and* Dialogue and Proclamation. Maryknoll, NYU: Orbis Books, 1994. x, 244 pp. Paper. 0883449358.

The complete text of the two most influential encyclicals by John Paul II on mission, evangelization, and dialogue with other faiths, with official commentaries plus shorter critiques by an international group of Catholic and Protestant scholars.

GW66 Jenkins, Paul et al.

Archivbeiträge: Artikel über Westafrika/Ghana auf Grund von Material im Archiv der Basler Mission. (Mitteilungen der Basler Afrika Bibliographien, 9). Basel, SZ: Basler Afrika Bibliographien; Schwabisch-Gmund, GW: Afrika-Verlag der Kreis bei Lempp, 1973. 86 pp. 392070715X.

Introductions, in either German or English, to the archival collections in the Basel Mission House, with special reference to Africa: the [Gold Coast] *Christian Messenger* 1883-1931, African studies in Swiss universities and polytechnics, and German colonial literature to 1914.

GW67 John Paul II, Pope

Encyclical Letter Redemptoris Missio *of the Supreme Pontiff on the Permanent Validity of the Church's Missionary Mandate.* Washington, DCU: USCC, 1991. 153 pp. Paper. 1555864244.

The text of Pope John Paul II's important 1990 encyclical on the church's missionary mandate.

GW68 John XXIII, Pope
L'oeuvre missionnaire de Jean XXIII: textes et documents pontificaux, 1958-1963, présentés par l'Union pontificale missionnaire. (Siège apostolique et les missions, 4). Paris, FR: Lethielleux, 1966. 223 pp. No ISBN.

The fourth volume of the statements of John XXIII on missions; published in the series *Le Siège Apostolique et les Missions.*

GW69 Schütte, Johannes, ed.
Mission nach dem Konzil. Mainz, GW: Matthias-Grünewald-Verlag, 1967. 344 pp. No ISBN.

This book is an introduction to, and commentary on, the missionary decree *Ad Gentes* by various authors who actually helped shape that Vatican II document.

GW70 Scherer, James A., and Stephen B. Bevans, eds.
New Directions in Mission and Evangelization 1: Basic Statements, 1974-1991. Maryknoll, NYU: Orbis Books, 1992. xx, 324 pp. Paper. 0883447924.

This first volume in a series of sourcebooks on contemporary mission contains official statements by global and regional bodies of Roman Catholic, Eastern and Oriental Orthodox, and conciliar and evangelical Protestant traditions.

GW71 Soetens, A.
Inventaire des archives Vincent Lebbe. (Cahiers de la Revue théologique de Louvain, 4). Louvain-la-Neuve, BE: Faculté de théologie, 1982. 124 pp. No ISBN.

Lebbe, of the Société des Auxiliaires des Missions (SAM), entered the China mission in 1895 and died in 1940.

GW72 Thomas, Norman E., ed.
Classic Texts in Mission and World Christianity. (American Society of Missiology Series, 20). Maryknoll, NYU: Orbis Books, 1995. xx, 346 pp. Paper. 1570750068.

One-hundred-eighty original source documents from the early church to the present, with contemporary voices of persons in mission—women and men, from Africa, Asia, the Americas, and Europe—published as a companion volume to David Bosch's *Transforming Mission* (1991).

Conferences and Congresses

See also GW265, HI243, CR70, and EV172.

GW73 *Acta Synodalia Sacrosancti Concilii Oecumenici Vaticana II*, 4 vols. in 20
Vatican City, IT: Typis Polyglottis Vaticanis, 1970-1977. 4 vols. No ISBN.

The official collection of all Vatican II documents.

GW74 Elliston, Edgar J., ed.
Teaching Them Obedience in All Things: Equipping for the 21st Century. (Evangelical Missiological Society Series, 7). South Pasadena, CAU: William Carey Library, 1999. vii, 286 pp. Paper. 0878083812.

The ten papers collected in this volume were originally presented at the Evangelical Missiological Society (Orlando, Florida, 1998).

GW75 Gheddo, Piero
Concilio e Terzo Mondo. (Crocevia dei Popoli). Milano, IT: Editrice Missionaria Italiana, 1964. 259 pp. No ISBN.

A series of interviews with mission leaders attending second Vatican Council, including Cardinals Agagianan, Ben, and Konig, giving detailed information about the position of the Roman Catholic Church in certain countries.

GW76 Glazik, Josef, ed.
Dekret über die Missionstätigkeit der Kirche: Mit den Ausführungsbestimmungen vom 6.8.1966; authentischer lateinischer Text, deutsche Übersetzung. Münster, GW: Aschendorff, 1967. 148 pp. No ISBN.

Text of *Ad Gentes*, the missionary decree of Vatican II, the norms for its implementation, and commentary.

GW77 International Association for Mission Studies Conference (6th, Harare, Zimbabwe, 1985)
Christian and Human Transformation. Edited by F. J. Verstraelen. (*Mission Studies*, 2: 1). Gweru, ZI: Mambo Press, 1985. 149 pp. Paper. No ISBN.

Proceedings, including all lectures and workshop reports, with extensive material on issues for the African churches.

GW78 IVCF Missionary Convention (10th, Urbana, Illinois, 27-31 Dec. 1973)
Jesus Christ: Lord of the Universe, Hope of the World. Edited by David M. Howard. Downers Grove, ILU: InterVarsity, 1974. 252 pp. Paper. 0877847360.

A compendium of the addresses given at the convention attended by over 14,000 students, graduates, and missionaries.

GW79 IVCF Missionary Convention (8th, Urbana, Illinois, 27-31 Dec. 1967)
God's Men from All Nations to All Nations. Chicago, ILU: InterVarsity, 1968. 351 pp. Paper. No ISBN.

A collection of the messages delivered by twenty-six speakers at the convention attended by over 9,200 students, graduates, and missionaries.

GW80 Kyle, John E., comp.
The Unfinished Task. Ventura, CAU: Regal Books, 1984. 280 pp. Paper. 0830709835.

Sixteen missionary addresses given at Haystack '81 (Williams College, August 1981) commemorating the 175th anniversary of the first haystack prayer meeting and challenging young adults called to overseas mission work.

GW81 Lande, Aasulv, and Werner Ustorf, eds.
Mission in a Pluralist World. (Studies in the Intercultural History of Christianity, 97). Frankfurt am Main, GW: Lang, 1996. 193 pp. Paper. 3631494300 (GER), 0820429732 (US).

Papers by ten British and Nordic missiologists on "Mission in a Pluralist World," the theme of the Anglo-Nordic Summer Seminary (Selly Oak Colleges, Birmingham, UK, 18-23 June 1994).

GW82 Lemopoulos, George, ed.
Your Will Be Done: Orthodoxy in Mission. Geneva, SZ: WCC Publications, 1989. 267 pp. Paper. 2825409510.

A collection of many of the presentations to the CWME consultation of Eastern Orthodox and Oriental Orthodox churches (Neapolis, Greece, 16-24 April 1988), offered in hope that new opportunities will be given to Orthodox clergy, theologians, and laypeople to engage in research and missiological endeavors.

GW83 Lindsell, Harold, ed.

The Church's Worldwide Mission: An Analysis of the Current State of Evangelical Missions and a Strategy for Future Activity. Waco, TXU: Word Books, 1966. 289 pp. No ISBN.

Proceedings of the Congress on the Church's Worldwide Mission held at Wheaton College in April 1966, including the "Wheaton Declaration."

GW84 Lindsell, Harold, ed.

La mission de l'Église dans le monde: une analyse de la situation actuelle des missions évangéliques, et proposition d'une stratégie future. Translated by Jacques Blocher. La Côte-aux-Fées: Éd. des Groupes Missionnaires; Féderation de Missions Évangéliques Francophones, 1968. 320 pp. No ISBN.

French translation.

GW85 Mission Symposium

Proceedings of the Mission Symposium: Celebrating Seventy-Five Years in Mission. [Maryknoll, NYU: Maryknoll Sisters], 1986. 166 pp. Paper. No ISBN.

Addresses and discussion notes from an important symposium, held 12-14 September 1986 at Maryknoll, sponsored by the Catholic Foreign Mission Society of America and the Maryknoll Sisters.

GW86 Rynne, Xavier

Vatican Council II. Maryknoll, NYU: Orbis Books, 1999. xiv, 594 pp. Paper. 1570752931.

A reprint of the 1968 edition (Farrar, Straus & Giroux) with a new introduction by the author, with background and explanation of his earlier resort to a pseudonym and an assessment of the legacy of the landmark council, including its impact on the church's renewal and mission.

GW87 Schütte, Johannes, ed.

L' Activité missionaire de l'Église décret "Ad Gentes." Paris, FR: Éditions du Cerf, 1967. 445 pp. No ISBN.

The Latin text and French translation of the Vatican II "Decree on Missions" (*ad gentes*), with thirteen commentaries by leading Catholic scholars.

GW88 Semana de Misionología de Bérriz (16th)

Misiones y desarrollo de los pueblos. (Coleccion Bérriz, 23). Bilbao, SP: Mensajero, 1969. 322 pp. Paper. No ISBN.

A collection of studies addressing some contemporary issues in missions: the problem of non-Christians, the new theology of missions, and the necessary development of peoples.

GW89 Stott, John R. W. et al.

Christ the Liberator. (IVCF Missionary Convention (9th, Urbana, Illinois, 1970)). Downers Grove, ILU: InterVarsity, 1971. 288 pp. Paper. 0877847576.

Addresses presented as challenges to mission for the 12,300 college-age youth at Urbana '70.

GW90 *Suomen lähetyskongressi 77 Helsingissä 25.-29.7.1977*

Helsinki, FI: Suomen kirkon seurakuntatoiminnan keskusliitto, 1978. 310 pp. Paper. 9519303243.

A congress report dealing with various activities in all fields of the Finnish missionary organizations.

GW91 Vatican Council (2nd: 1962-1965)

The Documents of Vatican II: In a New and Definitive Translation with Commentaries and Notes by Catholic, Protestant and Orthodox Authorities. Edited by Walter M. Abbott. New York, NYU: Crossroad Publishing, 1989. xxi, 792 pp. 0824509803.

All sixteen official texts promulgated by the Ecumenical Council, 1963-1965, with introductions and commentaries by Catholic bishops and specialists, and responses by Protestant and Orthodox scholars.

General Works: Scholarly

See also GW280, HI38, HI66, HI221, HI332, HI436, HI579, TH255, ME58, ME223, ME236, ME252, ME257, EC27, EV70, EV80, EV140, CH34, AS65, and AS968.

GW92 Aagaard, Johannes, and Borge Helleskov, eds.

Mission over alle grænser. Christiansfeld, DK: Forlaget Savanne; Christiansfeld, DK: Dansk Missionsråd, 1971. 131 pp. Paper. 8799709252.

Articles on Danish missionary activities in different parts of the world, with reflections on contemporary missiological issues, including relations to persons of other religions and ideologies.

GW93 Ageneau, Robert, and Denis Pryen

Un nouvel âge de la mission. Paris, FR: Revue Spiritus, 1973. 320 pp. Paper. No ISBN.

A well-documented survey of contemporary issues in the church's mission, including the political contexts of missionary activity, new objectives for missions, new approaches of the church, and reflections on the future of missions.

GW94 Anderson, Gerald H., and Thomas F. Stransky, eds.

Mission Trends, No. 1: Crucial Issues in Mission Today. New York, NYU: Paulist Press; Grand Rapids, MIU: Eerdmans, 1974. ix, 276 pp. Paper. 0802814832.

Twenty-three scholarly essays on rethinking mission, the message and goals of mission, the missionary, churches in mission, and humanization, dialogue, and liberation.

GW95 Bühlmann, Walbert

Courage, Church!: Essays in Ecclesial Spirituality. Translated by Mary Smith. Maryknoll, NYU: Orbis Books, 1978. 149 pp. Paper. 0883440687.

English translation from the Italian of *Coraggio, Chiesa!*, a series of essays from 1975 to 1976 in which the author develops the idea that salvation history is still in the making and that the church must continue to move forward into that history; also published under the title *Forward Church* (Slough, ENK: St. Paul Publications, 1977).

GW96 Bühlmann, Walbert

Wandlung zum Wesentlichen: Der Sinn der Evangelisierung. (Münsterschwarzacher Studien, 30). Münsterschwarzach, GW: Vier-Türme-Verlag, 1976. viii, 167 pp. Paper. 3878680872.

A *festschrift* compiled by the author himself on the occasion of his 60th birthday, with bibliography and excerpts from his writings.

GW97 Bates, M. Searle, and Wilhelm Pauck, eds.

The Prospects of Christianity throughout the World. New York, NYU: Scribner, 1964. 286 pp. No ISBN.

A concise, critical, and authoritative non-Roman Catholic survey of the state of Christianity throughout the world, by an international team of sixteen Protestant scholars.

GW98 Bavinck, Johan Herman

An Introduction to the Science of Missions. Philadelphia, PAU: Presbyterian and Reformed Publishing, 1960. xxi, 323 pp. No ISBN.

A comprehensive exposition of Christian missionary thought, with a keen awareness of contemporary problems, as well as a broad historical perspective; translated by David Hugh Freeman.

GW—GENERAL WORKS

GW99 Beckmann, Johannes
Weltkirche und Weltreligionen: Die religiöse Lage der Menschheit.
Freiburg i.Br., GW: Herder, 1960. 197 pp. Paper. No ISBN.

A study of the religious situation of humanity outside Christianity, the Catholic Church in non-Christian countries, and of problems and tasks for the future.

GW100 Berentsen, Jan-Martin et al., eds.
Misjonsengasjement og forskertrang: festskrift til professor dr. Ludvig Munthe på 70-årsdagen 22. April 1990. Oslo, NO: Universitetsforlaget, 1990. 124 pp. No ISBN.

Festschrift to Professor L. Munthe, missiologist, theological teacher, and former missionary to Madagascar, with outstanding knowledge of Malagasy culture, history, and religion, and with a special concern for historical archives related to Madagascar, with a bibliography of his published and unpublished works in Norwegian and Swedish, and a table of contents in English; a thematic issue of *Norsk Tidskrift for Misjon* 44, 1/2 (1990).

GW101 Bertelsen, Ole, ed.
Missionens krise. (Synspunkt). Hellerup, DK: DMS-Forlag, 1970. 56 pp. Paper. 8774310070.

A former missionary to India, Kaj Baagø, instigated the discussion reflected in these essays on the motivations of missions in the postcolonial era.

GW102 Bertetto, Domenico, ed.
Maria Ausiliatrice e le missioni. (Atti dell'Accademia mariana salesiana, 11). Rome, IT: Libreria Ateneo Salesiano, 1977. 364 pp. No ISBN.

A compendium of fifteen essays by Marianist scholars, published for the centenary of the Salesian orders (Holy Ghost Fathers, CSSP and Daughters of Mary Help of Christians, FMA).

GW103 Beyerhaus, Peter
Krise und Neuaufbruch der Weltmission: Vorträge, Aufsätze, Dokumente. (Edition C, A Evangelische Missionslehre, 80). Bad Liebenzell, GW: Liebenzeller Mission, 1987. xi, 316 pp. Paper. 3880023034.

An anthology of articles stating, unequivocally, the evangelical stand on mission ("Declaration of Frankfurt"), but also seriously attempting to clarify controversial missiological issues such as dialogue, world religions, and racism.

GW104 Beyerhaus, Peter, and Carl F. Hallencreutz, eds.
The Church Crossing Frontiers: Essays on the Nature of Mission in Honour of Bengt Sundkler. (Studia Missionalia Upsaliensia, 11). Lund, SW: Gleerup, 1969. xx, 282 pp. No ISBN.

Twenty-two essays by a diverse international panel of scholars on missiological theory honoring Sweden's major missionary scholar.

GW105 Bifet, Juan Esquerda
Pastorale per una Chiesa Missionaria. Rome, IT: Pontificia Universitas Urbaniana, 1991. 302 pp. Paper. 8428509751.

A Catholic exposition of the basis and goals of mission and of missionary spirituality; based on the papal encyclical *Redemptoris Missio* (1991) and earlier Vatican documents.

GW106 Billington, Antony, Tony Lane, and Max Turner, eds.
Mission and Meaning: Essays Presented to Peter Cotterell. Carlisle, ENK: Paternoster Press, 1995. xvi, 375 pp. Paper. 0853646767.

A *festschrift* by twenty colleagues of the former principal of London Bible College exploring a variety of missiological themes (biblical, historical, philosophical, and contextual).

GW107 Blaser, Klauspeter, and Jean Eric Bertholet
La mission: dialogues et défis. Geneva, SZ: Éditions Labor et Fides; Lausanne, SZ: Éditions du Soc, 1983. 101 pp. 2825900176.

This book deals with the reasons and necessity of the Christian/non-Christian dialogue, defining Christian missions and the mission of Christians, and the difference between mission and evangelization.

GW108 Bloch-Hoell, Nils, ed.
Misjonskall og forskerglede: festskrift til professor Olav Guttorm Myklebust på 70-årsdagen 24. Juli 1975. Oslo, GW: Universitetsforlaget, 1975. 287 pp. 8200048608.

A *festschrift* with seventeen essays by distinguished Norwegian and international scholars, honoring Professor O. G. Myklebust, the distinguished Norwegian missiologist, on the occasion of his 70th birthday.

GW109 Brennecke, Gerhard, ed.
Weltmission in ökumenischer Zeit. Stuttgart, GW: Evan Missionsverlag, 1961. 335 pp. Paper. No ISBN.

A 1960 world survey, by a team of twenty-eight specialists, examining challenges and problems in the Christian mission, existing situations in Africa, Asia, Oceania, and Latin America, the Western contribution to evangelistic achievement, and some changing backgrounds which call for a new approach.

GW110 Bria, Ion, ed.
Go Forth in Peace: Orthodox Perspectives on Mission. Geneva, SZ: WCC, 1986. 102 pp. Paper. 2825408611.

A revised edition of a 1982 collection of papers by the same title, with new chapters on the contextualization of mission and the history of Orthodox mission.

GW111 Bria, Ion, ed.
Martyria/Mission: The Witness of the Orthodox Churches Today. Geneva, SZ: WCC, CWME, 1980. xi, 255 pp. Paper. 2825406287.

A collection of articles, stimulated by the WCC's CWME, by members of the Orthodox Church discussing, out of their own situations, the concerns and challenges of mission in today's Orthodox world, with descriptions of various Eastern and Oriental Orthodox churches and reports of recent Orthodox consultations on mission.

GW112 Brown, John P.
The Nature and Calling of the Church Today. Delhi, II: ISPCK, 1990. 88 pp. Paper. No ISBN.

Five lectures on mission and church renewal, delivered at clergy conferences of the Mar Thoma Church in India in 1989, by the Director of the Commission for Mission of the Uniting Churches in Australia.

GW113 Brown, Robert McAfee
Frontiers for the Church Today. New York, NYU: Oxford University Press, 1973. xvii, 149 pp. No ISBN.

Rethinking the church and its structure in the light of the challenges of ecumenism and secularism, the author explores a wide range of images including the servant church, "counter-culture," pilgrim people, diaspora, and going "outside the camp."

GW114 Brown, Terry, and Christopher Lind, eds.
Justice as Mission: An Agenda for the Church. Ontario, ONC: Trinity Press International, 1985. 249 pp. Paper. 0920413129.

Twenty-five essays honoring Marjorie and Cyril Powles of Canada, on diverse mission themes—mission and cultures including Japan, mission theology, women, mission and economics, missions and war and peace.

GW115 Bue, Bjørn, Svein Langås Tore, and Arne B. Samuelsen, eds.
Misjon—en velsignelse til alle folkeslag: en missiologisk studiebok. (Presteforeningens studiebibliotek, 25). Oslo, No: Den norske kirkes presteforening, 1988. 195 pp. 8290561024.

A textbook on missiology containing fourteen articles by missiologists, mission leaders, and missionaries; prepared for use in continuing education courses for pastors and other church workers.

GW116 Carpenter, Harold R.
Mandate and Mission: The Theory and Practice of Assemblies of God Missions. Springfield, MOU: CBC Press, 1990. v, 318 pp. Paper. No ISBN.

A revised edition of a popular introduction to Assemblies of God theology, history, organization, strategies, and promotion of missions.

GW117 Chandran, J. Russell
The Church in Mission: Some Reflections. Madras, II: CLS, 1991. x, 189 pp. Paper. No ISBN.

A collection of articles on mission, the theology of mission, and Christian approaches to other faiths by the respected ecumenical leader and former President of EATWOT (1976-1981), principal and professor of theology and ethics at United Theological College, Bangalore.

GW118 *Chiesa e Missione*
(Studia Urbaniana, 37). Rome, IT: Pontificia Universitas Urbaniana, 1990. 645 pp. Paper. 8840110372.

Twenty scholarly essays on various aspects of Roman Catholic missiology since Vatican II, especially the theology of mission and the varied forms of mission.

GW119 Comblin, Joseph
Atualidade da Teologia da Missão. Petrópolis, BL: Editorial Vozes, 1980. 93 pp. No ISBN.

Study of new perspectives offered by a theology of missions, considered independently and in historical context.

GW120 Comblin, Joseph
The Meaning of Mission: Jesus, Christians, and the Wayfaring Church. Translated by John Drury. Maryknoll, NYU: Orbis Books, 1977. vi, 142 pp. 088344304X (hdbk), 0883443058 (pbk).
English translation.

GW121 Comblin, Joseph
Teologiá de la Misión: La Evangelización. Buenos Aires, AG: Latinoamerica Libros, 1974. 116 pp. No ISBN.
Spanish translation.

GW122 Copeland, E. Luther
World Mission and World Survival: The Challenge and Urgency of Global Missions Today. Nashville, TNU: Broadman, 1985. 156 pp. Paper. 0805463356.

An introduction to the authority, motives, and goals of world missions in the light of global social issues.

GW123 Costas, Orlando E.
The Church and Its Mission: A Shattering Critique from the Third World. Wheaton, ILU: Tyndale; London, ENK: Coverdale House Publishers, 1974. xviii, 313 pp. 0842302751.

A scholarly holistic interpretation of the church as an instrument of God's mission to the world; by a leading Latin American evangelical, focusing on the 1968-1973 conciliarevangelical debate.

GW124 Cotter, James P.
The Word in the Third World. Washington, DCU: Corpus Books, 1968. 285 pp. No ISBN.

A collection of papers discussing missionary activities in Africa, Asia, and Latin America.

GW125 Dörmann, Johannes, ed.
Weltmission in der Weltkrise: Vortragsreihe zum Monat der Weltmission in Münster, Oktober 1978. (Veröffentlichungen des Instituts für Missionswissenschaft Münster, 14). St. Augustin, GW: Steyler Verlag, 1979. 92 pp. Paper. 3877871275.

Six lectures giving an overview of the missionary situation of the time, organized by the Missiological Institute of the University of Münster, but also meant for the general public.

GW126 Davies, John Dudley
The Faith Abroad. (Faith and the Future Series). Oxford, ENK: Blackwell Publishers, 1983. xi, 163 pp. Paper. 0631131833 (hdbk), 063113221X (pbk).

A book relating overseas missions to important aspects of Christianity in the contemporary scene, drawing inspiration from the Catholic revival in the Anglican Communion, known in the 19th century as the Oxford Movement.

GW127 Dempster, Murray W., Byron D. Klaus, and Douglas Petersen, eds.
Called and Empowered: Global Mission in Pentecostal Perspective. Peabody, MAU: Hendrickson, 1991. xix, 321 pp. Paper. 0943575478.

Twelve essays by Pentecostal scholars and three responses by persons of other traditions, on Pentecostal theology and strategies of mission.

GW128 Dhavamony, Mariasusai
Prospettive di Missiologia, OGGI: Volume Commemorativo Del 50∘ Anniversario dello Facolta di Missiologia. Rome, IT: Universita Gregoriana, 1982. 418 pp. Paper. No ISBN.

Scholarly essays, in commemoration of the 50th anniversary of the Faculty of Missiology, on the theology of the universal mission of the church, the history of its expansion into the world, and the anthropology of the principal world religions and cultures.

GW129 Doyle, Dennis M.
The Church Emerging from Vatican II: A Popular Approach to Contemporary Catholicism. Mystic, CTU: Twenty-Third Publications, 1992. viii, 349 pp. Paper. 0896225070.

A Catholic lay theologian's analysis of the nature and mission of the Roman Catholic Church in the modern world, including chapters on ecumenism, religious pluralism, laity, spirituality, and liberation theology.

GW130 Eddleman, H. Leo
Missionary Task of a Church. Nashville, TNU: Convention Press, 1961. 123 pp. No ISBN.

In this work the President of New Orleans Baptist Theological Seminary (New Orleans, Louisiana) presents the Bible as a source for missions, discusses the history of missions, and addresses missions as an ongoing concern for the church in the world; in the format of a textbook for the Baptist Church Study Course for Teaching and Training.

GW131 Eden, Martyn, and David F. Wells, eds.
The Gospel in the Modern World: A Tribute to John Stott.
Leicester, ENK: InterVarsity, 1991. 279 pp. 0830817565 (US),
0851106447 (UK).

Thirteen essays by a cross section of world leaders in
mission and evangelism, honoring the noted Anglican evangelical on his 70th birthday; including sections on "the essential Gospel," "understanding the modern world," and "living
the Gospel."

GW132 Eidberg, Peder A. et al., eds.
*For kirke og misjon: festskrift til professor, dr. theol. Nils Egede
Bloch-Hoell pd 70-årsdagen 26. september 1985.* Oslo, NO:
Universitetsforlaget, 1985. n.p. pp. No ISBN.

A *festschrift* containing twelve scholarly articles honoring
Professor N. E. Block-Hoell, the first professor in missiology and
ecumenical theology at the University of Oslo, and noted scholar
of the Pentecostal movement; published as a thematic issue of
Tidsskrift for misjon 39, nos. 3/4 (1985): 125-287.

GW133 Elliston, Edgar J., and Stephen E. Burris, eds.
Completing the Task: Reaching the World for Christ. Joplin,
MOU: College Press, 1995. 307 pp. 0899007295.

An introductory text on missions for college students and
local church leaders designed as a companion to the *Perspectives on the World Christian Movement* sourcebook.

GW134 Evangelical Alliance Commission on World Mission
*One World, One Task: Report of the Evangelical Alliance
Committee on World Mission.* London, ENK: Scripture Union
for the Evangelical Alliance, 1971. 173 pp. 0854212973.

Report of a special commission covering the theology of
mission, with analyses of the contemporary world, of the
church, and existing and future patterns of partnership.

GW135 Evangelisches Missionswerk (Hamburg)
*Was heisst Mission?: Grundlagen und neue Aspekte einer The-
ologie der Mission; Dokumentation eines Seminars in Bossey/
Genf vom 4.-9. 9. 1989.* (Weltmission heute, 8). Hamburg,
GW: EMW, 1990. 124 pp. Paper. No ISBN.

Documentation of a 1989 seminar held at the Ecumenical
Institute of Bossey (Switzerland), on the meaning of mission
today; with contributions by various German Protestant and
Catholic missiologists.

GW136 Flanagan, Padraeg, ed.
A New Missionary Era. Maryknoll, NYU: Orbis Books, 1982.
ix, 180 pp. No ISBN.

A collection of articles by Roman Catholic leaders on
contemporary missiology.

GW137 Forman, Charles W.
*To Renew a Right Spirit: Fresh Challenges and Fresh Chan-
nels for Mission.* Atlanta, GAU: General Assembly Mission
Board., PCUSA, 1985. 47 pp. Paper. No ISBN.

Four lectures on facets of the contemporary missionary
vocation: mission and the church, mission and the religions,
mission and culture, and mission and liberation.

GW138 Francis, T. Dayanandan, and Israel Selvanayagam, eds.
*Many Voices in Christian Mission: Essays in Honour of J. E.
Lesslie Newbigin, World Christian Leader.* Madras, II: CLS,
1994. x, 240 pp. Paper. No ISBN.

A *festschrift* honoring a pioneer bishop of the Church of
South India, missiologist and ecumenical leader, that contains six
tributes by Indian church leaders, plus eleven short articles on
missiological themes, and a select bibliography of his writings.

GW139 Freitag, Anton
Mission und Missionswissenschaft. (Steyler Missionsschrift-
enreihe, 4). Kaldenkirchen, GW: Steyler Verlag, 1962. 136
pp. Paper. No ISBN.

A work by the first doctor of Catholic mission theology
dealing with the various concepts of mission and with missiology as an academic discipline.

GW140 Freytag, Justus, and Hans Jochen Margull, comps.
Junge Kirchen auf eigenen Wegen: Analysen und Dokumente.
(Perspektiven der Weltmission, 2). Neukirchen-Vluyn, GW:
Neukirchener Verlag, 1972. 146 pp. 3788703288.

Analyses and documentation from Zaire (EJCSK), East Asia,
Taiwan, Japan, and Togo; by the editors and Erich Viering.

**GW141 Freytag, Walter, Jan Hermelink, and Hans Jochen Mar-
gull, eds.**
Reden und Aufsätze. (Theologische Bücherei; 13.1-2: Missionswissenschaft). Munich, GW: Kaiser, 1961. 2 vols. No ISBN.

A collection of speeches and essays covering a wide range
of issues by the prominent missiologist and one-time President of the German Protestant Missionary Council [vol. 1, 293
pp; vol. 2, 236 pp.].

GW142 Gensichen, Hans-Werner
Living Mission: The Test of Faith. Philadelphia, PAU: Fortress Press, 1966. xiii, 114 pp. Paper. No ISBN.

Five lectures by the University of Heidelberg's professor
of missiology on mission: its crisis, basis, aim, work, and study.

GW143 Gensichen, Hans-Werner
Mission und Kultur: Gesammelte Aufsätze. Edited by Theo
Sundermeier. (Theologische Bücherei, 74: Religionen und
Mission). Munich, GW: Kaiser, 1985. 239 pp. 3459015950.

A collection of essays by the prominent German Protestant missiologist.

GW144 Gittins, Anthony J.
*Bread for the Journey: The Mission of Transformation and
the Transformation of Mission.* (American Society of Missiology Series, 17). Maryknoll, NYU: Orbis Books, 1993. xx,
187 pp. Paper. 0883448572.

Probing reflections by a Catholic missiologist on the aims
and methods of Christian mission with focus on issues of inculturation, contemporary spirituality, and the missionary vocation.

GW145 Glazik, Josef
*Mission, der stets größere Auftrag: Gesammelte Vorträge und
Aufsätze.* Aachen, GW: Missio Aktuell Verlag, 1979. 175 pp.
Paper. 3921626056.

Lectures and articles from 1958 to 1975, mirroring the
change in understanding of mission and mission priorities; with
bibliography of the author's work.

GW146 Greenway, Roger S.
Together Again: Kinship of Word and Deed. Monrovia, CAU:
MARC, 1998. 33 pp. Paper. 1887983082.

A biblically based argument for reuniting evangelism and
social action under the banner of evangelical missions, by the
professor of world missiology at Calvin Theological Seminary in Grand Rapids, Michigan.

GW147 Hallencreutz, Carl F., ed.
"Daring in Order to Know": Studies in Bengt Sundkler's Contribution as Africanist and Missionary Scholar. (Studia Missionalia Upsaliensia, 39). Uppsala, SW: Swedish Institute of Missionary Research, 1984. 60 pp. No ISBN.

Bishop Bengt G. M. Sundkler is here honored by a *festschrift*, consisting of four articles on his contribution as Africanist and missionary scholar.

GW148 Hallencreutz, Carl F.
Tro från tredje världen. Stockholm, SW: Proprius, 1983. 198 pp. 9171184716.

A textbook on world mission, missiology and the Third World churches of today, including a survey of Swedish mission history.

GW149 Harr, Wilber C., ed.
Frontiers of the Christian World Mission since 1938: Essays in Honor of Kenneth Scott Latourette. New York, NYU: Harper & Brothers, 1962. viii, 310 pp. No ISBN.

Collection of papers given in honor of Kenneth Scott Latourette at the Association of Professors of Mission in 1960, including studies on faith missions and on the life and writings of Latourette.

GW150 Hawthorne, Steven C.
Perspectives on the World Christian Movement: A Study Guide. Edited by Ralph D. Winter, and Stephen E. Burris. South Pasadena, CAU: William Carey Library, 1994. 342 pp. Paper. 0878087621.

An update of the 1992 study guide to *Perspectives on the World Christian Movement* with material presented in a fifteen-lesson sequence, plus eleven new articles on emerging mission issues in the 1990s.

GW151 Henry, Antonin Marcel
Grundzüge einer Theologie der Mission. Mainz, GW: Grünewald, 1963. 208 pp. No ISBN.
German translation.

GW152 Henry, Antonin Marcel
A Mission Theology. Translated by Albert J. LaMothe. Notre Dame, INU: Fides, 1962. 197 pp. No ISBN.

The English translation of *Esquisse d'une theologie de la mission* (Paris: Éditions du Cerf, 1959), a study by a French Dominican applying the "six-continent" concept of missionary obligation to the Roman Catholic Church.

GW153 Hermelink, Jan
Christ im Welthorizont. Stuttgart, GW: Kreuz-Verlag, 1962. 157 pp. No ISBN.

A collection of speeches, articles, and reports, by a Protestant missiologist, on various aspects of modern missions.

GW154 Hernández, Angel Santos
Misionología: Problemos Introductorios y Ciencias Auxiliares. Santander, SP: Editorial Sal Terrae, 1961. 570 pp. No ISBN.

A one-volume introduction to missiology for Catholic seminarians, including chapters on the theology, history, and practice of missions.

GW155 Hiebert, Paul G., and Frances F. Hiebert
Case Studies in Missions. Grand Rapids, MIU: Baker Books, 1987. 264 pp. Paper. 0801043085.

Sixty-one case studies, based on true experiences in the lives of missionaries and church leaders around the world, prepared to encourage discussion and the search for biblical solutions in the classroom setting.

GW156 Hogg, William Richey
Un mundo, una misión. Buenos Aires, AG: Editorial La Aurora—CUPSA, 1961. 172 pp. Paper. No ISBN.
Spanish translation.

GW157 Hogg, William Richey
One World, One Mission. New York, NYU: Friendship Press, 1960. ix, 164 pp. No ISBN.

A popular introduction to Christian mission, emphasizing its biblical foundations, ecumenism and mission, and new patterns of mission.

GW158 Italiaander, Rolf
Partisanen und Propheten: Christen für eine Welt. Erlangen, GW: Evangelical Lutheran Mission, 1972. 152 pp. Paper. 3872140345.

Profiles of ten distinguished contemporary Christians from all over the world.

GW159 Italiaander, Rolf
Profile und Perspektiven. (Erlanger Taschenbücher, 11). Erlangen, GW: Ev-Luth. Mission, 1971. 178 pp. 387214023X.

This collection of sketches from the lives and experiences of various evangelical Christians in Africa, Asia, and Latin America, focuses on their witness to Christ as leaders of church or of state.

GW160 Jacobs, Donald R.
Pilgrimage in Mission. Scottsdale, PAU: Herald Press, 1983. 162 pp. Paper. 0836133242.

An update on Anabaptist/Mennonite missiology in light of a half-century of Mennonite involvement in cross-cultural missions.

GW161 Johnson, Howard A.
Global Odyssey: An Episcopalian's Encounter with the Anglican Communion in Eighty Countries. New York, NYU: Harper & Row, 1963. 448 pp. No ISBN.
A global Anglican survey.

GW162 Jongeneel, J. A. B.
Missiologie. (Mission: Missiologisch Onderzoek in Nederland, 1). The Hague, NE: Boekencentrum, 1986-1991. 2 vols. 9023906403.

A two-volume introduction into missiology as an academic science, with special emphasis on methodological problems, bibliographical elaboration, and mission theology; by the professor of missiology at the State University of Utrecht [vol. 1: *Zendingswetenschap* (1986, 208 pp.); vol. 2: *Missionaire Theologie* (1991, 401 pp.)].

GW163 Kähler, Martin
Schriften zu Christologie und Mission: Gesamtausgabe der Schriften zur Mission; mit einer Bibliographie. Edited by Heinzgün Frohnes. (Theologische Bücherei, 42). Munich, GW: Chr. Kaiser Verlag, 1971. xxxvi, 574 pp. Paper. 345900617X.

A collection of essays, sermons, and other writings on mission by the prominent Protestant theologian, spanning the years 1893-1912.

GW164 Kane, J. Herbert
The Christian World Mission: Today and Tomorrow. Grand
Rapids, MIU: Baker Books, 1981. 294 pp. 0801054265.

A basic introduction to missiology including sections on
the biblical basis of missions, global dimensions, crucial issues, and continuing problems.

GW165 Kane, J. Herbert
Understanding Christian Missions. Grand Rapids, MIU: Baker
Books, 1982. 472 pp. 0801053447.

A third edition of an assessment of the global missionary
enterprise by a leading evangelical missiologist.

GW166 Kane, J. Herbert
Wanted: World Christians. Grand Rapids, MIU: Baker Books,
1986. 245 pp. Paper. 0801054745.

An introduction, for Christian students, to what it means
to be a world Christian, including chapters on the basis for
world missions, the challenges, and possible responses.

GW167 Karotemprel, Sebastian et al., eds.
*Following Christ in Mission: A Foundational Course in Mis-
siology.* Nairobi, KE: Paulines Publications Africa, 1995. 336
pp. Paper. 9966211667.

A basic introductory text on missiology prepared by an international team of specialists for use in Catholic major seminaries, formation centers, missiological and missionary institutes.

GW168 Kasdorf, Hans, and Klaus W. Müller, eds.
*Bilanz und Plan: Mission an der Schwelle zum Dritten Jahr-
tausend.* (Veröffentlichungen der Freien Hochschule für Mission, C1). Bad Liebenzell, GW: Verlag der Liebenzeller Mission, 1988. 504 pp. Paper. 3880023379.

A collection of forty-seven articles in English and German by twenty-three North American and European authors,
on contemporary issues in missiology; written to honor George
W. Peters on his 80th birthday.

GW169 Kasdorf, Hans, and Klaus W. Müller, eds.
Reflection and Projection: Missiology at the Threshold of 2001.
Bad Liebenzell, GW: Verlag der Liebenzeller Mission, 1988.
504 pp. Paper. 3880023387.

English edition.

GW170 Kniffka, Jörg, ed.
*Martyria: Festschrift zum 60. Geburtstag von Peter Beyer-
haus am 1.2.1989.* Wuppertal, GW: Brockhaus, 1989. 272
pp. Paper. 3417246059.

A collection of thirty-three essays published in honor of
the German evangelical missiologist Peter Beyerhaus.

GW171 Kollbrunner, Fritz
*The Splendour and Confusion of Mission Today: An Essay on
the Theology of Mission.* (Mambo Occasional Papers—Missio-Pastoral Series, 5). Gwelo, RH: Mambo Press, 1974. 63
pp. Paper. No ISBN.

Lectures on the origin, form, aim, and task of mission
today; originally given at the Faculty of Divinity, Lucerne,
Switzerland.

GW172 Kritzinger, J. J., and W. A. Saayman
Mission in Creative Tension: A Dialogue with David Bosch.
Pretoria, SA: South African Missiological Society, 1990. 269
pp. Paper. 0620148985.

Scholarly essays, originally presented at the 1990 congress of the Southern African Missiological Society, to honor

the noted South African missiologist on the occasion of his
60th birthday.

GW173 Kroeger, James H.
Living Mission: Challenges in Evangelization Today. Maryknoll, NYU: Orbis Books; Quezon City, PH: Claretian Publications, 1994. xii, 164 pp. Paper. 0883449218 (US),
9715015883 (PH).

The Asia-Pacific Area Assistant on the Maryknoll General Council develops contemporary themes in global mission,
combining the scholarship of a theologian with the practical
wisdom of a field missionary (Bangladesh and the Philippines).

GW174 Kroeger, James H.
Mission Today: Contemporary Themes in Missiology. (FABC
Papers, 61). Hong Kong: Federation of Asian Bishops' Conference; Davao City, PH: Mission Studies Institute, 1991. 31
pp. Paper. 9715011071.

Three lectures on mission spirituality, relating Scripture
with world religions; by a Maryknoll missionary recently based
at the Loyola School of Theology in Manila.

GW175 LaVerdiere, Eugene, ed.
*A Church for All Peoples: Missionary Issues in a World
Church.* Collegeville, MNU: Liturgical Press, 1993. 104 pp.
Paper. 0814621414.

Short papers and responses by distinguished Catholic theologians and educators, originally delivered at the symposium
on "The Church: Salvation and Mission" (Mundelein, Illinois,
11-13 October 1991), exploring issues treated in the encyclical *Redemptoris Missio* (1990) by Pope John Paul II.

GW176 Lewis, Jonathan, ed.
*Misión Mundial: Un Análisis del Movimiento Cristiano Mun-
dial.* South Pasadena, CAU: William Carey Library, 1986. 3
vols. Paper. 0878088059 (vol. 1), 0878088067 (vol. 2),
0878088075 (vol. 3).

Spanish translation.

GW177 Lewis, Jonathan, ed.
*World Mission: An Analysis of the World Christian Move-
ment.* South Pasadena, CAU: William Carey Library, 1987.
3 vols. Paper. 0878082085 (vol. 1), 0878082093 (vol. 2),
0878082107 (vol. 3).

A three-part study guide, integrating essential and relevant articles from *Perspectives on the World Christian Movement,* (1981) discussing Biblical/Historical Foundations (Part
One, 132 pp.), The Strategic Dimension (Part Two, 185 pp.),
and Cross-Cultural Considerations (Part Three, 170 pp.).

GW178 Lyon, David H. S.
How Foreign Is Mission? Edinburgh, STK: St. Andrew Press,
1978. x, 83 pp. Paper. 0715203703.

An introduction to contemporary issues in mission, with
pertinent biblical exegesis by the general secretary of the Overseas Council of the Church of Scotland.

GW179 Müller, Karl, ed.
Missionsstudien. (Studia Instituti Missiologici SVD, 1). Kaldenkirchen, GW: Steyler Verlag, 1962. viii, 275 pp. Paper. No ISBN.

A collection of missiological articles in German, English,
French, and Dutch missiological articles by Divine Word missionaries, inaugurating the "Steyler Missionswissenschaftliches Institut" (1962), covering topics in the history, theology,
spirituality, and praxis of mission.

GW180 Margull, Hans Jochen

Zeugnis und Dialog: Ausgewählte Schriften. (Perspektiven der Weltmisssion: Wissenschaftliche Beiträge, 13). Ammersbek bei Hamburg, GW: Verlag an der Lottbek, 1992. 375 pp. Paper. 3926987812.

Selections from the writings of H. J. Margull, presented around the themes of mission, reform of the church, church history in the Third World, and interreligious dialogue.

GW181 McGavran, Donald Anderson, ed.

Crucial Issues in Missions Tomorrow. Chicago, ILU: Moody, 1972. 272 pp. 0802416756.

A collection of scholarly essays, mostly by Protestant evangelicals, on a theology of mission, Gospel and culture, and selected practical issues of church growth.

GW182 Messer, Donald E.

A Conspiracy of Goodness: Contemporary Images of Christian Mission. Nashville, TNU: Abingdon, 1992. 176 pp. Paper. 0687094844.

An argument by the president of Iliff School of Theology, Denver, Colorado, that mission is the vocation of the entire community of faith, presenting new images of metaphors for missional ministry.

GW183 *Missiologia oggi*

(Subsidia Urbaniana, 14). Rome, IT: Urbaniana University Press, 1985. 401 pp. Paper. No ISBN.

A collection of sixteen essays by outstanding Roman Catholic missiologists, relating the vision of the papal encyclical *Ad Gentes* to contemporary issues in missions.

GW184 Myklebust, Olav Guttorm

Det store oppdrag: Artikler i utvalg, 1938-1988. Oslo, NO: Otto Falch, 1988. 194 pp. No ISBN.

Twenty important studies on the understanding of mission in a world of constant change, all previously published in various contexts, are here put together and published privately by the author, professor emeritus and for years the leading missiologist in Norway.

GW185 Nazir-Ali, Michael

From Everywhere to Everywhere: A World View of Christian Mission. London, ENK: Collins, 1992. 269 pp. Paper. 0005992222.

An introduction to contemporary goals for mission, and the theology which undergirds them, by the general secretary of the Church Missionary Society.

GW186 Neill, Stephen Charles

Salvation Tomorrow: The Originality of Jesus Christ and the World's Religions. Nashville, TNU: Abingdon, 1976. x, 150 pp. 0687367999.

Five essays on contemporary ecumenism (issues of ecumenical history, interreligious dialogue, moratorium on missionaries, the church and revolution, and mission training); originally given as the Chavasse Lectures at Wycliffe Hall, Oxford.

GW187 Newbigin, James Edward Lesslie

A Word in Season:Perspectives on Christian World Missions. Grand Rapids, MIU: Eerdmans; Edinburgh, STK: Saint Andrew Press, 1994. xi, 208 pp. Paper. 0802807305 (US), 0715207040 (UK).

A collection of seventeen never-before-published essays, sermons, and addresses on Christian mission; by the noted ecumenical leader in missions.

GW188 Ohm, Thomas

Ex contemplatione loqui: Gesammelte Aufsätze. (Missionswissenschaftliche Abhandlungen und Texte, 25). Munich, GW: Aschendorff, 1961. vii, 468 pp. No ISBN.

A collection of essays on mission theory, missionary methods, and comparative religion; written between 1927 and 1959, by a prominent Catholic missiologist; with a bibliography of his writings.

GW189 Ohm, Thomas

Machet zu Jüngern alle Völker: Theorie der Mission. Freiburg im Breisgau, GW: Wewel, 1962. 927 pp. No ISBN.

A detailed and scholarly introduction to missiology, including motives, rationale, aims, planning, accomplishments, fruits, and fulfillments of mission; by the distinguished professor of Missions of the Roman Catholic faculty at Münster University.

GW190 Ohm, Thomas, ed.

Faîtes des disciples de toutes les nations: théorie de la mission. Translated by Germain Varin and André Décamps. (In Domo Domini). Paris, FR: Éditions Saint-Paul, 1964-1967. 3 vols. No ISBN.

French translation.

GW191 Olson, C. Gordon

What in the World Is God Doing?: The Essentials of Global Missions, an Introductory Guide. Cedar Knolls, NJU: Global Gospel Publishers, 1989. 310 pp. Paper. 0962485004.

A survey text, with teaching aids, on world missions for college undergraduates; by the professor of missions and theology at Northeastern Bible College in Essex Fells, New Jersey, including sections on a biblical theology of missions, its history, the church in its context, and mission strategy.

GW192 Orchard, Ronald Kenneth

Missions in a Time of Testing: Thought and Practice in Contemporary Missions. Philadelphia, PAU: Westminster Press, 1964. 212 pp. No ISBN.

An introduction to the theoretical foundations and empirical processes of mission by the London Secretary of the IMC.

GW193 Pate, Larry D.

Misionología: Nuestro Cometido Transcultural. Miami, FLU: Editorial Vida, 1987. 447 pp. 0829709975.

A basic introduction to missiology prepared for theological students in Latin America.

GW194 Pate, Larry D.

Missiologia: A Missão Transcultural da Igreja. Translated by João Barbosa Batista. Miami, FLU: Editora Vida, 1987. 401 pp. 0829716203.

Portuguese translation.

GW195 Pentecost, Edward C.

Issues in Missiology: An Introduction. Grand Rapids, MIU: Baker Books, 1982. 205 pp. 0801070716.

An introduction to missiology emphasizing the contributions of the social science fields of anthropology, sociology, psychology, and communications.

GW196 Pittman, Don A., Ruben L. F. Habito, and Terry C. Muck, eds.

Ministry and Theology in Global Perspective: Contemporary Challenges for the Church. Grand Rapids, MIU: Eerdmans, 1996. xvii, 524 pp. Paper. 0802808441.

A reader on the theology of religions, mission amidst religious pluralism, and interreligious dialogue.

GW197 Prawdzik, Werner, ed.
Theologie im Dienste der Weltkirche: Festschrift zum 75-jäh-
rigen Bestehen des Missionspriesterseminars St. Augustin.
(Veröffentlichungen des Missionspriesterseminars, 38).
Nettetal, GW: Steyler Verlag, 1988. 321 pp. Paper.
380500219X.

A collection of thirteen papers revealing how a Catholic
missionary congregation (Society of the Divine Word) attempted to redefine its identity in a time of change.

GW198 Rétif, Louis, and André Rétif
The Church's Mission in the World. Translated by Reginald
F. Trevett. (Twentieth Century Encyclopedia of Catholicism,
102). New York, NYU: Hawthorn Books, 1964. 121 pp. No
ISBN.

English translation; first published in 1962.

GW199 Rahner, Karl, ed.
Re-Thinking the Church's Mission. (*Concilium*, 13). New
York, NYU: Paulist Press, 1966. viii, 152 pp. No ISBN.

Four essays on contemporary issues by leading Catholic
missiologists, plus commentaries on Vatican documents and a
bibliographic survey on mission as an ecclesiological theme.

GW200 Schmemann, Alexander
Church, World, Mission: Reflections on Orthodoxy in the West.
Crestwood, NYU: St. Vladimir's Seminary Press, 1979. 227
pp. Paper. 0913836494.

A book which answers the question: "What is the destiny
of the Orthodox Church in the second half of the twentieth
century in a world so radically different from that which shaped
its beginning?"

GW201 Schmitz, Josef et al., eds.
Das Ende der Exportreligion: Perspektiven für eine künftige
Mission. (Patmos paperback). Düsseldorf, GW: Patmos-Ver-
lag, 1971. 98 pp. Paper. 3491003113.

This short book, rather misleadingly named, contains four
essays by prominent German theologians on mission in the
New Testament and in the primitive Church, a situational analysis of Christian mission, mission and world cultures, and
motives for mission.

GW202 Semaine de missiologie (44th, 1974, Louvain)
Qui portera l'Évangile aux nations ?rapports, échanges et
points de vue de la XLIVe Semaine de missiologie de Lou-
vain,1974. (Museum Lessianum; Section Missiologique, 58).
[Brussels], BE: Desclée de Brouwer, 1974. 176 pp. No ISBN.

"Who Will Carry the Gospel to the Nations?" was the theme
of this 44th Louvain Seminar for Catholic missiologists.

GW203 Shenk, David W.
God's Call to Mission. Scottdale, PAU: Herald Press, 1994.
229 pp. Paper. 0836136691.

With biblical sources, as well as acecdotes from his work
as a Mennonite missionary in East Africa, mission executive
and teacher, Shenk shows how the Gospel is incarnated in cultures without being enslaved by them.

GW204 Shenk, Wilbert R., ed.
Mission Focus: Current Issues. Scottdale, PAU: Herald Press,
1980. 488 pp. Paper. 0836119371.

Thirty-five essays, mostly by Mennonites, on biblical and
theological perspectives, mission and the world, and mission
strategies and policies.

GW205 Sinclair, Maurice
Ripening Harvest, Gathering Storm: What Is the Relevance of
the Christian Faith in a World Sliding into Crisis? Bromley,
Kent, ENK: STL Books; London, ENK: MARC; London,
ENK: Church Missionary Society, 1988. 252 pp. Paper.
1850780463 (S), 0860656489 (M).

A call for missionary obedience in the light of the biblical teaching on world mission, its historical development, and
contemporary challenges on six continents; also published by
Evangelical Missionary Alliance, London, UK.

GW206 Smith, Eugene L.
God's Mission—and Ours. Nashville, TNU: Abingdon, 1961.
169 pp. No ISBN.

A Methodist world mission's executive challenges the
missionary movement to go beyond social service, to the root
causes of injustice, and to proceed from a well-grounded spiritual orientation.

GW207 Smith, Eugene L.
Mandate for Mission. New York, NYU: Friendship Press,
1968. 157 pp. Paper. No ISBN.

A reexamination of the rationale for mission in light of
the Gospel, as well as contemporary contrasts of affluence and
poverty, and the search for meaning; prepared as a mission
study book by the Executive Secretary in the United States for
the WCC.

GW208 Smith, Louis A., and Joseph R. Barndt
Beyond Brokenness. New York, NYU: Friendship Press, 1980.
125 pp. Paper. 0377001007.

A study guide attempting to explore the ways in which
the contemporary world and Scripture calls us to new understanding of Christian faithfulness.

GW209 Steuernagel, Valdir, comp.
La Misión de la Iglesia: Una Visión Panorámica. San José,
CR: Vision Mundial, 1992. 468 pp. Paper. 9977965218.

A series of essays by Latin American missiologists on
the mission of the church as it relates to fundamental biblical-
theological understandings, the search for unity, service, and
the church as a therapeutic agent addressing issues of health,
family, and children.

GW210 Stott, John R. W.
Christian Mission in the Modern World. London, ENK: Fal-
con Books/Church Pastoral Aid Society, 1977. 127 pp. Paper.
0854918558.

The biblical meanings of five key words—mission, evangelism, dialogue, salvation, and conversion—and their relationship to the contemporary understanding of the nature of
missions.

GW211 Stott, John R. W.
Gesandt wie Christus: Grundfragen christlicher Mission und
Evangelisation. (ABCTeam, A62). Wuppertal, GW: R. Brock-
haus Verlag, 1976. 138 pp. Paper. 3417005809.

German translation.

GW212 Stott, John R. W.
La Misión Cristiana Hoy. Translated by David Powell. Buenos Aires, AG: Ediciones Certeza, 1977. 171 pp. No ISBN.

Spanish translation.

GW213 Stott, John R. W.
Mission chrétienne dans le monde moderne. Translated by S. Dupertuis. Lausanne, SZ: Éditions des Groupes Missionnaires, 1977. No ISBN.
   French translation.

GW214 Strachan, Robert Kenneth
The Inescapable Calling: The Missionary Task of the Church of Christ in the Light of Contemporary Challenge and Opportunity. Grand Rapids, MIU: Eerdmans, 1968. 127 pp. No ISBN.
   A primer on the contemporary challenges to mission, their biblical bases, and contemporary methods of witness, including the "evangelism-in-depth" program pioneered by the author.

GW215 Sundkler, Bengt
Maailmanlähetys. Translated by Esko Rintala. Helsinki, FI: Suomen Luterilainen Evankeliumiyhdistys, 1965. 259 pp. No ISBN.
   Finnish translation.

GW216 Sundkler, Bengt
Missionens Värld: Missionskunskap och missionshistoria. (Scandinavian University Books). Stockholm, SW: Svenska Bokförlaget, 1970. 230 pp. No ISBN.
   Second revised edition of a textbook on the theology and history of the missionary church, with a central thesis that mission as translation involves risk, and numerous illustrations from the author's experience as a missionary in Africa; originally published in 1963.

GW217 Sundkler, Bengt
The World of Mission. Translated by Eric J. Sharpe. Grand Rapids, MIU: Eerdmans; London, ENK: Lutterworth Press, 1965. 318 pp. No ISBN.
   English translation.

GW218 Tallman, J. Raymond
An Introduction to World Missions. Chicago, ILU: Moody; Dubuque, IAU: Kendall/Hunt Publishing, 1989. 271 pp. 084035696X.
   An introduction to the study of missions by the Chairman of the Department of World Missions at Moody Bible Institute, covering theological bases, concerns of missionary candidates, and international challenges for world missions.

GW219 Thampu, Valson
Rediscovering Mission: Towards a Non-Western Missiological Paradigm. New Delhi, II: TRACI, 1995. 278 pp. Paper. No ISBN.
   A well-reasoned and persuasive non-Western biblical paradigm for Christian missions in a religiously plural world.

GW220 Tippett, Alan Richard
Introduction to Missiology. South Pasadena, CAU: William Carey Library, 1987. xxv, 457 pp. Paper. 0878082069.
   Forty articles on theological, anthropological, historical, and practical dimensions of world mission; by the Australian former professor at Fuller's School of World Mission and the Biola University School of Intercultural Studies.

GW221 *To the Ends of the Earth: A Pastoral Statement on World Mission*
(United States Catholic Conference Publication, 112-1). Washington, DCU: USCC, 1986. 26 pp. Paper. 1555861121.

A Roman Catholic statement providing a theological and pastoral instrument for mission in order to stimulate interest and personal responsibility for the church's mission to other peoples.

GW222 Trueblood, David Elton
The Validity of the Christian Mission. New York, NYU: Harper & Row, 1972. xi, 113 pp. 0060687401.
   The popular author and professor of Earlham College takes seriously the doubts of honest and good-hearted people as to the validity of missions, in a well-reasoned defense and theology of Christian missions.

GW223 Turner, Philip, and Frank Sugeno
Crossroads Are for Meeting: Essays on the Mission and Common Life of the Church in a Global Society. Sewanee, TNU: SPCK, 1986. xiv, 288 pp. Paper. 0933667019.
   A collection of twenty papers on the nature of the Church and its mission; originally presented at the Pan-Anglican Symposium on the Theology of Mission at Hartford, Connecticut, in 1984.

GW224 Urbina, Fernando
Misión: vocaciones para una comunidad misionera. (Cuadernos de pastoral, 70). Valencia, SP: Comercial Editora de Publicaciones, 1974. 209 pp. 8470501100.
   An analysis of the current situation in the world and how the church can move effectively in its missionary and other religious activities.

GW225 Van Rheenen, Gailyn
Missions: Biblical Foundations and Contemporary Strategies. Grand Rapids, MIU: Zondervan, 1996. 251 pp. 0310208092.
   An introductory missions textbook for persons preparing to be cross-cultural missionaries and church planters.

GW226 Verkuyl, Johannes
Contemporary Missiology: An Introduction. Translated by Dale Cooper. Grand Rapids, MIU: Eerdmans, 1978. xiv, 414 pp. 080283518X.
   English translation.

GW227 Verkuyl, Johannes
Inleiding in de nieuwere zendingswetenschap. Kampen, NE: Kok, 1976. 571 pp. 9024208513.
   An introduction to contemporary missiology concentrating on theological and missiological developments in Asia, Africa, Latin America, and the Caribbean and Pacific areas, with subject bibliographies.

GW228 Verstraelen, F. J. et al., eds.
Oecumenische inleiding in de missiologie: Teksten en konteksten van het wereldchristendom. Kampen, NE: Kok, 1988. 525 pp. 9024244900.
   This ecumenical introduction to missiology is the combined scholarly effort of twenty-one Dutch Protestant and Catholic missiologists, who wrestle with the basic tension of presenting one Christian faith in varied cultures, resulting in a polycentric and multifaceted Christianity.

GW229 Verstraelen, F. J. et al.
Missiology: An Ecumenical Introduction: Texts and Contexts of Global Christianity. Grand Rapids, MIU: Eerdmans, 1995. vii, 498 pp. Paper. 080280487X.
   Revised English translation.

GW—GENERAL WORKS

GW230 Vicedom, Georg F.
Die Mission am Scheideweg. (Missionierende Gemeinde, 14). Berlin, GW: Lutherisches Verlagshaus, 1967. 74 pp. No ISBN.

The noted German missiologist discusses mission at the crossroads of new theories and secular challenges.

GW231 Waack, Otto
So sende ich euch: Festschrift für Martin Pörksen zum 70. Geburtstag. Edited by Justus Freytag, and Gerhard Hoffman. Korntal bei Stuttgart, GW: Evan Missionsverlag, 1973. 344 pp. 377140178X.

A series of thirty essays on general missionary topics published in honour of Martin Pörksen, for many years the director of the Breklum Mission.

GW232 Waldenfels, Hans, ed.
"... denn ich bin bei euch" (Mt 28,20): Perspektiven im christlichen Missionsbewusstsein heute; Festgabe für Josef Glazik und Bernward Willeke zum 65. Geburtstag. Einsiedeln, SZ: Benziger, 1978. 461 pp. 3545240592.

A commemorative volume in honor of two Catholic missiologists, with thirty-seven essays covering a broad field of missiological interest.

GW233 WCC, Central Committee
Mission und Evangelisation: Eine ökumenische Erklärung. (Weltmission heute—zum Thema...). Hamburg, GW: EMW, 1982. 34 pp. Paper. No ISBN.

German translation.

GW234 WCC, Central Committee
Misión mundial y evangelización: Una afirmación ecuménica. Geneva, SZ: WCC, 1986. 47 pp. Paper. No ISBN.

Spanish translation.

GW235 WCC, Central Committee
Mission and Evangelism: An Ecumenical Affirmation: A Study Guide. Compiled by Jean Stromberg. Geneva, SZ: WCC, 1983. viii, 84 pp. Paper. 282540778X.

A study guide on the WCC's 1982 theology of mission.

GW236 Winter, Ralph D., and Steven C. Hawthorne, eds.
Perspectives on the World Christian Movement: A Reader. Third edition. South Pasadena, CAU: William Carey Library; Carlisle, ENK: Paternoster Press, 1999. xviii, 782 pp. Paper. 0853649995 (UK), 0878082891 (US).

A revised textbook for Protestant students of mission on biblical, historical, cultural, and strategic mission perspectives, with some updated articles; originally published in 1981.

GW237 Winterhager, J. W., and Arnold Brown, eds.
Vocation and Victory: An International Symposium Presented in Honour of Erik Wickberg. Basel, SZ: Brunnen-Verlag, 1974. 322 pp. 3765503266 (hdbk), 3765503274 (pbk).

A *festschrift* honoring the general of the Salvation Army with papers in French (8), German (7), Swedish (2), and English (13), including articles on mission by John Stott, J. Norman Anderson, Johannes Verkuyl, Donald Bloesch, William Barclay, and D. Elton Trueblood.

GW238 Zaplata, Feliks, ed.
Wspolezesne dzielo misyjne Kacciola. (Zeszyty Misjologiczne, 1). Warsaw, PL: Akademia Teologii Katholickiej, 1974. 3 vols. Paper. No ISBN.

The first two volumes contain papers of the Missiological Symposium of 1971 and 1972, [vol. 1: 215 pp.; vol. 2: 235 pp.], and the third essays by A. M. Henry, D. Colombo, A. Noser (on New Guinea), F. Zaplata, C. B. Alpuerto (on Philippines), and S. Achewa [vol. 3: 278 pp.]; with summaries in French.

General Works: Popular

See also ME67, ME103, ME187, and SP156.

GW239 Bertuzzi, Federico A.
El Despertar de las Misiones. Miami, FLU: Editorial Unilit/ COMIBAM Internacional, 1997. 137 pp. Paper. 0789904454.

A collection of twelve essays, all written by the author and prepared originally for either presentation at missionary conferences or for publication.

GW240 Brown, Alistair
I Believe in Mission. (I Believe Series). London, ENK: Hodder & Stoughton, 1997. 176 pp. Paper. 0340694270.

A biblical, practical call to mission for young adults by the General Director of the Baptist Missionary Society in Great Britain.

GW241 Brugnoli, Carlo, and Michèle Brugnoli
Erzählt es allen Völkern: Motivierende Perspektiven zum Thema Weltmission. Wiesbaden, GW: Projektion J. Buch—und Musikverlag, 1995. 185 pp. Paper. 3894900695.

German translation of *Progresser avec Dieu* (1992), a study book on motivations and perspectives on world mission.

GW242 Eastman, A. Theodore
Chosen and Sent: Calling the Church to Mission. Grand Rapids, MIU: Eerdmans, 1971. 144 pp. Paper. No ISBN.

A primer on the church's mission to the whole world, based on a three-fold foundation of biblical faith, historical precedent, and contemporary change.

GW243 Fjärstedt, Biörn
Missionen skiftar ansikte: Missionsteologi i tiden. Stockholm, SW: Verbum Förlag, 1991. 206 pp. 9152617424.

A popular study of the church's missional response to a changing world from a biblical and theological perspective, by Bishop Biörn Fjärstedt of the Church of Sweden.

GW244 Fletcher, Jesse C.
The Mission of the Church: Layman's Library of Christian Doctrine. (Layman's Library of Christian Doctrine, 14). Nashville, TNU: Broadman, 1988. 139 pp. 0805416447.

A popular theology of mission for laity; the fourteenth volume of sixteen on the major doctrines of Christian faith.

GW245 Galilea, Segundo
Los Ciegos Véran: La mística misionera en los relatos evangélicos. (Colección Iglesia Nueva, 66). Bogotá, CK: Indo-American Press Service, 1982. 58 pp. Paper. No ISBN.

Reflections on the meaning of mission.

GW246 Gijsen, J. M.
Missie is: de harten openen voor God: Het Rijk Gods is nabij; bekeert u en gelooft; gaat uit en verkondigt het evangelie. Roermond, NE: Stichting Verkondiging van het bisdom Roermond, 1982. 59 pp. Paper. 9065160132.

Two lectures read during courses of faith education in his diocese, in which Dr. J. M. Gijsen, then bishop of Roermond (now of Iceland), explains what mission should be; namely, the opening up of hearts for God.

GW247 Greenway, Roger S., John E. Kyle, and Donald Anderson McGavran

Missions Now: This Generation. Grand Rapids, MIU: Baker Books, 1990. 126 pp. Paper. 0801038383.

A primer for young people, on God's plan, the church's response, and the contribution of youth in world mission in the 1990s.

GW248 Grubb, Richard

Global God: Subduing the Earth with His Glory. Shippensburg, PAU: Destiny Image, 1990. 126 pp. Paper. 1560430273.

A popular challenge to evangelical Christians to "subdue the earth with the Gospel of the Kingdom of God."

GW249 Horton, Wade Henry

Unto the Uttermost. Cleveland, TNU: Pathway Press, 1973. 279 pp. No ISBN.

Sermons, missionary stories and biographies, statistics, mission travelogues, and personal experiences of a former Church of God missions executive and general overseer, including a number of biographical sketches of early Pentecostal missionaries.

GW250 John Paul II, Pope

The Pope Answers: Pope John Paul II's Encyclical "The Mission of Christ the Redeemer." Edited by Juliette Baker. Middlegreen, ENK: St. Paul Publications, 1992. 71 pp. Paper. 0854394052.

A popular presentation for Catholic study groups of the main themes of Pope John II's encyclical *Redemptoris Mission (The Mission of Christ the Redeemer*, 1990).

GW251 Johnson, E. H.

For a Time Like This: Studies for Salvation Today and Mission Today. New York, NYU: Friendship Press, 1973. 128 pp. Paper. 0377030015.

A popular introduction to mission themes (salvation, justice, poverty) designed to motivate individuals and congregations to greater mission involvement.

GW252 King, Philip

Good News for a Suffering World. Crownborough, ENK: Monarch Publications, 1996. 190 pp. Paper. 1854242776.

Helps for local church leaders on basic concepts in mission and evangelism, including the relation of evangelism to social action, healing, culture, and the church and other faiths, by the Secretary of Church of England's Board of Mission.

GW253 Kraus, C. Norman

An Intrusive Gospel?: Christian Mission in the Postmodern World. Downers Grove, ILU: InterVarsity, 1998. 141 pp. Paper. 0830815465.

Short essays on intervention as the contemporary goal of mission, based on the author's lecture-discussions with the staff of the Mennonite Central Committee in 1994.

GW254 Land, Sipke van der

Was für eine Welt: Eindrücke einer Weltreise um die Erde. Konstanz, GW: Christliche Verlagsanstalt, 1977. 157 pp. 3767321300.

What a World is the author's impression, from visits on six continents, to creative mission projects and leaders.

GW255 Oosterhouse, Kenneth

Born of a Glorious Thunder: Real Life Accounts of Foreign Christian Work. Highland, INU: West Indies Publishing, 1986. 302 pp. Paper. No ISBN.

Five popular accounts by Christian Reformed Church missionary families, of their adventures in New Guinea, Dominica, Haiti, Bangladesh, and Argentina.

GW256 Seamands, John T.

Harvest of Humanity. Wheaton, ILU: Victor Books, 1988. 213 pp. Paper. 0896934284.

A popular study guide discussing contemporary mission issues, environmental forces, and new movements shaping mission philosophy and strategy.

GW257 Starkes, M. Thomas

The Foundations for Missions. Nashville, TNU: Broadman, 1981. 192 pp. Paper. 0805463259.

A devotional guide from the Baptist perspective, which presents a plan or a view of mission as the redemption of humankind.

GW258 Sumrall, Lester, and Stephen J. Conn

Run with the Vision. South Bend, INU: LeSea Publishing, 1990. 185 pp. Paper. 0882702610.

An update of the 1986 edition of reflections on motivations to mission, based on sixty years of travel to more than 100 nations; by the founders of LeSEA (Lester Sumrall Evangelistic Association) and LeSEA Broadcasting, a world Christian radio and TV ministry.

GW259 Wagner, C. Peter

Stop the World, I Want to Get On. Glendale, CAU: Regal Books, 1975. iii, 136 pp. Paper. 0830702725 (hdbk), 0830702717 (pbk).

A popular introduction to contemporary issues of world mission, encouraging young people to make a missionary commitment; by the associate professor at the School of World Mission at Fuller Theological Seminary.

GW260 Walker, Alan

A Ringing Call to Mission. New York, NYU: Abingdon, 1966. 127 pp. No ISBN.

A call to mission as a servant church, offering both personal and social salvation; by the superintendent of the creative Central Methodist Mission in Sydney, Australia.

GW261 Wells, Tom

A Vision for Missions. Edinburgh, ENK: Banner of Truth Trust, 1985. 157 pp. Paper. 0851514332.

A popular primer on the inspiration for missions, including the 18th- and 19th-century examples of Brainerd, Carey, and Martyn.

GW262 Wilson, J. Christy

"More to Be Desired Than Gold": A Collection of True Stories as Told by J. Christy Wilson, Jr. Compiled by Ivan S. Chow. Edited by Helen S. Mooradkanian. South Hamilton, MAU: Gordon-Conwell Theological Seminary, 1994. viii, 179 pp. Paper. 0964091003.

Second edition of a collection of the real-life experiences of Christians in mission, including Afghanistan, where the author, professor emeritus of Evangelization at Gordon-Conwell Theological Seminary, served as a tentmaking missionary (1951-1974).

GW263 Yohannan, K. P.
The Coming Revolution in World Missions. Altamonte Springs, FLU: Creation House, 1986. 205 pp. Paper. 0884191958.

A popular presentation of the vision, call, and way of global missions by the President of Gospel for Asia.

Study and Teaching

See also GW128, GW154, GW191, GW226-GW227, HI566, HI701, TH89, EA209, ME239, SO27-SO28, SO73, EC65, EV215, CH438, AF816, and EU285.

GW264 *Antropología y Teología Misioneras*
Bogotá, CK: Ediciones Paulinas, 1975. 208 pp. Paper. No ISBN.

A textbook of theological anthropology and missiology developed by CELAM's Department of Missions at its course for active missionaries in Latin America (Caracas, Venezuela, 23 July-17 August 1974).

GW265 Becker, Dieter, and Andreas Feldtkeller, eds.
Es begann in Halle. . .: Missionswissenschaft von Gustav Warneck bis heute. (Missionswissenschaftliche Forschungen, 5). Erlangen, GW: Ev.-Luth. Mission, 1997. 208 pp. Paper. 3872143352.

These twelve significant essays from the 1996 Gustav Warneck-Symposium (Halle University), address the significance and impact of missiologist Warneck (1834-1910), in the development of mission theory and practice.

GW266 Borgenvik, Johannes, and Erik Larsen, eds.
I hellig oppdrag: festskrift ved Misjonshøgskolens 140-srsjubileum og innvielse av Fakultetsbygget. Stavanger, NO: Misjonshøgskolen forlag, 1983. 149 pp. 8272190354.

Essays written to commemorate the 140th anniversary of the School of Mission and Theology.

GW267 Bowen, Roger
"... So I Send You": A Study Guide to Mission. (SPCK International Study Guide, 34). London, ENK: SPCK, 1996. xiii, 248 pp. Paper. 0281049394.

This basic textbook on Christian mission for international use covers biblical foundations, issues of mission and culture, and movements in mission today, with helps in each chapter for related Bible study and contextual application.

GW268 Conn, Harvie M., and Samuel F. Rowen, eds.
Missions and Theological Education in World Perspective. Farmington, MIU: Associates of Urbanus, 1984. xli, 432 pp. Paper. 0930957008.

An important collection of twenty-five essays on the teaching of missions and evangelism, particularly in Third World churches.

GW269 Evans, Alice Frazer, Robert A. Evans, and David A. Roozen, eds.
The Globalization of Theological Education. Maryknoll, NYU: Orbis Books, 1993. xvii, 366 pp. Paper. 0883449188.

A basic resource on the major new emphasis in North American theological education in the 1990s, with essays, case studies, and commentaries on twelve subthemes by an international panel of thirty-nine theological educators.

GW270 Gensichen, Hans-Werner
Invitatio ad Fraternitatem: 75 Jahre Deutsche Gesellschaft für Missionswissenschaft (1918-1993). (Beiträge zur Missionswissenschaft und interkulturellen Theologie, 1). Munich, GW: Lit, 1993. 129 pp. Paper. 3894737735.

A brief history of the German Protestant missiological association and its endeavor to develop a science of mission studies.

GW271 Glazik, Josef, ed.
50 (Fünfzig) Jahre katholische Missionswissenschaft in Münster: 1911-1961; Festschrift. (Missionswissenschaftliche Abhandlungen und Texte, 26). Münster, GW: Aschendorff, 1961. 211 pp. No ISBN.

The first part of the book deals with the first fifty years of the chair of missiology in Münster, the "Internationales Institut für Missionswissenschaftliche Forschungen" and "Zeitschrift für Missionswissenschaft und Religionswissenschaft"; the second part contains eleven scholarly contributions on different topics.

GW272 Jongeneel, J. A. B.
Philosophy, Science, and Theology of Mission in the 19th and 20th Centuries: A Missiological Encyclopedia. (Studies in the Intercultural History of Christianity, 92, 106). Frankfurt am Main, GW: Lang, 1997. 2 vols. 3631483120 (pt. 1), 3631483139 (pt. 2,GW), 0820432997 (pt. 2,US).

A major attempt to define missiology as an academic discipline, based on a decade of curricular developments at Utrecht University; with definitions, brief histories, and bibliographies for each branch of missiology. [Part 1: *The Philosophy and Science of Mission*, 1995, xxiii, 403 pp.; Part 2: *Missionary Theology*, 1997, xxii, 428 pp.]

GW273 Lee, Ignatius Ting Pong
Facultates missionariae disciplinae vigenti accommodatae. (Institutum Iuridicum Claretianum). Rome, IT: Commentarium pro Religiosis, 1976. xv, 423 pp. No ISBN.

The instructions of the Propaganda Fide concerning required content for the training of Roman Catholic missionaries.

GW274 Lindgren, Juhani
Unity of All Christians in Love and Mission: The Ecumenical Method of Kenneth Scott Latourette. (Annales Academiae Scientiarum Fennicae; Dissertationes Humanarum Litterarum, 54). Helsinki, FI: Suomalainen Tiedeakatemia, 1990. 401 pp. Paper. 9514106180.

A scholarly study of the contribution to ecumenics, missiology, and a global understanding of world Christian history by Latourette (1884-1968), the preeminent Yale University historian and ecumenist.

GW275 Müller, Karl
Friedrich Schwager (1876-1929): Pionier katholischer Missionswissenschaft. (Studia Instituti Missiologici SVD, 34). Nettetal, GW: Steyler Verlag, 1984. 207 pp. Paper. 3877871801.

A scholarly biography of F. Schwager, one of the pioneers of Catholic missiology, who made a noteworthy contribution to the missionary movement in Germany in the first decades of this century and who, toward the end of his life, became a Protestant.

GW276 Müller, Karl
Josef Schmidlin (1876-1944): Papsthistoriker und Begründer der katholischen Missionswissenschaft. (Studia Instituti Missiologici SVD, 47). Nettetal, GW: Steyler Verlag, 1989. 441 pp. Paper. 3805002467.

A scholarly biography of J. Schmidlin, holder of the first Catholic chair of missiology, who had a decisive influence on missions and missiology in Germany and beyond, and achieved an enduring reputation through a number of fundamental publications.

GW277 Martin, Alvin, ed.

The Means of World Evangelization: Missiological Education at the Fuller School of World Mission. South Pasadena, CAU: William Carey Library, 1974. xix, 518 pp. Paper. 0878081437.

A handbook that describes missiology through the examination of course descriptions, research and writing objectives, and the dynamic interaction between intimately related situations facing missionaries and national church leaders, as they seek to advance the Christian movement throughout the world.

GW278 Martin, Earl R.

Passport to Servanthood. Nashville, TNU: Broadman, 1988. 190 pp. Paper. 0805472320.

A popular account of the influence and missionary involvement of the former professor of missions at Southwestern Baptist Theological Seminary, Thomas Buford Maston.

GW279 Mulders, Alphonsus

Missiologisch Bestek: Inleiding tot de katholieke missiewetenschap. (Bijdragen van het Missiologisch Instituut der R. K. Universiteit te Nijmegen, 6). Hilversum, NE: Paul Brand, 1962. xxi, 453 pp. No ISBN.

A systematic introduction and scientific exposition of Roman Catholic missiology by the esteemed professor of missiology at the Catholic University of Nijmegen, The Netherlands.

GW280 Myklebust, Olav Guttorm

Misjonskunnskap: en innføring. Oslo, NO: Gyldendal, 1976. 359 pp. 8205086893.

A comprehensive and learned textbook on missiology for theological students.

GW281 Neely, Alan

Christian Mission: A Case Study Approach. (American Society of Missiology Series, 21). Maryknoll, NYU: Orbis Books, 1995. xx, 295 pp. Paper. 0570750084.

Eighteen case studies to be used in teaching current issues in Christian mission by the Henry Luce Professor of Mission and Ecumenism at Princeton Theological Seminary.

GW282 Ritschl, Dietrich, and Werner Ustorf

Ökumenische Theologie. Missionswissenschaft. (Grundkurs Theologie, 10.2; Urban-Taschenbücher, 430.2). Stuttgart, GW: Verlag W. Kohlhammer, 1994. 144 pp. Paper. 3170115642.

A basic introduction to ecumenical theology by the professor of dogmatics and ecumenical theology at the University of Heidelberg in Germany, and to the discipline of missiology by the professor of missiology at the University of Birmingham in England.

GW283 Rivinius, Karl Josef

Errichtung des Lehrstuhls fur Missionswissenschaft in de Ludwig-Maximilians-Universitat München. Immensee, SZ: *NZM*, 1985. 66 pp. Paper. 3858240656.

The history of the establishment of a chair of missions-science at the Ludwig-Maximilians University, Munich, Germany.

GW284 Roozen, David A., Alice Frazer Evans, and Robert A. Evans

Changing the Way Seminaries Teach: Globalization and Theological Education. Hartford, CTU: Hartford Seminary, Center for Social and Religious Research; Simsbury, CTU: Plowshares Institute, 1996. iv, 206 pp. Paper. No ISBN.

A comprehensive report on how twelve diverse North American seminaries worked for five years to embody globalization in their curricular and institutional practices.

GW285 Shenk, Wilbert R.

The American Society of Missiology, 1972-87. Elkhart, INU: American Society of Missiology, 1987. 47 pp. Paper. No ISBN.

Brief history of the founding and first fifteen years of the ASM by its secretary-treasurer.

GW286 Stewart, Marjorie

Training in Mission: St. Colm's College Church of Scotland. Edinburgh, STK: St. Andrew Press, 1973. v, 138 pp. 0715202197.

A history of the Training College of the Church of Scotland for missionaries, 1894 to 1972.

GW287 Verkuyl, Johannes

Gedenken en verwachten: memoires. Kampen, NE: Kok, 1983. 348 pp. 9024225833.

Memoirs of the prominent Dutch missiologist (born 1908), with many detailed descriptions of church life and leaders in Indonesia, as well as the internal affairs of the (Protestant) Dutch Missionary Council.

GW288 Verstraelen, F. J.

Missiologie onderweg: een auto-bibliografie in kontekst. (IIMO Research Pamphlet, 2). Leiden, SZ: IIMO, 1980. vi, 112 pp. No ISBN.

A study of missiology based on European studies, field experience and studies in Ghana and Zambia, and analytical research undertaken in the Netherlands based on African field research.

GW289 Woodberry, John Dudley, Charles Edward van Engen, and Edgar J. Elliston, eds.

Missiological Education for the Twenty-First Century: The Book, the Circle, and the Sandals. (American Society of Missiology Series, 23). Maryknoll, NYU: Orbis Books, 1996. xxv, 310 pp. Paper. 1570750890.

Twenty-one essays by prominent world missiologists, on the past, present, and future of mission studies in confessional, regional, and interdisciplinary perspectives.

MISSIONS: HISTORY

Dana Robert, Subeditor

The history of mission is "the oldest branch of empirical mission studies" (Jongeneel, 1995:219). Many departments of mission studies have been placed under Church History in the curricula of universities and theological seminaries.

Kenneth Scott Latourette (1884-1968) was the first historian of mission to write the history of Christianity from a global perspective with cross-cultural sensitivity (1978). In a major essay on mission historiography, Mark Noll acknowledged the contributions of Western missiologists to the rewriting of world Christian history (1996:47-64). Third World church historians, with major collaborative projects in Latin America and India, have interpreted Christian missions from the perspectives of the indigenous church. These are building blocks for the writing of "a genuinely global history" (Noll, 1996:50). Jongeneel (1995:229-257) contains both an expanded mission historiography and citations of earlier pre-1960 works.

Works on mission history by country or continent have been placed within geographical chapters. Subsections on "history" are to be found also in chapters on Ecumenical Aspects, Education, Evangelism, and Church Renewal.

This chapter opens with resources for the study of the history of mission (bibliographies, reference works, documentation and archives, conferences and congresses). Many works listed in the corresponding subsections under "General Works" contain materials on mission history.

Next can be found general works on mission history, followed by groupings under periods of church history from the early church to the twentieth century. See Jongeneel (1995:229-236) for a helpful listing of the older histories. The rest of the chapter is organized by the major divisions of Christianity: Orthodoxy, Roman Catholicism, and Protestantism.

Students of the mission of Orthodox churches, both Eastern and Oriental, will begin with works in the next section. They will find additional resources under the history sections, by continent and in certain geographical areas (Eastern Europe, Middle East, etc.).

The history of Roman Catholic mission is well documented. Many archival sources have been published during the 1960 to 2000 period. Often they are to be found under specific geographical areas. The abundant "see also" citations under "Roman Catholic: General" will guide the reader to their locations in the bibliography. A short section on books concerning the Vatican's involvement in missions is followed by works on the various Catholic orders. They are grouped by men's and women's orders. Biographies of the founders of orders will be found here. The "see also" citations under each order are designed to guide the researcher to biographies of individual missionaries normally placed under the country of service.

The final divisions contain a listing of works on Protestant mission societies, in alphabetical order. Note that various confessional traditions have their own listings (Anglican, Lutheran, Pentecostal, Reformed, etc.) for histories not readily classified under particular mission societies.

Norman E. Thomas

Bibliographies

See also GW4 and GW12.

HI1 *Archivis et Biblothecis Missionibus atque Scientiae Missionum Inservientibus*

Rome, IT: Pontifical University Urbaniana, 1968. 612 pp. No ISBN.

Bibliographic sourcebook on Catholic missions and missionary archives, with twenty-seven scholarly essays in five languages.

HI2 Aulo, Thea

Suomenkielinen lähetyskirjallisuus 1800-luvulla. (Suomen lähetystieteellisen seuran julkaisuja, 11). Helsinki, FI: Suomen lähetystieteellinen seura, 1965. 120 pp. Paper. No ISBN.

A bibliography of the Finnish missionary literature in the 19th century.

HI3 Bangert, William V.
A Bibliographical Essay on the History of the Society of Jesus: Books in English. (Series IV: Study Aids on Jesuit Topics, 6). St. Louis, MOU: Institute of Jesuit Sources, 1976. xiv, 75 pp. Paper. 0912422165.

An annotated bibliography on Jesuit history organized primarily by geographical regions, with index of authors and names.

HI4 Brackney, William H.
Christian Voluntarism in Britain and North America: A Bibliography and Critical Assessment. (Bibliographies and Indexes in Religious Studies, 35). Westport, CTU: Greenwood, 1995. xiv, 306 pp. 0313284210.

An annotated bibliography of 981 books and periodical articles on the history of voluntary societies in Great Britain and the United States in the 19th and 20th centuries, including missionary societies.

Serials and Periodicals

See also TH4.

HI5 Atkinson, Ernest Edwin
A Selected Bibliography of Hispanic Baptist History. (Southern Baptist Convention). Nashville, TNU: Historical Commission, SBC, 1981. xiii, 88 pp. 0939804115.

Identifies works on Baptists, focusing on Southern Baptists, in Spanish-speaking Latin America, Spain, and the United States.

HI6 Polgár, Láslo
Bibliography of the History of the Society of Jesus. (Sources and Studies for the History of the Jesuits, 1). Rome, IT: Jesuit Historical Institute; St. Louis, MOU: St. Louis University, 1967. 207 pp. No ISBN.

A useful selection of items from a vast body of literature, arranged in chronological order with index.

HI7 Wares, Alan C., comp.
Bibliography of the Summer Institute of Linguistics: 1935-1975—volume 2: 1976-1982—supplement. Dallas, TX: SIL, 1979. xxvii, 649 pp. Paper. 0883129132 (vol. 1), 0883129140 (vol. 2), 0883129159 (vol. 3).

Three volumes of bibliographic information for books and articles published by the Summer Institute of Linguistics [Vol. 1, 1935-1975, xxvi, 317 pp.; vol. 2, 1976-1983, xx, 232 pp.; vol. 3, supplement, to December 1985, 100 pp.].

Reference Works

See also GW40, GW48, GW53, GW56, GW59-GW60, HI388, AF38, AM965, and AS1023.

HI8 Barrett, David B.
Cosmos, Chaos, and Gospel: A Chronology of World Evangelization from Creation to New Creation. (A.D. 2000 Series). Birmingham, ALU: New Hope, 1987. 105 pp. Paper. 093662518X.

A detailed chronology of 5,000 significant events in Christian history for the mission and expansion of the church, with statistical tables, an assessment of the status of Christianity in 1988, and a projection concerning the future of world evangelization in ten eras to come.

HI9 Burgess, Stanley M., Gary B. McGee, and Patrick H. Alexander, eds.
Dictionary of Pentecostal and Charismatic Movements. Grand Rapids, MIU: Zondervan, 1988. 911 pp. 0310441005.

A comprehensive dictionary with sixty-five contributors representing a variety of denominations, reflecting upon the spectrum of pentecostal and charismatic movements in North America and Europe.

HI10 Cross, F. L., and E. A. Livingstone, eds.
The Oxford Dictionary of the Christian Church. Oxford, ENK: Oxford University Press, 1997. xxxvii, 1,786 pp. 019211655X.

The contributions by 480 scholars in this standard reference work include brief articles and bibliographies on Christianity in each country, and on Western missionaries and missions; revised third edition.

HI11 Du Bose, Francis M., ed.
Classics of Christian Missions. Nashville, TNU: Broadman, 1979. 462 pp. 0805463135.

A single-volume introduction to literature from all periods of Christian mission history, including excerpts from histories, biographies, journals, letters, sermons, and conferences; each selection is prefaced by a valuable introduction.

HI12 Freitag, Anton
The Universal Atlas of the Christian World: The Expansion of Christianity through the Centuries. London, ENK: Burns & Oates, 1963. xi, 200 pp. No ISBN.

Translation of *Atlas du Monde Crétien* (1959), a historical atlas of the missionary work of the Catholic Church from the beginnings to 1960.

HI13 Ohm, Thomas
Wichtige Daten der Missionsgeschichte: Eine Zeittafel. (Veröffentlichungen des Instituts für Missionswissenschaft Münster, 4). Münster, GW: Aschendorff, 1961. 290 pp. No ISBN.

A very helpful chronological table of mission history with an emphasis on Catholic missions.

Documentation and Archives

See also GW72, HI1, HI41, HI186, HI510, and CR1011.

HI14 Amistad Research Center
Author and Added Entry Catalogue of the American Missionary Association Archives. Westport, CTU: Greenwood, 1970. 3 vols. 0837136024.

Archival resources for the major Protestant home mission organization of the 19th century, including mission to African Americans.

HI15 Bickers, Robert A., and Rosemary Seton, eds.
Missionary Encounters: Sources and Issues. Richmond, ENK: Curzon Press, 1996. vi, 255 pp. 0700703691 (hdbk), 0700703705 (pbk).

A collection of papers from a broad spectrum of disciplines, most having been presented at the workshop on missionary archives held at the University of London's School of Oriental and African Studies (July 1992), exploring questions concerning the variety of work that can be undertaken using mission resources.

HI16 Evangelische Missionsgesellschaft, Basel
Basel Mission Archive: Catalogue of the Printed Collection (Archiv-Bücherei). Basel, SZ: Die Gesellschaft, 1974. No ISBN.

Catalogue of a major mission archive.

HI17 Forman, Charles W., ed.
Christianity in the Non-Western World. Englewood Cliffs, NJU: Prentice-Hall, 1967. viii, 146 pp. 0836918061.

A sourcebook with interpretive introductions on the Christian encounter with Asia, the South Pacific, and Africa from the 16th to the mid-20th century.

HI18 Heuser, Frederick J.
A Guide to Foreign Missionary Manuscripts in the Presbyterian Historical Society. (Bibliographies and Indexes in World History, 11). New York, NYU: Greenwood/Presbyterian Historical Society, 1988. xxv, 108 pp. 0313262497.

An overview, organized by country of service, of foreign missionary manuscripts and archival collections acquired and processed through 1986.

HI19 Schurhammer, Georg
Varia. (Bibliotheca Instituti Historici Societatis Iesu, 23). Rome, IT: Institutum Historicum Societatis Iesu; Lisbon, PO: Centro de Estudos Históricos Ultramarinos, 1965. xxiii, 1055 pp. No ISBN.

Various documents related to Xavierian studies, including essays on oriental history and the history of missions, and book reviews and indexes (4 vols. in 2. Vol. IV/1 *Anhänge*; IV/2 *Besprechungen und Index*).

HI20 Shuster, Robert D., James Stambaugh, and Ferne Weimer, comps.
Researching Modern Evangelicalism: A Guide to the Holdings of the Billy Graham Center, with Information on Other Collections. (Bibliographies and Indexes in Religious Studies, 16). New York, NYU: Greenwood, 1990. xv, 353 pp. 0313264783.

Bibliographic guide to a collection that contains major holdings on Africa Inland Mission, Woman's Union Missionary Society, China Inland Mission, and other nondenominational missions.

Conferences and Congresses

See also GW85, HI509, HI598, and HI688.

HI21 Beaver, Robert Pierce, ed.
American Missions in Bicentennial Perspective. South Pasadena, CAU: William Carey Library, 1977. viii, 438 pp. Paper. 0878081534.

A collection of papers concerning the history and influence of 200 years of American missions; presented at the 1976 annual meeting of the American Society of Missiology.

HI22 Cuming, G. J., ed.
The Mission of the Church and the Propagation of the Faith: Papers Read at the Seventh Summer Meeting and the Eighth Winter Meeting of the Ecclesiastical History Society. (Studies in Church History, 6). Cambridge, ENK: Cambridge University Press, 1970. viii, 170 pp. 521077524 (SBN).

A collection of eleven papers relating to missions, from the early church to the 19th century.

HI23 Société d'histoire ecclésiastique de la France et le concours de la Société d'histoire du protestantisme français
Les Réveils missionnaires en France du Moyen-Âge à nos jours (XIIe-XXe siècles): actes du Colloque de Lyon, 29-31 mai 1980. Paris, FR: Beauchesne, 1984. 423 pp. 2701011019.

Papers from an important conference surveying eight centuries of French contributions to missionary awakenings.

HI24 Vischer, Lukas, ed.
Towards a History of the Church in the Third World: The Issue of Periodisation. (Veröffentlichung, 3). Bern, SZ: Evangelische Arbeitsstelle Ökumene Schweiz, 1985. 135 pp. Paper. No ISBN.

Papers and report of a consultation on the issue of periodization (Geneva, Switzerland, 17-21 July 1983) sponsored by the Working Commission on Church History of EATWOT.

General Works

See also GW216-GW217, TH72, ME108, SO36, SO436, SO484, PO149, CO136, MI34-MI35, MI163, MI166, AF1196, AM84, AM115, AS906, AS950, AS1011, AS1044, and EU135.

HI25 Albertson, Clinton, ed.
Anglo-Saxon Saints and Heroes. Bronx, NYU: Fordham University Press, 1967. xv, 347 pp. No ISBN.

A collection of medieval hagiography, including biographies of the missionaries Wilfred, Willibrord, and Boniface.

HI26 Berg, J. van den, and F. G.M. Broeyer
Geschiedenis der Kerk, IX and De jongste tijd: De jonge kerken op het zendingsveld. Edited by G. P. van Itterzon, and D. Nauta. Kampen, NE: Kok, 1967. 197 pp. Paper. No ISBN.

A combined publication of revised editions of two earlier works—that of Van den Berg (*Geschiedenis der Kerk*), updating the late Professor J. H. Bavinck's general church history dealing with churches in the former mission fields, and that of Broeyers (*De Jongsts Tijd*) on the church history of other countries in recent times; both originally published by Kok in 1946.

HI27 Birtwhistle, Norman Allen
They Who Will Hear. London, ENK: Epworth Press, 1961. xiii, 177 pp. No ISBN.

A discursive history of Christian missions, from New Testament times to the 20th century, with emphasis on the relationship of Christianity and culture.

HI28 Christensen, Torben, and Sven Góransson
Kyrkohistoria. (Scandinavian University Books). Stockholm, SW: Läromedelsförlaget; (Svenska bokförlaget), 1976. 814 pp. 9124256675.

A mammoth general church history, presented in three volumes and produced by the professors of church history at Copenhagen and Uppsala, which balances Third and First World history, and includes substantial chapters on the missionary movement and ecumenical developments (Vol. 1, *Era evangelium til den pavelige gudsstat*, by Torben Christensen; vol. 2, *Från pavens gudsstat till religionsfriheten*, by Sven Góransson; vol. 3, *Från västerns religion till världsreligion*).

HI29 Clouse, Robert G., Richard V. Pierard, and Edwin M. Yamauchi
Two Kingdoms: The Church and Culture through the Ages. Chicago, ILU: Moody, 1993. 672 pp. 0802485901.

A global history of the Christian church, from Pentecost to the present, focusing on the influence of the church on culture and the impact of society on the church; with numerous references to Christian missions.

HI30 Comby, Jean
Deux mille ans d'évangélisation: histoire de l'expansion chrétienne. (Bibliothèque d'histoire du Christianisme, 29). Paris, FR: Desclée, 1992. 327 pp. 2718905867.

A narrative history of missions from a Roman Catholic perspective with brief passages from representative source documents.

HI31 Comby, Jean
How to Understand the History of Christian Mission. Translated by John Bowden. London, ENK: SCM Press; New York, NYU: Continuum, 1996. xiv, 178 pp. Paper. 0334026156 (UK), 0826409091 (US).

English translation.

HI32 Comby, Jean
Para comprender dos mil ños de evangelización: Historia de la expansión cristiana. Translated by Alfonso Ortiz García. Estella, SP: Verbo Divino, 1994. 234 pp. Paper. 8471518988.

Spanish translation.

HI33 Cook, Harold R.
Highlights of Christian Missions: A History and Survey. Chicago, ILU: Moody, 1967. 256 pp. No ISBN.

A textbook for an introductory survey of Christian missions by a Moody Bible Institute professor.

HI34 Davison, Leslie
Sender and Sent: A Study in Mission. London, ENK: Epworth Press, 1969. 236 pp. Paper. 0716201224.

Exploration of the biblical understanding of mission, tracing mission history from the early church through the 20th century.

HI35 Fahlbusch, Erwin et al., eds.
The Encyclopedia of Christianity: Volume 1 (A-D). Translated by Geoffrey W. Bromiley. Grand Rapids, MIU: Eerdmans; Leiden, NE: E. J. Brill, 1999. xxxviii, 893 pp. 0802824137 (US), 9004113169 (NE).

English translation.

HI36 Fahlbusch, Erwin, ed.
Evangelisches Kirchenlexikon: internationale theologische Enzyklopädie. Göttingen, GW: Vandenhoeck & Ruprecht, 1986-. 5 vols. 3525501285 (v.1).

This international work, with articles written by scholars from various countries and cultural backgrounds, includes separate articles describing the history and current situation of Christian faith in over 170 countries.

HI37 Flachsmeier, Horst R.
Geschichte der evangelischen Weltmission. Giessen, GW: Brunnen-Verlag, 1963. xv, 597 pp. No ISBN.

A popular panegyrical history of Protestant missions, mostly devoted to the mission of pietism, the development of the Protestant missionary societies, and the world missionary conferences.

HI38 Glover, Robert Hall
The Progress of Worldwide Missions. New York, NYU: Harper & Row, 1960. 502 pp. No ISBN.

A summary of the expansion of world missions from the apostolic age to the early 20th century, with an analysis of missionary activity in the Two-Thirds World; revised and enlarged by Herbert Kane.

HI39 González, Justo L.
Historia de las Misiones. (Biblioteca de Estudios Teologics). Buenos Aires, AG: Editorial La Aurora, 1970. 477 pp. No ISBN.

A general history of missions from the New Testament to the present, both Catholic and Protestant.

HI40 Hastings, Adrian, ed.
A World History of Christianity. Grand Rapids, MIU: Eerdmans; London, ENK: Cassell, 1999. xiv, 594 pp. 0802824420.

An introduction to the global and ecumenical scope of Christianity through historical and analytical dimensions, from its beginnings to contemporary expressions in the Western and non-Western world.

HI41 Henkel, Willi, ed.
Ecclesiae Memoria. Rome, IT: Herder, 1991. 495 pp. Paper. No ISBN.

A *festschrift* containing thirty-one scholarly essays by Roman Catholic missiologists honoring Josef Metzler, O.M.I., Prefect of the Secret Vatican Archives and formerly of the Archives of the Propaganda Fide; many based on archival research using those primary sources.

HI42 Kane, J. Herbert
A Concise History of the Christian World Mission: A Panoramic View of Missions from Pentecost to the Present. Grand Rapids, MIU: Baker Books, 1982. 216 pp. 0801053951.

Revised edition of a classic survey of Christian missions from the New Testament to the 20th century, written for introductory courses in missiology; originally published in 1978.

HI43 Kane, J. Herbert
A Global View of Christian Missions: From Pentecost to the Present. Grand Rapids, MIU: Baker Books, 1975. xi, 590 pp. 0801053080.

Revised edition of a general survey of missions to 1800, with country-by-country reports on 19th-century missions.

HI44 Kee, Howard Clark et al.
Christianity: A Social and Cultural History. Upper Saddle River, NJU: Prentice-Hall, 1998. vii, 600 pp. Paper. 0135780713.

The second edition of a history of Christianity as a social-cultural movement, including chapters on the missionary movement and the growth of non-Western Christianity in the 20th century.

HI45 Keyes, Frances Parkinson
Tongues of Fire. New York, NYU: Coward-McCann, 1966. 327 pp. No ISBN.

Anecdotal history of missions primarily from a biographical perspective, emphasizing Catholic missionaries, with a chapter on the history of medical missions.

HI46 Latourette, Kenneth Scott
A History of the Expansion of Christianity. Grand Rapids, MIU: Zondervan, 1978. 7 vols. Paper.

Reprint, in seven volumes, of the most complete mission history, from the beginnings to 1945 update, *The 25 Unbelievable Years, 1945-1969* by Ralph D. Winter [vol. 1: *The First Five Centuries*, xxvi, 412 pp., 0310273617; vol. 2: *The Thousand Years of Uncertainty*, ix, 492 pp., 0310273714; vol. 3: *Three Centuries of Advance*, ix, 503 pp., 0310273811; vol. 4: *The Great Century: Europe and the United States*, viii, 516 pp., 0310273919; vol. 5: *The Great Century: The Americas, Australia, and Africa*, ix, 526 pp., 031027401X; vol. 6: *The Great Century: North Africa and Asia*, ix, 502 pp., 0310274117; vol. 7: *Advance Through Storm*, 570 pp., 0310274214]; originally published by Harper and Brothers (New York, 1937-1945) and Eyre and Spottiswoode (London, 1938-1947).

HI47 Leeuwen, Arend Theodor Van
Christianity in World History: The Meeting of the Faiths of the East and West. Translated by H. H. Hoskins. London, ENK: Edinburgh House Press; New York, NYU: Scribners, 1964. xi, 487 pp. No ISBN.

An imaginative and controversial interpretation of Christianity's history in relation to the biblical faith, the spread of Western culture, the impact of technology, and the meeting of world religions.

HI48 Mathews, Basil Joseph
Forward through the Ages. New York, NYU: Friendship Press, 1960. xii, 276 pp. No ISBN.

Second edition of a popular account of the whole of Christian mission history, with emphasis on the period 1800-1950 and the world scope of mission work; British edition titled *Disciples of All Nations*.

HI49 Mathews, Basil Joseph
En Marcha al traves de las Edades. México, MX: Casa Unida de Publicaciones; Bueno Aires, AG: La Aurora, 1960. 263 pp. No ISBN.

Spanish translation.

HI50 McManners, John, ed.
The Oxford History of Christianity. Oxford, ENK: Oxford University Press, 1993. viii, 770 pp. Paper. 0192852914.

A reprint of the text of *The Oxford Illustrated History of Christianity* (1990) which gives considerable treatment of Christianity since 1800 in a worldwide context.

HI51 Neill, Stephen Charles
Geschichte der christlichen Missionen. Edited by Niels Peter Moritzen. (Erlanger Taschenbücher, 14). Erlangen, GW: Ev.-Luth. Mission, 1974. 416 pp. Paper. 3872142283.

German translation and adaptation of *A History of Christian Missions* (1968).

HI52 Neill, Stephen Charles
A History of Christian Missions. (History of the Church, 6). London, ENK: Penguin Books, 1986. 528 pp. Paper. No ISBN.

Revised second edition by Owen Chadwick of a now-classic historical survey of the worldwide expansion of Christianity, including Catholic, Protestant, and Orthodox achievements; originally published in 1964.

HI53 Neill, Stephen Charles
Misjon i 2000 sr. Translated by Odd Kval Pedersen. Stavanger, NO: Nomi Förlag, 1972. 523 pp. 8250100409.

Norwegian translation.

HI54 Ohm, Thomas
Les Principaux faits de l'histoire des missions. (Historie de missions, 1). Tourai, FR: Casterman, 1961. 162 pp. No ISBN.

A detailed chronology of the history of missions; translation of *Wichtige Daten der Missionsgeschichte* (Münster: Aschendorff Verlagsbuchhandlung, 1961).

HI55 Rosenkranz, Gerhard
Die christliche Mission: Geschichte und Theologie. Munich, GW: Kaiser, 1977. 513 pp. 3459011068.

A "summa" of the scholarly work of this prominent Protestant missiologist, who follows "the way of mission" through history, and critically examines its biblical legitimacy.

HI56 Roux, André
Missions des églises, mission de l'Église: histoire d'une longue marche. ("Rencontres," 35). Paris, FR: Éditions du Cerf, 1984. 341 pp. 2204021644.

A general mission history emphasizing the shift from missions as a one-way sending to other continents, to the whole church as a community in mission.

HI57 Schlunk, Martin
Kristillisen lähetystyön historia. Translated by Matti Peltola. Helsinki, FI: Suomen Lähetysseura, 1973. 398 pp. 9516241212 (hdbk), 9516241204 (pbk).

Finnish translation of *Die Welt Mission der Kirche Christi* (Stuttgart, 1951), a general history of Christian missions.

HI58 Spickard, Paul R., and Kevin M. Cragg
God's Peoples: A Social History of Christians. Grand Rapids, MIU: Baker Books, 1994. 486 pp. 0801025850.

A narrative illustrated history of Christians from the 1st to the 20th century, focusing on key leaders on six continents, including both missionaries and Two-Thirds World church leaders.

HI59 Starkes, M. Thomas
God's Commissioned People: A Fresh History of Christian Missions. Nashville, TNU: Broadman, 1984. 380 pp. Paper. 0805463380.

General introduction to the whole of missions history, emphasizing modern missions beginning with William Carey.

HI60 Steuernagel, Valdir
Obediência misionera y práctica histórica. Grand Rapids, MIU: Eerdmans, 1996. 190 pp. Paper. 080280943X.

A Brazilian missiologist, following an analysis of the challenge of contextualization in Latin American mission, presents five historical approaches from Julian and St. Francis to Zinzendorf, Gustaf Warnek, and Walter Freytag; originally published in Portuguese in 1993 (ABU Editora S/C, Sao Paulo, Brazil).

HI61 Syrdal, Rolf A.
To the End of the Earth: Mission Concept in Principle and Practice. Minneapolis, MNU: Augsburg, 1967. xi, 177 pp. No ISBN.

A discussion of the nature of mission as found in the Bible, which traces the progress of missions through various periods of history, covering the objectives, methods, and procedures of missions in the successes and failures of the church.

HI—HISTORY

HI62 Van Dusen, Henry P., ed.
Christianity on the March. New York, NYU: Harper & Row, 1963. xii, 176 pp. No ISBN.
Seven essays on the historic development and spread of Christianity, including sections on the world Christian situation today and on Christianity's principal religious rivals.

HI63 Von Sicard, Harald, and Knut B. Westman
Den kristna missionens historia. Stockholm, SW: Diakonistyrelsens Bokförlag, 1960. 382 pp. No ISBN.
A textbook for theological students on missions history from the early church to modern times.

HI64 Walls, Andrew F.
A History of the Expansion of Christianity Reconsidered: The Legacy of George E. Day. (Yale Divinity School Library Occasional Publication, 8). New Haven, CTU: Yale Divinity School Library, 1996. 35 pp. Paper. No ISBN.
An appraisal of the mission historiography of Kenneth Scott Latourette on the occasion of the 50th anniversary of publication of his monumental seven-volume history of the expansion of Christianity.

HI65 Walls, Andrew F.
The Missionary Movement in Christian History: Studies in the Transmission of Faith. Maryknoll, NYU: Orbis Books; Edinburgh, ENK: T&T Clark, 1996. xix, 266 pp. Paper. 1570750599 (O), 0567085155 (T).
A collection of lectures and articles by the distinguished missiologist, former missionary to Sierra Leone, and professor emeritus of the Study of Christianity in the Non-Western World at the University of Edinburgh.

HI66 Warren, Max Alexander Cunningham
I Believe in the Great Commission. Grand Rapids, MIU: Eerdmans, 1976. 190 pp. Paper. 0802816592.
A realistic appraisal of Christian history, which emphasizes the role that economic, political, and cultural colonialism has had in undermining obedience to the Great Commission.

HI67 Westman, Knut B.
Den Kristna Missionens Historia. Stockholm, SW: Svenska Kyrkans Diakonistyrels es Bokförlag, 1960. 336 pp. No ISBN.
A one-volume textbook on the history of missions, both by historical periods and by country; with a chronology and bibliographic essay but no footnotes.

HI68 Westman, Knut B.
Geschichte der Christlichen Mission. Translated by Harald von Sicard. Munich, GW: Kaiser, 1962. 340 pp. No ISBN.
German translation.

HI69 WSCF
History's Lessons for Tomorrow's Mission: Milestones in the History of Missionary Thinking. Geneva, SZ: WSCF, 1960. 300 pp. Paper. No ISBN.
Collection of essays by prominent missions leaders on the essential historical background for understanding the life and mission of the church, including short annotated bibliographies of books on mission in French, English, and German.

General: Early

See also TH202, TH265, TH349, CR1213, EV229, CH498-CH499, AF271, AF773, AS48, AS949, AS1023, EU45, EU103, and EU217.

HI70 Bormann, Lukas, Kelly Del Tredici, and Angela Standhartinger, eds.
Religious Propaganda and Missionary Competition in the New Testament World: Essays Honoring Dieter Georgi. (Supplements to *Novum Testamentum*, 74). Leiden, NE: Brill, 1994. xiii, 570 pp. 9004100490.
Twenty-five scholarly essays in English and German, on the significance of missionary and propagandistic themes, as well as strategies, in the confrontation of Judaism and Christianity at the beginning of the common era; published as a *festschrift* honoring Professor Dieter Georgi of Harvard University on his 65th birthday.

HI71 Brown, Peter, and Robert Lamont
The Rise of Western Christendom: Triumph and Diversity, A.D. 200-1000. (The Making of Europe). Cambridge, MAU: Blackwell Publishers, 1996. xiii, 353 pp. 1557861366.
This history of Christianity's first centuries includes efforts to extend Christianity in northern Europe and Asia.

HI72 Daniélou, Jean, and Henri Marrou
The Christian Centuries: A New History of the Catholic Church, vol. 1: The First 600 Years. Translated by Vincent Cronin. London, ENK: Darton, Longman, & Todd, 1964. xxx, 522 pp. No ISBN.
The first in a series of five volumes designed for the general reader and non-specialist student, with an extensive bibliography.

HI73 Feldtkeller, Andreas
Identitätssuche des syrischen Urchristentums: Mission, Inkulturation und Pluralität im ältesten Heidenchristentum. (Novum Testamentum et Orbis Antiquus, 25). Freiburg, SZ: Universitätsverlag; Göttingen, GW: Vandenhoeck & Ruprecht, 1993. iv, 266 pp. Paper. 3727808721 (SZ), 3525539274 (GW).
A scholarly analysis of early church missions in Syria, arguing on the basis of biblical and other early sources that the new Christian identity had a plurality of expressions, as Christians engaged a variety of groups and cultural emphases.

HI74 Ferguson, Everett, ed.
Missions and Regional Characteristics of the Early Church. (Studies in Early Christianity, 12). New York, NYU: Garland, 1993. xiv, 367 pp. 0815310722.
A collection of fourteen scholarly essays on the expansion of Christianity into different regions of the ancient world; with an introductory survey by W. H. C. Frend on the "missions of the early church 180-700 AD."

HI75 Foster, John
The First Advance AD 29-500. (Church History, 1; TEF Study Guide, 5). London, ENK: SPCK, 1991. xiv, 186 pp. Paper. 0281045613 (UK).
A revised and updated edition, with additions by W. H. C. Frend, of a basic text on early church history prepared for use in the Two-Thirds World; originally published in 1972.

HI76 Fox, Robin L.
Pagans and Christians. San Francisco, CAU; 1988: Penguin Books; New York, NYU; 1987: Knopf, 1988. 799 pp. Paper. 0140097376 (P), 0394554957 (K).

A history of the early church as it struggled to grow from the 2nd century A.D. to the conversion of Constantine.

HI77 Frohnes, Heinzgünter, Hans-Werner Gensichen, and Georg Kretschmar, eds.
Kirchengeschichte als Missionsgeschichte. Munich, GW: Kaiser, 1974. 2 vols. 3459007729 (vol. 1), 3459011076 (vol. 2).

To date these are the only two parts of a planned multi-volume work about the ancient church ca. 30–600, and the early Middle Ages respectively, concerned with the history of the expansion of Christianity [vol. 1: *Die alte Kirche* (1974); vol. 2: *Die Kirche des früheren Mittelalters*].

HI78 George, K. M.
The Early Church. (Gospel and Cultures Pamphlet, 15). Geneva, SZ: WCC Publications, 1996. 37 pp. Paper. 2825412147.

An interpretive essay on the major encounter between Christian faith and secular culture during the Church's first four centuries, by the Vice Principal of the Orthodox Theological Seminary, Kottayam, Kerala, India.

HI79 Gnilka, Christian
Kultur und Conversion. (Chrêsis: Die Methode der Kirchenväter im Umgang mit der antiken Kultur, 2). Basel, SZ: Schwabe, 1993. 201 pp. 3796509517.

The second of three volumes of lectures dealing with three missiological problems of the early church (change, conversion, and purification) and how the Fathers dealt with them in the culture of their time.

HI80 Goulder, Michael
St. Paul Versus St. Peter: A Tale of Two Missions. Louisville, KYU: Westminster John Knox, 1995. xii, 196 pp. Paper. 0664255612.

An argument that the Apostolic Church was never a single, unified church, but instead two "competing" missions overseen by Peter and Paul; first published by SCM Press in 1994 under the title *A Tale of Two Missions.*

HI81 Harrison, Everett Falconer
The Apostolic Church. Grand Rapids, MIU: Eerdmans, 1985. xii, 251 pp. Paper. 0802800440.

A comprehensive and clearly written survey of the first-century Christian Church, based on evidence in the Book of Acts.

HI82 Hinson, E. Glenn
Evangelization of the Roman Empire: Identity and Adaptability. Macon, GA: Mercer University Press, 1981. x, 332 pp. 0865540144.

A detailed study of the contribution made by early Christianity's major ecclesiastical and theological forms to its work as a missionary people; based on an analysis of documents from 30 to 451 A.D.

HI83 Kasting, Heinrich
Die Anfänge der urchristlichen Mission: Eine historische Untersuchung. (Beiträge zur evangelischen Theologie, 55). Munich, GW: Kaiser, 1969. 158 pp. Paper. No ISBN.

An exegetical study on the beginnings of Jewish and early Christian mission, with special emphasis on the Easter reports, the call of Paul, and the historical importance of the inclusion of converts from the Hellenistic world.

HI84 Kreider, Alan
The Change of Conversion and the Origin of Christendom. (Christian Mission and Modern Culture). Harrisburg, PAU: Trinity Press International, 1999. xviii, 126 pp. Paper. 1563382989.

An examination of conversion in early Christianity—changes in belief, belonging, and behavior—with the argument that Christendom is the product of changes in the understandings and practices of conversion.

HI85 Lymann, Rebecca
Early Christian Tradition. (The New Church's Teaching Series, 6). Cambridge, MAU: Cowley Publications, 1999. xi, 178 pp. Paper. 1561011614.

Beginning with the Jewish, Greek, and Roman cultures at the time of Jesus, the author explores the development of a small group of believers on the margins of Judaism—their theology, worship, leadership, and moral life—and their growth up through the 6th century as the established religion of the Roman Empire.

HI86 MacMullen, Ramsay
Christianity and Paganism in the Fourth to Eighth Centuries. New Haven, CTU: Yale University Press, 1997. vi, 282 pp. 0300071485.

A scholarly analysis of the interchange of influence between paganism and Christianity from the 4th to the 8th century, including both Christian efforts to extripate all religious alternatives, and its inevitable absorption of pagan concepts and practices.

HI87 MacMullen, Ramsay
Christianizing the Roman Empire (A.D. 100-400). New Haven, CTU: Yale University Press, 1984. viii, 183 pp. 0300032161.

A history of the growth of the Church as seen from the outside, during the period when Christianity became dominant in Europe; with an analysis of points of contact between paganism and Christianity, both before and after 312 A.D.

HI88 McNeill, John T.
The Celtic Churches: A History A.D. 200 to 1200. Chicago, ILU: University of Chicago Press, 1974. xiii, 289 pp. 0226560953.

A comprehensive study of Celtic Christianity; a story of individuals, their achievements, and of monks who planted active colonies of religion and culture wherever they went (Britain, Ireland, Brittany).

HI89 Momigliano, Arnaldo, ed.
The Conflict between Paganism and Christianity in the Fourth Century. Oxford, ENK: Clarendon Press, 1963. 222 pp. No ISBN.

Eight scholarly essays on the struggle between paganism and Christianity during the decline of the Roman Empire.

HI90 Stark, Rodney
The Rise of Christianity: A Sociologist Reconsiders History. Princeton, NJU: Princeton University Press, 1996. xiv, 246 pp. 0691027498.

A highly readable account of the growth, social cohesion, and impact of the early church, 40 to 300 A.D., and of the mission to Jews, taking clues from sociological analysis of new religious movements in the present; with many insights for issues of renewal.

HI—HISTORY

HI91 Walsh, Michael
The Triumph of the Meek: Why Early Christianity Succeeded.
San Francisco, CAU: Harper & Row, 1986. 256 pp.
0060692545.

A narrative history of early missionary advance with
emphasis on the social reasons for the success of the Christian
movement.

General: Medieval

See also HI71, HI77, HI88, HI171, HI173, HI245, CR1011,
CR1016, CR1046, CR1120, CR1449, PO26, AS48, AS762, EU42-
EU43, EU66, EU103, EU126, and EU226.

HI92 Addison, James Thayer
*The Medieval Missionary: A Study of the Conversion of North-
ern Europe, A.D. 500-1300.* (Perspectives on European History Series, No.1). Philadelphia, PAU: Porcupine Press, 1976.
xiv, 176 pp. 0879916109.

An analysis of missionary methods and leading figures in
an often neglected period of mission history.

HI93 Angenendt, Arnold
*Kaiserherrschaft und Königstaufe: Kaiser, Könige und Päp-
ste als geistliche Patrone in der abendländischen Missionsgeschichte.* (Arbeiten zur Frühmittelalterforschung, 15). Berlin,
GW: Gruyter, 1984. xiii, 378 pp. 3110098989.

A scholarly history of the role of baptism and patronage
relationships in the missions history of the early Middle Ages.

HI94 Beunamm, Helmut, ed.
*Heidenmission und Kreuzzugsgedanke in der deutschen Ostpoli-
tik der Mittelalters.* (Wege der Forschung, 7). Darmstadt, GW:
Wissenschaftliche Buchgesellschaft, 1963. xii, 485 pp. No ISBN.

Various essays about the German medieval mission in
Eastern Europe, with special emphasis on the part played by
the Teutonic Order.

HI95 Christiansen, Eric
*The Northern Crusades: The Baltic and the Catholic Fron-
tier, 1100-1525.* (New Studies in Medieval History). Minneapolis, MNU: University of Minnesota Press; London, ENK:
Macmillan, 1980. xv, 273 pp. 0333262433 (hdbk, UK,
0333263952 (pbk, UK), 0816609942 (US).

A scholarly history of the crusades of northeastern Europe, from the end of the Viking Age until the early 16th century; with a discussion of the religious and political motivation behind the "northern" crusades.

HI96 Cusack, Carole M.
Conversion among the Germanic Peoples. (Cassell Religious
Studies). London, ENK: Cassell, 1998. x, 214 pp. 0304701556.

A scholarly study of the process of conversion among the
Germanic peoples from the 4th to 11th centuries; revision of
the author's Ph.D. dissertation (University of Sydney, 1995).

HI97 Duckett, Eleanor Shipley
The Wandering Saints of the Early Middle Ages. London,
ENK: Catholic Book Club, 1960. 319 pp. No ISBN.

A history of Celtic wayfaring missionary saints from the
5th to 9th centuries.

HI98 Finney, John
Recovering the Past: Celtic and Roman Mission. London,
ENK: Darton, Longman & Todd, 1996. viii, 148 pp. Paper.
0232520836.

A historical comparison and contrast of Celtic and Roman mission, with emphasis on the challenges they bring to
the way we evangelize today.

HI99 Fowden, Garth
*Empire to Commonwealth: Consequences of Monotheism in
Late Antiquity.* Princeton, NJU: Princeton University Press,
1993. xvii, 205 pp. 0691069891.

A provocative scholarly interpretation of religion in the
Middle East, from Constantine the Great to Caliph'Harun al-
Rashid (d. 809), arguing for a parity of Christianity and Islam
as products of a common momentum toward missionary monotheism and world empire.

HI100 Hillgarth, Jocelyn N., ed.
*Christianity and Paganism, 350-750: The Conversion of West-
ern Europe.* (The Middle Ages). Philadelphia, PAU: University of Pennsylvania, 1986. xvii, 213 pp. 081227993X (hdbk),
0812212134 (pbk).

An enlarged version of *The Conversion of Western Europe 350-750* (Prentice-Hall, 1969), a sourcebook for the period; with additional documents on Ireland and liturgy.

HI101 Huelin, Gordon
Saint Willibrord and His Society. Westminster, ENK: Faith
Press, 1960. 80 pp. No ISBN.

A brief introduction to the life and work of the pioneer
English missionary to northern Europe, St. Willibrord (658-
739), and to the work of the Society of St. Willibrord, 1908-
1958, as an Anglican mission among Old Catholics in The
Netherlands.

**HI102 *La Conversione al cristianesimo nell'Europa dell'Alto
Medioevo***
(Settimane di Studio del Centro Italiano di Studi sull'Alto
Medioevo, 14). Spoleto, IT: Presso la Sede del Centro, 1967.
865 pp. No ISBN.

A collection of scholarly essays on the conversion of the
Germanic, Celtic, and Slavic peoples to Christianity in Europe during the Middle Ages.

HI103 Lehane, Brendan
Quest of Three Abbots. New York, NY: Viking Press; London, ENK: Murray, 1968. 240 pp. 0719517710 (both).

An account of early Celtic Christians of the 5th and 6th
centuries, focusing on the biographies of Sts. Brendan, Columba, and Columbanus, Irish missionaries to England, Wales,
and continental Europe, and confrontation between Roman and
Celtic Christianity at the Synod of Whitby in 664 A.D.

HI104 Marnell, William H.
*Light from the West: The Irish Mission and the Emergence of
Modern Europe.* New York, NYU: Seabury Press, 1978. xi,
208 pp. 0816403899.

Scholarly history of the origin and development of the Celtic medieval mission to France, Belgium, Switzerland, and Germany; including chapters on Sts. Columbanus, Gall, and Virgil.

HI105 McMahon, Sean
Rekindling the Faith: How the Irish Re-Christianized Europe.
Dublin, IE: Mercer University Press, 1996. 80 pp. Paper.
1856351432.

The influence of Irish monasticism in Europe during the
"golden age of Ireland" abroad, when Irish monks went into
voluntary exile as pilgrims for Christ, from the 6th to the 12th
centuries.

HI106 Meryerson, Mark D., and Edward D. English, eds.
Christians, Muslims, and Jews in Medieval and Early Modern Spain: Interaction and Culture Change. (Notre Dame Conferences in Medieval Studies, 8). Notre Dame, INU: University of Notre Dame Press, 1999. xxi, 322 pp. 026802250X.

A collection of 15 scholarly essays spanning both the medieval and early modern period, illuminating ongoing complexities and subtleties of relations between Christians, Muslims, and Jews in Spain, from the 9th to the 17th centuries.

HI107 Muldoon, James, ed.
Varieties of Religious Conversion in the Middle Ages. Gainesville, FLU: University Press of Florida, 1997. viii, 208 pp. 081301509X.

Eleven scholarly essays on medieval conversions to Christianity of pagan invaders, Jews, and Muslims.

HI108 Padberg, Lutz von
Wynfreth-Bonifatius. (R. Brockhaus Taschenbuch, 1104). Wuppertal, GW: R. Brockhaus Verlag, 1989. 189 pp. Paper. 3417211042.

This study of the missionizing of Winfried (St. Boniface) (672/75-754) is enriched with thirty-four reproductions (black and white) of medieval artifacts and manuscripts.

HI109 Phillips, J. R. S.
The Medieval Expansion of Europe. Oxford, ENK: Oxford University Press, 1988. x, 303 pp. Paper. 0192192329.

An analysis of the extent and nature of the relations between western Europe and Asia, Africa, and America, from 1000 to 1500 A. D., including information on the Eastern mission and on missionary motivations in overseas exploration, exploitation, and settlement in the late Middle Ages.

HI110 Richard, Jean
La papauté et les missions d'Orient au Moyen Âge (XIIIe-XVe siècles). (Collection de l'École française de Rome, 33). Rome, IT: École française de Rome, 1977. xxxiv, 325 pp. No ISBN.

A history of French missions to the Orient from the 13th to 15th centuries, with a good bibliography.

HI111 Sierksma, Kl., ed.
Liudger 742-809: De confrontatie tussen heidendom en christendom in de Lage Landen. (Publicatie van de Stichting "Comité Oud Muiderberg," 19). Dieven, NE: Bataafsche Leeuw; Muiderberg, NE: Stichting Comité Oud Muiderberg, 1984. 132 pp. 9067070130.

The missionary Liudger at work in the Netherlands (742-809) and the confrontation between heathenism and Christianity.

HI112 Sullivan, Richard Eugene
Christian Missionary Activity in the Early Middle Ages. (Collected Studies Series, CS431). Aldershot, ENK: Variorum, 1994. x, 265 pp. 0860784029.

A collection of six articles, reprinted from various scholarly journals, exploring aspects of medieval missionary thought and practice, including the encounter of Christian missionaries with pagans and barbarians, the papacy and mission activity, and a comparison of Eastern and Western missionary methods.

HI113 Vlasto, A. P.
The Entry of the Slavs into Christendom: An Introduction to the Medieval History of the Slavs. Cambridge, ENK: Cambridge University Press, 1970. xii, 435 pp. No ISBN.

A general survey of Slavic Christendom from 500 to 1200

A.D. within the framework of Eastern European culture, emphasizing the work of early Byzantine missionaries.

HI114 Vodopivec, Janez
The Holy Brothers Cyril and Methodius, Co-Patrons of Europe: Cultural Link between the East and the West. (Studia Urbaniana, 25). Rome, IT: Urbaniana University Press, 1985. 218 pp. Paper. No ISBN.

A monograph in response to Pope John Paul II's proclamation of the Holy Brothers Cyril and Methodius as "co-patrons of Europe," arguing that they are the cultural link between East and West in Christian evangelization and in human promotion.

General: Modern

See also HI233, HI486-HI487, EA71, PO153, MI170, AM101, AS388, and EU149.

HI115 Öberg, Ingemar
Luther och Världsmissionen: Historisk-systematiska studier med särskild hänsyn till bibelutläggningen. (Studier utgivna av institutionen för systematisk teologi vid åbo akademi, 23). Åbo, FI: Åbo Akademis kopieringscentral, 1991. ix, 670 pp. Paper. 9516497829.

A scholarly study of the approach of Martin Luther to world mission, in theology and practice.

HI116 Beeching, Jack
An Open Path: Christian Missionaries, 1515-1914. London, ENK: Hutchinson, 1979. 325 pp. 0091400805.

A historical analysis of the international legacy of missionaries, especially their explorations and the political role that they played in the colonial world.

HI117 Bosch, David Jacobus
The Vulnerability of Mission. (Occasional Paper, 10). Birmingham, ENK: Selly Oak Colleges, 1991. 18 pp. Paper. No ISBN.

A lecture by the distinguished South African missiologist, delivered 30 November 1991 to mark the 25th anniversary of St. Andrew's Hall at Selly Oak Colleges, Birmingham, England.

HI118 Boxer, C. R.
The Church Militant and Iberian Expansion, 1440-1770. (Johns Hopkins Symposia in Comparative History, 10). Baltimore, MDU: Johns Hopkins University Press, 1978. xi, 148 pp. 0801820421.

An examination of the principal methods and impact of the Spanish and Portuguese overseas missions.

HI119 Boxer, C. R.
A igreja e a expansão ibérica, 1440-1770. (Lugar da historia, 11). Lisboa, PO: Edicões, 1981. 155 pp. No ISBN.
Portuguese translation.

HI120 Brandon, William
New Worlds for Old: Reports from the New World and Their Effect on the Development of Social Thought in Europe, 1500-1800. Athens, OHU: Ohio University Press, 1986. x, 226 pp. 0821408186 (hdbk), 0821408194 (pbk).

An examination of the influence of mission to the New World (America) on the Old World (Europe), tracing its impact through political, economic, philosophical, and religious thought from the 15th through the 18th centuries in France, Spain, and Italy.

HI—HISTORY

HI121 Christensen, Torben, and William R. Hutchison, eds.
Missionary Ideologies in the Imperialist Era, 1880-1920.
Arhus, DK: Aros, 1982. 248 pp. Paper. 8770034370.

A collection of essays concerning Protestant missionary motivation in Europe and America during the "high imperial" period; originally presented at the consultation of the International Commission for Comparative Church History (University of Durham, 1981).

HI122 Foster, John
To All Nations: Christian Expansion from 1700 to Today.
(World Christian Books, 35). New York, NYU: Association Press, 1961. 87 pp. Paper. No ISBN.

A brief history of the Western missionary advance over the last 250 years.

HI123 Gensichen, Hans-Werner
Missionsgeschichte der neueren Zeit. (Die Kirche in ihrer Geschichte, 4 T). Göttingen, GW: Vandenhoeck & Ruprecht, 1976. 66 pp. Paper. 3525523831.

A very concise summary of Roman Catholic, Protestant, and Russian-Orthodox mission history.

HI124 Gründer, Horst
Welteroberung und Christentum: Ein Handbuch zur Geschichte der Neuzeit. Gutersloh, GW: Gerd Mohn, 1992. 751 pp. 3579001361.

This "handbook" provides a historical overview of the role of the expansion of Christianity in relationship to the "globalization" of the world, from the time of the Portuguese explorations of the 15th century to the emancipation of black Africa in the 20th century, and is, therefore, a comprehensive history of missions in modern times.

HI125 Hutchison, William R.
Errand to the World: American Protestant Thought and Foreign Missions. Chicago, ILU: University of Chicago Press, 1987. xii, 227 pp. 0226363090.

A historical analysis of American foreign-mission thinking, from the post-Revolutionary period to the current era, illuminating dilemmas arising when one culture attempts to apply its ideals and technology to the supposed benefit of another.

HI126 Jarrett-Kerr, Martin
Patterns of Christian Acceptance: Individual Response to the Missionary Impact, 1550-1950. London, ENK: Oxford University, 1972. xviii, 342 pp. 0192139460.

A series of biographical sketches of non-Western Christians and Christian missionaries, designed to illuminate the indigenization of the Gospel from an international and personal perspective.

HI127 Jong, J. A. de
As the Waters Cover the Sea: Millennial Expectations in the Rise of Anglo-American Missions, 1640-1810. Kampen, NE: Kok, 1970. vii, 245 pp. Paper. 902420285X.

An investigation into the motivations and theology present in the development of English and American missions, from the turn of the 17th century through the founding of the American Board of Commissioners for Foreign Missions (ABCFM).

HI128 Latourette, Kenneth Scott
Christianity in a Revolutionary Age: A History of Christianity in the Nineteenth and Twentieth Centuries. New York, NYU: Harper and Brothers Publishers, 1973. 5 vols. 0837157005.

Thorough country-by-country analysis of contemporary, international Christianity, with reviews of churches and major mission events of the Roman Catholic, Protestant, and Orthodox churches [vol. 1: *The Nineteenth Century in Europe: Background and the Roman Catholic Phase* (1958, xiv, 498 pp.); vol. 2: *The Nineteenth Century in Europe: The Protestant and Eastern Churches* (1959, ix, 532 pp.); vol. 3: *The Nineteenth Century outside Europe: The Americas, the Pacific, Asia, and Africa* (1961, viii, 527 pp.); vol. 4: *The Twentieth Century in Europe: The Roman Catholic, Protestant, and Eastern Churches* (1961, vii, 568 pp.); vol. 5: *The Twentieth Century outside Europe: The Americas, the Pacific, Asia, and Africa: The Emerging World Christian Community* (1962, vi, 568 pp.)].

HI129 Müller, Karl, and Werner Ustorf, eds.
Einleitung in die Missionsgeschichte: Tradition, Situation und Dynamik des Christentums. (Theologische Wissenschaft, 18). Stuttgart, GW: Verlag W. Kohlhammer, 1995. 291 pp. Paper. 3170110802.

Seventeen short essays and bibliographies, by an international panel of Catholic and Protestant missiologists, on themes in the modern history of Christian missions on each continent.

HI130 Marty, Martin E.
Missions and Ecumenical Expressions. (Modern American Protestantism and Its World, 13). Munich, GW: K. G. Saur, 1993. xiii, 208 pp. 3598415443.

Twelve scholarly republished essays on 19th and 20th century Protestant motives and methods for mission.

HI131 Pirouet, M. Louise
Church History 4: Christianity Worldwide AD 1800 Onwards. (TEF Study Guide, 22). London, ENK: SPCK, 1989. x, 246 pp. Paper. 0281043612 (net ed.).

The fourth volume in the TEF Guide to Church History, carrying on the story from 1800; provides an overview of worldwide contextual background to further an appreciation of happenings in various parts of the church and a clearer understanding of the detailed studies in geographic areas (ISBN: 02821043604 non-net edition for Africa, Asia, S. Pacific, and Caribbean).

HI132 Pullapilly, Cyriac K., and Edwin J. Van Kley
Asia and the West: Encounters and Exchanges from the Age of Explorations. Notre Dame, INU: Cross-Cultural Publications, 1986. xv, 359 pp. 0940121042.

Fourteen essays, mainly on 16th- and 17th-century contacts between Asia and the West, including two on Protestant and Catholic missionary interest in India and China.

HI133 Silva, António da
Trent's Impact on the Portuguese Patronage Missions. Lisbon, PO: Centro de Estudios Históricos Ultramarinos, 1969. 244 pp. No ISBN.

An examination of the influence of the decisions of the Council of Trent on Portuguese missionary work, particularly with reference to the question of "accommodation."

HI134 Stolle, Volker, ed.
Kirche aus allen Völkern: Luther-Texte zur Mission. Erlangen, GW: Evangelical Lutheran Mission, 1983. 95 pp. Paper. 3872141619.

A collection of short passages from Martin Luther's writings related to mission, including his commentary on biblical passages, the practice of mission in his day, and mission principles.

HI135 Vicedom, Georg F.
Mission im ökumenischen Zeitalter. (Evangelische Enzyklopädie, 17/18). Gütersloh, GW: Gerd Mohn, 1967. 208 pp. No ISBN.

A survey of modern missions in the ecumenical era by the noted German Protestant missiologist, including the challenges of world religions, secularism, and syncretism.

General: Modern, Women

See also HI330, HI370-HI371, HI435, HI462, HI477-HI478, HI519, HI523, HI542, HI545, HI547, HI550-HI551, HI554-HI556, HI570, HI620, HI633, HI671, HI718, TH129, MI191, AF1027, AM1035, and AM1206.

HI136 Allen, Catherine B.
Laborers Together with God: 22 Great Women in Baptist Life. Birmingham, ALU: Woman's Missionary Union, 1987. 246 pp. Paper. No ISBN.

Twenty-two thoroughly researched biographical sketches of influential leaders in the Women's Missionary Union, and the affect they had on the Southern Baptist Convention.

HI137 Beaver, Robert Pierce
American Protestant Women in World Mission: History of the First Feminist Movement in North America. Grand Rapids, MIU: Eerdmans, 1980. 227 pp. Paper. 0802818463.

A revision of *All Loves Excelling* (Eerdmans, 1968) tracing 150 years of the history and influence of women's missionary societies.

HI138 Calkins, Gladys Gilkey
Follow Those Women: Church Women in the Ecumenical Movement. New York, NYU: United Church Women, 1961. 108 pp. Paper. No ISBN.

A narrative history of years of cooperation for missions by women in the United States, from the founding of a Union Missionary Society in 1861 to United Church Women, in which the author has been a leader for over twenty-five years.

HI139 Drummond, Lewis A., and Betty Drummond
Women of Awakenings: The Historic Contribution of Women to Revival Movements. Grand Rapids, MIU: Kregel Publications, 1997. 365 pp. Paper. 0825424747.

Popular short biographies of two biblical women (Deborah and Priscilla) and ten modern women (from Susanna Wesley and Catherine Booth to Ruth Bell Graham) who have fostered spiritual awakening and revival in the church.

HI140 Hill, Patricia R.
The World Their Household: The American Women's Foreign Mission Movement and Cultural Transformation, 1870-1920. Ann Arbor, MIU: University of Michigan Press, 1985. 231 pp. 0472100556.

An examination of the women's foreign missionary movement as a cultural and religious phenomenon; including its role in cultural imperialism and its symbiotic relationship with the changing cultural paradigms of ideal womanhood in America.

HI141 Montgomery, Helen Barrett
Western Women in Eastern Lands: An Outline Study of Fifty Years of Woman's Work in Foreign Missions. (Women in American Protestant Religion 1800-1930, 20). New York, NYU: Garland, 1987. xiv, 286 pp. 0824006704.

Reprint of the author's classic (Macmillan, 1910) on fifty years of women's work in the United States for foreign missions.

HI142 Porterfield, Amanda
Mary Lyon and the Mount Holyoke Missionaries. (Religion in America Series). New York, NYU: Oxford University Press, 1997. xi, 179 pp. 0195113012.

Critical study of early missionaries trained at Mount Holyoke Seminary (later College), and their effect on cultures in Persia, India, and South Africa.

HI143 Robert, Dana L.
American Women in Mission: A Social History of Their Thought and Practice. Macon, GAU: Mercer University Press, 1996. xxii, 444 pp. Paper. 0865545499.

A chronological overview of the mission thought and practice of American women in foreign missions—mainline Protestants, evangelicals, and Roman Catholics—from 1810 to 1980.

HI144 Tucker, Ruth A., and Walter L. Liefeld
Daughters of the Church: Women and Ministry from New Testament Times to the Present. Grand Rapids, MIU: Zondervan, 1987. 552 pp. Paper. 0310457416.

A popular account of women in church leadership over two thousand years—their aspirations, determination, disappointments, practice, and achievements; including their leadership in foreign missions and the churches of the Two-Thirds World.

HI145 Tucker, Ruth A.
Guardians of the Great Commission: The Story of Women in Modern Missions. Grand Rapids, MIU: Zondervan, 1988. 278 pp. Paper. 0310414717.

Biographical history of women's contributions and issues in modern missions; especially strong on conservative Protestant women; written as a companion volume to *From Jerusalem to Irian Jaya* (1983).

HI146 Wittenmyer, Annie
Women's Work for Jesus. New York, NYU: Garland, 1987. 240 pp. 0824006852.

Reprint of a 1873 work that emphasizes the role of women in both home and foreign missions, including a strong call for purity and temperance stances.

General: 18th Century

See also HI516, HI540, HI564, CH5, AM792, AM1150, AS975, and EU296.

HI147 Chaney, Charles L.
The Birth of Missions in America. South Pasadena, CAU: William Carey Library, 1976. xiv, 337 pp. 0878081461.

An analysis of the mission impulse in early America, (1790-1830), including an extensive bibliography.

HI148 Conforti, Joseph A.
Jonathan Edwards, Religious Tradition, and American Culture. Chapel Hill, NCU: University of North Carolina Press, 1995. xiv, 267 pp. 0807822248 (hdbk), 0807845353 (pbk).

A scholarly analysis of Jonathan Edwards' place in American cultural history, including motivation for missions and the First and Second Great Awakenings.

General: 19th Century

See also HI2, HI208, HI263, HI365, HI381, HI424, HI445, HI488, ME90, CR1462, EV233, EV238, AM986, AM1017, EU134, EU278, and OC165.

HI149 Corts, Thomas E., ed.
Henry Drummond: A Perpetual Benediction: Essays to Commemorate the Centennial of His Death. Edinburgh, ENK: T&T Clark, 1999. xxxiii, 141 pp. 0567086674.

This biography of Drummond includes his place in the rise of evangelicalism, his efforts to confront a new generation with a thoughtful, world-aware Christianity, and his work on science and Christian faith.

HI150 Harvey, Bonnie C.
Fanny Crosby. (Women of Faith Series). Minneapolis, MNU: Bethany House, 1999. 157 pp. Paper. 07642121661.

Blind from infancy, Crosby became one of the most prolific hymn writers of the 19th century with nearly 9,000 hymns, including "Blessed Assurance" and "To God Be the Glory."

HI151 Martin, Roger H.
Evangelicals United: Ecumenical Stirrings in Pre-Victorian Britain, 1795-1830. (Studies in Evangelicalism, 4). Metuchen, NJU: Scarecrow Press, 1983. xii, 230 pp. 0810815869.

Brief histories of the founding of four interdenominational organizations by British evangelicals during the 1795 to 1830 period, illustrating their "Catholic Spirit": The London Missionary Society, the Religious Tract Society, the British and Foreign Bible Society, and the London Society for Promoting Christianity amongst the Jews.

HI152 Nemer, Lawrence
Anglican and Roman Catholic Attitudes on Missions: An Historical Study of Two English Missionary Societies in the Late Nineteenth Century, 1865-1885. (Studia Instituti Missiologici SVD, 29). St. Augustin, GW: Steyler Verlag, 1981. 210 pp. Paper. 3877871410.

A scholarly comparison of two UK-based missionary societies (CMS and Mill Hill) in their backgrounds, missionary motivation, organization, personnel, and funding.

HI153 Williams, Walter L.
Black Americans and the Evangelization of Africa, 1877-1900. Madison, WIU: University of Wisconsin Press, 1982. xviii, 259 pp. 0299089207.

A scholarly investigation into the motivations and attitudes of black American missionaries working in Africa in the late 19th century; focuses on the source and rise of mission sentiment, the organization among black churches, missionary attitudes toward native African cultures, and the impact of the missions movement on the rise of pan-African sentiment.

General: 20th Century

See also HI135, HI607, SO222, EV240, AF1162, AM37, AM63, AM85-AM86, AM116, AM160, AM341, AM565, AS1015, AS1083, EU110, and OC165.

HI154 Baum, Gregory, ed.
The Twentieth Century: A Theological Overview. Maryknoll, NYU: Orbis Books; London, ENK: Cassell; Ottowa, ONC: Novalis, 1999. viii, 263 pp. Paper. 1570752826 (US), 0225668807 (UK), 2895070156 (CN).

Eighteen Christian scholars offer theological assessments of key moments in world history, and examine trends and movements of this century that have important bearing on the next century, such as globalization, the women's movement, and ecology.

HI155 Carpenter, Joel A., and Wilbert R. Shenk, eds.
Earthen Vessels: American Evangelicals and Foreign Missions, 1880-1980. Grand Rapids, MIU: Eerdmans, 1990. xviii, 350 pp. Paper. 0802804020.

Fourteen scholarly essays providing the first major historical treatment of the distinctly evangelical wing of 20th-century Protestant missions from North America.

HI156 Lotz, Denton
"The Evangelization of the World in This Generation": The Resurgence of a Missionary Idea among the Conservative Evangelicals. Hamburg, GW: By the author, Denton Lotz, 1970. x, 560 pp. No ISBN.

An analysis of the watchword for world evangelization from 1885 to 1938, and of its place in conservative evangelical missions since 1945; originally presented as a doctoral dissertation to the theology faculty of the University of Hamburg in Germany.

HI157 Robinson, Martin
To Win the West. Crowborough, ENK: Monarch Publications, 1996. 255 pp. Paper. 1854242512.

The director of mission and theology at the British Bible Society reviews major themes of the 20th-century mission, with the aim of developing a pan-evangelical coalition for evangelizing not only individuals, but also Western culture.

HI158 Ustorf, Werner
Christianized Africa—De-Christianized Europe?: Missionary Inquiries into the Polycentric Epoch of Christian History. (Perspektiven der Weltmission, 14). Ammersbek bei Hamburg, GW: Verlag an der Lottbek, 1992. 157 pp. Paper. 3926987928.

Ten scholarly essays on challenges to mission in the polycentric cultures of the 20th century, contrasting the religious vibrancy and church growth of Africa with the church's decline in Europe; by the distinguished professor of mission of Birmingham University and the Selly Oak Colleges.

Orthodox and Oriental Churches

See also GW82, HI113-HI114, TH90, EA87, EA125, EA244, CR1063, MI179, SP227, SP229, AF538, AM990, AM1172, AM1200, AS414, AS909, AS960, and AS964.

HI159 Aprem, Mar, and George Mooken
Nestorian Missions. (The Probe Series). Maryknoll, NYU: Orbis Books, 1980. vi, 129 pp. No ISBN.

A popular history of the expansion of the Nestorian Church in Asia and the Middle East from its beginnings until the end of the Medieval period, emphasizing the movement of the church into Persia, Arabia, India, China, and Japan, and its influence on the religious development in Asia; originally published in Kerala, India by the Mar Narsai Press in 1976.

HI160 Chakmakjian, Hagop A.
Armenian Christology and Evangelization of Islam: A Survey of the Relevance of the Christology of the Armenian Apostolic Church to Armenian Relations with its Muslim Environment. Leiden, NE: Brill, 1965. xiii, 146 pp. No ISBN.

This thesis is developed in a broad historical study, starting with Armenian theology (325-1410) and the impact of contemporary American Protestant missions on the Armenian Apostolic Church.

HI161 Drobena, Thomas John, and Wilma Kucharek
Heritage of the Slavs. Columbus, OHU: Kosovo, 1979. xvii, 168 pp. Paper. No ISBN.

A history of the political and religious events, A.D. 800-899, concerning the Christianization of the Slavs and the Great Moravian Empire, including the biography of missionaries Constantine and Methodius.

HI162 Dvornik, Francis
Byzantine Missions among the Slavs: Sts. Constantine-Cyril and Methodius. (Rutgers Byzantine Series). New Brunswick, NJU: Rutgers University Press, 1970. xviii, 484 pp. 0813506131.

A scholar of Byzantine Empire history explores the conversion of the Slavic peoples to Christianity, with emphasis on the roles of Sts. Cyril and Methodius, and the dissemination of Christian literature, art, law, and government to the tribes of Serbia, Croatia, Russia, and Bulgaria.

HI163 Gabrieli, Francesco, and E. J. Costello
Arab Historians of the Crusades. New York, NYU: Barnes & Noble, 1993. xxxvi, 362 pp. 0710028741.

Reprint of the translation of *Storici Arabi delle Crociate* (1957); originally published in 1969 (London, ENK: Routledge & K. Paul; Berkeley, CAU: University of California Press).

HI164 Gabrieli, Francesco, ed.
Chroniques arabes des Croisades. Translated by Viviana Pâques. (La Bibliothèque arabe). Paris, FR: Sindbad, 1996. 405 pp. 2742707913.

Second edition of the French translation.

HI165 Gabrieli, Francesco, ed.
Die Kreuzzüge aus arabischer Sicht. Translated by Barbara von Kaltenborn-Stachau. Munich, GW: Deutscher Taschenbuch Verlag, 1976. 456 pp. 3423041722.

Second edition of the German translation.

HI166 Gabrieli, Francesco, ed.
Storici arabi delle Crociate. (Nuova universale Einaudi, 34). Torino, IT: Einaudi, 1973. 353 pp. No ISBN.

Fourth edition of an extensive study on the Crusades from the Arab viewpoint, using original texts from 478 to 690; originally published in 1957.

HI167 Gregorios, Paulos
Introducing the Orthodox Churches. Delhi, II: ISPCK; Kerala, II: Mar Gregorios Foundation, 1999. x, 76 pp. Paper. 8172144873.

Historical, geographical, and cultural perspectives of the Orthodox churches which began in India when one of the original twelve apostles, St. Thomas, established churches there.

HI168 Kawerau, Peter
Ostkirchengeschichte, Vol. 1: Das Christentum in Asien und Afrika bis zum Auftreten der Portugiesen im Indischen Ozean. (Corpus Christianorum Orientalium, 451: Subsidia, 70). Louvain, BE: Peeters, 1983. lxxi, 204 pp. Paper. No ISBN.

A work dealing with the Oriental churches up to the 15th century.

HI169 Le Coz, Raymond
L'Église d'Orient: chrétiens d'Irak, d'Iran et de Turquie. Paris, FR: Éditions du Cerf, 1995. 441 pp. Paper. 2204051144.

A scholarly history of the Oriental churches of Iraq, Iran, and Turkey, from their origins to the present, with details on Christian-Muslim encounters.

HI170 Moravcsik, Gyula
Byzantium and the Magyars. Translated by Samuel R. Rosenbaum. Amsterdam, NE: Hakkert; Budapest, HU: Akadémiai Kiado, 1970. 147 pp. No ISBN.

A short summary of fifteen years of research by the author into the influence of Byzantium on the Magyars of Hungary, including their conversion to Christianity; originally published as *Bizanc es a Magyarsag* (Budapest, 1953).

HI171 Piffl-Percevic, Theodor, ed.
Der heilige Method, Salzburg und die Slawenmission. (Pro Oriente, 11). Innsbruck, AU: Tyrolia-Verlag, 1987. 470 pp. Paper. 3702216324.

A commemorative volume concentrating on the mission of Cyril and Methodius to the Slavs, also containing the papal documents *Egregiae virtutis* (1980) and *Slavorum apostoli* (1985).

HI172 Roberson, Ronald
The Eastern Christian Churches: A Brief Survey. (Orientalia Christiana). Rome, IT: Edizioni *Orientalia Christiana*, 1999. 276 pp. Paper. 8872103215.

An overview of the Eastern churches, placed in their historical, geographical, doctrinal, and liturgical contexts, for the non-specialist who might be bewildered by the array of the national churches and ethnic jurisdictions; a sixth and substantially revised edition.

HI173 Schütz, Joseph, ed.
Die Lehrer der Slawen Kyrill und Method: Die Lebensbeschreibungen zweier Missionare aus dem Altkirchenslawischen. Sankt Ottilien, GW: EOS Verlag, 1885. 152 pp. Paper. 3880964963.

A scientific edition of two old biographies of the Apostles to the Slavs: *Vita Constantii* (written soon after 1869) and *Vita Methodii* (shortly after 1885); with notes and translations by the editor and three shorter documents.

HI174 Schulte, Heinrich
Der Beginn: Eine Hilfsaktion für den christlichen Orient. (Das Werk des Katholischen Apostolats, 1). Limburg, GW: Lahn-Verlag, 1966. 240 pp. Paper. No ISBN.

A historical study of a relief campaign organized by St. Vincent Pallotti for the Chaldean Church, and a general picture of the problems of the Oriental churches before the First Vatican Council.

HI175 Smirnoff, Eugene
A Short Account of the Historical Development and Present Position of Russian Orthodox Missions. Welshpool, Powys, WLK: Stylite Pub., 1986. xiv, 85 pp. 0947805095.

A reprint of a 1903 history which traces Russian Orthodox missions from ancient Russia to the 19th century; also published in 1975 by Eastern Orthodox Books.

HI176 Stamoolis, James J.
Eastern Orthodox Mission Theology Today. (American Society of Missiology Series, 10). Maryknoll, NYU: Orbis Books, 1986. xiv, 194 pp. Paper. 0883442159.

A comprehensive survey of Eastern Orthodox missions, including history, background, aim, methods, motives, and the place of liturgy and theology.

HI—HISTORY

HI177 Stylianopoulos, Theodore, ed.
Orthodox Perspectives on Pastoral Praxis. Brookline, MAU: Holy Cross Orthodox Press, 1988. xiv, 202 pp. Paper. 0917651197.

Essays by fifteen Greek Orthodox educators and clerics, which reveal how Orthodox thinkers are grappling with new challenges in the North American milieu in pastoral care, education, the place of women in the church, divergent practices of receiving converts, and monasticism.

General Works

See also GW11, GW51, GW99, GW221, HI12, HI30-HI32, HI105, TH53, TH59, TH121, TH151, ME54, ME92, ME123, ME197, ME243, CR167, SO69-SO71, SO135, SO196, EC277, PO213, MI132, MI168, MI184, CH355, CH501, SP280, AF28, AF61, AF85, AF93, AF113, AF353, AF456, AF762, AF834, AF1216, AF1268, AF1313, AF1375, AM22, AM42, AM52, AM73, AM85-AM86, AM116, AM164, AM166, AM184, AM220, AM284, AM350, AM411, AM567, AM781, AM825, AM852, AM963, AM969, AM1081-AM1082, AM1189, AM1199, AM1301-AM1302, AM1368, AM1372, AM1379, AM1405, AS55, AS320, AS353-AS354, AS368, AS467, AS470, AS602, AS635-AS636, AS792, AS854, AS861, AS940, AS969, AS1046, AS1049-AS1050, AS1063, AS1103, AS1245-AS1246, AS1254, AS1260-AS1262, AS1336-AS1338, AS1344, AS1473, EU203-EU204, EU212, OC47, OC118, and OC300.

HI178 Camp, Richard L.
The Papal Ideology of Social Reform: A Study in Historical Development, 1878-1967. Leiden, NE: Brill, 1969. viii, 180 pp. No ISBN.

A scholarly history of the development of Roman Catholic social conscience in the 19th and 20th centuries through an analysis of papal writings.

HI179 Catholic Church. Congregation de Propaganda Fide
Sacrae Congregationis de Propaganda Fide memoria rerum, 1622-1972: 350 anni a servizio delle missioni. Edited by Josef Metzler. Rome, IT: Herder, 1975. 3 vols in 5. No ISBN (v. 1), 3451163527 (v. 2), 3451163535 (v. 3:1), 3451163543 (v. 3:2).

An encyclopedic history of Catholic missions from 1622 to 1972 in 4,500 pages, with entries in Italian, German, English, Spanish, and French, plus summaries in English or Italian [vol. 1: 1622-1700; vol. 2: 1700-1815; vol. 3: 1815-1972].

HI180 Consejo Superior de Misiones
España Misionera: Catálogo de los Misioneros y de los Religiosos Espaóoles en el Extranjero. Madrid, SP: Ediciones Españoles Misionera, 1962. 2 vols. No ISBN.

A directory of all the Spanish missionary orders around the world, including addresses, names of all missionaries, and other relevant data [vol. 1: 431 pp.; vol. 2: 499 pp.].

HI181 Dries, Angelyn
The Missionary Movement in American Catholic History. (American Society of Missiology Series, 26). Maryknoll, NYU: Orbis Books, 1998. xviii, 398 pp. Paper. 1570751676.

A pioneer history of Catholic missions in and from the United States, organized by historical periods, and developed as a history project of the United States Catholic Mission Association.

HI182 Euntes Docete: Commentaria Urbaniana
(Roma/XLIV/1991/2). Rome, IT: Pontificia Università Urbaniana, 1991. 338 pp. Paper. No ISBN.

This issue of the prestigious Catholic journal contains nine essays by prominent Catholic ecclesiastics (Ratzinger) and missiologists (Henkel), interpreting Pope John Paul II's encyclical, *Redemptoris Missio*, in the light of earlier Roman Catholic mission thought.

HI183 Giglioni, Paolo
La Missione Sulle Vie del Concilio: Il Pensiero Missionaro di Giovanni Paolo II. (Pontificia Universitas Urbaniana, 8043). Rome, IT: Pontificia Universitas Urbaniana, 1988. 209 pp. Paper. No ISBN.

An analysis of the principal themes in the missionary thought of Pope John Paul II upon the tenth anniversary of his papacy, with the texts of his annual messages for the World Mission Day.

HI184 Hastings, Adrian, ed.
Modern Catholicism: Vatican II and After. London, ENK: SPCK; New York, NYU: Oxford University Press, 1991. xvii, 473 pp. 0281044708 (UK), 0195206576 (US).

Fifty-five short summaries of various developments in the Roman Catholic Church since Vatican II, including chapters on missions, ecumenism, and Catholicism, in various countries and continents.

HI185 Huiskamp, Harrie
A Genealogy of Ecclesiastical Jurisdictions: Schematic Outline, Illustrating the Development of the Catholic Church in Territories Assigned to Portugal by the Treaty of Tordesillas in 1494. (Church and Theology in Context, 23). Kampen, NE: Uitgeverij Kok, 1994. xix, 315 pp. Paper. 9039005028.

A schematic outline, organized by present nation-states, of the development of the Roman Catholic Church in Brazil, Africa, Asia, and Oceania, from 1494 to the present, identifying church jurisdictions and areas of responsibility of missionary orders.

HI186 Kachel, Fabiano S.
As Missoes catolicas: Pronunciamentos dos Papas, desde Leao XIII ate Joao Paulo II, e documentos do Vaticano II. Petropolis, BL: Editora Vozes, 1980. 325 pp. Paper. No ISBN.

Texts of seventeen documents related to 20th-century Roman Catholic mission.

HI187 Leclercq, Jean
Nouvelle page d'histoire monastique: Histoire de l'A.I.M. 1960-1985. Ponte de Beauvoisin, FR: Abbaye de la Rochette, 1986. 222 pp. No ISBN.

A twenty-five-year history of Aide à l'Implantation Monastique (AIM), a program to assist Catholic monasteries in the Third World.

HI188 Lernoux, Penny
People of God: The Struggle for World Catholicism. New York, NYU: Viking Penguin, 1989. xii, 466 pp. 0670815292.

A journalist's detailed account of the twenty-five-year struggle in the Roman Catholic Church since Vatican II, between advocates of reform and of counter-reformation (restoration).

HI189 Millot, René Pierre
Missions d'aujourd'hui. (Je sais, je crois; 99). Paris, FR: Fayard, 1960. 124 pp. No ISBN.

A history of the development of Roman Catholic perspectives on missions and of the inception of Catholic missionary activity in several countries.

HI190 Millot, René Pierre
Missions in the World Today. Translated by J. Holland Smith. New York, NYU: Hawthorn Books, 1961. 139 pp. No ISBN.
English translation.

HI191 Moser, Bruno, ed.
Gehet hin in alle Welt: Ereignisse und Gestalten christlicher Missionsgeschichte. Munich, GW: Südwest Verlag, 1984. 415 pp. 3517008214.
Articles of various kinds (without footnotes and biographical references) by missiologists and missionary writers giving a rough overview of the history of Catholic missions and presenting personalities who dedicated themselves totally to the missionary cause.

HI192 Mulders, Alphonsus
Missionsgeschichte: Die Ausbreitung des katholischen Glaubens. Translated by Johannes Madey. Regensburg, GW: Verlag Friedrich Pustet, 1960. 535 pp. No ISBN.
A scholarly history of Catholic missions; originally published in Dutch with the title *Missiegeschiedenis* (1957, xxvi, 565 pp.; Uitgeverij Paul Brand, Bussum, NE).

HI193 Nedungatt, George
The Spirit of the Eastern Code. Rome, IT: Centre for Indian and Inter-religious Studies; Bangalore, II: Dharmaram Publications, 1993. xiv, 261 pp. Paper. No ISBN.
A detailed analysis and assessment of *The Code of Canons of the Oriental Churches* (1991), which provided for the first time a common canon law for the Eastern-rite churches (Roman Catholic).

HI194 Nygren, David J., and Miriam D. Ukeritis
The Future of Religious Orders in the United States: Transformation and Commitment. Westport, CTU: Praeger, 1993. xxvi, 313 pp. 0275946657.
A social-scientific study of the condition of Catholic religious orders in the United States, based on extensive interviews of leaders, and an attitudinal survey of members.

HI195 O'Bryan, James P.
Awake the Giant: A History of the Missionary Cenacle Apostolate. Holy Trinity, ALU: Missionary Cenacle Press, 1986. 376 pp. Paper. No ISBN.
A detailed history of the Missionary Cenacle Apostolate from its founding by Thomas Judge in 1910 to his death in 1933, based on community documents; written for Catholic laity.

HI196 Stoffel, Oskar
Die katholischen Missionsgesellschaften: Historische Entwicklung und konziliare Erneuerung in kanonischer Sicht. (Neue Zeitschrift für Missionswissenschaft: Supplementa XXXIII). Immensee, SZ: *Neue Zeitschrift für Missionswissenschaft*, 1984. xxxvi, 283 pp. Paper. 3858240621.
A scholarly study of the historical development of Catholic missionary orders and their contributions to conciliar renewal.

HI197 Theyssen, Hans-Josef
In alle Welt: Missionsberuf heute; Taschenbuch über die Missionen, Missionare und Missionsschwestern der katholischen Kirche. Cologne, GW: Wienand, 1965. 271 pp. Paper. No ISBN.
A publication of the Catholic Missionary Council of Germany giving short descriptions of 119 mission-sending religious congregations and institutes of men and women.

HI198 Vaulx, Bernard de
History of the Missions: From the Beginning to Benedict XV (1914). Translated by Reginald F. Trevett. (Faith and Fact Books, 98; *Twentieth Century Encyclopedia of Catholicism*, 99). New York, NYU: Hawthorn Books; London, ENK: Burns & Oates, 1961. 191 pp. No ISBN.
English translation.

HI199 Vaulx, Bernard de
Katholische Missionsgeschichte. (Christ in der Welt, 12-13). Aschaffenburg, GW: Pattloch, 1962. 179 pp. Paper. No ISBN.
German translation.

HI200 Vaulx, Bernard de
Les missions, leur histoire: des origines à Benoit XV (1914). (Je sais, je crois, 98). Paris, FR: Artheme Fayard, 1960. 126 pp. No ISBN.
An historical survey of Catholic missions, from Pentecost to the present, and twenty-seven articles by an international panel of mission historians; with annotated bibliographies of the most important books in English, French, and German, translated by Reginald F. Trevett.

Congregation for the Evangelization of Peoples (Congregatio de Propaganda Fide)

See also HI673 and CH469.

HI201 Catholic Church, Congregation for the Evangelization of Peoples
Acta pontificalium operum a Propagatione Fidei. Rome, IT: Sacrae Congretionis de Propaganda, 1933-. 114 pp. No ISBN.
Since 1933 the Propaganda Fidei has published periodically these reports in French and Italian of its activities as the coordinating body for Catholic missions.

HI202 Catholic Church. S. Congregazione per l'Evangelizzazione dei Popoli
La Sacra Congregazione per l'Evangelizatione dei Popoli nel decennio del decreto "Ad Gentes." Rome, IT: Sacra Congregazione pro Gentium Evangelizatione, 1975. 294 pp. No ISBN.
An analysis of ten years of work of the Sacred Congregation for the Evangelization of People in response to the decree on mission (*Ad Gentes*) of Vatican II.

HI203 Henkel, Willi
Die Druckerei der Propaganda Fide: Eine Dokumentation. (Communicatio Socialis, 5). Munich, GW: Schöningh, 1977. 109 pp. Paper. 3506738410.
Articles, reprinted from the review *Communicatio Socialis*, about the establishment and development of the Propaganda Fide printing press, on the occasion of its 350th anniver-sary; with eight historical documents (1638-1642 and 1759) printed in Italian, with translations and commentaries in German.

HI204 Prudhomme, Claude
Stratégie missionnaire du Saint-Siège sous Léon XIII (1878-1903): centralisation romaine et défis culturels. (Collection de l'École française de Rome, 186). Paris, FR: École française de Rome; Paris, FR: Palais Farnèse, 1994. 621 pp. Paper. 2728302901.
A detailed analysis of the missionary strategy of the Vatican (Propaganda Fide) during the papacy of Leo XIII, 1878 to 1903.

Missio

HI205 Simons, Konrad
Missio: Die Geschichte einer Bewegung; Das Internationale Katholische Missionswerk in Aachen von 1832 an. Aachen, GW: Missio, 1983. 367 pp. No ISBN.

The history of "Missio," founded in Aachen in 1832 as "Franziskus-Xaverius-Missionsverein," and incorporated into the Pontifical Society for the Propagation of the Faith (with headquarters in Rome) in 1922, reflecting the changing understanding of mission.

General Works

See also GW110-GW111, GW200, TH151, SO24, SP7, AM1010, AS1396, EU240-EU241, EU249, EU257, and OC89.

HI206 Bona, Candido, and Joseph Allamano
A Master of Missionary Life and a Father of Missionaries. London, ENK: Consolata Missionaries, 1986. 97 pp. No ISBN.

Biographical essays on the life and work of the founder of Consolata Missions.

HI207 Cummins, J. S.
Jesuit and Friar in the Spanish Expansion to the East. (Variorum Collected Studies Series, CS237). London, ENK: Variorum, 1986. ix, 246 pp. 0860781852.

Seven scholarly essays on Jesuit and Dominican missions in the 16th and 17th centuries, from Christopher Columbus to Japan, China, and the Philippines.

HI208 Feldmann, Christian
Adolph Kolping: Towards a Christian Society. (Challenge Series, 4). Nairobi, KE: Paulines Publications Africa, 1999. 112 pp. Paper. 9966214445.

The biography of a 19th-century advocate of the underprivileged, whose Catholic social initiative has blossomed from humble beginnings in the mid-1800s to a Kolping Society of 350,000 members in thirty-six countries; first published under the title *Adolph Kolping: Für ein soziales Christentum* by Verlag Herder (1991).

HI209 Loew, Jacques
Les cieux ouverts: chronique de la mission ouvriere Saints-Pierre-et-Paul, 1955-1970. (L'Évangile au vingtieme siècle). Paris, FR: Éditions du Cerf, 1971. 239 pp. No ISBN.

Letters to friends and supporters of the Mission Association of Sts. Peter and Paul.

HI210 Maestrini, Nicholas
P.I.M.E. in the United States: The First Twenty-Five Years 1947-1972. Detroit, MIU: PIME World Press, 1994. xxv, 398 pp. Paper. 0964201003.

A narrative history of the work of the Pontifical Institute for Foreign Missions (PIME) in the United States, 1947-1972, by one of its senior members.

HI211 Spink, Kathryn, and José Luis González-Balado
Spirit of Bethlehem: Brother Andrew and the Missionary Brothers of Charity. London, ENK: SPCK, 1987. xiii, 113 pp. Paper. 0281042578.

The first popular history of the Missionary Brothers of Charity founded by Mother Teresa for men in 1965.

HI212 Vugt, Joos P. A. van
Brothers at Work: A History of Five Dutch Congregations of Brothers and Their Activities in Catholic Education, 1840-1970. (Scrip-

ta of the Catholic Documentation Centre and the Catholic Study Centre, 8). Nijmegen, NE: Valkhof Pers, 1996. 126 pp. Paper. 905625006X.

An abridged history of the origins, development, accomplishments, and decline of four Dutch congregations of brothers engaged in Catholic education across the world.

HI213 Wittberg, Patricia
The Rise and Decline of Catholic Religious Orders: A Social Movement Perspective. (Religion, Culture, and Society). Albany, NYU: SUNY Press, 1994. xii, 423 pp. 0791422291 (hdbk), 0791422305 (pbk).

A sociological study of the growth and decline of Catholic religious orders in the United States and the consequences for the various missions of the Catholic Church.

Augustinians (Order of St. Augustine), O.S.A.

See also AM870, AM1467, AM1488, and AS1454.

HI214 Alonso, Carlos
Primer Viaje Misional Alrededor del Mundo (1542-1549): Una Gesta Agustiniana. (Monografías de Misiones y Misioneros Agustinos v Centenario del Descubrimiento y Evangelización de América, 4). Valladolid, SP: Ed. Estudio Agustiniano, 1989. 206 pp. 848598532X.

An account of the first voyage around the world of four Augustinian missionary monks from Mexico.

Benedictines (Order of St. Benedict), O.S.B.

See also CR846, SP31, SP94, AF664, AF797-AF798, AF1092-AF1093, AM1361, AS719, AS1215, and EU212.

HI215 Doppelfeld, Basilius
Mönchtum und kirchlicher Heilsdienst: Entstehung und Entwicklung des nordamerikanischen Benediktinertums im 19. Jahrhundert. (Münsterschwarzacher Studien, 22). Münsterschwarzach, GW: Vier-Türme-Verlag, 1974. xx, 381 pp. Paper. 3878680635.

A dissertation on the Bavarian and Swiss Benedictines who brought Benedictine monasticism to the United States, and were also engaged in missionary and pastoral work (dissertation University of Würzburg 1973).

HI216 Doppelfeld, Basilius, ed.
Mönche und Missionare: Wege und Weisen benediktinischer Missionsarbeit. (Münsterschwarzacher Studien, 39). Münsterschwarzach, GW: Vier-Türme-Verlag, 1988. 280 pp. 387868374X (hdbk), 3878683715 (pbk).

This work is a series of historical, systematical, and biographical essays on the development and work of the Benedictines of St. Ottilien during the first hundred years of their existence (1888-1988).

HI217 Hertlein, Siegfried, and Remigius Rudmann, eds.
Zukunft aus empfangenem Erbe: 100 Jahre benediktinische Missionsarbeit. St. Ottilien, GW: EOS Verlag, 1983. 223 pp. 3880961506.

A work published on the occasion of the centenary of the missionary Benedictines of St. Ottilien, with seventeen articles covering such themes as theological foundations, encounter with cultures and peoples, historical development, and specialized fields.

HI—HISTORY

HI218 Kardong, Terrence
The Benedictines. (Religious Order Series, 1). Collegeville, MNU: Liturgical Press, 1988. 208 pp. 0814656471.
An overview of the Rule of Benedict and of the history, organization, and spirituality of the Benedictine Order.

HI219 Renner, Frumentius
The Five-Branch Candlestick. Translated by Gertrude Brey and Ingeborg Schmitz. Rome, IT: Missionary Benedictine Sisters of Tutzing, 1984. 466 pp. No ISBN.
English translation of vol. 1 of *Der Fünfarmige Leuchter.*

HI220 Renner, Frumentius, ed.
Der Fünfarmige Leuchter: Beiträge zum Werden und Wirken der Benediktinerkongregation von St. Ottilien. St. Ottilien, GW: EOS Verlag, 1990. 4 vols. No ISBN.
A work in four volumes, based on extensive source materials, on the history of the congregation of the Benedictines of St. Ottilien, the first two describing its beginnings in Germany, and the development of the individual monasteries and missions established in Europe, Africa, Asia, and Latin America; the third dealing with its European foundations since the Second Vatican Council; the fourth with missions in Zululand, East Asia, and new work in North and South America [Vol. 1, xii, 383 pp., 388096047X; vol. 2, vi, 566 pp., 3880966443; vol. 3, 392 pp. 3880966990; vol. 4, 399 pp., 3880966338].

Bethlehem Missionaries, Society of (Societas Missionum Exterarum de Bethlehem im Helvetia), S.M.B.

See also GW14 and AF1142.

HI221 Baumgartner, Jakob, ed.
Vermittlung zwischenkirchlicher Gemeinschaft: 50 Jahre missionsgesellschaft Bethlehem, Immensee. Festschrift. (*NZM*, 17). Schoneck, GW: *NZM*, 1971. viii, 496 pp. Paper. No ISBN.
Twenty-two scholarly essays published on the 50th anniversary of the Bethlehem Fathers, with several articles on their work in Asia and Africa.

HI222 Heim, Walter
Geschichte de Instituts Bethlehem. Immensee, SZ: Missionsgesellschaft Bethlehem, 1982-1989. 5 vols. Paper. No ISBN.
A very detailed scholarly history of the Bethlehem Missionaries based in Immensee, Switzerland; the five volumes published to date dealing with the origins and developments up to 1920 [vol. 1: *Bethlehems Stiftungsdokument* (vii, 128 pp.); vol. 2: *Die Errichtung des Missionshäuser Bethlehem* (ii, 133 pp.); vol. 3: *Immensee 1896/97* (i, 265 pp.); vol. 4: *Die Entwicklung des Instituts Bethlehem 1897/1904* (i, 187 pp.); vol. 5: *Krise und Neugestaltung des Instituts Bethlehem 1905-1920* (ii, 207 pp.)].

HI223 Heim, Walter
Im Dienst weltweiter Solidarität: Aufgabe, Wesen, Geist und Arbeit der Missionsgesellschaft Bethlehem, Immensee nach dem 2. Vatikanischen Konzil. Immensee, SZ: Missionsgesellschaft Bethlehem, 1976. 150 pp. Paper. No ISBN.
The history and contemporary region-by-region work of the Bethlehem Fathers (SMB).

HI224 Rust, Ambros
Die Bethlehem-Missionare, Immensee (Schweiz). (Orden der Kirche, 5). Freiburg, SZ: Paulus Verlag, 1961. 245 pp. No ISBN.

A description of the development, organization, lifestyle, and activities of the Bethlehem Missionaries, with statistics and bibliography.

Carthusians, O.Cart.

HI225 *Poor, Therefore Rich: Carthusian Novice Conferences*
(Cistercian Studies Series, 184). London, ENK: Darton, Longman & Todd; Kalamazoo, MIU: Cistercian Publications, 1999. vi, 213 pp. Paper. 0879077840.
This further volume of Carthusian novice conferences offers the father-master's words of instruction on poverty to the men who are drawn to the Carthusian Order, that seeks Christ in simplicity and silence; translated by an Anglican solitary.

Columbans (Society of St. Columban), S.S.C.

See also AF635, AS338, AS611, AS1391, AS1461, and OC163.

HI226 Fischer, Edward
Journeys Not Regretted: The Columban Fathers' Sixty-Five Years in the Far East. New York, NYU: Crossroad Publishing, 1986. vi, 170 pp. Paper. 0824507355.
Twenty-eight vignettes of the dedicated men and women of the Society of St. Columban, and of the Missionary Sisters of St. Columban, and their service in Burma, China, Korea, Japan, Fiji, and the Philippines, from 1912 to 1977.

HI227 Smyth, Bernard T.
The Chinese Batch: The Maynooth Mission to China, Origins, 1911-1920. Dublin, IE: Four Courts Press, 1994. 128 pp. Paper. 1851821422.
A narrative history of the origins at Maynooth College in Dublin, Ireland, and early work in China of the missionaries of St. Columban; with extensive quotes from archival documents.

Comboni Missionaries of the Heart of Jesus (Verona Fathers), M.C.C.J.

See also SP69, AF630, AF765, and AM975.

HI228 Catrice, Paul
Un audacieux pionnier de l'Église en Afrique: Mgr. Comboni et l'évangélisation de l'Afrique centrale. Lyon, FR: Éditions Vitte, 1964. viii, 139 pp. No ISBN.
Biography of Daniele Camboni (1831-1881), pioneer Catholic missionary bishop to central Africa and founder of the Verona (Comboni) Fathers.

Congregation of the Immaculate Heart of Mary, C.I.C.M.

HI229 Verhelst, Daniël, and Hyacint Daniëls, eds.
Scheut, hier et aujourd'hui 1862-1987: histoire de la Congrégation du Coeur Immaculé de Marie C.I.C.M. (Ancorae, 12). Leuven, BE: Leuven University Press, 1993. 551 pp. Paper. 9061865271.
An illustrated history of the Congregation of the Immaculate Heart of Mary (CICM), also known as the Congregation of Scheut, from its foundation as a Belgian mission to China from 1862 to 1988.

HI230 Verhelst, Daniël, and Nestor Pycke, eds.
C.I.C.M. Missionaries, Past and Present 1862-1987. (AN-CORAE, 13). Leuven, BE: Leuven University Press, 1995. 551 pp. Paper. 9061866766.
   English translation.

Dominicans (Order of Friars Preachers), O.P.

See also HI207, PO26, PO61, AF810, AM23, AM44, AM182, AM357-AM358, AM743, AM759, AM803, AM898, AM959, AM1481, and AS329.

HI231 Ashley, Benedict M.
The Dominicans. (Religious Order Series, 3). Collegeville, MNU: Liturgical Press, 1990. 278 pp. 0814657230.
   A narrative history of the Order of Preachers—the Dominicans.

HI232 Charria, Angulo Beatríz
Primera Comunidad Dominicana en América: Defensora del Indígena. (V Centenario, 13). Bogotá, CK: CELAM, 1987. 273 pp. Paper. 9586250865.
   An account of Fray Pedro de Córdoba, the outstanding historical figure from the perspective of Dominican evangelization work, and of his defense of indigenous peoples.

HI233 Fernandez Navarrete, Domingo
The Travels and Controversies of Friar Domingo Navarrette, 1618-1686. Edited by J. S. Cummins. (Hakylut Society Works. 2nd ser., 118-119). Cambridge, ENK: Cambridge University Press for the Hakylut Society, 1962. 2 vols. No ISBN.
   A remarkable source of first-hand impressions of Catholic 17th-century missions in Mexico, the Philippines, Malacca (Singapore), Macao, and China visited 1646 to 1674, with insights on the Chinese Rites Controversy, and an interpretive essay by the editor.

HI234 González Vallés, Jesús, ed.
Cuatro Siglos de Evangelización (1587-1987): Rutas Misioneras de los Dominicos de la Provincia de Nuestra Señora del Rosario. (Orientalia Dominicana, General, 2). Madrid, II: Huellas Dominicanas, 1987. 488 pp. Paper. 8439890818.
   More than twenty authors offer a historical description of Dominican activities in the Philippines, Taiwan, Vietnam, Hong Kong, and Venezuela.

HI235 González, Pola Manuel et al.
Dominicos en Oriente. (Studium, 27:3 (1987) 387-629). Madrid, SP: Studium, 1987. No ISBN.
   A numbered monograph containing ten articles on the Dominicans of the Santo Rosario Province, and their missionary activities in the Philippines, Japan, China, and Vietnam between 1587 and 1987.

HI236 Loedding, Walter Johannes
Die schwarz-weisse Legion: Missionsgeschichte des Dominikanerordens. Cologne, GW: Albertus-Magnus-Verlag, 1974. 500 pp. Paper. No ISBN.
   A very informative account of the missionary work of the Dominicans from the 13th century to modern times, but without references or adequate bibliography.

HI237 *Mémoire Dominicaine: histoire—documents—vie dominicaine*
(Fondations et missions, 6). Paris, FR: Éditions du Cerf, 1995. 310 pp. Paper. 2204051918.

A collection of essays on the history and life of French-speaking Dominican brothers and sisters.

HI238 Parmisano, Fabian Stan
Mission West: The Western Dominican Province, 1850-1966. Oakland, CAU: Western Dominican Province, 1995. xv, 454 pp. Paper. No ISBN.
   A narrative history of the Dominican Fathers' Western Province, containing the texts of numerous source documents plus photos.

Franciscans-Capuchins (Order of Friars Minor Capuchin), O.F.M.Cap.

See also HI244, AF400, AF402, AF417, AF479, AF497, AF507, AM1385-AM1386, AM1394-AM1396, AM1527, AS637, AS941, and AS1131.

HI239 Bühlmann, Walbert, ed.
Ein Missionsorden fragt nach seiner Zukunft: Überlegungen zum Dokument "Missionarisch in Leben und Wirken" des 3. Plenarrates der Kapuziner (Mattli, 1978). Münsterschwarzach, GW: Vier-Türme-Verlag, 1979. x, 178 pp. Paper. 3878681143.
   Various documents and articles reflecting the discussions and resolutions of the Third Plenary Council of the Capuchins on missionary life today, and an appendix with reflections of the editor on the present situation of the order.

HI240 *Historia Missionum Ordinis Fratrum Minorum*
Rome, IT: Secretariatus Missionum O.F.M., 1974. 4 vols. No ISBN.
   A four-volume collection of historical essays in Latin on the history of Franciscan missions organized by continent and country [vol. 1: 350 pp.; vol. 2: 193 pp.; vol. 3: 112 pp.; vol. 4: 159 pp.; 1967-74].

HI241 *Miscellanea Melchor de Pobladura: Studia Franciscana Historica P. Melchiori a Pobladura Dedicata*
(Bibliotheca Seraphico-Capuccina; Sectio Historica, 23-24). Rome, IT: Institutum Historicum O.F.M. Cap, 1964. 2 vols. No ISBN.
   Commemorative volumes dedicated to the Capuchin who was so important for the missionary history of his order, including a number of articles on Capuchin missionary history in English, French, German, Latin, Spanish, and Catalan [vol.1: xxxv, 487 pp.; vol. 2: x, 557 pp.].

Franciscans-Friars Minor (Order of Friars Minor), O.F.M.

See also HI337, CR940, ED170, SP79, AM100, AM679, AM768-AM769, AM784, AM800-AM802, AM832, AM841, AM847, AM849, AM854, AM861, AM874, AM894, AM901, AM907-AM909, AM912, AM916-AM918, AM920-AM922, AM1137, AM1371, AM1374, AM1389, AM1393, AM1463-AM1464, AM1482, AM1510, AM1530, AS299, AS309, AS398, AS536, AS570, AS921, AS1020, AS1101, AS1403, and OC13.

HI242 Boff, Leonardo, and Walbert Bühlmann, comps.
Los Franciscanos ante os desafios do terceiro mundo. Petrópolis, BL: Editora Vozes; Santiago, CL: CEFEPAL, 1983. 250 pp. Paper. No ISBN.
   Spanish translation.

HI243 Boff, Leonardo, and Walbert Bühlmann, eds.
Baue meine Kirche auf: Franziskanische Inspirationen aus der Dritten Welt. Dusseldorf, GW: Patmos Verlag, 1983. 227 pp. 3491721245.

A collection of papers and documents resulting from a meeting of the Franciscan orders (Mattli, Swizterland, Sept. 1982), reflecting on the ideal of the founder in the light of the challenges of modern times, particularly in the Third World.

HI244 Camps, Arnulf, and Gerfried W. Hunold, eds.
Erschaffe mir ein neues Volk: Franziskanische Kirchlichkeit und missionarische Kirche. (Veröffentlichungen der Missionszentrale der Franziskaner, Bonn). Mettingen, GW: Brasilienkunde Verlag, 1982. 287 pp. 3885590034.

Franciscans and Capuchins attempt to make the heritage of their founder relevant for modern times by discussing Franciscan missiology, poverty, and brotherhood in relation to problems of the modern world.

HI245 Daniel, E. Randolph
The Franciscan Concept of Mission in the High Middle Ages. Lexington, KYU: University Press of Kentucky, 1975. xvi, 168 pp. 0813113156.

A brief investigation into the mission theory of Franciscans in the 13th century, stressing the continuity between the Franciscan monastic rule and the order's mission imperative.

HI246 Iriarte, Lazaro
Franciscan History: The Three Orders of St. Francis of Assisi. Translated by Patricia Ross. Chicago, ILU: Franciscan Herald Press, 1982. xxxvii, 603 pp. 0819908312.

A detailed history of the imprint left by St. Francis and his three orders, on church and social life throughout successive centuries.

HI247 Missionszentrale der Franziskaner
Bruder aller Menschen: Der missionarische Aufbruch in Franziskus von Assisi. Werl, GW: Dietrich-Coelde-Verlag, 1976. 182 pp. 3871631159.

Members of the Franciscan Order reflect on its understanding of mission, as expressed in the "Medellin Document," that "our entire brotherhood is missionary in nature and takes part in the missionary call."

HI248 Rotzetter, Anton, Roque Morschel, and Horst von der Bey, eds.
Von der Conquista zur Theologie der Befreiung: Der franziskanische Traum einer indianischen Kirche. Zürich, SZ: Benziger, 1993. 304 pp. Paper. 35452550938.

A collection of essays assessing the influence of Franciscan activity and spirituality in Central and South America from colonial times until today, arguing that Franciscan influence was less Eurocentric in the process of inculturation than that of other Catholic orders.

HI249 Short, William J.
The Franciscans. (Religious Order Series, 2). Collegeville, MNU: Liturgical Press, 1989. viii, 152 pp. 0814657222.

An introduction to the history, spirit, and present work of the various orders of Franciscan brothers and sisters.

HI250 Sylvest, Edwin Edward
Motifs of Franciscan Mission Theory in the Sixteenth-Century New Spain Province of the Holy Gospel. (Monograph Series—Academy of American Franciscan History, 11). Washington, DCU: Academy of American Franciscan History, 1975. xiv, 148 pp. No ISBN.

A scholarly analysis, with extensive quotes from primary source documents, of the dynamics of encounter of the traditional culture of central Mexico with that of 6th-century Franciscan missionaries.

Holy Cross, Congregation of the (C.S.C.)

See also AS866.

HI251 Connelly, James T.
Holy Cross in East Africa 1958-1980. (Preliminary Studies in the History of the Congregation of the Holy Cross in America, 1). Notre Dame, INU: Province Archives Center, 1981. 34 pp. Paper. No ISBN.

A preliminary history of mission work in Uganda, Kenya, and Tanzania by priests, brothers, and sisters of the Congregation of Holy Cross in America (C.S.C.).

HI252 Cullen, Franklin
Holy Cross on the Gold Dust Trail: And Other Western Ventures. (Preliminary Studies in the History of the Congregation of Holy Cross in America, 5). Notre Dame, INU: Indiana Province Archives Center, 1989. 93 pp. Paper. No ISBN.

Short histories of the Holy Cross 1850 expedition to California, the mission with the Pomo Indians of California (1881-1882), and to the Dakotas in the Black Hills (1878-1897).

Holy Ghost Fathers (Congregation of the Holy Ghost), C.S.Sp.

See also GW102, AF23, AF545, AF610-AF611, AF689, AF1316, and AF1338.

HI253 Burke, Christy
Morality and Mission: A Case Study: Francis Libermann and Slavery, 1802-1852. Nairobi, KE: Paulines Publications Africa, 1998. 93 pp. Paper. 9966213899.

A narrative assessment of the missionary methodology of Francis Libermann (1802-1852), a converted Jew, founder of the Holy Heart of Mary missionary society (later integrated into the Congregation of the Holy Spirit), and vigorous crusader against slavery; based on the author's Ph.D. dissertation.

HI254 Charrier, René
Les frères courage: variations sur les frères spiritains. (Mémoire Spiritaine, Études et Documents, 1). Paris, FR: Congrégation du Saint-Esprit, 1994. 236 pp. Paper. No ISBN.

A brief account of the formation in 1850 by the Spiritains of a lay order, Les Frères Courage (The Courageous Brothers), for the evangelization of Africa; with excerpts from their journals and testimonies over the ensuing century of work.

HI255 Coulon, Paul, and Paul Brasseur, eds.
Libermann 1802-1852: Une pensée et une mystique missionaires. Paris, FR: Éditions du Cerf, 1988. 938 pp. Paper. 2204029505.

A major collection of resources by which to assess the legacy of Fr. François Libermann (1802-1852), founder of the society (1841) and Congregation (1848) of the Holy Spirit; containing scholarly essays, source documents, chronology, and bibliography.

HI—HISTORY

HI256 Gay, Jean

François Libermann: les chemins de la paix. (Mémoire Spiritaine, Études et Documents, 2). Paris, FR: Congrégation du Saint-Esprit, 1995. 189 pp. Paper. 2900666104.

Third edition of reflection on the life, writing, and spirituality of Spiritain Father François Libermann (1802-1852), who served as spiritual director for novices, as missionary in the Caribbean and West Africa, and as Superior of the order.

HI257 Koren, Henry J.

Les Spiritains: trois siècles d'histoire religieuse et missionnaire : histoire de la Congrégation du Saint-Esprit. Translated by J. Bouchaud, and A. Grach. Paris, FR: Beauchesne, 1982. 633 pp. Paper. 2701010462.

French translation of *To the Ends of the Earth* (1983, with adaptations by the translators from the pre-publication text).

HI258 Koren, Henry J.

A Spiritan Who Was Who in North America and Trinidad, 1732-1981. Pittsburgh, PAU: Duquesne University Press, 1983. xiii, 442 pp. 0820701653.

A directory of members of the Holy Ghost Fathers (cssp).

HI259 Koren, Henry J.

To the Ends of the Earth: A General History of the Congregation of the Holy Ghost. Pittsburgh, PAU: Duquesne University Press, 1983. xiv, 548 pp. 0820701572.

An updated scholarly history of the Congregation of the Holy Ghost, with a brief survey of the eighty countries in which the congregation has worked.

HI260 Michel, Joseph

Claude-François Poullart des Places: fondateur de la Congrégation du Saint-Esprit, 1679-1709. Paris, FR: Éditions Saint-Paul, 1962. 349 pp. Paper. No ISBN.

Biography of the founder of the Congrégation du Saint-Esprit (Holy Ghost Fathers and Brothers) in 1703.

HI261 Michel, Joseph

L' influence de l'Association secrète de piété sur Claude François Poullart des Places: aux origines de la Congrégation du Saint-Esprit. Paris, FR: Beauchesne, 1992. 108 pp. Paper. 2701012708.

A monograph examining the possible influence of L'Aa, a 17th-century secret association to deepen spirituality, on the work of Claude Poullart des Places in founding the Holy Ghost missionary order and seminary.

HI262 Rath, Josef Theodor

Geschichte der Kongregation vom Heiligen Geist: (1703-1980). Knechtsteden, GW: Missionsverlag, 1971-1986. 5 vols. Paper. No ISBN.

A detailed scholarly history of the Congregation of the Holy Ghost Fathers and its work on five continents, including a biography of the founder (vol. 3), Fr. François Marie Paul Libermann (1803-1852); (vol. 1: 385 pp., vol. 2: 305 pp., vol. 3: 352 pp., vol. 4: 436 pp., vol. 5: 597 pp.; 1971-86).

Jesuits (Society of Jesus), S.J.

See also HI3, HI6, HI19, HI207, TH565, CR930, SO554, PO14, PO95, PO160-PO161, CO163, ED20, ED52, MI174, SP82, SP177, AF117, AF487-AF488, AF820, AF1141, AF1151, AM71, AM91, AM459, AM612, AM628, AM653, AM706, AM737, AM739, AM786, AM794-AM795, AM804, AM811-AM812, AM834, AM836, AM839, AM842, AM844-AM846, AM850-AM851, AM859, AM878-AM879, AM902, AM911, AM915, AM919, AM995, AM1008, AM1013, AM1019-AM1020, AM1024-AM1025, AM1124-AM1125, AM1138, AM1142, AM1155, AM1157, AM1177, AM1182, AM1190, AM1249, AM1254, AM1257-AM1259, AM1262, AM1264, AM1275, AM1293, AM1343, AM1397, AM1410, AM1439-AM1441, Am1444-AM1447, AM1449-AM1457, AM1459, AM1466, AM1472, AM1495, AM1502, AM1511, AM1528, AS9, AS37, AS40-AS41, AS45, AS298, AS327, AS329, AS332-AS334, AS349-AS350, AS365, AS383-AS384, AS391, AS397, AS404, AS504-AS505, AS511, AS526, AS532, AS567, AS585, AS590, AS612, AS642-AS644, AS665, AS668, AS679, AS683-AS685, AS695, AS699, AS821, AS872, AS905, AS919-AS920, AS1058, AS1064, AS1086, AS1117, AS1132, AS1141, AS1159, AS1195-AS1196, AS1200, AS1205, AS1218, AS1221, AS1313, AS1405, AS1417, AS1464, AS1470, AS1517, and OC15.

HI263 Amaladass, Anand, ed.

Jesuit Presence in Indian History. Anand, II: Gujarat Sahitya Prakash, 1988. xi, 379 pp. Paper. No ISBN.

Essays commemorating the Jesuit impact on Indian history; originally presented at the commemoration of the 150th anniversary of the New Madurai Mission, 1838-1988.

HI264 Bangert, William V.

A History of the Society of Jesus. (Series III: Original Studies, Composed in English, 3). St. Louis, MOU: Institute of Jesuit Sources, 1986. xii, 578 pp. 0912422734 (hdbk), 0912422742 (pbk).

The revised and updated edition of a comprehensive one-volume history of the Jesuits from 1540 to 1983; originally published in 1972.

HI265 Barthel, Manfred

Die Jesuiten: Legende und Wahrheit der Gesellschaft Jesu, gestern, heute, morgen. Düsseldorf, GW: Econ Verlag, 1982. 416 pp. 3430111722.

The first complete and balanced history of the Jesuits, from the 16th-century founding of the order to the present, examining its achievements and the frequent criticisms leveled against it.

HI266 Barthel, Manfred

The Jesuits: The History and Legend of the Society of Jesus. Translated by Mark Howson. New York, NYU: Morrow, 1984. 324 pp. 0688028616.

English translation.

HI267 Brodrick, James

The Origin of the Jesuits. Chicago, ILU: Loyola University Press, 1997. xi, 274 pp. 0829405224.

Reprint of a classic 1940 history of the early years of the Society of Jesus to the death of Ignatius, primarily concerning the life, character, and work of Francis Xavier and St. Ignatius of Loyola.

HI268 Caraman, Philip

Ignatius Loyola: A Biography of the Founder of the Jesuits. San Francisco, CAU: Harper & Row, 1990. xi, 222 pp. 0062501305.

A readable yet scholarly portrait of the founder of the Society of the Jesus, focusing on his background, personality, and motivations, and those of his contemporaries.

HI269 Chapple, Christopher, ed.
The Jesuit Tradition in Education and Missions: A 450-Year Perspective. Scranton, PAU: University of Scranton Press; London, ENK: Associated University Presses, 1993. 290 pp. 094086617X.

Sixteen scholarly essays commemorating the 450th anniversary of the founding of the Society of Jesus, focusing on contributions to education and to missions in Peru, Paraguay, Africa, India, and the United States.

HI270 Dalmases, Cándido de
Ignatius of Loyola, Founder of the Jesuits: His Life and Work. (Modern Scholarly Studies About Jesuits, II, 6). St. Louis, MOU: The Institute of Jesuit Sources, 1985. xxii, 362 pp. 0912422599 (hdbk), 0912422580 (pbk).

English translation.

HI271 Dalmases, Cándido de
El Padre Maestro Ignacio: Breve Biografía Ignaciana. (BAC Popular, 22). Madrid, SP: Biblioteca de Autores Cristianos, 1982. xiv, 258 pp. 8422009382.

Second edition of a biography of Ignatius of Loyola (1491-1556), founder of the Jesuit order; originally published in 1979.

HI272 Dehergne, Joseph
Répertoire des Jésuites de Chine de 1552 à 1800. (Bibliotheca Instituti Historici Societatis Iesu, 37). Rome, IT: Institutum Historicum Societatis Iesu; Paris, FR: Letouzey & Ané, 1973. 428 pp. No ISBN.

An index of Jesuit missionaries who served in China, 1552 to 1800.

HI273 Duclos, Paul, ed.
Les Jésuites. (Dictionnaire du Monde Religieux dans la France Contemporaine, 1). Paris, FR: Éditions Beauchesne, 1985. 269 pp. No ISBN.

Biographical information on Jesuits who were born or who worked in France from 1802 to 1960, including several missionaries; with a brief essay on Jesuit history, statistics on Jesuit missions and schools, and an extensive bibliography.

HI274 Echaniz, Ignacio
Passion and Glory: A Flesh-and-Blood History of the Society of Jesus. Anand, II: Gujarat Sahitya Prakash, 2000. 4 vols. Paper. No ISBN.

A narrative history of the Society of Jesus in four volumes [I: *Spring: 1592-1581*, xi, 216 pp.; II: *Summer: 1581-1687*, 325 pp.; III: *Autumn-Winter: 1687-1773-1814*, viii, 194 pp.; IV: *Second Spring: 1814-1965-1999*, 397 pp.].

HI275 Flores, Moacyr
Colonialismo e Missões Jesuíticas. Porto Alegre-RS, BL: EST/ Instituto de Cultura Hispânica do RS, 1983. 176 pp. Paper. No ISBN.

A narrative history, based on secondary sources, of the Jesuit missions to indigenous peoples in South America, and of Jesuit relations with Spanish and Portuguese colonialists.

HI276 Lacouture, Jean
Jesuits: A Multibiography. Translated by Jeremy Leggatt. Washington, DCU WAU: Counterpoint, 1995. x, 550 pp. 1887178058.

A well-researched and popularly written history of the Jesuits, focusing on outstanding individuals; translated and condensed from the two-volume French version.

HI277 Mitchell, David J.
The Jesuits: A History. New York, NYU: Franklin Watts, 1981. 320 pp. 0531099474.

A sympathetic history of the political and ideological dimensions of Jesuit missionary activites, highlighting their persecution and struggles.

HI278 Morrissey, Thomas
As One Sent: Peter Kenney SJ 1779-1841: His Mission in Ireland and North America. Dublin, IE: Four Courts Press; Washington, DCU: Catholic University of America Press, 1996. xii, 529 pp. 185182251X (F), 0813208807 (C).

A scholarly biography of the key figure in the reorganization of the restored Society of Jesus, both in Ireland and in the United States in the first half of the 19th century.

HI279 Ravier, André
Ignace de Loyola fonde la Compagnie de Jésus. (Collection Christus, 36: Histoire). Montréal, QUC: Bellarmin; Paris, FR: Desclée de Brouwer, 1974. 564 pp. No ISBN.

A detailed analysis of the early gradual development of the Society of Jesus into a missionary society, with a chronicle of its first seventeen years, and an assessment of the mentality, mystique, mission, and message of Ignatius of Loyola.

HI280 Ravier, André
Ignacio de Loyola Funda la Compañia de Jesús. Translated by María Aurrecoechea. (Biografías Espasa, Perfiles de Siempre). Madrid, SP: Espasa-Calpe; Mexico City, MX: Obra Nacional de la Buena Prensa, 1991. 596 pp. 842392257X (SP), 9686056416 (MX).

Spanish translation.

HI281 Ravier, André
Ignatius of Loyola and the Founding of the Society of Jesus. Translated by Maura Daly, Joan Daly, and Carson Daly. San Francisco, CAU: Ignatius Press, 1987. 504 pp. 0898700361.

English translation.

HI282 Schurhammer, Georg
Francis Xavier, His Life, His Times. Translated by M. Joseph Costelloe. Rome, IT: Jesuit Historical Institute, 1982. 4 vols. No ISBN.

English translation.

HI283 Schurhammer, Georg
Francisco Javier, su Vida y su Tiempo. Translated by Arixnabarreta Felix de Areitio. Bilbao, SP: Editorial Mensajero, 1992. 4 vols. 842711740X.

Spanish translation.

HI284 Schurhammer, Georg
Franz Xaver, sein Leben und seine Zeit. (His Franz Xaver, 1). Freiburg, GW: Herder, 1973. 4 vols. No ISBN.

The major scholarly biography of the pioneer Jesuit missionary to Asia; published as two volumes in four [I. Europe, 1506-1541; II: 1, India and Indonesia, 1541-1547; II: 2, India and Indonesia, 1547-1549; II: 3, Japan and China, 1549-1552].

HI285 Tylenda, Joseph N.
Jesuit Saints & Martyrs: Short Biographies of the Saints, Blessed, Venerables, and Servants of God of the Society of Jesus. Chicago, ILU: Jesuit Way, 1998. xvii, 478 pp. 0829404473.

Second edition of a collection of 160 short biographies which tell the stories of 323 Jesuits, arranged for reading on the date of their death or martyrdom; originally published in 1984 (Chicago, ILU: Loyola University Press).

HI–HISTORY

HI286 Woodrow, Alain
The Jesuits: A Story of Power. London, ENK: Chapman, 1996.
viii, 296 pp. 022566738X.
    Reflecting on the desire of recent Jesuit leaders that their
order renounce power and prestige, and return to their missionary roots; a religious journalist chronicles key episodes in
400 years of Jesuit involvement in power politics and revolutionary movements for social justice.

HI287 Xavier, Francis
The Letters and Instructions of Francis Xavier. Translated by M.
Joseph Costelloe. (Series I: Jesuit Primary Sources in English
Translation, 10). St. Louis, MOU: Institute of Jesuit Sources, 1992.
xxx, 488 pp. 188081000X (hdbk), 1880810018 (pbk).
    A scholarly translation from the Schurhammer-Wicki
Latin critical edition (Rome, 1944) with appropriate explanatory notes and related 16th-century documents, including one
letter more recently identified as Xavier's; published with an
extensive index and select bibliography.

HI288 Zambrano, Francisco
Diccionario-biográfico de la Compañia de Jesús en México.
México, MX: Editorial Jus, 1961-1977. 12 vols. No ISBN.
    A biographical dictionary of Jesuits who have served in
Mexico.

Mariannhill, Congregation of the Missionaries of, C.M.M.

See also AF915, and AF1041.

HI289 Balling, Adalbert Ludwig
Rebelde sin Causa? Translated by Robert R. Barr. Madrid,
SP: Misioneros de Marianhill, 1984. 143 pp. No ISBN.
    Spanish translation.

HI290 Balling, Adalbert Ludwig
*Der Trommler Gottes: Missionsabt Franz Pfanner—Abenteur-
er und Rebell (1825-1909).* Freiburg im Breisgau, GW: Herder, 1981. 350 pp. 3451191857.
    A very readable, but well-documented, book about the
life and work of Abbot Pfanner, who laid the foundations of
the Marianhill Missionaries in South Africa, raising the missiological issue of how the contemplative tradition can be reconciled with active missionary activity.

HI291 Mariannhill Missionaries
*Mariannhill und seine Sendung: Werden und Wachsen der
Mariannhiller Mission.* Reimlingen, GW: Sankt-Josefs-Ver-
lag, 1963. 288 pp. No ISBN.
    A well-illustrated, solid presentation of the achievements
of the congregation of the Mariannhill Missionaries (CMM),
which began as an off-shoot of a Trappist monastery, and eventually went its own way under the guidance of Abbot Franz
Pfanner in 1909.

Maryknoll Fathers (Catholic Foreign Missionary Society of America), M.M.

See also MI127, AS366, AS757, AS869, AS1445, and AS1500.

HI292 Kittler, Glenn D.
Maryknoll Fathers. Cleveland, OHU: World Publishing, 1961.
318 pp. No ISBN.

A popular history of the first half-century of Maryknoll
(Catholic Foreign Missionary Society of America), 1910-1960,
organized by decades.

HI293 Kroeger, James H.
Fourscore and More: Maryknoll's Asian Presence, 1917-1997.
Maryknoll, NYU: [Maryknoll Fathers and Brothers], 1997. 54
pp. Paper. No ISBN.
    A brief overview of eighty years of Maryknoll mission in
Asia.

HI294 Richardson, William J., ed.
The Church as Sign. Maryknoll, NYU: Maryknoll Publications, 1968. vii, 170 pp. No ISBN.
    Essays on mission in the post-Vatican II period, by Wil-
liam Frazier, Joseph A. Grassi, Stephen Neill, Joseph Newman, and J. J. Blomjous; with two appendices of reappraisal
by Maryknoll of its own activities.

HI295 Seddon, John T.
*When Saints Are Lovers: The Spirituality of Maryknoll Co-
Founder Thomas F. Price.* Collegeville, MNU: Liturgical
Press, 1997. x, 174 pp. Paper. 0814622283.
    A spiritual biography based on the diaries of Thomas Fre-
derick Price (1860-1919), co-founder of the Catholic Foreign
Missionary Society of America (Maryknoll).

Mercedarians (Order of Our Lady of Mercy), O. de M.

See also AM771.

HI296 Pérez Nolasco, Pedro
Historia de las Misiones Mercedarias en América. (Estudios,
22). Madrid, SP: Revista "Estudios," 1966. 487 pp. No ISBN.
    A history of the activities of Spanish Mercedarian mis-
sionaries in Central and South America in the 16th to 18th
centuries.

HI297 Pikaza, Xavier
Camino de liberación: El Modelo Mercedario. Estella, SP:
Verbo Divino, 1987. 277 pp. Paper. 847151527X.
    A discussion of the missionary activity of the La Merced
Order among the oppressed and imprisoned, from the thirteenth
century to the present; with proposals regarding the future of
the order.

Missionaries of Africa [White Fathers], M. Afr.

See also SO229, AF252, AF257, AF414, AF476, AF554, AF668,
AF670, AF676-AF677, AF719, AF733, AF735, AF747, and AF751.

HI298 Burridge, William
*Destiny Africa: Cardinal Lavigerie and the Making of the White
Fathers.* London, ENK: Chapman, 1966. 195 pp. No ISBN.
    Description of the early years of this Catholic missionary
order, emphasizing the spiritual leadership and principles of
its founder, Cardinal Lavigerie.

HI299 Burridge, William
The Missionary Principles and Work of Cardinal Lavigerie.
Dublin, IE: Chapman, 1965. 256 pp. No ISBN.
    A careful analysis of Cardinal Lavigerie's ideas and mis-
sionary principles.

HI300 Cuoq, Joseph
Lavigerie, les Pères Blancs et les Musulmans Maghrébins.
Rome, IT: Société des Missionnaires d'Afrique, 1986. 244 pp.
Paper. No ISBN.

An analysis of the mission to Muslims in North Africa (Algeria, Tunisia, and northern Sudan), by the White Fathers (now the Missionaries of Africa) and their founder Cardinal Lavigerie.

HI301 Lavigérie, Charles Martial Allemand
Écrits d'Afrique. Paris, FR: Grasset, 1966. iv, 263 pp. No ISBN.

The missionary letters of Charles Martial Allemand Lavigerie (1825-1892), founder of the order of Les Pères Blancs (White Fathers), with introduction and notes.

HI302 Lavigérie, Charles Martial Allemand
La mission universelle de l'Église. (Chrétiens de tous les temps, 27). Paris, FR: Éditions du Cerf, 1968. 207 pp. No ISBN.

An excellent selection from the writings of Cardinal Lavigerie, founder of the White Fathers, showing the extent of his missionary and church activities.

HI303 Montclos, Xavier de
Le Cardinal Lavigerie: la mission universelle de l'Église. (Foi vivante, 280). Paris, FR: Éditions du Cerf, 1991. 206 pp. Paper. 2204043869.

A new assessment of the theology of mission of Charles Lavigerie (1825-1892), cardinal, Archbishop of Carthage and Primate of Africa (1884), and founder of the Society of Missionaries of Africa (White Fathers) in 1868; with a selection of his writings.

HI304 Renault, François
Cardinal Lavigerie: Churchman, Prophet and Missionary. Translated by John O'Donohue. London, ENK: Athlone Press, 1994. vi, 470 pp. 0485114534.

The first biography, based on original research, of Cardinal Lavigerie (1825-1892), founder of the White Fathers (Missionaries of Africa) and the White Sisters.

Oblates of the Virgin Mary (Oblates of Mary Immaculate), O.M.V.

See also MI188, AF930, AM613-AM615, AM647, AM652, and AM661.

HI305 Pielorz, Jósef
Oblaci Polscy: Zarys Dziejów Prowincji Polskiej Misjonarzy Oblatów Maryi Niepokalanej z Okazji 50-lecia Istnienia. Rzym, IT: Dom Generalny, 1970. 185 pp. No ISBN.

A fifty-year history of the work of Polish Oblates of Mary Immaculate (OMI), with a list of their assignments throughout the world in 1971 (primarily in Europe, North America, Cameroun, Chile, and Sri Lanka).

HI306 Pielorz, Jósef
Les Oblats Polonais dans le monde: esquisse historique des Missionaires Oblats de Marie Immaculée d'origine polonaise, à l'occasion du cinquantenaire de la province de Pologne, 1920-1970. Rome, IT: Maison Generale of OMI, 1971. 254 pp. No ISBN.

French translation.

HI307 Woestman, William H.
The Missionary Oblates of Mary Immaculate: A Clerical Religious Congregation with Brothers. Ottawa, ONC: St. Paul University, 1995. xviii, 294 pp. 091926137X.

Published in second edition upon the canonization of the order's founder, Eugène de Mazenod, in 1995, this history of the order from its founding in 1826 was originally published as a doctoral dissertation (St. Paul University, 1985).

Passionists (Congregation of the Passion), C.P.

See also AM1490 and AS312.

HI308 Caulfield, Caspar, ed.
Missionlands of Saint Paul of the Cross. Rome, IT: Secretariatus Generalis Missionum Congregationis Passionis JesuChristi, 1976. 144 pp. Paper. No ISBN.

An atlas of the Passionist missions with a brief history of each; with Italian and English text.

HI309 Mercurio, Roger
The Passionists. (Religious Order Series, 7). Collegeville, MNU: Liturgical Press, 1992. 192 pp. 0814657257.

A short history of the Passionists based on secondary sources.

Salesians of St. John Bosco (Society of St. Francis de Sales), S.D.B.

See also AF13, AF442, AM587, AM1251, AM1261, AM1327, AM1360, AM1364, AS898, and AS1208.

HI310 Bosco, Giovanni
Epistolario: Introduzione, testi critici e note. Edited by Francesco Motto. (Instituto storico salesiano; Scritti editi e inediti, 6). Rome, IT: Libreria Ateneo Salesiano (LAS), 1991. 718 pp. Paper. 8821302261.

The first volume of a critical edition of the letters of St. Giovanni Bosco (1815-1888), founder of the Salesians; containing 726 letters from 1835 to 1863.

HI311 Tomatis, Domenico
Epistolario (1874-1903). Edited by Jesus Borrego. (Instituto storico salesiano; Scritti editi e inediti di salesiani, 2). Rome, IT: Libreria Ateneo Salesiano (LAS), 1992. 420 pp. Paper. 8821302253.

A critical edition of the letters of Domenico Tomatis (1849-1912), pioneer Salesian missionary to Argentina (1876-1887) and Chile (1888-1912).

Salvatorians (Society of the Divine Savior), S.D.S.

See also AS898.

HI312 Bornemann, Fritz
Der Pfarrer von Neuwerk Dr. Ludwig von Essen (gestorben 1886) und seine Missionspläne. (Studia Instituti Missiologici SVD, 8). St. Augustin, GW: Steyler Verlag, 1967. 232 pp. No ISBN.

A valuable contribution to the history of the Inland Mission in Germany during the 19th century, particularly in connection with the Salvatorian priests and nuns and the founding of the Steyler Missionary Society.

HI—HISTORY

Society for the Propagation of the Faith

See also HI205.

HI313 Bachmann, L. G.
Das reiche Fräulein Jaricot: Lebensbild einer apostolisch-sozialen Kämpferin. (Stirb und werde, 4). Mödling b. Wien, AU: Gabriel-Verlag, 1962. 232 pp. No ISBN.

A popular biography of Pauline M. Jaricot (1799-1862), founder of the Society for the Propagation of the Faith.

HI314 Hickey, Edward John
The Society for the Propagation of the Faith: Its Foundation, Organization and Success, 1822-1922. New York, NYU: AMS Press, 1974. x, 196 pp. 0404577539.

A reprint of the 1922 edition—originally the author's thesis for Catholic University of America.

Society of African Missions, S.M.A.

See also AF709, and AF1339.

HI315 Todd, John Murray
African Mission: A Historical Study of the Society of African Missions. London, ENK: Burns & Oates, 1962. vii, 230 pp. No ISBN.

A historical study of the Society of African Missions from 1856 to 1958, focusing on the founder, Melchior de Marion Bresilla, the society's work in West Africa, and on relations with native African cultures.

Society of the Divine Word, S.V.D.

See also SP293, AF1373, AM655-AM656, AM1241, AM1442, AS77, AS195, AS355-AS356, AS367, AS392-AS393, AS502-AS503, AS523, AS551, AS561, AS593, AS1345, AS1467-AS1468, EU265, OC178, OC204, OC206, and OC238.

HI316 Alt, Josef, ed.
Arnold Janssen SVD, Briefe nach Südamerika. (Studia Instituti Missiologici SVD, 44-45). Nettetal, GW: Steyler Verlag, 1989-9199. 4 vols. Paper. 3805002300 (set).

Further letters from the Society of the Divine Word missionary from 1900 to 1904; published in four volumes [Vol. 1: 1890-1899 (1989, 380502919); vol. 2: 1900-1902 (1991, xiv, 528 pp., 380500267X); vol. 3: 1903-1904 (1992, xii, 514 pp., 3805002920); vol. 4: 1905-1908 (1993, xviii, 529 pp., 3805003234)].

HI317 Bauer, Johannes A.
Das Presseapostolat Arnold Janssen (1837-1909): Seine Bedeutung für die Entfaltung der Gesellschaft des Göttlichen Wortes und die Ausbildung des Missionsbewusstseins. (Studia Instituti Missiologici SVD, 49). Nettetal, GW: Steyler Verlag, 1989. 100 pp. Paper. 3805002548.

The series continues research into the career and work of Arnold Janssen, founder of the SVD, by examining his apostolate of the press.

HI318 Bevans, Stephen B., and Roger Schroeder, eds.
Word Remembered, Word Proclaimed: Selected Papers from Symposia Celebrating the SVD Centennial in North America. (Studia Instituti Missiologici SVD, 65). Nettetal, GW: Steyler Verlag, 1997. vii, 255 pp. Paper. 3805003986.

Nine papers on the new evangelization, African American ministry, and multicultural education and ministry; originally presented at the symposium celebrating the Society of the Divine Word's centennial in 1994 and 1995.

HI319 Bornemann, Fritz
Arnold Janssen, der Gründer des Steyler Missionswerkes, 1837-1909: Ein Lebensbild nach zeitgenössischen Quellen. Steyl, NE: Missionsdruckerei, 1970. 532 pp. No ISBN.

A detailed biography, but without footnotes, of Arnold Janssen, the founder of the SVD missionary order.

HI320 Bornemann, Fritz
Arnold Janssen, Founder of Three Missionary Congregations, 1837-1909: A Biography. Edited by John Vogelgesang. Manila, PH: Arnoldus Press, 1975. 515 pp. No ISBN.

English translation.

HI321 Bornemann, Fritz
Arnoldo Janssen, Fundador de los Misioneros del Verbo Divino: su Vida y su Obra. Estella, SP: Verbo Divino, 1971. 584 pp. Paper. No ISBN.

Spanish translation.

HI322 Bornemann, Fritz, ed.
Erinnerungen an P. Arnold Janssen, Gründer des Steyler Missionswerkes. St. Augustin, GW: Steyler Verlag, 1974. 490 pp. 3805000382.

Second edition of reflections on the life and work of Fr. Arnold Janssen (1837-1909), founder of the SVD.

HI323 Bornemann, Fritz, ed.
Erinnerungen an P. Josef Freinademetz: Ein Sudtiroler in China. St. Augustin, GW: Steyler Verlag; Mödling, GW: Verlag St. Gabriel, 1974. 151 pp. Paper. 3805000391 (SV), 3852640709 (VSG).

Reflections on the life and work of Fr. Josef Frenademetz (1852-1908), pioneer SVD missionary and administrator in China (1879-1908).

HI324 Brandewie, Ernest
In the Light of the World: Divine Word Missionaries of North America. (American Society of Missiology Series, 29). Maryknoll, NYU: Orbis Books, 2000. xviii, 408 pp. Paper. 157075232X.

In this history of the Society of the Divine Word, the author tells of its expansion since 1900, its stimulation of American interest in overseas mission, and pioneer work among African Americans.

HI325 Brandewie, Ernest
When Giants Walked the Earth: The Life and Times of Wilhelm Schmidt, SVD. (Studia Instituti Anthropos, 44). Fribourg, SZ: University Press, 1990. 357 pp. Paper. 3727807121.

A scholarly biography of Wilhelm Schmidt, SVD (1868-1954), and assessment of his influence on Catholics in mission through his seminary teaching, his editorship of *Anthropos*, which he founded in 1906, his magnum opus *Der Ursprung der Gottesidee* (The Origin of the Idea of God), and his political involvements.

HI326 Divine Word Missionaries, eds.
The Word in the World: Divine Word Missionaries, 1875-1975. Techny, ILU: SVD, 1975. 191 pp. Paper. No ISBN.

A collection of articles on the worldwide missionary activity of the Society of the Divine Word on the occasion of its centenary.

HI327 Pöhl, Rudolf
Der Missionar zwischen Ordensleben und missionarischem Auftrag: Untersuchungen zur missionarischen Zielvorstellung und zur spirituellen Pluriformität in der Gesellschaft des Göttlichen Wortes (SVD). (Studia Instituti Missiologici SVD, 18). St. Augustin, GW: Steyler Verlag, 1977. 488 pp. Paper. No ISBN.

Analysis of a detailed questionnaire sent to all SVD members in 1971 revealing motivations, types of missionary spirituality, lifestyle issues, and the polarity in the SVD between membership of a "religious" order and of a missionary society in the light of official SVD documents.

Vincentians (Congregation of the Mission; Lazarists), C.M.

See also AF509, AF564, AF569, AF774, and AS537.

HI328 Redondo Rodrigues, José
Misionología de san Vicente de Pablo: Año tricentenario 1660-1960. México, MX: Porrúa Hermanos, 1960. xi, 354 pp. No ISBN.

A study of the writings of St. Vincent de Paul concerning missionary work, both theological and practical, including a listing of the past (since 1600) and present missions of his order around the world.

Xaverian Missionary Fathers, S.X.

See also AS342.

HI329 Mondin, Battista
Missione Annuncio di Christo Signore. (Collana studi saveriani, 6). Bologna, IT: Editrice Missionaria Italiana, 1994. 171 pp. Paper. 8830705306.

An analysis of the Christocentric theology of Guido Maria Conforti (1865-1931), founder of the Xaverian Missionary Fathers.

General Works

See also GW48, GW171, GW279, TH586, EA23, EA237, EA243, ME144, CR241, SO193, EC382, PO20, PO166, PO217, MI176, MI185, CH333-CH336, AF114, AF247, AF426, AF469, AF543, AF1147, AM93, AM114, AM122, AM130, AM134, AM185, AM207, AM231-AM232, AM348, AM597, AM697, AM793, AM1306-AM1307, AM1322, AM1484, AS75-AS76, AS343, AS491, AS608, AS639, AS913, AS979, AS1363, AS1480, EU4, and EU181.

HI330 Brown, Alden V.
The Grail Movement and American Catholicism, 1940-1975. Notre Dame, INU: University of Notre Dame Press, 1989. xl, 229 pp. 0268010153.

History of the Grail's apostolate to American Catholic laywomen, including discussion of mission vision.

HI331 McNamara, Jo Ann
Sisters in Arms: Catholic Nuns through Two Millennia. Cambridge, MAU: Harvard University Press, 1996. xi, 751 pp. 067480984X.

The first definitive history of Catholic nuns in the Western world, focusing on their multiple roles as scholars, mystics, artists, political activists, healers, and teachers.

HI332 Shields, Joseph J.
Attitudes of American Women Religious towards the Concept of Mission Research: Report Submitted to the United States Catholic Mission Council. Washington, DCU: United States Catholic Mission Council, 1977. i, 61 pp. Paper. No ISBN.

Results of an attitudinal survey among Catholic women religious in the United States concerning their understandings of mission as evangelization, liberation, or Christian witness.

HI333 Stewart, George C.
Marvels of Charity: History of American Sisters and Nuns. Huntington, INU: Our Sunday Visitor, 1994. 607 pp. 0879736488.

An overview history of American nuns, including those organized for missions.

Benedictines (various), O.S.B.

HI334 Walter, Bernita
Sustained by God's Faithfulness: The Missionary Benedictine Sisters of Tutzing. Translated by Matilda Handl. St. Otilien, GW: EOS Verlag, 1987. 2 vols. No ISBN.

This English translation of *Von Gottes Treuge getragen* is a two-volume illustrated history of the Missionary Benedictine Sisters of Tutzing founded in Bavaria, Germany in 1887, with special focus on their mission work in present Tanzania [vol. 1: *Founding and Early Development of the Congregation* (1987, x, 238 pp., 3880961972); vol. 2: *Proclaiming God's Faithfulness Preparing the Way for the Church in East Africa* (1992, viii, 401 pp., 3880966389)].

HI335 Walter, Bernita
Von Gottes Treue getragen: Die Missionsbenediktinerinnen von Tutzing. Vol.1: Gründung und erste Entwicklung der Kongregation. St. Ottilien, GW: EOS Verlag, 1985. x, 264 pp. 3880961433.

The first volume of a history of the congregation, from the beginnings to the transfer of the mother house to Tutzing (1904); with copious biographical and bibliographical references drawn from authentic archive material.

Charity of St. Vincent de Paul, Daughters of, D.C.

HI336 McKenna, Mary Olga
Charity Alive: Sisters of Charity of Saint Vincent de Paul, Halifax 1950-1980. Lanham, MDU: University Press of America, 1999. xxvi, 376 pp. 0761809864.

A history from 1950 to 1980; including sweeping reforms brought on by the Second Vatican Council, with its challenge to religious congregations to reclaim the charisma of their founders, the call to the missions, and the shaping of the future.

Franciscans (various)

See also HI246, HI249, AM666, AM962, AM1139, AM1153, AM1203, and AM1375.

HI337 Hubaut, Michel, and Marie-Therese De Maleissye
Two Gospel People: Francis of Assisi and Mary of the Passion, Experience of God is the Basis of Gospel Life. Macao, MH: Mandarin Printing Press, 1977. 188 pp. No ISBN.

Biographies of St. Francis (1186-1226) and Marie de la Passion (1839-1904) of the Franciscan Sisters of Mary.

HI338 Teresa, Frances
This Living Mirror: Reflections on Clare of Assisi. London, ENK: Darton, Longman, & Todd; Maryknoll, NYU: Orbis Books, 1995. xii, 131 pp. Paper. 0232520670(UK, hdbk), 0232520674 (UK, pbk), 1570750238 (US).

    An account of Clare of Assisi's journey to God, which led her outward in mission to the needy in 13th-century Italy; by a member of the Community of Poor Clares.

HI339 Willmann, Agnes
Everywhere People Waiting: The Life of Helen de Chappotin de Neuville (Mother Mary of the Passion) 1839-1904, Foundress of the Franciscan Missionaries of Mary. North Quincy, MAU: Christopher Publishing House, 1973. 376 pp. 0815802943.

    Biography of Hélène de Chappotin de Neuville (1839-1904), missionary of the Society of Mary Reparatrix (1864-1876) in the Madura missions of India, who in 1877 founded the Institute of Missionaries of Mary, which became the Franciscan Missionaries of Mary (FMM) in 1882.

Holy Spirit Missionary Sisters

See also AM1039.

HI340 Gier, Ann
This Fire Ever Burning: A Biography of M. Leonardo Lentrup. [n.p.]: Holy Spirit Missionary Sisters, 1986. xii, 330 pp. Paper. 0961772204.

    Biography of Elizabeth Lentrup (Sister Leonarda), founder in North America of the Holy Spirit Missionary Sisters.

HI341 Müller, Karl
Contemplation and Mission: Sister-Servants of the Holy Spirit of Perpetual Adoration, 1896-1996. Translated by Frank Mansfield. (Studia Instituti Missiologici SVD, 69). Nettetal, GW: Steyler Verlag, 1998. xi, 448 pp. 3805004192.

    The official centennial history by the noted German missiologist of the order founded 1896 in Holland, and in the United States from 1915.

HI342 Müller, Karl
Kontemplation und Mission: Steyler Anbetungsschwestern, 1896-1996. (Studia Instituti Missiologici SVD, 64). Nettetal, GW: Steyler Verlag, 1996. xii, 552 pp. Paper. 3805003749.

    A detailed centennial history of the Adoration Sisters of the Holy Spirit founded by Arnold Janssen, SVD, in 1896.

HI343 Zosso, Terisse, ed.
A Century of Mission Service. Chicago, ILU: G I A Publications, 1989. 175 pp. No ISBN.

    A commemorative album portraying in English, German, and Spanish, the hundred years' worldwide service of the Holy Spirit Missionary Sisters.

Immaculate Heart of Mary, Sisters of the

HI344 De Meester, Marie-Louise, and Cecile Sandra
Op weg met God. Beveren, NE: Emmaus for the Sisters Missionaries of the Immaculate Heart of Mary, 1981. 280 pp. 9026477406.

    Biography of Marie-Louise De Meester (1857-1928), foundress of the missionary congregation Canonnesses Missionaries of Saint-Augustin, now called Sisters Missionaries of the Immaculate Heart of Mary, who started missionary work in India, Philippines, the Caribbean, Belgian Congo, and China/Mongolia.

HI345 Verhelst, Daniël
La Congrégation du Coeur Immaculé de Marie (Scheut): édition critique des sources. (Symbolae Facultatis Litterarum et Philosophiae Lovaniensis Series A, 15). Leuven, FR: Leuven University Press, 1986. 367 pp. 9061862051.

    This first volume of documents from the archives of the Congregation of the Immaculate Heart of Mary covers the founding of the order for women religious.

Mary, Company of (Order of Notre Dame), O.D.N.

HI346 Foz y Foz, Pilar, and Estela Meija Restrepo
Fuentes primarias para la historia de la educación de la mujer en Europa y América: Archivos históricos Compañía de María Nuestra Señora 1607-1921. Rome, IT: Tipografía Políglota Vaticana, 1989. xxxii, 1445 pp. No ISBN.

    A compilation of archival documents in Spanish and French, including correspondence and photographs of the Company of Mary, also known as the Order of Notre Dame; covering their work as a complement to the Society of Jesus in educating youth in Europe and the Americas; with a history of the order from its founding in France in 1608 to 1921.

Maryknoll Sisters, M.M.

See also GW85, AM671, AM728, and AM756.

HI347 Kennedy, Camilla
To the Uttermost Parts of the Earth: The Spirit and Charism of Mary Josephine Rogers. Maryknoll, NYU: Maryknoll Sisters, 1987. 313 pp. No ISBN.

    History of the Maryknoll Sisters through the life of their founder, including primary documents by Mother Mary Joseph.

HI348 Lernoux, Penny
Hearts on Fire: The Story of the Maryknoll Sisters. Maryknoll, NYU: Orbis Books, 1993. xxxiii, 294 pp. 0883449250.

    A scholarly oral history by the acclaimed journalist of the Maryknoll Sisters from their founding in 1912; completed by Arthur Jones and Robert Ellsberg following the author's death in 1989.

HI349 Louise, Mary Francis
The Maryknoll Sisters: A Pictoral History. New York, NYU: Dutton, 1962. 184 pp. No ISBN.

    A history of the Maryknoll Sisters from 1906 to 1962.

HI350 Lyons, Jeanne Marie
Maryknoll's First Lady: The Life of Mother Mary Joseph, Foundress of the Maryknoll Sisters. Garden City, NYU: Doubleday, 1967. vi, 319 pp. No ISBN.

    A biography of Mother Mary Joseph Rogers (1882-1955), foundress of the Maryknoll Sisters of St. Dominic in 1920, an order which grew to number more than 1,100 at the time of her death; originally published in 1964 by Dodd, Mead and Maryknoll Sisters.

Medical Mission Sisters (Society of Catholic Medical Missionaries), S.C.M.M.

See also HI226.

HI351 Plechl, Pia Maria
Kreuz und Äskulap: Dr. med. Anna Dengel und die Missionsärztlichen Schwestern. Vienna, AU: Herold, 1967. 228 pp. No ISBN.

A biography of the foundress of the Medical Mission Sisters who, overcoming all obstacles posed by tradition, expanded the activity of women religious to all fields of medicine; with accounts of their work in Africa and Asia.

HI352 Plechl, Pia Maria
Die Nonne mit dem Stethoskop: Dr. med. Anna Dengel (Asien, Afrika), (1892-1980, Eine Tirolerin geht einen neuen Weg). (Missionare, die Geschichte machten). Mödling, AU: Verlag St. Gabriel; St. Augustin, GW: Steyler Verlag, 1981. 130 pp. Paper. 3852641738 (AU), 3877871453 (GW).

The story of Mother Dengel, foundress of the Medical Mission Sisters, who succeeded in reconciling medical and missionary work against the age-old prohibition of canon law.

Mercy, Sisters of the Union in the U.S.A., R.S.M.

HI353 Healy, Kathleen, ed.
Sisters of Mercy: Spirituality in America, 1843-1900. (Sources of American Spirituality). New York, NYU: Paulist Press, 1992. x, 393 pp. 0809104539.

A collection of spiritual writings of the Sisters of Mercy in the United States during the second half of the 19th century; including historical sketches of Mercy missions.

Missionaries of Charity, M.C.

See also SP9, SP150, SP187-SP189, SP191-SP195, AS997-AS998, AS1147-AS1148, AS1150, AS1189, AS1198, AS1211, AS1217, and AS1228.

HI354 Fischer, Werner
Mutter Teresa: Ein Heiligkeitsmodell kritisch betrachtet. Munich, GW: Deutscher Taschenbuch Verlag, 1985. 201 pp. Paper. 3423104449.

A critical and thought-provoking book about the idealization process of Mother Teresa, her "model of holiness" in the Indian context, and what lies behind the publicity connected with her person and work.

HI355 Le Joly, Edward
We Do It for Jesus: Mother Teresa and Her Missionaries of Charity. New Delhi, II: Oxford University Press, 1998. 201 pp. Paper. 0195645618.

The second edition of a book about the Missionaries of Charity, written with the blessing of Mother Teresa; now including important events in Mother Teresa's life until her death and state funeral in September 1997, as well as the *Prayer of Peace* inserted at her request.

HI356 Sebba, Anne
Mother Teresa: Beyond the Image. New York, NYU: Doubleday, 1997. xix, 297 pp. 0385489528.

A narrative biography of the founder of the Missionary Sisters of Charity, with analysis of her social, historical, and geographic context, and an assessment of the future of her order.

Missionaries of Mary Immaculate and St. Catherine of Siena

HI357 Mesa, Carlos E.
La Madre Laura: Misionera. Medellín, CK: Editorial Zuluaga, 1986. 142 pp. Paper. No ISBN.

A biography of Laura Montoya de Santa Catalina, foundress of the Missionaries of Mary Immaculate and St. Catherine of Siena.

HI358 Montoya, Santa Catalina Laura de
La Aventura Misional de Dabeiba o "brochazos," Históricos sobre los Orígenes de la Congregación. Bogotá, CK: Carlos E. Mesa, 1980. 532 pp. Paper. No ISBN.

A narrative of the missionary activities and beginnings of the Missionaries of Mary Immaculate and St. Catherine of Siena.

Sacred Heart, Society of the, R.S.C.J.

See also AM1014.

HI359 Sadoux, Dominique, and Pierre Gervais
La vie religieuse: premières constitutions des religieuses de la Société du Sacré Coeur. Paris, FR: Beauchesne, 1986. 362 pp. Paper. 270101123X.

The first constitutions (1815-1826) of the Nuns of the Society of Sacred Heart, with a detailed commentary.

HI360 William, Margaret Anne
The Society of the Sacred Heart: History of a Spirit, 1800-1975. London, ENK: Darton, Longman & Todd, 1978. 406 pp. Paper. 0232513953.

The 175-year history of the Society of the Sacred Heart (RSCJ), focusing on the spiritual continuity throughout the history of the order of Catholic women religious.

St. Joseph, Sisters of (various)

HI361 Moore, Brian
A Little Good: The Life of Blessed Anne Maria Javouhey, Foundress of the Sisters of St. Joseph of Cluny. Melbourne, AT: Polding Press, 1982. 161 pp. 0858843447.

A biography of Anne Marie Javouhey (1779-1851), who founded in France the missionary order of the Congregation of St. Joseph of Cluny.

General Works

See also GW149, HI37, TH11, TH107, TH167, ME90, ME231, CR1393, CR1413, SO443, SO603, EV97, MI74-MI75, AF656, AF857, AM140, AM197, AM575, AM1267, AM1319, AS722, AS816, AS839, AS896, AS959, AS1286, AS1332-AS1333, EU201, and OC274.

HI362 Allan, John D., comp.
The Evangelicals: An Illustrated History. Grand Rapids, MIU: Baker Books; Exeter, ENK: Paternoster Press, 1989. 154 pp. Paper. 0853644993.

An illustrated history of the evangelical movement and its activity throughout the world, from its roots in Jesus and the early Church to Lausanne 1974.

HI363 Davey, Cyril J.
Caring Comes First: The Story of the Leprosy Mission. Basingstoke, ENK: Marshall Pickering, 1987. 192 pp. Paper. 0551014342.
    Narrative history of the Leprosy Mission of Great Britain's more than a century of service in the world.

HI364 *Les missions protestantes et l'histoire: actes du 11e Colloque (4-9 Octobre 1971)*
(Étude des Colloques, 2). Paris, FR: Société de l'Histoire du Protestantisme Français, 1972. 144 pp. Paper. No ISBN.
    Nine scholarly essays reappraising various aspects of Protestant mission history, including Stephen Neill on syncretism, Bengt Sundkler on Zulu Messianism, and L. Joubert on missions and 19th-century colonialism in Africa.

HI365 Tracy, Joseph
History of American Missions to the Heathen, from Their Commencement to the Present Time. (Series in American Studies). New York, NYU: Johnson Reprint, 1970. lv, 726 pp. No ISBN.
    A reprint of the 1840 history of the American-based missionary societies (American Board, Baptist General Convention, Freewill Baptist, Methodist Episcopal, Protestant Episcopal, and Presbyterian).

Adventists: General

See also AF1035.

HI366 Pfeiffer, Baldur, Luther E. Träder, and George R. Knight, eds.
Die Adventisten Hamburg: Von der Ortsgemeinde zur internationalen Bewegung. Frankfurt am Main, GW: Lang, 1992. vii, 161 pp. Paper. 3631446357.
    A collection of essays on the rapid growth of the Seventh-day Adventist Church in Europe.

Africa Inland Mission, 1895-

See also AF428, AF470, and AF629.

HI367 Anderson, Dick
We Felt Like Grasshoppers: The Story of Africa Inland Mission. Nottingham, ENK: Crossway Books, 1994. 348 pp. 1856841073 (hdbk), 1856841065 (pbk).
    A collection of stories of the founding of Africa Inland Mission in 1895, and its subsequent ministries, primarily in East Africa; published for its centennial in 1995.

HI368 Richardson, Kenneth
Garden of Miracles: The Story of the Africa Inland Mission. London, ENK: Africa Inland Mission, 1976. 270 pp. 0854760075.
    A history of the Africa Inland Mission from its formation in 1895 to 1966, emphasizing the early pioneers and early church development in Africa.

African Methodist Episcopal Church, 1816-

See also EV272 and MI189.

HI369 Campbell, James T.
Songs of Zion: The African Methodist Episcopal Church in the United States and South Africa. New York, NYU: Oxford University Press, 1995. xv, 418 pp. 0195078926.
    A scholarly history, based on archival sources, of the African Methodist Church, of its absorption of an African "Ethiopian" church in South Africa in 1896, and of the resulting history of cross-Atlantic contacts which resulted from that merger.

HI370 Dandridge, Octavia W.
A History of the Women's Missionary Society of the African Methodist Episcopal Church, 1874-1987. [United States]: Women's Missionary Society, 1987. xiv, 175 pp. Paper. No ISBN.
    A commissioned history consisting primarily of short biographies of key leaders in each episcopal district.

African Methodist Episcopal Zion Church, 1796-

HI371 Rogerson, Idonia Elizabeth, comp.
Historical Synopsis of the Woman's Home and Foreign Missionary Society, African Methodist Episcopal Zion Church. Charlotte, NCU: AME Zion Publishing House, 1967. 88 pp. No ISBN.
    A popular history of the AME Zion Church's mission outreach by women.

HI372 Walls, William J.
African Methodist Episcopal Zion Church. Charlotte, NCU: AME Zion Publishing House, 1974. 669 pp. No ISBN.
    A history of the AME Zion Church, including information on its missions work in Africa to 1972.

American Baptist Churches in the U.S.A., 1972-

See also AM161, AM1128, AS692, AS895, AS940, AS1267, AS1271, AS1390, AS1392-AS1395, and AS1397.

HI373 Cattan, Louise Armstrong, and Helen C. Schmitz
One Mark of Greatness. Philadelphia, PAU: Judson Press, 1961. 173 pp. Paper. No ISBN.
    A history of American Baptist missions including both home and foreign missionary programs, emphasizing the work of early missionary to the Far East, Nathan Brown, and home mission pioneers John Peck, Jonathan Going, and Joanna Moore.

American Bible Society, 1816-

See also AM1388.

HI374 Lacy, Creighton
The Word Carrying Giant: The Growth of the American Bible Society (1816-1966). South Pasadena, CAU: William Carey Library, 1977. vii, 311 pp. 0878084258.
    An informative and readable chronicle of the American Bible Society's first 150 years based on ABS archives.

HI375 Taylor, Robert T.
Wings for the Word: A Short History of the American Bible Society. Plainfield, NJU: Logos International, 1978. vi, 161 pp. Paper. 088270298X.
    A popular history of the American Bible Society and its work of translation, publication, and distribution both in the United States and overseas.

HI—HISTORY

HI376 Wosh, Peter J.
Spreading the Word: The Bible Business in Nineteenth-Century America. Ithaca, NYU: Cornell University Press, 1994. xii, 271 pp. 0801429285.

The history of the American Bible Society in the 19th century by its Director of Archives and Library Services.

American Board of Commissioners for Foreign Missions, 1810-1961

See also EA97, ED42, SP170, AF804, AF947, AF953, AF981, AM1009, AM1115, AM1118, AM1147, AM1154, AM1179, AS307, AS339, AS400, AS529, AS560, AS694, AS785, AS858-AS859, AS1493, EU287, OC309, OC313, OC315, and OC317.

HI377 Anderson, Rufus
To Advance the Gospel: Selections from the Writings of Rufus Anderson. Edited by Robert Pierce Beaver. Grand Rapids, MIU: Eerdmans, 1967. 225 pp. No ISBN.

A reprint of important writings of Rufus Anderson, Corresponding Secretary of the ABCFM (1826-1866), on the call to mission, principles of mission, and the missionary; with an interpretive essay by the editor.

HI378 Andrew, John A.
Rebuilding the Christian Commonwealth: New England Congregationalists and Foreign Missions, 1800-1830. Lexington, KYU: University Press of Kentucky, 1976. vii, 232 pp. 0813113334.

Scholarly history of the relation of New England Congregationalists and foreign mission; specifically an inquiry into the social, political, economic, and religious environment which produced and supported the Sandwich Islands mission.

HI379 Bartlett, Samuel Colcord
Historical Sketches of the Missions of the American Board. (Religion in America Series II). New York, NYU: Arno Press, 1972. 161 pp. 0405040571.

Contains six sketches of the history of the ABCFM in Africa, China, India, North America, the Pacific Islands, and Turkey, which were published as separate tracts in 1876.

HI380 Goodsell, Fred Field
They Lived Their Faith: An Almanac of Faith, Hope and Love. Boston, MAU: ABCFM, 1961. xxi, 486 pp. No ISBN.

A collection of anecdotes, biographies, historical sketches, and vignettes, arranged day-by-day through the year for inspirational reading; by a former Executive Vice President of the ABCFM.

HI381 Harris, Paul William
Nothing but Christ: Rufus Anderson and the Ideology of Protestant Foreign Missions. (Religion in America Series). New York, NYU: Oxford University Press, 1999. viii, 204 pp. 019513172X.

As the corresponding secretary of the ABCFM from 1832 to 1866, Anderson laid the foundation for the development of indigenous Christianity through his goal for native churches to be self-supporting, self-governing, and self-propagating.

HI382 Phillips, Clifton Jackson
Protestant America and the Pagan World: The First Half Century of the American Board of Commissioners for Foreign Missions, 1810-1860. (Harvard East Asian Monographs, 32). Cambridge, MAU: Harvard University, East Asian Research Center, 1969. viii, 370 pp. 0674717805.

A history of the first fifty years of the ABCFM.

HI383 Strong, William Ellsworth
The Story of the American Board. New York, NYU: Arno Press; New York, NYU: *New York Times*, 1969. ix, 523 pp. No ISBN.

A reprint of a 1910 history of the first 100 years of the ABCFM, which demonstrates the growth of the mission in terms of a planting period (1810-1850), a watering period (1850-1880), and the increase (1880-1910).

HI384 Whipple, Charles K.
Relation of the American Board of Commissioners for Foreign Missions to Slavery. New York, NYU: Negro Universities Press, 1969. 247 pp. No ISBN.

Reprint of an 1861 collection of reports, letters, and other documents, reflecting different viewpoints of the ABCFM on the slavery issue, from its first mission to the Cherokees in 1817 to 1860.

American Lutheran Church, 1930-60; 1960-87

See also SO208, AF1289, AM996, and OC194.

HI385 Lagerquist, L. DeAne
From Our Mother's Arms: A History of Women in the American Lutheran Church. Minneapolis, MNU: Augsburg, 1987. 221 pp. Paper. No ISBN.

A history of the development of women's societies in the Lutheran churches, which came together to form the American Lutheran Church in 1960; with details concerning their missionary federations.

American Tract Society, 1825-

HI386 The American Tract Society Documents, 1824-1925
(Religion in America, Series 2). New York, NYU: Arno Press, 1972. various pp. 0405040555.

Collection of reprinted documents illustrating the history of the American Tract Society, including financial reports and lists of publications.

Anglicans: General

See also GW161, HI653, EA219, ME126, EV262, SP278, AF468, AF529, AF958, AF962, AF979, AF1005, AF1059, AF1063, AF1127, AF1131, AF1136, AF1160, AS419, AS954, AS1152, EU71, OC25, OC39, OC248-OC249, OC253, and OC270.

HI387 Anglican Consultative Council
Many Gifts, One Spirit: Report of ACC-7, Singapore 1987. London, ENK: Church House Publishing, 1987. ix, 167 pp. Paper. 0715147641.

Includes the resolutions of the seventh meeting of the Anglican Consultative Council, Singapore 1987 (mission and ministry, dogmatic and pastoral, Christianity and society) as well as reports of business conducted.

HI388 Anglican Religious Orders and Communities: A Directory
Cincinnati, OHU: Forward Movement, 1991. 117 pp. Paper. 088028126X.

A directory of 168 Anglican religious communities by country and type, with a brief history and description of each.

HI389 Griffiss, James E.

The Anglican Vision. (The New Church's Teaching Series, 1). Cambridge, MAU: Cowley Publications, 1997. xi, 148 pp. Paper. 1561011436.

An introduction to the Anglican tradition, including its origins, Catholic and Evangelical renewal movements of the 19th century, and a survey of Anglican mission, theology, and worship.

HI390 Herklots, Hugh G. G.

Frontiers of the Church: The Making of the Anglican Communion. London, ENK: Benn, 1961. 293 pp. No ISBN.

History of the worldwide missionary expansion of the Anglicans, from the Reformation to 1960, emphasizing the contributions of national churches to the Anglican communion.

HI391 Howe, John

Highways and Hedges: Anglicanism and the Universal Church. Toronto, ONC: Anglican Book Centre, 1985. 240 pp. Paper. 0919891306.

An overview of the changes in and development of the modern Anglican Communion; by Bishop Howe, the first Secretary General of the Anglican Consultative Council.

HI392 Mann, Wendy

An Unquenched Flame: A Short History of the South American Missionary Society. London, ENK: South American Missionary Society, 1968. 94 pp. Paper. No ISBN.

A short narrative history of the South American Missionary Society, founded in 1844 by Anglicans for mission to Indians and other inhabitants in Paraguay, Chile, and Argentina.

HI393 Marshall, Michael

Church at the Crossroads: Lambeth 1988. San Francisco, CAU: Harper & Row; London, ENK: Collins, 1988. xii, 178 pp. 0060654279 (H), 0005990920 (C).

An anecdotal account of the issues and discussions of the twelfth meeting of the bishops of the Anglican Communion, with background on the history of Lambeth conferences since 1867.

HI394 Steer, Roger

Guarding the Holy Fire: The Evangelicalism of John R. W. Stott, J. I. Packer and Alister McGrath. Grand Rapids, MIU: Baker Books, 1999. Paper. 0801058465.

From the days of Wycliffe and the Lollards to the era of the present Archbishop of Canterbury, the author captures the zeal, commitment, and burning spirituality characteristic of Anglican evangelicalism; first published by Hodder and Stoughton as *Church on Fire: The Story of Anglican Evangelicals* (1998).

HI395 Yates, Timothy E.

Venn and Victorian Bishops Abroad: The Missionary Policies of Henry Venn and Their Repercussions upon the Anglican Episcopate of the Colonial Period, 1841-1872. (Studia Missionalia Upsaliensia, 33). Uppsala, SW: Swedish Institute of Missionary Research; London, ENK: SPCK, 1978. 212 pp. Paper. 918542403X.

A study of the primary issues of Venn in his dealings with the episcopate at home and abroad, as he influenced the development of the CMS throughout the world.

Assemblies of God, 1914-

See also GW116, AF827, AF1294, AM1315, AS306, AS910, AS1138, and AS1274.

HI396 Blumhofer, Edith L.

The Assemblies of God: A Chapter in the Story of American Pentecostalism. Springfield, MOU: Gospel Publishing House, 1989. 2 vols. No ISBN.

Beginning with the thesis that Pentecostalism began as a restorationist movement, Blumhofer uses the history of the Assemblies of God to argue that Pentecostalism's identity has changed significantly as it has grown in numbers and influence, met the changing expectations of American culture, and engaged in mission; [Vol. 1, *To 1941*, 463 pp., 0882434578; vol. 2, *Since 1941*, 242 pp., 0882434586].

HI397 Booze, Joyce Wells

Into All the World: A History of Assembly of God Foreign Missions. Springfield, MOU: Gospel Publishing House, 1980. 73 pp. No ISBN.

A five-lesson correspondence study course on Pentecostal missions, designed to encourage awareness and participation in local AG missions programs.

HI398 Champion, Richard, Edward S. Caldwell, and Gary Leggett, eds.

Our Mission in Today's World: Council on Evangelism Official Papers and Reports. Springfield, MOU: Gospel Publishing House, 1968. 217 pp. No ISBN.

Proceedings of an historic Assemblies of God meeting in which the denomination re-examined the purposes and goals of its missionary outreach.

HI399 DeLeon, Victor

The Silent Pentecostals: A Biographical History of the Pentecostal Movement among the Hispanics in the 20th Century. Taylors, SCU: Faith Printing, 1979. ix, 206 pp. No ISBN.

A history of the Hispanic Assemblies of God both in the United States and Latin America; containing short sections on early Pentecostal missions to Hispanics, and on the missions work of the Latin American Assemblies of God.

HI400 McGee, Gary B.

This Gospel Shall Be Preached: A History and Theology of Assemblies of God Foreign Missions to 1959. Springfield, MOU: Gospel Publishing House, 1986. 288 pp. Paper. 0882435116.

Scholarly analysis of AG missions since 1959, including organizational structures and missiological principles.

HI401 Menzies, William

Annointed to Serve: The Story of the Assemblies of God. Springfield, MOU: Gospel Publishing House, 1971. 424 pp. No ISBN.

General history of the Assemblies of God, including a section on AG missions and outreach services to 1970.

HI402 Wilson, Everett A.

Strategy of the Spirit: J. Philip Hogan and the Growth of the Assemblies of God Worldwide, 1960-1990. Carlisle, ENK: Regnum Books, 1997. xiv, 214 pp. Paper. 1870345231.

An assessment of the contribution of J. Philip Hogan, executive director of the Assemblies of God's Division of Foreign Missions (1960-1989)—a period of the church's phenomenal global expansion.

Baptists: General

See also HI662, SO628, AF1237, AM321, AM960, AM1161, AM1276, AS375, AS700, AS1055, AS1181, and EU27.

HI403 Brackney, William H., ed.
Baptist Life and Thought: A Source Book. Valley Forge, PAU: Judson Press, 1998. 550 pp. Paper. 0817012664.

A substantially revised edition; originally published in 1983 as *Baptist Life and Thought: 1600-1980.*

HI404 Fitts, Leroy
A History of Black Baptists. Nashville, TNU: Broadman, 1985. 368 pp. Paper. 0805465804.

A history of the black Baptist experience including social, economic, and political aspects, and a section on the role of black Baptists in Christian missions.

HI405 Fitts, Leroy
The Lott Carey Legacy of African American Missions. Baltimore, MDU: Gateway Press, 1994. xix, 226 pp. Paper. 0942683137.

A biography of Lott Carey (1780?-1829), the first African American missionary to Africa, together with a history of African American Christian missions to 1979, and of the Lott Carey Baptist Foreign Mission Convention.

HI406 Freeman, Edward A.
The Epoch of Negro Baptists and the Foreign Mission Board. New York, NYU: Arno Press, 1980. xv, 301 pp. 0405124600.

A detailed narrative history of the development and expansion of black Baptists in foreign missions from 1619 to 1951.

HI407 Jones, Jeffery D.
Keepers of the Faith: Illustrated Biographies from Baptist History. Valley Forge, PAU: Judson Press, 1999. ix, 140 pp. Paper. 0817012923.

Cartoon stories of the actual history of seventy well-known Baptist figures, including Roger Williams, Joanna P. Moore, and Martin Luther King, Jr.; suggested use including church bulletins, Sunday school, membership classes, and newsletters.

HI408 Long, Dorothy Fisher
This Glad Year of Jubilee: Being a History of the Woman's Baptist Missionary Organization of the District of Columbia Baptist Association from 1888-1963. Singapore, SI: By the author, Dorothy Fisher Long, 1963. 71 pp. No ISBN.

A brief history of seventy-five years of mission education and action in the nation's capital.

HI409 Martin, Sandy D.
The Black Baptists and African Missions: The Origins of a Movement, 1880-1915. Macon, GAU: Mercer University Press, 1989. xv, 242 pp. 0865543534.

A scholarly study which traces the origins and developments of black Baptist interests in missions in the Southern states and their efforts to evangelize West Africa in particular.

HI410 Smith, Elliot
The Advance of Baptist Associations Across America. Nashville, TNU: Broadman, 1979. 184 pp. Paper. 0805465499.

History of the missionary outreach of Baptists as it was implemented through Baptist missionary associations, emphasizing the role of associations in both the geographical advance across America and in the initiation of Baptist foreign missions work.

HI411 Wardin, Albert W., ed.
Baptists Around the World: A Comprehensive Handbook. Nashville, TNU: Broadman, 1995. xxxii, 474 pp. 0805410767.

A one-volume reference work on Baptist history, belief, distinctiveness, and variations of groups; with a country-by-country description containing facts on mission origins and influences.

HI412 Wooley, Davis Collier, ed.
Baptist Advance: The Achievements of the Baptists of North America for a Century and a Half. Nashville, TNU: Broadman, 1964. xvi, 512 pp. Paper. No ISBN.

Brief historical essays by several authors, produced in conjunction with a five-year cooperative Baptist effort to mark the 150th anniversary of the foundation of the first national Baptist missionary organization in the United States.

Baptist Missionary Society [BMS, London, UK], 1792-

See also AF746, AF961, AF1226, AF1365, AM600, AS902, AS922, AS1052, AS1134, AS1139-AS1140, AS1149, AS1182, and AS1389.

HI413 Stanley, Brian
The History of the Baptist Missionary Society, 1792-1992. Edinburgh, ENK: T&T Clark, 1992. xix, 564 pp. 0567096149.

A major history commissioned by the Baptist Missionary Society to mark its bicentenary in 1992.

Berliner Missiongesellschaft, 1824-

See also AF708, AF935, and AS541.

HI414 Lehmann, Hellmut T.
150 (Hundertfünfzig) Jahre Berliner Mission. (Erlanger Taschenbücher, 26). Erlangen, GW: Ev.-Luth. Mission, 1974. 208 pp. Paper. 3872140574.

This work describes the history of the Berlin Mission Society, operating mostly in South Africa, Tanzania, and China, in its confrontation with the developments and problems of the last 150 years, and its eventual incorporation into the church.

HI415 Lehmann, Hellmut T.
Zur Zeit und zur Unzeit: Geschichte der Berliner Mission 1918-1972. Berlin, GW: Berliner Missionswerk, 1989. 3 vols. Paper. No ISBN.

A detailed history of the Berlin Mission Society from 1918 to 1972 focusing on the church's discovery of its responsibility for the universal mission of Christ.

Bethel Mission, 1920-

See also AF708.

HI416 Menzel, Gustav
Die Bethel Mission: Aus 100 Jahren Missionsgeschichte. Neukirchen-Vluyn, GW: Neukirchener Verlag; Wuppertal, GW: Vereinigte Evang. Mission; Bielefeld, GW: Bodelschwinghsche Anstalten, 1986. xiii, 658 pp. 3788712317 (N), 3921900093 (V), 3922463487 (B).

A history of the Bethel Mission founded in Berlin in 1886 for work in German East Africa, saved from collapse by Friedrich von Bodelschwingh, who joined the work in 1890, and forced to seek other mission fields after the First World War; in 1971 it merged with the Rhenish Mission Society to form the Vereinigte Evangelische Mission.

Bible Churchmen's Missionary Society, 1922-

HI417 Russell, Stanley Farrant
Full Fifty Years: The BCMS Story. London, ENK: Patmos Press, 1972. 89 pp. 0902475053.

A brief history of the work of the Bible Churchmen's Missionary Society, Anglican and evangelical, with brief sketches of each of the fields in which the BCMS has operated, and a list of the more than 500 missionaries who have served under it.

Brethren in Christ Church, 1863-

See also AS1137.

HI418 Wittlinger, Carlton O.
Quest for Piety and Obedience: The Story of the Brethren in Christ. Nappanee, INU: Evangel Press, 1978. x, 580 pp. No ISBN.

An official history of the Brethren in Christ Church including its missionary involvements.

British and Foreign Bible Society, 1804-

See also HI151.

HI419 Roe, James Moulton
A History of the British and Foreign Bible Society, 1905-1954. London, ENK: British and Foreign Bible Society, 1965. xii, 497 pp. No ISBN.

A detailed history including the home organization, the overseas administration, translations, and the work of distribution.

HI420 Smit, A. P.
God Made It Grow: History of the Bible Society Movement in Southern Africa, 1820-1970. Translated by W. P. De Vos. Cape Town, SA: Bible Society of South Africa, 1970. xii, 276 pp. No ISBN.

An English translation from Afrikaans of the history of the Bible Society of South Africa from its beginnings as the British and Foreign Bible Society in 1804.

Child Evangelism Fellowship, 1937-

See also AS1513.

HI421 Ervine, Vera Dorothy
Vera's Adventures. Franklin, TNU: Providence House, 1996. 224 pp. Paper. 1881576930.

The author in this autobiography recounts years of service with the International Child Evangelism Fellowship.

China Inland Mission, 1865-1964

See also MI167, AS433, AS497, AS506, AS515, AS562, AS579-AS581, AS583, and AS587.

HI422 Bacon, Daniel W.
From Faith to Faith: The Influence of Hudson Taylor on the Faith Missions Movement. (OMF Books Study Series). Singapore, SI: OMF, 1984. 198 pp. Paper. 9971972034.

A study of the missiological distinctives of Hudson Taylor and the CIM in relation to the wider faith missions movement.

HI423 Houghton, Frank, ed.
The Fire Burns On: CIM Anthology. London, ENK: CIM/OMF, 1965. 254 pp. No ISBN.

An anthology of extracts, articles, and addresses illustrating aspects of the work of the CIM during its first 100 years.

HI424 Thomson, Rod
Living Water: Hudson Taylor and the Call of Inland China. Fort Washington, PAU: CLC, 1999. 143 pp. Paper. 0875086667.

Hudson Taylor's response to the call of God to leave England 150 years ago and to battle sickness, danger, loneliness, Satanic oppression, and human opposition in the interior of China where CIM was conceived.

Christian and Missionary Alliance, 1897-

See also SO409, AF368, AF448-AF449, AM1401, AM1412, AS132, AS310, AS500, AS535, AS698, AS1173, AS1293, AS1308, AS1331, AS1510, and AS1514.

HI425 Evearitt, Daniel J.
Body and Soul: Evangelism and the Social Concern of A. B. Simpson. Camp Hill, PAU: Christian Publications, 1994. 164 pp. Paper. 0875095356.

An analysis of the theology and social thought of Albert Benjamin Simpson (1843-1919), pioneer of the Evangelical and Missionary Alliance, documenting how he was able to maintain an unusual balance between old-fashioned evangelism and active social concern.

HI426 Hartzfeld, David F., and Charles Nienkirchen, eds.
The Birth of a Vision. Alberta, ONC: Buena Book Services, 1986. xvi, 305 pp. 0889650748.

Essays by the members of the faculty of the Canadian Bible College and the Canadian Theological Seminary on the centennial of the Christian and Missionary Alliance, tracing the thought and impact of A. B. Simpson on various aspects of missionary work.

HI427 Hunter, James Hogg
Beside All Waters: The Story of Seventy-Five Years of Worldwide Ministry: The Christian and Missionary Alliance. Harrisburg, PAU: Christian Publications, 1964. 245 pp. No ISBN.

A geographical overview of the missionary work of the CMA, commissioned to commemorate its seventy-fifth anniversary.

HI428 Moothart, Lorene
Heartbeat for the World: The Story of Gustave and Pauline Woerner. (The Jaffray Collection of Missionary Portraits, 22). Camp Hill, PAU: Christian Publications, 1999. xv, 187 pp. Paper. 0875098185.

A biography of CMA missionaries in China and Indonesia in the early 1900s, and their subsequent missionary-sending ministry at Toccoa Falls College, Georgia.

HI429 Niklaus, Robert L., John S. Sawin, and Samuel J. Stoesz
All for Jesus: God at Work in the Christian and Missionary Alliance over One Hundred Years. Camp Hill, PAU: Christian Publications, 1986. xiii, 322 pp. 0875093833.

A commissioned centennial history written by three long-standing alliance ministers, emphasizing the global impact of the movement and the work and influence of A. B. Simpson, founder of the CMA.

HI430 Niklaus, Robert L.
To All Peoples: Missions World Book of the Christian and Missionary Alliance. Camp Hill, PAU: Christian Publications, 1990. xvii, 412 pp. 0875094325.

A popular illustrated overview of the history and contemporary mission work of 1,200 missionaries in fifty-one countries of the CMA, organized by continent and country.

HI431 Pardington, G. P.
25 Wonderful Years, 1889-1914: A Popular Sketch of the Christian and Missionary Alliance. New York, NYU: Garland, 1984. 238 pp. 0824064356.

A reprint of a 1914 history of the first twenty-five years of the CMA.

HI432 Pardington, G. P.
Twenty-Five Wonderful Years 1889-1914: A Popular Sketch of the Christian and Missionary Alliance. (Higher Christian Life Series, 34). New York, NYU: Garland, 1984. 238 pp. 0824064356.

Revised reprint of a 1914 history covering the CMA's first twenty-five years; by a friend and colleague of CMA founder A. B. Simpson.

Christian Church (Disciples of Christ), 1832-

See also AF4, AM1460, and AS656.

HI433 Harrison, Richard L.
From Camp Meeting to Church: A History of the Christian Church (Disciples of Christ) in Kentucky. Lexington, KYU: Christian Board of Publication, 1992. xiv, 343 pp. Paper. No ISBN.

An official state history containing much information on 19th-century evangelism and missions.

HI434 Hull, Debra B.
Christian Church Women: Shapers of a Movement. St. Louis, MOU: Chalice Press, 1994. vi, 180 pp. Paper. 0827204639.

Short biographics of women leaders of the Disciples of Christ in the United States as missionaries, Christian educators, reformers, preachers, pastors and evangelists.

HI435 Lollis, Lorraine
The Shape of Adam's Rib: A Lively History of Women's Work in the Christian Church. St. Louis, MOU: Bethany Press, 1970. 219 pp. No ISBN.

A chronological and thematic story of women's worldwide missionary work in the Christian Church from 1874 to 1969.

Christian Churches/Churches of Christ, 1927-

HI436 Priest, Doug, ed.
Unto the Uttermost: Missions in the Christian Churches/Churches of Christ. South Pasadena, CAU: William Carey Library, 1984. xiii, 313 pp. Paper. 0878081976.

A well-annotated and indexed college and seminary textbook on mission theology, history, anthropology, and theory, for interested persons of the Christian Churches and the Churches of Christ.

Church Army, The (London), 1882-

See also EU145.

HI437 Heasman, Kathleen
Army of the Church. London, ENK: Lutterworth Press, 1968. 180 pp. No ISBN.

A popular account of the history and contemporary ministries of the Church Army.

Church Missionary Society, 1799-

See also HI152, HI395, EA98, EA115, ME148, AF457, AF504, AF549, AF609, AF623, AF631, AF639, AF652, AF684, AF701, AF717, AF728, AF732, AF734-AF735, AF1292, AF1308, AF1339, AF1351, AM636, AM658, AM660, AS510, AS557, AS663, AS909, AS1193, OC79, OC96, OC113-OC114, OC120, OC129, and OC132.

HI438 Cole, Edmund Keith
A History of the Church Missionary Society of Australia. Melbourne, AT: Church Missionary Historical Publications, 1971. xii, 367 pp. 090982102X.

The official history of the CMS of Australia, its mission outreach, and its various state branches within Australia.

HI439 Haaramäki, Ossi
Max A. C. Warrenin missionaarinen ekklesiologia: systemaattinen selvitys vuosien 1942-1963 Warrentuotannosta. (Missiologian ja ekumeniikan seuran julkaisuja; 35). Helsinki, FI: Missiologian ja ekumeniikan seura, 1982. 160 pp. Paper. 9519520600.

A detailed study of the missionary ecclesiology of Max A. C. Warren (1904-1977), noted CMS secretary and ecumenical leader, based on an analysis of his writings from 1942 to 1963; originally presented as a thesis at the University of Helsinki.

HI440 Harris, John
We Wish We'd Done More: Ninety Years of CMS and Aboriginal Issues in North Australia. Adelaide, AT: Openbook Publishers, 1998. xii, 524 pp. Paper. 0859108961.

This study asks and answers the difficult questions about how CMS and its missionaries dealt with issues such as aboriginal cultures, land rights, the removal of children from their families, and the nature of the Gospel.

HI441 Hewitt, Gordon
The Problems of Success: A History of the Church Missionary Society, 1910-1942. London, ENK: SCM Press, 1971. 2 vols. 0334002524 (vol. 1), 0334013135 (vol. 2).

The official history of the CMS covering the society's work in tropical Africa, the Middle East, and at home (vol. 1: 1971, xx, 506 pp.), and in Asia and with overseas partners (vol. 2: 1977, xii, 424 pp.), with attention to government relations, the development of indigenous churches, organization, family care, missionary training, and financial policy.

HI442 Murray, Jocelyn
Proclaim the Good News: A Short History of the Church Missionary Society. London, ENK: Hodder & Stoughton, 1985. xiii, 304 pp. Paper. 0340445012.

A popular summary of nearly 200 years of CMS missions, showing its partnership with local Christians in many areas.

HI—HISTORY

HI443 Shenk, Wilbert R.
Henry Venn—Missionary Statesman. (American Society of Missiology Studies, 6). Maryknoll, NYU: Orbis Books; Ibadan, NI: Daystar Press, 1983. xvi, 175 pp. Paper. 0883441810 (O), 9781221666 (D).

The society's own short history and 1961 priorities and commitments in mission.

A detailed historical analysis of the life and work of the CMS's creative leader, 1841 to 1872, who championed indigenous churches based on "three-self" principles.

HI444 *The Church Missionary Society: A Manual Outlining its History, Organization and Commitments.*
London, ENK: Highway Press, 1961. 60 pp. Paper. No ISBN.

The society's own short history and 1961 priorities and commitments in mission.

HI445 Venn, Henry
To Apply the Gospel: Selections from the Writings of Henry Venn. Edited by Max Alexander Cunningham Warren. Grand Rapids, MIU: Eerdmans, 1971. 243 pp. No ISBN.

Seven major writings by the influential general secretary of the CMS (1841-1872), organized topically to disclose his views, convictions, and theories about mission; with an interpretative introduction by the editor.

Church of God (Anderson, Indiana), 1909-

See also AF596, and AF718.

HI446 Crose, Lester A.
Passport for a Reformation: A History of the Church of God Reformation Movement's Missionary Endeavors Outside North America. Anderson, INU: Warner Press, 1981. v, 271 pp. Paper. 0871622424.

Narrative history of the missionary work of the Church of God (Anderson, IN) from its inception in 1881 to 1980; written by the COG missions administrator.

Church of God (Cleveland, Tennessee), 1907-

See also GW249, and AM362.

HI447 Davidson, C. T.
Upon This Rock. Cleveland, TNU: White Wing Publishing House and Press, 1976. 3 vols. No ISBN.

A massive history of the Church of God of Prophecy, including information on its foreign missions work [vol. 1: (1973, 692 pp.); vol. 2: 1923-1943 (1974, 933 pp.); vol. 3: 1943-1953 (1976, 832 pp.)].

Church of Scotland, 1560-

See also AF539, AF605, AM654, and AS1251.

HI448 Hewat, Elizabeth G. K.
Vision and Achievement, 1796-1956: A History of the Foreign Missions of the Churches United in the Church of Scotland. London, ENK: Nelson, 1960. xii, 308 pp. No ISBN.

A comprehensive history of the foreign missions of the Church of Scotland, commissioned by the Foreign Missions Committee, with particular attention paid to the church's work in Africa, India, and Pakistan.

Church of the Brethren, 1708-

See also SO449, MI195, AF1332, and AS1136.

HI449 Marsh, Leslie A.
In His Name: A Record of Assembly Missionary Outreach from New Zealand. Palmerston North, NZ: Gospel Publishing House, 1974. 386 pp. No ISBN.

History of New Zealand Brethren missionary work.

HI450 Ronk, Albert T.
History of Brethren Missionary Movements. Ashland, OHU: Brethren Press, 1971. 152 pp. Paper. No ISBN.

A textbook on the mission outreach of the Brethren in the United States, with numerous quotations from church documents.

HI451 Ronk, Albert T.
History of the Brethren Church: It's Life, Thought, Mission. Ashland, OHU: Brethren Press, 1968. 524 pp. No ISBN.

An official history of the Brethren Church (Ashland, Ohio) from its organization in 1883; with coverage of its missionary ministries.

Church of the Nazarene, 1908-

See also EV594, AF1134, AM581, AM1023, and AS571.

HI452 Ford, Jack
In the Steps of John Wesley: The Church of the Nazarene in Britain. Kansas City, MOU: Nazarene Publishing House, 1968. 300 pp. No ISBN.

History of the Church of the Nazarene in Great Britain, the International Holiness Mission, and the Calvary Holiness Church, tracing their origins to the British Holiness movement.

HI453 Parker, J. Fred
Mission to the World: A History of Missions in the Church of the Nazarene through 1985. Kansas City, MOU: Nazarene Publishing House, 1988. 681 pp. 0834112094.

A thorough mission history of the Church of the Nazarene, organized according to geographic regions.

HI454 Purkiser, W. T.
Called Unto Holiness: The Story of the Nazarenes, Vol. II: The Second 25 Years. Kansas City, MOU: Nazarene Publishing House, 1983. 356 pp. 0834108682.

A history of the Nazarene Church from 1933 to 1958, containing much information on Nazarene foreign and home missions and on mission administration.

HI455 Smith, Timothy L., and W. T. Purkiser
Called unto Holiness. Kansas City, MSU: Nazarene Publishing House, 1962. 2 vols. 0834108682 (vol. 2).

A scholarly denominational history based on published sources often available only in archives, with good coverage of the church's evangelism and mission priorities; [vol. 1: *The Story of the Nazarenes: The Formative Years,* by Timothy L. Smith (1962, 413 pp.); vol. 2: *The Second Twenty-Five Years,* 1933-58 by W. T. Purkiser (1983, 356 pp.)].

Church World Service, 1946-

HI456 Stenning, Ronald E.
Church World Service: Fifty Years of Help and Hope. New York, NYU: Friendship Press, 1995. xii, 160 pp. Paper. 0377003182.

The story of fifty years of ecumenical relief efforts by US churches placed in the context of world events; by the former Associate Executive Director of CWS.

Conference of Missionary Societies in Great Britain & Ireland, 1912-

HI457 Hardyman, John T., and Ronald Kenneth Orchard
Two Minutes from Sloane Square: A Brief History of the Conference of Missionary Societies in Britain and Ireland, 1912-1977. London, ENK: CBMS, 1977. 56 pp. Paper. 0900540133.

Sketch of the institutional development of the CBMS; with illustrative examples of its activities and an appendix listing officers and member bodies.

Conservative Baptist Association of America, 1947-

See also SO512, AF422, AS325, and AS507.

HI458 Finzel, Hans W., ed.
Partners Together, 50 Years of Global Impact: The CBFMS Story, 1943-1993. Wheaton, ILU: Conservative Baptist Foreign Mission Society, 1993. 208 pp. No ISBN.

Stories of the work of the Conservative Baptist Foreign Mission Society in thirty-one countries and thirteen specialized ministries; with color illustrations, statistics, and lists of missionaries.

Dansk Forenet Sudan Mission

See also AF1328 and AF1335.

HI459 Bronnum, Niels Hogh, Gunnar Laursen, and Ernst I. Engskov
Sudanmissionens historie igennem 50 sr fortalt i tekst og billeder. Copenhagen, DK: Dansk Forenet Suda Missions Forlag, 1961. 48 pp. Paper. No ISBN.

Three different authors describe the development of the Danish United Sudan Mission during fifty years.

Danske Missionsselskab (DMS), 1821-

See also AS444, AS958, AS1113, and EU157.

HI460 Det Danske Missionsselskab
Mission er mennesker: Glimt fra Det danske Missionsselskabs arbeidsomrsder gennem 150 sr. Edited by Thorkild Grœsholt, and Egon Nielsen. Hellerup, DK: DMS-Forlag, 1971. 154 pp. 8774310194.

Descriptions of the work of the Danish Missionary Society in Asia, Africa, and the Middle East through 150 years.

Episcopal Church, The (USA), 1789-

See also ME81, ED12, CH55-CH56, CH259, AF1280, AM1016, AM1027, AM1114, AS501, AS513, and AS1459.

HI461 Addison, James Thayer
The Episcopal Church in the United States, 1789-1931. Hamden, CTU: Archon Books, 1969. xii, 400 pp. 0208007415.

This standard history of the Episcopal Church, originally published in 1951 by Charles Scribner's Sons, contains sections on the church's missionary outreach in each period.

HI462 Donovan, Mary Sudman
A Different Call: Women's Ministries in the Episcopal Church 1850-1920. Wilton, CTU: Morehouse Barlow, 1986. xi, 230 pp. 0819213969.

Ground-breaking history of the work of women in the Epis-

copal Church, with chapters on women in missions and the Woman's Auxiliary to the Board of Missions of the Episcopal Church.

HI463 Douglas, Ian T.
Fling Out the Banner!: The National Church Ideal and the Foreign Mission of the Episcopal Church. New York, NYU: Church Hymnal Corporation, 1996. viii, 341 pp. 0898692458.

A history of the foreign missionary enterprise of the Episcopal Church in the United States from 1821 to 1994; originally presented as a Ph.D. dissertation at Boston University.

HI464 Sumner, David E.
The Episcopal Church's History: 1945-1985. Wilton, CTU: Morehouse-Barlow, 1987. xiii, 221 pp. 0819214027.

An overview of issues and changes in the Episcopal Church since 1945, with attention to concerns before the church as it enters a global era.

HI465 Young, Frances Margaret
Thankfulness Unites: The History of the United Thank Offering 1889-1979. Edited by Ruth G. Cheney. Cincinnati, OHU: Forward Movement, 1979. 85 pp. Paper. No ISBN.

The ninety-year history (1889-1979) of the United Thank Offering, the major source of support for the global mission of the Episcopal Church, USA.

Evangelical Alliance Mission, The (TEAM), 1890-

See also AM1399, AM1434, AS1302, AS1372, AS1497, and EU88.

HI466 Mortenson, Vernon
God Made It Grow: Historical Sketches of TEAM's Church Planting Work. South Pasadena, CAU: William Carey Library, 1994. 1,003 pp. Paper. 0878082573.

The official centennial history of TEAM's church planting work on six continents.

HI467 Mortenson, Vernon
Light is Sprung Up. Chicago, ILU: Evangelical Alliance Mission, 1965. 159 pp. Paper. No ISBN.

A largely pictorial essay of the work of TEAM, with a short essay on the historical development of TEAM missions in various countries.

HI468 Woodward, David B.
Aflame for God: Biography of Fredrik Franson, Founder of the Evangelical Alliance Mission. Chicago, ILU: Moody, 1966. 190 pp. No ISBN.

A popular biography of Frederick Franson (1852-1908), who founded the Scandanavian Alliance Mission in 1980, which later became TEAM.

Evangelical Free Church of America, 1884-

See also AF427, AM1244, and AS47.

HI469 Norton, Hugo Wilbert
European Background and History of Evangelical Free Church Foreign Missions, 1887-1955. Moline, ILU: Christian Service Foundation, 1964. x, 289 pp. No ISBN.

A second edition that primarily concerns the missionary heritage and history of the Evangelical Free Church in Scandinavia and America, with emphasis on 19th-century revival movements in Sweden, Norway, and Denmark; includes a survey of foreign mission actitvity.

HI470 Torjesen, Edvard P.
A Study of Fredrik Franson: The Development and Impact of His Ecclesiology, Missiology, and Worldwide Evangelism. Ann Arbor, MIU: University Microfilms, 1984. xii, 855 pp. Paper. No ISBN.

A Ph.D. thesis study of a Lutheran from Sweden who came to the United States, affiliated with the Moody Bible Institute Church, and conducted evangelism crusades in many countries in the late 1800s.

Evangelical United Brethren Church, 1946-1968

See also AF1370 and AS697.

HI471 Reber, Audrie E.
Women United for Mission: A History of the Women's Society of World Service of the Evangelical United Brethren Church, 1946-1968. Cincinnati, OHU: UMC, Board of Missions, 1969. 134 pp. Paper. No ISBN.

A short survey of topics relating to the growth and development of women's missionary societies in the United Brethren and Evangelical churches from the mid-19th century to the 1960s.

Evangelisch-Lutherische Mission zu Leipzig, 1836-

See also AF648, AF674-AF675, AF679, and AF694.

HI472 Moritzen, Niels Peter
Werkzeug Gottes in der Welt: Leipziger Mission 1836-1936-1986. (Erlanger Taschenbücher, 76). Erlangen, GW: Ev.-Luth. Mission, 1986. 260 pp. Paper. 3872141767.

A scholarly history of the Leipzig Missionary Society, concentrating on the last fifty years of work, difficulties, and developments.

Evangelische Missiongesellshaft in Basel, 1815-

See also HI16, TH139, TH187, EC24, MI192, AF27, AF1217, AF1250, AF1256, AF1261, AF1266-AF1267, AS376, AS819, and AS1163.

HI473 Baumann, Franz, ed.
Kein Vogel fliegt mit einem Flügel: 12 Skizzen zu 175 Jahren Basler Mission. Basel, SZ: Basileia Verlag, 1990. 147 pp. Paper. 3855550360.
German translation.

HI474 Baumann, Franz, ed.
No Bird Flies with Just One Wing: Reflections on the History and Identity of the Basel Mission. Basel, SZ: Basel Mission, 1990. v, 104 pp. Paper. No ISBN.

Published for the 175th anniversary of the Basel Mission, this collection of articles explores the identity of the mission; translated by Franz Baumann.

HI475 Bieder, Werner
Erfahrungen mit der Basler Mission und ihrer Geschichte. (Neujahrsblatt/Gesellschaft für das Gute und Gemeinnutzige, 169). Basel, SZ: Helbing und Lichtenhahn, 1991. 210 pp. Paper. 3719011399.

In this study Werner Bieder, retired professor of New Testament and missiology at the University of Basel, and sometime director of studies at the Basler Missionshaus, outlines the history of the involvement of that institution with the Third World, and in particular with Cameroon, Ghana, India, and Korea.

HI476 Des missionnaires de la Mission de Bâle, J. Rossel
Mandat sans frontière. Edited by Fritz Raaflaub. Translated by Étienne de Peyer. (Collection missionnaire, 1). Geneva, SZ: Éditions Labor et Fides; Paris, FR: Diffusion en France, Librairie protestante, [1965]. 205 pp. No ISBN.
French translation.

HI477 Haas, Waltraud, and Ken Phin Pang
Mission History from the Woman's Point of View. (Texts and Documents, 13). Basel, SZ: Basel Mission, 1989. 52 pp. No ISBN.

Essays on the 19-th century Basel Mission and its women missionaries (Haas) and in China (Pang), with the texts of source documents.

HI478 Haas, Waltraud, and Ken Phin Pang
Missionsgeschichte aus der Sicht der Frau. (Edited by Basler Mission). (Texte und Dokumente, 12). Basel, SZ: Basler Mission, 1989. 64 pp. No ISBN.
German translation.

HI479 Jenkins, Paul
Texts and Documents: A Short History of the Basel Mission. (Texts and Documents Series, 10). Basel, SZ: Basel Mission, 1989. 25 pp. Paper. No ISBN.

A brief history of the Basel Mission written by the archivist in the Mission House, Basel.

HI480 Prodolliet, Simone
Wider die Schamlosigkeit und das Elend der heidnischen Weiber: Die Basler Frauenmission und der Export des europäischen Frauenideals in die Kolonien. Zürich, SZ: Limmat Verlag, 1987. 181 pp. Paper. 3857911301.

A copiously illustrated work examining how women missionaries of the Basel Mission during the colonial period "evangelized" non-Christian women, at the same time transferring the European ideal of womanhood for the supposed purpose of emancipating them.

HI481 Raaflaub, Fritz, ed.
Der bleibende Auftrag: 150 Jahre Basler Mission. Stuttgart, GW: Evan Missionsverlag; Basel, SZ: Basileia Verlag, 1965. 255 pp. No ISBN.

Forty-two accounts, illustrated with maps, of the work over 150 years of the Basel Mission in Ghana, Cameroon, northern Nigeria, India, Hong Kong, Indonesia, and Sabah.

HI482 Rennstich, Karl
Handwerker-Theologen und Industrie-Brüder als Botschafter des Friedens: Entwicklungshilfe der Basler Mission im 19. Jahrhundert. (ABC-Ieam, 358). Stuttgart, GW: Evan Missionsverlag, 1985. 207 pp. Paper. 3767523582.

This work, by a missiologist with many years of missionary experience in Asia, is a response to the discussion about the task of mission in development, exemplified by the history of the Basel Mission which, though never addressing the question theoretically, was always concerned about the improvement of the living conditions of the local Christians.

HI483 Witschi, Hermann von
Geschichte der Basler Mission, 1920-1940. Edited by Wilhelm Schlatter. Basel, SZ: Basileia Verlag, 1970. 423 pp. No ISBN.
Volume 4 of a projected five-volume history of the Basel Mission (volumes 1-3, written by Wilhelm Schlatter, cover the period 1815-1919 and were published by Verlag der Basler Missionsbuchhandlung beginning in 1916).

Evangeliska Fosterlands-Stiftelsen [ENMS]

See also AF480 and AS1000.

HI484 Evangeliska Fosterlands-Stiftelsen
Mission 100: Text och bilder kring Evangeliska Fosterlands-Stiftelsens yttre mission 1866-1966. Edited by Allan Hofgren. Stockholm, SW: Evangeliska Fosterlands-Stiftelsens bokförlag, 1966. 67 pp. No ISBN.
A history of the evangelical mission society Evangeliska Forsterlands-Stiftelsen and its missionary involvement in Ethiopia, Eritrea, India, and Tanzania.

Every Home for Christ, 1954-

HI485 Eastman, Dick
Beyond Imagination: A Simple Plan to Save the World. Grand Rapids, MIU: Chosen Books, 1997. 318 pp. Paper. 0800792505.
The international president of Every Home for Christ and originator of the Change the World School for Prayer introduces and relates experiences in its simple plan to save the world.

Faith Missions, various

See also GW149, HI20, and HI691.

HI486 Fiedler, Klaus
Ganz auf Vertrauen: Geschichte und Kirchenverständnis der Glaubensmissionen. (Monographien und Studienbücher). Giessen, GW: Brunnen-Verlag, 1992. 605 pp. 3765593753.
The original German edition of a comprehensive survey of the history, theology, and practice of the faith missions movement; originally submitted as a Th.D. dissertation at Heidelberg University.

HI487 Fiedler, Klaus
The Story of Faith Missions. Oxford, ENK: Regnum/Lynx Communications; Sutherland, AT: Albatross Books, 1994. 428 pp. Paper. 0745926878 (UK), 0732408512 (AT).
English translation.

HI488 Pierson, Arthur T.
Forward Movements of the Last Half Century. New York, NYU: Garland, 1984. xi, 428 pp. 0824064372.
A reprint of the classic 1905 history of current evangelical enterprises, including the emerging faith missions movement.

Far Eastern Broadcasting, 1945-

See also CO149.

HI489 Ledyard, Gleason H.
Sky Waves: The Incredible Far East Broadcasting Company Story. Chicago, ILU: Moody, 1965. 208 pp. No ISBN.

Second edition of a popular narrative history of the Far East Broadcasting Company, emphasizing the success and value of the work and its continued need for support.

Free Methodist Church of North America, 1860-

See also AF612, AF869, AM900, AS669, and AS780.

HI490 Fear, Leona K.
New Ventures: Free Methodist Missions, 1960-1979. Winona Lake, INU: Light & Life Press, 1979. 160 pp. 0893670367.
Details the work of FMM in Africa, Indonesia, and the Americas, emphasizing new directions, goals, and methods, as well as the ministries of literature, medicine, and education; with a list of missionaries who served in the years 1960-1979.

HI491 Lamson, Byron Samuel
To Catch the Tide. Winona Lake, INU: Free Methodist Church, General Missionary Board, 1963. 128 pp. No ISBN.
A survey of the spread of Free Methodism, especially the indigenization of Free Methodist missions, by the general missions secretary of the Free Methodist Church.

HI492 Lamson, Byron Samuel
Venture: The Frontiers of Free Methodism. Winona Lake, INU: Light & Life Press, 1960. 287 pp. No ISBN.
A history of Free Methodist missions from 1860 to 1960 by the general missions secretary of the Free Methodist Church, including sections on frontier missions, women in mission, and a detailed chronology of Free Methodist missionaries in their respective fields.

HI493 Marston, Leslie Ray
From Age to Age a Living Witness: A Historical Interpretation of Free Methodism's First Century. Winona Lake, INU: Light & Life Press, 1960. 608 pp. No ISBN.
A history of Free Methodism from 1860 to 1960 including chapters on Free Methodist world missions, evangelism, and press and radio outreach.

Free Will Baptists, 1935-

See also AM355, and AS1133.

HI494 Hanson, Eric O., ed.
Mission genom nittio sr: Fribaptistsamfundet yttre missiuon i Sydafrakanska republiken, Mocambique, Zambia, China och Hong Kong, 1892-1982. Habo, SW: Fribaptistsamfundets Förlag, 1982. 102 pp. No ISBN.
A history of the Swedish Free Baptist's foreign missions, 1892-1982.

HI495 Sollin, Rune, ed.
Öppna dörrar: Några glimtar från Fribaptistsamfundets mission i Afrika, Kina och Hong Kong, 1892-1967 Habo, SW: Fribaptistsamfundets Förlag, 1967. 129 pp. No ISBN.
A book about the Swedish Free Baptists (Fribaptisterna) and their foreign missions.

HI—HISTORY

Friends, Society of, 1652-

See also AM595, AM678, AS584, and AS1036.

HI496 Greenwood, John Ormerod
Quaker Encounters. York, ENK: William Sessions, 1975. 3 vols. 0900657294 (vol.1), 0900657413 (vol. 2), 0900657421 (vol. 3).

A three-volume history of world mission concerns by Quakers in Great Britain and Ireland from the 18th century to the present, including joint service with American Quakers in relief, mission, and international work, [vol. 1: Friends and Relief (1975, xii, 360 pp.); vol. 2: Vines on the Mountains (1977, x, 320 pp.); and vol. 3: Whispers of Truth (1978, vii, 400 pp.)].

HI497 Milligan, Edward Hyslop
The Past Is Prologue: 100 Years of Quaker Overseas Work, 1868-1968. London, ENK: Friends Service Council, 1968. 63 pp. Paper. 0852450001.

A brief, popular history of the foreign missions work of the English Quakers, including illustrations.

Gospel Recordings, 1939-

HI498 Barlow, Sanna Morrison
Arrows of His Bow. (A "One Evening" Condensed Book). Westchester, ILU: Good News Publishers, 1966. 96 pp. No ISBN.

Reviews the work of Gospel Recordings, a missionary enterprise devoted to the dissemination of the evangelical message through recordings in native languages; originally published by Moody Press, Chicago, IL (1960).

Gossnersche Missiongesellschaft, 1836-

See also AF755, AS972, and AS1002.

HI499 Stieglitz, Klaus von
Der unvollendete Auftrag: Mission am Beispiel der Gossner-Kirche in Indien. (Weltweite Reihe, 22/23). Stuttgart, GW: Evan Missionsverlag, 1969. 174 pp. Paper. No ISBN.

The official report of a visitation to the Gossner Mission in North East India,with a general history of that society.

IFMA (Interdenominational Foreign Mission Association), 1917-

HI500 Frizen, Edwin L.
75 Years of IFMA 1917-1992: The Nondenominational Missions Movement. South Pasadena, CAU: William Carey Library, 1992. 478 pp. Paper. 0878082352.

A narrative history of the IFMA, whose seventy-two evangelical faith missions enable more than 11,000 missionaries and staff from North America, plus 3,000 from other countries, to be in missionary service.

InterVarsity Christian Fellowship, 1939-

See also GW89, and ME183.

HI501 Hunt, Keith, and Gladys Hunt
For Christ and the University: The Story of InterVarsity Chris- tian Fellowship of the U.S.A., 1940-1990. Downers Grove, ILU: InterVarsity, 1991. 454 pp. Paper. 0830849963.

A narrative history of the most influential evangelical Protestant movement for evangelism and missions among college and university students in the United States.

HI502 Woods, C. Stacey
The Growth of a Work of God: The Story of the Early Days of the Inter-Varsity Christian Fellowship of the United States of America as Told by It's First General Secretary. Downers Grove, ILU: InterVarsity, 1978. 164 pp. 087784741X.

The early history of InterVarsity through 1965, with an assessment of its organizational strengths.

HI503 Woods, C. Stacey
Some Ways of God. Downers Grove, ILU: InterVarsity, 1976. 131 pp. 0877847150.

The personal memoirs of the former secretary of the Inter-Varsity Christian Fellowship of Canada, and founder in 1947 of the International Fellowship of Evangelical Students which he served until retirement in 1973.

Lebanon Evangelical Mission, 1860-1976

HI504 Scott, Frances E.
Dare and Persevere: The Story of One Hundred Years of Evangelism in Syria and Lebanon from 1860-1960. London, ENK: Lebanon Evangelical Mission, 1960. 143 pp. No ISBN.

A popular history of the work of the Anglican-supported Lebanon Evangelical Mission, which for a century worked for change through the ancient churches of the East in Syria and Lebanon, including schools and other ministries with women.

London Missionary Society, 1795-1966

See also HI151, ME33, CR462, CO128, AF31, AF33-AF36, AF256, AF258, AF260, AF570, AF572, AF575, AF752, AF804, AF806, AF808, AF824, AF832, AF846-AF847, AF849, AF851, AF980, AF1079, AF1088, AS575, AS956, AS990, EU243, OC67, OC135, OC280-OC281, OC288, OC294, OC320, and OC323.

HI505 Thorogood, Bernard, ed.
Gales of Change: Responding to a Shifting Missionary Context—The Story of the London Missionary Society 1945-1977. Geneva, SZ: WCC Publications, 1994. viii, 345 pp. 2825411264.

This third volume of the official history of the London Missionary Society was written by a team of authors to cover the period of transition culminating in its merger into the Council for World Mission in 1977.

HI506 Turtas, Raimondo
L'Attivita e la politica missionaria della direzione della London Missionary Society: 1795-1820. (Analecta Gregoriana, 182; Series Facultatis Historiae Ecclesiasticae, sec. B, 30). Rome, IT: Universita Gregoriana, 1971. xvi, 334 pp. No ISBN.

A history of the LMS during its first twenty-five years and analysis of its policies, with a résumé in English.

Lutherans: General

See also HI115, HI134, TH76, TH80, TH98, TH144, EA237, CR1141, EV150, AF511, AF679, AF688, AF698, AF710, AF883, AF922, AF968, AF990, AF1173, AM165, AM199-AM201, AM718, AM985, AM1049, AM1111, AM1187, AM1296, AM1305, AM1339-AM1340, AM1353, AM1377, AS455, AS742, AS1056, AS1111-AS1112, AS1357, EU71, OC191, OC198, OC207, OC209, OC225, and OC245.

HI507 Bachmann, E. Theodore, and Mercia Brenne Bachmann
Lutheran Churches in the World: A Handbook. Minneapolis, MNU: Augsburg, 1989. 631 pp. 0806623713.

A narrative description of all known Lutheran communions in the world by country, with a brief description of the religious situation in each, including mission information.

HI508 Henschen, Ernst
100 (Hundert) Jahre Mission unter der Losung Jesus allein: Eine Breklumer Chronik. Breklum, GW: Breklumer Verlag, 1976. 179 pp. Paper. 3779304090.

A history of the Breklumer Mission founded by Christian Jensen in 1876 (based in Schleswig-Holstein, since 1969 "Nordelbisches Missionszentrum"), clarifying the new departures and crises of mission during the last hundred years.

HI509 *Mission and Evangelism*
(LWF Report, 4). Geneva, SZ: LWF, 1979. viii, 127 pp. Paper. No ISBN.

Report of a LWF Consultation for North America, the Nordic Countries,and the Federal Republic of Germany (26 Nov.-2 Dec. 1978), emphasizing the recent history of worldwide Lutheran missions and its application to questions of future mission activity.

HI510 Raupp, Werner, ed.
Mission in Quellentexten: Geschichte der Deutschen Evangelischen Mission von der Reformation bis zur Weltmissionskonferenz Edinburgh 1910. Erlangen, GW: Ev.-Luth. Mission; Bad Liebenzell, GW: Verlag der Liebenzeller Mission, 1990. 479 pp. Paper. 3872142380 (E), 3880024243 (L).

This collection brings together the primary sources for a history of the missionary initiatives of the German Lutheran churches, from the time of the Reformation to Edinburgh in 1910.

HI511 Scherer, James A.
... dass das Evangelium rechtschaffen durch die Welt gepredigt werde: Mission und Evangelisation im 20. Jahrhundert; Ein Beitrag aus lutherischer Sicht. (LWB Report, 1982/11-12). Geneva, SZ: LWF, 1982. viii, 277 pp. Paper. No ISBN.

German translation.

HI512 Scherer, James A.
Mission and Unity in Lutheranism: A Study in Confession and Ecumenicity. Philadelphia, PAU: Fortress Press, 1969. xiv, 258 pp. No ISBN.

A thoroughly researched history of Lutheran world missions with particular attention to the tension between confessional and ecumenical approaches to mission.

HI513 Scherer, James A.
That the Gospel May Be Sincerely Preached throughout the World: A Lutheran Perspective on Mission and Evangelism in the 20th Century. Stuttgart, GW: Kreuz Verlag Erich Breitsohl, 1982. viii, 302 pp. Paper. No ISBN.

A LWF report focusing on the Lutheran missionary idea in historical perspective, the Lutheran mission in the 20th century, recent development (since 1947) in ecumenical missionary thinking, and the involvement of the LWF in missions and evangelism.

HI514 Stolle, Volker, ed.
Kirchenmission nach lutherischen Verständnis: Vorträge zum 100-jährigen Jubiläum der Lutherischen Kirchenmission (Bleckmarer Mission). (Beiträge zur Missionswissenschaft und Interkulturellen Theologie, 5). Münster, GW: Lit, 1993. iv, 215 pp. Paper. 3894738642.

A collection of nine talks given at the 100-year jubilee of the Lutheran Church Mission (Bleckmarer), grouped under historical, fundamental, and practical/experiential aspects.

HI515 Welz, Justinian von
Essays by an Early Prophet of Mission. Translated by James A. Scherer. (World Christian Books). Grand Rapids, MIU: Eerdmans, 1969. 111 pp. Paper. No ISBN.

Writings of the earliest Lutheran missionary (1621-1668) who, after trying to awaken German Lutherans to mission, left for Surinam in South America in 1666 and died there; with history of early Lutheran thought about missions by the translator.

HI516 Zimmerling, Peter
Pioniere der Mission in älteren Pietismus. Giessen, GW: Brunnen-Verlag, 1985. 58 pp. 3765590479.

A history of early Lutheran Pietist missions, emphasizing the influence of Franke and Zinzendorf.

Lutheran Church: Missouri Synod, 1847-

See also AM746-AM747, AS1021, AS1135, and AS1442.

HI517 Lueking, F. Dean
Mission in the Making: The Missionary Enterprise among Missouri Synod Lutherans, 1846-1963. St. Louis, MOU: Concordia Publishing, 1964. 354 pp. No ISBN.

A history of Missouri Synod Lutheran home missions (1846-1900) and foreign missions (1894-1963), arguing that missionary motives and practice were derived from a combination of both prevailing theologies of American evangelicalism and Lutheran confessionalism.

HI518 Meyer, Carl Stamm, ed.
Moving Frontiers: Readings in the History of the Lutheran Church-Missouri Synod. St. Louis, MOU: Concordia Publishing, 1964. x, 500 pp. No ISBN.

The chapter entitled "Into All the World" traces missions interest from early Indian missions in North America to the present worldwide program in eight fields.

HI519 Meyer, Ruth Fritz
Women on a Mission: The Role of Women in the Church from Bible Times up to and Including a History of the Lutheran Women's Missionary League during Its First 25 Years. St. Louis, MOU: Lutheran Women's Missionary League/Concordia Publishing House, 1967. 300 pp. No ISBN.

The history of the 200,000-member League of the Lutheran Church-Missouri Synod, and their work to educate the church and promote missions.

Lutheran Church in America, 1962-1987

See also CH136.

HI520 Hall, George Fridolph
The Missionary Spirit in the Augustana Church. (Augustana Historical Society Publication, 32). Rock Island, ILU: Augustana Historical Society, Augustana College Library, 1984. ix, 166 pp. 0091018431.

History of the missionary activity of the Augustana Synod, from its founding in 1860 until its merger in 1962 with the Lutheran Church in America, emphasizing important synods, missionary societies, and influential individuals.

HI521 Swanson, S. Hjalmar
Foundation for Tomorrow: A Century of Progress in Augustana World Misssions. Minneapolis, MNU: Augustana Lutheran Church, Board of World Missions, 1960. 370 pp. No ISBN.

A history of Augustana missionary service in Japan, China, South America, India, and Africa, from 1860 to 1960.

Mennonites: General

See also AF412, AF416, AF624, AF681, AM642, AM893, AS994, AS1003, and AS1031.

HI522 Kraybill, Paul N., ed.
Mennonite World Handbook: A Survey of Mennonite and Brethren in Christ Churches. Lombard, ILU: Mennonite World Conference, 1978. vi, 390 pp. Paper. No ISBN.

Traces the history of the WMC, the migrations of the Mennonites, and their growth through missions in Africa, Asia, Australia, Central and South America, Europe, North America, and the USSR.

HI523 Rich, Elaine Sommers
Mennonite Women: A Story of God's Faithfulness, 1683-1983. Scottdale, PAU: Herald Press, 1983. 257 pp. Paper. 0836133110.

An examination of all aspects of the work and role of Mennonite women, containing chapters on early overseas missions, home missions, health care ministries, and a history of the founding and development of the Woman's Missionary and Service Commission.

HI524 Schlabach, Theron F.
Gospel Versus Gospel: Mission and the Mennonite Church, 1863-1944. (Studies in Anabaptist and Mennonite History, 21). Scottdale, PAU: Herald Press, 1980. 352 pp. 0836112202.

A detailed study of the themes that motivated Mennonites in mission from the Civil War to World War II.

HI525 Schlabach, Theron F.
Gospel vs. Gospel: Mission and the Mennonite Church 1863-1944. (Studies in Anabaptist and Mennonite History, 21). Scottdale, PAU: Herald Press, 1980. 352 pp. 0836112202.

A scholarly history of the development and changes in the Mennonite Church and their effect on the church's missionary work.

HI526 Schlabach, Theron F.
A New Rhythm for Mennonites: The Mennonite Church and the Missionary Movement, 1860-1890. Elkhart, INU: Mennonite Board of Missions, 1975. 41 pp. Paper. No ISBN.

The first of a series of booklets produced by the Missions History Project of the Mennonite Board of Missions giving a brief account of the background (convictions, ideas, and influences) out of which the Mennonite Church began its missions, with an interpretation of results achieved by 1890.

HI527 Shenk, Wilbert R., ed.
Anabaptism and Mission. (Institute of Mennonite Missionary Studies, 10). Scottdale, PAU: Herald Press, 1984. 261 pp. Paper. 0836133676.

A collection of thirteen essays on Anabaptist mission theology, emphasizing the major role of missions in the thought of the radical Reformers and their influence throughout later Anabaptist history.

Mennonite Board of Missions, 1906-

See also GW160, AM1038, AM1263, AM1272, AS522, and AS1003.

HI528 Falcón, Rafael
The Hispanic Mennonite Church in North America, 1932-1982. Translated by Ronald Collins. Scottdale, PAU: Herald Press, 1986. 223 pp. 0836112822.

English translation.

HI529 Falcón, Rafael
La Iglesia Menonita Hispana en Norte América, 1932-1982. Scottdale, PAU: Herald Press, 1985. 191 pp. 0836112725.

A history of Spanish Mennonites in the United States and of fifty-seven local congregations.

HI530 Kraybill, Paul N., ed.
Called to Be Sent: Essays in Honor of the 50th Anniversary of the Founding of the Eastern Mennonite Board of Missions and Charities, 1914-1964. Scottdale, PAU: Herald Press, 1964. 238 pp. No ISBN.

A collection of essays by Mennonites concerning the development of mission activity of the Lancaster (PA) Mennonite Conference, including information on city and rural missions and benevolent institutions in America, and on foreign missions work (especially Africa).

HI531 Lapp, John Allen
"Through the Church the Song Goes On": MBM Celebrates 100 Years of International Ministries. (Mission Insight, 4). Elkhart, INU: Mennonite Board of Missions, 1999. 15 pp. Paper. 1877736252.

A pamphlet that highlights the 100-year history of the Mennonite Board of Missions in international ministries.

Mennonite Brethren Missions/ Services, 1878-

See also AF440, AM631, AM710, AM913, AS1511, and EU81.

HI532 Klassen, A. J., ed.
The Church in Mission. Fresno, CAU: Mennonite Brethren Church, Board of Christian Literature, 1967. xvi, 417 pp. No ISBN.

A collection of essays by Mennonite scholars dealing with mission history and theology in the Mennonite Brethren Church; with statistics on the work of the church at home and abroad.

HI533 Peters, George W.
Foundations of Mennonite Brethren Missions. Hillsboro, KSU: Kindred Press, 1984. v, 262 pp. Paper. 093519613X.

A 120-year (1860-1980) history of the Mennonite Brethren missions, including missions to Russia, and the theology, organization, and work of the church during that period.

Mennonite Central Committee (MCC), 1920-

HI534 Dyck, Cornelius J., ed.
The Mennonite Central Committee Story, Vol. 2: Responding to Worldwide Needs. Scottdale, PAU: Herald Press, 1980. 155 pp. 0836112296.

An institutional history of the MCC from 1920 to the 1970s (later period deals with Vietnam only); drawn from correspondence and committee documents.

HI535 Kreider, Robert S., and Rachel Waltner Goossen
Hungry, Thirsty, a Stranger: The MCC Experience. Scottdale, PAU: Herald Press, 1988. 391 pp. Paper. 0836112997.

A study guide from the Mennonite Central Committee (MCC), discussing its history and its international service projects on six continents; with case studies and an extensive bibliography.

Mennonite Church General Conference (Newton, Kansas), 1860-

See also AF388, AM1169, AM1191, and OC84.

HI536 Juhnke, James C.
A People of Mission: A History of General Conference Mennonite Overseas Missions. (Mennonite Historical Series). Newton, KSU: Faith and Life Press, 1979. xi, 280 pp. 0873030192.

The official history of more than eighty years of the overseas missions work of the General Conference Mennonite Church.

HI537 Pannabecker, S. F.
The Christian Mission of the General Conference Mennonite Church. Newton, KSU: Faith and Life Press, 1961. 80 pp. Paper. No ISBN.

A project by the General Conference Mennonite Church, summarizing reports of mission work, both at home and abroad.

Methodists, General

See also AF913, AF958, AM577, EU205, and OC326.

HI538 Doraisamy, Theodore R.
What Hath God Wrought: Motives of Mission in Methodism from Wesley to Thoburn. (An MBR Publication). Singapore, SI: Methodist Book Room, 1983. xix, 132 pp. No ISBN.

A thesis analyzing Methodist missionary motivations from John Wesley (1703-1791) to James M. Thoburn (1836-

1922), missionary bishop to India; by the bishop of the Methodist Church in Malaysia and Singapore.

HI539 Padgett, Alan G., ed.
The Mission of the Church in Methodist Perspective: The World Is My Parish. (Studies in the History of Missions, 10). Lewiston, NYU: E Mellen Press, 1992. v, 180 pp. 0773491570.

Eight essays by scholars of the Wesleyan tradition in the United States, on the theology, history, and contemporary emphases of Methodists in mission and evangelism.

HI540 Schmidt, Martin
Der junge Wesley als Heidenmissionar und Missionstheologe: Ein Beitrag zur Entstehungsgeschichte des Methodismus. (Deutsche Gesellschaft für Missionswissenschaft, 9). Gütersloh, GW: Gerd Mohn, 1973. 66 pp. 3579042653.

The story of young John Wesley as a missionary and theologian; with an extensive bibliography and letters in English between the Wesleys, father and son, and people in the American colonies who were requesting a missionary to the Indians.

HI541 Taggart, Norman W.
The Irish in World Methodism, 1760-1900. London, ENK: Epworth Press, 1986. xvii, 222 pp. 0716204231.

An examination of the role Irish Methodism played in overseas mission; including case studies of prominent Irish missionaries.

HI542 Thomas, Hilah F., and Rosemary Skinner Keller, eds.
Women in New Worlds: Historical Perspectives on the Wesleyan Tradition. Nashville, TNU: Abingdon, 1981. 2 vols. Paper. 0687459680 (vol.1), 0687459699 (vol.2).

Essays on the contribution of women in the Wesleyan tradition; including chapters on "National Missions and Social Reform" and "Foreign Missions and Cultural Imperialism" (vol. 1: 445 pp.; vol. 2: 445 pp.).

HI543 Vickers, John A.
Thomas Coke: Apostle of Methodism. (Wesley Historical Society Lecture, 30). Nashville, TNU: Abingdon, 1969. xiv, 394 pp. 0716201283.

A detailed biography, based on primary archival sources, of Thomas Coke (1747-1814), the extraordinary world missionary of the Wesleyan revival.

Methodist Church (U.K.), 1932-

See also EU215, OC12, OC116, and OC324.

HI544 Davey, Cyril J.
Mad about Mission: The Story of Dr. Thomas Coke. Basingstoke, Hants, ENK: Marshall Pickering, 1985. 127 pp. Paper. 0551012714.

A introductory history of the Methodist Missionary Society, from 1770 through the death of Coke in 1813, written as a celebration of the 200th anniversary of the beginning of the society now called the Methodist Church in Britain's Overseas Division.

HI—HISTORY

HI–HISTORY

Methodist Church (U.S.A.), 1939-1968

See also PO186, CO127, ED17, AF407, AF430-AF431, AF868, AF1148, AF1159, AF1168, AF1279, AF1283, AM142, AM643, AM958, AM988, AM1113, AM1123, AM1159, AM1381, AM1465, AS540, AS556, AS576-AS577, AS588, AS640, AS753, AS1074, AS1183, AS1185, AS1207, AS1383, and AS1477.

HI545 Baker, Frances J.

The Story of the Women's Foreign Missionary Society of the Methodist Episcopal Church, 1869-1895. (Women in American Protestant Religion, 1800-1930, 9). New York, NYU: Garland, 1987. 435 pp. Paper. 0824006585.

Reprint of the 1896 edition concerning the organization, literature, and missions work in India, China, Europe, and South America, of the Women's Foreign Missionary Society; including a statistical summary of institutions, finances, and women missionaries in 1896.

HI546 Barclay, Wade Crawford, and J. Tremayne Copplestone

History of Methodist Missions. New York, NYU: Methodist Church, Board of Missions, 1973. 4 vols. No ISBN.

A comprehensive mission history of the denominations that formed the Methodist Church in 1939 in the United States; with extensive bibliographies [vol. 1: *Early American Methodism, 1769-1844: Missionary Motivation and Expansion* by W. C. Barclay, 1949, xli, 449 pp.; vol. 2: *Early American Methodism, 1769-1844: To Reform the Nation* by W. C. Barclay, 1950, xi, 562 pp.; vol. 3: *Methodist Episcopal Church: Widening Horizons, 1845-1895* by W.C. Barclay, 1957, xv, 1,211 pp.; vol. 4: *Methodist Episcopal Church, 1896-1939* by J. T. Copplestone, 1973, xi, 1,267 pp.].

HI547 Born, Ethel W.

By My Spirit: The Story of Methodist Protestant Women in Mission, 1879-1939. Cincinnati, OHU: UMC, Board of Global Ministries, 1990. xi, 196 pp. Paper. No ISBN.

An illustrated history of women organized for mission within the Methodist Protestant denomination, a forerunner of the Women's Division of the United Methodist Church's Board of Global Ministries.

HI548 Carter, Ruth G. et al.

To a Higher Glory: The Growth and Development of Black Women Organized for Mission in the Methodist Church, 1940-1968. Cincinnati, OHU: UMC, Board of Global Ministries, 1980. 153 pp. Paper. No ISBN.

An account of the values that black women have historically brought to the church, giving young black people a sense of racial pride and loyalty to Christ, and inspiring all United Methodists to greater achievements as a multiracial church; findings of the Task Group on the History of the Central Jurisdiction Women's Organization.

HI549 Cobb, Alice

"Yes, Lord, I'll Do It": Scarritt's Century of Service. Nashville, TNU: Scarritt College, 1987. xviii, 206 pp. No ISBN.

A history of the Methodist Episcopal Church South's Bible and missionary training school for women.

HI550 McDowell, John Patrick

The Social Gospel in the South: The Woman's Home Mission Movement in the Methodist Episcopal Church, South, 1886-1939. Baton Rouge, LAU: Louisiana State University Press, 1982. x, 167 pp. 0807110221.

A scholarly history with emphasis on the social concern of the female leadership of the Methodist Episcopal Church, South, tracing the extension of Christianity into the home and workplace of immigrants, blacks, and women, especially as this intersected with social reform and ethical living.

HI551 Meeker, Ruth Esther

Six Decades of Service, 1880-1940: A History of the Women's Home Missionary Society of the Methodist Episcopal Church. Cincinnati, OHU: Steinhauser, 1969. v, 405 pp. Paper. No ISBN.

Commissioned history based on the minutes and publications of the WHMS, including a narrative history of the work by decade, an examination of specific projects (e.g. the deaconess work, social welfare, and outpost missions), and an examination of the various organizational and financial methods used.

HI552 Methodist Church (USA) Board of Missions, Joint Section of Education and Cultivation

The Christian Mission Today. New York, NYU: Abingdon, 1960. 288 pp. No ISBN.

A collection of essays by prominent missiologists written as a text for pastors' summer schools of the Methodist Church, emphasizing the contemporary worldwide missions situation in a historical perspective.

HI553 Neely, Thomas Benjamin

The Methodist Episcopal Church and Its Foreign Missions. New York, NYU: Gallimard, 1968. 341 pp. No ISBN.

Reprint of a 1923 history of the foreign missions of the Methodist Episcopal Church USA with focus on administrative structures including the role of bishops; originally published by the Methodist Book Concern.

HI554 Task Group on the History of the Central Jurisdiction Women's Organization, UMC

To a Higher Glory: The Growth and Development of Black Women Organized for Mission in the Methodist Church, 1940-1968. Cincinnati, OHU: Service Center, 1978. 153 pp. Paper. No ISBN.

A brief historical survey of the role of black women in the Methodist missions, with appendices noting specific individuals in leadership positions.

HI555 Tatum, Noreen Dunn

A Crown of Service: A Story of Women's Work in the Methodist Episcopal Church, South, from 1878-1940. Nashville, TNU: Parthenon Press, 1960. 418 pp. No ISBN.

The commissioned history of the home and worldwide missionary operations of women in the M. E. Church, South.

Methodist Church (Canada), 1884-1925

HI556 Gagan, Rosemary Ruth

A Sensitive Independence: Canadian Methodist Women Missionaries in Canada and the Orient, 1881-1925. (McGill-Queen's Studies in the History of Religion, 9). Montreal, QUC: McGill-Queen's University Press, 1992. xiii, 281 pp. 0773508961.

A history of the work of missionaries of the Women's Missionary Society (WMS) of the Methodist Church of Canada, primarily in the Northwest Territories, China, and Japan; originally submitted as a doctoral dissertation at McMaster University.

Mission Aviation Fellowship, 1973-

See also AM1426.

HI557 Buss, Dietrich G., and Arthur F. Glasser
Giving Wings to the Gospel: The Remarkable Story of Mission Aviation Fellowship. Grand Rapids, MIU: Baker Books, 1995. 377 pp. Paper. 0801052300.

A narrative illustrated history of the Mission Aviation Fellowship.

Mission to Lepers

HI558 Leprosy Mission
This Spreading Tree: The Story of the Leprosy Mission from 1918-1970. London, ENK: Leprosy Mission, 1974. 193 pp. 0902731122.

A narrative history of the Leprosy Mission, showing its growth from 1917; the continuation of Donald Miller's *An Inn Called Welcome* (1965).

HI559 Miller, A. Donald
An Inn Called Welcome: The Story of the Mission to Lepers, 1874-1917. London, ENK: Mission to Lepers, 1965. x, 241 pp. Paper. No ISBN.

A history of the Mission to Lepers, covering the period during which its founder, Wellesly Cosby Baily, led the work; written by a former director of the mission.

Missionsanstalt Hermannsburg, 1849-

See also AF92, AF506, AF650, AF852, AF1004, and OC85.

HI560 Harms, Hartwig F.
Concerned for the Unreached: Life and Work of Louis Harms, Founder of the Hermannsburg Mission. Hermannsburg, GW: Verlag Missionshandlung Hermannsburg; Addis Ababa, ET: Mekane Yesus Seminary, 1999. x, 102 pp. Paper. 3875461177.

The leader of a congregation in Germany stirs up his village and congregation, and the revival leads to the founding of a missionary-sending seminary to all continents, the founding of Hermannsburg Mission 150 years ago.

HI561 Wendlandt-Homann, Luise
Zugvögel kennen ihre Zeit: Als Missionarsfrau in vier Erdteilen, 1837-1932. (Erlanger Taschenbücher, 81; Quellen und Beiträge zur Geschichte der Hermannsburger Mission). Erlangen, GW: Ev.-Luth. Mission, 1987. 119 pp. Paper. 3872141813.

Reproduction of a manuscript of autobiographical material, written for her children by the author (born Henriette Elisabeth Luise Bensen), 1837-1932, who served beginning in 1859 with the Missionsanstalt Hermannsburg (Hermannsburg Mission) in southern India, then in South Africa, and later among the Aborigines of central Australia.

HI562 Wickert, Winfried
Männer und Zeiten: 50 Jahre Hermannsburger Missionsgeschichte; ein Rückblick. (Quellen und Beiträge zur Geschichte der Hermannsburger Mission, 2). Erlangen, GW: Ev.-Luth. Mission, 1987. 338 pp. Paper. 3872142143.

This work (without bibliographical references) by a director of the Hermannsburg Mission, continues Georg Haccius' four-

volume *Hannoversche Missionsgeschichte* (1909-1920), presenting the more recent history of the society, mainly through four prominent missionary personalities: Egmont Harms, Georg Haccius, Christoph Schomerus, and August Elfers.

Moravians: General

See also TH12, EA90, EC24, AF710, AF932-AF933, AM550, AM552, AM943-AM944, AM1140, AM1158, AM1173, AM1176, AM1515, and AM1523.

HI563 Beck, Hartmut
Brüder in vielen Völkern: 250 Jahre Mission der Brüdergemeine. Erlangen, GW: Ev.-Luth. Mission, 1981. 583 pp. 3872141244.

A solid history of the missionary work of the Moravians in four parts describing its beginnings, activities during the age of slavery, and the developments in the 19th and 20th centuries concentrating on typical aspects of each period.

HI564 Freeman, Arthur J.
An Ecumenical Theology of the Heart: The Theology of Count Nicholas Ludwig von Zinzendorf. Bethleham, PAU: Moravian Church in America, 1998. vi, 346 pp. Paper. 1878422383 (hdbk), 1878422367 (pbk).

The product of more than forty years of research on Zinzendorf, this systematic study of Zinzendorf's theology places it in the context of Moravian theology since the 15th century, and reflects on its contribution toward contemporary spiritual and ecumenical formation.

HI565 Lewis, A. J.
Zinzendorf: The Ecumenical Pioneer: A Study in the Moravian Contribution to Christian Mission and Unity. London, ENK: SCM Press, 1962. 208 pp. No ISBN.

An uncritical biography based on the best of secondary sources, with a brief survey of the Moravian Church from the death of Zinzendorf to 1961.

HI566 Linde, J. M. van der
Gods Wereldhuis: Voordrachten en opstellen over de geschiedenis van zending en oecumene. Amsterdam, NE: Ton Bolland, 1980. 219 pp. Paper. No ISBN.

A selection of articles by then-retiring professor of the history of mission at Utrecht University, about the history of the Moravian missions in Europe and the Caribbean, and the history of missiology in the Netherlands.

HI567 Linde, J. M. van der
Gods wereldhuis: Voordrachten en opstellen over de geschiedenis van zending en oecumene. Amsterdam, NE: Ton Bolland, 1980. 219 pp. No ISBN.

An introduction to Moravian world missions.

Moravian Church in America, 1734-

See also AM535, and AM1174.

HI568 Groenfeldt, John S.
The Moravian Church at Work around the World. (Book One). Bethlehem, PAU: Moravian Church in America, 1986. 51 pp. Paper. No ISBN.

A study guide written for Moravians detailing their mission work in Czechoslovakia, Western Europe, and Central America.

National Baptist Convention of America, 1880-

See also AM1051.

HI569 Harvey, William J.
Bridges of Faith Across the Seas. Philadelphia, PAU: National Baptist Convention, Foreign Mission Board, 1989. xv, 363 pp. 0962464902.

A history of Black Baptist missions by the executive secretary of the National Baptist Convention's Foreign Mission Board.

HI570 Higginbotham, Evelyn Brooks
Righteous Discontent: The Women's Movement in the Black Baptist Church 1880-1920. Cambridge, MAU: Harvard University Press, 1993. xii, 306 pp. Paper. 0674769775.

A study of black Baptist women's organizations for racial uplift and leadership development, including missionary societies.

HI571 Jordan, Lewis Garnett
Negro Baptist History, U.S.A.: 1750-1930. (E. C. Morris History of National Baptists Series, 2). Nashville, TNU: Townsend Press/Sunday School Publishing Board, 1995. xlviii, 464 pp. Paper. 0910683166.

A revised edition of the classic (1930) history of the National Baptist Convention, including the American Baptist Missionary Convention and the work among African Americans of the American Baptist Home Missionary Society.

Nederduitse Gereformeerde Kerk in Suid Afrika (NGK), 1652-

See also AF593, AF770, AF902, AF928, AF941, AF955-AF956, AF974, AF993, AF1052, AF1073, AF1077, AF1090, and AF1166.

HI572 Cronjé, J. M.
Born to Witness: A Concise History of the Churches Born out of the Mission Work of the Dutch Reformed Church (Nederduitse Gereformeerde Kerk) of South Africa. Pretoria, SA: N. G. Kerkboekhandel Transvaal, 1982. 228 pp. 0798703342.

History of cross-cultural missions of the Nederduitse Gereformeerde Kerk of South Africa, with photographs.

Nederlandsch Zendeling Genootschap, 1797-

See also AF980, AS429, AS1301, AS1318-AS1319, AS1329, and AS1366.

HI573 Boneschansker, Jan
Het Nederlandsch Zendeling Genootschap in zijn eerste periode: Een studie over opwekking in de Bataafse en Franse tijd. (Proefschrift Theol. Fac. Rijksuniversiteit Groningen). Leeuwarden, NE: Dykstra, 1987. 253 pp. Paper. 907052211X.

A detailed and scholarly history of the origins and early developments within the Dutch Missionary Society (founded 1797), covering the period 1773-1814.

HI574 Boone, A. Th., and J. van Ekeris
Zending tussen woord en daad: Twee hoofdstukken uit de geschiedenis van gereformeerd pidtisme en zending. Kampen, NE: Guitgeverij de Groot Goudriaan/Stichting Studie der Nadere Reformatie, 1991. 99 pp. Paper. 9061402921.

Two essays on the tensions between the mission goals of reformed pietism and the practices of early 19th-century missionaries of the Dutch Missionary Society (Nederlandisch Zendeling-Genootschap).

HI575 End, Th. van den, Chr. G. F. de Jong, A. Th. Boone, and P. N. Holtrop, eds.
Twee eeuwen Nederlandse zending 1797-1997: Twaalf opstellen. (Werkgroep voor de Geschiedenis van de Nederlandse Zending en Overzeese Kerken: Kleine Reeks, 3). Zoetermeer, NE: Boekencentrum, 1997. x, 248 pp. Paper. 9023905695.

Commemorating two-hundred years of Dutch Protestant mission work, this collection of articles on the beginnings of missions in Africa (1954-1965), deals with education, cultural change, nationalism, and changes in theological thinking.

HI576 Smit, Wouter
De islam binnen de horizon: Een missiologische studie over de benadering van de islam door vier Nederlandse zendingscorporaties (1797-1951). (Proefschrift Universiteit Utrecht). (MISSION, 11). Zoetermeer, NE: Boekencentrum, 1995. xix, 312 pp. Paper. 9023914813.

A doctoral dissertation on the approaches to Islam of four Dutch missionary societies, mainly operating in Indonesia.

Nederlandse Hervormde Kerk (c.690-)

See also HI576, CR1395, AF1254, AM1517, AS1298-AS1299, AS1320, AS1346, AS1348, and EU225.

HI577 Enklaar, Ido Hendricus
Kom over en help ons!: Twaalf opstellen over de Nederlandse zending in de negentiende eeuw. au-Gravenhage, NE: Boekencentrum, 1981. 173 pp. 9023902645.

A collection of twelve articles on the history of Dutch missions in the 19th century, with some articles on South Africa and Indonesia, but mostly on missionary thinking in the Netherlands.

HI578 Holtrop, P. N., ed.
ZGKN 100: Een bundel opstellen over de Zending van de Gereformeerde Kerken in Nederland ter gelegenheid van de honderdjarige herdenking van de Synode van Middelburg 1896. (Kleine Reeks, 3). Kampen, NE: WZOK, 1996. 200 pp. Paper. 907565104X.

A collection of articles on the mission of the Dutch Reformed Church (DRC) in the Netherlands, commemorating the centennial of the Synod of Middelburg in 1896, at which the DRC accepted the Calvinist principles as the basis for method and organization of its mission work.

Norddeutsche Missionsgesellschaft in Bremen, 1836-

See also AF1200, and AF1205.

HI579 Schöck-Quinteros, Eva, and Dieter Lenz, eds.
150 annees mission de l'Allemagne du Nord, 1836-1986. Bremen, GW: Roder-Druck, 1989. 85 pp. Paper. No ISBN.
French translation.

HI580 Schöck-Quinteros, Eva, and Dieter Lenz, eds.
150 Years of North German Mission, 1836-1986. Bremen,
GW: North German Mission, 1989. 83 pp. Paper. No ISBN.
   English translation.

HI581 Schöck-Quinteros, Eva, ed.
*150 (Hundertfünfzig) Jahre Norddeutsche Mission, 1836-
1986.* Bremen, GW: Norddeutsche Mission, 1986. 418 pp.
Paper. No ISBN.
   A volume commemorating 150 years of the Norddeutsche Mission with contributions by foreign and local missionary authors on the history of the society, critical questions about the period between the wars, the advancement
to partnership in mission, and what lessons can be learned
from the past.

Nordisk Misjonsrad, 1923-

**HI582 Hallencreutz, Carl F., Johannes Aagaard, and Nils
Bloch-Hoell, eds.**
*Missions from the North: Nordic Missionary Council, 50
Years.* (Studia Missionalia Upsaliensia, 20; Supplementa—
Norsk Tidsskrift for Misjon, 5). Oslo, NO: Oslo Univer-
sitetsforlaget, 1974. 170 pp. Paper. 8200093441.
   A collection of essays tracing the fifty-year history of
the Nordic Missionary Council; with emphasis on the role
played by each Scandinavian country, and on the recent
merger of Nordic missionary work.

Norsk Luthersk Misjonssamband (NLM), 1891-

HI583 Helland, Birger et al., eds.
*Misjonærer: Norsk Luthersk Mis jonssambands misjonær-
er, 1891-1986.* Oslo, NO: Norsk Luthersk Misjonssamband,
i kommisjon hos Lunde, 1986. 158 pp. 8252046584.
   A survey of all the missionaries of the Norwegian Lutheran Mission, with brief biographical data, 1891-1986; updates older editions with planned supplements in the yearbook of the society.

Norske Misjonsselskap, 1842-

See also AF567, AF1018, AF1045-AF1046, AF1094, AF1227-
AF1228, and AM1428.

HI584 Hauken, Tor, and Arne B. Samuelsen, eds.
*Forskere i misjonens tjeneste utgitt til Misjonshøgskolens
150-års jubieum 1993.* Stavanger, NO: Misjonshøgskolens
Forlag, 1993. v, 185 pp. Paper. 8277210000.
   Four scholarly essays on aspects of Norwegian mis-
sions, published to celebrate the 150th anniversary of the
School of Mission and Theology.

HI585 Jørgensen, Torstein, ed.
I tro og tjeneste: Det Norske Misjonsselskap,1842-1992.
Stavanger, NO: Misjonshøgskolen Forlag, 1992. 2 vols.
8272190788.
   The official history of the work of the Norwegian Missionary Society, 1842-1992; organized by country of service, with numerous photographs [vol. 1: 504 pp.; vol. 2:
450 pp.].

HI586 Meling, G. Andrea, ed.
Guds høstfolk: det Norske misjonsselskaps misjonærer,
1842-1977. Stavanger, NO: Norske misjonsselskap, Det,
1977. 143 pp. No ISBN.
   A survey of all the missionaries of the Norwegian Missionary Society, with brief biographical data, 1842-1977;
to be updated by supplements in the yearbook of the society.

HI587 Riisager, Filip
*Forventning og opfyldelse: Studier i Karl Ludvig Reichelts
liv og missionsforstselse indtil 1925—med sµrligt henblik
ps buddhistmissionens udskillelse fra Det norske Missionsselskab.* (Teologiske Studier, 1). Aarhus, DK: Forlaget Aros,
1973. 328 pp. Paper. 8770032262.
   This thesis describes Reichelt's theological development and his relationship with the Norwegian Mission Society and the foundation of the Nordic Mission to Buddhists.

HI588 Terray, László, G., and Õystein Õstenstad, eds.
Den Norske Israelsmisjon 125 år. Stavanger, NO: Nomi
Forlag for Den Norske Israelsmisjon, 1947-1969. 2 vols.
No ISBN.
   The 125-year history of the Norwegian Church Minis-
try to Israel; presented in two volumes [vol. 1, *histoire i
hundred, 1844-1944*; vol. 2, *histoire II, 1944-1969*].

O.C. Ministries, 1979-

HI589 Brown, Keith, and John Hoover
*It's Never Too Late to Say Yes!: Eleven Inspiring Accounts
of People Who Made Mid-Life Ministry Commitments.* Ventura, CAU: Regal Books, 1987. 192 pp. Paper. 0830712496.
   A popular account of the faith journeys of eleven couples who felt called to become missionaries and pastors; by
staff members of Overseas Crusades.

HI590 Winebrenner, Jan
Steel in His Soul. Chicago, ILU: Moody, 1985. 170 pp.
0802422020.
   The story of Dick Hillis's vision: the inception and
development of the Overseas Crusade ministry in China,
Taiwan, Vietnam, Argentina, Brazil, and other nations.

OMS International, 1973-

See also AS458, and AS533.

HI591 Huff, Alice, and Eleanor Burr, comps.
A Watered Garden: Devotional Stories from Missionaries. Grand
Rapids, MIU: Asbury Press, 1987. 192 pp. 0310393906.
   A unique daily devotional guide written by OMS In-
ternational missionaries reflecting experiences in their lives.

Operation Mobilization, 1957-

HI592 Meroff, Deborah
*Footsteps in the Sea: Adventures with Operation Mobilisa-
tion.* London, ENK: Hodder & Stoughton, 1994. 190 pp.
Paper. 0340612266.
   A popular account of the founding of Operation Mobi-
lization by Georg Verwer and of its global ministries.

HI593 Meroff, Deborah
*Huellas en el Mar: Aventuras con la Operación Moviliza-
ción.* Translated by Nellyda Pablovsky. Miami, FLU: Editorial Unilit, 1997. 232 pp. Paper. 0789901447.
   Spanish translation.

HI—HISTORY

HI594 Rhoton, Elaine
The Ship Called Logos. Chicago, ILU: Moody, 1989. 185 pp. Paper. 0802476910.

A popular account of the history of Operation Mobilization's ship *Logos*, which from 1971 to 1988 made 400 port visits in 103 countries for evangelical faith witness.

Örebromissionen, 1892-

HI595 Eriksson, Linné, ed.
I mänsklighetens tjänst: Örebromissionen i fyra världsdelar. Örebro, SW: Libris, 1971. 100 pp. No ISBN.

Eleven articles on the history and work of the evangelical mission society Örebromissionen, from 1890 to 1970.

Ostasien Mission, 1884-

HI596 Hahn, Ferdinand, ed.
Spuren...: Festschrift zum hundertjährigen Bestehen der Ostasienmission. Stuttgart, GW: EMW, 1984. viii, 256 pp. Paper. 3880963819.

A *festschrift* published on the occasion of the centenary of the German (and Swiss) Ostasien-Mission (formerly Allgemeiner Evangelisch-Protestantischer Missionsverein), with nineteen essays dealing with the theological foundations of the mission, the history of the society, and various concrete problems.

Pentecostals: General

See also HI9, HI397, HI447, HI696, TH357-TH358, TH364, CO164-CO165, EV240, EV256, MI180, AF406, AF444, AF907, AF1057, AF1066, AF1118, AM121, AM257, AM1242, AM1255, AM1279, AM1316-AM1317, AM1376, AM1381, AM1403, AM1411, AS768, AS843, AS1258-AS1259, EU92, and EU255.

HI597 Coggins, James Robert, and Paul G. Hiebert, eds.
Wonders and the Word. Winnipeg, MBC: Kindred Press, 1989. 162 pp. Paper. 0919797822.

A series of essays by prominent experts in theology, history, and mission, who critique some of the ideas raised by John Wimber, the founder of the Vineyard Movement for charismatic renewal.

HI598 Conference on Pentecostal and Charismatic Research in Europe (1989, Utrecht)
Experiences of the Spirit. Edited by J. A. B. Jongeneel. (Studien zur interkulturellen Geschichte des Christentums, 68). Frankfurt am Main, GW: Lang, 1991. xiv, 277 pp. Paper. 3631433115.

Papers and reports from the fifth Conference on Pentecostal and Charismatic Research, focusing on 20th-century developments in Europe, Africa, the Caribbean, and Latin America.

HI599 Cox, Harvey Gallagher
Fire from Heaven: The Rise of Pentecostal Spirituality and the Reshaping of Religion in the Twenty-First Century. Reading, MAU: Addison-Wesley, 1995. xviii, 346 pp. 020162656X.

A narrative history and assessment of contemporary world Pentecostalism by the Victor Thomas Professor of Religion at Harvard University.

HI600 Damboriena, Prudencio
Tongues as of Fire: Pentecostalism in Contemporary Christianity. Washington, DCU: Corpus Books, 1969. viii, 256 pp. No ISBN.

An overview of the holiness and Pentecostal movement, its history, and theology, with a survey of its involvements in mission and ecumenism.

HI601 Goff, James R.
Fields White Unto Harvest: Charles F. Parham and the Missionary Origins of Pentecostalism. Fayetteville, ARU: University of Arkansas Press, 1988. ix, 263 pp. 1557280258 (hdbk), 1557280266 (pbk).

An in-depth study of the origins of Pentecostalism in the American Midwest as seen through the life and evangelistic ministry of one responsible for giving that movement its identity.

HI602 Hollenweger, Walter J.
Enthusiastisches Christentum: Die Pfingstbewegung in Geschichte und Gegenwart. Wuppertal, GW: Theologischer Verlag Brockhaus; Zürich, GW: Zwingli-Verlag, 1969. xxiii, 640 pp. No ISBN.

An encyclopedic survey of the Pentecostal movement, featuring a detailed history of the movement in various parts of the world, especially Latin America, and a detailed exposition of the movement's many beliefs and practices; by the professor of missions at the University of Birmingham, England.

HI603 Hollenweger, Walter J.
El Pentecostalismo: Historia y Doctrinas. (Biblioteca de Estudios Teológicos). Buenos Aires, AG: La Aurora, 1976. 530 pp. No ISBN.

Spanish translation.

HI604 Hollenweger, Walter J.
The Pentecostals: The Charismatic Movement in the Churches. Translated by R. A. Wilson. Peabody, MAU: Hendrickson, 1988. xxix, 572 pp. 0943575028.

Reprint of the third edition of the English translation first published in 1972, with revisions by the author.

HI605 McClung, L. Grant, ed.
Azusa Street and Beyond: Pentecostal Missions and Church Growth in the Twentieth Century. South Plainfield, NJU: Bridge-Logos, 1986. xvi, 245 pp. Paper. 0882706071.

Fifteen essays and two documents which illustrate the history, theological motivations, and practical issues of Pentecostal missions.

HI606 Michel, David
Telling the Story: Black Pentecostals in the Church of God. Cleveland, TNU: Pathway Press, 2000. 163 pp. Paper. 0871489465.

Told from an academic and evangelical perspective, here are the untold stories of the Pentecostal movement, in particular those of African descent, in the United States, the Caribbean, Africa, Asia, and Europe.

HI607 Nichol, John T.
Pentecostalism: A Study of the Growth and Development of a New Force in American Protestantism. New York, NYU: Harper & Row, 1966. xvi, 264 pp. No ISBN.

A study of Pentecostals which includes a section on Central and South America; originally submitted as a Ph.D. dissertation (Boston University, 1965).

HI–HISTORY

HI608 Owens, Robert R.
Speak to the Rock: The Azusa Street Revival, Its Roots and Its Message. Lanham, MDU: University Press of America, 1998. viii, 140 pp. 076181101X.

A history of the Azusa Street Revival, its spread, schisms, and implications for the mainline social gospel response—all from a Pentecostal perspective.

HI609 Sahlberg, Carl-Erik
The Pentecostal Movement: Five Case Studies. Nairobi, KE: Evangel Publishing House, 1986. 69 pp. Paper. No ISBN.

Five scholarly interpretations of the general Pentecostal missions movement, including a brief history of the Pentecostal mission in Tanzania.

HI610 Suenens, Léon Joseph
¿Un Nuevo Pentecostés? Translated by José María de Llanos. (Nuevo biblioteca de teologia). Bilbao, SP: Desclée de Brouwer, 1975. 237 pp. 843300526X.

Spanish translation.

HI611 Suenens, Léon Joseph
Een nieuw Pinksteren? Brugge, NE: Desclée de Brouwer, 1974. 299 pp. 9026471653.

Dutch translation.

HI612 Suenens, Léon Joseph
A New Pentecost? Translated by Francis Martin. London, ENK: Darton, Longman & Todd; New York, NYU: Seabury Press, 1975. xiii, 239 pp. 023251335X (UK, hdbk), 0232513341 (UK, pbk), 0816402760 (US).

English translation.

HI613 Suenens, Léon Joseph
Une nouvelle Pentecôte? Paris, FR: Desclée de Brouwer, 1974. 271 pp. No ISBN.

A noted Belgian cardinal reconsiders the work of the Holy Spirit in the church, in the light of history, the charismatic renewal, and the Second Vatican Council.

HI614 Synan, Vinson
The Spirit Said "Grow"   : The Astounding Worldwide Expansion of Pentecostal and Charismatic Churches. (Innovations in Mission). Monrovia, CAU: MARC/World Vision, 1992. ii, 62 pp. Paper. 0912552735.

Seven brief lectures delivered at Fuller Theological Seminary, November 1990, on the history of Pentecostal church growth.

HI615 Synan, Vinson
The Twentieth Century Pentecostal Explosion: The Exciting Growth of Pentecostal Churches and Charismatic Renewal Movements. Altamonte Springs, FLU: Creation House, 1987. 235 pp. 0884192067.

A narrative history by denomination of the charismatic renewal movement and of Pentecostalism; with many references to missions.

Pentecostal Assemblies of Canada, 1919-

See also AS565.

HI616 Overseas Missions Department
Ripening Harvest: The Pentecostal Assemblies of Canada. Toronto, ONC: Pentecostal Assemblies of Canada, 1974. 64 pp. No ISBN.

A popular survey of the overseas missions work of the Pentecostal Assemblies of Canada.

Pilgrim Holiness Church, 1922-1968

HI617 Thomas, Paul Westphal, and Paul William Thomas
The Days of Our Pilgrimage: The History of the Pilgrim Holiness Church. Marion, INU: Wesley Press, 1976. xviii, 382 pp. No ISBN.

Official history of the Pilgrim Holiness Church including its missionary activities.

Presbyterian Church in Canada, 1925-

See also AM608, AS382, AS527, AS638, AS716, and AS908.

HI618 Johnston, Geoffrey
Unknown Country: A Centennial Account of Missions, the Presbyterian Church in Canada. Toronto, ONC: Presbyterian Church in Canada, 1973. 80 pp. No ISBN.

A history of the Presbyterian Church in Canada's stewardship in mission, showing the church's attempt to face its challenges and fulfill its opportunities.

Presbyterian Church in Ireland, 1642-

HI619 Thompson, T. Jack, ed.
Into All the World: A History of 150 Years of the Overseas Work of the Presbyterian Church in Ireland. Belfast, NIK: PCI, Overseas Board, 1990. 222 pp. Paper. 0951663704.

Twelve short essays, without documentation, on aspects of Presbyterian mission outreach from Northern Ireland; with illustrations and a listing of missionaries and their fields of service.

Presbyterian Church in the United States, 1861-1983

See also ME139, CO174, AF386, AF421, AF429, AF434, AF1284, AM604, AM688, AM862, AM904, AM1021, AM1077, AM1388, AS308, AS363, AS512, AS534, AS558, AS574, AS751, AS818, AS1214, and AS1446.

HI620 Boyd, Lois A., and R. Douglas Brackenridge
Presbyterian Women in America: Two Centuries of a Quest for Status. (Contributions of the Study of Religion, 9). Westport, CTU: Greenwood, 1983. xiv, 308 pp. 031323678X.

An overview of the role of women in North American Presbyterian denominations, including the growth of organized women's work, women's missionary societies, the quest for women's ordination, and the development of professional and lay participation of women in church careers.

HI621 Brown, G. Thompson
Presbyterians in World Mission: A Handbook for Congregations. Decatur, GAU: CTS Press, 1995. xi, 147 pp. Paper. No ISBN.

A practical study guide introducing global missions and presenting biblical and historical foundations of the Presbyterian missionary endeavors around the world.

HI–HISTORY

HI622 Coleman, Michael C.
Presbyterian Missionary Attitudes toward American Indians, 1837-1893. Jackson, MSU: University of Mississippi Press, 1985. x, 222 pp. 087805278X.

A scholarly history of the PCUSA, drawn from missionary correspondence, focusing primarily on missionary attitudes and rhetoric in regard to the cultures and peoples of the Native American Choctaw and Nez Perce.

HI623 Rycroft, William Stanley
The Ecumenical Witness of the United Presbyterian Church in the U.S.A. Philadelphia, PAU: COEMAR, 1968. 332 pp. No ISBN.

A historical and interpretative study which traces the development of a missionary church, and the emergence of national churches and of mission in unity.

HI624 Rycroft, William Stanley
Latin America and the United Presbyterians. New York, NYU: COEMAR, 1962. 43 pp. No ISBN.

Second edition of a popular history of United Presbyterian missions, their purposes, and effects.

Presbyterian Church of New Zealand, 1839-

See also AS1025, and AS1304.

HI625 Murray, John Stanley
A Century of Growth: Presbyterian Overseas Mission Work, 1869-1969. Christchurch, NZ: Presbyterian Bookroom, 1969. 112 pp. Paper. No ISBN.

A popular history of one hundred years of overseas missions, primarily in Oceania, by the Presbyterian Church of New Zealand.

Reformed: General

See also ME256, AM763-AM765, AM866, AM1328, AS340, AS508, AS746, AS1328, AS1369-AS1370, EU231, EU295, and OC269.

HI626 Bauswein, Jean-Jacques, and Lukas Vischer, eds.
The Reformed Family Worldwide: A Survey of Reformed Churches, Theological Schools, and International Organizations. Grand Rapids, MIU: Eerdmans, 1999. xiii, 740 pp. Paper. 0802844960.

A country-by-country survey of churches and theological schools in the Reformed tradition, with all its multiplicity, richness, weakness, and potential, worldwide.

Reformed Church in America, 1867-

See also EA103, AF60, AM838, AS331, AS654-AS655, AS696, AS704, AS807, AS813, AS822, AS853, AS856, AS1171, AS1206, and AS1226.

HI627 Hoff, Marvin D.
Structures for Mission: The Reformed Church in America. (The Historical Series of the Reformed Church in America, 14). Grand Rapids, MIU: Eerdmans, 1985. xxvii, 234 pp. Paper. 0802800815.

History of the missionary activity of the Reformed Church in America from 1628 to 1980, emphasizing the organizational history of Reformed Church ministries, including the United Advance, Stewardship Council, General Synod Executive Committee, and the General Program Committee.

Regions Beyond Missionary Union, 1878-

See also AM1504.

HI628 Pritchard, Elizabeth
For Such a Time. Eastbourne, ENK: Victory Press; Sussex, ENK: Regions Beyond, 1973. 125 pp. Paper. 085476187X.

A popular centennial history of the Regions Beyond Missionary Union (RBMU), 1873-1973, by one of their missionaries.

Rheinische Missionsgesellschaft, 1828-

See also TH137, PO134, AF875, AF878, AF881, AF890, AF892, AF897-AF898, AS1279, AS1330, and OC238.

HI629 Braun, Thomas
Die Rheinische Missionsgesellschaft und der Missionshandel im 19. Jahrhundert. (Erlanger Monographien aus Mission und Ökumene, 17). Erlangen, GW: Ev.-Luth. Mission, 1992. 208 pp. Paper. 3872143174.

This history documents the involvement of the Rheinische Missionsgesellschaft with trade in the last century in its several mission fields, including South West Africa (Namibia), and Borneo and Sumatra in Indonesia.

HI630 Gossweiler, Christian
Unterwegs zur Integration von Kirche und Mission: Untersucht am Beispiel der Rheinischen Missionsgesellschaft. (Erlanger Monographien aus Mission und Ökumene, 23). Erlangen, GW: Ev.-Luth. Mission, 1994. 433 pp. Paper. 3872143239.

A doctoral thesis (University of Tübingen, 1994) on issues of the relation of church and mission in Germany after World War II, as reflected in the history of the Rhenish Mission Society-RMG (Rheinische Missiongesellschaft) and of the United Evangelical Mission-UEM (Vereinigte Evangelische Mission) as its successor body.

HI631 Menzel, Gustav
Die Rheinische Mission: Aus 150 Jahren Missionsgeschichte. Wuppertal, GW: VEM, 1978. 463 pp. 392190000X.

A well-documented work by the director of the Rhenish Mission Society, describing its history up to the incorporation into the Vereinigte Evangelische Mission (1971), without much reference to general church and social history.

Salvation Army, 1865-

See also AS1164, EU105, and EU122.

HI632 Coutts, Frederick L.
Weapons of Good Will: The History of the Salvation Army. London, ENK: Hodder & Stoughton, 1986. 347 pp. 0340390875 (hbk), 0340390867 (pbk).

The seventh volume of the official history of the Salvation Army.

HI633 Larsson, Flora
My Best Men Are Women. London, ENK: Hodder & Stoughton; New York, NYU: Salvation Army, 1975. 222 pp. 0340182008.

Biographies of prominent women officers of the Salvation Army.

HI634 McKinley, Edward H.
Marching to Glory: The History of the Salvation Army in the United States, 1880-1992. Grand Rapids, MIU: Eerdmans, 1995. xix, 451 pp. 0802837611.

An expanded second edition of scholarly history based on archival research of the Salvation Army in the United States; originally published for the army's centennial in 1980.

HI635 McKinley, Edward H.
Somebody's Brother: A History of the Salvation Army Men's Social Service Department, 1891-1985. (Studies in American Religion, 21). Lewiston, NYU: E Mellen Press, 1986. xiii, 273 pp. 0889466653.

History of the social work of the Salvation Army in the United States by an officer of the Salvation Army, with primary concern for work with alcoholics.

HI636 Murdoch, Norman H.
Origins of the Salvation Army. Knoxville, TNU: University of Tennessee Press, 1994. xii, 241 pp. 0870498584.

A social history of the Salvation Army in Great Britain from its roots in Wesleyan revivalism (1829-1865), to the East London Home Mission (1865-1879), to national social reform (1880s).

HI637 Neal, Harry Edward
The Hallelujah Army. Philadelphia, PAU: Chilton, 1961. xiii, 261 pp. No ISBN.

Eighteen stories of the ministries of the Salvation Army, mostly in the United States in the late 19th and early 20th centuries.

HI638 Waldron, John D., comp.
Pioneering Salvationists: An Anthology of Selected Articles by Salvationist Authors, Past and Present, on the Pioneering Exploits the World Over. New York, NYU: Salvation Army, 1987. xii, 158 pp. Paper. 0892160748.

Twenty-five popular narratives recounting the lives and ministries of Salvation Army ministers and missionaries, 1885-1983.

HI639 Watson, Bernard
A Hundred Years' War: The Salvation Army. London, ENK: Hodder & Stoughton, 1968. 318 pp. 0340043806.

A description of the army's varied global ministries, demonstrating how it has adapted to new frontiers in mission; with numerous illustrations, photographs and case histories.

HI640 Wikfeldt, Sigfrid
Frälsningsarmén i världsmissionen: den svenska insatsen. Stockholm, SW: Frälsningsarméns högkvarter, 1961. 231 pp. No ISBN.

A book on missionary activities of the Swedish Salvationists.

HI641 Winston, Diane
Red-Hot and Righteous: The Urban Religion of the Salvation Army. Cambridge, MAU: Harvard University Press, 1999. viii, 290 pp. 0674867068.

A historical study of the Salvation Army's New York mission that in 1880 was called "vulgar" and "sensationalist" due to its eye-catching advertisements, brass bands, female preachers, and overheated services.

Santalmisjonen, 1876-

HI642 Eie, Oluf
En kirke bliver til: Santalkirken, dens vµkst og udvikling. Copenhagen, DK: Dansk Santalmission, 1967. 226 pp. Paper. No ISBN.

The author, a missionary to India from 1920 to 1964, describes in a personal way the growth of the Northern Evangelical Lutheran Church, an offspring of the Danish Santal Mission.

Scripture Gift Mission, 1888-

HI643 Baker, Ashley
Publishing Salvation: The Story of the Scripture Gift Mission. London, ENK: Scripture Gift Mission (SGM), 1961. 224 pp. No ISBN.

A popular history of the SGM from 1888 to 1958, emphasizing biographical information and anecdotes concerning the leaders of the mission.

Scripture Union, 1867-

HI644 Sylvester, Nigel
God's Word in a Young World: The Story of the Scripture Union. London, ENK: Scripture Union, 1984. 256 pp. Paper. 0862012597.

A popular history of the Scripture Union, from its foundation in 1867 to 1984, emphasizing the work of the Union in Bible translation and with children.

Seventh-day Adventist Church, 1863-

See also TH57-TH58, ME237, CR1108, SO589, AF1157, AF1222, AM1283-AM1284, AM1318, AM1369, AM1438, AS520, AS525, AS806, AS1295, AS1439, AS1488, EU28, EU44, EU78, EU164, OC18, OC28, and OC148.

HI645 Greenleaf, Floyd
The Seventh-day Adventist Church in Latin America and the Caribbean. Berrien Springs, MIU: Andrews University Press, 1992. 2 vols. 094387257X.

A full history in two volumes of a Protestant denomination's evangelism, church planting, and services in education and healthcare in the region from 1885 to the late 20th century [vol. 1: *Let the Earth Hear His Voice*, (iv, 470 pp.); vol. 2: *Bear the News to Every Land*, (ii, 542 pp.)].

HI646 Maxwell, C. Mervyn
Tell It to the World: The Story of Seventh-Day Adventists. Mountain View, CAU: Pacific Press, 1976. 287 pp. No ISBN.

This history of the Seventh-day Adventist Church includes a discussion of its substantial missionary expansion in the 1870s.

HI647 Oosterwal, Gottfried
Mission: Possible: The Challenge of the Mission Today. Nashville, TNU: Southern Publishing Association, 1972. 122 pp. 081270066X.

A series of articles and studies concerned with Seventh-day Adventist missionary work.

HI—HISTORY

HI—HISTORY

Seventh-day Baptist

See also AF587, and AF1095.

HI648 Sanford, Don A.
A Choosing People: The History of Seventh-Day Baptists. Nashville, TNU: Broadman, 1992. 448 pp. 0805460551.

An official history of the oldest sabbath-keeping Christian denomination, from its 17th-century origins to the present; containing extensive information on its missionary outreach.

Société des Missions Evangéliques de Paris, 1822-

See also AF744, AF854, and OC302.

HI649 Clavier, Henri
Thomas Arbousset: recherche historique sur son milieu, sa personnalité, son oeuvre parallèle avec Livingstone. Paris, FR: Société des Missions évangéliques, 1965. 429 pp. No ISBN.

A reprint of the biography of Thomas Arbousset (1810-1877), pioneer missionary of the Société des Missions Evangéliques of Paris to Basutoland (Lesotho) from 1833 to 1864; originally published under the title *Thomas Arbousset: Pioneer* (1964).

Society for the Propagation of the Gospel

See also ED19, MI187, AF609, AF999, AF1179, AS992, AS1146, and AS1222.

HI650 Dewey, Margaret
The Messengers: A Concise History of the United Society for the Propagation of the Gospel. London, ENK: Mowbray, 1975. vi, 158 pp. 0264663020 (hdbk), 0264660879 (pbk).

A history of the United Society for the Propagation of the Gospel, showing its ability to adapt itself to changing times and circumstances without compromising its aim of proclaiming the Gospel in foreign lands.

HI651 Humphreys, David
An Historical Account of the Incorporated Society for the Promotion of the Gospel in Foreign Parts. New York, NYU: Arno Press, 1969. xxxi, 356 pp. No ISBN.

A reprint of a 1730 publication concerning the foundation, proceedings, and missionary work of the society in the British colonies of North America until 1728.

HI652 Mayhew, Jonathan
Observations on the Charter and Conduct of the Society for the Propagation of the Gospel in Foreign Parts. (Religion in America Series, 2). New York, NYU: Arno Press, 1972. 176 pp. 0405040776.

Reprint of a 1763 work by a Boston pastor critical of the conduct of the SPG in New England.

HI653 Ritchie, Carson I. A.
Frontier Parish: An Account of the Society for the Propagation of the Gospel and the Anglican Church in America. Rutherford, NJU: Fairleigh Dickinson University Press; London, ENK: Associated University Presses, 1976. xiii, 210 pp. 0838617352.

A narrative history, 1690 to 1776, from the records of the bishop of London.

Southern Baptist Convention, 1845-

See also GW278, HI5, ME65, ME102, ME111, EC109, MI160, MI173, AF683, AF1207, AF1298, AF1301, AM762, AM791, AM961, AM998, AM1108, AM1266, AM1341, AM1400, AM1415, AS326, AS409, AS495, AS524, AS534, AS542, AS553, AS563-AS564, AS566, AS659, AS701, AS833, AS1361, AS1515, and EU7.

HI654 Allen, Catherine B.
A Century to Celebrate: History of Woman's Missionary Union. Birmingham, ALU: Woman's Missionary Union, 1987. 515 pp. 0936625163.

A comprehensive history of the Southern Baptist Woman's Missionary Union from 1888 to 1985, including a detailed chronology and lists of leaders.

HI655 Baldridge, Gary
Keith Parks: Breaking Barriers and Opening Frontiers. Macon, GAU: Smyth & Helwys, 1999. x, 102 pp. Paper. 1573122866.

Parks led Baptists to unprecedented engagement of the least-evangelized peoples of Asia and North Africa in the mid-1980s, when, at a time of upheaval in Baptist life, his leadership gave catalytic mission work the boost needed to evangelize hundreds of tribes and groups through non-traditional methods.

HI656 Belew, M. Wendell
A Missions People: The Southern Baptist Pilgrimage. Nashville, TNU: Broadman, 1989. 240 pp. Paper. 0805463453.

A popular introduction to mission history, and the understanding and practice of missions in the SBC.

HI657 Bobo, Nell Tant
Driven by a Dream: A History of Mission Service Corps. Atlanta, GAU: Home Missions Board of the Southern Baptist Convention, 1992. 140 pp. Paper. No ISBN.

A narrative history of the long-term volunteer program, from 1977 to 1991, of the Home Mission Board of the SBC.

HI658 Carpenter, Kathryn E.
Across the Years: In Louisiana Baptist Woman's Missionary Union. New Orleans, LAU: Woman's Missionary Union, Louisiana Baptist Convention, 1988. ii, 122 pp. Paper. No ISBN.

A brief history of the Southern Baptist Woman's Missionary Union in Louisiana.

HI659 Cauthen, Baker James et al.
Advance: A History of Southern Baptist Foreign Missions. Nashville, TNU: Broadman, 1970. 329 pp. No ISBN.

A comprehensive, popular historical analysis of Southern Baptist missions, organized by continent; including a chapter on administrative development.

HI660 Cauthen, Baker James, and Frank K. Means
Advance to Bold Mission Thrust: A History of Southern Baptist Foreign Missions, 1845-1980. Richmond, VAU: SBC, Foreign Mission Board, 1981. vi, 493 pp. Paper. No ISBN.

A sequel to *Advance: A History of Southern Baptist Foreign Missions* by Baker James Cauthen and others (Broadman, 1970), with introductions to each continent and detailed coverage of the work of the Foreign Mission Board during the 1970s.

HI661 Copeland, E. Luther

The Southern Baptist Convention and the Judgement of History: The Taint of an Original Sin. Lanham, MDU: University Press of America, 1995. xvii, 179 pp. 0819199346 (hdbk), 0819199354 (pbk).

A critical historical assessment of the SBC, including linkages among racism, sexism, imperialism, and the denomination's foreign missionary enterprises.

HI662 Cornelius, Janet Duitsman

Slave Missions and the Black Church in the Antebellum South. Columbia, SCU: University of South Carolina Press, 1999. x, 305 pp. 1570032475.

A scholarly study of the interaction of white missionaries and slaves in the 1840s and 1850s. The study describes ways in which blacks used the missions to nurture the formation of the organized black church by taking advantage of opportunities to create a small break in the oppression of slavery.

HI663 Crouch, Kate C. Maddry

The Magnificent Nobility: A History of Woman's Missionary Union of North Carolina, 1952-1972. Raleigh, NCU: Woman's Missionary Union of North Carolina, 1977. 125 pp. No ISBN.

A history of the Woman's Missionary Union, auxiliary to the North Carolina Convention (Southern Baptist).

HI664 Crow, Hilton Jones

God's Highway: Four Decades in Review. Phoenix, AZU: Woman's Missionary Union, 1968. 93 pp. No ISBN.

A history of the Woman's Missionary Union, auxiliary to the Arizona Convention (Southern Baptist).

HI665 Estep, William R.

Whole Gospel— Whole World: The Foreign Mission Board of the Southern Baptist Convention, 1845-1995. Nashville, TNU: Broadman, 1994. xx, 429 pp. 0805410414.

A thorough, popularly written, and lavishly illustrated history of Southern Baptist missions by an eminent church historian.

HI666 Fletcher, Jesse C.

Baker James Cauthen: A Man for All Nations. Nashville, TNU: Broadman, 1977. 272 pp. 0805472193.

A biography of Baker Kames Cauthen (b.1909), China missionary (1939-1945) and executive secretary of the SBC's Foreign Mission Board (1953-1976).

HI667 Fletcher, Jesse C.

The Southern Baptist Convention: A Sesquicentennial History. Nashville, TNU: Broadman, 1994. xiv, 463 pp. Paper. 0805411674.

An official narrative history of the SBC's first 150 years, with extensive coverage of its missionary efforts.

HI668 Gaskin, Jesse Marvin

Baptist Women in Oklahoma. Oklahoma City, OKU: Messenger Press, 1986. xix, 572 pp. No ISBN.

A history of Oklahoma Baptist women's work, tracing its development from its beginning with the Woman's Missionary Union in 1876.

HI669 Greene, Kathryn A.

The Eternal Now: A History of the Woman's Missionary Union, Auxiliary to the South. Columbia, SCU: Woman's Mission-ary Union, Carolina Baptist Convention, 1980. x, 250 pp. No ISBN.

A history of the South Carolina branch of the Southern Baptist women's mission organization.

HI670 Gruver, Kate Ellen

From This High Pinnacle: One Hundred Years with the Georgia Baptist Woman's Missionary Union. Decatur, GAU: Woman's Missionary Union of Georgia, 1983. 213 pp. No ISBN.

A history of the Georgia branch of the Southern Baptist women's mission organization.

HI671 Hunt, Alma

History of Woman's Missionary Union. Edited by Catherine B. Allen. Nashville, TNU: Convention Press, 1976. xiii, 241 pp. Paper. No ISBN.

Revised edition of a general history of the WMU of the SBC from 1813 to 1976, prepared as a SBC study course in missions.

HI672 Hunt, Inez Boyle

Century One: A Pilgrimage of Faith, Woman's Missionary Union of Texas, 1880-1980. Dallas, TXU: Woman's Missionary Union, 1979. 154 pp. Paper. No ISBN.

Officially sponsored institutional history with an emphasis on the work of key leaders; including numerous appendices and pictures.

HI673 Jackson, Hermione Dannelly

Women of Vision. Birmingham, ALU: Woman's Missionary Union, 1988. 177 pp. No ISBN.

Centennial edition of the commissioned history of the Alabama Woman's Missionary Union from 1889 to 1964; with appendices containing lists of officers and financial information.

HI674 Kilpatrick, Dorothy

The Golden Chain, or Called, Committed, Challenged: A History of California WMU. CAU: Woman's Missionary Union, 1986. 59 pp. Paper. No ISBN.

A history of the California WMU since 1941, written for the 1988 WMU Centennial.

HI675 Knight, Walker L.

Tell the People. Memphis, TNU: Home Missions Board of the SBC, 1986. vi, 107 pp. Paper. No ISBN.

A history of World Mission Conferences (1907-1985), a ministry of the SBC.

HI676 Lassiter, Lelia Boring

On This Foundation: History of the Woman's Missionary Union Auxiliary to the Florida Baptist Convention. Jacksonville, FLU: Woman's Missionary Union, 1966. vii, 144 pp. Paper. No ISBN.

A history of the Florida Woman's Missionary Union Auxiliary to the Florida Baptist Convention from 1888 to 1960.

HI677 Mylum, Dixie Bale

Proclaiming Christ: History of Woman's Missionary Union of Kentucky, 1878-1978. Louisville, KYU: Woman's Missionary Union of Kentucky, 1978. xi, 243 pp. No ISBN.

Centennial history of the Kentucky women's auxiliary to the Kentucky Baptist Convention.

HI—HISTORY

HI678 Patterson, Marjean
Covered Foundations: A History of Mississippi Woman's Missionary Union. [Jackson, MSU]: SBC, Mississippi Woman's Missionary Union, 1978. v, 160 pp. No ISBN.

A popular centennial history.

HI679 Rutledge, Arthur B., and William G. Tanner
Mission to America: A History of the Southern Baptist Home Missions. Nashville, TNU: Broadman, 1983. xxx, 277 pp. Paper. 080546526X.

Second revised edition of a detailed overview of SBC home missions from 1845 to 1975, including the development of the Home Mission Board.

HI680 South Carolina Woman's Missionary Union
Commemoration, Commission, Commitment: A Century of Service, Woman's Missionary Union of South Carolina, 1875-1975. Columbia, SCU: Woman's Missionary Union, 1974. 50 pp. No ISBN.

A history of the South Carolina SBC's Woman's Missionary Union.

HI681 Watkins, Rees
A Backward Glance: History of Woman's Missionary Union. Birmingham, ALU: Woman's Missionary Union, 1987. 96 pp. Paper. No ISBN.

A popular account of men and women who forged plans for world and national mission through their support of the Woman's Missionary Union (1800-1986) of the SBC.

HI682 Watson, Jane B.
Labourers Together...: A History of Arkansas Woman's Missionary Union. Little Rock, ARU: Woman's Missionary Union, 1987. 229 pp. Paper. 0874830575.

The centennial history (1888-1988) of the Arkansas Woman's Missionary Union of the SBC.

Student Foreign Missions Fellowship (SFMF), 1936-1946

See also HI685.

HI683 Norton, Hugo Wilbert
To Stir the Church: A Brief History of the Student Foreign Missions Fellowships, 1936-1986. Madison, WIU: Student Foreign Missions Fellowships, 1986. iii, 62 pp. Paper. No ISBN.

An introductory study to the origin and development of the Student Foreign Missions Fellowship (SFMF) from 1936 to 1986.

HI684 Poynor, Alice
From the Campus to the World: Stories from the First Fifty Years of Student Foreign Missions Fellowship. Downers Grove, ILU: InterVarsity, 1986. 156 pp. Paper. 0877849471.

A collection of twenty-four biographies of individuals involved with the Student Foreign Missions Fellowship since 1936.

Student Volunteer Movement (SVM), 1886-

See also EA145, and MI167.

HI685 Howard, David M.
Moving Out: The Story of Student Initiative in World Missions. Downers Grove, ILU: InterVarsity Press, 1984. 80 pp. Paper. 0877845654.

A concise history of both the SVM and the Student Foreign Missions Fellowship (SFMF), with analysis of the contemporary scene and its implications for student mission in the future.

HI686 Parker, Michael
The Kingdom of Character: The Student Volunteer Movement for Foreign Missions (1886-1926). Lanham, MDU: University Press of America, 1998. 250 pp. 0761810129 (hdbk), 0761810137 (pbk).

The first scholarly history of the SVM for the period from its founding in 1886 to 1926; originally presented as a Ph.D. dissertation at the University of Maryland.

HI687 Showalter, Nathan D.
The End of a Crusade: The Student Volunteer Movement for Foreign Missions and the Great War. (ATLA Monograph Series, 44). Lanham, MDU: Scarecrow Press, 1998. x, 241 pp. 0810833409.

Critical analysis of the SVM's interaction with issues of war and peace, leading ultimately to the failure of the movement; revision of a Harvard doctoral dissertation.

HI688 Student Volunteer Movement for Foreign Missions, International Convention, 1st, Cleveland, 1891
Student Mission Power: Report of the First International Convention of the Student Volunteer Movement for Foreign Missions, held at Cleveland, Ohio, USA, February 26, 27, 28, and March 1, 1891. South Pasadena, CAU: William Carey Library, 1979. xi, 235 pp. 0878087362.

A reprint of the first conference report of the SVM, at which evangelization of the world was affirmed as a missionary goal.

HI689 Wallstrom, Timothy C.
The Creation of a Student Movement to Evangelize the World: A History and Analysis of the Early Stages of the Student Volunteer Movement for Foreign Missions. Pasadena, CAU: William Carey International University, 1980. 95 pp. Paper. 0865850003.

A short history and analysis of the early stages of the SVM, 1880-1910.

Sudan Interior Mission (SIM), 1893-1982

See also AF491, AF493, AF496, and AF628.

HI690 Boer, Jan Harm
Missionary Messengers of Liberation in a Colonial Context: A Case Study of the Sudan United Mission. (Amsterdam Studies in Theology, 1). Amsterdam, NE: Rodopi, 1979. ix, 330 pp. Paper. 9062035612.

A doctoral thesis (Free University), based on archives and many other unpublished sources, concerning the relation between the Sudan United Mission, colonialism, and postcolonial Sudan, 1904-1960.

HI691 Carpenter, Joel A., ed.
Missionary Innovation and Expansion. New York, NYU: Garland, 1988. 269 pp. 0824050428.

Contains reprints of two early (1943) fundamentalist works, *Seven Sevens of Years and a Jubilee; The Story of the Sudan Interior Mission* and *Radio: The New Missionary.*

HI692 Fuller, W. Harold
Celebrate the God Who Loves:. Scarborough, ONC: SIM International Media, 1992. 136 pp. 0919470289.

A pictorial presentation of the current ministries of the Sudan Interior Mission, published for its centennial celebration.

Summer Institute of Linguistics (SIL), 1953-

See also AM1402, AM1494, and OC236.

HI693 Cano, Ginette et al.
Los Nuevos Conquistadores: El Instituto Lingüistico de Verano en América Latina. Quito, EC: Cedis and Fenoc, 1981. 385 pp. No ISBN.

An assessment critical of the Summer Institute of Linguistics' mission work in Latin America.

Suomen Lahetysseura Finska Missionssallskappet

See also TH362, ME22, ME77-ME79, MI136, AF649, AF685, AF699-AF700, AF707, AF874, AF880-AF882, AF894-AF895, AS401, AS678, AS770, EU166, and EU169.

HI694 Ihamäki, Kirsti, ed.
Matkoilla: Suomen Lähetysseura 125 vuotta. (Suomen Lähetysseuran julkaisu). Helsinki, FI: Kirjaneliö, 1983. 193 pp. 9516005985.

A collection of reports of Finnish missionaries on the occasion of the 125th anniversary of the Finnish Evangelical Lutheran Mission.

HI695 Väliaho, Juha, ed.
Näkyä toteuttamassa. (Tulevaisuus on Jumalan, 2; Lähetystrilogia, 2). Helsinki, FI: Uusi tie, 1987. 201 pp. 951619172X.

A history of the first twenty years of the Finnish Lutheran Mission (founded in 1967).

Suomen Vapaakirkko, 1878-

HI696 Ahonen, Lauri
Missions Growth: A Case Study on Finnish Free Foreign Mission. South Pasadena, CAU: William Carey Library, 1984. xi, 72 pp. Paper. 0878083359.

A former dissertation concerning factors that contributed to the growth of the Finnish Free Foreign Mission, the common missions board for the independent Pentecostal churches of Finland.

HI697 Björklund, Boris et al., comps.
Tro och liv. Helsinki, FI: Fria Missionsförbundets Forlag, 1989. 199 pp. Paper. 9529007906.

A history of the Finnish Free Church Mission (Fria Missionsförbundet), 1889-1989, including China and missionary activities in Finland.

HI698 *Kaikkeen maailmaan 1929-1989: 60 vuotta helluntaiseurakuntien lähetystyötä*
Vantaa, FI: RV-kirjat, 1989. 103 pp. Paper. 9516061176.

A history of the Finnish Pentecostal missions, 1929-1989.

Svenska Fria Missionen, 1907-

HI699 Hämelin, Eila, and Sisko Peltoniemi
Edelläkävijät: vuosisata vapaakirkollista lähetystyötä. Hämeenlinna, FI: Päivä, 1990. 379 pp. 9516224822.

A history of the missionary activities of the Evangelical Free Church in Finland.

Svenska Krykans Missions Styrelse, 1874-

See also GW148, SP294, AF361, AF378-AF379, AF502, AF512, AF702, AF1174, AS402, AS568, AS934, AS1153, and EU293.

HI700 Furberg, Tore
Kyrka ock Mission i Sverige 1868-1901: Svenska Kyrkans Missions tillkomst och första verksamhetstid. (Studia Missionalia Upsaliensia, 4). Uppsala, SW: Almqvist & Wiksell; Uppsala, SW: Svenska Institutet för Missions-forskning, 1962. 485 pp. No ISBN.

A doctoral dissertation on the origins and early years of the Church of Sweden Mission.

HI701 Hallencreutz, Carl F.
En missionerande församling: om mission på sex kontinenter. Stockholm, SW: Verbum, 1973. 71 pp. No ISBN.

A textbook on missions and missiology prepared for study groups in connection with the 100th anniversary of the Church of Sweden Mission.

HI702 Hallencreutz, Carl F.
Svensk mission över sex kontinenter. Stockholm, SW: Gummesson, 1970. 91 pp. No ISBN.

A survey of Swedish mission enterprises from the Middle Ages to 1970.

HI703 Hallencreutz, Carl F.
Swedish Missions. Stockholm, SW: Svenska Missions-rådet, 1968. 80 pp. Paper. No ISBN.

An introductory sketch of the worldwide work of Swedish missions, from the 19th century to the present, tracing factors that led to pluralism.

HI704 Kalm, Ingvar
Missionen i Linkopings stift: BitrSdesmissionssSllskapets verksamhet 1841-1875. (Studia Missionalia Upsaliensia, 38). Uppsala, SW: Svenska Institutet för Missions-forskning, 1977. 112 pp. No ISBN.

A study of the early beginnings of interest in missions in the Church of Sweden, focusing on the Diocese of Linkoping and the relation between mission society and church.

HI—HISTORY

Svenska Missionsförbundet, 1878-

See also CR1219, SP294, AF435, AF438, AS1087, and EU260.

HI705 Hultvall, John

Mission och revolution i Centralasien: Svenska Missions-förbundets mission i Östturkestan 1892-1938. (Studia Missionalia Upsaliensia, 35). Stockholm, SW: Gummesson, 1981. 288 pp. 9170706166.

A study of the Mission Covenant Church of Sweden in East Turkestan, 1892-1938.

Trinitarian Bible Society

HI706 Brown, Andrew J.

The Word of God Among All Nations: A Brief History of the Trinitarian Bible Society, 1831-1981. London, ENK: Trinitarian Bible Society, 1981. xi, 162 pp. 0907861016.

An institutional history, with emphasis on the key role played by controversy and individual leadership, examining work of Bible translation and distribution in Portugal, Spain, and Poland, as well as recent African work.

United Bible Societies, 1946-

HI707 Robertson, Edwin H.

Taking the Word to the World: Fifty Years of the United Bible Societies. Nashville, TNU: Nelson, 1996. xii, 338 pp. 0785272321.

The official jubilee history of the United Bible Societies, from its inception in 1946 to 1996, a movement supplying God's word in nearly every country in the world; written by the UBS's former study secretary.

United Church of Christ, 1957-

See also OC313.

HI708 Carter, Michael D.

Converting the Wasteplaces of Zion: The Maine Missionary Society (1807-1862). Wolfeboro, NHU: Longwood Academic, 1990. xx, 169 pp. Paper. 0893416339.

A scholarly history of the Maine Missionary Society, formed by Congregationalists to engage in home missions and church extension.

HI709 Dunn, David

A History of the Evangelical and Reformed Church. Philadelphia, PAU: Christian Education Press, 1961. 369 pp. No ISBN.

A history of the Reformed Church in the United States and the Evangelical Synod of North America, both before and after their union in 1929, including information on both home and foreign missions.

HI710 Rohrer, James R.

Keepers of the Covenant: Frontier Missions and the Decline of Congregationalism, 1774-1818. (Religion in America Series). New York, NYU: Oxford University Press, 1995. x, 201 pp. 0195091663.

A detailed analysis, based on archival research, of Congregationalist responses to frontier democracy fol-

lowing the American revolution; originally presented as a Ph.D. dissertation at Ohio State University.

HI711 Zikmund, Barbara Brown, ed.

Hidden Histories in the United Church of Christ. New York, NYU: United Church Press, 1987. 2 vols. Paper. 0829807047 (vol. 1), 0829807535 (vol. 2).

Twenty-two essays in two volumes on the histories of minority groups and movements within the United Church of Christ, including ministries among Native Americans, African Americans, and immigrant groups (Germans, Hungarians, and Japanese), and the work of women and men through missionary societies.

United Methodist Church, 1968-

See also HI539, SO413, PO71, CH183, AF392, AF868, AF1170, AF1281, AM1034, AM1062, AM1088, AS640, AS1176, EU262, and EU268.

HI712 *A Vision for New Hispanic Churches*

(National Mission Resources). New York, NYU: UMC, Board of Global Ministries, 1987. 86 pp. Paper. No ISBN.

Papers from the May 1985 National Program Division of General Board of Global Ministries' consultation on Hispanic congregational development in the UMC.

HI713 *An Enduring Legacy: Black United Methodists and the National Program Division*

Cincinnati, OHU: UMC, General Board of Global Ministries, 1985. 72 pp. Paper. No ISBN.

A listing and description of programs through the United States (1981-1984) which reflect the activity of the legacy and struggle of Black Methodists.

HI714 Daniels, George M.

Turning Corners: Reflections of African Americans in the United Methodist Church from 1961-1993. Dayton, OHU: UMC, General Council on Ministries, 1996. iii, 98 pp. Paper. No ISBN.

Milestones in the struggle for inclusivity in the UMC; including its Board of Global Ministries.

HI715 González, Justo L., ed.

Each in Our Own Tongue: A History of Hispanic United Methodism. Nashville, TNU: Abingdon, 1991. 176 pp. Paper. 0687114209.

Short appraisals of mission efforts by the dominant culture and the Hispanic response to these initiatives in five geographic jurisdictions of the United Methodist Church in the United States plus Puerto Rico; with a historical and cultural overview by the editor.

HI716 Hoover, Theressa

With Unveiled Face: Centennial Reflections on Women and Men in the Community of the Church. New York, NYU: UMC, Board of Global Ministries, 1983. 126 pp. Paper. No ISBN.

A case study of men/women relations through United Methodist Women and the Women's Division of the UMC; with copious notes indicating sources, chronologically arranged appendices giving a clearer understanding of the development of those relations, and a brief biography of the author.

HI717 Kehrberg, Norma
Love in Action—UMCOR: 50 Years of Service. Nashville, TNU: Abingdon, 1989. 140 pp. Paper. 0678228085.

A popular history of the United Methodist Committee on Relief (UMCOR) and its response to disasters and Third World development needs, by its chief executive.

HI718 Keller, Rosemary Skinner, ed.
Spirituality and Social Responsibility: Vocational Vision of Women in the United Methodist Tradition. Nashville, TNU: Abingdon, 1993. 336 pp. Paper. 0687392365.

Fourteen scholarly essays, with supporting primary source documents, on pioneering ministries of women of racial and ethnic diversity, from the 18th century to the present; including missionary founders of Ehwa Women's University (Korea), a contemporary Korean liberationist (Alice Yun Chai), and a mission society crusader for social reform (Thelma Stevens).

HI719 Magalis, Elaine
Missionaries of the United Methodist Church through the Camera's Eye. New York, NYU: UMC, Board of Global Ministries, 1988. vi, 160 pp. Paper. No ISBN.

A pictorial history of the missionary efforts of the UMC and its predecessor bodies, from 1819 to the present.

HI720 Stevens, Thelma
Legacy for the Future: The History of Christian Social Relations in the Woman's Division of Christian Service, 1940-1968. New York, NYU: UMC, Board of Global Ministries, 1979. 130 pp. Paper. No ISBN.

The history of the Department of Social Relations of the Women's Division (1940-1968), as it pioneered mission frontiers and helped to set exacting standards for Christian witness and service; by its department's senior staff executive during that period.

United Pentecostal Church International, 1945-

See also AF574, AF831, AF1366, AM555, AM1406, AS341, AS735, AS1178, AS1239, and AS1490.

HI721 *The Foreign Missions Story of the United Pentecostal Church International*
Hazelwood, MOU: United Pentecostal Church International, 1975. 96 pp. No ISBN.

A general survey of the foreign missions program, staff, and statistics of the United Pentecostal Church.

United Presbyterian Church in the United States of America, 1957-1983

See also HI621, EA100, SO596, ED24, AF441, AF443, AF791, AM1012, AM1035, AM1045, AM1130, AM1206, AS545, AS817, AS1175, and AS1248.

HI722 Black, Donald
Merging Mission and Unity. Philadelphia, PAU: Geneva Press, 1986. 180 pp. Paper. 066424047X.

The history of the Commission on Ecumenical Mission and Relations (COEMAR) of the UPCUSA from its founding in 1958 to 1972; focusing on issues of structure, mission-church relationships, methods, ecumenism, and social justice ministries.

HI723 *Journal of Presbyterian History*
United Presbyterian Church in Mission: An Historic Overview. Philadelphia, PAU: Journal of Presbyterian History, 1979. 240 pp. No ISBN.

A special issue (vol. 57, Fall 1979) containing historical overviews of important mission activities of the United Presbyterian Church.

HI724 Smith, John Coventry
From Colonialism to World Community: The Church's Pilgrimage. Philadelphia, PAU: Geneva Press, 1982. 333 pp. Paper. 0664244521.

Detailed reminiscences by the former general secretary of the Commission on Ecumenical Mission and Relations (COEMAR) of the UPCUSA, Presbyterian moderator, and WCC president, of his active involvements from 1927 to 1970 as pastor, missionary, denominational executive, and ecumenical leader.

Uniting Church of Australia, The, 1977-

See also OC35, OC81, OC98, and OC267.

HI725 Wright, Don
Mantle of Christ: A History of the Sydney Central Methodist Mission. Queensland, AT: University of Queensland Press, 1984. xii, 272 pp. 0702217395.

A scholarly account of the Australian Methodist Missionary Society, from its foundation under the direction of William George Taylor (1884), to the metropolitan and evangelistic ministries of Alan Walker in the 1970s.

Universities' Mission to Central Africa, 1857-1965

See also AF607, AF771, and AF819.

HI726 Anderson-Marshead, A. E. M., and A. G. Blood, eds.
History of the Universities' Mission to Central Africa. London, ENK: UMCA, 1955. 3 vols. No ISBN.

The official history of the mission, from its entry in Zanzibar to its spread and recent development in present Tanzania, Malawi, and Zambia; volume one being a reprint of the 1909 edition [vol. 1: *1859-1909* (313 pp.); vol. 2: *1907-1932* (326 pp.); vol. 3: *1933-1957* (468 pp.)].

Woman's Union Missionary Society of America, 1861-1972?

HI727 MacLeod, Judith
Woman's Union Missionary Society: The Story of a Continuing Mission. Upper Darby, PAU: InterServe, 1999. x, 85 pp. Paper. 0967516803.

The story of the first women only missionary organization in North America, which originated in the 1860s, became ecumenical, merged with the Bible and Medical Missionary Fellowship in 1976, and is directly related to InterServe.

World Gospel Mission, 1910-

See also SP132 and AF533.

HI728 Bushong, Burnis H.

R.U.N.: Reaching the Unreached Now: A Brief History of World Gospel Mission. Marion, INU: World Gospel Mission, 1995. x, 110 pp. Paper. 0962040657.

A popular history of the World Gospel Mission from 1910 to 1990.

World Vision, 1950-

HI729 Gehman, Richard J.

Let My Heart Be Broken with the Things That Break the Heart of God. New York, NYU: McGraw-Hill, 1960. 245 pp. No ISBN.

An account of the work of World Vision International and its founder, Bob Pierce.

HI730 Irvine, Graeme S.

Best Things in the Worst Times: An Insider's View of World Vision. Wilsonville, ORU: Book Partners, 1996. 285 pp. Paper. 1885221355.

A narrative account of four decades of global humanitarian ministries by World Vision; viewed through the lens of the author's twenty-eight-year involvement, and culminating when he became its international president (1989-1995).

Wycliffe Bible Translators, 1934-

See also HI7, CO93, CO122, AM140, AM837, AM877, AM895, AM910, AM1367, AM1480, AM1506, AS1510, OC176, and OC222.

HI731 Elson, Benjamin F., comp.

Language in Global Perspective: Papers in Honor of the 50th Anniversary of the Summer Institute of Linguistics 1935-1985. Dallas, TXU: SIL, 1986. xiii, 626 pp. Paper. No ISBN.

This volume of fifty essays is in honor of the beginning of field work in 1935 in Mexico, where Townsend and Pike began the Summer Institute of Linguistics.

HI732 Steven, Hugh

Wycliffe in the Making: The Memoirs of W. Cameron Townsend 1920-1933. Wheaton, ILU: Shaw Publishers, 1995. xxiii, 263 pp. Paper. 0877888906.

A narrative account of the work of W. Cameron Townsend (1896-1982) in founding the Wycliffe Bible Translators and its Summer Institute of Linguistics; based on his extensive letters, diaries, and public writings.

HI733 Stoll, David

¿Pescadores de hombres o fundadores de imperio? (El Instituto Lingüístico de Verano en América Latina). Translated by Flica Barclay. Lima, PE: Desco, 1985. 496 pp. No ISBN.

Spanish translation.

HI734 Stoll, David

Fishers of Men or Founders of Empire?: The Wycliffe Bible Translators in Latin America. London, ENK: Zed Books; Cambridge, MAU: Cultural Survival, 1982. vii, 344 pp. 0862321115 (hdbk), 0862321123 (pbk).

A history of the work of Wycliffe Bible Translators throughout the world (primarily Central America) emphasizing its destruction of indigenous belief systems, undermining the cohesion of native communities, and increasing their vulnerability to further exploitation.

HI735 Thompson, Phyllis

Matched with His Hour: The Story of the British Home Base of the Wycliffe Bible Translators. London, ENK: Word Books, 1974. 127 pp. Paper. 0850090490.

A narrative account of the recruitment and training of Wycliffe Bible Translators in Great Britain, 1953 to 1972, by a former China Inland Mission missionary.

Young Men's Christian Association (YMCA), 1844-

See also SO513, EV277, AS344, AS509, AS572, and AS927.

HI736 Mjagkij, Nina

Light in the Darkness: African Americans and the YMCA, 1852-1946. Lexington, KYU: University Press of Kentucky, 1994. x, 198 pp. 0813118522.

A detailed history of the evolution of African American YMCAs and their leadership from slavery to desegregation.

Young Women's Christian Association (YWCA), 1845-

See also AS702.

HI737 Boyd, Nancy

Emissaries: The Overseas Work of the American YWCA 1895-1970. New York, NYU: Woman's Press, 1986. xv, 337 pp. 0961487801.

An historical study of the worldwide work of the YWCA, including apprendices containing complete listings of officers and foreign secretaries (by field), with biographical sketches.

HI738 Wilson, Elizabeth

Fifty Years of Association Work among Young Women, 1866-1916. (Women in American Protestant Religion, 1800-1930; 34). New York, NYU: Garland, 1987. 402 pp. 0824006836.

Reprint of a history of the first fifty years of the YWCA, recounting the movement's beginnings in Great Britain and America, and the story of local and national organization; with a chronology, bibliography, and list of local associations and personnel; originally published by the YWCA in 1916.

Youth with a Mission (YWAM), 1960-

See also EV464 and EU72.

HI739 Wilson, R. Marshall

Youth with a Mission. Plainfield, NJU: Logos International, 1971. 170 pp. Paper. 0912106107.

A popular account of the early years of one of the largest Pentecostal-charismatic mission sodalities in the world today.

Zendingsgenootschap der Evangelische Broedergemeente

See also AM1514, AM1516, and AM1518.

HI740 Lenders, Maria

Strijders voor het Lam: Leven en werk van Herrnhutter Broeders en-Zusters in Suriname, 1735-1900. (Caribbean Series, 16). Leiden, NE: KITLV, 1996. xii, 451 pp. 9067180955.

A doctoral dissertation presented at the State University in Leyden on the missionary work in Surinam of the Mission Society of the Moravian Church (1735-1900), with special attention to the contributions of women.

HI741 Lyall, Leslie T.

A Passion for the Impossible: The Continuing Story of the Mission Hudson Taylor Began. London, ENK: OMF Books, 1976. 227 pp. 0853631166 (hdbk), 0853631158 (pbk).

A narrative centennial history of the China Inland Mission (now Overseas Missionary Fellowship); originally published in 1965, and now updated to 1976.

HI742 Lyall, Leslie T.

Urgent Harvest: Partnership with the Church in Asia. London, ENK: Lutterworth Press for the China Inland Mission, 1962. 223 pp. No ISBN.

A survey of the work in Asia of the CIM Fellowship since the mission's withdrawal from the Chinese mainland in 1951, based upon material and observations collected personally by the author during a visit to the area in 1960.

HI743 Overseas Missionary Fellowship

One Small Flame. Sevenoaks, ENK: OMF, 1978. 96 pp. No ISBN.

A popular survey of the work of the Overseas Missionary Fellowship in the past twenty-five years.

HI744 Sanders, John

Just the Same Today. London, ENK: OMF, 1975. 127 pp. Paper. 0853631050.

The former general director of the Overseas Missionary Fellowship testifies to God's guidance of the OMF (former China Inland Mission) especially since 1945.

HI—HISTORY

MISSIONS: THEOLOGY

Stephen Bevans, SVD, Subeditor

Gerald Anderson introduced *The Theology of the Christian Mission* with these words: "The fundamental task . . . of the missionary enterprise today is to clarify the nature and meaning of its being. This must be done in the realm of theological thought, not only to increase effectiveness in presenting the Gospel to the world, but also to give Christians a deeper understanding of what their task *is* in the world" (1961:4). In this chapter are to be found the responses to this challenge by missiologists during the 1960-2000 period.

Jongeneel divides missiology into the philosophical, the empirical, and the theological study of mission (1995:185). Under the latter he includes both the theory and practice of mission. Bibliographers prefer a more limited scope for mission theology. Vriens (1960) grouped both biblical and church teachings under "Mission Theory." Henkel, in *Bibliographia Missionaria*, places theology of mission, ecumenical dialogue and mission, and mission and dialogue in separate chapters—a typology followed in this bibliography. Walls, in the *International Review of Mission* under "History and Theology of Mission," groups "Mission in the Bible," "Theology of Mission," "Black Theology," "Liberation and Political Theologies," and "Charismatic Movement and Pentecostalism." I will follow this typology also.

As in the preceding chapter on the history of mission, readers are encouraged to extend their search for reference works beyond the listings in this chapter. They will find corresponding subsections in each chapter, and that those under "General Works" contain much that is relevant to mission theology.

The large subsection of "General Works" attests to the volume of recent scholarship in this field. One common theme is that of *liberation,* which has its own subsection. Here are grouped general works, as well as those from Europe and North America. Those from other continents will be found in subsections on African, Asian, Indian, Latin American, and Oceanian theologies in other chapters. In this chapter is found a distinct subsection on "Feminist/Womanist Liberation." *Praxis* (action/reflection) is at the core of liberation theologies—both God's action and the response by Christians and the church. The result is missiological by content if not by announced intention of the author.

"Bible and Missions" is one of the largest subsections of this chapter. It has been argued that every authentic Christian theology of mission "should take its inspiration and validation from the word of God expressed in the Scriptures" (Müller, 1997:44). The search for authentic mission leads mission leaders back to the study of biblical models. Conversely, missiologists also remind biblical scholars that the document they study originated in and addressed the work of early Christian missions (Soards, 1996).

Finally, this chapter contains subsections on "Pentecostalism" and the "Charismatic Movement." Readers with particular interest in these topics should see also the listings under "Pentecostal: General" in the History chapter, those on "Gifts of the Spirits" under Church Renewal, and those on the "Charismatic Movement" and "Spiritual Warfare" in the chapter on Spirituality, Worship, and Mission.

Norman E. Thomas

Bibliographies

See also GW4, TH5, TH341, SO2, ED108, AF2, and AM1.

TH1 Anderson, Gerald H., comp.
Bibliography of the Theology of Missions in the Twentieth Century. New York. NYU: MRL, 1966. ix,119 pp. Paper. No ISBN.

A third revised, enlarged edition of an international bibliography of more than 1,500 books and articles with some annotations.

TH2 Evans, James H., comp.
Black Theology: A Critical Assessment and Annotated Bibliography. (Bibliographies and Indexes in Religious Studies, 10). Westport, CNU: Greenwood, 1987. xii, 205 pp. 0313248222.

An annotated bibliography of 461 books and periodical articles, on the origin and development of black theology, and the dialogue of black theologians with other liberation theologians including feminists and those of the Two-Thirds World of Africa, Latin America, Asia, and Oceania.

TH3 Spindler, Marc, and P. R. Middelkoop, eds.
Bible and Mission: A Partially Annotated Bibliography, 1960-1980. (IIMO Research Pamphlet, 4). Leiden, NE: IIMO, 1981. xii, 96 pp. Paper. No ISBN.

A bibliographical contribution to the BISAM project, Biblical Studies and Missiology, initiated and sponsored by the International Association for Mission Studies (IAMS); presenting 1,069 items, some with short summaries in English and French.

Serials and Periodicals

TH4 *Studies in World Christianity.* Vol. 1, pt. 1 (1995) -. Semiannual
Edinburgh, STK: Edinburgh University Press; Maryknoll, NYU: Orbis Books, 1995-. ISSN 13549901.

An international forum in which scholars analyze the challenges of Western-dominated Christian theology and religious studies coming from the re-emergent religious cultures of the non-Western world and from other religions and ideologies.

TH5 *Theology in Context.* Vol. 1, no. 1 (1984) -. Semiannual
Aachen, GW: Institute of Missiology Missio, 1984-. ISSN 01761439.

This English edition of *Theologie im Kontext* intends to inform readers about current theological thinking outside Europe and North America, by providing an annotated bibliography of the contents of theological journals in Africa, Asia, Oceania, and Latin America, summaries of major articles, book reviews, and reports on recent theological conferences.

Reference Works

See also GW56.

TH6 Geisler, Norman L.
Baker Encyclopedia of Christian Apologetics. (Baker Reference Library). Grand Rapids, MIU: Baker Books, 1998. vii, 841 pp. 0801021510.

A comprehensive encyclopedia designed to equip believers for Christian defense against a full range of opposing arguments.

Documentation and Archives

See also GW72, TH586, and TH606.

TH7 Benedict XV, Pope, Pope Pius XI, and Pope Pius XII
Geht hin in alle Welt.... Die Missionsenzykliken der Papste Benedikt XV, Pius XI, Pius XII und Johannes XXIII. Edited by E. Marmy. Freiburg, GW: Paulus Verlag, 1961. 201 pp. No ISBN.

A modernized German translation of papal missionary encyclicals (*Maximum illud, Rerum ecclesiae, Evangelii praecones, Ad Sinarum gentem, Fidei donum, Ad Apostolorum Principis, Princeps pastorum*).

TH8 *Inventaris van het archief van Johannes Christiaan Hoekendijk, 1912-1975*
(Inventarissen van de afdeling handschriften van de Universiteitsbibliotheek Utrecht, 1). Utrecht, NE: Universiteitsbibliotheek, 1983. 113 pp. Paper. 9067010030.

A catalogue of the personal papers of the noted Dutch theologian and missiologist Johannes Christian Hoekendijk (1912-1975) housed at the library of the University of Utrecht in the Netherlands.

TH9 Masson, J., ed.
L' Attività missionaria della chiesa. (Collana Magistero Conciliare, 13). Torino-Leumann, IT: Elle Di Ci, 1966. 619 pp. No ISBN.

Second edition of the Latin and Italian texts (on facing pages) of Vatican II's "Decree on Missionary Activity" and several other documents; plus a detailed commentary on each document.

TH10 Retnowinarti, et al., eds.
Hendrik Kraemer—Bibliografie en Archief: Een uitgave ter gelegenheid van het 100e geboortejaar van Prof. H. Kraemer. (IIMO Research Publication, 22). Leiden-Utrecht, NE: IIMO, 1988. iv, 100 pp. Paper. 9064951632.

A bibliography of Hendrik Kraemer's writings with an inventory of his archives kept in the Hendrik Kraemer Institute in Oegstgeest, the Netherlands.

TH11 Welz, Justinian von
Justinian von Welz: Ein Österreicher als Vordenker und Pionier der Weltmission; seine Schriften. Edited by Fritz Laubach. (Monographien und Studienbücher). Wuppertal, GW: Brockhaus, 1989. 319 pp. Paper. 3417293480.

An edition of all extant writings of Justinian von Welz (d. 1668), a passionate promoter of the missionary idea and himself an active preacher of the Gospel in South America, at a time when missionary work was still frowned upon by Protestants.

TH12 Zinzendorf, Nikolaus Ludwig Graf von
Texte zur Mission: Mit einer Einführung in die Missionstheologie Zinzendorfs. Edited by Helmut Bintz. Hamburg, GW: Wittig, 1979. 119 pp. Paper. 3804841732.

A collection of texts on mission from sermons, letters, and instructions of Count Nikolaus Ludwig von Zinzendorf, the founder of the Moravian Missionary Movement.

Conferences and Congresses

See also GW69, HI318, TH9, TH368, TH494, TH524, TH537, TH539, TH543, TH548-TH549, EA134, CH9, SP13, AM206, and AM211.

TH13 Branson, Mark Lau, and C. René Padilla, eds.
Conflict and Context: Hermeneutics in the Americas. Grand Rapids, MIU: Eerdmans, 1986. xii, 323 pp. Paper. 0802801722.

A collection of papers, study group reports, and transcriptions of plenary discussions, from the Context and Hermeneutics in the Americas Conference (Tlayacapan, Mexico, 24-29 November 1983) sponsored by the Theological Students Fellowship and the Latin American Theological Fraternity.

TH14 Caudron, Marc, ed.
Faith and Society/Foi et société/Geloof en mattschappij: Acta Congressus Internationalis Theologici Lovaniensis. (Bibliotheca Ephemeridum Theologicarum Lovaniensium, 47). Gembloux, FR: Duculot, 1978. 299 pp. 2801101753.

Published work of twenty-one scholars attending the International Theological Congress in Louvain (1976), covering the themes of God and society, male-female relationships, and community.

TH15 EATWOT
Doing Theology in a Divided World. Edited by Virginia Fabella, and Sergio Torres. Maryknoll, NYU: Orbis Books, 1985. xix, 218 pp. Paper. 0883441977.

Papers from the Sixth International Conference of EATWOT (Geneva, Switzerland, 5-13 January 1983).

TH16 EATWOT

Herausgefordert durch die Armen: Dokumente der Ökumenischen Vereinigung von Dritte-Welt-Theologen, 1976-1986. (Theologie der Dritten Welt, 13). Freiburg im Breisgau, GW: Herder, 1990. 229 pp. Paper. 3451218755.

This volume provides the complete documentation of the seven conferences of EATWOT with suitable introductions of short chapter length.

TH17 EATWOT

Irruption of the Third World. Edited by Virginia Fabella, and Sergio Torres. Maryknoll, NYU: Orbis Books, 1983. xix, 280 pp. 0883442167.

Papers from the Fifth International Conference of EATWOT (New Delhi, India, 17-29 August 1981).

TH18 EATWOT

Teología desde el Tercer Mundo: Documentos finales de los cinco congresos internacionales de la Asociación Ecuménica de Teólogos del Tercer Mundo. San José, CR: DEI, 1982. 99 pp. Paper. No ISBN.

A collection of the final documents produced by EATWOT at five international congresses: Dar es Salaam, Tanzania-1976, Accra, Ghana-1977, Wennappuwa, Sri Lanka-1979, Sao Paulo, Brazil-1980, and New Delhi, India-1981.

TH19 EATWOT

Third World Theologies: Commonalities and Divergences. Edited by K. C. Abraham. Maryknoll, NYU: Orbis Books, 1990. xix, 216 pp. Paper. 0883446812.

Papers from the Seventh International Conference of the EATWOT (Oatepec, Mexico, 7-14 December, 1986), giving an overview of the state of theology and its political, economic, and social context in Africa, Asia, Latin America, and among minorities in the United States; ending with an evaluation of EATWOT.

TH20 Goldewijk, Berma Klein, Erik Borgman, and Fred van Iersel, eds.

Bevrijdingstheologie in West-Europa: teksten van het Symposium "Westeuropese Bevrijdingstheologie," gehouden op 12-13 november 1987 aan de Theologische Faculteit te Nijmegen. (Kerk en theologie in context, 2). Kampen, NE: Kok, 1988. 178 pp. 9024231957.

Essays on various aspects of liberation theologies, including approaches to contextualization and secularization; originally read at the symposium on "Western European Theology of Liberation" held 12-13 November 1987 at the theological faculty of the University of Nijmegen in the Netherlands.

TH21 Guillermo, Garlatti et al.

Evangelización y Liberación. (Sociedad Argentina de Teología (4th, 1985, Bueno Aires, Argentina)). (Teología, 1). Buenos Aires, AG: Sociedad Argentina de Teología, 1986. 249 pp. Paper. 9500906406.

A collection of seven conference papers on the general subject of liberation and its relation to the Pauline correspondence, Latin American church history, primitive church, anthropology, Christology, pastoral theology, etc.

TH22 Hunter, Harold D., and Peter Hocken, eds.

All Together in One Place: Theological Papers from the Brighton Conference on World Evangeiization. (*Journal of Pentecostal Theology* Supplement Series). Sheffield, ENK: JSOT Press-Sheffield Academic Press, 1993. 281 pp. Paper. 1850754063.

A selection of twenty-seven contributions by scholars and leaders of Pentecostal and charismatic movements from six continents; originally presented at "Brighton '91" (Brighton, England, 8-14 July 1991), an international conference on Pentecostal-charismatic theology planned by the International Charismatic Consultation on World Evangelization (IC-COWE).

TH23 Nieuwenhove, Jacques van, and Berma Klein Goldewijk, eds.

Popular Religion, Liberation and Contextual Theology. (Church and Theology in Context, 8). Kampen, NE: Kok, 1991. vii, 256 pp. Paper. 9024234999.

Papers by African, Latin American, Asian, and Eastern European theologians on liberation, spirituality, contextualization, and mission, in relation to popular religion in their respective regions; originally presented at a congress (Nijmegen, The Netherlands, 3-7 January 1990) honoring Arnolf Camps, OFM.

TH24 Torres, Sergio, and John Eagleson, eds.

Theology in the Americas. Maryknoll, NYU: Orbis Books, 1976. xxviii, 438 pp. 0883444798.

Report and papers of the important "Theology in the Americas: 1975" conference held in Detroit, Michigan, between prominent Latin American theologians and a cross-section of their counterparts in North America.

General Works

See also GW65, GW103, GW119-GW121, GW134-GW135, GW139, GW151-GW152, GW163, GW168-GW169, GW173, GW184, GW216-GW217, GW219, GW222, GW243, GW279-GW280, HI34, HI55, HI94, HI176, TH9, TH184, TH220, EA52, EA65, EA82, EA194, ME13, ME25, ME75, ME100, CR98, CR242, CR1423, SO102, EC20, PO13, EV73, EV120, EV158, EV186, EV198, EV413, MI25, MI95, SP64, SP229, AF95, AF895, AS180, and EU188.

TH25 Aagaard, Anna Marie, Hans Raun Iversen, and Michael Schelde, eds.

Fra europaeisk kirke til verdens kirke: Katolsk missionsteologi efter II Vatikanerkoncil. (Verdensdelenes teologi, 1). Aarhus, DK: Forlaget Anis, 1986. 119 pp. 8774570528.

Issues in Roman Catholic missiology since Vatican II, including inculturation and the universality and locality of the church.

TH26 Aagaard, Anna Marie

Helligånden sendt til verden. Aarhus, DK: Forlaget Aros, 1973. 299 pp. Paper. No ISBN.

A doctoral thesis on the theological concept of sending, as applied to the Holy Spirit in Catholic, Protestant, and Orthodox missiological thinking.

TH27 Adams, Daniel J., ed.

From East to West: Essays in Honor of Donald G. Bloesch. Lanham, MDU: University Press of America, 1997. x, 255 pp. 0761808019.

Fifteen essays contributed as a *festschrift* to honor evangelical theologian Donald Bloesch of the University of Dubuque; mostly on issues of mission, evangelism, and theology in East Asia, especially Korea.

TH28 Amstutz, Josef
Kirche der Völker: Skizze einer Theorie der Mission. (Quaestiones disputatae, 57). Freiburg, GW: Herder, 1972. 127 pp. Paper. 3451020572.

A theory of mission in which the focal point is the public, specific history of salvation between Christ and the coming of "the reign of God," during which time the Church must insert itself into the different cultures and religious situations and "gather the scattered children of God."

TH29 Anderson, Gerald H., ed.
Christian Mission in Theological Perspective: An Inquiry by Methodists. Nashville, TNU: Abingdon, 1967. 286 pp. No ISBN.

Twelve essays by North American theologians, plus D. T. Niles of Sri Lanka; originally presented at annual consultations sponsored by the Division of World Mission of the Methodist Church (US).

TH30 Anderson, Gerald H., ed.
The Theology of the Christian Mission. New York, NYU: McGraw-Hill; Nashville, TNU: Abingdon; London, ENK: SCM Press, 1961. xvii, 341 pp. No ISBN.

A monumental collection of essays on mission by twenty-five outstanding theologians and missiologists, e.g. Karl Barth, Paul Tillich, Oscar Cullman, Alexander Schmemann, R. Pierce Beaver, and Max Warren.

TH31 Bürkle, Horst
Missionstheologie. (Theologische Wissenschaft, 18). Stuttgart, GW: Kohlhammer, 1979. 212 pp. Paper. 3170011367.

With the thesis of "missionary outreach" as leitmotif running through his whole work, the author describes the various fields of tension in the present missionary situation, and systematically treats such questions as ethnos and ecclesia, mission and ecumenism, communication, context, and service.

TH32 Barr, William R., ed.
Constructive Christian Theology in the Worldwide Church. Grand Rapids, MIU: Eerdmans, 1997. xviii, 553 pp. Paper. 0802841430.

An anthology containing thirty-nine essays discussing themes of the Christian faith—many by prominent Catholic, Orthodox, and Protestant Third World theologians.

TH33 Barreda, Jesús Angel et al.
Iglesia misionera al servicio del reino de Dios. Madrid, SP: Instituto de Teología—Misionología, 1984. 166 pp. 8460034658.

A collection of papers by Europeans focusing on the connection between the church's missionary work and the coming of the Kingdom of God.

TH34 Berentsen, Jan-Martin
Teologi og misjon: trekk fra protestantismens historie fram til vsrt srhundre. Oslo, NO: Nye Luther, 1990. 183 pp. 8253142269.

A textbook for theological students on missiology, discussing issues in the development of Protestant thought until the turn of the 20th century.

TH35 Beyerhaus, Peter
Allen Völkern zum Zeugnis: Biblisch-theologische Besinnung zum Wesen der Mission. Wuppertal, GW: Brockhaus, 1972. 144 pp. Paper. 3797400411.

A collection of various texts (lectures, meditations, sermons) from an evangelical perspective, on the biblical foundation of mission, its realization, and the awakening of missionary responsibility.

TH36 Beyerhaus, Peter
Shaken Foundations: Theological Foundations for Mission. (Contemporary Evangelical Perspectives). Grand Rapids, MIU: Zondervan, 1972. 105 pp. No ISBN.

An analysis of contemporary theology and issues in mission, by the professor of missions at the University of Tubingen, West Germany; with an interpretation of the Frankfurt Declaration of German evangelicals critical of WCC priorities in mission.

TH37 Bifet, Juan Esquerda
Mariology for a Missionary Church. (Pontificia Universitas Urbaniana, 58). Rome, IT: Urbaniana University Press, 1994. 175 pp. Paper. 8840180583.

A noted Italian Catholic missiologist summarizes Marian doctrine and its significance for the church's theology of mission.

TH38 Billheimer, Paul E.
Love Covers: A Biblical Design for Unity in the Body of Christ. Minneapolis, MNU: Bethany House, 1981. 164 pp. Paper. 0871234009.

An analysis of the church's understanding of theological debate and how it causes disunity.

TH39 Bockmühl, Klaus
Was heisst heute Mission?: Entscheidungsfragen der neueren Missionstheologie. (ABC-Team, G & D 905). Giessen, GW: Brunnen-Verlag, 1974. 192 pp. Paper. 3765503398.

While the first part of this work is a revised edition of a previous work of the author on "the new mission theology" (1964), the second part explores the development of the understanding of mission from the WCC Assembly in New Delhi (1961) to the International Congress on World Evangelization in Lausanne (1974).

TH40 Boer, Harry R.
Pentecost and Missions. Grand Rapids, MIU: Eerdmans; London, ENK: Lutterworth Press, 1961. 270 pp. No ISBN.

The author argues that missionary witness is rooted in the very being of the church, and that we must witness in unity of the Spirit because that was the very nature of the church at Pentecost.

TH41 Bosch, David Jacobus
Dynamique de la mission chrétienne: histoire et avenir des modèles missionnaires. Paris, FR: Karthala; Geneva, SZ: Labor et Fides; Lomé, TG: Haho, 1995. 774 pp. Paper. 286537601X (FR), 2830907930 (SZ), 290671853X (TG).

French translation.

TH42 Bosch, David Jacobus
Transforming Mission: Paradigm Shifts in Theology of Mission. (American Society of Missiology Series, 16). Maryknoll, NYU: Orbis Books, 1991. xix, 587 pp. 0883447444 (hdbk), 0883447193 (pbk).

A monumental analysis of the history of mission theology from the New Testament to the present; analyzed as six historic paradigms.

TH—MISSIONS: THEOLOGY

TH43 Bosch, David Jacobus

Witness to the World: The Christian Mission in Theological Perspective. London, ENK: Marshall, Morgan and Scott; Atlanta, GAU: John Knox Press, 1985. x, 274 pp. 0551008237 (MMS).

A scholarly analysis of the biblical foundation of mission and of the development of mission theology throughout Christian history.

TH44 Braaten, Carl E.

The Apostolic Imperative: Nature and Aim of the Church's Mission and Ministry. Minneapolis, MNU: Augsburg, 1985. 206 pp. Paper. 0806621680.

A biblically based theology of mission, focusing on the nature and scope of the church's mission and ministry.

TH45 Braaten, Carl E.

The Flaming Center: A Theology of the Christian Mission. Philadelphia, PAU: Fortress Press, 1977. vi, 170 pp. 0800604903.

A call for a Christocentric theology of mission relating the Kingdom of God, the church, and the world.

TH46 Bsteh, Andreas

Zur Frage nach der Universalität der Erlösung: Unter besonderer Berücksichtigung ihres Verständnisses bei den Vätern des 2. Jahrhunderts. (Wiener Beiträge zur Theologie, 14). Vienna, AU: Herder, 1966. 188 pp. Paper. No ISBN.

An examination of the fundamental statement of the Christian faith in Romans 5:15, from the perspective of dogma.

TH47 Camps, Arnulf

De weg, de paden en de wegen: De christelijke theologie en de concrete godsdiensten. (Oekumene, 9. jaarg., 2). Baarn, NE: Bosch & Keuning, 1977. 103 pp. Paper. 9024630967.

The noted Dutch missiologist advocates a new Christian apologetic in response to various faiths and popular religiosity.

TH48 Castro, Emilio

Freedom in Mission: The Perspective of the Kingdom of God, an Ecumenical Inquiry. Geneva, SZ: WCC, 1985. vii, 348 pp. Paper. 2825408247.

A thesis presenting a biblical and theological discussion of the Kingdom of God and its missionary implications, with republished articles by the author on mission in Latin America.

TH49 Castro, Emilio

Llamados a liberar: Misión y unidad en la perspectiva del reino de Dios. Buenos Aires, AG: Ediciones La Aurora, 1985. 152 pp. Paper. 9505510500.

Spanish translation.

TH50 Christiansen, Paul Kofoed et al., eds.

Mission og fundamentalisme. (Nyt Synspunkt, 30). Hellerup, DK: DMS-Forlag, 1988. 70 pp. Paper. 8774311417.

This booklet deals with fundamentalism as a general phenomenon in relation to missions, with examples from Denmark, Central America, South Africa, the Middle East, and the United States.

TH51 Clasper, Paul D.

Theological Ferment: Personal Reflections. Quezon City, PH: New Day Publishers, 1982. 120 pp. 9711000423 (hdbk), 9711000431 (pbk).

A collection of essays from the 1970s and 1980s revealing a pilgrimage in missionary thinking.

TH52 Collet, Giancarlo

Das Missionsverständnis der Kirche in der gegenwärtigen Diskussion. (Tübinger Theologische Studien, 24). Mainz, GW: Grünewald, 1984. 308 pp. Paper. 3786711275.

This dissertation examines the problems and changing structures of mission today, post-conciliar papal documents and synodal declarations on mission, and five recent models of mission theology.

TH53 Colzani, Gianni

Teologia della Missione: Vivere la fede donandola. Padova, IT: Edizioni Messaggero Padova, 1996. 254 pp. Paper. 8825005466.

An introduction to official Catholic mission theology from the 16th century to the present, with extended analysis of the document *Ad Gentes* of Vatican II.

TH54 Consultation on Theology and Mission, School of World Mission and Evangelism

Theology and Mission: Papers and Responses Prepared for the Consultation on Theology and Mission, Trinity Evangelical Divinity School of World Mission and Evangelism, March 22-25, 1976. Edited by David J. Hesselgrave. Grand Rapids, MIU: Baker Books, 1978. 338 pp. Paper. 0801041317.

Papers by evangelical missiologists on charismatic theology and neo-Pentecostalism, the contextualization of theology, contemporary evangelism and Catholicism, the theology of church growth, dialogue with the non-Christian religious, and mission strategy and changing political situations.

TH55 Cotterell, Peter

Mission and Meaninglessness: The Good News in a World of Suffering and Disorder. London, ENK: SPCK, 1990. xii, 332 pp. Paper. 028104449X.

A detailed analysis of various approaches to the apparent meaninglessness of life (Christian, Jewish, Muslim, Marxist), with advocacy of an evangelical theology of mission.

TH56 Courth, Franz, Paul Eisenkopf, and Heinrich Hamm

Wie mich der Vater gesandt hat, so sende ich euch: Beiträge zur Theologie der Sendung. Edited by Heinrich M. Köster. (Glaube, Wissen, Wirken, 6). Limburg, GW: Lahn-Verlag, 1982. 120 pp. Paper. 3784020070.

Nine lectures in which Pallotine professors of various theological disciplines develop the idea of mission and "being sent" from their own specific standpoints.

TH57 Damsteegt, P. Gerard

Foundations of the Seventh-day Adventist Message and Mission. Berrien Springs, MIU: Andrews University Press, 1988. xv, 348 pp. No ISBN.

A detailed analysis of the developing Seventh-day Adventist theology of mission, 1850 to 1874; originally published in 1977 (Grand Rapids, MIU: Eerdmans).

TH58 Damsteegt, P. Gerard

Toward the Theology of Mission of the Seventh-day Adventist Church: Historical-Theological and Missiological Study of the Origins and Basic Structure of the Seventh-day Adventist Theology of Mission. Grand Rapids, MIU: Eerdmans, 1977. xv, 348 pp. Paper. No ISBN.

A doctoral dissertation originally presented to the theological faculty of the Free University in Amsterdam, the Netherlands.

TH—MISSIONS: THEOLOGY

TH59 Daniels, Eugene
The Catholic Church in Mission: Highlights of Church Teaching Since 1891. Monrovia, CAU: MARC, 1993. iv, 44 pp. Paper. 0912552808.

A concise summary for Protestants of the major Catholic documents leading up to the church's present teaching on the mission of the church.

TH60 Dapper, Heinz
Mission—Glaubensinterpretation—Glaubensrealisation: Ein Beitrag zur ökumenischen Missionstheologie. (Regensburger Studien zur Theologie, 16). Frankfurt am Main, GW: Lang, 1979. 319 pp. Paper. 3820463291.

Endeavoring to develop a missionary spirituality, the author examines the concept of mission in the documents of the WCC and of the Second Vatican Council, and compares it with Latin American liberation theology and the critical theology of E. Schillebeeckx.

TH61 Deminger, Sigfrid
Evangelist på indiska villkor: Stanley Jones och den indiska renässansen, 1918-1930. (Studia Missionalia Upsaliensia, 42). Örebrto, SW: Libris, 1985. 223 pp. 9171943927.

A doctoral dissertation on the theology of E. Stanley Jones and his approach to Indian religion, with a summary in English.

TH62 Driver, John
La Obra Redentora de Cristo y la Misión de la Iglesia. Buenos Aires, AG: Nueva Creación; Grand Rapids, MIU: Eerdmans, 1994. 294 pp. 080280926X.

Spanish translation.

TH63 Driver, John
Understanding the Atonement for the Mission of the Church. Scottsdale, PAU: Kitchner; Ontario, ONC: Herald Press, 1986. 286 pp. Paper. 0836134036.

A Mennonite perspective on the reconciling act of atonement, and the understanding of new creation through reconciling community; with a chapter on missiological reflections and implications.

TH64 Dunn, Edmond J.
Missionary Theology: Foundations in Development. Lanham, MDU: University Press of America, 1980. xiv, 395 pp. 0819112097 (hdbk), 0819112100 (pbk).

A theology of mission as a theology of development, with a detailed analysis of related theologies of liberation and revolution; given by a theological educator with experience as a papal volunteer in Peru.

TH65 Engen, Charles Edward van, Dean S. Gilliland, and Paul Pierson, eds.
The Good News of the Kingdom: Mission Theology for the Third Millennium. Maryknoll, NYU: Orbis Books, 1993. xv, 320 pp. 0883448645 (hdbk), 0883448637 (pbk).

A *festschrift* containing twenty-five scholarly essays on biblical, ecumenical, and contextual dimensions of theologies of mission, honoring Arthur F. Glasser, dean and professor emeritus of theology and East Asian studies at Fuller Theological Seminary.

TH66 Engen, Charles Edward van
Mission on the Way: Issues in Mission Theology. Grand Rapids, MIU: Baker Books, 1996. 306 pp. Paper. 0801020905.

A basic text on mission theology based on the author's earlier writings in journals and symposia.

TH67 Evers, Georg
Mission—nichtchristliche Religionen—weltliche Welt. (Missionswissenschaftliche Abhandlungen und Texte, 32). Münster, GW: Aschendorff, 1974. xxii, 232 pp. 3402035219.

A study dealing with the basic missiological problems in Catholic mission theology since Schmidlin, a theology of religions from a Catholic perspective, and the relationship of mission to a secularized world.

TH68 Gensichen, Hans-Werner
Glaube für die Welt: Theologische Aspekte der Mission. Gütersloh, GW: Gerd Mohn, 1971. 288 pp. 3579042114.

Basing his approach to a comprehensive Protestant theory of mission on the concepts of "dimension" and "intention," the author points out the critical situation of missionary work at the time of writing, and analyzes the foundation, goal, and work of mission.

TH69 Glasser, Arthur F., and Donald Anderson McGavran
Contemporary Theologies of Mission. Grand Rapids, MIU: Baker Books, 1983. 251 pp. Paper. 0801037905.

A description of four theories of mission—conciliar, liberationist, Roman Catholic, and evangelical—with an analysis of the historical development of each.

TH70 Grellert, Manfred, Bryant L. Myers, and Thomas H. McAlpine, comps.
Al Servicio del Reino. San José, CR: Visión Mundial, 1992. 301 pp. Paper. 997796520X.

Translations into Spanish of essays on the integral mission of the church, by missiologists from Africa (Bediako, Bosch, and Sanneh), Asia (Fung, Maggay, and Samuel), Yugoslavia (Kuzmic), the United Kingdom (Forster, Newbigin, and Sugden), and the United States (Myers and Yoder).

TH71 Gurp, Peter van
Kerk en zending in de theologie van Johannes Christiaan Hoekendijk, 1912-1975: een plaatsbepaling. Haarlem, NE: AcaMedia, 1989. 335 pp. Paper. 9071646041.

Doctoral dissertation on the relation between church and mission in the theology of Johannes Hoekendijk, on the basis of his publications and archival sources at the WCC (correspondence with Visser't Hooft), and the State University of Utrecht where the Hoekendijk archives are kept.

TH72 Haight, Roger
Jesus: Symbol of God. Maryknoll, NYU: Orbis Books, 1999. xiv, 505 pp. 1570752478.

A systematic approach to the discipline of Christology by a Jesuit priest and professor; includes the examination of soteriology, liberation theology, and religious pluralism.

TH73 Hall, Douglas John
Confessing the Faith: Christian Theology in a North American Context. Minneapolis, MNU: Fortress Press, 1996. xii, 534 pp. 0800625471.

The third volume of the author's systematic theology, containing a major section on the church and its mission.

TH74 Hall, Douglas John
Professing the Faith: Christian Theology in a North American Context. Minneapolis, MNU: Fortress Press, 1993. x, 566 pp. 0800625463 (hdbk), 080062548X (pbk).

In the second volume of a projected three-volume systematic theology in the North American context, Hall focuses on doctrines of God, humanity, and Jesus Christ as central for Christian witness.

TH75 Hall, Douglas John
Thinking the Faith: Christian Theology in a North American Context. Minneapolis, MNU: Augsburg, 1989. 476 pp. 0800625455 (hdbk), 0806623888 (pbk).

The first of a three-volume systematic theology in the North American context, with an in-depth introduction to the contextualization of theology and an analysis of classical themes in theologizing (nature, method, theological knowledge) in relation to the North American context.

TH76 Hess, Willy
Das Missionsdenken bei Philipp Nicolai. (Arbeiten zur Kirchengeschichte Hamburgs, 5). Hamburg, GW: Wittig, 1962. 248 pp. 3804840183.

This scholarly examination of the missionary idea in the writings of the 16th-century Lutheran theologian leads to a much more positive evaluation of Lutheran orthodoxy than was hitherto the case in Protestant missiology (dissertation University of Münster, Faculty of Protestant Theology, 1957).

TH77 Hodges, Melvin L.
A Theology of the Church and Its Mission: A Pentecostal Perspective. Springfield, MOU: Gospel Publishing House, 1977. 185 pp. Paper. 0882436074.

An account of the theology of the church and its missions, written from a Pentecostal perspective, explaining its growth particularly in Latin America.

TH78 Hoekendijk, Johannes Christian, L. A. Hoedemaker, and Pieter Tijmes, eds.
The Church Inside Out. Translated by Isaac C. Rottenberg. London, ENK: SCM Press, 1966. 212 pp. No ISBN.

A selection of writings by the influential Dutch missiologist who centered his argument on the concept of joining God in mission in the world through shalom.

TH79 Hollenweger, Walter J.
Interkulturelle Theologie. Munich, GW: Kaiser, 1979. 3 vols., 3459017341 (vol. 3).

A three-volume work within the framework of intercultural theology: Vol. 1 on experiential and phenomenological aspects [*Erfahrungen der Leibhaftigkeit* (1979, 381 pp., 3459011971)]; vol. 2 on the relationship between body and spirit, with focus on pneumatology [*Umgang mit Mythen* (1982, 276 pp., 3459014148)]; vol. 3 follows a modified Bultmann approach on biblical narratives and myth [*Geist und Materie* (1988, 415 pp., 3459017341)].

TH80 Holze, Henry
Kirche und Mission bei Ludwig Adolf Petri: Ein Beitrag zum Missionsgespräch des 19. Jahrhunderts. (Studien zur Kirchengeschichte Niedersachsens). Göttingen, GW: Vandenhoeck & Ruprecht, 1966. 232 pp. Paper. No ISBN.

A book about the ideas of L. A. Petri, a prominent promoter of mission in northern Germany, on the relationship between church, confession, and mission; based on diaries kept by the author (1877-1961) during twenty years of missionary activity in New Guinea and later as professor of theology at Neuendettelsau.

TH81 Horner, Norman A., ed.
Protestant Cross-Currents in Mission: The Ecumenical-Conservative Encounter. Nashville, TNU: Abingdon, 1968. 224 pp. No ISBN.

A symposium of contrasting perspectives on the mandate, design, and strategies of world mission.

TH82 Hunsberger, George R.
Bearing the Witness of the Spirit: Lesslie Newbigin's Theology of Cultural Plurality. Grand Rapids, MIU: Eerdmans, 1988. xii, 341 pp. Paper. 0802843697.

An in-depth study by the professor of missiology at Western Theological Seminary in Holland, Michigan.

TH83 Ice, Thomas, and Kenneth L. Gentry
Great Tribulation: Past or Future? The Two Evangelicals Debate the Question. Grand Rapids, MIU: Kregel Publications, 1999. 224 pp. Paper. 0825429013.

The authors debate the preterist view, that prophecies of the Great Tribulation were fulfilled in the early church, and the futurist view that Bible prophecy portrays the Great Tribulation as yet to come.

TH84 Institut for Missionsteologi og Ökumenisk Teologi, Aarhus Universitet
Missionsteologi og Ökumenisk Teologi: Hovedlinier. Åarhus, DK: Åarhus Universitet, det teologiske Fakultet, 1973. 149 pp. Paper. No ISBN.

This is an introduction to the field of missiology, containing some crucial texts.

TH85 Irvin, Dale T., and Akintunde E. Akinade, eds.
The Agitated Mind of God: The Theology of Kosuke Koyama. Maryknoll, NYU: Orbis Books, 1996. xvi, 239 pp. 157075084X.

A *festschrift* containing fourteen essays to honor the distinguished Japanese-born theologian upon his retirement as Rockefeller Professor of Ecumenics and World Christianity at Union Theological Seminary in New York; arranged under themes of "global community," "the crucified mind," and "neighborology."

TH86 Jansen, Schoonhoven E.
Variaties op het thema "zending." Kampen, NE: Kok, 1974. 207 pp. 9024205522.

Selected articles on "mission" by Jansen Schoonhoven, professor of missiology in Leiden (1962-1974), and first director of the missiological department of IIMO (1970-1974); presented at the occasion of his retirement.

TH87 Jeroense, P. J. G.
Theologie als zelfkritiek: Een onderzoek naar de missionaire theologie van Arend Th. van Leewen. (Mission—Missiologisch Onderzoek in Nederland, 7). Zoetermeer, NE: Boekencentrum, 1994. xi, 235 pp. Paper. 9023906470.

A dissertation analyzing the theology of the Dutch scholar Arend Th. van Leewen (1918-1993), focusing on his interpretations as mission theologian of secularization, Islam, and Marxism.

TH88 Joosse, L. J.
Reformatie en zending: Bucer en Walaeus: vaders van reformatorische zending. Goes, NE: Oosterbaan en Le Cointre, 1988. 160 pp. No ISBN.

A study of the concepts of mission in the first century of the Calvinist/Presbyterian reformation, especially with the German theologian Martin Bucer (1491-1551) and the Dutch professor Ant. Walaeus (1573-1639).

TH89 Kasdorf, Hans
Gustav Warnecks missiologisches Erbe: Eine biographisch-historische Untersuchung. Giessen, GW: Brunnen-Verlag, 1990. xviii, 488 pp. Paper. 3765593532.

This work is a critical reappraisal of the missiological legacy of Gustav Warneck (1834-1910), the founder of Protestant missiology, with special focus on his theory of mission, cosmic universalism, and the realization of discipleship within the framework of the local Christian community.

TH90 Keshishian, Aram
Orthodox Perspectives on Mission. Oxford, ENK: Regnum Books, 1992. 138 pp. Paper. 0745926851.

A collection of articles and papers by the archbishop of the Armenian Apostolic Church in Lebanon and current moderator of the WCC's Central Committee, in which he draws on the rich traditions of spirituality and theology of Orthodox Christians.

TH91 Kirk, J. Andrew, and Kevin J. Vanhoozer, eds.
To Stake a Claim: Mission and the Western Crisis of Knowledge. Maryknoll, NYU: Orbis Books, 1999. xvii, 254 pp. Paper. 1570752745.

This collection of eleven scholarly essays establishes a dialogue between philosophers and missiologists evaluating dominant positions in contemporary philosophy regarding truth, rationality, and pluralism.

TH92 Kirk, J. Andrew, ed.
Contemporary Issues in Mission. (Department of Mission Occasional Series, 1). Birmingham, ENK: Selly Oak Colleges, 1994. ix, 89 pp. Paper. 0900653191.

Eight short essays by staff members of the Department of Mission, Selly Oak Colleges, Great Britain, on key theological issues for contemporary mission

TH93 Kirk, J. Andrew
The Mission of Theology and Theology as Mission. (Christian Mission and Modern Culture Series). Valley Forge, PAU: Trinity Press International; Herefordshire, UK: Gracewing, 1997. viii, 71 pp. Paper. 1563381893 (T), 0852444206 (G).

Three essays showing why and how theology and mission are inextricably linked; by the dean and head of the Department of Mission at the Selly Oak Colleges, Birmingham, England.

TH94 Kirk, J. Andrew
What Is Mission?: Theological Explorations. Minneapolis, MNU: Fortress Press, 2000. viii, 302 pp. Paper. 0800632338.

An open and honest exploration of the meaning of making disciples of all nations in our post-Christian, multi-faith world.

TH95 Klaes, Norbert
Stellvertretung und Mission. Essen, GW: Ludgerus-Verlag, 1968. 118 pp. Paper. No ISBN.

A thorough study of the theology of mission, expressing the idea of substitution as a means of salvation, especially through the pronouncements of the Old and New Testaments (dissertation, University of Innsbruck, AU, 1966).

TH96 Kohler, Werner
Umkehr und Umdenken: Grundzüge einer Theologie der Mission. (Studies in the Intercultural History of Christianity, 56). Frankfurt am Main, GW: Lang, 1988. 292 pp. Paper. 3820411518.

Kohler's work, the title of which in translation reads "Conversion and Rethinking: Basic Features for a Theology of Mission," attempts to discover a theology of mission in dialogue with earlier figures of this century, such as R. Bultmann and E. Thurneysen.

TH97 Kramm, Thomas
Analyse und Bewährung theologischer Modelle zur Begründung der Mission: Entscheidungskriterien in der aktuellen Auseinandersetzung zwischen einem heilsgeschichtlich-ekklesiologischen und einem geschichtlich-eschatologischen Missionsverständnis. Aachen, GW: Missio Aktuell Verlag, 1979. 264 pp. Paper. 3921626048.

In an attempt to throw light on the discussion about the meaning of mission, the author compares two missiological models: that of Amstutz from the perspective of salvation history, and of Rütti with a more eschatological orientation.

TH98 Lazareth, William H., and Péri Rasolondraibe
Lutheran Identity and Mission: Evangelical or Evangelistic? Minneapolis, MNU: Fortress Press, 1994. 128 pp. Paper. 0800628373.

Lectures by two prominent Lutheran theologians from the United States and Madagascar, on the relationship between the Lutheran confessions of the 16th century and contemporary Lutheran identity and understandings of mission.

TH99 Liepold, Heinrich
Missionarische Theologie: Emil Brunners Weg zur theologischen Anthropologie. (Forschungen zur systematischen und ökumenischen Theologie, 29). Göttingen, GW: Vandenhoeck & Ruprecht, 1974. 298 pp. 3525562349.

A scholarly analysis of Emil Brunner's development of a theology of mission through his contacts with other peoples, cultures, and religions, especially those of Japan; and his dialogue with Karl Barth.

TH100 Lindsell, Harold
An Evangelical Theology of Missions. Grand Rapids, MIU: Zondervan, 1970. 234 pp. Paper. No ISBN.

Revised edition of a conservative theology of missions; originally published in 1949 with the title, *A Christian Philosophy of Missions* by Van Kampen Press.

TH101 Linz, Manfred
Anwalt der Welt: Zur Theologie der Mission. Stuttgart, GW: Kreuz-Verlag, 1964. 239 pp. No ISBN.

A dissertation asserting that, like Jesus, the church, and especially missions, must go out into the world, and criticizing such matters as the preoccupation of the church with itself, and the overemphasis on the geographical dimension of mission.

TH102 Müller, Karl
Missionstheologie: Eine Einführung mit Beiträgen von Hans-Werner Gensichen und Horst Rzepkowski. Berlin, GW: Dietrich Reimer Verlag, 1985. ix, 207 pp. Paper. 3496008229.

Conforming to the European tradition of an "introduction," this mission theology, written by a Roman Catholic, is commendably ecumenical in its approach to other religions, worldviews, and cultures.

TH103 Müller, Karl, Hans-Werner Gensichen, and Horst Rzepkowski
Mission Theology: An Introduction. (Studia Instituti Missiologici SVD, 39). Nettetal, GW: Steyler Verlag, 1987. 237 pp. Paper. 3805001916.

English translation.

TH104 Müller, Karl, Hans-Werner Gensichen, and Horst Rzepkowski
Teología de la misión. (Misión sin Fronteras). Estella, SP: Verbo Divino; Buenos Aires, AG: Editorial Guadalupe, 1988. 247 pp. Paper. 847151592X (SP).
Spanish translation.

TH105 Müller, Karl, Hans-Werner Gensichen, and Horst Rzepkowski
Teologia misji: Wprowadzenie. Warsaw, PL: Verbinum, 1989. 260 pp. Paper. 8385009426.
Polish translation.

TH106 Maimela, Simon S.
The Emergence of the Church's Prophetic Ministry: An Essay on Modern Trends in Theology. Johannesburg, SA: Skotaville Publishers, 1990. v, 208 pp. Paper. 0947479325.
Essays by the noted South African theologian on key issues in theology since the 18th century, including liberation theology.

TH107 Manecke, Dieter
Mission als Zeugendienst: Karl Barths theologische Begründung der Mission im Gegenüber zu den Entwürfen von Walter Holsten, Walter Freytag und Joh. Christian Hoekendijk. Wuppertal, GW: Brockhaus, 1972. 288 pp. Paper. 3797400403.
The author investigates the basis of the mission theologies of Holsten, Freytag, and Hoekendijk, and the possibility of a foundation for "mission as witness" in the theology of Karl Barth, in particular from the perspective of that theologian's teaching on reconciliation.

TH108 McConnell, C. Douglas, ed.
The Holy Spirit and Mission Dynamics. (Evangelical Missiological Society Series, 5). South Pasadena, CAU: William Carey Library, 1997. 207 pp. Paper. 0878083790.
Ten essays by evangelical missiologists on biblical, historical, and contemporary issues of the Holy Spirit in missions.

TH109 Mitterhöfer, Jakob
Thema Mission. (Thematische Verkündigung). Vienna, AU: Herder, 1974. 182 pp. Paper. 3210244669.
This work presents a summary of Catholic mission theology, and twenty-nine models of how to integrate the idea of mission in various pastoral services.

TH110 Newbigin, James Edward Lesslie
A Faith for This One World? London, ENK: SCM Press, 1961. 128 pp. No ISBN.
The noted missiologist's William Belden Noble Lectures given at Howard University in November 1958, based on materials originally written for the WCC's Amsterdam (1948) and New Delhi (1961) assemblies.

TH111 Newbigin, James Edward Lesslie
The Open Secret: An Introduction to the Theology of Mission. Grand Rapids, MIU: Eerdmans, 1995. viii, 192 pp. Paper. 0802808298.
A revised edition of an introduction to the contemporary theology of mission, by the noted ecumenical leader and missiologist; originally published in 1978.

TH112 Newbigin, James Edward Lesslie
Truth to Tell: The Gospel as Public Truth. (Osterhaven Lecture Series, 2). Grand Rapids, MIU: Eerdmans; Geneva, SZ: WCC Publications, 1991. v, 90 pp. Paper. 0802806074 (E), 2825410306 (W).
An apologetic for Christianity as *Truth*, both personal and public, in an increasingly secularized modern world; by the eminent missiologist; originally presented at the Osterhaven lectures at Western Theological Seminary, Holland, Michigan.

TH113 Niles, Daniel Thambyrajah
Feuer auf Erden: Gottes Sendung und das Missionswerk der Kirchen. Stuttgart, GW: Evan Missionsverlag, 1962. 282 pp. Paper. No ISBN.
German translation of *Upon the Earth* (1962).

TH114 Niles, Daniel Thambyrajah
Sur la terre: la mission de Dieu et de son Église. (Collection œcuménique, 5). Geneva, SZ: Éditions Labor et Fides, 1965. 294 pp. No ISBN.
French translation.

TH115 Niles, Daniel Thambyrajah
Upon the Earth: The Mission of God and the Missionary Enterprise of the Churches. New York, NYU: McGraw-Hill, 1962. 270 pp. No ISBN.
A penetrating analysis of the church's mission to the world by a leading Asian Christian.

TH116 Osthathios, Geevarghese
Sharing God and a Sharing World. Delhi, II: ISPCK; Kerala, II: Christava Sahitya Samithy (CSS), 1995. 156 pp. Paper. 8172142536.
A trinitarian theology of mission, by the noted Orthodox Indian theologian, with special attention to issues of religious pluralism in India; published as a sequel to *Theology of a Classless Society* (1978, 1980).

TH117 Padilla, C. René
Misión integral: Ensayos sobre el reino y la iglesia. Grand Rapids, MIU: Eerdmans; Buenos Aires, AG: Nueva Creación, 1986. xi, 211 pp. Paper. 0802809022.
Spanish translation.

TH118 Padilla, C. René
Mission Between the Times. Grand Rapids, MIU: Eerdmans, 1985. xi, 199 pp. Paper. 0802800572.
A Latin American perspective on diffferent aspects of the mission of the church, rejecting liberation theology as a secular ideology.

TH119 Paton, David MacDonald
Christian Missions and the Judgment of God. Grand Rapids, MIU: Eerdmans, 1996. xiv, 114 pp. Paper. 0802840876.
A reissue of the 1953 classic by a former China missionary and missiologist; with a new introduction and biography of the author by his son.

TH120 Piskaty, Kurt, and Horst Rzepkowski, eds.
Verbi Praecones: Festschrift für P. Karl Müller SVD zum 7. Geburtstag. (Studia Instituti Missiologici SVD, 56). Nettetal, GW: Steyler Verlag, 1993. 397 pp. Paper. 3805003242.
Twenty-one essays in German (13) and English (8) on various aspects of mission theology and issues of contextualization; published as a *festschrift* to honor Karl Müller SVD, the noted German missiologist, on his 75th birthday.

TH—MISSIONS: THEOLOGY

TH121 Piskaty, Kurt, ed.
Mission als Auftrag Gottes an uns: Das Missionsdekret des Zweiten Vatikanischen Konzils; Anhang: Übersicht über den personalen Missionseinsatz der Katholiken Österreichs. Vienna, AU: Zentrale der Päpstlichen Missionswerke Österreichs, 1966. 72 pp. Paper. No ISBN.

The German text of *Ad Gentes*, and an overview of Austrian missionary personnel.

TH122 Pobee, J. S.
Mission in Christ's Way. New Delhi, II: ISPCK, 1989. 61 pp. Paper. No ISBN.

Lectures on the theme of the WCC Conference on World Mission and Evangelism (San Antonio, 1989) delivered in Kerala, India, November 1988, by the associate director of the WCC's Programme on Theological Education.

TH123 Pomerville, Paul A.
The Third Force in Missions: A Pentecostal Contribution to Contemporary Mission Theology. Peabody, MAU: Hendrickson Publishers, 1985. xii, 208 pp. Paper. 3805001932.

A scholarly analysis of the contribution of Pentecostalism to mission theology and strategies, by a noted Assemblies of God missiologist.

TH124 Power, John
Mission Theology Today. Maryknoll, NYU: Orbis Books, 1971. 216 pp. Paper. No ISBN.

Lectures given to the Catholic SEDOS seminar on missiology, including the new vision of Vatican II, the biblical roots, and applications relating mission to development issues.

TH125 Rétif, André
La mission: éléments de théologie et de spiritualité missionaire. (Esprit et Mission). Paris, FR: Mame, 1963. 295 pp. No ISBN.

Collected essays on missionary theology and spirituality; originally published in French journals.

TH126 Rétif, André, and Louis Rétif
Teilhard et l'évangélisation des temps nouveaux. (Collection Points d'appui). Paris, FR: Éditions Ouvrieres, 1970. 200 pp. No ISBN.

An analysis of the relevance of the theology of Teilhard de Chardin for the church's universal mission, including his thought concerning church and world, other religions, mission, missionary spirituality, and mysticism.

TH127 Rütti, Ludwig
Zur Theologie der Mission: Kritische Analysen und neue Orientierungen. (Gesellschaft und Theologie: Systematische Beiträge, 9). Munich, GW: Kaiser; Mainz, GW: Grünewald Verlag, 1972. 362 pp. Paper. 3459008369 (K), 3786703795 (G).

Strongly criticizing traditional mission praxis and theory, this dissertation of the University of Münster maintains that mission is service to the world, and that Christians are "sent" to shape a more human future.

TH128 Reid, John, James Edward Lesslie Newbigin, and David Pullinger
Modern, Postmodern and Christian. (Lausanne Occasional Paper, 27). Carberry, STK: Handsel Press, 1996. 71 pp. Paper. 1871828317.

This short work consists of an introduction by Lesslie Newbigin, an essay on modernity by John Reid, an essay on communicating the Gospel to postmoderns by David Pullinger, and questions and Bible passages for group study.

TH129 Rooy, Sidney H.
The Theology of Missions in the Puritan Tradition: A Study of Representative Puritans: Richard Sibbes, Richard Baxter, John Eliot, Cotton Mather, and Jonathan Edwards. Grand Rapids, MIU: Eerdmans; Delft, NE: Meinema, 1965. 346 pp. Paper. No ISBN.

A detailed study of the thought of Richard Sibbes, Richard Baxter, John Eliot, Cotton Mather, and Jonathan Edwards as representative Puritans; originally submitted as a doctoral thesis at the University of Amsterdam.

TH130 Rosin, H. H., and Gerardus Adam Christiaan van Winsen
Missio Dei: Term en functie in de zendingstheologische discussie. Leiden, NE: IIMO, 1971. 57 pp. Paper. No ISBN.

A study by Protestant (Rosin) and Catholic (Van Winsen) missiologists about the concept of *missio dei* in theological studies of the 20th century.

TH131 Saayman, W. A., and J. J. Kritzinger, eds.
Mission in Bold Humility: David Bosch's Work Reconsidered. Maryknoll, NYU: Orbis Books, 1996. viii, 184 pp. Paper. 1570750874.

Thirteen essays by an international panel of missiologists assessing the life and work of the late David Bosch, the noted South African missiologist, including essays on themes relatively neglected in his work.

TH132 Sahlberg, Carl-Erik
Budskapets väg. Stockholm, SW: Verbum, 1988. 181 pp. 9152615804.

A study in missiology and the church's theology of mission taking into account the mission to the north.

TH133 Salvación y Construcción del Mundo
(Colección Andina, 8). Barcelona, SP: Editorial Nova Terra; Santiago, CL: Disapsa, 1968. 152 pp. Paper. No ISBN.

A collection of five articles by prominent Latin American theologians for presentation at "Word and Evangelization," a conference on Pastoral Theology in Santiago, Chile, July, 1966.

TH134 Scherer, James A., and Stephen B. Bevans, eds.
New Directions in Mission and Evangelization 2: Theological Foundations. (New Directions in Mission and Evangelization, 2). Maryknoll, NYU: Orbis Books, 1994. xiv, 215 pp. Paper. 0883449536.

An anthology of recent articles by missiologists and church leaders, exploring the various theological foundations on which the church's missionary efforts are based.

TH135 Scherer, James A.
Gospel, Church, and Kingdom: Comparative Studies in World Mission Theology. Minneapolis, MNU: Augsburg, 1987. 271 pp. Paper. 0806622806.

A comprehensive survey of 20th-century developments in mission theory, with separate chapters on ecumenical (conciliar), evangelical, Lutheran, and Roman Catholic mission theology.

TH136 Schmidt, Arne, G. E. Phillips, and Harald Nielsen
L. P. Larsen, a Theology for Mission: Selected Works and Letters Including Translations from the Danish, a Bibliography of Larsen's Writings, and Historical Essays. Edited by James M. Gibbs. Madras, II: CLS for United Theological College, Bangalore, 1978. viii, 436 pp. Paper. No ISBN.

A collection of the writings, including translations from the Danish, of the missionary to India (1889-1932) and former professor of the United Theological College, Bangalore, revealing his understanding of Christian mission.

TH–MISSIONS: THEOLOGY

TH137 Schmidt, Wolfgang R.

Mission, Kirche und Reich Gottes bei Friedrich Fabri. Wuppertal-Barmen, GW: Verlag der Rheinischen Mission, 1965. 242 pp. No ISBN.

A study of the mission theology of F. Fabri, general secretary of the Rheinische Mission (1857-1884), who, proceeding from the notion of the Kingdom of God and theosophical epistomology, championed the primacy of mission and the unity of church and mission.

TH138 Schreiter, Robert J.

The New Catholicity: Theology between the Global and the Local. (Faith and Cultures Series). Maryknoll, NYU: Orbis Books, 1997. xii, 140 pp. Paper. 157075120X.

Beginning with an analysis of new understandings of communication, culture, identity, and social movements, the professor of doctrinal theology at Catholic Theological Union in Chicago discusses implications for contextual and liberation theologies, and for a new catholicity.

TH139 Schwarz, Gerald

Mission, Gemeinde und Ökumene in der Theologie Karl Hartensteins. (Calwer Theologische Monographien, C 5). Stuttgart, GW: Calwer Verlag, 1980. 324 pp. Paper. 3766805649.

A detailed, systematic presentation of the missiological concept of K. Hartenstein (1894-1952), for many years director of the Basel Mission, from the perspective of his understanding of salvation history and eschatology.

TH140 Scott, Waldron

Bring Forth Justice: A Contemporary Perspective on Mission. Grand Rapids, MIU: Eerdmans, 1980. xvii, 318 pp. Paper. 080281848X.

A study (then-general secretary of the World Evangelical Fellowship) of the integral interrelatedness of three biblical themes—mission, discipleship, and justice—in the context of global economic and political realities.

TH141 Scott, Waldron

Karl Barth's Theology of Mission. Translated by M. Wieseler, and L. Laepple. (Outreach and Identity: Evangelical Theological Monographs, 1). Downers Grove, ILU: InterVarsity; Exeter, ENK: Paternoster Press, 1978. 47 pp. Paper. 0877845417 (I), 0852642346 (P).

English translation.

TH142 Scott, Waldron

Die Missionstheologie Karl Barths. (Theologie und Dienst, 12). Giessen, GW: Brunnen-Verlag, 1977. 48 pp. 3765504335.

An analysis of Karl Barth's theological presuppositions and his specific view of missions; by the former general secretary of the WEF.

TH143 Scudieri, Robert J.

The Apostolic Church: One, Holy, Catholic and Missionary. (Lutheran Society for Missiology Book Series). Fullerton, CAU: Lutheran Society for Missiology, 1995. iv, 86 pp. Paper. 096487640X.

A monograph on the original meaning of "the Apostolic Church" in the New Testament, the early church, and the creeds.

TH144 Sensche, Klaus

Christian Jensen und die Breklumer Mission: Der missionstheologische Ansatz Christian Jensens und seine Verwirklichung in der Breklumer Missionsgeschichte. (Studien und Materialien / veröffentlicht im Nodfriisk Institut, 10). Bräist/Bredstedt, GW: Nordfriisk Institut, 1976. iv, 200 pp. Paper. 388070504.

A dissertation presenting, on the basis of primary sources, the mission theology of C. Jensen (1839-1900) and its effects on the Breklum Mission he founded.

TH145 Servizio documentazione e studi

Foundations of Mission Theology. Translated by John Drury. (Maryknoll Documentation Series). Maryknoll, NYU: Orbis Books, 1972. xii, 168 pp. No ISBN.

Twelve essays written by theologians of various countries exploring the basic concerns of missionary institutes as to the "why?" of mission work; with discussion of questions concerning salvation through non-Christian religions, mission work, and development; originally presented at a SEDOS (Servizio documentazione e studi) conference (Rome, 1969) and published in French in *Spiritus* 39 (1969): 321-521.

TH146 Seumois, André

L' Anima dell'Apostolato Missionario. Bologna, IT: Editrice Missionaria Italiana, 1961. 222 pp. No ISBN.

A systematic introduction to missiology for Roman Catholics placing it within scholastic theology.

TH147 Seumois, André

Teologia missionaria. Bologna, IT: Edizioni Dehoniane, 1993. 315 pp. Paper. 8810503120.

A systematic theology of mission for Roman Catholics, relating the insights of scripture, the church fathers, and church traditions to the emerging issues since Vatican II (including the relation of the church and its mission to various cultures and religions); originally published in five parts in French (1973-1981).

TH148 Seumois, André

Théologie missionnaire. (Subsidia Missiologica, 1). Vatican City, VC: Urbaniana University Press; Rome, IT: Bureau de Presse O.M.I., 1981. 5 vols. No ISBN.

A detailed theology of mission prepared as lectures for Catholic missionary candidates with extensive footnotes to relevant literature [vol. 1: *Délimitation de la fonction missionnaire de l'Église* (1973, 1980, 179 pp.); vol. 2: *Théologie de l'implantation ecclésiale* (1974, 1980, 219 pp.); vol. 3: *Salut et religions de la gentilité* (1974, 1981, 203 pp.); vol. 4: *Église missionnaire et facteurs socio-culturels* (1978, 191 pp.); and vol. 5: *Dynamisme missionnaire du peuple de Dieu* (1981, 209 pp.)].

TH149 Shenk, Wilbert R., ed.

The Transfiguration of Mission: Biblical, Theological and Historical Foundations. (Institute of Mennonite Studies (IMS) Missionary Studies, 12). Scottdale, PAU: Herald Press, 1993. 256 pp. Paper. 0836136101.

Six essays by Mennonite missiologists examining current trends in missiological thought, and calling the church to renewal in mission based on the discipleship model of Jesus the Messiah.

TH150 Shorter, Aylward

Theology of Mission. Notre Dame, INU: Fides; Cork, IE: Mercier Press, 1972. 92 pp. Paper. 0853422990.

A brief theology of mission in the light of the Second Vatican Council.

TH151 Siepen, Karl, ed.
Das Konzil und die Missionstätigkeit der Orden. Cologne,
GW: Wienand, 1966. 107 pp. Paper. No ISBN.

The text of the Vatican II decree on missionary activity,
together with six lectures on that theme; delivered at a meeting of the German Catholic Missionary Council in June 1966.

TH152 Song, Choan-Seng, ed.
Doing Theology Today. Madras, II: CLS, 1976. xv, 126 pp.
Paper. No ISBN.

Papers by an international panel of theologians (Minear,
Cone, Song, Sauter, Cooke, and Nissiotis); originally presented at Bossey Ecumenical Institute in 1974 at a consultation on
how we can and should "do theology" in the different contexts
of our world today.

TH153 Spindler, Marc
La mission: combat pour le salut du monde. (Bibliothéque
théologique). Neuchatel, SZ: Delachaux et Niestlé, 1967. 272
pp. No ISBN.

A thesis, with detailed analysis of biblical and contemporary theological arguments, that the goal of mission is the struggle for the salvation of the world.

TH154 Starkes, M. Thomas
Toward a Theology of Missions. Aurora, ONC: AMG Publishers, 1984. 96 pp. Paper. 0899570550.

A popular account of the basic understanding of missions
theology from the perspective of a former director of the Department of Interfaith Witness for the Home Mission Board of
the SBC.

TH155 Sugden, Chris
Radical Discipleship. Basingstoke, ENK: Marshall, Morgan
and Scott, 1981. x, 214 pp. Paper. 0551009012.

A readable holistic theology of mission, with numerous
illustrations drawn from the author's mission experience in
England and India.

TH156 Sundermeier, Theo
Konvivenz und Differenz. (Missionswissenschaftliche Forschungen Neue Folge, 3). Erlangen, GW: Ev.-Luth. Mission,
1995. 247 pp. Paper. 3872143336.

Essays by the noted German missiologist on his 60th birthday, containing his theology of mission and analysis of Third
World theologies, with special emphasis on Africa.

**TH157 Sundermeier, Theo, Hans-Jürgen Becken, and
Bernward H. Willeke, eds.**
*Fides pro mundi vita: Missionstheologie heute, Hans-Werner
Gensichen zum 65. Geburtstag.* (Missionswissenschaftliche
Forschungen, 14). Gütersloh, GW: Gerd Mohn, 1980. 331 pp.
Paper. 3579040766.

An ecumenical commemorative volume for the author of
Glaube für die Welt, a standard work in mission theology, reflecting a cross section of recent missiological thought, with
impulses for theory and praxis.

TH158 Taylor, John Vernon
*The Go-Between God: The Holy Spirit and the Christian Mis-
sion.* London, ENK: SCM Press, 1972. ix, 246 pp. 334005574
(SBN).

A theology of Christian mission centered on the doctrine of
the Holy Spirit; originally presented as the 1967 Edward Cadbury Lectures in Theology at the University of Birmingham.

TH159 Thangaraj, M. Thomas
The Common Task: A Theology of Christian Mission. Nashville, TNU: Abingdon, 1999. 167 pp. Paper. 0687001447.

Exploration of a new starting point for a theology of mission in moral imperatives shared by all the world's religions.

TH160 Thomas, Madathilparapil M. et al.
Some Theological Dialogues. (Indian Christian Thought Series, 14). Madras, II: CLS, 1977. 157 pp. Paper. No ISBN.

Stimulating excerpts from the correspondence and writings of ten theologians and the author (moderator of the World
Council of Churches' Central Committee and director emeritus of the Institute for the Study of Religion and Society in
Bangalore, India), on issues pertaining to the theology of Christian mission.

TH161 Tippett, Alan Richard
Verdict Theology in Missionary Theory. South Pasadena, CAU:
William Carey Library, 1973. xix, 195 pp. Paper. 0878081054.

A collection of addresses prepared for a special week of
missionary presentations at Lincoln Christian College and
Seminary, Lincoln, Illinois, describing church growth as "direct change," including materials on the theology, theory, and
anthropology of Christian mission.

TH162 Van der Walt, B. J.
*Anatomy of Reformation: Flashes and Fragments of a Refor-
mational Worldview.* (Series F: Institute for Reformational
Studies F3: Colleción, 13). Potchefstroom, SA: Potchefstroom
University, 1991. iii, 581 pp. Paper. 1868220362.

A compilation of writings on Reformation theology with
application to the contemporary mission of the church in South
Africa; by the director of the Institute of the Potchefstroom
University for Christian Higher Education in South Africa.

TH163 Vasko, Timo
Luterilainen Lähetyskasitys: Foundations of Lutheran Mission.
Helsinki, FI: Kirjapaja, 1991. 90 pp. Paper. 9516250270.

A short trinitarian theology of mission by the director of
the Institute of Mission Theology in Helsinki, Finland.

TH164 Vicedom, Georg F.
Actio Dei: Mission und Reich Gottes. Munich, GW: Kaiser,
1975. 148 pp. 3459010134.

A monograph by the noted German missiologist, relating
two themes: the mission of God (*missio dei*) and the kingdom
of God.

TH165 Vicedom, Georg F.
*The Mission of God: An Introduction to a Theology of Mis-
sion.* Translated by Gilbert A. Thiele and Dennis Hilgendorf.
(Witnessing Church Series). St. Louis, MOU: Concordia Publishing, 1965. xiv, 156 pp. No ISBN.

A theological statement of the source, motive, and end of
missions, based on the assumption that the missionary movement is sourced in the triune God.

TH166 Weber, Christian
*Missionstheologie bei Wilhelm Löhe: Aufbruch zur Kirche der
Zukunft.* (Die Lutherische Kirche, Geschichte und Gestalten, 17).
Gütersloh, GW: Gerd Mohn, 1996. 576 pp. Paper. 3579001388.

A detailed evaluation of the life and mission theology of
Johann Konrad Wilhelm Loehe (1808-1872), distinguished German Lutheran pastor and founder of the Neuendettelsau Foreign
Mission Society, which trained and sponsored ministers to German immigrants in North America, Australia, and Brazil.

**TH—MISSIONS:
THEOLOGY**

TH167 Wiedenmann, Ludwig
Mission und Eschatologie: Eine Analyse der neueren deutschen evangelischen Missionstheologie. (Konfessionskundliche und kontroverstheologische Studien, 15). Paderborn, GW: Bonifacius-Druckerei, 1965. 209 pp. No ISBN.

Wiedenmann examines the relationship between mission and eschatology in the writings of Karl Hartenstein, Hendrik Kraemer, Walter Freytag, Gerhard Rosenkranz, Georg Vicedom, and Hans Jochen Margull, in light of the main currents of Protestant eschatological thinking in the 20th century (Barth Althaus, Cullmann).

TH168 Winsen, Gerardus Adam Christiaan van
Missio 1900-1970: Fasen van Rooms-katholieke bezinning op een kerngedachte. Leiden, NE: IIMO, 1971. 61 pp. Paper. No ISBN.

A survey of the various meanings of the word "mission" in Catholic theology since the beginning of the 20th century.

TH169 Yates, Timothy E.
Christian Mission in the Twentieth Century. New York, NYU: Cambridge University Press, 1994. xvi, 275 pp. 0521434939 (hdbk), 0521565073 (pbk).

A scholarly overview of the dominant themes in mission theology in the 20th century; focusing on debates at major mission conferences and personalities in conciliar Protestantism.

TH170 Zangger, Christian D.
Welt und Konversation: Die theologische Begründung der Mission bei Gottfried Wilhelm Leibniz. (Basler Studien zur historischen und systematischen Theologie, 21). Zürich, SZ: Theologischer Verlag, 1973. 238 pp. Paper. 3290133214.

This scholarly work, on the concept of mission in the writings of Leibniz, presents his basic idea that human beings must realize divine harmony in the world by means of concrete action (dissertation, University of Basel).

TH171 Zepp, Paul, ed.
Erstverkündigung heute. (Veröffentlichungen des Missionspriesterseminars, 34). Nettetal, GW: Steyler Verlag, 1985. 143 pp. Paper. 3877871887.

A series of essays by well-known German theologians on the preaching of the Gospel in light of mission, ecumenical concerns, and Third World theology.

TH172 Zuck, Roy B., ed.
Vital Missions Issues: Examining Challenges and Changes in World Evangelism. (Vital Issues Series). Grand Rapids, MIU: Kregel Resources, 1998. 288 pp. Paper. 0825440947.

Twenty articles, compiled from the theological journal *Biblioteca Sacra* of Dallas Theological Seminary, on the message, motive, and means of missions in a religiously pluralistic world.

Bible and Missions

TH173 Abesamis, Carlos H.
The Mission of Jesus and Good News to the Poor: Biblico-pastoral Considerations for a Church in the Third World. (Nagliliyab (The Burning Bush), 8). Quezon City, PH: Claretian Publications, 1991. x, 82 pp. Paper. 9715013945.

A brief analysis, by a founding member of EATWOT, of the biblical bases in the Gospels and Isaiah of the "preferential option for the poor."

TH174 Amirtham, Samuel, comp.
Stories Make People: Examples of Theological Work in Community. Geneva, SZ: WCC Publications, 1989. ix, 99 pp. Paper. 2825409634.

A collection of eleven stories from Asia, Africa, Europe, Latin America, and North America which demonstrate how real people are "doing theology" in their own contexts by the Bible stories and faith stories they tell and retell.

TH175 Anderson, Bernhard W.
Creation Theology as a Basis for Global Witness. (Mission Evangelism Series, 3). New York, NYU: UMC, Board of Global Ministries, 1999. 34 pp. Paper. 1890569127.

A re-examination of the foundation of evangelical strategy which reclaims and reaffirms its biblical foundations, moving beyond outmoded theological models, and beginning where the Bible and Apostles' Creed begins: with creation.

TH176 Arias, Mortimer
Venga tu Reino: La memoria subversiva de Jesús. (Praxis Bíblica, 4). México, MX: CUPSA, 1980. 174 pp. Paper. No ISBN.

Theological analysis of various historical concepts of the "Kingdom" and a new reading of the Gospels for Latin America, with four final theses: the Kingdom and human struggles, discerning signs of the Kingdom, the Kingdom and the poor, and Kingdom, church, and mission.

TH177 Arkkila, Reijo, Simo Kiviranta, and Seppo Suokunnas, eds.
Jumalan lähetys: lähetysteologian perusteita ja näköaloja. Helsinki, FI: Sley-kirjat, 1990. 154 pp. 9516179347.

A collection of articles concerning the Lutheran theology of missions.

TH178 Armstrong, Donald, ed.
Who Do You Say That I Am?: Christology and the Church. Grand Rapids, MIU: Eerdmans, 1999. xvi, 143 pp. Paper. 0802838650.

An antidote to inaccurate pictures of God, six internationally recognized New Testament scholars and church leaders seek to reclaim the biblical view of Jesus and the mission of the church in a postmodern age.

TH179 Asensio, Félix
Horizonte misional a lo largo del Antiguo y Nuevo Testamento. (Biblioteca Hispana Bíblica, 5). Madrid, SP: Consejo Superior de Investigaciones Científicas, 1974. 253 pp. 8400039599.

A discussion of missionary and prophetic themes in the Old and New Testaments and the relationship between the two.

TH180 Baker, Christopher J.
*Covenant and Liberation: Giving New Heart to God's Endan-
gered Family.* (European University Studies 23: Theology,
411). Frankfurt am Main, GW: Lang, 1991. 357 pp. Paper.
3631434790.
   A comparative study of the biblical ideal of covenant and
the Latin American goal of liberation; with a proposed synthesis by the author who worked for a decade with the poor struggling for liberation in Lima, Peru.

TH181 Banks, William L.
*In Search of the Great Commission: What Did Jesus Really
Say?* Chicago, ILU: Moody, 1991. 168 pp. Paper. 0802440061.
   Exegesis and interpretation of five post-resurrection say-
ings of Jesus, one each from the four Gospels and Acts, giving
a mandate for missions.

TH182 Beeby, H. D.
Canon and Mission. (Christian Mission and Modern Culture).
Harrisburg, PAU: Trinity Press International, 1999. x, 117 pp.
Paper. 156338258X.
   A call for the recovery of an explicit link between the
entire Bible and mission within a post-Christendom, postmod-
ern context.

TH183 Beeby, H. D.
*From Moses and All the Prophets: A Biblical Approach to
Interfaith Dialogue.* Elkhart, INU: Mission Focus Publications, 1990. 30 pp. Paper. No ISBN.
   A biblical apologetic for dialogue assuming that the Christian participant will make a faith witness consistent with the
historic creeds of the church.

TH184 Beyerhaus, Peter
*Er sandte sein Wort: Theologie der christlichen Mission Band
I: Die Bibel in der Mission.* (Heilsgeschichtliche Missionstheologie, 1). Wuppertal, GW: R. Brockhaus Verlag; Wuppertal, GW: Verlag der Liebenzeller Mission, 1996. xiv, 845
pp. 3417294126 (RB), 388002572X (L).
   This first of four volumes by the noted German missiologist on the theology of Christian mission, contains a detailed
historical analysis of the importance of the Bible in Protestant
German missiology, from Martin Luther to the present; with a
54-page bibliography and extensive indexing.

TH185 Bieder, Werner
*Gottes Sendung und der missionarische Auftrag der Kirche
nach Matthäus, Lukas, Paulus und Johannes.* (Theologische
Studien, 82). Zürich, SZ: EVZ-Verlag, 1964. 52 pp. No ISBN.
   Four lectures on the mission of God and the missionary
task of the church (Matthew, Luke, Paul, and John; by the
study secretary of the Basel Mission.

TH186 Bieder, Werner
*Das Mysterium Christi und die Mission: Ein Beitrag zur mis-
sionarischen Sakramentalgestalt der Kirche.* Zürich, SZ: EVZ-
Verlag, 1964. 115 pp. No ISBN.
   A comparative analysis of understandings of "mystery"
in the mystery-religions, with New Testament and early church
understandings of the mystery of Christ.

TH187 Bieder, Werner
*Segnen und Bekennen: Der Basler Mission zum Anlass des
150-jährigen Bestehens.* Basel, SZ: Basileia Verlag, 1965.
123 pp. No ISBN.

A discussion of the New Testament concepts of blessing
and witnessing and their implications for missionary service;
with particular reference to the history of the Basel Mission in
the 19th century on its 150th anniversary.

TH188 Blauw, Johannes
*Gottes Werk in dieser Welt: Grundzüge einer biblischen The-
ologie der Mission.* Munich, GW: Kaiser Verlag, 1961. 192
pp. No ISBN.
   An influential study of the biblical foundations of mission theology, based on Western European scholarship, including the Old Testament, New Testament, and intertestimental
periods.

TH189 Blauw, Johannes
*L'apostolat de l'Église: esquisse d'une theéologie biblique de
la mission.* (Foi vivante, 69). Paris, FR: Delachaux et Niestlé,
1968. 221 pp. No ISBN.
   French translation.

TH190 Blauw, Johannes
*The Missionary Nature of the Church: A Survey of the Bibli-
cal Theology of Mission.* Grand Rapids, MIU, 1974. 182 pp.
0802815774.
   Reprint of the 1962 English translation (New York:
McGraw Hill).

TH191 Blauw, Johannes
*A Natureza Missionaria da Igreja: Exame da teologia biblica
da missão.* São Paulo, BL: ASTE, 1966. 179 pp. Paper. No
ISBN.
   Portuguese translation.

TH192 Blount, Brian K.
*Go Preach!: Mark's Kingdom Message and the Black Church
Today.* (The Bible & Liberation Series). Maryknoll, NYU:
Orbis Books, 1998. xiii, 290 pp. Paper. 1570751714.
   A scholarly study of the apocalyptic message of Mark's
Gospel, and its relevance to principles and programs of socio-
cultural transformation in the life of the black church in the
United States.

TH193 Boesak, Allan Aubrey
*Comfort and Protest: Reflections on the Apocalypse of John
of Patmos.* Philadelphia, PAU: Westminster Press, 1987. 140
pp. Paper. 0664246028.
   Bible studies on the Book of Revelation, with exposition
of its relevance to the struggle against apartheid in South Africa.

TH194 Bonda, Jan
*The One Purpose of God: An Answer to the Doctrine of Eter-
nal Punishment.* Grand Rapids, MIU: Eerdmans, 1993. xxv,
278 pp. Paper. 0802841864.
   A detailed argument by a Dutch pastor-theologian against
the doctrine of eternal punishment; based on exegesis of Romans and other biblical passages.

TH195 Bowley, James E., ed.
*Living Traditions of the Bible: Scripture in Jewish, Christian,
and Muslim Practice.* St. Louis, MOU: Chalice Press, 1999.
ix, 206 pp. Paper. 0827221274.
   A collection of ten scholarly articles on what the Bible
means and how it has been used in Catholicism, Protestantism, Orthodoxy, Judaism, and Islam historically and in the
present.

**TH—MISSIONS:
THEOLOGY**

TH196 Breneman, J. Mervin
Cosmovisión, Historia y Sociedad en el Antiguo Testamento: Perspectivas Bíblicas Para la Mision de Dios Hoy. Lima, PE: Seminario Evangélico de Lima, Departamento de Misiología, 1982. 47 pp. Paper. No ISBN.

A collection of three scholarly articles: "Israel's Vision in a Pagan World," "A Vision of History in the Old Testament," and "God, Person, and Society."

TH197 Brennan, John P.
Christ, the One Sent. Collegeville, MNU: Liturgical Press, 1997. 191 pp. Paper. 0814624456.

A priest of the Society of African Missions, who spent twenty years in Latin America and Africa, argues that to rediscover Christ as the one sent by the Father for the salvation of the world is to rediscover our own sentness and mission.

TH198 Bretón, Santiago
Vocación y misión: Formulario profético. (Analecta bíblica, 111). Rome, IT: Editrice Pontificio Instituto Biíblico, 1987. xii, 267 pp. 8876531114.

A study of the genres of Hebrew words in the Old Testament used to describe the prophets and their work.

TH199 Brown, Robert McAfee
Unexpected News: Reading the Bible with Third World Eyes. Philadelphia, PAU: Westminster Press, 1984. 166 pp. Paper. 0664245528.

Exposition of ten Old and New Testament passages given fresh interpretations by liberation theologians of the Americas.

TH200 Brownson, James V.
Speaking the Truth in Love: New Testament Resources for a Missional Hermeneutic. (Christian Mission and Modern Culture). Harrisburg, PAU: Trinity Press International, 1998. vii, 86 pp. Paper. 1563382393.

An introduction to the ways in which the New Testament writers interpreted the Gospel across cultural boundaries, with discussion of contemporary use of such models in Christian mission.

TH201 Brox, Norbert et al.
Mission im Neuen Testament. Edited by Karl Kertelge. Freiburg, GW: Herder, 1982. 240 pp. 3451020939.

An exceptional collection of essays by leading German-speaking Catholic New Testament scholars on mission in New Testament teaching, including chapters on early church presuppositions and origins of mission, the "Great Commission," the "theologies of mission" from the viewpoints of Matthew, Mark, Luke, and Paul, and mission in the contexts of antiquity.

TH202 Bussmann, Claus
Themen der paulinischen Missionspredigt auf dem Hintergrund der spätjudisch-hellenistischen Missionsliteratur. (European University Studies, XXIII, 3). Bern, SZ: Lang, 1975. xix, 210 pp. Paper. 3261002352.

In this second edition the author makes a distinction between Paul's "missionary" and "pastoral" preaching, identifies, analyzes, and evaluates Pauline missionary passages, and compares them with late Jewish and Hellenistic mission literature.

TH203 Cardenal, Ernesto
Chrétiens du Nicaragua: l'évangile en révolution. Translated by Claire Wery and Charles Condamines. (Collection chré-tiens en liberté). Paris, FR: Karthala, 1980. 215 pp. 2865370070.

French translation.

TH204 Cardenal, Ernesto
El Evangelio en Solentiname. Salamanca, SP: Ediciones Sígueme; Managua, NG: Nueva Nicaragua, 1983. 4 vols. No ISBN.

A third edition of a remarkable transcription of commentaries by peasant farmers and fishermen in Solentiname, a remote archipelago on Lake Nicaragua, on the Sunday Gospel readings, a grassroots Catholic liberation theology in the making; originally published in Spain (Ediciones Sígueme) and Venezuela (Editorial Signo Contemporáneo) in 1976.

TH205 Cardenal, Ernesto
Das Evangelium der Bauern von Solentiname: Gespräche über das Leben Jesu in Lateinamerika. Translated by Anneliese Schwarzer de Ruiz. Wuppertal, GW: Jugenddienst, 1976. 4 vols. Paper. 377957604X.

A second edition of the German translation.

TH206 Cardenal, Ernesto
Love in Practice: The Gospel in Solentiname. Translated by Donald D. Walsh. Maryknoll, NYU: Orbis Books; London, ENK: Search Press, 1976-1982. 4 vols.

English translation of *El Evangelio en Solentiname* (1975); includes vol. 1: (x, 265 pp.; 0883441683 (hdbk); 0883441764 (pbk)); vol. 2: (viii, 250 pp., 0883441675 (hdbk); 0883441756 (pbk)); vol. 3: (viii, 312 pp., 0883441723 (hdbk); 0883441748 (pbk)); and vol. 4: (x, 278 pp., 088344173X).

TH207 Carriker, C. Timoteo
Missões na Biblia: Princípios Gerais. São Paulo, BL: Sociedade Religiosa Edições Vida Nova, 1992. 70 pp. Paper. No ISBN.

A popular general treatment on the mission of the church, developing a biblical basis for mission.

TH208 Carriker, C. Timoteo
Missao Integral: Uma Teologia Biblica. São Paulo, BL: Editora SEPAL, 1992. iv, 317 pp. Paper. No ISBN.

A biblical theology of mission focusing on the biblical-historical perspectives found in selected Old and New Testament passages.

TH209 Clifford, Paul Rowntree
The Reality of the Kingdom: Making Sense of God's Reign in a World Like Ours. Grand Rapids, MIU: Eerdmans, 1996. viii, 133 pp. Paper. 0802808670.

From an evaluation of Gospel evidence, the former president of Selly Oak Colleges in Birmingham, England, discusses what Jesus meant by his proclamation of the Kingdom and in what sense his promise has been fulfilled.

TH210 Colson, Charles, and Nancy Pearcey
Y Ahora... ¿Como Viviremos? Miami, FLU: Editorial Unilit, 1999. 60 pp. Paper. No ISBN.

A call for all Christians to understand the Bible as a vision for the whole world and a perspective for the whole life.

TH211 Comblin, Joseph
Clamor dos oprimidos, clamor de Jesus. Santiago, CL: Rehue, 1986. 57 pp. No ISBN.

Spanish translation.

TH—MISSIONS: THEOLOGY

TH212 Comblin, Joseph
Cry of the Oppressed, Cry of Jesus: Meditations on Scripture and Contemporary Struggle. Maryknoll, NYU: Orbis Books, 1988. v, 90 pp. Paper. 0883446138.
    English translation.

TH213 Comblin, Joseph
O clamor dos oprimidos, o clamor de Jesus. Petrópolis, BR: Vozes, 1984. 63 pp. No ISBN.
    Meditations on scripture and contemporary struggle by the noted liberation theologian.

TH214 Crawley, Winston
Biblical Light for the Global Task: The Bible and Mission Strategy. Nashville, TNU: Convention Press, 1989. 126 pp. Paper. No ISBN.
    Adult studies for Southern Baptists of the biblical bases for mission by a former missionary and Foreign Mission Board executive; based on lectures presented in 1987 at the Philippine Baptist Theological Seminary.

TH215 Culver, Robert Duncan
A Greater Commission: A Theology for World Missions. Chicago, ILU: Moody, 1984. xvi, 176 pp. Paper. 0802433022.
    A detailed analysis of biblical passages in the New Testament that provide a mandate for mission, mainly from the parables of Jesus in Matthew's and Mark's Gospels.

TH216 Dabelstein, Rolf
Die Beurteilung der "Heiden" bei Paulus. (Beiträge zur biblischen Exegese und Theologie, 14). Frankfurt, GW: Lang, 1981. 245 pp. Paper. 3820461922.
    Considering the unfortunate connotations of the modern word "heathen," this work, based on a doctoral dissertation (Heidelberg, 1976), investigates what exactly Paul meant by *ethne*.

TH217 Das, Somen
Bible Studies, Sermons, Prayers and Reflections. (Christian Emphasis Series: Bible Study Series, 3). Delhi, II: ISPCK, 1998. xii, 124 pp. Paper. 8172144628.
    Bible studies, sermons, and prayers by the principal of Bishop's College, Calcutta, focused on burning issues of justice and peace in our time.

TH218 De Ridder, Richard
Discipling the Nations. Grand Rapids, MIU: Baker Books; Taipei, CH: Chinese Evangelical Seminary, 1985. viii, 253 pp. Paper. 0801028450.
    A biblical theology of missions intepreting the Great Commission of Matthew 28:18-20 as a covenant against the background of Jewish pre-Christian proselyting and diaspora, and the apostleship of Jesus Christ; originally published as *The Dispersion of the People of God* (Kampen: Kok, 1971).

TH219 Di Gangi, Mariano
I Believe in Mission: A Biblical View of the Church as a Going and Growing Concern. Phillipsburg, NJU: Presbyterian & Reformed Publishing, 1979. iv, 123 pp. Paper. No ISBN.
    A primer on biblical motivations for mission; with study guide by the chairman of the International Council of the Bible and Medical Missionary Fellowship.

TH220 Dias, Patrick V.
Vielfalt der Kirche in der Vielfalt der Jünger, Zeugen, und Diener. (Oekumenische Forschungen, 2). Freiburg im Breisgau, GW: Herder, 1968. 407 pp. No ISBN.

A scholarly analysis of issues of ecclesiology in relation to the mission of the church, the New Testament, and the contemporary reality of a plurality of Christian confessions and of religions.

TH221 Dollar, Harold E.
A Biblical-Missiological Exploration of the Cross-Cultural Dimensions in Luke-Acts. San Francisco, CAU: Mellen Research University Press, 1993. vii, 435 pp. 0773422129.
    A sociological analysis of Luke-Acts by a North American missiologist exploring the cultic, geographical, ethnic, and relational dimensions of both Jewish and Gentile missions.

TH222 Dollar, Harold E.
St. Luke's Missiology: A Cross-Cultural Challenge. South Pasadena, CAU: William Carey Library, 1996. viii, 197 pp. Paper. 0878082670.
    The theology of mission in Luke-Acts prepared as a basic textbook by the professor of missiology in the Talbot School of Theology at Biola University.

TH223 Driver, John
Images of the Church in Mission. Scottdale, PAU: Herald Press, 1997. 245 pp. Paper. 0836190580.
    Theological and historical studies of twelve biblical images of the church, with focus on their socio-historical contents and their relevance for mission today; based on courses taught by the author in Central America and Uruguay.

TH224 Du Bose, Francis M.
God Who Sends: A Fresh Quest for Biblical Mission. Nashville, TNU: Broadman, 1983. 173 pp. 0805463313.
    A comprehensive and systematic study of the biblical concept of "sending," aimed at a better concept of biblical mission; including a list of relevant scriptures written especially for college and seminary students, professors, mission administrators, missionaries, pastors, and other Christian leaders.

TH225 Dyrness, William A.
Let the Earth Rejoice!: A Biblical Theology of Holistic Mission. Westchester, ILU: Crossway Books, 1983. 216 pp. Paper. 0891072829.
    A popular introduction to a biblical theology of missions, drawing on both Old and New Testament sources.

TH226 Engel, James F., and William A. Dyrness
Changing the Mind of Missions: Where Have We Gone Wrong? Downers Grove, ILU: InterVarsity, 2000. 192 pp. Paper. 0830822399.
    Written for those involved in Western missions and also applicable to missionary agencies worldwide, the authors seek to point a way forward by returning to the biblical ground on which Jesus walked as he established and extended his Kingdom on earth.

TH227 Filbeck, David
Yes, God of the Gentiles, Too: The Missionary Message of the Old Testament. Wheaton, ILU: BGC, 1994. viii, 228 pp. Paper. 1879089149.
    An analysis of Old Testament content regarding God's plan for salvation, and the imperative to preach the Gospel to all nations.

TH228 Fuellenbach, John
The Kingdom of God: The Message of Jesus Today. Maryknoll, NYU: Orbis Books, 1995. xi, 340 pp. Paper. 1570750289.
    A systematic treatment of the doctrine of the Kingdom of God by a Divine Word missionary concerned for its missiological dimensions.

TH229 Galilea, Segundo
The Beatitudes: To Evangelize As Jesus Did. Translated by Robert R. Barr. Maryknoll, NYU: Orbis Books; Dublin, IE: Gill & Macmillan, 1984. iii, 108 pp. Paper. 0883443449 (O), 0717113353 (G).

A profound study of the Beatitudes, applying the principles of Jesus' teaching to life today with warmth and openness that inspires one to a deeper reliance on the roots of our faith in Jesus; originally written in Spanish by a Chilean Roman Catholic priest under the title *La Mision Segun las Bienaventuranzas* (1984).

TH230 Gatti, Enzo
Rich Church—Poor Church?: Some Biblical Perspectives. Translated by Matthew J. O'Connell. Maryknoll, NYU: Orbis Books, 1974. xi, 127 pp. 0883444372.

English translation of *Colui che sa il dolore dell'uomo* (1973).

TH231 Gill, Athol
Life on the Road: The Gospel Basis for a Messianic Lifestyle. Scottdale, PAU: Herald Press, 1992. 335 pp. Paper. 0836135881.

A call to rediscover an authentic Christian lifestyle based on Jesus and the Gospels, grounded in the author's experience of living in Christian community and working with the poor; originally published by Lancer Books in 1989.

TH232 Gnanakan, Ken R.
Kingdom Concerns: A Biblical Exploration towards a Theology of Mission. Bangalore, II: Theological Book Trust, 1989. v, 208 pp. Paper. No ISBN.

A biblical theology of missions for the Asian context by the chairman of the Asia Theological Association and president of the Association of Evangelical Theological Educators in India.

TH233 God's Kingdom and Mission
(Studia Missionalia, 46). Rome, IT: Editrice Pontificia Università Gregoriana, 1997. 384 pp. Paper. 8876527419.

This collection of sixteen articles, written in many languages, covers a wide range of missiological approaches to the Kingdom; a publication of the Faculty of Missiology at Gregorian University, Rome.

TH234 González, Justo L.
For the Healing of the Nations: The Book of Revelation in an Age of Cultural Conflict. Maryknoll, NYU: Orbis Books, 1999. ix, 117 pp. Paper. 1570752737.

An analysis of the cultural and economic setting of Revelation and its promises for liberation from injustice, oppression, pain, and misery.

TH235 Gregorios, Paulos
The Meaning and Nature of Diakonia. (Risk Book Series, 38). Geneva, SZ: WCC, 1988. 44 pp. Paper. 282540926X.

A collection of biblical meditations and theological reflections on the twofold ministry of diakonia (service through sacrificial worship, and through sacrificial love); by the principal of the Orthodox Seminary, Kottayam, India, who is also a president of the WCC.

TH236 Grilli, Massimo
Comunità e Missione: Le Direttive di Matteo; Indagine es-egetica su Mt 9, 35-11, 1. (European University Studies, 23: Theology, 450). Frankfurt am Main, GW: Lang, 1992. 361 pp. Paper. 3631445873.

A detailed study of the issues for a theology of mission contained in Jesus' discourse on the work and behavior of special disciples in Matthew 9:35-11:1.

TH237 Groot, Aart de
The Bible on the Salvation of Nations. Translated by F. Vander Heijden. De Pere, WIU: St. Norbert Abbey Press, 1966. vi, 149 pp. No ISBN.

English translation.

TH238 Groot, Aart de
De Bijbel over het hail der volken. (De Bijbel over ... , 21). Roermond en Maaseik, NE: Romen and Zonen, 1964. 124 pp. No ISBN.

A Roman Catholic biblical theology of missions.

TH239 Guder, Darrell L.
The Incarnation and the Church's Witness. (Christian Mission and Modern Culture). Harrisburg, PAU: Trinity Press International, 1999. xiii, 66 pp. Paper. 1563383101.

Using literary, historical, and social approaches to Scripture, Guder argues that the incarnation of Jesus—the culmination of God's activity and presence in the world—provides the foundational model for the practice of Christian missions in the world today.

TH240 Haas, Odo
Paulus der Missionar: Ziel, Grundsätze und Methoden der Missionstätigkeit des Apostels Paulus nach seinen eigenen Aussagen. (Münsterschwarzacher Studien, 11). Münsterschwarzach, GW: Vier-Türme-Verlag, 1971. ix, 132 pp. Paper. 387868004X.

A licentiate thesis on St. Paul as missionary, accepted by the University of Würzburg in 1959/60.

TH241 Hahn, Ferdinand
Mission in the New Testament. London, ENK: SCM Press, 1965. 184 pp. No ISBN.

English translation.

TH242 Hahn, Ferdinand
Das Verständnis der Mission im Neuen Testament. (Wissenschaftliche Monographien zum AT und NT, 13). Neukirchen-Vluyn, GW: Neukirchener Verlag, 1963. 168 pp. No ISBN.

The author investigates the various approaches to mission in the New Testament, focusing on the expectation of the eschatological hour and the missionary mandate of Jesus Christ.

TH243 Hedlund, Roger E.
God and the Nations: A Biblical Theology of Mission in the Asian Context. (Indian Contextual Theological Education Series, 14). Delhi, II: ISPCK, 1997. xix, 380 pp. Paper. 8172143966.

A basic textbook for the study of mission in theological colleges in South Asia, with further reflection on contextual issues since its earlier publication as *Mission to Man in the Bible* (Madras, 1985), *The Mission of the Church in the World* (Baker, 1991), and *A Biblical Theology: The Mission of the Church in the World* (ELS, Madras, 1994).

TH—MISSIONS: THEOLOGY

TH244 Hendrickx, Herman
The Third Gospel for the Third World. (A Michael Glazier Book). Collegeville, MIU: Liturgical Press, 1998. 5 vols. Paper. 0814658725.

A five-volume commentary on the Gospel of Luke, with the premise that when Luke spoke of the poor he had in mind the urban poor of his time, which provides special relevance for the millions of urban poor in the Third World today [vol. 1-A: *Preface and Infancy Narrative* (Luke 1:1-2:52), 304 pp., 0814658709; vol. 2-A: *Ministry in Galilee* (Luke 3:1-6:49), 384 pp., 0814658717; vol. 2-B: *Ministry in Galilee* (Luke 7:1-9:50), 340 pp., 0814658725; vol. 3-A: *Travel Narrative-I* (Luke 9:51-13:21), 0814658733; vol. 3-B: *Travel Narrative-II* (Luke 13:22-17:10), viii, 279 pp., 0814658741].

TH245 Hertig, Paul
Matthew's Narrative Use of Galilee in the Multicultural and Missiological Journey of Jesus. (Mellen Biblical Press Series, 46). Lewiston, NYU: E. Mellen Press, 1998. ix, 189 pp. 077342444X.

An in-depth missiological perspective on the Gospel of Matthew from three horizons (Hebrew Bible, Jewish Christianity, and multicultural Galilee); originally presented as a Ph.D. dissertation at Fuller Theological Seminary.

TH246 Herzog, William R.
Jesus, Justice and the Reign of God: A Ministry of Liberation. Louisville, KYU: Westminster John Knox, 1999. xv, 316 pp. Paper. 0664256767.

In this sequel to *Parables as Subversive Speech*, Herzog bridges the gap between purely historical and theological interpretations of the life of Jesus through a synthesis of politics and theology, faith and history.

TH247 Howard, David M.
By the Power of the Holy Spirit. Downers Grove, ILU: InterVarsity, 1973. 172 pp. Paper. 0877843589.

A popular presentation of the biblical witness to the Holy Spirit as the power for world mission and evangelism.

TH248 Howard, David M.
The Great Commission for Today. Downers Grove, ILU: InterVarsity, 1976. 112 pp. 0877846464.

A guide for study of the Great Commission as part of the "warp and woof of the Gospel" that has deep significance for discipleship; by the assistant to the president of InterVarsity Christian Fellowship.

TH249 Hull, Bill
The Disciple-Making Church. Grand Rapids, MIU: Revell, 1990. 256 pp. 0800716418 (hdbk), 0800756274 (pbk).

A primer on the biblical foundation of discipleship, and the principles and priorities of the first-century church.

TH250 Izco Ilundain, José A.
¿Que misión quiere la Biblia?: Raices bíblicas de la misión cristiana. Madrid, SP: IEME, 1987. 141 pp. Paper. No ISBN.

A synthetic study of the theme of mission in the various traditions of the Old Testament and in each book of the New Testament.

TH251 Jauregui, José Antonio
Testimonio apostolado-misión: Justificación teológica del concepto lucano apostol-testigo de la resurrección ... (Teología-Deusto, 3). Bilbao, SP: Ediciones Mensajero—Universidad de Deusto, 1973. 252 pp. 8427106270.

Exegetical analysis of Acts 1:15-26 focusing on Luke's view of salvation history.

TH252 Jessen, Carl Christian, Johannes Nissen, and Yap Kim Hao
Mission og evangelisering. (Synspunkt, 22). Hellerup, DK: DMS-Forlag, 1975. 71 pp. Paper. 8774310453.

A collection of articles, edited by Max Kruse, Jens Chr. Nielsen, and Karsten Nissen, on mission and evangelism in relation both to the New Testament and the situation of national churches in Scandanavia; with Danish translations of the "Lausanne Covenant" and Bangkok Conference (WCC, 1972) documents.

TH253 Jonge, Marinus de
God's Final Envoy: Early Christology and Jesus' Own View of His Mission. (Studying the Historical Jesus Series). Grand Rapids, MIU: Eerdmans, 1998. x, 166 pp. Paper. 0802844820.

A rich and provocative study by one of Europe's leading New Testament scholars, drawing from early Christian sources.

TH254 Köstenberger, Andreas J.
The Missions of Jesus and the Disciples According to the Fourth Gospel: With Implications for the Fourth Gospel's Purpose and the Mission of the Contemporary Church. Grand Rapids, MIU: Eerdmans, 1998. xvi, 271 pp. 0802842550.

A dissertation (University of Bern, Faculty of Protestant Theology) by a Japanese exegete, on Jesus' mission to the Gentiles as reflected in St. Mark's Gospel.

TH255 Kane, J. Herbert
Christian Missions in Biblical Perspective. Grand Rapids, MIU: Baker Books, 1976. 328 pp. 0801053706.

An introduction to what the Scriptures say concerning unchanging aspects of the Christian mission, including theological imperatives, historical context, and spiritual dynamics.

TH256 Kato, Zenji
Die Völkermission im Markusevangelium: Eine redaktionsgeschichtliche Untersuchung. (European University Studies, XXIII, 252). Bern, SZ: Lang, 1986. 214 pp. Paper. 3261040408.

A dissertation (University of Bern, Faculty of Protestant Theology) on Jesus' mission to the Gentiles.

TH257 Kavunkal, Jacob, and F. Krangkhuma, eds.
Bible and Mission in India Today. Bombay, II: St. Pauls, 1993. 336 pp. Paper. 8171091792.

A collection of fifteen essays, mostly by Indian scholars, on various biblical themes and their relation to mission in the context of India.

TH258 Kinsler, F. Ross, and Gloria Kinsler
The Biblical Jubilee and the Struggle for Life: An Invitation to Personal, Ecclesial, and Social Transformation. Maryknoll, NYU: Orbis Books, 1999. xix, 170 pp. Paper. 1570752893.

A cross-disciplinary approach to the Jubilee traditions of the Bible as models for contemporary approaches to economic and social justice.

TH259 Kraan, J. D.
Bijbel en andersgelovigen: Naar een bijbelse basis voor de ontmoeting met andersgelovigen. Kampen, NE: Kok, 1987. 217 pp. Paper. 9024253713.

A biblical theology of non-Christian religions, written as contribution to the debate about the policy of Christian schools in the Netherlands having a large number of Muslim pupils.

TH260 Kuhl, Josef

Die Sendung Jesu und der Kirche nach dem Johannes-Evangelium. (Studia Instituti Missiologici SVD, 11). St. Augustin, GW: Steyler Verlag, 1967. xx, 242 pp. Paper. No ISBN.

This is a scholarly work on the mission theology of St. John's Gospel, and the background of its Christology and soteriology, focusing on the idea of "being sent."

TH261 La Iglesia y su Misión: Homenaje a Rubén Lores Zucarino en su Jubilación

(*Vida y Pensamiento*, 7:1/2). San José, CR: *Vida y Pensamiento*, 1987. 119 pp. No ISBN.

A numbered monograph containing seven articles written by colleagues of Ruben Lores Zucarino, and three of his own, on the Great Commission in Matthew 28:18-20.

TH262 LaGrand, James

The Earliest Christian Mission to "All Nations" in the Light of Matthew's Gospel. (International Studies in Formative Christianity and Judaism, 1). Atlanta, GAU: Scholars Press, 1995. xi, 290 pp. 1555409377.

A detailed examination of Matthew's Gospel in the context of Israel's literature, focusing on the theme of mission to all nations as the definitive sign of the coming Kingdom.

TH263 Lane, Thomas J.

Luke and the Gentile Mission: Gospel Anticipates Acts. (European University Studies, 23: Theology, 571). Frankfurt am Main, GW: Lang, 1996. 240 pp. Paper. 363149999X (GE), 082042997X (US).

A doctoral dissertation (Gregorian University, 1994) entitled "The Anticipation of the Gentile Mission of the Acts of the Apostles in the Gospel of Luke."

TH264 Larkin, William J., and Joel F. Williams, eds.

Mission in the New Testament: An Evangelical Approach. (American Society of Missiology Series, 27). Maryknoll, NYU: Orbis Books, 1998. xix, 266 pp. Paper. 1570751692.

Eleven New Testament scholars, associated with Columbia International University, combine to present a comprehensive articulation of the New Testament teaching on mission.

TH265 Le Grys, Alan

Preaching to the Nations: The Origins of Mission in the Early Church. London, ENK: SPCK, 1998. xx, 220 pp. Paper. 0281051488.

A study of the background of Christian mission with the premise that mission to the Gentiles was not introduced by Jesus or his first disciples, but was largely introduced by Paul.

TH266 Legrand, Lucien

Le Dieu qui vient: la mission dans la Bible. Paris, FR: Desclée de Brouwer, 1988. 235 pp. Paper. 2718903740.

A detailed analysis of biblical perspectives on mission including the Old Testament, the Good News of Jesus, and the Apostolic Church in mission; with discussion of both divergences and convergences between Old and New Testament perspectives.

TH267 Legrand, Lucien

Unity and Plurality: Mission in the Bible. Translated by Robert R. Barr. Maryknoll, NYU: Orbis Books, 1990. xv, 189 pp. Paper. 0883446928.

English translation.

TH268 Lohfink, Norbert

Option for the Poor: The Basic Principle of Liberation Theology in the Light of the Bible. Berkeley, CAU: BIBAL Press, 1987. vii, 78 pp. Paper. 0941937002.

Nine lectures presenting the biblical notion of God's love for the poor, focusing on its affinity to, and difference from, liberation theology.

TH269 Müller, Josef

Wozu noch Mission?: Eine bibeltheologische Überlegung. (Biblisches Forum, 4). Stuttgart, GW: Verlag Katholisches Bibelwerk, 1969. 86 pp. Paper. No ISBN.

Considering such problems as secularization, poverty, and the renaissance of non-Christian religions, the author advances, for a wider readership, solid arguments justifying missionary work today.

TH270 May, Roy H.

Joshua and the Promised Land. New York, NYU: UMC, Board of Global Ministries, 1997. xiv, 161 pp. Paper. No ISBN.

An adult mission study on the Book of Joshua and its relevance for contemporary justice issues concerning land; with a leader's guide by Annette Vanzant Williams and Dorothy G. Rowan.

TH271 Maynard-Reid, Pedrito U.

Poverty and Wealth in James. Maryknoll, NYU: Orbis Books, 1987. vii, 136 pp. Paper. 0883444178.

A survey of poor and rich in Jewish and Christian literature during the first century.

TH272 McKenna, Megan

Blessings and Woes: The Beatitudes and the Sermon on the Plain in the Gospel of Luke. Maryknoll, NYU: Orbis Books, 1999. v, 234 pp. Paper. 1570752214.

A call to genuine discipleship through Jesus' Kingdom message; illustrated with insightful stories from Jewish rabbis, Zen masters, Sufi mystics, Leo Tolstoy, and other renowned personalities.

TH273 McMann, Duncan

Mission in Unity: The Bible and Missionary Structures. (Latimer Studies, 33). Oxford, ENK: Latimer House, 1989. i, 29 pp. 0946307326.

A short introduction, from an evangelical perspective, to patterns, principles, and structures of mission in the New Testament, as related to the current Anglican debate on mission in Great Britain.

TH274 Mesters, Carlos

Defenseless Flower: A New Reading of the Bible. Translated by Francis McDonagh. Maryknoll, NYU: Orbis Books; London, ENK: CIIR, 1989. viii, 175 pp. Paper. 0883445964 (O), 1852870559 (C).

English translation.

TH275 Mesters, Carlos

Fiore senza difesa: Una spiegazione della Biblia a partire dal popolo. Translated by Enzo Demarchi. (Spiritualità del nostro tempo). Assisi, IT: Cittadella Editrice, 1986. 268 pp. No ISBN.

Italian translation.

TH—MISSIONS: THEOLOGY

TH276 Mesters, Carlos
Flor sem defesa: Uma explicação da Biblia a partir do povo.
Petrópolis, BL: Vozes, 1983. 206 pp. No ISBN.

A collection of articles intended to capture the joy, life, and suffering of the people of Brazil who are engaged in exegeting and using the Bible in a popular manner for the sake of applying biblical truths to the context of their own lives; by a Dutch missionary and Carmelite priest who has worked for the past twenty years among base Christian communities in Brazil.

TH277 Mesters, Carlos
Flor sin Defensa: Una Explicación de la Biblia a partir del Pueblo. (Colección Perspectivas-CLAR, 16). Bogotá, CK: CLAR, 1984. 225 pp. No ISBN.

Spanish translation.

TH278 Meyer, Regina Pacis
Universales Heil, Kirche und Mission: Studien über die ekklesial-missionarischen Strukturen in der Theologie Karl Rahners und im Epheserbrief. (Studia Instituti Missiologici SVD, 22). St. Augustin, GW: Steyler Verlag; Techny, ILU: Divine Word International, 1979. 234 pp. Paper. 3877871119.

A dissertation (University of Münster) comparing Rahner's ecclesiological understanding of the problem of "universal salvation and mission" and the relevant passages in the letter to the Ephesians.

TH279 Mosala, Itumeleng J.
Biblical Hermeneutics and Black Theology in South Africa. Grand Rapids, MIU: Eerdmans, 1989. xiv, 218 pp. Paper. 0802803725.

A scholarly argument for a black theology capable of becoming an effective weapon for liberation in South Africa, with "struggle" as its key hermeneutical factor in appropriating and interpreting the Bible; by a teacher of religious studies at the University of Cape Town.

TH280 Mosher, Steve
God's Power, Jesus' Faith, and World Mission: A Study in Romans. Scottdale, PAU: Herald Press, 1996. 360 pp. Paper. 0836290319.

A creative exegesis of Romans as the letter of a missionary prophet with a passion for justice and reconciliation; with extensive exposition on its relevance for mission today.

TH281 Mukonyora, Isabel, James L. Cox, and F. J. Verstraelen, eds.
"Rewriting" the Bible: The Real Issues: Perspectives from within Biblical and Religious Studies in Zimbabwe. (Religious and Theological Studies Series, 1). Gweru, ZI: Mambo Press, 1993. 309 pp. Paper. 0869225383.

In eight essays, members of the Religious Studies Faculty of the University of Zimbabwe discuss the importance of the Bible for Christians in various cultural contexts, responding to Canaan S. Banana's contention that the Bible should be rewritten.

TH282 Myers, Ched et al.
"Say to This Mountain": Mark's Story of Discipleship. Edited by Karen Lattea. Maryknoll, NYU: Orbis Books, 1996. xv, 240 pp. Paper. 1570751005.

A study guide to Mark's Gospel, with suggestions for reflective prayer and concerted action in church renewal, Christian discipleship, and work for peace and justice—a popular level version of Ched Myers' *Binding the Strong Man* (Orbis 1988).

TH283 Núñez C., Emilio Antonio
Hacia una Misionología Evangélica Latinoamericana: Bases bíblicas de la Misión (Antiguo Testamento). Miami, FLU: Editorial Unilit/COMIBAM Internacional, 1997. 317 pp. Paper. 0789904411.

This scholarly work examines the universality of the salvific message from the point of view of the Law, Prophets, and Writings, and relates it to the Latin American context.

TH284 Nacpil, Emerito P.
Mission and Change. Manila, PH: EACC, 1968. 142 pp. Paper. No ISBN.

A collection of the Bible study lectures given at the Consultation on Mission (Galveston, Texas, 29 March-5 April 1968), under the auspices of the mission boards of the Evangelical United Brethren Church and the Methodist Church (now known as the United Methodist Church), on the theme "God's Gift of Newness to Church and World."

TH285 Nakanose, Shigeyuki
Josiah's Passover: Sociology and the Liberating Bible. (The Bible and Liberation Series). Maryknoll, NYU: Orbis Books, 1993. xvi, 192 pp. Paper. 0883448505.

A Catholic priest studies the biblical Passover, including critical reflection on it by the Brazilian base communities with whom he works.

TH286 Newbigin, James Edward Lesslie
En mission sur le chemin du Christ. Translated by Anne-Françoise Gillièron. (Perspectives bibliques). Aubonne, SZ: Éditions du Moulin, 1989. 83 pp. Paper. No ISBN.

French translation.

TH287 Newbigin, James Edward Lesslie
Mission in Christ's Way: A Gift, a Command, an Assurance. (WCC Mission Series, 8). Geneva, SZ: WCC Publications; New York, NYU: Friendship Press, 1987. vii, 40 pp. Paper. 2825409006 (SZ), 0377001902 (US).

An address and Bible studies originally presented at the synod of the Church of South India, exploring the nature of mission modeled after Christ, that includes concerns both for evangelism and for social and political justice.

TH288 Newbigin, James Edward Lesslie
Mission pa Jesu satt: Bibelstudier. Translated by Torsten Norrfjard. Stockholm, SW: Verbum Förlag, 1990. 48 pp. Paper. 9152617068.

Swedish translation.

TH289 Nissen, Johannes
I Kristus—Et nyt Fælleskab: Om Ny Testamente og mission. Hellerup, DK: DMS-Forlag, 1986. 192 pp. 8774311263.

The author, a New Testament exegete, analyzes the missionary perspectives in the Gospel of St. John, 1st Corinthians, and Philippians, and deals with problems such as identity and openness, worship and mission, and mission and money.

TH290 Nissen, Johannes
Mission og medansvar: 5 bibelforedrag. Copenhagen, DK: Kirketjenesten i Danmark; Hellerup, DK: DMS Forlag, 1983. 85 pp. Paper. 8774311077.

Five lectures by a New Testament exegete on the following themes: mission and power, compassion, meal fellowship, environment, and martyrdom.

TH291 O'Brien, Peter T.
Gospel and Mission in the Writings of Paul: An Exegetical and Theological Analysis. Grand Rapids, MIU: Baker Books; Carlisle, ENK: Paternoster Press, 1995. xiv, 161 pp. Paper. 0801020522 (US), 0853646147 (UK).

A textbook introducing Paul's theology as a missionary theology, with Paul's own statement of the "Great Commission."

TH292 Okure, Teresa
The Johannine Approach to Mission: A Contextual Study of John 4:1-42. Tübingen, GW: J. C. B. Mohr (Paul Siebeck), 1988. xx, 342 pp. Paper. 3161450493.

A dissertation on the Johannine approach to mission, with special attention to John 4:1-42; by Sister Okure, who teaches at the Catholic Institute of West Africa in Port Harcourt, Nigeria.

TH293 Ollrog, Wolf-Henning
Paulus und seine Mitarbeiter: Untersuchungen zu Theorie und Praxis der paulinischen Mission. (Wissenschaftliche Monographien zum Alten und Neuen Testament, 50). Neukirchen-Vluyn, GW: Neukirchener Verlag, 1979. ix, 282 pp. 3788705485.

A dissertation of the University of Heidelberg (1974) exploring the activities and roles of Paul's forty or so close missionary co-workers, and investigating the theological implications of their collaboration.

TH294 Padilla, C. René, ed.
Bases Bíblicas de la misión: Perspectivas Latinoamericanas. Buenos Aires, AG: Nueva Creación; Grand Rapids, MIU: Eerdmans, 1998. xi, 474 pp. Paper. 0802809529.

In this original work in Spanish, biblical scholars affiliated with the Latin American Theological Fraternity explore the Scriptures from Genesis to Revelation for insight to help the church fulfill its mission in a world deeply affected by injustice and poverty.

TH295 Padilla, C. René, ed.
El Reino de Dios y América Latina. El Paso, TXU: Chalice Press, 1975. 160 pp. Paper. No ISBN.

A collection of the five "Biblical Seminar" papers given in Lima, Peru, 11-18 December 1972, in preparation for the second consultation of the Latin American Theological Fraternity.

TH296 Pak, James Yeong-Sik
Paul as Missionary: A Comparative Study of Missionary Discourse in Paul's Epistles and Selected Contemporary Jewish Texts. (European University Studies, 23: Theology, 410). Frankfurt am Main, GW: Lang, 1991. v, 208 pp. Paper. 3631434596.

A scholarly analysis comparing the context of Paul's missionary preaching to Gentiles with missionary preaching of Hellenistic Jews in his day; originally submitted as a doctoral thesis at the Pontifical Biblical Institute in Rome (1990).

TH297 Pallares, José Cárdenas
Un Pobre llamado Jesús: Reflectura del Evangelio de San Marcos. México, MX: CUPSA, 1982. 177 pp. 9687011033.

In a moving exegesis of the Gospel of Mark, the Mexican theologian and biblical scholar unravels the liberative dimensions of Jesus' words and actions (identifying with poor and outcast persons), judged by authorities to be subversive in his day.

TH298 Pallares, José Cárdenas
A Poor Man Called Jesus: Reflections on the Gospel of Mark.

Translated by Robert R. Barr. Maryknoll, NYU: Orbis Books, 1986. viii, 136 pp. Paper. 0883443988.

English translation.

TH299 Peters, George W.
A Biblical Theology of Missions. Chicago, ILU: Moody, 1972. 368 pp. 0802407099.

A conservative evangelical analysis of the biblical foundations and dynamics of missions.

TH300 Peters, George W.
Missionarisches Handeln und biblischer Auftrag: Eine Theologie der Mission. Translated by Helmuth Engelkraut. (Telos-Buch: Evangelikale Theologie, 1800). Bad Liebenzell, GW: Verlag der Liebenzeller Mission, 1977. 392 pp. Paper. 3880020337.

German translation.

TH301 Piper, John
Let the Nations Be Glad!: The Supremacy of God in Missions. Grand Rapids, MIU: Baker Books; Leicester, ENK: InterVarsity, 1993. 240 pp. Paper. 0801071240 (B), 085110990X (I).

The senior pastor of Bethlehem Baptist Church in Minneapolis, Minnesota, develops biblical motivations for missions, focused both on the mission of the local church and on cross-cultural missions.

TH302 Pope-Levison, Priscilla, and John R. Levison, eds.
Return to Babel: Global Perspectives on the Bible. Louisville, KYU: Westminster John Knox, 1999. xiv, 234 pp. Paper. 0664258239.

Thirty scholars from Latin America, Africa, and Asia interpret six texts from the Hebrew Scriptures, and six from the Christian Scriptures.

TH303 Priest, Doug
The Gospel Unhindered: Modern Missions and the Book of Acts. South Pasadena, CAU: William Carey Library, 1994. x, 225 pp. Paper. 0878082565.

Fifteen short essays by evangelical Protestant missionaries, applying the missionary methods of St. Paul to the challenges of mission today.

TH304 Raen, Guttorm
Bibelens misjonsbudskap. Oslo, NO: Lunde, 1976. 109 pp. Paper. 8252040926.

A study book on a biblical theology of missions.

TH305 Rodriguez Ruiz, Miguel
Der Missionsgedanke des Johannesevangeliums: Ein Beitrag zur johanneischen Soteriologie und Ekklesiologie. (Forschung zur Bibel). Würzburg, GW: Echter Verlag, 1987. 397 pp. Paper. 3429010500.

A dissertation (University of Würzburg, 1985) on the mission texts in the Gospel of John, the history of the Johannine community, and its special structure with respect to mission.

TH306 Roels, Edwin D.
God's Mission: The Epistle to the Ephesians in Mission Perspective. Franeker, NE: Wever, 1962. 303 pp. Paper. No ISBN.

A scholarly analysis of mission themes in Ephesians (the theological basis of the mission, its eschatological fullness, and the church as both goal and instrument of mission); presented as a thesis at the Free University of Amsterdam, the Netherlands.

TH—MISSIONS: THEOLOGY

TH307 Samartha, Stanley J.
The Pilgrim Christ: Sermons, Poems and Bible Studies. (ATC, 252). Bangalore, II: Asian Trading Corp, 1994. vii, 154 pp. Paper. 8170861780.

A collection of writings on biblical themes by the first director of the WCC's Dialogue Program; with black and white drawings by Asian artists.

TH308 Samuel, Vinay
The Meaning and Cost of Discipleship. Bombay, II: Bombay Urban Industrial League for Development, 1981. 56 pp. Paper. No ISBN.

A biblical call to a ministry for social justice presented in Bombay as the Bishop Joshi Memorial Lecture in 1980.

TH309 Sautter, Gerhard
Heilsgeschichte und Mission: Zum Verständnis der Heilsgeschichte in der Missionstheologie; am Beispiel der Weltmissionskonferenzen ... bis 1975 ... Giessen, GW: Brunnen-Verlag, 1985. x, 426 pp. Paper. 3765593214.

This dissertation (Tübingen, 1984) develops the historical and biblical notions of "salvation history," then studies its reception by various ecumenical congresses; in documents from Edinburgh (1910) through Nairobi (1975), and in the evangelical declarations of Wheaton, Frankfurt, Berlin, and Lausanne.

TH310 Schnackenburg, Rudolf
God's Rule and Kingdom. Translated by John Murray. New York, NYU: Herder and Herder; London, ENK: Burns & Oates, 1968. 400 pp. No ISBN.

Second enlarged edition of the English translation of *Gottes Herrschaft und Reich: Eine biblisch-theologische studie* (1965).

TH311 Schnackenburg, Rudolf
Gottes Herrschaft und Reich: Eine biblisch-theologische studie. Freiburg, GW: Herder, 1965. xvi, 275 pp. No ISBN.

A careful examination of the biblical doctrine of the Kingdom of God and the mission to Jews and Gentiles—an important work on the theology of mission.

TH312 Schnackenburg, Rudolf
Règne et royaume de Dieu: essai de théologie biblique. Translated by Rene Marle. (Études théologiques, 2). Paris, FR: Éditions de l'Orante, 1965. 325 pp. No ISBN.

French translation.

TH313 Schottroff, Luise, and Wolfgang Stegemann
Jesús de Nazaret: Esperanza de los pobres. Translated by Manuel Olasagasti. (Pedal, 141). Salamanca, SP: Edicione Sígueme, 1981. 225 pp. 8430108610.

Spanish translation

TH314 Schottroff, Luise, and Wolfgang Stegemann
Jesus and the Hope of the Poor. Translated by Matthew J. O'Connell. Marynoll, NYU: Orbis Books, 1986. ix, 134 pp. Paper. 0883442558.

English translation.

TH315 Schottroff, Luise, and Wolfgang Stegemann
Jesus von Nazareth, Hoffnung der Armen. (Urban-Taschenbücher, 639; T-Reihe). Stuttgart, GW: Köln; Mainz, GW: Kohlhammer, 1978. 164 pp. 3170048953.

A socio-historical study of the Jesus Movement, presenting Jesus as a Jew who proclaimed God in a unique way, and who was himself a symbol of hope for the poor and the oppressed of his time.

TH316 Schottroff, Willy, and Wolfgang Stegemann, eds.
God of the Lowly: Socio-Historical Interpretations of the Bible. Translated by Matthew J. O'Connell. Maryknoll, NYU: Orbis Books, 1984. iv, 172 pp. Paper. 0883441535.

English translation.

TH317 Schottroff, Willy, and Wolfgang Stegemann, eds.
Der Gott der kleinen Leute: Sozialgeschichtliche Bibelauslegungen. Munich, GW: Kaiser; Gelnhausen, GW: Burckhardthaus, 1979. 2 vols. 3459012005 (vol.1).

Old Testament (vol. 1) and New Testament (vol. 2) studies on God's relationship to the poor.

TH318 Schwantes, Milton
Am Amfang war die Hoffnung: Die biblische Urgeschichte aus der Sicht der Armen. Munich, GW: Claudius Verlag, 1992. 134 pp. Paper. 3532621398.

The author, a Lutheran pastor and professor of Old Testament in Brazil, reflects intensively on the first eleven chapters of Genesis, and provides a new insight into their meaning from the standpoint of the poor.

TH319 Segovia, Fernando F., and Mary Ann Tolbert, eds.
Reading from this Place, Volume 2: Social Location and Biblical Interpretation in Global Perspective. Minneapolis, MNU: Fortress Press, 1995. xv, 365 pp. Paper. 0800629493.

Papers presented at an international conference on this liberation theme, held at Vanderbilt Divinity School (Nashville, Tenn., 21-24 October 1993).

TH320 Senior, Donald, and Carroll Stuhlmueller
The Biblical Foundations for Missions. Maryknoll, NYU: Orbis Books, 1983. xii, 371 pp. 0883440466 (hdbk), 0883440474 (pbk).

An application of the latest biblical scholarship in a survey of Old and New Testament images, related to the theology of mission by two Roman Catholic scholars of the Old (Stuhlmueller) and New (Senior) Testaments.

TH321 Sider, Ronald J.
Good News and Good Works: A Theology for the Whole Gospel. Grand Rapids, MIU: Baker Books, 1999. 253 pp. Paper. 0801058457.

A biblical theology for the whole Gospel of evangelism and social action; previously published in 1993 under the title, *One-Sided Christianity? Uniting the Church to Heal a Lost and Broken World.*

TH322 *Spirit, Gospel, Cultures: Bible Studies on the Acts of the Apostles*
(WCC Mission Series, 4). Geneva, SZ: WCC, 1995. 44 pp. Paper. 2825411671.

Seven Bible studies on the book of Acts for worldwide study, leading up to the WCC's Conference on World Mission and Evangelism (Salvador, Brazil, 1995).

TH323 Steward, John
Biblical Holism: Where God, People and Deeds Connect. Burwood, AT: World Vision of Australia, 1994. v, 193 pp. 1875140123.

A twelve- to sixteen-hour interactive video workshop for individuals (three-hour video, workbook/facilitator's guide, two audio tapes, and wall chart), on biblical holism in relation to individual commitment and witness; by the Development Services manager of World Vision Australia.

TH—MISSIONS: THEOLOGY

TH324 Stott, John R. W., David Martyn Lloyd-Jones, and Jose Grau
La Evangelización y la Biblia. (Pensamiento Evangelico). Barcelona, SP: Ediciones Evangélicas Europeas, 1969. 138 pp. Paper. No ISBN.

A collection of studies on the theme of the "Great Commission," including that by Stott presented at the World Congress of Evangelization (Berlin 1966).

TH325 Stott, John R. W.
The Spirit, the Church, and the World: The Message of Acts. Downers Grove, ILU: InterVarsity, 1990. 428 pp. 0830817506 (hdbk), 0830817646 (pbk).

A commentary by the prominent evangelical Anglican, emphasizing the teaching in Acts concerning the mission of the church; also published in the UK as *The Message of Acts* (InterVarsity, 1990).

TH326 Stumme, Wayne, ed.
Bible and Mission: Biblical Foundations and Working Models for Congregational Ministry. Minneapolis, MIU: Augsburg, 1986. 206 pp. Paper. 0806622377.

Sixteen essays studying the missions carried out in the Bible by Paul, Matthew, Luke, and John, and how they relate to active congregational settings today.

TH327 Sugirtharajah, R. S., ed.
The Postcolonial Bible. (The Bible and Postcolonialism, 1). Sheffield, ENK: Sheffield Academic Press, 1998. 204 pp. Paper. 1850758980.

Essays by an international panel of biblical scholars, exploring the colonial assumptions embedded in earlier biblical interpretation, and alternative ways of interpreting the Bible in specific Third World contexts.

TH328 Sugirtharajah, R. S., ed.
Voices from the Margin: Interpreting the Bible in the Third World. Maryknoll, NYU: Orbis Books, 1995. ix, 484 pp. Paper. 1570750467.

A substantially revised edition of the 1991 collection which includes fifteen new articles by Third World scholars—all arranged thematically with concern to bring the Bible alive for those struggling with injustice, oppression, hunger, and exploitation.

TH329 Tamez, Elsa
La Bible des opprimés. Translated by Migele Bajard, and Jean Bajard. (Collection Bible et vie chrétienne, Nouvelle série). Paris, FR: Lethielleux, 1984. 139 pp. 2249610177.

French translation.

TH330 Tamez, Elsa
Bible of the Oppressed. Translated by Matthew J. O'Connell. Maryknoll, NYU: Orbis Books, 1982. vii, 88 pp. Paper. 0883440350.

English translation of *La Biblia de los Oprimidos* (1979), with two chapters from *La Hora de la vida* (1978).

TH331 Tamez, Elsa
La Biblia de los oprimidos: La Opresion en la Teología Bíblica. (Collección Aportes). San José, CR: DEI, 1987. 125 pp. No ISBN.

Fourth edition of an analysis of the experience of oppression as recorded in the Old Testament; by a professor of biblical studies at Seminario Bíblico Latinoamericano in San José, Costa Rica.

TH332 Tamez, Elsa
La Hora de la vida: Lecturas bíblicas. 2nd. ed. (Collección Aportes). San José, CR: DEI, 1980. 125 pp. No ISBN.

Second edition of a presentation of the Gospel as good news for the poor, and of conversion as an affirmation of life.

TH333 Tamez, Elsa
When the Horizons Close: Rereading Ecclesiastes. Translated by Margaret Wilde. Maryknoll, NYU: Orbis Books, 2000. vi, 170 pp. Paper. 157075313X.

A Mexican theologian finds a current message in an ancient book which reflects a time when utopian hopes had been crushed, when prospects for change seemed remote, and the challenge was how to live faithfully in the present while maintaining some openness to a different future; an English translation of *Cuando los horizontes se cierran* (1998).

TH334 Trimingham, J. Spencer
Two Worlds Are Ours: A Study of Time and Eternity in Relation to the Christian Gospel Freed from the Tyranny of the Old Testament Reference. Beirut, LE: Librairie du Liban, 1971. 174 pp. No ISBN.

A distinguished Christian Islamist seeks to disconnect the Gospel from the Hebrew Bible in order to present the uniqueness of Christ, especially to Muslims, untrammelled by its Judaistic setting.

TH335 Van Rheenen, Gailyn
Biblically Anchored Missions: Perspectives on Church Growth. Austin, TXU: Firm Foundation Publishing, 1983. xv, 155 pp. Paper. No ISBN.

A philosophy of missions in which concepts of culture, church growth, receptivity, and identification are related to biblical models from the ministries of Christ and Paul; with illustrations from the author's ministry to the Kipsigis Tribe of Kenya.

TH336 Veloso, Mario
El compromiso cristiano: Un estudio sobre la actualidad misionera del evangelio de San Juan. (Libro Nuevo). Buenos Aires, AG: Zunino Ediciones, 1975. 349 pp. Paper. No ISBN.

A biblical study on the theme of "sending" in John.

TH337 Wagner, C. Peter
Blazing the Way: A New Look at Acts—Sharing God's Power throughout the World. (Acts of the Holy Spirit Series, 3). Ventura, CAU: Regal Books, 1995. 255 pp. 0830717196.

Volume 3 of a new commentary on Acts, covering chapters 15 to 28.

TH338 Wagner, C. Peter
Iluminado el mundo. Miami, FLU: Editorial Unilit, 1996. 255 pp. Paper. 1560638478.

Spanish translation.

TH339 Wagner, C. Peter
Lighting the World. (Acts of the Holy Spirit Series, 2). Ventura, CAU: Regal Books, 1995. 240 pp. 0830717188.

Volume 2 of a new commentary on Acts, covering chapters 9 to 15.

TH340 Wagner, C. Peter
Spreading the Fire: A New Look at Acts—God's Training Manual for Every Christian. (Acts of the Holy Spirit Series, 1). Ventura, CAU: Regal Books, 1994. 240 pp. 0830717102.

Volume 1 of a new commentary on Acts, covering chapters 1 to 8, by Fuller Seminary's professor of church growth, emphasizing how the early missionaries overcame cultural barriers to the Gospel.

TH—MISSIONS: THEOLOGY

TH341 Walton, Martin
Witness in Biblical Scholarship: A Survey of Recent Studies, 1956-1980. (IIMO Research Pamphlet, 15). Leiden, NE: IIMO, 1986. iv, 79 pp. Paper. 9071387143.

A scholarly study on two basic words in the Bible, (the Hebrew *'ed* and the Greek *marturion*); with a critical survey of some twenty recent studies on topics related to these keywords.

TH342 Weber, Hans-Ruedi
La Invitación: La misión cristiana según San Mateo. (Paxis Bíblica). México, MX: Casa Unida de Publicaciones, 1979. 186 pp. Paper. No ISBN.

Spanish translation.

TH343 Weber, Hans-Ruedi
The Invitation: Matthew on Mission. New York, NYU: UMC, Board of Missions, 1971. xii, 147 pp. Paper. No ISBN.

Bible studies on the Matthean way of witnessing to Christ.

TH344 Weber, Hans-Ruedi
L'invitation au festin: Matthieu et la mission. Translated by Étienne de Peyer. Geneva, SZ: Labor et Fides, 1972. viii, 141 pp. No ISBN.

French translation.

TH345 Weber, Hans-Ruedi
Power: Focus for a Biblical Theology. Geneva, SZ: WCC Publications, 1989. xi, 204 pp. Paper. 2825409251.

A detailed analysis of how a biblical theology of power developed as an ordered bundle of faith traditions, which stand in tension with one another but converge in Jesus Christ; by the former director of biblical studies at the WCC.

TH346 West, Gerald O.
Biblical Hermeneutics of Liberation: Modes of Reading the Bible in the South African Context. (The Bible and Liberation Series). Pietermaritzburg, SA: Cluster Publications; Maryknoll, NYU: Orbis Books, 1995. vii, 2274 pp. Paper. 0958380791 (SA), 1570750203 (US).

Detailed development of a biblical hermeneutic for those committed to the poor and oppressed, with examples of interpretive approaches by black, feminist, and Latin American liberation theologians; originally published in 1991 (Pietermaritzburg, SA: Cluster Publications; Johannesburg, SA: Thorold's Africana Books).

TH347 Wildhaber, Bruno
Paganisme populaire et prédication apostolique: d'après l'exégèse de quelques séquences des Actes: éléments pour une théologie lucanienne de la mission. Geneva, SZ: Labor et Fides, 1987. 226 pp. Paper. 2830900456.

A scholarly study of the elements of popular paganism in the first century A.D. Graeco-Roman world, in relation to selected passages in the Book of Acts which reveal the Lucan theology of mission expressed in apostolic preaching.

TH348 Wilkins, John R., ed.
The Bible and God's Mission: An Adventure in Study to Rediscover and Rethink Some Biblical Motivations for the Christian Mission. New York, NYU: UMC, Board of Missions, 1962. 104 pp. Paper. No ISBN.

An eleven-session study guide on biblical motivations for the Christian mission in our world today.

TH349 Winter, Bruce W.
Seek the Welfare of the City: Christians as Benefactors and Citizens. (First Century Christians in the Graeco-Roman World Series). Grand Rapids, MIU: Eerdmans; Carlisle, ENK: Paternoster Press, 1994. ix, 245 pp. Paper. 0802840914 (US), 0853646333 (UK).

Scholarly analysis of evidence that early Christians were urged positively and unambiguously to do good, and thus contribute to the welfare of the city.

TH350 Wit, J. H. de
Leerlingen van de Armen. Amsterdam, NE: VU Uitgeverij, 1991. xvi, 383 pp. Paper. 9053830278.

A scholarly exploration of the question: "Can the reading of the Bible by common people contribute to a liberating exegesis?," with detailed analysis of the responses of Latin American biblical scholars C. Mesters, J. S. Croatto, and M. Schwantes.

TH351 Zinkuratire, Victor, and Angelo Colacrai, eds.
The African Bible: Biblical Text of the New American Bible. Nairobi, KE: Paulines Publications Africa, 1999. 2,176 pp. 996621450X.

In response to Pope John Paul II's initiative, the Daughters of St. Paul have collaborated with two general editors and over thirty biblical scholars to create a Bible that is "African" through study guides, introductions, notes, comments, cross-references, and illustrations.

TH352 Zorrilla, Hugo
La Fiesta de liberación de los oprimidos: Relectura de Jn 7:1-10:21. San José, CR: Ediciones SEBILA, 1981. 318 pp. Paper. No ISBN.

A biblical study on the Samaritan contribution to the evangelization of heterodox communities.

Pentecostalism

See also HI599, HI605, HI607, TH22, AM131, AM243, AM321, AM820, AM1102, and AM1381.

TH353 Aker, Benny C., and Gary B. McGee, eds.
Signs and Wonders in Ministry Today. Springfield, MOU: Gospel Publishing House, 1996. 128 pp. Paper. 0882433466.

Nine short essays by faculty members of the Assemblies of God Theological Seminary, on biblical, historical, and practical incentives to seek for signs and wonders in ministry.

TH354 Bomann, Rebecca Pierce
Faith in the Barrios: The Pentecostal Poor in Bogotá. Boulder, COU: Lynne Rienner Publishers, 1999. xiii, 162 pp. 155587827X.

An evangelical Christian, utilizing field research techniques, lives a simple life in the barrios of Columbia, and gains insights about the vibrancy of Pentecostal faith in the region.

TH355 Dayton, Donald W.
Raices Teológicas del Pentecostalismo. Translated by Elsa R. de Powell. Buenos Aires, AG: Nueva Creación; Grand Rapids, MIU: Eerdmans, 1991. xvi, 163 pp. Paper. 0802809219.

Spanish translation.

TH356 Dayton, Donald W.
Theological Roots of Pentecostalism. (Studies in Evangelicalism, 5). Grand Rapids, MIU: Asbury Press; Peabody, MAU: Hendrickson; Metuchen, NJU: Scarecrow, 1987. 199 pp. 031039371X (F), 0943565796 (H), 0810820374 (S).

A history of the roots and early theological development of Pentecostalism, based on the author's personal collection of more than 4,000 volumes related to this subject.

TH357 Dempster, Murray W., Byron D. Klaus, and Douglas Petersen, eds.
The Globalization of Pentecostalism: A Religion Made to Travel. Oxford, ENK: Regnum Books; Carlisle, ENK: Paternoster Press, 1999. xvii, 406 pp. Paper. 1870345290.

This ranging, scholarly collection of sixteen articles provides a window on contemporary Pentecostal scholarship from theological, missiological, hermeneutical, and social science perspectives.

TH358 Hollenweger, Walter J.
Pentecostalism: Origins and Developments Worldwide. Peabody, MAU: Hendrickson Publishers, 1997. xi, 495 pp. 0943575362.

A comprehensive assessment of the roots and development of Pentecostalism, including black, Catholic, evangelical, and ecumenical components, and of its significance in both religion and politics by the professor of mission at the University of Birmingham, England.

TH359 Jongeneel, J. A. B., ed.
Pentecost, Mission and Ecumenism: Essays on Intercultural Theology. (Studies in the Intercultural History of Christianity, 75). Frankfurt am Main, GW: Lang, 1992. x, 376 pp. 3631440103.

A *festschrift* in honor of Professor Walter J. Hollenweger containing twenty-six scholarly essays—six on Hollenweger's life and work as a professor of mission, and twenty on Pentecostalism and charismatic renewal in missiological and ecumenical perspective.

TH360 Moltmann, Jürgen, and Karl-Josef Kuschel, eds.
Pentecostal Movements as an Ecumenical Challenge. (*Concilium*, 1996/3). London, ENK: SCM Press; Maryknoll, NYU: Orbis Books, 1996. ix, 143 pp. Paper. 0334030382 (S), 1570750726 (O).

Seventeen short essays on distinctives of Pentecostalism by Catholic, conciliar Protestant, and Orthodox theologians.

TH361 Smith, Harold B., ed.
Pentecostals from the Inside Out. (Christianity Today Series). Wheaton, ILU: Victor Books, 1990. 153 pp. 0896935442.

A primer on Pentecostalism, with short essays by ten scholars; presenting to both outsiders and insiders the movement and its mission outreach.

Charismatic Movement

See also HI610-HI613, TH108, TH359, and EU111.

TH362 Koivisto, Juhani, ed.
Sitä lujempi on sana: näkökohtia uskon, elämän ja lähtyksen perusteista. (Tulevaisuus on Jumalan, 1; Lähetystrilogia, 1). Helsinki, FI: Uusi tie, 1987. 206 pp. 9516191711.

A description of the missiological thinking of the Finnish Lutheran Mission as a revivalist movement.

TH363 McDonnell, Kilian, ed.
Toward a New Pentecost for a New Evangelization: Malines Document I. Collegeville, MNU: Michael Glazier/Liturgical Press, 1993. vi, 72 pp. Paper. 0814658466.

A revised second edition of *Theological and Pastoral Orientations on the Catholic Charismatic Renewal* (1974), which came out of the pioneer international consultation of leaders in Catholic Charismatic Renewal held in Malines, Belgium, in 1974, under the sponsorship of Cardinal Suenens.

TH364 Poewe, Karla O., ed.
Charismatic Christianity as a Global Culture. (Studies in Comparative Religion). Columbia, SCU: University of South Carolina Press, 1994. xiv, 300 pp. 0872499960.

A collection of nine scholarly essays on contemporary charismatic Christianity, from perspectives of anthropology, sociology, history, theology, religious studies, and missiology.

TH365 Scotland, Nigel
Charismatics and the Next Millennium: Do They Have a Future? London, ENK: Hodder & Stoughton, 1995. viii, 296 pp. Paper. 0340627670.

An assessment of the Charismatic Movement (1975-1995)—its strengths and weaknesses.

TH366 Sjöberg, Kjell
Vision om mission. Örebro, SW: Evangeliipress, 1973. 123 pp. 9170380066.

A Bible study on missions today from a neo-Charismatic perspective.

TH367 Vines, Jerry
Spirit Works: Charismatic Practices and the Bible. Nashville, TNU: Broadman, 1999. 231 pp. Paper. 0805419969.

A study of the Charismatic Movement's past and present growth through historical, cultural, and scriptural perspectives on different manifestations of the Holy Spirit.

TH368 Wogen, Norris L., ed.
Jesus, Where are You Taking Us?: Messages from the First International Lutheran Conference on the Holy Spirit. Carol Stream, ILU: Creation House, 1973. 250 pp. No ISBN.

Ten papers from an inaugural conference on the Charismatic Movement for Lutherans, including those by Mel Tari on the Timor revival, and David du Plessis on the Holy Spirit in the ecumenical movement.

Liberation, General (including North America and Europe)

See also TH2, TH20, TH192, TH199, TH246, TH268, TH319, TH346, TH511, TH541, TH554, CR296, CR1173, EC100, EC208, EC243, CO140, ED145, ED148-ED149, SP24, SP27, AM239, AM380-AM381, AM391-AM394, AM405, AM426-AM427, AM466, AM469, AM495, AM511, AM1081-AM1082, AS143, and EU12.

TH369 Alfaro, Juan
Esperanza cristiana y liberación del hombre. Barcelona, SP: Editorial Herder, 1972. 250 pp. Paper. No ISBN.

A theological study on Christian hope as the only authentic liberation of humanity and the only true salvation of history.

TH370 Amirtham, Samuel, and J. S. Pobee, eds.
Theology by the People: Reflections on Doing Theology in Community. Geneva, SZ: WCC, 1986. x, 143 pp. Paper. 282540862X.

A collection of the papers presented at the Programme on Theological Education's consultation in Mexico in April 1985, which dealt with the understanding of "theology by the people."

TH371 Anderson, Gerald H., and Thomas F. Stransky, eds.
Mission Trends, no. 4: Liberation Theologies in North America and Europe. New York, NYU: Paulist Press; Grand Rapids, MIU: Eerdmans, 1979. xii, 289 pp. Paper. 0809121859 (P), 0802810792 (E).

Twenty-seven selections focusing on North American theologies relating mission and liberation, including black, feminist, Native American, Asian American, and Hispanic American voices.

TH372 Belli, Humberto, and Ronald H. Nash
Beyond Liberation Theology. Grand Rapids, MIU: Baker Books, 1992. 206 pp. Paper. 0801010225.

An evangelical critique of the "old" liberation theology of Latin America, and argument for a "new" liberation theology supportive of democratic capitalism; by the minister of education in democratic Nicaragua and the professor of philosophy and theology at Reformed Theological Seminary, Orlando, Florida.

TH373 Berghoef, Gerard, and Lester DeKoster
Liberation Theology: The Church's Future Shock. Grand Rapids, MIU: Christian's Library Press, 1984. 197 pp. 0934874077.

A polemical study guide based on the premise that liberation theology takes its structure from Marxism and rejects the authority of the Bible.

TH374 Beyerhaus, Peter
Theologie als Instrument der Befreiung: Die Rolle der neuen Volkstheologien in der ökumenischen Diskussion. (Theologie und Dienst, 49). Giessen, GW: Brunnen-Verlag, 1986. 54 pp. Paper. 3765590495.

An analysis by the noted German missiologist of the role of the new peoples' theologies of liberation in the Two-Thirds World in the ecumenical discussion of a theology of mission.

TH375 Biehl, João Guilherme
De igul pra igual: Um diálogo crítico entre a teologia da libertacao e as teologias negra, feminista e pacifista. Petrópolis, BL: Editora Vozes; Sao Leopoldo, BL: Editora Sinodal, 1987. 160 pp. Paper. No ISBN.

A critical comparative study of liberation, black, feminist, and peace theologies.

TH376 Boesak, Allan Aubrey, ed.
Om het zwart te zeggen: Een bundel opstellen over centrale thema's in de zwarte theologie. Kampen, NE: Kok, 1975. 133 pp. 9024202329.

A collection of writings by black theologians introduced by a South African "black" theologian to a Dutch audience.

TH377 Boff, Clodovis
Teología de lo Político: Sus Mediaciones. (Verdad e imagen, 61). Salamanca, SP: Ediciones Sígueme, 1980. 429 pp. 8430108009.

Spanish translation.

TH378 Boff, Clodovis
Teologia e prática: Teologia do político e suas mediações. (Publicações CID: Teologia, 15). Petrópolis, BL: Vozes, 1993. 407 pp. 8532609376.

A critical analysis of the epistemological presuppositions of any theology, clarifying the boundaries among theology, political and social sciences, hermeneutics, and praxis, by Brazil's leading liberation theologian; first published in 1978.

TH379 Boff, Clodovis
Theologie und Praxis: Die erkenntnis theoretischen Grundlagen der Theologie der Befreiung. Translated by E. Kuter and A. Johannemann. Munich, GW: Kaiser; Mainz, GW: Matthias-Grünewald, 1983. 357 pp. 3459015055 (K), 3786710651 (M).

German translation.

TH380 Boff, Clodovis
Theology and Praxis: Epistemological Foundations. Translated by Robert R. Barr. Maryknoll, NYU: Orbis Books, 1987. xxx, 379 pp. 088344416X.

English translation.

TH381 Boff, Leonardo
Church: Charism and Power: Liberation Theology and the Institutional Church. New York, NYU: Crossroad Publishing, 1986. 182 pp. Paper. 0824507266.

The controversial analysis by a leading liberation theologian of the oppression within the Catholic Church, and of its roots in present church structures.

TH382 Boff, Leonardo
Do Lugar do Pobre. (Publicáções CID, Teologia, 22). Petrópolis, BL: Vozes, 1984. 151 pp. No ISBN.

An exploration of the extensive and historic changes that must happen before peoples can live free of exploitation; a liberation theology which is a response to Vatican II, reflecting on the meaning of the Eucharist, the Cross, and the Resurrection in a world of injustice.

TH383 Boff, Leonardo
Teología desde el lugar del pobre. Translated by Jesús García-Abril. (Colección Presencia teológica, 26). Santander, SP: Sal Terrae, 1986. 148 pp. 8429307419.

Spanish translation.

TH384 Boff, Leonardo
When Theology Listens to the Poor. Translated by Robert R. Barr. San Francisco, CAU: Harper & Row, 1988. xi, 147 pp. 0062541625.

English translation.

TH385 Boff, Leonardo, and Clodovis Boff
Liberation Theology: From Dialogue to Confrontation. New York, NYU: Harper & Row; Toronto, ONC: Fitzhenry and Whiteside, 1986. 100 pp. Paper. 0866835288 (US).

A primer for understanding one of the controversial religious movements of today, with a precise summary of liberation theology by a Franciscan, and by a priest from the Order of Servants of Mary—both missionaries in Brazil.

TH386 Boff, Leonardo, and Clodovis Boff
Da Libertação: o sentido teológico das libertaçoes socio-históricas. (Publicaçóes CID. Teologia, 19). Petrópolis, BL: Editora Vozes, 1985. 114 pp. No ISBN.

In this monograph, the brother Brazilian liberation theologians strike a balance between the theological and political meanings of the concept of liberation; a fourth edition.

TH387 Boff, Leonardo, and Clodovis Boff
Libertad y Liberacion. (Pedal, 154). Salamanca, SP: Ediciones Sígueme, 1985. 169 pp. 843010884X.

Second edition of the Spanish translation.

TH388 Boff, Leonardo, and Clodovis Boff
Salvation and Liberation: In Search of a Balance between Faith and Politics. Maryknoll, NYU: Orbis Books; Melbourne, AT: Dove Communications, 1984. viii, 119 pp. Paper. 0883444518 (US), 0859243257 (AT).
English translation of *Da Libertaçao* (1979).

TH389 Borgman, Erik
Sporen van de bevrijdende God: Universitaire theologie in aansluiting op Latijnsamerikaanse bevrijdingstheologie, zwarte theologie en feministische theologie: een wetenschappelijke proeve op het gebied van de godgeleerdheid. (Kerk en theologie in context, 7). Kampen, NE: Kok, 1990. xviii, 360 pp. 902426510X.
A positive assessment of various theologies of liberation (Latin American, feminist, black American, and black South African), which affirms that God is present in all things and all places; with critique of all academic theologies and missiologies that lose these traces of God.

TH390 Brackely, Dean
Divine Revolution: Salvation and Liberation in Catholic Thought. Maryknoll, NYU: Orbis Books, 1996. xxiv, 197 pp. Paper. 157075055.
A scholarly analysis of the changes that have taken place in Catholic theology in its understanding of salvation and liberation in the last fifty years; with special attention to the thought of Jacques Maritain, Karl Rahner, and Gustavo Gutiérrez.

TH391 Brown, Robert McAfee
Liberation Theology: An Introductory Guide. Louisville, KYU: Westminster John Knox, 1993. xiii, 143 pp. Paper. 0664254241.
A lively explanation of liberation theology for North American readers who may have no previous knowledge of this dynamic recent Christian movement.

TH392 Brown, Robert McAfee
Theology in a New Key: Responding to Liberation Themes. Philadelphia, PAU: Westminster Press, 1978. 212 pp. Paper. 0664242049.
An overview of Latin American liberation theology and its relevance for North American Christians.

TH393 Cadorette, Curt et al., eds.
Liberation Theology: An Introductory Reader. Maryknoll, NYU: Orbis Books, 1992. viii, 307 pp. Paper. 0883448017.
A collection of readings from a cross section of the world's leading exponents of liberation; grouped under themes of methodology, Christology, ecclesiology, and spirituality.

TH394 Castillo, José Maria
Los Pobres y la Teología: Qué Queda de la Teología de la Liberación? (Collección Cristianismo y Sociedad, 49). Bilbao, SP: Desclée de Brouwer, 1997. 376 pp. 8433012681.
Exploration of the development of liberation theology in today's global context, including issues of ethics, justice, ecclesiology, dignity, and hope.

TH395 Ceresko, Anthony R.
Introduction to Old Testament Wisdom: A Spirituality for Liberation. Maryknoll, NYU: Orbis Books, 1999. xi, 205 pp. Paper. 157075277X.
A comprehensive coverage of wisdom literature within a liberative framework.

TH396 Chenu, Bruno, ed.
La théologie noire américaine. Translated by Françoise Reynaud. Lyon, FR: Faculté de théologie, 1982. v, 55 pp. Paper. 2853170284.
A sourcebook on black theology in North America; prepared by the Faculty of Theology, Lyon, France.

TH397 Chopp, Rebecca S.
The Praxis of Suffering: An Interpretation of Liberation and Political Theologies. Maryknoll, NYU: Orbis Books, 1986. xi, 178 pp. Paper. 0883442566.
A scholarly study of the fundamental characteristics of liberation theology which includes resources from Latin American liberation theology and German political theology.

TH398 Codina, Victor
Seguir a Jesús hoy: De la modernidad a la solidaridad. (Pedal, 187). Salamanca, SP: Ediciones Sígueme, 1988. 291 pp. Paper. 843011047X.
A discussion of the movement from secularism to liberation, and from development to justice, in the Roman Catholic Church in Latin America; originally published under the title *De la Modernidad a la Solidaridad: Seguir a Jesús hoy* (1984).

TH399 Cone, James H.
Black Theology and Black Power. New York, NYU: Seabury Press, 1969. x, 165 pp. No ISBN.
A pioneer development of themes in black theology.

TH400 Cone, James H.
A Black Theology of Liberation. (Twentieth Anniversary Edition). Maryknoll, NYU: Orbis Books, 1990. xx, 214 pp. Paper. 0883446855.
The third edition of this classic of black liberation theology (first, 1970; second, 1986); with critical reflections by six prominent scholars and an afterword by the author.

TH401 Cone, James H.
God of the Oppressed. New York, NYU: Seabury Press, 1975. viii, 280 pp. 0816402639.
A black theology of liberation relating the black experience to Scripture and Jesus Christ, by the prominent black theologian and professor of theology at Union Theological Seminary in New York.

TH402 Cone, James H.
Teologaia Negra de la Liberación. Translated by Manuel Mercader. Buenos Aires, AG: Lohlae, 1973. 180 pp. No ISBN.
Spanish translation.

TH403 Cone, James H.
Teologia Nera della Liberazione e Black Power. Translated by Bruno Corsani, and Mirella Corsani. Torino, IT: Claudiana, 1973. 224 pp. No ISBN.
Italian translation.

TH404 Cone, James H.
Théologie noire de la libération. Paris, FR: L'Harmattan, 1977. 100 pp. No ISBN.
French translation of *A Black Theology of Liberation* (1970).

TH405 Conference of European Churches
European Theology Challenged by the Worldwide Church: Study Material for Use in Churches and Theological Faculties, Seminaries and Congregations. (Occasional Paper, 8). Geneva, SZ: CEC, 1976. 145 pp. Paper. No ISBN.
Report and papers from a study consultation (Geneva, 29 March-2 April 1976).

TH—MISSIONS: THEOLOGY

TH406 Conn, Harvie M. et al.
Evangelicals and Liberation. Edited by Carl E. Armerding.
(Studies in the World Church and Missions, 6). Nutley, NJU:
Presbyterian & Reformed Publishing; Grand Rapids, MIU:
Baker Books, 1977. ix, 136 pp. Paper. No ISBN.

Seven essays by prominent evangelical theologians offering critical appreciation of Latin American and black theologies of liberation.

TH407 Damico, Linda H.
The Anarchist Dimension of Liberation Theology. (American
University Studies, 7: Theology and Religion, 28). New York,
NYU: Lang, 1987. xi, 213 pp. 0820404438.

A scholarly analysis of the parallels between themes in
20th-century Latin American liberation theology, and ideas
found in 19th-century European anarchism.

TH408 Dussel, Enrique D.
Philosophy of Liberation. Maryknoll, NYU: Orbis Books,
1985. vii, 240 pp. Paper. 0883444054.

A provisional philosophical framework for a theology of
liberation; by the president of the CEHILA.

TH409 Eicher, Peter, ed.
Theologie der Befreiung im Gespräch. Munich, GW: Kösel-
Verlag, 1985. 128 pp. Paper. 3466202752.

A series of dialogues with well-known liberation theologians (Leonardo Boff, Peter Eicher, Horst Goldstein, Gustavo
Gutiérrez, and Josef Sayer), addressing the issue of whether
liberation theology is consistent with the biblical Good News.

TH410 Ellis, Marc H., and Otto Maduro, eds.
*The Future of Liberation Theology: Essays in Honor of Gusta-
vo Gutiérrez.* Maryknoll, NYU: Orbis Books, 1989. xviii, 518
pp. 0883444216.

A collection of forty-two original essays on liberation
theology with the contributions of Gustavo Gutiérrez; originally presented in July-August 1988 at Maryknoll, New York.

TH411 Ferm, Deane William, ed.
Third World Liberation Theologies: A Reader. Maryknoll,
NYU: Orbis Books, 1986. xi, 386 pp. Paper. 0883445166.

A sourcebook of the writings of twenty-seven foremost
liberation theologians of Asia, Africa, and Latin America;
written as a companion volume to *Third World Liberation
Theologies: An Introductory Survey.*

TH412 Ferm, Deane William
Third World Liberation Theologies: An Introductory Survey.
Maryknoll, NYU: Orbis Books, 1986. ix, 150 pp. Paper.
0883445158.

An initial overview of the liberation theologies of Latin
America, Africa, and Asia, dealing with major themes and including summaries of the contributions and criticisms of seventy Third World theologians.

**TH413 Freire, Paulo, Eduardo I. Bodino-Malumba, James H.
Cone, Hugo Assmann Bodino-Malumba, Eduardo I., Cone,
James H., and Assmann, Hugo**
Teología Negra: Teología de la Liberación. (Estudios
Sígueme, 11). Salamanca, SP: Ediciones Sígueme, 1974. 136
pp. Paper. 8430106049.

Spanish translation of *A Symposium on Black Theology and
the Latin American Theology of Liberation* (Geneva, SZ: WCC).

TH414 Gardiner, James J., and James Deotis Roberts, eds.
Quest for a Black Theology. Philadelphia, PAU: Pilgrim Press,
1971. xiii, 111 pp. 0829801960.

Six essays by African American theologians originally
presented at the "Black Church/Black Theology" conference
at Georgetown University (Washington, DC, May 1969).

TH415 Getz, Lorine M., and Ruy O. Costa, eds.
Struggle for Solidarity: Liberation Theologies in Tension.
Minneapolis, MNU: Fortress Press, 1992. 171 pp. Paper.
0800625285.

A compendium of essays on issues and dilemmas posed
by the challenge of solidarity to five paradigms of liberation
theologies (North American black, feminist, Hispanic, post-
Holocaust Jewish, and Latin American).

TH416 Gibellini, Rosino
Il Dibattito sulla Teologia della Liberazione. (Giornale de
teologia, 166). Brescia, IT: Editrice Queriniana, 1986. vi, 146
pp. No ISBN.

A general overview of liberation theology with comments
on the seminal writings of major theologians, an examination
of Vatican documents on liberation theology, and responses
by its advocates.

TH417 Gibellini, Rosino
The Liberation Theology Debate. Maryknoll, NYU: Orbis
Books, 1988. vi, 120 pp. Paper. 088344271X.

English translation.

TH418 Goizueta, Roberto S.
*Caminemos con Jesús: Toward a Hispanic/Latino Theology
of Accompaniment.* Maryknoll, NYU: Orbis Books, 1995. xii,
224 pp. Paper. 1570750343.

The former president of the Academy of Catholic Hispanic Theologians of the United States links the socio-political approaches of liberation theologies with the aesthetic approaches to prayer and celebration of popular Catholicism in
his Hispanic/Latino theology.

TH419 Goizueta, Roberto S.
*Liberation, Method, and Dialogue: Enrique Dussel and North
American Theological Discourse.* (American Academy of
Religion Academy Series, 58). Atlanta, GAU: Scholars Press,
1988. xxiv, 174 pp. 1555401899 (hdbk), 1555401902 (pbk).

An analysis of the themes of domination and liberation in
the methodology of Enrique Dussel, their affinity to the thought
of Bernard Lonergan of North America, and their misinterpre-
tation by critics (Michael Novak, Dennis McCann, and Roger
Vekemans).

TH420 González, Justo L.
*Mañana: Theologie aus der Sicht der Hispanics Nordameri-
kas.* Translated by Hans-Werner Gensichen and Anneliese
Gensichen. (Theologie der Ökumene). Göttingen, GW: Vandenhoeck & Ruprecht, 1994. 162 pp. 3525563299.

German translation.

TH421 González, Justo L.
Mañana: Christian Theology from a Hispanic Perspective.
Nashville, TNU: Abingdon, 1990. 184 pp. Paper. 0687230675.

A concise systematic theology from US Hispanic perspective; by the noted Protestant Cuban American theologian and
historian of doctrine.

TH422 González, Justo L.
Out of Every Tribe and Nation: Christian Theology at the Ethnic Roundtable. Nashville, TNU: Abingdon, 1992. 128 pp. Paper. 0687298601.

A theology for "the whole people of God" presented as visions of catholicity, the Word, the world, salvation, and the church — developed by participants of the United Methodist Roundtable of Ethnic.Minority Theologians (1987-91).

TH423 Gottwald, Norman K., and A. Horsley Richard, eds.
The Bible and Liberation: Political and Social Hermeneutics. (The Bible and Liberation). Maryknoll, NYU: Orbis Books; London, ENK: SPCK, 1993. xxi, 558 pp. Paper. 0883448491 (O), 0281047197 (S).

A revised edition of a classic anthology, providing a social class analysis of the biblical texts; with mostly new selections by Asian, African, African American, Latin American, and feminist scholars.

TH424 Guerrero, Andres G.
A Chicano Theology. Maryknoll, NYU: Orbis Books, 1987. v, 186 pp. Paper. 0883444070.

An introduction to the history and experience of oppression, in both secular and religious symbolism of the Chicano in US society; with essential elements of a Chicano theology of liberation.

TH425 Hayes, Diana L.
And Still We Rise: An Introduction to Black Liberation Theology. Mahwah, NJU: Paulist Press, 1996. iii, 219 pp. Paper. 0809136228.

A primer on major sources, issues and concerns of black theology in the United States, including womanist and black Catholic theology.

TH426 Hennelly, Alfred T., ed.
Liberation Theology: A Documentary History. Maryknoll NYU: Orbis Books, 1990. xxvi, 547 pp. Paper. 0883445921 (hdbk), 088344593X (pbk).

A thorough reference work on the liberation theology movement—its background, origins, development, and surrounding controversy; bringing together fifty-nine important documents from many sources.

TH427 Hennelly, Alfred T.
Liberation Theologies: The Global Pursuit of Justice. Mystic, CTU: Twenty-Third Publications, 1995. 382 pp. Paper. 0896226476.

An introduction to various liberation theologies (Latin American, feminist, black, Hispanic, African, Asian, First World Ecotheology, and those of the world religions) and to principal theologians; designed as a textbook with study questions and suggested readings.

TH428 Hennelly, Alfred T.
Theology for a Liberating Church: The New Praxis of Freedom. Washington, DCU: Georgetown University Press, 1989. ix, 207 pp. Paper. 0878404732 (hdbk), 0878404740 (pbk).

A detailed analysis of the dialectic between theory and practice in Latin American liberation theology, relating it to recent Vatican documents on liberation theology, and needs for a new theology for North America.

TH429 Herzog, Frederick
God-Walk: Liberation Shaping Dogmatics. Maryknoll, NYU: Orbis Books, 1988. xxxii, 272 pp. 0883446073.

A text which lays the foundation for a North American theology of liberation, and the struggle for social justice focusing on Christian doctrine and dogma from the liberationist perspective.

TH430 Herzog, Frederick
Liberation Theology: Liberation in the Light of the Fourth Gospel. New York, NYU: Seabury Press, 1972. 272 pp. 0816402418.

Liberation themes developed for North American white Christians.

TH431 Hinkelammert, Franz J. et al.
Teología Alemana y Teología Latinoamerica de la liberación: Un esfuerzo de diálogo. (Historia del la iglesia y de la teología). San José, CR: DEI, 1990. 123 pp. Paper. 9977830142.

Nine short essays relating themes of liberation in Latin American liberation theology to the thought of German theologians (Luther, Müntzer, Melanchthon, Bonhoeffer, Rahner, Bultmann, and Moltmann).

TH432 Honig, A. G.
Jezus Christus, de bevrijder, de inhoud van de missionaire verkondiging. (Kamper Cahiers, 25). Kampen, NE: Kok, 1975. 40 pp. 9024205352.

A valuable survey in Dutch of developments to 1974 in liberation and black theology, arguing that their deeper dimensions come from biblical rather than Marxist thought.

TH433 Hopkins, Dwight N.
Black Theology USA and South Africa: Politics, Culture, and Liberation. (The Bishop Henry McNeal Turner Studies in North American Black Religion, 4). Maryknoll, NYU: Orbis Books, 1989. xi, 249 pp. Paper. 0882446391.

A scholarly introduction to the black theologies in the United States and South Africa, with an analysis of the contribution of eight theologians in each country, and of the dialogue that has taken place between them.

TH434 Hopkins, Dwight N.
Introducing Black Theology of Liberation. Maryknoll, NYU: Orbis Books, 1999. x, 237 pp. Paper. 1570752869.

Founded upon the religious experience of African Americans in slavery, this book provides a historical survey of various streams of black theology, including womanist theology.

TH435 Hopkins, Dwight N.
Shoes That Fit Our Feet: Sources for a Constructive Black Theology. Maryknoll, NYU: Orbis Books, 1993. xi, 242 pp. Paper. 0883448483.

An analysis of certain source documents for Black theology, including slave narratives, the novels of Toni Morrison, and the writings of W. E. B. DuBois, M. L. King, Jr., and Malcolm X.

TH436 Hundley, Raymond C.
Radical Liberation Theology: An Evangelical Response. Wilmore, KYU: Bristol Books, 1987. 141 pp. 0917851048.

An introduction to liberation theology for North American evangelicals by an OMF missionary to Colombia; organized around questions asked frequently concerning liberation theology; with an extensive bibliography.

TH437 Isasi-Díaz, Ada María, and Fernando F. Segovia, eds.
Hispanic/Latino Theology: Challenge and Promise. Minneapolis, MNU: Fortress Press, 1996. 382 pp. Paper. 0800629213.

Sources, the locus, and expressions of Hispanic/Latino theology in the United States by nineteen scholars from that tradition; originally presented at a conference at the Theological School of Drew University, 15-17 April 1994.

TH438 Kee, Alistair
Marx and the Failure of Liberation Theology. Philadelphia, PAU: Trinity Press International; London, ENK: SCM Press, 1990. xii, 302 pp. Paper. 0334024374.

An argument that the failure of liberation theology stems from a lack of commitment to Karl Marx and a reluctance to apply his philosophy to the contemporary situation.

TH439 Knitter, Paul F., ed.
Pluralism and Oppression: Theology in World Perspective. (The Annual Publication of the College Theology Society, 34). Lanham, MDU: University Press of America, 1993. xii, 278 pp. 0819179043 (hdbk), 0819179051 (pbk).

Essays by Raimundo Panikkar, Thomas Berry, Jon Sobrino, and Enrique Dussel, that explore possibilities of uniting concerns for religious pluralism, ecology, and human liberation.

TH440 Lane, Dermot A., ed.
Liberation Theology: An Irish Dialogue. Dublin, IE: Gill & Macmillan, 1977. 104 pp. 0717108627.

Introductions to the main themes of liberation theology; originally presented to the 1976 annual conference of the Irish Theological Association; including lectures by Bishop Francisco Claver of the Philippines.

TH441 Lehmann, Karl, Heinz Schürmann, and Olegario de González de Cardedal
Theologie der Befreiung. (International Theological Commission). (Sammlung Horizonte, 10). Einsiedeln, SZ: Johannes Verlag, 1977. 195 pp. 3265101932.

Papers on liberation theology read at the 1976 meeting of the International Theological Commission, together with the final document.

TH442 *Liberation Theology and the Vatican Document*
Quezon City, PP: Claretian Publications, 1988. 3 vols. 9715010237 (vol. 1), 9715011330 (vol. 2), 9715011616 (vol. 3).

Essays by Third World theologians in response to the Vatican document, "Instruction on Christian Freedom and Liberatio" [vol. 1, *A General Survey*, vii, 110 pp; vol. 2, *A Philippine Perspective*, viii, 170 pp; vol. 3, *Perspective from the Third World*, ix, 159 pp.]

TH443 Maimela, Simon S., and Dwight N. Hopkins, eds.
We Are One Voice. Braamfontein, SA: Skotaville Publishers, 1989. xix, 166 pp. Paper. 0947009795.

A compilation of papers by theologians and pastors reaffirming the thrust of the black poor, "God's chosen people," with an examination of how diverse black theologians continue to write about white theologians.

TH444 Massabki, Charles
Le Christ, libération du monde aujourd'hui. Paris, FR: Fayard, 1975. ix, 289 pp. Paper. No ISBN.

A French Catholic theologian's advocacy of liberation as a central theme for the church's mission and ministry in the world.

TH445 Massabki, Charles
Christ, Liberation of the World Today. Translated by Eloise Therese Mescall. New York, NYU: Alba House, 1978. xi, 312 pp. Paper. 0818903740.

English translation.

TH446 Massabki, Charles
Cristo liberazione del mondo oggi. Rome, IT: Città Nuova Editrice, 1977. 330 pp. Paper. No ISBN.

Italian translation.

TH447 McElvaney, William K.
Good News Is Bad News Is Good News. Maryknoll, NYU: Orbis Books, 1980. xii, 132 pp. Paper. 0883441578.

A primer for middle-class North American Christians on themes of liberation theologies (black, feminist, and Latin American).

TH448 McGlasson, Paul C.
Another Gospel: A Confrontation with Liberation Theology. Grand Rapids, MIU: Baker Books, 1994. 94 pp. Paper. 0801063159.

An evangelical theologian's critique of liberation theology, and of mainline Christianity's priority to contextualize the Gospel as a counter-cultural movement for political change.

TH449 McGovern, Arthur F.
Liberation Theology and Its Critics: Toward an Assessment. Maryknoll, NYU: Orbis Books, 1989. xxii, 281 pp. Paper. 0883445956.

A comprehensive and systematic explication of the diverse criticisms of liberation theology; with a historical overview and rigorous defense by the distinguished Jesuit Professor of Philosophy at the University of Detroit (US).

TH450 Metz, René
Idéologies de libération et message du salut. Edited by Jean Schlick. (Hommes et Église, 4). Strasbourg, FR: CERDIC-Publications, 1973. 222 pp. 2850970018 (fr).

Reports and papers by Protestant and Catholic theologians comparing liberation concepts in Marxism with those in ecumenical, feminist and Latin American theologies; originally presented at the fourth Cerdic Colloquium (Strasbourg, France, 10-12 May 1973).

TH451 Metz, René, and Jean Schlick, eds.
Liberation Theology and the Message of Salvation: Papers of the Fourth Cerdic Colloquium Strasbourg, May 10-12, 1973. Translated by David G. Gelzer. (Pittsburgh Theological Monograph Series, 20). Pittsburgh, PAU: Pickwick, 1978. ix, 150 pp. Paper. 0915138263.

English translation.

TH452 Min, Anselm Kyongsuk
Dialectic of Salvation: Issues in Theology of Liberation. Albany, NYU: SUNY Press, 1989. x, 207 pp. 0887069088 (hdbk), 0887069096 (pbk).

A scholarly examination of the philosophical sources of "theology of liberation," and of the polemical issues raised for and against it by Cardinal Ratzinger, Schubert Ogden, Dennis McCann, and others.

TH453 Núñez C., Emilio Antonio
Liberation Theology. Translated by Paul E. Sywulka. Chicago, ILU: Moody, 1985. 304 pp. 0802448933.

An introduction to liberation theology from an evangelical perspective.

TH454 Nnamani, Amuluche Gregory

The Paradox of a Suffering God: On the Classical, Modern-Western and Third World Struggles to Harmonise the Incompatible Attributes of the Trinitarian God. (Studies in the Intercultural History of Christianity, 95). Frankfurt am Main, GW: Lang, 1995. 428 pp. Paper. 3631490321 (GE), 082042935X (US).

A comparative study of the classical, Western, and Third World approaches to the reality of God, and particularly to the issue of divine suffering; originally submitted as a Th.D. dissertation at the University of Innsbruck, Austria, in 1994.

TH455 Novak, Michael

Will It Liberate?: Questions about Liberation Theology. Lanham, MDU: Madison Books, 1991. xxiv, 311 pp. Paper. 0819180602.

A revision of the first edition (Paulist Press, 1986) by liberation theology's sharpest North American critic, who asks, "How well does liberation theology free people from economic, political, and cultural bondage?"

TH456 Olivier, Bernard

Développement ou libération?: Pour une théologie qui prend parti. Brussels, BE: Éditions Vie Ouvrière, 1973. 181 pp. No ISBN.

An early argument for a theology of liberation rather than a theology of development, based on biblical and contemporary analysis by the Belgian National Commission on Justice and Peace of the Catholic Church.

TH457 Pernia, Antonio M.

God's Kingdom and Human Liberation: A Study of G. Gutiérrez, L. Boff and J. L. Segundo. Manila, PH: Divine Word Publications, 1990. x, 270 pp. Paper. 9715100465.

Originally presented as a doctoral dissertation at the Pontifical Gregorian University in Rome, this book attempts to shed light on the events of human liberation in history in relation to the Kingdom of God; represented by three of its most important personalities.

TH458 Persaud, Winston D.

The Theology of the Cross and Marx's Anthropology: A View from the Caribbean. (American University Studies, 7: Theology and Religion, 84). New York, NYU: Lang, 1991. xiii, 295 pp. 0820414093.

A scholarly analysis of Marx's anthropology, the theology of the Cross (Luther, Moltmann, Gutiérrez, and Sobrino), and the contemporary relationship of Christianity and Marxism in the Caribbean; originally presented as a Ph.D. thesis (University of St. Andrews, Scotland, 1980).

TH459 Peter-Raoul, Mar, Linda Rennie Forcey, and Robert Fredrick Hunter, eds.

Yearning to Breathe Free: Liberation Theologies in the United States. Maryknoll, NYU: Orbis Books, 1990. xiii, 242 pp. Paper. 0883447320.

Twenty-five essays by representatives of communities of Hispanics, African Americans, Native Americans, Asians, rural poor, and homeless in the United States, speaking out about their conditions, emerging theologies, and consequences of these theologies put into action.

TH460 Planas, Richardo

Liberation Theology: The Political Expression of Religion. Kansas City, MOU: Sheed & Ward, 1986. vi, 289 pp. Paper. 0934134995.

A presentation of liberation theology from the standpoint of political analysis, assessing its relationship to Marxism, the politics of social change, and the churches.

TH461 Richard, Pablo

El Movimento de Jesús: Después de su Resurrección y antes de la Iglesia: Una interpretación liberadora de los Hechos de los Apóstolos. (Colección Biblia, 71). Quito, EC: "Tierra Nueva" —Vicaría Sur de Quito; Cuenca, EC: EDICAY-Iglesia de Cuenca; Quito, EC: Centro Biblico "Verbo Divino," 1998. 192 pp. Paper. No ISBN.

A commentary on the Acts of the Apostles from the perspective of the church's mission, and of liberation theology.

TH462 Roberts, James Deotis

A Black Political Theology. Philadelphia, PAU: Westminster Press, 1974. 238 pp. 0664249884.

A theology "growing out of the experience of the black American"—a revisit of themes of reconciliation and liberation by the dean of the School of Theology at Virginia Union University.

TH463 Roberts, James Deotis

Black Theology in Dialogue. Philadelphia, PAU: Westminster Press, 1987. 132 pp. Paper. 0664240224.

Essays on the relationship of American black thought to African, liberation, feminist, Asian, and Euro-American theologies covering issues of love, justice, power, and evil.

TH464 Roberts, James Deotis

Liberation and Reconciliation: A Black Theology. Maryknoll, NYU: Orbis Books, 1994. xix, 119 pp. Paper. 088344951X.

A revised edition of a classic (1971) articulation of black theology, with new introduction and bibliography.

TH465 Rowland, Christopher

The Cambridge Companion to Liberation Theology. (Cambridge Companions to Religion). Cambridge, ENK: Cambridge University Press, 1999. xviii, 260 pp. 0521461448 (hdbk), 0521467071 (pbk).

An introduction in eleven essays to the history and characteristics of liberation theology in its various forms in different parts of the world.

TH466 Rowland, Christopher, and Mark Corner

Liberating Exegesis: The Challenge of Liberation Theology to Biblical Studies. Louisville, KYU: Westminster John Knox, 1989. viii, 205 pp. Paper. 066425084X.

An extensive study identifying the biblical and theoretical foundations of liberation theology, the ways in which it affects the reading of the canonical accounts of Jesus, and arguing for its universality.

TH467 Schipani, Daniel S., ed.

Freedom and Discipleship: Liberation Theology in an Anabaptist Perspective. Maryknoll, NYU: Orbis Books, 1989. ix, 188 pp. 0883445417.

Fifteen scholarly essays on liberation theology from an Anabaptist perspective, covering themes of discipleship, justice, peace, non-violence, freedom, and renewal.

TH468 Shaull, Richard
The Reformation and Liberation Theology: Insights for the Challenges of Today. Louisville, KYU: Westminster John Knox, 1991. 136 pp. Paper. 0664252222.

A reinterpretation out of the author's experience with Latin American liberation theology and Christian base communities, arguing that the 16th-century Protestant Reformation was a liberation movement analogous to that taking place in Christian communities in the Third World.

TH469 Sobrino, Jon
Liberación con espíritu: Apuntes para una nueva espiritualidad. (Coleccióm Teología latinoamericana, 9). San Salvador, ES: UCA Editores, 1987. 219 pp. 8484051021.

Second edition of a text coming out of the experience of El Salvador, dealing with spirituality and liberation historically, theologically, and politically; originally published by Editorial Sal Terrae (1985).

TH470 Sobrino, Jon
Spirituality of Liberation: Toward Political Holiness. Translated by Robert R. Barr. Maryknoll, NYU: Orbis Books, 1988. x, 189 pp. Paper. 0883446170 (hdbk), 0883446162 (pbk).
English translation.

TH471 Sobrino, Jon, and Attilio Cancian
Espiritualidade da Liberta ção: estrutura e conteúdos. São Paulo, BL: Ediçõ Loyola, 1992. 214 pp. 8515006804.
Portuguese translation.

TH472 Sponheim, Paul R.
The Pulse of Creation: God and the Transformation of the World. Minneapolis, MNU: Fortress Press, 1999. xii, 235 pp. Paper. 0800631889.

Utilizing concepts of interruption, calling, and relationship, the author formulates a theology of creative transformation, which is a North American version of liberation theology.

TH473 Tabb, William K., ed.
Churches in Struggle: Liberation Theologies and Social Change in North America. New York, NYU: Monthly Review Press, 1986. 331 pp. 0853456925 (hdbk), 0853456933 (pbk).

A collection of twenty-five essays by theologians and Christian social activists in North America who are committed to the struggle for social justice, and see the biblical message as profoundly radical.

TH474 Tamayo Acosta, Juan José
Para Comprender la Teología de la Liberación. Estella, SP: Verbo Divino, 1989. 295 pp. Paper. 8471515997.

A systematic presentation of liberation theology: its origins, content, reception and rejection, and its principal representatives.

TH475 Tesfai, Yacob, ed.
The Scandal of a Crucified World: Perspectives on the Cross and Suffering. Maryknoll, NYU: Orbis Books, 1994. ix, 155 pp. Paper. 0883449765.

Ten essays by theologians from five continents—mostly Third World understandings of the Cross and suffering—originally presented at a consultation (Nice, France, 1992) sponsored by the Institute for Ecumenical Research.

TH476 Théraios, Démetre
Le malaise chrétien: archétypes marxistes de la théologie de liberation. Geneva, SZ: Georg; Paris, FR: OEIL, 1987. 380 pp. 2825701432.*

A polemic against the use of Marxist categories of thought and social analysis by liberation theologians.

TH477 Verkuyl, Johannes
De boodschap der bevrijding in deze tijd. Kampen, NE: Kok, 1971. 132 pp. No ISBN.

Second edition of a popular exposition of the meaning of salvation for the world today: what it entails, how Christ can be savior and liberator in present world circumstances, and how the church should proclaim Christ the Savior and Liberator to modern persons; by the professor and head of the Department of Mission and Evangelism at the Free University, Amsterdam.

TH478 Verkuyl, Johannes
The Message of Liberation in Our Age. Translated by Dale Cooper. Grand Rapids, MIU: Eerdmans, 1972. 110 pp. Paper. 0802814379.
English translation.

TH479 Wilmore, Gayraud S., and James H. Cone, eds.
Black Theology: A Documentary History, 1966-1979. Maryknoll, NYU: Orbis Books, 1979. ix, 657 pp. Paper. 0883440415 (hdbk), 0883440423 (pbk).

An indispensable sourcebook on the development of black theology in the United States from 1964 to 1979, with fifteen essays on the relationship between black theology and Third World theologies.

TH480 Wilmore, Gayraud S., and James H. Cone, eds.
Teologia negra. Translated by Euclides Carneiro da Silva. (Colécao Pesquisa e projeto, 7). São Paulo, BL: Edições Paulinas, 1986. 566 pp. 850500342X.
Portuguese translation.

TH481 Witvliet, Theo
Een plaats onder de zon: bevrijdingstheologie in de derde wereld. Baarn, NE: Ten Have, 1984. 208 pp. Paper. 9025951317.

A survey of liberation theologies in North America (black theology), Africa, the Caribbean, Latin America, and Asia (esp. Korea, *minjung* theology) as the dawn of a new ecumenical theology.

TH482 Witvliet, Theo
A Place in the Sun: An Introduction to Liberation Theology in the Third World. Maryknoll, NYU: Orbis Books; London, ENK: SCM Press, 1985. ix, 182 pp. Paper. 0883444046.
English translation.

TH483 Witvliet, Theo
The Way of the Black Messiah: The Hermeneutical Challenge of Black Theology as a Theology of Liberation. (Proefschrift Theol. Fac. Universiteit van Amsterdam). Oak Park, ILU: Meyer-Stone Books, 1987. xx, 332 pp. 0940989093 (hdbk), 0940989042 (pbk).
English translation.

TH484 Witvliet, Theo
De weg van de zwarte Messias: De hermeneutische uitdaging van zwarte theologie als een theologie van bevrijding. (Proefschrift Theol. Fac. Universiteit van Amsterdam). Baarn, NE: Ten Have, 1984. 351 pp. No ISBN.

A doctoral thesis on the hermeneutics of black theology in the United States as a theology of liberation.

TH485 Witvliet, Theo, ed.
Berijdingstheologie in de Derde Wereld: Teksten uit Azië, Afrika en Latijns-Amerika. (Sleutelteksten in godsdienst en theologie, 9). Gravenhage, NE: Meinema, 1990. 310 pp. Paper. 9021161087.

Texts from theologies of liberation in Asia, Africa, and Latin America; chosen and introduced by a professor at the Theological Faculty of the University of Amsterdam.

TH486 Young, Josiah U.
Black and African Theologies: Siblings or Distant Cousins? (Bishop Henry McNeal Turner Studies in North American Black Religion, 2). Maryknoll, NYU: Orbis Books, 1986. xiii, 146 pp. Paper. 0883442523.

A detailed analysis of the relationship of black theology (US) to African theology; including both a historical background and a comparison and contrast of the writings of key theologians.

TH487 Young, Josiah U.
No Difference in the Fare: Dietrich Bonhoeffer and the Problem of Racism. Grand Rapids, MIU: Eerdmans, 1998. xiv, 178 pp. Paper. 0802844650.

A creative reflection on the intersections of the thought of Dietrich Bonhoeffer with that of Africans and African Americans engaged in the struggle against racism.

Feminist/Womanist Liberation

TH488 Ackermann, Denise, and Riet Bons-Storm, eds.
Liberating Faith Practices:Feminist Practical Theologies in Context. Leuven, Belgium: Peeters, 1998. viii, 200 pp. Paper. 9042900032.

A collection of nine articles by white women scholars who critique popular models of pastoral theology, proposing transformative practices based on lives of women.

TH489 Aldredge-Clanton, Jann
In Search of the Christ-Sophia: An Inclusive Christology for Liberating Christians. Mystic, CTU: Twenty-Third Publications, 1995. 189 pp. Paper. 0896226298.

A founder of the Inclusive Worship Community in Waco, Texas, shares her theology (which is inclusive of both male and female images), resources for inclusive worship, and their implications for the church's mission.

TH490 Baker-Fletcher, Karen, and Garth Baker-Fletcher
My Sister, My Brother: Womanist and XODUS God-Talk. (The Bishop Henry McNeal Turner/Sojourner Truth Series in Black Religion, 12). Maryknoll, NYU: Orbis Books, 1997. xii, 307 pp. Paper. 1570750998.

A lively dialogue between two creative African American theologians, organized around themes of God, Christ, humanity, generations, church, and last things—one a womanist and the other a self-named "Xodus" theologian.

TH491 Bekkenkamp, Jonneke et al., eds.
Proven van vrouwenstudies theologie. (Exchange, E595). Leiden, NE: IIMO; Utrecht, NE: Interuniversitaire Werkgroep Feminisme en Theologie, 1991. 309 pp. Paper. 9064952450.

A collection of scholarly essays by Dutch women theologians, members of the Interuniversity Work Group on Feminism and Theology, on the textual basis of Dutch feminist theology, and the self-image, objectives, and identity of its leaders.

TH492 Chopp, Rebecca S., and Sheila Greeve Davaney, eds.
Horizons in Feminist Theology: Identity, Tradition, and Norms. Minneapolis, MNU: Fortress Press, 1997. viii, 264 pp. Paper. 0800629965.

A collection of thirteen papers by feminist theologians; originally presented at the conference on Feminist Theology and the Role of Theory held at the Iliff School of Theology, Denver, Colorado, in 1994.

TH493 Esser, Annette, and Luise Schottroff, eds.
Feministische Theologie im europäischen Kontext/Feminist Theology in a European Context/Théologie féministe dans un contexte européen. (Jahrbuch der Europäischen Gesellschaft für die Theologische Forschung von Frauen, 1). Kampen, NE: Kok Pharos; Mainz, GW: Matthias-Grünewald, 1993. 255 pp. Paper. 9039000476 (NE), 3786717249 (GW).

This first yearbook of the European Society of Women in Theological Research contains essays in English (5), French (1), and German (6), plus book reviews and bibliography.

TH494 Fabella, Virginia, and Mercy Amba Oduyoye, eds.
With Passion and Compassion: Third World Women Doing Theology. Maryknoll, NYU: Orbis Books, 1988. xv, 192 pp. Paper. 0883446236.

Twenty-two original essays providing outlines of the common struggle of Third World women to forge their own liberation theology: discussing Christology, spirituality, and the Bible.

TH495 Fiorenza, Elisabeth Schüssler, and M. Shawn Copeland
Feminist Theology in Different Contexts. (Concilium, 1996/1). London, ENK: SCM Press; Maryknoll, NYU: Orbis Books, 1996. vi, 158 pp. Paper. 0334030366 (UK), 0883448882 (US).

Sixteen essays providing a ten-year update on developments in feminist theology, including regional and interfaith perspectives.

TH496 Fiorenza, Elisabeth Schüssler, ed.
The Power of Naming: A Concilium Reader in Feminist Liberation Theology. Maryknoll, NYU: Orbis Books; London, ENK: SCM Press, 1996. xxxix, 373 pp. Paper. 1570750947 (O), 0334026601 (S).

A compilation of thirty essays by feminist theologians; originally published in *Concilium*.

TH497 Gebara, Ivone
Longing for Running Water: Ecofeminism and Liberation. Translated by David Molineaux. Minneapolis, MNU: Fortress Press, 1999. ix, 230 pp. Paper. 0800631838.

A leading Latin American theologian and a Brazilian Sister of Our Lady shares her experiences with the Brazilian poor-women's movement, and develops a gritty urban ecofeminism, exploring its epistemology and articulating its worldview.

TH498 Hinsdale, Mary Ann, and Phyllis Kaminski, eds.
Women and Theology. (Annual Publication of the College Theology Society, 40-1994). Maryknoll, NYU: Orbis Books, 1995. xiii, 274 pp. Paper. 1570750351.

A collection of sixteen essays on "Women and Theology," including contributions from Asia and Latin America; originally presented at the 40th anniversary celebration of the College Theology Society in 1994.

TH499 Isasi-Díaz, Ada María, and Yolanda Tarango
Hispanic Women: Prophetic Voice in the Struggle. San Francisco, CAU: Harper & Row, 1988. xx, 123 pp. Paper. 0060640952.

A presentation of the voices of Hispanic women; a reflection of Hispanic women's experience and how it is intrinsic to the doing of theology.

TH500 Isasi-Díaz, Ada María
En la Lucha/In the Struggle: Elaborating a Mujerista Theology/A Hispanic Women's Liberation Theology. Minneapolis, MNU: Fortress Press, 1993. xxi, 226 pp. Paper. 0800626109.

The chief exponent of a distinctive theology for Hispanic women, develops that theology based on their struggle for survival and liberation; in Spanish and in English, with chapter summaries in Spanish.

TH501 Isasi-Díaz, Ada María
Mujerista Theology: A Theology for the Twenty-first Century. Maryknoll, NYU: Orbis Books, 1996. xi, 210 pp. Paper. 1570750815.

A collection of ten essays by the author on Hispanic feminist theology.

TH502 Keller, Rosemary Skinner, and Rosemary Radford Reuther, eds.
In Our Own Voices: Four Centuries of American Women's Religious Writing. Louisville, KYU: Westminster John Knox, 2000. viii, 542 pp. Paper. 0664222854.

A collection of 10 scholarly essays on multicultural women voices that become metaphor of women's efforts to speak and act as persons with authority in their own right, ushering in social reform.

TH503 King, Ursula, ed.
Feminist Theology from the Third World: A Reader. London, ENK: SPCK; Maryknoll, NYU: Orbis Books, 1994. xiii, 434 pp. Paper. 0281047367 (UK), 0883449633 (US).

Thirty-eight key texts representing the voices of women in Africa, Asia, Latin America, Oceania, and minority groups in the United States.

TH504 Kirk-Duggan, Cheryl A.
Exorcizing Evil: A Womanist Perspective on the Spirituals. (The Bishop Henry McNeal Turner/Sojourner Truth Series in Black Religion, 14). Maryknoll, NYU: Orbis Books, 1997. xx, 403 pp. Paper. 1570751463.

A womanist theologian analyzes the language of the spirituals, relating them to the historic struggles for justice and liberation of the slavery and civil rights eras in North America.

TH505 Moody, Linda A.
Women Encounter God: Theology across the Boundaries of Difference. Maryknoll, NYU: Orbis Books, 1996. viii, 184 pp. Paper. 1570750823.

An analysis of both commonalities and differences between white feminist, womanist, and *mujerista* theologies of liberation in the Americas.

TH506 Pobee, J. S., ed.
Culture, Women and Theology. Delhi, II: ISPCK, 1994. 188 pp. Paper. 8172142005.

Thirteen short essays by prominent women theologians, mostly from Africa and Asia, plus two by the editor who facilitated this WCC process of study.

TH507 Robins, Wendy S., and Musimbi R. A. Kanyoro, eds.
Speaking for Ourselves: Bible Studies and Discussion Starters by Women. Geneva, SZ: WCC, 1990. x, 106 pp. Paper. 2825409812.

Papers from a 1988 workshop sponsored jointly by the WCC and the LWF, at which issues of health, poverty, global economy, racism, and patriarchy were studied, relating women's experiences to those found in the Bible.

TH508 Russell, Letty M. et al., eds.
Inheriting Our Mother's Gardens: Feminist Theology in Third World Perspective. Philadelphia, PAU: Westminster Press, 1988. 181 pp. Paper. 066425019X.

A collection of eight articles by leading feminist theologians, giving personal histories and experiences of women in Africa, Asia, Anglo-America, and Latin America; including an annotated bibliography.

TH509 Sanders, Cheryl J., ed.
Living the Intersection: Womanism and Afrocentrism in Theology. Minneapolis, MNU: Fortress Press, 1995. 192 pp. Paper. 0800628527.

Essays by nine prominent African American women theologians on the contemporary intersections of womanist and Afrocentric thought, with assessments of the missional involvements of women in the United States.

TH510 Strahm, Doris
Vom Rand in die Mitte: Christologie aus der Sicht der Frauen in Asien, Afrika und Lateinamerika. (Theologie in Geschichte und Gesellschaft, 4). Luzern, SZ: Edition Exodus, 1997. 447 pp. 3905577119.

Results of an intensive research by a Swiss woman theologian on the various Christological contributions of feminist theologians from Asia, Africa, and Latin America.

TH511 Vuola, Elina
Limits of Liberation: Praxis as Method in Latin American Liberation Theology and Feminist Theology. (Annales Academiae Scientiarum Fennicae, Humaniora, 289). Helsinki, FI: Suomalainen Tiedeakatemia, 1997. 246 pp. Paper. 9514108256.

A critical examination of the methodological presuppositions of Latin American liberation theology and feminist theology; originally submitted as a doctoral dissertation at the University of Helsinki, Finland.

TH512 Welch, Sharon D.
Communities of Resistance and Solidarity: A Feminist Theology of Liberation. Maryknoll, NYU: Orbis Books, 1985. x, 102 pp. Paper. 0883442043.

A prolegomenon to liberation theology which focuses on the sociopolitical reality of a feminist, white, middle-class American Christian theologian who is both the oppressed and the oppressor.

TH513 Welch, Sharon D.
A Feminist Ethic of Risk. Minneapolis, MNU: Fortress Press, 2000. 206 pp. Paper. 0800631854.

A revised edition aimed toward learning ethical daily living—creative, responsible, and compassionate in contemporary global and political contexts.

Third World Theologies

See also TH15-TH19, TH25, TH156, TH244, TH302, TH354, TH442, TH458, TH481-TH482, ME257, CR132, SO190, PO47, PO125, AF1138, AS142, AS261, and AS265.

TH514 Anderson, Gerald H., and Thomas F. Stransky, eds.
Mission Trends, no. 3: Third World Theologies. New York, NYU: Paulist Press; Grand Rapids, MIU: Eerdmans, 1976. viii, 254 pp. Paper. 0809119846 (P), 0802816541 (E).

A collection of twenty-eight essays from Protestant, Roman Catholic, and evangelical perspectives, containing several views of the contextualization enterprise and articles on various questions from Latin America, Africa, and Asia.

TH515 Bertsch, Ludwig, ed.
Was der Geist den Gemeinden sagt: Bausteine einer Ekklesiologie der Ortskirchen. (Theologie der Dritten Welt, 15). Freiburg im Breisgau, GW: Herder, 1991. 214 pp. Paper. 3451222965.

These twelve essays center on the theme of the legitimacy of local churches throughout the world as expressions sof the universal church, which is seen as the ecclesiological heritage of the Second Vatican Council.

TH516 Boff, Leonardo, and Virgilio P. Elizondo, eds.
Teologías del Tercer Mundo: Convergencias y divergencias. (*Concilium*, 24, 219). Madrid, SP: Concilium, 1988. 166 pp. No ISBN.

A collection of twelve works addressing the theologies of Latin America, Africa, Asia, and the United States.

TH517 Boff, Leonardo, and Virgilio P. Elizondo, eds.
Theologies of the Third World: Convergences and Divergences. Edinburgh, STK: T&T Clark, 1988. xv, 144 pp. Paper. 056730079X.

Several important Third World theologians (e.g. Balasuriya, Cone, Upkong, Rayan) present overviews of the theological situation in their geographical areas, and provide helpful bibliographical essays on publications issued until the late 1980s.

TH518 Carro, Daniel, and Richard Francis Wilson, eds.
Contemporary Gospel Accents: Doing Theology in Africa, Asia, Southeast Asia, and Latin America. Macon, GAU: Mercer University Press, 1997. xv, 142 pp. Paper. 0865545057.

Essays from a two-day conference on "What Gospel Means to Us" (Buenos Aires, August 1995); by sixteen Baptist theologians from five continents.

TH519 Chandran, J. Russell, ed.
Third World Theologies in Dialogue: Essays in Memory of D. S. Amalorpavadass. Bangalore, II: EATWOT, 1991. ix, 212 pp. Paper. No ISBN.

Sixteen essays by members of EATWOT on themes common to the association, and in the thought of the late Fr. D.S. Amalorpavadass of India.

TH520 Chenu, Bruno
Teologías Cristianas de los Terceros Mundos: Teologías Latinoamericana, Negra Norteamericana, Negra Sudafricana, Africana y Asiática. Barcelona, SP: Herder, 1989. 244 pp. Paper. 8425416434.

Spanish translation.

TH521 Chenu, Bruno
Teologie cristiane dei terzi mondi: Teologia latino-americana, teologia nera americana, teologia nera sudafricana, teo- *logia africana, teologia asiatica.* (Giornale di teologia, 181). Brescia, IT: Queriniana, 1988. 312 pp. 8839906819.

Italian translation.

TH522 Chenu, Bruno
Théologies chrétiennes des tiers mondes: théologies latino-américaine, noire américaine, noire sud-africaine, africaine, asiatique. Paris, FR: Le Centurion, 1987. 213 pp. 2227315660.

A history of theologies which have developed since the 1950s in the Third World, including Latin American, African American, South African, and Asian.

TH523 Collet, Giancarlo, ed.
Theologien der Dritten Welt: EATWOT als Herausforderung westlicher Theologie und Kirche. (Supplementa, 37). Immensee, SZ: *NZM*, 1990. 359 pp. Paper. 3858240699.

Ten theologians report on the significance of the various theologies emerging from EATWOT as a research project of the Romero House of the Bethlehem Missions Society.

TH524 Duncan, Quince et al.
Cultura Negra y Teología. San José, CR: DEI, 1986. 184 pp. Paper. 9977904294.

A collection of papers presented at the Consultation on Black Culture and Latin American Theology (Rio de Janeiro, Brazil, 8-12 July 1985), organized by EATWOT.

TH525 Dyrness, William A., ed.
Emerging Voices in Global Christian Theology. Grand Rapids, MIU: Zondervan, 1994. 255 pp. Paper. 0310604613.

A sample of nine essays by younger evangelical theologians in Africa, Asia, Latin America, and Eastern Europe.

TH526 Dyrness, William A.
Invitation to Cross-Cultural Theology: Case Studies in Vernacular Theologies. Grand Rapids, MIU: Zondervan, 1992. 194 pp. Paper. 0310535816.

A popular presentation of ways in which lay communities of Christians endeavor to shape their world by their faith; with case studies from the Akamba (Kenya), Maya (Guatemala), house churches (China), squatters (Manila), and middle-class Americans (Northern California).

TH527 Dyrness, William A.
Learning About Theology from the Third World. Grand Rapids, MIU: Academie Books, 1990. ix, 221 pp. Paper. 0310209714.

A general introduction to the way Christians outside of Europe and North America think about their faith.

TH528 Ferm, Deane William
Profiles in Liberation: 36 Portraits of Third World Theologians. Mystic, CTU: Twenty-Third Publications, 1988. 193 pp. Paper. 0896223779.

Thirty-six short profiles of Third World liberation theologians of Africa, Asia, and Latin America, including the background, theological development, and distinctive contribution of each.

TH529 Górski, Jan
Misje w Teologii Kontekstualnej. (Dissertationen Theologische Reihe, 43). St. Ottilien, GW: EOS Verlag, 1991. 139 pp. 3880968438.

A *habilitation* thesis focused on the development since Vatican II of three distinct models of contextual theology among Roman Catholics in Asia, Africa, and Latin America.

TH530 Gensichen, Hans-Werner, and Gerhard Rosenkranz, eds.
Theologische Stimmen aus Asien, Afrika und Lateinamerika.
Munich, GW: Kaiser, 1968. 3 vols. No ISBN.

A series of three books with contributions by local authors in many parts of the world, presenting the theological situation of young churches [vol. 1, *Das Problem einer "einheimischem" Theologie*, 146 pp.; vol. 2, *Beiträge zur biblischen Theologie*, 192 pp.; vol. 3, *Beiträge zur systematischen Theologie*, 152 pp.].

TH531 Gibbs, Philip
The Word in the Third World: Divine Revelation in the Theology of Jean-Marc Éla, Aloysius Pieris and Gustavo Gutiérrez.
(Gregoriana Theology Series, 8). Rome, IT: Gregorian University Press, 1995. 447 pp. Paper. 8876526978.

A detailed comparative study of the understandings of revelation in the thought of three Third World theologians, the Second Vatican Council, and several Roman Catholic bishops' conferences.

TH532 Goldewijk, Berma Klein, and Jacques van Nieuwenhove, eds.
Theologie in de context van de Derde Wereld: Een vergelijkende studie. (Kerk en theologie in context, 21). Kampen, NE: Kok, 1993. 226 pp. 9024266726.

A collection of scholarly essays by Dutch Catholic theologians and missiologists on various Third World theologians and their contributions to contextual theologies, not only in their own countries, but also in Europe and the United States.

TH533 Hadjor, Kofi Buenor, and Brian Wren, eds.
Christian Faith and Third World Liberation. London, ENK: Third World Csommunications, 1985. 95 pp. Paper. No ISBN.

Thirty-nine brief essays and documents introducing Western readers to the concerns of a wide spectrum of liberation theologians; a special issue of a *Third World Book Review*, volume 1, numbers 4 and 5.

TH534 *Jahrbuch für kontextuelle Theologien/Yearbook of Contextual theologies ...*
(Missionswissenschaftliches Institut Missio, 5). Frankfurt, GW: IKO-Verlag für Interkulturelle Kommunikation, 1993. 214 pp. Paper. 3889392415.

Articles, discussions, bibliography, and book reviews on contextual theology issues in German, English, Spanish, and French.

TH535 Joseph, M. P., ed.
Confronting Life: Theology Out of the Context. (ISPCK Contextual Theological Education Series, 7). Delhi, II: ISPCK, 1995. 224 pp. Paper. 8172142552.

Essays by twelve outstanding international theologians and ecumenical leaders, written to honor M. M. Thomas of India and to speak to four central issues in his thought: responding to the political process, redefining ecumenism, rereading the Bible, and reconstructing theology.

TH536 Kirk, J. Andrew
Theology and the Third World Church. (Outreach & Identity; Evangelical Theological Monographs, 6). Downers Grove, ILU: InterVarsity Press; Exeter, ENK: Paternoster Press, 1983. 64 pp. Paper. 0877848920 (US), 0853643210 (UK).

An analysis of the revolution in Third World theological consciousness of essential conditions for Christian theology in that context; with implications for theological education.

TH537 Konferenz evangelikaler Missionstheologen (Bangkok, 22-25, März 1982)
Der ganze Christus für eine geteilte Welt: Evangelikale Christologien im Kontext von Armut, Machtlösigkeit und religiösem Pluralismus. Edited by Vinay Samuel, and Chris Sugden. Translated by Joachim Wietzke. (Erlanger Taschenbücher, 83). Erlangen, GW: Ev.-Luth. Mission, 1987. 283 pp. Paper. 387214183X.

German translation.

TH538 Míguez Bonino, José et al.
Christ and the Younger Churches: Theological Contributions from Asia, Africa, and Latin America. Edited by Georg F. Vicedom. (Theological Collections, 15). London, ENK: SPCK, 1972. 112 pp. 0281024774.

A collection of seven essays on Christian theology from the point of view of theologians from Asia, Africa, and Latin America.

TH539 Mbiti, John S., ed.
African and Asian Contributions to Contemporary Theology: Report of Consultation Held at the World Council of Churches' Ecumenical Institute, Bossey, 8-14 June 1976. Céligny, SZ: World Council of Churches Ecumenical Institute, 1977. 153 pp. Paper. No ISBN.

Papers from the pioneer consultation of African and Asian Theologians held at the WCC's Ecumenical Institute (Bossey, Switzerland, June 1976).

TH540 Opoku, Kofi Asare, Yong-Bock Kim, and Antoinette Clark Wire
Healing for God's World: Remedies from Three Continents. New York, NYU: Friendship Press, 1991. 159 pp. Paper. 0377002291.

The 1988 Cook lectures on "Responses in Faith to Broken Humanity: Contributors from Three Continents," given in Asia and North America by a Ghanaian scholar of African religions, a Korean *minjung* theologian, and an American feminist New Testament teacher.

TH541 Pero, Alberto, and Ambrose Moyo, eds.
Theology and the Black Experience: The Lutheran Heritage Interpreted by African and African American Theologians. Minneapolis, MNU: Augsburg, 1988. 272 pp. Paper. 0806623535.

A collection of fourteen essays that demonstrate how African and African American theologians interpret the Lutheran heritage; first presented to an international conference of black Lutheran theologians held in Zimbabwe in 1986.

TH542 Pope-Levison, Priscilla, and John R. Levison
Jesus in Global Contexts. Louisville, KYU: Westminster John Knox, 1992. 232 pp. Paper. 066425165X.

A global tour of the Christologies emerging in Latin America, Asia, and Africa, and those of North American feminist and African American theologies.

TH543 Samuel, Vinay, and Chris Sugden, eds.
Sharing Jesus in the Two Thirds World: Evangelical Christologies from the Contexts of Poverty, Powerlessness and Religious Pluralism. Grand Rapids, MIU: Eerdmans, 1982. x, 284 pp. Paper. 0802819974.

Report of the First Conference of Evangelical Mission Theologians from the Two-Thirds World (Bangkok, Thailand, 22-25 March 1982), including fourteen papers presented and conference findings.

TH544 Schrijver, George de, ed.
Liberation Theologies on Shifting Grounds: A Clash of Socio-Economic and Cultural Paradigms. (Bibliotheca Ephemeridum Theologicarum Lovaniensium, 135). Louvain, BE: Leuven University Press; Louvain, BE: Peeters, 1998. xi, 453 pp. Paper. 9061868831 (L), 9042903023 (U).

Papers and responses from around the world given at an international symposium (21-23 November 1996) in conjunction with a research project entitled "Paradigm-Shift in Third World Theologies of Liberation: From Socioeconomic Analysis to Cultural Analysis: Assessment and Status of the Question" based at the Faculty of Theology, Kuleuven.

TH545 Spencer, Aída Basançon, and William David Spencer, eds.
The Global God: Multicultural Evangelical Views of God. (A BridgePoint Book). Grand Rapids, MIU: Baker Books, 1998. 281 pp. Paper. 0801021634.

Eleven evangelical scholars write on attributes of God most understood and needing to be more fully apprehended in their diverse cultural contexts (US, Hispanic American, Caribbean, African, Chinese American, Chinese, Korean, and Korean American).

TH546 Sundermeier, Theo
Das Kreuz als Befreiung: Kreuzesinterpretationen in Asien und Afrika. (Kaiser-Traktate, 89). Munich, GW: Kaiser, 1985. 99 pp. Paper. 3459016221.

The beliefs and opinions of theologians from the African and East Asian churches, with a look at their own cultural heredity—an attempt to show the depth of Third World understandings of the Cross and Resurrection, which are often neglected by scholars.

TH547 Thistlethwaite, Susan Brooks, and Mary Potter Engel, eds.
Lift Every Voice: Constructing Christian Theologies from the Underside. Maryknoll, NYU: Orbis Books, 1998. xix, 339 pp. Paper. 1570751633.

A revised and expanded sourcebook on the methods and themes of Third World liberation theologies; originally published in 1990 by Harper San Francisco.

TH548 Torres, Sergio, and Virginia Fabella, eds.
Dem Evangelium auf der Spur: Theologie in der Dritten Welt. (Kirchlichen Entwicklungsdienst, 22). Frankfurt am Main, GW: Verlag Otto Lembeck, 1980. 267 pp. Paper. 3874761312.

German translation of *The Emergent Gospel* (1978).

TH549 Torres, Sergio, and Virginia Fabella, eds.
The Emergent Gospel: Theology from the Underside of History. Maryknoll, NYU: Orbis Books, 1978. xxiii, 275 pp. 0883441128 (hdbk), 0883441136 (pbk).

Papers and reports from the first consultation of Third World Theologians reflecting the ecumenical importance of theologies associated with Africa, Asia, and Latin America.

TH550 Waldenfels, Hans, ed.
Theologen der Dritten Welt: Elf biographische Skizzen aus Afrika, Asien und Lateinamerika. Munich, GW: Beck, 1982. 198 pp. Paper. 3406084605.

Eleven biographical sketches of Third World theologians: J. M. Bonino, L. Boff, S. Torres, C. Nyamiti, C. G. Baeta, T. Tshibangu Shishiku, A. A. Boesak, A. J. Appasamy, D. S. Amalorpavadass, Choan-Seng Song, and Seiichi Yagi.

TH551 Wessels, Antonie
Images of Jesus: How Jesus Is Perceived and Portrayed in Non-European Cultures. Translated by John Vriend. Grand Rapids, MIU: Eerdmans; London, ENK: SCM Press, 1990. ix, 195 pp. Paper. 0802802877 (US), 033400697X (UK).

English translation.

TH552 Wessels, Antonie
Jezus zien: hoe Jezus is overgeleverd in andere culturen. Baarn, NE: Ten Have, 1986. 174 pp. Paper. 902594292X.

Jewish, Muslim, Latin American, Asian, and African concepts of Jesus, elaborated through an analysis of theological texts and examples of Christian art.

TH553 Wietzke, Joachim, Frank Kürschner-Pelkmann, and Gisela Köberlin, eds.
Theologie als konziliarer Prozess: Chancen und Grenzen eines interkulturellen Dialogs zwischen Theologien der "Dritten" und "Ersten Welt." (Weltmission heute, 3). Hamburg, GW: EMW, 1988. 164 pp. Paper. No ISBN.

Nine essays which deal with the prospects and possibilities of dialogue between First World and Third World theologians.

Church and World; Social Justice

See also GW50, HI425, HI497, TH140, TH233-TH234, TH272, TH427, TH472, EA93, ME174, CR63, CR866, SO516, EC106, PO100, PO192, ED155, ED161, CH9, CH20, SP57, SP63, AF135, AF958, AF1119, AM172, AM315, AM357, AM501, AM503, AM564, AM730, AM1102, AM1327, AS114, AS144, AS255, AS883, and EU199.

TH554 Aman, Kenneth, ed.
Border Regions of Faith: An Anthology of Religion and Social Change. Maryknoll, NYU: Orbis Books, 1987. xvi, 528 pp. Paper. 0883444151.

A comprehensive collection of sixty-one essays focusing on six areas: feminism, civil rights and black theology, the New Right, the Third World, economics, peace, and anti-nuclear movements.

TH555 Balasuriya, Tissa
World Churches and Integral Liberation. (Quest, 78). Colombo, CE: Centre for Society and Religion, 1984. vii, 141 pp. Paper. No ISBN.

A collection of essays on mission and justice concerns by the noted Sri Lankan Catholic theologian and social activist.

TH556 Baum, Gregory
Compassion and Solidarity: The Church for Others. (CBC Massey Lectures Series). Mahwah, NJU: Paulist Press; Toronto, ONC: CBC Enterprises, 1990. 109 pp. Paper. 0809131412, 0887943357.

The noted Roman Catholic theologian presents the new Faith and Justice Movement in Canada, the Roman Catholic Church's considerable opposition to it, and the movement's spiritual content, all leading to the author's call for a new ecumenism which moves all Christians to work for liberation in the Third World and Canada; originally published in 1987 by CBC Enterprises, Toronto, Ontario, Canada.

TH557 Baum, Gregory, and Robert Ellsberg, eds.
The Logic of Solidarity: Commentaries on Pope John Paul II's Encyclical "On Social Concern." Maryknoll, NYU: Orbis Books, 1989. xv, 232 pp. Paper. 0883445786.

The complete text of Pope John Paul II's encyclical, followed by eleven commentaries by renowned theologians and social scientists.

TH—MISSIONS: THEOLOGY

TH558 Bennett, John C., ed.

Christian Social Ethics in a Changing World: An Ecumenical Theological Inquiry. (WCC Department on Church and Society, 1). New York, NYU: Association Press; London, ENK: SCM Press, 1966. 381 pp. No ISBN.

A preparatory volume for the WCC's 1966 Conference on Church and Society, including essays on the theological foundations of social ethics and regional issues.

TH559 Best, Thomas F., and Martin Robra, eds.

Ecclesiology and Ethics: Ecumenical Ethical Engagement, Moral Formation and the Nature of the Church. Geneva, SZ: WCC Publications, 1997. xiii, 121 pp. Paper. 2825412163.

Reports and papers from WCC consultations on "Costly Unity" (Ronde, Denmark, Feb. 1993), "Costly Commitment" (Jerusalem, Nov. 1994), and "Costly Obedience" (Johannesburg, June 1996)—part of a five-year study process on ecclesiology and ethics.

TH560 Bock, Paul

In Search of a Responsible World Society: The Social Teachings of the World Council of Churches. Philadelphia, PAU: Westminster Press, 1974. 251 pp. 0664207081.

An introduction to the social teachings of the 20th-century ecumenical movement and of the WCC; by a professor of religion who served for two years on the staff of the WCC.

TH561 Bockmühl, Klaus

Evangelicals and Social Ethics: A Commentary on Article 5 of the Lausanne Covenant. (Outreach and Identity: Evangelical Theol. Monographs, 4). Downers Grove, ILU: InterVarsity; Exeter, UK: Paternoster Press, 1979. 47 pp. Paper. 0877844917 (I), 0853642613 (P).

The text from the International Congress on World Evangelization (Lausanne, 1974), dealing with the social responsibility of Christians, with an analysis of it based on three addresses by René Padilla, Samuel Escobar, and Carl F. H. Henry given at the Congress.

TH562 Boesak, Allan Aubrey

The Finger of God. Maryknoll, NYU: Orbis Books, 1982. xii, 100 pp. Paper. 0883441357.

A dozen eloquent sermons bringing scripture to bear on the current socio-political realities of South Africa; by the well-known theologian and student chaplain at the University of the Western Cape.

TH563 Bonavía, Pablo, and Javier Galdona

Neoliberalismo y Fe Cristiana. Madrid, SP: Acción Cultural Cristiana, 1995. 83 pp. 8492032332.

A historical, theological and ethical analysis of the "option for the poor" as a Christian imperative; by the professors of theology and social moral theology at the Theological Institute of Uruguay.

TH564 Brown, Robert McAfee, ed.

Kairos: Three Prophetic Challenges to the Church. Grand Rapids, MIU: Eerdmans, 1990. vii, 158 pp. Paper. 0802805329.

A study guide on three recent *kairos* proclamations by church leaders (South Africa 1985, Central America 1988, and "The Road to Damascus" 1989); with introduction, text, and study questions on each document.

TH565 Calvez, Jean-Yves

Faith and Justice: The Social Dimension of Evangelization. Translated by John E. Blewett. St. Louis, MOU: Institute of Jesuit Sources, 1991. 193 pp. Paper. 0912422491.

Text and commentary on the important 1975 Jesuit document entitled "The Service of Faith and the Promotion of Justice," including historical elements, theological foundations, and its relationship to the work of the Society of Jesus.

TH566 Carmody, Denise Lardner, and John Carmody, eds.

The Future of Prophetic Christianity: Essays in Honor of Robert McAfee Brown. Maryknoll, NYU: Orbis Books, 1993. v, 170 pp. 0883448971.

A *festschrift* honoring the distinguished US theologian, social activist and prophet, containing eighteen essays on ecumenical relations, Jewish-Christian dialogue, liberation theology, social ethics, spirituality, and issues of war and peace.

TH567 Chiba, Shin, George R. Hunsberger, and Lester Edwin J. Ruiz, eds.

Christian Ethics in Ecumenical Context: Theology, Culture, and Politics in Dialogue. Grand Rapid, MIU: Eerdmans, 1995. xii, 385 pp. 0802837875.

A *festschrift* honoring Charles C. West on his retirement as Professor of Christian Ethics at Princeton Theological Seminary, focusing on theology, ethics, society, culture, and politics in global perspective.

TH568 Coleman, John Aloysius, ed.

One Hundred Years of Catholic Social Thought: Celebration and Challenge. Maryknoll, NYU: Orbis Books, 1991. ix, 364 pp. 0883447452.

Twenty-three short essays by Catholic scholars on one-hundred years of Catholic social teaching; with specific reference to issues of work, peace, and family life.

TH569 Davies, J. G.

Dialogue with the World. London, ENK: SCM Press, 1967. 79 pp. Paper. No ISBN.

Lectures on mission as a divine activity, and the church's true being occurring only through active participation in God's world; originally presented in La Paz and Montero, Bolivia.

TH570 De Vries, Egbert de, ed.

Man in Community: Christian Concern for the Human in Changing Society. (WCC Department on Church and Society, 4). New York, NYU: Association Press; London, ENK: SCM Press, 1966. 382 pp. No ISBN.

Essays by sociologists, anthropologists, psychologists, natural scientists, and theologians, analyzing contemporary crises in human communities, including racism and secularization, and seeking specific Christian contributions toward the renewal of community—preparatory papers for the WCC's 1966 Conference on Church and Society.

TH571 Desrochers, John

The Social Teaching of the Church. Bangalore, II: Desrochers, 1982. 783 pp. Paper. No ISBN.

A comprehensive study of the social teachings of the church based on significant papal encyclicals, key statements of the WCC, the Second Vatican Council, the Catholic episcopal conferences of Latin America, Asia and India, the CCA, the NCCI, and some of the churches of India.

TH572 Dorr, Donal

Option for the Poor: A Hundred Years of Vatican Social Teaching. Maryknoll, NYU: Orbis Books, 1992. ix, 433 pp. Paper. 0883448270.

This revised edition (first published in 1983) of a standard work on modern Catholic social teaching includes commentaries on recent documents from Latin America and the Vatican on justice, peace, ecotheology, etc.

TH573 Dorr, Donal

The Social Justice Agenda: Justice, Ecology, Power and the Church. Maryknoll, NYU: Orbis Books, 1991. 201 pp. Paper. 0883447223.

A general and fairly simple introduction to issues of justice and peace as they have emerged in the last thirty years in the RCC and the WCC; with options for what the church can do.

TH574 Dorr, Donal

Spirituality and Justice. Dublin, IE: Gill & Macmillan; Maryknoll, NYU: Orbis Books, 1984. 260 pp. Paper. 0717113760 (G), 0883444496 (O).

An integrated vision of faith and action for those social activists put off by a traditional disinterested spirituality, and for those deeply concerned with spirituality but intimidated by the demands of effective commitment to social justice.

TH575 Dussel, Enrique D.

Éthique communautaire. Translated by Francis Guibal. (Collection libération. Économie, société, théologie). Paris, FR: Éditions du Cerf, 1991. 256 pp. 2204042080.

French translation.

TH576 Dussel, Enrique D.

Ética comunitária. Translated by Jaime A. Clasen. (Coleção Teologia e libertação, Série III, Libertação na história, 8). Rio de Janeiro, BL: Editora Vozes, 1987. 285 pp. No ISBN.

Portuguese translation.

TH577 Dussel, Enrique D.

Ética Comunitaria. (Colección Cristianismo y Sociedad, 2). Florida, AG, and Madrid, SP: Ediciones Paulinas, 1986. 285 pp. 9500906465 (AG).

A comprehensive introduction to what liberation theology has to say about ethics and morals; by a leading Latin American church historian and liberation theologian.

TH578 Dussel, Enrique D.

Ethics and Community. Translated by Robert R. Barr. Maryknoll, NYU: Orbis Books, 1988. xii, 260 pp. Paper. 0883446197 (hdbk), 0883446189 (pbk).

English translation.

TH579 Dussel, Enrique D.

Ethik der Gemeinschaft. (Bibliothek Theologie der Befreiung: Die Befreiung in der Geschichte). Düsseldorf, GW: Patmos Verlag, 1988. 239 pp. No ISBN.

German translation.

TH580 Elliott, Clifford

With Integrity of Heart: Living Values in Changing Times. New York, NYU: Friendship Press, 1991. v, 138 pp. Paper. 0377002194.

A mission study for adults, examining contemporary value systems and proposing values based on Scripture to guide Christians seeking to carry out God's mission.

TH581 Escobar, Samuel E., and John Driver

Christian Mission and Social Justice. (Missionary Studies, 5). Scottdale, PAU: Herald Press, 1978. 112 pp. Paper. 0836118553.

Two theologians from Free Church (Baptist and Mennonite) traditions and Latin American mission experience, espouse mission and social justice in contrast to the common polarization of personal and social salvation.

TH582 Fowler, Stuart

The Church and the Renewal of Society. (Wetenskaplike Bydraes: Series F: Institute for Reformational Studies, F2 Brochures, 43). Potchefstroom, SA: Potchefstroom University, 1990. ii, 108 pp. Paper. 0869909738.

Five short essays on the meaning of the Gospel in various societal relations; by a leader of the Baptist Reformed Church of Australia, concerned for both personal piety and social justice; originally published in 1988.

TH583 Gallardo, José

The Way of Biblical Justice. Scottdale, PAU: Herald Press, 1983. 76 pp. 0836133218.

A Latin American interpretation of biblical teachings on social justice.

TH584 Gardner, E. Clinton

The Church as a Prophetic Community. Philadelphia, PAU: Westminster Press, 1967. 254 pp. No ISBN.

An intensive analysis of the relationship between the church and the secular world, including contemporary divisive factors of race and social class, the biblical vision of the church existing for humanity, and the necessity of the church's creative tension with society and culture; by the professor of Christian Ethics at Emory University.

TH585 Goodall, Norman

Christian Missions and Social Ferment. London, ENK: Epworth Press, 1964. 123 pp. No ISBN.

This book contains the Beckley Social Service Lecture, 1964, in which the writer explicitly related the missionary movement to social, industrial, economic, and international developments.

TH586 Gremillion, Joseph

The Gospel of Peace and Justice: Catholic Social Teaching since Pope John. Maryknoll, NYU: Orbis Books, 1976. xiv, 623 pp. 0883441659 (hdbk), 0883441667 (pbk).

A collection of twenty-five official Roman Catholic documents which reflect the church's social teachings from 1961 to 1975; with a penetrating analysis of their implications by the first secretary of the Pontifical Commission on Justice and Peace.

TH587 Harvey, Barry A.

Another City: An Ecclesiological Primer for a Post-Christian World. (Christian Mission and Modern Culture). Harrisburg, PAU: Trinity Press International, 1999. xi, 195 pp. Paper. 1563382776.

The author calls upon the church to remember that it is "Another City" in contrast to "the City," the world of hedonism, narcissism, and compromise to allegiance to any political entity.

TH588 Jacques, Geneviève
Beyond Impunity: An Ecumenical Approach to Truth, Justice, and Reconciliation. Geneva, SZ: WCC Publications, 2000. x, 61 pp. Paper. 2825413216.

Reflecting on the experiences of people around the world, the author challenges churches to reach across traditional boundaries and join others in the search for new paths toward genuine justice, repentance, reconciliation, and hope.

TH589 Küng, Hans, and Helmut Schmidt, eds.
A Global Ethic and Global Responsibilities: Two Declarations. London, ENK: SCM Press, 1998. viii, 152 pp. Paper. 0334027403.

On the fiftieth anniversary of the adoption of the United Nations' Declaration of Human Rights, the InterAction Council, a distinguished body of elder statesmen and other leading figures, first chaired by Helmut Schmidt and now by Malcolm Fraser, has produced a "Universal Declaration of Human Responsibilities," the text of which is provided and discussed in this book, along with the 1993 Declaration of the Parliament of the World's Religions.

TH590 Kasenene, Peter
Religious Ethics in Africa. Kampala, UG: Fountain Publishers, 1998. iv, 110 pp. Paper. 9970021338.

A comparison of traditional African religion, Christianity, Islam and Baha'i faiths on specific moral issues confronting every African, with the premise that Africans must rediscover their ethical and moral heritage because an immoral society is bound to disintegrate.

TH591 Kater, John L.
Finding Our Way: American Christians in Search of the City of God: Lessons from Panama. Cambridge, MAU: Cowley Publications, 1991. ix, 164 pp. Paper. 1561010294.

A study book for North American Christians relating contemporary issues of social justice to biblical values.

TH592 Kirk, J. Andrew
The Good News of the Kingdom Coming: The Marriage of Evangelism and Social Responsibility. Downers Grove, ILU: InterVarsity, 1985. 164 pp. Paper. 0877849382.

A call for a new consensus among evangelical, liberal, and radical Christians affirming the centrality of the themes of the Kingdom of God, response to the poor, and the task of evangelism; also published under the title, *A New World Coming* (IVP, 1983).

TH593 Kitagawa, Joseph Mitsuo
The Christian Tradition: Beyond Its European Captivity. Philadelphia, PAU: Trinity Press International, 1992. xii, 307 pp. Paper. 1563380412.

Essays by the distinguished professor of the history of religions at the University of Chicago on the relation of the Christian faith, piety, morality, and mission to the cultures of Asia, of Asian Americans, and of the West.

TH594 Mackay, John A.
Realidad e Idolatría en el Cristianismo Contemporáneo. (Conferences Carnahan). Buenos Aires, AG: Editorial La Aurora, 1970. 111 pp. No ISBN.
Spanish translation.

TH595 Maggay, Melba Padilla
Transforming Society. Oxford, ENK: Regnum/Lynx; Sutherland, AT: Albatross Books, 1994. 107 pp. Paper. 0745930611 (UK), 0732412161 (AT).

Out of her involvements with the poor through the Institute for the Study of Asian Church and Culture in her native Manila, the author develops a biblical rationale for Christian involvement in social transformation.

TH596 Mangalwadi, Vishal
Truth and Social Reform. London, ENK: Nivedit Good Books, 1996. 162 pp. Paper. 8186701003.

The founder of an Indian Christian community to serve the rural poor relates central themes on Christian theology to social reform; originally published in 1985.

TH597 Mendes, Candido
Justice faim de l'Église. Paris, FR: Desclée, 1977. 144 pp. 2718901004.

Out of the struggle against oppression during military rule, a Brazilian lay theologian calls the Catholic Church to leadership in social justice.

TH598 Moreno Rejón, Francisco
Moral Theology from the Poor: Moral Challenges of the Theology of Liberation. Quezon City, PH: Claretian Publications, 1988. xi, 203 pp. Paper. 9715013066 (np), 9715013074 (bp).
English translation.

TH599 Moreno Rejón, Francisco
Salvar la Vida de los Pobres: Aportes a la teología moral. (Experiencias Cristianas, 10). Buenos Aires, AG: Ediciones Paulinas, 1989. 198 pp. Paper. 9500907496.

A proposal for a method and perspective of moral reflection in Latin America that analyzes the existing relationship between ethics and utopia, and between ethics and spirituality.

TH600 Moreno Rejón, Francisco
Teología Moral desde los Pobres: La moral en la reflexión teológica desde América Latina. (Estudios de ética teológica, 6). Madrid, SP: Covarrubias, 1986. 229 pp. 8428403708.

An ethic and spirituality of liberation by one working with Gustavo Gutiérrez, among others, in Lima, Peru.

TH601 Moser, Antonio, and Bernardino Leers
Moral Theology: Dead Ends and Alternatives. (Theology and Liberation Series). Maryknoll, NYU: Orbis Books; Kent, ENK: Burns & Oates, 1990. xvi, 240 pp. 0883446804 (hdbk), 0883446650 (pbk).

A systematic treatment of moral theology from the perspective of liberation theology; by two Brazilian theologians surveying the evolution of Catholic moral theology, and laying the foundations for a Christian ethic in a world of injustice.

TH602 Nicolás, Adolfo de
Teología del Progreso: Génesis y desarrollo en los teólogos católicos contemporáneos. (Verdad e Imagen, 29). Salamanca, SP: Ediciones Sígueme, 1972. 416 pp. Paper. No ISBN.

A historical and systematic study of the theology of earthly realities, theology of history, political theology, and the theology of human progress.

TH603 Niles, D. Preman
Resisting the Threats to Life: Covenanting for Justice, Peace, and the Integrity of Creation. (Risk Book Series, 41). Geneva, SZ: WCC Publications, 1989. x, 85 pp. Paper. 2825409642.

An intense effort to convey the meaning of the call to "Justice, Peace, and the Integrity of Creation" issued at the Sixth Assembly of the WCC (Vancouver, Canada, 1983); written by the JPIC program director from Sri Lanka.

TH—MISSIONS: THEOLOGY

TH604 Noble, Lowell
Sociotheology: Thy Kingdom Come—On Earth. Jackson, MIU: Lowell Noble, 1987. xiii, 213 pp. Paper. No ISBN.

A textbook relating sociology and theology for evangelicals, calling them to combine biblical concerns for personal salvation and social justice, with special application for black Christians in the United States to issues of racism.

TH605 Nurnberger, Klaus
Ethik des Nord-Sud-Konflikts: Das globale Machtgefalle als theologisches Problem. (Missionswissenschaftliche Forschungen, 20). Gutersloh, GW: Gerd Mohn, 1987. 333 pp. Paper. 3579002406.

An examination of North-South socio-economic and political issues, with regard to implications for social action and theological ethics, as well as for mission and missiology.

TH606 O'Brien, David J., and Thomas A. Shannon, eds.
Catholic Social Thought: The Documentary Heritage. Maryknoll, NYU: Orbis Books, 1992. viii, 688 pp. 0883448033 (hdbk), 0883447878 (pbk).

Contains the complete text of every essential papal document on social thought, along with other important documents from the Vatican and the US Bishops.

TH607 Oglesby, Enoch H.
Born in the Fire: Case Studies in Christian Ethics and Globalization. New York, NYU: Pilgrim Press, 1990. x, 181 pp. Paper. 0829808493.

Twenty case studies from African American and African experiences, of moral issues of faith and cultural diversity; with an introduction to globalization ethics by a professor of theology and social ethics at Eden Theological Seminary, St. Louis, Missouri.

TH608 Ojakaminnor, Efeturi
Catholic Social Doctrine: An Introductory Manual. Nairobi, KE: Paulines Publications Africa, 1996. 158 pp. Paper. 966212523.

A simple manual introducing Catholic social doctrines, with special emphasis on human rights.

TH609 Stogre, Michael
That the World May Believe: The Development of Papal Social Thought on Aboriginal Rights. Sherbrooke, PQC: Éditions Paulines, 1992. 279 pp. Paper. 2890395499.

The first and only detailed study of the development of the papacy's social teaching on aboriginal rights; a revised version of the author's doctoral dissertation.

TH610 Walsh, John
Evangelization and Justice: New Insights For Christian Ministry. Maryknoll, NYU: Orbis Books, 1982. xiii, 107 pp. Paper. 0883441098.

A Maryknoll missionary reflects on the close relation of justice and peace ministries to evangelization in Christian mission.

TH611 Walsh, Michael, and Brian Davies, eds.
Proclaiming Justice and Peace: Documents from John XXIII-John Paul II. Mystic, CTU: Twenty-Third Publications, 1984. xxii, 345 pp. 089622239X (hdbk), 0896222365 (pbk).

A collection of ten papal statements issued between 1962 and 1981, in response to issues arising out of the struggle of the Third World to survive in a world dominated by the First and Second Worlds.

TH612 Walton, Martin
Marginal Communities: The Ethical Enterprise of the Followers of Jesus. Kampen, NE: Kok Pharos, 1994. 294 pp. Paper. 9039001162.

A scholarly review of the modern usage of the term *status confessionis*, from Bonhoeffer's opposition to Nazism, to its application to the challenges of apartheid, the nuclear threat, and world poverty; with advocacy of its usage in a church renewed in concern for the poor and the marginalized.

TH613 Webber, Robert E.
The Church in the World: Opposition, Tension, or Transformation? Grand Rapids, MIU: Zondervan, 1985. 333 pp. Paper. 0310366011.

A text for courses on church and society in colleges and seminaries, including the biblical basis, the historical background, and contemporary models.

TH614 Will, James E.
The Universal God: Justice, Love, and Peace in the Global Village. Louisville, KYU: Westminster John Knox, 1994. viii, 280 pp. Paper. 0664255604.

The Henry Pfeiffer Professor of Systematic Theology at Garrett Evangelical Theological Seminary in Evanston, Illinois, a process theologian, develops themes for a cross-cultural and relational understanding of God for a pluralistic and often divided world.

TH615 Wolfe, Regina Wentzel, and Christine E. Gudorf, eds.
Ethics and World Religions: Cross-Cultural Case Studies. Maryknoll, NYU: Orbis Books, 1999. ix, 419 pp. Paper. 1570752400.

Ethical issues of eighteen original cases of diverse people and religions around the world are followed by two commentaries that explore the issues, principles, and laws from two different religious perspectives.

TH616 Wolterstorff, Nicholas
Until Justice and Peace Embrace. Grand Rapids, MIU: Eerdmans; Kampen, NE: Kok, 1983. x, 197 pp. Paper. 0802833446, 9024225507.

After a brief analysis of the modern world system, the author examines the answers given by two contemporary versions of world-formative Christianity (liberation theologians and neo-Calvinists) to the problems of mass poverty, nationalism, and urbanization.

TH—MISSIONS: THEOLOGY

MISSIONS: ECUMENICAL ASPECTS

Norman E. Thomas, Subeditor

The term ecumenical, in theology today, generally refers to efforts to achieve greater unity among Christians and their churches. It comes from the Greek word *oikoumene,* meaning "the whole inhabited earth" in its New Testament usage (Lk. 4:5). By the fourth century it was used to refer to seven church councils recognized as authoritative by the then-undivided church.

In the last two centuries mission leaders often spearheaded efforts for greater Christian unity. William Carey, often recognized as the father of modern Protestant missions, proposed "a general association of all denominations of Christians from the four quarters of the world" to be held in Cape Town in 1810 or 1812 "to enter into one another's views" (Pierson 2000:301; Ritschl 1997:120).

In the last century many scholars narrowed the use of the term to efforts for conciliar unity (such as that represented by the WCC), and to organic church unity. A few, including Raimundo Pannikar, sought to recover the original Greek inclusiveness. Works on such a wider ecumenism will be included in a later chapter on "Christianity and Other Religions." This bibliography takes a middle position, using *ecumenical* to refer to all efforts to achieve greater Christian unity.

This is not an inclusive bibliography on ecumenism (see Fahey, 1992). Instead, it includes works that focus, in whole or in part, on mission and unity. Much literature on faith and order issues is excluded because its primary concern is for faith, ministry, church order, and sacraments in the gathered community of faith.

Works on national or regional mission and unity can be found in chapters on the various continents. The reader will find standard bibliographies and reference works on ecumenism. The section on "Conferences and Congresses" contains only general works, with most titles grouped under the sponsoring ecumenical bodies.

Many "General Works" contain useful sections on mission and unity. They are followed by historical sections and biographies of ecumenical leaders.

Separate subsections are provided on the "International Missionary Council" (IMC) and the "World Council of Churches" (WCC). Next, books on "World Denominational Fellowships" are included, containing sections on mission and unity.

The next section includes works on "World Evangelical Movements and Associations." Paul Pierson has called these "the most important manifestation of the ecumenical movement today" (Pierson 2000:302).

The following sections on "Inter-Confessional Conversations/Cooperation" and "Youth" are limited to works dealing with unity and mission. Books on "Plans of Church Unity and Reunion" tell of the efforts, primarily in the Third World, to overcome divisions. Often imposed from outside, they injured not only the visible unity of the Body of Christ, but also the credibility of its evangelistic witness in mission contexts.

Norman E. Thomas

Bibliographies

EA1 Beffa, Pierre
Bibliography on the Ecumenical Movement and the World Council of Churches: 1968-1995. (WCC Library Series, 5). Geneva, SZ: WCC Publications, 1995. 159 pp. Paper. No ISBN.

A comprehensive bibliography, organized by subject, of holdings in the library of the WCC.

EA2 *Doctoral Dissertations on Ecumenical Themes: A Guide for Teachers and Students*
Geneva, SZ: WCC, 1977. 70 pp. 2825405485.

A substantial list of dissertations on ecumenical topics available in the WCC library, including biographies of ecumenical leaders and theologians, plus suggested topics for further research.

EA3 Fahey, Michael Andrew, comp.
Ecumenism: A Bibliographical Overview. (Bibliographies and Indexes in Religious Studies, 23). Westport, CTU: Greenwood, 1992. xxi, 384 pp. 0313251029.

An annotated bibliography of books published from the 1950s to early 1990s in various European languages on ecumenism, focusing on faith and order concerns.

EA4 Puglisi, J. F., and S. J. Voicu
A Bibliography of Interchurch and Interconfessional Theological Dialogues. Rome, IT: Centro Pro Unione, 1984. 260 pp. Paper. No ISBN.

A comprehensive international bibliography of the texts and papers of interconfessional dialogues, 1965-1983, and of related periodical articles, arranged by subject without annotation.

EA5 Van der Bent, A. J.
Six Hundred Ecumenical Consultations, 1948-1982. Geneva, SZ: WCC, 1983. 246 pp. Paper. 282540764X.

Brief descriptions with bibliographical information on 633 ecumenical consultations sponsored by the WCC or its departments.

Serials and Periodicals

See also GW20, GW25, CR20, CR30, SO6-SO7, ED2, EV4, and EV9.

EA6 *Bulletin [WCC].* Vol. 1 (1955)-vol. 10, no. 1 (Spring 1964). Semiannual
Geneva, SZ: WCC, Division of Studies, 1955-1964. No ISSN.

Papers from the WCC's study projects; continued by *Study Encounter.*

EA7 *Ecumenical Review.* Vol. 1, no.1 (1948) -. Quarterly
Geneva, SZ: WCC, 1948-. ISSN 00130796.

This official journal of the WCC includes articles plus book reviews on central themes of ecumenical concern.

EA8 *Interchurch Aid Newsletter.* No. 1 (Jan.-Feb. 1955)-no. 6 (Nov.-Dec. 1971). Bimonthly
Geneva, SZ: WCC, CICARWS, 1955-1971. No ISSN.

Feature articles and news on issues and programs of relief and development; continued as *Justice and Service.*

EA9 *Journal of Ecumenical Studies.* Vol. 1, no. 1 (Winter 1964)- Quarterly
Philadelphia, PAU: Temple University, 1964-. ISSN 00220558.

Articles covering scholarly and grassroots concern for interreligious dialogue worldwide, including English language coverage of the literature and events from six continents, and extensive book reviews.

EA10 *Justice and Service.* Vol. 1, no. 1 (1973)-vol. 2 (1974). Quarterly
Geneva. SZ: WCC, CICARWS, 1972-1974. No ISSN.

News of development issues and the programs of relief and interchurch aid of the WCC and other agencies; superseded *Interchurch Aid Newsletter.*

EA11 *Occasional Papers [IMC/WCC].* Series 1, no. 1 (1958)- series 3, no. 6 (1964). Irregular
London, ENK: International Missionary Council, Dept. of Missionary Studies; Geneva, SZ: WCC, Division of Studies, 1958-1964. No ISSN.

Papers on topics of mission concern, with correspondence and discussion; superseded by *Study Encounter.*

EA12 *One World.* No. 1 (Nov. 1974-no. 211 (Dec. 1995). Monthly
Geneva, SZ: WCC, 1974-1995. ISSN 0303125X.

The news magazine of the WCC designed to provide a means for churches in every part of the world to speak to other churches about their convictions and activities concerning liberation, salvation, mission, and unity; news of WCC and other ecumenical initiatives.

EA13 *Student World.* Vol. 1, no. 1 (1908)-vol. 62, nos. 3-4 (1969). Quarterly
Geneva, SZ: WSCF, 1908-1969. No ISSN.

Thematic issues on theological, ecumenical, and global concerns of the world student movement, plus a chronicle of ecumenical student activites around the world; superseded by *WSCF Books* and *WSCF Newsletter.*

EA14 *Study Encounter.* Vol. 1, no. 1 (1965)-vol. 12, no. 4 (1976). Quarterly
Geneva, SZ: WCC, Staff Advisory Group on Studies, 1965-1976. No ISSN.

Thematic issues of papers and documents related to theological, ecumenical, and missiological concerns of the World Council of Churches; superseded *Occasional Papers* and its *Bulletin.*

Reference Works

See also EA20.

EA15 Friars of the Atonement
Ecumenism around the World: A Directory of Ecumenical Institutes, Centers and Organizations. Rome, IT: Centro Pro Unione, 1971. x, 211 pp. No ISBN.

An annotated directory of ecumenical study and research institutes and of action centers and organizations; with a union list of their serial publications, and the addresses of Roman Catholic episcopal conferences.

EA16 Kelliher, Alexander, ed.
International Directory of Ecumenical Research Centers and Publications. Rome, IT: Centro Pro Unione, 1986. 95 pp. Paper. No ISBN.

A revised edition of the directory of research centers and publications that focus on ecumenical (i.e., interchurch) dialogue; listed by country, with a directory of periodicals published by ecumenical centers.

EA17 Lossky, Nicholas et al., eds.
Dictionary of the Ecumenical Movement. Geneva, SZ: WCC; London, ENK: CCBI Publications; Grand Rapids, MIU: Eerdmans, 1991. xvi, 1196 pp. 282541025X (SZ), 0851692257 (UK), 0802824285 (US).

A comprehensive reference work on 20th-century ecumenism with more than 600 alphabetical entries on ecumenical themes, theology, events, organizations, personalities, ethical issues, and activities; by country, region, and confessional communion.

EA18 Van der Bent, A. J.
Historical Dictionary of Ecumenical Christianity. (Historical Dictionaries of Religions, Philosophies, and Movements, 3). Metuchen, NJU: Scarecrow Press, 1994. xxiii, 599 pp. 0810828537.

An indispensable handbook to 20th-century ecumenism with short and readable entries on significant persons, events, institutions, and activities, plus chronology and comprehensive bibliography; by the former librarian and research officer of the WCC (1963-1989).

EA19 *World Council of Churches Yearbook. 1995.* Annual.
Geneva, SZ: WCC Publications, 1995-. Paper. No ISSN.

Annual reviews of the WCC's involvements in ecumenism and mission, plus names and addresses of staff, member churches, and affiliated regional and national ecumenical bodies.

Documentation and Archives

EA20 Kinnamon, Michael, and Brian E. Cope, eds.
The Ecumenical Movement: An Anthology of Key Texts and Voices. Geneva, SZ: WCC Publications; Grand Rapids, MIU: Eerdmans, 1997. xiv, 548 pp. Paper. 2825411876 (SZ), 0802842631 (US).

An essential anthology with excerpts from the most important documents of the 20th-century ecumenical movement including mission, evangelism, and regional concerns; with introductions and a select bibliography.

EA21 Margull, Hans Jochen, ed.
Zur Sendung der Kirche: Material der Ökumenischen Bewegung. (Theologische Bücherei; Neudrucke und Berichte aus dem 20. Jahrhundert, 18; Mission und Ökumene). Munich, GW: Chr. Kaiser Verlag, 1963. 378 pp. No ISBN.

A sourcebook of key documents of the ecumenical movement from Edinburgh in 1910 to New Delhi in 1961.

EA22 Rusch, William G., and Jeffrey Gros, eds.
Deepening Communion: International Ecumenical Documents with Roman Catholic Participation. Washington, DCU: USCC, 1998. xxvi, 627 pp. Paper. 1574551647.

A collection of documents from bilateral dialogues of Roman Catholics with Protestants of the Reformed, Methodist, Baptist, Pentecostal, and Christian Church/Disciples of Christ traditions, including issues of common witness and service.

EA23 Stransky, Thomas F., and John B. Sheerin, eds.
Doing the Truth in Charity: Statements of Pope Paul VI, Popes John Paul I, John Paul II, and the Secretariat for Promoting Christian Unity, 1964-1980. (Ecumenical Documents, 1). New York, NYU: Paulist Press, 1982. xiv, 366 pp. Paper. 0809123983.

A sourcebook on the Vatican's position papers on ecumenism and interreligious dialogue, 1964 to 1980.

EA24 Van der Bent, A. J.
Vital Ecumenical Concerns: Sixteen Documentary Surveys. Geneva, SZ: WCC, 1986. vi, 333 pp. Paper. 2825408735.

A selection of official statements of the WCC (its assemblies, Central Committee, conferences, and consultations) and of regional ecumenical bodies arranged under sixteen themes, including mission and evangelism, Christianity and culture, and the dialogue with people of living faiths.

EA25 Wietzke, Joachim, comp.
Mission erklärt: Ökumenische Documente von 1972 bis 1992. Leipzig, GW: Evan Verlagsanstalt, 1993. xv, 454 pp. Paper. 3374014798.

This most useful handbook gathers official documents from around the world which relate to the nature and tasks of missionary work, and includes with each a historical introduction outlining the significance and effects.

Conferences and Congresses

See also GW91, HI387, TH252, EA85, EA170, EA208, and EA247.

EA26 International Ecumenical Consultation
Church History in an Ecumenical Perspective: Papers and Reports of an International Ecumenical Consultation held in Basel, October 12-17, 1981. Edited by Lukas Vischer. Bern, SZ: Evangelische Arbeitsstelle Ökumene Schweiz, 1982. 117 pp. Paper. No ISBN.

Papers and reports from an important international consultation designed to encourage church historians to write both with cultural sensitivities and ecumenical (global) perspectives.

EA27 Nilsson, Kjell Ove, ed.
Nåd för onådda: Missionsperspektiv från Melbourne och Pattaya. Stockholm, SW: Gummesson, 1981. 198 pp. 9170706204.

Reports and reflections from the CWME conference in Melbourne in 1980 and the Lausanne Committee for World Evangelization's conference in Pattaya in 1980.

EA28 Settimana di studi missionari, 10th, Milan, 1969
Le Missioni e l'unità dei cristiani: Atti della decima settimana di studi missionari, Milano, 8-12 Settembre 1969. Milan, IT: Vita e Pensiero, 1970. x, 188 pp. No ISBN.

Held at Sacred Heart University, Milan, Italy, this congress addressed the challenges of combining missionary evangelization with ecumenical awareness, with addresses on evangelization in orthodox theology (E. Timiadis) and ecumenism and evangelization in India (M. Dhavamony).

EA29 Smedjebacka, Henrik
Maailmanläetyksen kesä. Translated by Liisa Helminen. (Lähetys tänään, 3). Helsinki, FI: Kirjapaja, 1990. 156 pp. Paper. 9516219780.

A report of the congresses of the WCC and LCWE in 1989.

EA30 Till hela vSrlden—ps Kristi sStt: Frsn San Antonio 22 Maj—1 Juni 1989 och Manila 11 Juli 1989
Uppsala, SW: Swedish Mission Council, 1990. 172 pp. 918542420X.

Reports and reflections from the WCC Commission on World Mission and Evangelism's conference in San Antonio and the Lausanne Committee's congress in Manila in 1989.

General Works

See also GW156-GW157, GW184, GW282, HI623, ME23, ME115, PO13, EV133, CH122, CH162, SP272, AM1064, and AS63.

EA31 Amirtham, Samuel, and Cyris H. S. Moon, eds.
The Teaching of Ecumenics. Geneva, SZ: WCC, 1987. xii, 142 pp. Paper. 2825409073.

Ten papers and seven working group reports on teaching ecumenics within various theological disciplines—the results of a 1-11 July 1986 workshop held at the Ecumenical Institute in Bossey, Switzerland.

EA32 Bluck, John
Everyday Ecumenism: Can You Take the World Church Home? Geneva, SZ: WCC Publications, 1987. x, 70 pp. Paper. 2825408921.

Six popular essays exploring the meaning of "ecumenism" in the contexts of New Zealand and Australia.

EA33 Bruland, Esther Byle

Regathering: The Church from "They" to "We." Grand Rapids, MIU: Eerdmans, 1995. xv, 155 pp. Paper. 0802808662.

The personal stories of North American Christians of diverse confessional backgrounds who found the disunity of the churches to be a hindrance to its mission and advocated a renewed ecumenism.

EA34 Castro, Emilio

A Passion for Unity: Essays on Ecumenical Hopes and Challenges. Geneva, SZ: WCC Publications, 1992. xi, 94 pp. Paper. 2825410896.

Eight essays on themes of unity and mission by the WCC's General Secretary, published on the occasion of his retirement.

EA35 *Church and World: The Unity of the Church and the Renewal of Human Community*

(Faith and Order Paper, 151). Geneva, SZ: WCC, 1990. viii, 90 pp. Paper. 2825410047.

Findings from seven international consultations held on five continents, 1984-1989, sponsored by the WCC's Commission on Faith and Order to study "The Unity of the Church and the Renewal of Human Community."

EA36 Crow, Paul A.

Christian Unity: Matrix for Mission. New York, NYU: Friendship Press, 1982. iv, 119 pp. Paper. 0377001155.

A concise introduction to the ecumenical movement.

EA37 Cunningham, David S., Ralph Del Colle, and Lucas Lamadrid, eds.

Ecumenical Theology in Worship, Doctrine, and Life: Essays Presented to Geoffrey Wainright on His Sixtieth Birthday. New York, NYU: Oxford University Press, 1999. xxiv, 312 pp. 0195131363.

This collection of twenty-four scholarly essays includes studies on Lesslie Newbigin and Trinitarian ecclesiology, contextuality and catholicity, Methodism and ecumenism, Christ and culture, convincing unbelievers that the Bible is the Word of God, and spirituality and unity in South Africa.

EA38 Cunningham, Lawrence S., ed.

Ecumenism: Present Realities and Future Prospects: Papers Read at the Tantur Ecumenical Center, Jerusalem, 1997. Notre Dame, INU: University of Notre Dame Press, 1998. xi, 183 pp. 0268027528.

A collection of eleven scholarly papers presented at the Tantur Ecumenical Center conference in Jerusalem, held in the spring of 1997; the volume is a pledge for the future of Christian unity.

EA39 Derr, Thomas Sieger

Barriers to Ecumenism: The Holy See and the World Council of Churches on Social Questions. Maryknoll, NYU: Orbis Books, 1983. ix, 102 pp. Paper. 0883440318.

An expanded and updated version of a paper on the methodological differences, structural barriers, and substantive issues blocking the RCC and the WCC from ecumenical cooperation on social issues, by a professor of religion at Smith College.

EA40 Duchrow, Ulrich

Konflikte um die Ökumene: Christusbekenntnis—in welcher Gestalt der ökumenischen Bewegung? Munich, GW: Kaiser Verlag, 1980. 338 pp. 3459012617.

From a Lutheran perspective, and influenced by his seven-year service as director of the Student Office of the LWF, the author examines Lutherans' witness to/within ecumenism.

EA41 Durand, J. J. F.

Una Sancta Catholica in sendingperspektief: 'n analise van die probleme rondom kerklike pluriformiteit en ekumenisiteit in die sending. (Proefschrift Theol. Fac. Vrije Universiteit Amsterdam). Amsterdam, NE: Ten Have, 1961. 287 pp. Paper. No ISBN.

A doctoral thesis on the theology and reality of pluriformity in national churches, mostly in the Calvinist tradition, as well as the new denominationalism of AICs.

EA42 Durand, J. J. F.

Una Sancta Catholica in Sendingperspektief. Amsterdam, NE: Ten Have N.V., 1961. 287 pp. Paper. No ISBN.

A detailed study of the struggle for unity on the mission field, including the imperative in Reformation theology, the challenges on denominationalism, separation, indigenization, and 20th-century ecumenical efforts for unity in mission; originally submitted as a doctoral dissertation at the Free University of Amsterdam.

EA43 Ellis, Christopher J

Together on the Way: A Theology of Ecumenism. London, ENK: BCC, 1990. 146 pp. Paper. 0851692095.

A basic theology of ecumenism seeking answers from the Bible, church history, and the mission of the church to the question, "Is the search for the unity of the church important?"

EA44 George, K. M., and K. J. Gabriel, eds.

Towards a New Humanity: Essays in Honour of Dr. Paulos Mar Gregorios. Delhi, II: ISPCK, 1992. 162 pp. Paper. 8172140665.

Essays honoring a distinguished teacher, metropolitan of the Indian Orthodox Church, and ecumenical leader; by his friends and former students.

EA45 Goodall, Norman

The Ecumenical Movement: What It Is and What It Does. London, ENK: Oxford University Press, 1961. 240 pp. No ISBN.

An introduction to the history, organizational structures, problems, and programs of modern ecumenism.

EA46 Goodall, Norman

Ecumenical Progress: Decade of Change in the Ecumenical Movement, 1961-1971. London, ENK: Oxford University Press, 1972. x, 173 pp. 0192139541.

A sequel to Goodall's *The Ecumenical Movement* (1961), including updates on Eastern Orthodox representation in the WCC, changes in Roman Catholic positions regarding ecumenism, and WCC developments.

EA47 Lambert, Bernard

Ecumenism: Theology and History. New York, NYU: Herder and Herder; London, ENK: Burns & Oates, 1967. 533 pp. No ISBN.

English translation.

EA48 Lambert, Bernard

Le problème œcuménique. (L'Église en son temps. Série "études"). Paris, FR: Éditions du Centurion, 1962. 730 pp. No ISBN.

A substantial study of Catholic and Protestant principles of ecumenism as they relate to the problem of the church's mission, constitution, and worship.

EA49 Le Guillou, M. J.

Misión y Unidad. Barcelona, SP: Editorial Estela, 1963. 2 vols. No ISBN.

Spanish translation.

EA—MISSIONS: ECUMENICAL ASPECTS

EA50 Le Guillou, M. J.

Mission et unité: les exigences de la communion. (Unam Sanctam, 33-34). Paris, FR: Éditions du Cerf, 1960. 2 vols. No ISBN.

A detailed analysis of the history and current status of ecumenism written for Roman Catholics on the eve of Vatican II.

EA51 Le Guillou, M. J.

Sendung und Einheit der Kirche: Das Erfordernis einer Theologie der Communio. Mainz, GW: Matthias Grünewald, 1964. 686 pp. No ISBN.

German translation.

EA52 Limouris, Gennadios, ed.

Church, Kingdom, World: The Church as Mystery and Prophetic Sign. Geneva, SZ: WCC, 1986. 209 pp. Paper. 2825408476.

An account of the major contributions made at the WCC's Faith and Order consultation, held at Chantilly, France, January 1985, including discussions on church unity, church as mystery, and church as prophetic sign; edited by the Ecumenical Patriarchate of Constantinople.

EA53 Littell, Franklin H., ed.

A Half Century of Religious Dialogue, 1939-1989: Making the Circles Larger. (Toronto Studies in Theology, 46). Lewiston, NYU: E Mellen Press; Dyfed, ENK: Lampeter, 1989. 355 pp. 0889469261.

Twenty essays giving retrospective analyses of various aspects of ecumenism written to commemorate the First World Conference of Christian Youth (Amsterdam, 1939).

EA54 Marty, Martin E.

Church Unity and Church Mission. Grand Rapids, MIU: Eerdmans, 1964. 139 pp. No ISBN.

An appraisal by the eminent University of Chicago church historian of the trauma of contemporary ecumenism, in which international ecumenism is strong, but local ecumenism weak.

EA55 Michalon, Pierre

Œcuménisme et unité chrétienne. (Le Verbe fait chair, 9). Paris, FR: Éditions la Cordelle, 1968. 128 pp. No ISBN.

Instruction for Christians in the basic concepts of the *Oikumene* and of ecumenical work, emphasizing the great significance of missions for the concern of unity.

EA56 Michalon, Pierre

Ökumene und Einheit der Christen. Paderborn, GW: Schöningh, 1969. 104 pp. Paper. No ISBN.

German translation.

EA57 Potter, Philip

Life in All Its Fullness. Ann Arbor, MIU: University Microfilms, 1990. x, 173 pp. Paper. 2825406848.

Reprint of a collection of writings and speeches on ecumenical themes, by the then-general secretary of the WCC; first published in 1976 (Geneva, SZ: WCC).

EA58 Raiser, Konrad

Ecumenism in Transition: A Paradigm Shift in the Ecumenical Movement? Geneva, SZ: WCC Publications, 1991. viii, 132 pp. Paper. 2825409960.

A critical examination of the present-day problem areas in the ecumenical movement, including approaches to mission and interfaith dialogue, by a former deputy general secretary of the WCC.

EA59 Reuver, Marc, Friedhelm Solms, and Gerrit Huizer, eds.

The Ecumenical Movement Tomorrow: Suggestions for Approaches and Alternatives. Kampen, NE: Kok Publishing House; Geneva, SZ: WCC Publications, 1993. 410 pp. Paper. 9024262011 (NE), 2825411221 (SZ).

Twenty-nine essays by specialists from five continents on problems, currents, and issues of importance to the ecumenical movement, in future global economics, ecology, roles of women, health care, emerging theologies, justice and human rights, and violence/nonviolence.

EA60 Saayman, W. A.

Unity and Mission: A Study of the Concept of Unity in Ecumenical Discussions since 1961 and Its Influence on the World Mission of the Church. Pretoria, SA: University of South Africa, 1984. ix, 136 pp. Paper. 0869813137.

An analysis of the 20th-century debate among Roman Catholics, the Eastern Orthodox, and ecumenical and evangelical Protestants over issues of unity and mission.

EA61 Seumois, André

Œcuménisme missionnaire. (Urbaniana Nova Series, 4). Rome, IT: Pontificia Universitas Urbaniana, 1970. 234 pp. Paper. No ISBN.

An Oblate Catholic priest explores the missionary origins of the modern ecumenical movement and the impact that ecumenism has had on the way Catholic missions are conceived and operated.

EA62 Sobrino, Jon, and Juan Hernández Pico

Teología de la Solidaridad Cristiana. (Colección Dios habla en Centroamérica, 3). Managua, NQ: Instituto Histórico Centroamericano; Managua, NQ: Centro Ecuménico Antonio Valdivieso, 1983. 115 pp. No ISBN.

Two prophetic voices of the Church in Central America combine in a redefinition of Christian solidarity, based on insights from the churches in Latin America.

EA63 Sobrino, Jon, and Juan Hernández Pico

Theology of Christian Solidarity. Translated by Phillip Berryman. Maryknoll, NYU: Orbis Books, 1985. viii, 99 pp. Paper. 0883444526.

English translation.

EA64 Stirnimann, Heinrich, ed.

Ökumenische Erneuerung in der Mission. (Ökumenische Beihefte, 4). Freiburg, SZ: Paulus Verlag, 1970. 102 pp. No ISBN.

Four scholars and missiologists (Auf der Maur, P. Beyerhaus, H. Rickenbach, E. Wildbolz) focus on mission and church unity—the tensions, the conflicts, and most importantly, implications for universal church renewal.

EA65 Thomas, Madathilparapil M.

Towards a Theology of Contemporary Ecumenism: A Collection of Addresses to Ecumenical Gatherings, 1947-1975. Madras, II: CLS; Geneva, SZ: WCC, 1978. iv, 320 pp. Paper. No ISBN.

A collection of addresses to different ecumenical gatherings, reflecting on the relation between the universality of Jesus, the unity of the church, and the contemporary struggle for world community; by the director emeritus of the Christian Institute for the Study of Religion and Society (Bangalore, India) and Moderator of the WCC's Central Committee.

EA—MISSIONS:
ECUMENICAL ASPECTS

EA66 Van der Bent, A. J., ed.
Voices of Unity: Essays in Honour of Willem Adolf Visser 't Hooft on the Occasion of His 80th Birthday. Geneva, SZ: WCC, 1981. x, 101 pp. Paper. 2825406643.

Ten essays by an international panel of ecumenists, describing how the ecumenical movement has been shaped through recent conflicts and tensions in six continents.

EA67 Van Dusen, Henry P.
One Great Ground of Hope: Christian Missions and Christian Unity. Philadelphia, PAU: Westminster Press, 1961. 205 pp. No ISBN.

An eminent ecumenical leader's authoritative survey of the growth of Christian cooperation and unity within worldwide Protestantism, 1796-1960.

EA68 Webb, Pauline, ed.
Faith and Faithfulness: Essays on Contemporary Ecumenical Themes: A Tribute to Philip A. Potter. Geneva, SZ: WCC, 1984. xviii, 128 pp. Paper. 2825408123.

Fourteen ecumenical leaders from six continents celebrate the causes that have been integral to Philip Potter's ministry and ecumenical witness as general secretary of the WCC.

EA69 Wieser, Thomas, ed.
Whither Ecumenism?: A Dialogue in the Transit Lounge of the Ecumenical Movement. Geneva, SZ: WCC, 1986. 103 pp. Paper. 2825408751.

An account of the WCC's "Cultures In Dialogue" symposium held at Cartigny, France, in October 1984, to honor Dr. Philip Potter upon his retirement as general secretary.

History: General

See also HI135, EA49-EA51, EA61, and AS993.

EA70 Bassham, Roger C.
Mission Theology, 1948-1975: Years of Worldwide Creative Tension—Ecumenical, Evangelical, and Roman Catholic. South Pasadena, CAU: William Carey Library, 1979. xviii, 434 pp. 0878083308.

A study of interaction and reaction in three streams of Christian thought, in a period when each was developing conciliar modes of debate.

EA71 Beaver, Robert Pierce
Ecumenical Beginnings in Protestant World Mission: A History of Comity. New York, NYU: Nelson, 1962. 356 pp. No ISBN.

A history of one-and-one-half centuries of Protestant missions, focusing upon both the relationship among denominations manifested in their comity arrangements, and between new national churches and their parent denominations.

EA72 Fey, Harold E., ed.
The Ecumenical Advance: A History of the Ecumenical Movement, Vol. 2, 1948-1968. Geneva, SZ: WCC, 1986. 570 pp. Paper. 2825408727.

A second edition of the comprehensive history of the WCC and its programs and activities, with chapters on Orthodox and Roman Catholic involvement in the ecumenical movement, the growth of national and regional councils of churches, world confessionalism, and an extensive new ecumenical bibliography (1968-1985); first published in 1970 by SPCK, London, and Westminster Press, Philadelphia.

EA73 Hering, Wolfgang
Das Missionsverständnis in der ökumenisch-evangelikalen Auseinandersetzung: Ein innerprotestantisches Problem. (Studia Instituti Missiologici SVD, 25). St. Augustin, GW: Steyler Verlag, 1980. 180 pp. Paper. 3877871372.

A licentiate thesis on the history of the world missionary conferences, the WCC, and evangelical counter-movements, focusing especially on the concept of mission.

EA74 Hoekstra, Harvey T.
The World Council of Churches and the Demise of Evangelism. Wheaton, ILU: Tyndale, 1979. 300 pp. Paper. 0842385258.

An evangelical critique of changing WCC concerns for world mission and evangelism, 1948-1975.

EA75 Hudson, Darril
The World Council of Churches in International Affairs. Leighton Buzzard, ENK: Faith Press for the Royal Institute of International Affairs, 1977. 336 pp. Paper. 0716404656.

A study of the participation of international ecumenical organizations, including the WCC, in world affairs, 1907-1968.

EA76 Meyer, Harding, and William G. Rusch
That All May Be One: Perceptions and Models of Ecumenicity. Grand Rapids, MIU: Eerdmans, 1999. xvi, 156 pp. Paper. 0802843484.

A comprehensive study of the goal of church unity, from the beginning of the ecumenical movement to the present day; takes into account specific convictions of individual churches and denominations and offers a new vision for the future.

EA77 Neill, Stephen Charles
The Church and Christian Union. (The Bampton Lectures, 1964). London, ENK: Oxford University Press, 1968. ix, 423 pp. No ISBN.

An analysis of the theological climate affecting ecumenism, 1920-1960, especially related to ecclesiology.

EA78 Rouse, Ruth, and Stephen Charles Neill, eds.
A History of the Ecumenical Movement, 1517-1948, Vol. 1. Geneva, SZ: WCC, 1986. 838 pp. Paper. 2825408719.

A third edition of the official ecumenical history, covering four centuries of varied endeavors toward church unity in Europe, North America, and other continents; first published in 1954 by SPCK, London, and Westminster Press, Philadelphia.

19th Century

See also HI121.

EA79 Gordon, Marie Hale, and Adoniram Judson Gordon
Journal of Our Journey: Edited and Translated from Manuscript Notes by John Beauregard. Edited by John Beauregard. Wenham, MDU: Gordon College Archives, 1989. 289 pp. Paper. No ISBN.

The 1888 journals of Marie Hale Gordon and Adoniram Judson Gordon (1836-1895), newly rediscovered, a rich record of their participation in the great Centenary Missionary Conference (London, 1888), of preaching missions in Scotland, and plans to open the Boston Missionary Training Institute, the forerunner of the present Gordon College.

EA80 Hauzenberger, Hans

Einheit auf evangelischer Grundlage: Von Werden und Wesen der Evangelischen Allianz. Giessen, GW: Brunnen-Verlag; Zürich, SZ: Gotthelf Verlag, 1986. xviii, 513 pp. Paper. 3765593230 (B), 3857062355 (G).

This dissertation from Bern researches the conditions under which the Evangelical Alliance came to be, in the 19th century, through detailed examination of archival sources, of which ninety pages are reproduced in an appendix.

20th Century

See also GW274, HI156, HI511-HI513, TH39, TH603, EA46, EA127, EA147, EA231, CR148, CR248, EC167, PO189-PO190, PO224, EV153, AM969, AS269, and AS1097.

EA81 Bakker, J.

Œcumene, praktijk en probleem: Een vergelijkende sociologische beschouwing van hervormdgereformeerde verhoudingen in Nieuw-Guinea en Nederland. Meppel, NE: Boom, 1970. xi, 303 pp. No ISBN.

A detailed comparative study of ecumenical attitudes in first the Dutch Reformed Church of the Netherlands, which established mission work in New Guinea, and then of the Evangelical Christian Church as it developed there.

EA82 Beyerhaus, Peter

Mission in urchristlicher und endgeschichtlicher Zeit. (Theologie und Dienst, 4). Giessen, GW: Brunnen-Verlag, 1975. 40 pp. 3765503452.

A polemic against trends in ecumenical theology, contending that the WCC is in danger of replacing a biblical theology of the lordship of the risen Christ with a person-centered Marxist humanism.

EA83 Bilheimer, Robert S.

Breakthrough: The Emergence of the Ecumenical Tradition. Grand Rapids, MIU: Eerdmans; Geneva, SZ: WCC Publications, 1989. x, 235 pp. Paper. 0802802966 (E), 2825409553 (W).

A personal account of the ecumenical movement by a Presbyterian (US) minister who worked for the WCC (1948-1963) and directed the Institute for Ecumenical and Cultural Research (1963-1973); with intimate details of discussions and sketches of prominent ecumenical leaders.

EA84 Ellingsen, Mark

The Cutting Edge: How Churches Speak on Social Issues. Geneva, SZ: WCC; Grand Rapids, MIU: Eerdmans, 1993. xxiii, 370 pp. Paper. 2825410977 (SZ), 0802807100 (US).

An analysis of denominational and ecumenical statements made since 1964 on nine controversial issues related to racism, economic development, ecology, war and peace, marriage, abortion, genetic engineering, social justice, and sociopolitical idealogies; with a 46-page bibliography and subject index.

EA85 Hedlund, Roger E.

Roots of the Great Debate in Mission: Mission in Historical and Theological Perspective. (Theological Issues Series, 3). Bangalore, II: Theological Book Trust, 1993. xviii, 511 pp. Paper. No ISBN.

Revised edition of a detailed overview of the polarization, from 1910 to 1975, over the meaning of mission, including important documents in the debate; originally published in 1981 by Evangelical Literature Service.

EA86 Irvin, Dale T.

Hearing Many Voices: Dialogue and Diversity in the Ecumenical Movement. Lanham, MDU: University Press of America, 1994. 208 pp. 0819192619 (hdbk), 0819192627 (pbk).

A concise introduction to central themes of the 20th-century ecumenical movement (dialogue, mission, unity, community, faith, etc.), by a New York Theological Seminary professor.

EA87 Macris, George P.

The Orthodox Church and the Ecumenical Movement During the Period 1920-1969. Seattle, WAU: St. Nectarios Press, 1986. 185 pp. Paper. 0913026743.

Documentation of increasing Orthodox involvement in the ecumenical movement, 1920-1969, and resulting negative reactions; prepared by a Russian Orthodox priest who judges ecumenism to be the source of heresy and schism.

EA88 McGavran, Donald Anderson, ed.

The Conciliar-Evangelical Debate: The Crucial Documents, 1964-1976. South Pasadena, CAU: William Carey Library, 1977. 396 pp. No ISBN.

This second and expanded edition of *Eye of the Storm: The Great Debate in Mission* (Waco, TXU: Word Books, 1972) contains not only documents surrounding the WCC's Uppsala Assembly (1968), but also those of the Bangkok World Mission Conference (1972-1973), and the Nairobi Assembly (1975).

EA89 Nash, Margaret A.

Ecumenical Movement in the 1960s. Johannesburg, SA: Ravan Press, 1975. 430 pp. 08697504710.

A doctoral thesis analyzing the major priorities of the WCC and the Vatican in ecumenism in the 1960s.

EA90 Renkewitz, Heinz, ed.

Die Brüder-Unität. (Die Kirchen der Welt, 5). Stuttgart, GW: Evan Verlagswerk, 1967. 288 pp. No ISBN.

Twenty-two contributors from ten countries share their faith and experience as Moravians in this scholarly volume on the journey toward church unity, especially through Moravian missionary outreach worldwide.

EA91 Stadler, Anton Paul

Mission-Dialogue: A Digest and Evaluation of the Discussion in the Roman Catholic Church and within the World Council of Churches, 1965-1975. Ann Arbor, MIU: University Microfilms, 1977. viii, 399 pp. No ISBN.

A doctoral dissertation (Union Theological Seminary, 1977) comparing concepts of mission and interreligious dialogue in the RCC and the WCC.

EA92 Utuk, Efiong Sam

From New York to Ibadan: The Impact of African Questions on the Making of Ecumenical Mission Mandates, 1900-1958. (American University Studies, 7: Theology and Religion, 82). New York, NYU: Lang, 1991. xv, 350 pp. 0820414018.

A detailed analysis of African contributions to ecumenical thought on mission; originally presented as a doctoral dissertation at Princeton University in the United States.

EA93 Van der Bent, A. J.

Commitment to God's World: A Concise Critical Survey of Ecumenical Social Thought. Geneva, SZ: WCC Publications, 1995. xii, 243 pp. Paper. 2825411620.

A topical survey of the social thought of the WCC, with a concise history of the earlier 1850-1948 history, and of Roman Catholic social thought.

EA—MISSIONS: ECUMENICAL ASPECTS

EA94 Wind, A.

Zending en Œcumene in de twintigste eeuw: Handboek over de geschiedenis van zending en oecumene aan de hand van de grote conferenties en assemblées. (Deel 2a: Van Ghana 1957/58 tot en met Uppsala 1968). Kampen, NE: Kok, 1984, 1991. 2 vols.

A history of major ecumenical conferences of the 20th century, from Edinburgh in 1910 to Uppsala in 1968, focusing on the development of thought concerning mission and ecumenics; [vol. 1 Edinburgh (1910) to Evanston (1954), 434 pp., 9024231612; vol. 2 Ghana (1957) to Uppsala (1968), 536 pp., 9024230594].

Biography

See also HI439, TH71, EA193, CR172, EV280, AM364, AS277, AS287, AS1192, and EU143.

EA95 Bria, Ion, and Dagmar Heller, eds.

Ecumenical Pilgrims: Profiles of Pioneers in Christian Reconciliation. Geneva, SZ: WCC, 1995. viii, 257 pp. Paper. 2825411450.

Fifty short profiles of 20th-century ecumenical leaders—many of them leaders in mission and in the churches of the Two-Thirds World.

EA96 Clifford, Paul Rowntree

An Ecumenical Pilgrimage. London, ENK: West Ham Central Mission, 1994. viii, 184 pp. Paper. 0952452103.

An autobiography covering sixty years of ecumenical involvements by a prominent British Baptist minister, including wartime ministry at West Ham Central Mission (London), teaching at McMaster University (Canada), and the presidency of Selly Oak Colleges (Birmingham).

EA97 Davis, John Merle

An Autobiography. Tokyo, JA: Kyo Bun Kwan, 1960. 248 pp. No ISBN.

The life story of a noted missionary of the ABCFM, who later, as the first secretary of the IMC's research department, initiated a notable series of field studies of the economic and social conditions in "younger" churches.

EA98 Dillistone, F. W.

Into all the World: A Biography of Max Warren. London, ENK: Hodder & Stoughton, 1980. 251 pp. 0340254793.

An official biography of Max Alexander Cunningham Warren (1904-1977), who served as general secretary of the CMS (1942-1963) and as canon and sub-dean of Westminster (1963-1973); with an examination of his theology of mission.

EA99 Evans, G. R., Lorelei F. Fuchs, and Diane C. Kessler

Encounters for Unity. Norwich, ENK: Canterbury Press, 1995. vi, 234 pp. Paper. 1853110965.

Brief testimonies, by thirty-seven church leaders on six continents, of their pilgrimages of personal transformation through ecumenical encounters.

EA100 Flory, Margaret

Moments in Time: One Woman's Ecumenical Journey. New York, NYU: Friendship Press, 1995. xviii, 121 pp. Paper. 0377002984.

The founder of the Presbyterian Frontier Intern Program relates personal vignettes from fifty years of bridge-building on behalf of the world church.

EA101 Furtado, Christopher L.

The Contribution of Dr. D. T. Niles to the Church Universal and Local. Madras, II: CLS, 1978. xvi, 246 pp. Paper. No ISBN.

A dissertation analyzing the legacy as ecumenical church leader and theologian of Daniel Thambyrajah Niles (1908-1970)—Sri Lankan Methodist pastor and first general secretary of the EACC.

EA102 Gentz, Wiliam H.

The World of Philip Potter. New York, NYU: Friendship Press, 1974. 96 pp. Paper. 037700006X.

A brief popular account of the life of the WCC's general secretary, from his birth in the West Indies; organized around his qualities of leadership.

EA103 Goodall, Norman

Christian Ambassador: A Life of A. Livingstone Warnshuis. Manhasset, NYU: Channel Press, 1963. xi, 174 pp. No ISBN.

A popular biography of the US Secretary of the IMC (1924-1942), whose further leadership in Christian relief and reconstruction led to the emergence of Church World Service.

EA104 Grubb, Kenneth

Crypts of Power: An Autobiography. London, ENK: Hodder & Stoughton, 1971. 253 pp. 0340149639.

The autobiography and reflections of a Christian leader involved in many missionary and ecumenical activities, including missionary service and research in Latin America, the presidency of the CMS, and the chairmanship of the CCIA.

EA105 Hopkins, C. Howard

John R. Mott, 1865-1955: A Biography. Grand Rapids, MIU: Eerdmans, 1979. xvii, 816 pp. 0802835252.

A definitive biography of a leading ecumenical statesman in the first half of the 20th century.

EA106 Jackson, Eleanor M.

Red Tape and the Gospel: A Study of the Significance of the Ecumenical Missionary Struggle of William Paton (1886-1943). Birmingham, ENK: Phlogiston, 1980. 409 pp. 0906954010.

A detailed biography of William Paton (1886-1943), missionary statesman and ecumenical pioneer; based on an exhaustive analysis of archives of the Paton family, British SCM, WCC, and others.

EA107 Jacques, André

Madeleine Barot. Translated by Pat Nottingham and Bill Nottingham. Geneva, SZ: WCC Publications, 1991. viii, 88 pp. Paper. 2825409952.

English translation.

EA108 Jacques, André

Madeleine Barot: Une indomptable énergie. (L'histoire à vif, 0299-2833). Paris, FR: Éditions du Cerf; Genève, FR: Labor et Fides, 1989. 223 pp. 2204031976 (C), 283090589X (L).

The story of a half-century of courageous witness and action, 1940-1990, by the secretary-general of CIMADE (the French ecumenical committee to aid displaced people) and WCC staff member for youth, women, and development.

EA109 Neill, Stephen Charles

Brothers of the Faith. New York, NYU: Abingdon, 1960. 192 pp. No ISBN.

An account, published in 1960, of the struggle to form the WCC; told through the biographies of the men who worked for it, showing the issues, problems, successes, and failures through their experiences; by one who was a personal friend of many and much involved in the ecumenical movement.

EA110 Newbigin, James Edward Lesslie

Unfinished Agenda: An Autobiography. Grand Rapids, MIU: Eerdmans, 1985. 263 pp. Paper. 0802800912.

Autobiography of the Scotch Presbyterian missionary theologian, bishop of the Church of South India, and ecumenical leader.

EA111 Ranson, Charles W.

A Missionary Pilgrimage. Grand Rapids, MIU: Eerdmans, 1988. ix, 202 pp. Paper. 0802803199.

The autobiography of the late Charles W. Ranson, an Irish Methodist missionary to India, from 1929 to 1945, who later directed the IMC and the TEF.

EA112 Schmidt, William J.

Architect of Unity: A Biography of Samuel McCrea Cavert. New York, NYU: Friendship Press, 1978. vi, 330 pp. No ISBN.

A biography based on archives and oral interviews of the outstanding Presbyterian ecumenical leader (1888-1976) who served as general secretary of the Federal and National Council(s) of Churches (US), from 1921 to 1954.

EA113 Visser 't Hooft, Willem Adolph

Memoires: Een leven in de œcumene. Amsterdam, NE: Elsevier; Kampen, NE: Kok, 1971. 336 pp. 9010009793.

The original Dutch edition of the autobiography of the WCC's first general secretary, with detailed coverage of the ecumenical movement from 1937 to 1961.

EA114 Visser 't Hooft, Willem Adolph

Memoirs. Geneva, SZ: WCC Publications, 1987. x, 379 pp. 2825409057.

English translation.

EA115 Warren, Max Alexander Cunningham

Crowded Canvas: Some Experiences of a Life-Time. London, ENK: Hodder & Stoughton, 1975. 255 pp. 034018101X.

Reminiscences of Max Warren (1904-1977), from his childhood in India as the son of CMS missionaries, to his own missionary service in Nigeria, and twenty-one years as secretary of the CMS.

EA116 Weber, Hans-Ruedi

The Courage To Live: A Biography of Suzanne de Diétrich. Geneva, SZ: WCC Publications, 1995. x, 168 pp. Paper. 2825411566.

The story of Suzanne de Diétrich (1891-1981), a prominent leader in mission planning and reflection through the SCM, World YWCA, and WSCF.

EA117 Weber, Hans-Ruedi

Suzanne de Diétrich, 1891-1981: La passion de vivre. Paris, FR: Les Bergers et Les Mages, 1995. 285 pp. Paper. 2853041174.

French translation.

World Ecumenism: General

See also TH359, TH588, CR478, EC371, and PO209.

EA118 Aram I,

In Search of Ecumenical Vision. Antélias, LE: Armenian Catholicosate of Cilicia, 2000. 318 pp. Paper. No ISBN.

Advocates an ecumenism that transforms people, makes churches other-centered, provides mutual accountability, and turns toward the world in missionary engagement.

EA119 Bent, A. J. van der

God So Loves the World: The Immaturity of World Christianity. Maryknoll, NYU: Orbis Books, 1979. x, 150 pp. Paper. 0883441594.

A strong critique of the ecumenical movement by the librarian of the WCC's Ecumenical Centre in Geneva, for its failure to translate its words concerning a just, participatory, and sustainable society into deeds of mercy and justice; originally published by the CLS, Madras, India, in 1977.

EA120 Beyerhaus, Peter

Humanisierung, einzige Hoffnung der Welt? Bad Salzuflen, GW: MKB-Verlag, 1969. 69 pp. No ISBN.

Critique by a prominent evangelical German missiologist, of trends in the ecumenical movement's understanding of mission; plus the text of the Frankfurt Declaration.

EA121 Beyerhaus, Peter

Missions: Which Way? Humanization of Redemption. Translated by Margaret Clarkson. (Contemporary Evangelical Perspectives). Grand Rapids, MIU: Zondervan, 1971. 120 pp. No ISBN.

English translation.

EA122 Engel, Frank

Living in a World Community: An East Asian Experience of the World Student Christian Federation, 1931-1961. (Centennial Series, 18). Kowloon, HK: WSCF, 1994. xi, 123 pp. Paper. No ISBN.

A brief history, plus source documents, on the WSCF's work in East Asia; written by its former East Asian secretary.

EA123 Haque, A., ed.

Mission and Dialogue in the New Millennium. Delhi, II: ISPCK, 1999. xii, 88 pp. Paper. 8172145101.

This book traces and analyzes the understanding of dialogue among ecumenicals, Roman Catholics, and evangelicals, with a view to assess its relevance for Christian mission in India today.

EA124 Kärkkäinen, Veli-Matti

Ad ultimum terrae: Evangelization, Proselytism, and Common Witness in the Roman Catholic Pentecostal Dialogue, 1990-1997. (Studies in the Intercultural History of Christianity, 117). Frankfurt am Main, GW: Lang, 1999. 281 pp. Paper. 363135035X (GW), 0820443468 (US).

The second largest Christian constituency after the RCC, the Pentecostals are known for energetic evangelism and mission, but are accused of proselytism and lack of social concern in mission; this international dialogue between the two largest Christian families highlights similarities and differences in mission.

EA125 Limouris, Gennadios, comp.

Orthodox Visions of Ecumenism: Statements, Messages and Reports on the Ecumenical Movement 1902-1992. Geneva, SZ: WCC Publications, 1994. xii, 283 pp. Paper. 2825410802.

A sourcebook containing fifty texts of Orthodox church and conference statements on ecumenism and mission.

EA126 Philip, T. V., ed.
Edinburgh to Salvador: Twentieth Century Ecumenical Missiology, A Historical Study of the Ecumenical Discussions on Mission. Delhi, II: CSS/ISPCK, 1999. x, 265 pp. Paper. 8172145365.

This study is concerned with the missiological thinking expressed in conferences and assemblies of the IMC and the WCC, through the exploration of five major topics: church and mission; mission and unity; world, mission, and church; the Kingdom of God and mission; mission and the world of religions and cultures.

EA127 Van der Bent, A. J.
Incarnation and New Creation: The Ecumenical Movement at the Crossroads. Madras, II: CLS, 1986. viii, 171 pp. Paper. No ISBN.

A popular account of the evolution of the ecumenical movement through the eyes of the WCC librarian.

EA128 Visser 't Hooft, Willem Adolph
Auf dem Weg zur Einheit. Wetzhausen, GW: Kühne, 1970. 79 pp. No ISBN.

Lectures by the WCC's first General Secretary given at the Ecumenical Institute at Bossey, Switzerland, on the future of the ecumenical vision of unity and mission.

EA129 Visser 't Hooft, Willem Adolph
Hacia una Nueva Cristiandad. (Pensamiento Cristiano y Diálogo, 12). Bilbao, SP: Editorial Española Desclée de Brouwer, 1973. 84 pp. Paper. 8433004492.

Spanish translation.

EA130 Visser 't Hooft, Willem Adolph
Has the Ecumenical Movement a Future? Atlanta, GAU: John Knox Press, 1976. 97 pp. 0804209170.

Four lectures by the first General Secretary of the WCC, arguing that the ecumenical movement has a future as is "learns to realize more fully that the Lord gathers his people in order that they may be a light to the world."

EA131 Weber, Hans-Ruedi
Asia and the Ecumenical Movement, 1895-1961. London, ENK: SCM Press, 1966. 319 pp. No ISBN.

A detailed history of Asian contributions to the ecumenical movement including the student movement (WSCF, YM/YWCA), the IMC, Faith and Order, Life and Work, the WCC, and the EACC.

International Missionary Council

See also EA126, CR113, CR189, ED140, EV237, and AF744.

EA132 Günther, Wolfgang
Von Edinburgh nach Mexico City: Die ekklesiologischen Bemühungen der Weltmissionskonferenzen (1910-1963). Stuttgart, GW: Evan Missionsverlag, 1970. 279 pp. Paper. 3771400031.

A dissertation analyzing how the world missionary conferences struggled to integrate mission and church in the Protestant sphere (Dissertation, Univ. of Erlangen/Nürnberg, Fac. of Theology, 1968).

EA133 Hallencreutz, Carl F.
Kraemer towards Tambaran: A Study in Hendrik Kraemer's Missionary Approach. (Studia Missionalia Upsaliensia, 7). Uppsala, SW: Almqvist & Wiksell; Lund, SW: Gleerup, 1966. 340 pp. Paper. No ISBN.

The dissertation by the noted Swedish missiologist analyzing the development of Hendrik Kraemer's theology from his beginning student days in 1911 to his leadership at the Madras Conference in 1938, including Dutch missionary debate and his missionary service in Indonesia.

EA134 Hof, I. P. C. van't
Op zoek naar het geheim van de Zending: In dialoog met de Wereldzendingsconferenties 1910-1963. (Proefschrift Theol. Fac. Rijksuniversiteit Leiden). Wageningen, NE: Veenman, 1972. 242 pp. Paper. No ISBN.

A doctoral dissertation on the theology of mission as developed at the world missionary conferences, 1910-1963, based on minutes, archival, and other primary sources.

EA135 Karlström, Nils
Mission och ekumenik: Till frsgan om en integration mellan Internationella Missionsrsdet och Kyrkornas VSrldsrsd. Stockholm, SW: Diakonistyrelsens Bokförlag, 1960. 287 pp. No ISBN.

A study of the integration of the IMC and the WCC.

EA136 Nissen, Karsten
Mission og enhed: En undersogelse af de strukturelle, teologiske og politiske konsekvenser af Det internationale Missionsrsds integration med Kirkernes Verdensrad. Aarhus, DK: Karsten Nissen, 1973. 282 pp. Paper. No ISBN.

An analysis of the background, motivations and consequences of the integration in 1961 between the IMC and the WCC.

EA137 Schulz-Ankermann, Friederike
Die Boten Christi und ihr nichtchristliches Gegenüber auf den Weltmissionskonferenzen von 1910 bis 1963. Lübeck, GW: University of Hamburg, 1969. iii, 206 pp. Paper. No ISBN.

A dissertation on the encounter of missionaries with people of other religions according to the world missionary conferences from Edinburgh (1910) to Mexico City (1963).

EA138 Shivute, Tomas
The Theology of Mission and Evangelism in the International Missionary Council from Edinburgh to New Delhi. (Annals of the Finnish Society for Missiology and Ecumenics, 31). Helsinki, FI: Missiologian ja ekumeniikan seura; Helsinki, FI: Suomen Lähetysseura, 1980. x, 303 pp. 9519520562 (M), 9516241719 (S).

A study of missions and evangelism from 1910 to 1961, showing changes in the IMC until it became part of the ecumenical movement at New Delhi.

Student Associations

See also HI687, EA116, AM146, and EU233.

EA139 Adler, Elisabeth, ed.
Memoirs and Diaries: The World Student Christian Federation 1895-1990. (Centennial History Series, 3, 4). Geneva, SZ: WSCF, 1994. 221 pp. Paper. No ISBN.

A sourcebook of WSCF documents published for its centennial.

EA140 Antone, Hope S., ed.
Ecumenical Student Ministry in Asia-Pacific. Kowloon, HK: WSCF, 1995. iii, 177 pp. Paper. NO ISBN.

Eighteen short papers on ecumenical student ministries in the WSCF's Asia-Pacific region; originally presented at a CCA-WSCF Joint Program (Bangkok, 1-8 April 1995).

EA—MISSIONS: ECUMENICAL ASPECTS

EA141 Barclay, Oliver R.

Whatever Happened to the Jesus Lane Lot? Leicester, ENK: InterVarsity, 1977. 176 pp. 0851106242 (hdbk), 0851103960 (pbk).

A documented history of the Cambridge Intercollegiate Christian Union (CICCU) of Great Britain from its founding in 1877 through its separation from the SCM in 1910 to its metamorphosis into the InterVarsity Christian Fellowship in 1928, with an assessment of its worldwide influence on the growth of evangelical Christianity.

EA142 Dietrich, Suzanne de

Fifty Years of History: The World Student Christian Federation (1895-1945). Translated by Audrey Abrecht. (Centennial History Series, 2). Geneva, SZ: WSCF, 1993. 90 pp. Paper. No ISBN.

Reprint of a 1946 bird's-eye view of the life and witness of the WSCF by one of its prominent leaders.

EA143 Edwards, David L.

Movements into Tomorrow: A Sketch of the British SCM. London, ENK: SCM Press, 1960. 63 pp. No ISBN.

A short history of the Student Christian Movement of Great Britain and Ireland.

EA144 Howard, David M.

Student Power in World Evangelism. Downer's Grove, ILU: InterVarsity, 1970. 129 pp. 0877845395.

Inspiration for students interested in world mission including its biblical basis, a history of student power in world evangelism, and an assessment of the task that faces today's student generation.

EA145 Howard, David M.

Student Power in World Missions. Downers Grove, ILU: InterVarsity, 1979. 129 pp. Paper. 0877844933.

Begins with a biblical perspective of mission and in that context traces the student mission movement's history to the present with chapters on the movement's inception, the Haystack movement, the Student Volunteer Movement for Foreign Missions, and the Student Foreign Missions Fellowship.

EA146 Lehtonen, Risto

Story of a Storm: The Ecumenical Student Movement in the Turmoil of Revolution, 1968 to 1973. (Publications of the Finnish Society of Church History, 174). Helsinki, FI: Suomen kirkkohistoriallinen seura; Grand Rapids, MIU: Eerdmans, 1998. xxiv, 360 pp. 9525031063 (FI, hdbk), 0802844294 (US, pbk).

An insider's account of Christian student movements' involvement in the social protests of the 1960s and 1970s by the former General Secretary of the WSCF (1968-1972).

EA147 Lindner, John B., Alva I. Cox, and Linda-Marie Delloff

By Faith: Christian Students among the Cloud of Witnesses. New York, NYU: Friendship Press, 1991. 159 pp. Paper. 0377002364.

A study book exploring the history of the ecumenical student Christian movement in the United States in the 19th and 20th centuries and its major themes and passions.

EA148 Lowman, Pete

The Day of His Power: A History of the International Fellowship of Evangelical Students. Leicester, ENK: InterVarsity, 1983. 386 pp. Paper. 0851107133.

A popular account of the history and contemporary worldwide work of the International Fellowship of Evangelical Students (IFES).

EA149 Potter, Philip, and Thomas Wieser

Seeking and Serving the Truth: The First Hundred Years of the World Student Christian Federation. Geneva, SZ: WCC Publications, 1997. xi, 307 pp. Paper. 2825412104.

The official centennial history (1895-1995) of the World Student Christian Federation (WSCF) by two of its creative past leaders.

EA150 Selles, Johanna M.

Women's Role in the History of the World Student Christian Federation, 1895-1945. (Occasional Publications, 6). New Haven, CTU: Yale Divinity School Library, 1995. 26 pp. Paper. No ISBN.

An essay commissioned to commemorate the centennial of the founding of the WSCF.

EA151 Van der Bent, A. J.

From Generation to Generation: The Story of Youth in the World Council of Churches. Geneva, SZ: WCC, 1986. xi, 135 pp. Paper. 2825408441.

An interpretative survey of ecumenical youth work through the World Council of Churches and of international and regional youth movements from 1925 to the early 1980s.

EA152 Wieser, Thomas, ed.

Bible and Theology in the Federation: A Report. (Centennial History Series, 5). Geneva, SZ: WSCF, 1995. 71 pp. Paper. No ISBN.

Reflections on the relationship between the WSCF during its first one-hundred years and the Bible, based on papers and discussions at the WSCF's 1993 consultation held at the Ecumenical Institute, Bossey, Switzerland, on the theme.

EA153 WSCF Assembly (31st., Yamoussoukro, Côte d'Ivoire, 26 Aug.-10 Sept. 1995)

A Community of Memory and Hope: Celebrating God's Faithfulness. Edited by Jean-François Delteil. (*WSCF Journal* Dec. 1995). Geneva, SZ: WSCF, 1995. 89 pp. Paper. No ISBN.

Papers from the centennial gathering.

World Council of Churches

See also TH135, TH309, TH322, TH559-TH560, TH588, TH603, EA5, EA19, EA29, EA58, EA73-EA74, EA83, EA86, EA88, EA91, EA126-EA127, EA132, EA135-EA136, EA151, ME112, ME180, CR67, CR71, CR402, CR527, CR892, CR949, CR960, CR1220, CR1373, CR1458, SO23, SO31, SO78, SO133, SO186, SO210, SO226-SO227, SO230, SO232, SO236, SO401, SO430, SO435, SO438, SO448, SO504, SO550, EC13-EC14, EC17-EC18, EC30, EC38, EC99, EC197, EC221-EC222, EC259, EC327, EC330, EC335, EC342, EC368, PO7, PO38, PO63, PO81, PO191, PO217, CO15, EV14, EV103, EV113, EV237, CH477, SP232, AF813, AF1037, AF1042, AF1123-AF1124, AM673, AS74, AS803, AS1222, EU58, and OC74.

EA154 *Acting in Faith*

New York, NYU: WCC, nd. 29 mins pp. No ISBN.

A video overview of the varied ecumenical ministries of the World Council of Churches.

EA155 *And So Set Up Signs ... : The World Council of Churches' First 40 Years*

Geneva, SZ: WCC, 1988. 74 pp. Paper. 2825409413.

A popular portrait in photographs and words that tells the forty-year story of the World Council of Churches (WCC), 1948-1988.

EA156 Anderson, Gerald H., ed.
Witnessing to the Kingdom: Melbourne and Beyond. Maryknoll, NYU: Orbis Books, 1982. vi, 170 pp. Paper. 0883447088.

The reports of seven participants at the World Conference on Mission and Evangelism, held in Melbourne, Australia, in May 1980; they emphasize the poor in relation to the Kingdom, being Christ centered, and how these issues speak to North American Orthodox, Roman Catholic and Protestant people.

EA157 Arias, Mortimer
Salvação Hoje: Entre o Cativeiro e a Libertação. Petrópolis, BL: Editora Vozes, 1974. 172 pp. Paper. No ISBN.

Portuguese translation.

EA158 Arias, Mortimer
Salvación es Liberación: Reflexiones Latinoamericanas en Torno al Temario de la Conferencia Ecuménica Salvación Hoy Celebrada en Bangkok, en Diciembre de 1972 ... Buenos Aires, AG: Editorial La Aurora, 1973. xv, 183 pp. Paper. No ISBN.

Presentation and discussion of the themes of the Bangkok Conference (1972-1973), with practical appendices for reflection and study.

EA159 Bakare, Sebastian
The Drumbeat of Life: Jubilee in an African Context. (Risk Book Series, 80). Geneva, SZ: WCC Publications, 1997. ix, 52 pp. Paper. 2825412295.

An Anglican priest and senior chaplain at the University of Zimbabwe reflects on "Turn to God—Rejoice in Hope," the theme of the jubilee assembly of the WCC, held in his city in December 1998.

EA160 Bakare, Sebastian
Au son du tambour, danser la vie: Le jubilé dans un contexte africain. Geneva, SZ: WCC Publications, 1998. 65 pp. No ISBN.

French translation.

EA161 Bakare, Sebastian
Trommeln des Lebens: Das Erlassjahr im afrikanischen Kontext. Genf, GW: ÖRK, 1998. 66 pp. No ISBN.

German translation.

EA162 Best, Thomas F., ed.
Instruments of Unity: National Councils of Churches within the One Ecumenical Movement. Geneva, SZ: WCC, 1988. viii, 178 pp. Paper. 2825409367.

The report of an important WCC consultation with representives of national councils of churches (Geneva, Switzerland, 20-24 October 1986), which focused on the councils as agents of mission, service, and dialogue.

EA163 Best, Thomas F., ed.
Vancouver to Canberra, 1983-1990: Report of the Central Committee of the World Council of Churches to the Seventh Assembly. Geneva, SZ: WCC Publications, 1990. xxv, 275 pp. Paper. 2825409871.

Report includes major sections on mission, evangelism, justice ministries, and interreligious concerns; also published in French, German, and Spanish.

EA164 Beyerhaus, Peter
Bangkok '73: The Beginning or End of World Mission? Grand Rapids, MIU: Zondervan, 1973. 192 pp. Paper. No ISBN.

A description and criticism of the WCC's World Missionary Conference in Bangkok, attempting to prove that its understandings of salvation and mission were unbiblical, syncretistic, and ideologically biased.

EA165 Beyerhaus, Peter
Bangkok '73—Anfang oder Ende der Weltmission?: Ein gruppendynamisches Experiment. (Telos-Taschenbuch, 56). Bad Liebenzell, GW: Verlag der Liebenzeller Mission, 1973. 255 pp. 3921113393.

German translation.

EA166 Brinkman, Martien E.
Progress in Unity?: Fifty Years of Theology within the World Council of Churches, 1945-1995: A Study Guide. (Louvain Theological and Pastoral Monographs, 18). Grand Rapids, MIU: Eerdmans; Louvain, BE: Peeters Press, 1995. vii, 180 pp. Paper. 9068316842.

An assessment of the scope of the ecumenical agreement reached over fifty years, organized as a study guide around central themes.

EA167 Castro, Emilio, comp.
To the Winds of God's Spirit: Reflections on the Canberra Theme. Geneva, SZ: WCC, 1990. vii, 103 pp. Paper. 2825409944.

Ten theological reflections on the theme of the WCC's Canberra Assembly (1991), "Come Holy Spirit—Renew the Whole Creation"; originally published in *The Ecumenical Review.*

EA168 Castro, Emilio, ed.
Church and Society, Ecumenical Perspectives: Essays in Honor of Paul Abrecht. Geneva, SZ: WCC, 1985. xiii, 163 pp. Paper. 2825408190.

A special issue of *The Ecumenical Review*, Vol. 37:1 Jan. 1985, containing essays that give a variety of insights into the history and work of the WCC, especially in church and society issues.

EA169 CMI, Conferencia Mundial de Misiones y Evangelización, Melbourne, AT, 12-25 de mayo de 1980
Venga tu Reino: Perspectivas misioneras: Informe. (Nueva Alianza, 85). Salamanca, SP: Ediciones Sígueme, 1982. 349 pp. Paper. 8430108947.

Spanish translation.

EA170 Conference on World Mission and Evangelism (Salvador, Brazil, 24 Nov.-3 Dec. 1996)
Called to One Hope: The Gospel in Diverse Cultures. Edited by Christopher Duraisingh. Geneva, SZ: WCC Publications, 1998. xiv, 234 pp. Paper. 282541235X.

The official report and papers from the conference.

EA171 Conference on World Mission and Evangelism (San Antonio, Texas, 22 May-1 June 1989)
The San Antonio Report: Your Will Be Done; Mission in Christ's Way. Edited by Frederick R. Wilson. Geneva, SZ: WCC Publications, 1990. 214 pp. Paper. 282540974X.

The full report and papers of the conference.

EA172 Conference on World Mission and Evangelism (San Antonio, Texas, 22 May-1 June 1989)
Your Will Be Done: Mission in Christ's Way. Geneva, SZ: WCC, 1988. 80 pp. Paper. 2825409200.

Study and biblical reflection material.

EA173 *Die Kirche für andere und Die Kirche für die Welt*
Geneva, SZ: WCC, 1967. 152 pp. No ISBN.

German translation.

EA174 Early, Tracy
Simply Sharing: A Personal Survey of How Well the Ecumenical Movement Shares Its Resources. (Risk Book Series, 8). Geneva, SZ: WCC, 1980. v, 83 pp. Paper. 2825406449.

A popular presentation of the WCC's study on the ecumenical sharing of resources.

EA175 *Espíritu, Evangelio, Culturas: Estudios bíblicos sobre los Hechos de los Apóstoles*
Quito, EC: CLAI, 1996. 55 pp. Paper. No ISBN.

Spanish translation of *Spirit, Gospel, Cultures* (1995).

EA176 *Esprit, évangile, cultures: études bibliques sur les Actes des Apôtres*
Paris, FR: DEFAP, 1996. 55 pp. Paper. No ISBN.

French translation.

EA177 Fifth Faith and World Order Conference, Santiago de Compostela, 3-14 August 1993
Returning Pilgrims: Insights from British and Irish Participants in the Fifth World Faith and Order Conference, Santiago de Compostela 3-14 August 1993. London, ENK: CCBI, 1994. iv, 99 pp. Paper. 085169232X.

Reflections by twelve participants from Britain and Ireland, on themes of *koinonia*, witness in a multi-faith society, and contextual theology.

EA178 *From Canberra to Harare: An Illustrated Account of the Life of the World Council of Churches, 1991-1998*
Geneva, SZ: WCC Publications, 1998. 53 pp. Paper. 2825412600.

An illustrated report of the work of the WCC from 1991 to 1998, including areas of mission, evangelism, social justice, and service.

EA179 *Geist, Evangelium und Kulturen: Bibelarbeiten zur Apostelgeschichte*
(Weltmission heute Studienheft, 21). Hamburg, GW: EMW, 1996. 60 pp. Paper. No ISBN.

German translation.

EA180 *Hágase tu Voluntad: La misión conforme a Cristo*
Geneva, SZ: WCC, 1988. 88 pp. Paper. 2825409243.

Spanish translation.

EA181 Hallencreutz, Carl F., ed.
Frälsning i dag: Budskap från Bangkok 73. Stockholm, SW: Gummesson, 1973. 111 pp. 9170703574.

Reports and reflections from the World Mission Conference in Bangkok 1973, published by the Swedish Missionary Council's WCC section.

EA182 Hollenweger, Walter J.
Glaube, Geist und Geister: Professor Unrat zwischen Bangkok und Birmingham. Frankfurt am Main, GW: Lembeck, 1975. 124 pp. Paper. 3874760413.

Mission issues raised at the 1972-1973 Bangkok conference on "Salvation Today," presented as the conversations and reflections of an imaginary "Professor Unrat"; by the noted missiologist.

EA183 Howell, Leon
Acting in Faith: The World Council of Churches since 1975. Geneva, SZ: WCC, 1982. 120 pp. Paper. 2825407089.

A journalist assesses the work of the WCC during the 1975 to 1981 period, with focus on mission to the poor, education for renewal, and Christian unity.

EA184 Lefever, Ernest W.
Amsterdam to Nairobi: The World Council of Churches and the Third World. (Ethics and Public Policy Studies). Washington, DCU: Georgetown University, Ethics and Public Policy Center, 1979. xii, 114 pp. Paper. 0896330257 (hdbk), 0896330249 (pbk).

An analysis critical of the WCC's involvements in political issues, from its founding in 1948 to 1975; by the founding director of the Ethics and Public Policy Center at Georgetown University in Washington, DC.

EA185 Lefever, Ernest W.
Nairobi to Vancouver: The World Council of Churches and the World, 1975-1987. Washington, DCU: Ethics and Public Policy Center, 1987. xv, 149 pp. 0896331772 (hdbk), 0896331180 (pbk).

In this sequel to *Amsterdam to Nairobi: The World Council of Churches and the Third World* (1979), the author criticizes the WCC for its political stance, since the 1960s, of identification with liberation theology and revolutionary movements.

EA186 Müller, Jörg
Uppsala II. Erneuerung in der Mission: Eine redaktionsgeschichtliche Studie und Dokumentation zu Sektion II der 4. Vollversammlung des Ökumenischen Rates der Kirchen, Uppsala 1968. (Studies in the Intercultural History of Christianity, 10). Frankfurt am Main, GW: Lang, 1977. 381 pp. Paper. 3261022302.

A dissertation studying the various stages of the editorial process of the controversial Section II—"Renewal in Mission"—of the Fourth Assembly of the WCC in Uppsala.

EA187 Müller-Römheld, Walter
Zueinander, miteinander: Kirchliche Zusammenarbeit im 20. Jahrhundert. Frankfurt am Main, GW: Lembeck, 1971. 196 pp. No ISBN.

An introduction to the 20th-century ecumenical movement, with particular reference to the work of the WCC.

EA188 Morrison, Mary, ed.
Acting in Faithfulness: The San Antonio World Mission Conference 1989. London, ENK: BCC, 1989. iv, 44 pp. Paper. 0851692028.

An interpretation for European churches of the WCC/CWME Conference noting the continuing convergence that took place between "ecumenicals" and "evangelicals" concerned for world mission.

EA189 *Nairobi to Vancouver: 1975-1983 Report of the Central Committee to the Sixth Assembly of the World Council of Churches*
Geneva, SZ: WCC, 1983. xxv, 238 pp. Paper. 2825407593.

The Central Committee's report to the Sixth Assembly of the WCC, Vancouver 1983.

EA190 Orchard, Ronald Kenneth, ed.
Witness in Six Continents: Records of the Meeting of the Commission on World Mission and Evangelism of the WCC Held in Mexico City, December 8-19, 1963. London, ENK: Edinburgh House Press, 1964. x, 200 pp. No ISBN.

Provides addresses (including those by Alfonso Lloreda, Emilio Castro, and Gonzalo Castillo), list of participants, section reports, summary of committee work, and the message of this, the first meeting of the WCC's Commission on World Mission and Evangelism after the IMC/WCC merger.

EA—MISSIONS: ECUMENICAL ASPECTS

EA191 Paton, David MacDonald, ed.
Breaking Barriers: Nairobi 1975 (The Official Report of the Fifth Assembly of the World Council of Churches, Nairobi). London, ENK: SPCK; Grand Rapids, MIU: Eerdmans, 1976. xii, 411 pp. 0802816398 (E), 0281029229 (S).

The official report of the assembly, with the theme "Jesus Christ Frees and Unites."

EA192 Pranger, Jan Hendrik
Dialogue in Discussion: The World Council of Churches and the Challenge of Religious Plurality between 1967 and 1979. (IIMO Research Publication, 38). Utrecht, NE: IIMO, 1994. v, 198 pp. Paper. 9021170035.

A study of how the WCC, and the predecessor IMC, tried to deal with the challenge of religious pluralism; a revision of theses originally submitted at the universities of Groningen and Princeton.

EA193 Samartha, Stanley J.
Between Two Cultures: Ecumenical Ministry in a Pluralist World. Geneva, SZ: WCC Publications, 1996. xiii, 202 pp. Paper. 282541171X.

A first-person account of how interfaith dialogue gained a permanent place on the agenda of the WCC, by its first director of the subunit on Dialogue with People of Living Faiths.

EA194 Sovik, Arne
Salvation Today. Minneapolis, MNU: Augsburg, 1973. 112 pp. 0806613181.

A discussion of issues raised and debated at the World Conference on Salvation Today (Bangkok, Thailand, 29 Dec. 1972-8 Jan. 1973), sponsored by the WCC.

EA195 Study Process on Gospel and Cultures: Suggested Guidelines for Local Groups
Geneva, SZ: WCC Publications, 1995. 23 pp. Paper. No ISBN.

A brief description of the WCC's study process for local groups in preparation for the Conference on World Mission and Evangelism (Salvador, 1996).

EA196 The Church for Others and Church for the World: A Quest for Structures for Missionary Congregations
Geneva, SZ: WCC, Department on Studies in Evangelism, 1967. 133 pp. No ISBN.

The final reports of the Western European and North American working groups for the influential study by the WCC's Department on Studies in Evangelism on "The Missionary Structure of the Congregation."

EA197 Theology for Our Times: A Special Number on the Theme of the VIII Assembly of the World Council of Churches to Be Held at Harare (Zimbabwe) in 1998
(*Theology for Our Times*, 3/1996). Bangalore, II: Ecumenical Christian Centre, 1996. 112 pp. Paper. No ISBN.

Papers by eleven Indian theologians, originally presented in an ecumenical study group on "Turn to God and Rejoice in Hope," the theme of the eighth Assembly of the WCC (Harare, 1998), with special application to the Indian context.

EA198 Van der Bent, A. J.
Die Kirchen und die Eine Welt: Eine Herausforderung des Ökumenischen Rates der Kirchen. Translated by Walter Müller-Römheld. (Erlanger Taschenbücher, 31). Erlangen, GW: Ev.-Luth. Mission, 1974. 128 pp. Paper. 3872140612.

German translation.

EA199 Van der Bent, A. J.
The Utopia of World Community: An Interpretation of the World Council of Churches for Outsiders. London, ENK: SCM Press, 1973. x, 150 pp. 0334017246.

An introduction to the goals, program, and achievements of the WCC.

EA200 VanElderen, Marlin
Introducing the World Council of Churches. (The Risk Series, 46). Geneva, SZ: WCC Publications, 1990. vii, 174 pp. Paper. 2825409731.

A clear and concise introduction to the contemporary ecumenical movement in general, and to the WCC in particular, including its varied missional concerns.

EA201 Verkuyl, Johannes
Jezus Christus, de Bevrijder en de voortgaande bevrijdingen van mensen en samenlevingen: De betekenis van de Wereldconferentie voor zending en evangelisatie in Bangkok. Baarn, NE: Ten Have, 1973. 112 pp. Paper. 9025940315.

Personal impressions of the World Conference on Mission and Evangelization (Bangkok, 1973) by Verkuyl; with additional articles.

EA202 Vermaat, J. A. Emerson
The World Council of Churches and Politics: 1975-1986. (Focus on Issues, 6). New York, NYU: Freedom House, 1989. 128 pp. Paper. 0932088309 (hdbk), 0932088295 (pbk).

A critical analysis of WCC documents, 1975 to 1986, which illuminate the WCC's development of its political positions on some controversial international issues.

EA203 Vischer, Lukas
Veränderung der Welt, Bekehrung der Kirchen: Dekanstösse der Fünften Vollversammlung des Ökumenischen Rates der Kirchen in Nairobi. Frankfurt am Main, GW: Lembeck, 1976. 111 pp. 3874760499.

Four lectures by the WCC's chief resident theologian, giving a personal assessment of the WCC's Fifth Assembly (Nairobi), focusing on issues of witness, dialogue, social action, and unity.

EA204 Visser 't Hooft, Willem Adolph
The Genesis and Formation of the World Council of Churches. Geneva, SZ: WCC, 1982. ix, 130 pp. Paper. 282540733X.

The history of the ecumenical vision from the initial idea in 1919 to WCC formation in 1948, and to the definition of its nature in 1950, by the WCC's first general secretary.

EA205 WCC Assembly (6th., Vancouver, Canada, 24 July-10 August 1983)
Gathered For Life: Official Report ... Edited by David M. Gill. Geneva, SZ: WCC; Grand Rapids, MIU: Eerdmans, 1983. viii, 355 pp. Paper. 2825407798 (W), 0802819877 (E).

The official report of the Sixth Assembly, with the theme "Jesus Christ—the Life of the World."

EA206 WCC World Mission and Evangelism Assembly (Bangkok, Thailand, 9-12 Jan. 1973)
Bangkok Assembly 1973: Minutes and Reports. Geneva, SZ: WCC, 1973. 118 pp. No ISBN.

The official report and papers of the Bangkok Assembly of the WCC's Commission on World Mission and Evangelism.

EA—MISSIONS: ECUMENICAL ASPECTS

EA207 WCC, Central Committee
Uppsala to Nairobi, 1968-1975: Report of the Central Committee to the Fifth Assembly of the WCC. Edited by David Enderton Johnson. New York, NYU: Friendship Press; London, ENK: SPCK, 1975. 256 pp. Paper. No ISBN.

An insightful description and evaluation of the various programs of the WCC.

EA208 Webb, Pauline
Salvation Today. Naperville, ILU: SCM Press, 1974. x, 117 pp. Paper. No ISBN.

A popular interpretation of the deliberations of the WCC's conference on "Salvation Today" (Bangkok, 1973), by the Director of the Board of Lay Training of the Methodist Church (UK).

EA209 Weber, Hans-Ruedi
A Laboratory for Ecumenical Life: The Story of Bossey, 1946-1996. Geneva, SZ: WCC Publications, 1996. viii, 145 pp. Paper. 2825412155.

The story of the first fifty years of the WCC's Ecumenical Institute at Bossey, near Geneva.

EA210 Wietzke, Joachim
Dein Wille geschehe: Mission in der Nachfolge Jesu Christi. Frankfurt am Main, GW: Verlag Otto Lembeck, 1989. 302 pp. Paper. 3874762610.

Eleven short interpretive essays plus documents from the WCC's Conference on World Mission and Evangelism (San Antonio, Texas, 1989).

EA211 World Conference on Faith and Order (5th, Santiago de Compostela, 3-14 August 1993)
On the Way to Fuller Koinonia. Geneva, SZ: WCC Publications, 1994. xxx, 318 pp. Paper. 2825411272.

Official report and papers from the Fifth WCC Conference on Faith and Order, with positions on *koinonia*, common witness, reconciliation, and dialogue important for mission studies.

EA212 World Conference on Mission and Evangelism (Melbourne, Australia, 12-25 May 1980)
Your Kingdom Come: Mission Perspectives. Geneva, SZ: WCC, 1980. xvii, 283 pp. Paper. 2825406635.

The official report and papers of the Melbourne Conference of the WCC's Commission on World Mission and Evangelism.

EA213 World Conference on Mission and Evangelism, Bangkok, 1973
Das Heil der Welt heute: Ende oder Beginn der Weltmission? Dokumente der Weltmissionskonferenz, Bangkok, 1973. Edited by Philip Potter. Stuttgart, GW: Kreuz Verlag, 1973. 271 pp. Paper. 3783104084.

The documents emanating from the World Mission Conference of the WCC held in Bangkok, Thailand, in 1973, on the theme of "Salvation Today."

EA214 World Missionary Conference (1980: Melbourne, AT)
Dein Reich komme: Bericht der Weltkonferenz für Mission und Evangelisation in Melbourne 1980: Darstellung und Dokumentation. Edited by Martin Lehmann-Habeck. Frankfurt am Main, GW: Lembeck, 1980. 198 pp. Paper. 3874761320.

German translation of *Your Kingdom Come* (1980).

World Denominational Fellowships

See also CR1024, AF812, AF1030, and AS232.

EA215 Anglican Consultative Council (8th, Wales, 1990)
Mission in a Broken World: Report of ACC-8; Wales 1990. London, ENK: Church House Publishing, 1990. vi, 186 pp. Paper. 0715147978.

Addresses, papers, reports, minutes, and statements of the biennial council reflecting global Anglican concerns in mission.

EA216 Burgess, Andrew S., ed.
Lutheran Churches in the Third World. Minneapolis, MNU: Augsburg, 1970. 176 pp. No ISBN.

A survey of cooperation and joint action in mission among Lutheran bodies, with seven essays telling of the work of churches in Asia, Africa, and Latin America.

EA217 *Mission and Unity: The Reformed Family and its Mandate*
(John Knox Series, 6). Geneva, SZ: John Knox Centre International Réformé, 1989. 149 pp. Paper. No ISBN.

Report of the Consultation on Mission and Unity for Reformed Churches (Geneva, 21-27 August 1988) including twelve papers presented with French and German summaries.

EA218 Pradervand, Marcel
A Century of Service: A History of the World Alliance of Reformed Churches, 1875-1975. Grand Rapids, MIU: Eerdmans; Edinburgh, STK: St. Andrew Press, 1975. xv, 309 pp. 0802834663 (US), 0715203207 (UK).

The centennial history by WARC's general secretary.

EA219 Samuel, Vinay, and Chris Sugden
Lambeth: A View from the Two-Thirds World. London, ENK: SPCK, 1989. 158 pp. Paper. 0281044201(net), 0281044430.

An analysis of the Anglican Lambeth Conference of 1988 and what the presence of so many bishops from the Two-Thirds World signified, represented, and expressed.

EA220 *Towards a Common Testimony: Confessing the Faith Today, 17-24 August 1986*
(John Knox Series, 5). Geneva, SZ: John Knox Centre International Réformé, 1989. 299 pp. Paper. No ISBN.

Papers from the "Confessing the Faith Today" Consultation of Reformed Churches (Geneva, 17-24 August 1986) including issues of racism and church and state, which call forth new confessional statements.

EA221 Wingate, Andrew, Kevin Ward, Carrie Pemberton, and Wilson Sitshebo, eds.
Anglicanism: A Global Communion. New York, NYU: Church Publishing, 1998. xx, 416 pp. Paper 0898693047.

Seventy-five short essays by Anglican leaders, mostly from the Two-Thirds World, dealing with issues of faith, worship, spirituality, theology, culture, society, church, other faiths, and Anglican identity.

EA—MISSIONS: ECUMENICAL ASPECTS

World Evangelical Movements and Associations

See also TH561, EA73, and AF46.

EA222 Bakke, Corean
Let the Whole World Sing: The Story behind the Music of Lausanne II. Chicago, ILU: Cornerstone Press, 1994. xvi, 251 pp. Paper. 0940895188.

A chronicle of Christian witness through music from many cultures and confessions at Lausanne II (Manila 1989).

EA223 Fuller, W. Harold
People of the Mandate. Carlisle, ENK: WEF/Paternoster, 1996. xvi, 203 pp. Paper. No ISBN.

Stories of men and women involved in the WEF, including the work of its commissions and departments, as well as of national and regional fellowships.

EA224 Howard, David M.
The Dream That Would Not Die: The Birth and Growth of the World Evangelical Fellowship, 1846-1986. Exeter, ENK: Paternoster Press, 1986. xvi, 239 pp. Paper. 085364442X.

A history of the WEF by its general director; including information on its mission work.

EA225 Howard, David M.
The Elusive Dream: The Eventful Story of the World Evangelical Fellowship. Grand Rapids, MIU: Baker Books; Exeter, ENK: Paternoster Press, 1989. 128 pp. Paper. 0853644985.

A brief popular account of the beginnings of the WEF, written by its international director.

EA226 II Congresso Internacional de Evangelização Mundial, Lausanne, SZ, 1974
A Missão da Igreja no mundo de hoje: As palestras principais do Congresso Internacional de Evangelização Mundial realizado em Lausanne, Suiça. São Paulo, BL: ABU Editora; Belo Horizonte, BL: Visão Mundial, 1982. 248 pp. Paper. No ISBN.

Portuguese translation of *Alle Welt soll sein Wort hören* (1974).

EA227 International Congress on World Evangelization (1974, Lausanne, SZ)
Alle Welt soll sein Wort hören: Lausanner Kongress für Weltevangelisation. Edited by Peter Beyerhaus. (TELOS-Dokumentation, 901). Stuttgart, GW: Hanssler, 1974. 2 vol. Paper. No ISBN.

The presentations and reports of the influential congress of world evangelicals, held 16-25 July 1974.

EA228 International Congress on World Evangelization (1st, 1974, Lausanne, Switzerland)
Let the Earth Hear His Voice: Official Reference Volume, Papers and Responses. Edited by J. D. Douglas. Minneapolis, MNU: World Wide Publications, 1975. vii, 1471 pp. No ISBN.

English translation of *Alle Welt soll sein Wort hören* (1974).

EA229 International Congress on World Evangelization (2nd, 1989, Manila, Philippines)
Proclaim Christ until He Comes: Calling the Whole Church to Take the Whole Gospel to the Whole World. Edited by J. D. Douglas. Minneapolis, MNU: World Wide Publications, 1990. 463 pp. Paper. 0890661901.

The official record of the messages and presentations.

EA230 International Congress on World Evangelization (Manila, 1989)
The Manila Manifesto: An Elaboration of the Lausanne Covenant Fifteen Years Later. Pasadena, CAU: LCWE, 1989. vi, 69 pp. No ISBN.

The official text of the public declaration of Lausanne II, together with the corresponding manifesto of Lausanne I in 1974.

EA231 Kunneth, Walter, and Peter Beyerhaus
Reich Gottes oder Weltgemeinschaft?: Die Berliner Ökumene-Erklärung zur utopischen Vision des Weltkirchenrates. Bad Liebenzell, GW: Verlag der Liebenzeller Mission, 1975. 544 pp. 3880020159.

A collection of speeches and papers from the Berlin conference of evangelicals in 1974, with documentation of those policies, which were denounced at Berlin.

EA232 Nichols, Alan, ed.
The Whole Gospel for the Whole World. Charlotte, NCU: LCWE; Ventura, CAU: Regal Books, 1989. 144 pp. Paper. 9810012535.

A popular account of Lausanne II.

EA233 Padilla, C. René, ed.
The New Face of Evangelicalism: An International Symposium on the Lausanne Covenant. London, ENK: Hodder & Stoughton; Downers Grove, ILU: InterVarsity, 1976. 282 pp. Paper. 0340203242 (H), 0877847797 (I).

A symposium on the fifteen sections of the Lausanne Covenant formulated at the International Congress on World Evangelism held in 1974.

EA234 Poulsen, Peder
Lausannebevægelsen: Historie, Strategi, teologi. Aarhus, DK: Åarhus Universtet, Teologiske Fakultet, 1987. 86 pp. Paper. No ISBN.

This is a special study done by a student of the Faculty of Theology at the University of Aarhus, Denmark, dealing with the missionary principles of the Lausanne Movement.

EA235 Stott, John R. W., ed.
Making Christ Known: Historic Mission Documents from the Lausanne Movement, 1974-1989. Grand Rapids, MIU: Eerdmans, 1997. xxiv, 264 pp. Paper. 0802843158.

The Lausanne Occasional Papers compiled in book form with a historical introduction by the editor, plus the Lausanne Covenant (1974) and the Manila Manifesto (1989).

EA236 Stott, John R. W.
The Lausanne Covenant: An Exposition and Commentary. (Lausanne Occasional Papers, 3). Charlotte, NC: LCWE, 1986. 37 pp. Paper. No ISBN.

The declaration on evangelism resulting from the 150-nation International Congress on Evangelization in 1974, "a solemn covenant with God and each other, to pray, plan, and work together for the evangelization of the whole world"; originally published in 1975.

Interconfessional Conversations/ Cooperation

See also EA22, EA39, CH494, AM141, and AM970.

EA237 Birmele, André
Le salut en Jesus Christ: Dans les dialogues œcuméniques.
Paris, FR: Éditions du Cerf; Geneva, SZ: Labor et Fides, 1986.
513 pp. Paper. 2204026093 (FR), 2830900987 (SZ).

A two-part volume; the first, providing a history of the dialogue between the Roman Catholic and evangelical Lutheran churches, with particular reference to discussion of salvation; part two analyzes the significance of the RC dialogues with Reformed, Methodist, Pentecostal, Disciples of Christ, Anglican, and Orthodox churches.

EA238 Brown, Robert McAfee
The Ecumenical Revolution: An Interpretation of the Catholic-Protestant Dialogue. Garden City, NYU: Doubleday; London, ENK: Burns & Oates, 1967. xix, 388 pp. No ISBN.

A history and contemporary assessment of Protestant and Roman Catholic approaches to ecumenism by an American Protestant scholar and observer at Vatican II.

EA239 Ehrenstrom, Nils, and Günther Gassmann
Confessions in Dialogue: A Survey of Bilateral Conversations among World Confessional Families 1959-1974. (Faith and Order Paper, 74). Geneva, SZ: WCC, 1975. 266 pp. Paper. 2825405000.

This third edition is a revised and enlarged compendium of data concerning interconfessional dialogues.

EA240 Evangelical-Roman Catholic Dialogue on Mission
The Evangelical-Roman Catholic Dialogue on Mission, 1977-1984: A Report. Edited by Basil Meeking and John Robert Walmsley Stott. Grand Rapids, MIU: Eerdmans; Exeter, ENK: Paternoster Press, 1986. 96 pp. Paper. 0802801846 (US), 0853644373 (UK).

A full report of the three meetings of the Evangelical-Roman Catholic Dialogue on Mission, which took place in Venice (1977), Cambridge (1982), and Landevennec, France (1984).

EA241 McDonald, John J.
The World Council of Churches and the Catholic Church. (Toronto Studies in Theology, 21). New York, NYU: E. Mellen Press, 1985. 467 pp. 088946765X.

A scholarly comparison of Catholic and WCC theologies of ecumenism as represented by papal and WCC assembly documents, with a brief background to the ecumenical movement.

EA242 Meeking, Basil, and John Robert Walmsley Stott, eds.
Diálogo sobre la Misión: Informe sobre un diálogo entre evangélicos y católicorromanos (1977-1984). Buenos Aires, AG: Nueva Creación; Grand Rapids, MIU: Eerdmans, 1988. 88 pp. Paper. No ISBN.

Spanish translation.

EA243 Meeking, Basil, and John Robert Walmsley Stott, eds.
Der Dialog über Mission zwischen Evangelikalen und der Rómanisch-Katholischen Kirche, 1977-1984. (Theologie un Dienst, 52). Wuppertal, GW: R. Brockhaus Verlag, 1987. 79 pp. Paper. 341729052X.

German translation.

EA244 Meyendorff, John
Witness to the World. Crestwood, NYU: St. Vladimir's Seminary Press, 1987. 262 pp. Paper. 0881410691.

Editorials, written over a twenty-year period (1965-1984) for *The Orthodox Church* newspaper, which address the principles of Orthodox participation in the ecumenical dialogue (especially since Vatican II and with the polarizations in Protestantism), the Orthodox responsibilities in mission and education, and the state of the Orthodox Church in the Soviet Union in Gorbachev's era of leadership.

EA245 Tesfai, Yacob
Liberation and Orthodoxy: The Promise and Failures of Interconfessional Dialogue. Maryknoll, NYU: Orbis Books, 1996. xi, 196 pp. Paper. 1570750882.

A Third World critique of the ecumenical movement's interconfessional dialogue, by the Eritrean former research professor at the Institute for Ecumenical Research in Strasbourg, France.

Plans of Church Union and Reunion

See also EA77, AF740, AS63, and AS1476.

EA246 Berkhof, A. W., and H. H. van der Kloot Meyburg
Samen op weg in wereldperspektief: Een onderzoek naar hereeningen van kerken van hervormde signatuur. Utrecht, NE: IIMO, 1972. 403 pp. No ISBN.

An analysis of church union negotiations in various parts of the world and how they influenced each other.

EA247 Consultation of United and Uniting Churches (5th, Potsdam, GW, July 1987)
Living Today towards Visible Unity. Edited by Thomas F. Best. (Faith and Order Paper, 142). Geneva, SZ: WCC Publications, 1988. xii, 135 pp. Paper. 2825409170.

Papers reflecting on the possibilities of visible unity within the ecumenical movement.

EA248 Consultation of United and Uniting Churches (6th., Ocho Rios, Jamaica, 21-29 March 1995)
Built Together: The Present Vocation of United and Uniting Churches (Ephesians 2: 22). Edited by Thomas F. Best. Geneva, SZ: WCC Publications, 1996. 174 pp. Paper. 282541199X.

Papers revealing various approaches and initiatives in mission.

EA249 Ghana Church Union Committee
Proposals for Church Union in Ghana. Accra, GH: Ghana Church Union Committee, 1973. 194 pp. No ISBN.

A key document in the aborted negotiations to form a United Church in Ghana.

EA250 Gramberg, Th. B. W. G.
Œcumene in India en Ceylon: Op weg naar Gods ene Kerk. 's-Gravenhage, NE: Boekencentrum, 1962. xv, 366 pp. No ISBN.

A history of ecumenical endeavors in India and Sri Lanka since 1920, mostly based on published sources, but for the 1950s in Ceylon and North India based also on personal observations.

EA251 Hollis, Michael
The Significance of South India. (Ecumenical Studies in History, 5). Richmond, VAU: John Knox Press; London, ENK: Lutterworth Press, 1966. 82 pp. Paper. No ISBN.

A reevaluation of the pioneer church union in South India after twenty years; by the CSI's first moderator, including sections on its history, faith, worship, forms of ministry, and relationship with other churches.

EA252 Kalu, Ogbu U.
Divided People of God: Church Union Movement in Nigeria, 1875-1966. New York, NYU: Nok Publishers, 1978. xiv, 128 pp. 0883570483 (hdbk), 088357070X (pbk).

An analysis, by the senior lecturer in church history at the University of Nigeria, Nsukka, of why the church union movement failed in the 1960s.

EA253 Kinnamon, Michael, and Thomas F. Best, eds.
Called to Be One in Christ: United Churches and the Ecumenical Movement. (Faith and Order Paper, 127). Geneva, SZ: WCC, 1985. xiii, 77 pp. Paper. 2825408379.

Ten case studies originally presented at the Fourth Consultation of United and Uniting Churches (Colombo, Sri Lanka, 1981), together with a summary and bibliography.

EA254 Marshall, W. J.
A United Church: Faith and Order in the North India/Pakistan Unity Plan; A Theological Assessment. Delhi, II: ISPCK; London, ENK: Friends of CNI, 1987. xiii, 146 pp. Paper. No ISBN.

A detailed theological evaluation of the plan of union of the Church of North India as formed in 1970, and of results achieved in North India and Pakistan in the first decade.

EA255 Oosthuizen, G. C.
Theological Battleground in Asia and Africa and the Efforts to Overcome Western Divisions. London, ENK: Hurst, 1972. 900 pp. 0391002309.

An examination of the processes of confessional statement and union in some African and Asian churches, to 1971.

MISSIONS: METHODS

Mary Motte, FMM, Subeditor

Mission bibliographers differ widely in their classification of works dealing with the practice of mission. Vriens (1960:68) grouped together in a chapter on "Mission Methodology" works on practical methods for realizing the purpose of mission work as described in books on mission theory.

Andrew Walls, editor of the "Bibliography on Mission Studies" published quarterly in the *IRM*, includes under "The Structure of Mission" works on the church and mission, missions and the missionary, and financial aspects. *Bibliographia Missionaria*, published annually in Rome, lists under "Pastoral Topics" works on both methods and evangelization, with "Missionary Cooperation" as a separate chapter. Jongeneel, among eleven branches of missiology, includes "missionary cybernetics (government)" and "missionary catechetics (education)" (1997:155-211, 213-240).

In this bibliography, works on the practice of mission are found in several chapters. This chapter includes general works on mission strategies and issues of mission organization, planning, evaluation, finance, and education.

The first subsections include general works on methods of mission (bibliography, serials/periodicals, reference works, documentation, and conferences). Brought together under "General Works" are books on mission strategies from a variety of confessional positions.

Older classifications, "Home Missions" and "Foreign Missions" from the Library of Congress, are retained, but with few entries. Of greater usefulness is the rubric of "Third World Missions."

The next subsections include books on the organization and structure of the churches in mission. Under "Organization and Structure" are works on mission ecclesiology. Related to mutuality in mission are the next sections on "Cooperative Relationships" and "Indigenous Church Administration." Works on mission planning and evaluation are grouped under "Administration: Planning and Evaluation."

Education for mission is the focus of the next subsections. First are grouped general works on mission education. These are followed by the mission study literature, with books for adults distinguished from those for children and youth.

"Mission Finance" receives its own subsection, as does the "Future of Missions."

Norman E. Thomas

Documentation and Archives

ME1 Allen, Roland

The Compulsion of the Spirit: A Roland Allen Reader. Edited by David MacDonald Paton and Charles H. Long. Grand Rapids, MIU: Eerdmans; Cincinnati, OHU: Forward Movement, 1983. viii, 150 pp. Paper. 0802812619 (E), 0880280255 (F).

A compendium of nineteen passages from the writings of Roland Allen (1868-1947), a prophetic Anglican missiologist, concerning missionary methods and church growth, the law and the Spirit, and voluntary clergy.

ME2 *Crossroads in Missions*

(A William Carey Multibook). South Pasadena, CAU: William Carey Library, 1971. xxi, 182 pp. 0878087044.

A reprint of five classics of contemporary missiology: *The Missionary Nature of the Church* (J. Blauw, xxi, 182 pp.), *Missionary, Go Home!* (J. A. Scherer, 192 pp.), *The Responsible Church and the Foreign Mission* (P. Beyerhaus and H. Lefever, 199 pp.), *On the Growing Edge of the Church* (T. W. Street, 128 pp.), and *The Missionary between the Times* (R. P. Beaver, xii, 196 pp.).

ME3 Nevius, John Livingstone
Die Gründung und Entwicklung missionarischer Gemeinden.
Translated by Wolf Christian Jaeschke. (Edition afem). Bonn, GW:
Verlag für Kultur und Wissenschaft, 1993. 199 pp. 392610516X.
    German translation.

ME4 Nevius, John Livingstone
The Planting and Development of Missionary Churches. Philadelphia, PAU: Presbyterian & Reformed Publishing, 1958.
v, 92 pp. No ISBN.
    A reprint of the classic work (1886) on planting indige-
nous churches by the creative Presbyterian missionary to China; edited to be a textbook for mission study classes of the
Student Volunteer Movement for Foreign Missions.

Conferences and Congresses

See also GW90, ME134, ME147, ME250, ME256, and AM251.

ME5 Adrian, Victor, and Donald Loewen, eds.
*Committed to World Mission: A Focus on International Strat-
egy.* Hillsboro, KSU: Kindred Press, 1990. vi, 129 pp. Paper.
0921788002.
    Report and papers from the first worldwide conference
of the Mennonite Brethren (Curitiba, Brazil, 17-21 Feb. 1988).

ME6 Allan, Starling, ed.
*Seeds of Promise: World Consultation on Frontier Missions,
Edinburgh '80.* South Pasadena, CAU: William Carey Library,
1981. xiv, 258 pp. Paper. 0878081860.
    The papers and report of an influential consultation de-
signed to bring the hidden peoples of the world into sharp focus before representatives of 170 Protestant mission agencies.

ME7 Beek, Huibert van, ed.
*Sharing Life: Official Report of the WCC World Consultation
on Koinonia: Sharing Life in a World Community.* Geneva,
SZ: WCC Publications, 1989. x, 148 pp. Paper. 2825409596.
    The official report of a WCC consultation (El Escorial,
Spain, October 1987) at which 250 participants agreed on
guidelines and a discipline of sharing life in community.

ME8 Coggins, Wade T., and Edwin L. Frizen, eds.
Reaching Our Generation. South Pasadena, CAU: William
Carey Library, 1982. iv, 132 pp. Paper. 0878081887.
    Proceedings of a joint meeting of the Interdenomination-
al Foreign Mission Association (IFMA) and the Evangelical
Foreign Mission Association (EFMA) containing addresses
given at Overland Park, Kansas, 28 Sept.-2 Oct. 1981, on how
to share the gospel effectively in the contemporary world.

ME9 *Compassion and Fatigue*
Federal Way, WAU: World Vision, 1996. 78 pp. Paper. No
ISBN.
    Ten papers from the fifth [1996] Washington Forum, "Per-
spectives on Our Global Future," sponsored by World Vision.

ME10 Conn, Harvie M., ed.
Reaching the Unreached: The Old-New Challenge. Phillipsburg, NJU: Presbyterian & Reformed Publishing, 1984. x, 178
pp. Paper. 0875522092.
    Eleven papers from a 1983 consultation held at West-
minster Theological Seminary on goals, strategies, and structures for Christian witness to unreached peoples.

ME11 Fraser, David Allen, ed.
The Church on New Frontiers for Mission. Monrovia, CAU:
MARC, 1983. vii, 280 pp. Paper. 0912552409.
    Twenty papers originally presented at the Wheaton '83
consultation on various aspects of the nature and mission of
the church in new frontier missions.

**ME12 Global Consultation on World Evangelization by AD
2000 and Beyond (1989: Singapore)**
Countdown to AD 2000. Edited by Thomas Wang. Pasadena,
CAU: AD 2000 Movement, 1989. xx, 236 pp. Paper.
0878082239.
    Report and papers from an important conference of 314
evangelical mission leaders from fifty nations which evaluated proposals and recommended strategies for proclamation of
Christ to every person on earth by the year 2000.

ME13 Martinson, Paul Varo, ed.
*Mission at the Dawn of the 21st Century: A Vision for the
Church.* Minneapolis, MNU: Kirk House Publishers, 1999.
400 pp. Paper. 1886513309.
    A compilation of twenty-nine papers on contemporary
issues of mission, presented at the Congress on the World Mission of the Church at Luther Seminary in St. Paul, Minnesota
(23-27 June 1998).

**ME14 *Mission & Transformation in a Changing World: A
Dialogue with Global Mission Colleagues***
New York, NYU: UMC, Board of Global Ministries, 1998. ix,
118 pp. Paper. No ISBN.
    Papers from the United Methodist Board of Global Min-
istries' consultation (Kansas City, Kansas, April 1997).

ME15 Mozaz, Díaz et al.
*Las Misiones Populares, hoy: Conferencia de la Semana de
Estudios sobre Misiones Populares.* (Semana de Estudios sobre Misiones Populares (Madrid, 11-15 de septiembre de
1972)). Madrid, SP: La Milagrosa, 1973. 176 pp. 8430057145.
    Papers presented in Madrid at a conference of Roman
Catholic clergy and laity to review the current (1972) state of
missions and their relation to the church.

ME16 Sookhdeo, Patrick, ed.
New Frontiers in Mission. Exeter, ENK: Paternoster Press;
Grand Rapids, MIU: Baker Books, 1987. 190 pp. Paper.
0853644500 (P), 0801082846 (B).
    Sixteen papers from "Wheaton '83," an international evan-
gelical conference on "The Nature and Mission of the Church
in the New Frontier Mission," presenting a variety of viewpoints which define unfinished frontier tasks, unreached peoples, and resources to equip mission agencies.

ME17 Stockdale, Sharon, ed.
New Wineskins for Global Mission. South Pasadena, CAU:
William Carey Library, 1996. xv, 444 pp. Paper. 0878082697.
    Proceedings of the "New Wineskins for Global Mission"
conference (Ridgecrest, North Carolina, 27 April-7 May 1994)
sponsored by the Episcopal Church Missionary Community.

ME18 Winter, Ralph D.
Thy Kingdom Come. South Pasadena, CAU: William Carey
Library, 1995. 43 pp. Paper. 0878089632.
    Reprint of two articles on the historical origins and pur-
poses of the AD 2000 Movement prepared for the Second Glo-
bal Consultation on World Evangelization by AD 2000 (Seoul,
Korea, 17-26 May 1995).

ME19 World Consultation on Inter-Church Aid (Swanwick, Great Britain, 4-11 July 1966)

Digest of the 1966 World Consultation on Inter-Church Aid at Swanwick, Great Britain. Geneva, SZ: WCC, 1966. 135 pp. Paper. 2825403644.

Report of a major WCC-sponsored consultation with 239 participants from seventy-eight countries, the first with Roman Catholic Church representatives; edited by the Division of Inter-Church Aid, Refugee and World Service of the WCC.

ME20 Yuzon, Lourdino A., ed.

Called to Send and to Receive. Toa Payoh, SI: CCA, 1981. iv, 92 pp. Paper. 9971830469.

The addresses, workshop reports, bible studies, selected stories of missionary personnel, and papers from the consultation on the Asian Missionary Support Program held in Singapore on 20-24 September 1980, under the sponsorship of the Christian Conference of Asia.

General Works: Strategies

See also GW93, GW176-GW177, GW196, GW204-GW205, GW230, HI61, HI204, HI294, HI439, HI485, TH177, TH303, ME132, CR492-CR493, SO113, SO238, EC159, EV73, EV357-EV358, EV412, MI16, CH147, AF803, AF1204, AM991, AM1445, AS320, AS388, AS512, AS555, AS889, AS1060, and EU162.

ME21 Ageneau, Robert, and Pryen Denis

Les chemins de la mission d'aujourd'hui. Paris, FR: Revue Spiritus, 1972. 264 pp. Paper. No ISBN.

Second edition of an analysis of contemporary issues in Christian mission including issues of the liberation of peoples, the religious quest, new forms of Christian community, and forms of missionary service today.

ME22 Ahonen, Risto

Kenen vastuulla lähetys? (Lähetys tänään, 2). Helsinki, FI: Kirjapaja, 1989. 125 pp. Paper. 9516219144.

An analysis of the mission theology and missions methods in the Lutheran church, especially in Finland.

ME23 Ahrens, Theodor, ed.

Zwischen Regionalität und Globalisierung: Studien zu Mission Ökumene und Religion. (Perspektiven der Weltmission Wissenschaftliche Beiträge, Schriftenreihe der Missionsakademie an der Universität Hamburg, 25). Ammersbek bie Hamburg, GW: Verlag an der Lottbek, 1997. 468 pp. Paper. 3861300508.

Twenty-one essays organized around three themes: the tensions within regional and global missions; the ecumenical encounter and response between different cultures and religions toward organized evangelization; and the role of violence and religion in changing the relationship between church and state at the local and global levels.

ME24 Allen, Roland

Missionary Methods: St. Paul's or Ours? London, ENK: Lutterworth Press, 1969. 173 pp. No ISBN.

A reprint of the 1912 classic.

ME25 Allen, Roland

Missionary Principles. London, ENK (1969): Lutterworth Press; Grand Rapids, MIU (1964): Eerdmans, 1969. 168 pp. Paper. 0718812964.

A popular treatise on the impulse for missions in which the noted Anglican apologist for missions emphasized that the source of all missionary zeal is the presence of the living spirit of Christ.

ME26 Barres, Oliver

World Missions Windows. New York, NYU: Alba House, 1963. 209 pp. No ISBN.

A popular introduction to contemporary issues for world missions by a former Protestant missionary writing as a staff member of the Roman Catholic Society for the Propagation of the Faith.

ME27 Bavarel, Michel

New Communities, New Ministries: The Church Resurgent in Asia, Africa, and Latin America. Maryknoll, NYU: Orbis Books, 1983. 122 pp. Paper. 0883443376.

An account of the witness and growth of young Roman Catholic churches in the Two-Thirds World in situations of poverty and depression; translated from the French by Francis Martin.

ME28 Beals, Paul A.

A People for His Name: A Church-Based Missions Strategy. South Pasadena, CAU: William Carey Library, 1995. 259 pp. Paper. 0878087648.

An update of the author's 1985 sourcebook on the roles of local churches, mission boards, missionaries, and theological schools in the biblical fulfillment of the Great Commission.

ME29 Beck, Hartmut, ed.

Wege in die Welt: Reiseberichte aus 250 Jahren Brüdermission. (Erlanger Taschenbücher, 69). Erlangen, GW: Ev.-Luth. Mission, 1991. 300 pp. Paper. 3872141694.

Vignettes drawn from the experiences in mission of members of the Herrnhuter Brüdermission in various countries to honor the 250th anniversary of the society.

ME30 Bellagamba, Anthony

Mission and Ministry in the Global Church. Maryknoll, NYU: Orbis Books, 1992. ix, 150 pp. Paper. 0883448130.

Reflections by the former director of the US Catholic Mission Association on global megatrends and those creative strategies by which the church in mission can respond to them, including a spirituality for global ministries.

ME31 Benjamin, Medea, and Andrea Freedman

Bridging the Global Gap: A Handbook to Linking Citizens of the First and Third Worlds. Cabin John, MDU: Seven Locks Press, 1989. viii, 338 pp. Paper. 0932020739.

A guide to issues and resources for North Americans searching for non-violent ways to world peace and economic justice, and desiring through travel or volunteer service to link up with their Third World counterparts.

ME32 Blandenier, Jacques et al.

Mission renouvelée. La Côte-aux-Fées, SZ: Éditions des Groupes Missionnaires, 1975. 209 pp. No ISBN.

A call for a new mission contract, focusing on problems of church/mission relations, including new roles for expatriate missionaries.

ME33 Bonk, Jonathan J.

The Theory and Practice of Missionary Identification, 1860-1920. (Studies in the History of Missions, 2). Lewiston, NYU: E Mellen Press, 1989. xii, 364 pp. 088946071X.

A detailed scholarly examination of theory and practice of missionary identification with indigenous cultures and churches during the heyday of Western colonial expansion, focusing on data from Protestant international missionary conferences and London Missionary Society (LMS) practices in Central Africa and Central China.

ME—MISSIONS: METHODS

ME34 Campbell, Robert E., ed.
The Church in Mission. Maryknoll, NYU: Maryknoll Publications, 1965. x, 278 pp. No ISBN.

A collection of eleven articles by Roman Catholic missionary scholars, mostly written originally in French between 1958 and 1963, which provide background to the missionary documents of the Second Vatican Council.

ME35 Castro, Emilio
Hacia una Pastoral Latinoamericana. (Colección Iglesia y Misión, 2). San José, CR: Publicaciones INDEF, 1974. 156 pp. Paper. No ISBN.

Collection of conference papers given by the author at the Catedra Enrique Strachan of the Seminario Bíblico Latinoamericano in San José, Costa Rica, in April 1972.

ME36 Chang, Lit-sen
Strategy of Missions in the Orient: Christian Impact on the Pagan World. Philadelphia, PAU: Presbyterian & Reformed Publishing, 1970. 238 pp. Paper. No ISBN.

Exhortations on mission strategies in Asia originally provided for the Asia-South Pacific Congress on Evangelism (Singapore, Nov. 1968) by distinguished first-generation Chinese Christian educators.

ME37 Cheyne, John R.
Incarnational Agents: A Guide to Developmental Ministry. Birmingham, ALU: New Hope, 1996. xxii, 259 pp. Paper. 1563091682.

Biblical foundations for a holistic approach in missions, plus practical helps for planning responses to primary health care and other human needs by the former consultant on relief ministries of the Southern Baptist Foreign Mission Board.

ME38 Christiansen, Hendrik, Knud Ochsner, and A. Pilgaard Pedersen
Missionsselskab og kirke. (Nyt synspunkt, 2). Hellerup, DK: DMS-Forlag, 1976. 68 pp. Paper. 8774310569.

Several authors engaged in Danish missionary work discuss the relationship between missionary societies and the church, with special attention to mission as a concern of the whole church, and to the problem of urban mission; edited by Carl Chr. Jessen, Karsten Nissen, and Knud Ochsner.

ME39 Clark, Dennis E.
Missions in the Seventies. London, ENK: Scripture Union, 1970. 128 pp. Paper. 0854212906.

A popular presentation by a former India and Pakistan missionary of the need for new mission strategies for the 1970s.

ME40 Cook, Harold R.
Strategy of Missions: An Evangelical View. Chicago, ILU: Moody, 1963. 123 pp. No ISBN.

A primer on mission strategies originally presented at the Central American Mission's Inter-Republic Conference (Guatemala City, 1962).

ME41 Dayton, Edward R., and David Allen Fraser
Planning Strategies for World Evangelization. Grand Rapids, MIU: Eerdmans; Monrovia, CAU: MARC, 1990. xv, 349 pp. Paper. 0802804225 (M), 0802818323 (E).

A revised edition of the comprehensive guide to cross-cultural evangelization, including the perspectives, strategies, and management of missions to unreached people groups; originally published in 1980.

ME42 Fenton, Horace L.
Myths about Missions. Downers Grove, ILU: InterVarsity, 1973. 112 pp. 0877846650.

Seven short lectures on the myths of the limited call, the finished task, the unfinished task, the limited goal, the unqualified national, and the underpaid missionary; originally presented at the Conservative Baptist Theological Seminary, Denver, COU.

ME43 Fife, Eric S., and Arthur F. Glasser
Missions in Crisis: Rethinking Missionary Strategy. (IVP Series in Creative Christian Living). Chicago, ILU: InterVarsity, 1961. 269 pp. No ISBN.

A textbook on current mission strategies in relation to social changes which lead the church to be on the defensive, in tension, or on the offensive.

ME44 Glasser, Arthur F. et al., eds.
Crucial Dimensions in World Evangelization. South Pasadena, CAU: William Carey Library, 1976. x, 466 pp. Paper. 087808732X.

A sourcebook of key articles by twenty-seven missiologists on mission theology, anthropology, history, and contemporary strategies.

ME45 Goldsmith, Martin
God on the Move: Growth and Change in the Church Worldwide. Carlisle, ENK: OM Publishing, 1998. 186 pp. Paper. 1850783047.

The big picture for Christians of the North on the state of the church worldwide; originally published by MARC in 1991.

ME46 Goldsmith, Martin
What in the World Is God Doing? (An All Nations Series). Eastbourne, ENK: MARC-Monarch, 1991. 128 pp. Paper. 1854241389.

A succinct survey of the worldwide state of the church, pointing out challenges for mission and evangelization by a lecturer in mission studies at All Nations Christian College in England.

ME47 Grassi, Joseph A.
A World to Win: The Missionary Methods of Paul the Apostle. Maryknoll, NYU: Maryknoll Publications, 1965. viii, 184 pp. No ISBN.

A study relating the missionary methods of Paul to their applications in today's society by the Professor of New Testament Theology at the Maryknoll Major Seminary in the United States.

ME48 Griffiths, Michael
A Task Unfinished. Crownborough, ENK: Monarch Publications, 1996. 185 pp. Paper. 1854243136.

A primer for local publications on their roles in support of global mission by the former General Director of OMF International.

ME49 Hardin, Daniel
Mission: A Practical Approach to Church-Sponsored Mission Work. South Pasadena, CAU: William Carey Library, 1978. xii, 251 pp. Paper. 0878084274.

A basic overview of philosophies and strategies of mission prepared by a mission leader of the Church of Christ movement in North America.

ME50 Harjula, Raimo, Anne Jääskeläinen, and Harri Nurmi
Uskonnot kohtaavat: kristillinen lähetystyö tänään. Helsinki, FI: Kirjapaja, 1986. 126 pp. Paper. 9516216374.

A description of Christian missions among persons of other faiths.

ME—MISSIONS: METHODS

ME51 Horner, Norman A.

Cross and Crucifix in Mission: A Comparison of Protestant-Roman Catholic Missionary Strategy. New York, NYU: Abingdon, 1965. 223 pp. No ISBN.

A broad comparison of contemporary Roman Catholic and Protestant mission strategies based on the author's personal experience in Cameroon (1939-49) and travels in Latin America and Asia (1956-64).

ME52 Jenkinson, William, and Helene O'Sullivan, eds.

Trends in Mission: Toward the Third Millennium: Essays in Celebration of Twenty-Five Years of SEDOS. Maryknoll, NYU: Orbis Books, 1991. xx, 419 pp. Paper. 0883447665.

A compilation of forty-eight papers by international leaders in mission on "why mission?" and the contexts, models, peoples, and challenges in mission; published on the silver jubilee of SEDOS (Servizio de Documentazione e Studi)—an international research center in Rome.

ME53 Kane, J. Herbert

Winds of Change in the Christian Mission. Chicago, ILU: Moody, 1973. 160 pp. 0802495613.

An analysis of changes for missions in the turbulent '60s and '70s by the noted evangelical missiologist.

ME54 Kollbrunner, Fritz

Die Katholizität der Kirche und die Mission. (Schriftenreihe, 23). Immensee, SZ: NZM, 1973. xviii, 70 pp. Paper. No ISBN.

This is a reprint from the *Neue Zeitschrift für Missionswissenschaft* (1972/73) stressing the importance of a universal attitude, or "catholicity," in relation to missionary work, accommodation, and the local church (dissertation, part, Pontifical Univ. Gregoriana, Rome).

ME55 Kritzinger, J. J., Piet G. J. Meiring, and W. A. Saayman

You Will Be My Witness: An Introduction to Methods of Mission. Pretoria, SA: N. G. Kerkboekhandel Transvaal, 1984. 159 pp. Paper. 0798703946.

A textbook on the "who, what, where, and how" of missions for South African church leaders.

ME56 Lundy, David J.

We Are the Word: Globalization and the Changing Face of Missions. Carlisle, ENK: OM Publishing, 1999. xv, 174 pp. Paper. 185078342X.

An exploration of the concept of globalization in the world at large and in the world of missions, challenging the readers to make major paradigm shifts from a parochial to a wider outlook which does not automatically favor a Western approach to missions, co-workers, and the unevangelized world.

ME57 McAlpine, Thomas H.

By Word, Work and Wonder. (Cases in Holistic Mission). Monrovia, CAU: MARC, 1995. v, 151 pp. Paper. 0912552921.

Models of holistic mission which include both evangelism and social concern; originally published in *Transformation* by World Vision.

ME58 McGavran, Donald Anderson

Momentous Decisions in Missions Today. Grand Rapids, MIU: Baker Books, 1984. 231 pp. Paper. 0801061768.

A renewed call for the centrality of evangelization in Christian mission and analysis of four types of related decisions: theological, strategic, concerning missionary societies, and the ethnic mosaic of unreached peoples.

ME59 Menasce, Pierre Jean de

Permanence et transformation de la mission. (Parole et mission, 14). Paris, FR: Éditions du Cerf, 1967. 189 pp. No ISBN.

A study book on issues of mission methods for Roman Catholics.

ME60 Mission Institute (1970)

Mission in the '70s: What Direction? Edited by John T. Boberg and James A. Scherer. Chicago, ILU: Chicago Cluster of Theological Schools, 1972. 208 pp. Paper. No ISBN.

A collection of thirteen addresses presented at the 1971 Mission Institute sponsored by the Chicago Cluster of Theological Schools.

ME61 Motte, Mary

A Critical Examination of Mission Today: Research Project Report-Phase One. Washington, DCU: U.S. Catholic Mission Association, 1987. 86 pp. Paper. No ISBN.

An examination of emerging issues which may affect future mission thinking and activities in the world, identified by an international Catholic and Protestant panel of thirty-six-missiologists, written for the members of the US Catholic Mission Association.

ME62 Motte, Mary, and Joseph R. Lang, eds.

Mission Dialogue: The SEDOS Research Seminar on the Future of Mission, March 8-19, 1981, Rome, Italy. Maryknoll, NYU: Orbis Books, 1982. xv, 688 pp. 0883443325.

Forty-two papers from six continents on the mission of the local church.

ME63 Myers, Bryant L.

The New Context of World Mission. Monrovia, CAU: MARC, 1997. 61 pp. Paper. 1887983007.

A bird's-eye view of the historical, social, and religious contexts of mission, and of contemporary challenges.

ME64 Nielsen, Erik W.

Mission i en forandret verden. Edited by Svend Hauge. (Synspunkt, 1). Hellerup, DK: DMS, 1968. 37 pp. Paper. No ISBN.

The author, who has been a secretary of the Danish Missionary Society, the International Missionary Council, and the Theological Education Fund, deals with a number of questions related to missions in our time.

ME65 Parks, R. Keith

World in View. (AD 2000 Series). Birmingham, ALU: New Hope, 1987. 60 pp. Paper. 0936625082.

Seven popular essays on mission principles and methods governing the foreign missions effort of Southern Baptists by the President of the Foreign Missions Board, Southern Baptist Convention.

ME66 Rétif, Louis, and André Rétif

Pour une Église en état de mission. (Je sais—je crois: Encyclopédie du catholique au XX ème siècle, neuvième partie, les problèmes du monde et de l'Église). Paris, FR: Librairie Arthème Fayard, 1961. 142 pp. No ISBN.

Convinced that the modern missionary must belong to the particular world s/he is to evangelize, the authors urge the church to find open doors for mission in changing social movements, science, technology, etc.

ME—MISSIONS: METHODS

ME67 Rand, Stephen
Guinea Pig for Lunch: The Experiences of an Intrepid World Traveller. London, ENK: Hodder & Stoughton, 1998. ix, 239 pp. Paper. 0340721588.

Vignettes of the church in mission around the world based on the author's travel as part of the leadership team of Tearfund.

ME68 Rees, Paul S.
Don't Sleep through the Revolution. Waco, TXU: Word Books, 1969. 130 pp. No ISBN.

A study of mission theory, practice, and policy written by the Vice President at Large for World Vision International.

ME69 Robb, John D.
Focus! The Power of People Group Thinking: A Practical Manual for Planning Effective Strategies to Reach the Unreached. Monrovia, CAU: MARC, 1999. 167 pp. Paper. 0912552662.

An expanded edition of a practical manual for planning strategies to reach the unreached; originally published in 1989.

ME70 Santos Hernández, Angel
Derecho Misional. (Misionología, 7). Santander, SP: Editorial Sal Terrae, 1962. 588 pp. Paper. No ISBN.

A theoretical study of historical and juridical missional law.

ME71 Scherer, James A.
Missionary, Go Home! Englewood Cliffs, NJU: Prentice-Hall, 1964. 192 pp. No ISBN.

A reappraisal of mission strategies in the '60s.

ME72 Scott, Waldron, ed.
Serving Our Generation: Evangelical Strategies for the Eighties. Colorado Springs, COU: WEF, 1980. 281 pp. Paper. 0936444037.

Preparatory papers for the seventh General Assembly of the World Evangelical Fellowship (London 1980).

ME73 Settimana di Studi Missionari
Il Laicato cattolico dei paesi di missioni: atti della seconda Settimana di studi missionari, Milano, 4-8 settembre 1961. Milan, IT: Societî editrice Vita e pensiero, 1962. xiii, 298 pp. No ISBN.

Twenty-eight papers originally presented at the Second Week of Missionary Studies in Milan, Italy, on various aspects of the role of the Catholic laity in mission countries.

ME74 Sheen, Fulton J.
Missions and the World Crisis. Milwaukee, WIU: Bruce Publishing, 1963. viii, 273 pp. No ISBN.

An assessment of contemporary missions by the noted Catholic leader.

ME75 Shenk, Wilbert R.
Changing Frontiers of Mission. (American Society of Missiology Series, 28). Maryknoll, NYU: Orbis Books, 1999. xi, 207 pp. Paper. 1570752591.

A call for the renewal of the church through the recovery of a priority of mission in which the "frontier" is no longer a geographical location, but the outward movement away from the status quo and toward new challenges, growth, and opportunities.

ME76 Sjogren, Bob, Bill Stearns, and Amy Stearns
Run with the Vision: A Remarkable Global Plan for the 21st Century Church. Minneapolis, MNU: Bethany House, 1995. 288 pp. Paper. 1556613210.

A primer for evangelical Christians on global trends in mission and ways in which local churches can be missionary-sending without abandoning local concerns.

ME77 Smedjebacka, Henrik
Avartuva lähetys. Translated by Liisa Helminen. Helsinki, FI: Kirjapaja, 1988. 114 pp. Paper. 9516218563.

The author, Director of the Finnish Evangelical Lutheran Mission, describes the actual ways of missiological thinking in Finland and abroad.

ME78 Smedjebacka, Henrik
Vidgade missionsvyer. Helsinki, FI: Församlingsförbundets förlags AB, 1990. 78 pp. Paper. 9515504074.

Swedish translation.

ME79 Suomen Lähetysseura (The Finnish Evangelical Lutheran Mission)
Lähetettynä maailmaan: nykypäivän lähetystieto. Edited by Ritva Halmesmaa, and Ella Väänänen. Helsinki, FI: Kirjapaja, 1985. 220 pp. Paper. 9516215823.

A collection of Finnish missionaries' experiences from their work and from their encounters with other religions.

ME80 Syrjänen, Seppo, ed.
Ylitse kaikkien rajojen. Helsinki, FI: Kirjaneliö, 1979. 342 pp. 9516004725.

A collection of articles concerning the principles and methods of missions.

ME81 The Mission Information and Education Office World Mission in Church and Society
The World Mission Handbook: A Practical Guide to the Overseas Work of the Episcopal Church. New York, NYU: Episcopal Church Center, 1984. 157 pp. Paper. No ISBN.

A guide to the objectives, strategies and country involvements of the Episcopal Church (US) in world mission.

ME82 Wagner, C. Peter
Frontiers in Missionary Strategy. Chicago, ILU: Moody, 1971. 223 pp. Paper. 0802428819.

Guidelines for the development of missionary strategies which, while being evangelical and biblically oriented, are also pragmatic and effective.

ME83 Wiebracht, Dean
The World Beyond Your Walls: A Manual for Mobilizing Your Church in Missions. Manila, PH: Philippine Crusades/OMF Literature, 1992. 258 pp. Paper. 9715112536.

An easy-to-read book for Filipino congregations desiring to engage more effectively in missions.

ME84 Yohannan, K. P.
Why the World Waits: Exposing the Reality of Modern Missions. Lake Mary, FLU: Creation House, 1991. 244 pp. Paper. 0884193039.

A call for Protestants to rethink mission priorities, strategies, and the roles of missionaries in order to reach more effectively the unreached.

Home Missions

See also CH189 and EU168.

ME85 Gunther, Peter F., ed.
The Fields at Home: Studies in Home Missions. Chicago, ILU: Moody, 1963. 283 pp. No ISBN.

Twenty popular essays, mostly by evangelical Protestants, on various aspects of home missions in North America.

ME—MISSIONS: METHODS

ME86 Josgrilberg, Rui

Nós e a Missão: Um Texto Programado. Rudge Ramos, BL: Instituto Metodista de Ensino Superior, 1977. 184 pp. Paper. No ISBN.

Practical guide to the concepts and practice of mission today.

ME87 Madsen, Paul O.

Venture in Mission. New York, NYU: Friendship Press, 1968. 159 pp. Paper. No ISBN.

A short mission study on "New Forms of Mission" focusing on issues of urbanization, social relations, and institutionalism in home missions in the United States.

ME88 Olasky, Marvin

The Tragedy of American Compassion. Wheaton, ILU: Crossway Books, 1992. xvii, 299 pp. 0891076549.

A history of changing attitudes about the causes and remedies for poverty from the 1600s to the 1930s, including compassion for the homeless expressed through home missions.

ME89 Taylor, Wilma Rugh, and Norman Thomas Taylor

This Train Is Bound for Glory: The Story of America's Chapel Cars. Valley Forge, PAU: Judson Press, 1999. xiii, 382 pp. 0817012842.

The history of thirteen "churches on wheels," mission-bound vehicles, commissioned by the Baptist, Episcopal, and Roman Catholic churches to travel throughout the western United States between the 1890s and 1930s; includes photographs, train logs, historical data on towns of train routes, and information from survivors and descendants of those who experienced the missions firsthand.

Foreign Missions

See also HI130, HI553, HI574, MI69, and AS357.

ME90 Baumann, Andreas

Die "Apostelstrasse": Eine aussergewöhnliche Vision und ihre Verwirklichung. (Biblische Archäologie und Zeitgeschichte, 8). Basel, SW: Brunnen-Verlag, 1999. 180 pp. Paper. 376559430X.

This book describes a significant and influential, though unsuccessful, 19th-century experiment in Protestant mission strategy in which a "chain" of mission stations was established to serve as a pipeline for introduction of missionary personnel in a region from Jerusalem to Ethiopia.

ME91 Held, Helenis

Christendörfer: Untersuchung einer Missionsmethode. (Studia Instituti Missiologici SVD, 4). St. Augustin, GW: Steyler Verlag, 1964. xi, 96 pp. Paper. No ISBN.

A diploma thesis in missiology describing and evaluating critically the mission method of establishing Christian villages in Asia, South America, and Africa during the past century.

ME92 Society for the Propagation of the Faith, U.S. Mission Secretariat

Reappraisal: Prelude to Change. Edited by William J. Richardson. (World Horizon Books). Maryknoll, NYU: Maryknoll Publications, 1965. 125 pp. No ISBN.

Papers given at a symposium of the Mission Secretariat of the US Catholic Conference in 1965 which focuses on rethinking missions methods, training programs, and the nature of the missionary apostolate.

Third World Missions

ME93 Degrijse, Omer

Going Forth: Missionary Consciousness in Third World Catholic Churches. Maryknoll, NYU: Orbis Books, 1984. xi, 98 pp. Paper. 0883444275.

An introduction to the new understanding on mission and the rise of missionary consciousness among Roman Catholics in Africa, Asia, and Latin America.

ME94 Keyes, Lawrence E.

The Last Age of Missions: A Study of Third World Mission Societies. South Pasadena, CAU: William Carey Library, 1982. xiv, 238 pp. Paper. 0878084355.

A scholarly analysis of Third World mission societies, their nature and significance, with a complete 1980 directory of agencies and major research and study centers.

ME95 Lane, Denis

Tuning God's New Instruments. Singapore, SI: WEF, 1990. 100 pp. Paper. 9971972972.

A handbook for indigenous missions of the Two-Thirds World prepared by the Missions Commission of the World Evangelical Fellowship.

ME96 Larson, Peter A., comp.

Las Misiones del Tercer Mundo: Estudio mundial de las misiones no-occidentales en Asia, Africa y la América Latina. Buenos Aires, AG: Methopress, 1975. 160 pp. Paper. No ISBN.

Research into Protestant missionary work undertaken by Third World countries and not by Nordic nations.

ME97 Nelson, Marlin L., ed.

Readings in Third World Missions: A Collection of Essential Documents. South Pasadena, CAU: William Carey Library, 1976. x, 294 pp. Paper. 0878083197.

Thirty-one important articles on the "third wave" of missions by which Christians of Africa, Asia, Latin America, and Oceania reach out in mission; with an annotated bibliography of literature in the field.

ME98 Pate, Larry D.

From Every People: A Handbook of Two-Thirds World Missions with Directory/Histories/Analysis. Monrovia, CAU: MARC, 1989. xvi, 310 pp. Paper. 0912552670.

A handbook which illuminates the "Two-Thirds World" missions movement by way of critical analysis and case studies focusing on Malawi, Argentina, and India, with a directory of Two-thirds World mission agencies in Asia, Africa, the Middle East, Latin America, and Oceania.

ME99 Wong, James, ed.

Missions from the Third World: A World Survey on Non-Western Missions in Asia, Africa, and Latin America. Singapore, SI: Church Growth Centre, 1973. 135 pp. No ISBN.

An introduction with statistical summary, regional analyses, historical perspectives, and bibliography.

ME—MISSIONS: METHODS

Mission Organization/Structure

See also HI578, HI627, HI722, HI724, TH273, EA196, ME227, MI37, CH443, CH454-CH456, AM121, AM661, and AS1320.

ME100 Aagaard, Johannes
Mission, Konfession, Kirche: Die Problematik ihrer Integration im 19. Jahrhundert in Deutschland. (Studia Missionalia Upsaliensia, 8). Lund, SW: Gleerup, 1967. 2 vols. Paper. No ISBN.

A monumental thesis reworking the critical debate for Scandanavian Lutherans of whether there could be mission without church, church without mission, or both without confession, with extended analysis of the argument of Gustav Warneck in *Missionslehre* (1892-1903) and a summary in Danish.

ME101 Brent, Allen
Cultural Episcopacy and Ecumenism: Representative Ministry in Church History from the Age of Ignatius of Antioch to the Reformation with Special Reference to Contemporary Ecumenism. (Studies in Christian Missions, 6). Leiden, NE: Brill, 1992. xiv, 250 pp. 9004094326.

Out of the debate among Australian Anglicans over the form of episcopal supervision helpful to aboriginal peoples (cultural or territorial), the author provides a historical and theological analysis of the development of the episcopacy as a system of church oversight for diverse peoples.

ME102 Crawley, Winston
Global Mission. A Story to Tell: An Interpretation of Southern Baptist Foreign Missions. Nashville, TNU: Broadman, 1985. viii, 400 pp. 0805463402.

A comprehensive explanation in understandable terms of the complexity of Southern Baptist missions, including systems, personnel, objectives, and strategies.

ME103 *Facing Facts in Modern Missions: A Symposium*
Chicago, ILU: Moody, 1963. 141 pp. Paper. No ISBN.

Twelve scholarly evangelical mission leaders present in the light of Scripture the problems of interchurch cooperation, organization, alliance, and fellowship—a counter position to that of the ecumenical movement based on discussions at meetings of the Evangelical Foreign Missions Association.

ME104 Gillette, Arthur
One Million Volunteers: The Story of Volunteer Youth Service. Harmondsworth, ENK: Penguin Books, 1968. 258 pp. Paper. No ISBN.

A comprehensive history of the 20th-century movement for international volunteer service by youth from the first work camp during World War I to its multiplication into 250 agencies by 1967, many of them church related.

ME105 Kauppinen, Juha
Kansanlähetyksen alueellinen leviäminen: Tutkimus uskonnollisen innovaation hierarkkisesta diffuusiosta Suomessa vuosina 1967-1983. (Kirkon tutkimuskeskus. Sarja A, 52). Tampere, FI: Kirkon tutkimuskeskus, 1990. 333 pp. Paper. 9516961510.

Titled *The Spatial Diffusion of the Finnish Lutheran Mission*, this thesis is a study of religious innovation and its hierarchical diffusion in Finland from 1967 to 1983.

ME106 Lovell, George
Consultancy, Ministry and Mission: A Handbook for Practitioners and Work Consultants in Christian Organizations. New York, NYU: Burns & Oates, 2000. xii, 441 pp. Paper. 086012312X.

A handbook for practitioners and work consultants in Christian organizations, showing how work consultancy improves the performance of practitioners, churches, and Christian organizations.

ME107 Mageroy, Magnar
Misjonsperspektiv i praksis: Misjonsgrunnlag, misjonsorgan, misjonens midler og metoder, menigheten på misjonsmarken. Oslo, NO: Lunde, 1973. 249 pp. 8252046045.

A survey of the various ways in which Christian missions are organized.

ME108 Mellis, Charles J.
Committed Communities: Fresh Streams for World Missions. South Pasadena, CAU: William Carey Library, 1976. ix, 138 pp. Paper. 0878084266.

A popular exploration of the role of sodalities (committed communities) from the first to the 20th century (e.g. Catholic monastic orders, Moravians, Youth with a Mission) in the worldwide mission of the church.

ME109 Nasser, Antonio C.
Una Iglesia Apasionada por las Misiones: Una Aplicación de la teoría de lo obvio a la relación entre iglesias y agencias misioneras. Miami, FLU: Editorial Unilit/COMIBAM International, 1997. n.p. pp. Paper. 078990442X.

A pastor's plea to increase the effectiveness of mission work by letting the local church be the primary source of missionary preparation, sending, and support.

ME110 Townsend, Christopher
Stop Check Go. Carlisle, ENK: OM Publishing, 1996. 160 pp. Paper. 1850782407.

Practical helps for leaders of short-term mission projects by the leader of the British Tear Fund's Short-Term Overseas Programmes Unit.

ME111 Vestal, Daniel, and Robert A. Baker
Pulling Together. Nashville, TNU: Broadman, 1987. 117 pp. Paper. 0805464069.

A practical guide discussing "The Cooperative Program" in the Southern Baptist Church which allows local congregations to participate in Baptist missionary efforts while practicing autonomy and every member support.

ME112 Wieser, Thomas, ed.
Planning for Mission: Working Papers on the New Quest for Missionary Communities. New York, NYU: U.S. Conference for the WCC, 1966. 230 pp. Paper. No ISBN.

A selection of papers on the church's mission in the world produced for the World Council of Churches' study on "The Missionary Structure of the Congregation."

ME113 Willmer, Wesley K., J. David Schmidt, and Martyn Smith
The Prospering Parachurch: Enlarging the Boundaries of God's Kingdom. San Francisco, CAU: Jossey-Bass Publishers, 1998. xviii, 232 pp. 0787941980.

A study of the dramatic role of the parachurch in reshaping the religious world by providing infinite ways for people to find faith in God and have needs met—beyond the walls of the traditional church.

ME—MISSIONS: METHODS

ME114 Winter, Ralph D., and Robert Pierce Beaver

Warp and the Woof: Organizing for Mission. South Pasadena, CAU: William Carey Library, 1970. 63 pp. Paper. 0878081070.

A monograph presenting two parallel types of mission agencies—vertical church sponsored (modalities) and horizontal independent enterprises (sodalities).

Church to Church Relationships

See also GW223, EA71, ME103, ME217, MI53, AF102, AF107, AF369, AF672, AF684, AF768-AF769, AF1255, AM1277, AS72, AS1031, AS1061, AS1350, AS1402, and OC179.

ME115 Bauerochse, Lothar

Miteinander leben lernen: Zwischenkirchliche Partnerschaften als Ökumenische Lerngemeinschaften. (Erlanger Taschenbücher, 113). Erlangen, GW: Ev.-Luth. Mission, 1996. 491 pp. Paper. 3872145134.

A detailed study of historical understandings of partnership in missions, in the ecumenical movement, and in parish life, with a tjirty-four-page bibliography.

ME116 Bergquist, James A., and P. Kambar Manickam

The Crisis of Dependency in Third World Ministries: A Critique of Inherited Missionary Forms in India. Madras, II: CLS, 1974. 149 pp. No ISBN.

A critical examination of the forms and functions of the Protestant ministry as developed in India by 19th-century missionaries.

ME117 Beyerhaus, Peter

Die Selbständigkeit der jungen Kirchen als missionarisches Problem. Wuppertal-Barmen, GW: Verlag der Rheinischen Missionsgesellschaft, 1967. 393 pp. No ISBN.

The German missiologist's doctoral dissertation (University of Uppsala, 1959) under the direction of Bishop Sundkler entitled "The Independence of the Younger Churches as a Missionary Problem," with case studies of the Anglican Church in Nigeria, the Batak Lutheran Church (Indonesia), and the Korean Presbyterian Church.

ME118 Beyerhaus, Peter, and Henry Lefever

The Responsible Church and the Foreign Mission. Grand Rapids, MIU: Eerdmans; London, ENK: World Dominion Press, 1964. 199 pp. No ISBN.

Revised and condensed version of *Die Selbständigkeit der jungen Kirchen als missionaries Problem.*

ME119 Bush, Luis, and Lorry Lutz

Partnering in Ministry: The Direction of World Evangelism. Downers Grove, ILU: InterVarsity, 1990. 192 pp. Paper. 0830313322.

A primer on partner ministries between First World mission agencies and those of the Two-Thirds World of Africa, Asia, Latin America, and Oceania.

ME120 Consultation on the Exchange of Church Sendees (1976, Sukabumi)

Lord, Send Me: Report of the Consultation on the Exchange of Church Sendees Sukabumi, 5-10th April 1976. Jakarta, IO: Christian Publishing Board, 1977. 186 pp. Paper. No ISBN.

Papers discussing the patterns of mission, preparation, placement, pastoral care-finding, and lifestyle of church senders.

ME121 Elizondo, Virgilio P., Norbert Greinacher, and Marcus Lefébure, eds.

Tensions between the Churches of the First World and the Third World. (*Concilium*: Religion in the Eighties, 144). Edinburgh, STK: T&T Clark; New York, NYU: Seabury Press, 1981. ix, 94 pp. Paper. 0567300242 (UK), 0816423113 (US).

Eleven essays by an international panel of Catholic theologians who argue that the current theological tensions within the church in the midst of a divided world are signs of life and hope, stimulating creative new forms of Christian life and thought.

ME122 Enklaar, Ido Hendricus, and Johannes Verkuyl

Onze blijvende opdracht: De Nederlandse deelname aan wereldzending en werelddiakonaat in een nieuwe tijd. Kampen, NE: Kok, 1968. 252 pp. Paper. No ISBN.

A survey of concrete projects of cooperation between Dutch mission societies and churches in Indonesia, Pakistan, and some other countries during the 1960s.

ME123 Forster, Karl, and Gerhard Schmidtchen

Glaube und Dritte Welt: Ergebnisse einer Repräsentativumfrage über weltkirchliche Aufgaben und die Motive deutscher Katholiken. (Entwicklung und Frieden: Wissenschaftliche Reihe, 27). Munich, GW: Kaiser; Mainz, GW: Grünewald Verlag, 1982. 192 pp. Paper. 3459014741 (K), 3786710198 (G).

An investigation into the "Church of the Third World" and the responsibilities of German Catholics toward Third World peoples.

ME124 Harrison, Myron S.

Developing Multinational Teams: A Study of ... the Development of Multinational Team Ministry within the Association of Bible Churches. Singapore, SI: OMF, 1984. 179 pp. Paper. 9971972026.

A case study of the history, key factors, and specific recommendations which maintain the partnership between the Association of Biblical Churches of the Philippines, SEND-International, and the Overseas Missionary Fellowship.

ME125 Hodges, Melvin L.

The Indigenous Church and the Missionary: A Sequel to the Indigenous Church. South Pasadena, CAU: William Carey Library, 1987. viii, 99 pp. Paper. 0878081518.

An update of the author's now-classic guide for missionaries on evolving patterns of partnership between missions and national churches.

ME126 Horine, Robert B.

Partners in Mission USA II: A Popular Report. Cincinnati, OHU: Forward Movement, 1993. 79 pp. Paper. 0880281464.

Report of the Partners in Mission Consultation II (Mandelein, Illinois, 6-9 February 1993) in which Anglicans shared the fruits of yoking Episcopal dioceses in the United States with partners in other continents.

ME127 Jansen, Schoonhoven E.

Mutual Assistance of Churches in a Missionary Perspective: A Report on a Missiological Project. (IIMO Research Pamphlet, 1). Leiden, NE: IIMO, 1979. 40 pp. Paper. No ISBN.

English summary of *Wederkerige Assistentie van Kerken in Missionair Perspectief* (1977).

ME—MISSIONS: METHODS

ME128 Jansen, Schoonhoven E.
Wederkerige assistentie van kerken in missionair perspectief: Samenvatting en evaluatie van een studie-projekt van het Interuniversitair Instituut voor Missiologie en Oecumenica, afdeling Missiologie 1970-1976. Leiden, NE: IIMO, 1977. ix, 194 pp. Paper. No ISBN.

Final report of an IIMO research project on the concept of mutual assistance of churches.

ME129 Kraakevik, James H., and Dotsey Welliver, eds.
Partners in the Gospel: The Strategic Role of Partnership in World Evangelization. Wheaton, ILU: BGC, 1992. 203 pp. Paper. 1879089114.

Papers from an important Working Consultation on Partnership in World Mission held 9-11 May 1991, at the Billy Graham Center in Wheaton, Illinois.

ME130 Lagerwerf, Leny, Karel A. Steenbrink, and F. J. Verstraelen, eds.
Changing Partnership of Missionary and Ecumenical Movements: Essays in Honour of Marc Spindler. (IIMO Research Publication, 42). Leiden, NE: IIMO, 1995. 235 pp. Paper. 9021170116.

Seventeen essays in three languages (English—12, French—3, German—2) by missiologists on theological, historical, and contemporary missiological aspects of mission/church and missionary/national partnerships; published as a *festschrift* to honor the noted Dutch missiologist.

ME131 Margull, Hans Jochen, ed.
Keine Einbahnstrassen: Von der Westmission zur Weltmission. Korntal bei Stuttgart, GW: Evan Missionsverlag, 1973. 143 pp. Paper. 3771401747.

Taking up the discussion at the WCC's World Missionary Conference (Bangkok, 1973), this work rejects the one-sided polarization into givers and receivers, the haves and the have-nots, and appeals for partnership and exchange in mission.

ME132 Rickett, Daniel
Building Strategic Relationships: A Practical Guide to Partnering with Non-Western Missions. Pleasant Hill, CAU: Klein Graphics, 2000. iii, 74 pp. Paper. 0970054904.

Conceptual and practical tools for assessing intercultural partnerships and building collaborative relationships are provided to assist global outreach teams of local churches.

ME133 Ronsvalle, John, and Sylvia Ronsvalle
The Hidden Billions: The Potential of the Church in the U.S.A. Champaign, ILU: C-4 Resources, 1984. 185 pp. Paper. 0914527185.

Based on extensive research, the founders of Empty Tomb, Inc., in Urbana, IL, here show the potential of the US church to be in creative partnership with churches elsewhere in the world and the financial resources that could be released for this purpose.

ME134 Shenk, Wilbert R.
God's New Economy: Mission and Interdependence. Elkhart, INU: Mission Focus Publications, 1988. 69 pp. Paper. No ISBN.

A monograph on interdependence between churches as a strategy for mission, with statements on integration of mission structures from four consultations sponsored by the Mennonite World Conference, 1975-1987.

ME135 Somasekhar, Renuka Mukerji
Mission with Integrity in India: A Study in Changing Relationships between the Church and the Mission Boards. New York, NYU: Friendship Press, 1969. 56 pp. Paper. No ISBN.

An important study with some radical recommendations by the former principal of the Women's Christian College in Madras.

ME136 Steffen, Tom A.
Business as Usual in the Missions Enterprise? La Mirada, CAU: Center for Organizational & Ministry Development, 1999. 143 pp. Paper. 1882757041.

A challenge to assemblies, agencies, and academia—at home and abroad—to form creative partnerships toward fulfilling the Great Commandment and Great Commission through well-trained, cross-cultural Christian workers.

ME137 Taylor, William David, ed.
Kingdom Partnerships for Synergy in Missions. South Pasadena, CAU: William Carey Library, 1994. xix, 270 pp. Paper. 0878082492.

Twenty-two short essays on church-mission partnerships by mission leaders from around the world who are linked with the Missions Commission of the World Evangelical Fellowship.

ME138 *The Identity of the Church and Its Service to the Whole Human Being*
Geneva, SZ: LWF, 1977. 2 vols. Paper. No ISBN.

Reports on thirty-five self-study projects in forty-six national Lutheran churches on five continents, with summary reflections, in two volumes [vol. 1: 777 pp; vol. 2: 271 pp.].

ME139 United Presbyterian Church in the U.S.A., Commission on Ecumenical Mission and Relations, Advisory Study Committee
An Advisory Study. New York, NYU: UPSA, COEMAR, 1962. 94 pp. Paper. No ISBN.

Working paper on relations between a former part of the PCUSA and its related churches in mission and fellowship.

ME140 Verkuyl, Johannes
Daar en Nu: Over de assistentie aan de kerken in Azië, Afrika en Latijns Amerika in de huidige situatie. Kampen, NE: Kok, 1966. 134 pp. Paper. No ISBN.

Mission is examined within the biblical concept of the Kingdom of God and various forms of assistance to the now independent churches in Asia, Africa, and Latin America.

ME141 Verkuyl, Johannes
Zending in zes continenten: Wederkerige assistentie als opdracht. Leiden, NE: IIMO, 1973. 56 pp. Paper. No ISBN.

The new concept of "mutual assistance of churches" is related to the concept of "mission in six continents" and also to the idea of the diminishing difference between mission and evangelisation, with a general survey of ideas developed in an IIMO Research Project on Mutual Assistance of Churches.

ME142 Wagner, C. Peter, ed.
Church/Mission Tensions Today. Chicago, ILU: Moody, 1972. 238 pp. 0802415490.

Twelve key papers from the Green Lake 1971 Conference on church/mission tensions sponsored jointly by the IFMA and EFMA.

ME—MISSIONS: METHODS

ME143 Wakatama, Pius
Independence for the Third World Church: An African's Perspective on Missionary Work. Downers Grove, ILU: InterVarsity, 1976. 119 pp. Paper. 0877847193.

A critique of moratorium with advocacy of new relationships between nationals and missionaries.

ME144 Winsen, Gerardus Adam Christiaan van
L'assistance missionnaire catholique: étude historique sur les relations missionnaires dans l'Église d'après les documents officiels du XXe siècle. Leiden, NE: IIMO e, 1973. iii, 105 pp. No ISBN.

Historical study on the relations between sending and receiving local churches according to the official documents of the Catholic Church in the 20th century.

Indigenous Church Administration

See also HI491, ME127-ME128, ME143, SO164, ED120, EV423, AF102, AM169, and AS538.

ME145 Burrows, William R.
New Ministries: The Global Context. Maryknoll, NYU: Orbis Books, 1980. xiv, 178 pp. Paper. 0883443295.

Believing that the church in structure and ministry must be contextually relevant in each society, the author investigates new forms of ministry which could free Third World churches from the old dependency patterns.

ME146 Hodges, Melvin L.
The Indigenous Church. Springfield, MOU: Gospel Publishing House, 1976. 152 pp. Paper. 0882435272.

A study book by an Assembly of God missiologist comparing contemporary methods with biblical models of planting and developing churches.

ME147 Rickett, Daniel, and Dotsey Welliver
Supporting Indigenous Ministries: With Selected Readings. (BGC Monograph). Wheaton, ILU: BGC, 1997. xiii, 141 pp. Paper. 1879089262.

Papers from the inaugural Consultation on Support of Indigenous Ministries (Wheaton, Illinois, 17-20 October 1996), with four selected readings.

ME148 Williams, C. Peter
The Ideal of the Self-Governing Church: A Study in Victorian Missionary Strategy. (Studies in Christian Mission, 1). Leiden, NE: Brill, 1990. xv, 293 pp. 9004091882.

A scholarly analysis based on in-depth archival research concerning Henry Venn's ideal of the self-governing church and the attempts of the Church Missionary Society to implement it in Asia and Africa during the Victorian era to 1909.

ME149 Yaya, Louis Bala
Permanent Diaconate in the 1983 Code: Particular Reference to the Diocese of Jos (Nigeria). Rome, IT: Pontificia Universitas Urbaniana, 1989. 85 pp. Paper. No ISBN.

A study of the Roman Catholic rules and practice concerning leadership by permanent deacons with special reference to the Diocese of Jos in Nigeria, a doctoral dissertation at Urbaniana Pontifical University.

Administration: Planning and Evaluation

See also ME106, EC244, EC274, AF62, and OC47.

ME150 Camp, Bruce
Global Access Planner: Steps for Developing a Strategic Global Evangelism Plan for the Local Church. Peachtree City, GAU: ACMC, 1996. 48 pp. Paper. No ISBN.

Workbook for participants in a consultation to prepare a five-year mission plan for a local church.

ME151 *Church Missions Policy Handbook*
Peachtree City, GAU: ACMC, 1995. 77 pp. Paper. No ISBN.

A third edition detailed guide for churches to use in establishing a church missions policy, with such considerations as establishing a purpose, structure, responsibilities, and financial policies.

ME152 Hendrix, Olan
Management and the Christian Worker. Fort Washington, PAU: CLC, 1973. 165 pp. Paper. 0875082327.

Basic lectures on management for church administrators by the chairman of the Cooperation and Comity Committee of IFMA published for use by church workers in India; originally published by Living Books for All, Manila, Philippines (1972).

ME153 Mays, David
Building Global Vision: 6 Steps to Discovering God's Mission Vision for Your Church. Peachtree City, GAU: ACMC, 1996. 73 pp. Paper. No ISBN.

A six-step guide for local churches desiring to set new goals for mission outreach.

ME154 Schückler, Georg
Brücken zur Welt: 125 Jahre Aachener Missionszentrale. Aachen, GW: PWG, 1967. 58 pp. No ISBN.

A short illustrated history of 125 years of work of the Society of the Propagation of the Faith in Aachen, Germany.

ME155 Winter, Roberta H.
Once More Around Jericho: The Story of the US Center for World Mission. South Pasadena, CAU: William Carey Library, 1978. xiv, 234 pp. 0878081674.

A history of the US Center for World Mission, dedicated to evangelizing the hidden or unreached peoples of the world.

Education for Mission

See also HI577, TH109, EA157-EA158, ED74, AM143, AM982, and EU231.

ME156 Bühlmann, Walbert
Der ewige Auftrag in der heutigen Zeit: Ein aktuelles Bildungsbuch über die Fragen der Weltmission. Munich, GW: Rex, 1960. 117 pp. Paper. No ISBN.

Sketching the foundation, problems, and prospects of mission, this textbook calls for the "mobilization" of youth for the missionary cause.

ME157 Bauer, Arthur O. F.
Being in Mission: A Resource for the Local Church and Community. New York, NYU: Friendship Press, 1987. viii, 106 pp. Paper. 0377001732.

A handbook meant to assist the local church to have an effective program of education for mission.

ME—MISSIONS: METHODS

ME158 Bauer, Arthur O. F.
Making Mission Happen: Year-Round Program of Education for Mission in the Local Church and Community. New York, NYU: Friendship Press, 1974. 96 pp. Paper. 0377000191.

A basic resource for mission education in the local church and community.

ME159 Borthwick, Paul
How to Be a World-Class Christian. Wheaton, ILU: Victor Books, 1993. 108 pp. Paper. 1564762041.

The basic ABCs for North Americans on how to become a part of God's global action in missions.

ME160 Borthwick, Paul
A Mind for Missions: 10 Ways To Build Your World Vision. Colorado Springs, COU: Navpress, 1987. 167 pp. Paper. 0891091912.

A practical guide with ten building blocks for sensitizing people to the needs in mission beyond the borders of the United States, including current events, lifestyle choices, and case studies.

ME161 Caldwell, Larry W.
Missions and You: How You Can Be a Part of What God Is Doing in Today's World. Manila, PH: OMF Books, 1994. 84 pp. Paper. 9715113346.

How every Christian can be in missions both as a sender and as a sent one, by the Professor of Missions and Hermeneutics at Asian Theological Seminary in Manila.

ME162 Collins, Marjorie A., and Carl Blackburn
Missions on the Move in the Local Church: Promoting, Supporting Missions: Caring about the Missionary. Edited by Don Wardell and Paul Haney. Winona Lake, INU: Don Wardell, 1989. 224 pp. Paper. No ISBN.

Practical helps for local congregations desiring to be more effective in mission education and support of missionaries.

ME163 *Cultivating a Missions-Active Church*
Wheaton, ILU: ACMC, 1988. 112 pp. Paper. No ISBN.

A guidebook filled with practical, real-life examples of how churches can develop a "mind for missions" in their local communities.

ME164 De Ridder, Richard, and Roger S. Greenway
Let the Whole World Know: Resources for Preaching on Missions. Grand Rapids, MIU: Baker Books, 1988. 203 pp. Paper. 0801029775.

A practical resource featuring preaching outlines on great missionary texts from the Bible, mission mottos, and quotations from famous missionaries, by the Professor Emeritus of Church Polity at Calvin Seminary and Executive Director of Christian Reformed World Ministries.

ME165 End, Th. van den et al.
De heiden moest eraan gelovenGeschiedenis van zending, missie en ontwikkelingssamen-werking. Utrecht, NE: Stichting Het Catharijneconvent, 1983. 93 pp. Paper. No ISBN.

Richly illustrated catalogue of an exhibition in Utrecht (1983) on Dutch Protestant and Roman Catholic mission activities, including development work after World War II (Th.M.A. Claessens), with an overview of the various mission exhibitions in the Netherlands up to the 1950s.

ME166 Esquerda-Bifet, Juan
Espiritualidad Misionera. (BAC Minor, 49). Madrid, SP: Biblioteca de Autores Cristianos, 1982. xvi, 348 pp. 8422008823.

Second edition of a practical guide designed to awaken missionary enthusiasm in church-related persons and communities; originally published in 1978.

ME167 Fenton, Thomas P., ed.
Education for Justice: A Resource Manual. Maryknoll, NYU: Orbis Books, 1975. xvi, 464 pp. Paper. 0883441543.

A resource manual designed for Christian educators at all levels, containing program suggestions, background and resource materials, with an accompanying workbook for participants.

ME168 Gehris, Paul D., and Katherine A. Gehris, eds.
The Teaching Church—Active in Mission. Valley Forge, PAU: Judson Press, 1987. 98 pp. Paper. 0817010807.

A primer for local congregations desiring to be intentional in their education for mission.

ME169 Goiburu Lopetegui, Joaquín María
Animación Misionera: Vademecum. (Misión sin Fronteras, 2). Javier, SP: Centro Misional Javier; Estella, SP: Verbo Divino, 1985. 286 pp. Paper. 8471514303.

Manual dedicated to the promotion of missionary ideas among Roman Catholics: with thirty-eight topics, such as: concepts of mission, history of missions, missionary organizations, practical problems, etc.

ME170 Halvorson, Loren E.
Peace on Earth Handbook. Minneapolis, MNU: Augsburg, 1976. 128 pp. 0806615168.

An action guide with models for people who want to do something in their local churches about hunger, war, poverty, and other human problems, by a former staff member of the Lutheran World Federation.

ME171 Hampson, Tom, and Loretta Whalen
Tales of the Heart: Affective Approaches to Global Education. New York, NYU: Friendship Press, 1991. xv, 244 pp. Paper. 0377002232.

A resource manual for leaders of global awareness seminars.

ME172 *Make a World of Difference: Creative Activities for Global Learning*
New York, NYU: Friendship Press, 1989. 280 pp. Paper. 0377002117.

A handbook and "how to" manual for community education in global awareness developed by leaders of Church World Service, CROP, and denominational community educators in the United States.

ME173 *Missions Education Handbook*
Wheaton, ILU: ACMC, 1983. iv, 128 pp. Paper. No ISBN.

A step-by-step guide designed to help local churches integrate education for missions into their Christian education ministries.

ME174 O'Hare, Padraic, ed.
Education for Peace and Justice. San Francisco, CAU: Harper & Row, 1983. xvi, 240 pp. Paper. 0060663618.

Sixteen essays by Roman Catholic educators focusing on the theory, educational issues, and ministerial ramifications of educating persons for peace and justice with the intent of building a human community and enriching every person within it.

ME175 Pierce, Bob

Emphasizing Missions in the Local Church. Grand Rapids, MIU: Zondervan, 1964. 120 pp. No ISBN.

A primer on local church mission education by the President of World Vision, Inc.

ME176 Raymo, Jim

Marching to a Different Drummer: Rediscovering Missions in an Age of Affluence and Self-Interest. Fort Washington, PAU: CLC, 1996. 216 pp. Paper. 0875087191.

A compelling case to move people from self-centered narcissism to a biblically "others-directed" focus.

ME177 Ruf, Walther, ed.

Die Mission in der evangelischen Unterweisung: Ein Arbeitsbuch. Stuttgart, GW: Evan Missionsverlag, 1965. 452 pp. No ISBN.

Second edition of a handbook of mission for Protestant teachers of religion presenting theological questions, classroom materials, and methodological help.

ME178 Shoemaker, Dennis E.

The Global Connection: Local Action for World Justice. New York, NYU: Friendship Press, 1979. vi, 142 pp. Paper. 0377000698.

A handbook for consciousness-raising in the local church concerning justice issues.

ME179 Telford, Tom, and Lois Shaw

Missions in the 21st Century: Getting Your Church into the Game. Wheaton, ILU: Shaw Publishers, 1998. 171 pp. Paper. 0877885788.

A practical book for local church missions committees on how to ignite mission interest, recruit and support missionaries, and build partnerships in mission.

ME180 *The Christian Community in Mission ... in a Near and Global Context: European Seminar on Education for Mission, Aarhus, Denmark, May, 1977*

Geneva, SZ: WCC, CWME, 1978. 40 pp. Paper. 282540568X.

A collection of ideas on education for mission in the West that came out of a seminar organized by the Commission on World Mission and Evangelism of the World Council of Churches.

ME181 Watkins, Morris

Missions Resource Handbook: Ideas and Resources for Promoting Missions in the Local Church. Fullerton, CAU: R C Law & Co, 1987. vi, 144 pp. Paper. 0939925052.

A handbook for Protestant evangelicals that gives resources for understanding various aspects of Christian missions (prayer and intercession, the local church, home missions, etc.), with a list of missionary agencies for those who wish to serve as missionaries.

ME182 Wren, Brian

Education for Justice. London, ENK: SCM Press, 1986. xxi, 135 pp. Paper. 0334003563.

Second edition of a study book for persons desiring to become more involved in movements for social justice, with chapters on an appropriate theory of education (that of Paulo Freire) and the concept of justice in the Christian faith; originally published in 1986 (Maryknoll, NYU: Orbis Books; London, ENK: SCM Press).

Mission Study Literature: Adult

See also GW115, GW207-GW208, GW241, GW250, GW267, TH270, TH580, EA147, CR1114, SO425, SO431, EC105, EC154, PO222, AF228, AM182, AM1145, AS437, AS614, AS802, EU21, EU31, and EU103.

ME183 Bryant, David

In the Gap: What It Means to Be a World Christian. Ventura, CAU: Regal Books, 1984. 322 pp. Paper. 0830709525.

A popular classic written to motivate young adults toward full involvement in the cause of world evangelization by the Missions Specialist with InterVarsity Christian Fellowship.

ME184 Calver, Clive et al.

Dancing in the Dark?: Shining the Light on the Church. Oxford, ENK: Lynx Communications/Spring Harvest, 1994. 96 pp. Paper. 0745930301.

An adult study book on the church, its meaning, and models for ministry and mission, based on Paul's letter to the Philippians.

ME185 Calver, Clive, and Peter Meadows

Living on the Edge. Oxford, ENK: Lynx Communications/ Spring Harvest; Sutherland, AT: Albatross Books, 1993. 96 pp. Paper. 0745926894 (L), 0732407478 (A).

A study book on Christian living, making a difference in ethical and environmental issues, and in evangelism and spirituality.

ME186 Crisci, Elizabeth Whitney

Mission Made Exciting for Adults: Creative Ideas to Involve Adults in Missions. Colorado Springs, COU: Accent Publications, 1996. 127 pp. Paper. 0896363309.

Sixty interactive methods for use in mission education programs with adults.

ME187 Evers, Georg, and Dagmar Plum

Mission: Unterwegs zur Weltkirche. (Projekte zur theologischen Erwachsenenbildung, 6). Mainz, GW: Grünewald, 1977. 142 pp. Paper. 3786706301.

A textbook for promoting mission awareness among adult Christians explaining the meaning of mission, its worldwide dimension, how it differs from development aid, and the missionary task on the local parish level.

ME188 Griffiths, Michael

The Church and World Mission. Grand Rapids, MIU: Zondervan, 1982. 207 pp. Paper. 0310451116.

Six general lectures on world mission originally presented at Wycliffe Hall, Oxford, in 1978 by the former General Director of the Overseas Missionary Fellowship and principal of London Bible College; first published as *Shaking the Sleeping Beauty* by InterVarsity Press, Leicester, England, in 1980.

ME189 Obras Misionales Pontificias de España

La Misionología Hoy. (Misión sin fronteras, 5). Buenos Aires, AG: Editorial Guadalupe; Estella, SP: Verbo Divino, 1987. 599 pp. 8471515393.

Collection of twenty-one essays on the actual state of mission theology, missional studies, and the practical challenges that missionaries face.

ME190 Scherer, James A.
Global Living Here and Now. New York, NYU: Friendship Press, 1974. 128 pp. Paper. 0377000035.

A study book on mission as global consciousness, drawing heavily on ideas expressed at the World Conference on Salvation Today (Bangkok, 1973), by the professor of World Mission at the Lutheran School of Theology at Chicago.

ME191 Schlabach, Joetta Handrich
Extending the Table: A World Community Cookbook. Scottdale, PAU: Herald Press, 1991. 332 pp. Paper. 083613561X.

A unique international cookbook which includes stories and cultural traditions enabling readers to learn from the world community.

ME192 Vanderwerf, Nate
Common Ground Study Course: Global Awareness Program. Edited by Larry Ramey, and Dennis C. Benson. New York, NYU: CODEL, 1990. No ISBN.

A four-session course for church leaders designed to enhance global awareness through multi-media exposures including video and audio cassettes, a resource book, and a study guide.

ME193 Watkins, Morris
Seven Worlds to Win. Fullerton, CAU: R C Law & Co, 1987. viii, 228 pp. Paper. 0939925001.

A study guide for local church education and intercession for mission with country profiles grouped according to the dominant religion or ideology of each region.

ME194 Williamson, Roy
For Such a Time as This: Sharing in the Mission of God Today. London, ENK: Darton, Longman & Todd, 1996. 198 pp. Paper. 023252114X.

A seven-session study introducing biblical and contemporary motives for mission by the Anglican bishop of Southwark and former bishop of Bradford, England.

Mission Study Literature: Children and Youth

See also EC89, AF1156, AF1221, AM1281, AM1316, AM1367, and AM1436.

ME195 Borthwick, Paul
Youth and Missions: Expanding Your Students' World View. Wheaton, ILU: Victor Books, 1988. 160 pp. Paper. 0896935825.

A practical guide for cultivating a sense of mission and ministry in youth by using example, exposure, and experience, which will make youth into world Christians; written by the Minister of Missions at Grace Chapel in Lexington, Massachusetts.

ME196 Campbell, Barbara
I Don't Want to Wait until I'm Grown Up!: A Children's Mission Education Curriculum Development Guide. Wheaton, ILU: ACMC, 1991. 88 pp. Paper. No ISBN.

Practical helps for the development of a missions education program for children.

ME197 Catholic Church/Pontifical Work of the Holy Childhood (Germany-W)
Christi Wort für alle Zeit: Eine Geschichte der weltweiten Verkündigung der Frohbotschaft. (Schriften zur katechetischen Unterweisung, 12). Düsseldorf, GW: Patmos Verlag, 1965. viii, 182 pp. Paper. No ISBN.

A mission history for children with articles on basic missionary issues and sketches of great mission personalities.

ME198 Driskill, J. Lawrence
Misison Stories from around the World. Pasadena, CAU: Hope Publishing House, 1994. xi, 178 pp. 0932727727 (hdbk), 0932727719 (pbk).

Forty-four stories of Protestant missionaries written for children ages 7 to 12.

ME199 Dueck, Gerry
Kids for the World: A Guidebook to Children's Mission Resources. South Pasadena, CAU: William Carey Library, 1990. vii, 57 pp. Paper. 0878087559.

A resource guide with sample lesson plans, stories, games, and crafts meant to aid in planning a Sunday School curriculum which will give a mission vision to children.

ME200 Halverson, Delia
Helping Children Care for God's People: 200 Ideas for Teaching Stewardship and Mission. Nashville, TNU: Abingdon, 1994. 106 pp. Paper. 0687411033.

Resources for teaching elementary and middle school children Christian stewardship and mission as service.

ME201 Hopkins, Susan, and Jeffry Winters, eds.
Discover the World: Empowering Children to Value Themselves, Others and the Earth. Philadelphia, PAU: New Society Publishers; Philadelphia, PAU: Concerned Educators Allied for a Safe Environment, 1990. 157 pp. 0865711917 (hdbk US), 0865711925 (pbk US), 1550920081 (hdbk CA), 155092009X (pbk CA).

Resources on global awareness, peace, and conflict management for educational programs with children.

ME202 McElrath, William N.
Bold Bearers of His Name: Forty World Mission Stories. Nashville, TNU: Broadman, 1987. 274 pp. 0805443398.

A collection of forty world mission stories written as a resource for older children and their teachers of the Southern Baptist Convention.

ME203 Schultz, Dorothy Holsinger
Mini-Missions Conference: A Missions Adventure for Children. Fullerton, CAU: R C Law & Co, 1989. iv, 247 pp. Paper. 0939925435.

Thirty-two lessons compiled in seven volumes as an open-ended program in missions education for all ages, including lessons on new mission fields as well as other areas of ministry.

ME204 Spraggett, Daphne, and Jill Johnstone
You Can Change the World, Volume 2. Grand Rapids, MIU: Zondervan, 1996. 126 pp. 0310205654.

Mission education to help children and youth understand and pray for persons in twenty-six countries and twenty-six people groups—a children's version of *Operation World*.

ME205 Stearns, Bill
A Sunday for the World! Ventura, CAU: Gospel Light, 1996. 200 pp. Paper. 0830718249.

Helps for mission education activities for children.

ME206 Tower, Grace Storms

Growing Up in Mission: A Leader's Handbook on the Education of Children in the Mission of the Church. New York, NYU: Friendship Press, 1966. 175 pp. No ISBN.

A guide for parents and adults who work with children to help them, at varied ages, in their understanding of mission from the perspective of the Congregational Christian Churches.

Finance

See also HI465, ME9, ED139, MI102, AF1340, and EU229.

ME207 Baan, Antoon

SPL/PMP in Nederland 1920-1980: Zestig jaar geschiedenis van de Nederlandse afdeling van het Sint Petrus Liefdewerk/ Pauselijk Missiewerk voor Priesteropleiding overzee. Gravenhage, NE: PMW-Nederland, 1983. 380 pp. Paper. No ISBN.

The book describes sixty years (1920-1980) of organizing financial and spiritual support in the Netherlands for the training of local Roman Catholic priests in Africa and Asia; work started as a Dutch department of the international pontifical organization St. Peter's Charity (SPL), but continued later under the name Papal Mission Work for Own Priests (PMP).

ME208 Bonk, Jonathan J.

Missions and Money: Affluence as a Western Missionary Problem. (American Society of Missiology Series, 15). Maryknoll, NYU: Orbis Books, 1991. xxi, 170 pp. Paper. 0883447185.

A scholarly analysis of the historical and cultural context of Protestant missionary affluence in the 19th and 20th centuries, its consequences, and the theological, missiological, and strategic challenges that it presents for future effectiveness of missions from North America and other affluent regions.

ME209 Brown, Keith, and John W. Hoover

Faith Promise and Beyond: Unlocking the Resources of the Church to Help Fulfill the Great Commission. Keamey, NEU: Morris Publishing, 1995. 112 pp. Paper. 1575021013.

Practical helps for local churches in using the Faith Promise method of supporting missions.

ME210 Bush, Luis

Funding Two-Thirds World Missions. (World Evangelical Fellowship Missions Publications). Exeter, ENK: Paternoster Press, 1990. 31 pp. Paper. 0853645175.

A brief introduction to the history and future prospects for funding Two-Thirds World missions through First World financial support.

ME211 Carlson, Martin E.

Why People Give. New York, NYU: Council Press, 1968. xviii, 174 pp. Paper. No ISBN.

A practical exploration of motivations for giving to religious causes.

ME212 Karsten, Nissen, Knud Wumpelmann, and Frede Tramm

Mission og nodhjµlp. (Nyt synspunkt, 7). Hellerup, DK: DMS-Forlag, 1978. 64 pp. Paper. 8774310720.

Short essays edited by Carl Chr. Jessen, Karsten Nissen, and Knud Ochsner on the relationship between missions and interchurch aid, plus an interpretation of neighbor love in the New Testament.

ME213 Kotler, Philip

Marketing for Nonprofit Organizations. Englewood Cliffs, NJU: Prentice-Hall, 1995. 528 pp. No ISBN.

The third edition of this very instructional book treats marketing as a need satisfying activity for organizations such as schools, hospitals, and churches and as such provides a helpful guide to mission agencies in their efforts to raise support; originally published in 1974.

ME214 Krause, Evangeline

The Million-Dollar Living Room. Wheaton, ILU: Tyndale, 1984. 79 pp. Paper. 0842342850.

A popular account of the Missionary Fellowship which has raised $13 million for missions since 1955 from a living room in Minnesota.

ME215 Kroll, Woodrow

The Home Front Handbook: How to Support Missions behind the Lines. Lincoln, NEU: Back to the Bible, 1994. 69 pp. Paper. 0847408957.

Ten simple suggestions for laity desiring to support overseas missionaries through their local churches by the General Director of Back to the Bible.

ME216 Maiden, Peter

Take My Silver. Exeter, ENK: Send the Light; Exeter, ENK: Paternoster Press, 1988. 59 pp. Paper. 1850780390 (S), 085364473X (P).

Second edition of a practical survey on the whole subject of Christian giving; by the Associate International Coordinator of Operation Mobilization; originally published in 1982.

ME217 Millwood, David

Something to Share: The Who, What, Why, When and How of Ecumenical Resource Sharing. Uppsala, SW: Swedish Mission Council; Uppsala, SW: Church of Sweden International Study Department, 1989. 132 pp. Paper. 918542417X.

An enlarged study book to help lay Christians understand the concept of ecumenical resource sharing and how it might be promoted; originally published by the WCC in 1988.

ME218 Pospischil, Hans Thomas

Der solidarische Umgang mit Eigentum und Einkommen in christlichen Gemeinschaften und Gruppen. (Freiburger theologische Studien, 144). Freiburg im Breisgau, GW: Herder, 1990. xiii, 416 pp. Paper. 3451220695.

This dissertation is a study of the relationships of possessions to income in Germany for those who practice different types of personal "taxation" to support social justice causes through Christian communities and other organizations.

ME219 Quinn, Richard F., and Robert Carroll

The Missionary Factor in Irish Aid Overseas. Dublin, IE: Dominican Publications, 1980. 92 pp. Paper. 0950479780.

An economist evaluates the hidden contribution which Ireland, through the development work of missionaries, makes to the Third World.

ME220 Rust, Brian, and Barry McLeish

The Support-Raising Handbook: A Guide for Christian Workers. Downers Grove, ILU: InterVarsity, 1984. 119 pp. Paper. 0877843260.

A book of practical suggestions for Christian workers, especially those associated with para-church and independent mission agencies who have to raise their own support.

Future of Missions

See also HI8, HI509, ME62, ME75, ME77-ME78, SO205, SO256, EV219, MI56, AM987, EU13, and EU153.

ME221 Aeschliman, Gordon D.
Global Trends: Ten Changes Affecting Christians Everywhere.
Downers Grove, ILU: InterVarsity, 1990. 156 pp. Paper.
0830817328.

A popular presentation of ten trends affecting the future of the Christian world mission.

ME222 Amstutz, Josef, Giancarlo Collet, and Werner Zurfluh
Kirche und Dritte Welt im Jahr 2000. Zürich, SZ: Benziger, 1974. 252 pp. 3545240452.

Members of the Futures Group of the Swiss Catholic Missionary Council give their predictions for the year 2000.

ME223 Anderson, Gerald H., James M. Phillips, and Robert T. Coote, eds.
Mission in the Nineteen 90s. Grand Rapids, MIU: Eerdmans; New Haven, CTU: Overseas Ministries Study Center, 1991. 80 pp. Paper. 0802805426.

Seventeen essays by international mission leaders from eleven countries and five continents assessing the record, trends, and prospects for Christian world mission; originally published in the *International Bulletin of Missionary Research.*

ME224 Bühlmann, Walbert
The Church of the Future: A Model for the Year 2001. Translated by Mary Groves. Maryknoll, NYU: Orbis Books; Melbourne, AT: Dove Communications; Slough, ENK: St. Paul, 1986. xiii, 207 pp. Paper. 0883442531 (US), 0859246000 (AT), 0854392424 (UK).

English translation.

ME225 Bühlmann, Walbert
The Coming of the Third Church: An Analysis of the Present and Future of the Church. Maryknoll, NYU: Orbis Books, 1977. xi, 419 pp. Paper. 0883440709, 0883440695.

An overview by the Secretary-General of the Capuchins of social forces impacting the churches of Asia, Africa, and Latin America, and of emerging structures of mission in those lands.

ME226 Bühlmann, Walbert
Von der Kirche träumen: Ein Stück Apostelgeschichte im 20. Jahrhundert. Graz, AU: Verlag Styria, 1986. 269 pp. Paper. 3222117144.

A collection of essays by the noted German Catholic missiologist on the future of mission.

ME227 Bühlmann, Walbert
Weltkirche: Neue Dimensionen; Modell für das Jahr 2001. Graz, AU: Verlag Styria, 1984. 247 pp. Paper. 3222115125.

A vision of the Catholic Church in the year 2001 in which peoples of the Third World will predominate, advocating pluriform structures, a broadened understanding of ministry, and new values.

ME228 Bühlmann, Walbert
Wer Augen hat zu sehen: Was Gott heute mit uns Christen vorhat. Graz, AU: Styria, 1989. 271 pp. Paper. 3222118973.

A comprehensive and carefully developed prescription for the Roman Catholic Church if it is to be creatively in mission in the 21st century.

ME229 Bühlmann, Walbert
Wo der Glaube lebt: Einblicke in die Lage der Weltkirche. Freiburg, GW: Herder, 1974. 342 pp. Paper. 345117085X.

Considering the "new shape of the world" the Secretary-General for Capuchins throughout the world appeals to a wider audience for a new vision of church, the "Third Church," focusing on such matters as church ministries, laity, and local church.

ME230 Bühlmann, Walbert, and Robert R. Barr
With Eyes to See: Church and World in the Third Millennium. Maryknoll, NYU: Orbis Books, 1990. vi, 162 pp. Paper. 0883446839.

English translation.

ME231 Barna, George
The Frog in the Kettle: What Christians Need to Know about Life in the Year 2000. Ventura, CAU: Regal Books, 1990. 235 pp. 0830714499.

An insightful analysis of future trends in US society, and of the challenges and opportunities that they will bring for the churches.

ME232 Blair, Philip
Watching for the Morning: Global Chaos and Cosmic Hope. Cambridge, ENK: Lutterworth Press, 1999. 136 pp. Paper. 0718830008.

An analysis of past events, their future influences, and a scriptural challenge of hope in the "end time" climate.

ME233 Bryant, David
The Hope at Hand: National and World Revival for the 21st Century. Grand Rapids, MIU: Baker Books, 1995. 252 pp. Paper. 0801010993.

The founder and president of Concerts of Prayer International and of America's National Prayer Committee offers a popular summary of global trends and his expectation that "we are on the threshold of the greatest revival in the history of the church."

ME234 Bulman, Raymond F.
The Lure of the Millennium: The Year 2000 and Beyond. Maryknoll, NYU: Orbis Books, 1999. xvi, 238 pp. Paper. 1570752532.

An in-depth survey of responses to the new millennium, weaving in historical, biblical, and contemporary perspectives, including a challenge for a new global ethic.

ME235 Chandler, Russell
Racing toward 2001: The Forces Shaping America's Religious Future. Grand Rapids, MIU: Zondervan; San Francisco, CAU: HarperSanFrancisco, 1992. 367 pp. 0310541301 (Z), 0685553671 (H).

An analysis of twelve social trends in the new millennium with implications for church renewal in the United States based on interviews with seventy-five futurists.

ME236 Danker, William J., and Wi Jo Kang, eds.
The Future of the Christian World Mission: Studies in Honor of Pierce Beaver. Grand Rapids, MIU: Eerdmans, 1971. 181 pp. No ISBN.

Essays on the theory and practice of present and future mission activity honoring the University of Chicago's distinguished Professor of Missions.

ME237 Dunton, Hugh I., Baldur Pfeiffer, and Børge Schantz, eds.

Adventist Missions Facing the 21st Century: A Reader. (Archives of International Adventist History, 3). Frankfurt am Main, GW: Lang, 1990. xiii, 233 pp. Paper. 363142387X.

Major questions affecting all missionary sending agencies are treated here in the Adventist context.

ME238 Edwards, David L.

The Futures of Christianity. Wilton, CTU: Morehouse-Barlow; London, ENK: Hodder & Stoughton, 1987. 479 pp. Paper. 0819214213 (US), 0340407425 (UK).

A wide-ranging survey of present trends and likely future developments in the life of Christian churches around the world by the provost of the Anglican Southwark Cathedral and former editor of SCM Press.

ME239 Elmer, Duane, and Lois McKinney, eds.

With an Eye on the Future: Development and Mission in the 21st Century. Monrovia, CAU: MARC, 1996. x, 259 pp. Paper. 0912552999.

A *festschrift* containing twenty-nine short essays on the future of global mission, leadership development and theological education honoring Ted Ward, the Professor of International Studies and Mission at Trinity Evangelical Divinity School.

ME240 Fraser, Ian M.

The Fire Runs: God's People Participating in Change. London, ENK: SCM Press, 1975. 152 pp. 0334004837.

A reflection on the far-reaching mistakes of patronizing Western missions in the past, on signs of creative unrest of Christian communities in the Third World, and on the urgent need of a radical change of outlook among the churches in the West, by the Dean of Mission at the Selly Oak Colleges in Birmingham, England.

ME241 Freeman, J. Stephen, ed.

Shaping Our Future: Challenges for the Church in the Twenty-First Century. Cambridge, MAU: Cowley Publications, 1994. xiv, 193 pp. Paper. 1561010979.

Fifteen short essays on the challenges of structure, ministry, mission, culture, and leadership in the church's 21st century-mission; originally presented at the Episcopal Church's Shaping Our Future symposium (St. Louis, 1993).

ME242 Hall, Douglas John

The End of Christendom and the Future of Christianity. Valley Forge, PAU: Trinity Press International; Leominster, ENK: Gracewing, 1997. x, 69 pp. Paper. 1563381931 (T), 0852444214 (G).

A proposal that Christianity's future lies in making the disestablishment of churches work for good in Christian witness and service by the Professor of Christian Theology at McGill University in Montreal, Canada.

ME243 Harmer, Catherine M.

Religious Life in the 21st Century: A Contemporary Journey into Canaan. Mystic, CTU: Twenty-Third Publications, 1995. 136 pp. Paper. 0896226514.

An identification of key cultural and religious paradigm shifts that will necessitate Catholic religious orders to rethink their community life and ministry in church and world as they plan for mission in the 21st century.

ME244 Hesselgrave, David J.

Today's Choices for Tomorrow's Mission: An Evangelical Perspective on Trends and Issues in Missions. Grand Rapids, MIU: Zondervan, 1988. 272 pp. Paper. 0310368219.

An in-depth discussion of critical issues facing mission leaders and strategists today, with a survey of trends and concerns for tomorrow by the Director of the School of World Mission and Evangelism at Trinity Evangelical Divinity School (US).

ME245 Hopkins, Paul A.

What Next in Mission? Philadelphia, PAU: Westminster Press, 1977. 122 pp. Paper. 0664241433.

A discussion of the future of world mission by the Africa Secretary of the United Presbyterian Church (USA) focusing on issues of the moratorium and church-to-church relationships.

ME246 Houston, Tom

Scenario 2000. Monrovia, CAU: MARC, 1992. 47 pp. Paper. 0912552786.

Assessment in outline form by the international director of the Lausanne Committee for World Evangelization of Christian mission prospects in each part of the world dominated by another world faith or ideology, as well as in each continent.

ME247 Lohmann, Heinrich

Weltmission in der Krise?: Ein Arbeitsheft für alle, die von dieser Frage beunruhigt sind. Vom Generalsekretär der Evang. Arbeitsgemeinschaft fü Weltmission hrsg. in eigener Verantwortung. (Weltmission heute, 41/42). Stuttgart, GW: Evan Missionsverlag, 1970. 76 pp. 3771401569.

An assessment of whether world mission was in crisis as it entered the 1970s.

ME248 McKaughan, Paul, Dellanna O'Brien, and William O'Brien

Choosing a Future for U.S. Missions. Monrovia, CAU: MARC, 1998. ix, 114 pp. Paper. 1887983074.

Findings of the Task Force: 21st Century Missions project designed to help North American evangelical missions to engage in visionary planning.

ME249 Montgomery, Jim

Then the End Will Come: Great News about the Great Commission. South Pasadena, CAU: William Carey Library, 1997. xi, 209 pp. Paper. 0878082727.

The story of DAWN (Discipling a Whole Nation) with an update of developments in this world evangelization strategy from 1989 to 1995.

ME250 Mulholland, Kenneth B., and Gary Corwin, eds.

Working Together with God to Shape the New Millennium: Opportunities and Limitations. (Evangelical Missiological Society Series, 8). Pasadena, CAU: William Carey Library, 2000. 235 pp. Paper. 0878083820.

A collection of fourteen scholarly papers describing the opportunities and limitations for evangelical missions in the new millennium; originally presented at the EFMA/IFMA Triennial Leadership Conference (Virginia Beach, Virginia, September 1999).

ME251 Newbigin, James Edward Lesslie

The Other Side of 1984: Questions for the Churches. (Risk Book Series, 18). Geneva, SZ: WCC, 1983. 75 pp. Paper. 2825407844.

An invitation to the church to be bold in offering to all people of their culture a way of understanding based unashamedly in the revelation of God made in Jesus Christ and attested in Scripture and the tradition of the church.

ME—MISSIONS: METHODS

ME252 Phillips, James M., and Robert T. Coote, eds.

Toward the Twenty-First Century in Christian Mission: Essays in Honor of Gerald H. Anderson, Director, Overseas Ministries Study Center, New Haven, Connecticut, Editor, International Bulletin of Missionary Research. Grand Rapids, MIU: Eerdmans, 1993. x, 400 pp. Paper. 0802806384.

A comprehensive survey of the prospects and critical issues for the Christian world mission (for confessional families, geographic regions, and special ministries) with essays by an international team of thirty-eight missiologists.

ME253 Rétif, André

Mission-Heute noch? Cologne, GW: Bachem, 1968. 158 pp. Paper. No ISBN.

German translation.

ME254 Rétif, André

Un nouvel avenir pour les missions. Paris, FR: Éditions du Centurion, 1966. 179 pp. Paper. No ISBN.

A challenge to the Catholic churches of Europe to catch the missionary spirit of Vatican II including the urgency of the re-evangelization of Europe and zeal for the global mission of the church.

ME255 Raalt, Jannes van

De Wereld is van God en daarom van ons Allen: De pluralisering van de samenleving als oefenschool voor de toekomst. Kampen, NE: Kok Pharos, 1996. 267 pp. 9024222206.

The posthumous work of a Dutch missiologist who analyzed global trends in mobilization, technology, and politico-economic problems, and proposed missional responses based on biblical precedents.

ME256 Reformed Ecumenical Synod Missions Conference (1984: Chicago, ILU)

Mission and the Future: Charting New Strategies. Grand Rapids, MIU: Reformed Ecumenical Synod, 1985. ii, 69 pp. Paper. No ISBN.

Four papers reflecting upon missions in movement, challenges ahead, and interdependence at the cutting edge.

ME257 Samuel, Vinay, and Chris Sugden, eds.

A.D. 2000 and Beyond: A Mission Agenda. Oxford, ENK: Regnum Books, 1991. xii, 166 pp. Paper. 1870345096.

A collection of ten essays on holistic understandings of mission by leaders from four continents written by evangelical theologians of the International Fellowship of Mission Theologies to honor John Stott on his seventieth birthday.

ME258 Samuel, Vinay, and Chris Sugden

Christian Mission in the Eighties: A Third World Perspective. (Partnership Booklet, 2). Bangalore, II: Partnership in Mission-Asia, 1981. 32 pp. Paper. No ISBN.

A brief plea by two missioners in India stating that for missionaries to be effective in the '80s, events that shape the culture and lives of the people must be recognized.

ME259 Sine, Tom

Wild Hope. Dallas, TXU: Word Publishing, 1991. x, 343 pp. Paper. 0849931312.

A broad exposure to the thought of futurists concerning the 21st century, challenging the churches to creative futuring for the church and its mission in society.

ME260 Sine, Tom, ed.

Mustard Seed vs. McWorld: Reinventing Life and Faith for the Future. Grand Rapids, MIU: Baker Books, 1999. 249 pp. Paper. 0801090881.

In the midst of a contest between economic globalization (McWorld) and the "mustard seed" agenda of God, the author provides concrete ideas for acting out our faith, and anticipating and responding creatively to opportunities and challenges of our global future.

ME261 Smith, Joanmarie

A Context for Christianity in the 21st Century. Allen, TXU: Thomas More, 1995. 188 pp. Paper. 0883472929.

A primer for 21st-century Christians on how conversion and commitment are reconceived amidst religious pluralism and philosophical relativism.

ME262 Snyder, Howard A.

Earth Currents: The Struggle for the World's Soul. Nashville, TNU: Abingdon, 1995. 334 pp. 0687114497.

An analysis of global trends, shifting worldviews, and their implications for Christians by a noted missiologist.

ME263 Starkes, M. Thomas

Mission 2000. Chattanooga, TNU: AMG Publishers, 1979. 85 pp. Paper. 0899576125.

A study guide on the future of Christian missions containing biblical and theological foundations, a case study on the future of mission in Africa, and an exploration of issues for the 21st century.

ME264 Stocker, Christine, ed.

Dritte Welt im Jahr 2000. Compiled by Eugen Fehr. Zürich, SZ: Benziger, 1974. 304 pp. 3545240444.

A comprehensive study from the global perspective of population explosion, third world countries, and allocation of world's material and spiritual resources based on principles of Christian justice.

ME265 Sweet, Leonard I.

Faithquakes. Nashville, TNU: Abingdon, 1994. 237 pp. 0687126479.

A probing forecast of 21st-century beliefs and behaviors, with proposals for a renewed church in a postmodern era.

ME266 Sweet, Leonard I.

Soul Tsunami: Sink or Swim in New Millennium Culture. Grand Rapids, MIU: Zondervan, 1999. 446 pp. 0310227623.

A call for Christians to remove their tunnel-vision glasses and face the postmodern flood of issues such as globalization and modern technology.

ME–MISSIONS: METHODS

CHRISTIANITY AND OTHER RELIGIONS
Paul Knitter, Subeditor

David Bosch contended that since the 1960s the theology of religions has been the dominant theme in both missiological and general theological literature. This is attested by the "deluge of books" published on that subject (1991:477). The organizing principle of this chapter is what the noted missiologist called "mission as witness to people of other living faiths" (474).

While voluminous, I do not presume to include in this chapter a bibliography of world religions. The focus is on Christian understanding of other faiths and on Christian witness, dialogue, and mission among persons of other religions.

The chapter begins with several useful bibliographies on Christian encounter with other faiths. The subsection "Serials/Periodicals" provides a window to articles in the field.

Readers will find that standard reference works on world religions contain important articles related to the focus of this chapter. Useful sourcebooks have been grouped under "Documentation and Archives."

Numerous conferences have been held on the theme of this chapter. Many of their reports and papers include actual dialogues with persons of other faiths.

Jongeneel lists missionary apologetics as one of the eleven branches of missiology. He defines it as "the systematic and practical theological discipline which examines the missionary encounter between Christians and non-Christians" (1995: 339). Works on the theology of religions are found in the subsection on "General Works." Scholars studying world religions have produced many comparative studies. Many discuss themes useful in interreligious dialogue. General works on "Interreligious Dialogue" follow.

The rest of the chapter takes Christian encounters with each of the world religions in alphabetical order. First is "Christianity and African Religions." Additional content on this theme will be found in works under "African Theologies" in the Africa chapter. Next comes a subsection on "Christianity and Native American Religions."

Works on "Christianity and Buddhism" have been subdivided. First come general works. These are followed by books, in subsections, on "Missions to Buddhists" and "Buddhist Sources, Origins, and Impact." Next comes a grouping of works on Christianity and Chinese religions and philosophies (Taoism and Confucianism).

Students of Christianity and Hinduism will find the next sections rich with sources. The first is titled "Christianity and Hinduism." Books on "Hindu Sources, Origins, and Impact" are grouped together. Works under "Indian Christian Theologies" in the Asia chapter deal also with these themes.

Large subsections follow on "Christianity and Islam." Like those on Buddhism, they are subdivided into general works, missions to Muslims, and Islamic sources, origins, and impact.

Next come the writings on Christianity and Judaism. The biblical scholarship has not been included. Readers will find sources on the historical encounters of Christians and Jews. A small section follows on "Missions to Jews."

Continuing the coverage of Christian encounters with persons of other faiths, there follows a general subsection on "Christianity and Various Other Religions." The next subsections concern encounters with Japanese religions, Sikhism, and Zoroastrianism.

Difficult to categorize are those religious movements that arose out of a clash of cultures (Neill, et al., CDCWM: 154). Works in the final two subsections on "Cults and Sects" and "Post-Christian Religion" address that multi-faceted phenomenon. See also the large sections on new religious movements in the chapter on "Missions: Social Aspects."

Norman E. Thomas

Bibliographies

See also CR450 and CR1425.

CR1 Benz, Ernst, and Minoru Nambara
Das Christentum und die nicht-christlichen Hochreligionen: Begegnung und Auseinandersetzung, eine internationale Bibliographie. (Zeitschrift für Religious- und Geistesgeschichte, Beiheft, 5). Leiden, NE: Brill, 1960. 86 pp. Paper. No ISBN.

An international bibliography with about 2,400 entries of scholarly books and articles, mostly in English, French, or German, on the theology of religion and interreligious dialogue between 1925 and 1960.

CR2 Berthrong, John H., comp.
Interfaith Dialogue: An Annotated Bibliography. Wofford Heights, CAU: Multifaith Resources, 1993. ii, 30 pp. Paper. 0963737287.
A select bibliography of books and periodicals in English.

CR3 David, S. Immanuel, ed.
Christianity and the Encounter with Other Religions: A Select Bibliography. (UTC Publications). Bangalore, II: United Theological College, 1988. 107 pp. Paper. No ISBN.

A bibliography, without annotations, of 880 books and articles on the theme, based on theological library collections in Bangalore, India.

CR4 Educational Resources Committee of the Society for Buddhist-Christian Studies
Resources for Buddhist-Christian Encounter: An Annotated Bibliography. Wofford Heights, CAU: Multifaith Resources, 1993. iii, 27 pp. Paper. 0963737295.

A concise bibliography of books and media resources in English.

CR5 Jackson, Herbert C., ed.
Judaism, Jewish-Christian Relations and the Christian Mission to the Jews: A Selected Bibliography. New York, NYU: MRL, 1966. v, 69 pp. No ISBN.

An early bibliographic resource.

CR6 Pruter, Karl
Jewish Christians in the United States: A Bibliography. New York, NYU: Garland, 1987. xi, 192 pp. 0824087410.

A bibliography of the literature of groups engaged in missions to American Jews, with brief introductions to each group, including books, booklets, pamphlets, tracts, and periodicals published between 1960 and 1980.

CR7 *Religious Regimes in Contact: Christian Missions, Global Transformations, and Comparative Research: Bibliography*
Cambridge, MAU: Harvard University, Center for the Study of World Religions, 1993. 70 pp. Paper. No ISBN.

A selected bibliography of books and journal articles, mainly in English, from the 1954-1993 period, deemed important by faculty of the Harvard University Center for the Study of World Religions.

Serials and Periodicals

See also GW39, TH4, and EA9.

CR8 *Al-Basheer.* Vol. 1, no. 1 (Jan./Mar. 1972)-***
Hyderabad, II: Henry Martyn Institute of Islamic Studies, 1972-1976. No ISSN.

Superseded the *Bulletin of Christian Institutes of Islamic Studies*; changed back to the former title in 1978.

CR9 *Al-Mushir.* Vol. 1, no. 1 (Jan. 1959)-. Monthly (irregular)
Rawalpindi, PK: Christian Study Centre, 1959-. ISSN 02547856.

Articles in English and Urdu on the religions of Pakistan, with focus on Christian-Muslim relations.

CR10 *Areopagus: A Living Encounter with Today's Religious World.* Vol. 1, no. 1 (Fall 1987)-vol. 9, no. 4 (Winter-Spring 1997). Quarterly
Shatin, Hong Kong, CH: Tao Fang Shan Ecumenical Centre, 1987-1997. ISSN 10118101.

Initially published in cooperation with the Dialog Center International, in Aarhus, Denmark, this journal intends to provide a forum for communication between Christians professing faith in Jesus Christ with people of faith both in major world religions and in new religious movements; incorporated in 1987 *Update* (Aarhus) and *New Religious Movements Update.*

CR11 *Buddhist-Christian Studies.* Vol. 1 (1981) -. Annual
Honolulu, HIU: University of Hawaii, East-West Religions Project, 1981-. ISSN 08820945.

Articles, book reviews, and news items on Buddhism and Christianity; their interrelation, based on historical materials and contemporary experience.

CR12 *Bulletin of Christian Institutes of Islamic Studies* [Hyderabad]. Vol. 1, nos. 1-2 (Jan.-June 1978- vol. 8, no. 2 (Apr.-June 1985). Quarterly
Hyderabad, II: Henry Martyn Institute of Islamic Studies, 1978-1985. ISSN 09704698.

Superseded *Al-Basheer*; renamed *The Bulletin of the Henry Martyn Institute of Islamic Studies* [Hyderabad, India] in 1978.

CR13 *Bulletin of the Christian Institute of Religious Studies.* Vol. 19, no. 1 (Jan. 1990)-. Semiannual
Batala, Punjab, II: Christian Institute of Religious Studies, 1990-. No ISSN.

Short articles on issues of religion and society; superseded the *Bulletin of the Christian Institute of Sikh Studies.*

CR14 *Bulletin of the Christian Institute of Sikh Studies.* Vol. 1, no. 1 (Jan. 1972-vol. 18, no. 2 (July 1989). Semiannual
Batala, Punjab, II: Christian Institute of Sikh Studies, 1972-1989. No ISSN.

Contains short articles and papers on common concerns of Christians and Sikhs; continued as *Bulletin of the Christian Institute of Religious Studies.*

CR15 *Bulletin of the Christian Institutes of Islamic Studies* [Lucknow]. Vol. 1, no. 1 (July 1967-vol. 5, nos. 1-2 (July-Oct. 1971). Quarterly
Lucknow, II: Henry Martyn Institute of Islamic Studies, 1967-1971. No ISSN.

Reports and papers from Christian institutes of Islamic studies in India and Pakistan; superseded the *Bulletin of the Henry Martyn Institute of Islamic Studies*; continued by *Al-Basheer.*

CR16 *Bulletin of the Henry Martyn Institute of Islamic Studies* [Hyderabad]. Vol. 8, no. 3 (July-Sept. 1985)-. Quarterly
Hyderabad, II: Henry Martyn Institute of Islamic Studies, 1985. ISSN 09704698.

This quarterly publication of the Henry Martyn Institute, an international center for reconciliation and interfaith relations, aims to promote interreligious understanding with a special focus on the study of Islam; superseded by the *Bulletin of Christian Institutes of Islamic Studies.*

CR17 *Bulletin of the Henry Martyn Institute of Islamic Studies* [Lucknow]. Vol. 48, no. 1 (Jan./Mar. 1960)-vol. 56, no. 1 (Apr. 1967). Quarterly
Lucknow, II: Henry Martyn Institute of Islamic Studies, 1960-1967. ISSN 04406893.

Papers and reports from meetings and programs sponsored by the institute; succeeding *News and Notes* founded in 1912; superseded by the *Bulletin of Christian Institutes of Islamic Studies.*

CR18 *Ching Feng.* Vol. 8, no. 1 (Winter 1964)-. Quarterly
Hong Kong, CH: Christian Study Centre on Chinese Religion and Culture, 1964-. ISSN 00094668.

An international refereed journal on interreligious dialogue, Asian theologies, Christianity in China, and Christianity and Chinese culture; continues *Quarterly Notes on Christianity and Chinese Religion*; exists also in Chinese edition.

CR19 Contemporary Religions in Japan. Vol. 1 (1960)-vol. 11 (1970). Semiannual
Tokyo, JA: International Institute for the Study of Religions, 1960-1970. ISSN 03041042.
Presents academic studies of Japanese religions; continued as *Japanese Journal of Religious Studies.*

CR20 Current Dialogue. Vol. 1, no. 1 (Winter 1980/81) -. Semiannual
Geneva, SZ: WCC, Office of Interreligious Relations, 1980-. No ISSN.
Papers, documents, and correspondence related to concerns and conferences of the WCC's Office of Interreligious Relations (formerly the unit on Dialogue with Peoples of Living Faiths and Ideologies); superseded the *Church and the Jewish People.*

CR21 Dialogue. No. 1 (1964)-no. 28 (1973); New series vol. 1 (1974) -. Annual
Colombo, CE: Ecumenical Institute for Study and Dialogue, 1964-. ISSN 00122181.
This annual publication, edited by Aloysius Pieris, contains scholarly articles and book reviews on issues of Christian-Buddhist dialogue.

CR22 Immanuel: A Bulletin of Religious Thought and Research in Israel. No. 1 (Summer 1972) -. Semiannual
Jerusalem, IS: Ecumenical Theological Research Fraternity in Israel, 1972-. ISSN 03028127.
Presents to an international, non-Hebrew reading audience translations and summaries in English of recent Hebrew publications on Jewish-Christian relations, contemporary religious life and thought in Israel, Jewish thought and spirituality, the Hebrew Bible, and the New Testament and the first centuries of Judaism.

CR23 Japanese Journal of Religious Studies. Vol. 1, no. 1 (1974) -. Semiannual
Tokyo, JA: International Institute for the Study of Religions, 1994-. ISSN 03041042.
Scholarly articles on Japanese religions; supersedes *Contemporary Religions in Japan.*

CR24 Japanese Religions. Vol. 1 (1959) -. Quarterly
Kyoto, JA: Center for the Study of Japanese Religions, 1959- . ISSN 04488954.
Scholarly articles on religion in Japan and other Asian countries; published by the research institute of the National Christian Council in Japan to promote intercultural understanding and to make knowledge of religions in Japan available internationally.

CR25 Journal of Religion in Africa. Vol. 1 (1967) -. Quarterly
Leiden, NE: Brill, 1967-. ISSN 00224200.
A scholarly journal devoted to the scientific study of the forms and history of religion within the African continent, and in sub-Saharan Africa in particular; articles in English and French; superseded *African Religious Research.*

CR26 Muslim World. Vol. 1 (1911) -. Quarterly
Hartford, CT: Hartford Seminary, Duncan Black Macdonald Center, 1911-. ISSN 00274909.
A journal devoted to the study of Islam and Christian-Muslim relationships, past and present, containing scholarly articles, review articles, and shorter book reviews; founded in 1911 as *The Moslem World* (ISSN 03624641) and continued under that title until 1948.

CR27 Quarterly Notes on Christianity and Chinese Religion. Series 1 (Mar. 1957) - series 7 (Dec. 1963). Quarterly
Hong Kong, CH: Christian Study Centre on Chinese Religion and Culture, 1957-1963. ISSN 00094668.
Scholarly articles on Christianity and Chinese culture; also published in Chinese edition; continued as *Ching Feng.*

CR28 Shermis, Michael
Jewish-Christian Relations: An Annotated Bibliography and Resource Guide. Bloomington, INU: Indiana University Press, 1988. xv, 291 pp. 0253331536.
A reference work listing materials developed for and about Jewish-Christian dialogue and relations from 1963 to 1988, including resources in print, media, and interested organizations.

CR29 Studies in Interreligious Dialogue. Vol. 1, pt. 1 (1991) -. Semiannual
Kampen, NE: Kok Pharos; Maryknoll, NYU: Orbis Books, 1991-. ISSN 09262326.
Scholarly articles, book reviews and announcements, and a survey of conferences on interreligious dialogue.

CR30 The Church and the Jewish People. Vol. 1 (1965) - Vol. 16 (1980). Semiannual
Geneva, SZ: WCC, 1965-1980. No ISSN.
Papers and reports from consultations on Christian/Jewish relations, sponsored initially by the WCC's Committee on the Church and the Jewish People, and later by its unit on Dialogue with Peoples of Living Faiths and Ideologies; continued as *Current Dialogue.*

Reference Works

See also CR1170 and CR1310.

CR31 Adams, Charles J., ed.
A Reader's Guide to the Great Religions. New York, NYU: Free Press; London, ENK: Collier Macmillan, 1977. xvii, 521 pp. 0029002400.
Second edition of thirteen scholarly essays on the history, beliefs, and institutions of the world's religious traditions, with a concluding essay on the history of the history of religions.

CR32 Bishop, Peter D., and Michael Darton, eds.
The Encyclopedia of World Faiths: An Illustrated Survey of the World's Living Religions. London, ENK: Macdonald Orbis, 1987. 352 pp. 0356140628.
An introduction to the cultural and religious structures of twelve of the world's major living religions: Judaism, Zoroastrianism, Christianity, Islam, Babism and the Baha'i faith, Hinduism, Jainism, Buddhism, Confucianism, Taoism, and Shinto, as well as discussions of new religious movements in Western society and "among primal peoples."

CR33 Bowker, John, ed.
The Oxford Dictionary of World Religions. Oxford, ENK: Oxford University Press, 1997. xxiv, 1,111 pp. 0192139657.
A global panel of eighty scholars' comprehensive reference guide to world religions, sects, cults, texts, leaders, sacred sites, customs, beliefs, and ethics; with alphabetical organization of 13,000 entries plus topical index.

CR—CHRISTIANITY AND OTHER RELIGIONS

CR34 Crim, Keith, ed.
Abingdon Dictionary of Living Religions. Nashville, TNU: Abingdon, 1981. xviii, 830 pp. 0687004098.

A one-volume guide to the historical development, beliefs, and practices of the sometimes bewildering array of religions in today's world.

CR35 *Dialog der Religionen: Vol. 1, no. 1 (1991)-. Semiannual*
Munich, GW: Chr. Kaiser Verlag, 1991. Paper. ISSN 09395539.

This journal takes as its leitmotif the task of providing information on interreligious dialogue from a worldwide perspective, as well as a forum for interdisciplinary exchange among theologians, scholars in the field of history of religions, and the social sciences.

CR36 *Eerdman's Handbook to the World's Religions*
Grand Rapids, MIU: Eerdmans, 1994. 464 pp. Paper. 0802808530.

A revised edition of a clear and stimulating introduction and guide to the world's religions; originally published in 1982.

CR37 Eliade, Mircea, ed.
The Encyclopedia of Religion. New York, NYU: Macmillan, 1987. 16 vols. 0029094801 (set).

A comprehensive encyclopedia of the important ideas, beliefs, rituals, myths, symbols, and persons of each religion, with articles also on Christian missions and Christianity by continent.

CR38 Hinnells, John R., ed.
A New Handbook of Living Religions. Cambridge, MAU: Blackwell Publishers, 1997. x, 902 pp. 0631182756.

A team of twenty-five international scholars introduces major religions in the modern world and cross-cultural issues of their diaspora communities—their sources, history, teachings, practices, popular traditions, and 20th-century developments—an update of the Penguin *Handbook of Living Religions* (1984)

CR39 Jung, Moses, Swami Nikhilananda, and Herbert W. Schneider, eds.
Relations among Religions Today: A Handbook of Policies and Principles. Leiden, NE: Brill, 1963. xii, 178 pp. Paper. No ISBN.

A compilation of documents on principles for the improvement of interreligious relations from the official documents of various faiths, the statements of their leaders, and the writings of their scholars.

CR40 Khoury, Adel Théodore, ed.
Lexikon religiöser Grundbegriffe: Judentum, Christentum, Islam. Graz, AU: Verlag Styria, 1987. xlix, 1175 pp. 3222117179.

A one-volume encyclopedia of Judaism, Christianity, and Islam emphasizing central concepts.

CR41 Levinson, David
Religion: A Cross-Cultural Encyclopedia. (Encyclopedia of Human Experience). New York, NYU: Oxford University Press, 1998. xx, 288 pp. 0874368650 (hdbk), 0195123115 (pbk).

A dictionary providing a basic profile and chronology of sixteen world religions, plus indigenous religions.

CR42 Loth, Heinz-Jürgen, ed.
Christentum im Spiegel der Weltreligionen: Kritische Texte und Kommentare. Stuttgart, GW: Quell Verlag, 1979. 374 pp. Paper. 3791860046.

A compilation of texts on Christianity by Jews, Muslims, Hindus, Buddhists, and others, with commentaries by experts in comparative religion.

CR43 Parker, Philip M.
Religious Cultures of the World: A Statistical Reference. (Cross-Cultural Statistical Encyclopedia of the World, 1). Westport, CTU: Greenwood, 1997. xi, 144 pp. 0313297681.

Comparative tables presenting 329 variables for over 70 religious groups, developed to allow quantitative comparisons across non-national cultures.

CR44 Parrinder, Edward Geoffrey
A Dictionary of Non-Christian Religions. Philadelphia, PAU: Westminster Press, 1974. 320 pp. 0664209815.

A dictionary of names and terms of the non-Christian religions of the world, with special attention to Hinduism, Buddhism, and Islam; originally published in 1971 by Hulton Educational Publication, London (ISBN 0717505723).

CR45 Smith, Jonathan Z., ed.
The HarperCollins Dictionary of Religion. San Francisco, CAU: HarperSanFrancisco, 1995. xxviii, 115 pp. 0060675152.

A dictionary for the general reader on the world's religions, their beliefs, practices, and leaders, with 3,200 entries by 327 scholars.

CR46 Sutherland, Stewart et al., eds.
The World's Religions. Boston, MAU: G K Hall, 1988. xiv, 995 pp. 0816189781.

Fifty-eight articles providing history, theological basis and practice, the state of the study of religion and religions; also covering the topics of religion and the study of religions, Judaism and Christianity, Islam, religions of Asia, traditional religions, and new religious movements.

Documentation and Archives

See also CR42, CR184, and CR1027.

CR47 Flannery, Austin P., ed.
Missions and Religions. Dublin, IE: Scepter Books, 1968. 163 pp. No ISBN.

Texts and commentaries on Vatican II's "Decree on the Church's Missionary Activity" and "Declaration on the Relation of the Church to Non-Christian Religions."

CR48 Kramer, Kenneth
World Scriptures: An Introduction to Comparative Religions. New York, NYU: Paulist Press, 1986. v, 298 pp. Paper. 0809127814.

A guidebook to the primary sacred texts of Hinduism, Buddhism, Confucianism, Taoism, Judaism, Christianity, and Islam, with introductions and selected passages for those who have little background in the subject.

CR49 Pailin, David A.
Attitudes to Other Religions: Comparative Religion in Seventeenth and Eighteenth-Century Britain. Manchester, ENK: Manchester University Press, 1984. ix, 339 pp. 0719010659.

Following an extended introduction to 17th- and 18th century-English views on "other religions," thirty texts from the period are included with notes.

CR50 Peters, Francis E.
Judaism, Christianity, and Islam: The Classical Texts and Their Interpretation. Princeton, NJU: Princeton University Press, 1990. 3 vols. Paper. 0691020442 (vol. 1), 069102054X (vol. 2), 0691020558 (vol. 3).

A juxtaposition of extensive passages from Jewish, Christian, and Muslim traditions on central common themes, with commentary by the Professor of Near Eastern Languages and Judaic Studies at New York University; [vol. 1: *From Covenant to Community*, (xxv, 408 pp.); vol. 2: *The Word and the Law and the People of God*, (xxv, 395 pp.); vol. 3: *The Works of the Spirit*, (xxv, 408 pp.)].

CR51 Thyen, Johann-Dietrich
Bibel und Koran: Eine Synopse gemeinsamer Überlieferungen. (Kölner Veröffentlichungen zur Religionsgeschichte, 19). Cologne, GW: Böhlau Verlag, 1989. xxix, 349 pp. Paper. 3412010898.

Second edition of a page by page juxtaposition of parallel passages in the Bible and Qu'ran, with subject index and Qu'ran concordance, where the Koran reflects on biblical stories and traditions.

CR52 Van Voorst, Robert E.
Anthology of World Scriptures. Belmont, CAU: Wadsworth Publishing, 1994. xvi, 344 pp. Paper. 0534191762.

An anthology for university undergraduates of representative scriptures from major world religions, with an introduction on the function of such scriptures.

CR53 Viladesau, Richard, and Mark Massa, eds.
World Religions: A Sourcebook for Students of Christian Theology. New York, NYU: Paulist Press, 1994. ix, 276 pp. Paper. 0809134616.

A sourcebook of primary texts in Buddhism, Hinduism, Taoism, post-classical Judaism, and Islam; with introductions noting parallels and contrasts to the Christian tradition.

Conferences and Congresses

See also CR210, CR218, CR293, CR414, CR445, CR505, CR566, CR717, CR986, CR1072, CR1105, CR1125, CR1130, CR1186, CR1311, PO52, PO203, and EV27.

CR54 Anderson, Gerald H., and Thomas F. Stransky, eds.
Christ's Lordship and Religious Pluralism. Maryknoll, NYU: Orbis Books, 1981. viii, 209 pp. 0883440881.

Proceedings of an ecumenical conference held at Union Theological Seminary, Richmond, Virginia, with Roman Catholic, mainline Protestant, and conservative Evangelical presenters.

CR55 Angilella, Joseph T., and Alan Ziajka, eds.
Rediscovering Justice: Awakening World Faiths to Address World Issues. San Francisco, CAU: University of San Francisco, 1998. xiv, 133 pp. 0966405900 (hdbk), 0966405919 (pbk).

Proceedings and papers of the Interfaith Conference for Youth held on the fiftieth anniversary of the founding of the United Nations (University of San Francisco, 22-24 June 1995).

CR56 Beversluis, Joel D., ed.
A Sourcebook for the Community of Religions. Grand Rapids, MIU: CoNexus Press and Global Education Associates, 1995. x, 366 pp. Paper. 0963789716.

Revised edition of a compendium of addresses, papers, prayers, and reflective essays from the Parliament of the World's Religions (Chicago, 1993).

CR57 Braybrooke, Marcus
Pilgrimage of Hope: One Hundred Years of Global Interfaith Dialogue. New York, NYU: Crossroad Publishing, 1992. xvi, 368 pp. 0824509498.

A history of interfaith organizations, events, and trends, as well as the people and historical contexts which helped shaped the movement since the 1893 World's Parliament of Religions.

CR58 Carman, John Braisted, and Frederick J. Streng, eds.
Spoken and Unspoken Thanks: Some Comparative Soundings. (Studies in World Religions, 5). Boston, MAU: Harvard University, Center for the Study of World Religions; Dallas, TXU: Center for World Thanksgiving, 1989. xi, 170 pp. 0945454007 (H hdbk), 0945454015 (H pbk), 0962002607 (W hdbk), 0962002615 (W pbk).

Short presentations by Hindu, Buddhist, Muslim, and Christian scholars made at the Seminar on Acts of Thanksgiving and the Virtue of Gratitude (Dallas, Texas, December 1983); jointly sponsored by the Center for the Study of World Religions at Harvard University and the Center for World Thanksgiving.

CR59 Dawe, Donald G., and John Braisted Carman, eds.
Christian Faith in a Religiously Plural World. Maryknoll, NYU: Orbis Books, 1978. viii, 195 pp. 0883440830.

Papers from an influential symposium of Christian thinkers and concerned scholars from other religious traditions (Lexington, Virginia, 22-24 April 1976) exploring various bases for interreligious dialogue.

CR60 Heim, S. Mark, ed.
Grounds for Understanding: Ecumenical Resources for Responses to Religious Pluralism. Grand Rapids, MIU: Eerdmans, 1998. vi, 227 pp. Paper. 0802805930.

Thirteen papers on responses of varied Christian denominations to religious pluralism; originally presented at the "Theological Resources for Responses to Religious Pluralism" consultation (Newark, New Jersey, 13-14 October 1994).

CR61 Küng, Hans, and Karl-Josef Kuschel, eds.
Erklärung zum Weltethos: Die Deklaration des Parlamentes der Weltreligionen. (Serie Piper, 1958). Munich, GW: Piper, 1993. 138 pp. 3492119581.

German translation of the Parliament's "Declaration" with prologue by the editors.

CR62 Küng, Hans, and Karl-Josef Kuschel, eds.
Hacia una Etica mundial: Declaración del Parlamento de las Religiones del Mundo. Translated by José Maria Bravo Navalpotro. (Colección Estructuras y Procesos, serie Religión). Madrid, SP: Editorial Trotta, 1994. 109 pp. Paper. 8481640204.

Spanish translation.

CR63 Küng, Hans, ed.
Yes to a Global Ethic. Translated by John Bowden. New York, NYU: *Continuum*, 1996. xi, 239 pp. Paper. 0826409075.

The drafter of the "Declaration toward a Global Ethic" of the 1993 Parliament of the World's Religions offers the witness of leading world figures in politics, culture, and religion, to a new global awareness and ethical consensus.

CR—CHRISTIANITY AND OTHER RELIGIONS

CR64 Müller, Karl, and Werner Prawdzik, eds.
Ist Christus der einzige Weg zum Heil? (Veröffentlichungen des Missionspriesterseminars, 40). Nettetal, GW: Steyler Verlag, 1991. 199 pp. Paper. 380500270X.

Eight scholars from various disciplines within Catholic theology discuss the question, "Is Christ the only way to salvation?"; originally delivered for the missions study week at Sankt Augustin, 5-9 June 1990.

CR65 Nicholls, Bruce J.
The Unique Christ in Our Pluralist World. Carlisle, ENK: Paternoster Press; Grand Rapids, MIU: Baker Books, 1994. 288 pp. Paper. 0853645744 (UK), 0801020131 (US).

Twenty papers from the WEF sponsored congress on "The Unique Christ in Our Pluralistic World" (Manila, 16-20 June 1992), published as an evangelical response to the Parliament of the World's Religions (Chicago, 1993).

CR66 Parliament of the World's Religions (Chicago, 1993)
A Global Ethic: The Declaration of the Parliament of the World's Religions. Edited by Hans Küng and Karl-Josef Kuschel. New York, NYU: *Continuum*, 1993. 124 pp. Paper. 0826406408.

The text of the "Declaration toward a Global Ethic" approved at the Parliament of the World's Religions (Chicago 1993), with commentaries by Hans Küng and Karl-Josef Kuschel of the University of Tübingen.

CR67 Samartha, Stanley J., ed.
Towards World Community: The Colombo Papers. Geneva, SZ: WCC, 1975. iv, 164 pp. Paper. 282540506X.

A collection of papers presented by Hindus, Buddhists, Jews, Christians, and Muslims at a consultation in Sri Lanka in 1974; organized by the WCC to discuss "resources and responsibilities of living together."

CR68 Seager, Richard Hughes
The World's Parliament of Religions: The East/West Encounter, Chicago, 1893. (Religion in North America). Bloomington, INU: Indiana University Press, 1995. xxxi, 208 pp. 0253351375.

A reassessment of the significance of the 1893 World's Parliament of Religions after more than a century of subsequent interreligious encounters in North America.

CR69 Teasdale, Wayne R., and George F. Cairns, eds.
The Community of Religions: Voices and Images of the Parliament of the World's Religions. New York, NYU: *Continuum*, 1996. 259 pp. Paper. 0826408990.

A compilation of major addresses and shorter reflections by participants of several faiths at the Parliament of the World's Religions (Chicago, 1993).

CR70 Thanh, Phan Tan
Il Problema della religione e delle religioni nei dibattiti e documenti del Concilio Vaticano II. Rome, IT: Pontificia Studiorum Universitas a Sancto Thoma Aquinate in Urbe, 1982. 279 pp. No ISBN.

A detailed analysis of Vatican II's debate and statements on the relation of Christianity to other faiths; originally submitted as a doctoral dissertation in 1981 at the Pontifical University of St. Thomas Aquinas in Rome.

CR71 Theological Consultation (Chiang Mai, Thailand, 18-27 April 1977)
Dialogue in Community: Statement and Reports ... Geneva, SZ: WCC, 1977. 49 pp. Paper. 2825405523.

The report of one of the WCC's most important consultations on interreligious dialogue.

CR72 Thompson, Henry O., ed.
World Religions in Dialogue: Cooperating to Transform Society. Delhi, II: ISPCK, 1993. 176 pp. Paper. 8172140681.

Twenty-one short essays from around the world prepared for the Parliament of the World's Religions under the theme, "Interreligious Cooperation: Working Together to Transform Society."

CR73 World's Parliament of Religions (1893: Chicago, ILU)
The Dawn of Religious Pluralism: Voices from the World's Parliament of Religions, 1893. Edited by Richard Hughes Seager and Ronald R. Kidd. LaSalle, ILU: Open Court, 1993. xvii, 502 pp. 0812692225 (hdbk), 0812692233 (pbk).

A selection of the speeches and newspaper reports from the influential first World's Parliament of Religions; published as background reading for the second Parliament in Chicago in 1993.

CR74 Ziolkowski, Eric J., ed.
A Museum of Faiths: Histories and Legacies of the 1893 World's Parliament of Religions. (Classics in Religious Studies, 9). Atlanta, GAU: Scholars Press, 1993. xv, 366 pp. 1555409040 (hdbk), 1555409059 (pbk).

Sixteen scholarly essays on the proceedings, impact, and legacy of the World's Parliament of Religions (Chicago, 1893).

General Works

See also GW88, GW92, GW186, GW196, GW226-GW227, HI47, TH55, TH172, TH278, TH551-TH552, TH615, EA137, CR91, CR456, CR524, CR548, CR698, CR788, SO62, SO142, SO205, CO62, EV120, EV164, EV176, EV198, EV206, AM1109, AS136, AS209, AS951, EU33, and EU139.

CR75 Abeyasingha, Nihal
A Theological Evaluation of Non-Christian Rites. Bangalore, II: Theological Publications in India, 1979. xix, 250 pp. Paper. No ISBN.

Serious theological reflection about the place of non-Christian rites (rituals, forms of worship) in the salvific plan of God, with a history of Christian thought on this issue; originally presented as a doctoral dissertation to the Faculty of Theology of the Pontifical Athenaeum of Anselm in Rome.

CR76 Aldwinckle, Russell F.
Jesus—A Savior or the Savior?: Religious Pluralism in Christian Perspective. Macon, GAU: Mercer University Press, 1982. viii, 231 pp. 0865540233.

A critical evaluation of the approach of the science and phenomenology of religion that would treat all religious truth claims as relative, arguing for the unique and distinctive character of Christian salvation, by the Emeritus Professor of Systematic Theology at McMaster University in Hamilton, Ontario, Canada.

CR—CHRISTIANITY AND OTHER RELIGIONS

CR77 Allen, E. L.
Christianity among the Religions. London, ENK (1960): Allen and Unwin; Boston, MAU (1961): Beacon Press, 1961. 159 pp. No ISBN.

History and evaluation of the major attitudes taken toward the non-Christian religions in the course of Christian thought and Western philosophy since the 13th century; by a distinguished British scholar and former missionary.

CR78 Amalorpavadass, D. S.
Approaches in Our Apostolate among Followers of Other Religions. (Mission Theology for Our Times Series, 3). Bangalore, II: NBCLC, 1978. 51 pp. Paper. No ISBN.

A paper presented at the SEDOS Symposium on Mission Theology for Our Times (Rome, 26-31 March 1969) by the Director of the National Biblical, Catechetical, and Liturgical Centre in Bangalore, India.

CR79 Anderson, Gerald H., and Thomas F. Stransky, eds.
Mission Trends, no. 5: Faith Meets Faith. Ramsey, NJU: Paulist Press; Minneapolis, MNU: Eerdmans, 1981. x, 306 pp. Paper. 0809123568 (P), 0802818218 (E).

A basic sourcebook on mission and how religious pluralism, dialogue, and interfaith relations are put into practice.

CR80 Anderson, James Norman Dalrymple
Christianity and World Religions: The Challenge of Pluralism. Downers Grove, ILU: InterVarsity, 1984. 216 pp. 0877849811 (US), 0851113230 (UK pbk.).

Revised edition of an apology for the Christian faith in the incarnation as a unique, historical event which provides the *Kerygma* (proclamation) to persons of other faiths; originally published under the title *Christianity and Comparative Religion* (1970).

CR81 Anderson, James Norman Dalrymple
Jesus, Krishna, Mohammed: Christentum und Weltreligionen in der Auseinandersetzung. Translated by Gerhard Raabe. Wuppertal, GW: Oncken Verlag, 1972. 117 pp. 3789304433.

German translation of *Christianity and Comparative Religion* (1970).

CR82 Ariarajah, S. Wesley
The Bible and People of Other Faiths. Geneva, SZ: WCC, 1985. 71 pp. Paper. 2825408409.

A general introduction to Christian approaches to other faiths, based on a conviction that some of the common assumptions about the Bible and persons of other faiths can be questioned from within the Bible; by the Director of the Dialogue Subunit of the WCC.

CR83 Böld, Willy et al.
Kirche in der ausserchristlichen Welt. Regensburg, GW: Pustet, 1967. 141 pp. No ISBN.

A series of lectures by four leading Roman Catholic and Protestant scholars on the church in the non-Christian World.

CR84 Bühlmann, Walbert
Alle haben denselben Gott: Begegnung mit den Menschen und Religionen Asiens. Frankfurt am Main, GW: Josef Knecht, 1978. 223 pp. No ISBN.

The Secretary General of the Capuchin missions, a former missionary to Tanzania and Professor of Missiology, re-creates the encounters that have occurred in WCC-sponsored dialogues with persons of other faiths, and documents the progress that has been made.

CR85 Bühlmann, Walbert
God's Chosen Peoples. Translated by Robert R. Barr. Maryknoll, NYU: Orbis Books, 1982. xiv, 301 pp. Paper. 0883441500.

English translation of *Die auserwählten Völker*, a pioneer interdisciplinary study of the biblical theme of election and its contemporary relevance both for a Christian theology of the religions and for Christian approaches to persons of other faiths.

CR86 Bühlmann, Walbert
The Search for God: An Encounter with the Peoples and Religions of Asia. Translated by B. P. Krokosz, and A. P. Dolan. Maryknoll, NYU: Orbis Books; Slough, ENK: St. Paul Publications, 1980. 221 pp. 088344450X (US), 0854391606 (UK).

English translation.

CR87 Bühlmann, Walbert
Wenn Gott zu allen Menschen geht: Für eine neue Erfahrung der Auserwählung. Freiburg, GW: Herder, 1981. 292 pp. Paper. 3451191865.

A popular work pointing out how "being chosen" and "being sent" implies hope for all peoples, inquiring how the chosen people and other peoples see themselves, and presenting a new concept of missionary reflection on the theology of religions.

CR88 Bürkle, Horst
Einführung in die Theologie der Religionen. (Die Theologie). Darmstadt, GW: Wissenschaftliche Buchgesellschaft, 1977. x, 191 pp. Paper. 3534070437.

Examining various religions without comparing them to Christianity, the author attempts to make a contribution to genuine dialogue using Hinduism, Buddhism, and African tribal religions as paradigms.

CR89 Balchand, Asandas
The Salvific Value of Non-Christian Religions According to Asian Christian Theologians Writing in Asian-Published Theological Journals, 1965-1970. Manila, PH: East Asian Pastoral Institute, 1973. 81 pp. No ISBN.

An analysis of the themes of the presence of God and Christ, revelation, faith, and grace in non-Christian religions—a reprint from *Teaching All Nations* (1973, nos. 1 and 2).

CR90 Balthasar, Hans Urs von, Wilhelm Brening, and Horst Bürkle
Absolutheit des Christentums. Edited by Walter Kasper. (Quaestiones disputatae, 79). Freiburg, GW: Herder, 1977. 156 pp. Paper. 3451020793.

Theologians of international repute discuss central questions such as the absoluteness and universality of Christianity, religious freedom, and an adequate theology of religions.

CR91 Barnes, Michael
Christian Identity and Religious Pluralism: Religions in Conversation. Nashville, TNU: Abingdon, 1989. 200 pp. Paper. 0687072190.

The author, a lecturer in religious studies at Heythrop College, University of London, presents various Christian views on religious pluralism, and develops a Spirit-centered theology of religions as an effort to overcome the difficulties inherent in more traditional Christological approaches.

CR92 Bavinck, Johan Herman

The Church between Temple and Mosque: A Study of the Relationship between the Christian Faith and Other Religions. Grand Rapids, MIU: Eerdmans, 1981. 206 pp. No ISBN.

Reprint of the 1966 edition of a discussion of the relation between Christian faith and the world religions by a leading Dutch Professor of Mission.

CR93 Benz, Ernst

Ideen zu einer Theologie der Religionsgeschichte. Mainz, GW: Verlag der Akademie der Wissenschaften und der Literatur, 1961. 76 pp. No ISBN.

After sketching the harshly judgmental history of the non-Christian religions by Christians, Benz outlines the elements of both a New Testament and a more positive Christian theology of the history of religions.

CR94 Berentsen, Jan-Martin

Det moderne Areopagos: røster fra den religionsteologiske debatten i vårt århundre. Stavanger, NO: Misjonshøgskolens forlag, 1994. iii, 104 pp. Paper. 8277210051.

A survey of the 20th-century debate in Europe on a theology of the religions focused on key participants (Troeltsch, Hocking, Barth, Althaus, Rahner, Cragg, Hick, and W. C. Smith).

CR95 Bernhardt, Reinhold

Der Absolutheitsanspruch des Christentums: Von der Aufklärung bis zur pluralistischen Religionstheologie. Gütersloh, GW: Gerd Mohn, 1990. 263 pp. Paper. 3579002740.

A dissertation providing a systematic overview of the debate about the absolute claim of Christianity (in particular the models worked out by Troeltsch, Barth, and Rahner) and, considering the profound changes brought about by pluralistic theology of religions, inquiring whether this claim can still be upheld.

CR96 Bleeker, Claas Jouco

Christ in Modern Athens: The Confrontation of Christianity with Modern Culture and the Non-Christian Religions. Leiden, NE: Brill, 1965. xii, 152 pp. No ISBN.

An analysis of the confrontation of Christianity with modern culture, emphasizing missiological issues.

CR97 Bleeker, Claas Jouco

Christus in het moderne Athene: Confrontatie van het Christendom met de moderne cultuur en niet-christelijke godsdiensten. Wassenaar, NE: Servire, 1967. 137 pp. No ISBN.

Dutch translation.

CR98 Boublik, Vladimir

Teologia delle Religioni. Rome, IT: Editrice Studium, 1973. 342 pp. No ISBN.

A scholarly theology of religion for Christians desiring to witness to Christ in a religiously plural world.

CR99 Bowker, John

Licensed Insanities: Religions and Belief in God in the Contemporary World. London, ENK: Darton, Longman & Todd, 1987. x, 164 pp. Paper. 0232517258.

A popular essay on why religions as systems have such influence in our increasingly secular society, and why interreligious dialogue is often difficult.

CR100 Brück, Michael von

Möglichkeiten und Grenzen einer Theologie der Religionen. (Theologische Arbeiten, 38). Berlin, GW: Evan Verlagsanstalt, 1979. 246 pp. No ISBN.

After a detailed analysis and comparison of Karl Barth's and Rudolf Otto's theologies of religions, the author attempts to show their complementarities and then develops his own suggestions for a coherent theology of religions.

CR101 Braaten, Carl E.

No Other Gospel: Christianity among the World's Religions. Minneapolis, MNU: Fortress Press, 1992. ix, 146 pp. Paper. 0800625390.

A reassertion that Christ is the normative, decisive, and final self-revelation of God for the salvation of the world; by the Professor of Theology at the Lutheran School of Theology at Chicago, focusing on themes of justification, eschatological hope, and a new trinitarian understanding of God.

CR102 Brennan, Patrick J.

Christian Mission in a Pluralistic World. Slough, ENK: St. Paul Publications, 1990. x, 134 pp. Paper. 0854393269.

An introduction to a theology of the religions by a missionary priest of the SMA who currently teaches theology in Nigeria.

CR103 Carpenter, George Wayland

Encounter of the Faiths. New York, NYU: Friendship Press, 1967. 174 pp. No ISBN.

A popularly written apologetic for Christians facing the contemporary pluralism of faiths including secularism.

CR104 Carruthers, Gregory H.

The Uniqueness of Jesus Christ in the Theocentric Model of the Christian Theology of World Religions: An Elaboration and Evaluation of the Position of John Hick. Lanham, MDU: University Press of America, 1990. xii, 363 pp. 0819178896.

A dissertation at the Gregorian University in Rome analyzing and strongly criticizing the claims of John Hick that Jesus is one among many saving religious figures.

CR105 Carson, D. A.

The Gagging of God: Christianity Confronts Pluralism. Grand Rapids, MIU: Zondervan, 1996. 640 pp. 031047910X.

The research professor of New Testament at Trinity Evangelical Divinity School presents a detailed apologetic for the evangelical's exclusivist stance, providing a history of modern pluralism, key points in the inclusivist/exclusivist debate, and broader issues raised by contextualization and globalization.

CR106 Clarke, Andrew D., and Bruce W. Winter, eds.

One God, One Lord: Christianity in a World of Religious Pluralism. London, ENK: Paternoster Press; Grand Rapids, MIU: Baker Books, 1992. 256 pp. Paper. 0951835629 (P), 0801025710 (B).

A revised second edition containing twelve essays by British scholars offering biblical and evangelical approaches to religious pluralism.

CR107 Clendenin, Daniel B.

Many Gods, Many Lords: Christianity Encounters World Religions. Grand Rapids, MIU: Baker Books, 1995. 189 pp. Paper. 080102059X.

An overview of exclusivism and inclusivism as alternative Christian responses to religious pluralism, with study of biblical affirmations both of God's universal salvific love, and of the particularity of grace in Christ.

CR—CHRISTIANITY AND OTHER RELIGIONS

CR108 Cobb, John B.

Transforming Christianity and the World: A Way beyond Absolutism and Relativism. Edited by Paul F. Knitter. (Faith Meets Faith Series). Maryknoll, NYU: Orbis Books, 1999. v, 189 pp. Paper. 1570752710.

Emphasizing the transforming nature of Jesus in Christianity from a process-thought perspective, Cobb's essays assert that every religious tradition includes an ideal for transformation, and that religions are comprised not only of an internal identity, but are also formed by their relation with other religions.

CR109 Commission Théologique Internationale

Le Christianisme et les religions. Paris, FR: Éditions du Cerf; Paris, FR: Bayard-Éditions/Centurion, 1997. 101 pp. Paper. 2204058939 (C), 2227911115 (B).

The Roman Catholic International Theological Commission chaired by Cardinal Joseph Ratzinger presents its positions on theology of the religions and interreligious dialogue.

CR110 Conference on the Philosophy of Religion (Birmingham, 1970)

Truth and Dialogue in World Religions: Conflicting Truth-Claims. Edited by John Hick. Philadelphia, PAU: Westminster Press; London, ENK: Sheldon Press, 1974. vii, 164 pp. 0664207138 (US), 0859690121 (ENK).

Ten scholarly essays published in its UK edition under the title *Truth and Dialogue: The Relationship between World Religions.*

CR111 Cornille, Catherine, and Valeer Neckebrouck

A Universal Faith?: Peoples, Cultures, Religions, and the Christ. (Louvain Theological and Pastoral Monographs, 9). Louvain, BE: Peeters; Grand Rapids, MIU: Eerdmans, 1992. x, 198 pp. Paper. 9068314297.

A diverse collection of scholarly essays by Roman Catholic theologians, philosophers, and missiologists on themes of inculturation, the theology of religions, and interfaith dialogue; originally presented at a 1991 colloquium and published as a *festschrift* honoring Frank De Graeve, S. J., who introduced courses in these areas at the universities of Notre Dame and Leuven.

CR112 Cote, Richard G.

Universal Grace: Myth or Reality. Maryknoll, NYU: Orbis Books, 1977. 172 pp. 0883445212.

Exposition of a theology of universal grace as the appropriate theology of mission in the post-Vatican II period.

CR113 Cracknell, Kenneth

Justice, Courtesy and Love: Theologians and Missionaries Encountering World Religions, 1846-1914. London, ENK: Epworth Press, 1995. xviii, 459 pp. Paper. 0716205017.

A detailed analysis of the major shifts of thinking concerning other faiths in the Protestant missionary movement from 1800 to 1914, with special attention to the World Missionary Conference (Edinburgh, 1910).

CR114 Cragg, Kenneth

Christianity in World Perspective. New York, NYU: Oxford University Press, 1968. 227 pp. No ISBN.

After tracing the contrast between 19th-century Christian mission, which assumed Western cultural dominance, and its apostolic precedents, the noted Islamicist develops a theology of religious pluralism in which the Jewish sense of destiny, Islamic worship, and the African worldview can each contribute significantly.

CR115 Cyriac, M. V.

Meeting of Religions: A Reappraisal of the Christian Vision. (Dialogue Series, 3). Madras, II: Dialogue Series, 1982. xix, 214 pp. No ISBN.

A broad review of Christian attitudes toward other faiths beginning with the Bible and the Patristic Age, up to the Second Vatican Council, with special emphasis on the church as sacrament.

CR116 Damboriena, Prudencio

La Salvación en las Religiones no Cristianas.... (BAC, 343). Madrid, SP: EDICA, 1973. xxiv, 533 pp. 8422004240.

A broad study of the theological problem of the salvation of non-Christians, including the historical evolution of concepts related to the issue proposed by Catholics and Protestants, as well as a look at the theological question itself.

CR117 Danielou, Jean

The Advent of Salvation: A Comparative Study of Non-Christian Religions and Christianity. Translated by Rosemary Sheed. (Deus Books). New York, NYU: Paulist Press, 1962. 192 pp. Paper. No ISBN.

English translation of the French Catholic theologian's early biblical theology of the religions; originally published as *Le Mustere de l'Avent* (1948) and *Advent* (Sheed and Ward, 1950).

CR118 D'Costa, Gavin

John Hick's Theology of Religions: A Critical Evaluation. Lanham, MDU: University Press of America, 1987. xi, 239 pp. 0819166170 (hdbk), 0819166189 (pbk).

A doctoral thesis presented to the University of Cambridge in 1986, concentrating on the thought of John Hick, leader and influential representative of theological "pluralism."

CR119 D'Costa, Gavin

Theology and Religious Pluralism: The Challenge of Other Religions. Oxford, ENK: Blackwell Publishers, 1986. 155 pp. Paper. 0631145176 (hdbk), 0631145184 (pbk).

A study of the significance of pluralism, inclusivism, and exclusivism in today's theological understanding of the nature of missions.

CR120 D'Costa, Gavin, ed.

Christian Uniqueness Reconsidered: The Myth of a Pluralistic Theology of Religions. (Faith Meets Faith Series). Maryknoll, NYU: Orbis Books, 1990. xxii, 218 pp. Paper. 0883446871 (hdbk), 0883446863 (pbk).

An ecumenical response to J. Hick and P. Knitter's *The Myth of Christian Uniqueness* in fourteen essays by Roman Catholic and Protestant theologians arguing for the uniqueness of Christianity, with philosophical, theological, and hermeneutical considerations.

CR121 Dhavamony, Mariasusai

Christian Theology of Religions: A Systematic Reflection on the Christian Understanding of World Religions. (Studies in the Intercultural History of Christianity, 108). Bern, SZ: Lang, 1998. 242 pp. Paper. 3906760073 (SZ), 0820434361 (US).

A scholarly overview of the theological problem of the relation of other religions to Christianity, covering the salvific value of other faiths, the presence of Christ in them, the necessity of the church for salvation, and a theology of interreligious dialogue.

CR—CHRISTIANITY AND OTHER RELIGIONS

CR122 Dickson, Kwesi A.
Uncompleted Mission: Christianity and Exclusivism. Mary-knoll, NYU: Orbis Books, 1991. x, 177 pp. Paper. 0883447517.

A careful exploration of the biblical, theological, and historical origins of Christian attitudes of exclusivism in mission outreach to persons of other faiths, with a new perspective to overcome them by the noted African theologian and president of the Methodist Church in Ghana.

CR123 Dinoia, J. A.
The Diversity of Religions: A Christian Perspective. Washington, DCU: Catholic University of America Press, 1992. xii, 199 pp. 0813207630 (hdbk), 081320769X (pbk).

A careful philosophical account of the possibility of conversation among religions (primarily Buddhism, but also Hinduism, Islam, and Judaism), and a developed Christian theology of the religions.

CR124 Drummond, Richard Henry
Toward a New Age in Christian Theology. (American Society of Missiology Series, 8). Maryknoll, NYU: Orbis Books, 1985. 272 pp. Paper. 088344514X.

A review of past and current Christian attitudes toward other religions, urging a more open dialogue without losing the centrality of Christ.

CR125 Dunne, John S.
The Way of All the Earth: Experiments in Truth and Religion. Notre Dame, INU: University of Notre Dame Press, 1978. xiii, 240 pp. 0268019274 (hdbk), 0268019282 (pbk).

Records of a personal faith pilgrimage by a Christian theologian who encounters Islam, Buddhism, and Hinduism; originally published by Macmillan in 1972 and Sheldon Press in 1973.

CR126 Dupuis, Jacques
Jésus-Christ à la rencontre des religions. (Collection Jésus et Jésus-Christ, 39). Paris, FR: Desclée, 1989. 345 pp. Paper. 271890433X.

A Christian theology of religions out of the context of Hindu-Christian dialogue, with chapters on beliefs concerning universal salvation, the Christ of faith and historical Jesus, the universality of Jesus Christ, dialogue and evangelization, and a theology of dialogue.

CR127 Dupuis, Jacques
Jesus Christ at the Encounter of World Religions. Translated by Robert R. Barr. (Faith Meets Faith Series). Maryknoll, NYU: Orbis Books, 1991. ix, 296 pp. 088344724X (hdbk), 0883447231 (pbk).

English translation.

CR128 Dupuis, Jacques
Toward a Christian Theology of Religious Pluralism. Maryknoll, NYU: Orbis Books, 1997. xiv, 433 pp. 1570751250.

The *magnum opus* of the professor of theology at the Gregorian University in Rome providing an overview of Christian approaches to religions from the Hebrew Bible to the contemporary debate, followed by the author's constructive synthesis based on a trinitarian Christological model.

CR129 Dupuis, Jacques
Vers une Théologie Chrétienne du Pluralisme Religieux. Paris, FR: Éditions du Cerf, 1997. 655 pp. Paper. 2204057592.

French translation.

CR130 Euler, Walter Andreas
Unitas et Pax: Religionsvergleich bei Raimundus Lullus und Nikolaus von Kues. (Würzburger Forschungen zur Missions-und Religionswissenschaft, 2.15). Würzburg, GW: Echter Verlag; Altenberge, GW: Telos-Verlag, 1990. 296 pp. Paper. 3429013429 (E), 3893750290 (T).

A work investigating and comparing the medieval assessment of Christianity and the other religions, especially Islam and Judaism, by Raymond Lull and Nicholas of Cusa, attempting to elucidate such themes as the concept of religion, salvation, redemption, and the relationship of faith and reason.

CR131 Evangelischer Theologen-Kongress (Vienna, 1966)
Der christliche Glaube und die Religionen: Hauptvorträge des Evangelischen Theologenkongresses, Wien, 26-30.9.1966. Edited by Carl Heinz Ratschow. Berlin, GW: Töpelmann, 1967. 128 pp. Paper. No ISBN.

Five lectures on the non-Christian religions; also published in the *Neue Zeitschrift für systematische Theologie und Religionsphilosophie* (1967).

CR132 Fernando, Ajith
Jesus and the World Religions. London, ENK: MARC; Bromley, Kent, ENK: STL Books, 1988. 192 pp. Paper. 0860656403 (M), 1850780412 (S).

Reflections on interreligious relationships based on Paul's methods for dealing with other religions by a Sri Lankan evangelist and national director of Youth for Christ, International; originally published as *The Christian's Attitude toward World Religions* (Tyndak, 1987).

CR133 Forcinelli, Joseph
The Global Democratization of Religion and Theology: An Evolution of Spiritual Freedom. (Studies in American Religion, 54). Lewiston, NYU: E Mellen Press, 1990. 109 pp. 0889467404.

A closely reasoned argument that Western Christian theologies (Barth, Troeltsch, Hocking, Tillich, W. C. Smith, and the WCC) include a theology of mission increasingly open to other communities of faith.

CR134 Fornberg, Tord
The Problem of Christianity in Multi-Religious Societies of Today: The Bible in a World of Many Faiths. (Toronto Studies in Theology, 70). Lewiston, NYU: E Mellen Press, 1995. 304 pp. 0773488774.

A survey, by theologians in Asia and by biblical scholars, of thirty years (1961-1991) of debate on mission and non-Christian religions, by official church bodies (Catholic, Lutheran, Protestant, evangelical, and the WCC).

CR135 Fredericks, James L.
Faith among Faith: Christian Theology and Non-Christian Religions. New York, NYU: Paulist Press, 1999. vii, 188 pp. Paper. 080913893X.

A summary of the lively debate regarding the pluralistic theology of religions, suggesting comparative theology as an alternative path around the current impasse.

CR136 Friedli, Richard
Le Christ dans les cultures: carnets de routes et de déroutes. Fribourg, SZ: Éditions Universitaires; Paris, FR: Éditions du Cerf, 1989. 162 pp. Paper. 2827104512 (SZ), 2204040967 (FR).

A theology of religions, by the professor of the science of religions and of missionary theology at the University of Fribourg, Switzerland, in which he presents different theological approaches by which to interpret the presence of Christ in Hinduism, Buddhism, African traditional religion, and the Latin American context.

CR—CHRISTIANITY AND OTHER RELIGIONS

CR137 Fries, Heinrich
Jesus in den Weltreligionen. (Kirche und Religionen, Begegnung und Dialog, 1). St. Ottilien, GW: EOS Verlag, 1981. 190 pp. 3880961913.

Six articles based on lectures by board members of the Catholic Institute for Pure Research in Mission Theology—IMG (Fries, Koester), by the director (Wolfinger), and missiologists (Buerkle, Moritzen, and Willeke).

CR138 Gawronski, Raymond
Word and Silence: Hans Urs von Balthasar and the Spiritual Encounter between East and West. Grand Rapids, MIU: Eerdmans; Edinburgh, STK: T&T Clark, 1995. xiv, 233 pp. 0802838103 (USA), 0567097447 (UK).

A scholarly assessment of the theological contribution of Hans Urs von Balthasar (b.1905) to the encounter of Christianity with Asian worldviews, especially Buddhism.

CR139 Geffré, Claude, Jean-Pierre Jossua, and Marcus Lefébure, eds.
True and False Universality of Christianity. (*Concilium*: Religion in the Eighties). Edinburgh, ENK: T&T Clark; New York, NYU: Seabury Press, 1980. ix, 127 pp. Paper. 0567300153 (T), 081642277X.

A collection of ten essays on the issue of how Christians can affirm the universal vocation of the church as a witness to the salvation of all persons in Jesus Christ without encouraging forms of intolerance and domination.

CR140 Gerth, André A.
Theologie im Angesicht der Religionen: Gavin D'Costas Kritik an der pluralistischen Religionstheologie John Hicks. (Beiträge zur ökumenischen Theologie, 27). Paderborn, GW: Verlag Ferdinand Schöningh, 1997. 264 pp. Paper. 3506707779.

A Roman Catholic theologian, grounded in Karl Rahner's theology, analyzes and critiques the impact of pluralism on religion and theology by comparing the approaches of Gavin D'Costa and John Hick.

CR141 Gillis, Chester
Pluralism: A New Paradigm for Theology. (Louvain Theological and Pastoral Monographs, 12). Louvain, NE: Peeters; Grand Rapids, MIU: Eerdmans, 1993. 192 pp. Paper. 9068314688.

A theology of religions for Roman Catholics with implications for pastoral practice.

CR142 Giudici, Amilcare
Religioni e Salvezza: un confrento tre la teologia cattolica e la teologia protestante. Rome, IT: Borla, 1978. 217 pp. Paper. No ISBN.

A comparative analysis of Protestant and Catholic attitudes after Vatican II toward the salvation of persons of other faiths.

CR143 Gnanakan, Ken R.
The Pluralistic Predicament. (Theological Issues Series, 1). Bangalore, II: Theological Book Trust, 1992. viii, 234 pp. Paper. No ISBN.

A lucid description of various Christian theological approaches to other faiths from exclusivism to inclusivism, with a Christocentric viewpoint presented by the author, the general secretary of the Asia Theological Association.

CR144 Goldsmith, Martin
What about Other Faiths? London, ENK: Hodder & Stoughton, 1989. 183 pp. Paper. 0340510625.

A practical look at other religious practices in today's world, drawing both on biblical material and the author's expertise, with a brief explanation of other religions' concepts of God, revelation, and salvation.

CR145 Grünschloss, Andreas
Religionswissenschaft als Welt-Theologie: Wilfred Cantwell Smiths interreligiöse Hermeneutik. (Forschungen zur systematischen und ökumenischen Theologie, 71). Göttingen, GW: Vandenhoeck & Ruprecht, 1994. 360 pp. Paper. 3525562780.

A scholarly analysis of the interreligious hermeneutic of Wilfred Cantwell Smith, the noted Harvard University Professor of World Religions.

CR146 Gregson, Vernon
Lonergan, Spirituality, and the Meeting of Religions. (College Theology Society Studies in Religion, 2). Lanham, MDU: University Press of America, 1985. xvi, 154 pp. 0819146196 (hdbk), 081914260X (pbk).

An analysis of Bernard Lonergan's understanding of faith as a falling in love unrestrictedly, and the deciphering of such faith in the religious traditions of the world.

CR147 Griener, George E.
Ernst Troeltsch and Herman Schell: Christianity and the World Religions: An Ecumenical Contribution to the History of Apologetics. Frankfurt am Main, GW: Lang, 1990. 348 pp. Paper. 3631408587.

A detailed scholarly analysis of the progressive thought on non-Christian religions of Herman Schell (1850-1906) and Ernst Troeltsch (1865-1923), and of their contribution to a theology of religions.

CR148 Hallencreutz, Carl F.
New Approaches to Men of Other Faiths, 1938-1968: A Theological Discussion. (Research Pamphlet, 18). Geneva, SZ: WCC, 1970. 95 pp. Paper. No ISBN.

A brief summary of the discussion in the missionary and ecumenical movement on the relationship between Christians and persons of other faiths from the World Missionary Conference (Tambaram, 1938) to the WCC's Fourth Assembly (Uppsala, 1968), based on lectures given at Selly Oak Colleges, Birmingham.

CR149 Heim, Karl, and Friso Melzer, eds.
Das Heil der Welt: Die Botschaft der christlichen Mission und die nicht-christlichen Religionen. Moers, GW: Brendow Verlag, 1986. 187 pp. Paper. 3870672935.

A collection of essays by a prominant Tübingen theologian, systematically treating Christian mission and non-Christian religions.

CR150 Heim, S. Mark
Is Christ the Only Way?: Christian Faith in a Pluralistic World. Valley Forge, PAU: Judson Press, 1985. 159 pp. Paper. 0817010270.

How those who believe in the exclusivity of the Christian faith should deal with the facts of pluralism in our modern world, and how they can be open to meaningful dialogue with those of other faiths.

CR—CHRISTIANITY AND OTHER RELIGIONS

CR151 Heim, S. Mark
Salvations: Truth and Difference in Religion. (Faith Meets Faith Series). Maryknoll, NYU: Orbis Books, 1995. x, 242 pp. Paper. 1570750408.

A critical discussion of major types of pluralistic theology, with the author's alternative construct of theologies of religion focusing on the salvation theme in each.

CR152 Heislbetz, Josef
Theologische Gründe der nicht-christlichen Religionen. (Quaestiones disputatae, 33). Freiburg, GW: Herder, 1967. 231 pp. Paper. No ISBN.

While maintaining the superiority of Christianity, the author explores the common basis and the value of non-Christian religions in the idea of the general salvific will of God.

CR153 Hick, John
A Christian Theology of Religions: The Rainbow of Faiths. Louisville, KYU: Westminster John Knox, 1995. x, 160 pp. Paper. 0664255965.

Using a dialogue between "Phil" (philosophy) and "Grace" (theology), the noted theologian and philosopher of religion explores the validity of other religions and Christianity's place among them.

CR154 Hick, John
Disputed Questions in Theology and the Philosophy of Religion. New Haven, CTU: Yale University Press, 1993. xi, 198 pp. 0300053541.

Ten essays by the noted British theologian of world religions, developing alternative Christian perspectives on religious pluralism.

CR155 Hick, John
God and the Universe of Faiths: Essays in the Philosophy of Religion. New York, NYU: St. Martin's Press; London, ENK: Macmillan, 1973. xii, 201 pp. 0333150023.

Hick's pioneering book, proposing the famous "Copernican revolution" from a Christocentric to a theocentric theology in the understanding of religions.

CR156 Hick, John
God Has Many Names. Philadelphia, PAU: Westminster Press, 1982. 140 pp. Paper. 066424419X.

A persuasive and controversial argument for true religious pluralism, respectful of the non-Christian traditions that have persisted over time—Hinduism, Buddhism, Judaism, and Islam.

CR157 Hick, John
An Interpretation of Religion: Human Responses to the Transcendent. New Haven, CTU: Yale University Press, 1989. xv, 412 pp. 0300042485.

Hick's *magnum opus* in which he elaborates and expands his case for a pluralistic view of the world of religions in which both genuine diversity and unity are affirmed.

CR158 Hick, John
Problems of Religious Pluralism. New York, NYU: St. Martin's Press, 1985. x, 148 pp. 0312651546.

An exploration of themes and controversies encountered on the way to a more global perspective on religion, by a leading British philosopher of religion.

CR159 Hick, John, and Brian Hebblethwaite, eds.
Christianity and Other Religions: Selected Readings. Philadelphia, PAU: Fortress Press, 1981. 253 pp. Paper. 0800614445.

A sourcebook showing a diversity of positions by Christian theologians toward other faiths.

CR160 Hick, John, and Paul F. Knitter, eds.
The Myth of Christian Uniqueness: Toward a Pluralistic Theology of Religions. (Faith Meets Faith Series). Maryknoll, NYU: Orbis Books, 1987. xii, 227 pp. Paper. 0883446030 (hdbk), 0883446022 (pbk).

A collection of twelve essays by Christian thinkers with a pluralistic paradigm; exploring new attitudes toward other believers and traditions.

CR161 Hillman, Eugene
Many Paths: A Catholic Approach to Religious Pluralism. (Faith Meets Faith Series). Maryknoll, NYU: Orbis Books, 1989. xi, 95 pp. 0883445476.

An introduction to the "wider ecumenism" approach to interreligious dialogue, and to Roman Catholic sources for a new theology of religion, by a Holy Ghost Father with more than twenty years of missionary experience in East Africa.

CR162 Hunter, Alastair G.
Christianity and Other Faiths in Britain. London, ENK: SCM Press, 1985. xvi, 176 pp. Paper. 0334019249.

A Church of Scotland minister, out of cross-cultural experiences in Pakistan and Scotland, provides a practical introduction to how Christians may understand the relationship of the different faiths to one another.

CR163 Hutten, Kurt, and Siegfried von Kortzfleisch, eds.
Asien missioniert im Abendland. Stuttgart, GW: Kreuz-Verlag, 1962. 296 pp. No ISBN.

A series of essays on the "missionary" aspects of Eastern religions in Europe, this collection probes into the status of Christianity among the world religions.

CR164 Jackson, Carl T.
The Oriental Religions and American Thought: Nineteenth-Century Explorations. (Contributions in American Studies, 55). Westport, CTU: Greenwood, 1981. xii, 302 pp. 0313224919.

A history of perceptions in the United States of Asian religions from the 18th century to the 1893 World's Parliament of Religions.

CR165 Jackson, Herbert C.
Man Reaches Out to God: Living Religions and the Christian Missionary Obligation. Valley Forge, PAU: Judson Press, 1963. 126 pp. Paper. No ISBN.

A primer on Christian approaches to various world faiths by then-Director of the Missionary Research Library in New York City.

CR166 Jathanna, Origen Vasantha
The Decisiveness of the Christ-Event and the Universality of Christianity in a World of Religious Plurality. (Studies in the Intercultural History of Christianity, 29). Bern, SZ: Lang, 1981. xi, 574 pp. Paper. 326104974X.

A scholarly analysis of the debate over the decisiveness of the Christ-event, and the universality of Christianity in a world of religious plurality, in the thought of four 20th-century religionists (Hendrik Kraemer, Alfred George Hogg, William Ernest Hocking, and Pandipeddi Chenchiah); originally presented as a doctoral thesis at the University of Basel, Switzerland.

CR167 Köster, Heinrich M., Otmar Rieg, and Albert Walkenbach

Über die Religionsfreiheit und die nichtchristlichen Religionen. (Glaube, Wissen, Wirken, 5). Limburg, GW: Lahn-Verlag, 1967. 124 pp. Paper. No ISBN.

Drawing from *Nostra Aetate* and *Dignitatis Humanae*, the authors show how the Second Vatican Council opted for freedom and tolerance without detracting from the universal mandate of the Church.

CR168 Kaufman, Gordon D.

God, Mystery, Diversity: Christian Theology in a Pluralistic World. Minneapolis, MNU: Fortress Press, 1996. xii, 233 pp. Paper. 0800629590.

The noted professor of divinity emeritus at Harvard Divinity School faces the issues that religious pluralism and diversity raise concerning the status of truth claims, with special reference to Buddhism.

CR169 Kauuova, Werner

Religious Pluralism as a Challenge to the Church in Southern Africa. (Brochures of the Institute for Reformational Studies, 69). Potchefstroom, SA: Potchefstroom University, 1997. ii, 61 pp. Paper. 1868222756.

A primer on issues of religious pluralism and the ethical and dogmatic challenges that come with religious freedom in Namibia and South Africa.

CR170 Kim, Kyoung Jae

Christianity and the Encounter of Asian Religions: Method of Correlation, Fusion of Horizons, and Paradigm Shifts in the Korean Grafting Process. (Missiologisch Onderzoek in Nederland, 10). Zoetermeer, NE: Boekencentrum, 1994. 215 pp. 9023908317.

An application of Paul Tillich's method of correlation, H-G. Gadamer's fusion of horizons, and Thomas Kuhn's paradigm shifts to the theology of Korean religions, with comparisons to Chinese and Japanese worldviews.

CR171 Kirk, J. Andrew

Loosing the Chains: Religion as Opium and Liberation. London, ENK: Hodder & Stoughton, 1992. viii, 210 pp. Paper. 0340546182.

An apologetic for a Christ-centered rather than theocentric theology for Christians engaged in dialogue with secularists or persons of other faiths by the dean of the Department of Mission at Selly Oak Colleges, Birmingham, England.

CR172 Klootwijk, Eeuwout

Commitment and Openness: The Interreligious Dialogue and Theology of Religions in the Work of Stanley J. Samartha. Zoetermeer, NE: Boekencentrum B.V., 1992. xi, 380 pp. Paper. 9023908287.

A doctoral thesis analyzing the pluralist theology of religions of the former director of the WCC's Sub-unit on Dialogue with People of Living Faiths and Ideologies, with reference to the contexts both of Indian and ecumenical theology.

CR173 Klos, Frank W., Lynn Nakamura, and Daniel F. Martensen, eds.

Lutherans and the Challenge of Religious Pluralism. Minneapolis, MNU: Augsburg Fortress, 1990. viii, 197 pp. Paper. 0806624531.

Designed for both academic and congregational use, this text offers a Lutheran response to the challenges of religious pluralism in today's society.

CR174 Knitter, Paul F.

Ein Gott—viele religionen: Gegen den absolutheitsanspruch des Christentums. Munich, GW: Kösel-Verlag, 1988. 219 pp. 3466202957.

German translation of *No Other Name?* (1985).

CR175 Knitter, Paul F.

Horizonte der Befreiung: Auf dem Weg zu einer pluralistischen Theologie der Religionen. Edited by Bernd Jaspert. Frankfurt am Main, GW: Verlag Otto Lembeck; Paderborn, GW: Bonifatius, 1997. 423 pp. 3874763137 (O), 3870888873 (B).

A collection of twenty-two articles on a theology of religions and interreligious dialogue written from 1965 to 1984 by the noted Professor of Theology at Xavier University in Cincinnati, Ohio.

CR176 Knitter, Paul F.

Jesus and the Other Names: Christian Mission and Global Responsibility. Maryknoll, NYU: Orbis Books, 1996. xv, 193 pp. Paper. 157075053X.

The author of *No Other Name?*, a landmark work in interfaith dialogue, constructs what he calls a "correlational, globally responsible theology of religions" as an alternative to both traditional-pluralist and exclusivist approaches.

CR177 Knitter, Paul F.

No Other Name?: A Critical Survey of Christian Attitudes toward the World Religions. (American Society of Missiology Series, 7). Maryknoll, NYU: Orbis Books, 1985. xvi, 288 pp. Paper. 0883443473.

A survey of popular and Christian attitudes toward religious pluralism advocating an approach to authentic dialogue based on a theocentric Christology.

CR178 Knitter, Paul F.

Towards a Protestant Theology of Religions: A Case Study of Paul Althaus and Contemporary Attitudes. (Marburger Theologische Studien). Marburg, GW: N. G. Elwert Verlag, 1974. xii, 273 pp. 3770804856.

A detailed analysis of the theology of religions of Paul Alhaus, as a middle way between Ernst Troeltsch and Karl Barth, attractive for both Protestants and Roman Catholics; originally submitted as a Th.D. dissertation at Marburg University.

CR179 Kraemer, Hendrik

Godsdiensten en culturen: de komende dialoog. 's-Gravenhage, NE: Boekencentrum, 1963. 383 pp. No ISBN.

Dutch translation.

CR180 Kraemer, Hendrik

World Cultures and World Religions: The Coming Dialogue. Philadelphia, PAU: Westminster Press, 1960. 386 pp. No ISBN.

The Stone Lectures delivered at Princeton Theological Seminary in 1958 in which the noted Dutch missiologist analyzes the history of the relations of Eastern cultures and religions with the West, focusing on 20th-century interactions.

CR181 Kreeft, Peter

Ecumenical Jihad: Ecumenism and the Culture War. San Francisco, CAU: Ignatius Press, 1996. 172 pp. Paper. 0898705797.

A popular appeal for Christians, Jews, and Muslims to unite against the common enemies of godless secular humanism, materialism, and immorality.

CR—CHRISTIANITY AND OTHER RELIGIONS

CR182 Krieger, David J.

The New Universalism: Foundations for a Global Theology. (Faith Meets Faith Series). Maryknoll, NYU: Orbis Books, 1991. ix, 219 pp. 0883447282 (hdbk), 0883447274 (pbk).

Drawing on the work of Raimundo Panikkar and Ludwig Wittgenstein, the Professor of Theology in Lucerne, Switzerland, constructs a method and philosophical foundation for a universal theology of religion which resolves conflicts and appropriates insights from various faiths.

CR183 Kulandran, Sabapathy

The Bible and the People of Other Faiths: A Reply to Mr. Wesley Ariarajah. Chunnakam, CE: CISRS, 1991. ii, 23 pp. Paper. No ISBN.

An essay by the former bishop of the Church of South India in Jaffra, Sri Lanka, critical of the theocentric theology of the WCC's Secretary for Dialogue contained in his book, *The Bible and the People of Other Faiths* (1985).

CR184 Kuschel, Karl-Josef, ed.

Christentum und nichtchristliche Religionen: Theologische Modelle im 20. Jahrhundert. (WB-Forum, 91). Darmstadt, GW: Wissenschaftliche Buchgesellschaft, 1994. vi, 171 pp. Paper. 3534801695.

A collection of nine key 20th-century essays on Christendom and non-Christian religions (by Troeltsch, Barth, Tillich, Rahner, Knitter, Waldenfels, Pannenberg, Kuschel, and Küng), with an essay by the editor advocating that Christians move from exclusivity to an acceptance of religious pluralism as an expression of God's will for humanity.

CR185 Lai, Pan-Chiu

Towards a Trinitarian Theology of Religions: A Study of Paul Tillich's Thought. (Studies in Philosophical Theology, 8). Kampen, NE: Kok Pharos, 1994. 181 pp. Paper. 9039000255.

A study of the development of Paul Tillich's theology of the religions in relation to the thought of the period—a revision of a doctoral thesis originally submitted to King's College, University of London, in 1991.

CR186 Lakeland, Paul

Postmodernity: Christian Identity in a Fragmented Age. (Guides to Theological Inquiry). Minneapolis, MNU: Fortress Press, 1997. xiv, 130 pp. Paper. 080063098X.

A constructive theological apologetic for the church's mission amidst a plurality of religions in the postmodern world.

CR187 Lande, Aasulv, Jens Johansen, and Poul Exner

Kristendommen og de andre religioner. (Nyt Synspunkt, 16). Hellerup, DK: DMS-Forlag, 1982. 68 pp. Paper. 8774311042.

A brief introduction to the relationship of Christianity to other faiths by a Norwegian missionary to Japan, with examples from relations to Islam and new religious movements to interreligious dialogue in Japan; edited by Knud Sorensen, Karen Berntsen, and Hans Iversen.

CR188 Lightner, Robert P.

The God of the Bible and Other Gods: Is the Christian God Unique among World Religions? Grand Rapids, MIU: Kregel Publications, 1998. 216 pp. Paper. 0825431549.

The exclusiveness approach to other faiths and its biblical foundations; presented by the Emeritus Professor of Systematic Theology at Dallas Theological Seminary.

CR189 Lin, J. J. E. van

Protestantse theologie der godsdiensten: Van Edinburgh naar Tambaram (1910-1938). (Van Gorcum's Theologische Bibliotheek, 49). Assen, NE: Van Gorcum, 1974. xviii, 430 pp. 9023212002.

A detailed study of the Protestant theology of religions related to debates within the IMC between the conferences in Edinburgh and Tambaram (1910-1938), based on primary sources; presented as a doctoral thesis at the Catholic University of Nijmegen.

CR190 Lochhead, David

The Dialogical Imperative: A Christian Reflection on Interfaith Encounter. Maryknoll, NYU: Orbis Books, 1988. viii, 104 pp. Paper. 088344612X (hdbk), 0883446111 (pbk).

An exploration of both the sociological and theological dimensions of ideological stances (both exclusivity and inclusivity) that have defined Christian attitudes toward other faiths, with special reference to the thought of Barth, Plato, and Buber.

CR191 Müller, Karl

Die Kirche und die nicht-christlichen Religionen: Kommentar zur Konzilserklärung über das Verhältnis der Kirche zu den nicht-christlichen Religionen. (Der Christ in der Welt, 17.8). Aschaffenburg, GW: Pattloch, 1968. 175 pp. Paper. No ISBN.

This commentary on *Nostra Aetate* addresses the burning questions of the universality of salvation and the salvific value of non-Christian religions, and expounds the attitude of the Second Vatican Council to the religions.

CR192 MacPherson, Camilia Gangasingh

A Critical Reading of the Development of Raimon Panikkar's Thought on the Trinity. Lanham, MDU: University Press of America, 1996. xv, 158 pp. Paper. 0761801847.

A scholarly analysis and critical assessment of how the noted Catholic theologian of religions developed his thought on the Trinity.

CR193 Mann, Ulrich

Das Christentum als absolute Religion. Darmstadt, GW: Wissenschaftliche Buchgesellschaft, 1970. vii, 220 pp. Paper. No ISBN.

The author considers the problem of the "absoluteness of Christianity" by taking up reflections on the history of religion and depth psychology of a previous publication and, considering the dominance of scientific reasoning, calls for a dynamic, conscious religion.

CR194 Marshall, Molly Truman

No Salvation Outside the Church?: A Critical Inquiry. (NABPR Dissertation Series, 9). Lewiston, NYU: E Mellen Press, 1993. xii, 267 pp. 0773428524.

A doctoral dissertation (Southern Baptist Theological Seminary, 1983), comparing positions of Christian exclusivism (Emil Brunner), inclusivism (Karl Rahner), and relativism (John Hick) on the question of whether Christianity, as realized in the church through Christ, provides the only way to salvation.

CR195 Mooren, Thomas

Auf der Grenze: Die Andersheit Gottes und die Vielfalt der Religionen: Der interkulturelle Dialog aus anthropologischer Sicht als Anfrage an eine Theologie der Religionen. (European University Studies, 23: Theology, 434). Frankfurt am Main, GW: Lang, 1991. 201 pp. Paper. 3631442130.

An attempt to place the theology of religions within the purview of Christian theology using the model of intercultural understanding.

CR—CHRISTIANITY AND OTHER RELIGIONS

CR196 Morse, Merrill, and Kosuke Koyama

A Model for Intercultural Theology. (Studies in the Intercultural History of Christianity, 71). Frankfurt am Main, GW: Lang, 1991. xiv, 317 pp. Paper. 3631439628.

Essays on the challenge to Christianity of the highly pluralistic, intercultural nature of the modern world by a Lutheran missiologist who specializes in Asian religions, with chapters by the renowned Asian theologian on the methodology of Asian theology and a Christocentric yet open-ended approach for Christian encounters with the world's cultures and religions.

CR197 Mulder, Dirk Cornellis

Theologie en Godsdienstwetenschap. 's-Gravenhage, NE: Van Keulen, 1965. 24 pp. No ISBN.

The author's inaugural address on "Theology and Science of Religion" upon his installation as professor at the Free University in Amsterdam.

CR198 Mwakabana, Hance A. O., ed.

Andere Religionen aus theologischer Sicht: Auf dem Weg zu einer christlichen Theologie der Religionen. (LWF Documentation, 41). Geneva, SZ: LWF, 1997. 281 pp. Paper. 3906706575.

German translation.

CR199 Mwakabana, Hance A. O., ed.

Theological Perspectives on Other Faiths: Toward a Christian Theology of Religions: Documentation from a Consultation Held in Bangkok, 10-13 July 1996. (LWF Documentation, 41/1997). Geneva, SZ: LWF, 1997. 292 pp. Paper. 3906706443.

Report and papers from a global conference on "Theological Perspectives on Other Faiths" (Bangkok, 1996)—the climax of a five-year study of the major religious traditions encountered by Christian and Lutheran churches worldwide.

CR200 Nash, Ronald H.

Is Jesus the Only Savior? Grand Rapids, MIU: Zondervan, 1994. 188 pp. Paper. 0310443911.

A critique of the pluralism of John Hick, and of the inclusivism of Clark Pinnock and John Sanders, with espousal of exclusivism; by the professor of philosophy at Reformed Seminary in Orlando, Florida.

CR201 Netland, Harold A.

Dissonant Voices: Religious Pluralism and the Question of Truth. Grand Rapids, MIU: Eerdmans; Leicester, ENK: Apollos, 1991. xii, 323 pp. 0802806023 (E), 0851114261 (A).

A closely reasoned defense of Christian exclusivism: a contribution to the contemporary debate on issues of religious pluralism by one who grew up in Japan as the son of conservative-evangelical missionaries and now serves as assistant professor of religious studies at Tokyo Christian University.

CR202 Neuner, Josef, ed.

Christian Revelation and World Religions. London, ENK: Burns & Oates, 1967. 186 pp. Paper. No ISBN.

Four essays by Catholic theologians (Piet Fransen, Hans Küng, Joseph Masson, and Raimundo Panikkar) on Christian revelation and non-Christian religions.

CR203 Newbigin, James Edward Lesslie

The Gospel in a Pluralist Society. Grand Rapids, MIU: Eerdmans; Geneva, SZ: WCC Publications, 1989. xi, 244 pp. Paper. 0802804268 (E), 2825409715 (W).

An impassioned defense of the missionary mandate in the face of apparently threatening new theologies that affirm the equal value of other religions.

CR204 Nys, Hendrik

Le salut sans l'évangile: étude historique et critique du problème du "salut des infidèles" dans la littérature théologique récente (1912-1964). (Parole et Mission, 12). Paris, FR: Éditions du Cerf, 1966. 296 pp. No ISBN.

A historical study of Roman Catholic writings on the question of salvation for non-Christians, 1912-1964, with an extensive bibliography.

CR205 Okholm, Dennis L., and Timothy R. Phillips, eds.

Four Views on Salvation in a Pluralistic World. (Counterpoints). Grand Rapids, MIU: Zondervan, 1995. 283 pp. Paper. 0310212766.

Report of the 1992 Wheaton Theology Conference at which four viewpoints on a theology of religions were presented and debated: normative pluralism (John Hick), inclusivism (Clark Pinnock), particularist-salvation in Christ (Alister McGrath), and particularist-salvation in Christ alone (R. Douglas Geivett and W. Gary Phillips); originally titled *More Than One Way?*

CR206 O'Leary, Joseph Stephen

La vérité chrétienne à l'âge du pluralisme religieux. (Théologie et sciences religieuses: Cogitatio Fidei, 181). Paris, FR: Éditions du Cerf, 1994. 330 pp. Paper. 220404900X.

An analysis of questions raised by Western philosophers (Derrida, Foucault, and Wittgenstein) and the Japanese Buddhist Nàgàrjuna for Christian theology in an age of religious pluralism; by an Irish Catholic philosopher and theologian who teaches at Sophia University in Tokyo.

CR207 Oxtoby, Willard G., ed.

Religious Diversity: Essays by Wilfred Cantwell Smith. New York, NYU: Harper & Row, 1976. xxiv, 198 pp. Paper. 0060674644.

Essays by the noted Harvard University religionist on religious diversity and truth, modernity and mutual understanding, including a reexamination of the Christian missionary's interactions with other cultures.

CR208 Panikkar, Raimundo

The Cosmotheandric Experience: Emerging Religious Consciousness. Maryknoll, NYU: Orbis Books, 1993. xv, 160 pp. 0883448629.

From a lifetime of accumulated wisdom as a philosopher-theologian living on the boundaries between Euro-America and Asia, Panikkar provides a cross-cultural analysis of constant patterns of religious experience (cosmic, divine, human) as the building blocks for a meta-theology of religion.

CR209 Panikkar, Raimundo

Invisible Harmony: Essays on Contemplation and Responsibility. Edited by Harry J. Cargas. Minneapolis, MNU: Fortress Press, 1995. xiv, 210 pp. Paper. 0800626095.

A collection of nine essays in which the noted pioneer in East-West and interreligious dialogue develops themes for a meta-theology of the religions.

CR210 Pathil, Kuncheria, ed.

Religious Pluralism: An Indian Christian Perspective. Delhi, II: ISPCK, 1991. x, 349 pp. Paper. 8172140053.

Thirteen research papers originally presented at the 1988 and 1989 meetings of the Indian Theological Association, together with statements by the association on a theology of religions and an Indian Christian theology of religious pluralism.

CR—CHRISTIANITY AND OTHER RELIGIONS

CR211 Pinnock, Clark H.
A Wideness in God's Mercy: The Finality of Jesus Christ in a World of Religions. Grand Rapids, MIU: Zondervan, 1992. 217 pp. Paper. 0310535913.

An evangelical theology of religions professing both God's universal salvific will and Jesus Christ as the one mediator between God and humanity.

CR212 Prabhu, Joseph, ed.
The Intercultural Challenge of Raimon Panikkar. (Faith Meets Faith Series). Maryknoll, NYU: Orbis Books, 1996. xi, 307 pp. Paper. 1570750564.

Sixteen scholars, steeped in the multi-layered, multi-cultural texture of Panikkar's unique gifts, consider his profound contributions to philosophy of religions and interreligious dialogue.

CR213 Punt, Neal
Unconditional Good News: Toward an Understanding of Biblical Universalism. Grand Rapids: MIU: Eermans, 1980. x, 169 pp. Paper. 0802818358.

Punt argues that according to the Bible all are elected in Christ except those who are expressly declared by the Bible to be lost.

CR214 Röper, Anita
Die anonymen Christen. Mainz, GW: Grünewald, 1963. 154 pp. No ISBN.

Proceeding from the present situation of religions, the author presents an exposition of Karl Rahner's thesis of "anonymous Christians," and examines the relationship between anonymous Christians and explicit Christianity.

CR215 Race, Alan
Christians and Religious Pluralism: Patterns in the Christian Theology of Religions. Maryknoll, NYU: Orbis Books, 1983. xi, 176 pp. Paper. 0883441012.

A survey of exclusive and inclusive theologies of religions, with a proposal for a pluralist model for dialogue between Christianity and other religions.

CR216 Raguin, Yves
The Depth of God. Translated by Kathleen England. (Religious Experience Series, 10). Wheathampstead, ENK: Anthony Clark, 1979. xi, 145 pp. Paper. 085650050X.

English translation of *La profondeur de Dieu* (1973); originally published by Abbey Press, St. Meinard, Indiana (1975).

CR217 Raguin, Yves
La profondeur de Dieu. (Collection Christus, 33). Paris, FR: Desclée de Brouwer, 1973. 182 pp. No ISBN.

An invitation to find through human relationships with persons of varied faiths a greater knowledge of, and relationship to, God.

CR218 Rajashekar, J. Paul William, ed.
Religious Pluralism and Lutheran Theology. (LWF Report, 23/24). Geneva, SZ: LWF, 1988. 192 pp. Paper. No ISBN.

Papers from the seminar on "Religious Pluralism and Lutheran Response" (Geneva, Switzerland, 27 Oct. to 1 Nov. 1986) sponsored by the Office for Church and People of Other Faiths of the LWF.

CR219 Ramesh, Richard
The Population of Heaven. Chicago, ILU: Moody, 1994. 170 pp. Paper. 0802439462.

A critical evaluation of theological universalism by a professor at Dallas Theological Seminary.

CR220 Ratnasekera, Leopold
Christianity and the World Religions: A Contribution to the Theology of Religions. Kandy, SL: By the author, Leopold Ratnasekera, 1982. xviii, 247 pp. No ISBN.

From a historico-phenomenological perspective on Vatican II, a theological perspective, and a pastoral perspective as an Oblate priest in Sri Lanka, the author developed this major work; originally presented as a doctoral dissertation at the Institut Catholique de Paris in 1977.

CR221 Ratschow, Carl Heinz
Die Religionen. (Handbuch systematischer Theologie, 16). Gütersloh, GW: Gerd Mohn, 1979. 131 pp. 3579049453.

A review of attitudes toward other religions among the Reformers (Luther, Melanchthon, and Calvin), and among more recent systematicians (P. Altaus, W. Elert, K. Barth and O. Weber), with the author's own outline for a theology of religions.

CR222 *Religions: Fundamental Themes for a Dialogistic Understanding*
Rome, IT: Editrice Ancora, 1970. 602 pp. No ISBN.

Twenty-four essays edited by the Vatican Secretariat for Non-Christians on the meaning of religion, salvation, God or the Absolute, and good and evil, that together constitute a positive response to the Vatican II *Nostra Aetate* document.

CR223 Richards, Glyn
Towards a Theology of Religions. (Rautledge Religious Studies). London, ENK: Routledge, 1989. xi, 179 pp. 0415024501.

Twentieth-century responses in the West to the challenge of religious pluralism presented in a continuum of seven types, from the exclusivist to the universalist positions.

CR224 Rommen, Edward, and Harold A. Netland, eds.
Christianity and the Religions: A Biblical Theology of World Religions. (Evangelical Missiological Society Series, 2). South Pasadena, CAU: William Carey Library, 1995. 274 pp. Paper. 0878083766.

Members of the Evangelical Theological Society in North America provide thirteen essays giving biblical, historical, and doctrinal perspectives on contemporary questions raised by religious pluralism.

CR225 Rosenkranz, Gerhard
Religionswissenschaft und Theologie: Aufsätze zur evangelischen Religionskunde. (Veröffentlichungen zu Mission und Ökumene). Munich, GW: Kaiser, 1964. 361 pp. No ISBN.

An anthology of important essays of the well-known Protestant missiologist focusing particularly on the problems of religion in modern Asia.

CR226 Rousseau, Richard W., ed.
Christianity and the Religions of the East: Models for a Dynamic Relationship. (Modern Theological Themes, 2). Scranton, PAU: Ridge Row Press, 1982. xiii, 174 pp. Paper. 0940866013.

Ten short essays, mostly by prominent Christian scholars (Cobb, Elwood, Gilkey, Knitter, Lee, Martinson, etc.), on East-West religious relationships.

CR227 Ruokanen, Miikka
The Catholic Doctrine of Non-Christian Religions: According to the Second Vatican Council. (Studies in Christian Mission, 7). Leiden, NE: Brill, 1992. 169 pp. 9004095179.

A comprehensive analysis of conciliar teaching concerning the nature of other faiths, based on original Vatican II and pre-conciliar documents.

CR228 Saldanha, Chrys

Divine Pedagogy: A Patristic View of Non-Christian Religions. (Biblioteca di Scienze Religiose (Libreria Ateneo Salesiano), 57). Rome, IT: LAS, 1984. 192 pp. Paper. 882130079X.

A scholarly analysis of the theological appraisal of non-Christian religions by the early leaders of the Christian Church (Justin, Irenaeus, and Clement of Alexandria).

CR229 Salzburger Hochschulwoche (1979)

Jesus Christus und die Religionen. Edited by Ansgar Paus. Graz, SZ: Verlag Styria, 1980. 320 pp. Paper. 3766690922.

Nine lectures inquiring how the absolute claim of Christianity can be reconciled with modern principles such as freedom of religion, tolerance, and dialogue with other religions.

CR230 Samartha, Stanley J.

Ganges en Galilea: Een keuze uit het werk van Stanley J. Samartha. Edited by J. A. B. Jongeneel. Kampen, NE: Kok, 1986. 147 pp. Paper. 9024230810.

Ten scholarly articles, originally published between 1953 and 1981, now reissued to honor the founder-secretary of the Dialogue Subunit of the WCC (1968-1980), upon his receipt of an honorary doctorate from the Rijksuniversiteit in Utrecht, the Netherlands.

CR231 Samartha, Stanley J.

One Christ—Many Religions: Toward a Revised Christology. (Faith Meets Faith Series). Maryknoll, NYU: Orbis Books, 1991. xiv, 190 pp. 0883447347 (hdbk), 0883447339 (pbk).

A detailed argument for a revised Christology that in a religiously plural world can be judged to be biblically sound, spiritually satisfying, theologically credible, and pastorally helpful; by the former director of the dialogue programme of the WCC.

CR232 Santos Hernández, Angel

Salvación y Paganismo: El Problema Teológico de la Salvación de los Infieles. (Misionología, 6 / Biblioteca Comillensis). Santander, SP: Editorial Sal Terrae, 1960. vii, 756 pp. Paper. No ISBN.

A detailed textbook on the Roman Catholic theology of religions in both historical and dogmatic aspects.

CR233 Schebera, Richard L.

Christian, Non-Christian Dialogue: The Vision of Robert C. Zaehner. Washington, DCU: University Press of America, 1978. iv, 162 pp. 0819106291.

An analysis of the theology of the religions of Robert C. Zaehner (1913-1974), international linguist and Spaulding Professor of Eastern Religions and Ethics at All Souls College, Oxford.

CR234 Schlette, Heinz Robert

Die Religionen als Thema der Theologie: Überlegungen zu einer "Theologie der Religionen." (Quaestiones disputatae, 22). Freiburg, GW: Herder, 1964. 126 pp. Paper. No ISBN.

One of the first systematic presentations of the question of the salvific value of the non-Christian religions, this study rejects both traditional dialectical and fulfillment theology, and pleads for a "theology of salvation history which makes visible the unity of God's action towards human beings and the diversity of ways."

CR235 Schoen, Ulrich

Das Ereignis und die Antworten: Auf der Suche nach einer Theologie der Religionen heute. Göttingen, GW: Vandenhoeck & Ruprecht, 1984. 166 pp. Paper. 3525561769.

After reviewing the contemporary world's need for a greater dialogue between religions, the author reviews contemporary theologies of religions, finds them in great part wanting, and offers his own suggestions for a more open and transforming exchange between religious traditions.

CR236 Schwerdtfeger, Nikolaus

Gnade und Welt: Zum Grundgefüge von Karl Rahners Theorie der "anonymen Christen." (Freiburger Theologische Studien, 123). Freiburg, GW: Herder, 1982. xvi, 454 pp. Paper. 3451196352.

A dissertation on Karl Rahner's theory of "anonymous Christians" in which the author attempts to show the possibility of saving grace outside the structure of Christianity without, however, playing down the urgency of mission.

CR237 Shenk, Calvin E.

Who Do You Say That I Am?: Christians Encounter Other Religions. Scottdale, PAU: Herald Press, 1997. 294 pp. Paper. 0836190602.

After an assessment of contemporary theologies of religious pluralism, the former Mennonite missionary to Ethiopia and Professor of Religion and Mission at Eastern Mennonite University since 1976 presents a biblical perspective that views Christ as normative, with implications for Christian witness and dialogue.

CR238 Shim, Johannes Sang-Tai

Glaube und Heil: Eine Untersuchung zur Theorie von den "anonymen Christen" Karl Rahners. Tübingen, GW: Universität Tübingen, 1975. v, 391 pp. Paper. No ISBN.

A dissertation on Karl Rahner's theory of "anonymous Christians" granting the undeniable possibility of salvation outside empirical Christianity, nevertheless asserting that an ecclesiastical sacramental life is fundamental for Christians of mission countries.

CR239 Smith, Wilfred Cantwell

The Meaning and End of Religion. New York, NYU: Harper & Row, 1978. xviii, 340 pp. Paper. 0060674652.

A modern classic in which Smith succeeds in developing new categories of thought by which Christians may begin to do justice to the faith of other people.

CR240 Stowe, David M.

When Faith Meets Faith. New York, NYU: Friendship Press, 1972. 192 pp. Paper. No ISBN.

Second revised printing of a remarkably clear examination of other faiths and of "the distinctiveness of my own faith" as steps in the quest of encounter.

CR241 Straelen, H. van

The Catholic Encounter with World Religions. Westminster, MDU: Newman Press, 1966. 202 pp. No ISBN.

A scholarly response, by a veteran Catholic missionary to Japan, on the Vatican II decrees on Christianity and other faiths.

CR242 Studientagung (1975, St. Gabriel)

Universales Christentum angesichts einer pluralen Welt: Vörtrage. Edited by Andreas Bsteh. (Beiträge zu Religionstheologie, 1). Mödling, AU: Verlag St. Gabriel, 1976. 126 pp. Paper. 3852640849.

Five Roman Catholic theologians (Anton Vorbichler, Walter Kasper, Karl Rahner, Ferdinand Hahn, and Josef Glazik) discuss aspects of the particularity of Christ and the universality of salvation—the first volume in a series on "Contributions to the Theology of Religions."

CR243 Swidler, Leonard J., and Paul Mojzes, eds.
The Uniqueness of Jesus: A Dialogue with Paul F. Knitter.
(Faith Meets Faith). Maryknoll, NYU: Orbis Books, 1997. xi,
189 pp. Paper. 1570751234.

Twenty contributions by an international panel of theologians to a dialogue with Paul F. Knitter on the uniqueness of
Jesus in a religiously plural world.

CR244 Swidler, Leonard J., ed.
Toward a Universal Theology of Religion. (Faith Meets Faith
Series). Maryknoll, NYU: Orbis Books, 1987. viii, 256 pp.
Paper. 0883445808 (hdbk), 0883445557 (pbk).

Four scholarly essays by prominent Christian theologians
(Wilfred Cantwell Smith, John. B. Cobb, Jr., Raimundo Panikkar, and Hans Küng) on the concepts and problems of a universal theology of religion and interreligous dialogue, with
responses by representatives from major religions.

CR245 *Theology of Religions: Christianity and Other Religions*
(Studia Missionala, 42). Rome, IT: Editrice Pontificia Università Gregoriana, 1993. viii, 394 pp. Paper. 8876526579.

A compendium of essays in English (13), Italian (4), and
French (2) by a panel of nineteen international scholars and
missiologists.

CR246 Thils, Gustave
*Propos et problèmes de la théologie des religions non chréti-
ennes.* (Église vivante). Paris, FR: Casterman, 1966. 204 pp.
No ISBN.

A discussion of the theological problems involved in
Christian relationships with non-Christian religions, with a
valuable bibliography.

CR247 Thils, Gustave
Las Religiones no Critianas: Problemas y reflexiones. Translated by Josep A. Pombo. (Colección Peniamento cristiano,
14). Barcelona, SP: Editions Peninsula, 1967. 248 pp. No
ISBN.

Spanish translation.

CR248 Thomas, Madathilparapil M.
*Risking Christ for Christ's Sake: Towards an Ecumenical The-
ology of Pluralism.* Geneva, SZ: WCC, 1987. vii, 122 pp.
Paper. 2825408824.

A survey of Catholic and Protestant approaches to pluralism, particularly as these are represented in the writings of
Raimundo Panikkar and Paul Devanandan, with an analysis of
issues of Christology and ecclesiology and their importance
for the ecumenical movement.

CR249 Thomas, Owen C., ed.
*Attitudes Toward Other Religions: Some Christian Interpre-
tations.* (Harper Forum Books). London, ENK: SCM Press;
New York, NYU: Harper & Row, 1969. 236 pp. Paper. No
ISBN.

A sourcebook by leading Western philosophers and theologians of the 19th and 20th centuries showing their varied
attitudes toward world religions, with an introductory essay
by the editor.

CR250 Thunberg, Lars, Eric J. Sharpe, and Horst Bürkle
Religionsteologi. (Nyt Synspunkt, 29). Hellerup, DK: DMS-
Forlag, 1988. 80 pp. Paper. 8774311379.

A collection of essays on the problem of a Christian theology of religions, edited by Paul Kofoed Christiansen, Peter Lod-
berg, Michael Schelde, Knud Sorensen, and Lars Thunberg.

CR251 Tillich, Paul
Christianity and the Encounter of World Religions. (Fortress
Texts in Modern Theology). Minneapolis, MNU: Fortress
Press, 1994. xvi, 79 pp. Paper. 080062761X.

A reprint of the German-American theologian's influential Bampton Lectures at Columbia University in 1961, with a
new foreword on their significance by Krister Stendahl.

CR252 Tillich, Paul
The Encounter of Religions and Quasi-Religions. Edited by
Terence Thomas. (Toronto Studies in Theology, 37). Lewis-
ton, NYU: E Mellen Press, 1990. xxix, 170 pp. 0889467560.

A publication without critical notes of three late manuscripts (1957-1961) in which the noted theologian relates his
"Protestant Principle" to the encounter with world religions,
and shares in a Christian-Buddhist dialogue.

CR253 Troeltsch, Ernst
The Absoluteness of Christianity and the History of Religions.
Richmond, VAU: John Knox Press, 1971. 173 pp. 0804204624.

The English translation of *Die Absolutheit des Christentums und die Religionsgeschichte* (1901,1929), the German
theologian's influential contribution to a theology of religions.

CR254 van Stekelenburg, Laetitia E.
*Wegen naar Waarachtig Mens-Zijn: De invloed van het werk
van Wilfred Cantwell Smith op de hedendaagse theologie van
de godsdiensten.* (Kerk en Theologie in Context, 38). Kampen,
NE: Kok, 1998. xix, 179 pp. Paper. 9024262763.

A doctoral dissertation (Catholic University at Nijmegen)
on the contribution to a theology of religions of Wilfred
Cantwell Smith of Harvard University.

CR255 Veliath, Dominic
*Theological Approach and Understanding of Religions: Jean
Danielou and Raimundo Panikkar; A Study in Contrast.* Ban-
galore, II: Kristu Jyoti College, 1988. xvi, 407 pp. No ISBN.

A detailed examination of the theologies of both men and an
attempt to work out some sort of a loose synthesis between them.

CR256 Vicedom, Georg F.
Maailmanuskontojen nousu. Translated by Aaro Hurskainen,
and Matti Peltola. Helsinki, FI: Suomen Lähetysseura, 1967.
166 pp. Paper. No ISBN.

Finnish translation of *Die Mission der Weltreligionen*
(Kaiser,1959), an analysis of the religious situation of the world
and the prospects of Christian missions.

CR257 Viladesau, Richard
*Answering for Faith: Christ and the Human Search For Sal-
vation.* Mahwah, NJU: Paulist Press, 1987. xiii, 312 pp. Paper. 0809128829.

The second part of an introduction to a Christian theological anthropology—an attempt through a phenomenology of
religions to examine concrete claims of various faiths to have
encountered a saving word or illumination from God, including the affirmation of Jesus Christ as eschatological Savior.

CR258 Vroom, Hendrik M.
*No Other Gods: Christian Belief in Dialogue with Buddhism,
Hinduism, and Islam.* Translated by Lucy Jansen. Grand Rap-
ids, MIU: Eerdmans, 1996. viii, 174 pp. Paper. 0802840973.

An answer to the question, "For what reason would a person who has read extensively on Buddhist, Hindu, or Islamic
thought continue to be a Christian?" by the Professor of Religion at the Free University of Amsterdam.

CR–CHRISTIANITY AND OTHER RELIGIONS

CR259 Waldenfels, Hans
Begegnung der Religionen: Theologische Versuche I. (Begegnung, 1). Bonn, GW: Borengässer, 1990. xi, 377 pp. 392394618X.

The author presents his many studies on the theology of religions in the form of an anthology divided into three sections covering the theology of religions, specific questions concerning the religions, and the question of Christian self-understanding.

CR260 Waldenfels, Hans
Il fenomeno del cristianesimo: Una religione mondiale nel mondo delle religioni. (Giornale di teologia, 236). Brescia, IT: Queriniana, 1995. 192 pp. 883990736X.

Italian translation.

CR261 Waldenfels, Hans
Phänomen Christentum: Eine Weltreligion in der Welt der Religionen. Freiburg, GW: Herder, 1994. 187 pp. Paper. 3451233150.

An exposition of the Christian faith in the context of the religious pluralism of our times, including Judaism, Islam, Hinduism, and Buddhism, with treatment of fundamentalisms and syncretism.

CR262 Walgrave, Jan Hendrik
Un salut aux dimensions du monde. Translated by Emmanuel Brutsaert. (Cogitatio fidei, 46). Paris, FR: Éditions du Cerf, 1970. 192 pp. No ISBN.

A Belgian Dominican describes humanity's search for salvation within the great religions, especially within Christianity, but also outside it.

CR263 Watts, Alan
The Supreme Identity: An Essay on Oriental Metaphysic and the Christian Religion. New York, NYU: Pantheon Books, 1972. 204 pp. 0394482492.

A search for a common ground for Christians and persons of other faiths by a noted interpreter of Zen Buddhism and Indian and Chinese philosophy; originally published in 1949.

CR264 Whaling, Frank
Christian Theology and World Religions: A Global Approach. (Contemporary Christian Studies). Basingstoke, ENK: Marshall Morgan and Scott, 1986. xi, 192 pp. Paper. 0551013362.

The author, a lecturer in religious studies at the University of Edinburgh, proposes "renewing Christian theology through world religions."

CR265 Wiles, Maurice
Christian Theology and Inter-religious Dialogue. Philadelphia, PAU: Trinity Press International; London, ENK: SCM Press, 1992. viii, 90 pp. Paper. 1563380366 (T), 0334025230 (S).

Lectures on a Christian theology of interreligious dialogue, with special reference to the thought of Karl Rahner; originally presented at Manchester and Yale universities by the Regius Professor of Divinity Emeritus at Oxford.

CR266 Young, Pamela Dickey
Christ in a Post-Christian World: How Can We Believe in Jesus Christ When Those Around Us Believe Differently—Or Not at All? Minneapolis, MNU: Augsburg Fortress, 1995. ix, 162 pp. Paper. 0800629159.

After outlining the chief alternatives in current debates over religious pluralism, the Professor of Theology at Queen's Theological College in Kingston, Ontario offers a Christian feminist contribution.

CR267 Young, Robert Doran
Encounter with World Religions. Philadelphia, PAU: Westminster Press, 1970. 223 pp. 0664208762.

A study of the grounds for, and means to, dialogue between Christians and persons of other faiths, focusing upon the doctrines of revelation, God, and incarnation.

Religions: Comparative Studies

See also TH495, TH614, CR80-CR81, CR222, CR254, CR257, CR468, CR494, CR555, CR660, CR879, CR885, CR936, CR1448, SO434, EC84, EC276, EC295, PO30, PO35, ED151, EV202-EV203, EV211, MI33, SP2, SP89, SP113, SP319, AS1056, and EU15.

CR268 Antoun, Richard T., and Mary Elaine Hegland
Religious Resurgence: Contemporary Cases in Islam, Christianity, and Judaism. Syracuse, NYU: Syracuse University Press, 1987. xiii, 269 pp. 0815624093.

A scholarly examination of social, economic, and political factors which affect contemporary religious renascence, with an analysis of the complex personal reasons involved when individuals join religious movements; including case studies from the Middle East, Malaysia, United States, and Israel.

CR269 Barot, Rohit, ed.
Religion and Ethnicity: Minorities and Social Change in the Metropolis. Kampen, NE: Kok Pharos, 1993. vii, 203 pp. Paper. 9039000611.

Sixteen case studies of the significance of religion among immigrants (mostly Muslims and Hindus) to Europe.

CR270 Bergunder, Michael
Wiedergeburt der Ahnen: Eine religionsethnographische und religionsphänomenologische Untersuchung zur Reinkarnationsvorstellung. (Hamburger Theologische Studien, 6). Münster, GW: Lit Verlag, 1994. xii, 514 pp. 3894738006.

A wide-ranging study of views of reincarnation from tribal religions to religions in China, Indonesia, India, and Europe.

CR271 Biallas, Leonard J.
World Religions: A Story Approach. Mystic, CTU: Twenty-Third Publications, 1991. xii, 324 pp. Paper. 0896224937.

A study text on major religions of the modern world using stories from each tradition to introduce each faith; with study questions for Christian students.

CR272 Biggar, Nigel, Jamie S. Scott, and William Schweiker, eds.
Cities of Gods: Faith, Politics and Pluralism in Judaism, Christianity and Islam. (Contributions to the Study of Religion, 16). New York, NYU: Greenwood, 1986. viii, 244 pp. 031324944X.

Twelve scholarly essays on understandings of the state and political action in Judaism, Christianity, and Islam, half of which were originally presented at the conference on "Religious Conviction and Public Action: The Life of Faith in a Pluralistic World" (Divinity School of the University of Chicago, 1982.)

CR273 Bird, Michael S., ed.
Art and Interreligious Dialogue: Six Perspectives. Lanham, MDU: University Press of America, 1995. v, 159 pp. 0819195545 (hdbk), 0819195553 (pbk).

Based on the premise that there is a universal connection between art and religion, six scholars and their respondents explore visual art and architecture as vehicles of interreligious dialogue.

CR—CHRISTIANITY AND OTHER RELIGIONS

CR274 Bleeker, Claas Jouco, and Geo Widengren, eds.
Historia Religionum: Handbook for the History of Religions.
Leiden, NE: Brill, 1969-1971. 2 vols. No ISBN.

Thirty-one scholarly essays on the history of each of the world's religious traditions; [vol. 1: *Religions of the Past* (1969, viii, 690 pp.); vol. 2: *Religions of the Present* (1971, vi, 715 pp.)].

CR275 Bleeker, Claas Jouco, and Geo Widengren, eds.
Historia Religionum: Manual de historia de las religiones.
Madrid, SP: Cristiandad, 1973. 2 vols. 8470571427 (vol. 1), 8470571435 (vol. 2), 8470571419 (set).

Spanish translation.

CR276 Bowker, John
Problems of Suffering in Religions of the World. London, ENK: Cambridge University Press, 1970. xii, 318 pp. 521074126.

With extensive quotes from source materials, these Lectures in Divinity at the University of Cambridge provide a comparative study of the ways in which the problems of suffering are treated by the major world religions.

CR277 Bowker, John
The Religious Imagination and the Sense of God. Oxford, ENK: Clarendon Press, 1978. xii, 343 pp. 0198266464.

Scholarly examination of the distinctive sense of God found in four major religious traditions: Judaism, Christianity, Islam, and Buddhism.

CR278 Bracken, Joseph A.
The Divine Matrix: Creativity as Link between East and West. (Faith Meets Faith Series). Maryknoll, NYU: Orbis Books; Herefordshire, ENK: Gracewing, 1995. xi, 179 pp. Paper. 1570750041 (US), 0852443366 (UK).

Comparative theology from a process perspective designed to open up categories mutually acceptable in Eastern and Western thought.

CR279 Brandon, S. G. F., ed.
The Saviour God: Comparative Studies in the Concept of Salvation. Manchester, ENK: Manchester University Press; New York, NYU: Barnes & Noble, 1963. xxii, 242 pp. No ISBN.

Fifteen essays by European scholars on soteriology in various world faiths; written as a *festschrift* to honor Edwin Olives James, Professor Emeritus in the University of London.

CR280 Braswell, George W.
Understanding World Religions. Nashville, TNU: Broadman, 1983. xvi, 206 pp. Paper. 0805410686.

Revised edition of a basic textbook on world religions, with helps for Christians desiring to communicate their beliefs and faith to others.

CR281 Brown, David
All Their Splendor: World Faiths: A Way to Community. London, ENK: Fount, 1982. 223 pp. Paper. 0006264840.

A thematic approach to understanding similarities among world faiths by the Anglican bishop of Guildford.

CR282 Brown, David
A Guide to Religions. (TEF Study Guide, 12). London, ENK: SPCK; USCL for the Theological Education Fund, 1975. xiv, 271 pp. 0281028494.

A textbook for Third World seminarians by the bishop of Guildford (UK), with six chapters based on material supplied by nationals with whom he had missionary contact in Sudan and the Middle East.

CR283 Burnett, David
Clash of Worlds. Eastbourne, ENK: MARC, 1990. 255 pp. Paper. 1854241079.

An examination of the clash of traditional, modern, and postmodern religious worldviews, and of the biblical worldview and its transforming challenge to all of them.

CR284 Caldarola, Carlo, ed.
Religions and Societies: Asia and the Middle East. (Religion and Society, 22). Berlin, GW: Mouton, 1982. viii, 688 pp. 902793259X.

A comparative sociology of religion in Asia, providing profiles on the interaction of religions and societies in a number of countries of the Middle East, and of Central, East, South, and Southeast Asia.

CR285 Cannon, Dale
Six Ways of Being Religious: A Framework for Comparative Studies of Religion. Belmont, CAU: Wadsworth Publishing, 1996. xiv, 402 pp. Paper. 0534253326.

Comparative religion introduced through an analysis of six ways of being religious, with application in a comparison of Buddhism and Christianity.

CR286 Carman, John Braisted
Majesty and Meekness: A Comparative Study of Contrast and Harmony in the Concept of God. Grand Rapids, MIU: Eerdmans, 1994. ix, 453 pp. Paper. 0802806937.

A careful and sensitive account of ideas about God in Hinduism and Christianity, with complementary views in Buddhism, Islam, and Judaism; by the former director of the Center for the Study of World Religions at Harvard University.

CR287 Carmody, Denise Lardner, and John Carmody
How to Live Well: Ethics in the World Religions. Belmont, CAU: Wadsworth Publishing, 1988. xiii, 222 pp. Paper. 0534084729.

A textbook for undergraduate students giving an overview of ethical connections among Jews, Christians, Muslims, Hindus, and adherents of Chinese and Japanese religions.

CR288 Carmody, Denise Lardner, and John Carmody
In the Path of the Masters: Understanding the Spirituality of Buddha, Confucius, Jesus, and Muhammad. New York, NYU: Paragon House, 1994. ix, 232 pp. 1557784094.

The spiritual legacies of four founders of world faiths, divided into the major dimensions of spiritual life—nature, society, the self, and divinity.

CR289 Carmody, Denise Lardner, and John Carmody
Peace and Justice in the Scriptures of the World Religions: Reflections on Non-Christian Scriptures. New York, NYU: Paulist Press, 1988. iii, 191 pp. Paper. 0809130149.

A personal reflection on images of, and guidelines for, peace in Hinduism, Buddhism, Taoism, Islam, and Judaism.

CR290 Carmody, Denise Lardner, and John Carmody
Prayer in World Religions. Maryknoll, NYU: Orbis Books, 1990. viii, 168 pp. Paper. 0883446448.

A survey of the understandings of prayer in Hinduism, Islam, Buddhism, Judaism, African, and Native American faiths, and their relevance to interfaith understanding, dialogue, and spiritual life.

CR291 Carmody, Denise Lardner, and John Carmody
Religion, the Great Questions. New York, NYU: Seabury Press, 1983. ix, 182 pp. Paper. 0816424764.

On each of the great questions about the human quest (God, evil, and the good life), the authors summarize and compare answers from Hinduism, Buddhism, Taoism, Judaism, Islam, and Christianity.

CR292 Carmody, Denise Lardner, and John Carmody
Ways to the Center: An Introduction to World Religions. Belmont, CAU: Wadsworth Publishing, 1993. xi, 489 pp. Paper. 0534191827.

An updated fourth edition of the widely used textbook incorporating changes made in new editions of *Western Ways to the Center* (1991) and *Eastern Ways to the Center* (1992).

CR293 Carter, Robert E., ed.
God, the Self, and Nothingness: Reflections Eastern and Western. (A New ERA Book). New York, NYU: International Religious Foundation, 1990. xxxix, 291 pp. 0892260726 (hdbk), 0892260734 (pbk).

Essays by Eastern and Western scholars seeking commonalities in understandings of the ultimate; originally presented at conferences sponsored by the New Ecumenical Research Association (1986-1988), and the sixteenth International Conference on the Unity of the Sciences (Atlanta, 16-19 Nov. 1987).

CR294 Catholic Church, Secretariatus Pro Non Christianis
Religions in the World. Vatican City, IT: Palazzo San Calisto, n.d. 241 pp. No ISBN.

A survey of, and popular introduction to, world religions and to interreligious dialogue.

CR295 Clasper, Paul D.
Eastern Paths and the Christian Way. Maryknoll, NYU: Orbis Books, 1980. viii, 136 pp. Paper. 0883441004.

An introduction for Christians into the religious thought and experience of Hinduism, Theravada Buddhism, and Zen as an aid to sympathetic understanding and dialogue.

CR296 Cohn-Sherbok, Dan, ed.
World Religion and Human Liberation. (Faith Meets Faith Series). Maryknoll, NYU: Orbis Books, 1992. vii, 143 pp. 0883447967 (hdbk), 0883447959 (pbk).

Eight scholarly essays on the possible interconnections and discontinuities between Christian liberation theology and Judaism, Islam, Buddhism, Hinduism, and African traditional religions.

CR297 Corduan, Winfried
Neighboring Faiths: A Christian Introduction to World Religions. Downers Grove, ILU: InterVarsity, 1998. 363 pp. 0830815244.

An introduction for Christians to the major world religions, emphasizing not just formal religious teachings, but how each religion is practiced in daily life; with helps for Christians who engage in constructive dialogue.

CR298 Cornélis, Étienne
Christliche Grundgedanken in nicht-christlichen Religionen. Translated by Robert Maria Zadow. Paderborn, GW: Bonifacius-Druckerei, 1967. 195 pp. Paper. No ISBN.

German translation.

CR299 Cornélis, Étienne
Valeurs chrétiennes des religions non chrétiennes: histoire du salut et histoire des religions christianisme et Bouddhisme. (Cogitatio Fidei, 12). Paris, FR: Éditions du Cerf, 1965. 229 pp. No ISBN.

An introduction to a theology of religions, focusing on presentation of the Christian faith to Buddhists.

CR300 Cornélis, Étienne
Valores de las Religiones no Cristianas: Aproximación al budismo. Barcelona, SP: Editorial Nova Terra, 1970. 268 pp. No ISBN.

Spanish translation.

CR301 Corrigan, John et al.
Jews, Christians, Muslims: A Comparative Introduction to Monotheistic Religions. Upper Saddle River, NJU: Prentice-Hall, 1998. xvi, 542 pp. Paper. 0023250925.

The three religions are compared in light of monotheism, scripture and tradition, worship and ritual authority, ethics, material culture, and political order.

CR302 Coward, Harold G., ed.
Experiencing Scripture in World Religions. (Faith Meets Faith Series). Maryknoll, NYU: Orbis Books, 2000. ix, 178 pp. Paper. 1570752982.

This collection of six in-depth papers provides an inside view of how the scriptures of major world religions illuminate the lives and experience of their devotees.

CR303 Coward, Harold G., ed.
Life after Death in World Religions. (Faith Meets Faith Series). Maryknoll, NYU: Orbis Books, 1997. vii, 131 pp. Paper. 1570751196.

Six lectures on the answers given by six world religions to the question, "Is there life after death?"; originally presented in 1995 at the University of Victoria, British Columbia, Canada.

CR304 Coward, Harold G.
Pluralism: Challenge to World Religions. Maryknoll, NYU: Orbis Books, 1985. viii, 131 pp. Paper. 088344710X.

An introduction to the approaches to religious pluralism in Judaism, Christianity, Islam, Hinduism, and Buddhism; with new guidelines proposed for interreligious dialogue.

CR305 Coward, Harold G.
Sacred Word and Sacred Text: Scripture in World Religions. Maryknoll, NYU: Orbis Books, 1988. x, 222 pp. Paper. 0883446057 (hdbk), 0883446049 (pbk).

A study of the world's sacred texts, showing the importance of oral-aural experience of scripture, and how it is more transforming than the written word.

CR306 Cragg, Kenneth
The Privilege of Man: A Theme in Judaism, Islam and Christianity. (Jordan Lectures). London, ENK: Athlone Press, 1968. ix, 208 pp. No ISBN.

Essays on the comparative beliefs about humanity, with Abraham as the prototype in Judaism, Islam, and Christianity; originally presented in 1967 as the Jordan Lectures at London University's School of Oriental and African Studies.

CR—CHRISTIANITY AND OTHER RELIGIONS

CR307 Crawford, S. Cromwell, ed.
World Religions and Global Ethics. (A New Ecumenical Research Association (ERA) Book). New York, NYU: Paragon House, 1989. xvi, 306 pp. 0913757578 (hdbk), 0913757586 (pbk).

A collection of essays by eminent religious scholars on the specific values and insights that particular religious traditions bring to ethical inquiry.

CR308 De Gruchy, John W., and Martin Prozesky, eds.
A Southern African Guide to World Religions. Cape Town, SA: David Phillip, 1991. viii, 248 pp. Paper. 0864861729.

An introductory textbook for the teaching of comparative religion by scholars of religious studies in South African universities.

CR309 Dean, Thomas, ed.
Religious Pluralism and Truth: Essays on Cross-Cultural Philosophy of Religion. (Religious Studies). Albany, NYU: SUNY Press, 1995. xi, 271 pp. 0791421236 (hdbk), 0791421244 (pbk).

Fourteen scholarly essays on religious pluralism and cross-cultural truth by noted philosophers of religion today, including Ninian Smart, Raimundo Panikkar, and Harold Coward.

CR310 Denny, Frederick Mathewson, and Rodney L. Taylor, eds.
The Holy Book in Comparative Perspective. (Studies in Comparative Religion, 1). Columbia, SCU: University of South Carolina Press, 1985. viii, 252 pp. 0872494535.

Ten essays by North American biblical scholars on the ways in which scripture functions in various religious traditions.

CR311 Eck, Diana L., and Devaki Jain, eds.
Speaking of Faith: Global Perspectives on Women, Religion and Social Change. Philadelphia, PAU: New Society Publishers, 1987. ix, 296 pp. 0865711003 (hdbk), 0865711011 (pbk).

Twenty-six papers, including involvements of Christian women in social change; originally presented at an international, interreligious conference on "Women, Religion and Social Change" (Harvard University, June 1983); originally published in 1986 by Kali for Women.

CR312 Eck, Diana L.
On Common Ground: World Religions in America. (The Pluralism Project). New York, NYU: Columbia University Press, 1997. CD-ROM pp. 0231108982.

A CD containing insights into the history, beliefs, and current practices of fifteen religious traditions in the United States, through geographic portraits in eighteen cities and regions, the voices of people speaking about their faith traditions, and an anthology of documents on encountering religious diversity; users' guide available at http://www.columbia.edu/ocg/org.

CR313 Eigo, Francis A., ed.
Prayer: The Global Experience. Villanova, PAU: Villanova University Press, 1997. xi, 210 pp. Paper. 0877230900.

Six essays comparing Christian experiences of prayer with those of Hindus, Jews, Buddhists, Muslims, and Native Americans.

CR314 Eliade, Mircea
História das crenças e das idéias religiosas. (Espírito e matéria). Rio de Janeiro, BL: Zahar Editores, 1978. 3 vols. No ISBN.
Portuguese translation.

CR315 Eliade, Mircea
Histoire des croyances et des idées religieuses. (Bibliothèque historique Payot). Paris, FR: Payot, 1983. 3 vols. 2228881589 (vol. 1), 2228881597 (vol. 2), 2228881600 (vol. 3).

A survey by the distinguished Romanian-born historian of religions, of manifestations of the sacred and creative moments in varied religious traditions, from the Stone Age to the 18th century [vol. 1: *De l'âge de la pierre aux mystères d'Eleusis* (1976); vol. 2: *De Gautama Bouddha au triomphe du christianisme* (1978); vol. 3: *De Mahomet à l'âge de Réformes* (1983)].

CR316 Eliade, Mircea
Historia de las Creencias y de las Ideas Religiosas. Madrid, SP: Ediciones Cristiandad, 1978. 4 vols. 8470572822 (set).
Spanish translation.

CR317 Eliade, Mircea
A History of Religious Ideas. Translated by Willard R. Trask, Alf Hiltebeitel, and Diane Apostolos-Cappadona. Chicago, ILU: University of Chicago Press, 1978. 3 vols.
English translation.

CR318 Eliade, Mircea
Istoria creditelor si ideilor religioase. Translated by Cezar Baltag. Bucuresti, RM: Editura Stiintifica, 1991. 3 vols. 9734400274 (vol. 1), 9734400282 (vol. 2), 9734400290 (vol. 3).
Romanian translation.

CR319 Ellwood, Robert S.
The History and Future of Faith: Religion Past, Present, and to Come. New York, NYU: Crossroad Publishing, 1988. viii, 184 pp. 0824508793.

A scholarly reflection of what religion may become, based on historical studies of major religions by the Bishop W. Bashford Professor of Oriental Studies, University of California.

CR320 Falaturi, Abdoldjavad, Jakob Josef Petuchowski, and Walter Strolz, eds.
Three Ways to the One God: The Faith Experience in Judaism, Christianity, and Islam. Tunbridge Wells, ENK: Burns & Oates, 1987. 173 pp. Paper. 0860121585.

Twelve international theologians, representatives of Judaism, Christianity, and Islam, discuss the fundamental bases of their faiths.

CR321 Fernando, Antony
Christianity Made Intelligible: (as ONE of the World's Religions). Kadawata, CE: Intercultural Book Promoters, 1990. vi, 222 pp. Paper. 955903605X.

A deeply religious and ecumenical presentation of Christianity for non-Christians, bringing out Christian spirituality; by the head of the Department of Classical and Christian Studies at the Kelaniya University in Sri Lanka.

CR322 Frenz, Albrecht, ed.
Grace in Saiva Siddhanta, Vedanta, Islam and Christianity. Madurai, II: Tamil Nadu Theological Seminary, 1975. 128 pp. No ISBN.

Papers originally delivered at the "Seminar on Grace" at Tamil Nadu Theological Seminary (Madurai, India, 11 Oct. 1975).

CR—CHRISTIANITY AND OTHER RELIGIONS

CR323 Friedli, Richard
Zwischen Himmel und Holle—die Reinkarnation: Ein religions-wissenscchaftliches Handbuch. Freiburg, SZ: Universitatsverlag, 1986. 122 pp. Paper. 3727803614.

This handbook, which explicates texts and rites of rebirth out of the Hindu, Buddhist, Black African, and Christian contexts, demonstrates a dialogical process grounded in cultural anthropology, which enables persons of these faiths to cooperate responsibly.

CR324 González Vallés, Carlos
Dejar a Dios ser Dios: Imagenes de la Divinidad. (El Pozo de Siquem, 28). Santander, SP: Editorial Sal Terrae, 1987. 187 pp. Paper. 8429309656.

A study of the image of God in various cultures, particularly India.

CR325 Gordon, Haim, and Leonard Grob, eds.
Education for Peace: Testimonies from World Religions. Maryknoll, NYU: Orbis Books, 1987. viii, 240 pp. Paper. 0883443597.

Witness to the contribution to peacemaking from representatives of Hinduism, Buddhism, Judaism, Christianity, and Islam.

CR326 Gorospe, Vitaliano R., and Larry D. Shinn, eds.
Incarnation and Avatara in World Religions. (God: The Contemporary Discussion Series). New York, NYU: Paragon House, 1985. Paper. 0913757128 (hdbk), 0913757136 (pbk).

A collection of essays on beliefs concerning the descent and incarnation of the deity in various world faiths.

CR327 Graham, William A.
Beyond the Written Word: Oral Aspects of Scripture in the History of Religion. Cambridge, ENK: Cambridge University Press, 1987. xiv, 306 pp. 0521331765.

An analysis of the significant oral roles of written sacred texts in the history of religion, focusing on the Judaeo-Christian Scriptures and the Qu'ran.

CR328 Griffiths, Bede
A New Vision of Reality: Western Science, Eastern Mysticism and Christian Faith. Edited by Felicity Edwards. London, ENK: Collins, 1989. 304 pp. 0002153637.

A major study by the distinguished leader in Hindu-Christian dialogue, inviting us to look afresh at Christianity in the context of modern physics on the one hand, and Eastern mysticism on the other.

CR329 Griffiths, Paul J., ed.
Christianity through Non-Christian Eyes. (Faith Meets Faith Series). Maryknoll, NYU: Orbis Books, 1990. xiv, 286 pp. Paper. 0883446626 (hdbk), 0883446618 (pbk).

An anthology containing nineteen 20th-century analyses of Christianity by Jewish, Muslim, Buddhist, and Hindu scholars, with introductions and explanatory notes.

CR330 Häring, Hermann, and Johannes Baptist Metz, eds.
Reincarnation or Resurrection? London, ENK: SCM Press; Maryknoll, NYU: Orbis Books, 1993. x, 139 pp. Paper. 0334030218 (S), 0883448734 (O).

Six essays on ideas of reincarnation in various world religions, and seven essays on Christian theological orientations on resurrection.

CR331 Häring, Hermann, and Johannes Baptist Metz
The Many Faces of the Divine. (*Concilium*, 1995/2). London, ENK: SCM Press; Maryknoll, NYU: Orbis Books, 1995. ix, 142 pp. Paper. 0334030315 (UK), 0883448831 (US).

Twelve essays, mainly by First World theologians, on the multiplicity of religious images and experiences of God, in Christianity and other religious traditions.

CR332 Halverson, Dean C., ed.
The Compact Guide to World Religions. Minneapolis, MNU: Bethany House, 1996. 272 pp. Paper. 1556617046.

Brief profiles of various faiths prepared for Christians desiring to witness to international students.

CR333 Hanawalt, Emily Albu, and Carter Lindberg, eds.
Through the Eye of a Needle: Judeo-Christian Roots of Social Welfare. Kirksville, MOU: Thomas Jefferson University Press, 1994. viii, 256 pp. 0943549175.

Twelve scholarly essays on the history of Jewish and Christian social welfare, from ancient to modern times; originally presented as lectures at Boston University in 1990.

CR334 Heiler, Friedrich
Die Frau in den Religionen der Menschheit. (Theologische Bibliothek Töpelmann, 33). Berlin, GW: Gruyter, 1976. 194 pp. 3110065835.

A random collection of data gathered through the ages, mostly from secondary sources, concerning the image and status of women in different religious traditions.

CR335 Hernández, Alacalá Vicente
La Exposición de lo Divino en las Religiones no Cristianas. (BAC, 334). Madrid, SP: EDICA, 1972. xxiv, 331 pp. Paper. No ISBN.

An essay on religious phenomena which, according to the author, demonstrate a fundamental coincidence that is hidden beneath frequently contradictory forms.

CR336 Hick, John, and Edmund Meltzer, eds.
Three Faiths—One God: A Jewish, Christian, Muslim Encounter. Albany, NYU: SUNY Press, 1989. xiv, 240 pp. Paper. 0791400425 (hdbk), 0791400433 (pbk).

Eleven essays on beliefs concerning God, the earth, humanity, the land of Israel, and the Trinity; originally presented in Claremont, California, in a trialogue among Jewish, Muslim, and Christian scholars, with responses to each view from the other traditions.

CR337 Hick, John, and Hasan Askari, eds.
The Experience of Religious Diversity. Hampshire, ENK: Gower Publishing, 1985. 236 pp. 056605020X (hdbk), 0861271130 (pbk).

Buddhist, Christian, Hindu, Jewish, Muslim, and Sikh writers explore the resources of their own traditions in support of a pluralistic vision in which the Ultimate is humanly perceived in different ways.

CR338 Hinnells, John R., ed.
A Handbook of Living Religions. Middlesex, ENK: Penguin Books, 1985. 528 pp. Paper. 0140223428.

Sixteen essays on active 20th-century religions, including primal religions and new religious movements.

CR339 Hixon, Lex

Coming Home:The Experience of Enlightenment in Sacred Traditions. (The Library of Spiritual Classics). Los Angeles, CAU: Tarcher; New York, NYU: St. Martin's Press, 1989. xviii, 215 pp. 0874775035.

The experience of enlightenment as revealed in the lives and teachings of individuals from the traditions of the *I Ching*, Zen, Sufism, Hasidic Judaism, Tantric Buddhism, Ramana Maharishi, Advaita Vedanta, Greek and Christian mysticism; originally published in 1978.

CR340 Hospital, Clifford G.

Breakthrough: Insights of the Great Religious Discoverers. Maryknoll, NYU: Orbis Books, 1985. xi, 191 pp. Paper. 088344206X.

Popularly written summaries of the teachings of the Upanishadic seers, Buddha, Jesus, and Muhammad, with the purpose of suggesting what we all can learn from them.

CR341 Howard, Leslie G.

The Expansion of God. Maryknoll, NYU: Orbis Books, 1981. ix, 452 pp. Paper. 0883441217.

An Irish journalist with extensive experience in Asia writes of the modern spiritual crisis, with special reference to the contacts of Asian religions and cultures with Christianity; including chapters on China, Japan, Thailand, and India.

CR342 Ibish, Yusuf, and Ileana Marculescu, eds.

Contemplation and Action in the World Religions: Selected Papers from the Rothco Chapel Colloquim "Traditional Modes of Contemplation and Action." Houston, TXU: Rothko Chapel; Seattle, WAU: University of Washington Press, 1978. 274 pp. Paper. 0295956348.

Selected papers from a colloquium on "Traditional Modes of Contemplation and Action" held in Houston, Texas, in 1978.

CR343 IbnKammuna, Sadibn Mansur

Ibn Kammuna's Examination of the Three Faiths: A Thirteen-Century Essay in the Comparative Study of Religion. Translated by Moshe Perlmann. Berkeley, CAU: University of California Press, 1971. xi, 160 pp. 0520016580.

An important medieval Islamic essay comparing the concepts of prophecy in Judaism, Christianity, and Islam; translated from the Arabic with an introduction and notes.

CR344 Idel, Moshe, and Bernard McGinn, eds.

Mystical Union and Monotheistic Faith: An Ecumenical Dialogue. New York, NYU: Macmillan Publishing; London, ENK: Collier Macmillan, 1989. xi, 252 pp. 0028960319.

A comparative study of the concept of mystical union with the divine in Judaism, Christianity, and Islam.

CR345 Jennings, George James

All Things, All Men, All Means—to Save Some. Le Mars, IAU: Middle East Missions Research, 1984. x, 284 pp. Paper. No ISBN.

A Middle East missions consultant demonstrates through presentation of twenty-one different worldviews, that understanding them is a key to effective missions.

CR346 Jurji, Edward J., ed.

Religious Pluralism and World Community: Interfaith and Intercultural Communication. (Studies in the History of Religions, 15). Leiden, NE: Brill, 1969. viii, 3 pp. No ISBN.

Twelve papers on the worldviews, involvements in modern society, and cultural expressions of various world religions by an interfaith panel of scholars.

CR347 Küng, Hans, and Jürgen Moltmann, eds.

Fundamentalism as an Ecumenical Challenge. (*Concilium*, 1992/93). London, ENK: SCM Press, 1992. xiii, 128 pp. Paper. 0334030145.

Thirteen scholarly essays from the perspectives of theology and social psychology, on fundamentalism and its expressions in Christianity, Judaism, and Islam.

CR348 Keller, Carl A. et al.

Jesus außerhalb der Kirche: Das Jesusverständnis in neuen religiösen Bewegungen. (Weltanschauungen im Gespräch, 5). Freiburg, GW: Paulus Verlag, 1989. 159 pp. 3722801958, 3290100367 (TVZ).

Descriptions and evaluations of how Jesus is understood today by Buddhists, Muslims, contemporary gurus, and the followers of Sun Myung Moon.

CR349 Keller, Carl A. et al.

Reinkarnation—Wiedergeburt—aus christicher Sicht. (Weltanschauungen im Gespräch, 2). Freiburg, SZ: Paulas Verlag; Zürich, SZ: Theologischer Verlag, 1988. 148 pp. Paper. 3722801753 (P), 3290100081 (T).

A collection of five essays on the notions of reincarnation and rebirth in Hinduism, Mahayana Buddhism, New Age thought, and Christianity.

CR350 Kepel, Gilles

Die Rache Gottes: Radikale Moslems, Christen und Juden auf dem Vormarsch. Translated by Thorsten Schmidt. Munich, GW: Piper, 1991. 315 pp. 3492035086.

German translation.

CR351 Kepel, Gilles

La revanche de Dieu: Chrétiens, juifs et musulmans à la reconquête du monde. (Points Actuels, 117). Paris, FR: Éditions du Seuil, 1991. 282 pp. 2020129299.

A comparative study of the resurgence of belief as a reaction against modern secularism in Mediterranean Islam, European Catholicism, North American Protestantism, and Judaism (both in Israel and among Jews of the diaspora).

CR352 Kepel, Gilles

The Revenge of God: The Resurgence of Islam, Christianity and Judaism in the Modern World. Translated by Alan Braley. University Park, PAU: Pennsylvania State University Press, 1994. viii, 215 pp. 0271013133 (hdbk), 0271013141 (pbk).

English translation.

CR353 Khoury, Adel Théodore, ed.

Was ist Erlösung: Die Antwort der Weltreligionen. (Herderbücherei, 1181). Freiburg im Breisgau, GW: Herder, 1985. 155 pp. No ISBN.

Articles by experts such as E. Khoury, D. Meier, P. Vetter, Hünermann, and L. Hagemann on the meaning of salvation in Hinduism, Buddhism, Judaism, Islam, and Christianity.

CR354 King, Ursula

Towards a New Mysticism: Teilhard de Chardin and Eastern Religions. New York, NYU: Seabury Press, 1980. 318 pp. 0816404755.

A scholarly analysis of Teilhard de Chardin's reactions to Eastern religions based on unpublished sources.

CR355 King, Ursula, ed.

Women in World's Religion, Past and Present. (Ecumenical Research Association. A New Book/God, The Contemporary Discussion Series). New York, NYU: Paragon House, 1987. x, 261 pp. 0913757322 (hdbk), 0913757330 (pbk).

A diverse collection of fourteen essays analyzing both historical and contemporary perspectives on the roles of women in specific world religions, and the feminist issues raised by them.

CR356 Kitagawa, Joseph Mitsuo

The History of Religions: Understanding Human Experience. (AAR Studies in Religion, 47). Atlanta, GAU: Scholars Press, 1987. xix, 375 pp. 1555401279 (hdbk), 1555401287 (pbk).

A collection of twenty-two previously published essays on the history of religions, applied religious science, and on the author's mentors; with an autobiographical and bibliographical introduction.

CR357 Kitagawa, Joseph Mitsuo

Spiritual Liberation and Human Freedom in Contemporary Asia. (Rockwell Lectures, 1). New York, NYU: Lang, 1990. x, 213 pp. 0820413186.

Lectures, originally presented at Rice University in 1977, on religious trends in Asia, with special references to the interplay between religions of East and West.

CR358 Klostermaier, Klaus K.

Liberation—Salvation—Self-Realization: A Comparative Study of Hindu, Buddhist and Christian Ideas. Madras, II: University of Madras, 1973. 84 pp. Paper. No ISBN.

The Swamikannu Pillai Endowment Lectures (University of Madras, India, 5-7 March 1969).

CR359 Kooiman, Dick, Otto van den Muijzenberg, and Peter van der Veer, eds.

Conversion, Competition and Conflict: Essays on the Role of Religion in Asia. (Anthropological Studies Free University, 6). Amsterdam, NE: VU Uitgeverij/ Free University Press, 1984. ix, 216 pp. Paper. 9062560857.

Papers from the conference on "Religion and Social Change in Asia" held at the Free University in Amsterdam in May 1983 on three themes (Hindu values and politics in India, Islam and political conflict in Java, and Christian mission and political-economic expansion on Formosa and in South India/Ceylon).

CR360 *La réalité supreme dans les religions non-chrétiennes*

(Studia Missionalia, 17). Rome, IT: Press de l'Universite Gregorienne, 1968. 243 pp. No ISBN.

Eleven scholarly essays in French, Italian, and English, about awareness, position, and worship of the Supreme Being in the various non-Christian religions.

CR361 Levering, Miriam, ed.

Rethinking Scripture: Essays from a Comparative Perspective. Albany, NYU: SUNY Press, 1989. ix, 276 pp. 0887066135 (hdbk), 0887066143 (pbk).

Seven scholarly essays explaining how sacred texts function within each of the major world faiths.

CR362 Lewis, James F., and William G. Travis

Religious Traditions of the World. Grand Rapids, MIU: Zondervan, 1991. ix, 422 pp. 0310519004.

A textbook for evangelical Christians describing the important features of major religious traditions, and several contemporary Christian theologies of religion.

CR363 Little, David, and Summer B. Twiss

Comparative Religious Ethics. San Francisco, CAU: Harper & Row, 1978. xi, 266 pp. 0060652543.

A systematic introduction to the comparative study of religious ethics, with application to the religion and morality of the Navaho, in the Gospel of Matthew, and in Theravada Buddhism.

CR364 Little, David, John Kelsay, and Abdulaziz A. Sachedina

Human Rights and the Conflict of Cultures: Western and Islamic Perspectives on Religious Liberty. (Studies in Comparative Religion). Columbia, SCU: University of South Carolina, 1988. x, 112 pp. 0872495337.

An analysis of the ways that certain religious traditions may or may not provide support for ideas expressed in various international documents on religious liberty and freedom of conscience.

CR365 Lyden, John

Enduring Issues in Religion. (Enduring Issues Series). San Diego, CAU: Greenhaven Press, 1995. 312 pp. Paper. 1565102592.

Classic texts from 20th-century thinkers of various world faiths answering basic human questions including, "What should one think about religions other than one's own?"

CR366 Magida, Arthur J., ed.

How to Be a Perfect Stranger: A Guide to Etiquette in Other People's Religious Ceremonies. Woodstock, VTU: Jewish Lights Publishing, 1996. 417 pp. 1879045397.

A practical guide for persons desiring to participate with sensitivity in the worship, life cycle events, or home celebrations of faiths other than their own, with chapters on various Christian denominations and other faiths.

CR367 Markham, Ian S., ed.

A World Religions Reader. Malden, MAU: Blackwell Publishers, 1996. xvi, 368 pp. 063118239X (hdbk), 063118242X (pbk).

An introductory college text prepared for a course on "Christianity and Other Religions," with central texts of each faith, plus commentaries and questions for reflection covering the religious mind, worldviews, institutions, rituals, ethical expressions, and modern expressions of each faith.

CR368 Marty, Martin E., and Frederick E. Greenspahn, eds.

Pushing the Faith: Proselytism and Civility in a Pluralistic World. New York, NYU: Crossroad Publishing, 1988. xiv, 190 pp. 0824508718.

Theological, historical, and sociological perspectives on how proselytism is both being criticized and is enduring in our pluralistic world; special emphasis is given to Jewish and Christian religion.

CR369 Marty, Martin E., and R. Scott Appleby, eds.

Accounting for Fundamentalisms: The Dynamic Character of Movements. (The Fundamentalism Project, 4). Chicago, ILU: University of Chicago Press, 1994. ix, 852 pp. 0226508854.

A collection of twenty-eight scholarly essays on ideologies, behaviors, internal dynamics, and attitudes to the outside world in fundamentalist movements of the various world religions.

CR370 Matlins, Stuart M., and Arthur J. Magida, eds.

How to Be a Perfect Stranger, Vol. 2: A Guide to Etiquette in Other People's Religious Ceremonies. Woodstock, VTU: Jewish Lights Publishing, 1997. 396 pp. 187904563X.

Helps for understanding teachings and practices of seventeen smaller (50,000+ member) Christian denominations in the United States, plus Native American, Baha'i, and Sikh communities.

CR—CHRISTIANITY AND OTHER RELIGIONS

CR371 McMullen, Clarence O., ed.

The Nature of Guruship. Delhi, II: ISPCK, 1976. 219 pp. No ISBN.

Eighteen papers delivered at a seminar on the nature of guruship in the world's religions; organized by the Christian Institute of Sikh Studies, with the Punjab and Sikh notions figuring prominently in the papers.

CR372 Mensen, Bernhard, ed.

Recht auf Leben, Recht auf Toten: ein Kulturvergleich. (Vortragsreihe/Akademie Volker und Kulturen, 15). Nettetal, GW: Steyler Verlag, 1992. 162 pp. Paper. 3805003072.

Eight articles which attempt to explain the various factors in (mostly) non-Western cultures relating to the right to life or conversely, the right to kill.

CR373 Mensen, Bernhard, ed.

Die Schöpfung in den Religionen. (Vortragsreihe/Akademie Völker und Kulturen, St. Augustin, 13 (1989/90)). Nettetal, GW: Steyler Verlag, 1990. 111 pp. Paper. 3805002653.

These six essays, originally delivered as lectures at the Akademie Völker und Kulturen St. Augustin in 1989/90, discuss man's relationship with nature from the context of several of the world's religions.

CR374 Mensen, Bernhard, ed.

Schuld und Versöhnung in verschiedenen Religionen. (Vortragsreihe/Akademie Völker und Kulturen, 9 (1985/86)). Nettetal, GW: Steyler Verlag, 1986. 116 pp. Paper. 3877872107.

Six scholarly essays examining the concepts of offense and reconciliation in Buddhism, Judaism, Islam, Shintoism, and the secular society of West Germany, from the perspective of Roman Catholic theological developments since the Second Vatican Council.

CR375 Montgomery, Robert L.

The Diffusion of Religions: A Sociological Perspective. Lanham, MDU: University Press of America, 1996. xxii, 219 pp. 0761803440 (hdbk), 0761803459 (pbk).

A socio-historical study of variations in the diffusions of Buddhism, Christianity, and Islam, with the nature of intergroup relationships between sending, receiving, and surrounding groups judged to be the key factor.

CR376 Na'im, Abd Allah Ahmad, Jerald D. Gort, Henry Jansen, and Hendrik M. Vroom, eds.

Human Rights and Religious Values: An Uneasy Relationship? (Currents of Encounter, 8). Amsterdam, NE: Editions Rodopi; Grand Rapids, MIU: Eerdmans, 1995. xvii, 291 pp. Paper. 9051837771 (NE), 080280506X (US).

Eighteen papers by Hindu, Buddhist, Christian, Jewish, and Muslim scholars; originally presented at a workshop on "Human Rights and Religious Values" (Free University of Amsterdam, 1993).

CR377 Neill, Stephen Charles

The Supremacy of Jesus. (The Jesus Library). Downers Grove, ILU: InterVarsity, 1984. 174 pp. Paper. 0877849285.

The noted missiologist considers what distinguishes Christ from influential teachers of other faiths.

CR378 Neusner, Jacob, ed.

Sacred Texts and Authority. (The Pilgrim Library of World Religions). Cleveland, OHU: Pilgrim Press, 1998. xviii, 163 pp. Paper. 0829812490.

A comparative analysis of how five religions (Judaism, Islam, Hinduism, Buddhism, and Christianity) regard their sacred texts.

CR379 Neusner, Jacob, ed.

World Religions in America: An Introduction. Louisville, KYU: Westminster John Knox, 2000. xii, 271 pp. Paper. 0664258395.

Revised and expanded edition of an introduction and study guide of fourteen religious loyalties or expressions in the United States, seeking to clarify both how religion shapes American life and how it impacts politics; originally published in 1994.

CR380 Neville, Robert Cummings

Behind the Masks of God: An Essay toward Comparative Theology. Albany, NYU: SUNY Press, 1991. x, 200 pp. 0791405788 (hdbk), 0791405796 (pbk).

A comparative theology of world religions focusing on the concepts of divinity and creativity in Buddhism, Confucianism, and Christianity.

CR381 Neville, Robert Cummings

The Truth of Broken Symbols. (Religious Studies). Albany, NYU: SUNY Press, 1996. xxv, 320 pp. 0791427412 (hdbk), 0791427420 (pbk).

A cross-cultural analysis of how religious symbols function in both theological and philosophical perspectives.

CR382 Occhiogrosso, Peter

The Joy of Sects: A Spirited Guide to the World's Religious Traditions. New York, NYU: Image, 1996. xxx, 626 pp. Paper. 0385425651.

A readable introduction for the interested outsider to the histories, beliefs, laws, rituals, and terminologies of six major world faiths and related traditions from Sikhism to New Age.

CR383 Oddie, Geoffrey A., ed.

Religion in South Asia: Religious Conversion and Revival Movements in South Asia in Medieval and Modern Times. New Delhi, II: Manohar Publications, 1991. viii, 272 pp. 8185425469.

Revised and enlarged edition of twelve case studies of conversions to Islam, Christianity, Buddhism, and the Baha'i faith in India and Sri Lanka, and reconversions to Hinduism; originally published in 1977.

CR384 O'Neill, Maura

Women Speaking, Women Listening: Women in Interreligious Dialogue. Maryknoll, NYU: Orbis Books, 1990. x, 131 pp. 0883446987 (hdbk), 0883446979 (pbk).

O'Neill explains the fact that there are so few women engaged in interreligious dialogue, why such a fact is a liability, and how women can contribute to a more authentic encounter of religious believers.

CR385 Oxtoby, Willard G., ed.

World Religions: Eastern Traditions. Toronto, ONC: Oxford University Press, 1996. 554 pp. Paper. 0195407504.

An introduction to religious traditions of South Asian and East Asian origin, including primal traditions of Asia and the Pacific.

CR386 Oxtoby, Willard G., ed.

World Religions: Western Traditions. Toronto, ONC: Oxford University Press, 1996. 597 pp. Paper. 0195407512.

An introduction to religious traditions of Middle Eastern origin (Judaism, Christianity, and Islam), with chapters on Zoroastranism, Greek and Roman religion, African traditional religion, North American native traditions, religion in pre-Christian Europe, New Age spirituality, and interreligious dialogue.

CR387 Oxtoby, Willard G.
The Meaning of Other Faiths. (Library of Living Faith). Philadelphia, PAU: Westminster Press, 1983. 120 pp. Paper. 0664244432.

An introduction to the meaning for Christians today of the diversity of religions; by the Professor of Religious Studies at the University of Toronto in Canada.

CR388 Paden, William E.
Religious Worlds: The Comparative Study of Religion. Boston, MAU: Beacon Press, 1988. viii, 192 pp. 0807012106 (hbk), 0807012114 (pbk).

A concise and readable conceptual framework for understanding the central categories of thought and ritual of the world's religions.

CR389 Panikkar, Raimundo
Blessed Simplicity: The Monk as Universal Archetype. New York, NYU: Seabury Press, 1982. xi, 202 pp. 081640531X.

Report of a symposium on "The Monk as Universal Archetype" (Holyoke, Massachusetts, Nov. 1980) designed to help North American monks and nuns to discover spiritual values in other religious traditions, with presentations by the author and responses by partipants.

CR390 Panikkar, Raimundo
The Trinity and the Religious Experience of Man: Icon-Person-Mystery. Maryknoll, NYU: Orbis Books; London, ENK: Darton, Longman & Todd, 1973. xvi, 82 pp. Paper. 088344495X (O), 0232512000 (D).

In this monograph the distinguished professor of religious studies at the University of California (Santa Barbara) explores common themes in Hinduism and Christianity (spirituality, trinity and humanity as a "Theandric mystery"); originally published by CLS in 1970.

CR391 Parrinder, Edward Geoffrey
Encountering World Religions: Questions of Religious Truth. New York, NYU: Crossroad Publishing, 1987. vii, 232 pp. 0824508262.

Studies of Buddhism, Shinto, Hinduism, Sikhism, Islam, Judaism, and African religions, with particular reference to intergroup relations and missionary activity.

CR392 Parrinder, Edward Geoffrey
Mysticism in the World's Religions. London, ENK: Sheldon Press, 1976. viii, 210 pp. 0859690857 (hdbk), 0859690865 (pbk).

A survey of mysticism in the world's religions by the distinguished professor of the comparative study of religion at the University of London.

CR393 Parrinder, Edward Geoffrey
Worship in the World's Religions. (Littlefield, Adams Quality Paperback, 316). Totowa, NJU: Littlefield, Adams & Co., 1976. 239 pp. Paper. 0822603160.

A readable comparison of worship, practices, and beliefs in the world's religions.

CR394 Prickett, John, ed.
Initiation Rites: Living Faiths. Guildford, ENK: Lutterworth Educational, 1978. 99 pp. 0718823338.

A comparative study of initiation into adulthood as practiced by seven Christian denominations and seven other faiths in England.

CR395 Randall, Albert B.
Theologies of War and Peace among Jews, Christians, and Muslims. (Toronto Studies in Theology, 77). Lewiston, NYU: E Mellen Press, 1998. v, 476 pp. 0773482547.

Reflections by a Christian teacher of philosophy upon a lifetime of interfaith encounters, and the traditions concerning war and peace of the three Abrahamic faiths.

CR396 Rausch, David A., and Carl Hermann Voss
World Religions: Our Quest for Meaning. Minneapolis, MNU (1989): Fortress Press; Valley Forge, PAU (1991): Trinity Press International, 1989. xv, 212 pp. Paper. 0800623312, 1563380692.

An introductory text to Hinduism, Jainism, Buddhism, Confucianism, Taoism, Shinto, Judaism, Christianity, and Islam through an exploration of the basic belief structure, historical circumstance, and personal practices of adherents to each faith.

CR397 Reat, N. Ross, and Edmund F. Perry
A World Theology: The Central Spiritual Reality of Humankind. Cambridge, ENK: Cambridge University Press, 1991. xi, 314 pp. 0521331595.

A Christian theologian and an atheistic Buddhist philosopher examine five major world religions (Hinduism, Buddhism, Judaism, Christianity, and Islam) to demonstrate that each is a particular expression of one common "world theology."

CR398 Ring, Nancy C. et al., eds.
Introduction to the Study of Religion. Maryknoll, NYU: Orbis Books, 1998. x, 340 pp. Paper. 1570751838.

An introductory college textbook on basic questions that arise in the study of religion, including personal and communal religious change.

CR399 Rouner, Leroy S., ed.
Human Rights and the World's Religions. (Boston University Studies In Religion and Philosophy, 9). Notre Dame, INU: University of Notre Dame Press, 1988. xviii, 220 pp. 0268010862.

Twelve scholarly essays which together provide a comparative analysis of human rights perspectives in Buddhism, Confucianism, Hinduism, Islam, Judaism, Christianity, and Marxism.

CR400 Ruland, Vernon
Imagining the Sacred: Soundings in World Religions. (Faith Meets Faith Series). Maryknoll, NYU: Orbis Books, 1998. vii, 309 pp. Paper. 1570752095.

An introduction to what it means to live, wonder, think, and pray in eight religious traditions, from the primal way, to major world faiths, to humanism; designed for classroom use by the Jesuit Professor of World Religions at the University of San Francisco.

CR401 Sacerdoce et prophetie dans le Christianisme et les autres religions: Priesthood and Prophecy in Christianity and Other Religions
(Studia Missionalia, 22). Rome, IT: Gregorian University Press, 1973. 370 pp. Paper. No ISBN.

A collection of sixteen essays on priesthood and prophecy in Christianity and other religions, written in English, German, French, and Italian.

CR402 Samartha, Stanley J., ed.
Living Faiths and Ultimate Goals: A Continuing Dialogue. Geneva, SZ: WCC, 1974. xvii, 119 pp. Paper. 282540490X.

Nine papers by scholars of various faiths on the lasting values in their religious traditions; prepared as working documents for the WCC's World Conference on Mission and Evangelism (Bangkok, 29 December 1972 to 8 January 1973).

CR403 Schuon, Frithjof
Light on the Ancient Worlds. Translated by Lord Northbourne. Bloomington, INU: World Wisdom Books, 1984. 144 pp. Paper. 0941532038.

A second edition of the English translation of *Regards sur les mondes anciens* (1968).

CR404 Schuon, Frithjof
Regards sur les mondes anciens. Paris, FR: Éditions traditionnelles, 1976. 183 pp. No ISBN.

Second edition of an argument, by the noted philosopher of religion, that every healthy civilization is founded on an invisible or underlying religion; with comparative analyses of early Christian, Hellenistic, Hindu, Muslim, and Native American worldviews.

CR405 Schuon, Frithjof
Sobre los Mundos Antiguos. (Biblioteca de estudios tradicionales, 1). Madrid, SP: Taurus, 1980. 157 pp. 8430650016.
Spanish translation.

CR406 Schweizer, Gerhard
Ungläubig sind immer die anderen: Weltreligionen zwischen Toleranz und Fanatismus. Stuttgart, GW: Klett-Cotta, 1990. 364 pp. 3608931503.

Faced with the call of world religions for dialogue and openness, this work investigates the question of tolerance in religions, coming to the conclusion that, in the future, both dialogue and delimitation are necessary.

CR407 Scott, Jamie S., and Paul Simpson-Housley, eds.
Sacred Places and Profane Spaces: Essays in the Geographics of Judaism, Christianity, and Islam. (Contributions to the Study of Religion, 30). New York, NYU: Greenwood, 1991. xiv, 200 pp. 0313263299.

An interdisciplinary project in the study of religion and geography, in which nine scholars present essays on the symbolic role of particular sacred sites in Judaism, Christianity, and Islam.

CR408 Sharma, Arvind, ed.
Religion and Women. (McGill Studies in the History of Religions). Albany, NYU: SUNY Press, 1994. xi, 291 pp. 0791416895 (hdbk), 0791416909 (pbk).

Scholarly essays on women in the North American, African, Shinto, Jain, Zoroastrian, Sikh, and Baha'i religious traditions.

CR409 Sharma, Arvind, ed.
Today's Woman in World Religions. (McGill Studies in the History of Religions). Albany, NYU: SUNY Press, 1994. xii, 459 pp. 0791416879 (hdbk), 0791416887 (pbk).

Scholarly essays on women in seven traditions: Hinduism, Buddhism, Confucianism, Taoism, Judaism, Christianity, and Islam.

CR410 Shenk, David W.
Global Gods: Exploring the Role of Religions in Modern Societies. Scottdale, PAU: Herald Press, 1999. 400 pp. Paper. 0836190068.

Second edition of a comparative exploration of ten contemporary world religions, philosophies, and ideologies, asking how they are challenged, confronted, and sometimes transformed by realities of modernity and the search for quality global well-being; first published in 1995.

CR411 Siriwardena, Reggie, ed.
Equality and the Religious Traditions of Asia. New York, NYU: St. Martin's Press, 1987. 173 pp. 031200401X.

Eight essays exploring concepts and attitudes toward social equality in Hindu, Buddhist, Taoist, Muslim, and Jewish traditions.

CR412 Smart, Ninian
Religions of the West. Englewood Cliffs, NJU: Prentice-Hall, 1994. 272 pp. Paper. 0131568116.

A comparative analysis of the value systems of Judaism, Christianity, and Islam, using a typology of seven dimensions of religion.

CR413 Smart, Ninian
The Religious Experience of Mankind. New York, NYU: Scribner, 1983. xxii, 634 pp. 0684180774 (hdbk), 0684180782 (pbk).

Third edition of a standard introduction to the religions of each continent of the world.

CR414 Smart, Ninian, and B. Srinivasa Murthy, eds.
East-West Encounters in Philosophy and Religion. Long Beach, CAU: Long Beach Publications, 1996. xxii, 411 pp. 0941910075.

Thirty essays on comparative philosophies, religions, ethics, and cultures; originally presented at the East Meets West conferences (Mysore, India, 1991, and Long Beach, California, 1993).

CR415 Smith, Huston
The World's Religions. San Francisco, CAU: HarperSanFrancisco, 1991. xvi, 399 pp. 0062507990 (hdbk), 0062508113 (pbk).

A completely revised and updated edition of the most widely used introduction in English to the world's religions.

CR416 Smith, Wilfred Cantwell
Faith and Belief. Princeton, NJU: Princeton University Press, 1979. ix, 347 pp. 0691072329.

A comparative study of the nature of faith and belief in Buddhist, Hindu, Islamic, and Christian traditions by the noted Professor of the Comparative History of Religion at Harvard University.

CR417 Smith, Wilfred Cantwell
The Faith of Other Men. New York, NYU: New American Library, 1963. 140 pp. No ISBN.

Essays by the distinguished professor of religions at Harvard University, focusing on the religious qualities of the lives of believers of six faith traditions.

CR—CHRISTIANITY AND OTHER RELIGIONS

CR418 Smock, David R.
Perspectives on Pacifism: Christian, Jewish, and Muslim Views on Nonviolence and International Conflict. (Perspectives Series). Washington, DCU: United States Institute of Peace Press, 1995. ix, 74 pp. Paper. 1878379429.

Papers from a 1993 symposium on religious perspectives on pacifism, sponsored by the United States Institute of Peace.

CR419 Steenbrink, Karel A.
Adam Redivivus: Muslim Elaborations of the Adam Saga with Special Reference to the Indonesian Literary Traditions. (IIMO Research Publication, 49). Zoetermeer, NE: Meinema, 1998. 196 pp. Paper. 9021170191.

This study shows the similarity of developments between Jewish, Christian, and Muslim traditions based on the common concept of Adam, but includes the variety of religious cultures within each tradition.

CR420 Swidler, Leonard J., and Paul Mojzes, eds.
Attitudes of Religions and Ideologies toward the Outsider: The Other. (Religions in Dialogue, 1). Lewiston, NYU: E Mellen Press, 1990. x, 202 pp. 0889462704.

Twelve scholarly essays by representatives of the world's major faiths and ideologies—part of the GEO-DAPRI project on "Global Education on Dialogue and Peace among Religions and Ideologies."

CR421 Swidler, Leonard J.
The Meaning of Life at the Edge of the Third Millennium. New York, NYU: Paulist Press, 1992. v, 116 pp. Paper. 0809133156.

A concise comparative study of what various religious traditions say about "the ultimate reality," including what is universal and what is unique about the life and message of Yeshua of Nazareth; by the Professor of Catholic Thought and Interreligious Dialogue at Temple University (USA).

CR422 Thomas, Keith, ed.
Founders of Faith. Oxford, UNK: Oxford University Press, 1989. 376 pp. Paper. 019283066X.

Four self-contained studies of the founders of the world's great religious traditions (The Buddha, Confucius, Jesus, and Muhammad), with analysis of the traditions and ways in which men and women in both East and West have sought to make sense of the problems of human experience.

CR423 Thomas, Madathilparapil M.
Man and the Universe of Faiths. (Interreligious Dialogue Series, 7). Madras, II: CLS, 1975. xiii, 161 pp. Paper. No ISBN.

Analysis by the prominent Indian ecumenical leader of the transformations, both socio-political and religious, taking place in the modern world, with focus on the ways that the religions and ideologies are reinterpreting their understandings of God, humanity, and the world as they grapple with the forces and spirit of modernity.

CR424 Thottakkara, Augustine, ed.
Dialogical Dynamics of Religions. (Chavara Lectures, 3). Rome, IT: Centre for Indian and Interreligious Studies; Bangalore, II: Dharmaram Publications, 1993. iv, 156 pp. Paper. No ISBN.

Seven lectures by Catholic theologians (J. Pathrapankal, S. Thurathiyil, S. Elavthingal, and J. Dupuis) on various aspects of the relations among world religions; delivered as the Third Chavara Lectures (Rome, 1993).

CR425 Vroom, Hendrik M.
Religions and the Truth: Philosophical Reflections and Perspectives. (Currents of Encounter Series). Grand Rapids, MIU: Eerdmans; Amsterdam, NE: Rodopi, 1989. 388 pp. Paper. 0802805027.

The author, an Associate Professor of the Philosophy of Religion at the Free University in Amsterdam, seeks first to understand the nature of truth in interreligious perspective and Western philosophy, then to describe truth from Hindu, Buddhist, Jewish, Christian, and Islamic perspectives, and lastly to analyze "the meaning of truth in religion and interreligious encounter, describing religious traditions as 'multifaceted belief systems' which both overlap and exhibit differences."

CR426 Waardenburg, Jacques, ed.
Muslim Perceptions of Other Religions: A Historical Survey. New York, NYU: Oxford University Press, 1999. xv, 350 pp. 0195104722.

A scholarly collection of twenty articles on Muslim studies of other religions in early, medieval, and modern eras; includes a selected bibliography.

CR427 Wach, Joachim
Essays in the History of Religions. Edited by Joseph Mitsuo Kitagawa and Gregory D. Alles. New York, NYU: Macmillan; London, ENK: Collier Macmillan, 1988. xxii, 202 pp. 0029335205.

Eight articles (some previously unpublished) on the history of religions as presented from each phase of Wach's scholarly career, reflecting his intellectual pilgrimage from 1925 to 1962.

CR428 Ward, Keith
Images of Eternity: Concepts of God in Five Religious Traditions. London, ENK: Darton, Longman & Todd, 1987. viii, 197 pp. Paper. 0232516863.

Original interpretations of major texts by representative theologians of five world faiths, by the Professor of History and Philosophy of Religion at London University.

CR429 Westwood, Jennifer
Sacred Journeys: An Illustrated Guide to Pilgrimages around the World. New York, NYU: Henry Holt & Co., 1997. 223 pp. 0805048456.

A full-color introduction to major pilgrimage sites, mostly related to world faiths.

CR430 Whaling, Frank, ed.
Religion in Today's World: The Religious Situation of the World from 1945 to the Present Day. Edinburgh, ENK: T&T Clark, 1987. viii, 383 pp. 0567094529.

Thirteen essays designed as introductions to the five major religious traditions, religion in China and Japan, civil religion, cults and new religious movements, secular worldviews, spirituality, and the study of religion in today's world.

CR431 Wilson, Howard A.
Invasion from the East. Minneapolis, MNU: Augsburg, 1978. 160 pp. Paper. 0806616717.

A sympathetic analysis of the resurgence of Eastern religions, identifying their major features, interpreting their attractions for Westerners, and suggesting what Christians can learn from these developments.

CR432 Wilson, Rodney
Economics, Ethics and Religion: Jewish, Christian and Muslim Economic Thought. New York, NYU: New York University Press, 1997. ix, 233 pp. 0814793134.

A comparative study of economic ethics in Judaism, Christianity, and Islam.

CR433 Yeow, Choo Lak, ed.
Doing Theology with Religions of Asia. (ATESEA Occasional Papers, 4). Singapore, SI: ATESEA, 1987. 187 pp. Paper. No ISBN.

Fifteen scholarly papers dealing with theological interactions of Southeast Asian Christians with persons of other faiths, on levels affecting the lives of believers, their communities, and their nations.

CR434 Zaehner, Robert Charles
Christianity and Other Religions. (*The Twentieth Century Encyclopedia of Catholicism*, 146, Section 15: Non-Christian Beliefs). New York, NYU: Hawthorn Books, 1964. 148 pp. No ISBN.

An introduction for Roman Catholics to the religions of India, China, Japan, and the Islamic world to help the church make its message and life appealing to these other seekers after God; also published as *The Catholic Church and World Religions* (Burns & Oates, 1964).

CR435 Zaehner, Robert Charles
The Convergent Spirit: Towards a Dialetics of Religion. (Religious Perspectives, 8). London, ENK: Routledge, 1963. 210 pp. No ISBN.

The noted religionist attempts to show that the history of humankind, from its evolutionary beginnings, may be regarded as a vast *preparatio evangelica* for the union of all humankind within the mystical body of Christ.

CR436 Zaehner, Robert Charles
El Cristianismo y las Grandes Religiones de Asia. Barcelona, SP: Editorial Herder, 1967. 230 pp. Paper. No ISBN.

Spanish translation.

CR437 Zaehner, Robert Charles
Matter and Spirit: Their Convergence in Eastern Religions, Marx, and Teilhard de Chardin. (Religious Perspectives, 8). New York, NYU: Harper & Row, 1963. 210 pp. No ISBN.

A difficult but unique and significant study—important for all concerned with theology, the sociology of religion, and the Christian world mission in our era; originally published in Great Britain as *The Convergent Spirit: Towards a Dialetias of Religion.*

Interreligious Dialogue: General

See also HI106, TH183, TH195, TH259, TH439, TH589, EA91, EA192-EA193, EA201, CR2-CR3, CR59, CR71, CR99, CR111, CR121, CR141, CR172, CR212, CR233, CR244, CR248, CR258, CR265, CR420, CR446, CR703, CR721, CR860, CR885, CR1151, CR1448, CR1460, SO440, PO216, ED97, EV218, SP86, SP162, AF644, AM899, AS50, AS107, AS839, AS889, AS902, EU140, and EU147.

CR438 Åmell, Katrin
Contemplation et dialogue: quelques exemples de dialogue entre spiritualités après le concile Vatican II. (Studia Missionalia Upsaliensia, 70). Uppsala, SW: Swedish Institute of Missionary Research, 1998. 248 pp. Paper. 9185424501.

A dissertation (Uppsala University) surveying 20th century missiological theologies of interreligious dialogue, Benedictine initiatives from the 1960s to 1990s, Japanese Catholic dialogues with Zen Buddhists, and recent dialogues focusing on comparative religious experiences.

CR439 Amaladoss, Michael
Walking Together: The Practice of Interreligious Dialogue. (Jesuit Theological Forum Reflections, 7). Anand, II: Gujarat Sahitya Prakash, 1992. ix, 185 pp. No ISBN.

A collection of twelve essays by the noted Indian Jesuit theologian on various dimensions of contemporary interreligious dialogue.

CR440 Anawati, Georges C. et al.
Missionaire wegen voor morgen. (De grote oecumene: interreligieuze ontwikkelingen). Hilversum, NE: Paul Brand, 1967. 326 pp. No ISBN.

A survey of Roman Catholic relations with other faiths and with Protestant churches and missions.

CR441 Ariarajah, S. Wesley, ed.
Not Without My Neighbour: Issues in Interfaith Relations. (Risk Book Series, 85). Geneva, SZ: WCC Publications, 1999. 130 pp. Paper. 2825413089.

Drawing upon experiences as a participant in interfaith dialogue with the WCC, as a Methodist pastor in Sri Lanka and as a student of Hinduism, the author explores key issues that arise in interfaith dialogue.

CR442 Askari, Hasan
Spiritual Quest: An Interreligious Dimension. Pudsey, ENK: Seven Mirrors Publishing House, 1991. x, 139 pp. Paper. 1873685009.

Essays on major themes in interreligious dialogue by a prominent Muslim participant during the past twenty years.

CR443 Aubert, Jean Marie, and Gilles Couvreur
Mission et dialogue interreligieux. Lyon, FR: Profac, 1990. 217 pp. Paper. 285317042X.

The sourcebook for a course on "Mission and Interreligious Dialogue" in the Faculty of Theology of the University of Lyon in France, including fifteen short essays on various aspects (historical, theological, missiological, and ecclesiological) for the Catholic Church since Vatican II.

CR444 Aumann, Jordan et al.
Asian Religious Traditions and Christianity. (Thomasian Forum, 2). Manila, PH: University of Santo Tomas, Faculty of Theology, 1983. 272 pp. No ISBN.

Ten scholarly essays by Catholic theologians on Christian dialogue with the various religions of Asia, plus three documents by the Vatican and the Asian bishops on such dialogue.

CR445 Bühlmann, Walbert
Alle haben denselben Gott: Begegnung mit den Menschen und Religionen Asiens. Frankfurt am Main, GW: Knecht, 1978. 223 pp. 3782004140.

A narrative report by the secretary general of the Capuchin missions on the developing sensitivities of Asian theologians and missionaries to the great Asian religions, based on the documents of twenty years of interreligious dialogues and his acquaintance with the participants.

CR446 Bakker, R. et al., eds.

Religies in nieuw perspectief: Studies over interreligieuze dialoog en religiositeit op het grondvlak. Kampen, NE: Kok, 1985. 176 pp. Paper. 9024207312.

A *festschrift* for Prof. D. C. Mulder, with a number of articles on interreligious dialogue and popular religion by Stanley Samartha, Hasan Askari, and others.

CR447 Barbosa da Silva, António, and Hans Ucko

Mission-dialog: Förmedling av Evangelium i en sekulariserad värld. (KISA-rapport, 1). Uppsala, SW: Kyrkans internationella studieavdelning-KISA, 1988. 108 pp. No ISBN.

Five articles on interfaith dialogue and the Gospel in an age of secularization.

CR448 Barla, John Berchmans

Christian Theological Understanding of Other Religions according to D. S. Amalorpavadass. (Documenta Missionalia, 26). Rome, IT: Editrice Pontificia Università Gregoriana, 1999. 484 pp. Paper. 8876528199.

This theological inquiry into the question of religious pluralism is divided into three parts: the biblical and Vatican II sources with regard to other religions, Jesus Christ and religions, and the church and religions.

CR449 Barnes, Michael

Walking the City: Christian Discipleship in a Pluralist World. Delhi, II: ISPCK, 1999. xiii, 119 pp. Paper. 8172145357.

This study of the mission of Christianity in a world of many faiths calls for a process of communication by which people learn to live alongside and understand one another.

CR450 Basset, Jean-Claud

Le dialogue interreligieux: chance ou déchéance de la foi. (Cogitatio Fidei, 197). Paris, FR: Éditions du Cerf, 1996. 503 pp. Paper. 2204054070.

A historical and typological analysis of interreligious dialogues during the 1970-1990 period, including a fifty-page bibliography.

CR451 Berkey, Robert F., and Sarah A. Edwards, eds.

Christology in Dialogue. Cleveland, OHU: Pilgrim Press, 1993. viii, 390 pp. Paper. 0829809562.

Twenty-three scholarly essays on contemporary Christological affirmations as influenced by new scholarship in New Testament and classical studies, and the ongoing dialogue of Christians with persons of other faiths and with contemporary culture.

CR452 Berthrong, John H.

The Divine Deli: Religious Identity in the North American Cultural Mosaic. (Faith Meets Faith Series). Maryknoll, NYU: Orbis Books, 1999. xxvi, 163 pp. Paper. 1570752680.

In a day when individuals choose a combination of religious beliefs like a delicatessen menu, the author questions whether the combinations will have the power to stem the forces of impending ecological disaster, give strength in trials, and bring justice among the nations.

CR453 Brück, Michael von

Möglichkeiten und Grenzen einer Theologie der Religionen. (Theologische Arbeiten, 38). Berlin, GW: Evan Verlagsanstalt, 1979. 248 pp. Paper. No ISBN.

A dissertation (University of Rostock, 1995) addressing the problem of dialogue and the community of religions, not only on an intellectual level but also in everyday life and meditation.

CR454 Braybrooke, Marcus

Faith and Interfaith in a Global Age. Grand Rapids, MIU: CoNexus Press; Oxford, ENK: Braybrooke Press, 1998. 144 pp. Paper. 0963789724 (US), 0951688359 (UK).

A leader in international interfaith activities, the author tells the story of this world wide movement, which began with the 1893 World's Parliament of Religions; includes centennial events of 1993 and then focuses on the development of the movement through 1997.

CR455 Bryant, M. Darrol, and Frank K. Flinn, eds.

Interreligious Dialogue: Voices from a New Frontier. New York, NYU: Paragon House, 1989. xx, 234 pp. 089226067X.

Twenty-five essays by representatives of seven faiths; based on presentations made at the Assembly of the World's Religions (McAfee, New Jersey, US, Nov. 1985).

CR456 Bryant, M. Darrol, ed.

Pluralism, Tolerance and Dialogue: Six Studies. (Religion and Canadian Pluralism, 2). Waterloo, ONC: University of Waterloo Press, 1989. x, 150 pp. Paper. 0888980965.

Six scholarly papers with responses from an ongoing series of faculty colloquia, sponsored by the Department of Religious Studies at the University of Waterloo, Canada.

CR457 Camps, Arnulf

Christendom en godsdiensten der wereld: Nieuwe inzichten en nieuwe activiteiten. (Ökumene 6, 7). Baarn, NE: Bosch & Keuning, 1976. 104 pp. Paper. 902463086X.

Second part of a general study on the dialogue of religions, formulating concepts and strategies of dialogue with concrete religious traditions (Islam, Hinduism, Buddhism, as well as local traditions in Japan, Africa, Latin America, and China).

CR458 Camps, Arnulf

Geen doodlopende weg: Lokale kerken in dialoog met hun omgeving. (Ökumene 2, 10). Baarn, NE: Ten Have, 1978. 108 pp. Paper. 9025951058.

Third part of a study on the dialogue of religions, concentrating on local churches, inculturation, and pluriformity in theology and liturgy.

CR459 Camps, Arnulf

Partners in Dialogue: Christianity and Other World Religions. Maryknoll, NYU: Orbis Books, 1983. viii, 264 pp. 0883443783.

English translation.

CR460 Copeland, E. Luther

A New Meeting of the Religions: Interreligious Relationships and Theological Questioning. Waco, TXU: Baylor University Press, 1999. ix, 179 pp. 0918954711.

The author demonstrates that one can affirm the Christian mission internationally and interculturally, without diminishing either the importance of good interreligious relationships or the recognition of the worth of the major religions.

CR461 Cox, Harvey Gallagher

Many Mansions: A Christian's Encounter with Other Faiths. Boston, MAU: Beacon Press, 1988. 216 pp. 0807012084.

A collection of nine personal essays by the noted Harvard University theologian, arguing the importance of serious interfaith dialogue and investigating what pluralism of the postmodern world means for Christians.

CR462 Cracknell, Kenneth

Mission und Dialog: Für eine neue Beziehung zu Menschen anderen Glaubens. Frankfurt am Main, GW: Lembeck, 1990. 160 pp. Paper. 387476253X.

German translation of *Towards a New Relationship* (1986).

CR463 Cracknell, Kenneth

Towards a New Relationship: Christians and People of Other Faiths. London, ENK: Epworth Press, 1986. viii, 198 pp. Paper. 0716204215.

A BCC study on ethical issues in interfaith relations and how they confront Christians in their understandings of religious pluralism, by the Executive Secretary of the BCC Committee for Relations with People of Other Faiths.

CR464 Cragg, Kenneth

The Christ and the Faiths. Philadelphia, PAU: Westminster Press, 1987. xii, 360 pp. Paper. 0664250009.

A scholarly analysis of the frontiers of interreligious theological encounter of Christians with Muslims, Jews, Hindus, and Buddhists.

CR465 Cragg, Kenneth

The Christian and Other Religions: The Measure of Christ. London, ENK: Mowbrays, 1977. xiv, 138 pp. 0264664132 (hdbk), 0264662563 (pbk).

Reflections by the noted Christian Islamicist on themes and approaches by which Christians can present their faith to those of other religions.

CR466 Cragg, Kenneth

Faith and Life Negotiate: A Christian Story-Study. Norwich, ENK: Canterbury Press, 1994. 331 pp. Paper. 1853110884.

A personal reflection by Bishop Cragg on the theological and practical interrelation of religious faiths and their communities, including his own wide experience in Christian dialogue with Jews and Muslims.

CR467 Cragg, Kenneth

To Meet and to Greet: Faith with Faith. London, ENK: Epworth Press, 1992. 216 pp. Paper. 0716204835.

Guidance for Christians seeking to deepen relationships with persons of other faiths, based on the author's lifetime study of the teachings of Jesus, of Islam, and of interreligious dialogue.

CR468 Cragg, Kenneth

Troubled by Truth: Biographics in the Preserve of Mystery. Durham, ENK: Pentland Press, 1992; Cleveland, OHU: Pilgrim Press, 1994. viii, 320 pp. 1872793714 (Pentland, 0829810056 (Pilgrim).

Through telling the stories of the quest for truth in a religiously plural world by thirteen contemporary Christian, Jewish, and Muslim leaders, the noted Christian interpreter of Islam explores themes for interreligious dialogue.

CR469 D'Costa, Gavin, ed.

Faith Meets Faith: Interfaith Views on Interfaith. London, ENK: BFSS, 1988. 82 pp. No ISBN.

A valuable collection of essays from people of different faiths living in London, England.

CR470 Eck, Diana L.

Encountering God: A Spiritual Journey from Bozeman to Banaras. Boston, MAU: Beacon Press, 1993. xv, 259 pp. 0807073024 (hdbk), 0807073032 (pbk).

A collection of essays on interreligious dialogue by the Professor of Comparative Religion and Indian Studies at Harvard University, who for fifteen years has been involved in the interfaith dialogue program of the WCC.

CR471 Forward Studies Unit at the European Commission, ed.

The Mediterranean Society: A Challenge for Islam, Judaism and Christianity. (Forward Studies Series). New York, NYU: St. Martin's Press; Luxembourg City, LU: Office for Official Publications of the European Communities, 1998. viii, 87 pp. 0312216009.

Papers from the Toledo Conference (Toledo, Spain, 4-7 November 1995) sponsored by the European Commission to stimulate interreligious dialogue by representatives of all the religious and philosophical traditions of the Mediterranean basin, with special attention to the role of women.

CR472 Friedli, Richard

Fremdheit als Heimat: Auf der Suche nach einem Kriterium für den Dialog zwischen den Religionen. (Ökumenische Beihefte zur Freiburger Zeitschrift für Philosophie und Theologie, 8). Freiburg, SZ: Universitätsverlag, 1974. 214 pp. 3727801085.

An analysis by a missionary in Rwanda of the significance of cultural attitudes toward *der Fremde* (the alien, the stranger, the foreigner) as a significant factor in interreligious dialogue.

CR473 Fu, Charles Wei-hsun, and Gerhard E. Spiegler, eds.

Religious Issues and Interreligious Dialogues: An Analysis and Sourcebook of Developments since 1945. Westport, CTU: Greenwood, 1989. x, 693 pp. 0313232393.

A comprehensive collection of twenty-seven scholarly articles which attempt to force a reexamination of basic concerns in religion, religious belief, and religious studies, while reshaping attitudes toward meaningful dialogue among persons of different religious groups.

CR474 Gort, Jerald D. et al., eds.

Dialogue and Syncretism: An Interdisciplinary Approach. (Currents of Encounter Series). Grand Rapids, MIU: Eerdmans; Amsterdam, NE: Rodopi, 1989. 228 pp. Paper. 0802805019.

In this work seventeen world-renowned experts in theology, philology, comparative religion, and cultural anthropology seek first to fully understand the phenomenon of syncretism, then to present case studies of syncretism in interreligious encounter, and finally to draw some conclusions about interreligious dialogue and its relation to syncretism.

CR475 Gort, Jerald D. et al., eds.

On Sharing Religious Experience: Possibilities of Interfaith Mutuality. (Currents of Encounter, 4). Amsterdam, NE: Editions Rodopi; Grand Rapids, MIU: Eerdmans, 1992. xi, 304 pp. 9051832079 (R), 0802805051 (E).

Twenty-two scholarly essays on possibilities and practices of interreligious sharing of religious experience; originally presented at the second international workshop on this theme (Amsterdam; Free University, 1990).

CR476 Griffiths, Paul J.

An Apology for Apologetics: A Study in the Logic of Interreligious Dialogue. (Faith Meets Faith Series). Maryknoll, NYU: Orbis Books, 1991. xii, 113 pp. 0883447622 (hdbk), 0883447614 (pbk).

A rigorously-argued analysis of how apologetics is a vital component of any sound effort at interreligious dialogue.

CR—CHRISTIANITY AND OTHER RELIGIONS

CR477 Grose, George Benedict, and J. Benjamin Hubbard, eds.

The Abraham Connection: A Jew, Christian and Muslim in Dialogue. (The Church and the World Series, 6). Notre Dame, INU: Cross Cultural Publications, 1994. xxxiii, 243 pp. Paper. 0940121182.

Transcript of a live dialogue between representatives of Judaism (Gordis), Christianity (Grose), and Islam (Siddiqi); sponsored by the Academy for Judaic, Christian, and Islamic Studies in 1991.

CR478 Hallencreutz, Carl F.

Dialogue and Community: Ecumenical Issues in Inter-Religious Relationships. (Studia Missionalia Upsaliensia, 31). Uppsala, SW: Swedish Institute of Missionary Research; Geneva, SZ: WCC, 1977. 109 pp. Paper. 9185424021.

A missiological and theological study of interfaith dialogue as it has developed within the WCC and the Catholic Church since the 1960s.

CR479 *Heil voor deze wereld: Studies aangeboden aan prof. dr. A.G. Honig jr*

Kampen, NE: Kok, 1984. 213 pp. Paper. 9024230721.

A *festschrift* entitled "Salvation for this World" containing thirteen scholarly essays on understandings of salvation in interreligious and interfaith dialogue, honoring Professor A. G. Honig, Jr. of the Higher School of Theology, Kampen, the Netherlands.

CR480 Hengsbach, Franz, ed.

Nuovi orizzonti del dialoguo missionario. Parma, IT: Instituto Saveriano Missioni Estere, 1967. 332 pp. No ISBN.

Nineteen short essays by Roman Catholic missiologists on interreligious dialogue in various countries, in response to *Ad Gentes* of Vatican II.

CR481 Hoedemaker, L. A.

Met Christus bij anderen: Opmerkingen over dialoog en apostolaat. (Œkumene 4:9). Baarn, NE: Ten Have, 1978. 109 pp. Paper. 9025951023.

Dialogue of religions as one of the utmost consequences of a dialectical theology; a missiological study by one of the most prominent students of Prof. Hoekendijk.

CR482 Honig, A. G.

Meru en Golgotha: De veelheid der verlossingswegen en de belijdenis aangaande Jezus Christus als de enige verlosser. Franeker, NE: Wever, 1969. 355 pp. Paper. No ISBN.

Meru, a volcano in Indonesia, often considered as the dwelling place of the divinity in Javanese mythology, is placed opposite Golgotha in this theological confrontation between non-Christian religions and the message of the Gospel, with Honig taking a position somewhere between Van Leeuwen and John Hick.

CR483 Jai Singh, Herbert, ed.

Inter-Religious Dialogue. (Devanandan Memorial, 3). Bangalore, II: CISRS, 1967. viii, 237 pp. No ISBN.

Essays on dialogue by missionaries and Indian church leaders.

CR484 Jathanna, C. D., ed.

Dialogue in Community: Essays in Honour of Stanley J. Samartha. Mangalore, II: Karnataka Theological Research Institute, 1982. xii, 259 pp. Paper. No ISBN.

Sixteen essays on interfaith dialogue written as a *festschrift* honoring Dr. Stanley J. Samartha, Director of the WCC Programme on Dialogue with People of Living Faiths and Ideologies, and first Indian Principal of the Karnataka Theological College.

CR485 Küng, Hans et al.

Christianity & World Religions: Paths of Dialogue with Islam, Hinduism, and Buddhism. Translated by Peter Heinegg. Maryknoll, NYU: Orbis Books, 1993. xx, 460 pp. Paper. 0883448580.

Second edition of an English translation of *Christentum und Weltreligionen* (Piper Verlag, 1985).

CR486 Küng, Hans

Global Responsibility: In Search of a New World Ethic. Translated by John Bowden. New York, NYU: Crossroad Publishing, 1991. xix, 158 pp. 0824511026.

English translation.

CR487 Küng, Hans

Projekt Weltethos. Munich, GW: Piper, 1990. 191 pp. 349234268.

A call by the noted Catholic theologian to intensified interreligious dialogue for the sake of peace in the new polycentric, transcultural, and multireligious world.

CR488 Küng, Hans

Proyecto de una Ética Mundial. Translated by Gilberto Canal Marcos. (Colección Estructuras y Procesos, Serie Religión). Madrid, SP: Editorial Trotta, 1992. 174 pp. 848769912X.

Spanish translation.

CR489 Küng, Hans, and Jürgen Moltmann, eds.

Christianity among World Religions. (*Concilium*: Religion in the Eighties, 183). Edinburgh, STK: T&T Clark, 1986. xv, 130 pp. Paper. 0567300633.

Thirteen scholarly essays by noted religionists of various faiths on themes important for interreligious dialogue between Christians and followers of Islam, Hinduism, Buddhism, and Chinese religions.

CR490 Küng, Hans, Josef van Ess, and Heinrich von Stietencron

Christentum und Weltreligionen: Hinführung zum Dialog mit Islam, Hinduismus und Buddhismus. Munich, GW: Piper, 1984. 631 pp. 3492029356 (hdbk), 3492020396 (jacket).

As an introduction to the field of religions and a solidly based interreligious dialogue, this work comprises four articles each by three experts on Islam, Hinduism, and Buddhism, and Christian responses to them by Hans Küng.

CR491 Kasimow, Harold, and Byron L. Sherwin, eds.

No Religion Is an Island: Abraham Joshua Heschel and Interreligious Dialogue. Maryknoll, NYU: Orbis Books, 1991. xxv, 205 pp. Paper. 088344769X.

Thirteen reflective essays on Rabbi Abraham Joshua Heschel (1907-1972) and his thought concerning religious pluralism and interreligious dialogue.

CR492 Kerkhofs, Jan, and Antonin Marcel Henry, eds.

Dialogue d'aujourd'hui, mission de demain. Tours, FR: Mame; Paris, FR: Éditions du Cerf, 1968. 326 pp. No ISBN.

Eighteen essays by an international panel of Roman Catholic missiologists and church leaders, on dialogue with persons of varied faiths and ideologies, as well as training for dialogue in varied contexts.

CR493 Kerkhofs, Jan, ed.

Modern Mission Dialogue: Theory and Practice. New York, NYU: Newman Press, 1969. xxii, 263 pp. No ISBN.

English translation.

CR—CHRISTIANITY AND OTHER RELIGIONS

CR494 Kirste, Reinhard, Paul Schwarzenau, and Udo Tworuschka, eds.
Engel, Elemente, Energien. (Religionen im Gespräch, 2). Balve, GW: Zimmermann Druck, 1992. 716 pp. 3890530435.

A collection of scholarly articles by an international panel of religion specialists, including thirteen contributions on general questions of interreligious dialogue, plus essays on understandings of angels, elements, and energies in various religious traditions.

CR495 Kirste, Reinhard, Paul Schwarzenau, and Udo Tworuschka, eds.
Interreligiöser Dialog zwischen Tradition und Moderne. (Religionen im Gespräch, 3). Balve, GW: Zimmermann Druck, 1994. 512 pp. Paper. 3890530435.

A collection of essays by international scholars on fundamental problems of interreligious dialogue, and on the specific themes of tradition, modernity, and postmodernity, and their relationship with interreligious dialogue.

CR496 Kirste, Reinhard, Paul Schwarzenau, and Udo Tworuschka, eds.
Wertewandel und Religiöse Umbrüche. (Religionen im Gespräch, 4). Balve, GW: Zimmermann Druck, 1996. 671 pp. 3890530613.

A collection of essays by leading international scholars on fundamental problems of interreligious dialogue.

CR497 Knitter, Paul F.
One Earth Many Religions: Multifaith Dialogue and Global Responsibility. Maryknoll, NYU: Orbis Books, 1995. xiv, 218 pp. Paper. 1570750378.

A well-reasoned argument by the general editor of Orbis' Faith Meets Faith Series that a globally responsible interfaith dialogue should focus on issues of ecojustice.

CR498 Kroeger, James H., ed.
Interreligious Dialogue: Catholic Perspectives. Davao City, PH: Mission Studies Institute, 1990. 103 pp. Paper. 9715011071.

A collection of readings and documents, with study guide, designed to present the Roman Catholic position on interfaith dialogue as it is currently understood.

CR499 Kuttianimattathil, Jose
Practice and Theology of Interreligious Dialogue: A Critical Study of the Indian Christian Attempts since Vatican II. Bangalore, II: Kristu Jyoti Publications, 1995. xxiii, 757 pp. No ISBN.

A detailed history of developments in interreligious dialogue in India from 1965 to 1993.

CR500 Lamb, Christopher
Belief in a Mixed Society. Sutherland, AT: Lion Publishing, 1985. 160 pp. Paper. 0867605774, 0856482102.

An analysis of the cultural factors important in religious pluralism between Christians and Muslims, both in Asia and in Great Britain, including differing values and customs concerning food, health, morality, law, work, education, marriage, and sex roles.

CR501 Mercado, Leonardo N., and James J. Knight, eds.
Mission and Dialogue: Theory and Practice. (Asia-Pacific Missiological Series, 1). Manila, PH: SVD, 1989. x, 249 pp. Paper. 9715100422.

Papers given at an international symposium sponsored by the Society of the Divine Word (Tagaytay City, December 1988) dealing with the creative tensions between evangelization and dialogue with the poor, and with primal and world religions.

CR502 Mildenberger, Michael, ed.
Denkpause im Dialog: Perspektiven der Begegnung mit anderen Religionen und Ideologien. Frankfurt am Main, GW: Lembeck, 1978. 157 pp. 3874761045.

German translation of selected papers and documents from the WCC's consultation on "Dialogue with People of Living Faiths and Ideologies" (Chiang Mai, Thailand, 18-27 April 1977); published in *Faith In the Midst of Faiths* (1977).

CR503 Mojzes, Paul, and Leonard J. Swidler, eds.
Christian Mission and Interreligious Dialogue. (Religions in Dialogue, 4). Lewiston, NYU: E Mellen Press, 1990. 279 pp. 0889465207.

Roman Catholic and Protestant theologians respond positively and negatively to Cardinal Josef Tomko's criticism of the way new Christian theologies of other religions militate against missionary work.

CR504 Muck, Terry C.
Those Other Religions in Your Neighborhood: Loving Your Neighbor When You Don't Know How. Grand Rapids, MIU: Zondervan, 1992. 223 pp. Paper. 0310540410.

Practical helps for evangelical Protestants desiring to befriend and witness to the 10 percent of their neighbors in the United States who belong to other faiths.

CR505 Mulder, Dirk Cornellis
Ontmoeting van gelovigen: Over de dialoog tussen aanhangers van verschillende religies. (Œkumene nr. 5, jrg. 8). Baarn, NE: Bosch & Keuning, 1977. 100 pp. Paper. 9024630940.

An introductory book, written for lay members of Christian churches, about the theology of religions and interreligious dialogue, by the General Secretary of the Dutch Council of Churches, who at the time was also Chairman of the Section on Dialogue between Men of Living Faith and Ideologies in the WCC.

CR506 My Neighbour's Faith—and Mine: Theological Discoveries through Interfaith Dialogue
Geneva, SZ: WCC, 1986. xi, 52 pp. Paper. 2825480697.

A ecclesiastical study guide, prepared by the WCC's Dialogue Subunit, which urges Christians to witness to their non-Christian neighbors through deepening faith, experienced salvation, witness, spirituality, hope, and vision.

CR507 Neill, Stephen Charles
Christian Faith and Other Faiths. London, ENK: InterVarsity, 1970. vii, 245 pp. Paper. 0192830112.

Insights of the noted Anglican missiologist on what each of the major world faiths means to its adherents today, indicating fruitful themes for interreligious dialogue; second edition of the work first published in 1961.

CR508 Neill, Stephen Charles
Crises of Belief: The Christian Dialogue with Faith and No Faith. London, ENK: Hodder & Stoughton, 1984. 304 pp. Paper. 0340341564.

An introduction to the world's faiths, with guidance for Christians seeking to engage in interreligious dialogue or to witness others seeking meaning and a purpose in life; by the noted Anglican missionary bishop to India and missiologist.

CR509 Neill, Stephen Charles
Gott und die Götter: Christlicher Glaube und die Weltreligionen. Gütersloh, GW: Mohn, 1963. 223 pp. Paper. No ISBN.

German translation of *Christian Faith and Other Faiths* (1984).

CR510 Nwaiwu, Francis O.
Inter-Religious Dialogue in African Context. (Facultas Theologiae). Rome, IT: Pontificia Universitas Urbaniana, 1989. 212 pp. No ISBN.

A survey of various Christian approaches to religious pluralism with special treatment of the dialogue in Africa of Christians with Muslims and traditional religionists; a dissertation presented at the Urbaniana Pontifical University.

CR511 Oberhammer, Gerhard, ed.
Transzendenzerfahrung, Vollzugshorizont des Heils: Das Problem in indischer und christlicher Tradition: Arbeitsdokumentation eines Symposiums. (Publications of the de Nobili Research Library, 5). Vienna, AU: Institut für Indologie Universität, 1978. 253 pp. 3900271046.

Eleven scholars of spirituality discuss states of transcendance and mystical aspects of both Western Christianity and Eastern religions, presenting parallels, tensions, and contrasts.

CR512 O'Connor, Daniel
Relations in Religion: The Westcott Lectures 1992. New Delhi, II: Allied Publishers, 1994. xii, 57 pp. 8170231914.

Three essays on themes in interreligious dialogue (friendship, solidarity, and ecumenism); originally presented in India as the Westcott Memorial Lectures in 1992.

CR513 Panikkar, Raimundo
The Intrareligious Dialogue. New York, NYU: Paulist Press, 1999. xx, 160 pp. Paper. 0809137631.

Revised edition of a bold, creative outline of the nature of, and conditions for, interreligious dialogue; originally published in 1978, it contains new chapters on "ecumenical ecumenism," the "dialogical dialogue," and Christian dialogue with Hindus.

CR514 Panikkar, Raimundo
Der neue religiöse Weg: Im Dialog der Religionen leben. Munich, GW: Kösel, 1990. 188 pp. 3466203201.

German translation.

CR515 Phan, Peter C., ed.
Christianity and the Wider Ecumenism. New York, NYU: Paragon House, 1990. xix, 288 pp. Paper. 0892260742 (hdbk), 0892260750 (pbk).

Papers from the important "Christians and the Wider Ecumenism" Conference (Istanbul, Turkey, 8-14 May 1988), on attitudes by Christians of different denominations and theological orientations toward persons of other faiths; sponsored by the Council for the World's Religions.

CR516 Price, Lynne
Interfaith Encounter and Dialogue: A Methodist Pilgrimage. (Studies in the Intercultural History of Christianity, 70). Frankfurt am Main, GW: Lang, 1991. ix, 180 pp. Paper. 3631437358.

A case study among Methodists in Birmingham, England, of their attitudes toward interfaith encounters compared with the official statements of their church.

CR517 Räisänen, Heikki
Marcion, Muhammad and the Mahatma: Exegetical Perspectives on the Encounter of Cultures and Faiths. London, ENK: SCM Press, 1997. xi, 293 pp. Paper. 0334026938.

In light of cultural diversity in the Bible, and the historical consciousness of relativity of all cultures, the author calls for a radically new approach to religious dialogue; from the Edward Cadbury Lectures at the University of Birmingham 1995/96 in England.

CR518 Rao, Sreenivasa, ed.
Inter-Faith Dialogue and World Community. Madras, II: CLS, 1991. xxxix, 282 pp. Paper. No ISBN.

Selected papers originally presented at the International Seminar on "Inter-Faith Dialogue for National Integration and Human Solidarity" (Madras Christian College, 27-31 January 1986).

CR519 Rolston, Holmes
Religious Inquiry: Participation and Detachment. New York, NYU: Philosophical Library, 1985. xiv, 309 pp. 0802224504.

The author brings together the insights of Augustine, Ghazali, Sankara, and Nagarjuna in order to better understand both the difficulties and the promise of interreligious encounter.

CR520 Rosenkranz, Gerhard
Der Christliche Glaube angesichts der Weltreligionen. (Sammlung Dalp, 100). Bern, SZ: Francke Verlag, 1967. 328 pp. No ISBN.

A historical essay on the meetings of faiths, focusing on the attitudes of Christians toward the Jews and the "heathen" from the New Testament to the present, stressing the importance of honest dialogue.

CR521 Rousseau, Richard W., ed.
Interreligious Dialogue: Facing the Next Frontier. (Modern Theological Themes: Selections from the Literature, 1). Scranton, PAU: Ridge Row Press, 1981. x, 234 pp. 0940866005.

A selection of recent essays by Christian thinkers trying to elaborate a theology of interreligious dialogue.

CR522 Samartha, Stanley J., ed.
Living Faiths and the Ecumenical Movement. Geneva, SZ: WCC, 1971. 184 pp. Paper. No ISBN.

A collection of ten essays by an international panel of scholars, plus three key WCC documents, on the theme of Christians in dialogue with people of living faiths and ideologies.

CR523 Samartha, Stanley J.
Courage for Dialogue: Ecumenical Issues in Inter-Religious Relationships. Geneva, SZ: WCC; New York, NYU: Orbis Books, 1982. 172 pp. 0883440946.

Essays by the former Director of the WCC's unit on Dialogue with People of Living Faiths and Ideologies.

CR524 Schaeffler, Richard, George Chemparathy, and Eduard Schweizer
Dialog aus der Mitte christlicher Theologie. Edited by Andreas Bsteh. (Beiträge zur Religionstheologie, 5). Mödling, AU: Verlag St. Gabriel, 1987. 245 pp. Paper. 3852642884.

In this work attempting to fix the precise position of the Christian faith in the encounter with the religions of humanity, the authors attempt to work out a theology of dialogue in relationship to the focal point of the Christian faith, Jesus and his Cross.

CR525 Schwarzenau, Paul
Der grössere Gott: Christentum und Weltreligionen. (Radius-Bücher). Stuttgart, GW: Radius-Verlag, 1977. 253 pp. Paper. 3871735264.

Writing as a Christian but not from within a closed system, the author enters into dialogue with Judaism, Islam, Hinduism, Buddhism, and Chinese universalism.

CR—CHRISTIANITY AND OTHER RELIGIONS

CR526 Selvanayagam, Israel

A Dialogue on Dialogue: Reflections on Inter-Faith Encounters. Madras, II: CLS, 1995. xvi, 172 pp. Paper. No ISBN.

The coordinator of a program on interfaith dialogue at Tamilnadu Theological Seminary in Madurai, India, presents a summary of perspectives on dialogue and issues in dialogue for the Indian context.

CR527 Sheard, Robert B.

Interreligious Dialogue in the Catholic Church since Vatican II: An Historical and Theological Study. (Toronto Studies in Theology, Vol. 31). Queenstown, ONC: E Mellen Press, 1987. x, 419 pp. 0889467749.

A detailed history and assessment of the work in interreligious dialogue from 1964 to 1980 of the Vatican Secretariat for Non-Christians and the WCC's Subunit for Dialogue with People of Living Faiths and Ideologies.

CR528 Shenk, David W., and Linford Stutzman

Practicing Truth: Confident Witness in Our Pluralist World. Scottdale, PAU: Herald Press, 1999. 255 pp. Paper. 0836191072.

This collection of fourteen articles addresses issues of religious pluralism and truth in order to confront over-confident Christians who dismiss challenges of postmodern thought, and timid Christians who are eager to accept pluralism while reducing Jesus' claims to whatever is inoffensive.

CR529 Sherwin, Byron L., and Harold Kasimow, eds.

John Paul II and Interreligious Dialogue. (Faith Meets Faith Series). Maryknoll, NYU: Orbis Books, 1999. xv, 236 pp. Paper. 1570752605.

A collection of thirteen essays by John Paul II, with nine responses by leading scholars of Buddhism, Islam, Judaism, and Catholicism.

CR530 Slomp, Jan, ed.

Wereldgodsdiensten in Nederland: Christenen in gesprek met moslims, hindoes en boeddhisten. Amersfoort, NE: Horstink; Zoetermeer, NE: Publivorm, 1991. 234 pp. Paper. 9061843618 (H), 9064952469 (P).

Sixteen essays by Christian scholars, together with Muslims, Hindus, and Buddhists, seeking authentic encounter between Christians and adherents of the three major non-Christian faiths in the Netherlands.

CR531 Smart, Ninian

A Dialogue of Religions. (The Library of Philosophy and Theology). London, ENK: SCM Press, 1960. 142 pp. No ISBN.

An imaginary but brilliant dialogue between a Christian, a Jew, a Muslim, a Hindu, and two Buddhists (from Sri Lanka and Japan) is the format in which the noted religionist presents current issues in interreligious dialogue.

CR532 Smith, Wilfred Cantwell

Toward a World Theology: Faith and the Comparative History of Religions. Philadelphia, PAU: Westminster Press, 1981. vi, 206 pp. 0664213804.

A veteran of interreligious dialogue argues that all religions share a common history and can now enter a new dialogical unity.

CR533 Straelen, H. van

Our Attitude Towards Other Religions. Tokyo, JA: Enderle-Herder, 1965. 115 pp. Paper. No ISBN.

Reflecting on the debate concerning the mission schema at Vatican II, the author, an SVD missionary to Japan and Professor of Modern Philosophy and Comparative Religion at Nanzar University in Nagoya, proposes prerequisites for effective interfaith dialogue by Christians.

CR534 Sundermeier, Theo

Wenn Fremdes vertraut wird: Predigten im Gespräch mit anderen Religionen und Kulturen. (Erlanger Taschenbücher, 109). Erlangen, GW: Ev.-Luth Misson, 1994. 204 pp. Paper. 3872145096.

Twenty sermons in which a noted German missiologist and former southern Africa missionary uses a dialogical style in sermons to relate biblical texts to current issues of interreligious dialogue.

CR535 Swearer, Donald K.

Dialogue: The Key to Understanding Other Religions. (Biblical Perspectives on Current Issues). Philadelphia, PAU: Westminster Press, 1977. 174 pp. 0664241387.

An introduction to various contemporary approaches Christians have made to other religions, to conditions necessary for interreligious dialogue, and to dialogue with Theravada Buddhists as an example.

CR536 Swidler, Leonard J. et al.

Death or Dialogue?: From the Age of Monologue to the Age of Dialogue. London, ENK: SCM Press; Philadelphia, PAU: Trinity Press International, 1990. viii, 151 pp. Paper. 0334024455.

A collection of essays by four Christian scholars supporting interreligious dialogue and the necessity of open-mindedness and communication across cultural, social, political, economic, and religious barriers.

CR537 Swidler, Leonard J.

After the Absolute: The Dialogical Future of Religious Reflection. Minneapolis, MNU: Augsburg Fortress, 1990. xvi, 248 pp. Paper. 0800624238.

Present philosophical and theological reasons for the necessity of dialogue and the impossibility of using absolute claims within the dialogue, while endorsing an "ecumenical Esperanto" as the means and goal of dialogue.

CR538 Swidler, Leonard J.

Die Zukunft der Theologie: Im Dialog der Religionen und Weltanschauungen. Regensburg, GW: Verlag Friedrich Pustet; Munich, GW: Kaiser Verlag, 1992. 104 pp. Paper. 3791713426 (P), 3459019638 (K).

The noted Professor of the Scientific Study of Religion discusses the conditions, methods, partners, and consequences of present and future dialogue among persons of various religions and ideologies.

CR539 Thangaraj, M. Thomas

Relating to People of Other Religions: What Every Christian Needs to Know. Nashville, TNU: Abingdon, 1997. 112 pp. Paper. 0687051398.

Autobiographical, anecdotal, biblical, and practical reflections on approaches and attitudes Christians bring to encounters with persons of other faiths; prepared as a study book for individual and local church use.

CR540 Theological Consultation on Dialogue in Community (Chiang Mai, Thailand, 18-27 April 1977).
Faith in the Midst of Faiths: Reflections on Dialogue in Community. Edited by Stanley J. Samartha. Geneva, SZ: WCC, 1977. 200 pp. Paper. 2825405450.

The official report, including papers presented, of the influential WCC-sponsored Chiang Mai consultation.

CR541 Thompson, Norma H., ed.
Religious Pluralism and Religious Education. Birmingham, ALU: Religious Education Press, 1988. 330 pp. Paper. 0891350616.

Original essays by educators of the major world faiths, giving basic principles and practical guidelines for entering into shared learning, with and about other faith traditions

CR542 Thomsen, Mark W.
The Word and the Way of the Cross: Christian Witness among Muslim and Buddhist People. Chicago, ILU: Evangelical Lutheran Church in America, Div. for Global Mission, 1993. 189 pp. Paper. 0963663003.

A theology of dialogue presenting the way of the Cross as the entry point to engaging Muslims and Buddhists in dialogue and witness, by the Executive Director of the Division for Global Mission of the Evangelical Lutheran Church in America.

CR543 Thunberg, Lars, Pandit Lal, and Carl Vilhem Fogh-Hansen, eds.
Dialogue in Action, Essays in Honour of Johannes Aagaard. New Delhi, II: Prajna Publications, 1988. xii, 367 pp. No ISBN.

Essays by Bengt Sundkler, Stephen Fuchs, and other European and Indian scholars on aspects of contemporary Christianity and issues in religious dialogue.

CR544 Thundy, Zacharias P., Kuncheria Pathil, and Frank Podgorski, eds.
Religions in Dialogue: East and West Meet. Lanham, MDU: University Press of America, 1985. xiv, 314 pp. 0819144673 (hdbk), 0819144665 (pbk).

Nineteen scholarly articles on interreligious dialogue in global perspective in India and the United States; written as a *festschrift* honoring John Britto Chethimattam, former Dean of Studies at Dharmaram College, Bangalore, India.

CR545 *Towards a Theology for Inter-Faith Dialogue*
London, ENK: Church House Publishing, 1986. viii, 56 pp. Paper. 0715155253.

A second edition of a 1984 report to the General Synod of the Church of England exploring this new and sensitive area for Christians, with added study materials to be used in preparation for the Lambeth Conference of 1988.

CR546 Tracy, David
Dialogue with the Other: The Interreligious Dialogue. (Louvain Theological and Pastoral Monographs, 1). Grand Rapids, MIU: Eerdmans, 1991. xii, 123 pp. Paper. 0802805620.

Further analysis by the distinguished Professor of Theology at the University of Chicago, on dialogue between Buddhists, Jews, and Christians, and the contributions of figures as diverse as Meister Eckhart and William James, to appreciation of "the other"; also published by Peeters Press (1990).

CR547 Wessels, Antonie
Van Alkmaar begint de victorie...: Gastvriendschap, sleutel tot het verstaan van de verhouding van christenen en mensen van ander of "geen" geloof. Kampen, NE: Kok, 1979. 63 pp. 902420402X.

The Dutch Professor of Religions explores hospitality and friendship as keys to the understanding of the relationship between Christians and people of other religions, or of those professing no faith.

CR548 Woodberry, John Dudley, ed.
Reaching the Resistant: Barriers and Bridges for Mission. (Evangelical Missiological Society Series, 6). South Pasadena, CAU: William Carey Library, 1998. xii, 252 pp. Paper. 0878083804.

A study of the barriers erected by those considered resistant to the Gospel in Jewish, Muslim, and Japanese cultures, and bridges God is using to carry the Gospel to them.

Christianity and African Religions

See also TH590, ME263, CR510, SO75, SO356, SO625, ED153, ED159, AF69-AF70, AF77, AF104, AF111, AF134, AF168, AF198, AF200, AF263-AF264, AF277, AF316, AF343, AF464, AF559-AF560, AF704, AF739, AF851, AF987, AF998, AF1058, AF1143, AF1229, AF1240, AF1317, AF1323, AF1333, AF1363, AF1369, AM1040, and AM1060.

CR549 Aguilar, Mario I.
Dios en Africa: Elementos para una antropología de la religión. (Misión Sin Fronteras, 11). Navarra, SP: Verbo Divino, 1997. 143 pp. Paper. 8481691631.

A basic textbook on religion in Africa including traditional beliefs and rituals, conversation, Islam and Christianity, African theology, and mission and culture.

CR550 Anderson, David M., and Douglas Hamilton Johnson, eds.
Revealing Prophets: Prophecy in Eastern African History. (Eastern African Studies). London, ENK: Currey; Nairobi, KE: East African Educational Publishers; Kampala, UG: Fountain Publishers, 1995. x, 310 pp. 0821410881 (hdbk), 082141089X (pbk).

Eleven case studies of various prophets and prophetic movements in eastern Africa during the past century; also published by Ohio University Press, Athens, Ohio (1995).

CR551 Bastide, Roger
The African Religions of Brazil: Toward a Sociology of the Interpenetration of Civilizations. Translated by Helen Sebba. (Johns Hopkins Studies in Atlantic History and Culture). Baltimore, MDU: Johns Hopkins University Press, 1978. xxviii, 494 pp. 0801820561 (hdbk), 0801821304 (pbk).

English translation of *Les religions Africaines au Brésil* (1960).

CR552 Bastide, Roger
As Religiões africanas no Brasil: Contribução a uma sociologia das interpenetrações de civilizações. Translated by Maria Capellato and Olivia Krahenbuhl. (Biblioteca Pioneira de Ciências Sociais). São Paulo, BL: Libraria Pioneira Editôra/Editora da Universidade de São Paulo, 1971. 2 vols. Paper. No ISBN.

Portuguese translation of *Les religions Africaines au Brésil: Vers une sociologie des interpénétrations de civilizations* (vol. 1: 240 pp.; vol. 2: 327 pp.; 1960).

CR553 Bediako, Kwame

Jesus in African Culture: A Ghanaian Perspective. Accra, GH: Asempa Publishers, 1990. 49 pp. Paper. 9964781806.

A short essay showing how African (particularly Akan) religious concerns can help Africans understand some traditional Christian affirmations about Jesus Christ, such as his priestly role as mediator and his Lordship as King.

CR554 Beken, Alain van der

L'Evangile en Afrique, vécu et commenté par des Bayaka. (Studia Instituti Missiologici SVD, 38). Nettetal, GW: Steyler Verlag, 1986. 328 pp. Paper. 3877872042.

A scholarly monograph on the Africanization of the Gospel and the relationship of Christianity to African traditional religion—a case study among the Bayaka people of Zaire, with eighteen documents in Yaka and French translation illustrative of African spirituality.

CR555 Ben-Jochannan, Yosef, Charles Finch, and Modupe Oduyoye

The Afrikan Origins of the Major World Religions. London, ENK: Karnak House, 1988. iii, 98 pp. Paper. 0907015352.

Papers presented at the second International London Conference on the Afrikan Origins of Civilization in which the authors, African historians and linguists, bring their insights to purport that Judaism and Christianity both have Afrikan (Egyptian) origins.

CR556 Berglund, Axel-Ivar

Zulu Thought Patterns and Symbolism. London, ENK: Hurst; Bloomington, INU: Indiana University Press, 1976. 402 pp. 185065056X (UK, hdbk), 0903983486 (UK, pbk), 0253311756 (US, hdbk), 0253212057 (US, pbk).

A thesis by the Director of Theological Education of the SACC, based on twelve years of field research into Zulu culture and religion; originally published in 1976 (New York, NYU: Africana Publishing; London, ENK: C. Hurst; Uppsala, SW: Swedish Institute of Missionary Research).

CR557 Binsbergen, Wim M. J. van, and J. M. Schoffeleers, eds.

Theoretical Explorations in African Religion. London, ENK: KPI, 1985. x, 389 pp. 0710300492.

Twelve scholarly essays on classic and contemporary approaches to African religion (traditional, Christian, and Islamic) seeking greater methodological and theoretical precision and validity.

CR558 Booth, Newell S., ed.

African Religions: A Symposium. New York, NYU: NOK Publishers, 1977. vii, 390 pp. 0883570122.

Papers from the Colloquium on African Religion sponsored by Western College, Oxford, Ohio, in 1969-1970, including traditional African religion, Christianity, Islam, and the influence of African religion in the Americas.

CR559 Bourdillon, Michael F. C.

Religion and Society: A Text for Africa. Gweru, RH: Mambo Press, 1990. 406 pp. Paper. 0869224921.

An introduction textbook for university use on the sociology of religion, with special reference to African societies.

CR560 Catholic Church, Secretariat for Non-Christians

À la rencontre des religions africaines. Rome, IT: Ancora, 1969. 187 pp. No ISBN.

Second edition of the official guide, from the Vatican Secretariat for Non-Christians, giving doctrinal and practical guidelines for Christian dialogue with African traditional religionists, including a section of various African prayers as illustrations of African religious vitality; issued also under the title *Meeting the African Religions.*

CR561 Christensen, Thomas G.

An African Tree of Life. (American Society of Missiology Series, 14). Maryknoll, NYU: Orbis Books, 1990. xix, 184 pp. Paper. 0883446561.

A detailed case study of contextualization among the Gbaya people of the Cameroon and the Central African Republic, with a focus on their stories, rituals, and the peace-bringing tree of life.

CR562 Conference on World Evangelization (Pattaya, Thailand, 1980)

The Thailand Report on People of African Traditional Religions: Report of the ... Mini-Consultation on Reaching Traditional Religionists (Africa). (Lausanne Occasional Papers, 18). Wheaton, ILU: LCWE, 1980. 20 pp. Paper. No ISBN.

A general understanding of African traditional religions, with comparisons to Christianity, closing with practical recommendations for Christian witness to traditionalists.

CR563 Daneel, M. L.

The God of the Matopo Hills: An Essay on the Mwari Cult in Rhodesia. The Hague, NE: Mouton, 1970. 95 pp. Paper. No ISBN.

An essay on the belief and rituals of African traditional religion in Zimbabwe, focusing on tribal belief in a high god (*Mwari*) who influences political life both historically and in the present.

CR564 Davis, Kortright, and Elias Farajaje-Jones, eds.

African Creative Expressions of the Divine. Washington, DCU: Howard University School of Divinity, 1991. xi, 257 pp. Paper. No ISBN.

Thirteen scholarly essays on the survival of African religions in the Caribbean, Central and South America, and sub-Saharan Africa; originally presented at three conferences on the theme "African Religion: Creativity, Imagination, and Expression" in 1986-1987.

CR565 Drake, St. Clair

The Redemption of Africa and Black Religion. Chicago, ILU: Third World Press; Atlanta, GAU: Institute of the Black World, 1970. 80 pp. Paper. 0883780178.

An essay on the roots in Africa of African American religion in North America and the Caribbean, and the role of that religion in the struggles toward freedom, identity, and self-determination—part of a larger work on the black diaspora.

CR566 *Encounter of Religions in African Cultures*

Geneva, SZ: LWF, 1991. v, 65 pp. Paper. 3906706079.

Report and papers of a consultation sponsored by the LWF and the WCC (University of Malawi, September 1989).

CR567 Fisher, Robert B.

West African Religious Traditions: Focus on the Akan of Ghana. (Faith Meets Faith Series). Maryknoll, NYU: Orbis Books, 1998. xvi, 197 pp. Paper. 157075165X.

A case study of the Akan traditional religion of Ghana, developed with study guide to help readers understand the dynamics and structures of traditional West African religion, and to see its resonances in African American religious life today.

CR—CHRISTIANITY AND OTHER RELIGIONS

CR568 Froelich, Jean-Claude

Le nouveau dieu d'Afrique. Paris, FR: Orantew, 1969. 128 pp. No ISBN.

"The development of traditional religions through Islam, Christianity, messianism, and multiple syncretisms."

CR569 Gehman, Richard J.

African Traditional Religion in Biblical Perspective. Kijabe, KE: Kesho Publications, 1989. 310 pp. Paper. 996686007X.

A textbook on key issues facing the African Christian believers related to the traditional African religion.

CR570 Hexham, Irving

Texts on Zulu Religion: Traditional Zulu Ideas About God. (African Studies, 6). Lewiston, NYU: E Mellen Press, 1987. 488 pp. 0889461813.

Selected key writings on the Zulu people by Europeans during the first fifty years of their initial contact; edited to provide the reader with the earliest available texts on Zulu religion.

CR571 Idowu, E. Bolaji

African Traditional Religion: A Definition. London, ENK: SCM Press; Maryknoll, NYU: Orbis Books, 1973. xii, 228 pp. 0883440059.

A carefully reasoned argument for the serious inclusion of African traditional religion among the world's major faiths, with an analysis of its structure of beliefs and practices.

CR572 Idowu, E. Bolaji

Olodumare: God in Yoruba Belief. New York, NYU: Praeger, 1963. vii, 222 pp. No ISBN.

A pioneer scholarly study of Yoruba traditional religion including changes occuring with the advance of Islam and Christianity; also published by Longmans, London, UK (ISBN: 0582608031, 1962).

CR573 Imasogie, Osadolor

African Traditional Religion. Ibadan, NR: University Press, 1985. iv, 81 pp. Paper. 978154693X (NR), 0195758234 (non NR).

Second edition of an overview of African traditional religion with special reference to Nigeria.

CR574 Jenkins, Ulysses Duke

Ancient African Religion and the African-American Church. Jacksonville, NCU: Flame International, 1978. xvi, 158 pp. 0933184018.

The personal odyssey of an African American scholar who, through a pilgrimage to Ile-Ife, the holy city of the Yoruba people of Nigeria, examines the influences of traditional African religions on African American religious practices.

CR575 Jones, Major J.

The Color of God: The Concept of God in Afro-American Thought. Macon, GAU: Mercer University Press, 1987. xi, 124 pp. 0865542740 (hbbk), 0865542767 (pbk).

A broad review of the notion of God in African religions, and an application of its significance for Christian theology in Africa.

CR576 Kihara, James

Ngai, We Belong to You: Kenya's Kikuyu and Meru Prayer. (Spearhead Series, 89.). Eldoret, KE: Gaba Publications, 1985. vii, 48 pp. Paper. No ISBN.

An analysis of traditional understandings of God, humanity, and prayer among the Kikuyu and Meru peoples of Kenya, and how these can have a positive impact on Christian prayer.

CR577 King, Noel Q.

African Cosmos: An Introduction to Religion in Africa. (The Religious Life of Man Series). Belmont, CAU: Wadsworth Publishing, 1986. xiv, 149 pp. Paper. 0534053343.

A college text introducing African religions, with case studies of the Yoruba of Nigeria, the Akan of Ghana, the Dinka of Sudan, and the Acholi of Uganda.

CR578 Kirby, Jon P.

God, Shrines, and Problem-Solving among the Anufo of Northern Ghana. (Collectanea Instituti Anthropos, Vol. 34). Berlin, GW: Dietrich Reimer Verlag, 1986. 368 pp. Paper. 3496007850.

An extensive study of the social and religious beliefs and practices of the Anufo people of northern Ghana; by a Roman Catholic missionary-anthropologist who lived for several years among them.

CR579 Kirwen, Michael C.

The Missionary and the Diviner: Contending Theologies of Christian and African Religions. Maryknoll, NYU: Orbis Books, 1987. xxv, 134 pp. Paper. 0883445859 (hdbk), 0883445840 (pbk).

A well-researched presentation of issues arising in the interaction between Christian theology and African traditional religion presented as a conversation between a Western missionary and an African diviner in Tanzania.

CR580 Lagerwerf, Leny

Witchcraft, Sorcery and Spirit Possession: Pastoral Responses in Africa. (Mambo Occasional Papers—Missio Pastoral Series, 19). Gweru, RH: Mambo Press, 1987. 82 pp. 0869224387.

First published in *Exchange 41* 1985, this monograph deals with issues of pastoral theology in sub-Saharan Africa related to demonic possession, witchcraft, and magic.

CR581 Lawson, E. Thomas

Religions of Africa: Traditions in Transformation. San Francisco, CAU: Harper & Row, 1984. x, 106 pp. Paper. 006065211X.

A concise introduction to the complex diversity of African religions as practiced by peoples with vastly different cultures and languages, with special attention to the religions of the Yoruba of Nigeria and the Zulu of South Africa.

CR582 Lufuluabo, François Marie

Valeur des religions africaines selon la Bible et selon Vatican II. Kinshasa, CG: Éditions St. Paul Afrique, 1967. 95 pp. No ISBN.

A Congolese Catholic assessment of indigenization in relation to African religion.

CR583 MacGaffey, Wyatt

Religion and Society in Central Africa: The BaKongo of Lower Zaire. Chicago, ILU: University of Chicago Press, 1986. xi, 295 pp. Paper. 0226500292 (hdbk), 0226500306 (pbk).

A product of extensive research and fieldwork among the BaKongo people of Central Africa which reveals the fabric of the Kongo religion and culture, and how it has remained intact despite historical upheavals in that region.

CR584 Magesa, Laurenti

African Religion: The Moral Traditions of Abundant Life. Maryknoll, NYU: Orbis Books, 1997. xiv, 296 pp. Paper. 1570751056.

One of Africa's best-known Catholic theologians explores comprehensively the moral and ethical imperatives of African religion.

CR—CHRISTIANITY AND OTHER RELIGIONS

CR585 Mbiti, John S.

African Religions and Philosophy. Garden City, NYU: Doubleday; London, ENK: Heinemann, 1990. xiv, 288 pp. Paper. 0385037139 (D), 0435895915 (H).

A clear, sympathetic presentation of African religious thought as a basis for constructing an African Christianity:

CR586 Mbiti, John S.

Afrikanische Religionen und Weltanschauung. Translated by W. F. Feuser. (De Gruyter Studienbuch). Berlin, GW: Gruyter, 1974. xv, 375 pp. No ISBN.

German translation of *African Religions and Philosophy* (1970).

CR587 Mbiti, John S.

Introduction to African Religion. New York, NYU: Praeger, 1975. vi, 211 pp. No ISBN.

A comprehensive introduction to the beliefs and practices of African religion prepared for use as a college textbook.

CR588 Mbiti, John S.

The Prayers of African Religion. Maryknoll, NYU: Orbis Books, 1975. xii, 193 pp. 0883443945.

A rich collection of prayers from various African countries, traditions, and occasions, with commentary by one of Africa's best-known Christian theologians.

CR589 McVeigh, Malcolm J.

God in Africa: Conceptions of God in African Traditional Religion and Christianity. Cape Cod, MAU: Claude Stark, 1974. xix, 235 pp. 0890070032.

A scholarly study of the interactions between the concepts of God in African traditional religions and Christianity.

CR590 Mendelsonn, Jack

God, Allah, and Juju: Religion in Africa Today. Boston, MAU: Beacon Press, 1965. 245 pp. No ISBN.

An analysis of the spiritual conflicts between Christianity, Islam, and African traditional religion, emphasizing the African tendency to revive traditional customs and beliefs suppressed by missionaries.

CR591 Metuh, Emefie Ikenga

Comparative Studies of African Traditional Religions. Onitsha, NR: IMICO Publishers, 1987. xi,288 pp. Paper. 9782442089.

A textbook for graduate students of African traditional religions, organized thematically with numerous examples from varied African countries.

CR592 Metuh, Emefie Ikenga

God and Man in African Religion: A Case Study of the Igbo of Nigeria. London, ENK: Chapman, 1981. xiv, 181 pp. 0225662795.

A study of the place of God in the life and worship of the Igbo of southeastern Nigeria by the lecturer in religious studies at the University of Jos, Nigeria.

CR593 Moreau, A. Scott

The World of Spirits: A Biblical Study in the African Context. Nairobi, KE: Evangel Publishing House, 1990. xiii, 221 pp. Paper. 9966850910.

An examination of beliefs in spirits in the African context, and biblical teaching and practical guidelines for Christian workers dealing with spiritism in Africa.

CR594 Mudimbe, V. Y.

Parables and Fables: Exegesis, Textuality, and Politics in Central Africa. Madison, WIU: University of Wisconsin Press, 1991. xxii, 238 pp. Paper. 0299130606 (hdbk), 0299130649 (pbk).

An in-depth trialogue between the philosophical problems of otherness and identity as understood in Western philosophy, Catholic missionary theology, and the African "philosophy" of the Luba people of Zaire.

CR595 Mulago, Vicente

Simbolismo Religioso Africano: Estudio comparativo con el sacramentalismo cristiano. (BAC, 407). Madrid, SP: EDICA, 1979. xxxi, 366 pp. 8422009129.

A comparative analysis of African initiations, rites, and ceremonies and the Christian sacraments, plus a comparison of African solidarity with Christian co-responsibility.

CR596 Murphy, Joseph M.

Working the Spirit: Ceremonies of the African Diaspora. Boston, MAU: Beacon Press, 1994. xiii, 263 pp. 0807012203.

A scholarly examination of various religions of Africa extant in Haiti, Jamaica, Brazil, Cuba, and the United States, relating them to their history, interaction with Christianity, and shared African heritage.

CR597 Nkurunziza, Deusdedit R. K.

Bantu Philosophy of Life in the Light of the Christian Message: A Basis for an African Vitalistic Theology. (European University Studies, 23: Theology, 289). Frankfurt am Main, GW: Lang, 1989. 307 pp. Paper. 3631422288.

A dissertation exploring the African philosophy of life in the light of the Christian message, comparing the African worldview to Old and New Testament understandings.

CR598 Nyamiti, Charles

Christ as Our Ancestor: Christology from an African Perspective. (Mambo Occasional Papers—Missio-Pastoral Series, 11). Gweru, RH: Mambo Press, 1984. 151 pp. Paper. No ISBN.

Essays comparing African beliefs on ancestors with Christian beliefs concerning Christ and the saints as ancestors.

CR599 Obiego, Cosmas Okechukwu

African Image of the Ultimate Reality: An Analysis of Igbo Ideas of Life and Death in Relation to Chukwu-God. (European University Studies, 23: Theology, 237). Bern, SZ: Lang, 1984. 322 pp. Paper. 3820474609.

A detailed study of the traditional religion of the Igbo people of southeastern Nigeria, with a Christian theological perspective for dialogue.

CR600 O'Donohue, John

Spirits and Magic: A Critical Look. (Spearhead Series, 68). Eldoret, KE: Gaba Publications, 1981. 51 pp. Paper. No ISBN.

A critical analysis of African traditions of magic and belief in the spirits of the dead, arguing that Christian inculturation requires the transformation and regeneration, rather than total rejection, of these aspects of African culture.

CR601 Okorocha, Cyril C.

The Meaning of Religious Conversion in Africa: The Case of the Igbo of Nigeria. Aldershot, ENK: Avebury; Brookfield, VTU: Gower Publishing Company, 1987. xv, 352 pp. 0566050307.

A scholarly study of how Igbo conversion to Christianity, and present understandings of it, are influenced by the people's traditional concepts of salvation; originally presented as a Ph.D. thesis at the University of Aberdeen, Scotland.

CR602 Olowola, Cornelius
African Traditional Religion and The Christian Faith. (Theological Perspectives in Africa, 4). Achimota, GH: Africa Christian Press, 1993. 65 pp. Paper. 9964877986.

A constructive critical approach to African traditional religion from the standpoint of Christian faith by the acting provost of the ECWA Theological Seminary in Igbaja, Nigeria.

CR603 Olupona, Jacob Obafemi Kehinde, and Sulayman S. Nyang, eds.
Religious Plurality in Africa: Essays in Honour of John S. Mbiti. (Religion and Society, 32). Berlin, GW: Mouton, 1993. xxi, 455 pp. 3110122200.

A *festschrift* honoring the noted African theologian with twenty essays by African and European scholars on African traditional religion, African theology, Africa and Christianity, other world religions (Islam, Hinduism, Judaism) and Africa, and responses to John Mbiti's work.

CR604 Olupona, Jacob Obafemi Kehinde, ed.
African Traditional Religions in Contemporary Society. New York, NYU: Int. Relgous Foundation; Paragon House Publishers, 1991. 204 pp. 0892260777 (hdbk), 0892260793 (pbk).

Fourteen scholarly essays on African traditional religion including the impact of Christian mission and movements upon its revitalization.

CR605 Omari, Cuthbert Kashingo
God and Worship in Traditional Asu Society: A Study of the Concept of God and the Way He Was Worshipped among the Vasu. (Makumira Publications, 6). Erlangen, GW: Ev.-Luth. Mission, 1990. 348 pp. Paper. 3872142348.

Research conducted between 1967 and 1969 on God and worship among the Pare people in northeast Tanzania; subsequently submitted in 1970 as a thesis to the University of East Africa.

CR606 Ongong'a, Jude J.
Life and Death: A Christian/Luo Dialogue. (Spearhead, 78). Eldoret, KE: Gaba Publications, 1983. v, 65 pp. Paper. No ISBN.

A case study on the church's dialogue with the Luo of Kenya's traditional beliefs and rituals, with special reference to those concerning death and immortality.

CR607 Paris, Peter J.
The Spirituality of African Peoples: The Search for a Common Moral Discourse. Minneapolis, MNU: Fortress Press, 1995. xii, 194 pp. Paper. 0800628543.

A noted African American ethicist probes the religious and moral values embodied in African experience, and pervading traditional religious worldviews in Africa and the diaspora.

CR608 Parrinder, Edward Geoffrey
Religion in Africa. Baltimore, MDU: Penguin Books, 1969. 253 pp. Paper. No ISBN.

A history and study of major religious traditions, including traditional, Christian, and Islamic faiths; based on twenty years of teaching and traveling experience throughout Africa and India.

CR609 Parrinder, Edward Geoffrey
West African Religion: A Study of the Beliefs and Practices of Akan, Ewe, Yoruba, Ibo, and Kindred Peoples. London, ENK: Epworth Press, 1961. xv, 203 pp. No ISBN.

Originally written as a textbook of comparative religion in 1949, this second edition expands the range of West African religions analyzed as a result of further research and study by the author.

CR610 Pastoral Institute of Eastern Africa
Dialogue with the African Traditional Religions: A Selective Report.... (Gaba Institute Pastoral Papers, 37). Kampala, UG: Gaba Publications, 1975. 60 pp. Paper. No ISBN.

Selected papers and report from the meeting organized by the Vatican Secretariat for Non-Christians at the Pastoral Institute of Eastern Africa (Gaba), 5-7 August 1974.

CR611 Pheko, S. E. M.
African Religion Re-Discovered. Bulawayo, RH: Daystar Publications, 1965. 47 pp. Paper. No ISBN.

An evangelical Protestant primer relating biblical teachings to traditional African religion.

CR612 Pobee, J. S., ed.
Religion in a Pluralistic Society. Leiden, NEU: Brill, 1976. viii, 236 pp. 9004045562.

A collection of essays by nineteen scholars and churchpeople on various aspects of African religion, assessing the role of Christian missions on that continent.

CR613 Quarcoopome, Nii Otokunor
West African Traditional Religion. Ibadan, NR: African Universities Press, 1987. 200 pp. Paper. 9781482338.

An introduction to West African traditional religion with references to Christianity and Islam; prepared as a textbook for "A" level studies.

CR614 Ranger, Terence O., and I. N. Kimambo, eds.
The Historical Study of African Religion. Berkeley, CAU: University of California Press; London, ENK: Heinemann, 1972. ix, 307 pp. 0520022068 (US), 043532747X (UK hdbk), 0435327488 (UK pbk).

This volume grew out of the Dar es Salaam conference on the historical study of African religious systems, held in June 1970.

CR615 Ray, Benjamin C.
African Religions: Symbol, Ritual, and Community. (Prentice-Hall Studies in Religion Series). Upper Saddle River, NJU: Prentice-Hall, 2000. xii, 238 pp. 0130828424.

This revised edition includes substantial chapters on African Islam and Christianity, and a new chapter on traditional religious art; the author's premise is that popular culture and folk religion have provided the philosophical, religious, and ethical foundation for contemporary African societies; originally published in 1976.

CR616 Rivinius, Karl Josef, ed.
Schuld, Sühne und Erlösung in Zentralafrika (Zaire) und in der christlichen Theologie Europas. (Veröffentlichungen des Missionspriesterseminars, 33). St. Augustin, GW: Steyler Verlag, 1983. 298 pp. Paper. 387787164X.

Essays on the concepts of guilt, atonement, and redemption in the traditional African cultures of Zaire and in European Christian theologies; originally read at a missiological conference in Sankt Augustin in 1982.

CR617 Rwehumbiza, Philibert R. K.
Patriarchal and Bantu Cults Compared. (Spearhead, 103). Eldoret, KE: AMECEA Gaba Publications, 1988. 48 pp. Paper. No ISBN.

A treatment of three main cultic institutions—prayer, offerings, and altars and sanctuaries—common both to the Hebrew patriarchs and to Bantu-speaking peoples of Kenya, Tanzania, and Uganda.

CR—CHRISTIANITY AND OTHER RELIGIONS

CR618 Sawyerr, Harry
God: Ancestor or Creator?: Aspects of Traditional Belief in Ghana, Nigeria and Sierra Leone. London, ENK: Longman, 1970. 118 pp. 0582640571.
Essays by the noted Ghanaian theologian on traditional African understandings of God's ancestorship and creatorship.

CR619 Schoffeleers, J. M.
Religion and the Dramatisation of Life: Spirit Beliefs and Rituals in Southern and Central Malawi. (Kachere Monograph, 5). Blantyre, MW: CLAIM; Bonn, GW: Verlag für Kultur und Wissenschaft, 1997. 165 pp. Paper. 9990816069 (MW), 3926105828 (GW).
Six essays on African traditional religion in predominately Christian Malawi by the Professor of Religious Anthropology at the Free University of Amsterdam and the University of Utrecht in the Netherlands.

CR620 Schoffeleers, J. M.
River of Blood: The Genesis of a Martyr Cult in Southern Malawi, c. A.D. 1600. Madison, WIU: University of Wisconsin, 1992. xiii, 325 pp. Paper. 0299133206 (hdbk), 0299133249 (pbk).
A detailed scholarly reconstruction of the beginning of the Mbona martyr cult of Malawian traditional religion, revealing the intersections of an indigenous belief system with European Christianity.

CR621 Semaine d'Études Ethno-Pastorales, 3, Bandundu, 1967
Mort, funérailles, deuil et culte des ancêtres chez les populations du Kwango/Bas-Kwilu. Bandundu, CG: Centres d'Études ethnologiques, 1969. 240 pp. No ISBN.
Local studies from Kinshasa of traditional death and funeral practices establishing valuable links between Christian faith and traditional rites and beliefs.

CR622 Shorter, Aylward
African Christian Theolog—Adaptation or Incarnation? Maryknoll, NYU: Orbis Books, 1977. 167 pp. Paper. 0883440032.
An introduction to African traditional religion arguing that African Christian theology must grow out of a dialogue between Christianity and African religiosity.

CR623 Shorter, Aylward
Prayer in the Religious Traditions of Africa. New York, NYU: Oxford University Press, 1975. 145 pp. No ISBN.
A comprehensive study of prayer in various religions of Africa (traditional, Islam, mainline Christian, and African Independent) with the texts of 152 prayers.

CR624 Smit, J. H., M. Deacon, and A. Shutte
Ubuntu in a Christian Perspective. (Series F: Institute of Reformational Studies; Series F1: IRS Study Pamphlets, 374). Potchefstroom, SA: Institute for Reformational Studies/PU for CHE, 1999. 52 pp. Paper. 1868223299.
A Christian interpretation of the ethics of *ubuntu*, a traditional African moral concept that now has widespread usage in contemporary post-apartheid South Africa, and in business and management practice, globally, through the fundamental recognition of the central importance of the human being.

CR625 Stine, Philip C., and Ernst R. Wendland, eds.
Bridging the Gap: African Traditional Religion and Bible Translation. (UBS Monograph Series, 4). Reading, ENK: UBS, 1990. x, 226 pp. Paper. 0826704549.

A monograph on aspects of Central African traditional religion which should influence Bible translation, with case studies of the Turkana and Luo of Kenya, the Godié Kru of Ivory Coast, and the Gbaya of Cameroon.

CR626 Sundermeier, Theo
Nur gemeinsam können wir leben: Das Menschenbild schwarzafrikanischer Religionen. (GTB, 784). Gütersloh, GW: Gerd Mohn, 1990. 304 pp. Paper. 357900784X.
This work by a European with eleven years of experience in Africa is a study of African anthropology, and covers African consciousness, the ritual man, man as dependent, and ethics.

CR627 Taylor, John Vernon
Du findest mich, wenn du den Stein aufhebst: Christliche Präsenz im Leben Afrikas. Translated by Christoph Hahn and Gertrud Hahn. (Veröffentlichungen zu Mission und Ökumene). Munich, GW: Kaiser, 1965. 169 pp. Paper. No ISBN.
German translation.

CR628 Taylor, John Vernon
The Primal Vision: Christian Presence amid African Religion. (Christian Presence Series). London, ENK: SCM Press; Philadelphia, PAU: Fortress Press, 1982. 204 pp. 0334013062.
A classic analysis of African traditional religions and the importance of understanding them in order to communicate the Gospel effectively in Africa; originally published in 1963.

CR629 Towa, Marcien
Essai sur la problématique philosophique dans l'Afrique actuelle. (Point de vue, 8). Yaounde, CM: Éditions CLE, 1971. 77 pp. No ISBN.
A brief introduction to Bantu philosophy and the concept of *negritude* in relation to European philosophic traditions.

CR630 Turaki, Yusufu
Tribal Gods of Africa: Ethnicity, Racism, Tribalism and the Gospel of Christ. Jos, NR: Crossroads Media Services, 1997. viii, 168 pp. 9783402560.
The author traces the moral values and principles from African traditional religions, and uses them to help Africans understand the principles of Christ's redemption on the Cross in ethical as well as salvific terms.

CR631 Twesigye, Emmanuel K.
Common Ground: Christianity, African Religion and Philosophy. (American University Studies, 7: Theology and Religion, 25). Bern, SZ: Lang, 1987. xiv, 227 pp. 082040408X.
A comparative analysis of philosophical and theological traditions of both Africa and the Christian West, comparing the anthropology and soteriology of Karl Rahner with that of traditional African religion.

CR632 Verbeek, Léon
Le monde des esprits au sud-est du Shaba et au nord de la Zambie. (Biblioteca di Scienze Religiose, 89). Rome, IT: Libreria Ateneo Salesiano, 1990. 305 pp. Paper. 8821301923.
Original texts in chiBemba and other African languages, with French translations and interpretive commentary, on interviews conducted in 1986 with informants on traditional African religion in the Shaba Province of Zaire, and the Luapula Province of Zambia.

CR—CHRISTIANITY AND OTHER RELIGIONS

CR633 Weinecke, Werner A.
Die Bedeutung der Zeit in Afrika: In den traditionellen Religionen und in der missionarischen Verkündigung. (Studies in the Intercultural History of Christianity, 81). Frankfurt am Main, GW: Lang, 1992. 363 pp. Paper. 3631446313.

A European missionary to South-West Africa (Namibia) demonstrates how the African perception of time is a key concept in understanding African religion, with notable consequences for theology and for missionary work in that arena.

CR634 Westerlund, David
African Religion in African Scholarship: A Preliminary Study of the Religious and Political Background. (Studies Published by the Institute of Comparative Religion at the University of Stockholm, 7). Stockholm, NE: Almqvist & Wiksell, 1985. 104 pp. Paper. 9171463445.

An analytical survey of research by African scholars on African religion in West, East, and Central Africa.

Christianity and Native American Religions

See also CR1440, AM670-AM671, AM833, AM869, AM1165, AM1272, and AM1309.

CR635 Aberle, David F.
The Peyote Religion among the Navaho. Norman, OKU: University of Oklahoma Press, 1982. lii, 451 pp. Paper. 0806123826.

A comprehensive study of Navajo Peyotism in historical and contemporary practice, with discussion of Christian missions and both Peyotism and anti-Peyotism.

CR636 Carmody, Denise Lardner, and John Carmody
Native American Religions: An Introduction. Mahwah, NJU: Paulist Press, 1993. viii, 270 pp. Paper. 0809134047.

An introduction to the spiritual traditions of native Americans, from northern Alaska and Canada to the southernmost point of South America, with occasional references to the impact of Christian missions.

CR637 Carrasco, David
Religions of Mesoamerica: Cosmovision and Ceremonial Centers. (Religious Traditions of the World Series). San Fransisco, CAU: Harper & Row, 1990. xxviii, 174 pp. Paper. 0060613254.

Reviews the history and cosmovision of the region's religions with major attention to the Aztecs and Mayas, the impact of the Spanish conquest, and the post-conquest continuity of the native traditions.

CR638 Cervantes, Fernando
The Devil in the New World: The Impact of Diabolism in New Spain. New Haven, CTU: Yale University Press, 1994. viii, 182 pp. 0300059752.

Describes the encounter and interaction of religions, Spanish and Native American, during Mexico's colonial period; with special reference to beliefs about, and pacts with, the Devil.

CR639 Fornet-Betancourt, Raúl, ed.
Mystik der Erde: Elemente einer indianischen Theologie. (Theologie der Dritten Welt, 23). Freiburg, GW: Herder Verlag, 1997. 260 pp. 3451264129.

A collection of scholarly essays on Americo-Indian religions and Christianity, with implications for developing Americo-Indian theologies.

CR640 Gill, Sam D.
Native American Religions: An Introduction. (The Religious Life of Man Series). Belmont, CAU: Wadsworth Publishing, 1982. xvi, 192 pp. Paper. 0534009735.

An introduction to Native American religions with references to the impact of Christian missions.

CR641 Gill, Sam D.
Native American Traditions: Sources and Interpretations. (The Religious Life of Man Series). Belmont, CAU: Wadsworth Publishing, 1983. xii, 183 pp. Paper. 0534013740.

A sourcebook of writings by interpreters (including missionaries) of Native American religions and worldviews, containing the words of Native Americans wherever possible.

CR642 Gossen, Gary H., ed.
South and Meso-American Native American Spirituality: From the Cult of the Feathered Serpent to the Theology of Liberation. (World Spirituality: An Encyclopedic History of the Religious Quest, 4). New York, NYU: Crossroad Publishing, 1993. xii, 563 pp. 0824512243.

Explores religions of the region from the pre-Columbian period to the present, describing Amerindian state religions, varieties of transplanted Hispanic Catholicism, the meeting of these traditions, contemporary religions in the region, and the complex intermingling of ideas and beliefs.

CR643 Harrison, Sue
Mother Earth, Father Sky. New York, NYU: Doubleday, 1990. 320 pp. 0385411596.

A novel set in the Aleutian Islands (Alaska) in the 8th millennium B.C., which includes reflections on issues of the relation between the Christian Church and native traditions, including approaches to morality and women's concerns.

CR644 Hultkrantz, Åke
De amerikanska indianeras religioner. (Scandanavian University Books). Stockholm, SW: Svenska Bokförlaget, 1967. 276 pp. No ISBN.

A comprehensive survey of the indigenous religions of North, Meso-, and South America, with references to the impact of Christian missions.

CR645 Hultkrantz, Åke
The Religions of the American Indians. Translated by Monica Setterwall. (Hermeneutics: Studies in the History of Religions, 7). Berkeley, CAU: University of California Press, 1979. xiv, 335 pp. 0520026535.

English translation.

CR646 Luckert, Karl W.
The Navajo Hunter Tradition. Translated by John Cook, Victor Beck, and Irvy Goossen. Tucson, AZU: University of Arizona Press, 1975. viii, 239 pp. Paper. 0816505489 (hdbk), 0816504393 (pbk).

A sourcebook on Navajo hunter mythology by a leading authority on Native American religions, showing the continuity between the Navajo and Western religious traditions.

CR647 Schreijäck, Thomas, ed.
Die indianischen Gesichter Gottes. Frankfurt am Main, GW: IKO-Verlag für Interkulturelle Kommunikation, 1992. 307 pp. Paper. 388939051X.

German translation.

CR–CHRISTIANITY AND OTHER RELIGIONS

CR648 Marzal, Manuel M., ed.
El Rostro Indio de Dios. Lima, PE: Pontificia Universidad Católica del Perú, 1991. 448 pp. Paper. No ISBN.
One descriptive and four analytical articles, examining the actual religious practices and beliefs about God among the Rurámuri and Tseltales of Mexico, the Quechua of the south Peruvian Andes, the Aymara of Bolivia, Chile, and Peru, and the Guarani of Paraguay; written in preparation for the 500th anniversary of the first evangelization of the Americas.

CR649 Marzal, Manuel M.
Estudios sobre la religión campesina. Lima, PE: Pontificia Universidad Católica del Perú, 1977. 306 pp. Paper. No ISBN.
A study of indigenous religious concepts that are important for the evangelization of a predominantly rural country.

CR650 Marzal, Manuel M.
The Indian Face of God in Latin America. Translated by Penelope R. Hall. (Faith and Culture Series). Maryknoll, NYU: Orbis Books, 1996. x, 245 pp. Paper. 1570750548.
English translation.

CR651 Marzal, Manuel M.
O Rosto índio de Deus. Translated by Jaime A. Clasen. (Coleção Teologia e libertação, Serie VII: Desafios do Religião do povo, 1). São Paulo, BL: Vozes, 1989. 357 pp. No ISBN.
Portuguese translation.

CR652 Pflüg, Melissa A.
Ritual and Myth in Odawa Revitalization: Reclaiming a Sovereign Place. Norman, OKU: University of Oklahoma Press, 1998. xvi, 280 pp. 0806130075.
An ethnographic account of how myths and rituals helped the Odawa (Ottawa) people of the Great Lakes region to establish a strong tribal identity, which Christianity could not provide.

CR653 Ruiz de Alarcón, Hernando
Treatise on the Heathen Superstitions: That Today Live among the Indians Native to This New Spain, 1629. Translated by J. Richard Andrews, and Ross Hassig. (The Civilization of the American Indian Series, 164). Norman, OKU: University of Oklahoma Press, 1984. xxvi, 406 pp. Paper. 0806120312.
In this important surviving document of early colonial Mexico, written in 1629, the author meticulously records Nahuatl (Aztec) religious beliefs and practices as an aid to evangelization.

CR654 Starkloff, Carl F.
The People of the Center: American Indian Religion and Christianity. New York, NYU: Seabury Press, 1974. 144 pp. 0816492077.
An introduction to Native American religion for white Christians, including its mythical, doctrinal, ritual, ethical, social, and experiential dimensions.

CR655 Tedlock, Dennis, and Barbara Tedlock, eds.
Teachings from the American Earth: Indian Religion and Philosophy. New York, NYU: Liveright, 1975. xxiv, 279 pp. 0871405597 (hdbk), 0871400979 (pbk).
An anthology of seven writings by Native Americans, and seven by Anglo scholars, on various aspects of both Christianity and Native American myth and religion.

CR656 Vecsey, Christopher, ed.
Religion in Native North America. Moscow, IDU: University of Idaho Press, 1990. xiii, 201 pp. Paper. 0893011363.
Eleven scholarly case studies of the religion of various Native American tribes, including mission Christianity; by scholars from Canada, the United States, England, and Scandanavia.

CR657 Weaver, Jace, ed.
Native American Religious Identity: Unforgotten Gods. Maryknoll, NYU: Orbis Books, 1998. xiii, 242 pp. Paper. 1570751811.
Fifteen Native American scholars and writers combine to examine the issue of native religious identity today, including Christian, traditional, and "post-Christian" perspectives.

Christianity and Buddhism

See also CR4, CR138, CR168, CR285, CR295, CR513, CR782, CR1422, SP90, SP94-SP95, SP102, AS188, AS212, AS1266, and AS1508.

CR658 Åmell, Katrin
"Frsn solens uppgsng": Brev herm frsn Japan. Stockholm, SW: Proprius, 1989. 191 pp. 9171186573.
A book on the dialogue between Christianity and Buddhism in Japan.

CR659 Abe, Masao
Buddhism and Interfaith Dialogue: Part One of a Two-Volume Sequel to "Zen and Western Thought." Edited by Steven Heine. Honolulu, HIU: University of Hawaii Press; London, ENK: Macmillan, 1995. xx, 245 pp. 0824817516 (hdbk), 0824817524 (pbk).
Essays by the leading exponent of Zen Buddhism in the West on the Buddhist approach to interfaith dialogue, 20th-century theological issues, and the thought of Paul Tillich.

CR660 Abe, Masao
Zen and Western Thought. Edited by William R. LaFleur. Honolulu, HIU: University of Hawaii Press; London, ENK: Macmillan, 1985. xix, 308 pp. 0824809521.
Essays interpreting Zen Buddhism for Western readers, with a comparison of Zen and Christianity, by the well-known Professor of Japanese Philosophy at the University of Hawaii.

CR661 Amore, Roy C.
Two Masters, One Message. Nashville, TNU: Abingdon, 1978. 208 pp. 0687427509 (hbk), 0687427517 (pbk).
After showing the possibility that there may have been Buddhist influence on New Testament writers, Amore traces the similarities in the life-structure and teachings of Jesus and Buddha, and concludes that there may have been Buddhist influence on the formation of Q.

CR662 Appleton, George
On the Eightfold Path: Christian Presence Amid Buddhism. (Christian Presence Series). New York, NYU: Oxford University Press, 1961. 156 pp. No ISBN.
An introduction for Christians to Buddhism as a living faith, suggesting how Christians who seek to experience Buddhist spirituality may, by doing so, come to a new experience of Jesus Christ.

CR663 Berrigan, Daniel, and Thich Nhat Hanh
The Raft Is Not the Shore: Conversations toward a Buddhist/Christian Awareness. Boston, MAU: Beacon Press, 1975. 139 pp. 080701124X (hdbk), 0807011258 (pbk).
Both partners in this conversation draw on their traditions in order to show how they can make a contribution to the concrete social needs of humanity, expecially in light of the Vietnam War.

CR664 Bobilin, Robert

Revolution from Below: Buddhist and Christian Movements for Justice in Asia. Lanham, MDU: University Press of America, 1988. x, 180 pp. 0819170372 (hdbk), 0819170380 (pbk).

A compilation of four case studies concerning movements in Thailand and Sri Lanka, which provides an outline of the socio-economic teaching, the role of founders and leaders, and the social action of the four Christian and Buddhist movements.

CR665 Bruns, J. Edgar

The Christian Buddhism of St. John: New Insights into the Fourth Gospel. New York, NYU: Paulist Press, 1971. xiv, 80 pp. Paper. No ISBN.

Shows basic similarities in the way of life and notion of the Ultimate in Buddhism and John's Gospel, and argues that there may have been some Buddhist influence on the author of the Fourth Gospel.

CR666 Buri, Fritz

Der Buddha-Christus als der Herr des wahren Selbst: Die Religionsphilosophie der Kyoto-Schule und das Christentum. Bern, SZ: Haupt, 1982. 469 pp. 3258031622.

From the angle of comparative religion, this book inquires about the encounter of Christianity with Asia, in particular the philosophy of religion of the so-called Kyoto School of Buddhism.

CR667 Buri, Fritz et al.

Erlösung in Christentum und Buddhismus. (Religionstheologische Studientagung 3,). Edited by Andreas Bsteh. (Beiträge zur Religionstheologie, 3). Mödling, AU: Verlag St. Gabriel, 1982. 200 pp. Paper. 3852641861.

An introduction into the situation of the Christian-Buddhist dialogue of the present, an analysis of the human need for salvation, and basic reflections on the way of salvation in both traditions.

CR668 Burnett, David

The Spirit of Buddhism. Crowborough, ENK: MARC-Monarch Publications; Ware, ENK: All Nations Christian College, 1996. 288 pp. Paper. 1854242989.

An introduction to Buddhist traditions from a Christian perspective; by the Director of Studies at All Nations Christian College in England.

CR669 Callaway, Tucker N.

Zen Way: Jesus Way. Rutland, VTU: Tuttle, 1976. 263 pp. 0840811903.

A strong criticism of Zen metaphysics on the basis of Christian convictions and the author's dialogues as a Protestant missionary with Zen masters in Japan.

CR670 Cobb, John B., and Christopher Ives, eds.

The Emptying God: A Buddhist-Jewish-Christian Conversation. (Faith Meets Faith Series). Maryknoll, NYU: Orbis Books, 1990. xix, 212 pp. Paper. 0883446715 (hdbk), 0883446707 (pbk).

Nine critical and constructive essays on Buddhist-Christian relations, focused on the thought of Masao Abe whose Kyoto School of Buddhism rejects theism yet seeks dialogue with Christians.

CR671 Cobb, John B.

Beyond Dialogue: Toward a Mutual Transformation of Christianity and Buddhism. Philadelphia, PAU: Fortress Press, 1982. xiii, 156 pp. Paper. 0800616472.

Themes in the Christian-Buddhist (especially Mahayana) dialogue that prepare the way for transformative growth in both religions.

CR672 Cobb, John B.

Bouddhisme—Christianisme: au-delà du dialogue? Translated by Marc Deshays. (Lieux théologiques, 13). Geneva, SZ: Labor et Fides, 1988. 178 pp. Paper. 2830901177.

French translation.

CR673 Corless, Roger, and Paul F. Knitter, eds.

Buddhist Emptiness and Christian Trinity: Essays and Explorations. Mahwah, NJU: Paulist Press, 1990. iii, 109 pp. Paper. 0809131315.

Essays by Masao Abe, Michael von Brück, and Roger Corless, with responses by Hans Küng, Paul Ingram, and Durwood Foster, on what kind of positive relations one can or cannot make, between emptiness and a deeper understanding of the Trinity.

CR674 Dalai Lama XIV

The Good Heart. Edited by Robert Kiely. Translated by Geshe Thupten Jinpa. London, ENK: Rider, 1996. xiv, 207 pp. Paper. 0712672753.

Commentaries by the Dalai Lama on passages from the Gospels; originally presented at the John Main Seminar (London 1994), sponsored by the World Community for Christian Meditation to bring Christians and Buddhists together in friendship.

CR675 De Silva, Lynn A.

Reincarnation in Buddhist and Christian Thought. Colombo, CE: CLS, 1968. 176 pp. No ISBN.

Numerous well-documented quotations and testimonies by one who has been active for many years in Buddhist-Christian dialogue.

CR676 Dharmasiri, Gunapala

A Buddhist Critique of the Christian Concept of God. Antioch, CAU: Golden Leaves, 1988. xxi, 313 pp. Paper. 0942353013 (hdbk), 0942353005 (pbk).

In this work the Professor of Philosophy at the University of Sri Lanka provides a detailed comparison of contemporary Christian theological ideas with early Buddhist teachings, arguing that the Western concept of God is undeveloped and unrefined when compared with that in Eastern thought.

CR677 Drummond, Richard Henry

A Broader Vision: Perspectives on the Buddha and the Christ. Virginia Beach, VAU: ARE Press, 1995. xx, 341 pp. Paper. 0876043481.

A scholarly comparative study of the lives and teachings of the Buddha and Jesus Christ.

CR678 Drummond, Richard Henry

Gautama the Buddha: An Essay in Religious Understanding. Grand Rapids, MIU: Eerdmans, 1974. 239 pp. Paper. 0802834442.

A review of the life and teachings of the Buddha, followed by an analysis that points out areas where Christians might fruitfully dialogue with Buddhists.

CR679 Dumoulin, Heinrich, ed.

Buddhism in the Modern World. New York, NYU: Macmillan; London, ENK: Collier Macmillan, 1976. xii, 368 pp. 0025337904 (hdbk), 0020847904 (pbk).

English translation.

CR680 Dumoulin, Heinrich, ed.
Buddhismus der Gegenwart. (Weltgespräch). Freiburg, GW: Herder, 1970. 232 pp. No ISBN.

Twenty scholarly essays on contemporary Buddhism in fifteen countries of Asia, with five general essays on Buddhist teachings, movements, and societal impact.

CR681 Dunne, Carrin
Buda y Jesús: Diálogos. Madrid, II: Ediciones Paulinas, 1978. 173 pp. Paper. 8428506868.

Spanish translation.

CR682 Dunne, Carrin
Buddha and Jesus: Conversations. Springfield, ILU: Templegate, 1975. 112 pp. Paper. 87243057X (SBN).

Free-flowing, imaginary conversations between Buddha and Jesus in which they explore questions regarding God, self, the world, action in the world—and learn from each other.

CR683 Enomiya-Lassalle, Hugo M.
Leben im neuen Bewusstsein. Munich, GW: Kösel-Verlag, 1986. 3466202817.

Selections from the writings of Hugo Enomiya-Lassalle [Hugo Makibi]—a German Jesuit priest who is also a Zen master—on Christian spirituality through the practice of Zen meditation.

CR684 Enomiya-Lassalle, Hugo M.
Living in the New Consciousness. Edited by Roland Ropers. Translated by Paul Shepherd. Boston, MAU: Shambhala Publications, 1988. xix, 153 pp. Paper. 0877734496.

English translation.

CR685 Enomiya-Lassalle, Hugo M.
Zen Meditation for Christians. Translated by John C. Maraldo. (Religious Encounters: East and West). LaSalle, ILU: Open Court, 1974. 175 pp. 0875481515.

English translation.

CR686 Enomiya-Lassalle, Hugo M.
Zen-Meditation: Eine Einführung. Zürich, SZ: Einsiedeln; Cologne, GW: Benziger, 1975. 164 pp. 3545200531.

An introduction to Zen meditation for Christians with a comparison of Zen and Christian mysticism; originally published in 1968.

CR687 Eusden, John Dykstra
Zen and Christian: The Journey Between. New York, NYU: Crossroad Publishing, 1981. 189 pp. 0824500997.

An experiential introduction to Zen Buddhism by the professor of Christian theology at Williams College in the United States, a minister of the United Church of Christ who also became a member of a Zen Buddhist temple.

CR688 Fernando, Antony
Zu den Quellen des Buddhismus: Eine Einführung für Christen. (Topos Taschenbücher, 169). Mainz, GW: Grünewald, 1987. 191 pp. Paper. 3786713138.

German translation of *Buddhism and Christianity: Their Inner Affinity* (1981).

CR689 Fernando, Antony, and Leonard J. Swidler
Buddhism Made Plain: An Introduction for Christians and Jews. Maryknoll, NYU: Orbis Books, 1985. xxii, 138 pp. Paper. 0883441989.

Revised edition of a clear explanation of the heart of the teaching of Buddha, and comparison to the heart of the Judeo-Christian tradition; originally published as *Buddhism and Christianity : Their Inner Affinity* (Colombo: Ecumenical Institute for Study and Dialogue, 1981).

CR690 Fox, Douglas A.
Buddhism, Christianity, and the Future of Man. Philadelphia, PAU: Westminster Press, 1970. 190 pp. 0664209378.

In this work the author, an Associate Professor of Religion at Colorado College (US), examines Buddhism and Christianity to discover whether they really offer a framework by which people can confidently address the challenges and opportunities of the modern world.

CR691 Geffré, Claude, and Mariasusai Dhavamony, eds.
Buddhism and Christianity. (*Concilium*: Religion in the Seventies, 116). New York, NYU: Seabury Press, 1979. x, 126 pp. Paper. 0816403953 (hdbk), 0816426120 (pbk).

Thirteen essays by Christian specialists on the mainstream of Buddhist thought and practice, designed to aid interfaith understanding, and raise the theological problems involved in Buddhist-Christian dialogue.

CR692 Graham, Dom Aelred
Conversations: Christian and Buddhist Encounters in Japan. New York, NYU: Harcourt, Brace and World, 1968. xvi, 206 pp. No ISBN.

Thirteen discussions held by the Prior of the Benedictine Community in Portsmouth, Rhode Island, with representatives of the Buddhist faith in Japan.

CR693 Graham, Dom Aelred
Zen Catholicism: A Suggestion. (A Harvest Book). New York, NYU: Harcourt, Brace & World, Inc, 1963. xxv, 228 pp. Paper. No ISBN.

A Benedictine monk, educator, and writer reflects upon points of contact between Zen Buddhism and Catholicism.

CR694 Habito, Ruben L. F.
Total Liberation: Zen Spirituality and the Social Dimension. Maryknoll, NYU: Orbis Books, 1989. xviii, 110 pp. Paper. 0883445379.

Habito demonstrates the relevance of Zen to contemporary Christian spirituality, and to a socially active role in the world; a revised and expanded edition originally published by the Zen Center for Oriental Spirituality in the Philippines (1986).

CR695 Hackett, David G.
The Silent Dialogue: Zen Letters to a Trappist Abbot. New York, NYU: Continuum, 1996. 157 pp. 0826407803.

A Catholic practitioner of Zen meditation shares the journal relating two years of his participation in Christian-Buddhist dialogue in Japan and Southeast Asia, in the form of letters sent to Fr. Thomas Keating and the monks of his home St. Joseph's Abbey.

CR696 Hanh, Thich Nhat
Living Buddha, Living Christ. New York, NYU: Riverhead Books, 1995. xxvii, 208 pp. 1573220183.

Reflections on Buddhist-Christian dialogue by the noted Vietnamese monk, Zen master, and peace activist.

CR—CHRISTIANITY AND OTHER RELIGIONS

CR697 Hanh, Thich Nhat
Love in Action: Writings on Nonviolent Social Change. Berkeley, CAU: Parallax Press, 1993. 154 pp. Paper. 0938077635.

A collection of essays on nonviolence, peace, and reconciliation by a world leader of Engaged Buddhism who played a central role in the Buddhist non-violent movement for peace in Vietnam in the 1960s.

CR698 Henry, Patrick G., and Donald K. Swearer
For the Sake of the World: The Spirit of Buddhist and Christian Monasticism. Minneapolis, MNU: Fortress Press; Collegeville, MNU: Liturgical Press, 1989. 256 pp. 080062310X (F), 0814615880 (L).

A scholarly comparison of the monastic traditions in Christianity and Buddhism including such themes as contemplation and action, its ascetic ideal, the rule of life, the monk/nun as teacher, and attitudes to modernity.

CR699 Houston, G. W., ed.
The Cross and the Lotus: Christianity and Buddhism in Dialogue. Delhi, II: Motilal Banarsidass, 1985. 249 pp. 0895817675.

Ten scholarly essays to help people wrestle with what appear to be conflicting worldviews.

CR700 Houston, G. W., ed.
Dharma and Gospel: Two Ways of Seeing. (Bibliotheca Indo-Buddhica,13). Delhi, II: Sri Satguru Publications, 1984. vii, 124 pp. No ISBN.

Seven authors explore similarities and differences between the Christian and Buddhist notions of the ultimate; among the authors are John Cobb, Roger Corless, Massaki Honda, Jay McDaniel, and Seiichi Yagi.

CR701 Indapañño, Bhikkhu Buddhadasa
Christianity and Buddhism. (Sinclaire Thompson Memorial Lecture, 5). Bangkok, TH: Sublime Life Mission, 1967. 123 pp. Paper. No ISBN.

A Thai Buddhist scholar and monk's comparison of Thai Pali Buddhism with Christianity; originally presented as the Sinclaire Thompson Memorial Lectures at the Thailand Theological Seminary (Chiang Mai, 18-20 February 1967).

CR702 Ingram, Paul O., and Frederick J. Streng, eds.
Buddhist-Christian Dialogue: Mutual Renewal and Transformation. Honolulu, HIU: University of Hawaii Press, 1986. 248 pp. Paper. 0824808290.

Eleven essays on philosophical, theological, and structural aspects of contemporary Buddhist-Christian dialogue in an effort to assess its potential as a source for the renewal and transformation of both traditions.

CR703 Ingram, Paul O.
The Modern Buddhist-Christian Dialogue: Two Universalistic Religions in Transformation. (Studies in Comparative Religion, 2). Lewiston, NYU: E Mellen Press, 1988. xvii, 441 pp. 0889464901.

A discussion of contemporary Buddhist-Christian dialogue; and an analysis of their transformation and theological structures in the "post-Christian" era of religious and secular pluralism.

CR704 Italiaander, Rolf, ed.
Eine Religion für den Frieden: Die Rissho Kosei-kai: Japanische Buddhisten für die Ökumene der Religionen. (Erlanger Taschenbücher, 23). Erlangen, GW: Ev.-Luth. Mission, 1973. 170 pp. 3872140450.

Fourteen diverse essays arguing for continued dialogue between Buddhists and Christians including contributions about Rissho Kosei-kai, a Japanese lay movement for dialogue.

CR705 Johnston, William
Christian Zen. New York, NYU: Fordham University Press, 1997. 134 pp. 0823218007.

Third edition of a readable study of Zen meditation in the light of Christian mysticism with a Thomas Merton letter to the author; originally published by Harper & Row in 1971.

CR706 Johnston, William
The Still Point: Reflections on Zen and Christian Mysticism. New York, NYU: Harper & Row, 1971. 239 pp. Paper. 0800616472.

Insightful presentation of possibilities for Christians to profit from Zen practice and perspective.

CR707 Keenan, John P.
The Gospel of Mark: A Mahayana Reading. (Faith Meets Faith Series). Maryknoll, NYU: Orbis Books, 1995. viii, 423 pp. Paper. 1570750416.

The Professor of Religious Studies at Middlebury College, an Episcopal priest, provides a commentary on St. Mark's Gospel through the lens of Mahayana Buddhist philosophy.

CR708 Keenan, John P.
The Meaning of Christ: A Mahayana Theology. (Faith Meets Faith Series). Maryknoll, NYU: Orbis Books, 1989. viii, 312 pp. Paper. 0883446413 (hdbk), 0883446405 (pbk).

A reinterpretation of Christian tradition in the light of Mahayana Buddist philosophy, first examining the meaning of Christ as developed in the early church, and then applying the Mahayana approach to the doctrines of incarnation and Trinity.

CR709 Kern, Iso
Buddhistische Kritik am Christentum im China des 17. Jahrhunderts: Text von Yu Shunxi, (?-1621), Zhuhong (1535-1615), Yuanwu (1566-1642), Tongrong (1593-1679), Xingyaun (1611-1662), Zhixu (1599-1655). (Schweizer Asiatische Studien, 11). Frankfurt am Main, GW: Lang, 1992. 418 pp. Paper. 3261044950.

Texts from 17th-century Chinese Buddhism which provide substantial criticism of doctrines taught by the Jesuit missionaries, such as the creation of the world and the immortality of the human soul.

CR710 King, Winston Lee
Buddhism and Christianity: Some Bridges of Understanding. Philadelphia, PAU: Westminster Press; Greenwood, SCU: Attic Press; London, ENK: Allen and Unwin, 1963. 240 pp. No ISBN.

Working mainly with the Theravada tradition of Buddhism, King shows the points of convergence in the areas of God, love, conquest of self, grace, and faith.

CR711 Klimkeit, Hans-Joachim
Die Begegnung von Christentum, Gnosis und Buddhismus an der Seidenstrasse. (Geisteswissenschaften/Rheinisch-Westfälische Akademie der Wissenschaften; Vorträge, G283). Opladen, GW: Westdeutscher Verlag, 1986. 54 pp. 3531072838.

A scholarly essay on the historical encounter in central Asia along the Silk Road, between Christianity, Buddhism, and Manichaeism.

CR—CHRISTIANITY AND OTHER RELIGIONS

CR712 Krüger, J. S.
Metatheism: Early Buddhism and Traditional Christian Theism. Pretoria, SA: University of South Africa, 1989. ix, 142 pp. Paper. 0869816209.

A comparative study of the god-concept in Christianity, and in an early Buddhist *sutra*, the *Tevijja Sutta*.

CR713 Langer-Kaneko, Christiane
Das Reine Land: Zur Begegnung von Amida-Buddhismus und Christentum. (Zeitschrift für Religions- und Geistesgeschichte, 29). Leiden, NE: Brill, 1986. ix, 193 pp. 9004077863.

A work on Amida (Jodo) Buddhism—the first part dealing with core themes like suffering, faith, and liberation; the second with the history of its encounter with Christianity (dissertation, University of Tübingen 1982).

CR714 Lefebure, Leo D.
The Buddha and the Christ: Explorations in Buddhist and Christian Dialogue. (Faith Meets Faith Series). Maryknoll, NYU: Orbis Books, 1993. xxiii, 239 pp. Paper. 0883449242.

A scholarly analysis of similarities and differences between Shakyamuni, called the Buddha, and Jesus, called the Christ, and between traditions of theology and mysticism in Mahayana Buddhism and Christianity.

CR715 Lefebure, Leo D.
Life Transformed: Meditations on the Christian Scriptures in Light of Buddhist Perspectives. Chicago, ILU: ACTA Publications, 1989. xii, 186 pp. Paper. 0914070614.

The author, a Roman Catholic theologian and member of the Society for Buddhist-Christian Studies, experienced meditation practices of Theravada and Zen Buddhists, and then applied the wisdom of Buddhist perspectives on life in these short meditations on Old and New Testament passages.

CR716 Ling, Trevor
Buddha, Marx, and God: Some Aspects of Religion in the Modern World. London, ENK: Macmillan; New York, NYU: St. Martin's Press, 1966. xii, 227 pp. No ISBN.

After introducing contemporary Buddhist faith and practice, the author relates the growing appeal of Buddhism for Westerners to the Marxist critique of religion, suggesting the need for a Christian theology relevant to issues raised both by contemporary Buddhism and Marxism.

CR717 Lopez, Donald S., and Steven C. Rockefeller, eds.
The Christ and the Bodhisattva. Albany, NYU: SUNY Press, 1987. viii, 274 pp. 0887064019.

Nine essays by three eminent Christian theologians exploring both the significance of the Christ from the Roman Catholic contemplative tradition, modern depth psychology, and liberal Protestantism, and the significance of the Bodhisattva in India, East Asia, and Tibet.

CR718 Masutani, Fumio
A Comparative Study of Buddhism and Christianity. Tokyo, JA: Bukkyo Dendo Kyokai, 1967. iv, 193 pp. No ISBN.

A fifth edition in which a Taisho University (Japan) professor compares Buddhist and Christian answers to four basic questions: What is the nature of Man? What should I hope to be? What should I rely on? and What should I do?

CR719 May, John D'Arcy
Meaning, Consensus and Dialogue in Buddhist-Christian Communication: A Study in the Construction of Meaning.

(Studies in the Intercultural History of Christianity, 31). Bern, SZ: Lang, 1984. xi, 348 pp. Paper. 3261032871.

A scholarly comparative study of the systems of meaning in Buddhist and Judeo-Christian scriptures, with an analysis of the resulting hermeneutics, logic, and programs of contemporary Buddhist-Christian dialogue; presented as a doctoral thesis at the Johann Wolfgang Goethe University in Frankfurt am Main, Germany.

CR720 Meier, Erhard, and Adel Théodore Khoury
Buddha für Christen: Eine Herausforderung. (Herderbücherei, 1303). Freiburg im Breisgau, GW: Herder, 1986. 190 pp. Paper. 3451083035.

Meier describes the Buddha, his teachings, and their significance for Christians; Khoury provides an anthology of Buddhist texts and bibliography.

CR721 Melzer, Friso
Das Licht der Welt: Beiträge zur Begegnung mit asiatischer Hochreligion. Stuttgart, GW: Evan Missionsverlag, 1973. 195 pp. Paper. 3771401771.

After thirty years of reflection on Asian religions, this Protestant author presents his views on interreligious dialogue, asserting that Jesus Christ is the only light of the world and has brought to fulfillment the limited religious expressions found in Buddhism and its contemporary religious traditions.

CR722 Merton, Thomas
Mystics and Zen Masters. New York, NYU: Farrar, Straus and Giroux, 1967. x, 303 pp. No ISBN.

Merton, the Benedictine contemplative, analyzes both difficulties and opportunities in the Zen Buddhist-Christian dialogue on the level of mysticism.

CR723 Merton, Thomas
Zen and the Birds of Appetite. (A New Directions Book). New York, NYU: New Directions, 1968. ix, 141 pp. No ISBN.

The noted Trappist monk's reflections on Christianity and Zen Buddhism containing his dialogue with the Zen master, D. T. Suzuki.

CR724 Mitchell, Donald W.
Spirituality and Emptiness: The Dynamics of Spiritual Life in Buddhism and Christianity. New York, NYU: Paulist Press, 1991. xvi, 224 pp. Paper. 0809132664.

A detailed study of the archetypal theme of emptiness from the perspectives of deeply held commitments inside both the traditions of Zen and Pure Land Buddhism of The Kyoto School, and in Christianity.

CR725 Mommaers, Paul, and Jan van Bragt
Mysticism Buddhist and Christian: Encounters with Jan van Ruusbroec. (Nanzan Studies in Religion and Culture). New York, NYU: Crossroad Publishing, 1995. v, 302 pp. 0824514556.

A scholarly study of parallels and contradictions between Buddhist mysticism and that of Jan van Ruusbroec (1293-1381).

CR726 Niles, Daniel Thambyrajah
Buddhism and the Claims of Christ. Richmond, VAU: John Knox Press, 1967. 88 pp. Paper. No ISBN.

A Ceylonese Methodist minister's presentation of basic Christian beliefs in Buddhist idioms as catechetical tools for introducing Buddhists to the Christian faith.

CR—CHRISTIANITY AND OTHER RELIGIONS

CR727 O'Connor, Patrick, ed.

Buddhists Find Christ: The Spritual Quest of Thirteen Men and Women in Burma, China, Japan, Korea, Sri Lanka, Thailand, Vietnam. Rutland, VTU: Tuttle, 1975. viii, 180 pp. Paper. 0804811466.

Thirteen stories compiled by a Catholic priest and journalist, written by modern Asian men and women of Buddhist background who tell how their quest for enlightenment, an essential Buddhist goal, led them to Christ.

CR728 Pallis, Marco

A Buddhist Spectrum: Contributions to Buddhist-Christian Dialogue. New York, NYU: Seabury Press., 1981. ix, 163 pp. 0816404933.

Drawing on his thirty years of Buddhist practice, this Christian author explores a variety of Buddhist views and practices and their significance for Christian notions of the self, evil, grace, and theological reflection.

CR729 Panikkar, Raimundo

The Silence of God: The Answer of the Buddha. Translated by Robert R. Barr. (Faith Meets Faith Series). Maryknoll, NYU: Orbis Books, 1989. xxvi, 268 pp. 0883444661 (hdbk), 0883444453 (pbk).

A scholarly analysis of issues in Buddhist-Christian dialogue challenging the Western view of Buddhism as "atheistic."

CR730 Pieris, Aloysius

Fire and Water: Basic Issues in Asian Buddhism and Christianity. (Faith Meets Faith Series). Maryknoll, NYU: Orbis Books, 1996. xvi, 219 pp. Paper. 1570750556.

A wide-ranging discussion by the noted Sri Lankan theologian on authentic Asian perspectives on women's issues, feminist theology, spirituality and human liberation, mission, and Buddhist-Christian dialogue.

CR731 Pieris, Aloysius

Liebe und Weisheit: Begegnung von Christentum und Buddhismus. Translated by Wolfgang Siepen. Mainz, GW: Matthias-Grünewald-Verlag, 1989. 203 pp. 3786714126.

German translation.

CR732 Pieris, Aloysius

Love Meets Wisdom: A Christian Experience of Buddhism. (Faith Meets Faith Series). Maryknoll, NYU: Orbis Books, 1988. xii, 161 pp. Paper. 0883443724 (hdbk), 0883443716 (pbk).

An exploration of the social and spiritual dimensions of Buddhism, its doctrine and political vision, and issues pertinent to an interreligious understanding between Christians and Buddhists, by the director of Tulana Dialogue Center in Kelaniya, Sri Lanka.

CR733 Pieris, Aloysius, ed.

Woman and Man in Buddhism and Christianity. (Dialogue New Series, 19-20). Colombo, CE: Ecumenical Institute for Study & Dialogue, 1992-1993. vi, 254 pp. Paper. No ISBN.

Seven scholarly essays comparing the attitudes in Buddhism and Christianity towards women and the contemporary feminist critique; written to honor two Sri Lankan pioneers in Christian-Buddhist dialogue (Lynn A. Lakshmi and Lakshmi de Silva); published as a special issue of *Dialogue*.

CR734 Prothero, Stephen

The White Buddhist: The Asian Odyssey of Henry Steel Olcott. Bloomington, INU: Indiana University Press, 1996. xiii, 242 pp. 0253330149.

A scholarly biography of Colonel Henry Steel Olcott (1832-1907), the first American of European descent to make a formal conversion to Buddhism. He defended Asian religions against the missionaries as President-Founder of the Theosophical Society.

CR735 Ri, Jemin

Wonhyo und das Christentum: Ishim als personale Kategorie. (Würzburger Studien zur Fundamentaltheologie, 2). Frankfurt am Main, GW: Lang, 1987. 387 pp. 3820488219.

A comparison of Christian thought with that of the 7th-century Buddhist philosopher Wonhyo, and of the syncretic Popsong School of Korean Buddhist thought that he inspired.

CR736 Rupp, George

Beyond Existentialism and Zen: Religion in a Pluralistic World. New York, NYU: Oxford University Press, 1979. xiv, 113 pp. 0195024631 (hdbk), 0195024621 (pbk).

Using the Christian notion of the Kingdom of God, Rupp seeks to mediate between Zen, which affirms the meaning of reality but leads to an acceptance of the status quo, and existentialism, which calls for engagement in the world but cannot ground the ultimate significance of such activity.

CR737 Senécal, Bernard

Jésus le Christ à la rencontre de Gautama le Bouddha: identité chrétienne et Bouddhisme. Paris, FR: Éditions du Cerf, 1998. 252 pp. Paper. 2204057568.

From a lifetime of ministry in Korea, a Jesuit missioner presents how a journey to the heart of Buddhism evokes a Christological crisis and demands a new theology of religions.

CR738 Siegmund, Georg

Buddhism and Christianity: A Preface to Dialogue. Translated by Mary Frances McCarthy. Tuscaloosa, ALU: University of Alabama Press, 1980. vii, 197 pp. 0817367039.

English translation.

CR739 Siegmund, Georg

Buddhismus und Christentum: Vorbereitung eines Dialogs. Frankfurt am Main, GW: Josef Knecht, 1968. 313 pp. No ISBN.

A scholarly comparison of the beliefs and religious experiences of Buddhism and Christianity, based in part on the author's visit to five countries of eastern Asia in 1966.

CR740 Silber, Ilana Friedrich

Virtuosity, Charisma, and Social Order: A Comparative Sociological Study of Monasticism in Theravada Buddhism and Medieval Catholicism. (Cambridge Cultural Social Studies). New York, NYU: Cambridge University Press, 1995. x, 250 pp. 0521413974.

The lecturer in sociology at Hebrew University in Jerusalem presents a scholarly comparison of monasticism in Theravada Buddhism and medieval Catholicism.

CR741 Sivaraksa, Sulak

A Buddhist Vision for Renewing Society: Collected Articles by a Concerned Thai Intellectual. Bangkok, TH: Tienwan Publishing House, 1986. xxvii, 243 pp. Paper. 9747493411.

A Thai Buddhist educated in Protestant and Catholic schools presents his vision for a socially engaged Buddhism and a renewed Thai society.

CR—CHRISTIANITY AND OTHER RELIGIONS

CR742 Smart, Ninian

Beyond Ideology: Religion and the Future of Western Civilization. San Francisco, CAU: Harper & Row, 1981. 350 pp. 0060674024.

In these Gifford Lectures of 1979-1980, Smart attempts two formidable objectives: to show the complementarity between Christianity and Buddhism, and to argue that their combined vision can help the global village survive and prosper.

CR743 Smart, Ninian

Buddhism and Christianity: Rivals and Allies. Honolulu, HIU: University of Hawaii Press, 1993. viii, 157 pp. 082481519X (hdbk), 0824815203 (pbk).

An examination by the J. F. Rowny Professor of Comparative Religions at the University of California, Santa Barbara, of relations between Buddhism and Christianity in the context of our emerging world civilization.

CR744 Spae, Joseph John

Buddhist-Christian Empathy. Chicago, ILU: Chicago Institute of Theology and Culture; Tokyo, JA: Oriens Institute for Religious Research, 1980. 269 pp. 0936078022.

In this fifth volume in a series of studies related to the encounter of Christianity with Eastern cultures, the noted Catholic specialist on Japanese culture compares Buddhist and Christian mysticism, models of holiness, and themes for dialogue.

CR745 Takizawa, Katsumi

Reflexionen über die universale Grundlage in Buddhismus und Christentum. (Studien zur interkulturellen Geschichte des Christentums, 24). Frankfurt am Main, GW: Lang, 1980. viii, 195 pp. 3820464484.

Within an existential framework the author examines parallels between Buddhism and Christianity, with heavy reliance on Karl Barth as normative for Christianity.

CR746 Thelle, Notto R.

Buddhism and Christianity in Japan: From Conflict to Dialogue, 1854-1899. Honolulu, HIU: University of Hawaii Press, 1987. xi, 356 pp. 0824810066.

A scholarly account of cross-cultural interactions between Buddhists and Christians in the history of Japan, and how that history influences Buddhist-Christian dialogues today.

CR747 Toynbee, Arnold Joseph, and Daisaku Ikeda

Escolha a vida: Um diálogo sobre o futuro. Translated by Ruy Jungman. Rio de Janeiro, BL: Record, 1976. 346 pp. 8510345953.

Portuguese translation.

CR748 Toynbee, Arnold Joseph, and Daisaku Ikeda

The Toynbee-Ikeda Dialogue: Man Himself Must Choose. Tokyo, JA: Kodansha International, 1982. 348 pp. Paper. 0870115154 (US), 4770009984 (JP).

An East-West dialogue on scores of topics, including religion, between the eminent historian Arnold J. Toynbee and Daisaku Ikeda, religious leader of the Buddhist lay organization Soka Gokkai; first published in 1976.

CR749 Tweed, Thomas A.

The American Encounter with Buddhism, 1844-1912: Victorian Culture and the Limits of Dissent. (Religion in North America). Bloomington, INU: Indiana University Press, 1992. xxiv, 242 pp. 0253360994.

A detailed scholarly history of the early encounters of North American intellectuals with Buddhism, from Henry David Thoreau in 1844, to 1914; focusing on the debate which such contacts engendered concerning fundamental beliefs and values.

CR750 Waldenfels, Hans

Absolute Nothingness: Foundations for a Buddhist-Christian Dialogue. Translated by J. W. Heisig. New York, NYU: Paulist Press, 1980. ix, 214 pp. Paper. 0809123169.

English translation of *Absolutes Nichts* (1978).

CR751 Waldenfels, Hans

Absolutes Nichts: Zur Grundlegung des Dialogs zwischen Buddhismus und Christentum. Freiburg, GW: Herder, 1978. 222 pp. Paper. 3451176343.

This contribution to Christian-Buddhist dialogue compares the concept of "absolute nothingness" in the philosophy of Nishitani with "negative theology" of the Christian tradition.

CR752 Waldenfels, Hans

Faszination des Buddhismus: Zum christlichen-buddhistischen Dialog. Mainz, GW: Matthias-Grünewald Verlag, 1982. 194 pp. 3786709882.

A collection of historical and theological articles about some problems of dialogue between Buddhism and Christianity.

CR753 Walker, Susan, ed.

Speaking of Silence: Christians and Buddhists on the Contemplative Way. Mahwah, NJU: Paulist Press, 1987. viii, 327 pp. Paper. 0809128802.

An anthology of talks, conversations, poetry, and rituals shared by participants during informal conferences on Christian and Buddhist meditation; hosted by Naropa Institute, Boulder, Colorado, from 1981 to 1985.

CR754 Welbon, Guy Richard

The Buddhist Nirvāna and its Western Interpreters. Chicago, ILU: University of Chicago Press, 1968. xi, 320 pp. No ISBN.

An outline of the history of Western European and North American discussions on the meaning of the Buddhist concept of nirvana.

CR755 Williams, Jay G.

Yeshua Buddha: An Interpretation of New Testament Theology as a Meaningful Myth. (Quest Books). Wheaton, ILU: Theosophical Publishing House, 1978. 134 pp. 0835605159.

A free interpretation of the biblical stories and teachings of Jesus showing their basic agreement with the no-self doctrine of Buddha.

CR756 Yagi, Seiichi

A Bridge to Buddhist-Christian Dialogue. Translated by Leonard J. Swidler. New York, NYU: Paulist Press, 1990. x, 152 pp. Paper. 0809131692.

English translation by the professor of interreligious dialogue and Catholic thought at Temple University.

CR757 Yagi, Seiichi

Die Front-Struktur als Brücke vom buddhistischen zum christlichen Denken. (Ökumenische Existenz Heute, 3). Munich, GW: Kaiser, 1988. 101 pp. 3459017171.

A popular work which focuses on the relatedness of Buddhism and Christianity, and what it means to the Christian person in Japan.

CR758 Zürcher, Erik

Bouddhisme, Christianisme et société chinoise. (Conférences, essais et leçons du Collège de France). Paris, FR: Julliard, 1990. 93 pp. 2260006833.

A collection of papers on Buddhism and Christianity in China; originally given at the Collège de France in Paris.

CR759 Zago, Marcello
Buddhismo e Cristianesimo In Dialogo: Situazione-Rapporti-Convergenze. Rome, IT: Citta Nuova, 1985. 429 pp. 8831135317.

A scholarly presentation by the Secretary of the Vatican Office for Non-Christians, on the origins of Buddhism, the present state of Roman Catholic-Buddhist dialogue, and the type of dialogue possible on topics such as God, grace, prayer, and salvation.

Buddhist Sources, Origins, Impact

See also CR427 and CR720.

CR760 Eppsteiner, Fred, ed.
The Path of Compassion: Writings on Socially Engaged Buddhism. Berkeley, CAU: Parallax Press, 1988. xx, 219 pp. Paper. 0938077023.

A collection of writings by twenty-five leaders and interpreters of socially engaged Buddhism in Southeast Asia.

CR761 Iida, Shotaro
Facets of Buddhism. London, ENK: Kegan Paul International, 1993. vii, 166 pp. 0710304463.

Ten essays by the noted Buddhist scholar, mainly on Buddhism in Japan, including comparison with Judeo-Christian beliefs and religious practices.

CR762 Ozaki, Makoto
Introduction to the Philosophy of Tanabe: According to the English Translation of the Seventh Chapter of the Demonstratio of Christianity. (Currents of Encounter: Studies on the Contact between Christianity and Other Religions, Beliefs, and Cultures, 6). Amsterdam, NE: Editions Rodopi; Grand Rapids, MIU: Eerdmans, 1990. 258 pp. Paper. 9051832052.

A detailed study of the thought of the Japanese philosopher Tanabe Hajime (1885-1962), who synthesized Japanese Buddhism, Christianity, and Marxism; originally presented as a Ph.D. thesis at the University of Leiden.

CR763 Queen, Christopher S., and Sallie B. King, eds.
Engaged Buddhism: Buddhist Liberation Movements in Asia. Albany, NYU: SUNY Press, 1996. xii, 446 pp. 0791428435 (hdbk), 0791428443 (pbk).

Essays on the liberation movement within Buddhism that has been of high interest to Christian theologians in Asia.

CR764 *Walking with the Buddha*
(Maryknoll Video Magazine). Maryknoll, NYU: Maryknoll World Publications, 1993. 28:20 mins. No ISBN.

Filmed in Thailand, this video is an introduction for Christians to Buddhist beliefs, emphasizing compassion based on meditation.

Missions to Buddhists

See also HI587, CR767, AS574, and AS1489.

CR765 Conference on World Evangelization (Pattaya, Thailand, 1980)
The Thailand Report on Buddhists: Report of the ... Mini-Consultation of Reaching Buddhists. (Lausanne Occasional Papers, 15). Wheaton, ILU: LCWE, 1980. 26 pp. Paper. No ISBN.

The report gives a geographical and historical background of Buddhism, worldviews of Theravada and Mahayana Buddhists, and principles and practical strategies for reaching these groups.

CR766 Eilert, Håkan
Boundlessness: Studies in Karl Ludwig Reichelt's Missionary Thinking with Special Regard to the Buddhist-Christian Encounter. (Studia Missionalia Upsaliensia, 24). Aarhus, DK: Forlaget Aros, 1974. 253 pp. Paper. 8770032513.

A doctoral thesis by a Swedish missionary to Japan involved in the Nordic Mission to Buddhists, dealing with the principles about mission to Buddhists expressed by the Norwegian missionary Karl Ludvig Reichelt, founder of the Nordic Mission to Buddhists.

CR767 Tsering, Marku
Sharing Christ in the Tibetan Buddhist World. Upper Darby, PAU: Tibet Press, 1988. x, 205 pp. Paper. No ISBN.

A practical guide to sharing Christ with Tibetan Buddhists—through the approach of Paul to the Athenians; including a glossary of Chinese terms, as well as an analysis of past efforts to reach the Tibetan Buddhists.

Christianity and Confucianism, Taoism

See also SP106, AS16, AS327, AS335, AS358, AS367, AS381, AS384, AS463, and AS473.

CR768 Berling, Judith A.
A Pilgrim in Chinese Culture: Negotiating Religious Diversity. (Faith Meets Faith Series). Maryknoll, NYU: Orbis Books, 1997. xiii, 157 pp. Paper. 1570751528.

A thematic examination of Chinese religious diversity; by the Professor of History of Religions at the Graduate Theological Union, Berkeley, California.

CR769 Berthrong, John H.
All under Heaven: Transforming Paradigms in Confucian-Christian Dialogue. (SUNY Series in Chinese Philosophy and Culture). Albany, NYU: SUNY Press, 1994. viii, 273 pp. 079141857X (hdbk), 0791418588 (pbk).

A scholarly analysis of themes in the modern Confucian-Christian dialogue derived from neo-Confucianism and 20th-century Christian thought, especially Process theology.

CR770 Bush, Richard C.
Religion in Communist China. Nashville, TNU: Abingdon, 1970. 432 pp. Paper. 0687360153.

A summary of the insights of Western China watchers concerning the effect of the first twenty years of Communist rule on each of the religions of China.

CR771 Ching, Julia
The Butterfly Healing: A Life between East and West. Maryknoll, NYU: Orbis Books; Toronto, ONC: Novalis, 1998. xii, 220 pp. Paper. 1570752370.

The memoir of the noted scholar of Chinese religions who, as a several-time cancer survivor, explores the medical, philosophical, and spiritual responses to living and dying, from both East and West.

CR772 Ching, Julia
Chinese Religions. Maryknoll, NYU: Orbis Books, 1993. xv, 275 pp. Paper. 0883448750.

A comprehensive and concise history of Chinese religious traditions including Christianity.

CR—CHRISTIANITY AND OTHER RELIGIONS

CR773 Ching, Julia
Confucianism and Christianity: A Comparative Study. Tokyo, JA: Kodansha International / Institute of Oriental Religions, 1977. xxvi, 234 pp. 0870113038.

A history of the Confucian-Christian encounter, examining similarities and differences inherent in common thematic problems (of humanity, God, self-transcendence, and political relevance).

CR774 Ching, Julia
Konfuzianismus und Christentum. (Dialog der Religionen). Mainz, GW: Matthias-Grünewald-Verlag, 1989. 230 pp. 3786714428.

German translation.

CR775 Conference on World Evangelization (Pattaya, Thailand, 1980)
The Thailand Report on Chinese: Report of the ... Mini-Consultation on Reaching Chinese. (Lausanne Occasional Papers, 6). Wheaton, ILU: LCWE, 1980. 32 pp. Paper. No ISBN.

Factors in Chinese resistance to the Gospel, with ideas for reaching Chinese both on the mainland and in diaspora.

CR776 Haglund, Ake
Contact and Conflict: Studies in Contemporary Religious Attitudes among Chinese People. Lund, SW: Gleerups, 1972. 248 pp. Paper. No ISBN.

After a succinct historical description of the confrontation between Chinese and Western religion, the author, a former China missionary, compares contemporary attitudes to religion in China (based on written sources) to those among Chinese in Penang, Malaysia (based on interviews).

CR777 Hang, Thaddaeus T'ui-Chieh
Das kosmische Jen: Die Begegnung von Christentum und Konfuzianismus. (Theologie interkulturell, 7). Frankfurt am Main, GW: IKO-Verlag für Interkulturelle Kommunikation, 1993. 164 pp. Paper. 3889393705.

A critical study of Confucianism's all-encompassing "springtime impulse" in its historical roots and influence, its search for true humanity, and its encounter with the Christian image of the church as mystical body.

CR778 Küng, Hans, and Julia Ching
Christentum und Chinesische Religion. Munich, GW: Piper, 1988. 319 pp. 3492031781.

A scholarly dialogue between a noted theologian and a professor of religious studies, presenting Christianity and the Chinese religions (folk, Confucianism, Taoism, and Buddhism) as equal partners in dialogue.

CR779 Küng, Hans, and Julia Ching
Christianisme et religion chinoise. Paris, FR: Seuil, 1991. 324 pp. 2020114224.

French translation.

CR780 Küng, Hans, and Julia Ching
Christianity and Chinese Religions. New York, NYU: Doubleday, 1989. xxiv, 309 pp. 0385260229.

English translation.

CR781 Kim, Heup Young
Wang Yang-ming and Karl Barth: A Confucian-Christian Dialogue. Lanham, MDU: University Press of America, 1996. xii, 234 pp. 0761802266.

An analysis of the doctrines related to the issue of humanization in the thought of Wang Yang-ming (1472-1529) and Karl Barth (1886-1968), with implications for contemporary Confucian-Christian dialogue in Korea; revision of the author's Ph.D. dissertation (Graduate Theological Union, Berkeley, 1992).

CR782 Lee, Chwen Jiuan A., and Thomas G. Hand
A Taste of Water: Christianity through Taoist-Buddhist Eyes. New York, NYU: Paulist Press, 1990. iii, 224 pp. Paper. 0809131498.

Two Catholic missionaries reflect on the positive influence of Eastern philosophy (Taoism) and practice (Zen) on their spiritual formation.

CR783 Lee, Hwain Chang
Confucius, Christ and Co-Partnership: Competing Liturgies for the Soul of Korean-American Women. Lanham, MDU: University Press of America, 1994. 100 pp. 0819192236.

A Korean American Presbyterian Church deacon relates her struggle for self-identity amidst competing perspectives: Confucianism, liberationist, and feminist theologies.

CR784 Lee, Jung Young
Cosmic Religion. New York, NYU: Philosophical Library, 1973. 109 pp. 802221254.

A brief presentation of eighteen themes for a holistic religion, beginning with change as the ultimate reality, drawing upon wisdom from the *I Ching* (Book of Changes) and Christian theology.

CR785 Lee, Jung Young
Embracing Change: Postmodern Interpretations of the I Ching *from a Christian Perspective.* Scranton, PAU: University of Scranton Press; London, ENK: Associated University Presses, 1994. 251 pp. 0940866234.

A comprehensive interpretation of the Confucian classic *I Ching* (Book of Changes) for Christians, developing change as an important theme for Christian theology.

CR786 Lee, Peter K. H., ed.
Confucian-Christian Encounters in Historical and Contemporary Perspective. (Religions in Dialogue, 5). Lewiston, NYU: E Mellen Press, 1991. xiv, 479 pp. 0889465215.

Twenty-eight scholarly papers, most originally written and presented in Chinese at an international Confucian-Christian conference (Hong Kong, 8-15 June 1988).

CR787 Loya, Joseph A., Wan-Li Ho, and Chang-Shin Jih
The Tao of Jesus: An Experiment in Inter-Traditional Understanding. Mahwah, NJU: Paulist Press, 1998. xiii, 185 pp. Paper. 080913764X.

Christian and Taoist scholars combine to provide for Christians an introduction to Taoism and insight into the ethical wisdom of the *Tao Te Ching.*

CR788 Martinson, Paul Varo
A Theology of World Religions: Interpreting God, Self, and World in Semitic, Indian, and Chinese Thought. Minneapolis, MNU: Augsburg, 1987. 272 pp. 0806622539.

A creative analysis of theological themes meaningful in Chinese religious experience, and the impact of Buddhism, Hinduism, Islam, Judaism, and Christianity upon that experience.

CR789 Neville, Robert Cummings
The Tao and the Daimon: Segments of a Religious Inquiry. Albany, NYU: SUNY Press, 1982. xv, 281 pp. 0873956613 (hdbk), 0873956621 (pbk).

A comparative study of the notion of creation in Western and Eastern thought (Buddhism, Confucianism, and Taoism).

CR790 Overmyer, Daniel L.

Religions of China: The World as a Living System. Prospect Heights, ILU: Waveland Press, 1998. ix, 125 pp. Paper. 1577660005.

A primer on the religions of China in the 19th and 20th centuries, their beliefs and practices, with a brief history of earliest development; a reprint of the text edition (HarperSan-Francisco, 1986).

CR791 Petulla, Joseph

The Tao Te Ching and the Christian Way. Maryknoll, NYU: Orbis Books, 1998. ix, 132 pp. Paper. 1570752117.

A new English version of a reading from the Taoist *Tao Te Ching*, with reflections by the author on its significance for Christians.

CR792 Smith, D. Howard

Chinese Religions. (History of Religion Series). New York, NYU: Holt, Rinehart & Winston, 1968. xiii, 221 pp. No ISBN.

A scholarly introduction to the development of the various religions of China from 1000 B.C. to the present; by a former China missionary and later lecturer in comparative religion at the University of Manchester.

CR793 Taylor, Rodney L.

The Religious Dimensions of Confucianism. (Religious Studies). Albany, NYU: SUNY Press, 1990. xiii, 198 pp. Paper. 0791403114 (hdbk), 0791403122 (pbk).

A definitive study of the old question whether Confucianism is a "religion," with a comparative analysis of Christian and Confucianist responses to the problem of suffering.

CR794 Young, John D.

Confucianism and Christianity: The First Encounter. Hong Kong, HK: Hong Kong University Press, 1983. xi, 182 pp. 9622090370.

A serious and well-documented examination of the first encounter of Chinese literati with Matteo Ricci and other Jesuit missionaries of the 16th to 18th centuries, focusing on their contrasting worldviews.

Christianity and Hinduism

See also TH61, CR295, CR324, CR513, CR837, SO367, EC86, CO50, CH414, SP95, SP101, SP116, SP118-SP119, SP124, SP292, SP307, AS4, AS212, AS239, AS246, AS249-AS250, AS258-AS259, AS270, AS272, AS890, AS904, AS953, AS987, AS1043, AS1069, AS1086, AS1095, AS1196, AS1212, AS1215, AS1217, and AS1267.

CR795 Abhishiktananda, Swami

Ascent to the Depth of the Heart: The Spiritual Diary (1948-1973) of Swami Abhishiktananda (Dom H. le Saux). Edited by Raimundo Panikkar. Delhi, II: ISPCK, 1998. xxxvi, 410 pp. Paper. 8172144245.

The spiritual diary of the French Benedictine monk's twenty-five years of creative Hindu-Christian dialogue in India; translated by David Fleming and James Stuart.

CR796 Abhishiktananda, Swami

The Further Shore: Sanyassa and The Upanishads, An Introduction: Two Essays. Delhi, II: ISPCK, 1975. xii, 120 pp. No ISBN.

Exposition of the brahmanic ideal of saintliness by the French Benedictine missionary to India, Henri le Saux, who stands in the Roberto de Nobili, J. Monchanin, and Raimundo Panikkar traditions.

CR797 Abhishiktananda, Swami

Das Geheimnis des heiligen Berges: Als christlicher Mönch unter den Weisen Indiens. Freiburg, GW: Herder, 1989. 179 pp. 3451213893.

German translation.

CR798 Abhishiktananda, Swami

Gnânânanda: un maître spirituel du pays tamoul. (Le soleil dans le occur, 3). Chambéry, FR: Éditions Présence, 1970. 159 pp. No ISBN.

A straightforward account of the teaching and way of life of a Hindu sage.

CR799 Abhishiktananda, Swami

Guru and Disciple. Translated by Heather Sanderman. London, ENK: SPCK, 1974. xiii, 176 pp. 0281027773 (hdbk), 028102779X (pbk).

Translations from the French of *Gnánánanda* (1970) and *Une messe aux sources du Gange* (1967) in which Henri le Saux explores connections between Christian and Hindu traditions of pilgrimage and spirituality.

CR800 Abhishiktananda, Swami

Hindu-Christian Meeting Point: Within the Cave of the Heart. Translated by Sara Grant. Delhi, II: ISPCK, 1976. xiii,128 pp. Paper. No ISBN.

English translation of the revised 1969 edition.

CR801 Abhishiktananda, Swami

La rencontre de l'Hindouisme et du Christianisme. Paris, FR: Éditions du Seuil, 1966. 236 pp. No ISBN.

The story of a Christian group of theologians and contemplatives from Christian ashrams in India who sought to encounter the Hindu mystic experience of non-duality so as to deepen Hindu-Christian dialogue.

CR802 Abhishiktananda, Swami

Saccidananda: A Christian Approach to Advaitic Experience. Delhi, II: ISPCK, 1984. xv, 234 pp. No ISBN.

Revised edition of the wisdom of Henri le Saux, remarkable Benedictine missionary to India from 1977 to 1973, who went further than anyone else to live *advaita* as a Christian; originally published in 1974.

CR803 Abhishiktananda, Swami

The Secret of Aruneachala: A Christian Hermit on Shiva's Holy Mountain. Delhi, II: ISPCK, 1988. x, 144 pp. Paper. No ISBN.

English translation.

CR804 Abhishiktananda, Swami

Souvenirs d'Arunâchala: récit d'un ermite chrétien en terre hindoue. (L'homme du 8o jour). Paris, FR: Epi, 1978. 177 pp. 2704500827.

The autobiography of Dom Henri le Saux, OSB (1910-1973) who, after twenty years as a monk in France, founded the ashram of Shantivanam in South India with Fr. J. Monchanin, and lived the life of a hermit alongside noted Hindu sages, taking the name Swami Abhishiktananda.

CR805 Abraham, Koshy

Prajapathi, the Cosmic Christ. Delhi, II: ISPCK, 1997. xii, 72 pp. Paper. 8172143907.

An argument by a Kerala lay theologian that the cosmic Christ of the Bible is the Nishkaianka Purusha of the Rig-Veda.

CR806 Amaladoss, Michael
Towards Fullness: Searching for an Integral Spirituality. Bangalore, II: NBCLC, 1994. 101 pp. Paper. No ISBN.

Lectures by the noted Indian Jesuit interpreting his identity as "Hindu-Christian" as integration, not syncretism; originally given in Bangalore, India, in 1993 as the Fr. Amalor Memorial Lectures.

CR807 Appasamy, A. J.
The Theology of Hindu Bhakti. (Indian Theological Library, 5). Madras, II: CLS, 1970. iii, 130 pp. Paper. No ISBN.

A bishop of the Church of South India studies the *bhakti* (devotion) movement in Hinduism, asking whether Christians may absorb values and expressions from it into their own spirituality.

CR808 Ariarajah, S. Wesley
Hindus and Christians: A Century of Protestant Ecumenical Thought. (Currents of Encounter, 5). Amsterdam, NE: Rodopi; Grand Rapids, MIU: Eerdmans, 1991. x, 244 pp. Paper. 0802805043 (E), 9051832060 (R).

A detailed analysis of developments, within the 20th-century ecumenical movement, in the Christian attitude toward Hinduism, with a call for a theological reappraisal to enhance Christian-Hindu relationships; by the Director of the WCC's Subunit on Dialogue.

CR809 Arokiasamy, Soosai
Dharma, Hindu and Christian According to Roberto de Nobili: Analysis of Its Meaning and Its Use in Hinduism and Christianity. (Documenta Missionalia, 19). Roma, IT: Pontificia Università Gregoriana, 1986. 376 pp. Paper. 8876525653.

A scholarly study of the noted Jesuit's understanding and use of the Hindu concept of *dharma*, and of his pioneer adoption of the concept in 17th-century Catholic missions in India; presented as a doctoral thesis at the Gregorian University in 1986.

CR810 Bürkle, Horst
Dialog mit dem Osten: Radhakrishnans neuhinduistische Botschaft im Lichte christlicher Weltsendung. Stuttgart, GW: Evan Verlagswerk, 1965. 313 pp. No ISBN.

A thesis representing the best available discussion and critique of the thought of the noted contemporary Hindu philosopher, pointing out its challenge to current Christian theology.

CR811 Bassuk, David E.
Incarnation in Hinduism and Christianity: The Myth of the God-Man. London, ENK: Macmillan Press, 1987. xiii, 232 pp. 033341358X.

A comparative study of divine incarnation in Hinduism and Christianity.

CR812 Bhaktipada, Kirtanananda Swami
Christ and Krishna: The Path of Pure Devotion. Moundsville, WVU: Palace Publishing, 1987. xi, 182 pp. Paper. 0932215033.

A popular presentation of the relation between Christianity and Krishna Consciousness; based on 1987 conversations with Christians by a prominent Hari Krishna leader.

CR813 Bharati, Dayanand
Living Water and Indian Bowl: An Analysis of Christian Failings in Communicating Christ to Hindus, with Suggestions toward Improvements. Delhi, II: ISPCK, 1997. xviii, 127 pp. Paper. 8172143915.

A collection of essays critiquing past Christian mission to Hindus, with proposals for a more effective contextualized approach.

CR814 Brück, Michael von
Einheit der Wirklichkeit: Gott, Gotteserfahrung und Meditation im hinduistisch-christlichen Dialog. (Kaiser Traktate, 18). Munich, GW: Kaiser, 1986. 409 pp. Paper. 345901699X.

After five years of immersion in Hindu-Christian dialogue, the German Lutheran theologian offers this philosophical and theological study of basic trinitarian concepts in Christianity and Hinduism based on Hindu understanding of the Trinity, and not just Jewish or Greek categories and experience.

CR815 Brück, Michael von
The Unity of Reality: God, God-Experience and Meditation in the Hindu-Christian Dialogue. Translated by James V. Zeitz. New York, NYU: Paulist Press, 1986. vi, 340 pp. Paper. 0809132141.

English translation of *Einheit der Wirklichkeit* (1986).

CR816 Braun, Hans-Jür, and David J. Krieger
Indische Religionen und das Christentum im Dialog. Zürich, SZ: Theologischer Verlag, 1986. 148 pp. 3290115771.

Two essays explore methodological questions on religious and cultural pluralism, followed by four studies: salvation in Hinduism and Christianity, a vedic view of the Trinity, unity and plurality in *advaita*, and Nagarjuna's Middle Way.

CR817 Braybrooke, Marcus
The Undiscovered Christ: A Review of Recent Developments in the Christian Approach to the Hindus. (Inter-Religious Dialogue Series, 5). Madras, II: CLS, 1973. 119 pp. Paper. No ISBN.

A popular summation of recent developments in Hindu-Christian dialogue in India.

CR818 Brockington, John
Hinduism and Christianity. New York, NYU: St. Martin's Press, 1992. xiii, 215 pp. 0312084048.

Analysis of seven themes in religious thought and practice which are of central concern both to Hinduism and to Christianity; with a brief history of contacts and dialogue between adherents of these two faiths.

CR819 Bromley, David G., and Larry D. Shinn, eds.
Krishna Consciousness in the West. Lewisburg, PAU: Bucknell University Press; London, ENK: Associated University Presses, 1989. 295 pp. 083875144X.

Twelve scholarly papers originally presented at a 1985 multidisciplinary conference on the history, theology, and organization of the International Society for Krishna Consciousness (ISKCON), and public reaction to the Hare Krishna movement in the United States.

CR820 Carman, John Braisted
The Theology of Ramanuja: An Essay in Inter-Religious Understanding. New Haven, CTU: Yale University Press, 1974. 333 pp. 0300015216.

A revision of the author's Yale University dissertation (1962) drawing out similarities between Vaisnavism and Christianity.

CR821 Carpenter, David
Revelation, History and the Dialogue of Religions: A Study of Bhartrhari and Bonaventure. (Faith Meets Faith Series). Maryknoll, NYU: Orbis Books, 1995. xi, 208 pp. Paper. 1570750394.

An in-depth comparative study of the theories and practices related to revelation by two specific individuals—the Hindu grammarian and philosopher of language Bhartrhari (ca 450-500 CE), and the medieval scholastic St. Bonaventure (1221-1274).

CR—CHRISTIANITY AND OTHER RELIGIONS

CR822 Catholic Church, Secretariet for Non-Christians

For a Dialogue with Hinduism. Milan, IT: Editrice Ancora, 1972. 183 pp. No ISBN.

A guide for Roman Catholics desiring to respond to Vatican II's declaration *Nostra Aetate* through creative dialogue with Hindus.

CR823 Chatterjee, Margaret

Gandhi's Religious Thought. Notre Dame, INU: University of Notre Dame Press, 1983. xiv, 194 pp. 0268010099.

An examination of Gandhi's religious thought by a leading Indian philosopher who addresses interactions between the traditions of the Hindu and Christian communities in today's world.

CR824 Chemparathy, George

An Indian Rational Theology: Introduction to Udayana's Nyay-akusumanjali. (Publications of the de Nobili Research Library, 1). Leiden, NE: Brill; Vienna, AU: Gerold & Co.; Delhi, II: Motilal Banarsidass, 1972. 202 pp. No ISBN.

A detailed study of the Nyaya-Vaisesika School of Hindu philosophy and the relevance for Christianity of its central doctrine of rational monotheism.

CR825 Clooney, Francis X.

Theology after Vedanta: An Experiment in Comparative Theology. (Toward a Comparative Philosophy of Religions). Albany, NYU: SUNY Press, 1993. xviii, 265 pp. 0791413659 (hdbk), 0791413667 (pbk).

A detailed comparative analysis of the epistemologies and understandings of truth in *Advaita* Vendanta Hinduism and in the Christian theology of Thomas Aquinas' *Summa Theologiae.*

CR826 Conference on World Evangelization (Pattaya, Thailand, 1980)

The Thailand Report on Hindus: Report of the ... Mini-Consultation on Reaching Hindus. (Lausanne Occasional Papers, 14). Wheaton, ILU: LCWE, 1980. 24 pp. Paper. No ISBN.

The report gives the historical and biblical framework for Hindu evangelization, points out hindrances, gives case studies in Christian ministry and strategies and tools for the task of evangelism.

CR827 Coward, Harold G., ed.

Hindu-Christian Dialogue: Perspectives and Encounters. (Faith Meets Faith Series). Maryknoll, NYU: Orbis Books, 1989. xix, 281 pp. Paper. 0883446340 (hdbk), 0883446332 (pbk).

A collection of essays from eighteen various authors reviewing the interaction of these faith communities and, by extension, the interaction between India and the West.

CR828 Coward, Harold G., ed.

Modern Indian Responses to Religious Pluralism. Albany, NYU: SUNY Press, 1987. xii, 340 pp. Paper. 0887065716 (hdbk), 0887065724 (pbk).

Fourteen essays by Indian scholars (nine Hindus and five of other faiths) examining the way in which the various religions are responding to the challenge of living side by side with one another in modern India.

CR829 Das, Sisir Kumar

The Shadow of the Cross: Christianity and Hinduism in a Colonial Situation. New Delhi, II: Munshiram Manoharlal, 1974. x, 181 pp. No ISBN.

A scholarly analysis of the interaction of Western thought, both Christian and Humanist, with Hindu religion and culture, particularly in the intellectually fertile soil of 19th-century Bengal.

CR830 David, George

Communicating Christ among Hindu Peoples. Chennai, II: CBMTM Publications, 1998. vi, 183 pp. Paper. No ISBN.

Principles of Christian discipleship, communication, and apologetics in a Hindu context.

CR831 Devamani, B. S.

The Religion of Ramanuja: A Christian Appraisal. Madras, II: CLS, 1990. xi, 61 pp. Paper. No ISBN.

A dissertation on the religio-philosophic thought of Ramanuja (c.1017-1137) whose Vedanta theism and *bhakti* spirituality exhibit remarkable similarities to Christian religion.

CR832 Devanandan, Paul David, Nalini Devanandan, and Madathilparapil M. Thomas, eds.

Preparation for Dialogue: A Collection of Essays on Hinduism and Christianity in New India. (Devanandan Memorial, 2). Bangalore, II: CISRS, 1964. v, 193 pp. Paper. No ISBN.

A compilation of writings (1958-1962) on Hindu-Christian dialogue by the former Director of the Christian Institute for the Study of Religion and Society in Bangalore, India.

CR833 Devanandan, Paul David

Christian Concern in Hinduism. Bangalore, II: CISRS, 1961. xii, 142 pp. Paper. No ISBN.

A sincere effort to understand and interpret the living reality of Hinduism as a contemporary religion, and to formulate a Christian approach to the Hindu intellectuals, by the Director of the Christian Institute for the Study of Religion and Society.

CR834 Devaraja, N. K.

Hinduism and Christianity: Brahmananda Keshab Chandra Sen Memorial Lectures on Comparative Religion Delivered at Calcutta University. New York, NYU: Asia Publishing House, 1969. xi, 126 pp. No ISBN.

A scholarly comparison of the philosophies and values in Hinduism and Christianity, presented, by the Senior Professor of Philosophy at Banares Hindu University in 1967, as the Brahmananda Keshab Chandra Sen Memorial Lectures on Comparative Religion at Calcutta University.

CR835 Diehl, Carl Gustav, Bent Smidt Hansen, and Torben Christensen

Modet mellem hinduisme og kristendom: en indforing. Edited by Lars Thunberg. Aarhus, DK: TF-tryk, 1982. 209 pp. Paper. 8798127918.

This book emanates from a conference arranged by the Institute of Missiology and Ecumenical Theology, University of Aarhus, with papers on the Hindu renaissance of the 19th century, the Christian mass movements in India, Indian Christian theology, religious education in Indian schools, and guruism and its world mission.

CR836 D'Sa, Francis X.

Gott, der Dreieine und der All-Ganze: Vorwort zur Begegnung zwischen Christentum und Hinduismus. (Theologie interkulturell, 2). Düsseldorf, GW: Patmos Verlag, 1987. 155 pp. Paper. 3491776821.

A scholarly contribution to dialogue between Christianity and Hinduism, this work compares the two religions under such headings as worldview, prayer, and the concept of *moksha.*

CR—CHRISTIANITY AND OTHER RELIGIONS

CR837 Dunuwila, Rohan A.

Saiva Siddhata Theology: A Context for Hindu-Christian Dialogue. Delhi, II: Motilal Banarsidass, 1985. xiii, 231 pp. 089581675X.

A survey of the Saiva Siddhata tradition of South Indian Hinduism, focusing on Aghorasiva (C.E. 1100), the theologian who bridged the Sankrit and Tamil traditions with comparison to Catholic trinitarian thought.

CR838 Fakirbhai, Dhanjibhai, comp.

Shri Krist Gita: The Song of the Lord Christ. Bromley, ENK: Pilot Publications, n.d. 122 pp. Paper. 185859006X.

The sayings of Jesus presented in the style of Hindu *bhakti* poetry.

CR839 Francis, T. Dayanandan

The Relevance of Hindu Ethos for Christian Presence: A Tamil Perspective. Madras, II: CLS, 1989. vi, 120 pp. Paper. No ISBN.

A socio-theological examination of the influence of Hindu terminology on Indian Christianity, including a discussion of the chasm between scholarly consensus on dogma and precepts, and the religious experience of those not theologically trained; by the General Secretary of the Christian Literature Society in Madras.

CR840 Gamaliel, James Canjanam

Dharma in the Hindu Scriptures and in the Bible. Dehli, II: ISPCK, 1997. x, 81 pp. Paper. 8172143850.

A short synopsis of the author's doctoral thesis in which he compares and contrasts the key concept of dharma in the sacred scriptures of Hinduism and Christianity.

CR841 Gandhi, Mahatma

Gandhi on Christianity. Edited by Robert Ellsberg. Maryknoll, NYU: Orbis Books, 1991. xviii, 117 pp. Paper. 0883447568.

An anthology of Mohandas Gandhi's writings on Christianity, together with four scholarly articles on Gandhi's contributions to interreligious dialogue and attitudes toward Jesus and Christian mission.

CR842 Gelberg, Steven J., ed.

Hare Krishna, Hare Krishna: Five Distinguished Scholars on the Krishna Movement in the West. New York, NYU: Grove Press, 1983. 276 pp. Paper. 0394624548.

Dialogues between an articulate member of the Krishna movement and five eminent North American religious scholars: Harvey Cox, Larry D. Shinn, Thomas J. Hopkins, A. L. Basham, and Shrivatsa Goswani.

CR843 Gidoomal, Ram, and Margaret Wardell

Chapatis for Tea: Reaching Your Hindu Neighbour: A Practical Guide. Guildford, ENK: Highland Books, 1994. xi, 180 pp. Paper. 1897913079.

A primer for Christians desiring to understand their Hindu neighbors and to witness to them.

CR844 Gidoomal, Ram, and Mike Fearon

Karma 'n' Chips. London, ENK: Wimbledon, 1994. 222 pp. Paper. 1898855013.

How twelve central themes in Hinduism are being reinterpreted by Asian immigrants to Great Britain in their search for a new and relevant spirituality.

CR845 Gispert-Sauch, G., ed.

God's Word among Men: Papers in Honour of Fr. Joseph Putz, Frs. J. Bayart, J. Volkhaert, and P. de Letter. Delhi, II: Vidyajyoti, 1973. xxxi, 384 pp. No ISBN.

A *festschrift* honoring four venerable Jesuit missionaries who served in India, containing a variety of essays on a theology of religions and interreligious dialogue.

CR846 Griffiths, Bede

Christ in India: Essays towards a Hindu-Christian Dialogue. New York, NYU: Scribner, 1966. 251 pp. No ISBN.

Essays by the famed Benedictine monk who in 1958 founded the Kurisumala Ashram as a monastery of the Syrian Rite in Kerala for Hindu-Christian dialogue.

CR847 Griffiths, Bede

Expériénce chrétienne, mystique hindoue. Translated by Charles H. de Brantes. (Rencontres, 40). Paris, FRE: Éditions du Cerf, 1985. 202 pp. 2204023620.

French translation of *The Marriage of East and West* (1982)

CR848 Griffiths, Bede

Die Hochzeit von Ost und West: Hoffnung für die Menschheit. Salzburg, AU: Müller, 1983. 217 pp. Paper. 3701306672.

German translation of *The Marriage of East and West* (1982).

CR849 Griffiths, Bede

The Marriage of East and West: A Sequel to "The Golden String." Springfield, ILU: Templegate; London, ENK: Collins, 1982. 224 pp. Paper. 0872431053 (T), 000215529X (C).

Volume 2 of the Benedictine monk's spiritual autobiography covering his discovery of India from his arrival in 1955 through his participation in the Saccidananda Ashram in Tamil Nadu where, with Henry le Saux, he adapted to Hindu ways of life and thought, broadening his Christian understanding and commitment.

CR850 Griffiths, Bede

Vedanta and Christian Faith. Los Angeles, CAU: Dawn Horse Press, 1973. x, 89 pp. Paper. 0913922030.

A search for a new synthesis between the spiritual and mystical traditions of India and the Christian West by the Benedictine monk who since 1955 has led a contemplative community in India.

CR851 Healy, Kathleen

Christ as Common Ground: A Study of Christianity and Hinduism. Pittsburgh, PAU: Duquesne University Press, 1990. xiv, 218 pp. 0820702277.

A penetrating study of the Christian church today, bringing it in touch with the rich tradition of oriental Hinduism, a meeting of East and West, in hope of a future grounded in spirituality, equality, justice, and love.

CR852 Hooker, R. H.

Themes in Hinduism and Christianity: A Comparative Study. (Studies in the Intercultural History of Christianity, 53). Frankfurt am Main, GW: Lang, 1989. viii, 396 pp. Paper. 3631404166.

A scholarly comparative analysis of seven themes found both in Christianity and Hinduism: myth, time, evil, purity, images, renunciation, and woman.

CR853 Julian, A. Kulundaisamy

God Is More Loving than a Mother. Madras, II: CLS, 1991. xxi, 101 pp. Paper. No ISBN.

A comparative study of the motherly aspect of God in specific biblical texts of Hebrew poetry and in the *Tiruvacakam*, the ancient (9th century C.E.) Tamil classic of Saiva Bhakti poetry.

CR854 Klostermaier, Klaus K.

In the Paradise of Krishna: Hindu and Christian Seekers. Philadelphia, PAU: Westminster Press, 1971. ix, 118 pp. Paper. 0664249043.

A popular account of real dialogue with Hindus by a Roman Catholic monk who spent two years in Vrindaban, one of the most popular Hindu places of pilgrimmage in northern India; originally published in Great Britain as *Hindu and Christian in Vrindaban,* SCM Press, (1969).

CR855 Klostermaier, Klaus K.

Indian Theology in Dialogue. Madras, II: CLS, 1986. vii, 270 pp. Paper. No ISBN.

Thirteen essays on Christian-Hindu dialogue from J. M. Farquhar to M. M. Thomas, with emphasis on the use of Hindu terms to communicate Christian faith.

CR856 Kozhuppakalam, Mathew

Ethik im Dialog: Ansätze in der Bhagavadgita für eine Begegnung zwischen Hinduismus und Christentum. (Kirche und Religionen: Begegnung und Dialog, Sonderband 1). St. Ottilien, GW: EOS Verlag, 1984. viii, 300 pp. Paper. 3880963819.

A dissertation analyzing the concepts of God, creation and salvation, and the ethical code as expressed in dharma in the Bhagavad Gita, in order to find points of convergence leading towards a possible dialogue between Hinduism and Christianity.

CR857 Kulandran, Sabapathy

Grace: A Comparative Study of the Doctrine in Christianity and Hinduism. London, ENK: Lutterworth Press, 1964. 278 pp. No ISBN.

A comparative study of the concept of grace in Christian thought (New Testament, Augustine, and Luther) and in Hindu theism (Vaisnavism and Saivism), emphasizing special points of convergence.

CR858 Lutz, Lorry

Destined for Royalty: A Brahmin Priest's Search for Truth. South Pasadena, CAU: William Carey Library, 1985. xi, 138 pp. Paper. 0878082026.

Vignettes from the life and witness of Anand Chaudhari, radio-evangelist on Trans World Radio, presenting the Bible to a Hindu-speaking world.

CR859 Manickam, T. M.

Dharma According to Manu and Moses. Bangalore, II: Dharmaram Publications, 1977. xviii, 358 pp. No ISBN.

A comparative study of the social and moral ideas in the Hindu Dharmasastras and the Hebrew Bible (OT), with special reference to Manusmrti and Pentateuch.

CR860 Mataji, Vandana

Living with Hindus: Hindu-Christian Dialogues: My Experiences and Reflections. Bangalore, II: IJA; Delhi, II: ISPCK, 1999. xvi, 106 pp. Paper. 8172145098.

The author seeks a path of mutuality of relations on religious grounds with suggestions on how people of two different faiths might live amicably together.

CR861 Matus, Thomas

Yoga and the Jesus Prayer Tradition: An Experiment in Faith. Ramsey, NJU: Paulist Press, 1984. iii, 193 pp. Paper. 0809126389.

A careful examination of the relation between Tantric Yoga and Hesychasm in Eastern Orthodoxy based on the author's own journey from yoga to Christ.

CR862 Minz, Nirmal

Mahatma Gandhi and Hindu-Christian Dialogue. (Inter-Religious Dialogue Series, 3). Madras, II: CLS, 1970. vii, 202 pp. Paper. No ISBN.

The author, trained in theology and anthropology in India and the United States, deals with the relation among Christ, Christianity, and Hinduism, and how the life and thoughts of Gandhi are of great significance to the development of an Indian Christian theology.

CR863 Mitra, Kana

Catholicism-Hinduism: Vedantic Investigation of Raimundo Panikkar's Attempt at Bridge Building. Lanham, MDU: University Press of America, 1987. xxvi, 157 pp. Paper. 0819161586.

An examination by a Hindu scholar of the contribution of Raimundo Panikkar to interreligious dialogue, arguing that his integration of Hindu and Catholic insights makes possible communion between Catholicism and Hinduism.

CR864 Moder-Frei, Elfi

Reinkarnation und Christentum: Die verschiedenen Reinkarnationsvorstellungen in der Auseinandersetzung mit dem christlichen Glauben. (Dissertationen: Theologische Reihe, 67). St. Ottilien, GW: EOS Verlag, 1993. 288 pp. Paper. 3880967679.

A comparative study of perceptions of redemption and reincarnation in Hinduism and Christianity; written as a dissertation in theology.

CR865 Moffitt, John

Journey to Gorakhpur: An Encounter with Christ beyond Christianity. New York, NYU: Holt, Rinehart & Winston, 1972. xiv, 304 pp. 0030865778.

A personal introduction to the riches of Hinduism, challenging Christians to ask whether Christ is not already at work outside Christianity; by one who for twenty-five years was a Ramakrishnan monastic, but is now a Roman Catholic.

CR866 Moinz, John

'Liberated Society': Gandhian and Christian Vision: Comparative Study. (Documenta Missionalia, 23). Rome, IT: Editrice Potificia Università Gregoriana, 1996. 543 pp. Paper. 8876527001.

A detailed comparison of Gandhi's Hindu vision of a liberated society, with the Christian social visions as enunciated in 20th-century papal documents and by the Second Vatican Council.

CR867 Neuner, Josef, ed.

Hinduismus und Christentum: Eine Einführung. Freiburg im Breisgau, GW: Herder, 1962. xvi, 249 pp. No ISBN.

A symposium in which eight Jesuits with many years of working experience in India describe and examine contemporary Hindu beliefs and practices.

CR868 Oberhammer, Gerhard, ed.

Epiphanie des Heils: Zur Heilsgegenwart in indischer und christlicher Religion: Arbeitsdokumentation eines Symposiums. (Publications of the De Nobili Research Library, 9). Wien, AU: Institut für Indologie der Universität Wien, 1982. 256 pp. 3900271100.

Twelve scholars examine the experience and salvific significance of transcendence as it is manifested both in Eastern and Christian mystical traditions.

CR—CHRISTIANITY AND OTHER RELIGIONS

CR869 Oberhammer, Gerhard, ed.
Offenbarung, geistige Realität des Menschen: Arbeitsdokumen-tation eines Symposiums zum Offenbarungsbegriff in Indien. (Publications of de Nobili Research Library, 2). Leiden, NE: Brill; Vienna, AU: Indologisches Institut Universität Wien; Delhi, II: Motilal Banarsidass, 1974. 237 pp. 3900271003.

A collection of essays by Western scholars on aspects of Hinduism and the perspectives that Christian theologians bring to an encounter with Hinduism.

CR870 Oddie, Geoffrey A.
Hindu and Christian in Southeast India. (London Studies on South Asia, 6). London, ENK: Curzon Press; Wellesley Hills, MAU: Riverdale Company, 1991. x, 280 pp. 0700702245 (UK), 0913215554 (US).

A detailed case study of Hindu-Christian encounters in relation to colonial government policies in the late 19th and early 20th centuries in the Tanjore and Trichinopoly districts of southeastern India.

CR871 Pöhlmann, Horst Georg
Begegnungen mit dem Hinduismus: Dialoge, Bebachtungen, Umfragen und Grundsatzüberlegungen nach zwei Indi-enaufenthalten, ein Beitrag zum interreligiösen Gespräch. Frankfurt am Main, GW: Lembeck, 1995. 205 pp. 3874763099.

The Professor of Systematic Theology in the University of Osnabrück (Germany) shares experiences from more than one-hundred interviews with Hindus in and around Bangalore, India, with learnings concerning opportunities, limitations, and presuppositions of Christian-Hindu dialogue.

CR872 Pöhlmann, Horst Georg
Encounters with Hinduism: A Contribution to Interreligious Dialogue. Translated by John Bowden. London, ENK: SCM Press, 1996. vii, 121 pp. Paper. 0334026288.

English translation.

CR873 Panikkar, Raimundo
Christus der Unbekannte im Hinduismus. (Dialog der Reli-gionen). Mainz, GW: Matthias-Grünewald Verlag, 1986. 166 pp. 3786712174.

German translation.

CR874 Panikkar, Raimundo
El Cristo Desconocido del Hinduismo. Translated by Amador Lapuente. (Nuevas Fronteras). Madrid, SP: Ediciones Maro-va; Barcelona, SP: Editorial Fontanella, 1970. 206 pp. No ISBN.

Spanish translation.

CR875 Panikkar, Raimundo
Il Cristo sconosciuto dell'induismo. (Filosofia e scienze umane, 19). Milan, IT: Vita e Pensiero, 1976. 200 pp. No ISBN.

Italian translation.

CR876 Panikkar, Raimundo
Kerygma und Indien: Zur heilsgeschichtlichen Problematik der christlichen Begegnung mit Indien. Edited by Hans-Werner Bartsch and Bettina Bäumer. (Kerygma und Mythos, 5). Ham-burg-Bergstedt, GW: Reich, 1967. 154 pp. Paper. No ISBN.

Examining the encounter of the church with the non-Chris-tian environment of the East, the author analyzes Hindu phi-losophy from the Christian perspective, and suggests a Trini-tarian concept at the core of Hinduism.

CR877 Panikkar, Raimundo
Kultmysterium in Hinduismus und Christentum: Ein Beitrag zur vergleichenden Religionstheologie. Freiburg, GW: Alber, 1964. 232 pp. Paper. No ISBN.

The book analyzes the formal religious tradition and cul-tic practice in Hinduism—*karmamarga, jnanamarga, bhakti-marga*—and attempts to find points of comparison with reli-gious beliefs and rituals in Christianity.

CR878 Panikkar, Raimundo
The Unknown Christ of Hinduism: Towards an Ecumenical Christophany. Maryknoll, NYU: Orbis Books; London, ENK: Darton, Longman & Todd, 1981. xii, 195 pp. Paper. 0883445239 (O), 0232514968 (D).

The revised and enlarged edition of the 1964 classic (Lon-don: Darton, Longman & Todd) in which the renowned Ro-man Catholic philosopher of religions describes the Hindu-Christian encounter on both ontological and existential levels, analyzing complementary doctrinal relationships between Hin-duism and Christianity.

CR879 Parrinder, Edward Geoffrey
Avatar and Incarnation: The Wilde Lectures in Natural and Comparative Religion in the University of Oxford. New York, NYU: Barnes & Noble, 1970. 296 pp. 0389013587.

A critical study of the *avatar* beliefs in India, comparing them with the Christian doctrine of the incarnation and paral-lels in other faiths; originally presented as the Wilde Lectures in Natural and Comparative Religion at the University of Ox-ford.

CR880 Parrinder, Edward Geoffrey
Upanishads, Gita and Bible: A Comparative Study of Hindu and Christian Scriptures. London, ENK: Faber & Faber; New York, NYU: Harper & Row, 1962. 136 pp. 061316601 (SBN).

The distinguished Professor of Comparative Religion compares Hindu and Christian perspectives on such topics as creation, anthropology, future life, spirituality, suffering, reli-gion and society.

CR881 Peringalloor, Joseph
Salvation through Gita and Gospel. Bombay, II: Institute of Indian Culture, 1972. 109 pp. Paper. No ISBN.

An analysis by an Indian Catholic scholar of the doc-trine of salvation contained in the Bhagavad Gita and its differences from Christian viewpoints.

CR882 Prabhavananda, Swami
The Sermon on the Mount According to Vedanta. New York, NYU: New American Library; Madras, II: Sri Ramakrishna Math; New York, NYU: Mentor, 1972. 126 pp. No ISBNs.

A sensitive, but free-ranging, *advaitic* interpretation of the message and person of Jesus as presented in the Gospel of Matthew; originally published in 1964

CR883 Rao, Ch. G. S. S. Sreenivasa, ed.
S. Radhakrishnan: A World Philosopher. Madras, II: CLS, 1994. xiii, 239 pp. Paper. No ISBN.

A selection of papers assessing the life and work of the noted Indian philosopher, including his contributions to inter-faith understandings; originally presented at an international seminar on his philosophy at Madras Christian College (Tam-baram, 9-12 February 1988).

CR—CHRISTIANITY AND OTHER RELIGIONS

CR884 Rao, R. R. Sundara

Bhakti Theology in the Telugu Hymnal. (Confessing the Faith in India Series, 16). Madras, II: CLS, 1983. v, 129 pp. Paper. No ISBN.

A monograph on a significant contextualization of Christianity in India as Christians in Andrah Pradesh adapted the classical traditions of *bhakti* (devotion) for the nourishment of their spiritual lives.

CR885 Renard, John

Responses to 101 Questions on Hinduism. New York, NYU: Paulist Press, 1999. x, 179 pp. Paper. 080913845X.

One of three volumes by Renard on Eastern religions for the purpose of comparing Buddhism, Islam, and Hinduism and, in this volume, for Hindu-Christian dialogue.

CR886 Richard, Herbert L.

Christ-Bhakti: Narayan Vaman Tilak and Christian Work Among Hindus. Delhi, II: ISPCK, 1991. 130 pp. Paper. 8172140045.

A popular reappraisal of the contribution of Narayan Vaman Tilak (1862-1919) who, as a Hindu, explored many areas for social reform and, after his conversion in 1895, introduced *bhakti* poems as a way of personal devotion to God and of Christian witness to Hindus.

CR887 Robinson, Gnana, ed.

Influence of Hinduism on Christianity. (Tamil Nadu Theological Seminary Seminar Series, 3). Madurai, II: Tamil Nadu Theological Seminary, 1980. vii, 138 pp. Paper. No ISBN.

Papers presented at the Seminar on Hindu Influence on Christianity held at the Tamil Nadu Theological Seminary (Madurai, 20-22 Oct. 1978).

CR888 Robinson, John Arthur Thomas

Truth Is Two-Eyed. Philadelphia, PAU: Westminster Press; London, ENK: SCM Press, 1979. xi, 161 pp. 0664243169 (W), 0334016908 (S).

An argument by the innovative Church of England bishop that Christianity and Hinduism need each other in order to see more clearly key areas of religious experience and doctrine; originally presented at the Teape Lectures in Madras, Delhi, and Calcutta, India, in 1977.

CR889 Romanella, Joseph

Towards an Age of Enlightenment: A Prophetic Vision for Man and His World as Echoed through Judaism, Christianity, Islam, Hinduism and Buddhism. Dehli, II: ISPCK, 1997. xvi, 538 pp. Paper. 8172143885.

A Christian *sanyasi* develops an inclusive perspective in which every religion, creed, and philosophy in the world dedicated to the pursuit of the one reality through worship of self-realization is affirmed like a precious jewel.

CR890 Samartha, Stanley J.

The Hindu Response to the Unbound Christ. (Inter-Religious Dialogue Series, 6). Madras, II: CLS, 1974. vi, 202 pp. Paper. No ISBN.

English translation

CR891 Samartha, Stanley J.

Hindus vor dem universalen Christus: Beiträge zu einer Christologie in Indien. Stuttgart, GW: Evan Verlagswerk, 1970. 213 pp. 3771501008.

An analysis of the interpretations of the person and work of Jesus Christ by leaders of the Hindu Renaissance, including Ram Mohan Roy, Ramakrishna, Vivekananda, Gandhi, and Radhakrishnan, with a new constructive approach to an Indian Christology.

CR892 Samartha, Stanley J.

The Other Side of the River: Some Reflections on the Theme of the Vancouver Assembly. Madras, II: CLS, 1983. iv, 52 pp. Paper. No ISBN.

Reflections on bases for Hindu-Christian dialogue by the first Director of the WCC's Dialogue Programme, in response to the theme of the WCC's sixth Assembly, "Jesus Christ—The Life of the World."

CR893 Samuel, Vinay, and Chris Sugden, eds.

The Gospel among Our Hindu Neighbors. Bangalore, II: Partnership in Mission, 1983. vii, 211 pp. Paper. No ISBN.

A collection of papers presented at a conference jointly sponsored by the Association for Evangelical Theological Education in India (AETEI) and Partnership in Mission—Asia (Bangalore, November 1982) focusing on the nature of Christian witness among Hindus.

CR894 Satprakashananda, Swami

Hinduism and Christianity: Jesus Christ and His Teachings in the Light of Vedanta. St. Louis, MOU: Vedanta Society of St. Louis, 1975. 196 pp. 0916356531.

Lectures for Christians on Hinduism; by a senior Ramakrishna monk and founder of the Vedanta Society of St. Louis, Missouri, in the United States.

CR895 Scott, David C., ed.

Keshub Chunder Sen. (Library of Indian Christian Theology Companion Volume Series, 1). Madras, II: CLS, 1979. xv, 361 pp. Paper. No ISBN.

An anthology of writings by Keshub Chunder Sen (1838-1884)—leader of the New Dispensation of the Hindu Renaissance—which included admiration for Christian ideals and personal devotion to Christ.

CR896 Sequeira, A. Ronald

Gandhi für Christen: Eine Herausforderung. (Herderbücherei, 1345). Freiburg im Breisgau, GW: Herder, 1987. 222 pp. Paper. 3451083450.

An 128-page introduction to Gandhi, followed by 80 pages of selections from his writings, by a native Indian historian of religions; designed to make more familiar in the West "one of the most Christian of any figure in history."

CR897 Seunarine, James F.

Reconversion to Hinduism through Suddhi. Madras, II: CLS, 1977. x, 105 pp. Paper. No ISBN.

A study of the missionary activity of the Arya Samaj of Hinduism seeking the reconversion of Christians.

CR898 Sharma, Arvind, ed.

Neo-Hindu Views of Christianity. Leiden, NE: Brill, 1988. viii, 217 pp. 9004087915.

Nine scholarly essays on the interpretations of Christ and Christianity by leaders of the Hindu Renaissance from 1875 to 1914, including Ram Mohan Roy, Ramakrishna, Vivekananda, Gandhi, Radhakrishna, and Aurobindo.

CR899 Sharpe, Eric J.
Faith Meets Faith: Some Christian Attitudes to Hinduism in the Nineteenth and Twentienth Centuries. London, ENK: SCM Press, 1977. xiv, 178 pp. Paper. 0334004608.

An analysis of changing attitudes of Christians to Hinduism, and of Hindu views of Christianity by the Professor of Religious Studies at the University of Sydney, Australia.

CR900 Siddheswarananda, Swami
Hindu Thought and Carmelite Mysticism. Translated by William Buchanan. Delhi, II: Motilal Banarsidass, 1998. xiv, 172 pp. 8120815106.

English translation.

CR901 Siddheswarananda, Swami
Pensée indienne et mystique carmélitaine. Gretz-Armainvilliers, FR: Centre védantique Ramakrichna, 1974. vi, 203 pp. No ISBN.

Lectures on Christianity with appreciation of John of the Cross and the mystico-contemplative tradition of Christianity; by the founder of the Ramakrishna Center at Gretz, France.

CR902 Siddheswarananda, Swami
Pensiero indiano e mistica carmelitana. (Collezione Vidya, 11). Rome, IT: Asram Vidya, 1977. 197 pp. No ISBN.

Italian translation.

CR903 Smart, Ninian
The Yogi and the Devotee: The Interplay between the Upanishads and Catholic Theology. London, ENK: Allen and Unwin, 1968. 174 pp. No ISBN.

The Westcott Lectures for 1964 delivered at Bishop's College, Calcutta, exploring the relation between Christian belief and the great religious ideas of Hinduism.

CR904 Staffner, Hans
Dialogue, Stimulating Contacts with Hindus. Anand, II: Gujarat Sahitya Prakash, 1993. vii, 167 pp. Paper. No ISBN.

Reflections on over fifty years of active Christian-Hindu dialogue in India, with case studies.

CR905 Staffner, Hans
Jesus Christ and the Hindu Community: Is a Synthesis of Hinduism and Christianity Possible? (Series 7, Pastoral, 25). Anand, II: Gujarat Sahitya Prakash, 1988. xii, 253 pp. Paper. No ISBN.

After reviewing how modern Hindus view Christianity, Staffner summarizes the main elements in each religion and then attempts to show how they can complement each other.

CR906 Staffner, Hans
The Significance of Jesus Christ in Asia. (Gujarat Sahitya Prakash, 7. Pastoral, 11). Anand, II: Gujarat Sahitya Prakash, 1985. xvii, 264 pp. No ISBN.

Staffner summarizes how Christ is seen both by Hindus who were inspired by him but remained Hindu and those who became Christians, and then goes on to show how Christ does not destroy Hinduism but fulfills it.

CR907 Stark, Claude Alan
God of All: Sri Ramakrishna's Approach to Religious Plurality. Cape Cod, MAU: Claude Stark, 1974. xvii, 236 pp. 0890070008.

A sympathetic portrayal of Ramakrishna's life and thought based on both primary and secondary source documents.

CR908 Stewart, William
India's Religious Frontier: Christian Presence amid Modern Hinduism. London, ENK: SCM Press, 1964. 184 pp. No ISBN.

An analysis by the principal of Serampore College of recent developments within Hinduism, stressing the importance of having an indigenous church and a living of the Gospel in Christian witness to Hindus.

CR909 Teasdale, Wayne R.
Towards a Christian Vedanta: The Encounter of Hinduism and Christianity According to Bede Griffiths. New York, NYU: Fordham University, 1986. 306 pp. No ISBN.

A detailed critical analysis of the Christian Vedanta approach to Hinduism by Bede Griffiths; originally submitted as a Ph.D. dissertation at Fordham University (1985).

CR910 Thomas, Madathilparapil M.
The Acknowledged Christ of the Indian Renaissance. (Indian Theological Library, 4). Madras, II: CLS, 1976. xvi, 340 pp. Paper. No ISBN.

A survey by the prominent Indian ecumenist, focusing on the thoughts of 19th- and 20th-century leaders of the Indian Renaissance (Roy, Vivekananda, Radhakrishnan, Gandhi, etc.) and how they sought to understand the meaning of Christ and Christianity for the emerging new India.

CR911 Thomas, Madathilparapil M.
Christus im neuen Indien: Reform-Hinduismus und Christentum. (Theologie der Ökumene, 23). Göttingen, GW: Vandenhoeck & Ruprecht, 1989. 204 pp. Paper. 3525563272.

German translation.

CR912 Tornese, Nicola
Roberto de Nobili, 1577-1656: Contributo al dialogo con i non cristiani. Cagliari, IT: Pontificia Facolta Teologica del S. Cuore, 1973. 174 pp. No ISBN.

A detailed study, based on primary and secondary sources, of the ministry of de Nobili in Madurai among non-Christians, and his defense of his method citing the example of St. Paul.

CR913 Vekathanam, Mathew
Christology in the Indian Anthropological Context: Man-History-Christ: Christ, the Mystery of Man and of the Human History: An Evaluative Encounter with K. Rahner and W. Pannenberg. (European University Studies, 23: Theology, 287). Frankfurt am Main, GW: Lang, 1986. xxiii, 796 pp. Paper. 3820497765.

The Christological problem of God understood as both transcendent and historically immanent, analyzed in detail in an Indian cultural context of Vedantic philosophy, with discussion of the relevance to that debate of the Christologies of Karl Rahner and Wolfhart Pannenberg.

CR914 Vempeny, Ishanand
Krishna and Christ: In the Light of Some of the Fundamental Concepts and Themes of the Bhagavad Gita *and the New Testament.* Pune, II: Ishani Kendra; Anand, II: Gujarat Sahitya Prakash, 1988. xl, 498 pp. No ISBN.

A scholarly and reverential study by an Indian Jesuit who finds complementary and related themes and concepts concerning Lord Krishna and Lord Christ in the *Bhagavad Gita* and the New Testament.

CR—CHRISTIANITY AND OTHER RELIGIONS

CR915 Waspada, Ketut

Harmonie als Problem des Dialogs: Zur Bedeutung einer zentralen religiösen Kategorie in der Begegnung des Christentums mit dem Hinduismus auf Bali. (Religionswissenschaft, 1). Frankfurt am Main, GW: Lang, 1988. 314 pp. Paper. 3820400818.

Drawing on the religious background of the Balinese people, and taking the mission history of that island into account, the author presents the concept of "harmony" as the key to a realistic and biblically based encounter of Christianity with the people of Bali (dissertation, University of Munich).

CR916 Wolff, Otto

Christus unter den Hindus. Gütersloh, GW: Mohn, 1965. 222 pp. No ISBN.

A philosophical portrait of Christ as seen from the perspective of several Indian social reformers from Ram Mohan Roy to representatives of the Ramakrishna Movement today.

Hindu Sources, Origins, Impact

See also CR853.

CR917 Ayrookuzhiel, A. M. Abraham

Swami Anand Thirth: Untouchability, Gandhian Solution on Trial. Delhi, II: ISPCK, 1987. 144 pp. Paper. No ISBN.

The biography of Swami Anand Thirth (b. 1905), a Hindu reformer who struggled against the caste system by addressing the struggles of the Untouchables themselves, and by so doing critiqued Gandhi's approach to the removal of untouchability.

CR918 Burnett, David

The Spirit of Hinduism: A Christian Perspective on Hindu Thought. Turnbridge Wells, ENK: Monarch Publications, 1992. 286 pp. Paper. 185424194X.

A primer for Western Christians on Hinduism, its history, beliefs, customs, and movements as encountered in Europe.

CR919 Clooney, Francis X.

Hindu Wisdom for All God's Children. (Faith Meets Faith Series). Maryknoll, NYU: Orbis Books, 1998. xiv, 144 pp. Paper. 1570751641.

A thematic introduction to the spiritual riches of Hindu India; by a Jesuit theologian well-known for his ability to connect Hindu wisdom with Christian spirituality.

CR920 Clooney, Francis X.

Seeing through Texts: Doing Theology among the Srivaisnavas of South India. (Towards a Comparative Philosophy of Religions). Albany, NYU: SUNY Press, 1996. xxi, 351 pp. 0791429954 (hdbk), 0791429962 (pbk).

Through a study of 100 songs of the *Tiruvaymoli*, the 9th century masterpiece of the Hindu Vaisnavite saint Satkopan, the professor of comparative theology at Boston College develops themes for Hindu-Christian dialogue in South India.

CR921 Griffiths, Bede

The Cosmic Revelation: The Hindu Way To God. Springfield, ILU: Templegate, 1983. 136 pp. Paper. 0872431193.

A popular introduction to the Vedic tradition, by a Roman Catholic monk committed to understandings between Eastern and Western religions.

CR922 Griffiths, Bede

River of Compassion: A Christian Commentary on the Bhagavad Gita. New York, NYU: Continuum, 1995. 328 pp. Paper. 0826407692.

The noted scholar of East-West religious dialogue provides guidance for Christians open to the message of the Gita for their spiritual lives.

CR923 Huber, Friedrich

Die Bhagavadgita in der neueren indischen Auslegung und in der Begegnung mit dem christlichen Glauben. (Erlanger Monographien aus Mission und Ökumene, 12). Erlangen, GW: Ev.-Luth. Mission, 1991. x, 402 pp. Paper. 3872143123.

This *habilitationsschrift* undertakes a comprehensive study of the Bhagavad Gita through its modern interpreters insofar as it provides a basis for dialogue with Christianity.

CR924 Jacob, George

Religious Life of the Ilavas of Kerala: Change and Continuity. Delhi, II: ISPCK, 1995. viii, 216 pp. Paper. 8172141793.

A case study of the effects of modernization on the largest Hindu community in the Indian state of Kerala, of their struggles to overcome the strictures of the caste system upon them, and of their interactions with Christians.

CR925 Mathew, C. V.

Neo-Hinduism, a Missionary Religion. Madras, II: Church Growth Research Centre, 1987. 76 pp. Paper. No ISBN.

An analysis for Indian church leaders of the resurgence of Hindu fundamentalism and efforts to win converts within India from other faiths, including Christians to Hinduism.

CR926 Mathew, C. V.

The Saffron Mission: A Historical Analysis of Modern Hindu Missionary Ideologies and Practices. Delhi, II: ISPCK, 1999. xvi, 317 pp. Paper. 8172145373.

This study describes the missionary character of Hinduism, as well as the current nexus between religion and politics that has given rise to an intolerant and communalistic cultural nationalism bent on establishing a Hindu theocracy, and on providing an alternative to the Judeo-Christian culture of the West.

CR927 Mehta, Jaswant Lal

India and the West: The Problem of Understanding. (Studies in World Religions, 4). Chico, CAU: Scholars Press, 1985. xvii, 268 pp. 0891308261(hdbk), 089130827X (pbk).

Essays on the philosophy of religion and Indian religious traditions; by the Professor of Philosophy at Benares Hindu University and Visiting Professor at the Harvard University Center for the Study of World Religions.

CR928 Panikkar, Raimundo et al., eds.

The Vedic Experience Mantramañjari: An Anthology of the Vedas for Modern Man and Contemporary Celebration. Berkeley, CAU: University of California Press, 1977. xxxvi, 937 pp. 0520028546.

These engaging, amply annotated translations of selections from the Vedas, Upanishads, and Gita, together with extensive introductions and commentaries, are the means by which Panikkar seeks to present the Vedic experience as a possible "existential reenactment" for Western persons.

CR929 Ryerson, Charles
Regionalism and Religion: The Tamil Renaissance and Popular Hinduism. (Series on Religion, 27). Madras, II: CLS, 1988. xvi, 230 pp. Paper. No ISBN.

A historical study of the South Indian state of Tamil Nadu, focusing on the role of both Hinduism and Christianity in the growth of a regional consciousness (1949-1972), by a former missionary to India and faculty member at Princeton Theological Seminary.

CR930 The Sanskrit Grammar and Manuscripts of Father Heinrich Roth, S. J. (1620-1668)
Leiden, NE: Brill, 1988. 25, 166 pp. 9004086080.

A facsimile edition of the Sanskrit manuscripts of Fr. Heinrich Roth, S. J. (1620-1668) including his Sanskrit grammar, with an introduction analyzing their significance in understanding both the Mogul missions and the contribution of Fr. Roth in analysis of Sanskrit grammar.

CR931 Thompson, A. Frank
A New Look at Aurobindo. Delhi, II: CISRS/ISPCK, 1990. 106 pp. Paper. No ISBN.

Seven short essays on the understandings of science of Sri Aurobindo (1870-1950), the great Indian mystic and thinker, with parallels noted in his thought to classical Christian theology.

Christianity and Islam

See also HI160, HI163-HI166, HI169, HI576, TH334, TH590, CR51, CR320, CR327, CR336, CR1079, CR1100, CR1121, CR1181, CR1229, SP97, SP104, AF260, AF493, AF719, AF782, AF784, AF789, AF801, AF1201, AF1229, AF1314, AF1317, AF1333, AM1044, AS800, AS806, AS835, AS898, AS987, AS1055, AS1244, AS1318-AS1319, AS1362, AS1364, AS1373, AS1522, and EU281.

CR932 Abd-El-Jalil, Jean-Mohammed
L' Islam et nous. (Foi vivante, 268). Paris, FR: Éditions du Cerf, 1991. 129 pp. Paper. 2204043613.

Three texts originally written in 1938, 1955, and 1964, as introductions to the religious ideals of Islam; by a Roman Catholic priest who was born into the Muslim faith in 1904, baptized in 1928, and a priest of the Franciscan Order from 1935 until his death in 1979.

CR933 Accad, Fouad Elias
Building Bridges: Christianity and Islam. Colorado Springs, COU: NavPress, 1997. 158 pp. Paper. 0891097953.

Insights from the author's lifetime of experience building bridges between Muslims and Christians in Lebanon and other countries of the Middle East, with a comparison of Qu'ranic and biblical texts.

CR934 Amigo Vallejo, Carlos
Dios Clemente y Misericordioso: Experiencia religiosa de cristianos y musulmanes. Madrid, SP: Ediciones Paulinas, 1981. 150 pp. Paper. 8428508275.

An anthology of quotations from the Roman Catholic tradition, the Qu'ran, and contemporary authors on God's mercy and compassion.

CR935 Asin Palacios, Miguel
Saint John of the Cross and Islam. Translated by Howard W. Yoder and Elmer H. Douglas. New York, NYU: Vantage Press, 1981. 94 pp. 0533046254.

English translation of *Un precursor Hispano-Musulman de San Juan de la Cruz* (Madrid, SP: 1933).

CR936 Askari, Hasan, and Jon Avery
Towards a Spiritual Humanism: A Muslim-Humanist Dialogue. Pudsey, ENK: Seven Mirrors Publishing House, 1991. 145 pp. Paper. 1873685974.

A dialogue between a Muslim and a Christian humanist inviting readers to rethink their conceptions of anthropology and spirituality.

CR937 Baker, Dwight
Accessions to Islam in India. Andhra Pradesh, II: Henry Martyn Institute; Madras, II: Church Growth Research Centre, 1987. 20 pp. Paper. No ISBN.

A short essay on factors of immigration, conquest, and conversion in the growth of Islam in India during the early period of pre-European colonialism.

CR938 Basetti-Sani, Giulio
Louis Massignon, 1883-1962: Orientalista Cristiano. (Italia, Oriente, Mediterraneo, 2). Florence, IT: Alinea, 1985. 287 pp. No ISBN.

An interpretation of the life and thought of the great Islamist, 1883-1962; originally published in 1971 by Vita e Pensiero.

CR939 Basetti-Sani, Giulio
Louis Massignon, 1883-1962: Christian Ecumenist Prophet of Interreligious Reconciliation. Translated by Allan Harris Cutler. Chicago, ILU: Franciscan Herald Press, 1974. 262 pp. 0819904961.

English translation.

CR940 Basetti-Sani, Giulio
Per un dialogo cristiano-musulmano: Mohammed Damietta et La Verna. Milano, IT: Vita e Pensiero, 1969. x, 477 pp. No ISBN.

A handbook on Christian-Muslim dialogue by one with deep knowledge both of Islam and of Franciscan religious life.

CR941 Bennett, Clinton
In Search of Muhammad. London, ENK: Cassell, 1998. x, 276 pp. 0304337005 (hdbk), 0304704016 (pbk).

A critical study of the Muhammad of history which concludes with a postmodern theology of religions and explores a Christ-Muhammad option.

CR942 Borrmans, Maurice
Guidelines for Dialogue between Christians and Muslims. Translated by R. Marston Speight. (Interreligious Documents, 1). Mahwah, NJU: Paulist Press, 1990. vi, 132 pp. Paper. 0809131811.

English translation.

CR943 Borrmans, Maurice
Orientamenti per un dialogo tra cristiani e musulmani. Rome, IT: Pontifica Universitàs Urbaniana, 1988. 202 pp. No ISBN.

Italian translation.

CR944 Borrmans, Maurice
Orientations pour un dialogue entre Chrétiens et Musulmans. (Catholic Church/Secretariat for Non-Christians). Paris, FR: Éditions du Cerf; Rome, IT: Ancora, 1981. 191 pp. Paper. 2204017159.

A third edition of detailed guidelines prepared on behalf of the Pontifical Council in interreligious dialogue to aid Christians in forming relationships with Muslims.

CR945 Borrmans, Maurice
Wege zum christlich-islamischen Dialog. Frankfurt am Main, GW: CIBEDO, 1985. 167 pp. Paper. No ISBN.

German translation.

CR—CHRISTIANITY AND OTHER RELIGIONS

CR946 Bouman, Johna

Das Wort vom Kreuz und das Bekenntnis zu Allah: Die Grundlehren des Korans als nachbiblische Religion. Frankfurt am Main, GW: Verlag Otto Lembeck, 1980. 287 pp. 3874761452.

Recognizing the increasing numbers of Muslim guestworkers and refugees living in Germany, a Christian author examines Muslim beliefs and traditions, providing a basis for Muslim-Christian dialogue.

CR947 Brown, David

The Cross of the Messiah. (Christianity and Islam, 3). London, ENK: Sheldon Press, 1970. 80 pp. 281023247.

An exposition for Muslims with reference to Qu'ranic texts concerning the records and theology of the crucifixion.

CR948 Brown, Stuart E., ed.

Seeking an Open Society: Interfaith Relations and Dialogue in Sudan Today. (Faith in Sudan Series, 2). Nairobi, KE: Paulines Publications Africa, 1997. 104 pp. Paper. 9966213325.

Seven papers originally presented at a conference on "The Church in Sudan—It's Impact Past, Present and Future" (Limuru, Kenya, February 1997).

CR949 Brown, Stuart E.

Meeting in Faith: Twenty Years of Christian-Muslim Conversations Sponsored by the World Council of Churches. Geneva, SZ: WCC Publications, 1989. ix, 181 pp. Paper. 2825409499.

An introduction to thirteen Christian-Muslim dialogues held between 1969 and 1988, summarizing issues discussed, recommendations, and listing participants in each conversation.

CR950 Brown, Stuart E.

The Nearest in Affection: Towards a Christian Understanding of Islam. (Risk Book Series, 62). Geneva, SZ: WCC Publications, 1994. x, 124 pp. Paper. 2825409707.

The former Secretary for Christian-Muslim relations in the WCC (1983-1988) presents insights from Muslim-Christian conversations in more than fifty different countries on points of contact and divergences between the two faiths.

CR951 Bsteh, Andreas, ed.

Christlicher Glaube in der Begegnung mit dem Islam: Zweite Religionstheologische Akademie St. Gabriel: Referate, Anfragen, Diskussionen. (Studien zur Religionstheologie, 2). Mödling, AU: Verlag St. Gabriel, 1996. 616 pp. 3852644968.

Papers from a second workshop of Muslim and Christian scholars engaged in the study of Islam (Mödling, Austria, 1995).

CR952 Bsteh, Andreas, ed.

Der Gott des Christentums und des Islams. (Beiträge zur Religionstheologie, 2). Mödling, AU: Verlag St. Gabriel, 1978. 192 pp. Paper. 385264125X.

A book about the image of God of Christianity and Islam in their Scriptures and theology, and its consequences for the interpretation of the ultimate meaning of human existence.

CR953 Bsteh, Andreas, ed.

Hören auf sein Wort: Der Mensch als Hörer des Wortes Gottes in christlicher und islamischer Überlieferung. (Beiträge zur Religionstheologie, 7). Mödling, AU: Verlag St. Gabriel, 1992. 220 pp. Paper. 3852643988.

Eight scholarly essays on listening to the word of God in the traditions of Christianity and Islam.

CR954 Bsteh, Andreas, ed.

Der Islam als Anfrage an christliche Theologie und Philosophie. (Studien zur Religionstheologie, 1). Mödling, AU: Verlag St. Gabriel, 1994. 545 pp. 3852644577.

Papers from a workshop held at Mödling, Austria in 1994 as a meeting of Christian and Muslim scholars engaged in the study of Islam.

CR955 Busse, Heribert

Die theologischen Beziehungen des Islams zu Judentum und Christentum: Grundlagen des Dialogs im Koran und die gegenwärtige Situation. (Grundzüge, 72). Darmstadt, GW: Wissenschaftliche Buchgesellschaft, 1988. vi, 193 pp. Paper. 3534063945.

A monograph on the relationship between the three world religions—Islam, Judaism, and Christianity—in their scriptures and history, with a view to a possible dialogue.

CR956 Campbell, William

Le Coran et la Bible: à la lumière de l'histoire et de la science. Marne-la Vallé, FR: Éditions Farel, 1989. 328 pp. Paper. 2863140779.

In this work a medical doctor, after thirty years of practice in Morocco, Tunisia, and the Middle East, attempts a "scientific" comparison of the Bible and the Qu'ran, finding numerous analogies between them.

CR957 Cardaillac, Louis

Moriscos y Cristianos: Un Enfrentamiento Polémico, 1492-1640. Translated by Mercedes Garciá Arenal. (Fondo de Cultura Económica: Sección de Obras de Historia). Madrid, SP: Fondó de Cultura Económica, 1979. 567 pp. 8437501644.

Spanish translation of *Morisques et Chrétiens* (1977).

CR958 Cardaillac, Louis

Morisque et Chrétiens: un affrontement polémique, 1492-1640. (Témoins de l'Espagne: Série historique, 6). Paris, FR: Klincksieck, 1977. 543 pp. 2252019018.

A detailed analysis of the polemical manuscripts published 1492 to 1640 in the debate between the Moors and Spanish Christians, with conclusions concerning the significance of this literature and twenty representative primary source texts on which this work is based; also published in Arabic.

CR959 Chapman, Colin

Islam and the West: Conflict, Coexistence or Conversion? (Easneye Lectures Series). Carlisle, ENK: Paternoster Press, 1998. x, 198 pp. Paper. 085364781X.

A popular analysis of the three possible states of Christian-Muslim relations (conflict, coexistence, or conversion), and of key issues (education, mission, apologetics, human rights, secularization, etc.).

CR960 *Christians Meeting Muslims: WCC Papers on Ten Years of Christian-Muslim Dialogue*

Geneva, SZ: WCC, 1977. 158 pp. Paper. 2825405566.

A compilation of reports and papers from the 1966-1976 consultations sponsored by the WCC's Subunit for Dialogue with People of Living Faiths and Ideologies.

CR961 Chukwulozie, Victor

Muslim-Christian Dialogue in Nigeria. Ibadan, NR: Daystar Press, 1986. xviii, 201 pp. 9781221925.

A guide for Christians desiring to participate in Muslim-Christian dialogue in Nigeria, including chapters on the Nigerian history, principles, and practices of that dialogue.

CR962 Commission for Relations between Christians and Muslims (CERAO)
Connais-tu ton frère?: pour mieux comprende les Musulmans en Afrique. Bobo-Dioulasso, UV: Imprimerie de la Savane, 1981. 131 pp. No ISBN.

Helps for lay Christians in francophone Africa to understand their Muslim neighbors, principally the work of Fathers Augustin de Arteche of Burkino Faso.

CR963 Commission for Relations between Christians and Muslims (CERAO)
Let Us Understand Each Other: An Attempt at Fostering Mutual Understanding between Christians and Muslims. (Spearhead Series, 90-91). Eldoret, KE: Gaba Publications, 1986. 2 vols. Paper. No ISBN.

English translation.

CR964 Cooper, Anne, comp.
Ishmael My Brother: A Christian Introduction to Islam. Turnbridge Wells, ENK: MARC, 1993. 317 pp. Paper. 1854242334.

A revised and updated introduction to Islam for clergy and laypersons working with Muslim peoples, with a chapter on Muslim fundamentalism and case studies from different countries; originally published by MARC Europe, MARC International, EMA, and STL Books (1985).

CR965 Cragg, Kenneth
The Call of the Minaret. Maryknoll, NYU: Orbis Books, 1985. x, 358 pp. 0883442078.

An enlarged edition of Cragg's 1956 classic with new material on the contemporary setting, and the call to service and participation in Muslim-Christian dialogue; originally published in 1956 by Oxford University Press.

CR966 Cragg, Kenneth
Jesus and the Muslim: An Exploration. London, ENK: Allen & Unwin, 1985. xv, 315 pp. 0042970466.

A comparative study by the noted Christian interpreter of Islam, of the Islamic portrayal of Jesus in the Qu'ran and tradition in contrast to New Testament understandings; reprinted by Oneworld Publications in 1999.

CR967 Cragg, Kenneth
Muhammad and the Christian: A Question of Response. Oxford, ENK: Oneworld Publications, 1999. xii, 180 pp. Paper. 1851681795.

In this second edition, a leading Islamicist explores the Christian response to the Qu'ran, Christian reservations about Muhammad's life and claims, loyalty to the figure Christ, and the plea to Christians from the Qu'ran; originally published in 1984 (London, ENK: Darton, Longman & Todd).

CR968 Cragg, Kenneth, comp.
Alive to God: Muslim and Christian Prayer. London, ENK: Oxford University Press, 1970. xiv, 194 pp. Paper. 0192132202.

A collection of prayers and other passages from Muslim and Christian writers showing common elements and themes in prayer, with an introduction by the noted Christian scholar of Islam.

CR969 Damaskenos, Johannes, and Theodor Abu Qurra
Schriften zum Islam. (Corpus Islamo-Christianum: Series Graeca, 3). Würzburg, GW: Echter Verlag; Altenberge, GW: Oros Verlag, 1995. 222 pp. Paper. 3429015111 (E), 389375072X (O).

The texts in Greek, with German translation and commentary, of two important 8th-century documents for Christian-Muslim dialogue: the *Heresies* by Saint John of Damascus (675-740) and the *Opuscula Islamica* by Theodor Abu Zurra (750-825?).

CR970 DeCaro, Louis A.
Malcolm and the Cross: The Nation of Islam, Malcolm X, and Christianity. New York, NYU: New York University Press, 1998. xv, 270 pp. 0814718604.

Provides new insights into Malcolm X as a religious thinker and activist, including Christian influences on his life and mission.

CR971 Deshmukh, Ibrahimkhan O.
The Gospel and Islam. Bombay, II: Gospel Literature Service, 1982. x, 329 pp. Paper. No ISBN.

A book written for Muslims encouraging them to read the Scriptures of the Old Testament as understood in the Qu'ran; written by a Muslim who became a Christian in India.

CR972 Dharmaraj, Glory E., and Jacob S. Dharmaraj
Christianity and Islam: A Missiological Encounter. Delhi, II: ISPCK, 1998. x, 321 pp. Paper. 8172144113.

A basic introduction to Islam—its history, beliefs, and practices—for Christians concerned about mission to Muslims, with analysis of issues in dialogue, and missiological misunderstandings.

CR973 Dobers, H. et al., eds.
Development and Solidarity: Joint Responsibility of Muslims and Christians. Translated by Horst Schneider and Ulrike Schneider. (English series/Institut für internationale Solidarität, 12). Mainz, GW: Hase & Koehler, 1985. 246 pp. Paper. 3775810943.

The report from the second Christian-Islam Colloquium (Yaoundé, Cameroon, 21-24 February 1983), sponsored by the Konrad Adenauer Foundation, Dusseldorf; including papers on the respective concepts of man, solidarity, and development, and actual examples of common action.

CR974 *Ecumenical Considerations on Christian-Muslim Relations: Dialogue with People of Living Faiths*
Geneva, SZ: WCC Publications, 1990. 16 pp. Paper. 2825410209.

Guidelines for Christian-Muslim dialogue by the WCC's Subunit on Dialogue with People of Living Faiths.

CR975 Ellis, Kail C.
The Vatican, Islam, and the Middle East. Syracuse, NYU: Syracuse University Press, 1987. xviii, 344 pp. 0815624158.

Fifteen scholarly essays by noted theologians from Roman Catholic, Islamic, and Middle East perspectives on Christian-Muslim relations in the Middle East and the role of Vatican diplomacy.

CR976 Farrugia, Joseph
The Church and the Muslims: The Church's Consideration of Islam and the Muslims in the Documents of the Second Vatican Council. Gozo, MM: Media Center, 1988. 88 pp. Paper. No ISBN.

An analysis of Vatican II documents as they relate to Islam, focusing on theological themes with a juxtaposition of conciliar and Muslim responses to them.

CR—CHRISTIANITY AND OTHER RELIGIONS

CR977 Fitzgerald, Michael, ed.

Moslems und Christen—Partner? (Islam und westliche Welt, 1). Graz, AU: Styria, 1976. 205 pp. Paper. 3222109303.

A work on the basic principles of the Muslim way of life and thinking, and on the present state of the relationship between Islam and Christianity from a Muslim perspective.

CR978 Fitzgerald, Michael, ed.

Renaissance des Islams: Weg zur Begegnung oder zur Konfrontation? (Islam und westliche Welt, 4). Graz, AU: Styria, 1980. 189 pp. Paper. 3222112703.

Articles on the present development of Islam and the relationships between Christians and Muslims in Christian and Islamic societies.

CR979 Geisler, Norman L., and Abdul Saleeb

Answering Islam: The Crescent in Light of the Cross. Grand Rapids, MIU: Baker Books, 1993. 336 pp. Paper. 0801038596.

Two evangelical Christians (one a convert from Islam), present both a theological analysis and critique of Islam, and a Christian apologetic to Muslims.

CR980 Gerami, Shahin

Women and Fundamentalism: Islam and Christianity. (Reference Library of the Humanities, 1516; Women's History and Culture, 9). New York, NYU: Garland, 1996. xiii, 178 pp. 0815306636.

A comparative study of gender issues in Islamic and Protestant fundamentalism based on field research in Iran, Egypt, and the United States.

CR981 Gervers, Michael, and Ramzi Jibran Bikhazi, eds.

Conversion and Continuity: Indigenous Christian Communities in Islamic Lands, Eighth to Eighteenth Centuries. (Papers in Mediaeval Studies, 9). Toronto, ONC: Pontifical Institute of Mediaeval Studies, 1990. xi, 559 pp. Paper. 0888448090.

A collection of twenty-six scholarly essays on Christian-Muslim relations, 600-1500, including the rationale and polemics of conversion, the process of conversion and resistance to it, and implications for later relations; originally presented at a conference on Conversion and Continuity (University of Toronto, 23-25 October 1986).

CR982 Groupe de recherches islamo-chrétien

Ces écritures qui nous questionnent: la Bible et le Coran. Paris, FR: Le Centurion, 1987. 159 pp. Paper. 2227315652.

A summary of the initial years (1977-1982) of the Christian-Muslim dialogues, organized by the Group for Islamic-Christian Research; brings together scholars from Beirut, Brussels, Paris, Rabat, and Tunis, including two Islamic scholars commenting on the Bible, and comments on the Qu'ran by Christian scholars.

CR983 Groupe de recherches islamo-chrétien

The Challenge of the Scriptures: The Bible and the Qu'ran. Translated by Stuart E. Brown. (Faith Meets Faith Series). Maryknoll, NYU: Orbis Books, 1989. vii, 104 pp. Paper. 0883446510 (hdbk), 0883446502 (pbk).

English translation.

CR984 Höpfner, Willi, ed.

Der Islam als nachchristliche Religion. Wiesbaden, GW: Evangelische Mission in Oberägypten; Breklum, GW: Jensen, 1971. 100 pp. 3779304953.

Four scholars examine Islam's relationship to Eastern Christianity (W. Hage), Western Christianity (E. Dammann), Judaism (J. Bouman), and literary parallels between the Qu'ran and the Old Testament (S. Raeder).

CR985 Höpfner, Willi, ed.

Toleranz und Absolutheitsanspruch. (Christentum und Islam, 6). Wiesbaden, GW: Verlag der Evangelische Mission in Oberägypten; Breklum, GW: Breklumer Verlag, 1975. 93 pp. 3779304937.

A plea for tolerance by six scholars and church leaders within the framework of Christian-Muslim dialogue, drawing upon experiences and interpretations of Kraemer, Cragg, and Nicholas of Cuso.

CR986 Haddad, Yvonne Yazbeck, and Wadi Zaidan Haddad, eds.

Christian-Muslim Encounters. Gainesville, FLU: University Press of Florida, 1995. xi, 508 pp. 0813013569 (hdbk), 0813013593 (pbk).

Twenty-eight scholarly papers originally presented at a Hartford Seminary conference on "Christian-Muslim Encounter: The Heritage of the Past and Present Intellectual Trends" (Hartford, Connecticut, 7-9 June 1990).

CR987 Hagemann, Ludwig

Christentum für das Gespräch mit Muslimen. (Islam und Christentum, 1). Altenberge, GW: Verlag für Christlich-Islamisches Schrifttum, 1982. 166 pp. Paper. 3887330129.

This work draws from the Bible to present the fundamental tenets of the Christian faith and, against the background of the Qu'ran, examines the common elements and differences between Islam and Christianity.

CR988 Hagemann, Ludwig

Christentum und Islam zwischen Konfrontation und Begegnung. (Studien, 4). Altenberge, GW: Verlag für Christlich-Islamisches Schrifttum, 1983. 160 pp. Paper. 3887330218.

Proceeding from the self-understanding of Islam and recognizing the creative accomplishments of Muhummad, this book attempts to show common elements and differences between Islam and Christianity, and the way from the confrontations of the past toward encounter in our days.

CR989 Hagemann, Ludwig

Propheten—Zeugen des Glaubens: Koranische und biblische Deutungen. (Islam und westliche Welt, 7). Graz, AU: Styria, 1985. 207 pp. Paper. 3222116148.

This work describes the great prophetic figures (Abraham, Moses, Jesus, and Muhammad), as presented in the Qu'ran, in order to reveal the similarities and differences between Christianity and Islam.

CR990 Haines, Byron L., and Frank L. Cooley, eds.

Christians and Muslims Together: An Exploration by Presbyterians. Philadelphia, PAU: Geneva Press, 1987. 130 pp. Paper. 0664240615.

A study book on contemporary Islam, the Muslim world, and Christian-Muslim relations, with helps for constructive dialogue developed by the Islamic Advisory Study Committee of the PCUSA.

CR—CHRISTIANITY AND OTHER RELIGIONS

CR991 Hao, Yap Kim, ed.
Islam's Challenge for Asian Churches. Toa Payoh, SI: CCA, 1980. 50 pp. Paper. No ISBN.

Papers from a consultation held at Kuala Lumpur, Malaysia, in February 1980 with Muslim and Christian participants from six Asian countries.

CR992 Hock, Klaus
Der Islam im Spiegel westlicher Theologie: Aspekte christlich-theologischer Beurteilung des Islams im 20. Jahrhundert. (Kölner Veröffentlichungen zur Religionsgeschichte, 8). Cologne, GW: Böhlau Verlag, 1986. 403 pp. 3412002860.

A scholarly examination of 20th-century assessments of Islam by Western theologians; originally presented as a doctoral thesis (University of Hamburg, 1985).

CR993 Hoppenworth, Klaus
Islam contra Christentum—gestern und heute: Information für Christen zur Begegnung mit Moslems. (Telos-Dokumentation). Bad Liebenzell, GW: Verlag der Liebenzeller Mission, 1976. 141 pp. Paper. 3880020329.

Presents Islam as a world religion from both historical and cultural-demographic analysis with the goal of improving Christian-Muslim dialogue.

CR994 Hunwick, John O., ed.
Religion and National Integration in Africa: Islam, Christianity, and Politics in the Sudan and Nigeria. (Series in Islam and Society in Africa). Evanston, ILU: Northwestern University Press, 1992. xii, 176 pp. 0810110377.

Papers on Christian-Muslim relations and the struggles for political integration in Sudan and Nigeria; originally presented at the Seminar on Religion and National Integration in Africa (Northwestern University, 1988).

CR995 Jargy, Simon
Islam et chrétienté—les fils d'Abraham entre la confrontation et le dialogue. Geneva, SZ: Labor et Fides, 1981. 216 pp. Paper. No ISBN.

An account of the historical commonality between the religious and socio-political components of Islam and Christianity, as well as an understanding of conceptions that falsely separate them.

CR996 Jennings, Ronald C.
Christians and Muslims in Ottoman Cyprus and the Mediterranean World, 1571-1640. (New York University Studies in Near Eastern Civilization, 18). New York, NYU: New York University Press, 1993. xi, 428 pp. 0814741819.

A detailed social analysis of Christian-Muslim relations in Cyprus from the Ottoman Turks' victory over the majority Greek Orthodox community in 1570 to 1640.

CR997 Jensen, Johannes H., and Edv. Wulff Pedersen, eds.
Møde med Islam: Kristen mission blandt muslimer. Hellerup, DK: DMS-Forlag, 1973. 79 pp. Paper. 8774310321.

A primer introducing Islam to Dutch Christians, with study questions.

CR998 Johnson, James Turner, and John Kelsay, eds.
Cross, Crescent, and Sword: The Justification and Limitation of War in Western and Islamic Tradition. (Contributions to the Study of Religion, 27). New York, NYU: Greenwood, 1990. xviii, 236 pp. 0313273480.

Nine papers by Christian and Muslim scholars; originally presented at four conferences held at Rutgers University, 1988-89.

CR999 Joseph, Suad, and Barbara L. K. Pillsbury, eds.
Muslim-Christian Conflicts: Economic, Political, and Social Origins. Boulder, COU: Westview Press; Folkestone, ENK: Dawson, 1978. xxi, 245 pp. 0891582568 (US), 0712908846 (UK).

Seven scholarly essays on contemporary Muslim-Christian conflicts, with case studies from Lebanon, Egypt, Yugoslavia (Bosnia), Cyprus, and the Sudan.

CR1000 Küng, Hans, and Jürgen Moltmann, eds.
Islam: A Challenge for Christianity. (*Concilium*, 1994/3). Maryknoll, NYU: Orbis Books; London, ENK: SCM Press, 1994. viii, 163 pp. Paper. 0883448785 (US), 0334030269 (UK).

A collection of sixteen short essays seeking to move beyond the "clash of civilizations" interpretation of Christian-Muslim contacts to an ecumenical theology of a shared life and a theology of peace.

CR1001 Kateregga, Badru D., and David W. Shenk
Islam and Christianity: A Muslim and a Christian in Dialogue. Scottdale, PAU: Herald Press, 1997. 219 pp. Paper. 0836190521.

Two former lecturers at Kenyatta University in Nairobi, Kenya, open up basic questions of the human situation, and confront both similarities and differences in Muslim and Christian responses.

CR1002 Kelsay, John, and James Turner Johnson, eds.
Just War and Jihad: Historical and Theoretical Perspectives on War and Peace in Western and Islamic Traditions. (Contributions to the Study of Religion, 28). New York, NYU: Greenwood, 1991. xvi, 254 pp. 0313273472.

Eight essays by Western scholars of ethics, law, and Islamic studies; originally presented at Rutgers University, 1988-1989—a companion volume to *Cross, Crescent, and Sword* (1990).

CR1003 Kerr, David A., ed.
The Illuminated Manuscripts of Hartford Seminary: The Art of Christian-Muslim Relations. Hartford, CTU: Hartford Seminary, 1994. iv, 90 pp. Paper. 0964104806.

Color reproductions, with notes, of illuminated manuscripts, both Christian and Muslim, in the collection of the McDonald Center for the Study of Islam and Christianity in Hartford, Connecticut.

CR1004 Khoury, Adel Théodore, and Ludwig Hagemann
Christentum und Christen im Denken zeitgenössischer Muslime. (Studien, 7). Altenberge, GW: Christlich-Islamisches Schrifttum, 1986. 205 pp. Paper. 3887330676.

The book sketches a representative picture of the different views of Christianity within Islam today.

CR1005 Khoury, Paul
L' Islam critique de l'Occident dans la pensée arabe actuelle: Islam et sécularité, 1. (Religionswissenschaftliche studien, 35/1). Würzburg, GW: Echter Verlag; Altenberge, GW: Oros Verlag, 1994. 410 pp. Paper. 3429016509 (E), 3893751033 (O).

A thematic analysis of Islamic thought concerning secularization and other challenges of modern Western culture, with extensive bibliographic notations, but not quotations.

CR1006 Kimball, Charles A.
Striving Together: A Way Forward in Christian-Muslim Relations. Maryknoll, NYU: Orbis Books, 1991. xv, 132 pp. Paper. 088344691X.

A popular introduction for Christians to the history of Christian-Muslim relations and to the models in theology and practice for contemporary dialogue.

CR1007 King, Noel Q.
Christian and Muslim in Africa. New York, NYU: Harper & Row, 1971. xiv, 153 pp. No ISBN.

A survey of the successive advances and retreats of the two religions in Africa from the earliest times to the present, with extensive bibliographic notes.

CR1008 LaCocque, André, ed.
Commitment and Commemoration: Jews, Christians, Muslims in Dialogue. Chicago, ILU: Exploration Press, 1994. viii, 151 pp. 0913552542.

A selection of papers from trialogues sponsored by the Center for Jewish-Christian Studies of the Chicago Theological Seminary.

CR1009 Lazarus-Yafeh, Hava
Intertwined Worlds: Medieval Islam and Bible Criticism. Princeton, NJU: Princeton University Press, 1992. xiii, 178 pp. 0691073988.

A scholarly monograph by the professor of Islamic civilization of the Hebrew University of Jerusalem, tracing Jewish, Christian, and Hellenistic ideas reflected in Muslim writings on the Bible, and Muslim use of biblical texts.

CR1010 Leirvik, Oddbjørn
Images of Jesus Christ in Islam: Introduction, Survey of Research, Issues of Dialogue. (Studia Missionalia Upsaliensia, 76). Uppsala, SW: Swedish Institute of Missionary Research, 1999. 269 pp. Paper. 9185424536.

A general but thorough introduction and survey of research in the field, by a Christian theologian experienced in and committed to such dialogue.

CR1011 Lupprian, Karl-Ernst
Die Beziehungen der Päpste zu islamischen und mongolischen Herrschern im 13. Jahrhundert anhand ihres Briefwechsels. (Studi e Testi, 291.). Rome, IT: Biblioteca Apostolica Vaticana, 1981. 328 pp. 8821005755.

A sourcebook of correspondence between 13th century Catholic popes and Muslim and Mongol leaders, with an introductory essay and bibliography.

CR1012 Mallon, Elias D.
Neighbors: Muslims in North America. New York, NYU: Friendship Press, 1989. 104 pp. Paper. 0377001988.

A series of interviews with Muslims about their faith journeys, way of life, and challenges of being Muslims in North America; prepared as a mission study book.

CR1013 Manuel Palaeologus
Dialogue mit einem Muslim = Dialogos meta tinos Persou. (Corpus Islamo-Christianum: Series Graeca, 4). Würzburg, GW: Echter Verlag; Altenberge, GW: Oros Verlag, 1995. xxi, 341 pp. Paper. 3429016517 (E), 3893751041 (O).

The Greek text, with German translation, of *Dialogue with a Muslim*, an important 13th-century text containing both the Islamic critique of Christology and the Trinity and the Christian apologetic, with commentary by Karl Förstel.

CR1014 Marthelot, Pierre et al.
Islam, civilisation et religion. (Recherches et débats du Centre Catholique des Intellectuels Français, n.s., 51). Paris, FR: Fayard, 1965. 258 pp. No ISBN.

Ten contributions from Christian Islamicists and Muslims intended to prepare for dialogue.

CR1015 Martinson, Paul Varo, ed.
Islam: An Introduction for Christians. Translated by Stefanie Ormsby Cox. Minneapolis, MNU: Augsburg, 1994. 264 pp. Paper. 080662583X.

The first English-language edition of *Was Jeder vom Islam Wissen Muss* (1990), a primer for Christians on Islam prepared as a study book for use in the evangelical and Lutheran churches of Germany; with leader's guide by Irene R. Getz (ISBN 0806627026).

CR1016 Matar, Nabil
Islam in Britain, 1558-1665. Cambridge, ENK: Cambridge University Press, 1998. xi, 226 pp. Paper. 0521622336.

The transformation of British thought and society during the period from the accession of Elizabeth I to the death of Charles II; Christian-Muslim interaction was not, as often assumed, primarily adversarial and oppositional, but was engaged.

CR1017 McCurry, Don M.
Esperanza para los Musulmanes. Miami, FLU: Editorial Unilit, 1992. 468 pp. Paper. 0789901714.

A primer for Latin American Christians on Islam and witness to Muslims, by the Director of the Zwemer Institute.

CR1018 Mildenberger, Michael, ed.
Kirchengemeinden und ihre muslimischen Nachbarn. (Beiträge zur Ausländerarbeit, 13). Frankfurt am Main, GW: Lembeck, 1990. 104 pp. Paper. 3874762637.

Based on experiences in the Protestant church in Germany, this study attempts to provide a model for parish communities fostering acceptance and integration of Muslims in their neighborhoods.

CR1019 Milot, Jean-René
Musulmans et chrétiens: des frères ennemis? Montréal, QUC: Médiaspaul, 1995. 61 pp. 2894203187.

A brief historical study of Christian-Muslim relations.

CR1020 Milot, Jean-René
Muslims and Christians: Enemies or Brothers? New York, NYU: Alba House, 1997. v, 82 pp. Paper. 0818907797.

English translation.

CR1021 Mitri, Tarek, ed.
Religion, Law and Society: A Christian-Muslim Discussion. Geneva, SZ: WCC Publications; Kampen, NE: Kok Pharos, 1995. xvi, 137 pp. Paper. 2825411485 (SZ), 9039005141 (NE).

Seventeen short essays by Muslim and Christian scholars from a dozen countries on various aspects of Islamic law, human rights, religious freedom, and the challenge of secularism to both faiths.

CR1022 Mohammed, Ovey N.
Muslim-Christian Relations: Past, Present, Future. (Faith Meets Faith Series). Maryknoll, NYU: Orbis Books, 1999. 144 pp. Paper. 01570752575.

An introduction to Islam for Christians, with the examination of political, cultural, and economic Muslim-Christian differences, and a way forward in interfaith dialogue that seeks to be faithful to the Bible and the Qu'ran.

CR1023 Musk, Bill A.
Passionate Believing. Tunbridge Wells, ENK: Monarch Publications, 1992. 256 pp. Paper. 1854241729.

An introduction for Christians to contemporary Islamic fundamentalism, and its three distinct models in Pakistan, Egypt, and Iran, with beginning guidelines for a Christian response.

CR—CHRISTIANITY AND OTHER RELIGIONS

CR1024 *My Neighbour Is Muslim: A Handbook for Reformed Churches*
(John Knox Series, 7). Geneva, SZ: John Knox Centre International Réformé, 1990. 111 pp. Paper. 2884300066.

Papers from the second "Living Among Muslims" consultation for Reformed churches (Geneva, July 1990)

CR1025 Nazir-Ali, Michael
Frontiers in Muslim-Christian Encounter. Oxford, ENK: Regnum Books, 1987. 191 pp. Paper. 1870345053.

Essays on theological, missiological, or dialogical issues for Christians living in a Muslim environment, by the Director-in-Residence of the Oxford Centre for Mission Studies, assistant to the Archbishop of Canterbury, and bishop of the Church of Pakistan.

CR1026 Nazir-Ali, Michael
Islam: A Christian Perspective. Exeter, ENK: Paternoster Press, 1983. 185 pp. Paper. 0853643334.

A critical appraisal of facets of Islam by a Pakistani Anglican leader, with observations on the Christian-Muslim encounters.

CR1027 Newman, N. A., ed.
The Early Christian-Muslim Dialogue: A Collection of Documents from the First Three Islamic Centuries (632-900 A.D.). Hatfield, PAU: Interdisciplinary Biblical Research Institute, 1993. xvii, 776 pp. 0944788912.

Translations of the eight most important documents of Christian-Muslim dialogues from 632-900 AD, with commentary by the editor and full indexing of subjects, biblical and Qu'ranic references.

CR1028 Okafor, Gabriel Maduka
Christians and Muslims in Cameroon. (Religionswissenschaftliche Studien, 34). Würzburg, GW: Echter Verlag; Altenberge, GW: Oros Verlag, 1994. 144 pp. Paper. 3429016401 (E), 3893750991 (O).

A case study of Christian-Muslim relations in the Cameroon where one-fifth of the population is Muslim.

CR1029 Okafor, Gabriel Maduka
Development of Christianity and Islam in Modern Nigeria. Würzburg, GW: Echter Verlag; Altenberge, GW: Oros Verlag, 1992. 240 pp. Paper. 3429014743 (E), 3893750606 (O).

A critical appraisal of the religious forces of Christianity and Islam in modern Nigeria.

CR1030 Olupona, Jacob Obafemi Kehinde
Religion and Peace in Multi-Faith Nigeria. Ile-Ife, NR: By the author, Jacob K. Olupona, 1992. xiii, 203 pp. Paper. No ISBN.

Papers from an important conference on "Religion and Peace in Multi-Faith Nigeria" (Ile-Ife, 4-8 Dec. 1989), co-sponsored by the Council for the World's Religions and Obafemi Awolowo University.

CR1031 Parrinder, Edward Geoffrey
Jesus in the Qu'ran. New York, NYU: Oxford University Press; London, ENK: Sheldon Press, 1977. 187 pp. 0195199634 (O), 0859690695 (S).

A detailed examination of passages in fifty suras of the Qu'ran in which Jesus is mentioned; originally published by Barnes & Noble, New York (1965).

CR1032 Parshall, Phil
Beyond the Mosque: Christians within Muslim Community. Grand Rapids, MIU: Baker Books, 1985. 256 pp. Paper. 0801070899.

An analysis of the strong sense of Muslim community, which accounts for much of the Muslim's reluctance to consider the unique claims of Jesus Christ, and its implications for missions and the structures of Christian community.

CR1033 Partner, Peter
God of Battles: Holy Wars of Christianity and Islam. Princeton, NJU: Princeton University Press, 1997. xxvii, 364 pp. Paper. 0691002355.

A comparative study of Islamic *jihad* and the Christian crusades from the 7th century C.E. to the present.

CR1034 Phipps, William E.
Muhammad and Jesus: A Comparison of the Prophets and Their Teachings. New York, NYU: Paragon House; New York, NYU: *Continuum*, 1996. x, 304 pp. 1557787182 (P), 0826409148 (C).

A scholarly comparison of the lives, works, and contributions as prophets of Muhammad and Jesus.

CR1035 *Pistes de réponses aux questions qu'on nous pose: (par un groupe de chrétiens vivant en Tunisie)*
(Collection "Studi arabo-islamici del PISAI," 2). Rome, IT: Pontificio Instituto di Studi Arabi e d'Islamistica, 1987. 113 pp. Paper. 8885907016.

A practical help for Christians desiring to understand the belief system of Muslims so as to answer more helpfully their questions concerning Christian faith and life—the result of a twelve-year study project by Catholic clergy and laity in Tunisia.

CR1036 Poston, Larry
Islamic Da'wah in the West: Muslim Missionary Activity and the Dynamics of Conversion to Islam. New York, NYU: Oxford University Press, 1992. 224 pp. 0195072278.

An exploration of the concept of *da'wah*, Islamic missionary activity, as it has evolved in contemporary Western societies.

CR1037 Powell, James M., ed.
Muslims under Latin Rule, 1100-1300. Princeton, NJU: Princeton University Press, 1990. vii, 221 pp. 0691055866.

Five scholarly essays focusing on Muslim minorities living in Christian-dominated lands of the Mediterranean basin during the high Middle Ages.

CR1038 Rajashekar, J. Paul William, and H. S. Wilson, eds.
Islam in Asia: Perspectives for Christian-Muslim Encounter. Geneva, SZ: LWF/WARC, 1992. xvi, 227 pp. Paper. 3906707095.

Papers and area reports by fourteen Christians knowledgeable about Islam and Christian-Muslim relations; originally presented in Bangkok, Thailand, in June 1991, at a consultation jointly sponsored by the LWF Federation and the WARC.

CR1039 Rajashekar, J. Paul William, ed.
Christian-Muslim Relations in Eastern Africa. Geneva, SZ: LWF, 1988. vi, 134 pp. Paper. 2881900046.

Papers and report from the seminar/workshop sponsored by the LWF and the Project for Christian-Muslim Relations in Africa (Nairobi, Kenya, 2-8 May 1987).

CR1040 Register, Ray G.

Dialogue and Interfaith Witness with Muslims: A Guide and Sample Ministry in the U.S.A. Fort Washington, PAU: WEC, 1979. xii, 99 pp. Paper. 0960301801.

A book that attempts to understand and overcome the difficulties that block communications with Muslims; by one who served as Southern Baptist representative to Arabs in Israel, Nazareth, and Galilee.

CR1041 Renard, John

Responses to 101 Questions on Islam. (101 Questions Series). New York, NYU: Paulist Press, 1998. viii, 173 pp. Paper. 0809138034.

A primer for Christians on Islam, covering their beliefs and contemporary customs.

CR1042 Riedel, Siegfried

Sünde und Versöhnung in Koran und Bibel: Herausforderung zum Gespräch. Erlangen, GW: Evangelical-Lutheran. Mission, 1982. 105 pp. Paper. 3872141821.

Asserting that sin and reconciliation are the main themes of both the Bible and the Qu'ran, the author of this book compares what he regards as the basic tenets of faith in both holy books.

CR1043 Robinson, Neal

Christ in Islam and Christianity. Albany, NYU: SUNY Press, 1991. xi, 235 pp. 0791405583 (hdbk), 0791405591 (pbk).

A scholarly analysis of the different Christian approaches to Jesus in the Qu'ran and in the classical Muslim commentaries.

CR1044 Rousseau, Richard W., ed.

Christianity and Islam: The Struggling Dialogue. (Modern Theological Themes: Selections from the Literature, 4). Montrose, PAU: Ridge Row Press, 1985. 229 pp. Paper. 094086603X.

Twelve essays reporting on Muslim-Christian dialogues, 1968-1978, with an assessment of major issues.

CR1045 Samartha, Stanley J., and John B. Taylor, eds.

Christian-Muslim Dialogue: Papers Presented at the Broumana Consultation, 12-18 July 1972. Geneva, SZ: WCC, 1973. 167 pp. Paper. No ISBN.

Report and papers from an important WCC consultation on interfaith dialogue, bringing together almost an equal number of Muslims and Christians from twenty countries.

CR1046 Samir, Samir Khalil, and Jorgen S. Nielsen, eds.

Christian Arabic Apologetics during the Abbasid Period (750-1258). (Studies in the History of Religions, 63). Leiden, NE: Brill, 1994. xii, 250 pp. 9004095683.

Important papers from the First Mingana Symposium on Arabic Christianity and Islam (Woodbrooke College, Birmingham, England, 24-28 May 1990).

CR1047 Sanneh, Lamin

Piety and Power: Muslims and Christians in West Africa. (Faith Meets Faith Series). Maryknoll, NYU: Orbis Books, 1996. xv, 207 pp. Paper. 1570750904.

A scholarly analysis of the dynamics of Muslim-Christian relations in West African societies by the D. Willis James Professor of Missions and World Christianity at Yale University.

CR1048 Sanson, Henri

Dialogue intérieur avec l'Islam. (Religions en Dialogue). Paris, FR: Centurion, 1990. 210 pp. Paper. 2227363029.

The author, a Jesuit whose family has lived as Christians in Algeria since 1830, shows through twenty-eight short meditations on immanence and transcendence how Christianity and Islam become mirror images of each other, steeped both in Christian piety and Islamic culture.

CR1049 Schuon, Frithjof

Christianity/Islam: Essays on Esoteric Ecumenicism. Bloomington, INU: World Wisdom Books, 1985. vi, 270 pp. Paper. 9941532054.

Fourteen essays by a prominent scholar of comparative religion who, through a theocentric approach and philosophical categories, finds unity between Christianity and Islam; originally published in 1981.

CR1050 Schwartländer, Johannes

Freiheit der Religion: Christentum und Islam unter dem Anspruch der Menchenrechte. (Forum Weltkirche: Entwicklung und Frieden, 2). Mainz, GW: Matthias-Grünewald-Verlag, 1993. 474 pp. Paper. 3786713928.

A collection of essays by Muslim and Christian scholars on human rights, with a focus on issues of religious freedom and Islamic law (*sharia*).

CR1051 Shadid, W. A. R., and P. S. van Koningsveld

Religious Freedom and the Position of Islam in Western Europe: Opportunities and Obstacles in the Acquisition of Equal Rights (with an Extensive Bibliography). Kampen, NE: Kok Pharos, 1995. viii, 229 pp. Paper. 9039000654.

A collection of articles published between 1987 and 1994 on the public status of Islam in the various countries of Western Europe, including issues of religious education in schools.

CR1052 Shafaat, Ahmad

Islam, Christianity, and the State of Israel as Fulfillment of Old Testament Prophecy. Indianapolis, INU: American Trust Publications, 1989. iv, 102 pp. Paper. 0892590823.

A Muslim scholar interprets briefly the messianic tradition in the Old Testament and Jewish writings, and their later interpretation in the New Testament and the Qu'ran.

CR1053 Six, Jean-François

Louis Massignon. Paris, FR: Éditions de l'Herne, 1970. 520 pp. Paper. No ISBN.

A major retrospective work by scholars assessing the life and contribution of Louis Massignon (1883-1962), noted Islamicist and founder in 1929 of L'institut des Études Islamiques, with a selection from his major writings.

CR1054 Smith, Wilfred Cantwell

On Understanding Islam: Selected Studies. (Religion and Reason, 19). The Hague, NE: Mouton, 1981. xiii, 351 pp. 9027934487.

A collection of scholarly writings on Islam, including Muslim-Christian relations, by the Professor of World Religions at Harvard University.

CR—CHRISTIANITY AND OTHER RELIGIONS

CR1055 Speight, R. Marston
Christian-Muslim Relations: An Introduction for Christians in the United States of America. Hartford, CTU: NCCUSA, 1984. 96 pp. Paper. No ISBN.

Second edition of a practical introduction to Islam in the United States, with practical suggestions for Christian-Muslim dialogue; originally published in 1983.

CR1056 Stamer, Josef
Islam in Sub-Saharan Africa. Estella, SP: Verbo Divino, 1996. 156 pp. 8481690384.

A historical and contemporary study of Islam in sub-Saharan Africa, of interaction between Islam and Christianity in the region, with a challenge to the Catholic Church to fulfill her Second Vatican Council calling there.

CR1057 Steenbrink, Karel A.
Dutch Colonialism and Indonesian Islam: Contacts and Conflicts, 1596-1950. Translated by Jan Steenbrink and Henry Jansen. (Studies on the Contact between Christianity and Other Religions, Beliefs, and Cultures, 7). Amsterdam, NE: Rodopi, 1993. 170 pp. Paper. 9051832672.

A detailed study of perceptions of Islam by Dutch leaders in Indonesia—entrepreneurs, government officials, and missionaries during the colonial period.

CR1058 Sweetman, J. Windrow
Islam and Christian Theology. London, ENK: Lutterworth Press, 1945-1967. 4 vols. No ISBN.

A detailed historical theology of the interrelations of Islam and Christianity organized according to the philosophical and theological concepts at issue [2 parts in 4 volumes: I-1: xiv, 216 pp.; I-2: viii, 285 pp.; II-1: x, 354 pp.; II-2: viii, 356 pp.].

CR1059 Swidler, Leonard J., ed.
Muslims in Dialogue: The Evolution of a Dialogue. (Religions in Dialogue, 3). Lewiston, NYU: E Mellen Press, 1992. xviii, 536 pp. 0889464995.

A collection of twenty-eight essays by Muslim, Jewish, and Christian scholars on interreligious dialogue by Muslims with persons of other faiths; originally published in the *Journal of Ecumenical Studies*, or in other books.

CR1060 Thomas, Richard Walter
Islam: Aspects and Prospects—A Critical Analysis. Villach, AU: Light of Life, 1988. 200 pp. Paper. No ISBN.

An introduction to some of the basic tenets and practices of Islam for Christians concerned about outreach to Muslims, based on a deeper understanding of Islam, by a lecturer in Arabic at the Extra-Mural Department of the University of Glasgow, Scotland.

CR1061 Tolan, John Victor, ed.
Medieval Christian Perceptions of Islam: A Book of Essays. (Reference Library of the Humanities, 1768; Medieval Casebooks, 10). New York, NYU: Garland, 1996. xxi, 414 pp. 0815314264.

Fifteen essays focusing on unfamiliar texts from the 7th to 16th centuries that reflect the wide range of medieval Christian preoccupation with Islam.

CR1062 Tudtud, Bienvenido Solon
Dialogue of Life and Faith: Selected Writings of Bishop Bienvenido S. Tudtud. Quezon City, PH: Claretian Publications, 1988. xi, 189 pp. Paper. 9715012671 (pk), 971501268X (hdbk).

Selected writings from the 1971 to 1987 period by the first Roman Catholic bishop of Iligan in the Philippines, focusing on issues of Christian-Muslim dialogue.

CR1063 Vaporis, Nomikos Michael, ed.
Orthodox Christians and Muslims. Brookline, MAU: Holy Cross Orthodox Press, 1986. ix, 203 pp. Paper. 0917651340.

Thirteen papers by Orthodox and Muslim scholars originally presented at a joint symposium at Hellenic College/Holy Cross Greek Orthodox School of Theology, March 1985.

CR1064 Verkuyl, Johannes
Met moslims in gesprek over het evangelie. Kampen, NE: Kok, 1994. 162 pp. Paper. 9024227593.

Reflections on issues in Muslim-Christian dialogue by the noted Dutch missiologist; originally published in 1985.

CR1065 Vermeulen, U., and J. M. F. Van Reeth
Law, Christianity and Modernism in Islamic Society. (Orientalia Lovaniensia Analecta, 86). Leuven, Belgium: Peeters, 1998. xviii, 299 pp. 9068319795 (BE), 2877233936 (FR).

A collection of the proceedings of the eighteenth Congress of the Union Européenne des Arabisants et Islamisants held at the Katholieke Universiteit Leuven (3-9 September 1996).

CR1066 Waardenburg, Jacques
Islamisch-Christliche Beziehungen: Geschichtliche Streifzünge. (Religionswissenschaftliche Studien, 23). Würzburg, GW: Echter Verlag; Altenberge, GW: Oros Verlag, 1993. 232 pp. Paper. 3429014859 (EV), 3893750649 (OV).

A 1991 summer lecture series on Islamic-Christian connections throughout the centuries, with texts mainly translated from other languages.

CR1067 Waardenburg, Jacques, ed.
Islam and Christianity: Mutual Perceptions since the Mid-20th Century. Leuven, BE: Peeters, 1998. viii, 320 pp. Paper. 9042900040 (BE), 2877233898 (FR).

A collection of nine scholarly contributions, both in English and French, describing important changes which have taken place in Roman Catholic, Protestant, and Orthodox perspectives with appreciations of Islam; also contains a variety of recent Muslim views and appreciation of Christianity.

CR1068 Watt, William Montgomery
Islam and Christianity Today: A Contribution to Dialogue. London, ENK: Routledge, 1983. xiv, 157 pp. 0710097662.

A summary of doctrinal aspects of the contemporary meetings of followers of Islam and Christianity; based on the author's forty-year study of the subject while in the Department of Arabic and Islamic Studies at the University of Edinburgh, Scotland.

CR1069 Watt, William Montgomery
Muslim-Christian Encounters: Perceptions and Misperceptions. London, ENK: Routledge, 1991. 164 pp. 0415054109 (hdbk), 0415054117 (pbk).

An analysis of the myths and misperceptions that have blighted Muslim and Christian perceptions of each other, with proposals for a more fruitful understanding and cooperation by the Emeritus Professor in Arabic and Islamic Studies at the University of Edinburgh.

CR–CHRISTIANITY AND OTHER RELIGIONS

CR1070 Wessels, Antonie

De moslimse naaste: Op weg naar een theologie van de Islam.
Kampen, NE: Kok, 1978. 156 pp. Paper. 9024208610.

A historical and theological study of the special relationship between Christianity and Islam by a Professor of Missiology in Amsterdam who is a former professor at the Near East School of Theology in Beirut (1971-1978).

CR1071 Wessels, Antonie

De nieuwe arabische mens: Moslims en christenen in het arabische oosten vandaag. Baarn, NE: Ten Have, 1977. 118 pp. 9025940978.

A reflection on the current Muslim-Christian relationship among religious populations of the Middle East countries, referenced by the author's understanding of the Qu'ran and Muslim tradition.

CR1072 Wilson, H. S., ed.

Islam in Africa: Perspectives for Christian-Muslim Relations.
(WARC Studies, 29). Geneva, SZ: WARC, 1995. 106 pp. Paper. 9290750227.

Papers from a WARC-sponsored consultation (Blantyre, Malawi, 6-10 June 1994).

CR1073 Wingate, Andrew

Encounter in the Spirit: Muslim-Christian Meetings in Birmingham. (Risk Book Series, 39). Geneva, SZ: WCC, 1988. ix, 86 pp. 2825409448.

The record of Muslim-Christian dialogue as it occured in Birmingham, England, with reflections on issues of faith, prayer, and theology as people meet across cultural boundaries.

CR1074 Ye'or, Bat

Les Chrétientes d'Orient entre jihad et dhimmitude: VIIe-XXe siècle. (L'Histoire à vif). Paris, FR: Éditions du Cerf, 1991. 528 pp. Paper. 2204043478.

A scholarly history of fourteen centuries of the status of Christians living under Muslim rule from the threats of jihad to dhimmitude (the status of being protected peoples).

CR1075 Ye'or, Bat

The Decline of Eastern Christianity under Islam: From Jihad to Dhimmitude, Seventh-Twentieth Century. Translated by Miriam Kochan and David Littman. Madison, NJU: Fairleigh Dickinson University Press; London, ENK: Associated University Presses, 1996. 522 pp. 0838636780 (hdbk), 0838636888 (pbk).

English translation.

CR1076 Zananiri, Gaston

L' Église et l'Islam. (Collection la Barque de Saint Pierre). Paris, FR: SPES Editorial, 1969. 388 pp. No ISBN.

An introduction to the history of Christian-Muslim relations from the 6th century to the present.

CR1077 Zepp, Ira G.

A Muslim Primer: Beginner's Guide to Islam. Westminster, MDU: Wakefield Editions, 1992. xl, 292 pp. Paper. 0870611887.

A beginner's guide to Islam for Christians desiring to engage in Muslim-Christian dialogue.

CR1078 Zirker, Hans

Islam: Theologische und gesellschaftliche Herausforderungen.
Düsseldorf, GW: Patmos Verlag, 1993. 367 pp. 3491779375.

A critical study of Christian perceptions of Islam, with analysis of central themes in Christian-Muslim dialogue and a twenty-three-page bibliography.

Islamic Sources, Origins, Impact

See also CR268, CR327, CR1010, CR1038, CR1065, and CR1067.

CR1079 Braswell, George W.

Islam: Its Prophet, Peoples, Politics and Power. Nashville, TNU: Broadman, 1996. xii, 338 pp. Paper. 0805411690.

A comprehensive, readable introduction to Islam for Christians—its history, beliefs, practices, ethics, global and US presence, and the history and current state of Muslim-Christian encounters.

CR1080 Bucaille, Maurice

La Bible, le Coran et la science: Les écritures saintes examinées à la lumière des connaissances modernes. Paris, FR: Seghers, 1990. 254 pp. 2221501535.

A French surgeon's revised and expanded treatise (1st French edition, 1976) arguing that the Old Testament, Gospels, and Qur'an are revelations from the same God, that the Old Testament and Gospels are full of contradictions resulting from human imagination, and that the statements in the Qur'an on natural phenomena are entirely consistent with modern scientific knowledge; also available in Arabic, Turkish, Serbo-Croat, Indonesian, Urdu, Persian, Gujarati, German, and Bengali.

CR1081 Bucaille, Maurice

The Bible, the Qur'an and Science: The Holy Scriptures Examined in the Light of Modern Knowledge. Translated by Alastair D. Pannell. Paris, FR: Seghers, 1989. 272 pp. Paper. 2221012119.

A sixth revised and expanded edition of the English translation of *La Bible, le Coran et la science* (1976).

CR1082 Cohn-Sherbok, Dan, ed.

Islam in a World of Diverse Faiths. New York, NYU: St. Martin's Press, 1991. xv, 175 pp. 0312053487.

Thirteen essays by Muslim, Christian, and Jewish scholars exploring the nature of the Islamic religion and its impact on a pluralistic society.

CR1083 Cohn-Sherbok, Dan, ed.

The Salman Rushdie Controversy in Interreligious Perspective. (Symposium Series, 27). Lewiston, NYU: E Mellen Press, 1990. viii, 151 pp. 0889467196.

A volume of essays on the controversy surrounding the publication of *Satanic Verses* by Salman Rushdie, by distinguished Christian, Muslim, Jewish, and Hindu thinkers who explore the central issues arising from the controversy.

CR1084 Cragg, Kenneth

The Event of the Qu'ran: Islam in Its Scripture. Oxford, ENK: Oneworld Publications, 1994. 208 pp. Paper. 1851680675.

A new edition of the noted Christian Islamist's interpretation of the significant message of the Qu'ran in relation to the worldview at the time of its writing; originally published by Allen and Unwin in 1971.

CR1085 Cragg, Kenneth

The Pen and the Faith: Eight Modern Muslim Writers and the Qur'an. London, ENK: Allen & Unwin, 1985. viii, 180 pp. Paper. 004297044X.

Lectures analyzing eight Muslim writers' understanding of the Qu'ran, in terms of exegesis, sociology, literature, and political science; by the noted Christian Islamist.

CR1086 Esposito, John L.

Islam: The Straight Path. New York, NYU: Oxford University Press, 1991. xvi, 251 pp. 0195062256 (hdbk), 0195074726 (pbk).

An expanded edition of a survey introducing the faith, belief, and practice of Islam, from its earliest origins to its contemporary resurgence; with references to Christian/Muslim relations.

CR1087 Falaturi, Abdoldjavad

Der Islam im Unterricht: Beiträge zur interkulturellen Erziehung in Europa. Translated by Udo Tworuschka. (Beilage zu den Studien zur internationalen Schulbuchforschung). Braunschweig, GW: Georg-Eckert-Institut für Internationale Schulbuchforschung, 1992. 54 pp. No ISBN.

Standards for the writing or evaluation of European textbooks on Islam, its doctrines and history.

CR1088 Falaturi, Abdoldjavad, and Udo Tworuschka

A Guide to the Presentation of Islam in School Textbooks. Translated by Michael Walpole. (CSIC Papers: Africa, 8; CSIC Papers: Europe, 8). Birmingham, ENK: Centre for the Study of Islam and Christian-Muslim Relations, 1991. 69 pp. Paper. 0946931011.

English translation.

CR1089 Haddad, Yvonne Yazbeck, and Jane Idleman Smith

Mission to America: Five Islamic Sectarian Communities in North America. Gainesville, FLU: University Press of Florida, 1993. xii, 226 pp. 0813012163 (hdbk), 0813012171 (pbk).

A scholarly study of the history, teachings, practices, and impact, of five Islamic sects in North America (the Druze, Ahmadiyya, Moorish Science Temple of America, Ansaru Allah, and United Submitters International), including their interpretations of Christianity and approaches to Christians.

CR1090 Haddad, Yvonne Yazbeck, ed.

The Muslims of America. (Religion in America Series). New York, NYU: Oxford University Press, 1991. x, 249 pp. 0195067282.

Papers first presented at the "Muslims in America" Conference (Amherst, University of Massachusetts, 1989), including essays on perceptions of Muslims in the USA.

CR1091 Jomier, Jacques

How to Understand Islam. Translated by John Bowden. New York, NYU: Crossroad Publishing, 1991. 168 pp. Paper. 0824509811.

English translation of *Pour connaitre l'Islam* (1988); originally published in 1989 by SCM Press, London, UK (ISBN 0334020700).

CR1092 Jomier, Jacques

Para Conocer el Islam. Estella, Navarra, SP: Verbo Divino, 1989. 165 pp. 8471516411.

Spanish translation.

CR1093 Jomier, Jacques

Pour connaître l'Islam. Paris, FR: Éditions du Cerf, 1988. 194 pp. 2204029696.

A concise introduction to Islam, including how Islam sees Christianity, relations between Christians and Muslims, and the missionary activity of Islam.

CR1094 Lewis, Bernard

Islam and the West. New York, NYU: Oxford University Press, 1993. ix, 217 pp. 0195076192.

Eleven scholarly essays by the Cleveland E. Dodge Emeritus Professor of Near Eastern Studies at Princeton University, including five on Western views of Islam, four on Islamic response and reaction, and two on encounters of Muslim populations under non-Muslim rule.

CR1095 Miller, Roland E.

Muslim Friends: Their Faith and Feeling. St. Louis, MOU: Concordia Publishing, 1995. 429 pp. Paper. 0570046246.

A popular introduction to the beliefs and practices of Muslims written by an internationally known Islamicist who spent twenty-four years among Muslims in Kerala, India.

CR1096 Mujahid, Abdul Malik

Conversion to Islam: Untouchables' Strategy for Protest in India. Chambersburg, PAU: Anima Books, 1989. 159 pp. Paper. 0890120501.

A monograph on the conversions of Dalits to Islam among the Tamils of South India, with reflection on the changing nature of conversions from social mobility to protest.

CR1097 Parshall, Phil

Inside the Community: Understanding Muslims through Their Traditions. Grand Rapids, MIU: Baker Books, 1994. 240 pp. Paper. 0801071321.

An introduction for Christians to Muslim traditions contained in the *hadith*.

CR1098 Schumann, Olaf H.

Der Christus der Muslime: Christologische Aspekte in der Arabisch-Islamischen Literatur—2. Durchgesehene und Erweiterte Aufl. (Kölner Veröffentlichungen zur Religionsgeschichte, 13). Köln, GW: Bohlau Verlag, 1988. x, 294 pp. Paper. 341206386X.

A scholarly analysis, based on Arabic sources, of Muslim interpretations of Jesus Christ, including the 9th century text *Ali at-Tabari* (Confutation of the Christian); first published in 1959.

CR1099 Speight, R. Marston

God Is One: The Way of Islam. New York, NYU: Friendship Press, 1989. 139 pp. Paper. 0377001961.

A mission study in which the author examines Islam in detail, revealing both the differences between Christianity and Islam, and points at which Christians and Muslims share common beliefs; with study guide, *One God Two Faiths*, by Sarah Klos (ISBN 037700197X).

CR1100 *The Islamic Impact: Report of a Consultation on the Islamic Resurgence in Countries within the CCA Region*

Singapore, SI: CCA, 1979. iii, 47 pp. No ISBN.

This report of a CCA consultation in Singapore, 11-13 July 1979, has papers which deal with Christian responses in four areas of Islamic resurgence in Asia: India, Pakistan, Malaysia, and the Philippines.

CR1101 Wessels, Antonie

De Koran verstaan: Een Kennismaking met het boek van de Islam. Kampen, NE: Kok, 1986. 196 pp. 9024241154.

An introduction to the Qu'ran for Jews and Christians, in twelve lectures; originally presented on Dutch radio.

CR—CHRISTIANITY AND OTHER RELIGIONS

Missions to Muslims

See also HI300, CR426, CR1010, CR1022, CR1415, SO247, CO50, AF189, AF776, AF781, AF785, AS763, AS818, AS1243, and AS1251.

CR1102 Abdul-Haqq, Abdiyah Akbar
Sharing Your Faith with a Muslim. Minneapolis, MNU: Bethany House, 1980. 189 pp. Paper. 0871235536.

A tool for those called to witness to Muslims, and for the edification of Muslims who seek after God and salvation in Christ; by a Third World Christian who is an evangelist with Billy Graham and whose father was a convert from Islam.

CR1103 Cate, Patrick O., comp.
An Introduction to Muslim Evangelism. Grand Rapids, MIU: Institute of Theological Studies, 1996. 56 pp. Paper. No ISBN.

Materials for distance education courses for evangelical seminaries.

CR1104 Christensen, Jens
The Practical Approach to Muslims. Toronto, ONC: Fellowship of Faith for the Muslims, 1977. 644 pp. Paper. No ISBN.

A reprint of lectures by Bishop Christensen, who spent a lifetime working among Muslim Pathans in the North West Frontier Province of Pakistan.

CR1105 *Christian Presence and Witness in Relation to Muslim Neighbours: A Conference, Mombasa, Kenya, 1979*
Geneva, SZ: WCC, 1981. vi, 88 pp. Paper. 2825406821.

This is a full report on the conference on "Christian Presence and Witness in Relation to Muslim Neighbors" held in Kenya in December 1979, as part of the WCC's dialogue with people of living faiths.

CR1106 *Christian Witness among Muslims: A Handbook Written Especially for Christians of Africa*
Accra, GH: Africa Christian Press, 1971. 96 pp. No ISBN.

A practical guide to advise the ordinary Christian on how to behave toward his Muslim neighbors, and how better to witness to Jesus Christ among them.

CR1107 Clark, Dennis E.
The Life and Teaching of Jesus the Messiah: (Sirat-ul-masih, Isa, Ibn Maryam). Elgin, ILU: Dove, 1977. ix, 200 pp. Paper. No ISBN.

The life and teachings of Jesus prepared for Muslim readers.

CR1108 Cleveland, Clyde C.
Indonesian Adventure for Christ. Washington, DCU: Review and Herald, 1965. 191 pp. No ISBN.

A personal account of Seventh-day Adventist work among Muslims in Indonesia.

CR1109 Conference on World Evangelization (Pattaya, Thailand, 1980)
The Thailand Report on Reaching Muslims: Report of the ... Mini-Consultation on Reaching Muslims. (Lausanne Occasional Papers, 13). Wheaton, ILU: LCWE, 1980. 24 pp. Paper. No ISBN.

A call to reflect on the need for respect and for planning, for action in training local Christians to welcome Muslim believers, and in dialogue to restate their faith in words meaningful to those with a Muslim worldview.

CR1110 Dretke, James P.
A Christian Approach to Muslims: Reflections from West Africa. South Pasadena, CAU: William Carey Library, 1979. xviii, 261 pp. Paper. 0878084320.

A unique, in-depth study of Christian methods, motives, and attitudes in seeking to bring Christianity to Muslims.

CR1111 Gaudeul, Jean-Marie
Appelés par le Christ: ils viennent de l'Islam. (L'histoire à vif). Paris, FR: Éditions du Cerf, 1991. 344 pp. Paper. 2204043524.

An inquiry into the motivations and appeals that have attracted Muslims to become Christians, based on their writings and oral testimonies.

CR1112 Goble, Phillip E., and Salim Munayer
New Creation Book for Muslims. Pasadena, CAU: Mandate Press, 1989. 175 pp. 0878082212.

Practical helps and readings for use by Christians in a contextualized ministry to Muslims through house *masjid* fellowships.

CR1113 Goldsmith, Martin
Islam and Christian Witness. London, ENK: Hodder & Stoughton, 1982. 160 pp. Paper. 0340269685.

A popular introduction to Islam for Western Christians, with suggestions for practical ways for effective witness by one experienced in mission among Muslims in the United Kingdom.

CR1114 Graham, Finlay M.
Sons of Ishmael: How Shall They Hear? Nashville, TNU: Convention Press, 1969. 116 pp. Paper. No ISBN.

A study book for adults on missions to Muslims in Lebanon, Jordan, and Yemen.

CR1115 Hamada, Louis Bahjat
God Loves the Arabs, Too. Nashville, TNU: Winston-Derek Publishers, 1986. vi, 133 pp. Paper. 1555230008.

A guide for evangelical Christians interested in evangelization and apologetics among Arabs, comparing accounts of the origin and heritage of both Jews and Arabs in biblical texts and widely held myths.

CR1116 Hamada, Louis Bahjat
Understanding the Arab World. Nashville, TNU: Nelson, 1990. 216 pp. 0840731620.

The Lebanese-born Executive Director of Hamada Evangelistic Outreach, Inc., presents his rationale for Christian missions to Muslims.

CR1117 Hitching, Bob
McDonalds, Minarets and Modernity: The Anatomy of the Emerging Secular Muslim World. Sevenoaks, ENK: Spear Publishing, 1996. 79 pp. Paper. No ISBN.

Helps for Christians in witnessing to Muslims affected by modernity and secularization.

CR1118 Jomier, Jacques
Jésus: la vie du Messie. (Foi vivante, 14). Paris, FR: Éditions du Cerf, 1966. 190 pp. No ISBN.

The life of Jesus, intended for use in Christian-Muslim dialogue.

CR1119 Jomier, Jacques
Jesus: The Life of the Messiah. Madras, II: CLS, 1974. xvi, 196 pp. Paper. No ISBN.

English translation.

CR1120 Kedar, Benjamin Z.
Crusade and Mission: European Approaches toward the Muslims. Princeton, NJU: Princeton University Press, 1984. xiii, 246 pp. 069105424X.

A scholarly study of the attitude of the medieval church toward Muslims, probing the relationship between the goal of conversion and that of conquest by crusade; including a Muslim response to Christian missions.

CR1121 Lenning, Larry G.
Blessing in Mosque and Mission. South Pasadena, CAU: William Carey Library, 1980. xvi, 155 pp. Paper. 0878084339.

An exploration of the biblical and Islamic understanding of blessing (*baraka*) and its potential usefulness in Christian witness to Muslims, particularly in West Africa.

CR1122 Livingstone, Greg
Planting Churches in Muslim Cities: A Team Approach. Grand Rapids, MIU: Baker Books, 1993. 271 pp. Paper. 0801056829.

A blueprint for church planting in Muslim cities that is both biblically and culturally appropriate; by the Director of Frontiers, the largest mission agency of church-planting teams among Muslims.

CR1123 Mallouhi, Christine
Mini-Skirts, Mothers and Muslims: Modelling Spiritual Values in Muslim Culture. Tunbridge Wells, ENK: Spear Publications, 1994. 109 pp. Paper. No ISBN.

Practical helps for Christian women seeking to understand, identify, and witness to Muslim women; by an Australian Christian who lived twenty years among Muslims in North Africa and the Middle East.

CR1124 Marsh, Charles R.
Share Your Faith with a Muslim. Chicago, ILU: Moody, 1975. 95 pp. Paper. 0802479006.

Principles and practices for Christians seeking culturally sensitive ways to present the Gospel to Muslims; by a pioneer missionary to Muslims in Algeria and Chad.

CR1125 McCurry, Don M., ed.
The Gospel and Islam: A 1978 Compendium. Monrovia, CAU: MARC, 1979. 638 pp. Paper. 0912552263.

Papers from the influential 1978 conference, at which 150 representatives of evangelical mission agencies sought God's direction for proclaiming Jesus Christ to the then 720 million followers of Islam.

CR1126 Miller, William McElwee
A Christian's Response to Islam. Bromley, ENK: STL, 1986. 178 pp. Paper. 0903843560.

A primer for Christians seeking to evangelize Muslims or to pray for them, by a former Presbyterian missionary to Iran (1919-1962); originally published in 1976 (Nutley, NJU: Presbyterian and Reformed; Bromley, ENK: STL; Wheaton, ILU: Tyndale).

CR1127 Musk, Bill A.
Touching the Soul of Islam: Sharing the Gospel in Muslim Cultures. Crowborough, ENK: MARC, 1995. 256 pp. Paper. 1854243179.

Insights into the worldview of Muslims, how it differs from that of Westerners, yet has affinities to that of the writers of the Gospel which Christians desire to share with Muslims.

CR1128 Musk, Bill A.
The Unseen Face of Islam: Sharing the Gospel with Ordinary Muslims. Eastbourne, ENK: MARC, Evangelical Missionary Alliance; Sutherland, AT: Albatross Books, 1989. 315 pp. Paper. 1854240188 (M), 0732404096 (A).

An introduction to popular Islam for Christians who wish to share their faith more effectively with Muslims, introducing major themes of Muslim belief and practice in story form.

CR1129 Nickel, Gordon
Peaceable Witness among Muslims. Scottdale, PAU: Herald Press Trade Books, 1999. 151 pp. Paper. 0836191056.

This book provides a unique treatment of Christian engagement with Muslims, offering provocative, innovative proposals for drawing on the Anabaptist peacemaking heritage for communicating the gospel of peace among Muslims.

CR1130 North American Conference on Muslim Evangelization
The Glen Eyrie Report: Report of the North American Conference on Muslim Evangelization, October 15-21, 1978. (Lausanne Committee for World Evangelization Occasional Papers, 4). Wheaton, ILU: LCWE, 1978. 14 pp. Paper. No ISBN.

This report on Muslim Evangelism talks about a listening and planning process, and moves to an unfinished agenda of human rights, resources, communication, evangelism, theological study groups, and a review of the place of Muslims in North America.

CR1131 Parshall, Phil
Bridges to Islam: A Christian Perspective on Folk Islam. Grand Rapids, MIU: Baker Books, 1983. 161 pp. Paper. 0801070813.

An introduction to practical ways by which Christians can present Christ to Muslims through the bridge potential of Islamic mysticism.

CR1132 Parshall, Phil
The Fortress and the Fire: Jesus Christ and the Challenge of Islam. Bombay, II: Gospel Literature Service, 1975. x, 134 pp. Paper. No ISBN.

Religious and social obstacles and opportunities in Christian mission to Muslims, based on a biblical perspective and thirteen years of work as a missionary in Bangladesh.

CR1133 Parshall, Phil
New Paths in Muslim Evangelism: Evangelical Approaches to Contextualization. Grand Rapids, MIU: Baker Books, 1980. 280 pp. Paper. 0801070562.

A call for a new readiness to experiment with forms of cultural adaption which are both biblical and workable in sharing the truth of "God reconciling the world to Himself through Christ" with Muslims, using Eastern rather than Western patterns of worship.

CR1134 Saal, William J.
Reaching Muslims for Christ. Chicago, ILU: Moody, 1991. 223 pp. Paper. 0802473229.

A primer for evangelical Protestants containing facts, insights, analysis, and examples gleaned from men and women engaged in witness to Muslims in North America and abroad; written by the US Director of Arab World Ministries.

CR1135 Safa, Reza F.
Inside Islam: Exposing and Reaching the World of Islam. Orlando, FLU: Creation House, 1996. 201 pp. Paper. 0884194167.

The founder of Harvesters World Outreach, an evangelistic ministry to Muslims, writes as a former Shiite Muslim about Islamic fundamentalism and Christian response.

CR1136 Vander Werff, Lyle L.
Christian Mission to Muslims, The Record: Anglican and Reformed Approaches in India and the Near East, 1800-1938.
(William Carey Library Series on Islamic Studies). South Pasadena, CAU: William Carey Library, 1977. xi, 366 pp. Paper. 0878083200.

A scholarly analysis of 19th- and 20th century-missions to Muslims, designed to give encouragement to Christ's disciples now living and witnessing among their Muslim neighbors.

CR1137 Woodberry, John Dudley, ed.
Muslims and Christians on the Emmaus Road. (Critical Issues in Witness among Muslims). Monrovia, CAU: MARC, 1989. xv, 392 pp. Paper. 0912552654.

Nineteen papers on mission to Muslims from a conference sponsored by the LCWE in Zeist, The Netherlands, in 1987; with a detailed listing of bibliographic, research, and training resources.

Christianity and Judaism

See also HI70, CR5, CR28, CR320, CR336, CR368, CR1008, CR1395, CR1398, CR1411-CR1412, AS387, AS824, AS850, AS852, and EU281.

CR1138 Alzin, Josse
Juifs et Chrétiens en dialogue: tous leurs problèmes de A à Z. Paris, FR: SPES Editorial, 1966. 235 pp. Paper. No ISBN.

Themes in Christian-Jewish dialogue presented as short essays in a dictionary format.

CR1139 Amersfoort, J. van, and J. van Oort, eds.
Juden und Christen in der Antike. Kampen, NE: Kok, 1990. 150 pp. Paper. 9024249260.

Eight papers by Dutch and German scholars on Judaism and Christianity in the 1st-3rd centuries C.E.; originally presented to the Patristics Research Association (Utrecht, the Netherlands, January 1989).

CR1140 Awerbuch, Marianne
Christlich-jüdische Begegnung im Zeitalter der Frühscholastik. (Abhandlungen zum christlich-jüdischen Dialog, 8). Munich, GW: Chr. Kaiser Verlag, 1980. 242 pp. 3459012560.

Scholarly writing carefully examining the history of anti-Semitism through Jewish and Christian literature, beginning in the 11th century and revealing a time period when Jewish-Christian tolerance dominated over intolerance.

CR1141 Baumann, Arnulf H., Käte Mahn, and Magne Saebø
Luthers Erben und die Juden: Das Verhältnis lutherischer Kirchen Europas zu den Juden. Hannover, GW: Lutherisches Verlagshaus, 1984. 144 pp. Paper. 3785904975.

A book intended for pastoral *praxis* examining the relationship between Christians and Jews in Germany since the Reformation and pointing out the critical issues; together with a bibliography and other practical information for those engaged in Jewish-Christian dialogue.

CR1142 Bea, Augustin
La Chiesa e il popolo Ebraico. Brescia, IT: Morcelliana, 1966. 166 pp. No ISBN.

The title of this work denotes not an exhaustive treatise on the church and the Jewish people, but a commentary on the document of the Second Vatican Council "On the Relationship of the Church to the non-Christian Religions," insofar as it is a treatment of Jewish-Christian relations; by one of the Fathers of that council.

CR1143 Bea, Augustin
The Church and the Jewish People: A Commentary on the Second Vatican Council's Declaration on the Relation of the Church to Non-Christian Religions. Translated by Philip Loretz. New York, NYU: Harper & Row, 1966. 172 pp. No ISBN.

English translation.

CR1144 Bea, Augustin
Die Kirche und das jüdische Volk. Translated by Franz Johna. Freiburg im Breisgau, GW: Herder, 1966. 167 pp. No ISBN.

German translation.

CR1145 Beeck, Frans Jozef van
Loving the Torah More Than God?: Toward a Catholic Appreciation of Judaism. Chicago, ILU: Loyola University Press, 1989. xvii, 105 pp. 0829406204.

Text and commentary on two poignant Jewish writings out of the Warsaw ghetto during the Holocaust, with learnings for Christians by the John Cardinal Cody Professor of Sacred Theology at Loyola University, Chicago, Illinois.

CR1146 Bemporad, Jack, and Michael Shevack
Our Age: The Historic New Era of Christian-Jewish Understanding. Hyde Park, NYU: New City Press, 1996. 96 pp. Paper. 1565480813.

Two noted Jewish rabbis explain what the Catholic Church is doing to rid itself and the world of anti-Semitism.

CR1147 Benin, Stephen D.
The Footprints of God: Divine Accommodation in Jewish and Christian Thought. (Judaica). Albany, NYU: Press, 1993. xxi, 327 pp. 079140711X (hdbk), 0791407128 (pbk).

A scholarly history of development of the concept of divine accommodation (revelation attuned to the human condition) in Jewish and Christian thought, from the first to the nineteenth century.

CR1148 Berlin, George L.
Defending the Faith: Nineteenth-Century American Jewish Writings on Christianity and Jesus. Albany, NYU: SUNY Press, 1989. x, 207 pp. 0887069207 (hdbk), 0887069215 (pbk).

In this work the author, a professor at Baltimore Hebrew University presents 19-century Jewish writings from traditionalist and reformed perspectives, which reveal the American Jewish community's struggle to define its relationship to the predominantly Christian surroundings of American culture and society.

CR1149 Beuken, Wim, Seán Freyne, and Anton Weiler, eds.
Messianism through History. London, ENK: SCM Press; Maryknoll, NYU: Orbis Books, 1993. xiv, 141 pp. Paper. 0334030188 (UK), 0883448696 (US).

Eleven scholarly essays on the messianic consciousness in Judaic and Christian scriptures, history, and contemporary movements, in Marxism (Kee), El Salvador (Sobrino), Jewish-Christian relations (Ruether), and the church (Moltmann).

CR—CHRISTIANITY AND OTHER RELIGIONS

CR1150 Bienert, Walther
Martin Luther und die Juden: Ein Quellenbuch mit zeitge-nössischen Illustrationen, mit Einführungen und Erläuter-ungen. Frankfurt am Main, GW: Evan Verlagswerk, 1982. 240 pp. Paper. 3771502136.

A sourcebook of Martin Luther's writings about the Jews; with illustrations from the times, plus introductions and explanatory notes for each selection.

CR1151 Boys, Mary C.
Jewish-Christian Dialogue: One Woman's Experience. New York, NYU: Paulist Press, 1997. vi, 103 pp. Paper. 0809137380.

Presenting five diverse stories illustrating interreligious encounter, the McAlpin Professor of Practical Theology at Union Theological Seminary in New York reflects on her own encounters with Jews and Judaism; originally present-ed as a Madeleva Lecture on Spirituality at St. Mary's Col-lege, Notre Dame, Indiana.

CR1152 Bradshaw, Paul F., and Lawrence A. Hoffman, eds.
Life Cycles in Jewish and Christian Worship. (Two Litur-gical Traditions, 4). Notre Dame, INU: University of Notre Dame Press, 1996. ix, 303 pp. 0268013071.

Eight scholars explore the models of human life im-plicit in Judaism's and Christianity's life cycle liturgies.

CR1153 Bradshaw, Paul F., and Lawrence A. Hoffman, eds.
The Making of Jewish and Christian Worship. (Two Litur-gical Traditions, 1). Notre Dame, INU: University of Notre Dame Press, 1991. x, 211 pp. 0268012067 (hdbk), 0268012083 (pbk).

Eight scholarly papers on the comparative origins and historical evolution of Jewish and Christian worship; orig-inally presented at a conference on liturgy held at the Uni-versity of Notre Dame (June 1988).

CR1154 Braybrooke, Marcus
Time to Meet: Towards a Deeper Relationship between Jews and Christians. London, ENK: SCM Press; Philadelphia, PAU: Trinity Press International, 1990. xii, 180 pp. Paper. 0334024471 (T).

An introduction to twenty-five years of Jewish-Chris-tian dialogue, including official documents and analysis of key theological issues; by the former Executive Director of the Council of Christians and Jews in Great Britian.

CR1155 Brocke, Michael, and Herbert Jochum
Wolkensäule und Feuerschein: Jüdische Theologie des Ho-locaust. (Kaiser Taschenbücher, 131). Gütersloh, GW: Kaiser, 1982. 284 pp. 3459013788.

Thirteen Jewish authors, representing the spectrum of Jewish traditions and several academic disciplines, exam-ine their history and religion as a post-Holocaust people, offering a "Theology of the Holocaust"; first published in 1983.

CR1156 Brown, Michael L.
Answering Jewish Objections to Jesus: General and His-torical Objections. Grand Rapids, MIU: Baker Books, 2000. xxvii, 270 pp. Paper. 080106063X.

Combining scholarship and honest answers in an en-gaging style, the author answers thirty-five objections on general historical themes.

CR1157 Bunte, Wolfgang
Religionsgespräche zwischen Christen und Juden in den Nied-erlanden, 1100-1500. (Judentum und Umwelt, 27). Frankfurt am Main, GW: Lang, 1990. 812 pp. Paper. 3631429630.

A sourcebook of original texts in Latin and Dutch (with parallel German translations) on Jewish-Christian dialogue between 1100 and 1500, which refutes the common assump-tion that Christians of the Middle Ages were always anti-Jew-ish.

CR1158 Burrell, David B., and Yehezkel Landau, eds.
Voices from Jerusalem: Jews and Christians Reflect on the Holy Land. (Studies in Judaism and Christianity). New York, NYU: Paulist Press, 1992. vi, 176 pp. Paper. 0809132702.

Nine essays by Jewish and Christian leaders, most of whom have spent many years in Israel, on comparative under-standings of the Holy Land in the faiths.

CR1159 Charlesworth, James H., ed.
Jesus' Jewishness: Exploring the Place of Jesus within Early Judaism. (Shared Ground among Jews and Christians, 2). New York, NYU: Crossroad Publishing; Philadelphia, PAU: Amer-ican Interfaith Institute, 1991. 288 pp. 0824510615.

Ten essays by prominent Christian (Cox and Küng) and Jewish (Flusser, Segal, and Rivkin) scholars on aspects of the Jewishness of Jesus.

CR1160 Charlesworth, James H., ed.
Jews and Christians: Exploring the Past, Present, and Fu-ture. (Shared Ground Among Jews and Christians, 1). New York, NYU: Crossroad Publishing, 1990. 258 pp. 0824510127.

Nine scholarly essays by Christian professors on the his-tory of Christian-Jewish relations; originally presented at a conference in Philadelphia, United States, in May 1987.

CR1161 Charlesworth, James H., Frank X. Blisard, and Jerry L. Gorham, eds.
Overcoming Fear between Jews and Christians. (Shared Ground among Jews and Christians, 3). New York, NYU: American Interfaith Institute; New York, NYU: Crossroad Publishing, 1993. xix, 198 pp. 0824512650.

Papers by fifteen distinguished Christian and Jewish schol-ars exploring the historical, sociological, theological, and per-sonal impact of fear between the faiths, suggesting ways to confront and overcome it; originally presented at a 1987 sym-posium in Philadelphia sponsored by the American Interfaith Institute.

CR1162 Chilton, Bruce, and Jacob Neusner, eds.
Trading Places Sourcebook: Readings in the Intersecting His-tories of Judaism and Christianity. Cleveland, OHU: Pilgrim Press, 1997. ix, 293 pp. Paper. 0829811419.

A sourcebook written as a companion and complement to the authors' *Trading Places: The Intersecting Histories of Judaism and Christianity* (1997).

CR1163 Chilton, Bruce, and Jacob Neusner
Trading Places: The Intersecting Histories of Judaism and Christianity. Cleveland, OHU: Pilgrim Press, 1996. xxii, 268 pp. Paper. 0829811419.

A textbook on Jewish-Christian relations in which Epis-copal priest Chilton and Jewish rabbi Neusner contend that early Christianity and Rabbinic Judaism intersected and ul-timately traded places during the first four centuries of the common era.

CR1164 Cohen, Arthur A.
The Myth of the Judeo-Christian Tradition and Other Dissenting Essays. New York, NYU: Schocken Books, 1971. xxi, 223 pp. Paper. 0805202935.

Thirteen essays written between 1950 and 1970 by a prominent Jewish scholar, arguing that Jewish-Christian relations can best be advanced by honest acceptance of historic theological enmity, rather than a facade of seeming harmony; originally published in 1957.

CR1165 Cohen, Jeremy, ed.
Essential Papers on Judaism and Christianity in Conflict: From Late Antiquity to the Reformation. (Essential Papers on Jewish Studies). New York, NYU: New York University Press, 1991. xiv, 578 pp. 0814714420 (hdbk), 0814714439 (pbk).

A compendium of nineteen scholarly essays on Christian attitudes toward Jews in late antiquity, the Middle Ages, and the Reformation, as well as Jewish responses and participation in interreligious dialogue during those periods.

CR1166 Cohen, Mark R.
Under Crescent and Cross: The Jews in the Middle Ages. Princeton, NJU: Princeton University Press, 1994. xxi, 280 pp. Paper. 0691033781.

The first in-depth comparison of Jewish life in medieval Islam and Christendom.

CR1167 Cohen, Naomi W., ed.
Essential Papers on Jewish-Christian Relations in the United States: Imagery and Reality. (Essential Papers on Jewish Studies). New York, NYU: New York University Press, 1990. x, 377 pp. 0814714455 (hdbk), 0814714463 (pbk).

A reader for persons beginning study on Jewish-Christian relations in the United States, containing twelve essays on Christianity and American anti-Semitism, the Holocaust, Zionism and Israel, dialogue, and American-Jewish response to 19th-century Christian mission.

CR1168 Cohen, Naomi W.
Jews in Christian America: The Pursuit of Religious Equality. (Studies in Jewish History). New York, NYU: Oxford University Press, 1992. viii, 300 pp. 0195065379.

A detailed analysis of the responses of American Jews to church-state issues from colonial times to 1963, with special attention to issues that resulted in Supreme Court decisions between 1948 and 1963.

CR1169 Cohn-Sherbok, Dan
The Crucified Jew: Twenty Centuries of Christian Anti-Semitism. Grand Rapids, MIU: Eerdmans; Philadelphia, PAU: American Interfaith Institute and the World Alliance of Interfaith Org., 1997. xx, 258 pp. Paper. 0802843115.

A readable, comprehensive, and perceptive survey of twenty centuries of the persecution of Jews; originally published in Great Britain (HarperCollins Religious, 1992).

CR1170 Cohn-Sherbok, Dan
A Dictionary of Judaism and Christianity. Philadelphia, PAU: Trinity Press International, 1991. 181 pp. Paper. 1563380307.

A dictionary for the general reader on the key concepts, beliefs, and practices of both Judaism and Christianity.

CR1171 Cohn-Sherbok, Dan
Issues in Contemporary Judaism. New York, NYU: St. Martin's Press, 1991. xv, 175 pp. 0312056125.

Ten essays on Jewish beliefs and Christian-Jewish encounters by a prominent Jewish scholar who teaches Jewish theology at the University of Kent.

CR1172 Cohn-Sherbok, Dan
Judaism and Other Faiths. New York, NYU: St. Martin's Press; London, ENK: Macmillan, 1994. ix, 186 pp. 0312103840 (US), 0333575237 (UK).

A concise history of Jewish attitudes toward other religious traditions from biblical times to the present, with a new Jewish theology of religious pluralism.

CR1173 Cohn-Sherbok, Dan
On Earth as It Is in Heaven: Jews, Christians and Liberation Theology. Maryknoll, NYU: Orbis Books, 1987. viii, 136 pp. Paper. 0883444100.

An analysis of the correlation between the traditions of the Hebrew nation and the liberation theology of today, which may provide new approaches to Jewish-Christian dialogue.

CR1174 Cohn-Sherbok, Dan, and Lavinia Cohn-Sherbok
Jewish & Christian Mysticism: An Introduction. New York, NYU: Continuum, 1994. viii, 186 pp. 0826406955.

A scholarly comparison of the evolution of mystical thought in Judaism and Christianity from the post-biblical era to the present day.

CR1175 Conzelmann, Hans
Gentiles, Jews, Christians: Polemics and Apologetics in the Greco-Roman Era. Translated by M. Eugene Boring. Minneapolis, MNU: Fortress Press, 1992. xxxvii, 390 pp. 080062520X.

English translation.

CR1176 Conzelmann, Hans
Die Heiden: Juden, Christen und das Problem des Fremden. Edited by Reinhard Feldmeier and Ulrich Heckel. (Wissenschaftliche Untersuchungen zum Neuen Testament, 70). Tübingen, GW: Mohr, 1994. xviii, 449 pp. 3161461479.

The German New Testament scholar's final work on origins of anti-Semitism among Gentiles and Christians in the period 300 B.C.E. to 200 C.E.; originally published in 1981.

CR1177 Croner, Helga, and Leon Klenicki, eds.
Issues in the Jewish-Christian Dialogue: Jewish Perspectives on Covenant, Mission and Witness. (Studies in Judaism and Christianity). New York, NYU: Paulist Press, 1979. vii, 189 pp. Paper. 0809122383.

Seven essays by Jewish scholars on themes of covenant, witness, and mission.

CR1178 Croner, Helga, comp.
More Stepping Stones to Further Jewish-Christian Relations: An Unabridged Collection of Christian Documents, 1975-1983. (Studies in Judaism and Christianity). New York, NYU: Paulist Press, 1985. viii, 235 pp. 0809127083.

A compilation of thirty Protestant and Roman Catholic documents plus four interpretive essays.

CR1179 Croner, Helga, comp.
Stepping Stones to Further Jewish-Christian Relations. (Studies in Judaism and Christianity, 1). London, ENK: Stimulus Books, 1977. xv, 157 pp. 0905967003.

A compilation of thirty-nine official church statements, both Protestant and Roman Catholic, on Jewish-Christian relations in the 1965-1975 period.

CR—CHRISTIANITY AND OTHER RELIGIONS

CR1180 Cunningham, Philip A.
Education for Shalom: Religion Textbooks and the Enhancement of the Catholic and Jewish Relationship. Collegeville, MNU: Liturgical Press, 1995. xviii, 169 pp. Paper. 0814622488.

A critical evaluation of treatments of Judaism in Catholic religious textbooks in the United States in the light of changes in official Vatican guidelines.

CR1181 Cutler, Allan Harris, and Helen Elmquist Cutler
The Jew as Ally of the Muslim: Medieval Roots of Anti-Semitism. Notre Dame, INU: University of Notre Dame Press, 1986. 577 pp. 0268011907.

A well-researched revision of traditional explanations of the roots of anti-Semitism in Western Europe during the Middle Ages, focusing on the connections between anti-Muslim and anti-Jewish prejudices in medieval Spain.

CR1182 Davies, Alan, and Marilyn F. Nefsky
How Silent Were the Churches?: Canadian Protestantism and the Jewish Plight during the Nazi Era. Waterloo, ONC: Wilfrid Laurier University Press, 1997. xvi, 179 pp. 0889202885.

A detailed study of anti-Semitism in Canadian Protestantism during the 1930s and the 1940s, and analysis of its impact upon Canada's refusal to accept as immigrants Jews fleeing from Nazism.

CR1183 De Lange, N. R. M.
Origen and the Jews: Studies in Jewish-Christian Relations in Third-Century Palestine. (University of Cambridge Oriental Publications, 25). Cambridge, ENK: Cambridge University Press, 1976. x, 240 pp. 0521205425.

A detailed study of Jewish influence on Origen's biblical scholarship and exegesis, leading to a reassessment of the relationship between Jews and Christians in 3rd-century Palestine.

CR1184 Dietrich, Donald J.
God and Humanity in Auschwitz: Jewish-Christian Relations and Sanctioned Murder. New Brunswick, NJU: Transaction Pubs., 1995. xii, 355 pp. 156000147X.

A synthesis of the findings of the past thirty years of research on the rise of anti-Semitism in Europe, official Catholic Church attitudes, and Christian and Jewish theologies that developed after the Holocaust.

CR1185 Ditmanson, Harold H., ed.
Stepping-Stones to Further Jewish-Lutheran Relationships: Key Lutheran Statements. Minneapolis, MNU: Augsburg Fortress, 1990. 144 pp. Paper. 0806624612.

Analysis in seven essays of the major Lutheran statements on Jewish-Lutheran relationships, with three additional documents that survey its history, including analyses of Luther's writings on the Jews.

CR1186 Dunn, James D. G., ed.
Jews and Christians: The Parting of the Ways A.D. 70 to 135. (Wissenschaftliche Untersuchungen zum Neuen Testament, 66). Tübingen, GW: J. C. B. Mohr (Paul Siebeck), 1992. x, 408 pp. Paper. 3161459725.

The Second Durham-Tübingen Research Symposium on Earliest Christianity and Judaism (Durham, Sept. 1989), containing 13 scholarly essays, in English (10) and German (3).

CR1187 Eckardt, A. Roy
Jews and Christians: The Contemporary Meeting. Bloomington, INU: Indiana University Press, 1986. xii, 177 pp. 0253331625.

A multidirectional view of the contemporary encounter of Jews and Christians, analyzing social, psychological, moral, theological, and religious factors.

CR1188 Eckardt, A. Roy
Your People, My People: The Meeting of Jews and Christians. New York, NYU: Quadrangle, 1974. xiv, 275 pp. 0812904125.

A reasoned argument by an American Protestant scholar of Jewish-Christian relations that true Christianity renounces anti-Semitism, ends mission to Jews, and supports brotherliness and the state of Israel.

CR1189 Ellis, Marc H.
Ending Auschwitz: The Future of Jewish and Christian Life. Louisville, KYU: Westminster John Knox, 1994. xii, 162 pp. Paper. 0664255019.

A forceful essay by the noted contemporary Jewish theologian reflecting on his 1991 visit to Auschwitz, arguing that the current agenda must deal equally with the realities of both the state of Israel and the Palestinians.

CR1190 Ellis, Marc H.
Toward a Jewish Theology of Liberation. Maryknoll, NYU: Orbis Books, 1987. xii, 147 pp. Paper. 0883443589.

Examining themes from the historic realities of the Exodus, the Holocaust, and the State of Israel in the writings of ten Jewish leaders, Ellis compares the development of a Jewish theology of liberation with parallel developments in Christianity.

CR1191 Ellis, Marc H.
Unholy Alliance: Religion and Atrocity in Our Time. Minneapolis, MNU: Fortress Press, 1997. xviii, 214 pp. Paper. 0800630807.

Probing reflections by a Jewish theologian on the recurring acts of violence from the Holocaust and beyond which scarred Jewish-Christian relations.

CR1192 Eskenazi, Tamara C., Daniel J. Harrington, and William H. Shea, eds.
The Sabbath in Jewish and Christian Traditions. (University of Denver Center for Judaic Studies). New York, NYU: Crossroad Publishing, 1991. xvi, 272 pp. 0824510933.

Papers from the symposium on "The Sabbath in Jewish and Christian Traditions" (University of Denver, 24-26 May 1989) exploring biblical, rabbinic, historical, theological, liturgical, legal, and ecumenical perspectives.

CR1193 Fackenheim, Emil L.
The Jewish Bible after the Holocaust: Re-Reading. (Sherman Studies of Judaism in Modern Times). Bloomington, INU: Indiana University Press; Manchester, ENK: Manchester University Press, 1990. xii, 122 pp. 0253320976 (US), 0719030307 (UK).

Reflections on the gulf opened up by the Holocaust between Jews and Christians, and on the healing possible through reading together the Old Testament.

CR1194 Falk, Gerhard
The Jew in Christian Theology: Martin Luther's Anti-Jewish "Vom Schem Hamphoras." Jefferson, NCU: McFarland & Co., 1992. viii, 296 pp. 0899507166.

A compilation of Christian source documents from Martin Luther to 1991, previously unpublished in English, with commentary pointing out the anti-Jewish content, and other milestones in church doctrine concerning Judaism.

CR1195 Falk, Randall M., and Walter J. Harrelson
Jews and Christians in Pursuit of Social Justice. Nashville, TNU: Abingdon, 1996. 172 pp. Paper. 0687011221.

A rabbi and a Christian scholar examine moral and ethical issues of our day in the light of their respective faith traditions.

CR1196 Feldman, Egal
Dual Destinies: The Jewish Encounter with Protestant America. Urbana, ILU: University of Illinois Press, 1990. xi, 339 pp. 0252017269.

A scholarly history of Protestant-Jewish interactions in the United States from colonial days to the present.

CR1197 Fiorenza, Elisabeth Schüssler, David Tracy, and Marcus Lefébure, eds.
The Holocaust as Interruption. (*Concilium*: Religion in the Eighties). Edinburgh, ENK: T&T Clark, 1984. xi, 88 pp. Paper. 0567300552.

A collection of ten theological reflections on the Holocaust by Jewish and Christian scholars.

CR1198 Fisher, Eugene J., A. James Rudin, and Marc H. Tanenbaum, eds.
Twenty Years of Jewish-Catholic Relations. New York, NYU: Paulist Press, 1986. iv, 236 pp. Paper. 0809127628.

Thirteen essays responding to the Second Vatican Council's "Declaration on the Relationship of the Church to Non-Christian Religions" (*Nostra Aetate*) including papers on the roles of liturgy, scripture, and religious education in Catholic-Jewish relations.

CR1199 Fisher, Eugene J., and Leon Klenicki, eds.
In Our Time: The Flowering of Jewish-Catholic Dialogue. (Studies in Judaism and Christianity; The Stimulus Foundation). Mahwah, NJU: Paulist Press, 1990. vi, 161 pp. Paper. 080913196X.

Interpretations by a leading Roman Catholic participant in Jewish-Christian dialogue and his Jewish counterpart, of the most important statements and guidelines issued by the Vatican, including the text of the documents and an annotated bibiliography.

CR1200 Fisher, Eugene J., ed.
Interwoven Destinies: Jews and Christians through the Ages. (Studies in Judaism and Christianity). Mahwah, NJU: Paulist Press, 1993. viii, 154 pp. Paper. 0809133636.

Eight brief historical studies delineating six stages of Jewish-Christian relationships in the ancient, medieval, and modern periods.

CR1201 Fisher, Eugene J., ed.
The Jewish Roots of Christian Liturgy. Mahwah, NJU: Paulist Press, 1989. v, 202 pp. Paper. 0809131323.

Sixteen short essays on Jewish roots of Christian liturgy; useful as a handbook for liturgists and anyone interested in Jewish-Christian dialogue.

CR1202 Fisher, Eugene J., ed.
Visions of the Other: Jewish and Christian Theologians Assess the Dialogue. (Studies in Judaism and Christianity). New York, NYU: Paulist Press, 1994. vii, 106 pp. Paper. 0809134772.

Papers by two Jewish (Greenberg, Hartmann) and two Christian (Pawlikowski, van Buren) theologians; originally presented at the National Workshop on Christian-Jewish Relations (9 May 1986, Baltimore).

CR1203 Fisher, Eugene J.
Faith without Prejudice: Rebuilding Christian Attitudes toward Judaism. (Shared Ground among Jews and Christians, 4). New York, NYU: American Interfaith Institute; New York, NYU: Crossroad Publishing, 1993. 208 pp. 0824512669.

A revised primer for Christians designed to develop positive attitudes toward Christian-Jewish relations through a survey of biblical, historical, and contemporary thought, with the texts of 1974-1988 statements by the Vatican and US bishops; originally published in 1977.

CR1204 Fisher, Eugene J.
Seminary Education and Christian-Jewish Relations: A Curriculum and Resource Handbook. Washington, DCU: National Catholic Education Association, 1988. 102 pp. Paper. 1558330054.

A second edition expansion of the 1983 handbook for seminaries presenting Jews and Judaism, with bibliography and selected Roman Catholic documents.

CR1205 Fleischner, Eva
Judaism in German Christian Theology since 1945: Christianity and Israel Considered in Terms of Mission. (ATLA Monograph Series, 8). Metuchen, NJU: Scarecrow Press, 1975. xvi, 205 pp. 0810808358.

Detailed analysis of German Christian thought about Israel and Judaism, the synagogue, and the Jewish experience since 1945, focusing on the 1961 Kirchentag and a 1964 LWF consultation in Lgumkloster, Denmark; originally published in 1972.

CR1206 Flothkötter, Hermann, and Bernhard Nacke, eds.
Das Judentum eine Würzel des Christlichen: Neue Perspektiven des Miteinanders. Würzburg, GW: Echter Verlag, 1990. 223 pp. Paper. 3429013186.

Based on Martin Buber's motto, "All true life is in meeting," these contributions to the Jewish-Christian dialogue offer substantive material for its progress.

CR1207 Flusser, David
Bemerkungen eines Juden zur christlichen Theologie. (Abhandlungen zum christlich-jüdischen Dialog, 16). Munich, GW: Kaiser, 1984. 103 pp. Paper. 3459015381.

Six scholarly essays on Jewish sources for various Christian doctrines.

CR1208 Fornberg, Tord
Jewish-Christian Dialogue and Biblical Exegesis. (Studia Missionalia Upsaliensia, 47). Uppsala, SW: Uppsala University, 1987. 74 pp. Paper. 9185424145.

A monograph exegeting passages of scriptures which have been stumbling blocks in Jewish-Christian dialogue (the six antitheses in Matthew 5:21-48, New Testament anti-Pharasaic polemic, and Malachi 1:11 on the pure sacrifices of Gentiles).

CR1209 Freedman, Jonathan
The Temple of Culture: Assimilation and Anti-Semitism in Literary Anglo-America. Oxford, ENK: Oxford University Press, 2000. vi, 264 pp. 0195131576.

The author demonstrates that the position of Jews and their image are intertwined with the ambiguities of high culture that evolved from England and America in the past century and a half.

CR1210 Gager, John G.
The Origins of Anti-Semitism: Attitudes toward Judaism in Pagan and Christian Antiquity. New York, NYU: Oxford University Press, 1983. viii, 312 pp. 0195036077(hdbk), 0195033167(pbk).

From the earliest records of Judeo-Christian relationships, the author concludes that anti-Semitism was rare in Greco-Roman paganism and early Christianity.

CR—CHRISTIANITY AND OTHER RELIGIONS

CR1211 Gallagher, Philip F., ed.
Christians, Jews and Other Worlds: Patterns of Conflict and Accommodation. Lanham, MDU: University Press of America, 1988. xii,156 pp. 0819168947.

Five diverse scholarly essays dealing with Christian-Jewish relations in the 16th, 19th, and 20th centuries, that of the Hospitallers of Rhodes with the Turks in the 14th, and that of Jesuits with Chinese literati in the 17th century; originally presented at the Avery Lectures in History, Brooklyn College, 1987.

CR1212 Goldberg, Michael
Jews and Christians, Getting Our Stories Straight: The Exodus and the Passion-Resurrection. Nashville, TNU: Abingdon, 1985. 224 pp. Paper. 0687203309.

The Jay Phillips Professor of Jewish Studies at St. John's University in Collegeville, Minnesota, proposes a reexamination of the "master stories" in Exodus and Matthew as the way by which Christians and Jews can gain respect for each other's understandings of who God is, what humanity is, and how humanity should therefore act in God's world.

CR1213 Goodman, Martin
Mission and Conversion: Proselytizing in the Religious History of the Roman Empire. Oxford, ENK: Clarendon Press, 1994. xiv, 194 pp. 0198149417.

A probing analysis of the Jewish origins of early Christian attitudes toward mission and proselytizing; originally presented as the Wilde Lectures in Natural and Comparative Religion at Oxford University in 1992.

CR1214 Gottlieb, Roger S., ed.
Thinking the Unthinkable: Meanings of the Holocaust. New York, NYU: Paulist Press, 1990. ix, 446 pp. Paper. 0809131722.

A collection of twenty-six reflections on the Holocaust—mainly by prominent Jewish and Christian leaders (Wiesel, Heschel, Arendt, Pawlikoski, etc.).

CR1215 Greeley, Andrew M. et al.
Forging a Common Future: Catholic, Judaic, and Protestant Relations for a New Millennium. Cleveland, OHU: Pilgrim Press, 1997. xiii, 109 pp. Paper. 0829811702.

Reflections on the Jewish/early Christian and Catholic/Protestant schisms and their significance for the religious faithful in the 21st century, by a panel of distinguished Jewish and Christian scholars.

CR1216 Greeley, Andrew M., and Jacob Neusner
Common Ground: A Priest and a Rabbi Read Scripture Together. Cleveland, OHU: Pilgrim Press, 1996. xviii, 335 pp. Paper. 0829811206.

A thoroughly revised and updated edition of *The Bible and Us* (1990) in which a noted liberal Catholic priest and a well-known Conservative Jewish rabbi present their provocative interpretations of the same scripture passages.

CR1217 Gunner, Göran
När tiden tar slut: Motivförskjutningar i frikyrklig apokalyptisk tolkning av det judiska folket och staten Israel. (Studia Theologica Holmiensis, 1; Studia Missionalia Upsaliensia, 64). Uppsala, SW: Swedish Institute of Missionary Research, 1996. 394 pp. Paper. 9188906000 (STH), 9185424447 (SMU).

A doctoral thesis in which the author analyzes the role given to the Jewish people and the state of Israel in the millennial and apocalyptic writings produced from the 1880s to the 1990s in the Swedish Free Church Movement.

CR1218 Gushee, David P.
The Righteous Gentiles of the Holocaust: A Christian Interpretation. Minneapolis, MNU: Fortress Press, 1994. xiv, 258 pp. 0800629027 (hdbk), 0800628381 (pbk).

The Assistant Professor of Christian Ethics at Southern Baptist Theological Seminary in Louisville, Kentucky, examines the motivations of that small minority of Christians who risked their lives to rescue Jews in need during the Holocaust, and why the vast majority took no action.

CR1219 Gustafsson, Per Erik
Tiden och tecknen: Israelmission och Palestinabild i det tidiga Svenska Missionsförbundet: En studie apokalyptik och mission c:a 1860-1907. (Studia Missionalia Upsaliensia, 41). Stockholm, SW: Verbum, 1984. 289 pp. 9152612384.

A study of apocalyptic emphases in the involvement of emerging Swedish Free churches with the Jews, 1860-1907.

CR1220 Hammerstein, Franz Von, ed.
Christian-Jewish Relations in Ecumenical Perspective with a Special Emphasis on Africa. Geneva, SZ: WCC, 1978. vii, 146 pp. Paper. 2825405698.

A report on the WCC's Consultation on the Church and the Jewish People (Jerusalem, 16-26 June 1977).

CR1221 Hammerstein, Franz von, ed.
Von Vorurteilen zum Verständnis: Dokumente zum jüdische-christlichen Dialog. Frankfurt am Main, GW: Lembeck, 1976. 165 pp. 3874760529.

A collection of essays by both Christian and Jewish thinkers wrestling with a fuller understanding of each other's faith.

CR1222 Harrelson, Walter J., and Randall M. Falk
Jews and Christians: A Troubled Family. Nashville, TNU: Abingdon, 1990. 208 pp. Paper. 0687203325.

This eye-opening dialogue between a rabbi and a Christian scholar challenges Jews and Christians to reexamine their misconceptions and prejudices about each other's faith.

CR1223 Haynes, Stephen R.
Reluctant Witnesses: Jews and the Christian Imagination. Louisville, KYU: Westminster John Knox, 1995. xi, 221 pp. Paper. 0664255795.

A detailed analysis of a complex of Christian beliefs and assumptions concerning Jews, called the "witness-people myth" by the author, and their influence on Christian-Jewish relations including responses to the Holocaust.

CR1224 Herczl, Moshe Y.
Christianity and the Holocaust of Hungarian Jewry. Translated by Joel Lerner. New York, NYU: New York University Press, 1993. ix, 299 pp. Paper. 0814735037.

A detailed history of the Jews in Hungary, of the Holocaust in that country, and of Roman Catholic involvements during it.

CR1225 Hilton, Michael
The Christian Effect on Jewish Life: "Wie es sich Christelt, so Juedelt es sich." London, ENK: SCM Press, 1994. x, 309 pp. Paper. 0334025826.

A scholarly analysis of Christian influences throughout history on Jewish life—festivals, interpretations of scripture, and other practices—by the rabbi of the Cheshire Reform Congregation in Manchester, England.

CR1226 Hilton, Michael, and Gordian Marshall

The Gospels and Rabbinic Judaism: A Study Guide. Hoboken, NJU: KTAV Publishing House; New York, NYU: Anti-Defamation League B'nai B'rith; London, ENK: SCM Press, 1988. xi, 169 pp. Paper. 0881253030 (US), 0334020212 (UK).

An introduction by a Reform rabbi and a Dominican priest on how differently the two traditions handle scripture.

CR1227 Holwerda, David Earl

Jesus and Israel: One Covenant of Two? Grand Rapids, MIU: Eerdmans; Leicester, ENK: Apollos, 1995. xi, 193 pp. Paper. 0802806856 (US), 0851114393 (UK).

A scholarly analysis of uses in the New Testament of Old Testament themes of Israel (holy people), temple, land, and law, and their challenges for contemporary Jewish-Christian dialogue.

CR1228 Hood, John Y. B.

Aquinas and the Jews. (Middle Ages Series). Philadelphia, PAU: University of Pennsylvania Press, 1995. xiv, 145 pp. 0812233050 (hdbk), 0812215230 (pbk).

A scholarly analysis arguing that Aquinas remained resistant to, or skeptical of, anti-Jewish trends in 13th-century theology; originally published in 1991 as a thesis for the University of Kansas.

CR1229 Imbach, Josef

Wem gehört Jesus?: Sein Bedeutung für Juden, Christen, und Moslems. Munich, GW: Kösel, 1989. 175 pp. 3466203066.

The author reviews how Jesus is understood among Jews and Muslims, and on the basis of New Testament scholarship and contemporary theology enters into a dialogue with such views.

CR1230 International Academic Meeting between Orthodoxy and Judaism (3rd, Athens, 21-24 March 1993)

Orthodox Christians and Jews on Continuity and Renewal: The Third Academic Meeting between Orthodoxy and Judaism. Edited by Malcolm Lowe. Jerusalem, IS: Ecumenical Theological Research Fraternity in Israel, 1993. 255 pp. Paper. No ISBN.

Report of an important dialogue between Orthodox Christian and Jewish leaders, with bibliography; published as issue 26/27 of the journal *Immanuel.*

CR1231 Jacob, Walter

Christianity through Jewish Eyes: The Quest for Common Ground. Cincinnati, OHU: Hebrew Union College Press, 1974. x, 284 pp. 0870682571.

A historical and critical study by one of the most significant modern Jewish thinkers on Christianity.

CR1232 Jacobs, Steven L., ed.

Contemporary Christian Religious Responses to the Shoah. (Studies in the Shoah, 6). Lanham, MDU: University Press of America, 1993. 289 pp. 0819189847.

Eleven Christian scholars respond theologically and personally to the Holocaust.

CR1233 Jaher, Frederic Cople

A Scapegoat in the New Wilderness: The Origins and Rise of Anti-Semitism in America. Cambridge, MAU: Harvard University Press, 1994. viii, 339 pp. 0674790065.

A comprehensive history of anti-Semitism in the United States—its scope, intensity, change, and causes—including its precursors in early Christianity and Western Europe.

CR1234 Jocz, Jakob

The Jewish People and Jesus Christ after Auschwitz: A Study in the Controversy between Church and Synagogue. Grand Rapids, MIU: Baker Books, 1981. 273 pp. Paper. 0801051231.

Detailed analysis by an evangelical Protestant scholar of thirty years (1950-1980) of writings by Christians and Jews about the other's faith, including the new phenomenon of the rise of Jewish Christianity.

CR1235 John Paul II, Pope

Spiritual Pilgrimage: Texts on Jews and Judaism, 1979-1995. Edited by Eugene J. Fisher, and Leon Klenicki. (A Crossroad Herder Book). New York, NYU: Crossroad Publishing, 1995. xxxix, 208 pp. Paper. 0824515447.

A compilation of the Pope's writings, homilies, and speeches on the importance of Judaism and the Jewish people.

CR1236 Küng, Hans

Judaism: Between Yesterday and Tomorrow. Translated by John Bowden. New York, NYU: Crossroad Publishing, 1992. xxii, 753 pp. 0824511816.

English translation.

CR1237 Küng, Hans

Das Judentum. (Die religiöse Situation der Zeit). Munich, GW: Piper, 1991. 907 pp. 3492034969.

A major study of living Judaism by the prominent Catholic theologian, with special emphasis on issues for Jewish-Christian-Muslim dialogue.

CR1238 Küng, Hans, and Walter Kasper, eds.

Christians and Jews. (*Concilium*: Religion in the Seventies, 8, 10). New York, NYU: Seabury Press, 1974. 93 pp. Paper. 0816420955.

Parallel essays by Jewish and Christian scholars on issues of law, liturgy, religiousness, messianic hope, Jesus, and the future of Christian-Jewish dialogue.

CR1239 Kee, Howard Clark, and Irvin J. Borowsky, eds.

Removing Anti-Judaism from the Pulpit. (American Interfaith Institute and World Alliance of Interfaith Organizations, 6). Philadelphia, PAU: American Interfaith Institute; New York, NYU: *Continuum*, 1996. 140 pp. 082640927X.

Eight essays by North American scholars on anti-Semitism in the New Testament, plus five exemplary sermons addressing this issue.

CR1240 Keith, Graham

Hated without a Cause?: A Survey of Anti-Semitism. Carlisle, ENK: Paternoster Press, 1997. xii, 301 pp. Paper. 0853647836.

Through a theological and historical examination, the author provides a realistic evaluation of the many influences that have contributed to the present situation, with suggestions on how the church may respond positively and sensitively.

CR1241 Kellenbach, Katharina von

Anti-Judaism in Feminist Religious Writings. (American Academy of Religion Cultural Criticism Series, 1). Atlanta, GAU: Scholars Press, 1994. x, 173 pp. 0788500430 (hdbk), 0788500449 (pbk).

A German Christian feminist's detailed analysis of anti-Jewish elements in recent feminist theology in Europe and North America.

CR—CHRISTIANITY AND OTHER RELIGIONS

CR1242 Kenny, Anthony J.

Catholics, Jews and the State of Israel. (Studies in Judaism and Christianity). Mahwah, NJU: Paulist Press, 1993. vii, 157 pp. Paper. 0809134063.

Focusing on the unresolved question of the Vatican's full recognition of the State of Israel, the author analyzes Catholic theology, official teachings, and Jewish-Catholic relations during the past thirty years.

CR1243 Kern, Kathleen

We Are the Pharisees. Scottdale, PAU: Herald Press, 1995. 160 pp. Paper. 0836136713.

A study book on Christian attitudes toward the Pharisees in Scripture, and how those attitudes contributed to Christendom's horrible legacy of anti-Semitism.

CR1244 Kjær-Hansen, Kai, and Ole Chr. M. Kvarme

Messiaaniset juutalaiset: Kristitty vähemmistö Israelissa. Translated by Sointu Rø. Helsinki, FI: Kirjaneliö, 1981. 189 pp. Paper. 951600542X.

Finnish translation.

CR1245 Klappert, Bertold

Israel und die Kirche: Erwägungen zur Israellehre Karl Barths. (Theologische Existenz heute, 207). Munich, GW: Kaiser Verlag, 1980. 76 pp. 3459012749.

With hindsight of Auschwitz and within the realm of Jewish-Christian dialogue, the author examines Karl Barth's doctrine of Israel and the church, with implications for theological models today.

CR1246 Klenicki, Leon, and Geoffrey Wigoder, eds.

A Dictionary of the Jewish-Christian Dialogue. (Studies in Judaism and Christianity). Mahwah, NJU: Paulist Press, 1995. viii, 240 pp. Paper. 0809135825.

Short separate essays by a Jewish and a Christian scholar on thirty-nine shared theological and religious topics; an expansion of the 1984 edition.

CR1247 Klenicki, Leon, and Richard John Neuhaus

Believing Today: Jew and Christian in Conversation. Grand Rapids, MIU: Eerdmans, 1989. viii, 108 pp. Paper. 080280313X.

A digest of conversations between two prominent American religious leaders—a rabbi and a Lutheran pastor—written to advance the argument that if believing Jews and Christians are more faithfully Jewish and more faithfully Christian, the dialogue will take care of itself.

CR1248 Klenicki, Leon, ed.

Toward a Theological Encounter: Jewish Understandings of Christianity. (Studies in Judaism and Christianity). New York, NYU: Paulist Press, 1991. vi, 168 pp. Paper. 0809132567.

Themes for Jewish-Christian dialogue analyzed by eight Jewish scholars.

CR1249 Kohn, Johanna

Haschoah: Christlich-jüdische Verständigung nach Auschwitz. (Fundamentaltheologische Studien, 13). Munich, GW: Kaiser; Mainz, GW: Grünewald Verlag, 1986. 107 pp. Paper. 3459016345 (K), 3786712387 (G).

This study probes the context and meanings of Jewish-Christian dialogue in Germany in the light of the Holocaust, which burdens such dialogue with special problems and urgency.

CR1250 Kulka, Otto Dov, and Paul R. Mendes-Flohr

Judaism and Christianity under the Impact of National Socialism. Jerusalem, IS: Historical Society of Israel, 1987. 558 pp. 9652270415.

A comprehensive collection of twenty-nine essays by both Jewish and Christian scholars on the complex and often controversial relationship between Hitler's National Socialism and the churches.

CR1251 Kuschel, Karl-Josef

Abraham: Sign of Hope for Jews, Christians, and Muslims. Translated by John Bowden. New York, NYU: *Continuum*; London, ENK: SCM Press, 1995. xxix, 286 pp. 0826408087 (US), 0334025672 (UK).

English translation.

CR1252 Kuschel, Karl-Josef

La contraversia su Abramo: Ciò che divide, e ciò che unisce ebrei, cristiani e musulmani. (Giornale di teologia, 245). Brescia: Queriniana, 1996. 444 pp. 8839907459.

Italian translation.

CR1253 Kuschel, Karl-Josef

Streit um Abraham: Was Juden, Christen und Muslime trennt—und was sie eint. Munich, GW: Piper, 1994. 334 pp. 3492037399.

After analyzing the role Abraham has been made to play in each of the three religions, the University of Tübingen theologian proposes an "Abrahamic ecumenism" as a model for future understanding and cooperation between Jews, Christians, and Muslims.

CR1254 Lapide, Pinchas

Die Bergpredigt, Utopie oder Programm? (Grünewald Reihe). Mainz, GW: Matthias-Grünewald-Verlag, 1984. 153 pp. 3786709920.

An Orthodox Jewish scholar offers a sober evaluation of Jesus' Sermon on the Mount within the context of Rabbinic Judaism.

CR1255 Lapide, Pinchas

The Sermon on the Mount: Utopia or Program for Action? Translated by Arlene Swidler. Maryknoll, NYU: Orbis Books, 1986. vii, 148 pp. Paper. 0883442485.

English translation.

CR1256 Lapide, Pinchas, and Ulrich Luz

Der Jude Jesus: Thesen eines Juden: Antworten eines Christen. Zürich, SZ: Benziger, 1979. 174 pp. 3545250458 (sz).

The authors discuss the following questions: Did Jesus identify himself as the Messiah? How did people of Israel respond to Jesus? Did Jesus repudiate his own people?

CR1257 Leaman, James R.

Faith Roots: Learning from and Sharing Witness with Jewish People. Nappanee, INU: Evangel Press, 1993. 171 pp. Paper. 0916035573.

A study book to help Christians embrace their Jewish roots, and Jewish believers to feel at home in Christian congregations, with treatment of the modern messianic Jewish movement.

CR1258 Lee, Bernard J.
The Galilean Jewishness of Jesus: Retrieving the Jewish Origins of Christianity. (Studies in Judaism and Christianity). Mahwah, NJU: Paulist Press, 1988. vi, 158 pp. Paper. 0809130211.

The first in a three-volume series designed to contribute to Jewish-Christian dialogue by examination of the history, cultures, and religions of Galilee in the time of Christ, the Jewishness of Jesus, and his positive links with the Pharasaic movement.

CR1259 Lieu, Judith M.
Image and Reality: The Jews in the World of the Christians in the Second Century. Edinburgh, STK: T&T Clark, 1996. xiv, 348 pp. 0567085295.

A detailed analysis of 2nd century C.E. texts showing the changing attitudes of Christians toward Jews at the time of the Apologists.

CR1260 Locke, Hubert G., and Marcia Sachs Littell, eds.
Holocaust and Church Struggle: Religion, Power and the Politics of Resistance. (Studies in the Shoah, 16). Lanham, MDU: University Press of America, 1996. xii, 347 pp. 0761803750.

Twenty scholarly essays on the Holocaust, the churches' struggle against Nazism, and current reflections; originally presented at the 22nd Annual Scholars' Conference on the Holocaust and the German Church Struggle (University of Washington, 29 February-4 March 1992).

CR1261 Lodahl, Michael E.
Shekhinah/Spirit: Divine Presence in Jewish and Christian Religion. (Studies in Judaism and Christianity). New York, NYU: Paulist Press, 1992. vi, 234 pp. Paper. 0809133113.

A scholarly comparison of the spirituality of God's presence and spirit in Judaism and Christianity, with special reference to beliefs concerning election, evil, and eschatology.

CR1262 Lohfink, Norbert
The Covenant Never Revoked: Biblical Reflections on Christian-Jewish Dialogue. Translated by John J. Scullion. New York, NYU: Paulist Press, 1991. v, 96 pp. Paper. 0809132281.

English translation.

CR1263 Lohfink, Norbert
Der niemals gekündigte Bund: Exegetische Gedanken zum christlich-jüdischen Gespräch. Freiburg im Breisgau, GW: Herder, 1989. 120 pp. 3451215977.

An argument by the renowned German biblical scholar that Christians and Jews are united in one covenant that is acknowledged and accepted in two distinctly different manners.

CR1264 Lowe, Malcolm, ed.
The New Testament and Christian-Jewish Dialogue: Studies in Honor of David Flusser. Jerusalem, IS: Ecumenical Theological Research Fraternity in Israel, 1990. 317 pp. Paper. No ISBN.

Fourteen scholarly essays on New Testament themes that have featured prominently in Christian-Jewish dialogue; published as a special issue of *Immanuel* to honor the seventieth birthday of the renowned scholar and leader in that dialogue in Jerusalem.

CR1265 Lubarsky, Sandra B., and David Ray Griffin, eds.
Jewish Theology and Process Thought. (Constructive Postmodern Thought). Albany, NYU: SUNY Press, 1996. xii, 316 pp. Paper. 0791428109.

A collection of six essays by Jewish thinkers who use process thought to explore Judaism and its theology, plus six essays (three by Jewish and three by Christian scholars) on the appropriateness of process thought for Judaism.

CR1266 Lubarsky, Sandra B.
Tolerance and Transformation: Jewish Aproaches to Religious Pluralism. (Jewish Perspectives, 4). Cincinnati, OHU: Hebrew Union College Press, 1990. x, 149 pp. 0878205047.

A scholarly analysis of various approaches of seminal modern Jewish thinkers (Baeck, Rosenzweig, Buber, and Kaplan) to religious pluralism, with advocacy for a mutually transformative dialogue.

CR1267 Lundmark, John
Det splittrade gudsfolket och missionsuppdraget: En studie i relationen mellan kyrkan och judendomen. (Studia Missionalia Upsaliensia, 37). Stockholm, SW: EFS förlaget, 1983. 288 pp. 9170805784.

A theological study on the relation between the church and the Jewish people, and it's consequences for missions among Jews.

CR1268 Maduro, Otto, ed.
Judaism, Christianity, and Liberation: An Agenda for Dialogue. Maryknoll, NYU: Orbis Books, 1991. viii, 152 pp. Paper. 0883446936.

Ten original essays by Latin-American liberation theologians and North American Jewish and Christian scholars, calling for a new dialogue between Christians and Jews on the meaning of justice and compassion in today's world.

CR1269 Maguire, Daniel C.
The Moral Core of Judaism and Christianity: Reclaiming the Revolution. Minneapolis, MNU: Fortress Press, 1993. x, 286 pp. Paper. 0800626893.

A cogent argument by the distinguished Professor of Ethics at Marquette University, that Judaism and Christianity have a profound common source for both morality and religion that should impel both faith communities to work together for a new humanity.

CR1270 Marcus, Marcel, Ekkehard W. Stegemann, and Erich Zenger, eds.
Israel und Kirche heute: Beiträge zum christlich-jüdischen Dialog. Freiburg im Breisgau, GW: Herder, 1991. 439 pp. 3451223309.

This *festschrift* for Ernst Ludwig Ehrlich, a pioneer of the Jewish-Christian dialogue, continues the dialogue with contributions from both Christian and Jewish writers, and closes with Ehrlich's impressive bibliography.

CR1271 Martin, Vincent
A House Divided: The Parting of the Ways between Synagogue and Church. (Studies in Judaism and Christianity; A Stimulus Book). New York, NYU: Paulist Press, 1995. vii, 194 pp. Paper. 0809135698.

A detailed analysis of the first-century historical factors that led to disagreements and finally separation of Christianity from Judaism.

CR1272 McGarry, Michael B.
Christology after Auschwitz. New York, NYU: Paulist Press, 1977. 119 pp. Paper. 0809120240.

A survey of post-World War II opinions concerning Catholic-Jewish relations based on an analysis of formal church statements, including those of Vatican II, and of scholarly theological writings.

CR—CHRISTIANITY AND OTHER RELIGIONS

CR1273 McInnes, Val Ambrose, ed.

New Visions: Historical and Theological Perspectives on Jewish-Christian Dialogue. (Tulane Chair of Judeo-Christian Studies, 3). New York, NYU: Crossroad Publishing, 1993. 165 pp. 0824512464.

A Tulane Judeo-Christian Studies edition containing eight essays by prominent Christian and Jewish theologians in North America and Europe around the central question: "Can Jews and Christians accept one another's truth without abandoning their own religious beliefs and identities?"

CR1274 Michalczyk, John J., ed.

Resisters, Rescuers, and Refugees: Historical and Ethical Issues. Kansas City, MOU: Sheed & Ward, 1997. xii, 355 pp. Paper. 155612970X.

Twenty-five essays on Jewish and Christian efforts to resist, rescue, and care for refugees during the Holocaust.

CR1275 Miller, Ronald Henry

Dialogue and Disagreement: Franz Rosenzweig's Relevance to Contemporary Jewish-Christian Understanding. Lanham, MDU: University Press of America, 1989. xvii, 213 pp. 0819175390 (hdbk), 0819175498 (pbk).

A detailed analysis of the contribution of German Franc Rosenzweig (1886-1929) to Christian-Jewish dialogue comparing apostolic Church and contemporary approaches.

CR1276 Monti, Joseph E.

Who Do You Say that I Am?: The Christian Understanding of Christ and Anti-Semitism. New York,, NYU: Paulist Press, 1984. vii, 98 pp. Paper. 0809125986.

A Catholic theologian proposes a reconstructed Christology as the way forward for Christian participants in dialogue with Jews.

CR1277 Moore, James F.

Christian Theology after the Shoah. (Studies in the Shoah, 7). Lanham, MDU: University Press of America, 1993. xiii, 189 pp. 0819190748.

A theological reinterpretation of the difficult Passion narratives concerning the Jews in the light of the Holocaust and advances in Jewish-Christian dialogue.

CR1278 Moran, Gabriel

Uniqueness: Problem of Paradox in Jewish and Christian Traditions. (Faith Meets Faith). Maryknoll, NYU: Orbis Books, 1992. vi, 160 pp. 0883448300 (hdbk), 0883448297 (pbk).

An engaging study of "uniqueness" as a key concept in both Christian and Jewish traditions, both in history and in contemporary Christian-Jewish relations.

CR1279 Mussner, Franz

Dieses Geschlecht wird nicht vergehen: Judentum und Kirche. Freiburg im Breisgau, GW: Herder, 1991. 185 pp. 3451223058.

Essays by a New Testament scholar on Jewish-Christian relations.

CR1280 Mussner, Franz

Tractate on the Jews: The Significance of Judaism for Christian Faith. Translated by Leonard J. Swidler. London, ENK: SPCK; Philadelphia, PAU: Fortress Press, 1984. 339 pp. 0281040869 (UK), 0800607074 (US).

English translation.

CR1281 Mussner, Franz

Traité sur les Juifs. (Cogitatio Fidei, 109). Paris, FR: Éditions du Cerf, 1981. 439 pp. 2204017337.

French translation.

CR1282 Mussner, Franz

Traktat über die Juden. Munich, GW: Kösel, 1979. 398 pp. 346620190X.

A comprehensive scholarly analysis of all relevant biblical issues concerning the relationships between Christianity and Judaism.

CR1283 Mussner, Franz

Tratado sobre los Judíos. (Biblioteca de Estudios Bíblicos, 40). Salamanca, SP: Ediciones Sígueme, 1983. 391 pp. 8430109129.

Spanish translation.

CR1284 Neuenzeit, Paul

Juden und Christen: Auf neuen Wegen zum Gespräch. Würzburg, GW: Echter Verlag, 1990. 216 pp. Paper. 3429012759.

This work outlines the genesis of anti-Semitism among Christians and the contemporary position of the Catholic Church toward Jews, together with a description of using this material as a "learning project" with participants from both groups at Würzburg.

CR1285 Neusner, Jacob

Children of the Flesh, Children of the Promise: A Rabbi Talks with Paul. Cleveland, OHU: Pilgrim Press, 1995. xxv, 119 pp. Paper. 0829810269.

The noted Jewish scholar contends that the apostle Paul misunderstood the true nature of Judaism, thereby drawing new boundaries for Jewish-Christian dialogue.

CR1286 Neusner, Jacob

Jews and Christians: The Myth of a Common Tradition. London, ENK: SCM Press; Philadelphia, PAU: Trinity Press International, 1991. xi, 158 pp. Paper. 033402465X.

A detailed argument from history that Judaism and Christianity can most honestly be understood as two separate religious traditions, rather than as a combined religious heritage.

CR1287 Neusner, Jacob

Judaism and Christianity in the Age of Constantine: History, Messiah, Israel, and the Initial Confrontation. (Chicago Studies in the History of Judaism). Chicago, ILU: University of Chicago Press, 1987. xv, 246 pp. 0226576523.

A scholarly analysis of the 4th century-polemical dialogue between Christian and Jewish teachers, including Christian texts by Eusebius, Aphrahat, and Chrysostom, and Jewish works (the *Talmud of the Land of Israel,* the *Genesis Rabbah,* and the *Leviticus Rabbah*).

CR1288 Neusner, Jacob

Judaism in the Matrix of Christianity. Philadelphia, PAU: Fortress Press, 1986. xix, 148 pp. Paper. 0800618971.

Eight free-standing essays dealing with the 4th and 5th centuries as Judaism changed and took shape in the matrix of Christianity.

CR1289 Neusner, Jacob

A Rabbi Talks with Jesus: An Intermillennial, Interfaith Exchange. New York, NYU: Doubleday, 1993. xviii, 154 pp. 0385424663.

An imaginary dialogue between Jesus and a rabbi of his day; by the world's preeminent authority on Judaism in the first centuries of the Christian era, who desires to encourage creative Jewish-Christian dialogue today.

CR1290 Neusner, Jacob
Telling Tales: Making Sense of Christian and Judaic Nonsense: The Urgency and Basis for Judeo-Christian Dialogue. Louisville, KYU: Westminster John Knox, 1993. vi, 170 pp. Paper. 0664253717.

The renowned Judaic scholar proposes a new way of beginning dialogue by Jews and Christians exchanging stories.

CR1291 Neusner, Jacob, and Bruce Chilton
The Body of Faith: Israel and the Church. Valley Forge, PAU: Trinity Press International, 1996. xvi, 183 pp. Paper. 1563381575.

The second of three volumes (*Revelation, The Body of Faith, God in the World*) designed to compare and contrast the paramount theological categories of Judaism and Christianity.

CR1292 Novak, David
Jewish-Christian Dialogue: A Jewish Justification. New York, NYU: Oxford University Press, 1989. xiii, 194 pp. Paper. 0195050843.

A historically documented account of the relationship between Rabbinic Judaism and Gentile Christianity, presenting a philosophically formulated theological argument for Jewish-Christian dialogue; by the Edgar M. Bronfman Professor of Modern Jewish Thought at the University of Virginia at Charlottesville.

CR1293 Oberman, Heiko A.
The Roots of Anti-Semitism in the Age of Renaissance and Reformation. Translated by James I. Porter. Philadelphia, PAU: Fortress Press, 1984. xi, 163 pp. 0800607090.

A provocative study of the roots of anti-Semitism, focusing on the Renaissance and Reformation periods; by the Director of the Institute for Late Medieval and Reformation Studies at the University of Tübingen in Germany.

CR1294 Oesterreicher, John M., ed.
Brothers in Hope. (The Bridge: Judaeo-Christian Studies, 5). New York, NYU: Herder and Herder, 1970. 350 pp. No ISBN.

Papers from the 1965-1969 period, mostly by members of the Institute of Judaeo-Christian Studies in response to the Vatican II statement on the Jews.

CR1295 Oesterreicher, John M.
God at Auschwitz? South Orange, NJU: Institute of Judeo-Christian Studies, Seton Hall University, 1993. 73 pp. Paper. No ISBN.

For his reflection on the Holocaust, the noted leader in Christian-Jewish dialogue draws upon resources from the Talmud.

CR1296 Oesterreicher, John M.
The New Encounter between Christians and Jews. New York, NYU: Philosophical Library, 1986. 470 pp. 0802224962.

A collection of articles on the background, content, and implications of the Second Vatican Council's statement on "The Church and the Jewish People" by one of its architects.

CR1297 Oesterreicher, John M.
The Unfinished Dialogue: Martin Buber and the Christian Way. New York, NYU: Philosophical Library, 1985. 133 pp. Paper. 0802224954.

A discussion of Buber, the Jewish philosopher's role among the philosophers of dialogue, and his two-fold understanding of faith as trust and affirmation in God.

CR1298 O'Hare, Padraic
The Enduring Covenant: The Education of Christians and the End of Anti-Semitism. Valley Forge, PAU: Trinity Press International, 1997. xi, 195 pp. Paper. 1563381869.

Principles and recommended practices for a religious education program for interreligious reverence between Jews and Christians, based on the author's fifteen years of sustained study and engagement in Jewish-Christian relations.

CR1299 Opsahl, Paul D., and Marc H. Tanenbaum, eds.
Speaking of God Today: Jews and Lutherans in Conversation. Philadelphia, PAU: Fortress Press, 1974. xiii, 178 pp. 0800602757.

Papers from a 1969 Lutheran-Jewish colloquium on beliefs concerning God, law, grace, election, land, people, and the state.

CR1300 Osten-Sacken, Peter von der
Christian-Jewish Dialogue: Theological Foundations. Philadelphia, PAU: Fortress Press, 1986. xi, 220 pp. 0800607716.

A scholarly development of a Christology more open to Judaism based on an extensive analysis of biblical texts, arguing that the New Testament itself allows for the continuation of Judaism.

CR1301 Osten-Sacken, Peter von der
Grundzüge einer Theologie im christlich-jüdischen Gespräch. (Abhandlungen zum christlich-jüdischen Dialog, 12). Munich, GW: Kaiser, 1982. 240 pp. Paper. 345901377X.

Analyzing the fundamental theological background of Jewish-Christian dialogue, this work provides a Christological model attempting to overcome the traditional prejudice of church and theology against the Jewish people.

CR1302 Osten-Sacken, Peter von der
Katechismus und Siddur: Aufbrüche mit Martin Luther und den Lehrern Israels. (Veröffentlichungen aus dem Institut Kirche und Judentum, 15). Berlin, GW: Institut Kirche und Judentum, 1984. 372 pp. Paper. 3923095155.

This is a comparative study of the similarities between the five divisions of Luther's catechisms (the Ten Commandments, Apostles' Creed, Lord's Prayer, Baptism, and Eucharist) with the five elements of the *siddur*, or Jewish prayerbook (the ten words as part of the Torah, Shema prayer, eighteen petitions/Amida, circumcision, and Pasch).

CR1303 Papademetriou, George C.
Essays on Orthodox Christian-Jewish Relations. Bristol, INU: Wyndham Hall Press, 1990. i, 133 pp. 1556051654 (hdbk), 1556051646 (pbk).

Key issues and topics of convergence and difference between Orthodox Christianity and Judaism, presented as themes for dialogue.

CR1304 Parkes, James
The Conflict of the Church and the Synagogue: A Study in the Origins of Anti-Semitism. New York, NYU: Hermon Press, 1974. xx, 430 pp. 0872030431.

Reprint of the 1934 edition of a doctoral thesis tracing the roots of anti-Semitism from A.D. 70 to the early Middle Ages.

CR1305 Parkes, James
Prelude to Dialogue: Jewish-Christian Relationships. New York, NYU: Schocken Books, 1969. xi, 227 pp. No ISBN.

A collection of lectures and articles from the 1947-1966 period by a Church of England priest who specialized in the study of Jewish-Christian relations.

CR—CHRISTIANITY AND OTHER RELIGIONS

CR1306 Pawlikowski, John T.
Christ in the Light of the Christian-Jewish Dialogue: Exploration of Issues in the Contemporary Dialogue between Christians and Jews. (Studies in Judaism and Christianity). New York, NYU: Paulist Press, 1982. 168 pp. Paper. 0809124165.

Themes arising from Christian-Jewish dialogue for the rethinking of Christology, with a survey of the thoughts of representative theologians.

CR1307 Pawlikowski, John T.
Sinai and Calvary: A Meeting of Two Peoples. Beverly Hills, CAU: Benziger, 1976. 229 pp. Paper. No ISBN.

A concise summary of the basis of Judaism in the Bible, and of Christian-Jewish relations in the New Testament period, in church history, and today.

CR1308 Perelmuter, Hayim Goren
Siblings: Rabbinic Judaism and Early Christianity at Their Beginnings. Mahwah, NJU: Paulist Press, 1989. v, 217 pp. Paper. 0809131048.

A work which seeks to illumine Rabbinic Judaism for "the serious neophyte" by examining the great thinkers of Rabbinic Judaism, the Rabbinic texts of the Midrash and Talmud, and the common cultural roots of Rabbinic Judaism and early Christianity; by the Professor of Jewish Studies at the Catholic Theological Union in Chicago, Illinois.

CR1309 Perry, Marvin, and Frederick M. Schweitzer, eds.
Jewish-Christian Encounters over the Centuries: Symbiosis, Prejudice, Holocaust, Dialogue. (American University Studies, 9: History, 136). New York, NYU: Lang, 1994. x, 436 pp. 0820420824.

Papers from an important conference on Jewish-Christian relations (New York, 1-3 March 1989) jointly sponsored by Manhattan and Baruch colleges.

CR1310 Petuchowski, Jakob Josef, and Clemens Thoma
Lexikon der jüdisch-christlichen Begegnung: Hintergründe— Klärungen—Perspektiven. (Herder/Spektrum, 4181). Freiburg, GW: Herder, 1994. xv, 237 pp. Paper. 3451042819.

This short dictionary of Jewish-Christian relations does not aim at just informing, but is the product of ongoing dialogue.

CR1311 Petuchowski, Jakob Josef, ed.
When Jews and Christians Meet. Albany, NYU: SUNY Press, 1988. xi, 190 pp. 0887066313 (hdbk), 088706633X (pbk).

Papers presented at the second Bronstein Colloquium on Judaeo-Christian Studies at Hebrew Union College, 1986, focusing on the possibilities of using biblical texts to facilitate interfaith exchange.

CR1312 Phayer, Michael, and Eva Fleischner
Cries in the Night: Women Who Challenged the Holocaust. Kansas City, MOU: Sheed & Ward, 1997. xxi, 143 pp. Paper. 1556129777.

Stories of seven Catholic women who defied Hitler and the Nazis during the Holocaust by saving Jews.

CR1313 Porter, Stanley E., and Brook W. R. Pearson, eds.
Christian-Jewish Relations through the Centuries. (Journal for the Study of the New Testament Supplement Series, 192; Roehampton Papers, 6). Sheffield, ENK: Sheffield Academic Press, 2000. 503 pp. Paper. 1841270903.

Proceedings that include twenty-three papers given at a conference held at Digby Stuart College, University of Surrey Roehampton (London, 21 February 1999).

CR1314 Pratt, Douglas, and Dov Bing, eds.
Judaism and Christianity toward Dialogue: A New Zealand Contribution. Auckland, NZ: College Communications, 1987. iii, 169 pp. Paper. 0959777555.

A collection of eight papers concerning various facets of Jewish-Christian dialogue which were presented at the summer public lecture series, "Judaism and Christianity— A New Dialogue," held at the University of Waikato (New Zealand) in April 1985.

CR1315 Rausch, David A.
Building Bridges. Chicago, ILU: Moody, 1988. 251 pp. Paper. 0802410766.

In this work the Professor of Church History and Judaic Studies at Ashland College and Theological Seminary acquaints readers with the rituals and customs of Judaism, the history and psyche of the Jewish people, and elaborates on the history and traditions of the Jewish community in the United States.

CR1316 Rausch, David A.
Communities in Conflict: Evangelicals and Jews. Philadelphia, PAU: Trinity Press International, 1991. x, 204 pp. Paper. 1563380293.

A balanced analysis of the attitudes toward each other of Jewish and Protestant-evangelical communities in the United States, based on actual comments and writings by adherents of both traditions.

CR1317 Rausch, David A.
Fundamentalist-Evangelicals and Anti-Semitism. Valley Forge, PAU: Trinity Press International, 1993. x, 253 pp. Paper. 1563380498.

A history of the attitudes of North American fundamentalists and evangelicals toward the Jews, including both anti-Semitism and Christian Zionism.

CR1318 Rendtorff, Rolf, ed.
Die Kirchen und das Judentum: Dokumente von 1945-1985; gemeinsame Veröffentlichung der Studienkommission Kirche und Judentum der EKD ... Paderborn, GW: Verlag Bonifatius-Druckerei; Munich, GW: Kaiser, 1989. 746 pp. 3870885246 (B), 3459017120 (K).

Second edition of a collection of 85 Roman Catholic, 80 Protestant, 8 Jewish, and about 40 Christian-Jewish official statements on Jewish-Christian dialogue.

CR1319 Riggans, Walter
Jesus ben Joseph: An Introduction to Jesus the Jew. Tunbridge Wells, ENK: Marc-Monarch Publications; St. Albans, ENK: Olive Press, 1993. 151 pp. Paper. 185424227X (M), 0904054160 (O).

Jesus put back into his "kosher" setting in a popular examination of Christ's nature, mission, and message, demonstrating why many Jews have come to accept Jesus as Israel's Messiah.

CR1320 Rittner, Carol, and John K. Roth, eds.
From the Unthinkable to the Unavoidable: American Christian and Jewish Scholars Encounter the Holocaust. Westport, CTU: Praeger, 1997. xii, 220 pp. Paper. 0275957640.

Fifteen essays by well-known American Christian and Jewish scholars exploring Christian complicity, indifference, resistance, rescue, and other responses to the Holocaust.

CR1321 Rosenberg, Stuart E.

The Christian Problem: A Jewish View. New York, NYU: Hippocrene Books, 1986. xii, 241 pp. 0870522841.

The rabbi of Beth Torah Congregation in Toronto, Canada, answers Christian myths about Jews and Judaism, proposes restoring Jews to the mainstream of history, and discusses continuing problems in dialogue evoked by the Holocaust and the state of Israel.

CR1322 Rothschild, Fritz A., ed.

Jewish Perspectives on Christianity: The Views of Leo Baeck, Martin Buber, Franz Rosenzweig, Will Herberg, and Abraham J. Heschel. New York, NYU: Crossroad Publishing, 1990. x, 363 pp. 0824509374.

Writings on Christianity by five prominent Jewish scholars of the 20th century.

CR1323 Rousmaniere, John

A Bridge to Dialogue: The Story of Jewish-Christian Relations. Edited by James A. Carpenter and Leon Klenicki. (Studies in Judaism and Christianity). Mahwah, NJU: Paulist Press, 1991. v, 149 pp. Paper. 0809132842.

A Christian historian's history of twenty centuries of Christian misunderstandings of Judaism.

CR1324 Rousseau, Richard W., ed.

Christianity and Judaism: The Deepening Dialogue. Scranton, PAU: Ridge Row Press, 1983. 217 pp. Paper. 0940866021.

Fifteen essays by Jewish and Christian scholars on contemporary issues in Jewish-Christian dialogue.

CR1325 Rubenstein, Richard L., and John K. Roth

Approaches to Auschwitz: The Holocaust and Its Legacy. Atlanta, GAU: John Knox Press, 1987. ix, 422 pp. 080420778X (hdbk), 0804207771 (pbk).

Two scholars, a Jew and a Christian, collaborate in bringing a multidisciplinary analysis of the philosophical history of the Holocaust, including Christian-Jewish relations in history and today.

CR1326 Rudin, A. James, and Marvin R. Wilson, eds.

A Time to Speak: The Evangelical-Jewish Encounter. Grand Rapids, MIU: Eerdmans; Austin, TXU: Center Judaic-Christian Studies, 1987. xvi, 202 pp. Paper. 0802802818.

Nineteen papers originally presented at the "Evangelicals and Jews: Coming of Age" conference held at Gordon College, Wenham, Massachusetts, in 1984, co-sponsored by the college and the Interreligious Affairs Department of the American Jewish Committee.

CR1327 Sahas, Daniel J.

John of Damascus on Islam: The "Heresy of the Ishmaelites." Leiden, NE: Brill, 1972. xvi, 171 pp. No ISBN.

A study of John of Damascus (ca.655-750), his historical encounter with early Islam, and his polemical writings.

CR1328 Sanders, Jack T.

Schismatics, Sectarians, Dissidents, Deviants: The First One Hundred Years of Jewish-Christian Relations. Valley Forge, PAU: Trinity Press International, 1993. xxiii, 404 pp. Paper. 156338065X.

A comprehensive survey and analysis of all literary and archaeological evidence concerning relations between Judaism and Christianity in the latter's first 100 years.

CR1329 Sandmel, Samuel

Anti-Semitism in the New Testament? Philadelphia, PAU: Fortress Press, 1978. xxi, 168 pp. 0800605217.

A thorough and sensitive examination of this controversial question by a leading Jewish expert on the New Testament.

CR1330 Saperstein, Marc

Juifs et Chrétiens: moments de crise. Translated by Marie Brunet. Paris, FR: Éditions du Cerf, 1991. 100 pp. 2204042684.

French translation.

CR1331 Saperstein, Marc

Moments of Crisis in Jewish-Christian Relations. London, ENK: SCM Press; Philadelphia, PAU: Trinity Press International, 1989. xii, 84 pp. Paper. 033401025X.

An examination of five moments of crisis in Jewish-Christian history: Jews and Christians in antiquity, persecution in the high Middle Ages, the Reformation period, the Holocaust, and the present day, with attention on how to learn from past mistakes so we can positively change the future.

CR1332 Schoeps, Hans Joachim

Israel und Christenheit: Jüdisch-christliches Religionsgespräch in neunzehn Jahrhunderten. Munich, GW: Ner-Tamid Verlag, 1961. 230 pp. No ISBN.

Third edition of a survey of nineteen centuries of Jewish-Christian relations, with attention to key 20th-century German Jewish leaders; originally published in 1937 under duress and later revised by the author, an outstanding Jewish scholar and Professor of the History of Religion at the University of Erlangen, Germany.

CR1333 Schoeps, Hans Joachim

The Jewish-Christian Argument: A History of Theologies in Conflict. Translated by David E. Green. London, ENK: Faber & Faber, 1965. xviii, 208 pp. No ISBN.

English translation; also published by Holt, Rinehart & Winston, New York (1963).

CR1334 Schottroff, Willy

Das Reich Gottes und der Menschen: Studien über das Verhältnis der christlichen Theologie zum Judentum. (Abhandlungen zum christlich-jüdischen Dialog, 19). Munich, GW: Kaiser Verlag, 1991. 235 pp. Paper. 345901881X.

These six essays take the Christian task of understanding the Jewish underpinnings of Christian theology in this century to a deeper level than many of its teachers, such as Emanuel Horsch and Herbert Braun, whose work is explicitly discussed.

CR1335 Schreckenberg, Heinz

Die Christlichen Adversus-Judaeos-Texte (11.-13.Jh.): Mit einer Ikonographie des Judenthemas bis zum 4. Laterankonzil. (European University Studies, 23: Theology, 335). Frankfurt am Main, GW: Lang, 1991. 729 pp. Paper. 3631438249.

A sourcebook of Christian texts from the Middle Ages (from apologetics, exegesis, canon law, liturgy, history of religious orders, missions to the Jews, etc.) which relate to an adversarial attitude toward Jews, together with a study of Christian iconography along the same lines.

CR1336 Schreckenberg, Heinz

The Jews in Christian Art: An Illustrated History. New York, NYU: Continuum, 1996. 400 pp. 0826409369.

A history containing more than one thousand depictions of Jews in Christian art through the centuries.

CR1337 Schuster, Ekkehard, and Reinhold Boschert-Kimmig
Hope Against Hope: Johann Baptist Metz and Elie Wiesel Speak Out on the Holocaust. (Studies in Judaism and Christianity; A Stimulus Book). Mahwah, NJU: Paulist Press, 1999. vii, 106 pp. Paper. 0809138468.

A Christian theologian and a Jewish writer, bound together by their passion for remembrance and memory of suffering at the Holocaust, engage in reflection that has important implications today.

CR1338 Schwartz, G. David
A Jewish Appraisal of Dialogue: Between Talk and Theology. Lanham, MDU: University Press of America, 1994. xiii, 148 pp. Paper. 0819194131 (hdbk), 081919414X (pbk).

Essays by an active participant in Jewish-Christian dialogue groups in Cincinnati, Ohio, proposing ways in which Jewish participants can foster a deepening of the dialogues.

CR1339 Sell, Alan P. F., ed.
Reformed Theology and the Jewish People. (WARC Studies, 9). Geneva, SZ: WARC, 1986. 72 pp. Paper. 9290750049.

A study document resulting from a five-year international study sponsored by WARC, with four supporting essays by Reformed theologians.

CR1340 Seltzer, Sanford, and Max L. Stackhouse, eds.
The Death of Dialogue and Beyond. New York, NYU: Friendship Press, 1969. 192 pp. Paper. No ISBN.

Papers from a colloquium entitled "Israel, Jews and Christians: Reassessment in a Time of Crisis" held at Andover-Newton Theological School (Newton, Mass.) following the 1967 Arab-Israeli war.

CR1341 Setzer, Claudia J.
Jewish Responses to Early Christians: History and Polemics, 30-150 C.E. Minneapolis, MNU: Fortress Press, 1994. viii, 254 pp. Paper. 080062680X.

An analysis of trends in the responses of Jews to Christians and their faith in the first two centuries.

CR1342 Shain, Milton
The Roots of Anti-Semitism in South Africa. Johannesburg, SA: Witwatersrand University Press, 1994. x, 203 pp. Paper. 1868142515.

An original analysis of the sources and development of anti-Semitism in South Africa, emphasizing its 19th-century roots.

CR1343 Shermis, Michael, and Arthur E. Zannoni, eds.
Introduction to Jewish-Christian Relations. New York, NYU: Paulist Press, 1991. iv, 275 pp. Paper. 0809132613.

Ten scholarly essays representing Jewish, Protestant, and Catholic traditions, designed as a textbook for college or adult education.

CR1344 Siker, Jeffrey S.
Disinheriting the Jews: Abraham in Early Christian Controversy. Louisville, KYU: Westminster John Knox, 1991. 296 pp. Paper. 0664251935.

A detailed analysis of the changing early Christian use of Abraham (50-150 C.E.), first to argue for Gentile inclusion, and later to argue for Jewish exclusion from the Christian community.

CR1345 Silva, António Barbosa da
Is There a New Imbalance in Jewish-Christian Relations? (Studia Missionalia Upsaliensia, 56). Uppsala, SW: Uppsala University, 1992. xiv, 345 pp. Paper. 9185424307.

A revised and expanded edition of a 1985 analysis of the theoretical presuppositions and theological implications of the Jewish-Christian dialogue in the light of the WCC's and the RCC's conceptions of interreligious dialogue.

CR1346 Simon, Marcel
Versus Israel: étude sur les relations entre chrétiens et juifs dans l'empire romain (135-425). Paris, FR: Éditions de Boccard, 1964. 518 pp. No ISBN.

The study of the relationship between Jews and Christians in the Roman Empire from the Second Jewish War (A.D. 132-135) to the end of the Jewish Patriarchate (A.D. 425), with an analysis of Judaism as a missionary religion.

CR1347 Simon, Marcel
Versus Israel: A Study of the Relations between Christians and Jews in the Roman Empire (135-425). Translated by Henry McKeating. Oxford, ENK: Oxford University Press, 1986. xviii, 533 pp. 019710035X.

English translation.

CR1348 Slageren, Jaap van
Missiologie in Joods Perspectief: De plaats van Israël in de zending. (Verkenning en Bezinning: nieuwe reeks, 11). Kampen: Kok, 1996. 118 pp. Paper. 9024291291.

Analyzes the influence of the (re)discovery of the Jewish roots of Christianity for missiology, and gives an account of the discussion in Third World churches about Israel.

CR1349 Smelik, Klass A. D.
Anti-Judaisme an de kerk: een verkenning. Baarn, NE: Ten Have, 1993. 152 pp. 9025943233.

With the hypothesis that Christians need to drop their anti-Jewish attitudes, the author presents as a stimulus for discussion groups, twelve "typical" events in the church which reveal such attitudes with their backgrounds.

CR1350 Snoek, Johan M.
The Grey Book. New York, NYU: Humanities Press, 1970. xxvi, 315 pp. 391000047 (SBN).

Source documents from the 1933-1945 period on the protests of the non-Roman Catholic churches against the Nazi persecution of Jews; originally published in 1969 by Van Gorcum, Assen, NE.

CR1351 Sonderegger, Katherine
That Jesus Christ Was Born a Jew: Karl Barth's "Doctrine of Israel." University Park, PAU: Pennsylvania State University, 1992. viii, 191 pp. 0271008180.

A scholarly analysis of the thought of the influential Swiss theologian, that by its anti-Judaic character yet Christological concentration makes Jesus the Jew the foundation for Christian opposition to anti-Semitism and Nazism.

CR1352 Soulen, R. Kendall
The God of Israel and Christian Theology. Minneapolis, MNU: Fortress Press, 1996. xii, 195 pp. Paper. 0800628837.

A major effort to rethink how Christian theology is peculiarly and truly Christian, while thoroughly accountable to the Old Testament, and the continuing and primary place of Israel in salvation history.

CR1353 Spong, John Shelby, and Jack Daniel Spiro
Dialogue: In Search of Jewish-Christian Understanding. New York, NYU: Seabury Press, 1975. 109 pp. Paper. 0816421153.

The narrative account of a dialogue between a prominent Episcopal clergyman and a rabbi in Richmond, Virginia.

CR1354 Stöhr, Martin, ed.
Jüdische Existenz und die Erneuerung der Christlichen Theologie: Versuch der Bilanz des Christlich-jndischen Dialogs für die Systematische Theologie. (Abhandlungen zum christlich-jüdischen Dialog, 11). Munich, GW: Kaiser, 1981. 242 pp. 3459013761.

Twelve theologians examine the traditions held in common by Judaism and Christianity, and the significance of the state of Israel in light of anti-Semitism and the legacy of Auschwitz.

CR1355 Stanton, Graham N., and Guy G. Stroumsa, eds.
Tolerance and Intolerance in Early Judaism and Christianity. New York, NYU: Cambridge University Press, 1998. xiv, 370 pp. 052159037X.

Nineteen essays by Jewish and Christian scholars on issues of tolerance and intolerance faced by Jews and Christians between 200 B.C.E. and 200 C.E.

CR1356 Stow, Kenneth R.
Alienated Minority: The Jews of Medieval Latin Europe. Cambridge, MAU: Harvard University Press, 1992. 346 pp. 0674015924.

A narrative history, based on secondary sources, surveying Christian-Jewish interactions in Europe from the 5th to the 16th century.

CR1357 Strober, Gerald S.
Portrait of the Elder Brother: Jews and Judaism in Protestant Teaching Materials. New York, NYU: American Jewish Committee; New York, NYU: NCCJ, 1972. 56 pp. Paper. No ISBN.

A summary of findings from a study of the presentation of Jews and Judaism in the teaching materials of ten Protestant denominations and two independent publishing houses in the United States.

CR1358 Svidercoschi, Gian Franco
Letter to a Jewish Friend: The Simple and Extraordinary Story of Pope John Paul II and his Jewish School Friend. Translated by Gregory Dowling. New York, NYU: Crossroad Publishing, 1994. 96 pp. 0824514823.

The story of the wartime (1939-1945) friendship of Karol Wojtyla (Pope John Paul II) and Jerzy Kluger, with a prologue by Christian and Jewish leaders on its significance for Jewish-Roman Catholic relations.

CR1359 Swidler, Leonard J. et al.
Bursting the Bonds?: A Jewish-Christian Dialogue on Jesus and Paul. (Faith Meets Faith Series). Maryknoll, NYU: Orbis Books, 1990. viii, 224 pp. 0883447134 (hdbk), 0883447126 (pbk).

These scholars take seriously the historical fact that both Jesus and Paul were observant Jews, and show how such an approach can correct misunderstandings of both men.

CR1360 Talmage, Frank Ephraim, ed.
Disputation and Dialogue: Readings in the Jewish-Christian Encounter. New York, NYU: KTAV Publishing House, 1975. xix, 411 pp. 0870682849.

A reader for Christians preparing for dialogue, with thirty-three selections on themes of election of the Jews, messiah and Christ, law and gospel, the scepter of Judah, and coexistence; designed to present a cross section of the 2,000-year debate between Judaism and Christianity.

CR1361 Tanenbaum, Marc H., Marvin R. Wilson, and A. James Rudin, eds.
Evangelicals and Jews in an Age of Pluralism. Lanham, MDU: University Press of America, 1990. 285 pp. Paper. 0819176699.

A reprint of the 1984 Baker Book House edition of papers detailing the growing relationship between evangelical Christians and the Jewish community; originally presented at the second National Conference of Evangelicals and Jews (1980, Trinity Evangelical Divinity School).

CR1362 Tanenbaum, Marc H., Marvin R. Wilson, and A. James Rudin, eds.
Evangelicals and Jews in Conversation on Scripture, Theology, and History. Grand Rapids, MIU: Baker Books, 1978. xvi, 326 pp. 0801088348.

Papers from an important National Conference of Evangelical Christians and Jews.

CR1363 Taylor, Miriam S.
Anti-Judaism and Early Christian Identity: A Critique of the Scholarly Consensus. (Studia Post-Biblica, 46). Leiden, NE: Brill, 1995. ix, 207 pp. 9004101861.

A scholarly argument that patristic writers sought to distinguish Christianity from Judaism, rather than to provide polemic for an early church rivalry with Jews for converts.

CR1364 *The Theology of the Churches and the Jewish People: Statements by the World Council of Churches and Its Member Churches.*
Geneva, SZ: WCC, 1988. ix,186 pp. Paper. 2825409324.

A compilation of WCC and member church statements on Jewish-Christian relations (1948-1987), with an analysis of the theological issues raised.

CR1365 Thoma, Clemens
Christliche Theologie des Judentums. (Der Christ in der Welt VI, 4a/b). Aschaffenburg, GW: Pattloch, 1978. 300 pp. Paper. 3557941809.

A comprehensive theological assessment of Judaism, providing a very well-informed overview of different streams of Jewish thought.

CR1366 Thoma, Clemens
Theologische Beziehungen zwischen Christentum und Judentum. (WB-Forum, 35). Darmstadt, GW: Wissenschaftliche Buchgesellschaft, 1989. ix, 174 pp. Paper. 3534800494.

An analysis of the theological relationships between Christianity and Judaism—present and future points of separation and coming together—by the Professor of Biblical Studies and Judaism at the Theological Faculty, Lucerne, Switzerland, and Director of an Institute for Jewish-Christian research.

CR1367 Thoma, Clemens
Die theologischen Beziehungen zwischen Christentum und Judentum. (Grundzüge, 44). Darmstadt, GW: Wissenschaftliche Buchgesellschaft, 1982. ix, 174 pp. Paper. 3534085566.

This monograph gives a short historical and theological summary of Jewish-Christian contacts, from the beginnings of Christianity to modern times.

CR—CHRISTIANITY AND OTHER RELIGIONS

CR1368 Thoma, Clemens, and Michael Wyschogrod, eds.

Parable and Story in Judaism and Christianity. Mahwah, NJU: Paulist Press, 1989. vi, 258 pp. Paper. 0809130874.

A series of essays interpreting and examining selected parables from both Jewish and Christian experience, to discover ways they can enrich understanding; by renowned experts in biblical parable and narrative.

CR1369 Thoma, Clemens, and Michael Wyschogrod, eds.

Understanding Scripture: Explorations of Jewish and Christian Traditions of Interpretation. (A Stimulus Book). New York, NYU: Paulist Press, 1987. viii, 167 pp. Paper. 080912873X.

Ten papers originally presented in the discussion between Catholic and Jewish theologians at the symposium on "The Authority and Interpretation of Scripture in Judaism and Christianity" held in Lucerne, Switzerland, January 1984.

CR1370 Thoma, Clemens, ed.

Judentum und christlicher Glaube: Zum Dialog zwischen Christen und Juden. Vienna, AU: Klosterneuburger Buch- und Kunstverlag, 1965. 230 pp. Paper. No ISBN.

Essays by six authors on different aspects of the Jewish-Christian dialogue, including ecumenism and Christian anti-Semitism.

CR1371 Thompson, Norma H., and Bruce K. Cole, eds.

The Future of Jewish-Christian Relations. Schenectady, NYU: Character Research Press, 1982. xxi, 280 pp. 0915744279 (hdbk), 0915744287 (pbk).

Thirteen scholarly essays reflecting Christian-Jewish dialogue on issues of social justice, the Holocaust, future Jewish-Christian relations, tensions arising from mission and liturgy, and educational attitudes.

CR1372 Ucko, Hans

Common Roots—New Horizons: Learning about Christian Faith from Dialogue with Jews. (Risk Book Series, 61). Geneva, SZ: WCC Publications, 1994. xi, 100 pp. Paper. 2825411280.

A popular introduction to common Jewish and Christian themes by the WCC's executive secretary for Christian-Jewish relations.

CR1373 Ucko, Hans, ed.

The Jubilee Challenge: Utopia or Possibility?: Jewish and Christian Insights. Geneva, SZ: WCC Publications, 1997. vii, 197 pp. Paper. 2825412317.

Eighteen essays on the concept of jubilee; that have grown out of the Jewish-Christian dialogue at the WCC's Ecumenical Institute in Bossey, Switzerland.

CR1374 Ucko, Hans, ed.

People of God, Peoples of God: A Jewish-Christian Conversation in Asia. Geneva, SZ: WCC Publications, 1996. xxiii, 112 pp. Paper. 2825411728.

A first collection of essays on several areas in which Asian Christians and Jews could meet and share experiences, including papers presented at an Asian Christian-Jewish conference held in Cochin, India, in November 1993.

CR1375 Van Buren, Paul Mathews

A Theology of the Jewish-Christian Reality. New York, NYU: Seabury Press, 1980-1988. 3 vols. No ISBN.

A trilogy, by the Professor of Religious Studies at Temple University, arguing that the continuing witness to God of the Jewish people requires, for Christians, a new systematic theology concerning the nature of God, revelation, Christ, the Bible, the Trinity, the church, and hope; [I, *Discerning the Way*, 1980, 207 pp., 0816401241; II, *A Christian Theology of the People Israel*, 1983, xvii, 362 pp., 0816405484 (hdbk), 0816424772 (pbk); III, *Christ in Context*, 1988, xv, 312 pp.].

CR1376 Vasko, Timo

Die dritte Position: der jüdisch-christliche Dialog bei Schalom Ben-Chorin bis 1945. (Missiologian ja ekumeniikan seuran julkaisuja, 48). Helsinki, FI: Missiologian ja ekumeniikan seura, 1985. 379 pp. Paper. 9519520732.

An analysis of the contribution of the noted Jewish scholar, Schalom Ben-Chorin, to Jewish-Christian dialogue through 1945; originally submitted as a thesis at the University of Helsinki.

CR1377 Vogel, Rolf

Ernst Ludwig Ehrlich und der christlich-jüdische Dialog. Frankfurt am Main, GW: Josef Knecht, 1984. 206 pp. Paper. 378200504X.

An extended interview and a collection of essays on the contemporary Christian-Jewish dialogue movement by the European director of B'nai B'rith.

CR1378 Wiesel, Elie, and Albert H. Friedlander

The Six Days of Destruction: Meditations toward Hope. Mahwah, NJU: Paulist Press, 1988. viii, 112 pp. Paper. 0809104091 (hdbk), 080912999X (pbk).

Six chronicles of the Holocaust with liturgies for meditation of the Shoah, meant to be used by both Jews and Christians.

CR1379 Wigoder, Geoffrey

Jewish-Christian Relations Since the Second World War. Manchester, ENK: Manchester University Press, 1988. viii, 176 pp. 0719026393.

Lectures summarizing Christian attitudes toward Judaism and the Jews in the last forty years, Jewish attitudes toward the dialogue, and imputs from the Vatican and Israel, with key Vatican and WCC documents.

CR1380 Willebrands, J. G. M.

Church and Jewish People: New Considerations. New York, NYU: Paulist Press, 1992. xvi, 280 pp. 0809104563.

A collection of addresses and writings, 1974 to 1990, on relations between Christians and Jews; by Johannes Cardinal Willebrands, President of the Vatican Secretariat for Promoting Christian Unity and the Pontifical Council for Religious Relations with the Jews.

CR1381 Williamson, Clark M.

A Guest in the House of Israel: Post-Holocaust Church Theology. Louisville, KYU: Westminster John Knox, 1993. viii, 344 pp. Paper. 0664254543.

Beginning with official church statements on Christianity and Judaism (both Protestant and Catholic since World War II), the Professor of Theology at Christian Theological Seminary in Indianapolis restates central themes of the Christian faith with sensitivity to Jewish outlooks.

CR1382 Williamson, Clark M.

Has God Rejected His People?: Anti-Judaism in the Christian Church. Nashville, TN: Abingdon, 1982. 190 pp. Paper. 0687166497.

A critique of the alleged bases of anti-Semitism in scripture and church history.

CR—CHRISTIANITY AND OTHER RELIGIONS

CR1383 Williamson, Clark M.

When Jews and Christians Meet: A Guide for Christian Preaching and Teaching. St. Louis, MOU: Chalice Press, 1989. 126 pp. Paper. 0827242247.

An introduction to issues of Christian-Jewish coexistence from varied perspectives (biblical, theological, historical, and sociological), proposing new ways to envisage relationships between the two groups.

CR1384 Wilson, Marvin R.

Our Father Abraham: Jewish Roots of the Christian Faith. Grand Rapids, MIU: Eerdmans, 1989. xxi, 374 pp. Paper. 0802804233.

A biblical, historical, and cultural study of the Hebrew foundations of the Christian faith that calls Christians to reexamine their Jewish roots so that they might be able to effect a more authentically biblical lifestyle; by the Professor of Biblical and Theological Studies at Gordon College, Wenham, Massachusetts.

CR1385 Wilson, Stephen G.

Related Strangers: Jews and Christians 70-170 C.E. Minneapolis, MNU: Fortress Press, 1995. xvi, 416 pp. Paper. 0800629507.

A comprehensive survey of early Christian-Jewish relations based on a wide range of Christian and Jewish writings of the period.

CR1386 Wood, Diana, ed.

Christianity and Judaism: Papers Read at the 1991 Summer Meeting and the 1992 Winter Meeting of the Ecclesiatical History Society. (Studies in Church History, 29). Oxford, ENK: Blackwell Publishers, 1992. xvii, 493 pp. 063118497X.

Thirty-two scholarly historical case studies of Christian-Jewish relations, from the Byzantine Empire to Croatia during World War II.

CR1387 Wood, James Edward, ed.

Jewish-Christian Relations in Today's World. Waco, TXU: Baylor University Press, 1971. 164 pp. No ISBN.

Seven scholarly essays on the history of Jewish-Christian relations in the 20th century, with a selected and annotated bibliography.

CR1388 Zannoni, Arthur E., ed.

Jews and Christians Speak of Jesus. Minneapolis, MNU: Fortress Press, 1994. xiv, 191 pp. Paper. 0800628047.

Eight essays by Jewish and Christian scholars, presented in 1993 in symposia sponsored by the Center for Jewish-Christian Learning at the University of St. Thomas (St. Paul and Minneapolis, Minnesota).

CR1389 Zuidema, Willem

Gods Partner: ontmoeting met het jodendom. Baarn, NE: Ten Have, 1977. 289 pp. 902594115X.

This pleasing introduction to Judaism from a Christian standpoint grew out of innumerable conversations with Jews all around the world, who mostly speak for themselves.

CR1390 Zuidema, Willem

God's Partner: An Encounter with Judaism. London, ENK: SCM Press, 1987. 272 pp. Paper. 033400568X.

English translation.

CR1391 Zuidema, Willem

Gottes Partner: Begegnung mit dem Judentum. Neukirchen-Vluyn, GW: Neukirchener Verlag, 1983. 282 pp. 3788707003.

German translation.

Missions to Jews

See also CR5-CR6, and EU238.

CR1392 Aring, Paul Gerhard

Christen und Juden heute—und die "Judenmission"? Geschichte und Theologie protestantischer Judenmission in Deutschland, dargestellt und untersucht am Beispiel des Protestantismus im mittleren Deutschland. Frankfurt/M., GW: Haag und Herchen, 1987. x, 426 pp. Paper. 3892283958.

A critical analysis of the theological justification for the Protestant "mission to the Jews" and its historical development in Germany.

CR1393 Aring, Paul Gerhard

Christliche Judenmission: Ihre Geschichte und Problematik dargestellt und untersucht am Beispiel des evangelischen Rheinlandes. (Forschungen zum jüdisch-christlichen Dialog, 4). Neukirchen-Vluyn, GW: Neukirchener Verlag, 1980. ix, 283 pp. Paper. 3788706171.

A history of the relationship between the Protestant Church of the Rhineland and Jews in the 19th and 20th centuries.

CR1394 Bass, Martin Levi

Jesus für Israel: Aus Leben und Botschaft eines Judenmissionars. (Erlanger Taschenbücher, 46). Erlangen, GW: Ev.-Luth. Mission, 1978. 117 pp. Paper. 3872140949.

Biographical notes about, and lectures and sermons by, M. L. Bass (1906-1971), a convert from Judaism who wanted to build a bridge between Christians and Jews.

CR1395 Bastiaanse, J. F. L.

De Jodenzending en de eerste decennia van de Hervormde Raad voor Kerk en Israël, 1925-1965: Een generatie in dienst van de Joods-Christelijke toenadering (Proefschrift Rijksuniversiteit Leiden). Zoetermeer, NE: Boekencentrum, 1995. xxiii, 1163 pp. Paper. 9023900723.

A doctoral dissertation describing the history of the Mission to the Jews (1925-1941), and of the Council for Church and Israel of the Netherlands Reformed Church (1945-1965), showing the Jewish-Christian drawing together after the war.

CR1396 Chazan, Robert

Daggers of Faith: Thirteenth-Century Christian Missionizing and Jewish Response. Berkeley, CAU: University of California Press, 1989. vii, 226 pp. 1520062973.

A detailed account of Christian missions to Jews in 13th-century Europe and of Jewish responses to such missionizing, especially to the Christians' "Innovative Argumentation" and the *pugio fidei* (dagger of faith).

CR1397 Clark, Christopher M.

The Politics of Conversion: Missionary Protestantism and the Jews in Prussia, 1728-1941. Oxford, ENK: Clarendon Press, 1995. viii, 340 pp. 0198204566.

A scholarly analysis of two centuries of Protestant attempts to convert Jews in Prussia, and of the theological debates concerning those efforts.

CR—CHRISTIANITY AND OTHER RELIGIONS

CR1398 Cohen, Martin A., and Helga Croner, eds.
Christian Mission-Jewish Mission. (Studies in Judaism and Christianity). New York, NYU: Paulist Press, 1982. vi, 216 pp. Paper. 0809124750.

Eight scholarly essays exploring Jewish, Protestant, and Catholic historical and contemporary understandings of mission, including those of Christian churches toward the Jews, with essays by C. S. Song and Kwesi A. Dickson on the meaning of mission for churches in Asia and Africa.

CR1399 Conference on World Evangelization (Pattaya, Thailand, 1980)
The Thailand Report on Jewish People: Report of the ... Mini-Consultation on Reaching Jewish People. (Lausanne Occasional Papers, 7). Wheaton, ILU: LCWE, 1980. 24 pp. Paper. No ISBN.

A brief analysis of the why, what and how of Christian witness to Jews.

CR1400 De Ridder, Richard
My Heart's Desire for Israel: Reflections on Jewish-Christian Relationships and Evangelism Today. Nutley, NJU: Presbyterian & Reformed Publishing, 1974. xi, 126 pp. Paper. No ISBN.

Lectures on biblical answers to the question, "What relationship does God call for between Jew and Gentile in Christ?"

CR1401 Den danske Israelsmission
Den danske Israelsmission 1885-1975: Et jubilμumsskrift med glimt fra 90 srs missionshistorie. Copenhagen, DK: Den danske Israelsmission, 1975. 32 pp. Paper. No ISBN.

This booklet celebrates ninety years of Danish mission to Israel.

CR1402 Edvardsson, Lars
Kyrka och Judendom: Svensk judemission med särskild hänsyn till Svenska Isrealmissionens verksamhet 1875-1975. (Acta Universitatis Lundensis: I, 24; Bibliotheca Hisorico-Ecclesiastica Lundensis, 6). Lund, SW: Gleerup, 1976. 194 pp. 9140042170.

A doctoral dissertation on the Swedish mission among Jews, 1875-1975, with a summary in German.

CR1403 Eichhorn, David Max
Evangelizing the American Jew. Middle Village, NYU: Jonathan David, 1978. v, 210 pp. 0824602250.

Written by a Jewish author, this well-indexed book contains twelve documented chapters stressing the continuity of sometimes unwelcome Christian attempts to convert Jews to Christianity (1607-present), including specific denominational efforts toward that purpose.

CR1404 Endelman, Todd M., ed.
Jewish Apostasy in the Modern World. New York, NYU: Holmes and Meier, 1987. ix, 344 pp. 0841910294.

Twelve scholarly essays on missions to Jews in Europe and America, from 18th century to the present, and the dynamics of conversion/apostasy.

CR1405 Fieldsend, John
Messianic Jews: Challenging Church and Synagogue. Tunbridge Wells, ENK: Monarch Publications, 1993. 160 pp. Paper. 1854242288.

A popular introduction to the Messianic Jewish movement.

CR1406 Fischer, John
The Olive Tree Connection. Downers Grove, ILU: InterVarsity, 1983. 209 pp. Paper. 0877848483.

A popular guide for Christians wishing to witness to Jews by the deputy secretary in America for the International Hebrew Christian Alliance; originally published as *Sharing Israel's Messiah* (The Watchman Association, 1978).

CR1407 Goble, Phillip E.
Everything You Need to Grow a Messianic Yeshiva. South Pasadena, CAU: William Carey Library, 1981. xiii, 298 pp. Paper. 087808181X.

A comprehensive evangelistic tool designed to further the planting and growth of Messianic synagogues; a revision of *Everything You Need to Grow a Messianic Synagogue* (William Carey Library, 1974).

CR1408 Hornung, Andreas
Messianische Juden swischen Kirche und Volk Isreal: Entwicklung und Begründung ihres Selbstverständnisses. (Monographien und Studienbücher). Giessen, GW: Brunnen-Verlag, 1995. xvii, 125 pp. 3765593974.

A study of the history, theology, and witness of Messianic Jews of the Reformed tradition.

CR1409 Huisjen, Albert
The Home Front of Jewish Missions. Grand Rapids, MIU: Baker Books, 1962. 222 pp. No ISBN.

Principles, motivation and methods for mission and evangelism among those of Jewish faith by one who served in that field for thirty-two years.

CR1410 Kjær-Hansen, Kai
Joseph Rabinowitz and the Messianic Movement: The Herzl of Jewish Christianity. Translated by David Stoner and Birger Petterson. Edinburgh, ENK: Handsel Press; Grand Rapids, MIU: Eerdmans, 1995. x, 262 pp. Paper. 1871828376 (UK), 080280859X (US).

A scholarly biography of Joseph Rabinowitz (1837-1899), pioneer leader of Messianic Judaism, with an assessment of his contribution; by the international coordinator of the Lausanne Consultation on Jewish Evangelism; originally published in Danish in 1988.

CR1411 Kjær-Hansen, Kai, and Ole Chr. M. Kvarme
Messianische Juden: Judenchristen in Israel. Translated by Niels Peter Moritze, and Arnulf H. Baumann. (Erlanger Taschenbücher, 67). Erlangen, GW: Ev.-Luth. Mission, 1983. 194 pp. Paper. 3872141562.

German translation.

CR1412 Kjær-Hansen, Kai, and Ole Chr. M. Kvarme
Messianiske Jøder: En præsentation af de kristne jøder i Israel. Christiansfeld, DK: Svanne, 1979. 159 pp. 8785190624.

A study of the status, problems, and opportunities of Jewish Christians in Israel.

CR1413 Kremers, Heinz, ed.
Mission an Israel in heilsgeschichtlicher Sicht. Neukirchen-Vluyn, GW: Neukirchener Verlag, 1985. 134 pp. Paper. 3788707461.

A collection of essays on the attitudes and witness of Protestant Christians to Jews in Germany today.

CR1414 Kuiper, Arie de
Israël tussen zending en oecumene. (Proefschrift Theol. Fac. Rijksuniversiteit Utrecht). Wageningen, NE: Veenman, 1964. x, 190 pp. Paper. No ISBN.

The Christian church has to witness toward the Jews about Christ as Messiah, but has to learn from, and cooperate with, Judaism at the same time.

CR1415 Kvarme, Ole Chr. M., ed.
Let Jews and Arabs Hear His Voice: Christian Life and Ministry in the Encounter with Jews and Arabs in Israel Today. Jerusalem, IS: United Christian Council in Israel, 1981. 138 pp. Paper. No ISBN.

Ten essays on Christian life and ministry in the encounter with Jews and Arabs in Israel; originally presented 1976-1979 to annual conferences of the United Christian Council in Israel.

CR1416 Riggans, Walter
Yeshua Ben David: Why Do the Jewish People Reject Jesus as Their Messiah? Crowborough, ENK: MARC, 1995. 428 pp. Paper. 1854242873.

Systematic helps for Christians desiring to share their faith with Jews, and to understand Jewish rejections of Jesus as Messiah; by the General Director of the Church's Ministry among the Jews (CMJ).

CR1417 Rosen, Moishe, and Ceil Rosen
Share the New Life with a Jew. Chicago, ILU: Moody, 1976. 80 pp. Paper. 0802478980.

A handbook for evangelicals longing to witness to Jewish friends by the executive director of Jews for Jesus.

CR1418 Sigal, Gerald
The Jew and the Christian Missionary: A Jewish Response to Missionary Christianity. New York, NYU: KTAV Publishing House, 1981. xix, 311 pp. 0870688863.

A Jewish rebuttal of fundamentalist Protestant interpretations of sixty-eight passages of Scripture used by missionaries to Jews.

CR1419 Sobel, B. Zui
Hebrew Christianity: The Thirteenth Tribe. (A Wiley-Interscience Series). New York, NYU: Wiley, 1974. xi, 413 pp. 0471810258.

The first sociological study of the Hebrew-Christian movement, including Jews for Jesus in the United States and Israel, placed in the historical perspective of the 19th-century Christian efforts to evangelize the Jews.

CR1420 Telchin, Stan
Abandoned: What Is God's Will for the Jewish People and the Church? Grand Rapids, MIU: Chosen Books, 1997. 272 pp. Paper. 0800792491.

A theology and strategy for mission to Jews by one who believes that Yeshua is the Messiah.

CR1421 Verkuyl, Johannes, and Johan M. Snoek
Inter beraad in verband met de relatie tussen Kerk en Israel. Kampen, NE: Kok, 1988. 134 pp. 9024242363.

Background material for the training of Christian missionaries being sent to Israel, with an overview of biblical and historical relations between Jews and Christians, and of the need for mutual conversion in attitudes (Jews and Christians, Jews and Palestinians).

Christianity and Japanese Religions
See also CR187, CR438, CR713, AS648, AS663, and AS676.

CR1422 Dale, Kenneth J.
Circle of Harmony: A Case Study in Popular Japanese Buddhism with Implications for Christian Mission. South Pasadena, CAU: William Carey Library, 1975. xviii, 211 pp. 087808424X.

A detailed analysis of the daily practice of discussion and dialogue (*hoza*) of the Japanese new religious movement Rissho Koseikai, which is a key to its growth and a challenge to the Christian church; with a chapter by Susumu Akahoshi.

CR1423 Doi, Masatoshi
Search for Meaning through Interfaith Dialogue. Kyoto, JA: Kyobunkwan Book Company, 1976. 202 pp. No ISBN.

Essays on the theology of meaning as an introduction to the theology of mission, and on the types of interreligious encounter in Japan; by the Professor of Systematic Theology and History of Christian Thought at Doshisha University, and Director of the NCC Center for the Study of Japanese Religions.

CR1424 Earhart, H. Byron
Japanese Religion: Unity and Diversity. (Religious Life of Man). Belmont, CAU: Wadsworth Publishing, 1982. xii, 272 pp. Paper. 0534010288.

An introduction to persistent themes in Japanese religion through three historical periods and the changing patterns of the various religious traditions (Buddhism, Neo-Confucianism, Shinto, New Religions, and Christianity).

CR1425 Earhart, H. Byron
The New Religions of Japan: A Bibliography of Western-Language Materials. Tokyo, JA: Sophia University, 1970. xi, 96 pp. No ISBN.

An introduction to the new Japanese religions; with an annotated bibliography of 810 books and articles published since 1945 in various European languages.

CR1426 Eilert, Håkan
I regnbågens tecken: Dialoger, reflektioner, utmaningar. Stockholm, SW: Verbum, 1989. 191 pp. 9152616436.

A theological study on interfaith dialogue in a Japanese context.

CR1427 Ellwood, Robert S.
The Eagle and the Rising Sun: Americans and the New Religions of Japan. Philadelphia, PAU: Westminster Press, 1974. 224 pp. 0664207073.

An introduction to the history, forms of worship, teachings, and life in North America, of five new religions of Japan.

CR1428 Hayama Missionary Seminar (30th, 1989)
Showa, X-Day, and Beyond. Edited by Fritz Sprunger. Tokyo, JA: Amagi Sanso, 1989. v, 98 pp. Paper. No ISBN.

Eight papers that focus on the challenges of relating Christian mission to the changing times in Japan brought about by the passing of the Showa Era (the reign of Emperor Hirohito (1926-1989)), and the beginning of the reign of Emperor Akihito.

CR1429 Morioka, Kiyomi
Religion in Changing Japanese Society. Tokyo, JA: University of Tokyo Press, 1975. xvi, 231 pp. 0860081311.

A synthesis of twenty-five years of empirical studies of Japanese religion, focusing on the impact of population shifts, and of changes in family structure on Shrine Shinto, Buddhism, and Christianity.

CR1430 Murakami, Shigeyoshi
Japanese Religion in the Modern Century. Translated by H. Byron Earhart. Tokyo, JA: University of Tokyo Press, 1980. xvii, 186 pp. 0860082601.

English translation of *Nihon Hyakunen no Shukyo* (Kodansha 1968), a detailed analysis of the relationship of religion in Japan, to prevailing political, economic, and social conditions from the Meiji Restoration of 1868 to 1968.

CR1431 Norbeck, Edward
Religion and Society in Modern Japan: Continuity and Change. (Rice University Studies Monograph in Anthropology, 56, no. 1). Houston, TXU: William Marsh Rice University, 1970. vii, 232 pp. No ISBN.

An interpretation of the state of religion in modern Japan in its relationship to social and other cultural conditions that influence its forms and functions; with appendices on four of the new religions.

CR1432 Reader, Ian
Religion in Contemporary Japan. Honolulu, HIU: University of Hawaii Press, 1991. xv, 277 pp. Paper. 0824813537 (hdbk), 0824813545 (pbk).

A scholarly study of the role religion plays in contemporary Japanese society (rituals, the social system, beliefs and values), with a series of case studies of religion in action.

CR1433 Reader, Ian, Esben Andreasen, and Finn Stefansson
Japanese Religions: Past and Present. Honolulu, HIU: University of Hawaii Press; Folkestone, ENK: Japan Library, 1993. 189 pp. Paper. 0824815459 (H hdbk), 0824815467 (H pbk), 187341000X (J hdbk), 1873410018 (J pbk).

An overview of the entire range of contemporary Japanese religions (folk religion, Shinto, Buddhism, Christianity, and the "new" religions).

CR1434 Rzepkowski, Horst
Thomas von Aquin und Japan: Versuch einer Begegnung. (Studia Instituti Missiologici SVD, 9). St. Augustin, GW: Steyler Verlag, 1967. 75 pp. Paper. No ISBN.

A study of the possibility of an encounter between the philosophy and theology of Thomas Aquinas and Japanese ways of thinking.

CR1435 Shimizu, Masumi
Das "Selbst" im Mahayana-Buddhismus in japanischer Sicht und die "Person" Christentum im Licht des Neuen Testaments. (Beihefte der Zeitschrift für Religions- und Geistesgeschichte, 22). Leiden, NE: Brill, 1981. x, 223 pp. 9004064702.

Within the framework of Buddhist-Christian dialogue, the author compares and contrasts the Eastern understanding of the "True Self" with the Western idea of the "Person," in light of Johannine and Pauline writings; originally published as a thesis for the Friedrich Wilhelm Universität in 1979.

Christianity and Sikhism

CR1436 Cole, W. Owen, and Piara Singh Sambhi
Sikhism and Christianity: A Comparative Study. New York, NYU: St. Martin's Press, 1993. xii, 221 pp. 0312103654.

An exploration of the Sikh religion—its beliefs, practices, values, and parallels with Christianity.

CR1437 Cole, W. Owen, and Piara Singh Sambhi
The Sikhs: Their Religious Beliefs and Practices. (Library of

Beliefs and Practices). London, ENK: Routledge, 1978. xxvii, 210 pp. 0710088426 (hdbk), 0710088434 (pbk).

A multidimensional introduction to the Sikh faith developed out of the authors' own sharings as religious scholars in England.

CR1438 Gidoomal, Ram, and Margaret Wardell
Lions, Princesses, Gurus: Reaching your Sikh Neighbor. Godalming, STK: Highland Books, 1996. 224 pp. Paper. 1897913354.

Practical guidance for Christian witness to Sikhs.

CR1439 Webster, John C. B., ed.
Popular Religion in the Punjab Today. Delhi, II: ISPCK, 1974. 149 pp. Paper. No ISBN.

Twenty essays surveying religious beliefs, practices, and organizations in the Punjab; originally presented at a 1973 seminar on "Popular Religion in the Punjab Today."

Christianity and Various Other Religions

See also CR391, CR517, CR543, CR711, SO375, AM626, AM1131, AM1318, AM1468-AM1469, AS673, AS1331, AS1337, OC200, and OC224.

CR1440 Bailey, Keith M.
Strange Gods: Responding to the Rise of Spirit Worship in America. Camp Hill, PAU: Christian Publications, 1998. xii, 242 pp. Paper. 0875097707.

A Christian and Missionary Alliance pastor and missionary, in this introduction to animism and Native American religions, calls for a fresh affirmation of biblical truth as an antidote to the resurgence of Native American religions, and of New Age teachings in North America.

CR1441 Bastide, Roger
Les religions africaines au Brésil: Vers une sociologie des interpénétrations de civilisations. (Bibliothèque de sociologie contemporaine). Paris, FR: Presses universitaires de France, 1960. 578 pp. No ISBN.

The major work by the outstanding French sociologist of religion, analyzing within a single conceptual framework the historical, social, and religious dynamics of Afro-Brazilian religions.

CR1442 Buck, Christopher
Paradise and Paradigm: Key Symbols in Persian Christianity and the Baha'i Faith. Albany, NYU: SUNY Press, 1999. xvii, 402 pp. 0791440613 (hdbk), 0791440621 (pbk).

A comparison of the hymns of the great poet of early Christianity, Saint Ephrem the Syrian, and the imagistic writings of the late nineteenth century founder of the Persian Baha'i religion, Baha'u'llah; the symbolic center of compassion is the family of symbols having to do with paradise.

CR1443 Burnett, David
Unearthly Powers: A Christian's Handbook on Primal and Folk Religions. Nashville, TNU: Nelson, 1992. 288 pp. Paper. 0840796129.

The first American edition of a textbook designed to help the ordinary missionary, evangelist, and Christian to understand the complexity of rituals and symbols in primal religions, relating them to the biblical worldview; originally published in 1988 (London: Monarch Publications).

CR1444 Conference on World Evangelization (Pattaya, Thailand, 1980)

The Thailand Report on Traditional Religionists (Asia and Oceania): Report of the ... Mini-Consultation on Reaching Traditional Religionists (Asia and Oceania). (Lausanne Occasional Papers, 16). Wheaton, ILU: LCWE, 1980. 19 pp. Paper. No ISBN.

Helps for Christian witness (message and method) to traditional religionists of Asia and Oceania.

CR1445 Conference on World Evangelization (Pattaya, Thailand, 1980)

The Thailand Report on Traditional Religionists of Latin America and Caribbean: Report of the ... Mini-Consultation on Christian Witness to Traditional Religionists of Latin America and Caribbean. (Lausanne Occasional Papers, 17). Wheaton, ILU: LCWE, 1980. 20 pp. Paper. No ISBN.

Presuppositions of a Latin American mission strategy, with five case studies.

CR1446 Cox, Harvey Gallagher

Turning East: The Promise and Peril of the New Orientalism. New York, NYU (1977): Simon and Schuster; London, ENK (1979): Allen Lane, 1979. 192 pp. 067122851X (US), 0713911808 (UK).

Reflections by the noted Harvard University theologian on the fascination of many Westerners with Eastern religions, based on his own personal experience with the spirituality and devotees of these faiths.

CR1447 Ferguson, John

Gods Many and Lords Many: A Study in Primal Religions. Guildford, ENK: Lutterworth Educational, 1982. viii, 118 pp. Paper. 0718824962.

Using the creation myth and others like it, the President of Selly Oak Colleges in Birmingham, England, introduces the reader to countless expressions of faith in diverse parts of Africa, Australia, Asia, and the Americas.

CR1448 Jaoudi, Maria

Christian Mysticism East and West: What the Masters Teach Us. Mahwah, NJU: Paulist Press, 1998. v, 166 pp. Paper. 0809138239.

A scholar, mother, artist, and seeker of God explores mysticism across Hindu, Buddhist, Sufi, and Christian boundaries.

CR1449 Lieu, Samuel N. C.

Manichaeism in the Later Roman Empire and Medieval China: A Historical Survey. Manchester, NHU: Manchester University Press, 1985. xiii, 360 pp. 0719010888.

A detailed study of Manichaen missions in their spread from Mesopotamia to China, with reference to Christian influences and interactions.

CR1450 Marzal, Manuel M.

El Sincretismo Iberoamericano: Un estudio comparativo sobre los quechuas (Cusco), los mayas (Chiapas) y los africanos (Bahía). Lima, PE: Pontificia Universidad Católica del Peru, 1988. 235 pp. No ISBN.

Second edition of an academic investigation into syncretism in Latin America, defined as indigenous or black persons who were baptized and accepted the Christianity imposed by the missionaries, but who retained many elements of their original religion; with three case studies of the Quechua of Cusco,

Peru, the Maya of Chiapas, Mexico, and Africans of Bahía, Brazil.

CR1451 Maurier, Henri

Essai d'une théologie du paganisme. Paris, FR: Éditions de l'Orante, 1965. 327 pp. Paper. No ISBN.

Missionary practice and insight with sound theological thinking and knowledge on the question of the significance and theological value of pagan religions.

CR1452 Maurier, Henri

Theologie des Heidentums: Ein Versuch. Cologne, GW: Bachem, 1967. 293 pp. No ISBN.

German translation.

CR1453 Sabet, Huschmand

The Heavens are Cleft Asunder. Oxford, ENK: Ronald, 1975. xiii, 153 pp. 0853980551 (hdbk), 085398056X (pbk).

A layperson's presentation to Christians of the Baha'i faith, hailing it as the "rational faith" for modern humanity.

CR1454 Schaefer, Udo

The Light Shineth in Darkness: Five Studies in Revelation after Christ. Oxford, ENK: George Ronald, 1977. xi, 195 pp. 0853980721.

A translation, with new introduction of five studies of the Baha'i faith by a German lawyer, himself a Baha'i; originally published as *Wes es heisst, Baha'i zu Sein,* 1973; *Das missverstandene Religion,* 1968; *Baha'i Briefe,* 1969; and *Baha'i— Religion nach Mass?* 1970.

CR1455 Simpson, George Eaton

Black Religions in the New World. New York, NYU: Columbia University Press, 1978. ix, 415 pp. 0231045409.

A detailed study of black religious movements in the Caribbean and South America, their relation to African beliefs, and the economic and social environments in which they grew, by a scholar who has devoted four years to such study.

CR1456 Sontag, Frederick

Sun Myung Moon und die Vereinigungskirche. Krefeld, GW: SINUS Verlag, 1981. 191 pp. 3882898011.

German translation.

CR1457 Steyne, Philip M.

Gods of Power: A Study of the Beliefs and Practices of Animists. Houston, TXU: Touch Publications, 1990. 224 pp. Paper. No ISBN.

A thorough anthology of the beliefs and practices of animists, written to make Christian workers aware of the context in which they are seeking to apply the Christian message, and to propose a methodology for use in mission situations.

CR1458 Taylor, John B., ed.

Primal World-Views: Christian Involvement in Dialogue with Traditional Thought Forms. Ibadan, NR: Daystar Press, 1976. viii, 131 pp. No ISBN.

The report of an international conference on this theme, held at the Institute of Church and Society, Ibadan, Nigeria in September 1973, sponsored by the WCC's Subunit on Dialogue with People of Living Faiths and Ideologies.

CR1459 Townshend, George

The Heart of the Gospel, or, The Bible and the Baha'i Faith. Oxford, ENK: Ronald, 1995. 150 pp. 0853980209.

A Baha'i view of the Bible by the former Canon at St. Patrick's Cathedral in Dublin; originally published in 1939.

CR—CHRISTIANITY AND OTHER RELIGIONS

CR1460 Tweed, Thomas A., and Stephen Prothero, eds.
Asian Religions in America: A Documentary History. New York, NYU: Oxford University Press, 1999. xvi, 416 pp. Paper. 019511339X.

Ranging from 1784 to the present, this book reveals the depth and breadth of the American encounter with Asian religions through excerpts and illustrations drawn from literature, art, music, sports, philosophy, theology, politics, and law.

CR1461 Van Rheenen, Gailyn
Communicating Christ in Animistic Contexts. Grand Rapids, MIU: Baker Books, 1991. 342 pp. Paper. 0801093120.

A detailed analysis of animistic worldviews, practices, and powers, contrasting them with biblical perspectives; originally presented as a D.Miss. thesis at Trinity Evangelical Divinity School.

Cults and Sects

See also CR842, SO272, SO275, SO385-SO386, SO621, and AM1340.

CR1462 Avery, Valeen Tippetts
From Mission to Madness: Last Son of the Mormon Prophet. Urbana, ILU: University of Illinois Press, 1998. xii, 357 pp. Paper. 0252023994 (hdbk), 0252067010 (pbk).

A meticulously researched study of a poet, painter, singer, philosopher, naturalist, and effective missionary for the Reorganized Church of Jesus Christ and the Latter Day Saints; includes his struggle with mental illness until his death.

CR1463 Benkovic, Johnette S.
The New Age Counterfeit. Milford, OHU: Riehle Foundation, 1995. xii, 131 pp. Paper. 1877678368.

A Catholic laywoman's help for Christians to understand the many-faceted New Age movement; prepared as a thirteen-week study guide.

CR1464 Bowman, Robert M.
Jehovah's Witnesses. (Zondervan Guide to Cults and Religious Movements). Grand Rapids, MIU: Zondervan, 1995. 85 pp. Paper. 0310704111.

A concise guide for evangelical Christians desiring to witness to Jehovah's Witnesses.

CR1465 Braswell, George W.
Understanding Sectarian Groups in America. Nashville, TNU: Broadman, 1994. vii, 375 pp. Paper. 0805410473.

A revised edition of the author's guide to the history, major teachings, practices, and differences from historic Christianity, of Mormons, Jehovah's Witnesses, the Unification Church, Scientology, Satanism, Zen Buddhism, and New Age.

CR1466 Catholic Church Conferencia Nacional dos Bispos do Brasil
Macumba: Cultos Afro-Brasileiros: Candomblé, Umbanda, Observações pastorais. Edited by Cirilo Folch Gomes. São Paulo, BL: Edições Paulinas, 1976. 113 pp. No ISBN.

Second revised and enlarged edition of a symposium of scholarly papers by Catholic priests and academics on the range of spiritist cults in Brazil.

CR1467 Chandler, Russell
Understanding the New Age. Grand Rapids, MIU: Zondervan, 1993. 367 pp. Paper. 031038561X.

A revised and updated guide to understanding the New Age Movement and its impact on American society through music, medicine, business, politics, and religion.

CR1468 Chryssides, George D.
The Advent of Sun Myung Moon: The Origins, Beliefs, and Practices of the Unification Church. New York, NYU: St. Martin's Press, 1991. xii, 230 pp. 0312053479.

A phenomenological account of the Korean origins, teachings, and ceremonies of the Unification Church of Sun Myung Moon.

CR1469 Ellwood, Robert S.
Alternative Altars: Unconventional and Eastern Spirituality in America. (Chicago History of American Religion). Chicago, ILU: University of Chicago Press, 1979. xiii, 192 pp. 0226206181.

Occult, mystical, and Eastern movements in the United States interpreted in the context of the nation's religious heritage.

CR1470 Enroth, Ronald M., ed.
Evangelizing the Cults: How to Share Jesus with Children, Parents, Neighbors, and Friends Who Are Involved in a Cult. (Vine Books). Ann Arbor, MIU: Servant Publications, 1990. 195 pp. Paper. 0892836717.

Practical advice on how to present the Christian gospel to persons in nine different religions and cults in North America, by ten Protestant evangelicals who specialize in the study of new religious movements and ministry to persons influenced by them.

CR1471 Enroth, Ronald M.
The Lure of the Cults and New Religions: Why They Attract and What We Can Do. Downers Grove, ILU: InterVarsity, 1987. 140 pp. Paper. 0830817086 (hdbk), 0877849943 (pbk).

A popular introduction by a leading sociologists to the dynamics and core issues surrounding cults.

CR1472 Enroth, Ronald M.
Youth, Brainwashing, and the Extremist Cults. Grand Rapids, MIU: Zondervan; Exeter, ENK: Paternoster Press, 1977. 218 pp. No ISBN (Z; hdbk), 085364215X (P; pbk).

A sociologist and evangelical Christian's picture of seven cults in North America, based on in-depth interviews with dozens of former members and their relatives.

CR1473 Geisler, Norman L., and Ron Rhodes
When Cultists Ask: A Popular Handbook on Cultic Misinterpretations. Grand Rapids, MIU: Baker Books, 1997. 365 pp. 0801011493.

Identification of misinterpretations of scripture passages (Genesis to Revelation) by Jehovah's Witnesses, Mormons, and followers of New Age movements, with recommended corrections of them prepared by the Dean of Southern Evangelical Seminary, and the Executive Director of Reasoning from the Scriptures Ministries.

CR1474 Gesy, Lawrence J.
Today's Destructive Cults and Movements. Huntington, INU: Our Sunday Visitor, 1993. 315 pp. Paper. 0879734981.

A popular handbook, by the cult consultant for the Roman Catholic Archdiocese of Baltimore, on how to recognize cult groups (New Age movement, Satanism, KKK, Neo-Nazis, etc.), how they are structured, and how to seek counseling for persons involved in them.

CR1475 Gomes, Alan W.
Unmasking the Cults. (Zondervan Guide to Cults and Religious Movements). Grand Rapids, MIU: Zondervan, 1995. 93 pp. Paper. 0310704413.

An introduction to the Zondervan guides to cults and religious movements.

CR1476 Gorden, Kurt Van

Mormonism. (Zondervan Guide to Cults and Religious Movements). Grand Rapids, MIU: Zondervan, 1995. 94 pp. Paper. 0310704014.

A concise guide for evangelical Christians desiring to witness to Mormons.

CR1477 Hexham, Irving, and Karla O. Poewe

New Religions as Global Cultures: Making the Human Sacred. (Explorations: Contemporary Perspectives on Religion). Boulder, COU: Westview Press, 1997. xiv, 194 pp. 0813325072 (hdbk), 0813325080 (pbk).

An introduction for persons from Judeo-Christian backgrounds to religious movements, often called "cults," which have sprung up in the past twenty-five years.

CR1478 Hexham, Irving, and Karla O. Poewe

Understanding Cults and New Religions. Grand Rapdis, MIU: Eerdmans, 1986. xi, 170 pp. Paper. 0802801706.

An account by two respected Canadian professors of what is happening to North American society and its values during the past few decades that has helped create the climate conducive to the rise of cults and new religions.

CR1479 Hutchinson, Janis

The Mormon Missionaries: An Inside Look at Their Real Message and Methods. Grand Rapids, MIU: Kregel Resources, 1995. 272 pp. Paper. 0825428866.

A former Mormon gives an "insider's look" at the theology, politics, strategies, and tactics of Mormon missionaries.

CR1480 Hutchinson, Janis

Out of the Cults and into the Church: Understanding and Encouraging Ex-cultists. Grand Rapids, MIU: Kregel Resources, 1994. 222 pp. Paper. 0825428858.

Helps by a former Mormon for understanding problems experienced by ex-cultists during the first three years after their conversion to Christ.

CR1481 Kranenborg, R.

Een nieuw licht op de kerk?: Bijdragen van nieuwe religieuze bewegingen voor de kerk van vandaag. 's-Gravenhage, NE: Boekencentrum, 1984. 254 pp. 9023908090.

"A New Light on the Church?" analyzes the contribution of new religious (non-Christian) movements in the West to today's church, describing the contents of their message and their growth, and how the church may respond to them theologically and strategically.

CR1482 Kranenborg, R.

Zelfverwerkelijking: Oosterse religies binnen een westerse subkultuur. Kampen, NE: Kok, 1974. 332 pp. 9024203899.

An analysis of the growth in popularity of Eastern religious beliefs and practices in the West (TM, Yoga, Hare Krishna, etc.).

CR1483 LeBar, James J.

Cults, Sects, and the New Age. Huntington, INU: Our Sunday Visitor, Inc, 1989. 288 pp. Paper. 0879734310.

Four Roman Catholic priests in the United States introduce the Satanist movement, cult-like aspects of fundamentalism, and three cults that grew out of the Catholic Church itself; with Vatican documents and guidelines for group study.

CR1484 Lewis, James R.

Peculiar Prophets: A Biographical Dictionary of New Religions. St. Paul, MNU: Paragon House, 1999. xiii, 400 pp. Paper. 1557787689.

An authority on non-traditional religions captures a broad spectrum of backgrounds and diversity that undercuts some of the social prejudice against new religions; includes brief entries on over 300 religious leaders, over 75 photos, and a comprehensive index with over 2,300 entries.

CR1485 Lingle, Wilbur

Approaching Jehovah's Witnesses in Love: How to Witness Effectively without Arguing. Fort Washington, PAU: CLC, 1994. 240 pp. Paper. 0875087027.

A practical guide for evangelical Christians desiring to share their faith with Jehovah's Witnesses.

CR1486 Mather, George A., and Larry A. Nichols

Dictionary of Cults, Sects, Religions and the Occult. Grand Rapids, MIU: Zondervan, 1993. 384 pp. 0310531004.

A guide to the hundreds of religious groups in North America outside Protestantism, Catholicism, and Judaism, with short and long essays on their history, leaders, beliefs, practices, and influence.

CR1487 Mather, George A., and Larry A. Nichols

Masonic Lodge. (Zondervan Guide to Cults and Religious Movements). Grand Rapids, MIU: Zondervan, 1995. 83 pp. Paper. 0310704219.

Helps for evangelical Christians desiring to understand Freemasonry and its differences in beliefs from biblical Christianity; with selected bibliography.

CR1488 McDowell, Josh, and Don Stewart

The Deceivers: What Cults Believe; How They Lure Followers. San Bernardino, CAU: Here's Life Publishers, 1992. 311 pp. Paper. 0898403421.

A revised and updated version of *Understanding the Cults* (1982) with a new chapter on Scientology, including a comparison of their beliefs with orthodox Christianity, and suggestions for Christian witness to their followers.

CR1489 McDowell, Josh, and Don Stewart

The Occult: The Authority of the Believer over the Powers of Darkness. San Bernadino, CAU: Here's Life Publishers, 1992. 249 pp. Paper. 089840343X.

A revised and updated version of *Understanding the Occult* (1982) discussing the increase in occult activity in North America and the variety of occult beliefs and practices; with a comparison to biblical teachings.

CR1490 Mosatche, Harriet S.

Searching: Practices and Beliefs of the Religious Cults and Human Potential Groups. New York, NYU: Stravon Educational Press, 1983. 437 pp. 0873960920.

An analysis of nine groups that gained followers in the United States as part of the human potential movement, including Unification Church, Scientology, Divine Life Mission, and Hare Krishna.

CR1491 Nordquist, Ted A.

Ananda Cooperative Village: A Study in the Beliefs, Values, and Attitutes of a New Age Religious Community. (Skrifter utgivna av Religionshistoriska Institutionen i Uppsala [Hum. Fak.], 16). Uppsala, SW: Borgströms Tryckeri AB, 1978. 177 pp. 9150601520.

An in-depth investigation of Ananda Cooperative Village, its history and development as a New Age community in California since 1968, and present beliefs and commitments of its members.

CR—CHRISTIANITY AND OTHER RELIGIONS

CR1492 Passantino, Bob, and Gretchen Passantino
Satanism. (Zondervan Guide to Cults and Religious Movements). Grand Rapids, MIU: Zondervan, 1995. 96 pp. Paper. 0310704510.

A practical introduction to Satanism for evangelical Christians, including an overview of its theology and helps for witnessing effectively to its followers.

CR1493 Petersen, William J.
Those Curious New Cults. (A Pivot Family Reader). New Canaan, CTU: Keats Publishing, 1975. 272 pp. Paper. No ISBN.

A popular introduction for mainline Christians to nineteen groups, often called "cults," from Astrology to Satanism, Scientology to the Jesus Movement, and Hare Krishna to Baha'i.

CR1494 Powlison, David
Power Encounters: Reclaiming Spiritual Warfare. (Hourglass Books). Grand Rapids, MIU: Baker Books, 1995. 160 pp. Paper. 0801071380.

A popular presentation of a biblical approach for Christians to persons involved in New Age, the occult, and fascination with demons.

CR1495 Rhodes, Ron
New Age Movement. (Zondervan Guide to Cults and Religious Movements). Grand Rapids, MIU: Zondervan, 1995. 94 pp. Paper. 0310704316.

A concise introduction to the New Age movement and its differences from biblical Christianity, with helps for witnessing.

CR1496 Robert, R. Philip
Mormonism Unmasked: Confronting the Contradictions between Mormon Beliefs and True Christianity. Nashville, TNU: Broadman, 1998. viii, 184 pp. Paper. 0805416528.

Helps for Christians desiring to understand Mormonism and to witness to Mormons; by the Director of the Interfaith Witness Division, North American Mission of the Southern Baptist Convention.

CR1497 Sects and New Religious Movements: An Anthology of Texts from the Catholic Church, 1986-1994
Washington DCU: USCC, 1995. ix, 77 pp. Paper. 1574550233.

Selections from sixty-one Catholic documents on themes relevant to the pastoral challenges of sects and new religious movements; produced by the USCC's Working Group on New Religious Movements.

CR1498 Sontag, Frederick
Sun Myung Moon and the Unification Church. Nashville, TNU: Abingdon, 1977. 224 pp. 0687406226.

An early examination of the Unification Church by a seminary professor who participated in its seminars.

CR1499 Starkes, M. Thomas
Confronting Popular Cults. Nashville, TNU: Broadman, 1972. 122 pp. Paper. 0805418059.

Brief introduction to seven popular cults in America, presented as "Christian ... alternatives to discipleship," with helps for Christians desiring to communicate to their followers.

CR1500 Streiker, Lowell D.
The Cults Are Coming! Nashville, TNU: Abingdon, 1978. 127 pp. Paper. 0687100704.

A popular examination of three major cults—The Children of God, the Unification Church, and Krishna Consciousness—what they are, why they attract young people, and how Christians can combat them.

CR1501 Van der Walt, B. J., Stuart Fowler, and J. J. Venter
Die "New Age" Beweging/The "New Age" Movement. Potchefstroom, SA: Instituut vir Reformatoriese Studie, 1990. 79 pp. Paper. 1868220559.

A critical evaluation of the New Age movement by two South African and one Australian professors of theology in the Reformed tradition, with chapters in Afrikaans and English.

CR1502 Wikström, Lester
Nyandligt: En kartläggning och analys av nyreligiösa rörelser med särskild hänsyn till Luleå stift. Stockholm, SW: Verbum; Lund, SW: Håkon Ohlsson, 1978. 238 pp. No ISBN.

A survey of new religious movements in Lapland, northern Sweden, including Bible-, Hindu-, and Islamic-oriented groups.

CR1503 Yamamoto, J. Isamu
Unification Church. (Zondervan Guide to Cults and Religious Movements). Grand Rapids, MIU: Zondervan, 1995. 85 pp. Paper. 0310703816.

A concise guide for evangelical Christians desiring to witness to members of the Unification Church.

Post-Christian Religion

See also CR96-CR97, CR447, SO76, and EU267.

CR1504 Billington, Ray
The Christian Outsider. London, ENK: Epworth Press, 1971. 160 pp. Paper. 0716201682.

A frank assessment of the "non-church" movement in England, including parishes in Woolrich, and the attempts to find a common ground for Christians and humanists, following the earlier attempt in *Honest to God* (1963) by John Robinson, Bishop of Woolrich.

CR1505 Catholic-Humanist Dialogue (2nd, 1970, Brussels)
A Catholic/Humanist Dialogue: Humanists and Roman Catholics in a Common World. Edited by Paul Albert Kurtz and Albert Dondeyne. London, ENK: Pemberton Books; Buffalo, NYU: Promethea Books, 1972. xii, 117 pp. 030172041X (PE hdbk), 0301720428 (PE pbk), 0879750103 (PR hdbk), 0897950111 (PR pbk).

Papers from the second Catholic/Humanist Dialogue (Brussels, 2-4 October 1970) sponsored jointly by the International Humanist and Ethical Union and the Vatican Secretariat for Unbelievers.

CR1506 Conference on World Evangelization (Pataya, Thailand, 1980)
The Thailand Report on Marxists: Report of the ... Mini-Consultation on Reaching Marxists. (Lausanne Occasional Papers, 12). Wheaton, ILU: LCWE, 1980. 31 pp. Paper. No ISBN.

A brief look at Marxist characteristics and reasons for past failure or success, by Christians in witness to them, and a survey of strategies for Christian witness to Marxists in Western and Eastern Europe and in the Third World.

CR1507 Conference on World Evangelization (Pattaya, Thailand, 1980)

The Thailand Report on Christian Witness to Nominal Christians among the Orthodox: Report of the ... Mini-Consultation of Reaching Nominal Christians. (Lausanne Occasional Papers, 19). Wheaton, ILU: LCWE, 1980. 48 pp. Paper. No ISBN.

A short history of the development of Orthodox theology, review of contemporary orthodoxy in different countries, with strategies for witnessing to nominal Christians among the Orthodox.

CR1508 Conference on World Evangelization (Pattaya, Thailand, 1980)

The Thailand Report on Secularists: Report of the ... Mini-Consultation on Reaching Secularists. (Lausanne Occasional Papers, 8). Wheaton, ILU: LCWE, 1980. 31 pp. Paper. No ISBN.

Understandings of secularization with strategies for reaching secularized people.

CR1509 Gallagher, Michael Paul

Struggles of Faith. Dublin, IE: Columba Press, 1990. 141 pp. Paper. 0948183926.

Ways to enter into dialogue with people who have left the church or are undergoing a crisis in belief; by a staff member of the Pontifical Council for Dialogue with Non-Believers.

CR1510 González, Anleo

Banalización de la Vida e Increencia: Presentación. (Misión Abierta, 4). Madrid, SP: Misión Abierta, 1989. 145 pp. No ISBN.

A numbered monograph on postmodernity and religion.

CR1511 Hille, Rolf

Das Ringen um den säkularen Menschen: Karl Hems Auseinandersetzung mit der idealistischen Philosophie und den pantheistischen Religionen. (Monographien und Studienb cher). Giessen, GW: Brunnen-Verlag, 1990. 614 pp. Paper. 3765593605.

This Munich dissertation studies the work of Karl Heim, Professor of Systematics at the Evangelische Fakultät at Tübingen (1920-1939), insofar as it provides a meaningful Christian missionary apologetic versus idealistic and pantheistic forms of mysticism, as well as New Age thought, all of which are deficient in terms of positing a personal god, a need of redemption, or even a consciousness of sin.

CR1512 Instituto Fe y Secularidad

Fe y Sensibilidad Historica. (Verdad e Imagen, 26). Salamanca, SP: Ediciones Sígueme, 1972. 478 pp. Paper. No ISBN.

A collection of twelve papers written according to the institute's model and presented at the eighteenth Semana de Misionología de Berriz, organized by the Centro de Estudios Misionológicos of Berriz, Spain.

CR1513 Ramachandra, Vinoth

Gods That Fail: Modern Idolatry and Christian Mission. Downers Grove, ILU: InterVarsity, 1996. 226 pp. Paper. 0830818960.

Science, reason, and irrationality analyzed as secular false gods, by the regional secretary of South Asia of the International Fellowship of Evangelical Students.

CR1514 Reid, John

Man without God: An Introduction to Unbelief. (Theological Resources). New York, NYU: Corpus Instrumentorum; Philadelphia, PAU: Westminster Press, 1971. xix, 306 pp. No ISBN.

A systematic examination of the historical and philosophical bases and forms of atheism, with an approach to Christian witness, and dialogue with the unbeliever; by a consultant to the Vatican Secretariat for Non-Believers.

CR1515 Van de Weyer, Robert

Guru Jesus. London, ENK: SPCK, 1975. xi, 140 pp. Paper. 0281028737.

The author's faith journey from agnosticism to spiritual search in India, to discipleship as Christ's follower based on his personal diaries.

MISSIONS: SOCIAL ASPECTS

Paul Hiebert, Subeditor

This chapter of the bibliography covers two of Jongeneel's eleven branches of missiology—the ethnology and cultural anthropology of Christian mission (missionary anthropology) and the sociology of Christian mission (1995:284-305). In addition it includes sections on new religious movements, mission work among particular population groups, and the relation between mission and aspects of health and social welfare.

It begins with resources including bibliographies, periodicals, reference works, and sourcebooks. The papers of conferences on social aspects of mission are grouped here, or located through "see also" citations.

The subeditor has written an important essay on "Critical Issues in the Social Sciences and Their Implications for Mission Studies" (Hiebert, 1996). This chapter contains the theoretical works published since 1960. They are subdivided into "General Works," "Social Change," "Secularization," "Social Analysis," "Cultural Perspectives," and "Anthropology and Religion."

Books on "Gospel and Culture" follow, with many "see also" cross-references to works annotated under other headings, mostly geographical. Additional subsections are to be found on "Culture Conflict" and "Race."

"Unreached Peoples," the next subheading, has been a major concern of evangelical Christians. There follow works on "popular religiosity"—a theme found also in the literature on Christianity and the various religions.

New religious movements that arose from the clash of cultures have been a fascination for social scientists. Stud-ies of those groups having strong Christian roots are included in this chapter, under general works and by continent. See Harold Turner's six-volume *Bibliography of New Religious Movements in Primal Societies* for further citations, including periodical articles.

The next subgroup concerns "Special Types of Missions." Works that Jongeneel classified under missionary ethics (of marriage and family, and of ethnic and other groups) are to be found here (1997:120-123). These include work among children, youth, and adult age sets, and marriage and the family. Under the subheading on "Work among Women—Women in Christianity" are grouped books often scattered among other themes.

The chapter continues with literature on mission to other subpopulations (occupational groups, immigrants, refugees, ethnic or racial groups, prisoners, and handicapped persons).

"Urban Missions" is the next theme with books from various continents. See also subsections on church and society under each continent, and a special listing of "USA: City Missions" in the chapter on "Missions: The Americas."

Issues of health and social welfare conclude the chapter. Those concerning health have been subdivided into "Medical Missions," "Medicine and Religion," and "Spiritual Healing/Exorcism." Grundmann (1992) contains a longer bibliography. See also the subsection on "Spiritual Warfare" in the chapter on "Spirituality, Worship, and Mission." The final subsections are on "Social Work" and "Social Conflict."

Norman E. Thomas

Bibliographies

See also CR7, SO3, and AM1.

SO1 Hartley, Loyde H.
Cities and Churches: An International Bibliography. (ATLA Bibliography Series, 31). Metuchen, NJU: ATLA/Scarecrow Press, 1992. 3 vols. 081082583X.

A monumental bibliography with 18,500 citations, half of them annotated, covering church ministries in cities, 1800 to 1990 (vol. 1: 1800-1959; vol. 2: 1960-1979; vol. 3: 1980-1991).

SO2 Instituto Fe y Secularidad
Sociología de la religión y teología/Sociology of Religion and Theology: Estudio Bibliográfico/Bibliography. Madrid, SP: Editorial Cuadernos para el Diálogo, 1978. 2 vols. Paper. 8422960079 (vol. 1), 8422960214 (vol. 2).

A basic bibliography in two volumes (vol. 1: 1975, 474 pp; vol. 2: 1978, 215 pp.) that presents summaries of the sixty-four principal books in the field and a bibliographical file of 16,291 citations, concluding with indices of processed journals and authors.

SO3 Mitchell, Robert Cameron, and Harold W. Turner, eds.
A Comprehensive Bibliography of Modern African Religious Movements. Evanston, ILU: Northwestern University Press, 1966. 132 pp. No ISBN.

Contains 1,313 items dealing with the literature of non-Islamic modern African religious movements, i.e. the syncretic and independent church movements in Africa. Attempts to include every available reference in any language that has been published and has achieved more than local circulation.

SO4 Tippett, Alan Richard
Bibliography for Cross-Cultural Workers. South Pasadena, CAU: William Carey Library, 1971. 252 pp. 0878081097.

A bibliography of books and articles on social anthropology for the cross-cultural missionary, divided into general reference works, anthropological and religious dimensions, and research methods.

SO5 Turner, Harold W.
Bibliography of New Religious Movements in Primal Societies. (Bibliographies and Guides in African Studies, 1). Boston, MAU: G K Hall, 1991. 6 vols.

A six-volume bibliography of new religious movements in primal society; including annotated book and periodical entries grouped by geographical subregions, plus theoretical and general works [vol. 1: *Black Africa*, (1977, x, 277 pp., 0816179271); vol. 2: *North America*, (1978, x, 286 pp., 081617928X); vol. 3: *Oceania*, (1990, xii, 348 pp., 0816189846); vol. 4: *Europe and Asia*, (1991, xi, 279 pp., 0816179301); vol. 5: *Latin America*, (1991, xiii, 233 pp., 0816179298); vol. 6: *The Caribbean*, (1992, xiv, 303 pp., 0816190895)].

Serials and Periodicals

See also EA8 and EA10.

SO6 Contact. No. 1 (1971)-no. 126 (1992). Bimonthly
Geneva, SZ: WCC, Christian Medical Commission, 1971-1992. No ISSN.

Thematic issues on varied aspects of the community and churches' involvement in health issues throughout the world, with emphasis on innovative approaches, integral development, and ecumenical action; published also in French and Spanish, with selected issues in Portuguese, Kiswahili, and Arabic.

SO7 Exchange: Journal of Missiological and Ecumenical Rearch. No. 1 (April 1972) -. Quarterly
Leiden, NA: Brill with IIMO, 1972-. ISSN 01662740.

Scholarly articles, plus book reviews, on issues of Christian mission and culture, especially in the Two-Thirds World of Africa, Latin America, Asia, and Oceania.

SO8 Gospel in Context. Vol. 1, no. 1 (Jan. 1978)-vol. 2 (1979). Quarterly
Abington, PAU: Partnership in Mission, 1978-1979. ISSN 01938320.

Scholarly journal on gospel and culture issues; merged with *Occasional Bulletin of Missionary Research* to form the *International Bulletin of Missionary Research* in 1979.

SO9 Practical Anthropology. Vol. 1 (1953)-vol. 19 (1972). Bimonthly
Tarrytown, NYU: Practical Anthropology, 1953-1972. No ISSN.

A bulletin for Christian anthropologists, containing arti-cles and book reviews concerning the relation of Christian missions to diverse cultures; superseded by *Missiology: An International Review*.

SO10 Urban Mission. Vol. 1, no. 1 (Sept. 1983) -. Quarterly
Philadelphia, PAU: Westminister Theological Seminary, 1983-No ISSN.

Short articles, plus book reviews and lists of books received, concerning mission and ministries in the growing cities of the world.

Reference Works

See also EU225.

SO11 Directory of Protestant Church-Related Hospitals outside Europe and North America
(MRL Directory Series, 13). New York, NYU: MRL, 1963. vii, 159 pp. Paper. No ISBN.

Comprehensive directory giving names, addresses, and statistical information of 1,228 hospitals in 85 countries related in some way to Protestant churches; arranged geographically, and indexed under several headings.

SO12 Fenton, Thomas P., and Mary J. Heffron, eds.
Women in the Third World: A Directory of Resources. Maryknoll, NYU: Orbis Books, 1987. xvi, 141 pp. Paper. 0883445301.

A listing of organizations, books, periodicals, articles, and audiovisuals related to the role of women in Africa, Asia, and Latin America; compiled by the editors.

SO13 Starling, Allan, ed.
Peoplesfile Index: 1986 Edition. Pasadena, CAU: Global Mapping Project, 1986. vii, 381 pp. Paper. No ISBN.

A global index of 5,445 language groups by country, showing the extent that the Bible exists in recorded or printed form for their use, with a list of 3,800 unreached peoples.

Documentation and Archives

SO14 CELAM-Departamento de Misiones
Documentos de pastoral indígena, 1968-1985. (DEMIS, 9). Bogotá, CK: CELAM, 1989. 120 pp. Paper. 9586251462.

A collection of final documents from four meetings on pastoral indigenous work: Melgar (1968), Caracas (1969), Iquitos (1971), and Bogotá (1985).

SO15 Pirotte, Jean, and Claude Soetens
Évangélisation et cultures non européennes: Guide du chercheur en belgique francophone. (Cahiers de la Revue Théologique de Louvain, 22). Louvain-la Neuve, BE: Publication de la Faculté de Théologie, 1989. 179 pp. Paper. No ISBN.

Resources on the encounters of Belgian missionaries, both Roman Catholic and Protestant, with the cultures of Africa, Asia, and the Americas; including interpretive essays and an external bibliography.

SO16 Smalley, William A., ed.
Readings in Missionary Anthropology II. South Pasadena, CAU: William Carey Library, 1978. xxv, 913 pp. 0878087311.

An anthology of eighty-two articles originally published in *Practical Anthropology* (1954-1972), relating the insights of cultural anthropology to the tasks of cross-cultural missionaries.

SO17 Willard, Frances E.
Woman and Temperance: Or, the Work and Workers of the Woman's Christian Temperance Union. (Religion in America Series, 2). New York, NYU: Arno Press, 1972. 648 pp. 0405040938.

A reprint of the 1888 "field notes" of the famous President of the Woman's Christian Temperance Union (WCTU)—a valuable source document on the movement and about fifty of its leaders.

Conferences and Congresses

See also SO57, SO72, SO139, SO156, SO175, SO198, SO237, SO242, SO262, SO401, SO410, SO448, and EV27.

SO18 CELAM-Departamento de Pastoral
La Pastoral Social en América Latina: Documentos. (Documentos CELAM, 96). Bogotá, CK: CELAM, 1987. 150 pp. Paper. 9586250873.

A collection of papers and conclusions from the meeting of the presidents and secretaries of Catholic social/pastoral centers in Latin America (Bogotá, Colombia, 12-17 September 1986).

SO19 Consultation on the Role of the Churches in Social Service (Mülheim, Germany, 1962)
The Role of the Churches in Social Service: An International Perspective. Edited by Henry J. Whiting. Geneva, SZ: WCC, 1963. iv, 106 pp. Paper. No ISBN.

A study document as indicated in title.

SO20 InterVarsity Student Missions Convention (15th., Urbana, Il: University of Illinois, 27-31 December 1987)
Urban Mission: God's Concern for the City. Edited by John E. Kyle. Downers Grove, ILU: InterVarsity, 1988. 192 pp. Paper. 0830817115.

The messages focused on God's concern for the cities of the world.

SO21 *Pluralismo Socio-Cultural y Fe Cristiana*
(Teología Deusto, 22). Bilbao, SP: Mensajero, 1990. 444 pp. Paper. 8427116446.

Papers from the Congress of Theology (Bilbao-Vitoria, Spain, 12-16 February 1990) relating the Christian faith to issues of socio-cultural pluralism.

SO22 Vanhoozer, Kevin J., ed.
The Trinity in a Pluralistic Age: Theological Essays on Culture and Religion. Grand Rapids, MIU: Eerdmans, 1997. x, 166 pp. Paper. 0802841171.

Ten scholarly essays, by an international panel of theologians, exploring the Christian doctrine of the Trinity in the context of 20th-century cultural and religious pluralism; originally presented at the Fifth Edinburgh Dogmatics Conference (Edinburgh, 31 Aug.-3 Sept. 1993).

General Works

See also GW176-GW177, HI178, TH138, EA39, ME87, SO116, EC15, EC21-EC23, CO27, CH355, and AM850.

SO23 Ceccon, Claudius, and Kristian Paludan
My Neighbour—Myself: Visions of Diakonia. Geneva, SZ: WCC, 1988. 109 pp. Paper. 2825409103.

A complementary volume to the official report of the Larnaca Consultation 1986, designed to provoke local congregations into grappling with the meaning of service in today's world.

SO24 Harakas, Stanley Samuel
Let Mercy Abound: Social Concern in the Greek Orthodox Church. Brookline, MAU: Holy Cross Orthodox Press, 1983. 188 pp. Paper. 091658660X (hdbk), 0916586618 (pbk).

An analysis of the social concerns of Eastern Orthodoxy in the Americas (1958-1980); based on the encyclicals and speeches of Archbishop Iakovos and decisions and statements of the Clergy-Laity Congress' social and moral issues committees.

SO25 Kraemer, Hendrik
Uit de nalatenschap van Dr. H. Kraemer. Edited by B. J. Brouwer, E. Jansen Schoonhoven, and S. C. Graaf van Randwijck. Kampen, NE: Kok, 1970. 185 pp. 9024205727.

Essays on mission, religion, and culture written by the noted Dutch missiologist between 1940 and 1960.

SO26 Mbiti, John S., ed.
Confessing Christ in Different Cultures: Report of Colloquium Held at the World Council of Churches' Ecumenical Institute, Bossey, Switzerland, 2-8 July 1977. Céligny, SZ: Ecumenical Institute, 1977. 233 pp. Paper. No ISBN.

Speeches and reports from an important ecumenical consultation on issues of contextualization of the Christian witness in various cultures.

SO27 Missionswissenschaftliches Institut Missio, ed.
Ein Glaube in vielen Kulturen: Theologische und soziopastorale Perspektiven für ein neues Miteinander von Kirche und Gesellschaft in der einen Welt. Frankfurt am Main, GW: IKO-Verlag für Interkulturelle Kommunikation, 1996. 375 pp. 3889394213.

A collection of scholarly essays in English, Spanish, Portuguese, French, and German on the hermeneutics, theology, and praxis of contextual theologies; published to celebrate the 25th anniversary of the Institute of Missiology (Missio) in Aachen, Germany.

SO28 Rommen, Edward, and Gary Corwin, eds.
Missiology and the Social Sciences: Contributions, Cautions and Conclusions. (Evangelical Missiological Society Series, 4). South Pasadena, CAU: William Carey Library, 1996. 223 pp. Paper. 0878083782.

Ten essays by evangelical missiologists on the relationship of various social sciences to their discipline.

SO29 Shenk, Wilbert R.
Write the Vision: The Church Renewed. (Christian Mission and Modern Culture). Valley Forge, PAU: Trinity Press International; Leominster, ENK: Gracewing, 1995. viii, 119 pp. Paper. 1563381184 (US), 085244334X (UK).

Four lectures by the noted Mennonite missiologist on Christian mission and modern culture, with themes of integrity, mission, evangelization, and church.

SO30 Stutzman, Linford
With Jesus in the World: Mission in Modern Affluent Societies. Scottdale, PAU: Herald Press, 1992. 142 pp. Paper. 0836135997.

A provocative analysis of the social dimensions of Christian mission in modern affluent societies (to the marginalized, the establishment, and the majority), proposing models from Jesus and the early Anabaptists.

SO—MISSIONS: SOCIAL ASPECTS

SO31 World Consultation on Inter-Church Aid, Refugee and World Service (Larnaca, Cyprus, 1986)
Diakonia 2000. Called to Be Neighbors: Official Report. Edited by Klaus Poser. Geneva, SZ: WCC Publications, 1987. ix, 133 pp. Paper. 2825408883.

A report giving an overall description of twenty years of interchurch aid, emphasising the comprehensiveness of *diakonia* and the importance of the local church as a change agent.

Social Analysis

See also SO256, AS1053, AS1386, EU71, and EU124.

SO32 Holland, Joe, and Peter J. Henriot
Social Analysis: Linking Faith and Justice. Victoria, AT: Dove Communications; Maryknoll, NYU: Orbis Books, 1983. xxii, 118 pp. Paper. 0859242633 (D), 0883444623 (O).

Revised and enlarged edition of a widely used Catholic introduction to social science analysis, showing how it can be combined with theological reflection for a praxis-oriented approach to Christian action for social justice.

SO33 Maduro, Otto
Religion and Social Conflicts. Translated by Robert R. Barr. Maryknoll, NYU: Orbis Books, 1982. xxviii, 161 pp. Paper. 0883444283.

English translation.

SO34 Maduro, Otto
Religión y Lucha de Clases. (Colección Teoría Política). Caracas, VE: Editorial Ateneo; México, MX: CRT-CEE, 1979. 220 pp. No ISBN.

A scholarly study of the origin, structure, and social functions of religion in societies with social class conflicts, as in Latin America; also published as *Religión y Conflicto Social* by Centro de Reflexión Teológica.

Social Change

See also GW86, HI662, SO99, SO221, AF550, AM267, AM443, AM1037, AM1244, AS97, AS904, AS1183, and AS1415.

SO35 Jones, Arthur C.
Wade in the Water: The Wisdom of the Spirituals. Maryknoll, NYU: Orbis Books, 1999. xxi, 182 pp. Paper. 1570752885.

A celebration of the spirituals as a powerful cultural expression, with insights on freedom, resistance, deeper understanding, spiritual transformation, and social renewal; originally published in 1993.

SO36 Macy, Gary, ed.
Theology and the New Histories. (Annual Publication of the College Theology Society, 44). Maryknoll, NYU: Orbis Books, 1999. xiii, 262 pp. Paper. 1570752397.

Fourteen scholarly essays on how Christianity has historically responded to multiple readings from women, minority groups, non-Western peoples, and deconstructionalism; includes challenges posed to traditional theology and to the future.

SO37 O'Gorman, Frances
Charity and Change: From Bandaid to Beacon. Melbourne, AU: World Vision Australia, 1992. xii, 84 pp. Paper. 1875140107.

A Brazilian educator critiques five approaches to social change with examples from her own country and others.

SO38 Patterson, David
The Affirming Flame: Religion, Language, Literature. Norman, OKU: University of Oklahoma Press, 1988. x, 175 pp. 0806121092.

The examination of religious dimensions of language and literature, the linguistic elements of religion and literature, and the literary aspects of religion and language.

SO39 Perkins, John M.
A Quiet Revolution: The Christian Response to Human Need ... A Strategy for Today. Waco, TXU: Word Books, 1976. 226 pp. Paper. 0876807937.

Reflections on the church in evangelism, social action, economic development, and justice; by the noted African American Baptist evangelist and founder of Voice of Calvary Ministries in Mississippi.

SO40 Rossel, Jacques
Dynamik der Hoffnung: Eine zeitgemässe Studie zum Thema Christ und Welt. Translated by A. E. Vischer. Basel, SZ: Basileia Verlag, 1967. 176 pp. No ISBN.

German translation.

SO41 Rossel, Jacques
Mission dans une société dynamique. Geneva, SZ: Labor et Fides, 1967. 154 pp. No ISBN.

A challenging analysis, by the president of the Basel Mission, of the new social dynamic in which Christians are called to witness and serve (urbanization, secularization, mobility, pluralism, revolution, etc.).

SO42 Rossel, Jacques
Mission in a Dynamic Society. London, ENK: SCM Press, 1968. viii, 152 pp. 0334010241.

English translation.

SO43 Tychicus, Bakthan
Community Organization: Ideological Perspectives. Chennai, II: CLS, 1997. iv, 76 pp. Paper. No ISBN.

A three-part study on the 1) ideology and methodology of Saul Alinsky and Paulo Freire; 2) Christian perspectives on wholistic community organizing; and 3) reflection on means and ends in community organizing; with a perspective of the Kingdom of God.

SO44 Vries, Egbert de
Man in Rapid Social Change. London, ENK: WCC/SCM Press; Garden City, NYU: Doubleday, 1961. 240 pp. No ISBN.

A monumental analysis of the phenomena of rapid social change, its effects on the various institutions of society, and the resulting ethical decisions and new loyalties; prepared by the eminent Dutch social scientist for the WCC's study of Rapid Social Change.

Secularization

See also TH182, TH587, SO21, SO455, AM971, AM1516, AS1383, and EU192.

SO45 Braaten, Carl E., and Robert W. Jenson, eds.
Either/Or: The Gospel or Neopaganism. Grand Rapids, MIU: Eerdmans, 1995. vi, 123 pp. Paper. 0802808409.

Seven essays by North American scholars seeking to awaken the churches to pagan tendencies and return them to biblical orthodoxy; originally presented at the Center for Catholic and Evangelical Theology's Either/Or: The Gospel or Neopaganism Conference held at St. Olaf College (Northfield, Minnesota, April 1993).

SO—MISSIONS: SOCIAL ASPECTS

SO46 Henderson, David W.

Culture Shift: Communicating God's Truth to Our Changing World. Grand Rapids, MIU: Baker Books, 1998. 255 pp. Paper. 0801090598.

Insight on cultural shifts in North American popular culture, with practical suggestions on ways to witness, preach, and teach in light of those realities.

SO47 Henry, Carl F. H.

Gods of This Age or ... God of the Ages? Nashville, TNU: Broadman, 1994. x, 323 pp. Paper. 0805415483.

Essays by the founding editor of *Christianity Today* urging Christians to challenge contemporary paganism with evangelistic engagement and a theology relevant to new cultural themes.

SO48 Hiebert, Paul G.

Missiological Implications of Epistemological Shifts: Affirming Truth in a Modern/Postmodern World. (Christian Mission and Modern Culture Series). Harrisburg, PAU: Trinity Press International, 1999. xv, 135 pp. Paper. 1563382598.

The epistemological foundations for the translation and communication of the Gospel in the midst of an anti-colonial postmodern sea of religious relativism, and of accusations of Christian imperialism.

SO49 Hoedemaker, Bert

Secularization and Mission: A Theological Essay. (Christian Mission and Modern Culture). Harrisburg, PAU: Trinity Press International; Herefordshire, ENK: Gracewing, 1998. x, 82 pp. Paper. 1563382245 (US), 0852444818 (UK).

An introduction to what kind of rethinking of mission is necessary to take the implications and efforts of secularization seriously; by the professor of missions, ecumenics, and Christian ethics at the State University of Gronigen in the Netherlands.

SO50 Löffler, Paul, ed.

Secular Man and Christian Mission. (CWME Study Pamphlets, 3). Geneva, SZ: WCC; New York, NYU: Friendship Press, 1968. 48 pp. No ISBN.

Report of an international discussion among seven missiologists on the issue of the meaning of secularization for the mission of the church.

SO51 Newbigin, James Edward Lesslie

Honest Religion for Secular Man. (Adventures in Faith). Philadelphia, PAU: Westminster Press; London, ENK: SCM Press, 1966. 159 pp. Paper. No ISBN.

Lectures by the noted missiologist and bishop of Madras on the contemporary process of secularization and its challenges for Christians in their beliefs, values, spirituality, and mission.

SO52 Newbigin, James Edward Lesslie

Proper Confidence: Faith, Doubt, and Certainty in Christian Discipleship. Grand Rapids, MIU: Eerdmans, 1995. v, 105 pp. Paper. 0802808565.

The noted mission and ecumenical leader offers a Christian apology that he believes is more relevant to postmodern thought than either liberal or fundamentalist Christianity.

SO53 Newbigin, James Edward Lesslie

Religion Auténtica para el hombre Secular. (Frontera, 5). Madrid, SP: Editorial Razón y Fe, 1969. 221 pp. Paper. No ISBN.

Spanish translation.

SO54 Newbigin, James Edward Lesslie

Truth and Authority in Modernity. (Christian Mission and Modern Culture). Valley Forge, PAU: Trinity Press International; Leominster, ENK: Gracewing, 1996. ix, 85 pp. Paper. 1563381680 (TPI), 0852443773 (G).

Three essays by the noted missiologist and ecumenist on witnessing to divine authority in the context of modernity.

SO55 Robinson, Martin

The Faith of the Unbeliever. Crowborough, ENK: Monarch Publications; Westlea, ENK: Bible Society, 1994. 218 pp. Paper. 1854242350.

An analysis of components of the secular worldview in the West, and of how to communicate with persons holding such views.

SO56 Roxburgh, Alan J.

The Missionary Congregation, Leadership, and Liminality. (Christian Mission and Modern Culture). Harrisburg, PAU: Trinity Press International, 1997. viii, 71 pp. Paper. 1563381907.

Out of the Canadian churches' experience of marginality and secularization, the senior pastor of West Vancouver Baptist Church in British Columbia examines Victor Turner's work on liminality as suggestive in today's missionary congregations.

SO57 Sampson, Philip, Vinay Samuel, and Chris Sugden, eds.

Faith and Modernity. Oxford, ENK: Regnum Books; Oxford, ENK: Lynx Communications; Oxford, ENK: Paternoster Press, 1994. 352 pp. 1870345177 (hdbk), 0745930395 (pbk).

Fifteen scholarly essays on modernity and postmodernity and their impact on the church's life and mission; originally presented in Uppsala, Sweden, in 1993 at a conference sponsored by the LCWE.

SO58 Schillebeeckx, Edward

Wereld en kerk. (Theologische peilingen, 3). Bilthoven, NE: Nelissen, 1966. 278 pp. No ISBN.

An analysis by the distinguished professor of theology at the Catholic University of Nijmegen, Netherlands, of the situation of Christianity since World War II, the phenomenon of secularization, the dialectical tension between humanity and the church, and the roles of the church in modern social work, education, and interfaith dialogue.

SO59 Schillebeeckx, Edward, and N. D. Smith

World and Church. New York, NYU: Sheed and Ward, 1982. vii, 308 pp. 836213513 (hdbk), 072209812X (pbk).

English translation.

SO60 Scoville, Gordon

Into the Vacuum: Being the Church in an Age of Barbarism. (Christian Mission and Modern Culture). Harrisburg, PAU: Trinity Press International, 1998. ix, 102 pp. Paper. 1563382385.

Guidance for the post-Enlightenment church in North America in understanding the moral decline of its society and how cultural disintegration has contributed to church decline; with prescription for renewal.

SO61 Vela, Jesús Andrés

Reiniciación Cristiana: Respuesta a un bautismo "sociológico." (Misión sin fronteras, 3). Estella, SP: Verbo Divino, 1985. 395 pp. Paper. No ISBN.

Study of Christian re-initiation of those Christians who in reality have not overcome neopaganism and secularism—based on "Ordo Initiationis Christianae Adultorum" (OICA).

SO62 Ven, Johannes A. van der, and Hans-George Ziebertz, eds.

Religiöser Pluralismus und Interreligiöses Lernen. (Theologie and Empirie, 22). Kampen, NE: Kok; Weinheim, GW: Deutscher Studien Verlag, 1994. 291 pp. Paper. 9039005052 (NE), 3892714878 (GW).

A collection of nine essays by German and Dutch scholars on the twin challenges of secularization and religious pluralism.

SO63 Williams, Colin Wilbur

Faith in a Secular Age. (Chapel Books, 28). New York, NYU: Harper & Row, 1966. 128 pp. Paper. No ISBN.

After analyzing contributions of philosophers, social scientists, and theologians to our understanding of the rise of the secular society, the author draws implications for the church's contemporary mission and evangelism.

SO64 Wilson, Jonathan R.

Living Faithfully in a Fragmented World: Lessons for the Church from MacIntyre's After Virtue. (Christian Mission and Modern Culture). Harrisburg, PAU: Trinity Press International, 1997. x, 85 pp. Paper. 1563382407.

Analysis of several aspects of contemporary culture that create both opportunities and threats to Christian mission.

Cultural Perspectives: General

See also HI120, TH82, TH347, SO48, SO114, EC66, EC294, PO12, CO73, EV208, SP293, SP318, AF179, AF753, AM139, AM323, AM838, AM856, AM992, AM1033, AM1070, AM1456, and AS61.

SO65 Adeney, Bernard T.

Strange Virtues: Ethics in a Multicultural World. Downers Grove, ILU: InterVarsity, 1995. 286 pp. Paper. 0830818553.

An introduction to cross-cultural ethics based on the assumption that each culture gives rise to a distinctive value system; by one who draws upon three generations of missionary experience and currently teaches theology and ethics in Indonesia.

SO66 Augsburger, David W.

Pastoral Counseling across Cultures. Philadelphia, PAU: Westminster Press, 1986. 405 pp. 0664212727.

An in-depth exploration of the psychological, cultural, therapeutic, and theological complexity of doing counseling and psychotherapy across cultures.

SO67 Bosch, David Jacobus

Believing in the Future: Toward a Missiology of Western Culture. (Christian Mission and Modern Culture). Valley Forge, PAU: Trinity Press International; Leominster, ENK: Gracewing, 1995. x, 69 pp. Paper. 1563381176 (US), 0852443331 (UK).

In this essay written shortly before his death in 1992, the noted South African missiologist discusses steps needed to develop a missiology of Western culture.

SO68 Brown, Neil

Christians in a Pluralist Society. (Faith and Culture, 12). Manly, AT: Catholic Institute of Sydney, 1986. 145 pp. 0908224117.

A panoramic view of the social, political, and economic landscape of affluent nations within the English political tradition, with a description of an appropriate Christian response to those realities.

SO69 Carrier, Hervé

Évangile et cultures: De Léon XIII à Jean-Paul II. Cité du Vatican, VC: Libreria editrice vaticana; Montréal, PQC: Éditions Paulines, 1987. 276 pp. 8820915499, 2890393682 (E).

The present Secretary of the Pontifical Council for Culture traces the history of the contribution of the popes from Leo XIII to John Paul II on the issue of the relationship of Gospel message and human culture.

SO70 Carrier, Hervé

Evangelio y Culturas: De León XIII a Juan Pablo II. Translated by Angel Cortabarría Beitia, and Adolfo Varona López. (Patrimonio cultural de la iglesia, 2). Madrid, SP: Editorial EDICE, 1988. 194 pp. 8471412047.

Spanish translation.

SO71 Carrier, Hervé

Gospel Message and Human Cultures: From Leo XIII to John Paul II. Translated by John Drury. (Institute for World Concerns Series). Pittsburgh, PAU: Duquesne University Press, 1989. xiii, 178 pp. 0820702064 (hdbk), 0820702072 (pbk).

English translation.

SO72 CELAM-Sección para la Cultura, Seminario "Líneas para la Adveniente Cultura," Buenos Aires, AG, 21-27 de abril de 1986

¿Adveniente cultura? (Documentos CELAM, 87). Bogotá, CK: CELAM, 1987. 299 pp. Paper. 9586250644.

A collection of ten seminar papers.

SO73 Dellutri, Salvador

El Mundo Al que Predicamos. Miami, FLU: Logos International/Editorial Unilit, 1998. 245 pp. Paper. 07899906198.

A theological textbook, with study guide, in which an Argentinian pastor surveys the diverse Western views of humanity that have influenced Protestant witness and action in Latin America.

SO74 Doppelfeld, Basilius

Mission als Austausch. (Münsterschwarzacher Kleinschriften, 61). Münsterschwarzach, GW: Vier-Türme-Verlag, 1990. 68 pp. Paper. 3878684061.

Using examples from Africa, the author asserts that mission is, as the title suggests, a process of learning and an exchange between peoples and cultures.

SO75 Fahner, Chr., and W. van Laar, eds.

Evangelie als cultuur?: Het zendingswerk, de Bijbelse boodschap en de culturen. (Kijk op zending, 1). Kampen, NE: Kok, 1982. 102 pp. Paper. 902422182X.

A collection of articles on the relation between Gospel and culture, inculturation and indigenization, presenting general theories and case studies related to Indonesia and Africa; by authors belonging to the more conservative reformed churches.

SO76 Guinness, Os

The Dust of Death: A Critique of the Establishment and the Counter Culture—and a Proposal for a Third Way. Downers Grove, ILU: InterVarsity, 1973. 419 pp. 0877849560 (hdbk), 0877849110 (pbk).

A popular analysis of post-Christian movements in the United States, proposing the necessity of Christian radicalism as a missional response.

SO77 Hill, Harriet, and Jon Arensen, eds.
The Best of Ethno-Info. Nairobi, KE: SIL, 1995. xii, 138 pp.
Paper. No ISBN.

A selection of the best articles from Ethno-Info written
by missionaries examining socioculture aspects of life in different cultural settings.

SO78 Honig, A. G.
*Ontwikkeling en culturele identiteit: In twintig jaar oecume-
nische theologische bezinning.* (Kamper Cahiers, 44). Kampen,
NE: Kok, 1981. 51 pp. Paper. 9024221714.

A brief survey of ecumenical thought from 1948 to 1978
understanding missionary activity as encompassing human
development within local cultural contexts.

SO79 Hovey, Kevin
*Before All Else Fails, Read the Instructions: A Manual for
Cross Cultural Christians.* Brisbane, AT: Harvest Publica-
tions, 1995. xi, 298 pp. Paper. 0958831416.

Revised edition of insights on how to overcome cultural
barriers in communicating the Christian faith; based on the
author's ten years experience as an Australian Assemblies of
God missionary in Papua New Guinea and his mission studies
at Fuller; first published in 1986.

SO80 Inch, Morris A.
Doing Theology across Cultures. Grand Rapids, MIU: Baker
Books, 1982. 110 pp. Paper. 0801050324.

The author develops a general theory exploring both the
concept of revelation as the basis of theological endeavor and the
tension between biblical authority and cultural integrity, using
seven case studies to illustrate the Christian transformation of
culture.

SO81 Kraft, Charles H.
*Christianity with Power: Your Worldview and Your Experience
of the Supernatural.* Ann Arbor, MIU: Servant Publications, 1989.
xii, 230 pp. Paper. 0892833963.

A critique of the mechanistic Western worldview, advocating an alternative biblical understanding of signs and wonders.

SO82 Larkin, William J.
*Culture and Biblical Hermeneutics: Interpreting and Applying
the Authoritative Word in a Relativistic Age.* Grand Rapids, MIU:
Baker Books, 1988. 401 pp. Paper. 0801056519.

A detailed analysis of the current debate among evangelical
Protestants on the role of culture in biblical interpretation; with
development of a biblical theology of hermeneutics and culture.

SO83 Lingenfelter, Sherwood G., and Marvin K. Mayers
*Ministering Cross-Culturally: An Incarnational Model for
Personal Relationships.* Grand Rapids, MIU: Baker Books,
1986. 125 pp. 0801056322.

A revised and expanded analysis of Mayers' basic values
model for understanding intercultural relationships.

SO84 Lingenfelter, Sherwood G.
*Agents of Transformation: A Guide for Effective Cross-Cul-
tural Ministry.* Grand Rapids, MIU: Baker Books, 1996. 282
pp. Paper. 0801020689.

Research tools that will enable missionaries to ascertain
their own cultural biases, as well as those of persons among
whom they are ministering; written as a companion volume to
Transforming Culture (1992) by the professor of intercultural
studies at Biola University.

SO85 Lingenfelter, Sherwood G.
Transforming Culture: A Challenge for Christian Mission.
Grand Rapids, MIU: Baker Books, 1998. 190 pp. Paper.
0801021782.

A substantially revised second edition of the author's practical field manual for cross-cultural ministries, including case
studies from Africa, Asia, Latin America, and Oceania; originally published in 1992.

SO86 Mackay, John A.
Christian Reality and Appearance. Richmond, VAU: John
Knox Press, 1969. 108 pp. 0804205108.

Essays in which the president of Princeton Theological
Seminary analyzes the "modern idols" of doctrine, Christian
emotion, institutional religion, and legalism, recognizing the
powerful influences of Pentecostalism and renewed Roman
Catholic witness in Latin America; originally presented at
Austin Presbyterian Theological Seminary (1945) and at Highland Park Presbyterian Church in Dallas, Texas (1950, 1952).

SO87 Maurier, Henri
*Les missions: Religions et civilisations confrontées à
l'universalisme: Contribution à une histoire en cours.*
(L'histoire à vif). Paris, FR: Éditions du Cerf, 1993. 209 pp.
Paper. 2204047295.

Mature reflections on the struggle in Christian missions
to proclaim a universal faith amidst the particularity of human
cultures; by a former missionary in Burkina Faso of the Society of Missionaries of Africa (White Fathers).

SO88 McAlpine, Thomas H.
Facing the Powers: What Are the Options? (Innovations in Mission, 2). Monrovia, CAU: MARC, 1991. 103 pp. Paper.
0912552727.

An analysis of five traditions of interpreting "principalities
and powers" (biblical, Reformed, Anabaptist, Third Wave, and
social science), emphasizing the importance of this debate for
contemporary mission.

SO89 Mensen, Bernhard
*Die Begegnung des abendländischen Christentums mit anderen
Völkern und Kulturen.* (Akademie Völker und Kulturen). (Vor-
tragsreihe, 1978/79). St. Augustin, GW: Akademie Völker und
Kulturen, 1979. 112 pp. Paper. No ISBN.

Six lectures by prominent German missiologists on the encounter of Western Christianity with other peoples and cultures.

SO90 Mensen, Bernhard, ed.
Multikulturelle Gesellschaft. (Vortragsreihe, 1993/1994). Nettetal,
GW: Steyler Verlag, 1994. 118 pp. Paper. 3805003471.

A series of talks dealing with different aspects of multiculturalism with special application to Europe, including the
tensions between values of identity, preservation, and integration, interreligious dialogue, and the role of Christian churches in a changing society.

SO91 Montgomery, Robert L.
Introduction to the Sociology of Missions. Westport, CTU:
Praeger, 1999. xxi, 183 pp. 0275966917.

Recognizing the focus on anthropological insights in the
study of mission and the neglect of sociological perspectives,
the author seeks to increase dialogue between missiologists
and sociologists of religion by providing the former with a
sociological perspective and the latter with a deeper understanding of its missionary enterprise.

SO—MISSIONS: SOCIAL ASPECTS

SO92 Nichols, Aidan, ed.
Christendom Awake: On Re-Energising the Church in Culture.
Grand Rapids, MIU: Eerdmans, 1999. xiii, 255 pp. Paper.
0802846904.

A renowned Catholic theologian defends Orthodox faith,
seeks the recovery of the church's traditional mission to reener-
gize its witness, and argues that the church must regain confidence in its ability to transform daily life holistically if it is to
become a vital social force.

SO93 Nussbaum, Stan
*The ABC's of American Culture: Understanding the American
People through Their Common Sayings.* Colorado Springs, COU:
Global Mapping International, 1998. 55 pp. Paper. No ISBN.

The analysis of 234 proverbs in American culture which allows those new and familiar with the culture to probe more deeply into its worldview.

SO94 Sikkema, Mildred, and Agnes Niyekawa
Design for Cross-Cultural Learning. Yarmouth, MEU: Intercultural Press, 1987. 106 pp. 0933662637.

A text proposing structures for effective cross-cultural learning in high school and college, as well as graduate and professional training; endeavors to help individuals understand the meaning of cultural differences.

SO95 Sitton, David
To Every Tribe with Jesus! A Tribal Awareness Seminar. Los
Fresnos, TXU: Institute of Tribal Studies, 1998. 157 pp. Pa-
per. No ISBN.

A primer on reaching tribal peoples for Christ drawing
from the presence of many missionaries including the author's
own twenty years of church planting in Papua New Guinea.

SO96 Suess, Paulo
Culturas Indígenas y Evangelizacion. (CEP, 59). Lima, PE:
CEP, 1983. 102 pp. Paper. No ISBN.

Historical and ethnological analysis with a proposal for
an indigenous pastoral theology of liberation.

SO97 Sundermeier, Theo, ed.
Den Fremden wahrnehmen: Bausteine für eine Xenologie.
(Studien zum Verstehen fremder Religionen, 5). Gütersloh,
GW: Gerd Mohn, 1992. 230 pp. Paper. 357901787X.

Twelve authors discuss ecumenical thinking concerning
approaching and understanding strangers in our midst and their
distinct cultures.

SO98 Taber, Charles R.
*The World Is Too Much with Us: "Culture" in Modern Prot-
estant Missions.* (The Modern Mission Era, 1792-1992: An
Appraisal). Macon, GAU: Mercer University Press, 1991. xxiv,
208 pp. 0865543887.

A scholarly analysis of two-hundred years of discussion
on the relation of missions and culture, focusing on the interaction among Protestant missionaries, social scientists, and
indigenous peoples.

SO99 Thompson, Thomas R., ed.
The One in the Many: Christian Identity in a Multicultural World.
(Calvin Center Series). Lanham, MDU: University Press of Amer-
ica, 1998. xiv, 111 pp. 0716810684 (hdbk), 0761810692 (pbk).

A collection of essays on national and international understandings of cultural diversity; originating largely from a
faculty symposium on multiculturalism held at Calvin College, Grand Rapids, Michigan, 25-26 April 1997.

SO100 Yamamori, Tetsunao, and Charles R. Taber, eds.
Christopaganism or Indigenous Christianity? South Pasadena, CAU: William Carey Library, 1974. 262 pp. 0878084231.

A series of twelve lectures, the product of the William S.
Carter Symposium on Church Growth at Milligan College in
April of 1974, discussing the adjustments Christianity must
make as it spreads into the myriad cultures of the world, and
the limits of such adjustments.

Anthropology and Religion

See also GW264, CR323, CR375, CR549, CR596, CO68, AF553,
AF703, AM797, AM1261, AS157, AS935, AS949, AS985, AS1110,
AS1357, AS1415, EU159, OC56, and OC219.

**SO101 *Anthropology and Missionaries: Some Case-Studies
(Special Issue)***
(*Journal of the Anthropological Society of Oxford*, 23, 2 [1992]).
Oxford, ENK: JASO, 1992. iv, 196 pp. Paper. No ISBN.

Five case studies by anthropologists on the cultural effects
of missionary work; with an overview by W. S. F. Pickering.

SO102 Bochinger, Christoph
*Ganzheit und Gemeinschaft: Zum Verhältnis von theologischer
und anthropologischer Fragestellung im Werk Bruno Gutmanns.*
(Religionswissenschaft, 3). Frankfurt am Main, GW: Lang, 1987.
134 pp. Paper. 3820401245.

A master of arts thesis on the relationship between native
culture and the Christian message in the work of Bruno Gutmann.

SO103 Comblin, Joseph
Antropologia Cristã. (Teologia y liberación, 3). Petrópolis, BL:
Editora Vozes, 1985. 272 pp. Paper. No ISBN.

An exploration by the noted liberation theologian, of person
and personhood, soul and body, humankind in relation to time
and space, humanity and its liberation, humanity before God, and
of the person in relation to science, technology, and work; with
special attention to the poor.

SO104 Comblin, Joseph
Das Bild vom Menschen. (Bibliothek Theologie der Befreiung).
Düsseldorf, GW: Patmos Verlag, 1987. 246 pp. Paper.
3491777127.

German translation.

SO105 Comblin, Joseph
Retrieving the Human: A Christian Anthropology. (Theology
and Liberation Series). Maryknoll, NYU: Orbis Books; Kent,
ENK: Burns & Oates, 1990. ix, 259 pp. Paper. 0883446782 (US
hdbk), 088344657X (US pbk).

English translation.

SO106 Conn, Harvie M.
*Eternal Word and Changing Worlds: Theology, Anthropology,
and Mission in Trialogue.* Grand Rapids, MIU: Academie Books,
1984. 372 pp. Paper. 0310453216.

The recent history of thinking about cross-cultural mission,
including three periods of conversation between theology, anthropology (specifically cultural anthropology), and mission.

SO107 Franklin, Karl J., ed.
Current Concerns of Anthropologists and Missionaries. (In-
ternational Museum of Cultures, 22). Dallas, TXU: Internat'l
Museum of Cultures, 1987. vii, 163 pp. Paper. 088312176X.

Eleven papers from the 1986 SIL Anthropology Seminar
(Dallas, Texas, 17-22 March 1987).

SO—MISSIONS: SOCIAL ASPECTS

SO108 Fuchs, Stephen

Anthropology for the Missions. Allahabad, II: St. Paul Publications, 1979. 198 pp. No ISBN.

A basic text on mission anthropology, including Gospel and culture issues.

SO109 Grunlan, Stephen A., and Marvin K. Mayers

Cultural Anthropology: A Christian Perspective. (A Zondervan Publication). Grand Rapids, MIU: Academie Books, 1988. 309 pp. Paper. 0310363217.

Second edition of a scholarly discussion of "functional creationism," and the problems posed by biblical absolutism, cultural relativism, and how they relate to cultural diversity; originally published in 1979 (Grand Rapids, MIU: Zondervan).

SO110 Headland, Thomas N., Kenneth L. Pike, and Marvin Harris, eds.

Emics and Etics: The Insider/Outsider Debate. (Frontiers of Anthropology, 7). Newbury Park, CAU: Sage Publications, 1990. 226 pp. Paper. 0803937385 (hdbk), 0803937393 (pbk).

A dialogue between leading anthropologists and linguists over the meaning of "emic" and "etic," and their significance for the understanding of cultures.

SO111 Hedlund, Roger E., and Beulah Herbert, eds.

Culture and Evangelization: A Collection of Indian Anthropological Readings. Madras, II: Church Growth Research Centre, 1981. 164 pp. Paper. No ISBN.

A collection of Indian anthropological readings on aspects of ethnology, social life, and customs, and of Christianity and culture in the Indian context; includes complete indexes of persons and subjects.

SO112 Herbert, Christopher

Culture and Anomie: Ethnographic Imagination in the Nineteenth Century. Chicago, ILU: University of Chicago Press, 1991. x, 364 pp. 0226327388 (hdbk), 0226327396 (pbk).

Scholarly essays on several episodes in the 19th century emergence of the "anthropological" idea of culture, including one on Polynesia and the cultural perspectives of John Williams and other missionaries.

SO113 Hiebert, Paul G., and Eloise Hiebert Meneses

Incarnational Ministry: Planting Churches in Band, Tribal, Peasant, and Urban Societies. Grand Rapids, MIU: Baker Books, 1995. 405 pp. Paper. 0801020093.

Drawing upon the insights of cultural anthropology concerning various types of societies and cultures, two anthropologists discuss how these differences affect church planting in four different cultural settings.

SO114 Hiebert, Paul G., R. Daniel Shaw, and Tite Tiénou

Understanding Folk Religion: A Christian Response to Popular Beliefs and Practices. Grand Rapids, MIU: Baker Books, 1999. 412 pp. Paper. 0801022193.

An exploration of the characteristics of folk religions, the way religion is believed and practiced in daily life, with missiological implications.

SO115 Hiebert, Paul G.

Anthropological Insights for Missionaries. Grand Rapids, MIU: Baker Books, 1985. 315 pp. Paper. 0801042917.

A basic text in missionary anthropology designed to help young missionaries understand other cultures and themselves as they enter these cultures.

SO116 Hiebert, Paul G.

Anthropological Reflections on Missiological Issues. Grand Rapids, MIU: Baker Books, 1994. 272 pp. Paper. 0801043948.

A collection of essays by the noted missiologist and anthropologist, on conceptual issues relating theology, anthropology, and missiology, and practical issues in cross-cultural evangelization.

SO117 Kraft, Charles H.

Anthropology for Christian Witness. Maryknoll, NYU: Orbis Books, 1996. xvi, 493 pp. Paper. 1570750858.

A thorough basic introduction to the study of anthropology designed specifically for those who plan careers in mission or cross-cultural ministry.

SO118 Loewen, Jacob Abram

Culture and Human Values: Christian Intervention in Anthropology Perspective. South Pasadena, CAU: William Carey Library, 1975. 443 pp. 0878087222.

A reprint of articles originally published in *Practical Anthropology* based on mission experiences in Latin America.

SO119 Luzbetak, Louis J.

The Church and Cultures: New Perspectives in Missiological Anthropology. (American Society of Missiology Series, 12). Maryknoll, NYU: Orbis Books, 1988. xx, 464 pp. Paper. 0883446251.

A detailed introduction to missionary anthropology for those desiring a culturally sensitive ministry and witness—a complete revision of the 1963 classic in the light of contemporary anthropological and missiological thought and in face of current world conditions.

SO120 Luzbetak, Louis J.

La Iglesia y las Culturas: Antropología aplicada al servicio del apostado. (Colección FERES América Latina). Bogotá, CK: Tercer Mundo, 1968. xi, 261 pp. No ISBN.

Spanish translation of *The Church and Cultures: An Applied Anthropology for the Religious Worker* (1963).

SO121 Luzbetak, Louis J.

L'église et les cultures: Une anthropologie culturelle au service de l'ouvrier apostolique. Brusselles, BE: Lumen Vitae, 1967. 432 pp. No ISBN.

French translation.

SO122 Nida, Eugene Albert

Coutumes et cultures. Translated by Edouard Somerville. Cheseaux, SZ: Éditions Groupes Missionaires, 1978. 386 pp. No ISBN.

French translation.

SO123 Nida, Eugene Albert

Customs and Cultures: Anthropology for Christian Missions. South Pasadena, CAU: William Carey Library, 1975. 306 pp. 0878087230.

A now classic text on anthropology for persons preparing for cross-cultural missionary service; by the former Secretary for Translations of the American Bible Society; originally published by Harper (1954).

SO124 Schneider, Jane, and Shirley Lindenbaum, eds.

Frontiers of Christian Evangelism: Special Issue. Washington, DCU: American Anthropological Association, 1987. 190 pp. Paper. No ISBN.

A special issue of *American Ethnologist* (14 February 1987) exploring problematic aspects of Christian evangelism in various cultures; contains ten essays originally presented by anthropologists at the 1985 meeting of the American Ethnological Society

SO125 Sutlive, Vinson H. et al., eds.

Missionaries and Anthropologists, Part II: Studies in Third World Societies. Williamsburg, VAU: College of William and Mary, 1985. viii, 306 pp. Paper. No ISBN.

Ten case studies by anthropologists on the impact of missionaries on culture identity and change.

SO126 Whiteman, Darrell L. et al., eds.

Missionaries, Anthropologists, and Cultural Change. (Studies in the Third World Societies, 25). Williamsburg, VAU: College of William and Mary, 1985. xii, 424 pp. Paper. No ISBN.

Thirteen essays by mission scholars on the creative interaction between anthropology and missiology in theory and practice, with emphasis on issues of epistemology and cultural change.

SO127 Zahniser, A. H. Mathias

Symbol and Ceremony: Making Disciples across Cultures. (Innovations in Mission). Monrovia, CAU: MARC, 1997. x, 236 pp. Paper. 1887983058.

Helps for Western Christians to understand the functions of symbols and ceremonies within cultures, and to learn how to use them for cross-cultural disciple-making among Jews, Hindus, Muslims, and traditional religionists while avoiding syncretism.

Gospel and Culture

See also GW144, GW197, GW203, GW228-GW229, HI27, HI65, HI78, HI126, HI157, HI381, TH13, TH25, TH75, TH112, TH120, TH174, TH182, TH499, TH529, TH536, TH545, EA170, EA195, EA201, ME56, CR111, CR203, CR484, CR638, CR648, CR650-CR651, SO85, SO108, SO367, SO453, SO571, EC20, PO142, CO48, CO64, CO75, ED11, EV59, EV134-EV135, EV393, MI12, CH117, CH364, SP219, SP225-SP226, SP234, SP239, SP254, SP291, AF69-AF70, AF78, AF98, AF118, AF168, AF191, AF195, AF200, AF207-AF208, AF218, AF229, AF231, AF292, AF302, AF326, AF332, AF342, AF396, AF454, AF458, AF478, AF497, AF524, AF532, AF547, AF559, AF572, AF633, AF644, AF653-AF654, AF657-AF658, AF721, AF969, AF1059, AF1166, AF1170, AF1181, AF1200, AF1212, AF1262, AF1323, AF1326, AF1343, AF1349, AM127-AM129, AM238, AM433, AM443, AM554, AM610, AM624, AM632, AM791, AM897, AM961, AM974, AM977, AM980-AM981, AM999, AM1071, AM1080, AM1187, AM1361, AM1388, AM1506, AM1527, AS112, AS116, AS205, AS210, AS239, AS241, AS323, AS595, AS625, AS628, AS631, AS707, AS721, AS749, AS875, AS937, AS978, AS986, AS1003, AS1039, AS1041, AS1067, AS1072, AS1087, AS1134, AS1161, AS1197-AS1198, AS1270, AS1293-AS1294, AS1309, AS1327, AS1342, AS1358, AS1453-AS1454, AS1489, AS1496, EU9, EU42, EU100, EU130-EU131, EU163, EU189, EU193-EU194, EU237, EU283, OC38, OC45, OC55, OC101, OC156, OC234, and OC241.

SO128 Abraham, K. C., ed.

New Horizons in Ecumenism: Essays in Honor of Bishop Samuel Amirtham. Bangalore, II: Serampore College, Board of Theological Education of the Senate; Bangalore, II: Board for Theological Text Book Programme of South Asia, 1993. 155 pp. Paper. No ISBN.

A *festschrift* containing nine short essays on the Gospel and culture, with focus on the Indian context; written to honor the former Director of the WCC's Program for Theological Education and now bishop of the Church of South India in the Trivandrum Diocese.

SO129 Akwue, Matthew Anayo

Some Canonical Implications of Cultural Pluralism in the Church with Particular Application to Nigeria. (Faculty of Canon Law). Rome, IT: Pontificia Universitas Urbaniana, 1988. xxvi, 169 pp. Paper. No ISBN.

A scholarly analysis of support in Roman Catholic canon law for cultural pluralism, with applications for the church in Africa, especially Nigeria; a doctoral dissertation originally submitted at the Urbaniana Pontifical University.

SO130 Amaladoss, Michael

Beyond Inculturation: Can the Many Be One? Delhi, II: Vidyajyoti/ISPCK, 1998. xv, 148 pp. Paper. 8172144377.

A study of the complexity of inculturation, beginning with a series of poignant questions and leading to an exploration of divine-human encounter; by the noted Jesuit theologian/missiologist; based on his Indian experience.

SO131 Amalorpavadass, D. S.

Gospel and Culture: Evangelization, Inculturation and "Hinduisation." Bangalore, II: NBCLC, 1978. 55 pp. Paper. No ISBN.

An essay on contextualization from the perspective of a leading Indian Roman Catholic thinker.

SO132 Arbuckle, Gerald A.

Earthing the Gospel: An Inculturation Handbook for Pastoral Workers. London, ENK: Cassell; Maryknoll, NYU: Orbis Books, 1990. xi, 236 pp. Paper. 0225665840 (C), 088344643X (O).

A handbook for Christian workers in the First World (Australia, New Zealand, Britain, the United States, etc.) on issues of Gospel and culture, applying insights from social anthropology usually considered relevant only to overseas missions; with case history, personal stories, and other study helps.

SO133 Ariarajah, S. Wesley

Gospel and Culture: An Ongoing Discussion within the Ecumenical Movement. (Gospel and Cultures Pamphlet, 1). Geneva, SZ: WCC Publications, 1994. xv, 50 pp. Paper. 282541140X.

A brief survey of the main lines of the ecumenical Gospel-culture discussion by the WCC's Deputy General Secretary from Sri Lanka.

SO134 Azevedo, Marcello de Carvalho

Inculturation and the Challenges of Modernity. Rome, IT: Gregorian University, 1982. xii, 63 pp. Paper. No ISBN.

Papers from an interdisciplinary seminar on "The Nature and the Demands of Inculturation, as Seen in the Light of Holy Scriptures and of the Cultural Developments of Today" (Jerusalem, 16-26 June 1981).

SO—MISSIONS: SOCIAL ASPECTS

SO135 Bamat, Thomas, and Jean-Paul Wiest, eds.
Popular Catholicism in a World Church: Seven Case Studies in Inculturation. (Faith and Culture Series). Maryknoll, NYU: Orbis Books, 1999. xii, 315 pp. Paper. 1570752524.

Along with seven case studies on inculturation in specific regions of the world are four theological reflections on the studies by Kosuke Koyama, Ivone Gebara, Lamin Sanneh, and Michael Amaladoss.

SO136 Bosch, David Jacobus, ed.
Church and Culture Change in Africa. (Lux Mundi, 3). Pretoria, SA: N. G. Kerkboekhandel, 1971. 100 pp. No ISBN.

Papers read at the Third Annual Meeting of the South African Society for Missionary Studies, 1971.

SO137 Butselaar, Jan van, and Jan J. van Capelleveen, eds.
Evangelie en cultuur in de oecumenische discussie. Kampen, NE: Kok, 1989. 99 pp. Paper. 9024243483.

Eight short essays by missiologists and ecumenical church leaders analyzing ecumenical discussions on the relation of Gospel and culture in Africa, Asia, Latin America, and Europe.

SO138 Carrier, Hervé
Evangelizing the Culture of Modernity. (Faith and Culture Series). Maryknoll, NYU: Orbis Books, 1993. viii, 168 pp. Paper. 088344898X.

The noted Professor of the Sociology of Culture and Religion at the Gregorian University in Rome analyzes modernity as a dominant "superculture" in the First World, that profoundly impacts on all cultures, and develops an approach to evangelization which is responsive to it.

SO139 Costa, Ruy O., ed.
One Faith, Many Cultures: Inculturation, Indigenization, and Contextualization. (Boston Theological Institute Annual Volume 2). Maryknoll, NYU: Orbis Books; Cambridge, MAU: Boston Theological Institute, 1988. xvii, 162 pp. 0883445875 (O).

Sixteen scholarly essays by Protestant and Catholic theologians; originally presented at the dialogue on "Contextualization of the Faith: Past, Present, and Future," the Second Annual Consultation on Global Mission of the Boston Theological Institute (21-22 March 1986).

SO140 Cote, Richard G.
Re-Visioning Mission: The Catholic Church and Culture in Postmodern America. (Isaac Hecker Studies in Religion and American Culture). New York, NYU: Paulist Press, 1996. vi, 191 pp. Paper. 0809136457.

A Catholic Oblate missionary and missiologist contends that inculturation must be taken seriously as a missionary challenge for Roman Catholics in North America.

SO141 Dembrowski, Hermann, and Wolfgang Greive, eds.
Der andere Christus: Christologie in Zeugnissen aus aller Welt. (Erlangen Taschenbücher, 100). Erlangen, GW: Ev.-Luth. Mission, 1991. 230 pp. Paper. 3872145002.

A dozen representatives of different cultures present Christ as imagined and understood in their own ways.

SO142 Derrick, Christopher, ed.
Light of Revelation and Non-Christians. Staten Island, NYU: Society of St. Paul; Staten Island, NYU: Alba House, 1965. 141 pp. No ISBN.

A collection of essays by eight Catholic theologians on the indigenization of Christianity in Africa, Latin America, Israel, and China.

SO143 *Diverse Cultures, One Gospel*
Geneva, SZ: WCC Publications, 1995. 22 mins. No ISBN.

Part of the WCC study process on Gospel and Cultures, this twenty-two minute video includes case studies from the Philippines, Russia, Rwanda, Nicaragua, and Chicago, the United States.

SO144 Dumais, Marcel, R. M. Goldie, and Andrzej Swięcicki
Cultural Change and Liberation in a Christian Perspective. (Inculturation-Working Papers on Living Faith and Cultures, 10). Rome, IT: Gregorian University Press, 1987. xi, 63 pp. Paper. 8876525785.

Three diverse essays on the process of evangelization in cultural change (the Apostolic Church as a model of inculturation, the role of women in the process, and the moral implications of inculturation).

SO145 Dyrness, William A.
The Earth Is God's: A Theology of American Culture. (Faith and Culture Series). Maryknoll, NYU: Orbis Books, 1997. xvi, 208 pp. Paper. 157075151X.

A biblical theology of culture based on a theology of creation, with application to issues of ethnicity, ecology, and art in North America; by the Dean and Professor of Theology and Culture at Fuller Theological Seminary.

SO146 Fahner, Chr., ed.
Het Woord in de Context: Over het vraagstuk van de verinheemsing van kerk en theologie in zendingsgebieden. (Kijk op Zending, 2). Kampen, NE: Kok, 1984. 162 pp. Paper. 9024229227.

A collection of articles on the relation between Gospel and culture, inculturation and indigenization; presenting general theories and case-studies related to Indonesia, Peru, and the Caribbean.

SO147 Fleming, Bruce C. E.
Contextualization of Theology: An Evangelical Assessment. South Pasadena, CAU: William Carey Library, 1980. xii, 147 pp. Paper. 0878084312.

An evaluation, from an evangelical viewpoint, of varied understandings of "contextualization"; with selected source documents, by a missionary of the Evangelical Free Church of America, who is involved in theological education in Francophone Africa.

SO148 George, Francis E.
Inculturation and Ecclesial Communion: Culture and Church in the Teaching of Pope John Paul II. Rome, IT: Pontificia Universitas Urbaniana, 1990. 380 pp. Paper. 8840180516.

A detailed analysis situating the teaching of Pope John Paul II on culture and church within the preceding and contemporary debate on issues of Gospel and culture; originally presented as a doctoral thesis at the Urbaniana Pontifical University.

SO149 Gilbert, Maurice, Paul In-Syek Sye, and Théoneste Nkéramihigo
L'inculturation et la sagesse des nations. (Inculturation: études sur l'actualité de la rencontre entre la foi et les cultures, 4). Rome, IT: Pontifical Gregorian University, Centre "Cultures and Religions," 1984. ix, 52 pp. No ISBN.

Three essays on the Bible and inculturation (Gilbert), and inculturation in Korea (Sye), and Africa (Nkéramihigo).

SO150 Gilliland, Dean S., ed.
The Word among Us: Contextualizing Theology for Mission Today. Dallas, TXU: Word Publishing, 1989. viii, 344 pp. Paper. 0849931541.

Fourteen scholarly essays by thirteen faculty members of the School of World Mission of Fuller Theological Seminary, developing biblical and contemporary cross-cultural aspects of contextualization as a requirement for evangelical missions.

SO151 Gittins, Anthony J.
Gifts and Strangers: Meeting the Challenge of Inculturation. Mahwah, NJU: Paulist Press, 1989. xii, 144 pp. Paper. 0809130882.

A basic course for cross-cultural persons in mission from North America and Europe, seeking to understand the dynamics of belief and behavior in Third World communities; by the Associate Professor of Mission Theology at the Catholic Theological Union in Chicago, Illinois.

SO152 *Good News in Our Times: The Gospel and Contemporary Cultures*
(GS980). London, ENK: Church House Publishing, 1991. iv, 132 pp. Paper. 0715155296.

A report of the Mission Theological Advisory Group of the Board of Mission of the General Synod of the Church of England, on Gospel and culture issues and their application to mission in Great Britain.

SO153 Gorski, Juan F.
Las Situaciones Historicas como Contenido del Mensaje Evangélico: Pautas para la interpretacion de los signos de los tiempos y semillas del verbo como preparación evangélica. (Pastoral Popular, 8). Bogotá, CK: Ediciones Paulinas, 1975. 93 pp. Paper. No ISBN.

Essay on the contextualization of the Gospel as seen in Bolivia.

SO154 Greinacher, Norbert, and Norbert Mette, eds.
Christianity and Cultures: A Mutual Enrichment. (Concilium, 1994/2). London, ENK: SCM Press; Maryknoll, NYU: Orbis Books, 1994. x, 142 pp. Paper. 0334030250 (UK), 0883448777 (US).

Six essays by Catholic scholars on current issues in inculturation, with five case studies (Egypt, Zaire, Pakistan, Latin America, and French Canada).

SO155 Gremillion, Joseph, ed.
The Church and Culture since Vatican II: The Experience of North and Latin America. Notre Dame, INU: University of Notre Dame Press, 1985. xvii, 330 pp. Paper. 0268007535.

A collection of scholarly papers and discussion reports from a 1984 seminar on "*Guadiam et Spes* and Culture" held at Notre Dame University; co-sponsored by the Pontifical Council for Culture, with documents on the relation of the Catholic Church and culture from the 1965-1984 period.

SO156 Hayama Missionary Seminar (24th, 1983)
All Things to All Men: Interaction of Biblical Faith and the Surrounding Cultures. Edited by Carl C. Beck. Tokyo, JA: Hayama Missionary Seminar, 1983. iv, 60 pp. Paper. No ISBN.

Major papers on contextualization in Japan.

SO157 Hesselgrave, David J., and Edward Rommen
Contextualization: Meanings, Methods, and Models. Grand Rapids, MIU: Baker Books, 1989. xii, 281 pp. Paper. 0801043387.

A comprehensive text for evangelicals on contextualization, including historical background, contemporary regional understandings, frameworks for analysis, and six case studies of "authentic and relevant contextualization."

SO158 Hopler, Thom, and Marcia Hopler
Reaching the World Next Door: How to Spread the Gospel in the Midst of Many Cultures. Downers Grove, ILU: InterVarsity, 1993. 245 pp. Paper. 0830816615.

A primer on Gospel and culture for Christians, raised in North American homogeneous middle-class communities, who desire to spread the good news of Jesus Christ in urban multicultural settings.

SO159 Inch, Morris A.
Making the Good News Relevant: Keeping the Gospel Distinctive in Any Culture. Nashville, TNU: Nelson, 1986. 111 pp. 0840775407.

Six issues in contextualization with three illustrations of contextualization at work from the author's missionary experience in Africa; with a brief bibliography.

SO160 *Inculturation: The Faith That Takes Root in African Cultures*
(Missio-Pastoral Series, 24). Gweru, ZI: Mambo Press; Harare, ZI: IMBISA Secretariat, 1993. 67 pp. Paper. 0869225669.

A Catholic study document prepared by IMBISA (the Inter-Regional Meeting of Bishops of Southern Africa) for those involved in the process of inculturation of Christianity in Southern Africa.

SO161 José, Saraiva Martins
Missione e cultura. (Studia Urbaniana, 28). Roma, IT: Urbaniana University Press, 1986. 207 pp. Paper. No ISBN.

A scholarly analysis of Roman Catholic missiological understandings of inculturation in the light of the papal encyclicals *Gaudium et Spes* and *Ad Gentes*.

SO162 Küster, Volker
Theologie im Kontext: Zugleich ein Versuch über die Minjung-Theologie. (Studia Instituti Missiologici SVD, 62). Nettetal, GW: Steyler Verlag, 1995. 191 pp. Paper. 3805003625.

An analysis of the meaning and method of contextual theology, plus a study of the *minjung* theology of Korea.

SO163 Kaplan, Steven, ed.
Indigenous Responses to Western Christianity. New York, NYU: New York University Press, 1995. x, 183 pp. 0814746497.

Seven scholarly historical case studies on indigenous responses to Western Christianity in Africa, China, India, Japan, Mexico, Peru, and Thailand.

SO164 Kraft, Charles H., and Tom H. Wisley, eds.
Readings in Dynamic Indigeneity. South Pasadena, CAU: William Carey Library, 1979. xxxii, 547 pp. Paper. 0878087397.

A collection of twenty-four articles on the indigenous church—its theology and structure, in theory and practice.

SO165 Kraft, Charles H.
Christianity in Culture: A Study in Dynamic Biblical Theologizing in Cross-Cultural Perspective. Maryknoll, NYU: Orbis Books, 1979. xvii, 445 pp. 088344075X.

In this classic work on contextualization Kraft uses the dynamic equivalent method of biblical translation as a model for theologizing in various contexts, applies insights from anthropology and communication theory, and includes a large bibliography.

SO166 Lausanne Committee for World Evangelization

The Willowbank Report: Report of a Consultation on Gospel and Culture Held at Willowbank, Somerset Bridge, Bermuda, from 6th to 13th January 1978. (Lausanne Occasional Papers, 2). Wheaton, ILU: LCWE, 1978. 36 pp. Paper. No ISBN.

A report about culture in biblical revelation, understanding the Bible today, church and culture, and Christian ethics and lifestyle.

SO167 Müller, Josef

Missionarische Anpassung als theologisches Prinzip. (Missionswissenschaftliche Abhandlungen und Texte, 31). Münster, GW: Aschendorff, 1973. viii, 322 pp. Paper. 3402035200.

With arguments from the synoptic Gospels and the history of the canon, this dissertation asserts that accommodation is a theological, rather than merely a pedagogical, question because the Christian message can only be understood when communicated and interpreted in definite situations (dissertation, University of Münster).

SO168 Mayers, Marvin K.

Christianity Confronts Culture: A Strategy for Crosscultural Evangelism. Grand Rapids, MIU: Zondervan, 1987. xiv, 418 pp. Paper. 0310289017.

Revised and expanded edition of a basic textbook on effective communication in cross-cultural settings, including numerous case studies.

SO169 Missionswissenschaftliches Institut Missio e. V.

Yearbook of Contextual Theologies 99. Frankfurt am Main, GW: IKO-Verlag für Interkulturelle Kommunikation, 1999. 241 pp. Paper. 3889395139.

A collection of ten articles on contextual theologies, written mostly in English, and including issues related to politics and research in Brazil, Nigeria, Ethiopia, Palestine, and India.

SO170 Montefiore, Hugh, ed.

The Gospel and Contemporary Culture. London, ENK: Mowbray, 1992. viii, 182 pp. Paper. 0264672593.

Eight scholarly essays examining key areas of British cultural thought (history, science, the arts, epistemology, economics, education, health, and mass media) in the light of the Christian Gospel; a preparatory volume for the National Consultation on the Gospel and our Culture (Swanwick, 1992).

SO171 Neckebrouck, Valeer

La tierce Église devant le problème de la culture. (*Nouvelle Revue de Science Missionaire*: Supplément, 36). Immensee, SZ: Nouvelle revue de science missionnaire, 1987. 164 pp. Paper. 3858240672.

A series of essays on the Third World church: acculturation, adaptation, incarnation, contextualization, culture and liberation, explicitness of witness, religion and culture, "holy indifference," and the challenges of the postcolonial era.

SO172 Newbigin, James Edward Lesslie

Den Griechen eine Torheit: Das Evangelium und unsere westliche Kultur. Translated by Gerhard Koslowsky. Neukirchen-Vluyn, GW: Aussaat Verlag, 1989. 133 pp. Paper. 376154667X.

German translation.

SO173 Newbigin, James Edward Lesslie

Foolishness to the Greeks: The Gospel and Western Culture. Geneva, SZ: WCC, 1986. 156 pp. Paper. 282540859X.

An analysis of what would be involved in a genuine missionary encounter between the Gospel and the post-Enlightenment cultures shared by the peoples of Europe and North America, in order to re-establish a growing Christian church.

SO174 Nicholls, Bruce J.

Contextualization: A Theology of Gospel and Culture. (Outreach and Identity: Evangelical Theological Monographs, 3). Downers Grove, ILU: InterVarsity; Exeter, ENK: Paternoster Press, 1979. 72 pp. Paper. 0877844569 (I), 0853642621 (P).

An introduction to four Gospel and culture issues: cultural and supra-cultural factors, patterns in the movement from contextualization to syncretism, understanding biblical theology, and the dynamics of cross-cultural communication.

SO175 Piepke, Joachim G., ed.

Evangelium und Kultur: Christliche Verkündigung und Gesellschaft im heutigen Mitteleuropa. (Veröffentlichungen des Missionspriesterseminars, 45). Nettetal, GW: Steyler Verlag, 1995. 204 pp. Paper. 3805003579.

Nine German theologians present scholarly essays on issues of the Gospel and culture in middle-Europe.

SO176 Pontifical Council for Culture

Towards a Pastoral Approach to Culture. Washington, DCU: USCC, 1999. 50 pp. Paper. 1574553496.

This book challenges the church today to respond to the multi-cultural contexts and inculturate the Gospel.

SO177 Poupard, Paul

The Church and Culture: Challenge and Confrontation: Inculturation and Evangelization. Translated by John H. Miller. St. Louis, MOU: Central Bureau, CCVA, 1994. xii, 153 pp. Paper. 0962625779.

English translation.

SO178 Poupard, Paul

L'église au défi des cultures: inculturation et évangélisation. Paris, FR: Desclée de Brouwer, 1989. 181 pp. 2718904356.

Reflections on issues of inculturation and evangelization by the Cardinal President of the Pontifical Council for Culture.

SO179 Prawdzik, Werner, ed.

Wirklichkeit und Theologie: Theologische Versuche und pastorale Impulse aus der Weltkirche. (Veröffentlichungen des Missionspriesterseminars, 36). Nettetal, GW: Steyler Verlag, 1988. 164 pp. Paper. 3805001932.

Eight papers on new theological and pastoral approaches to present-day problems in the world church, throwing light on the questions of accommodation and inculturation.

SO180 Regan, Hilary D., Alan J. Torrance, and Antony Wood, eds.

Christ and Context: The Confrontation between Gospel and Culture. Edinburgh, STK: T&T Clark, 1993. v, 269 pp. Paper. 0567292355.

Essays on the place of Christ in our understanding of human contextuality by an international panel of theologians (John de Gruchy, Gustavo Gutiérrez, Daniel Hardy, Janet Martin Soskice, Johann Metz, Jürgen Moltmann, and Elisabeth Moltmann-Wendel).

SO—MISSIONS: SOCIAL ASPECTS

SO181 Ro, Bong Rin
Christian Alternatives to Ancestor Practices. (Asian Evangelical Theological Library, 1). Taichung, CH: Asia Theological Association, 1985. 332 pp. Paper. No ISBN.

Papers presented at the Consultation on the Christian Response to Ancestor Practices (Taipei, 1983) on the biblical analysis of ancestor practices, their historical backgrounds, and recommendations for Christian alternatives; includes the Joint Declaration of Ancestor Practices.

SO182 Roest Crollius, Ary A., and Théoneste Nkéramihigo
What Is So New about Inculturation? (Inculturation: Working Papers on Living Faith and Cultures, 5). Rome, IT: Pontifical Gregorian University, 1984. xi, 54 pp. Paper. No ISBN.

Three essays on inculturation in relation to theology and culture.

SO183 Roest Crollius, Ary A., ed.
Creative Inculturation and the Unity of Faith. (Inculturation, 8.). Rome, IT: Pontifical Gregorian University, 1986. xii, 76 pp. Paper. No ISBN.

Three scholarly papers originally presented at the 1985 Jerusalem Symposium on "Inculturation: The Christian Experience Amidst Changing Cultures," sponsored by the International Federation of Catholic Universities.

SO184 Roest Crollius, Ary A., ed.
Effective Inculturation and Effective Identity. (Inculturation:Working Papers on Living Faith and Cultures, 9). Rome, IT: Pontifical Gregorian University, 1987. xi, 129 pp. Paper. 887652567X.

Five working papers by Roman Catholic missiologists on issues of inculturation.

SO185 Roest Crollius, Ary A., ed.
L' Inculturation et la Sagesse des Nations. (Inculturation Series, 4). Rome, IT: Pontifical Gregorian University, 1984. ix, 52 pp. Paper. No ISBN.

Three essays on inculturation: (1) The book of Proverbs and inculturation; (2) problems of inculturation in Korea; and (3) culture and inculturation in Africa.

SO186 Russell, William P.
Contextualization: Origins, Meaning and Implications. Rome, IT: Pontifica, 1995. 515 pp. Paper. No ISBN.

A dissertation on what the WCC's Theological Education Fund originally understood by the term "contextualization" (1970-1972).

SO187 Sanneh, Lamin
Religion and the Variety of Culture: A Study in Origin and Practice. (Christian Mission and Modern Culture). Valley Forge, PAU: Trinity Press International; Leominster, ENK: Gracewing, 1996. viii, 87 pp. Paper. 1563381664 (TPI), 0852443781 (G).

A provocative analysis in which the D. Willis James Professor of Missions and World Christianity at Yale University advocates reconnecting religion and Christianity to culture.

SO188 Scherer, James A., and Stephen B. Bevans, eds.
New Directions in Mission and Evangelization 3: Faith and Culture. Maryknoll, NYU: Orbis Books, 1999. x, 240 pp. Paper. 1570752583.

Representing a variety of branches of the Christian church and located in areas around the world, the contributors express their views on issues of inculturation in this text designed for classroom use in mission and world Christianity courses.

SO189 Schineller, Peter
A Handbook on Inculturation. Mahwah, NJU: Paulist Press, 1990. iv, 141 pp. Paper. 0809131242.

In this basic introductory handbook on inculturation, the Superior of the Nigeria-Ghana Jesuit Mission discusses the "what and why" of inculturation, surveys its history, explores its theological basis and methods for carrying out inculturation, gives examples of inculturation in Africa and Latin America, and discusses inculturation's implications for a modern society (in this case, the United States).

SO190 Schreiter, Robert J.
Constructing Local Theologies. Maryknoll, NYU: Orbis Books, 1985. xiii,178 pp. Paper. 088344108X.

An interdisplinary and ecumenical introduction to issues which involve people in a community developing local theology, with regard for both the essence of the Gospel and church tradition.

SO191 Schreurs, Nico, and Huub van de Sandt, eds.
De ene Jezus en de vele culturen: Christologie en contextualiteit. (TFT Studies, 20). Tilburg, NE: Tilburg University Press, 1992. viii, 130 pp. Paper. 9036196744.

Presented at a congress on "Christology and Context," May 1992, on the occasion of the 25th anniversary of the Faculty of Theology at Tilburg University; papers on the experiences and interpretations of Christ in India (Amaladoss), South Africa (Mofokeng), Latin America (da Silva), Western Europe (Logister), and Western Feminism (de Haardt).

SO192 Shorter, Aylward
Evangelization and Culture. New York, NYU: Chapman, 1994. xi, 164 pp. Paper. 0225667231.

The noted anthropologist, a priest of the Society of Missionaries of Africa, argues for a new evangelization that takes cultural pluralism seriously.

SO193 Shorter, Aylward
Toward a Theology of Inculturation. Maryknoll, NYU: Orbis Books; London, ENK: Chapman, 1988. xii, 256 pp. Paper. 0883445360 (O), 0225665026 (C).

The author brings together the many strands of historic and contemporary Roman Catholic thought on the theology of inculturation, with the argument that faith must become culture in order to be fully received and lived.

SO194 Standaert, Nicolas
Inculturatie Evangelie en Cultuur. (Kerk en Wereld-Documentatie). Brugge, BE: Een uitgave van Kerk en Wereld, 1990. 94 pp. Paper. 9050690289.

A primer for Belgian Catholics on the meaning, history, and contemporary methods of inculturation of the Gospel in various cultures, as part of the church's missionary outreach.

SO195 Stott, John R. W., and Robert T. Coote, eds.
Down to Earth:Studies in Christianity and Culture. Grand Rapids, MIU: Eerdmans, 1980. x, 342 pp. Paper. 0802818277.

Important papers on culture and the Bible; culture, evangelism and conversion; and culture, churches, and ethics. An abbreviated form was published under the title *Gospel and Culture* in 1979 by William Carey Library.

SO196 Udoidem, S. Iniobong

Pope John Paul II on Inculturation: Theory and Practice.
Lanham, MDU: University Press of America, 1996. 141 pp.
0761805028.

A Nigerian priest analyzes views of Pope John Paul II on
inculturation, and the development of Catholic views during
his pontificate.

**SO197 Waliggo, John Mary, Ary A. Roest Crollius, Théoneste
Nkéramihigo, and John Mutiso-Mbinda**

Inculturation: Its Meaning and Urgency. (Christian Leadership in Africa, 1). Kampala, UG: St. Paul Publications-Africa,
1986. 83 pp. Paper. No ISBN.

Three essays on inculturation by Catholic scholars from
Uganda (Waliggo), Rwanda (Nkeramihigo), and Kenya (Mutiso-Mbinda), plus two by the organizer of working papers on
living faith and cultures (Crollius).

SO198 Wilson, H. S., ed.

Gospel and Cultures: Reformed Perspectives. (Studies from
the World Alliance of Reformed Churches, 35). Geneva, SZ:
World Alliance of Reformed Churches, 1996. 159 pp. Paper.
9290750308.

The papers and findings of a WARC-sponsored consultation (Tana Toraja, Sulawesi Selatan, Indonesia, 5-10 February 1996).

Culture Conflict

See also HI440, SO65, SO125-SO126, SO207, EC69-EC70,
PO40, PO116, EV196, MI111, AF164, AF376-AF377, AF551,
AF575, AF1016, AM282, AM302, AM662, AM762-AM763, AM833,
AM837, AM854, AM880, AM888, AM1125, AM1194, AM1199,
AS725, AS837, AS1006, AS1102, and OC133.

SO199 Carothers, J. Edward

The Churches and Cruelty Systems. New York, NYU: Friendship Press, 1970. 160 pp. Paper. 0377090212.

A sociological analysis of cruelty systems in the United
States, with proposals and theological justification for a new
style of ministry addressing them; by the head of the National
Division of the United Methodist Board of Global Ministries.

SO200 Cushner, Kenneth, and Richard W. Brislin

Intercultural Interactions: A Practical Guide. (Cross-Cultural Research and Methodology Series, 9). Beverly Hills, CAU:
Sage Publications, 1996. xiv, 365 pp. 0803959907 (hdbk),
0803959915 (pbk).

Second edition of a text to educate those preparing for
extensive interaction in other cultures, including case studies
of 100 exemplary critical incidents; originally published in
1986.

SO201 Gundry-Volf, Judith M., and Miroslav Volf

A Spacious Heart: Essays on Identity and Belonging. (Christian Mission and Modern Culture). Harrisburg, PAU: Trinity
Press International; London, ENK: Gracewing, 1997. viii, 71
pp. Paper. 1563382016 (T), 0852444656 (G).

Out of the ethnic genocides of Rwanda and Bosnia, the
authors explore key aspects of the problem of diverse group
identities, offering preliminary biblical and theological perspectives on the encounter with "others."

SO202 Lewis, Bernard

Cultures in Conflict: Christians, Muslims, and Jews in the Age

of Discovery. New York, NYU: Oxford University Press, 1995.
101 pp. 0195090268 (hdbk), 0195102835 (pbk).

The Cleveland E. Dodge Professor of Near Eastern Studies Emeritus at Princeton University reflects on the multiple
anniversaries of 1492—the Christian conquest of Granada (the
last Muslim outpost in Spain), the expulsion of the Jews from
all of Spain, and the voyage of Columbus.

SO203 Lewis, Norman

The Missionaries: God against the Indians. New York, NYU:
McGraw Hill; New York, NYU: Penguin Books, 1988. 245
pp. Paper. 0700376131 (M), 0140131752 (P).

An account of the tragic history of mistreatment of indigenous tribal peoples as part of the missionary conquest of Central and South America; with an exposé of continuing persecution based on the author's travels in the region from 1946 to
1987.

SO204 McGavran, Donald Anderson

The Clash between Christianity and Cultures. Washington,
DCU: Canon Press, 1974. 84 pp. Paper. 0913686123.

A contribution to the Gospel and culture debate by the
dean emeritus of the Fuller School of World Mission, who
argues for the inevitability of culture clash, opposes views that
would accommodate secularism, relativism, or pluralism, and
advocates for the authority of the Gospel within any culture.

SO205 Melander, Veronica, ed.

*Culture Confrontation and Local Mobilization: Essays in
Honour of Sigbert Axelson.* (Studia Missionalia Upsaliensia,
68). Uppsala, SW: Swedish Institute of Missionary Research,
1997. 253 pp. Paper. 918542448X.

A *festschrift* containing fifteen essays concerning the social and political functions of religion; to honor the noted Professor of Mission Studies at Uppsala University upon his retirement.

Social Conflict

See also SO35-SO36, and SO222.

SO206 Kenneson, Philip D.

Beyond Sectarianism: Re-Imaging Church and World. (Christian Mission and Modern Culture). Harrisburg, PAU: Trinity
Press International, 1999. x, 124 pp. Paper. 1563382784.

A model of the church in contemporary society as a "contrast society," and an answer to critics who regard this as sectarian and who operate with untenable understandings of rationality, culture, politics, religion, and critique.

SO207 Lederach, John Paul

The Journey toward Reconciliation. Scottdale, PAU: Herald
Press, 1999. 206 pp. Paper. 0836190823.

The author shares insights from years of work in international mediation and deep spiritual reflection on the task of
reconciliation through personal experiences and theological
reflection.

SO208 Reuss, Carl F., ed.

*Conscience and Action: Social Statements of the American
Lutheran Church, 1961-1970.* Minneapolis, MNU: Augsburg,
1971. 184 pp. Paper. 0806611065.

Formal social statements of the American Lutheran
Church as it sought to respond to, and act on, the social dilemmas prevalent in America between 1961 and 1970.

SO—MISSIONS: SOCIAL ASPECTS

SO209 Schrock-Shenk, Carolyn, and Lawrence Ressler, eds.
Making Peace with Conflict: Practical Skills for Conflict Resolution. Scottdale, PAU: Herald Press, 1999. 198 pp. Paper. 0836191277.

A collection of seventeen articles on walking conflict's holy ground in various settings and cultures, in relation to such issues as race, power, gender, family, global conflict, and decision making.

Race Relations

See also HI253, HI384, TH604, ED64, MI189, AF348, AF887, AF917, AF944, AF961-AF962, AF986, AF1019, AF1032, AF1037, AF1047, AF1073-AF1074, AF1076, AF1088, AF1096, AF1115, AF1122, AF1125, AM1034, EU110, EU116, EU134, OC99, and OC123.

SO210 Adler, Elisabeth
A Small Beginning: An Assessment of the First Five Years of the Programme to Combat Racism. Geneva, SZ: WCC, 1974. vi, 102 pp. Paper. No ISBN.

A first summary and evaluation, by the head of the Evangelical Academy in East Berlin, of the creative yet controversial work of the WCC's Programme to Combat Racism during the 1969-1974 period.

SO211 Barndt, Joseph R.
Liberating Our White Ghetto. Minneapolis, MNU: Augsburg, 1972. 128 pp. 0806612061.

A study book, with discussion guide, for white congregations and individual Christians in the United States, who desire to understand racism and rid themselves and their churches of it; by the founder of the Community Organization for Urban Progess in Oakland, California.

SO212 Best, Felton O., ed.
Black Religious Leadership from the Slave Community to the Million Man March: Flames of Fire. (Black Studies, 3). Lewiston, NYU: E Mellen Press, 1998. 262 pp. 0773483454.

Thirteen scholarly case studies examining the multifaceted means by which black religious leaders have embarked upon campaigns to eradicate social injustice.

SO213 Blaser, Klauspeter
Wenn Gott schwarz wäre: Das Problem des Rassismus in Theologie und christlicher Praxis. Zürich, SZ: Theologischer Verlag, 1972. 360 pp. 3290113108.

A standard theological text on questions of racism by one who has worked in South Africa.

SO214 Collum, Danny Duncan
Black and White Together: The Search for Common Ground. Maryknoll, NYU: Orbis Books, 1996. x, 133 pp. Paper. 1570750971.

Accounts of eight little-known episodes in United States' history in which black and white Americans found common cause, including contemporary church-based community organizations.

SO215 Davies, Susan E., and Paul Teresa Hennessee, eds.
Ending Racism in the Church. Cleveland, OHU: United Church Press, 1998. ix, 150 pp. Paper. 0829812385.

Diverse essays and case studies for equipping communi-

ty witness in the church's mission for the removal of racism from society and church.

SO216 Jones, Howard O.
White Questions to a Black Christian. Grand Rapids, MIU: Zondervan, 1975. 215 pp. Paper. No ISBN.

An associate evangelist with the Billy Graham Evangelistic Association answers questions on Christianity and race, asked at evangelistic crusades, Bible conferences, and missionary conventions.

SO217 Kitagawa, Daisuke
Race Relations and Christian Mission. New York, NYU: Friendship Press, 1964. 191 pp. Paper. No ISBN.

A mission study of racial tensions in Asia, Africa, and the United States; the nature of racism, the biblical basis for a Christian response, and alternatives for action.

SO218 Kitagawa, Daisuke
Rassenkonflikte und christliche Mission: Eine kritische Untersuchung der rassischen und völkischen Spannungen in Afrika, Asien und Amerika. Wuppertal, GW: Aussaat Verlag, 1968. 164 pp. Paper. No ISBN.

German translation.

SO219 K'Meyer, Tracy Elaine
Interracialism and Christian Community in the Postwar South: The Story of Koinonia Farm. Charlottesville, VAU: University Press of Virginia, 1997. x, 236 pp. 0813917123.

A detailed history of Koinonia Farm from its founding in 1942 by white Baptists as an interracial Christian cooperative to its metamorphosis into Koinonia Partners in 1968.

SO220 Linde, J. M. van der
Over Noach met zijn zonen: De Chamideologie en de leugens tegen Cham tot vandaag. (IIMO Research Publication, 33). Utrecht, NE: IIMO, 1993. 160 pp. 9021170019.

A historical study of how the identification of people of color as the children of Ham in Genesis was used to justify slavery and racism from biblical times to the present.

SO221 Matsuoka, Fumitaka
The Color of Faith: Building Community in a Multiracial Society. Cleveland, OHU: United Church Press, 1998. vii, 143 pp. Paper. 0829812814.

A theological study on racial and ethnic plurality which challenges the church to move beyond a segregated institution to become a catalyst for change.

SO222 McKivigan, John R., and Mitchell Snay, eds.
Religion and the Antebellum Debate over Slavery. Athens, GAU: University of Georgia Press, 1998. viii, 391 pp. 0820319724 (hdbk), 0820320765 (pbk).

Scholarly essays on the powerful pulls toward moderation and unity that existed within the institutional church in the antebellum sectional conflict over slavery, with emphasis on denominational schisms and diversity within religions, states, and denominations.

SO223 *Missioni e Razzismo*
Rome, IT: Lega Missionaria Studenti, 1965. 214 pp. No ISBN.

A collection of papers by Italian theological students on the racial problem in the light of missions.

SO224 Pannell, William E.

The Coming Race Wars?: A Cry for Reconciliation. Grand Rapids, MIU: Zondervan, 1993. 143 pp. Paper. 0310381819.

In response to the Los Angeles riot of 1992, the Professor of Preaching and Practical Theology at Fuller Theological Seminary pleads with white evangelicals to recognize the problems of institutional racism and injustice in the United States and to work actively to solve them.

SO225 Park, Andrew Sung

Racial Conflict and Healing: An Asian-American Theological Perspective. Maryknoll, NYU: Orbis Books, 1996. x, 198 pp. Paper. 1570750785.

In the aftermath of the Los Angeles riots of 1992 and the ensuing violence against Korean Americans, a Korean American theologian develops a theological model that will help transform a society of oppression, injustice, and violence into a community of equity, fairness, and mutual consideration.

SO226 Racism in Asia: Race and Minority Issues

(PCR Papers, 22). Geneva, SZ: WCC, Programme Unit on Justice and Service, 1986. 84 pp. Paper. No ISBN.

Articles on minority rights issues in Japan, India, Sri Lanka, and the Philippines, plus 1985 grants by the WCC Programme to Combat Racism.

SO227 Racism in Theology and Theology against Racism: Report of a Consultation Organized by the Commission on Faith and Order and the Programme to Combat Racism

Geneva, SZ: WCC, 1975. 20 pp. Paper. 2825405213.

A concise presentation on the ambiguity of racism, the Christian witness against racism, the search for a just society, and possible further actions by Christians.

SO228 Racism in Western Europe

(PCR Information, Reports and Background Papers, 21). Geneva, SZ: WCC, 1985. 74 pp. Paper. 2825405213.

Articles, reports, views, items, and book reviews concerning racism in Europe.

SO229 Renault, François

Lavigerie, l'esclavage africain, et l'Europe, 1868-1892. Paris, FR: Éditions de Boccard, 1971. 2 vols. No ISBN.

A dissertation detailing the struggle against African slavery between 1868 and 1892, the Arab-African contacts, the role of Europe in the African slave trade, and the struggle of Lavigerie and other missionaries against it [vol. 1: 433 pp.; vol. 2: 506 pp.].

SO230 Richardson, Neville

The World Council of Churches and Race Relations, 1960 to 1969. (Studies in the Intercultural History of Christianity, 9). Frankfurt am Main, GW: Lang, 1977. 78 pp. Paper. 326101718X.

A concise history of the decade in which the WCC moved from a general concern for race relations to develop a concrete Programme to Combat Racism.

SO231 Shearer, Jody Miller

Enter the River: Healing Steps from White Privilege toward Racial Reconciliation. Scottdale, PAU: Herald Press, 1994. 213 pp. Paper. 0836136608.

A popular study of the dynamics of racism and what can be done about it by Christian individuals and churches in the United States.

SO232 Van der Bent, A. J., ed.

Breaking Down the Walls: World Council of Churches Statements and Actions on Racism, 1948-1985. Geneva, SZ: WCC, 1986. 107 pp. Paper. 2825408662.

A compilation of the official responses of the WCC to issues of racism since its founding in 1948.

SO233 Verkuyl, Johannes

Break Down the Walls: A Christian Cry for Racial Justice. Translated by Lewis B. Smedes. Grand Rapids, MIU: Eerdmans, 1973. 166 pp. Paper. 0802814988 (hdbk), 0802814999 (pbk).

English translation.

SO234 Verkuyl, Johannes

Breek de muren af!: Om gerechtigheid in de rassenverhoudingen. (Ökumene). Baarn, NE: Bosch & Keuning, 1970. 158 pp. No ISBN.

A primer for Christians on contemporary race relations including a biblical perspective, a brief history of links between imperialism and racism, and recent issues (ecumenical declarations, South African apartheid, separtism in Rhodesia, and interracial marriage) by the Professor and Head of the Department of Mission and Evangelism at the Free University, Amsterdam, the Netherlands.

SO235 Vincent, John J.

The Race Race. New York, NYU: Friendship Press; London, ENK: SCM Press, 1970. xii, 116 pp. Paper. 0334013755.

A new style of ecumenical report on the Consultation on Race (London, May 1969), designed for the non-specialist who seeks understanding of contemporary issues of racism.

SO236 Walther, Christian, ed.

Rassismus: Eine Dokumentation zum ökumenischen Antirassismusprogramm. (Zur Sache, 6). Berlin, GW: Lutherisches Verlagshaus, 1971. 101 pp. Paper. No ISBN.

Volume six of the series "To the Point: Aspects of the Church Today," containing reports and white papers condemning racism by the WCC from 1954 to 1970.

Unreached Peoples

See also ME10, ME41, ME69, SO13, SO95, EV33, MI41, MI56, AS57, AS768, AS935, and AS1020.

SO237 Beaver, Robert Pierce, ed.

The Gospel and Frontier Peoples: A Report of a Consultation, December 1972. South Pasadena, CAU: William Carey Library, 1973. vii, 405 pp. Paper. 0878081240.

Fourteen papers by prominent missiologists, plus reports from the influential Consultation on Frontier Missions to tribal peoples, attended by ninety-seven leaders of North American mission boards, Catholic and Protestant.

SO238 Dayton, Edward R., and Samuel Wilson, eds.

The Future of World Evangelization: Unreached Peoples '84. (Unreached Peoples Series, 6). Monrovia, CAU: MARC, 1984. 717 pp. Paper. 0912552425.

A status report on the involvement of mission agencies in attempts to reach unreached people groups, indicating future plans. (An abbreviated version minus descriptions and registry of unreached peoples has been published separately under the title, *The Future of World Evangelization: The Lausanne Movement.*)

SO—MISSIONS: SOCIAL ASPECTS

SO239 Dayton, Edward R., and Samuel Wilson, eds.
The Refugees among Us: Unreached Peoples '83. (Unreached Peoples Series, 5). Monrovia, CAU: MARC, 1983. 523 pp. Paper. 0912552387.

The fifth volume of the Unreached Peoples Series containing a world overview of refugees, expanded descriptions of refugee people groups, and an updated registry of the unreached.

SO240 Dayton, Edward R., and Samuel Wilson, eds.
Unreached Peoples '82: The Challenge of the Church's Unfinished Business—Focus on Urban People. (Unreached Peoples Series, 4). Elgin, ILU: David C. Cook, 1982. 435 pp. 0891918388.

Essays on the evangelization of large cities with case studies and expanded descriptions of unreached peoples.

SO241 Dayton, Edward R.
That Everyone May Hear: Reaching the Unreached. Monrovia, CAU: MARC, 1983. 92 pp. Paper. 0912552352.

Third edition written to help people everywhere discover which people God wants them to reach, what they are like, and how to reach them; originally published in 1979.

SO242 *Inter-Agency Consultation for Resources and Information on Reaching the Unreached (Irving, Texas)*
Monrovia, CAU: MARC, 1988. 100 pp. Paper. No ISBN.

A consultation of twenty-eight denominations and Christian organizations, held in Dallas, Texas, to explore ways to share information on reaching unreached peoples.

SO243 *Missions Advanced Research and Communications Center: Unreached Peoples Directory*
Monrovia, CAU: MARC, 1974. 117 pp. Paper. No ISBN.

An initial directory of unreached peoples prepared for the International Congress on World Evangelization, Lausanne, 1974.

SO244 Pentecost, Edward C.
Reaching the Unreached: An Introductory Study on Developing an Overall Strategy for World Evangelization. South Pasadena, CAU: William Carey Library, 1974. xiv, 149 pp. Paper. 0878084185.

An introduction to methods by which to identify and evangelize peoples and groups largely unreached by the Gospel.

SO245 Schreck, Harley Carl, and David B. Barrett, eds.
Unreached Peoples: Clarifying the Task. (Unreached Peoples Series, 7). Monrovia, CAU: MARC, 1987. viii, 302 pp. Paper. 0912552581.

The seventh volume in the Unreached Peoples Series containing general articles and thirteen case descriptions of reaching peoples in Africa, plus a registry of the unreached.

SO246 Wagner, C. Peter, and Edward R. Dayton, eds.
Unreached Peoples '79: The Challenge of the Church's Unfinished Buisness. (Unreached Peoples Series, 1). Elgin, ILU: David C. Cook, 1979. 349 pp. Paper. 0891911464.

First volume in a series jointly inaugurated by the Strategy Working Group of the LCWE and MARC, containing general articles, case studies (Africa, UK), expanded descriptions of unreached peoples, and a registry of the unreached.

SO247 Wagner, C. Peter, and Edward R. Dayton, eds.
Unreached Peoples '80: The Challenge of the Church's Unfinished Business. (Unreached Peoples Series, 2). Elgin, ILU: David C. Cook, 1980. 383 pp. Paper. 089191837X.

Second book in the Unreached Peoples Series focusing on mission to Muslims, with case studies.

SO248 Wagner, C. Peter, and Edward R. Dayton, eds.
Unreached Peoples '81: The Challenge of the Church's Unfinished Business. (Unreached Peoples Series, 3). Elgin, ILU: David C. Cook, 1981. 467 pp. Paper. 0891913319.

Third book in the Unreached Peoples Series containing a special section on the peoples of Asia.

SO249 Wilson, Samuel, and Gordon D. Aeschliman
The Hidden Half: Discovering the World of Unreached Peoples. Monrovia, CAU: MARC, 1973. 152 pp. 0912552433.

A popular presentation of mission in areas not normally served by mission workers, including the biblical rationale for mission to unreached peoples.

SO250 Yamamori, Tetsunao
Penetrating Missions' Final Frontier: A New Strategy for Unreached Peoples. Downers Grove, ILU: InterVarsity, 1993. 213 pp. Paper. 0830813705.

A handbook on the whys and hows of mission strategies to people groups virtually untouched by Christianity.

Popular Religiosity

See also CR615, SO47, SO366, AM9, AM132, AM161, AM317-AM318, AM687, AM797, AM814, AM824-AM825, AM871, AM985, AM1060, AM1084, AM1103, AS292, AS912, AS1056, AS1064, and AS1439.

SO251 Bentué, Antonio, and Juan Carlos Scannone
Tercer Seminario Interamericano de Religiosidad Popular, Santiago, CL, 1986. (Teología y Vida, 28:1/2). Santiago, CL: Teología y Vida, 1987. 171 pp. No ISBN.

A collection of nine seminar papers whose principal themes are the concept of popular religiosity, religiosity and the cultural nucleus of a people, the value of popular religiosity, and evangelization and popular religion, with an extensive bibliography.

SO252 CELAM-Sección para No-creyentes, Seminario, Bogotá, CK, 19-24 de noviembre de 1981
Conflictos y no-creencia en América Latina: Hacia una superación a la luz de Puebla. (Documentos CELAM, 63). Bogotá, CK: CELAM, 1983. 244 pp. Paper. No ISBN.

Seminar materials.

SO253 Cox, Harvey Gallagher
La Seducción del Espíritu: El uso y el abuso de la religión del pueblo. (Punto limite, 8). Santander, SP: Editorial Sal Terrae, 1979. 364 pp. Paper. 8429305238.

Spanish translation.

SO254 Cox, Harvey Gallagher
The Seduction of the Spirit: The Use and Misuse of People's Religion. New York, NYU: Simon & Schuster, 1973. 350 pp. 0704500892.

Drawing upon life stories heard by the author on six continents, the Harvard Divinity School theologian and sociologist of religion outlines the sources and characteristics of new and vital popular religion.

SO255 Estrada, Juan Antonio
La Transformación de la Religiosidad Popular. (Materiales, 24). Salamanca, SP: Ediciones Sígueme, 1986. 136 pp. Paper. 8430110046.

Analysis of the theological significance of popular religiosity, with reflections particular to Andalucia, Spain, and guidelines for its transformation.

SO256 Kleinhenz, Christopher, and Fannie J. LeMoine, eds.
Fearful Hope: Approaching the New Millennium. Madison, WIU: University of Wisconsin Press, 1999. xiv, 222 pp. 0299164306 (hdbk), 0299164349 (pbk).

A collection of eleven essays, with appendices, on apocalyptic issues in religious and secular culture; illustrated from biblical prophets, medieval manuscripts, cult movements, and even current television shows, such as *The X-Files.*

SO257 Maldonado, Luis
Introducción a la Religiosidad Popular. (Presencia Teológica, 21). Santander, SP: Sal Terrae, 1985. 226 pp. Paper. 8429307214.

A comprehensive work that orders existing materials on popular religiosity and systematizes its fundamental categories and expressions.

SO258 Mouw, Richard J.
Consulting the Faithful: What Christian Intellectuals Can Learn from Popular Religion. Grand Rapids, MIU: Eerdmans, 1994. vi, 84 pp. Paper. 0802807380.

An essay calling upon the engagement of theological scholarship with contemporary popular religion in the United States by the president of Fuller Theological Seminary.

SO259 SELADOC
Religiosidad Popular. (Materiales, 13). Salamanca, SP: Ediciones Sígueme, 1976. 380 pp. Paper. 8430104224.

An anthology of documents, theological-pastoral reflections, interpretive analyses, and pastoral experiences.

SO260 Vidales, Raú, and Kudo Tokihiro
Práctica Religiosa y Proyecto Historico: Hipótesis para un estudio de la religiosidad popular en América Latina. (CEP, 13). Lima, PE: CEP, 1975. 132 pp. Paper. No ISBN.

A theoretical work of religious sociology directed toward the study of popular religiosity in Latin America.

New Religious Movements: General

See also CR835, CR1493, SO393, AF248, AF1242, and AM1476.

SO261 Beckford, James A., ed.
New Religious Movements and Rapid Social Change. Newbury Park, CAU: Sage Publications; Paris, FR: UNESCO, 1986. xv, 247 pp. 0803980038 (S), 923024027 (U).

A collection, sponsored by UNESCO, of nine essays on modern day religious movements in Third World countries.

SO262 Biezais, Haralds, ed.
New Religions. (Scripta Instituti Donneriani Aboensis, 7). Stockholm, SW: Almquist & Wiksell, 1975. 223 pp. Paper. No ISBN.

Sixteen essays by sociologists of religion on new religious movements and ideologies in Europe, Africa, Asia, and North America.

SO263 Brockway, Allen A., and J. Paul William Rajashekar
New Religious Movements and the Churches. Geneva, SZ: WCC, 1987. xix, 200 pp. Paper. 2825408905.

Report and papers of a consultation sponsored by the LWF and the WCC.

SO264 Bromley, David G., and Phillip E. Hammond, eds.
The Future of New Religious Movements. Macon, GAU: Mercer University Press, 1987. vi, 278 pp. Paper. 0865542376 (hdbk), 0865542384 (pbk).

Seventeen scholarly articles prepared for the Conference on the Future of New Religious Movements, held in October 1983 in Berkeley, California, sponsored by the New Ecumenical Research Association (New ERA).

SO265 Conference on World Evangelization (Pattaya, Thailand, 1980)
The Thailand Report on New Religious Movements: Report of the ... Mini-Consultation on Reaching Mystics and Cultists. (Lausanne Occasional Papers, 11). Wheaton, ILU: LCWE, 1980. 48 pp. Paper. No ISBN.

A look at the new religions and cults, their attraction for young people all over the world; with strategies for witness and counsel with those attracted by such groups.

SO266 Hesselgrave, David J., ed.
Dynamic Religious Movements: Case Studies of Rapidly Growing Religious Movements around the World. Grand Rapids, MIU: Baker Books, 1978. 326 pp. 0801041309.

Case studies designed to inform leaders of evangelical Christianity about twelve new religious movements and their significance.

SO267 Lane, David Christopher
Exposing Cults: When the Skeptical Mind Confronts the Mystical. (Reference Library of Social Science, 890; Religious Information Systems, 10). New York, NYU: Garland, 1994. xiv, 285 pp. 081531275X.

A collection of sixteen articles on new religious movements; originally published in the 1980s as the author's accounts of his experiences with various groups and their leaders.

SO268 Lanternari, Vittorio
Movimenti religiosi di libertà e di salvezza dei popoli oppressi. (I fatti e le idee, 27). Milano, IT: Feltrinelli, 1960. 365 pp. No ISBN.

A 20th-century survey of religious movements among colonial and semi-colonial peoples, including prophetic movements in the Americas, nativistic-religious movements in Africa, and messianic movements in Melanesia, Polynesia, Southeast Asia, and Japan.

SO269 Lanternari, Vittorio
Movimientos Religiosos de Libertad y Salvación en los Pueblos Oprimidos. Translated by Andrés Lupo. (Ciencias Humanas, 219). Barcelona, SP: Editorial Seix Barral, 1965. xi, 405 pp. No ISBN.

Spanish translation.

SO270 Lanternari, Vittorio, and Lisa Sergio
The Religions of the Oppressed: A Study of Modern Messianic Cults. New York, NYU: Knopf, 1963. 343 pp. No ISBN.

English translation.

SO—MISSIONS: SOCIAL ASPECTS

SO271 Margull, Hans Jochen
Aufbruch zur Zukunft: Chiliastisch-messianische Bewegungen in Afrika und Südostasien. (Missionswissenschaftliche Forschungen, 1). Gütersloh, GW: Gerd Mohn, 1962. 126 pp. No ISBN.

A wide-ranging survey of messianic movements, from the cargo cults of Southeast Asia to the prophet movements of South and West Africa, and the messianic ideology that surrounds Prime Minister Kwame Nkrumah of Ghana and some Indian leaders; with short biographies of more prominent prophetic leaders.

SO272 Needleman, Jacob, and George Baker, eds.
Understanding the New Religions. New York, NYU: Seabury Press, 1978. xxi, 314 pp. 0816404038 (hdbk), 0816421889 (pbk).

Twenty-five scholarly essays originally presented at the National Conference on the Study of New Religious Movements in America (Berkeley, California, 1977).

SO273 Nussbaum, Stan
New Religious Movements. Elkhart, INU: Mission Focus Publications, 1989. 36 pp. Paper. No ISBN.

Four essays focusing on the implications of the growth of new religious movements for missionary preparation and training; originally published in *Mission Focus* (June 1988-June 1989).

SO274 Oosterwal, Gottfried
Modern Messianic Movements as a Theological and Missionary Challenge. (Missionary Studies, 2). Elkhart, INU: Institute of Mennonite Studies, 1973. 55 pp. No ISBN.

An analysis of the nature of modern messianic movements and the challenge they pose for Christian missions.

SO275 Romarheim, Arild
The Aquarian Christ: Jesus Christ as Portrayed by New Religious Movements. New Territories, HK: Good Tidings, 1992. 112 pp. Paper. 962766801X.

A typology of the new religious concepts of Jesus Christ presented in diverse groups (Mormonism, Unification Church, The Way International, Rosecrucianism, T. M., Hare Krishna, Ahmadiiyya, Bahai, etc.).

SO276 Turner, Harold W.
Religious Movements in Primal Societies. Elkhart, INU: Mission Focus Publications, 1989. 31 pp. Paper. No ISBN.

Reprint of an introduction to new religious movements by the founder of the Centre for New Religious Movements (Birmingham, England); originally published in *Mission Focus*, September 1981.

SO277 Walls, Andrew F., and Wilbert R. Shenk, eds.
Exploring New Religious Movements: Essays in Honour of Harold W. Turner. Elkhart, INU: Mission Focus Publications, 1990. vi, 215 pp. Paper. 1877736082.

A *festschrift* containing sixteen scholarly essays in honor of the distinguished founder of the Centre for New Religious Movements.

SO278 Wilson, Bryan R.
The Social Dimensions of Sectarianism: Sects and New Religious Movements in Contemporary Society. Oxford, ENK: Clarendon Press; New York, NYU: Oxford University Press, 1990. xii, 299 pp. 0198273460.

Thirteen essays by the noted Oxford University sociologist, tracing the growth and expansion of various new religious movements in the West, relating them to their social contexts.

New Religious Movements: Africa

See also SO271, SO608, SO625, AF228, AF304, AF435, AF586, AF602, AF762, AF896, AF1270, AF1273-AF1275, and AS1497.

SO279 Adogame, Afeosemime U.
Celestial Church of Christ: The Politics of Cultural Identity in a West African Prophetic-Charismatic Movement. (Studies in the Intercultural History of Christianity, 115). Frankfurt am Main, GW: Lang, 1999. x, 251 pp. Paper. 3631348495 (GW), 082044331X (US).

The contemporary growth and development of a popular, widespread religious initiative in West Africa, the Celestial Church of Christ; includes the analysis of belief pattern and ritual structure within the context and continuum of African Christianity, and the tendency of the church toward globalization.

SO280 *And Some Fell on Good Ground*
(RISK, vol. 7, no. 3). Geneva, SZ: WCC, 1971. 63 pp. No ISBN.

Short illustrated essays introducing African independency with a Who's Who of leaders.

SO281 Baeta, C. G.
Prophetism in Ghana: A Study of Some "Spiritual" Churches. London, ENK: SCM Press, 1962. xiii, 169 pp. No ISBN.

A scholarly survey of five expressions of independency in Ghana: the Church of the Twelve Apostles, the Musama Disco Christo Church (Army of the Cross of Christ), the Saviour Church, the Apostolic Revelation Society, and the Prayer Healing Movement within the Evangelical Presbyterian Church.

SO282 Barrett, David B.
Schism and Renewal in Africa: An Analysis of Six Thousand Contemporary Religious Movements. London, ENK: Oxford University Press; Nairobi, KE: East African Publishing House, 1968. xx, 363 pp. Paper. No ISBN.

A comprehensive analysis of the vast number of movements of renewal, protest, and dissidence which have been taking place in Africa, inside and outside the Protestant and Catholic churches, in thirty-four nations and three-hundred tribes, over the past one-hundred years.

SO283 Becken, Hans-Jürgen
Theologie der Heilung: Das Heilen in den afrikanischen Unabhängigen Kirchen in Südafrika. (Verkündigung und Verantwortung, 1). Hermannsburg, GW: Verlag der Missionshandlung, 1972. 294 pp. Paper. No ISBN.

A dissertation, based on fieldwork, describing and interpreting the phenomenon of healing within the framework of the theology of the AICs; with detailed documentation.

SO284 Becken, Hans-Jürgen
Wo der Glaube noch jung ist: Afrikanische Unabhängige Kirchen im Südlichen Afrika. (Erlanger Taschenbücher, 73). Erlangen, GW: Ev.-Luth. Mission, 1985. 286 pp. Paper. 3872141732.

A study of the structure, forms, symbols and traditions of AICS in southern Africa, with the aim of encouraging dialogue and partnership with these groups.

SO285 Benz, Ernst et al., eds.

Messianische Kirchen, Sekten und Bewegungen im heutigen Afrika. (Beihefte der Zeitschrift für Religions- und Geistesgeschichte, 10). Leiden, NE: Brill, 1965. x, 128 pp. Paper. No ISBN.

Five articles and a bibliography comprise this short book on AICs: E. Damann on the Christology of post-Christian churches and sects; K. Schlosser on secular grounds for joining separatist churches; O. F. Raum on the Xhosa trajectory from tribal prophet to sect leader; H. W. Turner on the Aladura and analogous catechisms; and H. J. Greshat on witchcraft and separatism.

SO286 Bond, George, Walton R. Johnson, and Sheila S. Walker, eds.

African Christianity: Patterns of Religious Continuity. (Studies in Anthropology). New York, NYU: Academic Press, 1979. xvi, 175 pp. 0121134504.

Five scholarly case studies on Christian belief and worship in West and Central Africa: the Harrist churches of Ivory Coast and Ghana, The Church of the Messiah (Ghana), the African Methodist Episcopal Church (Zambia), the Apostolic Church of John Maranke (Zambia), and the Lumpa Church (Zambia).

SO287 Boschman, Don Rempel

The Conflict between New Religious Movements and the State in the Bechuanaland Protectorate Prior to 1949. (Studies on the Church in Southern Africa, 3). Gaborone, BS: University of Botswana, 1994. 46 pp. 9991220593.

A comprehensive and detailed study of the early history of independency in present Botswana, based on a doctoral thesis submitted at Harvard Divinity School in 1989.

SO288 Buell, Raymond Leslie

The Native Problem in Africa. Hamden, CTU: Archon Books; London, ENK: Cass, 1965. 2 vols. No ISBN.

Contains discussions on various separatist and independent church movements across the African continent.

SO289 Chirenje, J. Mutero

Ethiopianism and Afro-Americans in Southern Africa, 1883-1916. Baton Rouge, LAU: Louisiana State University Press, 1987. xii, 231 pp. 0807113190.

A scholarly history of the rise of AICs in southern Africa, focusing on the role African Americans played in that process.

SO290 Colloque International du CERA (4th, 1992, Kinshasa)

Sectes, cultures et sociétés: Les enjeux spirituels du temps présent. (Cahiers des Religions Africaines, 27-28 (1993-1994), 53-56). Kinshasa, CG: Facultés Catholiques de Kinshasa, 1994. 608 pp. No ISBN.

Papers from the Fourth International Colloquium of the Center for African Religious Studies (CERA) of the Catholic Faculty of Kinshasa, Zaire (14-21 Nov. 1992) focusing on sects and new religious movements.

SO291 Conference on Ministry to African Independent Churches: July, 1986, Abidjan, Côte d'Ivoire

Ministry of Missions to African Independent Churches: Papers presented at the Conference on Ministry to African Independent Churches, July 1986, Abidjan, Côte d'Ivoire. Edited by David A. Shank. Elkhart, INU: Mennonite Board of Missions, 1987. 291 pp. Paper. No ISBN.

A major conference on the AICs; with fourteen papers, mostly by prominent Western scholars.

SO292 Daneel, M. L.

Fambidzano: Ecumenical Movement of Zimbabwean Independent Churches. Gweru, RH: Mambo Press, 1989. xxvi, 645 pp. Paper. 0869224654.

The story of the development of the African (Shona) Independent Churches' Conference in Zimbabwe (FAMBIDZANO) and the men and women who began that ecumenical body; by the Professor of Missiology at the University of South Africa who was its founder.

SO293 Daneel, M. L.

Old and New in Southern Shona Independent Churches. (Change and Continuity in Africa). The Hague, NE: Mouton; Gweru, RH: Mambo Press, 1971. 3 vols. 9027977011 (vol. 2), 0869224433 (vol. 3).

Results of the most extensive study of AICs, covering their socio-economic background in Zimbabwe, related mission history, and typology [vol. 1: *Background and Rise of the Major Movements* (Mouton; 1971; xviii, 527 pp.; no ISBN); vol. 2: *Church Growth: Causative Factors and Recruitment Techniques* (Mouton; 1974; xviii, 373 pp.); and vol. 3: *Leadership and Fission Dynamics* (Mambo Press; 1988; xxi, 565 pp.)].

SO294 Daneel, M. L.

Quest for Belonging: Introduction to a Study of African Independent Churches. (Mambo Occasional Papers—Missio-Pastoral Series, 17). Gweru, RH: Mambo Press, 1987. 310 pp. Paper. 0869224263.

An introduction to African independency, arguing that as institutions in their own right, they provide havens of belonging through their intimate corporate life.

SO295 Daneel, M. L.

Zionism and Faith-Healing in Rhodesia: Aspects of African Independent Churches. Translated by V.A. February. (Communications, 2). The Hague, NE: Mouton, 1970. 64 pp. Paper. No ISBN.

A monograph based on field research into the attractions of Zionist churches in Zimbabwe as healing institutes.

SO296 Dillon-Malone, Clive M.

The Korsten Basketmakers: A Study of the Masowe Apostles, an Indigenous African Religious Movement. Denver, COU: International Academic Books, 2001. xi, 169 pp. 1588681181 (hdbk), 1588681173 (pbk).

A scholarly study of an AICh that originated in Zimbabwe, but whose members migrated to South Africa, Botswana, and Zambia; originally published in 1978 (Manchester, ENK: Manchester University).

SO297 Fogelqvist, Anders

The Red-Dressed Zionists: Symbols of Power in a Swazi Independent Church. (Uppsala Research Reports in Cultural Anthropology, 5). Uppsala, SW: University of Uppsala, 1986. 211 pp. Paper. 9150605054.

A detailed study of the Jericho Church in relation to African independency, traditional culture, and contemporary Swazi society; originally presented as a doctoral dissertation (Uppsala University, 1986).

SO298 Gifford, Paul, ed.

New Dimensions in African Christianity. (Africa Challenges Series, 3). Nairobi, KE: AACC, 1992. 215 pp. Paper. 9966987908.

Eight essays on various new religious movements in Africa, from a variety of approaches (sociological, historical, anthropological, and theological)—products of an AACC study project coordinated by the editor.

SO—MISSIONS: SOCIAL ASPECTS

SO299 Githieya, Francis Kimani
The Freedom of the Spirit: African Indigenous Churches in Kenya. (American Academy of Religion Academy Series, 94). Atlanta, GAU: Scholars Press, 1997. xiii, 304 pp. Paper. 0788501704.

An examination of the history and ecclesiology of two AICs in Kenya (African Orthodox Church and the Arathi/Agikuyu Spirit Churches) in the light of their socio-historical backgrounds; originally submitted as a Ph.D. dissertation (Emory University, 1992).

SO300 Graines d'Evangile: Aperçu des églises indépendantes africaines
Yaoundé, CM: Éditions Clé, 1973. 63 pp. No ISBN.

French translation of *And Some Fell on Good Ground* (1971).

SO301 Greschat, Hans-Jürgen
Kitawala: Ursprung, Ausbreitung und Religion der Watch-Tower-Bewegung in Zentralafrika. (Marburger theologische Studien, 4). Marburg, GW: Elwert Verlag, 1967. xii, 128 pp. Paper. No ISBN.

A dissertation investigating the orgin, history, expansion, and religion of Kitawala, a specifically African form of the Watch Tower Movement, no longer identical with the white-led Jehovah's Witnesses.

SO302 Greschat, Hans-Jürgen
West African Prophets: The Morphology of a Religious Specialisation. Translated by R. Rivers. (Marburger Studien zur Afrika- und Asienkunde; Serie A: Africa, vol. 4). Birmingham, ENK: Centre for New Religious Movements, 1985. 63 pp. Paper. No ISBN.

English translation.

SO303 Greschat, Hans-Jürgen
Westafrikanische Propheten: Morphologie einer religiösen Spezialisierung. (Marburger Studien zur Afrika—und Asienkunde, Ser. A, Africa, 4). Marburg an der Lahn, GW: Hans-Jürgen Greschat, 1974. 113 pp. No ISBN.

A summary of field research by the author among leaders of AICs in Nigeria in 1966-1967, focusing on self-understandings of their callings and leadership qualities.

SO304 Hackett, Rosalind I. J., ed.
New Religious Movements in Nigeria. (African Studies, 5). Lewiston, NYU: E Mellen Press, 1987. xvi, 245 pp. 0889461805.

Twelve scholarly essays focusing on the diversification and changes that have occurred in the new religious movements in Nigeria since the Civil War (1967-1970).

SO305 Haliburton, Gordon Mackay
Le prophète Harris. Translated by Marie-Noëll Faure. Abidjan, IV: Nouvelles éditions africaines, 1984. 143 pp. 2723606457.

French translation.

SO306 Haliburton, Gordon Mackay
The Prophet Harris: A Study of an African Prophet and His Mass-Movement in the Ivory Coast and the Gold Coast, 1913-1915. New York, NYU: Oxford University Press, 1973. xv, 155 pp. 0195016262.

A shortened version of the author's doctoral dissertation based on primary sources and oral interviews with those who experienced Harris' charismatic ministry in the Ivory Coast and western Ghana, where he succeeded in revitalizing churches and converting whole villages to Christ; originally published in 1971 (London, UK: Longman).

SO307 Hayward, Victor E. W., ed.
African Independent Church Movements. (Commission on World Mission and Evangelism Research Pamphlets, 11). London, ENK: Edinburgh House Press for the WCC, CWME, 1963. 94 pp. No ISBN.

A research pamphlet, stemming from a consultation (Mindolo Ecumenical Centre, Kitwe, Zambia, 6-13 Sept. 1962), on the struggle of the African spirit to express itself through the growth of the AIC movements, examining to what extent and for what reasons older churches are responsible for this development.

SO308 Hexham, Irving, and G. C. Oosthuizen, eds.
The Story of Isaiah Shembe: History and Traditions Centered on Ekuphakameni and Mount Nhlangakazi. Translated by Hans-Jürgen Becken. (Sacred History and Traditions of the Amanazaretha, 1). Lewiston, NYU: E Mellen Press, 1996. xxii, 258 pp. 0773487735.

Oral testimonies forming a history of the "ibandla lama Nazaretha" (the Nazareth Baptist Church) founded in the 1900s by the prophet Isaiah Shembe, and today the largest AIC among the Zulu-speaking people of southern Africa.

SO309 Hexham, Irving, ed.
The Scriptures of the amaNazaretha of Ekuphakameni: Selected Writings of the Zulu Prophets Isaiah and Londa Shembe. Translated by Londa Shembe, and Hans-Jürgen Becken. Calgary, ABC: University of Calgary, 1994. xlix, 143 pp. Paper. 1895176336.

Writings of one of South Africa's most famous African indigenous church leaders, Isaiah Shembe (1867?-1935) and his grandson Londa Shembe (d.1989) of the amaNazaretha; with an essay on their theology by the editor.

SO310 Jedrej, M. C., and Rosalind Shaw, eds.
Dreaming, Religion and Society in Africa. (Studies on Religion in Africa, 7). Leiden, NE: Brill, 1992. 194 pp. 9004089365.

Eleven scholarly essays on dreams and dreaming in various African cultures, with data on their importance in AICs.

SO311 Jules-Rosette, Bennetta
African Apostles: Ritual and Conversion in the Church of John Maranke. Ithaca, NYU: Cornell University Press, 1975. 302 pp. 0801408466.

A remarkable participant-observer account of the Church of John Maranke, one of the largest independent churches of Africa, by a North American sociologist who became a convert.

SO312 Jules-Rosette, Bennetta, ed.
The New Religions of Africa. (Modern Sociology). Norwood, NJU: Ablex Publishing, 1979. xxii, 248 pp. 0893910147.

A diverse collection of scholarly essays on new ritual and symbolic changes taking place in Africa, which find expression in new cults and religious movements adapting traditional African religion, Islam, and Christianity.

SO313 Kamphausen, Erhard
Anfänge der kirchlichen Unabhängigkeitsbewegung in Südafrika: Geschichte und Theologie der Äthiopischen Bewegung, 1872-1912. (Studies in the Intercultural History of Christianity, 6). Bern, SZ: Herbert Lang; Frankfurt am Main, GW: Peter Lang, 1976. 657 pp. Paper. 3261017139.

An attempt to reconstruct, on the basis of primary sources, the early history of the Ethiopian Movement, with special reference to its theological foundations.

SO314 Kasukuti, Ngoy
Recht und Grenze der Inkulturation: Heilserfahrungen im Christentum Afrikas am Beispiel der Kimbanguistenkirche. (Erlanger Monographien aus Mission und Ökumene, 13). Erlangen, GW: Ev. Luth. Mission, 1991. 165 pp. Paper. 3872143131.

Knowing intimately both the native religion of Zaire and the partial adoption of Christianity in his own family, this author discusses the possibilities and realities of inculturation.

SO315 Kealotswe, Obed N.
An African Independent Church Leader: Bishop Smart Mthembu of the Head Mountain of God Apostolic Church in Zion. (Studies on the Church in Southern Africa, 5). Gaborone, BS: University of Botswana, 1994. 37 pp. Paper. 9991220925.

Biography of the founder, in 1939, of the Head Mountain of God Church, based on oral research.

SO316 Kiernan, J. P.
The Production and Management of Therapeutic Power in Zionist Churches within a Zulu City. (Studies in African Health and Medicine, 4). Lewiston, NYU: E Mellen Press, 1990. vi, 277 pp. 0889462836.

A collection of essays on aspects of Zulu Zionism in South Africa (rules, resources and rewards, ritual and healing, leadership, and Zionists in the urban community); based on fieldwork conducted in KwaMashu near Durban, 1968-1970.

SO317 Kitshoff, M. C., ed.
African Independent Churches Today: Kaleidoscope of Afro-Christianity. (African Studies, 44). Lewiston, NYU: E Mellen Press, 1996. 310 pp. 0773487824.

Eighteen essays by southern African scholars on various aspects of the AICs today (history, healing, religious communication, orality, self-understanding, etc.); collected as a tribute to Professor G. C. Oosthuizen, a leading South African academic and researcher in the field of religion.

SO318 Korte, Werner
Wir sind die Kirchen der unteren Klassen: Entstehung, Organisation und gesellschaftliche Funktionen unabhängiger Kirchen in Afrika. (Studien zur interkulturellen Geschichte des Christentums, 15). Frankfurt am Main, GW: Lang, 1978. 134 pp. Paper. 3261023686.

Excerpt of a dissertation presenting a review of the literature on the historical, organizational, ideological, and political aspects of independent churches.

SO319 Krüger, Gesine
Zwischen Gott und Staat: Die Unabhängigen Kirchen in Südafrika. (Bibliothek Afrikanische Geschichte, 1). Hamburg, GW: Ergebnisse Verlag, 1989. 133 pp. Paper. 3925622551.

This book is about the positions taken toward the state by the "independent churches," which have sprung up since the end of the nineteenth century in South Africa (about 3,000 out of a total of 7,000 in all of Africa), often as a conscious rejection of the paternalistic and racist attitudes of missionaries.

SO320 Krabill, James R.
The Hymnody of the Harrist Church among the Dida of South-central Ivory Coast (1913-1949): A Historico-Religious Study. (Studies in the Intercultural History of Christianity, 74). Frankfurt am Main, GW: Lang, 1995. xv, 603 pp. Paper. 3631484046.

A detailed analysis of over 250 hymn texts, dating from 1913-1949, as a resource for understanding the early life, faith, and history of one of West Africa's largest independent churches.

SO321 Loth, Heinrich
Vom Schlangenkult zur Christuskirche: Religion und Messianismus in Afrika. Frankfurt am Main, GW: Fischer Taschenbuch Verlag, 1987. 270 pp. 3596243726.

A reinterpretation of African Christian history by a historian from Eastern Germany, with special emphasis on independent churches and prophetic movements, nearly exclusively interpreted as a religious protest against colonialism; also published in 1985 by Union Verlag.

SO322 MacGaffey, Wyatt
Modern Kongo Prophets: Religion in a Plural Society. (African Systems of Thought). Bloomington, INU: Indiana University Press, 1983. xiii, 285 pp. 0253338654 (hdbk), 0253203074 (pbk).

A scholarly study, based on intensive field research, of the relation to Kongo culture of the beliefs, rituals, and styles of leadership of the Church of Jesus Christ on Earth by Prophet Simon Kimbangu (Kimbanguists), the largest African independent church.

SO323 Manicom, Peter, ed.
Out of Africa: Kimbanguism. (CEM Student Theology Series). London, ENK: Christian Education Movement, 1979. 66 pp. Paper. 0905022556.

An introduction to the Church of Jesus Christ on Earth by the Prophet Simon Kimbangu, containing an English translation of the church's "Statement of Theology."

SO324 Martin, Marie-Louise
Kimbangu: An African Prophet and His Church. Translated by D. M. Moore. Grand Rapids, MIU: Eerdmans; Oxford, ENK: Blackwell Publishers, 1975. xxiv, 198 pp. 0802834833 (US), 0631160302 (UK).

English translation of *Kirche Ohne Weisse: Simon Kimbangu und seine Millionenkirche im Kongo* (1971).

SO325 Martin, Marie-Louise
Kirche ohne Weisse: Simon Kimbangu und seine Millionenkirche im Kongo. Basel, SZ: Reinhardt, 1971. 279 pp. Paper. 3724500107.

An insider's scholarly account of Simon Kimbangu (1889-1951), charismatic Zairois prophet, and of his movement, which became the largest African independent church on the continent; based on Kimbanguist documents, Protestant mission sources, and hitherto secret Belgian colonial records.

SO326 Martin, Marie-Louise
Simon Kimbangu: un prophète et son église. Translated by Christian Glardon, and Jacques Dépraz. Lausanne, SZ: Édition du Soc, 1981. 215 pp. No ISBN.

French translation.

SO—MISSIONS: SOCIAL ASPECTS

SO327 Mbon, Friday N.
Brotherhood of the Cross and Star: A New Religious Movement in Nigeria. (Studies in the Intercultural History of Christianity, 78). Frankfurt am Main, GW: Lang, 1992. xi, 350 pp. Paper. 3631441819.

A pioneer study of contemporary Nigeria's most controversial new religious movement—its history, beliefs, practices, and social impact in Africa and other continents—by the senior lecturer in comparative religion at the University of Calabar, Nigeria.

SO328 Muga, Erasto
African Responses to Western Christian Religion: A Sociological Analysis of African Separatist Religious and Political Movements in East Africa. Nairobi, KE: East African Literature Bureau, 1975. 216 pp. Paper. No ISBN.

An account of the clash of the European and African cultures in Kenya, Uganda, and Tanzania, and of why AICs developed as a reaction against Western European missionaries and European colonial ethnocentrism and dominance.

SO329 Mwene-Batende, Gaston
Le phénomène de dissidence des sectes religieuses d'inspiration kimbanguiste. (Cahiers du CEDAF 6/1971, Série 4 : Religion). Brussels, BE: CEDAF, 1971. 37 pp. Paper. No ISBN.

A brief history of the schism from the Kimbanguists of the Church of the Prophet Thomas Ntwalani in Congo [Zaire], with the texts of five key documents from that church.

SO330 Naudé, Piet
The Zionist Christian Church in South Africa: A Case-Study in Oral Theology. Lewiston, NYU: E Mellen Press, 1995. 159 pp. 0773491473.

A scholarly analysis of how hymns express both popular theology and spirituality in one of Africa's largest indigenous churches.

SO331 Ndiokwere, Nathaniel I.
Prophecy and Revolution: The Role of Prophets in the Independent African Churches and in Biblical Tradition. London, ENK: SPCK, 1981. xv, 319 pp. Paper. 028103737X (net), 0281037744 (non-net).

A comparative study of African prophetic movements and Old Testament prophecy by a Nigerian Roman Catholic theological educator.

SO332 Newman, Richard
Black Power and Black Religion: Essays and Reviews. West Cornwell, CTU: Locust Hill Press, 1987. 237 pp. 0933951035.

A collection of essays on new religious movements in Africa (Kimbanguists, African Orthodox Church) and among African Americans (African Universal Church); with bibliography.

SO333 Oosthuizen, G. C. et al., eds.
Afro-Christian Religion and Healing in Southern Africa. (African Studies, 8). Lewiston, NYU: E Mellen Press, 1989. 432 pp. 0889462828.

Nineteen scholarly essays, by academics from a variety of disciplines, on aspects of traditional healing and their incorporation in independent churches of South Africa.

SO334 Oosthuizen, G. C., and Irving Hexham, eds.
Afro-Christian Religion at the Grassroots in Southern Africa. (African Studies, 19). Lewiston, NYU: E Mellen Press, 1991. xvii, 412 pp. 0889462267.

Nineteen scholarly essays on the AICs of southern Africa; originally presented at the University of Zululand at the third New Religious Movements and Independent Churches' [NERMIC] Symposium.

SO335 Oosthuizen, G. C., and Irving Hexham, eds.
Empirical Studies of African Independent/Indigenous Churches. Lewiston, NYU: E Mellen Press, 1992. 345 pp. 0773495886.

Thirteen essays by South African scholars on various aspects of indigenization in AICs (oral history, theology, healing, worship, hymnody, and ethics).

SO336 Oosthuizen, G. C., ed.
Religion Alive: Studies in the New Movements and Indigenous Churches in Southern Africa. Johannesburg, SA: Hodder & Stoughton, 1986. ix, 262 pp. Paper. 0868501298.

Twenty-five papers on southern Africa's AICs; originally presented at a symposium held in February 1985, at the University of Zululand near Durban, South Africa.

SO337 Oosthuizen, G. C., M. C. Kitshoff, and S. W. D. Dube, eds.
Afro-Christianity at the Grassroots: Its Dynamics and Strategies. (Studies of Religion in Africa, 9). Leiden, NE: Brill, 1994. xii, 260 pp. 9004100350.

A collection of nineteen case studies by South African scholars on the history, values, changing patterns, women in ministry, and spirituality of various indigenous churches in southern Africa.

SO338 Oosthuizen, G. C.
Afro-Christian Religions. (Iconography of Religions 24, 12). Leiden, NE: Brill, 1979. ix, 40 pp. Paper. 9004059997.

Approximately 100 black-and-white photographs, presented with descriptions of origin and meaning; with a general introduction on symbols, liturgies, clothes, uniforms, and other visible aspects of Afro-Christian religions.

SO339 Oosthuizen, G. C.
The Healer-Prophet in Afro-Christian Churches. (Studies in Christian Mission, 3). Leiden, NE: Brill, 1992. xxvii, 200 pp. 9004094687.

A detailed study of the role of prayer healers in AICs, based on the author's thirty years of investigations in southern Africa.

SO340 Oosthuizen, G. C.
Post-Christianity in Africa: A Theological and Anthropological Study. Grand Rapids, MIU: Eerdmans; London, ENK: Hurst, 1968. xiv, 273 pp. No IBSN.

A scholarly analysis of theological challenges faced by the church in Africa as a result of the proliferation of AICs; with an introduction and classification.

SO341 Oosthuizen, G. C.
The Theology of a South African Messiah: An Analysis of the Hymnal of "The Church of the Nazarites." (Œkumenische Studien, 8). Leiden, NE: Brill, 1967. viii, 198 pp. No ISBN.

A linguistic and theological analysis of the Zulu hymns by Shembe and others; with many English translations.

SO342 Peel, J. D. Y.
Aladura: A Religious Movement among the Yoruba. London, ENK: Oxford University Press, 1968. xiii, 338 pp. No ISBN.

A revision of the author's thesis (University of London), a study of the development and growth of the Aladura Church and its relation to social change in Western Nigeria over fifty years.

SO343 Perrin-Jassy, Marie France
Basic Community in the African Churches. Translated by Jeanne Marie Lyons. Maryknoll, NYU: Orbis Books, 1973. xvi, 257 pp. Paper. 0883440253.

English translation.

SO344 Perrin-Jassy, Marie France
La communauté de base dans les Églises africaines. Bandundu, CG: Centre d' Études Éthnologiques, 1970. 231 pp. No ISBN.

A social anthropologist's study of AICs among the Luo of Tanzania.

SO345 Pobee, J. S., and Gabriel Ositelu
African Initiatives in Christianity: The Growth, Gifts and Diversities of Indigenous African Churches—A Challenge to the Ecumenical Movement. (Risk Book Series, 83). Geneva, SZ: WCC Publications, 1998. xiii, 73 pp. Paper. 2825412775.

An introduction to the phenomenon of the AICs, covering their key teachings, roots in African church history, and implications for the future of the ecumenical movement.

SO346 Pretorius, H. L.
Ethiopia Stretches out Her Hands unto God: Aspects of Transkeian Indigenous Churches. Pretoria, SA: Institute for Missiological Research, University of Pretoria, 1993. v, 126 pp. Paper. 0869798596.

Three essays on independency in South Africa: a biography of Nehemiah Tile (d.1891), the founder of the Ethiopian Church of Africa; the origin and history of the Transkei Church of Christ; and recent transformations in a rural Zionist church.

SO347 Pretorius, H. L.
Sound the Trumpet of Zion: Aspects of a Movement in Transkei. Pretoria, SA: Institute for Missiological Research-University of Pretoria, 1985. vi, 197 pp. Paper. 0869796283.

A case study of a Transkei Zionist Church founded in 1929, placed in the context of historical trends in the indigenous churches of the Transkei, South Africa.

SO348 Shank, David A., ed.
Ministry in Partnership with African Independent Churches. Elkhart, INU: Mennonite Board of Missions, 1991. ix, 436 pp. Paper. 1877736139.

Papers presented at the conference on this theme. (Kinshasa, Zaire, July 1989.)

SO349 Shank, David A.
Prophet Harris: The "Black Elijah" of West Africa. (Studies of Religion in Africa, 10). Leiden, NE: Brill, 1994. xv, 309 pp. 9004099808.

The only comprehensive study of the thought and influence of William Wade Harris (1860-1929), the Glebo (Liberia) loyalist whose prophetic mission from 1910 to 1929 moved tens of thousands out of traditional religion into Christian churches, mostly AICs, in West Africa—particularly the Ivory Coast.

SO350 Simbandumwe, Samuel S.
A Socio-Religious and Political Analysis of the Judeo-Christian Concept of Prophetism and Modern Bakongo and Zulu African Prophet Movements. (Africa Studies, 28). Lewiston, NYU: E Mellen Press, 1992. xviii, 434 pp. 0773491821.

A revision of the author's doctoral thesis (Edinburgh 1989) contrasting concepts of the holy mountain and the role of the prophet in the Old Testament with those of two prominent leaders of African independent churches—Simon Kimbangu (Zaire) and Isaiah Shembe (South Africa).

SO351 Sundkler, Bengt
Bantu Prophets in South Africa. London, ENK: Oxford University Press, 1961. 381 pp. No ISBN.

A second edition of the now-classic pioneer study on the proliferation of AICs in South Africa.

SO352 Sundkler, Bengt
Bantupropheten in Südafrika. (Die Kirchen der Welt, B 3). Stuttgart, GW: Evan Verlagswerk, 1964. 407 pp. No ISBN.

German translation.

SO353 Sundkler, Bengt
Zulu Zion and Some Swazi Zionists. (Studia Missionalia Upsliensia, 29). Lund, SW: Gleerup, 1976. 337 pp. 914004064X.

A scholarly study of the black Zion movement in southern Africa.

SO354 Sundkler, Bengt, Marie-Louise Martin, and G. C. Oosthuizen
Begegnung mit messianischen Bewegungen in Afrika. Edited by Peter Beyerhaus. (Weltmission heute, 33/34). Stuttgart, GW: Evan Missionsverlag, 1967. 72 pp. Paper. No ISBN.

A collection of essays intended as a contribution to a theological and sociological description and evaluation of messianic movements in Africa.

SO355 *The Rise of Independent Churches in Ghana*
Accra, GH: Asempa Publishers, 1990. 92 pp. Paper. 9964781822.

Six short essays assessing factors causing the rapid growth of AICs in Ghana.

SO356 Triebel, Johannes
Gottesglaube und Heronkult in Afrika: Untersuchungen zum Lwembe-Kult der Wakinga in Sudtanzania. (Erlanger Monographein aus Mission und Ökumene, 18). Erlangen, GW: Ev.-Luth. Mission, 1993. viii, 342 pp. Paper. 3872143182.

This *habilitationsschrift* (Erlangen, 1992) is a study of the cult of Lwembe in East Africa, from his deification through the cult's modifications as a result of contact with Christian missionaries, with missiological reflections on Christ as the "Proto-ancestor," and the world of the spirits in conjunction with the Holy Spirit.

SO357 Turner, Harold W.
History of an African Independent Church. Oxford, ENK: Clarendon Press, 1967. 2 vols. No ISBN.

A detailed and comprehensive study of the Church of the Lord Aladura from its origins in Nigeria to its spread throughout West Africa, including the background of prophet-healing movements, secession movements, the life of the church, and liturgical and theological developments within it [vol. 1: *The Church of the Lord (Aladura)* (xv, 217 pp.); vol. 2: *The Life and Faith of the Church of the Lord (Aladura)* (xviii, 391 pp.), with volume 2 also published under the title *African Independent Church*].

SO358 Turner, Harold W.
Religious Innovation in Africa: Collected Essays on New Religious Movements. Boston, MAU: G K Hall, 1979. x, 354 pp. 0816183031.

A collection of twenty-seven essays by the author covering twenty years (1957-1977) of his pioneer leadership in the study of new religious movements in primal societies.

SO—MISSIONS: SOCIAL ASPECTS

SO—MISSIONS: SOCIAL ASPECTS

SO359 Ustorf, Werner

Afrikanische Initiative: Das aktive Leiden des Propheten Simon Kimbangu. (Studies in the Intercultural History of Christianity, 5). Frankfurt, GW: Lang, 1975. 457 pp. Paper. 3261009489.

A scholarly history of the religious and social biography of Simon Kimbangu (1889-1951) and the origins of the Kimbanguist movement in the Belgian Congo.

SO360 Verryn, Trevor David

A History of the Order of Ethiopia. Cleveland, SA: Central Mission Press, 1972. iii, 193 pp. No ISBN.

Third edition of a history of one of the earliest AICs in South Africa.

SO361 Walker, Sheila S.

The Religious Revolution in the Ivory Coast: The Prophet Harris and the Harrist Church. (Studies in Religion). Chapel Hill, NCU: University of North Carolina Press, 1983. xvii, 206 pp. 0807815039.

A study of the origins, development, and present status of the Harrist Church of the Ivory Coast in Africa.

SO362 Webster, James Bertin

The African Churches among the Yoruba, 1888-1922. (Oxford Studies in African Affairs). Oxford, ENK: Clarendon Press, 1964. 217 pp. No ISBN.

A study of early African independency in Nigeria.

SO363 Welbourn, Frederick Burkewood, and Bethwell A. Ogot

A Place to Feel at Home: A Study of Two Independent Churches in Western Kenya. London, ENK: Oxford University Press, 1966. xv, 157 pp. No ISBN.

A scholarly study of the Church of Christ in Africa, of Anglican roots, and of the African Israel Church Nineveh, that sprang from the Pentecostal Mission.

SO364 Welbourn, Frederick Burkewood

East African Rebels: A Study of Some Independent Churches. (World Mission Studies). London, ENK: SCM Press, 1961. xiv, 258 pp. No ISBN.

A scholarly study of the history and social dynamics of African independency in Kenya and Uganda.

SO365 West, Martin

Bishops and Prophets in a Black City: African Independent Churches in Soweto Johannesburg. Cape Town, SA: David Philip; London, ENK: Rex Collings, 1975. xii, 225 pp. 0949968455 (SA), 901720933 (UK-SBN).

A 1969-1971 case study of fifty-eight AICs in fourteen sections of Soweto, Johannesburg, and of the rise and fall of the African Independent Churches' Association (AICA) there.

New Religious Movements: Asia

See also CR187, CR1422, SO5, SO271, AS1058, AS1319, and AS1343.

SO366 Fuchs, Stephen

Rebellious Prophets: A Study of Messianic Movements in Indian Religions. (Publication of the Indian Branch of the Anthropos Institute, 1). New York, NYU: Asia Publishing House, 1965. vix, 304 pp. No ISBN.

A study of the new messianic religious movements in India and their dynamics.

SO367 Hoerschelmann, Werner

Christliche Gurus: Darstellung von Selbstverständnis und Funktion indigenen Christseins durch unabhängige, charismatisch geführte Gruppen in Südindien. (Studien zur interkulturellen Geschichte des Christentums, 12). Frankfurt a.M., GW: Lang, 1977. 589 pp. Paper. 3261022930.

Sidestepping theological and ecumenical divergencies and considering the phenomenon of "Christian gurus," the author asserts that the work of the Holy Spirit affecting the lives of such charismatic persons is nothing but a full realization of the Gospel.

SO368 Kimura-Andres, Hannelore

Mukyokai: Fortsetzung der Evangeliumsgeschichte. (Erlanger Monographien aus Mission und Ökumene, 1). Erlangen, GW: Ev.-Luth. Mission, 1984. ix, 362 pp. Paper. 3872143018.

A detailed analysis of the history and social development of the Mukyokai "non-church" movement founded in Japan by Uchimura; with attention to the evolving ecclesial traditions during the group's third generation.

SO369 Mullins, Mark R.

Christianity Made in Japan: A Study of Indigenous Movements. (Nanzan Library of Asian Religion and Culture). Honolulu, HIU: University of Hawaii Press, 1998. x, 277 pp. 0824821149 (hdbk), 0824821327 (pbk).

A behind-the-scenes study of several indigenous Christian movements in Japan, giving voice to unheard perceptions of many Japanese Christians, while questioning the concept of Christianity as a truly "world religion."

SO370 National Consultation on New Religious Movements in the Philippines (Quezon City, 1988)

Exploring the New Religious Movements in the Philippines. Quezon City, PH: NCCP, Comm. on Evangelism & Ecumenical Relations, 1989. 91 pp. Paper. 9718548319.

Documents and relevant readings from an important consultation sponsored by the Commission on Evangelism and Ecumenical Relations of the NCCP.

New Religious Movements: Europe

See also SO5, and EU225.

SO371 Mirbach, Wolfram

Universelles Leben: Originalität und Christlichkeit einer Neureligion. (Erlanger Monographien aus Mission und Ökumene, 19). Erlangen, GW: Ev.-Luth Mission, 1994. viii, 328 pp. Paper. 3872143190.

A dissertation on the faith, teaching, and medicine of Universelles Leben (Universal Living), a new religion founded in Germany in 1984; with the author's thesis that UL is not a Christian religion although the group uses concepts from Christianity.

SO372 Olofson, Peter O. K.

Folkekirken og nyreligi sitet: Til modsigelse, inspiration og eftertanke. Fredericia, DK: Lohses Forlag, 1989. 61 pp. Paper. 8756450435.

This book deals in a very critical way with the challenge to traditional Christianity by new religious movements.

New Religious Movements: Latin America/Caribbean

See also AF304, AM591, AM596, AM1332, AM1336, AM1340, and AM1371.

SO373 Bastian, Jean-Pierre, ed.
Los Nuevos Movimientos Religiosos. (Cristianismo y Sociedad, 25, 93). México, MX: Cristianismo y Sociedad, 1987. 106 pp. No ISBN.

A numbered monograph with four socio-religious studies and the text of the "Cuenca Document" on new religious movements; produced by the Consultation of Catholic bishops and Protestant pastors of Latin America and the Caribbean (Cuenca, Ecuador, 4-10 Nov. 1986).

SO374 Chevannes, Barry
Rastafari: Roots and Ideology. (Utopianism and Communitarianism). Syracuse, NYU: Syracuse University Press, 1994. xiv, 298 pp. 081562638X (hdbk), 0815602960 (pbk).

A study of the cultural origins and roots of the Rastafari Movement in Jamaica, with an ethnographic description of the movement in the city of Kingston.

SO375 Desmangles, Leslie G.
The Faces of the Gods: Vodou and Roman Catholicism in Haiti. Chapel Hill, NCU: University of North Carolina Press, 1992. xiii, 218 pp. 0807820598 (hdbk), 0807843938 (pbk).

An anthropological study of the historical shaping of Voodoo and Roman Catholicism in Haiti and of the resulting mythology and folklore; by the Haitian-born Professor of Religion and Area Studies at Trinity College in Hartford, Connecticut.

SO376 Figge, Horst H.
Geisterkult, Besessenheit und Magie in der Umbanda-Religion Brasiliens. Freiburg, GW: Karl Alber, 1973. 340 pp. 3495472746.

The historical development, beliefs, cult elements, social roles, magical practices, possession phenomena, and socialization of Umbanda, exemplified by some groups in Rio de Janeiro.

SO377 Flasche, Rainer
Geschichte und Typologie afrikanischer Religiosität in Brasilien. (Marburger Studien zur Afrika- und Asienkunde; Seria A: Afrika, 1). Marburg, GW: Lahn, 1973. 302 pp. Paper. No ISBN.

A dissertation on the historical and systematic development of Afro-Brazilian religiosity, with special reference to Candomble, Makumba, and Umbanda.

SO378 Gerbert, Martin
Religionen in Brasilien: Eine Analyse der nicht-katholischen Religionsformen und ihrer Entwicklung im sozialen Wandel der brasilianischen Gesellschaft. (Bibliotheca Ibero-Americana, 13). Berlin, GW: Colloquim Verlag, 1970. 125 pp. Paper. No ISBN.

A sociological work describing non-Catholic religions in Brazil.

SO379 Landim, Leilah, ed.
Sinais dos tempos: Diversidade religiosa no Brasil. (Cadernos do ISER, 23). Rio de Janeiro, BL: Instituto de Estudos da Religião, 1990. 274 pp. No ISBN.

Twenty-nine studies on existing (mostly non-Christian) religions in Brazil.

SO380 Loth, Heinz-Jürgen
Rastafari: Bibel und afrikanische Spiritualität. (Kölner Veröffentlichungen zur Religionsgeschichte, 20). Cologne, GW: Bühlau Verlag, 1991. viii, 128 pp. Paper. 3412018899.

This short study attempts to correct the common stereotype of Rastafarians by exploring the deeper religious dimensions of this movement.

SO381 Moreira, Alberto, and Renée Zicman, eds.
Misticismo e Novas Religiões. Petrópolis, BL: Editora Vozes; Bragança Paulista, SP: USF/IFAN, 1994. 176 pp. 8532612431.

Papers from a national conference (Brazil, 21-24 May 1991) investigating new religious movements in contemporary Brazilian society.

SO382 Wulfhorst, Ingo
Der "Spiritualistisch-christliche Orden": Ursprung und Erscheinungsformen einer neureligiösen Bewegung in Brasilien. (Erlanger Monographien aus Mission und Ökumene, 2). Erlangen, GW: Ev.-Luth. Mission, 1985. xiv, 434 pp. Paper. 3872143026.

A dissertation dealing with syncretistic movements in Brazil, in particular the "Ordem Espiritualista Cristã," with documents on the Catholic Church's position in this respect.

SO383 Wulfhorst, Ingo
Discernindo os espíritos: O desafio do espiritismo e da religiosidade afro-brasileira. (Ecumenismo, 7). Petrópolis, BL: Editora Vozes; São Leopoldo, BL: Editora Sinodal, 1989. 250 pp. Paper. 8523301801.

Basic work for the study of spiritualism, Umbanda, and other religious sects in the light of current missiological reflection.

New Religious Movements: North America

See also SO332.

SO384 Groothuis, Douglas R.
Unmasking the New Age. Downers Grove, ILU: InterVarsity, 1986. 192 pp. Paper. 0877845689.

An analysis of the intrusion of New Age thinking into North American culture, and the challenge it poses for Christianity.

SO385 Hoyt, Karen, and J. Isamu Yamamoto, eds.
The New Age Rage: A Probing Analysis of the Newest Religious Craze. Old Tappan, NJU: Power Books, 1987. 263 pp. Paper. 0800752570.

Eleven chapters written by leading Christian scholars dealing with the New Age Movement; published by the Spiritual Counterfeits Project.

SO386 Kyle, Richard
The Religious Fringe: A History of Alternative Religions in America. Downers Grove, ILU: InterVarsity, 1993. 467 pp. Paper. 0830817662.

A short history of a wide range of new religious movements in North America from the colonial era to the present, with brief assessments of their influence on American culture; based on secondary sources.

SO387 La Barre, Weston
The Peyote Cult. Norman, OKU: University of Oklahoma
Press, 1989. xvii, 334 pp. Paper. 0806122145.

In this fifth expanded and updated edition of the author's
classic study on the plant peyote, and the Native American
tribes which use it in religious rituals, the author also discusses the progress of the Native American Church toward acceptance as a religious denomination, and the presumptions of the
Neo-American Church.

New Religious Movements: Oceania

See also OC136, OC152, OC174, OC286, and OC290.

SO388 Flannery, Wendy
*Religious Movements in Melanesia: A Selection of Case Stud-
ies and Reports.* Goroka, PP: Melanesian Institute, 1983. iv,
213 pp. Paper. No ISBN.

Eighteen papers of Melanesian Institute-sponsored research projects on movements of protest and revitalization in
Papua New Guinea and Irian Jaya, Indonesia, and on revivals
and "spirit" movements in Papua New Guinea; published as a
supplement to *Religious Movements in Melanesia Today, 1-3*
(Point Series, 2-4).

SO389 Gesch, Patrick F.
*Initiative and Initiation: A Cargo Cult-Type Movement in the
Sepik against its Background in Traditional Village Religion.*
(Studia Instituti Anthropos, 33). St. Augustin, GW: Anthro-
pos Institut, 1985. xv, 347 pp. Paper. 3921389968.

The doctoral dissertation (University of Sydney, 1982)
of a Divine Word missionary, based on field research on the
Mt. Rurun Movement, a cargo cult-type popular religious
movement since 1969, centered at Yangoru in the East Sepik
Province of Papua New Guinea.

SO390 Loeliger, Carl, and Garry W. Trompf, eds.
New Religious Movements in Melanesia. Suva, FJ: University of the South Pacific; Port Moresby, PP: University of Papua New Guinea, 1985. xvii, 188 pp. Paper. No ISBN.

Thirteen essays, eleven by Melanesian authors, on the traditional and transitional concerns of religions in New Guinea
and Papua New Guinea, including cargo cults.

SO391 Steinbauer, Friedrich
*Melanesian Cargo Cults: New Salvation Movements in the
South Pacific.* Translated by Max Wohlwill. St. Lucia, AT:
University of Queensland Press, 1979. xv, 215 pp.
0702210951.

English translation.

SO392 Steinbauer, Friedrich
*Melanesische Cargo-kulte: Neureligiöse Heilsbewegungen in
der Südsee.* London, ENK: Prior, 1979. 215 pp. No ISBN.

A survey of Melanesian cargo cults and their history, with
an assessment of their significance for the people of Melanesia, their governments and religious institutions; by an anthro-
pologist-missionary of the Lutheran Mission in Papua New
Guinea.

SO393 Trompf, Garry W., ed.
*Cargo Cults and Millenarian Movements: Transoceanic Com-
parisons of New Religious Movements.* (Religion and Society, 29). Berlin, GW: Mouton, 1990. xvii, 456 pp. 0899256015,
3110121662.

Ten scholarly essays on new religious movements in
Melanesia, Indonesia, Jamaica, black and white North America, and Namibia, with a major emphasis on cargo cults and
millenarianism in Melanesia.

SO394 Trompf, Garry W., ed.
Prophets of Melanesia: Six Essays. Port Moresby, PP: Institute of Papua New Guinea Studies; Suva, FJ: University of the
South Pacific, Institute of Pacific Studies, 1986. 162 pp.
9820200075.

Six scholarly essays on different new religious movements
in Melanesia; with discussion of the nature of prophecy and
the prophetic role.

Special Types of Missions: General

See also SO17, EV312, MI193, and AS421.

SO395 Conley, Paul C., and Andrew A. Sorensen
*The Staggering Steeple: The Story of Alcoholism and the
Churches.* Philadelphia, PAU: Pilgrim Press, 1971. xiv, 143
pp. 0829801952.

A study of the social and cultural role of the churches in
relation to alcoholism and alcohol-related problems in American society, from colonial times to 1971.

SO396 Elliott, Micheal
*Why the Homeless Don't Have Homes and What to Do About
It.* Cleveland, OHU: Pilgrim Press, 1993. xxv, 123 pp. Paper.
0829809651.

A penetrating analysis of the contemporary problem of home-
lessnesss in the United States, and of present inadequate responses by governmental and non-governmental agencies; by the Executive Director of Union Mission, Inc., a Southern Baptist minister who directs shelter programs for the homeless.

SO397 Grady, Duane
Helping the Homeless: God's Word in Action. Elgin, ILU:
Brethren Press, 1988. vii, 87 pp. Paper. 0871783495.

An eight-part Bible study, with worship resources, aimed
at sensitizing Christians to the problem of homelessness and
the need for a compassionate response.

SO398 Keller, John E.
Ministering to Alcoholics. Minneapolis, MNU: Augsburg,
1966. x, 158 pp. No ISBN.

Helps for pastors in understanding alcoholism, Alcoholics Anonymous, effective counseling with alcoholics and their
spouses, and alcohol education.

SO399 Sampley, DeAnn
A Guide to Deaf Ministry: Let's Sign Worthy of the Lord. Grand
Rapids, MIU: Zondervan, 1990. 155 pp. Paper. 0310521912.

A primer on local church ministry to the deaf presented
as cross-cultural communication; with a guide to available resources in the United States.

SO400 Wink, Walter
*Homosexuality and Christian Faith: Questions of Conscience
for the Churches.* Minneapolis, MNU: Fortress Press, 1999.
vi, 133 pp. Paper. 0800631862.

Sixteen essays from male and female, Protestant and Catholic, mainline and evangelical church leaders dealing with biblical
witness, sexual orientation, moral dilemmas of families and friends
of gays and lesbians, prodding the churches to wrestle with gay/
lesbian civil rights, ecclesial rights, and covenants.

Social Work and Missions

See also HI635, EC113, CH167, AM1221, AS692, and EU87.

SO401 *Contemporary Understandings of Diakonia: Report of a Consultation, Geneva, Switzerland, 22-26 November 1982*
Geneva, SZ: WCC, CICARWS, 1983. 67 pp. Paper. 2825407526.

A useful summary of ecumenical thinking concerning Christian service, containing a history of the work of the WCC's CICARWS, 1965-1982.

SO402 Coughlin, Bernard J.
Church and State in Social Welfare. New York, NYU: Columbia University Press, 1965. xii, 189 pp. No ISBN.

A study of the philosophies in social welfare of Protestant, Catholic, and Jewish groups in the United States, of their programs, and of sectarian agency-government relationships.

SO403 Garland, Diana S. Richmond, ed.
Church Social Work: Helping the Whole Person in the Context of the Church. St. Davids, PAU: North American Association of Christians in Social Work, 1992. vii, 119 pp. Paper. 0962363421.

A primer on local church-based social work—principles and practice in the United States.

SO404 Hayman, John
Doing Unto the Least of These: The Story of Birmingham's Jimmie Hale Mission. Montgomery, ALU: Black Belt Press, 1998. 151 pp. Paper. 1579660207.

A brief history of the mission begun in 1954 to provide drug and alcohol rehabilitation in Birmingham, Alabama.

SO405 Lindström, Sari, ed.
Kaukaisen lähimmäisen hyväksi: lähetystehtävän ja kansainvälisen diakonian esittelyä. Helsinki, FI: Kirjaneliö, 1981. 127 pp. Paper. 9516005381.

A collection of articles dealing with the relationship of missions and international diaconia.

SO406 Madigan, Dan, and Ann Bancroft
Many Hands, Many Miracles. Notre Dame, INU: University of Notre Dame Press, 1996. 141 pp. Paper. 0268014264.

The story of the Sacramento Food Bank's services and effective ministry to the poor and homeless of that California city.

SO407 Maule, Henry
Liebe zu den Leidenden: Das Leben der Eva den Hartog-Zeichen der Hoffnung in einer verzweifelten Welt. Konstanz, GW: Christliche Verlagsanstalt, 1978. 258 pp. 3767333482.

German translation.

SO408 Maule, Henry
Moved with Compassion: Eva den Hartog's World of Hope in the Midst of Despair. London, ENK: Souvenir Press, 1977. 288 pp. 0285622722.

A popular biography of Eva den Hartog (b.1923), a Dutch Salvation Army nurse in Congo [Zaire] 1958-1967, Bangladesh (1971-1975), and Vietnam (1973).

SO409 Westmeier, Arline
Healing the Wounded Soul: Ways to Inner Wholeness. Shippensburg, PAU: Companion Press, 1989. 152 pp. Paper. 1560434090.

A missionary with the Christian and Missionary Alliance in Columbia, South America, integrates secular psychology and religious healing to show how dysfunctional living can be changed.

Work for and among Children

See also AF554, AM618, AM1051, AS79, and AS1259.

SO410 *Children and Violence: The Washington Forum: Perspectives on Our Global Future*
Federal Way, WAU: World Vision, Office of Advocacy and Education, 1995. 88 pp. Paper. No ISBN.

Papers from the 1995 Washington Forum on "Children and Violence" sponsored by World Vision.

SO411 Daley, Shannon P., and Kathleen A. Guy
Welcome the Child: A Child Advocacy Guide for Churches. New York, NYU: Friendship Press; Washington, DCU: Children's Defense Fund, 1994. vi, 159 pp. Paper. 0377002666.

A revised and expanded edition of program helps for churches desiring to identify needs of children in their communities, and ways to cooperate in their assistance and advocacy; published in conjunction with the Children's Defense Fund.

SO412 Findley, Kathy Manis
The Survivor's Voice: Healing the Invisible Wounds of Violence and Abuse. Macon, GAU: Smyth & Helwys, 1999. xiii, 114 pp. Paper. 1573121959.

Voices of survivors of the anguish of domestic violence and sexual abuse in the home, along with voices crying out of the pages of the Bible calling the church to be a strong voice to the ministry of healing.

SO413 Friedrich, Laura Dean Ford
Putting Children and Their Families First: A Planning Handbook for Congregations. New York, NYU: UMC, Board of Global Ministries, 1997. vi, 90 pp. Paper. No ISBN.

A handbook designed for United Methodist local churches to assess needs, develop ministries, and support advocacy programs for children and their families.

SO414 Garland, Diana S. Richmond
Church Agencies: Caring for Children and Families in Crisis. Washington, DCU: Child Welfare League of America, 1994. xiv, 327 pp. Paper. 0878685324.

Resources for North American churches engaged in ministries to children and families in crisis (theological, historical, and strategic).

SO415 Grossoehme, Daniel H.
The Pastoral Care of Children. (Religion and Mental Health). New York, NYU: Haworth Pastoral Press, 1999. xiii, 152 pp. 0789006049 (hdbk), 0789006057 (pbk).

This volume addresses a variety of issues, including caring for children with psychiatric illness and overcoming anxiety, and of ministering to severely sick or injured children.

SO416 Hagstrom, Jane Stewart
The Young Witness: Evangelism to and by Children and Youth. Minneapolis, MNU: Augsburg, 1986. 47 pp. 0806622334.

A practical guide for congregational leaders and teachers concerned about evangelism to, with, and by children and youth.

SO417 Kena, Kirsti
Idän ja etelän lapsia. Helsinki, FIN: Kirjaneliö, 1979. 160 pp. Paper. 9516004687.

A description of the life of children and youth in the Finnish missionary fields.

SO418 Kilbourn, Phyllis, and Marjorie McDermid, eds.

Sexually Exploited Children: Working to Protect and Heal. Monrovia, CAU: MARC, 1998. xxi, 323 pp. Paper. 1887983090.

Twenty-two articles examining the exploitation of children, providing guidelines for ministries seeking to prevent and heal child abuse.

SO419 Kilbourn, Phyllis, ed.

Children in Crisis: A New Commitment. Monrovia, CAU: MARC, 1996. v, 272 pp. Paper. 0912552972.

Twenty-one short essays on children in crisis, a biblical response, strategies and opportunities, and equipping for ministry, with data on agencies engaged in such ministries.

SO420 Kilbourn, Phyllis, ed.

Healing the Children of War: A Handbook for Ministry to Children Who Have Suffered Deep Traumas. Monrovia, CAU: MARC, 1995. iv, 318 pp. Paper. 0912552875.

A panel of specialists from the United States (psychologists, educators, and social workers) provide practical guidance for Christians ministering to children who have been the victims of abuse and brutality.

SO421 Kilbourn, Phyllis, ed.

Street Children: A Guide to Effective Ministry. Monrovia, CAU: MARC, 1997. ix, 253 pp. Paper. 1887983015.

A primer for Christian workers among street children, in which twenty leaders from five continents share their insights and experiences.

SO422 Lindner, Eileen W., Mary C. Mattis, and June R. Rogers

When Churches Mind the Children: A Study of Day Care in Local Parishes. Ypsilanti, MIU: High Scope Press, 1983. xi, 176 pp. Paper. 0931114233.

A report on the findings of the most-extensive study ever undertaken of church-housed child day care in the United States; with insights into ways local parishes meet child care needs.

SO423 Myers, Glenn

Children in Crisis. (Briefings). Carlisle, ENK: OM Publishing, 1998. iv, 64 pp. Paper. 1850782709.

An introduction to the life of street children, child soldiers, children trapped in the sex industry, and child laborers; with an outline of some Christian responses.

SO424 Resener, Carl R., and Judy Hall, eds.

Kids on the Street: The Tragedy of Homeless Children ... and What You Can Do about It. Nashville, TNU: Broadmen, 1992. vi, 207 pp. Paper. 0805450912.

A popular account of the plight of the homeless in the United States, of causes, and of ministries of compassion to them; by two with sixty-four years (combined) of service in social work among the homeless.

SO425 *Welcoming the Children*

New York, NYU: Friendship Press, 1994. 24 mins pp. No ISBN.

A video presenting case studies in the United States of local churches addressing urgent needs of children; for use in the mission study on "Making the World Safe for Children."

Work among Women; Women in Christianity

See also HI144, HI480, HI740, TH488, TH503, TH506-TH508, CR311, CR334, CR409, CR730, SO12, EC109, EC296, EC308, EC351, EV190, EV224, EV433, MI12, MI192, CH383, SP65, AF146, AF151, AF180-AF181, AF197-AF198, AF379, AF593, AF749, AF789, AF899, AF929, AF1041, AF1210, AM250, AM324, AM368-AM369, AM525, AM527, AM642, AM705, AM719, AM721, AM945, AM1056-AM1057, AM1062, AM1328, AS80, AS128, AS155, AS753, AS756, AS909, AS1062, AS1205, AS1412, AS1487, EU63, EU222, and OC59.

SO426 Adeney, Miriam

A Time for Risking: Priorities for Women. Portland, ORU: Multnomah, 1987. 182 pp. Paper. 0880701927.

An inspiring account of what women have done, and can do, in varied efforts of Christian service; by a missiologist at Seattle Pacific University and Regent College; with insights into facing complex personal, ethical, and spiritual choices.

SO427 Balasundaram, F. J.

Women's Concerns in Asia. Madras, II: CLS, 1993. vi, 41 pp. Paper. No ISBN.

A research paper on Christian attitudes toward the role of women, with special reference to Asia; originally presented at the United Theological College in Bangalore, India.

SO428 Berkshire Conference on the History of Women (5th, Vassar College, 1982)

Women and the Structure of Society: Selected Research from the Fifth Berkshire Conference on the History of Women. Edited by Barbara Jean Harris, and Jo Ann McNamara. (Duke Press Policy Studies). Durham, NCU: Duke University Press, 1984. xi, 305 pp. Paper. 0822305585 (hdbk), 0822306034 (pbk).

Conference papers, including essays on the London Biblewomen and Nurses Mission, 19th-century women's home and foreign missions, and five black women preachers in the United States.

SO429 Bowie, Fiona, Deborah Kirkwood, and Shirley Ardener, eds.

Women and Missions: Past and Present: Anthropological and Historical Perceptions. (Cross-Cultural Perspectives on Women, 11). Providence, RI: Berg Publishers, 1993. xx, 279 pp. 0854967389 (hdbk), 0854968725 (pbk).

Thirteen scholarly essays by British and African anthropologists, missiologists, and historians on women missionaries, and on the effect of Christian missionary activity on women in Africa, Asia, and Latin America in the 19th and 20th centuries.

SO430 Brubaker, Pamela K.

Women Don't Count: The Challenge of Women's Poverty to Christian Ethics. (American Academy of Religion Academy Series, 87). Atlanta, GAU: Scholars Press, 1994. ix, 278 pp. 1555409571 (hdbk), 155540958X (pbk).

A scholarly exposé of the failures of Roman Catholic social teachings, the WCC, and the UNO to disclose the root causes of women's impoverishment, pauperization, and marginalization.

SO—MISSIONS: SOCIAL ASPECTS

SO431 Cunningham, Sarah, ed.

We Belong Together: Churches in Solidarity with Women. New York, NYU: Friendship Press, 1992. xii, 132 pp. Paper. 0377002429.

A mission study interpreting the perspectives of tradition, transition, justice, and promise in the Decade of the Churches in Solidarity with Women through short essays by feminist theologians, and other leading church women; with study guide entitled *Ours the Journey* by Barbara A. Horner-Ibler (ISBN 0377002437).

SO432 Flemming, Leslie A., ed.

Women's Work for Women: Missionaries and Social Change in Asia. Boulder, COU: Westview Press, 1989. vii, 174 pp. Paper. 0813377080.

Eight essays based on archival evidence, assessing the impact of women missionaries on social change for women in Asia in the late 19th and early 20th centuries.

SO433 Ghazan, Sunil Solomon

Tribute to the Prostitute. (Development Education Series, 23). Delhi, II: Navdin Prakashan Kendra, 1992. 52 pp. Paper. 8172140576.

Stories to raise the consciousness of Indian Christians concerning issues of prostitution.

SO434 Haddad, Yvonne Yazbeck, and Ellison Banks Findly, eds.

Women, Religion, and Social Change. Albany, NYU: SUNY Press, 1985. xxi, 508 pp. Paper. 0887060684 (hdbk), 0887060692 (pbk).

A focus on the way in which women from a number of religious traditions have been able to bring about change, which was either inhibitive or facilitating.

SO435 Herzel, Susannah

A Voice for Women: The Women's Department of the World Council of Churches. Geneva, SZ: WCC, 1981. viii, 197 pp. Paper. 2825406783.

The chronological history of the WCC Subunit on Women in Church and Society from 1949 to 1981; including ecumenical documents, thought-provoking citations, and personal interviews.

SO436 Jones, Kathleen

Women Saints: Lives of Faith and Courage. Maryknoll, NYU: Orbis Books, 1999. ix, 310 pp. Paper. 1570752915.

Grouped under the headings of visionaries, martyrs, collaborators, wives and mothers, penitents, outcasts, innovators, and missionaries, the lives forty women of extraordinary variety are explored.

SO437 Kanyoro, Musimbi R. A., ed.

In Search of a Round Table: Gender, Theology and Church Leadership. Geneva, SZ: WCC Publications, 1997. xii, 187 pp. Paper. 2825412090.

Twenty-five short papers in response to the Ecumenical Decade—Churches in Solidarity with Women; by a global cross-section of leaders concerned that the particular gifts of women be affirmed in the churches' life and witness.

SO438 *Living Letters: A Report of Visits to the Churches during the Ecumenical Decade — Churches in Solidarity with Women*

Geneva, SZ: WCC Publications, 1997. 50 pp. Paper. 2825412252.

An assessment of the findings of 75 ecumenical team visits to 330 churches, 68 national councils, and 650 women's groups during the Ecumenical Decade (1988-1997) of "Churches in Solidarity with Women."

SO439 Mananzan, Mary John et al., eds.

Women Resisting Violence: Spirituality for Life. Maryknoll, NYU: Orbis Books, 1996. viii, 184 pp. Paper. 1570750807.

Papers by fifteen of the world's outstanding women theologians; originally presented at the EATWOT-sponsored "Women's Resisting Violence" conference (San José, Costa Rica, 7-12 December 1994).

SO440 Mollenkott, Virginia Ramey, ed.

Women of Faith in Dialogue. New York, NYU: Crossroad Publishing, 1987. ix, 195 pp. Paper. 0824508238.

Essays by eighteen women of faith (Protestant, Catholic, Jewish, and Muslim) discussing challenges that confront women in their respective communities of faith.

SO441 Oduyoye, Mercy Amba

Who Will Roll the Stone Away?: The Ecumenical Decade of the Churches in Solidarity with Women. (Risk Book Series, 47). Geneva, SZ: WCC, 1990. 69 pp. Paper. 2825410187.

The story of the WCC's planning and implementation of the Ecumenical Decade of the Churches in Solidarity with Women (1988-1997).

SO442 Ortega, Ofelia, ed.

Women's Visions: Theological Reflection, Celebration, Action. Geneva, SZ: WCC Publications, 1995. xi, 182 pp. Paper. 2825411442.

Eighteen short essays by women theologians and church leaders from six continents; originally presented at the seminar on "Women in Dialogue: Wholeness of Vision towards the 21st Century" (Bossey, Switzerland, 29 April-8 May 1994).

SO443 Pasut, Ursula

Frauen in der Welt, Frauen in der Mission: Geschichte und Gegenwart des Deutschen Frauen-Missions-Gebetsbundes (DFMGB). (Telos-Taschenbuch, 419). Neuhausen-Stuttgart, GW: Hänssler-Verlag, 1985. 75 pp. 3775109951.

The history and present work of the German Women's Mission Prayer Band (DFMGB).

SO444 Pobee, J. S., and Bärbel von Wartenberg-Potter, eds.

New Eyes for Reading: Biblical and Theological Reflections by Women from the Third World. Geneva, SZ: WCC, 1986. viii, 106 pp. Paper. 2825408638.

Reflections and essays by women from Africa, Asia, and Latin America that are a significant contribution to women's theology, and part of their ongoing dialogue with others in the ecumenical movement.

SO445 Pobee, J. S., ed.

Komm, lies mit meinen Augen: Biblische und theologische Entdeckungen von Frauen aus der Dritten Welt. Translated by Bärbel von Wartenberg-Potter. Offenbach/M, GW: Burckhardthaus-Laetare Verlag, 1987. 144 pp. Paper. 3766492462.

German translation.

SO446 Ralte, Lalrinawmi, comp.

Women Re-Shaping Theology: Introducing Women's Studies in Theological Education in India. Bangalore, II: United Theological College; Delhi, II: ISPCK, 1998. xii, 116 pp. Paper. 8172144601.

Papers on women's issues; originally presented at the inaugural seminar of the Women's Studies Program at United Theological College (Bangalore, India, 21-23 February 1994).

SO447 Robins, Wendy S., ed.
Through the Eyes of a Woman: Bible Studies on the Experience of Women. Geneva, SZ: WCC Publications; Geneva, SZ: World YWCA Publications, 1995. xx, 145 pp. Paper. 2825411396.

A revised and abridged edition of the classic (1979) collection of Bible studies from the perspectives of women and the social issues they face; earlier published by the World YWCA in 1986.

SO448 *Sexism in the 1970s: Discrimination Against Women: A Report of a World Council of Churches Consultation, West Berlin, 1974*
Geneva, SZ: WCC, 1975. 150 pp. Paper. 2825404993.

The sharing by women from all over the world who met in 1974 to face what it means for their countries, families, and themselves to be engaged in a struggle for liberation.

SO449 Shull, Lois Netzley
Women in India Who Kept the Faith. North Manchester, INU: Lois N. Shull, 1985. 72 pp. Paper. No ISBN.

An account of Church of the Brethren women, both American and Indian, and their struggles from 1894 through 1984 to improve the quality of life of their Indian sisters.

SO450 Thomas, Juliet
After God's Own Heart. Bromley, ENK: Pilot Books, 1994. 102 pp. Paper. 1858590043.

A call for women to fulfill their callings as Christian leaders, especially in Asia; by the Founder and Director of Arpana Ministries (a national prayer network in India) and leader in the LCWE.

SO451 Vorster, W. S., ed.
Sexism and Feminism in Theological Perspective. (Miscellanea Congregalia, 24). Pretoria, SA: University of South Africa, 1984. 144 pp. 0869813188.

Proceedings of the eighth symposium of the Institute for Theological Research (UNISA) held at the University of South Africa (Pretoria, 5-6 September 1984).

SO452 Webster, John C. B., and Ellen Low Webster
The Church and Women in the Third World. Philadelphia, PAU: Westminster Press, 1985. 167 pp. Paper. 066424601X.

Eight essays on Christian images of women in the Third World, the role of women in the church, and the status of women; with an annotated bibliography on the theme.

SO453 *Women's Perspectives: Articulating the Liberating Power of the Gospel*
(Gospel and Culture Pamphlet, 14). Geneva, SZ: WCC Publications, 1996. 51 pp. Paper. 2825412082.

Seven essays based on WCC-sponsored presentations at the forum for non-governmental organizations during the UN's women's conference (Beijing, 1995).

Marriage and the Family

See also MI29, AF161, AF173, AF223, AF234, AF236, AF367, AF418, AF884, AF1066, AF1154, AF1182, AF1213, AF1248, AM1069, AS627, AS645, OC57, OC134, OC141, and OC146.

SO454 Blum, William G.
Forms of Marriage: Monogamy Reconsidered. (Spearhead, 105-107). Eldoret, KE: AMECEA Gaba Publications, 1989. xxiii, 317 pp. Paper. 9966836004.

A study of the two forms of African marriage, monogamy and polygamy, in light of traditional African society, biblical reflection, and pastoral practice; by the Academic Dean and Librarian at Tangaza College in Nairobi, Kenya.

SO455 Cragg, Kenneth
The Secular Experience of God. (Christian Mission and Modern Culture). Harrisburg, PAU: Trinity Press International; Herefordshire, ENK: Gracewing, 1998. viii, 82 pp. Paper. 1563382237 (US), 0852444826 (UK).

The noted Islamicist explores the ironies in the ways religions cope with secular dilemmas, focusing on sexuality as the core of cultural formation in birth, the family, and human relationships.

SO456 Fraser-Smith, Janet
Love across Latitudes. Loughborough, ENK: Arab World Ministries, 1993. ix, 155 pp. Paper. 0904971031.

A workbook of text, stories, and questions for those considering a life partner from a culture or social grouping other than their own.

SO457 Hillman, Eugene
Polygamy Reconsidered: African Plural Marriage and the Christian Churches. Maryknoll, NYU: Orbis Books, 1975. x, 266 pp. Paper. 0883443910.

A scholarly study of the anthropological and theological dimensions of polygamy, with discussion of the problems of evangelization and pastoral care in areas where simultaneous polygamy is both a traditional custom and a contemporary reality.

SO458 Hurley, Michael, ed.
Beyond Tolerance: The Challenge of Mixed Marriage: A Record of the International Consultation Held in Dublin, 1974. London, ENK: Chapman, 1975. xi, 193 pp. 0225660938.

The record of an international and ecumenical consultation on mixed marriage held by the Irish School of Ecumenics, which considered primarily marriages between Catholics and Protestants, but also interfaith marriages (with papers by Adrian Hastings and Kenneth Cragg).

SO459 Jeyaraj, Daniel
The Triumph over Dowry: A Real Story. (Development Education Series, 2). New Delhi, II: Navdin Prakashan Kendra, 1991. 43 pp. Paper. 8172410169.

Short case histories of harmful practices related to the Indian dowry system with suggestions for the role of the church.

SO460 Kanyadago, Peter M.
Evangelizing Polygamous Families; Canonical and African Approaches: Forms of Marriage, 2. (AMECEA Gaba Publications Spearhead, 116-18). Eldoret, KE: AMECEA Gaba Publications, 1991. xix, 230 pp. Paper. 9966836055.

A detailed analysis of canonical (1585-1983) and missional approaches to customary marriages, especially those of polygamous families of Africa.

SO461 Kimathi, Grace
Your Marriage and Family. (Series F2: Brochures of the Institute for Reformational Studies, 58). Potchefstroom, SA: Potchefstroom University; Potchefstroom, SA: Christian Literature Committee for Africa, 1994. i, 110 pp. Paper. 1868221865.

A family counselor with Family Life Mission, founded by Walter and Ingrid Trobisch, gives a Christian response to family issues in Africa today.

SO462 Masamba ma Mpolo, and Cecile de Sweemer, eds.
Families in Transition: The Case for Counselling in Context.
Geneva, SZ: WCC, 1987. viii, 148 pp. Paper. 2825409081.

Nine papers from the WCC Office of Family Education dealing with cultural and sociological contexts of family and pastoral counseling in Third World countries, including case studies.

SO463 Masamba ma Mpolo, ed.
Family Profiles: Stories of Families in Transition. Geneva, SZ: WCC, 1984. 96 pp. Paper. 282540814X.

Stories of family groups in different parts of the world as they talk of their parents and grandparents, their children and hopes for them, their own concerns and convictions—all families in transition.

SO464 McGrath, Michael, and Nicole Gregoire
Africa: Our Way to Love and Marriage. London, ENK: Chapman, 1977. ix, 201 pp. 0225661632.

A primer on Christian marriage for African Christians.

SO465 Nelson-Pallmeyer, Jack
Families Valued: Parenting and Politics for the Good of All Children. New York, NYU: Friendship Press, 1996. xii, 276 pp. Paper. 0377003093.

A father's reflection on parenting for personal and social transformation, with concern for global awareness, peace, and justice.

SO466 Osseo-Asare, Francislee
A New Land to Live In: The Odyssey of an African and an American Seeking God's Guidance on Marriage. Downers Grove, ILU: InterVarsity, 1977. 159 pp. Paper. 0877847223.

Letters and journal entries which share the struggles of a biracial couple (United States and Ghana) to grow in marriage, faith, and cross-cultural sensitivity.

SO467 Southard, Samuel
Family Counseling in East Asia. Manila, PH: EACC, 1969. 120 pp. No ISBN.

Practical insights for church leaders from the EACC Institute on Marriage and Family Counselling (Bangkok, Thailand, July 1968).

Work among Adult Age Sets

SO468 Bell, James
Bridge over Troubled Water: Ministry to Baby Boomers—A Generation Adrift. Wheaton, ILU: Victor Books, 1993. 251 pp. Paper. 1564761126.

A primer, with study helps, on the culture of the generation born in the United States from 1946 to 1964; with a biblical theology for the church's outreach and ministry to them.

SO469 Pontifical Council for the Laity
The Dignity of Older People and Their Mission in the Church and in the World. Washington, DCU: USCC, 1999. 51 pp. Paper. 1574553445.

An affirmation of the mission of "third age" people who have retired from active employment, yet have great inner resources for contributing to the common good.

SO470 Roof, Wade Clark, Jackson W. Carroll, and David A. Roozen, eds.
The Post-War Generation and Establishment Religion: Cross-Cultural Perspectives. Boulder, COU: Westview Press, 1995. xx, 291 pp. 0813389143.

Eighteen essays which together provide a comparative analysis of religious trends since World War II, in ten western countries of Europe, North America, and Australia; includes popular religiosity, the new spirituality, and levels of commitment by "baby boomers."

Work among Youth

See also EV509, EV523, EV569, EV576, AM1092-AM1093, AM1231-AM1232, AS1028, EU141-EU142, and EU183.

SO471 Kujawa, Sheryl A., ed.
Disorganized Religion: The Evangelization of Youth and Young Adults. Boston, MAU: Cowley Publications, 1998. xiv, 247 pp. Paper. 1561011495.

Twenty-five North Americans, mostly Episcopalians engaged in ministries to young people, share their challenges and approaches.

SO472 Lau, Lawson
The World at Your Doorstep: A Handbook for International Student Ministry. Downers Grove, ILU: InterVarsity, 1984. 144 pp. Paper. 0877845263.

A handbook for those who would institute Christian ministries among some of the more than 300,000 international students in the United States; by one such student from Singapore.

SO473 McKenna, David L.
The Coming Great Awakening: New Hope for the Nineties. Downers Grove, ILU: InterVarsity, 1990. 132 pp. Paper. 0830817352.

An appeal by the president of Asbury Theological Seminary to Christian college students, to lead in a religious awakening in the United States.

SO474 Phillips, Tom, Bob Norsworthy, and Terry Whalin
The World at Your Door. Minneapolis, MNU: Bethany House, 1997. 230 pp. Paper. 1556619642.

A primer by leaders of International Students Incorporated for those in ministry to international students in the United States.

SO475 Schieber, Andrea Lee, and Olson Ann Terman, eds.
What NeXt?: Connecting Your Ministry with the Generation formerly Known as X*. Minneapolis, MNU: Augsburg Fortress, 1999. 173 pp. Paper. 0806639687.

A primer for postmodern ministry written by contributors who are on the emerging edge of American culture through ministry to Generation X.

SO476 *Sons and Daughters of the Light*
Washington, DCU: USCC, 1997. vii, 59 pp. Paper. 1574551272.

The national plan for pastoral ministry to and with young adults, developed by the US Catholic Bishops' Committee on the Laity.

SO477 St. Clair, Barry, and Keith Naylor
Penetrating the Campus. Wheaton, ILU: Victor Books, 1993. 209 pp. Paper. 1564760855.

A practical guide for youth workers seeking to communicate God's love to high school students in the United States.

SO—MISSIONS: SOCIAL ASPECTS

Work among Occupational Groups

See also AM657 and EU286.

SO478 Bergmark, Ingemar
Kyrka och sjöfolk: En studie i Svenska kyrkans sjömansvård 1911-1933. (Studia Missionalia Upsaliensia, 23). Stockholm, SW: Verbum; Karlskrona, SW: Axel Abrahamsons Boktryckeri, 1974. 236 pp. No ISBN.

A study of the Church of Sweden's care for seamen, 1911-1933.

SO479 Cussiánovich, Alejandro
Nos ha Liberado. (Pedal, 12). Salamanca, SP: Ediciones Sígueme, 1973. 179 pp. Paper. 8430105360.

Reflections written for militant workers, to help them see Latin American reality through a faith perspective, and be able to name it and share this experience with others.

SO480 *En Marcha Hacia el Señor/Journeying Together toward the Lord*
Washington, DCU: USCC, 1993. 35 pp. Paper. 1555866568.

A bilingual catechetical resource offering support and direction for developing the faith life of migrant workers in Spanish and English.

SO481 Jacob, Micheal
The Flying Angel Story. London, ENK: Mowbrays, 1973. 129 pp. Paper. 0264646193.

A journalist's examination of the past, present, and possible future of the Missions to Seamen.

SO482 Kverndal, Roald
Seamen's Missions: Their Origin and Early Growth. South Pasadena, CAU: William Carey Library, 1986. xxviii, 901 pp. 0878084401.

Exhaustive scholarly history emphasizing British and American naval missions from 1779 to the mid-1800s, including historical studies of organizations such as the Naval and Military Bible Society, Marine Bible Society, Bethel Union, and the American Nautical Society; includes a section on maritime missiology, copius notes, and exhaustive bibliography.

SO483 National Catholic Conference of Airport Chaplains
Ministry of the Moment: A Manual for Developing an Airport Chaplaincy Program. Washington, DCU: USCC, 1997. xi, 49 pp. Paper. 1574551469.

A basic "how to" resource for establishing or enhancing Catholic airport ministries in the United States.

SO484 Smith, Waldo E. L.
The Navy and Its Chaplains in the Age of Sail. Toronto, ONC: Ryerson Press, 1961. xv, 197 pp. No ISBN.

A history of the role of the sea chaplain as preacher, counsellor, advocate, and missionary, from the sixth to the eighteenth centuries.

Work among Immigrants

See also EC334, AM1236, AM1351, EU108, EU166, and EU201.

SO485 Churches' Committee on Migrant Workers
Des femmes immigrées parlent: Textes présent és par Jean Guyot ... [et al.]. Paris, FR: Harmattan, 1978. 175 pp. No ISBN.
French translation, 2nd edition.

SO486 Churches' Committee on Migrant Workers
Migrant Women Speak. London, ENK: Search Press; Geneva, SZ: WCC, 1978. vii, 164 pp. 0855323914 (S), 2825405612 (W).
English edition.

SO487 Jacques, André
The Stranger within Your Gates: Uprooted People in the World Today. Geneva, SZ: WCC, 1986. viii, 87 pp. Paper. 2825408530.

A poignant picture of the different cruel aspects of uprootedness, with vignettes of Christian ministries among migrants and refugees.

SO488 Mensen, Bernhard, ed.
Minoritäten: Akademik Völker und Kulturen St. Augustin. (Vortragsreihe: Akademie Völker und Kulturen, 20). Nettetal, GW: Steyler Verlag, 1997. 137 pp. Paper. 3805004028.

These 1996-1997 lectures of the St. Augustine Academy in Nettetal, Germany, deal with the implications and impact of the new wave of worldwide migrations and cultural mobility for the peoples of color, and their different cultural and religious beliefs.

SO489 Mieth, Dietmar, and Lisa Sowle Cahill, eds.
Migrants and Refugees. London, ENK: SCM Press; Maryknoll, NYU: Orbis Books, 1993. x, 155 pp. Paper. 0334030226 (UK), 0883448726 (US).

Thirteen essays by European, Asian, and African Roman Catholic scholars, analyzing the facts of contemporary movements of immigrants and refugees, providing theological and ethical reflections with sensitivity to issues of racism.

SO490 National Conference of Catholic Bishops, Bishops' Committee on Migration
Today's Immigrants and Refugees: A Christian Understanding. Washington, DCU: USCC, 1988. iv, 147 pp. Paper. 1555872047.

Seven scholarly essays designed to provide a theology of pastoral care of immigrants, including two on Old Testament perspectives, one on the history of Roman Catholic ministries to immigrants in the United States, and four on contemporary issues of pastoral care.

Work among Refugees

See also SO239, SO420, SO487, SO489, SO637, EC38, PO173, AF210, AF470, AF616-AF617, AF846, and AS803.

SO491 Bau, Ignatius
This Ground Is Holy: Church Sanctuary and Central American Refugees. New York, NYU: Paulist Press, 1985. ix, 288 pp. Paper. 0809127202.

An account of the Sanctuary Movement in the United States in which, in defiance of federal law, ordinary citizens opened their homes, churches, and synagogues to illegal refugees fleeing terror and turmoil in Central America.

SO492 Canada-U.S. Church Consultation on Refugee Protection and Safe Haven
Building Bridges: Report and Recommendations. New York, NYU: NCCUSA, CWS, 1985. 41 pp. Paper. No ISBN.

A summary of the proceedings at the consultation (Washington, D.C., 11-12 April 1985), with recommendations and list of participants; published together with a fifty-eight-page supplement of theological reflections and responses.

SO493 Conference on World Evangelization (Pattaya, Thailand, 1980)
The Thailand Report on Refugees: Report of the ... Mini-Con-sultation on Reaching Refugees. (Lausanne Occasional Papers, 5). Wheaton, ILU: LCWE, 1980. 16 pp. Paper. No ISBN.

A review of the current situation of refugees, the biblical mandate, the role of local churches, and guidelines for responsible Christian action.

SO494 Dilling, Yvonne
In Search of Refuge. Scottdale, PAU: Herald Press, 1984. ix, 288 pp. Paper. 0806133641.

An intimate account by an international volunteer, of the suffering of El Salvadoran refugees on the Honduras border in 1981-1982 and ministries to them; with a brief appendix by Gary Mac Eoin giving historical background on Central America.

SO495 *Ecumenical Consultation on Asylum and Protection: (Zürich, 27 April-2 May 1986)*
Geneva, SZ: WCC, 1986. 73 pp. Paper. No ISBN.

Report of a conference sponsored jointly by the Refugee Service of WCC and Caritas-Switzerland.

SO496 Egan, Eileen
For Whom There Is No Room: Scenes from the Refugee World. New York, NYU: Paulist Press, 1995. v, 374 pp. 0809104733 (hdbk), 080913537X (pbk).

Stories from fifty years of ministry to refugees, 1943-1993, by Catholic Relief Services (CRS).

SO497 Ekin, Larry
Enduring Witness: The Church and the Palestinians. Geneva, SZ: WCC, 1985. xiv, 135 pp. Paper. 2825408433.

A detailed analysis of the WCC's policies in relation to the Palestinians from 1948 to 1980, and of the programs coordinated by the Middle East Council of Churches' Department of Service to Palestinian Refugees.

SO498 Ferris, Elizabeth G.
Beyond Borders: Refugees, Migrants and Human Rights in the Post-Cold War Era. Geneva, SZ: WCC Publications, 1993. xxxvi, 310 pp. Paper. 2825410950.

A thoroughly researched analysis of responses to needs of refugees by the UN, governments, and non-governmental organizations (NGOs), with a vision and plan of action for churches and other NGOs.

SO499 Golden, Renny
Sanctuary: The New Underground Railroad. Maryknoll, NYU: Orbis Books, 1986. ix, 214 pp. Paper. 0883444402.

The story of the Sanctuary Movement in North America, told by two members of the Chicago Religious Task Force on Central America, including both the first-person stories of refugees, and an analysis of the political and economic forces which try to stop the movement.

SO500 MacEóin, Gary, ed.
Sanctuary: A Resource Guide for Understanding and Participating in the Central American Refugees' Struggle. San Francisco, CAU: Harper & Row, 1985. 217 pp. Paper. 0060653728.

A collection of essays and lectures given at the Inter-American Symposium on Sanctuary (Tucson, Arizona, 23-24 January 1985), which gives theological, biblical, historical, ethical, and legal perspectives on sanctuary, in addition to stories from Latin American refugees seeking sanctuary in the United States, and the tasks by which the Sanctuary Movement challenges the American conscience.

SO501 Mayotte, Judy
Disposable People?: The Plight of Refugees. Maryknoll, NYU: Orbis Books, 1992. 316 pp. 0883448394.

Report of participant research, by the author, on the plight of long-term refugees in Cambodia, Afghanistan, and Somalia.

SO502 Moloney, Michael, ed.
Displaced in Africa. (One World Series, 5). Nairobi, KE: St. Paul Communications/Daughters of St. Paul, 1995. 52 pp. Paper. 9966210628.

A study book for African Christians on the contemporary refugee crisis of that continent.

SO503 Moussa, Helene, comp.
Stormy Seas We Brave: Creative Expressions by Uprooted People. Geneva, SZ: WCC Publications, 1998. 175 pp. Paper. 2825412813.

The voices of uprooted people/refugees, internationally displaced persons, and migrants, through poems, lyrics, reflections, dramas, and visual artwork.

SO504 Moussa, Helene, Patrick A. Taran, and Martin Robra, eds.
A Moment to Choose: Risking to Be with Uprooted People. Geneva, SZ: WCC, 1996. 90 pp. Paper. No ISBN.

A basic resource for Christians engaged in ministry with refugees and other displaced persons.

SO505 Mummert, John Ronald, and Jeff Bach
Refugee Ministry in the Local Congregation. Scottdale, PAU: Herald Press, 1992. 128 pp. Paper. 0836135806.

Inspiration and practical helps for local North American congregations considering sponsorship and ministry to refugees.

SO506 *Seeking Safe Haven: A Congregational Guide to Helping Central American Refugees in the United States*
New York, NYU: NCCUSA, CWS; New York, NYU: Lutheran Immigration and Refugee Service, 1986. 112 pp. Paper. No ISBN.

A updated edition of the manual for local churches interested in responding to the need for sanctuary of Central American refugees.

SO507 WCC Refugee Resettlement Consultation
Refugees Today and Tomorrow: New Directions for the WCC Refugee Resettlement Network. New York, NYU: CWS, 1986. 51 pp. Paper. No ISBN.

The report and recommendations of the consultation (Miami, Florida, 14-19 September 1986) sponsored jointly by the WCC and the CWS Immigration and Refugee Program.

SO508 World Council of Churches Consultation on Asylum and Protection (Niagara Falls, ONC, 14-18 May 1984)
Protection of Asylum Seekers in Western Countries: Report and Recommendations. New York, NYU: NCCUSA-CWS, 1984. 61 pp. Paper. No ISBN.

A summary, report, and recommendations of the consultation, addressing who the peoples are who need to be protected, their roots, and advocacy relationship with the church; including listing of participants.

SO—MISSIONS: SOCIAL ASPECTS

Work among Ethnic
and Racial Groups

See also HI232, SO14, AM120, AM151, AM216, AM242, AM280, AM806, AM853, AM1074, AM1116, AM1235, AM1255-AM1257, AM1262-AM1263, AM1307, AM1444, AM1448, AM1451, AM1459-AM1460, AS901, AS903, AS949, AS978, AS985, AS1004, AS1049, AS1080, AS1104, and AS1117.

SO509 Banks, William L.

The Black Church in the U.S.: Its Origin, Growth, Contributions, and Outlook. Shelbyville, TNU: Bible and Literature Missionary Foundation, 1983. 160 pp. No ISBN.

Revised edition of a general history including missions to and from African American Christians; originally published in 1969 (Macmillan).

SO510 Bentley, William Hiram

The National Black Evangelical Association: Reflections on the Evolution of a Concept of Ministry. Chicago, ILU: Bentley, 1979. 151 pp. Paper. No ISBN.

Revised edition of a brief history of the National Black Evangelical Association, founded in 1963 for meaningful fellowship among blacks of evangelical persuasion across denominational lines; with chapters on the changed understandings of ministry articulated at its annual conventions.

SO511 Davis, James H., and Woodie W. White

Racial Transition in the Church. Nashville, TNU: Abingdon, 1980. 142 pp. Paper. 0687352800.

The result of six years of research among hundreds of congregations in urban neighborhoods of the United States undergoing racial transition, this book offers both social analysis and strategies for such churches.

SO512 Duren, James, and Rodney Wilson

The Stranger Who Is among You: A Guide to Conservative Baptist Churches That Want to Reach out to the Ethnic Groups in Their Communities. South Pasadena, CAU: William Carey Library, 1983. x, 68 pp. Paper. 0878089209.

A short guide for Conservative Baptist churches that want to reach out to the ethnic groups in their communities.

Work among Prisoners

See also AS703.

SO513 Christiansen, Chris

Seven Years among Prisoners of War. Translated by Ida Egede Winther. Athens, OHU: Ohio University Press, 1994. xi, 221 pp. 0821410695.

The story of the YMCA's work among prisoners of war in Europe, 1942-1948; told by a Danish staff member.

SO514 Pace, Dale K.

A Christian's Guide to Effective Jail and Prison Ministries. Old Tappan, NJU: Revell, 1976. 318 pp. 080070844X.

A primer for those who would engage in prison ministries, including analysis of the criminal justice system and of existing correctional chaplaincies; with suggestions for effective ministry.

SO515 Raphael, Pierre

Inside Rikers Island: A Chaplain's Search for God. Maryknoll, NYU: Orbis Books, 1990. xvi, 140 pp. Paper. 088344674X.

The spiritual journey of a Catholic chaplain in Riker's Island, New York City, the largest prison colony in the world, telling of struggles for faith in the midst of darkness.

SO516 United States Catholic Conference

Responsibility, Rehabilitation, and Restoration: A Catholic Perspective on Crime and Criminal Justice. Washington, DCU: USCC, 2000. 69 pp. Paper. 1574553941.

Recognizing that human dignity applies to both victim and offender, the bishops utilize Scripture, sacramental and historical heritage, Catholic social teaching, and policy foundations to promote further dialogue and action.

SO517 Wiseman, Stella

Charles Colson. (Men of Faith). Minneapolis, MNU: Bethany House, 1995. 185 pp. Paper. 1556616295.

A popular account of the man who emerged from the Watergate scandal to found Prison Fellowship.

Work among Persons with
Handicapping Conditions

See also MI63 and AS750.

SO518 Mosteller, Sue

Body Broken Body Blessed: Reflections from Life in Community. Toronto, ONC: Novalis; Alexandria, AT: Dwyer, 1996. 128 pp. Paper. 2890887855 (N), 0855743905 (E).

The pastor at the Daybreak Community in Richmond, Ontario, recounts the high and low points of friendships with the disabled in L'Arche Daybreak ministries.

SO519 Nouwen, Henri J. M.

Adam: God's Beloved. Maryknoll, NYU: Orbis Books, 1997. 128 pp. 1570751331.

A moving final memoir by the noted Dutch theologian of his friendship with a severely handicapped young man as part of the ministry of the L'Arche Daybreak Community in Toronto, Canada.

SO520 Vanier, Jean

An Ark for the Poor: The Story of L'Arche. (L'Arche Collection). Toronto, ONC: Novalis; New York, NYU: Crossroad Publishing; London, UNK: Geoffrey Chapman, 1995. 125 pp. Paper. 2890887316 (N), 0824515382 (C), 0225668041 (G).

L'Arche's founder tells the story of the community's first thirty years of ministry to persons with physical and mental handicaps.

SO521 Vanier, Jean

Our Journey Home: Rediscovering a Common Humanity Beyond Our Differences. Translated by Maggie Parham. Maryknoll, NYU: Orbis Books; Ottawa, ONC: Novalis; London, ENK: Hodder & Stoughton, 1997. xix, 251 pp. Paper. 157075117X (OB/N), 0340661437 (HS).

English translation.

SO522 Vanier, Jean

Toute personne est une histoire sacrée. Paris, FR: Librairie Plon, 1994. 279 pp. 2259000967.

The founder of the L'Arche movement of communities for persons with mental handicaps in twenty-six countries sums up thirty years of learnings and wisdom.

SO—MISSIONS: SOCIAL ASPECTS

SO523 Wilke, Harold H.
Creating the Caring Congregation. Nashville, TNU: Abingdon, 1980. 110 pp. Paper. 0687098157.

A primer on the church's ministry to restore alienated and handicapped persons to the mainstream of community life.

Urban Missions

See also HI641, ME38, SO1, SO20, SO240, SO421, EC156, EV377, EV404, CH178, CH385, CH426, CH438, AF172, AF204, AF219, AF222, AF1228, AM277-AM278, AM1207-AM1208, AM1210, AM1212, AM1224, AM1228, AM1306, AM1495, AS110, AS635, AS740, AS764, AS971, AS1036, AS1436-AS1437, AS1485, EU32, EU82, EU84, EU102, EU106, EU118, EU120, EU122, EU129, EU144, EU149, EU166, and OC98.

SO524 Bakke, Raymond J.
A Theology as Big as the City. Downers Grove, ILU: InterVarsity, 1997. 221 pp. Paper. 0830818901.

A biblical theology for urban mission by the Executive Director of International Urban Associates in Chicago.

SO525 Bakke, Raymond J.
The Urban Christian: Effective Ministry in Today's Urban World. Downers Grove, ILU: InterVarsity, 1987. 200 pp. Paper. 0877845239.

Theological reflections on the opportunities and problems of ministry within the urban context with practical techniques and suggestions for ministry strategy.

SO526 Barrett, David B.
World Class Cities and World Evangelization. Birmingham, ALU: New Hope Press, 1986. 60 pp. Paper. 0936625007.

A well-researched study of the growth of world cities, their challenge to the churches, and strategies for evangelization; first of nine titles in the Global Evangelization Movement A.D. 2000 Series.

SO527 Brander, Bruce et al., eds.
Into the World's Cities: Report ... Monrovia, CAU: World Vision, 1990. 60 pp. Paper. No ISBN.

Findings of the International Urban Ministry Workshop (Forest Home, California, 19-20 March 1990) for World Vision leaders from five continents on "Equipping for Ministry in the World's Cities."

SO528 Cheuiche, Antônio do Carmo
Cultura Urbana; Reto a la evangelización: Seminario, Buenos Aires, AG, 30 de noviembre-4 de diciembre de 1988. (Documentos CELAM, 112). Bogotá, CK: CELAM, 1989. 250 pp. Paper. 9586251640.

A collection of eight biblical, pastoral, and sociological papers presented at the seminar on urban culture and evangelization.

SO529 Claerbaut, David
Urban Ministry. Grand Rapids, MIU: Zondervan, 1983. 230 pp. Paper. 0310459613.

One of the best overall introductions to urban ministry, combining theoretical perspectives with positive practical recommendations for dealing with issues such as social stratification, urban insecurity, and the poor.

SO530 Coffey, Ian et al.
No Stranger in the City: God's Concern for Urban People. Leicester, ENK: InterVarsity; Kent, ENK: STL Books, 1989. 159 pp. Paper. 0851108482.

Nine popular essays written by urban mission specialists on the factors and possibilities of communicating the Gospel with persons in the city.

SO531 Conference on World Evangelization (Pattaya, Thailand, 1980)
The Thailand Report on Large Cities: Report of the ... Mini-Consultation on Reaching Large Cities. (Lausanne Occasional Papers, 9). Wheaton, ILU: LCWE, 1980. 35 pp. Paper. No ISBN.

This report reviews the urbanization of the world, biblical mandates and resources for large city evangelism, and regional strategies.

SO532 Conn, Harvie M., ed.
Planting and Growing Urban Churches: From Dream to Reality. Grand Rapids, MIU: Baker Books, 1997. 271 pp. Paper. 080102109X.

A sourcebook containing seventeen short articles by specialists in urban mission, focusing on research, planning, and strategies in selected world cities.

SO533 Conn, Harvie M.
A Clarified Vision for Urban Mission: Dispelling the Urban Stereotypes. (Ministry Resources Library). Grand Rapids, MIU: Zondervan, 1987. 240 pp. Paper. 0310454417.

A preliminary look at urban realities for evangelical Christians desiring to break away from misunderstandings of the city in order to engage creatively in urban mission.

SO534 Damasio, Frank, ed.
Crossing Rivers, Taking Cities: Lessons from Joshua on Reaching Cities for Christ. Ventura, CAU: Regal Books, 1999. 303 pp. Paper. 0830723927.

This story shows how to interpret the times, the culture, the spiritual climate, and the prophetic signs of today to "strategically claim your town or city for Jesus Christ."

SO535 Dawson, John
Taking Our Cities for God: How to Break Spiritual Strongholds. Lake Mary, FLU: Creation House, 1989. 219 pp. Paper. 0884192415.

An inspirational book for urban lay missioners by the director of YWAM in Los Angeles.

SO536 Dougherty, James
The Fivesquare City: The City in the Religious Imagination. Notre Dame, INU: University of Notre Dame Press, 1980. xiii, 167 pp. 0268009465.

A scholarly analysis of the city as a symbol in the Bible and Western folklore and literature.

SO—MISSIONS: SOCIAL ASPECTS

SO537 Du Bose, Francis M.
How Churches Grow in an Urban World. Nashville, TNU:
Broadman, 1978. vii, 181 pp. 0805425314.

An assessment of the biblical understanding of urban-
ism and church growth, and its application to contemporary urban church life; with examples drawn largely from
American Baptist churches in North America, but also from
Western Europe, Japan, Brazil, and Africa.

SO538 Duncan, Michael
Costly Mission: Following Christ into the Slums. (Urban
Ministry, 2). Monrovia, CAU: MARC, 1996. vi, 135 pp.
Paper. 0912552964.

A testimony by a New Zealander of his work under
Servants to Asia's Poor in the Manila slum of Damayan
Lagi.

SO539 Engen, Charles Edward van, and Jude Tiersma, eds.
*God So Loves the City: Seeking a Theology for Urban Mis-
sion.* Monrovia, CAU: MARC, 1994. xiii, 313 pp. Paper.
0912552867.

Twelve short essays on urban mission (theology and
strategies); with extended bibliography.

SO540 Frenchak, David J., and Clinton E. Stockwell, comps.
Signs of the Kingdom in the Secular City. Edited by Helen
Ujvarosy. Chicago, ILU: Covenant Press, 1984. xii, 114 pp.
Paper. 0910452563.

A collection of thirteen essays concerned with urban
ministry which focus on global urbanization, the importance
of urban mission, and mission with Hispanics, blacks, and
Asians; originally presented at the 1980 SCUPE Congress
on Urban Ministry in Chicago, Illinois.

SO541 Greenway, Roger S., and Timothy M. Monsma
Cities: Mission's New Frontier. Grand Rapids, MIU: Baker Books, 2000. 280 pp. Paper. 0801022304.

A revised and expanded second edition of one of the
first major studies on urban missions, containing a biblical
framework for mission to cities, discussion of city issues
that need to be addressed by urban missions, and models of
urban mission in North America, Europe, Asia, Africa, and
Latin America; first published in 1989.

SO542 Greenway, Roger S., ed.
*Discipling the City: Theological Reflections on Urban Mis-
sion.* Grand Rapids, MIU: Baker Books, 1979. 286 pp.
Paper. 0801037271.

Nine essays by urban specialists from Reformed, Presbyterian, and Baptist traditions, who have been engaged in
urban mission on five continents.

SO543 Greenway, Roger S.
*Apóstoles a la Ciudad: estrategias bíblicas para misiones
urbanas.* Grand Rapids, MIU: Subcomisión de Literatura
de Iglesia Cristiana Reformada, 1981. 107 pp. Paper. No
ISBN.

Spanish translation.

SO544 Greenway, Roger S.
Apostles to the City: Biblical Strategies for Urban Missions.
Grand Rapids, MIU: Baker Books, 1978. 96 pp.
0801037247.

A study of various prophets and apostles called to minister in the urban centers of their day.

SO545 Grigg, Viv
Cry of the Urban Poor. Monrovia, CAU: MARC/World Vision, 1992. 295 pp. Paper. 0912552700.

A call for partnership with the poor for their evangelization based on the insights of anthropology and sociology, and
the author's experience in ten diverse cities as Director of the
Urban Leadership Foundation.

SO546 Haggard, Ted
*Primary Purpose: Making It Hard for People to Go to Hell
from Your City.* Orlando, FLU: Creation House, 1995. 178
pp. Paper. 0884193810.

Using Colorado Springs as a model of the contemporary
decaying urban city now experiencing changes, the author provides five practical principles tested and proven in that city
which can bring about necessary changes in the spiritual climate of any city.

SO547 Haggard, Ted
Primera Prioridad. Miami, FLU: Editorial Carisma, 1996.
196 pp. Paper. 9589354173.

Spanish translation.

SO548 Harper, Nile
Urban Churches, Vital Signs: Beyond Charity toward Justice.
Grand Rapids, MIU: Eerdmans, 1999. xv, 333 pp. Paper.
0802844413.

Stories of twenty-eight churches, including sixteen African American churches, in fifteen major cities across the United States that are making successful contributions to the transformation of inner-city communities.

SO549 Harvey, Anthony, ed.
Theology in the City. London, ENK: SPCK, 1989. ix, 132 pp.
Paper. 0281044171.

Seven essays responding to *Faith in the City*, written to
stimulate fresh and urgent theological thinking in the mission
and service of the church in urban Great Britain churches.

SO550 Howell, Leon
People Are the Subject: Stories of Urban Rural Mission. Geneva, SZ: WCC, CWME, 1980. viii, 80 pp. Paper. 2825406384.

A collection of stories of Christians related to the WCC's
Urban-Rural Network who seek missionary faithfulness in
urban, industrial, and rural settings.

SO551 Kratzig, Guillermo
*Urbangelización: Análisis de los obstaculos y ventajas que la
acción evangelística encuentra en los grandes centros urbanos.*
Buenos Aires, AG: Junta Bautista de Publicaciones, 1975. 126
pp. Paper. No ISBN.

A practical manual on urban evangelization.

SO552 Linthicum, Robert C., ed.
Signs of Hope in the City. (Urban Ministry). Monrovia, CAU:
MARC, 1995. 88 pp. Paper. 0912552956.

Urban theologians and practitioners discuss critical issues
which will surround urban mission into the 21st century.

SO553 Linthicum, Robert C.
*City of God, City of Satan: A Biblical Theology of the Urban
Church.* Grand Rapids, MIU: Zondervan, 1991. 330 pp. Pa-
per. 0310531411.

A biblical theology of the city, and the church's mission
within it, developed during four years of international workshops for urban pastors sponsored by World Vision.

SO—MISSIONS: SOCIAL ASPECTS

SO554 Lucas, Thomas M.

Landmarking: City, Church and Jesuit Urban Strategy. Chicago, ILU: Loyola Press, 1997. xiii, 245 pp. 0829409734.

The first in-depth study of St. Ignatius' revolutionary urban mission for the Jesuit order, with maps, illustrations, and comparison with earlier urban mission strategies.

SO555 Maust, John

Cities of Change: Urban Growth and God's People in Ten Latin American Cities. Coral Gables, FLU: Latin America Mission, 1984. 136 pp. Paper. No ISBN.

An introduction to ten Latin American cities to help evangelicals set priorities in their outreach.

SO556 McClung, Floyd

Seeing the City with the Eyes of God: How Christians Can Rise to the Urban Challenge. Tarrytown, NYU: Chosen Books, 1991. 180 pp. Paper. 0800791770.

A primer on urban mission aimed at motivating lay Christians to replace urban myths with a biblical theology of the city; originally published as *The Spirits of the City* (1990).

SO557 Meyers, Eleanor Scott, ed.

Envisioning the New City: A Reader on Urban Ministry. Louisville, KYU: Westminster John Knox, 1992. 363 pp. Paper. 0664253156.

Twenty-seven wide-ranging articles and case studies on urban ministry including biblical, contextual, ethical, pastoral, theological, and practical foundations.

SO558 Northcott, Michael

Urban Theology: A Reader. London, ENK: Cassell, 1998. xvii, 347 pp. 030470265X.

Urban social theory and analysis are combined with theological reflection in forty-eight essays, stories, and narratives on issues related to modern, postindustrial cities.

SO559 Plou, Dafne Sabanes

Peace in Troubled Cities: Creative Models of Building Community amidst Violence. (Risk Book Series, 84). Geneva, SZ: WCC Publications, 1998. 133 pp. Paper. 2825412562.

The courageous and imaginative work of local communities seeking to overcome violence in Belfast, Boston, Colombo, Durban, Kingston, Rio de Janeiro, and Suva—cities which have been part of the WCC's Peace to the City Campaign.

SO560 Rose, Larry L., and C. Kirk Hadaway

An Urban World: Churches Face the Future. Nashville, TNU: Broadman, 1984. 215 pp. Paper. 0805463399.

A helpful symposium written by some well-known writers on urbanization and Christian ministry worldwide.

SO561 Scanlon, A. Clark et al.

Con Cristo en la Ciudad: Indicaciones sobre el evangelismo urbano. El Paso, TXU: Chalice Press, 1976. 119 pp. Paper. No ISBN.

A manual using materials originating at the Conference on Urban Evangelism (Belo Horizonte, Brazil, August 1974).

SO562 Sheppard, David

Built as a City: God and the Urban World Today. London, ENK: Hoddard & Stoughton, 1974. 380 pp. Paper. 0340180099.

An analysis of the various problems of city life, the factors of power and powerlessness, and the strength and characteristics of urban churches; with suggestions as to how churches can reach out with the Gospel to those groups who feel most powerless; based on the bishop of Liverpool's pastoral experience in London, England.

SO563 Tonna, Benjamin

A Gospel for the Cities: A Socio-Theology of Urban Ministry. Translated by William E. Jerman. Maryknoll, NYU: Orbis Books, 1978. xvi, 203 pp. Paper. 0883441551.

English translation.

SO564 Tonna, Benjamin

Un vangelo per le città: Il pasaggio dalla missione urbana nel Terzo Mondo. Bologna, IT: EMI, 1978. 331 pp. No ISBN.

An introduction to urban sociology and the theology of urban mission in global perspective.

SO565 Wagner, C. Peter, Stephen Peters, and Mark Wilson, eds.

Förbön 100 nyckelstäder genom 10/40-fönstret. Kalmar, SW: WasaMedia, 1995. 68 pp. No ISBN.

Swedish translation.

SO566 Wagner, C. Peter, Stephen Peters, and Mark Wilson, eds.

Orando por las 100 Ciudades de Acceso a la Ventana 10/40. Miami, FLU: Unilit, 1995. 148 pp. Paper. 0789901455.

Spanish translation.

SO567 Wagner, C. Peter, Stephen Peters, and Mark Wilson, eds.

Praying through the 100 Gateway Cities of the 10/40 Window. Seattle, WAU: YWAM Publishing, 1995. 148 pp. 0927545802.

Four essays by evangelical missiologists (L. Bush, F. Markert, V. Gregg, C. P. Wagner) on strategies for reaching the unreached in cities with small Christian presence, focusing on the place of prayer.

SO568 Wessels, Antonie

Geloven in de stad. Antwerp, BE: Ten Have, 1997. 78 pp. Paper. 9025946968.

The noted Dutch missiologist examines biblical images of the city and their relevance for contemporary Christian approaches in Beirut, Jerusalem, and Athens.

SO569 White, Randy

Journey to the Center of the City: Making a Difference in an Urban Neighborhood. Downers Grove, ILU: InterVarsity, 1996. 143 pp. Paper. 083081129X.

A study book for a new generation of Christians desiring to move beyond charity to reconciling love, by the national director of urban projects for IVCF.

SO570 Yamamori, Tetsunao, Bryant L. Myers, and Kenneth L. Luscombe, eds.

Serving with the Urban Poor. (Cases in Holistic Ministry). Monrovia, CAU: MARC, 1998. ix, 234 pp. Paper. 1887983104.

Thirteen prominent urban practitioners explore the meaning, trends, and case studies of holistic urban mission, with emphasis on modernization, relief and development agencies, gender, and women's voices.

SO—MISSIONS: SOCIAL ASPECTS

Medical Missions

See also HI45, HI351-HI352, HI559, ME37, SO11, SO605, SO621, AF196, AF431-AF432, AF620, AF661, AF696, AF727, AF799, AF853, AF990, AF1233, AF1249, AF1316, AM590, AM606, AM744-AM745, AS315, AS359, AS564, AS750, AS851, AS1163, AS1166, AS1176, AS1203, AS1229, AS1232-AS1233, AS1245, AS1296, EU228, and OC316.

SO571 Breetvelt, J. N.
Dualisme en integratie: Een studie van de factoren die een rol spelen bij het hervinden van identiteit bij opgeleide Afrikanen. (Kerk en Theologie in Context, 3). Kampen, NE: Kok, 1989. xiii, 183 pp. Paper. 9024231957.

A theological dissertation (Theological Faculty, Catholic University of Nijmegen) by a medical doctor on psychological and cultural identity problems of the Western-educated African elite; based on interviews in Nigeria and analysis of the content of African novels and theological works, with discussion also of the organization and management of medical care in Africa.

SO572 Browne, Stanley G., Frank Davey, and William A. R. Thomson, eds.
Heralds of Health: The Saga of Christian Medical Initiatives. London, ENK: Christian Medical Fellowship for the Conference for World Mission, 1985. xii, 382 pp. Paper. 0906747171.

Twenty British medical missionaries who served in Africa or Asia present the history, and survey the present, of various aspects of medical missions.

SO573 Chon, Hikon
Health in Mission: The Church's Care for the Missionary and the Missionaries' Care for the Nationals. New York, NYU: Vantage Press, 1997. x, 245 pp. Paper. No ISBN.

A guide to medical mission work based on the author's extensive experience in the field.

SO574 *Cooperation towards Health: Planning and Evaluation of Health Care in the South*
Stockholm, SW: Swedish Mission Council, 1991. 128 pp. Paper. 9185424277.

A team project of the Swedish Mission Council's Working Group for Medical and Health Care, this volume is an introduction to the theology, issues, strategies, and resources for holistic health care ministries.

SO575 Dayton, Edward R., ed.
Medicine and Missions: A Survey of Medical Missions. Wheaton, ILU: Medical Assistance Programs, 1969. ix, 114 pp. Paper. No ISBN.

The results of a 1968 survey of over 1,000 medical missionaries.

SO576 Dodd, Edward M.
The Gift of the Healer: The Story of Men and Medicine in the Overseas Mission of the Church. New York, NYU: Friendship Press, 1964. 224 pp. Paper. No ISBN.

A popular account of the origins, development, and future of medical missions.

SO577 Erk, Wolfgang, ed.
Ärztlicher Dienst weltweit: 25 Beiträge über Heil und Heilung in unserer Zeit. Stuttgart, GW: Steinkopf, 1974. 327 pp. Paper. 3798402973.

Twenty-five articles based on the insight that Western medical practice needs to be reexamined in light of the psychological, sociological, and theological concrete realities in the Third World.

SO578 Ewert, D. Merrill, ed.
A New Agenda for Medical Missionries. Brunswick, GAU: MAP International, 1990. 136 pp. No ISBN.

Fifteen essays by medical practioners on medical missions and community-based health development, designed to show how the latter in theory and practice provides a new agenda for medical missions.

SO579 Fellowship of Christian Doctors
Christian Challenge in Medical Practice. Ibadan, NR: Institute of Church and Society, 1973. unknown pp. No ISBN.

The report of a conference held in 1972, sponsored by the Nigerian Voluntary Agencies Medical Committee, which discussed Christian medical ethics, relating with patients, responsibilities in government service and private practice, and the future of Christian hospitals in Nigeria.

SO580 Grundmann, Christoffer H.
Gesandt zu heilen!: Aufkommen und Entwicklung der arztlichen Mission im neunzehnten Jahrhundert. (Missionswissenschaftliche Forschungen, 26). Gutersloh, GW: Gerd Mohn, 1992. 395 pp. Paper. 3579002465.

A scholarly history since the 19th century of the medical missionary movement and of the medical missionary societies; with an extensive bibliography.

SO581 Hagen, Kristofer
Third World Encounters: Dreams of Development. Maple Grove, MNU: Nystrom Publishing Company, 1984. x, 308 pp. Paper. No ISBN.

A narrative about medical mission work in India, Ethiopia, Vietnam, Taiwan, and Honduras, dealing with Third World missionary service, cultural exchange, education for discipleship, global development, and evangelism.

SO582 Hefley, James C.
The Cross and the Scalpel. Waco, TXU: Word Books, 1971. 158 pp. No ISBN.

Fourteen brief sketches of the work of evangelical medical missionaries from the United States.

SO583 Hellberg, J. Hakan
Community Health and the Church. Geneva, SZ: WCC, 1971. 74 pp. Paper. No ISBN.

An introduction to the medical mission of the church with practical suggestions for church-related community health programs.

SO584 Jackson, Dave, Neta Jackson, and Beth Landis, eds.
The Gift of Presence: Stories That Celebrate Nurses Serving in the Name of Christ. Scottdale, PAU: Herald Press, 1991. 182 pp. Paper. 0836135660.

Fifty vignettes of Mennonite nurses from around the world serving in the name of Christ; published on the 50th anniversary of the Mennonite Nurses Association.

SO585 King, Maurice, ed.
Medical Care in Developing Countries: A Primer on the Medicine of Poverty and a Symposium from Makerere. Nairobi, KE: Oxford University Press, 1966. 1 vol. No ISBN.

A collection of articles on the planning, administration, and practice of medical ministries in less-developed countries, with sensitivity to cross-cultural issues.

SO586 McGilvray, James C.

The Quest for Health and Wholeness. Geneva, SZ: WCC; Tübingen, GW: German Institute for Medical Missions, 1981. xvi, 118 pp. Paper. No ISBN.

An overview of the churches' involvement in health care from medical missions to the work of the Christian Medical Commission resourcing community health care programs.

SO587 McGilvray, James C.

Die verlorene Gesundheit—das verheissene Heil. (Radius-Bücher). Stuttgart, GW: Radius-Verlag, 1982. 149 pp. Paper. 3871736287.

German translation.

SO588 Missionsärztliches Institut (Würzburg)

Heilung und Heil: 50 Jahre Missionsärztliches Institut, Würzburg, 1922-1972. Münsterschwarzach, GW: Vier-Türme-Verlag, 1972. 128 pp. Paper. No ISBN.

A *festschrift* dealing with the history and activities of the Würzburg Institute for Medical Missions.

SO589 Neff, Merlin L.

For God and C.M.E.: A Biography of Percy Tilson Magan upon the Historical Background of the Educational and Medical Work of Seventh-day Adventists. Mountain View, CAU: Pacific Press, 1964. 341 pp. No ISBN.

Story of the College of Medical Evangelists at Loma Linda, near Los Angeles, and of the physician and educationalist who was chiefly responsible for developing this institution as a missionary force and front-rank medical school; also published as *Invincible Irishman.*

SO590 Paterson, Gillian

Whose Ministry?: A Ministry of Health Care for the Year 2000. (Risk Book Series, 59). Geneva, SZ: WCC Publications, 1993. xi, 120 pp. Paper. 2825411183.

Dilemmas of health care delivery in the 1990s seen through a case study of the Christian Medical College in Vellore, India.

SO591 Pirotte, Jean, and Henri Derroitte, eds.

Églises et Santé dans le tier monde: Hier et aujourd'hui/ Churches and Health Care in the Third World Past and Present. (Studies in Christan Mission, 5). Leiden, NE: Brill, 1991. xxi, 176 pp. 9004094709.

Fifteen scholarly essays in French and English by theologians, historians, sociologists, and health care professionals assessing the results of health care by missionaries over three centuries.

SO592 Rowland, Stan

Multiplying Light and Truth through Community Health Evangelism. Nairobi, Kenya: Evangel Publishing House, 1990. vi, 201 pp. 9966850856.

An examination of the underlying philosophies, principles, and materials for establishing a community-based development program that integrates evangelism and health ministry.

SO593 Samuels-Grier, Marian E.

Wholistic Health: An African Christian Heritage. Conyers, GAU: SCP/Third World Literature Publishing House, 1992. 82 pp. Paper. 0913491217.

An African American pastor-educator reflects on sources of holism in African culture and Christianity based on mission

service in Liberia (1984-1987), and work in holistic health ministries in Mississippi.

SO594 Scheel, Martin

Partnerschaftliches Heilen: die Sozialmedizin in ökumenisch-diakonischer Sicht. Stuttgart, GW: Verlagswerk der Diakonie, 1987. 139 pp. Paper. 3923110219.

Second edition of a series of lectures on medical and health care in the context of the community.

SO595 Scheel, Martin, ed.

Ärztlicher Dienst im Umbruch der Zeit. Stuttgart, GW: Evan Missionsverlag, 1967. 269 pp. No ISBN.

The articles of this book promote the idea of Christian medical service in the missions, and point out the importance of adaptation to modern conditions.

SO596 Scott, Kenneth M.

Around the World in Eighty Years. Franklin, TNU: Providence House, 1998. xii, 276 pp. Paper. 157736077X.

A medical doctor recounts forty years of international service in China, Burma, India, and Korea, including as Director of the Christian Medical College and Hospital in Ludhiana, Punjab, India (1963-1974).

SO597 Svensson, Sven, ed.

Läkarmission: ett svar på människors nöd. Stockholm, SW: Svenska Journalens Forlag, 1969. 141 pp. No ISBN.

An anthology on missions and medical aid with contributors from ten mission societies.

SO598 Van Reken, David E.

Mission and Ministry: Christian Medical Practice in Today's Changing World Cultures. Wheaton, ILU: BGC, 1987. 75 pp. Paper. No ISBN.

An introduction, with bibliography, to current issues in medical missions, focusing on primary health care and the direction of international health ministries within the context of Christian missions; by a missionary physician in West Africa.

SO599 Vanderkooi, Mary

Village Medical Manual: A Layman's Guide to Health Care in Developing Countries. South Pasadena, CAU: William Carey Library, 1994. 2 vols. Paper. 0878082514 (vol. 1), 0878082522 (vol. 2).

A medical handbook for missionaries and community workers called upon to serve as village doctors in communities lacking trained health workers—a revision and update to the 1986 and 1992 editions; vol. 1: *Principles and Procedures,* (x, 250 pp.); vol. 2: *Diagnosis and Treatment,* (v, 444 pp.).

SO600 Werner, David

Where There Is No Doctor: A Village Health Care Handbook. Palo Alto, CAU: Hesperian Foundation; London, ENK: TALC Inst. of Child Health, 1977. 403 pp. Paper. 0942364013.

A practical manual for the treatment and prevention of diseases; prepared for use by non-medical personnel serving in areas where professional care is not available.

SO601 Werner, David, and Bill Bower

Helping Health Workers Learn: A Book of Methods, Aids and Ideas for Instructors at the Village Level. Palo Alto, CAU: Hesperian Foundation, 1982. 602 pp. Paper. 0942364090.

A well-illustrated sourcebook for missionaries and community development workers, of practical methods and aids for teaching health and health care in villages.

SO602 White, Paul Hamilton
Alias Jungle Doctor: An Autobiography. Exeter, UNK: Paternoster Press; Surry Hills, AT: Anzea Books; Greenwood, SCU: Attic Press, 1977. 227 pp. 0853642052 (PP), 0858920859 (AB), 0853642052 (AP pbk).

An engaging illustrated autobiography by the Australian medical missionary to East Africa, whose books and recordings in the Jungle Doctor Series have popularized medical missions.

SO603 Wilkinson, John
The Coogate Doctors: The History of the Edinburgh Medical Missionary Society, 1841 to 1991. Edinburgh, STK: Edinburgh Medical Missionary Society, 1991. ix, 86 pp. 0951867709 (hdbk), 0951867717 (pbk).

A brief illustrated history of the Edinburgh Medical Missionary Society, which has trained more than 400 medical missionaries and supported their work in the Middle East, in Nazareth and Damascus.

SO604 Willemsen, Jan A.
Van tentoonstelling tot wereldorganisatie: De geschiedenis van de stichtingen Memisa en Medicus Mundi Nederland 1925-1995. (KDSC Scripta). Nijmegen, NE: Valkhof Pers, 1996. 301 pp. Paper. 9056250132.

History of two Dutch Catholic organizations for medical mission, Memisa and Medicus Mundi Nederland, during the period 1925 to 1995—work which originated from activities of Catholic students in the years 1918 to 1921.

Medicine and Religion

See also SO283, SO316, SO333, SO339, SO646, ED155, AF175, AF221, AF691, AF755, AF880, AF1261, and AM588.

SO605 Aitken, J. T., H. W. C. Fuller, and D. Johnson, eds.
The Influence of Christians in Medicine. London, ENK: Christian Medical Fellowship, 1984. ix, 186 pp. Paper. 0906747112.

A survey of the impact of leading Christians on the development of Western medicine, from the 4th century to the present; including the spread of medical missions into Third World countries.

SO606 Allen, E. Anthony et al.
Health, Healing and Transformation: Biblical Reflections on the Church in Ministries of Healing and Wholeness. Monrovia, CAU: MARC; World Vision International, 1991. 109 pp. Paper. 0912552743 (M).

Four papers originally presented at the International Health Consultation sponsored by World Vision (Geneva, Switzerland, 2-9 Nov. 1989).

SO607 Appiah-Kubi, Kofi
Man Cures, God Heals: Religion and Medical Practice among the Akans of Ghana. Totowa, NJU: Allanheld, Osmun, 1981. xiv, 173 pp. 086598011X.

A richly documented survey of the religion and medical practices among the Akans of Ghana, including the faith healing and other practices of the African Christian Church, and the role of spirit possession in both Christian and non-Christian forms of healing.

SO608 Bate, Stuart C.
Inculturation and Healing: Coping-Healing in South African Christianity. Pietermaritzburg, SA: Cluster Publications, 1995. 317 pp. Paper. 1875053018.

An examination of sickness and healing from medical, psychological, cultural, socio-economic, philosophical, and theological perspectives, with special reference to "healing churches" in South Africa.

SO609 Berinyuu, Abraham Adu
Pastoral Care to the Sick in Africa: An Approach to Transcultural Pastoral Theology. (Studies in the Intercultural History of Christianity, 51). Frankfurt am Main, GW: Lang, 1988. xi, 136 pp. Paper. 3820416609.

A contribution to informed dialogue between African churches and societies on the one hand, and Western medicine and theology on the other, concerning understandings of sickness, medicine, healing, and spirituality in Africa.

SO610 Cahill, Kevin M., ed.
The Untapped Resource: Medicine and Diplomacy. Maryknoll, NYU: Orbis Books, 1971. 115 pp. No ISBN.

Nine short essays on the advantages and dangers of viewing medical assistance to developing countries as an arm of US diplomacy.

SO611 Carter, Nancy A.
Created and Loved by God: An HIV/AIDS Ministry Covenant to Care Handbook. New York, NYU: UMC, Board of Global Ministries, 1995. v, 89 pp. Paper. No ISBN.

Helps for persons engaged in HIV/AIDS ministries, including medical, biblical/theological, church, and program resources.

SO612 Center of Concern
Dimensions of the Healing Ministry. Edited by James E. Hug. St. Louis, MOU: Catholic Health Association of United States, 1989. xii, 222 pp. Paper. 0871251701.

Twenty essays giving retrospective analyses of various aspects of ecumenism written to commemorate the First World Conference of Christian Youth (Amsterdam, 1939).

SO613 Davidson, Lawrence
The Alexian Brothers of Chicago: An Evolutionary Look at the Monastery and Modern Health Care. New York, NYU: Vantage Press, 1990. vii, 214 pp. 0533086892.

The history of the Catholic Congregation of Alexian Brothers from their beginnings in charitable care for the sick in Aachen, Germany, in the Middle Ages, to their medical ministries through a modern hospital in Chicago in the 20th century.

SO614 *Facing AIDS: The Challenge, the Churches' Response*
Geneva, SZ: WCC Publications, 1997. ix, 116 pp. Paper. 2825412139.

Findings from a three-year broadly based study on AIDS sponsored by the WCC including scientific findings, theological and ethical issues, pastoral care, and the church as a healing community.

SO615 Fountain, Daniel E.
God, Medicine & Miracles: The Spiritual Factor in Healing. Wheaton, ILU: Shaw Publishers, 1999. 265 pp. Paper. 0877883211.

The author explores the underlying connection between faith, wholeness, and healing through research on the nature of healing, illness, medical caregiving, and scriptural faith.

SO616 Fountain, Daniel E.
Health, the Bible and the Church. (A BGC Monograph). Wheaton, ILU: BGC, 1989. xii, 226 pp. Paper. No ISBN.

A developed theology of human wellness that summons the church to recover its rightful role as partners with physicians, based on thirty years in medical missions in Central Africa.

SO617 Gammons, Peter

Christ's Healing Power Today. Tunbridge Wells, ENK: Monarch Publications, 1992. 240 pp. Paper. 1854241516.

A primer on healing ministries by the Director of Reach Out Ministries, with reports of evangelistic crusades which he led in various countries and continents.

SO618 Hetsen, Jac, and Raphael Wanjohi

Anointing and Healing in Africa. (Spearhead Series, 71). Eldoret, KE: Gaba Publications, 1982. i, 48 pp. Paper. No ISBN.

A biblical approach to healing and the Roman Catholic sacrament of the sick for Africa, with a supplement on medical and spiritual care among the Agikuyu of Kenya.

SO619 Kauffman, Christopher J.

Ministry and Meaning: A Religious History of Catholic Health Care in the United States. New York, NYU: Crossroad Publishing, 1995. xiv, 354 pp. 0824514599.

The first comprehensive history of Catholic health care in the United States that explores the religious self-understanding of caregivers, especially nuns.

SO620 Lyons, Cathie

Journey toward Wholeness: Justice, Peace, and Health in an Interdependent World. New York, NYU: Friendship Press, 1987. xii, 95 pp. Paper. 0377001716.

A study book on the international goal of "Health for All," with chapters on the biblical basis for Christian concern, the AIDS crisis, and the church as a healing community.

SO621 Numbers, Ronald L., and Darrel W. Amundsen, eds.

Caring and Curing: Health and Medicine in the Western Religious Traditions. Baltimore: MDU: Johns Hopkins University Press, 1998. xx, 601 pp. Paper. 0801857961.

Twenty original articles by notable scholars in the fields of history of religion and of history of medicine, demonstrating how religious values of various Christian traditions and sects affect medical practices; a reissue in paper of a classic originally published by Macmillan in 1986.

SO622 Paterson, Gillian

Love in a Time of AIDS: Women, Health, and the Challenge of HIV. (Risk Book Series, 72). Geneva, SZ: WCC Publications, 1996. xv, 114 pp. Paper. 2825411914.

Vivid accounts of women affected by the HIV/AIDS epidemic and the churches' ministries among them; from a WCC-sponsored conference (Vellore, South India, 1-7 September 1995).

SO623 Ram, Eric R., ed.

Transforming Health: Christian Approaches to Healing and Wholeness. Monrovia, CAU: MARC, 1995. v, 344 pp. Paper. 0912552891.

Leading Christian health care professionals from around the world share their insights on the practices of health and healing.

SO624 Rosny, Eric de

Healers in the Night. Translated by Robert R. Barr. Maryknoll, NYU: Orbis Books, 1985. x, 288 pp. Paper. 0883441993.
English translation.

SO625 Rosny, Eric de

L'Afrique des guérisons. Paris, FR: Éditions Karthala, 1992. 223 pp. Paper. 2865373274.

A collection of essays by the renowned French Jesuit based on his study of traditional and faith healing practices in the Cameroun and contact with AICs.

SO626 Rosny, Eric de

La nuit, les yeux ouverts: récit. Paris, FR: Éditions du Seuil, 1996. 283 pp. 2020285401.

A Catholic missionary/anthropologist in the Cameroon explains the importance of the traditional diviner/healer (*nganga*) in African society in a sequel to *Healers in the Night* (Orbis Books, 1985).

SO627 Rosny, Eric de

Les yeux de ma chèvre: sur les pas des maîtres de la nuit en pays douala (Cameroun). Paris, FR: Plon, 1996. 474 pp. 2259185223.

A priest's account of experiences and encounters with African traditional medical practitioners in Cameroon, Central Africa; originally published in 1981.

SO628 Snyder, Graydon F.

Health and Medicine in the Anabaptist Tradition: Care in Community. (Health/Medicine and the Faith Traditions). Valley Forge, PAU: Trinity Press International, 1995. xvi, 160 pp. 1563381206.

A primer on how the deep sense of community in their tradition leads Anabaptists (Brethren, Mennonites, etc.) to a holistic approach to health programs.

SO629 Stephens, A. John, ed.

African Attitudes to Health and Healing. (mimeo). Ibadan, NR: Christian Council of Nigeria, Institute of Church and Society, 1964. 71 pp. No ISBN.

Papers collected by a study group of the Christian Council of Nigeria.

SO630 Thampu, Valson

AIDS: Heresy and Prophecy; What the Virus Says. New Delhi, II: TRACI, 1993. 191 pp. Paper. No ISBN.

A call for a multi-disciplinary response to the HIV/AIDS pandemic with biblical/theological and strategic guidelines for response by Christians; based on the author's experience in India.

SO631 Thampu, Valson

Cross-Cultural Issues in AIDS: An Afro-Asian Advocacy. New Delhi, II: TRACI, 1995. x, 256 pp. Paper. No ISBN.

A primer on AIDS including medical, social, ethical, and cultural aspects, with helps for church responses by the chairman of the Theological Research and Communication Institute (TRACI) in New Delhi.

SO632 Vincent, V.

Healing beyond Medicines. Delhi, II: ISPCK, 1999. viii, 58 pp. Paper. 8172144792.

A medical doctor who has practiced in India, Kuwait, and Saudi Arabia applies spiritual principles to everyday life with simple psychological treatment modalities.

SO633 WCC/Christian Medical Commission

Healing and Wholeness: The Churches' Role in Health. Geneva, SZ: WCC, 1990. iv, 49 pp. Paper. No ISBN.

The summary of a global study on health and healing from the Christian perspective, including the roles of the churches and medical missions.

SO634 Wilson, Michael
The Church Is Healing. London, ENK: SCM Press, 1967. 128 pp. No ISBN.

Both pastor and physician, the author draws on experience of medical work in West Africa.

Spiritual Healing; Exorcism

See also CR771, SO114, SO295, SO607, SO632, EV285, SP322, AF747, AF1273, AM588, AM871, AM1310, and AS1497.

SO635 Chauvet, Louis-Marie, and Miklós Tomka, eds.
Illness and Healing. (*Concilium*, 1998/5). London, ENK: SCM Press; Maryknoll, NYU: Orbis Books, 1998. ix, 126 pp. Paper. 033403051X UK, 1570751919 US.

Thirteen scholarly essays on the various dimensions of religion and health today; with case studies on church practices in healing in India, Tanzania, and South Africa.

SO636 De Villiers, Pieter, ed.
Healing in the Name of God. Pretoria, SA: UNISA, C. B. Powell Bible Institute, 1986. 227 pp. 06620093145.

Articles by South African Protestants on healing in the Bible and spiritual healing today.

SO637 Grant, Robert
The Way of the Wound: A Spirituality of Trauma and Transformation. Burlingame, CAU: By the author, Robert Grant, 1998. x, 243 pp. Paper. No ISBN.

Helps in understanding the dynamics of trauma and how to cure the psychological and spiritual needs of trauma victims (the sexually abused, refugees, etc.), available from the author (P.O. Box 504, Burlingame, CA, 94010).

SO638 Lowe, Chuck
Territorial Spirits and World Evangelisation. Sevenoaks, ENK: Mentor/OMF, 1998. 189 pp. Paper. 1857923995.

A biblical, historical, and missiological critique of strategic level spiritual warfare.

SO639 Nevius, John Livingstone
Demon Possession. Grand Rapids, MIU: Kregel Publications, 1968. viii, 368 pp. 0825433029.

Reprint of Nevius' classical book orginally titled *Demon Possession and Allied Themes* (1894), which had a wide impact on mission thinking regarding demons in the 20th century.

SO640 Nyirongo, Lenard
Dealing With Darkness: A Christian Novel on the Confrontation with African Witchcraft. (Scientific Contribution of the Potchefstroom University for Christian Higher Education, Series F2). Potchefstroom, SA: Potchefstroom University, 1999. 125 pp. 1868223469.

Written for theologians, pastors, and lay people who find themselves confronted with issues of witchcraft; the author was born in a village of Zambia and is acquainted with the issues surrounding witchcraft.

SO641 Packer, J. I. et al.
The Kingdom and the Power: Are Healing and the Spiritual Gifts Used by Jesus and the Early Church Meant for the Church Today? Edited by Gary S. Greig and Kevin Springer. Ventura, CAU: Regal Books, 1993. 463 pp. 0830716343.

A sourcebook on healings, signs, and wonders in Scripture, and contemporary ministries of healing and exorcism.

SO642 Presler, Henry Hughes
A Search for Credible Religious Healing among Muslims, Hindus, Christians. Delhi, II: ISPCK, 1993. viii, 156 pp. Paper. 8172140738.

A missionary social scientist reports on field research among urban populations of various religions in mid-India concerning religious healing.

SO643 Reddin, Opal L., ed.
Power Encounter: A Pentecostal Perspective. Springfield, MOU: Central Bible College Press, 1989. viii, 291 pp. Paper. No ISBN.

Twelve essays by ten Pentecostal scholars on power encounters in biblical perspective, contemporary mission, and ministry.

SO644 Rommen, Edward, ed.
Spiritual Power and Missions: Raising the Issues. (Evangelical Missiological Society Series, 3). South Pasadena, CAU: William Carey Library, 1995. 163 pp. Paper. 0878083774.

Three influential essays for evangelicals on spiritual warfare and spiritual power in missions, authored by Robert J. Priest, Thomas Campbell, Bradford Mullen, Charles Kraft, and Patrick Johnstone; published as a preparatory study for the Evangelical Missionary Society's 1996 meeting on "The Holy Spirit and Missions."

SO645 Shay, Kenneth D., ed.
Conflict and Conquest: Power Encounter Topics for Taiwan. Taiwan, CH: O.C. International, 1990. 132 pp. No ISBN.

A reprint of nine articles on spirits, healing, demonization, and discernment by Protestant missiologists on power and power encounters in traditional religions.

SO646 Shorter, Aylward
Jesus and the Witchdoctor: An Approach to Healing and Wholeness. Maryknoll, NYU: Orbis Books; London, ENK: Chapman, 1985. x, 258 pp. Paper. 0883442256 (O), 0225664313 (C).

The author, an anthropologist, theologian, and missionary, draws on long experience in Africa and on biblical truth and sacraments to find a Christian guide to total healing including the physical, psychological, emotional, and spiritual dimensions of life.

SO647 Springer, Kevin, ed.
Power Encounters among Christians in the Western World. San Francisco, CAU: Harper & Row, 1988. xxxiv, 218 pp. Paper. 0060695374.

Testimonies by sixteen prominent Christian leaders, including C. Peter Wagner and Charles Kraft, compiled by the editor, about the impact of signs and wonders in their ministry and mission.

SO648 Ugwu, Chinonyelu Moses
Healing in the Nigerian Church: A Pastoral-Psychological Exploration. (Studies in the Intercultural History of Christianity, 109). Bern, SZ: Lang, 1998. 265 pp. Paper. 3906760111 (SZ), 082043437X (US).

A dissertation on healing among the Igbo people of Nigeria including traditional attitudes and practices, changes brought by the Catholic Church, and psychological dimensions of healing and exorcism today.

SO649 Wagner, C. Peter, and Fredrick Douglas Pennoyer, eds.
Wrestling with Dark Angels: Toward a Deeper Understanding of the Supernatural Forces in Spiritual Warfare. Ventura, CAU: Regal Books, 1990. 365 pp. Paper. 0830713859.

Thirteen papers and responses presented at the Academic Symposium of Fuller Seminary School of World Mission.

SO650 Wagner, C. Peter
Confronting the Powers: How the New Testament Church Experienced the Power of Strategic-Level Spiritual Warfare. (The Prayer Warrior Series). Ventura, CAU: Regal Books/ Gospel Light, 1996. 272 pp. 0830718192.

A primer on spiritual warfare in New Testament and contemporary experience, and the need of prayer for revival.

SO651 Wagner, C. Peter
Warfare Prayer: How to Seek God's Power and Protection in the Battle to Build His Kingdom. Ventura, CAU: Regal Books, 1992. 197 pp. 0830715347.

A guide to effective prayer for Christians engaged in the struggle against principalities and powers.

SO652 Wolford, Marvin S.
Free Indeed from Sorcery Bondage: A Proven Scriptural Ministry. San Rafael, CAU: Pathway Press, 1999. 258 pp. Paper. 0967091500.

Growing out of a ministry of Bible translation that spanned forty years in Africa, this study seeks a biblical response to sorcery and witchcraft.

MISSIONS AND ECONOMIC LIFE

Jonathan Bonk, Subeditor

After World War II, the scope of missionary economics was widened to include the churches' response to global economics, and their participation in its development. That will be the focus of this chapter (Jongeneel 1995, I:323-333).

Works are included that address the churches' involvement in economic life. Secular analyses of economic issues are excluded. Some books on economic ethics are included if they address the churches' response. Works on mission and economic life in specific continents and countries have their primary listing under the geographic area, with cross-references to topics in this chapter.

Following reference works, the chapter contains, under "Conferences and Congresses" and "General Works," the major studies on the churches and economic life. These are followed by short sections on "Economic Theory," including capitalism, socialism/Marxism, and communism.

Most books on Christian response to economic conditions are to be found under countries. In this chapter, however, you will find a large section on poverty and hunger, another on "Consumption/Lifestyle

Issues," and a third on "Ecology."

Works on the actual involvement of the churches in development issues are to be found in the next subsections. General works on church reflections on these issues are to be found under "Economic Policies: General" and "Development Issues" (Jongeneel 1997, II:309-317).

Missions pioneered in rural and agricultural development. Books on these efforts, as well as later action by churches, are to be found in the sections on "Rural Development" and "Agricultural Development/ Missions."

In response to the explosive growth of cities, churches became increasingly involved in urban mission. Works on these efforts are found not only in this chapter, but also in a section on "Urban Mission" in the chapter on "Missions: Social Aspects." See also "City Missions" under the USA in "The Americas." (Jongeneel 1997, II:328-335).

The chapter concludes with subsections on "Industrial Development/Missions," "Labor," "Technology," "Commerce/International Trade," and "Finance."

Norman E. Thomas

Bibliographies

EC1 Bauer, Gerhard
Towards a Theology of Development: An Annotated Bibliography. Geneva, SZ: SODEPAX; Geneva, SZ: Ecumenical Centre, Publications Department, 1970. viii, 201 pp. Paper. No ISBN.

An annotated bibliography prepared as a companion volume to *In Search of a Theology of Development* (1970).

EC2 Elliot, Mark R., ed.
Christianity and Marxism Worldwide: An Annotated Bibliography. Wheaton, ILU: Int. Society Christian Missions, 1988. 136 pp. Paper. No ISBN.

A selected annotated bibliography of works in English on Marxism in theory and practice in Eastern Europe, the Soviet Union, and Third World countries, with introductions for the layreader to each section.

Serials and Periodicals

See also EA8, EA10, and PO4.

EC3 *Jahrbuch Dritte Welt*
Munich, GW: Verlag C. H. Beck, 1983-. Paper. Annual.

This annual publication, edited by the staff of the Deutschen Ubersee-Institut, provides informative overviews and thematic contributions on the most important happenings, tendencies, and problems in the developing areas of the world.

Reference Works

See also MI3.

EC4 Benjamin, Bennet, comp.
Church in Development: A Directory of Development Activities of the Churches and Christian Organisations Related to the National Council of Churches in India (1989). Nagpur, II: NCCI, National Development Advisory Council, 1990. 130 pp. Paper. No ISBN.

The first edition of an intended annual directory of community development activities by the churches in India.

EC5 Boynes, Wynta, Florence M. Lowenstein, and Roger B. McClanahan, eds.
U.S. Non-Profit Organizations in Development Assistance Abroad: TAICH Directory 1983. New York, NYU: Technical Assistance Information Clearing House, 1983. xiv, 584 pp. 0932140025.

Revised eighth edition of a directory listing 456 organizations, of which 171 are voluntary; first published in 1956.

EC6 Fenton, Thomas P., and Mary J. Heffron, eds.
Food, Hunger, Agribusiness: A Directory of Resources. Maryknoll, NYU: Orbis Books, 1987. xvii, 131 pp. Paper. 088344531X.

An annotated guide to publications, organizations, audio-visuals, and other materials on economic development issues in the Third World.

EC7 Fenton, Thomas P., and Mary J. Heffron, eds.
Transnational Corporations and Labor: A Directory of Resources. Maryknoll, NYU: Orbis Books, 1989. xvi, 166 pp. Paper. 0883446359.

An exhaustive compilation of print, organization, and audio-visual resources devoted to investigating and reporting the impact of transnational corporations on Third World development, economics, and people.

Documentation and Archives

See also TH611.

EC8 Niles, D. Preman, comp.
Between the Flood and the Rainbow: Interpreting the Conciliar Process of Mutual Commitment (Covenant) to Justice, Peace and the Integrity of Creation. Geneva, SZ: WCC Publications, 1992. x, 192 pp. Paper. 2825410853.

A compilation of documents from the WCC's program in Justice, Peace, and the Integrity of Creation (JPIC) from its inception in 1983 to its closure in 1991.

EC9 Sider, Ronald J., ed.
Cry Justice: The Bible Speaks on Hunger and Poverty: A Bread for the World Reader. Downers Grove, ILU: InterVarsity; New York, NYU: Paulist Press, 1980. 220 pp. Paper. 0809123088 (P), 087784495X (I).

A classified compendium of biblical texts on justice-related topics, including peace, the poor, economic relationships among God's people, property and possessions, and justice.

Conferences and Congresses

See also GW88, ME19, SO23, SO31, EC186, EC235-EC237, EC273, EC303, EC307, EC311, EC339, EC357, EC364-EC365, EC370, AF241, and AM255.

EC10 Committee on Society, Development and Peace, Montreal, Canada, 9-12 May 1969
The Challenge of Development: A Sequel to the Beirut Conference of April 21-27, Montreal, Canada, 9-12 May, 1969. Geneva, SZ: SODEPAX, 1969. 37 pp. Paper. No ISBN.

The official report to the committee with a summary of recommendations.

EC11 Dams, Theodor, ed.
Entwicklungshilfe, Hilfe zur Unterentwicklung?: Eine Ausienandersetzung mit d. Thesen d. radikalen Kritik. (Reihe Entwicklung und Frieden, 5). Munich, GW: Kaiser; Mainz, GW: Matthias-Grünewald, 1974. 215 pp. 3459008776 (K), 378670418X (G).

Papers on Christian involvement in development and peace issues presented at a conference organized by the Katholischer Arbeitskreis Entwicklung und Friede (Walderberg, 1973).

EC12 Ferré, Frederick, and Rita H. Mataragnon, eds.
God and Global Justice: Religion and Poverty in an Unequal World. New York, NYU: Paragon House, 1985. ix, 214 pp. 0913757365 (hdbk), 0913757373 (pbk).

Twelve essays by philosophers, theologians, and social scientists presented at a conference on "God: The Contemporary Discussion" (Puerto Rico, 30 Dec. 1983 to 4 Jan. 1984), sponsored by the Unification Church.

EC13 Munby, Denys Lawrence, ed.
World Development: Challenge to the Churches. Washington, DCU: Corpus Books, 1969. xvi, 208 pp. Paper. No ISBN.

The official report and the papers of the SODEPAX conference held at Beirut, Lebanon, 21-27 April 1968, under the auspices of the Vatican Commission on Peace and Freedom and the WCC; with supporting documents and a list of participants.

EC14 Oracion, Levi ,
Ideologies and People's Struggles for Justice, Freedom, and Peace. (Occasional Study Pamphlet, 2). Geneva, SZ: WCC, 1990. 110 pp. Paper. No ISBN.

Report and papers from an important international consultation sponsored by the WCC's Commission on the Churches' Participation in Development.

EC15 Sine, Tom, ed.
The Church in Response to Human Need. Monrovia, CAU: MARC, 1983. vii, 487 pp. Paper. 0912552395.

Fifteen papers by well-known evangelical scholars and missiologists presented at the consultation on "The Church in Response to Human Need" of the I Will Build My Church—Wheaton '83 conference.

EC16 World Conference on Faith, Science and the Future (Cambridge, Mass., 12-24 July 1979)

Faith and Science in an Unjust World: Report of the World Council of Churches' Conference on Faith, Science and the Future. Edited by Roger Lincoln Shinn and Paul Abrecht. Geneva, SZ: WCC, 1980. 2 vols.

The papers and reports from a major international conference of scientists and church leaders, relating issues of science and technology to the WCC's concern for a just, participatory, and sustainable society [vol. 1: *Plenary Presentations*, xiv, 392 pp., 0800613902 (hdbk), 2825406295 (pbk); vol. 2: *Reports and Recommendations*, 214 pp., 0800613910 (hdbk), 282540635X (pbk)].

General Works

See also TH140, TH316-TH317, EA84, ME178, SO32, PO8, PO82, AM231-AM233, AM272, AM976, AM1054, and AS1450.

EC17 Abrecht, Paul

The Churches and Rapid Social Change. Garden City, NYU: Doubleday; London, ENK: SCM Press, 1961. 216 pp. No ISBN.

The summation of a six-year study sponsored by the WCC on "The Common Christian Responsibility towards Areas of Rapid Social Change" focusing on specific issues of politics, economics, industry, rural life, and morality, showing how these issues affect the churches in Asia, Africa, and Latin America.

EC18 Abrecht, Paul

Las Iglesias y los Ràpidos Cambios Sociales. Mexico City, MX: CUPSA; Buenos Aires, AG: Editorial La Aurora, 1963. 254 pp. Paper. No ISBN.

Spanish translation.

EC19 Bruwer, Eddie

Beggars Can Be Choosers: In Search of a Better Way out of Poverty and Dependence. (Institute for Missiological and Ecumenical Research). Pretoria, SA: University of Pretoria, 1996. 130 pp. Paper. 0869799851.

Revised edition of text on theology, principles, and strategies for breaking the cycle of poverty in rural South Africa; first published in 1994.

EC20 Collier, Jane, and Rafael Esteban

From Complicity to Encounter: The Church and the Culture of Economism. (Christian Mission and Modern Culture Series). Harrisburg, PAU: Trinity Press International, 1998. x, 118 pp. Paper. 1563382601.

A critique of the oppressive "culture of economism" of the West which has reared its ugly head in the church's history of conquest and oppression, but which presents a new opportunity for mission in the midst of paradigm shifts in the church and in economism.

EC21 Cosmao, Vincent

Changer le monde: Une tâche pour l'Église. Paris, FR: Éditions du Cerf, 1979. 189 pp. Paper. 2204013390.

A powerfully reasoned, and clearly argued presentation of the why and how of the church's involvement in the social and economic transformation of the world.

EC22 Cosmao, Vincent

Changing the World: An Agenda for the Churches. Translated by John Drury. Maryknoll, NYU: Orbis Books, 1984. xvii, 109 pp. Paper. 0883441071.

English translation.

EC23 Cosmao, Vincent

Transformar el Mundo: Una tarea para la Iglesia. (Colección Punto Limite, 13). Santander, SP: Editorial Sal Terrae, 1981. 196 pp. Paper. 842930598X.

Spanish translation.

EC24 Danker, William J.

Profit for the Lord: Economic Activities in Moravian Missions and the Basel Mission Trading Company. (Christian World Mission Books). Grand Rapids, MIU: Eerdmans, 1971. 183 pp. Paper. No ISBN.

A pioneer study of the economic dimensions of mission by Moravians in four continents (Europe, Africa, and North and South America), and by the Basel Mission Trading Company in India and Africa.

EC25 Duchrow, Ulrich

Global Economy: A Confessional Issue for the Churches? Translated by David Lewis. Geneva, SZ: WCC Publications, 1987. xiv, 231 pp. Paper. 282540876X.

English translation.

EC26 Duchrow, Ulrich

Weltwirtschaft heute: Ein Feld für Bekennende Kirche? Munich, GW: Kaiser, 1986. 312 pp. Paper. 3459016493.

A discussion of the problems, possibilities, and responsibilities faced by the church as it endeavors to decrease the destructiveness of the world economic order.

EC27 Edgington, David W.

Christians and the Third World. Exeter, ENK: Paternoster Press, 1982. 142 pp. Paper. 0853642869.

An examination of the practical implications of global poverty and underdevelopment for the church in general, and for Western missions in particular, with special reference to Great Britain.

EC28 Fortman, Bas de Gaay, and Berma Klein Goldewijk

God and the Goods: Global Economy in a Civilizational Perspective. Geneva, SZ: WCC Publications, 1998. 100 pp. Paper. 2825412643.

A reflection on the threefold crisis in the world today, on deepening poverty, environmental destruction, and social disintegration, and the past and present approaches of the churches to economic matters.

EC29 Haan, Roelf

The Economics of Honour: Biblical Reflections on Money and Property. Geneva, SZ: WCC, 1988. x, 71 pp. Paper. 2825409340.

A presentation of biblical passages alongside statements of economic problems, designed to give a spiritual critique of common economic assumptions; by the Director of General Affairs of the Dutch Interchurch Broadcasting Foundation (IKON).

EC30 Jeurissen, Ronald

Gods kinderen en de machten: Het Vaticann en de Wereldraad van Kerken over internationale economische verhoudigen, ontwikkeling bevrijding 1965-1985. (IIMO Research Pamphlet, 17). Utrecht, NE: IIMO, 1986. viii, 294 pp. Paper. 907138716X.

A comparative study of economic ethics of the Vatican and the WCC concerning issues of development, trade, and liberation.

EC—MISSIONS AND ECONOMIC LIFE

EC31 Krügel, Siegfried
Dienst im Zwielicht: Die Funktion kirchlicher Hilfsaktionen für die "Dritte Welt." (Fakten, Argumente). Berlin, GE: Union Verlag, 1976. 165 pp. Paper. No ISBN.

From a sociological perspective, the author examines the history and ideology of church development aid, Catholic and ecumenical, and advocates on an ecumenical "non-capitalist" form of development.

EC32 McCrae, Ian
Global Economics: Seeking a Christian Ethic. New York, NYU: Friendship Press, 1993. 120 pp. Paper. 0377002534.

A workbook for beginners, this text offers stories and exercises about our interdependent world, with biblical and ethical reflections, some teaching about basic ecomomic principles, and suggestions on how we can help create a new economic order; with study guide by Pamela Sparr (no ISBN).

EC33 Miller, Darrow L.
Discipling Nations: The Power of Truth to Transform Cultures. Seattle, WAU: YWAM Publishing, 1998. 308 pp. Paper. 1576580156.

Cogent arguments by a leader of Food for the Hungry that secular analyses and strategies of poverty and relief need to be challenged on the basis of Christian faith; written as a study book for concerned Christians.

EC34 National Conference of Catholic Bishops
Tenth Anniversary Edition of Economic Justice for All: Pastoral Letter on Catholic Social Teaching and the U.S. Economy. Washington, DCU: USCC; Washington, DCU: NCCB, 1997. vii, 152 pp. Paper. 1574551353.

A pastoral reflection applying the message of *Economic Justice for All*, the 1986 Pastoral Letter by the National Conference of Catholic Bishops [US], to the economy of the 1990s.

EC35 Nurnberger, Klaus, ed.
Affluence, Poverty and the Word of God: Interdisciplinary Study-Program of the Missiological Institute, Mapumulo. Durban, SA: Lutheran Publishing House, 1978. 270 pp. Paper. No ISBN.

From a Missiological Institute (Mapumulo, Natal) study program, twenty-one essays deal with a wide range of economic issues, at both personal and structural levels, suggesting a variety of biblically informed responses for Christians.

EC36 Reiss, Elizabeth Clark
The American Council of Voluntary Agencies for Foreign Service, ACVAFS: Four Monographs. New York, NYU: Carnegie Council on Ethics and International Affairs, 1985. 512 pp. No ISBN.

A history of the American Council of Voluntary Agencies for Foreign Services (ACVAFS), an organization that for nearly half a century has functioned as a coordinating and consultative body for American private voluntary organizations engaged in overseas relief, rehabilitation, and development work.

EC37 Rieger, Joerg, ed.
Liberating the Future: God, Mammon and Theology. Minneapolis, MNU: Fortress Press, 1998. viii, 168 pp. Paper. 0800631439.

Nine essays from prominent theologians such as Moltmann, Gutiérrez, and Cobb, exploring God and mammon, the global economy, poverty, liberation theology, postmodernism, and the church as alternative economy.

EC38 Slack, Kenneth, ed.
Hope in the Desert: The Churches' United Response to Human Need, 1944-1984. Geneva, SZ: WCC, 1986. xiii, 143 pp. Paper. 2825408646.

Historical and interpretative assessments of the WCC Commission on Inter-Church Aid, Refugee and World Service by people who, for the most part, were personally involved in that work.

EC39 Solberg, Richard W.
Also sind wir viele ein Leib: Vom weltweiten Dienst des Luthertums. Translated by Renate Zimmerman and Herbert Reich. Berlin, GW: Lutherisches Verlagshaus, 1960. 158 pp. Paper. No ISBN.

German translation of *As Between Brothers: The Story of Lutheran Response to World Need* (Augsburg, 1957).

EC40 *Theologie und Ökonomie: Der Nord-Süd-Konflikt als Herausforderung für Kirche und Mission*
(Weltmission heute, 12). Hamburg, GW: EMW, 1992. 86 pp. Paper. No ISBN.

Five essays from a September 1991 conference at the Ecumenical Institute, Bossey/Geneva, on the interrelationships of theology and economics with the interdependence of global and local realities.

Economic Theories

See also TH258, TH554, EC90, AM399, and AM1342.

EC41 Berger, Peter L.
Pyramids of Sacrifice: Political Ethics and Social Change. New York, NYU: Basic Books, 1974. xiv, 242 pp. 0465067786.

A comparison of capitalist and socialist approaches to development, with a call for a third alternative based on more Christian principles.

EC42 Carneiro de Andrade, Paulo Fernando
Capitalismo e socialismo: Diálogo entre a doutrina social da Igreja e a teologia da libertação. (Coleção Teologia e evangelização, 9). São Paulo, BL: Edições Loyola, 1993. 94 pp. 8515007517.

An examination of the positions of both Latin American liberation theology, and the Catholic Church's social teaching on capitalism and socialism.

EC43 Elwood, Douglas J.
Faith Encounters Ideology: Christian Discernment and Social Change. Quezon City, PH: New Day Publishers, 1985. xvi, 320 pp. Paper. 9711002019.

An exhaustive discussion on faith and ideology, looking into systems that are prevailing—status quo, capitalism, democratic socialism, Christian Marxists, liberation theology, and nonviolent change—in an attempt to understand other options.

EC44 Leatt, James, Theo Kneifel, and Klaus Nürnberger, eds.
Contending Ideologies in South Africa. Johannesburg, SA: David Philip; Grand Rapids, MIU: Eerdmans, 1986. x, 318 pp. Paper. 0864860382, 080280182X.

The report of a commission to study conflicting ideologies in South Africa (capitalism, socialism, nationalism, and Marxism) and the possible theological responses; sponsored by the National Conference of the SACC.

EC—MISSIONS AND ECONOMIC LIFE

EC45 McCarthy, George E., and Royal W. Rhodes
Eclipse of Justice: Ethics, Economics, and the Lost Traditions of American Catholicism. Maryknoll, NYU: Orbis Books, 1992. vi, 298 pp. 0883448068.

A scholarly critique by a sociologist and a church historian of "Economic Justice for All," the US bishops' Pastoral Letter on Catholicism and the US Economy (1986), with an analysis of earlier Catholic social critique and the current contributions of liberation theology.

EC46 Mott, W. King
The Third Way: Economic Justice According to John Paul II. Lanham, MDU: University Press of America, 1999. v, 169 pp. 0761812652.

Approaching the question of economic justice from the perspective of scholar and priest, the Pope articulates a view of economic justice to a world he considers marked by needless human suffering.

EC47 Novak, Michael, ed.
Liberation Theology and the Liberal Society. Washington, DCU: American Enterprise Institute, 1987. xiv, 238 pp. Paper. 0844722642.

Eight scholarly essays contrasting the ideals of Latin American liberation theology with those of the "liberal society" of North America, with commentary and discussion from oral presentations at the 1985 Summer Institute sponsored by the Center for Religion, Philosophy, and Public Policy of the American Enterprise Institute.

EC48 Nyirongo, Lenard
Should a Christian Embrace Socialism, Communism or Humanism? (Series F2: Brochures of the Institute for Reformational Studies, 57). Potchefstroom, SA: Potchefstroom University, 1994. v, 123 pp. Paper. 1868221709.

A Zambian evangelical Christian examines the historical roots of major ideologies (capitalism, socialism, communism, humanism) as "our modern idols," offering a biblical critique of each.

EC49 Strain, Charles R., ed.
Prophetic Visions and Economic Realities: Protestants, Jews, and Catholics Confront the Bishops' Letter on the Economy. Grand Rapids, MIU: Eerdmans, 1989. xiii, 257 pp. Paper. 0802800653.

Contributors from a variety of academic disciplines and representing four major North American religious traditions react to *Economic Justice for All: Catholic Social Teaching and the U.S. Economy* (1986) by the National Conference of Catholic Bishops.

EC50 Thomas, Madathilparapil M.
The Secular Ideologies of India and the Secular Meaning of Christ. (Confessing the Faith in India Series, 12). Madras, II: CLS, 1976. viii, 207 pp. Paper. No ISBN.

A scholarly study of Christian impact upon secular ideologies of India, including liberal nationalism, socialist humanism, Marxism-Leninism, and anti-Brahminism by the Director of the Christian Institute for the Study of Religion and Society.

Capitalism

See also AF1344.

EC51 Balleis, Peter
ESAP and Theology: Reflections on the Economic Structural Adjustment Programme in the Light of the Bible and the Social Teaching of the Catholic Church. (Silveira House Social Series, 1). Gweru, RH: Mambo Press, 1992. 40 pp. Paper. 0869225308.

A critique of capitalism based on the social teaching of the Catholic Church, written in response to the abandonment of socialism by the government of Zimbabwe and its espousal of a capitalist "Economic Structural Adjustment Programme" (ESAP).

EC52 Hinkelammert, Franz J.
Cultura de la Esperenza y Sociedad sin exclusión. (Colección Económica-Teología). San José, CR: DEI/Editorial Caminos, 1995. 387 pp. 9977830916.

An analysis, from a liberation theology perspective, of the development of capitalism into a global system following the fall from favor of state socialism in 1989.

EC53 Hinkelammert, Franz J.
The Ideological Weapons of Death: A Theological Critique of Capitalism. Maryknoll, NYU: Orbis Books, 1985. xxi, 282 pp. Paper. 0883442604.

A scholarly critique of both Marxist and capitalist economic theory from the perspective of a biblically based liberation theology, with implications for modern Catholic social thought.

EC54 Mueller, Franz H.
The Church and the Social Question. Washington, DCU: American Enterprise Institute, 1984. 158 pp. 0844735671.

A reprint of an extended essay, in which the Professor of Economics at the College of St. Thomas in St. Paul, Minnesota, traced the relation of Roman Catholism to three stages of capitalism; originally published in *The Challenge of Mater and Magistra* edited by J. N. Moody and J. G. Lavler (1963).

EC55 Sherman, Amy L.
Preferential Option: A Christian and Neo-Liberal Strategy for Latin America's Poor. Grand Rapids, MIU: Eerdmans, 1992. x, 230 pp. Paper. 0802806422.

An argument for democratic capitalism, rather than state socialism, as the most feasible strategy of holistic development for the poor of Latin America.

EC56 Tamez, Elsa, and Sául Trinidad, eds.
Capitalismo, Violencia y Anti-vida; La opresión de las mayorías y la domesticación de los dioses: Ponencias del Encuentro Latinoamericano de Científicos Sociales y Teólogos, San José, CR, 21-25 de febrero de 1978. San José, CR: EDUCA, 1978. 2 vols. Paper. No ISBN.

A collection of thirty-three papers analyzing the dominating, oppressive systems in Latin America and their modes of ideological legitimacy.

Socialism and Marxism

See also TH459, SO33-SO34, EC2, PO117, AF300, AM563, AM1280, and AS687.

EC57 Banana, Canaan Sodindo
Theology of Promise: The Dynamics of Self-Reliance. Harare, RH: College Press, 1982. 156 pp. Paper. 0869253794.

An African liberation theology attempting to reconcile the socialist revolution with the Christian faith; by the prominent Methodist minister and first President of Zimbabwe.

EC58 Banana, Canaan Sodindo
Towards a Socialist Ethos. Harare, RH: College Press, 1987. xi, 60 pp. Paper. 0869258249.

A popular essay by Zimbabwe's first President, a Methodist clergyman, designed to stimulate genuine debate by Christians and others on the challenges and imperatives of socialism.

EC59 Christians for Socialism (1st Latin American Conference, Santiago, Chile, 23-30 April 1972)

Los Cristianos y el Socialismo. Buenos Aires, AG: Siglo XXI Argentina Editores, 1973. 274 pp. Paper. No ISBN.

A collection of the conference's papers, reports, and conclusions.

EC60 Conway, James F.

Marx and Jesus: Liberation Theology in Latin America. New York, NYU: Carlton Press, 1973. 221 pp. No ISBN.

A general overview of the Marxist critique on religion which underlies the thought and method of Third World theologians, with detailed analysis of the contributions of Brazilian theologians in the light of that country's social reality.

EC61 Cort, John C.

Christian Socialism: An Informal History. Maryknoll, NYU: Orbis Books, 1988. xiii, 402 pp. 0883445743 (hdbk), 0883445735 (pbk).

A comprehensive survey of the Christian socialist movement—its theological foundations in scripture, history, and present expressions both in Catholicism and Protestantism, on several continents.

EC62 Coste, René

Marxist Analysis and Christian Faith. Maryknoll, NYU: Orbis Books, 1985. vii, 232 pp. Paper. 0883443422.

An analysis comparing essential features of Marxism to the foundations of Christian faith, noting points of conflict and convergence; translated from French by Roger A. Couture and John C. Cort.

EC63 Eagleson, John, ed.

Christians and Socialism: Documentation of the Christians for Socialism Movement in Latin America. Translated by John Drury. Maryknoll, NYU: Orbis Books, 1975. x, 246 pp. 0883440598 (hdbk), 088344058X (pbk).

Documents from the 1971-1973 period, telling the story of the Christians for Socialism Movement in Chile, which supported Salvador Allende's efforts at radical social and economic reform.

EC64 Míguez Bonino, José

Christians and Marxists: The Mutual Challenge to Revolution. Grand Rapids, MIU: Eerdmans; London, ENK: Hodder & Stoughton, 1976. 158 pp. 0802834779 (US), 0340193964 (UK).

The challenge to Christians by Marxism, by one of Latin America's leading Protestant thinkers; originally presented as the 1974 London Lectures in Contemporary Christianty.

EC65 Maczka, Romwald, and Mark R. Elliot, eds.

Christian/Marxist Studies in United States Higher Education: A Handbook of Syllabi. Wheaton, ILU: Wheaton College, Institute for the Study of Christianity and Marxism, 1991. xv, 233 pp. Paper. No ISBN.

A compendium of fifty-seven syllabi of college and seminary courses in the United States on various aspects of Christianity and Marxism, including liberation theology and churches under socialism in Eastern Europe and elsewhere.

EC66 Mathew, Philip, and Ajit Muricken, eds.

Religion, Ideology and Counter-Culture: Essays in Honor of S. Kappen. Bangalore, II: Horizon Books, 1987. 226 pp. Paper. No ISBN.

A volume which acknowledges Kappen's rethinking Christianity and Marxism in relation to social praxis, seeking to reflect on points of insertion for both Christ and Marx in the religious traditions of India.

EC67 McGovern, Arthur F.

Marxism: An American Christian Perspective. Maryknoll, NYU: Orbis Books, 1980. ix, 339 pp. 0883443015.

A reexamination of Marxism in the light of new Christian attitudes, including those of Latin American liberation theologians.

EC68 Metz, Johannes Baptist, and Jean-Pierre Jossua, eds.

Christianity and Socialism. (Concilium: Religion in the Seventies, 105). New York, NYU: Seabury Press, 1977. viii, 133 pp. Paper. 081642148X.

Sixteen theologians from Western capitalist, Eastern socialist, and Third World countries discuss the responsibility of Christianity to address issues of poverty and oppression.

EC69 Miranda, José Porfirio

Marx and the Bible: A Critique of the Philosophy of Oppression. Translated by John Eagleson. Maryknoll, NYU: Orbis Books, 1974. xxi, 338 pp. Paper. 0883443066 (hdbk), 0883443074 (pbk).

English translation.

EC70 Miranda, José Porfirio

Marx y la Biblia: Crítica a la Filosofía de la opresión. Salamanca, SP: Ediciones Sígueme, 1972. 342 pp. No ISBN.

A Mexican theologian's scholarly analysis of economic justice in the Old and New Testaments in comparison with Karl Marx's critique of the philosophy of oppression.

EC71 Mojzes, Paul

Christian-Marxist Dialogue in Eastern Europe. Minneapolis, MNU: Augsburg, 1981. 336 pp. 0806618957.

The first comprehensive interpretation of dialogue between Christians and Marxists in every Eastern European country.

EC72 Mojzes, Paul, ed.

Varieties of Christian-Marxist Dialogue. (*Journal of Ecumenical Studies,* vol. 15, no. 1). Philadelphia, PAU: Ecumenical Press, 1978. iv, 210 pp. Paper. 0931214025.

Eighteen short essays presenting the remarkable variety of forms and approaches to the Christian-Marxist dialogue during the past two decades.

EC73 Piediscalzi, Nicholas, and Robert G. Thobaben, eds.

Three Worlds of Christian-Marxist Encounters. Philadelphia, PAU: Fortress Press, 1985. xiv, 220 pp. Paper. 0800618408.

Nine scholarly essays on the varied patterns of Christian-Marxist encounter during the past two decades on five continents.

EC74 *The Arusha Declaration and Christian Socialism*

Dar es Salaam, TZ: Tanzania Publishing House, 1969. xi, 54 pp. Paper. No ISBN.

Six papers given at a two-day symposium addressing Roman Catholic social teachings as they relate to Tanzania's Arusha Declaration of 1967.

EC75 Verkuyl, Johannes

Voorbereiding voor de dialoog over het evangelie en de ideologie van het marxistisch Leninisme. Kampen, NE: Kok, 1976. 208 pp. 9024217792.

The eminent Dutch missiologist analyzes Marxism-Leninism as an ideology, identifying significant points for Christian-Marxist dialogue.

Communism

See also AS489, AS1225, and EU246.

EC76 Hoffmann, Gerhard, and Willie Wilhem, eds.
World Mission and World Communism. Translated by David Cairnos and Ingrid Stewart. Edinburgh, STK: St. Andrew Press; Richmond, VAU: John Knox Press, 1970. 142 pp. Paper. No ISBN.

English translation.

EC77 Hoffmann, Gerhard, ed.
Weltmission und Weltkommunismus. (Perspektiven der Weltmission, 1). Neukirchen-Vluyn, GW: Neukirchener Verlag, 1968. 122 pp. Paper. No ISBN.

A small volume concerned with the challenge for Christian witness posed by communism, reflecting on such topics as church and revolution, consequences for the universal mission of the church, and concrete examples from various parts of the world.

EC78 Miranda, José Porfirio
Communism in the Bible. Translated by Robert R. Barr. Maryknoll, NYU: Orbis Books; London, ENK: SCM Press, 1982. x, 85 pp. Paper. 0883440148 (US), 0334019451 (UK).

English translation.

EC79 Miranda, José Porfirio
Comunismo en la Biblia. (Sociología y política). Mexico City, MX: Siglo Veintiuno Editores, 1981. 86 pp. 9682314860.

A monograph by the prominent Mexican liberationist arguing that Marx did not invent the classless society, as it was an authentic emphasis in the teachings of Jesus Christ.

EC80 Verkuyl, Johannes
Evangelie en communisme in Azië en Afrika. Kampen, NE: Kok, 1966. 200 pp. No ISBN.

An essay on the threat and challenge of communism to church and mission in Asia and Africa, with extended treatment of developments in the Peoples Republic of China and Indonesia.

Economic History and Conditions

See also SO487, SP222, AM300, AM1401, AM1515, and AS1326.

EC81 Brunger, Scott
A Trade in Death: An Economics Mystery. New York, NYU: Friendship Press, 1994. x, 181 pp. Paper. 0377002658.

Africa's economic problems of international smuggling and government corruption presented in a novel by a former Frontier Intern in Benin and Togo.

EC82 Câmara, Hélder
Structures of Injustice. London, ENK: Justice and Peace Commission, 1972. 42 pp. Paper. No ISBN.

A Christian-Marxist analysis of sociological structural evil.

EC83 Countryman, Louis William
The Rich Christian in the Church of the Early Empire: Contradictions and Accommodations. (Texts and Studies in Religion, 7). New York, NYU: E Mellen Press, 1980. viii, 239 pp. 0889469709.

A useful piece of research, in view of the fact that Christian missionary teaching on the ethical implications of economics will prove at times (as inevitably as in the early centuries of the church!) to be awkwardly "out of this world."

EC84 Gremillion, Joseph
Food/Energy and the Major Faiths. Maryknoll, NYU: Orbis Books, 1978. ix, 293 pp. 0883441373 (hdbk), 0883441381 (pbk).

Papers of the Interreligious Peace Colloquium held in Bellagio, Italy, 26-30 May 1975, at which thirty-five prominent academics and world religious leaders called upon persons of all faiths to cooperate on issues on food, energy, and peace.

EC85 McCormack, Arthur
World Poverty and the Christian. (*Twentieth Century Encyclopedia of Catholicism*, 132). New York, NYU: Hawthorne Books, 1963. 158 pp. Paper. No ISBN.

A Christian response from a Catholic perspective to global social problems posed by poverty, population, and food supply.

Poverty and Hunger

See also HI355, HI717, TH173, TH271, TH313-TH315, TH382-TH384, ME170, SO430, EC6, EC235, EC241, EC262, EC385, CH337, SP79, SP184, SP245, AF514, AF1040, AF1119, AM249-AM250, AM349, AM379, AM587, AM723-AM724, AM894, AM1327, AM1481, AS237, AS348, AS842, AS939, AS1078, AS1522, EU138, and EU180.

EC86 Amalorpavadass, D. S.
Poverty of the Religious and the Religious as Poor. (Mission Theology for our Times Series, 14). Bangalore, II: NBCLC, 1984. 59 pp. Paper. No ISBN.

A guide to the study of poverty and the poor against a triple background: the cultural and religious traditions of India, the present social realities of India, and the Judeo-Christian heritage.

EC87 Atherton, John
The Scandal of Poverty: Priorities for the Emerging Church. (Mowbray's Emerging Church Series). London, ENK: Mowbray, 1983. vii, 131 pp. Paper. 0264668251.

An examination of what it is like to be poor in today's affluent society, with alternatives for the church's creative response by the Joint Director of the William Temple Foundation in Manchester, England.

EC88 Barreiro, Julio A., and Julio de Santa Ana
Separation without Hope?: Essays on the Relation between the Church and the Poor during the Industrial Revolution and the Western Colonial Expansion. Geneva, SZ: WCC, 1978. 192 pp. Paper. 2825405760.

This second volume of the CCPD study on "The Church and the Poor" contains ten essays covering church responses related to the industrial revolution, colonialism, and missions in Latin America and Africa.

EC89 Barrett, John M.
It's Hard Not to Worry: Stories for Children about Poverty. New York, NYU: Friendship Press, 1988. 51 pp. Paper. 0377001783.

A collection of six stories with Christian emphasis about North American children whose families are facing or living in poverty; written as a mission study for children in grades 1-6, with a teacher's guide (New York: Friendship Press, 1988, 26 pp. Paper. 0377001791).

EC90 Beckmann, David M., and Arthur R. Simon

Grace and the Table: Ending Hunger in God's World. Downers Grove, ILU: InterVarsity, 1999. iv, 219 pp. Paper. 0803822178.

Two leaders in the Christian response to reducing widespread hunger argue that, although the world has made progress, we have the ideas, experience, technology, and financing to eliminate it.

EC91 Boerma, Coenraad

The Poor Side of Europe: The Church and the (New) Poor of Western Europe. (Risk Book Series, 42). Geneva, SZ: WCC, 1989. x, 131 pp. Paper. 2825409693.

The head of the radio section of NCRV (the Netherlands) presents the reality of the existence of the poor in Europe, how European churches have lost these persons with a confusing message, how the gospel to the sinner is also the gospel to the poor, and how the poor can participate in the life of churches in Europe.

EC92 Boff, Leonardo, Virgilio P. Elizondo, and Marcus Lefébure, eds.

Option for the Poor: Challenge to the Rich Countries. (*Concilium*: Religion in the Eighties, 187). Edinburgh, STK: T&T Clark, 1986. xii, 131 pp. Paper. 0567300676.

Thirteen essays by an international panel of theologians interpreting the preferential option for solidarity with the poor, which is the trademark of the Catholic Church in Latin America.

EC93 Byron, William, ed.

The Causes of World Hunger. New York, NYU: Paulist Press, 1982. vi, 256 pp. Paper. 0809124831.

One of the most helpful introductions to the subject, with chapters contributed by eighteen former or present members of the Board of Directors of Bread for the World.

EC94 Caes, David, ed.

Caring for the Least of These: Serving Christ among the Poor. Scottdale, PAU: Herald Press, 1992. 176 pp. Paper. 0836135946.

First-person accounts of struggles for a quality of life written by poor people and those of the Christian Community Health Fellowship serving in settings of poverty.

EC95 Cherupallikat, Justinian

Witness Potential of Evangelical Poverty in India. (Neue Zeitschrift für Missionswissenschaft, 23). Immense, SZ: Nouvelle revue de science missionaire, 1975. xxxii, 215 pp. Paper. No ISBN.

After analyzing the ideal of evangelical poverty as found in the Old and New Testaments, the author, a Franciscan missionary to India, develops ways and means to incarnate the poverty of Christ as a mission mandate in the Indian cultural context.

EC96 Conference on World Evangelization (Pattaya, Thailand, 1980)

The Thailand Report on the Urban Poor: Report of the ... Mini-Consultation on Reaching the Urban Poor. Wheaton, ILU: LCWE, 1980. 40 pp. Paper. No ISBN.

An overview of the urban poor, biblical beliefs about them, and strategies for evangelism.

EC97 Cussiánovich, Alejandro

Desde los Pobres de la Tierra: Perspectivas de vida religiosa. (Pedal, 66). Salamanca, SP: Edicione Sígueme, 1977. 219 pp. 8430104771.

An argument for voluntary personal poverty, charity, and obedience as essential for effective mission service among the poor, by those with religious vocations.

EC98 Cussiánovich, Alejandro

Religious Life and the Poor: Liberation Theology Perspectives. Translated by John Drury. Maryknoll, NYU: Orbis Books, 1979. vii, 168 pp. 0883444291.

English translation.

EC99 De Gaspar, Diogo, Caesar Espiritu, and Reginald Herbold Green, eds.

World Hunger: A Christian Reappraisal. (An Ecumenical Approach to Economics, 3). Geneva, SZ: WCC, 1982. 63 pp. Paper. 2825407216.

Report of the Fourth Meeting of the WCC's Advisory Group on Economic Affairs (Washington, DC, 5-8 October 1981).

EC100 Dunnavant, Anthony L., ed.

Poverty and Ecclesiology: Nineteenth-Century Evangelicals in the Light of Liberation. Collegeville, MNU: Liturgical Press, 1992. 104 pp. Paper. 0814650244.

Case studies on 19th-century views of poverty and ecclesiology in three North American Protestant traditions (Baptist, Free Methodist, and Churches of Christ) as roots of recent Latin American expressions of God's "option for the poor."

EC101 Endersbee, Mary

They Can't Eat Prayer: The Story of TEAR Fund. London, ENK: Hodder & Stoughton, 1973. 160 pp. 0340156155.

The story of The Evangelical Alliance Relief Fund.

EC102 Freudenberger, C. Dean, and Paul Murray Minus, eds.

Christian Responsibility in a Hungry World. Nashville, TNU: Abingdon, 1976. 128 pp. Paper. 068707567X.

In this work the authors address the root causes of hunger, the reasons why Christians in America must respond to this worldwide problem, and specific steps for churches and Christians to take in conquering world hunger.

EC103 Garcia, Ana de, and George S. Johnson

Evangelism and the Poor: A Biblical Challenge for the Church. Minneapolis, MNU: Augsburg, 1986. 39 pp. Paper. No ISBN.

A study guide for adults focusing upon understandings and attitudes toward the poor, biblical awareness of God's love toward the poor, and ways in which Christians can experience growth and renewal through face-to-face encounter with poverty and solidarity with the poor.

EC104 Gheddo, Piero

Why Is the Third World Poor? Translated by Kathryn Sullivan. Maryknoll, NYU: Orbis Books, 1973. xv, 143 pp. Paper. 0883447576.

A simply written, but credible, non-ideological analysis of factors contributing to the creation and perpetuation of global poverty.

EC105 Gittings, James A.

Breach of Promise: Portraits of Poverty in North America. New York, NYU: Friendship Press, 1988. iv, 130 pp. Paper. 0377001813.

An examination of what it means to be poor in North America, featuring discussions with those in poverty; by a former editor of *Presbyterian Life, A. D. Magazine,* and *Seventh Angel.*

EC106 Goldewijk, Berma Klein, and Bas de Gaay Fortman

Where Needs Meet Rights: Economic, Social and Cultural Rights in a New Perspective. (Risk Book Series, 88). Geneva, SZ: WCC Publications, 1999. xiv, 146 pp. Paper. 2825413194.

Rooted in human needs, human dignity, and legitimacy, the authors base their premise on everyday realities of millions of people, realities that oblige fellow human beings to act.

EC—MISSIONS AND ECONOMIC LIFE

EC107 Gollwitzer, Helmut
Die reichen Christen und der arme Lazarus: Die Konsequen-zen von Uppsala. Munich, GW: Kaiser, 1969. 123 pp. No ISBN.

A treatise on Western Christian responsibility for the plight of the world's poor.

EC108 Gollwitzer, Helmut
The Rich Christians and Poor Lazarus. Translated by David Cairns. New York, NYU: Macmillan, 1970. xi, 108 pp. No ISBN.

English translation.

EC109 Gray, Charlene J., comp.
No Longer Forgotten: The Remarkable Story of Christian Women's Job Corps. Edited by Trudy O. Johnson. Birming-ham, ALU: New Hope Publishers, 1998. xii, 138 pp. Paper. 1563092506.

The story of a ministry of the Woman's Missionary Union, auxiliary to SBC, which began in 1993 and has grown into a nationally recognized program of women helping women in poverty to become equipped for life and employment.

EC110 Greinacher, Norbert, and Alois Müller, eds.
The Poor and the Church. (*Concilium*: Religion in the Seven-ties). New York, NYU: Seabury Press, 1977. vi, 119 pp. 08164036271 (hdbk), 0816421471 (pbk).

Fourteen essays exploring the many-sided Christian atti-tudes toward poverty.

EC111 Gushee, David P., ed.
Toward a Just and Caring Society: Christian Responses to Poverty in America. Grand Rapids, MIU: Baker Books, 1999. 574 pp. Paper. 0801022207.

In a collection of essays, sixteen evangelical scholars and teachers address the historical, political, and economic issues involved in the pervasive social problem of poverty in modern America.

EC112 Gutiérrez, Gustavo
The Power of the Poor in History: Selected Writings. Trans-lated by Robert R. Barr. Maryknoll, NYU: Orbis Books; Lon-don, ENK: SCM Press, 1983. xvi, 240 pp. Paper. 0883443880 (US), 0334012791 (UK).

A compilation of eight essays written from 1969 to 1979 by the pioneer of liberation theology in Latin America, focus-ing on social justice issues between the Medellin (1968) and Puebla (1979) conferences of Latin American bishops.

EC113 Harmer, Catherine M.
The Compassionate Community: Stategies that Work for the Third Millenium. Maryknoll, NYU: Orbis Books, 1998. xv, 205 pp. Paper. 157075196X.

Concrete strategies for combating major social injustice—endemic poverty, homelessness, domestic violence, and inad-equate health care—including the analysis of some strategies that persist despite their failure.

EC114 Henriot, Peter J.
Opting for the Poor: A Challenge for North Americans. (En-ergies for Social Transformation). Washington, DCU: Center of Concern, 1990. 62 pp. Paper. 0934255059.

A primer interpreting for North Americans, the rationale and imperative of the church's "option for the poor"; by the former Executive Director of the Center of Concern, with questions and scriptural references for individual reflection or group study.

EC115 Jennings, Anthony, ed.
Our Response to the Poorest of the Third World. Oxford, ENK: Pergamon Press, 1984. viii, 64 pp. 0080308228.

Papers presented at the colloquium formed by the Com-mission for International Justice and Peace of the Roman Cath-olic Bishops Conference of England and Wales at Westmin-ster in November 1982, with suggestions for action at the glo-bal, interregional, and national levels to reduce the gap be-tween the richest countries and the poorest.

EC116 Jennings, William H.
Poor People and Churchgoers. New York, NYU: Seabury Press, 1972. 128 pp. Paper. 0816420750.

A critical examination and assessment of responses by wealthy Christians to the poor.

EC117 Jimenez Liman, Javier, Jon Sobrino, and José Ignacio González
Opción por los Oprimidos y Evangelización. (Aportes CRT, 2). México, MX: CRT, 1978. 118 pp. Paper. No ISBN.

Theological essays on God's option for the poor and evan-gelization.

EC118 Kavanaugh, John F.
Faces of Poverty, Faces of Christ. Maryknoll, NYU: Orbis Books, 1991. xiii, 162 pp. Paper. 0883447258.

Five understandings of poverty represented in photo-graphs, scripture, and stories drawn from the author's own experiences on several continents.

EC119 Kelly, George Anthony
The Catholic Church and American Poor. New York, NYU: Alba House, 1976. xv, 206 pp. 081890321X.

A description of Church involvement with the victims of American socio-economic problems.

EC120 Kemp, Charles F.
Pastoral Care with the Poor. Nashville, TNU: Abingdon, 1972. 128 pp. Paper. 0687302951.

Basic principles that should govern pastoral care with the poor, developed out of a three-year study on pastoral care and poverty at Brite Divinity School, Texas Christian University, as part of the national ecumenical Ministry in the Seventies project.

EC121 Kim, Sebastian C. H., and Krickwin C. Marak, eds.
Good News to the Poor: The Challenge to the Church. Pune, II: Centre for Mission Studies; Delhi, II: ISPCK, 1997. viii, 285 pp. Paper. 8172143494.

A collection of thirteen essays from South India on the Nazareth Manifesto (Luke 4:16-30) of "good news to the poor" in biblical, socio-religious, historical, and ecclesiological per-spectives, with special application to India.

EC122 Kreider, Carl
The Rich and the Poor: A Christian Perspective on Global Economics. Scottdale, PAU: Herald Press, 1987. 168 pp. Pa-per. 0836134338.

A description of the main characteristics of less-devel-oped countries (LDCs) from a Christian perspective, and the major steps being taken to improve their economies.

EC123 Lapierre, Dominique
The City of Joy. Translated by Kathryn Spink. Garden City, NYU: Doubleday, 1985. 464 pp. 0385189524.

A book that succeeds in seeing life at the inside of one of Calcutta's most wretched slums from the perspectives of a few who were there by choice, and of the many who were there because there was no alternative.

EC—MISSIONS AND ECONOMIC LIFE

EC124 Lee, Peter K. H.
Poor Man, Rich Man: The Priorities of Jesus and the Agenda of the Church. London, ENK: Hodder & Stoughton, 1986. 239 pp. Paper. 034039305X.

A popular presentation of the biblical concept of the poor, with application to the South African context, by an evangelical Anglican priest in Johannesburg; with a foreword by Desmond Tutu.

EC125 Meeks, M. Douglas, ed.
The Portion of the Poor: Good News to the Poor in the Wesleyan Tradition. Nashville, TNU: Kingswood Books, 1995. 190 pp. Paper. 0687155290.

Eight scholarly essays on John and Charles Wesley's attitudes toward the poor, and their function as role models for those of the Wesleyan tradition, as they relate to poor and marginalized persons around the globe.

EC126 Minear, Larry
New Hope for the Hungry?: The Challenge of the World Food Crisis. New York, NYU: Friendship Press, 1975. 140 pp. Paper. 0377000434.

A brief discussion on world hunger, its causes, and the effects of the World Food Conference of 1974, with examples of constructive actions on the parts of churches, governments, and private organizations to alleviate world hunger.

EC127 Moomaw, I. W.
Crusade against Hunger: The Dramatic Story of the World-Wide Antipoverty Crusades of the Churches. New York, NYU: Harper & Row, 1966. vii, 199 pp. No ISBN.

In this first book about the work of Agricultural Missions, Inc., Mr. Moomaw, a farmer from Canton, Ohio, tells about the exciting experiences of unsung individual missionaries in alleviating hunger, by helping others to help themselves around the world over a forty-year period.

EC128 Mooneyham, W. Stanley
What Do You Say to a Hungry World? Waco, TXU: Word Books, 1975. 272 pp. Paper. No ISBN.

A sensitive examination by the President of World Vision International of the contexts of hunger, together with an analysis of Christian perspectives and appropriate responses.

EC129 Myers, Bryant L., ed.
Walking with the Poor: Principles and Practices of Transformational Development. Maryknoll, NYU: Orbis Books/World Vision, 1999. x, 279 pp. Paper. 0570752753.

How Christian mission can contribute to overcoming poverty and dismantling systematic social evil through the integration of theology, spirituality, and social science.

EC130 Neal, Marie Augusta
The Just Demands of the Poor: Essays in Socio-Theology. New York, NYU: Paulist Press, 1987. v, 142 pp. Paper. 0809128454.

Nine essays written for Americans by a prominent Catholic sociologist on issues of social justice for Third World peoples.

EC131 Nelson, Jack A.
Hunger for Justice: The Politics of Food and Faith. Maryknoll, NYU: Orbis Books, 1980. viii, 230 pp. Paper. 0883441969.

A superb analysis of the economic, political, and social roots of hunger, of biblical teaching, and of application to affluent "Christian" North Americans.

EC132 Nicholls, Bruce J., and Beulah Wood, eds.
Sharing Good News with the Poor. Carlisle, ENK: Paternoster Press; Grand Rapids, MIU: Baker Books, 1996. vii, 285 pp. Paper. 0853646961 (UK), 0801020999 (US).

Papers from the WEF-sponsored consultation on "Sharing Good News with the Poor" (New Delhi, India, 17-23 October 1993) on biblical and mission perspectives, plus case studies from four continents on evangelism, mission and the poor.

EC133 Nissen, Johannes
Poverty and Mission: New Testament Perspectives on a Contemporary Theme. (IIMO Research Pamphlet, 10). Leiden, NE: IIMO, 1984. iv, 208 pp. Paper. No ISBN.

An examination of the role of poverty in the missionary task of Jesus and the earliest churches, together with an exploration of the means whereby instruction on poverty and wealth was transmitted from one social setting to another at that time; with an extensive bibliography of little-known sources in German, Danish, Dutch, French, Swedish, and English.

EC134 Philp, Peter
Journey with the Poor. Victoria, AT: Collins Dove, 1988. 126 pp. Paper. 0859245624.

A popular account of a World Vision representative's life-changing encounter with poverty in Central and South America, and with Christians who are trying to change their oppressive circumstances.

EC135 Pixley, Jorge V., and Clodovis Boff
The Bible, the Church, and the Poor. Translated by Paul Burns. (Theology and Liberation Series). Maryknoll, NYU: Orbis Books, 1989. xvii, 266 pp. Paper. 0883446146 (hdbk), 0883445999 (pbk).

English translation.

EC136 Pixley, Jorge V., and Clodovis Boff
Opção pelos pobres. (Coleção Teologia e Libertação: Ser. 1, Experiéncia de Deus e justiça, 5). Petrópolis, BL: Editora Vozes, 1987. 280 pp. No ISBN.

A second edition of an analysis of what it means to make a preferential option for the poor, including pastoral and evangelical dimensions and personal and social consequences in Latin America, by two outstanding Latin American theologians, one Protestant and the other Roman Catholic.

EC137 Pixley, Jorge V., and Clodovis Boff
Opción por los Pobres. (Cristianismo y Sociedad, 1). Buenos Aires, AG: Ediciones Paulinas, 1986. 286 pp. Paper. 9500906457.

Spanish translation.

EC138 Pixley, Jorge V., and Clodovis Boff
Les pauvres: choix prioritaire. Translated by Charles Antoine. (Collection Libération: Économie, Société, Théologie). Paris, FR: Éditions du Cerf, 1990. xxv, 238 pp. Paper. 2204041882.

French translation.

EC139 Pobee, J. S.
Who Are the Poor?: The Beatitudes as a Call to Community. (Risk Book Series, 32). Geneva, SZ: WCC Publications, 1987. 71 pp. Paper. 2825408840.

A uniquely African perspective of community and blessedness in the understanding of the poor; originally presented at a seminar called "Ministry with the Poor" sponsored by the Ecumenical Institute at Bossey and the WCC's Programme on Theological Education.

EC—MISSIONS AND ECONOMIC LIFE

EC140 Pohier, Jacques, and Dietmar Mieth, eds.

The Dignity of the Despised of the Earth. (Concilium: Religion in the Seventies, *130*). New York, NYU: Seabury Press; Edinburgh, STK: T&T Clark, 1979. xi, 131 pp. 0816401314 (US hdbk), 0816420386 (US pbk), 0567300102 (UK).

Thirteen essays on biblical, historical, and contemporary attitudes of Christians toward poor or despised peoples in various societies.

EC141 Pontifical Council "Cor Unum"

World Hunger A Challenger for All: Development in Solidarity. Nairobi, KE: Paulines Publications Africa, 1996. 79 pp. Paper. 9966212981.

A Vatican document prepared at the request of Pope John Paul II to accompany his 1996 Lenten Message.

EC142 *Poverty in Southern Africa*

Potchefstroom, SA: Institute for Reformational Studies, 1991. 68 pp. Paper. 1868220842.

Papers on Christian perspectives on poverty, with reports on missional responses in Africa, Europe, and the Americas; originally presented at a conference hosted by the Reformed Ecumenical Council (Mamelodi, South Africa, 20 Feb.-2 March 1990).

EC143 Ramalho, Jether Pereira, ed.

Signs of Hope and Justice. Geneva, SZ: WCC, CCPD, 1980. ii, 134 pp. Paper. 2825406422.

Personal stories and church statements from six continents on solidarity with the poor as a sign of the renewal of the church.

EC144 Riddle, Katharine P., and R. D. Gatewood

Food with Dignity: A Survey Presentation of Major U.S. Protestant Efforts to Combat World Hunger. New York, NYU: NCCUSA, 1966. 68 pp. No ISBN.

A useful summary with a select list of books, periodicals, and other materials concerning world hunger.

EC145 Roberts, W. Dayton, ed.

Africa: A Season for Hope. Ventura, CAU: Regal Books, 1985. 125 pp. Paper. 0830711201.

A World Vision study book on famine in Africa with an update to 1987—problems, needs, and present Christian ministries to meet them, with helps for group discussions.

EC146 Ronsvalle, John, and Sylvia Ronsvalle

The Poor Have Faces: Loving Your Neighbor in the 21st Century. Grand Rapids, MIU: Baker Books, 1992. 156 pp. Paper. 0801077648.

A popular introduction showing how Christians can be mobilized to confront problems of poverty; based on actual situations faced by the authors in their worldwide ministry, Empty Tomb, Inc.

EC147 Samuel, Vinay, and Chris Sugden

Evangelism and the Poor: A Third World Study Guide. Oxford, ENK: Regnum Books, 1983. 163 pp. Paper. 0853643431.

Revised edition of a collection of three essays with summary discussing biblical studies, religious experiences of the poor, and strategies for Christian witness; originally published at the Fifth Conference of IAMS (Bangalore, India, 1982).

EC148 Santa Ana, Julio de, comp.

Hacia una Iglesia de los Pobres: Trabajo de un grupo ecuménico sobre la Iglesia y los pobres. Buenos Aires, AG:

Editorial La Aurora; Buenos Aires, AG: Editorial Tierra Nueva, 1983. 292 pp. Paper. 9505510071.

Spanish translation.

EC149 Santa Ana, Julio de, comp.

A Igreja dos pobres: Produzido por um grupo ecumênico de trabalho do Conselho Mundial de Igrejas. São Bernardo do Campo,: Imprensa Metodista/Ciências da Religião, 1985. 230 pp. Paper. No ISBN.

Portuguese translation.

EC150 Santa Ana, Julio de, ed.

Towards a Church of the Poor: The Work of an Ecumenical Group on the Church and the Poor. Geneva, SZ: WCC, 1982. xxiv, 236 pp. Paper. 2825406252.

Third volume of the trilogy, "Church and the Poor," prepared by the Commission on the Churches' Participation in Development (WCC).

EC151 Santa Ana, Julio de

El Desafío de los Pobres a la Iglesia. (Colección Testimonios). San José, CR: DEI, 1985. 141 pp. Paper. 9977904111.

An overview on the theme of poverty and the poor in the Bible and in the history of the church, by a Uruguayan theologian/sociologist who worked as study coordinator in the WCC's department for development; originally published in 1977.

EC152 Santa Ana, Julio de

Good News to the Poor: The Challenge of the Poor in the History of the Church. Translated by Helen Whittle. Geneva, SZ: WCC, 1982. xi, 136 pp. Paper. 282540540X.

English translation.

EC153 Santa Ana, Julio de

A Igreja e o desafio dos pobres: Um estudo sobre o desafio dos pobres e da pobreza à comunidade cristã, desde os primeiros séculos de sua história até o final da idade média. Translated by Edda Mastrangelo Dias. Petrópolis, BL: Vozes; Petrópolis, BL: Tempo e Presença Editora, 1980. 149 pp. No ISBN.

Portuguese translation.

EC154 Schlabach, Gerald

And Who Is My Neighbor?: Poverty, Privilege, and the Gospel of Christ. Scottdale, PAU: Herald Press, 1990. 212 pp. Paper. 0836135253.

A guide for studying scripture and helping groups to identify with the poor, with examples of personal encounters and resources for groups that wish to begin working for change, both locally and worldwide.

EC155 Shaull, Millard Richard

Heralds of a New Reformation: The Poor of South and North America. Maryknoll, NYU: Orbis Books, 1984. xiii, 140 pp. Paper. 0883443457.

A popular presentation of the theme of the poor in scripture, Christian tradition, contemporary liberation theology, and the life of basic Christian communities in Latin America.

EC156 Sheppard, David

Bias to the Poor. London, ENK: Hodder & Stoughton, 1983. 251 pp. Paper. 0340352779.

A challenge to churches to reflect God's bias to the poor in their attitudes, beliefs, and priorities; based on the author's experience of urban life.

EC157 Shorter, Aylward
Religious Poverty in Africa. Nairobi, KE: Paulines Pulications Africa, 1999. 36 pp. Paper. 996621447X.

This follow-up booklet of "Celibacy and African Culture" (Nairobi: Paulines Publications Africa) questions whether the vow of poverty can be lived without the religious engagement in a genuine and real solidarity with the African poor.

EC158 Sider, Ronald J.
Cristãos ricos em tempos de fome. São Leopoldo, BL: Editoral Sinodal, 1984. 240 pp. Paper. 8523300309.

Portuguese translation.

EC159 Sider, Ronald J.
Cup of Water, Bread of Life: Inspiring Stories about Overcoming Lopsided Christianity. Grand Rapids, MIU: Zondervan, 1994. 186 pp. Paper. 0310406013.

Ten case studies of ministries worldwide that help the poor and oppressed and integrate much-needed social action with evangelism.

EC160 Sider, Ronald J.
Just Generosity: A New Vision for Overcoming Poverty in America. Grand Rapids, MIU: Baker Books, 1999. 266 pp. Paper. 080106015X.

This holistic approach calls for faith-based groups to work with business, media, and government, uniting inner spiritual transformation with the addressing of structural injustice in order to end poverty in the world's richest nation.

EC161 Sider, Ronald J.
Rich Christians in an Age of Hunger: Moving from Affluence to Generosity. Dallas, TXU: Word Publishing, 1997. 329 pp. Paper. 0849914248.

A revised 20th-anniversary edition of the classic on how Christians can continue to address the worldwide problem of poverty.

EC162 Simon, Arthur R.
Bread for the World. New York, NYU: Paulist Press; Grand Rapids, MIU: Eerdmans, 1984. iii, 219 pp. Paper. 0809126702 (P), 0802800262 (E).

Revised and updated edition of a general introduction to world hunger especially addressed to North American readers; complete with numerous practical suggestions, group discussion questions, and sources for further information.

EC163 Sobrino, Jon
Resurrección de la Verdadera Iglesia: Los Pobres, Lugar Teológico de la Eclesiología. (Presencia Teológica, 8). Santander, SP: Sal Terrae, 1984. 349 pp. No ISBN.

Second edition of a biblical ecclesiology which focuses on the church *as* the poor, rather than merely *for* the poor.

EC164 Sobrino, Jon
The True Church and the Poor. Translated by Matthew J. O'Connell. Maryknoll, NYU: Orbis Books, 1984. x, 374 pp. Paper. 0883445131.

English translation.

EC165 Soper, Sharon E.
Soybeans and the Kingdom of God: An Approach to Holistic Mission. Winnipeg, MBC: Evangelical Mennonite Mission Conference, 1994. 159 pp. Paper. 1896257024.

A holistic approach to health for the world's hungry, combining the introduction of soybeans as a "miracle food" with cultural sensitivity and a kingdom theology.

EC166 Tamames, Ramón et al.
Esperanza de los Pobres, Esperanza Cristiana: II Congreso de Teología y Pobreza. (Misión Abierta, 75:4/5 493-783). Madrid, SP: Misión Abierta, 1982. 290 pp. No ISBN.

A monograph dedicated to the congress whose themes were the Gospel, church, and theology on the one hand, and poverty in Spain on the other.

EC167 Taylor, Michael
Not Angels but Agencies: The Ecumenical Response to Poverty—A Primer. (Risk Book Series, 69). London, ENK: SCM Press; Geneva, SZ: WCC Publications, 1995. viii, 174 pp. Paper. 0334026245 (UK), 282541168X (SZ).

A review and evaluation by the Director of Christian Aid, London, of fifty years of responses by churches and ecumenical agencies to poverty issues.

EC168 Toton, Suzanne C.
World Hunger: The Responsibility of Christian Education. Maryknoll, NYU: Orbis Books, 1982. xiv, 210 pp. Paper. 0883447169.

Using the methodology of liberation theology, the author works out the theory of educating for justice with respect to world hunger, examining causes of world hunger, Christian social teachings, and how educating for peace may take place in family, school, media, and church.

EC169 Vaughan, Benjamin Noel Young
The Expectations of the Poor: The Church and the Third World. London, ENK: SCM Press; Valley Forge, PAU: Judson Press, 1972. ix, 182 pp. Paper. 0334004314.

An introduction to issues of Third World poverty and the churches' response.

EC170 Yuzon, Lourdino A., ed.
Mission in the Context of Endemic Poverty. Toa Payoh, SI: CCA, 1983. iv, 131 pp. Paper. 997194815X.

Papers of a consultation on "Mission in the Context of Poverty and in Situations of Affluence" (Manila, 10-14 Dec. 1982).

Consumption and Lifestyle Issues

See also HI225, TH231, TH289, ME208, ME211, ME216, ME220, EC37, ED74, and CH423.

EC171 Fairfield, James G.T.
All That We Are We Give. Scottdale, PAU: Herald Press, 1977. 174 pp. Paper. 0836118391.

A book which grapples with the question of appropriate lifestyle not only for, but also as, Christian mission.

EC172 Finnerty, Adam Daniel
No More Plastic Jesus: Global Justice and Christian Lifestyle. Maryknoll, NYU: Orbis Books; New York, NYU: Dutton, 1977. xiv, 223 pp. 0883443406 (O, hdbk), 0883443414 (O, pbk).

A popular analysis of the growing global gap between rich and poor, and of alternatives for global economic justice, a church with holy poverty, and a simplified individual lifestyle based on the Shakertown Pledge.

EC173 Franz, Delton
Let My People Choose: Christian Choice Regarding Poverty, Affluence, Standard of Living. Scottdale, PAU: Herald Press, 1969. 156 pp. Paper. 0836163222.

An exploration of reflections on global poverty, with biblical implications for North American living standards; originally prepared as the 1969 Mission Study Course of the General Mennonite churches.

EC174 Fraser, Ian M., ed.
Leisure-Tourism: Threat and Promise. Geneva, SZ: WCC, 1970. 109 pp. Paper. No ISBN.

Report and papers of the pioneer World Consultation on Leisure-Tourism (Tutzing, Germany, 26 Sept.-2 Oct. 1969) sponsored by the WCC and attended by church leaders of twenty nations.

EC175 Gnuse, Robert
You Shall Not Steal: Community and Property in the Biblical Tradition. Maryknoll, NYU: Orbis Books, 1985. ix, 162 pp. Paper. 0883447991.

An argument that the Seventh Commandment was intended to ensure that no one should be in want of the essentials of life.

EC176 Halteman, James
The Clashing Worlds of Economics and Faith. Scottdale, PAU: Herald Press, 1995. 224 pp. Paper. 0836190149.

An Anabaptist critique of market capitalism with a biblically based alternative to conspicuous acquisition and consumption.

EC177 Hudnut-Beumler, James, ed.
Generous Saints: Congregations Rethinking Ethics and Money. (Money, Faith, and Lifestyle Series). Portland, MAU: Alban Institute, 1999. ix, 177 pp. Paper. 1566992109.

Provides theological links between faith and money, with a challenge toward individual and congregational generosity.

EC178 Kavanaugh, John F.
Following Christ in a Consumer Society: The Spirituality of Cultural Resistance. Maryknoll, NYU: Orbis Books, 1991. xxx, 194 pp. Paper. 0883447770.

A revision of the author's penetrating analysis of First World contemporary consumer culture, and of the power of the Gospel to critique that culture; with guidelines for First World missionaries and others making connections between their religious faith and economic and political issues; originally published in 1981.

EC179 Lockley, Andrew
Christian Communes. London, ENK: SCM Press, 1976. vii, 119 pp. Paper. 0334019273.

A useful introduction to this increasingly common phenomenon in Europe, tracing its origins in Christian history, surveying the development and lifestyle of contemporary communes, and assessing their significance for churches concerned for building Christian community.

EC180 McCleary, Paul F., and J. Philip Wogaman
Quality of Life in a Global Society. New York, NYU: Friendship Press, 1978. ii, 69 pp. Paper. 0377000701.

The 1976 Colliver Lectures at the University of the Pacific (Stockton, California) on issues of development and ecology; by a Professor of Christian Ethics and a church administrator with deep involvement in these issues.

EC181 Mullin, Redmond
The Wealth of Christians. Exeter, ENK: Paternoster Press; Maryknoll, NYU: Orbis Books, 1984. 256 pp. Paper. 0883447096.

An analysis of how Christians throughout history have dealt with the pursuit of wealth, arguing for greater connection between economic behavior and faith.

EC182 Munby, Denys Lawrence
God and the Rich Society: A Study of Christians in a World of Abundance. London, ENK: Oxford University Press, 1961. 209 pp. No ISBN.

An examination of ways in which rich Christians should, can, but often do not, respond to the poor.

EC183 Nichols, Alan
An Evangelical Commitment to Simple Life-Style. (Lausanne Occasional Papers, 20). Wheaton, ILU: LCWE, 1980. 5, 34 pp. Paper. No ISBN.

In urging evangelical commitment to simple lifestyle, such items as stewardship, poverty and wealth, lifestyle, justice and politics, evangelism, and the Lord's return are considered.

EC184 O'Grady, Ron
Tourism in the Third World. Maryknoll, NYU: Orbis Books, 1982. ix, 81 pp. Paper. 0883445077.

In this work the former Associate General Secretary of the CCA addresses the negative effects of tourism on poor countries and how the church can become involved in making tourism a more positive force for Third World development; also published as *Third World Stopover* (Geneva, SZ: WCC, 1981; Risk Book Series, 12; 2825407003).

EC185 Rifkin, Jeremy, and Ted Howard
The Emerging Order: God in the Age of Scarcity. New York, NYU: Putnam, 1979. xii, 303 pp. 0399123199.

An analysis of the shifts in charismatic and evangelical Protestantism in the United States in the mid-20th century, from a piety which accepted prevailing economic values, to one which sought to create a new covenant vision sensitive to limits to growth.

EC186 Sider, Ronald J., ed.
Lifestyle in the Eighties: An Evangelical Commitment to Simple Lifestyle. Philadelphia, PAU: Westminster Press, 1982. 256 pp. Paper. 0664244378.

Papers and testimonies by an international panel of evangelical leaders, presented at the International Consultation on Simple Lifestyle (High Leigh, England, 17-21 March,1980).

EC187 Taylor, John Vernon
Enough Is Enough. London, ENK: SCM Press; Naperville, IL: SCM Book Club, 221, 1975. 120 pp. Paper. No ISBN.

A clear outline and application of biblical teaching on excessive consumption and simple living by the former General Secretary of the CMS.

Ecology

See also ME185, CR108, CR497, SO145, EC321, SP108, and SP138.

EC188 Boff, Leonardo
Cry of the Earth, Cry of the Poor. Translated by Phillip Berryman. (Ecology and Justice Series). Maryknoll, NYU: Orbis Books, 1997. xii, 242 pp. Paper. 1570751366.

The noted theologian focuses on the threatened Amazon of his native Brazil in linking the spirit of liberation theology with the urgent challenge of ecology.

EC189 Boff, Leonardo
Ecologia, mundialização, espiritualidade: a emergência de um novo paradigma. (Série Religião e cidadania). São Paulo, BL: Editora Ática, 1993. 180 pp. 8508045026.

The noted Latin American liberation theologian critiques common approaches to ecology and offers a holistic and liberative ecotheology for the new millennium.

EC190 Boff, Leonardo

Ecology and Liberation: A New Paradigm. Translated by John Cumming. (Ecology and Justice Series). Maryknoll, NYU: Orbis Books, 1995. xi, 187 pp. Paper. 0883449781.

English translation.

EC191 Christiansen, Drew, and Walter Grazer, eds.

"And God Saw That It Was Good": Catholic Theology and the Environment. Washington, DCU: USCC, 1996. ix, 354 pp. Paper. 1574550896.

A reader containing eight essays by theologians and ethicists, plus documents from the Vatican and episcopal conferences on five continents, designed to address ecological issues in the light of Catholic tradition and teachings.

EC192 Daneel, M. L.

African Earthkeepers: Volume I: Interfaith Mission in Earth-Care. (African Initiatives in Christian Mission, 2). Pretoria, SA: University of South Africa, 1998. xx, 320 pp. Paper. 1868880508.

The author's intimate knowledge of traditional Shona culture, Shona religion, and Christianity, as well as his friendships with Shona tribespeople in Zimbabwe, enabled him to establish a tree-planting venture that has overcome religious differences and environmental devastation.

EC193 Dewitt, Calvin B., and Ghillean T. Prance, eds.

Missionary Earthkeeping. Macon, GAU: Mercer University Press, 1992. xii, 148 pp. 0865543909 (hdbk), 0865544042 (pbk).

Five essays by ethicists, professors, and practitioners of environmental conservation, developing an ecotheology for world missions; with case studies from Brazil, Ghana, and Zaire.

EC194 Dowd, Michael

Earthspirit: A Handbook for Nurturing an Ecological Christianity. Mystic, CTU: Twenty-Third Publications, 1991. viii, 117 pp. Paper. 0896224791.

A resource handbook for Christians desiring to bridge the gap between ecology and spirituality.

EC195 Du Preez, J.

Eschatology and Ecology: Perspectives from the Book of Revelation. (Third Lecture of the Institute of Missiological Research). Pretoria, SA: University of Pretoria, 1992. 32 pp. Paper. No ISBN.

The third lecture of the Institute of Missiological Research (ISWEN) by the Professor and Head of the Department of Missiology at the University of Stellenbosch in South Africa.

EC196 Duchrow, Ulrich, and Gerhard Liedke

Shalom: Biblical Perspective on Creation, Justice & Peace. Geneva, SZ: WCC Publications, 1989. 198 pp. Paper. 2825409626.

A detailed study book for congregations, groups, and synods by two German church specialists on environmental issues; designed to disclose causative factors of the ecological crisis, biblical perspectives, and appropriate action responses; with examples from around the world.

EC197 Gosling, David L.

A New Earth: Covenanting for Justice, Peace and the Integrity of Creation. London, ENK: CCBI, 1992. viii, 108 pp. Paper. 0851692222.

Reflections on the historical and theological development of concern for the environment in the ecumenical movement by the former Director of Church and Society of the WCC (1984-1989).

EC198 Granberg-Michaelson, Wesley

Redeeming the Creation: The Rio Earth Summit; Challenges for the Churches. (Risk Book Series, 55). Geneva, SZ: WCC Publications, 1992. xiv, 90 pp. Paper. 2825410918.

A Programme Secretary of the WCC's unit on Justice, Peace, and Creation gives a popular presentation of ecology issues arising from the Earth Summit (Rio de Janeiro, 1992), and ecumenical documents on a Christian theology of creation and sustainable society.

EC199 Granberg-Michaelson, Wesley, ed.

Tending the Garden: Essays on the Gospel and the Earth. Grand Rapids, MIU: Eerdmans, 1987. viii, 150 pp. Paper. 0802802303.

Eight short essays plus poetry on the relationship of God, humanity, and all creation; with focus on the churches' role in healing the earth.

EC200 Hall, Douglas John

Imaging God: Dominion as Stewardship. (Library of Christian Stewardship). Grand Rapids, MIU: Eerdmans; New York, NYU: Friendship Press, 1986. viii, 248 pp. Paper. 0802802443 (E), 037700166X (F).

In this his third book on mission and stewardship commissioned by the NCCUSA's Commission on Stewardship, McGill University's Professor of Christian Theology focuses on the implications of belief that human beings are created in the image of God (*imago Dei*).

EC201 Hallman, David G., ed.

Ecotheology: Voices from South and North. Geneva, SZ: WCC Publications; Maryknoll, NYU: Orbis Books, 1994. ix, 316 pp. Paper. 2825411310 (SZ), 0883449935 (US).

Twenty-six essays, by scholars and church leaders on six continents, on the biblical witness, theological challenges, insights from ecofeminism, insights from indigenous people, and ethical implications.

EC202 Hessel, Dieter T., ed.

Theology for Earth Community: A Field Guide. (Ecology and Justice Series). Maryknoll, NYU: Orbis Books, 1996. xii, 292 pp. Paper. 1570750521.

A collection of original essays assessing current resources on religion, ethics, and environmental challenges.

EC203 Jegen, Mary Evelyn, and Bruno V. Manno, eds.

The Earth Is the Lord's: Essays on Stewardship. New York, NYU: Paulist Press, 1978. ix, 215 pp. 0809120674.

Fifteen essays relating the Christian concept of stewardship to contemporary economic issues; originally presented at a seminar on "Stewardship: A Christian Perspective on Ownership and Use of Essential Resources" at the University of Dayton (Ohio) in 1976.

EC204 Limouris, Gennadios, ed.

Justice, Peace and the Integrity of Creation: Insights from Orthodoxy. Geneva, SZ: WCC, 1990. xiii, 126 pp. Paper. 2825409790.

A collection of the papers presented at two Orthodox consultations (Sofia, Bulgaria, 1987, and Minsk, USSR, 1989) celebrating a sacramental approach to creation, and providing theological rationale for a conscious commitment on the part of Christians to justice, peace, and the integrity of creation.

EC—MISSIONS AND ECONOMIC LIFE

EC205 McDaniel, Jay B.

With Roots and Wings: Christianity in an Age of Ecology and Dialogue. (Ecology and Justice). Maryknoll, NYU: Orbis Books, 1995. viii, 243 pp. Paper. 1570750017.

The Professor of Religion at Hendrix College in Arkansas presents an ecotheology which is both grounded in a Christian vision and appreciative of the spirituality of other faith traditions.

EC206 McDonagh, Sean

The Greening of the Church. Maryknoll, NYU: Orbis Books; London, ENK: Chapman, 1990. x, 227 pp. Paper. 0883446944 (O), 0225665867 (C).

An introduction to the global environmental crisis, with a biblical theology of creation and an analysis of responses by the Catholic Church, with special reference to the Philippines.

EC207 McDonagh, Sean

Passion for the Earth. (Ecology and Justice Series). Maryknoll, NYU: Orbis Books, 1994. viii, 164 pp. Paper. 1570750211.

An Irish Columban missionary who worked in the Philippines analyzes root causes of the planet's ecological devastation and suggests concrete paths to sustainable development and ecojustice.

EC208 Nalunnakkal, George Mathew

Green Liberation: Towards an Integral Ecotheology. Delhi, II: ISPCK/NCCI, 1999. xxiv, 303 pp. Paper. 8172145137.

Centered around the struggles of Dalits, tribals, fisherfolk, and women for ecojustice, the author takes Indian Christian theology toward a postmodern phase in a pioneering attempt to develop a green version of liberation theology.

EC209 Nehring, Andreas, ed.

Ecology: A Theological Response. Madras, II: Gurukul Institute, 1994. x, 344 pp. Paper. No ISBN.

Papers from the First Summer Institute in 1993 at Gurukul Lutheran Theological College, Madras, India, on the ecological crisis, the Adivasi and ecology, women and ecology, ecology and development, and theological responses.

EC210 Pitcher, Alvin

Listen to the Crying of the Earth: Cultivating Creation Communities. Cleveland, OHU: Pilgrim Press, 1993. x, 157 pp. Paper. 0829809619.

A call for the formation of "creation communities" based not only on listening to the earth, but also on listening to God; by the Professor Emeritus of Ethics and Society at the Divinity School, University of Chicago.

EC211 Rasmussen, Larry L.

Earth Community, Earth Ethics. (Ecology and Justice Series). Maryknoll, NYU: Orbis Books, 1996. xvi, 366 pp. 1570750866.

A comprehensive social analysis, theology, and ethic for creating a sustainable community by the Reinhold Niebuhr Professor of Social Ethics at Union Theological Seminary, who serves as Co-Moderator of the WCC's Commission on Justice, Peace, and the Integrity of Creation.

EC212 *Renewing the Face of the Earth: A Resource for Parishes*

Washington, DCU: USCC, 1994. 51 pp. Paper. 1555867669.

Resources for use by Roman Catholic parishes in the United States as part of a special three-year program on environmental justice.

EC213 Roberts, W. Dayton

Patching God's Garment: Environment and Mission in the 21st Century. Monrovia, CAU: MARC/World Vision, 1994. v, 168 pp. Paper. 0912552859.

A primer by mission specialists on issues of ecology and the deterioration of the global environment, with a biblical ecotheology and proposals for creative missional responses by the churches.

EC214 Rongsen, M.

Development and Ecology. Delhi, II: ISPCK, 1999. xi, 68 pp. Paper. 817214489X.

The dangers in models of modern development that uproot people from traditional cultural roots, destroy forests, dry up rivers, and pollute air and water; the author, a pastor, calls for a balance between ecology and people-centered development.

EC215 Ruether, Rosemary Radford, ed.

Women Healing Earth: Third World Women on Ecology, Feminism, and Religion. (Ecology and Justice Series). Maryknoll, NYU: Orbis Books, 1996. vi, 186 pp. Paper. 1570750572.

Fifteen case studies by women in Latin America, Asia, and Africa on the intersections of religion, ecology, and feminism in their respective countries.

EC216 *The Greening of Faith*

Manila, PH: NCCP, 1992. 191 pp. Paper. 9718548645.

A special edition on ecotheology of *Tugon* (vol. 12, no. 2), the ecumenical journal of the NCCP, with articles on the churches and environmental issues in Asia.

EC217 World Convocation on Justice, Peace, and the Integrity of Creation (Seoul, Korea, 1990)

Now Is the Time: Final Document & Other Texts. Geneva, SZ: WCC, 1990. 60 pp. Paper. No ISBN.

Report and documents from the WCC-sponsored World Convocation on Justice, Peace and the Integrity of Creation, Seoul, Korea, 5-12 March 1990.

EC218 Wright, Nancy G., and Donald Kill

Ecological Healing: A Christian Vision. Maryknoll, NYU: Orbis Books, 1993. ix, 161 pp. Paper. 0883449323.

An introductory text on ecology relating the worldwide, ecumenical experience of the Coordination in Development (CODEL) network to environmental insights from the world's religious traditions.

Economic Policies: General

See also TH258, ME31, SO37, EC8, EC25-EC26, EC37, AF1051, AM807, AM964, AS121, and EU227.

EC219 Arruda, Marcos, ed.

Ecumenism and a New World Order: The Failure of the 1970's and the Challenges of the 1980's. (An Ecumenical Approach to Economics, 1). Geneva, SZ: WCC, 1985. 97 pp. Paper. 2825406406.

Reports of two ecumenical consultations (Zürich, Switzerland, 5-10 June 1978, and Oaxtepec, Mexico, 18-21 April 1979) disclosing ecumenical thought on the development debate and the New International Economic Order (NIEO).

EC220 *Christian Faith and the World Economy Today: A Study Document from the World Council of Churches*
Geneva, SZ: WCC Publications, 1992. vii, 59 pp. Paper. 2825411000.

Signposts for Christian evaluation of the world economy, the values behind economic decision making, and the alternatives for Christian action to promote economic justice; prepared with helps for group discussion.

EC221 Dickinson, Richard D. N.
Poor, Yet Making Many Rich: The Poor as Agents of Creative Justice. Geneva, SZ: WCC, 1983. xi, 219 pp. Paper. 2825407321.

A review of how the WCC's thinking on development, liberation, and global justice continued to evolve between the Nairobi (1975) and Vancouver (1983) assemblies.

EC222 Dickinson, Richard D. N.
To Set at Liberty the Oppressed: Towards an Understanding of Christian Responsibilities of Development/Liberation. (CCPD Development Studies). Geneva, SZ: WCC, CCPD, 1975. x, 193 pp. Paper. 2825404985.

A preparatory volume for the Fifth Assembly of the WCC (Nairobi, Kenya, 1975) summarizing the world development debate and the Christian churches' responses since 1968, with comments by key leaders from the Two-Thirds World.

EC223 Drimmelen, Rob van
Faith in a Global Economy: A Primer for Christians. (Risk Book Series, 81). Geneva, SZ: WCC Publications, 1998. xiv, 156 pp. Paper. 2825412546.

An introduction to global economic issues for Christians desiring that their churches relate creatively to these issues.

EC224 Elliott, Charles
Inflation and the Compromised Church. Belfast, IE: Christian Journals, 1975. 148 pp. Paper. 090430213X.

A critical analysis of the effects and sources of inflation in developing countries.

EC225 Illich, Ivan D.
Tools for Conviviality. (World Perspectives, 47). New York, NYU: Harper & Row, 1973. xxv, 110 pp. 0060121386.

Incisive analysis of the usually unforseen social aspects of industrial and economic development.

EC226 Lindqvist, Martti
Economic Growth and the Quality of Life: An Analysis of the Debate within the World Council of Churches, 1966-1974. (Missiologian ja Ekumeniikan Seuran julkaisuja, 27). Helsinki, FI: Finnish Society for Missiology and Ecumenics, 1975. 227 pp. 951952052X.

A detailed analysis by the Finnish missiologist on the debate within the WCC on the two topics.

EC227 Martin-Schramm, James B.
Population Perils and the Churches' Response. (Risk Book Series, 76). Geneva, SZ: WCC Publications, 1997. xxiii, 56 pp. Paper. 2825412260.

A survey of the various "perils" of the population question, of responses already being made in the ecumenical family, and of theological resources and ethical guidelines.

EC228 Mensen, Bernhard, ed.
Die Zukunft der Menschheit als Gegenwartsaufgabe. (Vortragsreihe/Akademie Völker und Kulturen, 14). Nettetal, GW: Steyler Verlag, 1991. 107 pp. Paper. 3805002890.

Plans for the future in terms of nourishment, land reform, energy, political differences, migration, and population growth, are addressed by six authors.

EC229 Mulholland, Catherine, comp.
Ecumenical Reflections on Political Economy. Geneva, SZ: WCC, 1988. viii, 75 pp. Paper. 2825409308.

A summary of ten years of work by AGEM (the Advisory Group on Economic Matters, related to the WCC's Commission on the Churches' Participation in Development).

EC230 Munby, Denys Lawrence, ed.
Le développement économique dans une perspective mondiale. (Église et société, 3). Geneva, SZ: Éditions Labor et Fides, 1966. 272 pp. No ISBN.

French translation.

EC231 Munby, Denys Lawrence, ed.
Economic Growth in World Perspective. New York, NYU: Association Press; London, ENK: SCM Press, 1966. 380 pp. No ISBN.

The third of four study books prepared for the WCC Conference on Church and Society (Geneva, 1966) focusing on economic growth and welfare, technology and environmental control, the needs of developing countries, and the Christian ethical response to these issues.

EC232 Neal, Marie Augusta
A Socio-Theology of Letting Go: The Role of a First World Facing Third World Peoples. New York, NYU: Paulist Press, 1977. vii, 118 pp. Paper. 0809120127.

An analysis of that American civil religion unwittingly but nonetheless dangerously imbibed by many Western missionaries working among the world's poor.

EC233 Rumscheidt, Barbara
No Room for Grace: Pastoral Theology and Dehumanization in the Global Economy. Grand Rapids, MIU: Eerdmans, 1998. xii, 158 pp. Paper. 0802845479.

Critical faith development for the 21st century understood as an addressing of global issues of unfettered capitalism, dehumanization, and imperial Western cultures, and a listening to voices from the Two-Thirds World interpreting conscientization as re-evangelization.

EC234 *Sacrifice and Humane Economic Life*
(Occasional Study Pamphlet, 7). Geneva, SZ: WCC, CCPD, 1991. 80 pp. Paper. No ISBN.

Four papers by Latin American theological educators (Jorge Pixley, Julio de Santa Ana, and Franz J. Hinkelammert) relating the biblical theme of sacrifice to the contemporary economic policies in Latin America.

EC235 *Solidarity with the Poor: For Justice, Peace, and the Integrity of Creation (I)*
(CCPD Documents—Justice and Development, 9). Geneva, SZ: WCC, 1987. 64 pp. Paper. No ISBN.

Papers of a jointly sponsored consultation by the CCPD/WCC and the Federation of Evangelical Churches in Hirschluch, near Storkow/GDR, 21-28 May 1986; emphasis of encouraging churches, especially in the north, to identify with the poor.

EC236 WCC Commission on the Churches' Participation in Development
Dominación y Dependencia: Las iglesias y los cristianos en el contexto de las relaciones de dominación y dependencia. Translated by Hugo Assmann et al. Buenos Aires, AG: Editorial Tierra Nueva, 1975. 177 pp. Paper. No ISBN.

Spanish translation.

EC—MISSIONS AND ECONOMIC LIFE

EC237 WCC, Commission on the Churches' Participation in Development
To Break the Chains of Oppression: Results of an Ecumenical Study Process on Domination and Dependence. (CCPD Development Studies, 4). Geneva, SZ: WCC, 1975. viii, 113 pp. Paper. 2825405094.

Early papers from the WCC's CCPD calling churches and Christians to become active in liberating service for the victims of injustice and oppression.

Development Issues

See also HI482, TH124, TH270, ME37, ME212, CR973, SO405, SO592, EC1, EC11-EC13, EC55, EC104, EC122, EC129, EC160, EC214, EC221-EC222, EC372, EC384, PO42, SP81, SP158-SP160, AF148, AF176, AF179, AF399, AF464, AF527, AF821, AF971-AF972, AM335, AM542, AM672, AS328, AS924, AS959, AS976, AS1061, AS1110, AS1287, AS1330, EU202, EU204-EU205, and OC184.

EC238 Aaker, Jerry
Partners with the Poor: An Emerging Approach to Relief and Development. New York, NYU: Friendship Press, 1993. xiii, 158 pp. Paper. 0377002526.

An argument that genuine social transformation requires a lasting partnership, affirming that both the poor and the rich have resources, without which sustainable economic development is not possible; with reflections on church relief and development programs witnessed by the author in Vietnam, Peru, and Nicaragua as a representative of LWF, Heifer Project International, and CWS.

EC239 Abgasiere, Joseph Therese, and Boniface K. Zabajungu, eds.
Church Contribution to Integral Development. (African Theology in Progress, 2; Spearhead Series, 108-109). Eldoret, KE: Gaba Publications, 1989. ix, 262 pp. Paper. 9966836012.

A collection of twenty-four essays by Ugandan church leaders on church and society issues in their country, including development, education, health care, poverty, and church-state relations.

EC240 Achutegui, Pedro S. de
Mission and Development: Ecumenical Conversations. (Logos 5: Cardinal Bea Studies, I). Manila, PH: Loyola House of Studies, Ateneo de Manila University, 1970. 179 pp. No ISBN.

Papers from two 1970 symposia on "Development and the Churches" and "Mission of the Church to the Third World."

EC241 Adeney, Miriam
God's Foreign Policy. Grand Rapids, MIU: Eerdmans, 1984. 140 pp. Paper. 0802819680.

An examination of the weaknesses of current programs of relief and development, with recommendations to Christians interested in development without dehumanization, power aggrandizement, and other forms of exploitation.

EC242 Alexander, Robert Jackson
A New Development Strategy. Maryknoll, NYU: Orbis Books, 1976. x, 169 pp. 0883443287.

An analysis of economic development strategies in the 1970s with special reference to Latin America.

EC243 Andelson, Robert V., and James M. Dawsey, eds.
From Wasteland to Promised Land: Liberation Theology for a Post-Marxist World. Maryknoll, NYU: Orbis Books; London, ENK: Shepheard-Walwyn, 1992. xiv, 146 pp. 088344786X (hdbk), 0883447932 (pbk).

A critical evaluation of present systems of land tenure from a biblical and liberationist perspective, reviving the 19th-century perspective of Henry George, that justice requires sharing the wealth that the community creates from the land.

EC244 Boyd, Ben
Getting It There: A Logistics Handbook for Relief and Development. Monrovia, CAU: World Vision, 1987. 112 pp. Paper. 091255259X.

A practical guide to all aspects of relief and development logistics, including organization, coordination, procurement, transportation, materials management, maintenance, and personnel.

EC245 Bradshaw, Bruce, ed.
Bridging the Gap: Evangelism, Development and Shalom. (Innovations in Mission). Monrovia, CAU: MARC, 1993. vi, 183 pp. Paper. 0912552840.

Basic elements of a biblical view of holistic ministry (creation, redemption, and shalom), with examples from different countries of how the tension between evangelism and development is being resolved.

EC246 Byrne, Tony
The Church and the Development Dilemma. (Spearhead Series, 50). Eldoret, KE: Gaba Publications, 1977. 46 pp. Paper. No ISBN.

A study reflecting Christian motivation for development in African churches; discussing approaches, problems, politics, religious vocation, and education.

EC247 Byrne, Tony
Integral Development: Development of the Whole Person. Ndola, ZA: Mission Press, 1983. v, 108 pp. Paper. No ISBN.

A handbook on development for Christian workers (clergy and lay) to help in spiritual formation and practical training; based on existing Roman Catholic programs in Africa.

EC248 Câmara, Hélder
The Church and Colonialism: The Betrayal of the Third World. Denville, NJU: Dimension Books, 1969. vi, 181 pp. No ISBN.

In this work the archbishop of Olinda and Recife in northeast Brazil speaks out prophetically against the injustice of underdevelopment in the Third World, offers a Christian view of development, and suggests ways of genuine development.

EC249 *CCPD Perspectives*
(CCPD Documents: Justice and Development, 2). Geneva, SZ: WCC, CCPD, 1984. 59 pp. Paper. No ISBN.

An edition of texts on justice and service approved by the Central Committee, July 1984, followed by a description of the CCPD's activities.

EC250 Chakiath, Thomas
Value Clarification and Conscientization in Socio-Economic Development: The Role of the Church. (Pontifical Institute Publications, 15). Alwaye, II: Pontifical Institute of Theology and Philosophy, 1974. xxiii, 219 pp. No ISBN.

A scholarly introduction to issues in socioeconomic development, comparing "ideas" on development: materialistic, humanistic, and Christian.

EC251 Christian Conference of Asia
Report of an Asian Ecumenical Consultation on Development, Priorities and Guidelines. Singapore, SI: CCA, 1974. 97 pp. No ISBN.
Report of an important church consultation during the United Nation's Decade of Development.

EC252 Consultation on Ecumenical Assistance to Development Projects (Montreux, Switzerland, 26-31 January 1970)
Fetters of Injustice: Report ... Edited by Pamela H. Gruber. Geneva, SZ: WCC, 1970. 164 pp. Paper. 2825400602.
A Christian response to structural evil as it impedes development.

EC253 Consultation on Theology and Development, Cartigny, Switzerland,1969
In Search of a Theology of Development: Papers from a Consultation ... Geneva, SZ: SODEPAX, 1970. ii, 221 pp. Paper. No ISBN.
Papers from a Consultation on Theology and Development (Cartigny, Switzerland, Nov. 1969) sponsored by SODEPAX.

EC254 Crewe, Emma, and Elizabeth Harrison
Whose Development?: An Ethnography of Aid. London, ENK: Zed Books, 1998. x, 214 pp. 1856496058 (hdbk), 1856496066 (pbk).
The authors build upon their experiences in aid projects in Africa and Asia to examine flawed notions in the minds of developers about progress, gender, technology, partnership, motivation, culture, race, and power.

EC255 Crowley, Jerry
Go to the People: An African Experience in Development Education. London, ENK: CAFOD, 1988. ii, 70 pp. Paper. No ISBN.
A brief introduction to the Catholic Development Education Program in Kenya (1974-1984)—its evolution, program, and effects; originally published by Gaba Publications, Eldoret, Kenya (1985).

EC256 Dickinson, Richard D. N.
Cordel y Nivel: las iglesias y el desarrollo. Geneva, SZ: WCC, 1968. 114 pp. No ISBN.
Spanish translation.

EC257 Dickinson, Richard D. N.
Line and Plummet: The Churches and Development. Geneva, SZ: WCC, 1968. 112 pp. No ISBN.
A study of ways in which churches can address social problems rooted in economic underdevelopment.

EC258 Dickinson, Richard D. N.
La règle et le niveau: les Églises et le développement socio-économique dans le tiers monde. Geneva, SZ: WCC, 1968. 120 pp. No ISBN.
French translation.

EC259 Dickinson, Richard D. N.
Tiempos de Liberación: Hacia una comprensión de las responsabilidades cristianas para el desarrollo/liberación. Buenos Aires, AG: Editorial Tierra Nueva, 1976. 269 pp. Paper. No ISBN.
Spanish translation.

EC260 Doppelfeld, Basilius
In der Mitte—der Mensch: Wie Afrika Entwicklung versteht. (Münsterschwarzacher Studien, 43). Münsterschwarzach, GW: Vier-Türme-Verlag, 1994. 400 pp. 3878685025.

A critical analysis of understandings of development in Africa from statesmen to economists to African theologians, by a Benedictine monk with many years of experience in East African mission parishes.

EC261 Dunne, George Harold
The Right to Development. New York, NYU: Paulist Press, 1974. 141 pp. Paper. 0809118378.
A brief moral argument in support of the Third World's right to development.

EC262 Elliott, Charles
Comfortable Compassion?: Poverty, Power and the Church. London, ENK: Hodder & Stoughton; New York, NYU: Paulist Press, 1987. 194 pp. Paper. 0340407379 (H), 0809129361 (P).
An analysis of the past thirty years of church thinking on development issues by the noted Professor of Development Studies at the University of Bristol (UK) and former Director of Christian Aid.

EC263 Elliott, Charles
The Development Debate. New York, NYU: Friendship Press; London, ENK: SCM Press, 1971. 128 pp. Paper. 0377820618 (US), 0334002974 (UK).
A non-technical introduction to five perspectives on economic development, and theological approaches to development by the Assistant Secretary of SODEPAX.

EC264 Ellison, Marvin Mahan
The Center Cannot Hold: The Search for a Global Economy of Justice. Washington, DCU: University Press of America, 1983. xliii, 286 pp. Paper. 0819129631 (hdbk), 081912964X (pbk).
A scholarly analysis and evaluation of the "great economic debate" between Christian developmentalists and liberationists over issues of economic development in the Third World, by an ethics instructor at Bangor Theological Seminary, Bangor, Maine.

EC265 Elliston, Edgar J., ed.
Christian Relief and Development: Developing Workers for Effective Ministry. Dallas, TXU: Word Publishing, 1989. xiv, 351 pp. Paper. 084993155X.
A collection of nineteen essays which serve as an introduction to evangelical thinking about relief and development from a broad range of disciplines (sociology, history, ethics, economics, theology, and anthropology); designed to orient Christians who are working/dealing with relief and development issues.

EC266 Fordham-Rural Life Socioeconomic Conference (1958, Maryknoll Seminary)
The Missionary's Role in Socio-Economic Betterment. Edited by John J. Considine. New York, NYU: Newman Press, 1960. xi, 330 pp. No ISBN.
Bearing the *nihil obstat* of the then *censor deputatus*, Edward F. Malone, and the *imprimatur* of the archbishop of New York, Francis Cardinal Spellman, this volume, with its extensive classified bibliography, may be said to represent the model of the pre-Vatican II Catholic missiological thinking on the subject of socio-economic development.

EC267 Fuller, Millard, and Diane Scott
No More Shacks!: The Daring Vision of Habitat for Humanity. Waco, TXU: Word Books, 1986. 220 pp. 0849906040 (hdbk), 0849930502 (pbk).
An exposition of Habitat for Humanity's vision that "All of God's people should have at least a simple, decent place to live."

EC268 Fuller, Millard, ed.

More Than Houses: How Habitat for Humanity Is Transforming Lives and Neighborhoods. Nashville, TNU: Word Publishing, 2000. xiv, 303 pp. Paper. 0849937620.

Stories of people who had no hope until they had a home; stories of communities bonding together around an ethic of hard work and mutual respect; and stories of denominational, political, and racial barriers falling with every swing of the hammer.

EC269 Goudzwaard, Bob, and Harry de Lange

Beyond Poverty and Affluence: Toward an Economy of Care with a Twelve-Step Program for Economic Recovery. Translated by Mark R. Vander Vennen. Grand Rapids, MIU: Eerdmans; Geneva, SZ: WCC Publications, 1995. x, 165 pp. Paper. 0802808271 (US), 2825411388 (SZ).

Two Dutch economists active in church and secular agencies for development call for bold new economic practices in this English translation by Mark R. Vander Vennen of *Genoeg van te veel, genoeg van te weinig.*

EC270 Goulet, Denis

Incentives for Development: The Key to Equity. New York, NYU: New Horizons Press, 1989. xi, 196 pp. Paper. 0945257058 (hdbk), 0945257031 (pbk).

A closely reasoned argument, by the noted development economist and ethicist, that incentive systems can be effective policy instruments to achieve equitable development.

EC271 Goulet, Denis

A New Moral Order: Studies in Development Ethics and Liberation Theology. Maryknoll, NYU: Orbis Books, 1974. xiv, 142 pp. Paper. 0883443309.

Probing essays on the ethics of development, by a specialist on value conflict in technology transfers who argues that a radical transformation of the class society, rather than a liberal reformism, is required for justice in Latin America.

EC272 Goulet, Denis, and Michael Hudson

The Myth of Aid: The Hidden Agenda of the Development Reports. (Prepared by the Center for the Study of Development and Social Change). New York, NYU: IDOC-North America; Maryknoll, NYU: Orbis Books, 1971. 143 pp. No ISBN.

An exposé of the sad truth behind much of what Americans label "aid."

EC273 Hancock, Robert Lincoln, ed.

The Ministry of Development in Evangelical Perspective: A Symposium on the Social and Spiritual Mandate. South Pasadena, CAU: William Carey Library, 1979. viii, 109 pp. Paper. 087808164X.

Articles presented at a November 1977 symposium in Colorado Springs, sponsored by Development Assistance Services and convened by Carl F. H. Henry.

EC274 Hennes, Gerhard G.

Alone, You Get Nowhere: An Attempt at Assessing the Involvement of Personnel in the Sudan Relief and Rehabilitation Programs, 1972-75. Geneva, SZ: WCC, 1977. viii, 113 pp. Paper. 2825405361.

An assessment of the work of the Sudan Relief and Rehabilitation Programme from 1972-1975, with a discerning and sober analysis of motivations, problems, opportunities, roles, and of lessons still to be learned.

EC275 Hope, Anne, and Sally Timmel

Training for Transformation: A Handbook for Community Workers. Gweru, RH: Mambo Press, 1984. 3 vols. Paper. 0869222562 (vol. 1), 0869222554 (vol. 2), 0869222619 (vol. 3).

Using the approach of Paulo Freire, this basic and comprehensive course applying the Christian concept of transformation for the development of self-reliant creative communities, is designed for use by basic Christian community leaders, and adult education, community development, trade union, and social workers (vol. 1: 147 pp.; vol. 2: 131 pp.; vol. 3: 182 pp.).

EC276 Jameson, Kenneth P., and Charles K. Wilber, eds.

Religious Values and Development. (*World Development* 8,7/8). Oxford, ENK: Pergamon Press, 1981. 148 pp. 0080261078.

A reprint of articles from a special issue of the journal *World Development* (vol. 8, 1980) on the relationship between religion and development.

EC277 Klose, Dietmar

Kirchliche entwicklungsarbeit als Lernprozess der weltkirche: Dialog der Kirchen der Ersten und Dritten Welt als dynamische struktur in der Weltkirche. (Studien zur Praktischen Theologie, 30). Zürich, SZ: Benziger, 1984. 478 pp. Paper. 354521530X.

Having examined the historical experience of missions, this dissertation proceeds to demonstrate principles of church development work and some approaches and possibilities of dialogue between the local churches of the First World and Third World.

EC278 *Land is Our Life*

(PCR Information, 25). Geneva, SZ: WCC, PCR, 1989. 99 pp. Paper. No ISBN.

Three case studies, from Brazil, Australia, and Canada, of the struggle of indigenous peoples for their land rights, and of the churches' participation in that struggle.

EC279 Land, Philip, ed.

Theology Meets Progress: Human Implications of Development. (Studia Socialia). Rome, IT: Gregorian University Press, 1971. xv, 346 pp. No ISBN.

Eight essays by Jesuit scholars seeking a new methodology for analysis of development issues and a new theology of development.

EC280 Laurentin, René

Développement et salut. Paris, FR: Éditions du Seuil, 1969. 334 pp. No ISBN.

A detailed answer by a Catholic theologian to the question, "Does development have any significance in relation to salvation as proclaimed by Christ?" with special reference to Latin America.

EC281 Laurentin, René

Liberation, Development, and Salvation. Translated by Charles Underhill Quinn. Maryknoll, NYU: Orbis Books, 1972. xvii, 238 pp. No ISBN.

English translation.

EC—MISSIONS AND
ECONOMIC LIFE

EC282 Lean, Mary
Bread, Bricks, and Belief: Communities in Charge of Their Future. (Books for a World That Works). West Hartford, CTU: Kumarian Press, 1995. ix, 182 pp. Paper. 1565490460.

A journalist's account of how religious ethics and spirituality have made a significant impact on community development among the poor in postindustrial cities and Third World villages.

EC283 Lissner, Jørgen
The Politics of Altruism: A Study of the Political Behaviour of Voluntary Development Agencies. Geneva, SZ: LWF, 1977. 340 pp. No ISBN.

A critical assessment of the assumptions and behavior of Western development agencies by the General Secretary of Danchurchaid.

EC284 Lovell, George
The Church and Community Development: An Introduction. Middlesex, ENK: Grail Publications; London, ENK: Chester House Publications, 1972. xvi, 84 pp. Paper. 0901829080 (G), 0715000519 (C).

A nontechnical introduction to practical, theoretical, and theological aspects of the church in community development, based on the author's training in community development and his ministry experience in South London.

EC285 May, Roy H.
Los Pobres de la Tierra: Hacia una pastoral de la tierra. (Colección-Ecología-Teología). San José, CR: DEI, 1986. xvi, 133 pp. Paper. 9977904251.

Research into the issue of land in Latin America and the history and practice of the churches, with suggestions for a pastoral theology of the land.

EC286 May, Roy H.
The Poor of the Land: A Christian Case for Land Reform. Maryknoll, NYU: Orbis Books, 1991. xv, 139 pp. Paper. 0883447290.

English translation and revision of *Los pobres de la tierra* (1986).

EC287 May, Roy H.
Tierra: ¿Herencia o Mercancia?: Justicia, paz e integridad de la creación. (Colección ecología-teología). San José, CR: DEI, 1993. 94 pp. Paper. 9977830711.

A study book on land issues for Latin American Christians.

EC288 McGinnis, James B.
Bread and Justice: Toward a New International Economic Order. New York, NYU: Paulist Press, 1979. 358 pp. Paper. 0809195372.

A primer for Christians concerned about hunger and justice, with helps for understanding, evaluating, and acting on global economic issues, particularly the New International Economic Order (NIEO).

EC289 Nürnberger, Klaus
Die Relevanz des Wortes im Entwicklungsprozess: Eine systematisch-theologische Besinnung zum Verhältnis zwischen Theologie und Entwicklungstheorie. (Europäische Hochschulschriften, 23: Theologie, 200). Frankfurt am Main, GW: Lang, 1982. 440 pp. 3820472665.

Scholarly examination by a theologian of socio-economic models for developing countries in global perspective, addressing the theological tension between truth and reality, piety, and social engagement.

EC290 Olasky, Marvin, Herbert Schlossberg, Berthoud Pierre, and Clark H. Pinnock, eds.
Freedom, Justice, and Hope: Toward a Strategy for the Poor and the Oppressed. Westchester, ILU: Crossway Books, 1988. 171 pp. Paper. 0891074783.

A presentation of biblical and economic principles for effective work in relief and development, with practical guidelines, including the "Villars Statement on Relief and Development" (1987) by forty evangelical Christians.

EC291 Oommen, M. A., ed.
Development: Perspectives and Problems. Madras, II: CLS, 1973. vii, 120 pp. Paper. No ISBN.

Nine essays on development by scholars representing a variety of disciplinary perspectives.

EC292 Perkins, Harvey L., ed.
Guidelines for Development. Toa Payoh, SI: CCA, 1980. 95 pp. Paper. No ISBN.

The results of a 1979 workshop sponsored by the CCA which gives guidelines for defining development, motivating communities, analyzing social structures, and identifying the churches' role in the development process.

EC293 Perkins, Harvey L.
Roots for Vision: Reflections on the Gospel and the Churches' Task in Re-Peopling the De-Peopled. Singapore, SI: CCA, 1986. xxxix, 290 pp. Paper. 9971948389.

The distillation of creative thinking (biblical theology, sociocultural, and strategic) on the churches' mission to be with the poor and in the struggles for justice, peace, and freedom for all the human family; derived from five years (1976-1980) of workshops on development, sponsored by the CCA.

EC294 Poole, Richard, ed.
The Camel Strayed: An Aid Worker's View of Islam in the Modern World. Durham: Pentland Press, 1999. xiv, 203 pp. 185821677X.

This account of a development worker's encounter with the Sudanese people portrays them as deeply caring, tolerant, and unworthy of the hostility heaped upon them by the world media; includes a plea for new levels of cultural awareness and spirituality as the lasting solution to the contemporary worldwide predicament.

EC295 Quarles van Ufford, Philip, and J. M. Schoffeleers, eds.
Religion and Development: Towards an Integrated Approach. Amsterdam, NE: Free University Press, 1988. vii,293 pp. Paper. 9062566731.

Fourteen varied scholarly essays combined as case studies showing that religious anthropology and development studies are complementary disciplines.

EC296 Rebera, Ranjini, ed.
We Cannot Dream Alone: A Story of Women in Development. Geneva, SZ: WCC Publications, 1990. xiii, 125 pp. Paper. 2825409677.

The story of the Programme on Women and Rural Development of the WCC, 1974-1988, told through the experiences and evaluations by participants in some of the 230 projects.

EC297 Rennstich, Karl

Mission und wirtschaftliche Entwicklung: Biblische Theologie des Kulturwandels und christliche Ethik. (Gesellschaft und Theologie: Systematische Beiträge, 25). Munich, GW: Kaiser; Mainz, GW: Grünewald Verlag, 1978. 343 pp. Paper. 3459011815 (K), 3786706999 (G).

A dissertation (University of Basel) on understanding mission in the pietistic sense as a task encompassing all spheres of life—based on twelve years of scientific study and a report of development work in Malaysia and Singapore.

EC298 Roche, Douglas J.

Justice and Charity: A New Global Ethic for Canada. Toronto, ONC: McClelland & Stewart, 1976. 123 pp. 0771076800.

A study guide, prepared for use by Canadian Christians of six denominations, designed to present the problems of development to the person in the street, indicating potentials for response both by national governments and by nongovernment agencies including churches.

EC299 Rose, Stephen C., and Peter Paul van Lelyveld, eds.

The Development Apocalypse [or] *Will International Injustice Kill the Ecumenical Movement?* (*Risk* 3, nos. 1 and 2). New York, NYU: WCC, Youth Department; New York, NYU: WCCE, 1967. 152 pp. Paper. No ISBN.

A special edition of *Risk* published by the Youth Department of the WCC to awaken interest in global development issues and the churches' response.

EC300 Santa Ana, Julio de, ed.

Sustainability and Globalization. Geneva, SZ: WCC Publications, 1998. vii, 143 pp. Paper. 2825412651.

Biblical, biological, economic, and theological studies from diverse perspectives on the tensions between globalization and sustainability; first presented at the W.A. Visser't Hooft Consultations at the Ecumenical Institute of the WCC in Bossey, Switzerland.

EC301 Schwarz, John C.

Global Population from a Catholic Perspective. Mystic, CTU: Twenty-Third Publications, 1998. vi, 256 pp. Paper. 0896229327.

A survey of the RCC's stands on population issues in the light of the current global challenge, including official statements, its role in the United Nations, new emphases in moral theology, and the impact of Vatican II.

EC302 Shabecoff, Alice

Rebuilding Our Communities: How Churches Can Provide, Support, and Finance Quality Housing for Low-Income Families. Monrovia, CAU: World Vision, 1992. 280 pp. Paper. No ISBN.

Models and resources for church-sponsored groups interested in providing housing for low income families of the United States.

EC303 Sider, Ronald J., ed.

Evangelicals and Development: Toward a Theology of Social Change. Philadelphia, PAU: Westminster Press, 1982. 123 pp. Paper. 0664244459.

Four papers and the summary statement of intent from the Consultation on the Theology of Development (High Leigh, England, 10-14 March 1980), sponsored by the Unit on Ethics of the Theological Commission of the WEF.

EC304 SODEPAX

Partnership or Privilege?: An Ecumenical Reaction to the Second Development Decade. Geneva, SZ: SODEPAX, 1970. 118 pp. No ISBN.

Papers from an international colloquium held by SODEPAX to critique the preparatory papers for the second United Nations Development Decade, with the UNO strategy paper as an appendix.

EC305 Taylor, Michael

Good for the Poor: Christian Ethics and World Development. (Ethics: Our Choices). London, ENK: Mowbray, 1990. xi, 114 pp. Paper. 0264671902.

A primer for Christians on the problems of the Third World, development issues, and Christian response by the Director of Christian Aid.

EC306 Thimme, Hans, ed.

Im Dienst für Entwicklung und Frieden: In memoriam Bischof Heinrich Tenhumberg. (Entwicklung und Frieden: Dokumente, Berichte, Meinungen, 12). Munich, GW: Kaiser; Mainz, GW: Grünewald Verlag, 1982. 216 pp. Paper. 345901329X (K), 3786708525 (G).

Published in honour of the Catholic bishop of Münster who made an outstanding contribution to development and peace; the work includes papers and reports read at two study conferences, and various statements by the bishop himself.

EC307 *Training for Justice and Development*

(CCPD Reports and Background Papers, 3). Geneva, SZ: WCC, 1984. 66 pp. Paper. No ISBN.

The report of a workshop (Chiang Mai, Thailand, 3-9 June 1984), held in cooperation with Urban Rural Mission of the CCA, focusing on Asian experiences in training programs.

EC308 *Women, Work, and Economic Injustice*

(CCPD Documents—Justice and Development, 5). Geneva, SZ: WCC, 1985. 64 pp. Paper. No ISBN.

Fifteen essays expressing the economic plight of women, and injustices against women laborers on an international basis.

EC309 Wortham, Robert

Spatial Development and Religious Orientation in Kenya. (Distinguished Dissertations Series, 9). San Francisco, CAU: Mellen Research University Press, 1990. vii, 365 pp. Paper. 0773499547.

A scholarly application of spatial development theory to Kenya, with some considerations of religion as a factor in social and economic development.

Rural Development

See also EC19, EC330, CH187-CH188, AF759, AF1045, AM248, AM742, AM1297-AM1298, AM1417, AM1446, AM1471-AM1474, AS965, AS1111, AS1372, and AS1427.

EC310 Abel, M., ed.

Integrated Rural Development. Madras, II: Manohar Printers, 1982. 187 pp. Paper. No ISBN.

A collection of papers presented at a workshop on integrated rural development (Madras, India, 18-20 September 1980), focusing on trying to understand the basic causes and remedies of rural poverty in India.

EC311 Alianza Evangélica Costarricense-Comité de Obra Rural, Segunda Asamblea Evangélica de Obra Rural, San Carlos, CR, octubre de 1963

Tierra y espíritu de América. None: Alianza Evangélica Costarricense, 1963. 145 pp. Paper. No ISBN.

A collection of the papers and conclusions of the assembly.

EC—MISSIONS AND ECONOMIC LIFE

EC312 Batchelor, Peter
People in Rural Development. Carlisle, ENK: Paternoster Press, 1993. xii, 228 pp. Paper. 0853645418.

Revised and enlarged edition of practical approaches to rural development, with seven African case studies drawn from the author's forty-years experience on that continent.

EC313 Cogswell, James A., ed.
The Church and the Rural Poor. Atlanta, GAU: John Knox Press, 1975. 107 pp. Paper. 0804207976.

A resource based on workshops on rural poverty and economic development held across the American South, by the Rural Economic Development Task Force of the Southeastern Jurisdiction of the UMC and the Task Force on World Hunger of the PCUSA.

EC314 Fountain, Daniel E., ed.
Let's Build Our Lives. Brunswick, GAU: MAP International, 1990. 229 pp. Paper. No ISBN.

A book in basic English, translated by the editor, written collaboratively by the Team for Evangelism and Development of the Church of Christ of Zaire.

EC315 Misereor
Damit die Hoffnung lebt ... : 20 Jahre Fastenaktion Misereor. Edited by Winfried Kurrath. Aachen, GW: Misereor-Vertriebsgesellschaft, 1978. 172 pp. Paper. No ISBN.

Five articles on the German relief organization Misereor.

EC316 Mulwa, Francis Wambua
Participation of the Poor in Rural Transformation: A Kenyan Case. (Spearhead Series, 95). Eldoret, KE: Gaba Publications, 1987. viii, 83 pp. Paper. No ISBN.

A short summary of research concerning the causes of rural poverty, the situation of rural poor in Kenya, and responses to the problem by both government and the churches.

EC317 Sartorius, Peter
Churches in Rural Development: Guidelines for Action. (CCPD Development Studies). Geneva, SZ: WCC, 1975. 155 pp. Paper. 2825405035.

A primer to assist members of churches and development groups in understanding the main problems of rural development and solutions needed; complete with models of effective action programs, bibliography, and useful addresses of international organizations which assist with rural development projects.

EC318 SODEPAX
Development Projects: Examples of Church Involvement in Eastern Africa. (Gaba Institute Pastoral Papers, 18). Kampala, UG: Gaba Publications, 1972. xii, 65 pp. Paper. No ISBN.

Roman Catholic involvements in local development projects.

EC319 *The Christian Rural Mission in the 1980's—A Call to Liberation and Development of Peoples*
New York, NYU: Agricultural Missions, 1979. 28 pp. Paper. No ISBN.

Papers from a consultation on "Rural Mission in the 1980's" (Jayuya, Puerto Rico, 16-19 April 1979), the culmination of a three-year study of future directions by Agricultural Missions, Inc.

Agricultural Development/Missions

See also EC127, EC327, AF705, AM938, AS694, AS998, and AS1170.

EC320 *Cooperatives: An Ecumenical Perspective*
(*Tugon*, XII: 3). Manila, PH: NCCP, 1992. 84 pp. Paper. 9718548726.

A policy paper on cooperatives by the NNCCP.

EC321 Freudenberger, C. Dean
Global Dust Bowl: Can We Stop the Destruction of the Land Before It's Too Late? Minneapolis, MNU: Augsburg Fortress, 1990. 126 pp. Paper. 0806624485.

A critical examination of the crisis in world agriculture including promising alternatives for the future; by a trained agronomist and social ethicist.

EC322 Hessel, Dieter T., ed.
The Agricultural Mission of Churches and Land-Grant Universities: A Report of an Informal Consultation. Ames, IAU: Iowa State University Press, 1980. xiv, 146 pp. Paper. 0813809207.

Papers presented at the Informal Consultation on the Response of Land-Grant Universities to World Hunger (Ames, Iowa, 9-10 March 1978) revealing a lively awareness of the appropriate agricultural agenda for the last two decades of the 20th century, and how churches and the land-grant universities can cooperate in their responses.

EC323 Mosher, Arthur T.
Getting Agriculture Moving: Essentials for Development and Modernization. New York, NYU: Praeger, 1966. 191 pp. No ISBN.

A primer on agricultural missions by the former principal of the Allahabad Agricultural Institute, India.

EC324 Sen, Sudhir
A Richer Harvest: New Horizons for Developing Countries. Maryknoll, NYU: Orbis Books; New Delhi, II: Tata McGraw-Hill Publishing, 1974. xxiii, 573 pp. 0883444364.

A major study by an Indian agronomist, of prospects for the green revolution in developing countries, focusing on agricultural strategies.

EC325 Sobkoviak, Don, and Lois Sobkoviak
The Food Mission: Sustainable Food Production: A Manual of Sustainable Methods of Plant Production Helpful in Meeting Food Needs Everywhere. Milford, ILU: Sand Institutes International, 1995. iv, 84 pp. Paper. 0964583909.

Practical helps for an organic approach to sustainable food production by the Christian Institute for Social, Agricultural, and New-Life Development (SAND).

EC326 Wiser, William H., and Charlotte Viall Wiser
Behind Mud Walls, 1930-1960. Berkeley, CAU: University of California Press, 1964. xvii, 250 pp. No ISBN.

Reprint of a 1930 missionary classic on life in a North India village, with the authors' reflections on thirty years of changes.

Urban Development/Missions

See also SO558, AM1218-AM1219, AS108, AS751, and AS1042.

EC327 Butselaar, Jan van, G. J. C. van der Horst, and B. C. Lap
Met de zending bij de armen: 25 jaar Urban Rural Mission. Amsterdam, NE: ICCO, 1987. 74 pp. 9072030028.

Case studies from Hong Kong, Korea, and Japan to mark twenty-five years of urban-rural mission.

EC328 Churches Conference on Shelter and Housing (Washington, DC)
Making Room at the Inn: Congregational Investment in Affordable Housing. Washington, DCU: Churches Conference on Shelter and Housing, 1991. 64 pp. Paper. No ISBN.

Describes how congregations raise the money and build the team needed to create affordable housing, and profiles twelve faith-based housing programs illustrating development concepts and congregational roles in specific community settings.

EC329 Fry, John R., ed.
The Church and Community Organization. New York, NYU: NCCUSA, Division of Christian Life and Mission, 1965. viii, 179 pp. Paper. No ISBN.

A report of a NCCUSA-sponsored consultation on community organization and community development (Philadelphia, Pennsylvania, 7-10 December 1964), which examined models as an arm of Christian mission.

EC330 Lewin, Hugh, comp.
A Community of Clowns: Testimonies of People in Urban Rural Mission. Geneva, SZ: WCC, 1987. xiii, 303 pp. Paper. 2825408816.

Stories of the first twenty-five years (1961-1986) of the Urban Rural Mission (URM) department of the WCC, and the impact it has made in local and national struggles throughout the world.

EC331 Linthicum, Robert C.
Empowering the Poor: Community Organizing among the City's "Rag, Tag and Bobtail." (Innovations in Mission, 3). Monrovia, CAU: MARC, 1991. 118 pp. Paper. 0912552751.

A practical compendium of "how-to" stories and illustrations of what churches can do among and with the poor.

EC332 Perkins, John M., ed.
Restoring At-Risk Communities: Doing It Together and Doing It Right. Grand Rapids, MIU: Baker Books, 1995. 266 pp. Paper. 080105463X.

In this handbook for Christian community development, fourteen urban ministry professionals provide practical counsel for those ministering to at-risk communities in inner cities of the United States.

EC333 Reed, Gregory J.
Economic Empowerment through the Church: A Blueprint for Progressive Community Development. Grand Rapids, MIU: Zondervan, 1994. 224 pp. Paper. 0310489512.

A practical handbook on program development and fiscal management for local churches desiring to become a force for community revitalization through economic empowerment, with examples from African American parishes in the United States.

EC334 Väänänen, Ella, ed.
Kaupunkiin huomisen toivossa. Helsinki, FI: Kirjapaja, 1989. 205 pp. 951621991X.

A collection of articles dealing with urbanization and immigration and their impact on missions.

Industrial Development/Missions

See also AF744, AM1324, AS96, and AS1090.

EC335 Hargleroad, Bobbi Wells, ed.
Struggle to be Human: Stories of Urban-Industrial Mission. Geneva, SZ: WCC, CWME, 1973. 77 pp. Paper. 2825401188.

A booklet which relates specific cases of urban-industrial mission in the six continents, and introduces its basic perspectives and methods of operation.

EC336 Kane, Margaret
Gospel in Industrial Society. London, ENK: SCM Press, 1980. 179 pp. Paper. 0334020328.

A personal testimony, by a theological consultant to the churches in northeast England, of the reflections by Christians there on the tensions between the Christian faith and the realities of life in their industrial society.

EC337 *Mission Industry: Guidelines for the Development of the Church's Work in Asian Industrial Society*
Singapore, SI: EACC, Committee on Urban-Industrial Mission, 1969. 118 pp. Paper. No ISBN.

The operational handbook of the EACC's Urban-Industrial Mission Committee.

EC338 Poulat, Emile
Naissance de prêtres ouvriers. (Religion et sociétés). Paris, FR: Casterman, 1965. 538 pp. No ISBN.

A major study of the French worker priest movement including a literature review, the post-World War II social context, its development, and the tensions which finally broke it.

EC339 Rogerson, John W., ed.
Industrial Mission in a Changing World: Papers from the Jubilee Conference of the Sheffield Industrial Mission. Sheffield, ENK: Sheffield Academic Press, 1996. 195 pp. 1850756201 (hdbk), 1850757917 (pbk).

A collection of eighteen essays on the nature of mission, spirituality, and the Christian Gospel in today's society, with a review of the fifty-year history of the Sheffield [England] Industrial Mission.

EC340 Siefer, Gregor
The Church and Industrial Society: A Survey of the Worker-Priest Movement and Its Implications for the Christian Mission. Translated by Isabel McHugh, and Florence McHugh. London, ENK: Darton, Longman & Todd, 1964. xv, 335 pp. No ISBN.

English translation of *Die Mission der Arbeiterpriester* (1960).

EC341 *The Christian Witness in an Industrial Society*
Translated by Horst Symanowski, and George H. Kehm. Philadelphia, PAU: Westminster Press, 1964. 160 pp. No ISBN.

Theological, sociological, and ecclesiological perspectives on industrial mission by the esteemed pastor of the German Evangelical Church and officer of Gossner Mission in Mainz.

EC342 Todd, George, and Bobbi Wells Hargleroad, eds.
Mission and Justice: Urban Industrial Mission at Work. Geneva, SZ: WCC, CWME, 1977. 70 pp. Paper. 2825405493.

Articles on models of contemporary urban-industrial mission; previously published in the *International Review of Missions*, July 1976.

EC343 Velten, Georges
Mission in Industrial France. (SCM Book Club, 185). London, ENK: SCM Press, 1968. 126 pp. 0334010225.

A popular account of the work in French secular industrial communities of La Mission Populaire Evangelique de France.

Labor

See also EC7, EC308, AF1015, AM271, AS90, AS946, EU173, and EU176.

EC344 Antonides, H., and E. Vanderkloet
A Christian Labour Association. (Wetenskaplike bydraes of the PU for CHE: Series F: IRS-Study Pamphlets, 285). Potchefstroom, SA: Institute for Reformational Studies, 1991. ii, 23 pp. Paper. 186822080X.

Two essays on the Christian Labour Association of Canada (CLAC), published in South Africa to inform Christians there of this unique example of a trade union operating from an explicitly reformational viewpoint.

EC345 Assmann, Hugo
Crítica a lógica da exclusão: Ensaios sobre economia e teologia. (Coleçao Temas de atualidade). São Paulo, BL: Editorial Paulus, 1994. 144 pp. Paper. 8534901643.

A critique of the logic of exclusion and the social reality of marginalization, from the perspective of the preferential option for the poor and a theology of worldwide human solidarity; by one of the initiators of liberation theology, now professor at the Methodist University of Piracicaba, Brazil.

EC346 Bertran, Jorge
Los Difíciles Caminos de la Misión Obrera. (1968 Tiempos de Concilio, 19). Barcelona, SP: Editorial Nova Terra, 1968. 219 pp. Paper. No ISBN.

A study of the theology of mission, the role of the laity, and the mission of workers in particular.

EC347 Green, Reginald Herbold, ed.
Labour, Employment and Unemployment: An Ecumenical Reappraisal. (An Ecumenical Approach to Economics, 5). Geneva, SZ: WCC, 1987. 84 pp. Paper. 2825408956.

The report of the fifth meeting of the Advisory Group on Economic Matters (Geneva, Switzerland, 10-13 Oct. 1985) proposing Christian responses to the causes and effects of global unemployment.

EC348 Ike, Obiora F.
Value Meaning and Social Structure of Human Work. Frankfurt am Main, GW: Lang, 1986. xxx, 561 pp. Paper. 3820496408.

An academic thesis on the social ethic of human work as contained in the papal encyclical *Laborem Exercens* (1981) and its application to understandings of work in the Igbo society of Nigeria.

EC349 Loew, Jacques, and Paul Xardel
La flamme qui dévore le berger: éléments de spiritualité pour l'évangélisation. (Epiphanie Initiations). Paris, FR: Éditions du Cerf, 1993. 120 pp. Paper. 220404881X.

Pages from the journal of Paul Xardel (d. 1964), founder of Mission Saints-Pierre-et-Paul, a new community of worker priests, with commentary and reflections by Jacques Loew of that order on the spirituality and approach to the re-evangelization of the poor which it offers.

EC350 *Migrant Labour and Church Involvement: A Consultation Held in Umpumulo (Natal)*
Mapumulo, SA: LTC; Johannesburg, SA: Christian Academy in S. Africa, 1970. 210 pp. No ISBN.

Papers, church reports, and findings from an important consultation organized by the Missiological Institute at Umpumulo, South Africa.

EC351 Mizuno, Michelle, ed.
Women, Poverty and the Economy. (Ecumenical Decade Series, 1). Geneva, SZ: WCC, Subunit on Women in Church and Society, 1990. 55 pp. Paper. No ISBN.

A collection of short articles on women and the economy, with case studies from several countries and theological reflections.

EC352 Peabody, Larry
Secular Work Is Full-Time Service. London, ENK: CLC, 1974. 142 pp. 0900284366 (UK), 0875084486 (US).

A popular argument that one's work can be one's Christian calling.

EC353 Pierce, Gregory F. Augustine, ed.
Of Human Hands: A Reader in the Spirituality of Work. (The Christian at Work in the World). Minneapolis, MNU: Augsburg; Chicago, ILU: ACTA Publications, 1991. 124 pp. Paper. 080662504X (MN), 0879460571 (IL).

First-person reflections on the spiritual meaning of daily work by the former President of the Catholic National Center for the Laity.

EC354 *Poverty and Polarisation: A Call To Commitment*
Manchester, ENK: William Temple Foundation, 1988. 136 pp. Paper. 1870733169.

The final report of an international consultation organized by the West European Network on Work, Unemployment, and the Churches (Evangelische Akademie, Mulheim/Ruhr, Federal Republic of Germany, 20-24 April 1988).

EC355 Reindorp, Julian
Leaders and Leadership in the Trade Unions in Bangalore. (CISRS Social Research Series, 7). Madras, II: CLS, 1971. vii, 239 pp. Paper. No ISBN.

A study on the role of leaders and leadership in the trade unions of Bangalore, India, with a history of the trade union movement, showing how Christians in industry are called to exercise a prophetic ministry.

EC356 Siefer, Gregor
Die Mission der Arbeiterpriester: Ereignisse und Konsequenzen; ein Beitrag zum Thema: Kirche und Industriegesellschaft. Essen, GW: Driewer, 1960. 335 pp. No ISBN.

A detailed history and evaluation of the French Catholic Mission to the Workers, 1941-1959.

Technology

See also EC16, AF443, AS108, and AS620.

EC357 Abrecht, Paul, ed.
Faith, Science and the Future. Geneva, SZ: WCC, 1979. 244 pp. Paper. 2825405787.

A book of preparatory readings for the World Conference on Faith, Science, and the Future (Cambridge, Massachusetts, 12-24 July 1979), with contributions on technology, energy, food, resources, environment, population, and economic issues.

EC—MISSIONS AND ECONOMIC LIFE

EC358 Carothers, J. Edward et al., eds.
To Love or to Perish: The Technological Crisis and the Church-es. New York, NYU: Friendship Press, 1972. 152 pp. Paper. 0377020515.

The report of the USA Task Force on the Future of Mankind and the Role of the Christian Churches in a World of Science-Based Technology, co-sponsored by the NCCUSA and Union Theological Seminary of New York, which calls all humanity toward a new quality of life.

EC359 Charland, William A.
The Heart of the Global Village: Technology and the New Millennium. London, ENK: SCM Press; Philadelphia, PAU: Trinity Press International, 1990. 122 pp. Paper. 0334024382 (T).

Reflections by a Quaker member of the international development program, Right Sharing of World Resources, on the importance of people-centered development rather than high technology.

EC360 Consultation on New Technology, Work and the Environment
Technology from the Underside: Report of the Consultation... Geneva, SZ: WCC; Quezon City, PH: NCCP, 1986. xii, 107 pp. Paper. 9719104627.

The papers and report from the January 1986 consultation on technological issues in justice, peace, and environment in Southeast Asia.

EC361 Conway, Ruth
Choices at the Heart of Technology: A Christian Perspective. (Christian Mission and Modern Culture). Harrisburg, PAU: Trinity Press International, 1999. xii, 125 pp. Paper. 1563382873.

Critical of decisions made about and reasons for development of new technologies, the author encourages the Christian community to contribute to debates on these purposes and priorities, based on their deep involvement and biblical witness.

EC362 Davis, Howard, and David L. Gosling
Will the Future Work?: Values for Emerging Patterns of Work and Employment. Geneva, SZ: WCC, 1985. xvii, 123 pp. 2825408425.

A collection of the minor papers presented at workshops on Technology, Employment, and Rapid Social Change, composed in September 1984 by the Church and Society Subunit of the WCC and the Church of Scotland's Society, Religion, and Technology Project.

EC363 Galtier, Denis
Peut-on evangeliser des techniciens ?: Témoignage et réflexions. (Rencontres, 71). Paris, FR: Éditions du Cerf, 1966. 189 pp. No ISBN.

A record of the author's gropings, disappointments, and discoveries in a ministry to technicians.

EC364 Gill, David M.
From Here to Where?: Technology, Faith and the Future of Man. Geneva, SZ: WCC, 1970. 111 pp. Paper. No ISBN.

Report on a WCC-sponsored exploratory conference on the moral and ethical aspects of modern technology (Geneva, Switzerland, 28 June-4 July 1970).

EC365 Gill, David M.
Tecnología, Fe y Futuro del Hombre. Translated by Constantino Ruiz-Garrido. (Séptimo sello, 18). Salamanca, SP: Ediciones Sígueme, 1972. 131 pp. No ISBN.
Spanish translation.

EC366 Hall, Cameron P., comp.
Human Values and Advancing Technology: A New Agenda for the Church in Mission. New York, NYU: Friendship Press, 1967. 175 pp. No ISBN.

Major addresses and working group reports from a Consultation on Technology and Human Values held in Chicago, Illinois, 2-4 May 1967.

EC367 Leeuwen, Arend Theodor van
Prophecy in a Technocratic Era. New York, NYU: Scribner, 1968. 130 pp. No ISBN.

The noted Dutch theologian of history gives a cogent analysis of the undeniable reality of technocracy and secularization, suggesting a response by Christians consistent with their faith and commitment to the church's mission.

EC368 Pury, Pascal de
People's Technologies and People's Participation. Geneva, SZ: WCC, 1983. 164 pp. Paper. 2825407461.

An analysis and evaluation of thinking concerning "appropriate technologies" by the WCC's Technical Service and the CCPD from 1971 to 1981.

EC369 Stivers, Robert L.
Hunger, Technology and Limits to Growth: Christian Responsibility for Three Ethical Issues. Minneapolis, MNU: Augsburg, 1984. 175 pp. Paper. 0806620641.

A thoughtful analysis of appropriate Christian responses to the issues indicated in the title.

Commerce and International Trade

See also EC7 and EC288.

EC370 Arruda, Marcos, ed.
Transnational Corporations, Technology, and Human Development: Report of the Third Meeting of the Advisory Group on Economic Matters, Held in Rome, Italy, October 15-19, 1980. (An Ecumenical Approach to Economics, 2). Geneva, SZ: WCC, 1981. 65 pp. Paper. 282540683X.

An ecumenical approach to economic questions, with special emphasis on social aspects of international business enterprises.

EC371 Christiansen, Paul Kofoed et al., eds.
Mission, bekendelse og kirkens enhed. (Nyt Synspunkt, 23). Hellerup, DK: DMS-Forlag, 1986. 67 pp. Paper. 8774311239.

A collection of articles by Ulrich Duchrow and others on missions and world economics in the age of neo-colonialism.

EC372 *Churches' Report on Transnational Corporations*
(CCPD Documents Justice and Development, 7). Geneva, SZ: WCC, Programme Unit on Justice and Service, and CCPD, 1986. 80 pp. Paper. No ISBN.

Reports of the Fifth Assembly of the WCC in Nairobi 1975, discussing examples of ways in which WCC-member churches respond to WCC Central Committee recommendations.

EC—MISSIONS AND ECONOMIC LIFE

EC373 Evangelisches Missionswerk (Hamburg)

Kirche und Wirtschaft: Dokumentation über die Auswertungsphase des Studienprojektes "Herausforderungen für eine missionarische Kirche durch soziale Folgen bundesdeutscher Direktinvestitionen in Überse. Hamburg, GW: EMW, 1990. 135 pp. Paper. No ISBN.

With case studies from Brazil and South Korea, this ecumenical study, by the Gossner Mission in Germany, investigates effects which investments of German companies have on specific Third World countries and consequences drawn by churches.

EC374 Gallis, Marion

Trade for Justice: Myth or Mandate? Geneva, SZ: WCC, CCPD, 1972. 146 pp. No ISBN.

An analysis of the place of trade in the development puzzle from the perspective of the WCC's understanding of three objectives of development: justice, self-reliance, and economic growth.

EC375 MacDonald, Allen John

Trade Politics and Christianity in Africa and the East. New York, NYU: Negro Universities Press, 1969. xxi, 296 pp. 0837117550.

A revised edition of the 1916 original, discussing the problems raised by the contact of the West with Africa and the East, and the part that Christianity can play in the solutions.

EC376 Mensen, Bernhard, ed.

Globalisierung: Academie Völker und Kulturen St. Augustin. (Akademie Völker und Kulturen Vortragsreihe, 21 (1997/98)). Nettetal, GW: Steyler Verlag, 1998. 124 pp. Paper. 3805004230.

A collection of six scholarly essays by Catholic economists and political scientists on the moral issues in globalization.

EC377 Mieth, Dietmar, Jacques Pohier, and Marcus Lefébure, eds.

Christian Ethics and Economics: The North-South Conflict. (*Concilium*: Religion in the Eighties, 140). Edinburgh, STK: T&T Clark; New York, NYU: Seabury Press, 1980. xii, 114 pp. Paper. 056730020X (UK), 0816422826 (US).

Fourteen essays on economic and theoretical factors of the North-South conflict and attempts at a Christian response to the growing economic cleavage.

EC378 Millwood, David

Help or Hindrance?: Aid, Trade and the Rich Nations' Responsibility to the Third World. Geneva, SZ: SODEPAX, 1971. 42 pp. Paper. No ISBN.

A brief analysis of factors of poverty and the link between aid and trade, after two decades of development aid; by a staff member of the United Nations Conference on Trade and Development (UNCTAD).

EC379 Sullivan, Leon H.

Moving Mountains: The Principles and Purposes of Leon Sullivan. Valley Forge, PAU: Judson Press, 1998. xviii, 300 pp. 0817012893.

The black Baptist pastor tells the inside story of his work as a General Motors board member, and how his Sullivan Principles for industry played a key role in the downfall of apartheid in South Africa.

EC380 World Council of Churches CCPD

Churches and the Transnational Corporations: An Ecumenical Programme. Geneva, SZ: WCC, 1983. x, 145 pp. Paper. 2825407569.

A compilation of documents of the WCC's program on the churches and transnational corporations, including the report on the WCC's International Consultation on TNCs (Bad Boll, Germany, 23-28 November 1981).

International Finance

See also EC90 and EC373.

EC381 *Banking on Life and Debt*

Maryknoll, NYU: Maryknoll World Productions, 1995. 30 mins. No ISBN.

A documentary video on the human costs of the World Bank and International Monetary Fund (IMF) "solutions" to the debt crisis in developing countries.

EC382 Catholic Church. Pontificia Commissio Institia et Pax

At the Service of the Human Community: An Ethical Approach to the International Debt Question. London, ENK: Catholic Truth Society; Vatican City, IT: Pontifical Commission Justice and Peace; Washington, DCU: USCC, 1987. 30 pp. Paper. 0851836968 (C), 1555861490 (U).

A brief statement of six ethical principles to guide decision makers, both debtors and creditors (including the International Monetary Fund and the World Bank), as they seek to resolve the current debt crisis of many nations of the Two-Thirds World.

EC383 Sincere, Richard E.

The Politics of Sentiment: Churches and Foreign Investment in South Africa. Washington, DCU: Ethics & Public Policy Center, 1984. xii, 164 pp. Paper. 0896330885.

A critical evaluation of efforts by the churches (WCC, US, and South Africa) to curtail or stop outside investment in South Africa as a strategy to oppose apartheid.

EC384 *The Debt Crisis and the Third World*

(CCPD Documents Justice and Development, 6). Geneva, SZ: WCC, 1986. 54 pp. Paper. No ISBN.

A statement of the WCC's Central Committee on Third World debt, reflections on the world financial crisis, and reports of actions and campaigns in northern countries.

EC385 Vallely, Paul

Bad Samaritans: First World Ethics and Third World Debt. Maryknoll, NYU: Orbis Books, 1990. ix, 374 pp. Paper. 0883446685.

A journalist's comprehensive exposure of many facets of the Third World debt crisis from famine in Ethiopia to origins in colonialism, and policies of multinationals, governments, the World Bank and the International Monetary Fund, with a biblical theology and ethic of wealth and debt.

EC386 WCC, Commission on the Churches' Participation in Development

The International Financial System: An Ecumenical Critique: Report of the Meeting of the Advisory Group on Economic Matters Held in Geneva, Switzerland, November 1-4, 1984. Edited by Reginald Herbold Green. (An Ecumenical Approach to Economics, 4). Geneva, SZ: WCC, Commission on the Churches' Participation in Development, 1985. vii, 88 pp. Paper. 2825406360.

An analysis of concern, critique, and action by the churches concerning the international financial system, and the need for reforms sensitive to the needs of debtor nations.

MISSIONS AND POLITICAL LIFE

Alan Neely, Subeditor

Christian witness and service inevitably involve relations with those in political power. The Book of Acts is replete with accounts of Peter's and Paul's interactions with the rulers of their day. During the colonial period, government permission was required to engage in cross-cultural ministries, with partnerships offered in mission education. Governments practicing state socialism severely restricted the churches' public witness and service. The new millennium promises a heightened struggle for human rights (including religious liberty) in countries with authoritarian regimes or vocal religious fundamentalism.

This chapter includes works on many aspects of missions and political life. It includes the link between mission and law (Jongeneel 1995, I:306-319), but much more. Cross-referenced are books found in the geographical chapters on the churches and political life in various countries and continents.

Do not expect to find here a bibliography on political science. As with the chapter on "Missions and Economic Life," works on political ethics are included only if they include sections on the churches' response to political issues (Jongeneel 1997, II:134-153).

Some of the most creative thinking on the churches' relation to political life will not be found in this chapter.

Look for it instead in the subsection on "Liberation Theology" in the chapter on "Missions: Theology," and in those on the theologies of Africa, Latin America, Asia, and Oceania.

Following reference works, this chapter contains a large subsection on "General Works." In it have been grouped books on Christian ethics that deal with the churches' response to political issues. A short section follows on "Political Theory," and a longer one on "Human Rights," including issues of religious liberty.

Much cross-cultural mission takes place amidst political change and revolution, often including violence. How the churches have and ought to respond is the theme of the next subsections.

There are numerous "Church and State" issues in mission. Note the "see also" citations for various countries, as well as the general works included here. The next two subsections include specific works on "Missionaries and Political Activity" and "Colonialism and Missions."

Cross-cultural missions are affected by international relations. The final subsections of this chapter deal with these concerns, including "Peace," "War," and "International Organizations."

Norman E. Thomas

Bibliographies

See also AF10.

PO1 Church and Politics: A Current Bibliography on Social Issues Vol. 1 (1987/1988)-. Annual
London, ENK: BCC, 1987/88-. 0851692230.

An annual review of books in the area, including human rights and church and politics in Great Britain, with some coverage of the Two-Thirds World.

PO2 Fenton, Thomas P., and Mary J. Heffron, eds.
Human Rights: A Directory of Resources. Maryknoll, NYU: Orbis Books, 1989. xviii, 156 pp. Paper. 0883445344.

An annotated list of resources (books, pamphlets, organizations, etc.) for those who wish to study or engage in action on issues of human rights; prepared by Third World Resources.

PO3 Fenton, Thomas P., and Mary J. Heffron, eds.
Third World Resource Directory, 1994-1995: An Annotated Guide to Print and Audiovisual Resources from and about Africa, Asia and Pacific, Latin America and Caribbean, and the Middle East. Maryknoll, NYU: Orbis Books, 1994. xiv, 785 pp. Paper. 0883449412.

Focusing on problems in Third World countries (human rights abuses, poverty, racism, military repression, etc), this up-to-date directory contains 2,500 annotated entries for print and media resources, plus a directory of 2,300 international non-governmental organizations.

PO—MISSIONS AND POLITICAL LIFE

Serials and Periodicals

PO4 *IDOC International: North American Edition.* **No. 1 (April 4, 1970)-no. 69 (1975). Irregular**
Huntington, INU: IDOC-North America, 1970-1975. No ISSN.

Background documentation provided by more than 300 specialists, groups, and study centers in thirty-two countries on contemporary problems of human renewal, with special concern for political and economic developments, for the International Documentation on the Contemporary Church (IDOC).

PO5 *IDOC Internazionale.* **Vol. 1, no. 1 (1970)-. Bimonthly**
Rome, IT: IDOC Internazionale, 1970-. ISSN 025076431.

International documentation published simultaneously in English, Spanish, and Italian editions on problems of human renewal (political, economic, social, and religious).

PO6 *Journal of Church and State.* **Vol. 1, no. 1 (Jan. 1959)-. Quarterly**
Waco, TXU: Baylor University, J. M. Dawson Institute of Church-State Studies, 1959-. ISSN 0021969X.

Scholarly articles, documentation, book reviews, and a country-by-country update on church-state affairs.

PO7 *The Churches in International Affairs*
Geneva, SZ: WCC, CCIA, 1970-1990. 15 vols. Paper.

The reports of the influential ecumenical commission on international affairs, representing the churches at the United Nations, published annually at first (1949-1969), and later quadrennially (1970-1973, ISBN 2825404896; 1974-1978, ISBN 2825405914; 1979-1982, ISBN 2825407534; 1983-1986, ISBN 2825409146; 1987-1990, ISBN 2825410225), with the texts of WCC documents organized by international program emphases, regional issues, and national issues.

Reference Works

PO8 Corson-Finnerty, Adam Daniel
World Citizen: Action for Global Justice. Maryknoll, NYU: Orbis Books, 1982. xi, 178 pp. Paper. 0883447150.

A primer for the concerned US Christian on issues of economic and political justice, with sixty-one pages of resources (bibliography, action and information groups, and audio-visual resources).

PO9 Fenton, Thomas P., and Mary J. Heffron, eds.
Third World Struggle for Peace with Justice: A Directory of Resources. Maryknoll, NYU: Orbis Books, 1990. xviii, 188 pp. Paper. 088344660X.

An annotated directory of resources (books, articles, audiovisuals, and organizations) on the struggles of Third World peoples against economic and military repression, and for the rights of self-determination and peace.

Conferences and Congresses

See also EC14, AF129, AF138, AM255, and AS88.

PO10 Frizen, Edwin L., and Wade T. Coggins, eds.
Christ and Caesar in Christian Missions. Pasadena, CAU: William Carey Library, 1979. viii, 149 pp. Paper. 0878081690.

Addresses and discussions of the AEPM/EFMA/IFMA Study Conference (Overland Park, Kansas, 25-29 September 1978) on crucial issues facing Christian missions in relation to diverse political systems.

PO11 Hessel, Dieter T., ed.
The Church's Public Role: Retrospect and Prospect. Grand Rapids, MIU: Eerdmans, 1993. xiii, 309 pp. Paper. 0802806473.

Papers from an ecumenical symposium held at the Princeton Seminary Continuing Education Center, September 1990, on Christian involvements in public policy in the United States and Latin America.

General Works

See also HI188, TH345, EA84, EA202, ME31, ME178, CR379, EC8, EC17-EC18, PO8, PO86-PO89, MI164, SP240-SP241, SP317, AF165, AF183, AF1162, AM619, AM740, AM1287, AS1077, and EU131.

PO12 Axelson, Sigbert
Missionens ansikte. Lund, SW: Signum, 1976. 128 pp. 9185330094.

An analysis by the Swedish missiologist on missions, their political involvements and significance, and their cultural imperialism.

PO13 Beyerhaus, Peter
God's Kingdom and the Utopian Error: Discerning the Biblical Kingdom of God from Its Political Counterfeits. Wheaton, ILU: Crossway Books, 1992. x, 224 pp. Paper. 0891076514.

A critique by the noted German evangelical missiologist of thirty years (1961-1991), of political theologies by the WCC, and by liberation theologians that have linked struggles for social justice with the Kingdom of God.

PO14 Dear, John, ed.
Apostle of Peace: Essays in Honor of Daniel Berrigan. Maryknoll, NYU: Orbis Books, 1996. x, 245 pp. Paper. 1570750629.

Essays by forty friends celebrating Berrigan's life and gifts as peacemaker, prophet, poet, and priest, and "keeper of the word" on the occasion of his 75th birthday.

PO15 Fierro, Alfredo
El Evangelio Beligerante: introducción crítica a las teologías políticas. (Conciencia y revolución, 18). Estella, SP: Verbo Divino, 1975. 525 pp. 8471511630.

An introduction to contemporary Protestant and Roman Catholic political theologies.

PO16 Fierro, Alfredo
Introduzione alle teologie politiche. (Orizzonti nuovi). Assisi, IT: Cittadella Editrice, 1977. 376 pp. No ISBN.

Italian translation.

PO17 Fierro, Alfredo
The Militant Gospel: A Critical Introduction to Political Theologies. Translated by John Drury. Maryknoll, NYU: Orbis Books, 1975. xv, 459 pp. 0883443104 (hdbk), 0883443112 (pbk).

English translation.

PO18 Forman, Charles W.
The Nation and the Kingdom: Christian Mission in the New Nations. New York, NYU: Friendship Press, 1964. 174 pp. No ISBN.

A survey of the mutual impact of missions and the new independent nations of Asia and Africa.

PO19 Hallencreutz, Carl F. et al., eds.
Kristen Högervag I Amerikansk Mission?: Rapport fran ett missionsvetenskapligt faltstudium till USA varen 1990. Uppsala, SW: Teologiska Institutionen, 1990. viii, 240 pp. Paper. 9185424226.

A collection of nine scholarly essays by Swedish missiologists on the new religious right wing of Protestantism in the United States, its origins, and its impact on Protestant churches of Swedish origins, their missions, and local evangelical churches in the Third World.

PO20 Hanson, Eric O.
The Catholic Church in World Politics. Lawrenceville, NJU: Princeton University Press, 1987. x, 485 pp. 0691077290.

A scholarly analysis of the role of the church in national political consciousness, in relationship to socialism and capitalism, in regional alliances, and in issues of arms control.

PO21 Haynes, Jeff
Religion in Third World Politics. (Issues in Third World Politics). Boulder, COU: Lynne Rienner Publishers, 1994. ix, 166 pp. Paper. 1555874568.

Case studies of Christian and Muslim involvements in politics from Iran and Afghanistan to Latin America.

PO22 Jarrett-Kerr, Martin
Christ and the New Nations. New York, NYU: Morehouse-Barlow; London, ENK: SPCK, 1966. viii, 120 pp. No ISBN.

An engaging argument that the most important criteria for a renewal of mission is seeing God's mission through non-Western eyes, rather than material aid or new relationships of mutuality between First and Third World churches.

PO23 Libânio, J. B.
Discernimento e Política. (Coleção Vida Religiosa: Temas Atuais, 7). Petrópolis, BL: Editora Vozes, 1977. 167 pp. No ISBN.

Helps for Christians, especially members of religious orders or congregations, in choosing political programs to support, by the Professor of Theology at the Pontifical Catholic University in Rio de Janeiro, Brasil.

PO24 Libânio, J. B.
Spiritual Discernment and Politics: Guidelines for Religious Communities. Translated by Theodore Morrow. Maryknoll, NYU: Orbis Books, 1982. ix, 131 pp. Paper. 0883444631.

English traslation.

PO25 Míguez Bonino, José
Toward a Christian Political Ethics. Philadelphia, PAU: Fortress Press, 1983. 126 pp. Paper. 0800616979.

An introduction to ethical theory concerning politics by a major liberation theologian, with application to Latin American experience from the 15th century to the present.

PO26 Maier, Christoph T.
Preaching the Crusades: Mendicant Friars and the Cross in the Thirteenth Century. (Cambridge Studies in Medieval Life and Thought: Fourth Series, 28). New York, NYU: Cambridge University Press, 1998. x, 202 pp. Paper. 0521638739.

A scholarly evaluation of involvements by Franciscan and Dominican friars in the 13th century in propaganda for the crusades; originally submitted as a Ph.D. dissertation at the University of London in 1990; published in 1994.

PO27 Matthews, Zachariah Keodirelang, ed.
La responsibilité des governements à une époque révolutionnaire. (Église et société, 2). Geneva, SZ: Éditions Labor et Fides, 1966. 262p pp. No ISBN.

French translation.

PO28 Matthews, Zachariah Keodirelang, ed.
Responsible Government in a Revolutionary Age. New York, NYU: Association Press; London, ENK: SCM Press, 1966. 381 pp. No ISBN.

This second of four preparatory volumes for the WCC's Conference on Church and Society (Geneva 1966) is a collection of twenty-two substantive essays on contemporary politics, social change, and Christian involvements in diverse contexts.

PO29 Misztal, Bronislaw, and Anson Shupe, eds.
Religion and Politics in Comparative Perspective: Revival of Religious Fundamentalism in East and West. Westport, CTU: Praeger, 1992. xii, 223 pp. 027594218X.

Thirteen scholarly essays on religious fundamentalisms among Christians in the United States, Europe, and Latin America, and their contributions to social and political change.

PO30 Moen, Matthew C., and Lowell S. Gustafson, eds.
The Religious Challenge to the State. Philadelphia, PAU: Temple University Press, 1992. xi, 294 pp. 0877228566.

Twelve scholarly essays on the varied interaction with 20th-century state systems by Islam, Christianity, and Judaism.

PO31 Mouw, Richard J.
Political Evangelism. Grand Rapids, MIU: Eerdmans, 1973. 111 pp. Paper. 0802815448.

A monograph on political action as an aspect of the evangelistic task of the church, with a call to develop stronger reflections on ecclesiology and eschatology.

PO32 Nelson-Pallmeyer, Jack
The Politics of Compassion. Maryknoll, NYU: Orbis Books, 1986. viii, 132 pp. Paper. 0883443562.

Six essays calling on the non-poor Christians in North America to develop a politics of compassion rooted in biblical faith as a response to critical social problems, such as hunger, the arms race, and US policy in Central America.

PO33 Nichols, J. Bruce, and Gil Loescher, eds.
The Moral Nation: Humanitarianism and U.S. Foreign Policy Today. Notre Dame, INU: University of Notre Dame Press, 1989. 321 pp. 0268013721 (hdbk), 0268013985 (pbk).

Thirteen scholarly essays on the moral and political philosophy of humanitarianism, its relationship to the conduct of US foreign policy, and the political-legal factors which must be addressed in looking at US humanitarian policy today, including essays on church involvement in Central America (sanctuary, human rights) and in Ethiopia (famine relief, refugees).

PO34 Rajendra, Cecil
Dove on Fire: Poems on Peace, Justice, and Ecology. (Risk Book Series, 33). Geneva, SZ: WCC, 1987. ix, 82 pp. Paper. 2825408999.

Seventy-eight poems by one of Asia's best-known poets, reflecting human commitment to justice and mission concerns.

PO—MISSIONS AND POLITICAL LIFE

PO35 Rubenstein, Richard L., ed.
Spirit Matters: The Worldwide Impact of Religion on Contemporary Politics. (A Washington Institute Book). New York, NYU: Paragon House, 1987. xxvii, 384 pp. 0887022030 (hdbk), 0887022111 (pbk).

Collection of fifteen scholarly case studies on the interplay of religion and politics today in countries on five continents revealing six distinguishable patterns and regional differences.

PO36 Sahliyeh, Emile, ed.
Religious Resurgence and Politics in the Contemporary World. (Religion, Culture, and Society). Albany, NYU: SUNY Press, 1990. ix, 374 pp. 0791403815 (hdbk), 0791403823 (pbk).

Nineteen scholarly essays on highly politicized religious groups and movements that have surfaced since the late 1970s in the United States, the Philippines, India, and the Middle East.

PO37 Shenk, Calvin E.
When Kingdoms Clash: The Christian and Ideologies. (Peace and Justice Series, 6). Scottdale, PAU: Herald Press, 1988. 104 pp. Paper. 0836134818.

Description and discussion the major ideologies of our time—capitalism, Marxism, apartheid, and national security states—and how faith affects ideologies in a comparative arena.

PO38 Srisang, Koson, ed.
Perspectives on Political Ethics: An Ecumenical Enquiry. Geneva, SZ: WCC; Washington, DCU: Georgetown University Press, 1983. xiii, 193 pp. Paper. 2825407518 (W), 0878404074 (G).

Selected papers on current issues in political ethics on each of the six continents, with themes for Christian responses—part of an ongoing ecumenical study by the WCC.

PO39 Thunberg, Anne-Marie
Kontinenter i uppbrott: Kyrka och mission inför den afroasiatiska revolutionen. Stockholm, SW: Diakonistyrelsens Bokförlag, 1960. 291 pp. No ISBN.

A book on church and missions in newly independent countries of the Third World, including social ethics, politics, race relations, urbanization, and the technical revolution.

PO40 Tschuy, Théo
Ethnic Conflict and Religion: Challenge to the Churches. Geneva, SZ: WCC Publications, 1997. xv, 160 pp. Paper. 2825411906.

A veteran Swiss ecumenist presents case studies of nine 20th-century ethnic conflicts from Armenia to Bosnia, with an analysis of how ethnicity and nationalism challenge the churches.

PO41 Wallis, Jim, ed.
The Rise of Christian Conscience: The Emergence of a Dramatic Renewal Movement in the Church Today. San Francisco, CAU: Harper & Row, 1987. xxx, 290 pp. Paper. 0060690526.

A reprint of twenty-six visions, testimonies, and reflections by Christian leaders in the United States and other countries committed to justice and peace ministries; originally published in *Sojourners.*

PO42 Walt, B. J. van der
Religion and Society: Christian Involvement in the Public Square. (Institute for Reformational Studies, 50). Potchefstroom, SA: Potchefstroom University, 1999. iv, 86 pp. Paper. 186822337X.

A practical approach for equipping Christians in South Africa and in the world over, for active engagement in the "public square."

PO43 West, Charles C.
Power, Truth and Community in Modern Culture. (Christian Mission and Modern Culture). Harrisburg, PAU: Trinity Press International, 1999. xxi, 137 pp. Paper. 1563382970.

The Gospel as truth, community, power, and hope among the nations, rulers, and powers in our culture today.

PO44 Yoder, John Howard
Jesús y la Realidad Política. Buenos Aires, AG: Ediciones Certeza, 1985. 220 pp. Paper. 0830850570.

Spanish translation of *The Politics of Jesus* (1972).

PO45 Yoder, John Howard
The Politics of Jesus: vicit Agnus noster. Grand Rapids, MIU: Eerdmans; Carlisle, ENK: Paternoster Press, 1994. xiii, 257 pp. 0802807348 (E), 0853646201 (P).

Second edition of the classic work in which Yoder presses beyond the question of whether Jesus was political, to ask what sort of politics is the mark of Christian discipleship.

Political Theory

See also EC50, AF170, and AF272.

PO46 De Gruchy, John W.
Christianity and Democracy: A Theology for a Just World Order. (Cambridge Studies in Ideology and Religion). Cambridge, ENK: Cambridge University Press, 1995. xv, 291 pp. 0521452163 (hdbk), 0521458412 (pbk).

A scholarly study of the historic and contemporary roles of Christianity in the development of democracy, with case studies of church involvement in the United States, Nicaragua, sub-Saharan Africa, Germany, and South Africa.

PO47 Elmqvist, Karl-Axel, Per Frostin, Gunnar Gunnars, and Bo Nylund
Mission och politik: föredrag och diskussioner vid konferens i juni 1982. Uppsala, SW: Kristna socialdemokraterna Broderskapsrörelsen, 1983. 91 pp. No ISBN.

This volume discusses missions and liberation theology from a Christian social democratic standpoint.

PO48 *Religion, Politics and Ideology*
Manila, PH: NCCP, 1992. 206 pp. Paper. 9718548637.

A special issue of the Philippine ecumenical journal *TUGON* (vol.2, no. 1) with essays on religion and political theory, war and peace, and the Philippine General Election on 11 May 1992.

PO49 Witte, John, ed.
Christianity and Democracy in Global Context. Boulder, COU: Westview Press, 1993. xv, 327 pp. 0813318432.

A collection of eighteen scholarly essays on what Christianity has contributed in the past, and what it should contribute in the future to the shape of democratic governments, including Latin America (Lugo, McGrath, and Sigmund), Africa (Bediako, Joseph, Villa-Vincencio, Pobee, Tutu), and Asia (Thangaraj).

Human Rights

See also TH608, CR399, CR1050, CR1337, SO439, SO491, SO499, PO2, PO169, AF384, AF476, AF616-AF617, AF812, AF894, AF967, AF981-AF983, AF985, AF1030, AF1078, AF1112, AF1252, AF1314, AM4, AM13, AM26, AM30, AM32-AM33, AM52, AM120, AM249, AM268, AM294, AM337, AM663, AM705, AM711, AM728, AM746-AM747, AM756, AM765, AM919, AM1311-AM1312, AM1517, AS99, AS117, AS198, AS741, AS744, AS746, AS826, AS853, AS945, AS957, AS1105, AS1154, AS1420, AS1432, EU151, EU270, and OC100.

PO50 Baur, Jörg, ed.
Zum Thema Menschenrechte: Theologische Versuche und Entwürfe. Stuttgart, GW: Calwer Verlag, 1977. 112 pp. 3766805509.

Four scholarly essays on issues of human rights from the perspectives of the Old Testament (C. Westermann), New Testament (U. Luck), church history (M. Brecht), and systematic theology (J. Baur).

PO51 Billings, Peggy
Paradox and Promise in Human Rights. New York, NYU: Friendship Press, 1979. 126 pp. Paper. 0377000833.

A mission study book on sources of human rights, including their biblical and theological foundations, with an assessment of contemporary policies of the United States and Canadian governments, South Korea being a case study.

PO52 Braybrooke, Marcus, ed.
Stepping Stones to a Global Ethic. London, ENK: SCM Press, 1992. vi, 151 pp. Paper. 033401574X.

A compilation of thirteen international and interfaith statements on human rights, 1948 to 1990, with an introductory essay by the editor on the search for a global ethic.

PO53 Davidson, Miriam
Convictions of the Heart: Jim Corbett and the Sanctuary Movement. Tucson, AZU: University of Arizona Press, 1988. 187 pp. 0816510342.

The story of Jim Corbett, a Harvard-educated Quaker philosopher, and the beliefs with which he co-founded the Sanctuary Movement in the United States to shelter illegal aliens fleeing repression in Central America; and of the six-month, $2 million trial of the movement in which he was a defendant.

PO54 Dobrin, Arthur et al.
Gevangenen getuigen. Translated by A. Bok. Edited by Joke Glebbeek. (Bijeen publicatie, 23). 's-Hertogenbosch, NE: Stichting Gezamenlijke Missie Publiciteit, 1983. 154 pp. 9066780037.

Dutch translation.

PO55 Dobrin, Arthur, Lyn Dobrin, and Thomas F. Liotti
Convictions: Political Prisoners—Their Stories. Maryknoll, NYU: Orbis Books, 1981. xi, 100 pp. Paper. 088344089X.

A collection of true stories about eleven persons on five continents who have made their Christian witness while victims of human rights violations.

PO56 Dyck, Arthur J., ed.
Human Rights and the Global Mission of the Church. (Boston Theological Institute Annual Series, 1). Cambridge, MAU: Boston Theological Institute, 1985. 89 pp. Paper. No ISBN.

A collection of papers presented at a 1985 BTI Consulta-

tion on Human Rights, including viewpoints of women, Catholic, Protestant, and Third World scholars.

PO57 Evans, Robert A., and Alice Frazer Evans
Human Rights: A Dialogue between the First and Third Worlds. Maryknoll, NYU: Orbis Books; Guildford, ENK: Lutterworth Press, 1983. viii, 264 pp. Paper. 0883441942 (O), 01718825896 (L).

Eight human rights cases based on field research on six continents, with teaching notes and commentaries by a panel of theologians and missiologists from several countries.

PO58 Foxe, John
The New Foxe's Book of Martyrs. North Brunswick, NJU: Bridge-Logos, 1997. xx, 411 pp. Paper. 0882706721.

The 1570 classic rewritten in modern American English and updated to 1997, with chapters on the last ninety-seven years by Harold J. Chadwick.

PO59 Harper, Charles, ed.
Impunity: An Ethical Perspective. Geneva, SZ: WCC Publications, 1996. xviii, 141 pp. Paper. 2825412031.

Six case studies (Peru, Uruguay, Argentina, Chile, Bolivia, and El Salvador) of how churches and human rights organizations have struggled since the 1960s with the dilemmas of impunity for military leaders accused of gross human rights' violations.

PO60 Hennelly, Alfred T., and John Langan, eds.
Human Rights in the Americas: The Struggle for Consensus. Washington, DCU: Georgetown University Press, 1982. xiii, 291 pp. Paper. 0878404015 (hdbk), 0878404007 (pbk).

Eleven scholarly essays on the philosophical and theological roots and origins of human rights.

PO61 Hernández, Martín Ramón, ed.
Derechos Humanos en Francisco de Vitoria: Antología. (Biblioteca Dominicana, 4). Salamanca, SP: Editorial San Esteban, 1984. 234 pp. Paper. 8485045610.

An extensive introduction and anthology of selected writings of Francisco de Vitoria, a renowned Dominican jurist of 16th-century Spain and one of the founders of international law.

PO62 Kim, Chi Ha
The Gold-Crowned Jesus and Other Writings. Edited by Chong Sun Kim and Shelly Killen. Maryknoll, NYU: Orbis Books, 1978. xlvi, 131 pp. Paper. 0883441616.

The collected works of the writings of South Korea's leading writer and prisoner of conscience.

PO63 Koshy, Ninan
Religious Freedom in a Changing World. (Risk Book Series, 54). Geneva, SZ: WCC Publications, 1992. x, 115 pp. Paper. 2825410470.

A primer on the evolution of ecumenical thinking on religious liberty, with separate chapters detailing the advocacy of religious liberty by the WCC, the RCC, and the United Nations.

PO64 Lerner, Natan
Religion, Beliefs, and International Human Rights. (Religion and Human Rights Series). Maryknoll, NYU: Orbis Books, 2000. xii, 183 pp. Paper. 1570753016.

The author explores the interaction of religious ideas and institutions with human rights principles and practices, and seeks to discover the religious sources and practices of human rights.

PO65 Lochman, Jan Milíc, and Jürgen Moltmann, eds.
*Gottes Recht und Menschenrechte: Studien und Empfehlung-
en des Reformierten Weltbundes.* Neukirchen-Vluyn, GW:
Neukirchener Verlag, 1976. 104 pp. 3788705108.

A compilation of writings by theologians on human
rights, and statements by church and United Nations' conferences, prepared under the auspices of WARC.

PO66 Müller, Alois, and Norbert Greinacher, eds.
The Church and the Rights of Man. (*Concilium*: Religion
in the Seventies, 124). New York, NYU: Seabury Press;
Edinburgh, STK: T&T Clark, 1979. x, 124 pp. Paper.
0816404305 (US hdbk), 081642232X (US pbk), 0567300048
(UK).

A collection of essays on the biblical, historical, and
theological roots of Christian positions on human rights;
with case studies on actions by the Vatican, WCC, and the
churches of Latin America, the Philippines, and South Africa.

PO67 Mensen, Bernhard, ed.
Grundwerte und Menschenrechte in verschiedenen Kulturen.
(Vortragsreihe/Akademie Völker und Kultusen 1987/1988).
Nettetal, GW: Steyer Verlag/Wort und Werk, 1988. 113 pp.
Paper. 3805002203.

This collection of essays discusses human and fundamental rights in various contemporary situations, including
the Soviet Union, Africa, Islam, India, and Brazil.

PO68 Miller, Allen O., ed.
*A Christian Declaration on Human Rights: Theological
Studies of the World Alliance of Reformed Churches.* Grand
Rapids, MIU: Eerdmans, 1977. 190 pp. Paper. 0802817173.

Eleven essays giving the theological source of human
rights and dignity, and a summons to church action—the
result of a six-year study sponsored by WARC.

PO69 Nickel, James W.
*Making Sense of Human Rights: Philosophical Reflections
on the Universal Declaration of Human Rights.* Berkeley,
CAU: University of California Press, 1987. xiv, 253 pp.
Paper. 0520056884 (hdbk), 0520059948 (pbk).

A clarification of the meaning of human rights with a
persuasive defense of human rights as standards for international and domestic politics.

PO70 Power, David N., and F. Kabasele Lumbala, eds.
The Spectre of Mass Death. London, ENK: SCM Press;
Maryknoll, NYU: Orbis Books, 1993. x, 127 pp. Paper.
033403020X (UK), 0883448718 (US).

Ten essays on experiences of Christians in ministry to
persons in varied times and cultural situations grieving after mass deaths caused by natural disasters, war, or injustice, and focusing on use of the liturgy in Christian response.

PO71 *Principalities and Powers and People*
New York, NYU: UMC, Board of Global Ministries, 1979.
111 pp. Paper. No ISBN.

Stories of oppression and hope based on the personal
experiences of eighteen mission interns of the UMC in various countries.

PO72 Reuver, Marc, ed.
Human Rights: A Challenge to Theology. Rome, IT: IDOC

International; Geneva, SZ: WCC, 1983. 174 pp. Paper. No
ISBN.

A collection of papers, statements, and testimonies from
Latin America, Asia, Africa, and the Pacific, concerning
human rights issues—documents for an interconfessional
study project on the theological basis of human rights.

PO73 Santolaria Ruda, Juan José
*Los Sujetos de Derecho Internacional: El Caso de la Igle-
sia Católica y del Estado de la Ciudad del Vaticano.* Lima,
PE: Fondó Editorial de la Pontificia Universidad Católica y
del Estado de la Ciudad del Vaticano, 1995. 603 pp. Paper.
8483909774.

A scholarly analysis of the relationship between the
Catholic Church and the Vatican State and the role which
each plays in issues of human rights in the international
community.

PO74 Schreiter, Robert J.
The Ministry of Reconciliation: Spirituality & Strategies.
Maryknoll, NYU: Orbis Books, 1998. viii, 136 pp. Paper.
1570751684.

A noted missiologist looks at the spiritual dimensions
of reconciliation related both to Jesus' suffering and death,
and to the contemporary human rights struggles for justice
and reconciliation.

PO75 Short, Margaret I.
*Law and Religion in Marxist Cuba: A Human Rights Inqui-
ry.* Coral Gables, FLU: University of Miami, North-South
Center; New Brunswick, NJU: Transaction Publishers, 1993.
vii, 209 pp. Paper. 156000682X.

A case study on religious freedom in revolutionary
Cuba from 1959 to 1990, in connection with Cuban constitutional law, Marxist-Leninist ideology, and theological-
political diversity within the Cuban churches.

PO76 Swidler, Leonard J., ed.
*Religious Liberty and Human Rights in Nations and in Re-
ligions.* Philadelphia, PAU: Ecumenical Press; New York,
NYU: Hippocrene Books, 1986. xvi, 255 pp. Paper.
0931214068.

Seventeen scholarly papers on issues of religious liberty and human rights between nations, within nations, and
within religions; originally presented at an international
colloquium in Haverford, Pennyslvania, 3-8 Nov. 1985.

PO77 Tergel, Alf
Human Rights in Cultural and Religious Traditions. (Uppsala Studies in Faith and Ideologies, 8). Uppsala, SW: Uppsala University, 1998. 395 pp. Paper. 915544296X.

A detailed study of the evolution of thought concerning human rights in various Protestant confessional families and the WCC from 1945 to 1995; originally submitted
as a Ph.D. dissertation at the University of Uppsala.

PO78 Van Straaten, Werenfried
Where God Weeps. San Francisco, CAU: Ignatius Press,
1989. xviii, 250 pp. Paper. 0898702348.

A collection of short firsthand accounts of the author's
encounter with situations in which since 1945 Christians
have been persecuted and/or made to suffer in Europe, Asia,
Latin America, Africa, and Eastern Europe.

PO79 Villa-Vicencio, Charles

A Theology of Reconstruction: Nation-Building and Human Rights. (Cambridge Studies in Ideology and Religion). Cambridge, ENK: Cambridge University Press, 1992. xv, 300 pp. 0521416256 (hdbk), 0521426286 (pbk).

An interdisciplinary exploration of how theology on the one hand, and constitutional writing, lawmaking, economics, and the freedom of conscience on the other, can combine for nation-building and the promotion of human rights; with a focus on South Africa and Eastern Europe.

PO80 WCC, Human Rights Resources Office for Latin America

Behind the Mask: Human Rights in Asia and Latin America: An Inter-Regional Encounter. Edited by Erich Weingartner, and Mark R. Elliot. Geneva, SZ: WCC/HRROLA, 1988. xi, 99 pp. Paper. 2825409421.

A narrative account based on the experiences and findings of Asian and Latin American delegates to an interregional exchange program cosponsored by the WCC, the Latin American Council of Churches, and the CCA.

PO81 Weingartner, Erich

Human Rights on the Ecumenical Agenda: Report and Assessment. (CCIA Background Information 1983, 3). Geneva, SZ: CCIA/WCC, 1983. 73 pp. Paper. No ISBN.

An analysis of the development since 1948 of the WCC thought and action on human rights concerns, by the executive secretary of the CCIA.

PO82 White, C. Dale

Making a Just Peace: Human Rights and Domination Systems. Nashville, TNU: Abingdon, 1998. viii, 160 pp. Paper. 0687031338.

Out of his denominational and ecumenical leadership on human rights concerns, a United Methodist bishop develops a biblical and strategic response by the church in mission to issues of human rights, poverty, militarism, ecology, and patriarchy.

PO83 Witte, John, and Johan D. van der Vyver, eds.

Religious Human Rights in Global Perspective. The Hague, NE: Martinus Nijhoff Publishers, 1996. 2 vols. Paper. 9041101764 (I hdbk), 9041101799 (I pbk), 9041101772 (II hdbk), 9041101802 (II pbk).

Essays from the Emory University project on religion, democracy, and human rights, with nineteen essays by Christian, Jewish, and Muslim scholars of religion in North America (vol. 1: *Religious Perspectives,* xxxv, 597 pp.), and essays by an international panel of scholars on legal and ethical issues concerning freedom of religion, many of them national case studies (vol. 2: *Legal Perspectives,* xlvii, 670 pp.).

PO84 Zalaquett, José

The Human Rights Issue and the Human Rights Movement: Characterization, Evaluation, Propositions. Geneva, SZ: WCC-CCIA, 1981. 65 pp. Paper. No ISBN.

A brief summary of ten years of ecumenical thinking concerning human rights issues, with suggestions for future perspectives.

Political Change; Revolution

See also GW86, TH369, EC59, EC76-EC77, PO193, AF138, AF150, AF555, AF591, AF599, AF613, AF650, AF672, AF809, AF811, AF820, AF823, AF865, AF871, AF874, AF877, AF885, AF891, AF908-AF909, AF924-AF925, AF942, AF947, AF995, AF1018, AF1036, AF1053, AF1072, AF1100, AF1112, AF1122, AF1127, AF1137, AF1139, AF1157, AF1163, AF1177, AM12, AM16, AM130, AM207, AM210, AM256-AM258, AM265, AM267, AM287, AM297, AM306, AM311-AM314, AM338, AM560, AM562, AM564, AM568, AM579, AM598, AM667-AM668, AM672, AM681-AM683, AM716, AM719, AM725, AM727, AM731-AM732, AM737-AM738, AM749, AM758, AM780, AM894, AM922, AM924-AM925, AM929, AM931-AM933, AM935-AM937, AM940, AM943-AM944, AM950-AM953, AM1382, AM1403, AM1411-AM1412, AM1439, AM1498, AS104, AS378, AS385, AS418, AS456, AS815, AS828, AS831-AS832, AS850, AS915, AS1282, AS1328-AS1329, AS1416, AS1424-AS1426, AS1452, AS1473, AS1484, EU49, and EU53.

PO85 Barbé, Dominique

A Theology of Conflict and Other Writings on Nonviolence. Maryknoll, NYU: Orbis Books, 1989. xv, 181 pp. Paper. 0883445468.

Written by a man who lived, struggled, and wrote from the poverty of a Brazilian slum, this book explores the metaphysics, psychology, social, and political dimensions of conflict, and how nonviolent means may be applied in the struggle for liberation in Brazil.

PO86 Bigo, Pierre

Chiesa Rivoluzioni Sociali e Terzo Mundo. Rome, IT: Città Nuova Editrice, 1976. iv, 331 pp. No ISBN.

Italian translation.

PO87 Bigo, Pierre

The Church and the Third World Revolution. Translated by Jeanne Marie Lyons. Maryknoll, NYU: Orbis Books, 1977. iv, 316 pp. 0883440717 (hdbk), 0883440725 (pbk).

English translation.

PO88 Bigo, Pierre

La Iglesia y el Tercer Mundo. Salamanca, SP: Ediciones Sígueme, 1975. 303 pp. 8430106707.

Spanish translation.

PO89 Bigo, Pierre

L'Église et la révolution du Tiers Monde. Paris, FR: Presses Universitaires de France, 1974. 284 pp. No ISBN.

The Jesuit professor at the CELAM pastoral institute in Medellin, Columbia, offers Christians a multidisciplinary analysis of a world in revolution, including the social origins of revolution among marginalized and oppressed peoples, a theology of Christian involvement, the dialogue with Marxism, and alternative choices for a more just society.

PO90 Broucker, José de

Dom Helder Camara: la violence d'un pacifique. Paris, FR: Artheme Fayard, 1969. 221 pp. No ISBN.

A narrative introduction to the life and ministry of the remarkable Catholic bishop of Recife in Northeast Brazil.

PO91 Broucker, José de

Dom Helder Camara: The Violence of a Peacemaker. Translated by Herma Briffault. Maryknoll, NYU: Orbis Books, 1970. xiii, 154 pp. No ISBN.

English translation.

PO—MISSIONS AND POLITICAL LIFE

PO92 Broucker, José de
Dom Helder Camara: Die Leidenschaft des Friedensstifters.
Graz, AU: Verlag Styria, 1969. 245 pp. Paper. No ISBN.
German translation.

PO93 Broucker, José de
Dom Helder Camara: La Violencia de un Pacífico. Translated by P. José Carrillo. (Colección Nuestro Tiempo). Bilbao, SP: Desclée de Brouwer, 1971. 228 pp. No ISBN.
Second edition of the Spanish translation.

PO94 Brown, Robert McAfee
Religion and Violence. Philadelphia, PAU: Westminster Press, 1987. xxix, 114 pp. Paper. 066424078X.

The second edition of the widely used handbook (1st ed., 1973) on the imperative of just and necessary revolutions in Third World countries, the challenges of the '80s, and appropriate responses by North American churches.

PO95 Chatteris, Chris
Between a Rock and a Hard Place: Discernment in the Search for Justice: Some Concrete Issues. Pietermaritzburg, SA: Cluster Publications, 1995. 121 pp. Paper. 0958380775.

Guidance for Christians in mission amidst political upheavals, including those of the author as a Jesuit in South Africa.

PO96 Consultation on the Role of Religion in Conflict Situations (Cyprus, 23-27 April 1990)
The Role of Religion in Conflict Situations. Uppsala, SW: Life and Peace Institute, 1991. xxiv, 317 pp. Paper. No ISBN.

Papers from an important ecumenical consultation, with case studies from Northern Ireland, Palestine, Cyprus, Sudan, Lebanon, and South Africa.

PO97 Davies, J. G.
Christians, Politics and Violent Revolution. Maryknoll, NYU: Orbis Books; London, UK: SCM Press, 1976. 216 pp. 088344061X.

An argument that situations in which the masses are oppressed economically, politically, or racially, require a new Christian theology of social conflict, violence, and revolution that may include a redefinition of the just war tradition to include liberation wars.

PO98 *Directions of Change in South African Politics*
(Occasional Publications, 3). Johannesburg, SA: SPROCAS, 1971. 85 pp. No ISBN.
Papers of the SPROCAS Political Commission.

PO99 Dri, Rubén R.
La Utopía de Jesús. (Religión y Política, 4). México, MX: Ediciones Nuevomar, 1984. 302 pp. Paper. 9684690533.

An essay on the Kingdom of God and the praxis of Jesus of Nazareth in the light of the Latin American continent, which is considered dominated and oppressed.

PO100 Eigenmann, Urs
Politische Praxis des Glaubens: Dom Hélder Câmaras Weg zum Anwalt der Armen und seine Reden an die Reichen. Freiburg, SZ: Edition Exodus; Münster, GW: Edition Liberación, 1984. xxvi, 729 pp. Paper. 3905575108 (SZ), 392379214X (GW).

A dissertation on H. Camara; for the most part, an analysis of the lectures he delivered outside Brazil in order to promote conscientization concerning nonviolent change of unjust structures.

PO101 Eppstein, John
Does God Say Kill?: An Investigation of the Justice of Current Fighting in Africa. London, ENK: Tom Stacey, 1972. 138 pp. 085468204X.

A critique of the 1971 position of the Archbishop of Canterbury, sympathetic to liberation movements in Southern Africa; with an analysis of political developments in countries there.

PO102 Fragoso, Antônio Batista
Évangile et révolution sociale. (L'évangile au vingtieme siècle). Paris, FR: Éditions du Cerf, 1969. 173 pp. No ISBN.

A bishop from the northeast of Brazil advocates the urgent need for social improvements in the country, rejecting hatred and violence as contrary to the spirit of the Gospel.

PO103 Fragoso, Antônio Batista
Evangelõ e problemática social. Paris, FR: Éditions du Cerf, 1969. xciii, 166 pp. No ISBN.

Portuguese translation of *Évangile et révolution sociale* (1969).

PO104 Houtart, François, and André Rousseau
The Church and Revolution. Maryknoll, NYU: Orbis Books, 1971. xi, 371 pp. No ISBN.

A sociological study of revolution and the RCC's role therein as viewed by analyzing revolutionary movements in France from 1789 to contemporary revolutions in Cuba, South Africa, Vietnam, and Latin America.

PO105 Johnston, Douglas, and Cynthia Sampson, eds.
Religion, the Missing Dimension of Statecraft. (Center for Strategic and International Studies). New York, NYU: Oxford University Press, 1994. xviii, 350 pp. 0195087348.

Seven scholarly essays presenting case studies in which religious or spiritual influences have played a part in conflict resolution (Franco-German, Nicaragua, Nigeria, East Germany, Philippines, South Africa, and Zimbabwe), with eight essays assessing findings and implications.

PO106 Kirk, J. Andrew
Theology Encounters Revolution. Downers Grove, ILU: InterVarsity, 1980. 188 pp. Paper. 0877844682.

Describes the rise of theological interest in revolution and looks at various forms of revolutionary theology in different parts of the world (Western Europe, Eastern Europe, white North America, black North America, South America, and Latin America), and explores biblical and theological foundations of revolution (Rauschenbusch, R. Niebuhr, Barth, Bonhoffer).

PO107 Lacy, Creighton, ed.
Christianity amid Rising Men and Nations. New York, NYU: Association Press, 1965. 192 pp. No ISBN.

Nine essays by noted international scholars and church leaders, including Barbara Ward, M. Richard Shaull, Paul R. Abrecht, and Samuel D. Proctor on the relation between Christian mission and the social revolutions taking place in the nations of Africa, Asia, and Latin America.

PO108 Morris, Colin

Unyoung—Uncolored—Unpoor. Nashville, TNU: Abingdon, 1969. 158 pp. Paper. 0687431050.

An attempt at consciousness-raising among First World Christians concerning the plight of Third World poor and oppressed peoples, that leads them to use violence to achieve justice, by then-President of the United Church of Zambia.

PO109 Paoli, Arturo

Diálogo de la Liberación. Bueno Aires, AG: Ediciones Carlos Lohlé, 1970. 303 pp. No ISBN.

Spanish translation.

PO110 Paoli, Arturo

Dialogo della Liberazione. Brescia, IT: Morcelliana, 1970. 367 pp. No ISBN.

Expositions on eighteen dimensions of human freedom.

PO111 Paoli, Arturo

Freedom to Be Free. Translated by Charles Underhill Quinn. Maryknoll, NYU: Orbis Books, 1973. viii, 303 pp. 088344142X.

English translation.

PO112 Richard, Pablo et al.

Los Cristianos y la Revolución: Un debate abierto en América Latina. (Colección Camino Abierto, 1; Serie debates nacionales). Santiago, CH: Quimantú, 1973. 396 pp. No ISBN.

An exploration of the interconnections between Christianity, Marxism, and social revolution in Latin America.

PO113 Segundo, Juan Luis

Masas y Minorías en la Dialéctica Divina de la Liberación. Buenos Aires, AG: Editorial La Aurora, 1973. 110 pp. Paper. No ISBN.

A monograph on the revolutionary nature of the Christian message by the prominent Latin American theologian.

PO114 Segundo, Juan Luis

Massas e minorias na dialética divina da libertacão. São Paulo, BL: Edições Loyola, 1975. 99 pp. Paper. No ISBN.

Portuguese translation.

PO115 Sithole, Ndabaningi

Obed Mutezo: The Mudzimu Christian Nationalist. Nairobi, KE: Oxford University Press, 1970. x, 210 pp. Paper. No ISBN.

An exploration of the roots of African nationalism, including its spiritual roots both in Christian missions and traditional African religion, as told by a United Church of Christ minister who himself led the Zimbabwe African National Union (ZANU), through the biography of one Zimbabwe freedom fighter.

PO116 Sundström, Erland

Folkmord eller frigörelse?: Om mission och missionskritik. Herrljunga, SW: Interskrift, 1978. 124 pp. No ISBN.

This book deals with questions about missions and political and social liberation, and culture conflicts between missions and indigenous cultures.

PO117 *The Encounter of the Church with Movements of Social Change in Various Cultural Contexts*

Geneva, SZ: LWF, 1977. 2 vols. Paper. No ISBN.

Twenty-three national case studies from six continents presented as part of an LWF study of "The Encounter of the Church with Marxism in Various Cultural Contexts" at two seminars Bossey, Switzerland, 21-27 Sept. 1975; Glion, Switzerland, 4-11 July 1976 [vol. 1, 1975, 131 pp.; vol. 2, 1976, 238 pp.].

PO118 *The Road to Damascus: Kairos and Conversion*

Johannesburg, SA: Skotaville Publishers, 1989. 36 pp. Paper. 094700985X.

A document by Third World Christians in lands of violent political conflict (Philippines, South Korea, Namibia, South Africa, El Salvador, Nicaragua, and Guatemala) exploring causes of Christian divisions in such situations, and advocating a theology that sides with the poor and the oppressed.

PO119 *Vangelo violenza rivoluzione*

(IDOC Documentinuovi, 10). Milano, IT: Mondadori, 1969. 259 pp. No ISBN.

Essays edited by IDOC on theoretical and ideological issues in the relationships of the church and revolutions, together with three models by both European and Third World scholars, for interpreting the types, forms, and processes of revolutions.

PO120 Verkuyl, Johannes, and H. G. Schulte Nordholt

Responsible Revolution: Means and Ends for Transforming Society. Translated by Lewis B. Smedes. Grand Rapids, MIU: Eerdmans, 1974. 101 pp. Paper. 0802815464.

English translation.

PO121 Verkuyl, Johannes, and H. G. Schulte Nordholt

Verantwoorde revolutie: Over middelen en doeleinden in de strijd om transformatie van samenlevingen. Kampen: Kok, 1970. 144 pp. 9024228409.

In this second edition, the authors focus on the reality of revolution in modern times and offer a theology of transformation with which the church—and the individual Christian—can respond to this crisis.

PO122 Villa-Vicencio, Charles

Civil Disobedience and Beyond: Law, Resistance and Religion in South Africa. Cape Town, SA: David Philip; Grand Rapids, MIU: Eerdmans, 1990. xvi, 165 pp. Paper. 0864861443 (D), 0802805264 (E).

A discussion of some of the most important issues facing South Africa in the 1990s, including civil disobedience, armed conflict, and the task of government, with focus on the mission of the churches in the theological, legal, and political debate.

PO123 Von der Mehden, Fred R.

Religion and Nationalism in Southeast Asia: Burma, Indonesia, the Philippines. Madison, WIU: University of Wisconsin Press, 1963. 253 pp. No ISBN.

A scholarly study, based on firsthand investigation, of the role of religion (Buddhism, Islam, Catholicism) in creating new nations and their cultural patterns.

PO124 *When All Else Fails: Christian Arguments on Violent Revolution*

Philadelphia, PAU: Pilgrim Press, 1970. vi, 230 pp. 0829801871.

English translation edited by IDOC.

PO125 *With Raging Hope: Theology in the Third World Church and Social Transformation*

(SPI Series, Faith and Ideology, 1). Quezon City, PH: Socio-Pastoral Institute/Claretian Publications, 1983. i, 204 pp. 9715011039.

A compilation of fourteen essays on the church's responsibility to participate in the struggle for justice in situations of social revolution, with special reference to Nicaragua.

Violence and Nonviolence

See also EU125.

PO126 Câmara, Hélder

Spiral of Violence. Translated by Della Couling. Denville, NJU: Dimension Books, 1971. viii, 83 pp. No ISBN.

Writing in the tradition of Gandhi and Martin Luther King, Jr., the prophetic Archbishop of Olinda and Recife in northeast Brazil describes the fundamental conditions in society that spawn violence, protest, and repression, while opting for a nonviolent resolution of conflict.

PO127 Hope, Marjorie, and James Young

The Struggle for Humanity: Agents of Nonviolent Change in a Violent World. Maryknoll, NYU: Orbis Books, 1977. 305 pp. Paper. 0883444690.

Biographies of church, community, and national leaders, mostly in the Third World, who live out their commitments to nonviolent change; with a resource list of NGOs interested in nonviolent action and/or community formation.

PO128 O'Murchu, Diarmuid

Poverty, Celibacy, and Obedience: A Radical Option for Life. New York City, NYU: Crossword Publishing, 1999. vi, 135 pp. Paper. 0824514734.

A reclamation of the authentic tradition of the vowed life through the integration of the Eastern origin of nonviolence and Western spirituality; a study of vows as values rather than as laws.

PO129 Onderwys, Christelike Hoër

Venster op mag en geweld/Reflections on Power and Violence: Christelike Perspektiewe/Christian Perspective. Potchefstroom, SA: Potchefstroom University, 1990. ii, 303 pp. Paper. 1868220443.

Sixteen essays in Afrikaans (10) and English (6) by South African theologians on issues of power and violence with special reference to that country.

PO130 Reinders, Johannes Sjoerd

Violence, Victims and Rights: A Reappraisal of the Argument from Institutionalized Violence with Special Reference to Latin American Liberation Theology. Amsterdam, NE: Free University Press, 1988. 256 pp. 906256674X.

The author's Th.D. thesis at the Free University of Amsterdam.

PO131 Villa-Vicencio, Charles, ed.

Theology and Violence: The South African Debate. Grand Rapids, MIU: Eerdmans, 1988. 309 pp. Paper. 0802803598.

Nineteen essays by a cross section of South African church leaders and theologians on contemporary issues of violence in that country, and the theological debate on alternatives—a project of The Institute of Contextual Theology (ICT).

Colonialism and Missions

See also HI116, HI275, CR359, SO220, SO321, PO154, ED23, AF10, AF230, AF465, AF548, AF566, AF577, AF589, AF639, AF663, AF792, AF862, AF876, AF1174, AF1179, AF1199, AF1215, AF1217, AF1220, AF1235, AF1263, AF1281, AM17, AM84, AM98, AM559, AM769, AM1460, AM1479, AM1492, AS392-AS393, AS395, AS417, AS905, AS932, AS947, AS1006-AS1007, AS1012, AS1035, AS1084, AS1123, AS1164, AS1326, AS1388, EU187, EU282, and OC150.

PO132 Ahonen, Risto

Kristillisen lähetystyön ja amerikkalaisen imperialismin dilemma John R. Mott in ajattelussa. (Missiologian ja ekumeniikan seuran julkaisuja, 40). Helsinki, FI: Missiologian ja ekumeniikan seura; Helsinki, FI: Kirjapaja, 1983. 157 pp. Paper. 951952065I (M), 9516214541 (K).

An analysis of the dilemma of Christian mission and American imperialism in the thought of John R. Mott (1865-1955); originally presented as a thesis at the University of Helsinki.

PO133 Bade, Klaus J., ed.

Imperialismus und Kolonialmission: Kaiserliches Deutschland und koloniales Imperium. Wiesbaden, GW: Steiner, 1984. xiii, 333 pp. Paper. 3515043373.

A study of the relations between German imperialism and missions in the late 19th and early 20th centuries.

PO134 Bade, Klaus J.

Friedrich Fabri und der Imperialismus in der Bismarckzeit: Revolution, Depression, Expansion. (Beiträge zur Kolonial- und Überseegeschichte, 13). Freiburg im Breisgau, SZ: Atlantis, 1975. 579 pp. 3761104766.

A scholarly analysis of the impact on German colonial policy of Friedrich Fabri (1824-1891), an evangelical theologian who was the leading figure in the Rhineland Mission from 1857 to 1884.

PO135 Beck, Thomas, Annerose Menninger, and Thomas Schleich, eds.

Kolumbus' Erben: Europäische Expansion und überseeische Ethnien im Ersten Kolonialzeitalter, 1415-1815. Darmstadt, GW: Wissenschaftliche Buchgesellschaft, 1992. viii, 323 pp. Paper. 3534118723.

In nine essays in honor of mission scholar Eberhard Schmitt, German scholars discuss European expansion in Africa, the Americas, and the Orient, Europe's motivation, and the progressive involvement of the church.

PO136 Boxer, C. R.

The Portuguese Seaborne Empire, 1415-1825. (Aspects of Portugal). Manchester, ENK: Carcanet/Calouste Gulbenkian Foundation, 1991. xiii, 426 pp. 0856359629.

A survey of Portuguese imperialism from the 15th to 19th century in Brazil, Africa, and East Asia treated both chronologically and topically (the fleets, the church, ethnic relations, trade, etc.); originally published by Alfred A. Knopf, New York (1969).

PO137 Brufau Prats, Jaime

La Escuela de Salamanca ante el Descubrimiento del Nuevo Mundo. (Biblioteca de Teólogos Españoles, 33). Salamanca, SP: Editorial San Esteban, 1989. 179 pp. Paper. 8485045831.

A study of the legal doctrines of Francisco de Vitoria, Domingo de Soto, and other jurists of 16th-century Salamanca who made judgments concerning Spanish conquests in the New World.

PO138 Delavignette, Robert Louis

Christentum und Kolonialismus.... (Bibliothek Ekklesia, 21). Aschaffenburg, GW: Pattloch, 1961. 158 pp. Paper. No ISBN.

German translation.

PO139 Delavignette, Robert Louis

Christianisme et colonialisme. (Collection je sais je crois). Paris, FR: Édition Fayard, 1960. 127 pp. No ISBN.

Reflections on the attitudes adopted by Christians when confronted with the fact of colonialism, with special reference to Roman Catholic missions and papal missionary encyclicals of the 20th century.

PO140 Delavignette, Robert Louis

Christianity and Colonialism. Translated by J. R. Foster. (Twentieth Century Encyclopedia of Catholicism-The Church and the Modern World IX, 97). New York, NYU: Hawthorn Books, 1964. 172 pp. No ISBN.

English translation.

PO141 Dharmaraj, Jacob S.

Colonialism and Christian Mission: Postcolonial Reflections. Delhi, II: ISPCK, 1993. xx, 149 pp. Paper. 8172141009.

An exploration of the missiological thought and method of British missionary societies to India in the 19th century (William Carey to Alexander Duff), with focus on their colonial connections.

PO142 Gewecke, Helga et al.

Women Carry More than Half the Burden: Texts from a Workshop on the History of the Basel Mission and Its Partner-Churches in the 20th Century. (Texts and Documents, 2). Basel, SZ: Basel Mission, 1996. 78 pp. No ISBN.

A study of the Basel Mission project that promotes its identity, clarifies its history, and affirms in all its paradoxes a partnership with European women which evolved out of the colonial era.

PO143 Gründer, Horst

Christliche Mission und deutscher Imperialismus: Eine politische Geschichte ihrer Beziehungen während der deutschen Kolonialzeit (1884-1914) unter besonderer Berücksichtigung Afrikas und Chinas. (Sammlung Schöningh zur Geschichte und Gegenwart). Paderborn, GW: Ferdinand Schöningh, 1982. 444 pp. 3506774646.

A richly documented and precise history of the relationship of Christian missions with the German colonial authorities.

PO144 Grohs, Gerhard, and Harry Neyer, eds.

Die Kirchen und die portugiesische Präsenz in Afrika. (Entwicklung und Frieden, 2). Munich, GW: Chr. Kaiser Verlag; Mainz, GW: Matthias-Grünewald, 1975. 176 pp. Paper. 3459009950 (K), 3786704716 (G).

Papers from the 1973 Study Days in Bensberg about the church and the Portuguese colonies in Africa, including an overview of Portugal's political, economic and social situation, its overseas policies and church-state relations, with a fifty-page appendix of relevant pastoral letters and responses.

PO145 Höffner, Joseph

Kolonialismus und Evangelium: Spanische Kolonialethik im Goldenen Zeitalter. Trier, GW: Paulinus Verlag, 1972. vii, 455 pp. No ISBN.

A reprint of *Christentum und Menschenwürde* (1947), a scholarly analysis of the relation between Spanish missions and colonialism in Latin America in the 15th and 16th centuries.

PO146 Hammer, Karl

Weltmission und Kolonialismus: Sendungsideen des 19. Jahrhunderts im Konflikt. (Deutscher Taschenbuch Verlag, 4368; Wissenschaft). Munich, GW: Deutscher Taschenbuch Verlag, 1981. 348 pp. 3423043687.

An analysis of the 19th century conflicts between missions and colonialism; originally published in 1978 by Kösel.

PO147 Mehl, Roger

Decolonisation et missions protestantes. Paris, FR: Société des missions évangéliques, 1964. 134 pp. No ISBN.

An analysis of linkages between Protestant missions and colonialism.

PO148 Merle, Marcel

Les Églises chrétiennes et la décolonisation. Paris, FR: A. Colin, 1967. 520 pp. No ISBN.

A major study of the churches and colonialism.

PO149 Neill, Stephen Charles

Colonialism and Christian Missions. London, ENK: Lutterworth Press; New York, NYU: McGraw-Hill, 1966. 445 pp. No ISBN.

The first comprehensive survey of the historical relationship between colonialism and Christian missions to 1930, primarily concerning India, Eastern Asia, and Africa.

PO150 Paczensky, Gert von

Teurer Segen: Christliche Mission und Kolonialismus. Munich, GW: Goldmann, 1994. 544 pp. Paper. 3442125065.

A critical analysis of linkages between Christian mission and colonization from the crusades to the 20th century; originally published in 1991 (Munich, GW: A. Knaus).

PO151 Schwegmann, Barbara

Die protestantische Mission und die Ausdehnung des Britischen Empires. (Epistemata. Reihe Gesellschaftswissenschaften, 4). Würzburg, GW: Königshausen und Neumann, 1990. ii, 413 pp. Paper. 3884794949.

The author investigates the collaboration of Protestant missionaries with British colonialists in subjecting overseas peoples, concluding that most missionary societies and missionaries tried to avoid political matters but, nevertheless, played some part in extending the British Empire.

PO152 Stanley, Brian

The Bible and the Flag: Protestant Missions and British Imperialism in the Nineteenth and Twentieth Centuries. Leicester, ENK: Apollos, 1990. 212 pp. Paper. 0851114121.

A carefully built picture of the relationship between imperialism and mission, with special reference to Africa, attempting to establish that the general missionary motive was to promote Christianity, not to establish an empire.

PO153 Wright, Louis Booker

Religion and Empire. New York, NYU: Octagon Books, 1965. ix, 190 pp. No ISBN.

Second edition of a collection of seven lectures delivered at the University of Washington in 1942 concerning the influence of the clergy on the expansion of the British empire in the late 16th and early 17th centuries, concluding that the propaganda and influence of the clergy were powerful factors in building public sentiment in favor of overseas expansion.

Missionaries and Political Activity

See also HI121, HI506, PO10, MI170, AF615, AF742, AF756, AF888, AM288-AM289, AM675, AM689, AM739, AM752, AM771, AM775, AM1150, AS297, AS406, AS575, AS717, AS856, AS877, AS946, and AS1463.

PO154 Clymer, Kenton J.
Protestant Missionaries in the Philippines, 1898-1916: An Inquiry into the American Colonial Mentality. Chicago, ILU: University of Chicago Press; Champaign, ILU: University Press of Illinois, 1986. ix, 267 pp. 0252012100.

A study of US imperialism as personified in the Protestant missionaries who went to the Philippines, certain of the superiority of their faith and culture, and showing a clear linkage between politics and missionary activity in the US's Asian colony.

PO155 Grabill, Joseph L.
Protestant Diplomacy and the Near East: Missionary Influence on American Policy, 1810-1927. Minneapolis, MNU: University of Minnesota Press, 1971. x, 395 pp. 0816605750.

A detailed history based on archival research, of the impact Protestant missionaries and philanthropists had on the US foreign policy toward the Near East during World War I and its aftermath, including relief aid for Armenians in Turkey.

PO156 Graham, Stephen A., ed.
The Totalitarian Kingdom of God: The Political Philosophy of E. Stanley Jones. Lanham, MDU: University Press of America, 1998. vii, 173 pp. 0761812377.

A study of the deep and intimate involvement in politics of E. Stanley Jones throughout his adult life.

PO157 Jong, A. H. de
Missie en politiek in oostelijk Afrika: Nederlandse missionarissen en Afrikaans nationalisme in Kenya, Tanzania en Malawi 1945-1965. (Kerk en theologie in context, 25). Kampen, NE: Kok, 1994. xvi, 370 pp. Paper. 9039005079.

A scholarly assessment of the role of Dutch missionaries in African nationalism in Kenya, Tanzania, and Malawi between 1945 and 1965.

PO158 Lodwick, Kathleen L.
Crusaders Against Opium: Protestant Missionaries in China, 1874-1917. Lexington, KYU: University Press of Kentucky, 1996. xi, 218 pp. 0813119243.

A careful examination of the intersecting efforts of Protestant missionaries (particularly medical doctors), government officials, and commissions of inquiry, to end the importation of opium into China.

PO159 Neils, Patricia, ed.
United States Attitudes and Policies Toward China: The Impact of American Missionaries. (Studies on Modern China). Armonk, NYU: M. E. Sharpe, 1990. 289 pp. 0873326326.

Fifteen scholarly papers from an international conference held 23-24 October 1987 at the University of San Diego, US.

PO160 Vekemans, Roger
Caesar and God: The Priesthood and Politics. Translated by Aloysius Owen, and Charles Underhill Quinn. Maryknoll, NYU: Orbis Books, 1972. x, 118 pp. No ISBN.
English translation.

PO161 Vekemans, Roger
Iglesia y Mundo Político: Sacerdocio y política. (Colección Santo Toríío de Mogrovejo, 9). Lima, PE: Centro Arquidiocesano de Pastoral, 1970. 113 pp. No ISBN.

An argument that the engagement of a priest in politics must be both authentically priestly and realistically political, by the Director of CEDIAL (Centro de Estudio para el Desarrollo y la Integración de América Latina) based in Bogotá, Colombia.

Church and State

See also HI84, HI690, ME23, SO319, EC239, AF50, AF159, AF189, AF199, AF430, AF452, AF479, AF494, AF576, AF589, AF601, AF625, AF685, AF702, AF715, AF726, AF737, AF900, AF904, AF917, AF919, AF952, AF1020, AF1079, AF1081, AF1102-AF1103, AF1115-AF1116, AF1118, AF1152-AF1153, AF1159, AF1171, AF1176, AF1181, AF1264, AF1293, AF1322, AF1328, AF1355, AM97, AM269, AM290, AM295, AM304, AM307, AM322, AM335, AM569-AM570, AM576, AM605, AM688, AM694, AM774, AM777, AM787, AM794, AM823, AM955, AM1117, AM1244, AM1251, AM1288-AM1290, AM1343, AM1389-AM1390, AS88, AS102, AS634, AS648, AS652, AS718-AS719, AS1098-AS1099, AS1258, AS1283, AS1299, AS1417, AS1422, AS1521, EU155, EU180, EU195, EU221, EU247, EU253, EU274, and EU276.

PO162 Brown, Robert McAfee
Saying Yes and Saying No: On Rendering to God and to Caesar. Philadelphia, PAU: Westminster Press, 1986. 143 pp. Paper. 0664246958.

Eight contemporary political choices in which Christians saying "yes" to the God of the Bible say "no" to false gods of the state who crave our allegiance.

PO163 *Church and State: Opening a New Ecumenical Discussion*
(Faith and Order Paper, 85). Geneva, SZ: WCC, 1978. 183 pp. Paper. 2825405744.

Seven essays by church leaders from six continents presented at a WCC colloquium at Bossey, Switzerland (19-25 August 1976), together with Bible studies and the final report.

PO164 Coleman, John Aloysius, and Miklós Tomka
Religion and Nationalism. (*Concilium*, 1995/6). London, ENK: SCM Press; Maryknoll, NYU: Orbis Books, 1995. x, 116 pp. Paper. 0334030358 (UK), 0883448874 (US).

Ten essays on the challenge of nationalism to the churches, and on the varied roles of religions in national conflicts.

PO165 Comblin, Joseph
The Church and the National Security State. Maryknoll, NYU: Orbis Books, 1979. xiii, 236 pp. Paper. 0883440822.

An analysis of the national security system in Latin America, the religious sanction given to it by religious elites, and its critique from a liberation theology perspective.

PO166 Consejo Episcopal Latinoamerica
Relaciones Iglesia-estado: Análisis Teológico-Jurídico desde América Latina. Bogota, CK: CELAM; Quito, EC: Ediciones de la Pontificia Universidad Católica del Ecador, 1987. 386 pp. Paper. 9586250512.

Papers on church-state issues in Latin America covering historical themes, doctrinal foundations, human rights, and comparisons between church-state relations in Europe and Latin America, and human rights; prepared by the Latin American Conference of Bishops (RC) in collaboration with the Pontifical University in Zulto, Ecuador.

PO167 Heuvel, M. C., ed.

Rebuilding Our Nation: Participating in the Political Process from the Perspective of a Biblical Christian Worldview. (Series F2: Brochures of the Institute for Reformational Studies, 71). Potchefstroom, SA: Institute for Reformational Studies/PU for CHE, 1999. iv, 96 pp. Paper. 1868223345.

A call for Christians to be active in decision-making processes and mechanisms at grassroots and national levels of the new South Africa.

PO168 Hillekamps, Karl Heinz

Religion, Kirche und Staat in Lateinamerika. Munich, GW: Kösel Verlag, 1966. 185 pp. No ISBN.

The difficulties facing Latin America put into the perspective of past and present church-state relations, sketched by an author of vast experience on that continent.

PO169 Klaiber, Jeffrey L.

The Church, Dictatorships, and Democracy in Latin America. Maryknoll, NYU: Orbis Books, 1998. ix, 326 pp. Paper. 1570751994.

Twelve national case studies, from 1954 to the present, of the Catholic Church's involvement in Latin American struggles to defend human rights and achieve democracy.

PO170 Mignone, Emilio F.

Witness to the Truth: The Complicity of Church and Dictatorship in Argentina, 1976-1983. Translated by Phillip Berryman. Maryknoll, NYU: Orbis Books, 1988. xi, 162 pp. Paper. 0883446308 (hdbk), 0883446294 (pbk).

The account of the role of the RCC hierarchy in Argentina during the military dictatorship, 1976-1983, by an Argentinian lawyer, educator, and human rights advocate.

PO171 Nelson-Pallmeyer, Jack

War against the Poor: Low-Intensity Conflict and Christian Faith. Maryknoll, NYU: Orbis Books, 1989. xii, 98 pp. Paper. 09934445891.

A strong critique of the US government's policy of low-intensity conflict (LIC) by which it intervenes in the politics of Third World nations (e.g., Nicaragua), with proposals that U.S. churches oppose such policies as confessing churches.

PO172 Ngcokovane, Cecil

Demons of Apartheid: A Moral and Ethical Analysis of the N.G.K., N.P. and Broederbond's Justification of Apartheid. Braamfontein, SA: Skotaville Publishers, 1989. xiv, 249 pp. Paper. 0947009779.

An exploration of apartheid in an attempt to refute its sociopolitical legitimation and its Christian religious and moral justification, focusing on the history of the relationship between the Nederduitse Gereformeerde Kerk (NGK), the Nationalist Party, and the Broederbond.

PO173 Nichols, J. Bruce

The Uneasy Alliance: Religion, Refugee Work, and U.S. Foreign Policy. New York, NYU: Oxford University Press, 1988. xiv, 337 pp. 0195042743.

A detailed analysis of the complicated relationships between American religious organizations and the US government, with three case studies of their involvements in refugee assistance in Honduras, Thailand, and the Sudan.

PO174 Okullu, Henry

Church and State: In Nation Building and Human Development. Nairobi, KE: Uzima Press, 1984. xvi, 141 pp. Paper. No ISBN.

A discussion of the church's role in the development of political justice in the African nations.

PO175 Robbins, Thomas, and Roland Robertson, eds.

Church-State Relations: Tensions and Transitions. New Brunswick, NJU: Transaction Pubs., 1987. ix, 296 pp. Paper. 0887386512.

Nineteen scholarly articles on church-state relations in the United States and other nations, showing the variety of church-state and religious authority/political authority relationships.

PO176 Santos, Eduardo dos

L'état Portugais et le probleme missionnaire. Translated by Jean Haupt. Lisbon, PO: Junta de Investigacoes do Ultramar; Lisbon, PO: Centro de Estudos Históricos Ultramarinos, 1964. 162 pp. Paper. No ISBN.

A brief history of Portuguese government policies and regulation of missionaries in the 19th and 20th centuries, with special legislation affecting each territory (Macao, Angola, and Mozambique).

PO177 Schlossberg, Herbert

A Fragrance of Oppression: The Church and Its Persecutors. (The Turning Point Christian Worldview Series). Wheaton, ILU: Crossway Books, 1991. viii, 252 pp. Paper. 0891076263.

A popular analysis of contemporary persecutions of Christians by totalitarian and Islamic governments, from the perspective that conflicts between Christianity and totalitarian governments are inevitable.

PO178 Shiels, William Eugene

King and Church: The Rise and Fall of the Patronato Real. (Jesuit Studies). Chicago, ILU: Loyola University Press, 1961. xiii, 399 pp. No ISBN.

A history of relations between state and church in the Spanish colonies, with the texts of the main documents in the history.

PO179 Shupe, Anson, and Jeffrey K. Hadden, eds.

The Politics of Religion and Social Change. (Religion and the Political Order, 2). New York, NYU: Paragon House, 1988. xx, 284 pp. 0913757764 (hdbk), 0913757772 (pbk).

The second of three volumes examining the interactions of religion and politics around the globe, with essays by fourteen international scholars.

PO180 Sin, Jaime L.

Selected Writings on Church-State Relations and Human Development. (Inter-Faith Dialogue Series). Manila, PH: Centre for the Development of Human Resources in Rural Asia, 1984. 68 pp. Paper. No ISBN.

A collection of Cardinal Sin's major speeches on church-state questions from 1978 to 1984.

PO181 Thomas, Madathilparapil M., and M. Abel, eds.

Religion, State and Ideologies in East Asia: A Collection of Essays. Bangalore, II: EACC, 1965. xxvi, 160 pp. No ISBN.

Essays on church-state relations in nine Asian countries: Sri-Lanka (Ceylon), China, India, Indonesia, Japan, Korea, Malaysia, Pakistan, and the Philippines.

PO182 Villa-Vicencio, Charles

Between Christ and Caesar: Classic and Contemporary Texts on Church and State. Grand Rapids, MIU: Eerdmans; Claremont, SA: David Philip, 1986. xxvi, 269 pp. Paper. 0802802400 (US), 0864860706 (SA).

An introduction to the history of church-state relations, with key primary texts from the early church to the present.

International Relations: General

See also TH605, EA75, EC228, PO7, AF1042, AM229, AM286, AM582, AM964, AS106, AS411, AS414, AS724, AS794, and AS797.

PO183 Brown, Robert McAfee
Making Peace in the Global Village. Philadelphia, PAU: Westminster Press, 1981. 118 pp. Paper. 0664243436.

An introduction to issues of violence, the arms race, human rights, and global justice.

PO184 Kässmann, Margot
Overcoming Violence: The Challenge to the Churches in All Places. (Risk Book Series, 82). Geneva, SZ: WCC Publications, 1998. ix, 86 pp. Paper. 2825412287.

An introduction to the WCC's Programme to Overcome Violence, its rationale and opportunities.

PO185 Koshy, Ninan
Churches in the World of Nations: International Politics and the Mission and Ministry of the Church. Geneva, SZ: WCC Publications, 1994. x, 120 pp. Paper. 2825411361.

A primer on political involvement as part of the church's mission by the director of the WCC's Commission of the Churches on International Affairs.

PO186 MacKenzie, Kenneth M.
The Robe and the Sword: The Methodist Church and the Rise of American Imperialism. Washington, DCU: Public Affairs Press, 1961. 128 pp. No ISBN.

Original and somewhat critical research concerning the support which Methodist churches gave to American expansion and "manifest destiny" between 1865 and 1900.

PO187 Mische, Gerald, and Patricia Mische
Toward a Human World Order: Beyond the National Security Straitjacket. New York, NYU: Paulist Press, 1977. xiii, 399 pp. Paper. 0809102161 (hdbk), 0809119773 (pbk).

An analysis of why the nation state is an anachronism and the arms race evil, with advocacy for a new global consciousness, and multi-issue world coalitions, sanctioned by religious values as building blocks in an emerging new world order.

PO188 Roof, Wade Clark, ed.
World Order and Religion. (SUNY Series in Religion, Culture, and Society). Albany, NYU: SUNY Press, 1991. viii, 320 pp. 079140739X (hdbk), 0791407403 (pbk).

Fourteen scholarly essays on religion, especially Christianity, and international affairs, with essays by A. F. Walls, Lamin Sanneh, Michael A. Burdick, and Phillip E. Hammond on Christian missions and international politics.

PO189 Teinonen, Seppo A.
Kirkkojen yhteistyö ja kansainvälinen politiikka: The Cooperation of the Churches and International Politics, Summary. (Soumalaisen Teologisen Kirjallisuusseuran julkaisuja, 68). Helsinki, FI: Institute for Missiology and Ecumenics, University of Helsinki, 1960. 149 pp. No ISBN.

A monograph tracing the development of interchurch cooperation in international affairs in the 19th and 20th centuries, with an English summary.

PO190 Teinonen, Seppo A.
Missio Politica Oecumenica: A Contribution to the Study of the Theology of Ecumenical Work in International Politics. (Soumen Lähetystieteellisen Seuran Julkaisuja, 4). Helsinki,

FI: Finnish Society for Missiological Research, 1961. 86 pp. Paper. No ISBN.

English translation.

PO191 Van der Bent, A. J.
Christian Response in a World of Crisis: A Brief History of the WCC's Commission of the Churches on International Affairs. Geneva, SZ: WCC, 1986. viii, 80 pp. Paper. 2825408743.

A concise history of forty years' work of the WCC's Commission of the Churches on International Affairs.

PO192 Williams, Oliver F., and John W. Houck, eds.
Catholic Social Thought and the New World Order: Building on One Hundred Years. Notre Dame, INU: University of Notre Dame Press, 1993. xiv, 383 pp. Paper. 0268007977.

From their respective backgrounds in ecclesiology, theology, ethics, women's and minority studies, twenty leaders and scholars, mostly Roman Catholic, relate one-hundred years of Catholic social thought to the challenge of the new world order; originally presented at a symposium (1991) hosted by the University of Notre Dame Center for Ethics and Religious Values.

War

See also TH463, CR395, CR1033, and AF1285.

PO193 Conference on the Religious Contributions to War and Peace (May, 1984, University of Transkei, South Africa)
Religion, War and Peace. Edited by Ephriam K. Mosothoane, Luke Lungile Pato, and Louise Kretzschmar. Umtata, Transkei, SA: University of Transkei, 1984. xv, 152 pp. Paper. 0947029095.

Nine scholarly papers on responses by the churches in various historical periods to situations of political conflict, with special reference to the contemporary quest for peace in Southern Africa.

PO194 Hayama Missionary Seminar (26th., 1985)
Current Threats to God-Given Life: The Christian Response to Violence. Edited by Carl C. Beck. Tokyo, JA: Hayama Missionary Seminar, 1985. vi, 82 pp. Paper. No ISBN.

Major papers on Christian responses to various forms of violence, from abortion to nuclear war.

PO195 Linner, Rachelle
City of Silence: Listening to Hiroshima. Maryknoll, NYU: Orbis Books, 1995. xi, 146 pp. 1570750149.

Stories told by survivers of the first atomic bomb blast and those who joined them in ministries of reconciliation.

PO196 Minear, Larry, and Thomas G. Weiss
Mercy under Fire: War and the Global Humanitarian Community. Boulder, COU: Westview Press, 1995. xviii, 260 pp. 0813325668 (hdbk), 0813325676 (pbk).

Principles, guidelines and resources for those engaged in humanitarian relief operations in the post-Cold War era, based on interviews with 1,500 humanitarian workers and government officials in active war zones.

PO197 Shannon, Thomas A., ed.
War or Peace?: The Search for New Answers. Maryknoll, NYU: Orbis Books, 1980. xiv, 255 pp. Paper. 0883447509.

Thirteen scholarly contributions to the ongoing debate between pacifists and those who continue to support the just war tradition within American Catholicism, with reflections by leading Protestant ethicists.

PO—MISSIONS AND POLITICAL LIFE

PO198 Sider, Ronald J., and Richard K. Taylor
Nuclear Holocaust and Christian Hope: A Book for Christian Peacemakers. New York, NYU: Paulist Press; Downers Grove, ILU: InterVarsity, 1982. 368 pp. Paper. 0809125129 (P), 0877843864 (I).

A primer on nuclear war for Christians, including facts of nuclear destruction and deterrence, theological alternatives of just war or nonviolence, concrete ways to work for peace, and non-military means of national defense; with an extensive bibliography and resource guide.

PO199 *War and Conscience in South Africa: The Churches and Conscientious Objection*
Gweru, RH: Mambo Press; London, ENK: CIIR, 1983. 112 pp. Paper. No ISBN.

Case studies of South African conscientious objectors and the church debate on whether to provide chaplains to their members serving with liberation movements.

World Peace

See also ME170, ME234, CR395, CR418, SO559, PO9, PO198, SP78, SP183, AF363, AM565, AS1400, and EU117.

PO200 Barkat, Anwar M., ed.
Conflict, Violence, and Peace. Geneva, SZ: WCC, 1970. 163 pp. Paper. No ISBN.

The report of a Consultation on "Alternatives to Conflict in the Quest for Peace" held in the Ecumenical Institute at Bossey in summer 1969, including nine papers by international church leaders.

PO201 Beaver, Robert Pierce
Envoys of Peace: The Peace Witness in the Christian World Mission. Grand Rapids, MIU: Eerdmans, 1964. 133 pp. No ISBN.

Lectures by the noted missiologist and Professor of Missions at the University of Chicago Divinity School; originally presented at the 1962 conference on "The Christian Mission and the Peace Witness" (Germantown, Ohio), sponsored by the historic peace churches.

PO202 Branding, Ronice E.
Peacemaking: The Journey from Fear to Love. St. Louis, MOU: Chalice Press, 1987. 142 pp. Paper. 0827229402.

The author addresses the subject of peacemaking first by examining fear and insecurity, then, by setting out a way of transition from fear to love (the basis of peacemaking), and lastly by examining the process of building a peacemaking congregation.

PO203 Bsteh, Andreas, ed.
Friede für die Menschheit: Grundlagen, Probleme und Zukunftsperspektiven aus islamischer und christlicher Sicht. (Beiträge zur Religionstheologie, 8). Mödling, AU: Verlag St. Gabriel, 1994. 331 pp. Paper. 3852644569.

Papers on peace from the International Christian-Islamic Conference (Vienna, 30 March-2 April 1993).

PO204 Buttry, Daniel L.
Christian Peacemaking: From Heritage to Hope. Valley Forge, PAU: Judson Press, 1994. x, 214 pp. Paper. 0817012133.

An introduction to biblical peacemaking, the development of nonviolent direct action, and contemporary involvements

by the churches and other NGOs in conflict resolution and peacemaking.

PO205 Buttry, Daniel L.
Peace Ministry: A Handbook for Local Churches. Valley Forge, PAU: Judson Press, 1995. xiii, 224 pp. Paper. 0817012141.

A handbook for local church leaders in peacemaking ministries by the director of the Peace Program for American Baptists.

PO206 Friesen, Duane K.
Christian Peacemaking and International Conflict: A Realist Pacifist Perspective. (A Christian Peace Shelf Selection). Scottdale, PAU: Herald Press, 1986. 304 pp. Paper. 0836112733.

The author provides an interdisciplinary approach of social, political, and theological analysis on the issues of Christian peacemaking, develops a resource for discussion between the "peace" churches and mainstream Christianity, and stresses the relevance of the pacifist ethic for international order.

PO207 Gregorios, Paulos
Global Peace and Common Security. Delhi, II: Mar Gregorios Foundation; Delhi, II: ISPCK, 1998. 89 pp. Paper. 8172144679.

A call to save the planet from a Third World War and from complete annihilation, with specific interest in the Asia Pacific region; published by Rev. Ashish Amos for the Mar Gregorios Foundation of the Orthodox Theological Seminary and the ISPCK.

PO208 Herr, Robert, and Judy Zimmerman Herr, eds.
Transforming Violence: Linking Local and Global Peacemaking. Scottdale, PAU: Herald Press, 1998. 256 pp. Paper. 083619098X.

Short essays by leaders of the Fellowship of Reconciliation and the historic peace churches on local and global strategies for peacemaking; prepared as a resource for the WCC's proposed "Programme to Overcome Violence."

PO209 Jack, Homer A.
WCRP: A History of the World Conference on Religion and Peace. New York, NYU: World Conference on Religion and Peace, 1993. 595 pp. Paper. 093593409X.

The official history of a premier international interfaith organization founded in 1969, written by its first Secretary General (1969-1984).

PO210 Jeurissen, Ronald
Peace and Religion: An Empirical-Theological Study of the Motivational Effects of Religious Peace Attitudes on Peace Action. (Theologie und Empirie, 16). Kampen, NE: Kok; Weinheim, GW: Deutscher Studien Verlag, 1993. x, 353 pp. Paper. 9039000530 (NE), 3892713634 (GW).

A scholarly empirical study of goals and attitudes towards peacemaking in Dutch churches and peace movements, 1986-1990; originally submitted as a doctoral thesis at Nijmegen University.

PO211 Matsuki, Suguru, and David L. Swain, eds.
Called to Be Peacemakers. Tokyo, JA: Japan Ecumenical Books, 1989. xv, 157 pp. Paper. 4764299135.

Eight essays on contemporary peace issues; originally presented at Hiroshima Peace Seminars, 1983 to 1987.

PO—MISSIONS AND POLITICAL LIFE

PO212 Maxwell, Kenneth L.
Seek Peace and Pursue It. Valley Forge, PAU: Judson Press, 1983. 160 pp. Paper. 0817009922.

A primer for North American local churches seeking to move through greater understanding to action for peace.

PO213 Musto, Ronald G., ed.
Catholic Peacemakers: A Documentary History, Vol II: From the Renaissance to the Twentieth Century, Parts 1 and 2. (Reference Library, 1372). New York, NYU: Garland, 1996. xiv, 980 pp. Paper. 0815306059.

This sequel to *The Catholic Peace Tradition* (Orbis 1986) completes the narrative history of the concepts of peace and peace movements of the church, from the 15th to 20th centuries, including many missionary endeavors.

PO214 Musto, Ronald G.
The Catholic Peace Tradition. Maryknoll, NYU: Orbis Books, 1986. 365 pp. Paper. 0883442639.

A comprehensive survey of Catholicism's teachings, practices, and traditions with respect to war and peace.

PO215 Nouwen, Henri J. M.
The Road to Peace: Writings on Peace and Justice. Edited by John Dear. Maryknoll, NYU: Orbis Books, 1998. xxxvi, 220 pp. 1570751803.

This collection of writings by the noted Dutch priest/theologian highlights connections between intimacy with Christ and solidarity with a wounded world.

PO216 Panikkar, Raimundo
Cultural Disarmament: The Way to Peace. Translated by Robert R. Barr. Louisville, KYU: Westminister John Knox, 1995. ix, 142 pp. Paper. 0664255493.

The noted scholar of religions proposes that ongoing intercultural and interreligious dialogue can make a contribution toward world peace.

PO217 *Peace and Disarmament: Documents of the WCC Presented by the Commission of the Churches on International Affairs*
Geneva, SZ: WCC; Rome, IT: Pontifical Commission *Institia et Pax*, 1982. vii, 254 pp. Paper. 2825407151.

Documents of the WCC and the RCC informing Christians of the pastoral concern that peace will be found by turning away from the arms race, and by forging bonds of mutual respect and responsibility among nations.

PO218 Peachy, Paul, ed.
Peace, Politics, and the People of God. Philadelphia, PAU: Fortress Press, 1986. vii, 184 pp. Paper. 080061898X.

Ten papers expressing war-peace-violence concerns from both pacifist and non-pacifist perspectives, developed from a twenty-year conversation between members of the War-Nation-Church Study Group (WANACH), including both Protestant and Roman Catholic scholars.

PO219 Schreiter, Robert J.
Reconciliation: Mission and Ministry in a Changing Social Order. (The Boston Theological Institute Series, vol. 3). Maryknoll, NYU: Orbis Books; Cambridge, MAU: Boston Theological Institute, 1992. ix, 84 pp. Paper. 0883448092.

Lectures on reconciliation as rooted in Scripture and Christian theology, and as relevant in the vocation of peacemaking; by the Professor of Historical and Doctrinal Studies at the Catholic Theological Union in Chicago, Illinois.

PO220 Toews, John E., and Gordon Nickel, eds.
The Power of the Lamb. Hillsboro, KSU: Kindred Press, 1986. 183 pp. Paper. 0919797504.

A popular presentation by eight church leaders of scriptural teachings on peace and peacemaking, with an appendix containing Mennonite Brethren Church resolutions on peace issues from 1902 to 1984, and a separate leader's guide by Edith Ratzlaff for a thirteen-session study unit (ISBN 0919797725).

PO221 Yoder, John Howard
He Came Preaching Peace. (A Christian Peace Shelf Selection). Scottdale, PAU: Herald Press, 1985. 143 pp. Paper. 0836133951.

Biblical foundations for persons already engaged in the Christian peace movement.

International Organizations

See also AS186.

PO222 Adjali, Mia, and Deborah Storms, eds.
The Community of Nations. New York, NYU: Friendship Press, 1995. viii, 120 pp. Paper. 0377002925.

Basic information on the United Nations—its history, structure, conferences, past and present peacekeeping, and the involvement of the churches; prepared for adult mission education with *Study Guide* (0377002933).

PO223 Armstrong, Roger D.
Peace Corps and Christian Mission. New York, NYU: Friendship Press, 1965. 126 pp. No ISBN.

An analysis of the relationship of the Peace Corps to the Christian mission.

PO224 Zeilstra, Jurjen A.
European Unity in Ecumenical Thinking, 1937-1948. Zoetermeer, NE: Boekencentrum, 1995. xvii, 454 pp. Paper. 9023919556.

A detailed historical study of contributions by ecumenical bodies during and after the Second World War to the goal of European unity; submitted as a doctoral dissertation to the Theological Faculty of Utrecht University.

COMMUNICATIONS AND MISSIONS

Viggo B. Søgaard, Subeditor

"He appointed twelve . . . to be sent out to proclaim the message" (Mk. 3:14, NRSV). From the beginning the followers of Jesus linked mission and communication. The church began at Pentecost (Acts 2) as the apostles, filled with the Spirit, were able to witness in many languages.

Communications as an academic discipline within the social sciences emerged in the 1950s. Rapidly it gained acceptance in Anglo-American higher education (Kuper and Kuper 1989:32-33).

Within missiology communications has been subsumed under linguistics/philology (Jongeneel 1995, I:207-219) and under anthropology (DOM:28-29).

Any study of communications and the church's mission must include both communication theory and the changing techniques used. Eugene Nida in *Message and Mission* points out that "the whole movement of the expansion of the church, and the distinctly 'missionary outreach,' has been intrinsically bound together with secular phases of culture" (1990:9). Most books on communication theory, including the psychology of communication, as well as those on communication media, fall outside the scope of this bibliography.

Communication for Christian witness is the focus of this chapter. The section on "General Works" contains books by Eugene Nida, Charles Kraft, and others on the theory/theology of Christian communication and contemporary strategies for effective Christian witness.

Selected titles on "Sociolinguistics" guide the reader to that subdiscipline so essential in cross-cultural mission and Bible translation. Sections follow on language learning and teaching, bible translation, and the production and distribution of Christian literature.

Communication includes preaching or missionary homiletics (Jongeneel 1997, II:267-289). Works on this theme will also be found under "Pastoral/Parish Evangelism" in the chapter on "Evangelism and Missions."

The information revolution has challenged the church in every community to consider new methods of Christian witness. This challenge extends beyond the work of mission agencies to impact every church and para-church effort to communicate the Gospel. The final section on "Media" contains a selected list of important titles on Christian communication in this area.

Norman E. Thomas

Reference Works

See also SO13.

CO1 Eilers, Franz-Josef, and William R. Herzog
Catholic Press Directory: Africa/Asia. (Communicatio socialis: Beiheft, 4). Munich, GW: Paderborn; Munich, GW: Schöningh, 1975. 318 pp. 3506722123.

A source book on Roman Catholic involvements in communications in thirty-five countries of Africa and sixteen in Asia.

CO2 Grimes, Barbara F., ed.
Ethnologue: Languages of the World. Dallas, TXU: SIL, 1992. x, 938 pp. Paper. 0883128152.

A catalogue of the 6,170 identified languages of the world grouped by country in which spoken, with demographic and sociolinguistic data and the status of Bible translation for each language.

CO3 Grimes, Barbara F., ed.
Ethnologue Index. Dallas, TXU: SIL, 1992. 312 pp. Paper. 0883128195.

A twelfth new edition of the computer-produced index to 37,370 names of geographical places, people groups, languages and dialects found in the twelfth edition of *Ethnologue*.

CO4 Melton, J. Gordon, Phillip Charles Lucas, and Jon R. Stone, eds.
Prime-Time Religion: An Encyclopedia of Religious Broadcasting. Phoenix, AZU: Oryx Press, 1997. xvii, 413 pp. 0897749022.

This authoritative guide to religious media contains 396 entries on the history, organizations, programs, and personalities of religious radio and television in North America, and of missionary outreach across the world.

CO5 United Bible Societies

Scriptures of the World. London, ENK: UBS, 1986. 127 pp. Paper. 0826703038.

The eleventh biennial edition of a compilation of 1,848 languages in which at least one book of the Bible has been published since the first Gutenberg Bible.

Documentation and Archives

CO6 Phillipart, Michel, ed.

The African Church in the Communications Era: A Handbook of Source Texts for Christian Communicators in Africa. Nairobi, KE: St. Paul Publications-Africa, 1992. 160 pp. Paper. 996621027X.

A collection by the Catholic Media Council (CAMECO) of the major documents (ecumenical and Roman Catholic) on Christian communications in Africa from the 1970-1991 period.

Conferences and Congresses

CO7 Boisvert, Raymond, and Teresa Marcazzan, eds.

Publishing at the Service of Evangelization: Proceedings of the Seminar of the Catholic Publishers in Africa Nairobi, 12-24 February 1996. Nairobi, KE: Paulines Publications Africa, 1996. 192 pp. Paper. 9966212493.

Papers from an important Catholic seminary on Christian publishing in Africa.

CO8 Bunkowske, Eugene W., and Richard French

Receptor-Oriented Gospel Communication: Making the Gospel User-Friendly. Fullerton, CAU: R C Law & Co/Great Lakes Commission Resources Library, 1989. viii, 142 pp. Paper. 0939925419.

A collection of eleven essays delivered at the fourth annual Missions and Communication Congress (Ft. Wayne, Indiana, 28-30 September 1988).

CO9 CELAM-Departmento de Comunicación Social, Encuentro de Bogotá, 26 al 30 de enero de 1987

Comunicación-evangelización: Un reto para América Latina. (Documentos CELAM, 93). Bogotá, CK: CELAM, 1987. 149 pp. Paper. 9586250733.

A collection of materials from the meeting.

CO10 Gatwa, Tharcisse, and Teodoro Buss, eds.

Culture et communication œcuménique. Geneva, SZ: WCC, 1987. 80 pp. Paper. No ISBN.

The official report of an international seminar (Kigali, 13-21 January 1986) organized jointly by the Protestant Council of Rwanda and the Department of Communication of the WCC.

CO11 Massey, James, comp.

Communication and Community and Prophecy. Delhi, II: ISPCK, 1989. vi, 145 pp. Paper. No ISBN.

A collection of fourteen papers on effective and meaningful communication and Christian responsibility; presented at a consultation sponsored by WACC (New Delhi, India, 22-26 November 1988).

CO12 Okonkwo, Jerome Ikechukwu, ed.

Pastoral Management and Communication. Enugu, NR: Fourth Dimension Publishing, 1994. vi, 101 pp. Paper. 9781563931.

Papers on the priest as religious communicator; originally presented at a November 1992 seminar conducted by the Department of Social Development, Justice and Peace of the Catholic diocese of Okigwe in Nigeria.

CO13 Plou, Dafne Sabanes

Global Communication: Is There a Place for Human Dignity? (Risk Book Series, 71). Geneva, SZ: WCC Publications, 1996. xi, 74 pp. Paper. 2825411868.

Issues, challenges, and opportunities facing Christian communicators today as shared during the global congress of WACC (Metepec, Mexico, 7-11 October 1995).

CO14 Rinmawia, Lal, ed.

Credible Christian Communication: An Indian Perspective. Delhi, II: ISPCK, 1985. 102 pp. Paper. No ISBN.

A collection of eight essays discussing communication and Christianity in India, suggesting why some Christian communication agencies have failed in their mission; from the report of the NCCI Study Conference and Consultation (Nagpur, 28-30 November 1984).

CO15 SODEPAX Consultation on Church—Communication—Development (Driebergen, Holland, 12-16 March 1970)

Church—Communication—Development. Geneva, SZ: SODEPAX, 1970. 111 pp. Paper. No ISBN.

This 1970 SODEPAX report speaks to Roman Catholic and Protestant churches offering recommendations to assist in more effectively utilizing their extensive social communication media in building a better world, a more humane society, and a planetary community.

CO16 Thomas, Pradip, ed.

Communication and Human Dignity: Asian Christian Perspectives. Delhi, II: ISPCK, 1995. 130 pp. Paper. 8172142676.

Papers from two consultations (Delhi, India, Sept. 1993; Bali, Indonesia, Nov. 1994) on the theme "The Right to Communicate and Human Dignity," sponsored by the Asia Region of WACC and the CCA.

CO17 WACC

Misión de la Literatura Cristiana en América Latina: Ponencias, diálogos y documento final del I Seminario de evaluación de contenidos celebrado en Buenos Aires, del 16 al 20 de agosto de 1982. Buenos Aires, AG: WACC, 1982. 96 pp. Paper. No ISBN.

A collection of the eight papers and final document of a seminar on the mission of Christian literature in Latin America.

CO18 Yeow, Choo Lak, ed.

Theology and Communication: Equipping the Saints in the 1990's I. (ATESEA Occasional Papers, 9). Singapore, SI: ATESEA, 1990. xv, 160 pp. Paper. 981001175X.

Reports and papers from the 1989 General Assembly of ATESEA (Manila, 10-12 April 1989).

General Works

See also EV68.

CO19 Amalorpavadass, D. S.

Social Communication and Christian Communion: Reality, Theology, Pedagogy and Spirituality of Communication. (Mission Theology for Our Times Series, 16). Bangalore, II: NBCLC, 1984. 32 pp. Paper. No ISBN.

The keynote address delivered by the founder of the National Biblical, Catechetical, and Liturgical Centre in Bangalore, India, to the thirteenth Catholic World Congress of the Press (UCIP), October 1983, in Dublin, Ireland.

CO20 Balz, Heinrich

Theologische Modelle der Kommunikation: Bastian-Kraemer-Nida. (Missionswissenschaftliche Forschungen, 12). Gütersloh, GW: Gerd Mohn, 1978. 156 pp. 357904986.

A technical examination of communication theory, focusing on the models of Bastian, Kraemer, and Nida, with theological application, particularly as the theories relate to cross-cultural settings.

CO21 Bluck, John

Beyond Technology: Contexts for Christian Communication. (Risk Book Series, 20). Geneva, SZ: WCC, 1984. ix, 92 pp. Paper. 2825407925.

Ten brief essays by six authors on new media contexts for Christian communication and approaches to them; with contributions from the WCC's Sixth Assembly.

CO22 CELAM-Departamento de Comunicación Social

Teoría y praxis de la Iglesia latinoamericana en comunicaciones sociales: 25 años después de "Inter mirifica" (Dossier). (DECOS, 2). Bogotá, CK: CELAM, 1988. 426 pp. Paper. 9586251241.

An anthology of related works in Spanish and Portuguese.

CO23 Eilers, Franz-Josef

Communicating in Community: An Introduction to Social Communication. Manila, PH: LOGOS Publications, 1994. 342 pp. Paper. 9715100732.

A basic textbook on communication theory and the church and social communication, with selected documents by the SVD and WACC.

CO24 Engel, James F., and Hugo Wilbert Norton

What's Gone Wrong with the Harvest?: A Communication Strategy for the Church and World Evangelism. Grand Rapids, MIU: Academie Books, 1975. 171 pp. Paper. 0310241618.

A popular introduction relating communication theory to media ministries for evangelism—radio, television, literature, and preaching.

CO25 Engel, James F.

Contemporary Christian Communications: Its Theory and Practice. (A Chriscom Book). Nashville, TNU: Nelson, 1979. 344 pp. 0840751524.

In this major text on Christian communication the church is seen as both medium and message; with extensive references to the social and behavioral sciences, together with biblical citations.

CO26 Granfield, Patrick, ed.

The Church and Communication. (Communication, Culture and Theology). Kansas City, MOU: Sheed and Ward, 1994. vii, 237 pp. Paper. 1556126743.

Twelve papers by prominent Christian leaders in communication; originally presented at the Cavalletti Seminar on Ecclesiology and Communication (Rome, 24 Sept.-1 Oct. 1989).

CO27 Hesselgrave, David J.

Communicating Christ Cross-Culturally. Grand Rapids, MIU: Zondervan, 1978. 511 pp. 0310366917.

A comprehensive introduction to cross-cultural communication as it applies to Christian missions, with particular emphasis given to the communication of the Gospel in tribal, Hindu, Buddhist, and other cultural settings.

CO28 Hughes, Robert Don

Talking to the World in the Days to Come. Nashville, TNU: Broadman, 1991. 159 pp. 0805460373.

A popular introduction to future challenges for Christians as communicators, including missionaries and witnesses; by the Assistant Professor of Communication and Mass Media at the Southern Baptist Theological Seminary, Louisville, Kentucky.

CO29 James, Ross W., ed.

Case Studies in Christian Communication in an Asian Context. Manila, PH: OMF Books, 1989. 266 pp. Paper. 9715111548.

Two essays on biblical patterns and principles of communications, plus six Asian case studies and sample survey instruments.

CO30 Kraft, Charles H.

Communicating the Gospel God's Way. South Pasadena, CAU: William Carey Library, 1983. 60 pp. Paper. 0878087427.

A brief introduction to Christian communication theory advocating an incarnational model; by the Professor of Anthropology at the School of World Mission, Fuller Theological Seminary, Pasadena, California.

CO31 Kraft, Charles H.

Communication Theory for Christian Witness. Maryknoll, NYU: Orbis Books, 1991. xi, 180 pp. Paper. 0883447630.

An application of modern communication theory to the communication of the Gospel through skillful use of examples drawn from modern living and the Bible; originally published in 1983.

CO32 Lee, Philip, ed.

Communication for All: New World Information and Communication Order. Maryknoll, NYU: Orbis Books, 1986. xiii, 158 pp. Paper. 0883442469.

A collection of essays on the call for a New World Information and Communication Order that would provide a more participatory and democratic global communication system; with a chapter on "Communication and the Church in India."

CO33 Litteral, Robert L.

Community Partnership in Communications for Ministry. Wheaton, ILU: BGC, 1988. vi, 139 pp. Paper. No ISBN.

A monograph on the role of the community itself in communication relating it to culture and language in the development of cross-cultural Christian ministries; by a twenty-five-year veteran linguist who served with Wycliffe Bible Translators in Papua New Guinea.

CO34 Lochhead, David

Shifting Realities: Information Technology and the Church. (Risk Books Series, 75). Geneva, SZ: WCC Publications, 1997. xv, 110 pp. 282541221X.

Analysis of the implications for the Christian faith of the spread of computer technology and the "digitization" of reality; by the Professor of Systematic Theology at the Vancouver School of Theology, Vancouver, Canada.

CO35 Lowe, Kathy

Opening Eyes and Ears: New Connections for Christian Communication. Geneva, SZ: WCC/LWF/WACC, 1983. viii, 118 pp. Paper. 282540750X.

Nine case studies of creative ventures in communication by churches and church-related agencies that considered communication media to be potential instruments of liberation, change, and renewal.

CO36 Maggay, Melba Padilla, ed.
Communicating Cross-Culturally: Towards a New Context for Missions in the Philippines. Quezon City, PH: New Day Publishers, 1989. 61 pp. Paper. 9711003503.

A practical introduction to issues of communicating the Gospel in the Filipino context; written for Protestant missionaries.

CO37 Manuel, Albert D.
Communication and the Church. Delhi, II: ISPCK for the United Theological College, Bangalore, 1994. 96 pp. Paper. 8172142129.

A primer which explains the meaning of communication, and why the church should take communication in theological education seriously.

CO38 Martini, Carlo Maria
Communicating Christ to the World: The Pastoral Letters: "Ephphatha, Be Opened!," "The Hem of His Garment" and "Letters to a Family about TV." Translated by Thomas M. Lucas. Kansas City, MOU: Sheed and Ward, 1994. xxi, 192 pp. Paper. 1556126557.

English translations of three pastoral letters by the cardinal and bishop of Milan, critiquing present patterns of communication in the family, church, and media industry; offering a model of authentic communication.

CO39 Moore, Robert Laurence
Selling God: American Religion in the Marketplace of Culture. New York, NYU: Oxford University Press, 1994. 317 pp. 0195082281.

A cultural history of the commercialization of religion in the United States, from early-19th-century tracts to contemporary televangelism.

CO40 Muggeridge, Malcolm
Christ and the Media. (London Lectures in Contemporary Christianity; Ecclesia Books). Grand Rapids, MIU: Eerdmans; London, ENK: Hodder & Stoughton, 1977. 127 pp. Paper. 0802835082 (E), 034022438X (H).

Based on a series of lectures, the book gives a sharp and witty critique of our media-oriented culture, but provides a rather negative view of the possiblities for communicating truth through the media, with focus on the BBC in London.

CO41 Navone, John
Communicating Christ. Slough, ENK: St. Paul Publications, 1976. viii, 239 pp. Paper. 0854391274.

A guide for laypersons by a Jesuit theologian, explaining different dimensions of communicating Christ to others through the gifts of openness, friendship, healing, and enlightenment, emphasizing the importance of being a person transformed by Christ.

CO42 Nida, Eugene Albert
Message and Mission: The Communication of the Christian Faith. South Pasadena, CAU: William Carey Library, 1990. xviii, 300 pp. Paper. 0878087567.

A revised edition of the comprehensive classic analyzing both the technical and theological requirements of Christian communication, highlighting themes of particular relevance to students of missiology; originally published by Harper and Brothers in 1960.

CO43 Reid, Gavin
The Gagging of God: The Failure of the Church to Communi-

cate in the Television Age. London, ENK: Hodder & Stoughton, 1969. 126 pp. Paper. 0340106522.

A candid reflection on the church's failure to communicate its essential message to modern non-community people; a breakdown seen as the greatest threat to the Gospel.

CO44 Robinson, Gnana, ed.
Communicating the Gospel Today: Essays in Honour of the Rev. Dr. Albert Devasirvatham Manuel. Madurai, II: Tamil Nadu TheologicalSeminary, 1986. xv, 326 pp. Paper. No ISBN.

Twenty-one essays on various perspectives of Christian communication (biblical, theological, religious, cultural, and developmental), written to honor the Rev. Dr. A. D. Manuel, a Church of South India theologian and specialist in Christian communication.

CO45 Søgaard, Viggo B.
Applying Christian Communication. Ann Arbor, MIU: University Microfilms, 1986. xx, 467 pp. No ISBN.

An extensive treatment of communication theory, strategy, and research as applied to the use of media for effective Christian mission; a Ph.D. dissertation completed at Fuller Theological Seminary, School of World Mission, Pasadena, California.

CO46 Søgaard, Viggo B.
Research in Church and Mission. South Pasadena, CAU: William Carey Library, 1996. xviii, 260 pp. Paper. 0878082719.

A basic textbook for courses on social research in missiology and Christian communications.

CO47 Sample, Tex
Ministry in an Oral Culture: Living with Will Rogers, Uncle Remus, and Minnie Pearl. Louisville, KYU: Westminster John Knox, 1994. x, 100 pp. Paper. 066425506X.

An introduction to the world of oral culture in the United States, with implications for preaching, teaching, and counseling among those who are functionally illiterate.

CO48 Sanneh, Lamin
Translating the Message: The Missionary Impact on Culture. Maryknoll, NYU: Orbis Books, 1989. xiv, 255 pp. Paper. 0883443619.

A closely reasoned argument that in translating the Scriptures into vernacular languages, Christian missionaries have achieved significant contextualization of the faith; with detailed case studies, from the early church to contemporary West Africa.

CO49 Scholz, Marlene
Communication in Pastoral Work: Volume 9, Final Volume of an Experimental Source-Book for Religious Education. (AMECEA Pastoral Institute Spearhead Series, 64). Eldoret, KE: Gaba Publications, 1980. 97 pp. Paper. No ISBN.

The final volume of an experimentation sourcebook for religious education in East Africa, on various aspects of communication in the context of evangelization.

CO50 Seamands, John T.
Tell It Well: Communicating the Gospel Across Cultures. Kansas City, MOU: Beacon Hill Press, 1981. 236 pp. Paper. 0834106841.

A primer on communicating the Gospel to non-Christians by the Professor of Christian Missions at Asbury Seminary.

CO51 Smith, Donald K.
Creating Understanding: A Handbook for Christian Communication across Cultural Landscapes. Grand Rapids, MIU: Zondervan, 1992. 382 pp. Paper. 0310531217.

The Professor of International Communication at Western Seminary in Portland, Oregon, presents twenty-three basic propositions on the process of Christian communication, drawing upon resources developed during more than twenty years as a missionary communicator and teacher of communications in Southern and Eastern Africa.

CO52 Social Communication Departments, AMECEA and IMBISA
Basic Human Communication. (Communication for Pastoral Formation, 1). Nairobi, KE: Paulines Publications Africa, 1999. 70 pp. Paper. 9966214542.

The integration of communication into pastoral and seminary formation for varied situations of pastoral ministry in Africa; module one of a six module course.

CO53 Social Communication Departments, AMECEA and IMBISA
Communication in the Church and Society. (Communication for Pastoral Formation, 3). Nairobi, KE: Paulines Publications Africa, 1999. 175 pp. Paper. 9966214569.

This volume includes modules on pastoral communication, communications in church and society, and pastoral planning and policy for an African context.

CO54 Social Communication Departments, AMECEA and IMBISA
Communication, Culture and Community. (Communication for Pastoral Formation, 2). Nairobi, KE: Paulines Publications Africa, 1999. 125 pp. Paper. 9966214550.

The integration of communication into pastoral and seminary formation for varied situations of pastoral ministry in Africa; module two and three of six modules.

CO55 Soukup, Paul A.
Communication and Theology: Introduction and Review of the Literature. London, ENK: WACC; London, ENK: Centre for the Study of Communication and Culture, 1983. 114 pp. 0950878103.

A useful detailed organization of the literature in the field, with analysis of content and a thirty-two-page bibliography of works cited in the text.

CO56 Sweet, Leonard I., ed.
Communication and Change in American Religious History. Grand Rapids, MIU: Eerdmans, 1993. vi, 482 pp. Paper. 0802806821.

A collection of twelve essays by North American historians on the centrality of communications in shaping American religion; including religious revivals (18th-20th centuries), with a 125-page annotated bibliography.

CO57 Thomas, T. K., ed.
Ecumenical Communication in Asia. Toa Payoh, SI: CCA, 1981. 71 pp. Paper. 9971830442.

Major presentations made at a consultation of Christian journalists, convened by the CCA, 26 November to 2 December 1980.

CO58 Valle, Carlos A.
Challenges of Communication. Delhi, II: ISPCK, 1995. xii, 94 pp. Paper. 817214265X.

A primer on communication written for theological students in Bangalore, India, by the General Secretary of WACC.

CO59 Vassallo, Wanda
Church Communications Handbook: A Complete Guide to Developing a Strategy, Using Technology, Writing Effectively, Reaching the Unchurched. Grand Rapids, MIU: Kregel Publications, 1998. 303 pp. Paper. 0825439256.

A comprehensive study of structuring all forms of communication in the local church, from communication with the unchurched, to talking to the media, to utilizing technology; useful as a practical reference tool for church leaders.

CO60 Verstraelen, F. J.
Christianity in a New Key: New Voices and Vistas through Intercontinental Communication. (Religion and Theological Studies Series, 3). Gweru, RH: Mambo Press, 1996. xv, 321 pp. Paper. 0869226487.

A summary of the roles played by the "Third Church," that is Christians and their churches in Africa, Asia, Latin America, and Oceania, in vitalizing global Christianity; with special focus on their intercontinental communication.

CO61 Webber, Robert E.
God Still Speaks: A Biblical View of Christian Communication. Nashville, MIU: Nelson, 1980. 221 pp. 0840751893.

A theological treatment of Christian communication based on key passages of Scripture.

Sociolinguistics
See also HI731.

CO62 Biernatzki, William E.
Roots of Acceptance: The Intercultural Communication of Religious Meanings. (Inculturation Working Papers on Living Faith and Cultures, 13). Rome, IT: Editrice Pontificia Università Gregoriana, 1991. 186 pp. Paper. 8876526404.

A social-scientific analysis of the process and institutionalization of cross-cultural communication in religions in Asia; with case studies of the introduction of Buddhism into China, Islam into Indonesia, and Christianity into Korea.

CO63 Cotterell, Peter
Language and the Christian: A Guide to Communication and Understanding. London, ENK: Bagster, 1978. v, 179 pp. 0851501672.

An introduction to linguistics with special reference to literacy work and translation, particularly Bible translation.

CO64 Filbeck, David
Social Context and Proclamation: A Socio-Cognitive Study in Proclaiming the Gospel Cross-Culturally. South Pasadena, CAU: William Carey Library, 1985. Paper. 0878081992.

A good analysis of social systems, the ways these affect the communication of the Gospel in tribal, peasant, and modern societies, and how the ways in which a society is organized affect the place of religion in the lives of the people.

CO65 Griffin, Emory A.
The Mind Changers: The Art of Christian Persuasion. Wheaton, ILU: Tyndale, 1976. 228 pp. Paper. 0842342907.

A fine treatment of persuasion in Christian evangelism, its processes, techniques, and possibilities, as well as its problems and ethical questions; aimed at helping Christians share their faith with others.

CO—COMMUNICATIONS AND MISSIONS

CO66 Klem, Herbert V.

Oral Communication of the Scripture: Insights from African Oral Art. South Pasadena, CAU: William Carey Library, 1982. xxiv, 256 pp. Paper. 0878083324.

A convincing case for teaching and learning the message of Scripture without primary reliance on literacy.

CO67 Louw, Johannes P., ed.

Sociolinguistics and Communication. (UBS Monograph Series, 1). London, ENK: UBS, 1986. 146 pp. Paper. No ISBN.

The fifth in a series of monographs for Bible translators, focusing on sociolinguistic features which may have a direct effect on Bible translating.

CO68 Nida, Eugene Albert, and William D. Reyburn

Meaning Across Cultures. (American Society of Missiology Series, 4). Maryknoll, NYU: Orbis Books, 1981. vi, 90 pp. Paper. 0883443260.

A pioneering work that advances missiological theory, particularly in the areas of translation and contextualization.

CO69 Nida, Eugene Albert

Religion Across Cultures: A Study in the Communication of Christian Faith. New York, NYU: Harper & Row, 1968. vii, 111 pp. No ISBN.

An analysis of the psychological and dynamic factors in communication that can be applied universally.

CO70 Okonkwo, Jerome Ikechukwu, ed.

Pastoral Language and Evangelization 2000. Enugu, NR: Fourth Dimension Publishing, 1998. ix, 100 pp. Paper. 978156444X.

A collection of six articles on the choice of language, and on the language of the community, in the spread and propagation of the message of Christ.

CO71 Pike, Kenneth L.

Talk, Thought, and Thing: The Emic Road toward Conscious Knowledge. Dallas, TXU: SIL, 1993. xii, 85 pp. Paper. 0883126109.

A condensed philosophy of sociolinguistics by the one who first introduced the "emic\etic" distinction.

CO72 Renck, Günther

Contextualization of Christianity and Christianization of Language: A Case Study from the Highlands of Papua New Guinea. (Erlanger Monographien aus Mission und Ökumene, 5). Erlangen, GW: Ev-Luth Mission, 1990. xvi, 316 pp. Paper. 3872143050.

A detailed study in sociolinquistics conducted in the eastern highlands of Papua New Guinea, documenting issues in the contextualization of theology for the Evangelical Lutheran Church in its mission.

CO73 Rogers, Everett M., and Thomas M. Steinfatt

Intercultural Communication. Prospect Heights, ILU: Waveland Press, 1999. xiv, 292 pp. 1577660323.

This book utilizes the history of intercultural contact—for instance, in the spread of Islam, the Crusades, colonialism, and the slave trade—to emphasize the layers of collective consciousness that shape the attitudes and beliefs of various peoples.

CO74 Samarin, William J.

Field Linguistics: A Guide to Linguistic Field Work. New York, NYU: Holt, Rinehart & Winston, 1967. x, 246 pp. No ISBN.

A detailed guide for linguists collecting data for the analysis of a language, and for non-professionals faced with the task of learning a language, where the grammatical description is inadequate.

CO75 Shaw, R. Daniel

Transculturation: The Cultural Factor in Translation and Other Communication Tasks. South Pasadena, CAU: William Carey Library, 1988. xii, 300 pp. Paper. 0878082166.

A textbook on the cultural and non-verbal aspects of communication, by the Director of the Bible translation program at the Fuller Seminary School of World Mission; designed to help communicators who are not anthropologists present a message (including translated Scripture) effectively, within any culture.

Techniques

See also ED170 and AS748.

CO76 Cook, Bruce

Understanding Pictures in Papua New Guinea. Elgin, ILU: David C. Cook, 1981. 113 pp. Paper. 0891914889.

A book based on dissertation research, analyzing the use of pictures and illustrations as communication tools among illiterate people.

CO77 Dickerson, Wayne B., and Lonna J. Dickerson

Tips on Taping: Language Recording in the Social Sciences. South Pasadena, CAU: William Carey Library, 1977. x, 198 pp. 087808147X.

A great deal of technical information needed by linguists undertaking field recording in tropical countries.

CO78 Engel, James F.

How Can I Get Them to Listen? Grand Rapids, MIU: Zondervan, 1977. 185 pp. Paper. 0310241715.

An excellent introduction to research methods in communication studies, with ample case studies that demonstrate their function in effective use of media, and in the wider Christian mission.

CO79 Johnson, Douglas W., and Sarla E. Lall

Using Computers in Mission. (National Mission Resources). New York, NYU: UMC, Board of Global Ministries, 1985. 92 pp. Paper. No ISBN.

An introductory guide for local churches on use of the computer in various mission-related activities.

CO80 Steffen, Tom A.

Reconnecting God's Story to Ministry: Crosscultural Storytelling at Home and Abroad. La Habra, CAU: Center for Organizational and Ministry Development, 1996. 140 pp. Paper. 1882757033.

An introduction to the principles and methods of combining biblical storytelling with personal faith sharing.

CO81 Thomas, Richard Walter

An Introduction to Church Communication. Oxford, ENK: Lynx Communications; Sutherland, AT: Albatross Books, 1994. 160 pp. 0745928862 (UK), 0732408342 (AT).

A primer on techniques of church communication by the communications officer of the Anglican Diocese of Oxford, England.

CO—COMMUNICATIONS AND MISSIONS

CO82 Vierling, Hermann
Hermeneutik—Stammesreligion—Evangelium: Interkulturelle Kommunikation bei den Kendayan. (Missionswissenschaftliche Forschungen, 23). Gütersloh, GW: Mohn, 1990. 469 pp. Paper. 3579002430.

This work examines limitations of exclusively cognitive communication and the possibilities of non-verbal communication for missionary work especially among the Dayaks in Indonesia.

Language Learning and Teaching

See also MI107 and CH368.

CO83 Brewster, E. Thomas, and Betty Sue Brewster, eds.
Community Is My Language Classroom: Real-Life Stories from around the World of Language Learning and Missionary Ministry to Those Who Are Learning through Community Relationships. Pasadena, CAU: Lingua House Ministries, 1986. viii, 246 pp. Paper. 0916636062.

Twenty-two first-person accounts of the language learning experiences of missionaries in their first months of service, emphasizing language learning through cross-cultural relationships.

CO84 Brewster, E. Thomas, and Elizabeth S. Brewster
Language Acquisition Made Practical: Field Methods for Language Learners. Pasadena, CAU: Lingua House, 1982. xvi, 383 pp. Paper. 0916636003.

A unique approach to language learning, based on the concept of "bonding," where language is acquired through daily involvment with the people concerned.

CO85 Brewster, E. Thomas, and Elizabeth S. Brewster
Language Exploration and Acquisition Resource Notebook! Pasadena, CAU: Lingua House, 1986. xviii, 377 pp. Paper. No ISBN.

A revised edition of readings and exercises for a twelve-session course on "Language/Culture Learning and Mission."

CO86 Howell, Allison M.
A Daily Guide for Culture and Language Learning. Accra, GH: SIM Ghana, 1990. 180 pp. Paper. 9782668176.

A missionary anthropologist offers an easy-to-use guide for learning the language and culture of any people.

CO87 Larson, Donald N., and William A. Smalley
Becoming Bilingual: A Guide to Language Learning. Lanham, MDU: University Press of America, 1984. xv, 426 pp. Paper. 0819142468.

A detailed manual used by hundreds of missionaries, from its first draft in 1957 to the 1970s, as a handbook for language learning and applied linguistics; originally published by William Carey Library in 1972.

CO88 Larson, Donald N.
Guidelines for Barefoot Language Learning: An Approach through Involvement and Independence. St. Paul, MNU: Christian Missionary Society, 1984. 327 pp. Paper. 0932311008.

A guide for living and communicating with those who speak another language in your community.

Christian Literature: General

See also HI643, TH303, CO66, AS1318, AS1467, and EU190.

CO89 Chaplin, Joyce
Writers, My Friends. Elgin, ILU: David C Cook, 1984. 152 pp. 0891918094.

Reflections by the pioneer of Africa Christian Press.

CO90 Hesselgrave, David J.
Scripture and Strategy: The Use of the Bible in Postmodern Church and Mission. South Pasadena, CAU: William Carey Library, 1994. xiii, 192 pp. Paper. 0878083758.

Ten evangelical missiologists give popular essays on aspects of the use of the Bible in the church and in mission.

CO91 Makunike, Ezekiel C., ed.
Christian Press in Africa: Voice of Human Concern. Lusaka, ZA: Multimedia Publications, 1973. 61 pp. Paper. No ISBN.

Papers and church documents from a series of consultations held at the Africa Literature Centre, Kitwe, Zambia, in September 1973, on the church's ministry in the field of mass communications.

CO92 Wolfensberger, G. H.
Multiplying the Loaves: The Bible in Mission and Evangelism. London, ENK: Fontana, 1968. 191 pp. No ISBN.

A popular report on a study of the use of the Bible in various Third World countries; jointly sponsored by the UBS and the WCC.

Bible Translation

See also HI7, HI374, HI376, CR625, CO5, CO136, AF570, AM835, AM1200, AM1511, AS550-AS551, AS1368, OC4, OC176, OC222, and OC299.

CO93 *Any Given Day in the Life of the Bible*
Portland, ORU: Multnomah, 1992. 168 pp. Paper. 0880705132.

A quality pictoral essay on fifty different language projects undertaken by Wycliffe Bible Translators.

CO94 Beckmann, Johannes, Walbert Bühlmann, and Johann Specker, eds.
Die Heilige Schrift in den katholischen Missionen: Gesammelte Aufsätze. (*NZM*, 14). Schöneck-Beckenried, SZ: *NZM*, 1966. viii, 375 pp. Paper. No ISBN.

A systematic and scholarly study of the work of Bible translation in Roman Catholic missions in America, Asia, Oceania, the Arab world, and Africa.

CO95 Beekman, John, and John Callow
Translating the Word of God. Grand Rapids, MIU: Zondervan, 1974. 399 pp. 0310207711.

A comprehensive approach to translation theory and practice from an up-to-date perspective; by long term members of Wycliffe Bible Translators.

CO96 Cotterell, Peter, and Max Turner
Linguistics and Biblical Interpretation. London, ENK: SPCK, 1989. 348 pp. Paper. 0281043582.

A thorough non-technical presentation of aspects of linguistics relevant to Bible translating.

CO97 Dahlquist, Anna Marie
Trailblazers for Translators: The Chichicastenango Twelve. South Pasadena, CAU: William Carey Library, 1995. x, 159 pp. Paper. 0878082050.

A narrative account of the forerunners of Wycliffe Bible Translators (1934), traced back to Presbyterian and Central African Mission efforts to reach Indian tribes in Guatemala from 1921 onward.

CO-COMMUNICATIONS AND MISSIONS

CO98 Dammann, Ernst
Die Übersetzung der Bibel in afrikanische Sprachen. (Abhandlungen der Marburger Gelehrten Gesellschaft, Jahr 1972, 3). Munich, GW: Fink, 1975. 167 pp. Paper. 3770511220.

An examination of the questions faced by those who translate the Bible into African languages; with special reference to Bantu languages.

CO99 Dye, T. Wayne
Bible Translation Strategy: An Analysis of Its Spiritual Impact. Dallas, TXU: Wycliffe Bible Translators, 1988. iii, 382 pp. Paper. No ISBN.

A focus on the human factors that affect communication and influence translation of the Scriptures; originally published in 1980.

CO100 Grimes, Barbara F., ed.
Bible Translation Needs: Bulletin no. 1 (1988). Dallas, TXU: Wycliffe Bible Translators, 1988. xv, 270 pp. Paper. 0883127377.

A compendium of data produced by International Information Services on the status of Bible translation, or need of it, for each language of the world; taken from the archives of *Ethnologue: Languages of the World* (1988).

CO101 Gutt, Ernst-August
Translation and Relevance: Cognition and Context. Oxford, ENK: Blackwell Publishers, 1993. ix, 222 pp. 0631178570.

A scholarly elaboration of relevance theory and its application in the principles and guidelines of translation.

CO102 Larson, Mildred L.
Meaning-Based Translation: A Guide to Cross-Language Equivalence. Lanham, MDU: University Press of America, 1998. x, 586 pp. 0761809708 (hdbk), 0761809716 (pbk).

A second edition textbook on the principles and practice of translation, prepared for use in colleges and universities; with companion workbook (*Biblical Exercises*, xvi, 307 pp., 0761809481).

CO103 Larson, Mildred L.
La traducción basada en el Significado. Translated by Donald H. Burns, and Rodolfo von Moltke. Buenos Aires, AG: Editorial Universitaria de Buenos Aires, 1989. iv, 717 pp. 9502304675.

Spanish translation.

CO104 Louw, Johannes P., ed.
Meaningful Translation: Its Implications for the Reader. (UBS Monograph Series, 5). Reading, ENK: UBS, 1991. vii, 111 pp. Paper. 0826704557.

Papers from a convention for translators sponsored by the Bible Society of South Africa, addressing problems in Bible translation for both listening and reading; with examples from Genesis 15, Luke 1, and Romans 8.

CO105 Nida, Eugene Albert, and Charles R. Taber
The Theory and Practice of Translation. (Helps for Translators, 8). Leiden, NE: Brill, 1982. viii, 218 pp. No ISBN.

Volume 8 of *Helps for Translators*, prepared under the auspices of the UBS, designed to assist the translator in mastering the theoretical elements, as well as in gaining certain practical skills in translation; originally published in 1969.

CO106 Nida, Eugene Albert, ed.
The Book of a Thousand Tongues. New York, NYU: UBS, 1972. xviii, 536 pp. No ISBN.

Revised edition of a unique catalog of the 1,399 languages in which at least one complete book of the Bible has been published; with brief notes on the people who speak each language, and a history of Bible translation in the language; first published in 1938.

CO107 Nida, Eugene Albert
God's Word in Man's Language. South Pasadena, CAU: William Carey Library, 1973. 191 pp. No ISBN.

A reprint of the lucid introduction to Bible translation by the Secretary of the ABS; originally published in 1952 (San Francisco, CAU: Harper & Row).

CO108 Nida, Eugene Albert
Gott spricht viele Sprachen: Der dramatische Bericht von der übersetzung der Bibel für alle Völker. Translated by Karl-Heinz Kemmer. Stuttgart, GW: Evan Missionsverlag, 1966. 207 pp. Paper. No ISBN.

German translation.

CO109 Nida, Eugene Albert
La Palabra de Dios en la Lengua de los Hombres. Translated by Vivian M. Cruz Rivera. Río Piedras, PR: Universidad de Puerto Rico, 1994. xvii, 103 pp. No ISBN.

Spanish translation.

CO110 Nida, Eugene Albert
Signs, Sense, Translation. Cape Town, SA: Bible Society of South Africa, 1984. 143 pp. Paper. 0798206187.

Three technical essays relating communication theory to the practice of translating Greek texts; by the renowned Director of Translations and Executive Secretary of the ABS.

CO111 Nida, Eugene Albert
Toward a Science of Translating: With Special Reference to Principles and Procedures Involved in Bible Translating. Leiden, NE: Brill, 1964. x, 331 pp. No ISBN.

A scholarly textbook for Bible translators, with theory based on contemporary developments in the fields of linguistics, anthropology, and psychology; also relating to the wider activity of translating in general.

CO112 Persson, Janet
In Our Own Languages: The Story of Bible Translation in Sudan. (Faith in Sudan, 3). Nairobi, KE: Paulines Publications Africa, 1997. 46 pp. Paper. 996621349X.

A basic introduction by a twenty-year biblical translator in the Sudan under the SIL.

CO113 Poutanen, Mirja, and Kyllikki Valtonen, eds.
Kaikille kielille: Suomen Lähetysseuran raamatunkäännöstyötä eri puolilla maailmaa. (Suomen Lähetysseuran julkaisu). Helsinki, FI: Kirjaneliö, 1983. 127 pp. Paper. 9516006035.

A report of Bible translating organized by the Finnish Evangelical Lutheran Mission.

CO114 Schaaf, Ype
Hij ging zijn weg met blijdschap: Over de geschiedenis en de rol van de Bijbel in Afrika. Kampen, NE: Kok, 1990. 300 pp. Paper. 902424997X.

A journalistic description of how the Bible was translated and spread throughout Africa, and what influence the Bible and its message has had in the churches, the culture, education, and politics in Africa; with a review of the influence of the Qu'ran and other religious works.

CO115 Schaaf, Ype
L'histoire et le rôle de la Bible en Afrique. Translated by Antoinette Spindler and Marc Spindler. Nairobi, KE: CETA/HAHO; Lomé, TG: HAHO; Lavigny, SZ: Éditions de Groupes Missionnaires, 1994. 285 pp. 9966886729 (C), 2880500516 (G).

French translation; also published by Éditions Clé, Yaoundé, CM.

CO116 Schaaf, Ype
On Their Way Rejoicing: The History and Role of the Bible in Africa. Translated by Paul Ellingworth. (African Challenge Series of the AACC, 5). Carlisle, ENK: Paternoster Press; Nairobi, KE: AACC, 1994. xi, 254 pp. Paper. 0853645612 (UK), 9966886842 (KE).

English translation.

CO117 Shetler, Joanne, and Patricia Purvis
And the Word Came with Power: How God Met and Changed a People Forever. Portland, ORU: Multnomah, 1992. 164 pp. Paper. 0880704756.

Vignettes from the work of translating the New Testament among the Balangao people of northern Luzon in the Philippines, and its completion in 1981 by the Wycliffe Bible Translators' team.

CO118 Smalley, William A.
Translation as Mission: Bible Translation in the Modern Missionary Movement. (The Modern Mission Era, 1792-1992: An Appraisal). Macon, GAU: Mercer University Press, 1991. xiii, 287 pp. 0865543895.

A comprehensive account and appraisal of two hundred years of Bible translation and its centrality for Christian mission.

CO119 Stine, Philip C., ed.
Bible Translation and the Spread of the Church: The Last 200 Years. (Studies in Christian Mission, 2). Leiden, NE: Brill, 1990. xii, 154 pp. 9004093311.

Nine scholarly essays assessing the impact of Bible translation on the growth of the church, especially in the Two-Thirds World, in the last 200 years.

CO120 Tarr, Del
Double Image: Biblical Insights from African Parables. New York, NYU: Paulist Press, 1994. ix, 209 pp. Paper. 0809134691.

An introduction to how biblical truths can be communicated through African stories, proverbs, and legends; by a specialist in cross-cultural communications.

CO121 Waard, Jan de, and Eugene Albert Nida
From One Language to Another: Functional Equivalence in Bible Translating. Nashville, TNU: Nelson, 1986. 224 pp. Paper. 084075437X.

A scholarly discussion of new developments in translating, with special reference to insights from socio-semiotics and the concept of "functional equivalence"; with illustrative data from both the Old and New Testaments.

CO122 Wallis, Ethel Emily, and Mary Angela Bennett
Two Thousand Tongues to Go: The Story of the Wycliffe Bible Translators. New York, NYU: Harper & Row, 1964. ix, 272 pp. No ISBN.

A popular account of the adventures of various missionaries of the Wycliffe Bible Translators.

CO123 Wendland, Ernst R.
Comparative Discourse Analysis and the Translation of Psalm 22 in Chichewa, a Bantu Language of South-Central Africa. (Studies in the Bible and Early Christianity, 32). Lewiston, NYU: E Mellen Press, 1993. ix, 242 pp. 0773492895.

A detailed case study of the use of dynamic equivalence in biblical translation, in which the author translates Psalm 22 in the style of the Chichewa poetry of Malawi.

CO124 Wendland, Ernst R.
The Cultural Factor in Bible Translation: A Study of Communicating the Word of God in a Central African Cultural Context. (UBS Monograph Series, 2). London, ENK: UBS, 1987. xii, 221 pp. Paper. No ISBN.

The second monograph in a continuing series designed to provide significant technical help to translators; cultural-conditioning when translating biblical text, particularly for two East African languages chiChewa and chiTonga, is the focus of the study of Ruth.

Literature: Production and Distribution

See also HI203, AS869, AS1189, AS1201, and EU236.

CO125 A Miracle in China
New York, NYU: American Bible Society, 1995. Video pp. No ISBN.

The story, on video, of the efforts of the Amity Foundation to publish and distribute the scriptures in the People's Republic of China.

CO126 Andrew, Brother
The Ethics of Smuggling. Wheaton, ILU: Tyndale House; London, ENK: Coverdale House Publishers, 1974. 139 pp. 0842307303.

A narrative account by Brother Andrew, of his Bible smuggling activities in Eastern Europe under communism and their rationale.

CO127 Bennett, Adrian A.
Missionary Journalist in China: Young J. Allen and His Magazines, 1860-1883. Athens, GAU: University of Georgia Press, 1983. xii, 324 pp. Paper. 0820306150.

The detailed study of the career in China (1860-1883) of a Methodist Episcopal Church South missionary who, through two weekly magazines in Chinese, provided for the readers both new ideas and values concerning political systems, science, commerce, education, and Christianity.

CO128 Bradlow, Frank R.
Printing for Africa: The Story of Robert Moffat and the Kuruman Press. Kuruman, SA: Kuruman Moffat Mission Trust, 1987. vi, 36 pp. Paper. 0620114894.

Following a brief historical background on the work of the famous LMS missionary Robert Moffat, the author gives a history of the Kuruman Press, which Moffat founded, and a list of publications produced there between 1831 and 1870.

CO129 Coggan, Donald
Word and World. London, ENK: Hodder & Stoughton, 1971. 160 pp. 0340156090.

A popular history of the English Bible, its translation, and dissemination through the UBS and the former British Foreign Bible Society; originally presented by the author, the Anglican Archbishop of York, as the Duff Missionary Lectures.

CO130 Eilers, Franz-Josef
Christliche Publizistik in Afrika: Eine erste Erkundung.
(Veröffentlichungen des Missionspriesterseminars, 13). Sankt
Augustin, GW: Steyler Verlag, 1964. 103 pp. Paper. No ISBN.
   A scholarly study of the Christian and missionary press
in Africa.

CO131 Grubb, Norman P.
Leap of Faith. Fort Washington, PAU: CLC, 1971. 238 pp.
875082157 (SBN).
   A revised popular history of the Christian Literature Crusade.

CO132 Johnson, Carl E.
How in the World? Old Tappen, NJU: Revell, 1969. 125 pp.
No ISBN.
   A discussion of the production of Christian literature for
all the world.

CO133 Simonsson, Bengt K. D.
*The Way of the Word: A Guide for Christian Literature Work-
ers.* London, ENK: USCL; New York, NYU: Committee on
World Literacy and Christian Literature, 1965. xv, 206 pp.
Paper. No ISBN.
   A practical working manual for church literature secre-
taries and members of literature committees, by the former
Director of the Africa Literature Centre in Kitwe, Zambia.

CO134 Street, Harold B.
Distributing Christian Literature. Wheaton, ILU: Evangelical Literature Overseas, 1962. 141 pp. No ISBN.
   A practical manual for missionaries on effective book
distribution through mission bookstores.

CO135 Watkins, Lois
*The Strategic Use of Literacy and Literature in World Evan-
gelication.* South Pasadena, CAU: William Carey Library,
1978. n.p. pp. No ISBN.
   Practical helps by the co-founder of the Lutheran Bible
Translators (1964), and the All Nations Literacy Movement
(1972).

CO136 Watkins, Morris
Literacy, Bible Reading, and Church Growth through the Ages.
South Pasadena, CAU: William Carey Library, 1978. xiii, 224
pp. Paper. 0878083251.
   A study by the founder of Lutheran Bible Translators and
the All Nations Literacy Movement, of the major developments
in church history, from the beginning of the synagogue to the
present, showing the impact of Bible reading, or the lack of it,
on church growth or decline.

Communication and Missions

See also HI498, TH6, CR830, SO372, CO9, CO59, CO143, EV119,
AF632, AM309, AS1037, and AS1187.

CO137 Reisach, Christian
*Das Wort und seine Macht in Afrika: Probleme der Kommuni-
kation und Information für die Verkündigung.* (Münsterschwarzacher Studien, 34). Münsterschwarzach, GW: Vier-
Türme-Verlag, 1981. xx, 450 pp. Paper. 3878681380.
   A dissertation showing how the Africa of old lived by the
word, and what importance the word has in modern Africa; a
background for discussion on effectiveness of the word in
Christian proclamation.

Preaching

See also AF646.

CO138 Chartier, Myron R.
Preaching as Communication. Nashville, TNU: Abingdon,
1981. 127 pp. Paper. 0687338263.
   An excellent treatment of communication theory, demonstrating how preachers can greatly enhance ministry by utilizing its insights and techniques.

CO139 Duffett, Robert G.
A Relevant Word: Communicating the Gospel to Seekers.
Valley Forge, PAU: Judson Press, 1995. xvi, 166 pp. Paper.
0817012338.
   Helps for preaching to seekers from among the unchurched
in North America, by the Assistant Professor of Preaching and
Evangelism at Northern Baptist Theological Seminary.

CO140 Harris, James H.
Preaching Liberation. Minneapolis, MNU: Fortress Press,
1995. xii, 136 pp. Paper. 0800628411.
   Out of the African American experience of oppression,
the Professor of Pastoral Theology at Virginia Union School
of Theology in Richmond, Virginia, develops a homiletic bent
on liberating and transforming individuals and society.

CO141 Keevil, Philip W., ed.
*Preaching in Revival: Preaching and a Theology of Awaken-
ing.* Lanham, MDU: University Press of America, 1999. xi,
174 pp. 0761814930 (hdbk), 0761814949 (pbk).
   The author explores the central attributes of revival, biblical
and historical foundations, and the role of preaching in revival.

Media and Missions

See also HI489, HI691, CO4, CO35, CO59, ED168, EV139,
EV279, EV285, EV289, MI141, MI194, AM1431, and AS608.

CO142 Alexander, Bobby C.
*Televangelism Reconsidered: Ritual in the Search for Human
Community.* (American Academy of Religion Studies in Religion, 68). Atlanta, GAU: Scholars Press, 1994. x, 205 pp.
1555409067 (hdbk), 1555409075 (pbk).
   A sociological and psychological study of televangelism
and its function as redressive ritual for conservative Christians within a highly secularized society.

CO143 Arthur, Chris, ed.
*The Globalization of Communications: Some Religious Impli-
cations.* Geneva, SZ: WCC Publications; London, ENK:
WACC, 1998. 69 pp. Paper. 2825412880.
   The ethical and religious dimensions for Christian reflection on the roles of the media—constant exposures to the reality of human suffering far away, making us aware of the religious diversity of the human family, portrayal of religions and
religious people, and impacting faith traditions which have
focused on the spoken and written word.

CO144 Assmann, Hugo
*La Iglesia Electrónica y su Impacto en América Latina: invit-
ación a un estudio.* San José, CR: DEI, 1987. 170 pp.
9977904650.
   An analysis by the noted liberation theologian of the impact in Latin America of religious radio and television, especially the "electronic church" imports from the United States.

CO—COMMUNICATIONS AND MISSIONS

CO145 Benson, Dennis C.

The Visible Church. Nashville, TNU: Abingdon, 1988. 173 pp. Paper. 0687437709.

Creative new ideas for local church growth and outreach, with fourteen models in which interactive videos and other media techniques enable congregations to be more visible in their local communities.

CO146 Biener, Hansjörg

Christliche Rundfunksender weltweit: Rundfunkarbeit im Klima der Konkurrenz. (Calwer Theologische Monographien: C, Praktische Theologie und Missionswissenschaft, 22). Stuttgart, GW: Calwer Verlag, 1994. 336 pp. Paper. 3766832875.

A thorough introduction to Christian radio transmission worldwide—its history, sponsorship, content, and effectiveness, often in climates of opposition; with a guide to source documents and published works.

CO147 Bluck, John

Beyond Neutrality: A Christian Critique of the Media. (Risk Book Series, 3). Geneva, SZ: WCC, 1978. vii, 62 pp. Paper. 2825405957.

An entry point into the current media debate, written in popular style by an ecumenical journalist for the WCC, who is an Anglican priest from New Zealand.

CO148 Bruce, Steve

Pray TV: Televangelism in America. London, ENK: Routledge, 1990. xii, 272 pp. 0415030978 (hdbk), 0415030986 (pbk).

A detailed interpretation of the history and influence of televangelism in the United States.

CO149 Cousins, Peter, and Pam Cousins

The Power of the Air. (Hodder Christian Paperbacks). London, ENK: Hodder & Stoughton, 1978. 157 pp. Paper. 0340196521.

Following a popular introduction to Christian radio as mission around the world, the author relates the history of the Far East Broadcasting Association (FEBA).

CO150 Foege, Alec

The Empire God Built: Inside Pat Robertson's Media Machine. New York, NYU: Wiley, 1996. xi, 242 pp. 047115993X.

A critical analysis of the media ministry of Pat Robertson, the evangelist host of The 700 Club and head of the 1.7 million-member Christian Coalition.

CO151 Fore, William F.

Mythmakers: Gospel, Culture, and the Media. New York, NYU: Friendship Press, 1990. v, 150 pp. Paper. 0377002070.

An introduction to issues in contemporary Christian communication; prepared as a mission study text, with study guide entitled *The Mything Link* by Dave Pomeroy (0377002089).

CO152 Freed, Paul E.

Towers to Eternity. Cary, NCU: Trans World Radio, 1994. 191 pp. Paper. 0840757093.

Stories of the founding (in 1952) and work of Trans World Radio in Christian Broadcasting, told by its founder; originally published by Word Books in 1968.

CO153 Gibson, John, and Clair Dean Hutchins

Winning the World: A Proposal on How to Win the World for Christ: Now ... in Our Generation. Saint Petersburg, FLU: World Mission Crusade, 1985. vi, 266 pp. Paper. 0938351001.

A popular account of missionary work being done through mass media communication, particularly film evangelism called "the fourth dimension of evangelism."

CO154 Gilman, John

They're Killing an Innocent Man: The Cry of Those Who Have Never Heard. Milton Keynes, ENK: Word Publishing, 1992. 209 pp. Paper. 0850095689 (UK), 186258219X (AT).

A popular account by the founder of Dayspring International in 1979, of the use of films to present Christ in India.

CO155 Hadden, Jeffrey K., and Charles E. Swann

Prime Time Preachers. Reading, MAU: Addison-Wesley, 1981. xxi, 217 pp. 0201038854.

An insightful, piercing, and sometimes disturbing look at the major American television evangelists—their approaches, claims, and fund-raising, as well as their power and influence.

CO156 Head, Sydney W., ed.

Broadcasting in Africa: A Continental Survey of Radio and Television. (International and Comparative Broadcasting). Philadelphia, PAU: Temple University Press, 1974. xvi, 453 pp. 0877220271.

A major survey including chapter 11 on Religious Broadcasting.

CO157 Jørgensen, Knud

The Role and Function of the Media in the Mission of the Church: With Particular Reference to Africa. Ann Arbor, MIU: University Microfilms, 1986. xvii, 701 pp. No ISBN.

An excellent theological treatment of the incarnational model of communication, with special treatment of the function and possibilities of radio in mission; a Ph.D. dissertation completed at Fuller Theological Seminary, School of World Mission, Pasadena, California.

CO158 Jahn, Christoph, ed.

Frequenzen der guten Nachricht: Rundfunksender "Stimme des Evangeliums" Addis Abeba; Bilanz; Erfahrungen und Vorhaben eines gemeinsamen Projektes der Kirchen. (Erlanger Taschenbücher, 24). Erlangen, GW: Ev.-Luth. Mission, 1973. 192 pp. Paper. 3872140469.

An account of the first ten years (1963-1973) of Radio Voice of the Gospel, and of its pre-history in the 1948-1963 period; with selections illustrative of its program materials.

CO159 Johansson, Eskil

IBRA radio: Radiomission-varför? Stockholm, SW: IBRA Radio, 1971. 200 pp. No ISBN.

A book on the Swedish broadcasting mission IBRA and its activities.

CO160 McDonnell, James, and Frances Trampiets, eds.

Communicating Faith in a Technological Age. Middlegreen, ENK: St. Paul Publications, 1989. 175 pp. Paper. 0854393145.

Thirteen scholarly essays on issues facing Christian communicators in a society dominated by the technologies of mass communication; with suggestions for the church's mission and media ministries.

CO161 Milton, Ralph
Radio Programming: A Basic Training Manual. London, ENK: Geoffrey Bles for the World Association of Christian Broadcasting, 1968. 384 pp. Paper. 0713802162.

A basic, but excellent, step-by-step training manual for making radio programs; primarily as a self-study guide for people in developing countries where English is not the first language, and whose financial situation does not allow them to go to Europe or North America.

CO162 Peck, Janice
The Gods of Televangelism. (Hampton Press Communication Series). Cresskill, NJU: Hampton Press, 1993. xvii, 271 pp. 1881303659 (hdbk), 1881303667 (pbk).

An interdisciplinary study of evangelical television—its conception, aims, and methods; with some theoretical and practical concerns.

CO163 Renner, Louis L.
The KNOM/Father Jim Poole Story. Portland, ORU: Binford & Mort Publishing, 1985. 150 pp. Paper. 0832304441.

A heartwarming account of the history of a Roman Catholic missionary in Alaska, and his radio ministry to the Eskimo people since 1948.

CO164 Robertson, Pat
Julistakaa se Katoilta. Translated by Jamie Y. Buckingham. Tikkurila, FI: Ristin Voitto, 1974. 306 pp. 9516051243 (nid.), 9516051251 (sid.).

Finnish translation of the 1972 edition.

CO165 Robertson, Pat
Shout It from the Housetops. Virginia Beach, VAU: Christian Broadcasting Network, 1986. vii, 163 pp. No ISBN.

The story of "The 700 Club," a Pentecostal-charismatic sodality which has spread to many foreign countries; published as a revised edition for the 25th anniversary (1961-1986) of the Christian Broadcasting Network (CBN), and originally by Bridge Publishers (1972).

CO166 Søgaard, Viggo B.
Everything You Need to Know for a Cassette Ministry: Cassettes in the Context of a Total Christian Communication Program. Minneapolis, MNU: Bethany Fellowship, 1975. 221 pp. Paper. 0871231255.

A basic manual on Christian communication theory and strategy, and the application of such insights to the use of media, in particular the audio cassette, which is treated in the context of a total Christian communications strategy.

CO167 Søgaard, Viggo B.
Media in Church and Mission: Communicating the Gospel. South Pasadena, CAU: William Carey Library, 1993. xiv, 287 pp. Paper. 0878082425.

A basic text on the principles, guidelines, and techniques by which the church uses various media for Christian communication and mission.

CO168 Schultze, Quentin J., ed.
American Evangelicals and the Mass Media: Perspectives on the Relationship between American Evangelicals and the Mass Media. Grand Rapids, MIU: Academie Books, 1990. 382 pp. Paper. 0310272610.

A collection of sixteen essays covering the historical context between evangelicals and the media, contemporary media (books, magazines, music, and radio), televangelism, evangelical and secular news media, and their international influences on religious broadcasting.

CO169 Sellers, James E.
The Outsider and the Word of God: A Study in Christian Communication. New York, NYU: Abingdon, 1961. 240 pp. No ISBN.

An analysis of communicative techniques evolved by mass media, emphasizing their limits and potential for communicating the Word of God to the "outsider" (anyone not attuned to God's message).

CO170 Slaughter, Michael
Out on the Edge: A Wake-up Call for Church Leaders on the Edge of the Media Reformation. Nashville, TNU: Abingdon, 1998. 136 pp. Paper. 0687054532.

Stories, and resources on CD; from rapidly growing Ginghamsburg United Methodist Church, north of Dayton, Ohio, that embraces the media revolution in effective ministry to postmodern young adults.

CO171 Thompson, Phyllis
Capturing Voices: The Story of Joy Ridderhof. London, ENK: Hodder & Stoughton, 1978. 190 pp. 0340224479.

A popular account of the work of the foundress of Gospel Recordings, Inc., which today includes recordings of Scripture portions in more than 4,000 languages and dialects; American edition published under the title *Count It All Joy!*

CO172 Velacherry, Joseph
Social Impact of Mass Media in Kerala. (Social Research Series, 20). Delhi, II: ISPCK for CISRS, 1993. viii, 260 pp. Paper. 8172140649.

A sociological study of the impact of media on the highly literate society of Kerala, India, many of whom are Christians.

CO173 Whitehead, Briar
God Speaks from a Little Box. Eastbourne, ENK: MARC; Sutherland, AT: Albatross Books, 1989. 219 pp. Paper. 1854240579 (M), 0732404339 (A).

A Christian journalist's firsthand accounts of how broken men and women in Europe, South America, India, and the Middle East came to a deep faith in Christ through the ministry of Trans World Radio.

CO174 Wilson, Frederick R.
Without Communication Man Stands Alone: Mass Communications Overseas and the United Presbyterians. New York. NYU: COEMAR, 1964. 80 pp. No ISBN.

Describes how, why, and by whom the Gospel can be shared through mass media.

CO175 Anderson, Gerald H., ed.
Sermons to Men of Other Faiths and Traditions. Nashville, TNU: Abingdon; Ann Arbor, MIU: University Microfilms, 1977. 183 pp. No ISBN.

Fifteen sermons addressed either to persons of another faith, or to those of differing Christian traditions; with brief summaries for each of the supposed religious position of the person addressed.

EDUCATION AND MISSIONS

Lois McKinney-Douglas, Subeditor

"Education has always been an integral part of the missionary movement," J. Herbert Kane wrote in Understanding Christian Missions (1988:319). The sub-discipline of missiology which reflects on mission(ary) education is the pedagogics of mission *(Ger.: Missionspä dagogik)*.

Gustav Warneck introduced this term in the 19th century. Following that tradition, Jongeneel has identified the interdisciplinary scope of the pedagogics of mission. It "deals empirically and analytically with the link between education, on the one hand, and both the Christian mission and non-Christian missions and propaganda, on the other hand." It "describes and analyses the contribution of Christian mission to education and vice versa" (1995, I:346).

For an overview of this linkage see works listed under "General Works." The following section on "History" contains denominational and ecumenical surveys. This is then subdivided into the various types of education related to missions: "Formal Education" through Christian schools, "Secondary Education" through high schools, post-secondary or "Higher Education," and "Adult Education" often called non-formal or education by extension. Note the number of "see also" references in these sections, for local and national histories or studies have been placed in the appropriate geographic regions. Equipping of persons for ministry has been a priority in the shift from missions to mission in every continent.

The section on "Theological Education" brings together diverse publications on equipping for ministry, with special focus on Africa, Asia, Latin America, and Oceania.

Most of the literature on Christian education and religious education falls outside the scope of this bibliography as it concerns primarily the training of Christians concerning their own faith tradition and practice. Jesus' "Great Commission" to reach out to new believers, "teaching them to obey everything that I have commanded you" (Mt. 28:20) links mission to Christian education. Sections on "Christian Education," "Moral and Religious Education," "Sunday Schools," and "Catechetics" include works dealing with that linkage.

Other chapters of this bibliography contain works relating education and mission. Books on the study of missiology are found in the section on "General Study and Teaching" under "General Works." The section on "Recruitment and Training" under "Missionaries" covers the equipping of missionaries, while those on "Education for Mission" and "Mission Study Literature" under "Methods" contain works on teaching about the church's mission in local churches.

Norman E. Thomas

Bibliographies

ED1 Morris, Raymond P.
A Theological Book List. London, ENK: Theological Education Fund, 1960. xiv, 242 pp. Paper. No ISBN.

A listing of basic books in English, French, Spanish, and Portuguese for theological seminaries.

Serials and Periodicals

ED2 *Ministerial Formation.* No. 1 (1978)-. Quarterly
Geneva, SZ: WCC, Ecumenical Theological Education, 1978-. ISSN 02558777.

Articles on renewal of the churches through programs of ministerial formation, reports of consultations, and news of ecumenical and regional developments.

Reference Works

See also ED129.

ED3 Buker, Raymond B., and Ted Warren Ward, comps.
The World Directory of Mission-Related Educational Institutions. South Pasadena, CAU: William Carey Library, 1972. 880 pp. 0878081216.

Statistical data on 813 Protestant mission-related educational institutions in Africa, Asia, Latin America, and Oceania.

ED4 Smith, Charles Stanley, and Herbert F. Thomson, comps.
Protestant Theological Seminaries and Bible Schools in Asia, Africa, Middle East, Latin America and the Caribbean and Pacific Areas. Edited by Frank W. Price. (MRL Directory Series, 12). New York, NYU: MRL, 1960. viii, 50 pp. No ISBN.

A comprehensive directory.

Documentation and Archives

ED5 Cowan, L. Gray, James O'Connell, and David G. Scanlon
Education and Nation Building in Africa. New York, NYU: Praeger; London, ENK: Pall Mall Press, 1965. 403 pp. No ISBN.

A sourcebook of writings by African leaders and research specialists, 1948-1963, on interlocking relationships between politics, economics, and education in colonial and independent Africa.

Conferences and Congresses

See also ED94, ED115, and ED175.

ED6 All Africa Church Conference (Salisbury, Southern Rhodesia, 1963-63)
Christian Education in Africa: Report of a Conference Held at Salisbury, Southern Rhodesia, 29 December 1962 to 10 January 1963. London, ENK: Oxford University Press for the AACC, 1963. vii, 120 pp. Paper. No ISBN.

Brief surveys on the history of church participation in education in French and English-speaking countries of Africa, together with the report of this important conference of 130 Christian leaders from practically all countries and territories of the continent.

ED7 Beaver, Robert Pierce, ed.
Christianity and African Education: The Papers of a Conference at the University of Chicago. Grand Rapids, MIU: Eerdmans, 1966. 233 pp. Paper. No ISBN.

Thirteen scholarly papers presented at a conference on sub-Saharan education held at the University of Chicago, 19-22 October 1964, sponsored jointly by the Division of Overseas Ministries of the NCCUSA and the Divinity School of the University of Chicago.

General Works

See also SO43, ED39, AF176, AF656, AF736, and AF847.

ED8 *An Encounter with Education for Liberation and Community*
Singapore, SI: CCA, 1975. 70 pp. Paper. No ISBN.

Papers from the CCA Seminar for Liberation and Community held in Singapore, February 1975, in which twenty-five educators from twelve Asian countries presented their goals and guidelines for non-formal education through action-reflection programs.

ED9 Barman, Jean, Yvonne Hebert, and Don McCaskill, eds.
Indian Education in Canada—Volume 1: The Legacy. (Nakoda Institute Occasional Paper, 2). Vancouver, BCC: University of British Columbia Press, 1986. vii, 172 pp. Paper. 077480243X.

Eight scholarly essays on the education of Indians by whites since the arrival of the first Europeans in Canada, with special attention to the role of the churches, both Catholic and Protestant, in the 18th, 19th, and 20th centuries.

ED10 Consejo Episcopal Latinoamericano, Departamento de Educación
Colección Departamento de Educación: Un Desafío en América Latina. Bogotá, CK: CELAM, 1985. 184 pp. Paper. No ISBN.

A study commissioned at the Third General Conference of Latin American Bishops (Puebla, 1979), exploring the incarnation of Christian faith within the social realites of Latin America.

ED11 Cox, James L.
The Impact of Christian Missions on Indigenous Cultures: The "Real People" and the Unreal Gospel. (Studies in the History of Missions, 4). Lewiston, NYU: E Mellen Press, 1991. viii, 261 pp. 0889460728.

A detailed case study of educational strategies by Methodists and Presbyterians in Alaska, from the theology of cultural replacement for Eskimo peoples in the 1880s, to the diffusion theology of Alaska Methodist University in the 1980s.

ED12 Cully, Kendig Brubaker, ed.
The Episcopal Church and Education. New York, NYU: Morehouse-Barlow, 1966. 256 pp. No ISBN.

The first comprehensive review of all aspects of education with which the Episcopal Church in the United States is concerned.

ED13 Evans, Rob, and Tosh Arai, eds.
The Church and Education in Asia. Singapore, SI: CCA, 1980. 113 pp. Paper. No ISBN.

Brief reports on Christian education in fourteen Asian countries, including sections on general education, church-related schools, religious education in schools, Christian education in local congregations, and training for Christian education.

ED14 Palmer, Martin
What Should We Teach: Christians and Education in a Pluralist World. (Risk Book Series, 51). Geneva, SZ: WCC Publications, 1991. viii, 63 pp. Paper. 2825410403.

Findings from a 1986-1990 WCC project on "Learning in a World of Many Faiths, Cultures and Ideologies: A Christian Response," with case studies from Kenya, the Netherlands, the European Community, and the Philippines.

ED15 Verstraeten, A.
Ideas about Christian Education in India. Bangalore, II: Theological Publications in India, 1973. 218 pp. Paper. No ISBN.

An introduction to Christian education in India by a leading Roman Catholic educator relating the church's mission in that country to goals stated in Vatican II documents, papal encyclicals, the Kothari Report on education in India (1966), and the UNESCO Report on Education (1972).

ED16 WCC's Office of Education
Seeing Education Whole. Geneva, SZ: WCC, 1970. 126 pp. Paper. No ISBN.

Papers from the first consultation of the Office of Education of the WCC held at Bergen, the Netherlands, 17-22 May 1970, on the theme, "The World Educational Crisis and the Church's Contribution."

ED—EDUCATION AND MISSIONS

History

ED17 Brawley, James P.

Two Centuries of Methodist Concern: Bondage, Freedom and Education of Black People. New York, NYU: Vantage Press, 1974. 606 pp. 053300649X.

A history of educational ministries in the Methodist Episcopal Church for blacks in the United States, 1784-1974, with special reference to the histories of thirteen black colleges.

ED18 Brereton, Virginia Lieson

Training God's Army: The American Bible School, 1880-1940. Bloomington, INU: Indiana University Press, 1990. xix, 212 pp. 0253312663.

An in-depth look at the origin and development of Bible schools in the United States in which evangelicals and fundamentalists trained evangelists, pastors, missionaries, and teachers.

ED19 Calam, John

Parsons and Pedagogues: The S.P.G. Adventure in American Education. New York, NYU: Columbia University Press, 1971. xi, 249 pp. 0231033710.

A survey and reevaluation of the educational work of the SPG in Britain's North American colonies, 1702 to 1783.

ED20 Don Peter, W. L. A.

Xavier As Educator. Delhi, II: Jesuit Educational Association of India, 1974. x, 191 pp. No ISBN.

An analysis of the history and legacy in India of Francis Xavier as educator by a well-known Sri Lankan educationist.

ED21 Fenn, William Purviance

Ever New Horizons: The Story of the United Board for Christian Higher Education in Asia , 1922-1975. North Newton, KSU: Mennonite Press, 1980. x, 164 pp. Paper. No ISBN.

The story of the founding of the United Board for Christian Higher Education in Asia and its contribution to that cause.

ED22 Holden, Reuben

Yale in China: The Mainland, 1901-1951. New Haven, CTU: Yale in China Association, 1964. xii, 327 pp. No ISBN.

The scholarly history of fifty years of educational and medical missionary work by the Yale in China Association.

ED23 Koolen, G. M. J. M.

Een seer bequaen middel: Onderwijs en kerk onder de zeventiendeeeuwse VOC. (Kerk en theologie in context, 19). Kampen, NE: Kok, 1993. xiii, 287 pp. 9024266424.

An analysis of the involvement of the 17th-century missions in education under the Dutch East India Company.

ED24 Parker, Inez Moore

The Rise and Decline of the Program of Education for Black Presbyterians of the United Presbyterian Church U.S.A., 1865-1970. (Presbyterian Historical Society Publication Series, 16). San Antonio, TXU: Trinity University Press, 1977. ix, 319 pp. 0911536663.

Results of forty years of research in church archives documenting the contribution to the educational and cultural development of freed slaves by Presbyterian schools and colleges.

ED25 Ragsdale, John P.

Protestant Mission Education in Zambia, 1880-1954. Selinsgrove, PAU: Susquehanna University Press, 1986. 190 pp. 0941664090.

A detailed historical analysis of government/mission cooperation in education in colonial Northern Rhodesia (present Zambia).

ED26 Ringenberg, William C.

The Christian College: A History of Protestant Higher Education in America. St. Paul, MNU: Christian University Press; Grand Rapids, MIU: Eerdmans, 1984. x, 257 pp. Paper. 0802819966.

The first comprehensive history of Protestant higher education in what is now the United States, organized chronologically from the founding of Harvard College in 1636.

ED27 Wood, Robert D.

Teach Them Good Customs: Colonial Indian Education and Acculturation in the Andes. Culver City, CAU: Labyrinthos, 1986. v, 134 pp. Paper. 0911437177.

An analysis of the education provided by Catholic missionaries for Andean Indians from the Spanish conquest to 1800.

Formal Education: General

ED28 Berman, Edward H.

African Reactions to Missionary Education. New York, NYU: Teachers College Press, 1975. xxiv, 231 pp. 0807724459.

Seven scholarly case histories of Africans who went through mission-supported school systems in widely different settings, including an analysis of missionary education, with the historical forces that shaped it and led to its decline.

ED29 Cameron, John

The Development of Education in East Africa. New York, NYU: Teachers College Press, 1970. ix, 148 pp. No ISBN.

A history (1960s) of education, particularly teacher education, in Kenya, Tanzania, and Uganda; with a chapter on church-state relations.

ED30 Carper, James C., and Thomas C. Hunt, eds.

Religious Schooling in America. Birmingham, ALU: Religious Education Press, 1984. x, 257 pp. Paper. 0891350438.

Essays tracing the history and contemporary concerns of six major religious school movements in the United States—Roman Catholic, Lutheran, Calvinist, Seventh-day Adventist, and Jewish.

ED31 *Church Related Educational Institutions: Dossier*

(Vols. 2-5 (1970-1985)). Geneva, SZ: WCC, Sub-Unit on Education, 1970-1985. 5 vols. Paper. No ISBN.

Collections of case studies on church-related schools and actual approaches to Christian education in local situations in various countries.

ED32 Convey, John J., and Maria J. Ciriello

Strategic Planning for Catholic Schools: A Diocesan Model of Consultation. Washington, DCU: USCC, 1996. xii, 239 pp. Paper. 1574550551.

A comprehensive resource for strategic planning on the diocesan levels concerning the future of Catholic schools.

ED—EDUCATION AND MISSIONS

ED—EDUCATION AND MISSIONS

ED33 Devanesen, Chandran D. S.
Christ and Student Unrest: Thoughts on Christian Education.
Madras, II: CLS, 1982. vi, 93 pp. Paper. No ISBN.

A collection of twelve papers on the place of the church in formal education in India by the first Indian principal of the Madras Christian Institute for Development Education.

ED34 Dickson, Alec
A Chance to Serve. Edited by Mora Dickson. London, ENK: Dobson, 1976. 174 pp. 0234778881 (hdbk), 0234770225 (pbk).

Reflections by Alec Dickson, founder of "Community Service Volunteers," on curriculum, tutoring, and community development in Third World countries.

ED35 Fiévet, Michel
École, mission et l'Église de demain. (Parole et mission, nouv. ser., 18). Paris, FR: Éditions du Cerf, 1969. 138 pp. No ISBN.

As the result of his fourteen years of experience in Thailand, the author describes the "malaise" of the mission-schools today, indicating better ways of using educational opportunities for the purpose of evangelism.

ED36 Fowler, Stuart, Harro van Brummelen, and John van Dyk
Christian Schooling: Education for Freedom. (Institute for Reformational Studies F3: Collections, 39). Potchefstroom, SA: Potchefstroom University, 1990. vi, 198 pp. Paper. 1868220419.

A thoughtful examination, from a Reformed Protestant perspective, of the qualities of a Christian school, including chapters on social context, learning theory and practice, curriculum, and the teaching of Christianity.

ED37 Holmes, Brian, ed.
Educational Policy and the Mission Schools: Case Studies from the British Empire. London, ENK: Routledge; New York, NYU: Humanities Press, 1967. xv, 352 pp. 0710060025.

Eight scholarly essays on the results of colonial and missionary educational policies upon secondary education in former British colonies, including seven national case studies.

ED38 Illich, Ivan D.
Deschooling Society. London, ENK: Marion Boyars, 1996. viii, 116 pp. Paper. 0714508799.

A stinging critique of church-related educational institutions and methods in Latin America; originally published by Harper & Row, New York (1970).

ED39 Illich, Ivan D.
La Sociedad Desescolarizada. Translated by Gerardo Espinosa. (Breve biblioteca respuesta, 100). Barcelona, SP: Barral Editores, 1976. 148 pp. 8421103008.

Third edition of the Spanish translation.

ED40 Lutz, Jessie Gregory
China and the Christian Colleges, 1850-1950. Ithaca, NYU: Cornell University Press, 1971. xiii, 575 pp. 0801406269.

A scholarly history of the first century of Protestant mission education in China, focusing on those schools which became institutions of higher education.

ED41 Okpaloka, Pius Obi
The Role of the Church in Nigerian Education in the Light of Vatican Council II and the 1983 Code of Canon Law. (Facultas Iuris Conanici). Rome, IT: Pontificia Universitas Urbaniana, 1989. xvi, 352 pp. Paper. 8840133259.

A detailed study of Roman Catholic involvement in educa-

tion in Nigeria in the past thirty years; originally presented as a doctoral dissertation at the Urbaniana Pontifical University.

ED42 Stone, Frank A.
Academies for Anatolia: A Study of the Rationale, Program, and Impact of the Educational Institutions Sponsored by the American Board in Turkey, 1830-1980. Lanham, MDU: University Press of America, 1984. xx, 363 pp. 0819140643.

A scholarly, multidisciplinary study which describes and interprets rationales for educational programs initiated by the ABCFM.

ED43 Thompson, A. R. et al.
Church and Education in Tanzania: Report of the ISS/FERES Tanzania Project. Edited by Allan J. Gottneid. Nairobi, KE: East African Publishing House, 1976. xxi, 230 pp. Paper. No ISBN.

The report of a detailed field study in Tanzania of the relationships between the churches (both Catholic and Protestant) and the government in seeking to respond to educational needs in this developing nation.

ED44 Van der Laan, Henk J., Arnold H. De Graff, Harold W. Van Brummelen, et. al.
The Ideal of Christian Schools. (Institute for Reformational Studies, 358). Potchefstroom, SA: Institute for Reformational Studies, 1997. 80 pp. Paper. 1868222888.

Five essays on Christian schools with special reference to South Africa, Australia, Canada, and the United States, with a bibliography.

ED45 Walch, Timothy
Parish School: American Catholic Parochial Education from Colonial Times to the Present. New York, NYU: Crossroad Publishing, 1996. x, 301 pp. 0824515323.

A historical review of Catholic parochial education in the United States—its goals, methods, and impact.

Secondary Education

See also ED37, AF214, AF741, AF903, AF1144, AF1155, AM602-AM603, AM1491, and OC250.

ED46 Ciriello, Maria J., ed.
Expectations for the Catholic School Principal: A Handbook for Pastors and Parish School Committees. Washington, DCU: USCC, 1996. x, 148 pp. Paper. 1574550543.

A resource designed to help pastors and school board members learn about the scope of responsibilities entailed in the work of the Catholic school principal.

ED47 Kiriswa, Benjamin
Christian Counselling for Students. (Spearhead Series, 102). Eldoret, KE: Gaba Publications, 1988. vi, 81 pp. Paper. No ISBN.

A practical guide to train pastoral counselors to guide young people effectively, by the Roman Catholic Director of the Mitume Pastoral and Catechetical Centre in Kenya.

ED48 Mulligan, James T.
Evangelization and the Catholic High School: An Agenda for the 1990s. Ottawa, ONC: Novalis/St. Paul University, 1990. xiii, 296 pp. Paper. 2890884287.

A carefully argued case challenging Canadian Roman Catholics to maintain the special character of their schools, with numerous quotes from Catholic documents and interviews with pupils, teachers, and administrators.

ED49 Wagner, Jon
Misfits and Missionaries: A School for Black Dropouts. (The City and Society, 2). Beverly Hills, CAU: Sage Publications, 1977. 247 pp. 0803907222 (hdbk), 0803907230 (pbk).

The story of Mission Academy, an alternative high school for black public school dropouts in inner city Chicago in the 1960s, sponsored by an ecumenical organization of churches on Chicago's West Side.

Teacher

See also ED29, AF1271, and AS908.

ED50 Hughes, W.
Dark Africa and the Way Out: Or, a Scheme for Civilizing and Evangelizing the Dark Continent. New York, NYU: Negro Universities Press, 1969. xiv, 155 pp. 0837119901.

Reprint of a 1892 proposal for enhancing Africa missions through a Congo Training Institute.

Higher Education

See also ED21, ED26, ED40, AF1268, AM704, AM735, AM1493, AS337, AS655-AS656, AS822, AS876, AS1074, EU288, OC110, and OC148.

ED51 Abel, M.
Ideals and Reality: Reflections on Higher Education. Madras, II: CLS, 1995. xii, 178 pp. Paper. No ISBN.

Reflections on Indian developments in higher education since national independence in 1947, and the place of Christian institutions within those developments, by the former Principal of Madras Christian College.

ED52 Bonachea, Rolando E.
Jesuit Higher Education: Essays on an American Tradition of Excellence. Pittsburgh, PAU: Duquesne University Press, 1989. viii, 192 pp. 0820702080.

Fourteen essays by Jesuit scholars and campus ministers assessing the present state of Jesuit education, primarily in North America.

ED53 Burnstein, Ira Jerry
The American Movement to Develop Protestant Colleges for Men in Japan, 1868-1912. (University of Michigan Comparative Education Dissertation Series, 11). Ann Arbor, MIU: University of Michigan, School of Education, 1967. 158 pp. No ISBN.

A dissertation with extensive footnotes and bibliography.

ED54 Carpenter, Joel A., and Kenneth W. Shipps, eds.
Making Higher Education Christian: The History and Mission of Evangelical Colleges in America. Grand Rapids, MIU: Christian University Press, 1987. xvi, 304 pp. Paper. 0802802532.

Nineteen scholarly essays which document the history and character of American evangelical colleges and their development of a thoroughly Christian approach to contemporary higher education.

ED55 CCA-WSCF Joint Programme '95 (Bangkok, Thailand, 1-8 April 1995)
To Build and to Plant: Christian Witness in the 21st Century University Communities. Shatin, HK: CCA; Kowloon, HK: World Student Christian Federation, 1995. 2 vols. Paper. No ISBN.

Study papers on the mission of the church in Asian universities (vol. 1: 30 pp.; vol. 2: 36 pp.).

ED56 Cole, Charles E., ed.
Something More Than Human: Biographies of Leaders in American Methodist Higher Education. Nashville, TNU: UMC, Board of Higher Education, 1986. x, 243 pp. Paper. 0938162047.

Biographies of seventeen women and men who created Methodist schools, colleges, and universities in the United States, India (Isabella Thoburn), China, and Korea (Robert S. Maclay).

ED57 De Jong, Arthur J.
Reclaiming a Mission: New Direction for the Church-Related College. Grand Rapids, MIU: Eerdmans, 1990. xii, 169 pp. Paper. 0802804365.

A critical analysis of how church-related colleges came to adopt a public university educational philosophy, with a post-World War II overview of American society, and a design for pointing these colleges back to basic Christian tenets.

ED58 Dickinson, Richard D. N.
The Christian College in Developing India: A Sociological Inquiry. London, ENK: Oxford University Press, 1971. xx, 370 pp. 0195600665.

Report of a large 1964-1965 study of university level Christian colleges in India, with a critical appraisal and projection concerning their future.

ED59 Ducruet, Jean, et al.
Faith and Culture: The Role of the Catholic University. (International Federation of Catholic Universities). (Inculturation: Working Papers on Living Faith and Cultures, 11). Rome, IT: Pontifical Gregorian University, 1989. xi, 147 pp. Paper. No ISBN.

Fourteen papers from the sixteenth General Assembly of the International Federation of Catholic Universities that explore 1) cultural pluralism and diversity and the Catholic university's responses to it in different cultural contexts; 2) the challenges to the mission of the Catholic university presented by modern culture and the church; and 3) the tasks of the Catholic university in the "faith and culture" dialogue and in a multireligious society.

ED60 Elwood, Douglas J., ed.
The Humanities in Christian Higher Education in Asia: Ethical and Religious Perspectives. Quezon City, PH: New Day Publishers, 1978. x, 105 pp. Paper. No ISBN.

The proceedings of the All-Asia Workshop on the Humanities (Taipei, Formosa, April 1975) attended by representatives of twenty-four Protestant and Catholic colleges and universities in nine Asian countries.

ED61 Fowler, Stuart
A Christian Voice among Students and Scholars. (Wetenskaplike Bydraes; Series F: Institute for Reformational Studies, F2 Brochures, 51). Potchefstroom, SA: Potchefstroom University, 1991. vi, 231 pp. Paper. 0868220702.

Messages prepared for young Christians providing a perspective on Christians, their world, and life as students in the modern university, by the principal lecturer with the Institute for Christian Education, Melbourne, Australia.

ED—EDUCATION AND MISSIONS

ED62 Galligan-Stierle, Michael
The Gospel on Campus: A Handbook of Campus Ministry Programs and Resources. Washington, DCU: USCC, 1996. vii, 232 pp. Paper. 1574550314.

A resource manual for campus ministers, compiling insights from the work of hundreds in such ministries in the United States.

ED63 Iglehart, Charles W.
International Christian University: An Adventure in Christian Higher Education in Japan. Tokyo, JA: International Christian University, 1964. xii, 312 pp. No ISBN.

A detailed history of the beginnings and development of the university from 1945 to 1973.

ED64 Marais, J. L., S. C. du Toit, and J. H. Steyn
Onderwys in die Nuwe Suid-Afrika: Drie aktuele vraagstukke. (Reeks F1: Institut vir Reformatoriese Studie-Studiestuk, 375). Potchefstroom, SA: Potchefstroom University, 1999. 69 pp. Paper. 1868223353.

A collection of three articles on inclusive education, multicultural education, and the education of minority groups, written by two professors in the School of Education at Potschefstromse University and by the Rector at Potschefstroomse College in New South Africa.

ED65 Parsonage, Robert Rue, ed.
Church Related Higher Education: Perceptions and Perspectives. Valley Forge, PAU: Judson Press, 1978. 344 pp. 0817008314.

Report of a three-year study sponsored by the NCCUSA on the current state of church-related colleges and universities in that country.

ED66 Poorman, Mark L., ed.
Labors from the Heart: Mission and Ministry in a Catholic University. Notre Dame, INU: University of Notre Dame Press, 1996. xii, 278 pp. Paper. 0268014248.

Twenty-five short essays by faculty, administrators, and alumni of the University of Notre Dame, contributed as part of a fifteen-month study of the mission of the university.

ED67 Shockley, Donald G.
Campus Ministry: The Church Beyond Itself. Louisville, KYU: Westminster John Knox, 1989. v, 130 pp. Paper. 0804215839.

A mainline Protestant treatment of the history of campus ministry in the United States, of a theology of campus ministry, and of campus ministry as mission, by the chaplain of Emory University.

ED68 *The Christian College and National Development: The ISS-FERES Consultation of Principals of Christian Colleges, Tambaram, December 30th 1966-Jan 5th 1967*
Madras, II: CLS, 1967. 290 pp. Paper. No ISBN.

Papers and reports from the ISS-FERES joint project of the WCC and the Roman Catholic Church to reconsider the role of the churches in education in developing countries.

ED69 van der Walt, B. J., and Rita Swanepoel, eds.
Signposts of God's Liberating Kingdom: Perspectives for the 21st Century, Volume 1. (Orientation, 83-86). Potchefsfstroom, SA: Potchefstroom University, 1997. ix, 377 pp. No ISBN.

A reprint of short essays from *Orientation*, a publication of the Institute for Reformational Studies of Potchchefstroom University for Christian Higher Education, on the reign of God, social issues, and missions to Muslims.

ED70 van der Walt, B. J.
A Christian Worldview and Christian Higher Education for Africa. Potchefstroom, SA: Potchefstroom University, 1991. 124 pp. Paper. No ISBN.

Lectures relating African worldviews, the reformational worldview, and Christian higher education, by the Director of the Institute for Reformational Studies at the Potchefstroom University for Christian Higher Education in South Africa.

ED71 West, Philip
Yenching University and Sino-Western Relations, 1916-1952. (Harvard East Asian Series, 85). Cambridge, MAU: Harvard University Press, 1976. x, 327 pp. 0674965698.

A scholarly case study of Christianity and Chinese culture as seen through the interactions of Protestant missionaries with Chinese staff colleagues at Yenching University, from its founding in 1916 to the Communist takeover; with attention to the pivotal role of John Leighton Stuart, Yenching's longtime President (1919-1946) and American ambassador to China (1946-1953).

Special Aspects

See also EC168, ED49, and AF598.

ED72 Collins, Denis E.
Paulo Freire: His Life, Works, and Thought. (A Deus Book). New York, ENK: Paulist Press, 1977. 94 pp. 0809120569.

A biography of the influential educator, with an assessment of the main influences on his thought and of his pedagogy.

ED73 Dickerson, Lonna J., and Dianne F. Dow
Handbook for Christian ESL Teachers: Christian Teacher-Preparation Programs, Overseas Teaching Opportunities, Instructional Materials and Resources. (A BCG Monograph). Wheaton, ILU: Institute for Cross-Cultural Training; Evanston, ILU: Berry Publishing Services, 1997. 96 pp. Paper. 1879089254 (WE), 0963585614 (EV).

Resources for prospective teachers of English as a second language including training options, teaching opportunities, and instructional materials.

ED74 Evans, Alice Frazer, Robert A. Evans, and William Bean Kennedy
Pedagogies for the Non-Poor. Maryknoll, NYU: Orbis Books, 1987. xiv, 286 pp. Paper. 0883444097.

Case studies of eight models for transformative education of middle-class Americans, based upon Paulo Freire's liberation pedagogies for the oppressed.

ED75 Freire, Paulo
Cultural Action: A Dialectic Analysis. (CIDOC Cuaderno, 1004). Cuernavaca, MX: CIDOC, 1970. various pp. No ISBN.

Freire's distinction between education for liberation and education for domestication is the heart of this selection, in which he argues for radically changing the power structure in education to ensure education for liberation.

ED76 Freire, Paulo
Las Iglesias, la Educación y el Proceso de Liberación Humana en la Historia. Buenos Aires, AG: Editorial La Aurora, 1974. 48 pp. Paper. No ISBN.

Spanish translation of *Education, Liberation and the Church* (Geneva: WCC).

ED77 Freire, Paulo
Pedagogia del Oprimido. Translated by Jorge Mellado. Montevideo, UY: Tierra Nueva, 1970. 250 pp. No ISBN.
Spanish translation.

ED78 Freire, Paulo
Pedagogia do oprimido. (Série Ecumenismo e Humanismo, 16). Rio de Janeiro, BL: Paz e Terra, 1970. 218 pp. No ISBN.
The seminal work by the Brazilian educator, later a staff member for education of the WCC, proposing that the goals and methods of education raise the critical consciousness of men and women struggling for liberation.

ED79 Freire, Paulo
Pedagogy of the Oppressed. Translated by Myra Bergman Ramos. New York, NYU: *Continuum,* 1986. 186 pp. 0826400477.
English translation.

ED80 Freire, Paulo, and Antonio Faundez
Learning to Question: A Pedagogy of Liberation. Translated by Tony Coates. Geneva, SZ: WCC Publications, 1989. 142 pp. Paper. 2825408778.
A record of a free-flowing conversation between Paulo Friere, the Brazilian educator in exile known as author of *Pedagogy of the Oppressed,* and Antonio Faundez, a Chilean philosophy professor in exile, focusing on the importance of asking questions as a method of consciousness-raising in adult popular education.

ED81 Johnson, David M., ed.
Justice and Peace Education: Models for College and University Faculty. Maryknoll, NYU: Orbis Books, 1986. viii, 248 pp. Paper. 0883442477.
A collection of essays on peace and justice education in various academic disciplines; prepared as a resource for the 235 Catholic colleges and universities in the United States.

ED82 Preiswerk, Matías
Educación Popular y Teología de la Liberación. (Colección Sociología de la Religión). San José, CR: Editorial DEI; San José, CR: Seminario Bíblico Latinoamericano, 1994. 311 pp. Paper. 9977830789.
A systematic presentation of a philosophy of popular education, combining the values of Latin American liberation theology with the pedagogy of Paulo Freire; with application to both Christian education and theological education.

Literacy

ED83 Laubach, Frank C., and Robert S. Laubach
Toward World Literacy: The Each One Teach One Way. Durban, SA: Upgrade Literacy Press, 1984. xiv, 335 pp. Paper. No ISBN.
An edition, revised by Sandy and Louise D'Oliveira, of a training manual on the Laubach method of teaching those who are illiterate, including small articles for those newly literate; originally published in 1960 (Syracuse, NYU: Syracuse University Press).

ED84 Laubach, Frank C.
Forty Years with the Silent Billion: Adventuring in Literacy. Old Tappan, NJU: Revell, 1970. 501 pp. No ISBN.
The saga of the missionary pioneer of adult literacy, 1929 to 1968; originally published in 1959 covering the first thirty years.

ED85 Mason, David E.
Reaching the Silent Billion: The Opportunity of Literacy Missions. Grand Rapids, MIU: Zondervan, 1967. 190 pp. No ISBN.
A popular introduction to the goals and methods by which literacy education becomes a strategy for evangelistic outreach.

ED86 Shacklock, Floyd
Man of Two Revolutions: The Story of Justo González. (Bold Believers Series). New York, NYU: Friendship Press, 1969. 63 pp. 0377841617.
The life of a Methodist leader in Cuba (born 1902), and his wife Luisa, who became literacy experts and founders of ALFALIT after leaving Cuba in 1961.

ED87 Shacklock, Floyd
World Literacy Manual. (International Literacy Seminar (1965: Jerusalem)). New York, NYU: Committee on World Literacy & Christian Literature, 1967. xiv, 177 pp. Paper. No ISBN.
A handbook to the total process of literacy, from language analysis and primer making, through teaching and the training of teachers, to the production of the literature that new literates need.

Theological Education

See also GW268, TH370, TH536, CR1204, SO106, ED1, ED4, ED82, CH460, SP16, SP290, AF225, AF549, AF597, AM174, AM496, AM594, AM1229, AS127-AS128, and AS888.

ED88 Agbeti, John Kofi
West African Church History, II: Christian Missions and Theological Training, 1842-1970. Leiden, NE: Brill, 1991. xv, 262 pp. Paper. 9004091009.
A detailed scholarly case study of 138 years of theological training in West Africa.

ED89 Allen, Yorke
A Seminary Survey. New York, NYU: Harper, 1960. xxvi, 640 pp. No ISBN.
A comprehensive, detailed survey of Protestant, Roman Catholic, and Orthodox seminaries in Africa, Asia, and Latin America.

ED90 Amirtham, Samuel, and S. Wesley Ariarajah, eds.
Ministerial Formation in a Multifaith Milieu: Implications of Interfaith Dialogue for Theological Education. Geneva, SZ: WCC, 1986. 122 pp. Paper. 2825408697.
The report and papers from a WCC consultation of Asian theological educators (Kuala Lumpur, Malaysia,19-25 June 1985).

ED91 Anathil, George M.
The Theological Formation of the Clergy in India. Poona, II: Pontifical Athenaeum, 1966. xv, 262 pp. No ISBN.
A thorough study of the history of the training of the clergy in India, both under the Portuguese Padroado and under the Congregation for the Propagation of the Faith.

ED92 Banks, Robert
Reenvisioning Theological Education: Exploring a Missional Alternative to Current Models. Grand Rapids, MIU: Eerdmans, 1999. xii, 268 pp. 0802846203.
A revolutionary and biblical mandate for theological education that moves from abstract knowing to concrete leadership and character formation.

ED—EDUCATION AND MISSIONS

ED93 Bowers, Paul
Evangelical Theological Education Today: Vol. I—An International Perspective; Vol. II—Agenda for Renewal. Nairobi, KE: Evangel Publishing House, 1982. 2 vols. Paper. No ISBN.

Papers read at the First Consultation of the International Council of Accrediting Agencies (World Evangelical Fellowship) held 17-20 March 1980, in Hoddesdon, England, and the Second Consultation held 1-4 September 1981, in Chongoni, Malawi.

ED94 Consultation on Theological Education (2nd; 1966; Warwick, NY)
New Challenges to Seminary Teachers in a Rapidly Changing World: A Report. New York, NYU: NCCUSA, 1966. 79 pp. No ISBN.

Report of a consultation on theological education including a summary on Latin America.

ED95 Cook, Guillermo, and F. Ross Kinsler
Nuevos Caminos en la Educación Teológica: Educación teológica no-formal. (Serie: Ensayos ocasionales, 1). San José, CR: CELEP, 1989. 44 pp. Paper. No ISBN.

Two essays, written by members of the Latin American Evangelical Center for Pastoral Studies in San José, Costa Rica, entitled "Kairos In Theological Education" and "Non-Formal Theological Education."

ED96 Covell, Ralph R., and C. Peter Wagner
An Extension Seminary Primer. South Pasadena, CAU: William Carey Library, 1973. xii, 140 pp. 0878081062.

Nine lectures presented by the authors at 1970 workshops on TEE in Taiwan, Vietnam, Indonesia, Singapore, and central India; originally published in 1971.

ED97 Cracknell, Kenneth, and Christopher Lamb
Theology on Full Alert. London, ENK: BCC, Committee for Relations with People of Other Faiths, 1986. iv, 143 pp. Paper. 0851691811.

Revised and enlarged edition of a call for a reshaping of theological education in Great Britain to include encounters with persons of other faiths, with eighteen stories of such work in progress in various theological seminaries and colleges.

ED98 Ferris, Robert W.
Renewal in Theological Education: Strategies for Change. (A BGC Monograph). Wheaton, ILU: BGC, 1990. vi, 232 pp. Paper. 1879089033.

An evaluation of a variety of evangelical Protestant theological schools in Asia, Africa, and North America, with proposals to reform them so that they might be more responsive to the needs of the church.

ED99 Gerber, Vergil, ed.
Discipling through Theological Education by Extension: A Fresh Approach to Theological Education in the 1980s. Wheaton, ILU: Evangelical Missions Information Service, 1984. 191 pp. Paper. No ISBN.

Twelve essays by evangelical missiologists on the context of TEE that can equip participants for effective pastoral leadership in evangelism; originally published by Moody Press in 1980.

ED100 Hill, D. Leslie
Designing a Theological Education by Extension: A Philippine Case Study. South Pasadena, CAU: William Carey Library, 1974 x. i, 197 pp. 087808312X.

In this study the author sets forth basic principles of theological education by extension and applies them to the particular needs of Baptists in the Philippines.

ED101 Hoffman, Paul E., ed.
Theological Education in Today's Africa. Geneva, SZ: LWF, 1969. 176 pp. No ISBN.

Papers from the Theology Faculty Conference for Africa (Makumira, Tanzania, 15-22 July 1969) sponsored by the LWF.

ED102 Hogarth, Jonathan, Kiranga Gatimu, and David B. Barrett
Theological Education in Context: 100 Extension Programs in Contemporary Africa. Nairobi, KE: Uzima Press, 1983. 189 pp. Paper. No ISBN.

An interpretation of the theological education by extension movement in the African churches, including surveys.

ED103 *Issues in Theological Education 1964-1965, Asia, Africa, Latin America: A Report of the Theological Education Fund*
New York, NYU: TEF, 1968. v, 65 pp. No ISBN.

Report of an important survey of theological education in the Two-Thirds World.

ED104 Kemp, Roger, ed.
Text and Context in Theological Education. (ICAA Monograph Series, 5). Springwood, AT: ICAA for Evangelical Theological Education, 1994. iv, 117 pp. Paper. No ISBN.

Papers on contextualization in theological education; originally presented at a consultation on "From Text to Context in Evangelical Theological Education" (London, 1991).

ED105 Kinsler, F. Ross, and James H. Emery, eds.
Opting for Change: A Handbook on Evaluation and Planning for Theological Education by Extension. South Pasadena, CAU: William Carey Library; Geneva, SZ: WCC, Programme for Theological Education, 1991. vii, 104 pp. Paper. 0878082298 (US), 2825410268 (SZ).

Tools for reflection on basic issues in theological education, and for the evaluation and planning of TEE programs.

ED106 Kinsler, F. Ross, ed.
Ministry by the People: Theological Education by Extension. Maryknoll, NYU: Orbis Books; Geneva, SZ: WCC, 1983. xvi, 332 pp. Paper. 0883443341 (O), 2825407429 (W).

Twenty-eight local reports of theological education by extension as practiced in Latin America, the Caribbean, Africa, North America, Asia, Australia, and Europe; originally published in 1979 (New York: Auburn Theological Seminary).

ED107 Kinsler, F. Ross
The Extension Movement in Theological Education: A Call to the Renewal of the Ministry. South Pasadena, CAU: William Carey Library, 1981. vii, 288 pp. 0878087346.

Revised edition of fourteen papers on the history, philosophy, and practice in various countries of TEE, by one who has led in the movement from its inception in 1963; originally published in 1978.

ED108 Kirwen, Michael C., ed.
A Model Four Semester Syllabus for Transcultural Theology Overseas. Lewiston, NYU: E Mellen Press, 1986. x, 212 pp. 0889460477.

A detailed syllabus and readings designed to equip Maryknoll missioners for overseas ministries, especially in Africa.

ED109 Lienemann-Perrin, Christine
Training for a Relevant Ministry: A Study of the Contribution of the Theological Extension Fund. Madras, II: CLS; Geneva, SZ: WCC, Programme for Theological Education, 1981. xx, 252 pp. Paper. 2825406317.

A detailed history of the founding of the TEF and its development from 1958 to 1977, with case studies on Taiwan and theological education by extension.

ED110 Mazibuko, Bongani
Education in Mission/Mission in Education: A Critical Comparative Study of Selected Approaches. (Studies in the Intercultural History of Christianity, 47). Frankfurt am Main, GW: Lang, 1987. x, 401 pp. Paper. 3820497935.

A scholarly study of models of dialogical and intercultural theological education, comparing the Project in Partnership between Black and White in Birmingham, England, with similar projects in the United States, South Africa, and the WCC's Programme on Theological Education, relating theological education to the churches' involvement in social change.

ED111 *Ministry in Context: The Third Mandate Program of the Theological Education Fund, 1970-1977*
London, ENK: Theological Education Fund, 1972. 107 pp. Paper. No ISBN.

A brief history of the TEF, with a description of its current work and of key issues facing theological education in the Third World, especially Latin America; with appendices listing the members of the TEF committee, various associations of theological schools participating in the Theological Education Fund, and other information.

ED112 *Partners in Practice*
London, ENK: BCC, 1989. 43 pp. Paper. 0851691544.

Papers from a remarkable visit by five Third World theologicans to Great Britain in November 1987, to critically assess the theological education system there, where many Third World church leaders are educated.

ED113 Pobee, J. S., ed.
Ministerial Formation for Mission Today. Geneva, SZ: Asempa Publishers for the WCC Ecumenical Theological Education, 1993. v, 128 pp. Paper. 9964782144.

Report and papers from a consultation on "Ministerial Formation for Mission Today" (Limuru, Kenya, 3-8 January 1989) cosponsored by CEVAA, CWM, and the WCC.

ED114 Pobee, J. S., ed.
Theological Education by Extension in Africa, 1991. Geneva, SZ: Asempa Publishers for the WCC Ecumenical Theological Education, 1993. vi, 90 pp. Paper. 9964782195.

Ten short papers on TEE in Africa; originally presented at a consultation on Theological Education by Extension in Africa (Zambia, Malawi, 12-19 September 1991).

ED115 Pobee, J. S., ed.
Towards Viable Theological Education: Ecumenical Imperative, Catalyst of Renewal. Geneva, SZ: WCC Publications, 1997. xi, 164 pp. Paper. 2825412341.

Papers from a major global consultation on "Ecumenical Theological Education: It's Viability Today" (Oslo, Norway, 5-10 August 1996) sponsored by the WCC.

ED116 Poerwowidagdo, Judo
Towards the 21st Century: Challenges and Opportunities for

Theological Education. Geneva, SZ: WCC, 1993. 62 pp. Paper. No ISBN.

Lectures by the WCC's Executive Secretary for Ecumenical Theological Education; originally presented in 1993 at Tamilnadu Theological Seminary, Madurai, India.

ED117 Rajaratnam, K., and A. A. Sitompul, eds.
Theological Education in Today's Asia: Theological Education and Training for Witness and Service. Madras, II: CLS, 1978. 162 pp. Paper. No ISBN.

Report of the training and education consultation held in Manila by the LWF in 1976, emphasizing evangelism training in Asia, including case studies.

ED118 Richey, Russell E., ed.
Ecumenical and Interreligious Prespectives: Globalization in Theological Education. Nashville, TNU: *Quarterly Review*, 1992. xvii, 152 pp. Paper. 0938162128.

Papers from a consultation for faculty from United Methodist seminaries (Yahara, Wisconsin, March 1990) on the understandings and place of ecumenism, globalization, and interreligious dialogue in theological education.

ED119 Robinson, Gnana
A Journey through Theological Education. Madras, II: CLS, 1989. xiii, 190 pp. Paper. No ISBN.

A collection of essays published between 1962 and 1986 by the former Principal of Tamilnadu Theological Seminary in Madurai, South India, on issues of studying theology in the Indian context.

ED120 Shorter, Aylward, and Eugene Kataza, eds.
Missionaries to Yourselves: African Catechists Today. Maryknoll, NYU: Orbis Books; London, ENK: Chapman, 1972. x, 212 pp. 0225658623.

The report on research into the life, work, status, and training of catechists in the Roman Catholic Church in Eastern and Central Africa, with focus upon their training for effective ministry.

ED121 Snook, Stewart G.
Developing Leaders through Theological Education by Extension: Case Studies from Africa. (Monograph Series). Wheaton, ILU: BGC, 1992. xii, 228 pp. Paper. 1879089092.

A detailed assessment of the TEE programs in Africa—their aims, structure, curriculum, and relation to churches, including five descriptive case studies.

ED122 Stackhouse, Max L.
Apologia: Contextualization, Globalization, and Mission in Theological Education. Grand Rapids, MIU: Eerdmans, 1988. 237 pp. Paper. 0802802850.

Proposals for the reconstructing of theological education on foundations that are contextually alert, globally concerned, and mission-oriented, based on faculty conversations at Andover Newton Theological School (Newton, Massachusetts).

ED123 Theological Education Fund
Learning in Context: The Search for Innovative Patterns in Theological Education. Bromley, ENK: Theological Education Fund, 1973. 195 pp. Paper. 0902903047.

The second of three volumes published under the Third Mandate of the TEF, discussing perspectives on, and models for, the contextualization of theological education.

ED124 Thistlethwaite, Susan Brooks, and George F. Cairns, eds.

Beyond Theological Tourism: Mentoring as a Grassroots Approach to Theological Education. Maryknoll, NYU: Orbis Books, 1994. viii, 174 pp. Paper. 088344965X.

Ten reflections by Chicago area theological educators on overseas and local immersions, and other aspects of the area Globalization of Theological Education project.

ED125 Thornton, Margaret, ed.

Training T.E.E. Leaders: A Course Guide. Nairobi, KE: Evangel Publishing House, 1990. 108 pp. Paper. 9966850929.

A study guide for use in training local leaders in TEE.

ED126 *Visie & Missie/Vision & Mission: IRS 25 Jaar/Years (1962-1987)*

Kopiereg, SA: Institute for Reformational ST, 1989. 147 pp. Paper. 0869909940.

Seven lectures in both English and Afrikaans delivered at the silver jubilee of the Institute for Reformational Studies in Potchefstroom, South Africa (12-13 November 1987), which focus on relevant Christian theological education for Africa.

ED127 *Voice of the Church in Asia: Report and Proceedings*

(Asia Theological Association Consultation (1974, Hong Kong)). Hong Kong, HK: Christian Communications, 1975. viii, 168 pp. Paper. No ISBN.

Report of proceedings of an Asian Theological Association consultation (Hong Kong, 27 December 1973-4 January 1974)—Section I deals with theological education by extension; Section II discusses the development of evangelical theological education.

ED128 Welch, F. G.

Training for the Ministry in East Africa. Limuru, KE: Association of East African Theological Colleges, 1963. 219 pp. No ISBN.

Assessment of theological education and prospects for its development in East Africa by the former Secretary of the Association of East African Theological Colleges.

ED129 Weld, Wayne

The World Directory of Theological Education by Extension. South Pasadena, CAU: William Carey Library, 1973. xiii, 374 pp. 0878081348.

Information about more than 200 TEE programs and projects, plus the history and rationale for Theological Education by Extension.

ED130 Wingate, Andrew

Does Theological Education Make a Difference?: Global Lessons in Mission and Ministry from India and Britain. (Risk Book Series, 87). Geneva, SZ: WCC Publications, 1999. ix, 116 pp. Paper. 2825413208.

The author studies the influence of radical contextual theological education on ministry in the parish, and draws on extensive interviews with students of Tamilnadu Theological Seminary in Madurai, India.

ED131 Winter, Ralph D., ed.

Theological Education by Extension. South Pasadena, CAU: William Carey Library, 1969. xxvi, 589 pp. Paper. 0878081011.

A collection of thirty articles, essays, and reports on the first years of experiments with TEE, including principles, methods, case studies (Guatemala, Colombia, Bolivia, Brazil); with a management and curriculum manual for an extension seminary.

ED132 Yeow, Choo Lak, ed.

Challenges and Opportunities in Theological Education in Asia. (ATESEA Occasional Papers, 7). Singapore, SI: ATESEA, 1988. iii, 98 pp. Paper. 9810006667.

Papers on the challenges and opportunities facing theological education in Asia today, published to celebrate the thirtieth anniversary of the ATESEA.

ED133 Yeow, Choo Lak, ed.

Theological Education for Women. (ATESEA Occasional Papers, 1). Singapore, SI: ATESEA, 1983. 35 pp. Paper. No ISBN.

Important documents and reports, from the 1980 Planning Committee of ATESEA, review and assess theological education programs offered for women in Southeast Asia.

ED134 Yeow, Choo Lak, ed.

Theology and Ministry in S.E. Asia: Teaching Students Today for Ministry Tomorrow. Singapore, SI: Trinity Theological College, 1978. viii, 140 pp. Paper. No ISBN.

Papers by Asian theologians on mission and evangelism in their particular cultural contexts.

ED135 Yeow, Choo Lak

Church and Theology. Singapore, SI: ATESEA, 1985. 106 pp. No ISBN.

Popular presentations of issues in Asian theology and theological education by the Executive Director of the ATESEA.

ED136 Yeow, Choo Lak

Computer Crockery Cross. Madurai, II: Tamil Nadu Theological Seminary, 1986. vii, 76 pp. Paper. No ISBN.

Five lectures on theological education in Asia given at Tamil Nadu Seminary in India, arguing that there should be an integrated wholeness in life bridging computer and crockery.

ED137 Yeow, Choo Lak

Time for Action: Theological Education for Asia Today. Singapore, SI: ATESEA, 1988. x, 199 pp. 9810002378.

A collection of writings which focusing on challenges in theological education in Asia today; by the Executive Director of the ATESEA.

ED138 Youngblood, Robert L., ed.

Cyprus: TEE Come of Age. Exeter, ENK: Paternoster Press, 1984. 78 pp. Paper. 0853644438.

Three pages read at a consultation sponsored by the International Council of Accrediting Agencies (Cyprus, 2-6 July 1984), examining the past, present, and future of theological education by extension.

ED139 Zorn, Herbert M.

Viability in Context: A Study of the Financial Viability of Theological Education in the Third World, Seedbed or Shelter? Bromley, ENK: Theological Education Fund, 1975. i, 108 pp. Paper. No ISBN.

The report of a two-and-one-half-year study of the financial viability of theological education in the Third World, based on visitations and correspondence with mission boards.

ED—EDUCATION AND MISSIONS

Christian Education: General

See also ED82, ED176-ED177, AF520, AF648, AF751, AM227, and EU289.

ED140 Bjornberg, Anders
Teaching and Growth: Christian Religious Education in a Local and International Missionary Context 1900, till the Early 1930's. (Bibliotheca Historico-Ecclesiastica Lundensis, 29). Lund, SW: Lund University Press, 1991. 358 pp. Paper. 9179661726.

A detailed analysis of the type of Christianity presented, and methods used, in Christian religious education in Tamil Nadu, India, by the Lutheran Leipzig Mission (1900-1905) and the Church of Sweden Mission (1920-1935), in comparison with the religious education theory of the period.

ED141 George, Sherron K.
A Igreja ensinadora. Londrina, BL: By the author, Sherron K. George, 1987. iv, 211 pp. Paper. No ISBN.

A manual on biblical and theological bases and methodologies of Christian education.

ED142 Groome, Thomas H.
Christian Religious Education: Sharing Our Story and Vision. San Francisco, CAU: Jossey-Bass Publishers, 1999. xix, 296 pp. Paper. 0787947857.

A comprehensive integration of the history, theory, and practice of modern religious education for a new generation of educators utilizing a self-reflective and shared praxis approach; originally published in 1980 by Harper & Row.

ED143 Knoff, Gerald E.
The World Sunday School Movement: The Story of a Broadening Mission. (A Crossroad Book). New York, NYU: Seabury Press, 1979. xiv, 283 pp. 081640416X.

A carefully documented study of world cooperation in Christian education through Sunday Schools from the first World Sunday School Convention (1889) to the merger of the WCCE with the WCC (1971).

ED144 Megill, Esther L.
Education in the African Church. London, ENK: Chapman; Legon, GH: Trinity College, 1976. 222 pp. 0225662809.

A Christian education text for theological students in West Africa, with a bibliography including public reports, documents, and unpublished materials from English-speaking countries.

ED145 Pazmiño, Robert W.
Latin American Journey: Insights for Christian Education in North America. Cleveland, OHU: United Church Press, 1994. xxxi, 170 pp. Paper. 0829809937.

A North American religious educator recounts impressions of Costa Rica, Ecuador, and Nicaragua, and applies learnings from Latin American liberation theology and base Christian communities for Christian education in North America.

ED146 Preiswerk, Matías
Educar en la Palabra Viva: marco teórico para la Educación Cristiana. (Cuadernos de Estudio, 25). Lima, PE: CELADEC, 1984. 123 pp. No ISBN.

A contemporary model of liberative Christian education used in Latin America.

ED147 Preiswerk, Matías
Educating in the Living Word: A Theoretical Framework for Christian Education. Translated by Robert R. Barr. Maryknoll, NYU: Orbis Books, 1987. xii, 128 pp. Paper. 0883445727 (hdbk), 0883445719 (pbk).

English translation.

ED148 Schipani, Daniel S.
Religious Education Encounters Liberation Theology. Birmingham, ALU: Religious Education Press, 1988. iv, 276 pp. Paper. 0891350594.

An authoritative exploration of the fruitful interplay between religious education and liberation theology.

ED149 Schipani, Daniel S.
Teología del Ministerio Educativo: perspectivas latinoamericanas. Bueno Aires, AG: Nueva Creación; Grand Rapids, MIU: Eerdmans, 1993. 302 pp. Paper. 0802809197.

Spanish translation by the author.

Moral and Religious Education in Schools

See also CR541, AF371, AF973, AF1318, and AS362.

ED150 British Council of Churches
Worship in Education. London, ENK: BCC, 1989. xii, 36 pp. Paper. 0851692052.

A resource for British educators on creative approaches to worship in schools with a multi-faith constituency.

ED151 Fernando, Antony
Christian Path to Mental Maturity: A Lucid Exposition of Christianity for the Multi-Religious Classroom. Kadawata, CE: Inter-Cultural Book Promoters, 1998. iii, 262 pp. Paper. 9559036130.

An exposition of Christianity for the multireligious classrooms of secular schools and universities, by a Sri Lankan scholar with long experience in Buddhist-Christian dialogue.

ED152 Franzén, Allan
Missionsinslaget i finländska religionsläroböcker. (Institutionen för praktisk teologi vid Helsingfors universitet; Publikationer i praktisk teologi, C7). Helsingfors, FI: Helsingfors universitet, 1989. 82 pp. Paper. 9514550358.

This monograph titled *Teaching about Mission in Religion Textbooks in Finnish Schools* is a content analysis of official primary and secondary school textbooks in Finnish and Swedish.

ED153 Haar, Gerrie ter, Ambrose Moyo, and Simon J. Nondo, eds.
African Traditional Religions in Religious Education: A Resource Book with Special Reference to Zimbabwe. Utrecht, NE: Universiteit Utrecht, 1992. x, 224 pp. Paper. 9039300658.

This third and final publication of a joint University of Zimbabwe/Rijksuniversiteit Utrecht project on religious education in Africa contains a detailed rationale for a multifaith approach to the teaching of religious education in secondary schools, plus themes from African traditional religions to include in such a curriculum.

ED154 Haar, Gerrie ter
Faith of Our Fathers: Studies on Religious Education in Sub-Saharan Africa. (Utrechtse Theologische Reeks, 11). Utrecht, NE: Faculteit der Godgeleerdheid; Rijksuniversiteit Utrecht, 1990. 173 pp. Paper. 9072235134.

A review of the various forms of religious education in Africa south of the Sahara in the 20th century in traditional and Muslim contexts, and in both church and state schools.

ED155 Hobson, Peter R., and John S. Edwards
Religious Education in a Pluralist Society: The Key Philosophical Issues. London, ENK: Woburn Press, 1999. xvi, 184 pp. 0713002182 (hdbk), 0713040394 (pbk).

With a major shift towards multi-faith educationally oriented programs, the study of religion must now wrestle with the moral acceptability of religious truth claims, and differences of opinion on central moral problems such as birth control, abortion, and euthanasia.

ED156 Hofinger, Johannes, and Francis J. Buckley
The Good News and Its Proclamation. Notre Dame, INU: University Press, 1968. xii, 354 pp. No ISBN.

A new edition, published after the Vatican Council, including a consideration of the study-weeks on mission-history held since 1960; originally published as *Art of Teaching Religion* (1957).

ED157 Iheoma, Eugene O.
The Philosophy of Religious Education: An Introduction. Enugu, NR: Fourth Dimension Publishing, 1997. ix, 100 pp. Paper. 9781564407.

A study of the philosophical presuppositions of religion as belief and faith, and of education as reasoning and understanding; with a survey of modern methods and indoctrination in religious education, as well as education in a pluralist society.

ED158 Niblett, W. Roy
Christian Education in a Secular Society. London, ENK: Oxford University Press, 1960. 132 pp. No ISBN.

Analysis by a prominent British educator of the problem of introducing boys and girls to religious knowledge and Christian values in an educational system that is predominately secular.

ED159 Nondo, Simon J., ed.
Multifaith Issues and Approaches in Religious Education with Special Reference to Zimbabwe. Utrecht, NE: University of Utrecht, 1991. iv, 90 pp. Paper. 9172235509.

Proceedings of a December 1990 workshop focusing on teaching religious education in African secondary schools from a multi-faith perspective, with special concern for African traditional religious heritage.

ED160 Smith, Adrian B.
Interdenominational Religious Education in Africa: The Emergence of Common Syllabuses. (IIMO Research Pamphlet, 5). Leiden, NE: IIMO, 1982. iv, 90 pp. Paper. No ISBN.

A monograph on the common syllabi developed cooperatively by Catholics and Protestants for religious education in primary schools in Africa, including causative factors, aims, theology, and effects.

ED161 True, Michael
Ordinary People: Family Life and Global Values. Maryknoll, NYU: Orbis Books, 1991. xx, 140 pp. Paper. 088344738X.

A practical guide for US parents desiring to raise their children as "citizens of the world" with a commitment to the earth and a spirit of solidarity with others.

Sunday Schools

See also ED143 and OC326.

ED162 Bruce, Debra Fulghum, and Robert G. Bruce
Growing a Great Sunday School Class. Nashville, TNU: Abingdon, 1994. 88 pp. Paper. 0687121736.

Strategies for applying church growth principles through the Sunday School program.

ED163 Proctor, Frank
Growing through an Effective Church School. St. Louis, MOU: Chalice Press, 1990. 160 pp. Paper. 0827212356.

A primer for church leaders who desire to restore the partnership of education and evangelism, with principles and strategies for church school (including Sunday School) growth.

Catechetics: Membership Training

See also EV205, AF86, AF412, AF864, AF1039, AM865, AS659, AS721, and AS880.

ED164 Bailey, Keith M.
Care of Converts: A Comprehensive Training Tool for Discipling New Believers. Camp Hill, PAU: Christian Publications, 1997. ix, 192 pp. Paper. 0875097073.

A curriculum for discipling new believers based on biblical models; with the entire contents of *Learning to Live*, a manual for new believers, and a leader's guide.

ED165 Boston, Frances
Preparing for Christian Initiation. (Pastoral Papers, 26). Kampala, UG: Gaba Publications, 1973. 90 pp. No ISBN.

A program of preparation for Christian Baptism, Eucharist, and Confirmation for 9 to 13-year-old children, utilizing both traditional Christian and African values.

ED166 Catholic Church. Synod of Bishops (5th, 1977)
La Catequesis en Nuestro Tiempo: Documentos y estudios. Madrid, SP: Promotion Popular Cristiana, 1977. 70 pp. No ISBN.
Spanish translation.

ED167 Catholic Church. Synod of Bishops (5th, 1977)
Réalités et avenir de la catéchèse dans le monde: Principaux documents du Synode des Évêques 1977. Edited by Jacques Potin. (Documents d'Église). Paris, FR: Le Centurion, 1978. 238 pp. Paper. 2227425253.

French translation of the principal documents of the 1977 Synod of Bishops—the basis of John Paul II's apostolic exhortation *Catechesi Tradendae* (1979).

ED168 CELAM-Departamento de Catéquesis
Dieciocho años de producción catequética 1968-1986. (DECAT, 3). Bogotá, CK: CELAM, DECAT, 1987. 192 pp. Paper. 9586250563.

Lists of catechisms written for diverse situations: from magazines, audiovisual centers, and Latin American centers for catechetical formation.

ED—EDUCATION AND MISSIONS

ED169 CELAM-Departamento de Catequesis

Evangelización y catequesis: Documentos del magisterio eclesiástico con índice analítico. (DECAT, 2). Bogotá, CK: CELAM, 1986. 589 pp. Paper. 9586251845.

A collection of documents on evangelization: the Constitution *Dei Verbum*, the decree *Ad Gentes*, the chapter "Catequesis" from Medellín, the General Catechetical Directory, the encyclical *Evangelli Nuntiandi*, the 1977 Message from the Synod of Bishops, the chapter "Catequesis" from Puebla, the encyclical *Catequesis Tradendae*, the 1982 Document from Quito, and the "Libro III" from the new Code of Canon Law.

ED170 Cortes Castellanos, Justino

El Catecismo en Pictogramas de Fray Pedro de Gante: Estudio introductorio y desciframiento del Ms. Vit. 26-9 de la Biblioteca Nacional de Madrid. (Biblioteca Histórica Hispanoamericana, Serie V Centenario, 10). Madrid, SP: FUE, 1987. 500 pp. Paper. 8473922832.

An introductory study of the historical-catechetical context, and more particularly, the audiovisual method invented by the Franciscans and the Pedro de Ganto, OFM's pictogram catechism.

ED171 Crespo Ponce, María-Graciela

Estudio Histórico-teológico de la "Doctrina cristiana para instrucción e informació de los indios por manera de historia," de Fray Pedro Córdoba, O.P. (1521). (Colección teológica, 58). Pamplona, SP: Ediciones Universidad de Navarra, 1988. xxiv, 199 pp. 8431310421.

A study of the pre-16th-century Spanish catechisms, including two editions of a catechism used by Spanish missionaries to convert the Indians in Mexico, Central, and South America.

ED172 De Cordoba, Pedro

Christian Doctrine for the Instruction and Information of the Indians. Translated by Sterling A. Stoudemire. Coral Gables, FLU: University of Miami Press, 1970. 152 pp. 0870241591.

A translation, with interpretive introduction, of the earliest catechetics for the indigenous population of Espanola (present Haiti and Dominican Republic) by a Dominican who served there from 1510 until his death in 1521.

ED173 Fintan, McDonald

Adult Religious Education: People Do Matter. (Spearhead Series, 67). Eldoret, KE: GABA Publications, 1981. 81 pp. Paper. No ISBN.

A practical guide for Catholic religious educators in East Africa, advocating a life experience approach to adult catechesis.

ED174 Greinacher, Norbert, Virgilio P. Elizondo, and Marcus Lefébure, eds.

The Transmission of the Faith to the Next Generation. (Concilium: Religion in the Eighties). Edinburgh, STK: T&T Clark, 1984. x, 111 pp. Paper. 0567300544.

Ten essays and three case studies (the Philippines, East Germany, and the United States) on the task of catechesis in societies marked by rapid social change.

ED175 Hofinger, Johannes, and Terence J. Sheridan, eds.

The Medellin Papers: A Selection from the Proceedings of the Sixth International Study Week on Catechetics held at Medellin, Colombia, August 11-17, 1968. Manila, PH: East Asian Pastoral Institute, 1969. 222 pp. Paper. No ISBN.

English translations of papers and discussions from an important meeting of international specialists in catechetics focusing on problems of the church in Latin America and especially the teaching of religion.

ED176 International Study Week on Missionary Catechetics (Eichstätt, 1960)

Katechetik Heute: Grundsätze und Anregungen zur Erneuerung der Katechese in Mission und Heimat: Referate und Ergebnisse der Internet. Edited by Johannes Hofinger. Freiburg, GW: Herder, 1961. 368 pp. Paper. No ISBN.

Proceedings and papers from an international symposium on modern catechetics in the countries then referred to as "mission" countries.

ED177 International Study Week on Missionary Catechetics (Eichstätt, 1960)

Teaching All Nations. Edited by Johannes Hofinger. Translated by Clifford Howell. Freiburg, GW: Herder, 1961. xvi, 421 pp. No ISBN.

Revised English translation of *Katechetik Heute* (1961).

ED178 Johns, Cheryl Bridges

Pentecostal Formation: A Pedagogy among the Oppressed. (Journal of Pentecostal Theology Supplement Series, 2). Sheffield, ENK: Sheffield Academic Press, 1993. 154 pp. Paper. 1850754381.

An analysis of the powerful process of spiritual formation in Pentecostalism, contrasting it with the alternative "pedagogy of the oppressed" of Paulo Freire.

ED179 Medina, Miguel Angel

Doctrina Cristiana para Instrucción de los Indios. Edited by Pedro de Córdoba. (Los Dominicos y América/HIDEVA, 2). Salamanca, SP: Editorial San Esteban, 1987. 443 pp. 8485045793.

A basic catechism of the faith written by a Dominican to educate the native people of the Dominican Republic in the 16th century.

ED180 Oliveira, Ralfy Mendes de

O Movimento catequético no Brasil. São Paulo, BL: Editora Saleçiana Dom Bosco, 1980. 198 pp. Paper. No ISBN.

A comprehensive critical examination of the principal systems of catechesis in the last 400 years.

ED—EDUCATION AND MISSIONS

EVANGELISM AND MISSIONS

David Lowes Watson, Subeditor

Evangelization, the term more commonly used by Roman Catholics but also increasingly by Protestant evangelicals, is often used interchangeably with *evangelism*. See Barrett and Johnson, *World Christian Trends* (2001:675-757) for an exhaustive analysis of the use of both terms, and Jongeneel (1995:27-49) for an extended word study and bibliography.

Evangelism, however, has a varied place in the schema of mission bibliographers. Vriens (1960) does not include it. It is placed under "Pastoral Topics" in *Bibliographia Missionaria*, and under "The Practice of Missions: Forms of Ministry and Witness" in the *IRM*. Jongeneel discusses it under the *names* of missiology, but omits it from the *branches* of missiology.

The reference subsections of this chapter contain a few bibliographies, details of periodicals in the field, reference works, documentation, and citations for many conferences and congresses.

The subsection on "General Works" covers a variety of confessional and regional traditions. Next are found works on the theology of evangelism, with a separate subsection on "Conversion." Works on the psychology of evangelism will also be found there.

Scholars interested in the history of evangelism will find important works grouped in the next subsection. It is followed by biographies of evangelists, past and present.

"Church Growth," the next subsection, contains many works influenced by the thought of Donald McGavran of Fuller Theological Seminary. See also the section on "Unreached Peoples" in the chapter on "Missions: Social Aspects." Methods of church planting receive a separate grouping.

Remaining works on the practice of evangelism are divided under three subheadings: "Pastoral/Parish Evangelism," "Personal Evangelism/Witness," and "Prophetic Evangelism and Social Concerns." The latter subsection contains works by authors who articulate a holistic approach to evangelization.

Norman E. Thomas

Bibliographies

See also EV155.

EV1 *Évangélisation et mission: Bibliographie internationale 1975-1982*
(RIC Supplément, 74-77). Strasbourg Cedex, FR: CERDIC-Publications, 1982. 312 pp. Paper. 2850970336.

An international bibliography in two parts—books and periodical articles—with separate indexes for publications in French, German, Spanish, and Italian.

EV2 Paulist National Catholic Evangelization Association
Pentecost '88: The 1988/1989 Catholic Evangelization Resource Directory & Teleconference Program Guide. Washington, DCU: PNCEA, 1988. 110 pp. Paper. No ISBN.

The annual record of Roman Catholic judicatories and agencies in the United States involved in evangelization, with annotated list of print and electronic media resources, and a program guide for Pentecost '88, an event celebrating Catholic evangelization.

Serials and Periodicals

EV3 *Church Growth Bulletin*. Vol. 1, no. 1 (Sept. 1964)-vol. 16, no. 2 (1979). Bimonthly
Pasadena, CAU: Fuller Theological Seminary, 1964-1979. ISSN 00096385.

Bulletin of the School of World Mission, Donald A. Mc-Gavran, Director; continued as *Global Church Growth Bulletin*.

EV4 *Ecumenical Letter on Evangelism*. Nos. 5-6 (May/June 1994)-. Irregular (3-6 times per year)
Geneva, SZ: WCC, Desk on Evangelism, 1994-. No ISSN.

Continues *Monthly Letter about Evangelism*; reflections of the WCC Secretary for Evangelism, correspondence and guest articles.

EV5 *Global Church Growth Bulletin*. Vol. 17 (1980)-vol. 19, no. 2 (Mar.-Apr. 1982). Bimonthly
Santa Clara, CAU: O.C. Ministries, 1980-1982. ISSN 02737183.

Short articles and news on global evangelization and church growth; superseded *Church Growth Bulletin*; continued as *Global Church Growth*.

EV6 *Global Church Growth.* Vol. 19, no. 3 (May-June 1982)-.
Bimonthly (1982-1984); Quarterly (1985-)
Santa Clara, CAU: O.C. Ministries, 1982-1986; Corunna, INU:
Church Growth Center, 1987-, 1982-. ISSN 07311125.

Short articles and reports on world evangelization; superseded *Global Church Growth Bulletin.*

EV7 *India Church Growth Bulletin.* Vol. 1, no. 1 (Jan.-Mar. 1979)-.
Quarterly
Madras, II: Church Growth Association of India, 1979-. No ISSN.

A bulletin on evangelism and church planting for Indian
church leaders with articles by Indian and world leaders in church
growth, plus news and case studies on evangelization in India.

EV8 *Journal of the Academy for Evangelism in Theological
Education.* Vol. 1 (1985-1986)-. Annual
Atlanta, GAU: Academy for Evangelism in Theological Educa-
tion, 1985-. ISSN 08949034.

Articles by teachers and practitioners in evangelism, primarily in North America, plus book reviews.

EV9 *Monthly Letter about Evangelism.* 1956, no. 1-1994, no. 3/
4. Irregular
Geneva, SZ: WCC, CWME, 1956-1994. No ISSN.

Short articles and correspondence concerning ecumenical perspectives on evangelism; editions also in French and
German; continued as *Ecumenical Letter on Evangelism.*

EV10 *World Evangelization Information Bulletin.* Vol. 1, no. 1
(1976)-(1993). Quarterly (1976-1989); then irregular
Wheaton, ILU: LCWE, 1976-1993. No ISSN.

News of the efforts of the LCWE and other agencies and
national movements in world evangelization.

Reference Works

EV11 Krass, Alfred C.
Evangelizing Neopagan North America: The Word That Frees.
(Institute of Mennonite Studies, Missionary Studies, 9). Scottdale,
PAU: Herald Press, 1982. 250 pp. Paper. 0836119894.

An appeal for a holistic approach to evangelism by a leading Congregationalist, with eleven key source documents from
world conferences of the 1970s.

EV12 Towns, Elmer L., ed.
Evangelism and Church Growth. Ventura, CAU: Regal Books,
1995. 427 pp. 0830717420.

A combination glossary, encyclopedia on new areas of
evangelism, and biographical and historical dictionary.

Documentation and Archives

See also SO124, ED169, and EV163.

EV13 Finney, Charles G.
Lectures on Revival. Edited by Kevin Walter Johnson. Minneapolis, MNU: Bethany House, 1988. 288 pp. Paper.
1556610629.

A modified reissue (without commentary or notes) of
Lectures on Revivals of Religion (1853) by the outstanding
19th-century evangelist.

EV14 Fung, Raymond
*Evangelistically Yours: Ecumenical Letters on Contemporary
Evangelism.* Geneva, SZ: WCC Publications, 1992. viii, 260
pp. Paper. 2825410454.

An anthology, grouped by theme, of the ecumenical let-

ters on evangelism issued from 1982 to 1991 as the *Monthly
Letter on Evangelism*, by the author while Secretary for Evangelism of the WCC.

EV15 Instituto de Cultura Religiosa Superior
Evangelización Hoy. (Cuadernos del Instituto, 2). Buenos
Aires, AG: SEDOS, 1977. 292 pp. Paper. No ISBN.

Anthology of documents on the theme of evangelization
proceeding from the Holy See, CELAM, Latin American bishops, and from other regions that participated in the 1974 Synod of Bishops.

EV16 Macfarlan, Duncan
*The Revivals of the Eighteenth Century Particularly at Cam-
buslang: With Three Sermons by the Rev. George Whitefield.*
Wheaton, ILU: Richard Owen Roberts, 1980. vii, 312 pp. No
ISBN.

A reprint of the classic description of the 19th-century
evangelical revival in Church of Scotland parishes; originally
published in 1847 by Johnston and Hunter of Edinburgh.

EV17 Mahn-Lot, Marianne
*Las Casas: De l'unique manière d'évangéliser le monde enti-
er.* Paris, FR: Éditions du Cerf, 1990. 145 pp. Paper.
2204040754.

A French edition of *De unico modo vocationis omnes
gentes ad veram Religionem*, completed by the celebrated
Dominican in 1527, outlining the biblical argument for world
evangelization.

EV18 Reid, William
Authentic Records of Revivals. Wheaton, ILU: Richard Owen
Roberts, 1980. 478 pp. No ISBN.

Forty firsthand accounts of local church revivals in the
United Kingdom; originally published in 1860 by James Nisbet & Co. of London.

EV19 Shaw, S. B.
The Great Revival in Wales. Salem, OHU: Allegheny Publications, 1988. 152 pp. Paper. No ISBN.

Reprint of a 1905 compilation of source documents, mostly newspaper accounts, of the great Welsh revival of 1859-60.

EV20 Tyler, Bennet
*New England Revivals: As They Existed at the Close of the
Eighteenth and the Beginning of the Nineteenth Centuries.*
(Revival Library). Wheaton, ILU: Richard Owen Roberts,
1980. 378 pp. No ISBN.

These accounts of revivals in New England, mostly Connecticut, between 1790 and 1814, yield insight and encouragement on how young and middle-aged people experienced
conversion and commitment to family life and service.

Conferences and Congresses

See also TH22, TH295, EA27, EA29-EA30, EA85, EA157-EA158,
EA222, EA226-EA228, EA230, SO237, EV216, AM190, AM194,
AM213, AM220-AM221, AM990, and EU30.

EV21 Bales, Harold K., ed.
Bridges to the World. Nashville, TNU: Tidings, 1971. 109
pp. Paper. No ISBN.

Ten addresses given by resource persons at the United
Methodist Congress on Evangelism (New Orleans, 1971) to
provide insight and inspiration for those who look for expanded evangelism ministries.

EV22 Catholic Church. Synod of Bishops (4th, 1974)
I semi del Vangelo: Studi e interventi dei vescovi d'Asia. Bologna, IT: Editrice Missionari Italiani, 1975. 267 pp. Paper. No ISBN.

Italian translation of the preparatory documents from the churches of Asia for the 1974 Synod of Bishops.

EV23 Catholic Church. Synod of Bishops (4th, 1974)
Le nuove vie del Vangelo: I vescovi africani parlano a tutta la Chiesa. Bologna, IT: Editrice Missionari Italiani, 1975. 346 pp. Paper. No ISBN.

Italian translation of the preparatory documents from the churches of Africa for the 1974 Synod of Bishops.

EV24 Catholic Church. Synod of Bishops (4th, 1974)
Sínodo 1974: Predicación, evangelización. Madrid, SP: Palabra, 1974. 224 pp. No ISBN.

Spanish translation of the principal documents of the 1974 Synod of Bishops—the basis of Paul VI's *Evangelii Nuntiandi* (1975).

EV25 CELAM-Departamento de Vida Consagrada-CLAR, I Encuentro Latinoamericano de Obispos y Religiosos, Bogotá, CK, 26-31 de agosto de 1986
Evangelización, Jerarquía y Carisma. (Documentos CELAM, 91). Bogotá, CK: CELAM, 1987. 182 pp. Paper. 9586250636.

Materials and final document from the meeting.

EV26 Conference on World Evangelization (Pattaya, Thailand, 1980)
The Thailand Report on Roman Catholics: Report of the ... Mini-Consultation on Reaching Nominal Christians among Roman Catholics. (Lausanne Occasional Papers, 10). Wheaton, ILU: LCWE, 1980. 38 pp. Paper. No ISBN.

The report defines nominal Christians, gives a description of Roman Catholic Church and culture, and outlines strategies for reaching nominal Roman Catholics.

EV27 Congresso Internazionale scientifico di missiologia (Rome, 5-12 Oct. 1975)
Evangelizzazione e culture: Atti del Congresso internazionale scientifico di missiologia, Roma, 5-12 ottobre 1975. Rome, IT: Pontificia Università urbaniana, 1976. 3 vols. No ISBN.

The proceedings of an important Catholic conference on evangelization, gospel and culture, and Christianity and other faiths, with papers in English, French, German, Italian, Portuguese, and Spanish.

EV28 Cook, Guillermo, and Alvaro Vega, eds.
Movimiento de Lausana y Misión de la Iglesia: Aportes desde América Central. (Ensayos Ocasionales, 2). San José, CR: CELEP, 1989. 83 pp. Paper. No ISBN.

Analyses of Lausanne I and II and a collection of their documents, including "Pacto de Lausana," "Manifiesto de Manila," and others.

EV29 *Evangelization in the Culture and Society of the United States and the Bishop as Teacher of the Faith*
Washington, DCU: USCC, 1989. 169 pp. Paper. 1555862780.

Official documents presented at the 8-11 March 1989 meeting of Pope John Paul II with the archbishops of the United States, in which the role of the bishop in teaching as affected by cultural considerations of evangelization was discussed.

EV30 International Conference for Itinerant Evangelists (1st: Amsterdam, the Netherlands, 1983)
The Work of an Evangelist. Edited by J. D. Douglas. Minneapolis, MNU: World Wide Publications, 1983. xxiv, 888 pp. 0890660492.

A compendium of papers presented at Amsterdam 1983, exploring the personal, spiritual, and public ministry aspects of the evangelist's life.

EV31 International Conference for Itinerant Evangelists (2nd: Amsterdam, the Netherlands, July 1986)
The Calling of an Evangelist: The Second International Congress for Itinerant Evangelists Amsterdam, The Netherlands. Edited by J. D. Douglas. Minneapolis, MNU: World Wide Publications, 1987. xv, 430 pp. Paper. 0890660875.

The official report containing messages delivered, as well as workshops and seminar reports.

EV32 International Theological Conference, Nagpur, India, 1971
Evangelization, Dialogue and Development: Selected Papers of the International Theological Conference, Nagpur (India), 1971. Edited by Mariasusai Dhavamony. (Documenta Missionalia, 5). Rome, IT: Universita Gregoriana, 1972. viii, 358 pp. Paper. No ISBN.

A symposium from the Roman Catholic Church in India, in which the implications of Vatican II for world evangelization are examined in a cultural context of interreligious dialogue.

EV33 Kjær-Hansen, Kai, and Bodil Skjott
Forkynd Kristus indtil Han kommer: Udfordringer og glimt fra Lausanne II i Manila 11 - 21 juli 1989. (Den danske Lausanne-gruppe). Aarhus, DK: Forlaget OKAY-BOG, 1989. 84 pp. Paper. 8798259156.

A booklet about the 1989 Lausanne II Congress in Manila with Danish comments.

EV34 Kyle, John E., comp.
Finishing the Task: World Evangelism in Our Generation. Ventura, CAU: Regal Books, 1987. 215 pp. Paper. 0830712518.

Nine addresses presented at Celebration '86 (Asheville, North Carolina, 29 June-3 July 1986) commemorating the one-hundredth anniversary of the SVM and the fiftieth anniversary of the Student Foreign Missions Fellowship (SFMF).

EV35 Logan, James C., ed.
Christ for the World: United Methodist Bishops Speak on Evangelism. Nashville, TNU: Kingswood Books, 1996. 176 pp. Paper. 0687022061.

Papers from the second Consultation on Theology and Evangelism (Wesley Theological Seminary, Washington, DC, 9-12 March 1995) sponsored by the Foundation for Evangelism.

EV36 Lovell, Arnold B., ed.
Evangelism in the Reformed Tradition. Decatur, GAU: CTS Press, 1990. v, 147 pp. Paper. No ISBN.

A transcript of addresses from the Presbyterian Symposium on Evangelism (Charlotte, North Carolina, 23-26 October 1989).

EV37 Nicholls, Bruce J., ed.
In Word and Deed: Evangelism and Social Responsibility. Grand Rapids, MIU: Eerdmans, 1985. 238 pp. Paper. 0802819656.

Nine papers originally presented in June 1982, in Grand Rapids, Michigan, at a Consultation on the Relationship between Evangelism and Social Responsiblility; cosponsored by the LCWE and the WEF.

EV—EVANGELISM AND MISSIONS

EV38 Schmidt, Henry J., ed.
Witness of a Third Way: A Fresh Look at Evangelism. Elgin, ILU: Brethren Press, 1986. xii, 146 pp. Paper. 087178940X.

A collection of thirteen addresses given at the Brethren in Christ "Alive 85" event in Denver, Colorado, on biblical models of evangelism and contemporary understandings of conversion and discipling.

EV39 Seminario Latinoamericano de Evangelización
La Evangelización y el Reino de Dios: Expresiones Vibrantes en el Seminario Latinoamericano de Evangelización, Chaclacayo, Perú: Enero 25 al 5 Febrero 1986. Santiago, CL: CIEMAL, 1988. 155 pp. Paper. No ISBN.

Papers and reports from a consultation on "Evangelization and the Reign of God," with special references to the social realities of Latin America; sponsored by CIEMAL, the Council of Evangelical Methodist Churches in Latin America.

EV40 Synod of Bishops, Rome, 1974
Evangelisation of the Modern World. Edited by D. S. Amalorpavadass. (Mission Theology for Our Times Series, 9). Bangalore, II: NBCLC, 1975. 175 pp. Paper. No ISBN.

Documents from the Roman Catholic Synod of Bishops (Rome, 1974) on evangelization; with an evaluation of their significance by a leading Indian theologian.

EV41 Wells, David F.
God the Evangelist: How the Holy Spirit Works to Bring Men and Women to Faith. Grand Rapids, MIU: Eerdmans; Exeter, UK: Paternoster Press, 1987. x, 128 pp. Paper. 0802802710 (E), 0853644551 (P).

A summary of the papers, discussions, and exchanges by theologians and pastors working in the First, Second, and Third worlds at the Consultation on the Work of the Holy Spirit and Evangelization (Oslo, May 1985); sponsored by the Theology Working Group of the LCWE and the Theology Unit of the WEF.

EV42 World Congress on Evangelism (1966: Berlin, Germany)
One Race, One Gospel, One Task. Edited by Carl F. H. Henry and W. Stanley Mooneyham. Minneapolis, MNU: World Wide Publications, 1967. 2 vols. No ISBN.

The official report and papers of the first major international congress of Protestant evangelicals on world evangelization, attended by more than 1,200 delegates from 10 countries, containing 130 summaries of presentations, country profiles, discussion group reports, and interpretive essays [vol.1, 319 pp.; vol. 2, 527 pp.].

EV43 World Methodist Council, Consultation on Evangelism
Beginning in Jerusalem. Edited by Rueben P. Job. Nashville, TNU: Tidings, 1974. viii, 120 pp. Paper. No ISBN.

Eleven inspiring and definitive lectures delivered at the consultation by an international cross-section of Methodist leaders with the basic theme that mission does not go from "us" to "them," but from God to all of us.

General Works

See also GW214, HI98, TH21, EA124, EA233, ME233, SO46, SO55, SO192, SO471, SO617, CO169, EV525, EV548, EV569, CH23, AF342, AM19, AM147, AM149, AM223, AM965, AM987, AM998, AM1187, AS50, EU80, and EU284.

EV44 Anderson, Gerald H., and Thomas F. Stransky, comps.
Mission Trends, no. 2: Evangelization. New York, NYU: Paulist Press; Grand Rapids, MIU: Eerdmans, 1975. vii, 279 pp. Paper. 0809119005 (P), 080281624X (E).

A sourcebook of outstanding essays on theologies and strategies of evangelism on six continents.

EV45 Arnold, Walter, ed.
Evangelization im ökumenischen Gespräch: Beiträge eines Symposiums (Genf 1973). Erlangen, GW: Ev.-Luth. Mission, 1974. 112 pp. 3872140590.

Ten participants of the Genf symposium present different perspectives on evangelism today, from a journalist to a one-time general secretary of the WCC.

EV46 Avila P., Rafael
Elementos para una Evangelización Liberadora. (Temas Vivos, 9). Salamanca, SP: Ediciones Sígueme, 1971. 160 pp. Paper. No ISBN.

A scholarly examination of elements for a liberating evangelization. The author names seven necessary elements: five related to education for faith (or evangelization proper), and two related to education in faith (or catechism).

EV47 Baker, Gordon Pratt, ed.
Evangelism and Contemporary Issues. Nashville, TNU: Tidings, 1964. 158 pp. Paper. No ISBN.

This book, through experiences and insights of Christian leaders, explores the facets of our present-day revolution, delving into such topics as evangelism and contemporary theology, mission of the church, creative arts, secularism, leisure time, communism, and the ecumenical movement.

EV48 Barna, George
Evangelism That Works: How to Reach Changing Generations with the Unchanging Gospel. Ventura, CAU: Regal Books, 1995. 176 pp. 0830717390.

The founder and president of Barna Research Group applies his extensive research to strategies for reaching the unchurched in North America.

EV49 Barna, George
The Invisible Generation: Baby Busters. Glendale, CAU: Barna Research Group, 1992. 185 pp. Paper. 1882297008.

Findings of social researchers concerning the generation in the United States born between 1965 and 1983—their lifestyles, values, and religious perspectives.

EV50 Barrett, David B., and Todd M. Johnson
Our Globe and How to Reach It: Seeing the World Evangelized by AD 2000 & Beyond: A Manual for the Decade of Evangelization, 1990-2000. (The AD 2000 Series). Birmingham, ALU: New Hope, 1990. vii, 136 pp. Paper. 0936625929.

A master plan as well as a resource for all Christian groups who have plans for world evangelization during the 1990s.

EV51 Beougher, Timothy, and Alvin Reid, eds.
Evangelism for a Changing World: Essays in Honor of Roy Fish. Wheaton, ILU: Shaw Publishers, 1995. xv, 282 pp. Paper. 0877882401.

Sixteen short essays on the history of evangelism in the United States, its biblical bases and contemporary expressions; written to honor Dr. Roy Fish, Professor of Evangelism at Southwestern Baptist Theological Seminary.

EV52 Berg, J. van den et al., eds.

Christusprediking in de wereld: Studiën op het terrein van de zendingswetenschap gewijd aan de nagedachtenis van Professor Dr. Johan Herman Bavinck. Kampen, NE: Kok, 1965. 248 pp. No ISBN.

A *festschrift* for J. H. Bavinck (1895-1964), missionary in Java and Professor of Mission, with contributions of A. Pos and others.

EV53 Bonnke, Reinhard

Evangelism by Fire: Igniting Your Passion for the Lost. Laguna Hills, CAU: CfaN/Reihard Bonnke Ministries, 1993. 266 pp. Paper. 1882729005.

Revised edition of an illustrated account of the motivations and fruits of the author's worldwide evangelistic crusades; originally published in 1990 by Word Publishing.

EV54 Boyack, Kenneth, ed.

Catholic Evangelization Today: A New Pentecost for the United States. New York, NYU: Paulist Press, 1987. iv, 209 pp. Paper. 0809128462.

Fifteen original essays by noted church leaders, presenting a renewed vision of Catholic evangelization in the United States, applying *Evangeli Nuntiandi* to the United States context.

EV55 Boyack, Kenneth, ed.

The New Catholic Evangelization. New York, NYU: Paulist Press, 1992. v, 239 pp. Paper. 0809133105.

Sixteen essays by Catholic leaders in the United States, designed to highlight new ideas, strategies, methods, and the spirituality undergirding the "Decade of Evangelization" in the 1990s.

EV56 Brandon, Owen

Christianity from Within: A Frank Discussion of Religion, Conversion, Evangelism and Revival. London, ENK: Hodder & Stoughton, 1965. xii, 157 pp. No ISBN.

An analysis of the nature of religious experience, in particular of conversion, regeneration, and evangelism, with firsthand accounts by individuals of many different persuasions.

EV57 Bright, Bill

El Avivamiento que Viene: Un llamado a nuestro país para ayunar, orar, y "buscar el rostro de Dios." Miami, FLU: Editorial Unilit, 1996. 214 pp. Paper. 0789901803.

Spanish translation.

EV58 Bright, Bill

The Coming Revival: America's Call to Fast, Pray, and "Seek God's Face." Orlando, FLU: New Life Publications, 1995. 223 pp. 1563990652 (hdbk), 1563990644 (pbk).

A call for 21st-century revival in North America by the founder of Campus Crusade for Christ.

EV59 Butselaar, Jan van, ed.

Die van het kruis kun je vertrouwen: De communicatie van het evangelie in onze wereld. (Allerwegen, 17). Kampen, NE: Kok, 1995. 86 pp. 9024222281.

Essays by six international mission scholars on communicating evangelism in developing countries (Peru, Indonesia, Rwanda), stressing how the unique characteristics of the indigenous cultures, their social structures, and folk religions interplay with the Christian message.

EV60 Calver, Clive et al., eds.

A Guide to Evangelism. Basingstoke, ENK: Marshall, Morgan & Scott, 1984. 302 pp. Paper. 0551011114.

A primer on evangelism for Christians in Great Britain—foundations, strategies, and specific types of persons to be reached.

EV61 Cannon, William R.

Evangelism in a Contemporary Context. Nashville, TNU: Tidings, 1974. 110 pp. Paper. No ISBN.

Four practical lectures on evangelism by a United Methodist bishop seeing evangelism as mandatory if the church and the world are to survive.

EV62 Chaney, Charles L., and Watson Granville, comps.

Evangelism: Today and Tomorrow. Nashville, TNU: Broadman, 1993. 171 pp. Paper. 0805411585.

Short essays on evangelism by fourteen Southern Baptist leaders honoring Jack Stanton, Director of the Institute of Evangelism at Southwest Baptist University (1975-), who became known among Baptists as "Mr. Evangelism."

EV63 Coalter, Milton J., and Virgil Cruz, eds.

How Shall We Witness?: Faithful Evangelism in a Reformed Tradition. Louisville, KYU: Westminster John Knox, 1995. xx, 186 pp. 0664255752.

Eight theological educators suggest scriptural, historical, theological, and educational foundations for witness with integrity by churches of the Reformed and Presbyterian tradition.

EV64 Cocoris, G. Michael

Evangelism: A Biblical Approach. Chicago, ILU: Moody, 1984. 176 pp. Paper. 0802423965.

Popular lectures and sermons on evangelism—its biblical bases, message, principles, and methods—by the senior pastor of the Church of the Open Door of Los Angeles, California.

EV65 Coleman, Robert E., ed.

Evangelism on the Cutting Edge. Old Tappan, NJU: Revell, 1986. 156 pp. 0800714822.

A collection of essays that confront major issues that hinder the great commission.

EV66 Coleman, Robert E.

The Great Commission Lifestyle: Conforming Your Life to Kingdom Priorities. Grand Rapids, MIU: Revell, 1992. 126 pp. Paper. 0800754506.

A popular presentation of the affirmation, mandate, and promise for evangelism found in the Great Commission, with study guide.

EV67 Coleman, Robert E.

The Master Plan of Discipleship. Old Tappan, NJU: Revell, 1987. 156 pp. Paper. 0800715136 (hdbk), 0800752376 (pbk).

A study by the Director of the School of World Mission and Evangelism, Trinity Evangelical Divinity School, discerning how the apostolic church carried out the Great Commission using Acts as a reference.

EV68 Cook, Guillermo

Profundidad en la Evangelización: Reflexiones sobre la evangelización a la luz de la Biblia y de la ciencia de la comunicación. (Colección "Iglesia y misión," 4). San José, CR: Publicaciones INDEF, 1975. xx, 125 pp. Paper. No ISBN.

Manual for deepening various aspects of evangelization along the characteristic line of the Instituto de Evangelización.

EV—EVANGELISM AND MISSIONS

EV69 Costas, Orlando E.
Evangelización Contextual: Fundamentos Teológicos y Pastorales. San José, CR: Ediciones Sebila, 1986. 119 pp. Paper. 9977958009.

A collection of five lectures on the theme of contextual evangelism, offering biblical and theological foundations for proclaiming the Gospel in particular situations; originally presented as the Strachan Lectures at the Seminario Bíblico Latinoamericano in Costa Rica in 1985.

EV70 Das, Somen, ed.
Mission and Evangelism. Delhi, II: ISPCK, 1998. vii, 211 pp. Paper. 8172144490.

Nineteen papers by Asian theologians and church leaders from the "Mission and Evangelism" seminar at Bishop's College (Calcutta, India, February 1997).

EV71 Eller, Vernard
Proclaim Good Tidings: Evangelism for the Faith Community. Elgin, ILU: Brethren Press, 1987. ix, 52 pp. Paper. 0871784874.

A discussion on contemporary evangelism from the Anabaptist perspective, exploring "hospitality evangelism" and the evangelical heritage of the Church of the Brethren.

EV72 Fackre, Gabriel
Do and Tell: Engagement Evangelism in the '70s. Grand Rapids, MIU: Eerdmans, 1980. 106 pp. Paper. 0802814948.

In this reprint, the author tells us that nurture and sharing the faith is the way to evangelism, not involvement with the social struggle, and that we need to tell what God has done, is doing, and will do; originally published in 1973.

EV73 Farrell, Gerardo T. et al.
Comentario a la Exhortación Apostólica de Su Santidad Pablo VI "Evangelii Nuntiandi." Buenos Aires, AG: Editora Patria Grande, 1978. 288 pp. Paper. No ISBN.

Systematic commentary on the papal encyclical, *Evangelii Nuntiandi* (1975).

EV74 Ferm, Robert O., and Caroline M. Whiting
Billy Graham: Do the Conversions Last? Minneapolis, MNU: World Wide Publications, 1988. 153 pp. Paper. 0890661375.

A thorough investigation focusing on the effectiveness of mass evangelism through the Billy Graham ministry, with attention to the type of persons responding to this ministry, the role of emotion in the conversion experience, and the long-term impact of commitment on the individual's life.

EV75 Finney, John
Church on the Move: Leadership for Mission. London, ENK: Daybreak; London, ENK: Darton, Longman & Todd, 1992. x, 182 pp. Paper. 0232518890.

Principles and strategies for parish evangelism by the Church of England's officer for the National Decade of Evangelism.

EV76 Ford, Leighton
The Christian Persuader: The Urgency of Evangelism in Today's World. Minneapolis, MNU: World Wide Publications, 1988. 142 pp. Paper. 089066093X.

Second edition of an exploration of critical areas in the church's evangelistic mission by the well-known Christian communicator and partner to Billy Graham; originally published in 1966.

EV77 Ford, Leighton
La Gran Minoría: Evangelización dinámica para una Iglesia en crisis. San José, CR: Editorial Caribe, 1969. 170 pp. Paper. No ISBN.

Spanish translation.

EV78 Fung, Raymond, and George Lemopoulos, eds.
Not a Solitary Way: Evangelism Stories from Around the World. (WCC Mission Series). Geneva, SZ: WCC Publications, 1992. x, 80 pp. Paper. 2825410969.

Fifteen stories of Christian witnessing from different countries and confessional backgrounds (Orthodox, Protestant, and Roman Catholic).

EV79 Greinacher, Norbert, and Alois Müller, eds.
La Evangelización en el Mundo de Hoy. Madrid, SP: Concilium, 1978. 145 pp. No ISBN.

Spanish translation.

EV80 Greinacher, Norbert, and Alois Müller, eds.
Evangelization in the World Today. (*Concilium*, 114). New York, NYU: Seabury Press, 1979. ix, 123 pp. Paper. 0816403937 (hdbk), 0816426104 (pbk).

An international scholarly collection of fourteen short articles on different aspects of evangelization.

EV81 Hater, Robert J.
News That Is Good: Evangelization for Catholics. Notre Dame, INU: Ave Maria Press, 1990. 149 pp. Paper. 0877934347.

A balanced, readable, and holistic view of evangelization in the Catholic context prepared for North American laity and clergy.

EV82 Hedlund, Roger E.
Evangelization and Church Growth: Issues from the Asian Context. Madras, II: Church Growth Research Centre, 1992. xvi, 260 pp. Paper. No ISBN.

A collection of the author's writings on evangelization and mission issues in which biblical, theological, contextual, urban, and strategy questions are discussed.

EV83 Hendrick, John R.
Opening the Door of Faith: The Why, When, and Where of Evangelism. Atlanta, GAU: John Knox Press, 1977. 112 pp. 0804206759.

The purpose of this small book is to liberate and energize congregations for evangelism, beginning with testimonies of personal faith and closing with a discussion of the place of the congregation as an instrument of God for bringing persons to faith in Christ.

EV84 Hofinger, Johannes
Evangelization and Catechesis. New York, NYU: Paulist Press, 1976. v, 153 pp. 0809119285.

Because of ineffectiveness of modern-day preaching, there is great need for evangelization and catechesis.

EV85 Holton, Susan, and David L. Jones
Spirit Aflame: Luis Palau's Mission to London. Grand Rapids, MIU: Baker Books, 1985. 226 pp. Paper. 0801042933.

An account of the process of planning, executing, and evaluating this citywide evangelistic crusade.

EV—EVANGELISM AND MISSIONS

EV86 Horton, Michael Scott, ed.
Power Religion: The Selling Out of the Evangelical Church?
Chicago, ILU: Moody, 1992. 353 pp. 0802467741.

Views of twelve North American evangelical leaders pointing out serious distractions in the "power evangelism" movement from the core and message of the Christian faith in the "power evangelism" movement.

EV87 Houck, William et al.
John Paul II and the New Evangelization: How You Can Bring the Good News to Others. Edited by Ralph Martin, and Peter Williamson. San Francisco, CAU: Ignatius Press, 1995. 290 pp. Paper. 0898705363.

Seventeen short responses, mostly by North American Roman Catholics, to the call to evangelization by Pope John Paul II and the US Catholic bishops, designed as a resource for Catholic leaders at the parish or diocesan level.

EV88 Hunter, George G., ed.
Focus on Evangelism. Nashville, TNU: Discipleship Resources, 1978. 136 pp. Paper. No ISBN.

A collection of twelve articles by world leaders in evangelism who define evangelism, its message, and consider the roles of evangelistic proclamation, witness, counseling, and organizing the congregation for programatic outreach.

EV89 Hunter, George G.
How to Reach Secular People. Nashville, TNU: Abington, 1992. 192 pp. Paper. 0687179300.

Profiles of secular people in North America, and of effective means of communicating the Christian Gospel and ministering to them; by the Dean of the E. Stanley Jones School of Evangelism, Asbury Theological Seminary.

EV90 *Instruktionen der Kongregation für Evangelisation der Völker*
(Nach-Konziliar Dokumentation, 18). Trier, GW: Paulinus Verlag, 1970. No ISBN.

The Latin text, with a German translation, of two *Instructions of the Propaganda* of 1969, with a comprehensive commentary by Joseph Glazik.

EV91 John, Jeffrey, ed.
Living Evangelism: Affirming Catholicism and Sharing the Faith. London, ENK: Darton, Longman & Todd, 1996. vii, 102 pp. Paper. 0232521662.

Six essays by Anglo Catholics originally presented at the Church of England's Third National Affirming Catholicism Conference (York, England, July 1995).

EV92 Johnson, Ben Campbell
Rethinking Evangelism: A Theological Approach. Philadelphia, PAU: Westminster Press, 1987. 141 pp. Paper. 0664240607.

A popular account from the Presbyterian viewpoint on the place and understanding of evangelism in contemporary Christian discipleship.

EV93 Johnson, Ben Campbell
Speaking of God: Evangelism as Initial Spiritual Guidance. Louisville, KYU: Westminster John Knox, 1991. 188 pp. Paper. 0664252001.

A theological foundation with practical suggestions and a positive model for local congregations desiring to lead people into deeper commitments of faith and life.

EV94 Jonkers, J. B. G.
Doelen in de Evangelisatie: Een sociologische studie. (Proefschrift Soc. Wetenschappen Kath. Universiteit Nijmegen). Amsterdam, NE: Rodopi, 1986. 250 pp. Paper. 9090011528.

A doctoral thesis in the faculty of social sciences on the problem of defining concrete and specific goals for activities of evangelization.

EV95 Kew, Richard, and Cyril C. Okorocha
Vision Bearers: Dynamic Evangelism in the 21st Century. Harrisburg, PAU: Morehouse Publishing, 1996. 147 pp. Paper. 0819216569.

An introduction by two Anglican mission leaders, including global challenges to 21st-century mission and evangelism, and opportunities for pastoral care, social witness, and direct evangelistic outreach.

EV96 Krass, Alfred C.
Beyond the Either-Or Church: Notes toward the Recovery of the Wholeness of Evangelism. Nashville, TNU: Tidings, 1973. 104 pp. Paper. No ISBN.

This book is an appeal for the recovery of biblical evangelism in both the liberal and fundamental churches.

EV97 Ladd, Tony, and James A. Mathisen
Muscular Christianity: Evangelical Protestants and the Development of American Sport. (A BridgePoint Book). Grand Rapids, MIU: Baker Books, 1999. 288 pp. Paper. 0801058473.

The historical and sociological development of the evangelical protestant impact on American sports, including 19th- and 20th-century sports heroes and evangelists such as Billy Graham, Billy Sunday, Bill Glass, James Naismith, Eric Liddell, Amos Alonzo Stagg, and D. L. Moody.

EV98 Lageer, Eileen
New Life for All. London, ENK: Oliphants; Chicago, ILU: Moody Press, 1969. 144 pp. No ISBN.

The story of the inauguration of a major evangelistic campaign in Nigeria, with a foreword by Paul S. Rees.

EV99 Laney, James T., ed.
Evangelism: Mandates for Action. New York, NYU: Hawthorn Books, 1975. viii, 128 pp. Paper. 0801524105.

An urgent imperative, to relate individuals to their social contexts, even as they are brought into new relation with God, runs as a theme in addresses given by six religious leaders.

EV100 Latin America Mission
Evangelism-in-Depth: Experimenting with a New Type of Evangelism. Edited by Robert Kenneth Strachan. Chicago, ILU: Moody, 1961. 126 pp. No ISBN.

The story of the origin of this movement and the record of its first two campaigns in Nicaragua and Costa Rica.

EV101 Latin American Mission
Évangelisation totale! Edited by Robert Kenneth Strachan. Bruxelles, BE: La Mission Évangelique Belge, 1969. 136 pp. No ISBN.

French translation with adaptation by M. Demaude and J. Brepsant.

EV102 Linn, Jan G.
Reclaiming Evangelism: A Practical Guide for Mainline Churches. St. Louis, MOU: Chalice Press, 1998. vi, 152 pp. Paper. 0827232160.

A challenge for mainline Protestant churches in the United States to reclaim the vitality of their evangelistic outreach, with practical suggestions for local churches.

EV—EVANGELISM AND MISSIONS

EV103 Margull, Hans Jochen
Hope in Action: The Church's Task in the World. Philadelphia, PAU: Muhlenberg Press, 1962. xxi, 298 pp. No ISBN.

An evaluation of the history of the ecumenical discussion of evangelism, written by the author when Head of the Department of Evangelization of the WCC.

EV104 Marsh, Clinton M.
Evangelism Is ... Louisville, KYU: Geneva Press, 1997. xi, 137 pp. Paper. 0664500137.

A call for Presbyterians to confront their denomination's membership decline and to place evangelism at the heart of each congregation's life, by an African American pastor and former denominational staff member for evangelism.

EV105 Marshall, Michael
The Gospel Connection: A Study in Evangelism for the Nineties. London, ENK: Darton, Longman & Todd, 1991. xi, 209 pp. Paper. 0232519390.

The director of the Anglican Institute in St. Louis, Missouri, and former Bishop of Woolwich, issues an urgent call for Anglicans/Episcopalians to recover the biblical passion for evangelism as they participate in the Decade of Evangelism; originally published in 1990 by Morehouse Publishing.

EV106 Martín Velasco, Juan
Increencia y Evangelización: Del diálogo al testimonio. (Presencia Teológica, 45). Santander, SP: Editorial Sal Terrae, 1988. 252 pp. Paper. 8429308016.

An analysis of different types of unbelief and a systematic study of evangelization.

EV107 Martini, Carlo Maria
Once More from Emmaus. Translated by Matthew J. O'Connell. Collegeville, MNU: Liturgical Press, 1995. x, 109 pp. Paper. 0814621589.

English translation.

EV108 Martini, Carlo Maria
Ripartire da Emmaus. Milano, IT: Centro Ambrosiano; Casale Monferato, IT: Piemme, 1991. 127 pp. No ISBN.

The Catholic archbishop of Milan addresses the missionary dimension of the church to give witness to the world concerning God's plan for salvation, with biblical mandates for various aspects of the life of the parish.

EV109 Maynard-Reid, Pedrito U.
Complete Evangelism: The Luke-Acts Model. Scottdale, PAU: Herald Press, 1997. 184 pp. Paper. 0836190459.

An overview of Luke-Acts as a biblical basis for holistic evangelism where personal and social concerns are equally significant, with a brief historical overview by a Jamaican Seventh-day Adventist pastor-teacher.

EV110 McCulloch, Nigel
A Gospel to Proclaim. London, ENK: Darton, Longman & Todd, 1992. xii, 94 pp. Paper. 0232520070.

A primer on the six priorities in the Church of England's Decade of Evangelism by the Bishop of Wakefield, who chaired its Steering Group.

EV111 McIntosh, Gary
Make Room for the Boom ... or Bust: Six Church Models for Reaching Three Generations. Grand Rapids, MIU: Revell, 1997. 192 pp. Paper. 0800756142.

Six models for reaching the boomer and buster generations in North America for Christ.

EV112 Miles, Delos
Introduction to Evangelism. Nashville, TNU: Broadman, 1983. 386 pp. 0805462392.

An introductory textbook on evangelism with a balance between theory and practice, including sections on the meaning, message, models, the messenger, and the methods of evangelism.

EV113 Molendijk, Arie L.
Getuigen in missionair en oecumenisch verband: Een studie over het begrip "getuigen" in documenten van de Wereldraad van Kerken, de Rooms-Katholieke Kerk en de Evangelicalen, in de periode 1948-1985. (IIMO Research Pamplet, 16). Leiden, NE: IIMO, 1986. iv, 257 pp. Paper. 9081387208.

An analysis of the use of the term "witness" in official documents, 1948 to 1985, of the WCC, the Roman Catholic Church, and the Wheaton (1966) and Lausanne I (1974) conferences of evangelicals.

EV114 Padilla, C. René
El Evangelio Hoy. Buenos Aires, AG: Ediciones Certeza, 1975. 188 pp. Paper. No ISBN.

Collection of author's previously published articles, including the text of "Pacto de Lausana" with Padilla's response.

EV115 Pannell, William E.
Evangelism from the Bottom Up. Grand Rapids, MIU: Zondervan, 1992. 128 pp. Paper. 0310522218.

A call for a creative new approach to urban evangelism in the United States based on biblical integrity, cultural sensitivity to ethnic realities, and a passion for justice.

EV116 Percy, Harold
Good News People: An Introduction to Evangelism for Tongue-tied Christians. Toronto, ONC: Anglican Book Centre, 1996. 141 pp. Paper. 1551261650.

A primer on evangelism, with study guide, by the Anglican Director of the Institute of Evangelism at Wycliffe College in Toronto, Canada.

EV117 Peters, George W.
Evangelisation: Total—durchdringend—umfassend. Bad Liebenzell, GW: Liebenzeller Mission, 1977. 250 pp. 3880020442.

German translation.

EV118 Peters, George W.
Saturation Evangelism. (Contemporary Evangelical Perspectives). Grand Rapids, MIU: Zondervan, 1970. 237 pp. Paper. No ISBN.

A guide for a style of missionary evangelism designed to involve the entire membership of the church in evangelism, with analysis of two examples ("Evangelism in Depth" developed by the Latin American Mission, and "New Life for All" in Nigeria).

EV119 Pickard, Stephen K.
Liberating Evangelism: Gospel, Theology, and the Dynamics of Communication. (Christian Mission and Modern Culture). Harrisburg, PAU: Trinity Press International, 1999. ix, 108 pp. Paper. 1563382792.

A call for the church to be a community of the evangel and thus a community that seeks to embody the glad tidings of God in all its life.

EV—EVANGELISM AND MISSIONS

EV120 Pickard, William M.

Offer Them Christ: Christian Mission for the Twenty-First Century. Franklin, TNU: Providence House, 1998. xviii, 142 pp. Paper. 1577360907.

A Christian evangelism for the religiously plural 21st century following the model of E. Stanley Jones, centered on the presence of Jesus Christ as the model for a witness of faith, personal living, loving presence, and service.

EV121 Posterski, Donald C.

Reinventing Evangelism: New Strategies for Presenting Christ in Today's World. Downers Grove, ILU: InterVarsity, 1989. 202 pp. Paper. 0830912695 (US), 0889180024 (CN).

A popular work designed to give new meaning and strategies to evangelism by connecting the meaning of the Gospel with the language of modern culture, by a recognized expert on youth culture who is the Associate General Director of InterVarsity Christian Fellowship in Canada.

EV122 Rainer, Thom S., ed.

Evangelism in the Twenty-First Century: The Critical Issues. Wheaton, ILU: Shaw Publishers, 1989. xii, 227 pp. Paper. 087788238X.

Twenty-two essays by North American leaders in evangelism and professors honoring Lewis A. Drummond, a longtime professor of evangelism at Southern Baptist Theological Seminary.

EV123 Rainer, Thom S.

The Bridger Generation: America's Second Largest Generation; What They Believe; How to Reach Them. Nashville, TNU: Broadman, 1997. xii, 209 pp. 0805462961.

A survey of research on the 72 million children and youth born between 1977 and 1994 in the United States, their character and culture, with insights on how the church can reach them.

EV124 Read, David H. C.

Go and Make Disciples. Nashville, TNU: Abingdon, 1978. 110 pp. Paper. 0687148928.

A simple book addressed to those not sure what evangelism is, to church members who feel they ought to believe in it, and non-members who resist what looks like Christian aggression.

EV125 Reid, Alvin

Introduction to Evangelism. Nashville, TNU: Broadman, 1998. xvi, 362 pp. Paper. 0805411437.

A basic textbook covering the convictional, spiritual, and methodological bases of evangelism by the Professor of Evangelism at Southeastern Baptist Theological Seminary.

EV126 Reuter, Wilfred, ed.

Und bis ans Ende der Welt: Beiträge zur Evangelisation: Eine Festschrift zum 60. Neuhausen-Stuttgart, GW: Hänssler-Verlag, 1974. 269 pp. 3775101489.

A comprehensive compendium on evangelism, with chapters on its history, methods, and evangelism, in selected countries; written by German professors, evangelists of world stature (including Billy Graham), and pastors with keen evangelical interest.

EV127 Rosales, Ray S.

The Evangelism-in-Depth Program of the Latin American Mission: A Description and Evaluation. (Sondeos, 21). Cuernavaca, MX: Centro Intercultural de Documentacion (CIDOC), 1968. No ISBN.

The history, theory, procedures, and evaluation of the program with eight articles from the *International Review of Mission* in 1964 and 1965; originally presented as a STM thesis at Luther Theological Seminary in 1966.

EV128 Salter, Darius

American Evangelism: Its Theology and Practice. Grand Rapids, MIU: Baker Books, 1996. 426 pp. Paper. No ISBN.

A basic textbook on evangelism, its theology and practice, for North American church leaders.

EV129 Santos Hernández, Angel

Teología Bíblico-patrística de las Misiones. (Misionología, 4). Santander, SP: Sal Terrae, 1962. 242 pp. Paper. No ISBN.

Textbook on concepts of mission in the Bible and in the writings of the Church Fathers and early Popes; with many textual citations, clarifying footnotes, and bibliography.

EV130 Saxbee, John

Liberal Evangelism. London, ENK: SPCK, 1994. ix, 118 pp. Paper. 0281046913.

A theology and methodology of evangelism for liberal Christians in Great Britain, prepared as a resource for the Decade of Evangelism.

EV131 Shibley, David

A Force in the Earth: The Charismatic Renewal and World Evangelism. Altamonte Springs, FLU: Creation House, 1989. vi, 176 pp. Paper. 0884192490.

A popular presentation of the rationale for dynamic world evangelization by a leading charismatic pastor in the United States.

EV132 Smith, Glenn C., ed.

Evangelizing Blacks. Wheaton, ILU: Tyndale, 1988. 219 pp. Paper. 0842307877.

A collection of eleven papers giving an overview and case studies of evangelization, both Roman Catholic and Protestant, among African Americans.

EV133 Stowe, David M.

Ecumenicity and Evangelism. Grand Rapids, MIU: Eerdmans, 1970. 94 pp. Paper. No ISBN.

This book reflects the debate between conservative critics and ecumenists, relating it to evangelistic action and thought among Christians who do not participate in conciliar ecumenism.

EV134 Suess, Paulo

Evangelizar a partir dos Projetos Históricos dos Otros: Ensaios de Missiologia. São Paulo, BL: Paulus, 1995. 238 pp. 8534904472.

Ten scholarly essays on historical and cultural aspects of evangelization in Latin America.

EV135 Suess, Paulo

Evangelizar desde los Proyectos Históricos de los Otros: Diez Ensayos de Misionología. Quito, EC: Ediciones Abya-Yala, 1995. 210 pp. No ISBN.

Spanish translation of *Evangelizar a partir dos Projetos Históricos dos Otros: Ensaios de Missiología* (1995).

EV136 Sweazey, George Edgar

The Church as Evangelist. New York, NYU: Harper & Row, 1984. xii, 255 pp. 0060677767 (hdbk), 0060677775 (pbk).

Second edition of a basic textbook for mainline Protestants on evangelism in the local church; originally published in 1978.

EV—EVANGELISM AND MISSIONS

EV137 Torre Arranz, Jesús A. de la

Evangelización Inculturada y Liberadora: La praxis mision-era a partir de los encuentros latinoamericanos del postcon-cilio. Quito, EC: Abya-Yala, 1993. 154 pp. No ISBN.

Second edition of a text on Latin American views on evan-gelism since Vatican II—how it is perceived, and how it can im-prove to meet the needs of the people; first published in 1989.

EV138 Vadakumpadan, Paul

Evangelisation Today: Understanding the Integral Concept of Evangelisation in the Light of Contemporary Trends in the Theology of Mission. Shillong, II: Vendrame Missiological Institute, 1989. xviii, 337 pp. No ISBN.

A dissertation on Roman Catholic thought concerning evangelization since Vatican II, including themes of libera-tion, Gospel and culture, and interreligious dialogue.

EV139 Verkuyl, Johannes

Inleiding in de Evangelistiek. Kampen, NE: Kok, 1978. 284 pp. 9024208394.

A general introduction on the history, theory, and prac-tice of evangelism.

EV140 Walker, Alan

The New Evangelism. Nashville, TNU: Abingdon, 1975. 112 pp. 0687277361.

Five popular chapters on the motive, arena, message, method, and power of mission by United Methodism's world evangelist, who earlier demonstrated in ministries in Austra-lia, the integral link between mission and evangelism.

EV141 Walker, Christopher C.

Connecting with the Spirit of Christ: Evangelism for a Secu-lar Age. Nashville, TNU: Discipleship Resources, 1988. vii, 117 pp. Paper. 0881770566.

Written by a minister of the Uniting Church of Australia, this work focuses on helping congregations develop their own theology of evangelism, with chapters on the context of evan-gelism, how to communicate the Gospel with secular people, four contemporary theologies, and five principles of responsi-ble evangelism.

EV142 Watson, David

Creo en la Evangelización. (Creo). Miami, FLU: Editorial Caribe, 1978. 321 pp. Paper. No ISBN.

Spanish translation.

EV143 Watson, David

I Believe in Evangelism. Grand Rapids, MIU: Eerdmans, 1977. 188 pp. Paper. 0802816878.

An analysis of terms for proclamation and evangelization in the New Testament and their implications for parish life.

EV144 Wimber, John, and Kevin Springer

Power Evangelism. San Francisco, CAU: HarperSanFrancisco, 1992. 269 pp. Paper. 0060695420.

A revised and expanded edition, with study questions, of the influential work on signs, wonders, and evangelism; orig-inally published in 1985.

EV145 Wright, Christopher, and Chris Sugden, eds.

One Gospel—Many Clothes: Anglicans and the Decade of Evangelism. Oxford, ENK: EFAC/Regnum Books, 1990. 190 pp. Paper. 1870345088.

Sixteen essays honoring John Stott on his retirement as Founder-President of the Evangelical Fellowship in the An-glican Communion (EFAC), with national case studies from six continents.

Theology

See also TH98, TH249, TH565, EA138, SO649, EV35, EV39, EV105, EV218, EV254, EV343, EV513, EV550, AM489, and EU83.

EV146 Abraham, William J.

The Logic of Evangelism. Grand Rapids, MIU: Eerdmans; [London, ENK]: Hodder & Stoughton, 1989. ix, 245 pp. Pa-per. 0802804330 (E), 0340514515 (H).

A scholarly argument for evangelism as a serious topic of theological inquiry, with an understanding of evangelism as primary initiation into the Kingdom of God, and its implica-tions for the practice of evangelism in the contemporary church.

EV147 Amalorpavadass, D. S.

Approach, Meaning and Horizon of Evangelization. (Mis-sion Theology for Our Times Series, 8). Bangalore, II: NB-CLC, 1973. 107 pp. Paper. No ISBN.

This theological orientation speech at the All-India Con-sultation on Evangelization is an evaluation of the inadequacy of the theology of evangelization of the early 1970s, giving resources to remedy that deficiency.

EV148 Amateze, Simon Uchenna

The Prophetic Role of the People of God in Evangelization in the Light of Vatican II: Prophetic Evangelization. (Facultas Theolo-giae). Rome, IT: Pontificia Universitas Urbaniana, 1988. xviii, 195 pp. Paper. 8840133127.

A theology of "prophetic evangelization" offering witness to all humanity by the whole people of God; originally presented as a doctoral thesis at the Urbaniana Pontifical University.

EV149 Arias, Mortimer

Announcing the Reign of God: Evangelization and the Subver-sive Memory of Jesus. Philadelphia, PAU: Fortress Press, 1984. xviii, 155 pp. Paper. 0800617126.

The Bolivian former Methodist bishop and Professor of Hispanic Studies and Evangelism at Claremont School of The-ology, sets forth convincingly his understanding of the rela-tionship between a new Christ-centered evangelism and Chris-tian social ethics.

EV150 Arias, Mortimer, and Alan Johnson

The Great Commission: Biblical Models for Evangelism. Nash-ville, TNU: Abingdon, 1992. 142 pp. Paper. 0687157846.

A study book on the implications of Jesus' commissioning of the disciples for contemporary evangelism in each of the four gospels.

EV151 Arias, Mortimer, and Juan Damián

La Gran Comisión: Relectura desde América Latina: Estudio exegético y manual para talleres de evangelización. (Pensamiento Cristiano). Quito, EC: CLAI, 1994. vi, 148 pp. Paper. No ISBN.

Lectures by the noted Uruguayan Methodist theologian on the Great Commission in the four Gospels; with a study guide by the Secretary of Evangelización and Liturgy of the Latin American Council of Churches; also published in En-glish as *The Great Commission* in 1992.

EV152 Bowie, Richard W.

"Light for the Nations": (A Biblical Theology of Evangeliza-tion). Tanglin, SI: Haggai Centre for Leadership Studies, 1992. xii, 118 pp. 9810051956.

The Executive Director of Haggai Institute, Singapore, develops the biblical mandate for evangelism as the very rea-son for the church's existence.

EV153 Briese, Russell John

Foundations of a Lutheran Theology of Evangelism. (Regensburger Studien zur Theologie, 42). Frankfurt am Main, GW: Lang, 1994. ix, 304 pp. Paper. 3631463928.

A scholarly analysis of Lutheran understandings of evangelism from the time of Luther to the present, with a comparison of Lutheran themes with 20th-century emphases in mission theologies as expressed in IMC/WCC and evangelical mission conferences; originally presented in 1992 as a dissertation in Protestant theology at the University of Regensburg, Germany.

EV154 Brueggemann, Walter

Biblical Perspectives on Evangelism: Living in a Three-Storied Universe. Nashville, TNU: Abingdon, 1993. 139 pp. Paper. 0687412331.

A biblical theology of evangelism by the William Marcellus McPheeters Professor of Old Testament at Columbia Theological Seminary, Decatur, Georgia.

EV155 Costas, Orlando E., comp.

Hacia una Teología de la Evangelización. Buenos Aires, AG: Editorial La Aurora, 1973. 306 pp. Paper. No ISBN.

Nine studies on the theology, history, and contextualizations of missions, with a wide bibliography of works in English and Spanish.

EV156 Costas, Orlando E.

Liberating News: A Theology of Contextual Evangelization. Grand Rapids, MIU: Eerdmans, 1989. xiv, 182 pp. Paper. 0802803644.

A theology of holistic evangelism—from the standpoint of the poor, the powerless, and the oppressed—by the distinguished missiologist and former Dean of Andover-Newton Theological School in the United States.

EV157 Crockett, William V., and James G. Sigountos, eds.

Through No Fault of Their Own?: The Fate of Those Who Have Never Heard. Grand Rapids, MIU: Baker Books, 1991. 278 pp. Paper. 0801025621.

Twenty-two evangelical theologians, biblical scholars, and missiologists present a sturdy defense of the necessity of salvation through Christ.

EV158 Cserháti, Franz

Eingliederung in die Kirche um des Heiles willen: Eine Studie über die Vereinbarkeit der zwei katholischen Lehren: Heilsnotwendigkeit der Kirche und Heilsmoglichkeit ausserhalb ihr ... (European University Studies, 23, 228). Frankfurt, GW: Lang, 1984. xi, 257 pp. Paper. 3820479821.

Drawing on the New Testament, patristic documents, and the official teaching of the church, the author attempts to answer the difficult question of the necessity of the church for salvation (dissertation, University of Innsbruck, AU).

EV159 Drummond, Lewis A.

Eight Keys to Biblical Revival: The Saga of Scriptural Spiritual Awakenings, How They Shaped the Great Revivals of the Past, and Their Powerful Implications for Today's Church. Minneapolis, MNU: Bethany House, 1994. 222 pp. Paper. 1556614020.

An exposition of eight key factors found in the Bible that define the essence of a true spiritual awakening, with historical illustrations of each, by the Billy Graham Professor of Evangelism and Church Growth at Beeson Divinity School.

EV160 Drummond, Lewis A.

The Word of the Cross: A Contemporary Theology of Evangelism. Nashville, TNU: Broadman, 1992. 383 pp. 0805462554.

A biblical theology of evangelism for Protestant Christians by the {resident of Southeastern Baptist Theological Seminary in Wake Forest, North Carolina.

EV161 English, Donald, ed.

Windows on Salvation. London, ENK: Darton, Longman & Todd, 1994. xii, 194 pp. Paper. 0232520380.

Eleven essays by British theologians and church leaders designed to undergird that nation's Decade of Evangelism with insight into what salvation actually means.

EV162 Erickson, Millard J.

How Shall They Be Saved?: The Destiny of Those Who Do Not Hear of Jesus. Grand Rapids, MIU: Baker Books, 1996. 278 pp. Paper. 0801020654.

A survey of theological positions on salvation for those who have never heard the gospel by the Research Professor of Theology at Southwestern Baptist Theological Seminary.

EV163 Escobar, Samuel E.

Evangelio y Realidad Social: Ensayos desde una perspectiva evangélica. Lima, PE: Editorial Presencia Evangélica, 1985. 232 pp. Paper. No ISBN.

A collection of the author's papers presented in Bogotá 1969 (CLADE I), Cochabamba 1970, Lausanne 1974, and Lima 1979 (CLADE II), as well as a collection of texts of the following documents: "La Declaración Evangélica de Bogota," "La Declaración Evangélica de Cochabamba," and "El Pacto de Lausana."

EV164 Fackre, Gabriel

What about Those Who Have Never Heard?: Three Views on the Destiny of the Unevangelized. Edited by John Sanders. Downers Grove, ILU: InterVarsity, 1995. 168 pp. Paper. 0830816062.

Three theological views on the destiny of the unevangelized (inclusivism, divine perseverance, and restrictivism) presented as essays and responses by Fackre, Sanders, and Ronald H. Nash.

EV165 Fackre, Gabriel

Word in Deed: Theological Themes in Evangelism. Grand Rapids, MIU: Eerdmans, 1975. 109 pp. Paper. 0802816053.

A look at evangelism—the orientation, proclamation, authorization, action, and conversion.

EV166 Floristan, Casiano

La Evangelización, Tarea del Cristiano. (Epifanía, 47). Madrid, SP: Ediciones Cristiandad, 1978. 216 pp. Paper. 8470572334.

Analysis and definition of new concepts of evangelization in light of current research.

EV167 Häring, Bernhard

Evangelization Today. New York, NYU: Crossroad Publishing, 1991. x, 177 pp. Paper. 0824510968.

Inspired by the proclamation of the 1990s as the Decade of Evangelization, the prominent Catholic moral theologian revises his classic work (1974) on the morals of evangelization and the evangelization of morals; originally printed in 1974 (Notre Dame, INU: Fides; Slough, ENK: St. Paul Publications).

EV168 Henderson, Robert T.
Joy to the World: Spreading the Good News of the Kingdom.
Grand Rapids, MIU: Zondervan, 1991. 207 pp. Paper.
0310534410.

A reprint of the 1980 classic in which the senior pastor of
First Presbyterian Church, Hendersonville, North Carolina,
presents the Kingdom of God as the guiding principle for evangelism in the local congregation.

EV169 Hoekendijk, Hans
Horizons of Hope. Nashville, TNU: Tidings, 1970. 47 pp.
Paper. No ISBN.

This book takes a look at our modern world and with
integrity attempts to understand the ways God is leading us
through the last of the 20th century.

EV170 Holmes, Urban T.
*Turning to Christ: A Theology of Evangelization and Renew-
al.* Cambridge, MAU: Cowley Publications, 1994. xviii, 236
pp. Paper. 1561010987.

A reprint of the classic text (1981) providing an Anglican
theology and strategy for evangelization, with a new guide for
group study.

EV171 Hull, Bill
*New Century Disciplemaking: Applying Jesus' Ideas for the
Future.* Grand Rapids, MIU: Revell, 1997. 238 pp. Paper.
080075641X.

A study book on Jesus' discipling strategy and its application to 21st-century disciple-making.

EV172 Jong, Pieter de
A Theology of Evangelistic Concern. Nashville, TNU: Tidings, 1963. 72 pp. Paper. No ISBN.

An argument that evangelism is participation in God's
redemptive activity concerning the whole of creation, has cosmic complications, and aims at the transformation of the whole
of reality.

EV173 Klaiber, Walter
*Call and Response: Biblical Foundation of a Theology of Evan-
gelism.* Translated by Howard Perry-Trauthig and James A.
Dwyer. Nashville, TNU: Abingdon, 1997. 272 pp. Paper.
0687046025.

English translation.

EV174 Klaiber, Walter
*Ruf und Antwort: Biblische Grundlagen einer Theologie der
Evangelisation.* Stuttgart, GW: Christliches Verlagshaus;
Neukirchen-Vluyn, GW: Neukirchener Verlag, 1990. 303 pp.
Paper. 3767577429 (C), 3788713658 (N).

A comprehensive study of the biblical and theological
foundations of evangelism in relation to the contemporary
contexts in which the Gospel must be proclaimed and lived;
by the bishop of the Germany area of the United Methodist
Church.

EV175 Klinger, Elmar, ed.
Christentum innerhalb und ausserhalb der Kirche. (Quaes-
tiones disputatae, 73). Freiburg, GW: Herder, 1976. 293 pp.
Paper. 3451020734.

Proceeding from Rahner's concept of "anonymous Christians," these sixteen essays inquire about the salvation of those
who do not know the church but nevertheless live according
to Christian principles.

EV176 Kolb, Robert
Speaking the Gospel Today: A Theology for Evangelism. St.
Louis, MOU: Concordia Publishing, 1995. 278 pp. Paper.
0570042585.

An updated revised edition of the author's theology of
evangelism, which connects doctrine to everyday conversation with those who don't yet know Christ; by the Concordia
Seminary's Director of the Institute for Mission Studies in St.
Louis, Missouri; first published in 1984.

EV177 Legrand, Lucien, J. Pathrapankal, and M. Vellanickal
*Good News and Witness: The New Testament Understanding
of Evangelization.* Bangalore, II: Theological Publications in
India, 1974. vii, 179 pp. No ISBN.

A closely argued study of the meaning of mission in the
synoptic Gospels, the Johannine writings, and the thought of
Paul and the early church.

EV178 Logan, James C., ed.
Theology and Evangelism in the Wesleyan Heritage. Nashville, TNU: Kingswood Books, 1994. 223 pp. Paper.
0687413958.

Ten essays first presented at a symposium on "Theology
and Evangelism in the Wesleyan Heritage" (Emory University, Atlanta, Georgia, February 1992) sponsored by the United
Methodist Foundation for Evangelism.

EV179 Outler, Albert C.
Evangelism and Theology in the Wesleyan Spirit. Nashville, TNU:
Discipleship Resources, 1996. 144 pp. Paper. 0881771511.

A reissue of two short classics by the noted Wesley scholar
on John Wesley as evangelist and theologian.

EV180 Paul VI, Pope
On Evangelization in the Modern World: Evangelii nuntiandi.
Washington, DCU: USCC, 1976. 70 pp. No ISBN.

The influential Catholic encyclical on evangelization.

EV181 Paul VI, Pope
*Der Welt verpflichtet: Text und Kommentar des Apostolischen
Schreibens* Evangelii nuntiandi *über die Evangelisierung in
der Welt von heute.* Edited by Horst Rzepkowski. St. Augustin, GW: Steyler Verlag, 1976. 196 pp. Paper. 3877870872.

German text and commentary on the papal document
Evangelii nuntiandi concerning the evangelization of the world
today.

EV182 Poe, Harry L.
*The Gospel and Its Meaning: A Theology for Evangelism and
Church Growth.* Grand Rapids, MIU: Zondervan, 1996. 334
pp. Paper. 0310201721.

Drawing upon scholarship in both New Testament studies
and historical theology, the Associate Professor of Evangelism
and Church Growth at Southern Baptist Theological Seminary
develops the biblical and theological foundations for a Christian
apologetic to those outside the faith community.

EV183 Pope-Levison, Priscilla
Evangelization from a Liberation Perspective. (American
University Studies, 7: Theology and Religion, 69). New York,
NYU: Lang, 1991. xii, 201 pp. 0820411698.

An analysis of sources for a holistic model of evangelization from a liberation perspective found in Roman Catholic
and WCC's documents, and in the thought of ten representative Latin American theologians, both Roman Catholic and
Protestant.

EV—EVANGELISM AND MISSIONS

EV184 Sanders, John

No Other Name: An Investigation into the Destiny of the Unevangelized. Grand Rapids, MIU: Eerdmans, 1992. xviii, 315 pp. Paper. 0802806155.

A detailed theological treatise on the issues of the accessibility of salvation to the unevangelized and their eternal destiny, presenting both inclusive and exclusive arguments.

EV185 Stott, John R. W.

The Contemporary Christian: Applying God's Word to Today's World. Downers Grove, ILU: InterVarsity, 1992. 432 pp. 0830813160.

A major work by the noted evangelical theologian and churchman articulating a biblical theology of mission and evangelism for contemporary Christians.

EV186 Sullivan, Francis Aloysius

Salvation Outside the Church: Tracing the History of the Catholic Response. Mahwah, NJU: Paulist Press, 1992. v, 224 pp. Paper. 0809133040.

A thorough study of the history of Christian thought about the salvation of those "outside the church."

EV187 Taschner, Josef

Die Notwendigkeit des ausdrücklichen Glaubens an Christus: Eine geschichtlich-theologische Untersuchung im Anschluss an die Lehrmeinungen der Dogmatiker und Moraltheologen seit 1850. (Veroffentlichungen des Missionspriesterseminars, 6). Kaldenkirchen, GW: Steyler Verlag, 1960. xi, 96 pp. Paper. No ISBN.

A dissertation attempting to evaluate the different opinions on the necessity of explicit faith in Christ, and to prove that the theologies of Suarez and Valladarez are tenable.

EV188 Underwood, Byron E.

Sixteen New Testament Principles for World Evangelism. Franklin Springs, GAU: Advocate Press, 1988. 241 pp. Paper. 091186606X.

Brief notes on sixteen basic strategies for evangelization found in the Book of Acts, by the Vice Chairman of the Pentecostal Holiness Church.

EV189 Wisnefske, Ned

Preparing to Hear the Gospel: A Proposal for Natural Theology. Lanham, MDU: University Press of America, 1998. vii, 140 pp. 0761812342 (hdbk), 0761812350 (pbk).

Drawing on philosophical insights from Wittgenstein, the author points out that the natural form of life impresses a common morality that functions to prepare the way for the Gospel.

Conversion

See also HI84, HI96, HI107, EV224, EV548, CH119, SP244, AF1251, AF1352, AM1028, AS925, AS1009, and AS1065.

EV190 Connor, Kimberly Rae

Conversions and Visions in the Writings of African-American Women. Knoxville, TNU: University of Tennessee Press, 1994. x, 317 pp. 0870498185.

A psychosocial analysis of conversion experiences in the 19th- and 20th-century autobiographies and novels of African American women.

EV191 Erikson, Richard M.

Late Have I Loved Thee: Stories of Religious Conversion and Commitment in Later Life. New York, NYU: Paulist Press, 1995. v, 194 pp. Paper. 0809135949.

A groundbreaking study of the dynamics of conversion of older adult Catholics based on twenty-eight in-depth interviews with baptismal candidates in US parishes.

EV192 Fink-Dendorfer, Elisabeth

Conversio: Motive und Motivierung zur Bekehrung in der Alten Kirche. (Regensburger Studien zur Theologie, 33). Frankfurt am Main, GW: Lang, 1986. 358 pp. 3820487611.

A scholarly study of the theology of conversion as developed in the early church; originally presented as a doctoral thesis (University of Regensburg, 1984/85).

EV193 Fisk, Samuel, comp.

More Fascinating Conversion Stories. Grand Rapids, MIU: Kregel Publications, 1994. 186 pp. Paper. 0825426405.

Popular accounts of the life changing experiences of leading Protestants in the 16th to 19th centuries, including many missionaries and evangelists.

EV194 Gelpi, Donald L.

The Conversion Experience: A Reflective Process for RCIA Participants and Others. New York, NYU: Paulist Press, 1998. iii, 230 pp. Paper. 0809137968.

A practical, pastoral guide for introducing adult Christians to the dynamics of conversion, based on experiences of the author as a leader in the Roman Catholic Rite for the Christian Initiation of Adults (RCIA).

EV195 Gillespie, V. Bailey

The Dynamics of Religious Conversion: Identity and Transformation. Birmingham, ALU: Religious Education Press, 1991. 261 pp. Paper. 0891350845.

Drawing upon the latest research on biblical studies, systematic and pastoral theology, the social sciences, and literary studies, the author develops an interdisciplinary understanding of conversion, suggesting ministries through pastoral counseling and religious education to persons undergoing profound transformational changes.

EV196 Hawley, John C., ed.

Christian Encounters with the Other. New York, NYU: New York University Press, 1998. xiii, 197 pp. 0814735681 (hdbk), 081473569X (pbk).

Analyses of twelve diverse accounts in literature of Christian conversion, and of counter-conversion from the Renaissance Era to the present.

EV197 Hefner, Robert, ed.

Conversion to Christianity: Historical and Anthropological Perspectives on a Great Transformation. Berkeley, CAU: University of California Press, 1993. x, 326 pp. 0520078357 (hdbk), 0520078365 (pbk).

Eleven scholarly essays by anthropologists, sociologists, historians, and theologians; originally presented at a conference on "Conversion to World Religions: Historical and Ethnographic Interpretations" (Boston University, 14-15 April 1988).

EV198 Henkel, Willi

Die religiöse Situation der Heiden und ihre Bekehrung nach John Henry Newman. Rome, IT: Catholic Book Agency, 1967. 229 pp. Paper. No ISBN.

With Newman's understanding of conversion as point of departure, this dissertation investigates the "natural faith" of the heathen, the process of conversion, and the relationship of Christianity to non-Christian religions.

EV—EVANGELISM AND MISSIONS

EV199 Hill, Monica, ed.

Entering the Kingdom: A Fresh Look at Conversion. Bromley, ENK: MARC Europe; London, ENK: BCGA, 1986. 145 pp. Paper. 0947697349 (M), 0948704055 (B).

Papers on the current Protestant missiological debate on conversion, with emphasis on British and other European perspectives.

EV200 Holte, James Craig

The Conversion Experience in America: A Sourcebook on Religious Conversion Autobiography. New York, NYU: Greenwood, 1992. xiv, 228 pp. 0313266808.

A sourcebook for the study of American religious conversion narratives from Jonathan Edwards to Malcolm X, with critical commentary and bibliography for each of the thirty narratives.

EV201 Kasdorf, Hans

Christian Conversion in Context. Scottdale, PAU: Herald Press, 1980. 217 pp. Paper. 0836119266.

An analysis of conversion from an ethnotheological perspective, with a variety of case studies, showing that different types are consistent with biblical faith in the active working of the Holy Spirit.

EV202 Lamb, Christopher, and M. Darrol Bryant, eds.

Religious Conversion: Contemporary Practices and Controversies. (Issues in Contemporary Religion). London, ENK: Cassell, 1999. viii, 342 pp. 0304338427 (hdbk), 0304338435 (pbk).

This collection of twenty-one essays examines the practices of various world religions and highlights issues that cut across traditions, emerging in distinctive ways in different religions and cultural settings.

EV203 Malony, H. Newton, and Samuel Southard, eds.

Handbook of Religious Conversion. Birmingham, ALU: Religious Education Press, 1992. vi, 314 pp. 0891350861.

Seventeen essays on the theology and phenomenology of conversion in Christianity and other faiths.

EV204 Mattam, Joseph, and Sebastian C. H. Kim, eds.

Mission and Conversion. (FOIM Series, 4). Mumbai, II: St. Pauls, 1996. 234 pp. Paper. 8171092667.

Missiological essays addressing issues pertaining to conversion in the present Indian context; originally presented at the fourth annual meeting of the Fellowship of Indian Missiologists (Pune, 24-27 August 1995).

EV205 Nebreda, Alfonso M.

Kerygma in Crisis? Manila, PH: East Asian Pastoral Institute, 1971. xi, 140 pp. No ISBN.

An analysis, by a Jesuit missionary to Japan, of three stages of adult movement into Christian life: pre-evangelization, evangelization with the goal of personal conversion, and catechesis; also published by Loyola University Press Chicago, IL (1965) in the Loyola Pastoral Series.

EV206 Nietlispach, Freddy

Das Ende des Exportchristentums: Der Einfluss einer Neubewertung der nichtchristlichen Religionen auf die "Bekehrung" in und seit dem II Vatikanum. (European University Studies, XXIII, 94). Bern, SZ: Lang, 1977. 310 pp. Paper. 326103002X.

From the background of the understanding of conversion in the Bible and the primitive church, and also Thomas Ohm's

theology of conversion and salvation, this book examines the meaning of mission and conversion in and since Vatican II.

EV207 Oksanen, Antti

Religious Conversion: A Meta-Analytical Study. (Lund Studies in Psychology of Religion, 2). Lund, SW: Lund University Press; Bromley, ENK: Chartwell-Bratt, 1994. 175 pp. Paper. 9179662668 (SW), 0862383560 (UK).

A history of psychological research on the phenomena of religious conversion.

EV208 Olson, Lynette, ed.

Religious Change, Conversion, and Culture. (Sydney Studies in Society and Culture, 12). Sydney, AT: Sydney Studies, 1996. vii, 273 pp. Paper. 0949405108.

Twelve historical and contemporary case studies of conversion to Christianity, plus an article on the multiple causative factors.

EV209 Peace, Richard

Conversion in the New Testament: Paul and the Twelve. Grand Rapids, MIU: Eerdmans, 1999. xv, 397 pp. Paper. 0802842356.

This study on conversion integrates New Testament studies and practical theological experience of evangelism and discipleship.

EV210 Pokki, Tomi

America's Preacher and His Message: Billy Graham's View of Conversion and Sanctification. Lanham, MDU: University Press of America, 1999. xi, 353 pp. 0761814647.

This study of the theology of one of the most influential evangelical Protestants in the past five decades includes bibliographical references of Graham's works and primary sources, as well as indexes.

EV211 Rambo, Lewis R.

Understanding Religious Conversion. New Haven, CTU: Yale University Press, 1993. xx, 240 pp. 0300052839.

A scholarly analysis of the dynamics of conversion, presenting it as a multifaceted process of change (personal, cultural, social, and religious), with descriptions of how different religions and scholarly disciplines understand it.

EV212 Rzepkowski, Horst, ed.

Mission Präsenz, Verkündigung, Bekehrung? (Studia Instituti Missiologici SVD, 13). St. Augustin, GW: Steyler Verlag, 1974. 168 pp. Paper. No ISBN.

Lectures delivered at a mission study week held in Sankt Augustin in 1973 concerning mission and conversion.

EV213 Singh, Godwin R., ed.

A Call to Discipleship, Baptism and Conversion. Delhi, II: ISPCK for National Council of Churches in India, 1985. 217 pp. No ISBN.

Essays on baptism and conversion with special reference to the context of mission in India; originally presented at an ecumenical conference (Bangalore, India, 1982).

EV214 Smith, Rob

Leading Christians to Christ: Evangelizing the Church. Harrisburg, PAU: Morehouse Publishing, 1990. xvi, 146 pp. Paper. 0819215295.

A look at the meaning of evangelization and conversion, specifically in terms of the membership and environment of the Episcopal church, focusing on the difference between conversion to a church and conversion to Christ and his Gospel.

EV215 Triebel, Johannes
Bekehrung als Ziel der missionarischen Verkündigung: Die Theologie Walter Freytags und das ökumenische Gespräch. (Erlanger Taschenbücher, 35). Erlangen, GW: Ev.-Luth. Mission, 1976. 360 pp. Paper. 3872140663.

A thesis examining the theme of conversion in the ecumenical discussion, especially in the theology of the Protestant missiologist Walter Freytag, emphasizing the linkage of conversion, baptism, and formation of Christian community as the goal of missionary work.

EV216 Wells, David F.
Turning to God: Biblical Conversion in the Modern World. Exeter, ENK: Paternoster Press; Grand Rapids, MIU: Baker Books, 1989. 160 pp. Paper. 0801097002 (hdbk), 0863644969 (pbk).

Papers with interpretation of a consultation on the nature and necessity of Christian conversion held in Hong Kong, January 1988, under the joint sponsorship of the WEF and the LCWE.

EV217 Wenham, Clare, ed.
We Found the Living God: Five People Tell Their Own Stories. London, ENK: InterVarsity, 1974. 78 pp. 0851103790.

Short stories of five students from Hindu, Buddhist, Parsi, and nominal Christian backgrounds who found Christ.

EV218 Witte, John, and Richard C. Martin, eds.
Sharing the Book: Religious Perspectives on the Rights and Wrongs of Proselytism. (Religion and Human Rights Series). Maryknoll, NYU: Orbis Books, 1999. xviii, 423 pp. Paper. 1570752761.

Sixteen religious scholars and leaders offer authoritative statements and analyses of classic and contemporary perspectives on mission activity and conversion in Judaism, Christianity, and Islam.

History

See also HI98, HI148, ME105, EV19-EV20, EV51, EV159, EV305, CH235, AM128-AM129, AM1003, EU152, and EU276.

EV219 Barrett, David B., and James W. Reapsome
Seven Hundred Plans to Evangelize the World: The Rise of a Global Evangelization Movement. (The A.D. 2000 Series). Birmingham, ALU: New Hope, 1988. viii, 123 pp. Paper. 0936625554.

A comprehensive analysis of global evangelism movements with interpretive articles, statistics, chronology, and bibliography.

EV220 Barrett, David B.
Evangelize!: A Historical Survey of the Concept. (A.D. 2000 Series). Birmingham, ALU: New Hope, 1987. 92 pp. Paper. 0936625171.

A detailed examination of the root verb "evangelize," its usage in scripture and in Christian thought, especially in the 20th century.

EV221 Bell, Marion L.
Crusade in the City: Revivalism in Nineteenth-Century Philadelphia. Cranbury, NJU: Associated University Presses, 1977. 299 pp. 0838719295.

A detailed case study of revivalism in the city of Philadelphia from the arrival of Charles G. Finney in 1828 through Dwight L. Moody in 1875.

EV222 Blumhofer, Edith L., and Randall Balmer, eds.
Modern Christian Revivals. Urbana, ILU: University of Illinois Press, 1993. xvi, 232 pp. 0252019903 (hdbk), 0252062957 (pbk).

Twelve scholarly papers originally presented at a conference, "Modern Christian Revivals: A Comparative Perspective" (Wheaton College, 30 March-1 April 1989), covering 18th- to 20th-century revivals in the United States, Canada, Great Britain, and Norway, and 20th-century revivals in China and Latin America.

EV223 Boles, John B.
The Great Revival, 1787-1805: The Origins of the Southern Evangelical Mind. Lexington, KYU: University Press of Kentucky, 1972. xiii, 236 pp. 0813112605.

Beginning in Kentucky at the start of the 19th century and moving across the entire South, the revival was first thought to be the work of God. Some viewed it as ignorant fanaticism. Others thought of it as the Second Coming which prepared the way for the Shaker intrusion in 1805.

EV224 Brereton, Virginia Lieson
From Sin to Salvation: Stories of Women's Conversions, 1800 to the Present. (Midland Books, 636). Bloomington, INU: Indiana University Press, 1991. xvi, 152 pp. 0253312132 (hdbk), 0253206367 (pbk).

A multidisciplinary (literary, sociological, and theological) analysis of the narrative descriptions, by 19th- and 20th-century Protestant women in the United States, of their conversion experiences.

EV225 Cairns, Earle E.
An Endless Land of Splendor: Revivals and Their Leaders from the Great Awakening to the Present. Wheaton, ILU: Tyndale, 1986. 373 pp. 0842307702.

A global history of Protestant revivals from the 18th-century Great Awakening to the present, with analysis of the fruits of revival—missions, social reform, the holiness movement, etc.

EV226 Carwardine, Richard
Transatlantic Revivalism: Popular Evangelicalism in Britain and America, 1790-1865. (Contributions in American History, 75). Westwood, CTU: Greenwood, 1978. xviii, 249 pp. 0313203083.

This book focuses on the mainline British and American evangelical Protestant communities beginning in the United States, and affecting the British Evangelical Society as American evangelists preached in England.

EV227 Coleman, Robert E.
"Nothing to Do but to Save Souls": John Wesley's Charge to His Preachers. Grand Rapids, MIU: Zondervan, 1990. 107 pp. Paper. 0310754801 (hdbk), 031075481X (pbk).

A popular introduction to the theology and strategies of Wesleyan evangelism.

EV228 Colton, Calvin
History and Character of American Revivals of Religion. New York, NYU: AMS Press, 1973. xvi, 294 pp. 0404000185.

Reprint of a summary account of revivals that were taking place in the United States before 1832, when this book was written for British Christians at their request by an American preacher in London.

EV—EVANGELISM AND MISSIONS

EV229 Duewel, Wesley L.
Revival Fire. Grand Rapids, MIU: Zondervan, 1995. 382 pp. Paper. 0310496616.

Short accounts of thirty-five Protestant revivals from Whitefield and Wesley to Korea, East Africa, and Asbury College in 1970, with biblical precedents.

EV230 Fishwick, Marshall W.
Great Awakenings: Popular Religion and Popular Culture. (Haworth Popular Culture). New York, NYU: Harrington Park Press, 1995. xiv, 284 pp. Paper. 1560238585.

A narrative history of religious awakenings as aspects of popular culture from Jonathan Edwards to Billy Graham.

EV231 Garnett, Jane, and Colin Matthew, eds.
Revival and Religion since 1700: Essays for John Walsh. London, ENK: Hambledon Press, 1993. xi, 330 pp. 1852850930.

A *festschrift* honoring a noted historian of the Wesleyan movement, containing fourteen scholarly essays on revivalism (1700-1920) in Great Britain and the United States.

EV232 Green, Michael
Evangelism in the Early Church. Guildford, ENK: Eagle, 1995. xiv, 410 pp. Paper. 0863471579.

A scholarly examination of the history and methods of early church evangelists to approximately A.D. 250, written by an Anglican theologian and evangelist; originally published in 1970.

EV233 Green, Michael
La Evangelización en la Iglesia Primitiva. Buenos Aires, AG: Nueva Creación; Grand Rapids, MIU: Eerdmans, 1997. 490 pp. Paper. 0802809464.

Spanish translation of *Evangelism in the Early Church* (1970).

EV234 Hardman, Keith J.
Seasons of Refreshing: Evangelism and Revivals in America. Grand Rapids, MIU: Baker Books, 1994. 304 pp. Paper. 0801043891.

An illustrated narrative history of revivals in North America from the Puritans to the present.

EV235 Hordern, William
Evangelism, Luther and the Augsburg Confession. Minneapolis, MNU: American Lutheran Church, 1987. 32 pp. No ISBN.

A brief commentary on seven articles of the Augsburg Confession, and on several sayings of Martin Luther which relate to evangelism in our day.

EV236 Johnson, Todd M.
Countdown to 1900: World Evangelization at the End of the Nineteenth Century. (Global Evangelization Movement's AD 2000 Series). Birmingham, ALU: New Hope, 1988. 73 pp. Paper. 0936625694.

Analysis of rhetoric regarding the evangelization of the world by A.D. 1900, with a focus on A. T. Pierson.

EV237 Johnston, Arthur P.
World Evangelism and the Word of God. Minneapolis, MNU: Bethany Fellowship, 1974. 301 pp. Paper. 0871236001.

A prominent evangelical missiologist's history of the theology of evangelism of the IMC, arguing that it and the later merger into the WCC, made a tragic mistake of tying mission to unity.

EV238 Kent, John
Holding the Fort: Studies in Victorian Revivalism. London, ENK: Epworth Press, 1978. 381 pp. No ISBN.

Nineteenth-century revivalism in England is carefully reported and analyzed in its various manifestations—Anglo-Catholic, Wesleyan, through William Booth, D. L. Moody (and into the twentieth century, Billy Graham)—by a British Methodist professor of theology.

EV239 Long, Kathryn Teresa
The Revival of 1857-58: Interpreting an American Religious Awakening. (Religion in America Series). New York, NYU: Oxford University Press, 1998. viii, 256 pp. 0195112938.

The author, Assistant Professor of History at Wheaton College, thoroughly reexamines this ecumenical, urban awakening which has previously been overshadowed by historians' attention to the First and Second Great Awakenings.

EV240 McLoughlin, William Gerald
Revivals, Awakenings, and Reform: An Essay on Religion and Social Change in America, 1607-1977. (Chicago History of American Religion). Chicago, ILU: University of Chicago Press, 1978. xv, 239 pp. 0226560910.

A social-anthropological interpretation of religious revivals as revitalizations of culture.

EV241 Orr, J. Edwin
The Eager Feet: Evangelical Awakenings, 1790-1830. Chicago, ILU: Moody, 1975. viii, 248 pp. 080242287X.

A history of revival movements in England, Scandinavia, America, and Continental Europe, including information on the effect of awakenings on mission fields.

EV242 Orr, J. Edwin
The Fervent Prayer: The Worldwide Impact of the Great Awakening of 1858. Chicago, ILU: Moody, 1974. xx, 236 pp. 0802426158.

This is an indispensable book for those who really want to understand awakenings, especially the worldwide awakening of 1858, which extended through the ministry of D. L. Moody to 1899, and led to the formation of the China Inland Mission and the Salvation Army.

EV243 Orr, J. Edwin
The Flaming Tongue: The Impact of Twentieth Century Revivals. Chicago, ILU: Moody, 1973. vii, 241 pp. 0802428010.

An analysis of the impact of the early 20th-century revival movements on worldwide Christian missions, including a section on the theology and psychology of early Pentecostal missionary work.

EV244 Orr, J. Edwin
The Light of the Nations: Evangelical Renewal and Advance in the Nineteenth Century. Grand Rapids, MIU: Eerdmans; Exeter, ENK: Paternoster Press, 1965. 302 pp. No ISBN.

An historical study of the evangelistic work of the church in many countries during the 19th and early 20th centuries.

EV245 Outler, Albert C.
Evangelism in the Wesleyan Spirit. Nashville, TNU: Tidings, 1971. 109 pp. Paper. No ISBN.

Four popular lectures on the distinctive approach of John Wesley to evangelism and its relevance for Methodist renewal today.

EV246 Packard, William

Evangelism in America: From Tents to TV. New York, NYU: Paragon House, 1988. ix, 275 pp. 0913729736 (hdbk), 1557781796 (pbk).

A history of evangelism from the Reformation to the present, focusing on the celebrated mass evangelists of the 19th and 20th centuries in the United States.

EV247 Rawlyk, George A.

The Canada Fire: Radical Evangelicalism in British North America, 1775-1812. Kingston, PQC: McGill-Queen's University Press, 1994. xix, 244 pp. 0773512217 (hdbk), 0773512772 (pbk).

The history of the Second Great Awakening in northeast Canada, especially Nova Scotia, with biographies of five leading evangelists (Henry Alline, William Black, David George, Freeborn Garrettson, and Harris Harding).

EV248 Robertson, Darrell M.

The Chicago Revival, 1876: Society and Revivalism in a Nineteenth-Century City. (Studies in Evangelicalism, 9). Metuchen, NJU: Scarecrow Press, 1989. xi, 225 pp. 0810821818.

A detailed history of the three-month revival campaign by Dwight L. Moody and Ira D. Sankey in Chicago (USA) in 1876.

EV249 Rudnick, Milton L.

Speaking the Gospel through the Ages: A History of Evangelism. St. Louis, MOU: Concordia Publishing, 1984. 232 pp. 0570042046.

A history of evangelism from the early church to the present, with explanation of representative processes of Christianization employed at various times and plans.

EV250 Scharpff, Paulus

Geschichte der Evangelisation: driehundert Jahre Evangelisation in Deutschland, Grossbritannien und USA. (Herausgegeben durch das Elias-Schrenk-Institut). Giessen, GW: Brunnen-Verlag, 1964. 421 pp. No ISBN.

The now classic detailed history of evangelization from German Pietism to Billy Graham, 1091-1964.

EV251 Scharpff, Paulus

History of Evangelism: Three Hundred Years of Evangelism in Germany, Great Britain, and the United States of America. Translated by Helga Bender Henry. Grand Rapids, MIU: Eerdmans, 1966. xviii, 373 pp. No ISBN.

English translation.

EV252 Stallings, James O.

Telling the Story: Evangelism In Black Churches. Valley Forge, PAU: Judson Press, 1988. 127 pp. Paper. 0817011242.

A concise overview of religious movements in the 18th and 19th centuries highlighting social, political, cultural, and religious influences through which black churches of America emerged as separate and independent entities.

EV253 Stout, Harry S.

The Divine Dramatist: George Whitefield and the Rise of Modern Evangelism. (Library of Religious Biography). Grand Rapids, MIU: Eerdmans, 1991. xxiv, 301 pp. Paper. 0802801544.

An engaging biography of the great 18th-century revivalist, emphasizing his role as herald of the revival-centered voluntary movements that were to become characteristic of religion in the United States and United Kingdom.

EV254 Taylor, Mendell

Exploring Evangelism: History, Methods, Theology. Kansas City, MOU: Beacon Hill Press; Kansas City, MOU: Nazarene Publishing, 1964. 620 pp. No ISBN.

A detailed history of evangelism, with shorter sections on theology and North American methods, by the Dean of the Nazarene Theological Seminary in Kansas City, Missouri.

EV255 Terry, John Mark

Evangelism: A Concise History. Nashville, TNU: Broadman, 1994. v, 210 pp. 0805460446.

A concise history of evangelism from the New Testament church to the revivals in Great Britain and the United States, written with study helps by the Associate Professor of Missions and Evangelism at the Southern Baptist Theological Seminary, Louisville, Kentucky.

EV256 Weisberger, Bernard A.

They Gathered at the River: The Story of the Great Revivalists and their Impact upon Religion in America. Boston, MAU: Little, Brown, 1979. xii, 345 pp. 0374983380.

A balanced recounting of 19th-century revivals and revivalists, from the early camp meeting days through the growth of the revival movement in the cities.

EV257 Whittaker, Colin

Great Revivals: God's Men and Their Message. Basingstoke, ENK: Marshall Pickering, 1990. xix, 197 pp. Paper. 0551020687.

An account of great revivals around the world, beginning with New England in 1734, and ending about 1957 with the Scottish Hebrides, after recounting details of revivals in the British Isles, Latin America, Armenia, Africa, Indonesia, Korea, and China, with a final chapter discussing "What are the conditions for revival?"; originally published in 1984.

EV258 Wimberly, Edward P., and Anne Streaty Wimberly

Liberation and Human Wholeness: The Conversion Experience of Black People in Slavery and Freedom. Nashville, TNU: Abingdon, 1986. 143 pp. Paper. 0687216982.

A psychosocial analysis of the conversion experiences of slaves and ex-slaves in North America, 1750 to 1930, which documents the oneness of psychological, theological, and sociocultural worlds of blacks during this period.

Biography

See also HI655, AM697, AS1178, and EU141.

EV259 Blumhofer, Edith L.

Aimee Semple McPherson: Everybody's Sister. (Library of Religious Biography). Grand Rapids, MIU: Eerdmans, 1993. xiii, 431 pp. 0802837522 (hdbk), 0802801552 (pbk).

A narrative, yet well-researched, biography of Aimee Semple McPherson (1890-1944), the dynamic yet controversial Pentecostal evangelist and founder of The International Church of the Foursquare Gospel.

EV—EVANGELISM AND MISSIONS

EV260 Canclini, Arnoldo
Misión para el siglo XX: Billy Graham, sus amigos, sus métodos, sus resultados. Buenos Aires, AG: Junta Bautista de Publicaciones, 1962. 162 pp. Paper. No ISBN.

An essay on the person of Billy Graham and his evangelistic campaigns.

EV261 Denman, Harry
Prophetic Evangelist: The Living Legacy of Harry Denman. Edited by Earl G. Hunt and Ezra Earl Jones. Nashville, TNU: Upper Room Books, 1993. 392 pp. 0835806863.

A collection of writings of and about the world evangelist and Secretary of the Board of Evangelism of the Methodist Church, 1940-1965.

EV262 Dorsett, Lyle W.
Billy Sunday and the Redemption of Urban America. (Library of Religious Biography). Grand Rapids, MIU: Eerdmans, 1991. xii, 212 pp. Paper. 080280151X.

A popular biography of the US's tent and tabernacle revivalist who preached to over 100 million people between 1908 and 1920.

EV263 Dorsett, Lyle W.
A Passion for Souls: The Life of D. L. Moody. Chicago, ILU: Moody, 1997. 491 pp. 0802451942.

A scholarly biography of the noted 19th-century evangelist (1837-1899), with reflections on his contributions and legacy.

EV264 Drummond, Lewis A.
Spurgeon: Prince of Preachers. Grand Rapids, MIU: Kregel, 1992. 895 pp. 0825424720 (hdbk), 0825424739 (pbk).

The definitive biography of Charles Haddon Spurgeon (1834-92), the English Baptist pastor who was the foremost preacher/evangelist of his day.

EV265 Dudley-Smith, Timothy
John Stott, the Making of a Leader: A Global Ministry. Downers Grove, ILU: InterVarsity, 1999. 513 pp. 0830822070 (Early), 0830822089 (Later).

The influences that shaped John Stott, a shaper of evangelicalism around the world and key framer of the historic Lausanne Covenant (1974); described as "evangelicalism's premier teacher and preacher" by Christianity Today.

EV266 Epstein, Daniel Mark
Sister Aimee: The Life of Aimee Semple McPherson. New York, NYU: Harcourt Brace Jovanovich, 1993. x, 475 pp. 0151826889 (hdbk), 0156000938 (pbk).

Biography of the founder of the International Church of the Four Square Gospel and flamboyant evangelist of the 1915-1941 period in the United States.

EV267 Everett, Betty Steele
Ira Sankey: First Gospel Singer. Fort Washington, PAU: CLC, 1999. 107 pp. Paper. 0875084710.

The biography of a choir director and soloist who helped turn people to Jesus in Egypt, Jerusalem, Rome, Mexico, England, Scotland, and America, where he teamed up with evangelist Dwight L. Moody.

EV268 Frady, Marshall
Billy Graham: A Parable of American Righteousness. Boston, MAU: Little, Brown, 1979. 546 pp. 0316291307.

An intense personal portrait of Billy Graham from his parents' beginnings to shortly after the Nixon era, his mission and political involvements which bear witness to the preeminent position he has held in American popular life that will intrigue and fascinate followers and critics alike.

EV269 Graham, Billy
Just As I Am: The Autobiography of Billy Graham. San Francisco, CAU: HarperSanFrancisco; Grand Rapids, MIU: Zondervan, 1997. xxiii, 760 pp. 0060633875.

An illustrated autobiography and reflection on the work of The Billy Graham Evangelistic Association, by its founder and this generation's premier evangelist.

EV270 Graham, Franklin, and Jeanette W. Lockerbie
Bob Pierce, This One Thing I Do. Waco, TXU: Word Books, 1983. 220 pp. 0849900972.

An evangelical humanitarian whose life principles are used to illuminate evangelism, Bob Pierce was co-founder of Youth for Christ, founder of World Vision, Founder and President of Samaritan's Purse.

EV271 Gundry, Stanley N.
Love Them In: The Proclamation Theology of D. L. Moody. Chicago, ILU: Moody, 1976. 252 pp. 0802450261.

An historical analysis of the thought and theological content of the sermons of Dwight L. Moody, evaluating the relationship between his doctrine and his urban evangelism.

EV272 Hambrick-Stowe, Charles E.
Charles G. Finney and the Spirit of American Evangelicalism. (Library of Religious Biography). Grand Rapids, MIU: Eerdmans, 1996. xvii, 317 pp. Paper. 0802801293.

A major biography of the American evangelist of the mid-19th century who combined passion for personal and social salvation.

EV273 Hardman, Keith J.
Charles Grandison Finney 1792-1875: Revivalist and Reformer. Grand Rapids, MIU: Baker Books, 1990. xvii, 521 pp. 0815623976 (hdbk), 0801043484 (pbk).

A complete biography of a key figure in American religious history for the second quarter of the 19th century, most noted for his combining of evangelism and reform.

EV274 Humbard, Rex
To Tell the World. Englewood Cliffs, NYU: Prentice-Hall, 1975. 211 pp. 0139230947.

The autobiography of Rex Humbard, television evangelist and pastor of Calvary Temple, Akron, Ohio, and founder of the "Cathedral of Tomorrow" (1919-1975).

EV275 Israel, Adrienne M.
Amanda Berry Smith: From Washerwoman to Evangelist. (Studies in Evangelicalism, 16). Lanham, MDU: Scarecrow Press, 1998. xv, 181 pp. 0810835150.

Biography of Amanda Smith (1837-1915) who, as the outstanding African American woman evangelist of the late 19th century, led in the Holiness Movement, the Woman's Christian Temperance Union (WCTU), and the AME Church.

EV276 Lambert, Frank
"Pedlar in Divinity": George Whitefield and the Transatlantic Revivals, 1737-1770. Princeton, NJU: Princeton University Press, 1994. xii, 238 pp. 0691032963.

A fresh interpretation of the evangelistic techniques used by George Whitefield (1714-1770) in the 18th-century revivals in Great Britain and the North American colonies.

EV277 Martin, William

A Prophet with Honor: The Billy Graham Story. New York, NYU: Morrow, 1991. 735 pp. 0688068901.

A scholarly biography of the world evangelist based on archival research and nearly 200 interviews.

EV278 Minnix, Kathleen

Laughter in the Amen Corner: The Life of Evangelist Sam Jones. Athens, GAU: University of Georgia Press, 1993. xiv, 313 pp. 0820315397.

The first scholarly biography of Sam Porter Jones (1847-1906), an itinerant Methodist minister who became the best known southern evangelist of the late 19th century.

EV279 Morris, James

The Preachers. New York, NYU: St. Martin's Press, 1973. x, 418 pp. No ISBN.

Nine biographies of radio and TV evangelists telling where they came from, how they got started, how they attract millions of followers, and how they use the wealth and power they accrue from their success.

EV280 Nutt, Rick L.

The Whole Gospel for the Whole World: Sherwood Eddy and the American Protestant Mission. Macon, GAU: Mercer University Press, 1997. x, 379 pp. 0865545669.

A scholarly biography of Sherwood Eddy (1871-1963), international YMCA and SVM evangelist, missionary to India (1896-1911), and social activist.

EV281 Pollock, John Charles

Billy Graham: Evangelist to the World—An Authorized Biography of the Decisive Years. San Francisco, CAU: Harper & Row, 1979. x,324 pp. 0060666919.

The inside story of Billy Graham's ministries in the 1970s (a sequel to his earlier biography to 1969), including pictures and stories of crusades and family life.

EV282 Pollock, John Charles

Moody. Fearn, ENK: Christian Focus; Grand Rapids, MIU: Baker Books, 1997. 288 pp. Paper. 1857922700 (UK), 0801057868 (US).

Third edition of a readable biography of Dwight Lyman Moody (1837-1899), the outstanding 19th-century evangelist; originally published as *Moody: A Biographical Portrait*, (London, 1966), now reissued on the 160th anniversary of his birth.

EV283 Quebedeaux, Richard

I Found It!: The Story of Bill Bright and Campus Crusade. New York, NYU: Harper & Row, 1979. xiii, 202 pp. 0060667273.

A full scale account (for the general reader) of the life and mission of Bill Bright and his organization, Campus Crusade for Christ; with illustrations, pictures, and a bibliography.

EV284 Roberts, Oral

The Call: An Autobiography. London, ENK: Hodder & Stoughton, 1972. 216 pp. 0340163844.

An easily read autobiography of Oral Roberts and account of his ministry to both Christians and non-Christians through evangelism and healing.

EV285 Roberts, Oral

Expect a Miracle: My Life and Ministry. Nashville, TNU: Nelson, 1995. ix, 388 pp. 0785277528 (hdbk), 0785274650 (pbk).

The noted North American evangelist tells his own story of forty-eight years of television, healing, and educational ministry.

EV286 Rosell, Garth M., and Richard A. G. Dupuis, eds.

The Memoirs of Charles G. Finney: The Complete Restored Text. Grand Rapids, MIU: Zondervan, 1989. xivii, 736 pp. 0310459206.

A critical scholarly edition of the autobiography of the US's premier evangelist of the 19th century.

EV287 Smith, Amanda

An Autobiography: Amanda Smith's Own Story. Chicago, ILU: Afro-Am Press, 1969. 506 pp. 0841100802.

Reprint of the 1893 biography of the remarkable African American evangelist.

EV288 Stanley, Susie Cunningham

Feminist Pillar of Fire: The Life of Alma White. Cleveland, OHU: Pilgrim Press, 1993. xiv, 162 pp. Paper. 0829809503.

The biography of Alma White (1862-1946), a controversial fundamentalist yet feminist who pioneered in radio evangelism and founded her own pentecostal holiness church, the Pillar of Fire.

EV289 Swaggart, Jimmy, and Robert Paul Lamb

To Cross a River. Baton Rouge, LAU: Jimmy Swaggart Ministries, 1984. x, 244 pp. Paper. 0882702211.

A popular personal account by the well-known TV evangelist.

EV290 Warner, Wayne E.

The Woman Evangelist: The Life and Times of Charismatic Evangelist Maria B. Woodworth-Etter. (Studies in Evangelicalism, 8). Metuchen, NJU: Scarecrow Press, 1986. xii, 340 pp. 0810819120.

A candid definitive biography of Maria B. Woodworth-Etter (1844-1924), who broke the male domination of the Christian pulpit and made an important contribution not only to the Pentecostal Movement, but also to the Christian church worldwide; with eight interesting appendices, copious notes, and an extensive bibliography.

EV291 Williams, Herbert Lee

D. James Kennedy: The Man and His Ministry. Nashville, TNU: Nelson, 1990. 347 pp. 0840774753.

The biography of a man who has committed his life to proclaiming the gospel through the ministry of Coral Ridge Presbyterian Church, Evangelism Explosion International, and a thriving international television and radio ministry.

Church Growth: General

See also HI642, TH335, ME58, ME249, SO532, ED162-ED163, EV402, CH39, CH52, CH93, CH260, CH283, CH518, AF643, AF1319, AM170-AM171, AM181, AM895, AM968, AM1066, AM1354, AS459, AS742, AS957, AS963, AS967, AS1003, AS1036, AS1048-AS1050, AS1109, and EU145.

EV292 Adams, James R.

So You Can't Stand Evangelism?: A Thinking Person's Guide to Church Growth. Cambridge, MAU: Cowley Publications, 1994. xii, 193 pp. Paper. 1561010960.

The rector of St. Mark's Episcopal Church on Capital Hill in Washington, D.C., makes a case for a new evangelism relevant in our secular culture.

EV293 Anderson, Andy, and Linda Lawson
Effective Methods of Church Growth: Growing the Church by Growing the Sunday School. Nashville, TNU: Broadman, 1985. 120 pp. Paper. 080543237X.

A clear statement of the practices of Southern Baptist in achieving a spiral of congregational growth through an expanding Sunday School for all ages.

EV294 Barna, George
Marketing the Church: What They Never Taught You about Church Growth. Colorado Springs, COU: NavPress, 1988. 172 pp. Paper. 0891092501.

A primer for pastors and lay leaders desiring a new approach to building an effective church, applying to church ministry the principles and methods of marketing.

EV295 Barna, George
User Friendly Churches: What Christians Need to Know about the Churches People Love to Go To. Ventura, CAU: Regal Books, 1991. 191 pp. Paper. 0830714782.

Insights into principles behind successful, growing Protestant churches in North America today; by the founder and President of Barna Research Group.

EV296 Bartel, Floyd G., and Richard Showalter
A New Look at Church Growth. Newton, KSU: Faith and Life Press; Scottdale, PAU: Mennonite Publishing House, 1979. viii, 143 pp. Paper. 0873030273.

Helps for Mennonite local congregations desiring to rediscover the Anabaptist vision in which discipleship relates directly to the evangelistic mission of Jesus Christ.

EV297 Bontrager, G. Edwin, and Nathan D. Showalter
It Can Happen Today!: Principles of Church Growth from the Book of Acts. Scottdale, PAU: Herald Press, 1986. 96 pp. Paper. 0836134192.

A presentation in thirteen brief chapters of church growth dynamics in the book of Acts and guidelines on how each one can apply to the church today; with *Teacher's Manual* [335 pp., 0836112865].

EV298 Bradshaw, Malcolm R.
Church Growth through Evangelism-in-Depth. South Pasadena, CAU: William Carey Library, 1969. xvi, 127 pp. Paper. No ISBN.

The story of how Evangelism-in-Depth began and how it grew: the story of a man, a movement, an organization and outworkings in many lands, and how it affects church growth.

EV299 Bunkowske, Eugene W., and Gene K. Holtorf, eds.
Church Growth: A Biblical Perspective. Fullerton, CAU: Great Commission Resource Library/R. C. Law Publishers, 1990. 146 pp. Paper. 093992580X.

Papers, including lectures, sermons, and discussions, from Concordia Theological Seminary's Sixth Annual Missions and Communication Congress (Fort Wayne, Indiana, 10-12 Oct. 1990).

EV300 Burt, Robert L., ed.
Good News in Growing Churches. New York, NYU: Pilgrim Press, 1990. viii, 343 pp. Paper. 0829808728.

The stories of seventeen North American congregations of the United Church of Christ (African American, Anglo, Filipino, and Hispanic) that are growing in numbers, program, outreach, and devotion.

EV301 Cañizares, Antonio
La Evangelización Hoy. (Creer y comprender). Madrid, SP: Ediciones Marova, 1977. 155 pp. Paper. 8426903541.

A study situated in the missiological current, maintaining that all the church should be in a state of mission.

EV302 Cho, Yong-gi, and R. Whitney Manzano
More than Numbers. Waco, TXU: Word Books, 1984. 153 pp. 0849903661.

A guide to church growth, its motives and practices, by the pastor of the largest church in the world, the Yoido Full Gospel Church of Seoul, Korea.

EV303 Clapp, Steve
Plain Talk about Church Growth. Elgin, ILU: Brethren Press, 1989. 181 pp. Paper. 0871787089.

A revised edition of a study book for North American Protestants with practical suggestions for local churches.

EV304 Conn, Harvie M., ed.
Theological Perspectives on Church Growth. Nutley, NJU: Presbyterian & Reformed Publishing, 1977. vii, 154 pp. No ISBN.

Seven theological essays focusing on church growth in mission contexts.

EV305 Cook, Harold R.
Historic Patterns of Church Growth: A Study of Five Churches. Chicago, ILU: Moody, 1971. 128 pp. Paper. No ISBN.

Case studies in church history of rapid church growth (the Armenian Church, Celtic Church of Ireland, Hawaiian Church, Karen Church of Burma, and the Batak Church of Sumatra).

EV306 Coomes, David
The Flame Still Spreads. Guildford, ENK: Lutterworth Press, 1974. 127 pp. 0718819977.

Stories of contemporary church revival and growth in six continents.

EV307 Crawford, Dan R.
Church Growth Words from the Risen Lord. Nashville, TNU: Broadman, 1990. 176 pp. 0805462597.

In this work an Assistant Professor of Evangelism/Missions and Director of Evangelism and Missions Practica at Southwestern Baptist Theological Seminary (Fort Worth, Texas) studies New Testament passages centering on the resurrected Christ for sound wisdom for developing and maintaining vigorous church growth.

EV308 Dunagin, Richard L., and Lyle E. Schaller
Beyond These Walls: Building the Church in a Built-Out Neighborhood. (Innovators in Ministry Series). Nashville, TNU: Abingdon, 1999. 171 pp. Paper. 0687085969.

The author, pastor of Lake Highlands United Methodist Church in Dallas, shares by personal experience how God's Spirit can blow through churches in long established, stable communities, through bold and innovative programs and ministries that reinvigorate the spiritual life of the congregation, and draw in others from the community.

EV309 Easum, William M.
The Church Growth Handbook. Nashville, TNU: Abingdon, 1990. 176 pp. 0687081610.

A handbook by a United Methodist pastor in San Antonio, Texas, who outlines twenty church growth principles and provides questionnaires to help congregations analyze their strengths and weaknesses and develop a growth plan.

EV310 Elliot, Ralph H.

Church Growth That Counts. Valley Forge, PAU: Judson Press, 1982. 126 pp. Paper. 0817009434.

A critical evaluation of the church growth movement, its theological assumptions and strategies, by the senior pastor of North Shore Baptist Church, Chicago, Illinois.

EV311 Engen, Charles Edward van

The Growth of the True Church: An Analysis of the Ecclesiology of Church Growth Theory. (Amsterdam Studies in Theology, 3; Proefschrift Theol. Fac. Vrije Universiteit Amsterdam). Amsterdam, NE: Rodopi, 1981. 545 pp. Paper. No ISBN.

A doctoral dissertation, written under Prof. Joh. Verkuyl, by a former student and now Professor at Fuller Theological Seminary, on the ecclesiology and missiology of Donald McGavran and his school of church growth.

EV312 Exman, Gary W.

Get Ready ... Get Set ... Grow!: Church Growth for Town and Country Congregations. Lima, OHU: CSS Publishing, 1987. 148 pp. Paper. 089536865X.

A practical application of church growth principles to small town and rural churches in the United States.

EV313 Galloway, Dale E.

20/20 Vision: How to Create a Successful Church. Portland, ORU: Scott Publishing, 1997. 160 pp. 1885605005.

Twenty-one principles for growing local churches, with practical helps based on the author's ministry at New Hope Community Church in Portland, Oregon; originally published in 1993.

EV314 Galloway, Dale E.

Visión 20/20: Cómo crear una iglesia próspera con pastores laicos y grupos de células. Miami, FLU: Editorial Unilit, 1996. 187 pp. Paper. 1560639199.

Spanish translation.

EV315 George, Carl F., and Warren Bird

How to Break Growth Barriers: Capturing Overlooked Opportunities for Church Growth. Grand Rapids, MIU: Baker Books, 1993. 232 pp. Paper. 0801038537.

A practical study book for leaders (clergy and lay) who want their local churches to experience greater growth, yet have been frustrated by declining or static church membership; by a Professor of Church Growth at Fuller Seminary.

EV316 Gerber, Vergil

God's Way to Keep a Church Going & Growing. South Pasadena, CAU: William Carey Library, 1973. 95 pp. Paper. 0830702946.

A practical manual developed by the Fuller Institute for Church Growth as a textbook for evangelism/church growth workshops, with tools for evaluation and planning of local church evangelistic efforts.

EV317 Getz, Gene A., and Joe Wall

Effective Church Growth Strategies. (Swindoll Leadership Library). Nashville, TNU: Word Publishing, 2000. xv, 182 pp. 0849913632.

The author offers a fresh, new understanding of what constitutes a healthy, growing church, as opposed to the numbers game.

EV318 Gibbs, Eddie

I Believe in Church Growth. Grand Rapids, MIU: Eerdmans, 1982. 460 pp. Paper. 0802819214 (E).

A detailed introduction to church growth theory for the British churches, with numerous practical guidelines for implementation; also published by in 1981 by Hodder and Stoughton (0340263520).

EV319 Green, Hollis L.

Why Churches Die: A Guide to Basic Evangelism and Church Growth. Minneapolis, MNU: Bethany Fellowship, 1972. 219 pp. Paper. 0871236427.

An analysis giving thirty-five reasons why churches die, based on New Testament principles, with suggested remedial actions.

EV320 Guinness, Os

Dining with the Devil: The Megachurch Movement Flirts with Modernity. Grand Rapids, MIU: Baker Books, 1993. 113 pp. Paper. 0801038553.

A probing assessment of the megachurch movement in the United States and its inclination to compromise with modernity.

EV321 Guyton, J. Terry

Dynamics of Pentecostal Church Growth. (Pentecostal Church Growth Series). Cleveland, TNU: Pathway Press, 1989. 135 pp. Paper. 087148269X.

A popular presentation of biblical, theological, and ecclesiological factors in surging church growth among Pentecostals.

EV322 Hadaway, C. Kirk

Church Growth Principles: Separating Fact from Fiction. Nashville, TNU: Broadman, 1991. 203 pp. Paper. 0805460144.

An analysis of the results of efforts to test a wide variety of church growth hypotheses to show which principles are more important than others.

EV323 Hale, J. Russell

The Unchurched: Who They Are and Why They Stay Away. San Francisco, CAU: Harper & Row, 1980. xiv, 206 pp. 0060635606.

Case studies of some of the most unchurched counties in America, with data drawn from in-depth interviews.

EV324 Hedlund, Roger E., ed.

Church Growth in the Third World. Bombay, II: Gospel Literature Service, 1977. xx, 366 pp. Paper. No ISBN.

Seventeen short essays applying church growth principles to rural and urban ministries in Africa, Asia, and Latin America.

EV325 Hedlund, Roger E.

Building the Church. Madras, II: Evangelical Literature Service, 1982. vi, 142 pp. Paper. No ISBN.

An overview giving the imperative of church planting in India, from biblical premise and theological clarifications, to the practical situations of building new churches.

EV326 Hemphill, Ken

The Antioch Effect: 8 Characteristics of Highly Effective Churches. Nashville, TNU: Broadman, 1994. x, 228 pp. 0805430164.

Eight characteristics of growing churches by the Director of the Center for Church Growth of the (Southern) Baptist Home Mission Board.

EV327 Hemphill, Ken
The Bonsai Theory of Church Growth. Nashville, TNU: Broadman, 1991. 128 pp. Paper. 0805460454.

A popular application of church growth theory for small churches.

EV328 Hoge, Dean R., and David A. Roozen, eds.
Understanding Church Growth and Decline, 1950-1978. New York, NYU: Pilgrim Press, 1979. 398 pp. Paper. 0829803580.

A detailed analysis of national, contextual, denominational, and local factors affecting trends in membership and participation by mainline Protestants in the United States; with *Technical Appendix*, 116 pp.

EV329 Hunter, George G.
Church for the Unchurched. Nashville, TNU: Abingdon, 1996. 188 pp. Paper. 0687277329.

Models for North American local churches desiring to be "apostolic" like the early church in reaching the secular unchurched, based on field research among nine such local congregations.

EV330 Hunter, George G.
To Spread the Power: Church Growth in the Wesleyan Spirit. Nashville, TNU: Abingdon, 1987. 222 pp. Paper. 0687422590.

An analysis of the relation between contemporary church growth principles and those practiced by John Wesley, organized around six "mega-strategies" of church growth.

EV331 Hunter, Kent R., and David L. Bahn
Confessions of a Church Growth Enthusiast. Lima, OHU: Fairway Press, 1997. 277 pp. Paper. 0912961961.

An evangelical confessional Lutheran takes a hard look at the church growth movement.

EV332 Hunter, Kent R.
Foundations for Church Growth: Biblical Basics for the Local Church. Corunna, INU: Church Growth Center, 1994. 266 pp. Paper. 0912961996.

Basic principles of church growth by the President of the Church Growth Center in Indiana, senior editor of *Global Church Growth*, and prominent trainer in the field; originally published in 1983.

EV333 Jørgensen, Knud, Finn Ellerbek-Petersen, and Flemming Kramp
Evangelisation og kirkevækst: Replikker af Finn Ellerbek-Petersen, Flemming Kramp og Egon Nielsen. (Nyt synspunkt, 1). Hellerup, DK: DMS-Forlag, 1976. 53 pp. Paper. 8774310534.

Knud Jørgensen, a Danish Lutheran missionary in Addis Ababa, presents the problem of evangelism and church growth, edited with three articles by Carl Chr. Jessen, Karsten Nissen, and Knud Ochsner, responding to his analysis.

EV334 Kasdorf, Hans
Gemeindewachstum als missionarisches Ziel: Ein Konzept für Gemeinde- und Missionsarbeit. (TELOS-Skript). Bad Liebenzell, GW: Verlag der Liebenzeller Mission, 1976. 283 pp. 3880020345.

A missiologist examines the church growth movement—important figures, its history, theology, biblical interpretation of the Great Commission, and its relationship to the church, theology and to mission.

EV335 Kelley, Dean M.
Why Conservative Churches Are Growing: A Study in Sociology of Religion. New York, NYU: Harper & Row, 1977. xxi, 184 pp. Paper. 0060643013.

An influential sociological analysis of why mainline Protestantism declined in the 1960s and 1970s, with suggestive insights for church renewal.

EV336 Kraus, C. Norman, ed.
Missions, Evangelism, and Church Growth. Scottdale, . PAU: Herald Press, 1980. 165 pp. Paper. 0836119258.

Seven introductory essays for pastors and laypersons, giving general insights on mission theology and selective principles useful for church growth.

EV337 Lausanne Committee for World Evangelization
The Pasadena Consultation on the Homogeneous Unit Principle. (Lausanne Occasional Papers, 1). Wheaton, ILU: LCWE, 1978. 11 pp. Paper. No ISBN.

Papers from the Lausanne Theology and Education Group Consultation (Pasadena, California, June 1977) discussing points of agreement and tension around the "homogenous unit principle."

EV338 Logan, Robert E.
Beyond Church Growth: Action Plans for Developing a Dynamic Church. Grand Rapids, MIU: Revell, 1989. 220 pp. Paper. 0800753321.

A basic primer on ten principles for church growth, with local church action plans related to each principle.

EV339 MacArthur, John F.
Ashamed of the Gospel: When the Church Becomes Like the World. Wheaton, ILU: Crossway Books, 1993. 254 pp. 0891077294 (US), 1856840808 (UK).

A critique of evangelical "pragmatism," including the church growth movement, and call for faithful Christian apologetics by the pastor-teacher of Grace Community Church in Sun Valley, California.

EV340 Maier, Gerhard
Gemeindeaufbau als Gemeindewachstum: Eine praktisch-theologische Untersuchung zur Geschichte, Theologie und Praxis der "church growth" Bewegung. (Erlanger Monographien aus Mission und Ökumene, 22). Erlangen, GW: Ev.-Luth. Mission, 1994. 320 pp. Paper. 3872143220.

A scholarly study of the history, theology, and practice of the church growth movement; submitted as a doctoral dissertation at the University of Heidelberg in 1992.

EV341 Malphurs, Aubrey
Advanced Strategic Planning: A New Model for Church and Ministry Leaders. Grand Rapids, MIU: Baker Books, 1999. 288 pp. Paper. 0801090687.

A nine step strategic model for articulating the vision and carrying out the mission of the church.

EV342 Mathison, John Ed
Tried & True: Eleven Principles of Church Growth from Frazer Memorial United Methodist Church. Nashville, TNU: Discipleship Resources, 1992. viii, 116 pp. Paper. 0881771171.

The senior pastor of one of the fastest growing United Methodist churches in Montgomery, Alabama, relates their experience to eleven church growth principles.

EV—EVANGELISM AND MISSIONS

EV343 May, Flavius Joseph

The Book of Acts and Church Growth: Growth through the Power of God's Holy Spirit. (Pentecostal Church Growth Series). Cleveland, TNU: Pathway Press, 1990. 182 pp. Paper. 0871481138.

A popular presentation of the basic reasons for the explosive growth of the early church as recorded in the Book of Acts.

EV344 McGavran, Donald Anderson, and C. Peter Wagner, eds.

Understanding Church Growth. Grand Rapids, MIU: Eerdmans, 1990. xviii, 310 pp. Paper. 0802804632.

The third edition of the *magnum opus* of the father of the church growth movement with numerous case study illustrations from both Third and First World contexts, and an expanded annotated reading list; originally published in 1970.

EV345 McGavran, Donald Anderson, and George G. Hunter

Church Growth: Strategies That Work. (Creative Leadership Series). Nashville, TNU: Abingdon, 1980. 123 pp. Paper. 0687081602.

A "how-to" book applying church growth principles to the local church, with a focus on the motivation and training of the laity.

EV346 McGavran, Donald Anderson

Effective Evangelism: A Theological Mandate. Phillipsburg, NJU: Presbyterian & Reformed Publishing, 1988. xi, 162 pp. Paper. 0875522890.

A history of the "church growth" tradition with examination of the strengths and weaknesses of theological institutions in the area of evangelism, calling for a re-prioritizing of theological curricula.

EV347 McGavran, Donald Anderson

Ethnic Realities and the Church: Lesson from India. South Pasadena, CAU: William Carey Library, 1979. 262 pp. 0878081682.

A longer analysis on the factor of class and clan loyalties as they affect church growth strategies.

EV348 McIntosh, Gary, ed.

One Size Doesn't Fit All: Bringing Out the Best in Any Size Church. Grand Rapids, MIU: Revell, 1999. 174 pp. Paper. 0800756991.

The author explores how churches grow, and how church size determines effective strategy for ministry.

EV349 McQuilkin, J. Robertson

How Biblical Is the Church Growth Movement? Chicago, ILU: Moody, 1973. ix, 99 pp. 0802452191.

A series of lectures delivered by the author at Fuller Theological Seminary in 1973 intended as a critique of the church growth movement, examining the biblical validity of its basic presuppositions.

EV350 Mead, Loren B.

More Than Numbers: The Ways Churches Grow. Washington, DCU: Alban Institute, 1993. vii, 113 pp. Paper. 1566991099.

A primer on four types of church growth (numerical, maturational, organic, and incarnational); by an Episcopal priest with many years in parish ministry, who is the founder and President of The Alban Institute.

EV351 Miles, Delos

Church Growth: A Mighty River. Nashville, TNU: Broadman, 1981. 167 pp. Paper. 0805462279.

An overview of the church growth movement, from its beginnings to the present; by the Head of Evangelism at Midwestern Baptist Theological Seminary in Kansas City.

EV352 Miller, Herb

How to Build a Magnetic Church. (Creative Leadership Series). Nashville, TNU: Abingdon, 1987. 127 pp. Paper. 0687177626.

A study for both pastors and laypersons of the contemporary American church and an exposition of "nine essential factors" needed to facilitate church growth.

EV353 Moore, Waylon B.

Multiplicación de discípulos: Un método para el crecimiento de la iglesia. Translated by Rafael Enrique Urdaneta. El Paso, TXU: Casa Bautista de Publicaciones, 1981. 112 pp. Paper. 0311118178.

Spanish translation.

EV354 Morikawa, Jitsuo

Biblical Dimensions of Church Growth. Valley Forge, PAU: Judson Press, 1979. 95 pp. Paper. 081700839X.

A series of nine sermons which explore the biblical view of church growth, by the noted theologian of the American Baptist Churches in the United States.

EV355 Peters, George W.

A Theology of Church Growth. (Contemporary Evangelical Perspectives). Grand Rapids, MIU: Zondervan, 1981. 283 pp. Paper. 0310431018.

A systematic presentation of church growth principles with strong biblical foundations.

EV356 Pickett, Jarrell Waskom

The Dynamics of Church Growth. New York, NYU: Abingdon; Lucknow, II: Lucknow Publishing House, 1963. 124 pp. No ISBN.

Insights on church growth in principle and practice by the Methodist bishop to India who pioneered in church growth studies there; originally presented as the first Church Growth Series lectures at Northwest Christian College in 1961.

EV357 Pinola, Sakari

Church Growth: Principles and Praxis of Donald A. McGavran's Missiology. Åbo, FI: Åbo Akademi University Press, 1995. 311 pp. Paper. 952961652X.

A doctoral dissertation analyzing the missiological principles of Donald A. McGavran (1897-1990), especially his church growth theory.

EV358 Pinola, Sakari

Jumala antaa kasvun: kirkon kasvun missiologia. Helsinki, FI: Kirjaneliö, 1984. 137 pp. Paper. 9516006531.

An analysis of the missiological principles of Donald A. McGavran and the church growth movement.

EV359 Rainer, Thom S.

Eating the Elephant: Bite-Sized Steps to Achieve Long-Term Growth in Your Church. Nashville, TNU: Broadman, 1994. xii, 209 pp. 080546140X.

Out of his experience of helping a "traditional" and nine other churches to grow, the founding dean of the Billy Graham School of Missions at Southern Baptist Theological Seminary presents practical helps for sustained church growth.

EV—EVANGELISM AND MISSIONS

EV360 Roberts, W. Dayton
Revolution in Evangelism: The Story of Evangelism-in-Depth in Latin America. Chicago, ILU: Moody, 1967. 127 pp. Paper. No ISBN.

Beginning with the work of Kenneth Strachan, his first team and early experiments, the story follows the development of this plan of evangelism and gives an assessment.

EV361 Robinson, Martin
A World Apart: Creating a Church for the Unchurched. Tunbridge Wells, ENK: Monarch Publications; Bedford, ENK: BCGA, 1992. 222 pp. Paper. 1854241745 (M), 0948704373 (B).

The story of Willow Creek Community Church of South Barrington, Illinois, one of the fastest growing Protestant churches in North America, with suggested applications for Great Britain of its creative appeal for the unchurched.

EV362 Roozen, David A., and C. Kirk Hadaway, eds.
Church and Denominational Growth. Nashville, TNU: Abingdon, 1993. 392 pp. Paper. 0687159040.

Documented and reliable answers which penetrate many slogans and claims about growing or declining denominations and churches.

EV363 Schaller, Lyle E.
44 Steps Up Off the Plateau. Nashville, TNU: Abingdon, 1993. 144 pp. Paper. 0687132916.

The noted author and church growth consultant emphasizes quality, responsiveness, and productivity, and key steps to growth for a local church that has plateaued in membership and attendance.

EV364 Schaller, Lyle E.
Growing Plans. Nashville, TNU: Abingdon, 1983. 176 pp. Paper. 0687159628.

Church growth principles applied by size of congregation (small, medium, large) in the United States.

EV365 Schuller, Robert H.
Your Church Has Real Possibilities! Glendale, CAU: Regal Books, 1974. 180 pp. Paper. 0830703160.

Principles and strategies for church growth by the pastor of the Crystal Cathedral—Garden Grove Community Church in California.

EV366 Shenk, Wilbert R., ed.
The Challenge of Church Growth: A Symposium. (Inst. of Mennonite Studies, Missionary Study Series, 1). Scottdale, PAU: Herald Press, 1973. 109 pp. Paper. 0836112008.

Five papers prepared for use in the Mennonite Missionary Study Fellowship sessions of 1973, discussing various approaches and raising questions concerning the nature and mission of the church and church growth.

EV367 Shenk, Wilbert R., ed.
Exploring Church Growth. Grand Rapids, MIU: Eerdmans, 1983. viii, 312 pp. Paper. 0802819621.

Papers written by leading evangelical missiologists dealing with cases, methodological, and theological issues emerging out of the church growth movement.

EV368 Smith, Ebbie C.
Balanced Church Growth. Nashville, TNU: Broadman, 1984. 178 pp. Paper. 0805462465.

A study book on church growth by the Associate Professor of Christian Ethics and Missions at Southwestern Baptist Theological Seminary in the United States.

EV369 Smith, Richard K.
Making Your Church Grow: The Role of Leadership in Church Growth. Lima, OHU: Fairway Press, 1992. 137 pp. Paper. 1556734468.

A practical analysis of the key function of leadership in church growth, with a biblical theology of leadership.

EV370 Sullivan, Bill M.
Ten Steps to Breaking the 200 Barrier: A Church Growth Strategy. Kansas City, MOU: Beacon Hill Press, 1988. 99 pp. Paper. 083411223X.

Practical helps for congregations desiring to overcome the invisible barrier that North American churches often face in attempting to grow from 150 to 250 persons, including leadership, motivation, planning, and implementation; the sequel to *Toward a Theology of People Power* (1998) as a second volume on the People Power Movement in the Philippines.

EV371 Taylor, Richard S.
Dimensions of Church Growth: The Upward, Downward, Inward Factors. Grand Rapids, MIU: Asbury Press, 1989. xv, 204 pp. Paper. 0310754119.

A textbook for pastors on the theological outreach and nurturing dimensions of church growth, by the Professor Emeritus of Theology and Missions at Nazarene Theological Seminary.

EV372 Tippett, Alan Richard, ed.
God, Man and Church Growth: A Festschrift in Honor of Donald Anderson McGavran. Grand Rapids, MIU: Eerdmans, 1973. xii, 447 pp. 0802834248.

A *festschrift* in honor of Donald Anderson McGavran, the father of the church growth movement, on his 75th birthday; with twenty-nine essays by an international panel of his former students and colleagues.

EV373 Tippett, Alan Richard
Church Growth and the Word of God: The Biblical Basis of the Church Growth Viewpoint. Grand Rapids, MIU: Eerdmans, 1970. 82 pp. Paper. No ISBN.

An outline of the biblical foundations of church growth to show that the church established by Jesus Christ must be a growing church.

EV374 Towns, Elmer L., C. Peter Wagner, and Thom S. Rainer, eds.
The Everychurch Guide to Growth: How Any Plateaued Church Can Grow. Nashville, TNU: Broadman, 1998. x, 205 pp. Paper. 080540192X.

Helps for overcoming barriers to growth in small, middle-sized, and large churches, by three seasoned professors who are also experienced evangelical pastors.

EV375 Vaughan, John N.
The Large Church: A Twentieth-Century Expression of the First-Century Church. Grand Rapids, MIU: Baker Books, 1985. 144 pp. Paper. 0801092981.

An analysis of key issues related to the large church and its major strategy for extensive growth—the use of satellite groups.

EV376 Vaughan, John N.
Megachurches and America's Cities: How Churches Grow. Grand Rapids, MIU: Baker Books, 1993. 143 pp. Paper. 0801093155.

Nineteen indicators of growing urban ministries of large churches in the United States that reach out to the community with high impact concern.

EV377 Vaughan, John N.
The World's Twenty Largest Churches. Grand Rapids, MIU: Baker Books, 1984. 293 pp. Paper. 0801092973.

The aim of this book is to describe the twenty largest churches of the world, concentrating on their principles of church growth, their rates of growth, and their use of small groups to help build strong substructures, which encourage further growth.

EV378 Wagner, C. Peter, ed.
Church Growth: State of the Art. Wheaton, ILU: Tyndale, 1986. 318 pp. Paper. 0842302875.

A resource for pastors containing twenty-two articles by fifteen American church growth specialists discussing church growth principles and strategies.

EV379 Wagner, C. Peter
Church Growth and the Whole Gospel: A Biblical Mandate. Eugene, ORU: Wipf & Stock, 1998. xvi, 208 pp. Paper. 1579102018.

Theological reflections on the first twenty-five years of the church growth movement, including questions concerning the homogeneous unit principle, and the relation of social justice and church growth concerns; originally published in 1981 (San Francisco, CAU: Harper & Row).

EV380 Wagner, C. Peter
Leading Your Church to Growth: The Secret of Pastor/People Partnership in Dynamic Church Growth. Ventura, CAU: Regal Books, 1984. 224 pp. Paper. 0830709223.

An analysis of the variables that make church growth happen, focusing on the key role of the pastor as enabler.

EV381 Wagner, C. Peter
Strategies for Church Growth: Tools for Effective Mission and Evangelism. Ventura, CAU: Regal Books, 1987. 213 pp. 0830712453.

A practical guide to church growth, giving in concise form the research developed by the church growth movement, the LCWE, and the U.S. Center for World Mission on strategy, outreach, targeting, and related principles of evangelism and missions.

EV382 Wagner, C. Peter
Your Church Can Grow: Seven Vital Signs of a Healthy Church. Ventura, CAU: Regal Books, 1976. 176 pp. Paper. 0830704140.
Seven vital signs of a healthy local church.

EV383 Warren, Rick
The Purpose Driven Church: Growth without Compromising Your Message and Mission. Grand Rapids, MIU: Zondervan, 1995. 399 pp. 0310201063.

A model of church life that begins with defining the purpose, and includes ways of reaching out to people and building up the congregation; based in part on the experience of Saddleback Valley Community Church in California, a fast-growing Baptist Church.

EV384 Webster, Douglas D.
Selling Jesus: What's Wrong with Marketing the Church. Downers Grove, ILU: InterVarsity, 1992. 165 pp. Paper. 0830813179.

A hard-hitting critique of those who urge churches to model their mission on Madison Avenue selling methods, suggesting faithful and powerful alternatives to marketing the church.

EV385 Wedderspoon, Alexander, ed.
Grow or Die: Essays on Church Growth to Mark the 900th Anniversary of Winchester Cathedral. London, ENK: SPCK, 1981. ix, 141 pp. Paper. 0281037892.

Seven essays by prominent leaders of the Church of England, seeing hope for growth in a church that has been in steady decline for decades.

EV386 Weld, Wayne, and Donald Anderson McGavran
Principles of Church Growth. South Pasadena, CAU: William Carey Library, 1974. xii, 432 pp. 0878087206.

The English edition of a basic text on church growth for use in Latin America, especially in TEE.

EV387 Werning, Waldo J.
Vision and Strategy for Church Growth. Grand Rapids, MIU: Baker Books, 1984. 126 pp. Paper. 0801096588.

A practical guide for US congregations desiring to apply church growth principles, including forms and questionaires for congregational self-analysis.

EV388 Wetzel, Klaus
Wo die Kirchen wachsen: Der geistliche Aufbruch in der Zwei-Drittel-Welt und die Folgen für das Christentum. (TVG: Orientierung). Wuppertal, GW: R. Brockhaus Verlag, 1998. 117 pp. Paper. 3417290791.

A well-documented and scholarly study (with illustrative graphs) of the explosion of church growth in Third World countries, giving careful attention to the ways Christianity is transformed in its encounter with, and application within different cultures; with an excellent contemporary bibliography on church growth in the later 20th century.

EV389 Yamamori, Tetsunao, and E. LeRoy Lawson
Introducing Church Growth: A Textbook in Missions. Cincinnati, OHU: New Life Publications, 1975. 255 pp. 0872390004.

A workbook for individuals and study groups, with selected materials applying church growth principles to local US congregations.

EV390 Zunkel, C. Wayne
Church Growth Under Fire. Scottdale, PAU: Herald Press, 1987. 250 pp. Paper. 0836134281.

A practical study guide on understanding church growth principles and methods of new growth in the church.

EV391 Zunkel, C. Wayne
Growing the Small Church: A Guide for Church Members. Elgin, ILU: David C. Cook, 1983. 120 pp. Paper. No ISBN.

A practical eleven-week study including strategies for growth, diseases that prevent growth, and profiles of a growth pastor and congregation.

EV—EVANGELISM AND MISSIONS

Church Planting

See also SO113, EV325, AF819, AF1225, AF1251, AM781, AM861, AM995, AM1026, AM1278, AM1284, AM1378, AM1409, AS643, AS682, AS733, AS764, AS776, AS1018, AS1020, AS1363, AS1366, AS1399, and AS1485.

EV392 Amberson, Talmadge R., comp.
The Birth of Churches: A Biblical Basis for Church Planting. Nashville, TNU: Broadman, 1979. ix, 179 pp. 0805463178.

Nine essays in which the authors, all heavily involved in the missionary work of the Southern Baptist Convention, address different facets of church planting and development.

EV393 Apeh, John E.
Social Structure and Church Planting: A Study of Cultural Concerns of the Receptors of the Gospel. Shippensburg, PAU: Companion Press, 1989. 139 pp. Paper. 0914903853.

A study of cultural concerns, especially family, social, economic, and political structures, to be taken into account in cross-cultural evangelism.

EV394 Braun, Neil
Laity Mobilized: Reflections on Church Growth in Japan and Other Lands. Grand Rapids, MIU: Eerdmans, 1971. 224 pp. Paper. No ISBN.

Written from a Japanese setting, but speaking to the church on all six continents, Braun promotes the idea of the propagation of the Gospel, not by ordained ministers and missionaries, but chiefly by the laity.

EV395 Brock, Charles
The Principles and Practice of Indigenous Church Planting. Nashville, TNU: Broadman, 1981. 96 pp. Paper. 0805463283.

Practical helps for church planting experienced by the author among Southern Baptists in a semi-rural area of northern Philippines.

EV396 Bunch, David T., Harvey J. Kneisel, and Barbara L. Oden
Multihousing Congregation: How to Start and Grow Christian Congregations in Multihousing Communities. Atlanta, GAU: Smith Publishing, 1991. xxv, 153 pp. Paper. No ISBN.

Guidelines, with case studies based on Southern Baptist church planting experience in the United States, for reaching apartment dwellers for Christ.

EV397 Chaney, Charles L.
Church Planting at the End of the Twentieth Century. Wheaton, ILU: Tyndale, 1982. 175 pp. Paper. 0842302794.

Biblical principles and strategies for evangelicals desiring to reach the unchurched in North America through planting new congregations.

EV398 Compton, Stephen C., and G. Steven Sallee
Growing New Churches: A Manual for New Congregational Development. Nashville, TNU: Discipleship Resources, 1992. ix, 132 pp. Paper. 0881771155.

A step-by-step manual for new congregations by two United Methodist leaders in church planting in the United States.

EV399 *Evangelism in Depth: Experimenting with a New Kind of Evangelism*
Chicago, ILU: Moody, 1961. 126 pp. No ISBN.

Report by team members of the Latin American Mission, regarding their pioneer experiments in evangelistic techniques involving every church member, and directed toward the entire community.

EV400 Faircloth, Samuel D.
Church Planting for Reproduction. Grand Rapids, MIU: Baker Books, 1991. 206 pp. Paper. 0801035589.

A practical guidebook for evangelical Protestants desiring a more effective church growth strategy; by one who served for forty years as a missionary and church planter in Europe.

EV401 Fowler, Harry H.
Breaking Barriers of New Church Growth. Rocky Mount, NCU: Creative Growth Dynamics, 1990. 175 pp. Paper. No ISBN.

Practical helps, by the founder of Creative Growth Dynamics, Inc., for planters of new churches on how to overcome barriers to further growth at the 35, 75, and 125 levels of church attendance.

EV402 Francis, Hozell C.
Church Planting in the African-American Context. Grand Rapids, MIU: Zondervan, 1999. 122 pp. Paper. 0310228778.

A guide for shaping a vision for your church, formulating a plan for realizing your vision, cultivating strong community ties, developing an effective core of leaders, reaching families with the Gospel, and transcending cultural dividing lines.

EV403 Godwin, David E.
Church Planting Methods: A "How To" Book of Overseas Church Planting Crusades. DeSoto, TXU: Lifeshare Communications, 1984. 203 pp. Paper. No ISBN.

A handbook based on Assemblies of God experience in dozens of countries.

EV404 Greenway, Roger S., ed.
Guidelines for Urban Church Planting. Grand Rapids, MIU: Baker Books; Toronto, ONC: G. R. Welch; Johannesburg, SA: Word of Life Wholesale, 1978. 76 pp. Paper. 0801037077.

Strategies for urban mission in the Two-Thirds World, with concrete models from Asia, Africa, and Latin America; also published by S. John Bacon Pty (Melbourne, Australia) and G. W. Moore Ltd (Auckland, New Zealand).

EV405 Hesselgrave, David J.
Planting Churches Cross-Culturally: A Guide for Home and Foreign Missions. Grand Rapids, MIU: Baker Books, 1980. 462 pp. Paper. 0801042194.

A step-by-step approach for church planters on six continents, with guidance on how to transcend one's own cultural background.

EV406 Jones, Ezra Earl
Strategies for New Churches. New York, NYU: Harper & Row, 1976. xiv, 178 pp. 0060641835.

Insights on the context, principles, and process of church planting in the United States by the Associate Director of Research for the United Methodist Board of Global Ministries.

EV407 King, Fred G.
The Church Planter's Training Manual. Camp Hill, PAU: Christian Publications, 1992. 149 pp. Paper. 0875095267.

A step-by-step instructional guide for church planters by the Director of Church Growth for The Christian and Missionary Alliance.

EV—EVANGELISM AND MISSIONS

EV408 Licence, Graham
Rural Church Planting? (Church Growth Booklets). Bedford, ENK: BCGA, 1992. 40 pp. Paper. 0948704233.

Helps for evangelicals desiring to plant rural churches in Great Britain.

EV409 Lukasse, Johan
Churches with Roots. Translated by Machtteld Stassijns. Bromley, ENK: STL Books; Eastbourne, ENK: MARC-Monarch, 1990. 224 pp. Paper. 1850780730 (S), 1854240870 (M).

A practical guide for evangelical Christians desiring to plant churches in Great Britain.

EV410 Malphurs, Aubrey
Planting Growing Churches for the 21st Century: A Comprehensive Guide for New Churches and Those Desiring Renewal. Grand Rapids, MIU: Baker Books, 1998. 425 pp. Paper. 0801090539.

A revised and updated primer on church planting covering preparation, personnel, principles, and process; originally published in 1992.

EV411 Mannoia, Kevin W.
Church Planting: The Next Generation: Introducing the Century 21 Church Planting System. Indianapolis, INU: Light & Life Press, 1996. 156 pp. Paper. 0893671835.

An introduction to the Free Methodist's Century 21 Church Planting System.

EV412 Montgomery, Jim
Dawn 2000: 7 Million Churches to Go: The Personal Story of the DAWN Strategy for World Evangelization. South Pasadena, CAU: William Carey Library, 1989. ix, 230 pp. Paper. 0878082204.

A popular treatment of the DAWN (Discipling A Whole Nation) movement with strategies for mobilizing evangelical Christians in every country to plant new cells of believers.

EV413 Murray, Stuart
Church Planting: Laying Foundations. Cumbria, ENK: Paternoster Press, 1998. xii, 302 pp. Paper. 0853648255.

A thorough theological and strategic study which asks radical questions for church planters, warns against establishing clones of existing churches, and probes the kinds of churches needed in a post-Christian and postmodern society.

EV414 Patterson, George, and Richard Scoggins
Church Multiplication Guide: Helping Churches to Reproduce Locally and Abroad. South Pasadena, CAU: William Carey Library, 1994. 128 pp. Paper. 087808245X.

A practical study guide on church planting by two North American specialists, giving biblical principles and strategic plans.

EV415 Ratliff, Joe S., and Michael J. Cox
Church Planting in the African-American Community. Nashville, TNU: Broadman, 1993. 111 pp. Paper. 0805460713.

A popular account of Southern Baptist methods and approaches to church planting among African Americans, based on the author's experience in Houston, Texas.

EV416 Redford, Jack
Planting New Churches. Nashville, TNU: Broadman, 1978. 152 pp. 0805463143.

The author shares experiences of many persons engaged in starting new churches, biblical principles, nine steps in planting, and the role of mission pastors in starting new churches.

EV417 Robinson, Martin, and Stuart Christine
Planting Tomorrow's Churches Today: A Comprehensive Handbook. Tunbridge Wells, ENK: Monarch/BCGA, 1992. 353 pp. Paper. 1854241621 (M), 0948704209 (B).

A primer for church planters in Great Britain and elsewhere including theological rationale, historical contexts, and practical helps.

EV418 Schaller, Lyle E.
44 Questions for Church Planters. Nashville, TNU: Abingdon, 1991. 192 pp. Paper. 0687132843.

Helps for church planters based on the author's more than thirty years of consultations with leaders responsible for developing new churches.

EV419 Shenk, David W., and Ervin R. Stutzman
Creating Communities of the Kingdom: New Testament Models of Church Planting. Scottdale, PAU: Herald Press, 1988. 229 pp. Paper. 0836134702.

A thirteen-week study guide for developing New Testament models for new Christian communities, weaving biblical perspectives into the insights of contemporary theology, anthropology, sociology, psychology, communication theories, and church growth analysis.

EV420 Silvoso, Ed
That None Should Perish: How to Reach Entire Cities for Christ through Prayer Evangelism. Ventura, CAU: Regal Books, 1994. 295 pp. Paper. 0830716904.

The founder of Harvest Ministry's plan for urban evangelism through saturation church-planting and strategic-level spiritual warfare.

EV421 Smith, Ebbie C.
A Manual for Church Growth Surveys. South Pasadena, CAU: William Carey Library, 1976. xii, 130 pp. 0878081453.

A practical handbook for utilizing the theoretical concepts of church growth as developed by Donald A. McGavran and associates at Fuller Seminary.

EV422 Smith, Sid, comp.
Church Planting in the Black Community. Nashville, TNU: Convention Press, 1989. 160 pp. Paper. No ISBN.

A church study course for Southern Baptists, containing practical helps.

EV423 Steffen, Tom A.
Passing the Baton: Church Planting That Empowers. La Habra, CAU: Center for Organizational & Ministry Development, 1997. vi, 264 pp. Paper. 1882757025.

Helps for cross-cultural church planters, enabling national leaders to continue reproducing churches long after the missionary leaves; by the Associate Professor of Intercultural Studies at Biola University.

EV424 Steffen, Tom A.
Planned Phase-Out: A Checklist for Cross-Cultural Church Planters. San Francisco, CAU: Austin & Winfield, 1992. 54 pp. Paper. 1880921200.

An outline guide for church planters developed by the author during fifteen years as a church planter and consultant in the Philippines, and in teaching church planting as Professor of Intercultural Studies at Biola University.

EV425 Tidsworth, Floyd
Life Cycle of a New Congregation. Nashville, TNU: Broadman, 1992. xiv, 143 pp. Paper. 0805460691.

A model for church planting from birth to maturity to planting other new congregations.

EV426 Wagner, C. Peter
Church Planting for a Greater Harvest: A Comprehensive Guide. Ventura, CAU: Regal Books, 1990. 156 pp. Paper. 0830714359.

. A practical how-to manual for church planters, developed by the Professor of Church Growth at Fuller Theological Seminary out of his popular "How to Plant a Church" seminars.

EV427 Wagner, C. Peter
Plantando Iglesias para una Mayor Cosecha: Una Guía Exhaustiva. Translated by Nellyda Pablovsky. Miami, FLU: Editorial Unilit, 1997. 155 pp. Paper. 0789900386.

Spanish translation.

Personal Evangelism and Witness

See also TH6, ME185, CR528, SO477, SO525, CO80, CO139, EV67, EV518, EV578, CH238, CH518, SP261, AM584, AS624, and EU17.

EV428 Adsit, Christopher B.
Personal Disciplemaking: A Step-by-Step Guide for Leading a Christian from New Birth to Maturity. San Bernadino, CAU: Here's Life Publishers, 1988. 384 pp. Paper. 0898402131.

A practical yet thorough primer for discipleship, utilizing a step-by-step program, by a staff member of Campus Crusade for Christ.

EV429 Aldrich, Joseph C.
Gentle Persuasion: Creative Ways to Introduce Your Friends to Christ. Portland, ORU: Multnomah, 1988. 247 pp. Paper. 0880702532.

A primer on lay witnessing by the President of Multnomah School of the Bible in Portland, Oregon.

EV430 Aldrich, Joseph C.
Life-Style Evangelism: Crossing Traditional Boundries to Reach the Unbelieving World. Toorak, AT: Canterbury Press, 1988. 244 pp. 0930014464.

The author, President of the Multnomah School of the Bible, shows what he feels evangelism should be, how it relates to our culture, where we have failed in its practice and how we can reach out to those around us, as he relates evangelism to the local church, the individual member, church leadership, and the pastor; originally published in 1981 (Portland, ORU: Multnomah Press).

EV431 Armstrong, Richard Stoll
Service Evangelism. Philadelphia, PAU: Westminster Press, 1979. 198 pp. Paper. 0664242529.

Faith sharing in interpersonal witnessing—how to train Christians to become effective personal evangelists.

EV432 Becton, Randy
Everyday Evangelism: Making a Difference for Christ Where You Live. Grand Rapids, MIU: Baker Books, 1997. 127 pp. Paper. 080105740X.

Practical helps for persons desiring to share their faith with persons around them; with insights from the author's involvement in mass media evangelism.

EV433 Beougher, Sharon, and Mary Dorsett
Women and Evangelism: An Evangelistic Lifestyle from a Woman's Perspective. Wheaton, ILU: BGC, 1994. xi, 292 pp. Paper. 1879089157.

A self-study course consisting of six cassettes and a book designed to equip women to live an evangelistic lifestyle.

EV434 Billy Graham Evangelistic Association Spiritual Counselling Department
The Billy Graham Christian Worker's Handbook: A Layman's Guide for Soul Winning and Personal Counseling. Minneapolis, MNU: World Wide Publications, 1984. 270 pp. Paper. 0890660425.

Revised edition of a handbook originally compiled for a ministry of telephone counseling during telecasts of Billy Graham crusades; rewritten by Charles G. Ward.

EV435 Bleecker, Walter S., and Jan Bishop
The Non-Confronter's Guide to Leading a Person to Christ. San Bernardino, CAU: Here's Life Publishers, 1990. 160 pp. Paper. 0898402735.

A simple guide to personal evangelism by the Director of Harvesting Ministries.

EV436 Bright, Bill
Testificando Sin Temor: Cómo Compartir Su Fe Con Confianza. Translated by Hector L. Leyva. Miami, FLU: Unilit, 1998. 215 pp. Paper. 1560639202.

Spanish translation.

EV437 Bright, Bill
Witnessing without Fear. San Bernadino, CAU: Here's Life Publishers, 1989. 215 pp. Paper. 0898401763.

Reprint of the 1987 edition of a practical guide for learning to share the Christian faith without fear, with personal insights by the founder of Campus Crusade for Christ International.

EV438 Campolo, Tony, and Gordon D. Aeschliman
50 Ways You Can Reach the World. (Saltshaker Books). Downers Grove, ILU: InterVarsity, 1993. 148 pp. Paper. 0830813950.

Fifty practical ideas for individual Christians desiring to reach out in greater witness, caring, or mission to others in need, with a brief listing of resources for mission.

EV439 Campolo, Tony, and Gordon D. Aeschliman
50 Ways You Can Share Your Faith. Downers Grove, ILU: InterVarsity, 1992. 168 pp. Paper. 0830813934.

The ABCs on opportunities for personal faith sharing by two well-known public spokespersons for evangelical Christianity.

EV440 Chapman, John C.
Know and Tell the Gospel. Colorado Springs, COU: NavPress, 1985. 192 pp. Paper. 0891095349.

A popular training guide for personal evangelism; originally published in 1981 by Hodder and Stoughton, London, UK.

EV441 Coleman, Robert E. et al., eds.
Disciple Making: Training Leaders to Make Disciples. Wheaton, ILU: BGC, 1994. xiv, 231 pp. Paper. 1879089130.

Six cassette tapes and a twelve-lesson manual on the practical aspects of discipleship through mentor relationships.

EV—EVANGELISM AND MISSIONS

EV442 Coleman, Robert E.

The Master Plan of Evangelism. Grand Rapids, MIU: Revell, 1993. 200 pp. No ISBN.

Thirtieth-anniversary edition of a clear exposition of Jesus' principles and methods of evangelism, and of their relevance today; originally published by Asbury Theological Seminary in 1963.

EV443 Coleman, Robert E.

The Master's Way of Personal Evangelism. Wheaton, ILU: Crossway Books, 1997. 174 pp. Paper. 0891079122.

Twelve instructional pictures of how people were evangelized in scripture, written as a companion to the author's classic, *The Master Plan of Evangelism.*

EV444 Coleman, Robert E.

El Plan Maestro de la Evangelización. Translated by J. Vargas. Miami, FLU: Unilit, 1998. 184 pp. Paper. 0789903571.

Spanish translation.

EV445 DeSiano, Frank P., and Kenneth Boyack

Discovering My Experience of God: Awareness and Witness. New York, NYU: Paulist Press, 1992. v, 65 pp. Paper. 0809133008.

An evangelization training workbook designed especially to help Catholics know and affirm their personal stories of faith.

EV446 DeVille, Jard

The Psychology of Witnessing. Waco, TXU: SDA, General Conference, Ministerial Association, 1996. 91 pp. Paper. No ISBN.

An introduction to relational evangelism, with an exploration of the psychospiritual processes involved in communication and decision making, by a practicing psychotherapist; originally published in 1980 (Waco, TXU: Word Books).

EV447 Eisenman, Tom L.

Everyday Evangelism: Making the Most of Life's Common Moments. Downers Grove, ILU: InterVarsity, 1987. 152 pp. Paper. 0830817034 (hdbk), 0877849978 (pbk).

A study guide with practical and motivational information that can help make evangelism an everyday experience in family, neighbors, business, and all other relationships.

EV448 Fay, William, and Linda Evans Shepherd

Share Jesus without Fear. Nashville, TNU: Broadman, 1999. x, 195 pp. Paper. 0805418393.

Fay addresses the top six fears that keep most people from sharing their faith, and presents a formula for initiating non-confrontational, non-argumentative conversations with people who do not believe.

EV449 Fish, Roy J., and J. E. Conant

Every Member Evangelism for Today. San Francisco, CAU: HarperSanFrancisco, 1976. vii, 111 pp. Paper. 0060615516.

A revision and update by the Professor of Evangelism at Southwestern Baptist Theological Seminary of the 1922 classic on personal witnessing by J. E. Conant.

EV450 Fisher, Wallace E.

Because We Have Good News. Nashville, TNU: Abingdon, 1974. 128 pp. Paper. 068702532X.

This layman's guide for person-to-person evangelism in community is ecumenical in outlook, tested in a single church

by the author, and answers specific objections made by non-Christians.

EV451 Foster, John

God Has No Favourites: The Appeal of Christ to Men of Different Cultures. Edinburgh, STK: St. Andrew Press, 1968. 101 pp. 715200070 (SBN).

Short testimonies of faith by thirty-five Third World Christian leaders.

EV452 Fox, H. Eddie, and George E. Morris

Faith-Sharing: Dynamic Christian Witnessing by Invitation. Nashville, TNU: Discipleship Resources, 1996. 152 pp. Paper. 0881771589.

A revised and expanded edition of a best-selling primer on personal witnessing; originally published in 1986.

EV453 Fox, H. Eddie, and George E. Morris

Let the Redeemed of the Lord Say So!: Expressing Your Faith through Witnessing. Nashville, TNU: Abingdon, 1991. 191 pp. Paper. 0687213800.

A primer on verbal witnessing to the Gospel through preaching and testifying by two United Methodist leaders in world evangelism.

EV454 Fryling, Alice, ed.

Disciplemakers' Handbook. Downers Grove, ILU: InterVarsity, 1989. 211 pp. Paper. 0830812660.

A work which defines and describes disciple-making as a process, discusses essential skills, and gives practical ways in which individuals and groups can become effective disciplemakers.

EV455 Hanks, Billie, and William A. Shell, eds.

Discipleship: Great Insights from the Most Experienced Disciple Makers. Grand Rapids, MIU: Zondervan, 1993. 192 pp. Paper. 0310510015.

An updated edition of the classic (Zondervan, 1981), containing twelve short essays on aspects of personal evangelism and the discipling process; by North American evangelicals experienced in disciple-making.

EV456 Hawkins, O. S.

Drawing the Net: 30 Practical Principles for Leading Others to Christ Publicly and Personally. Nashville, TNU: Broadman, 1993. 143 pp. Paper. 080545358X.

Thirty practical principles for personal evangelism by the pastor of the large and growing First Baptist Church of Ft. Lauderdale, Florida.

EV457 Hershberger, Michele, ed.

A Christian View of Hospitality: Expecting Surprises. (The Giving Project Series, 2). Scottdale, PAU: Herald Press, 1999. 284 pp. 0836191099.

A practical approach to hospitality which breaks down walls that divide and views the stranger as one who brings the gift of hospitality.

EV458 Hewitt, Hugh

The Embarrassed Believer: Reviving Christian Witness in an Age of Unbelief. Nashville, TNU: Word Publishing, 1998. xv, 206 pp. 084991485X (hdbk), 0849914191 (pbk).

The co-host of a television nightly news show, author, and law professor challenges spiritually lethargic Christians in North America to witness boldly for Jesus Christ.

EV—EVANGELISM AND MISSIONS

EV459 Hoffman, Warren L.
The Secret of the Harvest: Mobilizing for Team Evangelism.
Nappanee, INU: Evangel Press, 1988. 239 pp. Paper. 0916035255.

A practical study guide for local church evangelism teams
including worksheets for each of the thirteen chapters; by a
church-planting pastor for the Brethren in Christ in Oklahoma
City, Oklahoma.

EV460 Hollis, James W.
*Beyond the Walls: A Congregational Guide for Lifestyle Rela-
tional Evangelism.* Nashville, TNU: Discipleship Resources,
1993. viii, 134 pp. Paper. 0881771244.

A training manual for leaders of local churches desiring to
train members through natural relationships with others, based on
models developed by the author in the North Georgia Conference
of The United Methodist Church.

EV461 Innes, Dick
*I Hate Witnessing: A Handbook for Effective Christian Commu-
nication.* Upland, CAU: ACTS Communications, 1994. 191 pp.
Paper. 0964252503.

A practical application of communication theory to personal
witnessing by the founder and International Director of ACTS
International; originally published by Regal Books in 1985.

EV462 Jacks, Bob, Betty Jacks, and Ron Wormser
Your Home a Lighthouse. Colorado Springs, COU: NavPress,
1987. 156 pp. Paper. 0891091270.

A revised edition of a practical guidebook for home Bible study groups with an evangelistic purpose; originally published in 1986 by Churches Alive International.

EV463 Johnson, Douglas W.
Reaching Out to the Unchurched. Valley Forge, PAU: Judson Press, 1983. 80 pp. Paper. 0817009787.

Creative suggestions for building appealing programs that
meet the needs of specific groups to find renewed life in Christ;
by the Executive Director of the Institute for Church Development, Inc.

EV464 Johnson, Ron, Joseph W. Hinkle, and Charles M. Lowry
Oikos: A Practical Approach to Family Evangelism. Nashville, TNU: Broadman, 1982. 91 pp. Paper. 0805462341.

A practical approach to family evangelism, from a Southern
Baptist perspective, which contains guidance and workable suggestions for reaching lost, unchurched, and hurting families.

EV465 Johnson, Ronald W.
How Will They Hear If We Don't Listen? Nashville, TNU:
Broadman, 1994. xii, 194 pp. Paper. 0805410678.

The Evangelism Director for the Georgia Baptist Convention advocates listening before telling, and dialogue in place
of monologue in personal witnessing.

EV466 Kendall, R. T.
*Stand Up and Be Counted: Calling for Public Confession of
Faith.* (Ministry Resources Library). Grand Rapids, MIU:
Zondervan, 1984. 127 pp. Paper. 031038351X.

The purpose of *Stand Up and Be Counted* is to convince
persons of the importance of public witness.

EV467 Kolb, Erwin J.
A Witness Primer. St. Louis, MOU: Concordia Publishing,
1986. 120 pp. Paper. 0570044413.

A study book on various aspects of personal witnessing

by the Executive Secretary for Evangelism of the Lutheran
Church-Missouri Synod.

EV468 Lehmann, Danny
Reaching People for Jesus. Edited by David Young. Manila,
PH: YWAM/OMF Literature, 1988. 171 pp. Paper.
9715111327.

A challenge to get involved in Great Commission witnessing by the Director of YWAM in Hawaii; also published
by Whitaker House, Springdale, PA, under the title *Bringing
'Em Back Alive* (1987).

EV469 Lischer, Richard
Speaking of Jesus: Finding the Words for Witness. Philadelphia, PAU: Fortress Press, 1982. x, 121 pp. Paper. 0800616316.

This book is principally about the words—and especially
the stories—that Christians speak to non-Christians in order
to call forth repentance, faith, and discipleship.

EV470 Little, Paul E.
How to Give Away Your Faith. Downers Grove, ILU: Inter-
Varsity, 1988. 192 pp. Paper. 0830812172.

A thorough revision for individual and group study of a
best-selling classic, giving a practical, biblical-based answer
on why and how to witness to people living in a 20th-century
world, by the former staff evangelist of InterVarsity Christian
Fellowship (1950-1975).

EV471 Lyon, Mary Jane
*Sharing Faith Stories: Thirty-Three Lay Witnesses Tell Their
Stories.* Nashville, TNU: Discipleship Resources, 1988. 32
pp. Paper. No ISBN.

Thirty-three intimate stories told by typical Christians, which
can be used as helps in witnessing and worship; by a leader in the
transdenominational Lay Witness Mission movement.

EV472 McCloskey, Mark
*Tell It Often—Tell It Well: Making the Most of Witnessing
Opportunities.* San Bernadino, CAU: Here's Life Publishers,
1986. 284 pp. Paper. 0898401240.

A popular account of the potential of effective personal
evangelism from both experiential and scholarly perspectives,
by an area director with the Campus Ministry of Campus Crusade for Christ.

EV473 Miles, Delos
Overcoming Barriers to Witnessing. Nashville, TNU: Broadman, 1984. 131 pp. Paper. 0805462457.

Practical answers to twelve common objections which
Christians themselves raise against sharing their faith, by the
Professor of Evangelism at Southeastern Baptist Theological
Seminary in the United States.

EV474 Mittelberg, Mark, Lee Patrick Strobel, and Bill Hybels
*Becoming a Contagious Christian: Communicating Your Faith
in a Style that Fits You.* Barrington, ILU: Willow Creek Resources; Grand Rapids, MIU: Zondervan, 1995. 2 vols. Paper.
0310500818 (Z v. 1), 2598650081 (W v. 1), 0310501016 (Z
v. 2), 2598650101 (W v. 2).

A multimedia resource containing videotape, overheads,
and manuals, field-tested with over 5,000 people at Willow
Creek Community Church, designed to equip believers for
effective evangelism in today's world [vol. 1: *Leader's Guide,*
287 pp; vol. 2: *Participant's Guide,* 127 pp.].

EV—EVANGELISM AND MISSIONS

EV475 Moyer, R. Larry
Free and Clear: Understanding & Communicating God's Offer of Eternal Life. Grand Rapids, MIU: Kregel Publications, 1997. 272 pp. Paper. 0825431778.

Practical helps for faith sharing by evangelical Christians prepared for individual or group study.

EV476 Neville, Joyce
How to Share Your Faith without Being Offensive. Wilton, CTU: Morehouse Publishing, 1989. iv, 162 pp. Paper. 0819214795.

Revised edition of the popular 1979 handbook for those desiring to provide effective verbal Christian witness through worship services, small groups, and one-on-one interaction.

EV477 Pawson, H. Cecil
Personal Evangelism. London, ENK: Epworth Press, 1968. 134 pp. 0716200406.

A primer for Christian laypeople on biblical motives and methods of personal evangelism by a pastor who has met weekly in Great Britian with men engaged in such witness.

EV478 Peace, Richard
Small Group Evangelism: A Training Program for Reaching Out with the Gospel. Downers Grove, ILU: InterVarsity, 1985. 190 pp. Paper. 0877843295.

A practical nine to thirteen-week training program, including explanations of group dynamics and guidelines to make the experience work.

EV479 Petersen, Jim
Living Proof: Sharing the Gospel Naturally. Colorado Springs, COU: NavPress, 1989. 251 pp. Paper. 0891095616.

A combination and revision of the author's previous works, *Evangelism as a Lifestyle* and *Evangelism for Our Generation*, offered to help witnessing Christians develop relationships with the unreached, model the Christian message, and present biblical claims in a non-threatening manner; by theAassistant to the General Director of The Navigators.

EV480 Pickard, Nellie
Just Say It: True Stories about Witnessing Opportunities. Grand Rapids, MIU: Baker Books, 1992. 195 pp. Paper. 0801071186.

The third book of the author's anecdotes about person-to-person evangelism on several continents.

EV481 Pickard, Nellie
What Do You Say When ...: An Inspirational Guide to Witnessing. Grand Rapids, MIU: Baker Books/Zondervan, 1988. 201 pp. Paper. 0801071062.

Thirty personal witnessing experiences of the author as an evangelist, demonstrating how a Christian can turn almost any situation into a faith sharing opportunity.

EV482 Pickard, Nellie
What Would You Have Said?: Witnessing with Confidence and Sensitivity. Grand Rapids, MIU: Baker Books, 1990. 174 pp. Paper. 0801071135.

A personal guide on how to comfortably turn any situation and personal encounter into a witnessing opportunity for sharing Christ's message in everyday situations.

EV483 Pippert, Rebecca Manley
Out of the Salt-Shaker and into the World: Evangelism as a Way of Life. Downers Grove, ILU: InterVarsity, 1999. 188 pp. Paper. 0877847355.

This revised and expanded edition presents Christ's method of conversational evangelism and helps for using this approach today.

EV484 Pollard, Nick
Evangelism Made Slightly Less Difficult: How to Interest People Who Aren't Interested. Downers Grove, ILU: InterVarsity, 1997. 178 pp. Paper. 0830819088.

Helps for Christian witnessing to those satisfied with their lives, content with their beliefs, and seeing no need to change.

EV485 Schneider, Floyd
Evangelism for the Fainthearted. Grand Rapids, MIU: Kregel Publications, 2000. 220 pp. Paper. 0825437954.

Developed while working on the mission field in Western and Eastern Europe, this resource is designed to help Christians become involved with friends who are not Christian by turning conversations toward spiritual things in a natural and comfortable way.

EV486 Schweer, G. William
Personal Evangelism for Today. Nashville, TNU: Broadman, 1984. 192 pp. 0805462144.

A book for everyone who witnesses for Christ—an appeal for responsible evangelism—a major evangelism textbook that should see many years of service.

EV487 Shaver, Charles
The Bible Speaks to Me about My Witness. Kansas City, MOU: Beacon Hill Press, 1991. 132 pp. 0834114046.

A practical guide for Nazarene Christians desiring to become more effective in their witness for Christ.

EV488 Smith, Daniel H.
How to Lead a Child to Christ. Chicago, ILU: Moody Press, 1987. 54 pp. Paper. 0802446221.

A practical guide for child evangelism including biblical bases, psychological needs, and methods with real life examples.

EV489 Stebbins, Thomas
Evangelism by the Book: 13 Biblical Methods. Camp Hill, PAU: Christian Publications, 1991. 337 pp. Paper. 0875094732.

A study book for the Evangelism Explosion approach to faith sharing, based on the author's training of pastors in evangelism on six continents and at Alliance Theological Seminary in Nyack, New York.

EV490 Stebbins, Thomas
Oikos—Outreach 4 Times a Year: The "Formula" for an Effective Strategy You Can Use to Mobilize Your Entire Congregation for Friendship Evangelism. Camp Hill, PAU: Christian Publications, 1992. 65 pp. Paper. 0875094996.

A reproduction in looseleaf notebook form of the worksheets and transparencies used in the 004 total-church evangelism strategy developed by the Outreach Council of Christ Community Church of Omaha, Nebraska.

EV491 Stiles, J. Mack
Speaking of Jesus: How to Tell Your Friends the Best News They Will Ever Hear. Downers Grove, ILU: InterVarsity, 1995. 196 pp. Paper. 0830816453.

Helps on how to speak about Jesus so people will listen; by the Kentucky area Director of InterVarsity Christian Fellowship.

EV—EVANGELISM AND MISSIONS

EV492 Strobel, Lee Patrick
Inside the Mind of Unchurched Harry and Mary: How to Reach Friends and Family Who Avoid God and the Church. Grand Rapids, MIU: Zondervan, 1993. 236 pp. Paper. 0310375614.

An action plan for personal witnessing to the unchurched by the teaching pastor at Willow Creek Community Church in South Barrington, Illinois.

EV493 Tapia, Andres, ed.
Campus Evangelism Handbook: A Practical Guide for Showing and Sharing God's Love. Downers Grove, ILU: InterVarsity, 1987. 155 pp. Paper. 083081213X.

A popular manual for campus ministry including narrative accounts of personal experiences, theological discussions, and practical techniques.

EV494 Tooley, Ross
We Cannot but Tell: A Practical Guide to Heart to Heart Evangelism. Manila, PH: YWAM/OMF Literature, 1990. 157 pp. Paper. 9715111807.

A practical handbook for personal evangelism (the "how" and the "what" of presenting the gospel message) by one who has been engaged in the Philippines for thirteen years in cross-cultural evangelism.

EV495 Wenger, A. Grace, Dave Jackson, and Neta Jackson
Witness: Empowering the Church through Worship, Community and Mission. Scottdale, PAU: Herald Press, 1989. 196 pp. Paper. 0836134826.

A revised study guide for individuals and groups taking basic "outreach" concepts and applying them to the church of today; originally published as *God Builds the Church through Congregational Witness* (1963).

EV496 Wiles, Jerry
How to Win Others to Christ: Your Personal Practical Guide to Evangelism. Nashville, TNU: Nelson, 1992. x, 180 pp. Paper. 0840796218.

A practical guide to help evangelical Protestants to be more effective in personal witnessing for Christ.

EV497 Wingeier, Douglas E.
Eight Ways to Become Christian: Sharing Your Story of Faith. Nashville, TNU: Discipleship Resources, 1988. 92 pp. Paper. 0881770604.

Drawing on forty-four faith stories, the Professor of Christian Education at Garrett-Evangelical Theological Seminary (Evanston, Illinois) delineates eight different paths that persons take as they come into a relationship with Christ and the church—four primarily individual journeys, and four in which formation in community is highlighted.

Pastoral/Parish Evangelism

See also SO416, CO70, EV102, EV104, EV308, CH47, CH118, CH247, CH408, CH431, CH511, SP202, SP213, SP216, SP296-SP297, AF258, AM992, AM1092-AM1093, AS986, and EU157.

EV498 Alessi, Vincie
Evangelism in Your Church School. Valley Forge, PAU: Judson Press, 1978. 63 pp. Paper. 0817007865.

A "how-to" book for Sunday school teachers in the United States based on Kenneth L. Cober's *Evangelism in the Sunday Church School* (Philadelphia, PAU: Judson Press, 1955).

EV499 Armstrong, Richard Stoll
The Pastor as Evangelist. Philadelphia, PAU: Westminster Press, 1984. 202 pp. Paper. 0664245560.

A very detailed book challenging pastors to utilize the evangelistic potential in each function of their ministries.

EV500 Armstrong, Richard Stoll
The Pastor-Evangelist in the Parish. Louisville, KYU: Westminster John Knox, 1990. 244 pp. Paper. 0664251315.

A thorough examination of specific ways in which a Protestant pastor in the United States does the work of an evangelist through visitation, counseling, teaching, discipling, administration, and public leadership.

EV501 Armstrong, Richard Stoll
The Pastor-Evangelist in Worship. Philadelphia, PAU: Westminster Press, 1986. 216 pp. Paper. 0664246931.

A practical down-to-earth guide for ministers who want to participate more fully in the church's mission of evangelism, through their roles as worship leader and preacher.

EV502 Arn, Win, and Charles Arn
The Master's Plan for Making Disciples: Every Christian an Effective Witness through an Enabling Church. Grand Rapids, MIU: Baker Books, 1998. 175 pp. Paper. 0801090512.

Second edition of a classic on principles and methods of disciplemaking; originally published in 1982.

EV503 Barna, George
Church Marketing: Breaking Ground for the Harvest. Ventura, CAU: Regal Books, 1992. 345 pp. Paper. 0830714049.

Practical help for North American parishes seeking biblically based, Christ centered ways of presenting the faith and the church to the wider public, through marketing strategies.

EV504 Bibby, Reginald Wayne
There's Got to be More!: Connecting Churches and Canadians. Winfield, BCC: Wood Lake Books, 1995. 159 pp. Paper. 1551450488.

The foremost expert on the sociology of religion in Canada challenges mainline churches in numerical decline to locate and minister to the unchurched.

EV505 Bisagno, John R.
How to Build an Evangelistic Church. Nashville, TNU: Broadman, 1971. x, 160 pp. 0805425241.

Practical methods for pastors, church leaders, and laypersons, by the pastor of the First Baptist Church in Houston, Texas (Southern Baptist Convention).

EV506 Brennan, Patrick J.
Re-Imagining Evangelization: Toward the Reign of God and the Communal Parish. New York, NYU: Crossroad Publishing, 1995. 170 pp. Paper. 0824514335.

The President of the National Center for Evangelization and Pastoral Renewal offers a blueprint for creating faith communities in the Roman Catholic "Decade of Evangelization."

EV507 Callahan, Kennon L.
Visiting in an Age of Mission: A Handbook for Person-to-Person Ministry. San Francisco, CAU: HarperSanFrancisco, 1994. xii, 141 pp. 0060612878.

A practical guide for local church and mission leaders on fourteen key forms of visiting, and how to use each effectively in ministries to both the churched and unchurched.

EV508 Celek, Tim, Dieter Zander, and Patrick Kampert
Inside the Soul of a New Generation: Insights and Strategies for Reaching Busters. Grand Rapids, MIU: Zondervan, 1996. 175 pp. Paper. 0310205948.

Practical helps for reaching the "generation X busters" based on the authors' pastoral experience in California and at Willow Creek Community Church in South Barrington, Illinois.

EV509 Chu, Thomas K., Sheryl A. Kujawa, and Anne Rowthorn
God Works: Youth and Young Adult Ministry Models ... Evangelism at Work with Young People. Harrisburg, PAU: Morehouse Publishing, 1997. 98 pp. Paper. 081921731X.

Eleven Episcopal parish models of youth/young adult ministries presented with pictures, stories, and how-to ideas.

EV510 Clarke, John
Evangelism That Really Works. London, ENK: SPCK, 1995. xi, 161 pp. Paper. 0281047936.

Suggestions to help a parish develop an evangelistic strategy, based on findings in a Church of England research project.

EV511 Clement, Shirley F., and Suzanne G. Braden
Caring Evangelism: A Visitation Program for Congregations. Nashville, TNU: Discipleship Resources, 1994. 2 vols. Paper. 0881771112 (vol. 1).

Training materials for Caring Evangelism teams in local churches which combine visitation evangelism with skilled caregiving, including both a leader's guide (Revised edition, 1994, 62 pp.) and a participant's workbook (1994, 38 pp.).

EV512 Clement, Shirley F., and Thomas L. Salsgiver, eds.
Youth Ministry and Evangelism: New Wine for a New Day. Nashville, TNU: Discipleship Resources, 1991. vi, 74 pp. Paper. 0881770949.

A challenge to old "myth-conceptions" about youth ministry, with stories of effective United Methodist youth groups using relational evangelism.

EV513 Click, E. Dale
Evangelism: The First Business of the Church. Lima, OHU: CSS, 1994. 282 pp. Paper. 1556739583.

A primer on the theology and practice of parish evangelism by the architect of the church-wide Lutheran Evangelism Mission of the United Lutheran Church in America.

EV514 Cowell, W. James
Extending Your Congregation's Welcome: Internal Climate and Intentional Outreach. Nashville, TNU: Discipleship Resources, 1989. vi, 90 pp. Paper. 088177068X.

Practical helps for congregations desiring to improve their welcome and hospitality to persons outside their fellowship by the United Methodist Director of Congregational Development.

EV515 Cowell, W. James
Incorporating New Members: Bonds of Believing, Belonging, and Becoming. Nashville, TNU: Discipleship Resources, 1992. vii, 85 pp. Paper. 0881771120.

Helpful ideas to enable new Christians to enter fully in the life of faith, Christian nurture, and mutual support of the faith community.

EV516 Dale, Robert D., and Delos Miles
Evangelizing the Hard-to-Reach. Nashville, TNU: Broadman, 1986. 129 pp. Paper. 0805462511.

A volume from the Baptist viewpoint, helping to tailor evangelism to those outside the church who are hard to reach—the left outs, the dropouts, the locked outs, and those who choose to opt out.

EV517 DeSiano, Frank P., and Kenneth Boyack
Creating the Evangelizing Parish. New York, NYU: Paulist Press, 1993. iv, 203 pp. Paper. 0809133873.

A primer for Roman Catholics open to an "encounter model" of evangelization, specifically placing the ministry into the framework of personal relationships.

EV518 DeSiano, Frank P.
The Evangelizing Catholic: A Practical Handbook for Reaching Out. Mahwah, NJU: Paulist Press, 1998. viii, 152 pp. Paper. 0809138360.

A practical handbook for Roman Catholics on both personal and parish evangelization.

EV519 DeSiano, Frank P.
Sowing New Seed: Directions for Evangelization Today. New York, NYU: Paulist Press, 1994. vii, 158 pp. Paper. 0809134799.

Helps for a theology and practice of evangelization in Catholic parishes by the president of the Paulist Fathers.

EV520 Dobson, Ed
Starting a Seeker Sensitive Service: How Traditional Churches Can Reach the Unchurched. Grand Rapids, MIU: Zondervan, 1993. 157 pp. Paper. 0310384818.

The story by the senior pastor of Calvary Church in Grand Rapids, Michigan, of how a traditional church launched a nontraditional service in order to open its doors to unchurched people.

EV521 Drummond, Lewis A.
Leading Your Church in Evangelism. Nashville, TNU: Broadman, 1975. 165 pp. Paper. 0805462104.

A guide for the pastor on the essential aspects of evangelism and foundation guidelines on how to evangelize the local church; first published in 1972 under the title *Evangelism: The Counter Revolution.*

EV522 Dunnam, Maxie D.
Congregational Evangelism: A Pastor's View. Nashville, TNU: Discipleship Resources, 1992. xiii, 55 pp. Paper. 0881771163.

Three lectures by the senior pastor of Christ United Methodist in Memphis, Tennessee, on the congregational basis of holistic evangelism; originally presented as Denman Lectures in Evangelism

EV523 Finley, Dean, comp.
Handbook for Youth Evangelism. Nashville, TNU: Broadman, 1988. 239 pp. Paper. 0805462562.

Thirteen short chapters by Southern Baptists on various aspects of youth work in US churches, with special attention to biblical bases, youth culture, and strategies for evangelizing youth.

EV524 Fish, Roy J.
Giving a Good Invitation. Nashville, TNU: Broadman, 1974. 55 pp. Paper. 0805421076.

This book discusses the reasons for, planning for, and how to offer the invitation, as well as the place of exhortation and psychology in giving the invitation to accept Christ.

EV525 Ford, Kevin Graham, and Jim Denney

Jesus for a New Generation: Putting the Gospel in the Language of Xers. Downers Grove, ILU: InterVarsity, 1995. 259 pp. Paper. 0830816151.

Out of his campus ministry and the InterVarsity Christian Fellowship's Baby Buster Consultation, the author provides practical guidance on postmodernism, narrative evangelism, life in cyberspace, and other themes important for those born after 1965.

EV526 Franco, Sergio

Evangelismo: Un concepto en evolucion. Kansas City, MOU: Casa Nazarena de Publicaciones, 1970. 144 pp. Paper. No ISBN.

A basic manual on evangelism for use by laity.

EV527 Fung, Raymond

The Isaiah Vision: An Ecumenical Strategy for Congregational Evangelism. (Risk Book Series, 52). Geneva, SZ: WCC Publications, 1992. ix, 55 pp. Paper. 2825410373.

A holistic strategy for congregational evangelism based on the agenda from Isaiah 64: 20-23, by the former Secretary for Evangelism of the WCC.

EV528 Geitz, Elizabeth Rankin

Entertaining Angels: Hospitality Programs for the Caring Church. Harrisburg, PAU: Morehouse Publishing, 1993. 142 pp. Paper. 0819216011.

Ideas for creating a successful newcomer ministry program in a local church with high lay involvement in outreach to youth, singles, young families, the sick, homeless, and the unemployed.

EV529 Green, Michael

Evangelism through the Local Church. Nashville, TNU: Nelson, 1992. xvi, 590 pp. 0840791593.

A detailed presentation of evangelistic principles and practices for parishes seeking meaningful outreach in a secular society by the former rector of St. Aldate's in Oxford, England, and current Professor of Evangelism at Regent College in Vancouver, Canada; originally published in Great Britain in 1990 by Hodder & Stoughton.

EV530 Green, Michael

La Iglesia Local, Agente de Evangelización. Grand Rapids, MIU: Nueva Creación, 1996. 616 pp. Paper. 0802809375.

Spanish translation.

EV531 Greenway, Roger S., ed.

The Pastor-Evangelist: Preacher, Model, and Mobilizer for Church Growth. Phillipsburg, NJU: Presbyterian & Reformed Publishing, 1987. viii, 205 pp. Paper. 0875522793.

A collection of fourteen short chapters by American pastor-evangelists giving practical helps for local churches on ways to share the Gospel with others.

EV532 Hadaway, C. Kirk

What Can We Do about Church Dropouts? (Creative Leadership Series). Nashville, TNU: Abingdon, 1990. 134 pp. Paper. 0687446058.

A readable study of persons who have drifted away, fled, or been "pushed out" of churches in the United States, with suggestions for outreach to them by a specialist in urban and church growth research for the Southern Baptist Convention.

EV533 Hanchey, Howard

Church Growth and the Power of Evangelism: Ideas That Work. Cambridge, MAU: Cowley Publications, 1990. xii, 247 pp. Paper. 1561010081 (hdbk), 1561010170 (pbk).

A primer for mainline Protestant churches in decline with multiple ideas on how to move a parish from maintenance to mission.

EV534 Harre, Alan F.

Close the Back Door: Ways to Create a Caring Congregational Fellowship. (Speaking the Gospel Series). St. Louis, MOU: Concordia Publishing, 1984. 127 pp. Paper. 0570039320.

Suggestions as to how clergy and laity can respond to those who have already "dropped out" of church life and become inactive members.

EV535 Hendee, John

Smart Fishing: Ways a Congregation Can Reach More People for Christ. Cincinnati, OHU: Standard Publishing, 1991. 160 pp. Paper. 087403857X.

An evangelism plan for the local church focusing on preprospects, prospects, plus new, active, and inactive members.

EV536 Hill, Richard O.

Training Evangelism Callers: Caller Manual. Minneapolis, MNU: Augsburg, 1986. 64 pp. 0806622288.

A training manual written by a pastor actively equipping laypersons for visitation ministry; designed as a ten-session series, focusing on the visitors and their relationship to those visited.

EV537 Hinson, William H.

A Place to Dig in: Doing Evangelism in the Local Church. Nashville, TNU: Abingdon, 1987. 139 pp. 0687315492.

Models for local church evangelism by the pastor of the 13,000-member First United Methodist Church of Houston, Texas.

EV538 Hunter, George G.

The Contagious Congregation: Frontiers in Evangelism and Church Growth. Nashville, TNU: Abingdon, 1979. 160 pp. Paper. 0687094909.

A combination of the insights of modern psychology and of church growth theory, for reaching the unchurched in a secular age.

EV539 Huston, Sterling W.

Crusade Evangelism and the Local Church. Minneapolis, MNU: World Wide Publications, 1984. 215 pp. Paper. 0890660484.

A readable analysis of the principles and practical methods of Billy Graham Crusades for North America, with emphasis on how these principles can be implemented in the evangelism program of the local churches of North America.

EV540 Jorstad, Eric et al.

What Lutherans Can Learn about Outreach: Why People Join and Why They Leave a Congregation. Minneapolis, MNU: American Lutheran Church, 1987. 46 pp. No ISBN.

This book is based on a 1985-1986 study of 131 congregations of The American Lutheran Church, which attempted to find why adults (other than transferees) were joining these congregations, why they were leaving, and which evangelism training activities were most effective in creating evangelistic zeal in a congregation.

EV541 Kallestad, Walt

Entertainment Evangelism: Taking the Church Public. Nashville, TNU: Abingdon, 1996. 144 pp. 0687054508.

Helps for designing and developing ministry and styles of worship that attract those tuned in on media and entertainment attractions, based on the author's experience as Senior Pastor of The Community [Lutheran] Church of Joy in Phoenix, Arizona.

EV542 Kallestad, Walt, and Tim Wright

Reaching the Unchurched: Creating the Vision: Planning to Grow. Minneapolis, MNU: Augsburg Fortress, 1994. 104 pp. No ISBN.

A four-part training program for local leaders of mainline churches, with workbook and video filmed at the Lutheran Community Church of Joy in Glendale, Arizona.

EV543 Keifert, Patrick R.

Welcoming the Stranger: A Public Theology of Worship and Evangelism. Minneapolis, MNU: Fortress Press, 1992. xi, 170 pp. Paper. 0800624920.

Theology and strategies for the practice of parish hospitality as expressed in the worship experience of Christians, by the Associate Professor of Systematic Theology at Luther Northwestern Theological Seminary in St. Paul, Minnesota.

EV544 Langford, Andy, and Sally Overby Langford

Worship and Evangelism. (Pathways to Church Growth). Nashville, TNU: Discipleship Resources, 1989. xii, 84 pp. Paper. 0881770744.

Resources for parish pastors desiring to climax worship with appropriate invitations to Christian discipleship, and to bring forth evangelistic emphases during the seasons of the Christian year.

EV545 Larsen, David L.

The Evangelism Mandate: Recovering the Centrality of Gospel Preaching. Wheaton, ILU: Crossway Books, 1992. 256 pp. Paper. 0891076786.

The nature, theology, urgency, and methods of evangelistic preaching in the local church, with the texts of five classic Gospel sermons.

EV546 Lewis, Larry L.

Organize to Evangelize. Nashville, TNU: Broadman, 1988. 132 pp. Paper. 0805462570.

A study guide for evangelistic progress in the local church, based on the "Flake Formula," by a former pastor and President of the Home Board of the Southern Baptist Convention.

EV547 Libert, Samuel O.

Más allá de lo imposible: La iglesia local evángelizando al mundo. Buenos Aires, AG: Casa Bautista de Publicaciones, 1973. 112 pp. Paper. No ISBN.

A manual for evangelism programming in the local church.

EV548 Lorentzen, Melvin E., ed.

Evangelistic Preaching: A Self-Study Course in Creating and Presenting Messages that Call People to Jesus Christ. Minneapolis, MNU: World Wide Publications, 1990. 175 pp. Paper. 089066210X.

Self-study manual and six cassette tapes which challenge people to make personal, eternal decisions about Jesus Christ through the evangelistic sermon; includes messages from Billy Graham, Charles Swindoll, and Luis Palau, as well as readings from sermons by John Wesley, Dwight L. Moody, and Charles H. Spurgeon.

EV549 Loscalzo, Craig A.

Evangelistic Preaching That Connects: Guidance in Shaping Fresh & Appealing Sermons. Downers Grove, ILU: InterVarsity, 1995. 177 pp. Paper. 0830818634.

Guidance in shaping evangelistic sermons that are fresh and appealing to today's unbeliever.

EV550 Lynch, Pat

Awakening the Giant: Evangelism and the Catholic Church. London, ENK: Darton, Longman & Todd, 1990. xii, 146 pp. Paper. 0232518661.

A well-known Roman Catholic preacher and evangelist in Britain and Ireland presents a biblical rationale and program goals for the Decade of Evangelization in the Roman Catholic Church.

EV551 Marshall, Michael

Great Expectations?: Preparing for Evangelism through Bible Study. Cambridge, MAU: Cowley Publications, 1991. xi, 145 pp. Paper. 1561010332.

Daily Bible studies of the Book of Acts designed for use in the six weeks after Easter, to prepare congregations for a new commitment to evangelism.

EV552 Martin, O. Dean

Invite: What Do You Do After the Sermon? Nashville, TNU: Tidings, 1973. 80 pp. No ISBN.

The author tries to help the reader (minister) find a way, at the close of each sermon, to challenge the hearers to some kind of commitment.

EV553 McIntosh, Gary

The Exodus Principle: A 5-Part Strategy to Free Your People for Ministry. Nashville, TNU: Broadman, 1995. iii, 204 pp. 0805461876.

Practical helps by an experienced North American church consultant, for local churches desiring to develop a "culture of service" to persons in need.

EV554 McIntosh, Gary, and Glen Martin

Finding Them, Keeping Them: Effective Strategies for Evangelism and Assimilation in the Local Church. Nashville, TNU: Broadman, 1992. 143 pp. Paper. 0805460519.

An introduction for laity to various strategies for evangelism, church growth, and the assimilation of new members.

EV555 Miller, Herb

Evangelism's Open Secrets. St. Louis, MOU: Bethany Press, 1977. 112 pp. Paper. 0827208030.

Practical inspiration and helps for pastors and laity based on study of nearly 500 churches, with an outline for a three-session church growth seminar.

EV556 Murren, Doug

The Baby Boomerang: Catching Baby Boomers as They Return to Church. Ventura, CAU: Regal Books, 1990. 287 pp. Paper. 0830713956.

Practical helps by the pastor of Eastside Foursquare Church in Kirkland, Washington, which grew from a few charter attendees in 1980 to nearly 4,000 in 1990, a primarily baby boomer congregation.

EV557 Oswald, Roy M., and Speed B. Leas
The Inviting Church: A Study of New Member Assimilation.
New York, NYU: Alban Institute, 1987. 113 pp. Paper. No
ISBN.

A joint effort by two experienced local church consultants reflecting on what happens to people as they discover, explore, and join a local Protestant congregation in
the United States.

EV558 Oswald, Roy M.
*Making Your Church More Inviting: A Step-by-Step Guide
for In-Church Training.* New York, NYU: Alban Institute,
1992. ix, 119 pp. Paper. 1566990556.

The essentials of new member outreach and assimilation, presented as a fifteen-session workshop based on the
"Inviting Church" materials of the Alban Institute.

EV559 Prior, David
*Creating Community: An Every-Member Approach to Min-
istry in the Local Church.* Colorado Springs, COU: Nav-
Press, 1992. 233 pp. Paper. 0891097139.

A popular exposition of principles and strategies for
strengthening Christian community, with experiences of the
author in ministry in England and South Africa.

EV560 Pritchard, Gregory A.
*Willow Creek Seeker Services: Evaluating a New Way of
Doing Church.* Grand Rapids, MIU: Baker Books, 1996.
330 pp. Paper. 0801052742.

A major study of what attracts the unchurched to fast-
growing Willow Creek Community Church in South Barrington, Illinois; originally submitted as a Ph.D. thesis at
Northwestern University in 1994.

EV561 Rainer, Thom S.
*Effective Evangelistic Churches: Successful Churches Re-
veal What Works and What Doesn't.* Nashville, TNU:
Broadman, 1996. xviii, 238 pp. Paper. 0805454020.

Results of a study of Southern Baptist churches in the
United States that reached at least one person for Christ in
1992/1993 for every twenty members.

**EV562 Ratz, Calvin C., Frank R. Tillapaugh, and Myron S.
Augsburger**
Mastering Outreach and Evangelism. (Mastering Ministry). Portland, ORU: Multnomah, 1990. 168 pp.
0880703636.

Identification of the challenges faced in leading a
church to significant, people-centered outreach, including
how to help motivate and deploy people to share the richness of the Gospel through ministries of compassion and
evangelism.

EV563 Rauff, Edward A.
Why People Join the Church. New York, NYU: Pilgrim
Press; Washington, DCU: Glenmary Research, 1979. viii,
212 pp. Paper. 0829803874.

An analysis of 180 interviews with formerly unchurched persons across the United States, revealing why
they dropped out of church, came back, and what the church
means to them now.

EV564 Robinson, Darrell W.
Total Church Life: Exalt, Equip, Evangelize. Nashville,
TNU: Broadman, 1993. 223 pp. Paper. 0805462503.

Revised edition of a practical guide by the Vice President for Evangelism of the Southern Baptist Convention's
Home Mission Board for church staff members and laypersons on how people can be reached effectively for Christ.

EV565 Scifres, Mary J.
*Searching for Seekers: Ministry with a New Generation of
the Unchurched.* Nashville, TNU: Abingdon, 1998. 177
pp. Paper. 0687005523.

Tools for reaching the new generation by understanding the various kinds of seekers such as "Sunday-Schooled
Seekers" and "Anti-Church Seekers," and creating "seeker-
friendly" worship services to reach them.

EV566 Senn, Frank C.
*The Witness of the Worshiping Community: Liturgy and the
Practice of Evangelism.* New York, NYU: Paulist Press,
1993. iii, 177 pp. Paper. 0809133687.

An argument by a Lutheran liturgist and pastor that an
experience of true worship, in word and sacrament, can draw
persons to new faith commitments.

EV567 Smith, Donald P.
How to Attract and Keep Active Church Members. Louisville, KYU: Westminster John Knox, 1992. 184 pp. Paper.
0664251404.

A review for mainline Protestant churches in the United States of issues of assimilation of new members, congregational vitality, church growth, conflict management,
and membership dropout, based on interviews with leaders
in 600 parishes.

EV568 Smith, Glenn C., ed.
Evangelizing Adults. Washington, DCU: Paulist National
Catholic Evangelization Association; Wheaton, ILU: Tyn-
dale House, 1985. 409 pp. Paper. 0842307931.

A handbook on the art of evangelism in the United
States from both Catholic and Protestant prospectives, containing contributions by nine evangelists, plus short descriptions of twelve outstanding evangelizing churches, nine
parachurch organizations, and seven resource agencies.

EV569 Smith, Glenn C., ed.
Evangelizing Youth. Washington, DCU: Paulist National
Catholic Evangelization Association; Wheaton, ILU: Tyn-
dale House, 1985. 366 pp. Paper. 0842307915.

A guidebook containing valuable information about
outstanding leaders, churches, organizations, and agencies,
both Catholic and Protestant, in the evangelization of youth
in the United States.

EV570 Southard, Samuel
Pastoral Evangelism. Atlanta, GAU: John Knox Press,
1981. 197 pp. 0804220379.

Revised edition of an independent analysis of the relationship between faith development and the work of the pastor as evangelist, by the Professor of Pastoral Theology at
Fuller Theological Seminary; originally published in 1962
(Broadman, Nashville, TNU).

EV571 Streett, R. Alan
The Effective Invitation. Old Tappan, NJU: Revell, 1984.
252 pp. 0800712412 (hdbk), 0800751701 (pbk).

A practical handbook used to develop an understanding, theology, and responses that revolve around the presentation of public invitations (altar calls).

EV—EVANGELISM AND MISSIONS

EV572 Stutzman, Ervin R.

Welcome!: A Biblical and Practical Guide to Receiving New Members. Scottdale, PAU: Herald Press, 1990. 174 pp. Paper. 083613530X.

A practical guide with numerous anecdotes on how any congregation can welcome newcomers.

EV573 Swanson, Roger K., and Shirley F. Clement

The Faith-Sharing Congregation: Developing a Strategy for the Congregation as Evangelist. Nashville, TNU: Discipleship Resources, 1996. viii, 107 pp. Paper. 0881771589.

A primer for mainline Protestant churches by two United Methodist church leaders in evangelism, on how to reclaim the local church congregation as the center of ministry and mission.

EV574 Terry, John Mark

Church Evangelism: Creating a Culture for Growth in Your Congregation. Nashville, TNU: Broadman, 1997. x, 227 pp. Paper. 0805410651.

A wide-ranging survey of techniques for the local church to mobilize for evangelistic outreach, by the Associate Professor of Evangelism and Missions at Southern Baptist Theological Seminary.

EV575 Turner, Gordon Bruce

Outside Looking In. Toronto, ONC: United Church Publishing House, 1987. viii, 133 pp. Paper. 0919000371.

A deliberate, yet compassionate, study of church dropouts and how to minister to them in a way that helps them reconsider coming back into the church, by the Secretary for Evangelism of the United Church of Canada.

EV576 Veerman, David R.

Youth Evangelism. Wheaton, ILU: Victor Books, 1984. 214 pp. 0896935698.

A practical step-by-step handbook for evangelical youth ministry in the USA by the National Campus Life Director for Youth for Christ/United States.

EV577 Walker, Alan

Evangelistic Preaching. Grand Rapids, MIU: Asbury Press, 1988. 110 pp. Paper. 0310752612.

An introductory textbook on evangelistic preaching and its place in a pluralistic society; by the evangelist from Australia who was Director of the World Evangelism for the World Methodist Council.

EV578 Webber, Robert E.

Celebrating Our Faith: Evangelism through Worship. San Francisco, CAU: Harper & Row, 1986. ix, 118 pp. 0060692863.

A call for "liturgical evangelism" among Protestants, which would restore the third-century practice of the adult catechumenate as Roman Catholics have done through the Rite of Christian Initiation of Adults (RCIA).

EV579 Weeden, Larry K., ed.

The Magnetic Fellowship: Reaching and Keeping People. (Leadership Library, 15). Waco, TXU: Word Books, 1988. 192 pp. 091746320X.

Fourteen short articles by leading evangelical Christians on attracting and keeping newcomers; originally published in the 1980s in *Leadership*.

EV580 Weeks, Andrew D.

Welcome!: Tools and Techniques for New Member Ministry. Washington, DCU: Alban Institute, 1992. xxvi, 123 pp. Paper. 1566990572.

A detailed how-to manual for parishes desiring a systematic approach for welcoming and tracking newcomers, based on the author's extensive knowledge and experience as a church consultant in the United States.

EV581 Willimon, William H., and Stanley Hauerwas

Preaching to Strangers: Evangelism in Today's World. Louisville, KYU: Westminster John Knox, 1992. vii, 144 pp. Paper. 0664251056.

Twelve sermons for those who have not yet heard or responded to the Gospel; by the Professor of Theological Ethics at Duke University, with commentary on preaching and evangelism in contemporary culture by Hauerwas, the Professor of Divinity and Law at Duke Divinity School.

EV582 Willimon, William H.

The Intrusive Word: Preaching to the Unbaptized. Grand Rapids, MIU: Eerdmans, 1994. viii, 144 pp. Paper. 0802807062.

Preaching presented as an act of evangelism in today's church; by the Dean of the Chapel and Professor of Christian Ministry at Duke University, Durham, North Carolina.

EV583 Winter, David

Communicating the Gospel Today. Oxford, ENK: Lynx Communications; Sutherland, AT: Albatross Books, 1993. 40 pp. Paper. 0745926916 (UK), 0732406692 (AT).

A nine-session bible study for small groups, with applications to church-based evangelism; includes audiocassette and study guide.

EV584 Wright, Tim

Unfinished Evangelism: More Than Getting Them in the Door. Minneapolis, MNU: Augsburg, 1995. 126 pp. Paper. 0806627948.

Practical helps for congregations seeking new ministries to secular people; by the Lutheran executive pastor of Community Church of Joy in Phoenix, Arizona.

Prophetic Evangelism and Social Concerns

See also HI149, TH117-TH118, ME57, ME234, EC245, PO43, EV37, EV109, EV156, EV258, CH168-CH169, AM13, AM30, AM32, AM445-AM446, AM450, AM1226, AS980, and AS1446.

EV585 Armstrong, James

From the Underside: Evangelism from a Third World Vantage Point. Maryknoll, NYU: Orbis Books, 1981. xiv, 93 pp. Paper. 0883441462.

A creative linking of evangelism and justice concerns, utilizing insights from Christians in Latin America, Africa, and Asia.

EV586 Brown, Fred

Libres para Comunicar: Una Nueva Visión de la Evangelización. México, MX: Casa Unida de Publicaciones, 1976. 144 pp. No ISBN.

Spanish translation.

EV587 Brown, Fred

Secular Evangelism. London, ENK: SCM Press, 1970. 126 pp. Paper. 0334014751.

A popular theology and strategy for evangelism forged by a Salvation Army major out of ministry in London's West End.

EV588 Conn, Harvie M.

Evangelism: Doing Justice and Preaching Grace. Grand Rapids, MIU: Zondervan, 1982. 112 pp. Paper. 0310453119.

A study relating evangelism and social justice concerns, with regard for prayer and spirituality; by a prominent evangelical Protestant missiologist.

EV589 Consultation on the Relationship between Evangelism and Social Responsibility (1982: Grand Rapids, Michigan)

Evangelism and Social Responsibility: An Evangelical Commitment. (Lausanne Occasional Papers, 21). Wheaton, ILU: LCWE, 1982. 64 pp. Paper. No ISBN.

The report and papers from an important consultation jointly sponsored by the LCWE and the WEF.

EV590 Miles, Delos

Evangelism and Social Involvement. Nashville, TNU: Broadman, 1986. 189 pp. 0805462481.

A basic text from a Protestant evangelical perspective on the relation between evangelism and social service, with biblical, theological, historical, and contemporary rationales for a holistic approach.

EV591 Moberg, David O.

The Great Reversal: Evangelism Versus Social Concern. (Evangelical Perspectives). Philadelphia, PAU: Lippincott, 1972. 194 pp. 0879810092.

A popular attempt to restore evangelical Christianity to a balanced emphasis on evangelism and social concern.

EV592 Richardson, William J.

Social Action vs. Evangelism: An Essay on the Contemporary Crisis. South Pasadena, CAU: William Carey Library, 1977. viii, 52 pp. Paper. 0878081607.

In this essay the Professor of New Testament and History at Northwest Christian College, Eugene, Oregon, sets forth the conviction that evangelism understood in biblical terms is not only compatible with, but is a necessary perspective, for social action.

EV593 Sider, Ronald J.

One-Sided Christianity?: Uniting the Church to Heal a Lost and Broken World. Grand Rapids, MIU: Zondervan; San Francisco, CAU: HarperSanFrancisco, 1993. 256 pp. Paper. 0310587611.

A prophetic call for Christians to combine evangelism with social concern in a style consistent with our larger understanding of Jesus, by the Professor of Theology and Culture at Eastern Baptist Theological Seminary.

EV594 Truesdale, Albert L., and Steve Weber, eds.

Evangelism and Social Redemption: Addresses from a Conference on Compassionate Ministry, November 1985. Kansas City, MOU: Beacon Hill Press, 1987. 150 pp. Paper. 0834111969.

Nine addresses by well-known mission leaders originally delivered at Nazarene Theological Seminary, Kansas City, 8-10 November 1985, with a selection of Nazarene documents on holistic mission.

EV595 Van Houten, Mark E.

Profane Evangelism: Taking the Gospel Into the "Unholy Places." Grand Rapids, MIU: Zondervan, 1989. 143 pp. Paper. 0310519519.

In this popular work a minister to the street people of Northside Chicago develops the thesis that Christians are able to evangelize most biblically and effectively as they incarnate Christ in profane settings.

EV596 Wallis, Jim

The Call to Conversion. Tring, ENK: Lion Publishing, 1986. xviii, 221 pp. 0745911390 (UK), 0867608412 (AT).

A call to the North American Church to be converted to costly discipleship and authentic community; by the editor of *Sojourners*; originally published in 1981 (San Francisco, CAU: Harper & Row).

EV597 Zorrilla, Hugo

The Good News of Justice: Share the Gospel: Live Justly. (Peace and Justice Series, 4). Scottdale, PAU: Herald Press, 1988. 86 pp. Paper. 0836134737.

A popular biblical exposition presenting evangelism as proclamation and lifestyle, justice as the cornerstone of the Gospel, and the relationship of justice to evangelism.

EV—EVANGELISM AND MISSIONS

MISSIONARIES

Joyce Bowers, Subeditor

Christian mission began with Christ's commissioning of the disciples to go and make disciples (Mt. 28:19). Soon the early church acknowledged that there were a variety of gifts for ministry (1 Cor. 12:4, 28-29). In the church in Antioch, where believers were first called "Christians," there were prophets and teachers, but also those set apart for cross-cultural mission (Acts 13:2). Today we call such persons *missionaries* or *persons in mission*.

The various dimensions of missionary service have been called *missionary diaconics* (Jongeneel, 1997:307-309). This chapter focuses upon the various aspects of such service.

Following reference works can be found "General Works" on missionary service. Next comes a subsection entitled "Types of Missionaries." While the full-time salaried missionary was once the norm, today there are a growing variety of forms of missionary service. The fastest growing type of cross-cultural workers are "Missionaries from the Third World."

Works in the next two sections concerning the life cycle of the missionary include recruitment, training, and in-service concerns, including the pastoral care of missionaries. Next is presented the considerable literature on missionary children.

The most numerous books on missionary service are biographies (collective or individual) and autobiographies. Most of these are to be found in geographical sections by country or subregion of service. This chapter contains only collected works, or biographies of persons in mission who served in several countries.

Norman E. Thomas

Bibliography

MI1 Austin, Clyde Neal
Cross-Cultural Reentry: An Annotated Bibliography. Abilene, TXU: ACU Press, 1983. xiv, 128 pp. Paper. 0915547007.

Literature on the problems of missionaries and others adjusting to western life after overseas service.

MI2 Missionary Research Library
Missionary Biography: An Initial Bibliography. New York, NYU: MRL, 1965. 151 pp. Paper. No ISBN.

A listing of 1,204 books and pamphlet titles of individual biographies, 486 articles on individual missionaries, 126 obituaries, and 339 titles dealing with multiple missionaries, with author/editor/compiler index.

Reference Works

See also GW40.

MI3 Beckmann, David M., Timothy J. Mitchell, and Linda L. Powers
The Overseas List: Opportunities for Living and Working in Developing Countries. Minneapolis, MNU: Augsburg, 1985. 224 pp. Paper. 0806621818.

The revised comprehensive handbook, with a collection of opportunities for working in developing countries by types of sending agencies, including church missions.

MI4 Lewis, Donald M., ed.
The Blackwell Dictionary of Evangelical Biography, 1730-1860. Oxford, ENK: Blackwell Publishers, 1995. 2 vols. 0631173846.

A biographical dictionary of Protestant evangelicalism, 1730-1860, with information on 1,100 key leaders including many missionaries and mission leaders.

MI5 Windsor, Raymond, ed.
World Directory of Missionary Training Programmes: A Catalogue of Over 500 Missionary Training Programmes from Around the World. South Pasadena, CAU: William Carey Library, 1995. vii, 333 pp. Paper. 087808259X.

The second edition of the WEF's handbook containing profiles of 514 missionary training programs in their network.

Documentation and Archives

See also HI723.

MI6 Hunter, Jane
The Gospel of Gentility: American Women Missionaries in Turn-of-the-Century China. New Haven, CTU: Yale University, 1984. xxi, 318 pp. 0300028784.

A historical analysis of the problems and opportunities facing both married and single women missionaries in China in the late 19th and early 20th centuries.

Conferences and Congresses

See also EV36.

MI7 Centre national des vocations, comp.
Missionaires pour demain: Session de Lyon, 1965. (Pour les appels de notre temps). Paris, FR: Éditions du Centurion, 1966. 207 pp. No ISBN.

Papers contributed to a conference on preparation for the missionary work of the Roman Catholic Church.

General Works

See also HI698, ME84, AF56, AF89, AF1256, AM152, and AS1051.

MI8 Almquist, Arden
Missionary, Come Back!. New York, NYU: World Publishing Company, 1970. xviii, 201 pp. No ISBN.

An apologetic for cross-cultural missions as "presence" and "cross" by the Executive Secretary of World Mission, Evangelical Covenant Church of America.

MI9 Austin, Clyde Neal, ed.
Cross-Cultural Reentry: A Book of Readings. Abilene, TXU: Abilene Christian University Press, 1986. xxix, 288 pp. Paper. 0915547740.

An anthology of twenty essays on issues of return to their culture by government employees, business personnel, missionaries, international students, and their children.

MI10 Bailey, Helen L., and Herbert C. Jackson
A Study of Missionary Motivation, Training, and Withdrawal, 1953-1962. New York, NYU: MRL, 1965. 99 pp. Paper. No ISBN.

An analysis of the motivation, training and reasons for termination covering responses of 670 North American Protestant missionaries who withdrew from service under thirty-six mission boards during the 1953-1962 period.

MI11 Beaver, Robert Pierce
The Missionary between the Times. Garden City, NYU: Doubleday, 1968. xiii, 196 pp. No ISBN.

A popular rationale for the continued sending of missionaries, developed in lectures to newly appointed and furloughed missionaries by the distinguished former Professor of Missions at Chicago Divinity School.

MI12 Brusco, Elizabeth, and Laura F. Klein, eds.
The Message in the Missionary: Local Interpretations of Religious Ideology and Missionary Personality. (Studies in Third World Societies, 50). Williamsburg, VAU: College of William and Mary, Department of Anthropology, 1994. viii, 146 pp. No ISBN.

Eight scholarly case studies on the impact of missionaries including four on women missionaries.

MI13 Burridge, Kenelm
In the Way: A Study of Christian Missionary Endeavours. Vancouver, BCC: UBC Press, 1991. xvi, 307 pp. 0774803762.

A detailed assessment of the contradictions and ambiguities of missionary service, building a theory about their role in Christianity and the building of Christian communities.

MI14 Cannon, Joseph L.
For Missionaries Only. Grand Rapids, MIU: Baker Books, 1969. 96 pp. No ISBN.

Forty-seven meditations for missionaries on themes connected with their life and work, from the author's experiences as a missionary in Japan and Okinawa.

MI15 Collins, Marjorie A.
Manual for Today's Missionary from Recruitment to Retirement. South Pasadena, CAU: William Carey Library, 1986. x, 390 pp. Paper. 0878082042.

A one-volume textbook on missionary preparation, orientation, training, field experience, furlough, and retirement, written from an evangelical Protestant perspective; includes material from several of the author's previous books.

MI16 Derroitte, Henri, and Claude Soetens
La mémoire missionnaire: les chemins sinueux de l'inculturation. (Théologies pratiques). Brussels, BE: Lumen Vitae, 1999. 196 pp. Paper. 2873241284.

An analysis of responses by 123 Belgian Catholic missionaries (men and women) to questions concerning missionary life, social relations, the transmission of the message, and inculturation, with chapters on missionary life in the Congo (former Zaire), and on the work of lay catechists in Burundi.

MI17 Doenig, Dennis A.
The Prophet's Return: God's Missions and the Manners of Men. East Aurora, NYU: Ionisus Press, 1996. iv, 666 pp. Paper. 0965422410.

A narrative account for future prophet-missionaries on biblical, historical, and contemporary models for such leadership.

MI18 Exley, Richard, and Helen Exley
The Missionary Myth: An Agnostic View of Contemporary Missionaries. Guildford, ENK: Lutterworth Press, 1973. 178 pp. 0718820266.

An assessment of missionary effectiveness in various countries of Africa based on in-depth interviews.

MI19 Jacobs, Sylvia M., ed.
Black Americans and the Missionary Movement in America. Westport, CTU: Greenwood, 1982. xii, 255 pp. 0313232806.

Twelve scholarly essays on the role of black Americans in the Protestant mission movement in Africa before 1960, focusing on their methods, interests, and activities.

MI20 Jordan, Peter
Re-Entry: Making the Transition from Missions to Life at Home. Seattle, WAU: YWAM Publishing, 1992. 150 pp. Paper. 0927545403.

A primer for missionaries on facing the emotional challenges of entry, cross-cultural service, and re-entry into the culture of birth, based on the author's experience of counseling with hundreds of returning missionaries.

MI—MISSIONARIES

MI21 Kane, J. Herbert
The Making of a Missionary. Grand Rapids, MIU: Baker Books, 1987. 115 pp. Paper. 0801054818.

Second edition of an orientation for new missionaries on what they will encounter in various settings.

MI22 Keidel, Levi O.
Stop Treating Me Like God. Carol Stream, ILU: Creation House, 1971. 223 pp. No ISBN.

A popular exposé of many of the stereotypes and time-honored images of the missionary (as person, in cultural settings, and with supporters), with alternate helpful images by a former Congo Inland Mission missionary.

MI23 Murphey, Cecil B.
But God Has Promised. Carol Stream, ILU: Creation House, 1976. 169 pp. 0884190021.

A first hand account by a missionary of the Elim Church in Kenya from 1961 to 1967 of his call, fund-raising, and service at the Suna Mission among the Luo people, with open acknowledgment of failures and problems in interpersonal relationships.

MI24 Neill, Stephen Charles
Call to Mission. Philadelphia, PAU: Fortress Press, 1970. v, 113 pp. No ISBN.

Neill clarifies the biblical basis of missionary endeavor and evaluates its past and future, recognizing the pitfalls of paternalism, sectarianism, and rejection of local customs, concluding that it is necessary to continue Christian witness on a worldwide basis.

MI25 Niles, Daniel Thambyrajah
The Message and Its Messengers. New York, NYU: Abingdon, 1966. 128 pp. No ISBN.

An essay on missionaries by the noted Sri Lankan Theologian.

MI26 Pettifer, Julian, and Richard Bradley
Missionaries. London, ENK: BBC Books; New York, NYU: Parkwest Publications, 1990. 272 pp. 0563207027.

An illustrated interpretive history of the impact of missionaries throughout Christian history, based on the six-part BBC television series by the same title.

MI27 Pirolo, Neal
Sirviendo al enviar Obreros: Cómo apoyar a sus misioneros. Miami, FLU: Editorial Unilit, 1991. 206 pp. Paper. 1880185059.

Spanish translation of *Serving As Senders* (Emmaus Road, Int'l., 1991).

MI28 Roundhill, Kenneth S.
Prescription for Today's Missionary. London, ENK: Marshall, Morgan & Scott, 1972. 157 pp. 0551051787.

A primer on the call and character of lay missionaries related both to the biblical guidance, and to the contemporary culture of Great Britain.

MI29 Semana Española de Misionología (1982, Burgos, Spain)
La Familia en una Églesia Misionera: Las vocaciones misioneras. (Biblioteca "Semanas Misionales"). Burgos, SP: Secretariado de Semanas Españolas de Misionología, Facultad deTeologí, 1984. ix, 378 pp. 8439816642.

A collection of papers (from two meetings in Spain) concerning the role of the family in the church, and the history and current status of lay and ordained missionaries.

MI30 Taylor, William David, ed.
Demasiado Valioso para que se Pierda: Exploración de las causas y curas del retiro misionero anticipado. (Serie sobre la globalización de la misión). Wheaton, ILU: WEF/Comibam International, 1997. 370 pp. Paper. No ISBN.

Spanish translation.

MI31 Taylor, William David, ed.
Too Valuable to Lose: Exploring the Causes and Cures of Missionary Attrition. (Globalization of Mission Series). South Pasadena, CAU: William Carey Library, 1997. xviii, 380 pp. Paper. 0878082778.

Findings of a fourteen-nation study by the World Evangelical Fellowship, with fifteen papers on the problem, the research, national case studies, and specific themes.

MI32 Thunberg, Lars, ed.
Missionaeren menighedens udsending. (Nyt Synspunkt, 26). Hellerup, DK: DMS-Forlag, 1987. 52 pp. Paper. 8774311328.

The main article, written by Knud Sorensen, General Secretary of the Danish Missionary Society, is about the role of the missionary in service of the local congregation/church, with three respondents.

MI33 Triebel, Johannes, ed.
Der Missionar als Forscher: Beiträge christlicher Missionare zur Erforschung fremder Kulturen und Religionen. (Missionswissenschaftliche Forschungen, 21). Gütersloh, GW: Mohn, 1988. 172 pp. Paper. 3579002414.

Nine lectures by a group of experts in comparative religion and missiology dealing mainly with Africa but also with religious manifestations in Asia and Oceania.

MI34 Tucker, Ruth A.
E até aos confins da terra: Uma história biográfica das missões cristãs. Edited by Barbara Burns. Translated by Neyd Siqueira. São Paulo, BL: Sociedade Religiosa Edições Vida Nova, 1986. 590 pp. No ISBN.

Portuguese translation.

MI35 Tucker, Ruth A.
From Jerusalem to Irian Jaya: A Biographical History of Christian Missions. (World Christian Series). Grand Rapids, MIU: Zondervan, 1983. 511 pp. Paper. 0310459311.

A series of vignettes which cover all periods of Christian missions, with an emphasis on the 19th and 20th centuries; contains sections on medical missions, translators, radio and recording ministries, and missionary aviation.

MI36 Warren, Max Alexander Cunningham
Social History and Christian Mission. London, ENK: SCM Press, 1967. 191 pp. No ISBN.

Eight lectures on missionaries in the British Empire in the 19th and 20th centuries focusing on social and economic background and impact of the missionaries, and church-state relations; by the former General Secretary of the Church Missionary Society (1942-1963).

Types of Missionaries

See also GW198, ME1, ME66, ME176, ED76, EV34, MI32, and AS1362.

MI37 Anthony, Michael J., ed.
The Short-Term Missions Boom: A Guide to International and Domestic Involvement. Grand Rapids, MIU: Baker Books, 1994. 236 pp. Paper. 0801002338.

A handbook on how a local church can organize, motivate, train, and finance short-term mission workers by sixteen specialists in the field.

MI38 Carter, Jeannine K.
Have Heart, Will Travel: Personal Experiences and Practical Guidelines for Volunteer Mission Trips. Franklin, TNU: Providence House, 1996. 128 pp. Paper. 1577360249.

The author's personal testimony on her sixteen international trips as a volunteer in mission.

MI39 Danielson, Edward E., Barbara Cummings, and Marion Fry
Lord, Send Me: A Handbook for Single Missionaries. Manila, PH: Faith Academy, 1984. 82 pp. Paper. No ISBN.

A practical guide for single missionaries based on the authors' thirty years of experience as counselors and psychologists among them.

MI40 Eaton, Chris, and Kim Hurst
Vacations with a Purpose: A Planning Handbook for Your Short-Term Missions Team. Colorado Springs, COU: NavPress, 1991. 220 pp. Paper. 0891096094 (LM), 0891096108 (TM).

A comprehensive planning guide (leader's manual) for leaders of short-term missions trips, including recruitment, site selection, relationships, and debriefing; with team member's manual.

MI41 Garrison, V. David
The Nonresidential Missionary: A New Strategy and the People It Serves. (Innovations in Missions Series, 1). Birmingham, ALU: New Hope; Monrovia, CAU: MARC, 1990. 161 pp. Paper. 0912552719.

The Director of Nonresidential Missions for the Foreign Mission Board of the Southern Baptist Convention examines the ministry of missionaries who work with unevangelized populations, but who are prohibited from living among them.

MI42 Gibson, Tim et al., eds.
Stepping Out: A Guide to Short Term Missions. Seattle, WAU: YWAM Publishing, 1992. 216 pp. Paper. 0927545292.

Forty-nine short articles prepared by members of The Fellowship of Short-Term Mission Leaders as a primer for those considering short-term mission service.

MI43 Griffiths, Michael
Tinker, Tailor, Missionary?: Options in a Changing World. Leicester, ENK: InterVarsity, 1992. 222 pp. Paper. 0851108601.

Guidance for those seeking to serve as part-time missionaries.

MI44 Haines, J. Harry
I'm Only One Person, What Can I Do? Nashville, TNU: Upper Room Books, 1985. 124 pp. Paper. 0835805212.

A very interesting collection of stories of what has been accomplished by persons in different parts of the world who, embued with a great faith in God, say with their actions, "I and my God together, we can do miracles."

MI45 Hamilton, Don
Tentmakers Speak: Practical Advice from over 400 Missionary Tentmakers. Ventura, CAU: GL/Regal Books, 1987. xvi, 99 pp. Paper. 0830713212.

An introduction for Christians considering being self-supporting lay missionaries in the secular world, with practical advice from over 400 tentmakers.

MI46 Hawthorne, Steven C., ed.
Stepping Out: A Guide to Short-Term Missions. Monrovia, CAU: Short-Term Missions Advocates, 1987. 144 pp. Paper. No ISBN.

A popular guide to the multifaceted world of short-term missions, with over sixty articles on the preparation, participation, and subsequent opportunity for this involvement.

MI47 Löffler, Paul
The Layman Abroad in the Mission of the Church: A Decade of Discussion and Experiment. (Research Pamphlets, 10). London, ENK: Edinburgh House Press; New York, NYU: Friendship Press, 1962. 96 pp. Paper. No ISBN.

A clearly organized summary of the philosophy and action of laity as cross-cultural missionaries, focusing on the history and discussion of issues during the previous decade.

MI48 Lewis, Jonathan, ed.
Working Your Way to the Nations: A Guide to Effective Tentmaking. South Pasadena, CAU: William Carey Library, 1993. x, 193 pp. Paper. 0878082441.

A self-help manual for tentmaking missionaries, with essays by mission specialists from around the world and a guide for a personal action plan.

MI49 Loew, Jacques
Comme s'il voyait l'invisible: un portrait de l'apôtre d'aujourd'hui. Paris, FR: Éditions du Cerf, 1964. 240 pp. Paper. No ISBN.

Drawing on the New Testament and his experiences as a worker-priest, the author gives a picture of the unselfish apostle in the modern, secularized European community, as well as in countries outside Europe.

MI50 Rétif, André
Laïcat missionnaire. Le Puy, FR: Mappus, 1966. 110 pp. No ISBN.

A basic primer on lay missionaries in the Roman Catholic Church in thought and contemporary practice.

MI51 Suter, Heinz, and Marco Gmür
Poder Empresarial en Misión Integral. Miami, FLU: Editorial Unilit/PM International, 1997. 112 pp. Paper. 0789904438.

This expanded master's thesis looks at tentmaking ministries as a mission strategy in countries that are difficult for traditional missionaries to enter.

MI52 Tanin, Vicki, Jim Hill, and Ray Howard, comps.
Sending out Servants: A Church-Based Short-Term Missions Strategy. Wheaton, ILU: ACMC, 1995. 89 pp. Paper. No ISBN.

A handbook for local churches sponsoring short-term missionaries.

MI53 Todd, Kathleen, comp.
Crossing Boundaries: Stories from the Frontier Internship in Mission Programme. (WCC Mission Series, 5). Geneva, SZ: WCC, 1985. vi, 108 pp. Paper. 2825408484.

A collection of stories on an experiment in ecumenical mission which crosses racial, cultural, economic, as much as physical and political frontiers, to minister with justice and mercy.

MI54 Van Cise, Martha
Successful Mission Teams: A Guide for Volunteers. Birmingham, ALU: New Hope, 1996. 231 pp. Paper. 1563091690.

A practical guidebook for volunteers involved in short-term mission work.

MI55 Wilson, J. Christy
Today's Tentmakers: Self-Support—An Alternative Model for Worldwide Witness. Wheaton, ILU: Tyndale, 1985. 165 pp. Paper. 0842372792.

A primer aimed to inspire, inform, encourage, and challenge persons interested in becoming self-supporting, cross-cultural missionaries.

MI56 Yamamori, Tetsunao
God's New Envoys: A Bold Strategy for Penetrating "Closed Countries." (New Perspectives on World Ministries). Portland, ORU: Multnomah, 1987. 190 pp. Paper. 0880701889.

A primer for tentmaking missionaries to unreached peoples dealing with motivation, training, strategies, and resources for volunteer, self-supporting missionaries.

Missionaries from the Third World

MI57 *Cry of the Unreached with K. P. Yohannan*
(GFA Video Library). Carrollton, TXU: Gospel for Asia, 1987. 45 mins pp. No ISBN.

On this video the Founder-President of Gospel for Asia argues for support of Asian missionaries to reach unreached peoples.

Recruitment and Training

See also GW225, GW266, HI143, HI593, ME136, ME155, CR442, SO78, SO249, SO478, EC271, ED21, EV438, EV468, MI5, MI15, MI123, MI133, MI143, SP178, and AS647.

MI58 Almquist, L. Arden
Debtor Unashamed: The Road to Mission Is a Two-Way Street. Chicago, ILU: Covenant Publications, 1993. vii, 150 pp. Paper. 0910452768.

Reflections, based on the author's lifetime of service as an ordained minister and medical doctor in Africa, on the importance of being, presence, community, and relationships for effective cross-cultural ministry.

MI59 Asay, Carlos E.
The Seven M's of Missionary Service. Salt Lake City, UTU: Bookcraft, 1996. viii, 146 pp. 1570082871.

Seven motivations to missionary service by a member of the Presidency of the Seventy of the Church of Jesus Christ of Latter-day Saints.

MI60 Barkman, Paul F., Edward R. Dayton, and Edward L. Gruman
Christian Collegians and Foreign Missions. Monrovia, CAU: MARC, 1969. xv, 424 pp. No ISBN.

Analysis of the responses of 5,000 delegates who attended the Ninth InterVarsity Missionary Convention (Urbana, Illinois, 27-31 December 1967), including 83 missionary candidates and 155 furlough missionaries, providing a profile of Protestant evangelicals motivated for missionary service.

MI61 Barton, Grady Carl
A Handbook for Missionaries. Cedarville, OHU: Christian Educational Publications, 1984. 77 pp. No ISBN.

A short guide for missionary candidates.

MI62 Bott, Randy L.
Prepare with Honor: Helps for Future Missionaries. Salt Lake City, UTU: Deseret Book Company, 1995. viii, 111 pp. Paper. 087579954X.

A primer on the essentials of preparing for mission service—physically, mentally, and spiritually.

MI63 Brewster, Dan
Only Paralyzed from the Neck Down: The Life and Ministry of Tom Brewster. South Pasadena, CAU: William Carey Library, 1997. xiii, 310 pp. Paper. 0878082751.

A key missionary strategist paralyzed from the neck down tells of his life story equipping persons for cross-cultural mission.

MI64 Christensen, Joe J., and Barbara K. Christensen
Making Your Home a Missionary Training Center. Salt Lake City, UTU: Desert Books, 1985. x, 102 pp. 087747589X.

A Mormon perspective on the way to teach children and adults in your home about how to prepare intellectually, physically, socially, and spiritually for missionary service.

MI65 Cunningham, Loren, and Janice Rogers
Making Jesus Lord: The Dynamic Power of Laying Down Your Rights. Seattle, WAU: YWAM Publishing, 1988. 156 pp. Paper. 1576580121.

Insights for cross-cultural persons in mission on servant leadership by the co-founders of Youth with a Mission.

MI66 Duncan, Michael
Move Out. Bromley, ENK: STL Books; London, ENK: MARC Europe, 1984. 170 pp. Paper. 0903843919 (S), 0947697020 (M).

A young New Zealand Baptist minister's challenge and guidance for persons considering cross-cultural ministry.

MI67 Engel, James F., and Jerry D. Jones
Baby Boomers and the Future of World Missions: How to Nurture and Channel the Involvement of this Generation for the Cause of World Evangelization. Orange, CAU: Management Development Associates, 1989. iii, 61 pp. No ISBN.

Practical helps for motivating a new generation for mission service.

MI68 Ferris, Robert W., ed.
Establishing Ministry Training: A Manual for Programme Developers. South Pasadena, CAU: William Carey Library, 1995. xviii, 189 pp. Paper. 087808262X.

A practical manual for trainers of cross-cultural missionaries.

MI69 Franzén, Allan
Missionärsutbildning i Norden: Sedd i relation till missionssituation och organisationsidentitet. (Missiologian ja ekumeniikan seuran julkaisuja, 49). Helsinki, FI: University of Helsinki, 1986. 428 pp. Paper. 9519520740.

A dissertation on missionary training models in Scandinavia as related to the missions' situation and the organizational identity, with English summary.

MI—MISSIONARIES

MI70 Godwin, Clement J.
Spend and Be Spent: A Reflection on Missionary Vocation, Spirituality, and Formation, with Particular Reference to India. (ATC Publication, 24). Bangalore, II: Asian Trading Corp, 1977. 209 pp. Paper. No ISBN.

The author, a missionary in India and a Professor of Social Sciences, attempts to reinterpret the missionary's call and spiritual formation in the light of Vatican II.

MI71 Goldsmith, Elizabeth
Getting There from Here: Mission Possible. Bromley, ENK: MARC Europe; London, ENK: Evangelical Missionary·Alliance; London, ENK: STL Books, 1986. 160 pp. Paper. 0947697233 (M), 0950296856 (E), 1850780153 (S).

A popular outline of the biblical basis for mission, with step-by-step directions for young missionary candidates by a former OMF missionary and staff member of All Nations Christian College.

MI72 Goldsmith, Martin
Don't Just Stand There ...: The Why and How of Mission Today. Leicester, ENK: InterVarsity, 1984. 128 pp. Paper. 085110391X.

A primer for the would-be missionary including chapters on the biblical basis for mission, evangelism and church growth, the call to missionary service, and the relationship of the foreign missionary to the recovering church; first published in 1976.

MI73 Gration, John A.
Steps to Getting Overseas. Downers Grove, ILU: InterVarsity, 1986. 31 pp. Paper. 0877842035.

Issues, answers, and advice given by an experienced missionary and teacher for those considering ministries overseas.

MI74 Griffiths, Michael
Give Up Your Small Ambitions. London, ENK: InterVarsity, 1993. 160 pp. 1562650173.

Revised edition of an introduction to the missionary life vocation by the General Director of the OMF, representing the tradition of spirituality which brought the China Inland Mission into being; originally published in 1971 (InterVarsity Press).

MI75 Griffiths, Michael
Laisser tomber vos petites ambitions. La Côte-aux-Fées: Groupes Missionaries and Romane; Lausanne, SZ: TEMA, 1977. 188 pp. No ISBN.
French translation.

MI76 Harley, C. David
Preparándolos para Servir: La capacitación del misionero transcultural. Wheaton, ILU: WEF, 1997. 192 pp. Paper. NO ISBN.
Spanish translation.

MI77 Harley, C. David
Preparing to Serve: Training for Cross-Cultural Mission. South Pasadena, CAU: William Carey Library, 1995. xiv, 156 pp. Paper. 0878082603.

Practical ideas on goals, strategies, and methods of missionary training, based on the author's experience as principal of All Nations Christian College in Kenya, and that of missionary training centers on several continents.

MI78 Harrison, Dan, and Gordon D. Aeschliman
Romancing the Globe: The Call of the Wild on Generation X. Downers Grove, ILU: InterVarsity, 1993. 132 pp. Paper. 0830813233.

A call to youth to live lives of sacrificial service and to consider cross-cultural mission service.

MI79 Hillis, Don W.
I Don't Feel Called (Thank the Lord!). Wheaton, ILU: Tyndale; London, ENK: Coverdale House Publishers, 1973. 128 pp. Paper. 0842315705.

Forthright answers to concerns of young people considering a missionary career by the Associate Director of the Evangelical Alliance Mission.

MI80 Howard, David M.
What Makes a Missionary? Chicago, ILU: Moody, 1987. 96 pp. Paper. 0802452043.

A popular study guide comparing the missionary call of Peter to the contemporary experience for women and men today, by the general director of the World Evangelical Fellowship.

MI81 Jong, A. H. de
De missionaire opleiding van Nederlandse Missionarissen. (Kerk en Theologie in Context, 29). Kampen, NE: Kok, 1995. xi, 109 pp. Paper. 9039005168.

A detailed study, based on archival research and oral interviews, of the preparation and training of Dutch Catholic missionaries of various orders for service in East Africa between 1930 and 1975.

MI82 Käser, Lothar
Fremde Kulturen: Eine Einführung in die Ethnologie für Entwicklungshelfer und kirchliche Mitarbeiter in Übersee. Bad Liebenzell, GW: Verlag der Liebenzeller Mission; Erlangen, GW: Ev.-Luth. Mission, 1997. 342 pp. Paper. 3880026440 (L), 3872142879 (E).

A training manual to acquaint and prepare missionaries and their assistants for overseas placements with understanding of social science methodologies, ethnology, psychology, and the role of cultures and languages.

MI83 Lewis, Norman
Priority One: What God Wants. South Pasadena, CAU: William Carey Library, 1988. 135 pp. Paper. 0878082158.

A popular exposition of the Great Commission aimed at motivating persons to be Christian witnesses, told through personal experiences of the author, with a challenge for complete globalization.

MI84 Lum, Ada
A Hitchhiker's Guide to Missions. Downers Grove, ILU: InterVarsity; Downers Grove, ILU: STL Books, 1985. 143 pp. Paper. 0877843287(IV hdbk), 0851104665 (IV pbk), 0903843951 (STL).

A step-by-step guide that seeks to abolish the myths and stereotypes of missionaries, and to offer practical insights and suggestions for someone considering missionary service.

MI85 Matos, Viriato et al.
Vocácões par a missão hoje. (Igreja e Missão, 33, 107/108). Valadares, PO: Igreja e Missão, 1981. 141 pp. No ISBN.

A monograph containing fifteen studies and proposals on different aspects of the missionary vocation.

MI—MISSIONARIES

MI86 Pirolo, Neal

Serving as Senders. San Diego, CAU: Emmaus Road, International, 1991. 207 pp. 1880185008.

A primer on the appointment, call, and election of missionaries.

MI87 Reed, Lyman E.

Preparing Missionaries for Intercultural Communication: A Bi-Cultural Approach. South Pasadena, CAU: William Carey Library, 1985. 208 pp. Paper. 087808438X.

An overview of what a prospective missionary should seek to understand such as international trends, social structure, worldview, and culture and language learning of the particular society being considered for missionary service.

MI88 Reformed Ecumenical Synod (RES) Missions Conference (1976, Cape Town)

Training for Missions. Grand Rapids, MIU: Reformed Ecumenical Synod, 1977. 143 pp. No ISBN.

A panel of ten mission leaders and missiologists, mainly from the United States and South Africa, consider issues in missionary training.

MI89 Rosengrant, John et al.

Assignment: Overseas. New York, NYU: Crowell, 1960. viii, 152 pp. No ISBN.

A collection of fifteen lectures on aspects of overseas service; originally presented at the Institute of Overseas Churchmanship by the Commission on Ecumenical Mission and Relations of the UPCUSA.

MI90 Rulla, Luigi M.

Anthropology of the Christian Vocation: Interdisciplinary Bases. Rome, IT: Gregorian University Press, 1986. 2 vols. Paper. 8876525718 (vol. 1), 887652598X (vol. 2).

English translation.

MI91 Rulla, Luigi M.

Antropologia della vocazione cristiana. (Psciologia e formazione, 17-18). Bologna, IT: EDB, 1997. 2 vols. 8801508173.

An interdisciplinary study of the psychological and social motivation that results in an individual choosing a priestly or religious life, this is the first of a two-volume work on the anthropology of Christian vocation [Vol. 1: *Basi interdisciplinari*, 512 pp.; vol. 2: *Conferme esistenziali*, no pp.].

MI92 Schlabach, Gerald

To Bless All Peoples: Serving with Abraham and Jesus. (Peace and Justice Series, 12). Scottdale, PAU: Herald Press, 1991. 103 pp. Paper. 0836135539.

A popularly written theology of servanthood in mission by an administrator with the Mennonite Central Committee.

MI93 Taylor, William David, ed.

Internationalizing Missionary Training: A Global Perspective. Exeter, ENK: Paternoster Press; Grand Rapids, MIU: Baker Books, 1991. xiv, 286 pp. Paper. 0853645205 (B), 0801089034 (L).

A compendium of twenty-three short essays on various aspects of the training of missionaries (both First and Two-Thirds World), representing the collective wisdom of the WEF's Missions Commission.

MI94 Thomson, Robin

The World Christian. Oxford, ENK: Lynx Communications/ St. Johns Extension Studies, 1991. 138 pp. Paper. 0745925405.

A workbook on biblical and cultural understandings needed to be a cross-cultural missionary today.

MI95 Tranholm-Mikkelsen, V., Lars Eckerdal, and Hans Raun Iversen

Under bon og hsndspsluggelse: Indivelse af missionurer, diakoner og pruser. Frederiksberg, DK: ANIS/Materialecentralen, 1989. 220 pp. Paper. 8787911523.

A cross-cultural study on the liturgical and theological aspects of ordination, specifically the problem of the ordination of missionaries as related to the ordination of priests and deacons, with special articles on ordination in the Methodist and the Baptist churches in Denmark, as well as on the deaconate of the Lutheran Church in Bangladesh and ordination in the Lutheran Church in Tanzania.

MI96 Unciti, Manuel de et al.

Seminarios Diocesanos y Misiones. (Misiones Extranjeras, 100, 237-335). Madrid, SP: Misiones Extranjeras, 1987. 98 pp. No ISBN.

A monograph with fifteen articles on fundamental aspects of missionary formation in Spanish seminaries.

MI97 Van Halsema, Dick Lucas, and Thea B. Van Halsema

Going and Growing: Is Cross-Cultural Mission for You? Grand Rapids, MIU: Baker Books, 1991. 95 pp. Paper. 0801093104.

A call for a new generation of college students to become cross-cultural missionaries; given first as the Baker Mission Lectures at the Reformed Bible College (Grand Rapids, Michigan, February 1990).

MI98 Williams, Derek, ed.

Prepared to Serve: A Practical Guide to Christian Service Overseas. London, ENK: Scripture Union, 1989. 224 pp. Paper. 0862015782.

A primer for short-term missionaries in which twenty-six missionaries give help from their experience on practical details of living and working as a Christian in a foreign culture.

MI99 Winter, Roberta H.

I Will Do a New Thing: The U.S. Center for World Mission ... and Beyond. South Pasadena, CAU: William Carey Library, 1987. xiv, 303 pp. Paper. 0878082018.

An expanded version of *Once More Around Jericho*— the historical account and visions of the U.S. Center for World Mission and its struggle to maintain and develop mission research, mobilization, and training.

In-Service

See also HI331, SO150, SO572, EC102-EC103, PO128, MI15-MI16, MI31, MI70, MI98, CH464, AS1133, and OC57.

MI100 Amalorpavadass, D. S.

Preaching the Gospel Today: Main Problems in Mission Lands. (Mission Theology for Our Times Series, 7). Bangalore, II: NBCLC, 1973. 39 pp. Paper. No ISBN.

This remarkable presentation of the main issues which hinder the proclamation and reception of the Gospel in mission lands focuses on the inevitable blunting of the living out of the Gospel by the missionary.

MI101 Aroney-Sine, Christine
Survival of the Fittest: Keeping Yourself Healthy in Travel and Service Overseas. Monrovia, CAU: MARC, 1999. 109 pp. Paper. 0912552883.

A primer for short-term or first-term missionaries on how to stay healthy—physically, emotionally, and spiritually; first published in 1994.

MI102 Barnett, Betty
Friend Raising: Building a Missionary Support Team That Lasts. Seattle, WAU: YWAM Publishing, 1991. 178 pp. Paper. 0927545101.

A practical handbook for workers in "faith missions" in which the author shares the methods that worked for her and others—the four practical pillars of lasting friend and support raising.

MI103 Bishop, Crawford M.
Missionary Legal Manual. Chicago, ILU: Moody, 1965. 158 pp. Paper. No ISBN.

A reference book for Protestant missionaries (US) on laws governing the foreign operations of US citizens, with special attention to national and international law concerning freedom of religion.

MI104 Bock, Valerie
P.S. Please Save the Stamps. London, ENK: Coverdale House Publishers, 1976. 128 pp. Paper. 0902088890.

Fictional letters from a new short-term missionary in Papua New Guinea to a friend in Australia designed to help candidates to understand the realities of missionary life.

MI105 Bott, Randy L.
Home with Honor: Helps for Returning Missionaries. Salt Lake City, UTU: Deseret Book Company, 1995. viii, 192 pp. Paper. 0875799566.

A comprehensive guide to post-mission life by a former missionary and mission president.

MI106 Bott, Randy L.
Serve with Honor: Helps for Missionaries. Salt Lake City, UTU: Deseret Book Company, 1995. viii, 214 pp. Paper. 0875799558.

Practical solutions for problems missionaries encounter during their years of service—part of a trilogy of helps for missionaries.

MI107 Brewster, E. Thomas, and Elizabeth S. Brewster
Bonding and the Missionary Task: Language Learning Is Communication—Is Ministry. Pasadena, CAU: Lingua House, 1982. 52 pp. Paper. 0916636006.

Two pamphlets published together—the first outlining a strategy for establishing a sense of belonging with people of a new society, and the second describing language learning as a social activity which facilitates communication.

MI108 Carvalho, Sarah de
A Survival Guide for Frontline Living: Working Out God's Calling—Wherever He's Placed You. London, ENK: Hodder & Stoughton, 1999. xii, 307 pp. Paper. 0340745452.

Drawing upon her redirection from film promoter and TV producer to missionary life among the discarded children of Brazil's slums, the author applies radical lessons learned on the mission field, at work, and at home.

MI109 Coffman, Carrie
Bored Readers Don't Pray Much: Three Simple Steps to Writing Newsletters That Recruit Prayer. Los Angeles, CAU: Apples of Gold, 1991. 112 pp. Paper. 0963328301.

Practical helps for writers of missionary letters.

MI110 Collins, Marjorie A.
Manual for Missionaries on Furlough. South Pasadena, CAU: William Carey Library, 1972. viii, 152 pp. Paper. 0878081194.

A popular guide in twenty-nine chapters covering reasons, preparation, finances, health, legal matters, speaking engagements, rest, and renewal for missionaires, by a former missionary to Pakistan.

MI111 Elmer, Duane
Cross-Cultural Conflict: Building Relationships for Effective Ministry. Downers Grove, ILU: InterVarsity, 1993. 189 pp. Paper. 0830816577.

Practical helps for persons in cross-cultural ministries for understanding the nature of culture and conflict, as well as creative ways to handle conflicts and build healthy relationships, with particular focus on Asian and Hispanic cultures.

MI112 Finton, Heather
Generous Living: The Joys and Heartaches of Ministry Overseas. Toronto, ONC: Anglican Book Centre, 1996. 95 pp. Paper. 1551261677.

Personal reflections of a volunteer in mission in southern Brazil on the joys and struggles of working in an international cross-cultural situation.

MI113 Foyle, Marjory F.
Honourably Wounded: Stress among Christian Workers. Bromley, ENK: MARC Europe; London, ENK: Evangelical Missi-onary Alliance; Wheaton, ILU: Evangelical Missions Information Service, 1987. 162 pp. Paper. 0947697306 (MARC), 0950296880 (EMA), 0961775106 (EMIS).

An experienced psychiatrist and former medical missionary in South Asia gives practical analysis of how stress affects missionaries, and guidance on how they can both cope with it and prevent it; also published by BMMF Interserve, London, UK (0990165170); titled *Overcoming Missionary Stress* by EMIS.

MI114 Friedmann, I. M.
Helping Resolve Conflict: True Experiences of a Christian Anthropologist. (Peace and Justice Series 10). Scottdale, PAU: Herald Press; Waterloo, ONC: Herald Press, 1990. 94 pp. Paper. 0836135210.

A simple, basic guide for those who suffer conflicts and want to resolve them more creatively and peacefully, with stories of the author's own personal growth through conflict including his work as an overseas missionary.

MI115 Gateley, I. M., and J. D. Gateley
My Reasonable Service?: Practical Suggestions for the Christian Working Overseas. Edinburgh, STK: Pentland Press, 1995. vi, 195 pp. Paper. 185821260X.

A primer for cross-cultural tentmaking missionaries.

MI116 Goldsmith, Martin, and Elizabeth Goldsmith
Finding Your Way: Guidance and the Will of God. Bromley, ENK: STL Books; Leicester, ENK: InterVarsity, 1987. 128 pp. Paper. 1850780242 (S), 0851104894 (I).

Out of their mission experience and Bible study the authors write spiritual helps for new persons in mission.

MI—MISSIONARIES

MI117 Goring, Paul

The Effective Missionary Communicator: A Field Study of the Missionary Personality. Wheaton, ILU: BGC, 1991. x, 111 pp. Paper. 1879089076.

A detailed analysis of responses from nearly 200 long-term evangelical missionaries in Africa and Latin America exploring such factors as personality type, dogmatism, acculturation, and language learning which affect their productivity and interpersonal relationships.

MI118 Hale, Thomas

On Being a Missionary. South Pasadena, CAU: William Carey Library, 1995. v, 422 pp. Paper. 0878082557.

Practical guidance for missionaries in service drawing upon the earlier experiences of more than one hundred missionaries, including the author in Nepal since 1970.

MI119 Illich, Ivan D.

Mission and Midwifery: Essays on Missionary Formation. (Mambo Occasional Papers: Missio-Pastoral Series, 4). Gwelo, RH: Mambo Press, 1974. 63 pp. Paper. No ISBN.

A selection of the early writings on missionary selection, formation, and life by the Catholic Co-Director of the Centre for Intercultural Documentation (CIDOC) in Cuernavaca, Mexico.

MI120 Janssen, Gretchen

Women Overseas: A Christian Perspective on Cross-Cultural Adaptation. Yarmouth, MEU: Intercultural Press, 1989. xiii, 144 pp. Paper. 0933662815.

The author, a PCUSA pastor, shares with other women what she has learned in living overseas as wife, mother, and witnessing Christian, and presents a faith perspective on such cross-cultural experiences.

MI121 Jessen, Carl Christian, Karsten Nissen, and Knud Ochsner, eds.

Missionæren-funktion og forventninger. (*Nyt Synspunkt*, 6). Hellerup, DK: DMS-Forlag, 1977. 64 pp. Paper. 8774310682.

A special issue of *Nyt Synspunkt* containing articles on the function of missionaries from the point of view of receiving churches, including a study guide.

MI122 Jones, Marge, and E. Grant Jones

Psychology of Missionary Adjustment. Springfield, MOU: Logion Press, 1995. 173 pp. 0882433210.

Practical helps for career missionaries, and those who support them, in their life cycle from mission board approval to preparation, first term stress, educating children, and final retirement.

MI123 Kane, J. Herbert

Life and Work on the Mission Field. Grand Rapids, MIU: Baker Books, 1989. xii, 366 pp. Paper. 0801052823.

A classic textbook written from a Protestant evangelical perspective for training prospective missionaries, dealing with the missionary's preparation, life, and work.

MI124 Keidel, Levi O.

Conflict or Connection: Interpersonal Relationships in Cross-Cultural Settings. Carol Stream, ILU: Evangelical Missions Information Service, 1996. 136 pp. Paper. 0961775122.

Practical advice for cross-cultural missionaries on dealing with mission issues and people, by a thirty-year Mennonite missionary to Zaire.

MI125 Kenney, Betty Jo

The Missionary Family. South Pasadena, CAU: William Carey Library, 1983. x, 110 pp. Paper. 0878081933.

A personalized and practical guide for the missionary family that covers issues ranging from choosing a mission board to furlough planning and retirement.

MI126 Kohls, L. Robert

Survival Kit for Overseas Living: For Americans Planning to Live and Work Abroad. Yarmouth, MEU: Intercultural Press, 1996. xvi, 165 pp. Paper. 1877864382.

An update of a practical, do-it-yourself guide for Americans living and working in cross-cultural contexts; originally published in 1984.

MI127 Lewis, Larry

The Misfit: Haunting the Human—Unveiling the Divine. Maryknoll, NYU: Orbis Books, 1997. xi, 187 pp. Paper. 1570751226.

A personal memoir by a Maryknoll missioner of how as a teacher of English in Wuhan, China, in 1988-1989 he grew from alienation to acceptance of the creative role of those whose lives and values challenge cultural norms.

MI128 Lockerbie, Jeannie

By Ones & By Twos: Single and Double Missionaries. South Pasadena, CAU: William Carey Library, 1983. 87 pp. Paper. 0878081933.

A realistic and practical handbook on issues relating to relationships among single missionaries, and problems that arise between them and their married counterparts.

MI129 Loss, Mario

Choque transcultural: La vida misionera en un contexto cultural diferente. Miami, FLU: Editorial Unilit, 1996. 138 pp. Paper. 0789902354.

A practical guide to help missionaries understand cross-cultural differences.

MI130 MacHarg, Kenneth D.

Don't Rush the Lord!: A Pilgrimage to God's Purpose. South Pasadena, CAU: William Carey Library, 1997. x, 88 pp. Paper. 0878082549.

An ordained United Church of Christ minister's narrative account of his first term of missionary service (1984-1990) in Ecuador with the World Radio Missionary Fellowship (HCJB).

MI131 McCarty, Doran C.

Supervision: Developing and Directing People on Mission. Nashville, TNU: Seminary Extension of the Southern Baptist Seminaries, 1994. viii, 151 pp. Paper. No ISBN.

A primer for those responsible for supervising mission personnel by an experienced Baptist leader in supervisory training.

MI132 Nunnenmacher, Eugen

Missionarisches Selbstverständnis nach dem Konzilsdekret "Ad Gentes" und nach persönlichen Änusserungen von Afrikamissionaren. (Studia Instituti Missiologici SVD, 33). Nettetal, GW: Steyler Verlag, 1984. xxxvi, 396 pp. Paper. 3877871798.

This dissertation compares the statements of the Vatican II missionary decree with the concrete motivation of missionaries in the Catholic diocese of Kenge, Zaire (Dissertation Pontifical Univ. Urbaniana, Rome).

MI—MISSIONARIES

MI133 O'Donnell, Kelly S., and Michele Lewis O'Donnell, eds.
Helping Missionaries Grow: Readings in Mental Health and Missions. South Pasadena, CAU: William Carey Library, 1988. xxi, 568 pp. Paper. 0878082164.

An anthology of fifty essays on missionary adjustment and growth designed to be a practical resource for missionaries and mission leaders wanting a greater understanding of how mental health concepts can be applied to mission settings.

MI134 O'Donnell, Kelly S., ed.
Missionary Care: Counting the Cost for World Evangelization. South Pasadena, CAU: William Carey Library, 1992. xvi, 360 pp. Paper. 0878082336.

A handbook for developing healthy and effective missionary personnel, containing twenty-five articles by twenty Protestant authors discussing issues, case studies, and personnel policies and strategies.

MI135 Palmer, Donald C.
Managing Conflict Creatively: A Guide for Missionaries and Christian Workers. South Pasadena, CAU: William Carey Library, 1990. iii, 116 pp. Paper. 087808231X.

A ten- fifteen-hour course in five sessions giving a biblical approach to conflict management, with special reference to cross-cultural conflict problems faced by missionaries and other Christian workers.

MI136 Salko, Jouni
Yksin vai yhdessä: naimattomuus ja perheellisyys Suomen ev. lut. kirkon lähetysjärjestöjen työnteki jöiden elämässä. (Käytännöllisen teologian julkaisuja, C9). Helsinki, FI: Helsingin yliopiston käytännöllisen teologian laitos, 1990. 147 pp. Paper. 9514554728.

This master's thesis titled "Singleness and Marriage in the Lives of Finnish Lutheran Missionaries" is an analysis of the opinions of 151 long-term missionaries (110 married, 65 single) representing four missionary organizations and ten different mission fields in Africa, Asia, and Europe.

MI137 Sands, Audrey Lee
Single and Satisfied. Wheaton, ILU: Tyndale House, 1971. 136 pp. Paper. 0842358900.

A forthright personalized account of issues and problems that face single women in overseas missionary service, from learning to live with a co-worker to grappling with sexual fantasies.

MI138 Sands, Audrey Lee
Soltera y Satisfecha. Translated by Angel Cazorla. Barcelona, SP: CLIE, 1971. 141 pp. 8472283402.

Spanish translation.

MI139 St. Kilda, Martin
Near the Far Bamboo: An Insightful Look at Cross-Cultural Clashes through the Eyes of a Tentmaking Missionary. Camp Hill, PAU: Christian Publications, 1993. 248 pp. Paper. 0875095100.

A tentmaking veterinarian missionary relates how he faced the culture shocks of service in another country (language study, dealing with poverty, child rearing, work pressures, etc.), with helpful suggestions for others.

MI140 Stafford, Tim
The Friendship Gap: Reaching Out across Cultures. London, ENK: MARC Europe, 1986. 146 pp. Paper. 0877849757 (US), 094769756X (UK).

A practical guide to interpersonal relationships for new missionaries based on the author's experience as a Protestant evangelical journalist in Kenya; originally published by Inter-Varsity Press in 1984.

MI141 Swanson, Jeffrey
Echoes of the Call: Identity and Ideology among American Missionaries in Ecuador. New York, NYU: Oxford University Press, 1995. viii, 204 pp. 0195068238.

A psycho-social analysis of the calling, work, self-identity, and social relationships of missionaries based on the personal histories of one-hundred missionaries of HCJB-World Radio in Ecuador; originally submitted as a doctoral dissertation at Yale University.

MI142 Tuggy, Joy Turner
The Missionary Wife and Her Work. Chicago, ILU: Moody, 1966. 191 pp. No ISBN.

An analysis of the multiple demands made upon missionaries, particularly those who are wives and mothers, and the search for spiritual and emotional rest which will make them most efficient in their roles, written by a missionary of the Orinoco River Mission in eastern Venezuela since 1943.

MI143 Ward, Ted Warren
Living Overseas: A Book of Preparations. New York, NYU: Free Press; London, ENK: Collier Macmillan, 1984. x, 358 pp. 002933960X (hdbk), 0029339405 (pbk).

An insightful, thought-provoking, comprehensive, and sometimes humorous overview of issues and problems that confront people living overseas, from coping with insects to maintaining an appropriate posture on political matters.

MI144 *When the Roof Caves In*
(Living Testimonies Series). Singapore, SI: OMF, 1985. 154 pp. Paper. 997197231X.

Simple testimonies by fourteen OMF missionaries of tragedies that have taken place in their lives, and how they coped with their feelings through trust in God.

Missionary Children

See also MI13 and AS1515.

MI145 Bell, Linda
Hidden Immigrants: Legacies of Growing up Abroad. (The West and the Wider World Series, 11). Notre Dame, INU: Cross Cultural Publications, 1997. xxv, 157 pp. Paper. 0940121352.

Thirteen North Americans who grew up overseas as children of diplomats, businessmen, and missionaries share their reflections on their bi-cultural adjustments.

MI146 Bowers, Joyce M., ed.
Raising Resilient MKs: Resources for Caregivers, Parents, and Teachers. Colorado Springs, COU: Association of Christian Schools International, 1998. xviii, 510 pp. Paper. No ISBN.

A comprehensive one-volume collection of essays on a wide range of topics dealing with the nurture and education of "missionary kids" (MKs).

MI147 Buffam, C. John
The Life and Times of an MK. South Pasadena, CAU: William Carey Library, 1985. 205 pp. Paper. 0878081984.

An overview of the various stages in the missionary child's life, with an emphasis on educational opportunities and problems, showing both the positive and negative side of the life of an MK.

MI148 Danielson, Edward E.

Missionary Kid—MK. South Pasadena, CAU: William Carey Library, 1984. xii, 91 pp. Paper. 0878087451.

An evaluation of educational options open to missionary children, concluding that boarding schools are generally a very positive aspect of MK development, and that missionary parents should prepare their children emotionally for the necessary adjustments.

MI149 Dyer, Jill, and Roger Dyer, eds.

And Bees Make Honey: An Anthology of Anecdotes, Reflections, and Poems by Third Culture Kids, Volume 2. Torens Park, AT: MK Merimna, 1994. 192 pp. Paper. 0646176293.

Fifty missionary children give short vignettes of their memories of missionary life.

MI150 Dyer, Jill, and Roger Dyer, eds.

Scamps, Scholars and Saints: An Anthology of Anecdotes, Reflections, Poems and Drawings by Third Culture Kids, Volume 1. Kingswood, AT: MK Merimna, 1991. 233 pp. Paper. 0646031449.

Stories, reflections, poems, and drawing by "Third Culture Kids," most of them from the world-wide community of missionary families.

MI151 Dyer, Jill, and Roger Dyer

What Makes Aussie Kids Tick? Kingswood, AT: MK Merimna, 1989. 293 pp. Paper. 0731654013.

A common-sense guide for cross-cultural missionaries on the special needs of their children, with special application for Australians, based on the authors' fifteen-year experience in a school for 600 missionary children near Manila in the Philippines.

MI152 Echerd, Pam, and Alice Arathoon, eds.

Planning for MK Nurture: Compendium of the International Conference on Missionary Kids, Quito, Ecuador, January 4-8, 1987. (International Conference on Missionary Kids (Quito, Ecuador, Jan. 1987)). South Pasadena, CAU: William Carey Library, 1989. 374 pp. Paper. 0878082263.

This second volume of conference papers contains essays which address the special needs of MKs for the benefit of teachers, counselors, school principals, house parents, mission board administrators, and other professionals who work with MKs.

MI153 Gordon, Alma Daugherty

Don't Pig Out on Junk Food: The MK's Guide to Survival in the U.S. Wheaton, ILU: Evangelical Missions Information Service, 1993. 160 pp. Paper. 0961775114.

Practical advice for the children of missionaries as they make their cross-cultural entry to the United States.

MI154 Gray, Charlene J.

Children of the Call: Issues Missionaries' Kids Face. Birmingham, ALU: New Hope, 1995. x, 118 pp. Paper. 1563091143.

Ten issues faced by the children of cross-cultural missionaries based on the author's own experiences as an MK in Africa, plus her continuing involvement with missionary children.

MI155 International Conference on Missionary Kids (Quito, Ecuador, Jan. 1987)

Understanding and Nurturing the Missionary Family: Compendium of the International Conference on Missionary Kids, Quito, Ecuador, January 4-8, 1987. Edited by Pam Echerd, and Alice Arathoon. South Pasadena, CAU: William Carey Library, 1989. 424 pp. Paper. 0878082247.

This first volume of the conference papers is a collection of presentations focused on the many different facets of the lives of MKs and their families, and how to care for their unique needs.

MI156 International Conference on Missionary Kids (Manila, Philippines, Nov. 1984)

New Directions in Missions: Implications for MKs. Edited by Beth A. Tetzel and Patricia Mortenson. West Brattleboro, VTU: ICMK, 1986. viii, 488 pp. Paper. No ISBN.

The text of forty-seven presentations on issues concerning missionary children (family, cross-culture experience, education, international education, and the care network).

MI157 Moessner-Stevenson, Jeanne

Theological Dimensions of Maturation in a Missionary Milieu. (European University Studies, 23: Theology, 346). Bern, SZ: Lang, 1989. 278 pp. Paper. 3261038977.

A dissertation on the attitudes and values of missionary children at Black Forest Academy, a Canadian religiously sponsored high school for missionary dependents in Germany, in relation to extant literature on the self-concept and personality development of missionary children.

MI158 Seaman, Paul Asbury, ed.

Far above the Plain: Private Profiles and Admissable Evidence from the First Forty Years of Murree Christian School, Pakistan, 1956-1996. South Pasadena, CAU: William Carey Library, 1996. vii, 298 pp. Paper. 0878082689.

Poignant vignettes on life for missionary children in a boarding school in Pakistan.

MI159 Seaman, Paul Asbury

Paper Airplanes in the Himalayas: The Unfinished Path Home. (The West and the Wider World Series, 13). Notre Dame, INU: Cross Cultural Publications, 1997. 287 pp. Paper. 0940121441.

An MK reconstructs his missionary childhood in Pakistan, 1963 to 1973, including life at Murree Christian School, and shares his struggle and those of other MKs who feel like global nomads without a cultural home.

MI160 Viser, William C.

It's O.K. to Be an MK. Nashville, TNU: Broadman, 1986. 231 pp. Paper. 0805463372.

An account of the reality of being a missionary kid, including their frustrations, loneliness, and honest feelings; based on interviews, conversations, and the author's observations among the children of Southern Baptist foreign missionaries.

MI161 Walters, Doris L.

An Assessment of Reentry Issues of the Children of Missionaries. New York, NYU: Vantage Press, 1991. x, 244 pp. 0533089603.

A thesis assessing problems faced by young people upon reentry into the United States after growing up overseas as missionary children, based on in-depth interviews and questionnaires to children of Christian and Missionary Alliance, Lutheran Church-Missouri Synod, and Southern Baptist missionaries.

MI—MISSIONARIES

Biography: Collective

See also HI25, HI45, HI127, HI172, HI174, HI275, HI289, HI432, ED59, EV193, MI34-MI35, MI193, AM340, AM1420, AS1035, AS1205, AS1330, AS1346, and AS1510.

MI162 Anderson, Gerald H., Robert T. Coote, Norman A. Horner, and James M. Phillips, eds.

Mission Legacies: Biographical Studies of Leaders of the Modern Missionary Movement. (American Society of Missiology Series, 19). Maryknoll, NYU: Orbis Books, 1994. xviii, 654 pp. 0883449641.

A reprint of seventy-five biographical articles on creative leaders in 19th- and 20th-century mission; originally published in the *International Bulletin of Missionary Research.*

MI163 Balasundaram, F. J., ed.

Martyrs in the History of Christianity. Delhi, II: ISPCK, 1997. xiv, 260 pp. Paper. 817214346X.

Twenty-five biographies of Christian martyrs from early Christianity to the present, written by Indian authors with affirmation that the blood of the missionary martyrs is the seed of the church.

MI164 Bergman, Susan, ed.

Martyrs: Contemporary Writers on Modern Lives of Faith. Maryknoll, NYU: Orbis Books, 1996. x, 333 pp. Paper. 1570751617.

Twenty accounts of 20th-century Christian martyrs from missionaries killed in the China Boxer Rebellion to Dietrich Bonhoeffer, M. L. King, Jr., Janani Luwum, Steven Biko, Oscar Romero, and others.

MI165 Creegan, Charles Cole, and Josephine A. B. Goodnow

Great Missionaries of the Church. (Essay Index Reprint Series). Freeport, NYU: Books for Libraries Press, 1972. xvi, 404 pp. 0836925416.

Reprint of the 1895 edition.

MI166 Eddy, Sherwood

Pathfinders of the World Missionary Crusade. Freeport, NYU: Books for Libraries Press, 1969. 319 pp. 083691127X.

Reprint of a 1945 biographical history of missions from the conversion of Europe to the 20th century, concentrating on the student missionary movement and missions work in India, China, and Africa.

MI167 Goldsmith, Elizabeth

Roots and Wings: Five Generations and Their Impact. Carlisle, UK: OM Publishing, 1998. xiii, 199 pp. Paper. 1850782806.

The author in this popular mission biography traces her family history from 1816 of five generations of missionaries who served under the American Board, the Student Volunteer Movement, and the China Inland Mission

MI168 Grulich, Rudolf

Der Beitrag der böhmischen Länder zur Weltmission des 17. und 18. Jahrhunderts. (Veröffentlichungen des Instituts für Kirchengeschichte von Böhmen-Mähren-Schlesien, NF 7). Königstein/Ts., GW: Institut für Kirchengeschichte von Böhmen-Mähren-, 1981. 232 pp. Paper. 3921344107.

An account of the work of missionaries from Bohemia and Moravia, especially Jesuits and Franciscans, during the 17th and 18th centuries.

MI169 Harvey, Edwin et al.

They Knew Their God. Stoke-on-Trent, ENK: MOVE Press, 1974. 2 vols. No ISBN.

A collection of biographical sketches of Christian heroes and heroines, some of them little-known missionaries [Book I, 159 pp.; Book II, 163 pp.].

MI170 Hefley, James C., and Marti Hefley, eds.

By Their Blood: Christian Martyrs of the Twentieth Century. (A Mott Media Book). Grand Rapids, MIU: Baker Books, 1996. 672 pp. Paper. 0801043956.

A major rewrite and update of a now classic compendium of hundreds of stories, organized by geographic regions, of 20t-century martyrs including many missionaries; originally published by Baker Books in 1979.

MI171 Holtrop, P. N.

Tussen Piétisme en Réveil: Het "Deutsche Christentumsgesellenschaft" in Nederland, 1784-1833. (Proefschrift Theol. Fac. Vrije Universiteit Amsterdam). Amsterdam, NE: Rodopi, 1975. 311 pp. 9062030599.

A detailed history of the "German Society for Christianity" in the Netherlands, including its role in the establishment and history of the "Nederlandsch Zendeling Genootschap" (Dutch Missionary Society) from its founding in 1797.

MI172 Houghton, S. M., ed.

Five Pioneer Missionaries: David Brainerd, William C. Burns, John Eliot, Henry Martyn, John G. Paton. Carlisle, PAU: Banner of Truth Trust, 1987. 345 pp. Paper. 0851511171.

Popular bibliographies of great missionaries, selected from the "The Banner of Truth" essay competition in 1962, of David Brainerd, William C. Burns, John Elliot, Henry Martyn, and John G. Paton; originally published in 1965 (London: Banner of Truth Trust).

MI173 McWilliams, Anne Washburn

Charles and Indy Whitten: Sent to Love. Birmingham, ALU: New Hope, 1988. xi, 237 pp. Paper. 093662521X.

An account of the pilgrimage of a Baptist missionary couple and their quest to evangelize Spanish-speaking people in America, Spain, South America, and Africa (1922-1987).

MI174 O'Malley, William J.

The Voice of Blood: Five Christian Martyrs of Our Time. Maryknoll, NYU: Orbis Books, 1980. 195 pp. Paper. 0883445395.

The stories of five Jesuit missionaries who died as martyrs in El Salvador, Rhodesia (now Zimbabwe), and Brazil in 1977-1978.

MI175 Perkiö, Pia

Pois en antaisi päivääkään: lähetystyön veteraaneja tapaamassa. (Suomen Lähetysseuran julkaisu). Helsinki, FI: Kirjaneliö, 1987. 192 pp. 9516007139.

Memories of Finnish missionaries.

MI176 Piggin, Stuart, and John Roxborogh

The St. Andrew's Seven: The Finest Flowering of Missionary Zeal in Scottish History. Edinburgh, STK: Banner of Truth Trust, 1985. 130 pp. Paper. 0851514286.

A history of the famous Scottish missionary movement founded by Thomas Chalmers of St. Andrews University, and six of his students (John Urquhart, Alexander Duff, Robert Nesbit, John Adams, David Ewart, and William Sinclair).

MI177 Scott, Dorothy E., and Ethel Trice, comps.
Great Women of Pentecost. Indianapolis, INU: By the authors, Dorothy E. Scott and Ethel Trice, 1983. 160 pp. Paper. No ISBN.

A first volume containing biographical sketches of pioneer women of the Pentecostal Assemblies of the World, Inc., many of whom were leaders of women's missionary societies.

MI178 Thompson, Phyllis
Each to Her Post: Six Women of the China Inland Mission. London, ENK: Hodder & Stoughton; London, ENK: Overseas Missionary Fellowship, 1982. 158 pp. Paper. 0340269332.

Biographical sketches of lives and ministries of Amelia Hudson Broomhall, Jennie Hudson Taylor, Margaret King, Jessie Gregg, Jessie McDonald, and Lillian Hamer.

MI179 Veronis, Luke Alexander
Missionaries, Monks and Martyrs: Making Disciples of All Nations. Minneapolis, MNU: Light & Life Press, 1994. vii, 153 pp. Paper. 1880971003.

Ten short biographies of missionaries honored in Orthodox churches from St. Paul to Bishop Anastasios in the 20th century.

MI180 Wallace, Mary H., comp.
Profiles of Pentecostal Missionaries. Hazelwood, MOU: Word Aflame Press, 1986. 352 pp. Paper. 0932581005.

A collection of fourteen popular stories of missionaries (both men and women) who served in the 1920s and 1930s in China, Japan, India, Africa, South America, and Jamaica.

MI181 Wallis, Jim, and Joyce Hollyday, eds.
Cloud of Witnesses. Maryknoll, NYU: Orbis Books; Washington, DCU: Sojourners, 1991. xvii, 292 pp. Paper. 0883447398.

A reprint of thirty-five interviews and biographical profiles of 20th-century Christian leaders in justice ministries; originally published in *Sojourners*.

MI182 Webb, Pauline
Women of Our Time. London, ENK: Cargate Press, 1963. 132 pp. No ISBN.

Stories of thr lives of Sister Elizabeth Stead, Miss Helen Dugdale, Sister Jessie Kerridge, Miss Helen Porter, Sisters Ethel Tomkinson, and Gladys Stephenson—all outstanding British Methodist missionaries of the 1930-1960 period.

MI183 Woodbridge, John D., ed.
Ambassadors for Christ. Chicago, ILU: Moody, 1994. 352 pp. 0802409393.

Sixty short illustrated biographies of 19th- and 20th-century missionaries, evangelists, and national church leaders from William Carey to Billy Graham and Festo Kivengere.

MI184 Zambon, Mariagrazia
A Causa de Gesú, Diciotto Missionari Martiri del PIME. Bologna, IT: EMI, 1994. No ISBN.

Profiles of eighteen 19th- and 20th-century missionary martyrs of the Pontifical Institute for Foreign Missions (PIME).

MI185 Zambon, Mariagrazia
Crimson Seeds: Eighteen PIME Martyrs. Translated by Steve Baumbusch. Detroit, MIU: PIME World Press, 1997. 212 pp. Paper. 0964201046.

English translation.

MI186 Zananiri, Gaston
Figures missionnaires modernes. Paris, FR: Casterman, 1963. 304 pp. No ISBN.

Brief biographies of twenty-four Catholic and Protestant missionaries of the 19th and 20th centuries, with a brief survey of the history of missions and of types of missionaries (hermits, intellectuals, and mystics).

Biography: Individual, Male

See also HI264, HI428, AF251, AF496, AF629, AF774, AF913, AM361, AM1453, AM1530, AS504, AS537, AS555, AS568, AS571, AS594, AS684, AS1140, AS1162, AS1181, AS1189, AS1208, AS1329, AS1444, OC191, and OC209.

MI187 Allen, Hubert J. B.
Roland Allen: Pioneer, Priest, and Prophet. Cincinnati, OHU: Forward Movement; Grand Rapids, MIU: Eerdmans, 1995. xv, 230 pp. Paper. 088028157X (F), 0802808972 (E).

A narrative biography of the noted Anglican SPG missionary to China (1895-1903) and missiologist by his grandson, with numerous quotes from his writings.

MI188 Schulte, Josef, and Hermann Lembeck
Der fliegende Pater Paul Schulte OMI. Aschaffenburg, GW: Pattloch, 1987. 120 pp. 355790900X.

A popular biography of a widely known Oblate missionary and pilot (1895-1977).

MI189 Seraile, William
Fire in His Heart: Bishop Benjamin Tucker and the A.M.E. Church. Knoxville, TNU: University of Tennessee Press, 1998. xiv, 242 pp. 1572330279.

The first full biography of one of the foremost clergy and editors in the AME Church, including his missional vision and his pioneering thought on what is now called the afrocentric school of theology.

MI190 Steele, Harvey, and Gary MacEóin
Agent for Change: The Story of Pablo Steele as told to Gary MacEóin. Maryknoll, NYU: Orbis Books, 1973. xvi, 175 pp. 08834440067.

The biography of Harvey (Pablo) Steele, a Roman Catholic priest whose life work involved him among miners in his native Nova Scotia, in China before and during World War II, and in the Dominican Republic and Panama, working to improve socio-economic conditions in ways that reflect the Christian gospel.

Biography: Individual, Female

See also HI146, HI151, HI355-HI356, HI359, HI438, MI6, SP42, AF245, AF552, AM1243, AM1487, AS695, AS812, AS1134, AS1210, AS1226, OC175, and OC309.

MI191 Cattan, Louise Armstrong
Lamps Are for Lighting: The Story of Helen Barrett Montgomery and Lucy Waterbury Peabody. Grand Rapids, MIU: Eerdmans, 1972. 123 pp. Paper. 0802814808.

Biographical sketches of two outstanding leaders of the Women's Baptist Foreign Missionary Society, 1889-1930, highlighting their leadership in the American women's missionary movement including their campaign to establish colleges for women in Asia.

MI192 Haas, Waltraud, and Ken Phin Pang

Texts and Documents: Mission History from the Woman's Point of View. (Texts and Documents Series, 13). Basel, SZ: Basel Mission, 1989. 52 pp. Paper. No ISBN.

The English version of three lectures by women about women in the work of the Basel Mission in Africa and India, originally given at a workshop on the History of the Basel Mission and its Partner Churches Overseas in 1988.

MI193 Markham, Bonnie

Sarah and Her Missionary Daughters. Hazelwood, MOU: Word Aflame Press, 1998. 271 pp. Paper. 1567222102.

The women included in these first-person accounts are from various regions.

MI194 Mitchell, Robert Bryant, and Marietta Mitchell Smith

Jennie and the Song of the Meadowlark. Des Moines, IAU: Open Bible Publishers, 1988. viii, 198 pp. Paper. 096081602X.

The biography of Jennie Clay Mitchell (1885-1978), founder of the Go-Ye Fellowship, and an early radio evangelist and world missioner.

MI195 Murray, Dorothy Garst

Sister Anna: God's Captive to Set Others Free. Elgin, ILU: Brethren Press, 1985. 176 pp. Paper. 0871787962.

The account of the major activities, beliefs, and interests of Anna Beahm Mow, as Church of the Brethren missionary in India (1923-1941), Bethany Theological Seminary professor, and associate of E. Stanley Jones in the Christian ashram movement.

Biography: National Workers

See also AS524 and AS690.

MI196 Rasooli, Jay M., and Cady H. Allen

Dr. Sa'eed of Iran: Kurdish Physician to Princes and Peasents, Nobles and Nomads. South Pasadena, CAU: William Carey Library, 1983. 189 pp. No ISBN.

A biography of a great Iranian Christian leader who faced many difficult struggles in his religious pilgrimage from Islam to a mature faith in Christ.

MI197 Seamands, John T.

Pioneers of the Younger Churches. Nashville, TNU: Abingdon, 1967. 221 pp. No ISBN.

Fourteen brief biographical sketches of outstanding Christians from the so-called "younger churches," written by the professor of mission at Asbury Seminary.

Autobiographies

See also HI565, AS1242, and EU160.

MI198 Winter, Miriam Therese

The Singer and the Song: An Autobiography of the Spirit. Maryknoll, NYU: Orbis Books, 1999. x, 180 pp. Paper. 1570752796.

A medical mission Sister, who has recorded a dozen music albums including *Joy Is Like the Rain*, shares her experiences in working with starving children in Ethiopia and with refugees in Cambodia, the mysteries of India, new aspects of community, and of having breast cancer and hope.

MISSION AND LOCAL CHURCH RENEWAL

Howard A. Snyder, Subeditor

"Missional Church: From Sending to Being Sent." With this title Darrell L. Guder introduced a new vision "for the sending of the church in North America." "Mission is not merely an activity of the church." Rather, mission is the result of God initiative (the *missio dei*). In response, local congregations need "to redefine themselves as missionary by their very nature" (1998:1,4,7).

"The church exists by mission, just as a fire exists by burning," wrote Emil Brunner (1931:108). This chapter includes works relating ecclesiology to the mission of the church (one aspect of the theology of mission) (Jongeneel, 1995: 88-97), those on renewal/revival movements, and those on the practical ways in which local churches are being renewed, with mission as their very reason for being.

Vriens included "Missionary Work at Home" as one of eight chapters in his mission bibliography. He described it as "the study of the methods of evoking and propagating missionary spirit among the faithful in non-mission lands," and of "stimulating their help by prayer, sacrifice, and contributions for the missions" (1960:94). His locus of mission remained in other countries. By contrast, the locus of mission in this chapter is the local church; that church can be renewed if mission becomes its raison d'être.

Following reference works, the reader will find two general sections: "General Works," and "Theology of Renewal." The latter contains books on ecclesiology and mission.

The next subsections concern renewal in various types of communities. Since renewal involves local action in mission, an understanding of the dynamic interrelationship of church and community is essential. Works on this theme will be found under the headings "Church Renewal and the Wider Community," "Church and Urban Community," and "Church and Rural Community."

Worship and prayer are at the heart of every renewal movement–both local and national. Books on this theme are grouped next, under three headings: "Renewal and Worship," "Liturgical Renewal," and "Charismatic Renewal."

Many persons leading in church renewal have been helped by their study of renewal movements. Those interested in this theme will find grouped together works on the "History of Renewal," and on "Creeds and Confessions."

Models for local church renewal are the focus of the next subsections. First are works on "Structures and Models for Renewal." They are followed by sections on specific models of renewal–"Base Christian Communities" and "House Churches." Next, the case study literature is grouped by "City Churches," "Suburban Churches," and "Rural Churches."

Leadership is a key topic for any church undergoing renewal. Following a general section on leadership, you will find subsections on "Renewal of Ministry" and "Pastoral Leadership." Jongeneel includes *missionary poimenics (pastoral care)* as one of his eleven branches of missiology. He defines it as the systematic study of the missionary office and functions of the pastor as shepherd (1997:291-306). This relates to this subsection and to that on "Mission and Pastoral Care."

Renewal in mission, however, involves more than the set-apart clergy. The church will be renewed only as the laity, both men and women, affirm that they are persons in mission, and not just supporters of mission. Sections on "Ministry of All Believers, Laity," and "Gifts of the Spirit" contain works from this perspective.

Norman E. Thomas

Serials and Periodicals

CH1 *Net Results*. Vol. 1, no. 1 (Jan. 1980)-. Monthly
Nashville, TNU: Cokesbury, 1980 -. ISSN 02704900.
Founded by Herb Miller, a noted church consultant and author, and now edited by consultant and author Tom Bandy, this newsletter aims to provide new ideas in church vitality for North American church leaders, with case studies and models for ministry contributed both by renowned leaders and local church pastors.

Documentation and Archives

See also GW65.

CH2 Finney, Charles G.
Reflections on Revival. Compiled by Donald W. Dayton. Minneapolis, MNU: Bethany Fellowship, 1978. 160 pp. 0871231573.

This collection of letters, written by the "father of modern revivalism" (1792-1875) and Oberlin Professor of Theology, show him to be an evangelist with a burning social passion, and one who believed that the spiritual vitality of the church is sapped not by her involvement in social reform, but by her avoidance of such issues; originally published under the title *Letters on Revivals* in 1845.

CH3 *Lectures on the Revival of Religion*
Wheaton, ILU: R. O. Roberts, 1980. xxiv, 444 pp. No ISBN.

Reprint of essays on the components of revival originally published in 1840 (Glasgow, STK: William Collins).

CH4 Penn-Lewis, Jessie, and Evan Roberts
War on the Saints: Unabridged Edition. Springdale, PAU: Whitaker House, 1996. 324 pp. Paper. 0948171103.

Writing in the aftermath of the Welsh Revival, Penn-Lewis collaborated with Evan Roberts in this discussion of false teaching, demonic influence, and genuine revival in the church; a reprint of the seventh edition of 1912.

CH5 Piper, John
God's Passion for His Glory: Living the Vision of Jonathan Edwards, with the Complete Text of "The End for Which God Created the World" by Jonathan Edwards. Wheaton, ILU: Crossway Books, 1998. xvii, 266 pp. 1581340079.

The author demonstrates the relevance of Jonathan Edward's radically God-centered view of virtue for cultural transformation and world evangelization today.

CH6 Schaller, Lyle E.
The Church Consultant: (The Collected Works on CD-Rom). Nashville, TNU: Abingdon, n.d. CD-ROM. 0687066891.

The collected works of North America's leading parish consultant (50 denominations, 5,000 congregations) on CD-ROM.

Conferences and Congresses

See also CH210, CH367, and CH479.

CH7 Baker, Derek, ed.
Renaissance and Renewal in Christian History: Papers Read at the Fifteenth Summer Meeting and the Sixteenth Winter Meeting of the Ecclesiastical History Society. (Studies in Church History, 14). Oxford, ENK: Blackwell for the Ecclesiastical History Society, 1977. xv, 428 pp. Paper. 0631177809.

Twenty-seven essays on a variety of renewal topics, including reform councils, primitivism, revival, and issues of worship.

CH8 Conference on World Evangelization (Pattaya, Thailand, 1980)
The Thailand Report on Christian Witness to Nominal Christians among Protestants: Report of the ... Mini-Consultation on Reaching Nominal Christians among Protestants. (Lausanne Occasional Papers, 23). Wheaton, ILU: LCWE, 1980. 16 pp. Paper. No ISBN.

A call for understanding of the causes of nominality, the need for renewed churches, and for everyday evangelism in local churches.

CH9 Nicholls, Bruce J., ed.
The Church: God's Agent for Change. Exeter, ENK: Paternoster Press for World Evangelical Fellowship, 1986. 299 pp. Paper. 0853644446.

Thirty-one essays centering on Third World or Eastern European understandings of the church in the world, exploring para-church agencies, church renewal, and the church under persecution—papers presented at the Wheaton '83 Conference on the Nature and Mission of the Church (Graham Center, Wheaton, Il., 20 June-1 July 1983).

CH10 Wilson, H. S., and Nyambura J. Njoroge, eds.
New Wine: The Challenge of the Emerging Ecclesiologies to Church Renewal: The Papers and Findings of the WARC Consultation and Women's Pre-Conference. (WARC Studies, 27). Geneva, SZ: WARC, 1994. 112 pp. Paper. 9290750162.

Papers and findings from an important WARC consultation (Kampen, the Netherlands, 18-23 October 1993).

General Works

See also ME62, ME265, EV306, EV495, CH6, CH373, AF203, and AM611.

CH11 Anderson, Leith
Dying for Change. Minneapolis, MNU: Bethany House, 1990. 208 pp. 1556611072.

A popular analysis of sociological and spiritual changes in US society, suggesting strategies for renewal for Protestant congregations and para-church ministries.

CH12 Anderson, Neil T., and Charles Mylander
Libertando a su Iglesia: Un Plan Biblico para Ayudar a su Iglesia. Translated by Héctor Aguilar. Miami, FLU: Editorial Unilit, 1997. 384 pp. Paper. 0789901684.

Spanish translation.

CH13 Anderson, Neil T., and Charles Mylander
Setting Your Church Free: A Biblical Plan to Help Your Church. Ventura, CAU: Regal Books, 1994. 352 pp. 0830716556.

A primer on the biblical bases for church renewal.

CH14 Barna, George
The Second Coming of the Church. Dallas, TXU: Word Publishing, 1998. 220 pp. 0849914906.

Summarizing cultural and demographic trends in US society, the noted church analyst provides biblical and programmatic perspectives for a renewed church of the 21st century.

CH15 Bayer, Charles H.
The Babylonian Captivity of the Mainline Church. St. Louis, MOU: Chalice Press, 1996. vii, 176 pp. Paper. 0827202210.

A study book on the 20th-century malaise of mainline Protestant churches in the United States, with guidelines for their renewal.

CH16 Blakemore, W. B., ed.
The Renewal of the Church: The Panel Reports. St. Louis, MOU: Bethany Press, 1963. 3 vols. No ISBN.

A panel of Disciples of Christ scholars discusses a wide range of renewal issues, including church structure, ministry, sacraments, evangelism, and "the restoration principle"; [vol. 1, 356 pp.; vol. 2, 347 pp.; vol. 3, 368 pp.].

CH—MISSION AND CHURCH RENEWAL

CH17 Bloesch, Donald G.
The Reform of the Church. Eugene, ORU: Wipf & Stock, 1998. 199 pp. 1579101747.

In this well-reasoned treatise, a prominent evangelical theologian calls for a new kind of evangelicalism that is ecumenical, biblical, and social as well as personal.

CH18 Buttry, Daniel L.
Bringing Your Church Back to Life: Beyond Survival Mentality. Valley Forge, PAU: Judson Press, 1988. 159 pp. Paper. 0817011439.

A practical guide for study groups in struggling churches encouraging revitalized worship, a holistic vision for mission, and a creative pastor's role, by the former pastor of the Dorchester Temple Baptist Church of Boston, Massachusetts.

CH19 Calian, Carnegie Samuel
Survival or Revival: Ten Keys to Church Vitality. Louisville, KYU: Westminister John Knox, 1998. xiv,150 pp. Paper. 0664257348.

A wake-up call for the vitality and vision of the church, for justice and responsibility in its mission.

CH20 Carroll, Jackson W.
Mainline to the Future: Congregations for the 21st Century. Louisville, KYU: Westminster John Knox, 2000. xiv, 130 pp. Paper. 0664222536.

With the premise that neither change nor tradition supercedes the other, the church needs to reclaim its interpretive power to make the Gospel relevant in every time and place.

CH21 Clark, Stephen B.
Building Christian Communities: Strategy for Renewing the Church. Notre Dame, INU: Ave Maria Press, 1972. 189 pp. Paper. 0877930430.

A brief but fairly comprehensive treatment of church renewal, including aspects of pastoral leadership, by a leader in the Catholic charismatic renewal.

CH22 Cobb, John B.
Reclaiming the Church. Louisville, KYU: Westminster John Knox, 1997. viii, 110 pp. Paper. 0664257208.

An analysis of the malaise of mainline Protestantism in the United States, with proposals for church renewal by the noted Professor Emeritus at the School of Theology at Claremont.

CH23 Coleman, Robert E.
The Coming World Revival: Your Part in God's Plan to Reach the World. London, ENK: Hodder & Stoughton, 1995. xv, 175 pp. 0891078401.

Revised edition of a biblically based primer on revival— what it is, what it does, how it comes about, when it may be expected—with practical suggestions for local churches by the director of the School of World Mission and Evangelism at Trinity Evangelical Divinity School; originally published as *The Spark That Ignites* (Minneapolis, MNU: World Wide, 1989).

CH24 Coleman, Robert E.
Dry Bones Can Live Again: Revival in the Local Church. Old Tappan, NJU: Revell, 1969. 127 pp. No ISBN.

One of the needs of today's church is to find effective means of reviving persons so that the reality of Pentecost becomes the reality of the modern church.

CH25 Cooke, Bernard J.
Christian Community: Response to Reality. New York, NYU: Holt, Rinehart & Winston, 1970. viii, 187 pp. Paper. 0030845572.

A general treatise on the church and its renewal, including a discussion of the church's internal life and mission to the world; by a Roman Catholic author.

CH26 Crabb, William, and Jeff Jernigan
The Church in Ruins: Foundations for the Future. Colorado Springs, COU: NavPress, 1991. 179 pp. Paper. 0891096515.

A primer exploring rebuilding the church through a biblical approach to mission, rather than by revamped methods or programs.

CH27 Dale, Robert D.
Keeping the Dream Alive. Nashville, TNU: Broadman, 1988. 155 pp. 0805425470.

In this sequel to *To Dream Again*, Dale stresses the importance of spirit and morale for a healthy congregation, giving practical suggestions for promoting congregational vitality and purpose.

CH28 Dawn, Marva J.
The Hilarity of Community: Romans 12 and How to Be the Church. Grand Rapids, MIU: Eerdmans, 1992. xvi, 303 pp. Paper. 0802806570.

An in-depth discussion of Romans 12 as a model for church life and renewal, with practical application to the church today.

CH29 Drummond, Lewis A.
The Awakening That Must Come: Beyond Renewal and Other Efforts, Believers Yearn for New Life in the Whole Church. Nashville, TNU: Broadman, 1978. 149 pp. Paper. 0805465359.

Principles and practices of church renewal from an evangelical perspective (Southern Baptist).

CH30 Easum, William M., and Thomas G. Bandy
Growing Spiritual Redwoods. Nashville, TNU: Abingdon, 1997. 215 pp. Paper. 0687336007.

The DNA of healthy churches defined by the Director of 21st Century Strategies, and by the Programme Officer of Congregational Mission and Evangelism for the United Church of Canada.

CH31 Edge, Findley B.
The Greening of the Church. Waco, TXU: Word Books, 1977. 195 pp. No ISBN.

Theological foundations and practical proposals for local church renewal by a Baptist seminary professor; affirms small groups and the priesthood (ministry) of all believers.

CH32 Eller, Vernard
The Outward Bound: Caravaning as the Style of the Church. Grand Rapids, MIU: Eerdmans, 1980. 104 pp. Paper. 0802818226.

Addresses to Christian congregations, this book calls for churches to be "risking communities" on a journey for God, and to be less concerned with security and success.

CH33 Engen, Charles Edward van
God's Missionary People: Rethinking the Purpose of the Local Church. Grand Rapids, MIU: Baker Books, 1991. 223 pp. Paper. 0801093112.

A fairly comprehensive and practical treatment of the church as a missionary community, drawing on Scripture, church history, and contemporary expressions of the church.

CH—MISSION AND CHURCH RENEWAL

CH34 Friedli, Richard
Mission oder Demission: Konturen einer lebendigen, weil missionarischen Gemeinde. Freiburg, SZ: Universitäts-Verlag, 1982. 166 pp. Paper. 3727802723.

A practical but solid work pointing out how a missionary spirit is absolutely essential for a truly Christian community.

CH35 Gamble, Robin
The Irrelevant Church. Tunbridge Wells, ENK: Monarch Publications; Bedford, ENK: BCGA, 1991. 192 pp. Paper. 185424163X (M), 0948704195 (B).

An analysis of a key challenge for church renewal—reaching the working class—with biblical, historical (19th-century Great Britain), and contemporary models.

CH36 Getz, Gene A.
Sharpening the Focus of the Church. Chicago, ILU: Moody; Wheaton, ILU: Victor Books, 1984. 359 pp. Paper. 0802479022 (M), 0896933938 (V).

An "extensively revised" update of the author's popular book on church renewal (Moody Press, 1974), viewing the church through the three "lenses": New Testament principles, contemporary needs, and church history; with a new introductory chapter charting the development of evangelical church renewal thinking over the previous decade.

CH37 Gibbs, Eddie
Winning Them Back: Tackling the Problem of Nominal Christianity. Tunbridge Wells, ENK: Marc-Monarch Publications, 1993. 319 pp. Paper. 1854242083.

A qualitative survey of nominality amongst churches in the English-speaking world by the former Professor of Church Growth at Fuller Theological Seminary.

CH38 Goodall, Norman
The Local Church: Its Resources and Responsibilities. London, ENK: Hodder & Stoughton, 1966. 63 pp. Paper. No ISBN.

Four lectures by a leader of the ecumenical movement, developing the Congregationalist view of the local church as the focal point of the church universal.

CH39 Goodwin, Steven J.
Catching the Next Wave: Leadership Strategies for Turn-Around Congregations. Minneapolis, MNU: Augsburg Fortress, 1999. iv, 132 pp. Paper. 0806638818.

This book assists individuals and communities in turning a declining or plateaued congregation toward health and vitality through creating a vision for mission, motivating lay leadership, connecting with community needs, addressing obstacles, and implementing a mission plan.

CH40 Green, Lynn, and Chris Forster
Small Church, Big Vision: How Your Church Can Change the World. London, ENK: Marshall Pickering, 1995. ix, 202 pp. Paper. 0551029048.

A manual on the renewal of the church's mission, showing how small churches can have a global impact, especially in evangelism.

CH41 Hadaway, C. Kirk, and David A. Roozen
Rerouting the Protestant Mainstream: Sources of Growth and Opportunities for Change. Nashville, TNU: Abingdon, 1995. 141 pp. Paper. 0687453666.

Two prominent church researchers analyze trends, markets, denominational influences, and directions for the future for mainline Protestants in the United States.

CH42 Hammett, Edward H.
The Gathered and Scattered Church: Equipping Believers for the 21st Century. Macon, GAU: Smyth & Helwys, 1999. xxiii, 104 pp. Paper. 1573122599.

With the thesis that Christianity penetrates the world when Christians learn to be and do church both inside and outside the walls, suggestions are offered about understanding, activating, and evaluating the church for effective ministry in the 21st century.

CH43 Hammett, Edward H.
Making the Church Work: Converting the Church for the 21st Century. Macon, GAU: Smyth & Helwys, 1997. ix, 113 pp. Paper. 1573121576.

Out of twenty years of work to reverse North American Protestant ineffectiveness in an unchurched culture, the guest lecturer at Southeastern Baptist Theological Seminary, Wake Forest, North Carolina, writes his prescription for congregation renewal.

CH44 Hanchey, Howard
From Survival to Celebration: Leadership for the Confident Church. Cambridge, MAU: Cowley Publications, 1994. 155 pp. Paper. 1561011002.

A study book for local churches desiring to move from maintenance-minded to mission-minded ministries, with practical suggestions based on Anglican/Episcopal ministries in Canada and the United States.

CH45 Harding, Joe A., and Ralph W. Mohney
Vision 2000: Planning for Ministry into the Next Century. Nashville, TNU: Discipleship Resources, 1991. x, 102 pp. Paper. 0881770981.

A planning book for United Methodist congregations desiring a biblically based and congregationally focused strategy for renewal.

CH46 Hauerwas, Stanley, and William H. Willimon
Resident Aliens: Life in the Christian Colony. Nashville, TNU: Abingdon, 1989. 175 pp. Paper. 0687361591.

Two United Methodist leaders analyze the church's changed cultural context, and call for a model of the church grounded firmly in the Gospel.

CH47 Hawkins, O. S.
Revive Us Again. Nashville, TNU: Broadman, 1990. 127 pp. Paper. 0805450963.

A popular presentation of four essential elements in church revival (participation, proclamation, preservation, and propagation); by the pastor of the growing First Baptist Church of Fort Lauderdale, Florida.

CH48 Henderson, Robert T.
A Door of Hope: Spiritual Conflict in Pastoral Ministry. Scottdale, PAU: Herald Press, 1997. 159 pp. Paper. 0836190653.

A challenge to Protestant pastors to forsake conformity to secularizing trends by focusing their ministries on church renewal and pastoral evangelism.

CH49 Hinkle, James, and Time Woodroof
Among Friends: You Can Help Make Your Church a Warmer Place. Colorado Springs, COU: NavPress, 1989. 230 pp. Paper. 0891095578.

A study guide providing biblically based guidelines for closer relationships in the local church, and the creative resolution of conflict.

CH—MISSION AND CHURCH RENEWAL

CH50 Hinson, E. Glenn
The Church: Design for Survival. Nashville, TNU: Broadman, 1967. 128 pp. Paper. No ISBN.

In this work the associate professor of church history at Southern Baptist Theological Seminary (Louisville, Kentucky) addresses how the church can "discard outdated institutions and practices and replace them with more relevant ones" as it repeatedly reevaluates its understanding of itself as the church.

CH51 Hull, Bill
Revival That Reforms: Making It Last. Grand Rapids, MIU: Revell, 1998. 239 pp. 080071752X.

Seeking to move beyond scheduled revivals, Cypress Evangelical Free Church pastor Bill Hull challenges the church to seek spiritual awakening that produces both revival and lasting reformation through dramatically transformed church structures, priorities, and roles.

CH52 Hunter, Kent R.
Your Church Has Personality: Find Your Focus—Maximize Your Mission. Corunna, INU: Church Growth Center, 1997. 147 pp. Paper. 0912961988.

A practical step-by-step process to help pastors and lay leaders to develop a philosophy of ministry and mission for the local church, by the President of the Church Growth Center in Corunna, Indiana.

CH53 Johnson, Douglas W.
Vitality Means Church Growth. (Creative Leadership Series). Nashville, TNU: Abingdon, 1989. 127 pp. Paper. 0687437997.

A practical introduction to factors that contribute to an active, vital church, by the Director of Research of the General Board of Global Ministries, the United Methodist Church.

CH54 Kassabián, Rubén
Avivamiento: ¿Bendición ... o Confusión? Miami, FLU: Editorial Unilit, 1996. 138 pp. Paper. 0789900580.

In this popular book *Revival: Blessing or Confusion?* the international evangelist and founder of Sepen (Seminary for Evangelists) considers the concept of revival and its characteristics, historical models, and results.

CH55 Kew, Richard, and Roger J. White
New Millennium, New Church: Trends Shaping the Episcopal Church for the Twenty-First Century. Cambridge, MAU: Cowley Publications, 1992. xiv, 177 pp. 1561010634 (hdbk), 1561010626 (pbk).

An application of megatrend thinking to issues of renewal of the Episcopal Church in the United States.

CH56 Kew, Richard, and Roger J. White
Toward 2015: A Church Odyssey. Boston, MAU: Cowley Publications, 1997. viii, 183 pp. Paper. 1561011371 (hdbk), 1561011363 (pbk).

A call to Episcopal/Anglican parishes to move beyond survival into a new era of spirituality, witness, and evangelism.

CH57 Kivengere, Festo
When God Moves You Move Too. Accra, GH: Asempa Publishers, 1973. 46 pp. No ISBN.

Four short talks on revival by the bishop of the Anglican Kigezi Diocese of the Church of Uganda, who has been both a spokesman for the East African Revival, and the best-known East African evangelist.

CH58 Kornfield, David
Church Renewal: A Handbook for Christian Leaders. Grand Rapids, MIU: Baker Books; Exeter, ENK: Paternoster Press, 1989. viii, 295 pp. Paper. 0853644454.

A manual with inductive Bible studies, designed to help church leaders work for local congregational renewal by helping them address thirteen important dimensions of church renewal in a systematic and deliberate manner; written by a member of the Commission on Church Renewal of the WEF.

CH59 Larson, Bruce, and Ralph Osborne
The Emerging Church. Waco, TXU: Word Books, 1970. 160 pp. No ISBN.

A consideration of the goals, resources, strategies, and opportunities of the church, including case studies, by leaders of Faith at Work.

CH60 Lecky, Robert S., and H. Elliot Wright
Can These Bones Live?: The Failure of Church Renewal. New York, NYU: Sheed and Ward, 1969. xviii, 201 pp. 083620364X.

A critique of most talk of church renewal in the United States as superficial, with a call for profound engagement with human needs as is happening in the black church.

CH61 Leith, John H.
From Generation to Generation: The Renewal of the Church According to Its Own Theology and Practice. (The 1989 Annie Kinkead Warfield Lectures). Louisville, KYU: Westminster John Knox, 1990. 223 pp. Paper. 0664251226.

An identification of the crisis facing today's church, and a challenge to those who lead congregations week-by-week to reclaim the preaching, teaching, and pastoral care roles of the clergy.

CH62 Long, Robert W., ed.
Renewing the Congregation. Minneapolis, MNU: Augsburg, 1966. ix, 213 pp. Paper. No ISBN.

Twenty short papers prepared for a conference on "The Role of the Congregation in the Mission of the Church," sponsored by the Division of American Missions of the National Lutheran Council.

CH63 Mallone, George
Furnace of Renewal. Downers Grove, ILU: InterVarsity, 1981. 201 pp. Paper. 0877846057.

An articulation of several principles of renewal in the local church, with particular focus on worship and leadership.

CH64 Malphurs, Aubrey
Developing a Vision for Ministry in the 21st Century. Grand Rapids, MIU: Baker Books, 1997. 256 pp. Paper. 0801062861.

Practical helps in goal setting for local church renewal by the professor and field education director at Dallas Theological Seminary.

CH65 Malphurs, Aubrey
Pouring New Wine into Old Wineskins: How to Change a Church without Destroying It. Grand Rapids, MIU: Baker Books, 1993. 212 pp. Paper. 0801063019.

Guides for a congregational revitalization program by the chairman of the Department of Field Education at Dallas Theological Seminary, with chapters on the problem, practice, and product of change, and on personnel for change.

CH—MISSION AND
CHURCH RENEWAL

CH66 Martin, Noah S.

Beyond Renewal. Scottdale, PAU: Herald Press, 1976. 211 pp. Paper. 0836119705.

Combines biblical, practical, and clinical pastoral insights, in calling for a church that responsibly lives out the Gospel on a day-by-day basis.

CH67 McBrien, Richard P.

The Remaking of the Church. New York, NYU: Harper & Row, 1973. xv, 175 pp. 0060653272.

An analysis of the institutional and charismatic aspects of the church, and of the church's need for renewal in light of the Vatican II Council; by the then President of the Catholic Theological Society of America, including in an "agenda for reform" more democratic structures, ordination of women, married clergy, and intercommunion with other Christians.

CH68 McLaren, Brian D.

Reinventing Your Church. Grand Rapids, MIU: Zondervan, 1998. 223 pp. Paper. 0310216540.

A call for new, reinvented churches in North America, in creative mission to an unchurched generation deeply affected by postmodernism.

CH69 Mead, Loren B.

The Once and Future Church: Reinventing the Congregation for a New Mission Frontier. Washington, DCU: Alban Institute, 1991. 92 pp. Paper. No ISBN.

The vision of mission for local churches for the 21st century by the distinguished President of the Alban Institute.

CH70 Mead, Loren B.

Transforming Congregations for the Future. (Once and Future Church Series, 3). New York, NYU: Alban Institute, 1994. xii, 139 pp. Paper. 1566991269.

This sequel to *The Once and Future Church* (1991) is a summary of recent research on the decline of mainline Protestantism in the United States, and a prescription for renewal by the founder of the Alban Institute, with study guide to the two books by Gilbert R. Rendle (1566991595).

CH71 Miller, C. John

Outgrowing the Ingrown Church. Grand Rapids, MIU: Zondervan Publishing House, 1986. 176 pp. Paper. 0310284112.

A handbook of practical helps for Protestant congregations that desire to change from being ingrown to being outward-looking and outward-moving, including biblical principles, objective analysis, and personal experiences.

CH72 Mission Study Week, (1961, Vienna)

Mission und Heimatseelsorge. Edited by Johannes Bettray. Vienna, AU: Päpstliche Missionswerke Österreichs, 1962. 239 pp. No ISBN.

Papers read at a study week emphasizing that mission not only involves material and moral support for foreign missionaries, but should penetrate the whole of Christian life.

CH73 Morris, George E., ed.

Rethinking Congregational Development. (World Evangelism Library, 3). Nashville, TNU: Discipleship Resources, 1984. viii, 96 pp. Paper. 0881770124.

Nine United Methodist Church leaders speak out on the revitalization of existing congregations and the development of new ones.

CH74 Nash, Robert N.

An 8-Track Church in a CD World: The Modern Church in the Postmodern World. Macon, GAU: Smyth & Helwys, 1997. xii, 132 pp. 1573120952.

An analysis of the painful culture divide which the North American church straddles between the modern and the postmodern worlds, with helps for answering the response of a young child, "Daddy, church is boring."

CH75 Nelson, C. Ellis

Congregations: Their Power to Form and Transform. Atlanta, GAU: John Knox, 1988. vi, 287 pp. Paper. 0804216010.

Eleven essays by American theological educators to help ministers, Christian educators, and lay leaders explore the major factors which create, sustain, critique, and transform the character and mission of congregations.

CH76 Newbigin, James Edward Lesslie

Sign of the Kingdom. Grand Rapids, MIU: Eerdmans, 1980. ix, 70 pp. Paper. 0802818781.

Newbigin argues that the church is not the Kingdom, but is to be a vital community that holds present reality and future hope in tension as a key to its mission in the world.

CH77 O'Brien, David J.

The Renewal of American Catholicism. New York, NYU: Oxford University Press; New York, NYU: Paulist Press, 1972. xiii, 302 pp. 0195016017 (O).

The author analyzes, from a historical perspective, issues of renewal facing contemporary North American Roman Catholicism.

CH78 Olthuis, James H. et al.

Will All the King's Men ... Out of Concern for the Church Phase II. Toronto, ONC: Wedge Publishing, 1972. iii, 255 pp. Paper. No ISBN.

Discusses problems of renewal in the institutional church, primarily from a Christian Reformed perspective.

CH79 Patterson, Bob E., ed.

The Stirring Giant: Renewal Forces at Work in the Modern Church. Waco, TXU: Word Books, 1971. 312 pp. No ISBN.

A sourcebook on Protestant church renewal literature from the 1960s in the United States.

CH80 Payne, Claude E., and Hamilton Beazley

Reclaiming the Great Commission: A Practical Model for Transforming Denominations and Congregations. San Francisco, CAU: Jossey-Bass, 2000. xx, 268 pp. 0787952680.

A practical and powerful model for transforming denominations and congregations into communities of miraculous expectation and spiritual transformation.

CH81 Plowman, Edward E.

The Underground Church: Accounts of Christian Revolutionaries in Action. Elgin, ILU: David C. Cook, 1971. 128 pp. Paper. No ISBN.

An account of the "Jesus Movement" in the United States by the former news editor of *Christianity Today.*

CH82 Rainer, Thom S.

Giant Awakenings: Making the Most of 9 Surprising Trends That Can Benefit Your Church. Nashville, TNU: Broadman, 1995. x, 198 pp. 0805461736.

A popular presentation of nine trends which can lead to renewal of traditional churches in the 21st century, focused on the United States.

CH—MISSION AND CHURCH RENEWAL

CH83 Regele, Mike, and Mark Schulz

Death of the Church. Grand Rapids, MIU: Zondervan, 1995. 279 pp. 0310200067.

A readable analysis of the various faces of change in North American culture, and their challenges to traditional church forms and structures; with implications for church renewal by the co-founders of the Percept Group, which assists local churches in analyzing their mission and ministry.

CH84 Riddell, Michael

Threshold of the Future: Reforming the Church in the Post-Christian West. London, ENK: SPCK, 1998. 194 pp. Paper. 0281050554.

A call to Christians in dying churches in the West to return to their radical biblical roots and essential character as a missionary body, by a lecturer in practical theology at Otago University in New Zealand.

CH85 Rose, Stephen C.

The Grass Roots Church: A Manifesto for Protestant Renewal. New York, NYU: Holt, Rinehart & Winston, 1966. xviii, 174 pp. No ISBN.

A call for a revitalized and reformed church in the United States with new structures to serve the emerging urban-technological society.

CH86 Roxburgh, Alan J.

Reaching a New Generation: Strategies for Tomorrow's Church. Downers Grove, ILU: InterVarsity, 1993. 140 pp. Paper. 0830813403.

The Director of the Center for Mission and Evangelism at McMaster Divinity College in Hamilton, Ontario, believes that the new generation yearns for community, spiritual experience, and an earth safe from ecological destruction, and that the church should respond with Christian community, ecology, and spirituality.

CH87 Schaeffer, Francis A.

The Church at the End of the Twentieth Century. Downers Grove, ILU: InterVarsity, 1971. 153 pp. Paper. 0877848890.

An analysis of the sociocultural challenges facing the church, and a proposed theology for corporate and personal church renewal.

CH88 Schaller, Lyle E.

The New Reformation: Tomorrow Arrived Yesterday. (Ministry for the Third Millennium). Nashville, TNU: Abingdon, 1995. 152 pp. Paper. 0687014743.

The noted church consultant's vision concerning 21st-century culture and church in the United States.

CH89 Seifert, Harvey

New Power for the Church. Philadelphia, PAU: Westminster Press, 1976. 175 pp. 0664247911.

Clear, positive suggestions for dealing with the problems and effectiveness of the declining mainline Protestant churches; based on research by the Professor of Christian Ethics, Claremont School of Theology.

CH90 Snyder, Howard A.

Radical Renewal: The Problem of Wineskins Today. Houston, TXU: Touch Publications, 1996. 223 pp. Paper. 1880828979.

A complete revision and update of the author's 1975 classic, challenging the churches to reexamine their structures in the light of 21st-century mission imperatives.

CH91 Spong, John Shelby

Why Christianity Must Change or Die: A Bishop Speaks to Believers in Exile. San Francisco, CAU: HarperSanFrancisco, 1998. xxiii, 257 pp. 0060675322 (hdbk), 0060675365 (pbk).

A new creed for a new millennium, from an outspoken advocate for a Christianity that is true to Jesus, and that brings a dying church back to life by courageously confronting anomalies that have driven many Christians into exile.

CH92 Stagg, Paul L.

The Converted Church: From Escape to Engagement. Valley Forge, PAU: Judson Press, 1967. 160 pp. Paper. No ISBN.

A contemporary approach to evangelism offering vistas for those who are eager to see the church move away from its much criticized self-centeredness toward one of engagement in the world.

CH93 Stewart, Carlyle Fielding

African American Church Growth: 12 Principles of Prophetic Ministry. Nashville, TNU: Abingdon, 1993. 160 pp. Paper. 0687164145.

Principles of prophetic ministry, understood as a concern for wholeness of the individual and community, applied to various ministry functions (worship, pastoral care, education, and evangelism) in the African American church.

CH94 Strommen, Merton P.

The Innovative Church: Seven Steps to Positive Change in Your Congregation. Minneapolis, MNU: Augsburg Fortress, 1997. 192 pp. Paper. 0806635738.

Analysis of the need for change in local churches and why change is difficult, with a practical seven-step strategy for innovation and renewal by the founder of Search Institute and the Augsburg Youth and Family Institute.

CH95 Tillapaugh, Frank R.

Unleashing the Church: Getting People Out of the Fortress and into Ministry. Ventura, CAU: Regal Books, 1982. 224 pp. Paper. 0830710248.

A popular challenge by the pastors of Bear Valley Baptist Church in California to local church renewal through every member ministry; originally published under the title *The Church Unleashed.*

CH96 Trueblood, David Elton

The Company of the Committed. New York, NYU: Harper & Row, 1961. 113 pp. No ISBN.

The noted Quaker scholar describes the church as a community called to effective witness and redemptive penetration of society, and marked by the key criterion of love.

CH97 Trueblood, David Elton

The Incendiary Fellowship. New York, NYU: Harper & Row, 1967. 121 pp. No ISBN.

Popular Quaker author Trueblood presents a case for the local church as a dynamic community based on the ministry of all believers and pastors as teachers and "coaches."

CH98 Vincent, John J., ed.

Stirrings: Essays Christian and Radical. London, ENK: Epworth Press, 1976. 128 pp. 0716202654.

A collection of essays by British clergy calling the church to rediscover the faith amidst the conflicts and tensions of the contemporary world.

CH99 Werning, Waldo J.
Renewal for the 21st Century Church. St. Louis, MOU: Concordia Publishing, 1988. 160 pp. Paper. 0570044901.

A Lutheran leader describes a process for church renewal based on rebuilding the church's spiritual and biblical foundations.

CH100 Westerhoff, John H.
Living the Faith Community: The Church That Makes a Difference. Minneapolis, MNU: Winston Press, 1985. 106 pp. Paper. 0866838708.

A noted North American religious educator envisions the church as the one community able to humanize society, nurture Christian growth, and create the kind of life God intends.

CH101 Wilke, Richard B.
Signs and Wonders: The Mighty Work of God in the Church. Nashville, TNU: Abingdon, 1989. 142 pp. Paper. 0687384486.

Popular helps for United Methodists seeking parish renewal, by the bishop of the Arkansas area.

CH102 Williamson, Clark M., and Ronald J. Allen
The Vital Church: Teaching, Worship, Community Service. St. Louis, MOU: Chalice Press, 1998. viii, 145 pp. Paper. 082724004X.

The authors state that revitalization can occur only when congregations reach back to basic core values and base their mission on the gospel of Jesus; the book ends with thumbnail sketches of six churches, thriving amid change and challenge.

CH103 Wilson, William J., ed.
Demands for Christian Renewal. Maryknoll, NYU: Maryknoll Publications, 1968. viii, 179 pp. No ISBN.

A series of studies by ten Roman Catholic laymen, on the meaning of mission in its various relations.

CH104 Wright, Tom
Bringing the Church to the World: Renewing the Church to Confront the Paganism Entrenched in Western Culture. Minneapolis, MNU: Bethany House, 1992. 221 pp. Paper. 1556613180.

A clear argument that the Western world is becoming increasingly and overtly pagan, that God in that context is reviving the church, and that new models of evangelism and mission are required.

CH105 Young, Doyle L.
New Life for Your Church: A Renewal Handbook for Pastors. Grand Rapids, MIU: Baker Books, 1989. 132 pp. Paper. 0801099234.

A handbook on church renewal for US Protestants, giving practical helps for serving the local church, with examples of churches that implement those ideas successfully; by the Professor of Church History at Southwestern Baptist Theological Seminary in Fort Worth, Texas.

Theology of Renewal

See also GW112, TH44, TH71, TH143, TH301, TH326, ME100, SO92, CO141, EV107-EV108, EV185, EV593, CH33, CH459, AM501, AM503, AM980, AS156, and EU54.

CH106 Amalorpavadass, D. S.
The Bible in Self-Renewal and Church-Renewal for Service to Society. (Mission Theology for our Times Series, 15). Bangalore, II: NBCLC, 1984. 16 pp. Paper. No ISBN.

The noted Indian Catholic leader in liturgical renewal outlines biblical and Indian cultural roots for church renewal and service to society.

CH107 Baker, Mark D.
Religious No More: Building Communities of Grace and Freedom. Downers Grove, ILU: InterVarsity, 1999. 187 pp. Paper. 0830815929.

Based on ten years of missionary experience in Honduras, at churches born out of North American missions, Baker detects fallacies in their "Gospel" played out amid the challenges of poverty, injustice, and entrenched religiosity, and calls for a refreshing approach to Christian community for laypersons, pastors, missionaries, and mission strategists.

CH108 Barr, William R., and Rena M. Yocom, eds.
The Church in the Movement of the Spirit. Grand Rapids, MIU: Eerdmans, 1994. xii, 136 pp. Paper. 080280554X.

Seven essays demonstrating the variety of ways in which the Spirit works to create, sustain, transform, and use the church in God's mission—a North American contribution to the ecumenical study of the "The Apostolic Faith Today."

CH109 Bloesch, Donald G.
Crumbling Foundations: Death and Rebirth in an Age of Upheaval. Grand Rapids, MIU: Academie Books, 1984. 168 pp. Paper. 0310298210.

Bloesch sees the church in disarray before the challenges of technological humanism, nihilism, and secularism, but suggests "new models for the church" marked by integrity, spiritual gifts, and costly discipleship.

CH110 Brow, Robert
The Church: An Organic Picture of Its Life and Mission. Grand Rapids, MIU: Eerdmans, 1968. 122 pp. No ISBN.

Noting unrest and stirrings of renewal in the church, the author's approach is "to look at the original and perennial forms of the church as a living organism," describing the church as a body of varied ministries and gifts.

CH111 Burns, Patrick J., ed.
Misión y Testimonio: La vida de la Iglesia. Santander, SP: Sal Terrae, 1969. 333 pp. No ISBN.

Spanish translation.

CH112 Burns, Patrick J., ed.
Mission and Witness: The Life of the Church. Westminster, MDU: Newman Press, 1964. xiii, 382 pp. Paper. No ISBN.

Seventeen essays by Roman Catholic scholars on ecclesiology and mission, written during Vatican II to give an ecumenical awareness.

CH113 Clapp, Rodney
A Peculiar People: The Church as Culture in a Post-Christian Society. Downers Grove, ILU: InterVarsity, 1996. 251 pp. Paper. 0830819908.

A comprehensive reevaluation of contemporary models of the church, and argument for the church to be God's people publicly in the world.

CH114 Dulles, Avery Robert
Modelos de la Iglesia: Estudio Crítico sobre la Iglesia en Todos Sus Aspectos. Translated by José A. Benito. (Colección "Teologia y mundo actual," 40). Santander, SP: Editorial "Sal terrae," 1975. 210 pp. No ISBN.

Spanish translation of *Models of the Church* (1974).

CH—MISSION AND CHURCH RENEWAL

CH115 Dulles, Avery Robert

Models of the Church. Garden City, NYU: Doubleday, 1987. 256 pp. 0385133685.

Expanded edition of an influential treatment of basic ecclesiology by a noted Jesuit theologian who explores six models of the church biblically and theologically; originally published in 1974.

CH116 Gerard, Francois C.

The Future of the Church: The Theology of Renewal of Willem Adolf Visser 't Hooft. (Pittsburgh Theological Monograph Series, 2). Pittsburgh, PAU: Pickwick, 1974. xii, 239 pp. Paper. 0915138018.

A detailed analysis of the thought of the WCC's first general secretary, based on his writings and private papers.

CH117 Guder, Darrell L., ed.

Missional Church: A Vision for the Sending of the Church in North America. (The Gospel and Our Culture Series). Grand Rapids, MIU: Eerdmans, 1998. viii, 280 pp. Paper. 0802843506.

A collaborative effort of The Gospel and Our Culture Network, this volume thoroughly explores the North American (including Canadian) cultural context and status of the church today, presenting a model for church renewal.

CH118 Guder, Darrell L.

Be My Witnesses: The Church's Mission, Message, and Messengers. Grand Rapids, MIU: Eerdmans, 1985. xiv, 237 pp. Paper. 0802800513.

A theology of mission for the local church, emphasizing incarnational witness.

CH119 Guder, Darrell L.

The Continuing Conversion of the Church. (The Gospel and Our Culture Series). Grand Rapids, MIU: Eerdmans, 2000. xvi, 222 pp. Paper. 080284703X.

The author demonstrates that the church's missionary calling, especially in Western society, requires that the theology and practice of evangelism be fundamentally rethought and redirected, focusing on the continuing conversion of the church for faithful witness in today's world.

CH120 Hathaway, Brian

Beyond Renewal: The Kingdom of God. Milton Keynes, ENK: Word Publishing, 1990. 233 pp. Paper. 0850093392 (UK), 186258091X (AT).

A theology of renewal by a New Zealand pastor based on the experience of his church, and reflection on the biblical call for the church to exist for God's Kingdom, not just for itself.

CH121 Jones, E. Stanley

The Reconstruction of the Church: On What Pattern? Nashville, TNU: Abingdon, 1992. 208 pp. 0687357314.

Reflections on a church renewed by the veteran India missionary and world evangelist, proposing the Antioch model and a federal union of presently divided churches; originally published in 1970.

CH122 Küng, Hans, ed.

The Church and Ecumenism. (*Concilium* Theology in the Age of Renewal: Ecumenical Theology, 4). New York, NYU: Paulist Press, 1965. viii, 215 pp. No ISBN.

An anthology of essays dealing with renewal in ecumenical perspective, including Kung's noted essay on "The Charismatic Structure of the Church."

CH123 Kaiser, Walter C.

Revive Us Again: Biblical Insights for Encouraging Spiritual Renewal. Nashville, TNU: Broadman, 1999. xii, 275 pp. Paper. 0805418199.

A study of sixteen revivals in Scripture as a means for preparing the way for revival on the verge of a new millennium.

CH124 Keyes, Dick

Chameleon Christianity: Moving Beyond Safety and Conformity. (Hourglass Books). Grand Rapids, MIU: Baker Books, 1999. 121 pp. Paper. 080105866X.

A call to unite a polarized understanding of God's holiness and love through a recovery of vital apologetics and the building of non-tribal communities.

CH125 Kochanek, Franz-Hermann

Theologie einer missionarischen Gemeinde: Studien zu einer praktisch-theoretischen Handlungstheorie. (Veröffentlichungen des Missionspriesterseminars, 39). Nettetal, GW: Steyler Verlag, 1990. xiii, 343 pp. Paper. 3805002602.

This dissertation provides the theoretical underpinnings for a theology of the local community as a missionizing existence.

CH126 Kraus, C. Norman

The Community of the Spirit: How the Church Is in the World. Scottdale, PAU: Herald Press, 1993. 221 pp. Paper. 0836136195.

A revised and updated edition of a church renewal classic, in which the former Mennonite missionary to Japan asks the church to become a dynamic "God movement" and "community of the Spirit"; originally published by Eerdmans in 1974.

CH127 Lloyd-Jones, David Martyn

Revival. Basingstoke, ENK: Marshall Pickering, 1986. 316 pp. Paper. 0551026405 (hdbk), 0720806526 (pbk).

A composite of twenty-four expository sermons examining the conditions for, and the nature of, revival in the Church of England.

CH128 Lovelace, Richard F.

Dynamics of Spiritual Life: An Evangelical Theology of Renewal. Downers Grove, ILU: InterVarsity, 1979. 455 pp. Paper. 087784626X.

An attempt to elaborate a "unified field theory" of spirituality, drawing on Scripture and a variety of sources, presenting a model of both cyclical and continuous renewal in the church.

CH129 Lovelace, Richard F.

Renewal as a Way of Life. Downers Grove, ILU: InterVarsity, 1985. 206 pp. Paper. 0877845948.

Further reflections on the dynamics of individual and corporate renewal in the church, with insights from Scripture and history; A condensation of the author's influential *Dynamics of Spiritual Life.*

CH130 Lyon, David, and Albert D. Manuel, eds.

Renewal for Mission. Madras, II: CLS, 1968. viii, 236 pp. No ISBN.

Revised second edition of papers and findings from the National Consultation on the Mission of the Church in Contemporary India (Nasrapur, 1966), plus essays written for the Sixteenth Assembly (Shillong, 1967) of the NCCI.

CH—MISSION AND CHURCH RENEWAL

CH131 Moltmann, Jürgen

Neuer Lebensstil: Schritte zur Gemeinde. Munich, GW: Kaiser, 1977. 152 pp. 345901105X.

An elaboration of several themes of church life, some of which are treated more fully in the author's *Kirche in der Kraft des Geistes* (1975) (*The Church in the Power of the Spirit*, 1977).

CH132 Moltmann, Jürgen

Un Nueva Estila de Vida: Sobre la Libertad, la Alegría y el Juego. Salamanca, SP: Sígueme, 1981. 182 pp. 8430108467.

Spanish translation.

CH133 Moltmann, Jürgen

The Passion for Life: A Messianic Lifestyle. Translated by M. Douglas Meeks. Philadelphia, PAU: Fortress Press, 1978. 128 pp. Paper. 080060508X.

A freely adapted translation of *Neuer Lebensstil, Schritte zur Gemeinde* (1977); also published in 1978 under the title *The Open Church* (London: SCM Press).

CH134 Nessan, Craig L.

Beyond Maintenance to Mission: A Theology of the Congregation. Minneapolis, MNU: Fortress Press, 1999. ix, 134 pp. Paper. 0800631528.

A model for mission-driven leadership for congregations wanting to move away from a maintenance mentality and turn toward powerful, creative engagement with the world.

CH135 Rahner, Karl

The Shape of the Church to Come. Translated by Edward Quinn. New York, NYU: Seabury Press, 1974. 136 pp. 0816411816.

The prominent Roman Catholic theologian offers a perceptive and incisive analysis of the Church today, with proposals for its renewal in Germany and other countries.

CH136 Reuman, John, ed.

The Church Emerging: A U.S. Lutheran Case Study. Philadelphia, PAU: Fortress Press, 1977. ix, 275 pp. 0800612590.

Four reflective essays on the ecclesiology and understandings of mission of Lutheran churches; written as a US contribution to the world Lutheran study of "The Identity of the Church and Its Service to the Whole Human Being."

CH137 Russell, Keith A.

In Search of the Church: New Testament Images for Tomorrow's Congregations. (Once and Future Church Series, 2). Bethesda, MDU: Alban Institute, 1994. viii, 107 pp. Paper. 1566991234.

The former President and Professor of Preaching at New York Theological Seminary explores the biblical record of the invention of congregations by the early church as a "daring creation of a new form of human community."

CH138 Sanks, T. Howland

Salt, Leaven, and Light: The Community Called Church. New York, NYU: Crossroad Publishing, 1992. xi, 251 pp. 0824511751.

An open and engaging survey of the theology of church in its biblical roots, historical development, and contemporary issues (ministry, liberation, inculturation, ecumenism, and interreligious dialogue), with special reference to the RCC in the United States.

CH139 Schaeffer, Francis A.

The Church before the Watching World: A Practical Ecclesiology. Downers Grove, ILU: InterVarsity, 1971. 105 pp. Paper. 0877845425.

In this brief book Schaeffer critiques theological liberalism, raises the issue of apostasy, and calls the church to a visible purity in life and doctrine.

CH140 Schillebeeckx, Edward

The Mission of the Church. Translated by N. D. Smith. New York, NYU: Seabury Press, 1973. ix, 244 pp. 0816411441.

English translation.

CH141 Schillebeeckx, Edward

De Zending van de Kerk. (Theologische peilingen, 4). Bilthoven, NE: Nelissen, 1968. 312 pp. No ISBN.

This work, written by one of the most effective interpreters of the decrees of Vatican II, is a detailed and thorough presentation of "the varieties of functions in the Church: laity, priests, and religious, and their mutual cooperation in service to the world."

CH142 Snyder, Howard A.

Liberating the Church: The Ecology of the Church and Kingdom. Downers Grove, ILU: InterVarsity, 1983. 288 pp. 0877848947 (hdbk), 0877843856 (pbk).

A theology of the church and church renewal based on ecological and organic models; includes chapters on witness, the ministry of all believers, lifestyle, and the role of women; also published by Wipf & Stock (1996).

CH143 Stedman, Ray C.

Birth of the Body. Santa Ana, CAU: Vision House, 1974. 200 pp. 088449019X (hdbk), 0884490130 (pbk).

A practical exposition of the life and functioning of the church based primarily on Acts 1-12 by the pastor of Peninsula Bible Church in California.

CH144 Stone, Bryan P.

Compassionate Ministry: Theological Foundations. Maryknoll, NYU: Orbis Books, 1996. xvi, 168 pp. Paper. 1570750696.

The compassion of God made real in the incarnation and ministry of Jesus, presented as the foundation for ministry today amidst suffering and poverty.

CH145 Suhard, Emmanuel-Célestin

The Responsible Church: Selected Texts of Cardinal Suhard. Translated by Patrick Hepburne-Scott. Compiled by Olivier de La Brosse. London, ENK: Chapman; Notre Dame, INU: Labor et Fides, 1967. 258 pp. No ISBN.

English translation.

CH146 Suhard, Emmanuel-Célestin

Vers une église en état de mission. Edited by Olivier de La Brosse. (Chrétiens de tous les temps, 8). Paris, FR: Éditions du Cerf, 1965. 364 pp. No ISBN.

A collection of the most important statements of the cardinal, whose name is connected with the Paris Mission and the worker-priest movement, and so with the missionary renewal of the ministry in France.

CH147 Talltorp, Çke
Sacrament and Growth: A Study in the Sacramental Dimension of Expansion in the Life of the Local Church, as Reflected in the Theology of Roland Allen. (Supplements to Annual Report of Uppsala Studies of Mission,1). Uppsala, SW: Swedish Institute of Missionary Research, 1989. 146 pp. Paper. 9185425188.

A dissertation on Roland Allen (1868-1947), independent mission strategist, who combined a catholic view of Anglicanism with a deliberate concern for developing the church as a network of local fellowships celebrating the sacraments.

CH148 Vajta, Vilmos, ed.
The Gospel and the Ambiguity of the Church. (The Gospel Encounters History Series). Philadelphia, PAU: Fortress Press, 1974. viii, 243 pp. 0800602781.

Seven essays by Lutheran theologians in Europe and North America on the nature, history, and structure of the church in relation to its mission.

CH149 Watson, David
I Believe in the Church. Grand Rapids, MIU: Eerdmans, 1979. 368 pp. Paper. 0802817882.

A comprehensive, biblically based theology of the church and its renewal by a widely influential charismatic Anglican priest; first published in London in 1978 (Hodder and Stoughton).

CH150 Watson, David Lowes
God Does Not Foreclose: The Universal Promise of Salvation. Nashville, TNU: Abingdon, 1990. 160 pp. Paper. 0687149649.

A theology of renewal and analysis of the vocation of Christian discipleship for individuals and congregations in contemporary culture.

CH151 Wessels, Cletus
The Holy Web: Church and the New Universe Story. Maryknoll, NYU: Orbis Books, 2000. x, 237 pp. Paper. 1570753024.

The author shows how the church's mission is to become a nurturing and dynamic web of relationships in which all humanity can find itself part of a wondrous whole.

CH152 Weth, Rudolf
Kirche in der Sendung Jesu Christi: Missionarische und diakonische Existenz der Gemeinde im nachchristlichen Zeitalter. Neukirchen-Vluyn, GW: Aussaat Verlag; Neukirchen-Vluyn, GW: Neukirchener Verlag, 1993. 127 pp. Paper. 3761548702 (A), 3788714735 (N).

A theological and biblical reflection on the missional and diaconal existence of the church in a post-Christian age, with reference to renewal in a unified Germany and Europe, by the director of a center for diaconal ministries.

Church Renewal and the Wider Community

See also TH612, ME133, SO60-SO61, SO92, EC146, EC333, CH25, CH291, CH420, AF1107, EU90, and EU175.

CH153 Allen, Jere, and George Bullard
Shaping a Future for the Church in the Changing Community. Atlanta, GAU: Home Mission Board, SBC, 1981. 99 pp. Paper. No ISBN.

A manual of resources to assist congregations in changing communities, with a step-by-step planning process.

CH154 Ammerman, Nancy Tatom, Arthur E. Farnsley et al.
Congregation and Community. New Brunswick, NJU: Rutgers University Press, 1997. xvi, 434 pp. 0813523346 (hdbk), 0813523354 (pbk).

Findings of a massive study of the relationship between social change and congregational life in the United States, with twenty-three case studies of Catholic and Protestant parishes.

CH155 Bühlmann, Walbert
Sorge für alle Welt: Pfarrei in neuer Verantwortung für die Mission der Kirche. Freiburg, GW: Seelsorge-Verlag, 1967. 94 pp. Paper. No ISBN.

This booklet gives practical advice on how the conciliar statement that the church is missionary by its very nature can be realized on a parish level.

CH156 Berger, Peter L.
The Noise of Solemn Assemblies: Christian Commitment and the Religious Establishment in America. Garden City, NJU: Doubleday, 1961. 189 pp. Paper. No ISBN.

Sociologist Berger critiques the US church for its compromises with culture, and calls the church to the "task of disestablishment," including internal renewal, social engagement, and new forms of the church.

CH157 Bos, A. David
A Practical Guide to Community Ministry. Louisville, KYU: Westminster John Knox, 1993. xii, 84 pp. Paper. 0664254055.

First edition of a primer for North American rural and urban parishes desiring to develop, on an ecumenical basis, a social and pastoral ministry.

CH158 Campolo, Tony, and Gordon D. Aeschliman
101 Ways Your Church Can Change the World: A Guide to Help Christians Express the Love of Christ to a Needy World. Ventura, CAU: Regal Books, 1993. 228 pp. 0830716505.

Practical helps for Christians and local churches desiring to focus their ministries outward to persons in need, with a complete thirteen-week study plan.

CH159 *Diagrammatic Modelling: An Aid to Theological Reflection in Church and Community Development Work*
(Occasional Papers, 4). Manchester, ENK: William Temple Foundation, 1980. 62 pp. Paper. No ISBN.

Reflections, by Methodists and others in Great Britain, on the theology and models for the church's involvement in community development.

CH160 Dudley, Carl S.
Next Steps in Community Ministry: Hands-on Leadership. Bethesda, MDU: Alban Institute, 1996. xviii, 138 pp. Paper. 1566991684.

Practical helps for those concerned to equip their local churches for community ministry, drawing upon twenty-five case studies of the Church and Community Project.

CH161 Evans, David, and Mike Fearon
From Strangers to Neighbors: How You Can Make the Difference in Your Community. London, ENK: Hodder & Stoughton, 1998. ix, 230 pp. Paper. 0340694556.

A powerful tool designed by the Director of Tear Fund's UK Action in Great Britain to encourage visionary Christians to get involved in their local communities.

CH—MISSION AND CHURCH RENEWAL

CH162 Hillman, Eugene
The Wider Ecumenism: Anonymous Christianity and the Church. (Compass Books). London, ENK: Burns & Oates; New York, NYU: Herder, 1968. 160 pp. 0223296457.

A call by a Roman Catholic missionary to the Masai tribe of East Africa for the church to rediscover its purpose in mission to the world, in the light of the post-Vatican II debate on universal salvation and "anonymous Christianity."

CH163 Hoyer, H. Conrad
Ecumenopolis U.S.A.: The Church in Mission in Community. Minneapolis, MNU: Augsburg, 1971. 159 pp. Paper. 0806611200.

Defining *ecumenopolis* as "one church, in mission, in community," the associate executive director of the NCCUSA's Commission on Regional and Local Ecumenism gives a holistic interpretation of the church's mission, to include both proclaiming the Gospel and serving the community, at all levels (geographical, political. and social).

CH164 Marcum, Elvis
Outreach: God's Miracle Business. Nashville, TNU: Broadman, 1975. 151 pp. 0805455566.

The story, written by its pastor, of how Graceland Baptist Church of New Albany, Indiana, grew from a small, struggling mission into a "miracle" church with various forms of outreach to its community.

CH165 Martin, Steele W., and Priscilla C. Martin
Blue Collar Ministry: Problems and Opportunities for Mainline "Middle" Congregations. Washington, DCU: Alban Institute, 1989. viii, 62 pp. Paper. No ISBN.

The author, an Episcopal priest who has served several working-class parishes in the United States, reveals ways to understand and bridge the gap between clergy and "blue collar" laity.

CH166 Paoli, Arturo
Gather Together in My Name: Reflections on Christianity and Community. Translated by Robert R. Barr. Maryknoll, NYU: Orbis Books, 1987. viii, 192 pp. Paper. 0883443570.

Reflections and meditations on community-building and its major obstacles, as presented to a young farmer in the western part of Venezuela, as a priest from the congregation of the Little Brothers of the Gospel of Charles de Foucauld introduces him to Christ.

CH167 Pohl, Christine D., ed.
Making Room: Recovering Hospitality as a Christian Tradition. Grand Rapids, MIU: Eerdmans, 1999. xiii, 205 pp. Paper. 0802844316.

Christian foundations for welcoming strangers and the necessity, difficulty, and blessing of hospitality today explored through biblical and historical research with extensive exposure to contemporary Christian communities such as L'Abr, L'Arche, and the Catholic Worker.

CH168 Sample, Tex
Blue-Collar Ministry: Facing Economic and Social Realities of Working People. Valley Forge, PAU: Judson Press, 1984. 192 pp. Paper. 0817010297.

Practical helps for pastors and religious professionals who work with blue-collar persons inside and outside the church, particularly in Protestant churches of the United States.

CH169 Sample, Tex
Hard Living People and Mainstream Christians. Nashville, TNU: Abingdon, 1993. 176 pp. Paper. 0687179319.

A revealing look, by the Professor of Church and Society at Saint Paul School of Theology in Kansas City, Missouri, at the church in the United States and its interactions and motivations for involvement with marginalized persons who are often social outcasts.

CH170 Schuller, Robert H.
Your Church Has a Fantastic Future: A Possibility Thinker's Guide to a Successful Church. Ventura, CAU: Regal Books, 1986. 359 pp. 0830711260.

A popular account of principles and guidelines to develop an active mission in your church and community, through finding and dealing with the needs of others; by the pastor of the Crystal Cathedral (Garden Grove Community Church).

CH171 Westerhoff, Caroline A.
Good Fences: The Boundaries of Hospitality. Boston, MAU: Cowley Publications, 1998. xiii, 172 pp. Paper. 1561011649.

The theological issues raised by boundaries that are blurred, shifted, moved, or "rigified," with practical help for exploring the identity of the church, defining social outreach, and practicing true hospitality.

CH172 Williams, Colin Wilbur
What in the World? London, ENK: Epworth Press, 1965. xxi, 105 pp. Paper. No ISBN.

A follow-up book to *Where in the World?* (1963), this study book is designed to help congregations search for an appropriate missionary relationship to the world.

CH173 Williams, Colin Wilbur
Where in the World?: Changing Forms of the Church's Witness. New York, NYU: NCCUSA, 1963. x, 116 pp. Paper. No ISBN.

A study book on local church life and witness developed as part of the WCC's long-range study on the missionary structure of the congregation.

CH174 Willie, Charles V.
Church Action in the World: Studies in Sociology and Religion. New York, NYU: Morehouse-Barlow, 1969. xv, 160 pp. No ISBN.

An analysis, by the distinguished Professor of Sociology at Syracuse University, of community structure and process, and how the church as a corporate body acts or fails to act in the world.

Church and Urban Community

See also SO548, CH405, AF182, AF204, and EU163.

CH175 Blumhorst, Roy
Faithful Rebels: Does the Old-Style Religion Fit the New Style of Life? St. Louis, MOU: Concordia Publishing, 1967. 100 pp. Paper. No ISBN.

A case study of mission outreach to residents of a high-rise apartment complex in Chicago, Illinois—one of the least "churched" sub-populations in the United States.

CH176 Cosby, Gordon
By Grace Transformed: Christianity for a New Millennium. New York, NYU: Crossroad Publishing, 1999. xiv, 210 pp. Paper. 0824517547.

A collection of sermons on servant leadership, forgiveness, renewal, and presence among the poor, by the founder and pastor of a fifty-year-old interracial congregation, the Church of the Savior in Washington, D.C.

CH—MISSION AND CHURCH RENEWAL

CH177 Gordon, Wayne L., and Randall Frame
Real Hope in Chicago: The Incredible Story of How the Gospel Is Transforming a Chicago Neighborhood. Grand Rapids, MIU: Zondervan, 1995. 220 pp. Paper. 0310205530.

The story of the Lawndale Community Church of Chicago, and of its part in rebuilding an inner-city neighborhood into a community of faith and hope.

CH178 Jefferson, Kinmoth W., and William E. Ramsden
Inner Vitality, Outward Vigor: The Missional Urban Church. New York, NYU: UMC, Board of Global Ministries, 1985. 96 pp. Paper. No ISBN.

Brief case studies of twenty-two United Methodist urban congregations.

CH179 Lee, Robert, ed.
The Church and the Exploding Metropolis: Theological, Biblical, and Sociological Perspectives on the Essence of the New Urban America. Richmond, VAU: John Knox Press, 1965. 125 pp. Paper. No ISBN.

Theological, biblical, and sociological perspectives on urbanization in the USA.

CH180 Lee, Robert, ed.
Cities and Churches: Readings on the Urban Church. Philadelphia, PAU: Westminster Press, 1962. 366 pp. No ISBN.

A sourcebook on readings of the role of religion in urban society in the United States.

CH181 Ortiz, Manuel
One New People: Models for Developing a Multiethnic Church. Downers Grove, ILU: InterVarsity, 1996. 158 pp. Paper. 0830818820.

A primer on multiethnic church development by the Professor of Ministry and Mission and Director of the Urban Program at Westminster Theological Seminary in Philadelphia, Pennsylvania.

CH182 Webber, George W.
Today's Church: A Community of Exiles and Pilgrims. Nashville, TNU: Abingdon, 1979. 160 pp. Paper. 0687423201.

Citing Jeremiah 29 as a prophetic call to God's people today, the President of New York Theological Seminary, and pioneer leader of the East Harlem Protestant Parish, encourages Christians to renew the urban church, through seeking the welfare of the city where God has placed them as his witnesses.

CH183 Wilson, Robert Leroy, and James H. Davis
The Church in the Racially Changing Community. Nashville, TNU: Abingdon, 1966. 159 pp. Paper. No ISBN.

Case studies of churches in racially changing communities in the United States, based on a study by the National Division of the Board of Missions of the Methodist Church.

CH184 Winter, Gibson
The New Creation as Metropolis. New York, NYU: Macmillan; London, ENK: Collier Macmillan, 1963. viii, 152 pp. No ISBN.

Proposals for a form of Christianity designed to shape the metropolis as a human community by a distinguished Professor of Ethics and Society at Chicago Divinity School.

CH185 Younger, George D.
From New Creation to Urban Crisis: A History of Action Training Ministries, 1962-1975. (Studies in Religion and Society). Chicago, ILU: Center for the Scientific Study of Religion, 1987. vi, 260 pp. 0913348252.

A detailed study of the development of "urban training programs" for US clergy beginning in 1962, and their coordination through the Action Training Coalition until its abandonment in 1975.

CH186 Ziegenhals, Walter E.
Urban Churches in Transition: Reflections on Selected Problems and Approaches to Churches and Communities in Racial Transition Based on the Chicago Experience. New York, NYU: Pilgrim Press, 1978. 201 pp. Paper. 0829803556.

A case study of the United Church of Christ's "Churches-in-Transition Project" in Chicago, highlighting the mission of congregations in areas of racial transition.

Church and Rural Community

CH187 Hinsdale, Mary Ann, Helen M. Lewis, and S. Maxine Waller
It Comes from the People: Community Development and Local Theology. Philadelphia, PAU: Temple University Press, 1995. xv, 400 pp. 156639211X (hdbk), 1566392128 (pbk).

A detailed case study of survival and renewal through community development in the Appalachian community of Ivanhoe, Virginia, focusing on the role of the churches in social transformation.

CH188 Jung, Shannon et al.
Rural Ministry: The Shape of the Renewal to Come. Nashville, TNU: Abingdon, 1998. 250 pp. Paper. 0687016061.

A primer on issues of renewal of rural churches and communities in the United States; findings of a three-year study by the Center for Theology and Land of the Rural Ministry Program at Wartburg Theological Seminary.

CH189 Pappas, Anthony, and Scott Planting
Mission: The Small Church Reaches Out. (Small Church in Action). Valley Forge, PAU: Judson Press, 1993. xii, 137 pp. Paper. 0817011749.

Out of their more than twenty years experience in small church and cooperative ministries in Maine and Rhode Island, the authors present models for effective local community ministries within the resources of small membership parishes.

Renewal and Worship

See also CO170, EV495, EV541, SP227, SP297, and AS886.

CH190 Arn, Charles
How to Start a New Service: Your Church Can Reach New People. Grand Rapids, MIU: Baker Books, 1998. 269 pp. Paper. 0801090377.

Resources for studying, planning, and implementing a new worship service in a new style, based on a seven-denomination study by the President of Church Growth, Inc.

CH191 Webber, Robert E.
Common Roots: An Call to Evangelical Maturity. Grand Rapids, MIU: Zondervan, 1978. 256 pp. 0310366305.

An examination of church life, particularly worship, in light of the early Christian tradition, with a critique regarding its "evangelical amnesia."

CH—MISSION AND CHURCH RENEWAL

CH192 Webber, Robert E.

Worship Old & New: A Biblical, Historical, and Practical Introduction. Grand Rapids, MIU: Zondervan, 1994. 287 pp. 0310479908.

Revised edition of a theology of worship that blends historical and traditional practices with contemporary elements and today's renewed interest in worship; first published in 1982.

Local Charismatic Renewal

See also HI597, HI608, CH21, AF1003, AM700, AS621, and EU178.

CH193 Byrne, James E.

Living in the Spirit: A Handbook on Catholic Charismatic Christianity. New York, NYU: Paulist Press, 1975. viii, 184 pp. Paper. 0809119021.

A practical guidebook for charismatic community within the local church, including a discussion on gifts and on guidance.

CH194 Gelpi, Donald L.

Charism and Sacrament: A Theology of Christian Conversion. New York, NYU: Paulist Press; London, ENK: SPCK, 1976. x, 258 pp. 0809119358 (US), 0281029776 (UK).

A serious essay on "fundamental theology" and the charismatic movement, by the Professor of Theology, Jesuit School of Theology, Berkeley, California.

CH195 Harris, Ralph W.

Spoken by the Spirit: Documented Accounts of "Other Tongues" from Arabic to Zulu. Springfield, MOU: Gospel Publishing House, 1973. 128 pp. No ISBN.

More than fifty testimonies to glossolalia from Africa, the Americas, Europe, and Asia, mostly from Assemblies of God sources.

CH196 Hummel, Charles E.

Fire in the Fireplace: Contemporary Charismatic Renewal. Downers Grove, ILU: InterVarsity, 1978. 275 pp. Paper. 0877847428.

An account of the rise of the charismatic movement and its impact on InterVarsity Christian Fellowship, with an exploration of the biblical and contemporary issues involved.

CH197 Kelsey, Morton T.

Tongue Speaking: An Experiment in Spiritual Experience. (Waymark Books). Garden City, NYU: Doubleday, 1968. xii, 252 pp. Paper. No ISBN.

Kelsey, an Episcopalian sympathetic to the charismatic movement, explores the phenomenon of tongues speaking biblically, historically, psychologically, and in contemporary expression; originally published in 1964.

CH198 Koberlein, Jean

A Church without Walls: Forgiveness and Healing from the Battlefield of Church Renewal to the Harvest Field of Love. Shippensburg, PAU: Destiny Image, 1990. 181 pp. Paper. 1560430540.

Personal testimonies by one who has participated in interdenominational charismatic renewal ministries in the United States since 1976.

CH199 Laurentin, René

Catholic Pentecostalism. London, ENK: Darton, Longman & Todd; Garden City, NYU: Doubleday, 1977. 239 pp. 0232513864 (UK), 0385121296 (US).

English translation.

CH200 Laurentin, René

Pentecôtisme chez les catholiquues: risques et avenir. Paris, FR: Beauchesne, 1974. 260 pp. No ISBN.

A careful examination of this contemporary phenomenon presenting the biblical, patristic, psychological, linguistic, and typological factors in the experience.

CH201 Lederle, Henry I.

Treasures Old and New: Interpretations of "Spirit-Baptism" in the Charismatic Renewal Movement. Peabody, MAU: Hendrickson Publishers, 1988. xx, 264 pp. Paper. 0913573752.

A detailed treatment of four different interpretations of "Spirit-Baptism" (pre-charismatic, neo-pentecostal, sacramental, and integrative) with a careful critique of each, thereby providing a survey of theologies of the charismatic renewal movement of Roman Catholics, Eastern Orthodox, Anglicans, and Protestants of a variety of denominations.

CH202 Mühlen, Heribert

A Charismatic Theology: Initiation in the Spirit. Translated by Edward Quinn and Thomas Linton. London, ENK: Burns & Oates; New York, NYU: Paulist Press, 1978. 360 pp. Paper. 0860120643.

English translation.

CH203 Mühlen, Heribert

Einübung in die christliche Grunderfahrung. (Topos-Taschenbücher, 40 & 49). Mainz, GW: Matthias-Grünewald-Verlag, 1976. 2 vols. 3786705305.

Helps for Catholics and Protestants desiring to enter the charismatic renewal movement; designed as a fourteen-week cycle of reading and devotions out of materials developed for seminars on faith, organized for parish missions [vol. 1: *Lehre und Zuspruch*; vol. 2: *Gebet und Erwartung*].

CH204 Mühlen, Heribert

Vous recevrez le don du Saint Esprit: le renouveau spirituel. Translated by Charles Baumgartner. Paris, FR: Le Centurion, 1982. 2 vols. 222734024X (vol. 1), 2227340258 (vol. 2).

French translation.

CH205 McDonnell, Kilian, ed.

The Holy Spirit and Power: The Catholic Charismatic Renewal. Garden City, NYU: Doubleday, 1975. 186 pp. Paper. 0385099098.

Eight Roman Catholic authors explore aspects of contemporary charismatic renewal, including baptism in the Holy Spirit, ecclesiological context, liturgy, and ecumenical concerns.

CH206 O'Connor, Edward D., ed.

Perspectives on Charismatic Renewal. Notre Dame, INU: University of Notre Dame Press, 1975. xv, 216 pp. Paper. 0268015171.

A professor at Notre Dame actively involved in the Catholic charismatic renewal edited this compendium, surveying the work of the Holy Spirit historically and theologically, and in Islam.

CH207 Ortiz, Juan Carlos

Disciple. Carol Stream, ILU: Creation House, [1975]. 158 pp. 088419101X.

A popular Argentinean charismatic pastor discusses church renewal as a call to discipleship and witness for the Kingdom, enabled by the Holy Spirit.

CH208 Pousson, Edward K.

Spreading the Flame: Charismatic Churches and Missions Today. Grand Rapids, MIU: Zondervan, 1992. 195 pp. Paper. 0310533317.

A popular description and analysis of the missionary activities of certain independent charismatic churches in the United States.

CH209 Pulkingham, W. Graham

Gathered for Power. New York, NYU: Morehouse-Barlow, 1972. 138 pp. Paper. 0819211303.

The story of charismatic renewal in the Episcopal Church of the Redeemer in Houston, Texas, told by the pastor.

CH210 Reformed Ecumenical Synod

The Holy Spirit Down to Earth. Grand Rapids, MIU: Reformed Ecumenical Synod, 1977. 80 pp. No ISBN.

Essays on the Holy Spirit and charismatic gifts (R. B. Gaffin), the church (K. Runia), and culture (G. C. Oosthuizen) with responses.

CH211 Rumble, Dale

Behold the Harvest. Shippensburg, PAU: Revival Press, 1998. xvii, 170 pp. Paper. 156043192X.

A call to charismatic renewal by the founder of the Fountain of Life Church in Kingston, New York.

CH212 Runyon, Theodore, ed.

What the Spirit Is Saying to the Churches. New York, NYU: Hawthorn Books, 1975. viii, 142 pp. Paper. 0801585465.

Papers from a conference held at Emory University in 1974, partly in response to the charismatic movement, with contributions by Krister Stendahl, Oral Roberts, Wayne Oates, David du Plessis, and others.

CH213 Samarin, William J.

Tongues of Men and Angels: The Religious Language of Pentecostalism. New York, NYU: Macmillan, 1972. xv, 277 pp. No ISBN.

A scholar in the area of sociolinguistics discusses the phenomenon of glossolalia in Christianity and gives some psychological explanations.

CH214 Schlink, Basilea

Ruled by the Spirit. Translated by John Foote, Mary Foote and Michael Harper. Basinstoke, ENK: Lakeland, 1970. 130 pp. Paper. 0551002077.

A discussion of charismatic renewal including spiritual gifts, the work of the Holy Spirit in history, and personal testimonies; originally published in 1969 (London, ENK: Oliphants); an English translation of *Wo der Geist weht* (1969).

CH215 Sherrill, John L.

They Speak with Other Tongues. Old Tappan, NJU: Revell; New York, NYU: McGraw-Hill, 1964. vii, 165 pp. Paper. No ISBN.

An influential, much-reprinted account of people experiencing charismatic renewal, including the author's own experience.

CH216 Slosser, Bob

Miracle in Darien. Plainfield, NJU: Logos International, 1979. 268 pp. 0882703552.

The engaging story of charismatic renewal in an Episcopal parish in Darien, Connecticut, in the 1970s.

CH217 Snyder, Howard A., and Daniel V. Runyon

The Divided Flame: Wesleyans and the Charismatic Renewal. Grand Rapids, MIU: Asbury Press; Grand Rapids, MIU: Zondervan, 1986. 120 pp. Paper. 0310751810.

Explores biblically and historically, the meaning of "charismatic," tracing similarities and differences in the Wesleyan, holiness, and charismatic movements.

CH218 Suenens, Léon Joseph

Œcuménisme et renouveau charismatique: orientations théologiques et pastorales. (Document de Malines, 2). Paris, FR: Le Centurion, 1978. 159 pp. 2227345128.

An outstanding leader in the Catholic charismatic movement shows what specific contribution charismatic renewal can make to the reuniting of divided Christendom.

CH219 Suenens, Léon Joseph

Ecumenism and Charismatic Renewal: Theological and Pastoral Orientations. (Malines Document 2). London, ENK: Darton, Longman & Todd; Ann Arbor, MIU: Servant Books, 1978. ix, 109 pp. Paper. 0232514305 (UK), 089283059X (US).

English translation.

CH220 Suenens, Léon Joseph

Hoffen im Geist: ein neues Pfingsten der Kirche. Salzburg, GW: Müller Verlag, 1976. 224 pp. 3701305145.

German translation.

CH221 Suenens, Léon Joseph

Renewal and the Powers of Darkness. Translated by Olga Prendergast. (Malines Document, 4). London, ENK: Darton, Longman & Todd, 1983. xv, 117 pp. Paper. 0232515913.

Discusses renewal in the Roman Catholic Church, particularly charismatic renewal, in the light of the problem of Satan, demons, and evil, and the practice of exorcism.

CH222 Synan, Vinson

Charismatic Bridges. Ann Arbor, MIU: Word of Life, 1974. xv, 57 pp. Paper. No ISBN.

The second edition of a brief, but informed and timely, call for charismatic fellowship across denominational lines and with Roman Catholics, including some historical perspective, by a key figure in the contemporary charismatic movement; originally published in 1971.

CH223 Wagner, C. Peter

The Third Wave of the Holy Spirit: Encountering the Power of Signs and Wonders Today. Ann Arbor, MIU: Servant Publications, 1988. 133 pp. Paper. 0892836016.

Based partly on his own experience, and the "Signs and Wonders" course at Fuller Theological Seminary, Wagner argues that the renewing work of God's Spirit is being extended to the whole church today.

CH224 White, John

When the Spirit Comes with Power: Signs and Wonders among God's People. Downers Grove, ILU: InterVarsity, 1988. 251 pp. Paper. 0830812229.

A historical and biblical examination of signs and wonders in the church in light of the contemporary Vineyard Movement.

CH—MISSION AND CHURCH RENEWAL

History of Renewal

See also HI90, EV231, EV239, and CH3.

CH225 Aubert, Roger, ed.
Historical Problems of Church Renewal. (*Concilium,* Theology in the Age of Renewal: Church History, 7). Glen Rock, NJU: Paulist Press, 1965. ix, 179 pp. No ISBN.

Eleven Roman Catholic authors consider church renewal historically, focusing on such issues as collegiality, church-state relations, Marxism, and the role of church councils.

CH226 Chenu, Marie Dominique
Nature, Man, and Society in the Twelfth Century: Essays on New Theological Perspectives in the Latin West. Translated by Jerome Taylor and Lester K. Little. (Medieval Academy Reprints for Teaching, 37). Toronto, ONC: University of Toronto, 1997. xxi, 361 pp. Paper. 0802071759.

English translation of nine selected essays from *La théologie au douzième siècle* (1957); originally published in English in 1957 (University of Chicago).

CH227 Chenu, Marie Dominique
La Teologia nel Dodicesimo Secolo. Milan, IT: Jaca Book, 1986. 481 pp. No ISBN.

Italian translation of *La théologie au douzième siècle* (1976); earlier published as *La Teologia nel medio evo* (1972).

CH228 Chenu, Marie Dominique
La théologie au douzième siècle. Paris, FR: J. Vrin, 1976. 413 pp. No ISBN.

Third edition of the noted French medievalist's scholarly history of medieval renewal currents, particularly the "evangelical awakening" of the 12th century; originally published in 1957.

CH229 Clark, Stephen B.
Unordained Elders and Renewal Communities. New York, NYU: Paulist Press, 1976. v, 105 pp. Paper. 0809119161.

A leader in the Catholic Charismatic Renewal studies the 4th-century ascetic movement for lessons about renewal, leadership, and the incorporation of renewal into the larger church.

CH230 Coalter, Milton J., John M. Mulder, and Louis B. Weeks, eds.
The Mainstream Protestant "Decline": The Presbyterian Pattern. (The Presbyterian Presence: The Twentieth-Century Experience). Louisville, KYU: Westminster John Knox, 1990. 263 pp. Paper. 0664251501.

Eight essays examining factors that energized growth and sustained membership of congregations when national membership in Presbyterian churches in the USA was in decline.

CH231 Davies, R. E.
I Will Pour Out My Spirit: A History and Theology of Revivals and Evangelical Awakenings. Tunbridge Wells, ENK: Monarch Publications, 1992. 288 pp. Paper. 1854241605.

A popular history of Protestant revivalism in Great Britain and the United States from Jonathan Edwards to the present.

CH232 Riss, Richard M.
A Survey of 20th-Century Revival Movements in North America. Peabody, MAU: Hendrickson Publishers, 1988. 202 pp. Paper. 0913573728.

An objective history of revival movements in the 20th century, including some contextual precursive influences, featuring the Pentecostal, Latter-Rain, healing, and charismatic movements.

CH233 Snyder, Howard A.
The Radical Wesley & Patterns of Church Renewal. Downers Grove, ILU: InterVarsity, 1980. 189 pp. Paper. 0877846251.

A historical study of John Wesley's radical Protestant roots, the early Methodist movement, and Wesley's theology of the church, with application to church renewal today.

CH234 Snyder, Howard A.
Signs of the Spirit. Grand Rapids, MIU: Academie Books, 1989. 336 pp. Paper. 0310515416.

A study of Montanism, Pietism, Moravianism, and early Methodism as renewal movements, with practical application to church life today.

CH235 Ward, W. Reginald
The Protestant Evangelical Awakening. Cambridge, ENK: Cambridge University Press, 1992. xviii, 370 pp. 0521414911.

A detailed scholarly survey of revival and renewal movements in Europe, England, and America in the 17th and 18th centuries, by a noted historian.

Structures and Models for Renewal: General

See also TH381, ME113, ME184, CO170, EV313-EV314, EV329, EV335, EV341, EV348, EV391, EV413, CH102, CH107, CH134, CH152, CH401, AF585, AF677, AM609-AM610, AM640, AS56, AS1128, EU20, EU148, EU297, OC91, and OC107.

CH236 Abrahamson, James O.
Put Your Best Foot Forward: How to Minister from Your Strength. (Ministry for the Third Millennium). Nashville, KYU: Abingdon, 1994. 128 pp. Paper. 0687004918.

Six models for local church renewal (worship-centered, Bible teaching, relational, market-driven, traditional, and social action); with case studies from growing Protestant parishes in the United States.

CH237 Ammerman, Nancy Tatom et al., eds.
Studying Congregations: A New Handbook. Nashville, TNU: Abingdon, 1998. 256 pp. Paper. 0687006511.

A thoroughgoing revision and update of the leading textbook in the field—*A Handbook for Congregational Studies*—utilizes a comprehensive systems approach to congregations, analyzing the ministries, stories, and processes that are at work in congregations.

CH238 Arnold, Jeffrey
Small Group Outreach: Turning Groups Inside Out. Downers Grove, ILU: InterVarsity, 1998. 138 pp. Paper. 0830811702.

This resource for various dimensions of small group outreach includes the development of a vision, multiplication, holistic care, evangelism, short-term mission, and community service.

CH239 Arnold, Jeffrey
Starting Small Groups: Building Communities that Matter. (Leadership Insight Series). Nashville, TNU: Abingdon, 1997. 142 pp. Paper. 0687018560.

Tools for designing and implementing a comprehensive and effective small group ministry.

CH240 Bandy, Thomas G.

Kicking Habits: Welcome Relief for Addicted Churches. Nashville, TNU: Abingdon, 1997. 231 pp. Paper. 0687031893.

A systematic approach to the organic transformation of local churches in decline; by the Programme Officer of Congregational Mission and Evangelism for the United Church of Canada.

CH241 Barna, George

Turn-Around Churches: How to Overcome Barriers to Growth and Bring New Life to an Established Church. Ventura, CAU: Regal Books, 1993. 122 pp. 0830715924.

A primer for North American congregations desiring to turn around from decline to growth; by the noted researcher on contemporary trends in North American culture and Christianity.

CH242 Beckham, William A.

The Second Reformation: Reshaping the Church for the Twenty-First Century. Houston, TXU: Touch Publications, 1995. 253 pp. Paper. 1880828901.

An informed, sustained argument for the New Testament pattern of large-group celebration wed to small-group discipleship.

CH243 Biersdorf, John E.

Hunger for Experience: Vital Religious Communities in America. New York, NYU: Seabury Press, 1975. xiii, 174 pp. 0816411980.

Case studies of religious renewal in North America, in thirty-five communities experiencing religious vitality within a wide variety of traditions (Roman Catholic, Protestant, Jewish, and other faiths).

CH244 Bloesch, Donald G.

Wellsprings of Renewal: Promise in Christian Communal Life. Grand Rapids, MIU: Eerdmans, 1974. 124 pp. 0802815006.

A historical and theological discussion of forms of community and discipleship, especially since the Reformation, with particular focus on new forms of Christian community life.

CH245 Boyd, Malcolm, ed.

The Underground Church. New York, NYU: Sheed and Ward, 1968. x, 246 pp. No ISBN.

Eighteen testimonies by leaders in the United States, in movements for Christian witness and mission outside the institutional churches.

CH246 Brennan, Patrick J.

Parishes That Excel: Models of Excellence in Education, Ministry, and Evangelization. New York, NYU: Crossroad Publishing, 1992. 130 pp. 0824511565.

Case studies of eighteen Catholic and Protestant parishes in the United States that are models of excellence in education, ministry, and evangelization.

CH247 Callahan, Kennon L.

Twelve Keys to an Effective Church. San Francisco, CAU: Harper & Row, 1983. 2 vols. 0060612975 (vol. 1), 0060612959 (vol. 2).

Twelve essential characteristics of effective growing churches and how they can be developed by any parish with long-term planning; based on data from more than 750 consultations with North American mainline Protestant congregations [vol. 1, *Strategic Planning for Mission*, xxxi, 127; vol. 2, *The Leader's Guide*].

CH248 Cho, Yong-gi, and Harold Hostetler

Successful Home Cell Groups. Plainfield, NJU: Logos International; South Plainfield, NJU: Bridge Publishing, 1981. ix, 176 pp. Paper. 088270513X.

Guidelines for successful home cell groups that can give every church member an opportunity to participate in the church's ministry and to bring revival to their neighborhood.

CH249 Clark, M. Edward, William L. Malcomson, and Warren Lane Molton, eds.

The Church Creative: A Reader on the Renewal of the Church. Nashville, TNU: Abingdon, 1967. 208 pp. No ISBN.

Eighteen exciting stories of new forms of ministry in eighteen churches in the United States, as they minister in new and more meaningful ways.

CH250 Cosby, Gordon

Handbook for Mission Groups. Waco, TXU: Word Books, 1975. 179 pp. No ISBN.

The founding pastor of the Church of the Savior in Washington, D.C., describes how mission groups for mutual support and ministry to the world can function effectively.

CH251 Craig, Robert H., and Robert C. Worley

Dry Bones Live: Helping Congregations Discover New Life. Louisville, KYU: Westminster John Knox, 1992. x, 114 pp. Paper. 0664253164.

A practical help for North American mainline Protestant parishes desiring revitalization, yet perceiving themselves as victims of outside forces.

CH252 Crandall, Ron

Turnaround Strategies for the Small Church. Edited by Herb Miller. (Effective Church Series). Nashville, TNU: Abingdon, 1995. 176 pp. Paper. 0687078555.

Twelve keys for renewal for small membership churches in the United States by the McCreeless Professor of Evangelism at Asbury Seminary.

CH253 Cronin, Deborah K. et al.

New Visions for Small-Membership Churches. (National Mission Resources). New York, NYU: UMC, Mission Education & Cultivation Program Department, 1992. iv, 95 pp. Paper. No ISBN.

Profiles of thirty small-membership United Methodist churches in the United States, both rural and urban, with effective ministries of nurture, outreach, and witness; published by the Mission Education and Cultivation Program Department of the GBGM.

CH254 Cushman, James E.

Beyond Survival: Revitalizing the Small Church. Parsons, WVU: McClain, 1981. v, 172 pp. Paper. 0870123912.

Guidance for small-church pastors and denominational leaders in the United States, seeking revitalization in both rural and urban settings.

CH255 Dale, Robert D.

To Dream Again: How to Help Your Church Come Alive. Nashville, TNU: Broadman, 1981. 154 pp. Paper. 0805425411.

A practical guide for ministers and lay leaders concerned for the health of their congregations or other voluntary organizations, and desiring to plan creatively for renewal.

CH—MISSION AND CHURCH RENEWAL

CH256 Donahue, Bill
The Willow Creek Guide to Leading Life-Changing Small Groups. (Willow Creek Resources). Grand Rapids, MIU: Zondervan, 1996. 191 pp. Paper. 0310205956.

Revised edition of a manual for leaders of the meta-church model for small group revitalization of the local church, based on the experience of Willow Creek Community Church in South Barrington, Illinois.

CH257 Dudley, Carl S., and Sally A. Johnson
Energizing the Congregation: Images That Shape Your Church's Ministry. Louisville, KYU: Westminster John Knox, 1993. xi, 116 pp. Paper. 0664253598.

Case studies showing how North American parishes are revitalized by claiming symbols that best articulate their self-identity (survivor, prophet, pillar, pilgrim, and servant); by two Chicago-based teachers of church and community ministries.

CH258 Episcopal Church, Task Force on Christian Education
To Seek and to Serve. Cincinnati, OHU: Forward Movement, 1991. x, 405 pp. Paper. 0880281227.

Case studies of how fourteen diverse parishes of the Episcopal Church (US), representing all nine provinces, discern and carry out their mission; with a "Revised Use Guide" by Adam McCoy and LaDonna Wind.

CH259 Fenhagen, James C., and Celia A. Hahn
Ministry for a New Time. Bethesda, MDU: Alban Institute/ Cornerstone Project, 1995. xiv, 175 pp. Paper. 1566991560.

The Director and founder of the Cornerstone Project of the Episcopal Church, and former Dean and President of General Theological Seminary, presents the project's case for renewal of Episcopal parishes, with a summary of responses by four leaders in renewal and mission of other denominations.

CH260 Forster, Roger, and John Richard, eds.
Churches That Obey: Taking the Great Commission Seriously. Carlisle, ENK: OM Publishing, 1995. 208 pp. 1850781966.

Leaders of twenty-one diverse Christian fellowships around the world share their strategies to fulfill the A.D. 2000 and Beyond movement goal of "a church for every people and a Gospel for every person by the year 2000."

CH261 Fray, Harold R.
Conflict and Change in the Church. Philadelphia, PAU: Pilgrim Press, 1969. xiv, 113 pp. Paper. No ISBN.

A case study of Eliot United Church of Christ in Newton, Massachusetts, which chose to use conflict constructively as a discipline for growth and renewal.

CH262 Frazee, Randy, and Lyle E. Schaller
The Come Back Congregation: New Life for a Troubled Ministry. (Innovators in Ministry). Nashville, TNU: Abingdon, 1995. 133 pp. 0687006201.

The story of how an independent church in decline and crisis, the Pantego Bible Church of Arlington, Texas, revisioned its ministries and mission through lay ministries and achieved sustained growth.

CH263 Friend, Howard E.
Recovering the Sacred Center: Church Renewal from the Inside Out. Valley Forge, PAU: Judson Press, 1998. xviii, 196 pp. Paper. 0817012745.

The story of the Pennsylvania Presbyterian Church in Gladwyne, and other local churches, seeking new inspiration and models for renewal.

CH264 Galloway, Dale E.
The Small Group Book: The Practical Guide for Nurturing Christians and Building Churches. Grand Rapids, MIU: Revell, 1997. 157 pp. Paper. 0800755707.

Practical helps on renewing the local church through small group ministry, drawing on the author's experience as a pastor and as Dean of the Beeson Center for Biblical Preaching and Church Leadership at Asbury Theological Seminary.

CH265 George, Carl F.
Prepare Your Church for the Future. Grand Rapids, MIU: Baker Books, 1991. 240 pp. Paper. 0800753658.

A noted church-growth consultant introduces the concept of "meta-church" through strategies for reaching the unchurched with ministries that combine large celebrative worship experiences and small caring fellowships.

CH266 Girard, Robert C.
Brethren, Hang Loose: Or, What's Happening to My Church? Grand Rapids, MIU: Zondervan, 1972. 220 pp. No ISBN.

Calling for the renewal and restructuring of the church on a more informal basis, this book had considerable influence in the 1970s, based largely on the author's pastoral experience and interaction with the New Testament.

CH267 Girard, Robert C.
Brethren, Hang Together: Restructuring the Church For Relationships. Grand Rapids, MIU: Zondervan, 1979. 331 pp. Paper. 0310390710.

Sees the church as an organic community under the headship of Christ, led by the Spirit to develop strong, loving relationships and facilitate the ministry of all believers through team pastoral leadership.

CH268 Gish, Arthur G.
Living in Christian Community. Scottdale, PAU: Herald Press, 1979. 379 pp. 0836118871.

A Church of the Brethren pastor, author, and activist describes various aspects of Christian community life, including mutual sharing, discipling, worship, nonconformity, and witness.

CH269 Goodman, Grace Ann
Rocking the Ark: Nine Case Studies of Traditional Churches in Process of Change. New York, NYU: UPCUSA, Board of National Missions, 1968. 214 pp. No ISBN.

Case studies of nine Protestant congregations in the United States, seeking to change in ways both faithful to Jesus Christ and relevant to their new social contexts.

CH270 Goslin, Thomas S.
The Church without Walls. Pasadena, CAU: Hope Publishing Company, 1984. 99 pp. Paper. 093272700X.

The vision of congregations free from the burden of buildings and nurtured to be a community of the redeemed.

CH271 Heinecke, Paul T., Kent R. Hunter, and David S. Luecke
Courageous Churches: Refusing Decline, Inviting Growth. St. Louis, MOU: Concordia Publishing, 1991. 160 pp. Paper. 0570045614.

Thirty-five principles for congregations in mission, including dimensions of outreach, spiritual growth, worship, and leadership; with examples from Missouri Synod Lutheran parishes in the United States.

CH—MISSION AND CHURCH RENEWAL

CH272 Howard, Walden

Nine Roads to Renewal. Waco, TXU: Word Books, 1967. 162 pp. No ISBN.

Case studies of nine churches of various denominations in North America that have experienced renewal, by the editor of *Faith at Work.*

CH273 Hull, Bill

Seven Steps to Transform Your Church. Grand Rapids, MIU: Revell, 1993. 194 pp. Paper. 0800756150.

From a platform of church history, biblical exegesis, and the latest information on church growth and leadership training, the President of T(raining)-Net International offers a primer for evangelical church renewal.

CH274 Hunter, Kent R.

Moving the Church into Action. St. Louis, MOU: Concordia Publishing, 1989. 152 pp. Paper. 0570045282.

Practical helps for congregations desiring to shift from institutional maintenance to positive growth, by the President of the Church Growth Center in Corunna, Indiana.

CH275 Hybels, Lynne, and Bill Hybels

Rediscovering Church: The Story and Vision of Willow Creek Community Church. (Willow Creek Resources). Grand Rapids, MIU: Zondervan, 1995. 213 pp. 0310593204.

The story of Willow Creek Community Church of South Barrington, Illinois, by its senior pastor and his wife, focusing on the strengths of this mega-church in mission and ministry.

CH276 Icenogle, Gareth Weldon

Biblical Foundations for Small Group Ministry: An Integrative Approach. Downers Grove, ILU: InterVarsity, 1994. 396 pp. Paper. 0830817719.

Biblical and theological foundations for small group ministries, presented with concern for their importance in parish renewal and mission.

CH277 Johnson, Douglas W., and Alan K. Waltz

Facts and Possibilities: An Agenda for the United Methodist Church. Nashville, TNU: Abingdon, 1987. 157 pp. 0687125413.

Two United Methodist denominational leaders analyze trends and challenges facing their church, and suggest an agenda for local churches, annual conferences, and the larger denominational organization.

CH278 Johnson, Douglas W.

A National Study of Congregations as Units of Mission: Survey Results. New York, NYU: UMC, Board of Global Ministries, 1985. iv, 56 pp. Paper. No ISBN.

The results of a national United Methodist Church study of 500 congregations and 3,000 pastors to discover what local churches were doing of a mission outreach nature, and how they thought of themselves as being in mission.

CH279 Kirkpatrick, Thomas G.

Small Groups in the Church: A Handbook for Creating Community. New York, NYU: Alban Institute, 1995. viii, 144 pp. Paper. 156699151X.

Practical helps for planning and training leaders for parish renewal through revitalized small groups.

CH280 Martin, Glen, and Gary McIntosh

Creating Community: Deeper Fellowship through Small Group Ministry. Nashville, TNU: Broadman, 1997. 179 pp. Paper. 0805461000.

How to plan for, promote, and nurture small groups; by two leading trainers in church growth.

CH281 Matheny, Judy C.

A National Study of Cooperative Parish Ministries as Units of Mission. New York, NYU: General Board of Global Ministries, 1985. v, 73 pp. Paper. No ISBN.

A summary of data from 255 cooperative parish ministries of the United Methodist Church in the United States, emphasizing their characteristics and involvement in local mission.

CH282 Mundey, Paul

Unlocking Church Doors: Ten Keys to Positive Change. Edited by Herb Miller. (Leadership Insight Series). Nashville, TNU: Abingdon, 1997. 165 pp. Paper. 0687030870.

Practical suggestions for leaders seeking to motivate their local churches for change and renewal.

CH283 Neighbour, Ralph Webster

Where Do We Go from Here?: A Guidebook for Cell Group Churches. Houston, TXU: Touch Publications, 1990. 463 pp. Paper. 1880828545.

A global consultant to cell group churches, now serving as President of Touch Outreach Ministries, Director of Church Planting for Columbia Biblical Seminary, and Associate Senior Pastor of Faith Community Baptist Church in Singapore, shares his understanding of cell group dynamics in growing churches.

CH284 Newby, James R.

Gathering the Seekers. Bethesda, MDU: Alban Institute, 1995. x, 85 pp. Paper. 1566991579.

Practical helps by the Director of Yokefellow Institute, for attracting and nurturing seekers after spiritual growth and renewal through small groups like the NET (Nurturing Experience Theologically) Groups.

CH285 Nichols, Roy C.

Doing the Gospel: Local Congregations in Ministry. Nashville, TNU: Abingdon, 1990. 191 pp. Paper. 0687110300.

A popular summary of findings from 140 congregations of the United Methodist Church in the USA, selected by their bishops as outstanding examples of vitality.

CH286 O'Connor, Elizabeth

Journey Inward, Journey Outward. New York, NYU: Harper & Row, 1968. x, 175 pp. No ISBN.

This engaging book tells the story of the innovative Church of the Savior in Washington, D.C., noting especially the development of "mission groups" committed both to mutual support and ministry outward to the world.

CH287 Oswald, Roy M., and Robert E. Friedrich

Discerning Your Congregation's Future: A Strategic and Spiritual Approach. Bethesda, MDU: Alban Institute, 1996. xvii, 174 pp. Paper. 1566991749.

A handbook for leaders of local churches desiring spiritual and strategic visioning for renewal in their planning process.

CH—MISSION AND
CHURCH RENEWAL

CH288 Posterski, Donald C., and Gary Nelson
Future Faith Churches: Reconnecting with the Power of the Gospel for the 21st Century. Winfield, BCC: Wood Lake Books, 1997. 256 pp. Paper. 1551450984.

Case studies of fourteen Canadian churches (evangelical, mainline Protestant, and Roman Catholic) that combine evangelism, social action, church growth, and strong leadership in worshiping communities that are life changing.

CH289 Potter, C. Burtt
The Church Reaching Out. Durham, NCU: Moore Publishing Company, 1976. xiii, 164 pp. 0877160627.

A former Southern Baptist missionary in Philadelphia gives many illustrations of bold, creative, and exciting ministries designed to meet "virtually every human need," as well as five ways for local churches to implement them through existing organizations with optimum effectiveness.

CH290 Raines, Robert A.
New Life in the Church. San Francisco, CAU: Harper & Row, 1961. x, 152 pp. Paper. 0060667737.

Renewal of the congregation through *koinonia* groups based on the author's experience at Aldersgate United Methodist Church in Cleveland, Ohio.

CH291 Raines, Robert A.
The Secular Congregation. New York, NYU: Harper & Row, 1968. viii, 144 pp. No ISBN.

The case study of First Methodist Church in Germantown, Pennsylvannia, seeking to become a secular congregation, a people of radically open to God, God's world, and to their neighbors; written by the pastor.

CH292 Ramey, Robert H.
The Dynamic Congregation: A Manual for Energizing Your Church. St. Louis, MOU: Chalice Press, 1999. xvi, 139 pp. Paper. 0827206267.

The author lays out a strategy by which pastors can energize lay leaders and create an effective, empowered church that serves inside and outside of the body of Christ.

CH293 Ratzmann, Wolfgang
Missionarische Gemeinde. (Theologische Arbeiten, 39). Berlin, GW: Evan Verlagsanstalt, 1980. 257 pp. Paper. No ISBN.

This book examines the structures of "missionary parish communities" according to the documents of the WCC and the LWF, and attempts to make applications for the German Democratic Republic.

CH294 Rausch, Thomas P.
Radical Christian Communities. Collegeville, MNU: Liturgical Press, 1990. 216 pp. Paper. 0814650082.

A succinct analysis of Christian communities, both historical and contemporary, both lay and religious, who responded to the Gospel call to discipleship in a radical way, whether by being communities of peace and reconciliation, of social ministry and solidarity with the poor, of service to the church, or of prayer and contemplation.

CH295 Reitz, Rüdiger
The Church in Experiment: Studies in New Congregational Structures and Functional Mission. Nashville, TNU: Abingdon, 1969. 205 pp. 0687081009.

An analysis of experiments in the United States during the 1960s, of church renewal through reconstruction of the congregation, and through forms of specialized ministries.

CH296 Rhodes, Stephen A.
Where the Nations Meet: The Church in a Multicultural World. Downers Grove, ILU: InterVarsity, 1998. 240 pp. Paper. 0830819363.

A nationally recognized United Methodist leader in multicultural ministries, out of a ministry in which thirty-two nationalities gather weekly in Falls Church, Virginia, provides a theological basis for multicultural ministry and practical suggestions for local churches.

CH297 Schaller, Lyle E.
Innovations in Ministry: Models for the Twenty-First Century. (Ministry for the Third Millennium). Nashville, TNU: Abingdon, 1994. 156 pp. Paper. 0687271053.

The noted authority on local church dynamics identifies new emerging models for ministry, with emphasis on laity-driven ministries; for Protestants in the United States.

CH298 Schaller, Lyle E.
The Small Membership Church: Scenarios for Tomorrow. (Ministry for the Third Millennium). Nashville, TNU: Abingdon, 1994. 142 pp. Paper. 0687387183.

A primer of options for renewal by a senior church planner in the United States.

CH299 Schowalter, Richard P.
Igniting a New Generation of Believers. Edited by Lyle E. Schaller. (Ministry for the Third Millenium). Nashville, TNU: Abingdon, 1995. 126 pp. Paper. 0687014921.

Practical helps for local church renewal through worship and music, large and small groups, and meeting the special needs and interests of children, youth, families, and the poor.

CH300 Schwarz, Christian A.
Natural Church Development: A Guide to Eight Essential Qualities of Healthy Churches. Translated by Lynn McAdam, Lois Wollin, and Martin Wollin. Carol Stream, ILU: ChurchSmart Resources, 1996. 128 pp. 1889638005.

Based on a comprehensive study of 1,000 churches in 32 countries, and published almost simultaneously in ten languages, this guidebook articulates useful principles for local church vitality.

CH301 Shoemaker, Samuel M.
With the Holy Spirit and with Fire. Waco, TXU: Word Books, 1973. 127 pp. No ISBN.

Shoemaker, an Episcopal priest and key figure in the founding of Alcoholics Anonymous and Faith at Work, outlines a practical theology of the Holy Spirit including implications for the life and reformation of the church; originally published in 1960 (New York: Harper & Row).

CH302 Slaughter, Michael
Spiritual Entrepreneurs: 6 Principles for Risking Renewal. Edited by Herb Miller. (Innovators in Ministry). Nashville, TNU: Abingdon, 1995. 160 pp. 0687005612.

Six principles of renewal illustrated through the high-commitment and innovative small-group structure of Ginghamsburg United Methodist Church in Tipp City, Ohio; originally published under the title *Beyond Playing Church: A Christ-Centered Environment for Church Renewal* (1994).

CH—MISSION AND CHURCH RENEWAL

CH303 Smith, Christian
Going to the Root: Nine Proposals for Radical Church Renewal. Scottdale, PAU: Herald Press, 1992. 176 pp. Paper. 0836135849.

Proposals for a radical church, emphasizing community, participation, relationships, discipleship, and spirituality; by a Professor of Sociology and a member of a house church based intentional Christian community in Salem, Massachusetts.

CH304 Smith, Luther E.
Intimacy and Mission: Intentional Community as Crucible for Radical Discipleship. Scottdale, PAU: Herald Press, 1994. 187 pp. Paper. 0836136624.

A study of five intentional religious communities in North America and their struggles for radical discipleship (Church of the Messiah, Koinonia Partners, Patchwork Central, Sojourners, and Voice of Calvary).

CH305 Snyder, Howard A.
The Community of the King. Downers Grove, ILU: InterVarsity, 1977. 216 pp. Paper. 0877847525.

Taking note of shifting models of the church, this book outlines the role of the church in God's plan, and presents insights from Scripture for vital church life.

CH306 Stockwell, Eugene L.
Claimed by God for Mission: The Congregation Seeks New Forms. New York, NYU: World Outlook Press, 1965. 159 pp. Paper. No ISBN.

An exploration of what it may mean for Christian congregations to participate effectively in God's mission, prepared as a study book for US Methodists.

CH307 Story, Betty Wilson
Seeds on Good Soil. Nashville, TNU: Abingdon, 1989. 66 pp. Paper. 0687371503.

Popular accounts of three United Methodist churches in the United States that grew by reaching out to multi-ethnic communities.

CH308 Sweet, Leonard I.
Eleven Genetic Gateways to Spiritual Awakening. Nashville, TNU: Abingdon, 1998. 192 pp. Paper. 0687051738.

Eleven keys to spiritual growth and meaningful ministry from the Wesleyan revival, with applications for twenty-first century ministries, by the Dean of Drew Theological Seminary, Madison, New Jersey.

CH309 Sweetser, Thomas P., and Patricia M. Forster
Transforming the Parish: Models for the Future. Kansas City, MOU: Sheed and Ward, 1993. ix, 241 pp. Paper. 1556126549.

A distillation of insights from twenty years of the Catholic Parish Evaluation Project in the United States, in areas of spirituality, small faith communities, liturgy, faith development, volunteers, and freeing structures.

CH310 Thatcher, Joan
The Church Responds. Valley Forge, PAU: Judson Press, 1970. 160 pp. Paper. 0817004661.

Case studies of Protestant churches in the United States, experiencing renewal through responses to fast-changing human needs.

CH311 Thung, Mady A.
The Precarious Organisation: Sociological Explorations of the Church's Mission and Structure. (Proefschrift Soc. Wetensch. Rijksuniversiteit Leiden). Den Haag, NE: Mouton, 1976. xiv, 347 pp. Paper. No ISBN.

Analysis of the missionary function of the church, including the concepts of organization, leadership, bureaucracy, and government, as developed in modern sociology; a doctoral thesis by then-Study Secretary of the (Protestant) Dutch Missionary Council.

CH312 Towns, Elmer L.
An Inside Look at 10 of Today's Most Innovative Churches: What They're Doing, How They're Doing It and How You Can Apply Their Ideas in Your Church. Ventura, CAU: Regal Books, 1990. 273 pp. Paper. 0830814057.

Case studies of ten innovative Protestant evangelical congregations in the United States, with an analysis of eight factors explaining their effectiveness in church renewal and church growth.

CH313 Trexler, Edgar R., ed.
Creative Congregations: Tested Strategies for Today's Churches. Nashville, TNU: Abingdon, 1972. 143 pp. Paper. 0687098246.

Case studies of sixteen mainline Protestant congregations in the United States noted for their creative approaches to local mission and ecumenical cooperation.

CH314 Vanier, Jean
La communauté: lieu du pardon et de la fête. Paris, FR: Éditions Fleurus; Montreal, PQC: Éditions Bellarmin, 1989. 333 pp. 2215013192 (FR), 2890076954 (CN).

The second French edition of a comprehensive discussion of factors that make for deep Christian community, based largely on the experience of the l'Arche community for the mentally challenged and their helpers; originally published in 1979 (Paris: Fleurus; Montreal: Éditions Bellarmin).

CH315 Vanier, Jean
Community and Growth. New York, NYU: Paulist Press; London, ENK: Darton, Longman & Todd, 1989. xv, 331 pp. Paper. 0809131358.

Second revised English edition—the author's translation of *La Communauté: Lieu du pardon et de la fête* (1979); first published in English in 1979 (London: Darton, Longman and Todd; New York: Paulist Press; Toronto: Griffin House).

CH316 Vanier, Jean
Comunidad: Lugar de Perdón y Fiesta. Translated by Maria Nieves López de la Vieja. Madrid, SP: Narcea, 1980. 221 pp. 8427704100.

Spanish translation.

CH317 Vanier, Jean
Gemeinschaft: Ort der Versöhnung und des Festes. Salzburg, GW: Otto Müller, 1983. 241 pp. No ISBN.

German translation.

CH318 Vanier, Jean
Wsp'ólnota miejscem radosci i przebaczenia. Translated by Lucyna Rutowska. Paris, FR: Éditions du Dialogue, 1985. 306 pp. 2853160475.

Polish translation.

CH319 Vaughan, Benjamin Noel Young
Structures for Renewal. London, ENK: Mowbray, 1967. ix, 156 pp. No ISBN.

A search for the renewal of the church's mission to the world by the Anglican bishop of Honduras.

CH320 Vendura, Nancy

Go! Do the Same: Developing Parish Outreach Programs.
New York, NYU: Paulist Press, 1992. ix, 149 pp. Paper.
0809133083.

Practical ideas for parishes to implement in reaching
out with compassion to the grieving, the homebound, the
poor, and the alienated.

CH321 Walker, Alan

*Como hacer Discipulos: Iglesias de diversas partes del mun-
do comparten sus métodos para formar cristianos nuevos.*
México, MX: CUPSA, 1980. 111 pp. Paper. No ISBN.

Spanish translation.

CH322 Walker, Alan

*Making Disciples: How Churches around the World Make
New Christians.* Nashville, TNU: Discipleship Resources,
1980. v, 106 pp. Paper. No ISBN.

The exciting true stories of successful evangelism in
ten different churches in various parts of the world, plus a
year-long plan involving church members in evangelism in
a local church setting.

CH323 Walrath, Douglas Alan

Leading Churches through Change. (Creative Leadership
Series). Nashville, TNU: Abingdon, 1979. 124 pp. Paper.
0687212707.

Six case studies of typical Protestant rural and urban
congregations in the United States, and how they faced rapid social change with strategies for renewal.

CH324 Washington, Preston Robert

God's Transforming Spirit: Black Church Renewal. Valley Forge, PAU: Judson Press, 1988. 143 pp. Paper.
0817011293.

The pastor of Memorial Baptist Church in Harlem, New
York City, outlines a model for church renewal that focuses on prayer, discipleship, congregational ministry, and reliance on the Holy Spirit.

CH325 Wesson, Anthony J., ed.

Experiments in Renewal. London, ENK: Epworth Press,
1971. 152 pp. Paper. 0716201798.

Thirteen experiments for the renewal of the church in
local communities in Great Britain; described by the people engaged in them.

CH326 White, James Emery

*Rethinking the Church: A Challenge to Creative Redesign
in an Age of Transition.* Grand Rapids, MIU: Baker Books,
1998. 142 pp. Paper. 0801090393.

A concise, readable presentation of the seeker-sensi-
tive model of church life by the pastor of Mecklenburg Community Church in North Carolina, where 80 percent of its
growth comes from the unchurched.

CH327 Young, David Samuel

*A New Heart and a New Spirit: A Plan for Renewing Your
Church.* Valley Forge, PAU: Judson Press, 1994. xviii, 107
pp. Paper. 0817012095.

A biblical basis for renewal and practical helps for local congregations; by an experienced Church of the Brethren pastor and teacher of church renewal courses at Eastern
Baptist Theological Seminary in Philadelphia.

Base Christian Communities

See also TH274-TH277, TH285, TH350, CR458-CR459, SO219,
EC155, EC275, EV139, CH375, SP223, AF137, AF385, AF664-
AF665, AF690, AF859, AF1063, AM340, AM418, AM717-AM718,
AM939, AM945, AM1286, AM1292-AM1293, AM1295-AM1296,
AM1321-AM1323, AM1330, AM1333, AM1344, AM1368, AS440-
AS441, and AS1433.

CH328 Baranowski, Arthur R.

*Creating Small Faith Communities: A Plan for Restructur-
ing the Parish and Renewing Catholic Life.* Cincinnati,
OHU: St. Anthony Messenger Press, 1988. x, 103 pp. Paper. 0867160977.

A Catholic priest in Troy, Michigan, tells how he successfully restructured the parish into small basic Christian
communities, with suggestions for others desiring to use
this model.

CH329 Barreiro, Alvaro

*Basic Ecclesial Communities: The Evangelization of the
Poor.* Translated by Barbara T. Campbell. Maryknoll, NYU:
Orbis Books, 1982. xiv, 82 pp. Paper. 0833440261.

English translation.

CH330 Barreiro, Alvaro

*Comunidades Eclesiais de Base e Evangelização dos Po-
bres.* São Paulo, BL: Edições Loyola, 1977. 95 pp. Paper.
No ISBN.

A comparison between God's good news to the poor
as found in the Gospels, and the experience of renewal and
liberation in base Christian communities in the Catholic
church in Brazil.

CH331 Boff, Clodovis

*Como Trabalhar Com o Povo: Metodologia do Trabalho
Popular.* (Colecao Fazer, 5). Petropolis, BL: Vozes, 1985.
118 pp. No ISBN.

Practical guidelines by the noted Brazilian priest-theo-
logican derived from the people-centered approach of base
Christian communities.

CH332 Boff, Clodovis

How to Work with People. Translated by Daniel R. Orpilla
and Tessa Cruz San Diego. (*Nagliliyab,* The Burning Bush
Series, 16). Quezon City, PH: Claretian Publications, 1988.
viii, 85 pp. Paper. 9715012965.

English translation.

CH333 Boff, Leonardo

*E a Igreja se fez povo: Eclesiogénese; Igreja que nasce da
fé do povo.* (Publicações CID, Teologia, 23). Petrópolis,
BL: Vozes, 1986. 199 pp. No ISBN.

Second edition that sees Latin American BECs as the
new form of the church of the future, and also deals with
questions of "lay" ministry and the priesthood of women;
first edition published in 1977 under the title *Ecclesiogénese.*

CH334 Boff, Leonardo

*Ecclesiogenesis: The Base Communities Reinvent the
Church.* (Collins Flame). Maryknoll, NYU: Orbis Books;
London, ENK: Collins, 1986. viii, 115 pp. Paper.
0883442140 (US), 000599926X (UK).

English translation.

CH335 Boff, Leonardo

Und die Kirche ist Volk geworden: Ekklesiogenesis. Düsseldorf, GW: Patmos Verlag, 1987. 248 pp. Paper. 349177685 (SBN).

German translation.

CH336 Boff, Leonardo

Y la Iglesia se Hizo Pueblo: "Eclesiogénesis": la Iglesia que Nace de la Fe del Pueblo. (Presencia teológica, 31). Santander, SP: Editorial Sal Terrae, 1987. 225 pp. Paper. 9586072398.

Spanish translation.

CH337 Boff, Leonardo, Virgilio P. Elizondo, and Marcus Lefébure, eds.

The People of God amidst the Poor. (*Concilium*: Religion in the Eighties, 176). Edinburgh, STK: T&T Clark, 1984. xiii, 112 pp. Paper. 0567300560.

Sixteen Catholic leaders, mostly from Latin America, describe aspects of BECs—the precedents for the people of God among the poor, the new roles involved in the church, and the contemporary dynamics of the movement.

CH338 Brennan, Patrick J.

Re-Imaging the Parish: Base Communities, Adulthood, and Family Consciousness. New York, NYU: Crossroad Publishing, 1990. x, 151 pp. 082451002X.

A new model for parish renewal, focusing on the generation of small, basic intentional communities, an emphasis on adult education, and the development of a family consciousness in ministry.

CH339 Caravias, José Luis

Living in Fellowship: Basic Christian Communities Reflect on Salvation History. Edited by Carlos Schauman. Quezon City, PH: Claretian Publications, 1986. xii, 142 pp. 9715011012 (hdbk), 9715011004 (pbk).

English translation.

CH340 Caravias, José Luis

Vivir como Hermanos: Reflexiones bíblicas sobre la hermandad. Edited by Carlos Schauman. Caacupé, PY: Carlos Schauman, 1989. 128 pp. No ISBN.

A basic text presenting the history of salvation of God's people in forty-six practical lessons, for use in Bible study groups of Christian base communities.

CH341 Clark, David

The Liberation of the Church: The Role of Basic Christian Groups in a New Re-Formation. Birmingham, ENK: National Centre for Christian Communities and Networks, 1984. 209 pp. Paper. 0946185050.

Develops a theology of community with particular emphasis on house churches and BCCs, and on the missionary structure of the church; an appendix compares "basic Christian groups" in Latin America with those in the United Kingdom.

CH342 *Communion and Mission/Communión y misión*

Washington, DCU: USCC, 1995. vi, 53 pp. Paper. 1547550071.

A guide for bishops and pastoral leaders of small church communities (BCCs), especially in Hispanic parishes, highlighting their emerging spirituality and rich cultural and faith expressions within them.

CH343 Comunidades Eclesiales de Base de Colombia

Hemos Vivido y Damos Testimonio: Teología popular. Bogotá, CK: Dimensión Educativa, 1988. 315 pp. Paper. No ISBN.

A systematic work on the theology of BCCs, based on narrative and testimony stimulating popular theological reflection.

CH344 Cook, Guillermo

The Expectation of the Poor: Latin American Base Ecclesial Communities in Protestant Perspective. (American Society of Missiology Series, 9). Maryknoll, NYU: Orbis Books, 1985. xix, 316 pp. Paper. 0883442094.

Based on the author's doctoral dissertation, this comprehensive study of Latin American BECs includes historical and theological analysis, drawing parallels with Protestant forms of grassroots community.

CH345 Cowan, Michael A., and Bernard J. Lee

Conversation, Risk, and Conversion: The Inner and Public Life of Small Christian Communities. Maryknoll, NYU: Orbis Books, 1997. x, 180 pp. Paper. 1570751498.

Analysis of the growth, development and impact of BCCs on Catholicism in the United States by two professors at Loyola University in New Orleans who are active in leading and evaluating such groups.

CH346 Deelen, Gottfried

Kirche auf dem Weg zum Volke: Soziologische Betrachtungen über kirchliche Basisgemeinden in Brasilien. Mettingen, GW: Brasilienkunde Verlag, 1982. 147 pp. 3885594129.

A sociological analysis of the Catholic BCCs in Brazil.

CH347 Gichuhi, George N.

The Spirituality of Small Christian Communities in Eastern Africa. (Spearhead Series, 85). Eldoret, KE: Gaba Publications, 1985. 57 pp. Paper. No ISBN.

An introduction for African Christians to the spiritual roots of the "small Christian communities" (SCCs) in the Acts of the Apostles, writings of St. Paul, and African concept of community; with application to the Roman Catholic SCCs in East Africa, from the Sudan to Zambia.

CH348 Goldewijk, Berma Klein

Praktijk of Principe: Basisgemeenschappen en de ecclesiologie van Leonardo Boff. (Kerk en theologie in context, 10). Kampen, NE: Kok, 1991. x, 372 pp. Paper. 9024234395.

A dissertation on the relevance, coherence, and consistency of Leonardo Boff's ecclesiological reflections on the identity of BECs; originally published at the Catholic University of Nijmegen.

CH349 Hebblethwaite, Margaret

Base Communities: An Introduction. Mahwah, NJU: Paulist Press, 1994. ix, 198 pp. Paper. 0809134098.

A primer on the characteristics of base communities in Latin America and their links to liberation theology, with texts of key documents, glossary of terms, and bibliography.

CH350 Hebblethwaite, Margaret

Basic Is Beautiful: Basic Ecclesial Communities from Third World to First World. London, ENK: HarperCollins, 1993. 202 pp. Paper. 0006274706.

An introduction for North American Christians to the BECs of Latin America.

CH—MISSION AND CHURCH RENEWAL

CH351 Hetsen, Jac, and James Holmes-Siedle
Aspects of Christian Community Building in Africa. (Spearhead, 75). Eldoret, KE: Gaba Publications, 1983. vi, 57 pp. Paper. No ISBN.

A brief analysis of the role of small Christian communities in Africa, why they fit Africa better than large parishes, how they function, and how they train people.

CH352 Hinton, Jeanne
Walking in the Same Direction: A New Way of Being Church. (Risk Book Series, 67). Geneva, SZ: WCC Publications, 1995. x, 106 pp. Paper. 2825411604.

A journalist's report on visits to BCCs on six continents.

CH353 Ingenlath, Hermann Josef
Bausteine für eine Theologie der Basisgemeinden. (European University Studies, 23: Theology, 567). Frankfurt am Main, GW: Lang, 1996. xv, 252 pp. Paper. 3631300336.

The author researches important themes for mission theology (presence and "immersion," open dialogue, inculturation, proclamation, participation, and church community), and explains their significance for the grassroots theologies of base communities.

CH354 Kleissler, Thomas A., Margo A. LeBert, and Mary C. McGuinness
Small Christian Communities: A Vision of Hope. New York, NYU: Paulist Press, 1991. xi, 284 pp. Paper. 0809132176.

A primer to foster development of small groups ("communities") for renewal within North American Catholic parishes by the founder of *Renew* and his associates.

CH355 Liehr, Wilfried
Katholizismus und Demokratisierung in Brasilien: Stimulierung von sozialen Lernprozessen als kirchliche Reformpolitik. (Forschungen zu Lateinamerika, 17). Saarbrücken, GW: Breitenbach, 1988. xvii, 468 pp. Paper. 3881564098.

This work investigates the role of the Catholic Church in Brazil, its aims in promoting social learning processes and conscientization by means of basic communities, and the consequences which result for the poorer classes in the development process.

CH356 Maney, Thomas
Basic Communities: A Practical Guide for Renewing Neighborhood Churches. Minneapolis, MNU: Winston Press, 1984. xiv, 101 pp. Paper. 0866838570.

Applying learnings from Latin American BECs, the book suggests methods for building BCCs in middle-class North American churches.

CH357 Marins, José, Teolide Maria Trevisan, and Carolee Chanona
The Church from the Roots: Basic Ecclesial Communities. London, ENK: CAFOD, 1989. xi, 70 pp. Paper. 1871549167.

A revised introduction, for English-speaking readers, to Latin American BECs by those who train leaders for them.

CH358 Mejia, Rodrigo
The Church in the Neighbourhood: Meetings for the Animation of Small Christian Communities. Nairobi, KE: St. Paul Publications-Africa, 1990. 124 pp. Paper. 9966210180.

The English edition of a Swahili text used as a primer for leaders of BCCs in Kenya and Tanzania.

CH359 Neo, Julma
Towards a Liberating Formation of Christian Communities. (*Nagliliyab*, The Burning Bush, 19). Quezon City, PH: Claretian Publications, 1988. xi, 185 pp. Paper. 9715013414.

Twenty-six value-formation sessions used in BCCs for integration of faith and life.

CH360 O'Halloran, James
Signs of Hope: Developing Small Christian Communities. Maryknoll, NYU: Orbis Books; Dublin, IE: Columba Press, 1991. viii, 168 pp. Paper. 0883447304 (US), 1856070107 (IE).

An analysis of the origin, nature, and theological context of small Christian community as experienced by the author, a Salesian priest, in Ireland, Sierra Leone, the United States, and Ecuador.

CH361 O'Halloran, James
Small Christian Communities: A Pastoral Companion. Maryknoll, NYU: Orbis Books; Blackrock, IE: Columba Press, 1996. 208 pp. Paper. 1570750777 (US), 1856071472 (IE).

Resources for small Christian communities around the world (theory, practice, and spirituality) by a Salesian priest who for twenty-five years has worked with them as member, coordinator, and promoter.

CH362 Olsen, Charles M.
The Base Church: Creating Community through Multiple Forms. Atlanta, GAU: Forum House, 1973. xvi, 167 pp. 0913618136.

Models for the renewal of the church through a multiplication of interdependent small, base groups for fellowship, prayer, mutual support, and missional action, both within and outside existing parishes.

CH363 Pelton, Robert S., ed.
Small Christian Communities: Imagining Future Church. Notre Dame, INU: University of Notre Dame Press, 1997. xi, 132 pp. Paper. 0268017611.

A collection of essays presented at the Third Notre Dame International Theological Consultation on Small Christian Communities (1996, University of Notre Dame).

CH364 Pinto, Joseph Prasad
Inculturation through Basic Communities: An Indian Perspective. Bangalore, II: Asian Trading Corp, 1985. xvi, 273 pp. Paper. No ISBN.

A Catholic theology and history of inculturation from an Indian perspective, with analysis of the contemporary importance of basic Christian communities.

CH365 Prior, David
Parish Renewal at the Grassroots. Grand Rapids, MIU: Asbury Press, 1983. 192 pp. 0310383706.

A popular comparison of the vitality of local Christian communities in early Methodism and contemporary Latin America, Africa, and Korea; originally published as *The Church in the Home* (Marshall, Morgan and Scott, 1983).

CH366 Santos, Fidelis Abad, and Oscar Camomot, comps.
Basic Christian Communities Journeying Together: Towards a New Way of Being Church. (*Nagliliyab*, 23). Quezon City, PH: Clarietian Publications; Quezon City, PH: Contak Philippines/BCC-CO Philippines; Quezon City, PH: Medical Mission Sisters, 1990. 83 pp. Paper. 9715014348.

Translation of the popular report of the Seventh Interecclesial Encounter of Basic Christian Communities (Rio de Janeiro, Brazil, 10-15 July 1989), including messages from key leaders to the BCCs of the Philippines.

CH367 Torres, Sergio, and John Eagleson, eds.
The Challenge of Basic Christian Communities. Translated by John Drury. Maryknoll, NYU: Orbis Books, 1981. xx, 283 pp. Paper. 0883445034.

Papers from the International Ecumenical Congress of Theology (São Paulo, Brazil, 20 February-2 March, 1980) sponsored by EATWOT, focusing on developments in the BCCs in Latin America, and their challenge to Christians of other continents.

CH368 Van Vugt, J. P. A. van
Democratic Organization for Social Change: Latin American Christian Base Communities and Literacy Campaigns. New York, NYU: Bergin & Garvey, 1991. xiv, 169 pp. 0897892453.

An analysis of the literary campaigns of Nicaragua and Brazil to assess the contributions of the BCCs to social transformation through democratic organization.

CH369 Vandenakker, John Paul
Small Christian Communities and the Parish: An Ecclesiological Analysis of the North American Experience. Kansas City, MOU: Sheed and Ward, 1994. xx, 260 pp. Paper. 155612709X.

An analysis of the pastoral and theological implications of a variety of small Christian communities in North American Catholic parishes.

CH370 Whitehead, Evelyn Eaton, and James D. Whitehead
Community of Faith: Crafting Christian Communities Today. Mystic, CTU: Twenty-Third Publications, 1992. ix, 157 pp. Paper. 0896225186.

A revised and enlarged edition by a Roman Catholic psychologist and a lay theologian (1st ed., New York: Seabury, 1982) reflecting ten additional years of serious Catholic experimentation with small Christian communities in the United States.

House Churches

CH371 Allen, Donald R.
Barefoot in the Church. Richmond, VAU: John Knox Press, 1972. 187 pp. 0804215405.

A description of vital house churches and house-church networks, based in part on the author's experience at Trinity Presbyterian Church, a cluster of house churches in Harrisonburg, Virginia.

CH372 Anderson, Philip, and Phoebe Anderson
The House Church. Nashville, TNU: Abingdon, 1975. 176 pp. 0687174376.

The goals, functions, and methods of the house church.

CH373 Banks, Robert
Paul's Idea of Community: The Early House Churches in Their Cultural Setting. Rev. ed. Peabody, MAU: Hendrickson Publishers, 1994. xiii, 233 pp. Paper. 1565630505.

Scholarly but accessible to the general reader, this book sets the experience of the New Testament church in the context of a variety of first-century forms of community, and shows the relevance for the church today.

CH374 Banks, Robert, and Julia Banks
The Church Comes Home. Peabody, MAU: Hendrickson Publishers, 1998. viii, 260 pp. Paper. 156563179X.

A handbook that describes how house churches can be formed, how they should grow, and how networks of home churches can develop.

CH375 Barrett, Lois
Building the House Church. Scottdale, PAU: Herald Press, 1986. 176 pp. Paper. 083613415X.

A manual for leaders of house churches based on the experience of five Mennonite house churches in Wichita, Kansas, with insights related to eleven characteristics of house churches in the book of Acts.

CH376 Birkey, Del
The House Church: A Model for Renewing the Church. Scottdale, PAU: Herald Press, 1988. 182 pp. Paper. 0836134672.

A reflection from personal experience, historical, and biblical study of the house church structure, arguing that it can be a continuing key to church renewal today.

CH377 Davies, William R.
Rocking the Boat: The Challenge of the House Church. Basingstoke, ENK: Marshall Pickering, 1986. 155 pp. Paper. 0551013354.

A popular account on the "House Church" movement within the Methodist Church in Great Britain.

CH378 Foster, Arthur L., ed.
The House Church Evolving. (Studies in Ministry and Parish Life). Chicago, ILU: Exploration Press, 1976. 126 pp. 0913552046 (hdbk), 0913552054 (pbk).

A collection of presentations made by house church leaders and scholars at the House Church III National Conference (Chicago Theological Seminary, April 1975), plus four case studies.

CH379 Hadaway, C. Kirk, Francis M. Du Bose, and Stuart A. Wright
Home Cell Groups and House Churches. Nashville, TNU: Broadman, 1987. 264 pp. 0805469443.

An overview and analysis of the home cell and house church movements, with case studies and chapters on the history, theology, problems of organization, and use of leadership and authority in house churches.

CH380 Hoffman, Virginia
Birthing a Living Church. New York, NYU: Crossroad Publishing, 1988. xiv, 183 pp. 0824509005.

A Roman Catholic writer involved in house churches presents an alternative to traditional, hierarchical models of the church.

CH381 Lee, Bernard J., and Michael A. Cowan
Dangerous Memories: House Churches and Our American Story. Kansas City, MOU: Sheed and Ward, 1986. vi, 201 pp. Paper. 0934134707.

The authors (one a theologian and the other a social scientist) examine the contemporary house church movement, particularly within Roman Catholicism, from the perspectives of Scripture, history, psychology, and social theory, and discuss the issue of servant leadership.

CH382 Noble, John
House Churches: Will They Survive? Eastbourne, ENK: Kingsway Publications, 1988. 125 pp. Paper. 0860656764.

A leader of the house church movement in England discusses the current status and emerging challenges facing the movement.

CH383 Robson, Brenda
The Turning Tide: Women in Leadership in the House Church. London, ENK: Marshall Pickering, 1989. 127 pp. Paper. 0551018976.

The author, a leader in the house church movement in England, presents the case for women in church leadership.

CH384 Vincent, John J.
Alternative Church. Belfast, IE: Christian Journals, 1976. 149 pp. Paper. 0904302229.

Case studies of four churches without church buildings in creative ministry in Great Britian (the Open Group in London, the Eucharist Congregation in Sheffield, the Corrymeela Community in Northern Ireland, and the House Church in Clapham).

City Church Renewal

See also SO557, EV376, EV595, CH176, EU92, EU94, and EU126.

CH385 Bakke, Raymond J., and Samuel K. Roberts
The Expanded Mission of "Old First" Churches. Valley Forge, PAU: Judson Press, 1986. 125 pp. Paper. 0817011005.

Case studies of American Baptist local churches that have been renewed, including concrete strategies, leadership requirements, inclusive theology needs, community analysis, and the development of a support system network to help in environmental dilemmas.

CH386 Cope, Gilbert, ed.
Cathedral and Mission. Birmingham, ENK: University of Birmingham, 1969. 118 pp. Paper. No ISBN.

The historical and contemporary challenges to mission by cathedral churches, with case study of Southwark Anglican Cathedral in England.

CH387 Driggers, B. Carlisle, comp.
Models of Metropolitan Ministry: How Twenty Churches Are Ministering Successfully in Areas of Rapid Change. Nashville, TNU: Broadman, 1979. 196 pp. Paper. 0805425330.

Case studies of twenty Southern Baptist churches in the United States ministering successfully in areas of rapid change.

CH388 Edington, Howard, and Lyle E. Schaller
Downtown Church: The Heart of the City. (Innovators in Ministry). Nashville, TNU: Abingdon, 1996. 157 pp. Paper. 0687054400.

Lessons for the renewal of downtown Protestant churches from the author's experience as senior pastor of First Presbyterian Church, Orlando, Florida.

CH389 Elizondo, Virgilio P., and Timothy M. Matovina
San Fernando Cathedral: Soul of the City. Maryknoll, NYU: Orbis Books, 1998. xv, 123 pp. Paper. 1570752176.

An illustrated Mexican-American history of a prominent cathedral built nearly two-and-a-half centuries ago, which remains a wellspring of life and renewal today.

CH390 Fisher, Wallace E.
From Tradition to Mission. Nashville, TNU: Abingdon, 1965. 208 pp. No ISBN.

The author's report of his own pastoral experiences in revitalizing the Evangelical Lutheran Church of the Holy Trinity in Lancaster, Pennsylvania (US), which moved from maintainance to mission goals.

CH391 Frenchak, David J., and Sharrel Keyes, eds.
Metro-ministry. Elgin, ILU: David C. Cook, 1979. 218 pp. Paper. 0891911014.

A collection of addresses given at the Congress on the Urban Church (Chicago, May 1978) designed as a guidebook for those who minister in the inner city.

CH392 Green, Laurie
Power to the Powerless: Theology Brought to Life. Basingstoke, ENK: Marshall Pickering, 1987. x, 148 pp. Paper. 0551015701.

An exploration of the meaning of parables as they relate to inner-city life with an analysis of the urban dilemma, seeking a theology with which to confront and change the problems which blight people's lives and make the teachings of Jesus live in their locality, with illustrations of the church in mission in a working-class parish of Birmingham, England.

CH393 Jones, Ezra Earl, and Robert Leroy Wilson
What's Ahead for Old First Church. New York, NYU: Harper & Row, 1974. xi, 132 pp. 0060642009.

Helps for congregations located in the central business districts of US cities as they seek renewal.

CH394 Leiffer, Murray H.
The Effective City Church. New York, NYU: Abingdon, 1961. 232 pp. No ISBN.

In this textbook a prominent church sociologist seeks to acquaint readers with patterns of city growth, influences of urbanization on people and the church, and effective methods of urban ministry.

CH395 Moore, Richard E., and Duane L. Day
Urban Church Breakthrough. New York, NYU: Harper & Row, 1966. xii, 183 pp. No ISBN.

The rationale for the renewal of Protestant urban ministries in the United States through increased social involvements.

CH396 Noyce, Gaylord B.
Survival and Mission for the City Church. Philadelphia, PAU: Westminster Press, 1975. 162 pp. Paper. 0664248136.

An analysis of factors in city life that point the downtown city church in the United States beyond mere survival to healthy growth.

CH397 Schaller, Lyle E., ed.
Center City Churches: The New Urban Frontier. (Ministry for the Third Millenium Series). Nashville, TNU: Abingdon, 1993. 187 pp. Paper. 0687048028.

Fourteen examples of mainline Protestant churches located in the center of US cities which are high-performance, missionary congregations.

CH398 Schaller, Lyle E.

Planning for Protestantism in Urban America. New York, NYU: Abingdon, 1965. 223 pp. No ISBN.

Practical guidance for urban church leaders in the United States on ways to plan for parish renewal, by the foremost US Protestant church planner of this generation.

CH399 Webber, George W.

The Congregation in Mission: Emerging Structures for the Church in an Urban Society. New York, NYU: Abingdon, 1964. 208 pp. No ISBN.

Deploring the present dichotomy between church and urban world the author, part of the group ministry in East Harlem (New York) Protestant Parish, suggests new structures to encourage the local congregation to exist in mission.

Suburban Church Renewal

See also EU121.

CH400 Bailey, Wilfred M., and William K. McElvaney

Christ's Suburban Body. Nashville, TNU: Abingdon, 1970. 208 pp. 068707858X.

A design for the missional engagement in their communities by suburban congregations in the United States, with five models and examples of each as practiced.

CH401 Becker, Penny Edgell

Congregations in Conflict: Cultural Models of Local Religious Life. Cambridge, ENK: Cambridge University Press, 1999. xii, 267 pp. 0521594448 (hkbk), 0521594626 (pbk).

A comparative study of twenty-three suburban churches and synagogues allows congregations of various persuasions to reflect on the tensions, vitality, makeup, social mission, and future prospects of religion in the face of a new millennium.

CH402 Bennett, F. Russell, comp.

Mission of the Suburban Church. Atlanta, GAU: Home Mission Board, Southern Baptist Convention, 1971. 119 pp. Paper. No ISBN.

Guidance for North American churches seeking to fulfill more effectively their mission in suburbia.

CH403 Costello, Tim, ed.

Ministry in an Urban World: Responding to the City. Canberra, AT: Acorn Press, 1991. x, 82 pp. Paper. 0908284101.

Helps for persons engaged in suburban ministry, with special reference to Australia.

CH404 Noyce, Gaylord B.

The Responsible Suburban Church. Philadelphia, PAU: Westminster Press, 1970. 176 pp. Paper. 0664249027.

Practical guidance for Christian witness and mission by Protestant parishes in suburban United States.

CH405 Winter, Gibson

The Suburban Captivity of the Churches: An Analysis of Protestant Responsibility in the Expanding Metropolis. Garden City, NYU: Doubleday, 1961. 216 pp. No ISBN.

A sociologist of religion's probing critique of mainline Protestantism's flight to the suburbs with corresponding neglect of ministries in the inner city.

Rural Church Renewal

See also EV408 and EU101.

CH406 Hunter, Kent R.

The Lord's Harvest and the Rural Church: A New Look at Ministry in the Agri-Culture. Kansas City, MOU: Beacon Hill Press, 1993. 144 pp. Paper. 0834115034.

Helps for renewal and growth of rural churches in the United States.

CH407 Richardson, John, ed.

Ten Rural Churches. Eastbourne, ENK: MARC; London, ENK: BCGA, 1988. vii, 150 pp. Paper. 0860656225 (M), 0948704101 (B).

Ten case studies of rural Protestant churches in England experiencing renewal.

CH408 Ruffcorn, Kevin E.

Rural Evangelism: Catching the Vision. Minneapolis, MNU: Augsburg, 1994. 128 pp. Paper. 0806626429.

Practical helps for parishes in small town and rural USA.

CH409 Wilkinson, Theodore S.

Churches at the Testing Point: A Study in Rural Michigan. (World Studies of Churches in Mission). New York, NYU: Friendship Press; London, ENK: Lutterworth Press, 1971. xviii, 200 pp. Paper. No ISBN.

A detailed study by the Head of the Department of Sociological Study in Nagpur University, India, of the churches in a small Midwest town in the United States (Hillsdale, Michigan), intended to discover the interrelatedness of the local church and the surrounding community.

Mission and Pastoral Care

See also EV534, AF980, and AM617.

CH410 Beek, Aart M. van

Cross-Cultural Counseling. (Creative Pastoral Care and Counseling). Minneapolis, MNU: Fortress Press, 1996. 108 pp. Paper. 0800626664.

A practical guide for caregivers sensitive to cross-cultural counseling issues, based on the author's experience in Indonesia and the southwestern United States.

CH411 Champlin, Joseph M.

The Marginal Catholic: Challenge, Don't Crush. Notre Dame, INU: Ave Maria Press, 1989. 155 pp. Paper. 0877934061.

Helps for Catholics who desire to reach out offering baptism and marriage to peripheral Catholics, rather than a crushing legalistic rejection.

CH412 Gilmour, Peter, and Patricia O'Connell Killen, eds.

Journeys in Ministry: Nine Memoirs from Around the World. Chicago, ILU: Loyola University Press, 1989. ix, 111 pp. Paper. 0829406220.

Nine firsthand accounts of persons doing active ministry in diverse cultural settings around the world following studies at Loyola University's Institute of Pastoral Studies in Chicago, Illinois.

CH413 Grose, G. H., and E. F. Grose

Called to Serve: A Practical Handbook for Pastors. Delhi, II: ISPCK, 1993. 100 pp. Paper. 8172141467.

A primer for pastors developed by the authors out of years of experience in church work in India.

CH414 Hein, Uwe
Indische christliche Seelsorge. (Erlanger Monographien aus Mission und ökumene, 14). Erlangen, GW: Ev.-Luth. Mission, 1991. 320 pp. Paper. 387214314X.

A dissertation on intercultural pastoral work in India, that emphasizes the assumptions of Indian culture, and challenges traditional German modalities in pastoral care.

CH415 Hoffman, Virginia
The Codependent Church. New York, NYU: Crossroad Publishing, 1991. 204 pp. Paper. 0824511158.

Beginning with recent insights on co-dependence within family relationships, Hoffman makes application to the local church, proposing that church renewal requires relationships of mutually respectful, co-responsible adults.

CH416 Taylor, Harold
Applied Theology 2: "Tend My Sheep." (TEF Study Guide, 19). London, ENK: SPCK, 1983. 305 pp. 0281040559 (net), 0281040567 (nonnet).

A basic textbook on pastoral care and counseling for Third World seminaries with abundant illustrations for parish life.

CH417 Watkins Ali, Carroll A.
Survival and Liberation: Pastoral Theology in African American Context. St. Louis, MOU: Chalice Press, 1999. xiii, 176 pp. Paper. 0827234430.

The author tests the theories of Seward Hiltner in relation to contemporary pastoral theory and practice, and brings together a womanist theology and traditional (male) black theology through the art of compassion and social justice in action, with the integration of psychological theory so that therapist and client become co-laborers in therapeutic experience.

CH418 Wicks, Robert J., and Barry K. Estadt, eds.
Pastoral Counseling in a Global Church: Voices from the Field. Maryknoll, NYU: Orbis Books, 1993. vi, 169 pp. Paper. 0883448653.

Ten pastoral counselors, mostly Roman Catholics, tell the stories of their experiences and approaches to cross-cultural counseling in ten countries on six continents.

CH419 Wilson, H. S. et al.
Pastoral Theology from a Global Perspective: A Case Study Approach. Maryknoll, NYU: Orbis Books, 1996. ix, 236 pp. Paper. 1570750793.

Fifteen case studies, with commentaries and teaching notes, designed for teaching pastoral care from a global perspective.

Mission and Justice Ministries

See also SO99, SO221, SO412, SO548, EC113, EC159, EC302, EV594, CH176, CH458, and EU95.

CH420 Bloom, Dorothy B.
Church Doors Open Outward: A Practical Guide to Beginning Community Ministry. Valley Forge, PAU: Judson Press, 1987. 78 pp. Paper. 081701117X.

A practical guide for American church leaders linking Bible study to greater sensitivity to the poor, the oppressed, and those of differing cultural backgrounds.

CH421 Christensen, Larry
A Charismatic Approach to Social Action. Minneapolis, MNU: Bethany Fellowship, 1974. 122 pp. 0871233894.

The author, a Lutheran pastor active in the charismatic movement, presents a biblical and pragmatic argument for Christian social action based on the Christian community as a "servant church" called to solve society's problems by helping to create a new society consistent with God's revelation.

CH422 Clark, Henry
Ministries of Dialogue: The Church Confronts the Power Structure. New York, NYU: Association Press, 1971. 224 pp. 080961829X.

A call for alternative models for local engagement of the church with social justice concerns, with an analysis of program activities, goals, targets and tactics, presuppositions, and evaluation of such ministries in ten US cities.

CH423 Hessel, Dieter T., ed.
Congregational Life-Style Change for the Lean Years: A Study Action Resource. New York, NYU: UPCUSA, Program Agency, 1981. xxii, 233 pp. No ISBN.

A resource designed to help groups in congregations and regional church bodies in the United States develop biblically based strategies for changing their institutional lifestyle from a corporate business model to a servant model which has its roots in the Gospel.

CH424 Hessel, Dieter T.
Social Ministry. Philadelphia, PAU: Westminster Press, 1982. 228 pp. Paper. 066424422X.

An exploration of how each of the central functions of parish life has a dynamic social significance, and can "meet human need with good Samaritan love while acting for justice with prophetic boldness."

CH425 Hug, James E., ed.
Tracing the Spirit: Communities, Social Action, and Theological Reflection. New York, NYU: Paulist Press, 1983. vi, 314 pp. Paper. 0809125293.

Thirteen theological reflections on the experience of small communities engaged in the struggle for social justice.

CH426 Mitchell, Ron
Organic Faith: A Call to Authentic Christianity. Chicago, ILU: Cornerstone Press, 1997. xv, 175 pp. Paper. 0940895404.

With a basis in the Sermon on the Mount and the Book of James, the author—director of a homeless shelter and former United Methodist missionary to Sierra Leone—seeks to move the reader beyond compartmentalized Christianity and into Christian community, cultural transformation, racial unity, urban mission, and the linkage of faith with human service professions.

CH427 National Conference of Catholic Bishops
Communities of Salt and Light: Parish Resource Manual. Washington, DCU: USCC, 1994. 73 pp. Paper. 1555867022.

Resources for Catholic parishes engaged in social justice ministries.

CH428 Wallis, Jim
Agenda for Biblical People. New York, NYU: Harper & Row, 1984. xv, 109 pp. Paper. 0060692340.

A new edition in which the editor of *Sojourners* presents a theology and call to discipleship in which the church is an alternative social reality committed to servanthood, justice, and identification with the poor; originally published in 1976.

Parish Missions

CH429 Briggs, Bill
Faith through Works: Church Renewal through Mission. Franconia, NHU: Thorn Books, 1983. 93 pp. No ISBN.

An account of two inner-city and one rural church as they experience both successes and failures while discovering integrity and effectiveness in their church renewal through missions.

CH430 Copenhaver, Martin B., Anthony B. Robinson, and William H. Willimon
Good News in Exile: Three Pastors Offer a Hopeful Vision for the Church. Grand Rapids, MIU: Eerdmans, 1999. xi, 116 pp. Paper. 0802846041.

The old-line "liberal" churches find themselves in a time of exile without privilege, advantage, or clout; but the authors, grounded in the realities of parishes where they serve, remind us that a time of exile can be rich and fertile.

CH431 National Conference of Catholic Bishops, Committee on Evangelization
A Time to Listen ... A Time to Heal: A Resource Directory for Reaching Out to Inactive Catholics. Washington, DCU: USCC, 1999. 36 pp. Paper. 1574553062.

Building on *Go and Make Disciples*, the bishops' pastoral plan for "evangel," this directory further develops Pope John Paul II's call for reconciliation in preparation for the Jubilee Year 2000; includes reflections, models, and faith sharing guides for evangelization staffs and all those involved in mission work.

CH432 Perry, John D.
The Coffee House Ministry. Richmond, VAU: John Knox Press, 1966. 127 pp. No ISBN.

The first book on this experimental movement, dealing with its theological grounds, staff, equipment, and daily operation.

Leadership: General

See also SO437, EV369, MI90-MI91, CH39, CH237, CH311, AF85, and AF934.

CH433 Arbuckle, Gerald A.
Refounding the Church: Dissent for Leadership. Maryknoll, NYU: Orbis Books, 1993. ix, 226 pp. Paper. 0883448983.

An analysis for Roman Catholics of alternative leadership styles, with advocacy of a collaborative model which appreciates the value of dissent in decision making as essential for effective mission today.

CH434 Becker, Palmer
Called to Care: A Training Manual for Small Group Leaders; Called to Equip: A Training and Resource Manual for Pastors. Scottdale, PAU: Herald Press, 1993. 2 vols. Paper. 0836136225 (vol. 1), 0836136233 (vol. 2).

A guide for lay leaders of "care groups" for nurture and outreach in the local church, with companion manual for pastors, including resources for recruiting, training and affirming a team of "care group" leaders.

CH435 Callahan, Kennon L.
Effective Church Leadership: Building on Twelve Keys. San Francisco, CAU: Harper & Row, 1990. xv, 268 pp. 0060612991.

A step-by-step guide to aid the leader with skills to become an effective missionary pastor by cultivating new understanding and practices in church leadership and management.

CH436 Cann, Gilbert
Liberating Leadership. North Bayswater, AT: TLC Publications, 1989. v, 115 pp. Paper. 0731672844.

An Australian pastor draws on Scripture and his experience in pastoral team leadership in discussing leadership that builds churches into ministering communities.

CH437 Croucher, Rowland
Your Church Can Come Alive: Strategies for Church Leaders. Melbourne, AT: JBCE, 1991. 136 pp. Paper. 0858198096.

A training manual for pastors and lay leaders to familiarize them with the latest theology and leadership ideas for congregational renewal.

CH438 Elliston, Edgar J., and J. Timothy Kauffman
Developing Leaders for Urban Ministries. (American Universities Studies 7: Theology and Religion, 147). New York, NYU: Lang, 1993. xx, 297 pp. Paper. 082042076X.

A practical guide for those equipping Christian leaders for urban ministry in varied cultural contexts, including foundational issues, educational principles, and curriculum content.

CH439 Elliston, Edgar J.
Home Grown Leaders. South Pasadena, CAU: William Carey Library, 1992. vii, 181 pp. Paper. 0878082360.

A primer for the development of Christian leaders including biblical values, patterns of spiritual leadership, the leader in the group, and cultural variables; by the Associate Professor of Leadership Selection and Training at the Fuller School of World Mission.

CH440 Greenleaf, Robert K.
Seeker and Servant: Reflections on Religious Leadership. Edited by Ann T. Fraker, and Larry C. Spears. San Francisco, CAU: Jossey-Bass Publishers, 1996. xix, 359 pp. 0787902292.

A selection from the writings of the late Robert Greenleaf contending that churches are key change agents in society, and that true leaders serve and empower others to achieve their potential.

CH441 Greenleaf, Robert K.
Servant Leadership: A Journey into the Nature of Legitimate Power and Greatness. New York, NYU: Paulist Press, 1977. x, 335 pp. Paper. 0809125277.

Drawing on his experience in businesss and his Christian commitment, the author describes and calls for servant leadership in all sectors of society, including the church.

CH442 Gunderson, Denny
The Leadership Paradox. Seattle, WAU: YWAM Publishing, 1997. 156 pp. Paper. 092754587X.

A study book on rethinking our leadership stereotypes on the basis of biblical leadership styles, by a Youth with a Mission staff member.

CH443 Jørgensen, Knud
Visjon og hverdag: Lederskap i misjon og menighet. Oslo, NO: Verbum, 1991. 249 pp. 8254305145.

A learned book on leadership in church and mission, discussing as well theories of leadership in relation to biblical conceptions as practical consequences.

CH444 Jacobs, Donald R.
From Rubble to Rejoicing: A Study in Effective Christian Leadership Based on Nehemiah. South Pasadena, CAU: William Carey Library, 1991. xi, 97 pp. Paper. 0878082131.

A popular study of biblical leadership, based on the book of Nehemiah, by the director of the Mennonite Christian Leadership Foundation and former Overseas Director of the Eastern Mennonite Board of Missions.

CH445 Malphurs, Aubrey
Developing a Dynamic Mission for Your Ministry: Finding Direction and Making an Impact as a Church Leader. Grand Rapids, MIU: Kregel Publications, 1998. 140 pp. Paper. 0825431891.

A "how-to" book for local churches desiring to develop their own mission statements.

CH446 Markham, Donna J.
Spiritlinking Leadership: Working Through Resistance to Organizational Change. Mahwah, NJU: Paulist Press, 1998. xiii, 143 pp. Paper. 0809138409.

Practical approaches for working through resistance to organizational transformation by building the circle of friends, fostering networks of compassion, and interweaving teams of relationships toward new ideas and ways of responding to mission.

CH447 McNeal, Reggie
Revolution in Leadership: Training Apostles for Tomorrow's Church. (Ministry for the Third Millennium). Nashville, TNU: Abingdon, 1998. 156 pp. Paper. 0687087074.

A study of management, lay, and paradigm issues of leadership rooted in the early church which drew upon the explicit model of Jesus.

CH448 Orr, Robert
The Essentials for Effective Christian Leadership Development. Linden, ABC: Leadership Essentials Press, 1994. v, 417 pp. Paper. 0969746431 (spiral), 0969746407 (pbk).

A resource textbook designed to make contemporary leadership and management training relevant for clergy, missionaries, and other Christian workers around the world.

CH449 Osei-Mensah, Gottfried
Wanted: Servant-Leaders: The Challenge of Christian Leadership in Africa Today. (Theological Perspective in Africa, 3). Achimota, GH: Africa Christian Press, 1990. 73 pp. Paper. 9964877978.

Lectures on the essential characteristics of Christian leadership; originally given to theological students in ten African countries.

CH450 Perrin-Jassy, Marie France
Leadership. (Pastoral Papers, 32). Kampala, UG: Gaba Publications, 1974. 100 pp. No ISBN.

An essay on African cultural dimensions of church leadership.

CH451 Schaller, Lyle E.
The Change Agent: The Strategy of Innovative Leadership. Nashville, TNU: Abingdon, 1972. 207 pp. 0687060427.

A practical discussion of innovation, and of power in the church that advocates a planned anticipatory approach to change, in which leaders know the potentials and problems of institutional change, and build a supporting group for implementation.

CH452 Spader, Dann, and Gary Mayes
Growing a Healthy Church. Chicago, ILU: Moody, 1991. 221 pp. Paper. 0802432352.

A popular presentation of four stages of a practical and simple strategy for rediscovering in the local church a balance of winning, building, and equipping disciples, as developing in North America by Sonlife Ministries.

CH453 Stevens, R. Paul, and Phil Collins
The Equipping Pastor: A Systems Approach to Congregational Leadership. Washington, DCU: Alban Institute, 1993. xxiv, 196 pp. Paper. 1566991080.

Drawing on social process, leadership styles, systems theory, and biblical insights, the authors show how to build a congregation that is liberated for mission.

CH454 Suenens, Léon Joseph
La coresponsabilité dans l'Église d'aujourd'hui. [Paris], FR: Desclée de Brouwer, 1968. 224 pp. No ISBN.

An analysis by a prominent Roman Catholic leader of the implications for the church's renewal and mission of the concept of co-responsibility in church leadership, as defined by Vatican II's *Constitution on the Church.*

CH455 Suenens, Léon Joseph
Coresponsibility in the Church. Translated by Francis Martin. New York, NYU: Herder, 1968. 218 pp. No ISBN.
English translation.

CH456 Suenens, Léon Joseph
La corresponsabilidad en la Iglesia de Hoy. (Colección Nueva biblioteca de teología). Bilbao, SP: Desclée de Brouwer, 1968. 199 pp. No ISBN.
Spanish translation.

CH457 Tiller, John, and Mark Birchall
The Gospel Community and Its Leadership. Basingstoke, ENK: Marshall Pickering, 1987. 168 pp. Paper. 0551013982.

An examination of the contemporary experiences of churches seeking renewal as they compare themselves with the radical definitions of priesthood, the temple, and sacrifice presented by Christ.

CH458 Weems, Lovett H.
Leadership in the Wesleyan Spirit. Nashville, TNU: Abingdon, 1999. 158 pp. Paper. 0687046920.

Walking the tightrope between continuity and change, Weems calls for a new vision of church leadership, drawing from principles of early Wesleyanism which began where the people, focused on service, remembered the poor, and lived in tension between the center and the edge.

CH459 Young, David Samuel
Servant Leadership for Church Renewal: Shepherds by the Living Springs. Scottdale, PAU: Herald Press, 1999. 176 pp. Paper. 0836191080.

Drawing upon his experience as a pastor and teacher, the author provides a practical and biblically based study on servant leadership which demands self-renewal, and produces church renewal.

CH—MISSION AND CHURCH RENEWAL

Renewal of Ministry

See also HI608, EV308, CH124, CH134, CH151, CH237, CH292, CH430, CH458-CH459, AM1066, AS622, AS884, AS1131, and EU154.

CH460 Calian, Carnegie Samuel
Where's the Passion for Excellence in the Church?: Shaping Discipleship through Ministry and Theological Education. Wilton, CTU: Morehouse Publishing, 1989. ix, 60 pp. Paper. 0819215007.

A call for a goal of excellence in leadership for seminary and church as the key to revitalization of mainline Protestant parishes in the United States, by the President and Professor of Theology at Pittsburgh Theological Seminary.

CH461 Centre national des vocations, comp.
Tomorrow's Priest. Edited by Raymond Izard. Translated by Albert J. Lamothe. Maryknoll, NYU: Maryknoll Publications, 1968. ix, 140 pp. No ISBN.

English translation.

CH462 De Gruchy, John W.
Theology and Ministry in Context and Crisis: A South African Perspective. Grand Rapids, MIU: Eerdmans, 1987. 183 pp. Paper. 0802802907.

A major theological study of ministry contextualized within the realities of the present South African situation.

CH463 John Paul II, Pope
The Consecrated Life: Vita Consecrata. Washington, DCU: USCC, n.d. 201 pp. Paper. 1574551221.

The text of *Vita Consecrata*, Pope John Paul II's 1996 Apostolic Exhortation on the consecrated life and its mission in the church and in the world.

CH464 Lèfebvre, Pierre
Ministries and Community: For a Church as a Family. Nairobi, KE: Paulines Publications Africa, 1998. 80 pp. Paper. 9966214011.

A primer on the development since Vatican II of Catholic perspectives on both "the priesthood of the faithful" and that of ordained clergy.

CH465 Newbigin, James Edward Lesslie
The Good Shepherd: Meditations on Christian Ministry in Today's World. Grand Rapids, MIU: Eerdmans; Bedfordshire, ENK: Faith Press, 1977. 158 pp. Paper. No ISBN.

Thirty meditations by the ecumenical mission leader calling all Christians to be in mission; originally published by the Christian Literature Society, Madras, in 1974.

CH466 Njino, Joseph K.
Institutes of Consecrated Life Religious and Secular. (Spearhead,104). Eldoret, KE: AMECEA Gaba Publications, 1988. viii, 79 pp. Paper. No ISBN.

An introduction to Vatican teachings and Catholic practice in "Institutes of Consecrated Life"—both those in contemplative monastic orders, and in institutes for clergy and laity in Christian witness and service in the "secular" world.

CH467 Paton, David MacDonald, ed.
Reform of the Ministry: A Study in the Work of Roland Allen. London, ENK: Lutterworth Press, 1968. 235 pp. No ISBN.

A disparate collection including Allen's own writings on the voluntary clergy, the eucharist as a family rite, and church policy for North China, plus a biographical and theological essay on Allen by the editor, and the story of the Survey Application Trust by Kenneth Drubb.

CH468 Winninger, Paul, Yves Congar, and Joseph Lecuyer, comps.
Le diacre dans l'Église et le monde d'aujourd'hui. (Unam Sanctam, 59). Paris, FR: Éditions du Cerf, 1966. 315 pp. No ISBN.

A symposium of enquiries into the diaconate in the history and teaching of the church, with some conclusions concerning its restoration both interesting and practical for the younger churches.

Pastoral Leadership in Renewal

See also EV348, CH447, CH451, AF94, and AS1323.

CH469 Congregation for the Evangelization of Peoples
Guide for Catechists: Document of Vocational, Formative and Promotional Orientation of Catechists in the Territories Dependent on the Congregation for the Evangelization of Peoples. Washington, DCU: USCC, 1993. 60 pp. Paper. 155586824X.

The Vatican's guidelines for lay catechists in mission dioceses.

CH470 Dawn, Marva J., and Eugene H. Peterson
The Unnecessary Pastor: Rediscovering The Call. Grand Rapids, MIU: Eerdmans, 2000. x, 256 pp. Paper. 0802846785.

A call for pastors to recover their gospel identity and clarify their vision of Christian leadership through biblical texts that equip them to be counter-cultural servants of the gospel.

CH471 Larom, Peter, George Enyagu, and Michael Hunter
Pastor: A Practical Guide for Church Leaders. Achimoto, GH: Africa Christian Press, 1989. 191 pp. Paper. 9964877013.

An easy-to-read practical guide for African pastors, set within a Ugandan context by a lecturer at Bishop Tucker College (Anglican).

CH472 Lesser, R. H.
You Who Are Sent: Helping Christians to Live Up to Their Vocation as Catechists. Bangalore, II: Theological Publications in India, 1988. 167 pp. Paper. No ISBN.

Practical admonitions for missionary catechists based on presentations to Catholic catechists-in-training in India.

CH473 Lobinger, Fritz
Katechisten als Gemeindeleiter: Dauereinrichtung oder Übergangslösung? (Münsterschwarzacher Studien, 24). Münsterschwarzach, GW: Vier-Türme-Verlag, 1973. xiv, 112 pp. Paper. 3878680538.

A scholarly work investigating the question of Catholic catechists as leaders of church communities, suggesting solutions and adding examples from Protestant churches.

CH474 Neighbour, Ralph Webster
The Shepherd's Guidebook. Houston, TXU: Touch Outreach Ministries, 1995. 218 pp. Paper. 1880828553.

Revised edition of a practical tool for pastoral leaders in cell churches, focusing on the life, and especially the tasks, of guiding cells; originally published in 1988.

CH475 Peterson, Eugene H.
The Contemplative Pastor: Returning to the Art of Spiritual Direction. Grand Rapids, MIU: Eerdmans, 1993. viii, 171 pp. Paper. 0802801145.

Drawing on his own pastoral experience, Peterson argues that effective pastors are "unbusy," "subversive," and "apocalyptic," and focuses on the importance of pastoral ministry "between Sundays."

CH476 Stabbert, Bruce
The Team Concept: Paul's Church Leadership Patterns or Ours? Tacoma, WAU: Hegg Brothers, 1982. 226 pp. Paper. No ISBN.

A detailed study of pastoral leadership in the New Testament which argues that team leadership (plurality of pastors) is the normative pattern; sees eldership as restricted to men.

Ministry of All Believers; Laity

See also TH293, TH488, EV441, EV457, MI92, CH31, CH63, CH297, CH447, CH453, SP169, AF391, AF1007, AF1028, AF1339, AM138, AS767, and EU133.

CH477 Apostola, Nicholas, ed.
A Letter from Christ to the World: An Exploration of the Role of the Laity in the Church Today. Geneva, SZ: WCC Publications, 1998. xi, 147 pp. Paper. 2825412805.

Papers from the WCC's consultation on "Towards a Common Understanding of the Theological Concepts of Laity/Laos: The People of God" (Geneva, Switzerland, 7-10 May 1997).

CH478 Ayers, Francis O.
The Ministry of the Laity: A Biblical Exposition. Evanston, ILU: Methodist Church, Board of the Lay Activities; Philadelphia, PAU: Westminster Press, 1962. 139 pp. No ISBN.

The author argues that all baptized believers are ministers called to serve God in the church and every area of life, and that the church presently is over-institutionalized in a way that restricts the effective ministry of men and women.

CH479 Bucy, Ralph D., ed.
The New Laity: Between Church and World. Waco, TXU: Word Books, 1978. 216 pp. Paper. 0849928338.

Eleven essays on the laity as the church in mission in the world—its biblical and theological foundations, and its historical and contemporary expressions; originally presented at the conference "The Laity—A New Direction" (University of Dallas, Texas, June 1976).

CH480 Crabtree, Davida Foy
The Empowering Church: A Guide for Group Exploration. New York, NYU: Alban Institute, 1990. 27 pp. Paper. No ISBN.

A study guide for use with *The Empowering Church* in six evening sessions or a weekend retreat.

CH481 Doohan, Leonard
Laity's Mission in the Local Church: Setting a New Direction. San Francisco, CAU: Harper & Row, 1986. ix, 146 pp. Paper. 0866834907.

A popular presentation from a Roman Catholic perspective on the mission of laity in the local church, including

worship, work, family and outreach in service, and social involvement.

CH482 Gibbs, Mark
Christians with Secular Power. (Laity Exchange Books). Philadelphia, PAU: Fortress Press, 1981. vii, 135 pp. Paper. 0800613899.

A theological rationale for the full ministry of the laity in politics, business, labor unions, the police and military, and the media.

CH483 Gibbs, Mark, and T. Ralph Morton
God's Frozen People: A Book for—and about—Ordinary Christians. London, ENK: Collins, 1964. 190 pp. Paper. No ISBN.

A primer on the importance of laity engaged in the church's ministries both within the gathered community of faith, and outside in a world needing Christian witness and service.

CH484 Gibbs, Mark, and T. Ralph Morton
God's Lively People. Philadelphia, PAU: Westminster Press, 1971. 212 pp. Paper. 0664249140.

Positive proposals for laity education as the channel that will give new strengths to the life of the whole worldwide church, arguing that "the theology of tomorrow depends upon the laity."

CH485 Hagstrom, Aurelie A.
The Concepts of the Vocation and the Mission of the Laity. San Francisco, CAU: Catholic Scholars Press, 1994. v, 224 pp. 1883255554 (hdbk), 1883255546 (pbk).

Scholarly analysis of four official Roman Catholic documents on the laity (Vatican II to 1988); originally submitted as a doctoral thesis at the Pontifical University.

CH486 Marney, Carlyle
Priests to Each Other. Valley Forge, PAU: Judson Press, 1974. 125 pp. Paper. 0817006281.

The book makes the case for the ministry of all believers to each other, and in the world, based on Christians' universal priesthood.

CH487 Mathison, John Ed
Every Member in Ministry. (Pathways To Church Growth). Nashville, TNU: Discipleship Resources, 1988. viii, 45 pp. Paper. No ISBN.

A collection of practical tools and advice from the pastor of Frazier Memorial United Methodist Church in Montgomery, Alabama, where nearly 90 percent of members are involved in various church ministries.

CH488 Menking, Stanley J., and Barbara Wendland
God's Partners: Lay Christians at Work. Valley Forge, PAU: Judson Press, 1993. xviii, 165 pp. Paper. 081701196X.

A study book on the theology and callings of laity to ministries in the church and wider community.

CH489 Neill, Stephen Charles, and Hans-Ruedi Weber, eds.
The Layman in Christian History: A Project of the Department on the Laity of the World Council of Churches. Philadelphia, PAU: Westminster Press; London, ENK: SCM Press, 1963. 408 pp. No ISBN.

This book depicts the place of the laity in Christian history as an undergirding for the role of the laity today in the renewal and outreach of the church.

CH—MISSION AND CHURCH RENEWAL

CH490 Ogden, Greg

The New Reformation: Returning the Ministry to the People of God. Grand Rapids, MIU: Zondervan, 1990. 224 pp. 0310310202.

A thoughtful, biblically founded review of key issues involved in equipping God's people for ministry, called the "New Reformation," with special attention to the enabling role of the pastor.

CH491 Pothirajulu, Doraisamy

Laity Formation: An Educational Model of Social-Self Actualization with Strategies of Adult Laity Formation and Ministry in the Church of South India. Madras, II: CLS, 1993. xiii, 221 pp. Paper. No ISBN.

Biblical and philosophical foundations and strategies for lay training, with special reference to the Indian situation; originally presented as a doctoral dissertation at Boston University in 1978.

CH492 Rademacher, William J.

Lay Ministry: A Theological, Spiritual, and Pastoral Handbook. New York, NYU: Crossroad Publishing, 1997. xiii, 321 pp. Paper. 0824515692.

A new edition, with a six-session study guide, of a basic book on the history, theology, and practice of lay ministry in local parishes; originally published in 1991.

CH493 Richards, Larry, and Gib Martin

Lay Ministry: Empowering the People of God. Grand Rapids, MIU: Ministry Resources Library, 1988. 332 pp. 0310521017.

The authors explore six biblical images for the church and draw out practical implications for the church today, giving examples from contemporary churches; previously published as *A Theology of Personal Ministry* (Zondervan, 1981).

CH494 Roman Catholic-Presbyterian/Reformed Consultation

Laity in the Church and in the World: Resources for Ecumenical Dialogue. Washington, DCU: USCC, 1998. vii, 117 pp. Paper. 1574552473.

This product of the fifth round of Roman Catholic/Presbyterian-Reformed dialogues (1992-1995) summarizes discussions on theology, ecumenism, and the role of the lay Christian.

CH495 Rowthorn, Anne

The Liberation of the Laity. Wilton, CTU: Morehouse-Barlow, 1986. 141 pp. Paper. 0819213950.

Drawing partly on history, the author argues that the key to church renewal is freeing the church's "lay majority" from clerical dominance and a rediscovery of the priesthood of believers.

CH496 Rweyemamu, Robert

People of God in the Missionary Nature of the Church: A Study of Concilian Ecclesiology Applied to the Missionary Pastoral in Africa. Beckenried, SZ: Schoneck, 1968. xiv, 132 pp. No ISBN.

The author, who comes from Tanzania, seeks in this dissertation to evaluate the concept of the people of God which was conceived at the Second Vatican Council, and to apply it to mission work in Africa.

CH497 Schaller, Lyle E.

44 Ways to Revitalize the Women's Organization. Nashville, TNU: Abingdon, 1990. 174 pp. Paper. 0687132886.

Hundreds of practical insights to promote growth and vitality in the women's fellowships of local churches, including their mission outreach.

CH498 Seumois, André

Apostolado: Estructura Teológica. (Diakonia: Temas de Teología Pastoral, 19). Estella, SP: Verbo Divino, 1968. 376 pp. Paper. No ISBN.

Spanish translation.

CH499 Seumois, André

Apostolat: structure theologique. (Urbaniana Nova, 1). Rome, IT: Universite Pontificale de Propaganda Fide, 1961. 222 pp. No ISBN.

A scholarly analysis, with extensive exegetical research, on the lay apostolate in the early church, including attitudes to conversion, baptism, and the catechumenate.

CH500 Slaughter, Michael, and Warren Bird

Real Followers: Beyond Virtual Christianity. Nashville, TNU: Abingdon, 1999. 203 pp. 0687033411.

A radical commitment to God's dream and mission for our lives involves cost and suffering that exposes the pretender inside each of us, and leads us into an engagement in contemporary culture; includes discussion and journaling questions with responsive prayer.

CH501 Specker, Johann, and Walbert Bühlmann, eds.

Das Laienapostolat in den Missionen. (Supplementa, 10). Schöneck-Beckenried, SZ: *NZM*, 1961. 383 pp. No ISBN.

A *festschrift* honoring the Catholic missiologist Johannes Beckmann on his 60th birthday, with tributes by W. Bühlmann and J. Specker, and seventeen essays by experts on various aspects of the lay apostolate in the Catholic missions.

CH502 Stevens, R. Paul

Liberating the Laity: Equipping All the Saints for Ministry. Downers Grove, ILU: InterVarsity, 1985. 177 pp. Paper. 0877846138.

Based on Scripture and pastoral experience, the author outlines theology, structures, and strategies for developing a congregation of ministries.

CH503 Thangasamy, D. A.

Towards Involvement: The Theory and Practice of Laity Education. Madras, II: CLS; Delhi, II: ISPCK, 1972. xii, 184 pp. No ISBN.

A serious endeavor to apply, in the context of the churches of South India, the insights from churches in other countries that involvement and training for the entire membership is an effective path to church renewal.

CH504 Vatican Council (2nd, 1962-1965)

L'Apostolat des Laïcs: Décret "Apostolicum Actuositatem." Edited by Yves Congar. Translated by M. Streiff. (Unam Sanctum, 75). Paris, FR: Éditions du Cerf, 1970. 311 pp. No ISBN.

An analysis in English of the Roman Catholic Church's problems and approaches to lay apostolic, with the Latin text, French translation, and commentary on the Vatican II decrees on the Lay Apostolate.

CH505 Weber, Hans-Ruedi

Cristianos Salados. San José, CR: Centro de Publicaciones Cristianas, 1967. 63 pp. Paper. No ISBN.

Spanish translation.

CH506 Weber, Hans-Ruedi
Salty Christians. New York, NYU: Seabury Press, 1963. 64 pp. Paper. No ISBN.

A creative study book on the role of the laity as the church in the world, originally prepared by the Secretary of the Department on the Laity of the WCC for the EACC.

CH507 Yoder, John Howard
The Fullness of Christ: Paul's Vision of Universal Ministry. Elgin, ILU: Brethren Press, 1987. iv, 105 pp. Paper. 0871784300.

The noted Mennonite theologian outlines the Pauline understanding of ministry in the church and sharply challenges the common professional model of the "religious specialist."

Gifts of the Spirit

CH508 Bugbee, Bruce
Auf mich kannst du bauen: Mein Dienst in der Gemeinde im Einklang von Neigungen, Stärken und Talenten. Wiesbaden, GW: Projektion J. Buch- und Musikverlag; Wuppertal, GW: R. Brockhaus Verlag, 1996. 151 pp. Paper. 3894901373 (P), 3417242657 (R).

German translation.

CH509 Bugbee, Bruce
What You Do Best in the Body of Christ: Discover Your Spiritual Gifts, Personal Style, and God-Given Passion. Grand Rapids, MIU: Zondervan, 1995. 144 pp. Paper. 0310494311.

A primer for laypersons seeking discernment of their spiritual gifts for lay ministry.

CH510 *Cómo hallar sus Dones Espirituales: Un cuestionario de uso facil para ayudarse a descubrir y entenderus dones espirituales*
Miami, FLU: Editorial Unilit, 1997. 17 pp. Paper. 0789901943.

Spanish translation by Néllyda Pablovsky of the questionnaire on spiritual gifts as modified by Richard Houts and C. Peter Wagner (1978, 1995).

CH511 Donnelly, Doris, ed.
Retrieving Charisms for the Twenty-First Century. Collegeville, MNU: Liturgical Press, 1999. x, 173 pp. Paper. 0814625401.

A collection of twelve articles on the gifts dispensed through the Holy Spirit in church and world as needed for the common good.

CH512 Hemphill, Ken
Mirror, Mirror on the Wall: Discovering Your True Self through Spiritual Gifts. Nashville, TNU: Broadman, 1992. 191 pp. 0805410376.

A revised edition of *Spiritual Gifts* (1988) providing an introduction to the discerning of spiritual gifts, by the pastors of First Baptist Church, Norfolk, Virginia.

CH513 Kinghorn, Kenneth Cain
Fresh Wind of the Spirit. Nashville, TNU: Abingdon, 1975. 128 pp. Paper. 0687134951.

Focuses especially on the work of the Holy Spirit in renewal, primarily in personal experience (sanctification and gifting), but also in church life.

CH514 Kinghorn, Kenneth Cain
Gifts of the Spirit. Nashville, TNU: Abingdon, 1976. 126 pp. Paper. 068714695X.

A popularly written overview of the New Testament teachings on spiritual gifts, including suggestions for discovering gifts and for using them in church ministry; includes a brief historical survey of how gifts have been understood in church history.

CH515 MacGorman, Jack W.
The Gifts of the Spirit. Nashville, TNU: Broadman, 1974. 124 pp. 0805413413.

In this work the author, a Professor of New Testament at Southwestern Baptist Theological Seminary (Fort Worth, Texas), presents an exposition of 1 Corinthians 12-14 in which he seeks to present a balanced perspective on the gifts of the Holy Spirit; written while the author was pastoring the Kanto Plains Baptist Church in Tokyo, Japan.

CH516 Murphy, Edward F.
Spiritual Gifts and the Great Commission. South Pasadena, CAU: Mandate Press, 1975. xv, 352 pp. 0878081445.

A popular account, reminiscent of the writings of Roland Allen, of how the gifts of the Spirit can contribute to the upbuilding of the church.

CH517 Neighbour, Ralph Webster
This Gift Is Mine. Nashville, TNU: Broadman, 1974. 122 pp. Paper. 0805452230.

The author, a prominent Baptist pastor, discusses the practical use of spiritual gifts in the local church as the basis for ministry, and sees new church forms emerging naturally as gift ministries are employed.

CH518 Wagner, C. Peter
Your Spiritual Gifts Can Help Your Church Grow. Ventura, CAU: Regal Books, 1994. 272 pp. Paper. 0803706445.

How to identify twenty-seven spiritual gifts found in scripture, and to use them effectively in one's own ministry; first published in 1974; with group study guide (Gospel Light, 1995, 119 pp., 0830717487).

CH519 Yohn, Rick
Discover Your Spiritual Gift and Use It. (Living Studies Edition). Wheaton, ILU: Tyndale, 1982. 154 pp. 0842306269.

A practical discussion of spiritual gifts and their role in the church by an Evangelical Free Church pastor; originally published in 1974.

SPIRITUALITY, WORSHIP, AND MISSION

Larry Nemer, SVD, Subeditor

Christian spirituality impacts the Christian mission at three key points. First, Christian mission is an extension of authentic spirituality. Second, spiritual vitality in the church sustains Christian mission. Third, mission is a calling of Christians to a true spirituality—life lived in submission to Christ and communion with Christ Jesus as Lord (Moreau, 2000:904).

This chapter combines topics listed by Jongeneel under both *missionary ascetics (spirituality)* and *missionary liturgics (worship)* (1997:19-48, 241-266). It includes works on spirituality, prayer and devotion, worship, and the arts related to mission.

The "Spirituality: General" section groups together works from a variety of confessional traditions. It is followed by "Comparative Studies." Those engaged in interfaith witness and dialogue will find these studies comparing and contrasting the spiritualities of living faiths to be insightful. Often such encounters take place in centers for spiritual renewal, which in India are called *ashrams*. A subsection is provided on this literature. There follows a subsection on "Works of Meditation and Devotion." Here are grouped works missional in theme and content. Some

are by famous missionaries (e.g. Mother Teresa, Carlo Carretto, Frank Laubach, Hudson Taylor). Others have been chosen for their missional themes (e.g. Henri Nouwen, Helder Camera, Ronald Sider).

In modern history, both Western missionaries and Third World theologians rediscovered the link between worship and mission (Jongeneel, 1997:241). These are found in the subsection titled "Worship: General." It is followed by more specialized literature on "Times and Seasons: The Church Year," "Liturgy and Ritual," and "Sacraments." See also the subsection on "Renewal and Worship" in the chapter on "Mission and Church Renewal."

Books on "Prayer and Mission" are to be found in the next subsection. These include both works about missional prayer and books of prayers. Of particular note are Patrick Johnstone's *Operation World* (1993) and the WCC's *With All God's People* (1990)—guides for praying for persons in mission, country by country, around the world.

The final grouping is of books relating mission to the arts. The first includes books on music, hymnology, and mission. The last groups together works relating art, architecture, and dance to Christian mission.

Norman E. Thomas

Reference Works

SP1 Carden, John, comp.
With All God's People: The New Ecumenical Prayer Cycle. Geneva, SZ: WCC, 1989. 2 vols. Paper. 2825409502.

Ecumenical resources for a fifty-two-week cycle of prayer for peoples of each country of the world [vol. 1, xv, 389 pp., 282540943X], and ecumenical orders of service [vol. 2, 133 pp., 2825409502]; successor to *For All God's People* published in 1978.

SP2 Griffiths, Bede, comp.
Universal Wisdom: A Journey through the Sacred Wisdom of the World. London, ENK: Fount; San Francisco, CAU: HarperSanFrancisco, 1994. 560 pp. 0006276792 (UK), 0006278159 (US).

This book contains writings from the Upanishads, Bhagavad Gita, *Dhammapada*, the *Tao Te Ching*, Sikh daily prayers, the Qu'ran and Sufi mystics, the wisdom literature of the Old

Testament and the New Testament, with an introduction by Bede Griffiths (1906-1993), the English Benedictine who spent most of his life in India.

SP3 Johnstone, Patrick J. St. G.
Operación Mundo: Guía diaria de oración por el mundo. Bogotá, CK: Centros de Literatura Cristiana, 1995. 729 pp. Paper. 9589149529.

Spanish translation.

SP4 Johnstone, Patrick J. St. G.
Operation World: The Day-by-Day Guide to Praying for the World. Grand Rapids, MIU: Zondervan, 1993. v, 662 pp. Paper. 0310400317.

An updated fifth edition of a world prayer calendar, giving basic statistics and evangelical prayer concerns for mission in each country; also published in electronic edition (1998); originally published in 1984 (Waynesboro, GAU: STL Books).

Documentation and Archives

SP5 Carmichael, Amy
Amy Carmichael: Fragments That Remain. Edited by Bee Trehane. London, ENK: Triangle/SPCK, 1987. x, 166 pp. Paper. 0281043116.

An inspirational collection of impressions, thoughts, and small episodes from the life and work of Amy Carmichael, who spent fifty-three years (1898-1951) in South India and founded the Dohnavur Fellowship there.

SP6 Carmichael, Amy
Candles in the Dark: Letters of Amy Carmichael. London, ENK: SPCK; Port Washington, PAU: CLC, 1981. x, 115 pp. Paper. 0281038147 (UK), 0875080855 (US).

A selection from the letters of the renowned Keswick missionary to South India (1895-1951), most written while an invalid between 1931 and 1951.

SP7 Oleksa, Michael J., ed.
Alaskan Missionary Spirituality. New York, NYU: Paulist Press, 1987. ix, 406 pp. 0809103869.

A first collection of documents, mainly from the 1795 to 1900 period, illustrating the spirituality of the Alaskan Orthodox missionaries.

SP8 Schweitzer, Albert
Reverence for Life: The Words of Albert Schweitzer. Compiled by Harold E. Robles. New York, NYU: HarperSanFrancisco, 1993. xxii, 177 pp. 0060670983.

Excerpts from the writings of Albert Schweitzer (1875-1965)—noted theologian, musician, medical missionary, and winner of the Nobel Peace Prize in 1952.

SP9 Teresa, Mother
Mother Teresa: Contemplative in the Heart of the World. London, ENK: Fount, 1986. 140 pp. Paper. 0006270735.

A collection of letters, spiritual retreats, and instructions introducing us to the life and spiritual vision of Mother Teresa; introduced by Brother Angelo Devananda.

Conferences and Congresses

See also AS166.

SP10 Colloque international de Kinshasa (10th, 1994)
La prière africaine: actes du Deuxième colloque international du 10 au 12 janvier 1994. Kinshasa, CG: Editions Baobob, 1994. 285 pp. No ISBN.

Papers from an international colloquium on Christian prayer and Carmelite spirituality in Africa.

SP11 Colloque international de Kinshasa (2nd, 1983)
Afrikanische Spiritualität und christlicher Glaube: Erfahrungen der Inkulturation. Edited by Mulago gwa Cikala Musharhamina. (Theologie der Dritten Welt, 8). Freiburg im Breisgau, GW: Herder, 1986. 198 pp. Paper. 3451206811.

German translation.

SP12 Colloque international de Kinshasa (2nd, 1983)
L'Afrique et ses formes de vie spirituelle: actes du deuxième colloque international, Kinshasa, 21-27 février 1983. (Cahiers de religions africaines, vol. 24, 47). Kinshasa, CG: Centre d'Études des Religions Africaines, 1990. 408 pp. No ISBN.

Second edition of eleven essays by African authors discussing the traditional religion and spirituality of their conti-

nent; originally presented at the Second International Colloquium for African Religions in February 1983 at Kinshasa, these essays indicate that a vital and authentic African Christianity can only be realized when it is rooted in a spirituality of African traditions; originally published in 1983.

SP13 EATWOT
Spirituality of the Third World: A Cry for Life. Edited by K. C. Abraham, and Bernadette Mbuy-Beya. Maryknoll, NYU: Orbis Books, 1994. vi, 214 pp. Paper. 0883449773.

Papers and reflections from EATWOT's Third General Assembly (Nairobi, Kenya, January 1992).

SP14 *Il Monachesimo nel Terzo mondo*
(Teologia, 27). Roma, IT: Edizioni Paoline, 1979. 288 pp. No ISBN.

A collection of essays concerning the congresses on monasticism and religious orders held in Africa, Latin America, and Asia.

Spirituality: General

See also GW105, GW144, GW174, HI353, TH60, TH125, TH469-TH471, TH574, ME30, CR146, CR730, EC349, PO23-PO24, PO74, MI70, MI198, CH107, CH128, SP13, AF147, AF513, AF513, AF549, AF755, AF773, AF780, AF783, AF1129, AM20, AM281, AM402-AM404, AM728, AM921, AM1099, AM1214, AM1329, and AM1366.

SP15 Amaladoss, Michael
Mission Today: Reflections from an Ignatian Perspective. Rome, IT: Centrum Ignatianum, 1988. 171 pp. Paper. No ISBN.

A hermeneutical reflection on the "mission centrality" of the Ignatian spiritual experience by the noted Indian Jesuit theologian and missiologist.

SP16 Amirtham, Samuel, and Robin Pryor, eds.
Resources for Spiritual Formation in Theological Education: The Invitation to the Feast of Life. Geneva, SZ: WCC, Programme on Theological Education, 1990. vii, 249 pp. Paper. No ISBN.

Papers from an important consultation on this theme (Jogyakarta, Indonesia, June 20-25, 1989) sponsored by the WCC's Programme for Theological Education; with an extensive annotated bibliography.

SP17 Arbuckle, Gerald A.
From Chaos to Mission: Refounding Religious Life Formation. Collegeville, MNU: Liturgical Press, 1996. ix, 211 pp. Paper. 0814624634.

An analysis of the changing needs and approaches to spiritual formation for Roman Catholic religious congregations, drawing upon both social anthropology and biblical studies of rites of passage.

SP18 Azevedo, Marcello de Carvalho, and Guillermo Cook
The Consecrated Life: Crossroads and Directions. Maryknoll, NYU: Orbis Books; Herefordshire, ENK: Gracewing, 1995. xv, 141 pp. Paper. 1570750033 (US), 0852443374 (UK).

English translation of *Vidas Consegrados* (1993).

SP19 Azevedo, Marcello de Carvalho
Les religieux, vocation et mission: une perspective actuelle et exigeante. Translated by Alexandre Bombieri. Paris, FR: Le Centurion, 1987. 187 pp. Paper. 2227340312.

French translation.

SP—SPIRITUALITY, WORSHIP, AND MISSION

SP20 Azevedo, Marcello de Carvalho

Os religiosos, vocação e missão: um enfoque exigente e atual. Rio de Janiero, BL: Conferência dos Religiosos do Brasil (CRBB), 1986. 218 pp. No ISBN.

A call for the renewal of the religious life in mission service, by the President of the Brazilian National Conference of Religious Men and Women, integrating the insights of spirituality, scripture, liberation theology, and cultural anthropology.

SP21 Azevedo, Marcello de Carvalho

Vocation for Mission: The Challenge of Religious Life Today. Translated by John W. Diercksmeier. New York, NYU: Paulist Press, 1988. xvi, 188 pp. Paper. 0809130246.

English translation.

SP22 Bakka, Peter

Talking to God: The Importance of Silence. Nairobi, KE: Paulines Publications Africa, 1999. 70 pp. Paper. 9966214402.

A "spiritual writer born in the heart of Africa" examines spirituality through recollection, meditation, and contemplation.

SP23 Baum, Horst

Mut zum Schwachsein—in Christi Kraft: Theologische Grundelemente einer missionarischen Spiritualität anhand von 2 Kor. (Studia Instituti Missiologici SVD, 17). St. Augustin, GW: Steyler Verlag, 1977. xxvi, 254 pp. Paper. No ISBN.

A dissertation on the missionary spirituality of the Second Letter to the Corinthians.

SP24 Bonnín, Eduardo, ed.

Espiritualidad y Liberación en América Latina. San José, CR: DEI, 1982. 204 pp. Paper. No ISBN.

A collection of major articles by fourteen authors on spirituality and liberation in Latin America, with annotated bibliographies.

SP25 Bonnín, Eduardo, ed.

Spiritualität und Befreiung in Lateinamerika. Würzburg, GW: Echter Verlag, 1984. 206 pp. Paper. 3429009006.

German translation.

SP26 Bosch, David Jacobus

A Spirituality of the Road. (Institute of Mennonite Studies Missionary Studies, 6). Scottsdale, PAU: Herald Press, 1979. 92 pp. Paper. 0836118898.

Five lectures on New Testament models for contemporary missionary spirituality; originally presented to the spring 1978 sessions of the Mennonite Missionary Study Fellowship.

SP27 Brown, Robert McAfee

Spirituality and Liberation: Overcoming the Great Fallacy. Philadelphia, PAU: Westminster Press, 1988. 158 pp. Paper. 0664250025.

A searching examination of the historic Christian dilemma which results when the spiritual and the temporal, when prayer and social involvement, are separated; with a new vision for Christian wholeness.

SP28 Caldwell, Larry W.

Sent Out!: Reclaiming the Spiritual Gift of Apostleship for Missionaries and Churches Today. South Pasadena, CAU: William Carey Library, 1992. xvi, 191 pp. Paper. 0878084428.

A careful examination of apostleship: its biblical and theological roots, historical development, and contemporary importance for missionary motivation.

SP29 Carmody, John

Holistic Spirituality. New York, NYU: Paulist Press, 1983. 145 pp. Paper. 0809125641.

Helps for Christians who desire a spirituality that relates to every aspect of life (economics, politics, health, recreation, education, etc.); by a noted scholar of world religions.

SP30 Cashmore, Gwen, and Joan Puls

Clearing the Way: En Route to an Ecumenical Spirituality. (Risk Book Series, 43). Geneva, SZ: WCC, 1990. xiv, 64 pp. Paper. 2825409804.

A collection of stories, reflections, and letters comprising the autobiographical journey of the co-directors of the new ecumenical spirituality project of the BCC.

SP31 Chittister, Joan D.

The Rule of Benedict: Insights for the Ages. New York, NYU: Crossroad Publishing, 1992. 180 pp. Paper. 0824525035.

An introduction to Benedictine spirituality, the source of strength in mission since the 6th century for one of the largest Roman Catholic orders.

SP32 Cho, Yong-gi

The Fourth Dimension. Plainfield, NJU: Logos International, 1983. 2 vols. Paper. No ISBN.

The pastor of the largest congregation in the world declares that, in addition to the three commonly accepted types (God's spirit, the devil, human spirit), there is a fourth: the human spirit allowing the Holy Spirit's order and direction [Vol. 1, vii, 186 pp., 0883703803; vol. 2, 186 pp., 088270561X]; originally published in 1979.

SP33 Clements, Teresa

Missionary Spirituality: For the Praise of His Glory. (Living Flame Series, 31). Dublin, IE: Carmelite Centre of Spirituality, 1987. 103 pp. Paper. 086088435X.

A brief reflection on modern day missionary experiences as they work in various countries, using discipleship, prayer, and compassion as central themes.

SP34 Comblin, Joseph

The Holy Spirit and Liberation. (Theology and Liberation Series). Maryknoll, NYU: Orbis Books, 1989. xvi, 213 pp. 0883443686 (hdbk), 0883443678 (pbk).

A systemic examination of the Holy Spirit in regard to liberation theology, moving inductively from experiential to doctrinal concerns, by one of Latin America's leading theologians.

SP35 Connolly, Finbarr B.

In the World: God and I. Bangalore, II: Theological Publications in India, 1977. 237 pp. No ISBN.

Irish Redemptorist's attempt at "modern spirituality," with a strong biblical basis and Christocentric emphasis, based on lectures given in India.

SP36 Crosby, Michael

Spirituality of the Beatitudes: Matthew's Challenge for First World Christians. Maryknoll, NYU: Orbis Books, 1981. ix, 244 pp. Paper. 0883444658.

Detailed exposition of the Beatitudes with application to the witness and mission of North American Christians.

SP37 David, Kenith A.

Sacrament and Struggle: Signs and Instruments of Grace from the Downtrodden. (WCC Mission Series, 3). Geneva, SZ: WCC Publications, 1994. xiv, 126 pp. Paper. 2825411434.

David, an Anglican priest from South Africa and WCC coordinator for Urban Rural Mission (1983-1993), explores five "visible signs of invisible grace" in Scripture and contemporary experience: life, land, community, name and identity, and the vision of "the new dawn."

SP38 De Mello, Anthony

Anthony de Mello: Writings. Selected with an Introduction by William Dych. (Modern Spiritual Masters Series). Maryknoll, NYU: Orbis Books, 1999. 141 pp. Paper. 1570752834.

The texts selected from this Indian Jesuit, with an introduction by William Dych, bring together the wisdom of East and West and challenge persons to have an encounter with God that moves beyond religious formulas.

SP39 Dinh, Joseph Duc Dao

La sposa sul monte: Il contributo dell'Asia per una Chiesa contemplativa e missionaria. (La Missione, 7). Bologna, IT: EMI, 1986. 143 pp. 8830700967.

A Vietnamese Catholic reflection on spirituality and mission.

SP40 Donders, Joseph G.

Charged with the Spirit: Mission Is for Everyone. Maryknoll, NYU: Orbis Books, 1993. viii, 156 pp. Paper. 0883449153.

Out of his experience of mission in Africa and teaching in the United States, Father Donders, a member of the Missionaries of Africa, wrote this guide for individual or group reflection on how Christians share Jesus' spirit so that we personally and in our communities become sacraments of Jesus' presence in the world.

SP41 Dorr, Donal

Integral Spirituality: Resources for Community, Peace, Justice, and the Earth. Maryknoll, NYU: Orbis Books; Dublin, IE: Gill & MacMillan; Melbourne, AT: Collins Dove, 1990. viii, 301 pp. Paper. 0883446588 (US), 0717117308 (IE), 0859249077 (AT).

Exposition of a holistic spirituality concerned for structural justice, interpersonal respect, and personal responsibility and integrity; with guided meditations, prayers, poems, and Scripture readings to enable the reader to explore and develop a new spiritual life, with an option for the poor.

SP42 Drummond, Lewis A., and Betty Drummond

The Spiritual Woman: Ten Principles of Spirituality and Women Who Have Lived Them. Grand Rapids, MIU: Kregel Publications, 1999. 300 pp. Paper. 0825424690.

Biblical principles are combined with life examples through the study of such women as Henrietta Means, Vonette Bright, Jill Briscoe, and Elisabeth Elliot Green.

SP43 Duquoc, Christian, and Gustavo Gutiérrez, eds.

Mysticism and the Institutional Crisis. (Concilium, 1994/4). London, ENK: SCM Press; Maryknoll, NYU: Orbis Books, 1994. xi, 111 pp. Paper. 0334030277 (UK), 0883448793 (US).

Eleven short essays on the recurring tension in the church between new forms of mysticism and spiritual experience on the one hand, and the institutional routinization of charisma on the other.

SP44 Esquerda-Bifet, Juan

Mariologia: Per una Chiesa Missionaria. Rome, IT: Urbaniana University Press, 1988. 221 pp. Paper. No ISBN.

Characteristics of a missionary church informed by a deeper study of Mariology, interpreted as the privilege of knowing the mystery of Christ, and of the church with a missionary perspective for the salvation of all people.

SP45 Esquerda-Bifet, Juan

Spiritualità e Animazione Missionaria. (Evangelizzazione e Cultura). Assisi, IT: EMIF, 1977. 161 pp. No ISBN.

The author, a lecturer at the Pontifical Urban University in Rome, explores the relationship between a missionary spirituality and missionary animation.

SP46 Esquerda-Bifet, Juan

Spirituality for a Missionary Church. (Pontificia Universitas Urbaniana, Subsidia Urbaniana, 54). Rome, IT: Urbaniana University Press, 1994. 233 pp. Paper. 8840120548.

Missionary spirituality presented as an existential function of the theology of evangelization by a noted Italian missiologist.

SP47 Galilea, Segundo

El Camino de la Espiritualidad. (Colección Actualidades Teológicas). Bogotá, CK: Ediciones Paulinas, 1987. 252 pp. 9586070298.

Third edition of a Chilean priest's vision of a truly contemporary spirituality of liberation and mission.

SP48 Galilea, Segundo

Espiritualidad de la Esperanza. Madrid, SP: ITVR, 1988. 116 pp. No ISBN.

Out of the background of base Christian communities in Latin America, the noted theologian finds the meaning of hope in living with joy and confidence in spite of great poverty and fear of persecution.

SP49 Galilea, Segundo

Espiritualidad de la Evangelización: Según las bienaventuranzas. Bogotá, CK: CLAR, 1981. 108 pp. Paper. No ISBN.

A popular presentation of a theology of spirituality and evangelization for the Latin American Church by a noted liberation theologian.

SP50 Galilea, Segundo

Spirituality of Hope. Translated by Terrence Cambias. Maryknoll, NY: Orbis Books, 1988. xi, 116 pp. 0883446367.

English translation.

SP51 Galilea, Segundo

The Way of Living Faith: A Spirituality of Liberation. Translated by John W. Diercksmeier. San Francisco, CAU: Harper & Row, 1988. x, 166 pp. 0060630825.

English translation of *El Camino de la Espiritualidad* (1982).

SP52 Gannon, Thomas M., and George W. Traub

The Desert and the City: An Interpretation of the History of Christian Spirituality. Chicago, ILU: Loyola University Press, 1984. xiii, 338 pp. No ISBN.

Reprint of a scholarly study of the history of spirituality, disclosing not only that each age had its own specific form of spirituality, but also the value of alternation between worldly involvement and the contemplative life; originally published in 1969 (New York: Macmillan).

SP—SPIRITUALITY, WORSHIP, AND MISSION

SP53 Gast, Douglas

Lost in the Woods: A 12 Step Approach to Spiritual Growth. Lima, OHU: Fairway Press, 1994. 196 pp. Paper. 1556738277.

A popular application of the Twelve Steps practiced by Alcoholics Anonymous (AA) to individual spiritual growth, and of the AA approach to caring outreach in local churches.

SP54 Gheddo, Piero

Quale Animazione Missionaria. Bologna, IT: EMI, 1989. 128 pp. Paper. 883070346X.

A popular account of the spiritual penetration of the missionaries told through vignettes of their daily experiences, by one personally involved in such ministries.

SP55 Hinson, E. Glenn, ed.

Spirituality in Ecumenical Perspective. Louisville, KYU: Westminster John Knox, 1993. xv, 200 pp. Paper. 0664253857.

Twelve essays by members of the Ecumenical Institute of Spirituality, written to honor Douglas V. Steere, its founder-leader, and to explore further themes found in his writings.

SP56 Hudson, Trevor

Christ-Following: Ten Signposts to Spirituality. Grand Rapids, MIU: Revell, 1996. 207 pp. Paper. 0800755758.

Out of the struggle for authentic mission in South Africa, a Methodist pastor develops a vision of an authentic spirituality that radiates outward as well as inward.

SP57 Hug, James E., and Rose Marie Scherschel

Social Revelation: Profound Challenge for Christian Spirituality. (Energies for Social Transformation). Washington, DCU: Center of Concern, 1987. 64 pp. Paper. 0934255059.

A study guide for Roman Catholics on the relationship, since Vatican II, between spiritual growth and the struggle for social justice.

SP58 Jaen, Nestor

Toward a Liberation Spirituality. Chicago, ILU: Loyola University Press, 1991. xvii, 123 pp. Paper. 0829406980.

An introduction to the close relationship between liberation and spirituality by a Jesuit priest who lives out that linkage through "Jesus in the Poor," a movement founded by him in the Catholic Church of Panama.

SP59 Judge, Thomas Augustine

The Apostolic Life: A Handbook for the Missionary Cenacle Apostolate. Holy Trinity, ALU: Missionary Cenacle Press, 1986. 185 pp. Paper. No ISBN.

A primary resource for Catholic spiritual formation, including the history and discipline of Cenacle Lay Missionaries.

SP60 King, Ursula

Christ in All Things: Exploring Spirituality with Teilhard de Chardin. Maryknoll, NYU: Orbis Books, 1997. ix, 181 pp. Paper. 1570751153.

Reflections on the implications of Teilhard's holistic vision for contemporary theological discussions concerning the sources of Christian spirituality, the role of mysticism, the dialogue among faiths, the voices of women, and the debates about environmental issues.

SP61 Kroeger, James H.

Aware We Are Sent: Exploring Mission Spirituality. Maryknoll, NYU: [Maryknoll Fathers and Brothers], 1997. 32 pp. Paper. No ISBN.

Introduction to a trinitarian mission spirituality.

SP62 McGinnis, James B.

Journey into Compassion: A Spirituality for the Long Haul. Bloomington, INU: Meyer-Stone Books; St. Louis, MOU: Institute for Peace and Justice, 1989. xii, 148 pp. Paper. 0940989557.

In this work the Co-Director of the Institute for Peace and Justice (Kansas City, US) incorporates the insights of Francis of Assisi, Gandhi, and Martin Luther King, Jr. into a practical spirituality which can be lived in an imperfect world.

SP63 Meehan, Francis Xavier

A Contemporary Social Spirituality. Maryknoll, NYU: Orbis Books, 1982. x, 133 pp. Paper. 0883440229.

Helps for US Christians who, tormented in their concern for peace and justice, seek global awareness with Christian spirituality, by the Associate Professor of Moral Theology at St. Charles Seminary, Philadelphia, Pennsylvania.

SP64 Monchanin, Jules

Théologie et spiritualité missionaires. Paris, FR: Beauchesne, 1985. 214 pp. Paper. 2701011043.

The first edition of lectures by Jules Monchanin (1895-1957), one of France's outstanding missiologists, on missionary theology and spirituality; given to missionary candidates going to India and Islamic countries.

SP65 Murk-Jansen, Saskia

Brides in the Desert: The Spirituality of the Benguines. London, ENK: Darton, Longman & Todd; Maryknoll, NYU: Orbis Books, 1998. 136 pp. Paper. 157075201X.

The voices of four Beguine women involved in a movement of 13th-century mystics, once hailed as the holiest way of Christian life and later condemned as heretical; the volume explains their experience of God in a world where suffering was commonplace.

SP66 Mwoleka, Christopher

Do This!: The Church of the Third Millenium—What Face Shall It Have? Ndanda, TZ: Benedictine Publications, 1988. 155 pp. Paper. 9976670230.

Pastoral reflections by the Roman Catholic Bishop of Rulenge, Tanzania, who seeks to develop an effective spirituality for building the Kingdom of God today.

SP67 Nolan, Albert

Biblical Spirituality. South Africa: OP, 1986. 72 pp. Paper. 0620059550.

Lectures on biblical spirituality originally given to Catholic religious in South Africa, seeking to integrate spirituality and social justice, prayers, and politics.

SP68 O'Reilly, Martin

The Formation of a Religious in Africa Today: A Handbook for Religious Formators. (Spearhead, 93). Eldoret, KE: Gaba Publications, 1986. vi, 53 pp. Paper. No ISBN.

A handbook for spiritual directors in the Roman Catholic Church in East Africa.

SP69 Pierli, Francesco

Be My Witnesses: Spirituality for Mission. Nairobi, KE: Paulines Publications Africa, 1996. 256 pp. Paper. 9966212825.

A basic introduction to mission spirituality based on the author's retreats with Comboni missionaries.

SP—SPIRITUALITY, WORSHIP, AND MISSION

SP70 Puls, Joan

Every Bush Is Burning: A Spirituality for Our Times. Geneva, SZ: WCC, 1985. 120 pp. Paper. 282540828X.

The search for a spirituality that embodies worship and prayer in the midst of the struggle for justice and peace.

SP71 Puls, Joan

Hearts Set on the Pilgrimage: The Challenge of Discipleship in a World Church. Mystic, CTU: Twenty-Third Publications, 1989. 117 pp. Paper. 0896224031.

A series of reflections which ask hard questions of all Christians about the meaning of discipleship and ministry in a world church, by a Franciscan nun who sees the church as pilgrim, servant, and hospitable community.

SP72 Puls, Joan

A Spirituality of Compassion. Mystic, CTU: Twenty-Third Publications, 1989. 134 pp. Paper. 0896223523.

A consideration of seven human situations, and the possibilities in each for incarnating the Gospel attitudes and responses of Jesus; by a Sister of St. Francis who ministers in interfaith dialogue and activity for spiritual growth and social concerns.

SP73 Raguin, Yves, and Kathleen England

I Am Sending You ... (John 22:21): Spirituality of the Missioner. Manila, PH: East Asian Pastoral Institute, 1973. v, 186 pp. No ISBN.

A translation of the French theologian's instructions for missionaries in training, stressing the Pauline idea of *kenosis* (self-emptying), which includes living on the frontier with persons of non-Christian religious traditions.

SP74 Rakoczy, Susan, ed.

Common Journey, Different Paths: Spiritual Direction in Cross-Cultural Perspective. Maryknoll, NYU: Orbis Books, 1992. viii, 175 pp. Paper. 0883447894.

Sixteen essays on basic cross-cultural issues, including the praxis of spiritual direction in Asia, Latin America, Africa, and the US Hispanic experience.

SP75 Reilly, Michael Collins

Spirituality for Mission: Historical, Theological, and Cultural Factors for a Present-Day Missionary Spirituality. Maryknoll, NYU: Orbis Books, 1978. 254 pp. Paper. 088344464X.

A scholarly analysis of some of the elements of a spirituality for mission, designed to be practical and personal, centering upon areas of inner life of the Christian in mission.

SP76 Roseveare, Helen

Living Holiness. London, ENK: Hodder & Stoughton, 1986. 188 pp. Paper. 0340383488.

A popular description of repentance, love of God, obedience, and service as four steps to Christian holiness, with illustrations from the experience of the author as a missionary of WEC International in the Congo (Zaire).

SP77 Rzepkowski, Horst, ed.

Allen alles werden: Beiträge zur missionarischen Spiritualität. (Studia Instituti Missiologici SVD, 21). St. Augustin, GW: Steyler Verlag, 1978. 163 pp. Paper. 3877871100.

Ten papers on missionary spirituality read at a study week in Sankt Augustin/Bonn, 1975.

SP78 Schreiter, Robert J.

In Water and in Blood: A Spirituality of Solidarity and Hope. New York, NYU: Crossroad Publishing, 1988. xii, 141 pp. Paper. 0824508777.

This book retrieves a major New Testament symbol, the blood of Jesus Christ, to sketch a spirituality for a world torn by conflicts and divisions.

SP79 Short, William J.

Poverty and Joy: The Franciscan Tradition. (Traditions of Christian Spirituality). London, ENK: Darton, Longman, & Todd; Maryknoll, NYU: Orbis Books, 1999. 143 pp. Paper. 1570752958.

Beginning with a historical account of the Franciscan order, the author reflects on key themes of the incarnation, poverty as a way to God, suffering and healing, and humanity and nature in the harmony of creation.

SP80 Sider, Ronald J.

Genuine Christianity. Grand Rapids, MIU: Zondervan, 1996. 183 pp. Paper. 0310201780.

A readable introduction to eleven basic, yet profound, ideals that spell the difference between nominal and genuine Christianity by the President of Evangelicals for Social Action.

SP81 Suderman, Robert J.

Calloused Hands, Courageous Souls: Holistic Spirituality of Development and Mission. Translated by W. Derek Suderman. Monrovia, CAU: MARC, 1998. xiii, 144 pp. Paper. 1887983112.

Christian mission defined as aligning the human task with the task of God, resulting in the inseparability of Christian spirituality and Christian mission.

SP82 Tetlow, Joseph A.

Ignatius Loyola: Spiritual Exercises. New York, NYU: Crossroad Publishing, 1992. 177 pp. Paper. 0824525000.

A popular presentation of the life and writings of Ignatius Loyola, founder of the Jesuits, with a modern translation of his famous *Spiritual Exercises.*

SP83 Van der Bent, A. J.

Simple Faith. Madras, II: CLS, 1992. vii, 87 pp. Paper. No ISBN.

A short exposition by the Dutch ecumenical leader on the meaning of "simple faith" interpreted as one that embraces concern for unity, mission, dialogue, and service all at the same time.

SP84 *When God Guides*

(Living Testimonies Series; An OMF Book). Singapore, SI: OMF, 1984. 212 pp. Paper. 9971972166.

A popular sharing, by twenty-seven members of the Oversees Missionary Fellowship, of how God guides in the lives of persons in mission.

SP85 Yohannan, K. P.

The Road to Reality: Coming Home to Jesus from the Unreal World. Altamonte Springs, FLU: Creation House, 1988. x, 203 pp. Paper. 0884192504.

A practical call, by the Founder-President of Gospel for Asia, to live a life of New Testament simplicity in order to fulfill the Great Commission.

SP—SPIRITUALITY, WORSHIP, AND MISSION

Comparative Studies

See also CR288, CR290, CR342, CR642, CR1174, PO128, ED150, SP11-SP12, AF41, AM375, and AS882.

SP86 Arai, Tosh, and S. Wesley Ariarajah, eds.
Spirituality in Interfaith Dialogue. Geneva, SZ: WCC Publications; Maryknoll, NYU: Orbis Books, 1989. xi, 103 pp. Paper. 2825409332 (SZ), 0883445247 (US).

Papers from a WCC consultation on "Spirituality in Interfaith Dialogue" (Kyoto, Japan, 1-5 Dec. 1987) exploring individual spiritual journeys which have led Christians (Roman Catholic, Orthodox, and Protestant) into the spiritual life of other religious traditions.

SP87 Bruteau, Beatrice
What We Can Learn from the East. New York, NYU: Crossroad Publishing, 1995. 126 pp. Paper. 0824514572.

A layperson's introduction to comparative spirituality (Christian, Buddhist, Hindu, and other Eastern traditions) by the founder of Schola Contemplationis, an interreligious network of contemplatives based in Pfafftown, North Carolina.

SP88 Carmody, Denise Lardner, and John Carmody
Catholic Spirituality and the History of Religions. (Catholic Spirituality in Global Perspective, 2). New York, NYU: Paulist Press, 1991. ix, 179 pp. Paper. 0809132850.

A balanced look at Catholic spirituality and its interaction with religious traditions throughout the world.

SP89 Carmody, John, and Denise Lardner Carmody
Christian Uniqueness and Catholic Spirituality. Mahwah, NJU: Paulist Press, 1990. vii, 182 pp. Paper. 0809131978.

An examination of Christ's uniqueness from a global perspective, including a comparative analysis of religions showing how Christ is not unique; written as a search for a Catholic spirituality open to interreligious dialogue.

SP90 Culligan, Kevin G., Mary Jo Meadow, and Daniel Chowning
Purifying the Heart: Buddhist Insight Meditation for Christians. New York, NYU: Crossroad Publishing, 1994. 239 pp. Paper. 0824514203.

Three North American Carmelites introduce "Christian Insight Meditation" which they believe provides a way to deepen prayer life through both Christian spirituality and Buddhist meditation.

SP91 Cuttat, Jacques Albert
Expérience chrétienne et spiritualité orientale. (Foi Vivante, 56). Paris, FR: Desclée de Brouwer, 1967. 376 pp. No ISBN.

The well-known Swiss diplomat and religious scholar has expanded his contribution to the compendium *La Mystique et les Mystiques* (1965) to a self-contained book, in which he attempts to fit into the pattern of Christian exercises in piety the positive values of the Asiatic religions.

SP92 Druille, Mayeul de, ed.
Christian Spirituality for India: A Symposium on Patristic and Indian Spirituality. (Supplement to Indian Theological Studies, 1). Bangalore, II: Asirvanam Benedictine Monastery, 1978. 129 pp. No ISBN.

Papers of a 1976 symposium; published also in *Indian Theological Studies* 15 (1978): 1-128.

SP93 Fleming, David A.
Pilgrim's Notebook: An Experience of Religious Life. Maryknoll, NYU: Orbis Books, 1992. vi, 97 pp. Paper. 0883447541.

Testimony by a Marianist priest active in formation work in Nepal that there are universal religious values in the particularity of religious life—in evangelical obedience, celibacy, and poverty—amidst religious pluralism.

SP94 Hardy, Gilbert G.
Monastic Quest and Interreligious Dialogue. New York, NYU: Lang, 1990. x, 285 pp. 0820412074.

Detailed comparative study of monasticism in Christianity (eg. St. Benedict) and Zen Buddhism (eg. Dgen Zenzi).

SP95 Healy, Kathleen
Entering the Cave of the Heart: Eastern Ways of Prayer for Western Christians. New York, NYU: Paulist Press, 1986. vi, 189 pp. Paper. 080912792X.

An exploration of Buddhist and especially Hindu forms of meditation with the purpose of stating what Christians might learn from them.

SP96 *Indian Spirituality in Action*
Bombay, II: Asian Trading Corp, [1973]. 191 pp. No ISBN.

A collection of papers by Bede Griffiths, Michael Amaladoss, and others on Hindu, Muslim, Buddhist and Christian sources of Indian spirituality; originally read at three seminars held at the Christa Prem Seva Ashram in Pune, India.

SP97 Jaoudi, Maria
Christian and Islamic Spirituality: Sharing a Journey. Mahwah, NJU: Paulist Press, 1993. iii, 103 pp. Paper. 0809134268.

A Christian teacher who has spent a great portion of her life in the Middle East finds a shared Muslim/Christian spirituality in the way of love, the need for purification, transformation, union with God, and a God-centered ecology.

SP98 Johnston, William
Mystical Theology: The Science of Love. Maryknoll, NYU: Orbis Books, 1995. x, 294 pp. Paper. 1570751757.

This wide-ranging study, of an Irish Jesuit who lived more than forty years in Japan, retrieves the riches of the Christian mystical tradition and points of connection with Buddhism and other faiths.

SP99 José, Susana
The Asian Religious Sensibility and Christian (Carmelite) Spirituality. Quezon City, PH: Carmelite Monastery of St. Therese, 1983. 504 pp. No ISBN.

Documents which contain conversations about the great Asian religions, Filipino religious sensibility, and Carmelite spirituality.

SP100 Kochumuttom, Thomas A.
Comparative Theology: Christian Thinking and Spirituality in Indian Perspective. Bangalore, II: Dharmaram Publications, 1985. x, 160 pp. No ISBN.

A comparative study of spirituality in Christianity, Hinduism, and Buddhism, with special reference to India.

SP101 Malpan, Varghese
A Comparative Study of the Bhagavad-gita and the Spiritual Exercises of Saint Ignatius of Loyola on the Process of Spiritual Liberation. (Documenta Missionalia, 22). Rome, IT: Editrice Pontificia Università Gregoriana, 1992. 442 pp. Paper. 887652648X.

A comparative study of the theme of spiritual liberation in the Bhagavad Gita and Ignatius' *Spiritual Exercises.*

SP102 Meadow, Mary Jo
Gentling the Heart: Buddhist Loving-Kindness Practice for Christians. New York, NYU: Crossroad Publishing, 1994. 178 pp. Paper. 0824514343.

Helps to realize the essential teaching of both Jesus and Buddha—universal, non-discriminating love.

SP103 *Meditation in Christianity and Other Religions/ Méditation dans le Christianisme et les autres religions*
(Studia Missionalia, 21). Rome, IT: Gregorian University Press, 1976. 336 pp. No ISBN.

Sixteen scholarly essays in French, English, and German, on meditation as practiced in various religions.

SP104 Parshall, Phil
The Cross and the Crescent: Reflections on Christian-Muslim Spirituality. Wheaton, ILU: Tyndale, 1989. 224 pp. Paper. 0842304738.

Helps for evangelicals desiring to understand Muslim thought and spirituality (in relation to that of Christians).

SP105 *Prayer in Christianity and Other Religions*
(Studia Missionalia, 24). Rome, IT: Gregorian University Press, 1975. 344 pp. No ISBN.

Fourteen scholarly essays in five languages on prayer in the various world religions.

SP106 Raguin, Yves
Ways of Contemplation East and West: Part One: The Structure of the Spiritual World. Taipei, CH: Ricci Institute for Chinese Studies, 1993. x, 200 pp. Paper. 9579185476.

The heart of lectures on contemplation in Western and Eastern spiritual traditions, given by the noted Sinologist at the Institute of East Asian Spirituality in Taipei, Taiwan.

SP107 *Saints: Christianity and Other Religions*
(Studia Missionalia, 35). Rome, IT: Gregorian University Press, 1986. 436 pp. No ISBN.

Seventeen scholarly essays (M. Watt, K. Cragg, H. Waldenfels, Y. Raguin, M. Dhavamony, and others) on approaches to sainthood and spirituality in various world religions.

SP108 Singh, David Emmanuel, ed.
Spiritual Traditions: Essential Visions for Living: A Book in Honour of David C. Scott. Bangalore, II: United Theological College; Delhi, II: ISPCK, 1998. x, 454 pp. Paper. 817214461X.

This collection of twenty-three scholarly papers covers world traditions of spirituality, including Sikh, modern Hindu, Advaita, and others, and their bearing on women's concerns, ecology, and interfaith issues; two papers provide explicit Christian perspectives in spite of a focus on other spiritual traditions.

SP109 *Spiritual Masters: Christianity and Other Religions*
(Studia Missionalia, 36). Rome, IT: Gregorian University Press, 1987. 364 pp. No ISBN.

Thirteen scholarly case studies on spiritual leaders in Judaism, Christianity, Hinduism, Buddhism, and African religions.

SP110 St. Romain, Philip A.
Kundalini Energy and Christian Spirituality: A Pathway to Growth and Healing. New York, NYU: Crossroad Publishing, 1991. 143 pp. Paper. 0824510623.

A popular explanation of the *Kundalini* experience or process in Tantric Yoga, and how it can be related to contemplative traditions in Christianity.

SP111 Stockton, Eugene
The Aboriginal Gift: Spirituality for a Nation. Alexandria, AT: Millennium Books, 1995. vii, 208 pp. Paper. 1864290269.

The author provides a concise description of Australian aboriginal spirituality, contending that modern Christianity in Australia and mainstream spiritual experience could be greatly enriched by it.

SP112 Tanghe, Omer
For the Least of My Brothers: The Spirituality of Mother Teresa and Catherine Doherty. New York, NYU: Alba House, 1989. xvi, 135 pp. Paper. 0818905654.

A comparison of the spirituality of Mother Teresa and Catherine Doherty (1900-1985), foundress of Madonna House in Combermere, Ontario, Canada, and its Little Mandate of spiritual disciplines.

SP113 Wilson, Roy I.
Medicine Wheels: Ancient Teachings for Modern Times. New York, NYU: Crossroad Publishing, 1994. 167 pp. Paper. 0824514165.

A guide to the Native American ritual of the medicine wheel, with reflections on parallel visions and practices in Judaism, Christianity, and other faiths.

Centers for Spiritual Renewal

See also CH284, AF773, AS886, and AS902.

SP114 Acharya, Francis, ed.
Kurisumala: A Symposium on Ashram Life. Kerala, II: Kurisumala Ashram, 1974. 173 pp. No ISBN.

A *festschrift* honoring the founder of the Kurisumala Ashram in Kerala, India, Francis Acharya (born Jean Mahieu), with reflections on monasticism in India and Asia by R. Tagore, Bede Griffiths, R. Panikkar, etc.

SP115 Chenchiah, P., V. Chakkarai, and A. N. Sudarisanam
Asramas Past & Present. Madras, II: Christian Literature Society, 1996. xxiv, 313 pp. Paper. No ISBN.

A reprint of the 1941 appraisal by three prominent Indian theologians.

SP116 Cornille, Catherine
The Guru in Indian Catholicism: Ambiguity or Opportunity of Inculturation? (Louvain Theological and Pastoral Monographs, 6). Louvain, BE: Peeters; Grand Rapids, MIU: Eerdmans, 1991. vii, 214 pp. Paper. 9068313096.

A scholarly reflection on the implications, problems, and possibilities of introducing the Hindu notion of the guru into the Catholic tradition through Christian ashrams in India, featuring the experience of Abhisiktananda (Henré Le Saux).

SP117 Gibello, Erika, ed.
Kleiner Führer durch christliche Ashrams in Indien. (Doku-
mentations-Edition, 3). Munich, GW: Verlag der Arbeitsgemeinschaft für Religions und Weltanschauungsfragen fragen,
1983. 100 pp. 392151360X.

A directory of Christian ashrams, organized by geographical area.

SP118 Griffiths, Bede
*Christian Ashram: Essays Towards a Hindu-Christian Dia-
logue.* London, ENK: Darton, Longman & Todd, 1966. 249
pp. No ISBN.

Essays by the leader of a Christian ashram, designed for
outreach to Hinduism, developing the thesis that only a meeting of Christianity with the religions of the East, at the deepest
level of the experience of God, can provide humanity with a
firm spirituality for the new technological age.

SP119 Jacquin, Françoise
Jules Monchanin Prêtre 1895-1957. Paris, FR: Éditions du
Cerf, 1996. 329 pp. Paper. 2204053198.

Biography of the Catholic priest who, with Henré Le Saux
(Abhishiktananda) and Bede Griffiths, led a Christian ashram,
Shantivanam, integrating Indian monasticism and Christiani-
ty.

SP120 Mataji, Vandana
Christian Ashrams: A Movement with a Future? Delhi, II:
ISPCK, 1993. 160 pp. Paper. 8172141300.

Twenty short reflections on the ministries and significance
of Christian ashrams in India; originally presented at meetings
of ashram leaders (*Satsang*) in 1991.

SP121 Melzer, Friso
*Christliche Ashrams in Südindien: Begegnung mit Bruder-
schaften.* (Erlanger Taschenbücher, 37). Erlangen, GW: Ev.-
Luth. Mission, 1976. 152 pp. Paper. 3872140752.

A description of the origins and philosophies of six Christian ashrams in India (Catholic, Syrian, Protestant), and of the
lifestyles and devotional practices of their members.

SP122 Noreen, Barbara
Crossroads of the Spirit. Delhi, II: ISPCK, 1994. xvi, 203 pp.
Paper. 8172142196.

The history of a Christian ashram community (*Christa
Sëva Sangha*) founded in 1922 by Jack Winslow, its participation in the Freedom Movement, its decline, and later reopen-
ing in 1972 as an ecumenical community.

SP123 Pulsfort, Ernst
*Christliche Ashrams in Indien: Zwischen dem religiösen Erbe
Indiens und der christlichen Tradition des Abendlands.* (Mün-
steraner Theologische Abhandlungen, 7). Altenberge, GW:
Telos-Verlag, 1989. xxi, 235 pp. Paper. 3893750169.

In this Münster dissertation, Pulsfort examines the significance of Christian ashrams in India, their theology and
spirituality, and tackles the ultimate question: "synthesis or
syncretism?"

SP124 Ralston, Helen
*Christian Ashrams: A New Religious Movement in Contempo-
rary India.* (Studies in Religion and Society, 20). Lewiston,
NYU: E Mellen Press, 1987. iii, 154 pp. 0889468540.

A sociologist's scholarly analysis of the development and
contemporary life of both Christian and Hindu ashrams based
on literature analysis and personal visits.

SP125 Vandana, Sister
Gurus, Ashrams and Christians. Madras, II: CLS, 1980. xviii, 131 pp. Paper. No ISBN.

An introduction to Indian spirituality, by the former Head
of the Sisters of the Sacred Heart in India, who has wide experience in both Hindu and Christian ashrams; also published in
1978 by Darton, Longman & Todd (023251416X).

Works of Meditation and Devotion

See also GW245, HI225, HI380, CR800-CR801, CR1378, EC118,
CH465, AF981-AF983, AF985, AM420-AM421, AM748, and
AS880.

SP126 Askew, Eddie
No Strange Land: Meditations and Prayers. London, ENK:
Leprosy Mission International, 1987. 85 pp. Paper.
0902731262.

Devotions by a leader of Leprosy Mission International.

SP127 Boff, Leonardo
Chemin de croix de la justice. Translated by François Malley.
(L'Évangile au XXe siècle). Paris, FR: Éditions du Cerf, 1984.
83 pp. 2204021296.

French translation.

SP128 Boff, Leonardo
Via Crucis de la Justicia. Madrid, SP: Paulinas, 1980. 175
pp. 8428507740.

Spanish translation.

SP129 Boff, Leonardo
Via-Sacra da justiça. Petrópolis, BL: Vozes, 1978. 95 pp. No
ISBN.

Meditations by the noted Brazilian theologian on the ten
Stations of the Cross, exploring justice issues.

SP130 Boff, Leonardo
Way of the Cross—Way of Justice. Translated by John Drury.
Maryknoll, NYU: Orbis Books, 1980. x, 127 pp. 0883447010.

English translation.

SP131 Bogo, Maria do Carmo
Led by Love: A Missionary Way of the Cross. Sunningdale,
ENK: Comboni Missionaries; Middlegreen, ENK: St. Paul
Publications, 1990. 61 pp. Paper. 0854393293.

Meditations on the Stations of the Cross for those desiring to be persons in missions.

SP132 Bushong, Burnis H.
The Best of the Story: Miraculous Answers to Prayer. Marion, INU: World Gospel Mission, 1993. ix, 235 pp.
0962040649.

True experience of missionaries of the World Gospel
Mission, presented as devotional readings with appropriate
scriptural texts.

SP133 Câmara, Hélder
The Desert Is Fertile. Maryknoll, NYU: Orbis Books, 1974.
vi, 61 pp. 0883440784.

A collection of prose and poetry by the Archbishop of
Olinda and Recife in northeast Brazil, through which he calls
for those who seek justice, peace, and love in the world (whom
he considers a minority) to become aware of one another, and
unite their aims and efforts in bringing about global justice
and peace.

SP—SPIRITUALITY,
WORSHIP, AND MISSION

SP134 Câmara, Hélder
Hoping Against All Hope. Maryknoll, NYU: Orbis Books; Melbourne, AT: Dove Communications; Dublin, IE: Gill and Macmillan, 1984. xiv, 82 pp. Paper. 0883441926 (US), 0859243095 (AT).

Short prose and poetry selections by the esteemed Catholic archbishop of Olinda and Recife in northeast Brazil, focusing on the theme of hope amidst suffering.

SP135 Câmara, Hélder
Indagações sobre uma vida melhor. Translated by Enio Silveira. São Paulo, BL: Civilização Brasileira, 1986. xii, 100 pp. No ISBN.

Portuguese translation.

SP136 Câmara, Hélder
Questions for Living. Maryknoll, NYU: Orbis Books, 1987. xii, 100 pp. Paper. 0883445581.

English translation.

SP137 Câmara, Hélder
Des questions pour vivre. Paris, FR: Éditions du Seuil, 1984. 104 pp. 2020068222.

Responses, by the beloved Catholic bishop of Olinda and Recife in northeast Brazil, to questions from his people concerning religious truth and justice issues.

SP138 Cane, Bill
Circles of Hope: Breathing Life and Spirit into a Wounded World. Maryknoll, NYU: Orbis Books, 1992. viii, 150 pp. Paper. 0883448165.

A study book, with helps for individual or group meditation and action, for those yearning for hope and healing through expanded circles of people concerned for renewal of spirit and renewal of the earth.

SP139 Carretto, Carlo
Carlo Carretto: Selected Writings. Edited by Robert Ellsberg. Maryknoll, NYU: Orbis Books, 1994. xiv, 166 pp. Paper. 0883449560.

A collection of the best devotional writings of the remarkable Italian Catholic who, at age forty-four, began ministry in the Saharan desert region of Algeria as a member of the Little Brothers of Jesus.

SP140 Carretto, Carlo
Cartas del Desierto. Translated by Alejo O. León. Caracas, VE: Ediciones Paulinas, 1966. 152 pp. 9802071501.

Spanish translation.

SP141 Carretto, Carlo
Letters from the Desert. Maryknoll, NYU: Orbis Books; London, ENK: Darton, Longman & Todd, 1972. xxi, 146 pp. Paper. 0232511780.

English translation of *Lettere del deserto* (Brescia, IT: La Scuola Editrice, 1964)—the meditations of a former Catholic Action leader who joined the Little Brothers in a life of contemplation and compassion at Tamanrasset in the Algerian Sahara, following in the footsteps of Charles de Foucauld.

SP142 Carretto, Carlo
Lettres du désert. Translated by J. Humbert. (Témoignages, 1). Paris, FR: Apostolat des éditions; Sherbrooke, PQC: Éditions Paulines, 1975. 207 pp. 2712200179 (FR), 0888400802 (PQC).

French translation.

SP143 Cassidy, Sheila
Sharing the Darkness: The Spirituality of Caring. Maryknoll, NYU: Orbis Books, 1991. xiii, 177 pp. Paper. 0883447797.

Meditations on the mystery of our wounded humanity by a physician who, from arrest and torture in Chile to directing a hospice for terminal cancer patients in Plymouth, England, has experienced grace, forgiveness, and the affirmation of humanity through Christian service.

SP144 Copan, Lil, and Elisa Fryling, comps.
Finding God between a Rock and a Hard Place: Stories of Gratitude and Grace. Wheaton, ILU: Shaw Publishers, 1999. 178 pp. Paper. 0877883297.

Personal stories from people around the globe on how God's grace shows up in airports, coffee shops, and hospital rooms; contributors include Corrie ten Boom, Madeleine L'Engle, and Larry Crab.

SP145 De Gruchy, John W.
Cry Justice!: Prayers, Meditations and Readings From South Africa. Maryknoll, NYU: Orbis Books, 1986. 261 pp. Paper. 088344223X.

Thirty-one sets of readings (each including a statement about the Christian life, Scripture reading, poetry, and hymn) on themes related to Christian life and mission in South Africa.

SP146 Donders, Joseph G., and Elizabeth Byrne, eds.
Original Joy: Free the Playful Child in You. Mystic, CTU: Twenty-Third Publications, 1989. 145 pp. Paper. 0896223884.

Creative poetry out of the authors' experiences of ministry in Kenya, Africa, inviting the adult reader to rediscover the unity with creation once experienced as children, as well as Jesus' fascination with childlike spirituality.

SP147 Donders, Joseph G.
Risen Life: Healing a Broken World. Maryknoll, NYU: Orbis Books, 1990. xii, 115 pp. Paper. 088344688X.

A member of the Missionaries of Africa, Fr. Donders offers meditations on Luke's Gospel, focused on the theme of healing as a metaphor for liberation in the search for an integral spirituality that unites spirit and body, individual and community, and church and world.

SP148 Dunne, John S.
The Church of the Poor Devil: Reflections on a Riverboat Voyage and a Spiritual Journey. New York, NYU: Macmillan; London, ENK: SCM Press, 1982. x, 180 pp. 0025339605 (US), 0334019400 (UK).

"I have named this book after a little chapel I found at the end of a riverboat voyage up the Amazon.... It sums up for me an adventure in passing over from personal religion to the religion of the poor and coming to a vision of human misery and the heart's longing."

SP149 Edwards, Tilden H., ed.
Living with Apocalypse: Spiritual Resources for Social Compassion. San Francisco, CAU: Harper & Row, 1984. xiii, 202 pp. 0060621230.

Contemporary readings by noted Protestant and Catholic leaders on spiritual foundations for compassionate social change, in the light of social and political upheavals and an escalating arms race.

SP—SPIRITUALITY, WORSHIP, AND MISSION

SP150 Egan, Eileen, and Kathleen Egan

Prayertimes with Mother Teresa: A New Adventure in Prayer Involving Scripture, Mother Teresa, and You. New York, NYU: Doubleday, 1989. ix, 166 pp. Paper. 0385262310.

A one-year devotional guide arranged under fifty-two themes, including scriptural passages, inspiring words of Mother Teresa, and anecdotes from her life's ministry.

SP151 Esquerda-Bifet, Juan

Te hemos Seguido: Espiritualidad Sacerdotal. (BAC Popular, 79). Madrid, II: EDICA, 1988. 175 pp. Paper. 8422012634.

Spiritual reflections on the evangelizing mission of Catholic priests.

SP152 Foucauld, Charles de

Inner Search: Letters (1889-1916). Translated by Barbara Lucas. Maryknoll, NYU: Orbis Books, 1979. 151 pp. Paper. 0883442817.

Abridged English translation; also published as *Letters from the Desert* (London: Burns and Oates, 1977, 0860120449).

SP153 Foucauld, Charles de

Lettres à mes frères de la Trappe. Paris, FR: Éditions du Cerf, 1991. 481 pp. 2204041432.

A collection of letters written between 1889 and 1916 by the noted Trappist from Algeria to France; originally published in 1969.

SP154 Foucauld, Charles de

Meditations of a Hermit. Translated by Charlotte Balfour. Maryknoll, NYU: Orbis Books; London, ENK: Burns & Oates, 1981. xx, 186 pp. Paper. 0883443252 (US), 0860121208 (UK).

The powerful spiritual writings of Charles Eugène de Foucauld (1858-1916), Christian hermit among the Muslim Tuareg tribes of North Africa.

SP155 Gnanabaranam, Johnson

Mein Jesus, mache mich neu: Gespräche mit Gott. (Erlanger Taschenbucher Band 80). Erlangen, GW: Ev.-Luth. Mission, 1986. 80 pp. Paper. 3872141805.

This is a German translation of poetry by the Indian theologian Johnson Gnanabaranam reflecting on his faith and the nature of mission.

SP156 Hall, Douglas John

The Stewardship of Life in the Kingdom of Death. Grand Rapids, MIU: Eerdmans, 1988. xvi, 144 pp. 0802803547.

Revised edition of meditations based on the belief that to engage in Christ's mission in the world today is to eschew triumphalism by living out a theology of the cross, and being stewards of life in the kingdom of death; originally published as *Christian Mission: The Stewardship of Life in the Kingdom of Death* by Friendship Press, New York (1985).

SP157 Hampton, Vinita, and Carol Plueddemann, comps.

World Shapers: A Treasury of Quotes from Great Missionaries. Wheaton, ILU: Shaw Publishers, 1991. xiv, 143 pp. Paper. 0877889465.

Short quotes by missionaries organized by inspirational themes.

SP158 Haug, Hellmut, and Jürgen Rump, comps.

Bibel provokativ: Gerechtigkeit für die Dritte Welt. Stuttgart, GW: Württembergische Bibelanstalt, 1969. 157 pp. No ISBN.

Brief biblical and contemporary readings on themes concerning justice and the Third World.

SP159 Haug, Hellmut, and Jürgen Rump, comps.

Biblia Inquietante: Justicia para el Tercer Mundo. Madrid, SP: Euramerica, 1970. 196 pp. No ISBN.

Spanish translation.

SP160 Haug, Hellmut, and Jürgen Rump, comps.

The Radical Bible. Translated by Erika J. Papp. Maryknoll, NYU: Orbis Books, 1972. vi, 161 pp. No ISBN.

English translation.

SP161 Hillsdon-Hutton, Val, ed.

Banners Unfurled!: Pilgrims in Today's World. Cincinnati, OHU: Forward Movement, 1991. vi, 101 pp. Paper. 0880281235.

A six-week cycle of daily meditations on mission themes including interviews with persons in mission, Bible readings, meditations, and prayer.

SP162 Johnston, William

Letters to Contemplatives. Maryknoll, NYU: Orbis Books, 1991. x, 112 pp. Paper. 0883447843.

Letters to friends by an Irish Jesuit teaching at Sophia University in Tokyo, exploring the relation between contemplation and action, and the interplay of Christian and Eastern mystical traditions.

SP163 Jones, Alfred H.

An Alphabet of Mission. New York, NYU: Friendship Press, 1991. 59 pp. Paper. 0377002380.

A help for twenty-six days of devotional reflection on contemporary Christian mission, including a Scripture passage, contemporary reading, and short prayer for each day.

SP164 Jones, E. Stanley

Sayings of E. Stanley Jones: A Treasury of Wisdom and Wit. Compiled by Whitney J. Dough. Franklin, TNU: Providence House, 1994. 144 pp. Paper. 1881576299.

A thematic arrangement of pithy quotes of E. Stanley Jones (1884-1973), Methodist missionary to India and leader of the Christian ashram movement.

SP165 Joseph, M. J.

Geben und empfangen. (Erlanger Taschenbücher, 48). Erlangen, GW: Ev.-Luth. Mission, 1978. 76 pp. 3872141015.

A sample of devotional writings by contemporary Indian theologians.

SP166 Kellermann, Bill Wylie

Seasons of Faith and Conscience: Kairos, Confession, Liturgy. Maryknoll, NYU: Orbis Books, 1991. xxviii, 228 pp. Paper. 0883447266.

Biblical and theological reflections on the connections between worship/liturgy and politics, with meditations for the seasons of the Christian year.

SP—SPIRITUALITY, WORSHIP, AND MISSION

SP167 Koyama, Kosuke
50 Meditations. Maryknoll, NYU: Orbis Books, 1979. 242 pp. Paper. 0883441349.

Meditations on various aspects of the Christian faith by a Japanese missionary to Thailand who also has taught theology in the United States and New Zealand, originally published in 1975 (Belfast: Christian Journals).

SP168 Koyama, Kosuke
Three Mile an Hour God: Biblical Reflections. Maryknoll, NYU: Orbis Books, 1979. viii, 146 pp. Paper. 0883444739.

Forty-five meditations by the eminent Japanese theologian and teacher at Union Theological Seminary in New York, applying biblical truths to Asian cultural realities.

SP169 Kraybill, J. Nelson
On the Pilgrim's Way: Conversations on Christian Discipleship. Scottdale, PAU: Herald Press, 1999. 239 pp. Paper. 0836190971.

A moving account of Kraybill and his walking partners who read a Psalm and pray in a local church, then hike 140 miles across England engaging in issues of Christian discipleship, prayer, celebration, community, money, doubt, risk-taking, and peacemaking.

SP170 Laubach, Frank C.
Man of Prayer: Selected Writings of a World Missionary. (The Heritage Collection). Syracuse, NYU: Laubach Literacy International, 1990. 330 pp. Paper. 0883365804.

A collection of the major devotional writings by the renowned missionary to the Philippines and world literacy pioneer.

SP171 Maggay, Melba Padilla
A Faith for the Emptiness of Our Time. Manila, PH: OMF Books, 1990. 122 pp. Paper. 9715111718.

The Christian story presented as an answer to the hollowness of much of contemporary life by the General Director of the Institute for Studies in Asian Church and Culture.

SP172 Martin, Earl R., and Pat Hostetter Martin, eds.
World Winds: Meditations from the Blessed of the Earth. Scottdale, PAU: Herald Press, 1990. 87 pp. Paper. 0836135350.

Short meditations, with photographs of Third World peoples and ministries, by former Mennonite volunteers in Vietnam and the Philippines.

SP173 Mathews, R. Arthur
Ready for Battle: 31 Studies in Christian Discipleship. Wheaton, ILU: OMF Books/Shaw Publishers, 1993. vii, 129 pp. Paper. 0877887276.

Thirty-one short meditations on Christian discipleship, including the call to missionary service by Robert Arthur Mathews (1912-1978), a China Inland Mission missionary (1938-1953).

SP174 Misioneral Siervas del Espíritu Santo
Devocionario Misional. Buenos Aires, AG: Editorial Guadalupe, 1983. 111 pp. Paper. 9505000553.

A book of meditations and prayers for missions.

SP175 Moses, Carl B.
Missionaries Are People Too. Orlando, FLU: Lock Haven Scripture Press, 1994. 366 pp. Paper. No ISBN.

Short meditations (365) with Scripture texts in which the author shares from over a half-century of experience as a pastor and missionary of CAM International to Latin America.

SP176 Nouwen, Henri J. M.
Walk with Jesus: Stations of the Cross. Maryknoll, NYU: Orbis Books, 1990. x, 98 pp. Paper. 0883446669.

Meditations inspired by a series of drawings by Sr. Helen David which represent the traditional Stations of the Cross through vignettes on the passion and suffering of the world's poor.

SP177 Nubiola, Ramon
Missionary Musings: A Search for Meaning. Anand, II: Gujarat Sahitya Prakash, 1991. ix, 110 pp. Paper. No ISBN.

The personal testimony of Ramon Nubiola (1907-1991), a Spanish Jesuit missionary to India, 1934-1991, focusing on the call to a missionary apostolate, and its biblical and spiritual groundings.

SP178 Oliana, Guido
Lectio Divina: Spirituality for the Mission. (Religious Life in Africa). Nairobi, KE: Paulines Publications Africa, 1998. 112 pp. Paper. 9966214143.

The integration of monastic tradition and mission rooted in the Gospel stories.

SP179 Oosterzee, Klaas van, ed.
"... en niemand zal met honger weggaan." (Allerwegen, 18). Kampen, NE: Kok, 1995. 77 pp. Paper. 9024224780.

Seven brief essays, previously published in mission journals or books, communicating particular Old and New Testament themes and biblical characters that become metaphors for the physical hunger and thirst experienced by peoples living south of the Equator.

SP180 Raschzok, Klaus, ed.
Die Welt ist heute an Bildern reich: 24 weihnachtliche Bilder aus aller Welt mit Informationen und Meditationen. Erlangen, GW: Ev.-Luth. Mission; Aachen, GW: Missio Aachen, 1997. 159 pp. 3872142747 (V), 393055612X (m).

A theologian and artist combine in this beautifully printed and richly illustrated book to present themes from the Old and New Testaments that portend the coming of Jesus in cross-cultural perspective.

SP181 Rauschenbusch, Walter
Walter Rauschenbusch: Selected Writings. Edited by Winthrop S. Hudson. New York, NYU: Paulist Press, 1984. vi, 252 pp. Paper. 0809103567.

Selected writings by the "Father" of the Social Gospel Movement in the United States on the relationship between social justice and Christian piety, 1897-1917.

SP182 Ruiz de Montoya, Antonio
Silex del Divino Amor. Lima, PE: Pontificia Universidad Católica del Perú, 1991. cxvi, 294 pp. Paper. No ISBN.

The writings of António Ruiz de Montoya (1586-1652), a Jesuit priest from Lima, Perú, who founded the mission to indigenous peoples in Paraguay, telling of his struggling youth, his conversion, mission to Paraguay, and appeal for a virtuous life, with an extended biographical introduction by José Luis Rouillon Arrospide.

SP183 Runcie, Robert, and Basil Hume
*Prayers for Peace: An Anthology of Readings and Prayers
Selected by Archbishop Robert Runcie and Cardinal Basil
Hume.* London, ENK: SPCK, 1987. x, 116 pp. Paper.
0281042659.

To extend Pope John II's vision for a Day of Prayer
for Peace at Assisi, the Archbishop of Canterbury and Cardinal Hume have gathered together this ecumenical and interfaith selection of readings and prayers.

SP184 Sider, Ronald J., ed.
*For They Shall Be Fed: Scripture Readings and Prayers
for a Just World.* Dallas, TXU: World Publishing, 1997.
xvi, 221 pp. Paper. 0849953146.

A revised edition of *Cry Justice* (1980), containing
Bible readings, prayers, and study questions pertaining to
hunger, justice, and the poor.

SP185 Sintas, Louis
Bonheur retrouvé. (Collection à pleine vie). Paris, FR: Éditions ouvrières, 1976. 158 pp. No ISBN.

A meditation on salvation history, in which the theme
of conversion is a unifying thread.

SP186 Steer, Roger
Hudson Taylor: Lessons in Discipleship. (OMF International). Crowborough, ENK: Monarch Publications, 1995.
153 pp. Paper. 1854243225.

One hundred lessons from the life and writings of the
founder of the China Inland Mission, on themes of holiness, prayer, knowing God, and the way of the cross; originally published in 1991 (London, ENK: Evangelical Library).

SP187 Teresa, Mother
Amor, un Fruto siempre maduro. Edited by Dorothy S.
Hunt. Translated by Dorotea Pläcking de Salcedo. Buenos
Aires, AG: Editorial Atlántida, [1998]. 253 pp. 9500808552.

Eleventh edition of the Spanish translation of *Love, a
Fruit Always in Season* (1987); first published in 1987.

SP188 Teresa, Mother
Beschaulich inmitten der Welt: Geistliche Weisungen. (Der
Neue Weg, 10). Freiburg, GW: Johannes Verlag Einsiedeln,
1990. 163 pp. Paper. 3894110228.

German translation.

SP189 Teresa, Mother
Con la parola e con l'esempio: Meditazioni spirituali.
Casale Monferrato, IT: Piemme, 1988. 156 pp. 8838420408.

Italian translation.

SP190 Teresa, Mother
*Daily Prayer with Mother Teresa: Prayers and Meditations
for Every Day of the Year.* Compiled by Angelo Devananda. London, ENK: Fount, 1994. xiv, 158 pp. Paper.
0006278353.

Quotes from Mother Teresa's sayings and writings providing wonderful tidbits of inspiration for each day of the
year; originally published in 1986.

SP191 Teresa, Mother
Gedanken für jeden Tag. (Herderbücherei, 1767). Freiburg
im Breisgau, GW: Herder, 1992. 183 pp. Paper.
3451087677.

German translation of *Jesus, the Word to Be Spoken*
(1986).

SP192 Teresa, Mother
*Love, a Fruit Always in Season: Daily Meditations from
the Words of Mother Teresa of Calcutta.* Edited by Dorothy S. Hunt. San Francisco, CAU: Ignatius Press, 1987.
260 pp. Paper. 0898701678.

The daily meditations by the founder of the order of
the Missionaries of Charity, arranged to coincide with the
seasons of the liturgical year.

SP193 Teresa, Mother
*Miloscowoc, który dojrzewa w kazdym czasie: rozwazania
na kazdy dzien.* Edited by Dorothy S. Hunt. Translated by
Halina Bramska. Warsaw, PL: Wydawnictwo Ksiezy Mari-
anów, 1991. 196 pp. 8385040269.

Polish translation of *Love, a Fruit Always in Season*
(1987).

SP194 Teresa, Mother
Mother Teresa, Contemplative in the Heart of the World.
Ann Arbor, MIU: Servant Books, 1985. 140 pp.
0892832797.

Meditations from Calcutta.

SP195 Teresa, Mother
Par la parole et par l'exemple. Translated by Jean-Marie
Wallet. (Spiritualité). Paris, FR: Nouvelle Cité, 1990. 182
pp. 2853132366.

French translation.

SP196 Thomas, M. A.
*About You and Me: Meditations on Mission and Message
for Our Time.* Madras, II: CLS, 1975. x, 78 pp. No ISBN.

Reflections by the Director of the Christian Ecumenical Centre in Bangalore, India, on how God's love in Christ
touches the lives of ordinary people.

SP197 Thomas, M. A.
*Weise den Weg: Sendung und Botschaft für unsere Zeit: neue
Meditationen und Gebete aus Indien.* (Erlanger Taschenbücher, 36). Erlangen, GW: Ev.-Luth. Mission, 1975. x, 79
pp. 3872140701.

German translation of *About You and Me* (1975).

SP198 Tucker, Ruth A.
*Parables of the Great Commission: A Daily Devotional for
World Christians.* Grand Rapids: MIU: Zondervan, 1989.
395 pp. 031051620X.

A 365-day devotional guide made up of historical and
contemporary testimonies of great Christians from around
the world, designed to deepen global understanding and
commitment to the Christian world mission; originally published as *Sacred Stories: Daily Devotions from the Family
of God.*

SP199 Verwer, George
The Revolution of Love. Bromley, ENK: STL Books, 1989.
128 pp. Paper. 1850780455.

Inspirational messages by the founder and International Co-Ordinator of Operation Mobilisation, a mission designed to train evangelical laity for personal witnessing and
church planting around the world.

SP—SPIRITUALITY,
WORSHIP, AND MISSION

SP200 Williamson, Clark M., and Ronald J. Allen
Dancing in the Margins: Meditations for People Who Struggle with Their Churches. New York, NYU: Crossroad Publishing, 1999. 159 pp. Paper. 0824518152.

The author invites reflections on heart-rending experiences that cause people to be weary, disoriented, and disappointed with their churches.

SP201 Yohannan, K. P.
Living in the Light of Eternity. Longwood, FLU: Longwood Communications, 1993. 266 pp. Paper. 0963219065.

Meditations by the international president and founder of Gospel for Asia calling Christians to a renewed passion and urgency for outreach to the millions who do not know Christ as Savior.

Worship: General

See also TH489, EV543-EV544, EV566, EV578, CH63, CH192, AF98, and OC45.

SP202 Benedict, Daniel C., and Craig Kennet Miller
Contemporary Worship for the 21st Century: Worship or Evangelism? Nashville, TNU: Discipleship Resources, 1994. viii, 128 pp. Paper. 0881771384.

Resources for, and examples of, contemporary worship services which both inspire believers and attract seekers.

SP203 Black, Kathy
Worship across Cultures: A Handbook. Nashville, TNU: Abingdon, 1998. 245 pp. Paper. 0687056527.

A practical guide to the basic worship and sacramental practices of twenty-one different ethnic and cultural groups in North American Protestantism.

SP204 Brenner, Scott Francis
Ways of Worship for New Forms of Mission. New York, NYU: Friendship Press, 1968. 96 pp. Paper. No ISBN.

A practical study guide for mainline Protestants in North America seeking ways by which worship can motivate for action in mission.

SP205 Brown, Paul B.
In and for the World: Bringing the Contemporary into Christian Worship. Minneapolis, MNU: Fortress Press, 1992. vii, 176 pp. Paper. 0800626575.

Lectures exploring ways in which the worship of today's church can reflect its engagement with the realities of its culture, including materials from the Two-Thirds World; originally given as the Bowen Lectures at Memphis Theological Seminary in 1990.

SP206 Carson, D. A., ed.
Worship: Adoration and Action. Grand Rapids, MIU: Baker Books; Carlisle, ENK: Paternoster Press, 1993. 256 pp. Paper. 0801025842 (US), 085364523X (UK).

This fifth and final volume of a series of studies produced by the Faith and Church Study Unit of the Theological Commission of the WEF contains essays on the biblical theology of worship and reflections on the practice of worship in different contexts: denominational, cultural (South America and the Two-Thirds World), the charismatic movement, and student groups.

SP207 Davies, J. G.
Worship and Mission. New York, NYU: Association Press, 1967. 159 pp. No ISBN.

A doctrinal study on the meaning of worship in terms of mission, with its implications for liturgical revision.

SP208 Dawn, Marva J.
A Royal "Waste" of Time: The Splendor of Worshiping God and Being Church for the World. Grand Rapids, MIU: Eerdmans, 1999. viii, 377 pp. Paper. 080284586X.

A sequel to *Preaching out without Dumbing Down,* this book explores the churches' need to engage in a serious process of community discernment concerning worship, to employ the best tools and forms, so that the splendor of God will nurture in believers a way of life that reaches out in mission to the world, and gives neighbors a warrant for belief.

SP209 Dournes, Jacques
L'offrande des peuples: recherches et remarques sur le binôme, activité missionnaire-action liturgique. (International Study Week on Mission and Liturgy (Nijmegen/Uden, 1959)). (Lex orandi, 44; Jeunesse de la liturgie). Paris, FR: Éditions du Cerf, 1967. 286 pp. No ISBN.

A detailed argument that in mission the activities of service and the action of the liturgy are one continuous encounter with God.

SP210 Hofinger, Johannes, ed.
Liturgy and the Missions: The Nijmegen Papers. New York, NYU: Kenedy; London, ENK: Burns & Oates, 1960. xii, 308 pp. No ISBN.

English translation.

SP211 International Study Week on Mission and Liturgy (Nijmegen/Uden, 1959)
Mission und Liturgie: Der Kongress von Nimwegen 1959. Edited by Johannes Hofinger. Mainz, GW: Grünewald, 1960. 203 pp. Paper. No ISBN.

Twenty-nine essays on liturgical renewal presented by an international team of Catholic missiologists and church leaders at The International Study Week on Mission and Liturgy (Nijmegen and Uden, the Netherlands, 12-19 September 1959).

SP212 Luykx, Boniface
Culte chrétien en Afrique après Vatican II. (Supplementa—Nouvelle revue de science missionnaire, 22). Immensee, SZ: Nouvelle revue de science missionaire, 1974. 190 pp. No ISBN.

A detailed analysis of changes made in Catholic liturgies in Africa after Vatican II.

SP213 Morgenthaler, Sally
Worship Evangelism: Inviting Unbelievers into the Presence of God. Grand Rapids, MIU: Zondervan, 1999. 320 pp. 031022649X.

With hands-on strategies for "worship that witnesses," Morgenthaler shows how to achieve worship appealing to non-believers that is both culturally relevant and authentic; first published in 1995.

SP214 Stauffer, S. Anita, ed.
Christian Worship: Unity in Cultural Diversity. (Lutheran World Federation Studies, 1/1996). Geneva, SZ: LWF, 1996. 145 pp. Paper. 3906706257.

Results of a 1993-1995 study sponsored by the LWF on global continuities and cultural diversities in Christian worship, with special attention to the Eucharist.

SP215 Stauffer, S. Anita, ed.
Worship and Culture in Dialogue: Reports of International Consultations, Cartigny, Switzerland, 1993, Hong Kong, 1994. (LWF Studies). Geneva, SZ: LWF, 1994. 247 pp. Paper. 3906706125.

An ecumenical examination of the contemporary, as well as historical relationships, between culture and Christian liturgy, church music, and church architecture; with case studies and bibliography.

SP216 Webber, Robert E.
Liturgical Evangelism: Worship as Outreach and Nurture. Harrisburg, PAU: Morehouse Publishing, 1993. viii, 118 pp. Paper. 0819215961.

A reprint of *Celebrating Our Faith* (Harper & Row, 1986) introducing the liturgical tradition to Protestants as a contemporary evangelism tool.

SP217 White, James F.
The Worldliness of Worship. New York, NYU: Oxford University Press, 1967. vii, 181 pp. No ISBN.

A primer for Protestants on the meaning of worship as equipping Christians for their life in the world, and for developing a worldly spirituality.

Times and Seasons: The Church Year

See also AF454 and OC58.

SP218 Bujo, Bénézet
Christmas: God Becomes Man in Black Africa. Nairobi, KE: Paulines Publications Africa, 1995. 88 pp. Paper. 9966211853.

A meditation by a Zairois Catholic theologian interpreting the message of the incarnation for an African continent in turmoil.

SP219 Burkhart, Louise M.
Holy Wednesday: A Nahua Drama from Early Colonial Mexico. (New Cultural Studies). Philadelphia, PAU: University of Pennsylvania Press, 1996. xii, 314 pp. 0812233425 (hdbk), 0812215761 (pbk).

A scholarly commentary on a Nahuatl Holy Week play, a drama translated by a native poet in the 16th century and adapted from the Spanish.

SP220 Doppelfeld, Basilius
Missionarisches Kirchenjahr. Münsterschwarzach, GW: Vier-Türme-Verlag, 1988. 175 pp. Paper. 3878683766.

A theology of mission throughout the liturgical year, as well as an animation for proclaiming the Gospel.

SP221 Gutiérrez, Gustavo
Sharing the Word through the Liturgical Year. Translated by Colette Joy Dees. Maryknoll, NYU: Orbis Books; London, ENK: Chapman; Alexandria, AT: E. J. Dwyer, 1997. xvi, 288 pp. Paper. 1570751382 (O), 0225668580 (C), 0855741198 (D).

Reflections on all three cycles (A-B-C) of scripture readings for the liturgical year, emphasizing themes of liberation and love; by the renowned Peruvian theologian.

SP222 Morley, Janet, ed.
Bread of Tomorrow: Prayers for the Church Year. Maryknoll, NYU: Orbis Books, 1992. 180 pp. Paper. 0883448319.

A selection of prayers from around the world and various confessional traditions centering on themes of poverty and ministry to the poor and grouped according to the seasons of the church year.

SP223 National Alliance for Parishes Restructuring into Communities
Faith Sharing for Small Church Communities: Questions and Commentaries on the Sunday Readings. Edited by Arthur R. Baranowski. Cincinnati, OHU: Anthony Messenger Press, 1993. iv, 132 pp. Paper. 0867161663.

Brief commentary on the Scripture readings of the three-year Common Lectionary for each Sunday, with life focus questions contributed by Catholic small church communities on six continents.

Liturgy and Ritual

See also EA52, CR877, CR1201, EV213, CH147, SP1, SP210-SP211, AF66, AF1337, AM779, AS644, and AS1001.

SP224 Amalorpavadass, D. S., ed.
Proceedings of the Second All-India Liturgical Meeting, Bangalore, 27th to 31st January 1969. Bangalore, II: St. Mary's Press, 1969. 116 pp. Paper. No ISBN.

A collection of papers given at a conference a few years after Vatican II, about some of the challenges faced in adaptation of the liturgy in the Indian cultural context.

SP225 Amalorpavadass, D. S.
Towards Indigenisation in the Liturgy. (Mission Theology for Our Times Series, 6). Bangalore, II: NBCLC, 1972. 176 pp. Paper. No ISBN.

The history, rationale, and practice of indigenization of the Catholic Mass in India by the director of NBCLC.

SP226 AMECEA Liturgical Colloquium
Liturgy: Towards Inculturation. (Spearhead, 92). Eldoret, KE: Gaba Publications, 1986. viii, 78 pp. Paper. No ISBN.

Papers and the report of an important Roman Catholic colloquium sponsored by AMECEA.

SP227 Bria, Ion
The Liturgy after the Liturgy: Mission and Witness from an Orthodox Perspective. Geneva, SZ: WCC Publications, 1996. viii, 88 pp. Paper. 2825411892.

The noted ecumenist and Romanian Orthodox theologian argues that in true Orthodoxy worship is inseparable from committed engagement in society and culture.

SP228 Chupungco, Anscar J.
Liturgies of the Future: The Process and Methods of Inculturation. New York, NYU: Paulist Press, 1989. iv, 220 pp. Paper. 0809130955.

The adaptation of the liturgy to various cultures and traditions, examined as the unfinished agenda of Vatican II, and contemporary task of Catholic local churches.

SP229 Dinteren, L. K. M. van
Opdat Gods glorie openbaar worde: De "lex orandi" als theologisch verantwoord fundament van orthodoxe missietheologie. (Kerk en theologie in context, 20). Kampen, NE: Kok, 1993. xvi, 256 pp. Paper. 9024280478.

An Orthodox theologian analyzes the glorification of God as celebrated in the liturgy as the theological basis of Orthodox mission theology; originally presented as a doctoral dissertation at the Catholic University of Nijmegen.

SP230 Egbulem, Nwaka Chris
The Power of Africentric Celebrations: Inspirations from the Zairean Liturgy. New York, NYU: Crossroad Publishing, 1996. 167 pp. Paper. 0824514890.

A guide to the roots of the Afri-Zairean worship experience that offers insights for developing authentic and sensitive worship celebrations in other parish contexts; by a Professor of Systematic Theology and Liturgical Studies in Nigeria and the United States.

SP231 Francis, Mark R.
Liturgy in a Multi-Cultural Community. (American Essays in Liturgy Series). Collegeville, MNU: Liturgical Press, 1991. 78 pp. Paper. 0814620469.

Helps for a multicultural community that worships together, including the Catholic guidelines for multilingual masses issued by the Federation of Diocesan Liturgical Commissions in the United States.

SP232 Harling, Per, ed.
Worshipping Ecumenically: Orders of Service from Global Meetings with Suggestions for Local Use. Geneva, SZ: WCC Publications, 1995. 183 pp. Paper. 2825411418.

Annotated orders of worship from WCC events adapted for use in local church or ecumenical settings, many with mission themes.

SP233 Jala, Dominic
Liturgy and Mission. (Bibliotheca "Ephemerides liturgicae" "subsidia," 41). Rome, IT: CLV—Edizioni Liturgiche, 1987. xviii, 343 pp. Paper. No ISBN.

A solid theological foundation for the relationship between liturgy and mission; originally submitted as a dissertation at the Pontifical Liturgical Institute in Rome.

SP234 Kabasele, François
Liturgies africaines: l'enjeu culturel, ecclésial et théologique. (Recherches africaines de théologie, 14). Kinshasa, CG: Facultés catholiques de Kinshasa, 1996. 159 pp. No ISBN.

An impassioned plea, by a well-known Catholic liturgist in Kinshasa, for liturgies attuned to African cultural realities.

SP235 Kanichikattil, Francis
To Restore or to Reform?: A Critical Study on Current Liturgical Renewal in the Syro-Malabar Church in India. Bangalore, II: Dharmaram Publications, 1992. xix, 230 pp. Paper. No ISBN.

A doctoral dissertation (Ph.D., University of London, 1991) on the search of the Syro-Malabar Church in India for authentic liturgical reform in the cultural context of today's India.

SP236 Missionswissenschaftlichen Institut Missio unter der Leitung von Ludwig Bertsch
Der Neue Messritus im Zaire: Ein Beispiel kontextueller Liturgie. (Theologie der Dritten Welt, 18). Freiburg im Breisgau, GW: Herder, 1993. 256 pp. Paper. 3451228904.

The new mass rite in Zaire as an example of contextualized liturgy; with official text and interpretation by the Zaire Bishop's Conference, plus five analytical essays by European and Zairois scholars.

SP237 Semaine de Missiologie
Liturgie en mission: rapports et compte rendu de la XXXIIe Semaine de missiologie, Louvain 1963. (Museum Lessianum: Section missiologique, 44). Paris, FR: Desclée de Brouwer, 1964. 287 pp. No ISBN.

Eighteen papers from the Thirty-Third Missiology Week (Louvain, Belgium, 1963) examining the rationale for, and attempts to adapt, liturgical practice to different cultural situations.

SP238 Tirabassi, Maren C., and Kathy Wonson Eddy
Gifts of Many Cultures: Worship Resources for the Global Community. Cleveland, OHU: United Church Press, 1995. xii, 260 pp. Paper. 0829810293.

An anthology of liturgical resources (prayers, poetry, stories, readings, art, and worship suggestions) from around the world; by two United Church of Christ pastors.

SP239 Uzukwu, E. Elochukwu
Liturgy: Truly Christian, Truly African. (Spearhead, 74). Eldoret, KE: Gaba Publications, 1982. ii, 73 pp. Paper. No ISBN.

This booklet describes the desire in African churches "to become truly African as well as truly Christian," with models for new forms of Christian worship in Africa.

Sacraments

See also SP214 and AS735.

SP240 Avila P., Rafael
Apuntes sobre las Implicaciones Socio-Políticas de la Eucaristía. Bogotá, CK: Policrom Artes Gráficas, 1977. 152 pp. No ISBN.

A critique of the Eucharist, including its history and a proposal to reform it to recover its true spiritual meaning for all people.

SP241 Avila P., Rafael
Worship and Politics. Translated by Alan Neely. Maryknoll, NYU: Orbis Books, 1981. xvii, 124 pp. Paper. 0838447142.

English translation.

SP242 Balasuriya, Tissa
The Eucharist and Human Liberation. Maryknoll, NYU: Orbis Books, 1979. xiii, 171 pp. 0883441187.

The author, one of Asia's foremost Christian theologians, challenges the reader to see the relation between the spiritual "bread of life" and the "staff of life" (food for the physically hungry).

SP243 Best, Thomas F., and Dagmar Heller
Eucharistic Worship in Ecumenical Context: The Lima Liturgy—And Beyond. Geneva, SZ: WCC Publications, 1998. 166 pp. Paper. 2825412325.

Of special interest to missiologists in this collection of papers and liturgies from a 1995 workshop held at the Ecumenical Institute, Bossey, Switzerland, are materials for eucharistic worship that lift up concerns for mission, justice, and service.

SP—SPIRITUALITY, WORSHIP, AND MISSION

SP244 Gelpi, Donald L.

Committed Worship: A Sacramental Theology for Converting Christians. (A Michael Glazier Book). Collegeville, MNU: Liturgical Press, 1993. 2 vols. Paper. 0814658253 (v. 1), 0814658261 (v. 2).

The Professor of Historical and Systematic Theology at the Jesuit School of Theology in Berkeley, California, examines the sacraments of marriage, ordination, baptism, and the eucharist, and how each contributes to ongoing Christian conversion, and the dynamics of adult Christian conversion [I, "Adult Conversion and Initiation," xvi, 278 pp.; II, "The Sacraments of Ongoing Conversion," viii, 312 pp.].

SP245 Grassi, Joseph A.

Broken Bread and Broken Bodies: The Lord's Supper and World Hunger. Maryknoll, NYU: Orbis Books, 1985. x, 116 pp. Paper. 0883441934.

Against the perennial temptation of Christians to separate worship and action, Professor Grassi shows that such attempts are a betrayal of the mission and message of Jesus, with a call to link the Eucharist and commitment to a lifestyle of service to the poor and hungry.

SP246 Kolb, Robert

Make Disciples Baptizing: God's Gift of New Life and Christian Witness. (Fascicle Series, 1). St. Louis, MOU: Concordia Seminary Publications, 1997. 105 pp. Paper. 0911770666.

A primer on the biblical teaching on baptism as a ritual of new birth, and on the incorporation of new believers into the Christian way of life.

SP247 Mathew, A. C.

Christian Baptism. Madras, II: CLS, 1992. xv, 128 pp. Paper. No ISBN.

A popular exposition for Indian Christians on who is to be baptized, modes of baptism, and the significance of baptism.

SP248 McKenna, Megan

Rites of Justice: The Sacraments and Liturgy as Ethical Imperatives. Maryknoll, NYU: Orbis Books, 1997. xii, 244 pp. Paper. 1570751080.

Combining the study of scripture and church teaching with storytelling, the author helps Catholic Christians to connect the rituals of the church, including the Rite for Christian Initiation of Adults, to the ethics of Jesus.

SP249 Nangelimalil, Jacob

The Relationship Between the Eucharistic Liturgy, the Interior Life, and the Social Witness of the Church According to Joseph Cardinal Parecattil. (Tesi Gregoriana Theology Series, 7). Rome, IT: Gregorian University Press, 1996. 222 pp. Paper. 8876526951.

A doctoral thesis (Pontifical Gregorian University, 1995) analyzing writings of Joseph Cardinal Parecattil (1912-1987) concerning the connection between the participation of Christians in the Eucharist, and their ensuing spirituality and social engagement.

SP250 Nouwen, Henri J. M.

With Burning Hearts: A Meditation on the Eucharistic Life. Maryknoll, NYU: Orbis Books, 1994. 95 pp. 0883449846 (hdbk), 1570751161 (pbk).

Meditations on the meaning of the Eucharist for ourselves and our communities in our brokenness; by the renowned Dutch priest and late pastor of the L'Arche Daybreak Community in Toronto, Canada.

SP251 Primavesi, Anne, and Jennifer Henderson

Our God Has No Favourites: A Liberation Theology of the Eucharist. Tunbridge Wells, ENK: Burns & Oates; San Jose, CAU: Resource Publications, 1989. xi, 107 pp. Paper. 0860121704 (UK), 0893901652 (US).

Examining biblical, historical and contemporary evidence, two British lay theologians (Catholic and Anglican) call for revival of a Eucharist that welcomes outsiders and motivates for mission.

SP252 Santa Ana, Julio de

Pan, Vino y Amistad. (Colección Aportes). San Jose, CR: DEI, 1985. 163 pp. Paper. 9977904189.

A scholarly reflection on the nature of the Eucharist, discussing Jesus' relationship with his disciples at the Last Supper, providing a basis for understanding the three essential elements of this sacrament (bread, wine, and friendship), that bind all communicants together in service.

SP253 Stromberg, Jean, ed.

Sharing One Bread, Sharing One Mission: The Eucharist as Missionary Event. (WCC Mission Series, 3). Geneva, SZ: WCC, 1983. viii, 79 pp. Paper. 2825407488.

Sharings by persons who believe that when properly done, the Eucharist is a missionary event, promoting unity and community and calling participants to costly witness.

SP254 Tovey, Phillip

Inculturation: The Eucharist in Africa. (Alcuin/GROW Liturgical Study, 55). Bramcote, ENK: Grove Books, 1988. 45 pp. Paper. 1851740910.

A short monograph on aspects of inculturation of worship and the Eucharist in mission and African independent churches.

Prayer

See also CR313, CR576, SO565, SO567, SO650-SO651, EV420, SP105, SP174, SP222, AF65, and AF178.

SP255 Boff, Leonardo

The Lord's Prayer: The Prayer of Integral Liberation. Maryknoll, NYU: Orbis Books; Melbourne, AT: Dove Communications, 1983. iv, 140 pp. Paper. 085924299X (US), 0859242374 (AT).

English translation.

SP256 Boff, Leonardo

O Pai-nosso: a oração da libertação integral. (Publicações CID: Espiritualidade, 2). Petrópolis, RJ, BL: Vozes, 1984. 150 pp. No ISBN.

Fourth edition of the call by the Brazilian Franciscan theologian for Christians to pray the "Our Father" in the context of oppression and the struggle for justice; originally published in 1979.

SP257 Bryant, David

With Concerts of Prayer: Christians Join for Spiritual Awakening and World Evangelism. Ventura, CAU: Regal Books, 1984. 250 pp. Paper. 0830709754.

A study guide exploring the power of concerted prayer and what it accomplishes for individuals, the church, and the world; with practical helps for mission prayer groups.

SP258 Carden, John, comp.

Another Day: Prayers of the Human Family. London, ENK: Triangle/SPCK, 1986. vii, 146 pp. Paper. 0281042519.

An ecumenical and international collection of prayers compiled by the former Asia Secretary of the CMS.

SP259 Castro, Emilio

When We Pray Together. (Risk Book Series, 40). Geneva, SZ: WCC Publications, 1989. 86 pp. Paper. 2825409537.

Some ecumenical suggestions for prayer, touching on traditions and practices, obstacles to contemporary prayer, relationships between personal and ecumenical spirituality, and the risks of intercessions that grow out of political situations; by the Methodist minister from Uruguay who was General Secretary of the WCC.

SP260 Cho, Yong-gi, and R. Whitney Manzano

Prayer: Key to Revival. Waco, TXU: Word Books, 1984. 177 pp. 0849904536.

A "how-to" book on prayer and how it is essential to genuine church growth, by the pastor of the world's largest church.

SP261 Christenson, Evelyn

A Time to Pray God's Way. Eugene, ORU: Harvest House, 1996. 254 pp. Paper. 1565073002.

Helps for pre-evangelism praying prepared for women responding to the "A.D. 2000 and Beyond" goal of reaching all the unreached in the world for Jesus in this decade; with study guide (1565075277).

SP262 Collins, Owen, ed.

2000 Years of Classic Christian Prayers: A Collection for Public and Personal Use. Maryknoll, NYU: Orbis Books, 1999. 342 pp. Paper. 1570753067.

Prayers for God's world and for the worldwide church are included.

SP263 Crosby, Michael

Thy Will Be Done: Praying the Our Father as Subversive Activity. Maryknoll, NYU: Orbis Books, 1977. viii, 254 pp. 0883444968 (hdbk), 0883444976 (pbk).

A fresh analysis of the Lord's Prayer by the Franciscan priest of an inner-city Milwaukee parish, who argues that it is prayed authentically only when we become God's conscious instruments to help fashion a society where peace and justice are the rule.

SP264 Dinh, Joseph Duc Dao

Preghiera Rinnovata per una Nuova Eva Missionaria in Asia. (Inculturation, 15). Roma, IT: Editrice Pontificia Università Gregoriana, 1994. xii, 214 pp. Paper. 8876526730.

The author, who lectures at the Urbanium University in Rome, presents the views of the Federation of Asian Bishops' Conference, William Johnston, and Yves Raguin on the importance of prayer for mission, evangelization, and inculturation of the Gospel in Asia.

SP265 Mhagama, Christian

God Bless Africa: Praying the Gospels for Africa's Wellbeing. Nairobi, KE: Paulines Publications Africa, 1996. 79 pp. Paper. 9966212841.

Litanies for African Christians to pray for God's blessings, based on central themes in each of the four Gospels.

SP266 Monloubou, Louis

Saint Paul et la prière: Prière et évangélisation. (Lectio divina, 110). Paris, FR: Éditions du Cerf, 1982. 137 pp. 2204017868.

A study of the importance of prayer in evangelization based on Paul's ministry and letters.

SP267 Nwankpa, Emeka

Redeeming the Land: Interceding for the Nations. Achimota, GH: Africa Christian Press, 1994. 130 pp. Paper. 9964877021.

A Ghanaian lawyer, and member of the Advisory Board of the International Fellowship of Intercessors, shares his concern and witness for prophetic prayer as spiritual warfare that has power to redeem the land.

SP268 Pawelzik, Fritz, comp.

I Sing Your Praise All the Day Long: Young Africans at Prayer. New York, NYU: Friendship Press, 1967. 62 pp. Paper. No ISBN.

English translation of *Ich singe dein Lob durch den Tag* (1965).

SP269 Pawelzik, Fritz, comp.

Ich singe dein Lob durch den Tag: Gebete junger Christen in Afrika. Wuppertal, GW: Aussaat Verlag, 1965. 70 pp. Paper. No ISBN.

A collection of psalm-like prayers that bring the reader into direct Christian fellowship with young Africans.

SP270 Pawelzik, Fritz, ed.

I Lie on My Mat and Pray: Prayers by Young Africans. Translated by Robbins Strong. New York, NYU: Friendship Press, 1964. vii, 63 pp. Paper. No ISBN.

English translation.

SP271 Pawelzik, Fritz, ed.

Ich liege auf meiner Matte und bete: Afrikanische Gebete. Wuppertal, GW: Aussaat Verlag, 1960. 58 pp. Paper. No ISBN.

A collection of contemporary prayers by Ghana's young Christians; illustrated by Gerg Lemke.

SP272 *Prayers Encircling the World: An International Anthology*

Louisville, KYU: Westminster John Knox, 1999. 278 pp. Paper. 0664258212.

Reflecting the ecumenical and international character of the Christian community, prayers from more than sixty countries and from all walks of life are included on topics of work and rest, war and peace, family and community, poverty and plenty, and church and mission.

SP273 Sand, Faith Annette

Prayers of Faith: On Learning to Trust God. Pasadena, CAU: Hope Publishing House, 1996. xvii, 206 pp. Paper. 0932727786.

Reminiscences by a former missionary to Brazil, of how in prayer she learned to trust God; organized around basic principles of prayer commended to all Christians.

SP274 Sanders, J. Oswald

World Prayer. Littleton, COU: OMF Books; Fort Washington, PAU: CLC, 1999. 124 pp. Paper. 9813009071 (O), 0875084915 (C).

A collection of teachings from spiritual giants, including the visionary prayer of J. Hudson Taylor, the practical prayer tools of Will Bruce, the life of abiding prayer of J. Oswald Sanders, and the prayer of faith of J. O. Fraser, encompassing the full scope of God's heart for the world.

SP—SPIRITUALITY, WORSHIP, AND MISSION

SP275 Singh, Herbert Jai

The Lord's Prayer. (Indian Christian Thought Series, 18). Delhi, II: ISPCK, 1985. 98 pp. Paper. No ISBN.

An interpretation of the Lord's Prayer in the context of contemporary Indian culture.

SP276 Wagner, C. Peter, ed.

Breaking Strongholds in Your City: How to Use Spiritual Mapping to Make Your Prayers More Strategic, Effective and Targeted. (The Prayer Warrior Series). Ventura, CAU: Regal Books, 1993. 240 pp. 0830715975.

An introduction to "spiritual mapping"—the focusing of prayer upon specific communities as a means for opening them up to the Gospel of Christ.

SP277 Wagner, C. Peter

Prayer Shield: How to Intercede for Pastors, Christian Leaders and Others on the Spiritual Frontlines. (The Prayer Warrior Series, 2). Ventura, CAU: Regal Books, 1992. 203 pp. 0830715738.

An instruction manual for pastors and laity on intercessory prayer.

Music; Hymnology

See also HI575, TH504, CR1442, SO35, SO320, SO330, SO341, EV267, AF1267, AM1264, AM1300, AS552, and OC189.

SP278 Castle, Brian C.

Hymns: The Making and Shaping of a Theology for the Whole People of God: A Comparison of the Four Last Things in Some English and Zambian Hymns in Intercultural Perspective. (Studies in the Intercultural History of Christianity, 6). Frankfurt am Main, GW: Lang, 1990. xi, 290 pp. Paper. 3631432682.

A detailed analysis of the theology of the four last things (death, judgment, heaven, and hell) as sung by Zambian Anglicans in Western and indigenous hymns.

SP279 Consociatio Internationalis Musicae Sacrae (Rome)

Musices aptatio: Liber annuarius = Jahrbuch 1982. Edited by Johannes Overath. (Musices aptatio, 1982). Rome, IT: CIMS, 1983. 172 pp. Paper. No ISBN.

Fifteen essays read at a symposium of the CIMS on the indigenization of liturgical music.

SP280 Consociatio Internationalis Musicae Sacrae; Symposium (Bonn, 1980)

Symposium Musico-Ethnologicum, Bonnae 1980. Compiled by Johannes Overath. (Musices Aptatio: Liber annuarius = Jahrbuch). Rome, IT: CIMS, 1981. 384 pp. Paper. No ISBN.

Papers in German, English, and French read at the Second Ethno-Musicological Symposium, in which African Catholic priests treated problems connected with church music in the evangelization of the Bantu peoples in East and Central Africa.

SP281 Corbitt, J. Nathan

The Sound of the Harvest: Music's Mission in Church and Culture. (A BridgePoint Book). Grand Rapids, MIU: Baker Books; Carlisle, ENK: Solway, 1998. 352 pp. Paper. 0801058295 (US), 1900507889 (UK).

From his experience working in Africa in cross-cultural communications and music, the professor of communications and music at Eastern College examines music's role in the church in mission in a multicultural world.

SP282 Gild-Bohne, Gerlinde

Das Lü Lü Zheng Yi Xubian: Ein Jesuitentraktat über die europäische Notation in China 1713. (Orbis Musicarum, 8). Göttingen, GW: Edition Re, 1991. 203 pp. Paper. 3927636290.

A dissertation investigating the "true importance of the 12 sounds" in Chinese music, and the possible influence of Western musical traditions introduced by Jesuit missionaries.

SP283 Henseler, Ewald

Katholische Kirchenmusik in Japan: Untersuchungen zu den Quellen und kommentierte Bibliographie. (Dissertationen: Theologische Reihe, 68). St. Ottilien, GW: EOS Verlag, 1994. 324 pp. Paper. 3880967687.

A dissertation tracing the historical sources of Catholic hymnody in Japan to its Western roots.

SP284 Hunt, T. W.

Music in Missions: Discipling through Music. Nashville, TNU: Broadman, 1987. 180 pp. Paper. 0805463437.

A basic text on music mission by the leading Protestant authority in the field, who serves as Professor of Church Music at Southwestern Baptist Theological Seminary.

SP285 Mbunga, Stephen B. G.

Church Law and Bantu Music: Ecclesiastical Documents and Law on Sacred Music as Applied to Bantu Music. (Neue Zeitschrift für Missionswissenschaft/Nouvelle Revue dem Missionnaire, 13). Schöneck-Beckenried, SZ: Nouvelle revue de science missionnaire, 1963. xxxi, 211 pp. No ISBN.

A thesis on canon law in the Roman Catholic Church concerning church music, and its application to the use of African music in the church, especially in Tanzania.

SP286 Pajamo, Reijo

Menkää maitten ääriin asti: suomalaisen virsikirjan lähetysvirsistä, niiden taustasta ja tekijöistä. (Suomen Lähetysseuran julkaisu). Helsinki, FI: Kirjaneliö, 1980. 95 pp. Paper. 9516005299.

A description of mission hymns in the previous hymnal of the Evangelical Lutheran Church in Finland.

SP287 Pajamo, Reijo, and Anna-Maija Raittila

Lähetä minut Herra: lähetysvirret ja lähetysajatus uudessa virsikirjassa. Helsinki, FI: Suomen Lähetysseura, 1989. 87 pp. Paper. 9516241883.

A description of mission hymns in the new hymnal of the Evangelical Lutheran Church in Finland.

SP288 *Sound the Bamboo: CCA Hymnal 1990*

Quezon City, PH: CCA, International Affairs, 1990. 442 pp. Paper. No ISBN.

The trial 1990 edition of the CCA's new hymnal, with many indigenous hymns expressing Asian spirituality.

SP289 Symposium musico-ethnologicum (Rome, 1975)

Musica indigena: Einheimische Musik und ihre mögliche Verwendung in Liturgie und Verkündigung. Edited by Johannes Overath. (Veröffentlichungen der Consociatio Internationalis Musicae Sacrae). Rome, IT: Sekretariat der CIMS, 1975. 170 pp. Paper. No ISBN.

The papers and results of the first international musico-ethnological symposium in Rome in 1975.

SP290 Temple, David G., and Arthur Morris Jones, eds.

Africa Praise: Hymns and Prayers for Schools. London, ENK: Lutterworth Press, 1969. x, 303 pp. No ISBN.

A collection including hymns from English-speaking sources, American spirituals, and African tunes and lyrics; with suggested orders for daily worship.

SP291 Weman, Henry

African Music and the Church in Africa. Translated by Eric J. Sharpe. (Studia Missionalia Upsaliensia, 3). Uppsala, SW: Svenska Institutet för Missionsforskning, 1960. 296 pp. No ISBN.

A musicologist's pioneer analysis of the structure and forms of expression of African folk music and their implications for the development of indigenous church music, based on field studies in South Africa and Southern Rhodesia (Zimbabwe).

Art; Architecture; Dance

See also TH551-TH552, CR273, SO503, CO49, SP180, AF105, AF498, AF1302, AM333, AM851, AM858, AM874, AS71, and AS1367.

SP292 Amalorpavadass, D. S.

Milieu of God-Experience: An Artistic Synthesis of Spirituality. Bangalore, II: NBCLC, 1982. 64 pp. Paper. No ISBN.

Interpretation of art and architecture at the NBCLC, Bangalore, India—a creative expression of Indian Christian theology and spirituality.

SP293 Börger, J. et al., eds.

Kunst met een missie: samenwerkingsproject Musea Missie Medemens. Maarheeze, NE: Werkgroep Musea-Missie-Medemens, 1988. 96 pp. Paper. 9090022082.

Art with a Mission resulted from a common project of the Catholic University in Nijmegen and four modernized museums (Styl, Nijmegen, Berg en Dal, Cadier en Keer), showing items formerly collected by SVD Roman Catholic missionaries.

SP294 Bohman, Barbro

Mission och GudstjSnstrum: Kyrkobyggnadsfrsgor i Svensk Mission 1870-1960. Lund, SW: Liber Forlag; Uppsala, SW: University of Uppsala; Lund, SW: CWK Gleerup, 1983. 261 pp. 9140048632.

A doctoral dissertation on architecture and theological aspects of churches built by Swedish missions, 1870-1960.

SP295 Butler, John Francis

Christian Art in India. Madras, II: CLS, 1986. xi, 187 pp. Paper. No ISBN.

A study of the contribution of Portuguese, French, and English artists to the Christian art, sculpture, and architecture of India.

SP296 Callahan, Kennon L.

Building for Effective Mission: A Complete Guide for Congregations on Bricks and Mortar Issues. San Francisco, CAU: HarperCollins, 1995. viii, 152 pp. 0060612800.

Helps for local churches desiring to clarify and prioritize their mission, and then site and build a facility consistent with that mission.

SP297 Campbell, John R.

Nonverbal Communication and Parish-Centered Programs of Evangelism: A Manual for Parish Clergy and Lay Leaders of the Episcopal Diocese of North Carolina. Washington, DCU: Alban Institute, 1990. ii, 47 pp. Paper. No ISBN.

Communication factors influencing a local church's evangelism efforts, with special reference to the influence of space (exterior and interior) and worship style.

SP298 Davies, J. G.

The Secular Use of Church Buildings. London, ENK: SCM Press; New York, NYU: Seabury Press, 1968. xiii, 305 pp. No ISBN.

A history of alternative community-centered use of church buildings from the Patristic to the Post-Reformation period, with an analysis of the problems for such usage in church buildings today.

SP299 Elavathingal, Sebastian

Inculturation and Christian Art: An Indian Perspective. Rome, IT: Urbaniana University Press, 1990. 342 pp. Paper. 8840180494.

A major treatise on the significance of art and symbolism in Christian life, with detailed application to the history and present realities of Indian Christian art.

SP300 Kubler, George, and Martin Soria

Art and Architecture in Spain and Portugal and Their American Dominions, 1500 to 1800. (Pelican History of Art, Z17). Baltimore, MDU: Penguin Books, 1969. xxviii, 445 pp. No ISBN.

A scholarly study of Hispanic, Lusitanian, and Latin American art and architecture, focusing on the wide array of influences which gave the Latin American arts their distinctiveness, including church art and architecture.

SP301 Lehmann, Arno

Afroasiatische christliche Kunst: Mit 282 Abbildungen. Berlin, GW: Evan Verlagsanstalt, 1966. 285 pp. No ISBN.

An illustrated collection of new expressions of the Christian faith in art (poetry, drama, dance, music, and architecture), with an index of captions in English, French, Russian, and Swedish.

SP302 Lehmann, Arno

Christian Art in Africa and Asia. St. Louis, MOU: Concordia Publishing, 1969. 283 pp. No ISBN.

English translation.

SP303 Linzenbach, Fritz

Kirchbau in heissen Klimata/Arquitectura religiosa en climas cßlidos/Church Construction in the Tropics: Handbuch des geistlichen Bauherrn und seines Architekten. Estella, SP: Verbo Divino, 1975. 288 pp. Paper. 8471511762.

Taking into consideration the norms of Vatican II, this book in Spanish, German, and English, including many useful drawings, suggests how church architecture can be adapted to tropical situations.

SP304 O'Grady, Ron, ed.

Christian Art in Asia. Toa Payoh, SI: CCA, 1979. 46 pp. Paper. No ISBN.

Report of a consultation held at Dhyana Pura (Bali, Indonesia, 24-30 August 1978) sponsored by the Christian Conference of Asia.

SP305 Peel, Joyce M., and Darius L. Swann

Drama for the Church: A Handbook on Religious Drama. Madras, II: CLS, 1962. vi, 121 pp. No ISBN.

The authors, both missionaries working to develop and improve Christian drama in India, give practical information on, and excerpts from, various types of dramatic production.

SP306 Sahi, Jyoti

Holy Ground: A New Approach to the Mission of the Church in India. Auckland, NZ: Pace Publishing, 1998. 200 pp. Paper. 095836320X.

The mission of Indian Christians throughout the centuries interpreted through church architecture of each period.

SP307 Sequeira, A. Ronald

Klassische indische Tanzkunst und christliche Verkündigung: Eine vergleichende religionsgeschichtlich-religionsphilosophische Studie. (Freiburger theologische Studien, 109). Freiburg, GW: Herder, 1978. 328 pp. Paper. 3451179482.

Examining the phenomenon and history of Indian classical dance, the author points out how this art form could be a valid medium for an ongoing dialogue between Christians and Hindus (Dissertation, Univ. of Munich, 1970).

SP308 Takenaka, Masao

Creation and Redemption through Japanese Art. Osaka, JA: Sogensha, 1966. 224 pp. No ISBN.

A theological interpretation of various works of Christian art in Japan, with illustrations.

SP309 Takenaka, Masao

The Place Where God Dwells: An Introduction to Church Architecture in Asia. Shatin, HK: CCA; Kyoto, JA: Asian Christian Art Association; Auckland, NZ: Pace Publishing, 1995. 111 pp. 0959797157.

The best on indigenous church architecture in Asia, with color illustrations and text by the honorary Founder-President of the Asian Christian Art Association.

SP310 Takenaka, Masao, and Ron O'Grady

The Bible through Asian Eyes. Auckland, NZ: Pace Publishing, 1991. 200 pp. 0959797106.

More than one-hundred reproductions of works of art from eighteen Asian countries, arranged by biblical theme (Old and New Testament), with complementary meditations by an Asian Christian and notes on each artist.

SP311 Takenaka, Masao, comp.

Christian Art in Asia. Tokyo, JA: Kyo Bun Kwan in association with Christian Conference of Asia, 1975. 171 pp. No ISBN.

A presentation of 120 recent works of art, with an analysis by the author, of their significance as signs of cultural and religious renewal in the churches of Asia.

SP312 Taylor, Richard W.

Jesus in Indian Paintings. (Confessing the Faith in India Series, 11). Madras, II: CLS, 1975. xiv, 184 pp. Paper. No ISBN.

An original attempt to interpret the Indian understanding of Jesus, which comes through Indian art forms as a living theology; with black-and-white illustrations.

SP313 Thiel, Josef Franz, and Heinz Helf

Christliche Kunst in Afrika. (Edited by Haus Völker und Kulturen, Steyler Missionare [St. Augustin, Germany]). Berlin, GW: Dietrich Reimer Verlag, 1984. 355 pp. 3496007451.

A geographically comprehensive study of Christian art in Africa by German ethnologists, including 603 images, a chapter on church architecture, and an extensive bibliography.

SP314 Wells, Ann E.

This Their Dreaming: Legends of the Panels of Aboriginal Art in the Yirrkala Church. St. Lucia, AT: University of Queensland Press, 1971. xiii, 76 pp. 070220692X.

Interpretations of traditional symbolism in the aboriginal art of the Yirrkala church in northeast Arnhem Land in Australia; photographed by James E. Wells.

SP315 Wray, Naomi

Frank Wesley: Exploring Faith with a Brush. Auckland, NZ: Pace Publishing, 1993. 224 pp. 0959797165.

The life and Christian art of Frank Wesley (b.1923), who expresses Indian, Japanese, and Australian influences in his more than 100 works in color interpreted in this book.

SP316 Wroth, William

Images of Penance, Images of Mercy: Southwestern Santos in the Late Nineteenth Century. Norman, OKU: University of Oklahoma Press, 1991. xvii, 196 pp. Paper. 0806123257.

The first systematic study of Hispanic religious images, or *santos*, of the late 19th century in the southwestern united States, with 147 illustrations.

SP317 Diamond, Sara

Spiritual Warfare: The Politics of the Christian Right. Boston, MAU: South End Press, 1989. ix, 292 pp. Paper. 0896083624 (hdbk), 0896083616 (pbk).

The scholarly work of an investigative reporter and doctoral student, thematically tracing the development of the Christian Right into a powerful but dangerous political force, in both the United States and the world, influencing churches and their missions.

SP318 Kraft, Marguerite G.

Understanding Spiritual Power:: A Forgotten Dimension of Cross-Cultural Mission and Ministry. (American Society of Missiology Series, 22). Maryknoll, NYU: Orbis Books, 1995. xi, 144 pp. pp. Paper. 115075036X.

The Professor of Intercultural Studies at Biola University in La Miranda, California, analyzes the dynamics of felt needs for spiritual power in various societies and how these relate to persons' worldviews; includes strategies for meaningful Christian witness in "power-oriented" societies.

SP319 Otis, George

The Twilight Labyrinth: Why Does Spiritual Darkness Linger Where It Does? Grand Rapids, MIU: Chosen Books, 1997. 414 pp. Paper. 0800792556.

The result of the author's seven-year journey in nearly fifty nations of the world, ascending sacred mountains, plumbing the depths of university libraries, paddling the holy Ganges River, venturing into crowded festivals, dark temples, and distant monasteries.

SP320 Wagner, C. Peter, ed.

Engaging the Enemy: How to Fight and Defeat Territorial Spirits. Ventura, CAU: Regal Books, 1991. xviii, 206 pp. 0830715169.

Nineteen short accounts by Christian leaders from several nations who believe that the Christian mission includes battle against Satanic forces, including territorial spirits.

SP321 Warner, Timothy M.
Spiritual Warfare: Victory over the Powers of This Dark World.
Wheaton, ILU: Crossway Books, 1991. 160 pp. Paper.
0891076077.

    Lectures on biblical teachings concerning confronting
forces of evil and their relevance for power encounter as a
necessary component in successful evangelism and church
planting.

SP322 Webster, Richard Alvis, and Flo Webster
Worship and Warfare: A Prayer Companion. South Pasadena, CAU: William Carey Library, 1990. vi, 41 pp. Paper.
0878089624.

Scripture verses to use in focused prayer—a companion to *Tearing Down Strongholds* by Richard A. Webster.

SP323 Webster, Richard Alvis
Tearing Down Strongholds. South Pasadena, CAU: William Carey Library, 1993. 366 pp. Paper. 0878082409.

    Revised edition of reflections on spiritual warfare by
Richard Alvis Webster (b.1920); originally published in
1990 with recollections from his missionary experiences in
China (1947-1950) and in building the Campus Evangelical Fellowship student movement in Taiwan during thirty
years of ministry.

SP—SPIRITUALITY, WORSHIP, AND MISSION

AFRICA

Walter Cason and Adrian Hastings, Subeditors

Africa defies generalizations. Its population of more than 824 million in 2000 spoke 1,320 languages. The boundaries of its 59 countries reflect colonial rather than ethnic boundaries (*WCE* 2:651; *World Book Encyclopedia,* 2000).

The growth of African Christianity has been one of the most surprising facts of 20th-century church history. The *WCE* numbered the continent's Christian community in 1900 at 8.7 million. By 1970 they estimated that there were 117 million professing Christians, and by 2000 there were 335 million—40 percent of the continent's population (*WCE* 1:12; *EDWM,* 37). Works on this history, continent-wide, will be found in the "History" section. You will find others by subcontinent and country.

Roman Catholics form the largest block of African Christians today (35.9% of the total). Protestants of historic denominations are 26.6 percent, Anglicans are 12.7 percent, and the Orthodox churches, 10.5 percent (primarily in Egypt and Ethiopia). The "independent" churches include 9,603 denominations in 59 countries. Many of these have no written histories. Works about the African initiated churches (AICs) are to be found in the chapter on "Missions: Social Aspects."

The chapter's subsections establish the pattern used in the five geographical chapters of this bibliography. Like preceding chapters, it begins with "Bibliography," "Periodicals," "Documentation and Archives," "History," and "General Works."

Next follows a section on "Conferences and Congresses"—works on the continent-wide meetings to discuss church renewal and mission. General works on "Church and Society" follow, including Gospel and culture, church and community, and church and state. See particular countries for more specific literature.

Biographies of both missionaries and national Christian leaders are found, generally, in the subsections on the countries in which they worked as mission leaders. Biographies of those who worked in a region (e.g. Livingstone) are to be found under the region, with the "General Biography" category retained for individuals of wider influence, or for collections of biographies.

The next subsection contains sources on African theologies—a growing literature since 1956. These are theologies that arise from the identity of African people and draw upon African categories of thought.

The growing literature on Christianity in relation to other faiths can be found in the chapter on "Christianity and Other Religions." See especially works on "Christianity and African Religions," and "Christianity and Islam."

The bulk of this chapter is geographical, with the fifty-nine countries of Africa grouped by subregions: central, eastern, North, southern, and West Africa.

Norman E. Thomas

Bibliographies

See also SO3, AF37, AF354, AF579, and AF646.

AF1 Chidester, David, Judy Tobler, and Darrel Wratten
Christianity in South Africa: An Annotated Bibliography. (Bibliographies and Indexes in Religious Studies, 43). Westport, CTU: Greenwood, 1997. ix, 489 pp. 0313304734.

An annotated bibliography of articles and books on the history and diversity of Christianity in South Africa.

AF2 Cochrane, James R., I. W. Henderson, and Gerald O. West, eds.
Bibliography in Contextual Theology in Africa: Volume 1. Pietermaritzburg, SA: Cluster Publications, 1993. 60 pp. Paper. 095831411X.

An annotated bibliography of books and journal articles on theological material from within or about the African context, including its cultural, social, political, and economic realities, 1986 to 1992.

AF3 Cowie, Margaret Jennifer, comp.
The London Missionary Society in South Africa: A Bibliography. (School of Librarianship Bibliographical Series, 44a). Cape Town, SA: University of Cape Town Libraries, 1969. vi, 81 pp. No ISBN.

A 370-entry bibliography on the LMS in South Africa, including books, reports, and periodical articles, indexed by author, missionary, and mission station, but excluding the biographies included in the 1952 bibliography by Margaret Brownlee.

AF4 Dargitz, Robert E.
A Selected Bibliography of Books and Articles in the Disciples of Christ Research Library in Mbandka, Demographic Republic of the Congo and the Department Africa and Jamaica of the UCMS. Indianapolis, INU: United Christian Mission Society, 1968. 431 pp. No ISBN.

An important bibliography on Disciples of Christ missions in Africa (especially the Congo) and the Caribbean.

AF5 Duignan, Peter, and L. H. Gann
A Bibliographical Guide to Colonialism in Sub-Saharan Africa. (Colonialism in Africa, 1870-1960, 5). Cambridge, ENK: Cambridge University Press, 1973. xii, 552 pp. 0521078598.

An international bibliography of 2,516 annotated titles grouped by subregion and country/colony.

AF6 Frost, Pamela J., comp.
A Bibliography of Missions and Missionaries in Natal. (Biographical Series, 74a). Cape Town, SA: Cape Town University, 1969. vi, 21 pp. No ISBN.

A bibliography, arranged by denomination, of books and bound pamphlet material concerned with mission activity in Natal and Zululand in the 19th and early 20th centuries.

AF7 Hofmeyr, J. W., and K. E. Cross, eds.
History of the Church in Southern Africa, Volume 1: A Select Bibliography of Published Material to 1980. Pretoria, SA: University of South Africa, 1986. xxi, 809 pp. 0869814354.

An extensive bibliography through 1980, dividing 5,735 entries by general history, denominations, missions and missionary societies, and selected topics, including materials on South Africa, Botswana, Lesotho, Swaziland, South West Africa/Nambia, and Zimbabwe.

AF8 Holter, Knut
Tropical Africa and the Old Testament: A Select and Annotated Bibliography. (Bibliography Series, 6). Oslo, NO: University of Oslo Faculty of Theology, 1996. 106 pp. Paper. 8299191378.

An annotated and well-indexed bibliography containing 232 titles, mostly journal articles, in various European languages.

AF9 Mieder, Wolfgang
African Proverb Scholarship: An Annotated Bibliography. Colorado Springs, COU: African Proverbs Project, 1994. 181 pp. Paper. No ISBN.

An annotated bibliography of 279 publications, mostly journal articles, on African proverbs, well-indexed by content, including religion.

AF10 Obdeijn, Herman L. M.
The Political Role of Catholic and Protestant Missions in the Colonial Partition of Black Africa: A Bibliographical Essay. (Intecontinenta, 3). Leiden, NE: [Leiden Centre for the History of European Expansion], 1983. 95 pp. Paper. No ISBN.

A bibliographic essay on colonialism and missions in Africa, organized by colonial powers and regions, with annotation of both archival and printed sources.

AF11 Ofori, Patrick E.
Christianity in Tropical Africa: A Selective Annotated Bibliography. Nendeln, LH: Kto Press, 1977. 461 pp. 3262000027.

A basic guide to the literature of the Christian religion in sub-Saharan Africa, bringing together 2,797 entries on 29 countries, from scattered sources (1841-1974), with a list of journals and periodicals, and an index of authors.

AF12 South African Theological Bibliography
Evanston, ILU: ATLA, 1985-1988. 0869815350.

A comprehensive database on theological literature in South Africa, including books and reviews (1956-1993), dissertations (1923-1993), and journal coverage (1923-1994); on CD-ROM with user's manual and reference guides; earlier published in book format (1983-1988) edited by C. F. A. Borchardt and W. S. Vorster.

AF13 Verbeek, Léon
Les salésiens de l'Afrique centrale: Bibliographie, 1911-1996. (Bibliographia/Instituto Storico Salesiano, 3). Rome, IT: Libreria Ateneo Salesiano, 1998. 239 pp. Paper. 8821304027.

An extensive well-indexed bibliography, mainly of periodical literature, related to the Catholic church in Central Africa and the mission work of the Salesians.

Serials and Periodicals

See also CR25.

AF14 AACC Bulletin. Vol. 1, no. 1 (October 1963)-vol. 12, no. 1 (1982). Irregular
Nairobi, KE: Information Department of the All Africa Conference of Churches, 1963-1982. No ISSN.

Information bulletin of the AACC primarily containing news of ecumenical relations in Africa, including the AACC's involvement in issues of church and society; also issued in French as the *CETA Bulletin.*

AF15 AFER: African Ecclesiastical Review. Vol. 1 (1959)-. Bimonthly
Eldoret, KE: AMECEA Gaba Publications, 1959-. ISSN 02504650.

A scholarly journal examining Scripture, religion, and development in Africa, sponsored by the Catholic pastoral institute AMECEA.

AF16 African Christian Studies. Vol. 1, no. 1 (Jan. 1985)-vol. 7, no. 4 (Dec. 1991). Semiannual (1985-86); quarterly (1987-91)
Nairobi, KE: Catholic Higher Institute of Eastern Africa, Faculty of Theology, 1985-1991. No ISSN.

Varied papers by Catholic theological educators in East Africa.

AF17 Henige, David P.
Catholic Missionary Journals Relating to Africa: A Provisional Checklist and Union List for North America. (The Archival and Bibliographic Series). [Los Angeles, CAU]: Crossroads Press; [Walthan, MAU]: African Studies Association, 1980. iii, 71 pp. Paper. No ISBN.

More than a bibliography of Africa mission journals, this is a comprehensive union list of more than 500 Catholic journals, containing articles related to Africa, including holdings in 85 locations and identification of sponsoring missionary orders.

AF18 *Journal of Theology for Southern Africa.* Vol. 1, no. 1 (Dec. 1972)-. Quarterly
Cape Town, SA: University of Cape Town, Department of Religious Studies, 1972-. ISSN 00472867.

Articles and book reviews intended to encourage theological reflection and dialogue within the southern African context.

AF19 *Pro Veritate.* Vol. 1 (1962)-vol. 16, no. 5 (Sept. 1977). Monthly
Braamfontein, Transvaal, SA: Christian Institute of Southern Africa, 1962-1977. No ISSN.

The prophetic voice of Christians opposed to apartheid, published in English and Afrikaans until banned by the South African government October 19, 1977.

AF20 *Sierra Leone Bulletin of Religion.* Vol. 1 (1959)-vol. 11 (1969). Semiannual
Freetown, SL: Fourah Bay College, 1959-1969. No ISSN.

Articles on the forms and history of religion in Sierra Leone, plus book reviews.

AF21 *The AACC Magazine.* Vol. 1, no. 1 (Mar. 1983)-vol. 3, no. 4 (Oct. 1985). Quarterly
Nairobi, KE: AACC, Communications Unit, 1983-1985. No ISSN.

Continues *AACC Bulletin* as a news magazine with text in English and French, on activities of the churches and of the AACC; continued as *The African Challenge.*

AF22 *The African Challenge.* Vol. 1, no. 1 (Jan. 1986)-vol. 3, no. 3 (Aug. 1989). Quarterly
Nairobi, KE: AACC, Communications Unit, 1986-1989. No ISSN.

Continues *AACC Magazine* with focus on the churches and social problems in Africa.

Documentation and Archives

See also AF947.

AF23 Brásio, Antonio, comp.
Monumenta Missionaries Africana: African Ocidental. Lisbon, PO: Agencia Geral do Ultramar, 1963. No ISBN.

A collection of documentary sources on the history of the Holy Ghost Fathers in Africa, published in thirteen volumes [Vol. 1: 1470-1531; vol. 2: 1532-1569; vol. 3: 1570-1599; vol. 4: 1469-1599; vol. 5: 1600-1610; vol. 6: 1611-1621. vol. 7: 1622-1630; vol. 8: 1631-1642; vol. 9: 1643-1646; vol. 10: 1647-1650; vol. 11: 1651-1655; vol. 12: 1656-1665; vol 13: 1666-1885].

AF24 Collins, Robert O., and Peter Duignan
Americans in Africa: A Preliminary Guide to American Missionary Archives and Library Manuscript Collections on Africa. (Hoover Institution Bibliographical Series, 12). Stanford, CAU: Hoover Institution on War, Revolution, and Peace, Stanford University, 1963. vii, 96 pp. Paper. No ISBN.

Descriptions of US mission societies working in Africa, their geographical fields of service, addresses, and archival holdings.

AF25 Fold, S. C. T., ed.
Cory Library for Historical Research. (Register of Documents, 28). Grahamstown, SA: Rhodes University, 1984. 122 pp. Paper. 0868101117.

A list of manuscripts [Shepherd Papers, Gold Fields Collection, Methodist Archives] in the archives of the Lovedale Press, 1823-1980—a pioneer in South Africa in the production of Christian literature in English and vernacular languages.

AF26 *Guide to the Basel Mission's Ghana Archive*
Basel, SZ: Basel Mission, 1985. 74 pp. Paper. No ISBN.

A second updated edition of a catalogue of the Ghana collection of unpublished materials related to the Basel Mission's work in Ghana, from 1828 to 1948.

AF27 Haas, Waltraud, and Paul Jenkins
Guide to the Basel Mission's Cameroon Archive. Basel, SZ: Basel Mission, 1988. xii, 159 pp. Paper. No ISBN.

A comprehensive bibliographic guide to the rich Cameroon Archive in the Mission House in Basel, Switzerland, designed to give scholars an overview of primary documents, largely in German.

AF28 Hickey, Raymond, ed.
Modern Missionary Documents and Africa. Dublin, IE: Dominican Publications, 1982. 265 pp. Paper. 090727109X.

A compilation of eleven documents by popes and Roman Catholic synods, on mission in Africa, 1919 to 1980, with a historical interpretation by the editor.

AF29 Johnson, William Percival
My African Reminiscenses, 1875-1895. Westport, CTU: Negro Universities Press, 1970. 236 pp. 0837132932.

Reprint of the 1924 reflections of African American missionary William Percival Johnson (1854-1928).

AF30 Livingstone, David
Church Missionary Society Archives Relating to Africa and Palestine, 1799-1923: Index to Records on Microfilm at the Center for Research Libraries. (Center for Research Libraries (US)). Chicago, ILU: Center for Research Libraries, 1968. 61 pp. No ISBN.

An important index to Anglican archives.

AF31 Livingstone, David
The Last Journals: David Livingstone, in Central Africa, from 1865 to His Death.... 2 vols. Edited by Horace Waller. Westport, CTU: Greenwood, 1970. 541 pp. 0403003598.

A facsimile reprint of the 1874 edition of Livingstone's last journal (1866-1873) with a narrative of his last moments and sufferings by Horace Waller

AF32 Livingstone, David
Letters and Documents 1841-1872: The Zambian Collection at the Livingstone Museum Containing a Wealth of Restored, Previously Unknown or Unpublished Texts. Edited by Timothy Holmes. Lusaka, ZA: Multimedia Zambia; Bloomington, INU: Indiana University Press; London, ENK: James Currey, 1990. xx, 202 pp. 0253335167 (US), 0852550413 (UK).

One-hundred-and-forty letters, fragments, and other pieces by the pioneer missionary explorer, arranged chronologically.

AF33 Livingstone, David
Livingstone's African Journal, 1853-1856. Edited by Isaac Schapera. Berkeley, CAU: University of California Press, 1963. 2 vols. No ISBN.

A scholarly edition by the professor of anthropology at the London School of Economics, who has also edited other parts of Livingstone's journals and correspondence [vol. 1: xxiv, 235 pp.; vol. 2: viii, 258 pp.].

AF34 Livingstone, David
Livingstone's Missionary Correspondence, 1841-1856. Edited by Isaac Schapera. London, ENK: Chatto & Windus, 1961. xxvi, 342 pp. No ISBN.

The critical edition of letters, with notes, written by the famous explorer missionary to the Directors of the London Missionary Society; from his early expeditions to the Bakgatta, Bakwena, Ngamiland, and the Makololo, to his epoch cross-continent exploration of 1853-56.

AF35 Livingstone, David
Livingstone's Private Diaries, 1851-1853. Edited by Isaac Schapera. London, ENK: Chatto and Windus, 1960. xxxvi, 341 pp. No ISBN.

The recently recovered notebooks covering Livingstone's journeys to the Makololo, the Cape, and Barotseland, with a scholarly introduction.

AF36 Livingstone, David
Some Letters from Livingstone, 1840-1872. Edited by David Chamberlin. New York, NYU: Negro Universities Press, 1969. xxvii, 280 pp. No ISBN.

A reprint of letters dated 1840 to 1872, from the first half of Livingstone's African career, which gives glimpses of his burning faith and heroic adventures, as he explored the heart of unknown Africa.

AF37 Nussbaum, Stan, ed.
African Proverbs: Collections, Studies, Bibliographies. (20: 21 Library, CD 3). Colorado Springs, COU: Global Mapping International, 1996. No ISBN.

A CD, version 1.0 for Windows, containing over 27,000 African proverbs, maps, annotated bibliography, and language and biographical directories, with user's guide.

AF38 Rego, António da Silva
Atlas Missionário Português. Lisbon, PO: Junta de Investigaçõcs do Ultramar, 1964. 198 pp. No ISBN.

An atlas of Portuguese missions from the 15th century to the present.

AF39 Schweitzer, Albert
Leben, Werk und Denken 1905-1965: Mitgeteilt in seinen Briefen. Edited by Hans Walter Bahr. Heidelberg, GW: Schneider, 1987. 454 pp. 3795306701.

A selection of the letters of Albert Schweitzer (1875-1965), noted medical missionary to Gabon in Africa, theologian, and musicologist; chosen to demonstrate his goals and lifework amid the social, intellectual, and spiritual problems of his time.

AF40 Schweitzer, Albert
Letters: 1905-1965. Edited by Hans Walter Bahr. Translated by Joachim Neugroschel. New York, NYU: Macmillan: Maxwell Macmillan International; Toronto, ONC: Maxwell Macmillan Canada, 1992. xxiii, 420 pp. 0026071711.

English translation.

AF41 Shorter, Aylward, ed.
African Christian Spirituality. Maryknoll, NYU: Orbis Books, 1980. xii, 160 pp. Paper. 0883440113.

A collection of twenty-six spiritual writings by a cross section of Africans, nearly all of them professing Christians, with an interpretive introduction by the editor, placing them in the context of contemporary African values.

History

See also HI65, HI153, HI158, HI298-HI299, HI448, EA92, CR1007, SO321, CO115-CO116, MI19, SP212, AF105, and AF231.

AF42 Adamo, David Tuesday
Africa and the Africans in the Old Testament. San Francisco, CAU: Christian Universities Press, 1998. viii, 208 pp. 1573092053 (hdbk), 1573092045 (pbk).

An examination of the role and contributions of Africa and Africans in the Old Testament and its environment.

AF43 Baur, John
2.000 Años de Cristianismo en Africa. Translated by P. Gabino Otero. Madrid, SP: Editorial Mundo Negro, 1996. 526 pp. Paper. 8472951421.

Spanish translation.

AF44 Baur, John
2000 Years of Christianity in Africa: An African History 62-1992. Nairobi, KE: Paulines Publications Africa, 1994. 560 pp. Paper. 9966211101.

The first complete African church history, from a Roman Catholic perspective, with a contemporary survey of Catholicism in each of the continent's fifty-five countries.

AF45 Blyden, Edward W.
Christianity, Islam and the Negro Race. Edinburgh, STK: Edinburgh University Press, 1967. xxvii, 407 pp. No ISBN.

A reprint of a 1887 classic collection of speeches, articles, and reviews by the black West Indian educator and diplomat whose distinguished career included government service in Liberia, Sierra Leone, and Nigeria.

AF46 Breman, Christina Maria
The Association of Evangelicals in Africa: Its History, Organization, Members, Projects, External Relations, and Message. (Missiological Research in the Netherlands Series, 13). Zoetermeer, NE: Boekencentrum, 1996. xxii, 601 pp. Paper. 9023903366.

A carefully documented history of the AEAM from its founding in 1966 to its present state as a major movement.

AF47 Falk, Peter
The Growth of the Church in Africa. (Contemporary Evangelical Perspectives). Grand Rapids, MIU: Zondervan, 1979. 554 pp. Paper. 0310375851.

A brief, non-technical history of African Christianity, organized by regions and written as a textbook for English-speaking Africa, to give an understanding of the Christword movement there; with extensive bibliography, indices, and study questions.

AF48 Gray, Richard
Black Christians and White Missionaries. New Haven, CTU: Yale University Press, 1990. viii, 134 pp. 0300049102.

A collection of essays by the distinguished former professor of the history of Africa at the University of London, focusing on new research on 17th-century missions, and summaries of research on Christianity and colonial rule in Africa.

AF—AFRICA

AF49 Hastings, Adrian

The Church in Africa, 1450-1950. (Oxford History of the Christian Church). Oxford, ENK: Clarendon Press, 1994. xiv, 706 pp. 0198269218.

A scholarly history of the development of African-led churches over 500 years, with concentration on Ethiopia, the Kingdom of the Kongo, West Africa, and South Africa.

AF50 Hastings, Adrian

A History of African Christianity, 1950-1975. (African Studies Series, 26). Cambridge, ENK: Cambridge University Press, 1979. xi, 336 pp. 0521222125 (hdbk), 0521293979 (pbk).

A scholarly survey of the development of African Christianity—Protestant, Catholic, and Independent—with special reference to parallel political developments and church-state relations.

AF51 Hildebrandt, Jonathan

History of the Church in Africa. Achimota, GH: Africa Christian Press, 1981. xi, 269 pp. Paper. 0853523207.

An introduction to the history of the church in Africa, written for secondary school students and focusing on the missionary introduction of Christianity in each country and subregion.

AF52 Isichei, Elizabeth

A History of Christianity in Africa: From Antiquity to the Present. Grand Rapids, MIU: Eerdmans; Lawrenceville, NJU: Africa World Press, 1995. xi, 420 pp. 0802808433(US,pbk), 0865434425(UK,hdbk), 0865434433(UK, pbk).

An introductory survey of the whole sweep of African Christian history from the early church to the present, focusing on expressions of indigenous African Christianity and church-state relations.

AF53 Kalu, Ogbu U., ed.

African Church Historiography: An Ecumenical Perspective. (Veröffentlichung, 4). Schweiz, GW: Evangelische Arbeitsstelle Ökumene Schweiz, 1988. 223 pp. Paper. No ISBN.

Twelve scholarly essays in English (10) and French (2; originally presented at a workshop on African Church History (Nairobi, 3-8 August 1986), designed to encourage the writing of church history by African historians from an ecumenical perspective.

AF54 MacDonald, Duff

Africana: Or the Heart of Heathen Africa. (The Colonial History Series). London, ENK: Dawsons of Pall Mall; New York, NYU: Negro Universities Press, 1969. 2 vols. 071290347X (UK, v. 1), 0712903488 (UK, v. 2), 083711523X (US).

A reprint of the 1882 edition, with a new introduction by George Shepperson; an early work on African ethnology (vol. 1: *Native Customs and Beliefs*) and the history of early missions (vol. 2: *Mission Life*).

AF55 Matheson, Elizabeth M.

African Apostles. Staten, NYU: Alba House, 1963. 224 pp. No ISBN.

The popular story of the White Fathers' work, as well as the work of others associated with them in Africa, focusing on the 1878 to 1899 period.

AF56 Moorhouse, Geoffrey

The Missionaries. New York, NYU: Lippincott; London, ENK: Eyre Methuen, 1973. 368 pp. 0397008015.

A scholarly assessment of missionary work in Africa during the 19th century, focusing on the achievements of the pioneers, both Catholic and Protestant.

AF57 Shaw, Mark

The Kingdom of God in Africa: A Short History of African Christianity. (A BGC Monograph). Grand Rapids, MIU: Baker Books; Wheaton, ILU: BGC, 1996. 328 pp. Paper. 0801020964 (BB), 1879089203 (BG).

An overview of the twenty-century history of Christianity on the African continent, based on the thesis that African Christianity has blended the sovereign rule of God, the redemptive reign of Christ, and the social emphasis of the Kingdom of justice; designed as a textbook for college and seminary use.

AF58 Simensen, Jarle, and Finn Fuglestad, eds.

Norwegian Missions in African History. Oslo, NO: Universitetsforlaget; London, ENK: Oxford University Press, 1986. 2 vols. 8200074188 (vol. 1), 8200074153 (vol. 2).

English translation of *Norsk misjon og afrikanske samfunn* (1984) including vol. 1: *South Africa, 1845-1906* (280 pp.); and vol. 2: *Madagascar* (155 pp.), a detailed study of Norwegian missionary interaction with the Malagasy people, from their arrival in 1866 to 1907; based on archival research in Africa and Europe—a Norwegian Missions in African History project at the University of Trondheim.

AF59 Sindima, Harvey J.

Drums of Redemption: An Introduction to African Christianity. (Contributions to the Study of Religion, 35). Westport, CTU: Greenwood, 1994. xiv, 211 pp. 0313290881.

Lectures on African church history and theology by the Assistant Professor of Philosophy and Religion at Colgate University.

AF60 Swart, Morrell F.

The Call of Africa: The Reformed Church in American Mission in the Sub-Sahara, 1948-1998. (The Historical Series of the Reformed Church in America, 29). Grand Rapids, MIU: Eerdmans, 1998. xvi, 536 pp. Paper. 0802846157.

The story of the RCA's first fifty years of mission in East Africa, from the Sudan south to Zambia.

General Works

See also TH351, SO74, SO286, SO298, SO312, SO358, SO640, EC157, CO52, CO54, CO98, CO130, CO137, ED102, ED121, MI18, CH449, CH464, CH473, CH496, SP22, SP68, SP226, SP239, SP265, SP280, SP313, AF134, and AF169.

AF61 Bühlmann, Walbert

Afrika. (Die Kirche unter den Völkern, 1). Mainz, GW: Grünewald, 1963. 339 pp. No ISBN.

A popular survey of pre-Christian, Christian, and anti-Christian Africa and the position of the Catholic Church on that continent.

AF62 Bühlmann, Walbert

The Missions on Trial-Addis Ababa, 1980: A Moral for the Future from the Archives of Today. Translated by A. P. Dolan, and B. P. Krokosz. (Archives of Today). Maryknoll, NYU: Orbis Books, 1979. 159 pp. 0883443163.

English translation.

AF63 Bühlmann, Walbert

Missionsprozess in Addis Abeba: Ein Bericht von morgen aus den Archiven von heute. Frankfurt am Main, GW: Knecht, 1977. 159 pp. 3782003896.

In the form of a fictitious trial, the author presents the more recent criticisms against mission work in Africa, and the defense of the missionary position by representatives of missionary societies, African scientists, and retired politicians.

AF64 Balling, Adalbert Ludwig

Wo Menschen lachen und sich freuen: Begegnungen in der Dritten Welt. (Herderbücherei, 1297). Freiburg im Breisgau, GW: Herder, 1986. 126 pp. Paper. 3451082977.

Reflections by a former German missionary to Rhodesia/Zimbabwe (1959-1965) on Christian life in Kenya, Tasmania, Zaire, Malawi, Zimbabwe, and Brazil.

AF65 Best, Kenneth Y., ed.

African Challenge. Nairobi, KE: Transafrica Pubs., 1975. viii, 183 pp. Paper. No ISBN.

Fifteen short essays by leading African Christians regarding the issues and challenges facing Christianity in Africa.

AF66 Bischofberger, Otto, and Fritz Kollbrunner, eds.

Mit afrikanischen Christen beten: Neue Gebetserfahrungen. Luzern, SZ: Rex-Verlag, 1978. 112 pp. 3725203229.

A collection of forty African prayers, mostly recorded in African independent churches, with commentary on the context of each prayer and the way they illustrate African spirituality.

AF67 Burki, Bruno

L' assemblée dominicale: introduction à la liturgie des églises protestantes d'Afrique. (Nouvelle revue de science missionnaire: Supplementa, 25). Immensee, SZ: Nouvelle revue de science missionaire, 1976. 200 pp. No ISBN.

Lectures on practical theology for Africa, focusing on liturgics; originally presented to Protestant seminarians in the Cameroun.

AF68 Dammann, Ernst

Das Christentum in Afrika. (Siebenstern-Taschenbuch, 116). Munich, GW: Siebenstern-Taschenbuch-Verlag, 1968. 190 pp. Paper. No ISBN.

This popular work provides an historical overview of the Christianization of Africa, simultaneously presenting the problems churches and Christians have to face today, such as those of language, local theology, and individual conversions in tightly knit tribal societies.

AF69 Dehoney, Wayne

African Diary. Nashville, TNU: Broadman, 1968. 157 pp. No ISBN.

A survey of Southern Baptist missions in Africa.

AF70 Eboussi Boulaga, F.

Christianisme sans fétiche: révélation et domination essai. (Situations et Perspectives). Paris, FR: Éditions Présence Africaine, 1981. 219 pp. 2708703935.

A penetrating analysis of the inculturation of Christianity in Africa, contrasting the missionary discourse with the constructive African alternative, by the Camerounian Professor of Philosophy at the National University of the Ivory Coast.

AF71 Eboussi Boulaga, F.

Christianity Without Fetishes: An African Critique and Recapture of Christianity. Translated by Robert R. Barr. Maryknoll, NYU: Orbis Books, 1984. xi, 238 pp. Paper. 0883444321.

English translation.

AF72 Ela, Jean-Marc, René Luneau, and Christiane Ngendakuriyo

Voici le temps des héritiers: églises d'Afrique et voies nouvelles. (Collection Chrétiens en liberté). Paris, FR: Karthala, [1981]. 269 pp. 2865370208.

Three West Africa Catholic theologians call upon the church both to affirm its heritage and to journey on new highways.

AF73 Fashole-Luke, Edward W. et al., eds.

Christianity in Independent Africa. Bloomington, INU: Indiana University Press, 1978. ix, 630 pp. 0253375061.

Forty-two scholarly papers analyzing religious and secular structures in independent African countries, and continuities and conflicts between traditional religion and Christianity; originally presented at a conference in Jos, Nigeria (September 1975).

AF74 Fuller, W. Harold

Run While the Sun Is Hot. New York, NYU: Sudan Interior Mission, 1966. 256 pp. No ISBN.

A popular account of the author's travels across Africa from Liberia to the Somali Republic, focusing upon the work of the Sudan Interior Mission and arguing that missions should work quickly while there is still time.

AF75 Fyfe, Christopher, and Andrew F. Walls, eds.

Christianity in Africa in the 1990s. Edinburgh, STK: University of Edinburgh Center of African Studies, 1996. iii, 160 pp. Paper. No ISBN.

Papers by twelve prominent historians and missiologists; originally presented at the University of Edinburgh in May 1992, at a conference jointly sponsored by its Center of African Studies and the Center for the Study of Christianity in the Non-Western World.

AF76 Geffré, Claude, and Bertrand Luneau, eds.

The Churches of Africa: Future Prospects. (*Concilium*: Religion in the Seventies). New York, NYU: Seabury Press, 1977. ix, 120 pp. Paper. 0816403643 (hdbk), 0816421501 (pbk).

Twelve articles by African theologians, educators, and journalists (mostly Roman Catholics), discussing the future of the black African church from various viewpoints.

AF77 Glélé, Maurice Ahanhanzo

Religion, culture et politique en Afrique noire. Paris, FR: Economica/Présence africaine, 1981. 206 pp. 2717802916 (E), 2708703854 (P).

An academic look at the impact and interactions of imported religion (Islam and Christianity) on the sociopolitical evolution of Africa, the place of traditional religion in this evolution, and the role these religions play vis-a-vis African political states.

AF78 Glasswell, Mark E., and Edward W. Fashole-Luke, eds.

New Testament Christianity for Africa and the World: Essays in Honour of Harry Sawyerr. London, ENK: SPCK, 1974. xxii, 221 pp. 0281027838.

Eighteen scholarly essays honoring the distinguished Sierra Leone theologian and educator on his 65th birthday, and his completion of forty years of service at Fourah Bay College; including two essays on missions, and seven on Christianity and African culture.

AF—AFRICA

AF79 Gutmann, Bruno

Afrikaner—Europäer in nächstenschaftlicher Entsprechung: Gesammelte Aufsätze anlässlich des 90. Edited by Ernst Jaeschke. Stuttgart, GW: Evan Verlagswerk, 1966. 234 pp. No ISBN.

A selection of essays by the ethnologist and Protestant missionary to Africa, Bruno Gutmann, under the three broad headings: social organization of the Bantu peoples, people as creatures and children of God, and structured community building, together with a bio-bibliography.

AF80 Hastings, Adrian

African Catholicism: Essays in Discovery. London, ENK: SCM Press; Philadelphia, PAU: Trinity Press International, 1989. xiv, 208 pp. Paper. 033400019X.

Twelve essays by the noted church historian, showing aspects of a church, working out its future in isolation, poverty, and faith on that continent.

AF81 Hastings, Adrian

African Christianity. New York, NYU: Seabury Press, 1976. vi, 105 pp. 0816403368.

A response, by a noted Roman Catholic historian and missiologist, to issues in contemporary African Christianity raised at two years of seminars in London and Jos, Nigeria, sponsored by the Christianity in Independent Africa project.

AF82 Hastings, Adrian

Church and Missions in Modern Africa. London, ENK: Burn & Oates; New York, NYU: Fordham University, 1967. 263 pp. No ISBN.

A personal assessment of the work of the Roman Catholic Church in Africa today.

AF83 Hastings, Adrian

Das schwarze Experiment: Kirche und Mission im modernen Afrika. Graz, AU: Styria, 1969. 348 pp. No ISBN.

German translation.

AF84 Hearne, Brian

Christian Unity in Africa: Some Underlying Issues. (Spearhead, 73). Eldoret, KE: Gaba Publications, 1982. 78 pp. Paper. No ISBN.

A reflective essay by a Catholic missiologist on the paradox facing African Christians who stress values of community, harmony, and neighborliness but respond slowly or resist calls for unity among divided Christians.

AF85 Hebga, Meinrad Pierre et al., eds.

Personnalité africaine et Catholicisme. Paris, FR: Présence Africaine, 1963. 293 pp. No ISBN.

A re-examination of the position of the Roman Catholic Church in Africa, along the same lines as *Des Prêtres noirs s'interrogent*, published in 1956 by the same publishers.

AF86 Hickey, Raymond

A Case for an Auxiliary Priesthood. Maryknoll, NYU: Orbis Books, 1982. 143 pp. Paper. 0883440210.

A Roman Catholic missionary in Nigeria proposes an auxiliary married priesthood, to help meet the need of ministering to the ever-growing number of Christians in Africa without minimizing the role of the existing celibate priesthood.

AF87 Köster, Fritz

Afrikanisches Christsein: Eine religionspädagogische Herausforderung; (Möglichkeiten der Integration afrikanischer Religiosität in den christlichen Glauben). (Studien zur Praktischen Theologie, 12). Zürich, SZ: Benziger, 1977. 412 pp. Paper. 3545215121.

A dissertation describing the spiritual and religious world of Africa and the theological and pedagogical principles for a reorientation in missionary catechesis.

AF88 Kanyoro, Musimbi R. A., Modupe Oduyoye, Andre Karamaga, et al.

Claiming the Promise: African Churches Speak. New York, NYU: Friendship Press, 1994. viii, 120 pp. Paper. 0377002674.

In this mission study text, fifteen African church leaders offer personal reflections, historical vignettes, and reports from major gatherings, to open windows on a continent full of determination and hope; with *Study Guide* by L. Cecile Adams [42 pp., 0377002682].

AF89 Kato, Byang H.

Biblical Christianity in Africa: A Collection of Papers and Addresses. (Theological Perspectives in Africa, 2). Achimota, GH: Africa Christian Press, 1985. vii, 54 pp. Paper. 9964877935.

A collection of papers given 1973-1975 by Byang H. Kato, African theologian and late general secretary of the Association of Evangelicals of Africa and Madagascar (AEAM), published to continue his vision for authenticity in African ecclesiology.

AF90 Kendall, Elliott

The End of an Era: Africa and the Missionary. London, ENK: SPCK, 1978. vii, 197 pp. Paper. 028102989X.

A scholarly analysis of two-hundred years of missionary involvement in Africa, calling for reassessment and redirection, and allowing the African churches to develop their own missionary nature and responsibility.

AF91 Luneau, René

Laissé aller mon peuple!: églises africaines au-delà des modèles? Paris, FR: Karthala, 1987. 193 pp. 2865371735.

A call for the Catholic Church in Africa to explore creative new models; with reflections on its recent history of indigenization.

AF92 Müller, Reinhart, ed.

Der Auftrag geht weiter: Beiträge zur Integration der Hermannsburger Mission in die lutherischen Kirchen im Südlichen Afrika und in Äthiopien; Festgabe für Hans Robert Wesenick. (Verkündigung und Verantwortung, 4). Hermannsburg, GW: Verlag Missionshandlung Hermannsburg, 1979. 223 pp. Paper. 3875460200.

A *festschrift* for the former Director of the Mission Institute of Hermannsburg; with essays dealing with the integration of the Hermannsburg Mission into the Lutheran churches in South Africa and Ethiopia.

AF93 Mroso, Agapit J.

The Church in Africa and the New Evangelisation: A Theologico-Pastoral Study of the Orientations of John Paul II. Rome, IT: Gregorian University Press, 1995. 456 pp. Paper. 8876526935.

A dissertation (Gregorian University, 1995) analyzing the theological and missiological thought of Pope John Paul II, its relevance to the Church in Africa, and its task of evangelization in the next century.

AF—AFRICA

AF94 Mugambi, J. N. Kanyua, and Laurenti Magesa
The Church in African Christianity: Innovative Essays in Ecclesiology. (AACC-African Challenge Series, 1). Nairobi, KE: Initiatives Publishers, 1990. vii, 205 pp. Paper. 9966420185.

Nine scholarly essays on various models of African ecclesiology, including that of African independent churches, as adaptations to particular cultural patterns of community life.

AF95 Mullin, Joseph
The Catholic Church in Modern Africa: A Pastoral Theology. New York, NYU: Herder Book Center, 1965. ix, 256 pp. No ISBN.

A basic pastoral theology for Roman Catholic priests in Africa developed by the author for use in Tanzania.

AF96 Muzorewa, Gwinyai H.
An African Theology of Mission. (Studies in History of Missions, 5). Lewiston, NYU: Edwin Mellen Press, 1990. xvi, 204 pp. 0889460736 (hdbk), 088946068X (pbk).

An African definition and critique of mission theologies and perspectives on evangelism by a Zimbabwe theologian.

AF97 Neckebrouck, Valeer
L' Afrique noire et la crise religieuse de l'Occident. Tabora, TZ: T.M.P. Book Department, 1970. 269 pp. No ISBN.

A Belgian Catholic missionary's analysis of the encounter between African religiosity and Western atheism.

AF98 Oehrig, Robert J., Rhena Taylor, and Diane Omondi, eds.
Crossing Cultures for Christ: The African Missionary Seminar, September 15-25th 1987, Nairobi, KE. Nairobi, KE: Daystar University College, 1987. 110 pp. Paper. No ISBN.

Report of a seminar in which twenty-eight Kenya church leaders considered missionary initiatives by Africa's churches.

AF99 Okure, Teresa et al.
32 Articles Evaluating Inculturation of Christianity in Africa. (Spearhead, 112-114). Eldoret, KE: AMECEA Gaba Publications, 1990. xii, 259 pp. Paper. 9966836039.

A sourcebook of thirty-two articles and documents on Vatican positions on acculturation, its biblical/theological bases, and applications in worship, music, dance, prayer, and Christian art.

AF100 Pierli, Francesco et al.
Missionary Ministry and Missiology in Africa Today. (Tangaza Occasional Papers, 1). Nairobi, KE: Paulines Publications Africa, 1994. 74 pp. Paper. 9966211322.

Five essays on various aspects of mission in Africa today (theological formation, relationship between expatriate and local pastoral agents, ecumenism and fundamentalism, mission ministry, and the churches and democratization); originally presented at a seminar opening the department of mission studies at Tangaza College in Nairobi, Kenya, in 1994.

AF101 Porro Cardeñoso, Julio
Cristo en el Continente Negro. Bilbao, SP: Ediciones Paulinas, 1964. 245 pp. No ISBN.

A primer on Catholic missions in Africa.

AF102 Ruggieri, Giuseppe, ed.
Église et histoire de l'Église en Afrique. (Bibliothèque Beauchesne : Religions, société, politique, 339-2279, 18). Paris, FR: Beauchesne, 1988. xxv, 393 pp. Paper. 2701012058.

Seventeen scholarly essays by historians and theologians interpreting various themes in African church history (missionary ideology and practice, rapport with Islam, Africanization, and problems of historical method); originally presented at the colloquy of Bologne, 22-25 October 1988.

AF103 Salvoldi, Valentino, and Renato Kizito Sesana
Africa: The Gospel Belongs to Us. Ndola, ZA: Mission Press, 1986. 187 pp. Paper. No ISBN.

An assessment by two Italian missionaries, of the state of the Roman Catholic Church in Africa, with a call for reconciliation and unity in diversity through an African council.

AF104 Sundermeier, Theo
Aus einer Quelle schöpfen wir: Von Afrikanern lernen. (Gütersloher Taschenbücher Siebenstern, 794). Gütersloh, GW: Gerd Mohn, 1992. 188 pp. Paper. 3579007947.

The author, Professor of the History of Religions and Missiology, presents here the fruit of ten years experience in Africa, in terms of how such basic human experiences as sorrow, joy, and suffering are dealt with in African religions, communities, and theologies.

AF105 Taryor, Nya Kwiawon
Impact of the African Tradition on African Christianity. Chicago, ILU: Strugglers' Community Press, 1984. xi, 309 pp. 0913491047 (hdbk), 0913491039 (pbk).

An examination of the impact of African traditions and contemporary political and social changes on African Christianity, including independent church movements, by a Liberian theological educator.

AF106 Thiel, Josef Franz
Christliches Afrika: Kunst und Kunsthandwerk in Schwarzafrika. St. Augustin, GW: Haus Völker und Kulturen, 1978. 96 pp. Paper. No ISBN.

A description of the objects displayed at an exhibition of African Christian art, together with contributions from various authors on the problems of Christian art in Africa.

AF107 Thielicke, Helmut
African Diary: My Search for Understanding. Waco, TXU: Word Books, 1974. 213 pp. No ISBN.

The renowned evangelical preacher and theologian lets readers share in the warmth and humor of his record of encounter with many Africans in South Africa, Mozambique, Tanzania, and Kenya, sharing their feelings and concerns.

AF108 Uka, Emele
Missionaries Go Home?: A Sociological Interpretation of an African Response to Christian Missions: A Study in Sociology of Knowledge. Berne, SZ: Lang, 1989. 313 pp. Paper. 3261038748.

A reworked doctoral dissertation (Drew University, US) tracing the socio-historical context of missionary-African encounters, which led to African dissatisfaction with the missionary impact, and the call in the 1970s for a moratorium on the further sending of missionaries to Africa.

AF109 Verstraelen-Gilhuis, Gerdien
A New Look at Christianity in Africa: Essays on Apartheid, African Education and a New History. (Occasional Papers, Missio-Pastoral Series, 22). Gweru, RH: Mambo Press, 1992. ix, 109 pp. Paper. 0869225189.

Essays on black theology and apartheid, missions and African education, Third World perspectives on mission history, and rewriting the history of Christianity in Africa.

AF—AFRICA

Conferences and Congresses

See also ED6-ED7, ED101, ED126, SP10, AF135, AF181, AF270, AF291-AF292, and AF1072.

AF110 AACC (1st Assembly, Kampala, Uganda, 20-30 April 1963)
Drumbeats from Kampala: Report.... London, ENK: USCL/ Lutterworth Press, 1963. 77 pp. No ISBN.

The report of the first AACC assembly under the theme, "Freedom and Unity in Christ."

AF111 Alberigo, Giuseppe, and A. Ngindu Mushete
Towards the African Synod. (*Concilium*, 1992/1). London, ENK: SCM Press, 1991. xiv, 160 pp. Paper. 0334030129.

Sixteen short essays on the political, social, and religious realities facing Catholicism as it prepared for the Africa Synod (Rome, 1993).

AF112 Blakely, Thomas D., Walter E. A. van Beek, and Dennis L. Thomson, eds.
Religion in Africa: Experience and Expression. (Monograph Series of the David M. Kennedy Center for International Studies at Brigham Young University, 4). London, ENK: Currey; Portsmouth, NHU: Heinemann, 1994. xvi, 512 pp. 0852552068 (J hdbk), 0852552076 (J pbk), 0435080814 (H hdbk), 0435080830 (H pbk).

Twenty scholarly essays on the dynamic expressions of religion in Africa (traditional, Christian, and Muslim); originally presented at a conference entitled "Religion in Africa: The Variety of Religious Experience in Sub-Saharan Africa" (Brigham Young University, Provo, Utah, 22-25 October 1986).

AF113 Cheza, Maurice, ed.
Le Synode africain: histoire et textes. (Collection Chrétiens en liberté, Questions disputées). Paris, FR: Éditions Karthala, 1996. 428 pp. Paper. 2865376486.

A collection of contributions out of Africa to the Vatican's "African Synod" (Catholic Church, Synodus Episcoporum, Special Assembly, Rome, 1994), and reflections on its significance by African church leaders.

AF114 Conus, Georges
L' Église d'Afrique au Concile Vatican II. (Cahiers de la Nouvelle revue de science missionnaire, 26). Immensee, SZ: Nouvelle revue de science missionnaire, 1975. 57 pp. No ISBN.

A meticulous study of African participation in the second Vatican Council.

AF115 Edinburgh University Centre for African Studies
Religion in Africa: Proceedings of a Seminar Held in the Centre of African Studies, University of Edinburgh, 10th-12th April, 1964. Edinburgh, STK: Edinburgh University Press, 1964. 130 pp. No ISBN.

A collection of eleven papers presented at the second annual seminar of the centre, by leading British scholars.

AF116 International African Seminar, 7th, University of Ghana, 1965
Christianity in Tropical Africa: Studies Presented and Discussed at the Seventh International African Seminar, University of Ghana, April 1965. Edited by C. G. Baeta. London, ENK: Oxford University Press for the International African Institute, 1968. xiii, 449 pp. No ISBN.

A collection of eighteen scholarly essays on early Catholic and Protestant missions, the engagement of Christianity with African concepts and ways of life, and trends and prospects in African Christianity.

AF117 Jesuit Conference on Africa and Madagascar (Kinshasa, Zaire, 5-8 October 1976)
Jesuit Response to the Challenge of Mission in Africa and Madagascar Today. Washington, DCU: Jesuit Missions, 1976. iv, 219 pp. No ISBN.

A major conference for Jesuits, planning for more effective promotion of mission in Africa.

AF118 John Paul II, Pope
The Church in Africa: Ecclesia in Africa and Its Evangelizing Mission towards the Year 2000. (Post-Synodal Apostolic Exhortation). Washington, DCU: USCC, 1994. 144 pp. Paper. 1574550594.

Pope John Paul II's apostolic exhortation, given in 1994 to the synod of African bishops.

AF119 Karamaga, André, comp.
Problems and Promises of Africa towards and beyond the Year 2000 in Mombasa in November, 1991: A Summary of the Proceedings of the Symposium Convened by the AACC. Nairobi, KE: AACC, 1991. 89 pp. Paper. 9966987983.

A summary of documents of a symposium convened by the AACC, in Mombasa, Kenya, in November 1991.

AF120 *Kultuurverskeidenheid in Afrika/Cultural Diversity in Africa: Verleentheid of geleentheid?/Embarrassment or Opportunity?*
Potchefstroom, SA: Potchefstroom University, 1991. ii, 261 pp. Paper. 1868220540.

A collection of papers (mainly in English, some in Afrikaans) delivered at a conference on "Cultural Diversity in Africa: Embarrassment or Opportunity?" held 12-14 May 1989 at Potchefstroom University in South Africa.

AF121 Makobane, Mohlomi, Bongani Sithole, and Matheadira Shiya, eds.
The Church and African Culture: Conference Papers. Germiston-Johannesburg, SA: Lukmo Institute, 1995. 185 pp. No ISBN.

Papers from a conference on inculturation (Germiston-Johannesburg, South Africa, 21-22 February 1995) attended by 140 laypeople, religious, and clergy, from different parts of southern Africa.

AF122 McGarry, Cecil, Rodrigo Mejia, and Valerian Shirima
A Light on Our Path: A Pastoral Contribution to the Synod for Africa. Nairobi, KE: St. Paul Publications—Africa, 1993. 148 pp. Paper. 9966210431.

Emphasizing the role of small Christian communities in the evangelizing mission of the Catholic Church, three Jesuit priests provide reflections on the teachings of Vatican II as preparatory reading for the Special Assembly for Africa of the Synod of Bishops (Rome, 1994).

AF123 Mushete, A. Ngindu
La Mission de l'Église aujourd'hui / The Mission of Church Today: La rencontre de Yaoundé 4-11 avril 1984: / Reports of the Yaounde Meeting 4-11 April 1984. (Bulletin of African Theology for the Ecumenical Association of African Theologians, 7, 13-14, 1985). Kinshasa, CG: Imprimerie Saint Paul, 1985. 446 pp. Paper. No ISBN.

The papers (in French and English) and report of a first encounter between African and European theologians; sponsored by the Ecumenical Association of African Theologians, and published as a special issue of *Bulletin of African Theology*.

AF124 Njoroge, Nyambura J., and Páraic Réamonn, eds.
La collaboration dans la mission de Dieu dans l'Afrique d'aujourd'hui. (Études de l'Alliance Réformée Mondiale, 28). Geneva, SZ: Alliance Réformée Mondiale, 1994. 102 pp. Paper. 9290750197.

French translation.

AF125 Njoroge, Nyambura J., and Páraic Réamonn, eds.
Partnership in God's Mission in Africa Today. (WARC Studies, 28). Geneva, SZ: WARC, 1994. 94 pp. Paper. 9290750189.

The papers and reports of the Consultation of African Women and Men of Reformed Tradition (Limuru, Kenya, 9-15 March 1994).

AF126 Pan African Christian Leadership Assembly (1976, Nairobi)
Facing the New Challenges: The Message of PACLA, December 9-19, 1976, Nairobi. Edited by Michael Cassidy and Luc Verlinden. Kisumu, KE: Evangel Publishing House, 1976. 662 pp. No ISBN.

A compilation of the speeches presented at PACLA in 1976.

AF127 Pan African Christian Leadership Assembly (1976, Nairobi)
Together in One Place: The Story of PACLA December 9-19, 1976, Nairobi. Edited by Michael Cassidy, and Gottfried Osei-Mensah. Kisumu, KE: Evangel Publishing House, 1978. 301 pp. Paper. No ISBN.

Report of the assembly, a remarkable meeting of 737 evangelical and ecumenical Protestants from forty-eight countries of Africa, seeking unity and a new passion for mission.

AF128 Rafransoa, Maxine
L' Église d'Afrique, qui es tu? (Voix d'Afrique). Lausanne, SZ: Éditions du Soc, 1983. 78 pp. Paper. No ISBN.

Texts of speeches by the General Secretary of the AACC, published on the occasion of its twentieth anniversary.

AF129 Semaine Théologiques de Kinshasa (17th: 1989)
Théologie africaine bilan et perspectives: actes de la dix-septième Semaine théologique de Kinshasa, 2-8 avril 1989. Kinshasa, CG: Facultés catholiques de Kinshasa, 1989. 441 pp. Paper. No ISBN.

Thirty-two Catholic theologians and church leaders present their evaluations of the state and impact of African theologies.

AF130 Semaines théologiques de Kinshasa (18th: 1991)
Quelle Église pour l'Afrique du Troisi̧me Millénaire?: contribution au synode spécial des évêques pour l'Afrique: actes de la dix-huitième Semaine théologique de Kinshasa du 21 au 27 avril 1991. Kinshasa, CG: Facultés catholiques de Kinshasa, 1991. 335 pp. Paper. No ISBN.

Proceedings of a consultation of Roman Catholic theologians and church leaders, with twenty-five papers reflecting on the contribution of the special Synod of Bishops for Africa, to new directions for the African church in the Third Millenium.

AF131 Semaines théologiques de Kinshasa (19th: 1993)
Églises et démocratisation en Afrique: actes de la dix-neuvième Semaine théologique de Kinshasa du 21 au 27 novembre 1993. Kinshasa, CG: Facultés catholiques de Kinshasa, 1994. 358 pp. Paper. No ISBN.

Proceedings of the 19th Kinshasa seminar, with ninteen papers on the churches, and on democratization in Africa.

AF132 Shorter, Aylward
The African Synod: A Personal Response to the Outline Document. Nairobi, KE: St. Paul Publications—Africa, 1991. 158 pp. Paper. 9966210128.

Out of his nearly thirty years in Africa as missionary theologian and anthropologist, Fr. Shorter responds to the Outline Document for the Special Assembly for Africa of the Synod of Bishops (Rome, 1994) and its theme, "The Church in Africa and her Evangelizing Mission towards the Year 2000."

AF133 *The African Synod: Documents, Reflections, Perspectives*
Maryknoll, NYU: Orbis Books, 1996. ix, 286 pp. Paper. 1570750386.

A sourcebook on the Synod of African Bishops (Rome, 1994)—its background, deliberations including documents, and assessment of its impact by a cross section of Roman Catholic interpreters; edited by Africa Faith and Justice Network.

AF134 Wilson, William J., ed.
The Church in Africa: Christian Mission in a Context of Change: A Seminar. Maryknoll, NYU: Maryknoll Publications, 1967. xii, 177 pp. Paper. No ISBN.

Papers from a seminar on "The Church in Africa" (Washington, DC, 22-23 September 1965) sponsored by the African Research and Information Center (AFRIC) and the Maryknoll Fathers.

Church and Society

See also CR549, CR580, CR973, SO136, SO160, SO318, SO454, SO457, SO460-SO461, SO502, SO593, SO609, EC80, EC145, EC246-EC247, EC260, EC312, EC375, PO139, PO144, PO174, CO1, CO6, CO53, CO114, ED28, ED154, ED160, CH351, SP285, SP290-SP291, SP301-SP302, AF88, AF116, AF121-AF122, AF326, AF454, AF459, AF462, AF535, AF541, AF622, AF823, AF901, AF1180, AF1183, AF1189, AF1195, AF1213, and AF1290.

AF135 Africa Diakonia Consultation (Nairobi, Kenya, 31 March-7 April 1989)
Towards Abundant Life: Official Report. Edited by Joshua N. Kudadjie, and Kakule Molo. Geneva, SZ: WCC, 1989. v, 103 pp. Paper. No ISBN.

A regional consultation for African church leaders designed to examine diaconal needs and activities in the light of the diverse social, economic, and political realities of the continent, sponsored by WCC-CICARWS as a follow-up to its world consultations on diakonia at Larnaca (1982) and El Escorial (1987); also published in French and Portuguese.

AF136 Agossou, Medewale-Jacob
Christianisme africain: une fraternité au-delà de l'ethnie. Paris, FR: Karthala, 1987. 217 pp. Paper. 2865371840.

A philosophy of religion for Africa that acknowledges distinctive elements in African religion and culture which impact Christian theology, by the Professor of Religious Anthropology and Theology at the Catholic Institute of West Africa in Abidjan, Ivory Coast.

AF137 Agostoni, Tarcisio
Every Citizen's Handbook. Nairobi, KE: Paulines Publications Africa, 1997. 447 pp. Paper. 9966213163.

A revised and enlarged edition of a basic textbook on Catholic social principles for African Christians; originally published in 1962.

AF138 Althausen, Johannes, ed.

Christen Afrikas auf dem Wege zur Freiheit. (Erlanger Taschenbücher, 17). Erlangen, GW: Ev.-Luth. Mission, 1971. 309 pp. Paper. 3872140302.

An ecumenical collection of thirty-seven church documents, many from the AACC and the WCC, plus others from regional church bodies or bishops' conferences, focusing on new freedom, theology, challenges, planning, rapid social change, political life, apartheid, and indigenous social perspectives.

AF139 AMECEA Pastoral Institute, 1979

The Community Called Church. (Experimental Source-Book for Religious Education, 5/ Spearhead, 60). Eldoret, KE: Gaba Publications, 1979. ii, 88 pp. Paper. No ISBN.

A sourcebook designed to provide leaders of small Christian communities (SCCs) insights from theology, the Bible, pastoral anthropology, and religious education supporting their vision of the church in renewal.

AF140 Assefa, Hizkias, and George Wachira, eds.

Peacemaking and Democratization in Africa: Theoretical Perspectives and Church Initiatives. Nairobi, KE: East African Educational Publishers, 1996. xiv, 242 pp. Paper. 9966468374.

Papers from the symposium on "The Role of Religious Leaders in Peacemaking and Social Change in Africa (Nyeri, Kenya, 18-23 July 1993), cosponsored by the Nairobi Peace Initiative (NPI), the AACC, and AMECEA.

AF141 Barrett, David B., ed.

African Initiatives in Religion: 21 Studies from Eastern and Central Africa. Nairobi, KE: East African Publishing House, 1971. xviii, 288 pp. No ISBN.

Twenty-one case studies on a variety of responses, choices, adaptations and initiatives by African Christians; originally presented at the Workshop in Religious Research (Nairobi, 27 Dec.-12 Jan. 1968).

AF142 Bediako, Kwame

Christianity in Africa: The Renewal of a Non-Western Religion. Edinburgh, STK: Edinburgh University Press; Maryknoll, NYU: Orbis Books, 1995. xii, 276 pp. Paper. 0748606254 (STK), 1570750483 (US).

Essays on Christianity in African life, Christianity as a non-Western religion, and Africa as a Christian continent by the director of the Akrofi-Christaller Memorial Centre in Ghana.

AF143 Beetham, Thomas Allan

Christianity and the New Africa. (Praeger Library of African Affairs). London, ENK: Praeger, 1967. x, 206 pp. No ISBN.

An overview of the prospects that a colonial religion can contribute to newly independent African countries, by a career Africa missionary and Africa secretary to the CBMS.

AF144 Bujo, Bénézet

African Christian Morality at the Age of Inculturation. (Christian Leadership in Africa Series). Nairobi, KE: St. Paul Publications, 1990. 137 pp. Paper. No ISBN.

Six short essays on the inculturation of Christian morals in Africa by the noted Zairois theologian and head of the Department of Moral Theology at the University of Freiburg in Switzerland; originally published in specialized journals and now made available to a wider African readership.

AF145 Bujo, Bénézet

The Ethical Dimension of Community: The African Model and the Dialogue between North and South. Nairobi, KE: Paulines Publications Africa, 1998. 237 pp. Paper. 9966213368.

In developing a social ethic for Africa, Bujo relates Euro-American ethics of communitarianism and the ethics of discourse to African social values.

AF146 Bujo, Bénézet

Morale africaine et foi chrétienne. (Église africaine en dialogue, 2). Kinshasa, CG: Faculté de théologie catholique, 1980. 54 pp. No ISBN.

Second edition of an essay on the relationship between Christian morality and African moral attitudes from the background of the Zairian campaign for "authenticity."

AF147 Chipenda, José B. et al.

The Church of Africa: Towards a Theology of Reconstruction. (African Challenge Book Series, 2). Nairobi, KE: AACC, 1991. vi, 63 pp. Paper. No ISBN.

Four short essays on the African context (José B. Chipenda), the Christian presence in Africa (Andre Karamanga), the future of the church in Africa (J. N. K. Mugambi), and church-state relations (C. K. Omari); originally presented to the AACC General Committee (Nairobi, March 1990).

AF148 Cummings, Mary Lou

Surviving Without Romance: African Women Tell Their Stories. Scottdale, PAU: Herald Press, 1991. 207 pp. Paper. 0836135385.

The best from twenty taped interviews in which African Christian women in Kenya and Tanzania tell their varied stories of love, relationships, and faith.

AF149 Curran, Tom, ed.

Spirituality and Reconciliation. (Tangaza Occasional Papers, 4). Nairobi, KE: Paulines Publications Africa, 1997. 54 pp. Paper. 9966213198.

Short essays on linkages between spirituality, reconciliation, liberation, justice, and peace in African society; by five Catholic missiologists.

AF150 Deng, Lual A.

Rethinking African Development: Toward a Framework for Social Integration and Ecological Harmony. Trenton, NJU: Africa World Press, 1998. 297 pp. Paper. 0865436088.

Critically reviewing the theory and practice of development in Africa during 1965-1994, the author identifies leading issues in African development and argues for a sustainable model of development, ensuring consistency between development policy and African thought, heritage, and institutions.

AF151 Desai, Ram, ed.

Christianity in Africa as Seen by Africans. Denver, COU: Allan Swallow, 1962. 135 pp. No ISBN.

Eleven essays by African intellectuals, including political leaders critical of missionary imperialism, with an introductory essay by the editor.

AF152 Dougall, James W. C.

Christians in the African Revolution. Edinburgh, STK: St. Andrew Press, 1963. 114 pp. No ISBN.

An analysis of the impact of Christian missions and leaders on the new independent states of Africa.

AF—AFRICA

AF153 Eastern & Central Africa Women in Development Network

Violence against Women: Trainers Manual. Nairobi, KE: Paulines Publications Africa, 1997. 54 pp. Paper. 996621321X.

An illustrated primer on violence against women in Africa—the result of a 1996 study by women leaders in East Africa.

AF154 Eboussi Boulaga, F.

À contretemps: l'enjeu de Dieu en Afrique. Paris, FR: Éditions Karthala, 1991. 264 pp. Paper. 286537307X.

A reassessment of Christianity in Africa, its contributions to the search for an African identity, to popular literature, and to postcolonial governments; by the distinguished Professor of Philosophy at the University of Yaoundé, the Cameroons.

AF155 Ela, Jean-Marc

African Cry. Translated by Robert R. Barr. Maryknoll, NYU: Orbis Books, 1986. vi, 154 pp. Paper. 0883442590.

English translation.

AF156 Ela, Jean-Marc

Le cri de l'homme africain: questions aux chrétiens et aux églises d'Afrique. Paris, FR: Librarie-Éditions l'Harmattan, 1980. 173 pp. 2858021457.

Essays by a rural-based Cameroonian priest on the interrelatedness of inculturation, liberation, and authenticity in developing a local African theology.

AF157 Ela, Jean-Marc

La plume et la pioche: réflexion sur l'enseignement et la société dans la développement de l'Afrique Noire. (Collection Point de Vue, 9). Yaounde, CM: Éditions Clé, 1971. 95 pp. Paper. No ISBN.

An early work on African education by the distinguished African theologian, calling for an egalitarian education for life, rather than the promotion of intellectual elitism.

AF158 Fenton, Thomas P., and Mary J. Heffron, eds.

Africa: A Directory of Resources. Maryknoll, NYU: Orbis Books, 1987. xiv, 144 pp. Paper. 0883445328.

The fifth in a series of annotated guides to publications, organizations, audiovisuals, and other materials and resources on the Third World, focused on justice issues and systems change.

AF159 Fowler, Stuart

The Oppression and Liberation of Modern Africa: Examining the Powers Shaping Today's Africa. (Brochures of the Institute for Reformational Studies, F2/63). Potchefstroom, SA: Potchefstroom University, 1995. 177 pp. Paper. 1868222225.

A critical study of the ideological and religious forces shaping today's Africa, with an appeal for the grassroots renewal of African society including the church.

AF160 Gifford, Paul

African Christianity: Its Public Role. Bloomington, INU: Indiana University Press, 1998. viii, 368 pp. 0253334179 (hdbk), 0253212049 (pbk).

A probing study of African Christianity in its contemporary social contexts, evaluating the churches' role in promoting a civil society, with case studies in Ghana, Uganda, Zambia, and Cameroon.

AF161 Gifford, Paul, ed.

The Christian Churches and the Democratisation of Africa. (Studies of Religion in Africa, 12). Leiden, NE: Brill, 1995. xi, 301 pp. 9004103244.

An important collection of eighteen essays by African, European, and North American scholars; originally presented for a conference on "The Christian Churches and Africa's Democratisation" (University of Leeds, 20-23 September 1993).

AF162 Häselbarth, Hans

Christian Ethics in the African Context. Ibadan, NR: Daystar Press, 1976. viii, 233 pp. 9781221151 (hdbk), 978122116X (pbk).

A textbook on basic and applied Christian ethics, developed on experiences gained in South Africa and Nigeria, but designed for use throughout the continent.

AF163 Hastings, Adrian

Christian Marriage in Africa: Being a Report Commissioned by the Archbishops of Cape Town, Central Africa, Kenya, Tanzania, and Uganda. London, ENK: SPCK, 1973. 185 pp. Paper. 0281027412, 0281028141.

A sociological and theological analysis of marriage patterns in Africa, commissioned by Anglican archbishops and carried out by the talented Roman Catholic church historian.

AF164 Hastings, Adrian

Mission and Ministry. (Sheed and Ward stagbooks). London, ENK: Sheed and Ward, 1971. ix, 214 pp. 0722006195.

A collection of essays by the noted Catholic historian on the Catholic Church and social problems in Africa.

AF165 Hatton, Desmond J., ed.

Missiology in Africa Today: Thought-Provoking Essays by Modern Missionaries. Dublin, IE: M H Gill, 1961. 151 pp. No ISBN.

Fourteen brief essays, with a final piece about the Society for the Propagation of the Faith, of which the editor is National Director, aimed to make readers more conscious of the tremendous apostolate of the missions of the church in general, and in South Africa in particular.

AF166 Haule, Cosmas

Bantu Witchcraft and Christian Morality: The Encounter of Bantu Uchawi with Christian Morality; an Anthropoligical and Theological Study. (Neue Zeitschrift für Missionswissenschaft Nouvelle Revue de Science Missionnaire, 16). Schöneck-Beckenried, SW: *Nouvelle Revue de Science Missionnaire,* 1969. xxviii, 187 pp. No ISBN.

A thesis, based on field research in southwestern Tanzania, on African beliefs and practices concerning sorcery (*uchawi*), and the confrontation resulting when Christian worldviews and moral values were introduced.

AF167 Haynes, Jeff

Religion and Politics in Africa. Nairobi, KE: East African Educational Publishers; London, ENK: Zed Books, 1996. 264 pp. 9966466576 (KE), 1856493911 (hdbk UK), 185649392X (pbk UK).

A comprehensive survey analyzing the impacts of both Christianity and Islam on the political processes in a wide variety of African societies.

AF168 Hebga, Meinrad Pierre

Afrique de la raison, Afrique de la foi. (Chrétiens en liberté). Paris, FR: Éditions Karthala, 1995. 206 pp. 2865325625 (hdbk), 2865375625 (pbk).

The Jesuit teacher at Yaoundé University in the Cameroon presents a critical reflection on the political, economic, and social development in some sub-Saharan countries since independence.

AF—AFRICA

AF169 Hertlein, Siegfried

Christentum und Mission im Urteil der neoafrikanischen Prosaliteratur. Münsterschwarzach, GW: Vier-Türme-Verlag, 1962. xxiii, 216 pp. Paper. No ISBN.

Drawing on recent black African literature, this dissertation investigates what African authors think about Christianity, how they judge missionary work, and what role they assign to Christianity in the construction of a new Africa.

AF170 Hillman, Eugene

Toward an African Christianity: Inculturation Applied. New York, NYU: Paulist Press, 1993. v, 101 pp. Paper. 0809133814.

A creative case study of the inculturation of Christianity with descriptions of the African Maasai tradition and how some of its forms lend themselves to the inculturation of Christian faith, practice, and worship.

AF171 Joinet, Bernard

Step by Step Towards Democracy. (Faith and Society Series, 2). Nairobi, KE: Paulines Publications Africa, 1997. 72 pp. Paper. 9966212949.

A primer for African Christians desiring insight into the nature of democracy and guidance for contributing to the building of a democratic society.

AF172 Kä Mana

L' Afrique va-t-elle mourir?: Bousculer l'imaginaire africain ; essai d'éthique politique. Paris, FR: Éditions du Cerf, 1991. 226 pp. Paper. 2204043990.

A theological reflection on the present travails of Africa; (corruption, dictatorial regimes, malnutrition, famine, AIDS, etc.), proposing a new political ethic as an alternative to numerous prevailing myths.

AF173 Kelley, John, ed.

The Church in the Town: Re-thinking the African Urban Apostolate. (Spearhead Series, 47). Eldoret, KE: Gaba Publications, 1977. ii, 60 pp. Paper. No ISBN.

Six case studies from Africa giving a broad spectrum of the models of urban ministries in Catholic parishes, with theological reflections on the church's urban mission.

AF174 Kisembo, Benezeri, Laurenti Magesa, and Aylward Shorter, eds.

African Christian Marriage. Nairobi, KE: Paulines Publications Africa, 1998. 256 pp. Paper. 9966123821.

Second edition with new introduction and update of the important report on the five-year Churches' Research on Marriage in Africa (CROMIA) project; originally published by Geoffrey Chapman in 1977.

AF175 Kyeyune, David, ed.

New Trends for the Empowerment of the People. Nairobi, KE: Paulines Publications Africa; Nairobi, KE: Catholic University of Eastern Africa, 1997. 205 pp. Paper. 9966213112.

Proceedings of the Catholic University of Eastern Africa's (CUEA) Third Interdisciplinary Study Session of the Faculty of Theology and the Department of Religious Studies (Nairobi, Kenya, 1-3 April 1996) focusing on prophetic and pastoral roles of the churches in relation to the struggles for democracy in eastern Africa.

AF176 Lartey, Emmanuel, Daisy Nwachuku, and Kasonga Wa Kasonga, eds.

The Church and Healing: Echoes from Africa. (African Pastoral Studies, 2). Frankfurt am Main, GW: Lang, 1994. 157 pp. Paper. 3631472277.

Essays by nine members of the African Association for Pastoral Studies and Counselling (AAPSC) on different aspects of the quest for health and wholeness in Africa today.

AF177 Makulu, Henry F.

Education, Development and Nation-Building in Independent Africa: A Study of the New Trends and Recent Philosophy of Education. London, ENK: SCM Press, 1971. xvi, 111 pp. 0334003628.

An analysis of the history and contemporary development of African education policies, including mission and church involvement, by a prominent Zambian educator and former Chairman of the AACC.

AF178 Masamba ma Mpolo, and Daisy Nwachuku, eds.

Pastoral Care and Counselling in Africa Today. (African Pastoral Studies, 1). Frankfurt am Main, GW: Lang, 1991. 194 pp. Paper. 3631441312.

This first volume in a special series by the African Association for Pastoral Studies and Counselling is an introduction to the major theoretical and practical issues of African specialists who contextualize their pastoral ministries to meet needs in various churches and cultures.

AF179 Masson, J.

Père de nos Pères. (Documenta Missionalia, 21). Rome, IT: Gregorian University, 1988. 284 pp. Paper. No ISBN.

An analysis of indigenous African prayer, with edited texts set in an interpretative framework.

AF180 Maurier, Henri

Religion et dévelopement: traditions africaines et catéchèses. (Esprit et mission). Paris, FR: Maison Mame, 1965. 190 pp. No ISBN.

A thoughtful analysis of African religion and society.

AF181 Mbugua, Judy, ed.

Our Time Has Come. Grand Rapids, MIU: Baker Books, 1994. 151 pp. Paper. 0853645256.

A collection of short papers originally presented at the Pan African Christian Women Assembly (Nairobi, Kenya, 6-12 August 1989) sponsored by the Association of Evangelicals of Africa and Madagascar (AEAM).

AF182 Mbuy-Beya, Bernadette, ed.

Woman, Who Are You?: A Challenge. (Challenge Series, 2). Nairobi, KE: Paulines Publications Africa, 1998. 158 pp. Paper. 9966214100.

A challenge for African Christians to help downtrodden women stand erect and knock down walls that separate the body of Christ; a call for conversion, justice, and love for one another in Christ.

AF183 Monsma, Timothy M.

An Urban Strategy for Africa. South Pasadena, CAU: William Carey Library, 1979. xv, 175 pp. Paper. 0878084304.

A primer on church growth in Africa including analyses of African urbanization, sources and structures for the church in urban Africa, and a program for growing urban churches.

AF184 Morris, Colin

Church and Challenge in a New Africa: Political Sermons. London, ENK: Epworth Press, 1964. 155 pp. No ISBN.

Clear statements of biblical teachings and practical guidelines for Christians in politics in contemporary Africa; by a Methodist missionary advisor to President Kenneth Kaunda of Zambia, as that state was founded in 1964.

AF—AFRICA

AF185 M'Timkulu, Donald
Beyond Independence: The Face of the New Africa. New York, NYU: Friendship Press, 1971. 64 pp. Paper. 0377110213.

A brief introduction for North Americans, to Christianity in the new Africa; by the noted South African educator and first General Secretary of the AACC.

AF186 Mulagogwa, Cikala M.
Un Visage africain du christianisme: L'Union vitale Bantu face à l'unité vitale ecclésiale. Paris, FR: Présence Africaine, 1965. 263 pp. No ISBN.

An appeal that authentic African spirituality become central in the Church in Africa.

AF187 Musopole, Augustine C.
Being Human in Africa: Toward an African Christian Anthropology. (American University Studies, 9: Anthropology; and Sociology, 65). New York, NYU: Lang, 1994. 261 pp. Paper. 0820423041.

An analysis of the dilemmas of identity, historical consciousness, cultural salvation, change and modernity, and epistemology that affect African self-understanding, plus a proposal for an African Christian anthropology; originally submitted as a dissertation at Union Theological Seminary (New York City).

AF188 Muyembe, Bernard Munono
Église, évangélisation et promotion humaine: le discours social des évêques africains. (Études d'éthique chrétienne: Studien zur theologischen Ethik, 63). Fribourg, SZ: Éditions Universitaires Fribourg; Paris, FR: Éditions du Cerf, 1995. 286 pp. Paper. 282710699X (EUF), 2204052833 (EDC).

A scholarly analysis of pastoral letters addressing social issues; by the episcopal conferences of African bishops, from Vatican II (1965) to the African Synod of Bishops (1994).

AF189 Myklebust, Olav Guttorm
Vindu mot Afrika: folk og kirke i oppbrudd. (Signalbøkene). Stavanger, NO: Nomi Forlag, 1971. 160 pp. 8250100085.

A popular presentation of issues facing the people and churches of Africa amidst rapid social change, with special reference to South Africa.

AF190 Na'im, Abd Allah Ahmad
Proselytization and Communal Self-Determination in Africa. Maryknoll, NYU: Orbis Books, 1999. x, 317 pp. Paper. 1570752613.

This collection of twelve essays, by Muslim and Christian, African and Western scholars, explores the question, "Where does one community's right to commend itself to others, leave off, and another community's right to be left alone, begin?"

AF191 Namwera, L.
Towards African Christian Liberation. Nairobi, KE: St. Paul Publications-Africa, 1990. 258 pp. Paper. No ISBN.

Fifteen lectures on various understandings of liberation, by the faculty of the Catholic Higher-Institute of Eastern Africa, in CHIEA's second extension program (1987-1988).

AF192 Neckebrouck, Valeer
Paradoxes de l'inculturation: les nouveaux habits des Yanomami. (Annua Nuntia Lovaniensia, 36). Leuven, BE: Leuven University Press; Leuven, BE: Peeters, 1994. 214 pp. Paper. 9061866111 (LU), 9068315994 (UP).

Eight scholarly essays on various issues in the inculturation of Christianity in Africa (liturgy, conversion, polygamy, and indigenous movements).

AF193 Nkafu Nkemnkia, Martin
African Vitalogy: A Step Forward in African Thinking. Nairobi, KE: Paulines Publications Africa, 1999. 239 pp. Paper. 0966214518.

This book explores the theme of African philosophy of thinking through historical, anthropological, cosmological, and metaphysical analyses.

AF194 Northcott, William Cecil
Christen in neuen Afrika. Basel, SZ: Basileia Verlag, 1965. 132 pp. No ISBN.

German translation.

AF195 Northcott, William Cecil
Christianity in Africa. (SCM Book Club, 152). London, ENK: SCM Press, 1963. 125 pp. Paper. No ISBN.

A popular introduction to African Christianity written during the first years of independence for many countries on the continent.

AF196 Ntetem, Marc
Die negro-afrikanische Stammesinitiation: Religionsgeschicht-liche Darstellung, theologische Wertung Möglichkeit der Christianisierung. (Münsterschwarzacher Studien, 36). Münsterschwarzach, GW: Vier-Türme-Verlag, 1983. xlvi, 381 pp. Paper. 3878681615.

A dissertation attempting to give a dogmatic basis for a reconciliation of African and Christian ways of living and thinking, with specific reference to the possible Christianization of tribal initiation.

AF197 O'Donohue, Maura, and Robert J. Vitillo
Caritas Training Manual on the Pandemic of HIV/AIDS. Nairobi, KE: Paulines Publications Africa, 1997. 142 pp. Paper. 9966212752.

A Caritas International primer for all those working with and taking care of HIV-AIDS patients in Africa.

AF198 Oduyoye, Mercy Amba, and Musimbi R. A. Kanyoro, eds.
The Will to Arise: Women, Tradition and the Church in Africa. Maryknoll, NYU: Orbis Books, 1992. viii, 230 pp. Paper. 0883447827.

Thirteen essays by African women theologians (twelve Christian, one Muslim), on women in African culture, issues of sexuality, and women within the Christian churches.

AF199 Oduyoye, Mercy Amba
Daughters of Anowa: African Women and Patriarchy. Maryknoll, NYU: Orbis Books, 1995. ix, 229 pp. Paper. 0883449994.

The noted Ghanaian Christian leader analyzes the influence of traditional African culture and Christianity on women's lives, including how myths, proverbs, and folktales reinforce patriarchy.

AF200 Omri, C. K., Julius Nyerere, and Peter Kijanga
Kirke og socialisme i Afrika. (Nyt synspunkt, 4). Hellerup, DK: DMS-Forlag, 1977. 64 pp. Paper. 8774310666.

On the basis of three African contributions, this booklet, edited by Carl Chr. Jessen, Karsten Nissen, and Knud Ochsner, discusses church and state in African states that have expressed their attachment to socialism (Tanzania, Ethiopia, etc.).

AF—AFRICA

AF201 Ott, Martin

Dialog der Bilder: Die Begegnung von Evangelium und Kultur in afrikanischer Kunst. (Freiburger theologische Studien, 157). Freiburg, GW: Herder, 1995. xv, 505 pp. Paper. 3451237431.

A study of Gospel and culture in African art, covering issues of inculturation, the break between evangelization and culture, myths and creation faith, a theology of the homeland, and African Christ symbols and Christ images.

AF202 Parsons, Robert Thomas, ed.

Windows on Africa: A Symposium. Leiden, NE: Brill, 1971. x, 202 pp. No ISBN.

Twelve case studies of contemporary church efforts at contextualization, including Angola, Ghana, Kenya, and Zaire.

AF203 Pato, Luke Lungile, ed.

Towards an Authentic African Christianity. Umtata, Transkei, SA: University of Transkei, 1989. 86 pp. Paper. 0947029281.

Seven papers by faculty of the department of Religious and Biblical Studies, University of Transkei, on issues of contextualization in southern Africa.

AF204 Paul, Leonard

Theology of the Church as Family of God. (Tangaza Occasional Papers, 3). Nairobi, KE: Paulines Publications Africa, 1997. 64 pp. Paper. 9966213104.

Five short essays on the image of the church as God's family, by Catholic leaders in their East African contexts.

AF205 Peil, Margaret et al.

African Cities and Christian Communities. (Spearhead, 72). Eldoret, KE: Gaba Publications, 1982. 88 pp. Paper. No ISBN.

Helps for urban parish leaders of eastern and central Africa, in understanding their urban apostolate, with seven case studies of pastoral experiences in building SCCs.

AF206 Pheko, S. E. M.

Christianity through African Eyes. Lusaka, ZA: Daystar Publications, 1969. 133 pp. No ISBN.

An examination of Scriptures from the perspective of an African worldview, and a challenge to the limitations of Western interpretations of the Gospel.

AF207 Pobee, J. S., ed.

Religion, Morality, and Population Dynamics. (University of Ghana Population Studies, 8). Legon, GH: University of Ghana, 1977. xii, 270 pp. No ISBN.

Proceedings of the Seminar on Moral and Religious Issues in Population Dynamics and Development (University of Ghana, Legon, 31 March to 4 April, 1974).

AF208 Pobee, J. S.

Skenosis: Christian Faith in an African Context. Gweru, ZI: Mambo Press, 1992. 174 pp. Paper. 0869225316.

Nine short lectures by the noted African biblical theologian, on how African Christians can remain faithful to their beliefs as well as their culture.

AF209 Rader, Dick Allen

Christian Ethics in an African Context: A Focus on Urban Zambia. (American University Studies Series 7: Theology and Religion, 128). New York, NYU: Lang, 1991. xii, 201 pp. 0820414530.

An introduction to issues of contextualization of Christianity in Africa, with chapters on biblical principles and application to urban Zambia; based on the author's decade of work as a theological educator in that country.

AF210 Robinson, John M.

The Family Apostolate and Africa. Dublin, IE: Helicon; Chicago, ILU: Christian Family Movement, 1964. xvi, 278 pp. No ISBN.

This study attempts to present a synthesis of the aspects and implications of the family apostolate—the effort to build up Christian married and family life in Africa, as well as a survey of its principal methods and organizations, with suggestions as to how to extend and improve family apostolate activity in Africa.

AF211 Rugema, Mike N., and Inge Tvedten

Survey of Posssible Expanded Education Assistance to Refugees from Angola and Mozambique. Nairobi, KE: AACC, 1991. 114 pp. Paper. 9966987940.

An assessment of educational needs of Angolan and Mozambican refugees in Malawi and Zambia.

AF212 Saayman, W. A., ed.

Embracing the Baobab Tree: The African Proverb in the 21st Century. (African Proverbs Series, 5). Pretoria, SA: UNISA, 1997. xiv, 269 pp. Paper. 0869819976.

Papers and proceedings from an Interdisciplinary Symposium on "The African Proverb in the 21st Century" (Pretoria, University of South Africa, 2-7 October 1996;) sponsored by the Pew Research Project on African Proverbs, with essays on the proverbs and Christianity.

AF213 Sanneh, Lamin

Encountering the West: Christianity and the Global Cultural Process: The African Dimension. (Christian Systematic Theology in a World Context; World Christian Theology Series). Maryknoll, NYU: Orbis Books; London, ENK: Marshall Pickering, 1993. 286 pp. 0883449293 (hdbk US), 088344934X (pbk US), 0551028114 (UK).

Six scholarly essays on the encounter of Africans and others with the modern West, including both Christian missions and intellectual traditions critical of religion, with positive assessment of the consequences of this interaction by the distinguished Yale University missiologist.

AF214 Sartorius, Joachim

Staat und Kirchen im francophonen Schwarzafrika und auf Madagaskar: Die religionsgeschichte. (Jus ecclesiasticum, 19). Munich, GW: Claudius Verlag, 1973. 220 pp. Paper. 3532714193.

The historical development of the legal aspects of missionary activity and freedom of religion in francophone Africa.

AF215 Scanlon, David G., ed.

Church, State, and Education in Africa. New York, NYU: Teachers College Press, 1966. iv, 313 pp. No ISBN.

An overview of the issues involved in transfer of schools in Africa, from management by churches and missionaries to government control, including seven national case studies.

AF216 Shorter, Aylward

The African Contribution to the World Church, and Other Essays in Pastoral Anthropology. (Gaba Institute Pastoral papers, 22). Kampala, UG: AMECEA Pastoral Institute, 1972. 73 pp. No ISBN.

Six essays about issues of African Christianity in response to culture.

AF—AFRICA

AF217 Shorter, Aylward
African Culture and the Christian Church. Maryknoll, NYU: Orbis Books, 1974. xi, 229 pp. Paper. 0883440040.

An introduction for African catechists to social and pastoral anthropology, with applications to Christian ministry in Africa.

AF218 Shorter, Aylward
Celibacy and African Culture. Nairobi, KE: Paulines Publications Africa, 1998. 48 pp. Paper. 9966213813.

Six talks, originally given to formators of the Holy Cross Congregation in Nairobi in 1997, based on the author's experiences and research as a social anthropologist in East Africa.

AF219 Shorter, Aylward
Christianity and the African Imagination: After the African Synod: Resources for Inculturation. Nairobi, KE: Paulines Publications Africa, 1996. 128 pp. Paper. 9966211678.

The noted Catholic missiologist proposes ways in which the Church can carry out the injunction of the African Synod to use resources from African oral traditions for the inculturation of the Gospel, based on his earlier unpublished lectures.

AF220 Shorter, Aylward
The Church in the African City. London, ENK: Chapman, 1991. vii, 152 pp. Paper. 0225666367.

A clear analysis of African urbanization and the church's mission in Africa's towns and cities by the president of the Catholic Missionary Institute in London and preeminent Catholic social anthropologist of East Africa.

AF221 Shorter, Aylward et al.
Towards African Christian Maturity. (Christian Leadership in Africa, 3). Nairobi, KE: St Paul Publications, 1987. 170 pp. Paper. No ISBN.

Nine lectures, by the faculty of the Catholic Higher-Institute of Eastern Africa (CHIEA), on contemporary Christian attitudes to African culture and African religions, other churches, the poor, the Bible, spirituality, liturgy, moral theology, and canon law.

AF222 Shorter, Aylward, and Edwin Onyancha, eds.
The Church and AIDS in Africa: A Case Study: Nairobi City. Nairobi, KE: Paulines Publications Africa, 1998. 141 pp. Paper. 996621384X.

The second Nairobi case study by two social anthropologists who live in that city, in which up to a third of the population is said to be infected with the AIDS virus.

AF223 Shorter, Aylward, and Edwin Onyancha
Secularism in Africa. A Case Study: Nairobi City. Nairobi, KE: Paulines Publications Africa, 1997. 144 pp. Paper. 9966213147.

Two noted Catholic anthropologists in East Africa living and working in Nairobi report on how secular values are eroding religious values in their city, suggesting methods of evangelization and social action which could counteract these secular influences.

AF224 Shorter, Aylward, ed.
Church and Marriage in Eastern Africa. Eldoret, KE: AMECEA Research Department, 1975. iii, 734 pp. Paper. No ISBN.

Twenty-four case studies on various aspects of marriage—part of the Roman Catholic and Anglican-sponsored Churches' Research on Marriage in Africa (CROMIA); a companion volume to *Church and Marriage in Modern Africa.*

AF225 Sindima, Harvey J.
Africa's Agenda: The Legacy of Liberalism and Colonialism in the Crisis of African Values. (Contributions in Afro-American and African Studies, 176). Westport, CTU: Greenwood, 1995. xvii, 256 pp. 0313294798.

A scholarly analysis of the current crisis of values in Africa, the past contribution of Christian missions in their formation, and of Christians today in their reconstruction.

AF226 Sundkler, Bengt
The Christian Ministry in Africa. (Studia Missionalia Upsaliensia, 2). Uppsala, SW: Swedish Institute of Missionary Research; London, ENK: SCM Press, 1962. 144 pp. No ISBN.

A study, written at the request of the IMC, on the problems of ministerial training, discussed in the wider context of social, political, and ecclesiastical developments; with statistics on theological schools and churches, plus field notes as appendices.

AF227 Tessier, Roger, ed.
Young People in African Towns—Their Pastoral Care. (Spearhead Series, 79). Eldoret, KE: Gaba Publications, 1983. 82 pp. No ISBN.

Background to the pastoral care of young people, pastoral activities and proposals for action for young people; with responses and experiences by A. Shorter, H. Burgman, Y. Durian, J.-L. Gouiller, G. Chabanon, "Youth of the Light" (Zaire), National Christian Council of Kenya, and M. Stetter.

AF228 Thompson, Henry O., Jan Knappert, and Helen Bell Feddema, eds.
Health Education and Welfare in Africa. Delhi, II: ISPCK, 1993. xiv, 114 pp. Paper. 8172141009.

Five essays (four on education in Africa and one on women's health) with references to missions and education.

AF229 *Today's Africa: The Church and the People*
New York, NYU: Friendship Press, 1993. 50 mins pp. No ISBN.

Two twenty-four minute programs, on video with study guide, for use in mission study on Africa—one on issues of economic development, and the other on the indigenous Christianity of the Harrist Church in the Ivory Coast.

AF230 Turkson, Peter, and Frans Jozef Servaas Wijsen, eds.
Inculturation: Abide by the Otherness of Africa and the Africans. (Kerk en theologies in context). Kampen, NE: Kok, 1994. x, 98 pp. 9039005060.

Essays by six African theologians on the future of inculturation in Africa.

AF231 Turner, Victor, ed.
Colonialism in Africa, 1870-1960: vol. 3: Profiles of Change: African Society and Rule. (Hoover Institution Publications). London, ENK: Cambridge University Press, 1971. viii, 455 pp. No ISBN.

Twelve scholarly essays on the interactions of African societies with colonialism, including missions, with an important chapter by F. B. Welbourn on "Missionary Stimulus and African Responses."

AF232 Ustorf, Werner, and Wolfram Weisse, eds.
Radiokolleg Kirchen in Afrika: Eine Sendereihe des Deutschlandfunks. (Erlanger Taschenbücher, 50). Erlangen, GW: Ev.-Luth. Mission, 1979. 103 pp. Paper. 3872141058.

A series of short essays on the decidedly "non-Western" character of African churches in various countries.

AF—AFRICA

AF233 Uzukwu, E. Elochukwu

A Listening Church: Autonomy and Communion in African Churches. Maryknoll, NYU: Orbis Books, 1996. x, 182 pp. Paper. 1570750602.

At the intersection of African and Roman traditions with the contemporary crisis of African society, the Nigerian Spiritan priest, liturgist, and ecclesiologist challenges the church in Africa to be an agent of social transformation.

AF234 van der Walt, B. J.

The Liberating Message: A Christian Worldview for Africa. (Institute for Reformational Studies, 44). Potchefstroom, SA: Potchefstroom University, 1994. v, 601 pp. Paper. 1868221407.

An introduction from the Reformed tradition of the Christian worldview, in relation to both traditional African culture and the presence of social change.

AF235 Verryn, Trevor David, ed.

Church and Marriage in Modern Africa. Groenkloof, SA: Ecumenical Research Unit, 1975. ii, 497 pp. Paper. No ISBN.

Fifteen essays by clerics in Southern Africa on various aspects of marriage—part of a continent-wide research project on marriage in Africa under Roman Catholic and Anglican leadership.

AF236 Villa-Vicencio, Charles, and John W. De Gruchy, eds.

Doing Ethics in Context: South African Perspectives. (Theology and Praxis, 2). Maryknoll, NYU: Orbis Books; Cape Town, SA: David Philip, 1994. xi, 221 pp. Paper. 0883449900 (US), 0864862660 (SA).

Twenty-two short essays by a wide range of South African theologians; prepared as an introduction to Christian ethics for South African theological students.

AF237 Wa Lele, Boniface

Family Spirituality In Africa. (Spearhead Series, 70). Eldoret, KE: Gaba Publications, 1982. 46 pp. Paper. No ISBN.

A short essay on how families can be truly Christian and truly African, affirming both traditional Kenyan values and Catholic teachings, as given in "A Message to Christian Families in the Modern World" by the 1980 Synod of Bishops.

AF238 Walt, B. J. van der

Leaders with a Vision: How Christian Leadership Can Tackle the African Crisis. (Institute for Reformational Studies, 59). Potchefstroom, SA: Potchefstroom University, 1995. 101 pp. Paper. 186822189X.

A South African Professor of Christian Philosophy reflects on the contemporary African crisis as one of leadership, based on his wide travels and interviews on the continent.

AF239 Waruta, Douglas W., ed.

African Church in the 21st Century: Challenges and Promises. Nairobi, KE: AACC, 1995. 155 pp. 996688601X.

A compilation of papers from the 1993 gathering of the Association of Theological Institutions in Eastern Africa, on the theme of the "African Church in the 21st Century."

AF240 Wilson, Monica Hunter

Religion and the Transformation of Society: A Study in Social Change in Africa. (The Scott Holland Memorial Lectures 1969). Cambridge, ENK: Cambridge University Press, 1971. 165 pp. 0521079918.

A personal examination by the prominent social anthropologist, of the effect and change occuring in the peoples of Africa as they are further exposed to European society, including the shift from group to personalized religion.

AF241 Wiredu, Kwasi

Cultural Universals and Particulars: An African Perspective. (African Systems of Thought). Bloomington, INU: Indiana University Press, 1996. ix, 237 pp. 0253332095 (hdbk), 0253210801 (pbk).

The eminent Ghanaian philosopher develops universal principles out of Akan thought and other African traditional philosophers, shows how they intersect with Western thought, including that introduced by missionaries, and applies it to current African political problems.

AF242 Yamamori, Tetsunao et al., eds.

Serving with the Poor in Africa. (Cases in Holistic Ministry). Monrovia, CAU: MARC, 1996. x, 230 pp. Paper. 0912552980.

Fourteen case studies and reflections on effective holistic ministry in Africa; originally presented at a World Vision-sponsored Africa Consultation on Holistic Ministry (Harare, Zimbabwe, November 1995).

Africa Biography: Collective

See also CO91, ED5, ED120, and AF736.

AF243 Bühlmann, Walbert

Sie folgten dem Ruf: Afrikanische Zeugen des Glaubens. (Topos-Taschenbücher, 119). Mainz, GW: Matthias-Grünewald-Verlag, 1982. 118 pp. Paper. 3786710058.

The biographies of exemplary African Christians, the "firstlings" of African missions, who persevered in their faith notwithstanding all kinds of difficulties and dangers.

AF244 Bartalsky, Kathy

Soaring on Broken Wings: A Story of Triumph in Tragedy. Chicago, ILU: Moody, 1990. 192 pp. 0802423159.

The inspiring story of a missionary family who served with Helimission (1980-1987), a Swiss-based ministry, flying food, medical supplies, and the Gospel to the needy people in Africa, and how Kathy's faith sustained her upon the deaths of her husband and two children.

AF245 Contran, Neno

They Are a Target. Nairobi, KE: Paulines Publications Africa, 1996. 207 pp. Paper. 9966212396.

Short biographies of forty Catholic priests martyred in Africa during the past forty years.

AF246 Oliver, Caroline

Western Women in Colonial Africa. (Contributions in Comparative Colonial Studies, 12). Westport, CTU: Greenwood, 1982. xv, 201 pp. 0313233888.

Scholarly accounts of five European women who distinguished themselves in Africa between 1850 and 1950, as explorer (Florence Baker), traveler (Alexandrine Tinne), scientist (Mary Kingsley), and missionary (Mary Slessor and Mother Kevin).

AF247 Russell, Henry

Africa's Twelve Apostles. Boston, MAU: St. Paul Editions, 1981. 387 pp. 0819807028 (hdbk), 0819807036 (pbk).

The story of how Catholicism has been planted in Africa since the middle of the nineteenth century; illustrated in the lives of twelve outstanding men who pioneered and left their impact on the African missions.

AF—AFRICA

AF248 Trobisch, Ingrid
On Our Way Rejoicing. Wheaton, ILU: Tyndale, 1986. 229 pp. Paper. 0842347453.

A firsthand account of mission service by Ingrid and Walter Trobisch and the Hult family in East and West Africa, 1941-1960.

AF249 Weaver, Edwin, and Irene Weaver
From Kuku Hill: Among Indigenous Churches in West Africa. (Missionary Studies, 3). Elkhart, INU: Institute of Mennonite Studies, 1975. 128 pp. Paper. No ISBN.

A personal record of the frustrations and victories of the Weavers as Mennonite missionaries seeking to establish meaningful relations with church elders and laymen in some of the indigenous churches in Ghana, 1959-1969, as they searched for answers to the question, "What does it mean for the church to be in mission today?"

Africa Biography: Individual

See also HI253, HI303, AF426, AF786, and AF1148.

AF250 De la Haye, Sophie
Byang Kato: Ambassador for Christ. Achimota, GH: Africa Christian Press, 1986. 126 pp. Paper. 9964875177.

A popular biography of Byang Kato (1936-1975) of Nigeria, the former General Secretary of the Association of Evangelicals of Africa and Madagascar (AEAM).

AF251 Fitts, Leroy
Lott Carey: First Black Missionary to Africa. Valley Forge, PAU: Judson Press, 1978. 159 pp. 0817008209.

The first scholarly study of this black ex-slave, who became the first American missionary to Africa, and of his impact on the evolution of black missionary theology and of the Lott Carey Baptist Foreign Missionary Convention, 1897-1977.

AF252 Gstrein, Heinz
Der Karawanenkardinal: Charles Lavigerie, Kardinalerzbischof von Algier und Carthago, Primas von Afrika sowie Gründer der Weissen Väter, (1825-1892, Auseinandersetzung mit dem Islam). (Missionare, die Geschichte machten). Mödling, AU: Verlag St. Gabriel, 1982. 110 pp. Paper. No ISBN.

A biography of Cardinal Lavigerie, Archbishop of Algiers and Carthage and Primate of Africa, who founded the White Fathers and Sisters for work among the Muslims.

AF253 Helly, Dorothy O.
Livingstone's Legacy: Horace Waller and Victorian Mythmaking. Athens, OHU: Ohio University Press, 1987. xviii, 404 pp. 0821408364.

A documented study of the creation of a Victorian legend, and of the identification of individual zeal and religious fervor with national self-interest; as portrayed in the relationship between Livingstone and Waller.

AF254 Honoré, Deborah Duncan, ed.
Trevor Huddleston: Essays on His Life and Work. Oxford, ENK: Oxford University Press, 1988. xv, 208 pp. 0198266928.

Essays offered to Trevor Huddleston on his 75th birthday that point to Huddleston's commitment to human rights and to eliminating racial discrimination during his forty years (1943-1983) of missionary service in South Africa, Tanzania, and Mauritius, and as an advocate to Great Britain.

AF255 Hunter, James Hogg
A Flame of Fire: The Life and Work of R. V. Bingham. Toronto, ONC: Sudan Interior Mission, 1961. 320 pp. No ISBN.

An official biography of Roland Victor Bingham (1872-1942), who founded the Sudan Interior Mission in Canada in 1893, to evangelize the interior of Africa between the Sahara and the equator; with a general history of the SIM's expansion, both in sending countries and in facets of its work to include medical work, education, Bible translation, and the printing of Christian literature.

AF256 Jeal, Tim
Livingstone. New York, NYU: Putnam, 1973. xv, 427 pp. 0399112154.

A biography of the pioneer missionary-explorer, published in 1973 to coincide with the centenary of his death; based on new source material.

AF257 Montclos, Xavier de
Le Cardinal Lavigerie, le Saint-Siège et l'Église: de l'avènement de Pie IX à l'avènement de Leon XIII, 1846-1878. Paris, FR: Éditions de Boccard, 1965. 666 pp. No ISBN.

A biography emphasizing Cardinal Lavigerie's concern for Muslims in North Africa and negroes in Central Africa.

AF258 Northcott, William Cecil
David Livingstone: His Triumph, Decline, and Fall. Philadelphia, PAU: Westminster Press, 1973. 140 pp. 0664209807.

A readable commentary on the life of the pioneer explorer-missionary; by the Secretary of the LMS Mission Board under which he served.

AF259 Ogola, Margaret, and Margaret Roche
Cardinal Otunga: A Gift of Grace. (Challenge Series, 3). Nairobi, KE: Paulines Publications Africa, 1999. 143 pp. Paper. 9966214267.

A biography of the youngest appointed and longest serving Catholic bishop, who served forty years until retiring as ordinary of the Archdiocese of Nairobi in 1997; includes his upbringing in a premier missionary school in the colony, and his commitment to evangelization and education.

AF260 Pachai, Bridglal, ed.
Livingstone: Man of Africa. London, ENK: Longman Group, 1973. 245 pp. 0582641357 (hdbk), 0582641365 (pbk).

These memorial essays provide a fresh appreciation of Livingstone's journeys in Africa, his work as a missionary doctor, his anti-slavery activities examined in the light of African history, and the impact he had on local affairs.

AF261 Schoen, Ulrich
Jean Faure, 1907-1967: Missionar und Theologe in Afrika und im Islam. Göttingen, GW: Vandenhoeck & Ruprecht, 1984. 207 pp. Paper. 3525553935.

Reflections on the life of a French missionary and theologian who served in New Guinea, Morocco, and black Africa for nearly forty years, and who had extensive contacts with African Muslims and Jews.

AF262 Taylor, Rhena
The Prisoner and Other Stories. Bromley, Kent, ENK: MARC Europe, 1987. 192 pp. Paper. 0947697578 (M).

A collection of ten stories which describe the immediacy of the mission world in Africa; from the experiences of the author, who worked in Ethiopia and Kenya from 1962 to 1987, supported by the Bible Churchmen's Missionary Society.

AF263 Veloso, Agostinho
D. Teodosio Clemente de Gouveia: Paladino de Portugal ao Servico de Deus. Lisboa, PO: Agencia Geral do Ultramar, 1965. 2 vols. No IBSN.

A two-volume biography, with illustrations of the first bishop south of the Sahara to become a cardinal (in 1946).

African Theologies

See also TH279, TH281, TH433, TH443, TH486, CR446, CR584, CR598, CR603, CR616, CR622, SO340, SO571, EC260, AF8, AF59, AF78, AF147, AF155-AF156, AF234, AF602, AF885, AF912, AF917, AF925, AF957, AF1033, AF1036, AF1053-AF1055, and AF1065.

AF264 Adeyemo, Tokunboh
Salvation in African Tradition. Nairobi, KE: Evangel Publishing House, 1997. 124 pp. Paper. 9966200630.

Second edition of a survey of African tradition as it relates to salvation, with a comparison of biblical and contemporary Christian concepts of salvation; by a leading African evangelical; originally published in 1979.

AF265 Bürkle, Horst, ed.
Theologie und Kirche in Afrika. Stuttgart, GW: Evan Verlagswerk, 1968. 311 pp. No ISBN.

Ten Protestant and eight Catholic theologians, eleven of them Africans, discuss the possibilities of an African theology, deriving from the encounter of Christianity with the historical heritage of Africa.

AF266 Bakole, Ilunga wa
Chemins de libération. Kananga, CG: Éditions de l'Archdiocèse, 1978. 350 pp. No ISBN.

Second edition of a liberation theology, ecclesiology, and spirituality for Africa, by the Roman Catholic Archbishop of Kananga, Congo.

AF267 Bakole, Ilunga wa
Paths of Liberation: A Third World Spirituality. Translated by Matthew J. O'Connell. Maryknoll, NYU: Orbis Books, 1984. viii, 215 pp. Paper. 0883444011.

English translation.

AF268 Banana, Canaan Sodindo
Come and Share: An Introduction to Christian Theology. Gweru, RH: Mambo Press, 1991. xxvii, 119 pp. Paper. 0869224956.

An invitation to Zimbabwe Christians to articulate their faith in an environment of both traditional African religion and Marxist socialism by the Methodist theological educator and first State President of Zimbabwe (1980-1988).

AF269 Battle, Michael
Reconciliation: The Ubuntu Theology of Desmond Tutu. Cleveland, OHU: Pilgrim Press, 1997. xvi, 255 pp. Paper. 0829811583.

A highly original analysis of Bishop Desmond Tutu's theology of *ubuntu*, its African roots, and application to facilitate interracial community and reconciliation in South Africa, based on a wide range of primary sources.

AF270 Becken, Hans-Jürgen, ed.
Relevant Theology for Africa: Report on a Consultation of the Missiological Institute at Lutheran Theological College, Mapumulo, Natal, 12-21 September, 1972. (Paperbacks of the Missiological Institute at LTC, Mapumulo, 1). Durban, SA: Lutheran Publishing House, 1973. 198 pp. Paper. No ISBN.

Twenty essays by black and white theologians on black theology, the encounter of the Old and New Testaments with African religious traditions, African independent churches, and other issues important to African Christianity.

AF271 Bediako, Kwame
Theology and Identity: The Impact of Culture upon Christian Thought in the Second Century and in Modern Africa. (Regnum Studies in Mission and Development). Oxford, ENK: Regnum Books, 1992. xviii, 507 pp. Paper. 187034510X.

A scholarly analysis of the question of identity as a key to understanding the concerns of Christian theology in modern Africa and in the 2nd century A.D.

AF272 Bettscheider, Heribert, ed.
Das Problem einer afrikanischen Theologie. (Veröffentlichungen des Missionspriesterseminars, 30). St. Augustin, GW: Steyler Verlag, 1978. 134 pp. Paper. 387787116X.

Papers on African theology read at the Missiological Conference (Sankt Augustin, West Germany, 1977).

AF273 Boesak, Allan Aubrey
Afscheid van de onschuld: een sociaal-ethische studie over zwarte theologie en zwarte macht. Kampen, NE: Kok, 1977. 154 pp. No ISBN.

Dutch translation.

AF274 Boesak, Allan Aubrey
Farewell to Innocence: A Socio-Ethical Study on Black Theology and Black Power. Maryknoll, NYU: Orbis Books, 1977. xii, 185 pp. 0883441306.

An African theology of liberation written by a black theologian out of the anguish of the black experience in South Africa; submitted as a doctoral dissertation at the Free University of Amsterdam.

AF275 Boesak, Allan Aubrey
Unschuld, die schuldig macht: Eine sozialethische Studie über Schwarze Theologie und Schwarze Macht. Translated by R. Sundermeier. Hamburg, GW: Lutherisches Verlagshaus, 1977. xiii, 210 pp. Paper. 378590424X.

German translation.

AF276 Bosch, David Jacobus
Het evangelie in Afrikaans gewaad. Kampen, NE: Kok, 1974. 119 pp. Paper. 902420237X.

A series of lectures, given at theological faculties in the Netherlands in 1973, on African/black theology and missionary dimensions of the church in Africa.

AF277 Bujo, Bénézet
African Theology in Its Social Context. Translated by John O'Donohue. (Faith and Culture Series, 4). Maryknoll, NYU: Orbis Books; Nairobi, KE: St. Paul Publications, 1992. 143 pp. Paper. 088344805X (O).

English translation.

AF278 Bujo, Bénézet
Afrikanische Theologie in ihrem gesellschaftlichen Kontext. (Theologie interkulturell, 1). Düsseldorf, GW: Patmos Verlag, 1986. 151 pp. Paper. 3491776546.

After sketching the religious tradition of Africa and the history of colonization and evangelization, the professor of moral theology in the Catholic Theological Faculty, Kinshasa, Zaire, presents examples of modern African Christology and ecclesiology and concludes with the question of the practical relevance of theology.

AF279 De Gruchy, John W., and Charles Villa-Vicencio, eds.
Doing Theology in Context: South African Perspectives. (Theology and Praxis, 1). Maryknoll, NYU: Orbis Books; Cape Town, SA: David Philip, 1994. xi, 236 pp. Paper. 0883449897 (US), 0864862652 (SA).

An introduction to theology by South African theologians from a wide range of traditions and perspectives, with special reference to the South African context.

AF280 De Gruchy, John W.
Liberating Reformed Theology: A South African Contribution to an Ecumenical Debate. Grand Rapids, MIU: Eerdmans; Cape Town, SA: David Philip, 1991. xviii, 291 pp. Paper. 0802805361 (US), 0864862024 (SA).

Out of the experience of South Africa the author seeks to develop a Reformed theology that can respond positively and critically to liberation theologies.

AF281 Dickson, Kwesi A., and Paul Ellingworth, eds.
Biblical Revelation and African Beliefs. London, ENK: Lutterworth Press; Maryknoll, NYU: Orbis Books, 1970. viii, 191 pp. 0718816528.

Eight papers by eminent African theologians; originally presented at a pioneer consultation on African Theology (Ibadan, Nigeria, 1966), sponsored by the AACC.

AF282 Dickson, Kwesi A., and Paul Ellingworth, eds.
Per una nuova teologia africana. Milano, IT: Jaca Book, 1973. 203 pp. No ISBN.
Italian translation.

AF283 Dickson, Kwesi A., and Paul Ellingworth, eds.
Pour une théologie africaine. (Collection théologique CLE, 1). Yaoundé, CM: Éditions Clé, 1969. 294 pp. No ISBN.
French translation.

AF284 Dickson, Kwesi A.
Theology in Africa. Maryknoll, NYU: Orbis Books; London, ENK: Darton, Longman & Todd, 1984. ix, 243 pp. Paper. 0883445085 (O), 0232515514 (D).

A Ghanaian theologian draws on African religiosity, the Hebrew Bible, and Christian experience to propose a distinctively African theology.

AF285 Donders, Joseph G.
Afrikanische Befreiungstheologie: Eine alte Kultur erwacht. Olten, SZ: Walter-Verlag, 1986. 219 pp. Paper. 3530168181.
German translation.

AF286 Donders, Joseph G.
Evangelizar ou colonizar?: Experiência africana de Jesus. São Paulo, BL: Edições Paulinas, 1987. 229 pp. Paper. No ISBN.
Portuguese translation.

AF287 Donders, Joseph G.
Non-Bourgeois Theology: An African Experience of Jesus. Maryknoll, NYU: Orbis Books, 1985. vii, 200 pp. Paper. 088344352X.

Themes in the developing African response to Christianity, interpreted by the former professor of philosophy at the University of Nairobi, Kenya, and Catholic chaplain to students there.

AF288 Dwane, Sigqibo
Issues in the South African Theological Debate: Essays and Addresses in Honor of the Late James Matta Dwane. Johannesburg, SA: Skotaville Publishers, 1989. 168 pp. Paper. 0947009671.

An analysis of key issues for black theology in South Africa, by a former Anglican theological educator who is now a bishop of the Order of Ethiopia.

AF289 EATWOT (1977: Accra, Ghana)
Libération ou adaptation?: La Théologie africaine s'interroge: Le Colloque d'Accra. Edited by Kofi Appiah-Kubi and Sergio Torres. Translated by R. Arrighi. Paris, FR: l'Harmattan, 1979. 239 pp. 2858021031.
French translation.

AF290 EATWOT (1977: Accra, Ghana)
African Theology en Route: Papers from Pan-African Conference of Third World Theologians, December 17-23, 1977, Accra, Ghana. Edited by Kofi Appiah-Kubi, and Sergio Torres. Maryknoll, NYU: Orbis Books, 1979. x, 214 pp. 0883440105.

Twenty contributions using black, African, and liberation categories in the search for a theology that arises from, and is accountable to, African people.

AF291 EATWOT
Église et théologie noire en Afrique du Sud (Church and Black Theology in South Africa). (Bulletin de Théologie Africaine, VI-12). Kinshasa, CG: Bulletin de Théologie Africaine, 1984. 197-415 pp. Paper. No ISBN.

Essays in French and English presented at an EATWOT conference (Yaoundé, Cameroun, 25-29 January 1984) on the challenge of black and African theology in southern Africa and other parts of Africa.

AF292 EATWOT
Culture, Religion and Liberation: Proceedings of the EATWOT Pan African Theological Conference, Harare, Zimbabwe, January 6-11, 1991. Edited by Simon S. Maimela. (African Challenges Series). Pretoria, SA: No publisher, 1994. ix, 171 pp. Paper. 062018762X.

Fifteen papers by African theologians and the final conference statement.

AF293 Ehusani, George Omaku
An Afro-Christian Vision "Ozovehe!": Toward a More Humanized World. Lanham, MDU: University Press of America, 1991. xi, 264 pp. 0819181145 (hdbk), 0819181153 (pbk).

A study by a Ghanaian Anglican priest on the contributions of both African traditional humanism and the Christian faith, to the inculturation of theology and values in Africa.

AF294 Ela, Jean-Marc
Ma foi d'africain. Paris, FR: Karthala, 1985. 224 pp. 2865371409.

In this call to reread the Gospel through African eyes, a Cameroonian pastor and theologian reveals how a theology of liberation, which truly stresses the liberation of the oppressed, has a real place in Africa.

AF295 Ela, Jean-Marc
Mein Glaube als Afrikaner: Das Evangelium in schwarzafrikanischer Lebenswirklichkeit. (Theologie der Dritten Welt, 10). Freiburg, GW: Herder, 1987. 197 pp. Paper. 3451210975.
German translation.

AF296 Ela, Jean-Marc
My Faith as an African. Translated by John Pairman. Maryknoll, NYU: Orbis Books; London, ENK: Chapman, 1988. xx, 187 pp. Paper. 0883446316 (US), 0225665662 (UK).
English translation.

AF297 Frostin, Per

Liberation Theology in Tanzania and South Africa: A First World Interpretation. (Studia Theologica Lundensia, 42). Lund, SW: Lund University Press; Bromley, Kent, ENK: Chartwell-Bratt, 1988. x, 283 pp. Paper. 9179660401 (L), 0862381599 (C).

Scholarly case studies of the development of African liberation theology in the contexts of Tanzania and South Africa, with extensive notes and bibliography.

AF298 Fulljames, Peter

God and Creation in Intercultural Perspective: Dialogue between the Theologies of Barth, Dickson, Pobee, Nyamiti, and Pannenberg. (Studies in the Intercultural History of Christianity, 86). Frankfurt am Main, GW: Lang, 1993. ix, 190 pp. Paper. 3631456093.

A comparative study of themes of community, life, and creativity in the writings of three contemporary African theologians (Kwesi Dickson, Charles Nyamiti, and John Pobee) and two European theologians (Karl Barth and Wolfhart Pannenberg).

AF299 Gibellini, Rosino, ed.

Paths of African Theology. Maryknoll, NYU: Orbis Books, 1994. vi, 202 pp. Paper. 0883449749.

Eleven Protestant and Catholic African theologians present original essays on various aspects of African Christian theology.

AF300 Goba, Bonganjalo

An Agenda for Black Theology: Hermeneutics for Social Change. Johannesburg, SA: Skotaville, 1988. vii, 126 pp. Paper. 0947009310.

A challenge to members of the black Christian community, to reflect critically about the relevance of their faith in the current oppressive situation of South Africa, including chapters on the nature, context, praxis, and goal of black theological reflection.

AF301 Govender, Shunmugam Perumal

In Search of Tomorrow: The Dialogue between Black Theology and Marxism in South Africa. Kampen, NE: Kok, 1987. 171 pp. Paper. 9024233348.

This doctoral dissertation presents a global view of the development of Marxism since the 1850s, culminating in an argument in favor of an integration of black theology and Marxist thought in South Africa.

AF302 Hallencreutz, Carl F., ed.

On Theological Relevance: Critical Interaction with Canaan Sodindo Banana. Uppsala, SW: Swedish Institute of Missionary Research, 1992. 52 pp. Paper. No ISBN.

Four short essays on the theology of Canaan Sodindo Banana, Methodist theologian and first President of Zimbabwe, by Carl F. Hallencreutz, John S. Pobee, Paul H. Gundani, and Carl R. Brakenhielm.

AF303 Healey, Joseph, and Donald Sybertz

Towards an African Narrative Theology. (Faith and Culture Series). Maryknoll, NYU: Orbis Books; Nairobi, KE: Paulines Publications Africa, 1996. 397 pp. Paper. 1570751218 (US), 996621187X (KE).

The fruit of years of work by the Sukuma Research Committee of the Catholic Church in Tanzania, this theology draws upon Africa's rich oral literature and traditions (proverbs, sayings, songs, etc.).

AF304 Heijke, J. P.

Kameroenese bevrijdingstheologie: Jean-Marc Ela: Theologie van onder de boom. (Kerk en Theologie in Context, 6). Kampen, NE: Kok, 1990. x, 226 pp. Paper. 9024253357.

A scholarly introduction to the theology of the Roman Catholic priest, Jean-Marc Ela (b.1936), Professor of Theology in Cameroon.

AF305 Hood, Robert E.

Must God Remain Greek?: Afro Cultures and God-Talk. Minneapolis, MNU: Fortress Press, 1990. xiii, 273 pp. Paper. 0800624491.

A detailed argument for the leavening and renewal of Christian concepts of God, Christ, the Spirit, and the saints, utilizing traditional African-based religions; with illustrations from African and Caribbean indigenous churches and religious movements.

AF306 Imasogie, Osadolor

Guidelines for Christian Theology in Africa. Achimota, GH: African Christian Press, 1983. 92 pp. Paper. 9964875126.

A brief contrast between Western and African worldviews, with guidelines for theologizing from an African worldview base; by the Principal of the Nigerian Baptist Theological Seminary.

AF307 Kabasélé, François et al.

Chemins de la christologie africaine. (Collection "Jésus et Jésus-Christ," 25). Paris, FR: Desclée, 1986. 317 pp. 2718902957.

A collection of essays by theologians in Francophone Africa, seeking an African Christology in which Christ is confessed in their own cultural terms, as chieftain, forefather, master of initiation, etc.

AF308 Kabasélé, François et al.

Christologia africana. (Saggi Teologici, 2). Milano, IT: Ed. Paoline, 1987. 277 pp. 8821513416.

Italian translation.

AF309 Kabasélé, François et al.

Der Schwarze Christus: Wege afrikanischer Christologie. (Theologie der Dritten Welt, 12). Freiburg im Breisgau, GW: Herder, 1989. 205 pp. Paper. 3451214776.

German translation.

AF310 Kato, Byang H.

Pièges théologiques en Afrique. Abidjan, IV: Centre de publication évangéliques, 1981. 231 pp. No ISBN.

French translation.

AF311 Kato, Byang H.

Theological Pitfalls in Africa. Kisumu, KE: Evangel Publishing House, 1975. 200 pp. Paper. No ISBN.

A critique of some trends in African theology, judged to be heretical by the author, the General Secretary of the Association of Evangelicals of Africa and Madagascar (AEAM).

AF312 Kä Mana

Foi chrétienne, crise africaine et reconstruction de l'Afrique: sens et enjeux des théologies africaines contemporaines. (Collections "Défi africain"). Nairobi, KE: CETA; Lomé, TG: HAHO; Yaoundé, CM: CLE, 1992. 220 pp. 9966987924.

A typology of African Christian theologies with proposals for a renewed "theology of reconstruction" by a Congolese Protestant theologian serving as a pastor in Dakar (Senegal).

AF—AFRICA

AF313 Kinoti, H. W., and John Mary Waliggo, eds.
The Bible in African Christianity: Essays in Biblical Theology. (African Christianity Series). Nairobi, KE: Acton Publishers, 1997. 209 pp. 9966888365.

A collection of nine essays by African scholars, on the impact of the Old and New Testaments on African societies, cultures, and peoples.

AF314 Kretzschmar, Louise
The Voice of Black Theology in South Africa. Johannesburg, SA: Ravan Press, 1986. xiii, 136 pp. Paper. 0869752693.

A presentation of the relationship between religion and politics, with particular attention paid to the impact of African, black, and liberation theologies on the experience of contemporary black South African Christians, and on the regional version of black theology that has emerged in the last decade.

AF315 Kurewa, John Wesley Zwomunondiita
Biblical Proclamation for Africa Today. Nashville, TNU: Abingdon, 1995. 112 pp. Paper. 0687014441.

Helps for the relevant communication of the Gospel in Africa through biblical preaching, by the Vice Chancellor of Africa University.

AF316 Martey, Emmanuel
African Theology: Inculturation and Liberation. Maryknoll, NYU: Orbis Books, 1993. xii, 176 pp. Paper. 0883448610.

A scholarly examination by the Ghanaian theologian and ordained Presbyterian minister of two major strands of African theology—inculturation and liberation.

AF317 Mbiti, John S.
Bibel und Theologie im afrikanischen Christentum. Translated by Bernard Ferrazzini. Edited by Gudrun Löwner. (Theologie der Ökumene, 22). Göttingen, GW: Vandenhoeck & Ruprecht, 1987. 212 pp. 3525563264.

German translation.

AF318 Mbiti, John S.
Bible and Theology in African Christianity. Nairobi, KE: Oxford University Press, 1986. xiv, 248 pp. Paper. 019572593X.

The well-known Kenyan theologian analyzes the dynamics of contemporary African Christianity, and defines its major terms (the Bible, theology, prayer, faith, salvation, and mission).

AF319 Mbiti, John S.
New Testament Eschatology in an African Background: A Study of the Encounter between New Testament Theology and African Traditional Concepts. London, ENK: Oxford University Press, 1971. xii, 216 pp. 0198216599.

A study by the noted African theologian comparing New Testament and Akamba (Kenya) religious beliefs.

AF320 Mofokeng, Takatso A.
The Crucified among the Cross Bearers: Towards a Black Christology. (Proefschrift Theol. Hogeschool Kampen). Kampen, NE: Kok, 1983. 263 pp. Paper. 9024230136.

In discussion with European theologians (first of all Karl Barth), Latin Americans (especially Sobrino), and African theologians, the ecclesiological and christological outlines of an African theology are developed.

AF321 Molynuex, K. Gordon
African Christian Theology: The Quest for Selfhood. San Francisco, CAU: Mellen Research University Press, 1993. 422 pp. Paper. 0773419462.

Case studies of the contextualization of theology in Zaire

by Roman Catholics, Protestants, and Kimbanguists; originally presented as a doctoral thesis at the School of Oriental and African Studies, University of London.

AF322 Moore, Basil, ed.
The Challenge of Black Theology in South Africa. Atlanta, GAU: John Knox Press; London, ENK: Hurst, 1973. xii, 156 pp. Paper. 0804207941 (US), 0900966971 (UK).

Seventeen essays banned by the South African goverment, which develop a black theology of liberation of the oppressed; originally published as *Essays in Black Theology.*

AF323 Moore, Basil, ed.
Schwarze Theologie in Afrika: Dokumente einer Bewegung. Translated by Ulrich Huhne. (Theologie der Ökumene, 14). Göttingen, GW: Vandenhoeck & Ruprecht, 1973. 178 pp. Paper. 3525563167.

German translation.

AF324 Mosala, Itumeleng J., and Buti Tlhagale, eds.
The Unquestionable Right to be Free: Black Theology from South Africa. Maryknoll, NYU: Orbis Books; Braamfontein, SA: Skotaville Publishers, 1986. xviii, 206 pp. Paper. 0883442515.

A collection of twelve significant essays by South African black theologians; originally presented in 1983 and 1984 at two conferences organized by the Black Theology Task Force of the Institute for Contextual Theology.

AF325 Mugambi, J. N. Kanyua
African Christian Theology: An Introduction. Nairobi, KE: Heinemann Kenya, 1989. xi, 152 pp. Paper. 9966468293.

A collection of essays on African theology, focusing on issues of Christology, ecclesiology, and eschatology, plus essays on missions, the church, and culture in East Africa; by the Chairman of the Department of Religious Studies, University of Nairobi.

AF326 Mugambi, J. N. Kanyua
From Liberation to Reconstruction: African Christian Theology after the Cold War. Nairobi, KE: East African Educational Publishers, 1995. xv, 258 pp. 9966465243.

Fourteen articles by the professor of philosophy and religious studies at the University of Nairobi, introducing "reconstruction" as a new paradigm for African Christian theology in the New World Order.

AF327 Mununguri, Masumbuko
The Closeness of the God of Our Ancestors: An African Approach to the Incarnation. (African Church: Inculturation 2, 4). Nairobi, KE: Paulines Publications Africa, 1998. 111 pp. Paper. 9966214119.

The interpretation of African traditional beliefs in God, in light of Christianity; part one develops the African view of God as creator and father, while part two deals with the African approach to the mystery of incarnation.

AF328 Muzorewa, Gwinyai H.
The Origins and Development of African Theology. Maryknoll, NYU: Orbis Books, 1985. xiv, 146 pp. Paper. 0883443511.

An informative survey of the sources of African theology and of the variety of its forms which have been developed in the past twenty years.

AF329 Ngewa, Samuel, Mark Shaw, and Tite Tiénou, eds.
Issues in African Christian Theology. Nairobi, KE: East African Educational Publishers, 1998. xiv, 329 pp. Paper. 9966467793.

A collection of twenty-three short essays by evangelical African theologians, many of them previously published in the *African Journal of Evangelical Theology.*

AF330 Nicolson, Ronald
A Black Future?: Jesus and Salvation in South Africa. London, ENK: SCM Press; Philadelphia, PAU: Trinity Press International, 1990. xvi, 265 pp. Paper. 033400120X.

A soteriology by the Professor in Religious Studies in the University of Natal, South Africa, seeking to build bridges between the theologies of Europe and America, on the one hand, and liberation and black South African theologies on the other.

AF331 Nolan, Albert, and Richard F. Broderick, eds.
To Nourish Our Faith: The Theology of Liberation in Southern Africa. South Africa: OP, 1987. v, 118 pp. Paper. 0620109424.

A study book for South African Christians based on lectures to Roman Catholic church leaders in 1986.

AF332 Nyamiti, Charles
African Tradition and the Christian God. (Spearhead Series, 49). Eldoret, KE: Gaba Publications, 1975. 76 pp. Paper. No ISBN.

A look at African theistic beliefs, relative to Christian beliefs, liberation theology in the African context, and the contributions of the African worldview understandings of God; first published in 1970.

AF333 Nyimi, Modeste Malu
Inversion culturelle et déplacement de la pratique chrétienne Africaine: préface à une théologie périphérique. (Kerk en theologie in context, 24). Kampen, NE: Kok, 1993. viii, 216 pp. Paper. 9039005036.

A scholarly analysis of the historical, cultural, economic, and theological influences on African worldviews that affect the development of African theology.

AF334 Oduyoye, Mercy Amba
Hearing and Knowing: Theological Reflections on Christianity in Africa. Maryknoll, NYU: Orbis Books, 1986. viii, 168 pp. Paper. 0883442582.

A scholarly reflection by a Ghanaian woman theologian on Christianity in Africa—its history, theology, and mission.

AF335 Oduyoye, Mercy Amba
Wir selber haben ihn gehört: Theologische Reflexionen zum Christentum in Afrika. Freiburg, SZ: Edition Exodus, 1988. 227 pp. Paper. 3905575396.

German translation.

AF336 Ogbonnaya, A. Okechukwu
On Communitarian Divinity: An African Interpretation of the Trinity. New York, NYU: Paragon House, 1994. xx, 124 pp. 1557787042.

An argument that the Christian idea of a God who is one-and-many is organically related to African communitarian understandings of reality, and community expressed in the theologies of Tertullian and other early fathers in North Africa.

AF337 Paratt, John
Reinventing Christianity: African Theology Today. Grand Rapids, MIU: Eerdmans; Trenton, NJU: Africa World Press, 1995. x, 217 pp. Paper. 0802841139 (E), 0865435235 (A).

The first comprehensive survey in English of Christian theology in Africa, covering historical development, methodology, types, central theological themes, and problematic issues.

AF338 Pobee, J. S., and Carl F. Hallencreutz, eds.
Variations in Christian Theology in Africa. Nairobi, KE: Uzima Press for WCC, 1986. viii, 111 pp. Paper. No ISBN.

Essays by John S. Pobee, Mercy A. Oduyoye, Lars Parkman, and Stina Karlten on variations between black and African theologies; originally presented at Uppsala University, Sweden in 1983.

AF339 Pobee, J. S., ed.
Exploring Afro-Christology. (Studies in the Intercultural History of Christianity, 79). Frankfurt am Main, GW: Lang, 1992. 155 pp. 3631444680.

Papers from an ecumenical encounter on the theme of Christology in Africa today, by scholars from Africa, the United States, and the West Indies.

AF340 Pobee, J. S.
Grundlinien einer afrikanischen Theologie. Göttingen, GW: Vandenhoeck & Ruprecht, 1981. 155 pp. Paper. 3525563213.

German translation.

AF341 Pobee, J. S.
Toward an African Theology. Nashville, TNU: Abingdon, 1979. 174 pp. Paper. 0687424208.

A prominent African theologian, Professor of New Testament and Church History at the University of Ghana at Legon, makes a case for translating Christianity into authentic African categories, with special reference to the Akan people of Ghana.

AF342 Rüucker, Heribert
"Afrikanische Theologie": Darstellung und Dialog. (Innsbrucker theologische Studien, 14). Innsbruck, AU: Tyrolia-Verlag, 1985. 271 pp. Paper. 3702215484.

A dissertation viewing African theology as an allegory including an overview of African realism, symbolic theology, and revelation theology.

AF343 Sawyerr, Harry
Creative Evangelism: Towards a New Christian Encounter with Africa. London, ENK: Lutterworth Press, 1968. 183 pp. 0718813294.

The distinguished West African theologian argues for the necessity of adopting a positive stance toward African traditions, and for Christianity to transcend cultural forms.

AF344 Sawyerr, Harry
The Practice of Presence: Shorter Writings of Harry Sawyerr. Edited by John Parratt. Grand Rapids, MIU: Eerdmans, 1996. xvi, 149 pp. Paper. 0802841155.

A collection of papers on West African religions and theological issues by Harry Sawyerr (1909-1987), the former Professor of Theology and Principal of Fourah Bay College, University of Sierra Leone.

AF345 Schreiter, Robert J., ed.
Faces of Jesus in Africa. (Faith and Cultures Series). Maryknoll, NYU: Orbis Books, 1991. xiii, 181 pp. Paper. 0883447681.

Eleven essays by African theologians, educators, and church leaders (mostly Roman Catholic), reinterpreting Christology within African cultures.

AF346 Semaine théologique de Kinshasa (4th: 1968)
Renouveau de l'église et nouvelles églises: colloque sur la théologie africaine. Inkisi, CG: Université Lovanium, 1969. 301 pp. No ISBN.

Papers from the 4th Theology Week (Kinshasa, 22-27 July 1968), originally published in the March and May 1969 issues of *Revue du Clergé Africain*, which reveal early ideas for an African theology.

AF347 Setiloane, Gabriel Molehe
African Theology: An Introduction. Johannesburg, SA: Skotaville Publishers, 1988. vi, 50 pp. Paper. 0947009140.

Nine brief lectures for African youth describing African theological structures.

AF348 Setiloane, Gabriel Molehe
Der Gott meiner Väter und mein Gott: Afrikanische Theologie im Kontext der Apartheid. Wuppertal, GW: Hammer, 1988. 122 pp. Paper. 3872943561.

The German translation of *African Theology: An Introduction* (Skotaville Publishers, 1986), plus three other essays by the author, with an introduction by Jürgen Moltmann.

AF349 Sundermeier, Theo, ed.
Christus, der schwarze Befreier: Aufsätze zum Schwarzen Bewütsein und zur Schwarzen Theologie in Südafrika. (Erlanger Taschenbücher, 25). Stuttgart, GW: Ev-Luth Mission, 1973. 156 pp. Paper. 3872140485.

A selection of texts by authors from southern Africa, elucidating the background and tendencies of black theology, and its relevance within the South African situation at the beginning of the seventies.

AF350 Sundermeier, Theo, ed.
Zwischen Kultur und Politik: Texte zur afrikanischen und zur Schwarzen Theologie. (Zur Sach-Kirchliche Aspekte heute, 15). Hamburg, GW: Lutherisches Verlagshaus, 1978. 173 pp. Paper. 3785904363.

A collection of articles by African authors on different aspects of African theology.

AF351 Tiénou, Tite
The Theological Task of the Church in Africa. (Theological Perspectives in Africa, 1). Achimota, GH: Africa Christian Press, 1990. 56 pp. Paper. 996487796X.

Second revised and expanded edition of a call to evangelicals to develop a positive theology for Africa; based on lectures delivered in Nigeria in 1978 and published in 1982 by Africa Christian Press.

AF352 Udoh, Enyi Ben
Guest Christology: An Interpretive View of the Christological Problem in Africa. (Studies in the Intercultural History of Christianity, 59). Frankfurt am Main, GW: Lang, 1988. xi, 284 pp. Paper. 3631407173.

A detailed analysis of the continuing disparity problem for Nigerian Christians who were first presented Christ within a Euro-Christian worldview, but who now wish to relate Christology to African cosmology.

AF353 Vähäkangas, Mika
In Search of Foundations for African Catholicism: Charles Nyamiti's Theological Methodology. Leiden, NE: Brill, 1999. vii, 326 pp. 9004113282.

This study explores the interaction between neo-Thomism and African traditional thinking in Charles Nyamiti's theological methodology; this first monograph published on the theological method of an African theologian has wide-ranging ramifications for Western philosophical/theological systems in a non-Western context.

AF354 Young, Josiah U.
African Theology: A Critical Analysis and Annotated Bibliography. (Bibliographies and Indexes in Religious Studies, 26). Westport, CTU: Greenwood, 1993. xiii, 257 pp. 0313264872.

The author, Professor of Systematic Theology at Wesley Theological Seminary in Washington, D.C., who writes extensively on Black and African theology, defines the scope of the field in five introductory essays, and gives extended annotation on 607 published books and articles in the field.

Central Africa: General Works

See also SO185 and SO245.

AF355 Balandier, Georges
Daily Life in the Kingdom of the Kongo from the Sixteenth to the Eighteenth Century. Translated by Helen Weaver. New York, NYU: Pantheon Books, 1968. 288 pp. No ISBN.

English translation.

AF356 Balandier, Georges
La vie quotidienne au royaume de Kongo du XVIe au XVIIIe siècle. Paris, FR: Hachette, 1965. 286 pp. No ISBN.

A well-researched history of the Bakongo kingdom of Central Africa during the period of pioneer Christianity there.

AF357 Heaton, Jane
Journey of Struggle, Journey in Hope: People and Their Pilgrimage in "Central Africa." New York, NYU: Friendship Press, 1983. vii, 92 pp. Paper. 0377001260.

Twenty-seven short articles prepared as a mission study on the multifaceted life of peoples and churches, from coast-to-coast in Africa south of the Sahara and north of the Zambezi River.

AF358 Moorehead, Alan
The White Nile. New York, NYU: Harper, 1960. 385 pp. No ISBN.

A dramatic study of the discovery of the source of the Nile and the opening up of Central Africa to European influence, 1850-1900; and the story of the missionaries, soldiers, diplomats, and merchants who made that exploration possible.

AF359 Ranger, Terence O., and John C. Weller, eds.
Themes in the Christian History of Central Africa. Berkeley, CAU: University of California Press, 1975. xvi, 285 pp. 0520025369.

A collection of twelve scholarly essays, plus introductions by the editors, providing case studies on historical confrontations between Christianity and central African religions, and the interaction between the churches and colonial society in the present Malawi, Zambia, and Zimbabwe.

AF360 Rowley, Henry
The Story of the Universities Mission to Central Africa: From Its Commencement under Bishop Mackenzie, to Its Withdrawal from the Zambesi. New York, NYU: Negro Universities Press, 1969. 424 pp. 0837112990.

A reprint of the 1866 edition of this pioneer history, by a participant in the missionary expedition from 1860 to 1864, undertaken in response to a 1857 appeal made by Livingstone at Cambridge and Oxford universities.

AF361 Söderberg, Gustav

Missionsresa i Centralafrika. Örebro, SW: Evangeliipress, 1970. 157 pp. No ISBN.

An assessment of Swedish Lutheran missions in central Africa.

Central Africa: Biography

See also HI228 and SO359.

AF362 Brabazon, James

Albert Schweitzer: A Biography. New York, NYU: Putnam, 1975. 509 pp. 0399114211.

A long and comprehensive biography giving a fully rounded portrait of Schweitzer and his accomplishments, showing him as father, husband, fund-raiser, friend, musician, and doctor; with pictures, extensive bibliography, index, and one of his articles.

AF363 Campbell, Dugald

In the Heart of Bantuland. New York, NYU: Negro Universities Press, 1969. 313 pp. No ISBN.

A record of twenty-nine years' pioneering in central Africa among the Bantu peoples, with a description of their habits, customs, secret societies, and languages; originally published in 1922 (Philadelphia, PAU: J. B. Lippincott; London, ENK: Seeley, Service & Co.).

AF364 Cousins, Norman

Albert Schweitzer's Mission: Healing and Peace. New York, NYU: Norton, 1985. 319 pp. 0393022382.

An intimate account, by the former editor of the *Saturday Review*, of his 1957 visit to Lambarene to see Schweitzer; with their correspondence, as well as with other prominent world leaders, 1955-1965, on the cause of world peace.

AF365 Harris, John

The Road to Kisumu. Arlington, TXU: John Harris, 1985. 143 pp. Paper. No ISBN.

An autobiographical account, by a United Pentecostal missionary, of work from 1970 to 1982, in Ethiopia, Kenya, Uganda, Tanzania, and Mauritius.

AF366 Marshall, George, and David Poling

Schweitzer: A Biography. Garden City, NYU: Doubleday, 1971. xviii, 342 pp. No ISBN.

A detailed biography of the missionary doctor, the first written since his death in 1965, designed to refute his critics.

AF367 Miller, David C., and James Pouilliard, eds.

The Relevance of Albert Schweitzer at the Dawn of the 21st Century. Lanham, MDU: University Press of America, 1992. x, 158 pp. 0819185256.

Papers presented at the International Albert Schweitzer Colloquium held 23-24 August 1990 at the United Nations at which twenty-three distinguished peacemakers, philosophers, environmentalists, medical innovators, and Nobel Prize winners spoke of how Albert Schweitzer's example has influenced their contributions to their fields and to the world; co-published by arrangement with Albert Schweitzer Institute for the Humanities.

AF368 Thompson, David C.

On Call. (Jaffray Collection of Missionary Portraits). Camp Hill, PAU: Christian Publications, 1991. 220 pp. Paper. 0875094430.

Adventures of a CMA medical missionary who grew up in Vietnam and served from 1977 in Gabon.

Central African Republic

See also CR561 and AF436.

AF369 Poli, Paolo

Chiesa e Poligamia in Africa: Fra tradizione e cambiamento. Bologna, IT: Editrice Missionaria Italiana, 1996. 327 pp. Paper. 8830706280.

A detailed sociological study of polygamy in the Central African Republic, and of responses (historical and contemporary, theological, ethical, and pastoral) by the Catholic Church.

AF370 Vallarino, Umberto, and Nicolas Godian

Centrafrica in bianco e nero. Genoa, IT: Procura Missioni Estere Cappuccini, 1970. 252 pp. No ISBN.

An illustrated popular report of visits to Roman Catholics missions in the Central African Republic.

AF371 Zarndé, René

Dépendance ou indépendance?: Une étude sur les structures, les fonctions et les finances de l'Église Baptiste de l'Ouest RCA. Central African Republic: Berbérati, 1996. 136 pp. No ISBN.

A study of mission/church relations in structure, function, and finance for the Baptist Church in the Central African Republic.

Chad

AF372 Clapham, J. W.

John Olley: Pioneer Missionary to the Chad. London, ENK: Pickering & Inglis, 1966. 139 pp. No ISBN.

Biography of a Christian Brethren missionary to Chad from 1925-1955, whose work concentrated on translation and Bible teaching, while using his profession as a doctor as a way to express his compassion to the local population.

AF373 Clauss, Mechthild

College in Koyom: Lehren und lernen im Tschad. (Erlanger Taschenbücher, 101). Erlangen, GW: Ev.-Luth Mission, 1992. 127 pp. Paper. 3872145010.

The author collects here, through her experience as teacher of French in a school in Chad, the reflections of her students on a variety of topics, such as the necessity of the bride price in that society.

Congo-Brazzaville

See also SO652.

AF374 Anderson, Efraim

Churches at the Grass-roots: A Study in Congo-Brazzaville. London, ENK: Lutterworth Press; New York, NYU: Friendship Press, 1968. 296 pp. 0718813308.

A scholarly study of the life and development of Protestant and Catholic churches in three districts of the Congo Republic, showing the importance of local, social, and cultural factors.

AF—AFRICA

AF375 Andersson, Efraim
Les Bongo-Rimba. (Occasional Papers, 9). Uppsala, SW: Almqvist & Wiksell, 1983. viii, 128 pp. Paper. No ISBN.

A report by the noted Swedish social anthropologist on field work carried out in 1931, 1934-1935, and 1949, among the Bongo-Rimba peoples in Gabon and Congo (Brazzaville), focusing on their religious beliefs and practices, including mission influences.

AF376 Andersson, Efraim
Ethnologie religieuse des Kuta II. (Occasional Papers, 14). Uppsala, SW: Almqvist & Wiksell, 1990. 225 pp. Paper. No ISBN.

The second part of the missionary anthopologist's study of the Kuta people of the Congo Republic, with analysis of new religious movements of the region, based on earlier research (1932-1960).

AF377 Andersson, Efraim
Ex oriente lux: Contribution a l'ethnographie des Kuta III. (Occasional Papers, 15). Uppsala, SW: Almqvist & Wiksell, 1991. 75 pp. Paper. No ISBN.

The final part of the social anthropologist's monograph on the Kuta people of the People's Republic of the Congo, including their religion.

AF378 Axelson, Sigbert
Culture Confrontation in the Lower Congo: From the Old Congo Kingdom to the Congo Independent State with Special Reference to the Swedish Missionaries in the 1880's and 1890's. (Studia Missionalia Uppsaliensia, 14). Stockholm, SW: Gummesson, 1970. 340 pp. No ISBN.

A detailed history, based on archival sources, of early missions in the Lower Congo River basin, from 1482 to 1900, including chapters on early Portuguese missions, later French Capuchin efforts, and 19th-century Swedish missions.

AF379 Axelson, Sigbert
Kulturkonfrontation i Nedre Kongo. Uppsala, SW: Tvåväga förlags AB, 1971. 194 pp. No ISBN.

Swedish translation.

AF380 Ernoult, Jean
Les Spiritains au Congo de 1865 à nos jours. (Mémoire spiritaine études et documents, 3). Paris, FR: Congrégation du Saint-Esprit, 1995. 461 pp. Paper. 2900666112.

A narrative illustrated account of the missionary work in the Congo, from 1865 to 1995, of the Congrégation du Saint-Esprit (Holy Ghost Fathers).

AF381 Johansson, Margareta
Kvinnoliv i Kongo. Stockholm, SW: Verbum Förlag, 1991. 104 pp. Paper. 9152617769.

An illustrated vignette of the lives of ten women in the Republic of the Congo, by a journalist who grew up there as a child of Swedish Lutheran missionaries.

Congo-Kinshasa [Belgian Congo; Zaire]

See also CR554, CR583, CR594, CR616, CR621, CR632, SO314, SO322-SO326, SO329, SO359, ED50, SP76, SP236, AF4, AF146, and AF834.

AF382 Anckaer, E. P. Leopold
De Evangelizatiemetode van de Missionarissen van Scheut in Kongo, 1888-1907. Brussels, BE: Koninklijke Academie voor Overzeese Wetenschappen, 1970. 307 pp. Paper. No ISBN.

A detailed history of the work of the Congregation of the Immaculate Heart of Mary (Scheutists) in the Belgian Congo from 1888 to 1907, written in Dutch with documentation in French.

AF383 Arnot, Frederick Stanley
Garenganze; Or Seven Years' Pioneer Mission Work in Central Africa. (Cass Lib. of African Studies, Miss. Researchers and Travels). London, ENK: Cass, 1969. xxiv, 276 pp. 0714618608.

New edition with a new introduction by Robert T. Rotberg.

AF384 Bartsch, Anna
Hidden Hand in the Story of My Life. Winnipeg, MBC: Christian Press, 1987. x, 234 pp. Paper. No ISBN.

A Mennonite Brethren woman of Russian descent tells of her calling from God and her experiences as mother and missionary wife in Africa, 1897-1988.

AF385 Bayly, Joseph T.
Congo Crisis: Charles and Muriel Davis Relive an Era of Missions during Weeks of Imprisonment in Stanleyville. London, ENK: Victory Press, 1966. 224 pp. No ISBN.

Popular account about the Congo uprising in 1964 in which thirty white missionaries and 10,000 Congolese Christians died at the hands of the rebels.

AF386 Benedetto, Robert, ed.
Presbyterian Reformers in Central Africa: A Documentary Account of the American Presbyterian Congo Mission and the Human Rights Struggle in the Congo, 1890-1918. Translated by Winifred Kellersberger Vass. (Studies in Christian Mission, 16). Leiden, NE: Brill, 1997. xxii, 580 pp. 9004102396.

A collection of 123 documents, including letters, diary extracts, reports, minutes of meetings, speeches, and published articles, that tell the story of the American Presbyterian Congo Mission, and its struggle for human rights in the Congo from 1890 to 1918; with introduction and notes by the editor.

AF387 Bertsch, Ludwig
Laien als Gemeindeleiter: Ein afrikanisches Modell; Texte der Erzdiözese Kinshasa. Translated by Ursula Faymonville. (Theologie der Dritten Welt, 14). Freiburg, GW: Herder, 1990. 237 pp. Paper. 3451218569.

The story of Cardinal Joseph Malula's establishing of lay leaders for base communities as an alternative to the traditional parish structures in Kinshasa, with all pertinent documentation leading to the movement's success.

AF388 Bertsche, Jim
CIM/AIMM: A Story of Vision, Commitment and Grace. Elkhart, INU: Fairway Press, 1998. xxvii, 855 pp. Paper. 0788014153.

An insider's history of Congo Inland Mission, later the African Inter-Mennonite Mission, pioneered by half a dozen Mennonite groups in the early 1900s.

AF389 Bormann, Martin
Zwischen Kreuz und Fetisch: Die Geschichte einer Kongomission. Bayreuth, GW: Hestia-Verlag, 1965. 386 pp. No ISBN.

Part history, part personal anecdote, part political commentary, the book narrates the adventures of a group of Sacred Heart missionaries in the period just prior to Vatican II in the heart of the central Congo (Zaire).

AF390 Braekman, E. M.
Histoire du Protestantisme au Congo. (Collection histoire du Protestanisme en Belgique et au Congo Belge, 5). Brussels, BE: Librairies des Éclaireurs Unionistes, 1961. 391 pp. No ISBN.

A history focusing solely on the evangelistic work of the Protestant churches in Congo during seventy-five years from the time of the independent state (1885-1908), through the Belgian colonial regime (1908-1960).

AF391 Burgess, Alan
Daylight Must Come: The Story of a Courageous Woman Doctor in the Congo. New York: Delacorte; London, ENK: Michael Joseph, 1975. vi, 297 pp. Paper. 0440033659 (US), 0718109996 (UK).

The account of Dr. Helen Roseveare and her medical ministry in the Congo (Zaire), especially during the years of the Simba rebellion.

AF392 Burrus, Barbara Howard
Sharing Four Cultures: A Journey of Love. Franklin, TNU: Providence House, 1997. 216 pp. 1577360451.

Reminiscences by the author (b.1931) of her life as a United Methodist missionary doctor's wife, and mother of seven children in India, Belgium, Zaire, and the United States.

AF393 Cappo, Salvatore
A Truly African Church. (Spearhead, 99). Eldoret, KE: Gaba Publications, 1987. iv, 42 pp. Paper. No ISBN.

A discussion of the role of laity in the RCC of Zaire including an exposition of Cardinal Malula's institution of the *Mokambi wa Paroise*; the rights and obligation of laypersons and reasons for the institution of the *bakambi* in the church in Zaire.

AF394 Carlson, Lois
Arzt im Kongo: Die Missionstätigkeit und das Martyrium des Dr. Paul Carlson. Freiburg, GW: Herder, 1967. 239 pp. No ISBN.
German translation.

AF395 Carlson, Lois
Monganga Paul: The Congo Ministry and Martyrdom of Paul Carlson, M.D. (Harper Jungle Missionary Classics). New York, NYU: Harper & Row, 1966. viii, 197 pp. No ISBN.

Story of the medical mission and martyrdom of Paul Carlson (1928-1964) as told by his widow.

AF396 Cavazzi, Giovanni Antonio
Descrição Histórica dos Três Reinos do Congo, Matamba e Angola. Translated by Graciano Maria de Leguzzano. (Estudos de Cartografia Antiga, 2-3). Lisboa, PO: Junta de Investigações do Ultramar, 1965. 2 vols. No ISBN.

A critical Portuguese edition in two volumes, of a work that first appeared in Italian in 1867; probably the best book ever written about the Congo Mission.

AF397 Crawford, John Richard
Protestant Missions in Congo 1878-1969. [Kinshasa, CG]: Librairie Evangelique du Congo, 1969. 26 pp. Paper. No ISBN.

A well-annotated, greatly condensed historical survey of the changing nature of Protestant witness in the Congo during its years of becoming established, developing a definite influence on the people through educational and medical institutions, and suffering persecutions during the rebellion of 1964-1965 and the subsequent upheavals in secular government.

AF398 Fabian, Johannes
Jamaa: A Charismatic Movement in Katanga. Evanston, ILU: Northwestern University Press, 1971. xii, 284 pp. 0810103397.

An extensive analysis of a charismatic movement within the Roman Catholic Church in Zaire, with special attention to the relationship between the social and the cultural aspects.

AF399 Filesi, Teobaldo
La relazioni tra il regno del Congo e la Sede apostolica nel XVI secolo. (Publicazioni dell'Instituto italiano per l'Africa, Serie 1: Quaderni d'Africa, 10). Como, IT: Cairoli, 1968. 249 pp. No ISBN.

A monograph on 16th-century relations between the Catholic Church and the Kongo Kingdom.

AF400 Filesi, Teobaldo, and Isidoro de Villapadierna
La Missio Antiqua dei Cappucini nel Congo (1645-1835): Studio preliminare e guida delle fonti. (Subsidia scientifica franciscalia, 6). Rome, IT: Instituto storico cappucini, 1978. 269 pp. No ISBN.

A guide to the mission of the Capuchins in the lower course of the River Zaire from its inception in 1618, with extensive reference to the writings of scholars in various languages.

AF401 Fuller, Millard
Bokotola. New York, NYU: Association Press; Piscataway, NJU: New Century Publishers, 1977. 174 pp. Paper. 0809619245 (A), 0832911798 (N).

A firsthand account by the Executive Director of Habitat for Humanity, of pioneer efforts to build houses for the poor in Zaire, 1973-1976.

AF402 Giovanni, Francesco Da Roma
Brève relation de la fondation de la Mission des frères mineurs Capucins du séraphique père St. François au Royaume du Congo. Louvain, BE: Nauwelaerts, 1964. xxviii, 149 pp. No ISBN.

Translation from Italian of a 1648 account of Capuchin pioneer missions in the Congo.

AF403 Goertzen, Anna Rose
Mama Nlundi—Our Adopted Mother. New York, NYU: Vantage Press, 1982. 155 pp. 0553050235.

Autobiography of a Mennonite missionary in Zaire.

AF404 Harrison, Mary
Mama Harri—and No Nonsense: Missionary Memories of a Congo Casualty. (Lakeland Publications, 140). London, ENK: Oliphants, 1969. 128 pp. 0551002557.

Reminiscences of a Congo missionary.

AF405 Hill, Brad, and Ruth Hill
Slivers from the Cross: A Missionary Odyssey. Chicago, ILU: Covenant Publications, 1990. 111 pp. Paper. 0910452717.

Vignettes by Evangelical Covenant Church missionaries in Zaire, 1973-1990.

AF406 Jacobsson, Per-Olaf
Hemma Hos Oss I Kongo. Stockholm, SW: Filadelfia, Solna, Seeling, 1968. 47 pp. No ISBN.

A brief account of Swedish Pentecostal missions and churches in the Democratic Republic of the Congo [Zaire].

AF—AFRICA

AF407 Kasongo, Michael
History of the Methodist Church in the Central Congo. Lanham, MDU: University Press of America, 1998. xi, 171 pp. 0761808825.

A history of the Methodist mission and church in the central Congo (Zaire), 1912 to 1996; based on the author's Ph.D. dissertation (University of Kentucky, 1982).

AF408 Keidel, Levi O.
Black Samson: An African's Astounding Pilgrimage to Personhood. Carol Stream, ILU: Creation House, 1975. 144 pp. 0884191168.

The moving story of Maweja Apollo, a Zairois criminal who converted to Christ and became a pastor—providing insights into missionary and Zairois attitudes toward culture and government during the last decades of Belgian colonial rule.

AF409 Keidel, Levi O.
War to be One. Grand Rapids, MIU: Zondervan, 1977. 239 pp. 031035370X (hdbk), 0310353718 (pbk).

Vignettes from the history of Mennonite missions in Congo(Zaire) from its development (1930-1950), transition (1950-1959), and trial by fire during the civil war (1960-1965).

AF410 Kratz, Michael
La Mission des rédemptoristes belges au Bas Congo: la période des semailes (1899-1920). Brussels, BE: Academie royale d'sciences d'outre-mer, 1970. 402 pp. No ISBN.

A detailed description in French, Flemish, and German, of the work of the Redemptorists in evangelizing hundreds of villages in the interior of the Bas Congo region of the Congo, its evolution and territorial extension up to 1920, with bibliographies.

AF411 Kremer, Eva Maria
Mutter am Kongo: Lebensbild der Geschwister Falter. Bayreuth, GW: Hestia-Verlag, 1963. 248 pp. No ISBN.

The youth and missionary lives of three sisters of the same family who became Sisters of the Precious Blood and worked in Central Congo for the Coquilhatville Diocese at the turn of the century.

AF412 Kroeker, Joanne
Shiny Shoes on Dusty Paths: The Polishing of Grace. Shippensburg, PAU: Treasure House, 1995. xvii, 274 pp. Paper. 1560438452.

A first-person account of missionary service in the Congo (1933-1943) by Abe Kroeker, a Canadian Mennonite who served with the Congo Inland Mission, as told to his daughter.

AF413 Lagergren, David
Mission and State in the Congo: A Study of the Relations between Protestant Missions and the Congo Independent State Authorities with Special Reference to the Equator District, 1885-1903. (Studia Missionalia Uppsaliensia, 13). Lund, SW: Gleerup, 1970. 365 pp. No ISBN.

A doctoral dissertation on the missionary critique of King Leopold I's exploitative policies in the Belgian Congo.

AF414 Lehr, Stephanie
"Wir leiden für den Taufschein!": Mission und Kolonialisierung am Beispiel des Landkatechumenates in Nordostzaire. (Studies in the Intercultural History of Christianity, 87). Frankfurt am Main, GW: Lang, 1993. 445 pp. Paper. 363145774X.

Following a brief history of the catechumenate of the White Fathers in northeast Zaire (1864-1963), the methods used, with special reference to baptism and confirmation, and the praxis in relation to traditional culture, is analyzed thoroughly for the 1930 to 1960 period.

AF415 Linder, Alois
Junge Kirche im afrikanischen Urwald: Aus der Geschichte der Diözese Bokungu-Ikela. Hallbergmoos, GW: Birkenverlag der Herz-Jesu Missionare, 1988. 283 pp. Paper. 3925263098.

A popular history of the Catholic diocese of Bokungu-Ikela, Zaire, on the occasion of its 25th anniversary.

AF416 Loewen, Melvin J.
Three Score. Elkhart, INU: Congo Inland Mission, 1972. 181 pp. No ISBN.

The history, 1911 to 1971, of what is now the African Inter-Mennonite Mission, formerly the Congo Inland Mission, in the Congo (Zaire).

AF417 Luca da Caltanisetta
Diaire congolais (1690-1701). Translated by François Bontinck. Louvain, BE: Nauwelaerts, 1970. liv, 250 pp. No ISBN.

New light is shed on a decade of mission and political history of the Congo through this excellent translation and interpretation of the notes of the Sicilian Capuchin (1644-1702).

AF418 Malula, Joseph-Albert
Œuvres complètes du Cardinal Malula:rassemblées et présentées par Léon de Saint Moulin. Edited by Antoine Matenkadi Finifini. (Documents du Christianisme Africain, 1-7). Kinshasa, CG: Imprimerie Saint Paul; Limete, CG: Facultés catholiques de Kinshasa, 1997. 7 vols. No ISBN.

A complete collection of the writings of the late Catholic Archbishop of Kinshasa, Joseph-Albert Cardinal Malula (1917-1989), with an introductory essay by the editors assessing his impact on African Christianity [vol.1. Introduction généale, tables et indes.; vol. 2. Textes biographiques et généraux; vol. 3. Textes concernant l'inculturation et les abbés; vol. 4. Directives diocésaines; vol. 5. Textes concernant la vie religieuse; vol. 6. Textes concernant le léicat et la société; vol. 7. Textes concernant la famille. Théatre et chants].

AF419 McGavran, Donald Anderson, and Norman Riddle
Zaire: Midday in Missions. Valley Forge, PAU: Judson Press, 1979. 252 pp. 0817008357.

A popular account of church growth in Zaire, seeking to answer the question, "Are missionaries still needed when 23 out of 25.5 million Zairois claim to be Christian?"

AF420 Mpongo, Laurent
Pour une anthropologie chrétienne du mariage au Congo: vers un rituel chrétien du mariage conformé au génie des Ntombe Njale. Kinshasa, CG: Éditions du CEP Limété, 1968. xxix, 201 pp. Paper. No ISBN.

A dissertation analyzing traditional marriage customs among the Ntomba people of Congo (Zaire), Christian marriage rituals and customs as introduced by Roman Catholic missionaries, and adaptations by which to reconcile the two.

AF421 Nelson, Henry S.
Doctor with Big Shoes: Missionary Experiences in China and Africa. (Tennessee Heritage Library Bicentennial Collection). Franklin, TNU: Providence House, 1995. 288 pp. Paper. 1881576450.

A Presbyterian Church US missionary recounts his and his wife's missionary experiences in China (1947-1951, 1986-1993) and in Congo/Zaire (1952-1982).

AF422 Nelson, Jack E.

Christian Missionizing and Social Transformation: A History of Conflict and Change in Eastern Zaire. New York, NYU: Praeger, 1992. x, 209 pp. 0275942465.

A detailed study of the animosities faced by Baptist missionaries, philosophically committed to the Three Self principles for development of an indigenous church, ironically resulting in a schism among Baptist churches in Kivu; based on archival research and oral interviews in northern Kivu, Zaire.

AF423 Nelson, Robert G.

Congo Crisis and Christian Mission. St. Louis, MOU: Bethany Press, 1961. 112 pp. No ISBN.

A report on the situation of missions and an emerging church in Zaire on the eve of its independence, and its implications both for the church in the Congo and its supporting churches in the North; based on the author's five visits to Africa, 1956-1960, as Africa Secretary of the United Christian Missionary Society (Disciples of Christ).

AF424 Noirhomme, G., W. de Craemer, and M. de Wilde d'Estmael

L' Église au Congo en 1963: Rapport d'une enquête socio-religieuse. Léopoldville, CG: Centre de recherches sociologiques, 1964. x, 188 pp. No ISBN.

A detailed report on the state of Catholicism in the newly independent country of Zaire.

AF425 Nsumbu, Josef

Culte et société: Le culte chrétien comme réflexion critique d'une société moderne africaine : cas du chant dans la Communauté évangélique du Zaïre. (Studia Missionalia Upsaliensia, 62). Uppsala, SW: Université d'Uppsala, Faculté de Théologie, 1995. 373 pp. Paper. 9185424200.

A dissertation analyzing worship and music patterns in the Protestant churches of Zaire, especially in the Communauté évangélique au Zaïre.

AF426 Otene, Matungulu

The Spiritual Journey of Anuarite. (Religious Life in Africa, 3). Nairobi, KE: Paulines Publications Africa, 1998. 143 pp. Paper. 9966214194.

Important stages of the life and martyrdom of Sister Marie Clémentine Anuarite in the context of the rebellions in Congo-Kinshasa.

AF427 Palmer, Bernard, and Marjorie Palmer

Mount to the Sky Like Eagles: The Story of Evangelical Free Church Missions in Africa and Europe. (Heritage Series, 9). Minneapolis, MNU: Free Church Publications, 1986. 356 pp. Paper. 0911802649.

The third book in a three-volume popular history of the Overseas Missions Department of the Evangelical Free Church (volume 9 of the ten-volume centennial history of the denomination,) including chapters on work in Germany, Belgium, and Zaire.

AF428 Petersen, William J.

Another Hand on Mine: The Story of Dr. Carl K. Becker of the Africa Inland Mission. New York, NYU: McGraw-Hill, 1967. viii, 228 pp. No ISBN.

A popular biography of Carl Becker (b.1894), covering stories of his medical missionary work in Congo (Zaire) from 1930 to 1964.

AF429 Phipps, William E.

The Sheppards and Lapsley: Pioneer Presbyterians in the Congo. Louisville, KYU: Presbyterian Church (US), 1991. 140 pp. Paper. No ISBN.

The story of the remarkable interracial team of William Henry Sheppard (1865-1927) and Samuel Lapsley (1866-1892) sent in 1890 as pioneer missionaries to the Congo Free State by the [Southern] Presbyterian Church in the United States.

AF430 Reid, Alexander James

Congo Drumbeat: History of the First Half Century in the Establishment of the Methodist Church among the Atetela of Central Congo. New York, NYU: World Outlook Press, 1964. 158 pp. No ISBN.

A history written by a career Methodist missionary.

AF431 Reid, Alexander James

The Roots of Lomomba: Mongo Land. Hicksville, NYU: Exposition Press, 1979. xiv, 194 pp. 0682490083.

A local history of the Mongo people (also known as the Otetela) of central Zaire, by a United Methodist missionary who worked for forty years among them; with special attention to their most illustrious son, Patrice Lumumba.

AF432 Roeykens, Auguste, ed.

La politique religieuse de l'État indépendant du Congo: documents. (Académie royale des sciences d'outre-mer; Classe des sciences morales et politiques, Nouv. sér., t. 32, fasc. 1.). Brussels, BE: Koninklijke Academie voor Overzeese Wetenschappen, 1965. v, 648 pp. No ISBN.

A collection of 552 documents from government and mission archives, illustrating the political policy of King Leopold II towards the Catholic missions.

AF433 Roseveare, Helen

Give Me This Mountain: An Autobiography. Grand Rapids, MIU: Eerdmans, 1966. 166 pp. No ISBN.

Autobiography of a twenty-year medical missionary in Congo (Zaire), with WEC International.

AF434 Rule, William

Milestone in Mission. Edited by Barbara Rule Sugue. Franklin, TNU: Providence House, 1998. xv, 336 pp. Paper. 1577360923.

A Presbyterian medical missionary to the Congo (Zaire), 1940 to 1980, tells his story.

AF435 Söderberg, Bertil

Karl Edvard Laman: Missionär, språkforskare, etnograf. Stockholm, SW: Svenska Missionsförbundet, 1985. 208 pp. 917070712X.

A biography of the missionary Karl Edvard Laman (1867-1944), of the Mission Covenant Church of Sweden, and an assessment of his contribution to Congo studies.

AF436 Samarin, William J.

The Black Man's Burden: African Colonial Labor on the Congo and Ubangi Rivers, 1880-1900. Boulder, COU: Westview Press, 1989. xii, 276 pp. 0813377404.

A thorough examination of French and Belgian colonization of central Africa (present Congo and Central African Republic) with a focus on labor policies, including those of Catholic and Protestant missions.

AF—AFRICA

AF437 Sinda, Martial
Le Messianisme Congolais et ses incidences politiques: Kimbanguisme, Matsouanisme, autres mouvements. (Bibliotheque historique). Paris, FR: Payot, 1972. 390 pp. No ISBN.

A detailed history of Belgian colonial repression of messianic movements in the Congo: primarily those of Simon Kimbangu and Matsoua Grenard, as well as a brief analysis of more recent movements such as *Mpeve Nzambi, N'zambi-Bougie (or Lassysme), Moounkoungouna,* and *Croix-Koma.*

AF438 Stenström, Arvid
Mission blir Kyrka. Stockholm, SW: Gummesson, 1977. 228 pp. Paper. 9170704929.

A history of the Mission Covenant Church of Sweden's mission in the Congo (Zaire).

AF439 Strijbosch, Alfons
Missionar im Tross der Kongo-Rebellen: Tatsachenbericht nach 33 Monaten Gefangenschaft bei den Simbas. (Kreuzring-Bücherei, 57). Trier, GW: Johann Joseph Zimmer, 1970. 211 pp. No ISBN.

Given up for dead as a victim of the rebellion in the Congo, Sacred Heart Father Strijbosch emerged from almost three years captivity in northeast Congo, and here tells his story.

AF440 Toews, John B.
The Mennonite Brethren Church in Zaire. Edited by Paul G. Hiebert. Fresno, CAU: Mennonite Church, General Conference, Board of Christian Literature; Hillsboro, KSU: Mennonite Brethren Publishing House, 1978. 255 pp. Paper. No ISBN.

A popular history, with study questions, of the growth from mission to indigenous church, beginning with Aaron Janzen's service with the Congo Inland Mission in 1913.

AF441 Vass, Winifred Kellersberger, and Lachlan C. Vass
The Lapsley Saga. Franklin, TNU: Providence House, 1997. xxi, 234 pp. 1577360230.

A narrative history of Samuel N. Lapsley (1868-1892) of the American Presbyterian Congo Mission, and of others who, with pioneer effort, opened up the central Congo to missions by navigating on the Zaire/Congo River.

AF442 Verbeek, Léon
Ombres et clairières: histoire de l'implantation de l'Église catholique dans le diocèse de Sakania, Zaïre (1910-1970). (Studi, Instituto Storico Salesiano, 4). Rome, IT: LAS, 1987. 422 pp. Paper. 8821301451.

A scholarly history of the establishment and development of the RCC in the Diocese of Sakania, Congo (Zaire), between 1910 and 1970; the volume examines the missiological, pastoral, social action, educational, and financial issues.

AF443 Williamson, Lamar
Ishaku: An African Christian between Two Worlds. Lima, OHU: Fairway Press, 1992. 134 pp. Paper. 1556733941.

The story of Ishaku (d.1964), an African Christian who died during the rebellion in the Kasai region of Zaire; focusing on the conflict of cultures in his life and the influence of Presbyterian and Christian Brethren missions on him and his contemporaries.

AF444 Womersley, Harold
Wm. F. P. Burton: Congo Pioneer. Eastbourne, ENK: Victory Press, 1973. 160 pp. 089476190X.

A popular biography of William F. P. Burton (1886-1971), noted British Pentecostal leader and founder of the Congo Evangelistic Mission.

AF445 Yrild, Joel
Mission och kommunikation: Den kristna missionen och transportnätets utveckling i Belgiska Kongo/Zaire 1878-1991. (Studia Missionalia Upsaliensia, 59). Göteborg, SW: Göteborg University, Department of Human and Economic Geography, 1994. xix, 459 pp. Paper. 9186472186.

A detailed study of the influence of the Christian missions in Congo (Zaire) on the forming of that nation's transportation systems (road, rail, river and air).

Equatorial Guinea

AF446 Crespo Prieto, Teodoro
Los Misioneros de Guinea Ecuatorial. Madrid, SP: Edicolor, 1964. 48 pp. No ISBN.

A brief introduction to Claretian missions in Equatorial Guinea.

Gabon

See also AF362, AF364, AF366, and AF375.

AF447 Klein, Carol M.
We Went to Gabon. Harrisburg, PAU: Christian Publications, 1974. 184 pp. No ISBN.

A popular autobiography of George and Carol Klein, pioneers of the CMA in Gabon, 1935-1963.

AF448 Rohrick, Lisa M.
Both Feet on God's Path: The Story of Julie Fehr. (The Jaffray Collection of Missionary Portraits, 16). Camp Hill, PAU: Christian Publications, 1996. xiii, 205 pp. Paper. 0875096727.

A popular illustrated biography of Julie Fehr (deceased 1994) who, from 1965 to 1993, served as a CMA missionary in Gabon, working as a Bible translator and as Director of TEE for West Africa.

AF449 Thompson, David C.
Beyond the Mist: The Story of Donald and Dorothy Fairley. Camp Hill, PAU: Christian Publications, 1998. ix, 229 pp. Paper. 0875097677.

The story of Don (1905-1990) and Dorothy (1908-1982) Fairley, pioneer CMA missionaries to Gabon, 1930 to 1954, and of the growth of the Gabon Christian Alliance Church to become that nation's largest Protestant denomination.

Eastern Africa: General Works

See also HI251, HI726, CR1039, SO328, SO646, EC254, EC318, PO157, CO49, ED29, ED128, ED165, MI81, CH347, AF60, AF98, AF186, AF224, and AF325.

AF450 Anderson, William B.
The Church in East Africa, 1840-1974. Dodoma, TZ: Central Tanganyika Press, 1977. 197 pp. Paper. No ISBN.

A first history of the spread of Christianity in Kenya, Tanzania, and Uganda; produced as a theological textbook in cooperation with the TEF.

AF451 Brown, Gerald Grover
Christian Response to Change in East African Traditional Societies. (Woodbrooke Occasional Papers, 4). London, ENK: Friends Home Service Committee for Woodbrooke College, 1973. 52 pp. No ISBN.

A short monograph on missions and responses to social change by the Kikuyu of Kenya and the Buganda of Uganda.

AF452 *Catholic Directory of Eastern Africa*
Tabora, TZ: T.M.P. Book Department, 1965. No ISBN.

A directory of Catholic churches and institutions.

AF453 Froise, Marjorie, ed.

World Christianity: South Central Africa: A Factual Portrait of the Christian Church. (World Christianity). Monrovia, CAU: MARC, 1991. iii, 164 pp. Paper. 091255276X.

Country profiles to show the progress of the Gospel and the state of Christianity in Angola, Comoros, Madagascar, Malawi, Mauritius, Mozambique, Reunion, Seychelles, St. Helena with Ascension and Tristan da Cunha, Zambia, and Zimbabwe.

AF454 Hansen, Holger Bernt, and Michael Twaddle, eds.

Religion and Politics in East Africa: The Period since Independence. (Eastern African Studies). London, ENK: Currey; Nairobi, KE: East African Educational Publishers; Kampala, UG: Fountain Publishers, 1995. ix, 278 pp. 0852553854 (UK hdbk), 0852553846 (UK pbk), 0821410857 (US hdbk), 0821410865 (US pbk).

Fourteen scholarly case studies on Muslim and Christian involvements in politics in eastern Africa and their interactions; also published by Ohio University Press, Athens, OHU (1995).

AF455 Healey, Joseph

What Language Does God Speak?: African Stories about Christmas and Easter. Nairobi, KE: St. Paul Publications, 1989. 80 pp. Paper. No ISBN.

Sixteen brief accounts shared in small Christian communities of Tanzania and Kenya of how lay Christians experience the Christmas and Easter faith.

AF456 Jong, A. H. de

De Uitdaging van Vaticanum II in Oost-Afrika: De bijdrage van Nederlandse missionarissen aan de doorvoering van Vaticanum II in Tanzania, Kenya, Uganda en Malawi 1965-1975. (Kerk en Theologie in Context, 30). Kampen, NE: Kok, 1995. xi, 196 pp. Paper. 903900515X.

Based on oral interviews with Dutch Catholic missionaries, the author analyzed the impact of Vatican II upon their efforts at adaptation to political and religious realities in East Africa.

AF457 Krapf, Ludwig

Travels, Researches, and Missionary Labours, during an Eighteen Years' Residence in Eastern Africa: Together with Journeys to Jagga, Usambara, Ukambani, Shoa, Abessinia and Khartum: and a Coasting Voyage from Mombaz to Cape Delgado. New York, NYU: Johnson Reprint, 1968. li, 566 pp. No ISBN.

Reprint of the 1860 edition of a mission classic, by the pioneer German Lutheran missionary and explorer in Kenya.

AF458 Miller, Paul M.

Equipping for Ministry in East Africa. Dodoma, TZ: Central Tanganyika Press; Scottdale, PAU: Herald Press, 1969. 231 pp. 0836116046.

A primer on Protestant theological education in East Africa.

AF459 Mugambi, J. N. Kanyua, ed.

Critiques of Christianity in African Literature: With Particular Reference to the East African Context. Nairobi, KE: East African Educational Publishers, 1992. vi, 166 pp. Paper. 9966465804.

Assessments of the relation of Christianity to African culture, by both Christian missionaries and African histori-

ans, novelists, and church leaders within East Africa, during the 1960s and 1970s.

AF460 Mugambi, J. N. Kanyua, John Mutiso-Mbinda, and Judith Vollbrecht

Ecumenical Initiatives in Eastern Africa. Nairobi, KE: AACC/ AMECEA, 1982. 188 pp. No ISBN.

The final report of the Joint Research Project of the AACC and AMECEA, 1976-1981.

AF461 New, Charles

Life, Wanderings, and Labours in Eastern Africa: With an Account of the First Successful Ascent of the Equatorial Snow Mountain, Kilima Njaro, and Remarks upon East African Slavery. (Cass Library of African Studies, Missionary Research and Travels, 16). London, ENK: Cass, 1971. 525 pp. No ISBN.

Third edition of a mission classic by Charles New (1840-1875), British Methodist missionary and explorer of East Africa from 1862 to 1875; with introduction by Alison Smith.

AF462 Okullu, Henry

Church and Politics in East Africa. Nairobi, KE: Uzima Press, 1974. 81 pp. Paper. No ISBN.

A brief essay by the Anglican bishop of Maseno South, Uganda, on why Christians should be involved in issues of development, tribalism, corruption, church and state, crime and punishment, democracy, and the indigenization of the church.

AF463 Pawelzik, Fritz

Mit Bibel, Ball und Badehose: Geschichten aus dem CVJM in Ostafrika. (Erlanger Taschenbücher, 32). Erlangen, GW: Ev.-Luth. Mission, 1975. 192 pp. Paper. 3872140655.

A descriptive account of a member's work with the YMCA in East Africa, with personal vignettes from Tanzania, Kenya, and Uganda.

AF464 Rudolph, Ebermut

Schwarze Völker suchen Gott: Afrikas Christen auf eigenen Weg. Munich, GW: Claudius Verlag, 1969. 256 pp. No ISBN.

Personal experiences and reflections from a two-year journey through eastern and southern Africa, visiting church personnel of every variety.

AF465 Schoffeleers, J. M. et al.

Missie en Ontwikkeling in Oost-Afrika: Een ontmoeting van culturen. (Publikaties van het Katholiek Studiecentrum). Nijmegen, NE: Katholiek Studiecentrum; Baarn, NE: Ambo, 1983. 167 pp. Paper. 9070713039 (K), 9026306148 (A).

A collection of articles on the relation between Christian mission and socioeconomic development in East Africa, with special reference to the Catholic church in Tanzania.

AF466 Strayer, Robert W., Edward I. Steinhart, and Robert M. Maxon

Protest Movements in Colonial East Africa: Aspects of Early African Response to European Rule. (Eastern African Studies, 12). Syracuse, NYU: Syracuse University, Program of Eastern African Studies, 1973. ix, 96 pp. No ISBN.

A monograph assessing the roots of African nationalism in East Africa, including influence of the missions.

AF467 Welbourn, Frederick Burkewood

East African Christian. (The Students' Library, 4). London, ENK: Oxford University Press, 1965. vi, 226 pp. Paper. No ISBN.

An introduction to the situation of Christians and the churches in East Africa in 1965.

AF—AFRICA

Eastern Africa: Biography

AF468 Coomes, Anne
Festo Kivengere: A Biography. Eastbourne, ENK: Monarch Publications, 1990. 478 pp. Paper. 1854240218.

The authorized biography of Festo Kivengere (1921-1988), evangelical Anglican bishop of Kigezi, Uganda (1972-1988), who was called both "the Billy Graham of Africa," and "a tireless campaigner for justice, integrity, and righteousness in Uganda."

AF469 Forristal, Desmond
Edel Quinn 1907-1944. Dublin, IE: Dominican Publications, 1994. 232 pp. Paper. 1871552370.

A popular biography of the pioneer Legion of Mary missionary from Ireland to East Africa (1936-1944), now nominated for canonization.

AF470 Holland, Frederick E.
Kulikuwa Hatari: A Way, a Walk, and a Warfare of Faith; Forty-Three Years in Africa as Nimrod, Nomad, and Missionary. New York, NYU: Exposition Press, 1963. 85 pp. No ISBN.

Reminiscences of forty-three years of service as a missionary in East Africa of the Africa Inland Mission.

AF471 Martin, James
This Our Exile: A Spiritual Journey with the Refugees of East Africa. Maryknoll, NYU: Orbis Books, 1999. xvii, 205 pp. Paper. 1570752508.

Spiritual and travel narratives of a young American Jesuit who works with refugees in the sprawling slums of Nairobi, Kenya, helping them to begin small businesses and earn a living.

AF472 Parsons, Anthea
Beyond the Horizon: The True Story of a Remarkable Young Missionary in Africa. London, ENK: Hodder & Stoughton, 1998. ix, 241 pp. Paper. 0340709898.

The story of Anthea Parsons (b.1968) and her remarkable ministry as a lay evangelist since 1990 in Nigeria, Burundi, and Uganda; supported by Kingdom Faith Ministries.

AF473 Wood, Michael
Go an Extra Mile: The Adventures and Reflections of a Flying Doctor. London, ENK: Fount, 1980. 160 pp. Paper. 0006259189.

The biography of Michael Wood—founder in 1958 of the African Medical and Research Foundation and the Flying Doctor Service assisting various missions in East Africa; first published in 1978 (London, ENK: Collins).

Burundi

See also AF612 and AF623.

AF474 Collart, René
Les débuts de l'évangélisation au Burundi: les grands moments du Buyogoma et du Buzige, 1896-1898. Bologna, IT: Editrice Missionaria Italiana, 1981. 2 vols. No ISBN.

A scholarly history of pioneer Catholic missions in Burundi, 1896 to 1898.

AF475 Hohensee, Donald
Church Growth in Burundi. South Pasadena, CAU: William Carey Library, 1977. vi, 153 pp. 0878083162.

A summary of the total Christian witness in Burundi since 1879, deriving lessons for further church growth.

AF476 Perraudin, Jean
Naissance d'une église: histoire du Burundi chrétien. Usumbura, BD: Presses Lavigerie, 1963. 228 pp. No ISBN.

History of the White Fathers' mission in Burundi.

AF477 Wingert, Norman A.
No Place to Stop Killing. Chicago, ILU: Moody, 1974. 125 pp. Paper. 0802459412.

A description of the effect of massacres on Burundi and its churches.

Comoros

AF478 Lloyd, Tom E.
The Forgotten Islands. London, ENK: African Inland Mission, 1976. 32 pp. No ISBN.

The story of how the African Island Mission began its work in the Comoro Islands, by providing medical and other services withdrawn by the French upon the islands' independence.

Ethiopia [Abyssinia]

See also HI484, PO33, CO158, EV329, and AF636.

AF479 Aimonetto, Lydia
Nell'Africa Inesplorata Con Guglielmo Massaja. Padova, IT: Edizioni Messaggero Padova, 1964. 232 pp. No ISBN.

The story of Guglielmo Massaja (1809-1889), a remarkable Italian Capuchin missionary in Ethiopia (1846-1886), whose creative inculturation of the faith reached the "Gallas" (Oromo).

AF480 Andersen, Knud Tage
A Brief History of the Mekane Yesus Church. Christiansfeld, DK: Forlaget Savanne, 1980. 75 pp. Paper. 8785190772.

A short history of the Lutheran Mekane Yesus Church in Ethiopia, with emphasis on the 1944-1969 period, and the church within the socialist state.

AF481 Arén, Gustav
Evangelical Pioneers in Ethiopia: Origins of the Evangelical Church Mekane Yesus. (Studia Missionalia Upsaliensia, 32). Stockholm, SW: EFS-Förlaget; Addis Abeba, ET: Evangelical Church Mekane Yesus, 1978. 486 pp. 9170803641.

A doctoral dissertation on the early history of the Evangelical Church Mekane Yesus (ECMY) in Ethiopia, 1826 to 1916.

AF482 Bakke, Johnny
Christian Ministry: Patterns and Functions within the Ethiopian Evangelical Church Mekane Yesus. Oslo, NO: Solum Forlag; Atlantic Highlands, NJU: Humanities Press, 1987. 297 pp. 8256004673 (S), 0391035444 (H).

A history of the ECMY, describing the religious background and the development from 1959 to 1984.

AF483 Beshah, Girma, and Merid Wolde Aregay
The Question of the Union of the Churches in Luso-Ethiopian Relations, 1500-1632. Lisbon, PO: Junta d'Investigações d'Ultramar; Lisbon, PO: Centro de Estudos Históricos Ultramarinos, 1964. 115 pp. No ISBN.

The history of Portuguese governmental and missionary involvements in Ethiopia in the 16th and 17th centuries, and of the abortive efforts to unite the Ethiopian Orthodox Church with the Roman Catholic Church.

AF484 Bidder, Irmgard
Lalibela: The Monolithic Churches of Ethiopia. Translated by Rita Grabham-Hartmann. New York, NYU: Praeger, 1960. 137 pp. No ISBN.
Descriptions of Lalibela, a historically and religiously important center of Orthodox Christianity during the Middle Ages, replete with photographs and drawings.

AF485 Bockelman, Wilfred, and Eleanor Bockelman
Ethiopia: Where Lutheran Is Spelled "Mekane Yesus." Minneapolis, MNU: Augsburg, 1972. 112 pp. 0806612053.
A popular history and description of the work of the Mekane Yesus Church in Ethiopia.

AF486 Brown, Clifton F.
The Conversion Experience in Axum during the Fourth and Fifth Centuries. (Second Series of Historical Publications, 13). Washington, DCU: Howard University, Department of History, 1973. 30 pp. No ISBN.
Attempts to examine the important early period in the history of the Ethiopian Orthodox Church

AF487 Caraman, Philip
L'empire perdu: l'histoire des jésuites en Éthiopie. Translated by Yves Morel. (Colección Christus, 67). Paris, FR: Desclée de Brouwer, 1988. 236 pp. 2220027112.
French translation.

AF488 Caraman, Philip
The Lost Empire: The Story of the Jesuits in Ethiopia 1555-1634. Notre Dame, INU: University of Notre Dame Press, 1985. viii, 176 pp. 0268012768.
A chronicle of the work of Pedro Paez and others who, from 1589 to 1633, attempted and failed to establish a permanent Jesuit mission in Ethiopia.

AF489 Cotterell, Peter
Born at Midnight. Chicago, ILU: Moody, 1973. 189 pp. 0802408893.
History of the Evangelical Church in southern Ethiopia.

AF490 Crummey, Donald
Priests and Politicians: Protestant and Catholic Missions in Orthodox Ethiopia, 1830-1868. (Oxford Studies in African Affairs). Oxford, ENK: Clarendon Press, 1972. xii, 176 pp. 0198216777.
Traces the development of relations between European missionaries and Orthodox Ethiopia during the period of Ethiopian history known as the Era of the Princess, and the subsequent reign of Emperor Tewodros.

AF491 Cumbers, John
Living with the Red Terror: Missionary Experiences in Communist Ethiopia. Kearney, NEU: Morris Publishing, 1996. vii, 296 pp. Paper. No ISBN.
The East African director of the Sudan Interior Mission (1973-1984) recounts the ordeal of Christians in Ethiopia under Marxist rule, 1974 to 1980.

AF492 Davis, Raymond J.
Fire on the Mountains: The Story of a Miracle—the Church in Ethiopia. New York, NYU: SIM International Publications, 1980. 253 pp. No ISBN.
A study of the establishment, expansion, and conversions of the Wollams Evangelical Church of Ethiopia, including accounts of prominent personalities and converts; originally published in 1966 (Grand Rapids, MIU: Zondervan; New York: SIM).

AF493 Davis, Raymond J.
The Winds of God. Cedar Grove, NJU: SIM International Publications, 1984. 148 pp. Paper. 0919470106.
A popular account of how the Gospel spread in the work of the Sudan Interior Mission among the Walayta people of southern Ethiopia; written as first-person accounts by nine Walayta Christians.

AF494 Donzel, E. J. van
Enbaqom, Anquasa Amin (la porte de la foi): apologie éthiopienne du christianisme contre l'Islam à partir du Coran. Leiden, NE: Brill, 1969. xviii, 303 pp. Paper. No ISBN.
The French translation and commentary on an anti-Islamic polemical treatise, written by the Ethiopian Christian theologian Enqabom ca.1530; originally submitted as a thesis at Rijksuniversity in Leiden.

AF495 Eide, Oyvind M.
Revolution and Religion in Ethiopia: A Study of Church and Politics with Special Reference to the Ethiopian Evangelical Church Mekane Yesus, 1974-1985. (Studia Missionalia Upsaliensia, 66). Stavanger, NO: Misjonshøgskolens forlag; Uppsala, SW: Uppsala Universitet, 1996. xv, 347 pp. Paper. 8277210167 (NO), 9185424463 (SW).
An analysis of the role of religion in Ethiopian politics and society, with a particular emphasis on the revolutionary period, 1974-1985; originally submitted as a Th.D. dissertation at the University of Uppsala, Sweden, in 1996.

AF496 Fargher, Brian L.
The Origins of the New Churches Movement in Southern Ethiopia, 1927-1944. (Studies of Religion in Africa, 16). Leiden, NE: Brill, 1996. xiv, 329 pp. 9004106618.
A detailed analysis of the background, beginnings, and early development of non-Orthodox churches in southern Ethiopia, especially the role of the Sudan Interior Mission; with an update to 1996.

AF497 Filosa, Rosalinda
In Gunst und Zorn des Negus: Guglielmo Massaia (Äthiopien); (1809-1889, Bahnbrecher im äthiopischen Süden). (Missionare, die Geschichte machten). Mödling, AU: Verlag St. Gabriel; St. Augustin, GW: Steyler Verlag, 1979. 143 pp. Paper. 3852641401 (AU), 3877871151 (GW).
The life of a Capuchin missionary and cardinal who spent thirty-five years in Ethiopia, and is regarded as one of the most successful African missionaries.

AF498 Forslund, Eskil
The Word of God in Ethiopian Tongues: Rhetorical Features in the Preaching of the Ethiopian Evangelical Church Mekane Yesus. Uppsala, SW: Swedish Institute of Missionary Research, 1993. 274 pp. Paper. 9185424358.
Content analysis of 232 sermons by 77 preachers of the Mekane Yesus Evangelical Church of Ethiopia, analyzing the extent to which the rhetoric and strategy of the preaching is linked, either to the evangelical missions, or to Ethiopian Orthodox traditions.

AF499 Gerster, Georg
Churches in Rock: Early Christian Art in Ethiopia. Translated by Richard Hosking. New York, NYU: Phaidon, 1970. 148 pp. No ISBN.
A lavish history, with many drawings and photographs, of the medieval rock churches of northern Ethiopia.

AF—AFRICA

AF500 Haile, Getatchew, Aasulv Lande, and Samuel Rubenson, eds.
The Missionary Factor in Ethiopia: Papers from a Symposium on the Impact of European Missions on Ethiopian Society, Lund University, August 1996. (Studies in the Intercultural History of Christianity, 110). Frankfurt am Main, GW: Lang, 1999. 215 pp. Paper. 3631332599 (GW), 0820435880 (US).

Includes discussions on the justification of foreign missionary activity in a country already Christian, the impact of Catholic missions in the 16th and 17th centuries, the impact of Europeans on social and intellectual developments, and the European influence on the evangelical churches.

AF501 Hega, Nathan B.
Beyond Our Prayers: Anabaptist Church Growth in Ethiopia, 1948-1998. Scottdale, PAU: Herald Press, 1998. 279 pp. Paper. 0836190858.

A Mennonite missionary to Ethiopia (1950-1974) tells the story of the outreach of the Lancaster Mennonite Conference into Ethiopia, beginning in 1948, and of the remarkable growth despite persecution of the Meserete Kristos Church.

AF502 Hellström, Ivan
Bland faror och nöd i Kunama. Uppsala, SW: EFS-förlaget, 1989. 189 pp. 9170808376.

The story of the work of Swedish Lutheran missionaries at Kunama, Ethiopia, during the 19th century.

AF503 Heyer, Friedrich
Die Kirche Äthiopiens: Eine Bestandsaufname. (Theologische Bibliothek Töpelmann, 22). Berlin, GW: de Gruyter, 1971. xviii, 360 pp. No ISBN.

A survey of the contemporary life of the Ethiopian Orthodox Church.

AF504 Isenberg, Karl Wilhelm
The Journals of C. W. Isenberg and J. L. Krapf Detailing Their Proceedings in the Kingdom of Shoa and Journeys in Other Parts of Abyssinia in the Years 1839, 1840, 1841 and 1842.... (Library of African Studies. Travels and Narratives, 34). London, ENK: Cass, 1968. 529 pp. No ISBN.

Reprint of the 1843 journals of pioneer Africa missionaries of the CMS, in which they told of missionaries' work, difficulties, and trials, including opposition from the Catholic Church to their reentry into Abyssinia in 1842.

AF505 Kaplan, Steven
The Monastic Holy Man and the Christianization of Early Solomonic Ethiopia. Wiesbaden, GW: Steiner, 1984. 150 pp. 3515039341.

A thesis examining the rise and function of the monastic holy men in Ethopia during the late 13th century, including important historical details.

AF506 Knoche, Elisabeth
Mais Lacht Noch auf dem Feuer: Als Ärtzin 1954-1984 in Äthiopien notiert. (Erlanger Taschenbucher, 72). Erlangen, GW: Ev.-Luth. Mission, 1985. 428 pp. Paper. 3872141724.

This volume presents the missiological reflections of Dr. Elisabeth Knoche, missionary doctor in Ethiopia (1954-1984) under the aegis of the Hermannsburger Mission; renamed Ev.-Luth. Missionswerk in Niedersachsen in 1977.

AF507 Lorit, Sergio C.
Abuna Messias. Costi quel che costi. (Minima di Citta Nuovo, 33). Rome, IT: Citta Nouva, 1968. 199 pp. No ISBN.

The history of missionary service in Ethiopia of the Italian Capuchin Guglielmo Massaja (1809-1889), and of his efforts from 1846 to extend the Latin Rite to non-Christians, with inculturation including married clergy.

AF508 Marwedel, Wolfgang
Äthiopien zuerst, 50 Jahre missionarischer Dienst-Revolution und Eigenständigkeit. Erlangen, GW: Ev.-Luth. Mission, 1978. 110 pp. Paper. 3872140973.

A historical review of Protestant Lutheran missions in Ethiopia, their relations with the ECMY (Evangelical Church Mekane Yesus), and with political developments.

AF509 Mazzarello, Maria Luisa, and Neghesti Micael
Giustino De Jacobis: Inculturasi per comunicare. (Orizzonti, 11). Rome, IT: LAS-Liberia Ateneo Salesiano, 1997. 155 pp. Paper. 8821303667.

A brief biography of Gusto de Jacobis (1800-1860)—bishop, first apostolic vicar of Ethiopia, and a member of the Congregation of the Missions of St. Vincent de Paul—who worked to establish the Roman Catholic Church in Ethiopia and was canonized in 1975 by Paul VI.

AF510 Molgaard, Lausten A.
Gammel kirke og ny mission i Ethiopien. Copenhagen, DK: Dansk Ethioper Mission, 1969. 81 pp. No ISBN.

The story of Danish missions in Ethiopia.

AF511 Saeveras, Olav
On Church-Mission Relations in Ethiopia, 1944-1969: With Special Reference to the Evangelical Church Mekane Yesus and the Lutheran Missions. (Studia Missionalia Upsaliensia, 27). Drammen, NO: Lunde Forlag og Bokhandel A/S, 1974. 215 pp. Paper. 8252046169.

A study of the role of missions in the development of the Ethiopian Evangelical Church to selfhood, with a preview sketching briefly mission activities in Ethiopia during the century before 1944.

AF512 Sandström, Allan
Per Stjärne-missionären. Stockholm, SW: EFS-Förlaget, 1988. 177 pp. 9170807183.

A biography of Per Stjärne (1895-1984), a Swedish missionary to Ethiopia.

AF513 Shepherd, Paul
Decade in the Desert: The Story of Haicota Hospital. Tunbridge Wells, ENK: Middle East Christian Outreach, 1977. 95 pp. No ISBN.

A vivid description of the first ten years (1964-1974) of the Middle East Christian Outreach's medical work in Eritrea, from its transfer from Egypt, to the hospital's evacuation under military orders.

AF514 Sidler, Werner
Mission in der Krise. Giessen, GW: Brunnen-Verlag, 1968. 118 pp. Paper. No ISBN.

This book is a history of the (Protestant) Chrischona Mission in Abyssinia in the 19th century, and answers questions concerning missionary spirituality, service, perseverance, and discernment of spirits.

AF—AFRICA

AF515 Solberg, Richard W.

Miracle in Ethiopia: A Partnership Response to Famine. New York, NYU: Friendship Press, 1991. 208 pp. Paper. 0377002151.

Careful research into relief agency archives and oral history interviews has documented the relief efforts of the Joint Relief Partnership of Lutheran, Catholic, and Ethiopian Orthodox churches, which distributed one-fourth of the total tonnage of relief food brought into a devastated Ethiopia; a cooperative effort by churches separated for 1,500 years.

AF516 Tamrat, Taddesse

Church and State in Ethiopia, 1270-1527. (Oxford Studies in African Affairs). Oxford, ENK: Clarendon Press, 1972. xv, 327 pp. 0198216718.

A detailed study, based on research done for the author's thesis (University of London), of the rise of the medieval Christian kingdom in Ethiopia, from the middle of the 13th century to the period just before the invasion of Ahmad Grahn.

AF517 Tolo, Arne

Sidama and Ethiopian: The Emergence of the Mekane Yesus Church in Sidama. (Studia Missionalia Upsaliensia, 69). Uppsala, SW: Uppsala University; Oslo, NO: Biblia/Fjellhaug Skoler, 1998. xviii, 312 pp. Paper. 9185424498 (SW), 8291911002 (NO).

A dissertation providing a detailed history, based on archival research, of the origin and development of the Ethiopian Evangelical Church Mekane Yesus among the Sidama people of southern Ethiopia.

AF518 Wesenick, Jürgen

Vitale Kirche in Äthiopien: Versuch einer Analyse des Aira District der Western Synod der Evangelical Church Mekane Yesus in Äthiopien. Hermannsburg, GW: Verlag der Missionshandlung, 1976. xvi, 458 pp. 3875460103.

A report in two parts of the West-Synod of the Evangelical Church Mekane Yesus in Ethiopia, with statistics and material of its churches and membership, 1962-1971.

AF519 Wilhelmsen, Bjørg

Dagbok fra en bambushytte. Oslo, NO: Lunde, 1977. 107 pp. 8252046266.

An account, with photos, of a visit in 1975 to Norwegian missions in Ethiopia.

AF520 Yeshag, Abuna

The Ethiopian Tewahedo Church: An Integrally African Church. New York, NYU: Vantage Press, 1989. xxiv, 244 pp. 0533075602.

An authorized history of the Ethiopian Orthodox Church, with an overview of the work of the church's diocese in the Western hemisphere, of which the author is the archbishop.

Kenya

See also CR576, CR606, SO299, SO363-SO364, EC255, EC309, EC316, PO174, ED47, AF148, AF259, and AF319.

AF521 Anderson, John E.

The Struggle for the School: The Interaction of Missionary, Colonial Government and Nationalist Enterprise in the Development of Formal Education in Kenya. London, ENK: Longman, 1970. 192 pp. 0582640644.

Examines the impact of the expatriate missionaries, government officials, traders, and technical experts, on African education in the Central Province of Kenya.

AF522 Barrett, David B. et al., eds.

Kenya Churches Handbook: The Development of Kenyan Christianity, 1498-1973. Kisumu, KE: Evangel Publishing House, 1973. xviii, 349 pp. Paper. No ISBN.

An illustrated history of the development of Christianity in Kenya, the rise of indigenous churchmanship and theology, and the extent of *harambee* (self-help) Christianity, with atlas, church directory, and bibliography.

AF523 Baur, John

The Catholic Church in Kenya: A Centenary History. Nairobi, KE: St. Paul Publications—Africa, 1990. 256 pp. Paper. No ISBN.

The official centennial history of the Roman Catholic Church in Kenya, with both a regional and a thematic survey; edited by members of the Assumptionist Community.

AF524 Bonzanino, Giovanni

Queste mie verdi colline: Profilo di Luigi Eandi. (Collana Incontri). Bologna, IT: EMI, 1977. 105 pp. No ISBN.

A popular appraisal of the missionary service of Fr. Luigi Eandi (d.1970) in Kenya.

AF525 Bottignole, Silvana

Kikuyu Traditional Culture and Christianity: Self Examination of an African Church. Nairobi, KE: Heinemann Educational Books, 1984. 233 pp. Paper. No ISBN.

The detailed case study of the ministries of the Roman Catholic diocese of Nyeri in Kenya, 1974-1976, using methods of radical-reflexive sociology to encourage self-evaluation, and the assessment of how traditional Kikuyu customs and values relate to Christianity.

AF526 Burgman, Hans

The Way the Catholic Church Started in Western Kenya. London, ENK: Mission Book Service; Nairobi, KE: Mill Hill Missionaries, 1990. viii, 336 pp. Paper. 0950788864 (UK).

A history of the work of Mill Hill Missionaries in western Kenya, 1895 to 1988.

AF527 Capon, M. G.

Towards Unity in Kenya: The Story of Co-Operation between Missions and Churches in Kenya, 1913-1947. Nairobi, KE: Christian Council of Kenya, 1962. 101 pp. No ISBN.

A narrative history of ecumenism in Kenya over thirty-five years of missionary work.

AF528 Chepkwony, Agnes

The Role of Non-Governmental Organizations in Development: A Study of the National Christian Council of Kenya (NCCK), 1963-1978. (Studia Missionalia Upsaliensia, 43). Uppsala, SW: University of Uppsaliensia, 1987. 393 pp. Paper. 9185424110.

A detailed case study of the nature and scope of the contribution to national development of the NCCK.

AF529 Church of the Province of Kenya, Provincial Unit of Research

Rabai to Mumias: A Short History of the Church of the Province of Kenya 1844-1994. Nairobi, KE: Uzima Press, 1994. xiv, 189 pp. Paper. 9966855327.

A narrative history of the first 150 years of the Anglican Church in Kenya.

AF—AFRICA

AF530 Conference on the Role of the Churches in Independent Kenya (1964: Limuru, Kenya)
The Role of the Church in Independent Kenya. Nairobi, KE: NCCK, 1964. 76 pp. Paper. No ISBN.

Proceedings of an important consultation held during Kenya's first year of independence (28-31 January 1964).

AF531 Donders, Joseph G.
Gathering All Nations. (Spearhead Series, 101). Eldoret, KE: Gaba Publications, 1988. vi, 44 pp. Paper. No ISBN.

The author's missiological reflection on his own missionary experience in Kenya as a Roman Catholic from the Netherlands.

AF532 Downes, Stan, Robert J. Oehrig, and John Shane
Summary of the Nairobi Church Survey. Nairobi, KE: Daystar University College, 1989. 100 pp. Paper. No ISBN.

Summary of the 1986 survey of Christianity in one of Africa's fastest growing cities, based on visits to over 600 Nairobi congregations, interviews with nearly 400 church leaders, and a survey of 1,500 church attendees.

AF533 Fish, Burnette C., and Gerald W. Fish
The Kalenjiin Heritage: Traditional Religious and Social Practices. Kericho, KE: Africa Gospel Church; Marion, INU: World Gospel Mission; Pasadena, CAU: William Carey Library, 1996. xxiii, 400 pp. Paper. 0962040665 (WG), 0878087699 (WC).

A popular presentation of the traditional ceremonies and religious practices of the Kipsigii people of Kenya, with "redemptive analogies" to make bridges for presenting the Christian message; based on understandings gleaned by the authors during forty years of service under the World Gospel Mission.

AF534 Fish, Burnette C., and Gerald W. Fish
The Place of Songs: A History of the World Gospel Mission and the Africa Gospel Church in Kenya. Marion, INU: World Gospel Mission; Kericho, KE: Africa Gospel Church, 1990. xvii, 564 pp. 0962040630.

An official history of the World Gospel Mission in Kenya, and of the development there of the Africa Gospel Church.

AF535 Gitari, David
In Season and Out of Season: Sermons to a Nation. Carlisle, ENK: Regnum Books, 1996. 155 pp. Paper. 1870345118.

A collection of twenty-five prophetic sermons preached between 1975 and 1994 by Anglican bishop Gitari in Kenya.

AF536 Haumann, Tjeu
Africa Give Me Your Eyes: Stories about Meeting People in Kenya. Translated by R. van Eyndhoven. Trabuco Canyon, CAU: Source Books, 1997. 135 pp. Paper. 0940147440.

English translation of *Achter de Bloemen van Nairobi* (1982); stories told by a Mill Hill missionary of the people he came to know in and around Mathare Valley, a huge slum in Nairobi, Kenya.

AF537 Horstmann, Regina, and Irmgard Horstmann
Ankomme Kenia morgen: Erlebnisse im Entwicklungsdienst. Erlangen, GW: Ev.-Luth. Mission, 1975. 128 pp. 387214068X.

A travel and work journal by a German woman who spent two years in voluntary service teaching in Kenyan schools and kindergartens.

AF538 Iltola, Maria
Tule ja katso: ortodoksista lähetystyötä Itä-Afrikassa. Helsinki, FI: Ortodoksinen lähetysry, 1983. 111 pp. Paper. 9519948511.

The history of the missionary work of the Orthodox Church of Finland in eastern Africa.

AF539 MacPherson, Robert
The Presbyterian Church in Kenya. Nairobi, KE: Presbyterian Church of East Africa, 1970. 151 pp. No ISBN.

An account of the origins from 1891 of the Church of Scotland Mission, and growth out of it of the Presbyterian Church of East Africa to 1963.

AF540 McAuliffe, Marius
Envoy to Africa: The Interior Life of Edel Quinn. Chicago, ILU: Franciscan Herald Press, 1975. 113 pp. 0819905607.

A popular biography (1907-1944) of the remarkable envoy of the Legion of Mary to East Africa now under consideration in Rome for beatification and canonization.

AF541 Mejia, Rodrigo, ed.
The Conscience of Society. (Hekima College Collection, 4). Nairobi, KE: Paulines Publications Africa, 1995. 240 pp. Paper. No ISBN.

A compilation of twenty-two pastoral letters (1960-1994) by the Catholic bishops of Kenya, with an analysis of the context and summary of each by the editor.

AF542 Mina, Gian Paola
I nomadi della Speranza. Bologna, IT: Editrice Missionaria Italiana, 1974. 219 pp. Paper. No ISBN.

Nine vignettes of the experiences of a Catholic missionary in Kenya, with biblical reflections.

AF543 Mina, Gian Paola
In Africa con amore: Profilo della missionaria medico suor Prisca Groppo. (Collana Incontri). Bologna, IT: EMI, 1977. 239 pp. No ISBN.

An illustrated biography of Prisca Groppo (1931-1971), an Italian medical missionary Consolata Sister in northern Kenya, 1964 to 1971, with excerpts from her journals.

AF544 Neckebrouck, Valeer
Le onzième commandement: étiologie d'une église indépendante au pied du Mont Kenya. (Neue Zeitschrift für Missionswissenschaft: Supplementa, 27). Immensee, SZ: Nouvelle revue de science missionnaire, 1978. lvi, 634 pp. 3858240532.

A scholarly study of independency among the Kikuyu and neighboring peoples (Chagga, Arusha, and Maasai) in Kenya.

AF545 Njoroge, Lawrence M.
A Century of Catholic Endeavour: Holy Ghost and Consolata Missions in Kenya. Nairobi, KE: Paulines Publications Africa, 1999. 272 pp. Paper. 9966214607.

A historical study of the Holy Ghost and Consolata Congregations since their arrival in Kenya one-hundred years ago; includes portraits of Anglican and Presbyterian evangelism and the work of brothers of St. Peter Claver and Mill Hill Mission, to provide an ecumenical touch.

AF546 Nthamburi, Zablon John
A History of the Methodist Church in Kenya. Nairobi, KE: Uzima Press, 1982. xviii, 162 pp. Paper. No ISBN.

A detailed history from the beginnings of the Methodist Church in Kenya, with maps, pictures, and tables.

AF547 Ohrt, Wallace

The Accidental Missionaries: How a Vacation Turned into a Vocation. Downers Grove, ILU: InterVarsity, 1990. 195 pp. Paper. 0830817417.

The fascinating story of how Denny and Jeanne Grindall of Seattle, Washington, moved from being tourists to becoming lay missionaries among the Maasai people of Kenya, 1968 to 1983.

AF548 Priest, Doug

Doing Theology with the Maasai. South Pasadena, CAU: William Carey Library, 1990. viii, 240 pp. Paper. 087808411X.

A case study of contextualization among the Maasai people of Kenya and Tanzania by a missionary-scholar among them, focusing on biblical and Maasai understandings of sacrifice.

AF549 Reed, Colin

Pastors, Partners and Paternalists: African Church Leaders and Western Missionaries in the Anglican Church in Kenya, 1850-1900. (Studies in Christian Mission, 17). Leiden, NE: Brill, 1997. xii, 202 pp. 9004106391.

A scholarly study tracing the relationships between missionaries and African church workers in Kenya, 1850-1900, as missionaries increasingly adopted imperial assumptions of Western superiority.

AF550 *Religious Formation in International Communities*

(Tangaza Occasional Paper, 6). Nairobi, KE: Paulines Publications Africa, 1998. 88 pp. Paper. 9966213996.

Five essays on the formation of young members of Catholic religious orders in East Africa, plus a 1996 survey of attitudes among them in Kenya.

AF551 Ryan, Patrick, ed.

Structures of Sin, Seeds of Liberation. (Tangaza Occasional Papers, 7). Nairobi, KE: Paulines Publications Africa, 1998. 120 pp. Paper. 9966214224.

This collection of seven essays from a Tangaza College project contributes to the debate on locating structures that maintain injustice and on discerning appropriate activity to bring about radical change.

AF552 Sandgren, David P.

Christianity and the Kikuyu: Religious Divisions and Social Conflict. (American University Studies 9: History, 45). New York, NYU: Lang, 1989. viii, 201 pp. 0820407321.

A scholarly analysis, based on archival sources, of the conflicts between missionary teachings and Kikuyu customs and leadership in Kenya, 1920-1945, including female circumcision, independent schools, the *Arathi*, and the *Kirore* revolt.

AF553 Shaffer, Ruth T.

Road to Kilimanjaro: An American Family in Maasailand. Grand Rapids, MIU: Four Corners Press, 1985. xii, 248 pp. 0961529725.

An account of the difficulties and triumphs that Ruth and Roy Shaffer confronted in their ministry with the Maasai in Kenya, beginning in the 1920s.

AF554 Shorter, Aylward

African Culture, An Overview: Socio-Cultural Anthropology. (Handbook / African Church, 7). Nairobi, KE: Paulines Publications Africa, 1998. 109 pp. Paper. 9966214127.

A seasoned author, teacher, and priest of the Society of Missionaries of Africa, examines religion, symbolism, ritual, marriage, family, community, creative arts, and contemporary urbanization in the African setting.

AF555 Shorter, Aylward, and Edwin Onyancha

Street Children in Africa: A Nairobi Case Study. Nairobi, KE: Paulines Publications Africa, 1999. 120 pp. Paper. 9966214488.

The symptoms and causes of the rise of street children in Nairobi, with studies of various organizations serving street children in order to map out a strategy for confronting the problem.

AF556 Smoker, Dorothy, comp.

Ambushed by Love: God's Triumph in Kenya's Terror. Fort Washington, PAU: CLC, 1993. 284 pp. Paper. 087508740X.

A collection of personal testimonies by participants in the East African Revival of how God sustained them during the Mau Mau struggle, 1952 to 1960.

AF557 Strayer, Robert W.

The Making of Mission Communities in East Africa: Anglicans and Africans in Colonial Kenya, 1875-1935. London, ENK: Heinemann; Albany, NYU: State University of New York Press, 1978. xiv, 174 pp. 0435948016 (UK), 0873952456 (US).

A detailed historical and cultural analysis of the attempt by the Anglican CMS to establish Christianity on the Kenya coast through the freed slave towns of Rabai and Freretown (1875-1900), and the resulting impact on Kenya's colonial society and church development in the 20th century.

AF558 Tablino, Paul

The Gabra: Camel Nomads of Northern Kenya. Translated by Cynthia Salvadori. (The African Church: Inculturation 1, 4). Nairobi, KE: Paulines Publications Africa, 1999. xxi, 434 pp. Paper. 9966214380.

An indepth study of Gabra culture for a better understanding of the people to whom the message of the Gospel has gone forth; originally published a *I Gabbra del Kenya* (1980).

AF559 Temu, A. J.

British Protestant Missions. London, ENK: Longman, 1972. 184 pp. 058264559X (hdbk), 0582645603 (pbk).

A study of Kenya missions from 1874 to 1929, claiming to reinterpret the role of the missions from an African perspective; based on the author's doctoral thesis at the University of Aberdeen.

AF560 Voshaar, Jan

Maasai: Between the Oreteti-Tree and the Tree of the Cross. (Church and Theology in Context, 34). Kampen, NE: Kok, 1998. 262 pp. Paper. 9024293707.

An in-depth case study of the inculturation of Christianity among the Maasai of Kenya, focusing on worldviews, myths, parables, and modernity.

AF561 Wanjohi, Gerald Joseph

The Wisdom and Philosophy of the Gikuyu Proverbs: The Kihooto World-View. Nairobi, KE: Paulines Publications Africa, 1997. 271 pp. Paper. 9966212868.

The former chairman of the Department of Philosophy at the University of Nairobi, Kenya provides a hermeneutical study of Kikuyu proverbs as a basis for an authentic African philosphy, with linkages to Judeo-Christian parallels.

AF—AFRICA

AF562 Wanyoike, E. N.
An African Pastor. Nairobi, KE: East African Publishing House, 1974. 255 pp. No ISBN.

A detailed biography of the author's grandfather who was an African pastor in the Gospel Missionary Society Fellowship, which later merged with the Presbyterian Church of East Africa.

AF563 Wolf, Jan de
Differentiation and Integration in Western Kenya: A Study of Religious Innovation and Social Change among the Bukusu. (Change and Continuity in Africa, 10). The Hague, NE: Mouton, 1977. xv, 231 pp. Paper. 9027976724.

A case study among the Bukusu of western Kenya, disclosing the mediating function of the churches in the process of social change, contributing both to structural political change and to individual social mobility.

Madagascar [Malagasy]

See also GW100, AF58, and AF1094.

AF564 Estrade, Jean-Marie
Aïna-la vie: Mission, culture et développement ô Madagascar. Paris, FR: L'Harmattan, 1996. 303 pp. 2738443567.

A Lazarist priest and missionary in Manakara, Madagascar, presents a summary of his mission work relative to historical issues of colonization and contemporary issues of indigenization.

AF565 Gow, Bonar A.
Madagascar and the Protestant Impact: The Work of the British Missions, 1818-95. (Dalhousie African Studies Series). New York, NYU: Africana Publishing; London, ENK: Longman/Dalhousie University Press, 1979. xvii, 266 pp. 0841904634.

An expansion of the author's Ph.D. thesis (Dalhousie University, 1972) on the general history of British missions in Madagascar in the 19th century.

AF566 Halverson, Alton C. O.
Madagascar: Footprint at the End of the World. Minneapolis, MNU: Augsburg, 1973. 112 pp. 080661319X.

Observations, directed to a popular readership of the American Lutheran Church on the Malagasy Republic, the Lutheran Church there, and those persons who make up both nation and church.

AF567 Johannes, Borgenvik
Bajonetter og demoner på Madagaskar: Fransk okkupas jon og gassisk samfunn i Johannes Einreims forfatterskap. Oslo, NO: Luther, 1979. 486 pp. 8253141319.

An analysis of the writings of Johannes Einrem, Norwegian missionary to Madagascar (1893-1933), with a special regard to his attitude to Malagasy society and culture, and to the French occupation and colonial government.

AF568 Jordaan, Bee
Splintered Crucifix: Early Pioneers for Christendom on Madagascar and the Cape of Good Hope. Cape Town, SA: Struik, 1969. xii, 276 pp. No ISBN.

The story of the early 19th-century pioneer missionaries, beginning with the Scottish missionary-artisan James Cameron (1800-1875) who served in Madagascar with the London Missionary Society (1826-1835, 1863-1875); and in the Cape of Good Hope (1835-1863).

AF569 Mélanges à l'occasion du centenaire de la reprise de l'évangélisation du sud de Madagascar par la Congrégation de la mission (Lazariste)
Le christianisme dans le sud de Madagascar. Fianarantsoa, MG: Baingan' Ambozontany, 1996. 410 pp. No ISBN.

A collection of short articles published to provide a short historical overview of the evangelization of southern Madagascar, and to celebrate the centenary of the Lazarists' work in that country.

AF570 Moss, Charles Frederick A.
A Pioneer in Madagascar: Joseph Pearse of the L. M. S. New York, NYU: Negro Universities Press, 1969. xvi, 261 pp. 0837127815.

Reprint of the 1913 biography of Joseph Pearse (1827-1911), an early (1863-1904) LMS missionary to Madagascar.

AF571 Munthe, Ludvig
La Bible à Madagascar: Les deux premières traductions du Nouveau Testament Malgache. (Avhandlinger utg. av Egede Instituttet, 10). Oslo, NO: Egede Instituttet, 1969. 244 pp. No ISBN.

The history of Bible translation into the Malgache language of Madagascar.

AF572 Price, Arnold H., ed.
Missionary to the Malagasy: The Madagascar Diary of the Rev. Charles T. Price, 1875-1877. (American University Studies, 9: History, 60). New York, NYU: Lang, 1989. xi, 261 pp. 0820410837.

The diary (without critical notes) of Charles Thomas Price (1847-1933), an account of his pioneer work under the auspices of the LMS in Madagascar in the 1870s.

AF573 Ramambason, Laurent W.
Missiology: Its Subject-Matter and Method: A Study of Mission-Doers in Madagascar. (Studies in the Intercultural History of Christianity, 116). Frankfurt am Main, GW: Lang, 1999. 208 pp. Paper. 3631346026 (GE), 0820443204 (US).

Missiology as the study of mission-doers who are potential facilitators or hinderers of the cause of Jesus Christ, since new contexts may require new people to carry out mission-in-action; illustrated with reference to the Church of Jesus Christ in Madagascar.

AF574 Richardson, Freida
Madagascar's Miracle Story. Hazelwood, MOU: Word Aflame Press, 1989. 176 pp. Paper. 0932581471.

The story of the missionary work of the author and her husband, United Pentecostal Church missionaries who built the United Pentecostal Church of Madagascar from nothing in 1969 to a denomination with more than 180 churches as of 1981.

AF575 Smith, F. G.
Triumph in Death: The Story of the Malagasy Martyrs. Welwyn, ENK: Evangelical Press, 1987. 128 pp. Paper. 085234242X.

A popular account of the beginnings of the LMS's work in Madagascar, and of the persecution and martyrdom of early converts, 1835-1857.

AF576 Tobiassen, Svein
Kulturkollisjon: Norske misjonaerers mote med Madagaskars innland, 1867-1883. (Maxipax 21). Oslo, NO: Pax Forlag, 1971. 189 pp. 8253000049.

An analysis of the cultural conflicts faced by pioneer Lutheran missionaries in Madagascar.

AF577 Vidal, Henri
La séparation des églises et de l'État à Madagascar, 1861-1968. (Bibliothêque africaine et malgache, droit et sociologie politique, 6). Paris, FR: Librairie générale de droit et de jurisprudence, 1970. 304 pp. No ISBN.

A detailed history of church-state relations in Madagascar during religious separation (1861-1913) and legal separation (1913-1968), with five related official documents as appendices.

Malawi [Nyasaland]

See also CR619-CR620, SO301, CO123, and AF1184.

AF578 Booth, Joseph
Africa for the African. Edited by Laura Perry. (Kachere Text, 6). Blantyre, MW: CLAIM; Bonn, GW: Verlag für Kultur und Wissenschaft, 1996. 114 pp. Paper. 9990816034 (C), 3926105682 (K).

Reprint of a classic 1897 text by the Australian missionary to Malawi, who criticized colonialism and led in advocating an African church led by Africans.

AF579 Chakanza, J. C., and Kenneth R. Ross, eds.
Religion in Malawi: An Annotated Bibliography. (Kachere Text, 7). Blantyre, MW: CLAIM; Bonn, GW: Verlag für Kultur und Wissenschaft, 1998. 160 pp. Paper. 9990816131.

The first attempt to provide a reasonably comprehensive bibliography of books and articles on religion in Malawi (traditional, Islam, and Christianity, including Catholic, Protestant, and African instituted churches).

AF580 Chakanza, J. C., ed.
Religion in Malawi. (Religion in Malawi, 5). Zomba, MW: University of Malawi, 1995. 48 pp. Paper. No ISBN.

The fifth in a series of annual publications devoted to the study of religious experience, with special reference to Malawi, by the Department of Theology and Religious Studies, Chancellor College, University of Malawi.

AF581 Elmslie, Walter Angus
Among the Wild Ngoni: Being Some Chapters in the History of the Livingstonia Mission in British Central Africa. (Cass Library of African Studies, Missionary Research and Travels, 12). London, ENK: Cass, 1970. xii, 319 pp. 0714618675.

A reprint of the 1899 history of the Ngoni people in their migration from South Africa to present Malawi, and of the pioneer missionary work among them, 1875 to 1897.

AF582 Forster, Peter G.
R. Cullen Young: Missionary and Anthropologist. Hull, ENK: Hull University Press, 1989. xv, 251 pp. Paper. 0859584852.

A scholarly analysis, from the perspective of social anthropology, of the work of Thomas Cullen Young, analyzing positively his contribution to the Tumbuka people through the Livingstonia Mission of the Free Church of Scotland.

AF583 Fraser, Donald
Winning a Primitive People: Sixteen Years' Work among the Warlike Tribe of the Ngoni and the Senga and Tumbuka Peoples of Cent. Westport, CTU: Negro Universities Press, 1970. 320 pp. 837137527.

A reprint of the 1914 description of people of Nyasaland as they were, and of the pioneer missionary work of the Livingstonia Mission among the Ngoni and the Tumbuka from 1896 to 1912; with an introduction by J. R. Mott.

AF584 Gelfand, Michael
Lakeside Pioneers: Socio-Medical Study of Nyasaland, 1875-1920. Oxford, ENK: Blackwell Publishers, 1964. x, 330 pp. No ISBN.

A detailed study of the efforts of both medical missions and the colonial government to provide health care services for both blacks and whites in present-day Malawi, by the esteemed specialist on medicine and social anthropology of the region.

AF585 Henderson, James
Forerunners of Modern Malawi: The Early Missionary Adventures of Dr. James Henderson, 1895-1898. Edited by M. M. S. Ballantyne, and R. H. W. Shepherd. Alice, SA: Lovedale Press, 1968. 297 pp. No ISBN.

A compilation of forty-two letters by James Henderson (1867-1930) to his then fiancée Margaret Davidson, about his life and work as a missionary-educator with the Livingstonia Mission of the Free Church of Scotland.

AF586 Kalilombe, Patrick A.
From Outstations to Small Christian Communities. (Spearhead, 82-83). Eldoret, KE: GABA Publications, 1984. ix, 93 pp. Paper. No ISBN.

A case study in the Roman Catholic diocese of Lilongwe, Malawi, of the history, nature, and functioning of two methods for evangelization and pastoral care—the outstation, and the small Christian community.

AF587 Langworthy, Harry
"Africa for the African": The Life of Joseph Booth. (Kachere Monograph, 2). Blantyre, MW: CLAIM; Bonn, GW: Verlag für Kultur und Wissenschaft, 1996. 520 pp. Paper. 9990816034 (C), 3926105674 (K).

A scholarly biography of a pioneer leader of African independency in Malawi.

AF588 Linden, Ian, and Jane Linden
Catholics, Peasants and Chewa Resistance in Nyasaland, 1889-1939. London, ENK: Heinemann Educational, 1974. xxi, 223 pp. 0435325302.

A study on the micro-events around Catholic mission stations and the interaction of European Catholic missionaries and African peasants, each with conscious aims and views of society.

AF589 McCracken, John
Politics and Christianity in Malawi, 1875-1940: The Impact of the Livingstonia Mission in the Northern Province. (Cambridge Commonwealth Series). London, ENK: Cambridge University Press, 1977. xv, 324 pp. 0521214440.

A detailed study of the impact of the Livingstonia Mission of the Free Church of Scotland, and of its interaction with African peoples up to the Second World War.

AF590 Mufuka, K. Nyamayaro
Missions and Politics in Malawi. (Modern Africa Series, 1). Kingston, ONC: Limestone Press, 1977. vii, 289 pp. 091964273X (hdbk), 0919642748 (pbk).

A detailed study of Scottish missionaries in Malawi, as both instruments and critics of British imperialism, and of their involvements in the struggle for African majority rule from 1927 to 1963.

AF—AFRICA

AF591 Ncozana, Silas S.
Sangaya: A Leader in the Synod of Blantyre Church of Central African Presbyterian. (Kachere Text, 2). Blantyre, MW: CLAIM; Bonn, GW: Verlag für Kultur und Wissenschaft, 1996. 56 pp. Paper. 999081600X (MW), 392610564X (GW).

An assessment of the contribution of Jonathan Sangaya (1907-1979), the first Malawian General Secretary of the Synod of Blantyre (1962), and Moderator of the General Synod of the Church of Central Africa Presbyterian.

AF592 Nzunda, Matembo S., and Kenneth R. Ross, eds.
Church, Law and Political Transition in Malawi, 1992-1994. (Kachere Series, 1). Gweru, ZI: Mambo Press/University of Malawi; Bonn, GW: Verlag für Kultur und Wissenschaft, 1995. 170 pp. Paper. 0869226029 (ZI), 3926105410 (GW).

Twelve short essays on the 1992-1994 transition of Malawi to multi-party democratic rule, focusing on the contributions by the churches and by lawyers in that transformation.

AF593 Pauw, Christoff Martin
Mission and Church in Malawi: The History of the Nkhoma Synod of the Church of Central Africa, Presbyterian, 1889-1962. Stellenbosch, SA: C M Pauw, 1980. x, 410 pp. Paper. No ISBN.

A doctoral thesis contributing to a study of the church in Africa, by an introductory survey of Malawi, a review of the Dutch Reformed Church Mission in Malawi, and a detailed survey of the development of the Nkhoma Synod from 1889 to 1962, when it became autonomous; with an extensive bibliography.

AF594 Phiri, Isabel Apawo
Women, Presbyterianism and Patriarchy: Religious Experience of Chewa Women in Central Malawi. (Kachere Monograph, 5). Blantyre, MW: CLAIM; Bonn, GW: Verlag für Kultur und Wissenschaft, 1997. 160 pp. Paper. 9990916069 (C), 3926105798 (K).

A Malawi woman theologian traces the contribution of Chewa women to the Church of Central Africa Presbyterian.

AF595 Reijnaerts, Hubert, Ann Nielsen, and J. M. Schoffeleers
Montfortians in Malawi: Their Spirituality and Pastoral Approach. (Kachere Text, 5). Blantyre, MW: CLAIM; Bonn, GW: Verlag für Kultur und Wissenschaft, 1997. xx, 496 pp. Paper. 9990816093 (C), 3926105801 (K).

A thorough documentation and history of the work of the Montfort missionary congregation in Malawi, told by two Montfort fathers and one sister of the Daughters of Wisdom congregation.

AF596 Ross, Andrew C.
Blantyre Mission and the Making of Modern Malawi. (Kachere Monograph, 1). Blantyre, MW: CLAIM; Bonn, GW: Verlag für Kultur und Wissenschaft, 1996. 216 pp. Paper. 9990816026 (C), 3926105658 (K).

A thorough examination of the foundation and early history of the Blantyre Mission of the Church of Scotland in Malawi.

AF597 Ross, Kenneth R., ed.
Christianity in Malawi: A Source Book. (Kachere Series, 3). Gweru, ZI: Mambo Press; Bonn, GW: Verlag für Kultur und Wissenschaft, 1996. 253 pp. Paper. 086922641X (ZI), 3926105577 (GW).

Twenty original source documents, 1888 to 1993, on Christian conversions, faith, culture and gender, the rise of independency, and church and state.

AF598 Ross, Kenneth R., ed.
Church, University and Theological Education in Malawi. (Kachere Series, 3). Zomba, MW: University of Malawi, Department of Theology and Religious Studies; Bonn, GW: Verlag für Kultur und Wissenschaft, 1995. 83 pp. Paper. 3926105496 (MW), 3926105496 (GW).

An introduction to theological education in Malawi today (institutions, degree programs, and courses).

AF599 Ross, Kenneth R., ed.
Faith at the Frontiers of Knowledge. (Kachere Book, 6). Blantyre, MW: CLAIM, 1998. 240 pp. Paper. 9990816115.

These papers explore issues of religion and values in the natural and social sciences, and in the humanities, with particular attention to Malawi; originally presented at the Faith and Knowledge Seminar, University of Malawi.

AF600 Ross, Kenneth R., ed.
God, People and Power in Malawi: Democratization in Theological Perspective. (Kachere Monograph, 3). Blantyre, MW: CLAIM; Bonn, GW: Verlag für Kultur und Wissenschaft, 1996. 272 pp. Paper. 9990816042 (C), 3926105712 (K).

Nine essays by theologians in Malawi, designed to construct a theology of power for today's Africa, in light of the Malawian struggle from dictatorship to democracy in 1992-1994.

AF601 Ross, Kenneth R.
Gospel Ferment in Malawi: Theological Essays. (Kachere Series, 2). Gweru, ZI: Mambo Press; Zomba, MW: University of Malawi Department of Theology and Religious Studies; Bonn, GW: Verlag für Kultur und Wissenschaft, 1995. 151 pp. Paper. 0869226150 (ZI), 3926105445 (GW).

A collection of six essays on the church and its mission in Malawian society, by the senior lecturer in theology and religious studies at Chancellor College, University of Malawi.

AF602 Ross, Kenneth R.
Here Comes Your King!: Christ, Church and Nation in Malawi. (Kachere Book, 5). Blantyre, MW: CLAIM, 1998. 200 pp. Paper. 9990816107.

A collection of essays by the Professor of Theology at Chancellor College, University of Malawi, on church and the nation, and the development of an African Christology in Malawi.

AF603 Schoffeleers, J. M.
Pentecostalism and Neo-Traditionalism: The Religious Polarization of a Rural District in Southern Malawi. (Anthropology Papers Free University, 1). Amsterdam, NE: Free University Press, 1985. 54 pp. Paper. 9062563961.

A religious history of the district of Nsanje (southern Malawi) since 1901, based on library sources and field research, with special attention to the causes of rivalry between several new churches, and a typology of the differing styles of Christianity of these new churches and the old missions.

AF604 Shepperson, George, and Thomas Price
Independent African: John Chilembwe and the Origins, Setting and Significance of the Nyasaland Native Rising of 1915. Edinburgh, ENK: University Press, 1987. xvi, 574 pp. Paper. 0852245408.

A history of an early African rising against European rule south of the Sahara, and the influence of black Americans on emergent African nationalism, especially in regard to the churches of the disinherited; originally published in 1958.

AF605 Sindima, Harvey J.
The Legacy of Scottish Missionaries in Malawi. (Studies in the History of Missions, 8). Lewiston, NYU: E Mellen Press, 1992. vi, 152 pp. 0773495746.

A history of Scottish missionary influence in Nyasaland (present Malawi) from David Livingstone's explorations in 1859 to Malawi's independence in 1964, with special reference to the work of missionaries of the Church of Scotland and the Free Church of Scotland.

AF606 Thompson, T. Jack
Christianity in Northern Malawi: Donald Fraser's Missionary Methods and Ngoni Culture. (Studies in Christian Mission, 15). Leiden, NE: Brill, 1995. xvii, 292 pp. 9004102086.

A detailed study of the inculturation of Christianity among the Ngoni people of northern Malawi in the late 19th and early 20th centuries, focusing on the policies of the Scottish missionary Donald Fraser (1870-1933) at Livingstonia Mission.

AF607 White, Landeg
Magomero: Portrait of an African Village. Cambridge, ENK: Cambridge University Press, 1987. xii, 271 pp. 0521321824 (hdbk), 0521389097 (pbk).

A detailed historical portrait of a village in the southern region of Malawi from 1859 to the present, based on archival and oral sources, with assessment of why the implementation of Livingstone's mission strategy of Christianity, commerce, and civilization failed at Magomero Mission.

AF608 Wishade, Robert Leonard
Sectarianism in Southern Nyasaland. London, ENK: Oxford University Press, 1965. 162 pp. No ISBN.

A study by a social anthropologist of the connection between the process of sectarianism and the mechanism of social organization in the southern part of Malawi.

Mauritius

AF609 Emmanuel, Ghislain
Diocese of Mauritius (1810-1973). Port-Louis, MF: By the author, Ghislain Emmanuel, 1975. 338 pp. No ISBN.

A first history of the Anglican diocese of Mauritius which served as a central depot for the Eastern missionary work of the church.

AF610 Michel, Joseph
Les auxiliaires laïcs du bienheureux Jacques Laval apôtre de l'île Maurice: de l'esclavage à l'apostolat. Paris, FR: Beauchesne, 1988. 151 pp. Paper. 2701011809.

The history of the remarkable experiment of Father Laval on the island of Mauritius, where from 1841 to 1869, with very few priests around, he trained freed slaves to serve as catechists and auxiliaries in the church's growing ministry.

AF611 Michel, Joseph
Le Père Jacques Laval: le "Saint" de l'île Maurice, 1803-1864. (Figures d'hier et d'aujourd'hui). Paris, FR: Beauchesne, 1976. 476 pp. Paper. No ISBN.

A biography of the pioneer Spiritain missionary to Mauritius.

Rwanda

AF612 Bilderback, Allen H., and Lillian A. Bilderback
Our African Journal, 1945-1950. Puyallup, WAU: ABCO Publishing, 1993. 155 pp. Paper. 0963071025.

Highlights from the journal of Free Methodist missionaries in Rwanda and Burundi, 1945 to 1950.

AF613 Church, John Edward
Forgive Them: The Story of an African Martyr. London, ENK: Hodder & Stoughton, 1966. 126 pp. No ISBN.

A popular memorial biography of Yona Kanamuzeyi (1918-1964), pioneer evangelist of the Rwanda Mission (CMS) by the author and mission colleagues of the Rwanda Mission (CMS).

AF614 Lawrence, Carl
Rwanda: A Walk through Darkness into Light. Gresham, ORU: Vision House, 1995. 189 pp. Paper. 1885305346.

A firsthand account of the Rwanda tragedy of 1994-1995, based on the journalist's visits and interviews.

AF615 Makower, Katherine
The Coming of the Rain: The Life of Dr. Joe Church: A Personal Account of Revival in Rwanda. Carlisle, ENK: Paternoster Press, 1999. xvi, 228 pp. Paper. 0853649685.

This study provides insights into Rwandan culture and conflicts, the great revival, and the pioneering missionary work of medical doctor Joe Church.

AF616 Mbanda, Laurent
Committed to Conflict: The Destruction of the Church in Rwanda. London, ENK: SPCK, 1997. xi, 147 pp. Paper. 0281050163.

An incisive analysis, by the Rwandan-born Director of Compassion International, of missionary church collusion in the corruption, violence, and ethnic tensions that were the seedbed of the Rwandan genocide.

AF617 McCullum, Hugh
The Angels Have Left Us: The Rwanda Tragedy and the Churches. (Risk Book Series, 66). Geneva, SZ: WCC Publications, 1995. xxiv, 115 pp. Paper. 282541154X.

A Canadian journalist analyzes the roots of the Rwanda human tragedy, the future of a shattered church in a shattered country, and the alternative ecumenical responses; based on hundreds of interviews with Rwandans.

AF618 McCullum, Hugh
Dieu était-il au Rwanda?: La faillite des églises. Translated by Michel Yves, and Monique Chajmowiez. Paris, FR: Éditions l'Harmattan, 1996. 230 pp. Paper. No ISBN.

French translation of *The Angels Have Left Us* (1995).

AF619 Overdulve, C. M.
Rwanda volk met een geschiedenis. (Allerwegen, 15). Kampen, NE: Kok, 1995. 60 pp. Paper. 9024221587.

A brief historical overview of Rwanda, from earliest oral traditions to 1994, including Catholic mission history.

AF620 Rapold, Walter F., ed.
Der Gott, der abends heimkommt: Die Inkulturation des christlichen Gottesbegriffs in Rwanda durch Ernest Johanssen (1864-1934) anhand der Imana-Vorstellung. Volketswil, GW: Verlagsgemeinschaft für Europäische Editionen, 1999. 642 pp. Paper. 3909093019.

This doctoral dissertation (University of Freiburg in Switzerland, 1999) is a rigorous study of the inculturation of the biblical concept of God in Rwanda in interaction with indigenous religious concepts.

AF—AFRICA

AF621 Snyder, C. Albert
On a Hill Far Away: Journal of a Missionary Doctor in Rwanda. Indianapolis, INU: Light & Life Press, 1995. 311 pp. Paper. 0896372025.

The 1993-1995 journal of a career medical missionary in Rwanda (1968-1990) who documents the 1993-1995 trauma of a nation facing genocide.

AF622 Spijker, Gerard Van't
Les Usages funéraires et la mission de l'église: Une Étude anthropologique et théologique des rites funéraire au Rwanda. Kampen, NE: Kok, 1990. x, 262 pp. Paper. 9024233208.

A dissertation examining both the anthropological and theological significance of funeral customs in Rwanda.

AF623 St. John, Patricia Mary
Breath of Life: The Story of the Rwanda Mission. London, ENK: Norfolk Press, 1971. 238 pp. 0852110049.

A popular account of the remarkable Anglican mission of the CMS in Rwanda and Burundi, 1921 to 1968.

Somalia

AF624 Eby, Omar
A Whisper in a Dry Land: A Biography of Merlin Grove, Martyr for Muslims in Somalia. Scottdale, PAU: Herald Press, 1968. 175 pp. No ISBN.

A biography of Merlin R. Grove, a Mennonite missionary, who lost his life among Muslims in Somalia.

Sudan

See also CR948, CR994, EC274, and CO112.

AF625 Ahmad, Hassan Makki Muhammad
Sudan: The Christian Design: A Study of the Missionary Factor in Sudan's Cultural and Political Integration, 1843-1986. Leicester, ENK: Islamic Foundation, 1989. 176 pp. Paper. 086037193X.

An Islamic interpretation of the roots and dimensions of Christian missions to the Sudan, and their impact in the period 1843 to 1986.

AF626 Barsella, Gino, and Miguel A. Ayuso Guixot
"Struggling To Be Heard": The Christian Voice in Independent Sudan, 1956-1996. (Faith in Sudan, 4). Nairobi, KE: Paulines Publications Africa, 1998. 126 pp. Paper. 9966213724.

A history of the efforts of Christians in modern Sudan to have their voices heard and to participate in politics.

AF627 *Black Book of the Sudan on the Expulsion of the Missionaries from Southern Sudan: An Answer*
Milan, IT: Istituto Artigianelli, 1964. 217 pp. No ISBN.

Documents related to the 1964 expulsion of Roman Catholic missionaries, including a refutation of the Sudanese government's memorandum.

AF628 Forsberg, Malcolm
Last Days on the Nile. Philadelphia, PAU: Lippincott; Chicago, ILU: Moody Press, 1970. 216 pp. No ISBN.

A firsthand account by a leader of the Sudan Interior Mission, of the relentless oppression of Christians by the Muslim majority in the Sudan, from national independence in 1956 to the expulsion of the remaining missionaries in 1965.

AF629 Green, Winifred, and Gayle Roper
Into Africa: A True Story of God's Faithfulness in a Dry and Needy Land. Camp Hill, PAU: Horizon Books, 1995. 200 pp. Paper. 0889651264.

A narrative account of service in Sudan by Africa Inland Mission missionaries, 1954 to 1992.

AF630 Gstrein, Heinz
Unter Menschenhändlern Sudan: Daniele Comboni (Sudan), (1831-1881; den Sklaven—ein Retter). (Missionare, die Geschichte machten). Mödling, AU: Verlag St. Gabriel; St. Augustin, GW: Steyler Verlag, 1978. 125 pp. Paper. 3852641195 (AU), 3877871038 (GW).

One of the greatest missionaries of the 19th century, Comboni struggled against the slave trade, evangelized by means of local personnel, and founded a missionary congregation, modeling for other missionaries.

AF631 Jackson, Herbert C.
Pastor on the Nile: A Memoir of Bishop L. H. Gwynne. London, ENK: ISPCK, 1960. ix, 270 pp. No ISBN.

A memoir of Llewellyn Henry Gwynne (1863-1957), beloved CMS missionary in the Sudan (1899-1914), bishop of Khartoum (1908-1920), and bishop of Egypt and the Sudan (1920-1945).

AF632 James, Wendy
The Listening Ebony: Moral Knowledge, Religion, and Power among the Uduk of Sudan. Oxford, ENK: Clarendon Press, 1988. xv, 391 pp. 0198234031.

A scholarly study of the worldview of the Uduk, a traditional hunting people of the Sudan, and of the impact and partial assimilation of fundamentalist Christianity, Islam, and Nilotic theocentric cults.

AF633 Lundström, Karl-Johan
The Lotuho and the Verona Fathers: A Case Study of Communication in Development. (Studia Missionalia Upsaliensia, 51). Uppsala, SW: EFS-Förslaget, 1990. 257 pp. 9170808910.

A doctoral dissertation on communication in development among the Lotuho people in southern Sudan.

AF634 McFall, Ernest A.
Approaching the Nuer of Africa through the Old Testament. South Pasadena, CAU: William Carey Library, 1970. iv, 99 pp. 0878081046.

A detailed comparison of Hebrew and Nuer social structure, social institutions, the extended family, and activities.

AF635 Morlang, Francesco
Missione in Africa Centrale: Diario 1855-1863. Translated by O. Huber Dellagiacoma and V. Dellagiacoma. (Museum Combonianum, 28). Bologna, IT: Edicione Nigrizia, 1973. xxxii, 426 pp. No ISBN.

A new critical edition of the 1855-1863 diary of Francesco Morlang (1828-1875), a pioneer missionary to Sudan of the Society of St. Columban.

AF636 Partee, Charles
Adventure in Africa: The Story of Don McClure. Grand Rapids, MIU: Zondervan, 1990. 464 pp. 0310519705.

A detailed biography of William Donald McClure (1906-1977), missionary of the American Mission to Sudan and Ethiopia from 1928 until his martyrdom in 1977, based on his letters.

AF637 Pierli, Francesco, Maria Teresa Ratti, and Andrew C. Wheeler, eds.
Gateway to the Heart of Africa: Missionary Pioneers in Sudan. (Faith in Sudan, 5). Nairobi, KE: Paulines Publications Africa, 1998. 160 pp. Paper. 9966213740.

Nine historical essays originally presented at a conference on "The Church in Sudan—Its Impact Past, Present, and Future" (Limuru, Kenya, February 1997).

AF638 Prina, Marco
Nel paese degli schiavi: Diario. Bologna, IT: EMI, 1976. 105 pp. No ISBN.

The diary of Marco Prina (1910-1970), a Catholic missionary to the Sudan.

AF639 Riley, Grace
No Drums at Dawn: A Biography of the Reverend Canon A. B. H. Riley, Pioneer Missionary in the Sudan. (Great Australian Missionaries, 3). Parkville, AT: Church Missionary Historical Publications, 1972. 84 pp. 0909821046.

The biography of a pioneer Anglican missionary (1926-1960) among the Zande and Dinka peoples of the Sudan.

AF640 Sanderson, Lilian Passmore, and Neville Sanderson
Education, Religion and Politics in Southern Sudan, 1899-1964. (Sudan Studies, 4). London, ENK: Ithaca Press; Khartoum, Sudan: Khartoum University Press, 1981. vi, 511 pp. 0903729636.

A detailed history, based on archival sources and interviews, of the relation of the colonial government (and later the national government) to the Christian missions and churches of the southern Sudan, with special reference to education.

AF641 Vandevort, Eleanor
A Leopard Tamed: The Story of an African Pastor, His People, and His Problems. New York, NYU: Harper & Row, 1968. xii, 218 pp. No ISBN.

How Christianity came to the Nuer tribe of the southern Sudan with changing allegiances, beliefs, and customs; told as the life story of a young boy, by a Presbyterian missionary who lived among the Nuer.

AF642 Vantini, Giovanni
Christianity in the Sudan. Bologna, IT: EMI, 1981. 302 pp. No ISBN.

This book, originally written in Arabic (1978), is a continuous narrative of Christianity in the Sudan, covering the rise and disappearance of Christianity in Ancient Nubia (Part I), and a survey of Christianity in the 19th and 20th centuries (Part II), with a chronology, thirty-five plates, and index of persons and places.

AF643 Vantini, Giovanni
The Excavations at Faras: A Contribution to the History of Christian Nubia. (Museum Combonianum, 24). Bologna, IT: Nigrizia, 1970. 311 pp. No ISBN.

English translation of *Il Contributo Degli Scavi di Faras alla Storia Della Nubia Cristiana.*

AF644 Wheeler, Andrew C., ed.
Land of Promise: Church Growth in a Sudan at War. (Faith in Sudan Series, 1). Nairobi, KE: Paulines Publications Africa, 1997. 152 pp. Paper. 9966213260.

Eight papers originally presented at a conference on "The Church in Sudan—Its Impact Past, Present, and Future" (Limuru, Kenya, February 1997).

AF645 Wheeler, Andrew C.
Announcing the Light: Sudanese Witnesses to the Gospel. (Faith in Sudan, 6). Nairobi, KE: Paulines Publications Africa, 1998. 288 pp. Paper. 9966214186.

A major collection of twenty-one papers in three parts: 1) liberation and alienation among early Sudanese Christians; 2) evangelists and teachers; and 3) martyrs and prophets; funded by the Pew Charitable Trust and arising from the Limuru, Kenya Conference "The Church in Sudan—Its Impact, Past, Present, and Future" (February 1997).

AF646 Yoh, John Gay, comp.
Christianity in the Sudan: An Annotated Bibliography. Amman, Jordan: Royal Institute for Inter-Faith Studies, 1999. ix, 153 pp. 1897750552.

An expanded bibliography of books and periodical articles; originally published in 1996.

Tanzania [Tanganyika]

See also HI334, HI472, HI609, CR579, CR605, SO343-SO344, SO356, SO602, EC74, ED43, SP66, SP285, AF166, AF254, AF297, and AF548.

AF647 Albrecht, Rainer
Eine Trommel allein singt kein Lied: "Engoma Emoi Tegamba Mulango": Predigt als dialogisches Geschehen in einer Kultur der Oralität; Untersuchungen zu Inhalt und Struktur evangelischer Predigt in Nordwest-Tanzania. (Missionswissenschaftliche Forschungen Neue Folge, 2). Erlangen, GW: Ev.-Luth. Mission, 1996. 373 pp. Paper. 3872143328.

A detailed study of preaching as the oral theology of African pastors in a Lutheran diocese of northwest Tanzania.

AF648 Althaus, Gerhard
Mamba-Anfang in Afrika. Edited by Hans-Ludwig Althaus. (Erlanger Taschenbücher, 5). Erlangen, GW: Ev.-Luth Mission, 1992. 136 pp. Paper. 3872142542.

This personal narration relates the experiences of the author and his wife during their seventeen years (1893-1910) as co-workers in the Leipziger Mission among the Chaggas in the shadow of Kilimanjaro (Tanzania).

AF649 Bahendwa, L. Festo
Christian Religious Education in the Lutheran Dioceses of North-Western Tanzania. (Annals of the Finnish Society for Missiology and Ecumenics, 56). Helsinki, FI: Finnish Society for Missiology and Ecumenics, 1990. xiv, 388 pp. Paper. 9519602011.

A detailed study of how Christian schools and Christian religious education influenced traditional Bahaya/Banyambo society in Tanzania; originally submitted as a dissertation at the University of Helsinki, Finland.

AF650 Bammann, Heinrich
Koinonia in Afrika: Koinonia bei Bruno Gutmann (Tanzania) und bei den Hermannsburger Missionaren im südlichen Afrika. (Veröffentlichungen der Freich Hochschule für Mission: Reihe C, 6). Bad Liebenzell, GW: Liebenzeller Mission, 1990. 127 pp. Paper. 3880024510.

A study of the theory and work of Bruno Gutmann (1876-1966) who, in what is now Tanzania, developed community as the focus of his missionary effort as a member of the Hermannsburg Mission.

AF—AFRICA

AF651 Baur, Etienne
Père Etienne Baur en de Arabische Opstand van 1888-1889.
Compiled by H. G. M. Tullemans. Nijmegen, NE: W. S. P.
Print, 1982. 2 vols. No ISBN.

A two-volume historical study, based on mission archives,
of the position of missionaries amidst slave traders, colonial
officials, and native peoples; focused on the role of French
missionary Fr. Etienne Baur, a go-between in the 1888-1889
Arab revolt against German colonial rule in East Africa; [vol.
1, Dutch, 212 pp.; vol. 2, "Transcribed Letters and Documents of the Bagamoyo Mission during the Arab Revolt, 1888-
1889," iii, 306 pp.].

AF652 Beidelman, T. O.
*Colonial Evangelism: A Socio-Historical Study of an East
African Mission at the Grassroots.* Bloomington, INU: Indi-
ana University Press, 1982. xix, 274 pp. Paper. 0253202787.

A detailed historical and ethnographic analysis of the
Kaguru people of Tanzania, and of the CMS's work among
them, by a distinguished anthropologist.

AF653 Bernander, Gustav
*Lutheran Wartime Assistance to Tanzanian Churches, 1940-
1945.* (Studia Missionalia Upsaliensia, 9). Lund, SW: Gleerup,
1968. 170 pp. No ISBN.

A history of the Tanzanian churches and relief work during the Second World War.

AF654 Donovan, Vincent J.
Africa, Comunidad Misionera: Los Masai. (Misión sin
Fronteras, 4). Estella, SP: Verbo Divino, 1987. 196 pp. Pa-
per. 8471515148.

Spanish translation.

AF655 Donovan, Vincent J.
Christianity Rediscovered. Maryknoll, NYU: Orbis Books,
1982. viii, 200 pp. Paper. 0883440962.

A culturally sensitive case study of the bringing of
Christianity to the Maasai people of Tanzania, in which the
contextualization of the message and structures is implemented
from the beginning; originally published by Fidas/Claretian,
Notre Dame, Indiana, in 1978.

AF656 Eggert, Johanna
*Missionsschule und sozialer Wandel in Ostafrika: Der Bei-
trag der deutschen evangelischen Missionsgesellschaften zur
Entwicklung des Schulwesens in Tanganyika 1891-1939.*
(Freiburger Studien zu Politik und Gesellschaft überseeischer
Länder, 10). Bielefeld, GW: Bertelsmann, 1970. 334 pp. Pa-
per. No ISBN.

A dissertation based on comprehensive source material,
investigating the extent to which German Protestant mission
schools brought about cultural change in Tanzania.

AF657 Fiedler, Irene
*Wandel der Mädchenerziehung in Tanzania: Der Einfluss von
Mission, Kolonialer Schulpolitik und nationalem Sozialismus.*
(Sozialwissenschaftliche Studien zu internationalen Proble-
men, 85). Saarbrücken, GW: Breitenbach, 1983. 449 pp. Pa-
per. 3881562524.

A dissertation describing traditional education of girls
in Tanzania, analyzing the values it had for traditional society, and giving extensive coverage to Catholic and Protestant
missionary activity, showing under what influences it further
developed.

AF658 Fiedler, Klaus
*Christentum und afrikanische Kultur: Konservative deutsche
Missionare in Tanzania , 1900-1940.* (Missionswissenschaft-
liche Forschungen, 16). Gütersloh, GW: Mohn, 1983. 218 pp.
Paper. 3579002368.

This dissertation examines the attempts made by German Protestant missionaries in Tanzania, 1900-1940, regarding the integration of African culture and the Gospel (dissertation, University of Daressalam, Fac. of Philosophy, 1977).

AF659 Fiedler, Klaus
*Christianity and African Culture: Conservative German Prot-
estant Missionaries in Tanzania, 1900-1940.* Leiden, NE:
Brill, 1996. xiii, 239 pp. Paper. 9004104976.

A detailed study of pioneer efforts by Bruno Gutmann
and other German missionaries in Tanzania to integrate Christianity with African culture.

AF660 Fleisch, Paul
*Lutheran Beginnings around Mt. Kilimanjaro: The First 40
Years.* Translated by Martin Jaeschke. (Makumira Publica-
tion, 10). Arusha, TZ: Erlanger Verlag für Mission und
Ökumene, 1998. 208 pp. Paper. 3872142917.

A historical account of the former Hersbruck Mission
Society and the Leipzig Mission, which were influenced by
rapid changes following the two world wars and in turn influenced the early Lutheran missions in Northern Tanzania; published by the Makumira University College, operated by the
Evangelical Lutheran Church of Tanzania.

AF661 Fletcher, Jesse C.
Wimpy Harper of Africa. Nashville, TNU: Broadman, 1967.
142 pp. No ISBN.

A popular biography of a Southern Baptist missionary to
Tanzania.

AF662 Fouquer, Roger P.
*Le docteur Adrien Atiman: Médicin-catéchiste au Tanganyi-
ka sur les traces de Vincent de Paul.* Paris, FR: SPES Editorial, 1964. 172 pp. Paper. No ISBN.

A popular biography of Adrien Atiman (1864-1956), a
remarkable medical doctor and catechist who served as a
medical missionary in Karema, Tanzania, for sixty-five years
beginning in 1891.

AF663 Grondin, Patricia A., and Paul A. Grondin
In His Time: A Family's Journey into the Heart of Africa.
Lima, OHU: Fairway Press, 1992. 124 pp. Paper. 1556734697.

First edition of a narrative account by short-term Roman
Catholic missionaries from Ohio to Tanzania, 1989-1990.

AF664 Gundolf, Hubert
*Maji-Maji—Blut für Afrika: Auf den Spuren des 1905 in Ost-
afrika ermordeten Missionsbischofs Cassian Spiss OSB.* St.
Ottilien, GW: EOS Verlag, 1984. 210 pp. 3880961662.

A chronicle about Bishop Spiss and the Maji-Maji Insurrection.

AF665 Healey, Joseph
*Auf der Suche nach dem ganzen Leben: Kleine christliche
Gemeinschaften in Tansania.* (Missio, 7). Aachen, GW: Mis-
sio Aktuell Verlag, 1984. 71 pp. Paper. No ISBN.

German translation.

AF—AFRICA

AF666 Healey, Joseph

A Fifth Gospel: The Experience of Black Christian Values. Maryknoll, NYU: Orbis Books; London, ENK: SCM Press, 1981. xvi, 203 pp. Paper. 088344013X (US), 0334004764 (UK).

A popular presentation on African Christian values and BCCs; originally presented to Catholic laity in Detroit by a Maryknoll missionary to Tanzania.

AF667 Hellberg, Carl J.

Missions on a Colonial Frontier West of Lake Victoria: Evangelical Missions in North-West Tanganyika to 1932. Lund, SW: Gleerup, 1965. 256 pp. No ISBN.

This historical study examines the first period of evangelical missions in northwest Tanganyika, to 1932, and the congregations founded as a result.

AF668 Heremans, Roger

Les établissements de l'Association internationale Africaine au lac Tanganika et les Péres Blancs: Mpala et Karéma. (Musée royal de l'Afrique Centrale, Tervuren, Belgique Annales. Sér. in-8j. Sciences historiques, 3). Tervuren, BE: Musée royal de l'Afrique Centrale, 1966. 139 pp. No ISBN.

A comparative historical study of the penetration of Tanganyika between 1877 and 1885, first by the International African Association, and then by the White Fathers.

AF669 Hertlein, Siegfried

Die Kirche in Tansania: Ein kurzer überblick über Geschichte und Gegenwart. (Münsterschwarzacher Studien, 17). Münsterschwarzach, GW: Vier-Türme-Verlag, 1971. xvi, 160 pp. Paper. 3878680082.

An introduction to the history of the Catholic Church in Tanzania including Tanzania's history and religions, the work of the Holy Spirit Fathers, White Fathers, and Benedictines, mission methods, growth toward indigenization, and collaboration with Protestant churches.

AF670 Hertlein, Siegfried

Wege christlicher Verkündigung: Eine pastoral-geschichtliche Untersuchung aus dem Bereich der Katholischen Kirche Tansanias. (Münsterschwarzacher Studien, 27-28). Münsterschwarzach, GW: Vier-Türme-Verlag, 1983. 2 vols. 3878681682.

An investigation, from the beginning of Catholic missionary work in Tanzania, to the development of an independent local church, mainly concentrating on the work of the Holy Ghost Fathers, White Fathers, and Benedictines of St. Ottilien; vol. 1: [1976; xix, 296 pp.; 3878680651]; vol. 2, pt. 1: [1983; xxiii, 267 pp.; 387868066X]; pt. 2: [1983; vii, 287 pp.; 387868164X].

AF671 Hess, Mahlon M.

The Pilgrimage of Faith of Tanzania Mennonite Church, 1934-83. Musoma, TZ: Tanzania Mennonite Church; Salinga, PAU: Eastern Mennonite Board of Missions and Charities, 1985. 175 pp. Paper. 096133682X.

A history of the experiences and viewpoints of many Mennonite workers in Tanzania, with statistics on congregational growth, schools, and leaders.

AF672 Hoffman, Stanley W.

To a Land He Showed Us. New York, NYU: Vantage Press, 1992. xiv, 222 pp. Paper. 0533103096.

Stories from nine years (1959-1968) of mission in Tanzania by a Canadian Church of God missionary couple.

AF673 Iversen, Hans Raun

Tanzania tur/retur: Syv tekster om socialisme og mission. Aarhus, DK: FK-Tryk, 1981. 287 pp. 8774570064.

Seven essays on relations between churches of the First and Third Worlds based on the author's two-year study visit to Tanzania.

AF674 Jaeschke, Ernst

Bruno Gutmann; His Life, His Thoughts and His Work: An Early Attempt at a Theology in an African Context. Erlangen, GW: Evangelical Lutheran Mission, 1985. xii, 466 pp. Paper. 3872142038.

A scholarly assessment for African readers of the contribution of Bruno Gutmann (1876-1966), who served as a missionary from 1902 to 1938 among the Chagga people in the Kilamanjaro area of what is now Tanzania; with extensive quotations from Gutmann's writings; based on lectures presented in 1968 at the Lutheran Theological College, Makymera, Tanzania.

AF675 Jaeschke, Ernst

Gemeindeaufbau in Afrika: Die Bedeutung Bruno Gutmanns für das afrikanische Christentum. (Calwer theologische Monographien, Reihe C: Praktische Theologie und Missionswissenschaft, 8). Stuttgart, GW: Calwer Verlag, 1981. 350 pp. 3766806912.

A scholarly assessment of the contribution of Bruno Gutmann (1876-1966), missionary to the Chagga people of Tanzania, focusing on his creative insights on inculturation for African Christianity, by his successor and pupil in the Leipzig Mission.

AF676 Joinet, Bernard

O Sol de Deus na Tanzânia. São Paulo, BL: Edições Paulinas, 1982. 134 pp. Paper. No ISBN.

Portuguese translation.

AF677 Joinet, Bernard

Le soleil de Dieu en Tanzanie. Paris, FR: Éditions du Cerf, 1977. 164 pp. 2204011363.

Contemporary missionary spirituality by a French White Father, highly supportive of church indigenization and Tanzanian socialism.

AF678 Kibira, Josiah M.

Church, Clan and the World. (Studia Missionalia Upsaliensia, 31). Lund, SW: Gleerup, 1974. 128 pp. No ISBN.

A longer essay on church, family, and clan in northwest Tanzania, and nine shorter articles on "A Living Church in a Changing World."

AF679 Kiel, Christel

Christen in der Steppe: Die Máasai-Mission der Nord-Ost-Diözese in der Lutherischen Kirche Tansanias. (Erlanger Monographien aus Mission und Ökumene, 25). Erlangen, GW: Ev.-Luth. Mission, 1996. 390 pp. Paper. 3872143255.

After an ethnographic study of the life cycle, social order, and faith of the Kisongo and Parakúyo peoples of northeast Tanzania, the author gives a centennial history of the Maasai Mission of the Lutheran Church in Tanzania, 1892 to 1992; originally submitted as a doctoral dissertation, University of Berlin, 1994.

AF680 Kiel, Christel

Christians in Maasailand: A Study of the History of Mission among the Máasai in the North Eastern Diocese of the Evangelical Lutheran Church in Tanzania. (Makumira Publications, 9). Usa River, TZ: Ev.-Luth. Mission, 1997. 313 pp. Paper. 3872142860.

An in-depth study of mission among the Maasai people of Tanzania by the Evangelical Lutheran Church of Tanzania.

AF681 Kisare, Z. Marwa

Kisare: A Mennonite of Kiseru. Salunga, PAU: Eastern Mennonite Board of Missions, 1984. 193 pp. Paper. 0961336811.

A first-person account of how a boy goat herder became the first African bishop in Tanzania of the Mennonite Church, as told to Joseph Shenk, who adds his remembrance.

AF682 Klobuchar, Jim

The Cross under the Acacia Tree: The Story of David and Eunice Simonson's Epic Mission in Africa. Minneapolis, MNU: Kirk House Publishers, 1999. 216 pp. Paper. 1886513228.

A well-known Minneapolis writer and adventurer, Jim Klobuchar, chronicles the lives of an entrepreneurial mission couple who founded and equipped 2,500 schools in Tanzania.

AF683 Knapp, Doug, and Evelyn Knapp

Thunder in the Valley. Nashville, TNU: Broadman, 1986. 240 pp. Paper. 0805463429.

An account of missionary success in Tanzania by two Southern Baptist agricultural missionaries, 1964-1986.

AF684 Knox, Elisabeth

Signal on the Mountain: The Gospel in Africa's Uplands before the First World War. Canberra, AT: Acorn Press, 1991. xix, 275 pp. Paper. 0908284063.

A narrative history, based on archival sources, of the CMS' Nyanza and Ussagara missions in northwest Tanganyika between 1876 and 1916.

AF685 Lindqvist, Ingmar

Partners in Mission: A Case-Study of the Missionary Practice of the Lutheran Foreign Mission Agency Involvement in Tanzania Since the Early 1960's Seen in a Historical and Theological Perspective. (Meddelanden frå stiftelsens för Åbo Akademi forskningsinstitut, 75). Åbo, FI: Åbo Akademi University Press, 1982. 268 pp. Paper. 9516488390.

A description of the Lutheran Foreign Mission Agency's mission involvement in Tanzania, discussing possible theological presuppositions of major aspects of this practice.

AF686 Ludwig, Frieder

Das Modell Tanzania: Zum Verhältnis zwischen Kirche und Staat während der Ära Nyerere. Berlin, GW: Dietrich Reimer Verlag, 1995. 290 pp. Paper. 3496025751.

A scholarly analysis of church-state relations in Tanzania during the Nyerere era (1961-1985) based on documents in English and oral interviews.

AF687 Magesa, Laurenti, ed.

The Prophetic Role of the Church in Tanzania Today. (AMECEA Gaba Publications, Spearhead, 115). Eldoret, KE: AMECEA Gaba Publications, 1991. 94 pp. Paper. 9966836047.

Five essays by Catholic scholars on the prophetic role of the church in Africa and the indigenous theology undergirding it.

AF688 Mellinghoff, Gerhard, Judah Kiwovele, and Sebastian Kolowa, eds.

Lutherische Kirche Tanzania: Ein Handbuch. Erlangen, GW: Ev.-Luth. Mission, 1976. 393 pp. Paper. 3872140779.

A handbook, with articles by Christians from East Africa, America, and Europe, describing the Evangelical Lutheran Church in Tanzania, its relationship to the African tradition, various missions, and the politics of Tanzania.

AF689 Mirtschink, Bernhard

Zur Rolle christlicher Mission in kolonialen Gesellschaften: Katholische Missionserziehung in "Deutsch-Ostafrika." (Berliner Studien zur Erziehung und Internationalität, 2). Frankfurt am Main, GW: Haag und Herchen, 1980. 148 pp. Paper. 3881293442.

A scholarly study of the educational work of the Holy Ghost Fathers and their relationship with the German colonial power in East Africa.

AF690 Mtaita, Leonard A.

The Wandering Shepherds and the Good Shepherd: Contextualization as the Way of Doing Mission with the Maasai in the Evangelical Lutheran Church in Tanzania, Pare Diocese. (Makumira Publication, 11). Arusha, TZ: Erlanger Verlag für Mission und Ökumene, 1998. 304 pp. Paper. 3872142909.

A historical and anthropological study of the Maasai people of Tanzania, the mission work of the Evangelical Lutheran Church there, and issues of contextualization.

AF691 Mwoleka, Christopher, and Joseph Healey, eds.

Ujamaa and Christian Communities. (Spearhead Series, 45). Eldoret, KE: Gaba Publications, 1976. 63 pp. Paper. No ISBN.

Reflections by Roman Catholic pastoral workers of Rulenge diocese in Tanzania, on efforts to build small Christian communities open to non-Christians, and integrated into their pluralistic surroundings; presented at the AMECEA Pastoral Institute (Nairobi, Kenya, July 1976).

AF692 Namata, Joseph A.

Edmund John, Man of God: A Healing Ministry. Translated by Marjory Stanway. Canberra, AT: Acorn Press, 1986. viii, 112 pp. Paper. 0908284179.

A popular biography of Edmund John (1922-1972), a Church of England evangelist in Tanzania who had a remarkable healing ministry.

AF693 Ngeiyamu, Joel, and Johannes Triebel, eds.

Gemeinsam auf eigenen Wegen: Evangelisch-Lutherische Kirche in Tanzania nach hundert Jahren. (Erlanger Taschenbücher, 99). Erlangen, GW: Ev.-Luth. Mission, 1994. 357 pp. Paper. 3872141996.

Twenty-five essays, mostly by Tanzanian authors, on various aspects of the church's mission and ministry in Tanzania (environment, tasks, challenges, and answers); published for the centennial of the Evangelical-Lutheran Church in Tanzania.

AF694 Parsalaw, Joseph Wilson

A History of the Lutheran Church, Diocese in the Arusha Region from 1904 to 1958. (Makumira Publications, 12). Erlangen, GW: Erlanger Verlag für Mission und Ökumene, 1999. 403 pp. Paper. 3872142992.

The continuation of historical studies dating back to 1893, when the first four pioneer missionaries from Liepzig Mission Society set foot on the slopes of Mt. Kilimanjaro.

AF—AFRICA

AF695 Ranger, Terence O.

The African Churches of Tanzania. (Historical Association of Tanzania, 5). Nairobi, KE: East African Publishing House, 1972. 28 pp. No ISBN.

A short pamphlet describing African Christian activity outside the mission churches, focusing on Watch Tower, The African National Church, The Last Church of God and His Christ, and the Malakite Church ("Dini ya Bapali"—The Polygamist Church) in an attempt to show the extent to which African Christians are responsible for most of the conversions that took place.

AF696 Sahlberg, Carl-Erik

From Krapf to Rugambwa: A Church History of Tanzania. Nairobi, KE: Evangel Publishing House, 1986. 190 pp. Paper. No ISBN.

A handbook on the mission history of all of the larger churches in Tanzania from 1844 to the present.

AF697 Schulpen, J. W. J.

Integration of Church and Government Services in Tanzania: Effects at District Level. Nairobi, KE: African Medical and Research Foundation, 1976. 301 pp. No ISBN.

A detailed thesis describing how churches and government cooperated in the Biharamulo district of Tanzania to improve health conditions of rural dwellers.

AF698 Smedjebacka, Henrik

Lutheran Church Autonomy in Northern Tanzania, 1940-1963. (Acta Academiae Aboensis series, A 44.3). Åbo, FI: Åbo Akademi University Press, 1973. 372 pp. 9516480357.

Detailed documentation by a Finnish Lutheran missionary of the development from the mission-ruled church of the pre-1940 period to the episcopally governed diocese (1963) of the Evangelical Lutheran Church of Tanzania.

AF699 Smedjebacka, Henrik

Tansaniasta tuli kutsu: Suomen Lähetysseuran työosuus, 1948-1973. Translated by Helinä Kuusiola. Helsinki, FI: Suomen Lähetysseura, 1976. 143 pp. 9516241530.

Finnish translation.

AF700 Smedjebacka, Henrik

Tjugofem år i Tanzania: Finska missionsshällskapets insats 1948-73. (Meddelanden/ Kyrkohistoriska arkivet vid Åbo Akademi, 3). Åbo, FI: Kyrkohistoriska arkivet vid Åbo Akademi, 1976. 130 pp. Paper. 9516482074.

A history of the work of the Finnish Evangelical Lutheran Mission in Tanzania, 1948-1973.

AF701 Stanway, Marjory

Alfred Stanway: The Recollections of a "Little M." Canberra, AT: Acorn Press, 1991. viii, 262 pp. Paper. 090828411X.

A biography of Alfred Stanway (1908-1989) by his wife, who served with him as an Australian Church Missionary Society missionary to Kenya and Tanzania (1937-1971).

AF702 Sundkler, Bengt

Bara Bukoba: Church and Community in Tanzania. London, ENK: Hurst, 1980. x, 229 pp. 0905838300.

A detailed case study of the Evangelical Lutheran diocese of Bukoba, Tanzania, by its former bishop (1961-1964), based on the author's personal interviews in the 1940s, 1960s, and early 1970s.

AF703 Swantz, Lloyd

Church, Mission, and State Relations in Pre- and Post-Independent Tanzania, 1955-1964. (Program of East Africa Studies: Occasional Paper, 19). Syracuse, NYU: Syracuse University, 1965. 50 pp. No ISBN.

A Lutheran missionary's analysis of changes in church-state relations between colonial Tanganyika and independent Tanzania.

AF704 Swantz, Marja-Liisa

Ritual and Symbol in Transitional Zaramo Society with Special Reference to Women. (Studia Missionalia Upsaliensia, 16). Lund, SW: Gleerup, 1970. 430 pp. No ISBN.

A detailed study, by a sensitive missionary anthropologist, of the Mwambao Zaramo people of Bunju district, 20-25 miles north of Dar-es-Salaam, among a traditional Muslim people.

AF705 Tanner, Ralph E. S.

Transition in African Beliefs: Traditional Religion and Christian Change; A Study of Sukumaland, Tanzania, East Africa. Maryknoll, NYU: Maryknoll Publications, 1967. xii, 256 pp. No ISBN.

A social-anthropological study of religious change among the Sukuma, from traditional beliefs and practices to conversion and new rituals, both Roman Catholic and Protestant.

AF706 *The Church's Contribution to Rural Development*

(Tanganyika Rapid Social Change Study—Commission "D"). Dodoma, TZ: Central Tanganyika Press, 1968. 55 pp. Paper. No ISBN.

A report on the contemporary rural situation in Tanzania, based on a Rapid Social Change Study (1962-1965) by the Christian Council of Tanzania, which stresses that the church must be a major change agent in Tanzanian rural development.

AF707 Urfer, Sylvain

Socialisme et Église en Tanzanie. Paris, FR: IDOC-France, 1975. 168 pp. 2858020051.

A careful study of the Catholic Church in independent Tanzania, and of attitudes toward Ujamaa socialism.

AF708 Von Sicard, Sigvard

The Lutheran Church on the Coast of Tanzania, 1887-1914: With Special Reference to the Evangelical Lutheran Church in Tanzania, Synod of Uzaramo-Uluguru. (Studia Missionalia Upsaliensia, 12). Lund, SW: Gleerup, 1970. 260 pp. Paper. No ISBN.

A detailed history based on archival sources, of the work of the Evangelical Missionary Society for German East Africa and the Berlin Mission Society in establishing the Lutheran Church on the coast of Tanzanika (Tanzania), and on Zanzibar.

AF709 Wijsen, Frans Jozef Servaas

"There Is Only One God": A Social-Scientific and Theological Study of Popular Religion and Evangelization in Sukumaland, Northwest Tanzania. (Kerk en theologie in context, 22). Kampen, NE: Kok, 1993. xv, 339 pp. 903900501X.

A dissertation interpreting popular religion as the counterpart of official religion in the Sukuma district of northwestern Tanzania.

AF—AFRICA

AF710 Wright, Marcia
German Missions in Tanganyika 1891-1914: Lutherans and Moravians in the Southern Highlands. (Oxford Studies in African Affairs). Oxford, ENK: Clarendon Press, 1971. xiv, 249 pp. 0198216653.

A scholarly study of the formative period of the Lutheran and Moravian churches and their involvement in the local and politico-religious conflicts of the southern highlands of Tanganyika/Tanzania, based on fieldwork and missionary and colonial archives.

Uganda

See also SO364, EC239, CH57, AF468, and AF613.

AF711 Ashe, Robert Pickering
Chronicles of Uganda. (Cass Library of African Studies, Mission Researches and Travels, 20). London, ENK: Cass, 1971. xvi, 480 pp. 0714618616.

A reprint of an early missionary journal (London: Hodder and Stoughton, 1894).

AF712 Bouchard, Richard, and Michel Lejeune
Eucharist and Community. (Gaba Institute Pastoral Papers, 28). Kampala, UG: Gaba Publications, 1973. 26 pp. No ISBN.

Report of an experiment in Christian growth in the Mushanga Roman Catholic parish.

AF713 Faupel, John Francis
African Holocaust: The Story of the Uganda Martyrs. Kampala, UG: St. Paul Publications, Africa, 1984. x, 245 pp. No ISBN.

The story of the widespread killing of Protestant and Catholic young men in Buganda in 1884-1886, and how their martyrdom became the seed of the church; originally published in 1962 (New York: P. J. Kenedy; London: G. Chapman).

AF714 Ford, Margaret
Janani: The Making of a Martyr. London, ENK: Lakeland, 1978. 93 pp. Paper. 055100794X.

The inside story of Janani Luwum, Anglican Archbishop of Uganda, who was shot by order of President Amin on 16 February 1977; also published as *Even unto Death* (Elgin, ILU: D. C. Cook, 1978, 0891911979).

AF715 Gruppo Uganda Terzo Mondo
Dove va la missione? La lezione dell'Uganda. Milan, IT: Jaca Book, 1969. 171 pp. No ISBN.

Report of a conference to reassess missions in Uganda.

AF716 Hansen, Holger Bernt
Mission, Church and State in a Colonial Setting: Uganda 1890-1925. London, ENK: Heinemann; New York, NYU: St. Martin's Press, 1984. xix, 649 pp. 0435945181 (UK), 0312534744 (US).

A study of colonialism vis-a-vis the missionary movement in one country but applicable to all Africa, by a recognized Danish authority on Third World missions, politics, race relations, and militarism.

AF717 Harrison, J. W.
A. M. Mackay: Pioneer Missionary of the Church Missionary Society to Uganda. (Cass Library of African Studies, Missionary Researches and Travel, 14). London, ENK: Cass, 1970. viii, 488 pp. 0714618748.

A reprint, with a new introductory note by D. A. Law, of an early biography of a pioneer CMS missionary (London: Hodder and Stoughton, 1890).

AF718 Hoffman, Stanley W.
Amid Perils Often. New York, NYU: Vantage Press, 1989. 231 pp. Paper. 053308492 (SBN).

An account by a Church of God missionary to East Africa (1959-1977), of his four added years in Uganda (1983-1987).

AF719 Hohmann, Horst
Ein Fels in der Brandung: Siméon Lourdel (Afrika); (1853-1890, der Apostel Ugandas). (Missionare, die Geschichte machten). Mödling, AU: Verlag St. Gabriel; St. Augustin, GW: Steyler Verlag, 1983. 112 pp. Paper. 3852641977 (AU), 3877871615 (GW).

A biography of the French White Father who died at the age of thirty-seven and is known as the "Apostle of Uganda."

AF720 King, Noel Q., Abdu B. K. Kasozi, and Arye Oded
Islam and the Confluence of Religions in Uganda, 1840-1966. (AAR Studies in Religion, 6). Tallahassee, FLU: American Academy of Religion, 1973. ix, 60 pp. Paper. 0884201058.

An interim report of a collaborative field research project, in which the authors, through archival research and oral interviews, present the historical course of conflict and accommodation among Islam, Christianity, and traditional African religions in Uganda.

AF721 Kivengere, Festo, and Dorothy Smoker
I Love Idi Amin: The Story of Triumph under Fire in the Midst of Suffering and Persecution in Uganda. (New Life Ventures). London, ENK: Marshall, Morgan and Scott; Old Tappan, NJU: Revell, 1977. 63 pp. 0551055774 (UK), 0800790049 (US).

A moving testimony, by the prominent Anglican bishop of Uganda, of his reactions to Idi Amin's dictatorship and persecution of the church from 1971 to 1977.

AF722 Kyewalyanga, Francis-Xavier Sserufusa
Traditional Religion, Custom, and Christianity in East Africa: As Illustrated by the Ganda with Reference to Other African Cultures (Acholi, Banyarwanda, Chagga, Gikuyu, Luo, Masai, Sukuma, Tharaka, etc.), and Reference to Islam. Hohenschäftlarn, GW: Klaus Renner, 1976. vii, 355 pp. 3876730481.

A native Ganda Catholic priest provides a useful summary of Ganda customs relating to birth, childhood, puberty, marriage, and death, identifying elements needed for the development of a genuinely African Christianity.

AF723 Ledogar, Robert J., ed.
Katigondo: Presenting the Christian Message to Africa. London, ENK: Chapman, 1965. xv, 139 pp. No ISBN.

Proceedings of the first Pan-African Catechetical Study Week, held at the Catholic Katigondo Seminary in Uganda from 27 August to 1 September, 1964.

AF724 Luck, A.
African Saint: The Story of Apolo Kivebulaya. London, ENK: SCM Press, 1963. 188 pp. No ISBN.

The first authoritative biography of a pioneer Ugandan Anglican missionary into the Congo.

AF725 Marie André de Coeur, Sacré Coeur, Sister
Uganda, terres de martyrs. (Église vivante). Paris, FR: Casterman, 1964. 295 pp. Paper. No ISBN.

Second edition of a narrative history of the events that led to the martyrdom of new Christians (Anglican and Roman Catholic) in Uganda in 1886, and of the later impact of that martyrdom, based on documents of the period.

AF726 Medeghini, Alessandro
Storia d'Uganda. (Museum Combonianum, 29). Bologna, IT: Nigrizia, 1973. 643 pp. No ISBN.

A chronological history of the Catholic Church in Uganda.

AF727 Mudoola, Dan M.
Religion, Ethnicity and Politics in Uganda. Kampala, UG: Fountain Publishers, 1996. vii, 126 pp. Paper. 9970020137.

Second edition of an analysis of the underlying causes of Uganda's political instability during the 1962-1971 period, with special attention to the role of the Catholic Church in the past, and its future potential for assisting in resolving political conflicts peacefully.

AF728 O'Brien, Brian
That Good Physician: The Life and Work of Albert and Katherine Cook of Uganda. London, ENK: Hodder & Stoughton, 1962. 264 pp. No ISBN.

An engaging biography of Sir Albert Ruskin Cook (1870-1951) and Katharine Timpson Cook (d.1938), who from 1896 until their deaths pioneered medical missions in Uganda under the CMS.

AF729 Pirouet, M. Louise
Black Evangelists: The Spread of Christianity in Uganda, 1891-1914. London, ENK: Rex Collins, 1978. xii, 255 pp. 0860360512.

A detailed study of early African initiatives in the spread of Christianity, from Buganda to the western and northern areas of Uganda, through the efforts of the CMS and the Native Anglican Church.

AF730 Potts, Mary
Ancestors in Christ: The Living Dead in African Traditional and Christian Religion. (Gaba Institute Pastoral Papers, 17). Kampala, UG: AMECEA Pastoral Institute, 1971. xii, 19 pp. No ISBN.

A brief essay on traditional African beliefs and rituals, important for contextualization of African Christianity in Uganda.

AF731 Russell, J. K.
Men without God?: A Study of the Impact of the Christian Message in the North of Uganda. London, ENK: Highway Press, 1965. 95 pp. No ISBN.

A study of the Anglican church in northern Uganda, its history and present situation, including social factors (education, politics, marriage, and death) and resources for ministry; written by the late bishop of the Upper Nile (1955-1960).

AF732 Taylor, John Vernon
Die Kirche in Buganda: Das Werden einer jungen afrikanischen Kirche. Translated by Erika Marie Mann. (Die Kirchen der Welt, 4). Stuttgart, GW: Evan Verlagswerk, 1966. 302 pp. No ISBN.

German translation of *The Growth of the Church in Uganda* (London, SCM Press, 1958), an in-depth case study of a few Anglican parishes in Uganda, from the introduction of Christianity in 1877 to the present.

AF733 Tourigny, Yves
So Abundant a Harvest: The Catholic Church in Uganda, 1879-1979. London, ENK: Darton, Longman & Todd, 1974. 224 pp. 0232514186.

A narrative centennial history of Catholicism in Uganda focusing on the work of the Missionaries of Africa (White Fathers).

AF734 Tuma, A. D. Tom, and Phares Mutibwa, eds.
A Century of Christianity in Uganda, 1877-1977: A Historical Appraisal of the Uganda Church over the Last 100 Years. Nairobi, KE: Uzima Press, 1978. xxiii, 189 pp. No ISBN.

A popular history written for the centenary celebrations of the (Anglican) Church of Uganda.

AF735 Tuma, A. D. Tom
Building a Ugandan Church: African Participation in Church Growth and Expansion in Busoga, 1891-1940. Nairobi, KE: Kenya Literature Bureau, 1980. viii, 231 pp. No ISBN.

A history of CMS (Anglican) and Mill Hill (Roman Catholic) missions and Ugandan leadership, based on oral interviews and archival sources; originally presented as a Ph.D. thesis at the University of London in 1973.

AF736 Vittorino, Delagiacoma
An African Martyrology. Verona, IT: Nigrizia, 1965. 243 pp. No ISBN.

Guidance for veneration of the saints, by African Catholics, including the Uganda martyrs; extracted from the 4th edition of *The Book of Saints* compiled by the Benedictine monks of St. Augustine's Abbey in Ramsgate, England.

AF737 Wandira, Asavia
Early Missionary Education in Uganda: A Study of Purpose in Ministry Education. Kampala, UG: Makerere University, 1972. 356 pp. No ISBN.

An account of the mission societies' dominant position and purposes in the management of mission education in Uganda, as well as the contributions of their work to the later adaption of education to the needs of society.

AF738 Welbourn, Frederick Burkewood
Religion and Politics in Uganda, 1952-1962. Nairobi, KE: East African Publishing House; London, ENK: Deutsch, 1965. iv, 78 pp. Paper. No ISBN.

A critical analysis of a politically volatile decade, tracing the rise to power of the Uganda People's Congress, the search for a new ethnic identity, and the role of both Muslims and Christians in Buganda society.

AF739 Wright, Michael
Buganda in the Heroic Age. Nairobi, KE: Oxford University Press, 1971. xvi, 244 pp. No ISBN.

A detailed history, based on archival and oral sources, of the Buganda kingdom of Uganda, 1888-1898, during the period of Muslim-Catholic-Anglican rivalries.

AF—AFRICA

Zambia [Northern Rhodesia]

See also CR632, SO301, ED25, SP278, AF209, AF1151, and AF1184.

AF740 Binsbergen, Wim M. J. van
Religious Change in Zambia: Exploratory Studies. (Monographs from the African Studies Centre). London, ENK: Kegan Paul International, 1981. x, 423 pp. 071030000X (hdbk), 0710300123 (pbk).

A collection of essays presenting a number of case studies on processes of change within Zambian religion, and a broad discussion of the theories for interpreting these changes, written by one of the leading anthropologists in the Netherlands.

AF741 Bolink, Peter
Towards Church Union in Zambia: A Study of Missionary Cooperation and Church-Union Efforts in Central Africa. (Proefschrift Theol. Fac. Vrije Universiteit Amsterdam). Franeker, NE: Wever, 1967. xvi, 430 pp. Paper. No ISBN.

A doctoral thesis, based on archives and interviews, presenting the history of schisms due to the division between missionary societies and the road toward the United Church of Zambia in 1965.

AF742 Carmody, Brendan Patrick
Conversion and Jesuit Schooling in Zambia. (Studies in Christian Mission, 4). Leiden, NE: Brill, 1992. xxix, 179 pp. Paper. 9004094288.

A detailed sociohistorical study of schooling at Chikuni, a Jesuit mission in southern Zambia, advocating a continuing function for church schools in the promotion of conversion and church growth.

AF743 Charlton, Leslie
Spark in the Stubble: Colin Morris of Zambia. London, ENK: Epworth Press, 1969. 158 pp. Paper. 0716201216.

A lightning sketch of one of Zambia's "political priests" in the years before and just after independence (1964), including his involvement in a church reconciliation team visiting the Lumpa Church of Alice Lenshina, prior to its violent oppression by government forces.

AF744 Colliard, François
On the Threshold of Central Africa: A Record of Twenty Years Pioneering Among the Batsi of the Upper Zambesi. Translated by Catherine Winkworth. (Cass Library of African Studies, Missionary Researches and Travels, 19). London, ENK: Cass, 1971. xxxiv, 663 pp. 0714618659.

English translation of the account of the pioneer Paris Evangelical Missionary Society's missionary to the Barotsi of Zambia; originally published as *Sur le haut Zambèze* in 1897.

AF745 Davis, John Merle
Modern Industry and the African: An Inquiry into the Effect of the Copper Mines of Central Africa Upon Native Society and the Work of Christian Missions. (International Missionary Council). New York, NYU: Negro Universities Press, 1969. xviii, 425 pp. 0837124263.

"Enquiry ... made in 1932 under the auspices of the Department of Social and Industrial Research of the IMC."

AF746 Doke, Clement M.
Trekking in South Central Africa, 1913-1919. Edited by Robert K. Herbert. Johannesburg, SA: Witwatersrand University Press, 1993. xl, 210 pp. Paper. 1868142310.

Based on diaries and notes of the missionary-linguist Dr. C. M. Doke and his father the Rev. J. J. Doke, pioneer of the Lambaland Mission in North Rhodesia.

AF747 Garvey, Brian
Bembaland Church: Religious and Social Change in South Central Africa 1891-1964. (Studies of Religion in Africa, 8). Leiden, NE: Brill, 1994. vii, 217 pp. 9004099573.

A detailed history of the Missionaries of Africa (formerly White Fathers) mission to the Bemba peoples of Zambia, based on archival sources.

AF748 Haar, Gerrie ter
Spirit of Africa: The Healing Ministry of Archbishop Milingo of Zambia. London, ENK: Hurst, 1992. ix, 286 pp. 1850651124 (hdbk), 1850651175 (pbk).

A multidimensional assessment of the controversial healing ministry of Catholic Archbishop Milingo of Zambia—historical, cultural, and theological—by the lecturer in the study of religions at the Catholic University of Utrecht in the Netherlands.

AF749 Henkel, Reinhard
Christian Missions in Africa: A Social Geographical Study of the Impact of Their Activities in Zambia. (Geographia Religionum, 3). Berlin, GW: Dietrich Reimer Verlag, 1989. 236 pp. Paper. 3496009349.

A detailed analysis of all the missions working in Zambia, their geographical distribution, and influence on settlement structure, education, and the economy.

AF750 Hinfelaar, Hugo F.
Bemba-Speaking Women of Zambia in a Century of Religious Change (1892-1992). (Studies of Religion in Africa, 11). Leiden, NE: Brill, 1994. xiv, 224 pp. 9004101497.

A detailed study of religious changes for the Bemba women of northern Zambia including their participation in Roman Catholic, Protestant, and African indigenous churches; based on a Ph.D. thesis completed in 1989 at the University of London.

AF751 Ipenburg, A. N.
"All Good Men": The Development of Lubwa Mission, Chinsali, Zambia, 1905-67. (Studies in the Intercultural History of Christianity, 83). Frankfurt am Main, GW: Lang, 1992. 345 pp. Paper. 3631453388.

A detailed history of the Presbyterian (now United Church of Zambia) Lubwa Mission in northeastern Zambia, founded in 1905 by David Julizya Kaunda, father of Kenneth Kaunda (first President of Zambia); focusing on involvements in education, the interplay of missionary Christianity with African cultures, rivalry with Roman Catholic White Fathers, the challenge of the Lumpa movement, and relations with the nationalist movement.

AF752 Jamieson, Gladys
Zambia Contrasts: A Page in the Story of Christian Education in Zambia. London, ENK: London Missionary Society, 1965. 87 pp. No ISBN.

Vignettes by the author on her service under the LMS at Malcolm Moffat Teacher Training College in Serenje, giving insight into race relations and the church's mission just before Zambia's independence.

AF753 Johnson, Walton R.
Worship and Freedom: A Black American Church in Zambia.
New York, NYU: Africana Publishing Company; London,
ENK: International African Institute, 1977. xx, 152 pp.
0841903158 (US), 0853020531 (UK).

A detailed study of the African Methodist Church in Zambia, its history, organization, and ministries in a situation of
social change.

AF754 Lane, James Eric
Moment of Encounter. New York, NYU: Lang, 1984. 163 pp.
Paper. 0820400904.

A historical analysis of cultural conflict among the Bemba people of Zambia, from David Livingstone to Alice Lenshina, with the European/African encounter understood as a
clash between two fundamentally different images of humanity.

AF755 Luig, Ulrich
Es ist heiss in Zambia: Partner in der Entwicklungsarbeit.
(Erlanger Taschenbücher, 102). Erlangen, GW: Ev.-Luth.
Mission, 1992. 113 pp. Paper. 3872145029.

The author, associated with the Gossner Mission, sketches daily life and his work for development of the people in the
Gwembe valley of Zambia.

AF756 Milingo, E.
*The World in Between: Christian Healing and the Struggle
for Spiritual Survival.* Edited by Mona Macmillan. London,
ENK: Hurst; Maryknoll, NYU: Orbis Books, 1984. vi, 137
pp. Paper. 1850650063 (H), 0883443546 (O).

Extracts from the writings of the archbishop of Lusaka
over the period 1976-1982; with introduction, commentary,
and epilogue by the editor.

AF757 Morris, Colin
*The End of the Missionary?: A Short Account of the Political
Consequences of Missions in Northern Rhodesia.* London,
ENK: Cargate Press, 1962. 61 pp. Paper. No ISBN.

A brief analysis of the history of missionary involvements
in politics in Northern Rhodesia (present Zambia), by one
who became advisor to President Kenneth Kaunda.

AF758 Mushindo, Paul Bwembya
*The Life of a Zambian Evangelist: The Reminiscences of Rev-
erend Paul Bwembya Mushindo.* (Communication—University of Zambia, Institute for African Studies, 9). Lusaka, ZA:
Institute for African Studies, University of Zambia, 1973. 60
pp. Paper. No ISBN.

This autobiography gives an insight into the role, the difficulties, and the ambivalences of the local Christian evangelists in relation to foreign missionaries.

AF759 O'Shea, Michael
*Missionaries and Miners: A History of the Beginnings of the
Catholic Church in Zambia with Particular Reference to the
Copperbelt.* Ndola, ZA: Mission Press, 1986. xv, 376 pp.
Paper. No ISBN.

The story of the beginnings of the Catholic church in the
Copperbelt mining communities of Zambia, focusing on the
Conventual Order of Franciscan's mission in the 1930s.

AF760 Poewe, Karla O.
Religion, Kinship, and Economy in Luapula, Zambia. (African Studies, 9). Lewiston, NYU: E Mellen, 1989. 265 pp.
0889461902.

A social anthropological case study on the functions of
kinship, and of evangelical and sectarian Christianity (Jehovah's Witnesses and Seventh-Day Adventists) affecting economic activities among the Luapula of Northern Zambia; based
on field research in the 1970s.

AF761 Randall, Max Ward
Profile for Victory: New Proposals for Missions in Zambia.
South Pasadena, CAU: William Carey Library, 1970. xxi, 204
pp. 0878084037.

A revision of the author's thesis (M.A.), Fuller Theological Seminary.

AF762 Reil, Sebald
Kleine Kirchengeschichte Sambias. (Münsterschwarzacher
Studien, 7). Münsterschwarzach, GW: Vier-Türme-Verlag,
1969. xx, 104 pp. Paper. No ISBN.

A study based on original sources, describing the development of the Catholic Church in Zambia.

AF763 Roberts, Andrew D.
The Lumpa Church of Alice Lenshina. Lusaka, ZA: Oxford
University Press, 1972. 56 pp. Paper. No ISBN.

An account of the rise and fall of the Lumpa church, a
religious protest movement that emerged in central Zambia
in the 1950s, and coincided, and finally clashed with the nationalist movement for political independence.

AF764 Rotberg, Robert I.
*Christian Missionaries and the Creation of Northern Rhode-
sia, 1880-1924.* Princeton, NJU: Princeton University Press,
1965. xi, 240 pp. No ISBN.

A survey of the history of the planting of Christianity in
the Republic of Zambia and the role of missionaries in the
introduction of Western civilization in that country

AF765 Santamarta, Sinesio R.
Diario de un Misionero. Madrid, SP: Mundo Negro, 1977.
221 pp. 8472950476.

The 1974-1976 diary of a missionary of the Comboni
order, to Zambia.

AF766 Shewmaker, Stan
Tonga Christianity. South Pasadena, CAU: William Carey
Library, 1970. xvi, 199 pp. 0878084096.

An important study of Christian missions and church
development among one of Zambia's major tribal groups.

AF767 Snelson, Peter
Educational Development in Northern Rhodesia, 1883-1945.
Lusaka, ZA: Kenneth Kaunda Foundation, 1990. xii, 324 pp.
9982000714.

A second edition of a detailed history of the contributions of missionaries to modern education in Zambia (formerly Northern Rhodesia); originally published in 1974.

AF768 Taylor, John Vernon
Christians of the Copperbelt. (World Mission Studies). London, ENK: SCM Press, 1961. 308 pp. No ISBN.

A detailed study of factors affecting the growth of Christian churches in the Copperbelt towns of Northern Rhodesia
(now Zambia), and of the church's response to the pressures
and demands of the urbanization taking place in so many parts
of Africa.

AF—AFRICA

AF—AFRICA

AF769 Verstraelen, F. J.
An African Church in Transition: From Missionary Dependence to Mutuality in Mission: A Case-Study on the Roman-Catholic Church in Zambia. Leiden, NE: IIMO, 1975. 2 vols. Paper. No ISBN.

A two-volume extensive survey of the Catholic Church in Zambia in the early 1970s, concentrating on the problems related to the diminishing role of expatriate missionaries and the dominating position of the indigenous clergy, with many statistics; vol. 1: (xxi, 348 pp.); vol. 2: (583 pp.).

AF770 Verstraelen-Gilhuis, Gerdien
From Dutch Mission Church to Reformed Church in Zambia: The Scope for African Leadership and Initiative in the History of a Zambian Mission Church. Franeker, NE: Wever, 1982. 366 pp. Paper. 9061353513.

History of the origins and development of the Reformed Church in Zambia, based on oral sources (interviews) and archival material, stressing the activities of indigenous believers from the very beginning of Christianity; doctoral dissertation at the Free University of Amsterdam.

AF771 Weller, John C.
The Priest from the Lakeside: The Story of Leonard Kamungu of Malawi and Zambia, 1877-1913. Blantyre, MW: CLAIM, 1971. 69 pp. Paper. No ISBN.

The life and ministry of the African Anglican priest, who was the pioneer of Msoro Mission in eastern Zambia.

North Africa: General Works

See also HI300.

AF772 Cooley, John K.
Baal, Christ, and Mohammed: Religion and Revolution in North Africa. New York, NYU: Holt, Rinehart and Winston, 1965. xiv, 369 pp. 815520115 (SBN).

A history of Christian-Muslim encounters in North Africa, with suggestions for the future of both Catholic and Protestant mission there.

AF773 Daniel, Robin
This Holy Seed. Harpenden, ENK: Tamarisk Publications, 1993. 493 pp. Paper. 0952043505.

A popular history of North African Christianity in its first ten centuries, focusing on reasons for its initial rapid growth but later slow decay and death.

North Africa: Biography

See also SP154.

AF774 Gstrein, Heinz
Der Heilige aus der Kanone: Jean Le Vacher, Apostel der Sklaven in Tunis und Algier, 1619-1683. (Missionare, die Geschichte machten). Mödling, AU: Verlag St. Gabriel; St. Augustin, GW: Steyler Verlag, 1980. 111 pp. Paper. 3852641446 (AU), 3877871216 (GW).

The life of one of the first and most renowned missionaries of the Congregation of the Vincentians, Vicar Apostolic of Algiers and Tunis, who died a martyr.

AF775 Vinatier, Jean
Le père Louis Augros: premier supérieur de la Mission de France (1898-1982). (L'histoire à vif). Paris, FR: Éditions du Cerf, 1991. 225 pp. Paper. 2204042935.

In this biography of the first superior of the seminary of the Mission of France, his co-worker and later Vicar-General of the Mission recounts his work as theological educator and later missionary in Algeria and Tunisia, with extensive excerpts from his letters.

AF776 Zwemer, Samuel Marinus
Raimundo Lulio: Primer Misionero entre los Musulmanes. Translated by Alejandro Brachmann. Madrid, SP: Sociedad de Publicaciones Religiosas, 1986. 141 pp. No ISBN.

Spanish translation of *Raimund Lull: First Missionary to the Muslims* (1902), the biography of the pioneer Catholic missionary and martyr (1315); written by the celebrated 20th-century Reformed missionary to Muslims in Arabia and Egypt.

Algeria

See also SP139-SP142, SP152-SP153, and AF775.

AF777 Carretto, Carlo
Letters to Dolcidia (1954-1983). Translated by Michael J. Smith and Gian Carlo Sibilia. Maryknoll, NYU: Orbis Books, 1991. 224 pp. Paper. 0883447207.

Letters from Carlo Carretto (1910-1988) to his sister Dolcidia, a Salesian nun, written mainly during the 1954-1965 period when he lived in the Algerian desert as a Little Brother of Jesus.

AF778 Castillon du Perron, Marguerite
Charles de Foucauld. Paris, FR: B. Grasset, 1982. 521 pp. 2246273617.

Biography of Charles Eugène de Foucauld (1858-1916), onetime Trappist monk and Christian hermit among the Muslim Tuareg tribes of North Africa.

AF779 Facelina, Raymond
Théologie en situation: une communauté chrétienne dans le tiers-monde (Algérie 1962-1974). (Hommes et Église, 5). Strasbourg, FR: CERDIC-Publications, 1974. 327 pp. 2850970026.

A scholarly study of the theology and ministry of the Catholic Church in Algeria in the twelve years following independence.

AF780 Foucauld, Charles de
Charles de Foucauld: Writings Selected with an Introduction by Robert Ellsberg. (Modern Spiritual Masters Series). Maryknoll, NYU: Orbis Books, 1999. 127 pp. Paper. 1570752443.

A biography of the modern mystic and martyr (1858-1916), a soldier, explorer, monk, and ultimately desert hermit who rediscovered the wisdom of the ancient desert fathers, and from whom evolved the Little Brothers and the Little Siters of Jesus.

AF781 Furioli, Antonio
L'amicizia con Cristo in Charles de Foucauld. Brescia, IT: Morcelliana, 1980. 190 pp. No ISBN.

A presentation of the concept of the friendship of Christ in the spirituality of Charles Eugène de Foucauld (1858-1916), Christian hermit among Muslim Tuareg tribes of North Africa.

AF782 Merad, Ali
Charles de Foucauld au regard de l'Islam. Paris, FR: Chalet, 1975. 130 pp. 2702302300.

A sensitive analysis by an Algerian Muslim of the impact of the "Hermit of the Sahara" upon Muslims in Algeria, understanding his life in relation to Islamic ideals.

AF783 Merad, Ali
Christian Hermit in an Islamic World: A Muslim's View of Charles de Foucauld. Translated by Zoe Hersov. New York, NYU: Paulist Press, 1999. iii, 115 pp. Paper. 0809139030.

English translation.

AF784 Quesnel, Roger
Charles de Foucauld: les ètapes d'une recherche. Tours, FR: Mame, 1966. xxiii, 310 pp. No ISBN.

Contributing to the discussion of the spiritual aspect of mission is this attempt, not only to describe, but also to explain various stages in the religious thought of the hermit of the Sahara.

AF785 Sanson, Henri
Christianisme au miroir de l'Islam: essai sur la rencontre des cultures en Algérie. (Rencontres). Paris, FR: Éditions du Cerf, 1984. 200 pp. Paper. 2204022780.

An essay on the encounter between Christianity and Islam in Algerian culture—a cohabitation in which Christianity is viewed through an Islamic looking glass; by a Jesuit priest who lived there from 1924 to 1984.

AF786 St. John, Patricia Mary
Until the Day Breaks....: The Life & Works of Lilias Trotter, Pioneer Missionary to Muslim North Africa. Bromley, Kent, ENK: OM Publishing, 1990. 222 pp. Paper. 1850780773.

A popular biography of Isabelle Lilias Trotter (1853-1928), who in 1888 began the Algiers Mission Band, a non-denominational society seeking to witness to Muslim women and children (later part of the North Africa Mission, which continues today as Arab World Ministries).

AF787 Trouncer, Margaret
Charles de Foucauld. London, ENK: George G. Harrap, 1972. 214 pp. 0245508406.

A quality biography of Charles Eugène de Foucauld (1858-1916), Trappist monk and missionary to the nomadic Tuaregs of North Africa (1904-1916), whose disciples formed the missionary orders of the Little Brothers of Jesus (1936) and Little Sisters of Jesus (1939).

Egypt [United Arab Republic]

See also AF631.

AF788 Altheim, Franz, and Ruth Stiehl
Christentum am Roten Meer. Berlin, GW: Gruyter, 1971. xv, 670 pp. 3110037904.

A collection of philological, archeological, and linguistic works by international scholars on themes related to ancient Christianity with origins in the Red Sea area—examinations of stone inscriptions and papyri.

AF789 Chitham, E. J.
The Coptic Community in Egypt: Spatial and Social Change. (Occasional Paper Series, 32). Durham, ENK: Centre for Middle Eastern and Islamic Studies, 1986. 121 pp. 0903011158.

A sociological survey of the Coptic minority in Egypt, demonstrating its importance in a region predominantly Arab in culture.

AF790 Höpfner, Willi, ed.
Die Frau bei den Kopten und Moslems in Ägypten. (Chris-

tentum und Islam, 13). Breklum, GW: Breklumen Verlag; Wiesbaden, GW: Orientdienst e.V., 1982. 71 pp. 3779304856.

Short papers providing a comparison of the status of Muslim and Coptic women in Egypt.

AF791 Kinnear, Elizabeth Kelsey
She Sat Where They Sat: A Memoir of Anna Young Thompson of Egypt. Grand Rapids, MIU: Eerdmans, 1971. 112 pp. Paper. No ISBN.

A popular biography of Anna Young Thompson (1851-1932), pioneer woman Presbyterian missionary in Egypt, from 1871 until her death there in 1932.

AF792 *Many Though One*
(Maryknoll Video Magazine). Maryknoll, NYU: Maryknoll World Productions, 1992. 28:30 mins. No ISBN.

Priest, bishop, and laypeople explain the practices and beliefs of seven different Catholic worship traditions (rites) in Cairo, Egypt.

AF793 McEwan, Dorothea
Habsburg als Schutzmacht der Katholiken in Ägypten: Kurzfassung der Studie über das österreichische Kirchenprotektorat von seinen Anfängen. (Schriften des Österreichischen Kulturinstituts Kairo, 3). Wiesbaden, GW: Harrasowitz, 1982. 174 pp. 3447020520.

A scholarly study of the role of the Hapsburg Empire to 1914 as a protective power for Catholicism in Egypt.

AF794 Meinardus, Otto F. A.
Christian Egypt Ancient and Modern. Cairo, UA: American University in Cairo, 1977. xxii, 708 pp. Paper. No ISBN.

A guide to Christianity in Egypt, including a historical outline, details on Coptic Christian life and liturgy, and a description of historic and contemporary sites of churches and monasteries.

AF795 Taylor, Howard
Borden of Yale. (Men of Faith). Minneapolis, MNU: Bethany House, 1988. 207 pp. Paper. 1556610149.

A popular biography narrating the experience of William Borden (1887-1913), who served widows, orphans, and the physically disabled of Chicago, before becoming a missionary to the Kansu people of Egypt, until his death in 1913.

AF796 Waters, John
Moving Mountains. London, ENK: Triangle, 1999. xiv, 130 pp. Paper. 0281050988.

A recounting of miracles and healing among rubbish collectors near Cairo, through the ministry of Father Simaan, a Coptic priest.

Morocco

AF797 Beach, Peter, and William Dunphy
Benedictine and Moor: A Christian Adventure in Moslem Morocco. New York, NYU: Holt, Rinehart & Winston, 1960. 214 pp. No ISBN.

An account of the founding and ministry of the only community of Christian monks in Muslim North Africa, the Toumliline Monastery, engaged in non-proselytizing Christian witness.

AF—AFRICA

AF798 Des Allues, Elisabeth
Das Buch von Toumliline: Benediktiner im Herzen des Islam.
Translated by Ludwig Fabritius. Vienna, AU: Herold, 1963.
205 pp. No ISBN.

An account of the Benedictine monastery in Morocco,
founded in 1951, and of the way its influence has spread
through witness to the Muslim population and establishment
of new monasteries among the African people in Bouaké (Ivory
Coast) and Koubri (Upper Volta).

AF799 Fisk, Eric G.
*The Cross Versus the Crescent: More Missionary Stories about
Work among Muslims.* London, ENK: Pickering & Inglis,
1971. 143 pp. 0720800595.

Testimonies of faith sharing with Muslims in Morocco.

AF800 Lafon, Michel
Le père peyriguere. Paris, FR: Éditions du Seuil, 1963. 188
pp. Paper. No ISBN.

A documented biography of "the Hermit of El Kbab"
(1883-1959), a follower of Charles de Foucauld, who devoted
his life to service and contemplation in Morocco.

AF801 St. John, Patricia Mary
*An Ordinary Woman's Extraordinary Faith: The Autobiogra-
phy of Patricia St. John.* Wheaton, ILU: Shaw Publishers,
1993. 305 pp. Paper. 0877887519.

The autobiography of Patricia Mary St. John (1919-1992),
focusing on her years of service as an OMF nurse in Morocco
(1949-1976).

Tunisia

See also CR1035 and AF775.

AF802 Garau, Marius
*La rose de l'imâm: L'amitié entre un chrétien et un musul-
man.* (Recontres Islam, 31). Paris, FR: Éditions du Cerf, 1983.
156 pp. 2204020125.

Story of the friendship of a priest and an imam in Tunisia.

**AF803 *Pistes de réponses aux questions qu'on nous pose,
par un groupe de chrétiens vivant en Tunisie***
(Collection "Studi arabo-islamici del PISAI," 2). Rome, IT:
Pontificio Istituto di Studi Arabi e d'Islamistica, 1987. 113
pp. 8885907016.

Results of a survey of Tunisian Christians on attitudes
toward Islam.

Southern Africa: General Works

See also HI420, CR169, SO160, SO284, SO336, EC142, PO42,
PO101, PO193, AF7, AF34, AF291, AF453, AF464, and AF1142.

AF804 Briggs, D. Roy, and Joseph Wing
*The Harvest and the Hope: The Story of Congregationalism
in Southern Africa.* Johannesburg, SA: United Congregational Church of Southern Africa, 1970. 344 pp. Paper. No ISBN.

A narrative history of the United Congregational Church
of Southern Africa and its predecessor missions, with photographs.

AF805 Carter, John Stanley
Methods of Mission in Southern Africa. London, ENK: SPCK,
1963. xiii, 150 pp. No ISBN.

A book for Anglican laity in South Africa, stressing
their role in evangelization and in being the church in the
world.

AF806 Comaroff, Jean, and John L. Comaroff
*Of Revelation and Revolution: Christianity, Colonialism,
and Consciousness in South Africa.* Chicago, ILU: University of Chicago Press, 1991. 2 vols. 0226114414 (vol.
1, hdbk), 0226114422 (vol. 1, pbk), 0226114430 (vol. 2,
hdbk), 0226114449 (vol. 2, pbk).

A scholarly, detailed study in two volumes, of the 19th-
century encounter between British missionaries of the London and Wesleyan missionary societies and the Southern
Tswana peoples of present South Africa and Botswana, as
well as the complex transactions between colonial officials,
capitalists, and British nonconformist missionaries (Moffat, Livingstone, etc.) among the Southern Tswana peoples
of the South African frontier [vol. 1, *Christianity, Colonialism, and Consciousness in South Africa* (1991, xx, 414
pp.); vol. 2, *The Dialectics of Modernity on a South African Frontier* (1997, xxiii, 588 pp]].

**AF807 Dachs, Anthony J., and Michael F. C. Bourdillon,
eds.**
Christianity South of the Zambezi. Gweru, RH: Mambo
Press, 1977. 2 vols. Paper. No ISBN.

A rich collection in two volumes (vol. 1: 1973, 213
pp.; vol. 2: 1977, 219 pp.) of scholarly essays on the impact of Christian missionary activity on the African people
of present Zimbabwe, with some references to South Africa.

AF808 Dachs, Anthony J., ed.
Papers of John MacKenzie. Johannesburg, SA: Witwatersrand University Press, 1975. xvi, 282 pp. 0854942432.

The writings of a LMS missionary-statesman who, from
1858 to 1899, not only worked to bring the Sotho-Tswana
peoples of southern Africa to Christ, but also sought to tem-
per English rule in the British territories in that region.

AF809 Daniels, George M., ed.
Southern Africa: A Time for Change. New York, NYU:
Friendship Press, 1969. 95 pp. Paper. No ISBN.

An illustrated collection of twenty essays by specialists designed to describe for North American Christians
the liberation struggles in southern Africa.

AF810 Denis, Philippe
*The Dominican Friars in Southern Africa: A Social Histo-
ry, 1577-1990.* (Studies in Christian Mission, 21). Leiden,
NE: Brill, 1998. xiii, 322 pp. 9004111441.

A detailed social and cultural history of the Dominicans in southern Africa, focusing on the 16th-century Zambezi Mission and the 19th- and 20th-century developments
in South Africa; by a Dominican scholar serving as Associate Professor of History at the School of Theology of the
University of Natal.

AF811 Florin, Hans W., ed.
Gewalt im südlichen Afrika: Ein Bericht. Translated by
Annemarie Oesterle. Frankfurt am Main, GW: Verlag Otto
Lembeck, 1971. x, 147 pp. 0874760081.

German translation of *Violence in Southern Africa: A
Christian Assessment* (1970).

AF812 Froise, Marjorie, ed.
World Christianity: Southern Africa: A Factual Portrait of the Christian Church in South Africa, Botswana, Lesotho, Namibia and Swaziland. (World Christianity). Monrovia, CAU: MARC, 1989. iii, 127 pp. Paper. 0912552638.

A volume by a native South African giving details and statistics on the background, living conditions, status of the Christian churches, their activities and needs in Botswana, Lesotho, Namibia, South Africa, and Swaziland.

AF813 Gifford, Paul
The New Crusaders: Christianity and the New Right in Southern Africa. Concord, MAU: Pluto Press, 1991. ix, 131 pp. 0745304567 (hdbk), 0745304575 (pbk).

A revised edition of *The Religious Right in South Africa* (1988) analyzing the impact of the right-wing politics of fundamentalists from the United States upon politics in Latin America and southern Africa, especially Zimbabwe and South Africa.

AF814 Hellberg, Carl J.
A Voice of the Voiceless: The Involvement of the Lutheran World Federation in Southern Africa, 1947-1977. (Studia Missionalia Upsaliensia, 34). Stockholm, SW: Verbum, 1979. 236 pp. No ISBN.

A study of the Lutheran churches in South Africa, the involvement of the LWF, and the struggle for racial equality.

AF815 Lagerwerf, Leny, ed.
Reconstruction: The WCC Assembly Harare 1998 and the Churches in Southern Africa. (IIMO Research Publication, 47). Zoetermeer, NE: Meinema, 1998. 200 pp. Paper. 9021170167.

Seven national case studies of mission challenges in the 1990s in southern Africa, as related to the theme of the 1998 jubilee assembly of the WCC meeting in Harare, Zimbabwe, "Turn to God—Rejoice in Hope."

AF816 Martin, Marie-Louise
The Biblical Concept of Messianism and Messianism in Southern Africa. Morija, LO: Morija Sesuto Book Depot, 1964. 207 pp. No ISBN.

A revision and expansion of the author's thesis (University of South Africa, 1962).

AF817 National Council of the Churches of Christ in the U.S.A., and the United States Catholic Conference
The Church and Southern Africa. Marcy, NYU: NCCUSA, 1977. 80 pp. Paper. No ISBN.

Report of an influential first Roman Catholic-Protestant joint discussion of southern Africa issues by church leaders of the subcontinent and North America.

AF818 Pretorius, H. L. et al., eds.
Reflecting on Mission in the African Context: A Handbook for Missiology. Bloemfontein, SA: Pro Christo Publications, 1987. viii, 196 pp. Paper. 1868040461.

An introductory handbook on missiology, with special reference to the southern Africa context.

AF819 Procter, Lovell J.
The Central African Journal of Lovell J. Procter, 1860-1864. Edited by N. Bennett and M. Ylvisaker. Boston, MAU: Boston University, African Studies Center, 1971. xvii, 501 pp. No ISBN.

The detailed journal of a member, and later leader, of the first expedition of the University's Mission to Central Africa, from South Africa to Magomere (present Malawi).

AF820 Rea, W. F.
The Economics of the Zambezi Missions, 1580-1759. (Bibliotheca Instituti Historici S. I., 39). Rome, IT: Institutum Historicum S. I., 1976. 189 pp. No ISBN.

A detailed comparative study of Dominican and Jesuit missions along the Zambezi River from the 16th to the 18th century.

AF821 Setiloane, Gabriel Molehe, and Ivan H. M. Peden, eds.
Pangs of Growth: A Dialogue on Church Growth in Southern Africa. Braamfontein, SA: Skotaville Publishers, 1988. viii, 229 pp. Paper. 0947009450.

A collection of short essays by thirteen men and women, concerned that the churches of Jesus Christ grow healthily as South Africa moves toward the 21st century.

AF822 Stack, Louise, and Don Morton
Torment to Triumph in Southern Africa. New York, NYU: Friendship Press, 1976. 143 pp. Paper. 0377000507.

A mission study book for North American Christians, with country profiles, focusing on the struggle against apartheid and for liberation of African peoples from white domination.

AF823 *The Role of the Church in Socio-Economic Development in Southern Africa: A Consultation held in Umpumulo (Natal) Africa*
Umpumulo, SA: Missiological Institute, 1972. 191 pp. No ISBN.

Papers from an important southern Africa consultation on the churches and development issues, including the basics of development, its theological dimensions (H. W. Gensichen), attitudes toward development, and case studies.

AF824 Thomas, Thomas Morgan
Eleven Years in Central Africa. (Cass Library of African Studies: Missionary Researches and Travels, 23). London, ENK: Cass, 1971. xx, 418 pp. 0714618802.

Reprint of the missionary classic of 1873, in which Thomas Morgan Thomas (1828-1884), LMS colleague of Robert Moffat, recounts the history of the Makololo and Zambezi missions, and that of the Ndebele people of Matabeleland (1859 to 1870) in present Zimbabwe.

AF825 *Violence in Southern Africa: A Christian Assessment*
London, ENK: SCM Press, 1970. x, 119 pp. 0334017408.

Report of a working party appointed by the Department of International Affairs, British Council of Churches, and the Conference of British Missionary Societies.

AF826 Walsh, Thomas G., and Frank Kaufmann
Religion and Social Transformation in Southern Africa. St. Paul, MNU: Paragon House, 1999. xx, 244 pp. Paper. 155778776X (hdbk), 1557787778 (pbk).

A spectrum of religious views from throughout southern Africa, in fifteen essays that intersect in religious, spiritual, political, social, and cultural dimensions.

AF827 Watt, Peter
From Africa's Soil: The Story of the Assemblies of God in Southern Africa. Cape Town, SA: Struik, 1992. 210 pp. Paper. 1868230597.

The first narrative history of the Assemblies of God in southern Africa, including the history, structure, and ministries of the movement, and its response to its religious and sociopolitical environment.

AF—AFRICA

Southern Africa: Biography

AF828 Crafford, D., ed.
Trail-Blazers of the Gospel: Black Pioneers in the Missionary History of Southern Africa. Bloemfontein, SA: Pro Christo Publications, 1992. viii, 203 pp. Paper. 1868041204.

Twenty-nine short biographies of black pioneer missionaries—all written by white South Africans.

AF829 Davies, Horton, ed.
Great South African Christians. Westport, CTU: Greenwood, 1970. vii, 190 pp. 837139163 (SBN).

Biographies of eighteen outstanding Christian leaders, mostly missionaries, of southern Africa; originally published in 1951 (Oxford University Press, London, UK).

AF830 Denniston, Robin
Trevor Huddleston: A Life. New York, NYU: St. Martin's Press, 1999. xxiii, 295 pp. 0312227094.

An Anglican monk and leader of the Anti-Apartheid Movement, Huddleston was a friend and hero to Nelson Mandela, Desmond Tutu, and others; the author draws upon Huddleston's extensive private archive of correspondence, speeches, and sermons.

AF831 Freeman, Nona
Bug and Nona on the Go. Hazelwood, MOU: Word Aflame Press, 1979. 169 pp. Paper. No ISBN.

A popular account of the experiences of a United Pentecostal missionary couple in Africa, primarily South Africa, from 1948 to 1974.

AF832 Northcott, William Cecil
Robert Moffat: Pioneer in Africa, 1817-1870. New York, NYU: Harper; London, ENK: Lutterworth Press, 1961. 357 pp. No ISBN.

A solid biography of the pioneer LMS missionary to southern Africa based on hitherto unpublished memoirs, letters, and journals.

Angola

See also AF396 and AF1168.

AF833 Brásio, António
Angola. (Spiritana Monumenta Historica: African Series, 1). Pittsburgh, PAU: Duquesne University Press; Louvain, BE: Nauwelaerts, 1971. 5 vols. No ISBN.

Documents in Portuguese related to the mission of the Congregation of the Holy Ghost in Angola, 1596 to 1967 [vol. 1: xxxii, 720 pp.; vol. 2: xxiii, 759 pp.; vol. 3: xxiii, 770 pp.; vol. 4: xxiv, 789 pp.; vol. 5: xxvii, 1,039 pp. (1966-1971)].

AF834 Brásio, António
História e Missiologia: Inéditos e esparsos. Luanda, AO: Instituto de Investigação Científica de Angola, 1973. viii, 929 pp. Paper. No ISBN.

A history of Portuguese Catholic missions in the Congo and Angola with the texts of source documents.

AF835 Chipenda, Eva de Carvalho
The Visitor: An African Woman's Story of Travel and Discovery. (Risk Book Series, 73). Geneva, SZ: WCC Publications, 1996. viii, 87 pp. Paper. 2825411922.

An Angolan Christian relates her life story based on her journal, with reflections on colonialism and development, missionaries and the church, and the role of women in a changing continent.

AF836 Gabriel, Manuel Nunes
Angola cinco séculos de cristianismo. Queluz, PO: Literal, 1978. 639 pp. No ISBN.

A history of Catholic missions to Angola from the 15th century to the present.

AF837 Henderson, Lawrence W.
The Church in Angola: A River of Many Currents. Cleveland, OHU: Pilgrim Press, 1992. xiii, 448 pp. 0829809384.

A comprehensive history of Christianity in Angola from 1866 to 1990 by a former missionary and staff member of the United Church Board for World Ministries; originally published as *A Igreja em Angola: Uno Rio Com Vrias Correntes* (Lisbon: Editorial Alem-Mar, 1990).

AF838 Neves, A. F. Santos
Ecumenismo em Angola: do ecumenismo cristão ecumenismo universal. (Editorial colóquios, 1). Nova Lisboa, AO: Instituto Superior Católico, 1968. 383 pp. No ISBN.

A full account of how ecumenical cooperation has been planned and carried out in the little diocese of Nova Lisboa in Angola.

AF839 Paas, S.
Tussen Wereldraad en concordaat: het Protestantisme in Angola. [De Bilt], NE: Internationale Raad van Christelijke Kerken, 1973. 64 pp. No ISBN.

A publication of the International Council of Christian Churches on Protestantism in Angola.

AF840 Samuels, Michael Anthony
Education in Angola, 1878-1914: A History of Culture Transfer and Administration. New York, NYU: Teachers College Press, 1970. xiii, 185 pp. Paper. No ISBN.

A detailed study, based on government and mission archives, of the policies of the Portuguese colonial administration and the missions.

AF841 Santos, Eduardo dos
Religiões de Angola. (Estudos missionários, 3; Religiões e missões, 3). Lisboa, AO: Junta de Investigações do Ultramar, 1969. 536 pp. No ISBN.

A thorough history of all religious groups in Angola (Catholic, Protestant, sectarian, and traditional African religions).

AF842 Tucker, John T.
A Tucker Treasury: Reminiscences and Stories of Angola, 1883-1958. Compiled by Catherine Tucker Ward. Winfield, BCC: Wood Lake Books, 1984. 221 pp. Paper. 091959929X.

Collected papers and reminiscenes of John Taylor Tucker (1883-1958), pioneer Angola missionary (1913-1951) of the United Church of Canada.

AF843 Wilson, Thomas Ernest
Angola Beloved. Neptune, NJU: Loizeaux Brothers, 1967. 254 pp. No ISBN.

A descriptive account of the principles and preaching of the Christian Brethren in mission in Angola.

Botswana [Bechuanaland]

See also SO287, SO315, and AF806.

AF844 Amanze, James
Botswana Handbook of Churches: A Handbook of Churches, Ecumenical Organisations, Theological Institutions and Other World Religions in Botswana. Gaborone, BS: Pula Press, 1994. xi, 316 pp. Paper. 9991261281.

An alphabetical directory of the many religious groups in Botswana, including African indigenous churches; with brief statements on their histories, objectives, theology, practices, and ethics.

AF845 Amanze, James
The Origin and Development of the Ecumenical Movement in Botswana, 1965-1994. (Studies on the Church in Southern Africa, 4). Gaborone, BS: University of Botswana, 1994. 71 pp. Paper. 9991220909.

A thirty-year history of ecumenism in Botswana based on interviews and archival research.

AF846 Hepburn, James Davidson
Twenty Years in Khama's Country; and, Pioneering among the Batauana of Lake Ngami, told in the Letters of J. D. Hepburn. Edited by C. H. Lyall. (Cass Library of African Studies, 7). London, ENK: Cass, 1970. xxxv, 397 pp. 0714618705.

Third edition of a reprint of the letters of James Davidson Hepburn (1840-1893), pioneer LMS missionary to the Ngwato people of Botswana; originally published in 1896.

AF847 Landau, Paul Stuart
The Realm of the Word: Language, Gender, and Christianity in a Southern African Kingdom. (Social History of Africa). Portsmouth, NHU: Heinemann; Cape Town, SA: David Philip; London, ENK: James Currey, 1995. xxix, 249 pp. 0435089633 (US, hdbk), 043508965X (US, pbk), 0852556705 (UK, hdbk), 0852556209 (UK, pbk).

A scholarly social history of Christianity and the Tswana of central Botswana, based on archival and field research, focusing on the roles of indigenous leaders, both women and men.

AF848 Meijers, Catrien
Werk aan de kerk in Etsha: Zendingswerk in de jaren tachtig van de twintigste eeuw. Leusden, NE: Centrum Zending en Diakonaat Geref. Kerken in Nederland; Oegstgeest, NE: Ned. Herv. Kerk, 1988. 60 pp. Paper. 9065721134.

Impressions of the author's first four years of missionary work among the Hambukushu in Etsha (1982-1986), refugees from Angola who started from scratch a new life in Botswana in the late 1960s, highlighting problems as well as promises for an independent and dynamic local church.

AF849 Mgadla, Part Themba
Missionaries and Western Education in the Bechuanaland Protectorate 1859-1904: The Case of the Bangwato. (Studies on the Church in Southern Africa, 2). Gaborone, BS: University of Botswana, 1994. 50 pp. Paper. 9991220275.

A short history of mission education under the LMS in Bechuanaland (present Botswana); published jointly by the Departments of History and of Theology and Religious Studies of the University of Botswana.

AF850 Potter, Jennifer
The Origins and Development of Methodist Mission Work in the Area of Present-Day Botswana. (Studies on the Church in Southern Africa, 6). Gaborone, BS: University of Botswana, 1995. v, 83 pp. Paper. 9991220917.

A narrative history, based on source documents, of British and South African Methodism's missionary work in Bechuanaland/Botswana from 1816 to 1986.

AF851 Price, Elizabeth Lees
The Journals of Elizabeth Lees Price, Written in Bechuanaland, Southern Africa, 1854-1883. Edited by Una Long. London, ENK: Arnold, 1962. No ISBN.

Journals of the daughter of Robert Moffat who lived from 1839 to 1919 and served, with her husband Roger, as pioneer missionaries of the LMS among the Tswana.

AF852 Proske, Wolfgang
Botswana und die Anfänge der Hermannsburger Mission: Voraussetzungen, Verlauf und Scheitern eines lutherischen Missionierungsversuches im Spannungsfeld divergierender politischer Interessen. (European University Studies 3: History and Allied Studies, 391). Frankfurt am Main, GW: Lang, 1989. 291 pp. Paper. 3631405464.

This thesis, dealing with the activities of the Hermannsburg Mission in Botswana from 1857 to 1864, places special emphasis on the controversy surrounding superintendent Hardeland and the involvement of the mission in the tensions between Tswana, Boers, and British.

AF853 Setiloane, Gabriel Molehe
The Image of God among the Sotho-Tswana. Rotterdam, NE: Balkema, 1976. x, 298 pp. Paper. 9061910072.

A detailed ethnographic and critical historical analysis of the religion of the Sotho-Tswana of Botswana and the Transvaal (South Africa), from their traditional beliefs through missionary impact to present expressions of Christianity.

Lesotho [Basutuland]

AF854 Arbousset, Thomas
Missionary Excursion into the Blue Mountains Being an Account of King Moshoeshoe's Expedition from Thaba-Bosiu to the Sources of the Malibamatso River in the Year 1840. Translated by Saint Ambrose and Albert Brutsch. Morija, LO: Morija Archives; Nairobi, KE: Centre de Recherche, d'Echanges et de Documentation Universitaire, 1991. 219 pp. Paper. No ISBN.

A critical edition in English, Lesotho, and French, of the account by Jean Thomas Arbousset (1810-1877), pioneer missionary of the Paris Evangelical Missionary Society, to Lesotho (1833-1860) and Tahiti (1863-1867), of travels with King Moshoeshoe of the Basuto; the English and Lesotho edition published by Morija Archives, and the French edition published by Centre de Recherche.

AF855 Baker, Jeff
African Flying Doctor: A Young Man's Living Journal. London, ENK: Allen, William H., 1968. 188 pp. 0491002106.

A first-person account of the work at the Albert Schweitzer Clinic in Lesotho, led by Dr. Carl van Aswegen under the auspices of the Basutoland Socio-Medical Services (BASOMED).

AF—AFRICA

AF856 Bernier, Cyrille
Plongée en afrique. Richelieu, QUC: Québec Imprimerie Notre Dame, 1969. 297 pp. No ISBN.
A missionary's reflection on Catholicism in Lesotho.

AF857 Casalis, Eugéne Arnaud
The Basutos or Twenty-Three Years in South Africa. Morija, LO: Morija Museum and Archives; London, ENK: Nisbet, 1992. xix, 355 pp. No ISBN.
A facsimile reprint of the classic 1861 English edition by the pioneer of the Société des Missions Evangeliques de Paris, with an interpretive essay by Stephen Gill and new comprehensive index.

AF858 Casalis, Eugéne Arnaud
My Life in Basutoland. Translated by J. Brierley. (Africana Collectanea Series, 38). Cape Town, SA: Struick, 1971. 300 pp. 0869770055.
A reprint of the 1889 translation of *Mes Souvenirs* [Paris, FR: Société des Missions Évangéliques, 1889], recollections by the author (1812-1891) who served under the Paris Missionary Society in planting Christian missions among the Basuto people in the middle part of the 19th century.

AF859 Dove, R.
Anglican Pioneers in Lesotho: Some Account of the Diocese of Lesotho, 1876-1930. Maseru, LO: Diocese of Lesotho, 1975. 216 pp. Paper. No ISBN.
An official diocesan history.

AF860 Froise, Marjorie, ed.
Lesotho Christian Handbook 1992-93. Johannesburg, SA: Christian Info, 1992. v, 67 pp. Paper. 0620167114.
A comprehensive directory of all Christian churches, missions, and agencies working in Lesotho, with a brief introductory profile.

AF861 Lapointe, Eugène
An Experience of Pastoral Theology in Southern Africa. Rome, IT: Pontifica Universita Urbaniana, 1986. 260 pp. Paper. No ISBN.
A detailed case study of the RCC in Lesotho, and the ways in which the "small Christian community" has enabled the church to be effective in ministry in the Lesotho sociocultural environment.

AF862 Lapointe, Eugène, ed.
Correspondance entre François Laydevant et Albert Perbal 1927-1952: dialogue du missionnaire et du missiologue. (Studies in Christian Mission, 12). Leiden, NE: Brill, 1994. viii, 262 pp. 9004101713.
A critical edition of the correspondence of Fr. François Laydevant, OMI, Catholic missionary to Lesotho (1905-1954) with Fr. Albert Perbal, OMI, a missiologist resident in Rome, covering missiological problems of the time.

AF863 Perrot, Claude H.
Les Sotho et les missionnaires européens au XIXe siècle. (Annales de l'Université d'Abidjan, Série F: Ethnosociologie, vol. 2, 1). Abidjan, IV: Université d'Abidjan, 1970. 185 pp. No ISBN.
Originally presented as the author's thesis (Paris, 1963), under the title: "Les Bassoutos et les missionaires europeens au XIXe siecle."

Mozambique [Portuguese East Africa]

AF864 Butselaar, Jan van
Africains, missionnaires et colonialistes: Les origines de l'Église Presbytérienne du Mozambique (Mission Suisse), 1880-1896. (Studies on Religion in Africa, Supplements to the *Journal of Religion in America*, 5). Leiden, NE: Brill, 1984. viii, 238 pp. Paper. No ISBN.
A scholarly and very detailed history of the beginnings of the Presbyterian Church of Mozambique, 1880-1896, focusing on the first conversions among the Tsonga tribe, resulting from the Christian witness of fellow tribesman converted to Christianity while in South Africa, and from activities of Swiss missionaries to Mozambique.

AF865 Garcia, Antônio
História de Mocambique Cristão. Lourenço Marques, MZ: Diario Grafica, 1969. 205 pp. No ISBN.
A short history of Catholic missions in Mozambique.

AF866 Grechane, Germano
A Nova figura do catequista leigo na igreja local moçambicana: Do concilio atéa renovação da catequese e a independência de Mocambique. Rome, IT: Pontificia Università Lateranensis, 1982. 123 pp. Paper. No ISBN.
Doctoral dissertation in two parts: the details of lay catechetical ministry in Roman Catholic documents, and catechetical practice in Mozambique.

AF867 Hastings, Adrian
Wiriyamu. London, ENK: Search Press, 1974. 158 pp. 0855323388.
Details of the 1971-1972 massacres of Frelimo supporters by the Portuguese, and of the responses by the church.

AF868 Helgesson, Alf
Church, State and People in Mozambique: An Historical Study with Special Emphasis on Methodist Developments in the Inhambane Region. (Studia Missionalia Uppsaliensia, 54). Uppsala, SW: Swedish Institute of Missionary Research, 1994. xiii, 436 pp. Paper. 9185424285.
A doctoral dissertation covering relations between the churches (Roman Catholic and Protestant) and the state in Mozambique, from colonial rule to the present.

AF869 Macy, Victor W., and Lela DeMilke
Discovery under the Southern Cross: Below the Equator: Missions Adventure in Mozambique and South Africa. Winona Lake, INU: Light & Life Press, 1984. 174 pp. Paper. 0893670936.
A popular history of the Free Methodist mission in the gold mining locations of South Africa, and in Mozambique, from Portuguese colonialism to Marxist rule.

AF870 Schebesta, Paul
Portugals Konquistamission in Südost-Afrika: Missionsgeschichte Sambesiens und des Monomotapareiches (1560-1920). (Studia Instituti Missiologici SVD, 7). St. Augustin, GW: Steyler Verlag, 1966. xiv, 487 pp. Paper. No ISBN.
A detailed history of Portugal's missionary work in South East Africa during the periods 1560-1830 and 1881-1935, attempting to throw light on the varied fortunes of the mission and its eventual failure due to the *conquista* system, with abundant citations from letters of missionaries.

AF871 Silva, António Barbosa da

Mentalidade missiológica dos Jesuítas em Moçambique antes de 1759: Esboço ideológico a partir do núcleo documental. (Estudos missisonários, 2). Lisbon, PO: n.p., 1967. 325 pp. No ISBN.

A detailed study of the motivations of Jesuit missions in Mozambique to 1759.

AF872 Silva, Manuel Ferreira da

Tríptco moçambicano: Sofala, Sabá, e Ofir; ensaio histórico-religioso das cristandades de Sofala e da localização de Ofir em Moçambique. Braga, PO: Gráfica de S. Vicente, 1967. 213 pp. No ISBN.

The story of early Catholic missions in Mozambique.

Namibia [South West Africa]

See also CR633.

AF873 Allison, Caroline

"It's Like Holding the Key to Your Own Jail": Women in Namibia. Geneva, SZ: WCC, 1986. x, 71 pp. Paper. 2825408417.

Moving testimonies by Namibian women who suffered the effects of war and repression, with a brief historical introduction.

AF874 Auala, Leonard, and Kirsti Ihamäki

Messlatte und Bischofsstab: Ein Leben für Namibia. (Erlanger Taschenbücher, 85). Erlangen, GW: Ev.-Luth. Mission; Wuppertal, GW: Verlag der VEM, 1988. 232 pp. Paper. 3872141856.

This autobiography of Leonard Auala (1908-) traces the career of the first native bishop of the Lutheran church, which developed out of the Finnish mission in northern Namibia.

AF875 Baumann, Julius

Mission und Ökumene in Südwestafrika: Dargestellt am Lebenswerk von Hermann Heinrich Vedder. (Ökumenische Studien, 7). Leiden, NE: Brill, 1965. xiii, 168 pp. No ISBN.

A dissertation on the understanding of mission of H. H. Vedder (b.1876), an important and politically committed member of the Rheinische Mission in South West Africa.

AF876 Beer, David de

The Way to Namibian Independence: UN Resolution 435. Edited by Eva Militz. Geneva, SZ: WCC, 1988. 45 pp. Paper. No ISBN.

A special issue of *PCR Information* (Programme to Combat Racism) on political issues concerning Namibian independence and the churches' involvement.

AF877 Diescho, Joseph, and Celeste Wallin

Born of the Sun: A Namibian Novel. New York, NYU: Friendship Press, 1988. x, 313 pp. 0377001880 (hdbk), 0377001872 (pbk).

A Michener-like novel of a young Namibian, educated in German Lutheran missionary schools, who as a miner becomes entangled in the South African apartheid system, and is later involved in the struggle for Namibian independence, while in Botswana.

AF878 Engel, Lothar

Kolonialismus und Nationalismus im deutschen Protestantismus in Namibia 1907 bis 1945: Beiträge zur Geschichte de deutschen evangelischen Mission und Kirche im ehemaligen *Kolonial- und Mandatsgebiet Südwestafrika.* (Studies in the Intercultural History of Christianity, 7). Bern, SZ: Herbert Lang; Frankfurt am Main, GW: Peter Lang, 1976. xxii, 612 pp. Paper. 3261017031.

A detailed study of the dynamic tensions from 1907 to 1945, between German colonial rule and the Protestant mission of the Rhenish Mission Society in Namibia.

AF879 Enquist, Roy J.

Namibia: Land of Tears, Land of Promise. Selinsgrove, PAU: Susquehanna University Press, 1990. 174 pp. 0945636091.

A creative analysis of the distinctly African Christian theology and ethic forged in the struggle of the Namibian people for liberation from colonial rule.

AF880 Hatakka, Kyllikki

Afrikka on minun peltoni: kuva lähetystyöntekijä Kalle Koivusta. (Suomen Lähetysseuran julkaisu). Helsinki, FI: Kirjaneliö, 1982. 132 pp. 9516005810.

A biography of a Finnish missionary, Kalle Koivu, who served for twenty-eight years in Namibia.

AF881 Hellberg, Carl J.

Mission, Colonialism and Liberation: The Lutheran Church in Namibia 1840-1966. (Studia Missionalia Upsaliensia, 63). Windhoek, SX: New Namibia Books; Stockholm, SW: Verbum, 1997. xi, 324 pp. Paper. 9991631593 (SX), 9152625354 (SW).

A detailed history of the Lutheran church in Namibia and its Rhenish and Finnish Lutheran mission antecedents, focusing on the relation of mission and church to the struggle for freedom and justice of the Namibian people.

AF882 Hiltunen, Maija

Witchcraft and Sorcery in Ovambo. Helsinki, FI: Finnish Anthropological Society, 1986. 178 pp. Paper. 951954349X.

A first presentation in English of original research by Finnish missionaries, concerning witchcraft and sorcery in Namibia at the turn of the 19th and 20th centuries.

AF883 Ihamäki, Kirsti

Leonard Auala: mustan Namibian paimen. Helsinki, FI: Kirjaneliö, 1985. 325 pp. 9516006779.

A biography of Leonard Auala, the first bishop of the Evangelical Lutheran Church in Namibia.

AF884 Kameeta, Zephania

Gott in schwarzen Gettos: Psalmen und Texte aus Namibia. (Erlanger Taschenbücher, 65). Erlangen, GW: Ev.-Luth. Mission, 1984. 99 pp. Paper. 387214149X.

German translation of *Why O Lord?* (1986).

AF885 Kameeta, Zephania

Why, O Lord? Psalms and Sermons from Namibia. (Risk Book Series, 28). Geneva, SZ: WCC, 1986. x, 62 pp. Paper. 2825408522.

Writings by a Lutheran minister born out of the reality of suffering and longing for liberation in Namibia.

AF886 Kampungu, Romanus

Concept and Aim of Okavango Marriages Investigated in the Light of Ecclesiastical Legislation. Rome, IT: Pontificia Universitas Urbaniana, 1966. 134 pp. No ISBN.

A detailed study of marriage practices among the Okavango of Namibia; originally submitted as a doctoral dissertation at the Pontifical Urban University in Rome in 1966.

AF—AFRICA

AF887 Katjavivi, Peter, Per Frostin, and Kaire Mbuende, eds.
Church and Liberation in Namibia. London, ENK: Pluto Press, 1989. xvii, 222 pp. 1853050733 (hdbk), 1853050784 (pbk).

Four scholarly essays, plus original source documents, detail how the churches in Namibia, once so closely identified with an oppressive colonial regime, became identified with the struggle for national liberation.

AF888 Klein, Hans de, and Sigfried Groth, eds.
Um Einheit und Auftrag: 125 Jahre Kirche und Mission in Südwestafrika. Eine Aufsatzsammlung. Wuppertal, GW: Rheinische Mission-Gesellschaft, 1968. 76 pp. No ISBN.

In observance of 125 years of missionary work by the Lutheran Rheinische Mission in South West Africa, and on the threshold of transition to indigenous church autonomy, this brochure examines the state of the church there, including essays on the struggles for church unity and political independence, apartheid, and against forced resettlement.

AF889 Krüger, Wolfgang Friedhelm
Schwarze Christen—weisse Christen: Lutheraner in Namibia und ihre Auseinandersetzung um den christlichen Auftrag in der Gesellschaft. (Erlanger Monographien aus Mission und Ökumene, 3). Erlangen, GW: Ev.-Luth. Mission, 1985. vii, 239 pp. Paper. 3872143034.

A scholarly analysis of positions on social issues in Namibia, of both black and white Christians, particularly concerning racism and apartheid; based on personal experience and the actions of Lutheran synods and conferences.

AF890 Loth, Heinrich
Die Christliche Mission in Südwestafrika: Zur destruktiven Rolle der Rheinischen Missionsgesellschaft beim Prozess der Staatsbildung in Südwestafrika (1842-1893). (Studien zur Kolonialgeschichte, 9). Berlin, GW: Akademie-Verlag, 1963. 180 pp. No ISBN.

An historical study from the Marxist point of view, of the destructive influence of the Rheinische Mission on the process of nation building in South West Africa; with a very critical analysis of the aims of the missionaries.

AF891 Loytty, Seppo
The Ovambo Sermon: A Study of the Preaching of the Evangelical Lutheran Ovambo-Kavango Church in South West Africa. (Publications of the Luther-Angricola Society, 7). Tampere, FI: Tampereen Keskuspaino, 1971. 173 pp. No ISBN.

Insights into the method, performance, and content of Ovambo preaching, and the problems of the daily life of the church (thesis—University of Helsinki, 1971).

AF892 Metzkes, J.
Otjimbingwe: Aus alten Iagen einer Rheinischen Missionsstation im Hererolande; Südwestafrika 1849-1890. Windhoek, SX: Südwestafrikanische Wissenschaftliche Gesellschaft, 1962. 136 pp. No ISBN.

A popular history of Otjimbingwe in South West Africa, the center of the Herero Mission of the Rheinische Mission.

AF893 Namibia in the 1980s
(A Future for Namibia, 1). London, ENK: CIIR/BCC, 1986. 83 pp. Paper. 0946848440.

Second edition of a summary of the history of Namibia's exploitation, the growth of the liberation movement SWAPO, and the Namibian churches' opposition to South African occupation.

AF894 Ongerki, Y.
Ambo-Kavangon kirkko: The Ovambo-Kavango Church. Aalongekidhi—Toim. Helsinki, FI: Suomen Lähetysseura, 1970. 32 pp. No ISBN.

A brief history of the Lutheran Ovambo-Kavango church in Namibia, which grew out of the Finnish Lutheran mission.

AF895 Saarisalo, Aapeli
Etelänristin mies Martti Rautanen. Porvoo, FI: Werner Söderström Osakeyhtiö, 1971. 245 pp. No ISBN.

An illustrated biography of Martti Rautanen (1845-1926), focusing on his service beginning in 1870, as a Finnish Lutheran missionary in Namibia.

AF896 Shamena, Magdalena, and Erastus Shamena
Wir Kinder Namibias: Eine Lebensgeschichte. Erlangen, GW: Ev.-Luth. Mission; Wuppertal, GW: Verlag der VEN, 1984. 167 pp. Paper. 3872141678.

A Namibian Christian couple describe their lives, caught up in the sociopolitical struggle of Namibia; German translation of *Perheemme ja Namibian tähden.*

AF897 Sundermeier, Theo
Mission, Bekenntnis und Kirche: Missionstheologische Probleme des 19. Jahrhunderts bei C. H. Hahn. Wuppertal-Barmen, GW: Verlag der Rheinischen Missionsgesellschaft, 1962. 215 pp. No ISBN.

A dissertation on the mission theology of C. H. Hahn, a missionary among the Herero in South West Africa, analyzing such themes as mission and vocation, mission and colonization, and mission and Kingdom of God (University of Heidelberg, Faculty of Theology, 1961).

AF898 Sundermeier, Theo
Wir aber suchten Gemeinschaft: Kirchwerdung und Kirchentrennung in Südwestafrika. (Erlanger Taschenbücher, 21). Witten, GW: Luther-Verlag; Erlangen, GW: Ev.-Luth. Mission, 1973. 357 pp. Paper. 3785801769 (LV), 3872140396 (VE).

An investigation into the causes and history of separatist movements from the Rheinische Mission in South West Africa and the challenges they pose to the mission church today.

AF899 Winter, Colin O'Brien
Namibia. Grand Rapids, MIU: Eerdmans; London ENK: Lutterworth Press, 1977. v, 234 pp. Paper. 0802816649 (US), 0718823257 (UK).

A readable firsthand account of the people's struggle against apartheid in Namibia; by the Anglican bishop-in-exile, focusing on the 1960 to 1972 period.

AF—AFRICA

South Africa

See also GW172, HI369, TH131, TH162, TH193, TH279, EA41, CR570, CR1342, SO233-SO234, SO283, SO308-SO309, SO313, SO319, SO330, SO333, SO341, SO346-SO347, SO351-SO352, SO360, SO365, SO608, EC19, EC44, EC124, EC350, EC379, PO46, PO79, PO98, PO122, PO129, PO131, PO167, PO172, PO182, PO199, CO128, CH462, SP145, AF1, AF3, AF6, AF12, AF165, AF189, AF203, AF236, AF254, AF269-AF270, AF273-AF275, AF279, AF297, AF301, AF314, AF320, AF322, AF324, AF348-AF349, AF568, AF746, AF810, AF853, AF869, and AM307.

AF900 Abraham, Garth
The Catholic Church and Apartheid: The Response of the Catholic Church in South Africa to the First Decade of National Party Rule, 1948-1957. Johannesburg, SA: Ravan Press, 1989. xiv, 161 pp. Paper. 0869753924.

The first detailed study of the response of the Catholic Church in South Africa to the Nationalist government's implementation of apartheid, 1948-1957, as the church moved from appeasement to resistance.

AF901 Ackermann, Denise, Jonathan A. Draper, and Emma Mashinini, eds.
Women Hold Up Half the Sky: Women in the Church in Southern Africa. Pietermaritzburg, SA: Cluster Publications, 1991. xix, 397 pp. Paper. 0958314152.

A collection of thirty-four essays by South African church women leaders on women and the Bible, theology, spirituality, the church, ministry, and the struggle for justice.

AF902 Adonis, J. C.
Die Afgebreekte Skeidsdmuur Weer Opgebou: Die Verstrengeling van die Sendingbeleid van die Nederduitse Gereformeerde Kerk In Suid-Afrika ... Aparteid in Historiese Perspektief. Amsterdam, NE: Rodopi, 1982. 238 pp. Paper. No ISBN.

A broad historical sketch of the white Dutch Reformed Church in South Africa from 1652 until 1978, stressing its mission policy as "deeply intertwined with the ideology and practice of apartheid"; doctoral dissertation at the Free University of Amsterdam under Prof. Jon. Verkuyl.

AF903 *Adventures of a Missionary: Or, Rivers of Water in a Dry Place*
Miami, FLU: Mnemosyne Publishing Company, 1969. 295 pp. No ISBN.

Reprint of the 19th-century account of the work of the English missionary Robert Moffat (1795-1883) in introducing the Gospel to South Africa; originally published in 1869 (Philadelphia: Presbyterian Board of Publications), and by other publishers.

AF904 Aeschliman, Gordon D.
Apartheid: Tragedy in Black & White. Ventura, CAU: Regal Books, 1986. 178 pp. Paper. 0830711783.

A first-person account for American Christians of how a Protestant evangelical raised in America's deep South experienced and interpreted South Africa's apartheid system.

AF905 Albers, Wolfgang
Schulen ohne Rassenschranken: Handeln nach dem Evangelium in Südafrika. (Erfahrung und Theologie, 13). Frankfurt am Main, GW: Lang, 1986. 331 pp. Paper. 3820495304.

This dissertation traces the history of the Catholic Church in education in South Africa, 1952-1983, including the decision to open its schools to children of whatsoever color, the difficulties encountered with this illegal act, and the victory to which it led in the name of the Gospel.

AF906 Albrecht, Gisela, and Hartwig Liebich, eds.
Bekenntnis und Widerstand: Kirchen Südafrikas im Konflikt mit dem Staat. Dokumente zur Untersuchung des Südafrikanischen Kirchenrats durch die Eloff-Kommission. Hamburg, GW: Missionshilfe Verlag, 1983. 560 pp. Paper. 3921620252.

Documents of the trial of the SACC before the Eloff Commission in 1983; published on the eve of the celebration of the 50th anniversary of the Barmen Confessions (1934).

AF907 Anderson, Allan, and Samuel Otwang
Tumelo: The Faith of African Pentecostals in South Africa. Pretoria, SA: University of South Africa, 1993. xi, 170 pp. Paper. 0869818341.

A detailed case study of Pentecostal mission churches and independent Pentecostal churches in Soshanguve township north of Pretoria—a project of the Institute for Theological Research at UNISA.

AF908 Ayliff, John
The Journal of John Ayliff, 1821-1830. Edited by Peter Bingham Hinchliff. (Graham's Town Series, 1). Cape Town, SA: Balkema for Rhodes University, 1971. 136 pp. No ISBN.

Ayliff was one of the early missionary settlers in the eastern Cape in 1820.

AF909 Bakker, Mewes Jans
Dagboek en brieven van Mewes Jans Bakker (1764-1824): Een Friese zendeling aan de zuidpunt van Afrika. Compiled by A. H. Huussen, and S. B. I. Veltkamp-Visser. (SAI-Reeks, 1). Amsterdam, NE: Suid-Afrikaanse Instituut, 1991. 336 pp. Paper. 9074112013.

The diary and letters of Mewes Jans Bakker (1764-1824), a Frisian sailor who, from 1798 to 1824, worked among the slaves in Stellenbosch as a missionary of the Zuid-Afrikaansche Genootschap (ZAG), the first South African missionary society.

AF910 Balcomb, Anthony
Third Way Theology: Reconciliation, Revolution, and Reform in the South African Church during the 1980s. Pietermaritzburg, SA: Cluster Publications, 1993. 291 pp. Paper. 0958314144.

An analysis of the attempt, during the 1980s in South Africa, to form a reconciliation movement between white and black power advocates, including themes of theology, power, conflict, and social transformation.

AF911 Baldwin, Lewis V.
Toward the Beloved Community: Martin Luther King, Jr. and South Africa. Cleveland, OHU: Pilgrim Press, 1995. xiv, 265 pp. Paper. 0829811028 (hdbk), 0829811087 (pbk).

A scholarly analysis of the relevance, implications, and influence of Martin Luther King, Jr.'s life and thought for the South African struggle against apartheid.

AF912 Balia, Daryl M., ed.
Perspectives in Theology and Mission from South Africa: Signs of the Times. Lewiston, NYU: E Mellen Press, 1993. 259 pp. Paper. 0773419500.

A collection of fourteen essays by South African theologians and missiologists on themes of mission, justice, and liberation, with applications to the South African context.

AF913 Balia, Daryl M.
Black Methodists and White Supremacy in South Africa.
Edited by Fatima Meer. Durban, SA: Madiba Publications,
1991. 112 pp. Paper. 0958316929.

The history of black leadership in the Methodist
Church of Southern Africa with biographies of early lead-
ers and an analysis of secessionist movements, based on
Methodist archival sources.

AF914 Balia, Daryl M.
*Christian Resistance to Apartheid: Ecumenism in South
Afrika, 1960-1987.* (Perspektiven der Weltmission, 8).
Hamburg, GW: Lottbek Jensen, 1989. 206 pp. Paper.
3926987138.

A detailed historical analysis of Christian challenges
to apartheid within South Africa; from the Cottesloe Consultation in 1960 to 1987.

AF915 Balling, Adalbert Ludwig
*Binde deinen Karren an einen Stern: Bernhard Huss (1876-
1948), Sozialreformer aus Liebe zu den Schwarzen.* Reimlingen, GW: Missionsverlag Mariannhill, 1981. 248 pp.
3922267165.

A popular account of the life and work of a Mariannhill missionary who worked in South Africa for fifty years
and has been characterized as "the most well-known Catholic priest among the non-Catholics of South Africa."

AF916 Bate, Stuart C., ed.
Serving Humanity: A Sabbath Reflection. Pietermaritzburg,
SA: Cluster Publications, 1996. 306 pp. Paper. 1875053077.

Thirty-seven insights and reflections on the 1989 Pastoral Plan of the Southern Africa Catholic Bishops' Conference with the theme "Community Serving Humanity."

AF917 Bate, Stuart C.
Evangelisation in the South African Context. (Inculturation: Working Papers Living Faith and Cultures, 12). Rome,
IT: Editrice Pontificia Università Gregoriana, 1991. xiii,
118 pp. Paper. 8876526358.

Examination of three emerging theologies in South Africa (prophetic, black, and African) and two emerging pastoral responses in African independent, white neo-pentecostal, and Roman Catholic churches.

AF918 Beckers, Gerhard
*Religiöse Faktoren in der Entwicklung der südafrikani-
schen Rassenfrage: Ein Beitrag zur Rolle des Kalvinismus
in kolonialen Situationen.* (Münchener Universitäts-
Schriften: Reihe der Philosophischen Fakultät, 7). Munich,
GW: Fink, 1969. 169 pp. No ISBN.

A scholarly study of religious factors in the development of apartheid in South Africa, especially the role of
Calvinist thought.

AF919 Bergh, Erik van den et al., eds.
*Met de moed der hoop: Opstellen aangeboden aan Dr. C.
F. Beyers Naudé.* Baarn, NE: Ten Have, 1982. 183 pp.
Paper. 9025942717.

Essays by European, Latin American, and South African
theologians honoring Beyers Naudé at his 70th birthday as a
symbol of hope inside and outside South Africa.

AF920 Birtwhistle, Norman Allen
William Threlfall: A Study in Missionary Vocation. Lon-

don, ENK: Marshall, Morgan and Scott, 1966. 168 pp. No
ISBN.

A picture of early English Methodism and the 1820 beginnings of mission work among settlers in South Africa.

AF921 Bloomberg, Charles, and Saul Dubow, eds.
*Christian-Nationalism and the Rise of the Afrikaner Broed-
erbond, in South Africa, 1918-48.* Bloomington, INU: Indiana University Press, 1989. xxviii, 250 pp. 0253312353.

A detailed study of the development of Christian na-
tionalism by Dutch Reformed clergy and laity in South
Africa, and their political involvement in the Afrikaner
Broederbond, which came to promote apartheid.

AF922 Bockelman, Wilfred, and Eleanor Bockelman
*An Exercise in Compassion: The Lutheran Church in South
Africa.* Minneapolis, MNU: Augsburg, 1972. 112 pp.
0806612045.

The story of Lutheran ministries to various racial
groups in South Africa.

**AF923 Boesak, Allan Aubrey, and Charles Villa-Vicencio,
eds.**
A Call for an End to Unjust Rule. Edinburgh, STK: St.
Andrew Press, 1986. 189 pp. Paper. 0715205943.

Reflections on two 1985 documents: *The Kairos Document* and *A Theological Rationale and a Call to Prayer
for the End to Unjust Rule* by nine South African church
leaders.

AF924 Boesak, Allan Aubrey, and Charles Villa-Vicencio
When Prayer Makes News. Philadelphia, PAU: Westminster Press, 1986. 187 pp. Paper. 0664240356.

Ten accounts of the events and theologies which led
South African Christians to a 1985 nationwide day of prayer,
and to make the Kairos Document a theological rationale
for the end to unjust rule.

AF925 Boesak, Allan Aubrey
*Black and Reformed: Apartheid, Liberation and the Cal-
vinist Tradition.* Maryknoll, NYU: Orbis Books, 1984. xix,
167 pp. Paper. 0883441489.

In this collection of sermons, letters, and essays, the
noted South African church leader exposes racism so long
disguised in Calvinist garb.

AF926 Boesak, Allan Aubrey
If This is Treason, I am Guilty. Grand Rapids, MIU: Eerd-
mans; Trenton, NJU: Africa World Press, 1987. ix, 134 pp.
Paper. 0802802516 (E), 0865430551 (A).

A collection of fifteen addresses and sermons by then-
President of the World Alliance of Reformed Churches,
showing all aspects of his involvement in the anti-apartheid movement in South Africa.

AF927 Boesak, Willa
*God's Wrathful Children: Political Oppression and Chris-
tian Ethics.* Grand Rapids, MIU: Eerdmans, 1995. xxi,
264 pp. Paper. 080280621X.

After reflecting on the history of vengeance in South
African society, and historical case studies of the Zealots,
Thomas Müntzer, and Malcolm X, the senior lecturer in
theological ethics at the University of the Western Cape in
Bellville, South Africa develops a sound practical ethic for
post-apartheid South Africa that sensitively challenges that
nation's blacks to channel their anger in constructive ways.

AF928 Bosch, David Jacobus, Adrio Konig, and Willem Nicol, eds.

Perspektief op die Ope brief. Kaapstad, SA: Human and Rousseau, 1982. 143 pp. 0798114584.

Perspectives on the "Open Letter" to the Dutch Reformed Church (NG Kerk), dated 9 June 1982, by 123 concerned DRC ministers.

AF929 Boulay, Shirley du

Tutu: Voice of the Voiceless. Grand Rapids, MIU: Eerdmans, 1988. 286 pp. 0802836496.

A biography of Desmond Tutu, narrating his emergence as a national and international figure in the context of the history of apartheid, and the conflict between the church and the South African government over the meaning of Christianity.

AF930 Brain, J. B.

Catholic Beginnings in Natal and Beyond Durban. Durban, SA: T. W. Griggs, 1975. xviii, 202 pp. Paper. 0621015462.

Traces the history of the Catholic church in the Natal Vicariate, from its earliest beginnings until 1885, when it included the Orange Free State, the Transvaal, the Transkei, and present-day Lesotho.

AF931 Brandel-Syrier, Mia

Black Woman in Search of God. London, ENK: Lutterworth Press, 1962. 251 pp. No ISBN.

A pioneer study on the role of church women's organizations in the self-affirmation of women in South Africa.

AF932 Bredekamp, Henry C., and Harold E. F. Plüddemann, eds.

The Genadendal Diaries: Diaries of the Herrnhut Missionaries H. Marsveld, D. Schwinn and J. C. Kühnel, Vol. 1, (1792-1794). (Publication Series, 4). Unibell, SA: University of the Western Cape, Institute for Historical Research, 1992. 291 pp. Paper. 186808115X.

Diaries of three Moravian missionaries at Genadendal in the Western Cape (1792-1794) who continued the mission to the Hottentots started by George Schmidt in 1737.

AF933 Bredekamp, Henry C., and J. L. Hattingh, eds.

Das Tagebuch und die Briefe von Georg Schmidt, dem ersten Missionar in Südafrika (1737-1744)/Dagboek en Briewe van George Schimdt: Erste sondeling in Süd-Africa. Translated by J. du P. Boeke. Unibell, SA: University of the Western Cape; Bellville, SA: Wes-Kaaplandse Instituut vir Historiese Navorsing, 1981. 504 pp. 0909075719.

The diary and letters of George Schmidt (1709-1785), the first missionary (Moravian) to South Africa, presented on facing pages for comparison purposes in modern German and 18th-century Dutch.

AF934 Bredekamp, Henry C., and Robert Ross, eds.

Missions and Christianity in South African History. Johannesburg, SA: Witwatersrand University Press, 1995. 260 pp. Paper. 1868142906.

Twelve scholarly essays originally presented at the "People, Power, and Culture: The History of Christianity in South Africa" conference (University of the Western Cape, August 1992).

AF935 Brennecke, Gerhard

Bruder in Schatten: Das bild einer Missionsreise durch Sudafrika gesehen bedacht und aufgezeichnet. Berlin, GW: Evan Verlagsantalt, 1974. 359 pp. No ISBN.

Report of a missionary journey through South Africa and Swaziland with reflection on the work of the Berlin Missionary Society there.

AF936 Brislin, Stephen

The Ministry of Deacons in an African Diocese. (Spearhead, 76). Eldoret, KE: Gaba Publications, 1983. vi, 56 pp. Paper. No ISBN.

A monograph on the theology of the diaconate, with an analysis of its practice and policy in the Roman Catholic diocese of Kroonstad in South Africa, which has a large proportion of permanent deacons.

AF937 Brown, Edward

A Historical Profile of the Nederduitse Gereformeerde Kerk (Dutch Reformed Church) in South Africa. (University of Zululand: Series 3, Specialized Publications, 8). Kwa Dlangezwa, SA: University of Zululand, 1973. 47 pp. 0949984191.

An interpretative and historical survey of the Dutch Reformed Church by a DRC minister; delivered originally as a lecture at the University of Aberdeen in 1972 in a series on Christianity and the non-Western World, with a ninety-eight-title bibliography.

AF938 Brown, Evelyn M.

Edel Quinn: Beneath the Southern Cross. New York, NYU: Vision Books; New York, NYU: Farrar; London, ENK: Burns & Oates, 1967. xv, 170 pp. No ISBN.

A biography of an Irish girl who dedicated her life to missionary service in South Africa.

AF939 Brown, William Eric

The Catholic Church in South Africa: From Its Origins to the Present Day. Edited by Michael Derrick. New York, NYU: Kenedy; London, ENK: Burns & Oates, 1960. 384 pp. No ISBN.

A factual account of the Roman Catholic Church's missionary activity in South Africa.

AF940 Brownlee, Charles Pacalt

Reminiscences of Kafir Life and History and Other Papers. (Reprint Series/Killie Campbell Africana Library, 1). Pietermaritzburg, SA: University of Natal Press, 1977. xliv, 475 pp. 086980104X.

A facsimile reproduction of the memoirs of Charles Brownlee (1821-1890), the Cape Colony's most important administrator in the 19th century, including details of missionary interaction with colonial officials; originally published in 1896 (Lovedale, SA: Lovedale Mission Press).

AF941 Bryan, G. McLeod

Naudé: Prophet to South Africa. Atlanta, GAU: John Knox Press, 1978. vii, 153 pp. 0804209421.

A moving account, with source documents, of the prophetic ministry of Beyers Naudé, the creative Dutch Reformed opponent of apartheid, from the founding of the Christian Institute in 1963 to his banning in 1977.

AF942 Bucher, Hubert

Youth Work in South Africa: A Challenge for the Church. (Neue Zeitschrift für Missionswissenschaft, Supplementa 21). Immensee, SZ: NZM, 1973. xxviii, 221 pp. No ISBN.

An inside interpretation of the Catholic Church's work with youth in apartheid South Africa, including Chiro, the Catholic Youth Movement.

AF—AFRICA

AF943 Cassidy, Michael
The Passing Summer: A South African's Response to White Fear, Black Anger, and the Politics of Love. Ventura, CAU: Regal Books; African Enterprise, 1989. xxiv, 534 pp. 0830714243.

A white South African Christian explores the Gospel and how it addresses the socio-political issues in South Africa, emphasizing the Christian responsibilities of all believers in the situation.

AF944 Cassidy, Michael
The Politics of Love: Choosing the Christian Way in a Changing South Africa. London, ENK: Hodder & Stoughton, 1991. 285 pp. Paper. 0340546093.

A popular account of the new political openings in South Africa since the release of Nelson Mandela in 1989, with proposals for political reform by the author, a well-known South African evangelical and Director of Africa Enterprise.

AF945 Cassidy, Michael
Prisoners of Hope: The Story of South African Christians at a Crossroads. Maseru, LO: Africa Enterprise, 1974. 183 pp. Paper. No ISBN.

An account for laypeople of the South African Congress on Mission and Evangelism (Durban, 1973) and its significance for the future of reconciliation in South Africa, by the congress' organizing secretary.

AF946 Cawood, Lesley
The Churches and Race Relations in South Africa. Johannesburg, SA: SAIRR, 1964. 140 pp. Paper. No ISBN.

An analysis of the attitudes of eleven Christian denominations in South Africa with regard to race relations, particularly recent apartheid legislation.

AF947 Champion, George
Journal of the Rev. George Champion, American Missionary in Zululand, 1835-9. Edited by Alan R. Booth. Cape Town, SA: Struik, 1967. xv, 149 pp. No ISBN.

Reprint of the journal of a pioneer American Board missionary in South Africa.

AF948 Chidester, David
Religions of South Africa. (Library of Religious Beliefs and Practices). London, ENK: Routledge, 1992. xvi, 286 pp. 041504779X (hdbk), 0415047803 (pbk).

The first comparative study of the diverse religions of South Africa (traditional, Roman Catholic, Protestant, independent, Judaism, Hinduism, Islam, etc.), with analysis of themes of pluralism, legitimation, and liberation.

AF949 Chidester, David
Shots in the Streets: Violence and Religion in South Africa. Boston, MAU: Beacon Press, 1991. xix, 220 pp. 0807002186.

A detailed analysis of ways in which South African violence in the service of nationalism is justified in religious terms.

AF950 Chikane, Frank
The Church's Prophetic Witness against the Apartheid System in South Africa. Johannesburg, SA: SACC, 1988. iv, 72 pp. Paper. No ISBN.

A collection of seventeen documents—the churches' response to the South African bannings and restrictions of eighteen nonviolent organizations on 24 February 1988.

AF951 Chikane, Frank
Mein Leben gehört nicht mir. Translated by Marie Dilger. (Erlanger Taschenbücher, 96). Erlanger, GW: Ev.-Luth. Mission, 1990. 178 pp. Paper. 3872141961, 3925263136.

German translation.

AF952 Chikane, Frank
No Life of My Own: An Autobiography. Maryknoll, NYU: Orbis Books; Braamfontein, SA: Skotaville Publishers; London ENK: CIIR, 1988. xvii, 132 pp. Paper. 0883445387 (US), 0947009515 (SA), 1852870117 (UK).

The autobiography of the general secretary of the SACC who has been one of the leading figures in the Christian resistance to apartheid.

AF953 Christofersen, Arthur Fridjof, and Richard Sales, eds.
Adventuring with God: The Story of the American Board Mission in South Africa. Durban, SA: Lutheran Publishing House, 1967. 183 pp. No ISBN.

A centennial history of the congregational mission to the Zulus, first written in 1935 and updated by the editor, containing numerous references to African church leaders.

AF954 Clayton, Geoffrey Hare
Where We Stand: Archbishop Clayton's Charges 1948-1957 Chiefly Relating to Church and State in South Africa. Edited by C. T. Wood. Cape Town, SA: Oxford University Press, 1960. 55 pp. No ISBN.

Eight declarations by Clayton (1884-1957), Anglican Archbishop of Capetown (1948-1957), to the provincial and diocesan aynods, plus his final letter to the Prime Minister, defining the church's stand against apartheid.

AF955 Cloete, G. D., and D. J. Smit, eds.
A Moment of Truth: The Confession of the Dutch Reformed Mission Church. Grand Rapids, MIU: Eerdmans, 1984. x, 161 pp. Paper. 0802800114.

English translation.

AF956 Cloete, G. D., and D. J. Smit, eds.
Oomblik van Waarheid: Opstelle rondom die NG Sendingkerk se afkondiging van 'n status confessionis en die opstel van 'n konsepdlydenis. Kaapstad, SA: Tafelberg, 1984. 160 pp. 0624020215.

The text of the 1982 confession of faith opposing apartheid, of the South African Dutch Reformed Mission Church, a model for the WARC's condemnation; with nine interpretive essays by South African Dutch Reformed theologians.

AF957 Cochrane, James R., John W. De Gruchy, and Robin Petersen, eds.
In Word and in Deed: Towards a Practical Theology of Social Transformation. (Cluster Studies, 1). Pietermaritzburg, SA: Cluster Publications, 1991. x, 129 pp. Paper. 0620110244.

The results of a three-year research project (1986-1988) in South Africa on the practice of mission and ministry in a context profoundly shaped by a liberative drive for social transformation.

AF958 Cochrane, James R.
Servants of Power: The Role of English-Speaking Churches in South Africa, 1903-1930. Johannesburg, SA: Ravan Press, 1987. xii, 278 pp. Paper. 0869752774.

Based on archival research and theoretical interpretation, the author tests the policy, practice, and theology of the English-speaking churches in the light of the history of socio-economic oppression in South Africa.

AF959 Concerned Evangelicals (Johannesburg, South Africa)

Evangelical Witness in South Africa: A Critique of Evangelical Theology and Practice by South African Evangelicals Themselves. Grand Rapids, MIU: Eerdmans; London, ENK: Evangelical Alliance, 1986. 48 pp. Paper. 0802802915 (US), 1870345002 (UK).

A critique by 132 South African church leaders, following the 1985 state of emergency, of the tendency of the evangelical community to support the status quo, recommending a stand against oppression and racism.

AF960 Connor, Bernard F.

The Difficult Traverse from Amnesty to Reconciliation. Pietermaritzburg, SA: Cluster Publications, 1998. 151 pp. Paper. 1875053131.

While the initial focus is on South Africa's Truth and Reconciliation Commission, these reflections draw on Catholic theology and explore the personal, social, and theological aspects of reconciliation.

AF961 Cross, K. E.

Ours Is the Frontier: A Life of G. W. Cross, Baptist Pioneer. Pretoria, SA: University of South Africa, 1986. xi, 253 pp. Paper. 0869813838.

A biography of G. W. Cross (1877-1920), the English Baptist missionary to South Africa who became influential in the development of religious education, social services, and the arts of his adopted land, and as the first President of the Baptist Union of South Africa.

AF962 De Blank, Joost

Out of Africa. London, ENK: Hodder & Stoughton, 1964. 160 pp. No ISBN.

Lectures and sermons by a prophetic Anglican churchman in South Africa.

AF963 De Gruchy, John W., and Charles Villa-Vicencio, eds.

Apartheid is a Heresy. Grand Rapids, MIU: Eerdmans; Cape Town, SA: David Philip; Guildford, ENK: Lutterworth Press, 1983. xx, 184 pp. Paper. 0802819729 (US), 0908396910 (SA), 0718825950 (UK).

Nine essays by South African church leaders, commenting on the 1982 decision of WARC that apartheid is sinful and its theological justification is heresy; also fourteen South African church statements on apartheid from the 1957-1982 period.

AF964 De Gruchy, John W., and Charles Villa-Vicencio, eds.

Wenn wir wie brüder Beieinander wohnten: Von der apartheid zur Bekennenden Kirche-Stellungnahmen südafrikanischer Theologen. Neukirchen-Vluyn, GW: Neukirchener Verlag, 1984. 217 pp. Paper. 3788707550.

German translation of *Apartheid Is a Heresy* (1983).

AF965 De Gruchy, John W.

The Church Struggle in South Africa. Grand Rapids, MIU: Eerdmans; London, EUK: Collins, 1986. xx, 290 pp. Paper. 0802802435 (E), 0005999545 (C).

Second edition of a scholarly exploration of the historical roots of the church in South Africa, its relation to apartheid, and the tensions between the church and society and within the church itself; originally published in 1979.

AF966 De Gruchy, John W.

Faith for a Time Like This. Cape Town, SA: Rondebosch United Church, 1992. vi, 132 pp. Paper. No ISBN.

Sermons preached in South Africa between 1988 and 1992, with application to struggles for justice during that period, by the Professor of Christian Studies at the University of Cape Town who is an ordained minister of the United Congregational Church of Southern Africa.

AF967 De Kock, Leon

Civilising Barbarians: Missionary Narrative and African Textual Response in Nineteenth-Century South Africa. Johannesburg, SA: Witwatersrand University Press, 1996. 231 pp. Paper. 1868142981.

A scholarly documentary analysis of attempts by English-speaking missionaries to inculcate a new normative worldview and morality in South Africa in the 19th century, and the responses by Africans to them through their writings.

AF968 Delft, Heinz von

Kirchbau am Kap: Als Hannoverscher Pastor 50 Jahre in Sndafrika. (Erlanger Taschenbücher, 105). Erlangen, GW: Ev.-Luth. Mission, 1993. 216 pp. Paper. 3872145053.

Reminiscences, of a German Lutheran pastor from Hamburg, of more than fifty years of ministry with conservative German Evangelical Lutheran congregations in South Africa, 1933 to 1987, relating his story to religious and political issues.

AF969 Denis, Philippe, Thulani Mlotshwa, and George Mukuka

The Casspir and the Cross: Voices of Black Clergy in the Natal Midlands. Pietermaritzburg, SA: Cluster Publications, 1999. 102 pp. 1875053174.

The author has compiled extracts from interviews with black clergy who ministered in the Natal Midlands in the apartheid era and negotiation period (1948-1994), showing how ordinary black ministers, ordained in a settler church or in an African-initiated church, reacted to discriminatory state policies and segregation patterns affecting their church.

AF970 Dickson, Mora

Beloved Partner: Mary Moffat of Kuruman. London, ENK: Dobson, 1976. 244 pp. 0234720158 (hdbk), 0234720174 (pbk).

A biography of Robert Moffat's wife (1795-1871) who served with him in South Africa north of the Orange River at Kuruman under the LMS from 1819 to 1871.

AF971 Dierks, Friedrich

Evangelium im afrikanischen Kontext: Interkulturelle Kommunikation bei den Tswana. (Missionswissenschaftliche Forschungen, 19). Gütersloh, GW: Mohn, 1986. 206 pp. Paper. 3579002392.

The main question discussed in this doctoral dissertation is how the Christian message can and must be communicated within the context of the traditional culture and religion of the Tswana in South Africa.

AF972 Dischl, Marcel

Two Missionary Bishops: Emmanuel Hanisch, Prefect and Vicar Apostolic of Umtata 1930-1940 and Joseph Grueter, Vicar Apostolic and Bishop of Umtata, 1940-1968: Their Lives and Deeds. Umtata, SA: Mariannhill Mission Institute, 1983. 132 pp. No ISBN.

A short biography of the lives and deeds of Hanisch (1882-1940) and Grueter (1896-1976), the first two Catholic bishops of Umtata in Transkei, South Africa.

AF—AFRICA

AF973 Donk, Mirjam van, comp.
Land Issues and Challenges to the Church: A Reader. (Relevant Church Series, 2). Cape Town, SA: Western Province Council of Churches, 1994. 177 pp. Paper. 095838682X.

A compilation of journal articles from the 1987-1994 period concerning South African land issues, prepared for use by pastors.

AF974 Donk, Mirjam van
Land and the Church: The Case of the Dutch Reformed Churches. (Relevant Church Series, 1). Cape Town, SA: Western Province Council of Churches, 1994. 87 pp. Paper. 0958386811.

A short history of the South African churches' involvement with racial land legislation, especially the Dutch Reformed churches.

AF975 du Toit, C. W., and J. S. Krüger, eds.
Multireligious Education in South Africa: Problems and Prospects in a Pluralistic Society. Pretoria, SA: University of South Africa, 1998. xix, 196 pp. Paper. 1868880540.

Papers from an important conference on multireligious education, held 3-4 July 1997 at the University of South Africa in Pretoria.

AF976 Dubb, Allie A.
Community of the Saved: An African Revivalist Church in the East Cape. Johannesburg, SA: Witwatersrand University Press for African Studies Institute, 1976. xvii, 175 pp. 0854942920.

A case study of the African Assembly of God in the East Bank Location, East London, South Africa.

AF977 Edgar, Robert R., and Hilary Sapire
African Apocalypse: The Story of Nontetha Nkwenkwe, a Twentieth-century South African Prophet. (Monographs in International Studies Africa Series, 72). Johannesburg, SA: Witwatersrand University Press; Athens, OHU: Ohio University Center for International Studies, 2000. xxiii, 190 pp. Paper. 0896802086 (US), 1868143376 (UK).

This volume consists of two stories; first, of the remarkable Xhosa prophetess Nontetha Nkwenkwe preaching that a day of judgment was drawing near and exhorting her followers to unite; second, of her incarceration in South Africa's notorious hospitals for the insane.

AF978 Elphick, Richard, and Rodney Davenport, eds.
Christianity in South Africa: A Political, Social, and Cultural History. Berkeley, CAU: University of California Press; Claremont, SA: David Philip; Oxford, ENK: James Currey Publishers, 1997. xiv, 480 pp. 0520209397 (U hdbk), 0520209400 (U pbk), 0864863063 (D pbk), 0852557515 (J pbk).

Twenty-five essays by South African scholars, exploring the intricate interplay of Christianity and the mainstream history of South Africa, with special attention to the missionary impact.

AF979 England, Frank, and Torquil Paterson
Bounty in Bondage: The Anglican Church in Southern Africa; Essays in Honour of Edward King, Dean of Cape Town. Johannesburg, SA: Ravan Press, 1989. vi, 222 pp. Paper. 0869753835.

Eleven essays by South African scholars from various disciplines, critically examining the life of the Anglican Church in Southern Africa; with a foreword by Archbishop Desmond Tutu.

AF980 Enklaar, Ido Hendricus
De levensgeschiedenis van Johannes Theodorus van der Kemp: Stichter van het Nederlandsch Zendeling-Genootschap, pionier van de London Missionary Society onder Kaffers en Hottentotten in Zuid-Afrika 1747-1811 tot zijn aankomst aan de Kaap in 1799. Wageningen, NE: Veenman, 1972. 168 pp. 9027810860.

An exhaustive biography of the founder of the Netherlands Missionary Society (1797) and his pioneer missionary work for the LMS in South Africa (1799-1811), where his non-conforming style drew widespread bewilderment and fierce criticism as he constantly battled for racial equality.

AF981 Etherington, Norman
Preacher, Peasants and Politics in Southeast Africa, 1835-1880: African Christian Communities in Natal, Pondoland, and Zululand. (Royal Historical Society Studies in History, 12). London, ENK: Royal Historical Society, 1978. xi, 230 pp. 0901050482.

A detailed case study of interactions in Natal, of American Board and Lutheran missionaries with Christian converts, African rulers, and colonial administrators.

AF982 Eybers, Howard H.
Pastoral Care to Black South Africans. (American Academy of Religion Academy Series, 67). Atlanta, GAU: Scholars Press, 1991. x, 237 pp. 1555404014 (hdbk), 1555404022 (pbk).

An ethical-psychological model for providing pastoral care within a context of racial and political oppression, adapting insights from H. Richard Niebuhr and Erik Erikson.

AF983 Farisani, Tshenuwani Simon, and Christian Frederic Beyers Naudé
Dagboek uit een Zuidafrikaanse gevangenis. Baarn, NE: Ten Have, 1988. 120 pp. 9025943764.

Dutch translation.

AF984 Farisani, Tshenuwani Simon
Diary from a South African Prison. Edited by John A. Evenson. Philadelphia, PAU: Fortress Press, 1987. 93 pp. Paper. 0800620623.

English translation.

AF985 Farisani, Tshenuwani Simon
In der Hölle, siehe, so bist Du auch da: Ein Tagebuch aus südafrikanischen Gefängnissen. (Erlanger Taschenbücher, 70). Erlangen, GW: Ev.-Luth. Mission, 1985. 119 pp. Paper. 3872141708.

This diary recounts the spiritual development of a young deacon unjustly imprisoned for terrorist activities in South Africa.

AF986 Farisani, Tshenuwani Simon
In Transit: Between the Image of God and the Image of Man. Grand Rapids, MIU: Eerdmans; Trenton, NJU: Africa World Press, 1990. xii, 251 pp. Paper. 0802804381 (E), 0865432074 (A).

An autobiographical account, using the story of his own life as a microcosm of the experience of blacks of oppression in South Africa, by a Dean and Deputy Bishop of the Evangelical Lutheran Church in South Africa.

AF987 Farisani, Tshenuwani Simon
Journal d'une prison sud-africaine. Translated by Alice Boggio. Paris, FR: Centurion, 1988. 168 pp. 2227355204.

French translation.

AF—AFRICA

AF988 Ffrench-Beytagh, Gonville
Encountering Darkness. New York, NYU: Seabury Press; London, ENK: Collins, 1973. 283 pp. 0816411492 (US), 0002152053 (UK).

The autobiography of the courageous Anglican Dean of Johannesburg, South Africa, focusing on his arrest in 1971 for supporting the black liberation struggle, his trial, conviction, and imprisonment.

AF989 Filter, H., comp.
Paulina Dlamini: Servant of Two Kings. Durban, SA: Killie Campbell Africana Library; Pietermaritzburg, SA: University of Natal Press, 1986. x, 135 pp. Paper. 0869805290 (hdbk), 0869805231 (pbk).

The reminiscences of Paulina Nomguqo Dlamini (1858?-1942), who served as part of the royal Zulu household during the 1870s, and from 1887 as a Christian missionary among her own Zulu people of South Africa.

AF990 Florin, Hans W.
Lutherans in South Africa. Durban, SA: Lutheran Publishing House, 1967. 180 pp. No ISBN.

An important survey of Lutheranism under apartheid in South Africa.

AF991 Froise, Marjorie, ed.
South African Christian Handbook, 1996/7. Welkom, SA: Christian Info, 1996. xii, 333 pp. Paper. 0620194685.

This 4th edition of the handbook updates the 1993/1994 edition with new statistics for 141 denominations and church groups, plus analysis of challenges for mission in the new South Africa; originally published in 1986 and 1990.

AF992 Gelfand, Michael
Christian Doctor and Nurse: The History of Medical Missions in South Africa from 1799-1976. Sandton, SA: Aitken Family and Friends; Atholl, SA: Mariannhill Mission Press, 1984. 346 pp. 0620077255.

A chronicle of 200 years of devotion to duty and the highest standards of medical achievements, often in the face of great personal hardship and difficult conditions.

AF993 General Synod of the Dutch Reformed Church
Human Relations and the South African Scene in the Light of Scripture. Cape Town, SA: Dutch Reformed Church, 1976. 100 pp. Paper. 0869911589.

The Dutch Reformed Church presents its convictions with regard to the problem of relationships in a multinational country from the viewpoint of the word of God; also published in Afrikaans.

AF994 Gerstner, Jonathan Neil
The Thousand Generation Covenant: Dutch Reformed Covenant Theology and Group Identity in Colonial South Africa, 1652-1814. (Studies in the History of Christian Thought, 44). Leiden, NE: Brill, 1991. xi, 280 pp. 9004093613.

A scholarly analysis of the religious origins of apartheid, especially its connection with Dutch Reformed theology; originally presented as a Ph.D. thesis at the University of Chicago in 1985.

AF995 Geyser, A. S. et al.
Delayed Action!: An Ecumenical Witness from the Afrikaans Speaking Church. Pretoria, SA: N. G. Kerkboekhandel, 1960. 168 pp. No ISBN.

English translation.

AF996 Geyser, A. S. et al.
Vertraagde aksie: 'n ekumeniese getuienis uit die Afrikaanssprekende Kerk. Pretoria, SA: N. G. Kerkboekhandel, 1960. 144 pp. No ISBN.

Eleven essays, mostly by Dutch Reformed theologians, advocating change from policies of apartheid.

AF997 Graybill, Lyn S.
Religion and Resistance Politics in South Africa. Westport, CTU: Praeger, 1995. vii, 157 pp. 0275951413.

A study of how religious beliefs shaped the political strategies of four South African political leaders and the organizations in which they were active (Albert Lutuli/ANC, Robert Sobukwe/PAC, Steve Biko/BCM, and Desmond Tutu/UDF).

AF998 Guma, Mongezi, and A. Leslie Milton, eds.
An African Challenge to the Church in the Twenty-First Century. Cape Town, SA: Salty Print, 1997. xi, 146 pp. 0620219246.

Twelve essays by South African theologians, published as a sequel to *Being the Church in South Africa Today* (1995); part of a project to draw up a theological manifesto for the new millennium.

AF999 Guy, Jeff
The Heretic: A Study of the Life of John William Colenso, 1814-1883. Johannesburg, SA: Ravan Press; Pietermaritzburg, SA: University of Natal Press, 1983. xii, 378 pp. Paper. 0869751689.

A scholarly biography of the controversial missionary bishop of Natal, South Africa, who stood up for justice for Africans in Natal and Zululand, but was found guilty of biblical heresy and excommunicated.

AF1000 Häselbarth, Hans
Die Auferstehung der Toten in Afrika: Eine theologische Deutung der Todesriten der Mamabolo in Nordtransvaal. (Missionswissenschaftliche Forschungen, 8). Gütersloh, GW: Mohn, 1972. 275 pp. No ISBN.

A theological interpretation of funeral rituals, and beliefs concerning the ancestors, of the Mamabolo of northern Transvaal, South Africa.

AF1001 Häselbarth, Hans
Lebenszeichen aus Afrika: Erfahrungen in Briefen. (Kaiser Traktate, 32). Munich, GW: Kaiser, 1978. 159 pp. 3459011483.

A German missionary couple recounts their years of service in Africa (1963-1977) based on their accumulated collection of personal and mission correspondence.

AF1002 Höckner, Elfriede
Die Lobedu Sudafrikas Mythos und Realität der Regenkönigin Modjadji. (Missionsgeschichtliches Archiv, 4). Stuttgart, GW: F. Steiner, 1998. 260 pp. Paper. 3515067949.

A published dissertation in ethnology seeking to reconstruct the evolution of South African culture on the basis of literature (both missionary correspondence and scientific research), of interest to historians of religion and of missions, ethnologists, and missiologists concerned for cultural context and impact.

AF1003 Hance, Gertrude Rachel
The Zulu Yesterday and Today: Twenty-Nine Years in South Africa. New York, NYU: Negro Universities Press, 1969. 274 pp. 0837117437.

Reprint of the 1916 edition of missionary activities among the Zulus.

AF—AFRICA

AF1004 Hasselhorn, Fritz
Mission, Land Ownership and Settlers' Ideology: Exemplified by the Hermannsburg Mission in South Africa. Johannesburg, SA: SACC, 1987. 40 pp. Paper. No ISBN.

An essay reporting the history and effects of land ownership in South Africa by the Lutheran Hermannsburg Mission, 1914-1955, which included support for apartheid policies.

AF1005 Hayes, Stephen
Black Charismatic Anglicans: The Iviyo loFakazi bakaKristu and Its Relations with Other Renewal Movements. Pretoria, SA: University of South Africa, 1990. xvi, 227 pp. Paper. 0869816314.

A study of Iviyo loFakazi bakaKristu (Legion of Christ's Witnesses), an Anglican charismatic renewal movement that began in Zululand, South Africa, in 1956, and has since spread to other parts of southern Africa; with texts of ten interviews with key leaders in the movement.

AF1006 Hinchliff, Peter Bingham
The Anglican Church in South Africa: An Account of the History and Development of the Church of the Province of South Africa. London, ENK: Darton, Longman & Todd, 1963. 266 pp. No ISBN.

An ecclesiastical and social history of Anglicanism in South Africa to 1935, with attention to its missionary efforts.

AF1007 Hinchliff, Peter Bingham
The Church in South Africa. London, ENK: SPCK for the Church Historical Society, 1968. xii, 116 pp. 0281022771.

A compilation of material from the works of others, in order to make a brief and coherent account of the history of Christianity in South Africa, from the middle of the 17th century with the arrival of the first Dutch settlers, to the 1960s.

AF1008 Hinchliff, Peter Bingham
John Williams Colenso, Bishop of Natal. London, ENK: Nelson, 1964. 199 pp. No ISBN.

A scholarly biography of Colenso (1814-1883), the bishop of Natal (1854-67) who was a representative of the "liberal" Anglican theology in the mid-19th century, a protagonist in the constitutional struggle taking place in South Africa at the time, and condemned for heresy by the church.

AF1009 Hirmer, Oswald
Die Funktion des Laien in der katholischen Gemeinde: Untersuchungen in der afrikanischen Mission unter Berücksichtigung entsprechender Erfahrungen nicht-katholischer Gemeinden im Xhosa-Gebiet der Republik Südafrika. (Münsterschwarzacher Studien, 23). Münsterschwarzach, GW: Vier-Türme-Verlag, 1973. 212 pp. Paper. 387868052X.

A dissertation on the different forms of church in various Christian denominations among the Xhosa (South Africa), seeking concrete possibilities for laypeople to cooperate and share responsibility in the Catholic Church.

AF1010 Hodgson, Thomas Laidman
The Journals of the Rev. T. L. Hodgson: Missionary to the Seleka-Rolong and the Griquas 1821-1831. Edited by R. L. Cope. Johannesburg, SA: Witwatersrand University Press for African Studies Institute, 1977. xvi, 435 pp. 0854943706.

The journal of T. H. Hodgson (1787-1850), pioneer Wesleyan Methodist missionary to the Seleka-Rolong and the Griquas of South Africa, 1821-1831, with annotations.

AF1011 Hofmeyr, J. W., J. H. H. du Toit, and C. J. J. Froneman, eds.
Perspektiewe op Kairos/*Perspectives on* Kairos. Kaapstad, SA: Lux Verbi, 1987. v, 200 pp. Paper. 0869972642.

Evaluations in Afrikaans and English by South African theologians and church leaders, mostly Dutch Reformed, of the controversial *Kairos Document* (1985).

AF1012 Hope, Anne
Torch in the Night: Worship Resources from South Africa. New York, NYU: Friendship Press; Washington, DCU: Center of Concern, 1988. iv, 134 pp. Paper. 0377001821.

Suggestions for twelve services based on themes from the South African liberation struggle, with readings in both poetry and prose from that country.

AF1013 Hope, Marjorie, and James Young
The South African Churches in a Revolutionary Situation. Maryknoll, NYU: Orbis Books, 1981. xi, 268 pp. Paper. 0883444666.

Two Quaker sociologists provide a 1979-1981 survey of the various denominational and ecumenical agencies in South Africa, with focus on their sociopolitical involvements.

AF1014 Huddleston, Trevor
Return to South Africa: The Ecstasy and the Agony. Grand Rapids, MIU: Eerdmans; Trenton, NJU: Africa World Press, 1992. 140 pp. Paper. 0802806457 (E), 0865433496 (A).

The moving diary of the Anglican bishop's return, in 1991, to South Africa, where he had served as a prophetic opponent of apartheid from 1943 until his expulsion in 1956.

AF1015 Hudson-Reed, Sydney, ed.
Together for a Century: The History of the Baptist Union of South Africa, 1877-1977. Pietermaritzburg, SA: South African Baptist Historical Society, 1977. 168 pp. No ISBN.

The official centennial history.

AF1016 Hulley, Leonard, Louise Kretzschmar, and Luke Lungile Pato, eds.
Archbishop Tutu: Prophetic Witness in South Africa. Cape Town, SA: Human and Rousseau, 1996. 264 pp. Paper. 0798136073.

A *festschrift* honoring Archbishop Tutu upon his retirement, with essays on "Who Is Desmond Tutu?" "Life and Faith in an African Context," and "Morality, Religion, and Society."

AF1017 Institute for Contextual Theology
The Church and Labour in South Africa. Compiled by James R. Cochrane. Johannesburg, SA: Skotaville Publishers, 1988. 54 pp. Paper. 0947009124.

A brief history of the relations between the South African churches and the labor movement in that country.

AF1018 Jørgensen, Torstein
Contact and Conflict: Norwegian Missionaries, the Zulu Kingdom, and the Gospel, 1850-1873. Oslo, NO: Solum Forlag, 1990. 393 pp. 8256007222.

Revised edition of a doctoral dissertation (University of Oslo, 1988), analyzing the cultural and religious encounter of the first Norwegian missionaries with the Zulu kingdom in South Africa.

AF—AFRICA

AF1019 Kairos '95 (Johannesburg, 22-25 Sept. 1995)

Kairos '95: At the Threshold of Jubilee—A Conference Report. Edited by Themba Dladla. Johannesburg, SA: Institute for Contextual Theology, 1996. 88 pp. Paper. 0620200618.

Report of a conference on the 10th anniversary of the *Kairos Document*, renewing commitment to the struggle for social justice in South Africa.

AF1020 Kansteiner, Walter H.

South Africa: Revolution or Reconciliation? Wilmore, KYU: Bristol Books, 1990. 208 pp. Paper. 0917851447.

An analysis of revolutionary change in South Africa arguing against justifying revolution on Christian just-war principles, and in favor of United States government support for a reformist policy working for a democratic future; originally published in 1988 by the Institute on Religion and Democracy, Washington, D.C.

AF1021 Khosa, Andreas Ruben

Deine Hand lag schwer auf mir: Mein Weg zu und mit Christus. (Erlanger Taschenbücher, 75). Erlangen, GW: Ev.-Luth. Mission, 1986. 210 pp. Paper. 3872141759.

Khosa, a black South African theologian and pastor, reflects upon his life, conversion, and ministry, providing an intimate view of South African life.

AF1022 Kistner, Wolfram

Hoffnung in der Krise: Dokumente einer christlichen Existenz in Südafrika. Wuppertal, GW: Hammer, 1988. 319 pp. Paper. 3872943626.

Festschrift in honor of Dr. Wolfram Kistner, Director of the Department of Justice and Reconciliation of the SACC, including Bible studies and other texts, by Kistner himself, as well as contributions by his colleagues, visitors, and friends.

AF1023 Kistner, Wolfram

Outside the Camp: A Collection of Writings. Edited by Hans Brandt. Johannesburg, SA: SACC, 1988. 223 pp. Paper. No ISBN.

A comprehensive collection of the writings of the Director of the Division of Justice and Reconciliation of the SACC, 1976-1988.

AF1024 Kritzinger, J. J.

The South African Context for Mission. Cape Town, SA: Lux Verbi, 1988. 148 pp. Paper. 0869972782.

Multi-volume study on missions in South Africa, tracing the history of South African missions, the status of the South African churches today, and their unfinished task in mission.

AF1025 Kruger, Bernhard

The Pear Tree Blossoms: A History of the Moravian Mission Stations in South Africa, 1737-1869. Genadenal, SA: Moravian Book Depot, 1966. 335 pp. No ISBN.

A dissertation history of the Moravian mission stations at the Cape, from the arrival of Georg Schmidt in 1737 until the division of the work into two provinces in 1869.

AF1026 Lückhoff, A. H.

Cottesloe. Cape Town, SA: Tafelberg, 1978. 197 pp. No ISBN.

An evaluation for South Africans of the important Cottesloe Conference of 1960 between WCC and South African church leaders.

AF1027 Landman, Christina

The Piety of Afrikaans Women: Diaries of Guilt. Pretoria, SA: University of South Africa, 1994. viii, 119 pp. Paper. 0869818538.

An analysis of the theology and piety of seven Afrikaner women of South Africa (several of them missionaries in the 18th to 20th centuries) as foremothers of contemporary feminism.

AF1028 Latrobe, Christian Ignatius

Journal of a Visit to South Africa in 1815 and 1816 with Some Account of Missionary Settlements of the United Brethren near the Cape of Good Hope. Cape Town, SA: Struick, 1969. 406 pp. No ISBN.

A reprint of the 1818 classic on the missionary travels of the author, describing with accuracy and impartiality the South African scene; with twelve hand-colored illustrations and four lithographs done by the author.

AF1029 Lee, Peter K. H.

Guard Her Children: Hope for South Africa Today. Eastbourne, ENK: Kingsway Publications, 1986. 256 pp. Paper. 0860654273.

A popular introduction to the church's involvement in justice and reconciliation ministries in South Africa today.

AF1030 Lobinger, Fritz, and Heinrich Aertker

Auf eigenen Füssen: Kirche in Afrika. Düsseldorf, GW: Patmos-Verlag, 1976. 120 pp. Paper. 3491774403.

A comparison of the work of Catholics in South Africa with the work of Anglicans and Methodists, in particular regarding voluntary community ministries by laypeople, in order to develop models of active, mature communities.

AF1031 Lockwood, Edgar

South Africa's Moment of Truth. New York, NYU: Friendship Press, 1988. vi, 183 pp. Paper. 0377001805.

The 1988 ecumenical mission study book on the churches and the struggle for justice in South Africa; with study guide, *Until We Are Free*, by John de Beer and Patricia de Beer (34 pp., 037700183X).

AF1032 Lodberg, Peter, and Erik Kyndal

Apartheid og de Lutherske kirker. (Ökumeniske studier, 1). Aarhus, DK: Forlaget Anis, 1988. 223 pp. Paper. 8774570811.

A prize-winning study of the attitude of the LWF and Lutheran churches toward apartheid in South Africa, including comparing the uses of the *status confessionis* in Germany (1930s) and South Africa (1980s).

AF1033 Logan, Willis H., ed.

The Kairos Covenant: Standing with South African Christians. New York, NYU: Friendship Press; Oak Park, ILU: Meyer-Stone Books, 1988. viii, 184 pp. Paper. 0377001899 (F), 0940989298 (M).

An introduction to the *Kairos Document* including the formal statements and responses from the Africa Committee of the National Council of Churches Convocation, November 1986, with study guide and annotated list of anti-apartheid agencies in the United States.

AF1034 Loubser, J. A.

A Critical Review of Racial Theology in South Africa: The Apartheid Bible. (Texts and Studies in Religion, 53). Lewiston, NYU: E. Mellen Press, 1987. xviii, 200 pp. 0889463840.

A history of the development of a theology of apartheid by Afrikaner Christians in South Africa, and of their recent repudiation of it.

AF—AFRICA

AF1035 Magethi, Pule B., and Thula M. Nkosi, eds.
God or Apartheid: A Challenge to South African Adventism.
(African Adventist Thought Series, 2). Braamfontein, SA:
Institute for Contextual Theology, 1991. 35 pp. Paper. No
ISBN.

A challenge to the Seventh-day Adventist Church in South
Africa to reposition itself in clear opposition to racism and
apartheid.

AF1036 Maimela, Simon S.
*Proclaim Freedom to My People: Essays on Religion and
Politics.* Braamfontein, SA: Skotaville, 1987. viii, 152 pp.
Paper. 0947009043.

Eleven essays by a Lutheran Professor of Theology at
the University of South Africa relating the central themes of
liberation and black theology to the South African system of
white racial domination and apartheid.

AF1037 Mayson, Cedric
*A Certain Sound: The Struggle for Liberation in South Afri-
ca.* Maryknoll, NYU: Orbis Books, 1985. xi, 145 pp. Paper.
0883442108.

The personal journey of a Methodist minister in South
Africa into the struggle against apartheid and, finally, to imprisonment and exile.

AF1038 Mayson, Cedric
*Jesus and the Holy Cows: The Message of Jesus for Today's
World.* London, ENK: Marshall Pickering, 1987. ix, 208 pp.
Paper. 055101444X.

A critique of South African political structures using reflections on the "historical Jesus," by a British Methodist
minister banned from South Africa in 1983 after thirty years
of mission work there.

AF1039 Mbali, Zolile
*The Churches and Racism: A Black South African Perspec-
tive.* London, ENK: SCM Press, 1987. xii, 228 pp. Paper.
0334019230.

A detailed case study of the WCC's Programme to Combat Racism, focusing on strategies developed to oppose apartheid and the competing liberation versus pro-apartheid theologies of the struggle in South Africa.

AF1040 Mears, William Gordon
Methodism in the Cape: An Outline. Cape Town, SA: Methodist Publishing House, 1973. ix, 194 pp. No ISBN.

An outline history of local church development among
Methodists in the Cape Province of South Africa in the 19th
century.

AF1041 Mettler, Lukas Anton
*Christliche Terminologie und Katechismus-Gestaltung in der
Mariannhiller Mission 1910-1920: Der grosse Wanger-Kate-
chismus von 1912 in Zulu und der um ihn entstandene Termi-
nologie- und Katechismus-Streit.* (Supplementa, 15). Immensee, SZ: *NZM,* 1967. xii, 284 pp. Paper. No ISBN.

A scholarly work describing the controversy about Christian terminology in the Zulu language, with special reference
to the catechism composed by Fr. Willibald Wanger of the
Mariannhill Missionaries.

AF1042 Meyer, Rudolph Adriaan
Poverty in Abundance or Abundance in Poverty? (C. I. Studies). Johannesburg, SA: Christian Institute of Southern Africa, 1973. 65 pp. 0620015071.

A study of the factor of poverty in race relations in South
Africa.

AF1043 Miller, Inger
The Light That Shines beyond the Grave. Philadelphia, PAU:
Continental Press, 1989. 80 pp. Paper. No ISBN.

A story based on the lives of actual Zulu women, telling
of their life, their sorrows, and eventual spiritual liberation
through the Christian Gospel.

AF1044 Mutambirwa, James, ed.
South Africa: The Sanctions Mission. Geneva, SZ: WCC;
London, ENK: Zed Books, 1989. xii, 135 pp. Paper.
0862329116 (UK pbk), 0862329108 (UK hdbk), 2825409766
(SZ pbk).

The report of a 1989 WCC-sponsored mission to seven
countries with high economic involvement in South Africa,
calling for mandatory economic sanctions until its government
negotiated with black majority leaders.

AF1045 Myklebust, Olav Guttorm
*Én var den første: studier og tekster til forståelse av H.P.S.
Schreuder: med bidrag av C.M. Doke og Ernst Dammann.*
(Avhandlinger utgitt av Egede Instituttet, 13). Oslo, NO: Gyl-
dendal, 1986. 320 pp. Paper. 8205166617.

This second part of the two-volume monumental work
on H. P. S. Schreuder, pioneer missionary of the Norwegian
Missionary Society to South Africa, is specially focused on
the person behind the missionary and excerpts from Schreuder's writings.

AF1046 Myklebust, Olav Guttorm
H. P. S. Schreuder: Kirke og misjon. (Land og kirke). Oslo,
NO: Gylden Norsk Forlag, 1980. 429 pp. 8205124515.

In this first part of his two-volume monumental work on
H. P. S. Schreuder, pioneer missionary of the Norwegian Missionary Society to South Africa, the author focuses on Schreuder's theological conception of church, ministry and mission,
and on his rupture with the sending society.

AF1047 Nürnberger, Klaus
Power and Beliefs in South Africa. Pretoria, SA: University
of South Africa, 1988. xiv, 334 pp. 0869815377.

A scholarly analysis of the interaction between economic power structures and patterns of conviction seen in the light
of a Christian ethic in South Africa.

AF1048 Nürnberger, Klaus, and John Tooke, eds.
The Cost of Reconciliation in South Africa. (NIR Reader, 1).
Cape Town, SA: Methodist Publishing House, 1988. v, 216
pp. Paper. 0949942960.

The first in a series of readers on justice and reconciliation issues in South Africa, published by the National Initiative for Reconciliation and designed for use by study and action groups.

**AF1049 Nürnberger, Klaus, John Tooke, and William Domeris,
eds.**
Conflict and the Quest for Justice. (NIR Reader). Pietermaritzburg, SA: Encounter Publications, 1989. 410 pp. Paper. 0620143150.

A reader designed for the use of study and action groups
concerned about issues of justice and reconciliation in South
Africa, with special emphasis on understanding violence in
that context, and the options for nonviolent action in the pursuit of justice.

AF1050 Nash, Margaret A., ed.

Rural Poverty Challenges the Church. Johannesburg, SA: SACC, 1984. 172 pp. Paper. 0949952137.

The report of a Northern Transvaal churches' workshop aimed at providing information and insight for those desiring to transform South Africa from a nation that displaces, impoverishes, and oppresses its black majority, to a nation "more conformed to God's will for liberation, justice, and peace."

AF1051 Naudé, Christian Frederic Beyers, and Dorothee Søelle

Hope for Faith: A Conversation. Geneva, SZ: WCC; Grand Rapids, MIU: Eerdmans, 1986. 41 pp. Paper. 2825408603 (SZ), 0802801919 (US).

A virtually unedited conversation between Christian Frederik Beyers Naudé (General Secretary of the South African Council of Churches) and Dorothee Sölle (Professor of Theology, Union Theological Seminary, US), discussing their conversion experiences, struggles, and commitments to ecumenical and justice concerns.

AF1052 Nederduitse Gereformeerde Kerk

Church and Society: A Testimony Approved by the Synod of the Dutch Reformed Church. Bloemfontein, SA: Pro Christo Publications, 1987. 58 pp. 1868040453.

Text of an important document by the synod of the Dutch Reformed Church on race relations in South Africa.

AF1053 Nolan, Albert

Dieu en Afrique du Sud. Translated by Philippe Denis. (Collection Théologies). Paris, FR: Éditions du Cerf, 1991. 300 pp. 2204043184.

French translation.

AF1054 Nolan, Albert

God in South Africa: The Challenge of the Gospel. Cape Town, SA: David Philip; Grand Rapids, MIU: Eerdmans, 1988. xiii, 241 pp. Paper. 0864860765 (SA), 0802804136 (US).

An attempt to reach South Africans with a new understanding of theology—its methodology and relevance, and how a new South African theology can be prophetic for the oppressed, by the former Master General of the Dominican Order in South Africa.

AF1055 Nolan, Albert

Gud I Sydafrika: Evangeliets utmaning. Translated by Pehr Edwall. Stockholm, SW: Verbum Förlag, 1990. 300 pp. Paper. 9152617491.

Swedish translation.

AF1056 Oosthuizen, G. C. et al.

Religion, Intergroup Relations, and Social Change in South Africa. (Contributions in Ethnic Studies, 24). Westport, CTU: Greenwood, 1988. xii, 237 pp. 0313263604.

A major scholarly study on the social role and significance of religion in intergroup relations of South Africans, drawing upon data from numerous local case studies.

AF1057 Oosthuizen, G. C.

Moving to the Waters: Fifty Years of Pentecostal Revival in Bethesda, 1925-1975. Durban, SA: Bethesda Publications, 1975. xvi, 239 pp. No ISBN.

A full history of the Full Gospel Church of God in mission and ministry among the Indian community of metropolitan Durban, South Africa.

AF1058 Oosthuizen, G. C.

Pentecostal Penetration into the Indian Community in Metropolitan Durban, South Africa. (Human Sciences Research Council Publications, 52). Durban, SA: Human Sciences Research Council, 1975. xi, 356 pp. No ISBN.

A detailed field research by the Professor of Comparative Religions at the University of Durban-Westville.

AF1059 Paton, Alan

Apartheid and the Archbishop: The Life and Times of Geoffrey Clayton, Archbishop of Cape Town. New York, NYU: Scribner; London, ENK: Cape, 1973. xiii, 311 pp. 0684137135 (US), 022400994X (UK).

A creative biography, by the noted South African author, of the former Anglican Bishop of Johannesburg (1934-1949) and Archbishop of Cape Town (1949-1957), focusing on his opposition to racism.

AF1060 Pauw, Berthold Adolf

Christianity and Xhosa Tradition: Belief and Ritual among Xhosa-Speaking Christians. Cape Town, SA: Oxford University Press, 1975. xiv, 390 pp. 0195700465.

A scholarly social-anthropological investigation of Christianity as practiced among Xhosa-speaking Africans in the Transkei and in Port Elizabeth, South Africa, with special reference to traditional religion and culture.

AF1061 Pauw, Berthold Adolf

Religion in a Tswana Chiefdom. London, ENK: Oxford University Press, 1960. xvi, 258 pp. No ISBN.

A detailed study of diverse religious interests (mainline and African independent churches and traditional religion) among the Tlaping section of the Tswana tribe, living in the north of South Africa's Cape Province; by a Dutch Reformed missionary and trained anthropologist.

AF1062 Peart-Binns, John S.

Ambrose Reeves. London, ENK: Gollancz, 1973. 303 pp. 0575016345.

A biography of the former Anglican Bishop of Johannesburg.

AF1063 Peart-Binns, John S.

Archbishop Joost de Blank: Scourge of Apartheid. London, ENK: Muller, Blond, & White, 1987. xv, 240 pp. 0584111304.

The biography of the controversial Anglican Archbishop of Capetown, South Africa (1908-1968), who became known as a revolutionary churchman against apartheid.

AF1064 Philip, John

Researches in South Africa. New York, NYU: Negro Universities Press, 1969. 2 vols. 0837114772.

Reprint of the 1828 edition of the journal and reflections of John Philip (1775-1851), Scottish superintendent of the London Missionary Society (LMS) in Southern Africa.

AF1065 Philpott, Graham

Jesus Is Tricky and God Is Undemocratic: The Kin-dom of God in Amawoti. Pietermaritzburg, SA: Cluster Publications, 1993. 204 pp. Paper. 0958380767.

Reflection on a bible study process by a base ecclesial community in Amawoti Inanda near Durban, South Africa, with transcripts of the dialogues and an analysis of the African liberation theology emerging from the experiences of oppressed people.

AF1066 Pillay, Gerald J.
Religion at the Limits?: Pentecostalism among Indian South Africans. Pretoria, SA: University of South Africa, 1994. xxxiii, 271 pp. Paper. 0869818554.

A scholarly study based on archival and field research of the development of the Pentecostal movement within the Indian community of South Africa, especially the large Bethesda Temple affiliated with the Full Gospel Church.

AF1067 Pityana, Barney N., and Charles Villa-Vicencio, eds.
Being the Church in South Africa. Johannesburg, SA: SACC, 1995. xiv, 173 pp. Paper. 0620194723.

Papers delivered at the consultation on "South Africa in Regional and Global Context: Being the Church Today" (Vanderbijlpark, 19-23 March 1995).

AF1068 Pretorius, H. L.
Swartman, seksualiteit en sending. Pretoria, SA: N. G. Kerkboekhandel, 1977. 161 pp. 079870103X.

A detailed study of attitudes toward sexuality, marriage, and polygamy among blacks in South Africa by a missionary of the Dutch Reformed Church.

AF1069 Prior, Andrew, ed.
Catholics in Apartheid Society. Cape Town, SA: David Philip, 1982. x, 197 pp. 0908396724.

Eleven essays on crucial areas of contemporary church-state conflict in South Africa, with an appendix containing statements since 1948 by the Catholic bishops of South Africa on church-state relations.

AF1070 Prozesky, Martin, and John W. De Gruchy, eds.
Living Faiths in South Africa. Cape Town, SA: David Philip; New York, NYU: St. Martin's Press; London, ENK: Hurst & Co., 1995. vi, 241 pp. Paper. 0864862539 (SA), 0312127766 (US), 185065249X (UK).

Thirteen essays surveying the range of faith perspectives in South Africa today, including African traditional religion, various forms of Christianity, and other faiths.

AF1071 Prozesky, Martin, ed.
Christianity amidst Apartheid: Selected Perspectives on the Church in South Africa. New York, NYU: St. Martin's Press, 1990. x, 244 pp. 0312035292.

Fourteen thoughtful essays by South African scholars and church leaders on the history of Christianity and the black people of South Africa, apartheid, other social issues, violence, religious pluralism, and the future of that country.

AF1072 Réamonn, Páraic, ed.
Farewell to Apartheid?: Church Relations in South Africa. (WARC Studies, 25). Geneva, SZ: WARC, 1994. 96 pp. Paper. 9290750146.

Papers on church relations in South Africa, especially the process of unification within the family of Dutch Reformed churches; originally presented at a WARC-sponsored consultation (Johannesburg, 3-5 March 1993).

AF1073 Randall, Peter
Prophet im eigenen Land: Beyers Naudé. Frankfurt am Main, GW: Lembeck, 1983. 143 pp. Paper. 3874762076.
German translation.

AF1074 Randall, Peter
A Taste of Power. (SPRO-CAS Publication, 11). Johan-

nesburg, SA: SPRO-CAS, 1973. 225 pp. Paper. 0869750259.

The final report of the South African-based Study Project on Christianity in Apartheid Society (SPRO-CAS), which sought alternatives for meaningful change for that country.

AF1075 Randall, Peter, ed.
Anatomy of Apartheid. (Occasional Publications, 1). Johannesburg, SA: SPRO-CAS, 1970. 88 pp. No ISBN.

Five essays on South African politics, economics, society, and race relations, used as study documents for the SPRO-CAS study.

AF1076 Randall, Peter, ed.
Apartheid and the Church: Report of the Church Commission of the Study Project on Christianity in Apartheid Society. (SPRO-CAS Publication, 8). Johannesburg, SA: SPRO-CAS, 1972. 91 pp. Paper. 0869750062.

Report of the Church Commission of the influential Study Project on Christianity in Apartheid Society (SPRO-CAS) jointly sponsored by the SACC and the Christian Institute of Southern Africa.

AF1077 Randall, Peter, ed.
Not without Honour: Tribute to Beyers Naudé. Johannesburg, SA: Ravan Press, 1982. viii, 107 pp. 0869751387.

A tribute to Beyers Naudé, an Afrikaner, who turned against many values and the political views of the majority of his community (compared to Solzhenitszyn) and led the Christian Institute until it was banned by the government in 1977.

AF1078 Regehr, Ernie
Perceptions of Apartheid: The Churches and Political Change in South Africa. Scottdale, PAU: Herald Press; Kitchener, ONC: Between the Lines, 1979. 309 pp. 0836118995 (US), 0919946127(CA-hdbk), 0919946119 (CA-pbk).

A detailed account of the various responses by South African Christians to apartheid since 1948, with a historical background to their racial involvement and attitudes.

AF1079 Ross, Andrew C.
John Philip (1775-1851): Missions, Race and Politics in South Africa. Aberdeen, STK: Aberdeen University Press, 1986. ix, 249 pp. Paper. 0080324576 (hdbk), 0080324673 (pbk).

A scholarly biography of the prophetic Resident Director for the LMS in South Africa, 1819-1851, with chapters on his Scottish background, the racial conflicts of the period, and a reassessment of Philip's missionary contribution.

AF1080 Rossouw, Pierre
Ecumenical Panorama: A Perspective from South Africa. Pretoria, SA: Pierre Rossouw, 1989. 398 pp. Paper. 0620127767.

A handbook on ecumenical bodies inside South Africa, and those outside but linked to South Africa, with the texts of eight international declarations on human rights.

AF1081 Rothe, Stefan
Der Südafrikanische Kirchenrat (1968-1988): Aus liberaler Opposition zum radikalen Widerstand. (Erlanger Monographien aus Mission und Ökumene, 11). Erlangen, GW: Ev.-Luth. Mission, 1990. xiii, 432 pp. Paper. 3872143115.

A political science dissertation about the South African Council of Churches, describing the political function and activities of Christian churches opposed to the regime.

AF1082 Ryan, Colleen
Beyers Naudé: Pilgrimage of Faith. Cape Town, SA: David Philip; Grand Rapids, MIU: Eerdmans; Trenton, NJU: Africa World Press, 1990. viii, 230 pp. Paper. 0864861567 (D), 0802805310 (W), 0865431906 (A).

The biography of the prophetic white Afrikaner who gained the respect of South Africans, both black and white, for his courageous resistance to apartheid.

AF1083 *Südafrikas Christen vor Gericht: Der Fall Beyers Naudé und das Christliche Institut*
Translated by Susanne Köhler. Wuppertal, GW: Jugenddienst-Verlag, 1977. 203 pp. 3779576260.

German translation of *The Trial of Beyers Naudé* (1975).

AF1084 Saayman, W. A.
Christian Mission in South Africa: Political and Ecumenical. Pretoria, SA: University of South Africa, 1991. xii, 128 pp. Paper. 0869816977.

An analysis of the mission of the Christian churches in South Africa from the perspective of the ecumenical and political dimensions of that mission.

AF1085 Saayman, W. A.
A Man with a Shadow: The Life and Times of Professor Z. K. Matthews. (African Initiatives in Christian Mission, 1). Pretoria, SA: UNISA Press, 1996. xxi, 108 pp. Paper. 0869819658.

A missiological interpretation of the life and work of Dr. Z. K. Matthews (1901-1968), based on published and archival sources by and about this prominent Christian educationalist in apartheid South Africa.

AF1086 Sales, Jane M.
The Planting of the Churches in South Africa. Grand Rapids, MIU: Eerdmans, 1971. 170 pp. Paper. No ISBN.

An indexed historical survey showing how the course of mission expansion in South Africa was affected by the constant antagonism between the Boer and British elements among the white settlers, by the white settlers' hunger for the land, and by the absence of a system of comity, which usually characterized mission in other parts of the world; with many notes and bibliography listing more than 250 titles.

AF1087 Schoeman, Karel, ed.
The Wesleyan Mission in the Orange Free State, 1833-1854, as Described in Contemporary Accounts. (Vrijstatia, 11). Cape Town, SA: Human and Rousseau, 1991. 144 pp. Paper. 0798128089.

An illustrated anthology of writings by pioneer Wesleyan missionaries to the Bechuana peoples, north of the Orange River, in what is now the Eastern Free State of South Africa.

AF1088 Schreiner, Gottlob
The Missionary Letters of Gottlob Schreiner, 1837-1846. Edited by Karel Schoeman. Cape Town, SA: Human and Rousseau, 1991. 160 pp. Paper. 0798128070.

The full text of nineteen official letters from South Africa by a LMS pioneer missionary in what is now the Orange Free State in South Africa, plus personal letters to the Basel Mission where he was trained.

AF1089 Semple, Duncan Wilkieson
A Scots Missionary in the Transkei: Recollections of Fieldwork. Lovedale, SA: Lovedale Press, 1965. xi, 74 pp. No ISBN.

Recollections of incidents and personalities between 1914 and 1947, in the intersection between the Khosa and the missionary, with a portrait of the mission work at the two Scottish stations of Sulenkama and Cunningham in the east of Cape Province.

AF1090 Serfontein, J. H. P.
Apartheid, Change, and the NG Kerk. Emmarentia, SA: Taurus, 1982. 295 pp. Paper. 062006157X.

A hastily written analysis of the events in and·around the Dutch Reformed Church (NG Kerk) in the period October 1981 to May 1982 (prior to the WARC Assembly of Ottawa), by a well-informed South African journalist; with twenty documents in the Annexures.

AF1091 Shaw, William
Never a Young Man: Extracts from the Letters and Journals of the Rev. William Shaw. Compiled by Celia Sadler. Cape Town, SA: H.A.U.M., 1967. 189 pp. No ISBN.

Vivid accounts by the John Wesley of South African Methodism, William Shaw (1798-1872), who served as a missionary in South Africa from 1820 to 1856; based heavily on Shaw's own works and his book, *The Story of My Mission* (1860).

AF1092 Sieber, Godfrey
Der Aufbau der Katholischen Kirche im Zululand: Von den Anfängen bis zur Gegenwart. (Münsterschwarzacher Studien, 21). Münsterschwarzach, GW: Vier-Türme-Verlag, 1976. xix, 314 pp. Paper. 3878680430.

A work outlining the contribution of the Benedictines to the evangelization of Zululand between 1922 and 1975 on the basis of copious primary sources.

AF1093 Sieber, Godfrey
The Benedictines of Inkamana. St. Ottilien, GW: EOS Verlag, 1995. xiv, 720 pp. 3880964807.

A thoroughly illustrated history of the Benedictines in Zululand, South Africa, from their founding in 1922.

AF1094 Simensen, Jarle, ed.
Norsk misjon og afrikanske samfunn: Sør-Afrika, ca. 1850-1900. Oslo, NO: Tapir, 1984. 227 pp. 8251906431.

A detailed study of the political and social interaction between Norwegian missionaries and Africans in South Africa; based on archival material in both countries—the first of two volumes of the Norwegian Missions in African History project at the University of Trondheim.

AF1095 Siwani, Nyaniso James
The Unknown Made Known: A History of Sabbathkeepers in South Africa. Port Elizabeth, SA: Seventh-Day Baptist Conference of South Africa; Janesville, WIU: Seventh-Day Baptist Historical Society, 1995. x, 118 pp. Paper. No ISBN.

A short history of the Seventh-Day Baptist Church in South Africa since its origin in 1909, with a brief history of other sabbath-keeping groups.

AF1096 South African Congress on Mission and Evangelism (Durham 1973)
I Will Heal Their Land....: Papers of the South African Congress on Mission and Evangelism, Durban, 1973. Edited by Michael Cassidy. Maseru, LO: Africa Enterprise, 1974. x 357 pp. No ISBN.

Papers from a major multi-racial congress on mission and evangelism in South Africa.

AF1097 *South Africa's Minorities*
(Occasional Publications, 2). Johannesburg, SA: SPROCAS, 1971. 77 pp. No ISBN.

Five short essays on South Africa's Indian, colored, Afrikaner, and English-speaking white communities.

AF1098 Spong, Bernard, and Cedric Mayson
Come Celebrate!: Twenty-Five Years of Work and Witness of the South African Council of Churches. Johannesburg, SA: SACC, 1993. 148 pp. Paper. No ISBN.

A brief narrative history, 1968 to 1993, by two leaders of the SACC.

AF1099 Strassberger, Elfriede
The Rhenish Mission Society in South Africa, 1830-1950. Cape Town, SA: Struick, 1969. xv, 109 pp. No ISBN.

The author's dissertation on the activities of the Rhenish Mission Society from its foundation until the work was handed over to the Dutch Reformed Church of South Africa.

AF1100 Study Project on Christianity in Apartheid Society, Social Commission
Towards Social Change: Report of the Social Commission of the Study Project in Christianity in Apartheid Society. (SPRO-CAS Publication, 6). Johannesburg, SA: SPRO-CAS, 1971. 197 pp. 0869750011.

A scholarly analysis of the nature of apartheid society, factors of injustice, the myths used to justify separation and domination, and strategies for change.

AF1101 Tatum, Lyle, ed.
South Africa: Challenge and Hope. New York, NYU: Hill and Wang, 1987. xii, 225 pp. Paper. 0809087502 (hdbk), 0809015307 (pbk).

Revised and expanded edition of South Africa's history and development, from a British colonial outpost, to white rule with apartheid; originally published by the American Friends Service Committee in cooperation with African Studies Progam, Indiana University (Philadelphia, PAU; 1982).

AF1102 Templin, J. Alton
Ideology on a Frontier: The Theological Foundation of Afrikaner Nationalism, 1652-1910. (Contributions in Intercultural and Comparative Studies, 11). Westport, CTU: Greenwood, 1984. xiii, 360 pp. 031324104X.

A scholarly study of the theological and historical origins of Afrikaner nationalism in South Africa, 1652-1910.

AF1103 *The Kairos Document—Challenge to the Church: A Theological Comment on the Political Crisis in South Africa*
Grand Rapids, MIU: Eerdmans; Braamfontein, SA: Skotaville Publishers, 1986. viii, 35 pp. Paper. 0802802729 (US), 0947009167 (SA).

Full text, with commentary, of South African theologians' and church leaders' challenge to existing church-state positions, advocating either conformity or moderate reform.

AF1104 *The Trial of Beyers Naudé: Christian Witness and the Rule of Law*
London, ENK: Search Press; Johannesburg, SA: Ravan Press, 1979. 188 pp. 0855323558 (UK).

Documentation from the 1973 trial in South Africa of the Director of the Christian Institute who, as an Afrikaner Dutch Reformed clergyman, rejected apartheid as "deeply inhuman and clearly unChristian"; edited by the International Commission of Jurists of Geneva, Switzerland, who monitored the trial.

AF1105 Thompson, Leonard Monteath
A History of South Africa. New Haven, CTU: Yale University Press, 1990. xxi, 288 pp. 0300048157.

A comprehensive and authoritative history of South Africa with details of historic missionary and contemporary church involvements in race relations in that country.

AF1106 Tingle, Rachel
Revolution or Reconciliation?: The Struggle in the Church in South Africa. London, ENK: Christian Studies Centre, 1992. 273 pp. Paper. 0951372114.

A narrative account of the various religious pressures for change in South Africa, both external (WCC) and internal, during the 1970 to 1990 period.

AF1107 Tlhagale, Buti, and Itumeleng J. Mosala, eds.
Hammering Swords into Ploughshares: Essays in Honour of Archbishop Mpilo Desmond Tutu. Grand Rapids, MIU: Eerdmans, 1987. 360 pp. Paper. 0802802699.

A *festschrift* of twenty-six essays in honor of Bishop Desmond Tutu, disclosing the tensions that exist in South Africa, the growing impatience with injustice, and the relevance of Christian hope and reconciliation; originally published in 1986 by Skotaville Publishers, Johannesburg, SA.

AF1108 Toit, C. W. du, ed.
Confession and Reconciliation: A Challenge to the Churches in South Africa. Pretoria, SA: University of South Africa, 1999. x, 155 pp. Paper. 1868880990.

The role played by religion, and specifically by church leaders in the apartheid era, their confession or absence of confession, and the future role of churches in fostering reconciliation; this is the outcome of a conference of the Research Institute for Theology and Religion at UNISA, Pretoria, on 23-24 March 1998 and a follow-up to the Open Letter of Confession sent to 12,000 ministers and church leaders.

AF1109 Tutu, Desmond
Crying in the Wilderness: The Struggle for Justice in South Africa. Grand Rapids, MIU: Eerdmans, 1982. 125 pp. Paper. 0802819400.

A collection of the most influential speeches, articles, press statements, and other writings by the General Secretary of the SACC from March 1978 to August 1980, revealing the role of the churches in the South African people's struggle against apartheid as it approached the 1980s.

AF1110 Tutu, Desmond
The Rainbow People of God: The Making of a Peaceful Revolution. Edited by John Allen. New York, NYU: Doubleday, 1994. xxii, 281 pp. 0385475462.

Selections from the speeches, letters, and sermons, 1976 to 1994, of the charismatic Anglican Archbishop of Cape Town who was awarded the Nobel Peace Prize for his contribution to peacemaking and racial reconciliation in South Africa.

AF1111 Van der Merwe, Willem Jacobus
The Road Ahead: Towards the Unity of the D. R. Family. Cape Town, SA: Lux Verbi, 1985. 55 pp. Paper. 086997176X.

A brief overview of the Dutch Reformed churches of South Africa by a senior missiologist who urges greater mutual understanding and trust, concerted witness and service, and a better expression of unity; originally published under the title *Die Pad vorentoe.*

AF1112 van der Walt, B. J.

Afrocentric or Eurocentric?: Our Task in a Multicultural South Africa. (Series F2: Brochures of the Institute for Reformational Studies, 67). Potchefstroom, SA: Potchefstroom University, 1997. ii, 190 pp. Paper. 186822256X.

A contribution to the debate on cultural diversity in South Africa by the Professor in Philosophy at the Potchefstroom University for Christian Higher Education, who warns against the extremisms both of Afrocentrism and Eurocentrism.

AF1113 Villa-Vicencio, Charles

The Spirit of Freedom: South African Leaders on Religion and Politics. (Perspectives on South Africa, 52). Berkeley, CAU: University of California Press, 1996. xxxii, 301 pp. 0520200446 (hdbk), 0520200454 (pbk).

A collection of twenty-one interviews that explore the lives of eminent South Africans who led the struggle against apartheid at great cost—Nelson Mandela, Chris Hani, Desmond Tutu, and Nadine Gordimer included.

AF1114 Villa-Vicencio, Charles

Trapped in Apartheid: A Socio-Theological History of the English-Speaking Churches. Maryknoll, NYU: Orbis Books; Cape Town, SA: David Philip, 1988. xiii, 250 pp. Paper. 0883445190 (US), 0864860986 (SA).

A profound analysis of those social and theological forces that led English-speaking churches of South Africa to compromise with apartheid, by the head of the Department of Religious Studies, University of Cape Town.

AF1115 Villa-Vicencio, Charles, and Carl Niehaus, eds.

Many Cultures, One Nation: A Festschrift for Beyers Naudé. Cape Town, SA: Human & Rousseau, 1995. 183 pp. Paper. 0798134127.

Fourteen essays by South African scholar-friends of Beyers Naudé, published as a *festschrift* on the occasion of his 80th birthday and focusing on the search for South African unity amidst cultural and racial diversity.

AF1116 Villa-Vicencio, Charles, and John W. De Gruchy, eds.

Resistance and Hope: South African Essays in Honour of Beyers Naudé. Grand Rapids, MIU: Eerdmans; Cape Town/Johannesburg, SA: David Philip, 1985. xii, 209 pp. Paper. 080280098X (US), 0864860323 (SA).

A *festschrift* honoring Dr. Beyers Naudé on his 70th birthday, as Afrikaner, theologian, ecumenist, and social prophet; with a bibliography of his publications.

AF1117 Villa-Vicencio, Charles, ed.

On Reading Karl Barth in South Africa. Grand Rapids, MIU: Eerdmans, 1988. xii, 172 pp. Paper. 0802803202.

Nine essays by South African theologians in the Reformed tradition, reflecting on the influence of Karl Barth's theology on their effort to reclaim the Christian heritage for the oppressed.

AF1118 Vincent, Eileen

I Will Heal Their Land: The Moving of God's Spirit in South Africa. Basingstoke, ENK: Marshall Pickering, 1986. 188 pp. Paper. 0551013311.

A popular account of modern-day Pentecostal ministries in South Africa, 1969-1979, and the prophetic leaders of this growing work.

AF1119 Vorster, W. S., ed.

Building a New Nation: The Quest for a New South Africa. Pretoria, SA: University of South Africa, 1991. x, 203 pp. Paper. 0869817280.

Fourteen scholarly essays, four specifically on the role of religion in the reconstruction of South African society; originally presented at the fifteenth symposium of the UNISA Institute for Theological Research (Johannesburg, 4-5 September 1991).

AF1120 Walker, David S.

Challenging Evangelicalism: Prophetic Witness and Theological Renewal. Pietermaritzburg, SA: Cluster Publications, 1993. 228 pp. Paper. 0958314128.

Revision of a doctoral thesis (University of Natal) on a theology of the poor, contextual method, and holistic mission in evangelical theology, with special reference to South Africa.

AF1121 Wallis, Jim, and Joyce Hollyday, eds.

Crucible of Fire: The Church Confronts Apartheid. Maryknoll, NYU: Orbis Books; Washington, DCU: Sojourners, 1989. xx, 169 pp. Paper. 0883446480.

A compendium of interviews, sermons, and letters by key church leaders struggling against apartheid in South Africa in 1988; many reprinted from *Sojourners* in 1989.

AF1122 Walshe, Peter

Church Versus State in South Africa: The Case of the Christian Institute. London, ENK: Hurst; Maryknoll, NYU: Orbis Books, 1983. xvi, 234 pp. 0905838815 (UK), 0883440970 (US).

A detailed history and appraisal of the Christian Institute of Southern Africa, from its founding by Rev. Beyers Naudé in 1963 to its banning in 1977.

AF1123 Walshe, Peter

Prophetic Christianity and the Liberation Movement in South Africa. Pietermaritzburg, SA: Cluster Publications, 1995. 180 pp. Paper. 0958380791.

An analysis of the role of the churches as they confronted racism and apartheid in South Africa from 1910 to the present; by a South African political scientist now teaching at the University of Notre Dame.

AF1124 Webb, Pauline, ed.

Ein langer Kampf: Der Ökumenische Rat der Kirchen und das Apartheidsregime in Südafrika. Mainz, GW: Plädoyer für eine ökumenische Zukunft, 1995. 201 pp. Paper. No ISBN.

German translation of *A Long Struggle* (1994).

AF1125 Webb, Pauline, ed.

A Long Struggle: The Involvement of the World Council of Churches in South Africa. Geneva, SZ: WCC Publications, 1994. xiv, 133 pp. Paper. 2825411353.

Eight essays reviewing the history of WCC involvement in South Africa from different perspectives.

AF1126 Weisse, Wolfram

Südafrika und das Antirassimusprogramm: Kirchen im Spannungsfeld einer Rassengesellschaft. (Studien zur interkulturellen Geschichte des Christentums, 1). Bern, SZ: Herbert Lang; Frankfurt am Main, GW: Peter Lang, 1975. 465 pp. Paper. 3261009764.

A study of reactions of individuals, churches, and governments in South Africa to the WCC's Programme to Combat Racism, with an extensive bibliography.

AF1127 Wepman, Dennis
Desmond Tutu: An Impact Biography. New York, NYU: Franklin Watts, 1989. 157 pp. 0531107809.

A popular illustrated biography of the Anglican archbishop of Cape Town, Nobel laureate, and leader in the struggle against apartheid.

AF1128 Wink, Walter
Violence and Nonviolence in South Africa: Jesus' Third Way. Philadelphia, PAU: New Society Publishers, 1987. viii, 98 pp. 086571116X (hdbk), 0865711178 (pbk).

A popular presentation by a leading biblical scholar from the USA, of nonviolent militant action as Jesus' alternative to passive nonviolence or violent revolution; with application to South Africa.

AF1129 World Council of Churches
Report on the World Council of Churches Mission in South Africa, April-December, 1960. Geneva, SZ: WCC, 1961. 36 pp. No ISBN.

The Cottesloe Consultation report including an assessment of the situation in South Africa immediately after the Sharpeville massacre in March 1960, a general overview of the work of the WCC and its member churches in South Africa, and the official documents of the consultation.

AF1130 Worsnip, Michael E., and Desmond van der Water, eds.
We Shall Overcome: A Spirituality of Liberation. Pietermaritzburg, SA: Cluster Publications, 1991. 139 pp. Paper. 0958314128.

Short essays by eight younger South African theologians, on contemporary liberation spirituality and the possibilities for its development; with special reference to southern Africa.

AF1131 Worsnip, Michael E.
Between the Two Fires: The Anglican Church and Apartheid, 1948-1957. Pietermaritzburg, SA: University of Natal Press, 1991. xvii, 202 pp. Paper. 0869807951.

A careful analysis of struggle between social activists and pietists in the Anglican Church of South Africa since the nationalists introduced apartheid in 1948.

AF1132 *Zending in Venda-land*
Dordrecht, NE: Brummen, 1975. 136 pp. Paper. No ISBN.

Dutch Reformed missionaries to the Venda people of northern Transvaal, South Africa, tell the stories of their work from 1960 to 1975.

Swaziland

See also SO297, and SO353.

AF1133 Froise, Marjorie, ed.
Swaziland Christian Handbook 1994. Welkom, SA: Christian Info, 1994. x, 115 pp. Paper. 0620167122.

A directory of Swaziland churches and Christian organizations with a brief history and analysis of their contexts for ministry.

AF1134 Parrott, Leslie
Sons of Africa: Stories from the Life of Elmer Schmelzenbach. Kansas City, MOU: Beacon Hill Press, 1979. 217 pp. Paper. 0834106019.

A biography of Harmon Schmelzenbach and his family, Nazarene missionaries to the Swazi people in the bushveldt of Swaziland and the eastern Transvaal in the Republic of South Africa.

AF1135 Scutt, J. F.
The Drums are Beating: Missionary Life in Swaziland. London, ENK: Africa Evangelical Fellowship, 1966. 132 pp. No ISBN.

A fictional biography, depicting the conversion of an African woman in Swaziland, by the name of 'Food-of-earth.'

Zimbabwe
[Southern Rhodesia, Rhodesia]

See also CR563, SO292-SO295, SO311, EC51, EC57-EC58, EC192, PO115, ED159, AF302, and AF824.

AF1136 Arnold, William E.
Here to Stay: The Story of the Anglican Church in Zimbabwe. Sussex, ENK: Book Guild, 1985. 159 pp. 086332102X.

A journalist's narrative history of Anglicanism in Zimbabwe from 1874 to 1980.

AF1137 Banana, Canaan Sodindo, ed.
A Century of Methodism in Zimbabwe 1891-1991. Harare, ZI: Methodist Church in Zimbabwe, 1991. ix, 234 pp. Paper. No ISBN.

Seven short reflective essays by Zimbabwe Methodist leaders celebrating the centenary of their church.

AF1138 Banana, Canaan Sodindo
The Church in the Struggle for Zimbabwe: From the Programme to Combat Racism to Combat Theology. (Studia Missionalia Upsalienia, 67). Gweru, ZI: Mambo Press for The Zimbabwe Centre of Research and Peace Studies; Uppsala, SW: Swedish Institute of Missionary Research, 1996. xi, 389 pp. Paper. 0869226940 (M), 9185424471 (S).

The first President of Zimbabwe, himself a Methodist pastor/theologian, gives an insider's account of the participation of the churches in the struggle for the liberation of Zimbabwe (1964-1980), and for authentic theology and justice in the independent nation (1980-1995), with special reference to the Methodist Church in Zimbabwe.

AF1139 Banana, Canaan Sodindo
The Gospel According to the Ghetto. Gwelo, ZI: Mambo Press, 1981. 156 pp. Paper. No ISBN.

Second revised edition of a work affirming the need for the ghetto masses to become co-partners with God, in his divine mission of moral, economic, political, and social revolution, by the first President of Zimbabwe; containing poems written and published under the same title while he was a student at Wesley Theological Seminary in Washington, D.C. (1974, 1977), and later prose writings.

AF1140 Banana, Canaan Sodindo
Politics of Repression and Resistance: Face to Face with Combat Theology. Gweru, ZI: Mambo Press, 1996. xiii, 335 pp. Paper. 0869226509.

The Methodist clergy-theologian and first President of Zimbabwe examines the political interface between the state, the church, and the individual in the evolution of Zimbabwe.

AF1141 Barr, Francis C.
Archbishop Aston Chichester, 1879-1962: A Memoir. Gwelo, RH: Mambo Press, 1978. vi, 97 pp. Paper. No ISBN.

The biography of Aston Sebastian Joseph Chichester (1879-1962), Jesuit missionary to Southern Rhodesia from 1929, and Bishop and first Catholic Archbishop of Salisbury (1931-1956).

AF—AFRICA

AF1142 Beckmann, Johannes
Tagebuch einer Reise ins südliche Afrika: 9 September 1938-26 März 1939. Edited by Jakob Baumgartner. (Schriftenreihe, 33). Immensee, SZ: *NZM,* 1993. ix, 200 pp. Paper. 3858240745.

The journal of Professor Johannes Beckman, SMB (1901-1971) as he traveled through southern Africa in 1938 and 1939 to explore the possibility of a Bethlehem Fathers mission in Southern Rhodesia.

AF1143 Bex, Anthony
St. Peter's Harare: Portrait of an African Town Parish. (Mambo Occasional Papers: Mission Pastoral Series, 7). Gwelo, RH: Mambo Press, 1976. 63 pp. No ISBN.

A vivid account of life in a Harare (former Salisbury) township, and of the work of a Catholic parish there.

AF1144 Bhebe, Ngwabi
Christianity and Traditional Religion in Western Zimbabwe 1859-1923. London, ENK: Longman, 1979. xiv, 190 pp. 058264237X.

A historical examination of the impact of Christianity upon Ndebele tribal society, culture, and religion, both before and after the first missionaries.

AF1145 Clinton, Iris
Hope Fountain Story: A Tale of One Hundred Years. Gwelo, RH: Mambo Press, 1969. 101 pp. No ISBN.

A short history of the first one hundred years of Hope Fountain Mission, established by the LMS in 1870, with accounts by early missionaries and nationals.

AF1146 Clutton-Brock, Guy, and Molly Clutton-Brock
Cold Comfort Confronted. London, ENK: Mowbrays, 1972. 201 pp. 0264646010.

The narrative autobiographical account of two Christians committed to racial justice and partnership, first in England, and from 1949 to 1971 in Rhodesia (present Zimbabwe).

AF1147 Dachs, Anthony J., and W. F. Rea
The Catholic Church and Zimbabwe, 1879-1979. (Zambeziana, 8). Gwelo, RH: Mambo Press, 1979. xiii, 260 pp. Paper. No ISBN.

The centennial history of the RCC in Zimbabwe, with special attention to church and society issues.

AF1148 Dodge, Ralph E.
The Revolutionary Bishop Who Saw God at Work in Africa. South Pasadena, CAU: William Carey Library, 1986. x, 211 pp. Paper. 0878082034.

The autobiography of a Methodist bishop in Africa, whose opposition to the racism of Ian Smith's Southern Rhodesian government (now Zimbabwe) led to his exile.

AF1149 Dove, John
Luisa: Dr. Luisa Guidotti 1932-1979. Gweru, RH: Mambo Press, 1992. 115 pp. Paper. 0869225235.

The biography of Dr. Luisa Guidotti (1932-1979), an Italian woman doctor martyred during the struggle for the liberation of Zimbabwe.

AF1150 Farrant, Jean Cecil
Mashonaland Martyr: Bernard Mizeki and the Pioneer Church. London, ENK: Oxford University Press, 1966. xxv, 258 pp. No ISBN.

A biography of Bernard Mizeki (1861-1896), the story of his martyrdom in the Mashonaland Rebellion of 1896, and of the early history of the Anglican church in Southern Rhodesia.

AF1151 Gelfand, Michael
Gubulawayo and Beyond: Letters and Journals of the Early Jesuit Missionaries to Zambesia (1879-1887). London, ENK: Chapman, 1968. 496 pp. 0225275465.

Letters and journals of early Jesuit missionaries to Zambesia (1879-1887), showing the significance played by early Jesuit missionaries who followed Livingstone in his call to introduce Christianity to Africa, specifically to Zimbabwe and Zambia.

AF1152 Gelfand, Michael
Mother Patrick and Her Nursing Sisters: Based on Extracts of Letters and Journals in Rhodesia of the Dominican Sisterhood, 1890-1901. Cape Town, SA: Juta, 1964. 281 pp. No ISBN.

A scholarly history of the medical work undertaken by the Dominican sisters in three of the main centers in Southern Rhodesia, and an attempt to depict, through letters, the type of life led by the first settlers in this area.

AF1153 Hallencreutz, Carl F., and Ambrose Moyo, eds.
Church and State in Zimbabwe. (Christianity South of the Zambezi, 3). Gweru, ZI: Mambo Press, 1988. ix, 507 pp. Paper. 0869224409.

Nineteen scholarly essays which chronicle the church/state relationship during the struggle for an independent Zimbabwe, the church's role in development, and the theological perspectives held during the struggle for independence and the post-independence period.

AF1154 Hallencreutz, Carl F.
Religion and Politics in Harare 1890-1980. (Studia Missionalia Upsaliensia, 73). Uppsala, SW: Swedish Institute of Missionary Research, 1998. 502 pp. Paper. 9185424528.

A scholarly history of the development of Christianity in Zimbabwe's capital city, with particular emphasis on issues of church and state.

AF1155 Hansson, Gurli
Mwana Ndi Mai: Toward an Understanding of Preparation for Motherhood and Child Care in the Transitional Mberengwa District, Zimbabwe. (Studia Missionalia Upsaliensia, 65). Uppsala, SW: Swedish Institute of Missionary Research, 1996. 358 pp. Paper. 9185424455.

A detailed case study of the interaction of medicine and religion in preparing women for motherhood and child care in the Mberengwa district of Zimbabwe; originally submitted as a doctoral dissertation at Uppsala University in 1996.

AF1156 Harlin, Tord
Spirit and Truth: Religious Attitudes and Life Involvements of 2,200 African Students. (Studia Missionalia Upsaliensia, 19). Uppsala, SW: University of Upsaliensia, 1973. 203 pp. No ISBN.

A doctoral dissertation studying religious attitudes among 2,200 high school students in Rhodesia (present Zimbabwe).

AF1157 Irland, Nancy Beck
Service and a Smile. Boise, IDU: Pacific Press, 1987. 75 pp. Paper. 0816307040.

A popular account of Seventh-day Adventist missionaries Harry and Nora Anderson, who initiated work at Solusi Mission, Southern Rhodeshia, from 1895 to 1948.

AF1158 Kapungu, Leonard T.
Rhodesia: The Struggle for Freedom. Maryknoll, NYU: Orbis Books, 1974. xii, 177 pp. 0883444356.

A lucid analysis by a Zimbabwean scholar, of the liberation struggle in his country and the churches' involvement, concentrating on the 1962-1973 period.

AF—AFRICA

AF1159 Kurewa, John Wesley Zwomunondiita

The Church in Mission: A Short History of The United Methodist Church in Zimbawe, 1897-1997. Nashville, TNU: Abingdon, 1997. 192 pp. Paper. 0687010330.

A centennial history of the origins and development of Methodism in Zimbabwe, by the Vice Chancellor of Africa University in that country.

AF1160 Lapsley, Michael

Neutrality or Co-Option?: Anglican Church and State from 1964 until the Independence of Zimbabwe. (Missio-Pastoral Series, 16). Gweru, ZI: Mambo Press, 1986. 106 pp. Paper. 0869224077.

An account of the role of the Anglican church leadership during the crucial phase of the Zimbabwean struggle for liberation and nationhood, 1964-1980.

AF1161 Linden, Ian

The Catholic Church and the Struggle for Zimbabwe. London, ENK: Longman Group, 1980. x, 310 pp. Paper. 0582643031.

A history of the ideological struggle over church-state issues in Zimbabwe within the RCC between 1959 and 1979; originally published as *Church and State in Rhodesia, 1959-1979* (Mainz, WG: Grunewald-Verlag, 1980).

AF1162 Maxwell, David

Christians and Chiefs in Zimbabwe: A Social History of the Hwesa People. Westport, CTU: Praeger, 1999. xii, 291 pp. 0275966267.

Explores the encounter of Christian missions with one another and with traditional culture and religion, as well as the conjunctions of the institutions of the colonial state with Hwesa political and religious institutions, from the precolonial to the postcolonial period (ca.1870s-1990s).

AF1163 McDonagh, Enda

Church and Politics: From Theology to a Case History of Zimbabwe. Notre Dame, INU: University of Notre Dame Press, 1980. 177 pp. 0268007349.

A study, by a University of Notre Dame professor, of the working theology of church and politics of Catholics in Rhodesia (present Zimbabwe), torn by racial conflict in 1978; with the author's theological reflection and original site visit report.

AF1164 McLaughlin, Janice

On the Frontline: Catholic Missions in Zimbabwe's Liberation War. Edited by John Conradie, and John Reed. Harare, ZI: Baobab Books, 1996. xvi, 352 pp. Paper. 0908311796.

A study of four Catholic missions in Zimbabwe during the 1965-1980 war of liberation; by a Maryknoll sister/scholar who was an active participant in that struggle; based on archives and interviews.

AF1165 McPherson, Alexander

James Fraser: The Man Who Loved the People: A Record of Missionary Endeavour in Rhodesia in the Twentieth Century. London, ENK: Banner of Truth Trust, 1967. ix, 224 pp. No ISBN.

A biography of a Scottish Presbyterian missionary (1913-1958), who served in Southern Rhodesia among the Matebele from 1938 until his death in 1958.

AF1166 Merwe, W. J. van der

From Missionfield to Autonomous Church in Zimbabwe. Pretoria, SA: N. G. Kerkboekhandel, 1981. 253 pp. No ISBN.

A historical survey of the Mashonaland missionfield of the Dutch Reformed Church Mission in Rhodesia, by a former DRC missionary.

AF1167 Moyo, Ambrose

Zimbabwe: The Risk of Incarnation. (Gospel and Culture Pamphlet, 8). Geneva, SZ: WCC Publications, 1996. ix, 49 pp. Paper. 2825411965.

The senior lecturer in religious studies at the University of Zimbabwe introduces various historical and contemporary responses by Christians to Gospel and culture issues.

AF1168 Mungazi, Dickson

The Honoured Crusade: Ralph Dodge's Theology of Liberation and Initiative for Social Change in Zimbabwe. Gweru, ZI: Mambo Press, 1991. xii, 142 pp. Paper. 0869225073.

An interpretive analysis of the work of Ralph Edward Dodge (b.1907), a crusader for social change while a Methodist missionary in Angola (1936-1950) and bishop of the Methodist Church in Rhodesia (1956-1968).

AF1169 Murphree, Marshall W.

Christianity and the Shona. (London School of Economics: Monographs on Social Anthropology, 36). London, ENK: Athlone Press; New York, NYU: Humanities Press, 1969. viii, 200 pp. No ISBN.

An analysis of the different forms of religious life found in contemporary Shona society in the Mutoko district.

AF1170 Muzorewa, Abel Tendekai

Rise Up and Walk: The Autobiography of Bishop Abel Tendekai Muzorewa. Edited by Norman E. Thomas. Nashville, TNU: Abingdon; London, ENK: Evans Brothers; London, ENK: Sphere, 1978-1979. xiv, 289 pp. 0687364507 (A), 0237503670 (E), 0722162901 (S).

The autobiography of the United Methodist bishop who became a leader in the struggle for liberation in Zimbabwe and that country's first black Prime Minister (1978-1979).

AF1171 Peaden, W. R.

Missionary Attitudes to Shona Culture, 1890-1923. (Local series, 27). Salisbury, RH: Central Africa Historical Association, 1970. 41 pp. No ISBN.

An abriged version of part of the author's thesis on the interaction of missionary activity and Shona culture in the first thirty years of European settlement in Southern Rhodesia.

AF1172 Ranger, Terence O.

Are We Not Also Men?: The Samkange Family and African Politics in Zimbabwe 1920-64. (Social History of Africa). Harare, RH: Baobab Books; Portsmouth, NHU: Heinemann; London, ENK: James Currey, 1995. x, 211 pp. 0435089757 (RH, hdbk), 0435089773 (RH, pbk), 0852556683 (UK, hdbk), 0852556187 (UK, pbk).

A scholarly biography of three Zimbabwe Methodists—Thompson Samkange (1893-1956), and his sons Sketchley (1936-) and Stanlake (1922-)—with analysis of the interplay of mission/church and government.

AF1173 Söderström, Hugo

God Gave Growth: The History of the Lutheran Church in Zimbabwe 1903-1980. (Studia Missionalia Upsaliensia, 40). Uppsala, SW: Swedish Institute of Missionary Research, 1984. x, 237 pp. Paper. No ISBN.

This history demonstrates how a mission became a church, and how this church (the Evangelical Lutheran Church in Zimbabwe) became indigenous and contributed to the spiritual growth of the whole nation, during the events which transformed Rhodesia into Zimbabwe.

AF1174 Söderström, Hugo

Kyrkväg 70 i Zimbabwe: Frsn svensk mission till afrikansk kyrka 1903-1975. Stockholm, SW: Verbum, 1977. 245 pp. 9901602068.

A history of the Swedish missionary contribution to the evolution of the Lutheran Church in Zimbabwe.

AF1175 Sauerwein, Astrid

Mission und Kolonialismus in Simbabwe 1840-1940: Kollisionen, Konflikte und Kooperation. (Focus Kritische Universität). Gieéen, GW: Focus, 1990. 227 pp. Paper. 3883493783.

A dissertation on the question of how Christianity could become a strong influence in Zimbabwe and the role played by the missions in the colonial process.

AF1176 Sisters of the Order of St. Dominic, Salisbury, Rhodesia

In God's White-Robed Army: The Chronicle of the Dominican Sisters in Rhodesia, 1890-1934. Cape Town, SA: M. Miller, 1951. 276 pp. No ISBN.

An account of the work and experiences of the first sisters, based on the diary of the Rev. Mother Patrick, as well as personal testimonies of surviving sisters.

AF1177 Skelton, Kenneth

Bishop in Smith's Rhodesia: Notes from a Turbulent Octave 1962-1970. Gweru, ZI: Mambo Press, 1985. 152 pp. Paper. No ISBN.

An account of an Anglican bishop's experiences in Matabeleland from 1962 to 1970, as he struggled to underline Christian witnessing against the racism and absolutism of the state.

AF1178 Spring, William

The Long Fields: Zimbabwe since Independence. (Pickering Paperbacks). Basingstoke, ENK: Pickering & Inglis, 1986. 191 pp. Paper. 0720806348.

A popular account of political conflicts and violence in Zimbabwe under Marxism and Mugabe, from 1983 to 1985, and of the involvement of Christians on both sides of the conflict.

AF1179 Steere, Douglas V.

God's Irregular: Arthur Shearly Cripps. London, ENK: SPCK, 1973. xv, 158 pp. Paper. 0281026750.

A biography of the remarkable Anglican missionary to Southern Rhodesia (1901-1952) known for his complete identification with the African people, his political championing of their interests, and for his poetry and novels.

AF1180 Summers, Carol

From Civilization to Segregation: Social Ideals and Social Control in Southern Rhodesia, 1890-1934. Athens, OHU: Ohio University Press, 1994. xv, 311 pp. 0821410741.

A social history of colonial Zimbabwe, including the interactions of missionaries with government and white settlers.

AF1181 Thompson, Phyllis

The Rainbow or the Thunder. Sevenoaks, ENK: Hodder & Stoughton; Cheltenham, ENK: Publications Board, Elim Pentecostal Church, 1979. 157 pp. Paper. 0340242086.

The story of the massacre, during the liberation struggle, of twelve Elim Pentecostal Church missionary adults and children in Zimbabwe in 1978.

AF1182 Verstraelen, F. J.

Zimbabwean Realities and Christian Responses: Contempo-

rary Aspects of Christianity in Zimbabwe. Gweru, ZI: Mambo Press, 1998. viii, 152 pp. Paper. 0869227297.

A study of the diversity of Christianity in Zimbabwe, its impact on the socioeconomic and culturo-religious contexts, and vice versa, with reference to church-state relations and missio-theological reflections in an African setting.

AF1183 Weinrich, A. K. H.

African Marriage in Zimbabwe and the Impact of Christianity. Gweru, ZI: Mambo Press; Edinburgh, STK: Holmes McDougall, 1982. xx, 212 pp. Paper. 0869222082.

A sociological study of the present marriage patterns in Zimbabwe, with suggestions for stemming the exodus of couples marrying outside the churches.

AF1184 Weller, John C., and Jane Linden

Mainstream Christianity to 1980 in Malawi, Zambia and Zimbabwe. Gweru, ZI: Mambo Press, 1984. viii, 224 pp. Paper. 0869223232.

A general history of the missions and churches in the area, designed as a theological school textbook.

AF1185 Zvobgo, Chengetai J. M.

A History of Christian Missions in Zimbabwe, 1890-1939. Gweru, ZI: Mambo Press, 1996. 412 pp. Paper. 0869226282.

A comprehensive study of early missions in Southern Rhodesia, with a focus on educational and medical work.

AF1186 Zvobgo, Chengetai J. M.

The Wesleyan Methodist Missions in Zimbabwe 1891-1945: Supplement to Zambezia, 1991 the Journal of the University of Zimbabwe. Edited by R. S. Roberts. Harare, ZI: University of Zimbabwe Publications, 1991. ix, 169 pp. Paper. 0908307187.

A scholarly history published for the centennial of the Wesleyan Methodist Church in Zimbabwe.

AF1187 Zvobgo, Rungano J.

Colonialism and Education in Zimbabwe. Harare, ZI: Sapes Books, 1994. x, 108 pp. Paper. 1779050259.

A brief history of education in Zimbabwe, from 1890 to 1979, including an evaluation of the contributions of Protestant and Catholic missions.

West Africa: General Works

See also HI254, HI315, HI409, CR609, CR1047, SO279, SO305-SO306, ED88, ED144, AF23, AF45, AF249, and AF1354.

AF1188 Agbeti, John Kofi

West African Church History: Christian Missions and Church Foundations, 1482-1919. Leiden, NE: Brill, 1986. xi, 175 pp. Paper. 9004071679.

Histories of the work in West Africa of Roman Catholic missionary orders and nine Protestant missionary societies from Western Europe and the United States.

AF1189 Assimeng, Max

Religion and Social Change in West Africa: An Introduction to the Sociology of Religion. Accra, GH: Ghana Universities Press, 1989. 327 pp. Paper. 9964301723.

A textbook on the complex relationships in West Africa, between religion and other social institutions; with focus on factors of religious and social change.

AF—AFRICA

AF1190 Bane, Martin J.
The Popes and Western Africa: An Outline of Mission History, 1460's-1960's. Staten Island, NYU: Alba House, 1968. xv, 187 pp. No ISBN.

An attempt to trace efforts to propagate the Christian faith in Upper and Lower Guinea since the days of Henry the Navigator, showing the lengths to which the popes and Holy See went, to establish the church in the newly discovered areas of western Africa.

AF1191 Barrow, Alfred Henry
Fifty Years in Western Africa: Being a Record of the Work of the West Indian Church on the Banks of the Rio Pongo. New York, NYU: Negro Universities Press, 1969. iv, 157 pp. 0837121930.

A reprint of the 1900 history (London: SPCK) of a pioneer Anglican mission from the West Indies, 1851-1900, to the west coast of Africa (now Guinea).

AF1192 Centre de hautes études administratives sur l'Afrique et l'Asie modernes
Cartes des religions de l'Afrique de l'ouest: Notice et statistiques. Paris, FR: Documentation française, 1966. ii, 135 pp. No ISBN.

A gazetteer of Islam, Christianity (Catholicism and Protestantism), and African traditional religion in West Africa, by country and district, with statistical summaries, maps, and notes based on studies of Christianity and Islam since 1954.

AF1193 Clarke, Peter Bernard
West Africa and Christianity. London, ENK: Arnold, 1986. vi, 271 pp. Paper. 0713182636.

A comprehensive study of the history of Christianity in West Africa, from the 15th century to 1985.

AF1194 Curtin, Philip D., ed.
Africa and the West: Intellectual Responses to European Culture. Madison, WIU: University of Wisconsin Press, 1972. x, 259 pp. 0299061213.

Seven essays, by North American historians, on intellectual responses to Europe during the colonial era, by West Africans in Ghana, Sierra Leone, and Senegal.

AF1195 Heijek, Jan et al.
In elkaars spiegel: Westers christendom in Afika. (Nijmegen: Katholiek Studiecentrum, 3). Nijmegen, NE: Katholiek Studiecentrum, 1993. 248 pp. Paper. 9070713349.

These seven insightful essays given at the Katholiek Studiecentrum (Nijmegen) deal with the mission, impact, and development of Christianity in West Africa, including issues of the encounter between Christianity and indigenous religions, spirituality, acculturation, the impact of technologies on traditional social structures and church governance.

AF1196 Jakobsson, Stiv
Am I Not a Man and a Brother?: British Missions and the Abolition of the Slave Trade and Slavery in West Africa and the West Indies, 1786-1838. (Studia Missionalia Upsaliensia, 17). Uppsala, SW: Gleerup, 1972. 661 pp. Paper. No ISBN.

A comprehensive, readable, and well-documented study of British involvements by government, abolitionists, and missionaries in the 18th- to 19th-century movement to abolish the slave trade in Africa and the Caribbean.

AF1197 Kalu, Ogbu U., ed.
The History of Christianity in West Africa. London, ENK: Longman, 1980. vi, 378 pp. 0582646936 (hdbk), 0582603595 (pbk).

A collection of twenty-one scholarly articles by leading historians designed to show how African communities, which had their own religions and established instruments of social order, came into contact with Christianity, and responded variously to this external agent of change.

AF1198 Maldant, Boris, Maxime Haubert, and Yves Breton
Croissance et conjoncture dans l'Ouest Africain. (Études Tiers Monde, croissance, développement, progrès). Paris, FR: Presses Universitaires de France, 1973. 350 pp. No ISBN.

Exploration of issues of religious faith and economic development in West Africa.

AF1199 Myers, Glenn
The Poorest of the Poor? The Peoples of the West African Sahel. (Briefings). Carlisle, ENK: OM Publishing, 1998. 64 pp. Paper. 1850782997.

An introduction to the challenges for Christian mission in West Africa.

AF1200 Pabst, Martin
Mission und Kolonialpolitik: Die Norddeutsche Missionsgesellschaft an der Goldküste und in Togo bis zum Ausbruch des I. Weltkrieges. Munich, GW: Anarche, 1988. 645 pp. 3927317004.

A solidly documented doctoral dissertation attempting to show the interdependence of Christian missions and colonialism in its different dimensions and historical and political effects, exemplified by the Norddeutsche Mission.

AF1201 Pobee, J. S.
West Africa: Christ Would Be an African Too. (Gospel and Culture Pamphlet, 9). Geneva, SZ: WCC Publications, 1996. xi, 52 pp. Paper. 2825411981.

A Ghanaian theologian and missiologist, the WCC's program coordinator for Ecumenical Theological Education reflects on issues of Gospel, culture, and mission in West Africa.

AF1202 Sanneh, Lamin
The Crown and the Turban: Muslims and West African Pluralism. Boulder, COU: Westview Press, 1997. xiii, 290 pp. 0813330580 (hdbk), 0813330599 (pbk).

This detailed study on the clash of civilizations between the secular government and Muslim traditions in West Africa, also discusses Christian-Muslim relations, past and present, in the region.

AF1203 Sanneh, Lamin
West African Christianity: The Religious Impact. Maryknoll, NYU: Orbis Books, 1983. xviii, 286 pp. Paper. 0883447037.

A collection of nine scholarly essays, on the origins and development of Christian missions and African independent churches, concentrating on the role of Africans as principal agents in the spread of Christianity there, and linking the Christian religious theme to local religious responses and attitudes.

AF1204 Thompson, George
The Palm Land: Or West Africa Illustrated: Being a History of Missionary Labors and Travels.... (The Colonial History Series). London, ENK: Dawsons, 1969. 456 pp. 071290350X.

Reprint of an 1858 history of early West Africa missions, plus a continent-wide survey.

AF—AFRICA

AF1205 Ustorf, Werner
Die Missionsmethode Franz Michael Zahns und der Aufbau kirchlicher Strukturen in Westafrika: Eine missionsgeschichtliche Untersuchung. (Erlanger Monographien aus Mission und Ökumene, 7). Erlangen, GW: Ev.-Luth. Mission, 1989. 337 pp. Paper. 3872143077.

A scholarly analysis of the work of Franz Michael Zahn who, from 1862 to 1900, as an inspector of missions for the Norddeutschen Mission (North German Mission) in West Africa, helped it move away from German *volkskirche* models toward indigenous African churches.

AF1206 Vanderaa, Larry
A Survey for Christian Reformed World Missions of Missions and Churches in West Africa. Grand Rapids, MIU: Christian Reformed World Missions, 1991. vi, 135 pp. Paper. No ISBN.

A survey of Francophone Africa to determine needs in mission, with a view to new openings for Christian Reformed World Missions.

West Africa: Biography

See also HI256, SO349, AF1283, and AF1308.

AF1207 Brown, Pam
It Was Always Africa. Nashville, TNU: Broadman, 1986. 192 pp. Paper. 0805443355.

A popular account by a Southern Baptist missionary of service in West Africa.

AF1208 Moore, Moses N.
Orishatukeh Faduma: Liberal Theology and Evangelical Pan-Africanism, 1857-1946. (ATLA Monograph Series, 40). Lanham, MDU: Scarecrow Press, 1996. xiii, 289 pp. 0810830914.

A penetrating analysis of the life and writings of a first-generation Sierra Leonean Christian who contributed to Pan-Africanism on two continents; based on the author's Ph.D. dissertation (Union Theological Seminary, 1987).

Benin [Dahomey]

See also AF1303.

AF1209 Salvadorini, Vittorio A.
Le Missioni a Benin e Warri nel XVII Secolo: La Relazione inedita di Bonaventura da Firenze. (Universita di Pisa. Facolta di Scienze politiche, 2). Milan, IT: Giuffre, 1972. 314 pp. No ISBN.

A scholarly history of Catholic missions, especially those of Bonaventura of Florence, to the kingdoms of Benin and Warri in West Africa; with selected source documents.

Burkina Faso [Upper Volta]

AF1210 Beraud-Villars, J.
Études sur les vocations religieuses en pays Mossi. Paris, FR: Mouton, 1964. No ISBN.

A study of Catholic religious vocations in Upper Volta (Burkina Faso).

AF1211 Doti-Sanou, Bruno
L'Émancipation des femmes Madare: L'impact du projet administratif et missionnaire sur une société africaine, 1900-1960. (Studies in Christian Mission, 2). Leiden, NE: Brill, 1994. xxxii, 254 pp. 9004098526.

A detailed analysis of the efforts of Catholic missions and French colonial administration for the emancipation of Bobo women in the west of Burkina Faso (formerly Upper Volta).

AF1212 Ki-Zerbo, Joseph
Alfred Diban: Premier chrétien de Haute-Volta. (Semeurs). Paris, FR: Éditions du Cerf, 1983. 148 pp. 2204020796.

The biography of Alfred Diban (1875-1980), a freed slave who became the first Christian in Upper Volta and, as a catechist, assisted the White Fathers (RC) in their missionary activities.

AF1213 Le Roy Laudrie, Marie
Pâques africaines: de la communauté clanique à la communauté chrétienne. (Le Monde d'outre-mer, passé et présent, 3e série : Essais, 7). Paris, FR: La Haye Mouton et Cie, 1965. 231 pp. No ISBN.

Case study of Catholic Christianity among the Mossi of Burkina Fasa (Upper Volta).

AF1214 Philippe, Ouédraogo N.
Polygamie traditionnelle des Moose et communauté ecclésiale: Aspects juridiques et implications pastorales. (Thése de Doctorat, 3317). Rome, IT: Pontificia Universitas Urbaniana, 1988. 329 pp. Paper. No ISBN.

A detailed study of polygamy among the Mossi people of Burkina Faso (traditional customs and the legal and pastoral responses of the RCC); originally submitted as a doctoral thesis at the Urbaniana Pontifical University.

AF1215 Sanon, Anselme Titianma
Tierce, église, ma mère: ou, la conversion d'une communaté païenne au Christ. Paris, FR: Institut Catholique de Paris; Bobo-Dioulasso, UV: Anselme Titianma Sanon, 1977. 294 pp. No ISBN.

A detailed study of contextualization in the Catholic parish of Tounou-Ma-nasso in Burkina Faso (former Ivory Coast), disclosing the struggle toward cultural conversion, an indigenous African theology, and authentic forms of Christian community; presented as a doctoral thesis to the Faculty of Theology of the Catholic Institute of Paris.

Cameroon

See also CR561, CR1028, SO624, CO114, AF27, AF248, and AF304.

AF1216 Abeng, Nazaire Bitoto
Von der Freiheit zur Befreiung: Die Kirchen- und Kolonialgeschichte Kameruns. (European University Studies, 23: Theology, 364). Frankfurt am Main, GW: Lang, 1989. xxii, 275 pp. Paper. 3820410473.

A dissertation investigating the history of colonialism and the Catholic Church in Cameroon, and its effects on the present situation, together with possibilities for political, economic, and theological liberation in Africa.

AF1217 Balz, Heinrich
Where the Faith Has to Live: Studies in Bakossi Society and Religion. Berlin, GW: Dietrich Reimer Verlag, 1995. Vol. 1. Paper. 3496025638.

Revised edition of a detailed 1984 study of the relation between religion and culture among the Bakossi people of the Cameroon, with special reference to the development of the Presbyterian Church out of the work of the Basel Mission (Part 1: Living Together).

AF1218 Berger, Heinrich
Mission und Kolonialpolitik: Die katholische Mission in Kamerun während der deutschen Kolonialzeit. (Supplementa, 26). Immensee, SZ: NZM, 1978. xxvii, 358 pp. Paper. 3858240524.

A work describing the genesis and working methods of the Catholic missions in Cameroon between 1890 and 1914, and the tensions existing between missions, colonial administration, and local culture.

AF1219 Booth, Bernard F.
Mill Hill Fathers in West Cameroon: Education, Health and Development, 1884-1970. Bethesda, MDU: International Scholars Publications, 1995. xvi, 284 pp. 1883255414 (hdbk), 1883255406 (pbk).

A detailed case study, based on archival and field research, of the work of the Mill Hill fathers in educational, medical, and other ministries of social development in former British Cameroon.

AF1220 Cereti, Giovanni
Rapporto sull'Africa nera: Impressioni di un viaggio in Cameroun. Milano, IT: Pontifico Instituto Missioni Estere, 1969. 117 pp. No ISBN.

A popular introduction to experiences of the Catholic Church in missions in the Cameroon.

AF1221 Essiben, Madiba
Colonisation et evangélisation en Afrique: l'héritage scolaire du Cameroun, 1885-1956. (Studies in the Intercultural History of Christianity, 23). Bern, SZ: Lang, 1980. 293 pp. 3261046112.

A scholarly analysis of the factors of colonialism and evangelization in the contributions of the missions to education in Cameroon.

AF1222 Fly, James L.
Africa Adopted Us. Boise, IDU: Pacific Press, 1987. 80 pp. Paper. 0816307377.

A popular biography of Aime and Madeleine Cosendai, Swiss Seventh-Day Adventist missionaries to the Cameroon, 1939-1982.

AF1223 Gravrand, Charbel
Fils de Saint Bernard en Afrique: une foundation au Cameroun, 1951-1988. Paris, FR: Beauchesne, 1990. 180 pp. Paper. 2701012228.

The history of the founding of Cistercian monasteries in Africa, with special attention to developments under African leadership in the Cameroon.

AF1224 Hallden, Erik
The Culture Policy of the Basel Mission in the Cameroons, 1886-1905. (Studia Ethnographica Uppsaliensia, 31). Uppsala, SW: Uppsala University; Lund, SZ: Berlingska Boktryckeriet, 1968. xvi, 142 pp. No ISBN.

A doctoral thesis originally presented at the University of Uppsala in 1968.

AF1225 Keller, W., Jörg Schnellbach, and J. R. Brutsch, eds.
The History of the Presbyterian Church in West Cameroon. West Cameroon, CM: Presbyterian Church West Cameroon, Radio and Literature Department, 1969. 154 pp. No ISBN.

A survey of the general development of the Presbyterian Church including the full integration of the Basel Mission projects in West Cameroon; with a history of church developments in East Cameroon after the First World War.

AF1226 Kwast, Lloyd Emerson
The Discipling of West Cameroon: A Study of Baptist Growth. Grand Rapids, MIU: Eerdmans, 1971. 205 pp. Paper. No ISBN.

A comprehensive study of multiple factors affecting growth in the Baptist Convention of the Cameroon during the 1947-1966 period.

AF1227 Larsen, Erik
Kamerum: Norsk Misjon gjennom 50 år. Stavanger, NO: Nomi Forlag, 1973. 144 pp. 8250101502.

An illustrated narrative history of fifty years of work in Cameroon by the Norwegian Missionary Society.

AF1228 Lode, Käre
Appelé à la liberté: histoire de l'Église Evangélique Luthérienne de Cameroun. Amstelveen, NE: Improcep Editions, 1990. 351 pp. Paper. 9071358089.

An important work on Lutheran mission and church history in Cameroon, with lists of all missionaries and indigenous pastors having served in the Evangelical Lutheran Church of Cameroon.

AF1229 Mbala-Kyé, Achille
La pastorale dans une ville d'Afrique: Yaoundé. (Recherches institutionelles, 22). Nordheim, FR: CERDIC-Publications, 1995. 339 pp. Paper. 2850970549.

A detailed case study from Yaoundé in Cameroon of urbanization and the church, suggesting new pastoral approaches for effective ministry.

AF1230 Mfochivé, J.
L' éthique chrétienne face a l'interconnexion culturelle et religieuse en Afrique: Exemple du pays Bamoun 1873-1937. (Proefschrift Theol. Fac. Rijksuniversiteit Leiden). Meppel, NE: Krips Repro, 1983. 300 pp. Paper. No ISBN.

A social and cultural history of the Bamoun people of the Cameroon, 1873-1937, including a description of the religious and legal thinking of the Muslim Sultan Njoya (born ca.1873), and the coming of the colonial powers of Germany, France, and Britain; with a comparative study of traditional, Muslim, and Christian ethics.

AF1231 Muyo, Joshua Ngwalem
Entlassen ins Nichts?: Jugenderlebnisse eines Kameruner Theologiestudenten. (Erlanger Hefte aus der Weltmission). Erlangen, GW: Ev.-Luth. Mission, 1979. 48 pp. 3872141090.

The autobiography of a young Presbyterian pastor in Cameroon; originally written (but not published) in English.

AF1232 O'Neil, Robert J.
Mission to the British Cameroons. London, ENK: Mission Book Service, 1991. xix, 185 pp. Paper. 0950788899.

A narrative account of the Mill Hill Missionaries' evangelizing work in the British Cameroons from 1921 to 1970.

AF1233 Philombe, René
Un sorcier blanc à Zangali. Yaoundé, CM: Éditions Clé, 1969. 187 pp. Paper. No ISBN.

A novel about the concomitance of evangelization and colonization in Cameroon.

AF—AFRICA

AF1234 Reyburn, William D.

Out of the African Night. New York, NYU: Harper & Row, 1968. xiv, 176 pp. No ISBN.

A popular account of medical missions in the Cameroon, 1930-1960, featuring that of the Presbyterian doctor George Thorne at Central Hospital in Bululand.

AF1235 Slageren, Jaap van

Les origines de l'Église Évangélique du Caméroun: Missions européennes et christianisme autochtone. Leiden, NE: Brill, 1972. xii, 297 pp. 9004034277.

A history of Protestant missions in Cameroon until the foundation of the autonomous Evangelical Church, 1957; presented as a doctoral dissertation at the Rijksuniversity in Leiden by a former missionary in the area.

AF1236 Stumpf, Rudolf

La politique linguistique au Cameroun de 1884 à 1960: Comparison entre les administrations coloniales allemande, française et britannique et du rôle joué par les sociétés missionaires. (Publications Universitaires Européennes, 27: Études asiatiques et africaines, 4). Bern, SZ: Lang, 1979. 157 pp. 3261031565.

A comparative study of British, French, and German colonial administration in the Cameroon, and of mission influences.

AF1237 Weber, Charles William

International Influences and Baptist Mission in West Cameroon: German-American Missionary Endeavor under International Mandate and British Colonialism. (Studies in Christian Mission, 9). Leiden, NE: Brill, 1993. xvi, 176 pp. 9004097651.

A history, based on original archival and primary source material, of the educational mission of German and British Baptists in West Cameroon, from 1922 to 1945.

Gambia

AF1238 Prickett, Barbara

Island Base: A History of the Methodist Church in the Gambia, 1821-1969. Bo, SL: Bunum Press for the Methodist Church in the Gambia, 1969. 246 pp. No ISBN.

A detailed chronological history.

Ghana [Gold Coast]

See also EA249, CR567, CR578, SO281, SO355, SO466, SO607, SP268-SP271, AF26, AF241, and EU190.

AF1239 Agyemfra, L. S. G.

Ghana Church Union: An Opinion. Accra, GH: Waterville Publishing House, 1969. 50 pp. No ISBN.

A Presbyterian critic of church union in Ghana, stressing that the churches in Ghana should pursue aspects of inward and spiritual unity instead of external ecclesiastical organization.

AF1240 Atiemo, Abamfo Ofori

The Rise of the Charismatic Movement in the Mainline Churches in Ghana. Accra, GH: Asempa Publishers, 1993. viii, 76 pp. Paper. 9964782098.

A short account of the history of charismatic renewal movements in mainline churches in Ghana; with an appraisal of their present significance, based on interviews with denominational leaders, pastors, and local prayer group leaders.

AF1241 Barker, Peter

Peoples, Languages and Religion in Northern Ghana: A Preliminary Report. Ghana: Ghana Evangelism Committee/ Asempa Publishers, 1986. 320 pp. Paper. 9964781539.

A handbook to the peoples of northern Ghana, by language group, including information about the churches that work in each area and what Scripture and literacy materials exist in each language; with summaries of Muslim and Christian outreach.

AF1242 Bartels, Francis Lodowic

The Roots of Ghana Methodism. Cambridge, ENK: Cambridge University Press, 1965. xiii, 368 pp. No ISBN.

This is the story of the growth of the Methodist Church in Ghana, which became autonomous in 1961 after 126 years with the British Methodist conference.

AF1243 Beckmann, David M.

Eden Revival: Spiritual Churches in Ghana. St. Louis, MOU: Concordia Publishing, 1975. 144 pp. Paper. 0570031974.

An introduction to the history and dynamics of the spiritual church movement as a cultural counterpart of political nationalism; with special attention to the Eden Revival Church.

AF1244 Beecham, John

Ashantee and the Gold Coast: Being a Sketch of the History, Social State and Superstitions of the Inhabitants of the Countries with a Notice of the State and Prospects of Christianity among Them. (Colonial History Series; Land Marks in Anthropology). London, ENK: Dawsons; New York, NYU: Johnson Reprint Corp., 1968. xix, 376 pp. No ISBN.

A reprint of the 1841 edition (London: John Mason), in which the author provided information concerning Christian mission and indigenous culture in Ghana (former Gold Coast); based on the writings of missionaries of the Wesleyan Mission.

AF1245 Burke, F. L., and F. J. McCreanor

Training Missionaries for Community Development: A Report on Experiences in Ghana. Princeton, NJU: National Conference of Catholic Charities, 1960. xvi, 86 pp. No ISBN.

North American trainers report on missions and development issues in Ghana.

AF1246 Butler, Grace L. Chavis

Africa: Religions and Culture with a Focus on the Ashanti People. Pittsburgh, PAU: Dorrance, 1994. xxii, 288 pp. 0805935010.

An introduction for African Americans, to the religions and cultures of Africa, with special reference to the Ashanti peoples of Ghana.

AF1247 Conference on the Mission of the Church in Ghana Today

God's Mission in Ghana: Talks Given at a Conference on the Mission of the Church in Ghana, held in Kumasi in January 1973. Accra, GH: Asempa Publishers, 1974. 96 pp. No ISBN.

Papers from an important conference sponsored by the Christian Council of Ghana.

AF1248 Debrunner, Hans W.

A History of Christianity in Ghana. Accra, GH: Waterville Publishing House, 1967. xi, 375 pp. No ISBN.

A comprehensive illustrated history of the work of the various missions in Ghana, 1470-1957.

AF1249 Dovlo, C. K.

Christianity and Family Life in Ghana. Accra, GH: Presbyterian Book Depot, 1962. 55 pp. Paper. No ISBN.

A popular introduction to Christian marriage principles and their application in modern Ghana.

AF1250 Fischer, Friedrich Hermann

Der Missionsarzt Rudolf Fisch und die Anfänge medizinischer Arbeit der Basler Mission an der Goldküste (Ghana). (Studien zur Medizin-, Kunst-, und Literaturgeschichte, 27). Herzogenrath, GW: Murken-Altrogge, 1991. 585 pp. Paper. 3921801613.

A biography of the missionary doctor, Rudolf Fisch, who was a representative of the Basel Mission in Ghana (Gold Coast), 1885-1911, with special sections on medical work in the mission and on the African understanding of sickness.

AF1251 Hall, Peter

Autobiography of Rev. Peter Hall: First Moderator of the Presbyterian Church of Ghana. (Pioneer Series). Accra, GH: Waterville Publishing House, 1965. 74 pp. Paper. No ISBN.

A popular account by Peter Hall (b.1851), the son of Jamaican missionaries to the Gold Coast, written after fifty years of his own mission service in that country.

AF1252 Howell, Allison M.

The Religious Itinerary of a Ghanaian People: The Kasena and the Christian Gospel. (Studies in the Intercultural History of Christianity, 102). Frankfurt am Main, GW: Lang, 1997. xx, 413 pp. Paper. 363131440X (GW), 0820432563 (US).

A detailed historical and socio-anthropological study of the encounter with Christianity of the Kasena people of northern Ghana, focusing on the dynamics of conversion and church growth.

AF1253 Howell, Allison M.

The Slave Trade and Reconciliation: A Northern Ghanaian Perspective. Navrongo, GH: Bible Church of Africa and SIM Ghana, 1998. ix, 86 pp. Paper. No ISBN.

With slave traders driven out only one-hundred years ago, the goal of this joint seminar of the Bible Church of Africa and SIM Ghana was not to stir up hatred and bitterness, but to bring forgiveness and reconciliation through the Good News of Jesus Christ.

AF1254 Kpobi, David Nii Anum

Mission in Chains: The Life, Theology and Ministry of the Ex-Slave Jacobus E.J. Capitein (1717-1747): With a translation of his major publications. (Serie MISSION, 3). Zoetermeer, NE: Boekencentrum, 1993. 273 pp. Paper. 9023907930.

A dissertation on the life, theology, and ministry of the first sub-Saharan African to study Protestant theology in a European university, and serve as a pioneer missionary to his native Ghana.

AF1255 Kpobi, David Nii Anum

Triple Heritage: Facts and Figures about the Presbyterian Church of Ghana. Accra, GH: Asempa Publishers, 1995. viii, 32 pp. Paper. 9964782349.

A brief insight into the involvement of the Presbyterian Church of Ghana in the nation's social and religious life.

AF1256 Miller, Jon

The Social Control of Religious Zeal: A Study of Organizational Contradictions. New Brunswick, NJU: Rutgers University Press, 1994. xvi, 238 pp. 0813520606.

A detailed analysis of the organizational style of the Evangelical Missionary Society of Basel, Switzerland, from 1828 to 1918, as it struggled to bring its Pietist religious beliefs to the people of the Gold Coast (present Ghana) in West Africa.

AF1257 Mobley, Harris W.

The Ghanaian's Image of the Missionary: An Analysis of the Published Critiques of Christian Missionaries by Ghanaians, 1897-1965. (Studies on Religion in Africa, 1). Leiden, NE: Brill, 1970. xi, 181 pp. No ISBN.

An analysis by a former Ghana missionary of the published critiques of Christian missionaries by Christian Ghanaians from 1897 to 1965, with resulting interpretation of the composite missionary image.

AF1258 National Seminar on Lay Apostolate (Kumasi, Ghana, 31 Aug.-5 Sept. 1967)

Christians in Ghanaian Life: A Report. Accra, GH: National Catholic Secretariat, 1968. 119 pp. No ISBN.

Report of the Seminar sponsored by the National Catholic Secretariat.

AF1259 Obeng, Pashington

Asante Catholicism: Religious and Cultural Reproduction among the Akan of Ghana. (Studies of Religion in Africa, 15). Leiden, NE: Brill, 1996. xi, 243 pp. 9004106316.

A detailed analysis of how Catholicism has been contextualized and institutionalized in the Asante (Akan) diocese of Ghana; originally submitted as a Ph.D. dissertation at Boston University in 1991.

AF1260 Odjidja, Edward Martinus Lartey, ed.

Mustard Seed: The Growth of the Church in Kroboland. Accra, GH: Waterville Publishing House, 1973. 162 pp. No ISBN.

Autobiographical sketches of Johannes Zimmermann, pioneer of the Basel Mission (1886-1917) among the Krobo, and of the early Ghanaian leaders of the Krobo Presbyterian Church.

AF1261 Osafo, Ernest A.

Der Beitrag der Basler Mission zur wirtschaftlichen Entwicklung Ghanas von 1828 bis zum Ersten Weltkrieg. [Cologne, GW]: [University of Cologne], 1972. 164 pp. No ISBN.

History of nearly a century (1828-1915) of work by the Basel Mission in Ghana; originally presented in 1972 as a thesis at the University of Cologne.

AF1262 Owoahene-Acheampong, Stephen

Inculturation and African Religion:Indigenous and Western Approaches to Medical Practice. (American University Studies, 21: Regional Studies, 16). New York, NYU: Lang, 1998. xv, 225 pp. 082043129X.

A detailed investigation of the traditional African healing practices among the Akan people of Ghana, and of their encounter with Western approaches to healing advocated by missionaries and colonial officials; originally presented as a Ph.D. dissertation at the University of Toronto.

AF1263 Parsons, Robert Thomas

The Churches and Ghana Society, 1918-1955: A Survey of the Work of Three Protestant Mission Societies and the African Churches Which They Established in Their Assistance to Societary Development. Leiden, NE: Brill, 1963. xvi, 240 pp. No ISBN.

A scholarly study of the work of three Protestant mission societies, of the African churches they established (Ghana Presbyterian, Methodist, and Evangelical Presbyterian), of the social outreach of these churches, and of their efforts to integrate Christianity in African society.

AF1264 Pobee, J. S.

Kwame Nkrumah and the Church in Ghana, 1949-1966: A Study in the Relationship between the Socialist Government of Kwame Nkrumah, the First Prime Minister and First President of Ghana, and the Protestant Christian Churches in Ghana. Accra, GH: Asempa Publishers, 1988. 222 pp. Paper. 9964781687.

A careful historical account of the relationship between the state of Ghana and its first President, Kwame Nkrumah, and the Protestant churches of that country.

AF1265 Pobee, J. S.

Religion and Politics in Ghana. Accra, GH: Asempa Publishers, 1991. 150 pp. Paper. 9964781792.

An analysis, by the noted Ghanaian theological educator, of the religious factor in the evolution of the political history of Ghana.

AF1266 Reindorf, C. C., and Samuel Johnson

The Recovery of the West African Past: African Pastors and African History in the Nineteenth Century. Edited by Paul Jenkins. Basel, SZ: Basler Afrika Bibliographien, 1998. 212 pp. Paper. 3905141701.

Papers from an international seminar (Basel, Switzerland, 25-28 October 1995) celebrating the centenary of the publication of a Ghanaian pastor's *History of the Gold Coast and Asante.*

AF1267 Smith, Noel

The Presbyterian Church of Ghana, 1835-1960: A Younger Church in a Changing Society. Accra, GH: Ghana Universities Press; London, ENK: Oxford University Press, 1966. 304 pp. No ISBN.

An account of the growth and development of the Basel Mission/Presbyterian Church of Ghana, upon a background of the social and religious life of the Akan peoples; with an appraisal of the church within the country.

AF1268 Vogels, Raimund

Tanzlieder und liturgische Gesänge bei den Dagaaba in Nordwestghana: Zur Verwendung einheimischer Musik im katholischen Gottesdienst. (Beiträge zur Ethnomusikologie, 18). Hamburg, GW: Wagner, 1988. 2 vols. Paper. 0889790364.

A study based on field work analyzing the musical, stylistic, and linguistic structures of female dancing among the Dagaaba and discussing musical adaptation for the Catholic liturgy; with a comprehensive collection of songs with musical notations, text, and German translation [vol. 1: viii, 259 pp; vol. 2: vii, 192 pp.].

AF1269 Ward, William Ernest Frank

Fraser of Trinity and Achimota. Accra, GH: Ghana Universities Press, 1965. vi, 328 pp. No ISBN.

A scholarly biography of mission educator Alexander Garden Fraser (1873-1962), CMS missionary to Uganda (1900-1903), Principal of Trinity College (Kandy, Sri Lanka, 1904-1924), and Principal of Prince of Wales College, (Achimota, Ghana, 1924-1935).

AF1270 Williamson, Sydney George, and Kwesi A. Dickson, eds.

Akan Religion and the Christian Faith: A Comparative Study of the Impact of Two Religions. Accra, GH: Ghana Universities Press, 1965. xvii, 186 pp. No ISBN.

A historical and contemporary sociological analysis of the two dominant religious systems among the Akan people of Ghana, based on a doctoral thesis.

AF1271 Wyllie, Robert W.

The Spirit-Seekers: New Religious Movements in Southern Ghana. (American Academy of Religion Studies in Religion, 21). Missoula, MTU: Scholars Press, 1980. viii, 139 pp. 0891303553 (hdbk), 0891303561 (pbk).

A study of the dynamics of Spiritism among the Effutu people of Winneba, a Ghanaian coastal town, analyzing the interplay between the traditional religious system, the missions, and the emerging African independent churches; also published as *Spiritism in Ghana: A Study of New Religious Movements.*

AF1272 Yeboa-Dankwa, J.

History of the Presbyterian Training College, Akropong-Akwapim: 125 Years Anniversary 1848-1973. Accra, GH: Waterville Publishing House, 1973. 95 pp. No ISBN.

History of the earliest teacher training college in West Africa.

Guinea-Bissau [Portuguese Guinea]

AF1273 Macindoe, Betty

Going for God: The Story of Bessie Brierley. London, ENK: Hodder & Stoughton, 1974. 128 pp. Paper. 0340165340.

A popular biography of Bessie Brierley (d.1969), pioneer missionary of the Worldwide Evangelization Crusade in Portuguese Guinea (present Guinea Bissau), 1936-1959; first published in 1972.

Ivory Coast

See also SO305-SO306 and SO361.

AF1274 Auge, Marc et al.

Prophètisme et thérapeutique: Albert Atcho et la communauté de Bregbo. (Collection Savoir). Paris, FR: Hermann, 1975. 324 pp. Paper. 2705657894.

A collaborative research by six sociologists of religion, analyzing aspects of the prophetic healing ministry of Albert Atcho (b.1903), begun in 1948 in his village of Bregbo in the Ivory Coast, and of its links to the Harris Movement.

AF1275 Holas, Bohumil

Le séparatisme religieux en Afrique Noire: L'exemple de la Côte d'Ivoire. Paris, FR: Presses Universitaires de France, 1965. 410 pp. No ISBN.

A detailed analysis of cultural factors spawning religious independency in the Ivory Coast.

AF1276 Roux, André

L'évangile dans la forêt: Naissance d'une église en Afrique noire. (L'Évangile au vingtième siècle). Paris, FR: Éditions du Cerf, 1971. 195 pp. Paper. No ISBN.

A popular introduction to the vitality of Christianity in the Ivory Coast: Roman Catholic, Protestant, and Harris Movement, emphasizing elements of African initiative and uniqueness.

AF1277 Trichet, Pierre

Côte d'Ivoire: Les premiers pas d'une église. Abidjan, IV: La Nouvelle, 1994. 171 pp. No ISBN.

The first volume of a multi-volume history of the Catholic Church in the Ivory Coast, covering the 1895-1914 period.

AF1278 Truby, David William

Not So Much a Story, More a Work of God. London, ENK: Unevangelized Fields Mission, 1968. 48 pp. 0854790608.

Story of missions in West Africa's Ivory Coast.

Liberia

See also AF251.

AF1279 Campor, Alexander Priestley
Missionary Story Sketches: Folklore from Africa. Freeport, NYU: Books for Libraries Press, 1971. 346 pp. No ISBN.

Reprint of the 1909 edition (Cincinnati: Jennings and Grosham; New York: Eaton and Mains) revealing perceptions of African culture; by an African American missionary to Liberia of the Methodist Episcopal Church.

AF1280 Dunn, D. Elwood
A History of the Episcopal Church in Liberia, 1821-1980. (ATLA Monograph Series, 30). Metuchen, NJU: ATLA/Scarecrow Press, 1992. xxii, 477 pp. 0810825732.

A scholarly history, by a Liberian political scientist, of the Episcopal Church in Liberia, of its origins as a mission from the church in the United States, to 1980.

AF1281 Fadely, Anthony B.
Godpower in Africa. Cocoa, FLU: Fadelys and Associates, 1983. 120 pp. Paper. No ISBN.

A popular account of contemporary vitality and growth of the United Methodist Church in Liberia by one of its missionaries.

AF1282 Gifford, Paul
Christianity and Politics in Doe's Liberia. (Cambridge Studies in Ideology and Religion). New York, NYU: Cambridge University Press, 1993. xvi, 349 pp. 0521420296.

A comprehensive study of the sociopolitical function of Christianity in Liberia (mainline, evangelical, new Pentecostal, and independent) under the oppressive regime of Samuel K. Doe (1980-1990).

AF1283 Harley, Winifred J.
A Third of a Century with George Way Harley in Liberia. (Liberian Studies Monograph Series, 2). Newark, DEU: Liberian Studies Association in America, 1973. ii, 90 pp. No ISBN.

A popular account of a missionary doctor and his wife, living in a remote area of Africa.

AF1284 Holden, Edith
Blyden of Liberia: An Account of the Life and Labours of Edward Wilmot Blyden, LL.D. New York, NYU: Vantage Press, 1966. 1,040 pp. No ISBN.

A documentary biography of Edward Wilmot Blyden (1832-1912), scholar, diplomat, journalist, and educator, active as a Presbyterian minister in the church's mission in Liberia, and acclaimed as a father of African nationalism.

AF1285 Konkel, Wilbur
Jungle Gold: The Amazing Story of Sammy Morris, and True Stories of African Life. Salem, OHU: Schmul Publishing, 1993. 64 pp. 088019314X.

The story of Sammy Morris (1873-1893) and his mission to Liberia; originally published in 1966 (London, ENK: Pillar of Fire Press).

AF1286 Kulah, Arthur F.
Liberia Will Rise Again: Reflections on the Liberian Civil Crisis. Nashville, TNU: Abingdon, 1999. 112 pp. Paper. 0687075947.

Bishop Arthur Kulah perceptively tells the story of war with no plan for improvement, power with no purpose but survival, and rulers who ignore their people out of self interest; yet the story is filled with hope and the conviction that God still guides Christians, in times of war to prepare for peace.

AF1287 Oldfield, John R.
Alexander Crummell (1819-1898) and the Creation of an African-American Church in Liberia. (Studies in the History of Missions, 6). Lewiston, NYU: E Mellen Press, 1990. 165 pp. 0889460744.

A detailed biography of a remarkable Protestant Episcopal missionary to Liberia, 1853-1872, and analysis of his place as a leading black intellectual of the 19th century. .

AF1288 Scott, Dorothy E., and Ethel Trice, comps.
Ellen of Ka-Ka-Ta. Indianapolis, INU: By the authors, Dorothy E. Scott and Ethel Trice, 1985. 138 pp. Paper. No ISBN.

The saga of an African woman, Dr. Ellen Moore Hopkins, who, after training, returned to Liberia as a medical missionary of the Pentecostal Assemblies of the World.

AF1289 Stakeman, Randolph
The Cultural Politics of Religious Change: A Study of the Sanoyea Kpelle in Liberia. (African Studies, 3). Lewiston, NYU: E Mellen Press, 1986. 255 pp. 0889461775.

A detailed study, based on American Lutheran missionary accounts and unpublished documents, of the history and impact of the mission on Kpelle religion and society in central Liberia.

AF1290 Taryor, Nya Kwiawon, ed.
Justice, Justice: A Cry of My People. Chicago, ILU: Strugglers' Community Press, 1985. 319 pp. 0913491012 (hbk), 0913491004 (pbk).

A collection of speeches, papers, and important documents from the Movement for Justice in Africa (MOJA/Liberia), including essays on religion, church, and society in Liberia by the editor.

AF1291 Wold, Joseph Conrad
God's Impatience in Liberia. (Church Growth Series). Grand Rapids, MIU: Eerdmans, 1968. 227 pp. Paper. No ISBN.

An analysis of the slow growth among churches in Liberia, intertwining mission fact and theory, considering what has happened and what should happen.

Nigeria

See also EA252, ME149, CR572, CR574, CR592, CR601, CR961, CR994, CR1029-CR1030, SO129, SO279, SO302-SO304, SO327, SO362, SO629, SO648, EC348, CO12, ED41, EV98, AF352, AF1001, AF1209, and AM553.

AF1292 Adebiyi, Bayo
The Beloved Bishop: The Life of Bishop A. B. Akinyoele, DD, CBE, 1875-1968. Ibadan, NR: Daystar Press, 1969. 102 pp. No ISBN.

A popular biography of the beloved Anglican Bishop of Yorubaland in Nigeria.

AF1293 Agu, Charles Chikezie
Secularization in Igboland: Socio-Religious Change and Its Challenges to the Church among the Igbo. (Studies in the Intercultural History of Chistianity, 50). Frankfurt am Main, GW: Lang, 1989. 455 pp. Paper. 3820411542.

A thesis on the concept of secularization, a theological appraisal, the official reaction of the RCC, particularly at Vatican II, and applications among the Igbo of Eastern Nigeria.

AF1294 Aigbe, Sunday A.
Theory of Social Involvement: A Case Study in the Anthropology of Religion, State, and Society. Lanham, MDU: University Press of America, 1993. 266 pp. 0819188735.

A case study in Nigeria of the dynamic interplay between church, state, and society; with focus on the Pentecostal churches, including the Assemblies of God.

AF1295 Ajayi, J. F. A.
Christian Missions in Nigeria, 1841-1891: The Making of a New Elite. (Idaban History Series). Evanston, ILU: Northwestern University Press; London, ENK: Longmans, 1965. xvi, 317 pp. 0582645344.

A pioneer work on the sociopolitical evolution of Nigeria, and the role played by Christian missions in the evolution of new elites.

AF1296 Amu, J. W. Omo
The Rise of Christianity in Mid-Western Nigeria. Yaba, NR: Pacific Printers, 1965. 177 pp. No ISBN.

A short history of middle-belt Christianity in Nigeria.

AF1297 Arinze, Francis A.
Answering God's Call. London, ENK: Chapman, 1983. vi, 121 pp. Paper. 0225663244.

The Roman Catholic archbishop of Onitsha, Nigeria, on his church and the challenges to it.

AF1298 Atanda, J. A., ed.
Baptist Churches in Nigeria 1850-1950: Accounts of Their Foundation and Growth. Ibadan, NR: University Press, 1988. xlii, 318 pp. Paper. 978154984X.

A centennial history of Baptist work in Nigeria linked with the Southern Baptist Convention (US), with brief histories of more than 150 local congregations and associations.

AF1299 Ayandele, Emmanuel Ayankanmi
Holy Johnson: Pioneer of African Nationalism, 1836-1917. (Cass Library of African Studies, African Modern Library, 13). New York, NYU: Humanities Press; London, ENK: Cass, 1970. 417 pp. 0391000411 (US), 0714617431 (UK).

A scholarly biography of James Johnson who, as an Anglican minister, journalist, educationalist, legislator and author, both in his native Sierra Leone and in Nigeria, became one of the earliest fathers of Pan-Africanism.

AF1300 Ayandele, Emmanuel Ayankanmi
The Missionary Impact on Modern Nigeria, 1842-1914: A Political and Social Analysis. (Idaban History Series). London, ENK: Longmans, 1966. xx, 393 pp. No ISBN.

A critical study on the reaction of Nigerians to the early missionaries.

AF1301 Bowen, T. J.
Adventures and Missionary Labours in Several Countries in the Interior of Africa from 1849 to 1856. (Cass Library of African Studies, Missionary Researches and Travels, 3). London, ENK: Cass, 1968. 359 pp. No ISBN.

A facsimile reprint of the 1857 account by the pioneer Southern Baptist Convention (US) missionary to the Yoruba of Western Nigeria.

AF1302 Buchan, James
The Expendable Mary Slessor. Edinburgh, STK: Saint Andrew Press; New York, NYU: Seabury Press, 1980. xii, 253 pp. 0715204149 (UK, hdbk), 0715204386 (UK, pbk), 0816423202 (US, pbk).

A scholarly biography of Mary Mitchell Slessor (1848-1915), pioneer Scottish missionary in eastern Nigeria (Calabar), noted for her example of Christian inculturation as she lived simply with the people.

AF1303 Carroll, Kevin
Yoruba Religious Carving: Pagan and Christian Sculpture in Nigeria and Dahomey. London, ENK: Chapman, 1967. xii, 172 pp. No ISBN.

Comparative analysis of Yoruba and Benin traditional sculptures and their later Christian experiences.

AF1304 *Christian Responsibility in an Independent Nigeria: A Report Prepared for the Christian Council of Nigeria*
Idaban, NR: Christian Council of Nigeria, 1962. 126 pp. Paper. No ISBN.

Results of an important study, completed on the eve of Nigeria's independence, calling for the churches to be prophetic in politics and concerned about every aspect of human life.

AF1305 Cooke, Colman M.
Mary Charles Walker: The Nun of Calabar. Dublin, IE: Four Courts Press, 1980. 207 pp. No ISBN.

Biography of an Irish nun and her service in Nigeria.

AF1306 Crampton, Edmund Patrick
Christianity in Northern Nigeria. London, ENK: Chapman, 1979. xiii, 238 pp. Paper. 0225662558.

An examination of the development of Christianity, from the coming of the various missions to the establishment of indigenous churches; originally published in 1975 by Gaskiya Corporation, Zaria, Nigeria.

AF1307 Crowther, Samuel, and John Christopher Taylor
The Gospel on the Banks of the Niger: Journals and Notices of the Native Missionaries Accompanying the Niger Expedition of 1857-1859. (Colonial History Series). London, ENK: Dawsons, 1968. xi, 451 pp. 0712902864 (hdbk), 083700764X (pbk).

A reprint of the 1859 edition (London: Church Missionary House), containing certain records of the third (East) Niger Expedition.

AF1308 Decorvet, Jeanne
Samuel Ajayi Crowther: Un père de L'Église en Afrique noire. (Bibliothèque chrétienne de Poche: Foi Vivante, 309). Paris, FR: Éditions des Groupes Missionnaires; Paris, FR: Éditions du Cerf, 1992. 214 pp. Paper. 2880500494 (E), 2204047163 (C).

The first complete biography in French of Samuel Ajayi Crowther, the freed slave who became a pioneer Anglican missionary and bishop in West Africa.

AF1309 Dickson, Herbert W.
All the Days of My Life. Belfast, IE: Qua Iboe Mission, 1981. 190 pp. 0950765708.

Recollections of a Scottish missionary to Nigeria as told to Jean S. Corbett.

AF1310 Echewa, T. Obinkaram
The Land's Lord. (African Writers Series, 168). London, ENK: Heinemann Educational; Westport, CTU: Hill, 1976. 145 pp. 0435901680 (UK), 0882080695 (US, hdbk), 0882080709 (US, pbk).

A vivid fictional account of the Gospel among the Igbo of Nigeria, told as the story of an isolated Catholic missionary and his Igbo servant-cum-catechist.

AF1311 Ekechi, Felix K.
Missionary Enterprise and Rivalry in Igboland, 1857-1914.
London, ENK: Cass, 1971. xv, 298 pp. 071462778X.

The author's revised doctoral dissertation (University of Wisconsin, 1969) in which he traces and analyzes the history of rivalry and competition between various Protestant missions and the Roman Catholic Holy Ghost Fathers in Igboland (eastern Nigeria).

AF1312 Ekechi, Felix K.
Tradition and Transformation in Eastern Nigeria: A Sociopolitical History of Owerri and Its Hinterland, 1902-1947. Kent, OHU: Kent State University Press, 1989. xi, 256 pp. 0873383680 (hdbk), 0873383834 (pbk).

An analysis of the dynamics of social and political change in the Owerri division of Eastern Nigeria, from the establishment of British rule in 1902, to 1947; with special attention to the roles of Christian missions.

AF1313 Enang, Kenneth
Nigerian Catholics and the Independent Churches: A Call to Authentic Faith. (Nigerian Catholics and the Independent Churches: A Call to Authentic Faith, 45). Immensee, SZ: *NZM*, 2000. 240 pp. Paper. 385824080X.

Addressed primarily to the Catholics, the author seeks to bring back the "strayed sheep" to their "one and true fold in Christ."

AF1314 Epelle, Emmanuel M. Tobiah
Bishops in the Niger Delta. Aba, NR: Diocese of the Niger Delta, 1964. 196 pp. No ISBN.

Biographies of six bishops of the diocese (S. A. Crowther, Herbert Tugwell, James Johnson, A. W. Howells, T. C. John, and A. C. Onyeabo), plus a constitutional history of the Delta church.

AF1315 Falola, Toyin
Violence in Nigeria: The Crisis of Religious Politics and Secular Ideologies. Rochester, NYU: University of Rochester Press, 1998. xxi, 386 pp. 1580460186.

A comprehensive study of the major cases of violence in Nigeria in the 1980s and 1990s, their causes and consequences, and the links between religion and politics, including Christian-Muslim relations.

AF1316 Forristal, Desmond
The Second Burial of Bishop Shanahan. Dublin, IE: Veritas Publications, 1990. 329 pp. Paper. 1853901954.

The biography of Joseph Shanahan, C.S.Sp. (1871-1943), Holy Ghost Congregation missionary to southern Nigeria (1902-1932), who after his death was acclaimed as the leader and father of the great 20th-century Irish missionary movement.

AF1317 Fuller, Aletha B.
More Than a Memory: A True Story of Missionary Nursing Spanning Fifteen Years in the Bush Country of the Niger Delta in Eastern Nigeria, West Africa. San Angelo, TXU: Anchor Publishing, 1986. 473 pp. Paper. 0961608501.

A collection of correspondence describing the experiences of a Southern Baptist missionary nurse in the Nigerian bush country, 1952-1967.

AF1318 Gilliland, Dean S.
African Religion Meets Islam: Religious Change in Northern Nigeria. Lanham, MDU: University Press of America, 1986. vii, 241 pp. Paper. 0819156345 (hdbk), 0819156353 (pbk).

A study of the phenomenology of religious change among twenty ethnic groups in northern Nigeria describing the factors of religious conversion, levels of response among different ethnic groups, and degrees of accommodation.

AF1319 Graham, Sonia F.
Government and Mission Education in Northern Nigeria 1909-1919: With Special Reference to the Work of Hanns Vischer. Idaban, NR: Idaban University Press, 1966. xxvii, 192 pp. No ISBN.

An authoritative account of the early days of Western education in northern Nigeria, which throws an interesting light on mission and government policy.

AF1320 Grimley, John B., and Gordon E. Robinson
Church Growth in Central and Southern Nigeria. (Church Growth Series). Grand Rapids, MIU: Eerdmans, 1966. 386 pp. No ISBN.

An optimistic and forward-looking study by Protestant missionaries.

AF1321 Hackett, Rosalind I. J.
Religion in Calabar: The Religious Life and History of a Nigerian Town. (Religion and Society, 27). Berlin, GW: Mouton, 1989. xviii, 481 pp. 311011481X (GW), 0899253946 (US).

An extensive description of the various forms of religious expression, including a history of Calabar, traditional religions, and the integration of Christianity into this pluralistic society.

AF1322 Idowu, E. Bolaji
Towards an Indigenous Church. London, ENK: Oxford University Press, 1965. 60 pp. Paper. No ISBN.

An expansion, by the Professor of Religious Studies of the University of Ibadan, of three broadcast talks on "The Problem of the Indigenization of the Church in Nigeria."

AF1323 Ilesanmi, Simeon O.
Religious Pluralism and the Nigerian State. (Monographs in International Studies: Africa Series, 66). Athens, OHU: Ohio University Center for International Studies, 1997. xxxi, 299 pp. Paper. 0896801942.

The author proposes a new philosophy or model of religio-political interaction that he calls dialogical politics, suggesting that religious institutions become mediating structures between individual citizens searching for meaning and cultural identity, and the impersonal state.

AF1324 Ilogu, Edmund
Christianity and Ibo Culture. Leiden, NE: Brill, 1974. xvi, 262 pp. 9004040218.

A detailed study of the interaction between Christian ethics as presented by the missionaries and Ibo traditional morality, and of the resulting values of Ibo Christianity; also published as the author's Ph.D. dissertation at the Rijksuniversiteit in Leiden under the title *Christian Ethics in an African Background: A Study of the Interaction of Christianity and Ibo Culture.*

AF—AFRICA

AF1325 Johnson, James, and H. J. Ellis

Two Missionary Visits to Ijebu Country, 1892: Report on a Missionary Tour through a Portion of Ijebu-Remo, Made between 3rd and 29th August 1892. (Documents of Nigerian Church History,1). Ibadan, NR: Daystar Press, 1974. 86 pp. No ISBN.

This first sourcebook in a series on Nigerian church history includes reports by James ("Holy") Johnson (Anglican) and H. J. Ellis (Wesleyan).

AF1326 Johnston, Geoffrey

Of God and Maxim Guns: Presbyterianism in Nigeria, 1846-1966. (Editions in the Study of Religion, 8). Waterloo, ONC: Wilfrid Laurier University Press, 1988. iv, 321 pp. Paper. 0889201803.

A narrative history of Presbyterianism in Calabar, Nigeria, from the initial mission by Jamaicans in 1846, to 1977, emphasizing the interplay between the missionary tradition and the Nigerian response.

AF1327 Justin, Ukpong S.

Ibibio Sacrifices and Levitical Sacrifices. (Facultas Theologiae, 3328). Rome, IT: Pontificia Universitas Urbaniana, 1990. vii, 230 pp. Paper. No ISBN.

A detailed comparison of traditional practices of sacrifice by the Ibibio people of Nigeria, and Old Testament practices; originally presented as a doctoral dissertation at the Urbaniana Pontifical University.

AF1328 Kastfelt, Niels

Kulturmøde i Nigeria: Mødet mellem Bachamafolket, engelske koloniembedsmænd og Dansk Forenet Sudan Mission. Edited by Margit Warburg. Copenhagen, DK: Gad, 1981. 94 pp. 8712454168.

A narrative account of the work of the Danish United Sudan Mission among the Bachama people of Nigeria.

AF1329 Kastfelt, Niels

Religion and Politics in Nigeria: A Study in Middle Belt Christianity. London, ENK: British Academic Press, 1994. xii, 204 pp. 1850437882.

A scholarly study of the Protestant missions and churches of Adamawa Province in Nigeria's struggle for independence, 1940 to 1960.

AF1330 Kjær, Mogens

Mission teoretisk og praktisk. Christiansfeld, DK: Forlaget Savanne, 1983. 126 pp. 8785190985.

Theory and practice of mission in northern Nigeria.

AF1331 Kraft, Marguerite G.

Worldview and the Communication of the Gospel: A Nigerian Case Study. South Pasadena, CAU: William Carey Library, 1978. xvi, 220 pp. 0878083243.

A detailed case study of the Kamwo people of northeast Nigeria, demonstrating that sensitivity to the hearer's worldview is essential for effective Christian witness.

AF1332 Kulp, Mary Ann Moyer

No Longer Strangers: A Biography of H. Stover Kulp. Elgin, ILU: Brethren Press, 1968. 188 pp. No ISBN.

A popular biography of H. Stover Kulp (1894-1964), one of the founders of the Church of the Brethren Mission in northeastern Nigeria, where he served from 1923 to 1963.

AF1333 Ludwig, Frieder

Kirche im kolonialen Kontext: Anglikanische Missionare und afrikanische Propheten im südöstlichen Nigeria. (Studies in the Intercultural History of Christianity, 80). Frankfurt am Main, GW: Lang, 1992. 405 pp. Paper. 3631443625.

A study of the phases of Christianization in an Anglican mission area in southeast Nigeria, 1879-1918, with special attention to the African reaction and initiative in terms of freedom and emancipation.

AF1334 McKenzie, P. R.

Inter-Religious Encounters in West Africa. (Leicester Studies in Religion, 1). Leicester, ENK: University of Leicester, 1976. 115 pp. Paper. 0905510003.

A scholarly monograph on the complex attitudes toward other faiths of Bishop Ajayi Crowther (c.1806-1891), focusing on the period when he was superintendent of the Niger Mission of the CMS and first African bishop of the Anglican communion.

AF1335 Nissen, Margaret

An African Church Is Born: The Story of the Adamawa and Central Sardauna Provinces in Nigeria. Nigeria, NR: Betel & Partners, 1993. 254 pp. No ISBN.

Reprint of a recounting of the story, district by district, of the work of the Lutheran Church of Christ in the Sudan, which developed out of the Danish Sudan Mission, founded in 1911; originally published in 1968 (Viby, DK: Purups grafiske hus).

AF1336 Obielu, Clement Ngirikanwa

Ethnisch bedingte Probleme der Ausbreitung des Christentums in Nigeria: Unter besonder Berücksichtigung der katholischen Mission. Mainz, GW: Johannes Gutenberg University, 1982. viii, 283 pp. No ISBN.

A dissertation describing the development of Nigerian society, and discussing the different problems confronting the expansion of Christianity, which were mostly determined by ethnic and cultural factors.

AF1337 Oduyoye, Modupe

The Planting of Christianity in Yorubaland, 1842-1888. Ibaban, NR: Daystar Press, 1969. 77 pp. No ISBN.

A brief account of the beginnings of Christianity among the Yoruba, from the arrival of CMS missionaries in 1842, to the rise of African independent churches in 1888.

AF1338 Ogudo, Donatus Emeka Onyemaobi

The Catholic Missionaries and the Liturgical Movement in Nigeria: An Historical Overview. (The Holy Ghost Fathers and Catholic Worship among the Igbo People of Eastern Nigeria, 1). Paderborn, GW: Verlag Bonifatius-Druckerei, 1988. xiii, 318 pp. Paper. 3870885386.

The first volume of a detailed history, documenting strategies of the Holy Ghost Fathers (Spiritans) among the Igbo people of eastern Nigeria, used to increase their participation in the liturgy, prior to the reforms instituted by Vatican II.

AF1339 Ohadike, Don C.

Anioma: A Social History of the Western Igbo People. Athens, OHU: Ohio University Press, 1994. xx, 249 pp. 0821410725 (hdbk), 0821410733 (pbk).

A social history of the Western Igbo people of Nigeria, focusing on the interactions between a dynamic precolonial society, and European colonialism, including CMS and Roman Catholic missions.

AF—AFRICA

AF1340 Okereke, Gregory

The Laity and the Law: A Survey of the Legal Status of the Laity in the Nigerian Church, Towards the Relevance of Law in Evangelization within the Context of a Developing Country. (European University Studies, 23: Theology, 336). Frankfurt am Main, GW: Lang, 1989. 267 pp. Paper. 382041407X.

A detailed study of options for lay leadership in the RCC in Nigeria, including relevance for the church's task of evangelization.

AF1341 Okoh, Innocent Ekumauche

The Equitable Sustenance of Diocesan Priests in the Light of the Code of Canon Law and the Norms of the Catholic Bishops' Conference of Nigeria. (Facultas Iuris Canonici). Rome, IT: Pontificia Universitas Urbaniana, 1991. ixx, 261 pp. Paper. No ISBN.

A detailed study of policies and practices of the RCC in Nigeria, in the remuneration of parish priests; originally presented as a doctoral dissertation at the Urbaniana Pontifical University.

AF1342 Okolugbo, Emmanuel

A History of Christianity in Nigeria: The Ndosumili and the Ukwuani. Ibadan, NR: Daystar Press, 1984. 100 pp. Paper. 9781221801.

A history of Christianity among the Ndosumili and Ukwuani peoples of the Niger Delta (Mid-Western State) from 1841 to 1970.

AF1343 Omenka, Nicholas Ibeawuchi

The School in the Service of Evangelism: The Catholic Educational Impact in Eastern Nigeria, 1886-1950. (Studies on Religion in Africa, 6). Leiden, NE: Brill, 1989. xv, 317 pp. 9004086323.

A detailed study of the history of Catholic education in eastern Nigeria.

AF1344 Onuh, Charles Ok

Christianity and the Igbo Rites of Passage: The Prospects of Inculturation. (European University Studies, 23: Theology, 462). Frankfurt am Main, GW: Lang, 1992. xviii, 263 pp. Paper. 3631449747.

A case study among the Igbo of Nigeria of the value and strategic importance of adapting traditional rites of passage for the firm rooting of the Christian faith among Igbo youth.

AF1345 Rasmussen, Lissi

Religion and Property in Northern Nigeria: Socio-Economic Development and Islamic and Christian Influence in Northern Nigeria, with Special Reference to the Rights and Views of Property among the Birom and Kilba. (Studia Missionalia Upsaliensia, 52). Copenhagen, DK: Academic Press, 1990. 290 pp. Paper. 8750029444.

A Ph.D. thesis (University of Copenhagen, 1989) analyzing the impact of three religious traditions (African traditional religion, Islam, and Christianity), on understandings and use of property in the colonial and independent Nigeria periods, among the Kilba (Gongola) and Birom (Plateau) peoples of northern Nigeria.

AF1346 Reuke, Ludger

Die Maguzawa in Nordnigeria: Ethnographische Darstellung und Analyse des beginnenden Religionswandels zum Katholizismus. (Freiburger Studien zu Politik und Gesellschaft über-seeischer Länder, 4). Bielefeld, GW: Bertelsmann Universitätsverlag, 1969. 135 pp. No ISBN.

Taking the Maguzawa tribe in northern Nigeria as an example, the author shows, by means of careful ethnological and sociological enquiries, the real reasons why this tribe was converted to Catholicism.

AF1347 Rubingh, Eugene

Sons of Tiv: A Study of the Rise of the Church among the Tiv of Central Nigeria. Grand Rapids, MIU: Baker Books, 1969. 263 pp. No ISBN.

The history of the Tiv Church, founded by Dutch Reformed Church missionaries from South Africa, focusing on issues of communicating the Gospel, church and culture, and problems of partnership.

AF1348 Scheytt, Wilhelm, and René Gardi

Gavva. (Brennpunkte, 1). Basel, SZ: Basileia Verlag, 1965. 72 pp. No ISBN.

A documentary report on pioneering mission work in northern Nigeria.

AF1349 Smith, Edgar H.

Nigerian Harvest: A Reformed Witness to Jesus Christ in Nigeria, West Africa, in the Twentieth Century.... Grand Rapids, MIU: Baker Books, 1972. 318 pp. 0801079640.

A Reformed witness to Jesus Christ in Nigeria, West Africa, in the 420th century, including a detailed history of the missionary ministry of the Christian Reformed Church in the Benue Province, from 1940 to 1970.

AF1350 Smith, Frances

Towards a Living Church in a Changing African Society. (Pastoral Papers, 15). Kampala, UG: Gaba Publications, 1970. 95 pp. No ISBN.

An essay on the contextualization of the Catholic church in the Yoruba society of Nigeria.

AF1351 Tasie, Godwin O. M.

Christian Missionary Enterprise in the Niger Delta, 1864-1918. (Studies on Religion in Africa, 3). Leiden, NE: Brill, 1978. xiii, 287 pp. 9004052437.

A detailed analysis of pioneer mission work by Anglicans (CMS), Roman Catholics, and Wesleyan Methodists in Nigeria, based on primary sources, a selection of which is included as appendices.

AF1352 Turner, Harold W.

Profile through Preaching: A Study of the Sermon Texts Used in a West African Independent Church. (CWME Research Pamphlets, 13). London, ENK: Edinburgh House Press for the WCC, CWME, 1965. 86 pp. Paper. No ISBN.

Thorough field research into the beliefs and practices of the Aladura Church of Nigeria, comparing them with those of the Anglican Church.

AF1353 Wambutda, Daniel Nimcir

A Study of Conversion among the Angas of Plateau State of Nigeria with Emphasis on Christianity. (European University Studies, 23: Theology, 389). Frankfurt am Main, GW: Lang, 1991. 238 pp. 3820497803.

A historical and anthropological study of a northern Nigeria people, with a multi-factor analysis of their process of conversion to Christianity in the early 20th century.

AF1354 Wellman, Sam
Mary Slessor: Queen of Calabar. (Heroes of the Faith Series). Uhrichsville, OHU: Barbour Publishing, 1998. 207 pp. Paper. 157748178X.

Surrounded by warring tribes governed by witchcraft and tribal rites, Slessor served where few dared in 19th-century West Africa where she thrived on a contagious sense of humor, and medical and language skills.

AF1355 Wheatley, William Lord
Sunrise in Nigeria: A Record of Missionary Service from 1920 to 1952. Belfast, IE: Qua Iboe Mission, 1977. 107 pp. Paper. No ISBN.

Reminiscences by the author on twenty-five years of missionary service (1920-1945) among the Ibo people of Nigeria, under the auspices of the Qua Iboe Mission.

AF1356 Yusuf, Jolly Tanko
That We May Be One: The Autobiography of Nigerian Ambassador Jolly Tanko Yusuf. Edited by Lillian V. Grissen. Grand Rapids, MIU: Eerdmans, 1995. xvi, 123 pp. Paper. 0802841392.

The popular illustrated story of a first-generation Christian (from Islam), who rose to positions of national and international leadership in Nigeria; as told to Lillian V. Grissen.

AF1357 Zandstra, Gerald L., and Winabelle Gritter
Daughters Who Dared: Answering God's Call to Nigeria. Grand Rapids, MIU: Calvin Theological Seminary, 1992. 104 pp. Paper. 1562120182.

A popular account of five Christian Reformed Church missionaries and their pioneer mission work among the Kuteb people of Nigeria, from 1920 to 1940.

Senegal

AF1358 Gravrand, Henri
Visage africain de l'Église: Une Expérience au Sénégal. (Lumière et Nations). Paris, FR: Éditions de l'Orante, 1961. 287 pp. No ISBN.

Reflections on evangelization and contextualization by a Roman Catholic missionary who worked for twelve years in villages of Senegal.

Sierra Leone

See also AF1208 and AF1299.

AF1359 Cook, Herbert R.
One Man's Walk with God: A Lifetime of Christian Witness. Kalamazoo, MIU: Oak Woods Media, 1995. 294 pp. Paper. 0881960063.

Reminiscences of an Evangelical United Brethren lay educator who served in Sierra Leone, 1956-1957.

AF1360 Cox, Emmett D.
The Church of the United Brethren in Christ in Sierra Leone. South Pasadena, CAU: William Carey Library, 1970. xi, 171 pp. Paper. 0878083014.

A Fuller School of World Mission thesis, applying church growth principles in a historical analysis of the United Brethren in Christ mission in Sierra Leone.

AF1361 Fitzjohn, William H.
Chief Gbondo: A Sierra Leone Story. Ibadan, NR: Daystar Press, 1974. 80 pp. No ISBN.

The autobiography up to 1948 of an Evangelical United Brethren pastor turned politician and diplomat.

AF1362 Foster, Raymond Samuel
The Sierra Leone Church: An Independent Anglican Church. London, ENK: SPCK, 1961. 76 pp. Paper. No ISBN.

A firsthand account by a short-term missionary (1956-1959) of the challenges in selfhood and mission of the Anglican church in Sierra Leone.

AF1363 Giorgi, Gello
La Società secreta del Poro (Sierra Leone). (Studi e saggi, 6). Bologna, IT: Editrice Missionaria Italiana, 1977. 155 pp. No ISBN.

A systematic study of a secret male initiation society in Sierra Leone, by a missionary doctor who reveals important educational, social, political, and religious functions of the Poro.

AF1364 Gittins, Anthony J.
Mende Religion: Aspects of Belief and Thought in Sierra Leone. (Studia Instituti Anthropos, 41). Nettetal, GW: Steyler Verlag, 1987. 258 pp. Paper. 3805001711.

A scholarly study of the KpaMende region of Sierra Leone, including a general historical survey, and a discussion of belief systems, Mende spirituality, and the power structures of their culture.

AF1365 Gordon, Grant
From Slavery to Freedom: The Life of David George, Pioneer Black Baptist Minister. (Baptist Heritage in Atlantic Canada: Documents and Studies, 14). Hansport, NSC: Lancelot Press, 1992. xvii, 356 pp. Paper. 0889995060.

The biography of David George (1743-1810), the black Baptist preacher who pioneered in establishing congregations among his people in Nova Scotia (1782-1792) and Sierra Leone (1792-1810), with fifteen original source documents.

AF1366 O'Keefe, Donald Hugh
Mountain of the Lion: The Great Revival in Sierra Leone, West Africa. Hazelwood, MOU: Word Aflame Press, 1996. 237 pp. Paper. 1567221920.

A United Penticostal Church missionary, in Sierra Leone since 1974, recounts how revival came out of adversity to the church there.

AF1367 Olson, Gilbert W.
Church Growth in Sierra Leone: A Study of Church Growth in Africa's Oldest Protestant Mission Field. (Church Growth Series). Grand Rapids, MIU: Eerdmans, 1969. 222 pp. Paper. No ISBN.

A thesis on church growth based on missionary research among the congregations in Sierra Leone, where 67 percent of the descendants of the freed slaves are Protestant Christians, compared to only 2.1 percent of other inhabitants.

AF1368 Pawelzik, Fritz
Das Glück in der Tüte: Zu Besuch in Deutschland. (R. Brockhaus Taschenbuch, 842). Wuppertal, GW: R. Brockhaus Verlag, 1993. 207 pp. 3417208424.

This work describes the experience of a native of Sima in Freetown, and eventually, in Germany.

AF1369 Pratt, W. E. Akinumi
Autobiography. Edited by Gershon F. H. Anderson. Freetown, SL: Methodist Church in Sierra Leone, 1973. 71 pp. No ISBN.

Biography of the first President of the Sierra Leone Methodist Conference.

AF—AFRICA

AF1370 Reeck, Darrell
Deep Mende: Religious Interactions in a Changing African Rural Society. (Studies on Religion in Africa, Supplement 4). Leiden, NE: Brill, 1976. ix, 102 pp. 9004047697.

A historical analysis of the interaction, between Christianity, Islam, and traditional culture among the Mende of Sierra Leone since 1875, especially in districts of the United Methodist Church (former United Brethren in Christ).

AF1371 Wyse, Akintola
The Krio of Sierra Leone: An Interpretive History. London, ENK: Hurst, 1989. xiv, 156 pp. 1850650314.

A history of the Creole people of Sierra Leone, from their early 19th-century migration from Nova Scotia and Jamaica, to the 1980s.

Togo

AF1372 Debrunner, Hans W.
A Church between Colonial Powers: A Study of the Church in Togo. Translated by Dorothea M. Burton. (World Studies of Churches in Mission). London, ENK: Lutterworth Press, 1965. xi, 368 pp. No ISBN.

A scholarly case study of the Evangelical Church of Togo, including its development out of the German Bremen and French Paris missions, the influence of three colonial powers (Great Britain, Germany, and France), the indigenous characteristics of the church, with an assessment of future prospects.

AF1373 Müller-Felsenburg, Alfred
Architekt Gottes: Leben und Werk des Bruders Johannes Hopfer SVD (1856-1936), Steyler Missionar und Baumeister in Togo/Afrika. (Gelebter Glaube, 2). Nettetal, GW: Steyler Verlag, 1985. 172 pp. Paper. 3877871909.

A popular biography of a pious and industrious SVD missionary brother, architect of the cathedral in Lomé, Togo.

AF1374 Müller, Karl
Geschichte der Katholischen Kirche in Togo. (Veröffentlichungen des Missionspriesterseminars, 4). Kaldenkirchen, GW: Steyler Verlag, 1958. 573 pp. No ISBN.

A history of the Roman Catholic Church in Togo.

AF1375 Müller, Karl
Histoire de l'église catholique au Togo, 1892-1967. Translated by G. Athanasiades. Lomé, TG: Librarie Bon Pasteur, 1968. 251 pp. Paper. No ISBN.

French translation and abridged edition of *Geschichte der Katholischen Kirche in Togo* (1958).

THE AMERICAS

H. McKennie Goodpasture (General Works, Mexico, Mesoamerica), Andrew Walls (The Caribbean, Canada, Native America), Eduardo Bierzychudek (South America), Subeditors

The Americas are becoming an increasingly self-conscious region of the world. Politically, they affirm their interconnectedness through the Organization of American States (OAS). The United States includes a Latin American territory, Puerto Rico, within its governance. In economics, the North and South (Americas) are increasingly interdependent. The North American Free Trade Agreement (NAFTA) links Canada, Mexico, and the United States, with other nations considering applying for membership. Socially, the movements of peoples have brought millions of immigrants and migrants from Latin America to the United States. The frontiers of mission today include ministries to these peoples. For these reasons, two continents are grouped in this chapter on "The Americas."

In 2000, the combined population of the Americas reached over 827 million. Of this number, over 480 million lived in North America, and almost 347 million live in 51 independent countries in South America (*World Book Encyclopedia,* 2000).

These are the most Christianized continents of the world today. Organized Christianity in 2000, according to the *WCE,* included more than 687 million adherents in the Americas, or 83.1 percent of the total population. Proportions by confessional groups are as follows: Roman Catholic 77.4 percent, Protestant 17.2 percent, Anglican

0.6 percent, and Orthodox 1.0 percent. "Independents" form the most rapidly growing bloc of Christians, in 6,406 denominations in 48 countries. "Marginal Christians" are 2.5 percent of the total. High religious mobility is evident in a total of 171 million persons *doubly affiliated*—baptized in two or more denominations (*WCE* 1:12).

Works on mission history, or church history, are to be found in several subsections. General works are grouped together. Those on subregions will be found in the "General" sections for each region. Others will be found under specific countries in this chapter, or under particular mission orders or societies in the chapter, "Missions: History."

Issues of "Church and Society" provide rich literature. Since "Latin American Theologies" contain many missional themes, they are included in this bibliography. See also the "Missions: Theology" chapter with its subsections on "Liberation," "Feminist/Womanist," and "Third World Theologies."

Countries of the region have been grouped as follows: Canada, Caribbean, Mesoamerica [Central America], South America, and the USA. The latter contains subsections on urban mission, ethnic minority missions (African American, Asian American, Hispanic American), missions to immigrants, and Native American missions.

Norman E. Thomas

Bibliographies

See also GW2, ED1, and AM700.

AM1 Bierzychudek, Eduardo, ed.

Bibliografía Teológica Comentada del Área Iberoamericana: Vol. 1 (1973)-. Annual. Buenos Aires, AG: ISEDET, 1973-. ISSN 03266680.

A comprehensive bibliography, with many entries annotated, on Latin American, Spanish, and Portuguese Christianity; project directed by Eduardo Bierzychudek.

AM2 Cardenas, Francisco José, and Maria Elena Cardenas, comps.

Author Index to Handbook of Latin American Studies, Nos. 1-28, 1936-1966. Gainesville, FLU: University of Florida, 1968. vi, 421 pp. No ISBN.

A cumulative author index to the first twenty-eight numbers of the *Handbook of Latin American Studies,* which includes over 50,000 entries, including many works on missionary activity.

AM3 Fenton, Thomas P., and Mary J. Heffron, eds.

Latin America and Caribbean: A Directory of Resources. Maryknoll, NYU: Orbis Books, 1986. xvi, 142 pp. Paper. 0862326370 (hbk), 0862326389 (pbk).

An annotated catalog of organizations, books, periodicals, pamphlets, audiovisuals, and other resources; listing academic, church, and other agencies and study centers, with focus on social justice concerns.

AM4 Library of Congress, Hispanic Division

Human Rights in Latin America, 1964-1980: A Selective Annotated Bibliography. Washington, DCU: Library of Congress, 1983. x, 257 pp. 0844404152.

Provides annotated bibliographic entries for a wide range of subjects related to human rights, such as the church, the OAS, and US policy; with a list of human rights organizations and an author index.

AM5 Pérez Fernández, Isacio

Inventario Documentado de los Escritos de Fray Bartolomé de las Casas. Edited by Helen Rand Parish. (Estudios monográficos, 1). Bayamón, PR: Centro de Estudios de los Dominicos del Caribe, 1981. xvi, 928 pp. 8430047336.

A chronological bibliography, including correspondence, of Bartolomé de Las Casas, a 16th-century missionary to Latin America.

AM6 Sinclair, John H., ed.

Protestantism in Latin America: A Bibliographical Guide. South Pasadena, CAU: William Carey Library, 1976. xxv, 414 pp. Paper. 0878081267.

This annotated bibliography of selected references, mainly in English, Spanish, and Portuguese, contains useful bibliographical aids to assist both the student and researcher in the general field of Latin American studies; replaces the 1967 edition.

AM7 Turner, Frederick C.

The Church in Latin America: A Bibliography. Stoors, CTU: University of Connecticut, 1972. 40 pp. No ISBN.

A brief forty-page bibliography on the subject.

AM8 University of Texas at Austin: Library, Latin American Collection

Catalog of the Latin American Collection. Boston, MAU: G K Hall, 1969. 31 vols. No ISBN.

Photo-offset reproduction of over 175,000 entries of the catalog of the Latin American collection; especially strong in Mexican materials, with author, subject, and title cards arranged alphabetically.

AM9 Weigle, Marta

A Penitente Bibliography. Albuquerque, NMU: University of New Mexico, 1976. xiv, 162 pp. 082630401X.

An extensive bibliography of over 1,200 writings, both popular and scholarly, on the Brotherhood of Our Father Jesus, a long-standing folk religious movement among Mexican Americans.

Serials and Periodicals

AM10 *Caribbean Journal of Religious Studies.* Vol. 1, no. 1 (Sept. 1975)-. Semiannual

Kingston, JM: United Theological College of the West Indies, 1975-. ISSN 0253066X.

A forum for discussion of religious and pastoral issues affecting the life of Caribbean peoples.

AM11 *LADOC.* Vol. 1, no. 1 (June 1970)-. Monthly (June 1970-May 1975); bimonthly (Nov.-Dec. 1975-)

Washington, DCU: USCC, 1970-1997; Lima, PE: Latin American Documentation, 1998-. ISSN 03603350.

Documentation on church and society issues in Latin America.

Documentation and Archives

See also HI316, ED172, EV17, AM11, AM259, AM868, AM887-AM888, and AM891.

AM12 Bishops' Commission for Social Action, Lima

Between Honesty and Hope: Documents from and about the Church in Latin America. Translated by John Drury. (Maryknoll Documentation Series). Maryknoll, NYU: Maryknoll Publications, 1970. xxiv, 247 pp. Paper. No ISBN.

Documents by bishops, priests, and laypeople, originally published in Peru, to acquaint a wider audience with how the Roman Catholic Church has been involved in reforming an unjust and inhuman world since Vatican II.

AM13 Gispert-Sauch, Ana, ed.

Signos de Vida y Fidelidad: Testimonios de la Iglesia en América Latina, 1978-1982. (CEP, 50). Lima, PE: CEP, 1983. 563 pp. Paper. No ISBN.

Anthology of Catholic and Protestant statements addressing specific and/or ecclesial situations in Latin America.

AM14 González, Angel Martín

Gobernación Espiritual de Indias: Código Ovandino, libro Io. (Publicaciones del Instituto Teológico Salesiano, 18/ Colección histórica, 4). Guatemala, GT: Instituto Teológico Salesiano, 1978. xlviii, 345 pp. No ISBN.

A reprint of the Book of Church Government, used by Spain in Latin America in the 16th century; with an analysis of its laws and subsequent developments through the 19th century.

AM15 Grieb, Kenneth J. et al., eds.

Research Guide to Central America and the Caribbean. Madison, WIU: University of Wisconsin Press, 1985. xv, 431 pp. 0299100502.

Eighty-three articles which describe major archival depositories of research centers; with essays that suggest further directions for research.

AM16 Gutiérrez, Gustavo et al.

Signos de Renovación: Recopilación de documentos post-conciliares de la Iglesia en América Latina. Lima, PE: Editorial Universitaria, 1969. 262 pp. Paper. No ISBN.

A collection of ecclesiastical documents, focusing on the Church in the midst of the process of change happening in Latin America, the renewal of the church, and the Medellín Conference.

AM17 Hanke, Lewis, and Jane M. Rausch, eds.

People and Issues in Latin American History: The Colonial Experience—Sources and Interpretations. New York, NYU: Markus Wiener Publishing, 1993. xi, 356 pp. 155876061X.

Revised edition of *History of Latin American Civilization: Sources and Interpretations*, vol. 1 (Little, Brown and Co., 1967), containing original source documents on colonialism, including missions; with interpretive introductions by the editors.

AM18 Hoyo, Eugenio del
Indios, Frailes y Encomenderos en el Nuevo Reino de León: Siglos XVII y XVIII. Monterrey, MX: Archivo General del Estado de Nuevo León, 1985. 247 pp. No ISBN.

A sourcebook of documents from 1622 to 1784 on missions to the Indians in New Spain (Mexico).

AM19 John Paul II, Pope et al.
V Centenario. (Nuevo Mundo, 40). San Antonio de Padua, AG: Nuevo Mundo, 1990. 320 pp. No ISBN.

A monograph with twenty-six documents, historical studies, and proposals for new evangelization of the future, including John Paul II's encyclical, *Redemptoris missio.*

AM20 Las Casas, Bartolomé de
Bartolomé de las Casas: The Only Way. Edited by Helen Rand Parish. Translated by Francis Sullivan. (Sources of American Spirituality). New York, NYU: Paulist Press, 1992. vi, 282 pp. 0809103672.

A critical edition, with new translation, of the pioneer missionary to the Indies' first work, *The Only Way to Draw All People to a Living Faith*; with a biographical introduction on "Las Casas' Spirituality: The Three Crises."

AM21 Las Casas, Bartolomé de
Brevísima relación de la destrucción de las Indias. Edited by André Saint-Lu. (Letras hispánicas, 158). Madrid, SP: Catedra, 1989. 186 pp. 8437603412.

In this, the most famous of his short treatises written in 1542, Bartolomé de Las Casas, O.P. (1474-1566) condemned the cruelty of the conquistadores in his campaign for new laws to protect indigenous peoples of the Caribbean.

AM22 Las Casas, Bartolomé de
History of the Indies. Translated by Andrée Collard. (A Torchbook Library Edition). New York, NYU: Harper & Row, 1971. 302 pp. 0061315400.

Greatly abridged translation of Las Casas' *Historia de las Indias*, based on the 1951 Spanish edition by Augustin Millares Carlo.

AM23 Las Casas, Bartolomé de
In Defense of the Indians: The Defense of the Most Reverend Lord, Don Fray Bartolomé de Las Casas, of the Order of Preachers, Late Bishop Chiapa.... Edited by Stafford Poole. DeKalb, ILU: Northern Illinois University Press, 1992. xxvi, 385 pp. Paper. 0875805566.

A new critical translation by Stafford Poole, from the 1552 Latin manuscript of the pioneer missionary's famous defense of the Indians, "against the persecutors and slanderers of the peoples of the New World discovered across the seas."

AM24 Las Casas, Bartolomé de
Kurzgefasster Bericht von der Verwustung der Westindischen Länder. Edited by Hans Magnus Enzensberger. Translated by D. W. Andrea. (Insel Taschenbuch, 553). Frankfurt am Main, GW: Insel·Verlag, 1981. 152 pp. Paper. 3458322531.

German translation.

AM25 Las Casas, Bartolomé de
Obras completas. (Fundación "Instituto Bartolomé deLas Casas," de los dominicos de Andalucía). Madrid, SP: Alianza, 1988-1998. 14 vols. 8420640751 (set).

A critical edition of fourteen volumes of the complete works of Bartolomé de Las Casas [vol. 1, *Vida y obras*, by Alvaro Huerga; vol. 2, *De único vocationis modo*; vols. 3-5, *Historia de las Indias*; vols. 6-8, *Apologética historia sumaria*, ed. Vidal Abril Castelló, et al.; vol. 9, *Apologia*, ed. Angel Losada; vol. 10, *Tratados de 1552, impresa por las casas en Seville*, ed. Ramón Hernández and Lorenzo Gálmes; vol. 11, *De thesauris*, by Angel Losada; vol. 12, *De regia potestate*, ed. Jaime González Rodríguez; vol. 13 *Cartas y memoriales*, ed. Paulino Castañeda; vol. 14, *Diario del primer y tercer viaje de Cristóbal Colón*, ed. Consuelo Varela].

AM26 Las Casas, Bartolomé de
Une plume à la force d'un glaive: lettres choisies. Edited by Charles Gillen. Paris, FR: Éditions du Cerf, 1996. 412 pp. Paper. 2204053538.

Selected letters by the noted Dominican 16th-century missionary to the Americas, revealing his passion for justice and human rights.

AM27 Las Casas, Bartolomé de
A Selection of His Writings. Translated by George Sanderlin. (Borzoi Books on Latin America). New York, NYU: Knopf, 1971. x, 209 pp. 039446978X, 0394315375 text ed.

Translated selections from Las Casas' *Historia de las Indias*, *Apologetica Historia*, and various shorter writings.

AM28 Las Casas, Bartolomé de
Très brève relation de la destruction des Indes. Translated by Franchita Gonzalez Batlle. (La Découverte, 6). Paris, FR: Maspero, 1981. 155 pp. Paper. 2707111147.

French translation.

AM29 Las Casas, Bartolomé de
Werkauswahl. Edited by Mariano Delgado. Paderborn, GW: Ferdinand Schöningh, 1994-. 4 vols.

A four-volume collection, in German, of the writings of Las Casas [Band 1: *Missionstheologische Schriften*, 1994, 456 pp., 3506751212; Band 2: *Historische und ethnographische Schriften*, 1995, 527 pp., 3506751220].

AM30 Las Casas, Bartolomé de
Witness: Writings of Bartolomé de Las Casas. Edited by George Sanderlin. Maryknoll, NYU: Orbis Books, 1992. xxii, 182 pp. Paper. 0883447908.

An anthology of the work of the 16th-century defender of the Indians; originally published as *Bartolomé de Las Casas* (New York: Knopf, 1971).

AM31 Leuridan, Juan et al., eds.
Signos de Liberación: Testimonios de la Iglesia en América Latina, 1969-1973. (CEP, 8). Lima, PE: CEP, 1973. 291 pp. Paper. No ISBN.

Anthology of documents published by Catholics and Protestants, addressing critical social and/or ecclesial situations in Latin America.

AM32 Limpic, Ted
Catálogo de Organizaciones Misioneras Iberoamericanas. Miami, FLU: Editorial Unilit/COMIBAM International, 1997. 211 pp. Paper. 0789904403.

This reference work is divided into three sections: a list of missionary organizations, a list of countries where Latin American missionaries serve, and a collection of statistics and graphs.

AM—THE AMERICAS

AM33 Lora, Carmen et al., eds.
Signos de Lucha y Esperanza: Testimonios de la Iglesia en América Latina, 1973-1978. (CEP, 25). Lima, PE: CEP, 1978. xlii, 356 pp. Paper. No ISBN.

Anthology of Catholic and Protestant statements addressing extreme social and/or ecclesial situations in Latin America.

AM34 Marins, José, Teolide Maria Trevisan, and Carolee Chanona
Praxis de los Padres de América Latina: Documentos de las Conferencias Episcopales de Medellín a Puebla (1968-1978). Bogotá, CK: Ediciones Paulinas, 1978. 1191 pp. Paper. No ISBN.

A collection of 114 texts on the church in Latin America and its activity in such areas as evangelization, human rights, social justice, etc.

AM35 Otte, Enrique, and James Lockhart, eds.
Letters and People of the Spanish Indies, Sixteenth Century. (Cambridge Latin American Studies, 22). Cambridge, ENK: Cambridge University Press, 1976. xiii, 267 pp. 0521208831 (hdbk), 0521099900 (pbk).

Thirty-eight letters from Spanish and some Indian participants in the first conquest, concerning various aspects of later colonial life, and the affairs of church and government; translated by the editors.

AM36 Perena Vincente, Luciano
La Carta Magna de los Indios: Comunidad hispánica de naciones (1534-1609). (Catedra V Centenario, 1). Salamanca, SP: Pontificia Universidad de Salamanca, 1987. xv, 296 pp. Paper. 8472991962.

A 16th-century essay on the project of colonial Indian reconversion, in light of the protests by Francisco de Vitoria and the recoveries of the school of Salamanca.

AM37 Prien, Hans-Jürgen, ed.
Lateinamerika: Gesellschaft, Kirche, Theologie. Göttingen, GW: Vandenhoeck & Ruprecht, 1981. 2 vols. Paper. 3525553811 (vol. 1), 3525553838 (vol. 2), 3525553846 (set).

While volume 1 of this study analyzes the development of Latin America, 1965 to 1979, from the economic, political, ecclesiastical, and social perspectives, as exemplified by Cuba, Chile, Argentinia, and Brazil, volume 2 deals with the Document of Puebla and the development of liberation theology [vol. 1: 346 pp.; vol. 2: 254 pp.].

AM38 Remesal, Antonio de
Historia General de las Indias Occidentales y particular de la Gobernación de Chiapa y Guatemala. ([Biblioteca Guatemalteca de cultura popular, 91-94 (Guat); Biblioteca Porrúa, 89-90 (Mex)]). Guatemala City, GT: Jose de Pineda Ibarra; México City, MX: Editorial Porrúa, 1988. 4 vols. 9684522800 (set/E), 9684522819 (v.1 /E), 9684522827 (v.2 /E).

First published in 1620 under the title *Historia*, one of the most important accounts of Dominican beginnings and friendly relations between the Indians and the missionaries, led by the Dominican bishop de Las Casas, in contrast to the hostility of the Spaniards.

AM39 Rogel, Isaac, comp.
Documentos sobre la Realidad de la Iglesia en América Latina, 1968-1969. (Sondeos, 54). Cuernavaca, ME: CIDOC, 1970. 410 pp. No ISBN.

A collection of articles concerning the life of the church in Latin America, including episcopal statements and other documents.

AM40 Sauer, Sabine
Gottes streibare Diener für Amerika: Missionsreisen im Spiegel der ersten Briefe niederländischer Jesuiten (1616-1618). (Weltbild und Kulturbegegnung, 4). Pfaffenweiler, GW: Centaurus-Verlagsgesellschaft, 1992. 114 pp. Paper. 3890857329.

A critical edition of the first letters by Dutch Jesuits from the Americas, 1616-1618, together with maps and illustrations, revealing observations of the people and their customs.

AM41 Serra, Juníper
Writings of Junípero Serra. Edited by Antonine Tibesar. Washington, DCU: Academy of American Franciscan History, 1966. 4 vols. No ISBN.

Letters and other documents, in Spanish and English, of the 18th-century Franciscan missionary to Mexico and California, noted for founding the historic chain of nine missions on the West Coast; with notes, bibliography, and index.

AM42 *Signos de Nueva Evangelización: Testimonios de la Iglesia en América Latina, 1983-1987*
(CEP, 92). Lima, PE: CEP, 1988. xxiii, 575 pp. No ISBN.

A collection of documents from Latin America concerning issues affecting, or being addressed by, the Roman Catholic Church in the 1980s.

AM43 Taylor, Clyde W., and Wade T. Coggins, eds.
Protestant Missions in Latin America: A Statistical Survey. Washington, DCU: Evangelical Foreign Missions Association, 1961. xxvi, 314 pp. No ISBN.

Twenty-three separate maps, along with statistics on all Latin American and Caribbean countries; covering primarily conservative evangelical missions, with lists of missionary bodies and addresses of some national churches.

AM44 Vitoria, Francisco de
Obras de Francisco de Vitoria: Relecciones Teológicas. Edited by Teófilo Urdanoz. Madrid, SP: Biblioteca de Autores Cristianos, 1960. viii, 1,386 pp. No ISBN.

A critical edition of the writings of Francisco de Vitoria (c.1483-1546), Spanish Dominican theologian and international jurist, who made major contributions to international law, just-war theory, and was a staunch advocate of the rights of Native Americans living under Spanish colonial rule; with a biographical introduction by the editor.

History

See also HI118-HI119, HI128, HI181, HI248, HI645, SO203, PO137, PO145, ED171, ED179, EV132-EV133, AM17, AM180, AM304, AM322, AM360, AM476, and AM497.

AM45 *500 Años: Presencia christiana en América Latina y el Caribe*
Quito, EC: CLAI, 1991. 62 pp. Paper. No ISBN.

A workbook designed for use with local church groups to promote discussion of historical facts of the past 500 years, traditions, legends, and memories of evangelization of the Christian churches in Latin America and the Caribbean, each including a biblical commentary, life application, questions, and liturgical props.

AM46 Aubert, Jean Marie, Jean Comby, and Bruno A. Van der Maat, eds.

1492-1992: Conquête et évangile en Amérique latine: Questions pour l'Europe aujourd'hui. Lyons, FR: Profac, 1992. 323 pp. Paper. 2853170462.

Papers of an important colloquy on "1492-1992: Conquest and the Gospel in Latin America," including papers by prominent Third World Catholic theologians (Beozzo, Gutiérrez, Mveng, Panikkar, etc.).

AM47 Barbieri, Sante Uberto

Land of Eldorado. New York, NYU: Friendship Press, 1961. xiii, 161 pp. LC61-6628.

A general sketch of Protestantism in Latin America, its history, and situation in 1960; prepared as a mission study book.

AM48 Barbieri, Sante Uberto

El País de Eldorado. Buenos Aires, AG: Editorial La Aurora, 1962. xiii, 129 pp. No ISBN.

Spanish translation,

AM49 Bastian, Jean-Pierre

Le protestantisme en Amérique latine: une approche socio-historique. (Histoire et Société, 27). Geneva, SZ: Éditions Labor et Fides, 1994. 324 pp. Paper. 2830906845.

A social history of 500 years of Protestantism in Latin America, by the professor of sociology of religions at the University of Humane Sciences in Strasbourg, France.

AM50 Bastian, Jean-Pierre

Protestantismo y Modernidad Latinoamericana: Historia de unas minorías religiosas activas en América Latina. Translated by José Esteban Calderón. Mexico D.F, MX: Fondo de Cultura Económica, 1994. 351 pp. Paper. 9681644573.

Spanish translation.

AM51 Belli, Gioconda et al., eds.

1492-1992: La Interminable Conquista: Emancipación e Identidad de América Latina, 1492-1992. (Nuestra América frente al V Centenario, 2). San José, CR: DEI, 1991. 304 pp. Paper. 9977830371.

Fifteen Latin American theologians and church leaders present, in short essays, their evaluation of 500 years of Western oppression of the continent, as their contribution to the international study, "Emancipación e Identidad de América Latina: 1492-1992."

AM52 Bethell, Leslie, ed.

The Cambridge History of Latin America. New York, NYU: Cambridge University Press, 1984. 11 vols. 0521232236.

A scholarly history of Latin America, from 1492 to 1990; with extensive regional coverage since 1930, including mission history, and a volume of bibliographical essays [vols. 1-2: *Colonial Latin America* (1984, 0521232236 (v. 1), 0521245168 (v. 2)); vol. 3: *From Independence to c1870* (1985, xv, 945 pp., 0521232244); vol. 4: *c1870 to 1930* (1986, xviii, 676 pp., 0521232252); vol. 5: *c1870 to 1930* (1986, xviii, 951 pp., 0521245176); vol. 6: *Latin America since 1930: Economy, Society, and Politics*; vol. 7: *Latin America since 1930: Mexico, Central America, and the Caribbean* (1990, xiv, 775 pp., 0521245184); vol. 8: *Latin America since 1930: Spanish South America* (1991, 0521266521); vol. 10: *Latin America since 1930: Ideas, Culture, and Society* (1995, xiv, 645 pp., 0521495946); vol. 11: *Bibliographical Essays*].

AM53 Boff, Leonardo, and Virgilio P. Elizondo, eds.

1492-1992: The Voices of the Victims. London, ENK: SCM Press; Philadelphia, PAU: Trinity Press International, 1990. xiii, 151 pp. Paper. 0334030056.

Eleven short essays, mainly by Latin American theologians, reflecting on the fifth centenary of the European conquest of the Americas, from the perspective of the victims: the social injustices done to them, their demand for recognition, and their original contribution to the human race and to the church.

AM54 Borges Morán, Pedro

El Envío de Misioneros a América durante la Epoca Española. (Biblioteca Salmanticensis, 18). Salamanca, SP: Universidad Pontificia, 1977. 595 pp. 8460009475.

A study of the sending of missionaries to the Americas, from the 16th to the 19th centuries.

AM55 Borges Morán, Pedro

Misión y Civilización en América. Madrid, SP: Editorial Alhambra, 1987. 296 pp. Paper. 842051568X.

A historical study of the relationship that existed between evangelism and the human advancement of the indigenous peoples of America.

AM56 Brufau Prats, Jaime, Joachim G. Piepke et al.

Evangelización y Cultura en la América del siglo XVI: Población y evangelización en Hispanoamérica. (Estudios de Misionología, 7-8). Burgos, SP: Ediciones Aldecoa, 1987. 317 pp. 8470092677.

A collection of papers concerning the coming of Christianity and European civilization to the Americas and the Philippines in the 16th century.

AM57 Bruno, Cayetano

El Derecho Público de la Iglesia en Indias: Estudio histórico-jurídico. Salamanca, SP: Consejo Superior de Investigaciones Científicas, 1967. xiv, 347 pp. No ISBN.

A study of the civil and church laws, both indigenous and imported, affecting the native populations, from the 16th to the 18th centuries, in Latin America.

AM58 Burrus, Ernest J., ed.

Homenaje a Don José de la Peña y Camara. Madrid, SP: José Porrua Turanzas, 1969. xi, 288 pp. No ISBN.

A *festschrift* in English and Spanish, containing fourteen scholarly essays on the history of Latin America, including mission history; to honor the Director of the Indias Archives in Seville.

AM59 Capdevila, Nestor

Las Casas une politique de l'humanité: L'homme et l'empire de la foi. (Passages). Paris, FR: Éditions du Cerf, 1998. 380 pp. Paper. 2204058327.

A detailed reflection on how Las Casas (1484-1566) was able to defend the rights of Native Americans within the limits of Spanish Catholic ideology, which legitimated conquest in the Americas.

AM60 CEHILA, I Encuentro Latinoamericano, Quito, EC, 1973

Para una Historia de la Iglesia en América Latina. (El Sentido de la Historia, 10). Barcelona, SP: Editorial Nova Terra, 1975. 324 pp. Paper. 8428008329.

A collection of the meeting's papers, with bibliographic studies, and suggestions for systematic area examination of the history of Catholic and Protestant churches.

AM—THE AMERICAS

AM61 CEHILA, II Encuentro Latinoamericano, Chiapas, MX, 1974
Bartolomé de Las Casas (1474-1974) e Historia de la Iglesia en América Latina. (El Sentido de la Historia, 11). Barcelona, SP: Editorial Nova Terra, 1976. 298 pp. Paper. 8428005826.

A collection of eight addresses on Las Casas, and other information about the meeting.

AM62 Congreso Teológico Internacional, Instituto Bartolomé de Las Casas, ed.
Las Casas entre dos Mundos. Lima, PE: Instituto Bartolomé de Las Casas/CEP, 1993. 433 pp. No ISBN.

Lectures given at the International Theological Congress for Theology (Lima, Perú, 1992) on the theme "Las Casas Between Two Worlds."

AM63 Costello, Gerald M.
Mission to Latin America: The Successes and Failures of a Twentieth Century Crusade. Maryknoll, NYU: Orbis Books, 1979. xii, 307 pp. 0883443120.

A study by a Catholic journalist of the response of the US Catholic Church to Pope John XXIII's call in 1961 for priests and religious to serve in Latin America, analyzing the reasons why those who went accomplished little.

AM64 Dussel, Enrique D., ed.
The Church in Latin America: 1492-1992. Tunbridge Wells, ENK: Burns & Oates; Maryknoll, NYU: Orbis Books, 1992. x, 501 pp. 0860121801 (UK), 0883448203 (US).

A collaborative history of the church in Latin America, including a chronological survey, regional surveys, and chapters on special topics; produced under the aegis of CEHILA, drawing on its eleven-volume general history that is being published in Spanish.

AM65 Dussel, Enrique D.
Les évêques hispano-américains: Défenseurs et évangélisateurs de l'Indien, 1504-1620. (Veröffentlichungen des Instituts für Europaische Geschichte Mainz, 58). Wiesbaden, GW: Franz Steiner Verlag, 1970. lxi, 286 pp. No ISBN.

A detailed study, based on archival records, of the Catholic bishops in Latin America in the 16th and 17th centuries, with special attention to the issue of their sensitivity to the concerns of indigenous peoples.

AM66 Dussel, Enrique D.
El Episcopado Latinoamericano y la Liberación de los Pobres, 1504-1620. (Historia Latinoamericana, 6). Mexico City, MX: CRT, 1979. 442 pp. Paper. No ISBN.

A documentary study of biographies of bishops, and the history of Hispanic American councils and synods, that reveal testimonies for the option for the indigenous, poor and oppressed in spite of the interests of the Spanish crown from 1504 to 1620.

AM67 Dussel, Enrique D.
Die Geschichte der Kirche in Lateinamerika. Mainz, GW: Matthias-Grünewald-Verlag, 1988. 435 pp. Paper. 3786713413.

German translation.

AM68 Dussel, Enrique D.
Historia de la Iglesia en América Latina: Coloniaje y liberacion, 1492-1983. Madrid, SP: Mundo Negro; Mexico City, MX: Esquila Misional, 1983. 482 pp. 8472950662 (SP).

Fifth edition of a comprehensive history of mission, church, and state relations in Latin America; written from a liberation theology perspective, by the President of CEHILA; originally published as *Hipotesis para una Historia de la Teologia en America Latina* (1967) and reprinted under that title in 1986, by Indo-American Press Service, Bogotá, Colombia.

AM69 Dussel, Enrique D.
A History of the Church in Latin America: Colonialism to Liberation (1492-1979). Translated by Alan Neely. Grand Rapids, MIU: Eerdmans, 1981. xxiii, 360 pp. 0802835481.

English translation.

AM70 Dussel, Enrique D.
The Invention of the Americas: Eclipse of "the Other" and the Myth of Modernity. Translated by Michael D. Barber. New York, NYU: Continuum, 1995. 224 pp. 082640796X.

A reinterpretation, from the view of the conquered, of the history of European conquest and colonialism in Latin America; by a noted professor at the Universidad Autónomo of Mexico.

AM71 Encuentro de Profesores e Investigadores de Historia de la Iglesia, Resistencia, AG
Las Misiones Jesuíiticas de Guaraníes como Experiencia de Evangelización. (*Teología* 24, n. 50 (1987) 125-281). Buenos Aires, AG: Teología, 1987. 281 pp. No ISBN.

Collection of six addresses about Jesuit missions, from the conference (Argentina, 7-11 September 1987), with a bibliography of works, published 1983-1986, about Jesuit missions.

AM72 Foubert, Charles et al., eds.
The Church at the Crossroads: Christians in Latin America: From Medellín to Puebla, 1968-1978. (IDOC Europe Dossier, 6). Rome, IT: IDOC International, 1978. vii, 239 pp. Paper. No ISBN.

The history of the development of a theology and style of ministry by which the Roman Church in Latin America came to side with the poor and oppressed.

AM73 Greenleaf, Richard E., ed.
The Roman Catholic Church in Colonial Latin America. Tempe, AZU: Arizona State University, 1977. 272 pp. Paper. 087918034X.

Twenty-three scholarly essays on the influence of the church on social, economic, political, and intellectual life, and conflict between church and state, and the Inquisition.

AM74 Gutiérrez, Gustavo
Dieu ou l'or des Indes occidentales: Las Casas et la conscience chrétienne 1492-1992. Paris, FR: Éditions du Cerf, 1992. 161 pp. Paper. 2204044539.

French translation.

AM75 Gutiérrez, Gustavo
Dios o el oro en las Indias, Siglo XVI. Lima, PE: Instituto Bartolomé de Las Casas, CEP; Salamanca, SP: Ediciones Sígueme, 1989. 162 pp. Paper. 8430110798 (SP).

Five penetrating essays, by the noted Peruvian liberation theologian, on the 16th-century theological debate between Fr. Bartolomé de Las Casas, defender of the rights of the Indians, and his contemporaries, concerning the goals of missions and colonialism, and the relevance of these issues today.

AM76 Gutiérrez, Gustavo
En Busca de los Pobres de Jesucristo: El pensamiento de Bartolomé de Las Casas. (CEP, 124). Lima, Perú: Instituto Bartolomé de Las Casas, 1992. 700 pp. No ISBN.

A profound social history of Latin America's poor in the 16th century, and evaluation of the missionary work of Bartolomé de Las Casas (1474-1566).

AM77 Gutiérrez, Gustavo
Gott oder das Gold: Der befreiende Weg des Bartolomé de Las Casas. Freiburg, GW: Herder, 1990. 217 pp. 3451219948.
German translation.

AM78 Gutiérrez, Gustavo
Las Casas: In Search of the Poor of Jesus Christ. Translated by Robert R. Barr. Maryknoll, NYU: Orbis Books, 1993. xxii, 682 pp. 0883448386.
English translation.

AM79 Hanke, Lewis
All Mankind Is One: A Study of the Disputation between Bartolomé de Las Casas and Juan Ginés de Sepúlveda in 1550 on the Intellectual and Religious Capacity of the American Indians. DeKalb, ILU: Northern Illinois University Press, 1994. xvi, 205 pp. Paper. 0875800432.

A scholarly analysis of Las Casas' treatise *Defense against the Persecutors and Slanderers of the Peoples of the New World Discovered across the Seas* (1550), and of the 1547-1551 disputation in Spain concerning it; originally published in 1974.

AM80 Hanke, Lewis
La Humanidad es Una: Estudio acerca de la querella que sobre la capacidad intelectual y religiosa de los indígenes americanos sostuvieron en 1550 Bartolomé de Las Casas y Juan Ginés de Sepúlv. Translated by Jorge Avendaño-Inestrillas, and Margarita Sepúlved Baranda. (Sección de obras de historia). México, MX: Fondo de Cultura Económica, 1985. 232 pp. 9681620291.
Second edition (revised) of the Spanish translation.

AM81 Herring, Hubert Clinton, and Helen Baldwin Herring
A History of Latin America from the Beginnings to the Present. New York, NYU: Knopf, 1972. xxii, 1002 pp. No ISBN.

An enlarged third edition of a comprehensive history of the region, by periods and by areas, with significant coverage of Catholic Church history in the colonial period, but little, specifically, on the churches after independence.

AM82 Hop, Nguyen Thai et al.
Evangelización y Teología en el Perú: Luces y Sombras en el Siglo XVI. Lima, PE: Instituto Bartolomé de Las Casas/CEP, 1991. 314 pp. No ISBN.

Papers from a 1991 conference organized by the Theological Faculty of the Instituto Bartolomé de Las Casas in Lima, Peru, on the occasion of the 500 years' centenary of evangelization in Latin America.

AM83 Katholisch-Theologische Fakultät der Universität Würzburg
Entdeckung—Eroberung—Befreiung: 500 Jahre Gewalt und Evangelium in Amerika. Edited by Wilhelm Dreier, et al. Würzburg, GW: Echter Verlag, 1993. 228 pp. Paper. 3429015049.

Fourteen historical essays by European and Latin American scholars, assessing 500 years of colonialism and Christian missions in Latin America; sponsored by the Catholic Theological Faculty of the University of Würzburg.

AM84 Langer, Erick, and Robert H. Jackson, eds.
The New Latin American Mission History. (Latin American Studies Series). Lincoln, NEU: University of Nebraska Press, 1995. xviii, 212 pp. 0803229119 (hdbk), 0803279531 (pbk).

Seven North American historians reassess missionary contacts with indigenous peoples; in case studies from the Andes to northern Mexico and California.

AM85 Latorre Cabal, Hugo
La revolución de la Iglesia latinoamericana. (Cuadernos de Joaquin Mortiz, 5). México, MX: Mortiz, 1969. 158 pp. No ISBN.

The author describes the revolution of the "young church" that has emerged over the past twenty years, and finds the revolution rooted in traditional Christian principles, the encyclicals of Pope John XVIII and Paul VII, and the documents of Vatican II.

AM86 Latorre Cabal, Hugo
The Revolution of the Latin American Church. Translated by Frances K. Hendricks, and Beatrice Berler. Norman, OKU: University of Oklahoma Press, 1978. vi, 192 pp. 0806114495.
English translation.

AM87 Lembke, Ingo
Christentum unter den Bedingungen Lateinamerikas: Die katholische Kirche vor den Problemen der Abhängigkeit und Unterentwicklung. (Studies in the Intercultural History of Christianity, 2). Bern, SZ: Herbert Lang; Frankfurt am Main, GW: Peter Lang, 1975. 361 pp. Paper. 3261009861.

A study of the development of Christianity in Latin America during the past five centuries, and of basic communities, liberation theology, and the social teaching of the Catholic Church as a response to underdevelopment and mass poverty.

AM88 Lippy, Charles H., Robert Choquette, and Stafford Poole
Christianity Comes to the Americas, 1492-1776. New York, NYU: Paragon House, 1992. xi, 400 pp. 1557782342 (hdbk), 1557785015 (pbk).

Three distinguished historians retell, from the vantage point of the latest historical scholarship, the history of the introduction of Catholicism and Protestantism in the Americas.

AM89 Lopetegui, León, Félix Zubillaga, and Antonio de Egaña
Historia de la Iglesia en la América Española. Madrid, SP: Biblioteca de Autores Cristianos, 1966. 2 vols. No ISBN.

A detailed history of the Roman Catholic missions and church in Spanish Latin America, from the 15th to the 18th centuries, with extensive bibliography and illustrations [vol. 1: lix, 945 pp.; vol. 2: 1,126 pp., (1965-1966)].

AM90 Lopetegui, León, Félix Zubillaga, and Antonio de Egaña
Historia de la Iglesia en América Española desde el descubrimiento hasta comienzos de siglo XIX: México, América Central y Antillas hasta comienzos del siglo XIX. (Biblioteca de autores cristianos, 248, 256). Madrid, SP: EDICA, 1965. 2 vols. No ISBN.

A historical study of the missions and organization of the Roman Catholic Church in Latin America; presented in two volumes, with an extensive bibliography [vol. 1, *México, América Central, Antillas*, by Lopetegui and Zubillaga; vol. 2, *Hemisferio Sur*, by A. de Egaña].

AM91 Mörner, Magnus, ed.
The Expulsion of the Jesuits from Latin America. (Borzoi Books on Latin America). New York, NYU: Knopf, 1967. 207 pp. Paper. No ISBN.

Eighteen essays on the expulsion of the Jesuits from Portuguese (1759) and Spanish (1767) America; with a competent, brief interpretative study of the events plus bibliography.

AM92 Müller-Fahrenholz, Geiko et al.
Christentum in Lateinamerika: 500 Jahre seit der Entdeckung Amerikas. Regensburg, GW: Verlag Friedrich Pustet, 1992. 175 pp. Paper. 3791713191.

Seven scholarly lectures, by Protestant and Catholic theologians from Germany and Latin American countries, reflecting on 500 years of Christianity in Latin America—the perspective of the "discovered," the contribution of Las Casas, the contemporary situation, liberation theology and pastoral care, mission and evangelization, and issues of inculturation.

AM93 MacEóin, Gary, and Nivita Riley
Puebla: A Church Being Born. New York, NYU: Paulist Press, 1980. 136 pp. Paper. 0809122790.

A popular account of the Catholic Church in Latin America, from the conference at Medellin, Colombia, in 1968, to the sequel meeting at Puebla, Mexico, in 1979; including the role of the new Polish pope and the effect of these gatherings on the universal Catholic Church.

AM94 McGlone, Mary M.
Sharing Faith: Across the Hemisphere. Maryknoll, NYU: Orbis Books, 1997. xiv, 302 pp. Paper. 1570751323.

A narrative history of the relationship between the Catholic church in the United States and the Church in Latin America, with study guide and results of a 1995 parish survey.

AM95 Mensen, Bernhard, ed.
Fünfhundert Jahre Lateinamerika. (Vortragsreihe/Akademie Völker und Kulturen (St. Augustin), 12). Nettetal, GW: Steyler Verlag, 1989. 152 pp. Paper. 3805002475.

Six lectures covering varied topics in Latin American church history, from Las Casas to Romero, from the relationship of modern Latin American countries to ethnic minorities, and the influence of North America on this continent.

AM96 Mires, Fernando
La Colonializacion de las Almas: Misión y Conquista en Hispanoamérica. (Colección universitaria). San José, CR: DEI, 1987. 228 pp. Paper. 9977904448.

Critical history of the church-state relations, and the function performed by the church at the time of the conquest of America.

AM97 Mires, Fernando
La Colonización de las Almas: Misíon y Conquista en Hispanoamérica. (Historia de la Iglesia y de la Teología). San José, CR: DEI, 1991. 228 pp. Paper. 9977830401.

In this second edition, the author examines the historical role that missions played during the military conquests of the Americas, and questions whether the mission was a religious legitimization of the military conquest, or a medium to protect the Indians from the conquerors.

AM98 Mires, Fernando
En Nombre de la Cruz: Discusiones teológicas y políticas frente al holocausto de los indios, período de Conquista. San José, CR: DEI, 1986. 219 pp. 9977904278.

An analysis of the political and theological debate in Europe in the early 16th century, in which Las Casas was a central figure, concerning the holocaust of indigenous peoples.

AM99 Neckebrouck, Valeer, F. Gistelinck, and Catherine Cornille, eds.
Het Christendom en de Conquista, 1492-1992. (Annua Nuntia Lovaniensia, 35). Leuven, BE: Leuven University Press; Leuven, BE: Peeters Press, 1992. 208 pp. Paper. 9061865050 (L), 9068314270 (U).

Twelve scholarly case studies on various impacts of Christianity on the peoples and cultures of Latin America, eight of which were originally presented at a colloquium on the theme, held 27-28 January 1992 at Maria-Theresia-College.

AM100 Phelan, John Leddy
The Millennial Kingdom of the Franciscans in the New World. Berkeley, CAU: University of California Press, 1970. 179 pp. 0520014049.

Revised second edition of discussion of 16th-century Spanish Franciscans' worldview, especially that of Jeromino de Mendieta; first published in 1956.

AM101 Prien, Hans-Jürgen
Die Geschichte des Christentums in Lateinamerika. Göttingen, GW: Vandenhoeck & Ruprecht, 1978. 1302 pp. 3525553579.

An ecumenical church history of Latin America, with comprehensive bibliography; attempting to show the tensions between social, political, economic, and cultural structures in the different epochs.

AM102 Ramos, Demetrio, and M. Gonzalez Monteagudo
Estudios sobre Política Indigenista Española en América. (Terceras Jornadas Americanistas de la Universidad de Valladolid). (Bernal, serie americanista, 5-7). Valladolid, SP: Seminario de Historia de América, Universidad de Valladolid, 1977. 3 vols. 8440091702 (vol. 1), 8440098364 (vol. 2).

A collection of articles about the interaction between the native peoples of the Americas, and the Spanish Church and culture (16th-18th centuries) [vol. 1: *Iniciación, pugna de ocupación, demografía, lingüística, sedentarización, condición jurídica del indio* (1975, 391 pp.); vol. 2: *Evangelización, régimen de vida y ecología, servicios personales, encomienda y tributos* (1976, 505 pp.); vol. 3: *Contacto, proteccionismo, reparta de mercaderías, propiedad indígena y resguardos, nativismo, asimilaciones técnicas, ejemplos asistenciales, sobre el nacimiento del P. Las Casas* (1977)].

AM103 Richard, Pablo, ed.
Materiales para una Historia de la Teología en América Latina: VIII Encuentro Latinoamericano de CEHILA, Lima. San José, CR: DEI, 1981. 452 pp. Paper. No ISBN.

A collection of fourteen scholarly essays on issues of church historiography in Latin America: theory, overview, specific issues related to the Roman Catholic and Protestant churches, and a proposed division of historic periods.

AM104 Rivera Pagán, Luis N.
Evangelización y Violencia: La Conquista de América. San Juan, PR: Editorial CEMI, 1991. 449 pp. No ISBN.

Second edition of a detailed history of the linkage between violence and evangelization in the 15th-16th century conquest of the Americas, including issues of slavery, land, tenure, and genocide; originally published in 1990.

AM—THE AMERICAS

AM105 Rivera Pagán, Luis N.

A Violent Evangelism: The Political and Religious Conquest of the Americas. Louisville, KYU: Westminster John Knox, 1992. xvii, 357 pp. Paper. 0664253679.

English translation.

AM106 Salas, Alberto M.

Tres Cronistas de Indias: Pedro Mártir de Angleria, Gonzalo Fernández de Oviedo, Fray Bartolomé de las Casas. (Sección de obras de historia). México, MX: Fondó de Cultura Económica, 1986. 347 pp. Paper. 9681611950.

A scholarly study of three principal chroniclers of the 16th-century Spanish conquest of the Americas—the Dominicans (Angleria and Las Casas), who defended the Indians, and Oviedo, who in his *Historia General de las Indias* (1535) and work as a Secretary of the Indies, opposed Las Casas.

AM107 Schneider, Reinhold

Bartolomé de las Casas frente a Carlos V. Translated by Jorge C. Lehmann. (Creación literaria, 2). Madrid, SP: Ediciones Encuentro, 1979. 190 pp. 847490014X.

Spanish translation.

AM108 Schneider, Reinhold

Las Casas vor Karl V: Szenen aus der Konquistadorenzeit. (Ullstein Buch, 9). Frankfurt am Main, GW: Ullstein, 1965. 187 pp. No ISBN.

An analysis of Bartolomé de Las Casas' defense of the Indians at the court of Charles V.

AM109 Sievernich, Michael, and Dieter Spelthahn, eds.

Fünfhundert Jahre Evangelisierung Lateinamerikas: Geschichte, Kontroversen, Perspektiven. Frankfurt am Main, GW: Vervuert Verlag, 1995. 323 pp. Paper. 3893543813.

Papers from an international symposium sponsored by *Adveniat*, and the Catholic academy Die Wolfsburg (Mülheim, Germany, 19-21 Nov. 1992), on the pros and cons of evangelization in the New World.

AM110 Sievernich, Michael, Arnulf Camps, Andreas Müller, and Walter Senner, eds.

Conquista und Evangelisation: 500 Jahre Orden in Lateinamerika. Mainz, GW: Matthias-Grünewald-Verlag, 1992. 486 pp. Paper. 3786716498.

A collection of nineteen scholarly essays by Catholic historians, theologians, and missiologists, of Germany and Latin America, on various aspects of 500 years of European conquest and missions in Latin America.

AM111 Silva, Antonio Aparecido da et al.

História da evangelização na América Latina. (Teologia em Diálogo). São Paulo, BL: Edições Paulinas, 1988. 86 pp. Paper. 8505008642.

Ten lectures by the prominent Brazilian liberation theologian, on the significance of Christ's suffering and death for the contemporary painful passion of the world.

AM112 Suess, Paulo, comp.

Quema y Siembra: De la conquista espiritual al descubrimiento de una nueva evangelización. Translated by Victoria de Vela. Quito, EC: Ediciones Abya-Yala, 1990. 317 pp. No ISBN.

A collection of articles that reexamine the history of missionary work in Latin America—its positive and negative attributes toward a new definition of evangelization.

AM113 Todorov, Tzvetan

The Conquest of America: The Question of the Other. Trans-

lated by Richard Howard. Norman, OKU: University of Oklahoma Press, 1999. xiii, 274 pp. Paper. 0806131373.

The republication of a book that offers an original interpretation of Columbus' discovery of America, and the Spaniards' subsequent conquest, colonization, and destruction of pre-Columbian cultures in Mexico and the Caribbean; originally pubished in French under the title *La conquete de l'Amerique* (1982).

AM114 Tormo, Leandro

La Historia de la Iglesia en América Latina. (Estudios socio-religiosos latino-americanos, 8-10). Freiburg, SZ: FERES; Madrid, SP: OCSHA, 1962. 3 vols. Paper. No ISBN.

A general history of the Catholic Church in Latin America [t.1: *La evangelización de la América Latina*; t. 3: *La Iglesia en la crisis de la Independencia*].

AM115 Traboulay, David M.

Columbus and Las Casas: The Conquest and Christianization of America, 1492-1566. Lanham, MDU: University Press of America, 1994. xiv, 226 pp. 081919641X (hdbk), 0819196428 (pbk).

Reflections on linkages between 16th-century Spanish colonialism, and mission; by a Professor of History at the City University of New York, who is a native of Trinidad and Tobago.

AM116 Vitalis, Hellmut Gnadt

The Significance of Changes in Latin American Catholicism Since Chimbote, 1953. (Sondeos, 51). Cuernavaca, MX: Centro Intercultural de Documentacíon (CIDOC), 1969. 1 vol. No ISBN.

An overview marking the Chimbote, Peru, conference of 1953 as a turning point in reform of the Latin American Church, that included CELAM, Catholic Action, and the Vatican II reform process.

AM117 Vitoria, Francisco de

Relectio de Iure Belli o Paz Dinamica: Escuela Espanola de la Paz; Primera generacion 1526-1560. (Corpus Hispanorum de Pace, 6). Madrid, SP: CSIC, 1981. 408 pp. 840004911X.

A bilingual collection of the published and non-published texts of the author, a member of the first generation of the Spanish School of Peace, whose interest revolved around themes of violence, just war, and peace in the Americas; with a long and valuable historical study written by Luciano Perena Vicenta.

General Works

See also GW47, GW123, HI602-HI604, HI624, HI693, HI733-HI734, TH48, CR596, CR642, CR648, CR650-CR651, SO251, SO555, EC311, ED38-ED39, ED111, EV134, EV356, SP300, AM188, AM197, AM206, AM214, AM413-AM417, and AM464.

AM118 Ökumenischer Ausschuss für Indianerfragen (Germany W)

Menschenrechte der Indianer und missionarische Verantwortung der Kirchen in Lateinamerika: Arbeitstagung des Ökumenischen Auschusses für Indianerfragen, 6.-9.12.1977 in Arnoldshain/Ts. (Weltmission heute, zum Thema). Hamburg, GW: Ökumenischer Ausschuss für Indianerfragen, 1978. 108 pp. Paper. No ISBN.

Texts of a conference organized by the Ecumenical Committee for Indian Affairs in Germany, and other relevant documents concerning the protection of Indians.

AM119 Alonso, Isidoro

La Iglesia en América Latina: Estructuras eclesiásticas. (Estudios Socio-religiosos Latino-americanos, 21). Friburgo, SZ: FERES, 1964. 223 pp. Paper. No ISBN.

A structural and quantitative study of the church in Latin America, plus a socioreligious analysis.

AM120 Alvarez, Carmelo, and Pablo Leggett, eds.

Lectura Teológica del Tiempo Latinoamericano. San José, CR: SBL, 1979. 254 pp. Paper. No ISBN.

A collection of thirteen scholarly articles written in honor of Walter M. Nelson, former Dean of the Latin American Biblical Seminary.

AM121 Alvarez, Carmelo, ed.

Pentecostalismo y Liberación: Una experiencia latinoamericana. (Colección tradición protestante). San José, CR: Editorial DEI, 1992. 260 pp. Paper. 9977830592.

Sixteen essays, by Latin American Pentecostal pastors and theologians, on the history, ministry, relations with other movements, and spirituality of Pentecostalism in Central and South America.

AM122 Ballán, Romeo

El valor de Salir: La apertura de América Latina a la misión universal. (Colección Buena Nueva, 4). Lima, PE: Ediciones Paulinas, 1990. 192 pp. No ISBN.

Twentieth-century missionary work, including papal messages to Latin American countries, a description of current missionary organizations, and an analysis of their work.

AM123 Berg, Clayton L., and Paul E. Pretiz

The Gospel People. Monrovia, CAU: MARC, 1992. 156 pp. Paper. 0912552778.

A popular introduction to the history, context, and issues faced by the rapidly growing evangelical movement in Latin America; by leaders of the Latin American Mission's "Christ for the City" movement.

AM124 Berg, Clayton L., and Paul E. Pretiz

Spontaneous Combustion: Grass Roots Christianity, Latin American Style. South Pasadena, CAU: William Carey Library, 1996. 296 pp. Paper. 0878082654.

A readable survey of key grassroots movements in the churches of Latin America, both Catholic and Protestant, by two senior leaders of the Latin America Mission.

AM125 Boff, Leonardo

New Evangelization: Good News to the Poor. Translated by Robert R. Barr. Maryknoll, NYU: Orbis Books, 1991. xvi, 128 pp. Paper. 0883447789.

English translation.

AM126 Boff, Leonardo

La nouvelle évangelisation: dans la perspective des opprimés. Translated by Maine Jarton and Michèle Jarton. Paris, FR: Éditions du Cerf, 1992. 176 pp. Paper. 220404573X.

French translation.

AM127 Boff, Leonardo

Nova evangelizacao: Perspectiva dos oprimidos. Fortaleza, BL: Editora Vozes, 1990. 126 pp. 8532603440.

The noted Brazilian liberation theologian critiques the evangelization of cultural displacement practiced in Latin America in the colonial era, and proposes a new evangelization for the continent which affirms oppressed peoples and their cultures.

AM128 Borratt, Héctor, Hiber Conteris et al.

Protestantes en América Latina. (Cuadernos de Marcha, 29). Montevideo, UY: Cuadernos de Marcha, 1969. 80 pp. No ISBN.

A numbered monograph with nine essays by important Latin Americans on significant aspects of Protestant work.

AM129 Boudewijnse, Barbara, A. F. Droogers, and Frans Kamsteeg, eds.

More Than Opium: An Anthropological Approach to Latin American and Caribbean Pentecostal Praxis. (Studies in Evangelicalism, 14). Lanham, MDU: Scarecrow Press, 1998. ix, 327 pp. 0810833905.

A collection of ten essays by Dutch anthropologists from the Free University of Amsterdam's Pentecostalism Study Group, based on an earlier book in Spanish entitled *Algo más que opio* (DEI, 1991)

AM130 Bruneau, Thomas C., Chester E. Gabriel, and Mary Mooney, eds.

The Catholic Church and Religions in Latin America. (Center for Developing-Area Studies, Monograph Series, 18). Montreal, QUC: McGill University, 1984. vi, 279 pp. Paper. 088819062X.

Seven scholarly essays on popular religiosity in Latin America—case studies of how the Catholic Church as an institution is undergoing fundamental change within the context of a de facto pluralistic religious situation, including cults.

AM131 Castro, Emilio

Amidst Revolution. Belfast, NIK: Christian Journals, 1975. 111 pp. 0904302075.

A succinct reappraisal of the church's mission and role in contemporary Latin American society; by the Director of the WCC's Commission on World Mission and Evangelism.

AM132 CEHILA, III Encuentro Latinoamericano, Santo Domingo, DR, 1975

Para una Historia de la Evangelización en América Latina. (El Sentido de la Historia, 12). Barcelona, SP: Editorial Nova Terra, 1977. 319 pp. Paper. 8428006075.

A collection of the meeting's papers on Catholic evangelization and the challenge of Protestantism in Latin America.

AM133 Cleary, Edward L., ed.

Shaping a New World: An Orientation to Latin America. Maryknoll, NYU: Orbis Books, 1971. xiv, 319 pp. Paper. No ISBN.

An introductory study of Latin America, for people who intend to reside there; with sections on history and the church by Jordan Bishop, culture and sociology by C. H. Geraets, development by Thomas Stanley, and politics by Michael Elmer.

AM134 Consejo Episcopal Latinoamericano

Discípulos de Cristo desde América Latina: El Pueblo de Dios Aporta al Sínodo de 1987, vol. II. Bogotá, CK: CELAM, 1987. 191 pp. Paper. No ISBN.

Papers prepared by the Latin American Conference of Bishops (RC) for the Synod on the Laity, including analyses of the history of lay movements in Latin America, the diverse theologies of the laity, and of present situations and popular church developments.

AM135 Converse, Hyla Stuntz, comp.
Raise a Signal: God's Action and the Church's Task in Latin America Today. New York, NYU: Friendship Press, 1961. 126 pp. No ISBN.

Studies by eight mission workers and educators in Latin America, out of particular situations and experiences, centering on the life and mission of the church, present conditions, the religious situation, race and prejudice, the university frontier, the church's task in politics, and new forms of church life in a new society.

AM136 Cook, Guillermo, ed.
New Face of the Church in Latin America: Between Tradition and Change. (American Society of Missiology Series, 18). Maryknoll, NYU: Orbis Books, 1994. xiv, 289 pp. Paper. 0883449374.

An important anthology of essays, by mission and church leaders, on the changing face of the church in Latin America (reassessment of mission history, the dynamics of change, popular religion and the future of the church), plus five national case studies.

AM137 Costas, Orlando E.
Christ Outside the Gate: Mission Beyond Christendom. Maryknoll, NYU: Orbis Books, 1982. xvi, 238 pp. Paper. 0883441470.

A sociological and theological analysis of the missiological issues involved in the transition from paternalism, to the contextualization of the gospel and the church in the Americas.

AM138 Costas, Orlando E.
Compromiso y Misión. (Colección CELEP). San José, CR: Editorial Caribe, 1979. 159 pp. Paper. 0899221653.

Essay on the work of Christian missions in Latin America today.

AM139 Costas, Orlando E.
Theology of the Crossroads in Contemporary Latin America: Missiology in Mainline Protestantism, 1969-1974. Amsterdam, NE: Rodopi, 1976. xiv, 413 pp. 9062032591.

Doctoral dissertation on the concept of mission in several Latin American Protestant churches, organizations and conferences, and in the writings of Justo Gonzalez, Emilio Castro, and Mortimer Arias.

AM140 Damboriena, Prudencio
El Protestantismo en América Latina. (Estudios socio-religiosos latino-americanos, 12-13). Freiburg, SZ: FERES, 1962-1963. 2 vols. Paper. No ISBN.

Vol. 1: Study of the methods and stages of Protestant evangelization, with a concentrated analysis of the work of the Wycliffe Bible Translators, and the initiatives of the Seventh-day Aventist Church (138 pp); vol. 2: History of Protestantism in Latin America (288pp).

AM141 *Dar Desde Nuestra Pobreza: Vocación Misionera de América Latina*
(Documentos CELAM, 76). Bogotá, CK: CELAM, Departamento de Misiones, 1986. 250 pp. Paper. 9586250067.

Exposition of fundamental aspects of mission since the Second Vatican Council: history of missions, the document *Ad Gentes*, theology of missions, and practical aspects; a final chapter is devoted to the universal missionary responsibility of all Christians in Latin America.

AM142 Derby, Marian, and James E. Ellis
Latin American Lands in Focus. Edited by Dorothy McConnell. New York, NYU: Methodist Church, Board of Missions, 1961. 147 pp. No ISBN.

Brief history and description of Methodist work in Latin America.

AM143 Downey, Steve
More Than I Imagined. Miami, FLU: Latin America Mission, 1987. 155 pp. Paper. No ISBN.

A popular autobiographical account by a Spearhead missionary, of short-term mission service in Mexico, Honduras, and Ecuador, focusing on person-to-person evangelism.

AM144 Escobar, Samuel E.
La Chispa y la Llama: Breve Historia de la Comunidad Internacional de Estudiantes Evangélicos en América Latina. Buenos Aires, AG: Ediciones Certeza, 1978. 120 pp. Paper. No ISBN.

A brief history of the International Association of Evangelical Students (CIEE) in Latin America from 1958 to 1976.

AM145 Garcia, Rubén Dário
La "Primera evangelización" y sus lecturas, Desafíos a la "Nueva Evangelización": Lectura latinoamericana de los discursos de Juan Pablo II en Zaragoza, Santo Domingo, San Juan de Puerto Rico, Roma (10.11.12.17 de Octubre de 1984). (Estudios Proyecto, 1). Buenos Aires, AG: Centro Salesiano de Estudios "San Juan Bosco," 1990. 155 pp. Paper. No ISBN.

Documented analysis of different interpretations of the value of evangelization in the three Americas, especially in light of the pope's reasoning on the subject.

AM146 Gheerbrant, Alain
The Rebel Church in Latin America. Translated by Rosemary Sheed. (The Pelican Latin American Library). Harmondsworth, ENK: Penguin Books, 1974. 357 pp. 0140218017.

English translation.

AM147 Gorski, Juan F.
El Desarrollo histórico de la misionología en América Latina: Orientaciones teológicas del Departamento de Misiones del CELAM (1966-1979). La Paz, BO: Colegio Don Bosco, Escuela de Artes Gráficas, 1985. xv, 326 pp. Paper. No ISBN.

Author's doctoral thesis on the evolution of missional ideas, in documents published by the Missions Department of CELAM.

AM148 Green, Dana S., ed.
Chasms in the Americas. New York, NYU: Friendship Press, 1970. 127 pp. Paper. 0377102512.

Eight essays introducing Latin America, its people and churches and inter-American relations; with focus on Protestants.

AM149 Gutiérrez, Gustavo et al.
Hacia el Quinto Centenario: caminos para la nueva evangelización. (Páginas, 14 n.99 (1989) 1-79). Lima, PE: Páginas, 1989. 79 pp. No ISBN.

A collection of seven articles on past and present evangelization in Latin America.

AM150 Isais, Juan M.
The Other Side of the Coin. Translated by Elisabeth F. Isais. Grand Rapids, MIU: Eerdmans, 1966. 104 pp. No ISBN.

An analysis, in fictional form, of the tensions between foreign missionaries and Latin American Christians.

AM151 John Paul II, Pope
Ecclesia in America. Washington, DCU: USCC, 1999. 135 pp. Paper. 1574553216.

Pope John Paul II's post-synodal apostolic exhortation to the Special Assembly for America of the Synod of Bishops (Mexico City, 22 January 1999).

AM152 John Paul II, Pope
La Iglesia en América. Washington, DCU: USCC, 1999. 139 pp. Paper. 1574558196.

Spanish translation.

AM153 Kiesler, John
Signs and Instruments of Liberation: The Confederation of Latin American Religious (CLAR) and a Contextual Theology of Religious Life from 1966 until 1991. (Church and Theology in Context, 33). Kampen, NE: Kok Pharos, 1996. xii, 337 pp. Paper. 9039005249.

A detailed study of the evolving understandings of religious life and evangelization of CLAR, inncluding BECs.

AM154 Lara-Braud, Jorge, ed.
Our Claim on the Future: A Controversial Collection from Latin America. New York, NYU: Friendship Press, 1970. 128 pp. Paper. 0377100714.

A collection of essays by Lara-Braud, Fals-Borda, Illich, Alves, and others analyzing the Protestant participation in the struggle for social and economic justice and the movement for better relations with the Catholic Church.

AM155 Münchener Theologische Zeitschrift: Vierteljahresschrift für das Gesamtgebiet der katholischen Theologie
St. Ottilien, GW: EOS Verlag, 1992. 122 pp. Paper. No ISBN.

This special issue of the prominent journal on Catholic theology contains six scholarly reflections (one by Leonardo Boff) on the sesquicentennial of missions in Latin America; (the Eurocentric evaluation of natives, the continuing challenge of evangelization in Latin America, the ideology of slavery, and the absolute claims of Christianity versus personal freedom).

AM156 Mackay, John A.
The Latin American Churches and the Ecumenical Movement. New York, NYU: CCLA, 1963. 33 pp. Paper. No ISBN.

An address by the noted president of Princeton Seminary and ecumenist, reappraising Latin American involvements in ecumenism within secular and religious contexts.

AM157 Martin, David
Tongues of Fire: The Explosion of Protestantism in Latin America. Oxford, ENK: Blackwell Publishers, 1990. xiii, 352 pp. 063117186X.

A British sociologist reviews the growth of Protestantism, especially Pentecostal groups, and examines their worship, individualized morality, and accommodation to capitalism.

AM158 Materne, Yves, ed.
The Indian Awakening in Latin America. New York, NYU: Friendship Press, 1980. 127 pp. Paper. 0377000973.

Describes predicament, aspirations, and demands of Indian communities throughout the region; a collection of documents and interviews.

AM159 Meyers, Albert, ed.
Volksreligiosität in Lateinamerika. (Anuario: Jahrbuch für Bildung, Gesellschaft und Politik in Lateinamerika, 14). Munich, GW: Universiät Münster, Forschungsgruppe Lateinamerika, 1985. x, 238 pp. Paper. No ISBN.

Six examples of Latin American popular religiosity from Bolivia, Mexico, Peru, and Brazil.

AM160 Miller, Daniel R., ed.
Coming of Age: Protestantism in Contemporary Latin America. (Calvin Center Series, 1). Lanham, MDU: University Press of America, 1994. xix, 234 pp. 0819194069 (hdbk), 0819194077 (pbk).

Eight essays by North American scholars, evaluating aspects of contemporary Latin American Protestantism.

AM161 Morales, Adam
American Baptists with a Spanish Accent. Valley Forge, PAU: Judson Press, 1964. 112 pp. Paper. No ISBN.

American Baptist missions in Spanish America.

AM162 Núñez C., Emilio Antonio, and William David Taylor
Crisis and Hope in Latin America: An Evangelical Perspective. South Pasadena, CAU: William Carey Library; Carlisle, ENK: WEF, 1996. xvi, 528 pp. 0878087664 (US), 1900890011 (UK).

Revised edition of an overview, for North American evangelicals, of Latin America's history, culture, social reality, and spiritual dynamics; with special emphasis on the challenge of Christian social responsibility in Latin America, including both Catholic and Protestant initiatives; originally published as *Crisis in Latin America* (Moody Press, 1989).

AM163 Nida, Eugene Albert
Understanding Latin Americans: With Special Reference to Religious Values and Movements. South Pasadena, CAU: William Carey Library, 1974. viii, 163 pp. Paper. 0878081178.

The prominent linguist and executive secretary of the American Bible Society offers a readable tour of the high points of contrast for North Americans, between their culture, values, and forms of Christianity and those of Latin America; revised edition of *Communication of the Gospel in Latin America* (CIDOC, 1969).

AM164 Pape, Carlos
Katholizismus in Lateinamerika. (Veröffentlichungen des Missionspriesterseminars, 11). Kaldenkirchen, GW: Steyler Verlag, 1963. xv, 262 pp. Paper. No ISBN.

A description of the development of Latin America since the beginnings of evangelization, with special reference to the shortage of priests, advancing Protestantism, and the threat of Spiritism.

AM165 Pfeiffer, Johannes
Auf Luthers Spuren in Lateinamerika. (Erlanger Taschenbücher, 6). Erlangen, GW: Ev.-Luth. Mission, 1969. 205 pp. Paper. No ISBN.

An account of the development of the Lutheran church in Latin America, published on the occasion of the Fifth General Assembly of the Lutheran World Council in Brazil, 1970.

AM166 Promper, Werner
Priesternot in Lateinamerika. Löwen, BE: Latein-Amerika-Kolleg der Katholischen Universität, 1965. 317 pp. Paper. No ISBN.

Dissertation on the development of shortages of priests in Latin America, the situation in the 1960s, an analysis of the causes, resulting consequences, and suggested solutions.

AM167 Read, William R., Victor M. Monterroso, and Harmon A. Johnson

Avance Evangélico en la América Latina. El Paso, TXU: CSB, 1970. 400 pp. Paper. No ISBN.

Spanish translation.

AM168 Read, William R., Victor M. Monterroso, and Harmon A. Johnson

Latin American Church Growth. (Church Growth Series). Grand Rapids, MIU: Eerdmans, 1969. xxiv, 421 pp. No ISBN.

The results of a major research project on patterns of church growth (Protestant and Roman Catholic) in seventeen countries of Central and South America.

AM169 Scannone, Juan Carlos

Teología de la Liberación y Doctrina Social de la Iglesia. Madrid, SP: Ediciones Cristiandad; Buenos Aires, AG: Editorial Guadalupe, 1987. 285 pp. Paper. 8470574094 (S), No ISBN (A).

New collection of various studies, previously published in the journal *Stromata* and others since 1976, concerning the social task of the church or its appearance in theological reflection.

AM170 Schooyans, Michael

Chrétienté en contestation: l'Amérique latine, essai de perspective pastoral. Paris, FR: Éditions du Cerf, 1969. 320 pp. No ISBN.

In this book, the author, who is Professor of Pastoral Theology in São Paulo, tries to apply the decisions and decrees of the Second Vatican Council to different situations in South America.

AM171 Scopes, Wilfred, ed.

The Christian Ministry in Latin America and the Caribbean: Report of a Survey Commission Authorized by the International Missionary Council. Geneva, SZ: WCC, CWME, 1962. 264 pp. Paper. No ISBN.

The report of a comprehensive survey, including sections on historical and social background, ministry, Latin American theology, and theological education.

AM172 Segundo, Juan Luis

Ação pastoral latino-americana: seus motivos ocultos. Translated by Benno Brod. São Paulo, BL: Edições Loyola, 1978. 117 pp. No ISBN.

Portuguese translation.

AM173 Segundo, Juan Luis

Acción Pastoral Latinoamericana: Sus Motivos Ocultos. Buenos Aires, AG: Ediciones Busqueda, 1972. 130 pp. Paper. No ISBN.

Study of the motives that impede the Latin American Church from choosing new strategies of mission that would address and/or overcome the deficiencies of the past four centuries.

AM174 Segundo, Juan Luis

The Hidden Motives of Pastoral Action: Latin American Reflections. Maryknoll, NYU: Orbis Books, 1978. viii, 141 pp. 0883441853 (hdbk), 0883441861 (pbk).

English translation.

AM175 Steuernagel, Valdir

Al Servicio del Reino en América Latina: Un compendio sobre la misión integral de la iglesia cristiana en Latinoamérica. San José, CR: Visión Mundial, 1991. 240 pp. Paper. 9977965110.

Thirteen essays and two church documents from Latin America, which focus on integral mission as the principal vocation of the church.

AM176 Stoll, David

Is Latin America Turning Protestant?: The Politics of Evangelical Growth. Berkeley, CAU: University of California Press, 1990. xxi, 424 pp. 0520064992.

An inquiry into the spread of conservative and fundamentalist Protestantism, especially in Central America, and its ties with the political right in the United States.

AM177 Vaquez, Diza

El Compromiso Ecuménico de la Iglesia Católica y el problema de las sectas en América Latina. (San Vicente a Medina, 139). Caracas, VE: Acción Ecuménica, 1988. 54 pp. Paper. 9803001698.

A short reflection on how contemporary Roman Catholic commitment to ecumenism relates to a 500-year emphasis in Latin America on Catholic evangelization, in which Protestant "sects" were the enemy.

AM178 Wagner, C. Peter

Spiritual Power and Church Growth. Altamonte Springs, FLU: Strang Communications, 1986. 160 pp. Paper. 0930525043.

A revised, popular account of why Pentecostal churches are growing rapidly in Latin America; originally published as *Look Out! The Pentecostals are Coming* (1973).

AM179 Wolff, Carman St. J.

Adult Guide on Latin American Countries. New York, NYU: Friendship Press, 1961. 48 pp. Paper. No ISBN.

Gives suggestions for classroom sessions in Protestant churches, based mainly on Sante U. Barbieri's *Land of Eldorado* (New York: Friendship Press, 1961) and Henry L. McCorkle's *The Quiet Crusaders* (New York: Friendship Press, 1961).

Conferences and Congresses

See also TH13, TH387, ED175, EV29, EV39, AM61-AM62, AM71, AM82, AM151-AM152, AM262, AM406, AM546, and AM1277.

AM180 *Autour de Las Casas: actes du colloque du Ve centenaire, 1484-1984, Toulouse, 25-28 octobre 1984*

(Collection In-texte). Paris, FR: Tallandier, 1987. 2448 pp. 2235017460.

Proceedings of an important colloquium assessing, after five centuries, the contribution to missions of Bartolomé de Las Casas; with titles in Latin and texts in French and Spanish.

AM181 Baptist Union of Latin America (5th Conference, Caracas, Venezuela, 29 April-3 May 1987)

Misiones y Discipulado Cristiano. Caracas, VE: UBLA, 1987. 56 pp. Paper. No ISBN.

A collection of reports, studies, and discussions of the conference.

AM182 Barrado, José, ed.

II Congreso Internacional sobre los Dominicos y el Nuevo Mundo, Salamanca, SP, 28 de marzo al 1 de abril de 1989: Actas. Salamanca, SP: Editorial San Esteban, 1990. 1037 pp. Paper. 8487557082.

A collection of thirty-six papers from the congress, addressing the principal theme of the beginnings of evangelization in America.

AM183 CELAM (3rd, Buenos Aires, Argentina, 1969)
Deudores del Mundo: Informes–Comentarios. Montevideo, UY: Comisión Provisoria por Unidad Evangélica Latinoamericana, 1969. 54 pp. Paper. No ISBN.
A collection of documents from CELA III.

AM184 CELAM (2nd., Medellin, 1968)
The Church in the Present-Day Transformation of Latin America in the Light of the Council. Washington, DCU: NCCB, 1968. 2 vols. Paper. No ISBN.
The official report of the influential Medellin Conference, which applied the recommendations of Vatican II to the Church of Latin America.

AM185 CELAM (3rd, Puebla, Mexico, 1979)
Puebla and Beyond: Documentation and Commentary. Edited by John Eagleson and Philip Scharper. Maryknoll, NYU: Orbis Books, 1979. xiii, 370 pp. Paper. 0883443996.
An authorized translation of the report and papers.

AM186 CELAM (4th, Santo Domingo, Dominican Republic, 1993)
Santo Domingo and Beyond: Documents and Commentaries from the Fourth General Conference of Latin American Bishops. Edited by Alfred T. Hennelly. Maryknoll, NYU: Orbis Books, 1993. xiv, 242 pp. Paper. 088344920X.
Documents and addresses, with commentaries, by six Catholic theologians and missiologists, and one Protestant missiologist.

AM187 CELAM
Nueva Evangelización: Génesis y líneas de un proyecto misionero. (Colección Documentos CELAM, 115). Bogotá, CK: CELAM, 1990. 299 pp. Paper. 9586251721.
Report and papers from an important seminar, convened by CELAM, to probe the new evangelization relevant to the new culture of Latin America, in preparation for the 500th anniversary, in 1992, of evangelization in Latin America.

AM188 CICOP, Annual Conference (3rd, Chicago, 1966)
The Religious Dimension in the New Latin America. Edited by John J. Considine. Notre Dame, INU: Fides, 1966. xviii, 238 pp. Paper. No ISBN.
Eighteen short essays, mostly by Roman Catholic leaders in Latin America, originally presented at the Third Annual Conference of the Catholic Inter-American Cooperation Program, focusing on contemporary religious challenges, the activities of religious personnel, and the new pastoral apostolate.

AM189 CLADE (3rd, Quito, Ecuador, 1992)
El Movimiento de Lausana al Servicio de Reino. San José, CR: Visión Mundial, 1992. 273 pp. Paper. 9977965196.
Spanish translations of four key documents from the International Congress of World Evangelization (Lausanne 1974), plus two documents from the Lausanne Movement, prepared as background reading for participants in the 1992 Latin American Congress.

AM190 CLADE (1st, Bogotá, Colombia) 1969
Acción en Cristo para un Continente en Crisis. San José CR: Editorial Caribe, 1970. 135 pp. Paper. No ISBN.
A digest of the reports, lectures, and Bible studies of the congress, the birthplace of the Fraternidad Teológica Latinoamericana.

AM191 CLADE (2nd, Lima, Peru, 1979)
América Latina y la Evangelización en los años 80. Buenos Aires, AG: Fraternidad Teológica Latinoamericana, 1979. 386 pp. Paper. No ISBN.
A collection of the reports, documents, and addresses of the CLADE II congress.

AM192 CLAI, Asamblea General (1st, Oaxtepec, Mexico, 19-26 Sept. 1978)
De Panamá a Oaxtepec: El protestantismo latinoamericano en busca de unidad. (Pastoralia, 1, 1). San José, CR: Pastoralia, 1978. 164 pp. No ISBN.
A collection of historical studies on Panamá 1916, Montevideo 1925, Havana 1929, Bogotá 1969, and CELAM III, as well as the Oaxtepec documents on the identity and work of Protestant churches in Latin America.

AM193 CLAI, Asamblea General (2nd, Indaiatuba, São Paulo, Brazil, 1988)
Cosecha de Esperanza: Iglesia, hacia una esperanza solidaria. Edited by Gérson Meyer. Quito, EC: CLAI, 1988. 2 vols. Paper. No ISBN.
A collection of the working documents on the life, aspirations, evangelizing mission, and commitments of the Protestant churches in Latin America [vol. 1: 321 pp.; vol. 2: 341 pp.].

AM194 CLAI, Asamblea General (2nd, Indaiatuba, São Paulo, Brazil, 1988)
Iglesia, Hacia una Esperanza Solidaria: Documento de estudio. Edited by A. Plutarco Bonilla. (Pastoralia, 9, 19). San José, CR: Pastoralia, 1987. 138 pp. No ISBN.
A collection of seven biblical and theological studies, written in preparation for the assembly.

AM195 CLAI, Asamblea General, (2nd, Indaiatuba (São Paulo), Brazil, 1988)
Indaiatuba, Celebrando la Esperanza: Documentos. Quito, EC: CLAI, 1989. 274 pp. Paper. No ISBN.
A collection of the assembly's papers and documents.

AM196 CLAI, Encuentro Continental (Cochabamba, Bolivia, 9-15 August 1992)
Síntesis de la Memoria del Encuentro Continental del programa 500 años. Quito, EC: CLAI, 1992. 99 pp. Paper. No ISBN.
Report of a Latin American encounter, part of the "500 Years Program" of CLAI.

AM197 CLAI
Oaxtepec 1978: Unidad y Misión en América Latina. San Pedro de Montes de Oca, CR: CLAI, Comité Editorial, 1980. 228 pp. Paper. No ISBN.
History of the development of Protestant evangelization, from Panama in 1916 to Oaxtepec in 1978, plus the text of the document released by the final assembly held in Oaxtepec, Mexico, in 19-26 November 1978.

AM198 Conferencia Evangelica Latinoamericana (2nd, Lima, Peru, 1961)
Cristo: La Esperanza para América Latina. Buenos Aires, AG: [Confederación Evangélica del Río de La Plata], 1962. 176 pp. Paper. No ISBN.
Collection of conference papers and reports, with additional commentary on the conference.

AM199 Congreso Luterano Latinoamericano (6th, Bogotá, Colombia, 1980)
Misión y Evangelización de las Iglesias Luteranas en América Latina. Edited by George Posfay. Ginebra, SZ: LWF, 1980. 159 pp. Paper. No ISBN.
Collection of papers prepared for the 6th congress.

AM200 Congreso Luterano Latinoamericano (6th, Bogotá, Colombia, 1980)
Nuestra Fe y Nuestra Misión en América Latina. Sao Leopoldo, BL: Editora Sinodal, 1981. 148 pp. Paper. 8523300074.
A collection of the addresses and conclusions of the congress.

AM201 Congreso Luterano Latinoamericano (6th, Bogotá, Colombia, 1980)
Misión y evangelización de la islesias luteranas en América Latina. Geneva, SZ: LWF, 1980. 159 pp. No ISBN.
Papers from meetings preparing for the Sixth Lutheran Latinamerican Congress (Porto Allegro, Brazil, 29-31 May 1978; and José C. Paz, Argentina, 12-14 November 1979).

AM202 Consultation of Latin American and Caribbean Bishops and Pastors (3rd, Río de Janeiro, Brazil, July 1993)
Democracia en Crisis y el Nuevo Orden Mundial: Desafío a las iglesias de América Latina y el Caribe. Quito, EC: CLAI, 1993. 73 pp. Paper. No ISBN.
Texts of debates and reflections made during the Third Consultation of Latin American and Caribbean Bishops and Pastors, as they explored challenges of the new economic world order, democracy in crisis, and the religious context of Latin America and the Caribbean.

AM203 CPID-CAISMR
Las Iglesias en la Práctica de la Justicia: Consulta latinoamericana sobre la "Participación de las Iglesias en Programas y Proyectos de Desarrollo" Itaicí-Brasil-Setiembre 1980. (Oikoumene). San José, CR: DEI, 1981. 171 pp. Paper. No ISBN.
A collection of study material gathered at a meeting of the Latin American Consultation on "Church Participation in Programs and Projects of Development" (Itaici, BL, September 1980), including four Bible studies, workgroup reports, and the final document, an open letter to churches and Christians in Latin America.

AM204 Encuentro Latinoamericano de Teología (1975: Mexico City)
Liberación y Cautiverio: Debates en Torno al Método de la Teología en América Latina. Mexico City, MX: Comité Organizador, 1976. 660 pp. Paper. No ISBN.
Collection of conference papers, whose central theme was "methods of theological reflection in Latin America and their pastoral, historical, social, political, and ecclesiological implications."

AM205 *Fe Cristiana y Revolución Sandinista en Nicaragua*
(Apuntes para el Estudio de la Realidad Nacional, 3). Managua, NQ: Instituto Histórico Centroamericano, 1980. 375 pp. Paper. No ISBN.
Collection of conference papers and responses, primarily focusing on the Nicaraguan process, but also on the experience of Christians in the revolutions of Cuba, Chile, and Latin America in general.

AM206 Gutiérrez, Gustavo, Francis McDonagh, Càndido Padin, and Jon Sobrino
Santo Domingo and After: The Challenge for the Latin American Church. London, ENK: CIIR, 1993. 68 pp. Paper. 1852871202.
Four reflections on the 4th Latin American Bishops' Conference (Santo Domingo, 1992) by two liberation theologians (Gutiérrez and Sobrino), a Brazilian bishop (Padin), and a British journalist who covered the conference (McDonagh).

AM207 Henkel, Willi
Die Konzilien in Lateinamerika—Teil 1: Mexiko 1555-1897. (Konziliengeschichte—Reihe A: Darstellungen). Paderborn, GW: Ferdinand Schöningh, 1984. xv, 272 pp. 3506746839.
A scholarly history of the Catholic councils held in Mexico, from 1555 to 1897, with an analysis of the foundation, growth, and expansion of the church in Mexico; the first volume of a multi-volume work on the various missionary synods.

AM208 I Consulta Evangélica sobre Iglesia y Sociedad, Huampaní, PE, 23-27 de julio de 1961
Encuentro y Desafío; La acción cristiana evangélica ante la cambiante situación social, polftica y económica: Conclusiones y resoluciones. Montevideo, UY: Iglesia y Sociedad en América Latina, 1961. 70 pp. Paper. No ISBN.
A collection of the studies, conclusions, and resolutions of the consultation ("La responsabilidad social de la Iglesia evangélica frente a los rápidos cambios sociales"), the birthplace of the Junta Latinoamericana de Iglesia y Sociedad en América Latina.

AM209 Jornadas Fe Cristiana y Cambio Social en América Latina (1972: El Escorial, SP)
Fede cristiana e cambiamento sociale in América latina. Translated by Benedettine di Rosano. Assisi, IT: Cittadella Editrice, 1975. 319 pp. No ISBN.
Italian translation.

AM210 Jornadas Fe Cristiana y Cambio Social en América Latina (Escorial, Spain 1972)
Fe Cristiana y Cambio Social en América Latina: Encuentro de El Escorial, 1972. Salamanca, SP: Ediciones Sígueme, 1973. 428 pp. Paper. 8430105077.
Collection of twelve papers shared at this conference, a significant milestone in the history of liberation theology.

AM211 Kunde, Carlos, ed.
La Evangelización en Mesoamérica. Quito, EC: CLAI, 1988. 151 pp. Paper. No ISBN.
A collection of papers from a conference held in Antigua, Guatemala, 15-20 July 1987, attended by seventy leaders of Protestant churches from Guatemala, Honduras, El Salvador, Nicaragua, Costa Rica, and Panama.

AM212 Latin American Conference on Church and Society (2nd, El Tabo, Chile, 1966)
América Hoy: Acción de Dios y Responsabilidad del Hombre. Edited by Luis E. Odell. Montevideo, UY: ISAL, 1966. 132 pp. No ISBN.
This report and interpretation considers the theological bases for the Protestant churches' concern and action in Latin American society.

AM—THE AMERICAS

AM213 Latin American Conference on Church and Society (2nd, El Tabo, Chile, 1966)
Social Justice and the Latin Churches: Church and Society in Latin America. Translated by Jorge Lara-Braud. Richmond, VAU: John Knox Press, 1969. 137 pp. Paper. 0804215057.

English translation.

AM214 Lozano Barragan, Javier et al.
La Evangelización Fundante en América Latina: Estudio historico del siglo XVI. (DEC, 4). Bogotá, CK: CELAM, 1990. 417 pp. Paper. 9586251713.

A collection of the twelve historical studies presented at the seminar organized by CELAM and held in Mexico, 8-11 November 1988.

AM215 Njoroge, Nyambura J., and Páraic Réamonn, eds.
Partnership in God's Mission: In Latin America. (WARC Studies, 37). Geneva, SZ: WARC, 1998. 104 pp. Paper. 9290750499.

The papers and reports of the Consultation on Women and Men of Reformed Tradition in Latin America (Caracas, Venezuela, 20-27 November 1996).

AM216 Oliveros, Roberto
Nueva Evangelización en el Hoy de América Latina: Mensaje de la Conferencia Episcopal de Santo Domingo. Mexico City, MX: Centro de Estudios Sociales y Culturales Antonio de Montesinos, 1994. 164 pp. No ISBN.

A critical evaluation of the documents of CELAM IV.

AM217 Perena Vincente, Luciano, ed.
La Ética de la Conquista de América: Francisco de Vitoria y la escuela de Salamanca. (Corpus Hispanorum de Pace, 25). Madrid, SP: CSIC, 1984. 724 pp. 8400055624.

A collection of fourteen papers of historical research and the final conclusion of the First Symposium (Salamanca, Spain, 2-5 November 1983).

AM218 Rodríguez Maradiga, Oscar Andrés
América, llegó tu hora de ser Evangelizadora: COMLA 3. Bogotá, CK: CELAM, 1987. 343 pp. Paper. 9586250997.

A collection of greetings, papers, appendices, and recommendations from the Third Latin American Missionary Conference (Bogotá, Colombia, 5-9 July 1987) under the direction of CELAM.

AM219 Ruiz García, Samuel et al.
América Latina Misionera: Realidades y experiencias. (Pastoral Latinoamericana, 2). Bogotá, CK: Ediciones Paulinas, 1975. 179 pp. Paper. No ISBN.

A collection of testimonies and experiences presented in a course coordinated by DEMIS on Anthropology and Theology for Missionary Activity in Latin America (Caracas, Venezuela, 23 July-17 August 1974).

AM220 Schöpfer, Hans, ed.
Kontinent der Hoffnung: Die Evangelisierung Lateinamerikas heute und morgen; Beiträge und Berichte zur 3. Generalversammlung des lateinamerikanischen Episkopats in Puebla 1979. (Entwicklung und Frieden: Dokumente, Berichte, Meinungen, 8). Munich, GW: Kaiser; Mainz, GW: Grünewald Verlag, 1979. 164 pp. Paper. 3459012471 (K), 3786707820 (G).

The first German commentary on the Third General Assembly of the Latin American Bishops in Puebla/Mexico, consisting of eleven articles, ranging from ecumenism to the rediscovery of the Bible in Latin America.

AM221 Semana de Estudos Teológicos (2nd, 1987, São Paulo, Brazil)
Queimada e semeadura: Da conquista espiritual ao descobrimento de uma nova evangelizapcao. Edited by Paulo Suess. Petrópolis, BL: Editora Vozes, 1988. 268 pp. No ISBN.

A collection of papers on evangelism and missions, and biblical studies by Latin American scholars.

AM222 Semana de Estudos Teológicos (2nd, São Paulo, Brazil, 1987)
Quema y siembra: De la conquista espiritual al descubrimiento de una nueva evangelización. Edited by Paulo Suess. Translated by Victoria de Vela. Quito, EC: Abya-Yala, 1990. 317 pp. No ISBN.

Second edition of the Spanish translation.

AM223 Simposio Internacional de Teología (10th, 1989, Universidad de Navarra)
Evangelización y Teología en América (Siglo XVI): X Simposio internacional de teología de la Universidad de Navarra. Edited by Josep-Ignasi Saranyana. (Colección Teológica, 68). Pamplona, SP: Servicio de Publicaciones de la Universidad de Navarra, 1990. 2 vols. 8487146333 (set), 8487146341 (vol. 1), 848714635X (vol. 2).

A collection of articles discussing the Roman Catholic Church in Spain, and its encounter with the native peoples of the Americas and the Philippines (16th-17th centuries).

AM224 WCCE
Encuentro: New Perspectives for Christian Education. (*World Christian Education*, 20, 3-4). Lancashire, ENK: F. H. Brown; Geneva, SZ: WCCE, 1971. 183 pp. No ISBN.

Addresses, reports on seventeen *encuentros* in Latin America, interviews with delegates, biographies of delegates, photos and cartoons, and an article on the impact of the meetings on Latin America.

AM225 Woerkom, Jehanne van et al.
Geen feest na vijfhonderd jaar: Godsdienst, grond en mensenrechten in Latijns-America. Nijmegen, NE: Katholiek Studiecentrum, 1993. 214 pp. Paper. 9070713330.

Ten essays on Christianity's encounter with indigenous peoples and their religions; issues of human rights, justice, and politics; and the religious influence of African and African American religions in the development of Christianity in Latin America, especially Brazil—originally presented at a Katholicke University symposium, celebrating the discovery and planting of Christianity in the New World (Nijmegen, Netherlands, 22-23 May 1992).

Church and Society

See also GW264, HI275, TH473, EA62-EA63, SO18, SO33-SO34, EC42, EC55, EC63, EC67, EC112, EC134, EC155, EC232, EC234, EC248, EC285-EC286, PO11, PO25, PO59-PO60, PO99, PO112, PO165-PO166, PO168-PO169, PO171, PO178, CO17, ED10, ED146-ED147, CH337, CH344, CH368, SP24, SP135-SP137, AM4, AM34, AM55, AM66, AM87, AM162, AM202-AM203, AM212-AM213, AM225, AM442, AM511, AM593, AM669, AM682, AM704, AM711, AM779, AM797, AM952, AM1004, AM1362, AM1372, and AM1496.

AM226 Adams, Richard N. et al.
Social Change in Latin America Today: Its Implications for United States Policy. New York, NYU: Vintage Books, 1961. xiv, 353 pp. No ISBN.

Discussion of Protestant influence and innovations as a factor in breaking down Indian culture and causing uncertainty in religion; originally published by Harper for the Council on Foreign Relations, New York (1960).

AM227 Alvarez, Carmelo
Una Iglesia en Diáspora: Apuntes para una eclesiología solidaria. (Aportes). San José, CR: DEI, 1991. 104 pp. Paper. 9977830487.

A collection of presentations which focus on the author's experiences and interchanges, while serving in 1984-1985 as secretary of Pastoral Service of Consolation and Solidarity for CLAI.

AM228 Antoncich, Ricardo
Christians in the Face of Injustice: A Latin American Reading of Catholic Social Teaching. Translated by Matthew J. O'Connell. Maryknoll, NYU: Orbis Books, 1987. xvi, 181 pp. Paper. 0883444135.

English translation.

AM229 Antoncich, Ricardo
Os Cristaos diante da injustica: Para uma leitura latino-americana da doutrina social da igreja. São Paulo, BL: Loyola, 1983. 232 pp. Paper. No ISBN.

Portuguese translation.

AM230 Antoncich, Ricardo
Los cristianos ante la injusticia. Bogotá, CK: Ediciones Grupo Social, 1983. 187 pp. Paper. No ISBN.

An interpretation of Catholic social teaching in the context of injustice in Latin America; originally published in 1980 (Bogotá, CK: Grupo Social 2).

AM231 Antoncich, Ricardo, and José Miguel Munárriz
La Doctrina Social de la Iglesia. (Colección Cristianismo y Sociedad, 3). Madrid, SP: Ediciones Paulinas, 1987. 292 pp. 8428511543.

A history of the evolution of Catholic social teaching in Latin America in the 19th and 20th centuries, the systematic theology behind it, and its contemporary applications.

AM232 Antoncich, Ricardo, and José Miguel Munárriz
La doctrine social de l'Église. (Collection libération). Paris, FR: Éditions du Cerf, 1992. 293 pp. Paper. 2204044725.

French translation.

AM233 Arias, Esther, and Mortimer Arias
El Clamor de mi Pueblo: Desde el cautiverio en América Latina. New York, NYU: Friendship Press; Mexico, MX: CUPSA, 1981. x, 156 pp. Paper. 0377001058.

Spanish translation.

AM234 Arias, Esther, and Mortimer Arias
The Cry of My People: Out of Captivity in Latin America. New York, NYU: Friendship Press, 1980. x, 146 pp. Paper. 0377000957.

The authors sketch the history of U.S. relations with Latin America, revealing the vast social, economic, and political injustice present there, tracing the causes of underdevelopment, examining the "captivity" of human rights in the region, discussing the role of women in liberation, and presenting the development of Christianity's rediscovery of the Gospel among the poor and oppressed, and the theology of liberation, which arises to address these problems.

AM235 Arnold, Simon Pedro
La Otra Orilla: Una espiritualidad de la inculturación. (CEP, 166). Lima, PE: CEP, 1996. 201 pp. No ISBN.

A Benedictine monk from Chucuito (Peru) urges evangelization that is incarnational, requires radical openness and respect to others, advocation for the oppressed, and intercultural dialogue toward inculturation of the Gospel in Andean culture.

AM236 Batstone, David, ed.
New Visions for the Americas: Religious Engagement and Social Transformation. Minneapolis, MNU: Fortress Press, 1993. viii, 272 pp. Paper. 0800626907.

Fourteen essays by North and Latin America leaders in justice ministries, on future themes for liberation theologies and justice ministries, confronting neocolonialism and injustices based on social class, gender, and race.

AM237 Beeson, Trevor, and Jenny Pearce
A Vision of Hope: The Churches and Change in Latin America. Philadelphia, PAU: Fortress Press, 1984. 290 pp. Paper. 0800617584.

A country-by-country analysis of how Catholic and Protestant churches are responding, in Latin America, to the crisis brought about by economic neocolonialism, and the emergence of the poor to influence in public life.

AM238 Berryman, Phillip
Religion in the Megacity: Catholic and Protestant Portraits from Latin America. Maryknoll, NYU: Orbis Books, 1996. vi, 210 pp. Paper. 1570750831.

Case studies of differential responses to the challenges of the city, from the megacities of São Paulo and Caracas.

AM239 Bottasso, Juan, ed.
Documentos Latinoamericanos del Postconcilio. (Iglesia, Pueblos y Culturas, 1). Quito, EC: Iglesia, Pueblos y Culturas, 1986. 173 pp. No ISBN.

A numbered monograph that offers a collection of documents prepared by the Catholic and Protestant churches, as well as civil bodies, in defense of indigenous peoples and cultures.

AM240 Boudewijnse, Barbara, A. F. Droogers, and Frans Kamsteeg, eds.
Algo Más Que Opio: Una lectura antropológica del pentecostalismo latinoamericano y caribeño. (Sociología de la religión). San José, CR: DEI, 1991. 176 pp. Paper. 9977830444.

A collection of essays by Latin American and Caribbean authors, examining the cultural anthropological dimensions of the Pentecostal movement in Latin America; with an extensive bibliography of more than 700 titles.

AM241 Brown, Lyle C., and William F. Cooper, eds.
Religion in Latin American Life and Literature. Waco, TXU:
Markham Press Fund of Baylor University Press, 1980. x, 426
pp. 0918954231.
    Thirty-three scholarly essays (four covering the whole re-
gion; twenty-nine on Mexico, Spanish South America, and Brazil), with perspectives from history, social science, and literature.

AM242 Câmara, Hélder
Révolution dans la paix. Translated by Conrad Detrez. (Livre de
vie, 103). Paris, FR: Éditions du Seuil, 1970. 147 pp. 2020005549.
    French translation.

AM243 Câmara, Hélder
Revolução dentõ da Paz. (Hora e vez do Brasil, 2). Rio de Janeiro, BL: Ed. Sabia, 1968. 203 pp. No ISBN.
    A collection of writings by the renowned Catholic Arch-
bishop of Recife and Olinda in northeastern Brazil, on the need
for the church to join in a peaceful revolution for justice; with
particular reference to Latin America, and especially Brazil.

AM244 Câmara, Hélder
Revolution through Peace. Translated by Amparo McLean.
(World Perspectives, 45). New York, NYU: Harper & Row,
1971. xix, 149 pp. 0060105976.
    English translation.

AM245 Caravias, José Luis
Religiosidad Campesina y Liberación. (Colección Experiencias, 21). Bogotá, CK: Indo-American Press Service, 1978.
157 pp. No ISBN.
    A study of the unique faith of Latin American peasants,
and of how Catholicism needs to be shaped in more liberating
ways in order to be meaningful for them.

AM246 Castillo Lagarrigue, Fernando et al.
La Iglesia de los Pobres en América Latina. Santiago, CL:
Programa Ecuménico de Estudios del Cristianismo, 1983. 436
pp. No ISBN.
    An anthology of articles by Latin American theologians con-
cerning politics, human rights, and the poor, and how they inform and are informed by Protestantism and Roman Catholicism.

AM247 CEHILA
A Mulher pobre na história da Igreja latino-americana. Edited by Maria Luiza Marcílio. (Estudos e debates latino-americanos, 12). São Paulo, BL: Edições Paulinas, 1984. 211 pp.
8505002172.
    A collection of essays on the place of women, in poverty,
in the history of the Latin American church.

AM248 CELAM
Hacia un Mapa Pastoral de América Latina. Bogotá, CK:
CELAM, 1987. 507 pp. Paper. 9586250652.
    A manual of reports on historical, geographical, socio-
political, cultural, and socioreligious aspects of Latin America; presented as source material for organizing pastoral programs in the region.

AM249 CICOP (1st., 20-21 January 1964)
The Church in the New Latin America. Edited by John J.
Considine. (Fides Paperback Textbook, PBT-6). Notre Dame,
INU: Fides, 1964. xv, 240 pp. Paper. No ISBN.
    These papers present the Catholic Church, preparing for
action in confronting the problems of the area.

AM250 CICOP (3rd, 1996)
*Social Revolution in the New Latin America: A Catholic Ap-
praisal.* Edited by John J. Considine. (Fides Paperback Textbook, 21). Notre Dame, INU: Fides, 1966. xv, 245 pp. No
ISBN.
    Papers reflecting on problems of the area.

AM251 CICOP (4th, 1967)
Integration of Man and Society in Latin America. Edited by
Samuel Shapiro. Notre Dame, INU: University of Notre Dame
Press, 1967. xiii, 356 pp. No ISBN.
    Twenty-seven addresses and papers, by Catholics and
Protestants, on family, education, churches, and national and
international conditions of the region.

AM252 CICOP (5th, 1968)
Cultural Factors in Inter-American Relations. Edited by Sam-
uel Shapiro. Notre Dame, INU: University of Notre Dame
Press, 1968. xiii, 368 pp. No ISBN.
    A collection of papers by Richard Shaull, Denis Goulet,
Ruben Alves, and others, on aspiration for, and barriers to,
development and political liberation in Latin America.

AM253 CICOP (6th, 1969)
Human Rights and the Liberation of Man in the Americas.
Edited by Louis M. Colonnese. Notre Dame, INU: University
of Notre Dame Press, 1970. xxvi, 278 pp. 0268004226.
    Twenty-three papers on economic problems, agrarian
patterns, militarism, and traditional education as the primary
barriers to Latin American liberation.

AM254 CICOP (7th, Washington, DC, 5-8 Feb. 1970)
*Conscientization for Liberation: New Dimensions in Hemi-
spheric Realities.* Edited by Louis M. Colonnese. Washington, DCU: USCC, Div. for Latin America, 1971. xxi, 305 pp.
Paper. No ISBN.
    Sixteen papers by early Catholic and Protestant leaders
in liberation theology.

AM255 CICOP (8th, 1971)
*Freedom and Unfreedom in the Americas: Towards a Theolo-
gy of Liberation.* Edited by Thomas E. Quigley. (An IDOC
Book). New York, NYU: LAB, United States Catholic Church,
1971. 139 pp. No ISBN.
    Fourteen papers on the religious dimensions of the strug-
gle for freedom in Latin America.

**AM256 Cleary, Edward L., and Hannah W. Stewart-Gambino,
eds.**
*Conflict and Competition: The Latin American Church in a
Changing Environment.* Boulder, COU: Lynne Rienner Publishers, 1992. v, 234 pp. 1555872514 (hdbk), 1555873324
(pbk).
    Eight case studies by Latin American specialists, on the
Roman Catholic church and politics in selected countries; with
reflections on factors of liberation theology and the surge of
evangelical Protestantism, and overviews by the editors.

**AM257 Cleary, Edward L., and Hannah W. Stewart-Gambino,
eds.**
Power, Politics, and Pentecostals in Latin America. Boulder,
COU: Westview Press, 1997. vii, 261 pp. Paper. 0813321298.
    Twelve scholarly essays, both regional and national case
studies, assessing the dynamics of the Pentecostal movement,
including gender relations, political influence, and ecumenical relations.

AM258 Cleary, Edward L., ed.

Born of the Poor: The Latin American Church since Medellín.
Notre Dame, INU: University of Notre Dame Press, 1990.
vii, 210 pp. 0268006830.

Thirteen essays on liberation theology, the Medellín and
Puebla conferences of bishops, church, and society issues, and
on two conferences in the contexts of the world church and
social justice.

AM259 Cleary, Edward L., ed.

Path from Puebla: Significant Documents of the Latin American Bishops since 1979. Translated by Phillip Berryman.
Washington, DCU: USCC, 1989. 435 pp. Paper. 155587225X.

English translations of the major documents and articles
published by members of the Bishops' Conferences of Latin
America (CELAM) since 1979, organized with interpretative
introductions around forty-five themes.

AM260 Cleary, Edward L.

Crisis and Change: The Church in Latin America Today.
Maryknoll, NYU: Orbis Books, 1985. vi, 202 pp. Paper.
0883441497.

A clear, well-documented analysis of Latin American
trends (military, political, and economic), and of creative
Roman Catholics responses to them; by a Dominican priest
active in Latin American studies.

AM261 Codina, Víctor

Seguir a Jesús Hoy: De la modernidad a la solidaridad. (Pedal, 187). Salamanca, SP: Ediciones Sígueme, 1988. 21 pp.
Paper. 843011047X.

A discussion of the movement from secularism to liberation, from development to justice in the Roman Catholic Church
in Latin America; originally published under the title *De la Modernidad a la Solidaridad: Seguir a Jesús Hoy* (1984).

AM262 Conferencia Cristiana por la Paz de América Latina y el Caribe, Encuentro Internacional de Teologías (Matanzas,CU, 25 de febrero al 2 de marzo de 1979)

Evangelización y Política. Matanzas, CU: Centro de Información Ecuménica "Augusto Cotto," 1981. 271 pp. Paper.
No ISBN.

A collection of nine addresses from the meeting attended by important theologians.

AM263 Damen, Frans, and Esteban Judd Zanon, eds.

Cristo Crucificado en los Pueblos de América Latina: Antología de la Religión Popular. Quito, EC: Ediciones Abya-Yala; Cusco, PE: Instituto de Pastoral Andina, 1992. 417 pp.
Paper. No ISBN.

An anthology that provides access to the honorable role
that faith in the crucified Christ has played in popular religiosity, in the villages of Latin America, with illustrations by
Peruvian artists Antonio and Antonio Huillca.

AM264 D'Antonio, William V., and Frederick B. Pike, eds.

*Religion, Revolution and Reform: New Forces for Change in
Latin America.* New York, NYU: Praeger; London, ENK:
Burns & Oates, 1964. 276 pp. No ISBN.

Thirteen leading Catholic churchmen, politicians, and
social scientists explore the relationship of religion to social
change in Latin America, and the consequent decisions facing the church; papers originally presented in 1963 at the Notre
Dame Conference on Religion and Social Change in Latin
America.

AM265 Dumas, Benoit A.

*Los Dos Rostros Alienados de la Iglesia Una: Ensayo de
teología política.* Buenos Aires, AG: Latinoamerica Libros,
1971. 255 pp. Paper. No ISBN.

An essay on the Gospel as it faces the challenge of history, the poor, suffering, and the responsibility of the church in
Latin America.

AM266 Espada-Matta, Alberto

*Church and State in the Social Context of Latin America:
Caesar or Christ—Which Way in Latin America?* New York,
NYU: Vantage Press, 1985. xiv, 79 pp. 0533065925.

A historical analysis of the struggle between church and
state in Latin America, with a sensitive, practical approach to
a serious problem.

AM267 Eychaner, Fred, ed.

Ivan Illich: The Church, Change and Development. Chicago,
ILU: Urban Training Center Press, 1970. 125 pp. No ISBN.

Papers from Ivan Illich's contributions to a dialogue with
the staff of the Chicago Urban Training Center in the 1960s,
on the problems of Christian ministry, in the context of multiple social changes.

AM268 Floridi, Alexis Ulysses, and Annette E. Stiefbold

*The Uncertain Alliance: The Catholic Church and Labor in
Latin America.* (Monographs in International Affairs). Coral
Gables, FLU: University of Miami, Center for Advanced International Studies, 1973. vii, 108 pp. No ISBN.

Analysis of relationship between the Catholic Church and
workers in Latin America, foreseeing increasing church difficulties in maintaining internal unity and rapport with labor.

AM269 Fornet-Betancourt, Raúl

Verändert der Glaube die Wirtschaft: Theologie und Ökonomie in Lateinamerika. (Theologie der Dritten Welt, 16).
Freiburg im Breisgau, GW: Herder, 1991. 189 pp. Paper.
3451224135.

A collection of essays by economists, theologians, and philosophers from Latin America, exposes the injustice and religious hypocrisy of existent socio-economic systems of the area.

AM270 García, Ismael

Justice in Latin American Theology of Liberation. Atlanta,
GAU: John Knox Press, 1987. iv, 210 pp. Paper. 0804205019.

A comprehensive overview of the economic context of
political justice in Latin America, as understood by four prominent liberation theologians (Hugo Assmann, José M. Bonino, Gustavo Gutiérrez, and J. P. Miranda).

AM271 Garrard-Burnett, Virginia, and David Stoll, eds.

Rethinking Protestantism in Latin America. Philadelphia,
PAU: Temple University Press, 1993. vi, 234 pp. 1566391024
(hdbk), 1566391032 (pbk).

Essays by a historian, two sociologists, five anthropologists,
and a team of four political scientists, addressing two main issues: how are evangelicals responding to social crisis in Latin
America, and how are they affecting the societies around them?

AM272 Gheerbrant, Alain

L' Église rebelle d'Amérique latine. (Combats). Paris, FR:
Éditions du Seuil, 1969. 375 pp. No ISBN.

A narrative account, with numerous documents, on the Roman Catholic Church's responses to Latin American social realities during the visit of Pope John XXIII to Colombia in 1968,
and the Médellín Conference of Latin American bishops.

AM273 Goff, James E., and Margaret Goff

In Every Person Who Hopes ... the Lord Is Born Every Day: A Book of Latin American Faces and Places. New York, NYU: Friendship Press, 1980. 120 pp. Paper. 0377000965.

A collection of vignettes of ordinary people amid injustice in social and economic life, including brief descriptions of the life of the Protestant and Catholic churches, poems, hymns, liturgies, and cartoons of protest and hope; prepared as a mission study resource.

AM274 Greenway, Roger S.

Una Estrategia Urbana para Evangelizar a América Latina. El Paso, TXU: Chalice Press, 1977. 340 pp. Paper. 031113825X.

Spanish translation.

AM275 Greenway, Roger S.

An Urban Strategy for Latin America. Grand Rapids, MIU: Baker Books, 1973. 282 pp. Paper. 0801036674.

A detailed examination of modern urbanization in Latin America, biblical models for urban ministry, and strategies for urban mission in Latin America, with a Mexico City case study.

AM276 Grellert, Manfred

Los Compromisos de la Misión. San José, CR: Visión Mundial, 1992. 85 pp. Paper. 9977965072.

In this second edition, the author explores the integral mission of the church, as it is called to be the body of Christ which serves the poor, and challenges readers not to compromise the purposes of the reign of God in living out love and justice for the poor.

AM277 Gutiérrez, Azopardo et al.

Los Afroamericanos. (*Misiones Extranjeras* nn.102/103, 429-580). Madrid, SP: Misiones Extranjeras, 1989. 151 pp. No ISBN.

A numbered monograph containing twelve works on blacks in Latin America, past and present.

AM278 Gutiérrez, Gustavo

We Drink from Our Own Wells: The Spiritual Journey of a People. Translated by Matthew J. O'Connell. Maryknoll, NYU: Orbis Books; Melbourne, AT: Dove Communications, 1984. xxi, 181 pp. Paper. 088344707X (O), 0859243087 (D).

Reflections by Latin America's pioneer liberation theologian on the contexts and main aspects of contemporary Latin American spirituality.

AM279 Houtart, François

La Iglesia Latinoamericana en la hora del Concilio. Bogotá, CK: FERES, 1963. 62 pp. Paper. No ISBN.

A socioreligious study of social change occuring in Latin America, within both rural masses and traditional social elites, and the attitudes the church should assume in the face of social change.

AM280 Houtart, François, and Emile Jean Pin

The Church and the Latin American Revolution. Translated by Gilbert Barth. New York, NYU: Sheed and Ward, 1965. viii, 264 pp. No ISBN.

English translation.

AM281 Houtart, François, and Emile Jean Pin

Los Cristianos en la Revolución de América Latina. Translated by Marie Mercedes Riani and Maria Delia Barassi. (Contemplación y acción, 1). Buenos Aires, AG: Editorial Guadalupe, 1966. 221 pp. Paper. No ISBN.

Spanish translation.

AM282 Houtart, François, and Emile Jean Pin

L'Église à l'heure de l'Amérique latine. (Église vivante). Tournai, BE: Casterman, 1965. 265 pp. No ISBN.

A study of the changing social conditions in Latin America and of the Roman Catholic Church's adjustment to these changes.

AM283 Inman, Samuel Guy

Inter-American Conferences, 1826-1954: History and Problems. Washington, DCU: University Press, 1965. xi, 282 pp. No ISBN.

History of the Inter-American System, which draws on the personal experiences and insights from the author's long career as director of the CCLA.

AM284 Keogh, Dermot, ed.

Church and Politics in Latin America. New York, NYU: St. Martin's Press, 1990. xvii, 430 pp. 0312028156.

Twenty-one essays, by prominent Latin Americanists, about the Catholic Church, constraints from the Vatican, theological perspectives, the Central American scene, and the church amid revolution and counterrevolution across the region.

AM285 López Trujillo, Alfonso

¿Liberación o Revolución? (Colección Estudios Sociales, 4). Bogotá, CK: Ediciones Paulinas, 1975. 143 pp. No ISBN.

An evaluation and exploration of the theology of liberation as a permanent value—by a Roman Catholic Bishop of Colombia.

AM286 López Trujillo, Alfonso

Liberation or Revolution?: An Examination of the Priest's Role in the Socioeconomic Class Struggle in Latin America. Huntington, INU: Our Sunday Visitor, 1977. 128 pp. Paper. 0879736844.

English translation.

AM287 Löwy, Michael

The War of Gods: Religion and Politics in Latin America. New York, NYU: Verso, 1996. 163 pp. 1859849075 (hdbk), 1859840027 (pbk).

Through the lens of the sociology of culture, the author examines relations between religion, politics, and social issues, 1975-1995, as liberation theology has affected the Roman Catholic Church, and as Protestants have increased their forms and presence.

AM288 Landsberger, Henry A., ed.

The Church and Social Change in Latin America. Notre Dame, INU: University of Notre Dame Press, 1970. xiii, 240 pp. No ISBN.

A collection of commissioned papers on the Catholic Church.

AM289 Lange, Martin, and Reinhold Iblacker, eds.

Christenverfolgung in Südamerika: Zeugen der Hoffnung. (Herderbücherei, 770). Freiburg im Breisgau, GW: Herder, 1980. 189 pp. 3451077701.

Describing how Christians of different countries of Latin America, from peasants to bishops, are being persecuted, abducted, or murdered, this study also shows the background of the ideology of National Security and the opposition to liberation theology.

AM290 Lange, Martin, and Reinhold Iblacker, eds.

Witnesses of Hope: The Persecution of Christians in Latin America. Maryknoll, NYU: Orbis Books, 1981. xx, 156 pp. Paper. 0883447592.

English translation.

AM291 Lernoux, Penny

Cry of the People: United States Involvement in the Rise of Fascism, Torture, and Murder and the Persecution of the Catholic Church in Latin America. Garden City, NYU: Doubleday, 1980. xiv, 535 pp. 038513150X.

This work depicts the shift of the Catholic Church in Latin America from centuries of backing the established governments and property-holding classes, to become "the new Catholic Church," with a role that may confront the United States with forces now changing the face of Latin America.

AM292 Levine, Daniel H., ed.

Churches and Politics in Latin America. (Sage Focus Editions, 14). Beverly Hills, CAU: Sage Publications, 1980. 288 pp. 0803912986 (hdbk), 0803912994 (pbk).

Eleven essays by scholars from both North and South America, focusing on the new social role of religion, and the conflicts it has brought with governments more interested in national security doctrines than in human rights and redistributive policies that affect the poor.

AM293 Levine, Daniel H.

Popular Voices in Latin American Catholicism. (Studies in Church and State). Princeton, NJU: Princeton University Press, 1992. xxii, 403 pp. 0691087547 (hdbk), 0691024596 (pbk).

A scholarly study, by the Professor of Political Science at the University of Michigan, of grassroots factors affecting the initiation, substance, and impact of religious and cultural change in Latin America; based on rich interviews and community studies in Venezuela and Colombia, and analysis of broad ideological and institutional transformations.

AM294 Levine, Daniel H.

Religion and Political Conflict in Latin America. Chapel Hill, NCU: University of North Carolina, 1986. xiii, 266 pp. Paper. 0807816892 (hdbk), 0807841501 (pbk).

Eleven essays generated by an interdisciplinary, international conference, in March 1982, on popular religion, politics, and the culture in Latin America.

AM295 Levine, Daniel H.

Religion and Politics in Latin America: The Catholic Church in Venezuela and Colombia. Princeton, NJU: Princeton University Press, 1981. xii, 342 pp. 0691076243 (hdbk), 0691022003 (pbk).

A detailed analysis showing that, after centuries of close intertwining of religion and politics in Latin America, there is now a profound transformation shaping an emerging new relation between religion and political beliefs, attitudes, and action.

AM296 Liggett, Thomas J.

Where Tomorrow Struggles to be Born: The Americas in Transition. New York, NYU: Friendship Press, 1970. 160 pp. Paper. 037710051X.

A call for the United States government and churches to respect Latin American desires for self-determination.

AM297 Littwin, Lawrence

Latin America: Catholicism and Class Conflict. Encino, CAU: Dickenson Publishing, 1974. viii, 135 pp. 0822101173.

A study of the historical relationship between the economic and social organization of Mexico, Chile, and Cuba and the Thomistic worldview.

AM298 Lynch, Edward A.

Religion and Politics in Latin America: Liberation Theology and Christian Democracy. New York, NYU: Praeger, 1991. xi, 200 pp. 0275937747.

An analysis of the relationship between Christianity and politics in Latin America, assessing the impact of the two most important Catholic lay movements of liberation theology, and Christian democracy, in Nicaragua and Venezuela.

AM299 Miguez Bonino, José, Carmelo Alvarez, and Roberto Craig

Protestantismo y Liberalismo en América Latina. San José, CR: DEI, 1985. 91 pp. Paper. 997790412X.

Three essays on the social history of Protestantism in Latin America: the social history of Protestantism (J. Miguez Bonino); the contrast between liberal and liberational Protestantism (C. Alvarez), and a Costa Rica case study (R. Craig).

AM300 MacEóin, Gary

Revolution Next Door: Latin America in the 1970's. New York, NYU: Holt, Rinehart & Winston, 1972. vii, 243 pp. 0030914825.

A study of the "Decade of Development," neocolonialism, the church, the armed forces, and the CIA.

AM301 Mainwaring, Scott, and Alexander Wilde, eds.

The Progressive Church in Latin America. Notre Dame, INU: University of Notre Dame Press, 1989. xii, 340 pp. 0268015732 (hdbk), 0268015740 (pbk).

Eight scholarly essays on the Catholic church in relation to 20th-century political and social changes in Nicaragua, El Salvador, Brazil, and Peru; with a comprehensive introductory essay by the editors.

AM302 McIntosh, G. Stewart

7 Ensayos sobre la Realidad Misiológica en América Latina. Lima, PE: PUCEMAA, 1990. 57 pp. Paper. 1871609135.

Seven short essays on social aspects of mission in Latin America.

AM303 McManus, Philip, and Gerald Schlabach, eds.

Relentless Persistence: Nonviolent Action in Latin America. Philadelphia, PAU: New Society Publishers Resource Center for Nonviolence, 1991. xi, 312 pp. 086571181X (hdbk.US), 155092012X (hdbk, CAN), 0865711828 (pbk, US), 1550920138 (pbk, CAN).

A collection of fourteen case histories and testimonies from Latin America, of the creative use by the oppressed, of active nonviolence in their struggle for justice and human dignity.

AM304 Mecham, J. Lloyd

Church and State in Latin America: A History of Politico-Ecclesiastical Relations. Chapel Hill, NCU: University of North Carolina Press, 1966. ix, 465 pp. No ISBN.

Revised edition of a scholarly history, arranged by regions, of the relationships between the Roman Catholic Church and political authorities in Latin America, from 1493 to 1965.

AM305 Mutchler, David E.

The Church as a Political Factor in Latin America: With Particular Reference to Colombia and Chile. (Praeger Special Studies in International Politics and Public Affairs). New York, NYU: Praeger, 1971. xxviii, 460 pp. No ISBN.

A doctoral study of conflicts and fragmentation within the Roman Catholic Church bureaucracy in the 1960s, as it dealt with general political factors in Latin America, and particular factors in Colombia and Chile.

AM306 Nida, Eugene Albert
Communication of the Gospel in Latin America. (Sondeos, 53). Cuernavaca, MX: CIDOC, 1969. 145 pp. No ISBN.

Anthropological analysis of major religious and social themes of Latin American life; also published under the title *Understanding Latin Americans* (1973).

AM307 Norman, Edward R.
Christianity in the Southern Hemisphere: The Churches in Latin America and South Africa. Oxford, ENK: Clarendon Press; Oxford, ENK: Oxford University Press, 1981. vi, 230 pp. 0198211279.

A comparative study of the relationships between ecclesiastical and socio-political developments in Latin America, and in South Africa.

AM308 Pérez Esquivel, Adolfo
Le Christ au poncho: suivi de témoignages de luttes non-violentes en Amérique latine. Edited by Charles Antoine. Paris, FR: Le Centurion, 1981. 148 pp. 2227004010.

An essay on nonviolence, plus concrete case histories of nonviolent resistance in Latin America; with a biographical sketch of the author, winner of the Nobel Peace Prize in 1980.

AM309 Pérez Esquivel, Adolfo
Christ in a Poncho: Testimonials of the Nonviolent Struggles in Latin America. Edited by Charles Antoine. Translated by Robert R. Barr. Maryknoll, NYU: Orbis Books, 1983. iv, 139 pp. Paper. 0883441047.

English translation.

AM310 Pérez Esquivel, Adolfo
Lucha no Violenta por la Paz. Translated by Angel S. Maranon. Bilbao, SP: Desclée de Brouwer, 1983. 157 pp. 8433006088.

Spanish translation.

AM311 Pérez Esquivel, Adolfo
O Cristo de poncho: Seguido de testemunhos de lutas não-violentas na América Latina. São Paulo, BL: Edicões Loyola, 1982. 141 pp. No ISBN.

Portuguese translation.

AM312 Padilla, C. René et al.
Fe Cristiana y Latinoamericana Hoy. Buenos Aires, AG: Ediciones Certeza, 1974. 214 pp. Paper. No ISBN.

A collection of papers from the First Protestant Consultation on Social Ethics (Lima, Peru, 5-8 July 1972), on the theme of the participation of Christians in society.

AM313 Parades A., Ruben
El Evangelio en Platos de Barro. (Serie Presencia Evangélica). Lima, PE: Fe y Misión Cristiana, Ciencias Sociales y Anthropología, 1989. 188 pp. Paper. 1871609062.

A reader on insights from social anthropology for Prostestants in mission, in both the Andean and the Amazonian regions of South America.

AM314 Parker, Cristián G.
Otra Lógica en América Latina: Religión popular y modernización capitalista. (Sección de obras de sociología). México D.F., MX: Fondo de Cultura Económica; Santiago, CL: Fondo de Cultura Económica Chile, 1993. 407 pp. No ISBN.

An important work, by one of the leading Latin American sociologists of religion, tracing the past and present religious culture of Latin America, with special reference to contextual hermeneutical issues associated with popular Catholicism.

AM315 Parker, Cristián G.
Popular Religion and Modernization in Latin America: A Different Logic. Translated by Robert R. Barr. Maryknoll, NYU: Orbis Books, 1996. xii, 292 pp. 157075067X.

English translation.

AM316 Pattnayak, Satya R., ed.
Organized Religion in the Political Transformation of Latin America. Lanham, MDU: University Press of America, 1995. xi, 239 pp. 0761800395 (hdbk), 0761800409 (pbk).

Nine scholarly essays on the relation between religion and politics in Latin America; originally presented at a conference sponsored by Villanova University in 1993.

AM317 Peña, Milagros
Theologies and Liberation in Peru: The Role of Ideas in Social Movements. Philadelphia, PAU: Temple University Press, 1995. xii, 222 pp. 1566392942.

A scholarly analysis of how social protest has become a significant aspect of religious ideology throughout Latin America, particularly with the emergence of liberation theology in Peru.

AM318 Petersen, Douglas
Not by Might nor by Power: A Pentecostal Theology of Social Concern in Latin America. Oxford, ENK: Regnum Books, 1996. xvi, 260 pp. Paper. 1870345207.

A multidisciplinary approach to the study of Pentecostal social concern in Latin America, by the Assembly of God's area director for mission in Central America.

AM319 Pike, Frederick B., ed.
The Conflict between Church and State in Latin America. (Borzoi Books on Latin America). New York, NYU: Knopf, 1964. ix, 239 pp. Paper. No ISBN.

A collection of previously published papers on the topic, divided chronologically, and dealing with the colonial, 19th century, and modern periods.

AM320 Pin, Emile Jean
Elementos para una Sociología del Catolicismo Latinoamericano. (Estudios Socio-religiosos Latino-americanos, 20). Fribourg, SZ: FERES, 1963. 120 pp. Paper. No ISBN.

A sociologist of religion develops a social analysis of Latin American Catholicism.

AM321 Pixley, Jorge V., ed.
La Mujer en la Construcción de la Iglesia: Una Perspectiva Bautista Desde América Latina y el Caribe. San José, CR: DEI, 1986. 120 pp. Paper. 9977904324.

A collection of four papers prepared for and given at a conference of twenty Latin American and Caribbean Baptists (San José, Costa Rica, 10-14 February 1986) that discussed the role and participation of women within the Baptist tradition.

AM322 Richard, Pablo
Death of Christendoms, Birth of the Church: Historical Analysis and Theological Interpretation of the Church in Latin America. Maryknoll, NYU: Orbis Books, 1987. x, 213 pp. Paper. 0883445573.

Essays on the disintegration of the old alliance between the Catholic church and the governments, the attempt at a new "Christendom" from 1930 to 1960, and the renewal after Vatican II.

AM323 Richard, Pablo

La Iglesia Latinoamericana Entre el Temor y la Esperanza: Apuntes Teológicos para la Década de los Años 80. San José, CR: DEI, 1981. 103 pp. Paper. No ISBN.

A collection of five articles, originally written between 1976 and 1980, defining liberation theology, presenting a theological reflection on Latin American history during the 1960s and 1970s, and considering Christian and ecclesial identity amidst the popular movement.

AM324 Richard, Pablo, and José de Assis Countinho

A Igreja latino-americana entre o temor e a esperança: Apontamentos teológicos para a década de 80. (Coleção "Libertação e teologia," 19). São Paulo, BL: Edições Paulinas, 1982. 122 pp. No ISBN.

Portuguese translation.

AM325 Rosales, Juan

Los Cristianos, los Marxistas y la Revolución. Buenos Aires, AG: Ediciones Silaba, 1970. 449 pp. Paper. No ISBN.

A Marxist examination of the role of the Roman Catholic Church in the revolution in Latin America, "Social Christianity" as formulated by Thomas Aquinas and others, and Soviet and Cuban influences in Latin American social Christianity, particularly in Chile and Venezuela.

AM326 Sølle, Dorothee

Gott im Müll: Eine andere Entdeckung Lateinamerikas. Munich, GW: Deutscher Taschenbuch Verlag, 1992. 174 pp. 342330040X.

Fifty vignettes of struggles, by the poor, for a fuller life; written by the noted theologian following a recent journey through Latin America.

AM327 Sølle, Dorothee

Stations of the Cross: A Latin American Pilgrimage. Minneapolis, MNU: Fortress Press, 1993. ix, 146 pp. Paper. 0800626885.

English translation.

AM328 Sanders, Thomas G.

Catholic Innovation in a Changing Latin America. (Sondeos, 41). Cuernavaca, MX: CIDOC, 1969. various pp. Paper. No ISBN.

Essays written in 1967 and 1968 on social involvements of the Catholic Church in Latin America, with special reference to issues of education and family planning in Chile.

AM329 Sawyer, Frank

The Poor Are Many: Political Ethics in the Social Encyclicals, Christian Democracy, and Liberation Theology in Latin America. (Church and Theology in Context, 15). Kampen, NE: Kok, 1992. x, 199 pp. Paper. 9024273714.

A scholarly analysis of the multidimensional characteristics of the development/liberation problem in Latin America, and of the contributions of "Christian Democracy" and liberation theology; originally presented as a Ph.D. thesis in ethics at the Theological University, Kampen, the Netherlands.

AM330 Schöpfer, Hans

Neue christliche Kunst in Lateinamerika: Bilder und Meditationen. Mainz, GW: Matthias-Grünewald-Verlag, 1989. 72 pp. Paper. 3786714150.

Themes of suffering in the Third World, as represent-ed through the art of Maximino Cerezo Barredos, and related meditative texts by the author.

AM331 Schmid, Viola

Gott schwitzt in den Strassen Lateinamerikas. Frankfurt am Main, GW: Lembeck, 1983. 228 pp. 3874762092.

The journalist-author explores the relationship between church and politics through ten interviews with influential people in Latin America, including José Miguez Bonino and Cardinal Paulo Evaristo Arns.

AM332 Schmitt, Karl M., ed.

The Roman Catholic Church in Modern Latin America. (Borzoi Books on Latin America). New York, NYU: Knopf, 1972. x, 225 pp. 0394473892 (trade), 0394313526 (text).

The author's introduction briefly surveys the church's activities in political and social spheres, from independence to 1970, with a selection of readings pertaining largely to 20th-century church and state, and church and development issues.

AM333 Schutte, Ofelia

Cultural Identity and Social Liberation in Latin American Thought. (Latin American and Iberian Thought and Culture). Albany, NYU: SUNY Press, 1993. x, 313 pp. 0791413179 (hdbk), 0791413187 (pbk).

A philosophical analysis of the relationship between liberation, cultural identity, and Latin American social reality; with critiques of the works of Gustavo Gutiérrez, Paolo Freire, and others.

AM334 Sigmund, Paul E., ed.

Religious Freedom and Evangelization in Latin America: The Challenge of Religious Pluralism. (Religion and Human Rights Series). Maryknoll, NYU: Orbis Books, 1999. 359 pp. Paper. 157075263X.

While growing religious pluralism in Latin America has influenced a trend toward democracy and the growth of Protestantism, the author notes that it has led to unresolved tensions; these are analyzed through a collection of sixteen articles on Catholic and Protestant perspectives, in contexts of Brazil, Argentina, Mexico, Nicaragua, Cuba, El Salvador, Guatemala, Chile, Colombia, Venezuela, and Peru.

AM335 Silva Gotay, Samuel

El Pensamiento Cristiano Revolucionario en América Latina y el Caribe: Implicaciones de la Teología de la Liberación para la Sociología de la Religión. Río Piedras, PR: Ediciones Huracán, 1989. 393 pp. Paper. 0904023897.

Third edition of a historical study of the development of Christian thought, and its contribution to sociology and theology in Latin America, between 1960 and 1973; one chapter is devoted to the presence of Christians in the revolutionary processes of the region.

AM336 Smith, Christian

The Emergence of Liberation Theology: Radical Religion and Social Movement Theory. Chicago, ILU: University of Chicago Press, 1991. xiv, 300 pp. 0226764095 (hdbk), 0226764109 (pbk).

A comprehensive social history, using a political process model of the liberation theology movement in Latin America, from 1930 to the present; based on interviews, the analysis of primary source documents, and other studies.

AM337 Souza, Luiz Alberto Gómez de
Classes Populares e Igreja nos Caminhos da História.
(Publicações CID: Sociologia Religiosa, 6). Petropolis, BL:
Vozes, 1982. 311 pp. Paper. No ISBN.

Collection of the author's articles, arranged thematically: 1) theoretical reflection and its interaction with social practice, 2) the problem of education, and 3) the problem of church-state relations in the Puebla document, in
BCCs, and in the witness of Camilo Torres, Oscar A. Romero, and Hélder Câmara.

AM338 Swatos, William H., ed.
Religion and Democracy in Latin America. New Brunswick, NJU: Transaction Pubs., 1995. x, 163 pp. Paper.
1560008059.

A collection of ten recent essays; originally published
in the journals *Sociological Analysis* and *Sociology of Religion.*

**AM339 Symposium on Inter-ethnic Conflict in South
America (Bridgetown, Barbados, 25-30 January 1971)**
*Die Situation der Indios in Sndamerika: Grundlagen der
interethnischen Konflikte der nichtandinen Indianer.* Edited by Walter Dostal. Wuppertal, GW: Hammer, 1976. 3
vols. 3872940732 (vol.1), 3872940872 (v. 2-3).

German translation.

AM340 Torres, Carlos Alberto
*The Church, Society, and Hegemony: A Critical Sociology
of Religion in Latin America.* Translated by Richard A.
Young. Westport, CTU: Praeger, 1992. xv, 223 pp.
0275937739.

An Argentinian sociologist of religion, now associate
professor of education at the University of California at
Los Angeles, reinterprets major theorists on the sociology
of religion (Marx, Durkheim, Weber, and Gramsci), and
analyzes the "popular church" in Latin America; with a
case study on church-state relations in Argentina, 1880 to
1983.

AM341 Turner, Frederick C.
Catholicism and Political Development in Latin America.
Chapel Hill, NCU: University of North Carolina Press,
1971. xv, 272 pp. 0807811645.

Analyzes perceptions of political and economic change
by Catholic leaders in Latin America, stressing diversity
in the church, and examining orientations toward major
policy issues, such as education, birth control, and church-
state relations; based on archival research and interviews.

AM342 Vélez Correa, Jaime
*La Cultura como Mediación para Evangelizar la No-creen-
cia en América Latina.* (Serie Fe y Cultura, 4). Bogotá,
CK: CELAM, 1991. 89 pp. No ISBN.

Second edition of an analysis of nonbelief, in Latin
America based, on the thesis that successful evangelism
must take into account the culture, as well as beliefs; first
published in 1989.

AM343 Vallier, Ivan
*Catholicism, Social Control, and Modernization in Latin
America.* Englewood Cliffs, NJU: Prentice-Hall, 1970. x,
172 pp. No ISBN.

A sociologist analyzes the influence of the Roman

Catholic church in Latin America, trying to identify factors that help free the church from unfruitful alliances, and
indicating alternatives that are emerging through special
emphasis on laity and congregation.

AM344 Weber, Wilfried
*Transzendentales und innerweltliches Heil im Christentum
Lateinamerikas und der Philippinen: Zur Interdependenz
von Religion und Gesellschaftspolitik.* (Europäische Hoch-
schulschriften, 23: Theologie, 220.). Frankfurt am Main,
GW: Lang, 1983. 321 pp. Paper. 382047739X.

The idea behind this book is the contextualization of
pastoral ministry and mission, meeting the demands of "holistic salvation," and leading to a mutually fruitful dialogue
between medieval integralism and the modern, total separation of faith and science, church and state, and religion
and politics.

AM345 Yamamori, Tetsunao et al., eds.
Serving with the Poor in Latin America. (Cases in Holis-
tic Ministry). Monrovia, CA: MARC, 1997. vi, 156 pp.
Paper. 1887983031.

Nine case studies and five reflections; first presented
at the Latin American Consultation on Holistic Ministry
(Quito, Ecuador, November 1996).

**AM346 Yamamori, Tetsunao, Gregorio Rake, and C. René
Padilla, eds.**
*Servir con los Pobres en América Latina: Modelos de min-
isterio integral.* Buenos Aires, AG: Ediciones Kairós, 1997.
156 pp. Paper. 9879591526.

A collection of ten articles, the first of the Latin American Council on the (Integrated) Mainstay, in Quito, Ecuador (November, 1996).

AM347 Zambrano, Luis
*Entstehung und theologisches Verständnis der Kirches des
Volkes: (Iglesia Popular) in Lateinamerike.* (Erfahrung und
Theologie, 6). Frankfurt am Main, GW: Lang, 1982. v, 396
pp. Paper. 3820472681.

A work describing the situation of Latin America
amidst the aspect of dependence and underdevelopment,
and the reform of the Latin American church into a "church
of the people."

General: Biography, Collective

See also AM106, AM928-AM930, AM932, and AM936.

AM348 Clissold, Stephen
The Saints of South America. London, ENK: Knight, 1972.
217 pp. 0853141622.

The biographies of ten Spanish missionary-saints in
South America in the 16th and 17th centuries.

AM349 Gaustad, Edwin S., ed.
Memoirs of the Spirit. Grand Rapids, MIU: Eerdmans,
1999. xix, 356 pp. 0802838677.

A diverse collection of twenty-six spiritual autobiog-
raphies, that cover a wide range of faiths and a glimpse of
America's rich religious traditions; includes memoirs from
Thomas Merton, Black Elk, Richard Rodriguez, Mary Row-
landson, William F. Buckley, Frederick Douglas, Harry
Emerson Fosdick, Billy Graham, and Dorothy Day.

AM350 Habig, Marion Alphonse
Saints of the Americas. Huntington, INU: Our Sunday Visitor, 1974. 384 pp. 0879738804.

Brief sketches, based on secondary accounts, of all persons in the Western Hemisphere who have been canonized or beatified by the RCC.

AM351 Keyes, Frances Parkinson
The Rose and the Lily: The Lives and Times of Two South American Saints. New York, NYU: Hawthorn Books, 1961. 253 pp. No ISBN.

Two separate biographies: Isabel de F'lores y Olivia, St. Rose of Lima (1586-1617), and Mariana Paredes y F'lores, the Lily of Quito (1619-1645), including much local color of 16th-, 17th-, and 20th-century Peru and Ecuador.

AM352 McCorkel, Henry L.
The Quiet Crusaders. New York, NYU: Friendship Press, 1961. 175 pp. No ISBN.

Biographical sketches of twelve contemporary Latin American Protestants, both leaders and followers.

AM353 Pereira Alves, Antonio
Semblanzas Evangélicas. El Paso, TXU: Chalice Press, 1963. 133 pp. Paper. No ISBN.

A collection of twenty-four biographies of Protestant leaders, known in Latin America as missionaries, intellectuals, writers, etc.

AM354 Stehle, Emil L., ed.
Zeugen des Glaubens in Lateinamerika: Von der Entdeckung bis zur Gegenwart. Mainz, GW: Matthias-Grünewald-Verlag, 1980. 112 pp. 3786708355.

Twenty-two short biographies, ranging from Christopher Columbus to Archbishop Romero, sketch how the Latin American church was always faced with the task of defending the poor against powerful economic, political, and social interests.

General: Biography, Individual

See also MI190, AM5, AM76, and AM78.

AM355 Ballard, Jerry
Never Say Can't. Carol Stream, ILU: Creation House, 1971. 172 pp. No ISBN.

A popular biography of Thomas H. Willey (1898-1968), a pioneer CMA missionary to Peru (1927-1935), and Free Will Baptist missionary to Panama (1936-1939) and Cuba (1940-1961).

AM356 Biermann, Benno M.
Las Casas und seine Sendung: Das Evangelium und die Rechte des Menschen. (Walberberger Studien: Theologische Reihe, 5). Mainz, GW: Grünewald, 1968. xv, 92 pp. No ISBN.

A critical, but positive, study of the life and missionary vision of Bartolomé de Las Casas, defender of the Indians.

AM357 Boria, Rubén
Fray Pedro de Córdoba, O.P., 1481-1521: Padre de los dominicos del nuevo mundo, maestro de Fray Bartolomé de Las Casas, O.P., primer indigenista de América. Tucumán, AG: Ediciones UNSTA, 1982. 190 pp. No ISBN.

A biography of this Dominican Spanish missionary, the first to arrive in the New World, who was a teacher of Bartolomé de Las Casas.

AM358 Friede, Juan, and Benjamin Keen, eds.
Bartolomé de Las Casas in History: Toward an Understanding of the Man and his Work. DeKalb, ILU: Northern Illinois University Press, 1971. xiii, 632 pp. Paper. 0875800254.

A translation of ten important interpretive essays out of Europe, on the life, work, ideology, and heritage of the 16th-century "Protector of the Indians"; with an extensive bibliography.

AM359 Kramar, Marilynn, and Robert C. Larson
The Marilynn Kramar Story: Joy Comes in the Morning. Ann Arbor, MIU: Servant Publications, 1990. 158 pp. Paper. 0892836555.

Testimonies by the founder and President of Charis Missions, to God's guidance of her, in this Catholic mission to Hispanics in the United States and Latin America.

AM360 Neumann, Martin
Las Casas: Die unglaubliche Geschichte von der Entdeckung der Neuen Welt. Freiburg im Breisgau, GW: Herder, 1990. 285 pp. 3451220660.

A biography of Bartolomé de Las Casas, who renounced all his possessions as an *encomendero*, became a Dominican and bishop of Chiapas, and spent the rest of his life fighting for the rights of the Indians of Latin America.

AM361 Pérez Fernández, Isacio
Cronología Documentada de los Viajes, Estancias y Actuaciones de fray Bartolomé de las Casas. (Estudios monográficos, 2). Bayamón, PR: Centro de Estudios de los Dominicos del Caribe, 1984. xvi, 1,024 pp. 8439825978.

The life of Bartolomé de Las Casas, a missionary to the Caribbean, Central America, and Mexico, from 1502-1547; presented in chronological format.

AM362 Scarborough, Peggy
J. H. Ingram, Missionary Dean: A Biographical Portrait. (Church of God Missions Series: Portraits of Missionary Saints who have Ministered in the Church of God). Cleveland, TNU: Pathway Press, 1966. 160 pp. Paper. No ISBN.

A narrative biography of the man who, more than anyone else, helped spread the ministry of the Church of God [Cleveland, Tenn.] to numerous fields in Latin America.

AM363 Sinclair, John H.
Juan A. Mackay: Un Escocés con Alma Latina. Mexico City, MX: CUPSA, 1990. 239 pp. Paper. 9687011270.

Biography of John A. Mackay (1889-1983), Presbyterian minister, theological educator, and ecumenical leader in Latin America and the United States; focusing on his contribution in Latin America.

AM364 Wagner, Henry Raup
The Life and Writings of Bartolomé de Las Casas. Albuquerque, NMU: University of New Mexico Press, 1967. xxv, 310 pp. No ISBN.

An original biography of Las Casas, emphasizing his later years as "Protector" and legal advocate of the Indians, instead of his earlier years as the "apostle" or missionary to them; with a critical catalogue of his writings.

Latin American Theologies

See also TH21, TH176, TH180, TH203-TH206, TH297-TH298, TH333, TH350, TH375, TH377-TH380, TH386, TH388, TH410, TH419-TH421, TH424, TH428, TH431, TH474, TH500-TH501, TH541, TH575-TH579, TH598, TH600-TH601, CR639, SO103-SO105, EC42, EC47, EC60, EC100, EC188, PO113-PO114, PO130, EV180, CH348, SP34, AM103, AM121, AM139, AM169, AM190, AM204, AM209-AM210, AM220, AM231-AM232, AM236, AM254, AM258, AM270, AM287, AM335, AM466, AM469, AM671, AM677, AM693-AM694, AM723, AM741, AM822, AM1073, AM1316-AM1317, AM1344, AM1351, AM1363, and AM1398.

AM365 Alves, Rubem A.

Religión, ¿opio o instrumento de liberación? Montevideo, UY: Editorial Tierra Nueva, 1970. xii, 257 pp. Paper. No ISBN.

Spanish translation.

AM366 Alves, Rubem A.

A Theology of Human Hope. New York, NYU: Corpus Books, 1969. xv, 199 pp. No ISBN.

A theological account of what it takes to make and keep human life humane in the world; by a noted Brazilian theologian, who contrasts "humanistic messianism" with the "messianic humanism" of liberation theology.

AM367 Aquino, María Pilar, ed.

Aportes para Una Teología Desde la Mujer. Madrid, SP: Editorial Biblia y Fe, 1988. 160 pp. Paper. No ISBN.

Essays on methodology, Christology, ecclesiology, and spirituality, from the perspective of Latin American women; originally presented at the International Congress of Women (Oaxtepec, Mexico, December 1986).

AM368 Aquino, María Pilar

Nuestro Clamor por la Vida: Teología Latinoamericana desde la Perspectiva de la Mujer. (Colección Mujer Latinoamericana). San José, CR: Editorial DEI, 1992. 244 pp. 9977830576.

In this pioneer work, the President of the Association of Catholic Hispanic Theologians in the United States develops the special features of a theology developed out of women's experiences of oppression and liberation in Latin America.

AM369 Aquino, María Pilar

Our Cry for Life: Feminist Theology from Latin America. Translated by Dinah Livingstone. Maryknoll, NYU: Orbis Books, 1993. viii, 254 pp. Paper. 0883448955.

English translation.

AM370 Araya, Victorio G.

El Dios de los Pobres: El Misterio de Dios en la Teología de la Liberación. San José, CR: DEI, 1983. 244 pp. Paper. 9977904138.

A scholarly study of the mystery of God in Latin American liberation theology, drawing principally from the thought of Gustavo Gutiérrez and Jon Sobrino.

AM371 Araya, Victorio G.

God of the Poor: The Mystery of God in Latin American Liberation Theology. Translated by Robert R. Barr. Maryknoll, NYU: Orbis Books, 1987. xv, 205 pp. 0883445662 (hdbk), 0883445654 (pbk).

An analysis of the basic content concerning God in Latin American liberation theology by the Professor of Theology at the Latin American Biblical Seminary in Costa Rica.

AM372 Assmann, Hugo

Opresión—Liberación: Desafío a los Cristianos. Montevideo, UY: Tierra Nueva, 1971. 208 pp. Paper. No ISBN.

Study of the political dimension of faith, as a praxis of human liberation in history—with particular attention to the advances of liberation theology.

AM373 Assmann, Hugo

Teología desde la Praxis de la Liberación: Ensayo Teológico desde la Amárica Dependiente, I. (Agora). Salamanca, SP: Ediciones Sígueme, 1975. 271 pp. No ISBN.

Second edition of essays on the fundamentals of theologies of liberation, by a major Brazilian architect of Latin American liberation theology; originally published in 1973.

AM374 Assmann, Hugo

Theology for a Nomad Church. Translated by Paul Burns. Maryknoll, NYU: Orbis Books; London, ENK: Search Press, 1976. 146 pp. 0883444933 (US hdbk), 0883444941 (US pbk), 0855323469 (UK pbk).

English translation of *Telogía desde la Praxis de la Liberación* (1973); also published under the title *Practical Theology of Liberation* (London, UK: Search Press, 1975).

AM375 Aulbach, Stefan

Spiritualität schafft Befreiung: Der Entwurf christlicher Existenz bei Juan Luis Segundo. (Würzburger Studien zur Fundamentaltheologie, 10). Frankfurt am Main, GW: Lang, 1992. ix, 152 pp. Paper. 3631450788.

This outline of the spirituality of Juan Luis Segundo shows how political action is joined with faith in his form of liberation theology, as it criticizes the religion and piety inherited from Europe.

AM376 Bañuelas, Arturo J., ed.

Mestizo Christianity: Theology from the Latino Perspective. Maryknoll, NYU: Orbis Books, 1995. vi, 278 pp. Paper. 1570750327.

Fourteen essays by prominent Hispanic American theologians, providing an excellent introduction to Latino theology in the United States.

AM377 Batstone, David

From Conquest to Struggle: Jesus of Nazareth in Latin America. Albany, NYU: SUNY Press, 1991. xiv, 224 pp. 0791404218 (hdbk), 0791404226 (pbk).

A detailed analysis of the role of Jesus of Nazareth in the thought of Latin American liberation theologians.

AM378 Berryman, Phillip

Liberation Theology: Essential Facts about the Revolutionary Movement in Latin America and Beyond. Philadelphia, PAU: Temple University Press; Oak Park, ILU: Meyer-Stone Books; New York, NYU: Pantheon Books, 1987. 231 pp. 087722479X (T), 0940989034 (M), 0394552415 (P hdbk), 039474652X (P pbk).

A concise basic text for the study of Latin American liberation theology, and how it functions at the village or barrio level to impact political systems; also published in London by Tauris [1850430519 (hdbk); 1850430543 (pbk)].

AM379 Boff, Leonardo

O Caminhar da Igreja com os oprimidos: Do vale de lágrimas à terra prometida. (Coleção Edições do Pasquim, 82). Rio de Janeiro, BL: CODECRI, 1980. 252 pp. No ISBN.

An analysis of the sociology of oppression and the church's work with the poor, by the noted Brazilian liberation theologian.

AM380 Boff, Leonardo

A fé na periferia do mundo. (Publicações CID: Teologia, 17). Petrópolis, BL: Editora Vozes, 1983. 128 pp. No ISBN.

Third edition of a sociological analysis of faith and marginality, by the noted Brazilian liberation theologian; originally published in 1978.

AM381 Boff, Leonardo

Faith on the Edge: Religion and Marginalized Existence. Translated by Robert R. Barr. Maryknoll, NYU: Orbis Books; San Francisco, CAU: Harper & Row, 1991. 212 pp. 0883447428 (O), 0060608129 (H).

An English translation of chapters originally published in Portuguese as *A fé na periferia do mundo* (1978) and *O Caminhar da Igreja com os oprimidos* (1980).

AM382 Boff, Leonardo

Jesucristo el Liberador: ensayo de Cristología crítica para nuestro tiempo. Translated by Jesús García-Abril. (Colección presencia teológica, 6). Santander, SP: Sal Terrae, 1994. 277 pp. 8429305807.

Fifth edition of the Spanish translation.

AM383 Boff, Leonardo

Jesus Christ Liberator: A Critical Christology for Our Time. Translated by Patrick Hughes. Maryknoll, NYU: Orbis Books, 1978. xii, 323 pp. 0883442361.

English translation of *Jesus Cristo Libertador* (1972), plus an epilogue on the work as a liberationist Christology.

AM384 Boff, Leonardo

Jesus Cristo Libertador: ensaio de cristologia crítica para o nosso tempo. (Publicações CID, Teologia, 2). Petrópolis, BL: Editora Vozes, 1972. 234 pp. No ISBN.

A presentation of Jesus Christ designed to motivate privileged Christians to join in the struggle to liberate all human beings from all that diminishes them and offends God.

AM385 Boff, Leonardo

Pasión de Cristo—Pasión del Mundo: (hechos, interpretaciones y significado ayer y hoy). (Colección Alcance, 18). Santander, SP: Sal Terrae, 1980. 238 pp. 842930584X.

Spanish translation.

AM386 Boff, Leonardo

The Path to Hope: Fragments from a Theologian's Journey. Maryknoll, NYU: Orbis Books, 1993. x, 134 pp. Paper. 0883448157.

Several hundred short excerpts from the writings of the noted Brazilian liberation theologian; organized thematically, together with autobiographical notes, showing his Franciscan sensitivity, his impatience with injustice, his Catholic sacramental imagination, and the centrality of the Kingdom of God in his thought.

AM387 Boff, Leonardo

A Trindade, a Sociedade e a Libertação. Petrópolis, BL: Vozes, 1986. 296 pp. No ISBN.

A guide through the historical controversies and heresies about the Trinity; by the well-known Brazilian liberation theologian, who develops a liberationist perspective, linking the Trinity to political, economic, and social justice.

AM388 Boff, Leonardo

La Trinidad, la Sociedad y la Liberación. Translated by Al-fonso Ortiz García. (Colección Cristianismo y Sociedad, 5). Madrid, SP: Ediciones Paulinas, 1987. 308 pp. 8428511721.

Spanish translation.

AM389 Boff, Leonardo

Trinité et société. Translated by François Malley. (Collection libération). Paris, FR: Éditions du Cerf, 1990. iv, 298 pp. Paper. 2204042072.

French translation.

AM390 Boff, Leonardo

Trinity and Society. Translated by Paul Burns. Maryknoll, NYU: Orbis Books, 1988. xv, 272 pp. 0883446227 (hdbk), 0883446235 (pbk).

English translation.

AM391 Boff, Leonardo, and Clodovis Boff

Cómo hacer Teología de la Liberación. (Colección "Teología y Pastoral"). Madrid, SP: Paulinas, 1986. 132 pp. 842851092X.

Spanish translation.

AM392 Boff, Leonardo, and Clodovis Boff

Como fazer teologia da libertação. (Coleção Fazer, 17-18). Petrópolis, BL: Vozes, 1986. 141 pp. No ISBN.

An explanation of liberation theology for lay persons, pastors, and students, from the Roman Catholic perspective.

AM393 Boff, Leonardo, and Clodovis Boff

Introducing Liberation Theology. Translated by Paul Burns. Maryknoll, NYU: Orbis Books, 1987. xi, 99 pp. Paper. 0883445751 (hdbk), 0883445506 (pbk).

English translation.

AM394 Boff, Leonardo, and Clodovis Boff

Wie treibt man Theologie der Befreiung? Düsseldorf, GW: Patmos Verlag, 1988. 117 pp. 4491776538.

German translation.

AM395 Boff, Leonardo, José Ramos Regidor, and Clodovis Boff

A Teologia da Libertação: Balannço e Perspectivas. (Serie Religião e Cidadania). São Paulo, BL: Editora Atica, 1996. 128 pp. 8508060890.

Reflections on twenty-five years of Latin American liberation theology, by three of its most noted advocates.

AM396 Brown, Robert McAfee

Gustavo Gutiérrez: An Introduction to Liberation Theology. Maryknoll, NYU: Orbis Books, 1990. xxiv, 224 pp. Paper. 0883445972.

An introduction to liberation theology through the life and work of its most significant proponent, Gustavo Gutiérrez of Peru; based on his writings and personal conversations.

AM397 Bussmann, Claus

Befreiung durch Jesus?: Die Christologie der lateinamerikanischen Befreiungstheologie. Munich, GW: Kösel, 1980. 181 pp. Paper. 3466202000.

Proceeding from the context of dependence and oppression, Latin American theologians express themselves on their understanding of Christ.

AM398 Bussmann, Claus

Who Do You Say?: Jesus Christ in Latin American Theology. Translated by Robert R. Barr. Maryknoll, NYU: Orbis Books, 1985. vi, 185 pp. Paper. 0883447118.

English translation.

AM399 Cadorette, Curt

From the Heart of the People: The Theology of Gustavo Gutiérrez. Oak Park, ILU: Meyer-Stone Books, 1988. xviii, 140 pp. Paper. 0940989182.

An analysis of the theology, social structures, and influences on the thought of Gutiérrez.

AM400 Candelaria, Michael R.

Popular Religion and Liberation: The Dilemma of Liberation Theology. (Religion, Culture, and Society). Albany, NYU: SUNY Press, 1990. xv, 194 pp. 0791402290 (hdbk), 0791402304 (pbk).

A comprehensive look at the issues, questions, and problems that emerge from the debate among liberation theologians in Latin America, focusing on a comparative analysis of the thought of Juan Carlos Scannone (Argentina) and Juan Luis Segundo (Uruguay).

AM401 Casaldáliga, Pedro

In Pursuit of the Kingdom: Writings 1968-1988. Maryknoll, NYU: Orbis Books, 1990. xvii, 254 pp. Paper. 0883446553.

An anthology of the works of Bishop Pedro Casaldáliga (RCC) of Brazil, who has earned much praise and condemnation for his forthright identification with the poor.

AM402 Casaldáliga, Pedro, and José María Vigil

Espiritualidad de la Liberación. (Colección Teología Latinoamericana, 19). San Salvador, ES: UCA Editores, 1993. 287 pp. 8484051927.

Second edition of a work in which a prophetic Brazilian bishop and a Nicaraguan theologian join to produce the first systematic treatment of the spirituality of Latin American liberation theology.

AM403 Casaldáliga, Pedro, and José María Vigil

Espiritualidade da libertação. Translated by Jaime A. Clasen. (Coleção Teologia e libertação, Série III, libertação história, 9). São Paulo, BL: Vozes, 1993. 247 pp. 8532609325.

Portuguese translation.

AM404 Casaldáliga, Pedro, and José María Vigil

Political Holiness. Translated by Paul Burns and Francis McDonagh. (Theology and Liberation Series). Maryknoll, NYU: Orbis Books, 1994. xxviii, 244 pp. Paper. 088344979X.

English translation; first published as *The Spirituality of Liberation* (Burns and Oates, 1994).

AM405 Castillo, Fernando, ed.

Theologie aus der Praxis des Volkes: Neuere Studien zum lateinamerikanischen Christentum und zur Theologie der Befreiung. (Gesellschaft und Theologie: Abt. Systematische Beiträge, 26). Munich, GW: Kaiser; Mainz, GW: Grünewald Verlag, 1978. 219 pp. Paper. 3459011793 (K), 3786706980 (G).

Excerpts of four dissertations dealing with different aspects of liberation theology: liberating praxis and theological reflection, Paulo Freire's pedagogy, church and popular Catholicism in Brazil, and popular pastoral ministry.

AM406 CELAM, Encuentro de Bogotá

Liberación: Diálogos en el CELAM. (Documentos CELAM, 16). Bogotá, CK: CELAM, Secretariado General, 1974. 444 pp. Paper. No ISBN.

A collection of sixteen papers presented at the Bogata conference (19-24 November 1973) on fundamental aspects of liberation theology.

AM407 Ching, Theresa Lowe

Efficacious Love: Its Meaning and Function in the Theology of Juan Luís Segundo. Lanham, MDU: University Press of America; London, ENK: University Press of America, 1989. x, 157 pp. 0819175617.

A concise introduction to the theology of Juan Luís Segundo, in terms of historical development of his work and the main influences on his thought.

AM408 Comblin, Joseph

Called For Freedom: The Changing Context of Liberation Theology. Translated by Phillip Berryman. Maryknoll, NYU: Orbis Books, 1998. xix, 252 pp. Paper. 1570751730.

Reflections on past, present, and future directions of Latin American liberation theology, by one of the pioneers of the movement.

AM409 Comblin, Joseph

El Clamor de los Oprimidos, el Clamor de Jesús. (Colección Teología latinoamericana, 2). Santiago, CL: Rehue, 1986. 57 pp. No ISBN.

Spanish translation.

AM410 Comblin, Joseph

O Clamor dos oprimidos, o clamor de Jesus. Petrópolis: Vozes, 1984. 63 pp. No ISBN.

An essay continuities among the cry of the people of the Old Testament, the cry of Jesus, and the cry of the poor and oppressed of today's world (especially in Latin America).

AM411 Cox, Harvey Gallagher

The Silencing of Leonardo Boff: The Vatican and the Future of World Christianity. Oak Park, ILU: Meyer-Stone Books, 1988. x, 208 pp. Paper. 0940989352.

A behind the scenes look at the attempt by the Vatican in 1984, to silence Brazil's most prominent liberation theologian; with an analysis of its consequences for the world church, by the Victor S. Thomas, Professor of Divinity at Harvard Divinity School.

AM412 Davis, Kortright

Emancipation Still Comin': Explorations in Caribbean Emancipatory Theology. Maryknoll, NYU: Orbis Books, 1990. xi, 164 pp. Paper. 0883446723.

A new socially conscious and active theology for the Caribbean, sensitive both to Caribbean religion and spirituality, and to the continual struggle for identity, independence, and social justice.

AM413 Dussel, Enrique D.

Caminõs de Liberação Latino-Americana. (Estudos e Debates Latino-Americanos, 6-9). São Paulo, BL: Edições Paulinas, 1985. 4 vols. No ISBN.

Revised edition of collected essays in four volumes, by the noted Latin American church historian, giving historical, theological, and ethical interpretations of Latin American liberation [t. 1 *Interpretação histórico-teológica*; t. 2 *História, colonialismo e libetação*; t. 3 *Interpretação ético-theológica*; t. 4 *Reflexões para uma teologia da libertação*].

AM414 Dussel, Enrique D.

Caminos de Liberación Latinoamericana: Teología de la liberación y ética; seis conferencias. (Cuadernos para la reflexion). Buenos Aires, AG: Latinoamérica Libros, 1974. 221 pp. No ISBN.

Spanish translation of vol. 3 of *Caminos de Liberación Latinoamericana* (1973).

AM415 Dussel, Enrique D.
Ethics and the Theology of Liberation. Translated by Bernard F. McWilliams. Maryknoll, NYU: Orbis Books, 1978. xiv, 177 pp. 0883441152 (hdbk), 0883441160 (pbk).
English translation of vol. 3 of *Caminos de Liberación Latino-Americana* (1973).

AM416 Dussel, Enrique D.
Histoire et théologie de la libération: perspective latino-américaine. (Collection Développement et Civilisations). Paris, FR: Éditions Économie et Humanisme; Paris, FR: Éditions Ouvrieres, 1974. 183 pp. No ISBN.
French translation of vol. 1 of *Caminos de Liberación Latino-Americana* (1973).

AM417 Dussel, Enrique D.
History and the Theology of Liberation: A Latin American Perspective. Translated by John Drury. Maryknoll, NYU: Orbis Books, 1976. xvi, 189 pp. 0883441799 (hdbk), 0883441802 (pbk).
English translation of vol. 1 of *Caminos de Liberación Latino-Americana* (1973).

AM418 Echegaray, Hugo
La Práctica de Jesús. Lima, PE: CEP, 1980. 222 pp. No ISBN.
A scholarly study of the attitude of Jesus to poverty, and its relevance today to the life and mission of BCCs, such as those among whom the author ministered in Peru.

AM419 Echegaray, Hugo
The Practice of Jesus. Maryknoll, NYU: Orbis Books; Melbourne, AT: Dove Communications, 1984. xxi, 122 pp. Paper. 088344397X (US), 0859242978 (AT).
English translation of *La Práctica de Jesus* (1980).

AM420 Elizondo, Virgilio P., ed.
La Via della croce: La Passione di Cristo nelle Americhe. Brescia, IT: Editrice Queriniana, 1992. 71 pp. No ISBN.
Meditations and prayers on the Stations of the Cross, mostly by Latin American liberation theologians, sharing the suffering, death, and new life in Christ of the peoples of Latin America over the past five hundred years.

AM421 Elizondo, Virgilio P., ed.
Way of the Cross: The Passion of Christ in the Americas. Translated by John Drury. Maryknoll, NYU: Orbis Books, 1992. xiv, 111 pp. Paper. 088344819X.
English translation.

AM422 Ellacuría, Ignacio
Conversión de la Iglesia al Reino de Dios para Anunciarlo y Realizarlo en la Historia. (Teología Latinoamericana, 5). San Salvador, ES: UCA Editores, 1985. 303 pp. Paper. 8484050742.
An essay on liberation theology by the prominent Basque Jesuit who has worked for more than twenty-five years in El Salvador.

AM423 Ellacuría, Ignacio
Escritos Filosóficos, Tomo I. (Colección Estructuras y Procesos, Serie Mayor, 13). San Salvador, ES: UCA Editores, 1996. 664 pp. 8484052230.
The first part of a trilogy, that will contain all the philosophical writings of the liberation philosopher and theologian assassinated in 1989.

AM424 Ellacuría, Ignacio
Freedom Made Flesh: The Mission of Christ and His Church. Translated by John Drury. Maryknoll, NYU: Orbis Books, 1976. ix, 246 pp. 0883441403 (hdbk), 0883441411 (pbk).
English translation of *Teología Política* (1973).

AM425 Ellacuría, Ignacio
Teología Política. San Salvador, ES: Ediciones del Secretariado Social Interdiocesano, 1973. ix, 127 pp. No ISBN.
A major work of liberation theology, including chapters on salvation history, the political character of Jesus' mission, the historicity of the church's mission, and violence and the Cross.

AM426 Ellacuría, Ignacio, and Jon Sobrino, eds.
Mysterium Liberationis: Fundamental Concepts of Liberation Theology. Maryknoll, NYU: Orbis Books; North Blackburn, AT: Collins Dove, 1993. xv, 752 pp. 088344917X (US), 1863713131 (AT).
English translation abridged to thirty-four essays.

AM427 Ellacuría, Ignacio, and Jon Sobrino
Mysterium Liberationis: Conceptos fundamentales de la teología de la liberación. (Colección Estructuras y Procesos: Serie Religió). Madrid, SP: Trotta, 1994. 2 vols. 8481640212.
Second edition of a collection of forty-six scholarly essays by Latin American liberation theologians, on the history, methodology, and distinctive features of theologies of liberation.

AM428 Encuentro de Teología Protestante (1st, 1983, San José, Costa Rica)
La Tradición Protestante en la Teología Latinoamericana: Primer Intento: Lectura de la Tradición Metodista. Translated by José Duque. San José, CR: DEI, 1983. xvi, 362 pp. Paper. No ISBN.
A collection of twenty-one articles on historical and theological aspects of the Methodist tradition in Latin America, four workshop reports, and an open letter to the Methodist churches of Latin America—all results of the First Meeting on Protestant Theology (San José, Costa Rica, 6-11 February 1983).

AM429 Erskine, Noel Leo
Decolonizing Theology: A Caribbean Perspective. Maryknoll, NYU: Orbis Books, 1981. vii, 130 pp. Paper. 0883440873.
A pioneer liberation theology for the Caribbean, relating experiences of black people in that region to Christian theology and the experiences of other Third World peoples.

AM430 Escobar, Samuel E.
La Fe Evangélica y las Teologías de la Liberacíon. El Paso, TXU: Casa Bautista de Publicaciones, 1987. 224 pp. Paper. 0311091075.
The noted Latin American missiologist traces the social and theological ferment from 1950 to 1980, giving reasons why evangelicals can respond positively to theologies of liberation.

AM431 Escobar, Samuel E.
De la Misión a la Teología. (Fraternidad Teológica Latinoamericana, 1). Buenos Aires, AG: Ediciones Kairó, 1998. 96 pp. Paper. 9879591542.
Three essays; two translated from English, on evangelical theology and mission in Latin America.

AM—THE AMERICAS

AM432 Espín, Orlando O., and Miguel H. Díaz, eds.
From the Heart of Our People: Latino/a Explorations in Catholic Systematic Theology. Maryknoll, NYU: Orbis Books, 1999. viii, 271 pp. Paper. 1570751315.

A collection of twelve essays and a selective bibliography, on Catholic systematics, from a Latino/a perspective; arising from a year-long symposium funded by the Lilly Endowment, and culminating in two week-long meetings, in San Diego, California, in January and July of 1997.

AM433 Flores Lizana, Carlos
El Taytacha Qoyllur Rit'iTeología India hecha por Communeros y Mestizos Quechuas. Sicuani, PE: IPA, 1997. 347 pp. No ISBN.

A study of Americo-Indian Christian theology, founded in the Quechua peoples' religious experience, and reflected in their customs, feasts, rites, and symbols.

AM434 Fornet-Betancourt, Raúl, ed.
Befreiungstheologie: Kritischer Rückblick und Perspektiven für die Zukunft. Mainz, GW: Matthias-Grünewald-Verlag, 1997. 3 vols. 3786719543 (vol. 1), 3786719551 (vol. 2), 378671956X (vol. 3).

The results, in three volumes, of a research project designed to take stock of the development, reception, and impact of Latin American liberation theology, and coordinated by COELI (Centre Oecuménique de Liaisons Internationales) in Brussels; [vol. 1: *Bilanz der letzten 25 Jahre (1968-1993)*; vol. 2: *Kritische Auswertung und neue Herausforderungen*; vol. 3: *Die Rezeption im deutschsprachigen Raum*].

AM435 García-Rivera, Alex
St. Martin de Porres: The "Little Stories" and the Semiotics of Culture. (Faith and Culture Series). Maryknoll, NYU: Orbis Books, 1995. xvii, 142 pp. Paper. 1570750335.

Using the semiotic method the Cuban-born Assistant Professor of Systematic Theology at the Jesuit School of Theology, Berkeley, California, analyzes the popular stories about Saint Martin de Porres (1575-1639) of Peru, as an early source for an indigenous Latin American theology.

AM436 Gebara, Ivone, and Maria Clara Bingemer
María, Mãe de Deus e Mãe dos Pobres. (Colecao Teologia e libertação, Série 4). Petrópolis, BL: Editora Vozes, 1987. 208 pp. No ISBN.

A thorough reflection on the importance of Mary, by two Brazilian women theologians writing from the perspective of Latin American liberation theology.

AM437 Gebara, Ivone, and Maria Clara Bingemer
Mary: Mother of God, Mother of the Poor. (Theology and Liberation Series). Maryknoll, NYU: Orbis Books, 1989. xii, 196 pp. 0883446383 (hdbk), 0883446375 (pbk).
English translation.

AM438 Geffré, Claude, and Gustavo Gutiérrez, eds.
The Mystical and Political Dimension of the Christian Faith. (*Concilium*: Religion in the Seventies). New York, NYU: Herder and Herder, 1974. 160 pp. Paper. 0816425809.

A collection of nine essays by prominent Latin American theologians, both Roman Catholic and Protestant, introducing liberation theology as a new way of theologizing, a new theology of salvation, and a new kind of spirituality.

AM439 Geffré, Claude, and Gustavo Gutiérrez, eds.
Praxis de Liberación y Fe Cristiana: El testimonio de los teólogos latinoamericanos. (Colección Lee y discute, Serie V, 48). Madrid, SP: Bilbáo, 1974. 56 pp. 8431702931.

Lectures on liberation theology, given by the noted liberation theologian at the Mexican American Cultural Center in San Antonio, Texas, in 1974.

AM440 Goldstein, Horst
Brasilianische Christologie: Jesus, der Severino heisst; eine Skizze. Mettingen, GW: Brasilienkunde Verlag, 1982. 169 pp. Paper. 3885590042.

By comparing Jesus to Severino, the exploited person of northeast Brazil, and drawing on primary materials such as meditation texts, popular prayers, and letters, the author sketches the focal points of a Latin American Christology.

AM441 Goldstein, Horst
"Selig ihr Armen": Theologie der Befreiung in Lateinamerika ... und in Europa? (WB-Forum, 40). Darmstadt, GW: Wissenschaftliche Buchgesellschaft, 1989. xii, 235 pp. Paper. 3534800575.

A historical survey of liberation theology in Latin America, its main representatives, purposes, and theological streams, and its relevance for Europe.

AM442 Gutiérrez, Gustavo
Densidad del Presente: Selección de Artículos. (CEP, 172). Lima, PE: Instituto de Bartolomé de Las Casas-RIMAC / CEP, 1996. 468 pp. No ISBN.

A collection of articles, by the noted Peruvian liberation theologian, on Catholic social teachings, church developments in Latin America, spirituality, and social issues in Peru.

AM443 Gutiérrez, Gustavo
The Density of the Present: Selected Writings. Maryknoll, NYU: Orbis Books, 1999. ix, 213 pp. Paper. 157075246X.

A collection of essays by the pioneer of Latin American liberation theology on social teachings, the "option for the poor," and the link between action and spirituality.

AM444 Gutiérrez, Gustavo et al., eds.
Convocados por el Evangelio: 25 Años de Reflexión Teológica, 1971-1995. (CEP, 142). Lima, PE: Pontificia Universidad Católica del Perú, Departamento d, 1995. xv, 331 pp. No ISBN.

A collection of papers by Peruvian theologians, on the Bible, the discipleship of Jesus, and the option for the poor; with an introduction by Gustavo Gutiérrez placing these areas of study in the present-day Latin American context.

AM445 Gutiérrez, Gustavo
Evangelización y Opción por los Pobres. Buenos Aires, AG: Ediciones Paulinas, 1987. 118 pp. Paper. 9500906503.

Collection of lectures given by the author at the Quilmes Seminary (Buenos Aires, March 1986) on themes related to the theology of liberation.

AM446 Gutiérrez, Gustavo
La Fuerza Histórica de los Pobres: Selección de trabajos. Lima, PE: CEP, 1979. 424 pp. Paper. No ISBN.

A new collection of the author's articles, previously published in *Páginas* (Lima, 1976-1979) and in *Concilium* (Madrid, 1979), in a revision of his book *Teología desde el Reverso de la Historia* (Lima, Perú: CEP, 1977), and in other books.

AM—THE AMERICAS

AM447 Gutiérrez, Gustavo

The God of Life. Translated by Matthew J. O'Connell. Maryknoll, NYU: Orbis Books, 1991. xviii, 214 pp. Paper. 0883447606.

A greatly expanded version of the work by the same title (Lima: CEP, 1982), in which the noted liberation theologian looks, from the standpoint of the struggling poor, at the questions, "Who and where is God?" and "How are we to speak of God?"

AM448 Gutiérrez, Gustavo

Gustavo Gutiérrez: Essential Writings. Edited by James B. Nickoloff. Maryknoll, NYU: Orbis Books, 1996. viii, 336 pp. Paper. 1570751013.

Forty-three selections from all of the noted liberation theologian's full-length theological monographs, arranged by subject.

AM449 Gutiérrez, Gustavo

Hablar de Dios desde el Sufrimiento del Inocente: Una reflexión sobre el libro de Job. (Pedal, 183). Salamanca, SP: Ediciones S gueme, 1995. 187 pp. Paper. 843011002X.

Third edition of lectures by the prominent Peruvian Catholic theologian, relating a study of the biblical book of Job to key issues in liberation theology; originally presented in 1980 at a conference organized by the Department of Theology of the Catholic University (Lima) and published in 1986.

AM450 Gutiérrez, Gustavo

Die historische Macht der Armen. (Fundamentaltheologische Studien, 11). Munich, GW: Kaiser Verlag; Mainz, GW: Matthias-Grünewald, 1984. 203 pp. Paper. 3786711216 (K), 3459015675 (M).

German translation of *La Fuerza historica de los Pobres* (1979).

AM451 Gutiérrez, Gustavo

Líneas Pastorales de la Iglesia en América Latina: Análisis teológico. (CEP, 1). Lima, PE: CEP, 1983. 88 pp. Paper. No ISBN.

A collection of several addresses given by the author in 1964 that later became a key source of liberation theology.

AM452 Gutiérrez, Gustavo

On Job: God-Talk and the Suffering of the Innocent. Maryknoll, NYU: Orbis Books, 1987. xix, 136 pp. Paper. 0883445778 (hdbk), 0883445522 (pbk).

English translation.

AM453 Gutiérrez, Gustavo

Teología de la Liberación: Perspectivas. (Verdad e Imagen, 30). Salamanca, SP: Ediciones Sígueme, 1990. 352 pp. Paper. 8430104828.

Fourteenth edition of one of the first works to appear on liberation theology.

AM454 Gutiérrez, Gustavo

Teologia da libertação: Perspectivas. Translated by Jorge Soares. Petrópolis, BL: Editora Vozes, 1979. 274 pp. No ISBN.

Portuguese translation.

AM455 Gutiérrez, Gustavo

Theologie der Befreiung. Translated by Horst Goldstein. (Gesellschaft und Theologie: Systematische Beiträge, 11). Munich, GW: Kaiser, 1979. xii, 287 pp. 3459008784.

German translation of *Teología de la Liberación* (1971).

AM456 Gutiérrez, Gustavo

A Theology of Liberation: History, Politics and Salvation. Translated by Caridad Inda, and John Eagleson. Maryknoll, NYU: Orbis Books; London, ENK: SCM Press, 1988. xlv, 264 pp. 0883445433 (O hdbk), 0883445425 (O pbk), 0334023564 (S pbk).

English translation of *Teología de la Liberación, Perspectivas* (1971), with a new introduction for the 25th anniversary of publication.

AM457 Gutiérrez, Gustavo

The Truth Shall Make You Free: Confrontations. Maryknoll, NYU: Orbis Books, 1990. xii, 204 pp. Paper. 0883446790 (hdbk), 0883446634 (pbk).

Building on the foundations of *A Theology of Liberation*, this work is, first, the defense made by the noted Peruvian liberation theologian before the theological faculty of the Catholic Institute of Lyons, and, second, an exploration of the role of social sciences and their methodologies in theology.

AM458 Hünermann, Peter, and Gerd-Dieter Fischer, eds.

Gott im Aufbruch: Die Provokation der lateinamerikanischen Theologie. Freiburg, SZ: Basel Mission; Vienna, AU: Herder, 1974. 204 pp. 3451169606.

Five essays by notable theologians from Argentina, Colombia, and Uruguay, on different aspects of modern Latin American theology.

AM459 Hassett, John, and Hugh Lacey, eds.

Towards a Society That Serves Its People: The Intellectual Contribution of El Salvador's Murdered Jesuits. Washington, DCU: Georgetown University Press, 1991. xiv, 406 pp. Paper. 0878405232.

A compilation of writings on liberation themes by the Jesuit theologians martyred, 16 November 1989, in El Salvador.

AM460 Hennelly, Alfred T.

Theologies in Conflict: The Challenge of Juan Luis Segundo. Maryknoll, NYU: Orbis Books, 1979. xxiii, 200 pp. 0883442876.

An analysis situating major themes in the theology of Juan Luis Segundo, within Latin American theologies of liberation.

AM461 Hewitt, Marsha Aileen

From Theology to Social Theory: Juan Luis Segundo and the Theology of Liberation. (American University Studies, 7: Theology and Religion, 73). New York, NYU: Lang, 1990. x, 184 pp. 0820412589.

A detailed examination of Segundo's social theory, and use of Marxism in his theology of liberation.

AM462 Hofmann, Manfred

Bolivien und Nicaragua: Modelle einer Kirche im Aufbruch. Münster, GW: Edition Liberación, 1987. 364 pp. Paper. 3923792220.

A history of liberation theology in Bolivia and Nicaragua, based on documents from bishops' conferences, and Christian revolutionary and basic community groups.

AM463 Hoy, Michael

The Faith That Works: The Relationships of Faith and Works in the Theology of Juan Luis Segundo, S.J. Lanham, MDU: University Press of America, 1995. xxiv, 257 pp. 0819198145.

A doctoral dissertation (Capital University, 1990) on the theology of the noted Latin American liberation theologian.

AM—THE AMERICAS

AM464 Kirkpatrick, Dow, ed.
Faith Born in the Struggle for Life: A Re-Reading of Protestant Faith in Latin America Today. Grand Rapids, MIU: Eerdmans, 1988. xv, 328 pp. Paper. 0802803555.

Twenty Latin American theologians (three Catholics and the rest from the historic Protestant churches) write from within "the struggle for life," and reflect on various theological and ethical issues, illustrating a Latin American interpretation of the Gospel.

AM465 Lois, Julio
Teología de la Liberación: opción por los pobres. Madrid, SP: IEPALA; Editorial Fundamentos, 1986. 506 pp. Paper. 8485436296 (I), 8424504453 (E).

A treatment of liberation theology for the poor of Latin America, offering an objective, complete synthesis of four different theologies of poverty.

AM466 Míguez Bonino, José
Doing Theology in a Revolutionary Situation. Philadelphia, PAU: Fortress Press, 1975. xxviii, 179 pp. Paper. 0800614518.

An analysis, by the noted Argentinian Protestant theologian, of the history of sociopolitical involvements by Latin American Christians, both Catholic and Protestant; with critical analysis of their contemporary involvements; also published as *Revolutionary Theology Comes of Age.*

AM467 Míguez Bonino, José
Espacio para ser Hombres: Una interpretación del mensaje de la Biblia para nuestro mundo. Buenos Aires, AG: Ediciones La Aurora, 1990. 108 pp. Paper. 9505510985.

An open inquiry on basic questions of faith for Christians and atheists alike, by the Dean of Studies at Union Theological Seminary, Buenos Aires, with a spiritual plea for all people to take part in establishing worldwide justice; originally published in 1975 (Buenos Aires, AG: Tierra Nueva).

AM468 Míguez Bonino, José et al., eds.
Jesus, ni Vencido ni Monarca Celestial: Imágenes de Jesucristo en América Latina. (Colección Jesús de Nazaret). Buenos Aires, AG: Tierra Nueva, 1977. 272 pp. No ISBN.

Twelve essays, by well-known Latin American theologians, on the images of Christ in Latin America, their theological meaning, and their impact, both on the church and on politics.

AM469 Míguez Bonino, José
La Fe en busca de Eficacia: Una Interpretación de la reflexión teológica latinoamericana de liberación. Salamanca, SP: Ediciones Sígueme, 1977. 204 pp. Paper. 8430104518.
Spanish translation.

AM470 Míguez Bonino, José
Room to be People: An Interpretation of the Message of Bible for Today's World. Translated by Vickie Leach. Philadelphia, PAU: Fortress Press; Geneva, SZ: WCC, 1979. 80 pp. Paper. 080061349X (F), 282540604X (W).
English translation.

AM471 Míguez Bonino, José
Theologie im Kontext der Befreiung. (Theologie der Ökumene, 15). Göttingen, GW: Vandenboeck & Ruprecht, 1977. 158 pp. Paper. 3525563191.
German translation of *Doing Theology in a Revolutionary Situation* (1975).

AM472 Míguez Bonino, José, ed.
Faces of Jesus: Latin American Christologies. Translated by Robert R. Barr. Maryknoll, NYU: Orbis Books, 1984. vi, 186 pp. Paper. 0883441292.
English translation.

AM473 Mesters, Carlos
Befreit-gebunden: Die 10 gebote das Bundesbuch. Erlangen, GW: Ev.-Luth. Mission, 1989. 117 pp. Paper. 3872141945.
German translation.

AM474 Mesters, Carlos
Os dez mandamentos, ferramenta da comunidade. São Paulo, BL: Edições Paulinas, 1986. 75 pp. 8505005899.
Reflections on the Lutheran Book on the Covenant, and the Ten Commandments, from the viewpoint of liberation theology.

AM475 Modehn, Christian
Der Gott, der befreit: Glaubensimpulse aus Lateinamerika. Meitingen-Freising, GW: Kyrios Verlag, 1975. 40 pp. 3783801230.
A concise, well-written introduction to Latin American theologies of liberation.

AM476 Moreno Rejón, Francisco
Historia de la Teología Moral en América Latina: Ensayos y materiales. (CEP, 136). Lima, PE: Instituto Bartolomé de las Casas; Lima, PE: CEP, 1994. 258 pp. No ISBN.
Essays and source documents illuminating the development of moral theology in Latin America, from the 16th-century conquest to 20th-century liberation theology.

AM477 Muñoz, Ronaldo
Dieu: j'ai vu la misère de mon peuple. (Collection Libération). Paris, FR: Éditions du Cerf, 1990. 237 pp. Paper. 220404184X.
French translation.

AM478 Muñoz, Ronaldo
Dios de los Cristianos. (Coleccion Cristianismo y Sociedad, 4). Madrid, SP: Ediciones Paulinas, 1987. 252 pp. 8428511535.
Essays relating the cultural analysis of Latin American liberation theology to questions of epistemology, the doctrine of God, the authority of Scripture, and spirituality.

AM479 Muñoz, Ronaldo
The God of Christians. Translated by Paul Burns. (Theology and Liberation Series). Maryknoll, NYU: Orbis Books, 1990. xv, 192 pp. 0883446960 (hdbk), 0883446952 (pbk).
English translation.

AM480 Muñoz, Ronaldo
O Deus dos Cristãos. Translated by Jaime A. Clasen. Rio de Janeiro, BL: Editora Vozes, 1986. 243 pp. No ISBN.
Portuguese translation.

AM481 Nieuwenhove, Jacques van
Bronnen van Bevrijding: Varianten in de Theologie van Gustavo Gutiérrez. (Kerk en Theologie in Context, 12). Kampen, NE: Kok, 1991. ix, 229 pp. Paper. 9024268036.
An analysis of the theology of the noted liberation theologian of Peru, with particular attention to the methodological basis of his thought, dominant themes, and the cultural context in which he developed his theology.

AM482 Nordstokke, Kjell
Council and Context in Leonardo Boff's Ecclesiology: The Rebirth of the Church among the Poor. Translated by Brian MacNeil. (Studies in Religion and Society, 35). Lewiston, NYU: E. Mellen Press, 1996. ix, 305 pp. 0773487840.
English translation.

AM483 Nordstokke, Kjell
Ekklesiogenese:Konsil og kontekst i Leonardo Boffs ekklesiologi. (Diakonhjemmets Høgskolesenter; Rapporter, 3). Oslo, NO: Diakonhjemmets Høgskolesenter, 1990. 307 pp. No ISBN.
A doctoral dissertation (University of Oslo, 1990) on liberation theology in Latin America, and, especially, on the ecclesiology of Leonardo Boff and his controversies with Rome.

AM484 Nowak, Jutta
Theorie der Befreiung: Struktur, Bedingungen und Resultat "theologischer Produktion" bei Clodovis Boff. (Dissertationen: Theologische Reihe, 50). St. Ottilien, GW: EOS Verlag, 1992. xi, 224 pp. Paper. 3880968500.
A doctoral dissertation situating Clodovis Boff's political theology within the context of Latin American liberation theology.

AM485 Oliveros Maqueo, Roberto
Liberación y Teología: Génesis y crecimento de una reflexión (1966-1976). Lima, PE: CEP; México, D.F., MX: Centro de Reflexión Teológica, 1970. 490 pp. No ISBN.
A detailed analysis of the developments in Latin American liberation theology, from 1966 to 1976.

AM486 Penner, Peter
Die Aussenperspektive des Anderen: Eine Formalpragmatische Interpretation zu Enrique Dussels Befreiungsethik. (Edition Philosophie und Sozialwissenschaften, 36). Hamburg, GW: Argument-Verlag, 1996. 319 pp. 3886196364.
A detailed analysis of the liberation ethics of Enrique Dussel; originally accepted as a Ph.D. dissertation at the University of Bremen, Germany.

AM487 Piar, Carlos R.
Jesus and Liberation: A Critical Analysis of the Christology of Latin American Liberation Theology. (American University Studies, 7: Theology and Religion, 148). New York, NYU: Lang, 1994. 178 pp. Paper. 0820420980.
A critical analysis of the method, presuppositions, and content of Latin American liberation theologies, with focus on their Christologies.

AM488 Pironio, Eduardo F.
Evangelización y Liberación. (Esperanza, 15). Buenos Aires, AG: Editora Patria Grande, 1976. 95 pp. Paper. No ISBN.
Essay on the work of the church in the world, in light of liberation theology.

AM489 Pixley, Jorge V. et al.
Praxis Cristiana y Producción Teológica. Salamanca, SP: Ediciones Sígueme, 1979. 276 pp. Paper. 8430107819.
A collection of ten papers presented at the Encuentro de Teologías, organized by the Theological Community of Mexico (Mexico City, 8-10 October 1977).

AM490 Pottenger, John R.
The Political Theory of Liberation Theology: Toward a Reconvergence of Social Values and Social Science. Albany, NYU: SUNY Press, 1989. x, 264 pp. Paper. 0791401189 (hdbk), 0791401197 (pbk).
An analysis of concepts from political theory, social theory, and ethics, that has been integrated into Latin American liberation theology.

AM491 Quiróz Magaña, Alvaro
Eclesiología en la Teología de la Liberación. (Verdad e Imagen, 78). Salamanca, SP: Ediciones Sígueme, 1983. 363 pp. Paper. 8430109048.
A documented study of ecclesiology in liberation theology.

AM492 Richard, Pablo et al.
The Idols of Death and the God of Life: A Theology. Translated by Barbara E. Campbell, and Bonnie Shepard. Maryknoll, NYU: Orbis Books, 1983. viii, 232 pp. Paper. 0883440482.
English translation.

AM493 Richard, Pablo et al.
La Lucha de los Dioses: Los ídolos de la opresión y la búsqueda del Dios liberador, Investigaciones. (Colección Teología Latinoamericana). San José, CR: DEI; Managua, NQ: CAV, 1986. 268 pp. Paper. 9977904936.
Third edition of a collection of ten essays by Latin American theologians, contrasting the false gods of systems of oppression with the biblical God of justice.

AM494 Richard, Pablo
Raices de la teología Latinoamericana: Nuevos materiales para la historia de la teología. San José, CR: DEI/CEHILA, 1985. xxi, 429 pp. Paper. 9977904146.
A collection of several studies on the development of theological reflection in Roman Catholic and Protestant churches of Latin America.

AM495 Rubenstein, Richard L., and John K. Roth, eds.
The Politics of Latin American Liberation Theology: The Challenge to U.S. Public Policy. Washington, DCU: Washington Institute Press, 1988. xxi, 360 pp. Paper. 0887020399 (hdbk), 0887020402 (pbk).
A collection of thirteen essays, by US academics, from a multidisciplinary meeting on The Political Significance of Latin American Liberation Theology, held 15-17 October 1987, in Washington, D.C.

AM496 Santa Ana, Julio de
Por las Sendas del Mundo Caminando hacia el Reino: Reorientación pastoral y renovación teológica en América Latina. (Colección Aportes). San José, CR: DEI, 1984. xiv, 144 pp. Paper. 9977904065.
A collection of conference papers given by the author, at the Catedra Enrique Strachan of the Seminario Bíblico Latinoamericano, in San José, Costa Rica, in March 1984.

AM497 Saranyana, Josep-Ignasi, ed.
Historia de la Teología Latinoamericana. Pamplona, SP: Ediciones EUNATE, 1996. 420 pp. 8477680728.
The first part of a projected multi-volume history of the development of theology in Latin America, covering the 16th and 17th centuries.

AM—THE AMERICAS

AM498 Schürger, Wolfgang
Theologie auf dem Weg der Befreiung: Geschichte und Methode des Zentrums für Bibelstudien / CEBI in Brasilien. (Erlanger Monographien aus Mission und Ökumene, 24). Erlangen, GW: Ev.-Luth. Mission, 1995. 280 pp. Paper. 3872143247.

A detailed study of the theology and Bible study methods of BECs in Brazil; presented as a doctoral dissertation in theology, at Erlangen, in 1994.

AM499 Schall, James V.
Liberation Theology in Latin America: With Selected Essays and Documents. San Francisco, CAU: Ignatius Press, 1982. ix, 402 pp. Paper. 089870006X.

Fourteen reflections by European and North American writers, on the nature and meaning of liberation theology and its orientations; with an extended interpretive essay by the author.

AM500 Schubeck, Thomas L.
Liberation Ethics: Sources, Models, and Norms. Minneapolis, MNU: Fortress Press, 1993. x, 266 pp. Paper. 0800627555.

The first comprehensive assessment of the ethical import of Latin American liberation theology, based on interviews with key theologians.

AM501 Segundo, Juan Luis
The Community Called Church. Translated by John Drury. (A Theology for Artisans of a New Humanity, 1). Maryknoll, NYU: Orbis Books, 1973. xi, 172 pp. 0883444801 (hdbk), 088344481X (pbk).

English translation.

AM502 Segundo, Juan Luis
El Dogma Que Libera: Fe, Revelación y Magisterio Dogmático. (Colección Presencia Teológica, 53). Santander, SP: Editorial Sal Terrae, 1989. 406 pp. 8429308261.

Foundational questions of faith addressed by one of the pioneers of Latin American theology; with a concluding theology of revelation attuned to the "signs of the times."

AM503 Segundo, Juan Luis
Esa Comunidad llamada Iglesia. (A Theology for Artisans for a New Humanity, 1). Buenos Aires, AG: Ediciones Carlos Lohlé, 1968. 258 pp. No ISBN.

In this first volume of the five-volume series, *A Theology for Artisans of a New Humanity*, the noted Uruguayan Jesuit, in collaboration with the staff of the Peter Faber Center in Montevideo, Uruguay, develops an ecclesiology for a church in dialogue with the world and engaged in mission.

AM504 Segundo, Juan Luis
El Hombre de Hoy Ante Jesús de Nazaret. (Fe e ideología, 1). Madrid, SP: Cristiandad, 1982. 2 v. in 3 pp. 847057311X.

In this work, the noted Uruguayan theologian develops a Christology for Latin America, contrasting it with contemporary European thought.

AM505 Segundo, Juan Luis
Jesus devant la conscience moderne: l'histoire perdue. Translated by Francis Guibal. (Cogitatio fidei, 148). Paris, FR: Éditions du Cerf, 1988. 399 pp. 2204028770.

French translation.

AM506 Segundo, Juan Luis
Jesus of Nazareth Yesterday and Today. Translated by John Drury. (Faith and Ideologies, 1). Maryknoll, NYU: Orbis Books; Melbourne, AT: Dove Communications; London, ENK: Sheed and Ward, 1984. xv, 352 pp. Paper. 0883441276 (US), 0859242986 (AT), 0722035187 (UK).

English translation.

AM507 Segundo, Juan Luis
The Liberation of Dogma: Faith, Revelation, and Dogmatic Teaching Authority. Translated by Phillip Berryman. Maryknoll, NYU: Orbis Books, 1992. viii, 307 pp. Paper. 0883448041.

English translation of *El Dogma Que Libera* (1989).

AM508 Segundo, Juan Luis
Signs of the Times: Theological Reflections. Edited by Alfred T. Hennelly. Translated by Robert R. Barr. Maryknoll, NYU: Orbis Books, 1993. 208 pp. Paper. 0883447916.

A selection of essays by the noted Uruguayan Jesuit and liberation theologian, exploring issues of Christology, revelation, the option for the poor, the future of liberation theology, and the meaning of the Columbian quincentenary.

AM509 Segundo, Juan Luis
Theology and the Church: A Response to Cardinal Ratzinger and a Warning to the Whole Church. Translated by John W. Diercksmeier. New York, NYU: Winston Press; London, ENK: Chapman, 1985. 188 pp. 0866834915 (W), 0225664801 (C).

A detailed rebuttal by a prominent Latin American Catholic theologian, of the 1984 criticism, "The Instruction on the Theology of Liberation," published by the Vatican's Congregation for the Doctrine of Faith.

AM510 SELADOC
Panorama de la Teología Latinoamericana. Vol. V: Puebla. (Materiales, 17). Salamanca, SP: Ediciones Sígueme, 1981. 544 pp. Paper. 843010836X.

An anthology of articles published in Latin American journals and representing important streams of opinion within the church.

AM511 Sigmund, Paul E.
Liberation Theology at the Crossroads: Democracy or Revolution? New York, NYU: Oxford University Press, 1990. viii, 255 pp. 0195060644.

An examination of the origins and development of liberation theology—its leaders, influence, case studies in Chile and Central America, and its shifts from Marxist rhetoric to grassroots populism.

AM512 Sobrino, Jon
Jésus en amérique latine: sa signification pour la foi et la christologie. Translated by Francis Guibal. (Cogitatio fidei, 140). Paris, FR: Éditions du Cerf, 1986. 277 pp. 2204025763.

French translation.

AM513 Sobrino, Jon
Jesús en América Latina: Su Significado para la Fe y la Cristología. (Colección Teología Latinoamericana, 1). San Salvador, ES: UCA Editores, 1989. 192 pp. 8484050165.

Second edition of guidelines for a Latin American Christology, and how they are rooted into the experiences of El Salvador and Latin America; by one of Latin America's leading Catholic theologians; originally published in 1982.

AM514 Sobrino, Jon

Jesucristo Liberador: Lectura histórico-teológica de Jesús de Nazaret. (Colección Estructura y Procesos; Colección Teología Latinoamericana, 17). Madrid, SP: Editorial Trotta; San Salvador, ES: UCA Editores, 1991. 455 pp. 8487699200 (SP), 8484051633 (ES).

The first of two volumes by the noted Spanish-born Jesuit and liberation theologian of El Salvador, on the message and mission of Jesus, and the meaning of his suffering and death for our time.

AM515 Sobrino, Jon

Jesus in Latin America. Maryknoll, NYU: Orbis Books, 1987. xvi, 189 pp. Paper. 0883444127.

English translation.

AM516 Sobrino, Jon

Jesus the Liberator: A Historical-Theological Reading of Jesus of Nazareth. Translated by Paul Burns, and Francis McDonagh. Maryknoll, NYU: Orbis Books, 1993. ix, 308 pp. Paper. 0883449307.

English translation.

AM517 Sobrino, Jon

El Principio-Misericordia: Bajar de la cruz a los pueblos crucificados. (Colección Presencia Teológica, 67). Santander, SP: Editorial Sal Terrae, 1992. 267 pp. Paper. 8429310630.

A collection of nine articles on themes of mercy, salvation, forgiveness, and grace in relation to the church's mission of solidarity in a suffering world; by the noted liberation theologian, who teaches at the Central American University in San Salvador.

AM518 Sobrino, Jon

The Principle of Mercy: Taking the Crucified People from the Cross. Maryknoll, NYU: Orbis Books, 1994. viii, 199 pp. Paper. 0883449862.

English translation.

AM519 Sobrino, Jon, and Ignacio Ellacuría, eds.

Systematic Theology: Perspectives from Liberation Theology. Maryknoll, NYU: Orbis Books, 1996. xiii, 302 pp. 1570750688.

An abridged paperback version of *Mysterium Liberationis* (1993), containing essays by Latin American theologians on sixteen key themes in theology.

AM520 Stefano, Frances

The Absolute Value of Human Action in the Theology of Juan Luis Segundo. Lanham, MDU: University Press of America, 1992. xxxi, 298 pp. 0819185116.

A detailed analysis of one of the central themes in the writings, from 1948 to 1988, of the noted Latin American liberation theologian.

AM521 Stone, Bryan P.

Effective Faith: A Critical Study of the Christology of Juan Luis Segundo. Lanham, MDU: University Press of America, 1994. xiii, 225 pp. 0819191051 (hdbk), 081919106X (pbk).

A detailed study of the Christology of one of Latin America's leading theologians; originally presented as a Ph.D. dissertation at Southern Methodist University in Dallas, Texas.

AM522 Tamez, Elsa

The Amnesty of Grace: Justification by Faith from a Latin American Perspective. Translated by Sharon H. Ringe. Nashville, TNU: Abingdon, 1993. 208 pp. Paper. 0687009340.

English translation of *Contra toda condena* (1991).

AM523 Tamez, Elsa

Contra Toda Condena: La justificación por la fe desde los excluidos. (Colección Teología Latinoamericana). San José: CR: Seminario Bíblico Latinoamericano, 1991. 196 pp. 9977830673, 9977830355.

A study of the New Testament letters of Paul, reflecting on a central theme and its liberating, humanizing power.

AM524 Tamez, Elsa

Santiago: Lectura latinoamericana de la epístola. (Colección Aportes). San Jose, CR: Editorial DEI, 1985. 110 pp. Paper. 9977904200.

An interpretive commentary on the Epistle of James, particularly the nature of faith, from a perspective of Latin American liberation theology.

AM525 Tamez, Elsa, comp.

Teólogos de la Liberación Hablan Sobre la Mujer. San José, CR: DEI, 1986. 183 pp. Paper. 9977904340.

A collection of interviews on the oppression of women, conducted by Elsa Tamez, with eighteen Catholic and Protestant liberation theologians (fifteen male, three female) during 1985 and 1986; concluding with a helpful commentary on major points, as well as directions for future dialogue.

AM526 Tamez, Elsa, ed.

Against Machismo. Oak Park, ILU: Meyer-Stone Books, 1987. ix, 150 pp. 0940989131 (hdbk), 0940989123 (pbk).

English translation.

AM527 Tamez, Elsa, ed.

Through Her Eyes: Women's Theology from Latin America. Maryknoll, NYU: Orbis Books, 1989. viii, 168 pp. Paper. 0883443732.

Nine creative essays by Latin American female theologians, writing and working in the liberation tradition.

AM528 Trigo, Pedro

Creación e Historia en el Proceso de Liberación. (Colección Cristianismo y Sociedad, 13). Madrid, SP: Ediciones Paulinas, 1988. 358 pp. Paper. 8428512329.

A scholarly treatise arguing that God's creative activity continues in history, and that human beings collaborate in the divine work of creation, as they struggle for a new world out of the chaos of injustice.

AM529 Trigo, Pedro

Creation and History. Translated by Robert R. Barr. (Theology and Liberation Series). Maryknoll, NYU: Orbis Books, 1991. xix, 267 pp. 0883447371 (hdbk), 0883447363 (pbk).

English translation.

AM530 Trigo, Pedro

Criação e historia. Petropolis, BL: Editora Vozes, 1988. 358 pp. No ISBN.

Portuguese translation.

AM531 Trigo, Pedro

Schöpfung und Geschichte. (Bibliothek Theologie der Befreiung). Düsseldorf, GW: Patmos Verlag, 1989. 319 pp. 3491777232.

German translation.

AM532 Vijver, Hendrik Willem

Theologie en bevrijding: Een onderzoek naar de relatie tussen eschatologie en ethiek in de theologie van G. Gutièrrez, J.C. Scannone en R. Alves. (Proefschrift Theol. Fac. Vrije Universiteit Amsterdam). Amsterdam, NE: VU Uitgeverij, 1985. 262 pp. Paper. 9062564070.

An inquiry into the relation between eschatology and ethics in the theologies of Gustavo Gutiérrez, J. C. Scannone, and R. Alves.

AM533 Vilela, Ernesto Suarez

Reflexiones de un Latinoamericano Evangélico. Scottdale, PAU: Herald Press, 1987. 172 pp. Paper. 0836112918.

This volume contains personal theological reflections on a wide range of social, political, and faith issues, by an Argentinian Mennonite theologian.

AM534 Wagner, C. Peter

Latin American Theology: Radical or Evangelical?: The Struggle for the Faith in a Young Church. Grand Rapids, MIU: Eerdmans, 1970. 118 pp. Paper. No ISBN.

Describes the development of theology among Latin American Protestants, from a conservative evangelical perspective.

AM535 Waltermire, Donald E.

The Liberation Christologies of Leonardo Boff and Jon Sobrino: Latin American Contributions to Contemporary Christology. Lanham, MDU: University Press of America, 1994. viii, 139 pp. 0819190187.

An analysis of the Christologies of two prominent Latin American liberation theologians; originally presented as a Ph.D. dissertation at Southern Baptist Theological Seminary in 1990.

AM536 Wheaton, Philip, ed.

500 Years Domination or Liberation?: Theological Alternatives for the Americas in the 1990's. Managua, NQ: Ediciones Nicarao; Ocean City, MDU: Skipjack Press, 1992. 143 pp. Paper. 1879535041.

Eight short essays by Latin American theologians (L. Boff, J. Sobrino, et al.) on theologies of domination and liberation in the Americas.

AM537 Williams, Lewin Lascelles

Caribbean Theology. (Research in Religion and Family: Black Perspectives, 2). New York, NYU: Lang, 1994. xiii, 231 pp. 0820418595.

A scholarly analysis of Caribbean theology, including its development as a mission theology, its essential characteristics, its unity and diversity, and its validity for an indigenous Caribbean church.

AM538 Wostyn, Lode L.

Exodus Towards the Kingdom: A Survey of Latin American Liberation Theology. Quezon City, PH: Claretian Publications, 1986. ix, 200 pp. 9715011446.

An introduction to the main themes of Latin American liberation theology for Asian Christians.

Caribbean: General Works

See also TH459, SO380, ED172, AM113, AM412, AM429, and AM681.

AM539 Bessil-Watson, Lisa, comp.

Handbook of Churches in the Caribbean. Bridgetown, BB: Cedar Press, 1982. 134 pp. Paper. No ISBN.

Second edition of a handbook listing the members of the Caribbean Conference of Churches, including short histories of churches and theological colleges, as well as statistical data.

AM540 Bolioli, Oscar L., ed.

The Caribbean: Culture of Resistance, Spirit of Hope. New York, NYU: Friendship Press, 1993. x, 118 pp. Paper. 0377002542.

A popular mission study on the history, societies, economics, politics, and cultures of the Caribbean region, and how they impact Christian mission today; with study guide.

AM541 Butselaar, Jan van

Goed Nieuws Onder De Zon: De zending van de kerk in het Caribisch gebied. Amsterdam, NE: Nederlandse Zendingsraad, 1996. 44 pp. Paper. 9072030117.

This pamphlet provides an overview of the mission efforts of the Protestant Reformed churches in the Netherlands to build relations with evangelical Christian churches throughout the Caribbean; including issues of evangelism, politics, economics, and indigenous culture and religion.

AM542 Cuthbert, Robert W. M.

Ecumenism and Development: A Socio-Historical Analysis of the Caribbean Conference of Churches. Bridgetown, BB: Caribbean Conf. of Churches, 1986. xii, 145 pp. Paper. No ISBN.

A study of the work of the Caribbean Conference of Churches from 1957 to 1977—its history, involvement in community development and social change, and projected visions for its future.

AM543 Davis, Kortright

Mission for Caribbean Change: Caribbean Development as Theological Enterprise. (Studies in the Intercultural History of Christianity, 28). Frankfurt am Main, GW: Lang, 1982. 259 pp. Paper. 3820457321.

An analysis of the work, during the 1970s, of the Caribbean Conference of Churches, to promote development; with an extended theological rationale for such involvement, understanding that liberation and the proclamation of salvation are inseparable for Christian witness.

AM544 Glazier, Stephen D., ed.

Perspectives on Pentecostalism: Case Studies from the Caribbean and Latin America. Washington, DCU: University Press of America, 1980. viii, 197 pp. Paper. 081911071X (hdbk), 0819110728 (pbk).

Essays by differing authors on Pentecostals in Haiti, Jamaica, Puerto Rico, Trinidad, Colombia, Belize, and Brazil; including special aspects of Pentecostalism.

AM545 González, Justo L.

The Development of Christianity in the Latin Caribbean. Grand Rapids, MIU: Eerdmans, 1969. 136 pp. Paper. No ISBN.

A brief introductory history of Catholic and Protestant missions and churches in Haiti, the Dominican Republic, Cuba, and Puerto Rico, from 1492 to the present.

AM546 Hoornaert, Eduardo, ed.
História da igreja na América Latina e no Caribe, 1945-1995: O debate metodológico. Translated by Ephraim Alves, Jaime A. Clasen, and Lúcia Mathilde Endlich Orth. Petrópolis, BL: Editora Vozes; São Paulo, BL: CEHILA, 1995. 214 pp. 8532614809.

Working papers on Caribbean church historiography; originally presented at the Second General Assembly of CEHILA (São Paulo, July 1995).

AM547 Lampe, Armando
Breve Historia del Cristianismo en el Caribe. San José, CR: CEHILA, 1997. 207 pp. 9686571353.

A Catholic priest from the Dutch Antilles documents the process of the development of Christianity in the Caribbean cultural world.

AM548 Meier, Johannes
Historia General de la Iglesia en América Latina, IV: Caribe. México, MX: Universidad de Quintana Roo; Salamanca, SP: Ediciones Sígueme, 1995. 443 pp. 8430112553.

A general history of Christianity in the Caribbean, from the earliest missions to the present day—volume 4 of the Latin American Church history; edited by CEHILA.

AM549 Mitchell, David I., ed.
New Mission for a New People: Voices from the Caribbean. New York, NYU: Friendship Press, 1977. 144 pp. Paper. 0377000620.

Fifteen Caribbean Protestant leaders combine in this mission study book, to present their region—its colonial legacy, economy, society, education, culture, and religion.

AM550 Oldendorp, Christina Georg Andreas
History of the Mission of the Evangelical Brethren on the Caribbean Islands of St. Thomas, St. Croix. Edited by Johann J. Bossard, Arnold R. Highfield, and V. Barac. Ann Arbor, MIU: Karoma Publishers, 1987. xxxv, 737 pp. Paper. 0897200756.

The first English translation of Christian Oldendorp's history of pioneer Moravian missions in the Caribbean, including geography, natural history, and political history of the islands; originally published in 1777.

AM551 Osborne, Francis J., and Geoffrey Johnston
Coastlands and Islands: First Thoughts on Caribbean Church History. Kingston, JM: United Theological College of the West Indies, 1972. 262 pp. No ISBN.

An outline history with extensive bibliographic notes.

AM552 Ramlov, Preben
Brodrene og slaverne. Copenhagen, DK: Kristeligt Dagblads Forlag, 1968. 222 pp. No ISBN.

The author, a well-known novel writer, describes the work of the Moravian Brethren on the Danish islands of the West Indies, and their attitude to slavery.

AM553 Waddell, Hope Masterton
Twenty Nine Years in the West Indies and Central Africa: A Review of Missionary Work and Adventure, 1829-1858. (Cass Library of African Studies, Missionary Researches and Travels, 11). London, ENK: Cass, 1970. xxvi, 681 pp. 0714618810.

Reprint of the 1863 edition of a missionary journal and travelogue, including Calabar (Nigeria); with a new introduction by G. I. Jones.

AM554 Williams, Lewin Lascelles
The Caribbean: Enculturation, Acculturation and the Role of the Churches. (Gospel and Cultures Pamphlet, 10). Geneva, SZ: WCC Publications, 1996. ix, 29 pp. Paper. 2825412015.

An overview of the tensions of faith for Caribbean Christians—the legacy of initial indigenization of the Gospel there, the continuing appeal of precolonial religions, and the radical disengagement from earlier cultural patterns taking place today.

Caribbean, Biography

See also HI256.

AM555 Smith, Glen, Rachel Smith, and Mary H. Wallace
Caribbean Call: The Missionary Story of Glen and Rachel Smith. Hazelwood, MOU: Word Aflame Press, 1991. 224 pp. Paper. 0932581889.

A popular account of the service of United Pentecostal missionaries Glen and Rachel Smith, in the Caribbean, 1959 to 1992; as told by their friend Mary H. Wallace.

AM556 Vernooij, Joop
Jacobus Groof (1800-1852): Apostolisch Missionaris, Prefekt, Vikaris en Visitator in de West, de Oost, de West. Paramaribo, SR: Paramaribo Bishopric, 1990. 131 pp. Paper. 9991494979.

A biography of an important papal visitor to Roman Catholic missions, in both the East Indies (Indonesia) and West Indies; with texts of important documents.

Antigua and Barbuda

AM557 Ferguson, Moira, ed.
The Hart Sisters: Early African Caribbean Writers, Evangelicals, and Radicals. Lincoln, NBU: University of Nebraska Press, 1993. ix, 214 pp. 0803219849.

A biographical essay assessing the contributions of Anne Hart Gilbert (1773-1833) and Elizabeth Hart Thwaites (1772-1833), the first educators (Methodist) of slaves and free blacks in Antigua, and among the first African Caribbean female writers.

Bahamas

AM558 Barry, Colman J.
Upon These Rocks: Catholics in the Bahamas. Collegeville, MNU: St. John's Abbey Press, 1973. ix, 582 pp. 0814608124.

A scholarly history by the Benedictine Professor of Church History and Dean of the School of Religious Studies in The Catholic University of America.

Barbados

AM559 Davis, Kortright
Cross and Crown in Barbados: Caribbean Political Religion in the Late 19th Century. (European University Studies, 23: Theology, 212). Frankfurt am Main, GW: Lang, 1983. iv, 187 pp. Paper. 3820477810.

A detailed study of the use of religion, by an elite of planters and colonial administrators, to control the black laboring classes of Barbados in the 19th century.

AM560 Lewis, Kingsley
The Moravian Mission in Barbados, 1816-1886: A Study of the Historical Context and Theological Significance of Minority Church among an Oppressed People. Frankfurt am Main, GW: Lang, 1985. 273 pp. Paper. 3820482245.

A scholarly study of Moravian efforts to improve the lot of Barbadian slaves and their descendants, through religion and education, avoiding conflict with British political authorities.

AM561 Titus, Noel F.
The Development of Methodism in Barbados, 1823-1883. Frankfurt am Main, GW: Lang, 1994. x, 292 pp. Paper. 3906752089.

A detailed historical and sociological analysis of the development of Methodism in Barbados, in the closing years of slavery and the early emancipation period; based on extensive archival research; originally submitted as a Ph.D. thesis at the University of the West Indies.

Cuba

See also PO75 and ED86.

AM562 Alvarez, Carmelo, ed.
Cuba: testimonio cristiano, vivencia revolucionaria. (Historia de la Iglesia y de la Teología). San José CR: DEI, 1990. 199 pp. Paper. 9977830169.

A collection of fifteen interviews with committed Christians on their relations with committed revolutionaries in Cuba.

AM563 Arce Martínez, Sergio
The Church and Socialism: Reflections from a Cuban Context. New York, NYU: Circus Publications, 1985. xxvi, 196 pp. Paper. 0936123001.

An absorbing collection of lectures by a leading Cuban theologian, answering how one can be a Christian in a socialist society, and demonstrating the ongoing vitality of the church in Cuba today; includes speeches on Christianity by Fidel Castro.

AM564 Arce Martínez, Sergio et al.
Cristo vivo en Cuba: Reflexiones teológicas cubanas. (Testimonios). San José CR: DEI, 1978. 181 pp. Paper. No ISBN.

A collection of eleven papers on the work of the church and theology in a socialist society.

AM565 Braun, Theodore A.
A Perspectives on Cuba and Its People. New York, NYU: Friendship Press; New York, NYU: NCCUSA, 1999. vi, 138 pp. Paper. 0377003263.

The struggle between foreign domination and Cuban independence is set in the context of the economics of sugar, the era of US penetration, and the achievements and failures of postrevolutionary society; special attention is given to the perspectives of the Taino people, black Cubans, Cuban émigrés, and Cuban Christians, with a concluding chapter urging joint stewardship of Cubans and North Americans, to achieve mutual understanding and the sharing of the earth's resources.

AM566 Cepeda, Rafael, ed.
La Herencia Misionera en Cuba: Consulta de las Iglesias Protestantes Realizada en Matanzas, Cuba, del 26 de Octubre al 3 de Noviembre de 1984. (Colección testimonios). San José, CR: DEI, 1986. 244 pp. Paper. 9977904219.

A collection of twenty-six papers given at a consultation of Protestant churches, on "The Missionary Legacy of the Cuban Churches," discussing history, theology, liturgy, and church structures.

AM567 Conferencia de Obispos Católicos de Cuba
La Voz de la Iglesia en Cuba: 100 Documentos Episcopales. Mexico City, MX: Obra Nacional de la Buena Prensa, 1995. 485 pp. 9686056904.

A compilation of one hundred documents, published between 1914 and 1994 by the Cuban Catholic bishops and the Cuban Bishops' Conference.

AM568 Dewart, Leslie
Christianity and Revolution: The Lesson of Cuba. New York, NYU: Herder and Herder, 1963. 320 pp. No ISBN.

An essay giving a positive evaluation of the Cuban revolution, challenging Christians to support it, rather than be counterrevolutionary.

AM569 Gómez Treto, Raúl
The Church and Socialism in Cuba. Translated by Phillip Berryman. Maryknoll, NYU: Orbis Books, 1988. xiii, 151 pp. Paper. 0883443627.

English translation.

AM570 Gómez Treto, Raúl
La Iglesia Católica durante la Construcción del Socialismo en Cuba. (Colección Historia de la Iglesia y de la Teología). San José, CR: CEHILA; San José, CR: DEI, 1989. 125 pp. 997783007X.

Second edition of an analysis of the interactions of the Catholic Church in Cuba and the Castro socialist government.

AM571 García, Palacios Juan de
Sínodo de Santiago de Cuba de 1681. (Colección Tierra Nueva y Cielo Nuevo, 7; Sínodos Americanos, 1). Madrid, SP: CSIC; Salamanca, SP: Instituto de Historia de la Teología, 1982. xxvi, 232 pp. 8400052196.

A reprint of the 1844 edition of the texts of the influential Synod of Santiago, Cuba (1681).

AM572 Hageman, Alice L., and Philip Wheaton, comps.
Cuba: La Religión en la Revolución. (Libertad y Cambio, 29). Buenos Aires, AG: Granica Editor, 1974. 304 pp. Paper. No ISBN.

Spanish translation.

AM573 Hageman, Alice L., and Philip Wheaton, eds.
Religion in Cuba Today: A New Church in a New Society. New York, NYU: Association Press, 1971. 317 pp. 0809618230.

A collection of short essays and source documents on the contemporary Cuban churches, their historical background, and their efforts to articulate their social responsibility in a Marxist society.

AM574 Herr, Theodor
Kirche auf Cuba: Christentum und Marxismus am Wendepunkt? St. Ottilien, GW: EOS Verlag, 1988. 229 pp. Paper. 3880967490.

A German traveler relates his impressions of Castro's Cuba, the place of the Catholic church there, and the outlook for Marxism.

AM575 Ischuy, Theo
Hundert Jahre kubanischer Protestantismus (1868-1961): Versuch einer kirchengeschichtlichen Deutung. (Studien zur interkulturellen Geschichte des Christentums, 14). Frankfurt am Main, GW: Lang, 1978. 489 pp. Paper. 3261023562.

A comprehensive description of the historical development of the four biggest Protestant churches in Cuba.

AM576 Kirk, John M.
Between God and the Party: Religion and Politics in Revolutionary Cuba. Tampa, FLU: University of South Florida Press, 1989. xxi, 231 pp. Paper. 0813008794.

A thorough look at the Roman Catholic Church in relation to political rulers in Cuba from 1492 to 1987, with special attention to relationships with Fidel Castro's revolutionary government.

AM577 Neblett, Sterling Augustus
Historia de la Iglesia Metodista en Cuba, Volume I. Buenos Aires, AG: Evangelista Cubano, 1973. 147 pp. Paper. No ISBN.

A historical essay on the beginnings, missionary initiatives, and the subsequent development of the Methodist Church in Cuba between 1899 and 1948.

AM578 Ramos, Marcos Antonio
Panorama del Protestantismo en Cuba: La presencia de los protestantes o evangélicos en la historia de Cuba desde la colonización española hasta la revolución. San José, CR: Editorial Caribe, 1986. 668 pp. Paper. 0899222412.

A comprehensive history of Protestantism in Cuba, focusing on the pre-1959 period.

AM579 Ramos, Marcos Antonio
Protestantism and Revolution in Cuba. Coral Gables, FLU: University of Miami, 1989. 168 pp. Paper. 0935501177.

A history of Protestantism in Cuba in the 19th and 20th centuries, focusing on the relation of the churches to the social and political revolution; by a well-trained and highly respected Cuban historian.

AM580 Teste, Ismael
Historia Eclesiástica de Cuba. Burgos, SP: Editorial Monte Carmelo, 1969. 527 pp. No ISBN.

A history of the Roman Catholic Church in Cuba, from its beginnings; including information on the clergy, parishes, and religious orders.

Dominican Republic

See also HI232.

AM581 Bustle, Louie, and Ellen Bustle
Miracles Are Happening in the Dominican Republic. (Missionary Resource Book, 1978-79). Kansas City, MOU: Nazarene Publishing House, 1978. 94 pp. Paper. 0834104997.

Stories of the work of the Church of the Nazarene in the Dominican Republic, from its beginning in 1975.

AM582 Clark, James A.
The Church and the Crisis in the Dominican Republic. Westminster, MDU: Newman Press, 1967. xxvii, 256 pp. No ISBN.

An account of the Dominican Republic, from the viewpoint of the Roman Catholic Church, and of the troubles in 1965, leading to United States intervention.

AM583 Hefley, James C.
Intrigue in Santo Domingo: The Story of Howard Shoemake, Missionary to Revolution. Waco, TXU: Word Books, 1968. viii, 184 pp. No ISBN.

An account, by a freelance journalist, of the life and medical work of a Baptist missionary in Santo Domingo, in the 1960s.

AM584 Isais, Juan M., comp.
The Other Revolution: The Dramatic Story of Another Revolution in the Dominican Republic. Waco, TXU: Word Books, 1970. 163 pp. No ISBN.

Twenty-two short accounts of various aspects of the Evangelism-in-Depth campaign in 1965.

AM585 Meier, Johannes
Die Anfänge der Kirche auf den Karibischen Inseln: Die Geschichte der Bistümer Santo Domingo, Concepción de la Vega, San Juan de Puerto Rico und Santiago de Cuba von ihrer Entstehung (1511/22) bis zur Mitte des 17. Jahrhunderts. (Neue Zeitschrift für Missionswissenschaft Supplementa, 38). Immensee, SZ: *Neue Zeitschrift für Missionswissenschaft*, 1991. xxxiii, 313 pp. Paper. 3858240702.

This *habilitationsschrift* is a substantial history of the church province of Santo Domingo, as well as of the other bishoprics (Concepción de la Vega, San Juan de Puerto Rico, and Santiago de Cuba), from the beginnings in the early 16th century, to the middle of the 17th century.

AM586 Wipfler, William
The Churches of the Dominican Republic in the Light of History. (Sondeos, 2). Cuernavaca, MX: CIDOC, 1967. 214 pp. No ISBN.

A study of the causes of church problems in this Caribbean nation; originally submitted as a STM thesis at Union Theological Seminary (New York) in 1964.

Haiti

See also SO375.

AM587 Aristide, Jean-Bertrand
In the Parish of the Poor: Writings from Haiti. Translated by Amy Wilentz. Edited by Amy Wilentz. Maryknoll, NYU: Orbis Books, 1990. xxiv, 112 pp. Paper. 0883446820.

Letters, sermons, and poems by the prophetic former Salesian priest, who rose from a ministry of championing the rights of Haiti's poor to become president of that country in 1990.

AM588 Conway, Frederick J.
Pentecostalism in the Context of Haitian Religion and Health Practice. Washington, DCU: American University, 1978. vii, 283 pp. Paper. No ISBN.

A detailed analysis of Haitian Pentecostalism—its distinctives in theology and practice—in relation to Haitian Protestantism, Catholicism, and Spiritism (voodoo); originally submitted as a Ph.D. dissertation at the American University in Washington, D.C., in 1978.

AM589 Gispert-Sauch, Ana
Haiti, Opresión y Resistencia: Testimonios de cristianos. (CEP, 56). Lima, PE: CEP, 1983. 127 pp. Paper. No ISBN.

An anthology of testimonies and Christian documents, dating between 1971 and 1983.

AM590 Nelson, G. Dudley
As the Cock Crows. Franklin, TNU: Providence House, 1997. ix, 148 pp. Paper. 1577360478.

The founder of medical work for West Indies Mission in Aux Cayeo, Haiti (1946-1969), tells his story.

AM591 Petit-Monsieur, Lamartine
La coexistence de types religieux différents dans l'Haïtien contemporain. (Nouvelle Revue de Science Missionnaire, 39). Immensee, SZ: *NZM*, 1992. xxxvi, 391 pp. Paper. 3858240710.

A doctoral thesis (Sorbonne, Paris) on the history and social analysis of the various forms of religious life (Roman Catholic, Protestant, and voodoo) in Haiti, from colonization to 1971, focusing on the search for Haitian cultural and religious identity.

AM592 *Présence de l'Église en Haïti: messages et documents de l'Épiscopat, 1980-1988*
Paris, FR: Éditions SOS, 1988. 351 pp. Paper. 2718509910.

A collection of documents of the Roman Catholic bishops of Haiti, from the turbulent years (1980-1988), grouped by pastoral and doctrinal concerns, and responses to sociopolitical events.

Jamaica

AM593 Austin-Broos, Diane J.
Jamaica Genesis: Religion and the Politics of Moral Orders. Chicago, ILU: University of Chicago Press, 1997. xxiii, 304 pp. 0226032841 (hdbk), 0226032868 (pbk).

A penetrating historical and sociological assessment of how Pentecostalism came to flourish among Jamaicans, predominately of African descent; written by the Radcliffe-Brown Chair of Anthropology at the University of Sydney, Australia.

AM594 Davis, Edmund
Theological Education in a Multi-Ethnic Society: The United Theological College of the West Indies and Its Four Antecedent Institutions, 1841-1966. (Missiologisch Onderzoek in Nederland, 25). Zoetermeer, NE: Boekencentrum, 1998. 269 pp. Paper. 9023903722.

The development of Protestant theological education in Jamaica, from 1841 to 1966, including the birth and growth of four denominations and their colleges: Presbyterian, Baptist, Anglican, and Methodist.

AM595 Langford, Mary Jones
"The Fairest Isle": History of Jamaica Friends. Richmond, INU: Friends United Press, 1997. 210 pp. Paper. 0944350429.

A narrative history of the missionary activity of Orthodox Quakers from the midwestern United States, in Jamaica from 1883 to the present.

AM596 Lawson, Winston Arthur
Religion and Race: African and European Roots in Conflict—A Jamaican Testament. (Research in Religion and Family: Black Perspectives, 4). New York, NYU: Lang, 1996. xiii, 220 pp. Paper. 0820430935.

A detailed study of the historical and theological roots of the Anglican, Methodist, and Baptist churches in 19th-century Jamaica, and how their theologies, cosmologies, and cultural norms influenced the development of Jamaican colonial society.

AM597 Osborne, Francis J.
History of the Catholic Church in Jamaica. Chicago, ILU: Loyola University Press, 1988. xi, 532 pp. 0829405445.

A detailed scholarly study, based on research from the Jesuit archives of Catholic missions, and church growth in Jamaica from 1492 to 1986.

AM598 Stewart, Robert J.
Religion and Society in Post-Emancipation Jamaica. Knoxville, TNU: University of Tennessee Press, 1992. xxi, 254 pp. 0870497480 (hdbk), 0870497499 (pbk).

A detailed scholarly analysis of the role of religion in Jamaica, 1831 to 1875, in the rebellions, emancipation, and formation of a Creole society.

AM599 Turner, Mary
Slaves and Missionaries: The Disintegration of Jamaican Slave Society, 1787-1834. Chicago, ILU: University of Illinois Press, 1982. 223 pp. 0252009614.

A detailed, scholarly study of the role played by missionaries in the struggle, by Jamaican slaves, for religious freedom and emancipation.

AM600 Wright, Philip
Knibb "the Notorious": Slaves' Missionary, 1803-1845. London, ENK: Sidgwick and Jackson, 1973. 264 pp. 0283978733.

A scholarly biography of William Knibb (1803-1843), Baptist missionary to Jamaica (1825-1843), abolitionist, and champion of the slaves.

Netherlands Antilles

AM601 Oirschot, A. van
De fraters van Swijzen: 100 jaar fraters op de Nederlandse Antillen. Zutphen, NE: Walburg Pers, 1986. 191 pp. Paper. 9060115104.

The history of the missionary activities of the Catholic order of the "Brethren of Zwijsen," founded by Joh. Zwijsen, Bishop of Utrecht, in the Dutch part of the Caribbean.

Puerto Rico

See also AM1460.

AM602 Beirne, Charles Joseph
The Problem of "Americanization" in the Catholic Schools of Puerto Rico. Rio Pedras, PR: Editorial Universidad de Puerto Rico, 1975. 144 pp. No ISBN.

An analysis of the cultural biases of Catholic educators, arguing that they did not consciously try to destroy Puerto Rican identity.

AM603 Beirne, Charles Joseph
El Problema de la "Americanización" en las Escuelas Católicas de Puerto Rico. Translated by María E. Estades de Cámara. Río Piedras, PR: Editorial, Universidad de Puerto Rico, 1976. xi, 154 pp. 0847727262.

Spanish translation.

AM604 Mount, Graeme S.
Presbyterian Missions to Trinidad and Puerto Rico. Hantsport, NSC: Lancelot Press, 1983. 356 pp. Paper. 0889991871.

A detailed account of efforts by the Canadian and American Presbyterian missionaries to Trinidad and Puerto Rico, paying attention to their motivation, methods, attitudes, their converts, and their role in the total context of those two societies.

AM605 Silva Gotay, Samuel

Protestantismo y Política en Puerto Rico, 1898-1930: Hacia una Historia del Protestantismo Evangélico en Puerto Rico. San Juan, PR: Editorial de la Universidad de Puerto Rico, 1997. 375 pp. Paper. 0847702707.

The history of Protestant churches of Puerto Rico, with special attention to their role in education, culture, and social politics, by a Protestant theologian, who is Professor of Religious Sociology at the University of Puerto Rico in San Juan.

AM606 Smith, John A.

Ryder Memorial Hospital: An Unfolding Story of Health Care. Humacao, PR: Ryder Memorial Hospital; Brunswick, OHU: King's Court Communications, 1989. xiv, 241 pp. Paper. 089139043X.

A history of an outstanding missionary health care facility in Puerto Rico, from its founding by the American Missionary Association to the present; written by the doctor who served there (1946-1976) as its Medical Superintendent.

AM607 Wagenheim, Olga Jimenez de

Puerto Rico: An Interpretive History from Pre-Columbian Times to 1900. Edited by Leon King. Princeton, NJU: Markus Wiener, 1997. ix, 291 pp. 1558761217 (hdbk), 1558761225 (pbk).

A history expressly composed from the viewpoint of those colonized, suppressed, and exploited; the author explores the fate and contributions of Africans who became instrumental in Puerto Rico's social and economic development, contributing to the multicultural traditions of the Caribbean island.

Trinidad and Tobago

See also AM604.

AM608 Hamid, Idris

A History of the Presbyterian Church in Trinidad, 1868-1968: The Struggles of a Church in Colonial Captivity. San Fernando, TR: St. Andrew's Theological College, 1980. 271 pp. Paper. No ISBN.

A thesis tracing the history of the island of Trinidad, the missions of the Presbyterian Church and the United Church of Canada, and the ensuing struggle for selfhood and indigeneity of the Trinidad church; by a scholar raised by that church.

Canada

See also HI556, HI618, TH556, EC298, EC344, ED9, ED48, CH288, SP112, AF1365, AM650, AM995, AM1001, AM1008, AM1156, AM1170, and AM1197.

AM609 Best, Marion

Will Our Church Disappear?: Strategies for the Renewal of the United Church of Canada. Winfield, BCC: Wood Lake Books, 1994. 137 pp. Paper. 1551450495.

Conversations on issues of renewal for the United Church of Canada.

AM610 Bibby, Reginald Wayne

Fragmented Gods: The Poverty and Potential of Religion in Canada. Toronto, ONC: Stoddart Publishing, 1990. xiii, 319 pp. Paper. 0773754229.

A sociological survey of changes in post-World War II religion in Canada, suggesting ways for church renewal.

AM611 Bibby, Reginald Wayne

Unknown Gods: The Ongoing Story of Religion in Canada. Toronto, ONC: Stoddart Publishing, 1993. xx, 359 pp. Paper. 077375606X.

Canada's preeminent sociologist of religion analyzes the exodus from the churches and the disarray of organized religion, and offers suggestions for church renewal.

AM612 Campeau, Lucien

Monumenta Novae Franciae. (Monumenta Historica Societatis Jesu 96, 116, 130, 135, 138, 144, 146, 149). Rome, IT: Institutum Historicum Societatis Jesu; Montréal, ONC: Presses de l'Université Laval (vols. 1-3); Montréal, ONC: Les Éditions Bellarmin (vols. 4-8), 1967-1996. 8 vols. Paper. 2890077020.

Texts, in Latin and French, of documents related to the Jesuit mission in Quebec Province of Canada, 1641-1656 [vol. 1, *La première mission d'Acadie, 1602-1616*; vol. 2, *Établissement à Québec, 1616-1634*; vol. 3, *Fondation de la mission huronn, 1635-1637*; vol. 4, *Les grande épreuves, 1638-1640*, 2890076849; vol. 5, *La bonne nouvelle reçue, 1641-1643*, 1990, 862 pp, 2890077020; vol. 6, *Recherche de la paix, 1644-1646*; vol. 7, *Le témoinage du sang, 1647-1650*; vol. 8, *Au bord de la ruine, 1651-1656*, 1996, liv, 1,045 pp., 8870411494 (I), 2890078205 (C)].

AM613 Carriere, Gaston

Histoire documentaire de la Congrégation des missionnaires oblats de Marie-Immaculée dans l'est du Canada. Ottawa, ONC: Éditions l'Université d'Ottawa, 1975. 12 vols. 0776650718 (vol. 11).

An extensive account of the work and influence of the Oblats in Canada, particularly among various Indian tribes (1957-75) [vol. 1: *De l'arrivée au Canada à la mort du fondateur, 1841-1861*; vol. 2: *Dans la seconde moitie du XIXe siècle, 1861-1900*; vols. 3-5: *Les Études de l'Institut d'histoire du Canada de l'Université d'Ottawa*].

AM614 Champagne, Claude

Les débuts de la mission dans le Nord-Ouest canadien: Mission et Église chez Mgr Vital Grandin, O.M.I., 1829-1902. Ottawa, ONC: Éditions de l'Université St-Paul; Ottawa, ONC: Éditions de l'Université d'Ottawa, 1983. 276 pp. 2760301052.

The history of the 19th-century mission by the Oblates of Mary Immaculate to Native Americans in Canada's Northwest Territories.

AM615 Choquette, Robert

The Oblate Assault on Canada's Northwest. (Religions and Beliefs Series, 3). Ottawa, CA: University of Ottawa, 1995. xiii, 258 pp. Paper. 0776604023.

A history, based on research in Catholic archives, of the 19th-century Oblate missions to Native Americans in Canada's north and west; and analysis of the prevailing love-hate relationships between Catholics and Protestants.

AM616 Dickason, Olive Patricia

Canada's First Nations: A History of Founding Peoples from Earlier Times. (The Civilization of the American Indian Series, 208). Norman, OKU: University of Oklahoma Press, 1992. 590 pp. 0806124385 (hdbk), 0806124393 (pbk).

A comprehensive history of Canada's native peoples, including their extended encounters with missionaries.

AM617 Fagan, Cary

The Fred Victor Mission Story: From Charity to Social Justice. Winfield, BCC: Wood Lake Books for the Fred Victor Mission, 1993. viii, 176 pp. 0929032764 (hdbk), 092903290X (pbk).

A popular centennial history of the Fred Victor Mission, begun by Mary Sheffield as a Sunday School outreach to poor children in 1886, and developed as a mission that moved from charity to include concern for justice for the poor and homeless of Toronto, Canada.

AM618 Fast, Kenneth

Beyond the Extra Mile: An Odyssey of Faith and Commitment. New York, NYU: Vantage Press, 1993. ix, 189 pp. 0533104734.

The story of alternatives in Christian Ministry—an outreach ministry to youth outside the reach of traditional church programming in the Saskatchewan and Ontario provinces of Canada.

AM619 Fraser, Brian J.

The Social Uplifters: Presbyterian Progressives and the Social Gospel in Canada, 1875-1915. Waterloo, ONC: Wilfrid Laurier University Press, 1988. xv, 212 pp. Paper. 0889209723.

A historical examination of the Social Gospel among Canadian Presbyterians prior to World War I, exploring the theology, social context, and the strategies of the leaders of the Presbyterian Board of Evangelism and Social Service, by the Dean of St. Andrew's Hall, University of British Columbia.

AM620 Fumoleau, René

Here I Sit. Ottawa, ONC: Novalis, 1996. 192 pp. 289088791X (hdbk), 2890888142 (pbk).

Poetry by an Oblate priest, sharing his insights into the life of the Dene people of northern Canada, among whom he has lived as a missionary since 1953.

AM621 Graham, Elizabeth

Medicine Man to Missionary: Missionaries as Agents of Change among the Indians of Southern Ontario, 1784-1867. (Canadian Experience Series). Toronto, ONC: Peter Martin Associates, 1975. xi, 125 pp. 0887780776 (hdbk), 0887780784 (pbk).

A short history of Protestant and Catholic missions among the Mississaugas of Southern Ontario; originally part of a thesis prepared at the University of Toronto.

AM622 Grant, John Webster, ed.

The History of the Christian Church in Canada. Toronto, ONC: Ryerson Press, 1966-1972. 3 vol. No ISBN.

A detailed study of religious origins and patterns of Canadian society, presented in three volumes [vol. 1, H. H. Walsh, *The Church in the French Era: From Colonization to the British Conquest*, xiv, 212 pp.; vol. 2, John S. Moir, *The Church in the British Era: From British Conquest to Confederation*, xiii, 230 pp., 0070929599; vol. 3, John Webster Grant, *The Church in the Canadian Era: The First Century of Confederation*, xi, 241 pp., 0070929971].

AM623 Grant, John Webster

Moon of Wintertime: Missionaries and the Indians of Canada in Encounter since 1534. Toronto, ONC: University of Toronto Press, 1984. viii, 315 pp. 0802056431 (hdbk), 0802065414 (pbk).

A narrative scholarly account of 400 years of encounter between missionaries and Native Americans in Canada.

AM624 Gualtieri, Antonio R.

Christianity and Native Traditions: Indigenization and Syncretism among the Inuit and Dene of the Western Arctic. Notre Dame, INU: Cross Roads Books, 1984. 176 pp. 0940121034.

Volume II in the series, The Church and the World, which records missionary attitudes and judgments toward native traditions in the Canadian Western Arctic.

AM625 Hendry, Charles E.

Beyond Traplines: Does the Church Really Care?: Towards an Assessment of the Work of the Anglican Church of Canada with Canada's Native Peoples. Toronto, ONC: The Anglican Church of Canada, 1969. xi, 102 pp. Paper. No ISBN.

A church-sponsored, yet critical, assessment of the Anglican Church of Canada's work among native peoples.

AM626 Hodgson, Janet, and Jayant S. Kothare

Vision Quest: Native Spirituality and the Church in Canada. Toronto, ONC: Anglican Book Centre, 1990. 213 pp. Paper. 0921846045.

Sponsored by the Council on Native Affairs of the Anglican Church of Canada, this study is a survey of new vision and involvements of mainline Christian churches with Canada's native peoples.

AM627 Jaenen, Cornelius J.

The Role of the Church in New France. (The Frontenac Library, 7). Toronto, ONC: McGraw-Hill, 1976. x, 182 pp. Paper. 0070822581.

A basic history of Catholic missions in New France (Canada) from 1541 to 1760.

AM628 Jones, Elizabeth

Gentlemen and Jesuits: Quests for Glory and Adventure in the Early Days of New France. Buffalo, NYU: University of Toronto Press, 1986. xiii, 293 pp. 0802025943.

A soundly researched narrative history of the first French settlement in the New World, in Nova Scotia; and of Jesuit missionary work, both among the settlers and the Micmac Indians.

AM629 Kawano, Roland M.

Global City: Multicultural Ministry in Urban Canada. Winfield, BCC: Wood Lake Books, 1992. 144 pp. Paper. 092903256X.

A popular account of the history and sociology of multiculturalism in Canada, with theological and strategic rationales for missional ministries.

AM630 Kennedy, J. H.

Jesuit and Savage in New France. Hamden, CTU: Archon Books, 1971. vii, 206 pp. 0208010467.

A reprint of the 1950 edition, detailing French Catholic missions to Native Americans in Canada in the 17th and 18th centuries, and missionary perceptions of native culture.

AM631 Klassen, Herbert, and Maureen Klassen

Ambassador to His People: C. F. Klassen and the Russian Mennonite Refugees. Winnipeg, MBC: Kindred Press, 1990. xvii, 261 pp. Paper. 092178810X.

A chronicle by C. F. Klassen and the Mennonite Central Committee, of the emigration of Russian Mennonites to Canada (1928-1945) and Europe (1945-1954), and the ministry to these refugees.

AM632 McKay, Stan, and Janet Silman

The First Nations: A Canadian Experience of the Gospel-Culture Encounter. (Gospel and Cultures Pamphlet, 2). Geneva, SZ: WCC Publications, 1995. x, 53 pp. Paper. 2825411760.

Gospel and culture issues in Canada, told from the perspective of the country's first inhabitants.

AM633 Moir, John S., and C. T. McIntire, eds.

Canadian Protestant and Catholic Missions, 1820s-1960s: Historical Essays in Honour of John Webster Grant. (Toronto Studies in Religion, 3). Frankfurt am Main, GW: Lang, 1988. xiv, 266 pp. 0820404659.

Twelve essays, including biographical and historical studies of the history of missions in Canada, from the 1870s to the 1920s.

AM634 Mullins, Mark R.

Religious Minorities in Canada: A Sociological Study of the Japanese Experience. (Canadian Studies, 4). Lewiston, NYU: E Mellen Press, 1989. vii, 211 pp. 0889461953.

A sociological case study of religion in the Japanese Canadian community, including both foreign-oriented and native-oriented churches, their organizational dilemmas, and functions in the process of assimilation.

AM635 Murphy, Terrence, and Roberto Perin, eds.

A Concise History of Christianity in Canada. Toronto, ONC: Oxford University Press, 1996. xii, 456 pp. Paper. 019540758X.

A general history of the development of Christianity in Canada, containing much mission history.

AM636 Nock, David A.

A Victorian Missionary and Canadian Indian Policy: Cultural Synthesis vs Cultural Replacement. (Editions SR, 9). Waterloo, ONC: Wilfrid Laurier University Press, 1988. x,194 pp. Paper. 0889201536.

A case study in mission contextualization—the story of the efforts of E. F. Wilson, (1844-1915), an English CMS missionary to Canada, to promote Indian self-government and cultural synthesis.

AM637 Patterson, E. Palmer

Mission on the Nass: The Evangelization of the Nishga (1860-1890). Waterloo, ONC: Eulachon Press, 1982. 189 pp. Paper. No ISBN.

The history of Christian missions among the Nishga Native Americans of the Nass River Valley in British Columbia, from the arrival of a CMS Anglican missionary (William Duncan) in 1864, to the present.

AM638 Peelman, Achiel

Le Christ est Amérindien: Une réflexion théologique sur l'inculturation du Christ parmi les Amérindiens du Canada. Ottawa, ONC: Novalis, 1992. 346 pp. 2890886558.

Beginning with an overview of the Amerindian reality in Canada, based on field research across Canada in 1982, the Oblate missionary/theologian analyzes Amerindian responses to Christianity, and develops an Amerindian theology and Christology that is both contextual and liberative.

AM639 Peelman, Achiel

Christ Is a Native American. Toronto, ONC: Novalis/St. Paul University; Maryknoll, NYU: Orbis Books, 1995. 253 pp. Paper. 289088743X (CA), 1570750475 (US).

English translation.

AM640 Posterski, Donald C., and Irwin Barker, eds.

Where's a Good Church? Winfield, BCC: Wood Lake Books, 1993. 270 pp. Paper. 0929032942.

A Canadian survey with inputs from twenty-five focus groups and seventy-five interviews, to learn where spiritual vitality is evident and churches healthy, vital, and involving increasing numbers of people.

AM641 Rétif, André

Marie de l'incarnation et la mission. Paris, FR: Mame, 1964. 176 pp. No ISBN.

The first book published on the missionary work and concepts of the Ursuline Convent of Tours, that conducted a fruitful mission in Canada for thirty-three years, from 1639.

AM642 Redekop, Gloria Neufeld

The Work of Their Hands: Mennonite Women's Societies in Canada. (Studies in Women and Religion, 2). Waterloo, ONC: Wilfrid Laurier University Press, 1996. xv, 172 pp. Paper. 0889202702.

A history based on primary source documents of the establishment, in the 1870s, by Russian immigrant women, of societies for mission and spiritual strengthening, of their flowering in the 1950s and 1960s, and of their decline in the 1980s and 1990s.

AM643 Semple, Neil

The Lord's Dominion: The History of Canadian Methodism. (McGill-Queen's Studies in the History of Religion, 21). Montreal, PQC: McGill-Queen's University Press, 1996. x, 565 pp. 0773513671 (hdbk), 0773514007 (pbk).

The first comprehensive history of Canadian Methodism, including missionary work, both overseas and in Canada, among native peoples and immigrants.

AM644 Stanley, Laurie

The Well-Watered Garden: The Presbyterian Church in Cape Breton, 1798-1860. Cape Breton, NSC: University College of Cape Breton Press, 1983. 239 pp. No ISBN.

A detailed history originally presented as a M.A. thesis at Dalhousie University in 1980.

AM645 Walsh, H. H.

The Church in the French Era: From Colonization to the British Conquest. (A History of the Christian Church in Canada, 1). Toronto, ONC: Ryerson Press, 1966. xv, 221 pp. No ISBN.

A scholarly history of early Roman Catholic and Protestant missions in Canada, to 1763.

AM646 Weir, Joan

Catalysts and Watchdogs: B.C.'s Men of God, 1836-1871. Victoria, BCC: Sono Nis Press, 1995. 116 pp. Paper. 1550390554.

Chronicles a thirty-five year period in the pioneer history of British Columbia, Canada, during which a handful of missionaries from four different denominations succeeded in influencing every facet of the province's development—political, social, cultural, and educational.

AM647 Whitehead, Margaret

The Cariboo Mission: A History of the Oblates. Victoria, BCC: Sono Nis Press, 1981. 142 pp. 091946291X.

A history of the mission of the French order of the Oblates of Mary Immaculate to the numerous peoples (settlers and Native Americans) of British Columbia from 1866 to 1957.

AM648 Wilson, Douglas J.

The Church Grows in Canada. Toronto, ONC: Canadian Council of Churches, Committee on Missionary Education; New York, NYU: Friendship Press, 1966. x, 224 pp. Paper. No ISBN.

A brief, readable study book on the main outlines of Canadian church development.

Canada: Biography

See also AM636 and AM1023.

AM649 Brown, Bern Will

Arctic Journal. Toronto, ONC: Novalis, 1998. xii, 226 pp. 2890889017.

Fifty years of adventures in the Canadian Arctic of a missionary priest/artist of the Oblates of Mary Immaculate, who chose to live like the Inuit of Colville Lake, among whom he ministered.

AM650 Craig, Terrence L.

The Missionary Lives: A Study in Canadian Missionary Biography and Autobiography. (Studies in Christian Mission, 19). Leiden, NE: Brill, 1997. xvii, 169 pp. 9004108157.

A comparative analysis of more than 100 biographies and autobiographies of missionaries, to and from Canada, over the last 130 years, with a general introduction to Canadian missionary history.

AM651 Dempsey, Hugh A., ed.

The Rundle Journals, 1840-1848. (Historical Society of Alberta, 1). Calgary, ABC: Historical Society of Alberta, 1977. lxiv, 414 pp. No ISBN.

The letters and journal (1846-1848) of Robert Terrill Rundle, the pioneer missionary of the Wesleyan Missionary Society (UK) to the Indian tribes and fur traders of the province of Alberta, Canada.

AM652 Dolphin, Frank J.

Indian Bishop of the West: The Story of Vital Justin Grandin, 1829-1902. Ottawa, ONC: Novalis, 1986. 207 pp. Paper. 2890882772.

A biography of the "Indian bishop," a French Oblate Missionary of Mary Immaculate, who pioneered, from 1852 to 1902, in developing Catholic missions, schools, hospitals, and seminaries in western Canada.

AM653 Donnelly, Joseph P.

Jean de Brebeuf, 1593-1649. Chicago, ILU: Loyola University Press, 1975. 346 pp. Paper. 0829402330.

The biography of Jean de Brebeuf, including the history of the Christianization of the Huron nation in Midland, Ontario, by Jesuit missionaries, from 1639 through his canonization in 1930.

AM654 Gill, Stewart D.

The Reverend William Proudfoot and the United Secession Mission in Canada. (Studies in History of Missions, 7). Lewiston, NYU: E Mellen Press, 1991. vi, 248 pp. 0773494464.

A scholarly history, based on archival research, of the pioneer missionary work of William Proudfoot (1788-1851), of the Church of Scotland, and the United Secession in Canada, from 1832 to 1851.

AM655 Gstrein, Heinz

Entre pieles roja y esquimales: Apóstol de Athabasca, Émile Grouard (1840-1922). (Misioneros que hicieron historia, 6). Buenos Aires, AG: Editorial Guadalupe, 1982. 133 pp. 9500000024.

Spanish translation of *Ich scheue keine Mühe* (1977), a biography of Émile Jean Baptiste Marie Grouard, pioneer missionary bishop to the Athabasca Indians of Canada.

AM656 Gstrein, Heinz

Ich scheue keine Mühe: Emil Grouard, Apostel von Athabasca (Kanada). (Missionare, die Geschichte machten). Mödling, AU: Verlag St. Gabriel; St. Augustin, GW: Steyler Verlag, 1977. 131 pp. Paper. 3852641071 (AU), 387787097X (GW).

A biography of Bishop E. Grouard, who for sixty years (1862-1922) endured unbelievable hardship in the Indian and Eskimo missions in northwest Canada.

AM657 Mulhall, David

Will to Power: The Missionary Career of Father Morice. Vancouver, BCC: University of British Columbia, 1986. xii, 221 pp. 0774802545.

A study of British Columbia's most famous missionary—a meek and selfless priest who worked among the Carrier Indians between 1885 and 1903.

AM658 Murray, Peter

The Devil and Mr. Duncan. Victoria, BCC: Sono Nis Press, 1985. 341 pp. 091920368X.

The biography of William Duncan (1832-1918), pioneer CMS missionary (1857-1918) to the Tsimshian Native Americans of the Canadian Northwest and Alaska.

AM659 Rompkey, Ronald

Grenfell of Labrador: A Biography. Toronto, ONC: University of Toronto Press, 1993. xv, 350 pp. 0802059198 (hdbk), 0802077889 (pbk).

A scholarly biography of Sir Wilfred Thomason Grenfell (1865-1940), pioneer medical missionary to Newfoundland and Labrador; based on archival sources.

AM660 Usher, Jean

William Duncan of Metlakatla: A Victorian Missionary in British Columbia. (National Museum of Man Publications in History, 5). Ottawa, ONC: National Museum of Man, 1974. xii, 163 pp. No ISBN.

A case study of the CMS missionary William Duncan (1832-1918), the first Protestant missionary to the Native Americans of British Columbia, who from 1856 to 1887 worked to build the model Christian utopia of Metlakatla among the Tsimshian Nation.

AM661 Waugh, Earle H.

Dissonant Worlds: Roger Vandersteene among the Cree. Waterloo, ONC: Wilfrid Laurier University Press, 1996. xii, 344 pp. 0889202591.

The remarkable story of an Oblate missionary among the Cree in northern Canada, 1946-1976, who upon his death received burial as a Cree chief for his achievements in grounding Christian ideas in Cree imagery and spirituality.

AM662 Whitehead, Margaret, ed.

They Call Me Father: Memoirs of Father Nicholas Coccola. (Recollections of the Pioneers of British Columbia, 7). Vancouver, BCC: University of British Columbia Press, 1988. xi, 203 pp. Paper. 0774803134.

The memoirs of Father Nicholas Coccola, a Corsican-born Oblate Father, who worked for sixty-three years (1850-1934) among the native peoples of British Columbia, Canada.

Meso-America: General Works

See also SO491, SO500, PO32-PO33, EV125, EV395, and AM544.

AM663 Alonso, Isidoro, and Ginés Garrido
La Iglesia en América Central y el Caribe: Estructuras Eclesiásticas. (Estudios Socio-religiosos Latino-americanos, 4). Freiburg, SZ: FERES, 1962. 282 pp. Paper. No ISBN.

Brief introductions to the social structures of each nation plus a detailed exposition of its ecclesiastical structure.

AM664 Alvarez, Carmelo
People of Hope: The Protestant Movement in Central America with Selected Statements from the Churches. Translated by John Eagleson. New York, NYU: Friendship Press, 1990. v, 114 pp. Paper. 0377002127.

A historical account of the Protestant movement in Central America, from 19th-century mission effort through the church's growing autonomy, to the costly faithfulness amid the struggles of today; including six ecumenical statements from churches and Christians of Central America; translated from an unpublished Spanish manuscript.

AM665 Amerongen, Theo C. van
De bergen dragen vrede: geloof, lijden en verzet in Midden-Amerika. Amstelveen, NE: Luyten, 1984. 186 pp. 9064160627.

"The mountains will carry peace: faith, suffering, and resistance in Meso-America" describes the reactions of revolutionary Christians to political oppression since the mid-1960s: including the BCCs and their challenge for theology, the question of the legitimacy of violence, the option for the poor and Marxism, and the onslaught on the Indians of Guatemala.

AM666 Bacigalupo, Leonard
The American Franciscan Missions in Central America: Three Decades of Christian Service. Andover, MAU: Charisma Press, 1980. xix, 483 pp. 0933402201 (hdbk), 093340221X (pbk).

A chronological account, from 1944 to 1975, of the missionary activities of the friars of the Immaculate Conception Province in the United States, in Guatemala, Honduras, and El Salvador.

AM667 Ballin, Monika
Die politische Rolle der Kirche in Zentralamerika: Eine vergleichende Länderanalyse. (Kieler Schriften zur politischen Wissenschaft, 5). Frankfurt am Main, GW: Lang, 1990. v, 285 pp. Paper. 3631424485.

Inasmuch as the Catholic Church exercises the most significant sociopolitical criticism in Latin America, this study concentrates on that phenomenon in Costa Rica, Honduras, and Guatemala, with some subsections taking up similar Protestant activities.

AM668 Berryman, Phillip
Inside Central America: The Essential Facts Past and Present on El Salvador, Nicaragua, Honduras, Guatemala, and Costa Rica. New York, NYU: Pantheon Books, 1990. 166 pp. 0679729739.

A revised and updated edition of an introduction to the political conflict in Central America.

AM669 Berryman, Phillip
The Religious Roots of Rebellion: Christians in Central American Revolutions. Maryknoll, NYU: Orbis Books; London, ENK: SCM Press, 1984. xii, 452 pp. Paper. 0883441055 (US), 0334002060 (UK).

A detailed account of how Christians became involved in the Marxist-led revolutions in Nicaragua, El Salvador, and Guatemala; by a former Central American representative for the American Friends Service Committee (1976-1980).

AM670 Berryman, Phillip
Stubborn Hope: Religion, Politics, and Revolution in Central America. Maryknoll, NYU: Orbis Books; New York, NYU: New Press, 1994. viii, 276 pp. 0883449625 (O), 1565841360 (N).

A comprehensive analysis of the interplay between religion and politics in Central America in the 1980s.

AM671 Bonpane, Blase
Guerrillas of Peace: Liberation Theology and the Central American Revolution. Boston, MAU: South End Press, 1985. 119 pp. Paper. 0896083101.

Observations of a former Maryknoll missionary in Guatemala, on the realities of the Central America liberation struggle, 1962-1985.

AM672 Bricker, Victoria Reifler
El Cristo Indígena, el Rey Nativo: El sustrato histórico de la mitología del ritual de los mayas. Translated by Cecilia Paschero. (Sección de obras de antropología). México, MX: Fondo de Cultura Económica, 1989. 525 pp. No ISBN.

Spanish translation.

AM673 Bricker, Victoria Reifler
The Indian Christ, the Indian King: The Historical Substrate of Maya Myth and Ritual. Austin, TXU: University of Texas Press, 1981. xiv, 368 pp. 0292738242.

A scholarly study showing how the Maya used their cosmology to interpret the conquest and assimilate Christianity.

AM674 Calvin College, The Fellows of the Calvin Center for Christian Scholarship
Let My People Live: Faith and Struggle in Central America. Compiled by Gordon Spykman. Grand Rapids, MIU: Eerdmans, 1988. xvi, 271 pp. Paper. 0802803733.

Protestant scholars review Central American societies, politics, and economics in light of their faith, seeking to view the conflicts from the perspective of the oppressed, and to enable readers to grasp "the horror and the hope" of the situation.

AM675 CMI-Iglesias latinoamericanas
América Central: Textos y declaraciones. Ginebra, SZ: CMI-Iglesias latinoamericanas, 1981. 68 pp. No ISBN.

A collection of documents written between 1975 and 1981 in support of the poor and oppressed in Central America.

AM676 Cook, Guillermo, ed.
Crosscurrents in Indigenous Spirituality: Interface of Maya, Catholic and Protestant Worldviews. (Studies in Christian Mission, 18). Leiden, NE: Brill, 1997. xvii, 331 pp. 9004106227.

Eighteen essays on the clash of cultures and worldviews, the Maya culture and strategies of resistance, the rise of indigenous theology, and issues in dialogue and evangelization.

AM677 De Lella, Cayetano, comp.
Cristianismo y Liberación en América Latina, Vol. 1. (Colleción "Religión y Política", 5). Mexico City, MX: Claves Latinoamericanas; México, D.F., MX: Ediciones Nuevomar, 1984. Paper. 0968469055.
    Collection of twenty-eight essays and documents previously published elsewhere, that address the relationship between Church and politics in Central America, and in liberation theology.

AM678 Enyart, Paul C.
Friends in Central America. South Pasadena, CAU: William Carey Library, 1970. xii, 186 pp. 0878084053.
    Recounts the growth of the work of the California Friends Yearly Meeting, with a comparison to other evangelical churches in Guatemala, Honduras, and El Salvador.

AM679 Espinosa, Isidro Félix de
Crónica de los Colegios de Propaganda Fide de la Nueva España. (Fransciscan Historical Classics, 2). Washington, DCU: Academy of American Franciscan History, 1964. cii, 972 pp. No ISBN.
    New edition of an important historical work, which describes the spread of Catholic Christianity in Meso America, as far north as Texas, during the late 17th and early 18th centuries; first published in Mexico in 1746.

AM680 Hallum, Anne Motley
Beyond Missionaries: Toward Understanding of the Protestant Movement in Central America. (Religious Forces in the Modern Political World). Lantham, MDU: Rowman & Littlefield, 1996. xiii, 150 pp. 0847682978 (hdbk), 0847682986 (pbk).
    An overview of the complex phenomenon of Protestant, and especially Pentecostal, growth in traditionally Catholic Central America, including social and political implications.

AM681 Holland, Clifton L., ed.
World Christianity, Volume 4: Central America and the Caribbean. Monrovia, CAU: MARC, 1981. 240 pp. Paper. 0912552360.
    The status of Christianity in sixteen independent nations of Central America and the Caribbean, with a listing of people groups having less than 20 percent as practicing Christians.

AM682 Meléndez, Guillermo
América Central: Religión y conflicto social. (Cristianismo y Sociedad, 28, 103). México, MX: Cristianismo y Sociedad, 1990. 121 pp. No ISBN.
    A monograph containing six studies on the Roman Catholic church and Protestantism in Meso-America.

AM683 Meléndez, Guillermo
Seeds of Promise: The Prophetic Church in Central America. New York, NYU: Friendship Press, 1990. vi, 125 pp. Paper. 0377002046.
    An examination of the seeds of poverty and militarism sown in Central America for centuries, and a tracing of new seeds springing from the faith of Central America's people, which promise hope, justice, and love; written by the Catholic lay theologian and historian as a mission study for youth and adults; with study guide, *Sow in Tears, Reap in Joy* by Elise Higginbotham and David Kalke (44 pp., 0377002054).

AM684 Melville, Thomas, and Marjorie Melville
¿Para Quién es el cielo?: La transformación de un sacerdote y una monja norteamericanos de misioneros a revolucionarios
a través de su compromiso con los pobres y desheredados de Guatemala....* Translated by Teresa Pamies. México, MX: Roca, 1975. 301 pp. No ISBN.
    Spanish translation.

AM685 Melville, Thomas, and Marjorie Melville
Whose Heaven, Whose Earth? New York, NYU: Pocket Books, 1973. 274 pp. 671783475 (SBN).
    Story of the Melvilles' transformation from missionaries to revolutionaries through their commitment to the dispossessed of Guatemala; originally published by Knopf, New York (1971).

AM686 Nelson, Wilton M.
Protestantism in Central America. Grand Rapids, MIU: Eerdmans, 1984. vi, 90 pp. Paper. 0802800246.
    English translation.

AM687 Nelson, Wilton M.
El Protestantismo en Centroamérica. San José, CR: Editorial Caribe, 1982. 102 pp. 0899222110.
    A history of Protestantism in Central America from the 17th century to the present, focusing on the evangelical churches.

AM688 PCUSA (195th Assembly, 1983)
Adventure and Hope, Christians and the Crisis in Central America: Reports.... New York, NYU: PCUSA, General Assembly, 1983. 115 pp. Paper. No ISBN.
    Combined reports of task forces appointed by the Presbyterian Church (US) and the United Presbyterian Church (USA), with background material on the social, political, and economic history, country-by-country studies, evaluation of the policy of the United States, and recommendations to the churches.

AM689 Richard, Pablo, and Diego Irarrázaval
Religión y Política en América Central: Hacia una Nueva Interpretación de la Religiosidad Popular. San José, CR: DEI, 1981. 61 pp. Paper. No ISBN.
    A scholarly overview of popular religiosity in Latin America, and a detailed Nicaragua case study.

AM690 Richard, Pablo, and Guillermo Meléndez, eds.
La Iglesia de los Pobres en América Central: Un análisis socio-político y teológico de la iglesia centroamericana. (Colección Centroamerica). San José, CR: DEI, 1982. 345 pp. Paper. No ISBN.
    Research carried out by teams from each of the studied countries, on the relation of the hierarchical church with state, dominant classes, and popular movements.

AM691 Schäfer, Heinrich
Protestantismo y Crisis Social en América Central. (Colección sociología de la religión). San José, CR: DEI, 1992. 267 pp. Paper. 9977830614.
    A detailed study of the social and political involvements of Protestants in Central America, based on field research in Guatemala and Nicaragua in 1985-1986.

AM692 Schäfer, Heinrich
Protestantismus in Zentralamerika: Christliches Zeugnis im Spannungsfeld von US-amerikanischem Fundamentalismus, Unterdrückung und Wiederbelebung indianischer Kultur. (Studies in the Intercultural History of Christianity, 84). Frankfurt am Main, GW: Lang, 1992. 350 pp. Paper. 3631446551.
    A critique of Protestantism in Central America, focusing on the problems which have arisen, especially in churches of a Pentecostal and fundamental orientation, founded from North America.

AM693 Seminario Zubiri-Ellacuría (1st, 1993, Managua, Nicaragua), ed.
Voluntad de Arraigo: Ensayos filosóficos. (Colección Pensamiento, 2). Managua, NQ: Centro de Electrónica, Departmento de Filosofía e Histor, 1994. 258 pp. No ISBN.

An interdisciplinary collection of thirteen essays by Nicaraguan scholars, assessing the approaches of the Spanish philosopher Xavier Zubiri and the liberation theologian Ignacio Ellacuría to the search for contextualization.

AM694 Vigil, José María, comp.
El Kairos en Centroamérica. Managua, NQ: Ediciones Nicarao, 1990. 192 pp. Paper. No ISBN.

A collection of the *Kairos* documents from Central America, Guatemala, and Panama, accompanied by an analysis, and consideration of the *Kairos* theological method.

AM695 *When Christians Meet across North-South Barriers: The Affluent Church Meets Central America*
San José, CR: CELEP, 1989. 130 pp. Paper. No ISBN.

Twelve articles and poems originally presented at seminars of the Centro Evangelico Latinoamericano de Estudios Pastorales (CELEP) in San José, Costa Rica.

AM696 Wilgus, A. Curtis, and K. Meyer Harvey, eds.
Church and State in Central America: The Caribbean: The Central American Area. (The Central American Area: Series 1, 9). Gainesville, FLU: University of Florida Press, 1961. No ISBN.

Analyzes the interplay of church and state, with a focus on the church's role in education and health services.

Meso-America: Biography

AM697 Brett, Donna Whitson, and Edward T. Brett
Murdered in Central America: The Stories of Eleven U.S. Missionaries. Maryknoll, NYU: Orbis Books, 1988. xii, 366 pp. Paper. 0883446243.

A collection of eleven biographies of American missionaries martyred in Central America, from the Protestant and Roman Catholic churches.

AM698 Elliot, Elisabeth
Who Shall Ascend: The Life of R. Kenneth Strachan of Costa Rica. New York, NYU: Harper & Row, 1968. xiv, 171 pp. Paper. No ISBN.

A popular biography of the American founder of the Latin American Evangelization Campaign (LAEC) in Central America.

AM699 Roberts, W. Dayton
Strachan of Costa Rica: Missionary Insights and Strategies. Grand Rapids, MIU: Eerdmans, 1972. 187 pp. No ISBN.

A popular account of the work of R. Kenneth Strachan (1910-1965), General Director of the Latin America Mission and originator of Evangelism-in-Depth, with information on Protestantism in Costa Rica.

Belize [British Honduras]

See also AM893.

AM700 Bradley, Leo H., L. G. Vernon, and A. A. Dillet, eds.
A Bibliography of Published Material on British Honduras as Found in the National Collection. Belize, BH: British Honduras Library Service, 1960. 54 pp. No ISBN.

An earlier bibliography on Belize including works on missions.

AM701 Johnson, Wallace R.
A History of Christianity in Belize, 1776-1838. Lanham, MDU: University Press of America, 1985. xvii, 279 pp. Paper. 081914553X.

A scholarly examination of British missionary influence on the development of the Central American country of Belize, from the arrival of the first Anglican chaplain in 1776, to slave emancipation in 1838.

Costa Rica

See also ED145, EV99-EV100, AM299, and AM957.

AM702 Cook, Guillermo
Análisis Socio-Teológico del Movimiento de Renovación Carismática con Referencia especial al Caso Costarricense. San José, CR: Publicaciones INDEF, 1973. 244 pp. Paper. No ISBN.

A case study of Protestant charismatic renewal in San José, Costa Rica, emphasizing social and theological dimensions; written as a thesis for the Latin American Biblical Seminary.

AM703 Cruz Aceituno, Rodolfo
Reminiscencias de la Evangelización en Costa Rica. San José, CR: Publicaciones INDEF, 1984. vi, 185 pp. No ISBN.

The reminiscences concerning evangelization of a Guatemalan pastor who lived and worked in Costa Rica, 1920 to 1950.

AM704 Richard, Pablo, ed.
La Pastoral Social en Costa Rica: Documentos y Comentarios acerca de la Polémica entre la Iglesia Católica y el Periódico La Nación. (Colección cuadernos). San José, CR: DEI, 1987. 84 pp. Paper. 9977904464.

Documents and commentary on the 1987-1988 polemic of the journal *The Nation* in Costa Rica, against the social activism of the Catholic Church.

AM705 Solis, Javier
La Herencia de Sanabria: Análisis político de la iglesia Costarricense. (Colección Centro America). San José, CR: DEI, 1983. xviii, 173 pp. Paper. No ISBN.

A cogent examination of the legacy inherited by the Roman Catholic church in Costa Rica, following the death of Monsignor Victor Sanabria, Archbishop of San José, in the 1940s; including the role and influence of the church in Costa Rican society, from Vatican II and CELAM II (Medellín) to the present.

El Salvador

See also TH469-TH471, SO494, AM459, and AM665.

AM706 Beirne, Charles Joseph
Jesuit Education and Social Change in El Salvador. (Reference Library of Social Science, 1055; Studies in Higher Education, 5). New York, NYU: Garland, 1996. xvi, 259 pp. 081532121X.

A historical analysis of the development of the University of Central America by Jesuits in El Salvador, as a unique model of education for social change; covering the period from 1967 to the assassination of six of its leaders in 1989.

AM707 Best, Marigold, and Pamela Hussey
Life out of Death: The Feminine Spirit in El Salvador. London, ENK: CIIR, 1996. 210 pp. Paper. 185287189X.

An anthology of conversations with women from Christian communities, women's groups, and political organizations, who lived through El Salvador's bloody civil war.

AM708 Bogdahn, Martin, and Immanuel Zerger, eds.
Ich habe das Schreien meines Volkes gehört: Die Kirchen in El Salvador 10 Jahre nach der Ermordung von Oscar Arnulfo Romero. Munich, GW: Claudius Verlag, 1990. 168 pp. Paper. 3532620960.

Written ten years after the murder of Archbishop Oscar Romero, this book contains some of his more important statements, together with documents from the Lutheran communion about the state of Christians in El Salvador.

AM709 Brockman, James R.
Romero: A Life. Maryknoll, NYU: Orbis Books, 1989. xii, 284 pp. Paper. 0883446529.

A revised edition of *The Word Remains: A Life of Oscar Romero* (1982), a complete and authoritative biography of Archbishop Oscar Romero, taking account of sources not earlier available.

AM710 Classen, Susan
Vultures and Butterflies: Living the Contradictions. Scottdale, PAU: Herald Press, 1992. 183 pp. Paper. 0836136071.

Narrative recall by a registered nurse and Mennonite Central Committee worker, with excerpts from her daily journal, of identification, from 1982 to 1991, with people in Bolivia and El Salvador, whose lives were disrupted by poverty, oppression, and war.

AM711 Collet, Giancarlo, ed.
Vergessen heisst verraten: Erinnerungen an Oscar A. Romero zum 10. Todestag. (Peter Hammer Taschenbuch, 62). Wuppertal, GW: Hammer, 1990. 196 pp. Paper. 3872944274.

A collection of essays commemorating Archbishop Oscar Romero of San Salvador, and pointing out what the preferential option for the poor entails for Christian communities.

AM712 Dennis, Marie, Renny Golden, and Scott Wright
Oscar Romero: Reflections on His Life and Writings. (Modern Spiritual Masters Series). Maryknoll, NYU: Orbis Books, 2000. 127 pp. Paper. 1570753091.

On the 20th anniversary of his death, this volume celebrates the life, spirit, and legacy of Oscar Romero, the martyred Archbishop of San Salvador.

AM713 Equipo Tierra dos Tercios
El Evangelio Subversivo: Historia y documentos del encuentro de Riobamba, 9 a 16 de agosto de 1976. (Tierra dos Tercios, 3). Salamanca, SP: Ediciones Sígueme, 1977. 200 pp. Paper. 8430104585.

The working documents and chronicle of events of an *encuentro* held in Riobamba, El Salvador, 9-16 August 1976, which was interrupted by police as part of the church-state conflict in that country.

AM714 Erdozaín, Plácido
Archbishop Romero, Martyr of Salvador. Translated by John McFadden and Ruth Warner. Maryknoll, NYU: Orbis Books, 1981. xxiii, 98 pp. Paper. 0883440199.

English translation.

AM715 Erdozaín, Plácido
Monseñor Romero, Mártir de la Iglesia Popular. (Colección Centroamérica). San Salvador, ES: EDUCA; San José, CR: DEI, 1980. 159 pp. Paper. No ISBN.

A biography of Archbishop Oscar Arnulfo Romero, written by a colleague.

AM716 Erdozaín, Plácido
Monseigneur Romero, martyr de l'Église populaire. Translated by Denis Fontaine and Jean Villemaire. Montréal, PQC: Comité chrétien pour les droits humains en Amérique latine, 1983. 117 pp. No ISBN.

French translation.

AM717 Erdozaín, Plácido
San Romero de America: Das Volk hat dich heiliggesprochen; die Geschichte des Bischofs Oscar A. Romero von San Salvador. Wuppertal, GW: Jugenddienst Verlag, 1981. 122 pp. Paper. 3779573490.

German translation.

AM718 Gómez, Ernesto Medardo, and William Dexheimer
Five Against Five: Christian Ministry Face to Face with Persecution. Translated by Mary M. Solberg. Minneapolis, MNU: Augsburg Fortress, 1990. 94 pp. 0806624914.

English translation of a pastoral letter from a Lutheran bishop in El Salvador, who writes of the power of the Holy Spirit amid the fires of a repressive system in the 1970s and 1980s.

AM719 Galdamez, Pablo
Faith of a People: The Story of a Christian Community in El Salvador, 1970-1980. Translated by Robert R. Barr. Maryknoll, NYU: Orbis Books; London, ENK: CIIR; Melbourne, AT: Dove Publications, 1986. xviii, 91 pp. Paper. 0883442701 (US), 0946848483 (UK), 0859244431 (AT).

English translation of *La Fe de un pueblo* (1983).

AM720 Galdamez, Pablo
La Fe de un Pueblo: historia de una comunidad cristiana en El Salvador, 1970-1980. (Colección La Iglesia en América Latina, 8). San Salvador, ES: UCA Editores, 1983. 119 pp. No ISBN.

An account of the life of a Roman Catholic base Christian community in El Salvador telling of the struggles and hopes of the peoples of this country.

AM721 Golden, Renny
The Hour of the Poor, the Hour of Women: Salvadoran Women Speak. New York, NYU: Crossroad Publishing, 1991. 207 pp. 0824510887.

Testimonies of seventeen Salvadoran women from the war zone of El Salvador, including those active in BCCs.

AM722 Hatler, Grace
Land of the Lighthouse: As Told to Dorothy Molan. Valley Forge, PAU: Judson Press, 1966. 110 pp. No ISBN.

The personal memoir of American Baptist work in El Salvador, concentrating on educational aspects.

AM723 Hayes, Kathleen
Women on the Threshold: Voices of Salvadoran Baptist Women. Macon, GAU: Smyth & Helwys, 1996. ix, 134 pp. Paper. 1573120189.

The author interviews over ten Baptist women who, amid a destructive tradition of *machismo*, tell of the rise of feminism and hope for change.

AM724 Hussey, Pamela
Free from Fear: Women in El Salvador's Church. London, ENK: CIIR, 1989. ix, 59 pp. Paper. 1852870265.

An observation on the revolution in the role of women in El Salvador since 1980, which is seen as a contribution to an emerging liberation tradition, by a popular speaker of the Catholic Institute for International Relations.

AM725 López Vigil, Maria
Don Lito of El Salvador. Maryknoll, NYU: Orbis Books, 1990. xvi, 104 pp. Paper. 0883446693.

English translation.

AM726 López Vigil, María
Don Lito del Salvador: Proceso de una fe martirial. (Colección Servidores y testigos, 13). Santander, SP: Sal Terrae; Barcelona, SP: Claret, 1982. 85 pp. 842930620X.

The biographical sketch of a campesino from El Salvador, that reveals the awakening of a church and people committed to working together for peace and justice, from the perspective of the poor themselves.

AM727 Montgomery, Tommie Sue
Revolution in El Salvador: Origins and Evolution. Boulder, COU: Westview Press, 1982. xiv, 252 pp. 0865310491 (hdbk), 0865313865 (pbk).

A description of (1) the political and economic history of the country, (2) role played by the Catholic Church in 1960-1980, (3) the revolutionaries, and (4) the conflict of 1980-1982.

AM728 Noone, Judith M.
The Same Fate as the Poor. Maryknoll, NYU: Orbis Books, 1995. xiii, 170 pp. Paper. 1570750319.

A revised edition of the inspiring account of three Maryknoll Sisters, whose "option for the poor" in El Salvador led to their martyrdom; originally published in 1984.

AM729 Peterson, Anna L.
Martyrdom and the Politics of Religion: Progressive Catholicism in El Salvador's Civil War. Albany, NYU: SUNY Press, 1997. xxiv, 211 pp. 0791431819 (hdbk), 0791431827 (pbk).

A study of the way progressive Catholics of "the popular church" developed a theological ethic for interpretation and response to the political violence in the 1970s and 1980s.

AM730 Romero, Oscar A.
Archbishop Oscar Romero: A Shepherd's Diary. Translated by Irene B. Hodgson. Cincinnati, OHU: St. Anthony Messenger Press; Montreal, ONC: Novalis; London, UK: CAFOD, 1993. 542 pp. 0867161701 (US), 2890885917 (CA), 1852871091 (UK).

The personal diary, translated from Spanish, of the martyred bishop of San Salvador, from 1978 to four days before his murder in 1980; with content on human rights and other issues.

AM731 Romero, Oscar A.
In meiner Bedrängnis: Tagebuch eines Martyrerbischofs, 1978-1980. Edited by Emil L. Stehle. Freiburg im Breisgau, GW: Herder, 1993. 338 pp. Paper. 345123095X.

German translation.

AM732 Romero, Oscar A.
The Violence of Love. Translated by James R. Brockman.

Farmington, PAU: Plough Publishing House, 1998. xvii, 216 pp. Paper. 087468951X.

Selections from the writings of the martyred Roman Catholic Archbishop of San Salvador, on themes of salvation, justice, evangelization, and church renewal; originally published in 1988 (San Francisco, CAU: Harper & Row).

AM733 Romero, Oscar A.
Voice of the Voiceless: The Four Pastoral Letters and Other Statements. Translated by Michael J. Walsh. Maryknoll, NYU: Orbis Books, 1985. v, 202 pp. Paper. 0883445255.

English translation.

AM734 Romero, Oscar A.
La voz de los sin voz: la palabra viva de monseñor Oscar Arnulfo Romero. (Colección La Iglesia en América Latina, 6). San Salvador, ES: UCA Editores, 1987. 466 pp. No ISBN.

Third edition of book containing two interpretive essays and four pastoral letters of Archbishop Oscar Romero, who was martyred in El Salvador in 1980; originally published in 1980.

AM735 Santiago, Daniel
The Harvest of Justice: The Church of El Salvador Ten Years after Romero. New York, NYU: Paulist Press, 1993. iv, 195 pp. Paper. 0809134462.

Eighteen vignettes on the faithful endurance and witness of Roman Catholics seeking peace with justice in El Salvador, following the assassination of Archbishop Oscar Romero in 1979.

AM736 Sobrino, Jon
Archbishop Romero: Memories and Reflections. Translated by Robert R. Barr. Maryknoll, NYU: Orbis Books, 1990. ix, 214 pp. Paper. 0883446677.

A theological analysis of Archbishop Romero's person and work, by the prominent liberation theologian who knew him well.

AM737 Sobrino, Jon et al., comps.
Companions of Jesus: The Jesuit Martyrs of El Salvador. Maryknoll, NYU: Orbis Books, 1990. xxviii, 180 pp. Paper. 0883446695.

A memoir honoring the six Jesuit priests murdered in El Salvador on 16 November 1989, including excerpts from their writings and a reflection on the continuing mission of a Christian university.

AM738 Sobrino, Jon
Oscar Romero, Profeta y Mártir de la Liberación: Testimonios de mons. German Schmitz y mons. Jesús Calderón. (CEP, 41). Lima, PE: CEP, 1982. 189 pp. Paper. No ISBN.

A biography of Oscar Arnulfo Romero (1917-1980),archbishop of El Salvador, distinguished prophet in the church and in the social life of his country.

AM739 Whitfield, Teresa
Paying the Price: Ignacio Ellacuría and the Murdered Jesuits of El Salvador. Philadelphia, PAU: Temple University Press, 1995. xx, 505 pp. 1566392527 (hdbk), 1566392535 (pbk).

Examines the causes and consequences of the assassination, by government forces in 1989, of six Jesuit priests and two women, with special attention to Ignacio Ellacuría, S.J., rector of the University of Central America.

AM740 Wright, Scott et al., eds.

El Salvador: A Spring Whose Waters Never Run Dry. Washington, DCU: Ecumenical Program on Central America and the Caribbean; London, ENK: CAFOD, 1990. 95 pp. Paper. 0918346096 (US), 1852870796 (UK).

A collection of testimonies from Christian base communities in El Salvador in the 1980s, amidst repression and war; originally published in Spanish in *Carta a las iglesias.*

AM741 Wright, Scott

Promised Land: Death and Life in El Salvador. Maryknoll, NYU: Orbis Books, 1994. xl, 229 pp. Paper. 0883449552.

A Catholic lay missioner recounts his observations and participation from 1981 to 1991, with the church and the poor, amid the hopes, fears, and destruction of civil war and the encouraging influence of liberation theology.

Guatemala

See also CO97 and AM910.

AM742 Adams, Richard N.

Crucifixion by Power: Essays on Guatemalan National Social Structure, 1944-1966. Austin, TXU: University of Texas Press, 1970. xiv, 553 pp. 0292700350.

Emphasizes power relations between the United States and various sectors of Guatemalan society, and explores the interrelationships between the development of the military, the renaissance of the Guatemalan Church, the expansion of upper sector interest groups, the growth of campesino organizations, and the social organizations of low income urban families.

AM743 Aguilar, Francisco

History of the Foundation of the Town of Chamiquin in the Province of Verapaz. Translated by Lawrence H. Feldman. Culver City, CAU: Labyrinthos, 1988. x, 142 pp. Paper. 0911437304.

A translation of the original history of the new town of Chamiquin, Guatemala, 1819-1823; a case study of a pioneer mission effort among the Indians by Dominican friars.

AM744 Annis, Sheldon

God and Production in a Guatemalan Town. Austin, TXU: University of Texas Press, 1987. xiii, 195 pp. 0292727364.

An analysis of the emergence of Protestantism in rural Guatemala as a major force in political and economic life.

AM745 Arceyuz Zapata, Virgilio

Historia de la Iglesia Evangélica en Guatemala. Guatemala, GT: Génesis Publicidad, 1982. xii, 198 pp. No ISBN.

A history of Protestant denominations in Guatemala from 1882 to 1982, with many photographs.

AM746 Barton, Edwin

Arzt unter Mayas: Dr. Carroll Behrhorst's Leben für die Indianer Guatemalas. Basel, SZ: Reinhardt, 1974. 198 pp. No ISBN.

German translation.

AM747 Barton, Edwin

Physician to the Mayas: The Story of Dr. Carroll Behrhorst. Philadelphia, PAU: Fortress Press, 1970. 208 pp. No ISBN.

A popular account of the origin and growth of the medical mission work of Dr. Carroll Behrhorst of the Lutheran Church-Missouri Synod, the first M.D. among the Calchikel Indians of Guatemala from 1962 to 1969.

AM748 Bermúdez López, Fernando

Cristo muere y resucita en Guatemala. (Voces cristianas latinoamericanas, 2). Mexico City, MX: Casa Unida de Publicaciones, 1985. 68 pp. No ISBN.

A Roman Catholic missionary among the Pocomchi Amerindians tells of faith experiences and grim realities amidst warfare and oppression by the national army.

AM749 Bermúdez López, Fernando

Death and Resurrection in Guatemala. Maryknoll, NYU: Orbis Books, 1986. xv, 77 pp. Paper. 088344268X.

English translation.

AM750 Caldwell, Dondeena

If Quetzals Could Cry: A Guatemalan Scrapbook with Designs for Worship. New York, NYU: Friendship Press, 1990. iv, 80 pp. Paper. 0377002062.

Legends, history, poems, songs, and testimonies of suffering, injustice, faith, and hope for use in worship by church groups.

AM751 Esquivel, Julia

Threatened with Resurrection: Prayers and Poems from an Exiled Guatemalan. Elgin, ILU: Brethren Press, 1982. 128 pp. Paper. 0871788446.

Fourteen poems by a liberation theologian, to uplift Guatemala's persecuted and oppressed, who live in ressurrection hope; published in both Spanish and English.

AM752 Falla, Ricardo

Quiché Rebelde: Estudio de un movimiento de conversión religiosa rebelde a las creencias tradicionales en San Antonio Ilotenango, Quiché, (1948-1970). (Colección "Realidad Nuestra," 7). Guatemala, GT: Editorial Universitaria, 1980. 574 pp. No ISBN.

A study of a village in the state of Quiché, Guatemala, including its social and political systems, economy, indigenous religion and conversion of its inhabitants to Christianity; first published in 1978.

AM753 Falla, Ricardo

Quiché rebelde: Religious Conversion, Politics, and Ethnic Identity in Guatemala. Translated by Phillip Berryman. (LLI-LAS Translations from Latin America Series). Austin, TXU: University of Texas Press, 2001. [574] pp. 0292425310 (hdbk), 0292725329 (pbk).

English translation.

AM754 Frank, Luisa, and Philip Wheaton

Indian Guatemala: Path to Liberation: The Role of Christians in the Indian Process. Washington, DCU: EPICA Task Force, 1984. 112 pp. Paper. 0918346061.

A review of the history, including church participation in the democratic revolution and development failure, the efforts at community organizing, armed resistance to the government, the "Indian genocide," and the ongoing struggle.

AM755 Hinshaw, Robert E.

Panajachel: A Guatemalan Town in Thirty-Year Perspective. (Pitt Latin American Series). Pittsburgh, PAU: University of Pittsburgh Press, 1975. xxvii, 203 pp. 0822932962.

This study is based on data gathered by Sol Tax in the 1930s, and on fieldwork done by Hinshaw in the 1960s; a rigorous analysis of social change brought on by Protestantism, rapid population growth, lack of land, tourism, and industrialism.

AM756 Kita, Bernice

What Prize Awaits Us: Letters from Guatemala. Maryknoll, NYU: Orbis Books, 1988. xxiii, 231 pp. Paper. 0883442736.

The personal letters of Bernice Kita, Maryknoll missionary to the Mayan peoples of San Jeronimo, Guatemala, from 1977 to 1983.

AM757 Lutz, Christopher H.

Santiago de Guatemala, 1541-1773: City, Caste, and the Colonial Experience. Norman, OKU: University of Oklahoma Press, 1994. xx, 346 pp. 0806125977.

A scholarly history, based on archival research, of the most important urban center of Spanish Central America, from its establishment in 1541, to its destruction in the earthquakes of 1773.

AM758 Nouwen, Henri J. M.

Love in a Fearful Land. Notre Dame, INU: Ave Maria Press, 1985. 116 pp. Paper. 0877932948.

A simple, powerful story of the love, ministry, martyrdom, prayers, and friendship of two North American Catholic priests in Guatemala.

AM759 Oss, Adriaan C. van

Catholic Colonialism: A Parish History of Guatemala, 1524-1821. (Cambridge Latin American Studies, 57). Cambridge, ENK: Cambridge University Press, 1986. xx, 248 pp. 0521320720.

A detailed case study tracing the origins and developments of Roman Catholic parishes in Guatemala, from conquest (1493) to independence (1821).

AM760 REMHI

Guatemala: Never Again!. Translated by Gretta Tovar Siebentritt. Maryknoll, NYU: Orbis Books; London, ENK: CIIR/LAB, 1999. xli, 332 pp. Paper. 1899365443.

This report of the Interdiocesan Recovery of the Historical Memory Project, includes 6,500 personal testimonies of the victims and survivors of Guatemala's thirty-six long years of war.

AM761 Saenz de Santa María, Carmelo

El Licenciado don Francisco Marroquín: Primer Obispo de Guatemala (1499-1563). Madrid, SP: Ediciones Cultura Hispanica, 1964. 371 pp. No ISBN.

A biography of the first RC bishop of Guatemala, Francisco Marroquín, including all of his letters.

AM762 Scanlon, A. Clark

Hope in the Ruins. Nashville, TNU: Broadman, 1978. 175 pp. 0805463070.

The author describes the earthquake in Guatamala on 4 February 1976, and the kinds of help sent from many North American churches.

AM763 Schäfer, Heinrich

Befreiung vom Fundamentalismus: Entstehung einer neuen kirchlichen Praxis im Protestantismus Guatemalas; eine Fallstudie. (Theologie und Kirche im Prozess der Befreiung, 5). Münster, GW: Edition Liberación, 1988. 189 pp. Paper. 3923792301.

Description of the development and present situation of the Presbyterian Church in Guatemala, mirroring the great steps in the history of the country.

AM764 Schäfer, Heinrich

Beifreiung vom Fundamentalismus: Entstehung Einer neuen kirchlichen Praxis im Protestantismus Guatemalas: eine Fallstudie. (Reihe Theologie und Kirche im Prozess der Befreiung, 5). Münster, GW: Edition Liberación, 1988. 189 pp. 3923792301.

A history of the *Iglesia Evangelica Nacional Presbiteriana* (Presbyterian Church of Guatemala), including challenges of Pentecostals, political insurrection, intercultural tensions, and the search for theological identity.

AM765 Schäfer, Heinrich

Church Identity between Repression and Liberation: The Presbyterian Church in Guatemala. Translated by Craig Koslofsky. Geneva, SZ: WARC, 1991. v, 178 pp. Paper. 929075009X.

English translation.

AM766 Schotzko, Philip

Simple Faith: Stories from Guatemala. Kansas City, MOU: Sheed & Ward, 1989. xii, 91 pp. Paper. 1556122659.

A collection of popular stories about various aspects of life among the highlands Indians of Guatemala; from the author's pastoral experience at the San Lucas Mission (Roman Catholic).

AM767 Tooley, Michelle

Voices of the Voiceless: Women, Justice, and Human Rights in Guatemala. Scottdale, PAU: Herald Press, 1997. 232 pp. Paper. 0836190572.

An analysis of injustice in Guatemala, with stories of women there who have suffered and died in the struggle for human rights.

AM768 Tovar Astorga, Romeo, ed.

Documentos para la Historia de la Orden Franciscana en América Central. (Colección Centroamericana, 2). Guatemala, GT: Ministerio de Gobernación, Tip. Nacional, 1986. 719 pp. No ISBN.

Documents from the *Libro Becerro*, the manual governing Franciscan activities in a province of Guatemala between 1767 and 1817 (Spanish and Latin).

AM769 Vázquez de Herrera, Francisco

Vida y Virtudes del Venerable Hermano Pedro de San José de Betancur: Ampliaciones a la Relación de la Vida y Virtudes del Venerable Hermano, escrita por el R. P. Manuel Lobo, S.J. Translated by Lázaro Lamadrid Jiménez. Guatemala, GT: Licencia de la Orden, 1962. xxvii, 361 pp. Paper. No ISBN.

Writings of Fr. Pedro Betancur of San José (1626-1667), the Franciscan founder of a hospital, school, and homes for the poor in Guatemala; later used to argue for his beatification.

AM770 Wilson, Richard Francis

Maya Resurgence in Guatemala: Q'eqchi' Experiences. Norman, OKU: University of Oklahoma Press, 1995. xiv, 373 pp. 0806126906.

An analysis of cultural renewal among the Q'eqchi'-speaking Mayas of the Guatamalan province of Alta Verapaz, focusing on Roman Catholic, Protestant, and traditional influences.

Honduras

See also SO494.

AM771 Black, Nancy Johnson
The Frontier Mission and Social Transformation in Western Honduras: The Order of Our Lady of Mercy, 1525-1773. (Studies in Christian Mission, 14). New York, NYU: Brill, 1995. xii, 194 pp. Paper. 9004102191.

An anthropological history of nearly 250 years of Mercedarian mission among the Lenca Indians of western Honduras, focusing on organization, operation, goals, and changes.

AM772 Blanco, Gustavo, and Jaime Valverde
Honduras: Iglesia y Cambio Social. (Colección Sociología de la Religión). San José, CR: Editorial DEI, 1990. 228 pp. Paper. 9977830215.

The history of the 1957 to 1975 struggle for reform in Honduras, and of the participation by the churches (Catholic and Protestant) in that struggle that included fierce church-state conflicts.

AM773 Carney, J. Guadalupe
To Be a Revolutionary: An Autobiography. San Francisco, CAU: Harper & Row, 1987. xxi, 473 pp. Paper. 006061322X.

The author tells of his life as a Jesuit priest and missionary in Honduras during the 1960s and 1970s working for base communities, land reform and cooperatives, being forced into exile, and being called a "Christian revolutionary."

AM774 Winn, Wilkins B.
Pioneer Protestant Missionaries in Honduras: A. E. Bishop and J. G. Cassel and the Establishment of the Central American Mission in Western Honduras, 1896-1901. (Sondeos, 88). Cuernavaca, MX: CIDOC, 1973. 1 vol. No ISBN.

Edited diaries of two pioneer Protestant missionaries that reveal both problems and progress of missionary work, the attitudes and emotions of the missionaries, and comments on social conditions.

Mexico

See also HI214, HI250, HI288, CR637-CR638, CR647, CR653, SP219, AM18, AM41, AM113, AM275, and AM853.

AM775 *Alcancemos las Etnias de México*
Toluca, MXU: Operación Samaria, 1993. 111 pp. Paper. No ISBN.

Capsule introductions to fifty-four "people groups" in Mexico, produced to encourage Mexican young people to fulfill the Great Commission.

AM776 Bailey, David C.
Viva Cristo Rey!: The Cristero Rebellion and the Church/State Conflict in Mexico. Austin, TXU: University of Texas Press, 1974. 346 pp. 0292787006.

A scholarly history of the 1926-1929 rebellion, led by Catholic militants in an unsuccessful effort to overthrow the Mexican government.

AM777 Baldwin, Deborah J.
Protestants and the Mexican Revolution: Missionaries, Ministers, and Social Change. Urbana, ILU: University of Illinois Press, 1990. xii, 203 pp. 0252016599.

A detailed study, based on archival research, of Protestant involvements in the Mexican revolution of 1910, and the social ferment preceding and following it.

AM778 Basalenque, Diego
Historia de la Provincia de San Nicolás de Tolentino de Michoacán. (Colección Documentos y Testimonios). Morelia, MX: Balsal Editores, 1989. xv, 479 pp. 968600940X.

A reprint of the 1673 history of the Augustinian province of Saint Nicholas of Tolentino, of the state of Michoacán in Mexico.

AM779 Bastian, Jean-Pierre et al.
Religión y Sociedad en México. (Cristianismo y Sociedad, 27, 101). México, MX: Cristianismo y Sociedad, 1989. 110 pp. No ISBN.

A numbered monograph with eight studies of religious sociology, plus a bibliography on church-state relations in Mexico.

AM780 Bastian, Jean-Pierre
Protestantismo y Sociedad en México. México, MX: CUPSA, 1983. 241 pp. Paper. 9687011084.

A historical-sociological study of Protestantism and its development in Mexico.

AM781 Baumgartner, Jakob
Mission und Liturgie in Mexico. (Supplementa, 18-19). Immensee, SZ: NZM, 1971. 2 vols. Paper. No ISBN.

A dissertation based mainly on the first councils and synods (up to 1585), concerning the methods, difficulties, and achievements of the first missionaries in Mexico, with regard to the sacraments and the liturgy; the second part deals with the first two liturgical manuals of Latin America, the *Manuale de Adultos* (1549) and the *Manuale Sacramentorum* (1560), giving an extensive commentary on the latter [vol. 1: *Der Gottesdienst in der jungen Kirche Neuspaniens*, (xxiv, 422 pp.); vol. 2: *Die ersten liturgischen Bücher in der Neuen Welt*, (viii, 399 pp.)].

AM782 Bazant, Jan
Alienation of Church Wealth in Mexico: Social and Economic Aspects of the Liberal Revolution, 1856-1875. Edited by Michael P. Costeloe. Translated by Michael P. Costeloe. (Cambridge Latin American Studies, 11). London, ENK: Cambridge University Press, 1971. xvi, 332 pp. 0521078725.

English translation of *Los biense de la Iglesia en México (1856-1875)*, a scholarly examination of the conflict over the nationalization of ecclesiastical holdings, especially between 1856 and 1875.

AM783 Bennett, Charles
Tinder in Tabasco: A Study of Church Growth in Tropical Mexico. Grand Rapids, MIU: Eerdmans, 1968. 213 pp. Paper. No ISBN.

A historical study of the growth of the Evangelical church since 1881 in the tropical swamplands of southeast Mexico.

AM784 Bey, Horst von der, ed.
"Auch wir sind Menschen so wie ihr!": Franziskanische Dokumente des 16. Jahrhunderts zur Eroberung Mexikos. Paderborn, GW: Ferdinand Schöningh, 1995. 402 pp. Paper. 3506707841.

Sixteenth-century correspondence by Franciscans in Mexico, illuminating the variety of their roles, from punishing inquisitor to enthusiastic protector of the Indians.

AM785 Boersma, Franciscus F. van der Hoff
Organizar la Esperanza: Teología India Rural. (Kerk en Theologie in Context-Iglesia y Teologia en Contexto, 14). Kampen, NE: Kok, 1992. xi, 311 pp. Paper. 9024266351.

A detailed study of the religiosity and popular theology of rural Catholics in the diocese of Tehuantepec, Oaxaca, Mexico; submitted as a dissertation at the Catholic University of Nimegen, the Netherlands, in 1992.

AM786 Bolton, Herbert Eugene
The Padre on Horseback: A Sketch of Eusebio Francisco Kino, S.J., Apostle of the Pimas. Chicago, ILU: Loyola University Press, 1986. xiii, 84 pp. Paper. 0829400044.

A reprint of the biography of a Jesuit missionary to the Pima Indians of northern Mexico (and present state of Arizona), 1681-1711; originally published in 1932 by The Sonora Press, San Francisco.

AM787 Bowen, Kurt
Evangelism and Apostasy: The Evolution and Impact of Evangelicals in Modern Mexico. (McGill-Queen's Studies in the History of Religion, 23). Montreal, PQC: McGill-Queen's University Press, 1996. xiii, 270 pp. 0773513795.

A sociological survey of evangelicals and Pentecostals in Mexico, including the conversion process, commitment mechanisms, schisms, distinct beliefs, and the religious, social, and political influence of American missionaries.

AM788 Braden, Charles Samuel
Religious Aspects of the Conquest of Mexico. New York, NYU: AMS Press, 1966. xv, 344 pp. No ISBN.

An analysis of Aztec religious background, the work of 16th-century Catholic missions, and the mutual influences of Christianity and native religions; a reprint of the original 1930 edition.

AM789 Brading, D. A.
Church and State in Bourbon Mexico: The Diocese of Michoacán, 1749-1810. New York, NYU: Cambridge University Press, 1994. xiii, 300 pp. 0521460921.

A detailed case study, based on archival sources, highlighting the clash between grassroots Catholics and the civil and religious elite in a Mexican 18th-century diocese.

AM790 Bridges, Julián C.
Expansión Evangélica en México. El Paso, TXU: Editorial Mundo Hispano, 1973. 87 pp. Paper. No ISBN.

An analysis of the importance of the evangelical churches in Mexico, their geographical distribution, and their numerical increase since 1957.

AM791 Bridges, Julián C.
Into Aztec Land. Nashville, TNU: Convention Press, 1968. viii, 104 pp. Paper. No ISBN.

A mission study booklet on the work of the Southern Baptists in Mexico.

AM792 Bringas y Encinas, Diego Miguel
Friar Bringas Reports to the King: Methods of Indoctrination on the Frontier of New Spain, 1796-97. Edited by Daniel S. Matson and Bernard L. Fontana. (The Documentary Relations of the Southwest; The Franciscan Relations). Tucson, AZU: University of Arizona Press, 1977. ix, 177 pp. 0816505993 (hdbk), 0816505241 (pbk).

Useful translation of a manuscript dealing with the Franciscan missions, from 1768 to 1796.

AM793 Burkhart, Louise M.
The Slippery Earth: Nahua-Christian Moral Dialogue in Sixteenth-Century Mexico. Tuscon, AZU: University of Arizona Press, 1989. xii, 242 pp. 0816510881.

A detailed analysis of 16th-century catechistic literature by Franciscan friars in the Nahuatl (Aztec) language, interpreting the cross-cultural transition of religious concepts that took place.

AM794 Burrus, Ernest J., and Félix Zubillaga
El Noroeste de México: Documentos sobre las misiones jesuíticas, 1600-1769. (Serie documental/Instituto de Investigaciones Históricas, 18). México, MX: Universidad Nacional Autónoma de México, 1986. xli, 674 pp. 9688375292.

Documents concerning the founding and early history of Jesuit missionaries to northern Mexico and New Mexico.

AM795 Burrus, Ernest J.
Kino and Manje, Explorers of Sonora and Arizona: Their Vision of the Future. (Sources and Studies for the History of the Americas, 10). Rome, IT: Jesuit Historical Institute; St. Louis, MOU: St. Louis University, 1971. xi, 793 pp. No ISBN.

Study of Eusebio Kino's expeditions with Juan Mateo Manje into northern Sonora and southern Arizona between 1694 and 1701, with introductory chapters on both Kino and Manje.

AM796 Callcott, Wilfrid Hardy
Church and State in Mexico, 1822-1857. New York, NYU: Octagon Books, 1965. 357 pp. No ISBN.

An analysis of church-state relations at a time when pressure was growing to restrict the privileges of the Roman Catholic Church, and remove it from power and influence in government.

AM797 Camp, Roderic Ai
Crossing Swords: Politics and Religion in Mexico. New York, NYU: Oxford University Press, 1997. xi, 341 pp. 0195107845.

A scholarly study of the role of Catholicism in Mexican society, from the 1970s to 1995.

AM798 Canedo, Lino Gomez
Pioneros de la Cruz en México: Fray Toribio de Motolina y sus Compañeros. (Grande Evangelizadores de América). Madrid, SP: Biblioteca de Autores Cristianos, 1988. 221 pp. 8422013312.

An introduction to pioneer Franciscan missions in Mexico, in the 16th century, focusing on the collective work of twelve friars from Spain, as well as the evangelistic endeavors of Fray Toribio de Motolinía, known for his selflessness and humility.

AM799 Carmichael, Elizabeth, and Sayer Chloë
The Skeleton at the Feast: The Day of the Dead in Mexico. Austin, TXU: University of Texas Press, 1991. 160 pp. Paper. 0292776586.

A description of the history, art, and celebrations of the "Day of the Dead" (Todos Santos) as practiced in contemporary Mexico.

AM800 Cayota, Mario
Siembra entre Brumas: Utopia franciscana y humanismo renacentista, una alternativa a la conquista. Montevideo, UY: Instituto San Bernardino de Montevideo, 1990. 539 pp. Paper. No ISBN.

A historical, documentary study of the Franciscans, first evangelizers of America; their humanity and their missionary experiences, especially in Mexico, as opposed to the spirit of conquest and dominion seen in many Spaniards of the time.

AM801 Cervantes, Rafael
Fray Simón del Hierro, 1700-1775, y el Norte de México: Presentación historiográfica del Colegio Apostólico de Guadalupe, Zacatecas. (Serie Antropológica: Etnología, 52). Mexico City, MX: Universidad Nacional Autónoma de México, 1986. 407 pp. 9688376973.
Biography of an important 18th-century Franciscan missionary to Mexico.

AM802 Chávez, Angelico
Coronado's Friars. (Publications of the Academy of American Franciscan History; Monograph Series, 8). Washington, DCU: Academy of American Franciscan History, 1968. xx, 106 pp. No ISBN.
Identifies and provides biographical information on the six friars who accompanied Coronado.

AM803 Chance, John K.
Conquest of the Sierra: Spaniards and Indians in Colonial Oaxaca. Norman, OKU: University of Oklahoma Press, 1989. xvii, 233 pp. 0806122226.
A scholarly ethnohistory of the Spanish conquerors, the Dominican missionaries, and the Indians in the Oaxaca region of Mexico, from the time of Spanish conquest in 1521 through the mid-19th century; by the Associate Professor of Anthropology at Arizona State University.

AM804 Churruca, Pelaez Agustín
Primeras Fundaciones Jesuitas en Nueva España, 1572-1580. (Biblioteca Porrua, 75). México, MX: Porrua, 1980. lvi, 504 pp. 9684325681.
An historical study, with extensive documentary references, of Jesuit missions in New Spain in the 16th century.

AM805 Clavigero, Francisco Saverio, and Miguel León-Portilla
Historia de la Antigua o Baja California. (Colección Sepan cuantos, 143). México, MX: Porrua, 1982. xli, 262 pp. No ISBN.
Reprint of the classic 18th-century account of the Spanish conquest and rule in Baja California, including the missions; originally published in 1789.

AM806 Clavigero, Francisco Saverio
Historia de la Antigua o Baja California. Edited by Xavier Chaco Vazquez. Coyoacán, MX: Universidad Iéroamericana, Departamento de Historia y Plantel Noroeste, 1986. xlv, 345 pp. 968859010X.
Spanish translation.

AM807 Clavigero, Francisco Saverio
The History of Lower California. Translated by Sra E. Lake. Edited by A. A. Gray. Riverside, CAU: Manessier Publishing, 1971. liii, 413 pp. No ISBN.
English translation.

AM808 Conferencia del Episcopado Mexicano, Comisión Episcopal para Indígenas
Fundamentos Teológicos de la Pastoral Indígena en México. México, MX: Conferencia del Episcopado Mexicano, 1988. 178 pp. Paper. No ISBN.
A systematic treatment of doctrine and pastoral practice that integrates several proposals from current missiology.

AM809 Costeloe, Michael P.
Church Wealth in Mexico: A Study of the "Juzgado de Capellanias" in the Archbishopric of Mexico, 1800-1856. (Cambridge Latin American Studies, 2). London, ENK: Cambridge Univerity Press, 1967. ix, 139 pp. 0521047293.
Systematic examination of the Mexican church's credit monopoly, which concludes that it was not feudal, but an efficient commercial operation.

AM810 Crow, John Armstrong
Mexico Today. New York, NYU: Harper & Row, 1972. xiv, 369 pp. 0060109238.
Vivid observations introducing both Mexican history and modern life; revised edition.

AM811 Donohue, John Augustine
After Kino: Jesuit Missions in Northwestern New Spain, 1711-1767. (Sources and Studies for the History of the Americas, 6). Rome, IT: Jesuit Historical Institute; St. Louis, MOU: St. Louis University, 1969. iv, 183 pp. Paper. No ISBN.
A history of Jesuit activities in Sinaloa, Sonora, and southern Arizona during the years between the death of the missionary Eusebio Kino in 1711, and the Jesuits' expulsion from the Spanish dominions in 1767.

AM812 Ducrue, Benno Franciscus
Ducrue's Account of the Expulsion of the Jesuits from Lower California (1767-1769): An Annotated English Translation of Benno Ducrue's Relatio expulsionis. Edited by Ernest J. Burrus. (Sources and Studies for the History of the Americas, 2). Rome, IT: Jesuit Historical Institute; St. Louis, MOU: St. Louis University, 1967. vii, 212 pp. No ISBN.
An account of the expulsion of the Jesuits from Baja California; first published in 1784, with Latin text and other documents.

AM813 Durán, Diego
The Aztecs: The History of the Indies of New Spain. Translated by Doris Heyden, and Fernando Horcasitas. New York, NYU: Orion Publishing, 1964. xxxi, 381 pp. No ISBN.
English translation of *Historia de la Indias de Nueva España y islas de tierra firme* (1967).

AM814 Durán, Diego
Historia de las Indias de Nueva España e Islas de la Tierra Firme. (Biblioteca Porrúa, 36-37). México, MX: Editorial Porrúa, 1984. 2 vols. 9684329318.
Second edition of a history of the native people of Mexico, written in the 16th century by a Dominican; including a description of their history, from the beginning of creation to their involvement with Spain [vol. 1, xlvii, 341 pp., 9684329326; vol. 2, 641 pp., 9684329334].

AM815 Durán, Diego
The History of the Indies of New Spain. Translated by Doris Heyden. (Civilization of the American Indian Series, 210). Norman, OKU: University of Oklahoma Press, 1994. xxxvi, 642 pp. 0806126493.
A new translation and critical edition of a remarkable 16th century history of the Aztecs, by a Dominican friar who was fluent in the Nahuatl language and the most knowledgeable of the missionary ethnographers in New Spain.

AM816 Elizondo, Virgilio P.
Guadalupe: Mother of the New Creation. Maryknoll, NYU: Orbis Books, 1997. xx, 139 pp. Paper. 1570751102.
The noted Chicano theologian tells the story and meaning of the most powerful symbol of popular religiosity in Mexico—Our Lady of Guadalupe.

AM817 Espinosa, Isidro Félix de

Misioneros Valencianos en Indias. Valencia, SP: Generalitat Valenciana, 1989. 2 vols. 8475797482 (set), 8475797466 (vol.1).

The accounts of three missionaries' travels in the 18th century, and work with the native people of Guatemala and Mexico, including the present southwestern United States.

AM818 Farriss, Nancy M.

Crown and Clergy in Colonial Mexico, 1759-1821: The Crisis of Ecclesiastical Privilege. (University of London Historical Studies, 21). London, ENK: University of London/Athlone Press, 1968. xii, 288 pp. 0485131218.

A detailed study examining the Crown's indirect control over the activities of the Mexican clergy.

AM819 Gaxiola, Manuel J.

La Serpiente y la Paloma: Análisis del Crecimiento de la Iglesia Apostólica de la Fe en Cristo Jesus de México. South Pasadena, CAU: William Carey Library, 1970. xiv, 177 pp. 0878088024.

A thesis on the life and growth of a church in Mexico, probably the first scholarly work written by a Latin American Pentecostal on Pentecostalism.

AM820 Gerhard, Peter

The North Frontier of New Spain. Norman, OKU: University of Oklahoma Press, 1992. xiv, 456 pp. 0806125446.

Revised edition of a detailed history of the advance of Spanish control and influence, including that of missions, in northern Mexico from 1519 to 1821.

AM821 Gerhard, Peter

The Southeast Frontier of New Spain. Norman, OKU: University of Oklahoma Press, 1993. xi, 219 pp. 0806125438.

Revised edition of a detailed history of Spanish conquest and control in southeast Mexico (the Yucatan and the provinces of Tabasco, Luguna de Terminos, Chiapa, and Socunusco), including missionary influence, from 1511 to 1821.

AM822 Gill, Kenneth D.

Toward a Contextualized Theology for the Third World: The Emergence and Development of Jesus' Name Pentecostalism in Mexico. (Studies in the Intercultural History of Christianity, 90). Frankfurt am Main, GW: Lang, 1994. xi, 311 pp. Paper. 3631470967.

A scholarly study of Jesus' Name Pentecostalism in Mexico as a contextualized theology; originally presented as a Ph.D. dissertation at the University of Birmingham in 1989.

AM823 Gonzalez, Peter Asael, and Dan Wooding

Prophets of Revolution. London, ENK: Hodder & Stoughton, 1982. xviii, 192 pp. 0340323728.

Story of a Mexican family and attitudes toward liberation, conversion, Scripture distribution, and social action.

AM824 Goodman, Felicitas D.

Speaking in Tongues: A Cross-Cultural Study of Glossolalia. Chicago, ILU: University of Chicago Press, 1974. xxii, 175 pp. Paper. 0226303268.

A study based on research with apostolic congregations in Mexico City, in the Yucatan with Maya Indians, and visits with a congregation in Indiana.

AM825 Grayson, George W.

The Church in Contemporary Mexico. (Significant Issues Series). Washington, DCU: Center for Strategic and International Studies, 1992. xiii, 101 pp. Paper. 0892061820.

History of relations between the Catholic Church to the state, 1958 to 1991 in particular, and ending when President Salinas initiated a lifting of civic restrictions, long imposed on all religious bodies and their clergy.

AM826 Greenberg, James B.

Religión y Economía de los Chatinos. Translated by Jaime Rivero Toscana. (Colección INI, 77; Serie de anthropología social). México, MX: Instituto Nacional Indigenista, 1987. 311 pp. 968822071X.

Spanish translation.

AM827 Greenberg, James B.

Santiago's Sword: Chatino Peasant Religion and Economics. Berkeley, CAU: University of California Press, 1981. xii, 227 pp. 0520041356.

Analysis of Chatino folk Catholicism and socio-economic organization, focusing on rituals (including the concepts of house, cross, candle, rites of passage, and festivals) in a closed community (such as home, village, and region), and its effect on the wider economic order; including the economic and demographic dimensions of ritual behavior.

AM828 Greenleaf, Richard E.

La Inquisición en Nueva España, siglo XVI. Translated by Carlos Valdés. (Sección de Obras de Historia). México City, MX: Fondo de Cultura Económica, 1981. 246 pp. 9681607414.

Spanish translation of *The Mexican Inquisition of the Sixteenth Century* (1969).

AM829 Greenleaf, Richard E.

The Mexican Inquisition of the Sixteenth Century. Albuquerque, NMU: University of New Mexico Press, 1969. x, 242 pp. 0826301304.

Examines specific cases to argue that the Inquisition fell the hardest on Indians and foreigners.

AM830 Greenleaf, Richard E.

Zumárraga and the Mexican Inquisition, 1536-1543. (Academy of American Franciscan History; Monograph Series, 4). Washington, DCU: Academy of American Franciscan History, 1961. viii, 155 pp. No ISBN.

An analysis based on Mexican archival data from the inquisitorial cases of the 1530s and 1540s, detailing acts against Indian heretics, Lutherans, Judaizers, and sorcers of the inquisitorial authority of Juan de Zumarraga.

AM831 Greenleaf, Richard E.

Zumárraga y la Inquisición Mexicana, 1536-1543. Translated by Victor Villela. (Sección de obras de historia). México, MX: Fondo de Cultura Económica, 1988. 181 pp. 9681630041.

Spanish translation.

AM832 Griffen, William B.

Indian Assimilation in the Franciscan Area of Nueva Vizcaya. (Anthropological Papers of the University of Arizona, 33). Tucson, AZU: University of Arizona Press, 1979. vii, 122 pp. 0816505845.

Survey of the history of the Concho Indians from early 17th century through 1816.

AM833 Gruzinski, Serge
Man-Gods in the Mexican Highlands: Indian Power and Colonial Society, 1520-1800. Translated by Eileen Corrigan. Stanford, CAU: Stanford University Press, 1989. viii, 223 pp. 0804715130.

A reflective, richly documented essay on the concepts of power and man-god tradition in Mexican colonial history, examining the indigenous population's reaction to the cultural upheavals of the Spanish conquest and its aftermath.

AM834 Gutiérrez, Casillas José
Mártires Jesuitas de los Tepehuanes. México, MX: Edición Tradición, 1981. 93 pp. No ISBN.

The story of Jesuits martyred during the Tepehuan insurrection in Mexico in 1616.

AM835 Gutiérrez, Ramón A.
When Jesus Came, the Corn Mothers Went Away: Marriage, Sexuality, and Power in New Mexico, 1500-1846. Stanford, CAU: Stanford University Press, 1991. xxxi, 424 pp. 0804718164 (hdbk), 0804718326 (pbk).

A social history of the impact of the Spanish conquest on the Pueblo Indians, using marriage as a window for viewing the social, political, and economic arrangements of society, and the relations between the sexes and the races.

AM836 Hausberger, Bernd
Jesuiten aus Mitteleuropa im kolonialen Mexiko: Eine Bio-bibliographie. (Studien zur Geschichte und Kultur der Iberischen und Iberoamerikanischen Länder, 2). Munich, GW: R. Oldenbourg Verlag, 1995. 436 pp. Paper. 3486561510.

Analysis of the historical background and development of the Jesuit mission in colonial Mexico, with short biographies, significant correspondence, and an extensive bibliography.

AM837 Hefley, James C., and Hugh Steven
Miracles in Mexico. Chicago, ILU: Moody, 1972. 126 pp. Paper. 0802454100.

Popular accounts of twelve Mexican Christians, who turned to Christ after being able to read the Bible, newly translated into their languages by Wycliffe Bible Translators.

AM838 Hofman, J. Samuel
Mission Work in Today's World: Insights and Outlooks. South Pasadena, CAU: William Carey Library, 1993. ix, 210 pp. Paper. 0878082344.

Short articles on various aspects of mission and the life of a missionary; based on the author's thirty-year ministry (1959-1989) in Chiapas, Mexico, among the Tzeltal tribe, under the National Presbyterian Church of Mexico.

AM839 Hu-DeHart, Evelyn
Missionaries, Miners, and Indians: Spanish Contact with the Yaqui Nation of Northwestern New Spain, 1533-1820. Tucson, AZU: University of Arizona Press, 1981. 152 pp. Paper. 0816507406 (hdbk), 0816507554 (pbk).

Clearly written account of the way the Yaqui's combined work in the mines and residence in the missions to avoid assimilation during the Spanish colonization of Mexico.

AM840 Ingham, John M.
Mary, Michael, and Lucifer: Folk Catholicism in Central Mexico. (Latin American Monograph/Institute of Latin American Studies, 69). Austin, TXU: University of Texas Press, 1986. x, 216 pp. 0292750897 (hdbk), 0292751109 (pbk).

An ethnographic study of folk Catholicism, in a village of Spanish-speaking peasants of Morelos, Mexico, that highlights the centrality and pervasiveness of Catholic themes and symbols in the culture of that village, and the process of religious syncretism.

AM841 Kessell, John L.
Friars, Soldiers, and Reformers: Hispanic Arizona and the Sonora Mission Frontier, 1767-1856. Tucson, AZU: University of Arizona Press, 1976. xv, 347 pp. 0816505470 (hdbk), 0816504873 (pbk).

Popular history, based on primary sources, of the region around Tumacacori mission, between the expulsion of the Jesuits and the establishment of the territory.

AM842 Kessell, John L.
Mission of Sorrows: Jesuit Guevavi and the Pimas, 1691-1767. Tucson, AZU: University of Arizona Press, 1970. xvi, 224 pp. 0816501920.

History of the Jesuit mission at Guevavi, which was situated south of Tucson, near the international border.

AM843 Kessell, John L.
The Missions of New Mexico since 1776. Albuquerque, NMU: University of New Mexico Press, 1980. xii, 276 pp. 0826305148.

A review of the history of New Mexico's missions, from their foundation to 1980, with particular emphasis on 19th-century documents.

AM844 Kino, Eusebio Francisco
First from the Gulf to the Pacific: The Diary of the Kino-Antondo Peninsular Expedition, December 14, 1684-January 13, 1685. Edited by W. Michael Mathes. (Baja California Travels Series, 16). Los Angeles, CAU: Dawsons, 1969. 60 pp. No ISBN.

The diary deals with marches and halts, terrain, animals, Indians, and the events of Eusebio Francisco Kino, S.J. and Isidro de Atondo y Antillon's journey across Baja California; transcribed and translated by W. Michael Mathes.

AM845 Kino, Eusebio Francisco
Kino Escribe a la Duquesa: Correspondencia del P. Eusebio Francisco Kino con la Duquesa de Aveiro y otros documentos. Edited by Ernest J. Burrus. (Colección Chimalistac de libros y documentos acerca de la Nueva España, 18). Madrid, SP: Porrúa Turanzas, 1964. xxxii, 545 pp. No ISBN.

A collection of letters to his Spanish patroness, the Duchess of Aveivo, from Eusebio Francisco Kino, a Jesuit missionary to present New Mexico and Arizona (1680-1687).

AM846 Kino, Eusebio Francisco
Vida del P. Francisco J. Saeta, S.J.: Sanare misionera en Sonora. (Figuras y episodios de la historia de México, 102). México, MX: Editorial Jus, 1961. 213 pp. No ISBN.

A biography of Fr. Francisco J. Saeta, Jesuit, who brought Christianity to the Pima Indians of Northern Mexico in the 17th century; written by a Jesuit contemporary (with documents and maps).

AM847 Klor de Alva, J. Jorge, H. B. Nicholson, and Eloise Quiñones Keber, eds.
The Work of Bernadino de Sahagun: Pioneer Ethnographer of Sixteenth-Century Aztec Mexico. (Studies on Culture and Society, 2). Albany, NYU: Institute for Mesoamerican Studies, University at Albany SUNY, 1988. xiv, 372 pp. Paper. 0942041119.

Twenty-one scholarly essays on the remarkable ethnographic contributions of Bernardino de Sahagún (1529-1590), pioneer Franciscan missionary to the Nahuatl (Aztecs) of Mexico.

AM848 Knowlton, Robert J.

Church Property and the Mexican Reform, 1856-1910. (The Origins of Modern Mexico). DeKalb, ILU: Northern Illinois University Press, 1976. xii, 265 pp. 0875800556.

Traces the mid-century restrictions on the extensive wealth of the Catholic church and the historical aftermath of civil war, nationalization, the French presence, the restored republic, and the Dias era.

AM849 Kobayashi, José María

La Educación como Conquista: Empresa franciscana en México. (Colección "Biblioteca Abya-Yala," 40). México, MX: Colegio de México, 1996. 295 pp. No ISBN.

A study of pre-Columbian Mexico, the coming of Franciscan missionaries in the 16th century, and how they taught the native Mexican people about Christianity; first published in 1972.

AM850 Konrad, Herman W.

Una Hacienda de los Jesuitas en el México Colonial: Santa Lucía, 1576-1767. (Sección de obras de historia). México, MX: Fondo de Cultura Económica, 1989. 434 pp. 9681632761.

Spanish translation.

AM851 Konrad, Herman W.

A Jesuit Hacienda in Colonial Mexico: Santa Lucfa, 1576-1767. Stanford, CAU: Stanford University Press, 1980. xii, 455 pp. 0804710503.

Seminal history and analysis of the functioning of a complex of haciendas, which extended north from Mexico City to the Zacatecas region, and of agrarian issues, profitability, administration, daily life, slavery, and the Jesuits.

AM852 Kruip, Gerhard

Entwicklung oder Befreiung?: Elemente einer Ethik sozialer Strukturen am Beispiel ausgewählter Stellungnahmen aus der katholischen Kirche Mexikos (1982-1987). (Forschungen zu Lateinamerika, 19). Saarbrücken, GW: Breitenbach, 1988. vi, 597 pp. Paper. 3881564268.

A dissertation, with comprehensive bibliography, on the position of the Catholic Church of Mexico, regarding the social, political, and economic development of the country, stressing the need for a deeper dialogue between Catholic social teaching and liberation theology.

AM853 Kubler, George

Religious Architecture of New Mexico. Albuquerque, NMU: University of New Mexico Press for the School of American Research, 1972. xxviii, 232 pp. No ISBN.

Reprinting of Kubler's classic and important study of the missions, brought up-to-date by a "Preface to Fourth Edition," listing and abstracting the main literature since 1940.

AM854 León-Portilla, Miguel

Los Franciscanos Vistos por el Hombre Nahuatl: Testimonios indígenas del siglo XVI. México, MX: Universidad Nacional Autónoma de México, 1985. 87 pp. 9688375764.

A study of the writings and painting of the Nahuatl people of Mexico, concerning their view of the Franciscan missionaries who visited them in the 16th century.

AM855 Llaguno Farías, José A., ed.

500 años de Evangelización en México: Consulta indígena. (Cuadernos Estudios Indígenas, 3). México, MX: Cuadernos Estudios Indígenas, 1987. 204 pp. No ISBN.

A monograph designed to record missionary activities in general, and to track projects for the future of Mexico; with special attention to opinions of the indigenous peoples themselves.

AM856 Loewen, Jacob Abram

Developing Moralnets: Twenty-Five Years of Culture Change among the Choco. Williamsburg, VAU: College of William and Mary, Department of Anthropology, 1983. 42 pp. No ISBN.

A case study reviewing results of Protestant mission efforts, and the assumptions underlying programs of induced cultural change.

AM857 MacEóin, Gary

The People's Church: Bishop Samuel Ruiz of Mexico and Why He Matters. New York, NYU: Crossroad Publishing, 1996. v, 174 pp. Paper. 0824515765.

The story of the Catholic Church's involvements in the struggle for justice by Indian peasants of the Mexican state of Chiapas, and of the leadership of Bishop Samuel Ruiz in that struggle.

AM858 Masden, William

The Virgin's Children: Life in an Aztec Village Today. Austin, TXU: University of Texas Press, 1960. 248 pp. No ISBN.

A study of Nahuatl-speaking San Francisco Tecospa in the valley of Mexico, with special emphasis on differences between Christian and Aztec beliefs and ritual.

AM859 Mathes, W. Michael

Obras Californianas del Padre Miguel Venegas, S.J. La Paz, MX: Universidad Autónoma de Baja California Sur, 1979-1983. 5 vols. No ISBN.

The complete reproduction of *Noticia de la California* (1757), the work of an 18th-century Jesuit missionary, concerning the secular and spiritual conquest, by Spain, of California and northern Mexico.

AM860 McAndrew, John

The Open-air Churches of Sixteenth-Century Mexico: Atrios, Posas, Open Chapels, and Other Studies. Cambridge, MAU: Harvard University Press; London, ENK: Oxford University Press, 1965. xxxi, 755 pp. No ISBN.

Study of the ecclesiastical architecture of Mexico in the early colonial period, which includes analyzing the political and religious context, city planning, single-cell chapels, portico chapels, the "basilica" of Cuilapan, and the cathedral of Patzcuaro.

AM861 McCarty, Kieran

A Spanish Frontier in the Enlightened Age: Franciscan Beginnings in Sonora and Arizona, 1767-1770. (Monograph Series/Academy of American Franciscan History, 13). Washington, DCU: Academy of American Franciscan History, 1981. 116 pp. 0883830633.

History of the process of replacement of Jesuit missionaries by Franciscans after the Jesuits were expelled from the Spanish colonies.

AM862 McClelland, Alice J., and Ethel Taylor Wharton

Mission to Mexico. New York, NYU: PCUSA, Board of World Mission, 1960. 90 pp. No ISBN.

Popular history of Presbyterian missions to Mexico.

AM863 McGavran, Donald Anderson, John Huegel, and Jack E. Taylor
Church Growth in Mexico. Grand Rapids, MIU: Eerdmans, 1963. 136 pp. Paper. No ISBN.

Case studies of church growth in Mexico, dividing the country into ten subpopulations, according to receptivity to Protestant evangelization.

AM864 Megged, Amos
Exporting the Catholic Reformation: Local Religion in Early-Colonial Mexico. (Cultures, Belief, and Traditions, 2). Leiden, NE: Brill, 1996. x, 191 pp. 9004104003.

A detailed study of the contextualization of worldviews, norms, and mores, by Spanish mendicant priests in 16th- and 17th-century Mexico; based on archival sources.

AM865 Mendieta, Gerónimo de
Historia Eclesiástica Indiana. (Biblioteca de autores españoles, 260). Madrid, SP: Atlas, 1973. xlv, 790 pp. No ISBN.

An account of the coming of Christianity to Mexico, including a discussion of the native religion, by a Spanish Franciscan who wrote during the 16th century.

AM866 Mitchell, James E.
The Emergence of a Mexican Church: The Associate Reformed Presbyterian Church of Mexico. South Pasadena, CAU: William Carey Library, 1970. 183 pp. Paper. 0878083030.

Ninety years (1879-1969) of the history, and of relevant insights into the nature, of Protestant evangelism in Mexico, and relations among the church, the government, and the missionary societies.

AM867 Monsiváis, Carlos
Nuevo Catecismo para Indios Remisos. México, D.F., MX: Ediciones Era, 1989. 140 pp. 9682311926.

Revised and illustrated edition of a book of short folk stories and sayings, with themes of faith and morality based in Mexico; originally published in 1982 (México, D.F., MX: Siglo XXI Editores).

AM868 Mounce, Virginia N.
An Archivists Guide to the Catholic Church in Mexico. Palo Alto, CAU: R&E Research Associates, 1979. vii, 90 pp. 0882475703.

Designed as an aid to archivists, historians, and other researchers studying the organization and function of the Catholic Church in Mexico, from the colonial period to the present.

AM869 Murray, Paul V.
The Catholic Church in Mexico: Historical Essays for the General Reader, vol. 1 (1519-1910). México, MX: Editorial, 1965. 398 pp. No ISBN.

A comprehensive ecclesiastical history in Mexico, to the 1910 Revolution, with most attention given to the 19th century.

AM870 Navarrete, Nicolás P.
Los Agustinos en Querétaro: Su Obra Espiritual, Artística y Cultural: Ensayo Histórico. (Monografias Históricas de la Diocesis de Querétaro; Colección Primer Centenario 1863-1963, 5). México, MX: Editorial Jus, 1963. 125 pp. Paper. No ISBN.

An historical assessment of the spiritual, artistic, and cultural contributions of the Augustinians to the diocese of Querétaro in Mexico, 1724 to 1962; published for the centennial of the diocese in 1963.

AM871 Nebel, Richard
Altmexikanische Religion und christliche Heilsbotschaft: Mexiko zwischen Quetzalcóatl und Christus. (Supplementa, 31). Freiburg, SZ: *NZM*, 1983. xxxvii,393 pp. Paper. 3858240605.

A scholarly monograph on the history of attempts to relate the Christian faith to Aztec religion, from the 16th century to the present.

AM872 Nebel, Richard
Santa Maria Tonantzin Virgen de Guadalupe: Religiöse Kontinuität und Transformation in Mexiko. (*Neue Zeitschrift für Missionswissenschaft* Supplementa, 40). Immensee, SZ: *Neue Zeitschrift für Missionswissenschaft*, 1992. 372 pp. Paper. 3858240729.

In this Würzburg *Habilitationsschrift*, Nebel outlines the enormous consequences for Mexican self-understanding brought about by the Guadalupe experience of the 16th century.

AM873 Oktavec, Eileen
Answered Prayers: Miracles and Milagros Along the Border. Tuscon, AZU: University of Arizona Press, 1995. xxvi, 239 pp. Paper. 0816515573 (hdbk), 0816515816 (pbk).

A popular study of the custom of offering *milagros* (votive offerings requesting divine help), a practice often found on the Sonora and Arizona border.

AM874 Oroz, Pedro
The Oroz Codex: Relation of the Description of the Holy Gospel Province in New Spain, and the Lives of the Founders and Other Noteworthy Men of Said Province. Translated by Angelico Chávez. (Publications of the Academy of American Franciscan History Documentary Series, 10). Washington, DCU: Academy of American Franciscan History, 1972. xiv, 393 pp. No ISBN.

Translation of a version of biographies of early Franciscans of Mexico, written between 1584 and 1586, showing close relationship with a series of biographies that appear in the works of Friar Jerónimo de Mendieta, with extensive annotation of the text.

AM875 Palmer, Colin A.
Slaves of the White God: Blacks in Mexico, 1570-1650. Cambridge, MAU: Harvard University Press, 1976. viii, 234 pp. 0674810856.

Study, based on archival evidence, of slave life, which centers on societal status of slaves, their religious practices, the church's attitudes, and the process and effects of manumission.

AM876 Pickens, Buford, ed.
The Missions of Northern Sonora: A 1935 Field Documentation. (The Southwest Center Series). Tucson, ARU: University of Arizona Press, 1993. xxxii, 198 pp. 0816513422 (hdbk), 0816513562 (pbk).

The first publication of a detailed, illustrated 1935 National Park Service report, on the history and architecture of sixteen missions in northern Mexico and Arizona, founded by Padre Eusebio Kino during the 1690s and early 1700s.

AM877 Pike, Eunice V.
An Uttermost Part. Chicago, ILU: Moody, 1971. 192 pp. No ISBN.

A vivid firsthand account of pioneer work as Wycliffe translators among the Mazatec people of Mexico.

AM878 Polzer, Charles W. et al., eds.
The Jesuit Missions of Northern Mexico. (Spanish Borderlands Sourcebooks, 19). New York, NYU: Garland, 1991. xiii, 579 pp. 0824020960.

Sixteen essays by Jesuit scholars on the earliest period of Jesuit missions.

AM879 Polzer, Charles W.
Rules and Precepts of the Jesuit Missions of Northwestern New Spain. Tucson, AZU: University of Arizona Press, 1976. x, 141 pp. Paper. 0816505519 (hdbk), 0816504881 (pbk).

A critical scholarly reappraisal of Jesuit missions in northwestern Mexico, by a Jesuit church historian, focusing on their administration and inner workings, in comparison to Franciscan models of mission.

AM880 Poole, Stafford
Our Lady of Guadalupe: The Origins and Sources of a Mexican National Symbol, 1531-1797. Tucson, AZU: University of Arizona Press, 1995. xiii, 325 pp. 0816515263.

The first systematic and scholarly study of devotion to Our Lady of Guadalupe, which has become a source and symbol of Mexican national identity and liberation, as well as a factor in evangelization.

AM881 Quirk, Robert E.
The Mexican Revolution and the Catholic Church, 1910-1929. Bloomington, INU: Indiana University Press, 1973. 276 pp. 025333800X.

Examines church involvement in the cause, realities, and consequences of the revolution, focusing on the evolving roles and interplay between successive governments, revolutionary parties, and the Catholic Church.

AM882 Ramírez, Susan E., ed.
Indian-Religious Relations in Colonial Spanish America. (Foreign and Comparative Studies/Latin American Series, 9). Syracuse, NYU: Syracuse University, Maxwell School of Citizenship and Public Affairs, 1989. 102 pp. 0915984326.

Four scholarly essays (three on colonial Mexico and one on 18th-century Paraguay) on attitudes and relations of the Catholic Church to the Indians.

AM883 Ramos, Rutilio et al.
La Iglesia en México: Estructuras eclesiásticas. (Estudios Socio-Religiosos Latino-Americanos, 7). Madrid, SP: OCSHA; Bogotá, CK: FERES, 1963. 119 pp. Paper. No ISBN.

A sociological study of the milieu and ecclesiastical structures of the church in Mexico.

AM884 Redfield, Robert
A Village That Chose Progress: Chan Lom Revisited. (The University of Chicago Publications in Anthropology: Social Anthropology Series). Chicago, ILU: University of Chicago Press, 1970. xiv, 187 pp. No ISBN.

A now-classic sociological study of a 20th-century Mayan community, including the influence of Protestantism.

AM885 Ricard, Robert
The Spiritual Conquest of Mexico: An Essay on the Apostolate and the Evangelizing Methods of the Mendicant Orders in New Spain, 1523-1572. Translated by Byrd Simpson Lesley. London, ENK: Cambridge University Press, 1967. 423 pp. No ISBN.

The English translation of *Conquête Spirituelle du Mexique* (University of Paris, 1933), which describes the work of the early missionaries (Franciscans, Augustinians, Dominicans, and others) and their methods, theology, and social services during their evangelization of central Mexico, 1524-1572.

AM886 Rivera, Pedro R.
Instituciones Protestantes en México. México, MX: Editorial Jus, 1962. 188 pp. No ISBN.

A compilation of facts about Protestantism in Mexico, including a listing of institutions, churches, and seminaries; with discussion of their economic bases and successes.

AM887 Sahagún, Bernardino de
Historia General de las Cosas de Nueva España. (Sepan cuantos, 300). Mexico City, MX: Editorial Porrúa, 1985. x, 1,093 pp. 9684322658.

A contemporary Franciscan missionary's history of Spain's 16th-century conquest of Mexico, including early mission history.

AM888 Sahagún, Bernardino de
A History of Ancient Mexico, 1547-1577. Translated by Fanny R. Bandelier. (A Rio Grande Classic). Glorieta, NMU: Rio Grande Press, 1976. 362 pp. 0873801083.

English translation of Books 1-4; a reprint of the edition published by Fisk University Press in 1971.

AM889 Sahagún, Bernardino de
Primeros Memoriales. (Civilization of the American Indian Series, 200 part 1). Norman, OKU: University of Oklahoma Press, 1993. 190 pp. 0806125330.

A remarkable ethnography of the 16th-century Aztec culture, particularly the religious/ritual system. Eighty-eight folios of illustrations by eyewitnesses; prepared by Spanish Franciscan missionary Fray Bernardino de Sahagun, from 1559 to 1561.

AM890 Salmón, Roberto Mario
Indian Revolts in Northern New Spain: A Synthesis of Resistance, 1680-1786. Lanham, MDU: University Press of America, 1991. 145 pp. 0819179825 (hdbk), 0819179833 (pbk).

Examines the relations among indigenous people, settlers, and missionaries that led to rebellion on the frontier; based on archival material and secondary sources.

AM891 Salvatierra, Juan Marãa de
Selected Letters about Lower California. Translated by Ernest J. Burrus. (Baja California Travel Series, 25). Los Angeles, CAU: Dawsons, 1971. 279 pp. 087093225X.

Twenty-two letters by the founders of Loreto, the first permanent mission settlement in Baja California.

AM892 Sandstrom, Alan R.
Corn Is Our Blood: Culture and Ethnic Identity in a Contemporary Aztec Indian Village. Norman, OKU: University of Oklahoma Press, 1991. xxvii, 420 pp. 0806123990 (hdbk), 0806124032 (pbk).

A detailed case study of the struggle and success of a Nahua village to maintain their ancient Aztec culture in modern-day Mexico, with attention to religious beliefs and practices (traditional, Catholic, and Protestant).

AM893 Sawatzky, Harry Leonard
They Sought a Country: Mennonite Colonization in Mexico with an Appendix on Mennonite Colonization in British Honduras. Berkeley, CAU: University of California Press, 1971. xi, 387 pp. 0520017048.

A study of the survival and apparent success of Mennonite colonies in Mexico and Belize, analyzing their inability to remedy growing economic and social ills.

AM894 Sheridan, Thomas E., Charles W. Polzer, Thomas H. Naylor, and Diana W. Hadley, eds.
The Franciscan Missions of Northern Mexico. (The Spanish Borderlands Sourcebooks, 20). New York, NYU: Garland, 1991. xxii, 360 pp. 0824025997.

Reprints of fourteen scholarly essays on Franciscan mission strategies and ministries, on the northern frontier of old Mexico.

AM895 Steven, Hugh
They Dared to be Different. Huntington Beach, CAU: Wycliffe Bible Translators, 1991. 160 pp. 089081029X.

Stories of pioneer evangelism among the Chamula people of the Chiapas highlands in southern Mexico, by Wycliffe missionaries; originally published by Harvest House Publishers in 1976.

AM896 Tangeman, Michael
Mexico at the Crossroads: Politics, the Church, and the Poor. Maryknoll, NYU: Orbis Books, 1995. xiv, 138 pp. 1570750181.

Describes the Zapatista uprising, in Chiapas in 1994, its historical and social background, and the Catholic Church as a part of both the repressive elite and the passion for change.

AM897 Taylor, Jack E.
God's Messengers to Mexico's Masses: A Study of the Religious Significance of the Braceros. Eugene, ORU: Institute of Church Growth, 1962. vii, 82 pp. No ISBN.

A study of the religious significance of the *braceros.*

AM898 Torre, Tomás de la
Diario de Viaje de Salamanca a Ciudad Real de Chiapa, 1544-1545. (Colección Guzmán, 5). Burgos, SP: OPE, 1985. 164 pp. 8471881551.

The diary of a Dominican brother, who traveled from Spain to Mexico as a missionary in 1544; with entries concerning his trip and encounters with the native people.

AM899 Wasserstrom, Robert
Class and Society in Central Chiapas. Berkeley, CAU: University of California Press, 1983. x, 357 pp. 0520046706.

Argues that contemporary ethnicity and communal organization result from recent socioeconomic processes; that indigenous Christianity is a continuation of medieval tendencies, and of Las Casas's efforts to create and defend Christian communities.

AM900 Willard, F. Burleigh
Idol of Clay. Winoan Lake, INU: Light & Life Press, 1985. 94 pp. Paper. 0893671053.

A story about three young Mexican men and the impact that the Free Methodist missions had upon their lives, and those of other graduates of the Nogales Bible School and Light and Life Institute.

AM901 Wissmann, Hans
Sind doch die Götter auch gestorben: Das Religionsgespräch der Franziskaner mit den Azteken von 1524. (Missionswissenschaftliche Forschungen, 15). Gütersloh, GW: Mohn, 1981. 155 pp. Paper. 357900235X.

A dissertation on the opportunities and difficulties of missionary dialogue in the 16th century, based on the religious discussions between Franciscans and Aztecs in Mexico, in 1524.

AM902 Zubillaga, Félix, ed.
Monumenta Mexicana. (Monumenta Historica Societatis Jesu: 97, 104, 106, 114, 122, 139; Monumenta Missionum Societatis Jesu: 24, 29, 31, 36, 42, 54). Rome, IT: Institutum Historicum Societatis Jesu; Rome, IT: Instituto Histórica de la Compañía de Jesus, 1991. 8 vols. Paper. 8870411222 (vol. 7), 8870411397 (vol. 8).

A multi-volume collection of Jesuit source documents, in Spanish and Latin, from the 16th- and 17th-century mission to Mexico, including annual reports, letters, and accounts by missionaries [vol. 3: *1585-1590* (1968, 860 pp.); vol. 4: *1590-1592* (1971, xxx, 841 pp.); vol. 5: *1592-1596* (1973, xxviii, 793 pp.); vol. 6: *1596-1599* (1976, xxxi, 818 pp.); vol. 7: *1599-1602* (1981, xxvi, 866 pp.); vol. 8: *1603-1605* (1991, xxi, 73, 683)]; published from 1956-1991, with vols. 1 and 2 published before 1960; also published in the series Missiones Occidentales.

Mexico: Biography

AM903 Boyce, Marguerite P.
Captain Brenton's Heritage: The Gospel Message for Southwest Mexico. Franklin, TNU: Providence House, 1994. 96 pp. Paper. 1881576345.

The story of a high-ranking official of the Royal British Marines, credited with being the "father of the Mexican Navy," who returned to rural southwest Mexico as a missionary evangelist, 1904 to 1921.

AM904 Boyce, Marguerite P.
I Heard the Donkeys Bray: Thirty Years in the Mission Field. Franklin, TNU: Providence House, 1992. 192 pp. Paper. 1881576027.

Two career Presbyterian Church (US) missionaries to Mexico (1940-1970) recount their experiences in medical and educational work in rural Ometepec.

AM905 Dame, Lawrence
Maya Mission. Garden City, NYU: Doubleday, 1968. 252 pp. No ISBN.

A popular account of the service of two United Presbyterian missionaries, David and Elva Legters, among the Maya of Yucatan, 1936 to 1968.

AM906 Dame, Lawrence
Der Oschungelmissionar: David und Elva Legters Leben für die Mayas in Yucatan. Basel, SZ: Reinhardt, 1971. 203 pp. No ISBN.

German translation.

AM907 Englebert, Omer
The Last of the Conquistadors, Junípero Serra, 1713-1784. Translated by Katherine Woods. Westport, CTU: Greenwood, 1974. ix, 368 pp. 0837175232.

English translation; originally published in 1956 (New York: Harcourt, Brace).

AM908 Englebert, Omer
Le dernier des conquistadores, Junipero Serra, apôtre et fondateur de la Californie, 1713-1784. Paris, FR: Librairie Plon, 1956. ii, 342 pp. No ISBN.

A popular biography of an influential pioneer missionary friar in northwest Mexico (present state of California).

AM909 Geiger, Maynard J.
Franciscan Missionaries in Hispanic California, 1769-1848: A Biographical Dictionary. San Marino, CAU: Huntington Library, 1969. xiv, 304 pp. No ISBN.

Biographical data on the 142 Franciscan missionaries in California, from 1769 to 1848.

AM910 Hefley, James C.
Peril by Choice: The Story of John and Elaine Beekman, Wycliffe Bible Translators in Mexico. Lewisville, TXU: School of Tomorrow, 1995. 289 pp. 1562650556.

A reprint of a popular illustrated biography of Wycliffe Bible Translators in Guatemala and Mexico (1948-1968), who helped translate the Bible into the Chall Indian language; originally published by Zondervan in 1968.

AM911 Kino, Eusebio Francisco
Kino's Biography of Francisco Javier Saeta, S.J. Translated by Charles W. Polzer. (Sources and Studies for the History of the Americas, 9). Rome, IT: Jesuit Historical Institute; St. Louis, MOU: St. Louis University, 1971. xv, 363 pp. No ISBN.

The text describes Jesuit activities in the Pimeria Alta between 1687-1695, and analyzes the Pima rebellion and pacification of 1695; originally published in Spanish under the title *Kino Escribe a la Duquesa*, edited by Ernest J. Burrus (Madrid, SP: Porrúa Turanzas, 1964).

AM912 Lamadrid, Lázaro Jiménez
El Alavés Fray Fermín Francisco de Lasuén, O.F.M. (1736-1803); fundador de misiones en California. Vitoria, SP: Diputación Foral de Alava, Consejo de Cultura, 1983. 2 vols. No ISBN.

A biography of the Franciscan who founded nine missions between San Diego and San Francisco, with maps and illustrations [vol. 1, 483 pp.; vol. 2, 528 pp.].

AM913 Miller, Vernell Klassen
Anywhere with You. Scottdale, PAU: Herald Press, 1989. 192 pp. Paper. 0836135059.

A popular account of three years (1973-1975) of service with her husband, as faith missionaries in Mexico with the Mennonite Central Committee.

AM914 Newton, Norman
Thomas Gage in Spanish America. (Great Travellers). New York, NYU: Barnes & Noble; London, ENK: Faber, 1969. 214 pp. 0389010138 (B), 057108799X (F).

Biography of Thomas Gage, the English priest who lived and traveled in Mexico and Central America in the 17th century.

AM915 Och, Joseph
Missionary in Sonora: The Travel Reports of Joseph Och, S.J., 1755-1767. Translated by Theodore E. Treutlein. (California Historical Society Special Publication, 40). San Francisco, CAU: California Historical Society, 1965. xviii, 196 pp. No ISBN.

Travel account by a German Jesuit, describing his journey from Wurzburg to the Sonora missions, the expulsion of the Jesuits, and the return to Wurzburg; with descriptions of Mexico City, small towns, and the Indians of Sonora.

AM916 Palóu, Francisco
Biografía de fray Junípero Serra, O.F.M....: (1713-1784). Palma de Mallorca, SP: Cort, 1977. xxiv, 366 pp. 8485049497.

A biography of the Franciscan missionary who travelled from Spain to North America in the 18th century and established many missions in California.

AM917 Palóu, Francisco
Relación Histórica de la Vida y apostólicas Tareas del Venerable Padre Fray Junípero Serra y Misiones que fundó en la California Septentrional y Nuevos Establecimientos de Monterrey. Palma de Mallorca, SP: Cort, 1977. xxiv, 366 pp. 8485049497.

The 1787 biography of the Franciscan, Fr. Junipero Serra, who founded the missions in California (1713-1784).

AM918 Palóu, Francisco
Junipero Serra y las Misiones de California. Edited by José Luis Anta Félez. (Hermanos García Noblejas, 41). Madrid, SP: Historia 16, 1988. 352 pp. 8476791151.

A biography of Junipero Serra, the founder of the Spanish missions in California; written by an 18th-century contemporary.

AM919 Perez de Ribas, Andres
My Life among the Savage Nations of New Spain. Translated by Tomas Antonio Robertson. Los Angeles, CAU: Ward Ritchie Press, 1968. xvi, 256 pp. No ISBN.

A firsthand autobiographical account of Jesuit mission work in northwest Mexico; originally published in 1645.

AM920 Rasmussen, Jørgen Nybo
Broder Jakob den Danske, kong Christian II's yngre broder. Odense, DK: Odense Universitetsforlag, 1986. 143 pp. 8774925830.

An investigation of the 16th-century missionary service of Jacobus Danianus, in Mexico, and the claim that he belonged to the Danish royal family.

AM921 Rasmussen, Jørgen Nybo
Bruder Jakob der Däne OFM Als Verteidiger der religiösen Gleichberechtigung der Indianer in Mexiko im XVI. Jahrhundert. (Institut für europäische Geschichte, Mainz, 58). Wiesbaden, GW: Franz Steiner Verlag, 1974. 117 pp. Paper. 3515019464.

A biography about the Danish Benedictine who defended the religious equality of Indians in Mexico in the 16th century.

AM922 Stagg, Albert
The First Bishop of Sonora: Antonio de los Reyes, O.F.M. Tucson, AZU: University of Arizona Press, 1976. ix, 109 pp. Paper. 0816505497 (hdbk), 0816504865 (pbk).

Brief study of a friar who defended the Indians, worked as a missionary after the 18th Jesuit expulsion, and achived a position in the hierarchy.

AM923 Tavard, George H.
Juana Inéz de la Cruz and the Theology of Beauty: The First Mexican Theology. Notre Dame, INU: University of Notre Dame Press, 1991. 239 pp. 0268012067.

A study of the writing of Sister Juana (1651-1695), with special attention to her esthetic, moral, and religious thought.

Nicaragua

See also TH203-TH206, PO125, EV99-EV100, AM205, AM298, and AM462.

AM924 *Anecdotes and Analysis from Nicaragua*
New York, NYU: Circus Publications, 1988. 94 pp. 0936123044.

Essays, by Thomas Montgomery-Fate and Rafael Aragon, with José Maria Vigil, describing the people in the revolution, and the ideological struggle within the Catholic Church.

AM925 Belli, Humberto
Christians under Fire. San José, CR: Instituto Puebla, 1984. 151 pp. Paper. No ISBN.

A former Nicaraguan Marxist and collaborator with the Sandinistas writes, as a new Christian, this condemnation of the Nicaragua government as Marxist-Leninist and atheist.

AM926 Borge, Tomás
Christianity and Revolution: Tomas Borge's Theology of Life. Edited by Andrew Reding. Translated by Andrew Reding. Maryknoll, NYU: Orbis Books, 1987. ix, 166 pp. Paper. 0883444119.

Selected speeches and writings, from 1969 to 1986, by Nicaragua's Minister of the Interior; with an introduction interpreting the development of his liberation theology.

AM927 Cabestrero, Teófilo
Blood of the Innocent: Victims of the Contras' War in Nicaragua. Translated by Robert R. Barr. Maryknoll, NYU: Orbis Books; London, ENK: CIIR, 1985. vii, 104 pp. Paper. 0883442116 (O), 0946848114 (C).

English translation.

AM928 Cabestrero, Teófilo
Ministers of God, Ministers of the People: Testimonies of Faith from Nicaragua. Maryknoll, NYU: Orbis Books, 1983. xiv, 130 pp. 0862321921 (hdbk), 086232193X (pbk).

English translation.

AM929 Cabestrero, Teófilo
Ministros de Deus, ministros do povo: Testemunho de três sacerdotes no governo revolucionário da Nicarágua: Ernesto Cardenal, Miguel d'Escoto, Fernando Cardenal. Translated by Edyla Mangabeira Unger. Petrópolis, BL: Vozes, 1983. 134 pp. No ISBN.

Portuguese translation.

AM930 Cabestrero, Teófilo
Ministros de Dios, Ministros del Pueblo: Testimonio de 3 sacerdotes en el Gobierno Revolucionario de Nicaragua. (Colección Testimonio, 1). Bilbao, SP: Desclée de Brouwer, 1983. 137 pp. 843300607X.

The author, a priest-journalist working in Nicaragua, shares interviews with three priests in the Nicaraguan government, who explain how they combine their priesthood and their political involvement.

AM931 Cabestrero, Teófilo
Nicaragua: Crónica de una sangre inocente: La guerra sucia de los "paladines de la libertad." (Realidad social, 7). México, MX: Editorial Katún, 1985. 135 pp. 9688500399.

A Spanish priest and journalist visited towns in the war zone and interviewed people, who related their stories of suffering, faith, and hope.

AM932 Cabestrero, Teófilo
Des prêtres au gouvernement: L'expérience du Nicaragua. Paris, FR: Karthala, 1983. 133 pp. No ISBN.

French translation.

AM933 Cabestrero, Teófilo
Revolucionários por causa do evangelho. Translated by Romeu Teixeiro Campos. Petrópolis, BL: Vozes, 1985. 366 pp. No ISBN.

Portuguese translation.

AM934 Cabestrero, Teófilo
Revolucionarios por el Evangelio: Testimonio de 15 Cristianos en el Gobierno Revolucionario de Nicaragua. (Colección Testimonio, 4). Bilbao, NQ: Desclée de Brouwer, 1983. 348 pp. 8433006258.

Testimonies by fifteen committed Catholic lay Christians in leadership roles, who are working out the implications of the Gospel in the Nicaraguan revolution, as they improve the quality of life for the poor.

AM935 Cabestrero, Teófilo
Revolutionaries for the Gospel: Testimonies of Fifteen Christians in Nicaraguan Goverment. Maryknoll, NYU: Orbis Books, 1986. xxiii, 148 pp. Paper. 0883444062.

English translation.

AM936 Cabestrero, Teófilo, ed.
Priester für Frieden und Revolution: Ernesto Cardenal, Miguel d'Escoto, Fernando Cardenal. Translated by Gerta Simon. Wuppertal, GW: Hammer, 1983. 124 pp. 3872942190.

German translation.

AM937 Dodson, Michael, and Laura Nuzzi O'Shaughnessy
Nicaragua's Other Revolution: Religious Faith and Political Struggle. Chapel Hill, NCU: University of North Carolina Press, 1990. xii, 279 pp. 080781881X (hdbk), 0807842664 (pbk).

A scholarly study of the religious roots of democratic revolutions in England (1640s), the United States (1770s), and Nicaragua (1970s); the rise of the prophetic church amid the traditional one in Nicaragua; and the central role of religion in the revolution of 1979.

AM938 Everett, Melissa
Bearing Witness, Building Bridges: Interviews with North Americans Living & Working in Nicaragua. Philadelphia, PAU: New Society Publishers, 1986. xviii, 169 pp. Paper. 086571066X (hdbk), 0865710651 (pbk).

A collection of accounts by seventeen people who lived in Nicaragua during the Sandinista revolution, providing a variety of perspectives on the people's struggle in that troubled country.

AM939 Foroohar, Manzar
The Catholic Church and Social Change in Nicaragua. Albany, NYU: SUNY Press, 1989. xiv, 262 pp. 0887068642 (hdbk), 0887068650 (pbk).

A historical study of the involvement of the Catholic Church in the political, social, and religious issues of Nicaragua, focusing on the post-1979 period.

AM940 Gittings, James A., ed.
"God, King, and Campesino in the Vineyard of Naboth": A Report of the Agricultural Missions, Inc. Study Group in Nicaragua, November 10-17, 1982. New York, NYU: Agricultural Missions, 1983. 48 pp. Paper. No ISBN.

A collection of reflections about agriculture, landholding, production, and marketing structures in Nicaragua, and the means by which North American church, farm, and government leaders can assist and support agricultural and economic reform in that country.

AM941 Harst, Paul van der
Kerk Steeds Opnieuw: Vragen aan Kerk en Zending Vanuit een Pastoraal Experiment in Nicaragua. (Raad voor de Zending der Nederlandse Hervormde Kerk, 3). Oegsygeest, NE: Hervormde Kerk, 1991. 139 pp. Paper. 9071316114.

A reflection on church renewal based on a Catholic pastoral experiment in a slum area of Managua, Nicaragua, with the conclusion that new churches should develop as a result of compassion and understanding, rather than fitting these feelings into established church structures.

AM942 Haslam, David
Faith in Struggle: The Protestant Churches in Nicaragua and their Response to the Revolution. London, ENK: Epworth Press, 1987. x, 144 pp. Paper. 0716204363.

A staff member of the BCC spent three months in Nicaragua in 1986, and describes the history of the Protestants, their theology, their struggles over the revolution, and what outside churches might learn from them.

AM943 Helms, Mary W.
Asang: Adaptations to Culture Contact in a Miskito Community. Gainesville, FLU: University of Florida Press, 1971. viii, 268 pp. 0813002982.

Anthropological and sociological interpretation of the Miskito culture, using the village of Asang as a basis; with discussion of adaption amid 150 years of Moravian missions.

AM944 Helms, Mary W.
Asang: Adaptaciones al contacto cultural en una sociedad misquito. Translated by José Avila Arévalo, and Carola Russo de Cisneros. (Instituto Indigenista Interamericano; Ediciones especiales, 75). México, MX: Instituto Indigenista Interamericano, 1976. xx, 289 pp. No ISBN.

Spanish translation.

AM945 Heyward, Carter et al.
Revolutionary Forgiveness: Feminist Reflections on Nicaragua. (The Amanecida Collective). Maryknoll, NYU: Orbis Books, 1987. xxxvii, 150 pp. Paper. 0883442647.

A collection of observations by thirteen US citizens, sharing their experiences of the Nicaraguan Revolution from a Christian feminist perspective, with the Amanecida Collective.

AM946 *Kairos Central America: A Challenge to the Churches of the World*
(Amanecer, 3). New York, NYU: Circus Publications, 1989. 46 pp. 0936123052.

Third edition of a manifesto, produced and signed by over one hundred priests, pastors, theologians, and lay leaders in Nicaragua, April 1988, which sought to describe the current situation, speak to it from the perspective of faith, and call for action on the part of the Christian communities.

AM947 Linkogle, Stephanie
Gender, Practice and Faith in Nicaragua: Constructing the Popular and Making "Common Sense." Aldershot, ENK: Avebury, 1996. ix, 265 pp. 1859722989.

A sociological case study of the political and religious consciousness of women in Nicaragua in the 1990-1993 period, including the place of Christian base communities.

AM948 McGinnis, James B.
Solidarity with the People of Nicaragua. Maryknoll, NYU: Orbis Books, 1985. xiii, 162 pp. Paper. 0883444488.

A narrative account of the author's life with Nicaraguans,

working through peaceful means to rebuild their war-torn country; with a critical assessment of US policy toward that country.

AM949 Medcalf, John
Letters from Nicaragua. London, ENK: CIIR, 1988. 57 pp. Paper. 1852870311 (hdbk), 1852870222 (pbk).

A collection of letters which form a moving plea for the right of Nicaragua to its own form of social and religious development, by a Roman Catholic missionary in close proximity to the effects of Contra activity.

AM950 Mulligan, Joseph E.
The Nicaraguan Church and the Revolution. Kansas City, MOU: Sheed & Ward, 1991. xvi, 303 pp. Paper. 1556124112.

A political history of the Catholic church in Nicaragua in the 19th and 20th centuries, with special attention to Christian involvement in the Sandinista revolution and movements opposing it.

AM951 Newson, Linda A.
Indian Survival in Colonial Nicaragua. Norman, OKU: University of Oklahoma Press, 1987. xiv, 466 pp. 0806120088.

A detailed account, based on field work and archival research in both Central America and Spain, which describes the native cultures of the eastern region of Nicaragua and how the Spanish rule, including missionary effort, impacted their lifestyles from 1522 to 1821.

AM952 O'Shaughnessy, Laura Nuzzi, and Luis H. Serra
The Church and Revolution in Nicaragua. (Latin American Series, 11). Athens, OHU: Ohio University, 1986. x, 118 pp. Paper. 0896801268.

This volume addresses the complex issue of Christian response to the Nicaraguan revolution, and the role of the church in revolutionary times, from a perspective generally sympathetic to the Sandinista's goals.

AM953 Pochet, Rosa María, and Abelino Martínez
Nicaragua, Iglesia: ¿manipulación o profecía? (Colección sociología de la religión: Iglesia y pueblo). San José, CR: DEI, 1987. xxi, 179 pp. Paper. 9977904405.

An analysis of relations between the Catholic Church and the Sandinista government of Nicaragua during the 1968 to 1984 period.

AM954 Randall, Margaret
Christians in the Nicaraguan Revolution. Translated by Mariana Valverde. Vancouver, BCC: New Star Books, 1983. 207 pp. 0919573142 (hdbk), 0919573150 (pbk).

English translation.

AM955 Randall, Margaret, comp.
Cristianos en la Revolución: Del Testimonio a la Lucha. (Ediciones Monimbó). Managua, NQ: Editorial Nueva Nicaragua, 1983. 191 pp. No ISBN.

Through interviews and testimonies, the author describes the life and reflections in Christian-based, rural, and urban communities.

AM956 Robertson, C. Alton
The Moravians, the Miskitu, and the Sandinistas on Nicaragua's Atlantic Coast: 1979-1990. Bethlehem, PAU: Moravian Church in America, 1998. viii, 88 pp. Paper. 1878422375.

A concise scholarly account of the conflict between the Miskitu people of Nicaragua and the Sandinistas, exploring the mediating role of Moravian church leaders.

AM957 Williams, Philip J.
The Catholic Church and Politics in Nicaragua and Costa Rica. Pittsburgh, PAU: University of Pittsburgh Press, 1989. xvi, 228 pp. 0822911558.

A scholarly analysis of the interactions of politics and the Roman Catholic Church in Nicaragua and Costa Rica, revealing similar patterns of action in these two dissimilar contexts, by an assistant professor of political science at Northeast Missouri State University.

Panama

See also AM355.

AM958 Alfonse, Efraim S.
God at the Helm. London, ENK: Epworth Press, 1967. 139 pp. No ISBN.

The story of the Valiente Indian Methodist Mission of Northwest Panama.

AM959 Ariza S., Alberto E.
Los Dominicos en Panamá. Bogotá, CK: Convento-Seminario de Santo Domingo, 1964. 95 pp. No ISBN.

A short history of the Dominican order in Panama, from the 16th to the early 20th century.

AM960 Iglesias, Margaret G.
Messenger to the Golden People: The Story of Lonnie Iglesias. Nashville, TNU: Broadman, 1968. 64 pp. No ISBN.

Brief and popular study of Baptist work on the San Blas Islands near Panama.

AM961 Knight, Walker L.
Panama, the Land Between. Atlanta, GAU: Home Mission Board, Southern Baptist Convention, 1965. 106 pp. No ISBN.

A description of Southern Baptist work in Panama.

U.S.A.: General Works

See also HI21, HI125, HI130, HI137, HI140, HI147, HI181, HI194, HI215, HI238, HI252, HI318, HI365, HI378, HI464, HI496, HI550, HI652, ME85, CR312, CR452, CR1233, SO17, SO140, SO158, SO395, SO402, EC111, EC160, EC313, PO132, PO186, ED19, ED26, ED30, ED54, EV227, EV231, EV331, CH15, CH60, CH88, CH117, CH163, CH409, CH425, and AM811.

AM962 Almaraz, Felix D.
The San Antonio Missions and Their System of Land Tenure. Austin, TXU: University of Texas Press, 1989. xv, 100 pp. 0292746539.

A well-researched volume on the unique role of five Franciscan missions in a Spanish frontier society, focusing on 18th- and 19th-century changes, as mission lands passed to secular owners.

AM963 Avella, Stephen M., and Elizabeth McKeown, eds.
Public Voices: Catholics in the American Context. (American Catholic Identities: A Documentary History). Maryknoll, NYU: Orbis Books, 1999. xxiv, 375 pp. 1570752672 (hdbk), 1570752664 (pbk).

This volume of original documents on the political and social history of Catholics, from colonial America to the present, including issues of church and society (slavery, race, war, peace, etc.).

AM964 Axelson, Sigbert, and Carl F. Hallencreutz, eds.
Kristen högervåg i amerikansk mission?: Rapport från ett missionsvetenskapligt fältstudium till USA, våren 1990. Uppsala, SW: Uppsala Universiteit, Teologiska Institutionen, 1990. 240 pp. 9185424226.

Report from a missionary research field-study to the United States in 1990, entitled "Right-Wing Wave in American Mission?" with English summaries.

AM965 Beaver, Robert Pierce, ed.
Pioneers in Mission: The Early Missionary Ordination Sermons, Charges, and Instructions. Grand Rapids, MIU: Eerdmans, 1966. vi, 291 pp. No ISBN.

A sourcebook of the ordination sermons, charges, and instructions given to fourteen Protestant missionaries in New England, 1733 to 1812, including Daniel Brainerd and Andoniran Judson; with an essay analyzing how the emerging missionary movement is revealed through these documents.

AM966 Billingsley, K. L.
From Mainline to Sideline: The Social Witness of the National Council of Churches. Washington, DCU: Ethics & Public Policy Center, 1990. ix, 209 pp. 0896331415 (hdbk), 0896331423 (pbk).

An analysis of the social policies of the National Council of Churches in the United States since 1950, with particular reference to political and economic issues.

AM967 Bohr, David
Evangelization in America: Proclamation, Way of Life and the Catholic Church in the United States. New York, NYU: Paulist Press, 1977. xiii, 289 pp. Paper. 0809120399.

A detailed analysis of Roman Catholicism in America, its theology and its practice of evangelization.

AM968 Burrell, David B., and Franzita Kane, eds.
Evangelization in the American Context. Notre Dame, INU: University of Notre Dame, 1976. xiii, 183 pp. 0268009015.

Papers and reports from an important symposium, Notre Dame, 11-13 January 1976, which brought together Roman Catholic bishops and scholars to consider evangelization, through parish and university.

AM969 Butler, Anne M., Michael E. Engh, and Thomas W. Spalding, eds.
The Frontiers and Catholic Identities. (American Catholic Identities: A Documentary History). Maryknoll, NYU: Orbis Books, 1999. xxxii, 221 pp. 1570752702 (hdbk), 1570752699 (pbk).

This anthology of nearly 100 documents, selected with sensitivity to issues of gender, ethnicity, and multiculturalism, shows how Catholic clergy and laypeople participated in America's changing frontiers, from Kentucky to Hawaii and Alaska.

AM970 Campolo, Tony
Can Mainline Denominations Make a Comeback? Valley Forge, PAU: Judson Press, 1995. xvi, 205 pp. Paper. 0817012346.

The popular evangelical Baptist sociologist diagnoses the causes of denominational decline, and argues that restructuring, plus a recovery of balance between evangelism and social action, can bring 21st-century renewal.

AM971 Cavert, Samuel McCrea
Church Cooperation and Unity in America: A Historical Review, 1900-1970. New York, NYU: Association Press, 1970. 400 pp. 0809617803.

A survey of seventy years of cooperative endeavors in American Christianity, including world mission.

AM972 Colson, Charles, and Richard John Neuhaus, eds.
Evangelicals and Catholics Together: Toward a Common Mission. Dallas, TXU: Word Publishing, 1995. xxxv, 236 pp. Paper. 0849938600.

Papers from a creative interconfessional working group of theologians in the United States, including their 1994 statement, "Evangelicals and Catholics Together: The Christian Mission in the Third Millennium."

AM973 Dempsey, Ron D.
Faith Outside the Walls: Why People Don't Come and Why the Church Must Listen. Macon, GAU: Smyth & Helwys, 1997. viii, 132 pp. Paper. 1573120960.

An analysis of the religiosity and faith of the unchurched in the United States, of the cultural processes of secularization, and of proactive changes needed by churches in ministry to them; based on the author's doctoral dissertation.

AM974 Douglas, Jacobsen, and William Vance Trollinger, eds.
Re-Forming the Center: American Protestantism, 1900 to the Present. Grand Rapids, MIU: Eerdmans, 1998. xvi, 492 pp. Paper. 0802842984.

Essays on historical aspects of renewal in American Protestantism, including missionary outreach; originally prepared for the "Re-Forming the Center" project, funded by the Lilly Endowment.

AM975 Durchholz, Patricia
Defining Mission: Comboni Missionaries in North America. Lanham, MDU: University Press of America, 1999. xiv, 353 pp. 0761814272.

The Comboni mission to North America began in 1939 in ghetto parishes, then in California Indian missions, discovering both the country's diversity and its racism.

AM976 Dyrness, William A.
How Does America Hear the Gospel? Grand Rapids, MIU: Eerdmans, 1989. xi, 164 pp. Paper. 0802804373.

A study of the relationship of Gospel and culture in North America, with an analysis of how the dominant culture has shaped the Gospel message, by values of optimism, prosperity, and individualism, whereas minority cultures have stressed oppression and brokenness.

AM977 Elsbree, Oliver Wendell
The Rise of the Missionary Spirit in America, 1790-1815. (Perspectives in American History, 55). Philadelphia, PAU: Porcupine Press, 1980. 187 pp. 0879913762.

A detailed analysis, from archival sources, of changes in missionary motivation and action during the quarter century before 1815; originally submitted as a Ph.D. dissertation at Columbia University in 1928.

AM978 Fey, Harold E.
Cooperation in Compassion: The Story of Church World Service. New York, NYU: Friendship Press, 1966. 175 pp. Paper. No ISBN.

A popular history of the inception and growth of Church World Service, the cooperative relief and rehabilitation agency of the NCCUSA, representing both Protestant and Orthodox churches.

AM979 Fitzpatrick, Joseph P.
One Church, Many Cultures: Challenge of Diversity. Kansas City, MOU: Sheed and Ward, 1987. 208 pp. Paper. 0934134634.

An analysis of how Catholic Christians through history have related Gospel and culture, with particular reference to the United States, including the Hispanic churches.

AM980 Grindel, John A.
Whither the U.S. Church?: Context, Gospel, Planning. Maryknoll, NYU: Orbis Books, 1991. vii, 216 pp. Paper. 0883447762.

A challenge to the Catholic Church in the United States to engage in thorough social analysis (socio-economic, cultural, and political), and to develop a national pastoral plan for the church's mission.

AM981 *Heritage and Hope: Evangelization in the United States*
Washington, DCU: NCCB/USCC, 1991. 50 pp. Paper. 1555863868.

A pastoral letter of the NCCB, published in preparation for the 500th anniversary of the encounter between Europe and the Americas, in both English and Spanish.

AM982 Hunsberger, George R., and Craig Van Gelder, eds.
The Church between Gospel and Culture: The Emerging Mission in North America. Grand Rapids, MIU: Eerdmans, 1996. xix, 369 pp. Paper. 0802841090.

Drawing on some of the discussions in "The Gospel and Our Culture Network," this multi-author compendium focuses on assessing contemporary culture, discerning the Gospel, and defining the church.

AM983 Jennings, George James
Prairie Evangelicals and Christian Missions: A Study in Cultural Ecology. Le Mars, IAU: Middle East Missions Research, 1992. vi, 219 pp. Paper. No ISBN.

A study in words and numerous photographs of the environmental influences in the prairie states of the midwestern United States., which prompt Christians toward evangelicalism and world missions.

AM984 John, Thomas
A Strange Accent: The Reflections of a Missionary to the United States. Louisville, KYU: PCCUSA, Worldwide Ministries Division, 1996. vii, 84 pp. Paper. No ISBN, P.

An educator and pastor of the Church of South India, reflects, as a missionary to the United States, on his year's service as a PCUSA Mission Partner in Residence.

AM985 Klaas, Alan C.
In Search of the Unchurched. (Once and Future Church Series). Bethesda, MDU: Alban Institute, 1996. x, 132 pp. Paper. 1566991692.

A concise, easily read summary of a two year, million dollar study in twelve parts, of the unchurched, and of membership decline among North American Lutherans.

AM986 Kuykendall, John W.
Southern Enterprize: The Work of National Evangelical Societies in the Antebellum South. Westport, CTU: Greenwood, 1982. xv, 188 pp. 0313232121.

A study of how missionary and religious societies affected the antebellum South between 1815 and 1865.

AM987 Lippy, Charles H.
Being Religious, American Style: A History of Popular Religiosity in the United States. (Contributions to the Study of Religion, 37). Westport, CTU: Greenwood, 1994. x, 284 pp. 0313278954.

The noted sociologist of religion analyzes 350 years of popular religion in the United States, reflecting upon mission and evangelization.

AM988 Loewenberg, Robert J.

Equality on the Oregon Frontier: Jason Lee and the Methodist Mission, 1834-43. Seattle, WAU: University of Washington Press, 1976. xi, 287 pp. 0295954914.

A detailed account of a controversial period in the history of Oregon, when Jason Lee and other pioneer Methodist missionaries were torn between a their fervent wish to convert the Indians, and their belief that Indians must be "civilized" first.

AM989 Malphurs, Aubrey

Vision America: A Strategy for Reaching a Nation. Grand Rapids, MIU: Baker Books, 1994. 233 pp. Paper. 0801063132.

In this study book, the President of Vision Ministries International and Chairman of the Department of Field Education at Dallas Theological Seminary presents the impact of secularism on North American society, and offers both a vision, and strategies for 21st-century evangelistic outreach.

AM990 Oleksa, Michael J.

Orthodox Alaska: A Theology of Mission. Crestwood, NYU: St. Vladimir's Seminary Press, 1992. 252 pp. Paper. 0881410926.

A history of the Orthodox mission to Alaska over two centuries; originally presented as a doctoral dissertation at the Orthodox Theological Faculty, Presov, Czechoslovakia (1988).

AM991 Parvin, Earl

Missions USA. Chicago, ILU: Moody, 1985. xi, 381 pp. Paper. 0802459757.

A comprehensive volume on evangelical Christian mission in the United States, including descriptions and histories of 45 unchurched people groups, and listing 228 mission agencies serving them.

AM992 Rausch, John S., ed.

Mission 2009: The Future of the Catholic Church in the South. Atlanta GAU: Glenmary Research Center, 1990. 150 pp. Paper. 0914422197.

Papers from the home mission symposium "Mission 2009," convened to address the future of the Catholic Church in the South in the next twenty years, with focus on evangelization among African Americans, Hispanics, and white Protestants.

AM993 Rommen, Edward

Die Notwendigkeit der Umkehr: Missionsstrategie und Gemeindeaufbau in der Sicht evangelikaler Missionswissenschaftler Nordamerikas. (Monographien und Studienbücher). Gießen, GW: Brunnen-Verlag, 1987. x, 284 pp. Paper. 376559332X.

A dissertation investigating the basic theological assumptions of North American evangelical missiologists, and examining how they determine the practical shape of mission work.

AM994 Sample, Tex

U.S. Lifestyles and Mainline Churches: A Key to Reaching People in the 90s. Louisville, KYU: Westminster John Knox, 1990. ix, 171 pp. Paper. 0664250998.

A sociological analysis of the divergent values and lifestyles of persons on the cultural left, right, and middle in the United States, suggesting effective methods of Christian outreach to each group.

AM995 Schoenberg, Wilfred P.

Paths to the Northwest: A Jesuit History of the Oregon Province. Chicago, ILU: Loyola University Press, 1983. 647 pp. 0829404058.

A detailed history of Jesuit home mission work, 1831-1981, in the Oregon Province, which included western Canada and the present states of Oregon, Washington, Idaho, Montana, and Alaska.

AM996 Sen Gupta, Gunja

For God and Mammon: Evangelicals and Entrepreneurs, Masters and Slaves in Territorial Kansas, 1854-1860. Athens, GAU: University of Georgia, 1996. xi, 219 pp. 0820317799.

A new historical perspective on "bleeding Kansas," including examination of the antislavery ends and means of the American Missionary Association and the American Home Missionary Society.

AM997 Shannon, Foster H.

The Growth Crisis in the American Church: A Presbyterian Case Study. South Pasadena, CAU: William Carey Library, 1977. xv, 159 pp. No ISBN.

A statistical analysis of declining membership in the United Presbyterian Church (US), arguing that internal, rather than external, factors are more important in the growth or decline of local parishes.

AM998 Tanner, William G., comp.

From Sea to Shining Sea. Nashville, TNU: Broadman, 1986. 147 pp. Paper. 0805456678.

Eighteen short sermons and illustrations from the Home Mission Board of the Southern Baptist Convention, to help Christians win the United States to Christ.

AM999 *The American Catholic Heritage: Reflections on the Growth and Influence of the Catholic Church in the United States*

Rome, IT: Pontifical North American College, 1992. 131 pp. Paper. 1555865445.

Six lectures reflecting on 200 years of Roman Catholic mission and ministry in the United States.

AM1000 *Unmarried America: How Singles Are Changing and What It Means for the Church*

Glendale, CAU: Barna Research Group, 1993. 109 pp. Paper. 1882297032.

A sociological analysis of the growing contingents of unmarrieds in the United States, their lifestyles, interests, and values, with suggestions for church outreach ministries to them.

AM1001 Van Gelder, Craig, ed.

Confident Witness, Changing World: Rediscovering the Gospel in North America. (The Gospel and Our Culture Series). Grand Rapids, MIU: Eerdmans, 1999. xvii, 313 pp. Paper. 0802846556.

Twenty-one theologians, missiologists, and practitioners explore the radical cultural shift that has reshaped North American culture and church, and also explore new ways of presenting the Gospel in one of today's most important mission fields.

AM1002 Warner, Bowden Henry, and P. C. Kemeny, eds.

American Church History: A Reader. Nashville, TNU: Abingdon, 1998. 406 pp. Paper. 0687025443.

Thirty-three essays by noted church historians, on American religion and culture, ethnicity, religious thought, mainstream and other religious alternatives; including essays on revivals and mission outreach.

AM1003 Webb, Melody

Yukon: The Last Frontier. Lincoln, NBU: University of Nebraska Press, 1993. xviii, 416 pp. Paper. 0803297459.

Second edition of a scholarly, yet readable, history of the 2,000 mile-long Yukon River basin of Alaska, including mission history; originally published as *The Last Frontier: A History of the Yukon Basis of Canada and Alaska* (University of New Mexico Press, 1985).

AM1004 White, Ronald C., and C. Howard Hopkins

The Social Gospel: Religion and Reform in Changing America. Philadelphia, PAU: Temple University Press, 1976. xix, 306 pp. 0877220832 (hdbk), 0877220840 (pbk).

A new interpretation of the social Gospel movement in the United States, from its birth in the post-Civil War period to its reemergence during the social activism of the 1960s, with numerous references to churches' involvements in home missions.

AM1005 White, Ronald C., Louis B. Weeks, and Garth M. Rosell, eds.

American Christianity: A Case Approach. Grand Rapids, MIU: Eerdmans, 1986. xv, 188 pp. Paper. 0802802413.

A textbook containing twenty cases in American religious history, from the early 1600s to the present, including four on religious revivals and one on missions to Native Americans.

AM1006 Willis, John Randolph

God's Frontiersmen: The Yale Band in Illinois. Washington, DCU: University Press of America, 1979. 245 pp. Paper. 0819107816.

A detailed history, based on archival research, of home mission service in the frontier Illinois Territory, by Yale College graduates, mostly under the American Home Missionary Society, from 1829 to 1861.

U.S.A.: Biography

See also EV197 and AM1155.

AM1007 Armstrong, William Howard

A Friend to God's Poor: Edward Parmelee Smith. Athens, GAU: University of Georgia Press, 1993. xiii, 518 pp. 0820314935.

The first scholarly biography of Edward Parmelee Smith (1827-1876), a Congregational minister from New England, influential in the post-Civil War period in mission to freed slaves through the American Missionary Association, and with native Americans as Commissioner of Indian Affairs.

AM1008 Donnelly, Joseph P.

Jacques Marquette, S.J., 1637-1675. Chicago, ILU: Loyola University Press, 1985. x, 395 pp. 0829400249.

The first scholarly biography of the most prominent of the Jesuit missionaries in New France, 1666-1675; originally published in 1968.

AM1009 Drury, Clifford Merrill, ed.

On to Oregon: The Diaries of Mary Walker and Myra Eells. Lincoln, NEU: University of Nebraska Press, 1998. 382 pp. Paper. 0803266138.

The edited diaries of Myra Fairbanks Eells (1805-1878) and Mary Richardson Walker (1811-1897), covering the 1838-1848 period when they traveled to the Oregon Territory as pioneer American Board missionaries, to work among the Spokane people.

AM1010 Gambera, Giacomo

A Migrant Missionary Story: The Autobiography of Giacomo Gambera. Edited by Mary Elisabeth Brown. Translated by Serafina M. Clarke, and Thomas F. Carlesimo. New York, NYU: Center for Migration Studies, 1994. 295 pp. Paper. 0934733856.

Memoirs of an Italian missionary priest of the Scalabrinian order, Giacomo Gambera (1856-1934), focusing on his ministry among Italian immigrants in Boston and Chicago, 1889 to 1921.

AM1011 Kauffman, Christopher J.

Mission to Rural America: The Story of W. Howard Bishop, Founder of Glenmary. New York, NYU: Paulist Press, 1991. x, 298 pp. Paper. 0809132133.

The biography, based on archival research, of W. Howard Bishop (1885-1953), with an appraisal of the Glenmary Home Missioners he founded.

AM1012 Lazell, J. Arthur

Alaskan Apostle: The Life Story of Sheldon Jackson. New York, NYU: Harper, 1960. 218 pp. No ISBN.

A popular biography of Sheldon Jackson (1834-1909), who established the first Presbyterian mission in Alaska in 1878, and served there until 1907, as explorer, statesman, educator, and mission leader.

AM1013 Müller, Herman J.

Bishop East of the Rockies: The Life and Letters of John Baptist Miege, S.J. (A Campion Book). Chicago, ILU: Loyola University Press, 1994. xvii, 198 pp. Paper. 0829407804.

A narrative biography of John Baptist Miege (1815-1884), the German-born Jesuit bishop of the Indian Territory (1848-1854) and of Kansas (1854-1857), and founding father of the University of Detroit.

AM1014 Mooney, Catherine M.

Philippine Duchesne: A Woman with the Poor. New York, NYU: Paulist Press, 1990. xv, 259 pp. Paper. 0809131161.

A historical biography of the French Society of the Sacred Heart missionary (1769-1852), whose pioneer work on the midwest frontier of the United States, especially among poor immigrants and Native Americans (1818-1852), resulted in her canonization as a saint in 1988.

AM1015 Moore, Paul

Presences: A Bishop's Life in the City. Cambridge, MAU: Cowley Publications, 1997. 344 pp. Paper. 1561011681.

Personable and inspiring memoirs of a bishop and a father of nine, war hero, and peace activist.

AM1016 Morrett, John J.

Soldier Priest. Roswell, GAU: Old Rugged Cross Press, 1993. 312 pp. Paper. 1882270010.

Reminiscences of an Episcopal priest/missionary (b.1916) from his military service and imprisonment in the Philippines in World War II, to missionary service in China, Hawaii, and Thailand.

AM1017 Parman, Donald L., ed.

Window to a Changed World: The Personal Memoirs of William Graham. Indianapolis, INU: Indiana Historical Society, 1998. xxix, 289 pp. Paper. 0871951274.

Ordained as an itinerant Methodist preacher in 1844, and serving in that capacity for fifty years, Graham also worked as an apprentice carpenter, a missionary/teacher among the Choctaws for two years, and a Methodist circuit rider in western Arkansas.

AM1018 Peterson, James
More I Could Not Ask: Finding Christ in the Margins, A Priest's Story. New York, NYU: Crossroad Publishing, 1999. ix, 181 pp. Paper. 0824517725.

The autography of a priest who meets Christ in every person, including the prisoners, people on the street, ex-convicts, and addicts, helped by his fifty-year ministry of support and redemption in Erie, Pennsylvania.

AM1019 Renner, Louis L.
"Father Tom" of the Arctic. Portland, ORU: Binford & Mort Publishing, 1985. xi, 163 pp. 083230445X (hdbk), 0832304433 (pbk).

The biography of Father Thomas Patrick Cunningham, S.J., 1906-1959, who served for thirty years as a missionary in northern Alaska.

AM1020 Renner, Louis L.
Pioneer Missionary to the Bering Strait Eskimos: Bellarmine Lafortune, S.J. Portland, ORU: Binford & Mort Publishing, 1979. xv, 207 pp. 0832303437.

The first account about the pioneer Jesuit missionary, Bellarmine Lafortune, and his work with the Eskimos of Bering Strait, Alaska, from 1902 to 1947.

AM1021 Rogal, Samuel J.
The Educational and Evangelical Missions of Mary Emilie Holmes (1850-1906): "Not to Seem, But to Be." (Studies in Women and Religion, 34). Lewiston, NYU: E Mellen Press, 1994. iii, 105 pp. 0773490957.

An assessment of the contributions of one of the first four women to hold the Ph.D. in the United States (University of Michigan, 1887, in geology and paleontology), who established a seminary for black women in Mississippi, and helped to organize the Woman's Home Missionary Society in the Presbyterian Church in Illinois and the nation.

AM1022 Steckler, Gerard G.
Charles John Seghers: Priest and Bishop in the Pacific Northwest, 1839-1886: A Biography. Fairfield, WAU: Ye Galleon Press, 1986. 321 pp. 0877703752.

The scholarly biography of a Belgian Catholic priest, whose life's work centered on establishing the Catholic faith among the peoples of the Pacific Northwest.

AM1023 Swarth, Dowie, and John C. Oster
Ever the Pioneer: The Romance of Home Missions. (Missionary Resource Book, 1978-79). Kansas City, MOU: Nazarene Publishing House, 1978. 104 pp. Paper. 0834105047.

Reminiscences of the author, who served as a pastor, evangelist, and district superintendent of the Alberta, Canada, and Arizona, US, districts of the Church of the Nazarene.

AM1024 Terrell, John Upton
Black Robe: The Life of Pierre-Jean de Smet, Missionary, Explorer and Pioneer. Garden City, NYU: Doubleday, 1966. 279 pp. No ISBN.

A popular biography of the famous Jesuit missionary Pierre-Jean de Smet (1801-1873), whose pioneer contacts with the Plains Indians, from St. Louis to Oregon, between 1838 and 1842, led to thirty additional years of missionary service and advocacy for Native Americans.

AM1025 Terrell, John Upton
Robe noire: Vie de Pierre de Smet, missionnaire et explorateur. Namur, FR: Wesmael Charlier, 1969. 600 pp. No ISBN.

French translation of *Black Robe: The Life of Pierre-Jean de Smet: Missionary, Explorer and Pioneer* (1966).

AM1026 Thornbury, John
David Brainerd: Pioneer Missionary to the American Indians. Durham, ENK: Evangelical Press, 1996. 318 pp. Paper. 0852343485.

A popular biography of a pioneer 18th-century missionary to Native Americans, whose personal holiness and devotion to God was to inspire thousands to missionary service.

AM1027 Tuttle, Daniel Sylvester
Missionary to the Mountain West: Reminiscences of Episcopal Bishop Daniel S. Tuttle, 1866-1886. Salt Lake City, UTU: University of Utah Press, 1987. 498 pp. Paper. 0874803055.

A reprint of the autobiographical account by the pioneer bishop to Montana, Idaho, and Utah; originally published as *Reminiscences of a Missionary Bishop* (New York: T. Whittaker, c.1906).

U.S.A.: Ethnic Minorities

See also SO224, CH307, AM991, AM1108, AM1111, and AM1231.

AM1028 Appleby, Jerry L.
Missions Have Come Home to America: The Church's Cross-Cultural Ministry to Ethnics. Kansas City, MOU: Beacon Hill Press, 1986. 120 pp. Paper. 0834111322.

In this work the author, a former Nazarene missionary in American and Western Samoa, raises the question of cross-cultural evangelism in the American context, and addresses himself to the inherent challenges of cross-cultural evangelism in planting ethnic churches.

AM1029 Cenkner, William, ed.
The Multicultural Church: A New Landscape in U.S. Theologies. New York, NYU: Paulist Press, 1996. iii, 202 pp. Paper. 0809136074.

Papers and responses from a symposium on the "Implications of the Multicultural Dimensions of The Catholic Church in the United States" held at the Catholic University of America (Washington, D.C., April 1993).

AM1030 DeBoer, Clara Merritt
His Truth is Marching On: African Americans Who Taught the Freedmen for the American Missionary Association 1861-1877. New York, NYU: Garland, 1995. xx, 401 pp. 0815317883.

A detailed record from archival sources, of the "Crusade of Brotherhood," that prepared millions of former slaves for citizenship, before the withdrawal of federal troops and the dismantling of the Freedman's Bureau.

AM1031 Johnson, Clifton H., ed.
God Struck Me Dead: Voices of Ex-Slaves. (William Bradford Collection from the Pilgrim Press). Cleveland, OHU: Pilgrim Press, 1993. xxix, 171 pp. Paper. 0829809457.

Reprint of an invaluable collection of conversion narratives and autobiographies, by illiterate, but powerfully articulate, ex-slaves; originally published by Pilgrim Press in 1969, with a new introduction by Albert J. Raboteau.

AM1032 Moorman, Donald
Harvest Waiting. Saint Louis, MOU: Concordia Publishing, 1993. 222 pp. Paper. 0570099366.

Practical helps for local churches in the United States, desiring to undertake cross-cultural ministries; by a Missouri Synod Lutheran pastor who has been engaged in such ministries since 1977.

AM1033 Stories to Tell: Multicultural Ministry in Action
Chicago, ILU: Commission for Multicultural Ministries Evangelical Lutheran Church, 1991. 103 pp. Paper. No ISBN.

Forty-three short cases of multicultural ministries by parishes of the Evangelical Lutheran Church in America.

AM1034 The Joy of Service: Life Stories of Racial and Ethnic Minority Deaconesses and Home Missionaries
New York, NYU: UMC, Board of Global Ministries, 1992. 56 pp. Paper. No ISBN.

United Methodist ethnic minority deaconesses and home missionaries briefly tell their stories of mission service in the United States.

AM1035 Yohn, Susan M.
A Contest of Faiths: Missionary Women and Pluralism in the American Southwest. Ithaca, NYU: Cornell University Press, 1995. xi, 266 pp. 0801429641 (hdbk), 0801482739 (pbk).

A sociohistorical analysis of the late 19th-century work of Presbyterian women missionaries, in New Mexico and Colorado, among Hispanic women, focusing on the cultural values they sought to introduce in an "Americanizing" process.

AM1036 Yoo, David K., ed.
New Spiritual Homes: Religion and Asian Americans. (Intersections, Asian and Pacific American Transcultural Studies). Honolulu, HIU: University of Hawaii Press; Los Angeles, CAU: UCLA Asian American Studies Center, 1999. vii, 323 pp. Paper. 082482072X.

Eight essays, five creative works of poetry and story, and a selected bibliography on a wide range of topics, including a Christian theology of marginality, Taiwanese Buddhism in Southern California, Filipino Americans, folk religion, and voices of churched Korean American women.

African Americans and Mission

See also HI14, HI153, HI409, HI548, HI714, TH192, TH509, CR565, CR970, SO39, SO212, SO214, SO219, SO231, SO511, ED17, ED49, EV130, EV187, EV249, EV255, EV272, EV398, EV411, EV418, CH93, CH417, and AM1007.

AM1037 Beals, Ivan A.
Our Racist Legacy: Will the Church Resolve the Conflict? (The Church and the World Series, 9). Notre Dame, INU: Cross Cultural Publications, 1997. xvi, 228 pp. Paper. 0940121360.

A popular history of responses by churches to the race issue in the United States from the first colonies to 1995.

AM1038 Bechler, LeRoy
The Black Mennonite Church in North America, 1886-1986. Ontario, CNU: Herald Press, 1986. 109 pp. 0836112873.

A comprehensive history of Mennonite Church missions among blacks in the United States (1898-1950), and of the resulting churches to 1980.

AM1039 Best, Mary E.
Seventy Septembers. Techny, ILU: Holy Spirit Missionary Sisters, 1988. iv, 400 pp. 0961772212.

A history of the Holy Spirit Missionary Sisters' work in Mississippi and Arkansas, among African Americans.

AM1040 Billingsley, Andrew
Mighty Like A River: The Black Church as Agent of Social Reform. New York, NYU: Oxford University Press, 1999. xxiv, 262 pp. 0195106172.

An expert in African American culture surveys nearly 1,000 black churches across the country, their roots extending back to antebellum times and including their confrontation with social, economic, and political problems.

AM1041 Bishop, William Howard
Moving beyond Confined Circles: The Home Mission Writings of William Howard Bishop. Edited by Lou McNeil. Atlanta, GAU: Glenmary Research Center, 1990. xii, 116 pp. Paper. 0914422200.

Seventeen scholarly essays by historians and theologians, interpreting various themes in African church history (missionary ideology and practice, rapport with Islam, Africanization, and problems of historical method); originally presented at the colloquy of Bologne, 22-25 October 1988.

AM1042 Clemmons, Ithiel C.
Bishop C. H. Mason and the Roots of the Church of God in Christ. (Centennial Edition). Bakersfield,CAU: Pneuma Life Publishing, 1996. 208 pp. Paper. 1562294512.

History of the major black denomination founded in 1897, including its impact through the Asuza Street revival of 1906 on Pentecostalism and its mission outreach.

AM1043 Dash, Michael I. N., L. Rita Dixon, Darius L. Swann, and Ndugu T'Ofori-Atta, eds.
African Roots: Towards an Afrocentric Christian Witness. Lithonia, GAU: SCP/Third World Literature Publishing House, 1994. 221 pp. Paper. 0913491306.

In these papers from the Pan African Christian Church Conference I (PACCCI) held at the Interdenominational Theological Center, Atlanta, in July 1988, African and African American scholars develop the bases for Afrocentric Christian witness and mission; published with a study guide.

AM1044 Davis, Cyprian
The History of Black Catholics in the United States. New York, NYU: Crossroad Publishing, 1990. xvii, 347 pp. 0824510100.

A detailed history, including the contributions of numerous religious orders and congregations in evangelization, reform, and empowerment of African American Catholics.

AM1045 duCille, Frank O.
Indigenization: How to Grow Black Churches in White Denominations. Pineville, NCU: Frank O. duCille & Co., 1983. x, 135 pp. Paper. No ISBN.

A study of methods by which ethnic minority congregations, in mainline Protestant denominations in the United States, become indigenous. Includes a case study of Trinity Community Presbyterian Church pastored by duCille, in Detroit, Michigan.

AM1046 Finkelman, Paul, ed.
Religion and Slavery. (Articles on American Slavery, 16). New York, NYU: Garland, 1989. xviii, 706 pp. 0824067967.

An anthology of thirty-five scholarly essaysm, published 1930 to 1983, on the role of religion in the history of slavery; including articles on 19th-century missions to slaves and Native Americans.

AM1047 Haney, Marsha Snulligan
Islam and Protestant African-American Churches: Responses and Challenges to Religious Pluralism. San Francisco, CAU: International Scholars Publications, 1999. xvii, 304 pp. 1573093009.

This book demonstrates the contextualized missional response that the African American Protestant churches need to take, in order to lead to an authentic and biblical response to religious pluralism.

AM1048 Harrison, William Pope, comp.
The Gospel among the Slaves: A Short Account of Mission-ary Operations among the African Slaves of the Southern States. New York, NYU: AMS Press, 1973. 394 pp. 0404002633.

A history of mission work among slaves in the South, from 1829 to 1864, by the northern Methodist Episcopal Church; reprint of the 1893 edition.

AM1049 Johnson, Jeff G.
Black Christians: The Untold Lutheran Story. (Concordia Scholarship Today). St. Louis, MOU: Concordia Publishing, 1991. 262 pp. Paper. 0570045584.

A history of black Lutheranism in all branches in the United States, including mission.

AM1050 Johnson, Paul E., ed.
African-American Christianity: Essays in History. Berkeley, CAU: University of California Press, 1994. xi, 189 pp. 0520075935 (hdbk), 0520075943 (pbk).

Seven scholarly essays on various aspects of African American Christianity, including missions to slaves and to Africa.

AM1051 Jordan, Lewis Garnett
Up the Ladder in Foreign Mission. (The Baptist Tradition). New York, NYU: Arno Press, 1980. xiii, 269 pp. 0405124635.

Reprint of the 1901 classic on African American missions; published originally by the National Baptist Publishing Board.

AM1052 *Many Rains Ago: A Historical and Theological Reflection on the Role of the Episcopate in the Evangelization of African American Catholics*
Washington, DCU: NCCB/USCC, 1990. 64 pp. Paper. 1555863191.

Three historical essays by African American Catholic scholars, commemorating contributions by their people in the Catholic Church in the United States.

AM1053 Montgomery, William E.
Under Their Own Vine and Fig Tree: The African American Church in the South, 1865-1900. Baton Rouge, LAU: Louisi-ana State University Press, 1993. xiii, 358 pp. 0807117455.

A scholarly history of the black church in the post-eman-cipation era, with analysis of the role of missionaries in orga-nizing the church in the South.

AM1054 Newman, Susan D.
With Heart and Hand: The Black Church Working to Save Black Children. Valley Forge, PAU: Judson Press, 1995. xiii, 81 pp. Paper. 0817012230.

A practical resource profiling two national and eight lo-cal ministries in the United States, established specifically to affect the lives of children.

AM1055 Nieman, Donald G., ed.
Church and Community among Black Southerners, 1865-1900. (African American Life in the Post-Emancipation South, 9). New York, NYU: Garland, 1994. x, 409 pp. 0815314469.

A reprint of twenty essays, including two on missions, two on women's leadership, and several on evangelism, edu-cation, and church development.

AM1056 Perkins, James C.
Building Up Zion's Walls: Ministry for Empowering the African American Family. Edited by Jean Alicia Elster. Valley Forge, PAU: Judson Press, 1999. ix, 101 pp. Paper. 0817013377.

This resource assists in developing effective ministry in light of issues facing African American families today.

AM1057 Perkins, John M.
Beyond Charity: The Call to Christian Community Develop-ment. Grand Rapids, MIU: Baker Books, 1993. 192 pp. Pa-per. 0801071224.

Reflections on issues of biblical justice and the econom-ic development of the black community, by one who modeled creatively holistic mission in the southern United States.

AM1058 Richardson, Joe M.
Christianity Reconstruction: The American Missionary As-sociation and Southern Blacks, 1861-1890. Athens, GAU: University of Georgia Press, 1986. ix, 348 pp. 0820308161.

A history of the American Missionary Association, with emphasis on its role as an antislavery society, its work in the field of education, and its relationship to both the black and the white communities in the South.

AM1059 Riggs, Marcia Y., ed.
Can I Get a Witness?: Prophetic Religious Voices of African American Women: An Anthology. Maryknoll, NYU: Orbis Books, 1997. xv, 200 pp. Paper. 1570751137.

With short biographical sketches, twenty-eight African American women, from slavery times to the present, speak of the prophetic dimensions of the Gospel and of women's in-volvement in mission and justice ministries.

AM1060 Riggs, Marcia Y.
Awake, Arise, and Act: A Womanist Call for Black Libera-tion. Cleveland, OHU: Pilgrim Press, 1994. xiii, 149 pp. Paper. 0829810099.

A sociological analysis of the constraints and strengths of African American women as they strived for communal liberation and social betterment in the 19th and 20th centu-ries, by the Associate Professor of Christian Ethics at Colum-bia Theological Seminary.

AM1061 Sawyer, Mary R.
Black Ecumenism: Implementing the Demands of Justice. Valley Forge, PAU: Trinity Press International, 1994. xx, 251 pp. Paper. 1563380927.

This story of the cooperative, interdenominational efforts of black church leaders in North America, to address social, political, and economic inequities, reveals much concerning understandings of the churches' mission.

AM1062 Shockley, Grant S., ed.
Heritage and Hope: The African American Presence in Unit-ed Methodism. Nashville, TNU: Abingdon, 1991. 350 pp. Paper. 0687168988.

A comprehensive history and interpretation of the partici-pation of African Americans in the growth, development, and witness (including mission) of North American Methodism.

AM1063 Stevens Arroyo, Antonio M., and Andres I. Pérez y Mena, eds.
Enigmatic Powers: Syncretism with African and Indigenous Peoples' Religions among Latinos. (PARAL Studies Series, 3; Bildner Center Series on Religion, 3). New York, NYU: Bildner Center for Western Hemisphere Studies, 1995. 208 pp. 0929972112 (hdbk), 096578391X (pbk).

Eight essays by social-anthropologists on aspects of in-digenous and African popular religion among Latinos in the United States.

AM1064 Thomas, George B.

Young Black Adults: Liberation and Family Attitudes. New York, NYU: Friendship Press, 1974. 95 pp. Paper. 0377000019.

A probing analysis of the new black consciousness, which arose out of the civil rights struggles of the 1960s, and its implications for church ministries to African American young adults.

AM1065 Townes, Emilie M., ed.

Embracing the Spirit: Womanist Perspectives on Hope, Salvation, and Transformation. (Bishop Henry McNeal Turner/Sojourner Truth Series in Black Religion, 13). Maryknoll, NYU: Orbis Books, 1997. xix, 300 pp. Paper. 1570751404.

Essays by seventeen womanist theologians in the United States, on a variety of themes important for African American women, in personal and social transformation.

AM1066 Van Horne, John C., ed.

Religious Philanthropy and Colonial Slavery: The American Correspondence of the Associates of Dr. Bray, 1717-1777. Chicago, ILU: University of Illinois Press, 1985. xxii, 370 pp. 0252011422.

A sourcebook of 18th-century correspondence (1717-1777) by Anglicans of the philanthropic associates of Dr. Bray, telling of their efforts to convert and educate blacks in the American colonies.

AM1067 Watley, William D.

Singing the Lord's Song in a Strange Land: The African American Churches and Ecumenism. (Risk Book Series, 57). Geneva, SZ: WCC Publications; Grand Rapids, MIU: Eerdmans; Trenton, NJU: Africa World Press, 1993. xi, 69 pp. 2825411043 (W), 0802807119 (E), 0865433925 (A).

A popular introduction to the worship life, international mission, theological enterprise, and ecumenical relationships of the seven, so-called historic, black churches in the United States.

AM1068 Wilmore, Gayraud S.

Black Religion and Black Radicalism: An Interpretation of the Religious History of African Americans. Maryknoll, NYU: Orbis Books, 1998. xvi, 328 pp. Paper. 157075182X.

Revised and enlarged edition of a classic treatment of African American religious history, containing numerous references to the black churches' involvements in mission issues in North America and Africa; originally published in 1972 (Garden City, NYU: Doubleday).

Asian Americans and Mission

See also TH593.

AM1069 Fong, Ken Uyeda

Pursuing the Pearl: A Comprehensive Resource for Multi-Asian Ministry. Valley Forge, PAU: Judson Press, 1999. xii, 242 pp. Paper. 0817013040.

In a completely updated and revised version of his self-published *Insights for Growing Asian-American Ministries*, Fong examines current trends, models, and cultural realities in Asian American churches, for effective church growth and renewal.

AM1070 Hayashi, Brian Masaru

"For the Sake of Our Japanese Brethren": Assimilation, Nationalism, and Protestantism among the Japanese of Los Angeles, 1895-1942. (Asian American Series). Stanford, CAU: Stanford University Press, 1995. xvi, 217 pp. 0804723745.

An in-depth case study of Protestant mission to first and second generation Japanese Americans in Los Angeles before World War II; a revision of the author's Ph.D. dissertation at the University of California, Los Angeles.

AM1071 Kim, Illsoo

New Urban Immigrants: The Korean Community in New York. Princeton, NJU: Princeton University Press, 1981. xvi, 329 pp. 0691093555.

An account of the sociological techniques and assimilations developed by the 80,000 "new immigrants" from South Korea in the New York metropolitan area since 1967, with a chapter on the church as a basis for the community.

AM1072 Kim, Jung Ha

Bridge-Makers and Cross-Bearers: Korean-American Women and the Church. (American Academy of Religion Academy Series, 92). Atlanta, GAU: Scholars Press, 1997. viii, 168 pp. 0788501658 (hdbk), 0788501666 (pbk).

A sociological study of what it means to be a woman in the context of the Korean American church.

AM1073 Lee, Jung Young

Marginality: The Key to Multicultural Theology. Minneapolis, MNU: Fortress Press, 1995. vii, 208 pp. Paper. 0800628101.

A sociological analysis and theological reflection on marginality and multiculturalism in the United States, with special reference to the Asian American experience and church.

AM1074 Lundell, In-Gyeong Kim

Bridging the Gaps: Contextualization among Korean Nazarene Churches in America. (Asian Thought and Culture, 18). New York, NYU: Lang, 1995. xii, 155 pp. 0820425419.

A Korean American Nazarene pastor's thesis on multiple factors (historical, theological, and cultural) that influence the contextualization of Christianity among her members in Los Angeles, California.

AM1075 Matsuoka, Fumitaka

Out of Silence: Emerging Themes in Asian American Churches. Cleveland, OHU: United Church Press, 1995. x, 168 pp. Paper. 0829810250.

A candid sociological analysis of the experiences of Asian American Christians, with models for renewal in theology and mission; by the academic dean of the Pacific School of Religion in Berkeley, California.

AM1076 Ng, David, ed.

People on the Way: Asian North Americans Discovering Christ, Culture, and Community. Valley Forge, PAU: Judson Press, 1996. xxix, 300 pp. Paper. 0817012427.

Stories about experiences of Asian North American Christians as they are shaped by, and claim their identity, within their rich Asian religious and cultural heritage; prepared as a study book.

Hispanic Americans and Mission

See also HI528-HI529, HI715, TH420-TH421, TH424, TH437, TH500, SO506, and AM9.

AM1077 Brackenridge, R. Douglas, and Francisco O. Garcia-Treto
Iglesia Presbiteriana: A History of Presbyterians and Mexican Americans in the Southwest. (Presbyterian Historical Society Publications, 15). San Antonio, TXU: Trinity University Press, 1987. xiv, 278 pp. Paper. 0911536531 (hdbk), 0939980185 (pbk).

A study providing a context to describe the effect of Protestantism, in general, on Hispanic identity, as well as emphasizing ideological and cultural changes that have come about in the Southwest, as a result of the Mexican Revolution of 1910.

AM1078 Díaz-Stevens, Ana María, and Antonio M. Stevens Arroyo
Recognizing the Latino Resurgence in U.S. Religion: The Emmaus Paradigm. (Explorations: Contemporary Perspectives on Religion). Boulder, COU: Westview Press, 1998. xxi, 272 pp. 0813325099 (hdbk), 0813325102 (pbk).

Summarizing twenty years of research on Latino religious resurgence in the United States, two professors of church and society argue against an assimilation model, and for a church-based model of multicultural pluralism.

AM1079 Deck, Allan Figueroa
The Second Wave: Hispanic Ministry and the Evangelization of Cultures. New York, NYU: Paulist Press, 1989. xvi, 191 pp. Paper. 0809130424.

An analysis of the historical, cultural, and missiological factors to be considered by Roman Catholics, in creating strategies for Hispanic ministry and evangelization in the USA.

AM1080 Dolan, Jay P., and Allan Figueroa Deck, eds.
Hispanic Catholic Culture in the U.S.: Issues and Concerns. (The Notre Dame History of Hispanic Catholics in the U.S., 3). Notre Dame, INU: University of Notre Dame Press, 1994. vii, 457 pp. 0268011052.

Eleven scholarly essays on key issues for evangelization, mission, and church development among Catholic Hispanics in the United States.

AM1081 Dolan, Jay P., and Gilberto M. Hinojosa, eds.
Mexican Americans and the Catholic Church, 1900-1965. (The Notre Dame History of Hispanic Catholics in the U.S., 1). Notre Dame, INU: University of Notre Dame Press, 1994. vii, 380 pp. 0268014094.

A detailed history focusing on Catholic faith communities of Mexican Americans in the Southwest, California, and the Midwest of the United States.

AM1082 Dolan, Jay P., and Jaime R. Vidal, eds.
Puerto Rican and Cuban Catholics in the U.S., 1900-1965. (The Notre Dame History of Hispanic Catholics in the U.S., 2). Notre Dame, INU: University of Notre Dame Press, 1994. vii, 259 pp. 0268038058.

The first in-depth historical analysis of the Puerto Rican and Cuban American Catholic experience.

AM1083 Elizondo, Virgilio P.
Christianity and Culture: An Introduction to Pastoral Theology and Ministry for the Bicultural Community. Huntington, INU: Our Sunday Visitor, 1975. 199 pp. Paper. 0879738634.

A first attempt by a Mexican American to articulate a theology rooted in the unique bicultural experience of that community.

AM1084 Elizondo, Virgilio P.
The Future Is Mestizo: Life Where Cultures Meet. Bloomington, INU: Meyer-Stone, 1988. xii, 111 pp. Paper. 094098928X.

The faith journey of the founding president of the Mexican American Cultural Center in San Antonio, Texas, presented as an affirmation of United States Hispanic theology and culture.

AM1085 Elizondo, Virgilio P.
Galilean Journey: The Mexican-American Promise. Maryknoll, NYU: Orbis Books, 2000. xviii, 155 pp. Paper. 1570753105.

This revised and expanded version of the author's groundbreaking work in Hispanic theology, which relates the story of the Galilean Jesus to the story of the *mestizo* people, includes a new autobiographical introduction, and a concluding chapter on developments in Hispanic/Latino theology in the United States.

AM1086 Equipo Editorial de Profetas de Esperanza
La Juventud Hispana y la Respuesta Pastoral de la Iglesia. (Profetas de Esperanza, 1). Winona, MNU: Saint Mary's Press/Christian Brothers Publications, 1994. 289 pp. Paper. 088489326X.

Spanish edition of *Hispanic Young People and the Church's Pastoral Response* (1994).

AM1087 Espín, Orlando O.
The Faith of the People: Theological Reflections on Popular Catholicism. Maryknoll, NYU: Orbis Books, 1997. xxii, 186 pp. Paper. 1570751110.

Theology, spirituality, and evangelization in Latino popular Catholicism, analyzed by the director of the Center for the Study of Latino Catholicism at the University of San Diego.

AM1088 González, Justo L., ed.
En Nuestra Propia Lengua: Una historia del Metodismo unido hispano. Nashville, TNU: Abingdon, 1991. 192 pp. Paper. 0687114217.

A history and interpretation of the participation of Hispanic Americans in the growth, development, and witness (including mission) of United Methodism, in the USA and Puerto Rico.

AM1089 Haselden, Kyle
Death of a Myth: New Locus for Spanish American Faith. New York, NYU: Friendship Press, 1964. 175 pp. Paper. No ISBN.

A primer for Protestants in the United States, designed to introduce Spanish Americans and Anglo-Americans to one another, in such a way as to destroy the myth that Spanish Americans are loyally and predominantly Roman Catholic.

AM1090 Lucas, Isidro
The Browning of America: The Hispanic Revolution in the American Church. Chicago, ILU: Fides/Claretian, 1981. xiii, 146 pp. 0819006424.

A primer on challenges to effective mission among Hispanic Americans for Roman Catholics, with reference to Protestant ministries and government policies.

AM1091 National Conference of Catholic Bishops
Hispanic Ministry: Three Major Documents. Washington, DCU: USCC, 1995. v, 99 pp. Paper. 1555861970.

A bilingual (English and Spanish) publication of three major documents on Hispanic mission and ministry in the United States—the 1983 pastoral letter, the 1986 "Prophetic Voices," and the 1987 "National Pastoral Plan for Hispanic Ministry."

AM1092 Nostrand, Richard L.

The Hispano Homeland. Norman, OKU: University of Oklahoma Press, 1992. xiv, 281 pp. 0806124148.

A carefully delineated interpretation of the distinctive Spanish American subculture surviving in northern New Mexico and southern Colorado, among Pueblo Indians, nomad Indians, Anglos, and Mexican Americans; with references to Catholic (especially Franciscan) and Mormon influences.

AM1093 Ortiz, Manuel

The Hispanic Challenge: Opportunities Confronting the Church. Downers Grove, ILU: InterVarsity, 1993. 194 pp. Paper. 0830817735.

A primer on mission among Hispanic Americansn focusing on needs, key missiological issues, models for ministry, and leadership training.

AM1094 Pineda, Ana Maria, and Robert J. Schreiter, eds.

Dialogue Rejoined: Theology and Ministry in the United States Hispanic Reality. Collegeville, MNU: Liturgical Press, 1995. viii, 187 pp. Paper. 0814622062.

Ten scholarly essays, mostly by Hispanic Americans, on Hispanic realities relative to ministry and theology.

AM1095 Prophets of Hope Editorial Team

Evangelización de la Juventud Hispana. (Profetas de Esperanza, 2). Winona, MNU: Saint Mary's Press; Winona, MNU: Christian Brothers Publications, 1995. n.p. pp. Paper. No ISBN.

Spanish translation.

AM1096 Prophets of Hope Editorial Team

Evangelization of Hispanic Young People. (Prophets of Hope, 2). Winona, MNU: Saint Mary's Press/Christian Brothers Publications, 1995. 286 pp. Paper. 0884893278.

Volume 2 of the Catholic pastoral plan for ministry to young Hispanics in the United States, focusing on the evangelization process, models for small communities, and the role of Mary.

AM1097 Prophets of Hope Editorial Team

Hispanic Young People and the Church's Pastoral Response. (Prophets of Hope, 1). Winona, MNU: Saint Mary's Press/Christian Brothers Publications, 1994. 291 pp. Paper. 0884893251.

The first of a two-volume series, published in both English and Spanish, this book develops the Catholic "National Pastoral Plan for Hispanic Ministry" by dealing with the personal, relational, cultural, and religious realities of Hispanic young people in the United States.

AM1098 Recinos, Harold J.

Hear the Cry!: A Latino Pastor Challenges the Church. Louisville, KYU: Westminster John Knox, 1989. 156 pp. Paper. 0664250351.

The personal testimony of a Puerto Rican raised in the drug culture of New York City, who found Christ and later developed a creative ministry to Latinos, as pastor of the Church of All Nations, on the Lower East Side of Manhattan.

AM1099 Rodríguez-Díaz, Daniel R., and David Cortés-Fuentes, eds.

Hidden Stories: Unveiling the History of the Latino Church. Decatur, GAU: Asociación para la Educación Teológica Hispana, 1994. xviii, 165 pp. Paper. No ISBN.

Thirteen papers originally presented at the first North American conference for the study of Latino church history (McCormack Seminary, Chicago, 1993).

AM1100 Sandoval, Moises

On the Move: A History of the Hispanic Church in the United States. Maryknoll, NYU: Orbis Books, 1990. xvi, 152 pp. Paper. 0883446758.

A broad introduction to the origins and growth of the churches, both Catholic and Protestant, among Hispanic Americans in the southwestern United States; with focus on the struggle for rights and recognition.

AM1101 Sandoval, Moises, ed.

The Mexican American Experience in the Church: Reflections in Identity and Mission. New York, NYU: Sadlier, 1983. 125 pp. Paper. 0821598848.

A popular report of ideas shared by Mexican American Catholic leaders at a 1982 Mexican American Cultural Center tenth anniversary forum.

AM1102 Solivan, Samuel

The Spirit, Pathos and Liberation: Toward an Hispanic Pentecostal Theology. (Journal of Pentecostal Theology Supplement Series, 14). Sheffield, ENK: Sheffield Academic Press, 1998. 160 pp. Paper. 1850759421.

From a Hispanic American perspective, the author explores Hispanic diversity, its common roots and struggles, and the growth of the Pentecostal movement among the poor and disenfranchised of society.

AM1103 Stevens Arroyo, Antonio M.

Prophets Denied Honor: An Anthology on the Hispano Church of the United States. Maryknoll, NYU: Orbis Books, 1980. xvi, 379 pp. Paper. 0883443953.

An anthology of one hundred documents (essays, sermons, addresses, and poems) by Catholic Hispanic Americans.

AM1104 *Strangers and Aliens No Longer: Part One: The Hispanic Presence in the Church of the United States*

Washington, DCU: USCC, 1993. 133 pp. Paper. 1555865941.

The first of a series of findings from a Lilly Endowment-funded study of the multicultural phenomenon, as experienced by U.S. Catholics, focusing on issues confronting Hispanics.

AM1105 Villafañe, Eldin

The Liberating Spirit: Toward an Hispanic American Pentecostal Social Ethic. Grand Rapids, MIU: Eerdmans, 1993. xiii, 257 pp. Paper. 0802807283.

A social ethic for Hispanic American Pentecostals as a church of the poor and oppressed, by the Professor of Christian Social Ethics at Gordon-Conwell Theological Seminary, and founding director of the Center for Urban Ministerial Education in Boston, Massachusetts; originally published by University Press of America in 1992.

AM1106 Weigle, Marta

Brothers of Light, Brothers of Blood: The Penitentes of the Southwest. Albuquerque, NMU: University of New Mexico Press, 1976. xix, 300 pp. No ISBN.

A sourcebook tracing the history of the Brotherhood of Our Father Jesus from the 1770s to the 1970s.

U.S.A.: Missions to Immigrants

See also HI399, HI399, HI470, and CO163.

AM1107 Axtell, James
The Invasion Within: The Contest of Cultures in Colonial North America. New York, NYU: Oxford University Press, 1985. xv, 389 pp. 0195035968.

A detailed ethnohistory of the colonial French, English, and Indian efforts to convert one another; the first of three volumes on eastern North America.

AM1108 Belew, M. Wendell, comp.
Missions in the Mosaic. Atlanta, GAU: Home Mission Board of SBC, 1974. vi, 93 pp. Paper. No ISBN.

A collection of popular accounts of how Southern Baptists are ministering with Native Americans, Blacks, Hispanics, Asian Americans, and European language groups in the United States.

AM1109 Dolan, Jay P.
Catholic Revivalism: The American Experience, 1830-1900. Notre Dame, INU: University of Notre Dame Press, 1978. xx, 248 pp. 0268007225.

A history of Catholic parish missions in the United States in the 19th century, which were more successful than parallel Protestant efforts at reaching working class immigrants.

AM1110 Liptak, Dolores
Immigrants and Their Church. New York, NYU: Macmillan Publishing Company, 1989. xviii, 221 pp. 0029192315.

A detailed history of the churches of Catholic immigrants in the United States, 1790-1950, revealing multiple mission strategies.

AM1111 Lutheran Historical Conference (16th, Chicago, Illinois, 1992)
Missionary to America: The History of Lutheran Outreach to Americans. (The Lutheran Historical Conference, 15). Minneapolis, MNU: Augsburg Fortress, 1994. vi, 314 pp. Paper. No ISBN.

Essays and reports on the conference theme, "Missionary to America: The History of Lutheran Outreach to Americans."

AM1112 Warner, R. Stephen, and Judith G. Wittner, eds.
Gathering in Diaspora: Religious Communities and the New Immigration. Philadelphia, PAU: Temple University Press, 1998. vi, 409 pp. Paper. 1566396131 (hdbk), 156639614X (pbk).

Scholarly case studies of post-1965 immigrant communities in the United States and their diverse religious identities (Keralite, Korean and Chinese Christians, Iranian Jews, Muslims, Rastafarians, and Haitian followers of Voodoo in New York City, and Hindu and Mayan religion in Los Angeles).

AM1113 Whyman, Henry C.
The Hedstroms and the Bethel Ship Saga: Methodist Influence on Swedish Religious Life. Carbondale, ILU: Southern Illinois University Press, 1992. xvi, 183 pp. 0809317621.

A scholarly biography of Olof Gustaf Hedstrom (1803-1877) and Jonas Hedstrom (1813-1855) and their ministries to Swedish immigrants to the United States, primarily through Bethel Ship, a floating chapel in New York harbor.

U.S.A.: Missions to Native Americans

See also HI622, CR635-CR636, CR640-CR641, CR643, CR655-CR656, SO387, ED11, ED24, SP7, SP316, AM620, AM623, AM658, AM916, AM918, AM975, AM1003, AM1007, AM1019-AM1020, AM1024-AM1026, AM1046, AM1092, and EU278.

AM1114 Anderson, Owanah
400 Years: Anglican/Episcopal Mission among American Indians. Cincinnati, OHU: Forward Movement, 1997. xii, 401 pp. Paper. 0880281820.

A narrative history by the Choctaw Head of the Episcopal Church's Office of Indian Ministry.

AM1115 Andrew, John A.
From Revivals to Removal: Jeremiah Evarts, The Cherokee Nation, and the Search for the Soul of America. Athens, GAU: University of Georgia Press, 1992. x, 434 pp. 0820314277.

A scholarly history of the efforts, on behalf of the Cherokees, led by Jeremiah Evarts (1781-1831), Secretary of the ABCFM, from 1815 to 1829, that failed to block passage of the Indian Removal Bill in 1830.

AM1116 Bahr, Diana Meyers
From Mission to Metropolis: Cupeno Indian Women in Los Angeles. Norman, OKU: University of Oklahoma Press, 1993. xii, 184 pp. 0806125497.

Through in-depth interviews with Cupeno women of three generations now living in Los Angeles, the author discovers how urban Native Americans redefine themselves and their values (both tribal and Christian).

AM1117 Banker, Mark T.
Presbyterian Missions and Cultural Interaction in the Far Southwest, 1850-1950. Urbana, ILU: University of Illinois Press, 1993. xiv, 225 pp. 0252019296.

A detailed analysis of a mid 19th-century attempt to bring Native Americans, Hispanic Catholics, and Mormons into the American mainstream, by education in mission boarding schools.

AM1118 Bass, Althea
Cherokee Messenger. (The Civilization of the American Indian Series, 12). Norman, OKU: University of Oklahoma Press, 1996. 348 pp. Paper. 0806128798.

A reprint of the 1936 biography of Rev. Samuel Austin Worcester (1798-1859), missionary to the Cherokees from 1825 to 1859, under the auspices of the American Board.

AM1119 Beaver, Robert Pierce, ed.
The Native American Christian Community: A Directory of Indian, Aleut, and Eskimo Churches. Monrovia, CAU: MARC, 1979. 395 pp. 0912552255.

A directory of ministries with and by Native Americans, Aleuts, and Eskimos in the United States in the 1970s.

AM1120 Beaver, Robert Pierce
Church, State, and the American Indians: Two and a Half Centuries of Partnership in Missions between Protestant Churches and Government. St. Louis, MOU: Concordia Publishing, 1966. 230 pp. No ISBN.

A scholarly, readable history of the partnership between church and state in maintaining the Protestant mission to Native Americans, 1641 to 1890.

AM1121 Berkhofer, Robert F.

Salvation and the Savage: An Analysis of Protestant Missions and American Indian Response, 1787-1862. Westport, CTU: Greenwood, 1977. xiv, 186 pp. 0837197457.

A scholarly study, based on archival research, of the relationship of Protestant missions to Native Americans; originally published in 1965 by the University of Kentucky Press.

AM1122 Bowden, Henry Warner

American Indians and Christian Missions: Studies in Cultural Conflict. (Chicago History of American Religion). Chicago, ILU: Chicago University Press, 1981. xix, 255 pp. 0226068110.

A short history of American, Spanish, French, and English missions among the natives of North America, from the 16th to the 20th centuries, emphasizing intergroup social conflicts in a religious context; including an overview of American Indian religion.

AM1123 Boyd, Robert

People of the Dalles: The Indians of Wascopam Mission: A Historical Ethnography Based on the Papers of the Methodist Missionaries. (Studies in the Anthropology of North American Indians). Lincoln, NEU: University of Nebraska Press; Bloomington, INU: Indiana University, American Indian Studies Research Institute, 1996. xi, 396 pp. 0803212364.

A detailed history, with source material, of the Methodist mission from 1805 to 1848, to the Chinookan (Wasco-Wishram) and Sahaptin peoples of the Dalles area of the Columbia River basin.

AM1124 Burns, Robert Ignatius

The Jesuits and the Indian Wars of the Northwest. (Yale Western Americana Series, 11). Moscow, IDU: University of Idaho Press; New Haven, CTU: Yale University Press, 1966. xvi, 512 pp. No ISBN.

A scientific enquiry into the activity of Jesuit missionaries in the Oregon Territory, in particular, their role as peacemakers between Indians and whites.

AM1125 Carriker, Robert C.

Father Peter John de Smet: Jesuit in the West. (Oklahoma Western Biographies, 9). Norman, OKU: University of Oklahoma Press, 1995. xx, 266 pp. 0806127503.

A narrative biography of Father Pierre-Jean deSmet (1801-1873), who, from 1840 to 1873, labored to bring peace and Christianity to Native Americans of the Pacific Northwest and upper Missouri River.

AM1126 Conley, Robert J.

Mountain Windsong: A Novel of the Trail of Tears. Norman, OKU: University of Oklahoma Press, 1992. 218 pp. 0806124520 (hdbk), 0806127465 (pbk).

A Cherokee novelist recreates the tragic events of the Cherokees' removal from their traditional lands in North Carolina to Indian Territory [Oklahoma], between 1835 and 1838, citing historic documents referring to missionary involvement in the struggle.

AM1127 Cook, Sherburne Friend

The Conflict between the California Indian and White Civilization. Berkeley, CAU: University of California Press, 1976. xi, 522 pp. 0520031431.

A collection of essays that analyze the effects of disease, nutrition, forced labor, and foreign culture on mission Indians, including a comparison with non-mission Indians.

AM1128 Crawford, Isabel

Kiowa: A Woman Missionary in Indian Territory. Lincoln, NEU: University of Nebraska Press, 1998. xxx, 242 pp. Paper. 0803263872.

A Bison Books edition of the journal of Isabel Alice Hartley Crawford (1865-1961), founder of the Saddle Mountain Baptist Mission of the Kiowa-Comanche Reservation in Oklahoma; covering her work there, from her arrival in 1896 as an American Baptist home missionary, to 1906.

AM1129 Crying Wind,

Crying Wind. Chicago, ILU: Moody, 1987. 188 pp. 0854215514.

Autobiography of a Navaho Christian woman.

AM1130 Day, Richard Ellsworth

Flagellant on Horseback. (Broad Rim Books). Lewisville, TXU: Accelerated Christian Education, 1994. 253 pp. 1562650246.

Reprint of a popular biography of David Brainerd (1718-1747), New England missionary to Native Americans; originally published by Judson Press in 1950.

AM1131 Deloria, Vine

Custer Died For Your Sins: An Indian Manifesto. Norman, OKU: University of Oklahoma Press, 1988. xiii, 278 pp. Paper. 0806121297.

Revised edition of a 1969 publication, with updated information about the continuing plight of the American Indian, and the misconceptions and misdirected efforts of those who have tried to help them.

AM1132 Deloria, Vine

The Indian Affair. New York, NYU: Friendship Press, 1974. 95 pp. Paper. 037700023X.

A critical evaluation of the treatment of Native Americans by Anglos, including missionaries, by a theologically trained Sioux spokesman for North American Native Americans.

AM1133 DeMallie, Raymond J., and Douglas R. Parks, eds.

Sioux Indian Religion: Tradition and Innovation. Norman, OKU: University of Oklahoma Press, 1987. viii, 243 pp. 080612055X (hdbk), 0806121661 (pbk).

Twelve essays, by tribal religious leaders, scholars, and other members of the Sioux communities in North and South Dakota, on issues of Sioux ritual and belief, in relation to the history, tradition, and mainstream of American life; including four essays on Christian missions (Catholic, Protestant, and Mormon) among the Sioux.

AM1134 Devens, Carol

Countering Colonization: Native American Women and Great Lakes Missions, 1630-1900. Berkeley, CAU: University of California Press, 1992. xi, 185 pp. 0520075579.

A well-documented history of Native American women of the Ojibwa, Cree, and Montagnais-Naskapi peoples of the Upper Great Lakes region, showing how, to preserve their culture, they actively shaped successive encounters with Christian missionaries, from the 16th (Jesuit) to the 19th centuries (Wesleyan and others).

AM1135 Dolaghan, Thomas, and David Scates

The Navajos Are Coming to Jesus. South Pasadena, CAU: William Carey Library, 1978. xiii, 176 pp. Paper. 0878081623.

An analysis of factors affecting Navaho receptivity to Christianity, with a brief secular and church history, and 1976 survey of churches in the Navaho reservation.

AM1136 Dwight, Sereno Edwards
Memoirs of the Rev. David Brainerd: Missionary to the Indians on the Border of New York, New Jersey, and Pennsylvania. St. Clair Shores, MIU: Scholarly Press, 1970. 504 pp. 0403002338.

Papers of the pioneer missionary (1742-1747), including his diary and sermons preached at his ordination, and funeral (by Jonathan Edwards); reprint of 1822 edition.

AM1137 Emerson, Dorothy
Among the Mescalero Apaches: The Story of Father Albert Braun, O.F.M. Tucson, AZU: University of Arizona Press, 1973. xiii, 224 pp. 0816503214.

A popular biography of a Franciscan missionary priest to the Apaches, based at St. Joseph's mission, Mescalero, New Mexico, beginning in 1916.

AM1138 Enochs, Ross Alexander
The Jesuit Mission to the Lakota Sioux: Pastoral Theology and Ministry, 1886-1945. Kansas City, MOU: Sheed and Ward, 1996. x, 178 pp. Paper. 1556128134.

Archival and oral history research on the struggles over issues of contextualization by the Jesuit mission to the Lakota Sioux on the Pine Ridge and Rosebud reservations of South Dakota.

AM1139 Espinosa, J. Manuel, ed.
The Pueblo Indian Revolt of 1696 and the Franciscan Missions in New Mexico: Letters of the Missionaries and Related Documents. Norman, OKU: University of Oklahoma Press, 1988. xviii, 313 pp. 0806121394.

A well-researched presentation, from the view of the Spanish Franciscan missionaries, of Pueblo culture, with insights into the causes and results of the Pueblo revolt of Northern New Spain; including original documents.

AM1140 Fienup-Riordan, Ann
The Real People and the Children of Thunder: The Yup'ik Eskimo Encounter with Moravian Missionaries John and Edith Kilbuck. Norman, OKU: University of Oklahoma Press, 1991. x, 420 pp. 080612329X.

A cultural anthropologist recounts the history of the 1885 presentatioon of Christianity, to the Yup'ik people of western Alaska, by John Kilbuck and his family who were Native Americans of the Delaware tribe, and were Morovian missionaries.

AM1141 Goddard, Ives, and Kathleen J. Bragdon
Native Writings in Massachusetts (Parts One and Two). Philadelphia, PAU: American Philosophical Society, 1988. xxiv,x, 791 pp. 087169185X.

Two volumes of 18th- and 19th-century documents by the Massachusett tribe in southeastern Massachusetts, with facsimiles, translations, critical notes, and an interpretive essay on their significance for the understanding of early missions to Native Americans.

AM1142 Greer, Allan, ed.
The Jesuit Relations: Natives and Missionaries in Seventeenth-century North America. (The Bedford Series in History and Culture). Boston, MAU: Bedford/St. Martin's Press, 2000. xiii, 226 pp. 0312227442 (hdbk), 0312167075 (pbk).

Documents, colorful journal entries, and background information on French Jesuit missions to Native Americans.

AM1143 Grumet, Robert S.
Historic Contact: Indian People and Colonists in Today's Northeastern United States in the Sixteenth through Eighteenth Centu-

ries. (Contributions to Public Archeology, 1). Norman, OKU: University of Oklahoma Press, 1995. xxx, 514 pp. 0806127007.

A basic reference work on Native American and white (including missionary) relations in the northeast colonies, giving the history of thirty-four "Indian countries" from Maine to Virginia, and from the Atlantic coast to Ohio.

AM1144 Hann, John H.
A History of the Timucua Indians and Missions. (The Ripley P. Bullen Series). Gainesville, FLU: University of Florida Press, 1996. xvi, 399 pp. 0813014247.

A detailed history of the original Timucua people of Florida, from their first contact with European explorers in 1513, and their organization in mission villages by Spanish Franciscan priests in the 1580s, to their exile to Cuba in 1763, and their final eradication.

AM1145 Harrod, Howard L.
Mission Among the Blackfeet. (The Civilization of the American Indian Series No. 112). Norman, OKU: University of Oklahoma Press, 1971. xxi, 218 pp. 0806109661.

A detailed history, based on archival sources, of the Blackfeet Native Americans of the northern plains, from 1840 to the present; with a sociological assessment of the positive and negative effects of Protestant and Roman Catholic missions.

AM1146 Hummelen, Remmelt, and Kathleen Hummelen, eds.
Stories of Survival: Conversations with Native North Americans. New York, NYU: Friendship Press, 1985. 76 pp. Paper. 0377001503.

Twenty-one first person life stories and concerns by Native Americans; prepared as an adult mission study, with study guide, *Hear the Creator's Song* (44 pp., ISBN 0377001511).

AM1147 Jeffrey, Julie Roy
Converting the West: A Biography of Narcissa Whitman. (Oklahoma Western Biographies, 3). Norman, OKU: University of Oklahoma Press, 1991. xvii, 238 pp. 0806123591.

The biography of Narcissa Prentice Whitman (1808-1847), pioneer American Board missionary to the Cayuse Indians in the Oregon Territory.

AM1148 John, Elizabeth A. H.
Storms Brewed in Other Men's Worlds: The Confrontation of Indians, Spanish, and French in the Southwest, 1540-1795. Norman, OKU: University of Oklahoma Press, 1996. xxi, 805 pp. Paper. 0806128690.

Second edition of a 255-year history of encounters between Europeans and the native peoples of the Southwest, including early Catholic mission history; with a new preface and afterword by the author, discussing current research issues; originally published in 1975.

AM1149 Johnston, Basil H.
Indian School Days. Toronto, ONC: Key Porter Books; Norman, OKU: University of Oklahoma Press, 1988. 250 pp. Paper. 1550130722 (CA), 0806122269 (US).

The autobiography of a North American Ojibway, taken from his family in 1939 at age ten and placed in a Jesuit boarding school; revealing how he and others created a subculture of survival to resist cultural assimilation.

AM1150 Kellaway, William

The New England Company, 1649-1776: Missionary Society to the American Indians. London, ENK: Longmans, 1961. 303 pp. No ISBN.

A scholarly history, based on manuscript sources, of the first English Protestant missionary society, originally called the Society for Propagation of the Gospel in New England, assessing the work of John Elliott and others as a substantial accomplishment.

AM1151 Keller, Robert H.

American Protestantism and United States Indian Policy, 1869-1882. Lincoln, NEU: University of Nebraska Press, 1983. xiii, 359 pp. 080322706X.

A scholarly study, based on both denominational and government archives, of President Ulysses S. Grant's radical reform, placing administration of Native Americans under the churches.

AM1152 Kessell, John L., and Rick Hendricks, eds.

The Spanish Missions of New Mexico. (Spanish Borderlands Sourcebooks, 17-18). New York, NYU: Garland, 1991. 2 vols. 0824020952 (vol. 1), 0824023498 (vol. 2).

These sourcebooks contain primary source documents and scholarly essays, and focus on Franciscan missions among the Pueblo Indians of New Mexico after 1680 [vol. 1: *Before 1680* (1991, 490 pp.); vol. 2: *After 1680* (1991, xxii, 504 pp.)].

AM1153 Kessell, John L.

Kiva, Cross, and Crown: The Pecos Indians and New Mexico, 1540-1840. Albuquerque, NMU: University of New Mexico Press, 1987. xiii, 587 pp. Paper. 0826309682.

A thoroughly researched account of the Pecos area, written in a narrative style; including much detail on the Franciscans and valuable information on architecture.

AM1154 Kidwell, Clara Sue

Choctaws and Missionaries in Mississippi, 1818-1918. Norman, OKU: University of Oklahoma Press, 1995. xvi, 271 pp. 0806126914.

A detailed examination based on archival sources of the influence of Christian missionaries (primarily American Board, Methodist, and Roman Catholic) on the Choctaw in central Mississippi.

AM1155 Killoren, John J.

"Come, Blackrobe": De Smet and Indian Tragedy. Norman, OKU: University of Oklahoma Press, 1994. xv, 448 pp. Paper. 0806126159.

An in-depth analysis of two competing approaches to Anglo-Native American relations on the Western frontier—the government's policies of assimilation or extermination versus the Indian advocacy of Fr. Peter John De Smet, S.J.; told as a narrative biography of the latter, from 1823 to 1873.

AM1156 Lillard, Charles, ed.

Warriors of the North Pacific: Missionary Accounts of the Northwest Coast, the Skeena and Stikine Rivers, and the Klondike, 1829-1900. Victoria, BCC: Sono Nis Press, 1984. 280 pp. 0919203485.

A collection of 19th-century accounts by missionaries to Native Americans in British Columbia and Alaska, with an introduction and annotations by the editor.

AM1157 Llorente, Segundo

Memoirs of a Yukon Priest. Washington, DCU: Georgetown University Press, 1990. xiii, 223 pp. 0878404945.

The autobiography of a Jesuit priest from Spain, who spent forty years (1935-1975) enduring the hardships, challenges, and rewards of a life lived wholly in the presence of God, and at the service of the Eskimo people of Alaska.

AM1158 Loskiel, Georg Heinrich

Geschichte der Mission der Evangelischen Brüder unter den Indianern in Nordamerika. (Nikolaus Ludwig von Zinzendorf: Materialien und Dokumente, Reihe 2, 21). Hildesheim, GW: Georg Olms Verlag, 1989. 100, 783 pp. 3487092433.

A reprint of the 1789 edition of the famous history of Moravian missions among Indians of North America, with a substantial introduction and six newly collected plates.

AM1159 Marsh, Thelma R.

Moccasin Trails to the Cross: A History of the Mission to the Wyandott Indians on the Sandusky Plains. Upper Sandusky, OHU: UMC, Historical Society of Ohio, 1974. 150 pp. No ISBN.

A local history of the work of missionaries of the Methodist Episcopal Church among the Wyandott Indians in Ohio, 1824-1843.

AM1160 McLoughlin, William Gerald, Walter H. Conser, and Virginia Duffy McLoughlin

The Cherokee Ghost Dance: Essays on the Southeastern Indians, 1789-1861. Macon, GAU: Mercer University Press, 1984. xxiv, 512 pp. 0865541280.

A collection of eighteen essays on the Cherokee by the noted historian, including nine on missionary activity.

AM1161 McLoughlin, William Gerald

Champions of the Cherokees: Evan and John B. Jones. Princeton, NJU: Princeton University Press, 1990. xiv, 498 pp. 0691047707.

The scholarly biography of two extraordinary Northern Baptist missionaries, father and son, who lived with the Cherokee Indians from 1821 to 1876; a narrative of the Cherokee's suffering, and an analysis of ethnic relations in the United States.

AM1162 McLoughlin, William Gerald

The Cherokees and Christianity, 1794-1870: Essays on Acculturation and Cultural Persistence. Edited by Walter H. Conser. Athens, GAU: University of Georgia Press, 1994. xi, 347 pp. 0820316393.

Eleven essays by the distinguished historian, focusing on the imperialistic attempts at "Christianization" of the Cherokee civilization.

AM1163 McLoughlin, William Gerald

Cherokees and Missionaries, 1789-1839. Norman, OKU: University of Oklahoma Press, 1995. xvii, 375 pp. Paper. 0806127236.

A reprint of the noted Brown University historian's first of four volumes on the Cherokees and missionaries, with a new foreword by William L. Anderson; originally published in 1984.

AM1164 Merrell, James H.

The Indian's New World: Catawbas and Their Neighbors from European Contact through the Era of Removal. Chapel Hill, NCU: University of North Carolina Press, 1989. xv, 381 pp. 0807818321.

An eloquent account of the native peoples (the Carolina Piedmont), who came to be known as the Catawba Nation; with numerous references to their contacts with Christian missionaries.

AM1165 Mihesuah, Devon Abbott

Cultivating the Rosebuds: The Education of Women at the Cherokee Female Seminary, 1851-1909. Urbana, ILU: University of Illinois Press, 1993. xii, 212 pp. 0252019539.

A detailed history of the nondenominational Cherokee Female Seminary, which provided no instruction in the Cherokee language or culture, but was instead designed to assimilate full- and mixed-blood Cherokee girls into the dominant white culture, in present-day eastern Oklahoma.

AM1166 Miller, Christopher L.

Prophetic Worlds: Indians and Whites on the Columbia Plateau. New Brunswick, NJU: Rutgers University Press, 1985. x, 174 pp. 0813510848.

A history, based on archival research, of contacts by Native Americans of the Columbia River Valley in the Pacific Northwest, with whites, especially missionaries, between 1825 and 1855.

AM1167 Milner, Clyde A., and Floyd A. O'Neil, eds.

Churchmen and the Western Indians, 1820-1920. Norman, OKU: University of Oklahoma Press, 1985. xvi, 264 pp. 0806119500.

Papers from a conference held at Utah State University, 6-7 August 1982, on the work of six diverse missionaries (Presbyterian, Methodist, Mormon, Catholic, Quaker, and Episcopal) among Indians in Minnesota, Oklahoma, and Utah.

AM1168 Milner, Clyde A.

With Good Intentions: Quaker Work Among the Pawnees, Otos, and Omahas in the 1870s. Lincoln, NEU: University of Nebraska Press, 1982. xiii, 238 pp. 0803230664.

A detailed, scholarly study, based on archival sources, of the varied responses to the Quakers' attempts at implementing the government's program for assimilation among the tribes of the Northern Superintendency (Nebraska).

AM1169 Mitchell, Joseph, ed.

The Missionary Pioneer or a Brief Memoir of the Life, Labours, and Death of John Stewart, (Man of Colour) Founder, under God of the Mission Among the Wyandotts at Upper Sandusky, Ohio. (Negro Heritage Series, 3). New York, NYU: Pemberton Press; Austin, TXU: Jenkins Publishing, 1969. viii, 96 pp. No ISBN.

Reprint of an 1827 biography of a black Methodist missionary (1786-1823), who established a mission among the Wyandott Indians at Upper Sandusky, Ohio.

AM1170 Moore, James T.

Indian and Jesuit: A Seventeenth-Century Encounter. Chicago, ILU: Loyola University Press, 1982. 267 pp. 0829403957.

A well-documented history of the French Jesuits and their many missions begun in North America among the Indian nations.

AM1171 Morrison, Dane

A Praying People: Massachusett Acculturation and the Failure of the Puritan Mission, 1600-1690. (American Indian Studies, 2). New York, NYU: Lang, 1995. xxxi, 265 pp. 0820418080.

A detailed history of the development and end of the 17th-century Puritan mission to the Algonquins in Massachusetts.

AM1172 Mousalimas, S. A.

The Transition from Shamanism to Russian Orthodoxy in Alas-

ka. Providence, RIU: Berghahn Books, 1994. viii, 254 pp. 1571810064.

A detailed history, based on archival sources, of how Russian Orthodoxy became the Aleut and Alutiiq peoples' religion; originally submitted as a D. Phil. dissertation at Oxford University.

AM1173 Olmstead, Earl P.

Blackcoats Among the Delaware: David Zeisberger on the Ohio Frontier. Kent, OHU: Kent State University Press, 1991. xviii, 283 pp. 0873384229 (hdbk), 0873384342 (pbk).

A detailed history of David Zeisberger (1721-1808), Moravian missionary to the Delaware Indians in the Ohio country, and of the missions that he and other Moravians founded as Christian villages for Native Americans, between 1740 and 1821.

AM1174 Olmstead, Earl P.

David Zeisberger: A Life among the Indians. Kent, OHU: Kent State University Press, 1997. xxiv, 441 pp. 0873385683.

A narrative biography of David Ziesberger (1721-1808), a Moravian missionary, who for sixty-three years (1745-1808), lived and worked among the Iroquois and Delaware nations in New York, Pennsylvania, Ohio, Michigan, and Upper Canada; based on his diaries.

AM1175 Oswalt, Wendell H.

Bashful No Longer: An Alaskan Eskimo Ethnohistory, 1778-1988. Norman, OKU: University of Oklahoma Press, 1990. xviii, 270 pp. 0806122560.

A detailed ethnohistory of the Eskimos of the Kuskokwin River valley of southwestern Alaska; based on primary sources, including Russian Orthodox and Mennonite mission records.

AM1176 Oswalt, Wendell H.

Mission of Change in Alaska: Eskimos and Moravians on the Kuskokwim. San Marino, CAU: Huntington Library, 1963. 170 pp. No ISBN.

A scholarly study of eighty years of cultural interaction between the Kuskokwim River Eskimos of western Alaska and Moravian missionaries; based on oral histories, the author's field notes, and the diaries of William Henry Weinland, the pioneer missionary.

AM1177 Peterson, Jacqueline

Sacred Encounters: Father de Smet and the Indians of the Rocky Mountain West. Norman, OKU: University of Oklahoma Press, 1993. 192 pp. 0806125756 (hdbk), 0806125764 (pbk).

This catalogue of the International Sacred Encounters Exhibition, containing 200 full color illustrations, plus photographs and text, documents similarities and differences between European Christianity, introduced among the Coeur d'Alene Salish Indians of northern Idaho and western Montana by Fr. Pierre-Jean de Smet, S.J., in 1841, and Native American beliefs and customs.

AM1178 Phillips, George Harwood

Indians and Intruders in Central California, 1769-1849. (The Civilization of the American Indian Series, 207). Norman, OKU: University of Oklahoma Press, 1993. 270 pp. 0806124466.

A cultural history of central California, 1769-1849, with considerable attention given to the role of Spanish missions.

AM1179 Phillips, Joyce B., and Paul Gary Phillips, eds.
The Brainerd Journal: A Mission to the Cherokees, 1817-1823.
(Indians of the Southwest Series). Lincoln, NEU: University
of Nebraska Press, 1998. xix, 584 pp. 0803237189.

A scholarly edition of the journal of the American Board's
pioneer mission to the Cherokees, by a descendant of the superintendent of the Brainerd Mission.

AM1180 Prucha, Francis Paul
*American Indian Policy in Crisis: Christian Reformers and
the Indian, 1865-1900.* Norman, OK: University of Oklahoma Press, 1976. xii, 456 pp. 0806112794.

A detailed history of the efforts of "humanitarians," including many church leaders, to reform U.S. Indian affairs
during the post-Civil War period.

AM1181 Prucha, Francis Paul
The Churches and the Indian Schools, 1888-1912. Lincoln, NEU:
University of Nebraska Press, 1979. xii, 278 pp. 0803236573.

An analysis of tension and conflict between Protestants
and Catholics over Indian mission schools, at the end of the
19th and beginning of the 20th century.

AM1182 Río, Ignacio del
Conquista y Aculturación en la California Jesuítica, 1697-1768.
(Serie Historia novohispana, 32). México, D.F., MX: Univer-
sidad Nacional Autónoma de México, 1998. 242 pp. 9683671977.

A history of the entrance of Jesuit missionaries into Baja
California in the 18th century, the situation they found, and
their relations with native peoples; first published in 1984.

AM1183 Rausch, David A., and Blair Schlepp
Native American Voices. Grand Rapids, MIU: Baker Books,
1994. 180 pp. Paper. 0801077737.

An introduction to Native American culture, religion, and
history (including mission history), by a historian at Ashland
University in Ohio, and a counselor from the Lakota Sioux
heritage.

AM1184 Ruby, Robert H., and John A. Brown
A Guide to the Indian Tribes of the Pacific Northwest. (The
Civilization of the American Indian Series, 173). Norman,
OKU: University of Oklahoma Press, 1992. xx, 289 pp.
0806119675 (hdbk), 0806124792 (pbk).

Revised edition of short introductions to the 150 tribes
of Native Americans in the northwest United States, with
notations of mission influence in their history—a companion
volume to *Indians of the Pacific Northwest: A History* (1981).

AM1185 Ruby, Robert H., and John A. Brown
Indians of the Pacific Northwest: A History. (The Civilization of the American Indian Series). Norman, OKU: University of Oklahoma Press, 1988. viii, 294 pp. Paper. 0806121130.

A scholarly history of the Indians of the Pacific Northwest, from their first contact with Europeans through the
1890s, giving considerable attention to relationships with
Christian missionaries from various churches.

AM1186 Ruby, Robert H., and John A. Brown
John Slocum and the Indian Shaker Church. Norman, OKU:
University of Oklahoma, 1996. xx, 300 pp. 0806128658.

A detailed, well-documented history of the nativistic Indian Shaker Church, founded by the Squaxin spiritual leader,
John Slocum, in the Pacific Northwest, in 1882.

AM1187 Schmutterer, Gerhard Martin
Tomahawk und Kreuz: Fränkische Missionare unter Prärie-

Indianern 1858-1866; zum Gedenken an Moritz Bräuninger.
(Erlanger Taschenbücher, 79). Erlangen, GW: Ev.-Luth. Mis-
sion; Neuendettelsau, GW: Freimund Verlag, 1987. 198 pp.
Paper. 3872141791 (E), 3772601286 (F).

The author describes a difficult episode in the history of
the Neuendettelsau mission among the Indians, when the intertwining of missionary and political interests resulted in tragic consequences for the missionaries.

AM1188 Sevillano, Mando
Evangelizing the Culturally Different. Shippensburg, PAU:
Destiny Image, 1997. xix, 138 pp. Paper. 1560432918.

An intimate look at Hopi religion, customs, and ways of
life, as a case study of evangelistic principles and methods
effective in cross-cultural evangelism.

AM1189 Shea, John Gilmary
*History of the Catholic Missions among the Indian Tribes of
the United States, 1529-1854.* New York, NYU: Arno Press,
1969. 514 pp. No ISBN.

Reprint of an important early history (New York: P.J.
Kenedy, 1854).

AM1190 Smet, Pierre-Jean de
Western Missions and Missionaries: A Series of Letters. Shannon, IE: Irish University Press, 1972. xiii, 532 pp. No ISBN.

Reprint of the original 1859 edition of the letters of Rev.
Peter John de Smet, S.J. (1801-1873), pioneer missionary to the
Oregon Territory (1823-1846) and peacemaker missionary-statesman, recalling the increasing tensions between whites and Native Americans on the Western frontier (1846-1857).

AM1191 Smith, Donald B.
*Sacred Feathers: The Reverend Peter Jones (Kahkewaquona-
by) & the Mississauga Indians.* (American Indian Lives).
Lincoln, NEU: University of Nebraska Press; London, ENK:
University of Toronto Press, 1987. xix, 372 pp. 0803241739
(US), 0802057551 (UK, hdbk), 0802067328 (UK, pbk).

A scholarly biography of a remarkable Ojibwa Indian
leader and Methodist missionary (1802-1856), who struggled
to secure equality for his people with the white settlers; based
on his letters, diaries, sermons, and his history of the Ojiba-
was of Upper Canada.

AM1192 Steltenkamp, Michael F.
Black Elk: Holy Man of Oglala. Norman, OKU: University
of Oklahoma Press, 1993. xxiii, 211 pp. 0806125411.

A scholarly biography of Black Elk (1863-1950), a renowned ritual leader of the Lakota Sioux, focusing on his spiritual autobiography, including his conversion to Catholicism
in 1904, and service as a devoted catechist and missionary to
his fellow Native Americans.

AM1193 Stolzman, William
The Pipe and Christ. Chamberlain, SDU: Tipi Press, 1986. v,
222 pp. Paper. No ISBN.

The experiences of struggle and healing, and the spiritual journey of the author while living with the Lakota Indians
of South Dakota.

AM1194 Szasz, Margaret Connell
Indian Education in the American Colonies, 1607-1783. Albuquerque, NMU: University of New Mexico Press, 1988. x,
333 pp. 0826311032 (hdbk), 0826311040 (pbk).

A detailed monograph, based on archival research, on
the efforts of missionaries and teachers to bring Christianity
and civilization to Native Americans.

AM—THE AMERICAS

AM1195 Terrell, John Upton

The Arrow and the Cross: A History of the American Indian and the Missionaries. Santa Barbara, CAU: Capra Press, 1979. 253 pp. 088496132X (hdbk), 0884961338 (pbk).

A history about Christian missionary activity and conflict with the Indians in the American West, from Arizona to Washington, critical of methods used both by Protestant and Catholic missionaries to crush the Indians' resistance to Christianity.

AM1196 Tinker, George E.

Missionary Conquest: The Gospel and Native American Cultural Genocide. Minneapolis, MNU: Fortress Press, 1993. ix, 182 pp. Paper. 0800625765.

A Native American scholar, and associate professor of cross-cultural ministries at Iliff School of Theology in Denver, critiques four noted Christian missionaries to Native Americans (Eliot, Serra, de Smet, and Whipple) for their complicity in Anglo cultural imperialism.

AM1197 Treat, James, ed.

Native and Christian: Indigenous Voices on Religious Identity in the United States and Canada. New York, NYU: Routledge, 1996. viii, 248 pp. Paper. 041591373X.

An anthology of recent short essays by Native Americans in the United States and Canada, focusing on the problem of native Christian identity.

AM1198 Vaughan, Alden T.

New England Frontier: Puritans and Indians, 1620-1675. Norman, OKU: University of Oklahoma Press, 1995. lxxiii, 430 pp. Paper. 080612718X.

A third-edition reissue, with new introduction, of the standard authority on Puritan-Indian relations, from the landing of the Mayflower through the King Philip's War.

AM1199 Vecsey, Christopher

On the Padres' Trail. (American Indian Catholics, 1). Notre Dame, INU: University of Notre Dame Press, 1996. xvii, 440 pp. 0268037027.

The first of a three-volume historical study of Catholic mission and ministry among Native Americans in the United States, covering Catholic 16th-century expansion in New Spain and missions to the Pueblo peoples of New Mexico, and to Native Americans in California.

AM1200 Veniaminov, Ioann

Journals of the Priest Ioann Veniaminov in Alaska, 1823-1836. Translated by Jerome Kisslinger. (The Rasmuson Library Historical Translation Series, 7). Fairbanks, AKU: University of Alaska Press, 1993. xxxix, 220 pp. Paper. 0912006641.

These journals of the Orthodox priest Ivan Veniaminov (1797-1879) reveal details of the Aleut Mission.

AM1201 Walker, Edward E.

Conflict and Schism in Nez Perce Acculturation: A Study of Religion and Politics. Moscow, IDU: University of Idaho Press, 1985. xxvi, 171 pp. Paper. 0893011053.

A scholarly account of the effect of religious conflict between Catholics and Protestants, including Pentecostalists, upon the acculturation of the Nez Perce peoples.

AM1202 Wallis, Ethel Emily

God Speaks Navajo. New York, NYU: Harper & Row, 1968. xiv, 146 pp. No ISBN.

A popular biography of Faye Edgerton, who devoted her life to the Navajo Indians in the western United States, translating the New Testament into their language.

AM1203 Weddle, Robert S.

The San Saba Mission: Spanish Pivot in Texas. Austin, TXU: University of Texas Press, 1988. xiii, 238 pp. Paper. 0292776160.

A detailed account of the San Saba Mission in south Texas, from its founding as a Franciscan mission to the Apache Indians in 1757, to its destruction by the Comanches in 1879.

AM1204 Westmeier, Karl-Wilhelm

The Evacuation of Shekomeko and the Early Moravian Missions to Native North Americans. (Studies in the History of Missions, 12). Lewiston, NYU: E Mellen Press, 1994. ix, 444 pp. Paper. 0773491414.

A detailed analysis and history, from 1740, of the pioneer Moravian mission to the Scaticook Native Americans at Shekomeko, New York, including its practice of radical indigenization and forced closure by white authorities in 1745.

AM1205 Widder, Keith R.

Battle for the Soul: Métis Children Encounter Evangelical Protestants at Mackinaw Mission, 1823-1837. East Lansing, MIU: Michigan State University Press, 1999. xxiv, 254 pp. Paper. 0870134914.

A carefully researched biography of enthusiastic missionaries, uncompromising in religious devotion, who brought about transformation of the Métis of the upper Great Lakes, through their children and through holding different worldviews in tension.

AM1206 Willard, Carrie M.

Carrie M. Willard among the Tlingits: The Letters of 1881-1883. Sitka, AKU: Mountain Meadow Press, 1995. x, 222 pp. Paper. 0945519206.

Letters of a pioneer Presbyterian missionary to Alaska, with a brief historical introduction by Borg Hendrickson.

U.S.A.: Urban Mission

See also HI641, SO396, SO540, SO546-SO547, SO557, EC332, EV113, EV218, CH175, CH182, CH389, and AM1015.

AM1207 Burger, Delores T.

Women Who Changed the Heart of the City: The Untold Story of the City Rescue Mission Movement. Grand Rapids, MIU: Kregel Publications, 1997. 157 pp. Paper. 0825421462.

Stories of women leaders, beginning with Frances Nasmith, who led in inner-city rescue missions for the poor, in the early 1800s.

AM1208 Campolo, Tony

Revolution and Renewal: How Churches are Saving our Cities. Louisville, KYU: Westminster John Knox, 2000. xi, 286 pp. Paper. 066422198X.

Inspiring stories of faith-based social action, in apparently hopeless urban communities, provide a blueprint for reclaiming the future of our cities.

AM1209 Carle, Robert D., and Louis A. Decaro, eds.

Signs of Hope in the City: Ministries of Community Renewal. Valley Forge, PAU: Judson Press, 1999. xii, 281 pp. Paper. 0817013245.

Revised edition of a collection of eighteen articles on New York City mission in African American, Latino, and Asian American contexts, from a church-based community-organizing perspective; originally published in 1997.

AM1210 Christensen, Michael J.

City Streets, City People: A Call for Compassion. Nashville, TNU: Abingdon, 1988. 254 pp. Paper. 0687083958.

A practical manual for those desiring to minister to street people in North American cities by the founder/Director of Golden Gate Ministries in San Francisco.

AM1211 Conn, Harvie M.

The American City and the Evangelical Church: A Historical Overview. Grand Rapids, MIU: Baker Books, 1994. 232 pp. Paper. 0801025907.

A historical and sociological analysis of urban mission in the United States by the Professor of Missions at Westminster Seminary in Philadelphia.

AM1212 Davidson, James D.

Mobilizing Social Movement Organizations: The Formation, Institutionalization, and Effectiveness of Ecumenical Urban Ministries. (Society for the Study of Religion Monograph Series, 6). Storrs, CTU: SSSR, 1985. x, 210 pp. Paper. 0932566057.

A detailed evaluation of the Lafayette, Indiana, Urban Ministry, 1962-1971, which fostered social change, despite the fact that the majority of its church members opposed such change.

AM1213 Day, Dorothy

Loaves and Fishes. Maryknoll, NYU: Orbis Books, 1997. xviii, 221 pp. Paper. 1570751560.

A reprint of the 1963 classic by the founder of the Catholic Worker Movement in the United States.

AM1214 Ellison, Craig W., ed.

The Urban Mission: Essays on the Building of a Comprehensive Model for Evangelical Urban Ministry. Grand Rapids, MIU: Eerdmans, 1974. 230 pp. Paper. 080281560X.

Twenty-three essays by prominent American evangelicals, exploring the biblical, theological, historical, and cultural bases of urban mission, and challenging Protestant evangelicals to active involvement in various aspects of urban society in the United States.

AM1215 Frisbie, Margery

An Alley in Chicago: The Ministry of a City Priest. Kansas City, MOU: Sheed & Ward, 1991. xi, 298 pp. Paper. 1556124635.

A narrative biography of Monsignor John Joseph Egan, who, from his ordination in 1943, was known as a leader among Chicago's Roman Catholics in social justice ministries.

AM1216 George, Denise

An Unexpected Christman: The Story of Johnny Cornflakes. Birmingham, AL: New Hope Publishers, 1999. 89 pp. 156309715X.

This little book is based on the true story of a Southern belle, who moves to the inner city and befriends an outrageous, humorous homeless person, dubbed "Johnny Cornflakes" by the locals.

AM1217 Green, Clifford J., ed.

Churches, Cities, and Human Community: Urban Ministry in the United States, 1945-1985. Grand Rapids, MIU: Eerdmans, 1996. xiv, 378 pp. Paper. 0802842089.

Thirteen scholarly essays by mainline denomination leaders, reflecting on forty years of urban ministries in the United States.

AM1218 Huggins, Nathan Irvin

Protestants against Poverty: Boston's Charities, 1870-1900. Westport, CT: Greenwood, 1971. xiv, 225 pp. 0837133076.

A scholarly examination of various philanthropic movements in Boston, Massachusetts, at the beginning of the age of industrialization.

AM1219 Kenrick, Bruce

Come Out the Wilderness. London, ENK: Collins, 1963. 254 pp. No ISBN.

Twenty-four vignettes of the ministries of the East Harlem Protestant Parish, an innovative cooperative mission in the inner city.

AM1220 Laurentin, René

Miracle á El Paso ? Paris, FR: Desclée de Brouwer, 1981. 151 pp. 2220023745.

An account of the startling effects of the Good News, proclaimed to the poor, who live out their lives in the garbage and refuse dump of El Paso, along the border of the United States and Mexico.

AM1221 Laurentin, René

Miracles in El Paso? Translated by John Otto. Ann Arbor, MIU: Servant Books, 1982. 137 pp. 0892831052 (hdbk), 0892831502 (pbk).

English translation.

AM1222 Longo, Vinny, and Lloyd B. Hildebrand

Victory in Jesus: Living Answers for a Dying World. North Brunswick, NJU: Bridge-Logos, 1996. xxiii, 232 pp. Paper. 0882706942.

Stories of Jesus Christ transforming the lives of alcoholics, homosexuals, gang members, homeless people, prostitutes, drug addicts, and AIDS patients; by the founder and Director of Victory in Jesus, a ministry to the unchurched and downtrodden in the inner city.

AM1223 Magnusom, Norris

Salvation in the Slums: Evangelical Social Work, 1865-1920. Grand Rapids, MIU: Baker Books, 1990. xx, 299 pp. Paper. 0801062616.

Analysis of the urban welfare activities of the Salvation Army, the Volunteers of America, the CMA, multiple rescue missions and homes, and the religious journal *Christian Herald* during the time period; originally published in 1977 by Scarecrow Press, Metuchen, NJU.

AM1224 McNamee, John P.

Diary of a City Priest. Kansas City, MOU: Sheed and Ward, 1993. 258 pp. Paper. 155612662X.

An account, by a Catholic parish priest, of more than twenty-five years of ministry in poorer neighborhoods of Philadelphia.

AM1225 Moore, Paul

The Church Reclaims the City. New York, NYU: Seabury Press, 1964. xiii, 241 pp. No ISBN.

A practical handbook on urban inner-city mission, filled with examples from the author's experiences in Jersey City (New Jersey) and Indianapolis (Indiana) as an Episcopal priest and bishop.

AM—THE AMERICAS

AM1226 Phillips, Keith W.
They Dare to Love the Ghetto. Los Angeles, CAU: World Impact, 1976. 192 pp. Paper. 0830705112.

    The story of incarnational mission among the inner-city poor of the United States.

AM1227 Rosenberg, Carroll Smith
Religion and the Rise of the American City: The New York City Mission Movement, 1812-1870. Ithaca, NYU: Cornell University Press, 1971. x, 300 pp. 0801406595.

    A study of how religious sentiment, poverty, and the growth of cities interacted to shape the patterns of benevolence in America, 1812-1870.

AM1228 Scheuring, Tom, Lyn Scheuring, and Marybeth Greene, eds.
The Poor and the Good News: A Call to Evangelize. New York, NYU: Paulist Press, 1993. v, 162 pp. Paper. 0809133598.

    A narrative account of nine years (1983-1991) of a Catholic ministry in the New York area, told by the founders of LAMP (Lay Apostolic Ministry "With" the Poor).

AM1229 Stumme, Wayne, ed.
The Experience of Hope: Mission and Ministry in Changing Urban Communities. Minneapolis, MNU: Augsburg Fortress, 1991. 144 pp. Paper. 0806625465.

    Twelve essays describing Lutheran efforts in the United States to carry out the church's mission, and to exercise creative ministries in changing urban communities.

AM1230 Van Houten, Mark E.
God's Inner-City Address: Crossing the Boundaries. Grand Rapids, MIU: Zondervan, 1988. 139 pp. Paper. 0310520118.

    A practical help for people who are serious about living out the Gospel through inner-city ministry; by a minister to homeless youth through the Northside Ecumenical Night Ministry in Chicago, Illinois.

AM1231 Villafañe, Eldin
Seek the Peace of the City: Reflections on Urban Ministry. Grand Rapids, MIU: Eerdmans, 1995. xiv, 146 pp. Paper. 0802807291.

    A collection of essays on urban sociotheology, urban ministry, and urban theological education, by the Director of Gordon-Conwell Theological Seminary's program of contextualized urban theological education in Boston.

AM1232 Webber, George W.
God's Colony in Man's World. Nashville, TNU: Abingdon, 1960. 155 pp. No ISBN.

    A thoughtful, sincere, and powerful book about the Christian mission on the New York frontier, by a leader of the East Harlem Protestant Parish.

AM1233 Wilkerson, David, John L. Sherrill, and Elizabeth Sherrill
The Cross and the Switchblade. Grand Rapids, MIU: Chosen Books, 2000. 217 pp. Paper. 0800790707.

    A narrative account of a creative ministry to street gangs by a Pentecostal pastor in New York City; originally published in 1963 (New York: Pillar Books).

AM1234 Wilkerson, David, John L. Sherrill, and Elizabeth Sherrill
La Cruz y el Puñal. Translated by Banjamín E. Mercado. New York, NYU: Teen Challenge, 1969. 206 pp. No ISBN.

    Spanish translation.

AM1235 Woodworth, Ralph
Light in a Dark Place: "The Story of Chicago's Oldest Rescue Mission." Winona Lake, INU: Light & Life Press, 1978. 127 pp. Paper. 0893670227.

    A centennial history of Chicago's oldest rescue mission, the Free Methodist's Olive Branch Mission, established on the near-west side of Chicago in 1876.

South America: General Works

See also AM431, AM533, and AM544.

AM1236 Capelle, M. C.
Christen in Zuid-Amerika. Amsterdam, NE: Buijten en Schipperheijn, 1977. 239 pp. 9060640586.

    An introduction, with illustrations, to the history and present vitality of Protestantism in South America.

AM1237 CELAM, Departamento de Misiones
Pastoral Indígena hoy, en la Amazonia. (Colección Demis, 10). Bogotá, CK: CELAM, 1989. 148 pp. Paper. 9586251489.

    A collection of papers and conclusions from the Episcopal Convocation on Indigenous Pastoral Work in the Amazon, (Fusagasuga, Colombia, 23-28 August 1988).

AM1238 Favero, Luigi, ed.
Religión e Inmigración. (Estudios Migratorios Latinoamericanos, 5, n.14). Buenos Aires, AG: Estudios Migratorios Latinoamericanos, 1990. 250 pp. Paper. No ISBN.

    A monograph with nine historical and thematic studies of Catholic and Protestant immigration to South America.

AM1239 Fuller, W. Harold
Tie Down the Sun: Adventure in Latin America. Scarborough, ONC: SIM Publications, 1990. xviii, 364 pp. Paper. 0919470262.

    Vignettes of evangelical missions in South America, based on the author's travels of over 20,000 miles on the continent as deputy general director for SIM; includes related literature.

AM1240 Hamilton, Keith E.
Church Growth in the High Andes. Eugene, ORU: Institute of Church Growth, 1962. vii, 146 pp. No ISBN.

    Factors affecting response to its Gospel among Quechua- and Aymara-speaking inhabitants of Ecuador, Peru, and Bolivia; by a missionary who worked among them.

AM1241 Janssen, Arnold
Briefe nach Südamerika. (Studia Institute Missiologici SVD, 43-44). Nettetal, GW: Steyler Verlag, 1991. xiv, 528 pp. Paper. 380500267X (vol. 1), 380500267X (vol. 2), 3805002300 (set).

    A scholarly edition of letters by Arnold Janssen (edited by Josef Alt) to members of his missionary society (SVD) in Latin America, written 1890-1899 (vol. 1) and 1900-1902 (vol. 2); reflect not only the personality of the author, but also the situation of the Latin American churches at that time.

AM1242 Kliewer, Gerd Uwe
Das neue Volk der Pfingstler: Religion, Unterentwicklung und sozialer Wandel in Lateinamerika. (Studies in the Intercultural History of Christianity, 3). Frankfurt am Main, GW: Lang, 1975. 229 pp. Paper. 3261009969.

    A sociological study of the development of social concerns among Pentecostals in Brazil and Chile.

AM1243 Link, Hans-Georg, ed.
Confessing Our Faith around the World: IV, South America.
(Faith and Order Paper, 126). Geneva, SZ: WCC, 1985. xi,
111 pp. Paper. 2825408395.

Part IV of a WCC series, "Confessing Our Faith Around
the World," that contains contemporary expressions of faith
from nine countries of South America, useful both for personal devotion and liturgically.

AM1244 Palmer, Bernard, and Marjorie Palmer
*While the Sun Is High: The Story of Evangelical Free Church
Missions in South America.* (Heritage Series, 7). Minneapolis, MNU: Free Church Publications, 1984. 493 pp. Paper.
0911802606.

The second in a three-volume popular history of the Overseas Mission Department of the Evangelical Free Church, telling of the work done in Venezuela and Peru.

AM1245 Sand, Faith Annette
Travels of Faith. Pasadena, CAU: Hope Publishing House,
1986. iv, 138 pp. Paper. 0932727034.

Reminiscences of twenty years (1962-1982) of mission
encounters, from Spain, Brazil, Peru, Thailand, Colombia,
and Guatemala, by a second generation missionary, who grew
in cultural sensitivity and justice concerns.

AM1246 Smith, Brian H.
*Religious Politics in Latin America, Pentecostal vs. Catho-
lic.* (The Helen Kellog Institute for International Studies).
Notre Dame, INU: University of Notre Dame Press, 1998.
vii, 126 pp. Paper. 0268016623.

A study of the intersection of Catholicism and Pentecostalism; newly appointed conservative bishops feel obliged to
preach a social doctine on behalf of the oppressed, while Pent-
costals are becoming more active in politics and social issues.

AM1247 Turvasi, Francesco
*Giovanni Genocchi and the Indians of South America, 1911-
1913.* (Pontificia Universitas Gregoriana Miscellanea Historiae Pontificiae, 55). Rome, IT: Pontifical Gregorian University, 1988. xix, 152 pp. Paper. 8876525858.

A monograph of the missionary activity of Father Genocchi, a Sacred Heart priest, who was an advocate for the oppressed Indians of the Putumayo River basin in northwest
South America.

AM1248 Winter, Derek
Hope in Captivity: The Prophetic Church in Latin America.
London, ENK: Epworth Press, 1977. 136 pp. 0716202832.

A narrative account of how a former Baptist missionary
to Brazil discovered the Latin American prophetic church
through personal interviews with, and readings of, Latin
American theologians.

South America: Biography

See also AM289 and AM1348.

AM1249 McNaspy, C. J.
*Conquistador without Sword: The Life of Roque Gonzales,
S.J.* Chicago, ILU: Loyola University Press, 1984. 206 pp.
0829404554.

A biography of an American-born priest, who founded
the famed "Reductions," liberated thousands of Guaraní Indians of Paraguay, and was martyred there.

Argentina

See also HI311, PO170, AM325, and AM340.

**AM1250 Albergucci, Roberto, Carlos Alberto Javier Chiesa,
and Francisco J. Piñón**
*Cristianos para el Proyecto Educativo Nacional: Reflexiones
desde los valores cristianos presentes en nuestra cultura, a
la luz de la enseñanza de la Iglesia sobre educación.* (Colección Comunión y participación: Cuadernos de "comunión y
participación," 6). Buenos Aires, AG: Editorial Guadalupe,
1986. 220 pp. Paper. 9505001428.

Analysis of the place of the educational mission of the
Catholic Church in national reconstruction in Argentina.

AM1251 Belza, Juan Esteban, Raúl Agustín Entraigas et al.
La Expedición al Desierto y los Salesianos, 1879. Buenos
Aires, AG: Ediciones Don Bosco, 1979. 240 pp. Paper. No
ISBN.

A collection of four essays on the beginnings and development of the Salesian missions in Patagonia.

AM1252 Bonino, Elva C., de
Maravillas Misioneras en Tierra del Fuego. Buenos Aires,
AG: Fundación Cristiana de Evangelización, 1976. 141 pp.
Paper. No ISBN.

Biographies of two missionaries, Allen Francisco Gardiner and Carlos Rogers.

AM1253 Burdick, Michael A.
*For God and the Fatherland: Religion and Politics in Argen-
tina.* (SUNY Series in Religion, Culture, and Society). Albany, NYU: SUNY Press, 1995. xi, 283 pp. 0791427439 (hdbk),
0791427447 (pbk).

A history of Roman Catholic challenges to right-wing
politics in Argentina, from the 1880s to the present, with special attention to the Movement of Priests for the Third World/
Movimiento de Sacerdotes para el Tercer Mundo (MSTM),
in the 1968 to 1975 period.

AM1254 Campos Menchaca, Mariano José
Naheulbuta. (Biblioteca Francisco de Aguirre, 41). Buenos
Aires, AG: Francisco de Aguirre, 1972. xxiv, 592 pp. Paper.
No ISBN.

Stories and legends of the Araucanian people, and of the
missionary work of Jesuits there.

AM1255 de Gonzáles, Sara A., and Daniel Hallberg
Don Esture: Svensk missionspionjär i Argentina. Stockholm,
SW: Den kristna bokringen, 1982. 169 pp. 9153650565.

A biography on the Swedish Pentecostal missionary in
Argentina, Sture Andersson (1901-).

AM1256 Enns, Arno W.
*Man, Milieu, and Mission in Argentina: A Close Look at
Church Growth.* Grand Rapids, MIU: Eerdmans, 1971. 258
pp. Paper. No ISBN.

A comparative study of ten Protestant denominations in
Argentina, focusing on factors affecting church growth.

AM1257 Furlong, Guillermo
Antonio Ruiz de Montoya y su Carta a Comental, 1645. (Es-
critores Coloniales Rioplatenses, 17). Buenos Aires, AG:
Ediciones Teoría, 1964. 174 pp. Paper. No ISBN.

History of the missionary activities of Antonio Ruiz de
Montoya in the Jesuit reductions, including the text of his
letter to Father Pedro Comental.

AM—THE AMERICAS

AM1258 Furlong, Guillermo
Antonio Sepp S. J. y su "Gobierno Temporal" (1732). (Escritores Coloniales Rioplatenses, 12). Buenos Aires, AG: Ediciones Teoría, 1962. 130 pp. Paper. No ISBN.

History of the missionary activity of Antonio Sepp among the Guaranís of northern Argentina, including the text of his *Gobierno Temporal.*

AM1259 Furlong, Guillermo
Nicolás Mascardi S. J. y su "Carta Relación" (1670). (Escritores Coloniales Rioplatenses, 15). Buenos Aires, AG: Ediciones Teoría, 1963. 138 pp. Paper. No ISBN.

History of the missionary activity of Nicolás Mascardi among the Araucanos and other native people of southern Argentina, including the text of his *Carta y Relación.*

AM1260 Hux, Meinrado
Una Excursión Apostólica del Padre Salvaire a Salinas Grandes según un Esbozo de Diario. Buenos Aires, AG: Ediciones Culturales Argentinas, 1979. 146 pp. No ISBN.

The diary of a French missionary priest, regarding his journey to the Namuncurá tribe in Argentina, during October and November 1875.

AM1261 Massa, Lorenzo
Historia de las Misiones Salesianas en la Pampa, República Argentina. Buenos Aires, AG: Editorial Don Bosco, 1968. 2 vols. Paper. No ISBN.

A history of Salesian missions in the Pampas of Argentina [vol. 1: 442 pp.; vol. 2: 574 pp.].

AM1262 Millé, Andrés
Derrotero de la Compañia de Jesús en la conquista del Perú, Tucumán y Paraguay y sus iglesias del antiguo Buenos Aires, 1567-1768. Buenos Aires, AG: EMECE Editores, 1968. 539 pp. Paper. No ISBN.

A detailed analysis of the mission strategies of the Jesuits in Peru, Paraguay, and Argentina, from their beginnings in the 16th century to their expulsion in 1768.

AM1263 Miller, Elmer S.
Nurturing Doubt: From Mennonite Missionary to Anthropologist in the Argentine Chaco. Urbana, ILU: University of Illinois Press, 1995. xi, 225 pp. 025202155X (hdbk), 0252064550 (pbk).

A first-person account, documenting the transformational effects upon a Mennonite missionary turned anthropologist, of field experience among the Toba people of the Argentine Chaco, 1959 to 1988.

AM1264 Moncaut, Carlos Antonio
Reducción Jesuítica de Nuestra Señora de la Concepción de los Pampas, 1740-1753: Historia de un Pueblo Desaparecido a Orillas del Río Salado Bonaerense. La Plata, AG: Ministerio de Economía de la Provincia de Buenos Aires, 1981. 141 pp. Paper. No ISBN.

A detailed local mission history, with considerable documentation.

AM1265 Montes de Oca, Alba Leticia
Mi Dios y mis Tobas. Buenos Aires, AG: Junta Bautista de Publicaciones, 1976. 175 pp. Paper. No ISBN.

The author's personal testimony of missionary work carried out among the indigenous peoples of northern Argentina.

AM1266 Nash, Joy Balyeat
God's Gaucho: The Life Story of Kent Windsor Balyeat, Mu-
sic Missionary to Argentina. Fort Worth, TXU: Stonehaven Publishers, 1989. vii, 177 pp. Paper. 0962302600.

The story of the musicologist-missionary who established the School of Church Music of the International Baptist Seminary in Buenos Aires, Argentina, written by his sister.

AM1267 Powell, David R.
Historia que Faltaba: El Cristianismo Protestante o Evangélico en Tucumán. Buenos Aires, AG: Editorial Kairós; Tucumán, AG: Instituto de Historia y Pensamiento Argentinos, 1998. 220 pp. Paper. 9879591550.

An exploration of evangelical missionary work and its interaction with Catholicism in Argentina.

AM1268 Szabó, Ladislao
El Hungaro Ladislao Orosz en Tierras Argentinas, 1729-1767. Buenos Aires, AG: FECIC, 1984. 190 pp. Paper. 9509149209.

The story of a remarkable, 18th-century Hungarian Catholic mission to Native Americans, in lands now called Argentina, Uruguay, and Paraguay.

Bolivia

See also SO153, EC60, AM462, and AM710.

AM1269 Adelmann, Sigmund Graf, ed.
Gemeinsam unterwegs: Partnerschaft mit der Kirche Boliviens. Hildesheim, GW: Bernward, 1990. 238 pp. Paper. 3870655461.

Various texts on the present situation in Bolivia and possibilities of partnership with the Catholic Church there.

AM1270 Alonso, Isidoro, Ginés Garrido et al.
La Iglesia en Perú y Bolivia: Estructuras eclesiásticas. (Estudios Socio-religiosos Latino-americanos, 3/II). Friburgo, SZ: FERES, 1962. 271 pp. Paper. No ISBN.

A socioreligious study of social and ecclesiastical structures in Peru and Bolivia.

AM1271 Bösl, Antonio Eduardo
Bolivien-Report: Erlebnisberichte und Situationsbilder aus einer Franziskaner-Mission in Boliviens Urwald. (Edited by Franziskaner Missions-Verein in Bayern e.V.). Munich, GW: Franziskaner Missions-Verein in Bayern, 1975-1988. 4 vols. Paper. No ISBN.

Reports by the local bishop on the missionary activities of the Franciscans from Bavaria, who have worked in the Vicariate Apostolic Ñuflo de Chávez in Bolivia since 1951; presented in four volumes (vol. 1: 1975, 144 pp., No ISBN; vol. 2: 1982, 232 pp., No ISBN; vol. 3: 1984, 163 pp., 3890040314; vol. 4: 1988, 302 pp., 3890040349).

AM1272 Barkman, Betty
Anna: A Life of Stubbornness Made into Joyous Service. Winnipeg, MBC: Kindred Press, 1985. x, 171 pp. Paper. 0919797105.

The story of a remarkable Mennonite missionary to Bolivia, told perceptively, without sentimentality, and with a grasp of the issues involved.

AM1273 Bell, Inez Josephine, ed.
The Kantuta Blooms in Bolivia. Wolfville, NSC: Gaspereau Press, 1997. 152 pp. Paper. No ISBN.

Reprint of a narrative history of the Baptist Church in Bolivia; originally published in 1971 (Toronto, ONC: Canadian Baptist Overseas Mission Board).

AM1274 Berg, Hans van den
La Tierra no da así no más: Los ritos agrícolas en la religión de los aymara–cristianos. (Yachay, Temas monográficos, 5). La Paz-Cochabamba, BO: HISBOL-UCB/ISET, 1990. 352 pp. Paper. No ISBN.

An anthropological study of the encounter of the Aymara culture with Christianity; also published by CEDLA, Amsterdam, the Netherlands (1989, 291 pp.) in the Latin American Studies Series, 51.

AM1275 Block, David
Mission Culture on the Upper Amazon: Native Tradition, Jesuit Enterprise, and Secular Policy in Moxos, 1660-1880. Lincoln, NBU: University of Nebraska Press, 1994. xiii, 240 pp. 0803212321.

A pioneer ethnohistory of the Moxos people, of what is now northern or lowland Bolivia, from the arrival of the Jesuits in 1660, through the development of a distinctive mission culture, to the cataclysm of Jesuit expulsion, exploitation by rubber barons, and conflict.

AM1276 Brackney, William H., ed.
Bridging Cultures and Hemispheres: The Legacy of Archibald Reekie and Canadian Baptists in Bolivia. Macon, GAU: Smyth & Helwys, 1997. xviii, 341 pp. 1573121659.

Stories of pioneer and, later, Canadian Baptist missionaries in Bolivia, 1897 to 1996.

AM1277 Conferencia Episcopal de Bolivia a la IV Conferencia del Episcopado Latino Americano S. Domingo 1992
Nueva Evangelización Promoción Humana Cultura Cristiana. Santa Domingo, BO: La Paz, 1992. iv, 164 pp. Paper. No ISBN.

The report of the Episcopal Conference of Bolivia to the 4th Conference of Latin American bishops (CELAM IV, Santo Domingo, 1992).

AM1278 Gruber, Ludwig
Ich denke an Bolivien: Begegnungen mit der Welt der Aymara-Indianer. Munich, GW: Pfeiffer, 1988. 182 pp. 3790405256.

The thirteen chapters of this narrative reflect the author's experiences during two stays among the Aymara Indians, in Bolivia (1970-1972 and 1985), which were sponsored by Misereor.

AM1279 Johansson, Goran
More Blessed to Give: A Pentecostal Mission to Bolivia in Anthropological Perspective. (Stockholm Studies in Social Anthropology, 30). Stockholm, SW: Stockholm University, 1992. xi, 254 pp. Paper. 9171530169.

A detailed analysis, based on field research in 1987-1989, of the interactions between the Nordic Pentecostal Mission to Bolivia during its seventh decade, and the native church; originally presented as a doctoral dissertation at Stockholm University.

AM1280 Nordyke, Quentin
Animistic Aymaras and Church Growth. Newburg, ORU: Barclay Press, 1972. xiv, 200 pp. 0913342017.

A psychological and anthropological study in Bolivia and Peru.

AM1281 Palcio, Eudoxio, and José Brunet
Los Mercedarios en Bolivia. La Paz, BO: Universidad Mayor de San Andrés/H. Alcaldía Municipal de la Paz, 1977. 404 pp. No ISBN.

A collection of documents concerning the activities of the Order of Our Lady of Mercy (Mercedavians), in Bolivia from 1535 to 1975; including photographs.

AM1282 Peritore, Patrick N.
Socialism, Communism, and Liberation Theology in Brazil: An Opinion Survey Using Q-Methodology. (Monographs in International Studies; Latin America Series, 15). Athens, OHU: Ohio University, 1990. xviii, 245 pp. 089680156X.

A study seeking to discover the major currents of opinion concerning liberation theology, in the twelve parties of the socialist and communist left, as well as in the Catholic Church, and the extent to which they incorporate the thought and practice of Paulo Freire.

AM1283 Rizzo, Kay D.
Determined to Love: The Story of Ferdinand and Ana Stahl. Boise, IDU: Pacific Press, 1988. 80 pp. Paper. 081630727X.

Stories written in a popular style of the work of pioneer Seventh-day Adventist missionaries, Ferdinand and Ana Stahl; in Peru, 1917 to 1939.

AM1284 Ströbele-Gregor, Juliana
Dialektik der Gegenaufklärung: Zur Problematik fundamentalistischer und evangelikaler Missionierung bei den urbanen Aymara in La Paz (Bolivien). (Mundus Reihe Ethnologie, 24). Bonn, GW: Holos Verlag, 1988. xi, 369 pp. Paper. 3926216239.

A description and analysis of social and religious data collected during a twelve-month stay in an Adventist community in La Paz.

AM1285 Wagner, C. Peter
Defeat of the Bird God. South Pasadena, CAU: William Carey Library, 1975. 256 pp. 0878087214.

An account of the work of the South American Mission among the nomadic Ayore people of eastern Bolivia and northern Paraguay, mid-1940s to mid-1960s.

AM1286 Wagner, C. Peter
The Protestant Movement in Bolivia. South Pasadena, CAU: William Carey Library, 1970. xxii, 240 pp. 0878084029.

A revision of the missiologist's master's thesis (Fuller), surveying factors affecting Protestant church growth in Bolivia.

Brazil

See also TH285, TH497, TH597, CR551-CR552, CR1441, CR1466, SO37, SO376-SO379, EC188, EC278, PO85, PO90-PO93, PO100, PO136, ED75, CH344, CH346, SP134, AM24, AM238, AM242-AM244, AM379, AM381, AM401, AM411, and AM1412.

AM1287 Adriance, Madeleine
Opting for the Poor: Brazilian Catholicism in Transition. Kansas City, MOU: Sheed and Ward, 1986. vii, 200 pp. Paper. 0934134758.

An analysis of change within the Roman Catholic Church in Brazil, from charity understood as almsgiving, to participation in the struggle for social justice, which includes conflict with political authorities.

AM1288 Adriance, Madeleine
Promised Land: Base Christian Communities and the Struggle for the Amazon. Albany, NYU: SUNY Press, 1995. xxii, 202 pp. 0791426491 (hdbk), 0791426505 (pbk).

A socio-anthropologist's firsthand study of the involvement of Catholic base communities in northern Brazil in the struggle of indigenous peoples for land rights.

AM1289 Alves, Rubem A.
Protestantism and Repression: A Brazilian Case Study. Translated by John Drury. Maryknoll, NYU: Orbis Books, 1985. 256 pp. 0883440989.

A sociological and theological analysis of the Presbyterian church in Brazil, which, through a "Right-Doctrine" Protestantism, came to support the national security system, and repression of movements for social change.

AM1290 Antoine, Charles
Church and Power in Brazil. Translated by Peter Nelson. Maryknoll, NYU: Orbis Books; London, ENK: Sheed & Ward, 1973. xi, 275 pp. Paper. 0722073003.

English translation.

AM1291 Antoine, Charles
Kirche und Macht in Brasilien. [Graz], AU: Verlag Styria, 1972. 292 pp. 3222107211.

German translation.

AM1292 Antoine, Charles
L'Église et le pouvoir au Brésil: naissance du militarisme. Paris, FR: Desclée de Brouwer, 1971. 269 pp. No ISBN.

An insider's account of the first five years of military rule (1964-1996), and the responses to it by Roman Catholics; by a Catholic missionary who served as student chaplain and newspaper editor until exiled from Brazil.

AM1293 Azevedo, Ferdinand
Ensino, Jornalismo e Missões Jesuíticas em Pernambuco, 1866-1874. Recife, BL: Fundaçcão Antônio dos Santos Abranches, 1983. 163 pp. Paper. No ISBN.

Second edition of a history of Jesuit 19th-century mission work in Pernambuco, Brazil.

AM1294 Azevedo, Marcello de Carvalho
Basic Ecclesial Communities in Brazil: The Challenge of a New Way of Being Church. Translated by John Drury. Washington, DCU: Georgetown University Press, 1987. xiii, 304 pp. Paper. 0878404309 (hdbk), 0878404481 (pbk).

An English translation.

AM1295 Azevedo, Marcello de Carvalho
Communidades eclesiais de base e inculturação da fé: a realidade das CEBs e sua tematizao teórica, na perspectiva de uma evangelização inculturada. (Coleção "Fé e realidade," 19). São Paulo, BL: Edições Loyola, 1986. 416 pp. No ISBN.

An analysis of the basic elements underlying the present-day reality of BECs (theologically, pastorally, and institutionally), with projections of their future development.

AM1296 Bachmann, E. Theodore
Lutherans in Brazil: A Story of Emerging Ecumenism. Minneapolis, MNU: Augsburg, 1970. 79 pp. Paper. No ISBN.

A popular introduction to Brazil, its history, sociology, and religious trends.

AM1297 Barbé, Dominique
La grâce et le pouvoir: Les communautés de base au Brésil. (Rencontres International, 27). Paris, FR: Éditions du Cerf, 1982. 213 pp. 2204018708.

A wide range of information about Brazilian struggles for liberation, as seen through the eyes of a French priest working among the poor of São Paulo.

AM1298 Barbé, Dominique
Grace and Power: Base Communities and Nonviolence in Brazil. Translated by John Pairman Brown. Maryknoll, NYU: Orbis Books, 1987. x, 150 pp. Paper. 0883444186.

English translation.

AM1299 Benton, Peggie
Um Homem contra a sêca: Luta e realizaçâo no Brasil. Rio de Janeiro, BL: AGIR Editora, 1973. 216 pp. Paper. No ISBN.

Portuguese translation.

AM1300 Benton, Peggie
One Man against the Drylands: Struggle and Achievement in Brazil. London, ENK: Collins & Harvill, 1972. 223 pp. 000262608X.

A popular account of a Catholic priest's involvement in community development in northeast Brazil.

AM1301 Beozzo, José Oscar
A Igreja do Basil: De João XXIII a João Paulo II, de Medellin a Santo Domingo. (Coleção Igreja do Brasil). Petrópolis, BL: Editores Vozes, 1994. 324 pp. 8532611273.

A thirty-five year history (1958-1993) of the Catholic Church in Brazil, by the Chairman of CEHILA.

AM1302 Bispo, Antonio Alexandre et al.
Collectanea musicae sacrae Brasiliensis. (Musices aptatio: Liber annaurius, 1981). Rome, IT: Sekretariat der CIMS, 1981. 341 pp. Paper. No ISBN.

Historical and ethnographical articles in German, Portuguese, English, French, and Italian, on Brazilian church music.

AM1303 Boff, Clodovis
Feet-on-the-Ground Theology: A Brazilian Journey. Translated by Phillip Berryman. Maryknoll, NYU: Orbis Books, 1987. xv, 185 pp. Paper. 0883445794 (hdbk), 0883445549 (pbk).

English translation.

AM1304 Boff, Clodovis
Teologia pé-no-chão. (Publicações CID. Pastoral, 9). Petrópolis, BL: Editora Vozes, 1984. 230 pp. No ISBN.

A day-to-day account of a five-month missionary journey, among people of western Brazil, giving a portrait of the church of the poor.

AM1305 Brakemeier, Gottfried, ed.
Glaube im Teilen bewahrt: Lutherische Existenz in Brasilien. (Erlanger Taschenbücher, 92). Erlangen, GW: Ev.-Luth. Mission, 1989. 259 pp. Paper. 3872141929.

A series of essays on the Lutheran presence in Brazil: the land, churches, and theology; Lutheran church; and Lutheran confessions.

AM1306 Bruneau, Thomas C.
The Church in Brazil: The Politics of Religion. (Latin American Monographs, 56). Austin, TXU: University of Texas Press, 1982. xvi, 237 pp. 0292710712.

A first attempt in Brazil, to assess the influence of the Roman Catholic Church, through a survey, in-depth interviews, participant observation, and an analysis of documents.

AM1307 Bruneau, Thomas C.
The Political Transformation of the Brazilian Catholic Church. (Perspectives on Development, 2). London, ENK: Cambridge University Press, 1974. xiv, 270 pp. 0521202566 (hdbk), 0521098483 (pbk).

This analysis of the Brazilian church focuses, in particular, on its political role in relation to church and society issues.

AM1308 Burdick, John
Looking for God in Brazil: The Progressive Catholic Church in Urban Brazil's Religious Arena. Berkeley, CAU: University of California Press, 1993. xii, 280 pp. 0520080009.

Based on extensive fieldwork, a social-anthropologist analyzes why the radical Catholicism of the base communities is losing followers among the urban poor of Rio de Janeiro, while Pentecostalism and Umbanda are gaining.

AM1309 Cabestrero, Teófilo
Diálogos en Mato Grosso con Pedro Casaldáliga. (Tierra Dos Tercios, 7). Salamanca, SP: Ediciones Sígueme, 1978. 188 pp. Paper. 8430107169.

Texts of interviews conducted with Bishop Casaldáliga, in which he discusses his efforts on behalf of campesinos, workers, and indigenous peoples, as well as the repression he has endured.

AM1310 Cabestrero, Teófilo
Mystic of Liberation: A Portrait of Pedro Casaldaliga. Translated by Donald D. Walsh. Maryknoll, NYU: Orbis Books, 1981. xxii, 200 pp. Paper. 0883443244.

English translation.

AM1311 Chamarro, Graciela
Kurusu ñe ëngatu: Palabras que la historia no podria olvidar. (Biblioteca paraguaya de antropología, 25). Asunción, PY: Universidad Católica, Centro de Estudios Antropológicoss; São Leopoldo, BL: Instituto Ecuménico de Posgrado, Escuela Superior de Teología; São Leopoldo, BL: Consejo de Misión entre Indios, 1995. 235 pp. No ISBN.

A case study of indigenous expressions of faith through song, by the Kaiová-Guaraní indigenous people of Mato Grosso do Sul, Brazil.

AM1312 Chestnut, R. Andrew
Born Again in Brazil: The Pentecostal Boom and the Pathogens of Poverty. New Brunswick, NJU: Rutgers University Press, 1997. x, 203 pp. 0813524059 (hdbk), 0813524067 (pbk).

After tracing the historical development of Pentecostalism in Brazil, and its social and economic context, the author shares the findings of his ethnographic research, showing the relationship between faith healing and illness in a conversion process integral to the popularity of Pentecostalism among Brazil's poor.

AM1313 Christo, Carlos Alberto Libanio
Against Principalities and Powers: Letters from a Brazilian Jail. Maryknoll, NYU: Orbis Books, 1977. xiii, 241 pp. Paper. 0883440075 (hdbk), 0883440083 (pbk).

A collection of the letters of a Dominican seminarian, in a Brazilian jail from 1969 to 1973, that reveal his spiritual journey to a commitment to live and work among the poor in Vitoria, Brazil; also published as *Letters from a Prisoner of Conscience* (London: Lutterworth).

AM1314 Christo, Carlos Alberto Libanio
Dai sotterranei della storia. Milan, IT: Mondadori, 1971. 241 pp. No ISBN.

The personal observations and correspondence of a prisoner of conscience in Brazil.

AM1315 Conde, Emilio
História das Assembléias de Deus no Brasil. Rio de Janeiro, BL: CPAD, 1984. 368 pp. Paper. No ISBN.

Second edition of a detailed chronicle of events since 1910; first published in 1960.

AM1316 Corten, André
Le pentecôtisme au Brésil: Émotion du pauvre et romantisme théologique. Paris, FR: Editions Karthala, 1995. 307 pp. 2865375633.

A political scientist explores a utopia of equality, love, and emotion, staged during the worship service, as well as wider contextual issues such as liberation theology, piety, and prosperity, authoritarianism, and the marketing of the faith.

AM1317 Corten, André
Pentecostalism in Brazil: Emotion of the Poor and Theological Romanticism. Translated by Arianne Dorval. London, ENK: Macmillan Press; New York, NYU: St. Martin's Press, 1999. xix, 206 pp. 033374473X (UK), 0312225067 (US).

English translation.

AM1318 Day, Dan
Burning Hope. Boise, IDU: Pacific Press, 1987. 80 pp. Paper. 0816307237.

Stories of the pioneer mission work along the Amazon River of Brazil, during the 1920s and 1930s, by Hans Mayr, a German missionary of the Seventh-day Adventist church.

AM1319 Dias, Zwinglio
Krisen und Aufgaben im brasilianischen Protestantismus: Eine Studie zu den sozialgeschichtlichen Bedingungen und volkspädagogischen Möglichkeiten der Evangelisation. (Studies in the Intercultural History of Christianity, 18). Frankfurt am Main, GW: Lang, 1978. 369 pp. Paper. 3261026502.

An analysis of the historical context of Protestantism in Brazil, with a critical reflection on a renewal of the traditional church praxis.

AM1320 Droogers, A. F.
Macht in Zin: Een drieluik van Braziliaanse religieuze verbeelding. Amsterdam, NE: VU Uitgeverij, 1990. 56 pp. Paper. 9062568912.

A lecture at the Free University on the "symbolism of religious strength," as expressed in symbolism relating the human to the strength and power of the divine; with examples of three religious groups in Brazil (Umbanda, Pentacostal churches, and BCCs), in which each talk about religious strength.

AM1321 Edwards, Fred E.
The Role of the Faith Mission: A Brazilian Case Study. South Pasadena, CAU: William Carey Library, 1971. xxiii, 139 pp. 0878084061.

A brief history, statistical survey, and comparative analysis of mission and church growth strategies.

AM1322 Farace, Frederick A.
Love's Harvest: The Life of Blessed Pauline. Milford, OHU: Riehle Foundation, 1994. viii, 112 pp. Paper. 1877678317.

The story of Mother Pauline—the Mother Teresa of Brazil—who founded the Little Sisters of the Immaculate Conception and worked with the poor.

AM—THE AMERICAS

AM1323 Fragoso, Antônio Batista
Cercando un volto nuovo: Esodo di una chiesa latinoameri-cana. (Quaderni ASAL, 37). Bologna, IT: EMI, 1984. 137 pp. No ISBN.
    Italian translation.

AM1324 Fragoso, Antônio Batista
Face of a Church: A Nascent Church of the People in Cra-teus, Brazil. Translated by Robert R. Barr. Maryknoll, NYU: Orbis Books, 1987. xii, 164 pp. Paper. 088344576X (hdbk), 0883445514 (pbk).
    English translation.

AM1325 Fragoso, Antônio Batista
O rosto de uma igreja. São Paulo, BL: Edições Loyola, 1982. 153 pp. No ISBN.
    An historical account by the first Catholic bishop of the new rural diocese of Crateus, with personal testimonies of co-workers in the BECs of northeastern Brazil.

AM1326 Gates, Charles W.
Industrialization: Brazil's Catalyst for Church Growth: A Study of the Rio Area. South Pasadena, CAU: William Carey Library, 1972. xi, 78 pp. Paper. 0878084134.
    A case study of Protestant church growth in metropoli-tan Rio de Janeiro, demonstrating that industrialization re-sults in social mobility, with new openings for religious change.

AM1327 Giacone, Antonio
Trentacique anni fra le tribù del Rio Uapès (Amazonia—Brasile). Rome, IT: LAS, 1976. 239 pp. No ISBN.
    An illustrated history of Salesian missions among tribal groups along the Uaupe River in Amazonia, Brazil, from 1924 to 1960; with ethnographic and linguistic data.

AM1328 Gillies, John
The Martyrs of Guanabara. Chicago, ILU: Moody, 1976. 174 pp. 080245187X.
    A novel, based on fact, about the Hugenot involvement in 16th-century Brazil.

AM1329 Goss-Mayr, Hildegard
Die Macht der Gewaltlosen: Der Christ und die Revolution am Beispiel Brasiliens. Graz, AU: Verlag Styria, 1968. 284 pp. No ISBN.
    The causes of mass poverty in Latin America, exempli-fied by northeast Brazil, and the role of Christians in the strug-gle, violent and non-violent, for justice.

AM1330 Guider, Margaret Eletta
Daughters of Rahab: Prostitution and the Church of Libera-tion in Brazil. (Harvard Theological Studies, 40). Minneap-olis, MNU: Fortress Press, 1995. xiv, 235 pp. Paper. 0800670930.
    An analysis of 500 years of prostitution in Brazil—its history, social meaning, and responses by the Catholic Church; based on primary source documents and field research with marginalized women.

AM1331 Hall, Mary
The Impossible Dream: The Spirituality of Dom Helder Cà-mara. Maryknoll, NYU: Orbis Books, 1980. 96 pp. Paper. 0883442124.
    Eighteen vignettes on the prophetic ministry of the Ro-man Catholic Archbishop of Recife, Brazil, based on inter-views with him.

AM1332 Hartmann, Günter
Christliche Basisgruppen und ihre befreiende Praxis: Erfahr-ungen im Nordosten Brasiliens. (Gesellschaft und Theolo-gie: Fundamentaltheologische Studien, 2). Munich, GW: Kai-ser; Mainz, GW: Grünewald Verlag, 1981. 213 pp. Paper. 3459012633 (K), 3786707936 (G).
    Descriptions and reflections by a team consisting of (priest, religious sister, and social worker), in the state of Bahia, between 1966 and 1972, and the consequences for Christian commitment today.

AM1333 Hemming, John
Amazon Frontier: The Defeat of the Brazilian Indians. Cam-bridge, MAU: Harvard University Press, 1987. xv, 647 pp. 0674017250.
    A detailed narrative account of European exploitation and Indian resistance in Brazil, 1755-1910, with special at-tention to the roles of missionaries and anthropologists.

AM1334 Hess, David J.
Spirits and Scientists: Ideology, Spiritism, and Brazilian Culture. University Park, PAU: Pennsylvania State Univer-sity Press, 1991. xii, 260 pp. 0271007249.
    Detailed case studies of Brazilian spiritism and its roots in popular Catholicism, West African religion, and European parasciences; based on the author's doctoral dissertation (Cor-nell University, 1987).

AM1335 Hewitt, W. E.
Base Christian Communities and Social Change in Brazil. Lincoln, NEU: University of Nebraska Press, 1991. xvi, 150 pp. 0803223560.
    A critical, comprehensive, and detailed social scientific analysis of the BCCs of Brazil, focusing on their origins and organizational structures, as well as their present and poten-tial sociopolitical impact.

AM1336 Hofius, Erna, ed.
Mein Herz gehört den Indianern. Metzingen, GW: Brunnquell-Verlag der Bibel- und Missions-Stiftung, 1977. 110 pp. Pa-per. 3765600253.
    Third edition of a biography of Gisela Kruck, Wycliff Bible translator, who lost her life in an airplane accident while on the Brazilian mission field; also includes the eulogy by Wycliff translator H. Gaertner; first published in 1972.

AM1337 Hoornaert, Eduardo et al.
História da Igreja no Brasil. São Paulo, BL: Petrópolis; Edições Paulina: Editora Vozes, 1985. 2 vols. Paper. No ISBN.
    The CEHILA history of Christianity in Latin America, covering Roman Catholicism in Brazil during the colonial era [vol. 2/1: *Historia da Igreja no Brasil: Ensaio de interpreta-cao a partir do pove (Primera epoca)* by Eduardo Hoormaert, Riolando Azzi, and others (1983, 442 pp.); vol. 2/2: *Ensaio de interpretacao a partir do povo; segunda epoca: A Igreja no Brasil no seculo XIX* by Klaus van der Grijp, Benno Brod, and others (1985, 322 pp.]; originally published in 1977 (Petrópolis: Editora Vozes).

AM1338 Ireland, Rowan
Kingdoms Come: Religion and Politics in Brazil. (Pitt Latin American Series). Pittsburgh, PAU: University of Pittsburgh Press, 1991. xi, 262 pp. 0822936968.
    An in-depth field study, in northeast Brazil, of popular religion in a town near Recife, including folk Catholicism, Protestant Pentecostalism, and Afro-Brazilian spiritism.

AM1339 Jahn, Christoph, ed.
Es begann am Rio dos Sinos: Geschichte und Gegenwart der Ev. Kirche Lutherischen Bekenntnisses in Brasilien. (Erlanger Taschenbücher, 9). Erlangen, GW: Ev.-Luth. Mission, 1970. 207 pp. Paper. 3872140086.

Second edition, in which twenty-four German and German-Brazilian authors provide an introduction to the Evangelical Lutheran church in Brazil, covering such fields as history, pastoral priorities, and ministry to the Indians.

AM1340 Krause, Henrique
Lutherische Synode in Brasilien: Geschichte und Bekenntnis der Evangelisch-Lutherischen Synode von Santa Catarina, Parana und anderen Staaten Brasiliens. (Erlanger Monographien aus Mission und Ökumene, 10). Erlangen, GW: Ev.-Luth. Mission, 1993. 345 pp. Paper. 3872143107.

A history of the Evangelical Lutheran Synod of Santa Catarina, Parana, and other states of Brazil, and of support from the Lutherische Gotteskastenvereine (later the Martin-Luther-Bund), as well as from synods in Ohio and Iowa; based on archival material on two continents.

AM1341 Lancaster, Daniel B.
The Bagbys of Brazil: The Life and Work of William Buck and Anne Luther Bagby. (Texas Baptist Leaders, 3). Austin, TXU: Eakin Press, 1999. xv, 160 pp. 1571682511.

The missionary struggles and triumphs of the Bagbys in Brazil and in San Salvador, 1881 to 1939, where they founded the first Brazilian Baptist church in Salvador, Bahía; based on their personal letters and reports.

AM1342 Landim, Leilah, ed.
Igrejas e seitas no Brasil. (Cadernos do ISER, 21). Rio de Janeiro, BL: Cadernos do ISER, 1989. 114 pp. No ISBN.

A monograph containing the four central themes of a seminar on the church and sects in Brazil (Rio de Janeiro, July 1987); convened at the initiative of the Conselho Nacional de Igrejas Cristas.

AM1343 Leite, Serafim, ed.
Monumenta Brasiliae. (Monumenta Historica Societatis Jesu, 87, 99; Monumenta Missionum Societatis Jesu, 17, 26). Rome, IT: Institutum Historicum Societatis Jesu, 1960. 2 vols. Paper. No ISBN.

A multi-volume collection of documents in Portuguese, Spanish, and Latin, pertaining to the 16th-century Jesuit missions in Brazil [vol. 4: *1563-1568* (1960, 637 pp.); vol. 5: *sive Complementa Azevediana 1: 1539-1565* (1968, 513 pp.)]; also published in the series *Missiones Occidentales*—other volumes published before 1960.

AM1344 MacLean, Iain S.
Opting for Democracy?: Liberation Theology and the Struggle for Democracy in Brazil. (Studies in Religion, Politics, and Public Life, 2). New York, NYU: Lang, 1999. xv, 264 pp. 0820440116.

Through an analysis of Brazilian liberation theologians, Catholic social teaching, and BCCs (1964-1992), the author challenges the notion that liberation theology rejects democracy and embraces a new form of socialism.

AM1345 Mainwaring, Scott
The Catholic Church and Politics in Brazil, 1916-1985. Stanford, CAU: Stanford University Press, 1986. xv, 328 pp. 0804713200.

The first of a trilogy, dealing with the social and political realities of three large Brazilian states, as well as an analysis of radical Catholicism in Brazil, from 1916 to 1985.

AM1346 Mariz, Cecília Loreto
Coping with Poverty: Pentecostals and Christian Base Communities in Brazil. Philadelphia, PAU: Temple University Press, 1994. ix, 195 pp. 1566391121 (hdbk), 156639113X (pbk).

A Brazilian sociologist, through observation, interviews, and document analysis, studies the place of religion in the lives of Brazil's poorest citizens, contrasting the influence of Assembly of God churches and Roman Catholic BCCs, as well as other Pentecostal churches, folk Catholic tradition, and Afro-Brazilian spiritism.

AM1347 Mizuki, John
The Growth of Japanese Churches in Brazil. South Pasadena, CAU: William Carey Library, 1978. xxii, 213 pp. Paper. 0878083235.

A detailed historical and sociological study.

AM1348 *Paulo Evaristo Arns: cardeal da esperança e pastor da Igreja de São Paulo*
(Série Teologia em diálogo). São Paulo, BL: Edições Paulinas, 1989. 105 pp. 850501054X.

A human and spiritual portrait of the Archbishop of São Paulo, tireless campaigner against exploitation, and protector of the poor and marginalized; originally published by Alfa-Omega in 1979.

AM1349 *Paulo Evaristo Arns: Kardinal der Ausgebeuteten*
(Repräsentanten der Befreiungstheologie). Olten, SZ: Walter-Verlag, 1987. 218 pp. Paper. 3530023655.

German translation from the 1979 Portuguese edition, edited by Horst Goldstein.

AM1350 Peters, John F.
Life Among the Yanomami: The Story of Change Among the Xilixana on the Mucajai River in Brazil. Peterborough, ONC: Broadview Press, 1998. 292 pp. Paper. 1551111934.

A detailed account of traditions and social change among the Mucajai Yanomami people of Brazil's Amazon region; by a social anthropologist who lived among them as an Unevangelized Fields Mission International worker, from 1958 to 1967.

AM1351 Piepke, Joachim G.
Die Kirche auf dem Weg zum Menschen: Die Volk-Gottes-Ekklesiologie in der Kirche Brasiliens. (*Neue Zeitschrift für Missionswissenschaft* Supplementa, 34). Immensee, SZ: *Neue Zeitschrift für Missionswissenschaft*, 1985. 358 pp. Paper. 385824063X.

Piepke, a European theologian, with extensive experience in Brazil, examines the Second Vatican Council's concept of the "People of God," as it relates both to the mission work of the Catholic Church in Brazil, and to the thought of Leonardo Boff and other liberation theologians.

AM1352 Potrick, María Bernarda et al.
Dom Helder Câmara: Testigo del Evangelio en América Latina. (Experiencias Cristianas, 5). Buenos Aires, AG: Ediciones Paulinas, 1986. 200 pp. Paper. 9500906082.

A comprehensive look at the life, and leadership on behalf of the poor, of Dom Helder Câmara, bishop of San Salvador, Brazil.

AM1353 Prien, Hans-Jürgen

Evangelische Kirchwerdung in Brasilien: Von den deutsch-evangelischen Einwanderergemeinden zur Evangelischen Kirche Lutherischen Bekenntnisses in Brasilien. (Die Lutherische Kirche: Geschichte und Gestalten, 10). Gütersloh, GW: Mohn, 1989. 640 pp. Paper. 3579001191.

First chapters describe the arrival of German immigrants in Brazil, from 1824 onward, and the development of Lutheran communities; other chapters deal with the strong link with Germany and National Socialism, which led to a radical reappraisal of theological thinking after the Second World War.

AM1354 Puleo, Mev

The Struggle Is One: Voices and Visions of Liberation. Albany, NYU: SUNY Press, 1994. xiii, 247 pp. 0791420132 (hdbk), 0791420140 (pbk).

Understandings of liberation theology and the church's mission in Brazil, presented from interview transcripts and photos of sixteen laypersons, priests, and theologians.

AM1355 Rayment, Anne

A Hundred Houses: The Story of Irene Rowley. Fearn, ENK: Christian Focus, 1991. 160 pp. Paper. 1871676770.

A popular account of the life of Irene Rowley and her family in Brazil, 1966-1990, as missionaries of the Unevangelized Fields Mission, based on her letters and interviews with the author.

AM1356 Read, William R., and Frank A. Ineson

Brazil 1980: The Protestant Handbook. Monrovia, CAU: MARC, 1973. xxx, 405 pp. Paper. 0912552042.

An extensively documented analysis of Protestant church growth in Brazil, in the 1950s and 1960s, and of potential for growth in the 1970s.

AM1357 Read, William R.

Fermento religioso nas massas do Brazil. Campinas, BL: Livraria Cristã Unida; São Bernardo do Campo, BL: Imprensa Metodista, 1967. 250 pp. No ISBN.

Portuguese translation.

AM1358 Read, William R.

New Patterns of Church Growth in Brazil. Grand Rapids, MIU: Eerdmans, 1965. 240 pp. Paper. No ISBN.

A comparative study of Protestant church growth patterns in Brazil, contrasting the slow growth of mainline denominations with the meteoric rise of Pentecostal churches.

AM1359 Regozini, Georg Maria

August Comtes "Religion der Menschheit" und ihre Ausprägung in Brasilien: Eine religionsgeschichtliche Untersuchung über Ursprung, Werden und Wesen der "Positivistischen Kirche" Brasiliens. (Europäische Hochschulschriften, 23: Theologie, 88). Frankfurt am Main, GW: Lang, 1977. 237 pp. Paper. 3261029617.

An examination of Brazil's "Positivist church," from its origins in August Comte's "Religion of Humanity," and its founding by Miguel Lemos in 1881, to its period of greatest influence, 1889-1915.

AM1360 Salamone, Frank A.

The Yanomami and their Interpreters: Fierce People or Fierce Interpreters? Lanham, MDU: University Press of America, 1997. 117 pp. 0761806547.

A detailed analysis of the dispute among scholars and political leaders, concerning the culture of the Yanomami peo-ple of the Amazon, slaughtered by Brazilian miners in 1993; with special attention to the roles of the Catholic Salesian Mission and the Protestant New Tribes Mission.

AM1361 Scherer, Michael Emilio

Domingos Machado, der Restaurator: Beitrag zur Geschichte der Benediktiner in Brasilien. Munich, GW: Verlag der Bayerischen Benediktinerakademie, 1965. 162 pp. Paper. No ISBN.

A biography of D. Machado (1824-1908), the last Abbot General of the Brazilian Congregation of the Benedictines; a reprint of *Studien und Mitteilungen zur Geschichte des Benediktinerordens* (1964).

AM1362 Schermann, Rudolf

Die Guerilla Gottes: Lateinamerika zwischen Marx und Christus. Düsseldorf, GW: Econ Verlag, 1983. 319 pp. Paper. 3430179475.

A description of the two extreme theological streams within the Roman Catholic Church in Latin America, since the Medellin Conference (1968)—conservatives and liberationists—illustrated by concrete examples, emphasizing the difficulties encountered by a church, when it sides with the poor.

AM1363 Schoenborn, Ulrich

Gekreuzigt im Leiden der Armen: Beiträge zur kontextuellen Theologie in Brasilien. (Brasilien Taschenbuch, 7). Mettingen, GW: Brasilienkunde Verlag, 1986. 204 pp. Paper. 3885590301.

Contributions to the theme of inculturation of the Gospel in Brazil: basic communities, reading the bible from the perspective of the oppressed, and the image of Christ in Brazilian folk music.

AM1364 Silva, Antenor de Andrade

Os salesianos e a educação na bahia e em Sergipe—Brazil, 1897-1970. (Studi, 14). Rome, IT: Istituto Storico Salesiano, 2000. 431 pp. Paper. 8821304655.

A seventy-three year history of educational work by Salesians in the Bahia state of Brazil; published for the centenary of the Colégio do Salvador.

AM1365 Spellmeier, Arteno

Sprich mit den Sprachlosen ein Wort: Schicksale am Amazonas. (Erlanger Taschenbücher, 71). Kassel, GW: Gustav-Adolf-Werk; Erlangen, GW: Ev.-Luth. Mission, 1985. 119 pp. Paper. 3872141716.

Reflections in narrative form, which give flesh to the suffering and silent people of the interior of Brazil, on the Amazon.

AM1366 Stawinski, Alberto V., and Félix F. Busatta

Josué Bardin: História e Religião das Colônias Polonesas. (Coleção Imigração italiana, 45). Porto Alegre-RS, BL: Escola Superior de Teologia São Lourenço de Brindes; Caxias do Sul-RS, BL: Universidade de Caxias do Sul-RS, 1981. 111 pp. Paper. No ISBN.

The story of an Italian priest's ministry to Polish immigrants in Rio Grande de Sul, in the late 19th century.

AM1367 Steven, Hugh

To the Ends of the Earth. Huntington Beach, CAU: Wycliffe Bible Translators, 1986. 142 pp. 0915684365.

Second edition of a journalist's stories of five North American families, in northwest Brazil, working with Wycliffe Bible Translators; originally published in 1978 (Chappaqua, NYU: Christian Herald Books).

AM1368 Suss, Gunter Paulo

Volkskatholizismus in Brasilien: Zur Typologie und Strategie gelebter Religiosität. (Gesellschaft und Theologie: Abt. Systematische Beiträge, 24). Munich, GW: Kaiser; Mainz, GW: Grünewald Verlag, 1978. 200 pp. Paper. 3459011394 (K), 3786706735 (G).

A dissertation about the phenomenon of popular piety in the Catholic Church in Brazil, and a possible pastoral response.

AM1369 Tonn-Oliver, Katie

Lightbearer to the Amazon. Boise, IDU: Pacific Press, 1987. 79 pp. Paper. 0816306907.

The popular account of thirty years (1926-1956) of ministry to the people of the Amazon River in Brazil, by pioneer Seventh-day Adventist missionaries, Leo and Jessie Halliwell, serving both their physical and spiritual needs.

AM1370 Vásquez, Manuel A.

The Brazilian Popular Church and the Crisis of Modernity. (Cambridge Studies in Ideology and Religion, 11). Cambridge, ENK: Cambridge University Press, 1998. xv, 302 pp. 0521585082.

Through a longitudinal study in Nova Iguaçu, a working-class satellite city of Rio de Janeiro, a Brazilian sociologist of religion maps the crisis of progessive Catholicism, facing both the challenges of modernity and challenges from Pentecostalism.

AM1371 Vicente, do Salvador

História do Brasil, 1500-1627. (Coleção Reconquista do Brasil: Nova Série, 49). Belo Horizonte, BL: Editora Itatiaia; São Paulo, BL: Editora da Universidade de São Paulo, 1982. 437 pp. No ISBN.

Seventh edition of a 17th-century history of early Brazil, including very valuable sections on Franciscan missions and newly discovered manuscripts.

AM1372 Wegener, Stephan

Die katholische Kirche und der gesellschaftliche Wandel im brasilianischen Nordosten. (Materialien des Arnold-Bergstraesser-Instituts). Freiburg i.Br., GW: Arnold-Bergstraesser-Institut für kulturwissenschaftliche Forschungen, 1965. 264 pp. Paper. No ISBN.

A study of the position of the Catholic Church, regarding social change in northeast Brazil, with a historical reflection.

AM1373 Weingartner, Lindolfo

Umbanda: Synkretistische Kulte in Brasilien, eine Herausforderung für die christliche Kirche. (Erlanger Taschenbücher, 8). Erlangen, GW: Ev.-Luth. Mission, 1969. 230 pp. Paper. No ISBN.

A dissertation concerning the phenomenology of the Umbanda cult in Brazil, and the attitudes of the Catholic and Lutheran churches toward it.

AM1374 Willeke, Venâncio

Franziskanermissionen in Brasilien 1500-1966. (Schriftenreihe der *Neuen Zeitschrift für Missionswissenschaft,* 24). Immensee, SZ: *Neue Zeitschrift für Missionswissenschaft,* 1974. xii, 108 pp. No ISBN.

A compendium of articles published in *Neue Zeitschrift für Missionswissenschaft,* from 1967 to 1973, on the history of Franciscan missions in Brazil, 1500-1966.

AM1375 Willeke, Venâncio

Missões Franciscanas no Brasil. Petrópolis, BL: Editora Vozes, 1978. 197 pp. Paper. No ISBN.

Second edition of a history of Franciscan missions in Brazil.

AM1376 Willems, Emilio

Followers of the New Faith: Culture Change and the Rise of Protestantism in Brazil and Chile. Nashville, TNU: Vanderbilt University Press, 1967. x, 290 pp. 0816511066.

An analysis of the role of religion in the process of socio-cultural modernization, in this case Pentecostalism in Brazil and Chile; with numerous quotes from the personal testimonies of converts.

AM1377 Wirth, Lauri Emilio

Protestantismus und Kolonisation in Brasilien: Der evangelische Gemeindeverband in Brasilien: Kontextualität, Ekklesiologie und Institutionalisierung einer deutschen Einwandererkirche in Santa Catarina. (Erlanger Monographien aus Mission und Ökumene, 15). Erlangen, GW: Ev.-Luth. Mission, 1992. 198 pp. Paper. 3872143158.

This history of German-founded Protestantism in Santa Catarina, Brazil, until the formation of the modern Lutheran church there, in 1949, is based on Lutheran archival material of the Berlin, Basel, and Herrnhuter missions, and Brazilian church archives.

Chile

See also HI311, EC59, EC63, AM305, and AM1376.

AM1378 Alonso, Isidoro, Renato Poblete et al.

La Iglesia en Chile: Estructuras eclesiásticas. (Estudios Socio-religiosos Latino-americanos, 4). Fribourg, SZ: FERES, 1962. 282 pp. Paper. No ISBN.

Socioreligious study of economic and ecclesiastical structures in Chile.

AM1379 Barrios Valdés, Marciano

Pensamiento Teológico en Chile: Contribución a su estudio, VI: La Iglesia en la Historiografía de los Civiles, 1848-1988. (Anales de la Facultad de Teología, 46). Santiago, CL: Pontifica Universidad Católica de Chile, 1995. 127 pp. No ISBN.

A monograph on the reception of ecclesial and theological themes by 19th- and 20th-century secular historians in Chile—part of a larger project for reconstruction of the history of the Catholic Church in Chile.

AM1380 Cooper, Alf, and Jane Collins

It Shouldn't Happen to a Missionary. (All Nations Series). Tunbridge Wells, ENK: MARC-Monarch, South American Missionary Society; Easneye, ENK: AACC, 1993. 157 pp. Paper. 1854241680.

A popular account by a British missionary, who worked in Chile with the South American Missionary Society, pioneering novel approaches to evangelism and church planting.

AM1381 Epinay, Christian Lalive d'

Haven of the Masses: A Study of the Pentecostal Movement in Chile. (World Studies of Churches in Mission). London, ENK: Lutterworth Press, 1969. 263 pp. No ISBN.

A sociological field study, with a brief history of Chilean Pentacostalism, commissioned by the WCC's Commission on World Mission and Evangelism.

AM—THE AMERICAS

AM1382 Guerrero, J. Bernardo
A Dios Rogando ... Los pentecostales en la sociedad aymara de norte grande de Chile. Amsterdam, NE: Free University Press, 1995. 265 pp. 9053836091.

A scholarly assessment of the remarkable progress of the Pentecostal movement among the Aymara of northern Chile.

AM1383 Kamsteeg, Frans
Prophetic Pentecostalism in Chile: A Case Study on Religion and Development Policy. (Studies in Evangelicalism, 15). Lanham, MDU: Scarecrow Press, 1998. viii, 283 pp. 0810834405.

A detailed case study of Pentecostalism in Chile—its history and social participation.

AM1384 Kessler, Juan B. A.
A Study of the Older Protestant Missions and Churches in Peru and Chile: With Special Reference to the Problems of Division, Nationalism, and Native Ministry. Goes, NE: Oosterbaan & Le Cointre, 1967. xii, 369 pp. Paper. No ISBN.

Doctoral thesis on the missionary work of several Protestant denominations in Peru and Chile during the first half of the 20th century, with special attention to the causes of religious divisions, the rise of nationalism, and the development of indigenous church leadership; by a physical engineer who worked for ten years as a missionary in the area; based on extensive use of archives and interviews.

AM1385 Noggler, Albert
Cuatrocientos Años de Misión entre los Araucanos. Santiago, CL: Padre las Casas, 1983. 214 pp. No ISBN.
Spanish translation.

AM1386 Noggler, Albert
Vierhundert Jahre Araukanermission: 75 Jahre Missionsarbeit der bayerischen Kapuziner. (NZM, 20). Schöneck, GW: NZM, 1973. xxvi, 505 pp. No ISBN.

A history of missions by Capuchins to the Araucan people of south-central Chile, from 1600 to the present, including information on their culture, language, and religion.

AM1387 Ossa, Leonor
Christliche Basis-Gemeinden und die Zuspitzung sozialer Auseinandersetzungen in Chile: Untersuchungen zur Ideologie der "Christen fnr den Sozialismus" in Chile zur Zeit der Volksregierung (1970-1973). (Europäische Hochschulschriften, 23: Theologie, 92). Frankfurt am Main, GW: Lang, 1977. 336 pp. No ISBN.

A scholar's sociological analysis of "Christians for Socialism" ideology in Chile, 1970-1973, during the reign of Salvador Allende, separating its Marxist and Christian elements and analyzing their consequences.

AM1388 Paul, Irven
A Yankee Reformer in Chile: The Life & Works of David Trumbull. South Pasadena, CAU: William Carey Library, 1973. xiv, 157 pp. Paper. 0878084142.

A reassessment of the life of David Trumbull (1819-1889), pioneer Reformed missionary to Chile (1845-1889), where he labored for evangelical truth and religious liberty under the combined auspices of the Bible Society, the Seamen's Mission, and the Chile Mission of the American Presbyterian church.

AM1389 Rodríguez, Jorge Pinto, Holdenis Casanova Guarda, and Sergio M. Uribe Gutiérrez
Misioneros en la Araucanía, 1600-1900: Un Capítulo de historia fronteriza en Chile. (V Centenario, 38/1-2). Bogotá, CK: CELAM, 1990. 2 vols. 9586251756 (vol. 38), 9586250202 (comb. ed.).

A history of the Franciscan and Jesuit missions to the Araucan people of southern Chile, from the late 16th through the 19th centuries, including three documents written by missionaries about their experiences [vol. 1: *Estudios* (303 pp.); vol. 2: *Documentos* (238 pp.)].

AM1390 Sepúlveda, Juan
The Andean Highlands: An Encounter with Two Forms of Christianity. (Gospel and Cultures Pamphlets, 17). Geneva, SZ: WCC Publications, 1997. x, 44 pp. Paper. 2825412376.

Lessons from the encounters of the Aymara people of the Andean highlands of northern Chile; first, with Iberian Christianity and, more recently, with Pentecostalism.

AM1391 Smith, Brian H.
The Church and Politics in Chile: Challenges to Modern Catholicism. Princeton, NJU: Princeton University Press, 1982. xiii, 383 pp. Paper. 0691076294 (hdbk), 0691101191 (pbk).

A detailed examination of church/state issues in Chile from 1920 to 1980.

AM1392 Stewart-Gambino, Hannah W.
The Church and Politics in the Chilean Countryside. Boulder, COU: Westview Press, 1992. vii, 200 pp. 0813377242.

A scholarly analysis of the Roman Catholic Church's agrarian policy, between 1925 and 1964, and role in peasant mobilization, in areas of regressive land distribution.

AM1393 Valdés Subercaseaux, Francisco
Fray Francisco Valdé Subercaseaux, Misionero de la Araucanía y Primer Obispo de Osorno. Santiago, CL: Editorial Andrés Bello, 1985. xv, 156 pp. No ISBN.

A collection of writings and letters of a Franciscan missionary to the Araucan people of central Chile, and bishop of their diocese (1940-1982).

Colombia

See also TH354, SO409, AM295, and AM305.

AM1394 Bonilla, Víctor Daniel
Serfs de Dieu et maitres d'Indiens: histoire d'une mission capucine en Amazonie. Translated by Alain Gheerbrant. (Anthropologie critique). Paris, FR: Fayard, 1972. 335 pp. No ISBN.
French translation.

AM1395 Bonilla, Víctor Daniel
Servants of God or Masters of Men?: The Story of a Capuchin Mission in Amazonia. Translated by Rosemary Sheed. Harmondsworth, ENK: Penguin Books, 1972. 304 pp. 0140214364.
English translation.

AM1396 Bonilla, Víctor Daniel
Siervos de Dios y Amos de Indios: El Estado y la Misión Capuchina en el Putumayo. Bogotá, CK: By the author, V. D. Bonilla, 1969. 336 pp. No ISBN.

An exposé of the collaboration of Capuchin missionaries with the Colombian state in a 20th-century crusade to "civilize" the native peoples of Amazonia.

AM1397 Briceño Jáuregui, Manuel
Los Jesuitas en el Magdalena: Historia de una Misión.
Bogotá, CK: Editorial Kelly, 1984. 456 pp. Paper. No ISBN.
History of missions from the late 19th century to 1962.

AM1398 Castillo Cárdenas, Gonzalo
Liberation Theology from Below: The Life and Thought of Manuel Quintín Lame. Maryknoll, NYU: Orbis Books, 1987.
viii, 200 pp. Paper. 0883444089.
An introduction to the life and theology of this Colombian Andes Indian leader, with the full English text of his book, *The Thoughts of the Indian Educated in the Colombian Forests.*

AM1399 Constance, Helen
Stepping Out on Faith: The Story of Colombia Missionaries George and Helen Constance. Camp Hill, PAU: Christian Publications, 1988. 157 pp. Paper. 0875094090.
The popular story of pioneer evangelical and alliance missionaries to Colombia, 1935 to 1953.

AM1400 Corley, Marion
Doña Maria and Friends: Stories from 20 years of Missions Work in Colombia. Birmingham, ALU: New Hope, 1991. 129 pp. Paper. 1563090082.
Vignettes by a Southern Baptist missionary in Colombia, 1962-1982.

AM1401 Curtis, Carolyn
A Man for All Nations: The Story of Clyde and Ruth Taylor.
(The Jaffray Collection of Missionary Portraits). Camp Hill, PAU: Christian Publications, 1998. xii, 195 pp. Paper. 0875097685.
Christian and Missionary Alliance missionaries to Colombia tell their story of planting 100 house churches in and around the city of Armenia (1932-1942), with an introduction on Clyde Taylor's later work as Executive Director of the National Association of Evangelicals (NAE, 1944-1974).

AM1402 Estes, Steve
Called to Die: The Story of American Linguist Chet Bitterman, Slain by Terrorists. Grand Rapids, MIU: Zondervan, 1986. 198 pp. Paper. 0310283817.
The dramatic account of the kidnap, negotiations for release, and final martyrdom of an SIL missionary in Colombia in 1981.

AM1403 Flora, Cornelia Butler
Pentecostalism in Colombia: Baptism by Fire and Spirit.
Rutherford, NJU: Fairleigh Dickinson University Press, 1976.
288 pp. 0838615783.
A sociological study, based on careful field studies of economic conditions, concluding that Protestantism has not meant upward mobility and accumulation of capital.

AM1404 Howard, David M.
The Costly Harvest. Wheaton, ILU: Tyndale, 1975. xv, 207 pp. 0842304452.
The story of the planting and development of evangelical Christian churches in northern Colombia; originally published as *Hammered as Gold* in 1969, by Harper and Row.

AM1405 Krumwiede, Heinrich-W.
Politik und katholische Kirche im gesellschaftlichen Modernisierungsprozess: Tradition und Entwicklung in Kolumbien.
(Historische Perspektiven, 16). Hamburg, GW: Hoffmann und Campe, 1980. 308 pp. Paper. 3455092470.

A historical analysis of the political development of Colombia, and the politically relevant aspects of the process of change in the Catholic Church, after the Second Vatican Council.

AM1406 Morley, Lewis
Out of Weakness ... Strength: Miracles in the Life of a Missionary. Hazelwood, MOU: Word Aflame Press, 1987. 159 pp. Paper. 0932581021.
A popular account of a missionary family, who worked in Colombia in the United Pentecostal church from 1957 to 1977.

AM1407 Olson, Bruce
For This Cross I'll Kill You. Carol Stream, ILU: Creation House, 1973. 221 pp. 0884190382.
A vivid account of pioneer mission among the Motilones tribe in Venezuela and Colombia.

AM1408 Olson, Bruce
"Ich schwöre bei diesem Kreuz—ich töte euch!": Mission unter Indianerstämmen Südamerikas, ein Kampf auf Leben und Tod.
(Telos, 2017). Bad Liebenzell, GW: Verlag der Liebenzeller Mission, 1977. 213 pp. Paper. 388003043 (SBN).
German translation.

AM1409 Olson, Bruce
Por Esta Cruz te Amaré. Miami, FLU: Editorial Vida, 1973. 219 pp. Paper. No ISBN.
Spanish translation.

AM1410 Pacheco, Juan Manuel
Los Jesuitas en Colombia. Bogotá, CK: Editorial San Juan Eudes, 1962. 2 vols. No ISBN.
A historical study of the founding missions and their social, catechetical, missional, and cultural activities [vol. 1: *1567-1654* (1959, 622 pp.); vol. 2: *1654-1696* (1962, 542 pp.)].

AM1411 Palmer, Donald G.
Explosion of People Evangelism. Chicago, ILU: Moody, 1974. 191 pp. 0802424139.
An analysis of Pentecostal church growth in Colombia; originally presented as a master's thesis at Trinity Evangelical Divinity School.

AM1412 Peters, David, and Arlene Peters
By an Unfamiliar Path: The Story of David and Arlene Peters. (The Jaffray Collection of Missionary Portraits, 13).
Camp Hill, PAU: Christian Publications, 1994. 164 pp. Paper. 0875095801.
Reminiscences by church planters of the CMA in Colombia and Brazil, 1971-1984.

AM1413 Torres, Camilo
La Revolución: Imperativo Cristiano. Bogotá, CK: Ediciones del Caribe, 1965. 58 pp. Paper. No ISBN.
Essay in which the author proposes his thesis on the essence of the apostolate—with concrete suggestions for social, economic, and political change in Colombia.

AM1414 Torres, Camilo
Revolutionary Priest: The Complete Writings and Messages of Camilio Torres. New York, NYU: Random House, 1971.
xi, 460 pp. 0394462483.
The complete writings of the Colombian priest-guerrilla, with letters and writings by other Latin Americans, who also reveal the injustice perpetrated against the poor, and their struggles against oppression in Latin America.

AM1415 Turnage, Loren C.
Island Heritage: A Baptist View of the History of San Andrés and Providencia. Cali, CK: Historical Commission of the Colombia Baptist Mission, 1975. 138 pp. No ISBN.
  A narrative history, based on archival sources, of Baptist missions, since 1850, on the two islands off the coast of Colombia.

AM1416 Valtierra, Angel, and Rafael María de Hornedo
San Pedro Claver: Esclavo de los esclavos. (BAC popular, 69). Madrid, SP: EDICA, 1985. 232 pp. Paper. 8422012030.
  An accurate, popular account of the life and activity of Peter Claver (1580-1654), in Colombia, on behalf of black slaves.

AM1417 Walton, Jim, and Janice Walton
Sent to the River God Forgot. Wheaton, ILU: Tyndale, 1995. xv, 181 pp. Paper. 084235977X.
  A narrative account, by two SIL workers, of their life-changing experiences, from 1964 to 1981, among the Muinanes of Colombia's interior.

AM1418 Westmeier, Karl-Wilhelm
Reconciling Heaven and Earth: The Transcendental Enthusiasm and Growth of an Urban Protestant Community, Bogotá, Columbia. (Studies in the Intercultural History of Christianity, 41). Frankfurt am Main, GW: Lang, 1986. 462 pp. Paper. 3261035471.
  A scholarly study of Colombian Protestantism and how people act religiously in times of accelerated social change in large urban centers today.

Ecuador

See also MI130, MI141, AM351, and AM1526.

AM1419 Caravias, José Luis
Luchar por la tierra: Inspiraciones bíblicas para las comunidades campesinas. (Iglesia Nueva, 69). Bogotá, CK: Indo-American Press Service, 1984. 111 pp. Paper. No ISBN.
  Short reflections for the campesino communities of Ecuador.

AM1420 Drown, Frank, and Marie Drown
Misión entre Cazadores de Cabezas. Buenos Aires, AG: Editorial de Ediciones Selectas, 1962. 318 pp. No ISBN.
  Spanish translation.

AM1421 Drown, Frank, and Marie Drown
Mission to the Head-Hunters. New York, NYU: Harper, 1961. 252 pp. No ISBN.
  Narrative of a young couple, who served under the Gospel Missionary Union as pioneer missionaries among the Jivaro people of eastern Ecuador (1946 to 1960), and brought to fruition a vision to establish an indigenous church.

AM1422 Elliot, Elisabeth
Through Gates of Splendor. Wheaton, ILU: Tyndale, 1981. 273 pp. Paper. 0842371524.
  An updated account of the massacre of five missionaries in 1956, by Auca Indians of Ecuador.

AM1423 Garcia Villalba, Lorenzo
Historia de las Misiones en la Amazonia Ecuatoriana. Quito, EC: Ediciones Abya-Yala, 1985. 450 pp. Paper. No ISBN.
  A history of the activities of religious congregations that worked in the Amazon region of Ecuador for four centuries.

AM1424 Goffin, Alvin M.
The Rise of Protestant Evangelism in Ecuador, 1895-1990. Gainesville, FLU: University Press of Florida, 1994. xxiv, 189 pp. 0813012600.
  A scholarly history of North American fundamentalist Protestant missions in Ecuador.

AM1425 Grassiano, Maria Domenica
Beloved Jungle: Sister Maria Troncatti Daughter of Mary Help of Christians, the Kivaros' Sister Missionary. Rome, IT: Daughters of Mary Help of Xian, 1971. 387 pp. No ISBN.
  The biography of a beloved pioneer medical worker and educator among the Kivaro people of Ecuador.

AM1426 Hitt, Russell T.
Jungle Pilot: The Gripping Story of the Life and Witness of Nate Saint, Martyred Missionary to Ecuador. Grand Rapids, MIU: Discovery House, 1997. 320 pp. Paper. 1572930225.
  A reprint of the 1959 edition of the story of a Missionary Aviation Fellowship (MAP) missionary, martyred by the Waodani (Auca) Indians in Ecuador in 1956; with an update on that mission by Stephen F. Saint.

AM1427 Liefeld, Olive Fleming
Unfolding Destinies: The Untold Story of Peter Fleming and the Auca Mission. Grand Rapids, MIU: Zondervan, 1990. 245 pp. Paper. 0310540011.
  Reminiscences by the widow of missionary martyr Peter Fleming of the Auca Mission in the 1950s, with a narrative account of her return to Ecuador in 1989.

AM1428 Møller, Arvid
Señorita Sigrid. Oslo, NO: Luther Forlag, 1985. 192 pp. 8253141882.
  Biography of a Norwegian Lutheran missionary, who worked with Indians in Ecuador.

AM1429 Maust, John
New Song in the Andes. South Pasadena, CAU: William Carey Library, 1992. xiii, 143 pp. Paper. 0878082190.
  A missionary journalist's account of the rapid spread of evangelical Protestantism among the Zuichuas of Ecuador's Chimborazo Province.

AM1430 *Memorias de Frontera: Misioneros en el río Aguarico (1954-1984)*
Quito, EC: CICAME; Vicariato Apostólico de Aguarico, 1989. 319 pp. No ISBN.
  An account of the experiences of different Catholic missionaries who worked with the Siana, Secoya, and other native peoples in northeastern Ecuador, from 1954 to 1984.

AM1431 Padilla, Washington
La Iglesia y Los Dioses Modernos. Quito, EC: Corporación Editora Nacional, 1989. 455 pp. Paper. No ISBN.
  A carefully researched history of Protestantism in Ecuador, with preliminary material on the pre-Protestant indigenous and colonial Catholic history.

AM1432 Rosner, Enrique, ed.
Leonidas Proaño, Freund der Indianer: Ein Porträt des Bischofs der Diözese Riobamba in Ecuador. Freiburg, SZ: Edition Exodus, 1986. 208 pp. Paper. 3905575191.
  Various texts on the life and work of Bishop Proano (b. 1910, in Ecuador), a committed representative of the "preferential option for the poor."

AM1433 Savage, Stephen E.
Rejoicing in Christ: The Biography of Robert Carlton Savage. Reading, VTU: Shadow Rock Press, 1990. xiv, 367 pp. Paper. 096278480X.

The biography of Robert Carlton Savage (1914-1987), Baptist missionary in South America (1942-1968), known as an evangelist, and for radio ministry through "The Voice of the Andes," station HCJB, in Quito, Ecuador.

AM1434 Shepson, Charles W.
A Heart for Imbabura: The Story of Evelyn Rychner. Camp Hill, PAU: Christian Publications, 1992. 182 pp. Paper. 0875094821.

Vignettes from the work of Evelyn Rychner, a CMA missionary to Ecuador, 1950-1990.

AM1435 Wallis, Ethel Emily
Aucas Downriver: Dayuma's Story Today. London, ENK: Hodder & Stoughton, 1973. x, 126 pp. 0340180811.

The continuing story of Auca/missionary interactions, following the killing of five missionaries in 1956.

Guyana

AM1436 Dowdy, Homer
Christ's Jungle. Gresham, ORU: Vision House, 1995. 357 pp. Paper. 1885305176.

In this sequel to *Christ's Witchdoctor* (1964, 1994), the evangelical journalist recounts the development of Christianity among the Wai Wai people of Guyana through the life story of Elka, a former witchdoctor.

AM1437 Dowdy, Homer
Christ's Witchdoctor. Gresham, ORU: Vision House, 1994. vi, 241 pp. Paper. 1885305087.

A reissue of the 1964 Harper classic on pioneer work by Unevangelized Fields Missions (now UFM International) among the Wai Wai Indians of British Guiana (Guyana).

AM1438 Lantry, Eileen
Jungle Adventurer. Boise, IDU: Pacific Press, 1987. 79 pp. Paper. 0816307202.

The popular account of the struggles and death of O. E. Davis, a Seventh-day Adventist who established a mission station among the Mount Roraima Indians in Western British Guiana, 1910-1911.

Paraguay

See also SP182, AM882, and AM1280.

AM1439 Abou, Sélim
The Jesuit "Republic" of the Guaranís (1609-1768) and Its Heritage. Translated by Lawrence J. Johnson. New York, NYU: Crossroad Publishing, 1997. 160 pp. 0824517067.

A UNESCO-sponsored illustrated history of the Jesuit missions to the Guaranís and their cultural adaptation in present-day Paraguay, Argentina, and Brazil.

AM1440 Baucke, Florian P.
Zwettler-Codex 420. Edited by Etta Becker-Donner, and Gustav Otruba. (Veröffentlichungen zum Archiv für Völkerkunde, 4). Wien, AU: Braumüller, 1966. 2 vols. No ISBN.

Descriptions of life among the Paraguayan Indians and of Jesuit work among them by an Austrian Jesuit, expelled in 1769.

AM1441 Becker, Felix
Die politische Machtstellung der Jesuiten in Südamerika im 18 Jahrhundert: Zur Kontroverse um den "Jesuitenkönig" Nikolaus I. von Paraguay; mit einem Faksimile der "Histoire de Nicolas I" (1756). (Lateinamerikanische Forschungen, 8). Cologne, GW: Böhlau Verlag, 1980. vii, 357 pp. 3412072796.

The book deals with the 18th- and 19th-century controversies surrounding the Jesuits in Paraguay, examining the historicity or non-historicity of the controversial "King Nicholas of Paraguay."

AM1442 Bockwinkel, Juan
Steyler Indianermission in Paraguay, 1910-1925. (Studia Instituti Missiologici SVD, 55). Nettetal, GW: Steyler Verlag, 1992. 180 pp. Paper. 3805003056.

A critical analysis of SVD Indian missions in Paraguay, 1910 to 1925, including aims and strategies, material and spiritual development, and influence.

AM1443 Cano, Luis et al.
La Evangelización en el Paraguay: Cuatro siglos de historia. Asunción, PY: Ediciones Loyola, 1979. 218 pp. No ISBN.

A collection of articles concerning evangelism in Paraguay, from the 16th century to the present.

Am1444 Caraman, Philip
Ein verlorenes Paradies: Der Jesuitenstaat in Paraguay. Munich, GW: Kösel Verlag, 1979. 329 pp. No ISBN.

German translation.

AM1445 Caraman, Philip
The Lost Paradise: An Account of the Jesuits in Paraguay, 1607-1768. London, ENK: Sidgwick and Jackson, 1975. 341 pp. 0283982128.

The history of the beginnings, development, and forced closure of Jesuit missions among the Guarani of Paraguay.

AM1446 Cardiel, José
Compendio de la Historia del Paraguay, 1780. Buenos Aires, AG: Fundación para la Educación, la Ciencia y Ia Cultura, 1984. 214 pp. Paper. 9509149195.

First edition of the text of *Compendio*, with an introduction written by José M. Mariluz Urquijo.

AM1447 Dignath, Stephan
Die Pädagogik der Jesuiten in den Indio-Reduktionen von Paraguay, 1609-1767. (Eruditio, 9). Frankfurt a.M., GW: Lang, 1978. 174 pp. Paper. 3261026391.

A study of pedagogy in the Jesuit Reductions in Paraguay, and its effects on the life of the Guarani Indians.

AM1448 Equipo, Expa
En Busca de "la Tierra sin Mal": Movimientos campesinos en el Paraguay, 1960-1980. (Iglesia Nueva, 65). Bogotá, CK: Indo-American Press Service, 1982. 195 pp. Paper. No ISBN.

A testimonial history of the Christian "agrarian leagues" in Paraguay, their repression, and the expulsion of their leaders.

AM1449 Furlong, Guillermo
Bernardo Nusdorffer y su "Novena Parte" (1760). (Escritores Coloniales Rioplatenses, 22). Buenos Aires, AG: Ediciones Teoría, 1971. 176 pp. Paper. No ISBN.

History of the activities of Nusdorffer (or Neusdorfer), who was Superior of the Jesuit Reductions and Provincial Superior of the Jesuit Province of Paraquay, including the text of his *Novena Parte*.

AM1450 Furlong, Guillermo
Misiones y Sus Pueblos de Guaraníes. Buenos Aires, AG: Imprenta Balmes, 1962. 790 pp. No ISBN.

An illustrated history of the 16th- and 17th-century Jesuit mission to the Guarani Indians of Paraguay.

AM1451 Gutiérrez, Ramón
The Jesuit Guaraní Missions. Rio de Janeiro, BL: UNESCO Secretaria do Patrimonio Historico e Artistico National, 1987. 110 pp. No ISBN.

Motivated by UNESCO interest in conservation and restoration of building of the 17th- to 18th-century Jesuit mission to the Guaraní (modern day Paraguay), this book contains a brief history, but focuses upon architecture.

AM1452 Haubert, Maxime
La vie quotidienne au Paraguay sous les Jésuites. (La Vie quotidienne). Paris, FR: Hachette, 1967. 319 pp. No ISBN.

A detailed survey of the daily life of the Indians of Paraguay in the Jesuit missions of the 17th and 18th centuries.

AM1453 Hoffmann, Werner
Las Misiones Jesuíticas entre los Chiquitanos. Buenos Aires, AG: FECIC, 1979. 202 pp. Paper. No ISBN.

A documented historical study of Jesuit missions in Paraguay.

AM1454 Maeder, Ernesto J. A.
Cartas Anuas de la Provincia del Paraguay, 1637-1639. Buenos Aires, AG: FECIC, 1984. 192 pp. Paper. No ISBN.

Translations from Latin of the annual reports from Jesuit missionaries in Paraguay to their superiors in Rome—the continuation of a project begun by Emilio Ravignani in 1927.

AM1455 Mayr, Johann
Anton Sepp, ein Südtiroler im Jesuitenstaat. Bozen, SZ: Athesia, 1988. 480 pp. 8870144992.

A well documented biography, based on contemporary sources of Anton Sepp (1655-1733), a trailblazing missionary in Paraguay.

AM1456 McNaspy, C. J.
Lost Cities of Paraguay: Art and Architecture of the Jesuit Reductions, 1607-1767. Chicago, ILU: Loyola University Press, 1982. 160 pp. 0829403965.

An account of the thirty lost cities developed by the Jesuits, in Paraguay, Argentina, and Brazil, for the protection of primitive Indians from Spanish colonists and Portugese slave traders; photographs by J. M. Blanch.

AM1457 McNaspy, C. J.
Roque González de Santacruz: Un Conquistador Sin Espada. Asuncion, PY: Loyola, 1983. 92 pp. No ISBN.

Biography of an early Jesuit missionary.

AM1458 Melía, Bartomeu
El Guaraní Conquistado y Reducio: Ensayos de Etnohistoria. (Biblioteca Paraguaya de Antropología, 5). Asunción, PY: Universidad Católica, 1986. 304 pp. Paper. No ISBN.

A socio-anthropological analysis of the Jesuit mission to the Guaraní Indians of Paraguay.

AM1459 Montoya, Antonio Ruiz de
The Spiritual Conquest Accomplished by the Religious of the Society of Jesus in the Provinces of Paraguay, Parana, Uruguay, and Tape: A Personal Account of the Founding and Early Years of the Jesuit Paraguay Reductions. Translated by C. J. McNaspy, John P. Leonard, and Martin E. Palmer.

(Jesuit Primary Sources in English Translations Series I, 11). St. Louis, MOU: Institute of Jesuit Sources, 1993. 223 pp. 1880810026 (hdbk), 1880810034 (pbk).

English translations of *Conquista Espiritual* (1639) by Antonio Ruiz de Montoya (1585-1652), the Peruvian-born Jesuit, whose account of pioneer missions in Paraguay and Uruguay is one of the most important primary source documents for that period.

AM1460 Morton, C. Manly
Somewhere a Voice Is Calling: The Story of the Life of One Who Listened. Fort Lauderdale, FLU: Forman Christian Foundation, 1972. xvi, 146 pp. Paper. No ISBN.

Reminiscences of C. Manly Morton, pioneer Disciples of Christ missionary to Paraguay (1918-1923), founder of the International College there (1920), and educational missionary in Puerto Rico (1923-1950).

AM1461 Plett Welk, Rodolfo
El Protestantismo en el Paraguay: Su aporte cultural, económico y espiritual. Asunción, PY: Facultad Latinoamericana de Estudios Teológicos, 1987. 170 pp. Paper. No ISBN.

An historical study on the various existing Protestant churches in Paraguay, and their missionary activities among indigenous peoples.

Peru

See also CR649, ED27, SP182, AM235, AM317, AM351, AM418, AM433, AM435, AM442, AM444, AM1270, and AM1384.

AM1462 Alvarez Lobo, Ricardo
TSLA: Estudio Etno-histórico del Urbamba y Alto Ucayali. Salamanca, SP: Editorial San Estaban, 1984. 352 pp. Paper. 8485045602.

A study of Catholic missions to Indians of the Ucayali River Valley of Peruvian Amazonia, and of the missionaries' role as representatives for the Indians to the colonial authorities.

AM1463 Amich, José
Historia de las Misiones del Convento de Santa Rosa de Ocopa. (Monumenta Amazónica, Serie, b). Iquitos, PE: IIAP/CETA, 1988. 590 pp. 8489295050, 8489295557.

A history of the Franciscan convent of Ocopa, in Central Peru, one of the most important missionary centers in the 18th century.

AM1464 Biedma, Manuel
La Conquista Franciscana del Alto Ucayali. (Monumenta amazónica, 5; Serie V centenario, franciscanos evangelizadores del Perú, 2). Inquitos, PE: CETA/IIAP; Lima, PE: Provincia Franciscana de San Francisco Solano del Perú, 1989. 292 pp. 8489295050, 8489295476.

A history of the entrance of Franciscan missionaries into the eastern section of Peru in the 16th century, written in the 17th century; originally published in 1981 (Lima, PE: Editorial Milla Batres).

AM1465 Bruno-Jofre, Rosa del Carmen
Methodist Education in Peru: Social Gospel, Politics, and American Ideological and Economic Penetration, 1888-1930. (Comparative Ethics Series, 2). Waterloo, ONC: Wilfred Laurier University Press, 1988. xiii, 223 pp. Paper. 0889209545.

An analysis of the socioeconomic and political values transmitted by the North American missionaries, and the impact of these on Peruvian culture.

AM1466 Burgaleta, Claudio M.

José de Acosta, S.J., 1540-1600: His Life and Thought. Chicago, ILU: Jesuit Way/Loyola Press, 1999. xxxviii, 20 pp. Paper. 0829410635.

A narrative of an early Jesuit, who distinguished himself as a proto-evolutionist and sacred orator, a theologian and playwright, a missionary to Amerindians on the shores of Lake Titicaca in Peru, an economist, jurist, administrator, and a diplomat at the court of Philip II.

AM1467 Calancha, Antonio de la, and Bernardo de Torres

Crónicas Agustinianas del Perú. (Biblioteca Missionalia Hispánica, 17). Madrid, SP: CSIC, 1972. 2 vols. No ISBN.

A history of the Augustinian mission to Peru, from its beginning through the 17th century, including short biographies of many of the significant members of the order [vol. 1: xli, 943 pp.; vol. 2: xv, 837 pp.]; originally published under the title *Coronica Moralizada del Orden de San Agustin el Perú.*

AM1468 Concilio Nacional Evangélico del Perú

Consulta Nacional sobre la Misión, Lima, PE 28 de septiembre al 2 de octubre de 1987. Lima, PE: Concilio Nacional Evangélico del Perú, 1987. 279 pp. Paper. No ISBN.

A collection of seventeen papers presented at the consultation on missions in Peru, as well as the text of the "Declaración de Lima-87 sobre la misión de la Iglesia."

AM1469 Duviols, Pierre

Cultura Andina y Represión: Procesos y visitas de idolatrías y hechicerías. (Archivos de historia andina, 5). Cuzco, PE: Centro de Estudios Rurales Andinos "Bartolomé de las Casas," 1986. lxxxvi, 570 pp. No ISBN.

A collection of letters and other documents concerning the repression of native culture and religious beliefs by Spanish missionaries in the Cajatambo province of Peru.

AM1470 Duviols, Pierre

La Destrucción de las Religiones Andinas: Conquista y colonia. Translated by Albor Maruenda. (Serie de historia general—Instituto de Investigaciones Históricas, 9). México, MX: Universidad Nacional Autónoma de México, 1977. 479 pp. No ISBN.

Spanish translation of *La Lutte contre les religions autochtones dans le Pérou colonial* (1971).

AM1471 Duviols, Pierre

La lutte contre les religions autochtones dans le Perou colonial: "l'extirpation de l'idolâtrie" entre 1532 et 1660. (Travaux de l'Institut Français d'Études Andines, 13). Lima, PE: Institut Français d'Études Andines, 1971. 428 pp. No ISBN.

A detailed history of the struggle by the Spanish against indigenous religion in Peru, from the Spanish conquest of the Incas in 1532, to 1660, with an analysis of relevant political, economic, legal, and theological factors.

AM1472 Egaña, Antonio de, ed.

Monumenta Peruana. (Monumenta Historica Societatis Jesu, 95, 102, 110, 12, 128; Monumenta Missionum Societatis Jesu, 22, 27, 33, 40, 45). Rome, IT: Institutum Historicum Societatis Jesu, 1966. 5 vols. Paper. 8470411206 (vol. 7), 8870411281 (vol. 8).

A multi-volume collection of documents, in Spanish and Latin, pertaining to 16th-century Jesuit missions in Peru [vol.

4: *1586-1591* (1966, xix, 908 pp.); vol. 5: *1592-1595* (1970, xix, 986 pp.); vol. 6: *1596-1599* (1974, xx, 839 pp.); vol. 7: *1600-1602* (Edited by Antonio de Egaña and Enrique Fernández, 1981, no pages); vol. 8: *1603-1604* (1986, xxiv, 680 pp.)]; also published in the series Missiones Occidentales—other volumes published before 1960.

AM1473 Equipo Pastoral de Bambamarca, ed.

Trabaladores rurais animados pela fe. Translated by Adriana Zuchetto. São Paulo, BL: Paulinas, 1987. 616 pp. No ISBN.

Portuguese translation.

AM1474 Equipo Pastoral de Bambamarca, ed.

Vamos Caminando: A Peruvian Catechism. Translated by John Medcalf. Maryknoll, NYU: Orbis Books; London, ENK: SCM Press, 1985. x, 373 pp. Paper. 0883445263 (US), 0334017440 (UK).

English translation of *Vamos Caminando: Los Campesinos Buscamos con Cristo el Camino de Nuestra Liberacion,* 1983).

AM1475 Equipo Pastoral de Bambamarca, ed.

Vamos Caminando: Los campesinos buscamos con Cristo el camino de nuestra liberación. (CEP, 18). Lima, PE: CEP, 1983. 399 pp. No ISBN.

A collection of the actual study materials of a small group of Peruvian Christians, illustrating the capacity of the post-conciliar Catholic Church in Latin America to adapt to the Amerindian population.

AM1476 Equipo Pastoral de Bambamarca, ed.

Vamos caminando: Machen wir uns auf den Weg!: Glaube Gefangenschaft und Befreiung in den peruanischen Anden. Freiburg, SZ: Edition Exodus, 1983. xv, 430 pp. Paper. 390557502.

German translation.

AM1477 Gimpl, Herbert

Volksreligiosität und Pastoral im andinen Peru: Zugänge und Perspektiven einer Pastoral der Volksreligiosität. (Dissertationen Theologische Reihe, 60). St. Ottilien, GW: EOS Verlag, 1993. xiii, 354 pp. Paper. 3880964505.

Scholarly analysis of the interaction of the Catholic Church in its pastoral ministries with the popular religious consciousness of the Indian population of Peru, by a Comboni Father who served there (1973-1982), and presented this dissertation at the University of Innsbruck, Austria.

AM1478 Gow, David Drummond

The Gods and Social Change in the High Andes. Madison, WIU: University of Wisconsin, 1976. viii, 300 pp. No ISBN.

A scholarly study of new religious movements, since the 16th century, in the high Andes, and of the syncretistic cult of El Senor de Qoyllur Rit'i near Cuzco, Peru, showing how the NRM aided the peasants in their struggle for land reform and social justice; University of Wisconsin (at Madison) Ph.D. dissertation (anthropology).

AM1479 Griffiths, Nicholas

The Cross and the Serpent: Religious Repression and Resurgence in Colonial Peru. Norman, OKU: University of Oklahoma Press, 1996. xii, 355 pp. 0806128003.

A detailed archival study of the systematic assault on Andean traditional religion by Spanish missionaries in the 16th to 18th centuries, and how Andeans responded to it.

AM—THE AMERICAS

AM1480 Hefley, James C., and Marti Hefley
*Dawn over Amazonia: The Story of Wycliffe Bible Transla-
tors in Peru.* Waco, TXU: Word Books, 1972. 193 pp. No
ISBN.
    Vivid accounts of pioneer mission work.

AM1481 Hehrlein, Yacin
*Mission und Macht: Die politisch-religiöse Konfrontation
zwischen dem Dominikanerorden in Peru und dem Vizekönig
Francisco de Toledo (1569-1581).* (Walberberger Studien
der Albertus-Magnus-Akademie: Theologische Reihe, 16).
Mainz, GW: Matthias-Grünewald-Verlag, 1992. 173 pp.
Paper. 3786716455.
    Working from the voluminous archives relating to the
Spanish viceroy Francisco de Toledo, in Peru in the sixteenth century, this very readable historical study disclos-
es how thinly hidden, under the guise of Christianization,
were the real Spanish policies of economic and political
exploitation, when confronted by the Las Casas-inspired
Dominicans.

AM1482 Heras Diez, Julián
Los Franciscanos y las Misiones Populares en el Perú.
Madrid, SP: Editorial Cisneros, 1983. xiv, 338 pp. Paper.
8470470353.
    A historical study of the years 1725 to 1967, with an
appendix of documents.

AM1483 Irarrázaval, Diego
Religión del Pobre y Liberación en Chimbote. Lima, PE:
CEP, 1978. 482 pp. No ISBN.
    A recent history of Christianity in a Peruvian favela
and what meaning it has for the poor in that area.

AM1484 Kaiser, Friedrich
*Der Ruf aus den Anden: Aus dem Leben und Wirken einer
jungen peruanischen Schwesterngemeinschaft.* Paderborn,
GW: Verlag Bonifatius-Druckerei, 1988. 220 pp.
3870885394.
    Circular letters of Bishop Kaiser, reporting on his work
in South Peru, particularly with the congregation of the
Misioneras de Jesus Verbo y Victima, which he founded.

AM1485 Kessler, Juan B. A.
Historia de la Evangelización en el Perú. Lima, PE: Inca,
1987. 436 pp. Paper. No ISBN.
    A historical study of Protestant missionary work in
Peru, with an extensive bibliography.

AM1486 Klaiber, Jeffrey L.
*The Catholic Church in Peru, 1821-1985: A Social Histo-
ry.* Washington, DCU: Catholic University of America,
1992. xi, 417 pp. 0813207479.
    English translation.

AM1487 Klaiber, Jeffrey L.
*La Iglesia en el Perú: Su historia social desde la indepen-
dencia.* Lima, PE: Pontificia Universidad Católica del Perú,
1988. 530 pp. 8489292779.
    A general history, based on archival research, of the
Catholic Church in Peru, since independence.

AM1488 López, Teófilo Aparicio
*Fray Diego Ortíz, Misionero y Mártir del Perú: Un Proce-
so Original del Siglo XVI.* (Monografías de Misiones y
Misioneros Agustinos, 5). Valladolid, SP: Estudio Agustiniano, 1989. 331 pp. 8485985338.
    A biography of the Augustinian missionary, Diego
Ortíz, who was martyred in Peru in 1571, including eyewitness accounts used in his beatification process.

AM1489 Larson, Mildred L., and Lois Dodds
Treasure in Clay Pots. Dallas, TXU: Person to Person
Books, 1985. x, 306 pp. 0933973012.
    The account of Mildred Larson's work with the
Aguaruna people of northern Peru, who were struggling
with the rapid changes being brought on by forces of mod-
ernization entering the region.

AM1490 Lizarraga, Carlos
*En las Fuentes del Amazonas: Mons. Jauregui, obispo mi-
sionero.* Roma, IT: PP. Pasionistas, 1981. 236 pp. Paper.
8474070874.
    A popular historical work on the person and activities
of Atanasio Celestino Jauregui y Goiri, a Passionist missionary and bishop of Yurimaguas, Peru.

**AM1491 Lobo Guerrero, Bartolomé, and Fernando Arias de
Ugarte**
Sínodos de Lima de 1613 y 1636. (Tierra Nueva e Cielo
Nuevo, 22; Sínodos Americanos, 6). Madrid, SP: CSIC;
Salamanca, SP: Universidad Pontificia de Salamanca, 1987.
ciii, 459 pp. 8400067088.
    A reprinting of the 1754 edition, with a historical study
of both synods serving as a general introduction.

AM1492 MacCormack, Sabine
*Religion in the Andes: Vision and Imagination in Early
Colonial Peru.* Princeton, NJU: Princeton University Press,
1991. xv, 488 pp. 0691094683 (hdbk), 0691094687 (pbk).
    A monumental study of Incan and Andean religion, as
impacted by Spanish conquest and Catholic missions, 1532
to 1653.

AM1493 MacPherson, John M.
*At the Roots of a Nation: The Story of Colegio San Andres,
a Christian School in Lima, Peru.* Edinburgh, STK: Knox
Press, 1993. x, 230 pp. Paper. 0904422518.
    The story of Colegio San Andres, a Christian school
founded in 1917, in Lima, Peru, by the Free Church of Scotland; as told by one who served as a mission teacher (1959-
1977) and as a school headmaster (1988-1992).

AM1494 Marin Gonzales, José
*Peuples indigènes, missions religieuses et colonialisme in-
terne dans l'Amazonie péruvienne.* (Studia missionalia Upsaliensia, 55). Uppsala, SW: Uppsala universitat, Svenska
institutet för missionsforskning, 1992. xv, 277 pp.
9185424293.
    A scholarly study of missions to the Ashaninca Indi-
ans of Peru by Roman Catholics and the SIL; with emphasis on mission/state relations.

AM1495 Martin, Luis
*The Intellectual Conquest of Peru: The Jesuit College of
San Pablo 1568-1767.* New York, NYU: Fordham Univer-
sity Press, 1968. xiii, 194 pp. No ISBN.
    A detailed study of the first Jesuit college in Spanish
America and its role in colonial society, from its founda-
tion in 1568 to the expulsion of the order in 1767.

AM1496 Marzal, Manuel M., and José Sánchez Paredes

Religión y Sociedad en el Perú. (Cristianismo y Sociedad, 28, 106). México, MX: Cristianismo y Sociedad, 1990. 129 pp. No ISBN.

A monograph containing eight studies on specific topics concerning religion and society in Peru.

AM1497 Marzal, Manuel M.

Los Caminos Religiosos de los Inmigrantes en la Gran Lima: El Caso de El Agustino. Lima, PE: Pontificia Universidad Católica del Perú, 1989. 452 pp. Paper. No ISBN.

Second edition of a scholarly examination of rural immigrants and their religion in Lima, Peru, based on studies of the parish of El Agustino.

AM1498 Marzal, Manuel M.

Estudios Sobre Religión Campesina. Lima, PE: Pontifica Universidad Católica del Perú, 1988. 294 pp. No ISBN.

Second edition of three scholarly articles by a Jesuit priest and social anthropologist, on the religious thought and ritual of the Peruvian campesino (the image of God among the Ayaviri, the Andean matrimonial custom of *servinaku*, and the religious system of the campesino in Bajo Piura).

AM1499 Marzal, Manuel M.

La Transformación Religiosa Peruana. Lima, PE: Pontificia Universidad Católica del Perú, 1988. 458 pp. No ISBN.

Second edition of a historical-anthropological examination of the religious transformation of the Peruvian people, occasioned by the Spanish conquest of 1531, analyzing Andean beliefs, rituals, organization, and ethics, in relation to evangelization during the colonial era.

AM1500 Maust, John

Peace and Hope in the Corner of the Dead. Miami, FLU: Latin America Mission, 1987. 189 pp. Paper. No ISBN.

A journalist's account of Christian suffering and mission relief effort among evangelical Christians caught between Maoist guerrillas and goverment soldiers in Peru.

AM1501 McCarthy, Dan B.

Mission to Peru: A Story of Papal Volunteers. Milwaukee, WIU: Bruce Publishing, 1967. xii, 164 pp. No ISBN.

An account of the work done in Peru, by the author and his wife, as representatives of the lay organization, "The Papal Volunteers."

AM1502 McIntosh, G. Stewart

Acosta and the "De Procuranda Indorum Salute": A Sixteenth Century Missionary Model with Twentieth Century Implications. Tayport, STK: MAC Research, 1989. 45 pp. Paper. 1871609070.

Reflections on the atypical ministry of Father José de Acosta, SJ (1540-1600) in Peru (1572-1586), where he chose to identify with the common people, rather than serve as a religious agent of the Spanish conquistadors.

AM1503 McIntosh, G. Stewart

Introducción a la Misiología Latino-Americana. Lima, PE: PUCEMAA, 1990. 96 pp. Paper. 1071609127.

Second edition of an introductory textbook on Latin American missiology, including definitions of missiology and mission, role of missionaries, mission in urban, rural, and indigenous settings, and mission in the third millennium; with a special focus on mission in Peru.

AM1504 McIntosh, G. Stewart

The Life and Times of John Ritchie, Scotland and Peru, 1878-1952. Fife, STK: MAC Research Monographs, 1988. 108 pp. Paper. 1871609003.

A monograph, based on archival sources, analyzing the life and missionary contribution of John Ritchie (1878-1952), pioneer Scottish evangelical missionary to Peru (1906-1952), of the Regions Beyond Missionary Union and the Evangelical Union of South America.

AM1505 Money, Herbert

The Money Memoirs: New Zealand and Peru. Edited by G. Stewart McIntosh. Fife, STK: MAC Research, 1989. 3 vols. Paper. 1871609046.

The memoirs of Herbert Money (b.1899), Australian-born missionary of the Free Church of Scotland, 1927-1967, and first Executive Secretary of the National Evangelical Council of Peru (CONEP), 1940 to 1967 [vol. 1: 1930, 110 pp.; vol. 2: 1941, 115 pp.; vol. 3: 1967, 120 pp.].

AM1506 Rossi, Sanna Barlow

God's City in the Jungle. Wheaton, ILU: Tyndale; London, ENK: Coverdale House Publishers, 1975. 156 pp. Paper. 0842310703.

From among the Ticuna people of Peru, the Wycliffe Bible Translators tell their story.

AM1507 Sánchez Prieto, Nicolás

Santo Toribio de Mogrovejo: Apóstol de los Andes. (BAC Popular, 78). Madrid, SP: Biblioteca de Autores Cristianos, 1986. 211 pp. 8422012553.

Biography of Toribio Alfonso de Mogrovejo (1535-1606), second archbishop of Lima, who was responsible for reorganizing the Peruvian church and systematizing the evangelization of the Indians.

AM1508 Schlegelberger, Bruno

Unsere Erde lebt: Zum Verhältnis von altandiner Religion und Christentum in den Hochanden Perus. (NZM, 41). Immensee, SZ: NZM, 1992. 366 pp. Paper. 3858240737.

On the basis of numerous personal interviews, the author sketches the blending of native religion with imported Christianity, among the Quechua-speaking people of the southern and central Andes of Peru.

AM1509 Thielman, Jeff, and Raymond A. Schroth

Volunteer: With the Poor in Peru. New York, NYU: Paulist Press, 1991. iii, 112 pp. Paper. 0809132435.

A readable account, by a Boston College international volunteer, of his experiences at the Jesuit Cristo Rey Center for the Working Child in Tacna, Peru, 1988-1989.

AM1510 Unanue, Hipolito, and Fray Manuel Sobreviela

Historia de las Misiones de Caxamarquilla y Reducción de la Manoa. (Biblioteca Tenanitla: Libros Españoles e Hispanoamericanos, 6). Madrid, SP: Ediciones José Porrua Turanzas, 1963. 155 pp. No ISBN.

A history of the Franciscan missionaries, who introduced Christianity into the northern section of Peru in the 17th and 18th centuries.

AM1511 Uriarte, Manuel Joaquín
Diario de un Misionero de Maynas. (Monumenta Amazónica, B, Misioneros, 2). Iquitos, PE: IIAP-CETA, 1986. 686 pp. 8489295050 (set), 8489295077.
    Revised edition of the diary of Manuel Uriarte, a Jesuit missionary to the Maynas of northern Peru, 1750-1770.

AM1512 Vázquez, Jesus María
Pucallpa: Estudio socio-religioso de una ciudad del Perú. Madrid, SP: Editorial OPE, 1962. 232 pp. Paper. No ISBN.
    This pioneering work in religious sociology in Peru contains maps and statistics.

AM1513 Whalin, Terry, and Chris Woehr
One Bright Shining Path: Faith in the Midst of Terrorism. Wheaton, ILU: Crossway Books, 1993. ix, 223 pp. Paper. 0891077324.
    A popular biography of a Quechua Bible translator and his faithful Christian witness and final martyrdom by the Shining Path in 1989 in Peru.

Suriname [Dutch Guiana]

See also GW28 and HI740.

AM1514 Doth, R. E. C.
Kondre sa jere (het land zal het horen): 200 jaar zending onder de bosnegers van Suriname. (Boeken der Broeders, 4). Zeist, NE: Seminarie der Evangelische Broedergemeente, 1965. 66 pp. Paper. No ISBN.
    A concise general history of Protestant mission amongst the original black population of inland Suriname, 1765-1965.

AM1515 Fontaine, Jos
Onderweg van afhankelijkheid naar zelfstandigheid: 250 jaar Hernhutterzending in Suriname, 1735-1985. Paramaribo, SR: Evangelische Broedergemeente in Suriname, 1985. 140 pp. No ISBN.
    This richly illustrated book describes 250 years of Moravian mission in Suriname (1735-1985).

AM1516 Lamur, Humphrey E.
De kerstening van de slaven van de Surinaamse plantage Vossenburg, 1847-1878. (Vakgroep CA-NWS, 23). Amsterdam, NE: Anthrop.-Sociol. Centrum, 1985. 68 pp. Paper. No ISBN.
    A case study about the ideas of the Moravian brothers on slavery, through the story of the conversion of slaves on a sugar plantation in Suriname, 1847-1878; based on reports of the missionaries.

AM1517 Linde, J. M. van der
Surinaamse suikerheren en hun kerk: Plantagekolonie en handselskerk ten tijde van Johannes Basseliers, predikant en planter in Suriname, 1667-1689. Wageningen, NE: H. Veenman, 1966. 263 pp. No ISBN.
    "Suriname sugar-masters and their church" describes the plantation colony (1667 to 1689), its slavery, and the role of the Protestant church; with the life of minister and planter Johannes Basseliers as a starting point.

AM1518 Raalte, Jannes van
Secularisatie en zending in Suriname: Over het secularisatieproces in verband met het zendingswerk van de Evangelische Broedergemeente in Suriname. (Proefschrift Theol.

Hogeschool Geref. Kerken Kampen). Wageningen, NE: H. Veenman, 1973. 276 pp. Paper. No ISBN.
    Opposing A. Th. van Leuwen, the author states that secularization is not an irreversible process; shown through a case study of the Moravian mission in Suriname, 1770-1970.

AM1519 Vernooij, Joop
Aktie Grond-Rechten Binnenland. Paramaribo, SR: Stichting Wetenschappelijke Informatie, 1989. 24 pp. Paper. 9991490051.
    Background regarding a "Declaration for Human Rights" by Indians residing in the Apoera, Lower Marowijne, and Santigron areas in the interior of Suriname.

AM1520 Vernooij, Joop
Indianen en Kerken in Suriname: Identiteit en Autonomie in het Binnenland. Paramaribo, SR: Stichting Wetenschappelijke Informatie, 1989. 178 pp. Paper. 999149006X.
    Exploration of relationships between the Suriname Indian tribes, their autonomies and senses of identity, as they relate to the religious influences of Evangelical brothers, the Catholic Church, and the American missionaries.

AM1521 Vernooij, Joop
De rooms-Katholieke Kerk in Suriname vanaf 1866. Paramaribo, SR: J. Vernooij, 1974. 246 pp. No ISBN.
    A thesis containing the history of the Roman Catholic church in Suriname, from 1866.

AM1522 Zamuel, Hesdie Stuart
Johannes King: Profeet en apostel van het Surinaamse Bosland. (Mission-Missiologisch Onderzoek in Nederland, 6). Zoetermeer, NE: Boekencentrum, 1994. vi, 241 pp. Paper. 9023919505.
    A dissertation on the life and work of Johannes King (c1830-1898), whose theology combined his African heritage as a Maroon in Suriname with Moravian doctrine.

AM1523 Zeefuik, K. A.
Hernhutter Zending en Haagsche Maatschappij 1828-1867: Een hoofdstuk uit de geschiedenis van zending en emancipatie in Suriname. (Proefschrift Theol. Fac. Rijksuniversiteit Utrecht). Utrecht, NE: Drukkerij Elinkwijk, 1973. 192 pp. Paper. No ISBN.
    A detailed study of the complex relation between the Moravian Mission in Suriname and the humanitarian "Society for the Advancement of Religious Education among the Slaves and other heathen people in Suriname," 1828-1867, presenting a chapter in the history of the emancipation of slaves, and the role of Christian missions in this process.

Uruguay

See also AM298, AM1268, and AM1459.

AM1524 Cheuiche, José
Sepé Tiaraju Der Ietze Häuptling. Translated by Helmut Burger. Erlangen, GW: Ev.-Luth. Mission; Mettingen, GW: Brasilienkunde-Verlag, 1996. 287 pp. 3872142704 (V), 3885590646 (B).
    German translation of an eighteenth century book entitled *Sepé Tiaraju*, chronicling the struggle by rural Jesuits and native Guarini, led by this folk hero, to preserve both their independence and their indigenous religion, in the battle between Spain and Portugal for supremacy.

AM1525 Ferrando, Jorge, and María Bonino

Presencia Cristiana en las Experiencias de Promoción Popular. (Serie Investigaciones). Montevideo, UY: Ediciones de Observatorio del Sur, 1994. 140 pp. 9974597080.

Collaborators of the Centre of Research and Documentation (Observatorio del Sur—OBSUR) of Montevideo, Uruguay, investigate the concrete experiences of Christian groups committed to integral development and liberation of the poor in Uruguay.

Venezuela

See also HI234, CH166, AM238, AM295, and AM1407.

AM1526 Alonso, Isidoro, Medardo Luzardo et al.

La Iglesia en Venezuela y Ecuador: Estructuras eclesiásticas. (Estudios Socio-religiosos Latino-americanos, 3/I). Friburgo, SZ: FERES; Madrid, SP: OCSHA, 1962. 201 pp. Paper. No ISBN.

Research on social, economic, and ecclesiastical conditions in Venezuela and Ecuador, with statistics and graphs.

AM1527 Carrocera, Buenaventura de

Misión de los capuchinos en Guayana. (Biblioteca de la Academia Nacional de la Historia/Fuentes para la historia colonial de Venezuela, 139-141). Caracas, VE: Academia Nacional de la Historia, 1979. 3 vols. No ISBN.

A history of the Capuchin Franciscan mission among the Guayana of present-day Venezuela, including documents, from 1760 to 1819 [vol. 1: *Introducción y resumen histórico: Documentos (1682-1758)*, (xxxvii, 414 pp.); vol. 2: *Documentos (1760-1785)*, (406 pp.); vol. 3: *Documentos (1785-1819)*, (368 pp.)].

AM1528 Pelleprat, P. Pierre

Relato de las Misiones e los Padres de la Compañía de Jesús en las Islas y en Tierra Firme de América Meridional. Edited by José del Rey. (Biblioteca de la Academia Nacional de la Historia, 77). Caracas, VE: Fuentes para la Historia Colonial de Venezuela, 1965. lxi, 112 pp. No ISBN.

The story, by a French Jesuit, of the missions to Venezuela and the nearby Caribbean Islands in the 17th century.

AM1529 Ritchie, Mark Andrew

Spirit of the Rainforest: A Yanomamö Shaman's Story. Chicago, ILU: Island Lake Press, 1996. 271 pp. 0964695219.

An excellent presentation of a shamanistic worldview, and of the power of the Gospel to transform lives, as a Yanomamö shaman tells the story of his life and dealings with the spirits, of the coming of anthropologists and missionaries, and of their impact on his culture.

AM1530 Torrubia, Padre José

Crónica de la Provincia Franciscana de Santa Cruz de la Española y Caracas: Libro Primero de la Novena Parte de la Crónica General de la Orden Franciscana. (Biblioteca de la Academia Nacional de la Historia, 108). Caracas, VE: Fuentes para la Historia Colonial de Venezuela, 1972. 803 pp. No ISBN.

A chronicle, by a contemporary Franciscan priest, of missionary activities in a northern province of Venezuela during the 18th century.

ASIA

David Bundy (Middle East), Roger Hedlund (South Asia), James M. Phillips (East Asia), John Roxborogh (Southeast Asia), Subeditors

Asia, by geography and population, is the giant among the world's continents. It stretches east to west from Japan to Turkey, and north to south from the Russian arctic region to Indonesia and Sri Lanka. Its population of 3,747 million in 2000 was 60 percent of the world's population. It includes the two largest population concentrations—China and India.

By contrast, Christians are a small minority among Asia's peoples. Numbering just over 307 million in 2000, they were but 8.2 percent of the total. Only the Philippines has a majority Christian population (90 percent).

Asia has the largest number of unreached peoples in the world. In 27 of 49 Asian nations, Christians are less than 2 percent of the population. In countries such as Mongolia, Maldives and Bhutan, they are not even 0.3 percent of the population (Athyal, 1996:1, 7).

Unique among the continents, churches independent of historic Christianity contain the majority of Asia's Christians. They are found in 3,308 denominations in 49 countries. The number of evangelicals in Asia is greater than the combined total in North America, Europe, and Oceania (Athyal, 2). Proportions in Asian Christianity of other confessional groups are as follows: Roman Catholics 36 percent, Protestants 16.3 percent, Orthodox percent, Anglicans 0.2 percent, and marginal Christians 0.8 percent. A smaller proportion of Christians than in other continents are *double-affiliated* 8.2 percent (*WCE*, 1:12).

One anomaly of Asian Christianity is that it is still viewed by the general populace as a *Western* religion, although Christianity originated in Asia, and most of its missionaries today are Asians. An estimated 25,000 nationals from Asian countries serve as cross-cultural missionaries. Many, as in India, cross-cultural boundaries within their own country. Others, in increasing numbers, from South Korea, China, India, the Philippines, and other countries, cross national borders in mission (*EDWM*, 85). This bibliography includes works on this phenomenon both in subsections by country, and under "Third World Missions," in "Missions: Methods."

The subsection on "History" contains general works on mission in the continent. Other works on mission history are found under subregions and countries. Documents from Asian conferences concerning mission are to be found under "Conferences and Congresses."

Works on church and society issues are found primarily by country. Regional and continent-wide works are grouped in the subsection on "Church and Society." Since many works on Asian theology are missional in content, they are included under two subheadings: "Asian Theologies" and "Indian Christian Theologies."

The rich literature on Christian approaches to other faiths in Asia is found, mainly, in the chapter on "Christianity and Other Religions," with its subsections on Buddhism, Chinese religions, Hinduism, Islam, and Japanese religion.

Most biographies of mission and national leaders are found by country, with separate subsections for China, India, and Korea. Biographies of persons whose ministry reached several countries are grouped under "General: Biography," either individual or collective.

Works on mission are listed by country, where possible, with a secondary listing in the "History" chapter by missionary order or society. The Asian countries are grouped in four subregions: East Asia, Middle East, South Asia, and Southeast Asia.

Norman E. Thomas

Bibliographies

See also AS316.

AS1 Anderson, Bernard W., and John Correia-Afonso, comps. *Annual Bibliography of Christianity in India, 1981-.* Bombay, II: Heras Institute of Indian History and Culture, 1985. 65 pp. Paper. No ISBN.

An annual listing of books, pamphlets, and periodical articles, without annotation, but with name and subject indexes.

AS2 Ebisawa, Arimichi, comp.

Christianity in Japan: A Bibliography of Japanese and Chinese Sources, Part 1 (1543-1858). Tokyo, JA: International Christian University, Committee on Asian Cultural Studies, 1960. xxvii, 171 pp. No ISBN.

Volume 1 of a projected Bibliography of Christianity in Asia covers publications in Japan, from the entry of the Jesuit fathers in 1543 to the year before the arrival of the first Protestant missionaries in 1859; includes books both directly and indirectly related to Christianity and a number in which Christian influence is apparent.

AS3 Fenton, Thomas P., and Mary J. Heffron, eds.

Asia and Pacific: A Directory of Resources. Maryknoll, NYU: Orbis Books; London, ENK: Zed Books, 1986. xx, 137 pp. 088344528X (O), 0862326354 (Z hdbk), 0862326362 (Z pbk).

This volume, a directory of resources on Asia and the Pacific, is in a series of twelve, on Third World regions and issues, compiled by Data Center's Third World Resources Project; also compiled by the editors.

AS4 Mac, M. R., ed.

Conversion, Protest Movements and Change: A Select Bibliography (with Special Reference to Christianity in India). (CSS, 6). Surat, II: Centre for Social Studies, 1989. xii, 45 pp. Paper. No ISBN.

An important bibliography of 424 entries on change of religion in India, distributed under six subthemes: conversion and social movement, some aspects of conversion to Christianity, Christianity and the scheduled castes, Christianity and the scheduled tribes, conversion to non-Christian religions, and caste, class, and Christianity.

AS5 Peking Pei-t'ang

Catalogue de la Bibliothèque du Pei-t'ang. Paris, FR: Les Belles Lettres, 1969. iv, 1,334 pp. No ISBN.

New edition of the 1949 catalogue of one of the most valuable Christian libraries in the Far East.

AS6 Roxborogh, John

A Bibliography of Christianity in Malaysia. (Malaysian Church History Series, 2). Kuala Lumpur, MY: Seminari Theoloji Malaysia; Kuala Lumpur, MY: Catholic Research Centre, 1990. 68 pp. Paper. No ISBN.

A comprehensive resource guide to the writings about the history of the church in Malaysia.

AS7 Satyaprakash, comp.

Christianity: A Select Bibliography. (Subject Bibliography Series, 10). Haryana, II: Indian Documentation Service, 1986. 162 pp. Paper. No ISBN.

This 10th volume, in the Indian Documentation Service's Subject Bibliography Series, lists 1,534 research and general interest articles from 120 journals and two daily publications; published in India during the years 1962-1985, for use by librarians, researchers, and students of Christianity and comparative religion.

AS8 Yu, David C., comp.

Religion in Postwar China: A Critical Analysis and Annotated Bibliography. (Bibliographies and Indexes in Religious Studies, 28). Westport, CTU: Greenwood, 1994. xviii, 365 pp. 0313267324.

An annotated bibliography of 1,005 books and articles published in English and Chinese, from 1945 to 1990; with two brief overview chapters on religion in pre-modern and modern China.

AS9 Zürcher, Erik, Nicolas Standaert, and Adrianus Dudink, eds.

Bibliography of the Jesuit Mission in China (ca.1580-ca.1680). (CNWS Publications, 5). Leiden, NE: Leiden University, Centre of Non-Western Studies, 1991. iv, 136 pp. Paper. 9073782058.

About 1,000 scholarly books and articles in major Western languages, on the early, 17th-century Jesuit mission in China, and the Chinese reaction to it.

Serials and Periodicals

See also EV7 and AS416.

AS10 *Asia Journal of Theology.* Vol. 1, no. 1 (Apr. 1987)-. Semiannual

Singapore, SI: North East Asian Association of Theological Schools; Singapore, SI: Association for Theological Education in South East Asia, 1987-. ISSN 02171244.

Essays on Asian biblical scholarship and theological thinking with special relation to the cultures of Asia, issues in theological education, and concerns of member schools of the sponsoring associations; continues the *East Asia Journal Theology.*

AS11 *Bangalore Theological Forum.* Vol. 1, no. 1 (Jan. 1967)-. Semiannual

Bangalore, II: United Theological College, 1967-. ISSN 02539365.

Essays and book reviews by faculty and friends of the United Theological College, with focus on theological concerns in India.

AS12 *Bridge: Church Life in China Today.* No. 1 (Sept. 1983)-no. 64 (Mar.-Apr. 1994). Bimonthly

Kowloon, HK: Christian Study Centre on Chinese Religion and Culture, 1983-1994. No ISSN.

Results of the centre's research to understand Chinese society, culture, and religions, from an ecumenical perspective.

AS13 *CCA News.* Vol. 1, no. 1 (Mar. 15, 1975)-. Monthly

Hong Kong, CH: CCA, 1975-. ISSN 01299891.

This official organ of the CCA contains news on church and society issues in Asia, global currents, and the programs of the CCA.

AS14 *China and the Church Today.* Vol. 1, no. 1 (Jan. 1979)-vol. 8, no. 4 (Oct. 1986). Bimonthly

Shatin, N.T., HK: Chinese Church Research Center, 1979-1986. No ISSN.

In this newsletter, the Research Center, directed by Jonathan Chao, sought to provide to the church worldwide with accurate information concerning the church in the People's Republic of China.

AS15 *China Notes.* Vol. 1, no. 1 (Sept. 1962)-vol. 30, no. 3-4 (Summer & Autumn 1992). Quarterly published semiannually

New York, NYU: NCCUSA, CWS, 1962-199. No ISSN.

News and reflections on developments of the church in China, plus book reviews.

AS16 *Chinese Theological Review.* Vol. 1 (1985)-. Annual

Holland, MIU: FTESA, 1985. 4 vols. Paper. ISSN 08967660.

Articles and sermons by Chinese Christians, providing a broad spectrum of current theological writings; edited by Janice Wickeri.

AS17 *Dansalan Quarterly.* Vol. 1, no. 1 (Oct. 1979)-vol. 10, no. 4 (1989). Quarterly
Marawi City, PH: Dansalan Research Center, Dansalan Junior College, 1979-1989. No ISSN.

Short essays on issues of religion and culture, and Christian mission to Muslims in Mindanao, the Philippines; superseded the center's *Occasional Papers, DRC Reports, and Bibliographical Bulletin.*

AS18 *East Asia Journal of Theology.* Vol. 1, no. 1 (1983)-vol. 4, no. 2 (Oct. 1986). Semiannual
Singapore, SI: *East Asia Journal of Theology*, 1983-1986. ISSN 02173859.

The organ of the associations for theological education in Northeast and Southeast Asia; successor to the *Northeast Asia Journal of Theology* and the *South East Asia Journal of Theology*; continued as the *Asia Journal of Theology*.

AS19 *Gleanings.* Vol. 1, no. 1 (Jan. 1982)-. Quarterly
Colombo, CE: Ecumenical Institute for Study and Dialogue, 1982-. No ISSN.

Extracts and summaries from books, articles, and conference reports, designed to keep readers informed about current social issues and movements, and Christian thought and action concerning them.

AS20 *Gurukul Journal of Theological Studies.* Vol. 1, no. 1 (1989)-. Semiannual
Madras, II: Gurukul, 1989-. No ISSN.

Papers from Gurukal staff seminars and other academic gatherings, with focus on theology and culture in India.

AS21 *Indian Church History Review.* Vol. 1. no. 1 (June 1967)-. Semiannual
Bangalore, II: Church History Association of India, 1967-. ISSN 00194530.

Articles and book reviews on the church history of India; supersedes the *Bulletin of the Church History Association of India.*

AS22 *Indian Journal of Theology.* Vol. 1 (1952)-. Semiannual
Serampore, II: Serampore College, Theology Department, 1952-. ISSN 00195685.

Articles by Indian theologians, mainly on issues of theology, culture, and the religions of India.

AS23 Lodwick, Kathleen L., comp.
The Chinese Recorder Index: A Guide to Christian Missions in Asia, 1867-1941. Wilmington, DEU: Scholarly Resources, 1986. 2 vols. 0842022503.

A complete person, subject, and missions/organization index to the seventy-two year journal that became the major voice of Protestant missionaries in China [vol. 1: lviii, 544 pp.; vol. 2: 552 pp.].

AS24 *Religion and Society.* Vol. 1 (1954)-. Quarterly
Bangalore, II: CISRS, 1954-. ISSN 00343591.

Articles and book reviews on issues of religion and society and social justice in South Asia.

AS25 *S E Asia Journal of Theology.* Vol. 1 (1959/60)-vol. 9 (1967/68). Annual
Singapore, SI: ATESEA, 1959-1968. ISSN 00383406.

A scholarly journal to encourage Southeast Asian biblical scholarship and theological thinking; titled *The South East Asia Journal of Theology* from vol. 10 (1968).

AS26 *The Bulletin [Philippines].* Vol. 1 (1967)-vol. 4, no. 1-2 (Aug. 1970). Quarterly
Manila, PH: Christian Institute for Ethnic Studies in Asia, 1967-1970. No ISSN.

Papers on issues of Christianity and culture by participants in St. Andrew's Theological Seminary's Christian Institute for Ethnic Studies in Asia.

AS27 *The Japan Christian Quarterly.* Vol. 1 (1926)-vol. 57 (1991); suspended 1942-1950. Annual
Tokyo, JA: CLS, 1926-1991. ISSN 00214361.

Initially sponsored by the Fellowship of Christian Missionaries in Japan, this journal included a broad range of articles on Christianity in Japan.

AS28 *The Japan Christian Review.* Vol. 58 (1992)-vol. 64 (1998). Annual
Tokyo, JA: Kyo Bun Kwan (The Christian Literature Society of Japan), 1992-1998. ISSN 0918516X.

Published in English, this journal provided a wide range of articles and reviews of books in English, on Christianity in relation to Japanese religions, culture, and social issues.

AS29 *The Northeast Asia Journal of Theology.* No. 1 (Mar. 1968)-no. 28 (Sept. 1982). Semiannual
Tokyo, JA: North East Asian Association of Theological Schools, 1968-1982. ISSN 05498899.

Essays by Northeast Asian theological educators, often papers read at the annual meetings of the Northeast Asia Association of Theological Schools and its student conferences; continued as the *East Asia Journal of Theolgy.*

AS30 *The South East Asia Journal of Theology.* Vol. 10 (1968)-vol. 23 (1982). Semiannual
Manila, PH: ATESEA, 1968-1982. ISSN 00383406.

Essays by Southeast Asian theological educators, with special issues by countries in the region; continues the *S E Asia Journal of Theology*; continued as the *East Asia Journal of Theology.*

AS31 *Theological Review: The Near East School of Theology.* Vol. 1, no. 1 (April 1978)-. Semiannual
Beirut, LE: Near East School of Theology, 1978-. ISSN 03799557.

Essays, mostly by theological educators in the Middle East, on biblical and theological themes, plus book reviews.

Documentation and Archives

See also AF30, AS664-AS665, AS668, AS740, AS1101, AS1118, and AS1312.

AS32 Chatterjee, Sunil Kumar, comp.
The Carey Library Pamphlets: Religious Series: A catalogue. Serampore, II: Council of Serampore College, 1982. 55 pp. No ISBN.

A listing of rare archival documents at the William Carey Library in Serampore, India.

AS33 Crouch, Archie R. et al., eds.
Christianity in China: A Scholars' Guide to Resources in the Libraries and Archives of the United States. Armonk, NYU: M. E. Sharpe, 1989. lvi, 709 pp. 0873324196.

A comprehensive guide to resources in libraries and archives of the United States, dealing with the existence and progress of Christianity and Christian missions in China; including books, serial holdings, manuscripts, minutes/records/reports, maps, and audio-visual materials, both in Chinese languages and English.

AS34 Eilers, Franz-Josef, ed.

*For All the Peoples of Asia: Federation of Asian Bishops'
Conferences Documents from 1992 to 1996.* Quezon City,
PHU: Claretian Publications; Maryknoll, NYU: Orbis
Books, 1992-1997. 2 vols. Paper.

A collection of documents from general sessions and
special conferences, of, or sponsored by, the Roman Catholic Federation of Asian Bishop's Conferences [vol. 1, *From
1970 to 1991,* 1992, xxx, 356 pp., 9715015220 (PH),
0883448378 (US); vol. 2, *From 1992 to 1996,* 1997, xi,
319 pp., 9715017347 (PH)].

AS35 Gnanapiragasam, John, and Felix Wilfred, eds.

*Being Church in Asia: Theological Advisory Commission
Documents (1986-92).* Quezon City, PHU: Claretian Publications, 1994. xi, 140 pp. Paper. 9715016014.

A collection of three documents from the Theological
Advisory Commission of the Federation of Asian Bishops'
Conferences, on interreligious dialogue, the local church,
and the church and politics.

AS36 Lai, John Yung-Hsiang, comp.

*Protestant Missionary Works in Chinese [at the] Harvard-
Yenching Library, Harvard University.* Zug, SZ: IDC, 1983.
40 pp. Paper. No ISBN.

An important collection of hundreds of missionary-au-
thored writings in Chinese, published in the 19th and early
20th century at mission presses in Canton, Macao, Foochow, and Shanghai, mainly by American Board missionaries; with the full text available on IDC microfiche in Zug,
Switzerland.

AS37 Nobili, Roberto de

Roberto de Nobili on Indian Customs. Edited by Svarimuthu Rajamanickam. Palayamkottai, II: De Nobili Research Institute, 1972. xxii, 168 pp. No ISBN.

Writings by the noted 17th-century Jesuit missionary
to India.

AS38 Ray, N. R., and N. S. Bose, eds.

*A Descriptive Classified Catalogue of Christian Mission-
ary Records in Calcutta and Around.* Calcutta, II: Institute of Historical Studies, 1988. 2 vols. No ISBN.

A detailed catalogue with descriptions of contents of
documents in the Protestant missionary archives located in
Calcutta, and Bengal Province in India [vol. 1: 1986, xxxiii, 359 pp.; vol. 2: 1988, 247 pp.].

AS39 Rosales, Gaudencio B., and C. G. Arévalo, eds.

*For All the Peoples of Asia: Federation of Asian Bishops'
Conferences Documents from 1970 to 1991.* Maryknoll,
NYU: Orbis Books; Quezon City, PH: Claretian Publica-
tions, 1992. xxx, 356 pp. 0883448378 (O), 9715015220
(C).

A collection of documents from general sessions and
special conferences of, or sponsored by, the Roman Catholic Federation of Asian Bishops' Conferences.

AS40 Wicki, Josef, and John Gomes, eds.

Documenta Indica. (Monumenta Historica Societatis Jesu).
Rome, IT: Institutum Historicum Societatis Jesu, 1966-
1981. 16 vols. 8870411324 (vol. 1), 8870411332 (vol. 2).

A multi-volume collection of documents, mostly in
Spanish, Portuguese, and Latin, on Jesuit missions in India and Goa in the 16th century (1563-1597) [VI, (1563-
1566), 1960, xxv, 954 pp.; VII (1566-1569), 1962, xxv, 760
pp.; VIII (1569-1573), 1964, xxvi, 833 pp.; IX (1573-1575),
1966, xxiv, 775 pp.; X (1575-1577), 1968, xxiv, 1,125 pp.;
XI (1577-1580), 1970, xxxii, 923 pp.; XII (1580-1583),
1972, xxix, 1,041 pp.; XIII (1583-1585), 1975, xxi, 946
pp.; XIV (1585-1588), 1979, xxxviii, 1,015 pp.; XV (1588-
1592), 1981, xxvii, 914 pp.; XVI (1592-1594), 1984, xxvi,
1,161 pp.; XVII (1595-1597), 1988, xix, 446 pp.; XVIII
(1595-1597), 1988, x, 518 pp.]; other volumes published
before 1960.

History

See also HI128, HI159, HI235, HI293, CR711, CR1449, and
AS806.

AS41 De Souza, Teotonio R., ed.

Discoveries, Missionary Expansion and Asian Cultures. New
Delhi, II: Concept Publishing, 1994. 215 pp. 8170224977.

Seventeen papers by Indian scholars reassessing 450 years
of Roman Catholic, especially Jesuit, missions in Asia.

AS42 EATWOT: Working Commission on Church History

Asia and Christianity. Edited by M. D. David. Bombay, II:
Himalaya Publishing House, 1985. xiii, 196 pp. No ISBN.

Papers of the second consultation of the Working Commission on Church History of the Ecumenical Association of
Third World Theologians, including thirteen essays by Asian
historians rewriting the history of the church in their respective countries.

AS43 England, John C.

*The Hidden History of Christianity in Asia: The Churches of
the East before the Year 1500.* Dehli, II: ISPCK; Hong Kong,
JA: CCA, 1996. xvi, 203 pp. 8172142420.

A survey of Christianity from the 2nd to the 15th century
(pre-colonial) by the CCA's leader in its Programme for Theology and Culture in Asia.

AS44 Hao, Yap Kim

*From Prapat to Colombo: History of the Christian Confer-
ence of Asia (1957-1995).* Shatin, HK: CCA, 1995. 205 pp.
Paper. No ISBN.

A narrative history by the CCA's former General Secretary (1973-1985).

AS45 Jacques, Roland

*De Castro Marim à Faïfo: Naissance et développement du
padroado portugais d'Orient des origines à 1659.* Lisbon,
PO: Fundação Calouste Gulbenkian Serviço de Educação,
1999. 215 pp. 9723108445.

The history of the patronage given by the Pope to the
Portuguese crown in the Orient, from 1500 to 1659, with focus on the development of the missions in Malacca, Macao,
and Vietnam.

AS46 Moffett, Samuel Hugh

A History of Christianity in Asia: Vol. I: Beginnings to 1500.
Maryknoll, NYU: Orbis Books, 1998. xxvi, 560 pp. Paper.
1570751626.

Second revised edition of the first of two volumes of a
comprehensive history of Christianity in Asia, covering the
expansion of Christianity to Persia and India in the first century A.D., and its later outreach to China; originally published
in 1991 by HarperSan Francisco.

AS—ASIA

AS47 Palmer, Bernard, and Marjorie Palmer
Light a Small Candle: The Story of Evangelical Free Church Missions in the Orient. (Heritage Series, 5). Minneapolis, MNU: Free Church Publications, 1982. 460 pp. Paper. 0911801541.

The first book in a three-volume popular history of the Overseas Mission Department of the Evangelical Free Church (volume 5 of the ten-volume centennial history of the denomination), focusing on work in China, the Philippines, Malaysia, and Singapore.

AS48 Philip, T. V.
East of the Euphrates: Early Christianity in Asia. Delhi, II: CSS/ISPCK, 1998. xii, 192 pp. Paper. 8172144415.

Evidence for the first century advancement of Christianity in southeast and east Asian countries, such as Ceylon, Burma, Indonesia, and Korea, including the theology and missionary impulses of the early Asian Christian communities.

AS49 Wetzel, Klaus
Kirchengeschichte Asiens. (Monographien und Studienbücher). Wuppertal, GW: R. Brockhaus Verlag, 1995. xii, 605 pp. Paper. 3417293987.

A narrative history of Christianity in Asia, from the New Testament to the present; written as a textbook for theological students.

General Works

See also HI234, CR225, SO248, SO450, ED21, ED117, ED127, MI57, SP264, and AS72.

AS50 Amaladoss, Michael
Making All Things New: Dialogue, Pluralism, and Evangelization in Asia. Maryknoll, NYU: Orbis Books, 1990. x, 203 pp. Paper. 0883446774.

Essays by the noted Indian Jesuit missiologist on the future of the church in Asia, focusing on themes of dialogue, pluralism, and evangelization.

AS51 Athyal, Saphir, ed.
Church in Asia Today:Challenge and Opportunities. Singapore, SI: Asia LCWE, 1996. 539 pp. Paper. 9812202161.

Essays on the status of Christianity in every Asian country, from an evangelical perspective.

AS52 Beyerhaus, Peter
In Ostasien erlebt. (Weltweite Reihe, 26). Stuttgart, GW: Evan Missionsverlag, 1972. 124 pp. 3771401682.

A travel account by the Tubingen missiologist, as he taught, preached, and reported on various mission aspects during a trip to the Far East.

AS53 Buultjens, Ralph
Rebuilding the Temple: Tradition and Change in Modern Asia. Maryknoll, NYU: Orbis Books, 1974. xvi, 236 pp. 0883444305 (hdbk), 0883444313 (pbk).

An overview of continuities and change in Asian societies, including religion, development, and modernization, by a Sri Lankan-born scholar of Asian politics and philosophy.

AS54 Christian Conference of Asia
CCA Directory 1991. Kowloon, HK: CCA, 1991. 71 pp. Paper. No ISBN.

A concise directory with addresses of CCA organizations, leadership, programs, and member churches.

AS55 Clark, Francis X.
An Introduction to the Catholic Church of Asia. (Ateneo University Publications; Cardinal Bea Studies, 9). Manila, PH: Cardinal Bea Institute, Loyala School of Theology; Manila, PH: Ateneo de Manila University, 1987. xii, 150 pp. Paper. No ISBN.

The first concise introduction in English to the Catholic Church of Asia as a whole, organized around ten themes; with an appendix on mission and dialogue.

AS56 Fleming, John, and Ken Wright
Structures for a Missionary Congregation: The Shape of the Christian Community in Asia Today. Singapore, SI: EACC, 1964. viii, 123 pp. Paper. No ISBN.

An Asian contribution to the ecumenical study on "The Missionary Structure of the Congregation."

AS57 *Glad Sacrifice*
Carrollton, TXU: Gospel for Asia, n.d. 22:43 mins. No ISBN.

Stories on video of how native Asian evangelists are reaching unreached peoples on that continent.

AS58 Hoke, Donald E., ed.
The Church in Asia. Chicago, ILU: Moody, 1975. 703 pp. 0802415431.

A comprehensive country-by-country Protestant survey written by missiologists with close personal experience in the areas concerned; includes bibliographies and index.

AS59 Izco Ilundain, José A.
Retos a la Iglesia de Asia en los años 90: V Asamblea Plenaria de Obispos Asiáticos. (Misiones Extranjeras, 120). Madrid, SP: Misiones Extranjeras, 1990. 95 pp. Paper. No ISBN.

A monograph containing studies, testimonies, and documents, including the final document of the Fifth Plenary Assembly of the FABC (Federation of Episcopal Conference of Asia) and the 31 December 1989 Declaration of the Association of Indian Theologians.

AS60 John, Clement
Seoul to Manila: The Christian Conference of Asia from 1985 to 1990. Kowloon, HK: CCA, 1990. iii, 153 pp. Paper. 9627439045.

The report of the program activities of the CCA, from 1985 to 1990, to its 9th General Assembly (Manila, 1990), showing extensive joint action by the churches in justice ministries.

AS61 Ohm, Thomas
Asiens Nein und Ja zum westlichen Christentum. (2nd Edition). Munich, GW: Kosel, 1960. 242 pp. No ISBN.

A revised and expanded edition of *Asiens Kritik am abendländischen Christentum* (1948), this book asserts that much of Asian criticism of Christianity is founded on ignorance and misunderstanding, and emphasizes the importance of a fusion of the truths of revelation with the language, thought patterns, and experience of Asia.

AS62 Palmer, Spencer J.
Church Encounters Asia. Salt Lake City, UTU: Deseret Book Company, 1970. 201 pp. 087747365X.

A narrative survey of Mormon missions in Asia in 1970.

AS–ASIA

AS63 Philip, T. V.
Ecumenism in Asia. Delhi, II: ISPCK and CSS, 1994. ix, 174 pp. Paper. 8172141920.

A collection of essays by an Indian church leader on various aspects of ecumenism in Asia, including church union negotiations and the history of the CCA.

AS64 Schmidt, Wolfgang R.
Der lange Marsch zurück: Der Weg der Christenheit in Asien. (Lese-Zeichen). Munich, GW: Kaiser, 1980. 310 pp. Paper. 3459012811.

Focusing on specific Asian countries such as Thailand, Vietnam, and Korea, the author demonstrates how the Christian religion, founded in Asia and later completely Europeanized, can only become genuinely Asian by returning to the local cultures and taking into account the concerns of the poor.

AS65 Song, Choan-Seng
Christian Mission in Reconstruction: An Asian Analysis. Maryknoll, NYU: Orbis Books, 1977. xvi, 276 pp. 0883440733.

A creative reconsideration of Christian mission in Asia, developed with interaction between the biblical text and the Asian context, by the Principal of Tainan Theological College.

AS66 Titze, Kurt
Christen in Asien: Bericht über eine Pilgerreise. Trier, GW: Spee Verlag, 1977. 139 pp. 3877600182.

The journalist-author reports over his pilgrimmage to Christian sites and shrines throughout Asia, beginning in India with an ancient Catholic cemetery, to Sumatra and its Batak-Christian heritage.

Conferences and Congresses

See also EA140, CO57, ED55, SP304, AS166, AS360, AS607, AS631, AS788, and OC52.

AS67 Achutegui, Pedro S. de, ed.
Towards a "Dialogue of Life": Ecumenism in the Asian Context: First Asian Congress of Jesuit Ecumenists, Manila, June 18-23, 1975. (Cardinal Bea Studies, 4). Manila, PH: Cardinal Bea Institute, Loyola School of Theology, 1976. xii, 336 pp. No ISBN.

An important introduction to how Asian Catholic leaders approach interfaith dialogue.

AS68 Asian Monastic Conference (2nd: Bangalore, India, 1973)
Christian Monks and Asian Religions: Proceedings.... (Cistercian Studies, 9). Chimay, BE: Abbaye Notre Dame de la Paix, 1974. 336 pp. No ISBN.

Proceedings of the Second Asian Monastic Conference, 14-22 October 1973.

AS69 Asian Monastic Congress (2nd: Bangalore, India, 1973)
Les moines chrétiens face aux religions d'Asie. Vanves, FR: Aide Impantation Monastique, 1974. 366 pp. No ISBN.
French edition.

AS70 CCA
Building a Just and Convivial World: Niles Memorial Lectures. Kowloon, HK: CCA, 1990. 51 pp. Paper. 9627439053.

Three lectures on aspects of Christian mission in Asian society (post-Cold War politics, women and men in community, and Asia in the new world economy); originally presented at the 9th Assembly of the Christian Conference of Asia in June 1990 by Toshiki Mogami, Ranjini Rebera, and Levi Oracion.

AS71 Consultation of Asian Christian Women Artists (1992: Hong Kong)
Creation and Spirituality: Asian Women Expressing Christian Faith through Art. Edited by Rebecca Lozada, and Alison O'Grady. Shatin, HK: CCA, Women's Concerns Desk; Kyoto, JA: Asian Christian Art Association, 1995. 79 pp. Paper. No ISBN.

The illustrated report of the First Consultation of Asian Christian Women Artists (Hong Kong, September 1992).

AS72 EACC (1971, Kuala Lumpur, Malaya)
Missionary Service in Asia Today: A Report on a Consultation Held by the Asia Methodist Advisory Committee February 18-23, 1971. Kuala Lumpur, AM: University of Malaya, 1971. iv, 156 pp. Paper. No ISBN.

Papers and reports from an influential consultation held in cooperation with the Life, Message, Unity Committee of the EACC, which called for new missionary structures and for Asian churches to express their selfhood by assuming responsibility for mission in Asia.

AS73 Gnanakan, Ken R., ed.
Salvation: Some Asian Perspectives. Bangalore, II: Asia Theological Association, 1992. v, 190 pp. Paper. No ISBN.

Eleven papers plus the report of the congress on "Salvation in Asian Contexts" (Yang Peong, Korea, Sept. 1990), sponsored by the Asia Theological Association.

AS74 Jesus Christ with People in Asia: Report of the Asian Consultation in Singapore, July 5-11, 1982
Geylang, SI: Stamford Press, 1982. 71 pp. Paper. No ISBN.

The report of an Asian consultation on the theme "Jesus Christ—the Life of the World" of the WCC's 6th Assembly (Vancouver, 1983).

AS75 Metzler, Josef
Die Synoden in China, Japan und Korea, 1570-1931. (Konziliengeschichte, Reihe A: Darstellungen). Paderborn, GW: Ferdinand Schöningh, 1980. xvii, 324 pp. 3506746804.

A volume in the history of the Catholic synods, with a concentration on those in China, Japan, and Korea, from 1570 to 1931, and the missionary work of the councils.

AS76 Metzler, Josef
Die Synoden in Indochina, 1625-1934. (Konziliengeschichte, Reihe A: Darstellungen). Paderborn, GW: Ferdinand Schöningh, 1984. xxii, 407 pp. 3506746820.

A volume in the history of the Synods, centering on the councils in Indochina from 1625 to 1934, throwing new light on their development, as well as the inner pastoral life of the congregations and their spiritual relationships.

AS77 Seigel, Michael T., and Leonardo N. Mercado, eds.
Towards an Asian Theology of Mission. (Asia-Pacific Missiological Series, 5). Manila, PH: Divine Word Publications, 1995. viii, 141 pp. Paper. 9715700988.

Papers from the 1993 Divine Word Asia-Pacific Zone missiological symposium (Bali, Indonesia, October 1993) on a theology of mission for the Asia-Pacific region.

Church and Society

See also TH571, ME36, CR284, CR357, CR359, CR1100, SO181, SO226, SO427, SO432, SO630, EC80, EC184, EC216, EC251, EC292-EC293, EC337, EC360, EC375, PO123, PO181, CO1, ED13, ED55, ED60, ED132, SP301-SP302, SP309, SP311, AS34, AS51, AS70, AS149, AS237, AS286, AS622, AS625, AS637, AS789, AS880, AS915-AS916, AS925-AS926, AS932, AS948, AS1012, AS1042, AS1057, AS1080, AS1089-AS1090, AS1096, AS1306, AS1319, AS1359, AS1432, and AS1440.

AS78 Amirtham, Samuel, ed.
A Vision for Man: Essays on Faith, Theology and Society. Madras, II: CLS, 1978. v, 416 pp. No ISBN.

A *festschrift* honoring the Indian theologian, ecumenist, and Principal of United Theological College, Bangalore, containing thirty-eight short essays on Russell Chandran's life and work, theology and theological education, church and mission, and faith and society.

AS79 Arai, Tosh
Children of Asia. Singapore, SI: CCA, 1979. 52 pp. No ISBN.

These papers dealing with issues facing children in Asia, were given at the CCA Consultation on the Child (Kuala Lumpur, Malaysia, 28 November-2 December 1978), and from other Asian sources, as CCA's contribution to the International Year of the Child, 1979.

AS80 Atone, Hope S., and Yong Ting Jin
Our Stories, Our Faith. Kowloon, HK: WSCF, 1992. 159 pp. Paper. No ISBN.

Resources from the *Women Doing Theology Workshop* (Taiwan, 1-12 February 1991) culminating ten years of work by the women's program of the WSCF Asia-Pacific Region, to help Asian women tell their personal stories and reread the Bible from their perspectives.

AS81 Carr, Dhyanchand, ed.
God, Christ & God's People in Asia. Shatin, HK: CCA, Theological Concerns, 1995. 143 pp. Paper. No ISBN.

Papers from a working seminar in which twenty-two Asian theologians reflected on God's mission amidst the groaning nations of Asia.

AS82 CCA Youth Tarakwon, Korea April 19-26, 1983
Tarakwon '83. Tarakwon, KO: CCA, 1984. 120 pp. Paper. 9971948206.

Report of an Asian Ecumenical Youth Leader's Seminar (Tarakwon, Korea, 19-26 April 1983), focusing on the involvement of Christian youth in justice concerns in various countries.

AS83 CCA, Urban Rural Mission
Towards a Theology of People: I. Tokyo, JA: CCA, Urban Rural Mission, 1977. ii, 189 pp. Paper. No ISBN.

Reflections by members of the CCA's Urban/Rural action groups, some of them prominent Asian leaders (M. M. Thomas, Raymond Fung, Masao Takenaka, Francisco Claver, Kim Yong Bock, etc.), on Christian witness in the midst of the struggles of downtrodden peoples of Asia.

AS84 Chatterji, Saral K., ed.
The Asian Meaning of Modernization: East Asian Christian Conference Studies. Delhi, II: ISPCK; Madras, II: CLS; Lucknow, UP: Lucknow Publishing House, 1972. 147 pp. Paper. No ISBN.

Nine scholarly essays on the modernization process in Asia, prepared at the request of the Fourth General Assembly of the EACC (1968) to guide that body in its social thinking and mission programs.

AS85 *Christian Action in the Asian Struggle*
Toa Payoh, SI: CCA, 1973. 100 pp. Paper. No ISBN.

Lectures and papers on church and society concerns, with focus on Asia, compiled to honor the great Asian Christian D. T. Niles (1908-1970), including lectures given at the 5th Assembly of the EACC (Singapore, 1973).

AS86 Christian Conference of Asia Youth
Profit at Gunpoint. Toa Payoh, SI: CCA, 1984. viii, 188 pp. Paper. 9971948214.

Papers of the Fourth Asia Youth Resource Conference (Mindanao, Philippines, 15-30 May 1983), focusing on the dangers of militarization for economic development and human rights, with special reference to Mindanao.

AS87 Christian Conference of Asia, Assembly (7th, Bangalore, India, 1981)
A Call to Vulnerable Discipleship. Toa Payoh, SI: CCA, 1982. 115 pp. Paper. 9971948079.

Papers from the 7th Assembly, including the D. T. Niles Memorial Lectures, Bible studies, and testimonies related to the theme, "Living in Christ with People."

AS88 Christian Conference of Asia-International Affairs
The Church and Political Reform: A CCA-IA Consultation Report. Kowloon, HK: CCA-IA, 1989. iii, 123 pp. Paper. No ISBN.

Setting the scene with the expulsion of CCA from Singapore on charges of political involvement, this consultation focuses on the Asian churches' perceptions of their political roles.

AS89 Colaco, J. M.
Jesus Christ in Asian Suffering and Hope. Madras, II: CLS, 1977. viii, 95 pp. Paper. No ISBN.

Eight papers by Indian church leaders on the theme of the 6th Assembly of the CCA (Penang, Malaysia, 1977).

AS90 Committee for Asian Women
Beyond Labour Issues: Women Workers in Asia. Kowloon, HK: CAW, 1988. 71 pp. Paper. No ISBN.

A popular report of the regional conference (Hong Kong, 4-11 Oct. 1987), sponsored by the Committee for Asian Women (CAW), with the title as its theme.

AS91 Corwin, Charles
East to Eden?: Religion and the Dynamics of Social Change. Grand Rapids, MIU: Eerdmans, 1972. 190 pp. 0802814441.

Results of a seminar on Asian social problems, with reference to China, India, and Japan, and a brief history of Western (including missionary) impact.

AS92 Digan, Parig
Churches in Contestation: Asian Christian Social Protest. Maryknoll, NYU: Orbis Books, 1984. x, 214 pp. Paper. 0883441020.

A concise historical and social analysis of attitudes of Asian Christians toward major social problems of the continent, focusing on the development of a significant Asian Christian social witness during the 1945-1982 period.

AS—ASIA

AS93 Federation of Asian Bishop's Conferences, Office for Human Development

Becoming the Church of the Poor. (Nagliliyab (The Burning Bush), 17). Quezon City, PH: Claretian Publications, 1988. xii, 69 pp. Paper. 9715012973.

Reflections on the theme, "Becoming the Church of the Poor with Special Reference to Urban Workers," from the first Catholic Asian Institute for Social Action (Antipolo, Rizal, Philippines, 1987).

AS94 Fernando, J. Basil

Asian Refugees: A Search for Solutions: A Study Based on the Experiences of Burmese and Sri-Lankan Refugees. (Asian Issues 2, no. 14). Kowloon, HK: CCA-International Affairs, 1991. 51 pp. Paper. No ISBN.

Case studies of Burmese and Sri-Lankan refugees and the options for Asian solutions of such refugee problems.

AS95 Francis, T. Dayanandan, ed.

Our Daily Rice: Asian Poems on Freedom and Justice. Madras, II: CLS, 1992. xi, 79 pp. Paper. No ISBN.

Poems, songs, and hymns by Asian Christians, on God, creation, and society.

AS96 Fukada, Robert M., ed.

God's People in Asian Industrial Society. Kyoto, JA: Doshisha University School of Theology, 1967. 198 pp. No ISBN.

Report and papers from the EACC Conference concerning Christians in Industry and Lay Training (Kyoto, Japan, May 1966).

AS97 Haas, H.

Revolutie en kerk: De christenen in Azië. (De grote oecumene. Interreligieuze ontwikkelingen). Hilversum, NE: Brand, 1967. 94 pp. Paper. No ISBN.

The advisor to the Catholic Union of Students, Pax Romana, foresees possibilities for Christianity in Asia as a major force for economic and social revolution.

AS98 Hao, Yap Kim

Doing Theology in a Pluralistic World. Singapore: Methodist Book Room, 1990. 222 pp. Paper. 9810024037.

A wide-ranging study of issues (cultural, political, ecological, and religious) that Asian Christians face in the contextualization of theology, by the distinguished first Asian bishop of the Methodist church in Malaysia and Singapore and former General Secretary of the CCA.

AS99 Italiaander, Rolf

Wer seinen Bruder nicht liebt: Begegnungen und Erfahrungen in Asien. (Erlanger Taschenbücher, 45). Erlangen, GW: Ev. Luth. Mission, 1978. 188 pp. 3872140647.

Case studies of Asian Christians' involvement in national issues of justice, human rights, and religious liberty.

AS100 Mathew, George, ed.

Struggling with People is Living in Christ. Tokyo, JA: CCA, Urban Rural Mission, 1981. 154 pp. Paper. No ISBN.

Report and papers from a Theology and Ideology consultation of seventy Asian church leaders from eleven countries (Manila, Philippines, 24-31 October 1980) sponsored by the Urban Rural Mission program of the CCA.

AS101 O'Grady, Alison, ed.

Inheritors of the Earth: Report of the People's Forum on People, Land and Justice. Kowloon, HK: CCA, 1981. 114 pp. Paper. No ISBN.

Report of the Third People's Forum on "People, Land, and Justice" (Berastagi, Indonesia, 8-14 March 1981), including testimonies by participants from ten Asian countries concerning marginalization of people through deprivation of their land.

AS102 O'Grady, Ron

Banished: The Expulsion of the Christian Conference of Asia from Singapore and Its Implications. Kowloon, HK: CCA, International Affairs, 1990. 103 pp. Paper. 9627439037.

An analysis of the 1987 conflict with the government of Singapore that led to the expulsion of the CCA, by the former Associate General Secretary; with key source documents.

AS103 O'Grady, Ron

Singapore to Penang. Toa Payoh, SI: CCA, 1977. 62 pp. Paper. No ISBN.

A summary of five years of work of the CCA, prepared for its 6th Assembly (Penang, Malaysia, 1977).

AS104 Oh, Jae Shik, ed.

Escape from Domination: A Consultation Report on Patterns of Domination and People's Movements in Asia. Tokyo, JA: CCA, International Affairs, 1980. 110 pp. No ISBN.

This consultation of the CCA's International Affairs Group (Manilla, Philippines, 31 August-3 September 1979) focused on political struggles of Christian groups in various parts of Asia.

AS105 Pan Asian Catholic Students' Seminar (Colombo, 1967)

Christian Students and the Asian Revolution: Report of the Pan Asian Catholic Students' Seminar. Colombo, CE: Pax Romana, 1967. 200 pp. No ISBN.

Report and papers from a seminar supported by Pax Romana, the International Movement of Catholic Students.

AS106 Perkins, Harvey L.

Theological Guidelines for Christian Participation. Kowloon, HK: CCA, International Affairs, 1990. 96 pp. Paper. No ISBN.

An attempt to clarify and elaborate on the Christian basis for the work of the CCA in international affairs, tracing its history since its inception, and analyzing it in the theological and biblical context of the mission of the church.

AS107 Peter, Anton, ed.

Christlicher Glaube in mutireligiöser Gesellschaft: Erfahrungen, Theologische Reflexionen, Missionarische Perspektiven. (NZM, Supplementa, 44). Freiburg, SZ: Immensee, 1996. 422 pp. Paper. 3858240788.

Twenty scholarly essays on interreligious encounters and the Christian impact on India, Pakistan, Sri Lanka, Taiwan, Japan, and other Asian countries.

AS108 Razu, I. John Mohan

Transnational Corporations as Agents of Dehumanization in Asia: An Ethical Critique of Development. New Delhi, II: ISPCK, 1999. xxviii, 273 pp. Paper. 817214492X.

The author raises fundamental questions about transnational corporations, the prime movers of the process of globalization, and about the goal of development from a holistic, Christian perspective.

AS109 Ro, Bong Rin, ed.

Christian Suffering in Asia: "The Blood of the Martyrs Is the Seed of the Church." Taichung, CH: Evangelical Fellowship of Asia, 1989. ii, 228 pp. Paper. No ISBN.

Papers from the Consultation on the Church in the Midst of Suffering (Hong Kong, 24-27 Febrary 1988), sponsored by the Evangelical Fellowship of Asia.

AS110 Ro, Bong Rin, ed.
Urban Ministry in Asia/Cities: The Exploding Mission Field. Taiwan, CH: Asia Theological Association, 1989. iii, 248 pp. Paper. No ISBN.

A collection of papers on the biblical and historical roots of urban ministry, with a number of helpful case studies in urban ministry.

AS111 Robinson, Gnana, ed.
For the Sake of the Gospel. Madurai, II: T. T. S. Publications, 1980. viii, 284 pp. Paper. No ISBN.

Twenty essays on themes of Gospel and Asian culture, by Asian and Western scholars honoring the first principal of the Tamil Nadu Theological Seminary in Madurai, India.

AS112 Roest Crollius, Ary A., ed.
Building the Church in Pluricultural Asia. (Working Papers on Living Faith and Cultures, 7). Rome, IT: Pontifical Gregorian University, 1986. x, 171 pp. Paper. No ISBN.

Seven essays on the contextualization of Christianity in Asia (India, Indonesia, Japan, and the Philippines).

AS113 Sugden, Chris
Seeking the Asian Face of Jesus. (Regnum Studies in Mission). Oxford, ENK: Regnum Books, 1997. xix, 496 pp. Paper. 1870345266.

A critical and comparative study of the practice and theology of Christian social witness in Indonesia and India between 1974 and 1996, with special reference to the work of Wayan Mastra in the Protestant Christian Church of Bali, and of Vinay Samuel in the CSI.

AS114 Tai, Michael Cheng-Teh
In Search of Justice: The Development of the Social Teachings in Asian Churches. Chilliwack, BCC: Julia Griffin Insticol of Language Arts, 1985. xviii, 213 pp. 0969204205.

Centering on the work of the EACC and its successor, the CCA, this study traces the course of Christian social thought in Asian countries from 1949 to 1980, with reference to the work of the WCC during this period.

AS115 Takenaka, Masao
Cross and Circle. (URM Series, 1). Kowloon, HK: CCA, Urban Rural Mission, 1990. xiv, 417 pp. Paper. 9627250074.

A compilation of the addresses and short writings of the distinguished Japanese Christian ethicist, written since the 1950s on themes of Asian theology, urban and industrial mission, church and state, mission, and cultural expressions of Christianity, including art.

AS116 Takenaka, Masao
God Is Rice: Asian Culture and Christian Faith. Geneva, SZ: WCC, 1986. 83 pp. Paper. 2825408549.

Four short essays on the interaction between Christ and culture in Asia, with special reference to Japan.

AS117 Thalman, Eugene, ed.
Let Your Heart Be Bold: A Study on Church and National Security in Korea, Philippines, and Taiwan. Kowloon, HK: Center for the Progress of Peoples, 1985. lv, 256 pp. Paper. 9627261033.

An abridged edition showing, through interviews with Catholic church workers, the reality of the many pressures and injustices under which they work.

AS118 Thampu, Valson
The Word and the World: A Biblical Perspective on Contemporary Issues. New Delhi, II: TRACI, 1997. x, 277 pp. Paper. 8170085409.

Essays on justice issues (violence, corruption, religious fundamentalism, etc.) from a biblical perspective and Indian context.

AS119 Thomas, Madathilparapil M.
Asien und seine Christen in der Revolution. (Theologische Existenz heute, 145). Munich, GW: Kaiser, 1968. 104 pp. No ISBN.

German translation.

AS120 Thomas, Madathilparapil M.
The Christian Response to the Asian Revolution. London, ENK: SCM Press, 1966. 128 pp. No ISBN.

The Duff Missionary Lectures (Edinburgh and Glasgow, 1965) by the noted Asian ecumenist, analyzing the life and mission of the church in the midst of Asian revolutions and struggles for new societies with new spiritual foundations.

AS121 Thomas, Madathilparapil M.
Religion and the Revolt of the Oppressed. Delhi, II: ISPCK, 1981. 69 pp. No ISBN.

These 1980 lectures deal with the mission of Christian ecumenism in India as it faces issues of technology, revolt of the poor and oppressed, spiritual ferment created by the scientific-technical worldview, political ideologies, and resurgent religions.

AS122 Thomas, T. K., ed.
Testimony amid Asian Suffering. (Asia Focus Series). Toa Payoh, SI: CCA, 1977. 102 pp. Paper. No ISBN.

The four Niles Memorial lectures, plus thirteen testimonies on themes of evangelism, human rights, women, and struggles for justice; presented at the 6th Assembly of the CCA (Penang, 1977).

AS123 Villalba, Noel, ed.
Dialog-Asia. Kowloon, HK: CCA, 1986. 158 pp. Paper. No ISBN.

Report of *Dialog-Asia*, the Dialogue of Indigenous and Land-Deprived and Oppressed Groups in Asia (Manila, 20-30 October 1984) sponsored by the CCA's Urban-Rural Mission Department.

AS124 Wilfred, Felix
Sunset in the East?: Asian Challenges and Christian Involvement. (Asian Theological Search, 2). Madras, II: University of Madras, 1991. viii, 358 pp. No ISBN.

Scholarly reflections on how Christianity, an ancient Asian religion, can respond today to various social challenges in dialogue and collaboration with the believers of other religious traditions and with secular ideologies; by the Professor of Systematic Theology at St. Paul's Catholic Seminary, Tiruchirapalli, India.

AS125 Yamamori, Tetsunao, Bryant L. Myers, and David Conner, eds.
Serving with the Poor in Asia: Cases in Holistic Ministry. (Cases in Holistic Ministry). Monrovia, CAU: MARC, 1995. vii, 208 pp. Paper. 0912552905.

Papers from a 1994 consultation on holistic ministry held in Chiang Mai, Thailand; containing seven case studies, plus reflections by evangelical missiologists on combining the proclamation of the Gospel with practical service alongside the poor.

AS126 Yeow, Choo Lak, ed.
Doing Theology and People's Movements in Asia. (ATESEA Occasional Papers, 3). Singapore, SI: ATESEA, 1987. 250 pp. Paper. No ISBN.

Nineteen short essays by younger theologians affiliated with the ATESEA, focusing on doing theology in the midst of various people's movements throughout Asia.

AS127 Yeow, Choo Lak, ed.
Doing Theology with Cultures of Asia. (ATESEA Occasional Papers, 6). Singapore, SI: ATESEA, 1988. iv, 148 pp. Paper. 9810003099.

The compilation of papers and responses of the inaugural meeting of the Programme for Theological Cultures in Asia (PTCA), examining various facets of doing theology among the many cultures in Asia.

AS128 Yeow, Choo Lak, ed.
Women Participation and Contributions in Asian Churches. (ATESEA Occasional Papers, 5). Singapore, SI: ATESEA, 1988. xii, 108 pp. Paper. No ISBN.

A collection of reports, essays, findings, and statements intended to examine the state of theological education for women in Southeast Asia, and how women surmount obstacles hindering their Christian ministries in that region.

Asia: Biography, Collective

See also AS432.

AS129 Hinton, Linnet
Never Say Can't. Singapore, SI: OMF, 1987. 204 pp. Paper. 9971972565.

A popular biography of Norman and Amy McIntosh, OMF missionaries from New Zealand to China and Malaysia, 1936-1971.

Asia: Biography, Individual

See also AS356, AS840, OC66, and OC96.

AS130 Goldsmith, Elizabeth
God Can Be Trusted. Bromley, Kent, ENK: STL Books; Singapore, SI: OMF Books, 1989. 209 pp. Paper. 0903843854 (UK), 9971972786 (SI).

The revised edition of a popular autobiography of a woman raised by missionary parents in China, and of her service in Indonesia with the OMF (1960-1980), where her own faith was tested many times; originally published in 1974.

AS131 Oury, Guy Marie
Mgr François Pallu, ou, les missions étrangères en Asie au XVIIe siècle. Paris, FR: Éditions France-Empire, 1985. 216 pp. 2704804192.

A biography of François Pallu (1626-1684), Catholic Vicar Apostolic for East Asia, with an assessment of his contribution to 17th-century Catholic missions.

AS132 Tozer, A. W.
Let My People Go: The Life of Robert A. Jaffray. Camp Hill, PAU: Christian Publications, 1990. 135 pp. Paper. 0875094279.

The popular biography of Robert A. Jaffray (1873-1945), the pioneer Christian and Missionary Alliance missionary who, from China, opened work in French Indochina (1916) and Indonesia (1928).

Asian Theologies

See also TH27, TH244, TH442, CR89, CR433, CR783, SO162, ED135, CH353, AS34-AS35, AS39, AS42, AS73, AS77, AS98, AS126, AS405, AS675, AS729, AS733, AS746, AS748, AS782, AS824, AS1252, AS1309, AS1357, AS1385, AS1421, AS1450, and AS1478.

AS133 Adams, Daniel J.
Cross-Cultural Theology: Western Reflections in Asia. Atlanta, GAU: John Knox Press, 1987. vi, 124 pp. Paper. 0804206856.

Ten short essays on developing theology in an Asian context, based on the author's experience as a theological educator in Chinese, Korean, and middle-class American cultures.

AS134 Ahn, Byung-Mu
Draussen vor dem Tor: Kirche und Minjung in Korea; theologische Beiträge und Reflexionen. Edited by Winfried Glüer. (Theologie der Ökumene, 20). Göttingen, GW: Vandenhoeck & Ruprecht, 1986. 156 pp. Paper. 3525563248.

Essays and lectures by the leading representative of *minjung* theology, arising from the reality of dictatorship and oppression, and formulating the Christian position in the struggle for justice and human rights.

AS135 Ahn, Jae-woong
God in Our Midst. (World Student Christian Federation, 19). Kowloon, HK: WSCF Asia-Pacific Region, 1995. ii, 117 pp. Paper. No ISBN.

Reflections by the former Asia Region Secretary of the WSCF and present secretary for Urban Rural Mission of the CCA, on biblical themes and contemporary Asian issues related to WSCF and CCA ministries.

AS136 Amaladoss, Michael
Life in Freedom: Liberation Theologies from Asia. (Jesuit Theological Forum Studies, 6). Maryknoll, NYU: Orbis Books, 1997. xii, 180 pp. Paper. 1570751242.

A noted Indian Jesuit missiologist discusses current liberation movements and thought in Korea, the Philippines, India, and in the awakening of Asian women, plus approaches to human liberation in other Asian religions; with a prophetic overview of prospects for interreligious cooperation.

AS137 Amaladoss, Michael
Vivre en liberté: les théologies de la libération en Asie. Translated by Edouard Boné. Brussels, BE: Lumen Vitae; Paris, FR: Éditions du Cerf; Geneva, SW: Labor et Fides; Ontario, ONC: Novalis, 1997. 255 pp. Paper. 2873240989 (BE), 2204059609 (FR), 2830908856 (SZ), 2890889505 (CAN).

French translation.

AS138 Anderson, Gerald H., ed.
Asian Voices in Christian Theology. Maryknoll, NYU: Orbis Books, 1976. 321 pp. 0883440172 (hdbk), 0883440164 (pbk).

Nine essays, plus church confessional statements and bibliography, on the task of theology in the Asian churches.

AS139 Antone, Hope S., and Yong Ting Jin
Re-Living Our Faith Today: A Bible Study Resource Book. Kowloon, HK: WSCF, 1992. 180 pp. Paper. No ISBN.

Thirteen short Bible studies on liberation themes by Asian Christians active in justice ministries.

AS140 Arokiasamy, Soosai, and G. Gispert-Sauch, eds.

Liberation in Asia: Theological Perspectives. (Series XI. Jesuit Theological Forum, Reflections, 1). Delhi, II: Vidyajyoti; Gujarat, II: Gujarat Sahitya Prakash, 1987. xi, 269 pp. No ISBN.

Twelve essays by Asian Roman Catholic theologians, responding to 1984 and 1986 documents critical of a theology of liberation by the Sacred Congregation for the Doctrine of the Faith in Rome.

AS141 Balasundaram, F. J.

Contemporary Asian Christian Theology. Delhi, II: ISPCK for the United Theological College, Bangalore, 1995. 217 pp. Paper. 8172142331.

A collection of nine articles, by a noted Indian church historian, on seven theologians, plus two themes (the prophetic office and feminist concerns).

AS142 Balasundaram, F. J.

EATWOT in Asia: Towards a Relevant Theology. Bangalore, II: Asian Trading Corp, 1994. iv, 342 pp. Paper. 8170861640.

A scholarly history of the EATWOT and assessment of its impact on Asian theology; originally submitted as a doctoral dissertation at Hamburg University.

AS143 Balasuriya, Tissa

Mary and Human Liberation: The Story and the Text. Edited by Helen Stanton. London, ENK: Mowbray; Harrisburg, PAU: Trinity Press International, 1997. x, 262 pp. Paper. 0264674596 (UK), 1563382253 (US).

This collection of documents from the Sri Lankan priest's controversial essay to his excommunication in 1997 reveals how Asian liberation theologies challenge traditional viewpoints.

AS144 Balasuriya, Tissa

Planetary Theology. Maryknoll, NYU: Orbis Books, 1984. vi, 282 pp. Paper. 0883444003.

A theology related to social analysis of the de facto world system of order and disorder, with special reference to Asia, action-oriented and mission-oriented; by the noted Sri Lankan Catholic theologian and social activist.

AS145 Banawiratma, Johannes Baptista, and Johannes Müller

Kontextuelle Sozialtheologie: Ein indonesisches Modell. (Theologie der Dritten Welt, 20). Freiburg im Breisgau, GW: Herder, 1995. 237 pp. Paper. 3451236311.

Two Catholic theologians, after introducing the methods of social theology and social analysis, provide a social theology for the Indonesian context; originally published in Indonesian as *Bertologi Sosial Lintas Ilmu* (1993).

AS146 Battung, Mary Rosario et al., eds.

Religion and Society: Towards a Theology of Struggle, Book 1. Manila, PH: Fides, 1988. xx, 269 pp. Paper. 9718584005.

Twenty-eight short essays and statements on doing theology in the context of the struggle for justice in the Philippines.

AS147 Battung, Mary Rosario

Theologie des Kampfes: Christliche Nachfolgepraxis in den Philippinen. Translated by Liberato C. Bautista and Sophia Lizares-Bodegon. (Theologie und Kirche im Prozess der Befreiung, 8). Münster, GW: Edition Liberación, 1989. 240 pp. Paper. 3923792336.

German translation.

AS148 Batumalai, S.

An Introduction to Asian Theology: An Asian Story from a Malaysian Eye for Asian Neighbourology. Delhi, II: ISPCK, 1991. xii, 457 pp. Paper. 8172140150.

Lectures originally given in a course on Asian theology by the Dean of the Seminari Theologi Malaysia in Kuala Lumpur, surveying the new developments in the countries of East, Southeast, and South Asia.

AS149 Beltran, Benigno P.

Philippinische Theologie in ihrem kulturellen und gesellschaftlichen Kontext. (Theologie interkulturell, 3). Düsseldorf, GW: Patmos Verlag, 1988. 172 pp. Paper. 3491777070.

A series of lectures delivered by the author at the University of Frankfurt, 1987/1988, aiming at a critical dialogue between the European form of theology and a new theology developed within the framework of Philippine culture and society.

AS150 Bettscheider, Heribert, ed.

Das asiatische Gesicht Christi. (Veröffentlichungen des Missionspriesterseminars, 25). St. Augustin, GW: Steyler Verlag, 1976. 101 pp. Paper. 3877870854.

Five papers attempting to show how to do "indigenous theology," with examples from Christology in Japan and India.

AS151 Bock, Kim Yong, ed.

Minjung Theology: People as the Subjects of History. Toa Payoh, SI: CCA, 1981. iv, 196 pp. Paper. 9971948052.

Nine essays on Korea's liberation theology by Korean theologians—the first extensive presentation in English.

AS152 Boff, Leonardo, and Virgilio P. Elizondo, eds.

Any Room for Christ in Asia? Maryknoll, NYU: Orbis Books; London, ENK: SCM Press, 1993. xi, 152 pp. Paper. 088344870X (US), 0334030196 (UK).

Twelve papers by prominent Asian Catholics, originally presented at the Consultation on African and Asian Spirituality (Colombo, Sri Lanka, 18-25 June 1992).

AS153 Chai, Soo-Il

Die messianische Hoffnung im Kontext Koreas. (Perspektiven der Weltmission, 10). Ammersbek bei Hamburg, GW: Verlag an der Lottbek, 1990. 185 pp. Paper. 3926987421.

This dissertation, submitted by a South Korean, studies the concept and development of Korean messianism, attempting to discover common factors in traditional messianism and *minjung* theology.

AS154 Chang Ch'un-shen, A. B.

Dann sind Himmel und Mensch in Einheit: Bausteine chinesischer Theologie. (Theologie der Dritten Welt, 5). Freiburg, GW: Herder, 1984. 141 pp. Paper. 3451199769.

This anthology of selected essays by a Chinese theologian shows the development of an original Chinese theology in the Catholic Church of Taiwan during the past twenty-five years.

AS155 Chung, Hyun Kyung

Struggle to be the Sun Again: Introducing Asian Women's Theology. Maryknoll, NYU: Orbis Books, 1990. xiii, 146 pp. Paper. 0883446847.

A readable introduction to emerging feminist theologies in Asia, including their historical and social contexts, major themes, and an assessment of the contributions of Asian women's theology to contemporary theology.

AS—ASIA

AS156 CTC/CAA
Tradition and Innovation: A Search for a Relevant Ecclesiology in Asia. Singapore, SI: CCA, Commission on Theological Concerns, 1983. ii, 136 pp. 9971948141.

These papers report on two CTC-CCA consultations (Hong Kong, May 1982, and Kandy, Sri Lanka, 23-29 August 1982), dealing with ecclesiological issues that have arisen in various Asian contexts.

AS157 Davis, Richard H.
Images, Miracles, and Authority in Asian Religious Traditions. Boulder, COU: Westview Press, 1998. 239 pp. 0813334632.

This collection of nine articles examines how religious images are understood by practitioners in Asia, how the "miracles" associated with those images are, to some degree, programmed by expectations and responses, and how such religious events interrelate with political and social change and conflict.

AS158 Diaz, Hector
A Korean Theology: Chu-Gyu Yo Ji: Essentials of the Lord's Teaching by Chong Yak-jong Augustine (1760-1801). Immensee, SZ: *NZM*, 1986. 466 pp. Paper. 3858240648.

A scholarly analysis of the life, writings, and work of one of Korean Catholicism's first theologians and martyrs; including a historical survey of the introduction of the Catholic Church into Korea.

AS159 Elwood, Douglas J., ed.
Asian Christian Theology: Emerging Trends. Philadelphia, PAU: Westminster Press, 1980. 342 pp. Paper. 0664243541.

An expanded edition of *What Asian Christians Are Thinking* (Quezon City, PH: New Day, 1976), containing twenty-nine essays and five confessional statements on themes in Asian Christian theology (man in nature and history, God and revelation, Christ and the Christian life, and the theologies of mission, development, liberation, and religious pluralism).

AS160 Elwood, Douglas J., ed.
Wie Christen in Asien denken: Ein theologisches Quellenbuch. Frankfurt am Main, GW: Lembeck, 1979. viii, 317 pp. Paper. 3874761290.

German translation of *What Asian Christians Are Thinking* (1978).

AS161 England, John C., and Alan J. Torrance, eds.
Doing Theology with the Spirit's Movement in Asia. (ATESEA Occasional Papers, 11). Singapore, SI: ATESEA, 1991. vi, 204 pp. Paper. 9810026412.

Fifteen essays by Asian theologians, on the Holy Spirit and Asian mission; originally presented at the 8th Theological Seminar-Workshop sponsored by ATESEA.

AS162 England, John C., and Archie C. C. Lee, eds.
Doing Theology with Asian Resources: Ten Years in the Formation of Living Theology in Asia. Auckland, NZ: Pace Publishing for the Programme for Theology and Cultures in Asia, 1993. 265 pp. Paper. 0959797181.

Fifteen scholarly essays providing an overview of the program, plus selected papers from research groups on "Doing Theology with Women's History," "The Spirit's Movement in Asian History," and "Religion and Cultures of Asia."

AS163 England, John C., ed.
Living Theology in Asia. London, ENK: SCM Press; Maryknoll, NYU: Orbis Books, 1982. x, 242 pp. Paper. 0883442981.

Twenty-four Asian theologians write on doing theology amidst the struggle for human justice.

AS164 Fabella, Virginia, and Sun Ai Lee Park, eds.
We Dare to Dream: Doing Theology as Asian Women. Kowloon, HK: AWCCT; Greenhills, PH: EATWOT, 1989. x, 156 pp. Paper. 0883446731.

Papers by fourteen Asian women theologians; originally presented at conferences sponsored by the Women's Commission of the EATWOT and the Asian Women's Resource Centre for Culture and Theology.

AS165 Fabella, Virginia, ed.
Asia's Struggle for Full Humanity: Towards a Relevant Theology: Papers from the Asian Theological Conference, January 7-20, 1979, Wennappuwa, Sri Lanka. Maryknoll, NYU: Orbis Books, 1980. vi, 202 pp. Paper. 0883440156.

Report and papers from the Asian Theological Conference (Wennappuwa, Sri Lanka, 7-20 Jan. 1979) sponsored by EATWOT to promote Asian theologies and dialogue among Third World Christians.

AS166 Fabella, Virginia, Peter K. H. Lee, and David Kwang-sun Suh, eds.
Asian Christian Spirituality: Reclaiming Traditions. Maryknoll, NYU: Orbis Books, 1992. vi, 159 pp. Paper. 0883448009.

Papers presented to the 3rd Asian Theological Conference (Suanbo, Korea, 3-8 July 1989), showing how a spirituality, both faithful to a common Christian heritage and rooted in particular cultures and traditions, can animate Christianity in Asia.

AS167 Federschmidt, Karl H.
Theologie aus asiatischen Quellen: Der theologische Weg Choan-Seng Songs vor dem Hintergrund der asiatischen Ökumenischen Diskussion. (Beiträge zur Missionswissenschaft und interkulturellen Theologie, 7). Münster, GW: Lit, 1994. xiii, 304 pp. Paper. 38258220610.

A dissertation on Asian theology—its main contours, themes, sources, and contribution to inculturation within Asian contexts, e.g. Taiwan.

AS168 Fernandez, Eleazar S.
Towards a Theology of Struggle. Maryknoll, NYU: Orbis Books, 1994. vi, 193 pp. Paper. 088344982X.

A theology of struggle with special reference to the history of colonial and political oppression in the Philippines, and the popular movement for liberation there.

AS169 Fjärstedt, Biörn
Asiatisk gryning Kristen teologi från Öst. Stockholm, SW: Proprius, 1984. 67 pp. 9171184708.

A booklet presenting trends in contemporary Christian theology in Asia.

AS170 Francis, T. Dayanandan, and F. J. Balasundaram, eds.
Asian Expressions of Christian Commitment: A Reader in Asian Theology. Madras, II: CLS, 1992. ix, 416 pp. Paper. No ISBN.

Thirty-nine short essays designed to introduce some Asian Christians thinkers and the key themes in their theologies.

AS—ASIA

AS171 Furuya, Yasuo, ed.

A History of Japanese Theology. Grand Rapids, MIU: Eerdmans, 1997. v, 161 pp. Paper. 0802841082.

A first history by a Japanese scholar of theological developments in his country.

AS172 *Gentle but Radical: Korean Theologian Chung Hyun Kyung*

Geneva, SZ: WCC, n.d. 32:45 mins. No ISBN.

The noted Korean theologian is seen and heard in the multifaceted Asian and Korean experiences that have impacted her theology; captured on video.

AS173 Germany, Charles H.

Protestant Theologies in Modern Japan: A History of Dominant Theological Currents from 1920-1960. Tokyo, JA: IISR Press, 1965. xv, 239 pp. No ISBN.

A detailed history of 20th-century developments in Japanese Protestant theology; originally presented as a Ph.D. dissertation at Union/Columbia in New York.

AS174 Glüer, Winfried

Christliche Theologie in China: T. C. Chao, 1918-1956. (Missionswissenschaftliche Forschungen, 13). Gütersloh, GW: Mohn, 1979. 300 pp. Paper. 3579044907.

A dissertation showing how Tzu-ch'en Chao tried to harmonize Christian theology with the concrete historical situation in China in the various phases of his life.

AS175 Hao, Yap Kim, ed.

Asian Theological Reflections on Suffering and Hope. Toa Payoh, SI: CCA, 1977. 79 pp. Paper. No ISBN.

Report and papers from a consultation of younger Asian theologians (Hong Kong, 10-15 October 1976), who analyzed crucial issues confronting Asian societies and the challenge to reflect theologically on these issues.

AS176 Hargreaves, Cecil

Asian Christian Thinking: Studies in a Metaphor and Its Message. Delhi, II: ISPCK, 1979. ix, 185 pp. Paper. No ISBN.

Analysis of thematic aspects of Asian Christian theology (indigenous theology, modern spirituality, the meaning of mission, the shape of the church, social involvement, and the dimension of prayer) by the former Vice Principal of Bishop's College, Calcutta.

AS177 Heinrichs, Maurus

Katholische Theologie und Asiatisches Denken. Mainz, GW: Matthias-Grünewald-Verlag, 1963. 270 pp. No ISBN.

Having previously published handbooks of dogmatics (1954) and fundamental theology (1958) for Chinese and Japanese seminarians, the author here points out the possibilities of positive and informed contact and theological confrontation between Western and Asian ways of thinking.

AS178 Heinrichs, Maurus

Théologie chrétienne et pensée asiatique. Tournay, FR: Casterman, 1965. 296 pp. No ISBN.

French translation.

AS179 Hoffmann-Richter, Andreas

Ahn Byung-Mu als Minjung-Theologe. (Missionswissenschaftliche Forschungen, 24). Gütersloh, GW: Mohn, 1990. 176 pp. Paper. 3579002449.

A dissertation on *minjung* theology in South Korea on the basis of the life and writings of Ahn Byung-Mu, one of the more important East Asian theologians today.

AS180 Hwa, Yung

Mangoes or Bananas?: The Quest for an Authentic Asian Christian Theology. (Regnum Studies in Mission). Oxford, UIK: Regnum Books, 1997. xi, 273 pp. Paper. 1870345150.

A dissertation (Asbury) originally entitled "Theology and Mission in the Asian Church," in which the author, Principal of the Seminari Theoloji Malaysia in Kuala Lumpur, evaluates twenty years of Asian ecumenical and conservative theologies.

AS181 Kitamori, Kazoh

Teología del Dolor de Dios. Translated by Juan José Coy. (Verdad e imagen, 39). Salamanca, SP: Ediciones Sígueme, 1975. 241 pp. 8430106316.

Spanish translation.

AS182 Kitamori, Kazoh

Teologia del dolore di Dio. Edited by Hubert S. Takayanagi. Translated by Giovanni Moretto and Cheruino Guzzetti. (Giornale di teologia, 90). Brescia, IT: Queriniana, 1975. 265 pp. No ISBN.

Italian translation.

AS183 Kitamori, Kazoh

Theologie des Schmerzes Gottes. (Theologie der Ökumene, 11). Göttingen, GW: Vandenhoeck & Ruprecht, 1972. 172 pp. Paper. 3525563140.

German translation (1966).

AS184 Kitamori, Kazoh

Theology of the Pain of God. Richmond, VAU: John Knox Press, 1965. 183 pp. No ISBN.

The first work on Japanese theology introduced to the English-speaking world, a theology of the Cross in the light of the present-day situation; a translation of the 5th edition of *Kami no Itami ni Shingaku* (1958).

AS185 Koyama, Kosuke

Das Kreuz hat keinen Handgriff: Asiatische Meditationen. (Theologie der Ökumene, 16). Göttingen, GW: Vandenhoeck & Ruprecht, 1978. 111 pp. Paper. 3525563183.

German translation of *No Handle on the Cross* (1977).

AS186 Koyama, Kosuke

Mount Fuji and Mount Sinai: A Critique of Idols. Maryknoll, NYU: Orbis Books, 1985. x, 278 pp. Paper. 0883443538.

A profoundly biblical Asian theology of the Cross by the Professor of Ecumenics and World Christianity at Union Theological Seminary, New York, with a focus on world peace concerns developed from the tragedy of World War II in Japan to the present nuclear peril.

AS187 Koyama, Kosuke

No Handle on the Cross: An Asian Meditation on the Crucified Mind. Maryknoll, NYU: Orbis Books, 1977. ix, 119 pp. 0883443384 (hdbk), 0883443392 (pbk).

A meditation on Christianity from Southeast Asia, written out of the experience of the Japan-born theologian as a missionary in Thailand, exposing the paradox that Asians customarily feel that Western Christians preach and live a Christianity without the Cross.

AS—ASIA

AS188 Koyama, Kosuke

Water Buffalo Theology: Twenty-Fifth Anniversary Edition, Revised and Expanded. Maryknoll, NYU: Orbis Books, 1999. xvi, 187 pp. Paper. 1570752567.

A substantially revised edition of Koyama's classic collection of short essays, originally published in 1974, when the noted Asian theologian was a missionary from Japan to Thailand, interpreting Christianity in a way meaningful to Asian Christians living in Buddhist societies.

AS189 Kwok, Pui-lan

Discovering the Bible in the Non-Biblical World. (Bible & Liberation Series). Maryknoll, NYU: Orbis Books, 1995. xvi, 136 pp. Paper. 0883449978.

The foremost Chinese feminist theologian develops a new biblical hermeneutic, considering Asian religious traditions as well as the social biography of Asian peoples, especially women.

AS190 Lee, Jung Young, ed.

An Emerging Theology in World Perspective: Commentary on Korean Minjung Theology. Mystic, CTU: Twenty-Third Publications, 1988. viii, 211 pp. Paper. 0896223787.

Twelve essays presenting the *minjung* theology of South Korea, by ten world-renowned theologians, who include personal stories of the *minjung* people.

AS191 Lee, Jung Young

The Trinity in Asian Perspective. Nashville, TNU: Abingdon, 1996. 255 pp. Paper. 0687426375.

Utilizing both the Asian philosophical construct of *yin* and *yang* and the Christian doctrine of the Trinity, the noted Asian American theologian seeks to develop a more inclusive conception of God.

AS192 Lee, Sang-Bok, ed.

Asian Thought and Culture: A Comparative Study between Minjung Theology and Reformed Theology from a Missiological Perspective. (Asian Thought and Culture, 22). NYU: Lang, 1996. vx, 183 pp. Paper. 0820427020.

This study answers the questions of how Reformed theology compares with liberation theology in the Protestant church's mission in Korea, and why the Korean conservative church lost its social impact in its mission.

AS193 Lee, Sunhee

Die Minjung-Theologie Ahn Byungmus von ihren Voraussetzungen her dargestellt. Frankurt am Main, GW: Lang, 1992. xvii, 266 pp. Paper. 3631444591.

A detailed analysis of the *minjung* theology of Ahn Byungmu as it developed within the context of political resistance against a repressive regime.

AS194 Lukito, Daniel Lucas

Making Christology Relevant to the Third World: Applying Christopraxis to Local Struggle. (European University Studies, 23: Theology, 630.) Bern, SZ: Lang, 1998. 266 pp. Paper. 3906760278 (SW), 0820434426 (US).

Construction of a Christology of action for the Indonesian context of struggle, in which truth is done and applied by mirroring the ministry and humanity of Christ, based on the Christology of Choan-Seng Song; originally submitted as a D. Theol. thesis at the South East Asia Graduate School of Theology in Singapore.

AS195 Mercado, Leonardo N.

Inculturation and Filipino Theology. (Asia Pacific Missiological Series, 2). Manila, PH: Divine Word Publications, 1992. xi, 164 pp. Paper. 9715100562.

Reflections on mission and inculturation in theory and Filipino practice by an SVD theologian.

AS196 Michalson, Carl

Japanese Contributions to Christian Theology. Philadelphia, PAU: Westminster Press, 1960. 192 pp. No ISBN.

An introduction for Western readers of the major theologians (Uchimura, Watanabe, Kumano, Kitamori, and Hatani) and theological movements in Japan.

AS197 Michalson, Carl

Japanische Theologie der Gegenwart. (Missionswissenschaftliche Forschungen, 2). Gütersloh, GW: Mohn, 1962. 142 pp. No ISBN.

German translation.

AS198 Moltmann, Jürgen, ed.

Minjung: Theologie des Volkes Gottes in Südkorea. Neukirchen-Vluyn, GW: Neukirchener Verlag, 1984. 250 pp. Paper. 3788707259.

Texts by Christians from South Korea, who organize themselves into self-help groups in opposition to the military dictatorship, and identify with the *minjung*, the suffering people.

AS199 Moon, Cyris H. S.

A Korean Minjung Theology: An Old Testament Perspective. Maryknoll, NYU: Orbis Books; Kowloon, HK: Plough, 1985. vii, 83 pp. Paper. 0883442507 (US), 9627043109 (HK).

A creative comparative study of the theology of liberation of oppressed people (*minjung*) in the Old Testament with that of the *minjung* in contemporary Korea.

AS200 Nacpil, Emerito P., and Douglas J. Elwood, eds.

The Human and the Holy: Asian Perspectives in Christian Theology. Quezon City, PH: New Day Publishers, 1978. x, 367 pp. No ISBN.

Addresses, workshop reports, and papers of the Consultation on Theological Education for Christian Ministry in Asia (Makati, Metro-Manila, Philippines, March 1977).

AS201 Niles, D. Preman, and T. K. Thomas, eds.

Varieties of Witness. Toa Payoh, SI: CCA, 1980. 139 pp. Paper. No ISBN.

Four articles on aspects of Christian theology in Asia: Christ-centered syncretism (M. M. Thomas), guidelines for an Asian liberation theology (A. Pieris), a parable of Chinese theology (C. S. Song), a black American perspective (J. H. Cone), plus Bible studies on human development (H. Perkins), and short meditations on Korea (W. S. Han).

AS202 Oguro-Opitz, Bettina

Analyse und Auseinandersetzung mit der Theologie des Schmerzes Gottes von Kazoh Kitamori. (European University Papers: XXIII Theology, 133). Frankfurt a.M., GW: Lang, 1980. 131 pp. Paper. 3820466584.

A dissertation discussing the relationship between Japanese and universal theology, on the basis of the writings of the Japanese theologian Kitamori.

AS203 Osthathios, Geevarghese

Theology of a Classless Society. Maryknoll, NYU: Orbis Books, 1980. 159 pp. 088344500X.

The well-reasoned argument, by the metropolitan in Kerala, South India of the Orthodox Syrian Church, that sin results in a lack of solidarity among fallen humanity, but that redemption bringing reconciliation with God and humanity leads ultimately to a classless society.

AS204 Park, Andrew Sung

The Wounded Heart of God: The Asian Concept of Han and the Christian Doctrine of Sin. Nashville, TNU: Abingdon, 1993. 202 pp. Paper. 0687385369.

A detailed analysis of the Korean concept of *han*, relating this understanding of the depths of human suffering to ideas from both Eastern and Western religious traditions, with implications for interreligious dialogue.

AS205 Patmury, Joseph, and John C. England, eds.

Doing Theology with the Festivals and Customs of Asia. (ATE-SEA Occasional Papers, 13). SI: ATESEA, 1994. viii, 135 pp. Paper. 9810048599.

Papers on the Gospel and Asian cultures from the tenth seminar of the Programme for Theology and Cultures in Asia (Manila, June 1992).

AS206 Pieris, Aloysius

An Asian Theology of Liberation. (Faith Meets Faith Series). Maryknoll, NYU: Orbis Books; London, ENK: T&T Clark, 1988. xv, 144 pp. 0883446278 (hdbk), 088344626X (pbk).

English translation.

AS207 Pieris, Aloysius

Theologie der Befreiung in Asien: Christentum im Kontext der Armut und der Religionen. (Theologie der Dritten Welt, 9). Freiburg, GW: Herder Verlag, 1986. 270 pp. Paper. 3451208105.

A selection of thirteen essays, written since Vatican II, that focus on the theology of liberation in Asia, and reflect Christianity's response to the concerns of poverty and other religions in the Asian context.

AS208 Rajashekar, J. Paul William, and Satoru Kishii, eds.

Theology in Dialogue: Theology in the Context of Religious and Cultural Plurality in Asia. Geneva, SZ: LWF, 1987. vi, 123 pp. Paper. 2881900038.

Papers from the "Theology in Dialogue" seminar (Seoul, Korea, 11-17 Dec. 1987) sponsored by the Asian Programme for Advancement of Training and Studies (APATS) of the LWF.

AS209 Ramachandra, Vinoth

The Recovery of Mission: Beyond the Pluralist Paradigm. Carlisle, ENK: Paternoster Press, 1996. xiii, 293 pp. Paper. 0853647399.

A critique of the religious pluralism of three noted Asian theologians (Stanley Samartha, Aloysius Pieris, and Raimundo Panikkar), with a defense of the alternative exclusivist theology by the author, who is the regional secretary for South Asia of the International Fellowship of Evangelical Students.

AS210 Ro, Bong Rin, and Ruth Eschenaur, eds.

The Bible and Theology in Asian Contexts: An Evangelical Perspective on Asian Theology. Taichung, CH: Asia Theological Association, 1984. vii, 404 pp. Paper. No ISBN.

Eighteen addresses discussing Asian understandings of biblical texts and how they relate to Hindu, Buddhist, and Islamic cultures; originally presented at the Sixth Asia Theological Association Consultation (Seoul, Korea, 23-31 August 1982) and the Third World Theologians Consultation (Seoul, Korea, 27 Aug.-5 Sept. 1982).

AS211 Sadayandy, Batumalai

A Prophetic Christology for Neighbourology: A Theology for a Prophetic Living. Kuala Lumpur, MY: Seminari Theoloji Malaysia, 1986. xxii, 277 pp. Paper. No ISBN.

A theology for Christ's people in Malaysia; originally submitted as a dissertation at Birmingham University in the UK (1984).

AS212 Schelde, Michael

Udenfor byporten: Udviklingsliniier i asiatisk teologi. (Verdensdelenes teologi series, 2). Frederiksberg, DK: ANIS/Religionspadagogisk Ctr., 1989. 136 pp. Paper. No ISBN.

A study of Asian-Christian theologies in encounter with Hinduism and Buddhism, underlining the concept of the suffering God.

AS213 Schuttke-Scherle, Peter

From Contextual to Ecumenical Theology?: A Dialogue between Minjung Theology and "Theology after Auschwitz." (Studies in the Intercultural History of Christianity, 60). Frankfurt am Main, GW: Lang, 1989. xi, 232 pp. Paper. 3631418906.

A comparative survey of two contemporary contextual theologies: *minjung* in South Korea and the German "theology after Auschwitz," with possible contributions of that dialogue for the development of an ecumenical theology.

AS214 Song, Choan-Seng

The Compassionate God. Maryknoll, NYU: Orbis Books, 1982. xiii, 284 pp. Paper. 0883440954.

A creative exposition of what theology will look like when transposed to Asia, looking at the disruptions in the Old Testament faith in God, those for Jesus' disciples in the Cross and Resurrection, and those in Asia which disclose the heart of God in agony and compassion.

AS215 Song, Choan-Seng

Jesus and the Reign of God. Minneapolis, MNU: Fortress Press, 1993. xvi, 304 pp. Paper. 0800626710.

Drawing upon a vast storehouse of Asian wisdom, ancient and modern, the distinguished Asian theologian evokes the vision and reality of God's reign and its possibilities for the "transfiguration of life" in faith.

AS216 Song, Choan-Seng

Jesus in the Power of the Spirit. Minneapolis, MNU: Fortress Press, 1994. xiv, 335 pp. Paper. 0800627903.

The third volume in a trilogy on the person and message of Jesus Christ, by the noted Asian theologian, with reflections on the contextualization of theology in the Asian context, and on the significance of Jesus for a post-Christian world.

AS217 Song, Choan-Seng

Jesus, the Crucified People. (Cross in the Lotus World, 1). New York, NYU: Crossroad Publishing, 1990. xii, 239 pp. Paper. 0824510534.

In the first of a trilogy on *The Cross in the Lotus World*, the noted Asian theologian struggles to discern the meaning of the passion of Christ for suffering Asian women, men, and children, struggling for life.

AS—ASIA

AS218 Song, Choan-Seng

The Tears of Lady Meng: A Parable of People's Political Theology. (Risk Book Series, 11). Geneva, SZ: WCC, 1981. vii, 69 pp. Paper. 2825406864.

In an expanded version of a lecture given by a staff member of the Faith and Order Commission of the WCC at the Seventh Assembly of the CCA (Bangalore, India, May 1981), he develops a "people's political theology" by analyzing a Chinese parable.

AS219 Song, Choan-Seng

Tell Us Our Names: Story Theology from an Asian Perspective. Maryknoll, NYU: Orbis Books, 1984. xi, 212 pp. Paper. 0883445123.

Ten essays based on folk tales and fairy stories from different countries, but designed to throw light on five themes: methods in theology, the ecumenical movement, Christian mission, political theology, and dialogue with persons of other faiths.

AS220 Song, Choan-Seng

Theologie des Dritten Auges: Asiatische Spiritualität und christliche Theologie. Translated by Wolfgang Gern. (Theologie der Ökumene, 19). Göttingen, GW: Vandenhoeck & Ruprecht, 1989. 256 pp. Paper. 3525563221.

German translation of *Third-Eye Theology* (1979).

AS221 Song, Choan-Seng

Theology from the Womb of Asia. Maryknoll, NYU: Orbis Books, 1985. xiv, 241 pp. Paper. 0883445182.

A further reconstruction of Christian theology in relation to Asian culture, religions, and history, emphasizing intuition as well as reason, Eastern as well as Western spirituality; by the prominent Taiwanese theologian.

AS222 Song, Choan-Seng

Third-Eye Theology: Theology in Formation in Asian Settings. Maryknoll, NYU: Orbis Books, 1991. xv, 302 pp. Paper. 0883447355.

A revised edition of the author's classic (Orbis, 1979) in which he argued that Asian folklore, mythology, and tradition function in relation to Asian theology, like early Israelite religion, in relation to Judaism and Christianity.

AS223 Stults, Donald Leroy

Developing an Asian Evangelical Theology. Manila, PH: OMF Books, 1989. 233 pp. Paper. 9715111505.

An introductory textbook for Asian theological students to help them think theologically in contexts of Asian societies.

AS224 Sugirtharajah, R. S., ed.

Frontiers in Asian Christian Theology: Emerging Trends. Maryknoll, NYU: Orbis Books, 1994. viii, 263 pp. Paper. 0883449544.

Twenty essays by Asian theologians, demonstrating the rich variety of personal encounters, cultural dynamics, and theological concerns that enliven Asian Christian theologies today.

AS225 Sugirtharajah, R. S.

Asian Biblical Hermeneutics and Postcolonialism: Contesting the Interpretations. (The Bible and Liberation Series). Maryknoll, NYU: Orbis Books, 1998. xii, 148 pp. Paper. 1570752052.

An introduction to contemporary Asian biblical hermeneutics, applying postcolonial theory to biblical interpretation; by the senior lecturer in Third World theologies at Selly Oak Colleges in Birmingham, England.

AS226 Takizawa, Katsumi

Das Heil im Heute: Texte einer Japanischen Theologie. Edited by Theo Sundermeier. (Theologie der Ökumene, 21). Göttingen, GW: Vandenhoeck & Ruprecht, 1987. 220 pp. Paper. 3525563256.

A collection of texts by one of the most original representatives of Japanese theology ("Immanuel theology").

AS227 Thumma, Anthoniraj

Springs from the Subalterns: Patterns and Perspectives in People's Theology. Delhi, II: ISPCK, 1999. viii, 114 pp. Paper. 8172145330.

The author's goal is to liberate theological faculties from their scheduled ghettos, becoming more critical, conscientious, and participatory in the concreteness of peoples' lives and languages.

AS228 Torrance, Alan J., and Salvador T. Martinez, eds.

Doing Christian Theology in Asian Ways. (ATESEA Occasional Papers, 12). SI: ATESEA, 1993. iv, 73 pp. Paper. 981004478X.

Six essays exploring ways and means of doing theology, using Asian resources in Indonesia, New Zealand, Taiwan, and Thailand.

AS229 Wostyn, Lode L.

Doing Ecclesiology: Church and Mission Today. Quezon, PH: Claretian Publications, 1990. xi, 146 pp. Paper. 9715014135.

A critique of recent Roman Catholic ecclesiology and missiology by a Professor of Systematic Theology, who does theology using a *See-Judge-Act* method among the poor of Manila in the Philippines.

AS230 Yatco, Nicomedes T.

Jesus Christ Today for Today's Filipino. Quezon City, PH: New Day Publishers, 1983. vii, 120 pp. Paper. 9711001128 (hdbk), 9711000539 (pbk).

An attempt to show a Christ who responds to the needs of Filipinos in the 1980s, through a comparison of Christ as portrayed in the writings of the theologian Hans Küng and the Filipino playwright Aurelio Tolentino.

AS231 Yeo, Khiok-Khng

What Has Jerusalem to Do with Beijing?: Biblical Interpretation from a Chinese Perspective. Harrisburg, PAU: Trinity Press International, 1998. x, 325 pp. Paper. 1563382296.

Ten essays interpreting the Bible, both from Chinese cultural perspectives toward wisdom, and in the light of current sociopolitical realities; by the Assistant Professor of New Testament Interpretation at Garrett-Evangelical Theological Seminary, Evanston, Illinois.

AS232 Yeow, Choo Lak, and H. S. Wilson, eds.

Being Reformed Christians in Asia Today. Singapore, SI: ATESEA, 1994. iv, 58 pp. Paper. 9810048580.

Six essays by Asian theologians, originally presented at the Consultation on Reformed Self-Identity (Singapore, 14-17 April 1993), sponsored by WARC.

AS233 Yeow, Choo Lak, and John C. England, eds.

Doing Theology with People's Symbols & Images. (ATESEA Occasional Papers, 8). Singapore, SI: ATESEA, 1989. iv, 198 pp. Paper. 9810009321.

Papers by Asian theologians, demonstrating how Christian theology relates to the numerous symbols and images of spirituality commonly found in Asia.

AS234 Yeow, Choo Lak, ed.

Doing Theology with God's Purpose in Asia. (ATESEA Occasional Papers, 10). Singapore, SI: ATESEA, 1990. v, 154 pp. Paper. 9810018614.

Thirteen short papers from the ATESEA Theological Seminar-Workshop on "Doing Theology with God's Purpose in Asia" (Hong Kong, June 1989).

AS235 Yeow, Choo Lak, ed.

Theology and Religious Plurality. (Doing Theology with Asian Resources, 3). Singapore: ATESEA, 1996. vii, 192 pp. Paper. 9810040245.

An anthology of eighteen significant essays, by Asian theologians, on themes of religious pluralism.

AS236 Yeow, Choo Lak

To God be the Glory!: Doctrines on God and Creation. Singapore, SI: Trinity Theological College, 1981. x, 194 pp. No ISBN.

Essays by the principal of Trinity Theological College, Singapore, on doing theology in Asia; with focus on the doctrines of revelation, God, the Trinity, creation, humanity, and the world.

AS237 Yewangoe, Andreas Anangguru

Theologia Crucis in Asia: Asian Christian Views on Suffering in the Face of Overwhelming Poverty and Multifaceted Religiosity in Asia. (Amsterdam Studies in Theology, 6). Amsterdam, NE: Rodopi, 1987. vi, 352 pp. Paper. 9062036104.

A revision of the author's doctoral dissertation, which not only addresses the Asian Christian views on suffering in the midst of poverty, and in the presence of other faiths, but also reveals how a Christian faith, with which suffering people in Asia can live, is being constructed and articulated; with emphasis on theologians in India, Korea, Japan, and Indonesia.

Indian Christian Theologies

See also TH257, CR920, EC66, CH106, SP165, AS78, AS1015, and AS1060.

AS238 Ahlstrand, Kajsa

Fundamental Openness: An Enquiry into Raimundo Panikkar's Theological Vision and its Presuppositions. (Studia Missionalia Upsaliensia, 57). Uppsala, SW: Swedish Institute of Missionary Research, 1993. 209 pp. Paper. 9185424331.

A detailed analysis of the theology of religion of the noted Spanish-Indian theologian Raimundo Panikkar in relation to the traditions important to him; originally presented as a doctoral dissertation at Uppsala University in 1993.

AS239 Aleaz, K. P.

The Gospel of Indian Culture. Calcutta, II: Punthi Pustak, 1994. xiii, 344 pp. 8185094748.

An in-depth study of the Gospel and Indian culture, dealing with issues of religious pluralism and contextualization; commissioned by the World Council of Churches as part of its Gospel and Culture study.

AS240 Aleaz, K. P.

Sermons for a New Vision. Delhi, II: ISPCK, 1994. xi, 162 pp. Paper. 8172142307.

Forty-seven sermons delivered at Bishops' College, Calcutta, that express the author's struggle for an Indian hermeneutics articulating the meaning of Jesus in the Indian cultural context.

AS241 Amaladoss, Michael

Becoming Indian: The Process of Inculturation. (Chavara Lectures, 1). Rome, IT: Centre for Indian and Interreligious Studies; Bangalore, II: Dharmaram Publications, 1992. 114 pp. Paper. No ISBN.

In seven 1989 lectures, the noted Jesuit missiologist introduced inculturation as a process.

AS242 Amaladoss, Michael, Francis X. D'Sa, and Christopher Duraisingh

Wir werden bei ihm wohnen: Das Johannesevangelium in indischer Deutung. Edited by George M. Soares-Prabhu. (Theologie der Dritten Welt, 6). Freiburg im Breisgau, GW: Herder, 1984. 184 pp. Paper. 3451202778.

German translation, by Ursula Faymonville, of articles originally written in English by Indian scholars, reflecting on specifically Indian approaches to John's Gospel, offering commentaries on individual texts and pericopes.

AS243 Arokiasamy, Soosai, ed.

Responding to Communalism: The Task of Religions and Theology. (Jesuit Theological Forum Reflections, 6). Anand, II: Gujarat Sahitya Prakash, 1991. xv, 357 pp. No ISBN.

Papers and reports by South Asian theologians and sociologists; originally presented at a seminar on "Communalism and the Responsibility of the Religious Intellectuals (theologians)."

AS244 Azariah, M.

A Pastor's Search for Dalit Theology. Delhi, II: DLET/ISPCK, 2000. xx, 191 pp. Paper. 8172145810.

This collection of the author's Bible studies, essays, and articles, concerns the themes of caste discrimination, caste oppression, and Dalit liberation.

AS245 Bürkle, Horst, and Wolfgang M. W. Roth, eds.

Indian Voices in Today's Theological Debate. Translated by Klaus K. Klostermaier and Wolfgang M. W. Roth. Lucknow, II: Lucknow Publishing House; Delhi, II: ISPCK; Madras, II: Christian Literature Society, 1972. xix, 224 pp. No ISBN.

English translation.

AS246 Bürkle, Horst, and Wolfgang M. W. Roth, eds.

Indische Beiträge zur Theologie der Gegenwart. Stuttgart, GW: Evan Verlagswerk, 1966. 284 pp. No ISBN.

Scholarly papers highlighting the contributions that Hindu philosophy, mysticism, and metaphysics can make to Christianity, in the context of the historical Jesus and the Christ of faith.

AS247 Baago, Kaj

Pioneers of Indigenous Christianity. (Confessing the Faith in India Series, 4). Madras, II: CLS, 1969. vii, 214 pp. Paper. No ISBN.

A survey of late 19th- and early 20th-century indigenous movements and Christian theologies in India, with selections from the writings of key leaders (K. M. Banerjea, A. S. Appasamy, B. Upadyay, Sadhu Sundar Singh, and others).

AS248 Banerjee, Brojendra Nath

Jesus My Faith. Delhi, II: ISPCK for CISRS, 1999. xviii, 322 pp. Paper. 8172144830.

Patterns of mission faith from Abraham, Moses, Paul, and Jesus, in relation to India and Pakistan; written by a scholar in economic development.

AS249 Biehl, Michael

Der Fall Sadhu Sundar Singh: Theologie zwischen den Kulturen. (Studies in the Intercultural History of Christianity, 66). Frankfurt am Main, GW: Lang, 1990. 393 pp. Paper. 3631430132.

A doctoral dissertation in which the author attempts to show how local theology leads Christian theology into an intercultural encounter, exemplified by the controversial figure of Sundar Singh (1888-1929).

AS250 Boyd, Robin H. S., ed.

Manilal C. Parekh, 1885-1967; Dhanjibhai Fakirbhai, 1895-1967: A Selection. (Library of Indian Christian Theology, 2). Madras, II: CLS, 1974. x, 303 pp. Paper. No ISBN.

Selections from the writings of two first-generation Christians from Gujarat, who sought to develop a Christian *Bhakti* form of spirituality and thought.

AS251 Boyd, Robin H. S.

India and the Latin Captivity of the Church: The Cultural Context of the Gospel. (Monograph Supplements to the Scottish Journal of Theology, 3). London, ENK: Cambridge University Press, 1974. xiv, 151 pp. 0521203716.

A call by the vice-principal of the Gujarat United School of Theology in Ahmedabad, India, for a genuine Indian Christian theology, expressed in a form appropriate to Indian culture and modes of thought.

AS252 Boyd, Robin H. S.

An Introduction to Indian Christian Theology. Madras, II: CLS, 1975. xii, 361 pp. No ISBN.

An analysis of 20th-century developments in Indian Christian theology, its principal leaders, and its relation to the life and mission of the Indian church.

AS253 Boyd, Robin H. S.

Khristadvaita: A Theology for India. Madras, II: CLS, 1977. xxii, 435 pp. No ISBN.

A textbook for Indian students of Christian theology, which takes the Indian cultural background very seriously.

AS254 Chethimattam, J. B., ed.

Unique and Universal: Fundamental Problems of an Indian Theology. Bangalore, II: Dharmaram College, Centre for the Study of World Religions, 1972. vii, 230 pp. Paper. No ISBN.

Sixteen short essays by Indian theologians constituting an introduction to theology in the Indian context.

AS255 Dehn, Ulrich M.

Indische Christen in der gesellschaftlichen Verantwortung: Eine theologische und religionssoziologische Untersuchung zu politischer Theologie im gegenwärtigen Indien. (Studies in the Intercultural History of Christianity , 38). Frankfurt am Main, GW: Lang, 1985. x, 363 pp. Paper. 3820484760.

A dissertation examining how Christianity in India, in the early seventies, taking its cue from Latin America, began to develop a liberation theology within the Indian sociopolitical context.

AS256 Devanandan, Paul David

Paul D. Devanandan. Edited by Joachim Wietzke. (Library of Indian Christian Theology, 4-5). Madras, II: CLS, 1983-1987. 2 vols. Paper. No ISBN.

A sourcebook, in two volumes, of the articles, book reviews, and unpublished manuscripts of Paul David Devanan-

dan (1901-1962), noted Indian theologian, Professor in History of Religions at the United Theological College, Bangalore (1934-49), and first Director of the CISRS (1957-1962) [vol. 1: xii, 392 pp., 1983; vol. 2: viii, 383 pp., 1987].

AS257 Fakirbhai, Dhanjibhai

Khristopanishad (Christ-Upanishad). Bangalore, II: CISRS, 1965. xvi, 44 pp. No ISBN.

An attempt at indigenizing Christian theology, using Hindu religious terms and ideas, to discuss the nature of Jesus, man, salvation, and the meaning of the Christian life.

AS258 Francis, T. Dayanandan, ed.

The Christian Bhakti of A. J. Appasamy: A Collection of His Writings. Madras, II: CLS, 1992. xx, 349 pp. Paper. No ISBN.

Lectures and articles by Appasamy, showing his radical Hindu sympathies and his evangelical advocacy of Jesus Christ.

AS259 Jaswant Raj, Joseph

Grace in Saiva Siddhantham and in St. Paul: A Contribution in Inter-faith Cross-Cultural Understanding. Madras, II: South Indian Salesian Society, 1989. xxix, 743 pp. 8190009206.

A comparative study of the concept of grace as found in South Indian Saivite philosophy and in the theology of St. Paul.

AS260 Jesudasan, Ignatius

A Gandhian Theology of Liberation. Maryknoll, NYU: Orbis Books, 1984. xi, 179 pp. Paper. 0883441543.

A scholarly exposition of Gandhi's theology of liberation, vision of a liberated society, social strategies for achieving it, and challenge to Christianity; by an Indian Jesuit theologian.

AS261 John, T. K., ed.

Bread and Breath: Essays in Honour of Samuel Rayan S.J. (Jesuit Theological Forum Reflections, 5). Anand, II: Gujarat Sahitya Prakash, 1991. xii, 336 pp. No ISBN.

A *festschrift* honoring the noted Indian Jesuit theologian, with twenty-four essays—on liberation theologies, spirituality, and theology in dialogue—by his Indian colleagues (Amaladoss, M. M. Thomas, Wilfred, etc.) and fellow members of EATWOT (Gutiérrez, Sobrino, Cone, Koyama).

AS262 Kavunkal, Jacob

The "Abba" Experience of Jesus: Model and Motive for Mission in Asia. Indore, II: Satprakashan Sanchar Kendra, 1995. 176 pp. Paper. 8185428522.

A mission paradigm for the Indian context, postulated on John 20:21-23 as the starting point.

AS263 Kavunkal, Jacob, and F. Hrangkhuma, eds.

Christ and Cultures. (Fellowship of Indian Missiologists (2nd, Nagpur, August 1993)). Bombay, II: St. Pauls, 1994. 238 pp. Paper. 8171092144.

A collection of essays on Christology in the Indian context

AS264 Massey, James

Roots of Dalit History, Christianity, Theology and Spirituality. Delhi, II: ISPCK, 1996. 102 pp. 8172140347.

A revised and enlarged edition of *Roots: A Concise History of Dalits* (1991), by the well-known author and specialist in the field of Dalit theology.

AS265 Massey, James, ed.
Contextual Theological Education. (ISPCK Contextual Theological Education, 1). Delhi, II: ISPCK, 1993. viii, 99 pp. Paper. 8172141424.

Ten papers on contextual theology with special reference to India; originally presented in the ISPCK Contextual Theological Education consultation series at the Union Biblical Seminary, Pune, from 10-13 June 1992.

AS266 Massey, James, ed.
Indigenous People: Dalits: Dalit Issues in Today's Theological Debate. (ISPCK Contextual Theological Education Series, 5). Delhi, II: ISPCK, 1994. viii, 345 pp. Paper. 8172141548.

A collection of twenty-two short essays, by both Dalit activists, and non-Dalit scholars, on the major issues debated in the area of Dalit theology during the past decade.

AS267 Mizo Theological Conference
Towards a Tribal Theology: The Mizo Perspective. Edited by K. Thanzauva. Assam, II: Eastern Theological College, 1989. 115 pp. Paper. No ISBN.

Ten scholarly essays on developing a tribal Christian Theology in India by eight Mizo leaders, exploring traditional Mizo concepts and present trends.

AS268 Mookenthottam, Antony
Indian Theological Tendencies: Approaches and Problems for Further Research as Seen in the Works of Some Leading Indian Theologians. (Studies in the Intercultural History of Christianity, 21). Bern, SZ: Lang, 1978. 319 pp. Paper. 3261046139.

A survey of the leading Indian theological tendencies, from the beginning of Christianity in India to the 20th century, focusing on pluri-dimensional approaches, relating the concepts of truth and reality in Christian scriptures with those in Hinduism, Jainism, and Buddhism.

AS269 Philip, T. M.
The Encounter between Theology and Ideology: An Exploration into the Communicative Theology of M. M. Thomas. Madras, II: CLS, 1986. xvi, 160 pp. Paper. No ISBN.

An analysis of the liberation theology of M. M. Thomas (1916-1996), the eminent Indian ecumenical leader, focusing on the communicability of his radical Christocentric theology in the Asian context of religious and ideological pluralism.

AS270 Raja, R. J.
The Gospels with an Indian Face. Madras, II: CLS, 1996. viii, 81 pp. Paper. No ISBN.

A well-known Catholic biblical scholar relates the Gospel narratives to the three Hindu paths to salvation (wisdom, action, and devotion).

AS271 Rajasekaran, Vengal Chakk
Reflections on Indian Christian Theology. Madras, II: CLS, 1993. xii, 223 pp. Paper. No ISBN.

Theological reflections by an Indian lay theologian, drawing heavily on the 20th-century contributions of V. Chakkarai, P. Chenchiah, and other lay theologians of the "Rethinking Group of Madras."

AS272 Rao, Mark Sunder
Concerning Indian Christianity. New Delhi, II: YMCA Press, 1973. iv, 129 pp. No ISBN.

A search for those foundations of a genuine Indian Christian theology with which to enter into Hindu-Christian dialogue, by the well-known journalist and secretary of the National Missionary Society of India.

AS273 Rao, O. M.
An Asian's Christological Perspectives. Delhi, II: ISPCK, 1994. ix, 66 pp. Paper. 8172141807.

An Indian professor of the New Testament's Christology in relation to the contemporary Indian reality.

AS274 Selvanayagam, Israel
Towards a Humanist Theology of Religious Harmony: Insights from the Writings of Dayanandan Francis. Madras, II: CLS, 1994. 62 pp. Paper. No ISBN.

Indian Christian theology in dialogue with secular humanism, as reflected in the thought of T. Dayanandan Francis, general secretary of the CLS since 1979; with short selections from his poetry and other writings.

AS275 Sharpe, Eric J.
The Theology of A. G. Hogg. (Confessing the Faith in India Series, 7). Madras, II: CLS, 1971. xiii, 254 pp. No ISBN.

A scholarly introduction to the thought of Alfred George Hogg (1875-1954) who, as teacher and principal of Madras Christian College, influenced Hindu-Christian dialogue; with lengthy extracts from eleven of his writings.

AS276 Sugirtharajah, R. S., and Cecil Hargreaves, eds.
Readings in Indian Christian Theology, 1. (ISPCK Study Guide, 29). Delhi, II: ISPCK, 1993. x, 261 pp. Paper. 8172141394.

This, the first of two sourcebooks, covers methods and ways of doing theology, Indian-Christian understandings of Jesus, people's stories and their theologies, and Indian biblical hermeneutics.

AS277 Sumithra, Sunand
Revolution as Revelation: A Study of M. M. Thomas's Theology. New Delhi, II: ICN and TRACI, 1984. xii, 387 pp. Paper. No ISBN.

This evangelical analysis of the thinking of Dr. M. M. Thomas deals with critical issues in the relationship of biblical revelation and contemporary revolution.

AS278 Thangaraj, M. Thomas
The Crucified Guru: An Experiment in Cross-Cultural Christology. Nashville, TNU: Abingdon, 1994. 165 pp. Paper. 0687100089.

A careful examination of how the Indian concept of *guru*, as used in the Saiva Siddhanta philosophy of Tamilnadu, can contribute significantly to Christological thinking, both in India and in the West.

AS279 Thangasamy, D. A.
The Theology of Chenchiah. (Confessing the Faith in India, 1). Bangalore, II: CISRS, 1967. xxiv, 329 pp. No ISBN.

An analysis of the contribution of Pandippedi Chenchiah (1886-1959) to Indian Christian theology, with selections from his writings organized by subject.

AS280 Upadhyay, Brahmabandhab
The Writings of Brahmabandhab Upadhyay. Edited by Julius Lipner and G. Gispert-Sauch. (Library of Indian Christian Theology, 6). Bangalore, II: United Theological College, 1991. xlvi, 298 pp. Paper. 8185526001 (hdbk), 818552601X (pbk).

The first volume of the collected writings of Brahmabandhab Upadhyay (1861-1907), the self-styled "Hindu Catholic" pioneer in interreligious dialogue, with a résumé of his life and thought by the editors.

AS—ASIA

AS281 Wagner, Herwig
Erstgestalten einer einheimischen Theologie in Südindien: Ein Kapitel indischer Theologiegeschichte als kritischer Beitrag zur Definition von "einheimische Theologie." München, GW: Kaiser, 1963. 306 pp. Paper. No ISBN.

This book deals with Indian Christian theology, focusing specifically on the reflections of A. J. Appasamy ("mystical theology"), P. Chenchiah ("speculative theology"), and V. Chakkaray ("theology of experience"), with an evaluation and criticism by the author.

AS282 Wietzke, Joachim
Theologie im modernen Indien: Paul David Devanandan. (Studies in the Intercultural History of Christianity, 4). Bern, SZ: Herbert Lang; Frankfurt am Main, GW: Peter Lang, 1975. iv, 272 pp. Paper. 3261017007.

Analysis of how Devanandan's thought evolved as first Director of the CISRS in Bangalore, India.

AS283 Wilfred, Felix
Beyond Settled Foundations: The Journey of Indian Theology. (Asian Theological Search, 3). Madras, II: University of Madras, Dept. of Christian Studies, 1993. xii, 288 pp. Paper. No ISBN.

A survey of Catholic theological attempts to articulate the meaning of Jesus Christ in the Indian context.

AS284 Wilfred, Felix, ed.
Leave the Temple: Indian Paths to Human Liberation. (Faith Meets Faith Series). Maryknoll, NYU: Orbis Books, 1992. viii, 199 pp. Paper. 0883447940 (hdbk), 0883447819 (pbk).

Ten essays by Indian Catholic theologians, relating the theme of human liberation to India's varied religions and social realities.

AS285 Wilfred, Felix, ed.
Verlass den Tempel: Antyodaya–indischer Weg zur Befreiung. (Theologie der Dritten Welt, 11). Freiburg im Breisgau, GW: Herder, 1988. 208 pp. Paper. 3451212161.

In this collection of essays, nine Indian theologians and sociologists develop an indigenous theology of liberation, arguing that liberation in this world, despite common misperceptions, has often been a theme in the history and struggles of India.

AS286 Wilson, H. S., ed.
Indian Theological Case Studies. Madurai, Il: Tamil Nadu Theological Seminary, 1986. viii, 120 pp. Paper. No ISBN.

Nine cases, with theological reflections by Indian educators, on issues of marital and interpersonal relationships, as well as church and politics and human rights in India.

AS287 Wolters, Hielke T.
Theology of Prophetic Participation: M. M. Thomas' Concept of Salvation and the Collective Struggle for Fuller Humanity in India. Delhi, II: ISPCK, 1996. viii, 329 pp. Paper. 8172142463.

A detailed study of the development of thought of Madathiparampil Mammen Thomas (1916-1996) of India, from his upbringing in the Mar Thoma Church, to his personal involvement in the struggle for prophetic witness to the Gospel in student movements, and Indian and global ecumenism.

AS288 Younger, Paul
Theology of Bread, Vision, and Politics: The Indian Ethos and Christian Faith. Delhi, II: ISPCK, 1986. 58 pp. Paper. No ISBN.

A prolegomena to an Indian Christian theology by the Professor of Religions at McMaster University, Canada, delivered as special lectures at Mar Thoma Theological Seminary in Kottayam, India, in 1984.

East Asia: General Works

See also EA122, CR767, SO467, PO181, and AS157.

AS289 Flinn, Frank K., and Tyler Hendricks, eds.
Religion in the Pacific Era. (Studies in the Pacific Era Series). New York, NYU: Paragon House, 1985. xiv, 228 pp. Paper. 0913757195.

Scholarly papers on Western missionizing in Asia (from Nestorian missions and de Nobili to the present) and Eastern responses—most of which were originally presented at the new ERA Winter Seminar on "Religion in the Pacific Era," Nassau, the Bahamas, 23-27 February 1983.

AS290 Grueber, Johannes
Als Kundschafter des Papstes nach China 1656-1664: Die 1. Durchquerung Tibets; nach den Briefen J. Gruebers und den Berichten seiner Biographen, Athanasius Kircher und Melchisedeck Thevenot. Edited by Franz Braumann. (Alte abenteuerliche Reiseberichte). Stuttgart, GW: Thienemann, 1985. 199 pp. 3522607104.

The travel reports of an Austrian Jesuit, who was commissioned by the Pope to explore the land route from Europe to the East, and on the return journey visited Tibet, up to then unknown to the Western world.

AS291 Hanson, Eric O.
Catholic Politics in China and Korea. (American Society of Missiology Series, 2). Maryknoll, NYU: Orbis Books, 1980. xiii, 140 pp. Paper. 0883440849.

A well-documented study of Roman Catholic politics in the PRC, Taiwan, and South Korea, from 1580 through the late 1970s.

AS292 Heissig, Walther, and Hans-Joachim Klimkeit, eds.
Synkretismus in den Religionen Zentralasiens: Ergebnisse eines Kolloquiums vom 24.5. bis 26.5.1983 in St. Augustin bei Bonn. (Studies in Oriental Religions, 13). Wiesbaden, GW: Harrassowitz, 1987. viii, 226 pp. Paper. 3447026200.

Fifteen scholarly essays on aspects of popular religion/syncretism (Christian and Buddhist) among the Turkish, Chinese, and Tibetan peoples of Central Asia.

AS293 Ion, A. Hamish
The Cross and the Rising Sun: The Canadian Protestant Missionary Movement in the Japanese Empire, 1872-1931. Waterloo, ONC: Wilfrid Laurier University Press, 1990. 304 pp. 0889209774.

The first volume of a multi-volume history of Protestant missions in Japan, Korea, and Taiwan, covering missions from Canada, 1872 to 1931.

AS294 Ion, A. Hamish
The Cross and the Rising Sun, Volume 2: The British Protestant Missionary Movement in Japan, Korea, and Taiwan, 1865-1945. Waterloo, ONC: Wilfrid Laurier University Press, 1993. xii, 324 pp. 0889202184.

A narrative, yet scholarly, history of eighty years of British Protestant missions in East Asia, with focus on the Western cultural values they introduced, and how, in turn, they were affected by the response of East Asians to Western ideas.

AS295 Liao, David C. E., ed.

World Christianity, Volume 2: Eastern Asia. Monrovia, CAU: MARC, 1979. 198 pp. Paper. 091255231X.

Profiles of the status of Christianity in 1979, in eighteen countries of eastern and southeastern Asia, with a listing of people groups where less than 20 percent of the population are practicing Christians.

AS296 Mullins, Mark R., and Richard Fox Young, eds.

Perspectives on Christianity in Korea and Japan: The Gospel and Culture in East Asia. Lewiston, NYU: E Mellen Press, 1995. xxiii, 230 pp. 0773488685, E.

Fourteen scholarly essays based on papers prepared for the "Christianity in East Asia" project, co-sponsored by the Meiji Gakuin University's Institute for Christian Studies and the Global Mission Unit of the PCUSA.

AS297 Reed, James

The Missionary Mind and American East Asia Policy, 1911-1915. (Harvard East Asian Monographs, 104). Cambridge, MAU: Harvard University Press, 1983. xiv, 258 pp. 0674576578.

A detailed study of the role of US missionaries to China and Japan in their government's foreign policy formation during the presidency of Woodrow Wilson.

AS298 Ross, Andrew C.

A Vision Betrayed: The Jesuits in Japan and China (1542-1742). Maryknoll, NYU: Orbis Books, 1994. xvii, 216 pp. 0883449919.

The first comprehensive account in English of early Jesuit missions in Japan and China, with emphasis on their creative approaches to contextualization, and the reasons for their suppression.

AS299 Sánchez, Víctor, and Cayetano S. Fuertes, eds.

España en Extremo Oriente: Filipinas, China, Japón: Presencia Franciscana, 1578-1978. Madrid, SP: Cisneros; Madrid, SP: Publicaciones Archivo Ibero-Americano, 1979. xiv, 671 pp. 8470470213.

A collection of articles (in Spanish, English, and Italian) concerning Spanish missionary efforts, especially of the Franciscan order, in the Far East.

AS300 Thomas, T. K., ed.

Christianity in Asia: North-East Asia. Toa Payoh, SI: CCA, 1979. 112 pp. Paper. No ISBN.

A first ecumenical effort for Asians to write short histories of Christianity in their respective countries (China, Japan, Korea, and Taiwan).

China: General

See also HI132, HI227, HI272, HI428, HI477-HI478, HI699, ME3-ME4, CR709, CR758, CR776, PO158-PO159, ED22, ED40, MI6, SP282, SP323, AS5, AS8-AS9, AS33, AS36, AS154, AS291, and AS728.

AS301 Aambo, Kjetil

Kampen om "gullmannen": Fra letingen etter misjonær Knut Samset, bortført av røverere i Kina 1936. Oslo, NO: Lunde, 1977. 126 pp. Paper. 8252026290.

Letters of the Norwegian missionary Knut Samset, martyred in Central China in 1936.

AS302 Austin, Alvyn J.

Saving China: Canadian Missionaries in the Middle Kingdom, 1888-1959. Toronto, ONC: University of Toronto Press, 1986. 395 pp. 0802056873.

A comprehensive history of seventy-two years of China missions by Roman Catholics, and evangelical and liberal Protestants, giving a detailed picture of the religious and cultural face of Western imperialism in China.

AS303 Barr, Pat

To China with Love: The Lives and Times of Protestant Missionaries in China, 1860-1900. Garden City, NYU: Doubleday, 1973. xiii, 210 pp. 038503864X.

The story of the first impact of Protestant missionaries upon China, and of that legendary country's impact upon the missionaries, who rejected the securities of their Western world and chose to live, and often die, in the cause of their Christian faith.

AS304 Bays, Daniel H., ed.

Christianity in China: From the Eighteenth Century to the Present. Stanford, CAU: Stanford University Press, 1996. xxii, 483 pp. 0804726094.

Twenty original essays on Christianity and Chinese culture, from the 18th century to the present, with sections on women and the rise of an indigenous Chinese Christianity.

AS305 Bergeron, Marie-Ina

Le christianisme en Chine: approches et stratégies. Lyon, FR: Chalet, 1977. 155 pp. 2702302920.

Reflections on the various mission strategies of Roman Catholics in China, from Matteo Ricci to the present.

AS306 Bolton, Leonard

China Call: Miracles Among the Lisu People. Springfield, MOU: Gospel Publishing House, 1984. 221 pp. Paper. 0882435094.

The personal account of Leonard and Ada Bolton, missionaries among the Lisu people of Yunnan province in western China, as they struggled to build the Assemblies of God Church from the 1920s to the 1980s.

AS307 Brandt, Nat

Massacre in Shansi. Syracuse, NYU: Syracuse University Press, 1994. xxii, 336 pp. 0815602820 (hdbk), 0815602839 (pbk).

A narrative history, based on archival research, designed to uncover the life, attitudes, and Christianity of Oberlin College graduates who served as American Board missionaries in China, from the late 1880s until their martyrdom during the 1900 Boxer Rebellion.

AS308 Brown, G. Thompson

Earthen Vessels and Transcendent Power: American Presbyterians in China, 1837-1952. (American Society of Missiology Series, 25). Maryknoll, NYU: Orbis Books, 1997. xxiii, 428 pp. 1570751501.

A definitive chronological history of American Presbyterian missions in China, with appendices, listing institutions and personnel, numerous illustrations, and extensive endnotes and bibliography.

AS309 Camps, Arnulf, and Pat McCloskey

The Friars Minor in China, 1294-1955: Especially the Years 1925-55. St. Bonaventure, NYU: St. Bonaventure University Franciscan Institute Press, 1995. xviii, 316 pp. 157659002X.

The culmination of a fifteen-year research by the OFM on their missionary endeavors in China over seven centuries.

AS310 Carlsen, William D.

Tibet: In Search of a Miracle. Nyack, NYU: Nyack College, 1985. 70 pp. Paper. No ISBN.

A popular introduction to the history of missionary work of the Christian and Missionary Alliance church in Tibet, 1896-1940, as told by the author who retraced his steps in the 1980s.

AS—ASIA

AS311 Carlson, Ellsworth C.

The Foochow Missionaries, 1847-1880. (Harvard East Asian Monographs, 51). Cambridge, MAU: Harvard University, East Asian Research Center, 1974. i, 259 pp. 0674307336.

A detailed case study, based on archival research, of the first thirty-four years of missions in Foochow, an early center of Protestant missions in Fukien province of southeast China.

AS312 Caulfield, Caspar

Only a Beginning: The Passionists in China, 1921-1931. Union City, NJU: Passionist Press, 1990. xv, 296 pp. Paper. 0962611905.

A history of the first years of work by the Passionate Fathers in central China, including details of political conflicts in western Hunan and the murder of three priests by the communists in 1929.

AS313 Centre de Recherches Interdisciplinaire de Chantilly

Actes du Colloque International de Sinologie: la mission française de Pékin aux XVIIe et XVIIIe siècles ... 20-22 Septembre 1974. Paris, FR: Les Belles Lettres, 1976. 164 pp. No ISBN.

Fourteen scholarly papers on French Jesuit missions in China in the 17th and 18th centuries, including their relation to Chinese thought, artistic activity, and the Rites Controversy.

AS314 Chao, Jonathan

A History of the Church in China Since 1949: A Reader: An Expanded Study Guide (to Accompany the Programmed Syllabus). Grand Rapids, MIU: Institute of Theological Studies, 1995. 2 vols. Paper. No ISBN.

Readings, including study guides, for courses on China in evangelical seminaries, offered as distance education.

AS315 Cheung, Yuet-wah

Missionary Medicine in China: A Study of Two Canadian Protestant Missions in China before 1937. Lanham, MDU: University Press of America, 1988. xii, 179 pp. 0819169013.

A revision of the author's Ph.D. dissertation, highlighting the impact of Western medical missionaries on China's early stages of medical modernization, through a detailed examination of the medical work of two Canadian missions (Presbyterian and Methodist).

AS316 Chu, Clayton H.

American Missionaries in China: Books, Articles and Pamphlets Extracted from the Subject Catalogue of the Missionary Research Library. (Research Aids for American Far Eastern Policy Studies, 2). Cambridge, MAU: Harvard University, Committee on American Far Eastern Policy Studies, 1960. 3 vols. Paper. No ISBN.

A typescript catalogue of holdings on China in the Missionary Research Library in New York—much of it unpublished [vol. 1: 139 pp.; vol. 2: 200 pp.; vol. 3: xxiv, 509 pp.].

AS317 Clark, William H.

The Church in China: Its Vitality; Its Future? New York, NYU: Council Press, [1969]. xii, 212 pp. No ISBN.

A history of Christianity in China, from the Nestorian missions to 1969, by a United Presbyterian missionary to China, 1925-1949, who shares in the reappraisal of China missions.

AS318 Cliff, Norman

Courtyard of the Happy Way. Evesham, ENK: James, 1977. ix, 144 pp. Paper. 0853051917.

A former CIM educator at Chefoo School in China recounts his 1937-1945 experiences, including internship under Japanese occupation.

AS319 Cohen, Paul A.

China and Christianity: The Missionary Movement and the Growth of Chinese Antiforeignism, 1860-1870. (Harvard East Asian Series, 11). Cambridge, MAU: Harvard University Press, 1977. xiv, 392 pp. No ISBN.

A scholarly pioneer study based on archival research.

AS320 Collani, Claudia von

Die Figuristen in der Chinamission. (Würzburger Sino-Japonica, 8). Frankfurt, GW: Lang, 1981. iv, 124 pp. Paper. 3820462139.

A monograph about a group of French China missionaries of the 17th and 18th centuries, who based their missionary method on a Christian, figurative interpretation of the Chinese classical books.

AS321 Costantini, Celso

Réforme des missions au XXe siècle. Translated by Jean Bruls. (Église vivante). Tournai, BE: Casterman, 1960. 280 pp. No ISBN.

Extracts from the journal (1922-1953) of the apostolic delegate to China, who in the 1920s and 1930s was instrumental in higher education, and in advancing Chinese clergy and laity to leadership.

AS322 Costantini, Celso

Reforma de las Misiones en el siglo XX. (La Aventura humana: Serie Crónica, 1). Barcelona, SP: Editorial Fontanella, 1962. 353 pp. Paper. No ISBN.

Spanish translation of *Reforme ses missions au XXe. Siecle* (1960).

AS323 Covell, Ralph R.

Confucius, the Buddha, and Christ: A History of the Gospel in Chinese. (American Society of Missiology Series, 11). Maryknoll, NYU: Orbis Books, 1986. 285 pp. Paper. 0883442671.

A thoroughly documented, in-depth case study of contextualization in the history of missionary activity in China.

AS324 Covell, Ralph R.

The Liberating Gospel in China: The Christian Faith among China's Minority Peoples. Grand Rapids, MIU: Baker Books, 1995. 318 pp. Paper. 0801025958.

Eleven missiological case studies of how China's minority peoples received the Gospel prior to 1949, by a former Conservative Baptist missionary among them.

AS325 Covell, Ralph R.

Mission Impossible: The Unreached Nosu on China's Frontier. Pasadena, CAU: Hope Publishing House, 1990. x, 309 pp. Paper. 0932727352.

A popular account of the efforts of a group of young Conservative Baptist missionaries, among the independent Nosu minority people of Xikang Province in northwest China, in the days of China's civil war and the end of Western missionary influence (1946-1951).

AS326 Crawley, Winston
Partners across the Pacific: China and Southern Baptists: Into the Second Century. Nashville, TNU: Broadman, 1986. 140 pp. Paper. 0805463410.

A brief history of the 150-year involvement of Southern Baptist in China.

AS327 Criveller, Gianni
Preaching Christ in Late Ming China: The Jesuits' Presentation of Christ from Matteo Ricci to Giulio Aleni. (Variétés Sinologiques-New Series, 86). Taipei, CH: Ricci Institute for Chinese Studies; Brescia, IT: Fondazione Civiltà Bresciana-Annali 10, 1997. xxiv, 479 pp. Paper. 2910969029.

An original in-depth analysis of the Christology pursued by the first Jesuits in China, especially Matteo Ricci and Giulio Aleni.

AS328 Cui, Dan
The Cultural Contribution of British Protestant Missionaries and British-American Cooperation to China's National Development during the 1920's. Lanham, MDU: University Press of America, 1998. xxii, 405 pp. 0761810293.

A detailed historical study, based on archival sources, of the impact of the Social Gospel and British Protestant missions on Chinese national development and modernization in the 1920s.

AS329 Cummins, J. S.
A Question of Rites: Friar Domingo Navarrete and the Jesuits in China. Hants, ENK: Scolar Press; Brookville, VTU: Ashgate Publishing, 1993. xv, 349 pp. 0859678806.

The 17th-century Chinese Rites controversy, analyzed from the perspective of the Spanish Dominican, Domingo Navarrete (1618-1686), who was in conflict with the Jesuits.

AS330 Curwen, Charles Anthony
Taiping Rebel: The Deposition of Li Hsiu-Ch'eng. (Cambridge Studies in Chinese History, Literature, and Institutions). Cambridge, MAU: Cambridge University Press, 1977. viii, 357 pp. 0521210828.

A scholarly analysis of the "largest civil war in history" of importance to missiologists in the debate whether the Taiping movement was a notable example of contextualization; English translation of *Li, Hsiu-ch'eng Kung.*

AS331 De Jong, Gerald Francis
The Reformed Church in China, 1842-1951. (The Historical Series of the Reformed Church in America, 22). Grand Rapids, MIU: Eerdmans, 1992. xiii, 385 pp. Paper. 0802806619.

An overview of missionary work in China by the Reformed Church in America, based on church reports and periodicals in English.

AS332 Dunne, George Harold
Chinois avec les Chinois: Le père Ricci et ses compagnos Jésuites dans la Chine du XVIIe. Translated by G. Serve. (L'Église en son temps). Paris, FR: Éditions du Centurion, 1964. 415 pp. No ISBN.

French translation.

AS333 Dunne, George Harold
Generation of Giants: The Story of the Jesuits in China in the Last Decades of the Ming Dynasty. Notre Dame, INU: University of Notre Dame Press; London, ENK: Burns & Oates, 1962. 389 pp. No ISBN.

A scholarly study, drawn from some sources not previously used, significant for its treatment of Matteo Ricci (1552-1610) and the Rites Controversy about missionary methods.

AS334 Dunne, George Harold
Das grosse Exempel: Die Chinamission der Jesuiten. Translated by Margarethe Diemer. (Peter Paul Bücherei). Stuttgart, GW: Schwabenverlag, 1965. 496 pp. No ISBN.

German translation.

AS335 Eichhorn, Werner
Die Religionen Chinas. (Die Religionen der Menschheit, 21). Stuttgart, GW: Kohlhammer, 1973. 420 pp. 3172160319.

The most comprehensive description in German of the history of religion in China, from the beginnings to the present, including Christian missions.

AS336 Fairbank, John K., ed.
The Missionary Enterprise in China and America. (Harvard Studies in American-East Asian Relations, 6). Cambridge, MAU: Harvard University Press, 1974. 442 pp. 0674576551.

Fourteen scholarly essays on missionary roles in the United States and in China, 1840 to 1950.

AS337 Fenn, William Purviance
Christian Higher Education in Changing China, 1880-1950. Grand Rapids, MIU: Eerdmans, 1976. 256 pp. 0802834787.

A scholarly reassessment of the contributions of Christian colleges in China.

AS338 Fischer, Edward
Maybe a Second Spring: The Story of the Missionary Sisters of St. Columban in China. New York, NYU: Crossroad Publishing, 1983. 200 pp. Paper. 0824506154.

A narrative illustrated history of twenty-five years (1926-1951) of mission in China, primarily in education, health, and social welfare.

AS339 Forsythe, Sidney A.
An American Missionary Community in China, 1895-1905. (Harvard East Asian Monographs, 43). Cambridge, MAU: Harvard University, East Asian Research Center, 1971. viii, 146 pp. 0674026268.

A descriptive case study of how 103 missionaries of the ABCFM interpreted the settings and problems of their work in China.

AS340 Fulton, Austin
Through Earthquake, Wind and Fire: Church and Mission in Manchuria. Edinburgh, STK: St. Andrews Press, 1967. 416 pp. No ISBN.

A history of the work of the United Presbyterian Church, the United Free Church of Scotland, the Church of Scotland, and the Presbyterian Church in Ireland with the Chinese church in Manchuria.

AS341 Gamblim, Eleanor, and Joyce Morehouse
The Sparrow's Song. Hazelwood, MOU: Word Aflame Press, 1984. 192 pp. Paper. 0912315687.

A first-person account of the experiences and dedication of a United Pentecostal missionary in China, 1931-1938.

AS342 Garbero, Pietro
I missionari Saveriani in Cina: cinquant'anni de apostolato. Parma, IT: Istituto Saveriano per le Missioni Estere, 1965. 373 pp. No ISBN.

A detailed history of fifty years of work by the Xaverian Missionary Fathers in Honan Province.

AS343 Gardini, Walter
El Cristianismo Llega a China. Buenos Aires, AG: Editorial Guadalupe; Buenos Aires, AG: Obras Misionales Pontificias, 1983. 217 pp. Paper. 9505000650.
A historical examination of the entrance of Christianity into China, beginning with the arrival of Nestorian monks during the rule of the Tang dynasty, concluding with the author's thoughts regarding the future of Christianity in China.

AS344 Garrett, Shirley S.
Social Reformers in Urban China: The Chinese Y.M.C.A., 1895-1926. (Harvard East Asian Series, 56). Cambridge, MAU: Harvard University Press, 1970. 221 pp. 0674812204.
A detailed analysis based on primary sources.

AS345 Gernet, Jacques
China and the Christian Impact: A Conflict of Cultures. Translated by Janet Lloyd. Cambridge, ENK: Cambridge University Press; Paris, FR: Maison des Sciences de l'Homme, 1985. 310 pp. 0521266815 (C hdbk), 0521313198 (C pbk), 2735101169 (M hdbk), 273510138X (M pbk).
English translation.

AS346 Gernet, Jacques
Chine et Christianisme: action et réaction. (Bibliothèque des histoires). Paris, FR: Gallimard, 1982. 342 pp. 2070263665.
A detailed scholarly analysis of Chinese responses to Western mission impact in the seventeenth century, from the sympathetic reception of the Jesuit missionaries Ruggieri and Ricci, to later hostility.

AS347 Gernet, Jacques
Christus kam bis nach China: Eine erste Begegnung und ihr Scheitern. Zürich, SZ: Artemis Verlag, 1984. 341 pp. 3760806260.
German translation.

AS348 Gewurtz, Margo S.
Famine Relief in China: North Henan in the 1920s. (Working Papers Series, 50). Toronto, ONC: University of Toronto-York University Joint Centre of Asia Pacific Studies, 1987. 23 pp. Paper. 0921309791.
A short essay on contributions of Canadian missionaries.

AS349 Golvers, Noël
The Astronomia Europaea of Ferdinand Verbiest, S.J. (Dillingen, 1687): Text, Translation, Notes and Commentaries. (Monograph Series, 28). Nettetal, GW: Steyler Verlag, 1993. 547 pp. 3805003277.
A critical edition of *Astronomia Europaea* (1687) in which the Jesuit missionary to China, Ferdinand Verbiest (1623-1688), recounted developments that led to the reinstatement of European astronomy in China in 1668, and the subsequent mathematical and scientific contributions of Jesuit missionaries.

AS350 Golvers, Noël
François de Rougemont, S.J., Missionary in Ch'ang-Shu (Chiang-Nan): A Study of the Account Book (1674-1976) and the Elogium. (Louvain Chinese Studies, 7). Leuven, BE: Leuven University Press/Ferdinand Verbiest Foundation, 1999. xvii, 794 pp. Paper. 9058670015.

This book reconstructs missionary life in China through documents of a Jesuit missionary and his ten journeys to a small island residence.

AS351 Graham, Gael
Gender, Culture, and Christianity: American Protestant Mission Schools in China, 1880-1930. (Asian Thought and Culture, 25). New York, NYU: Lang, 1995. 231 pp. 0820427675.
A general survey of Protestant mission schools in China, 1880 to 1930, focusing on efforts to affect reform of Chinese gender beliefs and customs; originally submitted as a doctoral dissertation at the University of Michigan.

AS352 Gratuze, Gaston
Un pionnier de la mission tibétaine: le père Auguste Desgodins (1826-1913). Paris, FR: Apostolat des éditions, 1969. 365 pp. No ISBN.
The biography of the pioneer Roman Catholic missionary to Tibet (1865-1913) who, by his scholarly, linguistic, and geographical writings, made the closed plateau widely known.

AS353 Gundolf, Hubert
China zwischen Kreuz und Drachen: 650 Jahre katholische Mission im Reich der Mitte. Mödling, AU: St Gabriel-Verlag, 1969. 284 pp. No ISBN.
A popular illustrated history of the Catholic China mission, focusing on the 19th and 20th centuries.

AS354 Hang, Thaddaeus T'ui-Chieh
Die katholische Kirche im chinesischen Raum: Geschichte und Gegenwart. Munich, GW: Pustet, 1963. 224 pp. No ISBN.
After introductory chapters about Chinese history, culture, and the Chinese personality, this book gives an outline of the history of Christianity in China, the Catholic Church in the PR of China, Taiwan, Hong Kong, Macao, and the situation of the Catholic overseas Chinese.

AS355 Hartwich, Richard
Steyler Missionare in China: Beiträge zu einer Geschichte. (Studia Instituti Missiologici SVD, 32, 36, 40, 42, 48, 53). Nettetal, GW: Steyler Verlag, 1983. 6 vols. Paper.
A collection of documentary sources on the history of Divine Word missionaries in China, from 1879 onwards, presented in six-volumes [vol. 1: *Missionarische Erschliessung Südshantungs, 1879-1903* (1983, no pp., 387771666); vol. 2: *Bischof A. Henninghaus ruft Steyler Schwestern, 1904-1910* (1985, 626 pp., 3877871895); vol. 3: *Republik China und Erster Weltkrieg, 1911-1919* (1987, 638 pp., 3805001800); vol. 4: *Geistlicher Führer seiner Chinamissionare Rev.mus P. Wilhelm Gier SVD, 1922* (1988, 110 pp., 3805002025); vol. 5: *Aus Kriegsruinen zu neuen Grenzen, 1920-1923* (1989; xiv, 528 pp., 3805002424); vol. 6: *Auf den Wogen des Chinesischen Bürgerkrieges, 1924-1926* (1991; x, 713 pp., 3805002882)].

AS356 Heiar, James A., ed.
My China Memoirs, 1928-1951: Rev. Joseph Henkels, SVD. Techny, ILU: SVD, 1988. xi, 222 pp. Paper. No ISBN.
The memoirs of the first SVD missionary to China (1928-1951), reflecting on the experiences of everyday life, relationships, and the events in developing and maintaining Roman Catholic societies.

AS357 Hood, George A.

Mission Accomplished?: The English Presbyterian Mission in Lingtung, South China: A Study of the Interplay between Mission Methods and Their Historical Context. (Studies in the Intercultural History of Christianity, 42). Frankfurt am Main, GW: Lang, 1986. viii, 437 pp. Paper. 3820489959.

A well-documented study of the work of the English Presbyterian Mission begun in 1858, and of the development of a truly Chinese Three-Self church, to 1984.

AS358 Huang, Wen-chih

Das Taiping-Christentum: Eine Analyse seiner Entstehung, Entwicklung sowie seiner Lehre mit besonderer Berücksichtigung seiner Einflüsse auf die Revolutionsbewegung der Taipings. Erlangen, GW: University of Erlangen-Nürnberg, 1973. 147 pp. Paper. No ISBN.

This author investigates the Christian teaching of the religious and revolutionary Taiping Movement (1850-1864), asserting that Christianity was, indeed, the motivating factor of this movement.

AS359 Hueck, Otto

Zwischen Kaiserreich und Kommunismus: Als Missionsarzt in China. n.p.: By the author, Otto Hueck, 1977. 288 pp. No ISBN.

Reminiscences of a German missionary doctor who worked for fifty years in China (1921-1951) and North Sumatra (1951-1971).

AS360 International Conference on the Historiography of the Chinese Catholic Church (1st., Louvain, Belgium, Sept. 1990)

Historiography of the Chinese Catholic Church: Nineteenth and Twentieth Centuries. Edited by Jerome Heyndrickx. (Louvain Chinese Studies, 1). Leuven, BE: Ferdinand Verbiest Foundation, 1994. 511 pp. 9080183326.

Forty-seven papers on specific themes in the history of Catholicism in mainland China and Hong Kong, studies in process, and methods used.

AS361 Jen, Yu-wen, and Adrienne Suddard

The Taiping Revolutionary Movement. New Haven, CTU: Yale University Press, 1973. xxiii, 616 pp. 0300015429.

A detailed history of the Taiping Rebellion; based on archival research, including Christian mission influences upon the movement.

AS362 Johnston, Geoffrey, ed.

Happy Childhood: Moral Tales for Christian Children in China. Montreal, PQC: Presbyterian College, 1994. 117 pp. Paper. No ISBN.

Stories for Chinese children from three sources: the Christian *Happy Childhood* magazine, published by the China Sunday School Union (1915-1950), Confucian literature, and literature of the Communist era.

AS363 Kessler, Lawrence D.

The Jiangyin Mission Station: An American Missionary Community in China, 1895-1951. (The James Sprunt Studies in History and Political Science, 61). Chapel Hill, NCU: University of North Carolina Press, 1996. xiv, 212 pp. Paper. 0807850624.

A scholarly case study of a Presbyterian mission station in the Shanghai region, analyzing its program, which combined evangelism and social welfare, and the Chinese-American cultural interactions it fostered.

AS364 Krüssmann, Ingrid, Wolfgang Kubin, and Hans-Georg Möller, eds.

Der Abbruch des Turmbaus: Studien zum Geist in China und im Abendland—Festschrift für Rolf Trauzettel. (Monumenta Serica Monograph Series, 34). Sankt Augustin, GW: Institut Monumenta Serica; Nettetal, GW: Steyler Verlag, 1995. 314 pp. Paper. 3805003609.

Seventeen essays on Chinese worldview/spirit in philosophy and literature; published as a *festschrift* honoring the Professor of Sinology at the University of Bonn.

AS365 Krahl, Joseph

China Missions in Crisis: Bishop Laimbeckhoven and His Times, 1738-1787. (Analecta Gregoriana, vol. 137. Series Facultatis Historiae Ecclesiasticae; B, no. 24). Rome, IT: Gregorian University Press, 1964. xi, 383 pp. Paper. No ISBN.

Biography of one of the greatest missionaries to China in the 18th century, depicting his arrival in Macao in 1738 and his work as a missionary in Hukwang until he became bishop of Nanking in 1752.

AS366 Kroeger, James H., ed.

On the Maryknoll Road in China. Maryknoll, NYU: [Maryknoll Fathers and Brothers], 1997. 48, 56, 56, pp. No ISBN.

A narrative account of the early Maryknoll mission in China, 1917 to 1951, published in four booklets.

AS367 Kuepers, Jacobus J. A. M.

China und die katholische Mission in Süd-Shantung, 1882-1900: Die Geschichte einer Konfrontation. (Proefschrift Theol. Fac. Katholieke Universiteit Nijmegen). Steyl, NE: Missiehuis, 1974. 232 pp. Paper. No ISBN.

History of the SVD mission in southern Shandong between 1882 and 1900 (Boxer Rebellion), based on reports and letters from the missionaries, as well as official records of the Chinese Ministry of Foreign Affairs.

AS368 Ladany, L.

The Catholic Church in China. (Perspectives on Freedom, 7). New York, NYU: Freedom House, 1987. 110 pp. Paper. 0932088120.

A history, from both Communist and non-Communist views, of the Catholic Church in China, from its Jesuit beginnings to the days of the Communist takeover.

AS369 Lam, Wing-hung

Chinese Theology in Construction. South Pasadena, CAU: William Carey Library, 1983. viii, 308 pp. Paper. 0878081801.

A historical investigation of the response of the Protestant churches to the challenge of the anti-Christian movement in China in the 1920s.

AS370 Latourette, Kenneth Scott

The Chinese: Their History and Culture. New York, NYU: Macmillan; London, ENK: Collier Macmillan, 1964. xii, 714 pp. No ISBN.

Fourth edition of the definitive study in English of Chinese history and culture, placing Christian mission in that wider context, with major revisions to include the post World War II era; originally published in 1934.

AS371 Latourette, Kenneth Scott

A History of Christian Missions in China. Tai-pei, CH: Cheng Wen Publishing, 1973. xii, 930 pp. No ISBN.

A classic history by the noted Yale University historian; originally published in 1929 (London: SPCK); also reprinted in London in 1980 by Hodder & Stoughton and the Overseas Missionary Fellowship.

AS—ASIA

AS372 Lian, Xi
The Conversion of Missionaries: Liberalism in American Protestant Missions in China, 1907-1932. University Park, PAU: Pennsylvania State University Press, 1997. xiv, 247 pp. 027101606X.

A penetrating historical study of the development of a broad theological and cultural liberalism within American Protestant missions to China in the first third of the 20th century, beginning with biographical essays on Edward H. Hume, Frank J. Rawlinson, and Pearl S. Buck.

AS373 Ling, Oi Ki
The Changing Role of the British Protestant Missionaries in China, 1945-1952. Madison, WIU: Fairleigh Dickinson University Press, 1999. 303 pp. 0838637760.

A detailed study of the complexities and contradictions between the missionaries' own perceptions of their roles and Chinese realities, in the change from Nationalist to Communist rule.

AS374 Liu, Kwang-Ching, ed.
American Missionaries in China: Papers from Harvard Seminars. (Harvard East Asian Monographs, 21). Cambridge, MAU: Harvard University Press, 1970. 310 pp. Paper. No ISBN.

Seven scholarly essays on aspects of Protestant missions in China, 1860 to 1939, including missionary attitudes to nationalism, communism, and rural problems, and an assessment of their contribution to China.

AS375 Lotz, Denton, ed.
Spring Has Returned Listening ... To the Church in China. McLean, VAU: Baptist World Alliance, 1986. xii, 119 pp. Paper. No ISBN.

Addresses, testimonies, and Bible studies by Chinese Christians, presented at the Baptist World Alliance World Friendship Tour to China, 8–13 July 1986, Nanjing, China.

AS376 Lutz, Jessie Gregory, and Rolland Ray Lutz
Hakka Chinese Confront Protestant Christianity, 1850-1900: With the Autobiographies of Eight Hakka Christians, and Commentary. (Studies on Modern China). Armonk, NYU: M. E. Sharpe, 1998. xv, 293 pp. Paper. 0765600374 (hdbk), 0765600382 (pbk).

A history of the Basel Society's China mission in the late 19th century, among the Hakka of Kwangtung Province in South China; featuring the centrality in evangelization of eight pioneer Chinese as missionaries.

AS377 Lutz, Jessie Gregory, ed.
Christian Missions in China: Evangelists of What? (Problems in Asian Civilizations). Boston, MAU: Heath, 1965. xx, 108 pp. Paper. No ISBN.

Reprints of eighteen short essays by Chinese and Western scholars, originally published from 1878 to 1962, reevaluating the goals and methods of Christian missions in China.

AS378 Lutz, Jessie Gregory
Chinese Politics and Christian Missions: The Anti-Christian Movements of 1920-28. (The Church and the World, 3). Notre Dame, INU: Cross Cultural Publications, 1988. xiv, 410 pp. 0940121050.

Volume 3 of "The Church and the World" Series, analyzing the Kuomintang and Chinese Communist parties and their reaction to the Christian movement during the two decades before World War II, showing parallels to the growth of nationalist movements in African, and other Asian, countries.

AS379 Malek, Roman, ed.
Western Learning and Christianity in China: The Contribution and Impact of Johann Adam Schall von Bell, S.J., 1592-1666. (Monumenta Serica Monograph Series, 35, Vols 1, 2). St. Augustin, GW: China-Zentrum/Monumenta Serica Institute, 1998. xivi, 1259 pp. 3805004095.

This two-volume collection comprises fifty-one scholarly articles printed in their original languages (English, Chinese, German, and French), resulting from the proceedings of the international conference held in Saint Augustine, Germany in 1992, in commemoration of the 400th anniversary of the birth of German-born Jesuit China missionary, Johann Adam Scholl von Bell.

AS380 Merwin, Wallace C.
Adventure in Unity: The Church of Christ in China. Grand Rapids, MIU: Eerdmans, 1974. 232 pp. Paper. 0802834418.

A narrative history of the movements toward unity among Christians in China in the 20th century, the Church of Christ in China, and the model provided of an indigenous church.

AS381 Minamiki, George
The Chinese Rites Controversy: From Its Beginning to Modern Times. Chicago, ILU: Loyola University Press, 1985. xvi, 353 pp. 0829404570.

The first detailed historical account of the controversy over whether Catholic converts should honor Confucius and their own family ancestors, from the entry of Matteo Ricci into Peking in 1601 to the condemnation of such rites by Pope Benedict XIV in 1742.

AS382 Mitchell, Peter M.
Canadian Missionaries and Chinese Rural Society: North Honan in the 1930s. North York, ONC: University of Toronto-York University Joint Centre of Asia Pacific Studies, 1990. 43 pp. Paper. 0921309856.

An essay on contributions of missionaries of the Presbyterian church in Canada to rural reconstruction in China.

AS383 Mungello, David E.
Curious Land: Jesuit Accomodation and the Origins of Sinology. Honolulu, HIU: University of Hawaii Press, 1989. 405 pp. Paper. 0824812190.

A detailed scholarly analysis of Jesuit contextualization of Chinese Christianity by Fr. Matteo Ricci and his successors, and its influence on Chinese studies in Europe.

AS384 Mungello, David E.
The Forgotten Christians of Hangzhou. Honolulu, HIU: University of Hawaii Press, 1994. xii, 248 pp. 0824815408.

A detailed history of efforts by Jesuit missionaries and Chinese literati at Hangzhou to inculturate Christianity in the 17th century, based on manuscripts in the former Jesuit library in Shanghai.

AS385 O'Reilly, Luke
The Laughter and the Weeping: An Old China Hand Remembers. Dublin, IE: Columba Press, 1991. 203 pp. Paper. No ISBN.

Focused on the 1945-1951 period, this is an account of missionary encounters during a time of revolution, and of faith in the midst of suffering and persecution.

AS386 Pendergast, Mary Carita
Havoc in Hunan: The Sisters of Charity in Western Hunan, 1924-1951. Morristown, NJU: College of Saint Elizabeth Press, 1991. xvi, 249 pp. Paper. 0962611921.

A narrative account of the work of Sisters of Charity in the Western part of Hunan province in central China, from 1924 to 1951.

AS387 Pollak, Michael
Mandarins, Jews, and Missionaries: The Jewish Experience in the Chinese Empire. Philadelphia, PAU: Jewish Publication Society of America, 1980. xviii, 436 pp. 0827601204 (hdbk), 0827602294 (pbk).

An 800-year history (10th to 19th century) of the Jews of Kaifeng in Honan Province of China, including their relations with Christian missionaries.

AS388 Rabe, Valentin H.
The Home Base of American China Missions, 1880-1920. (Harvard East Asian Monographs, 75). Cambridge, MAU: Harvard University, Council on East Asian Studies, 1978. x, 299 pp. 0674405811.

A scholarly study concerning the development of American missionary interest in China, concentrating on home support issues, such as organizational development, missionary recruitment, and fund-raising.

AS389 Rennstich, Karl
Die zwei Symbole des Kreuzes: Handel und Mission in China und Südostasien. Stuttgart, GW: Quell Verlag, 1988. 280 pp. Paper. 3791814044.

The author traces the history of Christianity in China, from its earliest contacts with the West, to modern times.

AS390 Ricci, Matteo
The True Meaning of the Lord of Heaven (T'ien-chu Shih-i). Edited by E. J. Malatesta. Translated by Douglas Lancashire and Peter Hu Kuo-chen. (Series I: Jesuit Primary Sources, in English Translations, 6), (Variétés sinologiques, nouvelle sér., 72). St. Louis, MOU: Institute of Jesuit Sources; Taipei, CH: Institut Ricci, 1985. xiv, 485 pp. 0912422785 (hdbk), 0912422777 (pbk).

Parallel texts, in Chinese and English, of the influential work of Matteo Ricci, the Italian Jesuit in China, based on his dialogues with Chinese scholars in the 16th century.

AS391 Rienstra, M. Howard, ed.
Jesuit Letters from China, 1583-84. Minneapolis, MNU: University of Minnesota Press, 1986. 47 pp. 0816614318.

The first English translation of the letters from Michele Ruggieri and Francesco Pasio—two Jesuit missionaries in mainland China from 1582 to 1610.

AS392 Rivinius, Karl Josef
Die katholische Mission in Süd-Shantung: Ein Bericht des Legationssekretärs Speck von Sternburg aus dem Jahr 1895 über die Steyler Mission in China. (Studia Instituti Missiologici SVD, 24). St. Augustin, GW: Steyler Verlag, 1979. 144 pp. Paper. 3877871178.

The focal point of this study is the report of a German diplomat on a visit to the SVD mission in South Shantung in 1895, touching upon Germany's taking over of the protectorate of the Catholic mission.

AS393 Rivinius, Karl Josef
Mission und Politik: Eine unveröffentlichte Korrespondenz zwischen Mitgliedern der "Steyler Missionsgesellschaft" und dem Zentrumspolitiker Carl Bachem. (Veröffentlichungen des Missionspriesterseminars, 28). St. Augustin, GW: Steyler Verlag, 1977. 179 pp. Paper. 3877871003.

A critical edition of previously unpublished documents in the historical archives of Cologne, throwing light on the political background of the German Catholic mission in South Shantung at the turn of the century.

AS394 Rivinius, Karl Josef
Traditionalismus und Modernisierung: Das Engagement von Bischof Augustin Henninghaus auf dem Gebiet des Bildungs-und Erziehungswesens in China (1904-1914). (Veröffentlichungen des Missionspriesterseminars, 44). Nettetal, GW: Steyler Verlag, 1994. 244 pp. Paper. 3805003269.

This historical study traces the efforts of Bishop Augustin Henninghaus, apostolic vicar of the province of South Shantung in the early years of this century, in his efforts to shape and influence educational policy, following up the beginnings made by Bishop Johann Baptist Anzer.

AS395 Rivinius, Karl Josef
Weltlicher Schutz und Mission: das deutsche Protektoratüber die katholische Mission von Süd-Shantung. (Bonner Beiträge zur Kirchengeschichte, 14). Cologne, GW: Böhlau Verlag, 1987. xliv, 599 pp. 3412009873.

A detailed history of the linkages in the South Shantung province of China, between the Catholic missions and the German government protectorate, beginning in the 1880s.

AS396 Robinson, Lewis Stewart
Double-Edged Sword: Christianity and 20th Century Chinese Fiction. Shatin, HK: Tao Fong Shan Ecumenical Centre, 1986. vii, 384 pp. Paper. No ISBN.

A scholarly analysis, by historical periods from 1919 to 1949, of fictional presentations of Christianity through the eyes of Chinese and Taiwanese writers.

AS397 Ronan, Charles E., and Bonnie B. C. Oh, eds.
East Meets West: The Jesuits in China, 1582-1773. Chicago, ILU: Loyola University Press, 1988. xxxiii, 332 pp. 0829405720.

A collection of nine scholarly essays covering the period from the pioneer mission of Matteo Ricci to 1773; originally presented to the China Jesuit Symposium (Loyola University of Chicago, 7-9 October 1982), with updated bibliography.

AS398 Rosso, P. Antonius S., ed.
Relationes et Epistolas: Fractum Minorum Hispanorum in sinis qui 1696-98 missionem ingressi sunt. (Sinica Franciscana, 10). Rome, IT: OFM, 1997. lxxvii,1104 pp. 8470470620.

The writings, letters, and reports, in two volumes, of the four Spanish Franciscan missionaries who came to Imperial China in 1696, and labored on there until the persecution of 1732; with indexes of names and terms, in Chinese and Spanish.

AS399 Rubinstein, Murray A.
The Origins of the Anglo-American Missionary Enterprise in China, 1807-1840. (ATLA Monograph Series, 33). Lanham, MDU: Scarecrow Press, 1996. xi, 399 pp. 0810827700.

A monograph, based on extensive archival research, on Canton as the missionary door to China, 1782 to 1840; including the work of Robert Morrison and the American Board mission.

AS400 Ruoff, E. G., ed.
Death Throes of a Dynasty: Letters and Diaries of Charles amd Bessie Ewing, Missionaries to China. Kent, OHU: Kent State University Press, 1990. x, 276 pp. 0873384148.

Excerpts from the letters and diaries of American Board missionaries in North China from 1894 to 1913, including the Boxer uprising.

AS401 Saarilahti, Toivo
Suomen Lähetysseuran työ Kiinassa vuosina 1901-1926. (Sata vuotta suomalaista lähetystyötä, 3). Helsinki, FI: Suomen Lähetysseura, 1960. 283 pp. No ISBN.

A history of the Finnish Evangelical Lutheran Mission in China, 1901-1926; a part of the history series of the society.

AS402 Schlyter, Herman
Der China-Missionar Karl Gützlaff und seine Heimatbasis: Studien über das Interesse des Abendlandes an der Mission des China-Pioniers Karl Gützlaff und über seinen Einsatz als Missionserwecker. (Studia Missionalia Upsaliensia, 30). Lund, SW: Gleerup, 1976. 262 pp. 9140043738.

A study on the first Lutheran missionary to China, Karl Gützlaff (1803-1851), and his work to establish a base at home for his missionary enterprise.

AS403 Soetens, Claude, ed.
Pour l'Église Chinoise: recueil des archives Vincent Lebbe. (Cahiers de la Revue théologique de Louvain, 5, 7, 9). Louvain-la-Neuve, BE: Faculté de théologie, 1982. 3 vols. No ISBN.

Important Roman Catholic archives of the mission/church in China in the early 20th century [vol. 1: *La Visite apostolique des missions de Chine, 1919-1920* (337 pp.); vol. 2: *Une nonciature à Pékin en 1918?* (113 pp.); and vol. 3: *L'encyclique maximum illud.* (183 pp.); (1982-1983)].

AS404 Spence, Jonathan D.
The Memory Palace of Matteo Ricci. New York, NYU: Viking Penguin; Middlesex, ENK: Penguin Books, 1985. xiv, 350 pp. Paper. 0140080988.

A creative account of how the pioneer Jesuit missionary to China reached leaders of the Ming dynasty by developing a memory system superior to theirs.

AS405 Standaert, Nicolas
The Fascinating God. (Inculturation: Working Papers on Living Faith and Cultures, 17). Rome, IT: Pontifical Gregorian University, 1995. ix, 153 pp. Paper. 8876526803.

A scholarly analysis of the issue of names for God in 17th-century China, based on little-known texts by Chinese lay theologians; originally written as a dissertation at Fujen Catholic University in China.

AS406 Thomson, James Claude
While China Faced West: American Reformers in Nationalist China, 1928-1937. (Harvard East Asian Series, 38). Cambridge, MAU: Harvard University Press, 1969. xv, 310 pp. 0674951352.

An in-depth study of U.S.-China relations during the 1928-1937 period, when both missionaries and foundation representatives tried to help the Chinese government and Chinese reformers undertake a transformation of rural society.

AS407 T'ien, Ju-k'ang
Peaks of Faith: Protestant Mission in Revolutionary China. (Studies in Christian Mission, 8). Leiden, NE: Brill, 1993. vii, 161 pp. 9004097236.

A pioneer historical study of the Protestant churches' impact on seven minority groups noted for their conversion and devotion to Christianity in China's Yunnan province.

AS408 Ting, K. H. et al.
Chinese Christians Speak Out: Addresses and Sermons. (China Spotlight Series). Beijing, CC: New World Press, 1984. 140 pp. Paper. No ISBN.

Testimonies of faith and statements on the history and mission of the church by Chinese Christians from the 1980-1983 period.

AS409 Towery, Britt
The Penglai-Pingdu Baptist Memorials: Stories of Baptist Pioneers in Shandong China. Waco, TXU: Long Dragon Books, 1989. iii, 56 pp. Paper. No ISBN.

A sketch of a few of the early Southern Baptist missionaries who began their ministry in the northern province of Shandong in the early 1860s.

AS410 Wagner, Rudolf G.
Reenacting the Heavenly Vision: The Role of Religion in the Taiping Rebellion. (China Research Monograph, 25). Berkeley, CAU: Institute of East Asian Studies, University of California; Berkeley, CAU: University of California, Center for Chinese Studies, 1982. vii, 134 pp. Paper. 0912966602.

A scholarly reconstruction of the thought of the leaders of the Taiping rebellion in China (1851-1864), based on their writings and other primary source documents of the period.

AS411 Wehrle, Edmund S.
Britain, China, and the Antimissionary Riots, 1891-1900. London, ENK: Oxford University Press; Minneapolis, MNU: University of Minnesota Press, 1966. xii, 223 pp. No ISBN.

A scholarly study of British diplomatic history, with a thesis that vacillating British policy in China was one factor leading to the rising tide of anti-foreignism that climaxed in the Boxer Rebellion.

AS412 Wei, Louis Tsing-Sing
Le Saint-Siège et la Chine de Pie XI à nos jours. Sotteville-les-Rouen, FR: Allais, 1968. 470 pp. No ISBN.

A detailed history of relations between Chinese leaders of church and state and the papacy in Rome.

AS413 Whyte, Bob
Unfinished Encounter: China and Christianity. London, ENK: Collins Fount Paperbacks; Harrisburg, PAU: Morehouse Publishing, 1988. 537 pp. Paper. 0006271421 (C), 0819215279 (M).

A scholarly, comprehensive survey of Christianity in China, from the 7th to the 20th centuries, emphasizing past Chinese contributions to Western cultures and possible future contributions; largely Chinese sources used to chronicle the 1949 to 1987 time period.

AS414 Widmer, Eric
The Russian Ecclesiastical Mission in Peking During the Eighteenth Century. (Harvard East Asian Monographs, 69). Cambridge, MAU: Harvard University, 3062 East Asian Research Center, 1976. xi, 262 pp. 0674781295.

A scholarly history of a little-known Russian Orthodox mission effort.

AS415 Wiest, Jean-Paul
Maryknoll in China: A History, 1918-1955. Armonk, NYU: M. E. Sharpe, 1988. xxiii, 591 pp. 0873324188.

The monumental history of the work of Maryknoll missionaries in China—the culmination of the eight-year Maryknoll China History Project, with analysis of extensive written and oral sources by Maryknoll fathers, brothers, and sisters.

AS—ASIA

AS416 Wiest, Jean-Paul, ed.
Collectanea Commissionis Synodalis: Digests of the Synodial Commission of the Catholic Church in China, 1928-47 with Bibliographic Guide. Bethesda, MDU: Congressional Info Service, 1988. xvii, 93 pp. Paper. 0886921473.

A bibliographic guide to a multilingual journal which, from 1928 to 1947, contained the best of Roman Catholic scholarship on the church in mission in China.

AS417 Wirth, Benedicta
Imperialistische Übersee-und Missionspolitik: dargestellt am Beispiel Chinas. (Veröffentlichungen des Instituts für Missionswissenschaft, 13). Münster, GW: Aschendorff, 1968. 78 pp. No ISBN.

The author deals with the question of the linkage of foreign and mission policies of the Western powers, with respect to China, and the development of anti-Christian and anti-missionary feelings in that country.

AS418 Yi, Ka-che
Religion, Nationalism and Chinese Students: The Anti-Christian Movement of 1922-1927. (Studies on East Asia, 15). Bellingham, WAU: Center for East Asian Studies, 1980. iii, 133 pp. Paper. 0914584154.

A detailed study of the anti-Christian student movement as a manifestation of modern Chinese student nationalism; a revision of a doctoral dissertation (Department of History, Columbia University).

China: Hong Kong

See also AS573.

AS419 Brown, Deborah Ann
Turmoil in Hong Kong on the Eve of Communist Rule: The Fate of the Territory and Its Anglican Church. San Francisco, CAU: Mellen Research University Press, 1993. xxx, 447 pp. 0773422420.

A detailed survey of the history of the Anglican church in Hong Kong, its ministries, and future as Hong Kong became part of the PRC.

AS420 Constable, Nicole
Christian Souls and Chinese Spirits: A Hakka Community in Hong Kong. Berkeley, CAU: University of California Press, 1994. xv, 233 pp. 0520083849.

A scholarly case study by the assistant professor of snthropology at the University of Pittsburgh, of the intersection between religion and ethnic identity among Hakka migrants to Hong Kong, who sought to construct an "ideal" Chinese and Christian village.

AS421 Jarva, Ritva
Finska missionssällskapets verksamhet i Hongkong 1952-80. (Meddelanden/Kyrkohistoriska arkivet vid Åbo Akademi, Meddelanden, 15). Åbo, FI: Kyrkohistoriska arkivet vid Åbo Akademi, 1982. 97 pp. Paper. 9516488722.

A history of the work of the Finnish Evangelical Lutheran Mission in Hong Kong, 1952-1980.

AS422 Smith, Carl T.
Chinese Christians: Elites, Middlemen, and the Church in Hong Kong. Hong Kong: Oxford University Press, 1985. xvii, 252 pp. 0195839730.

An examination of the cultural bifurcation of Chinese Christian converts and their roles in Chinese and colonial society, as a case study in the socioeconomic implications of mission activity.

China: PRC

See also HI705, CR770, CO125, AS16, AS305, AS317, and AS412.

AS423 Adeney, David H.
China: The Church's Long March. Ventura, CAU: Regal Books; Singapore, SI: OMF Books, 1986. 256 pp. Paper. 0830710965.

An assessment of developments in Chinese Christianity since the 1949 revolution, by the North American Coordinator for the OMF China program.

AS424 Akademie Völker und Kulturen—St. Augustin
China, sein neues Gesicht. Edited by Bernhard Mensen. (Vortragsreihe, 10). Nettetal, GW: Steyler Verlag, 1987. 184 pp. Paper. 3805001967.

A collection of lectures on matters such as the German perception of China, China's mental picture of Europe, the situation of Christianity, and Chinese religious policy.

AS425 *Asian Christian Leaders in China: Impressions and Reflections of a Visit to China, June 1-14, 1983*
Toa Payoh, SI: CCA, 1983. 72 pp. Paper. 9971948222.

Report of the historic 1-14 June 1983 visit to China by a team of Asian church leaders.

AS426 Bates, M. Searle, ed.
China in Change: An Approach to Understanding. New York, NYU: Friendship Press, 1969. 191 pp. Paper. 0377190012.

A study book for North American Christians, containing seven essays, by China specialists, on the past and present revolutions affecting the Chinese people and the Christian churches there.

AS427 Beechy, Winifred Nelson
The New China. Scottsdale, PAU: Herald Press, 1982. 263 pp. Paper. 0836133102.

An introduction, for North Americans, to the PRC—its hopes, problems, fears, culture, and history; based on the author's experiences in China during 1980 as a Co-Director of a Goshen student exchange program.

AS428 Brown, G. Thompson
Christianity in the People's Republic of China. Atlanta, GAU: John Knox Press, 1986. xii, 248 pp. Paper. 0804214859.

The revised edition of a popular account of Christianity in China since 1949, with updated information on liberalization and church growth in the past eight years; originally published in 1983.

AS429 Butselaar, Jan van
Godsdienstvrijheid als mensenrecht: De zending van de kerk in China. Kampen, NE: Kok, 1993. 64 pp. Paper. 9024282055.

Reflections on the mission of the church in China by a secretary of the Dutch Mission Society, based on a 1993 visit to that country.

AS430 *CCA Consultation with Church Leaders from China: Hong Kong, March 23-26, 1981*
Toa Payoh, SI: CCA, 1981. iv, 80 pp. Paper. 9971948028.

Report and papers from an important consultation on Christian Witness (Hong Kong, 23-26 March 1981) attended by Protestant leaders from the PRC and other Asian countries.

AS—ASIA

AS431 Chan, Kim-Kwong, and Alan Hunter, comps.
Prayers and Thoughts of Chinese Christians. Boston, MAU: Cowley Publications, 1991. 105 pp. Paper. 1561010391.

A compendium, for Western Christians, of short writings (prose, poetry, prayers) representative of contemporary Chinese spirituality, with an interpretive introduction by the compilers.

AS432 Chao, Jonathan, and Richard L. Van Houton
Wise as Serpents, Harmless as Doves: Christians in China Tell Their Story. South Pasadena, CAU: William Carey Library; New Territories, HK: Chinese Church Research Center, 1988. xxxiv, 248 pp. Paper. 0878082123.

A chronologically arranged collection of interviews, reports, and testimonies of the growing Christian movement in China, outside the official Three-Self Patriotic Movement (TSPM).

AS433 Choy, Leona
Touching China: "Close Encounters of the Christian Kind". Paradise, PAU: Ambassadors for Christ, 1992. xv, 239 pp. Paper. 1882324005.

Written for potential visitors to China, the cofounder of Ambassadors for Christ, Inc. shares her experiences during fourteen visits since 1979.

AS434 *Christianity and the New China*
South Pasadena, CAU: Ecclesia Publications, 1976. 2 vols. 0878087265.

Papers on "Theological Implications of the New China" presented at an ecumenical seminar (Bastad, Sweden, January 1974, 200 pp.), and on "Christian Faith and the Chinese Experience" from an ecumenical colloquium (Louvain, Belgium, September 1974, 204 pp.), each cosponsored by the LWF and Pro Mundi Vita.

AS435 Chu, Michael, ed.
The New China: A Catholic Response. New York, NYU: Paulist Press, 1977. 165 pp. Paper. 0809120046.

Seven papers by Protestant and Catholic theologians on the theological implications of the new China; originally presented in 1974 at seminars held in Bastad (Sweden) and Louvain (Belgium).

AS436 Chu, Theresa, and Christopher Lind, eds.
A New Beginning: An International Dialogue with the Chinese Church. Montreal, QUC: Canadian Council of Churches, Canada China Programme, 1983. viii, 186 pp. Paper. 096912600X.

Report and papers from a historic meeting in Montreal, Canada, in 1981, of Catholic and Protestant leaders from China with 150 other Christians from around the world.

AS437 Coulson, Gail V., Christopher Herlinger, and Camille S. Anders
The Enduring Church: Christians in China and Hong Kong. New York, NYU: Friendship Press, 1996. vi, 121 pp. Paper. 0377003069.

The ecumenical mission study for adults in 1996-1997, with glimpses of present-day church life in China, on the eve of reunification with Hong Kong; with *Leader's Guide* by Camille S. Anders (29 pp., 0377003077).

AS438 Dehoney, Wayne
The Dragon and the Lamb. Nashville, TNU: Broadman, 1988. 176 pp. Paper. 0805463445.

A popular account of the resurgence of Christianity in China since 1949, by a Baptist teacher and pastor.

AS439 Freytag, Justus, ed.
China und die Christen: Beiträge aus der ökumenischen Studienaribeit. (Texte zum kirchlichen Entwicklungsdienst, 20). Frankfurt am Main, GW: Lembeck, 1979. 111 pp. 3874761363.

Nine scholarly works, originally in English, by missiologists and missionaries (J. Freytag, D. MacInnis, A. Sovik, E. Stockwell, P. Shen, C. West, J. T. Chao, C. S. Song, and J. Jonson), focusing on mission methodologies in China.

AS440 Fung, Raymond, comp.
Households of God on China's Soil. (WCC Mission Series, 2). Geneva, SZ: WCC, 1982. x, 78 pp. Paper. 282540716X.

Fourteen stories told by Chinese Christians, presenting firsthand experiences of how the church in China, through suffering, found its roots in Chinese soil during the Cultural Revolution.

AS441 Fung, Raymond, ed.
Graswurzel-Gemeinden auf Chinas Boden: 14 Berichte: Kirche im Sturm der Kulturrevolution. (Erlanger Taschenbücher, 66). Erlangen, GW: Ev.-Luth. Mission, 1983. 141 pp. Paper. 3872141554.

German translation.

AS442 Geffré, Claude, and Joseph John Spae, eds.
China as a Challenge to the Church. (*Concilium*: Religion in the Seventies). New York, NYU: Seabury Press; Edinburgh, STK: T&T Clark, 1979. ix, 123 pp. Paper. 0816422346 (US), 0567300064 (UK).

Eight reflective essays by scholars in the West on religious and theological implications of the Chinese revolution, with an update as of 1977 on research concerning Christianity in China.

AS443 Høgsgaard, Jens L.
Folk og kirke i Maos Kina. Translated by Svein Johs Ottesen. Oslo, NO: Luther Forlag, 1975. 213 pp. 8253141122.

Norwegian translation of *Midtens rige efter 1949* (Hellerup, DK: DMS, 1975), an assessment of Christian life and work in Mao's China since 1949.

AS444 Høgsgaard, Jens L.
Midtens rige efter 1949: Det nye Kinas folk og kirke. Hellerup, DK: DMS-Forlag, 1975. 168 pp. 8774310488.

A popular appraisal of developments since 1949 in Chinese Christianity by one who served in China under the Danish Missionary Society, from 1929 to 1947.

AS445 Hanson, Irene, and Bernard Palmer
The Wheelbarrow and the Comrade. Chicago, ILU: Moody, 1973. 187 pp. 0802494285.

Vivid stories from the authors' twenty-five years (1926-1951) of service as Presbyterian missionaries in China's Shantung Province, before and after the communist takeover.

AS446 Hayward, Victor E. W.
Christians and China. Belfast, IE: Christian Journals, 1974. 127 pp. Paper. 0904302040.

A popular presentation of the rethinking of the church's mission in China following the communist takeover and suppression of the church.

AS447 Hediger, Peter
Das Christentum in China seit 1949. Zollikon, SZ: Glaube in der 2. Welt, 1980. 58 pp. Paper. 3857100064.

This short work presents texts about the development of the Catholic, and especially the Protestant, churches in China, since 1949, and the attitude of Chinese communism toward religion and Christianity.

AS—ASIA

AS448 Hood, George A.

Neither Bang nor Whimper: The End of a Missionary Era in China. Singapore, SI: Presbyterian Church in Singapore, 1991. xviii, 288 pp. 9810028377.

A historical account, with appraisal of the missionary withdrawal from China during the years 1949 to 1953, by a British participant and later mission historian.

AS449 Hunter, Alan, and Don Rimmington, eds.

All under Heaven: Chinese Tradition and Christian Life in the People's Republic of China. (Kerk in Theologie in Context, 17). Kampen, NE: Kok, 1992. 142 pp. Paper. 9024273811.

Articles investigating the changing role of Christianity in China in the 1980s; by twelve scholars of both Chinese and British descent.

AS450 Hunter, Alan, and Kim-Kwong Chan

Protestantism in Contemporary China. (Cambridge Studies in Ideology and Religion). Cambridge, ENK: Cambridge Universtiy Press, 1993. xx, 291 pp. 0521441617.

Two social scientists, based at the University of Leeds, assess the dynamic resurgence of Protestantism in China in the 1980s through a review of English language publications of the period.

AS451 Jones, Francis Price, ed.

Documents of the Three-Self Movement: Source Materials for the Study of the Protestant Church in Communist China. New York, NYU: NCCUSA, Division of Foreign Missions, 1963. ix, 209 pp. No ISBN.

Fifty-two original texts by Chinese Protestants from the 1948 to 1962 period.

AS452 Jones, Francis Price

The Church in Communist China: A Protestant Appraisal. New York, NYU: Friendship Press, 1962. viii, 180 pp. Paper. No ISBN.

A concise assessment of the first thirteen years of Christianity under Communism in China; prepared as a mission study book for North Americans.

AS453 Jonson, Jonas

Kina: Kyrka-samhälle-kultur. Stockholm, SW: SKEAB, 1980. 101 pp. 9152600262.

A book for study groups on church, culture, and society in China.

AS454 Jonson, Jonas

Kina, Kyrkan och Kristen tro. (Gummessons kursiv). Stockholm, SW: Gummesson, 1975. 135 pp. 9170704376.

Reflections on the challenge by the Chinese revolution to Christian missions.

AS455 Jonson, Jonas

Lutheran Missions in a Time of Revolution: The China Experience, 1944-1951. (Studia Missionalia Upsaliensia, 18). Uppsala, SW: Tvåväga förlags AB, 1972. 230 pp. No ISBN.

A doctoral dissertation on the Lutheran missions in China, from optimistic new orientations in 1944, to the evacuation and the breakdown of the cooperation with the Chinese church seven years later.

AS456 Kauffman, Paul E.

China the Emerging Challenge: A Christian Perspective. Grand Rapids, MIU: Baker Books, 1982. 317 pp. Paper. 0801054427.

A popular introduction to Chinese political and mission history by the Founder-President of Asian Outreach and editor of *Asian Report*; with adaptation of materials previously published in a trilogy of *China Yesterday, China Today*, and *China Tomorrow*, written by the author.

AS457 Lacy, Creighton

Coming Home—To China. Philadelphia, PAU: Westminster Press, 1978. 156 pp. Paper. 0664242014.

The 1977 travelogue and reflections of a third-generation China missionary, on observed continuities and contrasts between the old and new China.

AS458 Lambert, Tony

China's Christian Millions: The Costly Revival. London, ENK: Monarch Publications, 1999. 254 pp. Paper. 1854244310.

Gripping accounts of courage, vision, and faith, along with carefully researched documentation on China's unprecedented spiritual revival and church growth.

AS459 Lambert, Tony

The Resurrection of the Chinese Church. (An OMF Book). Wheaton, ILU: Shaw Publishers, 1994. xiii, 353 pp. Paper. 0877887284.

A narrative account of the revival and rapid development of Christianity in China, 1974-1994, by the Director of China research for the OMF; based on Chinese documents, letters from Chinese Christians, and personal interviews.

AS460 Lawrence, Carl

The Church in China. Minneapolis, MNU: Bethany House, 1985. 169 pp. Paper. 0871238152.

A popular account of the Chinese churches; by a missionary in Southeast Asia for almost twenty years, with the Far Eastern Broadcasting Company; published also as *Against All Odds: The Church in China* (Aylesbury, UK: Marshall-Pickering, 1985).

AS461 Lawrence, Carl, and David Wang

The Coming Influence of China. Gresham, ORU: Vision House, 1996. 207 pp. Paper. 1885305508.

Popular reflections on the changing scene in China, with projections of what the dynamic growth of Christianity in China holds for the future of missions.

AS462 Lee, Shiu Keung

The Cross and the Lotus. Hong Kong, HK: Christian Study Centre on Chinese Religion and Culture, 1971. vi, 125 pp. Paper. No ISBN.

Lectures on the interaction of Christian missions and Chinese culture, given under the auspices of Hong Kong University.

AS463 Luo, Zhufeng, ed.

Religion under Socialism in China. Translated by Donald E. MacInnis and Zheng Xi'an. (Chinese Studies on China). Armonk, NYU: M. E. Sharpe, 1991. xxiii, 254 pp. 0873326091.

A detailed study of religion in contemporary China, of both governmental policies and popular practices, based on field research by Chinese social scientists.

AS464 MacInnis, Donald E.

Religion im heutigen China: Politik und Praxis. (Monograph Series, 31). Nettetal, GW: Steyler Verlag, 1993. 619 pp. 3805003307.

German translation.

AS465 MacInnis, Donald E.
Religion in China Today: Policy and Practice. Maryknoll, NYU: Orbis Books, 1989. xx, 458 pp. 0883445948 (hdbk), 0883446456 (pbk).

An extensive work revealing what has happened to religious believers and their churches and institutions in China since the end of the Cultural Revolution, providing 130 primary source documents of the five officially recognized religions—Protestant Christianity, Buddhism, Islam, Catholic Christianity, and Daoism.

AS466 MacInnis, Donald E.
Religious Policy and Practice in Communist China. New York, NYU: Macmillan; London, ENK: Collier Macmillan, 1972. xxiv, 392 pp. No ISBN.

A collection of 116 documents from the 1927 to 1970 period, by communist Chinese leaders, theoreticians, and the party, gathered by the Director of the China Program of NCCUSA.

AS467 Malek, Roman, and Werner Prawdzik, eds.
Zwischen Autonomie und Anlehnung: Die Problematik der katholischen Kirche in China, theologisch und geschichtlich gesehen. (Veröffentlichungen des Missionspriesterseminars, 37). Nettetal, GW: Steyler Verlag, 1989. 203 pp. Paper. 3805002181.

Papers from the China Colloquium (Sankt Augustin, 11-13 November 1987), which address the relationship of the Catholic Church with the government of China, with special emphasis on the issues arising from the unauthorized naming and consecrating of bishops apart from Rome; with a comprehensive international bibliography.

AS468 Malek, Roman, ed.
"Fallbeispiel" China: Ökumenische Beiträge zu Religion, Theologie und Kirche im chinesischen Kontext. Nettetal, GW: Steyler Verlag, 1996. 693 pp. 3805003854.

A collection of scholarly essays on religion, theology, and the church in China; published as a *festschrift* to honor the chairpersons of the Ecumenical China Study Group of Germany.

AS469 Moritzen, Niels Peter, ed.
China—Herausforderung an die Kirchen. (Erlanger Taschenbücher, 27). Erlangen, GW: Ev.-Luth. Mission, 1974. 95 pp. Paper. 3872140604.

Report of the first joint China consultation of the Catholic and Protestant missionary councils of Germany (1973), dealing with political and religious themes; in particular, the situation of the churches under Mao, and the possibilities of communication between the churches of China and the universal church.

AS470 Moser, Georg, Roman Malek, and Manfred Plate, eds.
Chinas Katholiken suchen neue Wege. Freiburg im Breisgau, GW: Herder, 1987. 192 pp. Paper. 3451211041.

The religious situation of Roman Catholics in post-Maoist China, particularly since 1976, is surveyed and critically evaluated in eight essays edited by a Sinologist and a journalist, with official church documents and a bibliography of recent literature.

AS471 Nelsson, Solveig, and Per-Çke Wahlström, eds.
Levande Kyrka i Kina. Örebro, SW: Libris, 1985. 106 pp. 9171943919.

Eight articles on the church in China, discussing the Three-Self Movement and the church and the communist state.

AS472 Orr, Robert G.
Religion in China. New York, NYU: Friendship Press, 1980. 144 pp. Paper. 0377001031.

A primer on the various religions of China prepared as a mission study book.

AS473 Pas, Julian F., ed.
The Turning of the Tide: Religion in China Today. New York, NYU: Oxford University Press, 1989. xi, 378 pp. Paper. 0195841018 (hdbk), 019584117X (pbk).

Fifteen essays by an international team of scholars on various aspects of China's contemporary religious pluralism.

AS474 Paterson, Ross, and Elisabeth Farrell
China: The Hidden Miracle: The Extraordinary Tale of Two Ordinary People. Tonbridge, ENK: Sovereign World, 1993. 189 pp. Paper. 1852401303.

The stories of a Chinese family's witness during the Cultural Revolution, and of the ongoing work of Chinese Church Support Ministries and Derek Prince Ministries in China.

AS475 Patterson, George
Christianity in Communist China. Waco, TXU: Word Books, 1969. xii, 174 pp. No ISBN.

A Christian journalist's assessment of church-state relations in the PRC, 1949 to 1968, and of future church strategies.

AS476 Richardson, William J., ed.
China and Christian Responsibility: A Symposium. New York, NYU: Friendship Press; New York, NYU: Maryknoll Publications, 1968. vi, 144 pp. Paper. No ISBN.

Six scholarly essays on the past, present, and future of Christianity in mainland China; originally presented at a 1967 China Consultation called by the Presbyterian (US) Board of World Mission on the centennial of their church's mission work in China.

AS477 Schilling, Werner
Das Heil in Rot-China?: Der "neue Mensch" im Maoismus und im Christentum. (Telos Dokumentation). Bad Liebenzell, GW: Verlag der Liebenzeller Mission, 1975. 167 pp. 388002023X.

An examination into Maoist ideology (new humanity, new life, the Spirit of the Tiger and the Ape) and its incompatibility with the Christian understanding of salvation and a new humanity.

AS478 Spae, Joseph John
Church and China: Towards Reconciliation? Chicago, ILU: Chicago Institute of Theology and Culture, 1980. 167 pp. Paper. 0936078014.

A review of the sociological changes occurring in China in the 1970s, and their implications for Christianity and the church in China.

AS479 Spae, Joseph John
Kirche unterm roten Stern: Neue Hoffnung für Chinas Christen? Translated by G. Evers. Aachen, GW: Missio Aktuell Verlag, 1980. 145 pp. 3921626153.
German translation.

AS480 Tang, Edmond, and Jean-Paul Wiest, eds.
The Catholic Church in Modern China: Perspectives. Maryknoll, NYU: Orbis Books, 1993. xvii, 260 pp. Paper. 0883448343.
Seventeen essays, by Sinologists and Chinese Catholics, on the history of tensions between church and state since 1979, and major issues facing the Catholic Church in China, today and tomorrow.

AS481 Ting, K. H.
Christian Witness in China Today: The Sixth Neesima Lectures. Kyoto, JA: Doshisha University Press, 1985. 49 pp. Paper. 4924608157.
The sixth Neesima Lectures at Doshisha University, by the President of the China Christian Council.

AS482 Ting, K. H.
No Longer Strangers: Selected Writings of Bishop K. H. Ting. Maryknoll, NYU: Orbis Books, 1989. xii, 199 pp. Paper. 0883446537.
Forty-seven writings, spanning the 1947 to 1987 period, by the internationally renowned Protestant leader (Principal of Nanjing Theological Seminary, Chairman of the Three-Self National Committee, and President of the China Christian Council), grouped by themes to highlight Ting's theological development in the areas of embodying Christianity, serving people, confronting the world, and affirming the church.

AS483 Towery, Britt
The Churches of China: Taking Root Downward, Bearing Fruit Upward. Waco, TXU: Baylor University Press, 1990. xvi, 242 pp. Paper. 0933335091.
This revised 3rd edition examines with new light how Christianity in China met the challenges of the 1950s, survived the Cultural Revolution of the 1960s, and evolved in the 1980s into one of the fastest growing churches in the world.

AS484 Wallis, Arthur
China Miracle: A Silent Explosion. Columbia, MOU: Cityhill Publishing, 1986. 171 pp. Paper. 0939159007.
A firsthand look at China's house churches, peering at the persecution, courage, and conviction of Chinese Christians.

AS485 Weth, Gustav
Zwischen Mao und Jesus: Die grosse Revolution Chinas fordert die Christenheit. Wuppertal, GW: Brockhaus, 1968. 118 pp. No ISBN.
An assessment of the impact of the Chinese Revolution and Maoism on Protestants in China in the light of mission history there.

AS486 Whitehead, James D., Yu-ming Shaw, and N. J. Girardot, eds.
China and Christianity: Historical and Future Encounters. Notre Dame, INU: University of Notre Dame, Centre for Pastoral and Social Ministry, 1979. xv, 293 pp. Paper. 0268007306.

Papers from an important interdisciplinary, ecumenical conference on "China: The Religious Dimension" (University of Notre Dame, 29 June-2 July 1977), attended by forty theologians, historians, social scientists, educators, and church leaders.

AS487 Whitehead, Raymond L., and Rhea M. Whitehead
China: Search for Community. New York, NYU: Friendship Press, 1978. ix, 68 pp. Paper. 0377000728.
Positive images of the revolution in the PRC and the churches' response there; published as a mission study book.

AS488 Whitehead, Raymond L.
Love and Struggle in Mao's Thought. Maryknoll, NYU: Orbis Books, 1977. xx, 166 pp. 0883442892 (hdbk), 0883442906 (pbk).
A positive reassessment of Mao Tse-tung by the onetime Asia Research Consultant for the NCCUSA, and missionary of the United Church Board for World Ministries in Hong Kong.

AS489 Wickeri, Philip L.
Seeking the Common Ground: Protestant Christianity, the Three-Self Movement, and China's United Front. Maryknoll, NYU: Orbis Books, 1988. xxviii, 356 pp. 0883444410.
A detailed account of four decades, 1949-1989, of dialogue and dialectics between Protestant Christians of the Three-Self Movement and Marxian communists.

AS490 Willis, Helen
Through Encouragement of the Scriptures: Recollections of Ten Years in Communist Shanghai. Hong Kong, HK: Christian Book Room, 1961. iv, 214 pp. No ISBN.
Recollections of an American missionary who returned to Shanghai after the Sino-Japanese War, and reopened and maintained a Christian bookshop under Communist rule for the next years, 1949 to 1959, providing an informative and stimulating picture of daily life, for Christians in those conditions.

AS491 Wurth, Elmer, ed.
Papal Documents Related to the New China, 1937-1984. Maryknoll, NYU: Orbis Books, 1985. 182 pp. Paper. 0883444038.
A sourcebook containing forty-six Vatican documents concerning China, the Catholic Church in China, and the Vatican's relationship with them.

AS492 Yinhan, Peng, and Charles Corwin
Return of a Chinese Patriot. Torrance, CAU: Tyrannus Halls of Asia, 1989. 208 pp. Paper. No ISBN.
The personal account of Taiwan-born Peng Yinhan, from his return in 1953 to help rebuild the new China, through his twenty-year detention (1960-1979), which included three years in a labor re-education camp, showing how his faith in God was awakened in the midst of hardships.

AS493 Zhao, Fusan
Christianity in China: Three Lectures. Edited by Theresa Carino. Manila, PH: La Salle University, 1986. v, 44 pp. Paper. 9711180456.
Three lectures on the Chinese cultural and religious setting, the history, and the prospects for Christianity by the Vice President of the Chinese Academy of Social Sciences.

AS—ASIA

China: Biography

See also HI666, CR766, CO127, MI127, MI187, MI190, AF421, AS174, and AS372.

AS494 Aitchinson, Margaret
The Doctor and the Dragon. Basingstoke, ENK: Pickering & Inglis, 1983. 159 pp. 0720805457.

A popular biography of Thomas Cochrase (1866-1953), a pioneer LMS medical missionary in Mongolia and Peking.

AS495 Allen, Catherine B.
The New Lottie Moon Story. Nashville, TNU: Broadman, 1980. 320 pp. 0805463194.

A well-documented biography of Lottie Moon (1840-1912), who was closely associated with the development of women's involvement and leadership in Southern Baptist missions and with mission work in China (1873-1912).

AS496 Anderson, Ken
Bold as a Lamb: Pastor Samuel Lamb and the Underground Church of China. Grand Rapids, MIU: Zondervan, 1991. 176 pp. Paper. 0310532213.

A popular account of Pastor Samuel Lamb (b.1924), a house church leader, who spent twenty years (1958-1978) imprisoned for his faith.

AS497 Armitage, Carolyn
Reaching for the Goal: The Life Story of David Adeney. Wheaton, ILU: OMF Books/Shaw Publishers, 1993. viii, 246 pp. Paper. 0877887128.

A popular biography of David Adeney (b.1912), a China Inland Mission (later OMF) missionary to China (1934-1950) who, with his wife Ruth, worked with students of the IVCF, and, thereafter, in leadership training in Hong Kong, Taiwan, and Singapore (1950-1976).

AS498 Benge, Janet, and Geoff Benge
Gladys Aylward: The Adventure of a Lifetime. (Christian Heroes: Then & Now). Seattle, WAU: YWAM, 1998. 205 pp. Paper. 1576580199.

A popular biography of Gladys Aylward (1902-1970), independent British missionary in China from 1930, known for her ministry to children, especially orphans.

AS499 Bohr, Paul Richard
Famine in China and the Missionary: Timothy Richard as Relief Administrator and Advocate of National Reform, 1876-1884. (Harvard East Asian Monographs, 48). Cambridge, MAU: Harvard University Press, 1972. xviii, 283 pp. 0674294254.

The scholarly biography, based on voluminous Chinese documentation, of the remarkable Baptist Missionary to China (1870-1916), who ardently advocated scientific and technological education as an answer to China's recurring cycles of famine and poverty.

AS500 Bollback, Anthony
To China and Back. (Jaffray Collection of Missionary Portraits). Camp Hill, PAU: Christian Publications, 1991. 130 pp. Paper. 0875094449.

A first-person account of adventures of a Christian and Missionary Alliance couple, as missionaries in China, Hong Kong, and Hawaii, 1946-1977.

AS501 Boone, Muriel
The Seed of the Church in China. Edinburgh, STK: St. Andrew Press; Boston, MAU: Pilgrim Press, 1974. 287 pp. 0715202359 (STK), 0829802649 (US).

A biography of Episcopal bishop W.J. Boone in China, 1837-1864.

AS502 Bornemann, Fritz
Entre Mandarines y Bandoleros: Jose Freinademetz, misionero del Verbo Divino en China por espacio de 28 años. Santiago, CL: Ediciones Mundo, 1984. 330 pp. Paper. No ISBN.

Spanish translation.

AS503 Bornemann, Fritz
Der selige P(ater) J. Freinademetz: 1852-1908; ein Steyler China-Missionar; ein Lebensbild nach zeitgenössischen Quellen. (2nd Edition). Bozen, IT: Freinademetz-Haus, 1977. 1217 pp. No ISBN.

A detailed biography of a Divine Word missionary to China, with numerous notes, bibliography, illustrations, and a report on the beatification process.

AS504 Bortoné, Fernando
Il 'Saggio d'Occidente'; il P. Matteo Ricci S.J. (1552-1610): Un grande Italiano nella Cina Impenetrabile. Rome, IT: Desclée de Brouwer, 1965. xxiii, 484 pp. No ISBN.

The revised and enlarged edition of a biography of the famed China missionary, with maps and illustrations; originally published in 1953.

AS505 Bossierre, Yves de Thomaz de
Jean-François Gerbillon, S.J. (1654-1707): Un des cinq mathématiciens envoyés en Chine par Louis XIV. (Louvain Chinese Studies, 11). Leuven, BE: Ferdinand Verbiest Foundation, 1994. 211 pp. Paper. 9080183318.

The travels and life of Jean-Francois Gerbillon, S.J., mathematician to Louis XIV, who was sent by the King to China in 1685, and later became the first Superior General of the French Jesuits in China (1700-1707); based on his journal and letters.

AS506 Broomhall, A. J.
Hudson Taylor and China's Open Century. London, ENK: Hodder & Stoughton; London, ENK: Overseas Missionary Fellowship, 1981. 7 vols. Paper.

A seven-volume history of the life and times of Hudson Taylor (1832-1905), founder of the China Inland Mission [vol. 1: *Barbarians at the Gates* (1981, 432 pp., 0340262109); vol. 2: *Over the Treaty Wall* (1982, 461 pp., 0340275618); vol. 3: *If I Had a Thousand Lives* (1982, 528 pp., 0340323922); vol. 4: *Survivors' Pact* (1984, 477 pp., 0340349220); vol. 5: *Refiner's Fire* (1985, 512 pp., 0340368667); vol. 6: *Assault on the Nine* (1988, 539 pp., 0340426292); vol. 7: *It Is Not Death to Die!* (1989, 718 pp., 0340502703).

AS507 Carr, Daniel L.
Me? A Missionary?: The Saga of a First Term Missionary. New York, NYU: Vantage Press, 1991. xv, 233 pp. Paper. 0533093678.

Reminiscences of a Conservative Baptist missionary to West China (1946-1951) and Taiwan (1951-1971).

AS508 Chao, Charles H., and Gordon Duncan, eds.
Out of the Tiger's Mouth: The Autobiography of Dr. Charles H. Chao. Fearn, ENK: Christian Focus, 1991. 158 pp. Paper. 1876676592.

The readable account by Charles H. Chao (b.1916) of his lifetime ministry to Chinese people in China, Taiwan, and the United States, as a Reformed Presbyterian pastor.

AS509 Chen, Chi Rong

Wu Yao-Tsung: Ein Theologie im Sozialistischen China, 1920-1960. (Beiträge zur Missionswissenschaft und Religionsgeschichte, 2). Münster, GW: Lit, n.d. iii, 185 pp. Paper. 3894736062.

The dissertation describes the life, work, and theology of YMCA leader Wu Yao-Tsung (1893-1979), and provides a rich knowledge of the Chinese history between 1920 and 1960, concerning politics and Christian religion.

AS510 Cole, Keith, ed.

Letters from China, 1893-1895: The Story of the Sister Martyrs of Ku Cheng. Victoria, AT: St. Hilary's Anglican Church, 1988. x, 136 pp. Paper. 0731619102.

The stories of Eleanor Saunders (1871-1895) and Elizabeth Saunders (1873-1895), told through their letters, from their departure from Melbourne, Australia, as the first missionaries of the Victorian Branch of the Church Missionary Association (Anglican) to their martyrdom in Ku Cheng, China, in 1895.

AS511 Collani, Claudia von

P(ater) Joachim Bouvet S.J.: Sein Leben und sein Werk. (Monumenta Serica, 17). Nettetal, GW: Steyler Verlag, 1985. xii, 269 pp. Paper. 3877871976.

Biography of a French Jesuit missionary (1656-1730) with a description of his missionary method known as "figurism," according to which, traces of a Christian primitive revelation can be found in the Chinese classics.

AS512 Covell, Ralph R.

W. A. P. Martin: Pioneer of Progress in China. Washington, DCU: Christian University Press, 1978. viii, 303 pp. 0802817157.

A scholarly biography of William Alexander Parson Martin, better known as W. A. P. Martin (1827-1916), brilliant Presbyterian missionary scholar and educator (1850-1916), with a concise history of China's political evolution, foreign relations, and educational system, as influenced by Martin.

AS513 Craighill, Marian G.

The Craighills of China. Ambler, PAU: Trinity Press International, 1972. xii, 285 pp. Paper. 0912046082.

A biography of Lloyd Rutherford Craighill (1886-1971), Anglican bishop of Anking, China (1940-1949); by his wife, based on their papers and her reminiscenses.

AS514 Crossman, Eileen Fraser

Mountain Rain: A Biography of James O. Fraser, Pioneer Missionary of China. Wheaton, ILU: Shaw Publishers, 1994. viii, 246 pp. Paper. 0877885516.

A popular biography by the daughter of James O. Fraser, pioneer missionary of the China Inland Mission to the Lisu people of Yunnan Province, China.

AS515 Dick, Lois Hoadley

Isobel Kuhn. Minneapolis, MNU: Bethany House, 1987. 157 pp. Paper. 0871239760.

A popular account of the life of a Canadian Moody Bible Institute graduate, who served as missionary to the Lisu in China, 1928-1950, and Thailand, 1951-1954.

AS516 Donnelly, Mary Rose, and Heather Dau

Katharine: Katharine Boehner Hockin, A Biography. Winfield, BCC: Wood Lake Books, 1992. 189 pp. Paper. 0929032756.

A biography of Dr. Katharine Boehner Hockin, from her birth in 1910, in Sichuan, China, to her own service as a Canadian Methodist missionary (later United Church of Canada) in West China (1939-1951), and her return to Canada to become an influential missiologist.

AS517 Drummond, Lewis A.

Miss Bertha: Women of Revival. Nashville, TNU: Broadman, 1996. x, 292 pp. Paper. 080541164X.

A biography of Bertha Smith (1888-1988), Southern Baptist missionary to China (1917-1948) and Taiwan (1948-1959), including her part in the Shantung revival.

AS518 Duan, Zhi-Dao "Julia", and Judith Palpant

Journey Against One Current: The Spiritual Autobiography of a Chinese Christian. South Pasadena, CAU: William Carey Library, 1997. x, 187 pp. Paper. 0878082735.

A Chinese Christian teacher (b.1920) describes the pain and suffering of the church in China through her life story.

AS519 Eber, Irene

The Jewish Bishop and the Chinese Bible: Schereschewsky (1831-1906). (Studies in Christian Mission, 22). Leiden, NE: Brill, 1999. xvi, 287 pp. 9004112669.

A study of Bishop Schereschewsky and his translation of the Hebrew Scriptures into northern vernacular (Mandarin) Chinese; based on missionary records and letters, including an analysis of the translated Chinese text, together with Schereschewsky's explanatory notes.

AS520 Edwards, J. Cunningham

Pioneers Together: A Biography of the Roy F. Cottrells. Nashville, TNU: Southern Publishing Association, 1967. 238 pp. No ISBN.

A popular account of the life of Seventh-day Adventist missionaries in China, 1908-1919.

AS521 Edwards, Lee

Missionary for Freedom: The Life and Times of Walter Judd. New York, NYU: Paragon House, 1990. xv, 364 pp. 1557780315.

The biography of a man who has been a medical missionary in China, Minnesota congressman, anti-communist crusader, and shaper of US foreign policy in the latter half of the 20th century.

AS522 Epp, Margaret

This Mountain Is Mine. Chicago, ILU: Moody, 1969. 191 pp. No ISBN.

A biographical account of the work done in China by Henry Bartel, who served under the China Mennonite Mission Society, 1901-1951.

AS523 Fleckner, Johannes

Thomas Kardinal Tien. (Studia Instituti Missiologici SVD, 16). St. Augustin, GW: Steyler Verlag, 1975. 138 pp. Paper. 3877870806.

The life of the first Chinese, and indeed non-white, cardinal, based on all sources available at the time, i.e. outside of China.

AS524 Fletcher, Jesse C.

Bill Wallace of China. Edited by Timothy George and Denise George. (Library of Baptist Classics, 9). Nashville, TNU: Broadman, 1996. xi, 276 pp. 080541259X.

A reprint, with a new introduction by the author, of the 1963 account of the SBC's famous medical missionary; martyred during the communist takeover of China in 1951.

AS525 Ford, Herbert
For the Love of China: The Life Story of Denton E. Rebok. Mountain View, CAU: Pacific Press, 1971. 127 pp. Paper. No ISBN.

A popular account of the adventures of Seventh-day Adventist missionaries Denton and Florence Rebok in China, 1917 to 1940.

AS526 Ghestin, Anatole
Désormais, je m'appelle Ting Ming-Cheng. Paris, FR: Éditions du Cerf, 1997. v, 306 pp. Paper. 2204057169.

The life of a remarkable Jesuit missionary in China, told through the letters which he wrote to his family in France, from 1907 until his death in 1961.

AS527 Goforth, Rosalind
Jonathan Goforth. Minneapolis, MNU: Bethany House, 1986. 157 pp. Paper. 087123842X.

A popular version of the classic 1937 biography of a pioneer missionary of the Presbyterian Church of Canada, who served in China from 1888 to 1934.

AS528 González, José María
El Primer Obispo Chino: Fray Gregorio Lo o López. (Colección OPE, 16). Pamplona, CK: Editorial OPE, 1966. 286 pp. No ISBN.

The biography of the Chinese Dominican Lo Wen-tsao (Gregory Lopez) who became the first Chinese bishop when consecrated in 1685.

AS529 Gulick, Edward V.
Peter Parker and the Opening of China. (Harvard Studies in American-East Asian Relations, 3). Cambridge, MAU: Harvard University Press, 1973. xi, 282 pp. 0674663268.

A scholarly biography of Peter Parker (1805-1888), pioneer prototype of medical missions overseas, who went to China in 1834 under the ABCFM, founded a hospital and the Medical Missionary Society of Canton, and lived to see Western medicine established in China under both church and state support.

AS530 Hamilton, Florence Olivia
To the Ends of the Earth. Franklin Springs, GAU: Advocate Press, 1965. 133 pp. No ISBN.

The autobiography of a Pentecostal Holiness missionary in China, 1923 to 1951.

AS531 Harris, Lillian Craig
Sins of the Fathers. (The Church and the World Series, 4). Notre Dame, INU: Cross Cultural Publications, 1988. xiv, 193 pp. 0940121085.

The painful story of Herndon Mason Harris, Jr. (1916-1981), a second generation Southern Baptist missionary to Confucian China who struggled with a dual identity as Southern Baptist missionary and Confucian "Eldest Son," until his suicide in 1981.

AS532 Heyndrickx, Jerome, ed.
Philippe Couplet, S.J. (1623-1693): The Man Who Brought China to Europe. (Monograph, 22). Nettetal, GW: Steyler Verlag; St. Augustin, GW: Institut Monumenta Serica; Louvain, SZ: Ferdinand Verbiest Foundation, 1990. 260 pp. Paper. 3805002661.

Twelve scholarly essays related to the contribution of the Jesuit missionary to China, Philippe Couplet (1623-1693), the first to introduce Chinese Confucian thinking to Europeans in a European language.

AS533 Hunt, Carroll F.
From the Claws of the Dragon. Grand Rapids, MIU: Zondervan, 1988. 134 pp. Paper. 0310515114.

A popular biography of Harry Lee (1925-) focusing on his

persecution during the Chinese cultural revolution and later service as an OMS international missionary.

AS534 Hyatt, Irwin T.
Our Ordered Lives Confess: Three Nineteenth-century American Missionaries in East Shantung. (Harvard Studies in American-East Asian Relations, 8). Cambridge, MAU: Harvard University Press, 1976. xv, 323 pp. 0674647351.

Case studies of the adjustments to life of three 19th-century missionaries in the city of Tengchow in northeast China—Tarleton Perry Crawford and Charlotte Diggs Moon (Southern Baptist), and Calvin Wilson Mateer (PCUSA).

AS535 Jacobson, S. Winifred
The Pearl and the Dragon: The Story of Alma and Gerhard Jacobson. (The Jaffray Collection of Missionary Portraits). Camp Hill, PAU: Christian Publications, 1997. x, 198 pp. Paper. 0875097006.

The story of a missionary couple's ministry in central China, 1918 to 1941, as Christian and Missionary Alliance missionaries.

AS536 Jochum, Alfons
Beim Grosskhan der Mongolen: Johannes von Monte Corvino (1247-1328), der erste Franziskaner in China. (Missionare, die Geschichte machten). Mödling, AU: Verlag St. Gabriel; St. Augustin, GW: Steyler Verlag, 1982. 127 pp. Paper. 3852641896 (AU), 3877871526 (GW).

The interesting life of an official of the Kingdom of Sicily who became a Franciscan, went as missionary to Armenia, in 1289 was appointed Papal Legate to Asia Minor and the Great Khan, and became first Archbishop of Peking.

AS537 Jochum, Alfons
Donner in Fernen Osten: Vincent F. Lebbe (China), (1877-1940, Vorkämpfer für eine chinesische Kirche). (Missionare, die Geschichte machten). Mödling-Wien, AU: Verlag St. Gabriel; Nettetal, GW: Steyler Verlag, 1984. 157 pp. Paper. 3852642140 (AU), 3877871704 (GW).

The portrait of a controversial missionary pioneer who championed the cause of a truly Chinese church at a time when Christianity in China was still very European.

AS538 Kinnear, Angus I.
Against the Tide: The Story of Watchman Nee. Eastbourne, ENK: Victory Press, 1973. xiv, 191 pp. 0854762019.

A biography of Ni Duosheng (1903-1972), founder of the "Little Flock" of indigenous local Chinese churches, whose courageous witness for Christ exerted nationwide influence on the churches of China.

AS539 Kinnear, Angus I.
Watchman Nee: Ein Leben gegen den Strom. Translated by Irmgard Muske. Eastbourne, ENK: Victory Press, 1973. 200 pp. 3417004721.

German translation.

AS540 Lane, Ortha May
Under Marching Orders in North China. Tyler, TXU: Story-Wright, 1971. iii, 276 pp. No ISBN.

From her perspective as a Methodist missionary to China from 1920 to 1948, the author presents a series of human interest stories, along with an account of the mission work in which she was involved, training young Chinese women for Christian leadership.

AS541 Lehmann, Emily
Scheitern, um zu begreifen: Als Missionarin und Pfarrfrau in China 1936 bis 1949. (Congnoscere, 11). Berlin, GW: Edition ost, 1997. 387 pp. 3932180259.

Autobiography of a Berlin Mission (Berliner Missionsgesellschaft) missionary wife in South China, from 1936 to 1949, that conveys an excellent understanding of the missionary work carried out in China prior to her arrival, and projects a deep empathy for China's rich, cultural heritage in the midst of civil unrest and war.

AS542 Leonard, Charles Alexander
Repaid a Hundred Fold. Grand Rapids, MIU: Eerdmans, 1969. 363 pp. No ISBN.

The autobiography of a Southern Baptist missionary who served in the Shantung Province of China (1910-1924), in Manchuria (1924-1937), and in Hawaii.

AS543 Li, Jeanette (Wan Wait Kit)
Jeanette Li: The Autobiography of a Chinese Christian. Translated by Rose A. Huston. London, ENK: Banner of Truth Trust, 1971. xvii, 360 pp. No ISBN.

The autobiography of Wan Wai Kit (1899-1968), a courageous Bible woman of South China, associated in her later years with the Reformation Translation Fellowship.

AS544 Locke, Mary
My China, the Way It Was. Santa Barbara, CAU: Fithian Press, 1992. 96 pp. Paper. 0931832950.

Family recollections from the 1916-1930 period by the daughter of Protestant missionaries in China.

AS545 Lodwick, Kathleen L.
Educating the Women of Hainan: The Career of Margaret Moninger in China, 1915-1942. Lexington, KYU: University Press of Kentucky, 1995. xv, 255 pp. 0813118824.

The biography of Mary Margaret Moninger (1891-1950), a pioneer Presbyterian woman missionary to Hainan Island, 1915 to 1942, based on a scholarly analysis of her letters and other writings.

AS546 Lyall, Leslie T.
Flame for God: John Sung and Revival in the Far East. London, ENK: OMF, 1976. xvii, 208 pp. Paper. 0853630267.

A popular biography of John Sung (1901-1944), whom the author called "the greatest evangelist China has ever known"; originally published in 1954.

AS547 Lyall, Leslie T.
Kaukoidän suuri herättäjä. Translated by Kalle Korhonen. Helsinki, FI: Ristin Voitto, 1962. 183 pp. No ISBN.

Finnish translation of *A Biography of John Sung* (4th edition, London, 1961).

AS548 Lyall, Leslie T.
Three of China's Mighty Men. Fearn, ENK: Christian Focus/OMF Publishing, 2000. 155 pp. 0853630909.

Popular biographies of three outstanding Chinese Christians: Yang Shao-T'ang, Watchman Nee, and Wing Ming-Dao; originally published in 1973.

AS549 Maberly, Allan
God Spoke Tibetan: The Epic Story of the Man Who Gave the Bible to Tibet, the Forbidden Land. Orange, CAU: Evangel Bible Translators, 1995. 96 pp. 0890810966.

A popular account of Yoseb Gergan and his struggle to provide the Bible in Tibetan; originally published in 1971 (Mountain View, CAU: Pacific Press).

AS550 Maberly, Allan
Heltedåd i Tibets fjellverdan: Bibelens eventyrlige vei til Dalai Lamas lukkede land. Translated by Eivind Keyn. Oslo, NO: Norsk Bokforlag, 1983. 140 pp. 8270070335.

Norwegian translation.

AS551 Macheiner, Alois
Kein fremder Teufel!: Fritz Kornfeld SVD, Missionar mit besonderer Sendung. Wien, AU: SVD, 1987. 78 pp. Paper. No ISBN.

The history of a China missionary (1904-1961) who devoted all his energies to the development of genuine Chinese church music.

AS552 Maestrini, Nicholas
China: Lost Mission? Detroit, MIU: PIME World Press, 1992. xv, 374 pp. Paper. 0940543230.

A first-hand account by a retired Catholic PIME missionary, of his service in Hong Kong and China, 1931 to 1949; first published by Magnificat Press in 1991 under the title *My Twenty Years with the Chinese, Laughter and Tears.*

AS553 McClain, Theresa
Never Too Late: One Woman's Journey in Mission Service. Birmingham, ALU: New Hope, 1988. 83 pp. Paper. 0936625457.

The life of Lola Mae Daniel (1903-), mission volunteer and teacher, as she struggled to fulfill her calling from God to work in Taiwan and China as a Baptist missionary.

AS554 Metzner, Hans Wolfgang
Roland Allen: Sein Leben und Werk; kritischer Beitrag zum Verständnis von Mission und Kirche. (Missionswissenschaftliche Forschungen, 6). Gütersloh, GW: Mohn, 1970. 298 pp. Paper. No ISBN.

A dissertation on the missionary of the Church of England in North China and Kenya (1869-1947), who believed that the founding of self-supporting and self-expanding local churches is the main goal of missionary activity.

AS555 Munro, John
Beyond the Moon Gate: A China Odyssey, 1938-1950. Vancouver, BCC: Douglas and McIntyre; Winfield, BCC: Wood Lake Books, 1990. xvii, 269 pp. Paper. 0888946848 (D), 0929032187 (W).

Excerpts from the China diaries of Margaret Outerbridge (1909-1984), from her arrival in war-torn west China as a United Church of Canada missionary in 1938, to departure under communist pressure in 1950.

AS556 Park, Polly, ed.
"To Save Their Heathen Souls": Voyage to and Life in Fouchow, China Based on Wentworth Diaries and Letters, 1854-1858. (Pittsburgh Theological Monographs Series, 9). Allison Park, PAU: Pickwick, 1984. xxxi, 173 pp. Paper. 0915138662.

A collection of the letters and diaries of Anna M. Wentworth and Erastus Wentworth, Sr., written between 1854 and 1858, giving a first-person account of their life as Methodist missionaries to China, and throwing light on the China they called "a fabulous empire in decay."

AS—ASIA

AS557 Pollock, John Charles

The Cambridge Seven. (An OMF Book). Basingstoke, ENK: Marshalls, 1985. 127 pp. Paper. 0551011742.

Brief biographies of seven famous Cambridge University athletes who went into China as missionaries in 1885; originally printed in 1966 (London, ENK: InterVarsity Press).

AS558 Pollock, John Charles

A Foreign Devil in China: The Story of Dr. L. Nelson Bell. Minneapolis, MNU: World Wide Publications, 1988. 355 pp. Paper. 0890661413.

The revised biography of a Presbyterian Church (US) medical missionary, who served in the Kiangsu Province of China from 1921 to 1941.

AS559 Pollock, John Charles

Hudson Taylor and Maria: Pioneers in China. New York, NYU: McGraw-Hill, 1962. 212 pp. No ISBN.

A biography of the founders of the China Inland Mission.

AS560 Price, Eva Jane

China Journal, 1889-1900: An American Missionary Family during the Boxer Rebellion: With the Letters and Diaries of Eva Jane Price and Her Family. New York, NYU: Scribner, 1989. xxiii, 289 pp. 0684189518.

Letters and journals of ABCFM missionaries in which they tell of their brief work in China's Shansi province, with vivid details of the Boxer Rebellion in which they were martyred.

AS561 Puhl, Stephan

Georg M. Stenz, SVD (1869-1928): Chinamissionar im Kaiserreich und in der Republik. Edited by Roman Malek. Nettetal, GW: Steyler Verlag, 1994. 317 pp. Paper. 3805003501.

A biographical essay on the life and thirty-five-year ministry in China of Rev. George M. Stenz, SVD; with an analysis of the mission/political context in southern Shantung on the eve of the Boxer Rebellion, and a selection of Stenz's letters.

AS562 Rae, Muriel W.

His Banner over Us Is Love. Willowdale, ONC: By the author, Muriel W. Rae, 1995. 267 pp. Paper. No ISBN.

Reminiscences of service by William (d.1972) and Muriel Rae, focusing on their work as CIM pioneers among the Miao people of central China, 1935 to 1942.

AS563 Raley, Helen Thames

Doctor in an Old World: The Story of Robert Earl Beddoe, Medical Missionary to China. Waco, TXU: Word Books, 1969. 156 pp. No ISBN.

A popular biography of Beddoe (1882-1952), a missionary physician and administrator who served in China under the Southern Baptist Mission during the period of the two World Wars and the communist takeover in that country, 1909 to 1947.

AS564 Rankin, Jerry

A Journey of Faith and Sacrifice: Retracing the Steps of Lottie Moon. Birmingham, ALU: New Hope Publishers, 1996. xii, 110 pp. 1563091887.

A photographic essay on the pioneer Southern Baptist missionary to China, with historic and contemporary photographs of sites in China.

AS565 Ratz, Calvin C.

They Call Him Pastor Wheat. Toronto, ONC: Testimony Press, 1970. 115 pp. Paper. NO ISBN.

The story of J. Ken Mcgillivray's missionary service in Inner Mongolia (1940-1941) as an Elim Mission associate, his internment by the Japanese (1941-1945), and his work in China (1945-1950), and Taiwan and Hong Kong (1951-1969); Far East Secretary of the Pentecostal Assemblies of Canada.

AS566 Rawlinson, John Lang

Rawlinson the Recorder and China's Revolution: A Topical Biography of Frank Joseph Rawlinson, 1871-1937. (Church and the World, 5). Notre Dame, INU: Cross Cultural Publications, 1990. v, 789 pp. 0940121123 (vol. 1), 0940121131 (vol. 2).

A scholarly biography of Frank Joseph Rawlinson (1871-1937), Southern Baptist missionary to China (1902-1937) and editor of the prestigious *The Chinese Recorder* (1914-1937).

AS567 Reil, Sebald

Kilian Stumpf, 1655-1720: Ein Würzburger Jesuit am Kaiserhof zu Peking. (Missionswissenschaftliche Abhandlungen und Texte, 33). Münster, GW: Aschendorff, 1978. xxxii, 207 pp. Paper. 3402035227.

The first detailed biography, based on archival materials, of a missionary who went to China in 1694, became President of the Mathematical Tribunal in Peking, and exercised great influence over Emperor Kanghi.

AS568 Schlyter, Herman

Erik Folke: Kyrkogrundare i Kina. Lund, SW: Gleerup, 1964. 144 pp. No ISBN.

A biography of the Swedish China missionary, Erik Folke (1862-1939).

AS569 Schmidt, William J., and Edward Ouellette

What Kind of a Man?: The Life of Henry Smith Leiper. New York, NYU: Friendship Press, 1986. xv, 307 pp. Paper. 0377001651.

A popular biography of Henry Smith Leiper (1891-1975), United Church of Christ pastor, China missionary, ecumenical leader, author, and Field Secretary of the American Bible Society.

AS570 Schneider, Herbert W.

" Und dennoch wird Gott siegen!": Cyrillus Jarre OFM, Martyr-erbischof aus Ahrweiler in China. Sinzig, GW: Sankt-Meinrad-Verlag, 1989. 172 pp. Paper. 3925793141.

A scholarly biography of the German-born Archbishop Jarre, who lectured on mission law and mission pastoral theology at the Antonianum in Rome, from 1924 to 1929, before being nominated Vicar Apostolic of North Shantung, China.

AS571 Scott, Mary L.

Kept in Safeguard: Mary Scott Tells the Story of Her Experiences in Old China. Kansas City, MOU: Nazarene Publishing House, 1977. 116 pp. Paper. 0834104628.

Wartime experiences of a Nazarene missionary in China from 1940 to 1949.

AS572 Service, John S., ed.

Golden Inches: The China Memoir of Grace Service. Los Angeles, CAU: University of California Press, 1989. xxvi, 346 pp. 0520066561.

The memoirs of Grace Service (1879-1954), who first went to China with her husband, Robert, as Student Volunteers under the YMCA in 1905, and served there through revolutionary changes until 1937.

AS573 Sharpe, Eric J.
Karl Ludvig Reichelt: Missionary, Scholar and Pilgrim. Hong Kong, HK: Tao Fong Shan Ecumenical Centre, 1984. iv, 210 pp. Paper. No ISBN.

A critical biographical study of the work and humanness of Dr. Karl Ludwig Reichelt, a Norwegian Lutheran missionary to China (1903-1952), who led in creative initiatives of mission to Chinese Buddhists and founded the Tao Fong Shan Ecumenical Centre in Hong Kong.

AS574 Shaw, Yu-ming
An American Missionary in China: John Leighton Stuart and Chinese-American Relations. (Harvard East Asian Monographs, 158). Cambridge, MAU: Harvard University, Council on East Asian Studies, 1992. xv, 381 pp. 0674478355.

A scholarly biography of John Leighton Stuart (1876-1962), Presbyterian missionary to China (1904-1941) who sought to apply the Christian Social Gospel in the uplifting of China as President of Yenching University (1919-1941) and US Ambassador to China (1946-1952).

AS575 Smith, Bertha
Bertha Smith: Go Home and Tell. Edited by Timothy George and Denise George. Nashville, TNU: Broadman, 1995. xix, 278 pp. 0805412581.

Selections from the writings of Bertha Smith (1888-1988), Southern Baptist missionary to China (1917-1948) and Taiwan (1948-1959), with questions for group study.

AS576 Stockwell, Esther Beck
Asia's Call: My Life As a Missionary In China and Singapore. San Francisco, CAU: Stockwell Press, 1988. 222 pp. Paper. No ISBN.

The memories (1900-1981) of Esther and Olin Stockwell, last exiled missionaries from China; Methodist missionaries to Korea, China, and Singapore, and developers of Trinity Theological Seminary in Singapore.

AS577 Swenson, Sally
Welthy Honsinger Fisher: Signals of a Century, the Life and Learning of an American Educator, Literacy Pioneer, and Independent Reformer in China and India, 1879-1980. Stittsville, ONC: By the author, S. Swenson, 1988. xx, 517 pp. Paper. 0969368402.

A biography of a former China missionary educator (1906-1917) of the Women's Foreign Missionary Society of the Methodist church, and founder in 1953 of Literacy House at Allahabad, India, where her husband, Fred Fisher, had been Methodist bishop (1924-1938).

AS578 Taylor, Howard
By Faith: Henry W. Frost and the China Inland Mission. Singapore, SI: OMF, 1988. xvii, 364 pp. 9971972654.

Biography of Henry Weston Frost (1858-1945), North American Director of the CIM and cofounder of the IFMA; originally published by the CIM in 1938.

AS579 Taylor, Howard, and Geraldine Taylor
Biography of James Hudson Taylor. London, ENK: OMF Books, 1965. vii, 366 pp. No ISBN.

An abridged edition of an earlier two-volume standard biography of James Hudson Taylor, founder of the China Inland Mission; produced for the centennial of the mission.

AS580 Taylor, Howard, and Geraldine Taylor
Hudson Taylor: Ein Mann, der Gott vertraute. Giessen, GW: Brunnen-Verlag, 1977. 334 pp. 3765504483.

Second edition of the German translation of *Biography of James Hudson Taylor* (1965).

AS581 Taylor, Howard, and Mary Geraldine Taylor
Spiritual Secret of Hudson Taylor. New Kensington, PAU: Whitaker House, 1996. 396 pp. Paper. 0883683873.

Reissue of reflections on the faith and missionary service of the founder of the CIM, by his son and daughter-in-law; originally published by the CIM in 1932.

AS582 Tharp, Robert N.
They Called Us White Chinese: The Story of a Lifetime of Service to God and Mankind. Charlotte, NCU: Tharp, 1994. xviii, 845 pp. 0963942506.

A narrative illustrated autobiography of Robert Tharp (b.1913), including his childhood in Manchuria as son of Plymouth Brethren missionaries, later service (1933-1941, 1946-1947) with his wife Eva in North China, and later work in the United States as a Chinese language teacher.

AS583 Thompson, Phyllis
Pilgrim in China: A Memoir. East Sussex, ENK: Highland Books, 1988. 219 pp. Paper. 0946616396.

The noted writer of mission biographies recalls, in letters to a friend, her own service in China as a CIM worker (1936-1951).

AS584 Tyzack, Charles
Friends to China: The Davidson Brothers and the Friends' Mission to China, 1886 to 1939. York, ENK: William Sessions, 1988. vi, 215 pp. Paper. 1850720312.

The story of the founding of the Society of Friends' mission in the western Province of Szechwan, China, in 1886, and its subsequent development, to 1942, by Robert Davidson, with Chinese Christians and three of his brothers.

AS585 Väth, Alfons
Johann Adam Schall von Bell, S.J.: Missionar in China, kaiserlicher Astronom und Ratgeber am Hofe von Peking. (Monumenta Serica, 25). Nettetal, GW: Steyler Verlag, 1991. xx, 421 pp. 3805002874.

This reprint of the 1933 first edition is a welcome reappearance of the most authoritative biography of Schall von Bell in any language, and is now enlarged with an updated bibliography (which also covers the Jesuit missions in China) and an index that includes Chinese characters.

AS586 Wang, Mary, Gwen England, and Edward England
Stephen the Chinese Pastor: The Life of Stephen Wang Is Part of the Heroic Story of the Chinese Church. (Hodder Christian Paperbacks). London, ENK: Hodder & Stoughton, 1975. 192 pp. 0340179848.

Reminiscences of the life and courageous witness of Stephen Wang (1900-1971); originally published in 1973 (0340147482).

AS587 Waston, Jean
Bosshardt: A Biography. Crowborough, ENK: Monarch Publications/OMF International, 1995. 247 pp. Paper. 1854242970.

The remarkable story of Alfred Bosshardt (1897-1993) and his wife Ruth, who, as CIM missionaries, were captured by the Red Army and taken on the Long March, 1934-1936.

AS588 Watters, Hyla S.
Hyla Doc: Surgeon in China through War and Revolution,
1924-1949. Edited by Elsie H. Landstrom. Fort Bragg,
CAU: QED Press, 1991. xxi, 288 pp. Paper. 0936609192.

    The letters and memoirs of Hyla S. Watters (1893-
1987), Methodist medical missionary to China (1924-1949),
containing insights into Chinese society, medicine, and
politics of the period.

AS589 Wellman, Sam
Gladys Aylward: Missionary to China. (Heroes of Faith
Series). Uhrichsville, OHU: Barbour Publishing, 1998. 204
pp. Paper. 1577482220.

    After CIM turned her down as a missionary, Aylward
found her own way there in 1932, and with simple dependence on God, would remain until her death in 1970, in
spite of a ten-year interruption during the communist takeover.

AS590 Witek, John W.
Controversial Ideas in China and in Europe: A Biography
of Jean-Francois Foucquet, S.J. (1665-1741). (Bibliotheca Instituti Historici S.I. Vol. XLIII). Rome, IT: Institutum
Historicum S.I., 1982. xv, 494 pp. Paper. 8870413438.

    A scholarly biography of the controversial French Je-
suit who worked in China during the Chinese Rites controversy, giving insight into the Jesuit presence in China during the early China period, and their impact in Europe on
the eve of the Enlightenment; with extensive bibliography.

AS591 Wu, Yuen-Lin
He Holds My Hand. Translated by David Wong. Camp
Hill, PAU: Horizon House Publishers, 1991. 158 pp. Pa-
per. 0889650969.

    The Founder-Director of Immanuel Orphanage in
Shanghai, Yuen-Lin Wu (1900-1982), tells her life story.

AS592 Yule, Jean
About Face in China: Eight Australians' Experience of the
Chinese Revolution, 1945-1951. Melbourne, AT: JBCE,
1995. xviii, 284 pp. Paper. 1864070404.

    Six Australian missionaries tell the story of their work
with the Church of Christ in China, amidst revolution.

AS593 Zmarzly, August, and Alois Macheiner
Georg Froewis SVD: 40 Jahre Missionar im Umbruch Chi-
nas. Wien-Mödling, AU: St. Gabriel-Verlag, 1960. 392
pp. No ISBN.

    The life and work of the Austrian G. Froewis (1865-
1934), the first Prefect Apostolic of Sinyang, China; written by fellow missionaries.

Japan

See also HI117, CR746, SO156, SO368-SO369, PO194-
PO195, ED53, EV390, MI14, SP283, SP308, AS2, AS116,
AS171, AS173, AS186, AS196-AS197, AS226, AS296, AS298,
and AS718.

AS594 Berentsen, Jan-Martin
Grave and Gospel. (Beihefte der Zeitschrift für Religions-
und Geistesgeschichte, 30). Leiden, NE: Brill, 1985. x, 306
pp. Paper. 9004078517.

    A systematic analysis of basic religious and ethical premises
underlying Japanese ancestor worship, and of the theological and
missiological responses approproate for Christians.

AS595 Boardman, Robert
A Higher Honor. Colorado Springs, COU: NavPress, 1986.
197 pp. Paper. 0891095527.

    Reminiscences of his service there, from 1956 to 1985,
by the former Director of Navigator ministries in Japan and
Okinawa.

AS596 Bollinger, Edward E.
The Cross and the Floating Dragon: The Gospel in Ryukyu.
Pasadena, CAU: William Carey Library, 1983. xviii, 345 pp.
Paper. 0878081909.

    The story of Christian missions in the Ryukyu Islands
(Okinawa), from 1624 to the present, by an American Baptist
missionary who served there since 1955.

AS597 Bollinger, Edward E.
On the Threshold of the Closed Empire: Mid-19th Century
Missions in Okinawa. South Pasadena, CAU: William Carey
Library, 1991. xxv, 249 pp. Paper. 0878082301.

    The history of missions in Okinawa developed by Dr.
Bernard J. Bettelheim of the British Seaman's Mission, and
French Catholic missionaries of the *Société des Mission Étran-*
geres.

AS598 Boxer, C. R.
The Christian Century in Japan. (California Library Reprint
Series). Berkeley, CAU: University of California Press, 1974.
xv, 535 pp. No ISBN.

    Reprint of a narrative account of 1549-1638 when Ca-
tholicism was planted in Japan by Jesuits and others, and of
the persecutions that drove the Christian community into hiding; first published in 1951.

AS599 Branley, Brendan R.
Christianity and the Japanese. (World Horizon Books). Mary-
knoll, NYU: Maryknoll Publications, 1966. x, 271 pp. Paper.
No ISBN.

    A narrative description, by a Catholic missionary in Ja-
pan, of Christian missionary work encountering Japanese society and Japanese cultural values.

AS600 Caldarola, Carlo
Christianity: The Japanese Way. (Monographs and Theoretical Studies in Sociology and Anthropology in Honour of Nels
Anderson, 15). Leiden, NE: Brill, 1979. viii, 234 pp.
9004058427.

    A scholarly analysis of the Japanese way of interpreting
Christianity in two indigenous Christian groups—the Mukyokai (non-church Christians) and Makuya (Tabernacle Christians).

AS601 Cary, Otis
A History of Christianity in Japan: Protestant Missions. Richmond, Surrey, ENK: Curzon Press, 1996. 2 vols. 0700702628.

    Reprint of a classic 1909 history of Protestant, Roman
Catholic, and Orthodox missions [vol. 1: 367 pp.; vol. 2: 423
pp.].

AS602 Cieslik, Hubert
"Das Blut der Märtyrer ist Samen der Christen": Bilder aus
der japanischen Kirchengeschichte. Bergisch-Gladbach, GW:
Heider-Verlag, 1988. 100 pp. Paper. 3873141981.

    A compilation of essays originally written for the review
Aus dem Land der aufgehenden Sonne, describing historical
events and personalities of the Catholic mission in Japan in
the 16th and 17th centuries.

AS603 Dalid, Gudrun
Tro eller tradition: en bok om mission i Japan. Örebro, SW: Libris, 1990. 189 pp. 9171947590.
A book on missions in Japan.

AS604 Danker, William J., and Kiyoko Matsuda
More Than Healing: The Story of Kiyoko Matsuda. St. Louis, MOU: Concordia Publishing, 1973. 4 vols. 0570031613.
The personal story of Kiyoko Matsuda, a Christian woman worthy of admiration.

AS605 Driskill, J. Lawrence, and Lillian Cassel Driskill
Japan Diary of Cross-Cultural Mission. Pasadena, CAU: Hope Publishing House, 1993. xvii, 172 pp. 0932727638 (hdbk), 093272762X (pbk).
The diary of Presbyterian missionaries to Japan (1951-1970), covering their first term of service in education and church development (1951-1955).

AS606 Drummond, Richard Henry
A History of Christianity in Japan. (Christian World Mission Books). Grand Rapids, MIU: Eerdmans, 1971. 397 pp. Paper. No ISBN.
A survey of Roman Catholic, Protestant, and Orthodox Christianity in Japan, from the 16th century to the present.

AS607 Dufty, Cynthia, ed.
Missionary Communication in a Visual Age: Taking Every Thought Captive to Christ. (Hayama Missionary Seminar (39th, 1998)). Tokyo, JA: Hayama Missionary Seminar, 1998. iii, 106 pp. Paper. No ISBN.
Missionary communication in Japan and issues of mass media and the church.

AS608 Durix, Claude
De la Gaule au Japon par les Chemins de Dieu: L'aventure heroïque de quelques femmes. (L'histoire à vif). Paris, FR: Éditions du Cerf, 1999. 350 pp. Paper. 2204063029.
A history of the work in Japan of the Sisters of Saint-Enfant-Jésus de Chauffailes, in education and health care, from 1977 to 1945, with comparisons to earlier work by Catholics in central France, and by Francis Xavier in Japan.

AS609 Elison, George
Deus Destroyed: The Image of Christianity in Early Modern Japan. (Harvard East Asian Series, 72). Cambridge, MAU: Harvard University Press, 1973. xiv, 542 pp. 0674199618.
A detailed study, based on archival research, of early Christian missions in Japan, from the arrival of Saint Francis Xavier in 1549,through their widespread acceptance, to the 1639 edict banning further contact with Catholic lands.

AS610 Endo, Shusaku
Stained Glass Elegies. Translated by Van C. Gessel. New York, NYU: Dodd, Mead, 1985. 165 pp. 0396086438.
Eleven short stories, by Japan's foremost living novelist, with the struggle to maintain Christian faith in a Japanese context as one common theme.

AS611 Fischer, Edward
Japan Journey: The Columbian Fathers in Nippon. New York, NYU: Crossroad Publishing, 1984. 165 pp. Paper. 0824506561.
A narrative account of the author's 1983 visit to the Columbian Fathers in mission in Japan; with reflections on their earlier work there, beginning in 1934.

AS612 Fröis, Luís
Historia do Japaõ. Lisboa, PO: Biblioteca Nacional de Lisboa, 1976. 4 vols. No ISBN.
Reprinting the monumental 16th-century history of the Jesuit mission in Japan, with a masterful introduction by the foremost scholar of Jesuit mission history [vol. 1, *1549-1564*; vol. 2, *1565-1578*; vol. 3, *1578-1582*, vol. 4, *1583-1587*].

AS613 Francis, Carolyn Bowen, and John Masaaki Nakajima
Christians in Japan. New York, NYU: Friendship Press, 1991. 2 vols. Paper. 037700216X.
The story of Japan's Christians, past and present, prepared as an adult mission study, with study guide (*The Way of Faithfulness: Study Guide to Christians in Japan* by Patricia J. Patterson; 0377002208).

AS614 Fujita, Neil S.
Japan's Encounter with Christianity: The Catholic Mission in Pre-Modern Japan. Mahwah, NJU: Paulist Press, 1991. viii, 294 pp. Paper. 0809132060.
A narrative history of contacts from the 16th to the 19th century, between Catholic missionaries and Japanese political and religious leaders.

AS615 Germany, Charles H., ed.
The Response of the Church in Changing Japan. New York, NYU: Friendship Press, 1967. 175 pp. Paper. No ISBN.
A comprehensive study of the past, present, and future of the Christian movement in Japan, by five Protestant leaders, missionaries, and national Japanese.

AS616 Gossmann, Elisabeth
Religiöse Herkunft, profane Zukunft?: Das Christentum in Japan. Munich, GW: Hueber, 1965. 296 pp. No ISBN.
A well-documented analysis of the past and present political and religious situation in Japan, raising the question of the meaningfulness of mission in a country showing so little "missionary success."

AS617 Grieco, Gianfranco
Giappone duemila. (Collana "Nostro tempo," 39). Milano, IT: Massimo, 1977. 144 pp. No ISBN.
A popular introduction for Catholics to Japanese society, culture, and the life and work of the Catholic Church in Japan.

AS618 Harrington, Ann M.
Japan's Hidden Christians. Chicago, ILU: Loyola University Press, 1993. xv, 208 pp. Paper. 0829407413.
A popular introduction to the beliefs and practices of the *Kakure Kirishitan* (hidden Christians) of Japan, descendants of the underground Catholic Church that survived persecution from 1639 to 1873.

AS619 Hayama Missionary Seminar (11th, 1970)
The Christian's Responsibility in Political Affairs in Japan. Edited by Carl C. Beck. Tokyo, JA: Hayama Missionary Seminar, 1970. vi, 136 pp. Paper. No ISBN.
Eight papers dealing theologically with the ethical questions raised by the modern political and social revolution, with insights on the Christian's responsibility in political affairs in Japan.

AS—ASIA

AS620 Hayama Missionary Society (12th, 1971)
The Church's Role in Urbanized Japan: Christian Witness in a Transitional Society. Edited by Carl C. Beck. Tokyo, JA: Hayama Seminar, 1971. vii, 147 pp. Paper. No ISBN.

Eight study papers with critiques on the implications, pressures, and forces at work among Japanese urban populations; with suggestions for appropriate ministries by Christians.

AS621 Hayama Missionary Seminar (13th, 1972)
The Mandate of the Gospel to Technological Society. Edited by Carl C. Beck. Tokyo, JA: Hayama Seminar, 1972. iv, 89 pp. Paper. No ISBN.

Seven thoughtful papers on the Christian's role and responsibility in creating and maintaining a human society, with special reference to Japan.

AS622 Hayama Missionary Seminar (14th, 1973)
The Contemporary Work of the Holy Spirit. Edited by Carl C. Beck. Tokyo, JA: Hayama Seminar, 1973. iv, 141 pp. Paper. No ISBN.

Eight varied papers on the work of the Holy Spirit, with special reference to Japanese society.

AS623 Hayama Missionary Seminar (15th, 1974)
Changing Patterns in the Church's Ministry. Edited by Carl C. Beck. Tokyo, JA: Hayama Seminar, 1974. iv, 113 pp. Paper. No ISBN.

Eight papers on new concepts and forms of Protestant ministry in the Japanese church.

AS624 Hayama Missionary Seminar (16th, 1975)
Christian Perspectives on Death: East and West. Edited by Carl C. Beck. Tokyo, JA: Hayama Seminar, 1975. 141 pp. Paper. No ISBN.

Papers on death and dying as they are viewed by the Japanese and by the Western world, exploring ethical problems associated with abortion, euthanasia, and suicide.

AS625 Hayama Missionary Seminar (17th, 1976)
Personal Evangelism in Today's Japan. Edited by Carl C. Beck. Tokyo, JA: Hayama Seminar, 1976. iv, 119 pp. Paper. No ISBN.

Nine papers on historical, biblical, theological, and practical aspects of personal witness by missionaries.

AS626 Hayama Missionary Seminar (18th, 1977)
Barriers and Bridges to Gospel Outreach in Japan. Edited by Carl C. Beck. Tokyo, JA: Hayama Seminar, 1977. iv, 70 pp. Paper. No ISBN.

A look at culture, language, and other barriers, and how they can be transformed to become bridges.

AS627 Hayama Missionary Seminar (21st, 1980)
The Christian Gospel and its Ethical Implications for Japanese Society. Edited by Marion F. Moorhead and Beryle C. Lovelace. Tokyo, JA: Hayama Seminar, 1980. iv, 104 pp. Paper. No ISBN.

Papers discussing the ethical issues confronting Christian missionaries in Japan, with in-depth discussion of the political, domestic, personal, social, and educational aspects.

AS628 Hayama Missionary Seminar (22nd, 1981)
The Christian Family in Japan. Edited by Beryle C. Lovelace and Marion F. Moorhead. Tokyo, JA: Hayama Seminar, 1981. iv, 59 pp. Paper. No ISBN.

Six papers on various aspects of the Japanese family and their significance for Christian witness and family life—each with a critique.

AS629 Hayama Missionary Seminar (23rd, 1982)
Can the Gospel Thrive in Japanese Soil?: Guilt, Shame, and Grace in a Unique Culture. Edited by Carl C. Beck. Tokyo, JA: Hayama Missionary Seminar, 1982. vi, 133 pp. Paper. No ISBN.

Major papers and critiques on the Gospel and particular emphases in Japanese culture.

AS630 Hayama Missionary Seminar (25th, 1984)
God at Work in Contemporary Japan: A Twenty-Fifth Anniversary Reflection. Edited by Carl C. Beck. Tokyo, JA: Hayama Seminar, 1984. iv, 56 pp. Paper. No ISBN.

Thirteen papers looking back at twenty-five years of growth, victories, and mistakes of the church in Japan and prospects for the future.

AS631 Hayama Missionary Seminar (27th, 1986)
Church Planting Patterns in Japan. Edited by Carl C. Beck. Tokyo, JA: Hayama Seminar, 1986. iv, 68 pp. Paper. No ISBN.

Ten papers on biblical and cultural factors affecting church growth in Japan.

AS632 Hayama Missionary Seminar (28th, 1987)
The Gospel Encounters the Japanese Worldview: Bridges or Barriers. Compiled by Fritz Sprunger. Tokyo, JA: Hayama Missionary Seminar, 1987. 82 pp. Paper. No ISBN.

Nine papers on issues and customs that are barriers to cross-cultural communication with the Japanese.

AS633 Hayama Missionary Seminar (29th, 1988)
Incarnating the Gospel in the Japanese Context. Edited by Fritz Sprunger. Tokyo, JA: Hayama Missionary Seminar, 1988. vi, 96 pp. Paper. No ISBN.

Eight papers describing spirituality, loyalty, contextualization, family, education, and cultural perspectives of Japan.

AS634 Hayama Missionary Seminar (31st, 1990)
Heisei: A New Era of More of the Same?: Missiological Issues in the '90s. Edited by Robert Lee and Barry L. Ross. Tokyo, JA: Tokyo Mission Research Institute, 1990. 120 pp. Paper. No ISBN.

Essays on the implications for Christian mission in Japan, of the new political era, of new Japanese religions, and of "new age" thought.

AS635 Hayama Missionary Seminar (32nd, 1991)
The Enigma of Japanese Society. Edited by Robert Lee and Barry L. Ross. Tokyo, JA: Tokyo Mission Research Institute, 1991. 111 pp. Paper. No ISBN.

Papers by a journalist, a constitutional law expert, and a pastor/counselor, on characteristics of Japanese civil society and personality—particularist, yet expecting conformity.

AS636 Hayama Missionary Seminar (33rd, 1992)
A World in Shambles in an Ordered Universe: Renewing Mission Engagement. Edited by Robert Lee. Tokyo, JA: Hayama Seminar, 1992. 120 pp. Paper. No ISBN.

Papers relating recent political and social changes in Japan to Christian mission, and the role of the missionary as catalyst for change.

AS637 Hayama Missionary Seminar (36th, 1995)

Leadership: The Church in Japan and the Missionary. Edited by Russell Sawatsky and Gregg Hutton. Tokyo, JA: Tokyo Mission Research Institute, 1995. 130 pp. Paper. No ISBN.

Papers on biblical leadership within the church in the Japanese setting, with special attention to the continuing role of the missionary.

AS638 Hayama Missionary Seminar (37th, 1996)

Reaching the Secular Mind for Christ: Practical Help for Evangelism in Japan. Edited by Tim Boyle. Tokyo, JA: Tokyo Mission Research Institute, 1996. 100 pp. Paper. No ISBN.

Report on "Young-Earth Creationism vs. Old-Earth Creationsim: How They Can Be Used as Tools for Evangelism."

AS639 Hayama Missionary Seminar (38th, 1997)

Revival and Renewal. Compiled by Tim Boyle and Cynthia Dufty. Tokyo, JA: Hayama Seminar Annual Report, 1997. iv, 98 pp. Paper. No ISBN.

Papers on revival in the Japan mission context.

AS640 Hecken, Joseph Leonard van

The Catholic Church in Japan since 1859. Translated by John van Hoydonck. Tokyo, JA: Herder Agency, 1963. vi, 317 pp. No ISBN.

A corrected and enlarged English translation.

AS641 Hecken, Joseph Leonard van

Un siècle de vie catholique au Japon, 1859-1959. (Missionary Bulletin Series, 9). Tokyo, JA: Committee of the Apostolate, 1960. 286 pp. No ISBN.

An encyclopedic summary of one hundred years of Japan Catholicism (1859-1959), with capsule histories of dioceses and church institutions.

AS642 Heinrichs, Maurus

Der grosse Durchbruch: Franziskus von Assisi im Spiegel japanischer Literatur. Werl, GW: Dietrich Coelde, 1969. 254 pp. Paper. No ISBN.

A detailed analysis, based on Japanese sources, of how St. Francis' teachings have been incorporated into Zen philosophy, thereby providing an indirect Christian influence on Japanese culture.

AS643 Ion, A. Hamish

The Cross in the Dark Valley: The Canadian Protestant Missionary Movement in the Japanese Empire, 1931-1945. Waterloo, ONC: Wilfrid Laurier University Press, 1999. xvi, 428 pp. 088920294X (vol. 3).

Volume three of a series titled *The Cross and the Rising Sun*, this pioneer and scholarly study sheds new light on the dramatic dynamics of Christianity, culture, education, and politics faced by missionaries and Japanese Christians, in a watershed period in the religious history of 20th-century East Asia.

AS644 Jennes, Jozef

A History of the Catholic Church in Japan: From Its Beginnings to the Early Meiji Era (1549-1873): A Short Handbook. Tokyo, JA: Oriens Institute for Religious Research, 1973. viii, 277 pp. No ISBN.

The expanded version of a handbook for newly arrived missionaries in Japan, covering Catholic missions from the arrival of Francis Xavier in 1549 to the end of the period of seclusion and prohibition in 1873.

AS645 Krummel, John W., ed.

A Biographical Dictionary of Methodist Missionaries to Japan: 1873-1993. Tokyo, JA: Kyo Bun Kwan, 1996. xiii, 342 pp. 476424019X.

A comprehensive, illustrated biographical dictionary of all persons who served in Japan under the Methodist churches that are members of the World Methodist Council, as well as their predecessor denominations.

AS646 Krummel, John W.

Letters from Japan, 1956-1997. Kearney, NEU: Morris Publishing, 1999. xi, 208 pp. Paper. No ISBN.

A collection of all of the general letters sent out through the Board of Missions to supporting churches and interested individuals by this forty-year Methodist missionary in Japan, who taught at Aoyama Gakwin University and was Dean of Chaplains upon retirement.

AS647 Lande, Aasulv

Meiji Protestantism in History and Historiography: A Comparative Study of Japanese and Western Interpretation of Early Protestantism in Japan. (Studies in the Intercultural History of Christianity, 58). Frankfurt am Main, GW: Lang, 1989. v, 177 pp. Paper. 3631406703.

A scholarly analysis of the formation of Protestantism in Japan during the Meiji period, 1872-1905, and its later interpretation, by both Japanese and Western historians.

AS648 Laplante, A., and C. J. Witte, eds.

Working for Christ in Japan: Initiation Guide to Missionary and Pastoral Work in Japan. Tokyo, JA: Oriens Institute for Religious Research, 1969. xvi, 280 pp. No ISBN.

Twenty-five essays by outstanding Sino-Japanese, seeking to provide newly arrived Catholic missionaries with insights into the missionary situation in Japan, and to facilitate their settling-in period and their work in the country.

AS649 Lee, Kun Sam

The Christian Confrontation with Shinto Nationalism: A Historical and Critical Study of the Conflict of Christianity and Shinto in Japan in the Period between the Meiji Restoration and the End of World War II, 1868-1945. (International Library of Philosophy and Theology; Philosophical and Historical Studies). Philadelphia, PAU: Presbyterian & Reformed Publishing, 1966. xi, 270 pp. No ISBN.

Detailed descriptions of old and new manifestations of Shinto are followed by the history of Protestant Christianity in Japan since the first half of the 19th century, focusing on Christian resistance against the mixture of Shinto and nationalism in Japan and Korea.

AS650 Lee, Robert

The Clash of Civilizations: An Intrusive Gospel in Japanese Civilization. (Christian Mission and Modern Culture). Harrisburg, PAU: Trinity Press International, 1999. xv, 128 pp. Paper. 1563383047.

This survey of the historical, political, social, cultural, and religious developments in Japan, from the time of Xavier, who established the Christian church (1549), to the present; includes a critique of the individualism that missionaries brought, and its clash with collectivism in Japanese culture.

AS—ASIA

AS651 Lee, Robert, ed.

The Japanese Emperor System: The Inescapable Missiological Issue. Tokyo, JA: Tokyo Mission Research Institute, 1995. 147 pp. Paper. 4101741058.

Five essays, by Japanese missiologists, on the emperor system as a missiological issue; originally published in Japanese as *Tennosei no kensho*, in 1990, by the Tokyo Mission Research Institute.

AS652 López-Gay, Jesús

El Catecumenado en la Misión del Japón del s. XVI. (Studia Missionalia—Documenta et Opera, 2). Roma, IT: Libreria dell'Università gregoriana, 1966. viii, 252 pp. Paper. No ISBN.

A historical study of conversions, the catechumenate, and baptisms in Japan, to 1597, during the Jesuit Mission.

AS653 López-Gay, Jesús

La Liturgia en la Misión del Japón del Siglo XVI. (Studia Missionalia: Documenta et opera, 4). Rome, IT: Libreria dell Università Gregoriana, 1970. viii, 329 pp. Paper. No ISBN.

A doctoral dissertation analyzing the liturgical developments in the 16th-century Jesuit mission in Japan, including sacraments and music.

AS654 López-Gay, Jesús

El Matrimonio de los Japoneses: Problema, y Soluciones. (Studia Missionalia, Documenta et Opera, 1). Roma, IT: Libreria dell/Università gregoriana, 1964. 185 pp. Paper. No ISBN.

A detailed study of the efforts of Gil Martínez de la Mata (1547-1599), a Jesuit missionary, to develop a Christian approach to marriage in Japan, with original source documents.

AS655 Loucky, John Paul, ed.

Famous Leaders Who Influenced Japan's Internationalization. Kitakyushu, JA: Seinan Women's Junior College, 1994. 334 pp. Paper. 9810054696.

A reader prepared for college use in Japan, containing source documents from 1547 to 1945 concerning contacts between Japanese leaders—many of them Christians—and the West.

AS656 Mensendiek, C. William

A Dream Incarnate: The Beginnings of Miyagi Gakuin for Women. Sendai, JA: Miyagi Gakuin, 1986. v, 135 pp. No ISBN.

A history of the foreign mission schools of Miyagi Gakuin and Tohoku Gukuin in Japan, a dream which began in 1883.

AS657 Mensendiek, C. William

Not without Struggle: The Story of William E. Hoy and the Beginnings of Tohoku Gakuin. Sendai, JA: Tohoku Gakuin, 1986. iv, 235 pp. No ISBN.

The biography of a missionary founder of Tohuku Gakuin, published for the university's centennial celebration.

AS658 Minton, Wilson P.

A Tour of Japan in 1920: An American Missionary's Diary with 129 Photographs. Edited by David W. Carstetter. Jefferson, NCU: McFarland & Co., 1992. xi, 316 pp. 0899505937.

The 1920 diary of Wilson Park Minton (1888-1969), written during his visit to Japan as the newly appointed foreign missions secretary for the Christian Church of America, with photos and index, but no content analysis.

AS659 Miyata, Mitsuo

Mündigkeit und Solidarität: Christliche Verantwortung in der heutigen japanischen Gesellschaft. (Missionswissenschaftliche Forschungen, 17). Gütersloh, GW: Mohn, 1984. 191 pp. Paper. 3579002376.

Written by a Japanese Protestant and authority in political science, this is a description of Japan's society, business, and religion inquires how Shintoism and nationalism can be reconciled with Christianity.

AS660 Mueller, George A.

The Catechetical Problem in Japan, 1549-1965. Tokyo, JA: Oriens Institute for Religious Research, 1967. ix, 230 pp. No ISBN.

A detailed historical study with bibliography of Catholic missionary catechesis in Japan.

AS661 Parker, F. Calvin

The Southern Baptist Mission in Japan, 1889-1989. Lanham, MDU: University Press of America, 1991. xiv, 346 pp. 0819181072 (hdbk), 0819181080 (pbk).

A comprehensive centennial study of Southern Baptist missions in Japan.

AS662 Phillips, James M.

From the Rising of the Sun: Christians and Society in Contemporary Japan. (American Society of Missiology Series, 3). Maryknoll, NYU: Orbis Books, 1981. xii, 307 pp. Paper. 0883441454.

The result of a ten-year study on the history of Christian churches in Japan since 1945, which reveals the successes and struggles of Christianity in its Japanese context.

AS663 Picken, Stuart D. B.

Christianity and Japan: Meeting, Conflict, Hope. Tokyo, JA: Kodansha International, 1983. 80 pp. 0870115898 (US), 4770010893 (JA).

Christian influence in Japan presented through beautiful color illustrations, brief text, and introductory essay by Edwin O. Reischauer, one of the best-known Western authorities on Japan.

AS664 Piryns, Ernest

Japan en het christendom: Naar de overstijging van een dilemma. (Proefschrift Theol. Fac. Katholieke Universiteit Nijmegen). Utrecht, NE: Lannoo, 1971. 2 vols. Paper. No ISBN.

On the basis of an extensive survey of the religious history of Japan and conflicts of Catholic and Protestant missions with the religions of Japan, the author of this doctoral dissertation defends his thesis that this longstanding conflict can only be solved by indigenization of Christianity [vol. 1: 287 pp; vol. 2: 394 pp.].

AS665 Powles, Cyril Hamilton

Victorian Missionaries in Meiji Japan: The Shiba Sect: 1873-1900. (Publications Series, 4/1). Toronto, ONC: University of Toronto-York University, Joint Centre on Modern East Asia, 1987. viii, 162 pp. Paper. 0921309082.

A scholarly analysis of the work of Canadian Church Missionary Society workers in Japan.

AS666 Ruíz de Medina, Juan G., ed.

Documentos del Japón, 1547-1557. (Monumenta Histórica Societatis Iesu, 137). Rome, IT: Instituto Histórico de la Compañía de Jesú, 1990. 791 pp. Paper. 8870411370.

A scholarly edition of 131 documents of Francis Xavier and other Jesuit missionaries.

AS—ASIA

AS667 Ruíz de Medina, Juan G., ed.

Monumenta Historica Japoniae: Documentos del Japón.
(Monumenta historica Societatis Iesu, 111, 137, 148; Monumenta missionum Societatis Iesu, 34, 52, 61). Rome, IT: Instituto Histórico de la Compañía de Jesús, 1975-1995. 3 vols. Paper. 8870411486 (vol. 2).

A multi-volume collection of documents in Spanish, Italian, Latin, and Portuguese, on Jesuit missions in Japan from 1549 to 1654 [vol. 1, *(1549-1654)*, 1975, xxvi, 1,333 pp.; vol. 2, *(1547-1557)*, 1990, 791 pp.; vol. 3, *(1558-1562)*, 1995, 743 pp.].

AS668 Scheiner, Irwin

Christian Converts and Social Protest in Meiji Japan. Berkeley, CAU: University of California Press, 1970. x, 268 pp. 0520015851.

The first major assessment of the impact of Christianity on Japanese thought and history during the Meiji period (1867-1912).

AS669 Schutte, Josef Franz

Introductio ad historiam Societatis Jesu in Japonia, 1549-1650: Ac prooemium ad catalogos Japoniae edendos ad edenda Societatis Jesu monumenta historica Japoniae propylaeum. Rome, IT: Apud Institum Historicum Societatis Jesu, 1968. xliv, 1,039 pp. No ISBN.

The sourcebook of all letters and reports to the Vatican, in Latin and Italian.

AS670 Snider, K. Lavern

Ten More Growing Churches in Japan Today. Osaka, JA: Japan Free Methodist Mission, 1985. ix, 173 pp. Paper. No ISBN.

A popular account of the history of growth in ten churches, from 1958 to 1985, of the Japan Free Methodist Mission.

AS671 Spae, Joseph John

Catholicism in Japan: A Sociological Study. Tokyo, JA: Oriens Institute for Religious Research, 1964. xii, 111 pp. No ISBN.

Second edition of the finest and most concise sociological study of Japan Catholicism in the 1960s.

AS672 Spae, Joseph John

Christian Corridors to Japan. Tokyo, JA: Oriens Institute for Religious Research, 1967. 265 pp. No ISBN.

A series of studies which investigate, from the perspectives of both theology and Japanese culture, the conditions for a fruitful meeting of Christianity with Japan.

AS673 Suggate, Alan

Japanese Christians and Society. (Studies in the Intercultural History of Christianity, 98). Bern, SZ: Lang, 1996. 285 pp. Paper. 3906755843.

A detailed analysis of the struggles of modern Japanese Christians for political, economic, and environmental justice.

AS674 Takenaka, Masao

Reconciliation and Renewal in Japan. New York, NYU: Friendship Press, 1967. 126 pp. No ISBN.

A study book on Protestant responses to the challenges of industrialization, nationalism, and sectarianism in contemporary Japan; an enlarged and revised edition of the original 1957 publication.

AS675 Terazono, Yoshiki, and Heyo E. Hamer, eds.

Brennpunkte in Kirche und Theologie Japans: Beiträge und Dokumente. Neukirchen-Vluyn, GW: Neukirchener Verlag, 1988. xi, 235 pp. Paper. 3788712244.

Articles and other documents, by twenty-one Japanese authors, on important aspects of Japanese life, such as emperor worship, peace and justice, relationship to neighboring countries, and the responsibility of the churches in their mission.

AS676 *The Beginning of Heaven and Earth: The Sacred Book of Japan's Hidden Christians*

Translated by Christal Whelan. Honolulu, HIU: University of Hawaii Press, 1996. xii, 135 pp. 0824818067 (hdbk), 0824818245 (pbk).

An English translation, with commentary, of *Tenchi Hajimari no Koto*, the sacred tale of the Kakure Kirishtan (Hidden Christians) of Japan.

AS677 Trevor, Hugh

Japan's Post-War Protestant Churches. Monrovia, CAU: MARC, 1995. 138 pp. Paper. No ISBN.

Research tracing the development of Japanese Protestant churches since 1945, with a brief history, description of each church, and statistics.

AS678 Uski, Jaakko

Uskontojen Japani. Hämeenlinna, FI: Evankelisluterilainen Lähetysyhdistys Kylväjä, 1979. 176 pp. Paper. 9519920420.

A description of the religious situation in Japan and of the activities of the Finnish Lutheran Mission there.

AS679 *Valignano's Mission Principles for Japan*

Translated by Josef Franz Schutte and John J. Coyne. (Series II—Modern Scholarly Studies about the Jesuits, 3, 5). St. Louis, MOU: Institute of Jesuit Sources, 1980. 1 vol. in 2. 091242236X (hdbk pt 1), 0912422351 (pbk pt 1), 0912422769 (hdbk pt 2), 0912422750 (pbk pt 2).

Two parts of a detailed historical study of the chief organizer of the Jesuit Far East mission, defining principles, methods, and procedures of evangelization: "From His Appointment as Visitor Until His First Departure from Japan (1573-1582)" [part 1: The Problem (1573-1580); part 2: The Solution (1580-1582)].

AS680 Webb, Keith E.

Overcoming Spiritual Barriers in Japan: Identifying Strongholds and Redemptive Gifts. Kearney, NE: Next Church Resources, 1999. 57 pp. Paper. 0966565800.

The author explores the invisible spiritual reality behind the 17th-century persecution of Christians in Japan, and the subsequent spiritual strongholds that continue to be barriers today.

AS681 Yamamori, Tetsunao

Church Growth in Japan: A Study in the Development of Eight Denominations, 1859-1939. South Pasadena, CAU: William Carey Library, 1974. xi, 185 pp. 0878084126.

A comparative study of eight Protestant denominations, concluding that their slow growth was due to their "school" approach; originally presented as a doctoral thesis at Duke University.

AS—ASIA

AS682 Yoshinobu, Kumazawa, and David L. Swain, eds.
Christianity in Japan, 1971-90. Tokyo, JA: Kyo Bun Kwan (The Christian Literature Society of Japan), 1991. xx, 369 pp. Paper. No ISBN.

Twenty-eight essays on ecumenism, Roman Catholicism, and evangelicalism—a major contribution to the understanding of the contemporary church in Japan, and worthy successor to *The Japan Christian Yearbook.*

Japan: Biography

See also AS202 and AS653.

AS683 Aoyama Gen, Paul
Die Missionstätigkeit des heiligen Franz Xaver in Japan aus japanischer Sicht. (Studia Instituti Missiologici SVD, 10). St. Augustin, GW: Steyler Verlag, 1967. xv, 182 pp. Paper. No ISBN.

A dissertation which attempts to supplement, from a Japanese perspective and with Japanese sources, the reports of European missionaries about the work of St. Francis Xavier in Japan.

AS684 Arrupe, Pedro
Als Missionar in Japan. Translated by Maria González-Haba and Kuno Küster. Munich, GW: Hueber, 1967. 275 pp. No ISBN.

German translation.

AS685 Arrupe, Pedro
Este Japon Increíble: Memorias del P. Arrupe. (Colección "Luz de las gentes"). Bilbao, SP: Siglo de las Misiones, 1965. 305 pp. No ISBN.

Third edition of the Jesuit General's recollections of his twenty-seven-year missionary activity in Japan.

AS686 Bikle, George B.
The New Jerusalem: Aspects of Utopianism in the Thought of Kagawa Toyohiko. (Monographs of the Association for Asian Studies, 30). Tucson, AZU: University of Arizona Press, 1976. 343 pp. 0816505500 (hdbk), 0816505314 (pbk).

A presentation of the aspects of utopianism in Kagawa's view of the future and his ideals for human achievement, shown in the personal response of this great Asian Christian to the issues raised by Japanese modernization.

AS687 Cole, Leone
Sentenced to Life. Huntington Beach, CAU: National Design Associates, 1987. 287 pp. Paper. 0961802618.

The biography of Leone and Harold Cole, missionaries of the Churches of Christ to Japan (1946-1986) and founders of Osaka Bible Seminary.

AS688 Diharce, Xavier
Sauveur Candau: apôtre du Japon et de l'amitié universelle (1897-1955). Urt, FR: Éditions Ezkila, 1966. 247 pp. No ISBN.

A biography of one of the most influential modern (1925-1940) Roman Catholic missionaries to Japan.

AS689 Drey, Carl van
Toyohiko Kagawa: Ein Samurai Christi. (ABCTeam, B 405). Stuttgart, GW: Evan Missionsverlag, 1988. 207 pp. Paper. 3767524058.

The story of Kagawa (1888-1960), baptized into the Presbyterian church at the age of sixteen, who decided some years later to live in the slums, where he worked tirelessly as missionary and social reformer.

AS690 Glynn, Paul
A Song for Nagasaki. Grand Rapids, MIU: Eerdmans, 1988. 267 pp. Paper. 0802836704 (hdbk), 0802804764 (pbk).

The moving biography of Takashi Nagai, M.D., pioneer professor of radiology at the University of Nagasaki, who, in his spiritual pilgrimage, journeyed from atheistic rationalism to a lively Christian faith, but who died of radiation sickness in 1951.

AS691 Hendricks, Kenneth C.
Shadow of His Hand: The Reiji Takahashi Story. St. Louis, MOU: Bethany Press, 1967. 202 pp. No ISBN.

The life of a disciple of Kagawa who laboured for the creation of a Christian social work centre in Tokyo.

AS692 Hine, Leland D.
Axling: A Christian Presence in Japan. Valley Forge, PAU: Judson Press, 1969. 205 pp. 0817004165.

A full-length biography of William Axling (1873-1963), eminent missionary of the American Baptist Foreign Mission Society to Japan (1901-1943) and secretary of the National Christian Council.

AS693 Ijiri, Toshiyuki
Paul Rusch: The Story of KEEP: and What a Man with Vision Can Do. Translated by Ben Kobashigawa and Osamu Wakugami. Cincinnati, OHU: Forward Movement, 1991. xii, 283 pp. Paper. 0880281219.

A tribute to Paul Rusch (1879-1979), Episcopalian missionary to Japan (1925-1942), known for his founding of the Kiyosato Educational Experiment Project (KEEP) in Yamanashi prefecture; with details of the post-war development of that project and of Paul Rusch's continued support of Japan and Japanese American ministries.

AS694 Kilson, Marion
Mary Jane Forbes Greene (1845-1910), Mother of the Japan Mission: An Anthropological Portrait. (Studies in Women and Religion, 30). Lewiston, NYU: Edwin Mellen Press, 1991. x, 137 pp. 0773497285.

A portrait and analysis of the missionary contribution of Mary Jane Forbes Greene (1845-1910), founder, with her husband, Cosby, in 1869, of the Japan Mission of the AB-CFM, under which she served in Japan until her death there in 1910.

AS695 Lourenço, J. Machado
Beato João Baptista Machado de Távora: Màrtir do Japão. Angra, PO: União Grafica Angrense, 1965. xv, 310 pp. No ISBN.

First reliable biography of the Portuguese Jesuit missionary to Japan who died during the persecution of Christians in 1617.

AS696 Mensendiek, C. William
A Man for His Times: The Life and Thought of David Bowman Schneder, Missionary to Japan, 1887-1938. Sendai, JA: North Japan University, 1972. ii, 194 pp. No ISBN.

The account of two dedicated mission educators, written to mark the 85th anniversary of the university founded by Schneder—North Japan College.

AS697 Messerschmidt, Lowell

Bauern-Sensei: The Story of Susan Bauernfeind, Pioneer Missionary to Japan. Lima, OHU: Fairway Press, 1991. 158 pp. Paper. 1556733319.

A narrative account of the missionary work of Susan Bauernfeind (1870-1945) who went to Japan in 1900 as the first single woman missionary of the Evangelical church, and served in industrial chaplaincy, education, and care for orphans until 1941.

AS698 Neudorf, Eugene

A Light to All Japan: The Story of Susan Dyck. Camp Hill, PAU: Christian Publications, 1998. xi, 206 pp. Paper. 0875097243.

A popular biography of Susan Dyck (b.1922), a Christian and Mission Alliance missionary to Japan from 1953 to 1983.

AS699 Pacheco, Diego

El Hombre que Forjó a Nagasaki: Vida del P. Cosmé de Torres, S.J. Madrid, SP: Apostolado de la Prensa, 1973. 160 pp. 8421303600.

A biography of Father Cosmede Torres, SJ, who, as a Spanish missionary to Japan, helped to found Nagasaki as a major port in the 16th century.

AS700 Parker, F. Calvin

Jonathan Goble of Japan: Marine, Missionary, Maverick. Lanham, MDU: University Press of America, 1990. xiii, 337 pp. 0819176397.

The first biography of the most colorful and eccentric missionary in 19th-century Japan, who first visited that country in 1853-1854 as a marine in Commodore Matthew Perry's expedition, returning in 1860 as a missionary of the American Baptist Free Mission Society, to serve until 1883 as Bible translator, interpreter, and builder.

AS701 Parker, F. Calvin

Precious Mother, Precious Crown: The Life and Mission of Elizabeth Taylor Watkins. Chapel Hill, NCU: Professional Press, 1997. xiv, 306 pp. Paper. 1570873437.

Biography of a Southern Baptist educational missionary to Japan (1929-1941, 1948-1970), based on her private papers.

AS702 Prang, Margaret

Caroline Macdonald and Prison Work in Japan. (Working Papers Series, 51). Toronto, ONC: University of Toronto-York University Joint Centre of Asia Pacific Studies, 1988. 34 pp. Paper. 0921309791.

An essay assessing the work of the Canadian missionary Caroline Macdonald (1874-1931), the first national secretary of the YWCA in Japan (1904-1915), and social worker among prisoners (1916-1931).

AS703 Rodrigo, Romualdo

Fuentes sobre Misioneros Agustinos Recoletos Martirizados en Japón. (Institutum Historicum Augustinianorum Recollectorum). Roma, IT: Institutum Historicum Augustinianorum Recollectorum, 1985. 323 pp. Paper. No ISBN.

A collection of texts from the first half of the 16th century.

AS704 Rosenstone, Robert A.

Mirror in the Shrine: American Encounters with Meiji Japan. Cambridge, MAU: Harvard University Press, 1988. xiv, 315 pp. Paper. 0674576411.

Daily life of three Americans in Meiji Japan—a scientist, a writer, and a Reformed Church missionary—retold vividly from their diaries of the 1870 to 1917 period.

AS705 Schildgen, Robert

Toyohiko Kagawa: Apostle of Love and Social Justice. Berkeley, CAU: Centenary Books, 1988. xvi, 340 pp. Paper. 0962053708 (hdbk), 0962053716 (pbk).

A detailed biography of Toyohiko Kagawa (1888-1960), outstanding Japanese Christian mystic and social reformer, with special emphasis on the social and historical setting of Kagawa's work, and his successful post-World War II intervention with US occupying forces, to relieve suffering and begin reconstruction.

Korea: General

See also TH27, CR170, CR735, SO185, SO225, AS134, AS192-AS193, AS291, and AS296.

AS706 Chong, Chae-sik

Korea: The Encounter between the Gospel and Neo-Confucian Culture. (Gospel and Cultures Pamphlets, 16). Geneva, SZ: WCC Publications, 1997. ix, 44 pp. Paper. 2825412368.

Presentation of the Gospel as the transformer of Korean animist and Confucianist traditions, by the Muelder Professor of Social Ethics at Boston University School of Theology.

AS707 Chun, Sung-Chun

Schism and Unity in the Protestant Churches of Korea. Seoul, Korea: CLS of Korea, 1979. 307 pp. No ISBN.

The sources of both church divisions and unity examined in this doctoral dissertation focusing mainly on the period from the 1880s to 1945; with an appendix by Glenn S. Fuller, that deals with Chun's urban ministry in the Seoul area, 1970-1971.

AS708 Clark, Allen D.

A History of the Church in Korea. Seoul, KO: CLS of Korea, 1971. 479 pp. No ISBN.

The standard textbook in Korea on Protestant missions and churches, from their founding to 1970.

AS709 Clark, Donald N.

Christianity in Modern Korea. (Asian Agenda Report, 5). Lanham, MDU: University Press of America; New York, NYU: Asia Society, 1986. xiii, 55 pp. 0819153842 (hdbk), 0819153850 (pbk).

A brief history of the development of Christianity in Korea from 1784 to the present, including such 1980s' developments as *minjung* theology, the Dissenting Church, church-state relations, and United States-Korean relations and the church.

AS710 Gardini, Walter

El Cristianismo en Corea: Historia y actualidad. (Coleccion "Mision"). Buenos Aires, AG: Obras Misionales Pontificias, 1984. 195 pp. Paper. 9505000936.

A basic introduction to Christianity in Korea, its history and contemporary situation in both North and South Korea, with special attention to cultural and political factors, and a chapter on Korean Christians in Latin America.

AS711 Grayson, James Huntley

Early Buddhism and Christianity in Korea: A Study in the Emplantation of Religion. Leiden, NE: E. J. Brill, 1985. vii, 164 pp. 9004074821.

A scholarly case study of the religious diffusion of Buddhism, Catholic and Protestant Christianity, to Korea.

AS712 Grayson, James Huntley

Korea: A Religious History. New York, NYU: Oxford University Press, 1989. xii, 319 pp. 0198261861.

The first detailed scholarly survey of the history of religion in Korea from c.600 CE to the present day, with chapters on Protestantism and Catholicism.

AS713 Ham, Sok Hon

Queen of Suffering: A Spiritual History of Korea. London, ENK: Friends, World Committee, 1985. xvii, 187 pp. Paper. No ISBN.

A translation from Korean of a concise history, emphasizing the seminal function of truths of Confucianism, Buddhism, and Christianity in the formation of the Korean national character and response to suffering.

AS714 Hunt, Everett Nichols

Protestant Pioneers in Korea. (American Society of Missiology Series, 1). Maryknoll, NYU: Orbis Books, 1980. xiii, 109 pp. Paper. 0883443961.

A scholarly analysis of the nature of Protestant beginnings in Korea, 1884-1900, and of the first missionaries (their backgrounds, attitudes, early work) in a rapidly changing Korea, by a veteran Korea missionary.

AS715 Huntley, Martha

Caring, Growing, Changing: A History of the Protestant Mission in Korea. New York, NYU: Friendship Press, 1984. 204 pp. Paper. 0377001457.

A timely and dramatic history (1884-1919) that documents the heroism and courage of Korean Christians, as they struggle to live out their faith in the midst of tremendous change and oppression; written in a novel-like form, by a Presbyterian missionary of twenty years in Korea.

AS716 Johnston, Geoffrey, and A. Hamish Ion

Canadian Missionaries and Korea: Two Case Studies in Public Opinion. (Working Papers Series, 52). Toronto, ONC: University of Toronto-York University Joint Centre of Asia Pacific Studies, 1988. 69 pp. Paper. 0921309813.

Two case studies of attitudes toward Korean politics, Japanese rule, and the Korean independence movement during the 1898-1931 period; by missionaries of the Presbyterian church in Canada.

AS717 Kang, Wi Jo

Christ and Caesar in Modern Korea: A History of Christianity and Politics. Albany, NYU: SUNY Press, 1997. viii, 214 pp. Paper. 0791432483.

A clear and concise survey of the events and issues of church-state relations in Korea, from the first Roman Catholic contacts (18th century) to the present politics of reunification.

AS718 Kang, Wi Jo

Religion and Politics in Korea under the Japanese Rule. (Studies in Asian Thought and Religion, 5). Lewiston, NYU: E Mellen Press, 1987. x, 113 pp. 0889460566.

A documented study of major religions and their relationship to politics in Korea from 1910 to 1945.

AS719 Kaspar, Adelhard, and Placidus Berger

Hwan Gab: 60 Jahre Benediktinermission in Korea und in der Mandschurei. (Münsterschwarzacher Studien, 15). Münsterschwarzach, GW: Vier-Türme-Verlag, 1973. xi, 368 pp. Paper. 3878680066.

Various authors, mostly Benedictines of St. Ottilien, paint an historical picture of the work of the Benedictines in Korea.

AS720 Kim, Andreas Jeong-soo

Katechese und Inkulturation: Dargestellt am Beispiel der Geschichte der katholischen Kirche in Korea 1603-1983. (European University Studies, 23. 319). Frankfurt a.M., GW: Lang, 1987. viii, 409 pp. Paper. 3820410171.

Proceeding from the history of the Catholic church in Korea, which the author bases mainly on five catechisms, he works out the relationship of catechesis and inculturation, particularly in the encounter with Confucianism, and formulates perspectives for a future model of Christianity.

AS721 Kim, In Soo

Protestants and the Formation of Modern Korean Nationalism, 1885-1920: A Study of the Contributions of Horace G. Underwood and Sun Chu Kil. (Asian Thought and Culture, 16). New York, NYU: Lang, 1996. viii, 215 pp. 0820425702.

A study of the contributions of Horace G. Underwood and Sun Chu Kil to Korean nationalism; originally submitted as a doctoral dissertation at Union Theological Seminary in Richmond, Virginia.

AS722 Kim, Yung-Jae

Der Protestantismus in Korea und die calvinistische Tradition der Presbyterianischen Kirche in Korea: Eine geschichtliche Untersuchung über Entstehung und Entwicklung. (European University Studies, XXIII, 140). Frankfurt am Main, GW: Lang, 1981. 211 pp. Paper. 382046736X.

A history of Protestantism in Korea, describing its beginnings since 1884; the consolidation of the young churches;the problems during the Japanese occupation; and the period after independence, characterized by rapid growth and internal conflict (Dissertation University of Marburg, Faculty of Protestant Theology, 1980).

AS723 Koshy, Ninan, ed.

Peace and the Reunification of Korea. Geneva, SZ: WCC, CCIA, 1990. 67 pp. Paper. No ISBN.

An update on the story of involvement by churches in Korea and the WCC's Commission of the Churches on International Affairs in processes supporting efforts for peace and the reunification of Korea.

AS724 Lee, Jung Young, ed.

Ancestor Worship and Christianity in Korea. Lewiston, NYU: E Mellen Press, 1988. 94 pp. 0889460590.

Seven essays by Korean scholars and church leaders, giving answers from varied perspectives to the question, "Can a Christian conscientiously participate in the practice of ancestor worship?"

AS725 Moffett, Samuel Hugh

The Christians of Korea. New York, NYU: Friendship Press, 1962. 174 pp. No ISBN.

A popular mission study of events which influenced the growth of Christianity in Korea by a senior Presbyterian missionary there.

AS—ASIA

AS726 Owens, Donald D.
Revival Fires in Korea. Kansas City, MOU: Nazarene Publishing House, 1977. 80 pp. Paper. 0834104555.

A narrative account of early growth of the Nazarene church in Korea.

AS727 Paik, Lak-Geoon George
The History of Protestant Missions in Korea, 1832-1910. (A Series of Reprints of Western Books on Korea, 6). Seoul, KO: Yonsei University Press, 1987. 23, 469 pp. No ISBN.

A reprint and fourth edition of the author's doctoral thesis at Yale University—a scholarly analysis of the cultural impact of early Christian missions in Korea in relation to political and social changes of the period; originally published in 1927.

AS728 Palmer, Spencer J.
Korea and Christianity: The Problem of Identification with Tradition. (Royal Asiatic Society Korea Branch Monograph Series, 2). Seoul, KO: Hollym Corporation, 1967. x, 174 pp. No ISBN.

A comparative study of Christianity and the traditions of China and Korea, seeking to understand why Christianity has gained a greater response in Korea than in China.

AS729 Rhee, Jung Suck
Secularization and Sanctification: A Study of Karl Barth's Doctrine of Sanctification and its Contextual Application to the Korean Church. Amsterdam, NE: VU University Press, 1995. xi, 324 pp. 9053833803.

A scholarly application of Karl Barth's theology of sanctification to the contemporary Korean theological and cultural context, arguing that the Korean church needs to recover the *theologia crucis* if it is to avoid secularization and the allure of a shamanistic gospel of blessing.

AS730 Ruíz de Medina, Juan G.
The Catholic Church in Korea: It's Origins, 1566-1784. Translated by John Bridges. [Seoul, KO: Seoul Computer Press for the Royal Asiatic Society, 1991]. 380 pp. No ISBN.

English translation.

AS731 Ruíz de Medina, Juan G.
Orígenes de la Iglesia Católica Coreana desde 1566 hasta 1784: Según Documentos Inéditos de la Epoca. (Bibliotheca Instituti Historici S.I., 45). Roma, IT: Institutum Historicum Societatis Jesu, 1986. xxiii, 206 pp. Paper. 8870413454.

A scholarly history of the origins of the Catholic Church in Korea, 1566-1784, with a selection of twenty-two previously unpublished documents from the Jesuit archives, 1571-1644, which throw light on the work of Francis Xavier and other early Jesuit missionaries.

AS732 Shearer, Roy E.
Wildfire: Church Growth in Korea. (Church Growth Series). Ann Arbor, MIU: University Microfilms, 1980. 242 pp. Paper. No ISBN.

A study of the religious, social, political, and geographical factors in church growth; originally published by Eerdmans, Grand Rapids, MIU (1966).

AS733 Yoo, Boo-Woong
Korean Pentecostalism: Its History and Theology. (Studies in the Intercultural History of Christianity, 52). Frankfurt am Main, GW: Lang, 1988. 283 pp. Paper. 3820416641.

A scholarly study of the roots, originality, and relation to *minjung* theology of Korean Pentecostalism, differentiating it from the movement both in Europe and the Americas.

Korea: North

See also AS713.

AS734 Yim, Hee-Mo
Unity Lost—Unity to be Regained in Korean Presbyterianism. (European University Studies, 23: Theology, 553). Frankfurt am Main, GW: Lang, 1996. xvii, 249 pp. Paper. 363148738X.

A dissertation (Erlangen University, 1994) on divisions and movements for unity among Presbyterians in Korea, with particular focus on the ecumenical and missiological significance of the eucharist.

Korea: South

See also PO51, PO62, EV298, CH248, SP32, SP260, AS151, AS158, AS190, and AS198.

AS735 Bernard, Elton D.
The Korean Frontier: A Story of Pentecostal Revival. Hazelwood, MOU: Word Aflame Press, 1989. 240 pp. Paper. 0932581439.

A popular account of the founding and growth of the United Pentecostal Church of Korea, 1965-1985, by its pioneer missionary.

AS736 Biernatzki, William E., Luke Jin-chang Im, and Anselm Kyongsuk Min
Korean Catholicism in the 1970's: A Christian Community Comes of Age. Maryknoll, NYU: Orbis Books, 1975. xv, 172 pp. 0883442655.

A sociological study of Korean Catholicism by a team from the Social Research Institute of Sogang University.

AS737 Billings, Peggy et al.
Fire Beneath the Frost: The Struggles of the Korean People and Church. New York, NYU: Friendship Press, 1984. 88 pp. Paper. 037700135X.

An ecumenical mission study text on human rights issues in South Korea.

AS738 Bong-Rin, Ro, and Marlin L. Nelson, eds.
Korean Church Growth Explosion. Taichung, CH: Asia Theological Association; Seoul, KO: Word of Life Press, 1983. 374 pp. Paper. No ISBN.

Twenty-three essays by leading Korean pastors, teachers, and veteran missioners, presenting factors that have contributed to the rapid growth of Protestant churches in Korea.

AS739 Capelleveen, Jan J. van
Minjung: Kerk in de sloppenwijken. Kampen, NE: Kok, 1987. 104 pp. Paper. 902424739X.

After a fact-finding visit to South Korea in 1986, the author describes how, starting from the daily experiences of the exploited industrial laborers in the slums of Seoul and other big cities, pastors, theologians, and the people, themselves *minjung*, responded to the Gospel message.

AS740 Emergency Christian Conference on Korean Problems
Documents on the Struggle for Democracy in Korea. Tokyo, JA: Shinkyo Shuppansha, 1975. xi, 288 pp. Paper. No ISBN.

Seventy-two documents from the 1969-1975 period when Christians led in the struggle to defend democracy and to establish human rights during the oppressive rule of the Park Chung-Hee government in South Korea.

AS741 Han, Gil Soo

Social Sources of Church Growth: Korean Churches in the Homeland and Overseas. Lanham, MDU: University Press of America, 1994. xi, 208 pp. 0819197580.

A scholarly comparative study of social factors affecting church growth in South Korea and among immigrant Koreans in Sydney, Australia.

AS742 Ji, Won Yong

A History of Lutheranism in Korea: A Personal Account. (Concordia Seminary Monograph Series, 1). St. Louis, MOU: Concordia Seminary, 1988. 347, 20 pp. 0911770550.

The first history of Lutheranism in Korea (1958-1987), told as an autobiographical account by one of its first missionary team; with photos and source documents.

AS743 K., T.

Letters from South Korea. Edited by *Sekai*. Translated by David L. Swain. New York, NYU: IDOC-North America; Tokyo, JP: Iwanami Shoten, 1976. xxi, 428 pp. 0890210403.

Anonymous letters by a well-known, informed Christian participant in the human rights struggle under martial law, 1973-1975; originally published in Japanese in *Sekai* [World] magazine.

AS744 Kang, Won Yong

Zwischen Tiger und Schlange: Beiträge aus Korea zu Christentum, Entwicklung und Politik. Edited by Rolf Italiaander. (Erlanger Taschenbücher, 19). Erlangen, GW: Ev.-Luth. Mission, 1975. 144 pp. 387214040X.

A collection of speeches, sermons, and articles presented over a twenty-year span by the Korean author, pastor, and Vice President of the EACC.

AS745 Ogle, George E.

Liberty to the Captives: The Struggle against Oppression in South Korea. Atlanta, GAU: John Knox Press, 1977. 188 pp. Paper. 0804214948.

A personal account by a United Methodist missionary in South Korea (1961-1971) of his entry into human rights advocacy from a background of urban-industrial mission work, focusing on the struggle against the Park dictatorship (1972-1974) that led to his deportation.

AS746 Oosterom, Leo

Contemporary Missionary Thought in the Republic of Korea: Three Case-Studies on the Missionary Thought of Presbyterian Churches in Korea. (IIMO Research Publication, 28). Leiden, NE: IIMO, 1990. viii, 136 pp. 9064952299.

An analysis of the idea of mission in three Korean Presbyterian churches that believe in a messianic role for Korean Christians; based on interviews and English-language publications.

AS747 Park, Chung-Se

A Model of Cross-Cultural Mission in Korea: A Comparative Study of Bible Stories and Korean Legend. San Francisco, CAU: San Francisco Theological Sem., 1990. 192 pp. Paper. No ISBN.

A thesis giving a comparative analysis of Bible stories and Korean legends concerning creation, punishment, sacrifice, a baby messiah, victimization, and resurrection.

AS748 Park, Il-Young

Minjung, Schamanismus und Inkulturation: Schamanistische

Religiosität und christliche Orthopraxis in Korea. Seoul, KO: II-Young Park, 1988. ix, 441 pp. Paper. No ISBN.

This dissertation (Freiburg, Switzerland, 1987) is a comprehensive attempt, by a native Korean Christian, to integrate *minjung* theology within the shamanistic traditional religion of Korea, in terms of "inculturation" rather than "accommodation."

AS749 Seel, David John

Suffer the Children. Franklin, TNU: Providence House, 1996. x, 54 pp. Paper. 157736029X.

The story of the Korean Children's Fund at the "Jesus Hospital" in Chonju, Korea, established by Presbyterians from Bradenton, Florida, to help children with handicapping conditions.

AS750 White, Margaret B., and Herbert D. White, eds.

The Power of People: Community Action in Korea. Tokyo, JA: EACC, Urban Industrial Mission, 1973. vi, 92 pp. No ISBN.

Case studies by trainees of the Institute of Urban Studies and Development, Yonsei University, Seoul, Korea, based on their daily diaries.

Korea: Biography

See also AS179.

AS751 Campbell, Arch

For God's Sake. Philadelphia, PAU: Dorrance, 1970. x, 203 pp. 805914161 (SBN).

Autobiographical reminiscences of a Presbyterian missionary in Korea, 1916-1966, recounted with zest and wit.

AS752 Cho, Wha Soon

Let the Weak Be Strong: A Woman's Struggle for Justice. Bloomington, INU: Meyer-Stone Books, 1988. viii, 168 pp. Paper. 0940989379.

The autobiography of an ordained Methodist minister engaged in urban-industrial mission in South Korea, and the fight for women's global solidarity; with seven reflections by members of the Korean Association of Women Theologians.

AS753 Davies, Daniel M.

The Life and Thought of Henry Gerhard Appenzeller (1858-1902): Missionary to Korea. (Studies in the History of Missions, 1). Lewiston, NYU: E Mellen Press, 1988. xv, 461 pp. 0889460698.

A dissertation on the life and work of the pioneer missionary of the Methodist Episcopal Church (US) to Korea, 1885-1902.

AS754 Kennedy, Nell L.

Dream Your Way to Success: The Story of Dr. Yonggi Cho and Korea. Plainfield, NJU: Logos International, 1980. xiii, 248 pp. Paper. 0882704079.

The authorized biography of Paul Yonggi Cho, pastor of the Full Gospel Central Church in Seoul, Korea.

AS755 Kim, Helen

Grace Sufficient: The Story of Helen Kim by Herself. Edited by J. Manning Potts. Nashville, TNU: Upper Room Books, 1964. x, 199 pp. No ISBN.

The autobiography of Helen Kim and the story of her fight for the emancipation and higher education of Korean women.

AS756 Kim, Jin-Hong
I Will Awake the Dawn. Translated by Myo Sik Park and Heran Yoo. Lima, OHU: Fairway Press, 1991. 177 pp. Paper. 1556733658.

A firsthand account by the founder-pastor of "Robin Hood Church" in a Seoul shanty town.

AS757 Morris, John E.
Father John E. Morris, M.M.: The Second Prefect Apostolic of Peng Yang, Korea and Founder of the Sisters of Our Lady of Perpetual Help. Edited by Jung Soon Lee and Tae Ho Lee. Seoul, KO: Sister of Our Lady of Perpetual Help, 1994. xiv, 564 pp. Paper. No ISBN.

A collection of the writings, correspondence, diaries, reports, and articles by John E. Morris, M.M. (1889-1987).

AS758 Shin, Young Keol
Yawoldo: A Story of Faith and Freedom. Translated by Song Soon Kim. DeBary, FLU: Longwood Communications, 1995. 144 pp. Paper. 1883928168.

A Presbyterian elder born in Manchuria in 1915 recounts persecution under Japanese occupation and his later ministry as an evangelist on the Korean island of Yawoldo.

Mongolia

See also AS292 and AS494.

AS759 Melckebeke, Carlo van
Service social de l'Église en Mongolie. Brussels, BE: Éditions de Scheut, 1969. 140 pp. No ISBN.

An illustrated history of the heroic work of Catholic missionaries in Mongolia from 1865 until 1939.

AS760 Payne, Joseph, and Wilhelmine Payne
I Beheld the Mountains. New York, NYU: Vantage Press, 1969. 142 pp. No ISBN.

Second edition of the story of a missionary couple of the CIM in Mongolia.

AS761 Racheiviltz, Igor de
Papal Envoys to the Great Khans. London, ENK: Faber & Faber; Stanford, CAU: Stanford University Press, 1971. 230 pp. 0571082939 (F), 0804707707 (S).

A narrative history, based on archival sources, of the medieval friars who visited Central Asia as papal envoys and missionaries just before, and soon after, Marco Polo.

AS762 Ruysbroeck, Willem van
The Mission of Friar William of Rubruck: His Journey to the Court of the Great Khan Möngke, 1253-1255. Translated by Peter Jackson. (Hakluyt Society Series 2, 173). London, ENK: Hakluyt Society, 1990. xvi, 312 pp. 0904180298.

A new annotated translation of the Franciscan friar's report of his travels across Mongol Asia and his visit to the Great Khan Möngke, over two decades before the latter's brother Qubilai received Marco Polo.

Taiwan

See also SO645, SP323, and AS575.

AS763 Bolton, Robert J.
Treasure Island: Church Growth among Taiwan's Urban
Minnan Chinese. South Pasadena, CAU: William Carey Library, 1976. xxi, 396 pp. 0878083154.

A chronicle of church growth among the dominant ethnic group on Taiwan, describing their moderate growth, and making suggestions for the future.

AS764 Covell, Ralph R.
Pentecost of the Hills in Taiwan: The Christian Faith among the Original Inhabitants. Pasadena, CAU: Hope Publishing House, 1998. xv, 302 pp. Paper. 0932727905.

The first systematic history of Christian missions among the indigenous hill peoples of Taiwan, by a former Conservative Baptist missionary among them.

AS765 Eberhard, Wolfram
Predigten an die Taiwanesen. (Asian Folklore and Social Life Monographs). Stuttgart, GW: Kommission Evangelischer Missionsverlag; Taipei, CH: Orient Cultural Service, 1972. 168 pp. Paper. No ISBN.

A collection of fifty sermons preached in Taiwan by various Christian preachers and Buddhists, with a content and theological analysis by the author, with his general conclusions.

AS766 Fischer, Brigitte
Neue Dienste in der katholischen Kirche Taiwans. (Supplementa, 42). Immensee, SZ: *NZM*, 1994. 382 pp. Paper. 3858240761.

A history of the Catholic Church in Taiwan, from the 17th century to the present, with a closing focus on a new model of ministry called "volunteer lay-apostle" and the goal of becoming an independent and self-supporting church before the next millenium; originally published as a doctoral dissertation in missiology at the Gregorian University in Rome, Italy.

AS767 Liao, David C. E.
The Unresponsive: Resistant or Neglected?: The Homogeneous Unit Principle Illustrated by the Hakka Chinese in Taiwan. South Pasadena, CAU: William Carey Library, 1972. 168 pp. Paper. 0878087354.

Using the Hakkas of Taiwan as an example, David C. E. Liao focuses on reasons for lack of responsiveness among the two billion persons on six continents who are not attracted to the Christian religion.

AS768 Marttinen, Eero
Sen Jumala teki: muistoja Taiwanista. Vantaa, FI: RV-kirjat, 1989. 208 pp. 9516061486.

An autobiography of Eero Marttinen, a Pentecostal missionary in Taiwan from 1963 to 1973.

AS769 Pagel, Arno
Licht über den Bergen: Bilder aus dem Reich Gottes und der Mission in Taiwan. Marburg a.d.L., GW: Francke-Buchhandlung, 1970. 103 pp. Paper. No ISBN.

A general history of Formosa mission work, with a descriptive report of the various mission sites of "The Marburger Mission" on Formosa, emphasizing the mountain region.

AS770 Pesonen, Mirja
Taiwan Suomen Lähetysseuran työalueena 1956-1986. Helsinki, FI: Kirjaneliö, 1990. 320 pp. Paper. 9516008022.

Taiwan as a field of the Finnish Evangelical Lutheran Mission, 1956-1986.

AS771 Raber, Dorothy A.
Protestantism in Changing Taiwan: A Call to Creative Response. South Pasadena, CAU: William Carey Library, 1978. x, 353 pp. Paper. 0878083294.

An in-depth survey of factors affecting receptivity and church growth patterns in Taiwan, 1964-1974, by an experienced Protestant missionary there.

AS772 Rubinstein, Murray A.
The Protestant Community on Modern Taiwan: Mission, Seminary, and Church. (Taiwan in the Modern World). Armonk, NYU: M. E. Sharpe, 1991. xi, 199 pp. 087332658X.

A sociological and missiological study of the shifts in self-understanding within Protestantism in Taiwan—as mission, cultural bridge, and indigenous church.

AS773 Swanson, Allen J.
The Church in Taiwan, Profile 1980: A Profile of the Past, a Projection of the Future. South Pasadena, CAU: William Carey Library, 1981. xxv, 440 pp. 0878081844.

A study of several Protestant churches in Taiwan from about 1954 until 1979, from the perspective of church growth analysis.

AS774 Swanson, Allen J.
Mending the Nets: Taiwan Church Growth and Loss In the 1980's. South Pasadena, CAU: William Carey Library, 1986. xvi, 267 pp. 0878082077.

An in-depth study in patterns of evangelism, conversion, and church growth in an Asian context; based on field research, with population figures, tables, and questionnaires.

AS775 Swanson, Allen J.
Taiwan: Mainline Versus Independent Church Growth: A Study in Contrasts. South Pasadena, CAU: William Carey Library, 1971. 300 pp. Paper. 0878084045.

Facts concerning both introversion and growth in various churches in Taiwan, demonstrating that churches can be planted that are both ardently Christian and thoroughly Chinese.

AS776 Trefren, Doris
From Headhunters to Hallelujahs. Chattanooga, TNU: AMG Publishers, 1980. 219 pp. 089957047X.

A narrative description of the historical and cultural background of the Ami and Jarako tribes in the mountains of Taiwan, and of lives transformed by Christ.

AS777 Vicedom, Georg F.
Ein Volk findet Gott: Erweckung in Formosa. Bad Salzuflen, GW: MBK-Verlag, 1962. 184 pp. No ISBN.

The story of church growth among the native peoples of Taiwan (Formosa).

AS778 Wilson, Kenneth L.
Angel at Her Shoulder: Lillian Dickson and Her Taiwan Mission. New York, NYU: Harper & Row, 1964. xiv, 256 pp. No ISBN.

A popular account of the medical mission of Lillian Dickson (1901-) to the hill tribes of Taiwan, beginning in 1927, and becoming Mustard Seed Care after 1954.

AS779 Wilson, Kenneth L.
Ein Engel ihr zur Seite: Lillian Dickson und ihr Leben für die Ärmsten von Taiwan. Translated by Eva Guldenstein-Holzer. Basel, SZ: Reinhardt, 1972. 272 pp. No ISBN.

German translation.

AS780 Winslow, Ruth
The Mountains Sing: God's Love Revealed to Taiwan Tribes. Winona Lake, INU: Light & Life Press, 1984. 168 pp. Paper. 0893670944.

A popular account of Free Methodist missions among tribal peoples in Taiwan, concentrating on its 1957-1982 period.

Middle East: General Works

See also HI160, HI169, SO497, SO603, PO155, AS836, and EU266.

AS781 Arberry, A. J., ed.
Religion in the Middle East: Three Religions in Concord and Conflict. London, ENK: Cambridge University Press, 1969. 2 vols. No ISBN.

A collection of scholarly essays on the contemporary situation of various branches of Judaism, Christianity, and Islam in several countries of the Middle East [vol. 1: xii, 595 pp.; vol. 2: 750 pp.].

AS782 Ateek, Naim Stifan, Marc H. Ellis, and Rosemary Radford Ruether, eds.
Faith and the Intifada: Palestinian Christian Voices. Maryknoll, NYU: Orbis Books, 1992. xv, 207 pp. Paper. 0883448084.

Papers from the important First International Symposium on Palestinian Liberation Theology (Tantur, 10-17 March 1990).

AS783 Barnes, Trevor
Terry Waite: Man with a Mission. Grand Rapids, MIU: Eerdmans; London, ENK: Fontana; Oxford, ENK: Isis, 1987. 142 pp. 0802803326 (E), 0006272355 (F), 1850892016 (I).

A popular biography of Terry Waite, international negotiator for freedom in the Middle East.

AS784 Betts, Robert Brenton
Christians in the Arab East. Athens, GR: Lycabettus Press, 1975. xvii, 293 pp. No ISBN.

A comprehensive study of the varying roles Arabic-speaking Christians have played in Islamic society since the Muslim conquests and in the states of the Arab East since independence; written by a lecturer in European and Middle Eastern history in Athens, Greece, since 1969.

AS785 Blincoe, Robert
Ethnic Realities and the Church: Lessons from Kurdistan: A History of Mission Work, 1668-1990. Pasadena, CAU: Presbyterian Center for Mission Studies, 1998. xv, 265 pp. Paper. 0965253325.

A history of Protestant mission work among the Kurds of present Turkey, Iraq, and Iran from the 17th to 20th centuries, with a brief missiology for persons in mission to Kurds today.

AS786 Coakley, J. F.
The Church of the East and the Church of England: A History of the Archbishop of Canterbury's Assyrian Mission. Oxford, ENK: Oxford University Press; Oxford, ENK: Clarendon Press, 1992. x, 422 pp. 0198267444.

A detailed history, based on archival sources, of the Church of England's mission of help, from 1884 to 1915, to the Assyrian Church of the East (popularly known as the Nestorian church) in its then-homeland in eastern Turkey and northwestern Persia (Iran).

AS787 Cragg, Kenneth
The Arab Christian: A History in the Middle East. Louisville, KYU: Westminster John Knox, 1991. ix, 336 pp. 0664219454.

An in-depth study of the identity and history of the people who are both Arab and Christian.

AS788 Douglass, Jane Dempsey, and Páraic Réamonn, eds.
Partnership in God's Mission: In the Middle East. (WARC Studies, 36). Geneva, SZ: WARC, 1998. 72 pp. Paper. 9290750472.

The papers and report of the Consultation on Women and Men of Reformed Tradition in the Middle East (Ayia Napa, Cyprus, 2-8 June 1996).

AS789 Haddad, Robert M.
Syrian Christians in Muslim Society: An Interpretation. Princeton, NJU: Princeton University Press, 1970. viii, 118 pp. 0691030863.

An analysis, based on archival research, of two periods of political change in Syria in the 18th and 19th centuries, when minority Christian communities were able to be politically influential.

AS790 Hefley, James C., and Marti Hefley
Arabs, Christians, & Jews: Whose Side Is God On? Hannibal, MSU: Hannibal Books, 1991. 223 pp. Paper. 0929292200.

A readable introduction to the Middle East conflicts for evangelical Christians, presenting both dispensational and non-dispensational interpretations of biblical prophecy; revised and updated (1st ed., Logos International, 1978).

AS791 Hefley, James C., and Marti Hefley
The Liberated Palestinian: The Anis Shorrosh Story. Wheaton, ILU: Victor Books, 1975. 172 pp. 0882076523.

The popular account of a Palestinian Christian, befriended by Baptists while in exile, who became a worldwide evangelist.

AS792 Heyberger, Bernard
Les Chrétiens du Proche-Orient: Au temps de la Réforme catholique: Syrie, Liban, Palestine, XVII-XVIII siècles. (Bibliothèque des écoles françaises d'Athènes et de Rome). Paris, FR: École française de Rome; Paris, FR: Palais Farnèse, 1994. 665 pp. 2728303096.

A scholarly history of the Eastern rite churches of Syria, Lebanon, and Palestine in the 17th and 18th centuries, and of French Catholic missions among them; with a detailed registry of archival sources.

AS793 Hopwood, Derek
The Russian Presence in Syria and Palestine: Church and Politics in the Near East. Oxford, ENK: Clarendon Press, 1969. 232 pp. No ISBN.

Russian mission involvements in the Middle East (18th-20th centuries) including the Ottoman Empire, missions in Jerusalem, the Imperial Orthodox Palestinian Society (1882-1917), and relations with Orthodox Arab nationalism.

AS794 Horner, Norman A.
A Guide to Christian Churches in the Middle East: Present-day Christianity in the Middle East and North Africa. Elkhart, INU: Mission Focus Publications, 1989. 128 pp. Paper. 1877736007.

A survey of the Christian churches of the Middle East, with an account of their origins and present-day distribution, and a discussion of the churches, in the area's present-day turmoil.

AS795 Horner, Norman A.
Rediscovering Christianity Where It Began: A Survey of Contemporary Churches in the Middle East and Ethiopia. Beirut, LE: Near East Council of Churches, 1974. 110 pp. Paper. No ISBN.

A handbook of churches in the Middle East, with brief histories and statistics; based on the author's extended visits to fourteen countries between 1969 and 1972.

AS796 Irani, George Emile
The Papacy and the Middle East: The Role of the Holy See in the Arab-Israeli Conflict, 1962-1984. Notre Dame, INU: University of Notre Dame Press, 1986. 218 pp. 0268015600.

An analysis of the policies of the Vatican on three major Middle East issues: the Israeli-Palestinian dispute, the status of Jerusalem and the Holy Places, and the Lebanese war.

AS797 Jennings, George James
Hadith: Composite Middle Eastern Village under a Missions Consultant's Gaze. Le Mars, IAU: Middle East Missions Research, 1983. xii, 265 pp. Paper. No ISBN.

A composite picture of village life in the Middle East by a professional missionary anthropologist.

AS798 Jennings, George James
A Missions Consultant Views Middle Eastern Culture and Personality. Le Mars, IAU: Le Mars Daily Sentinel Job, 1983. vii, 103 pp. Paper. No ISBN.

Reflections by a professional anthropologist who identifies with evangelical Christianity and has specialized in psychological anthropology to understand Middle Eastern peoples.

AS799 Joseph, John
Muslim-Christian Relations and Inter-Christian Rivalries in the Middle East: The Case of the Jacobites in an Age of Transition. Albany, NYU: SUNY Press, 1983. xviii, 240 pp. 0873956117 (hdbk), 0873956125 (pbk).

A modern history since the early 1800s of the Syrian Orthodox (Jacobite) and Syrian Catholic (formerly Jacobite) Christians of the Middle East, utilizing them as a case study in Christian-Muslim relations and inter-Christian rivalries in modern times.

AS800 Joseph, John
The Nestorians and Their Muslim Neighbors: A Study of Western Influence on Their Relations. (Princeton Oriental Studies, 20). Princeton, NJU: Princeton University Press; London, ENK: Oxford University Press, 1962. xv, 281 pp. No ISBN.

A detailed study of the adverse effect on Nestorian-Muslim relations in the near East, because of the arrival of Protestant and Roman Catholic missions in the 19th century.

AS801 Kimball, Charles A.
Angle of Vision: Christians and the Middle East. New York, NYU: Friendship Press, 1992. vii, 120 pp. Paper. 0377002402.

A mission study book focusing on the present life and mission of Middle East Christians in situations of conflict; with study guide, *From the Beginning*, by Betty Jane Bailey (60pp., 0377002410).

AS802 King, Michael Christopher
The Palestinians and the Churches. Geneva, SZ: WCC, CICARWS, 1981. 2 vols. Paper. 2825406759.

History of ecumenical work with Palestine refugees from 1948 to 1974; presented in two volumes [vol. 1: *1948-1956*; vol. 2: *Enduring Witness*].

AS—ASIA

AS803 McCurry, Don M., ed.
World Christianity, Volume 1: Middle East. Monrovia, CAU: MARC, 1979. 144 pp. Paper. 0912552271.

Profiles of the status of Christianity in the sixteen countries of the Middle East, with a listing of people groups in which less than 20 percent of the population are practicing Christians.

AS804 Meyer, Karl
Armenien und die Schweiz: Geschichte der schweizerischen Armenierhilfe: Dienst an einem christlichen Volk. Bern, SZ: Blaukreuz Verlag, 1974. 288 pp. No ISBN.

A scholarly history of the Armenian people, with details of Swiss mission relief work from 1894 to 1963; by one who served as a missionary among the Armenians in Lebanon and Syria, from 1927 to 1963.

AS805 Pacini, Andrea, ed.
Christian Communities in the Arab Middle East: The Challenge of the Future. Oxford, ENK: Clarendon Press, 1998. xiii, 365 pp. 0198293887.

Fourteen scholarly essays on Eastern Christian communities in Middle Eastern Arab societies—their decline and their social, political, and economic dynamics in relation to the Muslim majority culture.

AS806 Pfeiffer, Baldur, ed.
The European Seventh-day Adventist Mission in the Middle East, 1879-1939. (European University Studies, 23: Theology, 161). Frankfurt am Main, GW: Lang, 1981. 123 pp. Paper. 3820459189.

A brief history of the development by initiative of missionaries from Europe, 1879-1939, of Seventh-day Adventism in Turkey, Egypt, Mesopotamia, Palestine, and Syria.

AS807 Scudder, Lewis R.
The Arabian Mission's Story: In Search of Abraham's Other Son. (Historical Series of the Reformed Church in America, 30). Grand Rapids, MIU: Eerdmans, 1998. xxvi, 578 pp. Paper. 0802846165.

The history of the Arabian Mission, launched in 1889 and adopted by the Reformed Church of America in 1894, and continuing in mission in the Arab Gulf and southern Iraq until 1973.

AS808 *Turning Over a New Leaf: Protestant Missions and the Orthodox Churches of the Middle East: The Final Report of a Multi-Mission Study Group on Orthodoxy*
London, ENK: Interserve; Lynnwood, WAU: Middle East Media, 1992. xii, 122 pp. Paper. No ISBN.

Second edition of a study project by evangelical Protestant missionaries who served in the Middle East, calling for new patterns of Protestant mission cooperation with Orthodox churches.

AS809 Valognes, Jean-Pierre
Vie et mort des chrétiens d'Orient: Des origines à nos jours. Paris, FR: Fayard, 1994. 972 pp. 2213030642.

A voluminous survey of Christians in the Middle East—their state-by-state history, internal and external relations with other Christians and Muslims, and rituals.

AS810 Wessels, Antonie
Arab and Christian?: Christians in the Middle East. Kampen, NE: Kok Pharos, 1995. 255 pp. Paper. 9039000719.

A scholarly account of the positions and backgrounds of various Christian groups in the Middle East, with an assessment of their future.

AS811 Wessels, Antonie
Arabier en Christen: Christelijke kerken in het Midden-Oosten. Baarn, NE: Ten Have, 1986. 236 pp. Paper. 9025942466.

A survey of Christian churches in the Middle East and the ambivalence of being a Christian in the Arab world.

Afghanistan

See also GW262.

AS812 Laugierde Beaurecueil, Serge de
Prêtres des non-chrétiens. (Parole et mission, 15). Paris, FR: Éditions du Cerf, 1968. 112 pp. No ISBN.

The only Catholic priest in Afghanistan writes of his religious experiences in the capital city of Kabul, where he is a professor.

Bahrain

See also AS853.

AS813 Dalenberg, Cornelia
Sharifa. Grand Rapids, MIU: Eerdmans, 1983. xvi, 233 pp. Paper. 0802819737.

The autobiography and missionary experiences of a Reformed Church in America nurse, who served in Bahrain between 1921 and 1962.

Iran

See also MI196, AS1204, and EU260.

AS814 Dehqani-Tafti, H. B.
The Hard Awakening. New York, NYU: Seabury Press; London, ENK: Triangle SPCK, 1981. ix, 116 pp. 0816404968 (US), 028103104 (UK SBN).

The suffering and persecution occasioned by the Iranian Revolution is concisely narrated, giving an account of the pressures on individuals and the church during that chaotic time, resulting ultimately in the exile and death of the bishop's son.

AS815 Donaldson, Bess Allen
Prairie Girl in Iran and India. Galesburg, ILU: Mother Bickerdyke Collection, 1972. 425 pp. No ISBN.

An autobiographical account of missionary service, 1910 to 1951, first among Armenians in Teheran, and later at the Henry Martyn School of Islamic Studies.

AS816 Lyko, Dieter
Gründung, Wachstum und Leben der evangelischen christlichen Kirchen im Iran. (Ökumenische Studien, 5). Leiden, NE: Brill, 1964. vii, 285 pp. No ISBN.

A sociohistorical investigation of the problems of Christian churches in Iran and their relationship with the Islamic state.

AS817 Miller, William McElwee
My Persian Pilgrimage. South Pasadena, CAU: William Carey Library, 1995. ix, 376 pp. Paper. 0878082433.

Revised edition of the detailed and colorful autobiography of a missionary of the PCUSA to Iran, focusing on his forty-three-year effort (1919-1962) to evangelize Muslims.

AS818 Voorhees, Elizabeth C. Kay

Is Love Lost: Mosaics in the Life of Jane Doolittle "Angel Mother" in a Muslim Land. South Pasadena, CAU: William Carey Library, 1988. xi, 168 pp. Paper. 0878082182.

Vignettes from Jane Doolittle's (b.1899) remarkable fifty-eight year service (1921-1979) in Iran (formerly Persia), under the Board of Foreign Missions of the Presbyterian Church of the United States.

AS819 Waldburger, Andreas

Missionare und Moslems: Die Basler Mission in Persien 1833-1837. Basel, SZ: Basileia Verlag, 1983. 190 pp. Paper. 385555028X.

Drawing on the extensive sources in the archives of the Basel Mission, this scholarly analysis of that society's work in Persia reveals the diversity in the understanding of mission held by the missionaries involved (Dissertation, University of Zurich, 1982).

AS820 Waterfield, Robin E.

Christians in Persia: Assyrians, Armenians, Roman Catholics, and Protestants. New York, NYU: Barnes & Noble, 1973. 192 pp. 006497488X.

A general history of Christianity in present-day Iran, based on secondary sources, including chapters on Roman Catholic and Protestant missionary efforts.

Iraq

See also AS807 and AS856.

AS821 MacDonnell, Joseph F.

Jesuits by the Tigris: Men for Others in Baghdad. Boston, MAU: Jesuit Mission Press, 1994. xvii, 328 pp. Paper. No ISBN.

The thirty-seven-year history of the Jesuit educational mission in Iraq (1932-1969) through two Jesuit schools—Baghdad College and Al-Hikma University.

AS822 Van Ess, Dorothy

Pioneers in the Arab World. (The Historical Series of the Reformed Church in America, 3). Grand Rapids, MIU: Eerdmans, 1974. 188 pp. 0802815855.

The story of Dorothy and John van Ess, missionaries of the Reformed Church in America, who served as educators in the Arabian Mission in Basra in Arabia (present Iraq), from 1909 to 1956.

Israel

See also HI588, CR1189, CR1244, CR1376, CR1401, CR1421, AS790, and AS1173.

AS823 Österbye, Per

The Church in Israel: A Report on the Work and Position of the Christian Churches in Israel, with Special Reference to the Protestant Churches and Communities. Translated by Richard Webb. (Studia Missionalia Upsaliensia, 15). Lund, SW: Gleerup, 1970. 231 pp. Paper. No ISBN.

A report on the work and position of the Christian churches in Israel, with special reference to Protestant churches and communities and their understandings of their mission; originally presented as a thesis for the Licentiate at the University of Aarhus in Denmark.

AS824 Ateek, Naim Stifan

Justice, and Only Justice: A Palestinian Theology of Liberation. Maryknoll, NYU: Orbis Books, 1989. xvi, 229 pp. 0883445409 (hdbk), 088344540X (pbk).

This work, written by a Palestinian Christian clergyman, develops a Palestinian theology of liberation using Jewish theological paradigms to create an atmosphere of solidarity between Jews and Palestinians.

AS825 Bergen, Kathy, David Neuhaus, and Ghassan Rubeiz, eds.

Justice and the Intifada: Palestinians and Israelis Speak Out. New York, NYU: Friendship Press; Geneva, SZ: WCC Publications, 1991. 160 pp. Paper. 0377002372 (US), 2825410284 (SZ).

Twenty-four interviews with Israelis and Palestinians, including religious leaders, on issues of justice raised by the Palestinian protest movement begun in 1987, and the repression of it by the government of Israel.

AS826 Birkland, Carol J.

Unified in Hope: Arabs and Jews Talk about Peace. New York, NYU: Friendship Press, 1987. xiv, 160 pp. Paper. 0377001775.

Nineteen interviews with Jews and Palestinians in Israel exposing a diversity of views on the Arab/Israeli situation by articulate leaders, and a common longing for peace and reconciliation.

AS827 Chacour, Elias

Auch uns gehört das Land: Ein israelischer Palästiner kämpft für Frieden und Gerechtigkeit. Translated by Ursula Schneider. Frankfurt am Main, GW: John Knecht, 1993. 287 pp. 3782006631.

German translation.

AS828 Chacour, Elias, and David Hazard

Blood Brothers. Tarrytown, NYU: Revell; Grand Rapids, MIU: Chosen Books, 1984. x, 224 pp. Paper. 0800790960 (F), 0310608104 (C).

An autobiographical account, by a leading Palestinian Christian, of the struggle between Jews and Palestinians over the same homeland.

AS829 Chacour, Elias, and David Hazard

Frères de sang. Translated by Jérôme Bodin. (Collection "Pour quoi je vis"). Paris, FR: Éditions du Cerf, 1988. 204 pp. 2204024414.

French translation.

AS830 Chacour, Elias, and Mary E. Jensen

Nous sommes tous des fils du pays. Translated by Alain Archidec. Paris, FR: Desclée de Brouwer, 1992. 255 pp. 222003321X.

French translation.

AS831 Chacour, Elias, and Mary E. Jensen

We Belong to the Land: The Story of a Palestinian Israeli Who Lives for Peace and Reconciliation. San Francisco, CAU: HarperSanFrancisco, 1992. vii, 216 pp. 0060613521 (hdbk), 0060614153 (pbk).

A Palestinian parish priest's account of his efforts to work for peace, justice, and reconciliation, in Ibillin, Galilee, Israel, in the midst of escalating and excruciating conflicts.

AS832 Colbi, Saul P.
A History of the Christian Presence in the Holy Land. Lanham, MDU: University Press of America, 1988. xiv, 377 pp. 0819170364.

A history of Christian missions and churches in Israel from 280 A.D. to 1982.

AS833 Dorr, Roberta Kells
Alice. Nashville, TNU: Broadman, 1989. 143 pp. 0805450807.

A vivid first-person account of the life and work of a Baptist woman missionary in the Gaza strip as told through the testimony of a woman who came to know Christ through her ministry.

AS834 Ellis, Marc H.
Beyond Innocence and Redemption: Confronting the Holocaust and Israeli Power: Creating a Moral Future for the Jewish People. San Francisco, CAU: Harper & Row Publishers, 1990. xvi, 214 pp. 0060622156.

As an alternative to the Holocaust theology of militant Zionism, the noted Jewish scholar and social critic provides a radical moral vision of the Jewish people acting in solidarity with justice-seeking Palestinians.

AS835 Emmet, Chad F.
Beyond the Basilica: Christians and Muslims in Nazareth. (University of Chicago Geography Research Paper, 237). Chicago, ILU: University of Chicago Press, 1995. xix, 303 pp. Paper. 0226207110.

A detailed analysis of the patterns of cooperation by Christians and Muslims in Nazareth, while living in segregated quarters in the town.

AS836 Feldtkeller, Andreas
Die "Mutter der Kirchen" im "Haus des Islam": Gegenseitige Wahrnehmung von arabischen Christen und Muslimen im West—und Ostjordanland. (Missionswissenschaftliche Forschungen, Neue Folge, 6). Erlangen, GW: Erlanger Verlag für Mission und Ökumene, 1998. viii, 509 pp. Paper. 3872143360.

This ecumenical and historical study is an account of the development of Palestinian Christianity in a dominant Muslim culture, seeking to understand the character and significance of the ongoing conflicted relationship.

AS837 Frutiger, Uarda
Ärztin im Orient auch wenn's dem Sultan nicht gefällt: Josephina Th. Zürcher (1866-1932). (Neue Folge, Fasc. 1). Basel, SZ: Schwabe, 1987. 164 pp. Paper. 3796508618.

A biography of Josephina Theresia Zürcher, the first woman to practice medicine and psychiatry in the Near East, in Urfa, Aleppo, Marasch, Antioch, Haifa, and Jerusalem between 1897 and 1930, under the Deutscher Hilfsbund fur Christliches Liebeswerk im Orient.

AS838 Gordon, Haim, and Rivca Gordon, eds.
Israel/Palestine: The Quest for Dialogue. Maryknoll, NYU: Orbis Books, 1991. vi, 170 pp. Paper. 0883447312.

Twelve essays by Jewish, Muslim, and Christian leaders in Israel, on dialogue as the best approach to the Israeli-Palestinian conflict.

AS839 Hanselmann, Siegfried
Deutsche evangelische Palästinamission: Handbuch ihrer Motive, Geschichte und Ergebnisse. (Erlanger Taschenbücher, 14). Erlangen, GW: Ev.-Luth. Mission, 1971. 252 pp. Paper. 3872140272.

This work describes the theological foundations and history of the German Protestant missions in Palestine in connection with their various kinds of pastoral ministry.

AS840 Hurnard, Hannah
Thou Shalt Remember: Lessons of a Lifetime. San Francisco, CAU: Harper & Row, 1988. 201 pp. Paper. 0060640944.

A biography of the conversion and positive lessons used by the author to overcome her handicaps and become a missionary in Israel during World War II.

AS841 Kreiger, Barbara, and Shalom Goldman, eds.
Divine Expectations: An American Woman in 19th Century Palestine. Athens, OHU: Ohio University Press, 1999. xvii, 199 pp. 0821412949 (hdbk), 0821412957 (pbk).

An account of Clorinda Minor who was religiously motivated to teach poverty-stricken Jews of Palestine, but who operated in the social realm through her farm, a unique settlement where Christians, Muslims, and Jews labored alongside one another.

AS842 Kreutz, Andrej
Vatican Policy on the Palestinian-Israeli Conflict: The Struggle for the Holy Land. (Contributions in Political Science, 246). New York, NYU: Greenwood, 1990. xii, 196 pp. 0313268290.

A scholarly analysis of the foreign relations of the Vatican, concerning Jewish and Palestinian rights and claims in the 20th century.

AS843 Kunnas, Unto
Kaarlo Syväntö—tienraivaaja. Vantaa, FI: RV-kirjat, 1978. 272 pp. 9516055354.

A biography of Kaarlo Syväntö, a Pentecostal missionary in Israel.

AS844 LeLong, Michel
Guerre ou paix à Jérusalem? Paris, FR: Albin Michel, 1982. 185 pp. 2226016368.

Jerusalem in relation to Christians and Muslims.

AS845 Prince, Lydia, and Derek Prince
Appointment in Jerusalem. Waco, TXU: Word Books, 1979. 189 pp. Paper. 0849941091.

Second edition of a personal odyssey, from a Pentecostal experience of faith in Denmark to Christian witness in Jerusalem; originally published in 1975 (Old Tappan, NJU: Chosen Books).

AS846 Prior, Michael, and William Taylor, eds.
Christians in the Holy Land. London, ENK: World of Islam Festival Trust, 1994. xviii, 235 pp. Paper. 0905035321.

Papers from an ecumenical (Anglican/Roman Catholic/Orthodox) seminar held at Canterbury Lodge, London, in 1993, on the present welfare of Christians in a predominately Muslim and Jewish society.

AS847 Raheb, Mitri
I Am a Palestinian Christian. Translated by Ruth C.L. Gritsch. Minneapolis, MNU: Fortress Press, 1995. xi, 164 pp. Paper. 080062663X.

Lectures by a Palestinian Arab Lutheran pastor from Bethlehem, on being a Palestinian Christian and interpreting the Bible in the Israeli-Palestinian context.

AS—ASIA

AS848 Raheb, Mitri

Ich bin Christ und Palästinenser: Israel, seine Nachbarn und die Bibel. (Gütersloher Taschenbücher, 1307). Gütersloh, GW: Gerd Mohn, 1994. 125 pp. Paper. 3579013076.

In this booklet, a Lutheran pastor at the Nativity Church in Bethlehem addresses tasks and challenges of a contextualized Palestinian theology.

AS849 Ruether, Rosemary Radford, and Marc H. Ellis, eds.

Beyond Occupation: American Jewish, Christian, and Palestinian Voices for Peace. Boston, MAU: Beacon Press, 1990. ix, 319 pp. 0807069000.

A compilation of fourteen essays by American theologians, scholars, and activists of various ethnic, political, and religious backgrounds, exploring different frameworks for peace amidst the Israeli-Palestinian conflict.

AS850 Shafik, Farah

What Shall I Do With My Life? North York, ONC: By the author, Farah Shafik, 1995. xiii, 265 pp. Paper. 0969845006.

Stories of the Nazareth Hospital in Palestine, founded by the Edinburgh Medical Missionary Society in 1866, focusing on the 1969-1988 period in which Dr. Hans Bernath of Switzerland was administrator.

AS851 Ucko, Hans, ed.

The Spiritual Significance of Jerusalem for Jews, Christians, and Muslims: Report on a Colloquium. Geneva, SZ: WCC, 1994. 81 pp. Paper. No ISBN.

Papers and reports from an important Jewish-Christian dialogue sponsored by the Vatican, WCC, and LWF, held in Glion, Switzerland, 2-6 May 1993.

AS852 Wagner, Donald E.

Anxious for Armageddon: A Call to Partnership for Middle Eastern and Western Christians. Scottdale, PAU: Herald Press, 1995. 253 pp. Paper. 0836136519.

Out of his experience as director of Mercy Corps International's Middle East Program, and former Director of the Palestine Human Rights Campaign, the author calls for Christians to understand the pain of Middle East Jews and Palestinians.

Kuwait

AS853 Allison, Mary Bruins

Doctor Mary in Arabia: Memoirs by Mary Bruins Allison, M.D. Edited by Sandra Shaw. Austin, TXU: University of Texas Press, 1994. xxvii, 329 pp. 0292704542 (hdbk), 0292704569 (pbk).

Memoirs of a pioneer woman doctor of the Arabian Mission of the Reformed Church in America, covering her service in Kuwait (1934-1939, 1945-1967), Oman (1968, 1971-1973), and Bahrain (1968-1970).

Lebanon

See also HI504.

AS854 Moosa, Matti

The Maronites in History. Syracuse, NYU: Syracuse University Press, 1986. 391 pp. 0815623658.

A detailed study and analysis of the Uniate Roman Catholics of Lebanon, including Franciscan missions to the Maronite community.

AS855 Weir, Ben, Carol Weir, and Dennis C. Benson

Hostage Bound Hostage Free. Philadelphia, PAU: Westminster Press, 1987. 183 pp. 0664213227.

The first-person account by the moderator of the Presbyterian church, and former missionary to Lebanon, of his sixteen month (1984-1985) imprisonment by Shiite Muslims in Beirut.

Oman

AS856 Boersma, Jeanette, and David DeGroot

Grace in the Gulf: The Autobiography of Jeanette Boersma, Missionary Nurse in Iraq and the Sultanate of Oman. (The Historical Series of the Reformed Church in America, 20). Grand Rapids, MIU: Eerdmans, 1991. xix, 296 pp. Paper. 0802806031.

The autobiography of a missionary nurse of the Reformed Church in America who served in Iraq (1944-1948) and Oman (1948-1986).

Turkey

See also ED42, AS785, and EU73.

AS857 Farnham, Bruce

My Big Father. Waynesboro, GAU: OM Lit; Bromley, ENK: STL Books, 1985. 206 pp. Paper. 0963090828 (US), 0903843897 (UK).

The story of a young Armenian Christian in Turkey who grew in witness to his Muslim neighbors in the 1970s.

AS858 Leavy, Margaret R.

Looking for the Armenians: Eli Smith's Missionary Adventure, 1830-1831. (Part 4 of the Transactions of the Connecticut Academy of Arts and Sciences, 50). New Haven, CTU: Connecticut Academy of Arts and Sciences, 1992. 79 pp. Paper. 1878508075.

A monograph on the journey in 1830-1831, of a missionary of the ABCFM to the Armenian Christians in the Ottoman Turkish Empire; with extended excerpts from his letters and journal.

AS859 Martin, Edwin W.

The Hubbards of Sivas: A Chronicle of Love and Faith. Santa Barbara, CAU: Fithian Press, 1991. 318 pp. Paper. 0931832853.

An illuminating account of twenty-six years (1873-1899) of mission among Armenian Protestants in Sivas, Central Turkey, by American Board missionaries Albert (1841-1899) and Emma Hubbard (1851-1943).

South Asia: General Works

See also HI448, HI538, EA250, CR383, EC254, EV82, and EV321.

AS860 Chase, Barbara H., and Martha L. Man, eds.

Spirit and Struggle in Southern Asia. New York, NYU: Friendship Press, 1986. i, 105 pp. Paper. 0377001570.

A mission study book reflecting the stories of persons from Bangladesh, India, Nepal, Pakistan, and Sri Lanka as they struggle to relate their Christian faith to Asian culture; with a study-action guide entitled "Trust the Spirit, Share the Struggle" by William A. Dudde (52pp., 0377001589).

AS—ASIA

AS861 Costa, Cosme Jose

A Missiological Conflict between Padroado and Propaganda in the East. Goa, India: Pilar Publications, 1997. vi, 111 pp. Paper. No ISBN.

A short assessment of the conflict in Roman Catholic missions in South Africa from 1637 to 1857, between two papally-authorized evangelizing agencies—the Padroado and the Propaganda.

AS862 Devanandan, Paul David

Christian Issues in Southern Asia. New York, NYU: Friendship Press, 1963. 174 pp. Paper. No ISBN.

An excellent introduction, by an outstanding Indian church leader, to Christianity in relation to resurgent religions and social turmoil in Asia.

AS863 Hedlund, Roger E., ed.

World Christianity, Volume 3: South Asia. Monrovia, CAU: MARC, 1980. 320 pp. Paper. 0912552336.

Profiles of Christianity in the seven countries of South Asia, with detailed profiles for each state of India.

AS864 Neill, Stephen Charles

The Story of the Christian Church in India and Pakistan. Grand Rapids, MIU: Eerdmans, 1970. 183 pp. Paper. No ISBN.

A popular history of Christianity in the Indian subcontinent by the noted mission historian.

Bangladesh

AS865 Beurle, Klaus

Über schwankende Brücken: Hoffnungsfunken in Bangladesh. Aachen, GW: Missio Aktuell Verlag, 1990. 246 pp. Paper. 3921626889.

The author, a German Catholic priest, describes experiences from his fifteen-year involvement with the people of Bangladesh, through the "Dipshikha" initiative for the development of villages.

AS866 Goedert, Edmund N.

Holy Cross Priests in the Diocese of Dacca, 1853-1981. (Preliminary Studies in the History of the Congregation of Holy Cross in America, 3). Notre Dame, INU: Province Archives Center, 1983. 62 pp. Paper. No ISBN.

A brief history of 128 years of mission work in Bangladesh by priests of the Congregation of Holy Cross in America.

AS867 Lockerbie, Jeannie

On Duty in Bangladesh. Grand Rapids, MIU: Zondervan, 1973. 191 pp. No ISBN.

Dramatic journaling of experiences for missionaries and nationals during the 1971 war.

AS868 Lockerbie, Jeannie

Write the Vision. South Pasadena, CAU: William Carey Library, 1989. vii, 145 pp. Paper. 0878082220.

The autobiography of a registered nurse who became a missionary nurse and literature specialist in Bangladesh for the Association of Baptists for World Evangelism, 1963-1989.

AS869 McCahill, Bob

Dialogue of Life: A Christian among Allah's Poor. Maryknoll, NYU: Orbis Books, 1996. xiv, 109 pp. Paper. 1570750661.

A Maryknoll priest's testament of twenty years (1975-1995) of witness among the Muslim poor of Bangladesh.

AS870 McNee, Peter

Crucial Issues in Bangladesh: Making Missions More Effective in the Mosaic of Peoples. South Pasadena, CAU: William Carey Library, 1976. xx, 282 pp. 0878083170.

An evangelical's argument that near-neighbor evangelism among homogeneous units can be effective in Bangladesh and result in growth to one million Christians by 1990.

AS871 Walsh, Jay

Against All Odds: A Venture of Faith with the Hill Tribes of Bangladesh. Harrisburg, PAU: ABWE Publishing, 1996. 154 pp. Paper. 1888796006.

Baptist missionaries to Bangladesh (1960-1994) in evangelism, leadership training, and administration, tell their story.

Bhutan

AS872 Solverson, Howard

The Jesuit and the Dragon: The Life of Father William Mackey in the Himalayan Kingdom of Bhutan. Montreal, ONC: Davies Publishing, 1995. 299 pp. Paper. 1895854377.

The life and work of Jesuit Father William Mackey (b.1915) in northeast India (1947-1963) and Bhutan (1963-1993), based on his reminiscences.

India

See also HI132, HI167, HI263, HI472, HI484, HI499, TH308, TH571, EA123, EA251, EA254, ME135, CR78, CR499, CR543, CR835, CR866, CR937, SO111, SO128, SO131, SO366, SO449, SO459, SO590, EC4, EC50, EC95, EC121, EC310, EC355, PO141, PO156, CO14, CO32, CO44, CO154, CO172, ED15, ED33, ED51, ED58, ED91, ED119, ED130, ED140, EV32, EV71, EV144, EV201, EV210, CH364, CH492, CH503, SP9, SP92, SP96, SP112, SP114, SP120-SP121, SP123-SP125, SP188-SP189, SP194-SP195, SP224-SP225, SP235, SP295, SP306-SP307, SP312, AS1, AS4, AS7, AS40, AS78, AS113, AS118, AS248, AS259, AS262, AS264, and AS863.

AS873 Abhishiktananda, Swami

Towards the Renewal of the Indian Church. Cochin, II: K. C. M. Press, 1970. 99 pp. Paper. No ISBN.

An early writing on Christian encounter with Hinduism by the French Benedictine Henri Le Saux, who, from his Saccidananda Ashram, has led in interreligious dialogue.

AS874 Abraham, K. C., and Jeevan Babu, eds.

An Indian Encounter. (Gospel and Cultures). Delhi, II: ISPCK, 1996. vi, 44 pp. Paper. 8172143346.

A response by Indian church leaders as part of the WCC's study of the Gospel and cultures.

AS875 Adinarayan, S. P.

The Hilt and the Sword. Madras, II: CLS, 1986. iv, 225 pp. Paper. No ISBN.

A novel telling the story of a British missionary professor who taught from 1947 to 1977 at a mission college in South India.

AS876 Ali, Muhammad Mohar

The Bengali Reaction to Christian Missionary Activities, 1833-1857. Chittagong, BG: Mehrub Publications, 1965. xii, 243 pp. No ISBN.

A case study of the mid-19th century conflict in Bengal between missionaries seeking converts and social justice, and the Hindu reform movement (Tattvabodhini Sabha, the Brahma Samaj, and the landed aristocracy); based on mission archives and Indian court records.

AS877 Alter, James P. et al.

The Church as Christian Community: Three Studies of North Indian Churches. Edited by Victor E. W. Hayward. (World Studies of Churches in Mission). London, ENK: Lutterworth Press, 1966. viii, 353 pp. No ISBN.

Three detailed studies of the churches in the city of Delhi, the Punjab region, and the Kond Hills, commissioned as part of the WCC's project on "Churches in the Missionary Situation: Studies in Growth and Response."

AS878 Alter, James P.

In the Doab and Rohilkhand: North Indian Christianity, 1815-1915. Delhi, II: ISPCK, 1986. 264 pp. Paper. No ISBN.

A study of the history of the Christian community of North India, in Meerut, Farrukhabad, and Moradabad (now Uttar Pradesh), and how Christianity affected society, nationalism, liberty, equality, and fraternity, with special attention to Anglicans, Presbyterians, and Methodists.

AS879 Amaladass, Anand, and Richard Fox Young

The Indian Christiad: A Concise Anthology of Didactic and Devotional Literature in Early Church Sanskrit. Anand, II: Gujarat Sahitya Prakash, 1995. xviii, 378 pp. No ISBN.

This anthology of 18th- and 19th-century writings in Sanskrit by Indian Christians provides unique source material for a historical study of contextualization of the faith in Indian culture.

AS880 Amaladoss, Michael

A Call to Community: The Caste System and Christian Responsibility. (Series X, Jesuit Theological Forum, Studies, 5). Gujarat, II: Gujarat Sahitya Prakash, 1994. xv, 159 pp. Paper. No ISBN.

Reflections (theological, sociological, and strategic) on the church, the liberation of the Dalits, and the abolition of India's caste system.

AS881 Amalorpavadass, D. S., ed.

Indian Christian Spirituality. Bangalore, II: NBCLC, 1982. 384 pp. Paper. No ISBN.

Proceedings and papers from an important Seminar on Indian Christian Spirituality (Bangalore, India, 20-30 June 1981).

AS882 Amalorpavadass, D. S., ed.

The Indian Church in the Struggle for a New Society. Bangalore, II: NBCLC, 1981. 1,104 pp. No ISBN.

Report and papers from an influential interdisciplinary seminar (Bangalore, 18-24 Oct. 1981) on a theology and ecclesiology for a church engaging the sociopolitical realities of Indian society.

AS883 Amalorpavadass, D. S., ed.

Ministries in the Church in India: Research Seminar and Pastoral Consultation. New Delhi, II: CBCI Centre, 1976. xvi, 775 pp. No ISBN.

The documents from a comprehensive conference on "Ministry and Ministries" (Bangalore, India, June 1976) by the Roman Catholic National Biblical, Catechetical, and Liturgical Centre; with 31 research papers and an analysis of 450 field responses to them.

AS884 Amalorpavadass, D. S.

L'Inde à la recontre du Seigneur. (Christianisme contemporain). Paris, FR: Éditions Spes, 1964. 367 pp. No ISBN.

Surveys the history and position of the Catholic Church in India and methods used for the evangelization of the country, and urges a more active participation in this work by the Indian church and its members.

AS885 Appasamy, A. J.

A. J. Appasamy Speaks to the Indian Church. Madras, II: CLS, 1993. xiv, 184 pp. Paper. No ISBN.

The late bishop of the Church of South India presents a model for spirituality and renewal for mission; originally published in 1935 under the title *Christ in the Indian Church.*

AS886 Aprem, Mar

Indian Christian Directory: A Companion Volume to the Indian Christian Who is Who. Bangalore, II: Bangalore Parish Church of the East, 1984. 264 pp. Paper. No ISBN.

A collection of information about Christian leaders and Christian organizations in India, including aims, activities, and addresses.

AS887 Arles, Siga

Theological Education for the Mission of the Church in India: 1947-1987. (Studies in the Intercultural History of Christianity, 76). Frankfurt am Main, GW: Lang, 1991. xx, 558 pp. Paper. 3631441290.

A study of how theological education helped identify the task of mission and develop ministries in India, 1947-1987, with special reference to the Church of South India.

AS888 Athyal, Abraham P., and Dorothy Yoder Nyce, eds.

Mission Today: Challenges and Concerns. Chennai, II: Gurukul, 1998. viii, 230 pp. Paper. No ISBN.

Fourteen essays, mostly by the faculty of Gurukul Lutheran Theological College in India, on mission theology, spirituality, and methodology in the Indian context.

AS889 Ayrookuzhiel, A. M. Abraham

The Sacred in Popular Hinduism: An Empirical Study in Chirakkal, North Malabar. Madras, II: CLS for CISRS, 1983. x, 198 pp. Paper. No ISBN.

Everyday Hindu beliefs and practices as observed in Kerala.

AS890 Azariah, M.

Mission in Christ's Way in India Today. Madras, II: CLS, 1989. ix, 115 pp. Paper. No ISBN.

A collection of essays by the General Secretary of the Church of South India.

AS891 Azariah, M.

Witnessing in India Today. Madras, II: United Evangelical Lutheran Churches in India, 1983. x, 178 pp. Paper. No ISBN.

Collection of Bible studies and articles on four dimensions of Christian witness (evangelistic, social, political, and global) by the General Secretary of the Church of South India Synod.

AS892 Ballhatchet, Kenneth

Caste, Class and Catholicism in India, 1789-1914. (London Studies on South Asia, 17). Richmond, ENK: Curzon Press, 1998. xxi, 175 pp. 0700710957.

Meticulous research into the varied responses among Roman Catholic missionary orders in India, to issues of caste; by the Emeritus Professor of the History of South Asia at the University of London.

AS893 Banerjee, Brojendra Nath

Religious Conversions in India. New Delhi, II: Harnam Publications, 1982. xi, 384 pp. No ISBN.

Reflections on Christian attitudes toward religious conversions in India, with documents from the 1979-1980 period when 2,598 Harijans and Christians became Muslims in Tamil Nadu state.

AS—ASIA

AS894 Banerjee, Brojendra Nath

Struggle for Justice to Dalit Christians. New Delhi, II: New Age International, 1997. xi, 123 pp. 8122410820.

A narrative history of the people's movement for Dalit Christian rights in India, since independence.

AS895 Barpujari, H. K.

The American Missionaries and North-east India, 1836-1900 A.D.: A Documentary Study. Guwahati, II: Spectrum Publications, 1986. lvii, 322 pp. No ISBN.

A comprehensive study of American Baptist missionaries in northeast India in the 19th century, based on their reports, correspondence, and other archival records.

AS896 Barr, Margaret

A Dream Come True: The Story of Kharang. Edited by Roy W. Smith. London, ENK: Lindsey Press, 1974. viii, 117 pp. No ISBN.

Reminiscences by a beloved Unitarian missionary among the Khasi of Assam, India, 1933 to 1973.

AS897 Bayly, Susan

Saints, Goddesses and Kings: Muslims and Christians in South Indian Society 1700-1900. (Cambridge South Asian Studies, 43). New York, NYU: Cambridge University Press, 1989. xv, 504 pp. 0521372011.

A detailed history, based on archival sources and interviews, of the interaction of Christianity and Islam in ideology, literature, and social custom with the dominant Hinduism of South India.

AS898 Becker, C.

History of the Catholic Missions in Northeast India, 1890-1915. Edited by G. Stadler and Sebastian Karotemprel. Calcutta, II: Firma KLM, 1980. xii, 439 pp. No ISBN.

The first English translation, by G. Stadler and S. Karotemprel, of *Im Stromtal des Brahmaputra* (1923, 1927), a narrative history of the work of German Salvatorian missionaries in Assam (1890-1922), and that of the Salesians of Don Bosco (1922-1927).

AS899 Becker, C., F. Leicht, and Sebastian Karotemprel, eds.

Early History of the Catholic Missions in Northeast India, 1598-1890. Shillong, II: Firma KLM, 1989. xix, 251 pp. No ISBN.

A translation of the complete text of *Im Stromtal des Brahmaputra* (Munich, 1923), the first serious work in English on the early history of the Catholic Church in northeast India, including data on the geography, peoples, and religious practices of the region.

AS900 Behera, Deepak Kumar

Ethnicity and Christianity: Christians Divided by Caste and Tribe in Western Orissa. Delhi, II: ISPCK, 1989. 128 pp. Paper. No ISBN.

A revised version of the author's doctoral dissertation, in which he attempts to identify the acculturative influences of both Hindu and tribal cultures on Christian understandings and practice of inclusiveness or ethnic/caste exclusiveness in the Indian state of Orissa.

AS901 Bergen, Lutz F. M. van

Licht op het leven van religieuzen: Sannyasa-Dipika. (Proefschrift Theol. Fac. Katholieke Universiteit Nijmegen). Nijmegen, NE: Thoban Offset, 1975. 408 pp. Paper. No ISBN.

A descriptive, as well as evaluative, study of experiments of monastic life in India, especially monastic life where Christians and Hindus are living together; based on field research and primary sources.

AS902 Boal, Barbara M.

Fire is Easy: The Tribal Christian and His Traditional Culture. Manila, PH: Christian Instutute for Ethnic Studies in Asia, 1973. viii, 309 pp. Paper. No ISBN.

Anthropological study of the Kui people of Orissa and their Christian faith within the traditional setting.

AS903 Boel, J.

Christian Mission in India: A Sociological Analysis. (Proefschrift Sociale Wetensch. Vrije Universiteit Amsterdam). Amsterdam, NE: Academische Pers, 1975. x, 131 pp. Paper. No ISBN.

An analysis, with four case studies, of the social implications of conversion to Christianity among outcaste or low caste communities in India.

AS904 Borges, Charles J., and Helmut Feldmann, eds.

Goa and Portugal: Their Cultural Links. (XCHR Studies Series, 7). New Delhi, II: Concept Publishing, 1997. 319 pp. 8170226597.

A collection of twenty-one papers presented at the symposium on "Intercultural Relations: Portugal and Goa" (University of Cologne, Germany, 29 May-1 June 1996).

AS905 Borges, Charles J.

The Economics of the Goa Jesuits, 1542-1759: An Explanation of Their Rise and Fall. New Delhi, II: Concept Publishing, 1994. 215 pp. 8170225051.

A social and economic history, by a Jesuit priest, of the Goa Province of the Goan Christian community, from its inception in 1540 to the expulsion of the Jesuits in 1759.

AS906 Boyd, Robin H. S.

A Church History of Gujarat. Madras, II: CLS, 1981. xv, 264 pp. Paper. No ISBN.

An overview of how the Christian churches came to be established in Gujarat state, from the time of the Nestorians to the coming of the Roman Catholics and Protestants, leading to the present Indian churches.

AS907 Brockway, K. N., and Marjorie Sykes

Unfinished Pilgrimage: The Story of Some South Indian Schools. Madras, II: CLS, 1973. vii, 114 pp. No ISBN.

The fifty-year history of two schools founded by Scottish missionaries, with an assessment related to the evolution of Indian educational policies during the period (St. Christopher's Training College Golden Jubilee Volume, 1923-1973).

AS908 Brouwer, Ruth Compton

New Women for God: Canadian Presbyterian Women and India Missions, 1876-1914. (Social History of Canada, 44). Toronto, ONC: University of Toronto Press, 1990. xi, 294 pp. Paper. 0802027180 (hdbk), 0802067506 (pbk).

A detailed exploration of Canadian Presbyterian women in mission in Central India, focusing on the background and motivation of the well-educated, generally small town and rural women, who became career missionaries.

AS909 Brown, Leslie

The Indian Christians of St. Thomas. Madras, II: B. I. Publications, 1990. xii, 327 pp. No ISBN.

A revised study of the history, social life, and religious ceremonies of the Orthodox Syrian Christian community in Kerala, with an overview of present rites and ecclesiastical divisions; originally published in 1956.

AS910 Buntain, Fulton, and Hal Donaldson

One Man's Compassion. Springdale, PAU: Whitaker House, 1989. 249 pp. Paper. 0883682141.

Testimonies of thirteen residents of Calcutta, whose lives were touched by the ministry of Mark Buntain and the Mission of Mercy.

AS911 Caplan, Lionel

Class and Culture in Urban India: Fundamentalism in a Christian Community. Oxford, ENK: Clarendon Press; New York, NYU: Oxford University Press, 1987. ix, 296 pp. 0198234023.

A study of Christian fundamentalism in Madras, South India.

AS912 Caplan, Lionel

Religion and Power: Essays on the Christian Community in Madras. Madras, II: CLS, 1989. ix, 169 pp. Paper. No ISBN.

A collection of essays, originally published between 1980 and 1988, which focus on issues relating to denominationalism, ethnicity, and caste within the Protestant churches and community of Madras, India, noting the effects of fundamentalism on South India, particularly in the cities of Tamil Nadu.

AS913 Catholic Bishops' Conference of India

The Catholic Directory of India. Annual. 1912- . Madras, II: Catholic Supply Society; New Delhi, II: CBCI Centre, 1984. xxxii, 840 pp. No ISBN.

An annual compendium of information about the Roman Catholic Church in India, for each ecclesiastical unit, major organization, institution, order, and personnel; with names and addresses.

AS914 Chandy, K. K.

A Quest for Community and Dynamic Non-Violence. (Indian Christian Thought Series, 19). Delhi, II: ISPCK, 1990. 434 pp. Paper. No ISBN.

An account by an outstanding Mar Thoma clergyman and Christian leader of Kerala of Christian involvement using nonviolent methods in the pre- and post-independence struggles for social justice in India.

AS915 Chatterji, Saral K., and Hunter P. Mabry, eds.

Culture Religion and Society: Essays in Honor of Richard W. Taylor. Delhi, II: ISPCK, 1996. x, 310 pp. Paper. 817214170X.

Seventeen essays mostly by Indian scholars published to honor Richard W. Taylor, on issues of the relation of Christianity to Indian culture.

AS916 Chatterji, Saral K., ed.

Essays in Celebration of the CISRS Silver Jubilee. Madras, II: CLS, 1983. x, 262 pp. Paper. No ISBN.

Essays that raise social, political, and religious concerns about development and modernization, Third World problems, the role of women in India, and interreligious dialogue in Asia; written especially to honor the CISRS in Bangalore, India, on the occasion of its 25th anniversary.

AS917 Chatterji, Saral K., ed.

Society and Culture in North-East India: A Christian Perspective. Delhi, II: ISPCK, 1996. vii, 154 pp. Paper. 8172142447.

Fourteen short essays by scholars concerned that the Christian community in northeast India assert its presence intellectually, without disparaging its cultural identity; originally presented at a CISRS seminar (Shillong, 21-22 February 1992).

AS918 Clarke, Sundar

Let the Indian Church Be Indian. Madras, II: CLS, 1985. vii, 146 pp. Paper. No ISBN.

Practical guidance for indigenization and mission in the Church of South India by the Bishop of Madras.

AS919 Correia-Afonso, John

The Jesuits in India, 1542- 1773: A Short History. (Studies in Indian History and Culture of the Heras Institute, 25). Anand, II: Gujarat Sahitya Prakash, 1997. ix, 284 pp. No ISBN.

A study of Jesuit involvement and contributions in India.

AS920 Correia-Afonso, John, ed.

Letters from the Mughal Court: The First Jesuit Mission to Akbar (1580-1583). St. Louis, MOU: Institute of Jesuit Sources, 1981. xi, 136 pp. 0912422572.

An English translation of the letters to Goa and Europe, 1580-1583, of the first Jesuits at the court of Akbar the Great.

AS921 Creemers, W. H. M., Oswald Dijkstra, and Louis Mascarenhas

Dutch Franciscans and Their Missions. Utrecht, NE: Provincialate Dutch Franciscans, 1995. 2 vols. Paper. 9080269816.

Three narrative illustrated histories of the work of Dutch friars in India, Pakistan, and Japan [vol. I: *India: The Making of a Province*, and *Pakistan: The Story Unfolds....*, xxii, 186 pp.; vol. II: *Japan: Christianity in Search of Roots*, iv, 72 pp.].

AS922 Daniel, J. T. K., and Roger E. Hedlund, eds.

Carey's Obligation and India's Renaissance. Serampore, West Bengal, II: Council of Serampore College, 1993. xiv, 363 pp. No ISBN.

Articles by thirty Indian and international scholars, showing the impact of the Serampore Mission in the culture renewal of 19th-century Bengal, as well as the formation of the Christian church in eastern regions of India.

AS923 Daniel, K. G.

Let the Hills Rejoice: The Conversion of the Hill Arrians of Kerala and Its Effect on Evangelism. Delhi, II: ISPCK, 1998. xiii, 86 pp. Paper. 8172144164.

A Kerala-born missionary reflects on the process of conversion from animism to Christianity, 1848 to 1878, of the Hill Arrian tribe in Kerala, and its relevance as a model for cross-cultural mission today.

AS924 Das, Bhagwan, and James Massey, eds.

Dalit Solidarity. Delhi, II: ISPCK, 1995. xvi, 221 pp. Paper. 8172142498.

Ten papers plus the reports from the first national consultation of the Dalit Solidarity Programme (Nagpur, Dec. 1992), detailing leadership by Christians in the movement.

AS—ASIA

AS925 Das, Somen
Christian Ethics and Indian Ethos. (ISPCK Contextual Education Series, 3). Delhi, II: ISPCK, 1994. 202 pp. Paper. 8172141688.
    Revised and expanded edition of a text on contemporary ethical issues in the social, economic, and political spheres of life, especially in Indian society, as examined from a theological-ethical perspective.

AS926 Das, Somen, ed.
Women in India: Problems and Prospects. Delhi, II: ISPCK, 1989. v, 97 pp. Paper. No ISBN.
    Papers and reports from an interdisciplinary seminar on "Women in India" (Bishop's College, Calcutta, 24-25 January 1989), held to increase understanding of issues related to women in India, the World Decade for Women, and the Ecumenical Decade of the Churches in Solidarity with Women.

AS927 David, M. D.
The YMCA and the Making of Modern India: A Centenary History. New Delhi, II: National Council of YMCAs in India, 1992. xvi, 518 pp. No ISBN.
    A well-researched and documented study of the varied contributions of the YMCA to the development of modern secular India, by the Professor and Head of the Department of History at Wilson College, Bombay, and President of the Church History Association of India.

AS928 D'Costa, Anthony
The Christianisation of the Goa Islands 1510-1567. Bombay, II: Heras Institute St. Xavier's College, 1965. ix, 234 pp. No ISBN.
    A thesis presented at the Gregorian University in Rome—a critical survey by an Indian Jesuit of the history and conversion of the people of Goa.

AS929 Debbarma, Sukhendu
Origin and Growth of Christianity in Tripura: With Special Reference to the New Zealand Baptist Missionary Society, 1938-1988. New Delhi, II: Indus Publishing, 1996. 112 pp. 8173870381.
    A first history of the origin and growth of Christianity in the Tripura state of northeast India during and after the work of the New Zealand Baptist Missionary Society.

AS930 Dena, Lal
Christian Missions and Colonialism: A Study of Missionary Movement in Northeast India with Particular Reference to Manipur and Lushai Hills, 1894-1947. Shillong, II: Vendrame Missiological Institute, 1988. xvi, 131 pp. No ISBN.
    A history of Christian missions in Manipur State; originally submitted as a doctoral thesis at Jawaharlal Nehru University in New Delhi.

AS931 Devadason, E. D.
A Study on Conversion and its Aftermath. (Face to Face Series, 4). Madras, II: CLS, 1982. 66 pp. Paper. No ISBN.
    A brief study by an Indian Christian lawyer on the Harijans (Dalits) and the political, legal, and religious factors affecting the option of their conversion to Christianity.

AS932 Devanandan, Paul David, and Madathilparapil M. Thomas, eds.
Changing Pattern of Family in India. Bangalore, II: CISRS, 1967. x, 288 pp. No ISBN.

Results of a 1959-1960 study project on Indian family life, with a new chapter on mental health aspects; enlarged and revised by Richard W. Taylor.

AS933 Dhasmana, M. M.
The Ramos of Arunachal: A Socio-Cultural Study. New Delhi, II: Concept, 1979. 298 pp. No ISBN.
    An illustrated, empirical study of the customs and beliefs, social institutions, religion, law, and justice of an Arunachal frontier tribe.

AS934 Diehl, Carl Gustav
Arvet från Tranquebar: Kyrka och miljö i södra Indien. Stockholm, SW: Verbum, 1974. 136 pp. No ISBN.
    A historical study of the Evangelical-Lutheran Tamil Church in Tranquebar, South India.

AS935 Diehl, Carl Gustav
Church and Shrine: Intermingling Patterns of Culture in the Life of Some Christian Groups in South India. (Acta Universitatis Upsaliensis. Historia religionum, 2). Uppsala, SW: Hakan Ohlssons Boktryckeri, 1965. 203 pp. No ISBN.
    An anthropological study of intermingling cultural patterns in the life of Christians in South India.

AS936 Dietrich, Gabriele
Religion and People's Organization in East Thanjavur. Madras, II: CLS for CISRS, 1977. xvi, 169 pp. Paper. No ISBN.
    A case study of the role of religion in development, in a district of India's Tamil Nadu state, with detailed comparison of Marxist, Gandhian, and Christian influences in peoples' organization, and of the ambiguity of cultural factors in development.

AS937 Dixon, Grahame
The Blessings Came India-Shaped. Edinburgh, STK: Pentland Press, 2000. xix, 124 pp. Paper. 1858217369.
    This account of the author's two-month visit to India, at the invitation of Rev. David Raju in the area of the Bay of Bengal, describes the work of social and spiritual service in poverty-striken regions and leper colonies.

AS938 Downs, F. S.
Christianity in North East India: Historical Perspectives. Delhi, II: ISPCK, 1983. xi, 309 pp. Paper. No ISBN.
    A study of the Christian movement in Assam, Meghalays, Nagaland, Manipur, Tripura, Mizoram, and Arunachal Pradesh in the 19th and 20th centuries.

AS939 Downs, F. S.
Essays on Christianity in North-East India. Edited by Milton S. Sangma and David R. Syiemlieh. (NEHU History Series, 4). New Delhi, II: Indus Publishing, 1994. 270 pp. 8173870217.
    A collection of fifteen essays by the eminent Professor of History of Christianity at United Theological College in Bangalore, India.

AS940 Downs, F. S.
The Mighty Works of God: A Brief History of the Council of Baptist Churches in North East India, The Mission Period 1836-1950. Gauhati, II: Christian Literature Centre, 1971. vi, 252 pp. No ISBN.
    Studies of the origins of Christianity in northeast India, including numerical growth and emerging structures.

AS941 D'Souza, Daniel Anthony

The Growth and the Activities of the Catholic Church in North India, 1757-1858: A Historical Study. Mangalore, II: Vitus Prabhudas; Mangalore, II: Sharada Press, 1982. xv, 220 pp. No ISBN.

A study of the religious, educational, medical, and social activities of the Catholic Church and how the masses benefitted during the time of theEast India Company.

AS942 Dubois, Abbe J. A.

Letters on the State of Christianity in India in which the Conversion of the Hindoos Is Considered as Impracticableto Which Is Added a Vindication of the Hindoos Male and Female in Answer to a Severe Attack Made upon Both by the Reverend. Edited by Sharda Paul. (Associated Reprint, 9). New Delhi, II: Associated Publishing House, 1977. vii, 122 pp. No ISBN.

Missionary letters from the 1815-1821 period, opposing conversion of the Hindus; republished without notes or commentary.

AS943 Durrany, K. S.

State Measures for the Welfare of Minorities. Delhi, II: ISPCK, 1997. xii, 158 pp. Paper. 8172143575.

An assessment of the impact of the 15 Point Program for the Welfare of Minorities (1983), with special attention to Christian minorities in India.

AS944 Dutta, Abhijit

Christian Missionaries on the Indigo-Question in Bengal, 1855-1861. Calcutta, II: Minerva Associates, 1989. x, 163 pp. 8185195234.

A detailed case study based on archival records, of missionary opposition to exploitations of workers in the indigo plantations of Bengal, in the mid-19th century.

AS945 Emilsen, William W.

Violence and Atonement: The Missionary Experiences of Mohandas Gandhi, Samuel Stokes and Verrier Elwin in India before 1935. (Studies in the Intercultural History of Christianity, 89). Frankfurt am Main, GW: Lang, 1994. xiii, 391 pp. Paper. 3631470401.

A detailed historical study of two missionaries to India— Samuel Evans Stokes, Jr. (1882-1946), and Harry Verrier Holman Elwin (1902-1964), who embraced Mohandas Gandhi's challenge in the 1920s to make atonement for the wrongs of British imperialism.

AS946 Estborn, Sigfrid

The Church among Tamils and Telugus: Reports of Some Aspect Studies. (IMC Study Series on the Churches in India). Lucknow, II: NCCI, 1961. vi, 78 pp. Paper. No ISBN.

A local study of evangelism and conversion, growth in autonomy and independence, and growth in indigenous expression in Lutheran churches and the Church of South India.

AS947 Fürer-Haimendorf, Christoph von, and Elizabeth von Fürer-Haimendorf

The Gonds of Andhra Pradesh: Tradition and Change in an Indian Tribe. (Studies on Modern Asia and Africa, 12). New Delphi, II: Vikas; London, ENK: George Allen & Unwin, 1979. xii, 569 pp. 0706907183 (II), 0043010903 (UK).

Anthropological study of social and cultural life among the largest tribal group in India, as observed in Adilabad District during thirty-eight years.

AS948 Fernandes, Angelo

The Christian Way Today. Anand, II: Gujarat Sahitya Prakash, 1988. xv, 189 pp. Paper. No ISBN.

Collected essays on the Indian church, justice, and peace, by the Roman Catholic Archbishop of Delhi and chairman of the Commission for Development, Justice, and Peace of the Catholic Bishops' Conference of India (CBCI).

AS949 Fernando, Leonard

Christian Faith Meets Other Faiths: Origen's "Contra Celsum" and Its Relevance for India Today. (Contextual Theological Education, 17). Delhi, II: ISPCK and Vidyajyoti Education and Welfare Society, 1998. xvi, 261 pp. Paper. 8172144466.

Founded upon Origen's presentation of Christianity in the context of religious pluralism, this study seeks to bridge the gap between Christianity in its early phase in the Roman Empire and Christianity in the multi-religious nation of India.

AS950 Firth, Cyril Bruce

An Introduction to Indian Church History. (Christian Students Library, 23). Madras, II: CLS, 1983. xi, 304 pp. Paper. No ISBN.

A textbook for Indian theological students, outlining Indian Christian history from the beginning to the present time.

AS951 Forrester, Duncan B.

Caste and Christianty: Attitude and Policies on Caste of Anglo-Saxon Protestant Missions in India. (London Studies on South Asia, 1). London, ENK: Curzon Press; Atlantic Highlands, NJU: Humanities Press, 1979. viii, 227 pp. 070070129X (UK), 0391017853 (US).

A study of the Protestant critique of caste and its impact for behaviour modification, far beyond boundaries of the churches.

AS952 George, K. M.

Church of South India: Life in Union, 1947-1997. Delhi, II: ISPCK/ICSS, 1999. x, 290 pp. Paper. 8172145128.

The author highlights various facets of the life of the Church of South India, from union in 1947 to 1997.

AS953 George, V. C.

The Church in India before and after the Synod of Diamper. Alleppey, II: Prakasam Publications, 1977. xvi, 208 pp. Paper. No ISBN.

Indian church history from the perspective of St. Thomas Christians of Malabar, showing periods of vigor as well as decline prior to the coming of Western missionaries, interpreting the Synod of Diamper (1599) as a setback for Indian Christianity.

AS954 Gibbs, Mildred E.

The Anglican Church in India, 1600-1970. New Delhi, II: ISPCK, 1972. xvi, 437 pp. No ISBN.

History of the activities of the Church of England in India.

AS955 Gladstone, J. W.

Protestant Christianity and People's Movements in Kerala: A Study of Christian Mass Movements in Relation to Neo-Hindu Socio-Religious Movements in Kerala, 1850-1936. (Seminary Publications). Trivandrum, II: Kerala United Theological Seminary, 1984. xii, 479 pp. No ISBN.

An authentic account of struggles for emancipation from social and religious bondage.

AS—ASIA

AS956 Gnanadason, Joy

A Forgotten History: The Story of the Missionary Movement and the Liberation of People in South Travancore. Madras, II: Gurukul, 1994. vii, 182 pp. Paper. No ISBN.

The story of 19th- and 20th-century Protestant missions in the Kanyakumari district of South Travancore, India, and the continuing concern of the Church of South India there, for social liberation of men and women.

AS957 Gohla, Hans-Peter, ed.

Entwicklung für die Armen—Beispiel Indien: Ziele, Strategien und Arbeitsfelder kirchlicher Entwicklungsarbeit. (Entwicklung und Frieden: Dokumente, Berichte, Meinungen, 19). Mainz, GW: Grünewald; Munich, GW: Kaiser, 1986. 238 pp. Paper. 3786712352 (G), 3459016442 (K).

A collection of articles about the basic problems and goals of church development work in India, with descriptions of specific projects throughout the subcontinent.

AS958 Græsholt, Thorkild

Tilbage til Indien. Hellerup, DK: DMS-Forlag, 1979. 176 pp. 8774310828.

The former missionary to India (now bishop in the Danish national church) returns to India and to the Arcot church, grown out of Danish mission in South India.

AS959 Grafe, Hugald, ed.

Evangelische Kirche in Indien: Auskunft und Einblicke. (Erlanger Taschenbücher, 51). Erlangen, GW: Ev.-Luth. Mission, 1981. 427 pp. Paper. 3872141023.

This work depicts the salient features of Indian culture and religion; presents a detailed historical development of the Protestant church particularly in South India; reflects on the understanding of mission in the Protestant church in India; and finally, focuses on its one and only aim: proclamation.

AS960 Gregorios, Paulos

Die Syrischen Kirchen in Indien. Edited by Paul Verghese. (Die Kirchen der Welt, 13). Stuttgart, GW: Evan Verlagswerk, 1974. 222 pp. 3771501563.

Examining the Syrian Orthodox Church in India, from a historical perspective, this volume highlights the conflict of the Thomas Christians with the Portuguese, the church's subsequent inegalitarian difficulties, its liturgical traditions and missionary activities; with an appendix about revisions in the constitutions of the Syro-Malankara church in 1969.

AS961 Hedlund, Roger E. et al., eds.

India Church Growth. (*India Church Growth Quarterly,* 1-5). Madras, II: Church Growth Research Centre, 1984. ix, 319 pp. Paper. No ISBN.

Volumes 1-5 (1979-1983) of *India Church Growth Quarterly* containing eighty-six articles, case studies, reports, and book reviews, from different Christian perspectives, on India's church growth.

AS962 Hedlund, Roger E., and F. Hrangkhuma, eds.

Indigenous Missions of India. Madras, II: Church Growth Research Centre, 1980. x, 184 pp. Paper. No ISBN.

A directory of seventy-five indigenous Indian mission agencies, with seven short articles on their history and cultural contexts.

AS963 Heredia, Rudolf C.

Tribal Education for Community Development: A Study of

Schooling in the Talasari Mission Area. New Delhi, II: Concept Publishing, 1992. 247 pp. 817022425X.

Results of a 1983-1985 comparative study of mission and government schools in the Thane district of Maharashtra, India.

AS964 *History of Christianity in India*

Bangalore, II: Church History Association of India; Erlangen, GW: Ev.-Luth. Mission, 1984-1990. 6 vols. No ISBN.

Definitive scholarship by Indian church historians on the origins and development of the various forms of Christianity in their country [vol. 1: *From the Beginning up to the Middle of the Sixteenth Century* (up to 1542) by A. Mathias Mundadan (1984, xxii, 567 pp.); vol. 2: *From the Middle of the Sixteenth to the End of the Seventeenth Century (1542-1700)* by Joseph Thekkedath (1982, xviii, 529 pp.); vol. 4, pt. 2: *Tamilnadu in the Nineteenth and Twentieth Centuries* by Hugald Grafe (1990, xix, 325 pp., 3872143093 (Ev.-Luth)); vol. 5, pt. 5: *Northeast India in the Nineteenth and Twentieth Centuries* by F. S. Downs].

AS965 Hminga, Chhangte Lal

The Life and Witness of the Churches in Mizoram. Serkawn, II: Baptist Church of Mizoram, Literature Committee, 1987. xxiii, 365 pp. Paper. No ISBN.

A definitive study of the conversion and transformation of the entire Mizo people, the work of Welsh Presbyterian Mission and the British Baptist Mission, the emergence of the Presbyterian church in North Mizoram, the Baptist church, and other churches in their mission outreach; originally a dissertation at the Fuller Theological Seminary, School of World Mission.

AS966 Hoefer, Herbert E., ed.

Debate on Mission. Madras, II: Gurukul, 1979. xix, 470 pp. No ISBN.

A record of one theological institution's attempt to face issues of Christian mission in the Indian context, based on papers from study seminars and training workshops conducted by the Gurukul Lutheran Theological College and Research Institute in 1976 and 1977.

AS967 Hoefer, Herbert E.

Churchless Christianity. Madras, II: APATS College and Research Institute; Madras, II: Gurukul Lutheran Theological College, 1991. xix, 304 pp. Paper. No ISBN.

A report of research among non-baptised believers in Christ, in rural and urban Tamilnadu, India; with practical and theological reflections.

AS968 Hoefer, Herbert E.

Church-State-Society: Issues of Mission in India from the Perspective of Luther's Two-Kingdom Principle. Madras, II: CLS, 1982. 79 pp. Paper. No ISBN.

Lectures on the relevance of the Reformation for the life of the Indian church, focusing on Luther's Two-Kingdom distinction and church-state relations in India.

AS969 Houghton, Graham

The Impoverishment of Dependency: The History of the Protestant Church in Madras, 1870-1920. (Jubilee Year Series, 1). Madras, II: CLS, 1983. x, 277 pp. Paper. No ISBN.

Traces the development of Protestant missions and discusses issues of poverty, caste, dependence, paternalism, and other failures.

AS970 Hrangkhuma, F., and Sebastian C. H. Kim, eds.
The Church in India: Its Mission Tomorrow. (ISPCK Contextual Theological Education Series, 10). Delhi, II: ISPCK; Pune, II: Church Missionary Society, 1996. xiv, 249 pp. Paper. 8172142684.

Fourteen papers, plus recommendations from two consultations in 1994 and 1995, on "The Church in India: Its Mission Tomorrow" sponsored by the Centre for Mission Studies of Union Biblical Seminary in Pune.

AS971 Hrangkhuma, F., ed.
Christianity in India: Search for Liberation and Identity. (Contextual Theological Education, 17). Delhi, II: CMS/ISPCK, 1998. xxii, 337 pp. Paper. 8172144571.

Fourteen case studies of Christianity among people groups of India, mainly Dalits, written by Indian Christian leaders with a concern for a genuine Indian Christian theology and a new paradigm of Christian mission.

AS972 Jacob, Willibald
Trittsteine im Fluss: Aus der indischen Gossner Kirche. (Erlanger Taschenbücher, 103). Erlangen, GW: Ev.-Luth. Mission, 1992. 168 pp. Paper. 3872145037.

This narrative chronicles the life and struggles of the Gossner church and Lutheran mission in India, as experienced by the author since 1983.

AS973 Jayaprakash, L. Joshi
Evaluation of Indigenous Missions in India. Madras, II: Church Growth Research Centre, 1987. vii, 74 pp. Paper. No ISBN.

A report, with statistics, of a survey of eighty-two indigenous mission agencies in India.

AS974 Jayaweera, Neville
Some Reflections on the Theme of Continuity and Change in Indian Culture. New Delhi, II: ISPCK, 1990. 76 pp. Paper. No ISBN.

An attempt to explain the nature of continuity and change in India, and the history of Christian missionary involvement, by one who calls himself a Vedantin Christian.

AS975 Jeyaraj, Daniel
Inkulturation in Tranquebar: Der Beitrag der frühen dänisch-halleschen Mission zum Werden einer indisch-einheimischen Kirche, 1706-1730. (Missionswissenschaftliche Forschungen; Neue Folge, 4). Erlangen, GW: Ev.-Luth. Mission, 1996. xvi, 367 pp. Paper. 3872143344.

A detailed study of the 18th-century Danish-Halle Mission's work at Tranquebar, in South India, under the leadership of Ziegenbelg and Plütschau; originally submitted in 1995 as a dissertation at the University of Halle.

AS976 Kanjamala, Augustine
Religion and Modernization of India: A Case Study of Northern Orissa. (Studia Instituti Missiologici Societatis Verbi Divini, 27). Pune, II: Satprakashan Sanchar Kendra, 1981. St. Augustine, GW: Steyler Verlag, 1981. xiv, 371 pp. No ISBN.

A detailed study of interactions between Christianity, Hinduism, and forces of modernization, showing the impact of Christianity in tribal society.

AS977 Kanjamala, Augustine, ed.
Integral Mission Dynamics: An Interdisciplinary Study of the Catholic Church in India. New Delhi, II: Intercultural Publications, 1996. 656 pp. 8185574154.

An interdisciplinary study of the Catholic Church in India, from 1900 to 1990, covering church history, missionary activities, the place of the laity, and the church and social issues.

AS978 Karokaran, Anto
Evangelization and Diakonia. Bangalore, II: Dharmaram Publications, 1978. 285 pp. Paper. No ISBN.

An in-depth study of the Indian church on the relationships between evangelization and missionary involvement in the socioeconomic uplift of the poor; written by the professor of missiology at Dharmaram College, Bangalore, India.

AS979 Karotemprel, Sebastian
Albizuri among the Lyngäams: A Brief History of the Catholic Mission among the Lyngams of Northeast India. Calcutta, II: Firma KLM, 1986. xiv, 108 pp. No ISBN.

A monograph that touches upon the important aspects of the Lyngäam culture and the history of Catholic missions, amidst the social customs and habits of this Indian area.

AS980 Karotemprel, Sebastian
The Challenges Facing the Religious Life in the Context of the Church and the Society in Asia. Shillong, II: FABC Office of Evangelization, 1994. 48 pp. Paper. No IBSN.

A thoughtful essay on contemporary challenges for those in Catholic religious orders in India.

AS981 Karotemprel, Sebastian
The Impact of Christianity on the Tribes of Northeast India. Shillong, II: Sacred Heart Theological College, 1994. 63 pp. Paper. No ISBN.

An evaluation of Catholic mission strategies in northeast India, by the noted missiologist teaching at Sacred Heart Theological College in Shillong.

AS982 Karotemprel, Sebastian, ed.
The Catholic Church in Northeast India, 1890-1990: (A Multidimensional Study). Calcutta, II: Firma KLM, 1993. xxvii, 576 pp. NO ISBN.

The first and only comprehensive study of the Catholic church in northeast India.

AS983 Karotemprel, Sebastian, ed.
The Tribes of Northeast India. Calcutta, II: Firma KLM, 1984. xi, 435 pp. No ISBN.

A collection of papers presented by scholars at a seminar on "The Tribes of Northeast India" (1980: Shillong, II), devoted to tribal anthropology, culture, and religion of the northeast.

AS984 Kavunkal, Jacob
To Gather Them into One: Evangelization in India Today; A Process of Building Community. Indore, II: Satprakashan Sanchar Kendra, 1985. xviii,226 pp. No ISBN.

A careful discussion of Indian postcolonial missiological issues, including societal divisions, community, social transformation, dialogue, conversion, and baptism.

AS985 Khan, Mumtaz Ali
Mass Conversion of Meenakshipuram: A Sociological Enquiry. Madras, II: CLS, 1983. xii, 169 pp. Paper. No ISBN.

Background, consequences, and conclusions drawn from conversion of Harijans to Islam in Tamil Nadu, South India, during 1981.

AS986 Khiyalie, Vinod K.

Hundred Years of Baring's Mission to Batala: Christian Education and Change in a Punjabi Countryside. Delhi, II: ISPCK, 1980. viii, 100 pp. Paper. No ISBN.

A research project that shows the development of an institution, instrumental in bringing about a change in the habits, customs, lifestyles, and values to the people of Batala town.

AS987 Kochuparampil, Xavier

Evangelization in India: A Theological Analysis of the Missionary Role of the Syro-Malabar Church in the Light of the Vatican II and Post-Conciliar Documents. (OIRSI Publications, 162). Kerala, II: ORISA, 1993. xxvi, 556 pp. No ISBN.

A well-documented study of understandings of mission and interreligious dialogue of the Syro-Malabar (St. Thomas Christians) Church of Kerala, compared with Roman Catholic perspectives; originally presented as a dissertation at the University of Louvain in Belgium.

AS988 Koilpillai, J. Victor, ed.

"For All That Has Been-Thanks!": Life and Commitment of Daisy Gopal Ratnam. Madras, II: CLS, 1987. xviii, 190 pp. Paper. No ISBN.

A felicitation volume of the work of Daisy Gopal Ratnam, General Secretary of the Synod of the Church of South India (1972-1980), and pioneering leader for equal rights and full participation for women in the church; including her speeches, papers, and reflective letters of friends.

AS989 Koilpillai, J. Victor

The SPCK in India, 1710-1985: An Account of the Work of the Society for Promoting Christian Knowledge, London, and the Indian SPCK. Delhi, II: ISPCK, 1985. 80 pp. Paper. No ISBN.

A narrative of the ways in which the SPCK has participated in the spread of knowledge, especially of the Christian faith, in India.

AS990 Kooiman, Dick

Conversion and Social Equality in India: The London Mission Society in South Travancore in the 19th Century. New Delhi, II: Manohar Publications, 1989. xi, 236 pp. 8185054789.

From the archives of the LMS and others, the author depicts how 19th-century British missionaries preached an apolitical version of Christianity to untouchables in India, became socially involved, and founded mission stations as important centers of schooling and economic development.

AS991 Kuriakose, M. K., comp.

History of Christianity in India: Source Materials. (Indian Theological Library). Delhi, II: ISPCK, 1999. xix, 465 pp. Paper. 8172144938.

Second edition of a comprehensive sourcebook for students, including important developments in the modern period; with special emphasis on ecumenical and national materials that reflect the attitude of other faiths toward Christianity; compiled by the Church History Department of the United Theological College, Bangalore, and originally published in 1982.

AS992 Laird, M. A., ed.

Bishop Heber in Northern India: Selections from Heber's Journal. Cambridge, ENK: University Press, 1971. x, 324 pp. 0521078733.

A reprint of the 1828 journal of the pioneer Anglican bishop of Calcutta (1823-1827), whose record of life in North India was judged as the most perceptive contemporary account in its day.

AS993 Laird, M. A.

Missionaries and Education in Bengal, 1793-1837. Oxford, ENK: Clarendon Press, 1972. xiv, 300 pp. 0198215525.

A scholarly analysis of the contributions of Christian missionaries from England and Scotland to education in Bengal, India, in the early 19th century.

AS994 Lapp, John Allen

The Mennonite Church in India, 1897-1962. Scottdale, PAU: Herald Press, 1972. 278 pp. 0836111222.

A thesis providing a detailed documented history.

AS995 Lavan, Spencer

Unitarians and India: A Study in Encounter and Response. Chicago, ILU: Exploration Press, 1991. xiv, 217 pp. 0913552461.

Third edition of a scholarly and detailed history of Unitarianism in India, including not only ecclesiastical development, but also intellectual influence.

AS996 Lawrence, J.

An Ethical Critique of Land Reform with Special Reference to the Kerala Land Reform (Amendment) Act, 1969. Bangalore, II: CISRS; Delhi, II: ISPCK, 1998. ix, 128 pp. Paper. 8172144598.

An ethical critique on agrarian policies and land reforms in India.

AS997 Le Joly, Edward

La Madre Teresa: Lo Hacemos por Jesús. Translated by Joaquin Esteban Perruca. Madrid, SP: Ediciones Palabra, 1987. 285 pp. 8471185067.

Spanish translation.

AS998 Le Joly, Edward

We Do It for Jesus: Mother Teresa and her Missionaries of Charity. Oxford, ENK: Oxford University Press, 1999. 192 pp. Paper. 0195645618.

Second edition of a narrative account of the beginnings, aim, and spirit of the Missionaries of Charity as seen by one who was connected during many years with Mother Teresa's foundation; originally published in 1977 (London, ENK: Darton, Longman & Todd; Calcutta, II: Oxford University Press).

AS999 Leeuwen, J. A. G. Gerwin van

Fully Indian, Authentically Christian: A Study of the First Fifteen Years of the NBCLC (1967-1982), Bangalore-India in the Light of the Theology of its Founder, D.S. Amalorpavadass. (Kerk en Theologie in Context, 4). Kampen, NE: Kok, 1990. xv, 357 pp. Paper. 9024249066.

Doctoral dissertation on the (Catholic) National Biblical Catechetical and Liturgical Centre in Bangalore, India, concentrating on the work of its founder, D. S. Amalorpavadass; by a Catholic priest who was on the staff of the institute.

AS1000 Linder, Lennart, ed.

I andens förliga vind: Evangeliska Fosterlands-Stiftelsens Indienmission 100 år. Stockholm, SW: EFS-förlaget, 1977. 112 pp. 9170803412.

A history of the evangelical Evangeliska Fosterlands-Stiftelsen's missions in India, 1877-1977.

AS1001 Luke, P. Y., and John Braisted Carman

Village Christians and Hindu Culture: Study of a Rural Church in Andhra Pradesh South India. (World Studies of Churches in Mission). London, ENK: Lutterworth Press; New York, NYU: Friendship Press, 1968. xv, 246 pp. Paper. No ISBN.

A sociological study of village churches in the Medak Diocese of the Church of South India, raising key questions about church life in a non-Christian environment.

AS1002 Mahto, S.

Hundred Years of Christian Missions in Chotanagpur since 1845. Ranchi, II: Chotanagpur Christian Publishing House, 1971. 268 pp. Paper. No ISBN.

Establishment of the Gossner Lutheran, and other, missions, their humanitarian role and methods, subsequent tribal response, and social transformation

AS1003 Malagar, P. J.

The Mennonite Church in India. (The Churches in India Series). Nagpur, II: NCCI, 1981. 75 pp. Paper. No ISBN.

The historical background, origins, distinctives, and contributions of the Mennonite church in India.

AS1004 Mangalwadi, Vishal

India: The Grand Experiment. Farnham, ENK: Pippa Rann Books, 1997. xvii, 365 pp. Paper. 0951308955.

A Christian social reformer's social history of modern India with important reflections on missionary influence.

AS1005 Mangalwadi, Vishal

Missionary Conspiracy: Letters to a Postmodern Hindu. Mussoorie, II: Nivedit Good Books, 1996. 488 pp. Paper. 8186701001.

A new interpretation of the 18th- and 19th-century linkages between missions and British colonialism in Bengal.

AS1006 Manickam, Sundararaj

The Social Setting of Christian Conversion in South India: The Impact of the Wesleyan Methodist Missionaries on the Trichy-Tanjore Diocese with Special Reference to the Harijan Communities of the Mass Movement Area, 1820-1947. (Beiträge zur Südasienforschung, 33). Wiesbaden, GW: Franz Steiner Verlag, 1977. viii, 296 pp. 3515026398.

A detailed history of development of the Methodist church in the area of South India of Tiruchirapalli and Thanjavur, with special reference to the mass movement among the Harijans; originally submitted as a doctoral dissertation at the University of Heidelberg.

AS1007 Marak, Krickwin C., and Plamthodathil S. Jacob, eds.

Conversion in a Pluralistic Context: Perspectives and Perceptions. (ISPCK CTE, 20). Delhi, II: CMS/ISPCK, 2000. xviii, 230 pp. Paper. 817214556X.

This collection of seven papers on conversion in modern day India, begins with biblical perspectives and concludes with post-conversion pastoral care.

AS1008 Massey, James

Down Trodden: The Struggle of India's Dalits for Identity, Solidarity and Liberation. (Risk Book Series, 79). Geneva, SZ: WCC Publications, 1997. ix, 82 pp. Paper. 2825412309.

A Dalit Christian uncovers the religious roots of this system of oppression in India, traces its 3,500 year history, and the beginnings of the Dalits' struggle for liberation.

AS1009 Massey, James

Panjab: The Movement of the Spirit. (Gospel and Cultures Pamphlet, 5). Geneva, SZ: WCC Publications, 1996. viii, 34 pp. Paper. 2825411779.

A brief introduction to historical and cultural factors affecting the church in mission in North India.

AS1010 Mathew, A.

Christian Missions, Education and Nationalism: From Dominance to Compromise, 1870-1930. Delhi, II: Anamika Prakashan, 1988. vi, 261 pp. 8185150036.

A scholarly assessment of the Protestant mission strategy in India, of evangelization through education, and the introduction of Western thought and cultural influences for reaching India's intelligensia; based on a doctoral dissertation at Jawaharial Nehru University.

AS1011 Mathew, C. P., and Madathilparapil M. Thomas

The Indian Churches of Saint Thomas. Delphi, II: ISPCK, 1967. vi, 168 pp. Paper. No ISBN.

Traces the Thomas tradition, early Malabar Church, Portuguese period, Jacobite connection, CMS impact, schism, the Mar Thoma Church, and Orthodox and Jacobite factions.

AS1012 Mathew, C. V., and Charles Corwin

Area of Light: The Indian Church and Modernisation. (ISPCK Contextual Theological Education Series, 6). Delhi, II: ISPCK, 1994. viii, 139 pp. Paper. 8172141661.

A revised proposal of ways in which the Indian church can be more relevant to social issues, including a new chapter on "The Church and Hindu Militancy"; originally published in 1990 by Tyrannus Halls of Asia.

AS1013 Mattam, Abraham

The Indian Church of St. Thomas Christians and Her Missionary Enterprises before the Sixteenth Century. (ORISA Publications, 92). Vadavathoor, II: ORISA, 1985. 66 pp. No ISBN.

A pilot study on the missionary activities of the Thomas Christians before the arrival of the Portuguese in India.

AS1014 Mattam, Joseph, and Sebastian C. H. Kim, eds.

Dimensions of Mission in India. (FOIM Series, 3). Bombay, II: St. Pauls, 1996. 216 pp. Paper. 8171092428.

Essays on aspects of mission in India; originally presented at the 3rd annual meeting of the Fellowship of Indian Missiologists (Bangalore, 26-28 August 1994).

AS1015 Mattam, Joseph, and Sebastian C. H. Kim, eds.

Mission Trends Today: Historical and Theological Perspectives. (FOIM Series, 5). Mumbai, II: St. Pauls, 1997. 215 pp. Paper. 8171093132.

Essays on various historical and theological trends in mission in India; originally presented at the 5th annual meeting of the Fellowship of Indian Missiologists (Pune, 16-19 August 1996).

AS1016 Matthews, Desmond S.

The Joyful Kingdom of Raj Anandpur. Maryknoll, NYU: Maryknoll Publications, 1967. viii, 114 pp. No ISBN.

A vivid account of the life of a Roman Catholic missionary among the Adivasi people of the Ranchi district of India in the 1960s.

AS1017 Maw, Martin
Visions of India: Fulfillment Theology, the Aryan Race Theory & the Work of British Protestant Missionaries in Victorian India. (Studies in the Intercultural History of Christianity, 57). Frankfurt am Main, GW: Lang, 1990. xiv, 396 pp. Paper. 3631405448.

A detailed history of missionary attitudes in India in the late 19th and early 20th centuries, and of the extent to which they subscribed, either to the Aryanism of Frederick Max Muller, or to the fulfillment theology of Bishop Brooks Foss Westcott.

AS1018 McGavran, Donald Anderson
The Satnami Story: A Thrilling Drama of Religious Change. South Pasadena, CAU: William Carey Library, 1990. xiii, 177 pp. Paper. 0878082255.

A narrative description of missionary communication of the Gospel in mid-India during the 1950s, together with McGavran's missionary principles.

AS1019 McMahon, Robert J.
To God be the Glory: An Account of the Evangelical Fellowship of India's First Twenty Years, 1951-1971. New Delhi, II: Masihi Sahitya Sanstha/Christian Literature Institute, 1970. x, 76 pp. No ISBN.

A brief history, chronology, and the organization's Statement of Faith.

AS1020 Meersman, Achilles
The Franciscans in Tamilnad. (Neue Zeitschrift für Missionswissenschaft, 12). Schoneck-Beckenried, SZ: Nouvelle revue de science missionaire, 1962. xii, 133 pp. Paper. No ISBN.

The first history of Franciscan missions in South India, from 1550 to 1847.

AS1021 Meinzen, Luther W.
A Church in Mission: Identity and Purpose in India. Vaniyambadi, II: IELC Concordia Press and Training Institute, 1981. xvii, 285 pp. Paper. No ISBN.

After an outline of the social and religious context of mission in India, a career missionary of the Lutheran Church-Missouri Synod analyzes the mission affirmations and forms of ministry in the India Evangelical Lutheran Church.

AS1022 Menachery, George, ed.
The Nazranies. (Indian Church History Classic, 1). Paulinada, II: SARAS, 1998. 605 pp. 8187133058.

A sourcebook on the origins, history, culture, personalities, divisions and unions, spread, difficulties, and achievements of the Nazraney Christians of Kerala, who claim the apostle Thomas as their founder.

AS1023 Menachery, George, ed.
The St. Thomas Christian Encyclopaedia of India. Kerala, II: St. Thomas Christian Encyclopaedia of India, 1973-1982. 2 vols. No ISBN.

The first two volumes of a three-volume encyclopedia of Christianity in India, with major articles on the apostle Thomas, Kerala and Malabar Christianity, the indigenization of Christianity, Christian influences on Hinduism (vol. 1: 1973, 273 pp.), and Roman Catholic ecclesiastical divisions and Protestant churches (vol. 2: 1982, 218 pp.).

AS1024 Millington, Constance M.
An Ecumenical Venture: The History of Nandyal Diocese in Andra Pradesh, 1947-1990. (ATC Publication, 214). Bangalore, II: Asian Trading Corp, 1993. xvi, 283 pp. Paper. 8170861535.

A carefully-researched history of the Nandyal Diocese of the Church of South India in Andhra Pradesh and its Anglican roots; originally submitted as a Ph.D. dissertation at the University of Leeds.

AS1025 Morris, John Hughes
The History of the Welsh Calvinistic Methodists' Foreign Mission, to the End of the Year 1904. (NEHU History Series, 7). New Delhi, II: Indus Publishing, 1996. 336 pp. 8173870497.

A narrative history of the Welsh Presbyterian Mission in the Khasi and Jaintia Hills of Mizoram state, in northeast India.

AS1026 Moses, Y., ed.
Beyond Ourselves: Some New Perspectives for Christian Youth. Delhi, II: ISPCK for the National Council of Churches in India, 1985. 89 pp. No ISBN.

Papers and reports from a consultation of Christian youth leaders (Nagpur, India, 1984), focusing on youth involvements in the struggles for justice.

AS1027 Moses, Y., ed.
Following Jesus Christ In Our Times. Delhi, II: ISPCK, 1985. 88 pp. Paper. No ISBN.

The report of the Leadership Training Programme by the NCCI (Bangalore, India, 27-31 May 1985), that focused on inculcating in Indian Christian youth the means by which to make their faith more relevant and meaningful in their own context.

AS1028 Mundadan, A. Mathias
The Arrival of the Portuguese in India and the Thomas Christians under Mar Jacob, 1498-1552. (Dharmaram College Studies, 2). Bangalore, II: Dharmaram College, 1967. xxiii, 163 pp. No ISBN.

A detailed history of the first fifty-four years of contacts by St. Thomas Christians with the Portuguese; presented as a doctoral thesis at the Gregorian University of Rome.

AS1029 Mundadan, A. Mathias
Indian Christians: Search for Identity and Struggle for Autonomy. (Placid Lecture Series, no. 4). Bangalore, II: Dharmaram Publications, 1984. ix, 224 pp. Paper. No ISBN.

Nine lectures on the selfhood of the Indian churches, with a concentration on the six ancient churches preceding the modern missionary movement.

AS1030 Mundadan, A. Mathias
Sixteenth Century Traditions of St. Thomas Christians. (Dharmaram College Studies, 5). Bangalore, II: Dharmaram College, 1970. xxiv, 190 pp. No ISBN.

A critical analysis of the St. Thomas traditions in India, including his tomb in Mylapore near Madras, and the history of the Christians of St. Thomas, up to the arrival of the first Latin missionaries in the Middle Ages.

AS1031 Nørgaard, Anders
Mission und Obrigkeit: Die Dänisch-hallische Mission in Tranquebar, 1706-1845. Translated by Eberhard Harbsmeier. (Missionswissenschaftliche Forschungen, 22). Gütersloh, GW: Gerd Mohn; Gütersloh, GW: Gütesloher Verlagshaus, 1988. 312 pp. Paper. 3579002422.

This presentation of the history of the Danish-Halle Mission, that is, the Lutheran Mission (1706-1825) at Tranquebar, on the east coast of India, is a study of the ways European trade and missionary activity influenced each other; with a summary in Danish.

AS1032 National Council of Churches in India

Experiments in Christian Unity. Delhi, II: ISPCK, 1983. 56 pp. Paper. No ISBN.

A study book on contemporary ecumenism with special reference to the Indian ecumenical reality.

AS1033 Neill, Stephen Charles

A History of Christianity in India. Cambridge, ENK: Cambridge University Press, 1985. 2 vols. 0521243513 (vol. 1), 0521303761 (vol. 2).

A scholarly history of Christianity in India by the noted missionary and mission historian; in two volumes [vol. 1: *The Beginnings to AD 1707* (1984, xxi, 583 pp.); vol. 2: *1707-1858* (1985, xvii, 578 pp.)].

AS1034 Nelson, Amirtharaj

A New Day in Madras: A Study of Protestant Churches in Madras. South Pasadena, CAU: William Carey Library, 1975. xxvi, 340 pp. Paper. 0878084207.

Research into sociological and other factors influencing church growth and non-growth including urban evangelistic strategies; originally submitted as a doctoral dissertation (Fuller Theological Seminary, 1974).

AS1035 Nicholls, Bruce J., and Christopher S. Raj, eds.

Mission as Witness and Justice: An India Perspective. New Delhi, II: TRACI, 1991. 246 pp. No ISBN.

A varied collection of articles on the Bible and mission, cross-cultural evangelism, and justice in the biblical and Indian context; originally published from 1975 to 1985, in TRACI, the Journal of the Theological Research and Communication Institute in New Delhi.

AS1036 Nixon, E. Anna

A Century of Planting: A History of the American Friends Mission in India. Canton, OHU: Friends Foreign Missionary Soc, 1985. xviii, 493 pp. Paper. 0913342548 (P), 0913342548 (C).

A history of the Friends' mission and church in Bundelkhand (Madha Pradesh) from 1896 to 1984, emphasizing the pioneering ministry of women missionaries of the Evangelical Friends Church—Eastern Region.

AS1037 Oddie, Geoffrey A.

Social Protest in India: British Protestant Missionaries and Social Reforms, 1850-1900. New Delhi, II: Manohar, 1979. vi, 283 pp. Paper. No ISBN.

Scholarly study, from original source materials, of reform movements and issues such as caste, early marriage, oppression, land reform, opium, and the impact of the missions; originally published by South Asia Books (Columbia, MOU, 1978).

AS1038 Orr, J. Edwin

Evangelical Awakenings in Southern Asia. Minneapolis, MNU: Bethany Fellowship, 1975. x, 240 pp. 0871231271.

Revised edition of details of evangelical revivals in India, from 1860 to the present; an expansion of *Evangelical Awakenings in India* (1970).

AS1039 Padinjarekuttu, Isaac

The Missionary Movement of the 19th and 20th Centuries and Its Encounter with India: A Historico-Theological Investigation with Three Case Studies. (European University Studies 23: Theology, 527). Frankfurt am Main, GW: Lang, 1995. xiii, 305 pp. Paper. 3631474156.

A doctoral dissertation surveying various theologies of mission in relation to culture brought by Roman Catholic missionaries to India; those of Alfons Väth, Josef Schmidlin, and Thomas Ohm given extensive analysis.

AS1040 Patel, Hutokhshi, and Nafisa Goga D'Souza

A Review of "PROUD": A People's Organisation in Dharavi. Delhi, II: ISPCK, 1987. 55 pp. Paper. No ISBN.

A sociological study and assessment of the People's Responsible Organisation of United Dharavi in Bombay, India, in which a team from the CISRS trained leaders of Asia's largest slum, in community organizing, and struggling for basic human rights.

AS1041 Pathak, Sushil Madhava

American Missionaries and Hinduism: A Study of Their Contacts from 1813 to 1910. Delhi, II: Munshiram Manoharlal, 1967. xvi, 283 pp. No ISBN.

An analytical study of the role played by American Protestant missionaries in evangelism, education, medicine, and social reform; in India, in Hindu-Christian relations, and in interpreting India to the West.

AS1042 Paul, Thomas, ed.

Justice and Development in the Indian Context. (Pontifical Institute Publications, 27). Kerala, II: Pontifical Institute, 1976. 115 pp. Paper. No ISBN.

Eleven lectures by Indian scholars, mostly Roman Catholic, on the challenge to achieve justice and genuine positive development for the Indian people.

AS1043 Penner, Peter

Russians, North Americans and Telugus: The Mennonite Brethren Mission in India, 1885-1975. (Perspectives on Mennonite Life and Thought, 10). Winnipeg, MBC: Kindred Productions; Hillsboro, KSU: Kindred Productions, 1997. xi, 413 pp. Paper. 0921788401.

A history based on archival research, of mission to the Telegu-speaking peoples of India by Mennonite Brethren missionaries, first from Russia, and later from North America.

AS1044 Perumalil, H. C., and E. R. Hambye, eds.

Christianity in India: A History in Ecumenical Perspective. Alleppey, II: Prakasam Publications, 1972. 355 pp. Paper. No ISBN.

Twelve chapters by various contributors on early, Roman Catholic, Orthodox, Anglican, and Protestant Christianity, up to 1970.

AS1045 Perumthottam, Joseph

A Period of Decline of the Mar Thoma Christians (1712-1752). Kerala, II: ORISA, 1994. xvi, 307 pp. 8186063270.

A detailed study of how Portuguese colonialism, political intrigue, and insistence on Latinization of the church weakened the Mar Thoma church in the early 18th century.

AS1046 Philip, Puthuvail Thomas

The Growth of Baptist Churches in Nagaland. Gauhati, II: Christian Literature Centre, 1983. ix, 228 pp. No ISBN.

Second edition of a study of the progress of Christianity among the tribes of Nagaland; originally published in 1976.

AS1047 Pickett, Jarrell Waskom et al.

Church Growth and Group Conversion. South Pasadena, CAU: William Carey Library, 1973. xii, 116 pp. 0878071255.

Fifth edition of a collection of early writings on church growth by group conversion in contrast to the institutional mission compound approach; originally published in 1935 (Lucknow, II: Lucknow Publishing House).

AS—ASIA

AS1048 Pickett, Jarrell Waskom

Christian Mass Movements in India: A Study with Recommendations. (National Christian Council of India). Lucknow, II: Lucknow Publishing House, 1969. 370 pp. No ISBN.

The now-classic analysis of the impact and integrity of mass movements on the church in India; reprint of the second edition, originally published in 1933 (Lucknow: Lucknow Publishing House; and New York: Abingdon Press).

AS1049 Plattner, Felix Alfred

The Catholic Church in India: Yesterday and Today. Allahabad, II: St. Paul Publications, 1964. v, 158 pp. Paper. No ISBN.

English translation.

AS1050 Plattner, Felix Alfred

Die Kirche unter den Völkern: Indien. (Die Kirche unter den Völkern, 2). Mainz, GW: Grünewald, 1963. 238 pp. No ISBN.

This Jesuit scholar discusses the course Catholic mission activity had taken prior to Indian independence (1947), and sketches the task of building the "local church."

AS1051 Pothen, K. P.

A Socio-Economic Survey of the Christian Community in Malwa. (CISRS Social Research Series, 12). Madras, II: CLS for CISRS, 1975. ix, 244 pp. Paper. No ISBN.

Origins and growth of the church in Malwa Pradesh (central India), from the beginning in 1976, of the Canadian Presbyterian and subsequent United Church of Canada Mission, showing population aspects, economic conditions, family life, social conditions, and religious life.

AS1052 Potts, E. Daniel

British Baptist Missions in India, 1793-1837: The History of Serampore and its Missions. Cambridge, ENK: University Press, 1967. vii, 276 pp. No ISBN.

Activities and concepts of Carey, Marshman, and Ward, including medicine, agriculture, education, and especially, social reform.

AS1053 Powell, Avril A.

Muslims and Missionaries in Pre-Mutiny India. (London Studies on South Asia, 7). Richmond, ENK: Curzon Press, 1993. ix, 339 pp. 0700702105.

A detailed history of Muslim-Christian encounters in India, from the 7th to 20th centuries; focusing on the period leading to the Indian "Mutiny" of 1857; originally prepared as a Ph.D. thesis at the University of London.

AS1054 Presler, Henry Hughes

Primitive Religions in India: A Textbook on the Primitive Religous Type among India's Tribals. (Indian Theological Library, 6). Madras, II: CLS, 1971. xvi, 349 pp. Paper. No ISBN.

Pioneering missionary textbook on the nature of tribal religions and folk Hinduism in India, with recommendations for ministry to tribal peoples.

AS1055 Puthenpurakal, Joseph

Baptist Missions in Nagaland: A Study in Historical and Ecumenical Perspective. Calcutta, II: Firma KLM, 1984. xxii, 286 pp. No ISBN.

The history of the development of the Baptist church in Nagaland (India) and the contribution of American Baptist missions to the religious, cultural, educational, and economic life of the people.

AS1056 Raj, P. Solomon

A Christian Folk-Religion in India: A Study of the Small Church Movement in Andhra Pradesh, with a Special Reference to the Bible Mission of Devadas. (Studies in the Intercultural History of Christianity, 40). Frankfurt am Main, GW: Lang, 1986. ix, 375 pp. Paper. 382048924X.

A critical evaluation of independent church movements in India, focusing upon the Bible Mission of Fr. Devadas, which began as a breakaway from the Lutheran church in Andhra Pradesh; originally presented as a University of Birmingham (UK) thesis.

AS1057 Raj, Paul R.

Salvation and Secular Humanists in India. Madras, II: CLS, 1988. xvi, 222 pp. Paper. No ISBN.

A comparative study of understandings of salvation in Christianity and secular humanism, with implications for Christian mission in South India as it relates to the secular Dravida Kazhagam Movement in Tamilnadu.

AS1058 Rajamanickam, Svarimuthu

Roberto de Nobili on Adaptation. Palyamkottai, II: De Nobili Research Institute, 1972. xvi, 216 pp. No ISBN.

A scholarly examination of the 1619 conference at Goa about the Madurai Mission, including an examination of de Nobili's basic treatise on conversion work and controversial practices.

AS1059 Rajaratnam, K., and Bennet Benjamin

Sharing Life: An Alternative Paradigm of Development Partnership. Madras, II: Centre for Research on New International Economic Order, 1994. 73 pp. Paper. No ISBN.

Report of an international consultation on partnership between NGOs (including church agencies) and development projects by the churches in India.

AS1060 Ralte, Lalrinawmi et al., eds.

Envisioning a New Heaven and a New Earth. Nagpur, II: NCCI; Delhi, II: ISPCK, 1998. xviii, 306 pp. Paper. 8172144709.

Forty biblical devotions, sprinkled with artistic drawings, composed by Christian women from India on the occasion of the conclusion of the WCC's Ecumenical Decade for the Churches in Solidarity with Women.

AS1061 Rao, O. M.

Focus on North East Indian Christianity. Delhi, II: ISPCK, 1994. vii, 94 pp. Paper. 8172141254.

A primer on church and community in North East India from biblical, social, economic, and political perspectives.

AS1062 Robinson, Gnana, ed.

Religions of the Marginalised: Towards a Phenomenology and the Methodology of Study. Delhi, II: ISPCK; Bangalore, II: United Theological College, 1998. xi, 100 pp. Paper. 817214458X.

Papers on folk religion, defined as the religious practice of those marginalized by the dominant groups which control culture and religion; originally published at the consultation on "The Phenomenology and Methodology of Studying Folk Religions" at United Theological College, Bangalore, India, 17-22 October 1995.

AS—ASIA

AS1063 Robinson, Rowena, ed.

Conversion, Continuity and Change: Lived Christianity in Southern Goa. Walnut Creek, CAU: AltaMira Press; New Delhi, II: Sage Publications, 1998. 236 pp. Paper. 0761992294 (US), 8170366836 (II).

Located at the intersection of the sociology of popular religion and the dynamics of social transformation, this book examines the processes of conversion, as well as continuity and change, in a Goan Catholic community within the context of a wider Hindu society.

AS1064 Sa, Fidelis de

Crisis in Chota Nagpur: With Special Reference to the Judicial Conflict between Jesuit Missionaries and British Government Officials, November 1889-March 1890. Edited by Alvino Noronha. Bangalore, II: Redemptorist Publications, 1975. lx, 357 pp. No ISBN.

A detailed case study of the spectacular early advance of the Jesuit Mission in Chota Nagpur, focusing on the work of Fr. Lievens, of his championing of land rights for tribal peoples, and of conflicts with Lutheran missionaries.

AS1065 Sahay, Keshari N.

Christianity and Culture Change in India. New Delhi, II: Inter-India Publications, 1986. 328 pp. 8121001730.

Ten scholarly essays by a prominent Indian social anthropologist, on Christianity as an agency of cultural change in India, in general, and the state of Bihar, in particular.

AS1066 Sahu, Dhirendra Kumar

The Church of North India: A Historical and Systematic Theological Inquiry into an Ecumenical Ecclesiology. (Studies in the Intercultural History of Christianity, 88). Frankfurt am Main, GW: Lang, 1994. xii, 354 pp. Paper. 363146908X.

After chapters on mission, nationalism, and Christian identity in North India, the author analyses the history, theology, and ecclesiology behind this major organic union of churches in 1970.

AS1067 Saldanha, Julian

Conversion and Indian Civil Law. Bangalore, II: Theological Publications in India, 1981. v, 245 pp. Paper. No ISBN.

A study of conversion as a political and legal issue in India today, as well as a social and spiritual event.

AS1068 Sargant, Norman Carr

From Missions to Church in Karnataka, 1920-1950. Madras, II: CLS, 1987. xiv, 220 pp. Paper. No ISBN.

The history of the beginnings of the Mysore diocese of the Church of South India, relating the lives and faith journeys of English missionaries and Indian converts.

AS1069 Savariaradimai, Emmanuel

Culture, Gospel and Parish: An Integral Approach to Parish Renewal in South India. (Dissertationen: Theologische Reihe, 70). Ottilien, GW: EOS Verlag, 1994. xvii, 306 pp. Paper. 3880967709.

A detailed study of the Gospel-culture encounter in Catholic parishes in Tamilnadu, South India; originally submitted as a Th.D. dissertation to the Faculty of Theology, Vallendar, Germany.

AS1070 Selvanayagam, Israel

Tamilnadu: Confrontation, Complementarity, Compromise. (Gospel and Cultures Pamphlet, 7). Geneva, SZ: WCC Publications, 1996. 57 pp. Paper. 2825411957.

The coordinator of the program on interfaith dialogue, and lecturer in religions, mission, and dialogue at Tamilnadu Theological Seminary in Madras, traces aspects of Gospel and culture in South India, in historical perspective.

AS1071 Sen Gupta, Kanti Prasanna

The Christian Missionaries in Bengal, 1793-1833. Calcutta, II: K. L. Mukhopadhyay, 1971. xv, 245 pp. No ISBN.

An analysis of the first forty years of Protestant missionary work in Bengal, India, intended to throw light on some unexplored aspects of missionary activities; mainly based on original sources, listing the missionaries who served, tracts published, and a detailed bibliography of sources.

AS1072 Serampore College

The Story of Serampore and its College. Edited by William S. Steward. Calcutta, II: Baptist Mission Press; Serampore, II: Council of Serampore College, 1961. 121 pp. No ISBN.

Revised edition of an official history of Serampore College in India; originally written by George Howells in 1927.

AS1073 Seybold, Theodore C.

God's Guiding Hand: A History of the Central India Mission, 1868-1967. New York, NYU: United Church Board for World Ministries, 1967. x, 179 pp. No ISBN.

An account of a century of missionary work in the central provinces of India by one who had a considerable part in it.

AS1074 Sharma, Raj Bahadur

Christian Mission in North India, 1813-1913: A Case Study of Meerut Division and Dehra Dun District. Delhi, II: Mittal Publications, 1988. viii, 257 pp. 8170990831.

The history of Catholic and Protestant missions (Church of England, American Presbyterian, and American Methodist) in two districts of the present Uttar Pradesh State of India, including church-state relations.

AS1075 Shiri, Godwin

Karnataka Christians and Politics. (CISRS Social Research Series, 13). Madras, II: CLS, 1978. 95 pp. Paper. No ISBN.

An investigation into the low level of political participation by Protestants in the South Indian state of Karnataka, where they represent less than one percent of the population.

AS1076 Shiri, Godwin

The Plight of Christian Dalits: A South Indian Case Study. Bangalore, II: Asian Trading Corp, 1997. 270 pp. Paper. 8170862094.

This empirical case study gives evidence of the social degradation and economic disabilities suffered by the Christian Dalits, and seeks to create an awareness of their suffering in the public, in general, and in the Christian community in particular.

AS1077 Shourie, Arun

Missionaries in India: Continuities, Changes, Dilemmas. New Delhi, II: ASA Publications, 1994. xii, 305 pp. 8190019945.

A critical assessment of 150 years of Roman Catholic missions and influence in India, written by a Hindu economist well known as a commentator on current and political affairs.

AS1078 Simhadri, Y. C.

The Ex-Criminal Tribes of India. New Delhi, II: National Publishing House, 1979. xiv, 185 pp. No ISBN.

Analysis of the activities and rehabilitation of one ethnic (caste) group, the Yerukulas, and the role of the Salvation Army and other factors; originally submitted as a doctoral thesis (Case Western University, 1973).

AS—ASIA

AS1079 Singh, Godwin R.

In Search of Communal Harmony. Delhi, II: ISPCK, 1985. 75 pp. Paper. No ISBN.

A study book for Indian Christians concerned about the wave of intra-communal violence, and desiring to work for peace and communal harmony.

AS1080 Singh, Ram, ed.

Christian Perspectives on Contemporary Indian Issues: A National Colloquium. Madras, II: Institute for Development Education, 1983. xix, 252 pp. Paper. No ISBN.

Proceedings and papers from an important colloquium (Madras, 17-20 Dec. 1982) on contemporary Indian issues, and the Christian response.

AS1081 Slade, Herbert Edwin William

A Work Begun: The Story of the Cowley Fathers in India, 1874-1967. London, ENK: SPCK, 1970. 126 pp. 028102491X.

A narrative account focusing on the life and work of individual missionaries, with minimal documentation.

AS1082 Studdert-Kennedy, Gerald

British Christians, Indian Nationalists and the Raj. Oxford, ENK: Oxford University Press, 1991. x, 274 pp. 0195627334.

A scholarly study of the attitudes of British Christians toward India, the colonial administration, and rising Indian nationalism between the world wars (1919-1939); by the senior lecturer, Department of Political Science, University of Birmingham.

AS1083 Studdert-Kennedy, Gerald, ed.

Providence and the Raj: Imperial Mission and Missionary Imperialism. Walnut Creek, CAU: AltaMira Press; New Delhi, II: Sage Publications, 1998. 273 pp. 0761992774.

A study of the Christian component of British imperialism, its complex roots in British domestic politics, and its pervasive influence in the evolution of the Raj, India.

AS1084 Subbamma, B. V.

New Patterns for Disciplining Hindus: The Next Step in Andhra Pradesh, India. South Pasadena, CAU: William Carey Library, 1970. xiii, 194 pp. 0878083065.

A book of practical suggestions for the winning of "caste people" to Christianity, in which the author, a converted Lutheran, draws upon her own unusual training and experience.

AS1085 Sumithra, Sunand, and F. Hrangkhuma, eds.

Doing Mission in Context. (Centre for Mission Studies, 1). Bangalore, II: Theological Book Trust, 1995. vi, 148 pp. Paper. 8174750053.

Essays on mission in the present Indian context, presented at the 1st consultation of the Centre (Union Biblical Seminary, Pune, 1991).

AS1086 Suriá, Carlos

History of the Catholic Church in Gujarat. Anand, II: Gujarat Sahitya Prakash, 1990. xxii, 432 pp. No ISBN.

A detailed history of Catholic missions in the Gujarat state of India from 1893 to 1934, with an analysis of the contributions of the Jesuits and other missionary orders.

AS1087 Svärd, Lydia

Förbundskyrkan i Indien. Stockholm, SW: Gummesson, 1979. 162 pp. 9170705690.

A book on the Mission Covenant Church of Sweden's missions in India and the Hindustani Covenant Church.

AS1088 Taylor, Richard W., and Madathilparapil M. Thomas

Mud Walls and Steel Mills: God and Man at Work in India. New York, NYU: Friendship Press, 1963. 128 pp. Paper. No ISBN.

A mission study book on the Church in India in relation to radical social changes resulting from rapid industrialization and urbanization.

AS1089 Taylor, Richard W., ed.

Religion and Society: The First Twenty-Five Years, 1953-1978. Madras, II: CLS, 1982. vii, 374 pp. Paper. No ISBN.

Thirty-one articles on the interrelationship between religion and social realities in India; originally published in *Religion and Society* between 1953 and 1978.

AS1090 Taylor, Richard W.

Acknowledging the Lordship of Christ:Selected Writings of Richard W. Taylor. Delhi, II: ISPCK for Christian Institute for the Study of Religion and Society, 1992. xii, 225 pp. Paper. 8172140614.

A selection of writings by the distinguished missionary staff member of the CISRS (Bangalore, India) on his concerns for indigenous Christian art, ashrams, the church, dialogue, Indian theology, and society.

AS1091 Taylor, Richard W.

A Remembered Parish: St. Mark's Cathedral, Bangalore. (CISRS Social Research Series, 17). Delhi, II: ISPCK for CISRS, Bangalore, 1986. ii, 109 pp. Paper. No ISBN.

A study looks at the structures, methods of worship, fellowship, outreach, leadership, and community of one of the most innovative parishes in South India, St. Mark's Cathedral, Bangalore (CSI).

AS1092 Tete, Peter

A Missionary Social Worker in India: J. B. Hoffmann, the Chota Nagpur Tenancy Act and the Catholic Co-Operatives, 1893-1928. (Documenta Missionalia: 18). Rome, IT: Universita Gregoriana, 1984. xix, 191 pp. Paper. 8876525394.

A detailed history of the Catholic Mission by Belgian Jesuits among the tribal people of Chota Nagpur in northern India, focusing on the work of J. B. Hoffman, 1893 to 1928, to apply Catholic social principles of total salvation for these people, including political and economic justice; originally submitted as a doctoral dissertation at the Gregorian University in Rome.

AS1093 Thampu, Valson, Kathleen Nicholls, and Christopher S. Raj, eds.

Kristiya Drishtanta: A Christian Viewpoint. New Delhi, II: TRACI, 1989. iii, 122 pp. Paper. No ISBN.

Nine essays by Indian Christian leaders published as an annual by the TRACI, which is committed to interpreting and communicating the Christian faith in the context of Indian culture for strengthening the life and witness of the churches in India.

AS1094 Thangaraj, C. P.

Whither Indian Christianity. Madras, II: CLS, 1990. xvi, 87 pp. Paper. No ISBN.

An impassioned advocacy of social justice for Dalit Christians, arguing that Christianity is in decline in India because it has not championed the cause of the outcasts.

AS—ASIA

AS1095 Thangasamy, D. A.

India and the Ecumenical Movement. Madras, II: CLS, 1973. xii, 56 pp. Paper. No ISBN.

A resume of Indian participation in the 20th-century ecumenical movement, with a call for increased involvement by the late editor of *The South Indian Churchman.*

AS1096 Thomas, Abraham Vazhayil

Christians in Secular India. Cranbury, NJU: Associated University Presses, 1974. 246 pp. 0838610218.

A detailed study of the meaning and practice of the secular-state ideal, and of the mutual relationship between the state and the Christian community in India.

AS1097 Thomas, Madathilparapil M., and Paul David Devanandan

Christian Participation in Nation-Building: The Summing Up of a Corporate Study on Rapid Social Change. (Social Concerns Series, 9). Bangalore, II: NCCI; Bangalore, II: CISRS, 1960. xi, 325 pp. Paper. No ISBN.

The report, by the directors of the newly formed CISRS, of India's participation in the WCC study of rapid social change.

AS1098 Thomas, Madathilparapil M.

A Diaconal Approach to Indian Ecclesiology. (Chavara Lecture Series, 6). Bangalore, II: CSS Tiruvalla and DP, 1995. 87 pp. No ISBN.

Six lectures by the well-known ecumenical Indian theologian, exploring Indian modernization and the search for a new Indian contextual ecclesiology; originally delivered in December 1994, at the Centre for Indian and Inter-Religious Studies in Rome, Italy.

AS1099 Thomas, Madathilparapil M.

Salvation and Humanisation: Some Crucial Issues of the Theology of Mission in Contemporary India. (Indian Christian Thought Series, 11). Madras, II: CLS, 1971. iv, 64 pp. Paper. No ISBN.

A prominent Indian theologian and ecumenist brings out specific features of the debate as it has developed in modern Indian Christianity, renascent Hindu religion; and Indian secularism.

AS1100 Thomas, Madathilparapil M.

Towards an Evangelical Social Gospel: A New Look at the Reformation of Abraham Malpan. Madras, II: CLS, 1977. v, 39 pp. Paper. No ISBN.

Reflections on the Mar Thoma reformation in the ancient Syrian Othodox Church of India, within the context of the total cultural renaissance of Kerala in the 19th century.

AS1101 Trinidade, Paulo da

Conquista espiritual do Oriente: em que se dá relato de algumas cousas mais notàveis que fizeram os Frades Monores de Santa Provincia de S. Tomé da India Oriental.... Edited by Félix Lopes. Lisboa, PO: Centro de Estudios Históricos Ultramarinos, 1962. 3 vols. No ISBN.

A 17th-century chronicle of the Franciscan Province of Saint Thomas, India, based on texts from the Vatican Archives that constitute an indispensable reference work for the history of Portuguese missions from India to the Far East [vol. 1: xxxi, 414 pp.; vol. 2: xv, 456 pp.; vol. 3: xx, 606 pp.].

AS1102 Troisi, J.

Tribal Religion: Religious Beliefs and Practices Among the Saints. New Delphi, II: South Asia Books/ Manohar Publishing, 2000. xi, 294 pp. 0836401972.

A systematic study of traditional Santali beliefs and practices; originally submitted as a thesis at the University of Delhi and published in 1977.

AS1103 Tucker, Paul H. von

Nationalism, Case and Crisis in Missions: German Missions in British India, 1939-1946. Erlangen, GW: Tucher, 1980. iv, 698 pp. Paper. No ISBN.

History and experiences of the German missionary families interned by the British in India during World War II.

AS1104 Turaicami, Calamon

Christianity in India: Unique and Universal Mission. Madras, II: CLS, 1986. xii, 284 pp. Paper. No ISBN.

A study of Christianity in India, reflecting upon the evangelistic educational, healing, and social development ministries of the churches; by the former bishop of Tiruchi-Tanjore and moderator of the Church of South India (1980-82).

AS1105 Urquhart, Anne M.

Near India's Heart: An Account of Free Church of Scotland Mission Work in India during the 20th Century. Edinburgh, STK: Knox Press, 1990. 209 pp. Paper. 0904422259.

A narrative history of Free Church of Scotland missions in Madhya Pradesh province of India in the 20th century, by one who served there as a medical missionary, from 1962 to 1984.

AS1106 Varghese, V. Titus, and P. P. Philip

Glimpses of the History of the Christian Churches in India. Madras, II: CLS, 1983. viii, 174 pp. Paper. No ISBN.

A brief introduction to the history of Christianity in India, focusing upon the Syrian Orthodox and Mar Thoma church traditions.

AS1107 Vasantharaj, Albert, and Roger E. Hedlund, eds.

India Church Growth II, 1984-1988. Madras, II: Church Growth Research Centre, 1989. xv, 332 pp. Paper. No ISBN.

A five-year compilation of the *India Church Growth Quarterly,* together with a foreword, a preface, an introductory essay, table of contents, index of subjects, and index of names.

AS1108 Vidyarthi, Lalita Prasad, ed.

Applied Anthropology in India: Principles, Problems, and Case Studies. Allahabad, II: Kitab Mahal, 1987. vii, 533 pp. No ISBN.

Third edition of thirty-eight essays on aspects of holistic development, including planning and research, tribal change and needs, and Christianity as an agency of tribal welfare; originally published in 1968.

AS1109 Vincent, Kaushal

Socio-Economic study of Bhoilymbong: A Village in Meghalaya. (CISRS Social Research Series, 14). Madras, II: CLS, 1978. xiii, 378 pp. No ISBN.

A detailed local study of a largely Christian village in northeastern India, determining the extent to which Christianity has reshaped attitudes and behavior toward development and change.

AS—ASIA

AS1110 Visvanathan, Susan
*The Christians of Kerala: History, Belief and Ritual among the
Yakoba.* Madras, II: Oxford University Press, 1993. xiii, 279 pp.
0195631897.
    A detailed socio-anthropological study of the practice of
Christianity by Syrian Christians (both Orthodox and Jacobite)
in a village in Kerala, India.

AS1111 Waack, Otto
*Church and Mission in India: The History of the Jeypore Church
and the Breklum Mission (1876-1939).* Translated by Cynthia
C. Lies. Delhi, II: ISPCK for Northelbian Centre for Worldmis-
sion and Church World Service, 1997. 2 vols. No ISBN.
    English translation [vol. 1, *1876-1914*, xxii, 566 pp.,
8172143478; vol. 2, *1914-1939*, xvi, 332 pp., 8172143982].

AS1112 Waack, Otto
Indische Kirche und Indien-Mission. (Erlanger Monographien
aus Mission und Ökumene, 20-21). Erlangen, GW: Ev.-Luth.
Mission, 1994-1996. 2 vol. Paper. 3872143204.
    A scholarly, two-volume history of the Jeypore Church and
Breklumer Mission in the Koraput District of Madhya Pradesh,
India, covering the period 1876 to 1939; written by a former mis-
sionary teacher in India, with contributions by his Indian and
German co-workers [vol. 1, *Die Geschichte der Jeypore-Kirche
und der Breklumer Mission (1876-1914)*, xxiii, 491 pp.,
3872143204; vol. 2, *Die Geschichte der Jeypore-Kirche und der
Breklumer Mission (1914-1939)*, xii, 241 pp., 3872143212].

AS1113 Wandall, Povl
The Origin and Growth of the Arcot Lutheran Church. Madras,
II: CLS, 1978. vii, 189 pp. Paper. No ISBN.
    A short history of the Danish Mission in India, and of the
Arcot Lutheran Church, from its beginnings in 1863, to 1950.

AS1114 Webster, John C. B.
*The Christian Community and Change in Nineteenth Century
North India.* Delhi, II: Macmillan Company of India, 1976. xii,
293 pp. 0333901231.
    A detailed study, based on archival research, of the 19th-
century movements from mission to church among Protestants in
the Punjab and United provinces of British India; a revision of
the author's Ph.D. dissertation (University of Pennsylvania, 1971).

AS1115 Webster, John C. B.
The Dalit Christians: A History. (ISPCK Contextual Theological Education Series, 4). Delhi, II: ISPCK, 1994. xiii, 275 pp.
Paper. 8172141602.
    An updated second edition of a history of Dalit Christianity,
with new sections on Dalit social activism; originally published
in 1998 (Mellen Research University Press).

AS1116 Webster, John C. B.
The Pastor to Dalits. (ISPCK Contextual Theological Education Series, 8). Delhi, II: ISPCK, 1995. xi, 144 pp. Paper.
8172142773.
    An empirical study of the pastor and pastoral ministry to
Dalits in India today.

AS1117 Wicki, Josef
*Missionskirche im Orient: Ausgewählte Beiträge über Portugie-
sisch-Asien.* (*NZM*, 24). Immensee, SZ: *NZM*, 1976. 317 pp.
Paper. No ISBN.
    Mission history of the Catholic Church in India during the
Portuguese colonial period; documented by a Jesuit scholar, who

includes important correspondence and decisions that enhanced
Jesuit mission work.

AS1118 Wicki, Josef, ed.
O Livro do "pai dos cristõos." Lisboa, PO: Centro de Estudios Históricos Ultramarinos, 1969. xix, 446 pp. No ISBN.
    The text of a codex, discovered by the author in Goa,
containing state and church documents relating to the conversion, instruction, and pastoral care of new Indian Christians;
includes an interpretive introduction.

AS1119 Wilson, H. S., ed.
The Church on the Move: A Quest to Affirm the Biblical Faith.
Madras, II: CLS, 1988. vii, 160 pp. Paper. No ISBN.
    Fifteen scholarly essays reflecting international perspec-
tives on the roles of leadership, mission, education, pluralism, women, and liberation, given in honor of the Most Reverend Dr. P. Victor Premasagar, Bishop in Medak and Moderator of the Church of South India, on the completion of his
60th year.

AS1120 Wingate, Andrew
*The Church and Conversion: A Study of Recent Conversions
to and from Christianity in the Tamil Area of South India.*
Delhi, II: ISPCK, 1997. xiv, 306 pp. Paper. 8172143842.
    A scholarly study of Dalit conversions in South India;
originally submitted in 1995 as a Ph.D. thesis at the University of Birmingham in England.

AS1121 Witz, Cornelia
*Religionspolitik in Britisch-Indien, 1793-1813: Christliches
Sendungsbewusstsein und Achtung hinduistischer Tradition
im Widerstreit.* (Beiträge zur Südasienforschung, 98). Stuttgart, GW: Steiner, 1985. viii, 137 pp. Paper. 3515045287.
    This dissertation (Freiburg, 1981) is based on archival
research in England, and studies the missionary activity by
the British in India between 1793 and 1813, especially of the
evangelical Clapham sect.

AS1122 Zachariah, Mathai
The Christian Presence in India. Madras, II: CLS, 1981. viii,
145 pp. Paper. No ISBN.
    A selection of editorials, by the General Secretary of the
NCCI, published 1968 to 1980 as comments on current events
in church, society, and politics in India.

AS1123 Zachariah, Mathai
Inside the Indian Church. Delhi, II: ISPCK, 1994. x, 106 pp.
Paper. 8172142293.
    A frank and open assessment of the state of the church in
India, by the former General Secretary of the NCCI.

AS1124 Zachariah, Mathai, ed.
The Church: A People's Movement. Nagpur, II: NCCI, 1975.
119 pp. Paper. No ISBN.
    Nine essays by Indian church leaders, on a theology for
the church's mission in Indian society; planned as the preparatory study book for the 18th assembly of the NCCI (Nagpur
1975).

AS1125 Zachariah, Mathai, ed.
The Indian Church: Identity and Fulfilment. Madras, II: CLS;
Delhi, II: ISPCK; Lucknow, II: Lucknow Publishing House,
1971. xii, 220 pp. No ISBN.
    Twenty-one short essays written as a preparatory study
book for the 1971 assembly of the NCCI.

AS1126 Zachariah, Mathai, ed.
The Local Congregation: Its Mission in India. Delhi, II: ISPCK, 1982. viii, 140 pp. Paper. No ISBN.

Brief essays on the local congregation, its role and mission, plus case studies and workshop reports on developing missionary congregations.

AS1127 Zachariah, Mathai, ed.
Seeking Christ in India Today. Nagpur, II: NCCI, 1979. 103 pp. Paper. No ISBN.

A study book on the theme of the 1979 assembly of the NCCI.

India: Biography

See also HI339, HI354, TH61, EA110, CR795, CR896, MI195, SP5, AF392, AS247, AS258, AS577, and AS1092.

AS1128 Adhav, Shamsundar Manohar, ed.
Pandita Ramabai. (Confessing the Faith in India Series, 13). Madras, II: CLS, 1979. xi, 242 pp. Paper. No ISBN.

A celebration of the life and work of Pandita Ramabai (1858-1922), pioneer crusader for women's rights in India, with excerpts from her writings and a detailed chronology and bibliography.

AS1129 Appasamy, A. J.
A Bishop's Story. Madras, II: CLS, 1969. v, 185 pp. No ISBN.

Autobiography of the CSF bishop and spiritual leader best known for his Bhakti theology.

AS1130 Aprem, Mar
Indian Christian Who Is Who. Bombay, II: Bombay Parish Church of the East, 1983. 210 pp. No ISBN.

A directory, with short biographical notes, on contemporary Indian Christian leaders.

AS1131 Bühlmann, Walbert
Pionier der Einheit: Bischof Anastasius Hartmann. (Franziskanische Lebensbilder, 7). Zürich, SZ: Thomas Verlag; Paderborn, GW: Schöningh, 1966. 248 pp. No ISBN.

The biography of a Swiss Capuchin who became bishop in India, written on the 100th anniversary of his death.

AS1132 Bachmann, Peter R.
Roberto Nobili, 1577-1656: Ein missionsgeschichtlicher Beitrag zum christlichen Dialog mit Hinduismus. (Bibliotheca Instituti Historici S.I., 32). Rome, IT: Institutum Historicum S.I., 1972. xxxii, 271 pp. Paper. No ISBN.

This doctoral dissertation is a scholarly biography of Roberto de Nobili, with special reference to the controversy about accommodation and caste.

AS1133 Barnard, Laura Belle
Touching the Untouchables. Wheaton, ILU: Tyndale, 1985. 170 pp. Paper. 0842372962.

The autobiography of a pioneer Free Will Baptist missionary among the Harijans and Kota tribe in South India, 1935 to 1983.

AS1134 Beck, James R.
Dorothy Carey: The Tragic and Untold Story of Mrs. William Carey. Grand Rapids, MIU: Baker Books, 1992. 254 pp. Paper. 0801010306.

The story of Dorothy Carey (1756-1807), the first wife of William Carey, with source documents concerning her mental illness; written by the Associate Professor of Counseling at Denver Seminary.

AS1135 Brauer, Janice Kerper, ed.
A Rainbow of Saris: Four True Stories of Missionary Women in India. St. Louis, MOU: International Lutheran Women's Missionary League, 1996. 156 pp. Paper. 0961495553.

Four true stories of women missionaries, in India, of the Lutheran Church, Missouri Synod, and of the lives they touched through their dedication, service, and love.

AS1136 Brooks, Harlan J.
Call to India: The Missionary Journey of Harlan and Ruth Forney Brooks. North Manchester, INU: Glen and Betty Campbell, 1991. xii, 155 pp. Paper. No ISBN.

An autobiographical account of one family's service as Church of the Brethren missionaries in India, 1924-1960.

AS1137 Buckwalter, Leoda
Silhouette: Colonial India as We Lived It. Nappanee, INU: Evangel Press, 1988. 192 pp. Paper. 0916035247.

Firsthand accounts by the author, concerning the India she lived in as a Brethren in Christ missionary in Bihar State, from 1939 to 1948, during the conclusion of British rule and the Indian struggle for independence.

AS1138 Buntain, Huldah
Treasures in Heaven. Springdale, PAU: Whitaker House, 1989. 218 pp. Paper. 0883682176.

Reminiscences by an Assembly of God missionary to India (1954-1989) and cofounder of the Calcutta Mission of Mercy; as told to B. W. Corpany and Hal Donaldson.

AS1139 Chatterjee, Sunil Kumar
Felix Carey: A Tiger Tamed. West Bengal, II: Sunil Kumar Chatterjee, 1991. 122 pp. No ISBN.

A popular biography of Felix Carey (1786-1822), known as a missionary printer and author, and as the eldest son of William Carey.

AS1140 Chatterjee, Sunil Kumar
Hannah Marshman, the First Woman Missionary in India. Hoogly, II: Sunil Kumar Chatterjee, 1987. 106 pp. No ISBN.

Popular biography of Hannah (Shepherd) Marshman (1767-1847), wife of Joshua Marshman and mother of the Baptist Serampore Mission in India.

AS1141 Clarysse, L.
Father Constant Lievens, S.J. Ranchi, II: Satya Bharati, 1985. xii, 453 pp. Paper. No ISBN.

Historical study of the contribution of Father Constant Lievens to the evangelization and social transformation of the Chota Nagpur people of Bihar State in India.

AS1142 Daniel, Mathew
Sadhu Kochukunju: A Biography. Madras, II: CLS, 1996. 57 pp. Paper. No ISBN.

A short biography of Sadhu Kochukunju (1883-1920), a leader in the spiritual renewal of the indigenous church of Malabar in Kerala.

AS1143 Das, R. C.
Evangelical Prophet for Contextual Christianity. Edited by Herbert L. Richard. (Confessing the Faith in India, 19). Delhi, II: ISPCK, 1995. 302 pp. Paper. 8172142358.

A collection of the writings of R. C. Das (1908-1976), who devoted forty-six years of ministry at the Khristpanthi Ashram in Varanasi, reaching Hindus with the Gospel of Jesus Christ.

AS—ASIA

AS1144 Datta, Kitty Scoular, ed.

Science, Education, and Faith: H. John Taylor (1906-1996) and India. Delhi, II: ISPCK, 1999. x, 129 pp. Paper. 8172145144.

This biography is drawn from letters, reminiscences, lectures, sermons, poems, and hymns by a Professor of Physics in India, who believed wholeheartedly in open dialogue between religious faiths, as well as in dialogue between religion and science.

AS1145 Devadas, V. Henry

Christ Inspires Human Struggle for Freedom and Justice: A Freedom Fighter's Testimony. Delhi, II: ISPCK/CISRS, 1993. xii, 80 pp. Paper. 8172141211.

The former general secretary of the ISPCK recounts his active involvements in the life and mission of the YMCA and the Church of North India (church union negotiations, peace and justice concerns, producing Christian literature).

AS1146 Dharmagnani, P., ed.

Sister Carol Graham: The Beloved "Amma." Madras, II: CLS, 1989. vi, 92 pp. Paper. No ISBN.

A biography of the life and work of a woman who served all of her active life in South India (1898-1989), as foundress of the Order of Sisters in the CSI, and of the Farnscombe Community in Great Britain.

AS1147 Doig, Desmond

Mother Teresa: Her People and Her Work. San Francisco, CAU: Harper & Row, 1980. 175 pp. Paper. 0060619414.

English translation.

AS1148 Doig, Desmond

Mutter Teresa: Ihr Leben und Werk in Bildern. Freiburg, GW: Herder, 1977. 187 pp. 3451175215.

A sensitive portrayal by a journalist who had known her for well over twenty-seven years.

AS1149 Drewery, Mary

William Carey: A Biography. Grand Rapids, MIU: Zondervan, 1979. 224 pp. 0310388503.

A balanced appraisal of William Carey's life and ministry that credits him with great success and influence as the "Father of Modern Missions," while not ignoring his failures and character flaws.

AS1150 Egan, Eileen

Such a Vision of the Street: Mother Teresa—the Spirit and the Work. Garden City, NYU: Image Books, 1986. 522 pp. Paper. 0385174918.

A definitive account of the Calcutta nun, encompassing the worldwide character of her missionary activity; written by one of her lay co-workers of three decades.

AS1151 Elliot, Elisabeth

A Chance to Die: The Life and Legacy of Amy Carmichael. Old Tappan, NJU: Revell, 1987. 382 pp. 0800715357.

A chronicle of the life of the saintly Irish CMS missionary, founder of the Dohnavur Fellowship in South India, who spent fifty-three years there (1898-1951) without furlough.

AS1152 Elwin, Verrier

Din-Sevak: Verrier Elwin's Life of Service in Tribal India. (Confessing the Faith in India, 17). Delhi, II: ISPCK for CISRS, 1993. 285 pp. Paper. 817214069X.

Selections from the writings of Verrier Elwin (1902-1964) who lived in India from 1927 until his death in 1964—first as an Anglican missionary, then as one identified with Ghandi and Indian nationalism, and finally, as one devoted to the welfare and development of India's tribal peoples; with a biographical introduction by Daniel O'Connor.

AS1153 Estborn, Sigfrid

Johannes Sandegren och hans insats i Indiens kristenhet. (Studia Missionalia Upsaliensia, 10). Lund, SW: Gleerup, 1968. 255 pp. No ISBN.

A biography on Johannes Sandegren (1883-1962), missionary to India and the third bishop of the Tamil Evangelical Lutheran Church.

AS1154 Fauconnet-Buzelin, François

Les porteurs d'espérance: La mission du Tibet-sud, 1848-1854. (Cerf-Histoire). Paris, FR: Éditions du Cerf, 1999. 256 pp. Paper. 2204062391.

The story of two pioneer missionary priests of the Foreign Mission of Paris (Missions étrangères de Paris), martyred in 1854, in northeast India, on their way to Tibet, and now revered as the spiritual patrons of the strong Catholic Church in the Indian state of Arunachal Pradesh.

AS1155 Finnie, Kellsye M.

Beyond the Minarets: A Biography of Henry Martyn. Bromley, ENK: STL Books, 1988. 154 pp. Paper. 1850780269.

A popular biography of the missionary pioneer to British India and the interior of Persia (1781-1812), laying the foundations for the Urdu and Persian New Testaments.

AS1156 Francis, T. Dayanandan, ed.

The Christian Witness of Sadhu Sundar Singh: A Collection of His Writings. Madras, II: CLS, 1989. iii, 628 pp. Paper. No ISBN.

A comprehensive collection, without commentary, of all the writings of Sadhu Sundar Singh, the wandering Indian "Christian friar"; edited by the General Secretary of the CLS in Madras, India.

AS1157 Francis, T. Dayanandan

Vedanayagam Sastriyar and Krishna Pillai. Chennai, II: CLS, 1998. xi, 54 pp. Paper. No ISBN.

Three lectures on two great Christian Tamil poets; originally published in 1978 under the title *Christian Poets and Tamil Culture.*

AS1158 Gandhi, Mahatma, and Charles Freer Andrews

Gandhi and Charlie: The Story of a Friendship. Edited by David M. Gracie. Cambridge, MAU: Cowley Publications, 1989. 211 pp. 0936384743 (hdbk), 0936384719 (pbk).

A collection of writings and letters between Mohandas K. Gandhi and Rev. Charles F. Andrews, the Church of England educator-missionary, revealing the manner in which they met, became close friends, and engaged in the struggle against injustice and oppression in South Africa and India.

AS1159 Gnanapragasam, V. M.

Der grosse heroische Asket: Josef Constantius Beschi (Indien); (1680-1747, Gelehrter und Dichter der Tamilsprache). (Missionare, die Geschichte machten). Mödling-Wien, AU: Verlag St. Gabriel; St. Augustin, GW: Steyler Verlag, 1983. 117 pp. Paper. 3852642019 (AU), 3877871607 (GW).

The life of an Italian Jesuit in India who, like de Nobili, promoted the Indianization of Christianity, especially in art and literature.

AS1160 Goodwin, Alys

Sadhu Sundar Singh in Switzerland (His Sojourn as Record-ed by Alys Goodwin in Switzerland, March 1922). Edited by A. F. Thyagaraju. Madras, II: CLS, 1989. xviii, 63 pp. Paper. No ISBN.

The 1922 personal diary of the personal secretary of the Indian Christian mystic, as he sojourned in Switzerland; with a biographical introduction by Bishop A. J. Appasamy.

AS1161 Graham, Barbara

Jackfruit and Wild Honey. Delhi, II: ISPCK, 1996. xviii, 301 pp. Paper. 8172143060.

The story of Ebenezer Rajaratnam Sabhapathy (1917-1983), a doctor disciple of Mahatma Gandhi, who had a lifetime of rural medical ministry in the Mysore State of India.

AS1162 Guha, Ramachandra

Savaging the Civilized: Verrier Elwin, His Tribals, and India. Chicago, ILU: University of Chicago Press; New Delhi, II: Oxford University Press, 1999. xii, 398 pp. 0226310477 (hdbk), 0226310485 (pbk).

A meticulous study of Harry Verrier Elwin (1902-1964), an Anglican priest, evangelist, social worker, political activist, poet, and government worker, who "went native" with a vengeance in India; sheds light on contemporary India, the future of development, cultural assimilation versus cultural difference, the political practice of postcolonial as opposed to colonial governments, and the moral practice of writers and intellectuals.

AS1163 Gundert, Hermann

Tagebuch aus Malabar: 1837-1859. Stuttgart, GW: Steinkopf, 1983. 399 pp. 3798405697.

This book presents, in the form of a diary, the missionary life and achievements of Hermann Gundert (1814-1893), a German member of the Basel Mission who can be regarded as founder of the Protestant Church of Malabar (South India).

AS1164 Hansen, Lillian E.

The Double Yoke: The Story of William Alexander Noble, M.D. New York, NYU: Citadel Press, 1968. 268 pp. No ISBN.

A popular account of a lifetime spent in the building of the Salvation Army's extensive and well-equipped medical work in the State of Kerala, India.

AS1165 Harper, Susan Billington

In the Shadow of the Mahatma: Bishop V. S. Azariah and the Travails of Christianity in British India. (Studies in the History of Christian Missions). Grand Rapids, MIU: Eerdmans; Richmond, ENK: Curzon Press, 2000. xxi, 462 pp. 080283874X (US), 0700712321 (UK).

The first Indian bishop of an Anglican diocese and successful leader of rural conversion movements to Christianity in modern India, 1874-1945; negotiated within complex cultural, social, political, and economic pressures, with exceptional skill and diplomacy in a non-Christian context.

AS1166 Hefley, James C., and Marti Hefley

God's Tribesman: The Rochunga Pudaite Story. Lewisville, TXU: Accelerated Christian Education, 1994. 144 pp. 1562650033.

Reprint of a popular biography of a noted Indian evangelist, based on his unfinished autobiographical manuscript; originally published by A. J. Holman Company in 1974.

AS1167 Heiler, Friedrich

The Gospel of Sadhu Sundar Singh. Delhi, II: ISPCK, 1989. 277 pp. Paper. No ISBN.

A new Indian centenary edition of an outstanding biography of the Indian Christian saint (1889-1929?); originally published in German in 1924, under the title *Sadhu Sundad Singh: Ein Apostel des Ostens und Westens.*

AS1168 Hess, Gary R.

Sam Higginbottom of Allahabad: Pioneer of Point Four to India. Charlottesville, VAU: University Press of Virginia, 1967. ix, 177 pp. No ISBN.

A scholarly biography of Sam Higginbottom (1874-1958), founder of the Allahabad Agricultural Institute; with a survey of the development of Christian agricultural missions in India.

AS1169 Hoch, Erna M.

Hypocrite or Heretic: To Pretend or to Protest. (Indian Christian Thought Series, 17). Madras, II: CLS, 1983. viii, 192 pp. Paper. No ISBN.

A Swiss psychiatrist, Methodist missionary to India since 1956, and Director of the Nur Manzil Psychiatric Centre in Lucknow, reflects on the stages in the development of her thinking, values, and convictions, relative to the world of Indian thought and culture in which she lived and worked.

AS1170 Hodne, Olav

L.O. Skrefsrud: Missionary and Social Reformer among the Santals of Santal Parganas. (Studies of the Egede Institute, 9). Oslo, NO: Egede Instituttet, 1966. 362 pp. No ISBN.

A thesis detailing the creative ministry of the Norwegian missionary of the Santal Mission among the Santals of Bihar State from 1867 to 1881.

AS1171 Immanuel, David S.

Reformed Church in America Missionaries in South India, 1839-1938: An Analytical Study. Bangalore, II: Asian Trading Corp; St. Louis, MOU: South Asia Books, 1986. x, 184 pp. No ISBN.

An analysis of the attitudes, objectives, and achievements of Reformed Church in America (RCA) missionaries in India; based on the author's Th.D. thesis (Lutheran School of Theology at Chicago).

AS1172 Jacob, Plamthodathil S., ed.

The Experiential Response of N. V. Tilak. (Confessing the Faith in India Series, 14). Madras, II: CLS, 1979. xi, 127 pp. Paper. No ISBN.

A short biography of Narayan Vaman Tilak (1862-1919), pioneer Indian theologian, poet, and crusader for indigenous Indian Christianity, with selections of his poetry.

AS1173 Jacober, Virginia

The Promise: The Story of Ed and Virginia Jacober. (The Jaffray Collection of Missionary Portraits). Camp Hill, PAU: Christian Publications, 1994. 212 pp. Paper. 087509547X.

Reminiscences by a Christian and Missionary Alliance missionary of service for twenty-two years (1950-1971) in India and ten (1975-1985) in Israel.

AS1174 Jameson, Carol E.

Be Thou My Vision. Vellore, II: Carol E. Jameson, 1983. 252 pp. Paper. No ISBN.

The remarkable story of a missionary to South India, 1923-1963, and her work as Professor of Obstetrics and Gynecology at Vellore Christian Medical College.

AS1175 Johnson, Rachel Kerr

Affectionately, Rachel: Letters from India, 1860-1884. Edited by Barbara Mitchell Tull. Kent, OHU: Kent State University Press, 1992. xv, 351 pp. 0873384636.

Excerpts from the lifetime collection of letters by Rachel Kerr Johnson (1837-1888), focusing on her years in northwest India as the wife of a missionary with the PCUSA.

AS1176 Jones, E. Stanley

A Song of Ascents: A Spiritual Autobiography. Nashville, TNU: Abingdon, 1979. 400 pp. Paper. 0687391008.

Autobiography of Eli Stanley Jones (1884-1973), American Methodist missionary to India, global evangelist, and author; originally published in 1968.

AS1177 Joseph, Vasanth D.

Satya Joseph: The Service of Mr. Valiant-for-Truth. Chennai, II: CLS, 1997. xxx, 109 pp. Paper. No ISBN.

An illustrated biography of Rev. Satya Joseph (1900-1955), the first Indian missionary of the CSI to Papua New Guinea (1946-1955).

AS1178 Lerthansung

Lera. Hazelwood, MOU: Word Aflame Press, 1987. 272 pp. Paper. 0932581242.

A popular account of the life of one of the early Pentecostal revivalists in northeast India, including Bangladesh, Bhutan, and the Andaman Islands (1927-1986), as told to Stanley Scism.

AS1179 LungMuana, K.

A Pilgrimage to the Ecumenical World: (In Search of New Paradigms). Delhi, II: ISPCK, 1994. xi, 73 pp. Paper. 8172142420.

The personal odyssey of a pastor of the Presbyterian Church of Mizoram, who was General Secretary of the NCCI.

AS1180 MacNicol, Nicol

Pandita Ramabai: A Builder of Modern India. Mussoorie, II: Nivedit Good Books, 1996. 205 pp. Paper. 8186701002.

Reprint of a classic biography (Association Press, 1926) of Pandita Ramabai Sarasivati (1858-1922), India's pioneer Christian woman leader, with a new introduction by Vishal Mangalwadi.

AS1181 Mangalwadi, Ruth, and Vishal Mangalwadi

Carey, Christ and Cultural Transformation: The Life and Influence of William Carey. Carlisle, ENK: OM Publishing, 1997. xii, 142 pp. Paper. 185078258X.

A reevaluation of the contribution of William Carey to the modernization of India, by one well-known in India and the West as a political campaigner and champion of social reform.

AS1182 Mangalwadi, Vishal, and Ruth Mangalwadi

The Legacy of William Carey: A Model for the Transformation of a Culture. Wheaton, ILU: Crossway Books, 1999. 159 pp. Paper. 1581341121.

Described as the central character of India's modernization, this biography explores the silent revolution initiated by Carey, the industrialist, economist, medical humanitarian, educator, botanist, media pioneer, moral reformer—Christian missionary; originally published by William Carey (1993).

AS1183 Martin, Paul A. J.

Missionary of the Indian Road: The Theology of Stanley Jones.

Bungler, II: Theological Book Trust, 1996. viii, 299 pp. Paper. 8174750126.

A detailed analysis of the thought and missiological contributions of the noted American Methodist missionary to India; presented as a Ph.D. dissertation at Cambridge University.

AS1184 Mathew, E. V.

The Secular Witness of E. V. Mathew. (Confessing the Faith in India, 8). Madras, II: CLS, 1972. xx, 267 pp. Paper. No ISBN.

A study of the life and thought of E. V. Matthew (1917-1971), who took to the legal profession as Christian vocation, and was committed to the radical transformation of Indian society through law and politics; with selections from his writings.

AS1185 McEldowney, James E.

The Making of a Missionary: The Story of My Life. Bradenton, FLU: McEldowney, 1993. 378 pp. Paper. No ISBN.

The autobiography of an American Methodist missionary to India (1935-1967) active in theological education and Christian media development.

AS1186 Mongour, Paul

De l' Himalaya au Golfe de Bengali: monseigneur Louis Mathias. Tournai, BE: Oeuvre de Saint-Paul, 1969. 134 pp. No ISBN.

L. Mathias (1887-1965), from Alsace, was one of the men who gave guidance and direction to the Catholic Church in independent India, as Archbishop of Madras.

AS1187 Morris, Henry

The Life of John Murdoch, LL.D.: The Literary Evangelist of India. Madras, II: CLS, 1995. vi, 178 pp. Paper. No ISBN.

A reprint of a 1906 biography of John Morris (1819-1904) who, after educational work in Ceylon (1844-1854), devoted the remaining fifty years of his life to Christian literature development in India, becoming the first General Secretary of the CLS for India in 1891.

AS1188 Moyer, Samuel Tyson

They Heard the Call. Newton, KSU: Faith and Life Press, 1970. 171 pp. Paper. 0873038347.

Stories of General Conference Mennonite missionary pioneers in India.

AS1189 Murthy, B. Srinivasa

Mother Teresa and India. Long Beach, CAU: Long Beach Publications, 1983. xi, 131 pp. Paper. 0941910008.

An Indian philosopher's analysis of the Nobel Peace Prize winner's powerful spiritual message of Christian love in action, and of India's unique social problems, including the desperate plight of the poorest of the poor, to which she has responded.

AS1190 Neill, Stephen Charles, and Eleanor M. Jackson, eds.

God's Apprentice: The Autobiography of Stephen Neill. London, ENK: Hodder & Stoughton, 1991. 349 pp. 0340544902.

Recollections by the reowned missionary-missiologist (1900-1984), edited and abridged for posthumous publication.

AS1191 O'Connor, Daniel

Gospel, Raj and Swaraj: The Missionary Years of C. F. Andrews 1904-1914. (Studies in the Intercultural History of Christianity, 62). Frankfurt am Main, GW: Lang, 1990. xii, 366 pp. Paper. 3631420552.

A study tracing the development of the profound and original theological reflection through a formative decade of C. F. Andrews' life, his contribution to the making of an Indian church, and his friendship with Gandhi and people of other faiths.

AS1192 O'Connor, Daniel, ed.
The Testimony of C. F. Andrews. (Confessing the Faith in India Series, 10). Madras, II: CLS, 1974. xvi, 280 pp. Paper. No ISBN.

A sensitive study of the life and work of Charles Freer Andrews (1871-1940), Anglican missionary in India (1904-1940), with extensive excerpts from his writings showing his total identification with Indian life and the aspirations of the Indian people.

AS1193 Penner, Peter
Robert Needham Cust, 1821-1909: A Personal Biography. (Studies in British History, 5). Lewiston, NYU: E. Mellen Press, 1987. xiv, 357 pp. 0889464561.

Biography of a British colonial administrator in India (1843-1868) who, as philologist, linguist, and missionary statesman active in the CMS, influenced British opinion toward missions.

AS1194 Philip, T. V.
Krishna Mohan Banerjea: Christian Apologist. (Confessing the Faith in India, 15). Bangalore, II: CLS, 1982. viii, 201 pp. Paper. No ISBN.

A biography of the first Indian clergyman entrusted with an Episcopal church in Bengal who, during his life (1813-1885), made major contributions to the Bengali Renaissance and to Hindu-Christian dialogue; with selections from his writings.

AS1195 Plechl, Pia Maria
Con Trenza y Emplema de Casta; El misionero del Escandalo: Roberto de Nobili (1577-1656). (Misioneros Que Hicieron Historia, 5). Buenos Aires, AG: Editorial Guadalupe, 1982. 159 pp. Paper. 9500000016.

Spanish translation.

AS1196 Plechl, Pia Maria
Mit Haarschopf und Kastenschnur: Roberto de Nobili (Indien). (Missionare, die Geschichte machten). Mödling, GW: Verlag St. Gabriel; St. Augustin, GW: Steyler Verlag, 1977. 140 pp. 385264108X.

An analysis of the radical accommodation to Indian culture of the pioneer Jesuit missionary.

AS1197 Porter, David
Mother Teresa: The Early Years. Grand Rapids, MIU: Eerdmans, 1986. xii, 100 pp. Paper. 0802801854.

A popular account of Mother Teresa's early life, and call to become a nun to minister to the poorest of the poor in India; based on an Albanian biography by her cousin Lush Gjerji.

AS1198 Pucci, Mario V.
Madre Teresa di Calcutta: Un cuore grande come il mondo. (Figure della Chiesa). Padova, IT: Messaggero, 1990. 157 pp. 887026971X.

Enlarged third edition of a popular biography of Mother Teresa.

AS1199 Pudaite, Mawii
Beyond the Next Mountain: The Story of Rochunga Pudaite. Lewisville, TXU: Accelerated Christian Education, 1997. 152 pp. 156265019X.

Reprint of a popular biography of Rochunga Pudaite, Indian founder of Bibles for the World Ministries; first published by Tyndale House Publishers in 1982.

AS1200 Rajamanickam, Svarimuthu
The First Oriental Scholar: Robert de Nobili alias Tattuva Podagar, the Father of Tamil Prose. Tirunelveli, II: De Nobili Research Institute; : St. Xavier's College, 1972. xi, 279 pp. No ISBN.

A doctoral thesis reevaluating the life and work of Robert de Nobili, S.J. (1577-1656), with an extended analysis of his work as a scholar and writer of Tamil prose.

AS1201 Reynolds, Charles
Punjab Pioneer. Waco, TXU: Word Books, 1968. 183 pp. No ISBN.

A popular biography of Dr. Edith Brown (1864-1956), Baptist Zenana Mission Society doctor in India (1891-1956) and founder of Ludhiana Hospital and Medical College.

AS1202 Rowe, David Johnson
Consider Jesus: Lessons from the Life and Ministry of an Indian Evangelist Called Azariah. Bombay, II: David Johnson Rowe, 1994. vi, 215 pp. Paper. No ISBN.

The challenge of rural development in Andra Pradesh, India, and the partnership of the Indian church with Habitat for Humanity and Friends of Christ in India, told through the ministry of a South Indian itinerant evangelist, Korabandi Azariah Rajasekhararao.

AS1203 Sargant, Norman Carr
Mary Carpenter in India. Bristol, ENK: A.J. Sargant, 1987. 139 pp. No ISBN.

An account of the efforts of Mary Carpenter (1807-1877) to help Indian women, inspired by Raja Ram Mohan Roy and her father.

AS1204 Sargent, John
The Life and Letters of Henry Martyn. Edinburgh, STK: Banner of Truth Trust, 1985. xiv, 463 pp. Paper. 0851514685.

A reprint of the classic biography of a pioneer missionary to India (first published in 1819).

AS1205 Saulière, A.
His Star in the East. Edited by Svarimuthu Rajamanickam. Gamdi-Anand, II: Gujarat Sahitya Prakash, 1995. xxviii, 530 pp. No ISBN.

Revised edition of a definitive study of the life and contributions of Robert de Nobili, S.J., the controversial advocate of radical adaptation, and brilliant Tamil scholar in 17th-century South India; originally published in 1955.

AS1206 Scudder, Dorothy Jealous
A Thousand Years in Thy Sight: The Story of the Scudder Missionaries of India. New York, NYU: Vantage Press, 1984. xix, 356 pp. 0533057604.

An account of the first medical mission sent abroad by the ABCFM, and of four generations of Scudder family missionaries to India.

AS1207 Seamands, John T., and Ruth Seamands
Engineered for Glory. Wilmore, KYU: Francis Asbury Society, 1984. 171 pp. Paper. 0915143011.

Biography of Earl Arnett Seamands (1891-1984), an outstanding Methodist missionary evangelist in India (1919-1957), with tributes, including one by his son, who authored this narrative biography.

AS—ASIA

AS1208 Serreau, Yann, and Veronique Serreau

Tel un bon jardinier: François Guezou missionnaire en Inde. (Signatures). Paris, FR: Éditions du Cerf, 1993. 155 pp. Paper. 2204049336.

A popular biography of Francois Guezon (b.1924), a Salesian missionary in India (Kerala and Tamil Nadu) since 1952 who, like Mother Teresa, sought to minister to the poorest of the poor.

AS1209 Settgast, Ann-Charlott

Der Mann in Tranquebar: Ein Porträt des Bartholomäus Ziegenbalg, gestaltet nach alten Urkunden und Briefen. Berlin, GE: Evan Verlagsanstalt, 1981. 206 pp. No ISBN.

A portrait of B. Ziegenbalg (1682-1719), pioneer Protestant missionary in India.

AS1210 Sharpe, Eric J.

Not to Destroy But to Fulfill: The Contribution of J.N. Farquhar to Protestant Missionary Thought in India before 1914. (Studia Missionalia Upsaliensia, 5). Uppsala, SW: Almqvist & Wiksell; Lund, SW: Gleerup, 1965. 387 pp. No ISBN.

A scholarly analysis of the thought of John Nicol Farquhar (1861-1929), Madras Christian College teacher, YMCA Secretary, and later Professor of Comparative Religion in the University of Manchester, and of his influence on two generations of missionaries and Christian leaders in India.

AS1211 Spink, Kathryn

A Chain of Love: Mother Teresa and Her Suffering Disciples. London, ENK: SPCK, 1984. 117 pp. 0281040990.

Excerpts from letters of Mother Teresa, Jacqueline de Decker (a Belgian co-worker), and some of her 3,000 sick and suffering co-workers, providing insight into Mother Teresa's understanding of suffering.

AS1212 Spink, Kathryn

Mere Teresa: De la souffrance à la joie. Paris, FR: Éditions du Cerf, 1993. 157 pp. Paper. No ISBN.

French translation.

AS1213 Spink, Kathryn

A Sense of the Sacred: A Biography of Bede Griffiths. Maryknoll, NYU: Orbis Books; London, ENK: SPCK, 1989. viii, 214 pp. 0883444429 (US).

The biography of the remarkable English Benedictine monk (b.1906) who, since 1955, has witnessed in India that marriage of East and West made possible when persons seek the universal and eternal truth at the heart of all religions.

AS1214 Stokes, Samuel

The India of My Dreams: Samuel Stokes's Challenge to Christian Mission. Edited by William W. Emilsen. Delhi, II: ISPCK, 1995. xi, 210 pp. Paper. 8172142579.

Selections from the writings of Samuel (Satyanand) Stokes (1882-1946), with an interpretive essay by the editor on his contribution to mission in India, from his entry as a "freelance" American Presbyterian missionary in 1904, to his leadership in the 1920s and 1930s in Christian ashrams, the freedom struggle, and dialogue with Hindus.

AS1215 Stuart, James

Swami Abhishiktananda: His Life Told through His Letters. Delhi, II: ISPCK, 1989. xvi, 384 pp. Paper. No ISBN.

A full account of the life of Dom Henri Le Saux (Swami Abhishiktananda), showing the tensions in his double loyalty to Christianity and to Advaita philosophy, during twenty-five years in India.

AS1216 Taylor, Richard W., ed.

The Contributions of E. Stanley Jones. (Confessing the Faith in India Series, 9). Madras, II: CLS, 1973. vii, 120 pp. Paper. No ISBN.

This small volume introduces us to the work of Dr. Jones as he tried to relate the Gospel of Jesus Christ to the sociopolitical and cultural realities of India.

AS1217 Teresa, Mother

My Life for the Poor: Mother Teresa of Calcutta. Edited by José Luis González-Balado and Janet N. Playfoot. San Fransico, CAU: Harper & Row, 1985. xi, 107 pp. 006068237X.

Mother Teresa telling her own story in her own words as in an autobiography.

AS1218 Tete, Peter

Father Edward de Meulder, S. J. Bihar, II: Ranchi Jesuit Society, 1994. xv, 166 pp. No ISBN.

A biography of Edward de Meulder, S.J. (1904-1983), a Belgian Jesuit who spent fifty-seven years in India (1927-1983), mainly in ministry to tribals in the Ranchi district of Bihar state.

AS1219 Thomas, M. A.

A Leap into the Unknown: Autobiographical Anecdotes. Bangalore, II: Asian Trading Corp, 1992. 242 pp. Paper. 8170861586.

Reminiscences by the Rev. Dr. M. A. Thomas (b.1913), founder of the world-renowned Ecumenical Christian Centre at Whitefield, Bangalore, and of the Vigil India Movement.

AS1220 Thomas, Madathilparapil M.

My Ecumenical Journey, 1947-1975. Trivandrum, II: Ecumenical Publishing Centre, 1990. 467 pp. Paper. No ISBN.

The story by the ecumenical Indian theologian and moderator of the WCC's Central Committee (1968-1975), of his personal involvement in the ecumenical movement from Oslo (1947) to Nairobi (1975).

AS1221 Thomas, O. M.

Bishop Severin, SJ: Great Benefactor of the Tribals and Champion of Freedom of Conscience. Allahabad, II: Christian Agency, 1963. xvi, 340 pp. Paper. No ISBN.

A sympathetic account of the struggles to gain religious freedom for missionaries and Indian nationals, especially of the tribal groups, by Bishop Oscar Sevrin (b.1884), a Belgian Jesuit, missionary to India (1908-1957), and bishop in Madhiya Pradesh (1933-1957).

AS1222 Tinker, Hugh

The Ordeal of Love: C. F. Andrews and India. Delhi, II: Oxford University Press, 1979. xxii, 334 pp. No ISBN.

A scholarly biography of C. F. Andrews, who went to India as an Anglican priest, and became both a close friend of Gandhi and Tagore and a mediator between the Indian nationalists and the British.

AS1223 Vadakkan, Joseph

A Priest's Encounter with Revolution: An Autobiography. (Studies on Indian Marxism Series, 1). Madras, II: CLS, 1974. 159 pp. Paper. No ISBN.

An abridged version in English of the author's autobiography, published in 1974 in Malayalam, in which he describes his struggle of commitment to the poor as a Roman Catholic parish priest and his encounters with Communism in Kerala, India.

AS—ASIA

AS1224 Vandana, Sister, ed.
Swami Abhishiktananda: The Man and His Message. Delhi, II: ISPCK, 1993. 82 pp. Paper. 8172141203.

Revised second edition of reflections on the life and work of Swami Abhishiktananda (Dom Henri Le Saux, O.S.B.) by ten close friends.

AS1225 Wiebe, Viola Bergthold, and Marilyn Wiebe Dodge
Sepia Prints: Memoirs of a Missionary in India. Winnipeg, MBC: Kindred Press, 1990. xvii, 173 pp. Paper. 0921788037.

Illustrated memoirs of a Mennonite Brethren missionary, from her birth in India in 1903 to missionary parents, through her service in the Mahbubnagar region from 1927 to 1970.

AS1226 Wilson, Dorothy Clarke
Doktor Ida: Fünzig Jahre als Missionsärztin in Indien: Dr. Ida Scudder, 1870-1961. Translated by Ruth Rostock. Wuppertal, GW: R. Brockhaus Verlag, 1995. 239 pp. Paper. 3417219027.

German translation of *Dr. Ida* (New York: McGraw-Hill, 1959), the biography of Ida S. Scudder (1870-1959), outstanding medical missionary and founder of Vellore Christian Medical Centre in India.

AS1227 Wilson, Dorothy Clarke
Palace of Healing: The Story of Dr. Clara Swain, First Woman Missionary Doctor, and the Hospital She Founded. New York, NYU: McGraw-Hill, 1968. x, 245 pp. No ISBN.

A popular account of the work of the Clara Swain Hospital in Bareilly, North India, and of the Methodist missonary foundress who was the first woman physician to the Orient in 1869.

AS1228 Zambonini, Franca
Teresa of Calcutta: A Pencil in God's Hand. Translated by Jordan Aumann. Staten Island, NYU: Alba House, 1993. xviii, 189 pp. Paper. 0818906707.

A readable account, by a highly regarded Italian journalist, of the life and work of Mother Teresa, based on interviews and eyewitness accounts.

Nepal

See also HI699 and MI118.

AS1229 Cundy, Mary
Better than the Witch Doctor. Crowborough, ENK: MARC-Monarch, 1994. 288 pp. Paper. 1854242679.

The story of a pioneer ministry of healing in Nepal by an English social worker, Mary Cundy, from 1957 to 1989, and of the Christian community that grew out of it.

AS1230 Fletcher, Grace Nies
The Fabulous Flemings of Kathmandu: The Story of Two Doctors in Nepal. New York, NYU: Dutton, 1964. 219 pp. No ISBN.

A popular account of the pioneer medical mission of Drs. Robert and Bethel Fleming in Nepal, 1949 to 1964, under the United Mission to Nepal.

AS1231 Hale, Thomas
Don't Let the Goats Eat the Loquat Trees. Grand Rapids, MIU: Zondervan, 1986. 257 pp. Paper. 0310213010.

A personal account of an American physician working as a missionary at AMP Pipal Hospital, Nepal, 1970-1982.

AS1232 Hale, Thomas
Living Stones of the Himalayas: Adventures of an American Couple in Nepal. Grand Rapids, MIU: Zondervan, 1993. 255 pp. Paper. 0310385113.

The firsthand account of medical missionaries, Thomas and Cynthia Hale, who served, from 1970, under the United Mission to Nepal, in rural and urban communities and in medical education.

AS1233 Hankins, Gerald W.
A Heart for Nepal: The Dr. Helen Huston Story. Winnipeg, MBC: Windflower Communications, 1992. 245 pp. Paper. 1895308097.

Vignettes of the life and medical mission work of Helen Huston, a Canadian doctor at AMP Pipal Hospital of the United Mission to Nepal, 1953 to 1989.

AS1234 Hawker, David B. G.
The Story of Ruth Watson of Nepal. London, ENK: Scripture Union, 1984. 127 pp. Paper. 0862012171.

The biography of a pioneer British doctor who served in the United Mission to Nepal, 1951 to 1976.

AS1235 Lindell, Jonathan
Nepal and the Gospel of God. Kathmandu, NP: United Mission to Nepal; New Delhi, II: Masihi Sahitya Samstha, 1979. 279 pp. No ISBN.

A narrative official history of missions to Nepal, focusing on the work of the United Mission to Nepal since 1954.

AS1236 Lindell, Jonathan
Nepal ja Jumalan evankeliumi. Translated by Tellervo Ihalainen. Hämeelinna, FI: Päivä, 1981. 257 pp. Paper. 9516222471.

Finnish translation.

AS1237 Perry, Cindy L.
A Biographical History of the Church in Nepal. Kathmandu, NP: Nepal Church History Project, 1993. 155 pp. No ISBN.

Second edition of the history of the Christian church in Nepal, told through the biographies of its principal missionary and national leaders.

AS1238 Perry, Cindy L.
Nepali Around the World: Emphasizing Nepali Christians of the Himalyas. Kathmandu, NP: Ekta Books, 1997. xi, 463 pp. Paper. No ISBN.

A detailed survey of Christian ministries among Nepalis in diaspora; originally presented as a Ph.D. dissertation at the University of Edinburgh in Scotland in 1994.

Pakistan

See also MI158-MI159 and AS921.

AS1239 Corcoran, Lois
He Leadeth Me: An Autobiography of a Missionary to Pakistan. Hazelwood, MOU: Word Aflame Press, 1991. 268 pp. Paper. 0932581862.

Vignettes by United Pentecostal missionaries to Pakistan and other Asian countries since 1970.

AS1240 Daniels, L. T.

Frontier Challenge: "There Was a Man Sent from God Whose Name Was John." Penistone, ENK: Bridge Publications, 1987. xv, 172 pp. Paper. 0947934146 (hdbk), 0947934138 (pbk).

The life of Jack Ringer (1904-1985), a British Coldstream Guard who became a missionary to the staunchly Muslim Pathan tribes in northwest Pakistan as part of the Afghan Border Crusade (renamed the North West Frontier Fellowship in 1986).

AS1241 Esther, Gulshan, Sister, and Thelma Sangster

The Torn Veil: The Story of Sister Gulshan Esther as Told to Thelma Sangster with Noble Din Interpreter. Fort Washington, PAU: CLC, 1989. 155 pp. Paper. 0875084737.

The personal experience of a crippled, high-caste, Pakistani, Shia Muslim girl, healed by Christ.

AS1242 Larson, Warren Fredrick

Islamic Ideology and Fundamentalism in Pakistan: Climate for Conversion to Christianity? Lanham, MDU: University Press of America, 1998. xviii, 281 pp. 0761810943.

A scholarly study of Islamic theology and fundamentalism in Pakistan and its impact on possible conversions to Christianity; originally presented as a doctoral dissertation at Fuller Theological Seminary, Pasadena, California.

AS1243 Pfau, Ruth

Wenn du deine grosse Liebe triffst: Das Geheimnis meines Lebens. Freiburg, GW: Herder, 1985. 158 pp. Paper. 3451202591.

The account of a Catholic convert from Protestantism (b.1929), who studied medicine, entered a religious congregation, and devoted her life to the lepers of Pakistan.

AS1244 Rooney, John

The Hesitant Dawn: Christianity in Pakistan, 1579-1760. (Pakistan Christian History Monograph, 2). Rawalpindi, PK: Christian Study Centre, 1984. vi, 120 pp. Paper. No ISBN.

The history of Christianity under the Mughals, 1579-1760, in what is now known as Pakistan.

AS1245 Rooney, John

Into Deserts: A History of the Catholic Diocese of Lahore, 1886-1986. (Pakistan Christian History Monograph, 4). Rawalpindi, PK: Christian Study Centre, 1986. 149 pp. Paper. No ISBN.

Development of the Catholic Diocese of Lahore, illustrating the growth of an indigenous element in an uprooted people; utilizing published, unpublished, and oral sources.

AS1246 Rooney, John

On Heels of Battles: A History of the Catholic Church in Pakistan, 1780-1886. (Pakistan Christian history Monograph, 3). Rawalpindi, PK: Christian Study Centre, 1986. 129 pp. Paper. No ISBN.

History of the Catholic Church to the establishing of the hierarchy in 1886 and the beginning of the diocese of Lahore.

AS1247 Rooney, John

Shadows in the Dark: A History of Christianity in Pakistan up to the 10th Century. (Pakistan Christian History Monograph, 1). Rawalpindi, PK: Christian Study Centre, 1984. 120 pp. Paper. No ISBN.

The history, to the 10th century, of the beginnings of Christianity in what is now Pakistan.

AS1248 Stock, Frederick

People Movements in the Punjab: With Special Reference to the United Presbyterian Church. South Pasadena, CAU: William Carey Library, 1975. xxii, 364 pp. 0878084177.

A scholarly analysis of outreach to unreached people groups in the Punjab; originally submitted as a master's thesis at Fuller Theological Seminary.

AS1249 Syrjänen, Seppo

In Search of Meaning and Identity: Conversion to Christianity in Pakistani Muslim Culture. (Annals of the Finnish Society for Missiology and Ecumenics, 45). Helsinki, FI: Finnish Society for Missiology and Ecumenics, 1984. 246 pp. Paper. 9519520708.

This volume presents a phenomenological analysis of conversion to Christianity in an Islamic culture, using Pakistan as a case study, based on interviews of thirty-six converts.

AS1250 Vemmelund, Laurits

The Christian Minority in the North West Frontier Province of Pakistan. (C.S.C. Series, 6). Rawalpindi, PK: Christian Study Centre, 1973. 202 pp. No ISBN.

A 1972 sociological and statistical report on Christians in the NWFP of Pakistan; reprinted from AL-MUSHIR 15 (4-6), 1973.

AS1251 Young, William G.

Days of Small Things?: A Narrative Assessment of the Work of the Church of Scotland in the Punjab in "The Age of William Harper, 1873-85." (Pakistan Church History Monograph, 8). Rawalpindi, PK: Christian Study Centre, 1991. ii, 150 pp. Paper. No ISBN.

Details, based on archival records, of the mission service under the Church of Scotland Mission in the Punjab of Rev. William Harper (b.1845) from 1874 to 1893 and Rev. John Youngson (b.1852) from 1875 to 1886.

Sri Lanka [Ceylon]

See also EA101, SP242, AF1269, and AS248.

AS1252 Abeyasingha, Nihal

The Radical Tradition: The Changing Shape of Theological Reflection in Sri Lanka. Colombo, CE: Ecumenical Institute for Study and Dialogue, 1985. vi, 232 pp. No ISBN.

A survey of Catholic contextual theology in Sri Lanka—its origins, development, major theologians, and models in relation to Sinhalese Buddhism.

AS1253 Boudens, Robrecht

Catholic Missionaries in a British Colony: Successes and Failures in Ceylon, 1796-1893. (Schriften der *Neuen Zeitschrift für Missionswissenschaft,* 28). Immensee, SZ: Nouvelle revue de science missionaire, 1979. 181 pp. Paper. 3858240559.

A scholarly analysis of the strengths and weaknesses of Catholic missions in Ceylon under British rule, 1796 to 1893.

AS1254 Chandrakanthan, A. J. V.

Catholic Revival in Post-Colonial Sri Lanka: A Critique of Ecclesial Contextualization. Colombo, CE: Social and Economic Development Centre, 1995. xxxv, 260 pp. 9559576704.

A revised and updated version of the author's dissertation (Ottawa University 1987) analyzing the multifaceted issues of contextualization for the churches in postcolonial Sri Lanka.

AS1255 Don Peter, W. L. A.

Education in Sri Lanka under the Portuguese. Colombo, SL: Colombo Catholic Press; Bolawalana, CE: Don Peter, 1978. xiii, 342 pp. No ISBN.

A detailed analysis of how the Portuguese, from 1505 to 1658, used adult, elementary, and higher education in Ceylon for Christian influence and evangelization.

AS1256 Houtart, François

Religion and Ideology in Sri Lanka. Bangalore, II: TPI, 1974. xvi, 541 pp. Paper. No ISBN.

A sociology of the religions of Sri Lanka by a noted Belgian sociologist, with special focus on the interrelationship of religion and politics.

AS1257 Miller, Deo, and Susan F. Titus

You Start with One. Nashville, TNU: Nelson, 1990. 143 pp. Paper. 0840731493.

Vignettes of the ministry since 1978, of Deo and Elaine Miller in Sri Lanka through HOPE Child Care International, caring for more than 2,000 poverty-stricken children each year.

AS1258 Somaratna, G. P. V.

Origins of the Pentecostal Mission in Sri Lanka. Nugegoda, CE: Margaya Fellowship of Sri Lanka, 1996. 99 pp. Paper. No ISBN.

An historical study of the beginnings of the Pentecostal movement in Sri Lanka.

AS1259 Somaratna, G. P. V.

Walter H. Clifford: The Apostle of Pentecostalism in Sri Lanka. Nugegoda, CE: Margaya Publishers, 1996. xii, 116 pp. Paper. No ISBN.

A well-documented account of the life and work of the founder of Pentecostalism in Sri Lanka.

AS1260 *The Catholic Church in Sri Lanka: The British Period*

Translated by V. Perniola. (The Ceylon Historical Journal Monograph Series, 17-19). Dehiwala, CE: Tisara Prakasakayo, 1992-1995. 3 vols. No ISBN.

A full documentation in three volumes, of the British period of the Catholic Church in Ceylon [vol. 1: *The Colombo Vicarate, 1795-1844*; vol. 2: *The Vicarates of Colombo and Jaffna, 1845-1849*; vol. 3: *The Vicarates of Colombo and Jaffna, 1850-1855*].

AS1261 *The Catholic Church in Sri Lanka: The Portuguese Period*

Translated by V. Perniola. (The Ceylon Historical Journal Monograph Series, 12). Dehiwala, CE: Tisara Prakasakayo, 1989. 3 vols. No ISBN.

A full documentation in three volumes, of the Portuguese period of the Catholic Church in Ceylon [vol. 1: *1505-1565*; vol. 2: *1566-1619*; vol. 3: *1620-1658*].

AS1262 *The Catholic Church in Sri Lanka: The Dutch Period*

Translated by V. Perniola. (Ceylon Historical Journal Monograph Series, 3, 5). Dehiwala, CE: Tisara Prakasakayo, 1983-1985. 3 vols. No ISBN.

A full documentation in three volumes, of the Dutch period of the Catholic Church in Ceylon [vol. 1: *1658-1711*; vol. 2: *1712-1746*; vol. 3: *1747-1795*].

AS1263 Wilson, D. Kanagasabai

The Christian Church in Sri Lanka: Her Problems and Her Influence. Colombo, CE: Study Centre for Religion and Society, 1975. 144 pp. No ISBN.

A textbook on church and society issues in Sri Lanka, including issues of church and state, education, church union, caste, evangelism, and relation to other faiths.

AS1264 Young, Richard Fox, and G. P. V. Somaratna

Vain Debates: The Buddhist-Christian Controversies of Nineteenth-Century Ceylon. (Publications of the De Nobili Research Library, 23). Vienna, AU: Sammlung De Nobili, 1996. 236 pp. Paper. 3900271283.

A detailed analysis of the 19th-century debates between Christians and Buddhists in Ceylon.

AS1265 Young, Richard Fox, and S. Jebanesan

The Bible Trembled: The Hindu-Christian Controversies of Nineteenth-Century Ceylon. (Publications of the De Nobili Research Library, 22). Vienna, AU: Sammlung De Nobili, 1995. 204 pp. Paper. 3900271275.

A scholarly history of the clashes between Hindus and Christians in North Ceylon (present Sri Lanka); based on archival research, with bibliography.

Southeast Asia: General Works

See also ED133-ED134, ED136-ED137, SP39, SP168, and AS35.

AS1266 Anderson, Gerald H., ed.

Christ and Crisis in Southeast Asia. New York, NYU: Friendship Press, 1968. 176 pp. Paper. No ISBN.

A mission study book designed as a country-by-country report on the present state of the churches in Southeast Asia.

AS1267 Brown, Russell F.

How the Gospel Spreads: in Indonesia, Singapore, and the Philippines. Valley Forge, PAU: International Ministries, ABC/USA, 1982. 127 pp. Paper. No ISBN.

A study on the southeastern Asian islands where American Baptists are involved in challenging church relationships; including letters and writings from church workers.

AS1268 Koyama, Kosuke

Theology in Contact: Six Reflections on God's Word and Man's Life in God's World. (Word for the World, 4). Madras, II: CLS, 1975. vii, 87 pp. No ISBN.

Six meditations using contemporary parables in relating the Gospel to cultural realities in Southeast Asia.

AS1269 Myers, Glenn

The Rim of Fire: Indonesia and the Malay-Speaking Muslim World. (Briefings). Carlisle, ENK: OM Publishing, 1998. 64 pp. Paper. 1850782989.

An introduction to the challenge of Christian witness among Muslims in Indonesia and Malaysia.

AS1270 Ramientos, Nene

Contemporary Christian Issues. Quezon City, PH: New Day Publishers, 1982. 72 pp. Paper. 971100013X.

A Filipino Christian leader addresses himself to world evangelization, particularly the Asian situation, and challenges Filipinos to accept leadership through the Phillipine Association of Christian Education.

AS1271 Rose, Kurt

The Islands of the Sulu Sea. Palo Alto, CAU: Glencannon Press, 1993. 216 pp. Paper. 0963758616.

Adventures of a young German seaman in the Orient, including time spent as a crew member of the Fukuin Maru (Gospel Ship), an evangelization project of the Baptist Mission in the Philippines, 1932-1936.

AS1272 Stafford, Ann
Saigon Journey. London, ENK: Champion Press; New York, NYU: Taplinger Publishing, 1960. 188 pp. No ISBN.

The unusual journey of a Roman Catholic woman to twelve countries of Southeast Asia, and her conversations with representative Eastern women, paying high tribute to Roman Catholic missionaries.

AS1273 Von der Mehden, Fred R.
Religion and Modernization in Southeast Asia. Syracuse, NYU: Syracuse University Press, 1986. viii, 240 pp. Paper. 0815623615.

A scholarly analysis of the interrelationships of religion and modernization in Burma, Thailand, Malaysia, Indonesia, and the Philippines, in light of the theoretical assumptions presented by pos-twar social scientists.

Cambodia [Kampuchea]

See also AS1509.

AS1274 Burke, Todd, and DeAnn Burke
Annointed for Burial. Plainfield, NJU: Logos International; Oklahoma City, OKU: New Covenant Commission, 1977. v, 259 pp. 0882702459 (hdbk), 0882704850 (pbk).

Two short-term missionaries with the Khmer church in Cambodia in 1973-1975, before the nation fell to the communist Khmer Rouge, tell their story.

AS1275 Cormack, Don
Killing Fields Living Fields: An Unfinished Portrait of the Cambodian Church — the Church That Would Not Die. Grand Rapids, MIU: Monarch Publications, 2001. 463 pp. Paper. 0825460026, 1854244876.

Updated edition of a gripping narrative history of the church in Cambodia, its trauma during the Pol Pot terror of the 1970s, and its rebirth among refugees, and now, in Cambodia; first published in 1997 by Monarch Books, 1854244876.

AS1276 Ens, Mary
A Time for Mercy: Touching Stories of Open Arms and God's Love in the Streets and Alleys, Homes and Hospitals of Cambodia. (Walk Around the World Series, 2). Camp Hill, PAU: Christian Publications, 1998. 168 pp. Paper. 0875097871.

Stories told by a Christian and Missionary Alliance missionary of her coming home to Cambodia in 1994, recalling ministries there from 1961 to 1971.

Indonesia

See also GW28, GW287, EA133, ME120, CR915, CR1057, CR1108, AS113, AS145, AS194, and EU227.

AS1277 Akkeren, Philip van
Sri and Christ: A Study of the Indigenous Church in East Java. Translated by Annebeth Mackie. (World Studies of Churches in Mission). Cambridge, ENK: Lutterworth Press; New York, NYU: Friendship Press, 1970. xxiv, 229 pp. Paper. No ISBN.

A socioreligious study of popular religion and Protestant Christianity in rural East Java, Indonesia.

AS1278 Algra, A.
De Gereformeerde Kerken in Nederlands-Indië/Indonesië (1877-1961). Franeker, NE: Wever, 1968. 358 pp. No ISBN.

Detailed history of the Christian congregations in Indonesia related to the Reformed churches in the Netherlands.

AS1279 Aritonang, Jan S.
Mission Schools in Batakland (Indonesia) (1861-1940). Translated by Robert R. Boehlke. (Studies in Christian Mission, 10). Leiden, NE: Brill, 1994. xii, 379 pp. 9004099670.

A detailed study of mission schools pioneered by the Rhenish Mission (Rheinische Missions-Gesellschaft) among the Bataks of Indonesia—a major factor in the growth of the Lutheran Batak Church to become the largest Protestant church in that country.

AS1280 Bank, J.
Katholieken en de Indonesische revolutie. (Publicaties van het Katholiek Documentatie Centrum, Nijmegen, 11). Baarn, NE: Amboboeken, 1983. 576 pp. Paper. 9026305974.

A detailed history of the attitudes of Catholics in the Netherlands toward the Indonesian struggle for independence, 1945-1950, with attention to the conflict between the pro-colonial Catholic Party in the Netherlands and the missionaries in Indonesia who supported this struggle.

AS1281 Becker, Dieter
Die Kirchen und der Pancasila-Staat: Indonesische Christen zwischen Konsens und Konflikt. (Missionswissenschaftliche Forchungen Neue Folge, 1). Erlangen, GW: Verlag der Ev.-Luth. Mission, 1996. 327 pp. Paper. 387214331X.

A detailed analysis of the history and structure of church-state relations in Indonesia, including issues of religious freedom and the place of religious communities; with a thirty-eight-page bibliography.

AS1282 Becker, Dieter, ed.
Mit Worten kocht man keinen Reis: Beiträge aus den Batak-Kirchen von Nordsumatra. (Erlanger Taschenbücher, 84). Erlangen, GW: Ev.-Luth. Mission; Wuppertal, GW: Verlag der VEM, 1987. 227 pp. Paper. 3872141848.

A collection of essays, written mostly by Indonesians, on the occasion of the 125th anniversary of the foundation of the Batak mission, covering church structures, church and culture, and the church's future.

AS1283 Bentley-Taylor, David
Java Saga: Christian Progress in Muslim Java. London, ENK: OMF Books, 1976. xi, 148 pp. Paper. 085363100X.

A comprehensive account of the church in East Java, composed chiefly of converts from Islam and their descendants; originally published as *The Weathercock's Reward.*

AS1284 Bentley-Taylor, David
The Prisoner Leaps: A Diary of Missionary Life in Java. London, ENK: CIM, 1961. 352 pp. No ISBN.

The account by a CIM missionary, of his imprisonment by the Japanese in 1944, and subsequent ministry in Borneo and Java (1956-1959).

AS1285 Beyer, Ulrich
Entwicklung im Paradies: Sozialer Fortschritt und die Kirchen in Indonesien. Frankfurt am Main, GW: Lembeck, 1974. 253 pp. Paper. 3874760324.

The author descibes the socioeconomic, political, and cultural developments in independent Indonesia.

AS1286 Beyer, Ulrich

Und viele wurden hinzugetan: Mission und Gemeindewachstum in der Karo-Batak-Kirche/Indonesien. (Erlanger Taschenbücher, 63). Wuppertal, GW: Verlag der Rheinischen Missionsgesellschaft; Erlangen, GW: Ev.-Luth. Mission, 1982. 144 pp. Paper. 3872141481.

Drawing mainly on his own observations, the author describes a church in an animistic milieu that expanded twentyfold within a period of twenty years, mostly through the efforts of local co-workers.

AS1287 Beyerhaus, Peter

In der Inselwelt Südostasiens erlebt: Zweiter Teil des Reiseberichts. (Weltweite Reihe, 27-28). Stuttgart, GW: Evang. Missionsverlag, 1973. 160 pp. 3771401739.

The well-informed travel report, by the noted German evangelical missiologist, on the state of the church and mission in Indonesia in 1972.

AS1288 Boelaars, Huub J. W. M.

Indonesianisasi: Het omvormingproces van de katholieke kerk in Indonesië tot de Indonesische katholieke kerk. (Kerk en Theologie in Context, 13). Kampen, NE: Kok, 1991. xi, 472 pp. Paper. 9024268028.

A detailed study of the process of indigenization of theology, church structure, and cultural outreach of Roman Catholicism in Indonesia, as it moved from mission to church.

AS1289 Cooley, Frank L.

The Growing Seed: The Christian Church in Indonesia. Jakarta, MAU/IO: Christian Publishing House; New York, NYU: NCCUSA, Division of Overseas Ministries; Wuppertal-Barmen, GW: European Commission for Church and Mission in Indonesia, 1982. xv, 356 pp. No ISBN.

The final report (abbreviated English edition) of the comprehensive survey of churches in Indonesia carried out from 1967 to 1975, by the Department of Study and Research of the Council of Churches in Indonesia.

AS1290 Cooley, Frank L.

Indonesia: Church & Society. New York, NYU: Friendship Press, 1968. 128 pp. Paper. No ISBN.

An introduction to the churches of Indonesia and their cultural contexts; prepared as a mission study book for North American Christians.

AS1291 Coomans, Michael C. C.

Evangelisatie en kultuurverandering: Onderzoek naar de verhouding tussen de evangelisatie en de socio-kulturele veranderingen in de adat van de Dajaks van Oost-Kalimantan (bisdom Samarinda) Indonesië. (Studia Instituti Missiologici SVD, 28). St. Augustin, GW: Steyler Verlag, 1980. 327 pp. Paper. 3877871402.

A detailed study of issues in contextualization of the Gospel among the Dajaks of East Kalimantan, Indonesia; originally presented as a doctoral dissertation to the Theological Faculty at the Catholic University in Nijmegen, the Netherlands.

AS1292 Cornelissen, J. F. L. M.

Pater en Papoea: Ontmoeting van de Missionarissen van het heilig hart met de cultuur der Papoea's van Nederlands Zuid-Nieuw-Guinea (1905-1963). (Proefschrift Theol. Fac. Kath. Universiteit Nijmegen; Kerk en Theologie in Context, 1). Kampen, NE: Kok, 1988. ix, 256 pp. Paper. 9024232252.

Detailed description of the attitudes of Catholic Missionaries of the Sacred Heart toward native people in Southern Irian Jaya (Indonesia), on the basis of archives, private letters, and articles in missionary journals.

AS1293 Cutts, William A.

Weak Thing in Moni Land: The Story of Bill and Gracie Cutts. (Jaffray Collection of Missionary Portraits). Camp Hill, PAU: Christian Publications, 1990. viii, 164 pp. Paper. 0875094295.

A dramatic, popular autobiography by a veteran missionary of the Christian and Missionary Alliance, telling of work in Irian Jaya, Indonesia, 1950 to 1985.

AS1294 Dake, W. J. L.

Het medisch werk van de zending in Nederlands Indië. Kampen, NE: Kok, 1972. 222 pp. Paper. 9024200555.

A history of the medical work of missionary societies in the eastern part of the Dutch East Indies, 1855-1962.

AS1295 Davis, Thomas A.

Island of Forgotten Men. Washington, DCU: Review and Herald, 1967. 128 pp. No ISBN.

A popular account of the work of Dr. Gottfried (b.1930) and Emilie Oosterwal, as researchers and Seventh-day Adventist missionaries in Netherlands New Guinea (now West Irian), from 1957 to 1973.

AS1296 Dekker, John

Torches of Joy. Westchester, ILU: Crossway Books, 1985. 198 pp. Paper. 0891073396.

The story of pioneer missionary work, by the author and others of the Canadian Regions Beyond Missionary Union, among the Dani people of Irian Jaya, 1960-1981.

AS1297 Dietrich, Stefan

Kolonialismus und Mission auf Flores (ca. 1900-1942). (Münchner Beiträge zur Süd-Südostasienkunde, 1). Hohenschäftlarn, GW: Renner, 1989. 347 pp. Paper. 3876731305.

The first part of this work treats the period of transition from traditional tribal societies to colonialism; and the second part, the actual colonial rule, in which the Christian mission was an important factor, especially in connection with religious and educational policy.

AS1298 End, Th. van den, ed.

De Gereformeerde Zending op Sumba 1859-1972: Een bronnenpublicatie. (Project kerkhistorische Uitgaven Indonesië, 2). Oegstgeest, NE: Netherlands Reformed Church, Mission Council; Leusden, NE: Mission of the Reformed Churches in the Netherlands; Driebergen, NE: Reformed Mission League in the Netherlands Reformed Church, 1987. xiv, 726 pp. 906572110X.

A scholarly publication of selected documents from the archives of the mission of the Reformed Churches in the Netherlands in the island of Sumba, Indonesia, 1859-1972; by three Protestant churches (through their mission boards).

AS1299 End, Th. van den, ed.
De Gereformeerde Zendingsbond 1901-1961: Nederland-Tanah Toraja een bronnenpublicatie. (Project Kerkhistorische Uitgaven Indonesië, 1). Oegstgeest, NE: Netherlands Reformed Church, Mission Council; Leusden, NE: Mission of the Reformed Churches in the Netherlands; Driebergen, NE: Reformed Mission League in the Netherlands Reformed Church, 1985. xvii, 782 pp. 9071316017.

A scholarly publication of selected archival sources on the activities of the "Reformed Mission League in the Netherlands Reformed Church" in Tanah Toraja (Sulawesi/Indonesia), 1901-1961; published by the three Protestant churches (through their mission boards).

AS1300 End, Th. van den, J. A. B. Jongeneel, and Marc Spindler
Indonesische Geloofsbelijdenissen. (IIMO Research Pamphlet, 20). Leiden, NE: IIMO, 1986. iii, 231 pp. Paper. 9071387194.

A compendium of the confessions of faith in the various churches of Indonesia, with a history of their development.

AS1301 Enklaar, Ido Hendricus
Joseph Kam, "Apostel der Molukken." ("Bijdragen tot de Zendingswetenschap" Ned. Zend. Raad.). 's-Gravenhage, NE: Boekencentrum, 1963. xvi, 186 pp. No ISBN.

The life and work of Joseph Kam, missionary in the Moluccas (1815-1833); based on extensive research in archives of LMS and other societies.

AS1302 Gibbons, Alice
The People Time Forgot. Camp Hill, PAU: Christian Publications; Chicago, ILU: Moody Press, 1981. 346 pp. 0875094058 (C), 0802486886 (M, hdbk), 0802486924 (M, pbk).

A narrative account of pioneer missions among the Damal people of Irian Jaya (Indonesia), 1958 to 1978, by TEAM missionaries.

AS1303 Gih, Andrew
Revival Follows Revolution in Indonesia. London, ENK: Lakeland, 1973. ix, 150 pp. Paper. 0551004762.

The story of revival amidst revolution among Chinese Christians in Indonesia in the 1960s; with eleven personal testimonies.

AS1304 Gray, Marie
Tamu: A New Zealand Family in Java. Tauranga, NZ: Moana Press, 1988. 287 pp. Paper. 0908705344.

A popular illustrated account of the life and work of a New Zealand medical missionary family, as Presbyterian missionaries in Bandung, West Java, from 1959 to 1971.

AS1305 Hämmerle, Johannes Maria
Nias—eine eigene Welt: Sagen, Mythen, Überlieferungen. (Collectanea Instituti Anthropos, 43). St. Augustin, GW: Academia Verlag, 1999. 407 pp. Paper. 3896651471.

This first of a two-volume work, written by a Franciscan (Capuchin) missionary on the basis of his observation and presentation of folklore from the Indonesian island of Nias, deals with south and central parts of the island; ethnology, anthropology, history of religion, and missiology (especially as related to contextualization) are emphasized.

AS1306 Hayward, Douglas James
The Dani of Irian Jaya before and after Conversion. Sentani, IO: Regions Press, 1980. x, 223 pp. Paper. No ISBN.

Presented in three parts, this book tells the events that surrounded the turning to Christ of the Dani of Irian Jaya; part one gives an extensive overview of Dani culture, part two records Dani conversion, and part three records the struggles of Christian Danis.

AS1307 Hayward, Douglas James
Vernacular Christianity among the Mulia Dani: An Ethnography of Religious Belief among the Western Dani of Irian Jaya, Indonesia. Lanham, MDU: American Society of Missiology/University Press of America, 1997. ix, 329 pp. 0761807608 (hdbk), 0761807616 (pbk).

A meticulously researched case study of Dani traditional religion and the process of indigenization or contextualization of Christian beliefs and practices.

AS1308 Hitt, Russell T.
Cannibal Valley. New York, NYU: Harper & Row; Grand Rapids, MIU: Zondervan, 1970. 253 pp. No ISBN.

Story of the work of the Christian and Missionary Alliance among the primitive people of the interior of western New Guinea, and of the transformation of life that has resulted for those who have become Christians.

AS1309 Hoekema, A. G.
Denken in dynamisch evenwicht: De wordingsgeschiedenis van de nationale protestantse theologie in Indonesië (ca, 1860-1960). (Mission—Missiologisch Onderzoek in Nederland, 8). Zoetermeer, NE: Boekencentrum, 1994. 350 pp. Paper. 9023905385.

A dissertation analyzing the historical development of a Protestant theology in Indonesia between 1860 and 1960.

AS1310 Horne, Shirley
An Hour to the Stone Age. Chicago, ILU: Moody, 1974. 208 pp. Paper. 0802436900.

A popular account of work by the Missionary Aviation Fellowship in bringing the Gospel to the remote Dani people of West Irian (Indonesia).

AS1311 Houliston, Sylvia
Borneo Breakthrough. London, ENK: CIM; London, ENK: Lutterworth Press, 1963. 204 pp. No ISBN.

The story of a movement that resulted, from the work of the OMF, in the birth of new churches among the Chinese of West Borneo.

AS1312 Jacobs, Hubert, ed.
Documenta Maluncencia. (Monumenta Historica Societatis Jesu). Rome, IT: Institutum Historicum Societas Jesu, 1974-1984. 3 vol.

A three-volume collection of documents, mostly in Portuguese, on Jesuit missions in the Moluccas (Spice Islands) of East Indonesia in the 16th and 17th centuries [I (1542-1577), 1974, xlii, 842 pp.; II (1577-1606), 1980, xxxi, 859 pp., 8870411192; III (1606-1682), 1984, xxiii, 831 pp., 8870411265].

AS1313 Jacobs, Hubert, ed.
The Jesuit Makasar Documents (1615-1682). (Monumenta Historica Societatis Jesu, 134). Rome, IT: Institutum Historicum Societatis Jesu, 1988. xv, 285 pp. Paper. 8870411346.

A collection of documents in Italian, Dutch, Spanish, Latin, and especially, Portuguese, on Jesuit missions in the city of Makasar (South Sulawesi/Celebes, Indonesia).

AS1314 Jacobs, Hubert, ed.

A Treatise on the Moluccas (c. 1544): Probably the Preliminary Version of Antonio Galvao's Lost História das Molucas. (Sources and Studies for the History of the Jesuits, 3). Rome, IT: Jesuit Historical Institute, 1971. viii, 402 pp. No ISBN.

The original text, in both Portuguese and English, of a key 16th-century document for understanding early European contacts with Indonesia; edited, annotated, and translated into English from the Portuguese manuscript in the Archivo General de Indias, Seville; with bibliography.

AS1315 Jensma, Th. E.

Doopsgezinde Zending in Indonesië. (Proefschrift Theol. Fac. Universiteit van Amsterdam). 's-Gravenhage, NE: Boekencentrum, 1968. x, 181 pp. Paper. No ISBN.

A history of the missionary activities of Dutch Mennonites in Indonesia, 1821-1963; based on primary sources.

AS1316 Jong, C. A. M. de

Kompas 1965-1985: Een algemene krant met een katholieke achtergrond binnen het religieus pluralisme van Indonesië. (Kerk en Theologie in Context, 5). Kampen, NE: Kok, 1990. xxiii, 439 pp. Paper. 9024254159.

A dissertation to the Theological Faculty of the Catholic University of Nijmegen, analyzing the attitudes toward religious pluralism of KOMPAS, the most prominent Indonesian newspaper (Catholic in background), and its influence among the largely Muslim intellectual elite; based on interviews and content analysis.

AS1317 Jong, S. de

Een Javaanse levenshouding. (Proefschrift Theol. Fac. Vrije Universiteit Amsterdam). Wageningen, NE: Veenman, 1973. 193 pp. Paper. No ISBN.

A doctoral dissertation on Javanese culture and the new religious movement of Pangestu, resulting in a missiological approach; based on Indonesian and Javanese sources, as well as observations, as a Protestant minister in the area.

AS1318 Jongeling, M. C.

Het zendingsconsulaat in Nederlands-Indië, 1906-1942. (Proefschrift Theol. Fac. Rijksuniversiteit Leiden). Arnhem, NE: Van Loghum Slaterus, 1966. 371 pp. Paper. No ISBN.

A doctoral thesis about the office of the *Zendingsconsul,* the intermediary between Protestant mission societies and the Dutch colonial government of Indonesia; based on extensive research in the archives.

AS1319 Kamma, Freerk Ch.

"Dit wonderlijke Werk": Het probleem van de communicatie tussen oost en west gebaseerd op de ervaringen in het zendingswerk op Nieuw-Guinea (Irian Jaya) 1855-1972: een socio-missiologische benadering. Oegstgeest, NE: Ned. Hervormde Kerk, Raad voor de Zending, 1977. 2 vols. No ISBN.

A sociomissiological study of the personal experiences and approaches of Western missionaries to the tribal society of Dutch New Guinea (now the Indonesian province of Irian Java), 1855-1972, by a former missionary to the area; based mostly on reports in mission bulletins; in two volumes [vol.1: (xxiv, 836 pp.); vol 2: (xiv, 835 pp.)].

AS1320 Kipp, Rita Smith

The Early Years of a Dutch Colonial Mission: The Karo Field. Ann Arbor, MIU: University of Michigan Press, 1990. ix, 257 pp. 0472101765.

A detailed history of the first fifteen years (1889-1904) of the Dutch Reformed mission among the Karo People of North Sumatra (Indonesia).

AS1321 Kirchberger, Georg

Neue Dienste und Gemeindestrukturen in der katholischen Kirche Indonesiens. (Veröffentlichungen des Missionspriesterseminars, 35). Nettetal, GW: Steyler Verlag, 1986. 254 pp. Paper. 3877872018.

Confronted by the difficult situation in the Catholic Church in Indonesia caused by the shortage of priests, and with reference to the new insights emerging from Vatican II, this author suggests how new community structures and ministries could foster more lay responsibility in parish activities, without depriving the parish priest of overall responsibility.

AS1322 Kirk, Margaret

Let Justice Flow: An Asian Woman Works Creatively for the Liberation of Her People. Delhi, II: ISPCK, 1997. xvi, 224 pp. Paper. 817214394X.

Stories of the life work for justice and reconciliation of Agustina Lumentut, the first woman moderator of a church in Sulawesi.

AS1323 Kirk, Margaret

That Greater Freedom. Singapore, SI: OMF, 1986. vii, 203 pp. 9971972344.

Stories of courage of the Christians of Sulawesi amidst persecution, both by communists and Islamic fundamentalists.

AS1324 Knaap, G. J.

Kruidnagelen en Christenen: De Verenigde Oost-Indische Compagnie en de bevolking van Ambon, 1656-1696. (Verhandelingen van het Koninklijk Instituut voor Taal-, Land-, en Volkenkunde, 125). Dordrecht, NE: Foris Publications, 1987. xii, 323 pp. 9067652202.

"Cloves and Christians" analyzes how the Dutch East-Indian Company ruled the isle of Ambon from 1656 to 1696, in the sociopolitical, religious, demographic, and economic fields.

AS1325 Kobong, Theodorus

Evangelium und Tongkonan: Eine Untersuchung über die Begegnung zwischen christlicher Botschaft und der Kultur der Toraja. (Perspektiven der Weltmission, 7). Ammersbek bei Hamburg, GW: Verlag an der Lottbek, 1989. 338 pp. Paper. 3926987111.

This work explores the possibilities of adequately contextualizing the Christian message among the Toraja people on Sulawesi (Celebes) by taking into account the *tongkonan,* an institution constituting the backbone of the local society.

AS1326 Koch, Kurt Emil

The Revival in Indonesia. Grand Rapids, MIU: Kregel Publications, 1972. 310 pp. 0825430070.

English translation.

AS1327 Koch, Kurt Emil

Der Wein Gottes. Berghausen, GW: Evangelization Publishers, 1970. 310 pp. No ISBN.

An eyewitness account, by a visiting US pastor, of the explosive growth of the churches in Indonesia, in the years (1966-1968), following the defeat of a planned communist revolution.

AS1328 Koetsier, C. H.
Zending als dienst aan de samenleving: Over de houding van zending en kerk ten opzichte van sociaal-econoische vraagstukken in Indonesië in het bijzonder op Midden-Java. (Proefschrift Theol. Fac. Vrije Universiteit Amsterdam). Delft, NE: Meinema, 1975. 166 pp. Paper. 9021140101.

A case study about the relation between mission and socioeconomic development among Protestants in Central Java, 1950-1968, by a former missionary in the area.

AS1329 Kruyt, Jan
Het zendingsveld Poso: Geschiedenis van een konfrontatie. Kampen, NE: Kok, 1970. 378 pp. Paper. No ISBN.

History of the work of the pioneering missionary in central Sulawesi, in the early 20th century; written by his son, based on family archives and other primary sources.

AS1330 Landgrebe, Wilhelm
Ludwig Nommensen: "Mit Gott rechnen wie mit Zahlen." (Zeugen des gegenwärtigen Gottes; ABCTeam, B 3807). Giessen, GW: Brunnen-Verlag, 1986. 109 pp. Paper. 3765538078.

The life and work of L. Nommensen, pioneer of the Rheinische Mission among the Batak, and a great promoter of church self-sufficiency.

AS1331 Lewis, A. Rodger
The Battle for Bali: The Story of Rodger and Lelia Lewis. (The Jaffray Collection of Missionary Portraits, 23). Camp Hill, PAU: Christian Publications, 1999. xv, 213 pp. Paper. 0875098274.

A biography telling of the spiritual battles of Christian and Missionary Alliance missionaries in Bali, Indonesia.

AS1332 Müller-Krüger, Theodor
Der Protestantismus in Indonesien: Geschichte und Gestalt. (Die Kirchen der Welt, B 5). Stuttgart, GW: Evan Verlagswerk, 1968. 388 pp. No ISBN.

German translation of a work describing the history of Protestantism in Indonesia; originally written in Bahasa Indonesian.

AS1333 Müller-Krüger, Theodor, ed.
Indonesia Raja: Antlitz einer grossen Inselwelt. Bad Salzuflen, GW: MBK-Verlag, 1966. 231 pp. No ISBN.

Concentrating, for the most part, on the Protestant church in Indonesia, this compilation of articles by both Indonesian and non-Indonesian authors, describes the political, economic, cultural, and, in particular, the religious developments in the newly independent state.

AS1334 McKenzie, Douglas G.
The Mango Tree Church: The Story of the Protestant Church in Bali. Brisbane, AT: Boolarong Publications, 1988. vi, 81 pp. Paper. 0864390394.

A brief popular history of the Christian Protestant Church in Bali, 1597 to 1988.

AS1335 Middelkoop, Pieter
Curse—Retribution—Enmity: As Data in Natural Religion, Especially in Timor, Confronted with the Scripture. (Proefschrift Theol. Fac. Rijksuniversiteit Utrecht). Amsterdam, NE: Van Kampen, 1960. 168 pp. Paper. No ISBN.

A doctoral thesis relating biblical concepts to Timorese culture and religion.

AS1336 Muskens, Martin P. M.
Indonesië: Een strijd om nationale identiteit: Nationalisten, Islamisten, katholieken. (De grote oecumene: Interreligieuze ontwikkelingen). Bussum, NE: Paul Brand, 1969. 597 pp. No ISBN.

Dutch translation with English summary.

AS1337 Muskens, Martin P. M.
Partner beim Aufbau: Die Katholische Kirche in Indonesian. Aachen, GW: Missio Aktuell Verlag, 1979. 327 pp. 3921626064.

German translation.

AS1338 Muskens, Martin P. M.
Partner in Nation Building: The Catholic Church in Indonesia. Translated by Yoachim van de Linden. Aachen, GW: Missio Aktuell Verlag, 1979. 339 pp. 392162603X.

A revision, with additions up to 1978, of the Indonesian edition (*Sejarah Gereja Katolic Indonesia*); a dissertation describing the development of the modern Indonesian state, and the role of the Catholic Church in that process and in contemporary Indonesian society.

AS1339 Ogawa, Joshua K.
Unlimited Purpose: An Asian Missionary Tells His Story. Singapore, SI: OMF, 1986. ix, 144 pp. 9971972468.

An account, by an OMF's Japanese missionary, to Indonesia of his fourteen-year experience there.

AS1340 Parkin, Harry
Batak Fruit of Hindu Thought: A Thesis Presented to the Senate of Serampore College for the Degree of Doctor of Theology. Madras, II: CLS, 1978. xxii, 287 pp. Paper. No ISBN.

A detailed study of the traditional religion of the Toba-Batak people of North Sumatra in Indonesia, showing the incursion of Indian/Hindu elements; originally presented as a Th.D. thesis at Serampore College.

AS1341 Partonadi, Sutarman Soediman
Sadrach's Community and Its Contextual Roots: A Nineteenth Century Javanese Expression of Christianity. (Currents of Encounter, 3). Amsterdam, NE: Editions Rodopi, 1990. xiv, 317 pp. Paper. 9051830947.

Second edition of a scholarly description and very positive evaluation of the work of Sadrach (ca.1835-1924), a Javanese Christian and missionary, who came into conflict with the Dutch leadership of the Reformed church on Java (Indonesia), and then continued the building up of an independent Christian community.

AS1342 Pedersen, Paul Bodholdt
Batak Blood and Protestant Soul: The Development of National Batak Churches in North Sumatra. (A Christian World Mission Book). Grand Rapids, MIU: Eerdmans, 1970. 212 pp. Paper. No ISBN.

A study of the transitional stages leading to independent Batak churches that are developing their own application of Christian theology in an Indonesian national context.

AS1343 Peterson, Robert L.
The Demon Gods of Thorny River: A True-to-Life Story of a Chinese Family in West Kalimantan, Indonesian Borneo. London, ENK: OMF, 1974. 158 pp. Paper. 0853630984.

An OMF missionary in West Kalimantan (Borneo), Indonesia, describes life and customs among overseas Chinese through the story of the Lin family.

AS—ASIA

AS1344 Piskaty, Kurt

Die katholische Missionsschule in Nusa Tenggara (Südost-Indonesien): Ihre geschichtliche Entfaltung und ihre Bedeutung für die Missionsarbeit. (Studia Instituti Missiologici SVD, 5). St. Augustin, GW: Steyler Verlag, 1964. xxiv, 277 pp. Paper. No ISBN.

This work describes the role of the Catholic schools in the missions in southeast Indonesia.

AS1345 Piskaty, Kurt, ed.

Nusa Tenggara: 50 Jahre Steyler Missionare in Indonesien (1913-1963). St. Augustin, GW: Steyler Verlag, 1963. 175 pp. Paper. No ISBN.

This work presents the history of fifty years of mission work by SVM missionaries in southeast Indonesia.

AS1346 Plaisier, B.

Over bruggen en grenzen: De communicatie van het evangelie in het Torajagebied (1913-1942). (Mission—Missiologisch Onderzoek in Nederland, 5). Zoetermeer, NE: Boekencentrum, 1993. xiv, 701 pp. Paper. 9023912160.

A scholarly history of the GZB (the Reformed Mission League in the Netherlands Reformed Church) among the Toraja of South Sulawesi, Indonesia, and the rise of the Toraja church, 1913 to 1942.

AS1347 Prent, K., ed.

Missie verhalen: Interviews met missionarissen; Deel 1: Indonesië. (KDC Cursor, 4). Nijmegen, NE: KDC, 1989. 206 pp. Paper. No ISBN.

In-depth interviews with 235 Roman Catholic missionaries who served in Indonesia, organized by main topics from their life stories; the first report from a larger project, interviewing 902 Catholic missionaries sent from the Netherlands to a variety of countries.

AS1348 Quarles van Ufford, Philip

Grenzen van internationale hulpverlening: Een onderzoek naar de samenhang van de aard en effecten van de hulprelatie tussen de Javaanse Kerk van Midden-Java en de zending van de Gereformeerde Kerken in Nederland. Assen, NE: Van Gorcum, 1980. x, 344 pp. Paper. 9023217500.

A sociological study on the relation between a sending and spending church, the Reformed churches in the Netherlands, and a receiving community, the Christian church of Central Java, 1861-1978, with special emphasis on the period after 1965.

AS1349 Rae, Simon

Breath Becomes the Wind: Old and New in Karo Religion. Dunedin, NZ: University of Otago Press, 1994. viii, 306 pp. Paper. 0908569610.

A sociological study of the religion of the Karo people of the highlands of North Sumatra in Indonesia, including traditional, Muslim, and Christian influences, the latter including both Protestant missions and indigenous church developments.

AS1350 Richardson, Don

Friedens-Kind: Wandlung einer Dschungelkultur grausamer Tücke in Neuguinea. Translated by Markus Witte. Bad Liebenzell, GW: Liebenzeller Mission, 1976. 240 pp. Paper. 3880020302.

German translation of *Peace Child* (1974).

AS1351 Richardson, Don

Hijo de Paz. Translated by José D. Silva. Miami, FLU: Editorial Unilit, 1996. 317 pp. Paper. 0789903555.

Second edition of the Spanish translation of *Peace Child* (1974).

AS1352 Richardson, Don

L'enfant de paix. Translated by Nicole Lefévre. Miami, FLU: Éditions Vida, 1981. 256 pp. 0829708138.

French translation of *Peace Child* (1974).

AS1353 Richardson, Don

Lords of the Earth. Glendale, CAU: Regal Books, 1977. 368 pp. 0830705446.

The story of Stan and Pat Dale, pioneer missionaries to the Yali tribe, in the Snow Mountains of the eastern highlands in Netherlands New Guinea, now Irian Jaya.

AS1354 Richardson, Don

Peace Child. Ventura, CAU: Regal Books, 1976. 288 pp. 0083704159.

Firsthand narration of how the *Peace Child* brought true peace at last to the Sawi people of Irian Jaya.

AS1355 Schiller, Anne Louise

Small Sacrifices: Religious Change and Cultural Identity among the Ngaju of Indonesia. New York, NYU: Oxford University Press, 1997. xii, 178 pp. 019509557X (hdbk), 0195095588 (pbk).

A social anthropological exploration of rituals, beliefs, and attitudes associated with treatment of the dead among an indigenous rain forest people of Central Kalimantan, Indonesia, and of their Hindu and Christian reformulations.

AS1356 Schreiner, Lothar

Adat und Evangelium: Zur Bedeutung der altvölkischen Lebensordnungen für Kirche und Mission unter den Batak in Nordsumatra. (Missionswissenschaftliche Forschungen, 7). Gütersloh, GW: Gerd Mohn, 1972. 316 pp. Paper. 3579042300.

A detailed historical study of the culture conflict between the values of German Pietist missionary and Batak tribal customary law (*adat*) in northern Sumatra.

AS1357 Schreiner, Lothar

Das Bekenntnis der Batak-Kirche: Entstehung, Gestalt, Bedeutung und eine revidierte Übersetzung. (Theologische Existenz heute, Neue Folge 137). Munich, GW: Kaiser, 1966. 72 pp. Paper. No ISBN.

This work is about the creed of the Huria Kristen Batak Protestant church in North Sumatra, which, having overcome many initial difficulties, developed into an independent church, theologically anchored in the "Confession Augustana."

AS1358 Sidjabat, Walter Bonar

Religious Tolerance and the Christian Faith. Djakarta, IO: Badan Penerbit Kristen; Jakarta, IN: Gunung Mulia, 1982. 284 pp. No ISBN.

Second edition of a dissertation on problems of religious tolerance in Indonesia, including the concepts of both tolerance and intolerance in Islam and Christianity

AS1359 Simatupang, Tahi Bonar

Gelebte Theologie in Indonesien: Theologische Beiträge eines Nichttheologen zur gesellschaftlichen Verantwortung der Christen. Edited by Olaf H. Schumann and Heinz Joachim Fischer. (Theologie der Ökumene, 24). Göttingen, GW: Vandenhoeck & Ruprecht, 1992. 171 pp. Paper. 3525563280.

This posthumous collection of essays by Simatupang is intended to apprise a wider audience of the insightfully original ecumenical and social ethics work of the Indonesian author.

AS1360 Siregar, Susan Rodgers
Adat, Islam, and Christianity in a Batak Homeland. (Papers in International Studies Southeast Asia Series, 57). Athens, OHU: Ohio University Center for International Studies, 1981. v, 108 pp. Paper. 0896801101.

An ethnographic study of the interface between the traditional Batak cultural system (*adat*) and Christianity and Islam; based on the author's anthropological research in the Sipirok area of Sumatra, Indonesia, from 1974 to 1977.

AS1361 Smith, Ebbie C.
God's Miracles: Indonesian Church Growth. South Pasadena, CAU: William Carey Library, 1970. xv, 217 pp. Paper. 0878083022.

A church-growth survey of the seventeen-year-old Indonesian Baptist Mission of the SBC—a working document for planning, against the background of Indonesian life, culture and other churches.

AS1362 Steenbrink, Karel A.
Pesantren, madrasah, sekolah: Recente ontwikkelingen in Indonesisch islamonderricht. (Proefschrift Theol. Fac. Katholieke Universiteit Nijmegan). Meppel, NE: Krips Repro, 1974. xii, 366 pp. Paper. No ISBN.

A study of the changes within Islamic education in Indonesia 1900 to 1970, with a discussion of the impact of Western culture and secularization upon Muslim practice and belief; based on field research.

AS1363 Stegmaier, Ortrud
Der missionarische Einsatz der Schwestern auf den Inseln Flores und Timor: (Südostindonesien). (Studia Instituti Missiologici SVD, 15). St. Augustin, GW: Steyler Verlag, 1974. 118 pp. Paper. 3877870753.

The author describes the history and activities of twelve congregations of Sisters working on the islands of Flores and Timor, and reflects on the possibilities of ministry for Sisters in non-Christian contexts and young churches.

AS1364 Sunda, James
Church Growth in the Central Highlands of West New Guinea. Eugene, ORU: Institute of Church Growth, 1964. vi, 51 pp. No ISBN.

A case study of church growth among the tribal peoples of the New Guinea highlands of West Irian, now part of Indonesia, including important insights into people group evangelism and the encounter of Christianity with pagan religion; also published in 1963 by Lucknow Publishing House.

AS1365 Sundermeier, Theo, and Volker Küster, eds.
Das Schöne Evangelium: Christliche Kunst im balinesischen Kontext. (Studia Instituti Missiologici SVD, 51). Nettetal, NE: Steyler Verlag, 1991. 98 pp. Paper. 3805002858.

Exhibition catalogue for an eight-city German tour of the works of Nyoman Darsane, an outstanding Balinese Christian artist; includes eight color reproductions of his paintings.

AS1366 Swellengrebel, J. L.
In Leijdeckers voetspoor: Anderhalve eeuw bijbelvertaling en taalkunde in de Indonesische talen. (Verhandelingen van het Koninklijk Instituut voor Taal-, Land-, en Volkenkunde, 68, 82). 's-Gravenhage, NE: Martinus Nijhoff; Amsterdam, NE: Nederlands Bijbelgenootschap, 1974-1978. 2 vols. Paper. 9024716233 (vol. 1), 9061267129 (vol. 2).

Detailed and comprehensive study of the translation of the Bible into the languages of Indonesia, from the end of the 17th to the beginning of the 20th centuries [vol. 1: *1820-1900* (1974, vii, 255 pp.); vol. 2: *1900-1970* (1978, xi, 340 pp.)].

AS1367 Tari, Mel, and Cliff Dudley
Like a Mighty Wind. Carol Stream, ILU: Creation House, 1971. 173 pp. No ISBN.

A first missionary testimony of witnessing in Indonesian Timor, which helped move a people from resistance, to the Gospel, to revival.

AS1368 Tari, Mel, and Nona Tari
The Gentle Breeze of Jesus. Carol Stream, ILU: Creation House; London, ENK: Coverdale House Publishers, 1974. 191 pp. 0884190579 (US), 0902088831 (UK).

A popular account by an Indonesian Christian leader, of the spontaneous revival begun in 1965 in East Timor, Indonesia.

AS1369 Vreugdenhil, C. G.
Medeburgers der Heiligen: Een jonge Zendingskerk op weg naar de volwassenheid. Houten, NE: Den Hartog, 1983. 335 pp. 9033103346.

A rather detailed description of the mission work in Irian Jaya of the Reformed Congregations in the Netherlands, and of the church resulting from it, in various locations in the central mountains.

AS1370 Vries, Tjerk S. de
Zending in ontwikkeling: Evangelieverkondiging in Indonesië. (ND cahier, 4). Groningen, NE: Vuurbaak, 1984. 122 pp. Paper. 9060156242.

Mission in Development is a collection of articles originally published in the *Nederlands Dagblad*, on mission work of the Dutch Reformed church (liberated) in Kalimantan and Irian Jaya (Indonesia), established twenty-five years ago.

AS1371 Wawer, Wendelin
Muslime und Christen in der Republik Indonesien. (Beiträge zur Südasienforschung, 7). Wiesbaden, GW: Steiner, 1974. 326 pp. Paper. 351502042X.

From the background of the history of Muslims and Christians in Indonesia and difficult attempts to work out a constitution that does justice to both sides, this book describes the positions of both groups and problems in the field of missionary proclamation and religious education.

AS1372 Wick, Robert S.
God's Invasion: The Story of Fifty Years of Christian and Missionary Alliance Missionary Work in Irian Jaya. Camp Hill, PAU: Buena Book Services/Christian Publications, 1990. 219 pp. Paper. 0875094414.

A popular history of the first fifty years (1938-1988) of mission in Irian Jaya, Indonesia, by the Christian and Missionary Alliance.

AS1373 Willis, Avery T.
Indonesian Revival: Why Two Million Came to Christ. South Pasadena, CAU: William Carey Library, 1977. xviii, 263 pp. Paper. 0878084282.

A perceptive report of the remarkable Java revival of 1965 to 1971; originally presented as a Th.D. dissertation at Southwestern Baptist Theological Seminary.

AS1374 Woga, Edmund

Der parentale Gott: Zum Dialog zwischen der Religion der indonesischen Völker Sumbas und dem Christentum. (Studia Instituti Missiologici SVD, 59). Nettetal, GW: Steyler Verlag, 1994. 439 pp. Paper. 3805003447.

A theological dissertation on the concept of God in the "parental theology" of the Sumba people of Indonesia.

AS1375 Zollner, Siegfried

Lebensbaum und Schweinekult: Die Religion der Jali im Bergland von Irian-Jaya (West-Neu-Guinea). Wuppertal, GW: R. Brockhaus Verlag, 1977. 646 pp. 379746861X.

A detailed study of the beliefs and practices of the Yali people of Irian Jaya, Indonesia, and the effects of proclaiming the Gospel to them.

AS1376 Zollner, Siegfried

The Religion of the Yali in the Highlands of Irian Jaya. Translated by Jan A. Godschalk. (Point Series, 13). Goroka, PP: Melanesian Institute, 1988. x, 207 pp. Paper. No ISBN.

English translation by Jan A. Godschalk of *Lebensbaum und Schweinekult* (1977).

Laos

AS1377 Pitt, Jan, and Dan Wooding

Laos, No Turning Back: The Story of Lungh Singh. (The Church in Areas of Conflict). Basingstoke, ENK: Marshalls and Open Doors International, 1985. 127 pp. Paper. 0551012463.

A popular account of a Laotian Christian family and their struggle during the violent revolutionary takeover in Southeast Asia.

Malaysia

See also EC297, AS6, and AS211.

AS1378 Goh, Keat Peng, ed.

Readings in Malaysian Church and Mission. Selangor, MY: Pustaka SUFES, 1992. 163 pp. Paper. No ISBN.

Eight essays by Malaysian Protestant leaders, on contemporary issues of spiritual formation, religious pluralism, church and state, ecumenism, and the charismatic movement in their country.

AS1379 Hunt, Robert

William Shellabear: A Biography. Kuala Lumpur, MY: University of Malaya Press, 1996. xi, 373 pp. Paper. 9679940926.

An interpretive biography of William Girdlestone Shellabear (1862-1947), Methodist missionary to Malays in Singapore and Malaya (1890-1920), Bible translator, founder of the Malaya Publishing House, and advocate for the cultural affirmation of the Muslim Malay people.

AS1380 Hunt, Robert, Lee Kam Hing, and John Roxborogh

Christianity in Malaysia: A Denominational History. Selangor Darul Ehsan, MY: Pelanduk Publications, 1992. xiii, 396 pp. 9679784088 (hdbk), 967978407X (pbk).

Essays on twelve major denominations in Malaysia, with general essays on churches and social problems, ecumenism, and church growth.

AS1381 Lee, Raymond L. M., and Susan E. Ackerman

Sacred Tensions: Modernity and Religious Transformations in Malaysia. (Studies in Comparative Religion). Columbia, SCU: University of South Carolina Press, 1997. xi, 172 pp. 1570031673.

A sociological analysis of the resurgence of religion (Christianity, Islam, Buddhism and Hinduism) in Malaysia, particularly of charismatic practices, in light of the importance of modernity, rationalism, and bureaucracy.

AS1382 Lees, Bill, and Shirley Lees

Is It Sacrifice?: Experiencing Mission and Revival in Borneo. Robesonia, PAU: OMF Books; Leicester, ENK: InterVarsity, 1987. 192 pp. Paper. 9971972530 (O), 0851104878 (I).

A popular account of the authors' work in medical service and Bible translation, with the OMF in Sabah, East Malaysia (once known as the Borneo Evangelical Mission).

AS1383 Marsh, Mabel

Service Suspended. New York, NYU: Carlton Press, 1968. 180 pp. No ISBN.

The personal experiences of a Methodist educational missionary in Malaysia (1932-1942); written in the form of a series of letters to a dear friend.

AS1384 Russell, Sue A., ed.

Conversion, Identity, and Power: The Impact of Christianity on Power Relationships and Social Exchanges. Lanham, MDU: American Society of Missiology/University Press of America, 1999. xiv, 186 pp. Paper. 076181440X.

How the introduction of the church as a new social institution affects social exchanges, power relationships, and social identity in Sagal communities, where relationships are formed to gain supernatural resources, and the relationship between wife-giver and wife-taker is formed through the payment of bridewealth.

AS1385 Sadayandy, Batumalai

A Malaysian Theology of Muhibbah: A Theology for a Christian Witnessing in Malaysia. Kuala Lumpur, MY: Seminari Theoloji Malaysia, 1990. ii, 195 pp. Paper. No ISBN.

A collection of short articles on mission in Malaysia, suggesting themes for a relevant theology for Christians in that predominantly Muslim country; by an Anglican priest and theological educator.

AS1386 Saunders, Graham

Bishops and Brookes: The Anglican Mission and the Brooke Raj in Sarawak, 1848-1941. (South-East Asian Historical Monographs). Singapore: Oxford University Press, 1992. xvii, 290 pp. 019588566X.

A scholarly history, based on archival sources, of the USPG's mission in British Sarawak, with focus on church and state relations.

AS1387 Teixeira, Manuel

The Portuguese Missions in Malacca and Singapore, 1511-1958. Macau, MH: Instituto Cultural de Macau, 1987. 3 vols. No ISBN.

Second edition of a monumental history of Catholic missions in the gateway to the East, based on primary sources [vols. 1-2, *Malacca*; vol. 3, *Singapore*; originally published in Lisbon (Agência Geral do Ultramar, 1961-1963)].

AS1388 Vierow, Duain, and Jack M. Shelby

Malaysian Christian Handbook. (Compiled by by the Malaysian Church Growth Committee). Selangor, MY: Glad Sounds, 1979. 144 pp. No ISBN.

Directories and brief histories of the denominations at work in Malaysia, with special ministries noted, and a statistical essay; compiled by the Malaysian Church Growth Committee.

AS—ASIA

Myanmar [Burma]

See also EA79.

AS1389 Anderson, Courtney
To the Golden Shore: The Life of Adoniram Judson. Valley Forge, PAU: Judson Press, 1987. xviii,530 pp. Paper. 0817011218.

A carefully researched history of Ann and Adoniram Judson (1788-1854), two of the first missionaries to go out from North America as pioneer Baptist missionaries to Burma.

AS1390 Brumberg, Joan Jacobs
Mission for Life: The Story of the Family of Adoniram Judson. New York, NYU: Free Press; London, ENK: Collier Macmillan, 1980. xvi, 302 pp. 0029051002 (F), 0029051002 (C).

A well-researched history of two generations of the family of Adoniram Judson, the first American foreign missionary, relating biographies to the course of American cultural development and the persistence of evangelical traditions.

AS1391 Fischer, Edward
Mission in Burma: The Columban Fathers' Forty-Three Years in Kachin Country. New York, NYU: Seabury Press, 1980. vi, 164 pp. 081640464X.

A narrative history of the work of fifty-one Columban Fathers among the Kachins and Shans in upper Burma, from 1936 to 1979.

AS1392 Hubbard, Ethel Daniels
Ann of Ava. Lewisville, TXU: Accelerated Christian Education, 1996. 184 pp. 1562650599.

Reprint of a popular biography of Ann Judson (1789-1826), pioneer Baptist missionary to Burma; originally published by the Missionary Education Movement of the United States in 1913.

AS1393 Morrow, Honoré Willsie
An den Stufen des goldenen Thrones. Basel, SW: Basler Missionsbuchhandlung, 1942. 436 pp. No ISBN.

German translation.

AS1394 Morrow, Honoré Willsie
Guds herlighet. Translated by Helene Thu. Oslo, NO: Lutherstiftelsens Forlag, 1937. 213 pp. No ISBN.

Norwegian translation.

AS1395 Morrow, Honoré Willsie
Splendor of God: The Life of Adoniram Judson. Grand Rapids, MIU: Baker Books, 1982. 376 pp. 0801061296.

Reprint of a biography first published in 1929 (New York: Grosset & Dunlap).

AS1396 Pitrone, Jean Maddern
The Touch of His Hand: Colombo, a Modern Day Damien in Burma. Staten Island, NYU: Alba House, 1970. viii, 161 pp. 0818901950.

A biography of Father Cesar Colombo, a dedicated and resourceful PIME missionary, and his work through the Leprosy Colony at Keng Tung in northern Burma, 1935-1966.

AS1397 Tegenfeldt, Herman G.
A Century of Growth: The Kachin Baptist Church of Burma. South Pasadena, CAU: William Carey Library, 1974. xxv, 512 pp. 0878084169.

This is a history, of the Baptist church in Burma beginning in 1837, of how it became a people's movement and grew rapidly until 1942, when war engulfed the nation and church.

Philippines

See also ME83, ME124, CR1062, SO370, EC206, PO48, PO154, PO180, CO36, ED100, CH353, CH366, SP99, AM56, AM344, AS93, AS146-AS147, AS149, AS168, AS195, AS230, AS1270, and AS1513.

AS1398 *A Vision of Peace, an Agenda for Justice*
Kalookan City, PH: NCCP, 1991. 213 pp. Paper. 9718548556.

The key documents of the "peace program" of the National Council of Churches in the Philippines initiated in 1989; published as TUGON, vol. 11, no. 1 (1991).

AS1399 Allan, John D.
Poor Is No Excuse: The Story of Jun Vencer. Grand Rapids, MIU: Baker Books; Exeter, ENK: Paternoster Press, 1989. 108 pp. Paper. 0853644977.

A popular account of a poor Filipino runaway boy who, when Christ transformed his life, became a lawyer and evangelical pastor involved in aid and development projects in the Philippines and the Third World, through the WEF.

AS1400 Allen, Franklin W.
Breaking the Barriers: A History and Model of Church/ Mission Relationships in the Philippines. Singapore, SI: OMF, 1990. x, 146 pp. Paper. 9971972913.

How the Alliance of Bible Christian Communities of the Philippines came into being and relates to its founding missions; with source documents.

AS1401 Alonso, Isidoro et al.
The Catholic Church in the Philippines Today. Manila, PH: Historical Conservation Society, 1968. viii, 131 pp. Paper. No ISBN.

A factual survey of the state of Philippine Catholicism in both religious and non-religious aspects, plus short essays on missionary efforts to the Negritos, to Olutanga, and to the Cursillos de Cristiandad.

AS1402 Anderson, Gerald H., ed.
Studies in Philippine Church History. Ithaca, NYU: Cornell University Press, 1969. xiv, 421 pp. 0801404851.

Nineteen scholarly essays covering 400 years of Christianity in the Philippines, including the Spanish church in the Philippine setting, nationalism, dissent and disestablishment, and Protestant pluralism.

AS1403 Ante, Oscar A.
Contextual Evangelization in the Philippines: A Filipino Franciscan Experience. (Church and Theology in Context, 11). Kampen, NE: Kok, 1991. viii, 196 pp. Paper. 9024234093.

An exploratory study of the ongoing evangelization efforts of the Friars Minor (OFM) in the wider context of Philippine society.

AS1404 Apilado, Mariano C.
Revolutionary Spirituality: A Study of the Protestant Role in the American Colonial Rule of the Philippines, 1898-1928. Quezon City, PH: New Day Publishers, 1999. xx, 316 pp. Paper. 971101033X.

What begins as an obsessive search by the author for his "identity and authenticity" as a Filipino, and as a Christian, ends as a comprehensive historical account of the Protestant role in colonial rule by the USA in the Philippines.

AS1405 Arcilla, José S., ed.
Jesuit Missionary Letters from Mindanao, Volume Two: The Zamboanga-Basilian-Joló Mission. Quezon City, PH: Philippine Province Archives, 1993. xxxii, 564 pp. Paper. 9715500951.

One-hundred-seventy-two letters by Jesuit missionaries from Mindanao, 1880-1893, showing their serious concern for volatile political realities.

AS1406 Arienda, Roger, and Marichelle Roque-Lutz
Free within Prison Walls. London, ENK: Pickering & Inglis, 1982. 150 pp. 0720804957.

Personal observations on the Christian conversions of political prisoners in the Philippines.

AS1407 Asedillo, Rebecca C., and B. David Williams, eds.
Rice in the Storm: Faith in Struggle in the Philippines. New York, NYU: Friendship Press, 1989. viii, 182 pp. Paper. 0377001929.

A mission study in which nine Filipino Christian leaders describe the history of their people and their church, their joint struggle for peace and justice in politics, economics, and development; with a challenge to North American Christians to recognize how their national policies affect the lives of Filipinos, and to translate their Christian concern into action.

AS1408 Asedillo, Rebecca C., and B. David Williams, eds.
The Sari-Sari Store: A Philippine Scrapbook. New York, NYU: Friendship Press, 1989. 74 pp. Paper. 0377001953.

A rich and informative collection of examples of Filipino culture, history, and ways of life, including a detailed history of the Philippines' relationship with the United States, prepared as a mission study book for North American Christians.

AS1409 Barker, Jared
Assignment in the Philippines. Chicago, ILU: Moody, 1984. 158 pp. Paper. 0802402658.

Reminiscences by a founder of the Philippine Evangelical Enterprises, Incorporated (PEEI), of his missionary service in the Philippines from 1953 to 1981.

AS1410 Bautista, Liberato C., and Elizabeth Rifareal, eds.
And She Said No!: Human Rights, Women's Identities and Struggles. Quezon City, PH: NCCP, 1990. xviii, 189 pp. Paper. 9718548505.

Moving stories of witnesses to the suffering and struggles for dignity of Filipino women.

AS1411 Bernad, Miguel Anselmo
The Christianization of the Philippines: Problems and Perspectives. (Filipiniana Book Guild Publications, 20). Manila, PH: Filipiniana Book Guild, 1972. xix, 396 pp. No ISBN.

Lectures on the origins of Philippine Catholic Christianity and its development, especially in relation to native culture and leadership, by the rector of the Divine Word Seminary in Tagaytay.

AS1412 Brooks, Cyril H.
Grace Triumphant: The Triumph of God's Grace in the Philippines. Kansas City, KSU: Walterick Publishers, 1985. 266 pp. Paper. 0937396664.

The reminiscences of sixty years (1922-1982) of missionary service, mostly in the Philippines, with Christian Missions in Many Lands and the Bible School of the Air.

AS1413 Cannell, Fanella
Power and Intimacy in the Christian Philippines. (Cambridge Studies in Social and Cultural Anthropology, 109). New York, NYU: Cambridge University Press, 1999. xxiv, 316 pp. Paper. 0521646227.

Combining a strong theoretical basis in the anthropology of religion with a broader comparative attention to recent developments in Southeast Asian studies, the author offers a powerful alternative to the relationships between culture and tradition in the region and beyond.

AS1414 Carino, Feliciano V.
The Sacrifice of the Innocent: Themes on Christian Participation in the Philippine Struggle. Hong Kong, HK: WSCF, Asia/Pacific Region, 1984. 165 pp. Paper. No ISBN.

Frrom the pivotal point of the assassination of Benigno S. Aquino, this slim volume provides an analysis and theological reflection, from a Protestant point of view, on the radical revisioning of faith required for social transformation in the Philippine struggle for freedom and justice, as evidenced in the revolutionary lifestyle of the priest, Conrado Bolweg.

AS1415 Catholic Bishops' Conference of the Philippines
Responses to the Signs of the Times: Selected Documents. Edited by Abdon Ma.C. Josol. Quezon City, PH: Claretian Publications; Cebu City, PH: Redemptorist Publications, 1991. xiii, 380 pp. Paper. 9715014755 (C).

A selection of pastoral letters, published since 1967 by the CBCP, on issues of social ethics (social justice, rights of the poor, church-state relations, etc.).

AS1416 Chapman, Isabel, and Lucy Elphinstone
Arise and Reap. London, ENK: Marshall, Morgan and Scott, 1986. 191 pp. 0551013648.

A missionary testimony on work in an aboriginal area in the Philippines; originally published in 1984 (London, ENK: Hodder & Stoughton).

AS1417 Chirino, Pedro
Relación de las Islas Filipinas: The Filippines in 1600. Translated by Ramón Echevarria. (Biblioteca de la "Revista Católica de Filipinas"). Rome, IT: Estevan Paulino, 1979. xv, 200 pp. No ISBN.

The work of Jesuit missionaries in the Philippines in 1600, including information on the native alphabet and language.

AS1418 Claver, Francisco F.
The Stones Will Cry Out: Grassroots Pastorals. Maryknoll, NYU: Orbis Books, 1978. xii, 196 pp. 0883444712.

Thirty-eight pastoral letters and ten occasional lectures and letters by the prophetic Philippine Roman Catholic bishop, calling on both church and state to uphold fundamental human rights.

AS1419 Costa, Horacio de la
The Jesuits in the Philippines, 1581-1768. Cambridge, MAU: Harvard University Press, 1967. xiii, 702 pp. No ISBN.

A detailed history, based on archival sources, of the Society of Jesus in the Philippines, from their arrival in 1581 to their expulsion in 1768.

AS1420 Deats, Richard L.
Nationalism and Christianity in the Philippines. Dallas, TXU: Southern Methodist University Press, 1967. xii, 207 pp. No ISBN.

A comparative study of the influence of four churches (Roman Catholic, Philippine Independent, United Church of Christ, and Methodist) on Philippine nationalism from 1899 to 1964.

AS—ASIA

AS1421 Dominguez, Arsenio, and Edith Dominguez
Theological Themes for the Philippine Church. Quezon City,
PH: New Day Publishers, 1989. x, 258 pp. Paper. 9711002744.

The rural missionary founders of the Philippine Missionary Institute (1961) relate theological themes (liberation, the
person and mission of Jesus, etc.) to the mission of the church
in the Philippine setting.

AS1422 Elwood, Douglas J., ed.
*Alternatives to Violence: Interdisciplinary Perspectives on
Filipino People Power.* Quezon City, PH: New Day Publish-
ers, 1989. xiv, 110 pp. Paper. 9711003155.

Eleven essays by Silliman University staff (and one student), suggesting various alternatives to violence by which
the Filipino people can work for fundamental social change;
the second volume of a study on People Power in the Philippines.

AS1423 Elwood, Douglas J., ed.
*Toward a Theology of People Power: Reflections on the Phil-
ippine February Phenomenon.* Quezon City, PH: New Day
Publishers, 1988. viii, 132 pp. Paper. 9711002672.

Nine short essays on the development of a Philippine
theology of people power as a genuinely indigenous approach
to theological reflection; the first of two volumes on the People Power Movement in the Philippines.

AS1424 Elwood, Douglas J.
Philippine Revolution 1986: Model of Nonviolent Change.
Quezon City, PH: New Day Publishers, 1986. vi, 60 pp. Pa-
per. 9711003031.

A historical account of the events leading up to the election and transfer of power to Corazon Aquino in 1986, with
special focus on the role of the church, and the Reform the
Armed Forces Movement.

AS1425 Flavier, Juan M.
Back to the Barrios. Quezon City, PH: New Day Publishers,
1978. vii, 150 pp. Paper. No ISBN.

A collection of eighty true incidents of people and places
in the barrios of the rural Philippines by the medical missionary and president of the International Institute for Rural Reconstruction.

AS1426 Flavier, Juan M.
*Doctor to the Barrios: Experiences with the Philippine Rural
Reconstruction Movement.* Quezon City, PH: New Day Pub-
lishers, 1970. iv, 208 pp. Paper. No ISBN.

An account of the many events, experiences, and observations the President of the International Institute for Rural
Reconstruction encountered in his work among the barrio people of the rural Philippines.

AS1427 Flavier, Juan M.
My Friends in the Barrios. Quezon City, PH: New Day Publishers, 1974. xiv, 190 pp. Paper. No ISBN.

Vignettes of Philippine village life by a medical missionary who worked with the Philippine Rural Reconstruction Movement.

AS1428 Friesen, Dorothy
Critical Choices: A Journey with the Filipino People. Grand
Rapids, MIU: Eerdmans, 1988. viii, 284 pp. Paper.
0802803717.

A reflection on ten years' experiences in the Philippines
(1977-1987), focusing on the church's involvement in poli-

tics and justice issues; by the Co-Director of the Mennonite
Central Committee program in the Philippines and founder
of Synapses in Chicago, Illinois.

AS1429 Gaspar, Karl
*Friede den Bäumen!: Philippinische Basisgemeinden kämpfen
für die Schöpfung.* Translated by Petra Müller. (Erlanger
Taschenbücher, 111). Erlangen, GW: Ev.-Luth. Mission, 1996.
208 pp. Paper. 3872145118.

German translation.

AS1430 Gaspar, Karl
How Long?: Prison Reflections from the Philippines. Maryknoll, NYU: Orbis Books; Melbourne, AT: Dove Communications, 1986. xx, 171 pp. Paper. 0883442264.

Letters from prison (1983-1985) by a Filipino lay theologian, dramatist, and poet who became an advocate of human rights during the Marcos dictatorship.

AS1431 Gaspar, Karl
A People's Option: To Struggle for Creation. Quezon City,
PH: Claretian Publications, 1990. xx, 184 pp. Paper.
9715014259.

The journal of a Redemptorist Brother reflecting on the
experience of the birth of grassroots Christian communities
in the parish of San Fernando Bukidnon on the island of Mindanao in the Philippines, 1987-1989, and on social justice
issues they faced.

AS1432 Giordano, Pasquale T.
*Awakening to Mission: The Philippine Catholic Church, 1965-
1981.* Quezon City, PH: New Day Publishers, 1988. xv, 376
pp. Paper. 9711002663.

A revised version of the author's 1983 doctoral dissertation, which traces the conscientization of the Roman Catholic
Church in the Philippines from 1965 to 1981, the oppression
of authoritarian rule, the development of a Philippine ecclesiology to meet the country's concrete needs, the church's concern for human rights and its struggles over political involvement and violence.

AS1433 Gowing, Peter G.
*Islands under the Cross: The Story of the Church in the Phil-
ippines.* Manila, PH: NCCP, 1967. xvi, 286 pp. No ISBN.

A basic history of both Catholic and Protestant missions
and churches; based on secondary sources, with bibliography.

AS1434 Grigg, Viv
Companion to the Poor. Monrovia, CAU: MARC; Sutherland,
AT: Albatross Books, 1990. iii, 205 pp. Paper. 0912552697.

Revised edition of a narrative account of mission, since 1979,
in a Manila squatter settlement, by the founder of the New
Zealand-based mission called "Servants to Asia's Urban Poor."

AS1435 Grigg, Viv
Siervos entre los Pobres. (Nueva Creación). Grand Rapids,
MIU: Eerdmans, 1994. 246 pp. Paper. 0802809251.

Spanish translation.

AS1436 Hardy, Richard P.
Holiness for Today: A Filipino Martyr's Story. Quezon City,
PH: Claretian Publications, 1989. xxvi, 113 pp. Paper.
971501349X.

The life and martyrdom of Sofronio Roxas (1938-1984),
a leader of Catholic BECs and social action coordinator in the
Diocese of Kidapawan.

AS1437 Henry, Rodney L.

Filipino Spirit World. Manila, PH: OMF Books, 1986. 155 pp. Paper. 9715110886.

An analysis of the Filipino spirit world, and the impact of Christianity and modernity on the traditional Filipino worldview; challenging theologians to include the spirit-world in the scope of their doctrines; and missionaries to present God's power against demonic spirits.

AS1438 Holder, Philip

Captain Mahjong. London, ENK: OMF, 1976. 157 pp. Paper. 0853631131.

The story of how a Filipino village headman came to Christ.

AS1439 Holmes, C. Raymond

Boiled Rice and Gluten. Berrien Springs, MIU: Raymond C. Holmes, 1986. 134 pp. Paper. No ISBN.

A realistic, yet humorous, account of the author's mission and teaching service as a Seventh-day Adventist missionary to the Philippines, 1978-1981.

AS1440 Köster, Fritz, ed.

Macht und Ohnmacht auf den Philippinen: Kirche der Befreiung als einende Kraft. Olten, SZ: Walter-Verlag, 1986. 180 pp. Paper. 3530543519.

A work in which German observers and a Filipino bishop provide insights into the Philippine situation after the end of the Marcos dictatorship, and the resulting challenges for the church.

AS1441 Kinne, Warren

A People's Church?: The Mindanao-Sulu Church Debacle. (Studies in the Intercultural History of Christianity, 64). Frankfurt am Main, GW: Lang, 1990. xvii, 324 pp. Paper. 3631426216.

A thesis documenting the attempt at greater lay participation within and between local Catholic churches in Mindanao-Sulu, the Philippines, from 1971 to 1983.

AS1442 Kretzmann, Herbert

Lutheranism in the Philippines, 1952-1966. St. Louis, MSU: Concordia Theological Seminary, 1966. 168 pp. No ISBN.

A detailed analysis by regions and types of ministry of the Lutheran church in the Philippines.

AS1443 Kroeger, James H.

Church Truly Alive: Journey to the Filipino Revolution. Davao City, PH: Mission Studies Institute, 1986. 68 pp. Paper. 9715011071.

A Maryknoll missioner's account of how the interaction/collision of church and society in the Philippines, during the twenty-year Marcos regime, forged a vision of evangelization fitted to the Philippine context.

AS1444 Kroeger, James H.

Human Promotion as an Integral Dimension of the Church's Mission of Evangelization 1965-1984: A Philippine Experience and Perspective Since Vatican II, 1965-1984. Rome, IT: Pontificia Università Gregoriana, 1985. 595 pp. Paper. No ISBN.

A detailed analysis of the Roman Catholic Church's vision of evangelization in the Philippines, 1965-1984, including the development of its understanding that human promotion-development-liberation is an integral dimension of the church's very evangelizing mission; with a cover title "The Philippine Church and Evangelization 1965-1984."

AS1445 Kroeger, James H.

Remembering Our Bishop Joseph W. Regan, M.M. Quezon City, PH: Claretian Publications, 1998. viii, 235 pp. Paper. 9715018157.

Overviews, interviews, testimonies, and other documents of a priest, missioner, Maryknoller, and bishop, originally from Wisconsin, who left a lasting legacy of sixty-six years of service in China and the Philippines.

AS1446 Kwantes, Anne C.

Presbyterian Missionaries in the Philippines: Conduits of Social Change (1899-1910). Quezon City, PH: New Day Publishers, 1989. xvi, 238 pp. Paper. 9711003600.

The author's doctoral dissertation, in which she examines the activities of Presbyterian missionaries in the Philippines between 1899 and 1910, as "conduits of social change."

AS1447 Labayen, Julio X.

Revolution and the Church of the Poor. (Yapak Series, 1). Manila, PH: Socio-Pastoral Institute; Quezon City, PH: Claretian Publications, 1995. ix, 170 pp. Paper. 9715016553.

A prophetic Filipino Catholic bishop clarifies the meaning of the Philippine bishops' call for the whole Catholic community in that country "to be a Church of the Poor."

AS1448 Labayen, Julio X.

To Be the Church of the Poor. Edited by Denis Murphy. Metro Manila, PH: Communication Foundation for Asia, 1986. vii, 135 pp. Paper. 9711550989.

Talks on development and justice issues by the Catholic bishop and former Director of the Philippine Bishops' National Secretariat of Social Action (1966-1981).

AS1449 Mananzan, Mary John

The Woman Question in the Philippines. Pasay City, PH: Saint Paul Publications, 1991. 32 pp. Paper. 9715900023.

A brief introduction to justice issues for women in the Philippines by a leader in the women's movement there.

AS1450 Mendoza, Everett

Radical and Evangelical: Portait of a Filipino Christian. Quezon City, PH: New Day Publishers, 1999. ix, 276 pp. Paper. 9711005301.

The author explores the nature and task of evangelical theology in the Philippine context, in dialogue with Latin American liberation theology.

AS1451 Mesa, José M. de

In Solidarity with the Culture: Studies in Theological Rerooting. (Maryhill Studies, 4). Quezon City, PH: Maryhill, 1987. 223 pp. No ISBN.

Essays which open perspectives on the inculturation of the faith in the context of Filipino house churches and life.

AS1452 Mesa, José M. de

Maginhawa-Den Gott des Heils erfahren: Theologische Inkulturation auf den Philippinen. Translated by Ursula Faymonville. (Theologie der Dritten Welt, 17). Freiburg im Breisgau, GW: Herder, 1992. 240 pp. Paper. 3451226049.

German translation.

AS1453 Miranda-Feliciano, Evelyn, ed.
All Things to All Men: An Introduction to Missions in Filipino Culture. Quezon City, PH: New Day Publishers, 1988. vii, 54 pp. Paper. 9711003872.

An anthology of essays written for first-term missionaries to the Philippines, designed to increase their sensitivity to Filipino culture, and skills in cross-cultural communication.

AS1454 Mitchell, Mairin
Friar Andrés de Urdaneta, O.S.A. (1508-1568): Pioneer of Pacific Navigation from West to East. London, ENK: Mac-Donald and Evans Ltd, 196. ix, 182 pp. No ISBN.

The first scientific biography, in English, of a Spanish Augustinian, one of the first missionaries to the Philippines, and a famous navigator.

AS1455 Montgomery, Jim
Fire in the Philippines. Carol Stream, ILU: Creation House, 1975. 140 pp. 0884191060.

A study for members of the International Church of the Foursquare Gospel on their church's mission in the Philippines; originally published under the title *New Testament Fire in the Philippines.*

AS1456 Montgomery-Fate, Tom
Beyond the White Noise: Mission in a Multicultural World. St. Louis, MOU: Chalice Press, 1997. xiii, 152 pp. Paper. 0827202237.

Insights on how to replace old neocolonial concepts of mission—vignettes and reflections by the author on his short-term mission service in the Philippines, in the 1970s, as a Presbyterian fraternal worker.

AS1457 Nelson, Lincoln D.
With Scalpel and the Sword: An American Doctor's Odyssey in the Philippines. Harrisburg, PAU: ABWE Publishing, 1997. vii, 198 pp. Paper. 188879612X.

Reminiscences of an Association of Baptists for World Evangelism (ABWE) medical missionary to the Philippines, 1949 to 1987.

AS1458 Neo, Julma, and Eileen Laird, eds.
Prophets for the Third Millennium. Quezon City, PH: Claretian Publications, 1990. vii, 317 pp. Paper. 9715013759.

Report and papers from the 1989 Religious Life Week for Roman Catholic missioners in the Philippines, under the theme, "Religious Life and Its Mission in the Philippines Today."

AS1459 Nobes, Clifford E. Barry
Apo Padi: An Autobiography. Quezon City, PH: New Day Publishers, 1988. 168 pp. Paper. 9711003694.

An autobiographical account of the author's work as an Episcopal missionary among Igorot people of northern Luzon in the Philippines, 1931 to 1945.

AS1460 Nuval, Leonardo Q., and Beulah D. Nuval
The Claretians in the Philippines, 1946-1986. Quezon City, PH: Claret Seminary Foundation, 1986. xvi, 216 pp. Paper. 9715011675.

A collection of reminiscences by members of the Claretian order concerning their missionary work over forty years.

AS1461 O'Brien, Niall
Island of Tears, Island of Hope: Living the Gospel in a Revolutionary Situation. Maryknoll, NYU: Orbis Books, 1993. xiv, 234 pp. Paper. 0883449277.

The story of the struggle for justice of poor sugar workers on the island of Negros in the Philippines, told by an Irish-born Columban priest who was imprisoned and exiled by the Marcos dictatorship because he ministered together with them.

AS1462 O'Brien, Niall
Revolution from the Heart. New York, NYU: Oxford University Press, 1987. ix, 310 pp. Paper. 0195049500.

Account of the author's mission work in Negros, Philippines, where he was led to combat injustices suffered by the poor, creating a new kind of church.

AS1463 Pertierra, Raul
Religion, Politics, and Rationality in the Philippine Community. Honolulu, HIU: University of Hawaii Press, 1988. 207 pp. Paper. 0824812123.

A social anthropologist's detailed case study in a northern Luzon municipality, showing the social and cultural influence of Catholicism, American Protestantism, and Filipino independency.

AS1464 Puig, Francisco Xavier, and Nicholas P. Cushner, eds.
Philippine Jesuit in Exile: The Journals of Francisco Puig, S.J (1768-1770). (Bibliotheca Instituti Historici S.I., 24). Rome, IT: Institutum Historicum, 1964. xvi, 202 pp. No ISBN.

The Spanish text and English translation of the diary of Father Puig, leader of the Jesuits, who were driven from the Philippines back to Europe, 1768-1770; with a thorough introduction and commentary, and appendixes containing several documents not previously published.

AS1465 Rafael, Vicente L.
Contracting Colonialism: Translation and Christian Conversion in Tagalog Society under Early Spanish Rule. Ithaca, NYU: Cornell University Press, 1988. xiii, 230 pp. 0801420652.

A detailed analysis of the ways in which Spanish Christian doctrines were translated into the Tagalog language of the Philippines during the Spanish rule (1580-1705), with consequences both for acceptance of colonial rule, and resistance to it.

AS1466 Rosales, Antonio-Maria
A Study of a 16th Century Tagalog Manuscript on the Ten Commandments: Its Significance and Implications. Quezon City, PH: University of the Philippines Press; Honolulu, HIU: University of Hawaii Press, 1984. xvi, 149 pp. 9711050129 (UP), 0824809718 (UH).

A detailed study of an early 16th-century manuscript revealing early Catholic approaches to evangelization and catechesis in the Philippines.

AS1467 Schmitz, Josef
The Abra Mission in Northern Luzon, Philippines, 1598-1955: A Historical Study. Translated by John Vogelgesang. Cebu City, PH: University of San Carlos, 1971. ix, 240 pp. No ISBN.
English translation.

AS1468 Schmitz, Josef
Die Abra-Mission auf Nordluzon/Philippinen von 1598-1955: Eine missionsgeschichtliche Untersuchung. (Studia Instituti Missiologici SVD, 3). St. Augustin, GW: Steyler Verlag, 1964. 216 pp. No ISBN.

One of the few publications in German on Philippine mission history, this work deals with the development of the Abra Mission in North Luzon from 1598 to recent times.

AS1469 Schreurs, Peter

Caraga Antigua, 1521-1910: The Hispanization and Christianization of Agusan, Surigao, and East Davao. (San Carlos Humanities Series, 18). Cebu City, PH: San Carlos Publications, 1989. viii, 475 pp. 9711000555 (hdbk), 9711000547 (pbk).

A detailed mission history of the eastern third of the island of Mindanao in the Philippines, from the arrival of Magellan in 1521 to 1908.

AS1470 Schumacher, John N.

Father José Burgos: Priest and Nationalist. Manila, PH: Ateneo University Press for the Knights of Columbus, 1972. xvi, 273 pp. No ISBN.

A collection of the known writings of Fr. José Burgos, S.J. (1837-1872), Filipino priest-nationalist, executed with two other priests as "prime movers" of the 1872 mutiny; with an historical assessment by the author in Spanish, with the English translation following.

AS1471 Scott, William Henry

Cracks in the Parchment Curtain and Other Essays in Philippine History. Quezon City, PH: New Day Publishers, 1982. 300 pp. Paper. 9711000016.

Seventeen essays discussing the Philippine society as experienced by Filipinos as they struggle for emancipation, by the "Filipino nationalist with a white skin" lay missionary of the Philippine Episcopal Church.

AS1472 Scott, William Henry

A Missionary Prophet: The Church and Colonialism in the Philippines. Cincinnati, OHU: Forward Movement, 1989. 57 pp. Paper. 0880280956.

Occasional papers of an Episcopalian lay missionary who, after brief service in China (1946-1949), became a teacher in the Philippines (1953-1988), and an outspoken defender of Filipino youth in their struggle for peace and democracy.

AS1473 Sin, Jaime L.

Menschwerdung der Kirche. (Repräsentanten der Befreiungstheologie). Olten, SZ: Walter-Verlag, 1988. 220 pp. Paper. 3530821519.

Selected addresses delivered by the Archbishop of Manila in different countries, portraying him as a spiritual and political representative of the Catholic Church.

AS1474 Sitoy, T. Valentino

Comity and Unity: Ardent Aspirations of Six Decades of Protestantism in the Philippines (1901-1961). (TUGON: An Ecumenical Journal of Discussion and Opinion, vol. 9, nos 1-2, 1989.). Quezon City, PH: NCCUSA, 1989. v, 147 pp. Paper. 9718548467.

An introductory history of Protestantism in the Philippines, 1898 to 1963, focusing on efforts for Christian cooperation in mission and church union.

AS1475 Sitoy, T. Valentino

A History of Christianity in the Philippines: The Initial Encounter. (A History of Christianity in the Philippines, 1). Quezon City, PH: New Day Publishers, 1985. x, 384 pp. Paper. 971100254X.

The first of a projected three-volume history of Philippine Christianity, covering the 16th-century Spanish missionary effort.

AS1476 Sitoy, T. Valentino

Several Springs, One Stream: The United Church of Christ in the Philippines. (Heritage and Origins (1898-1948), 1). Quezon City, PH: United Church of Christ in the Philippines, 1992. 2 vols. Paper. No ISBN.

A history of Presbyterian, Congregational (American Board), United Brethren, and Disciples of Christ missions in the Philippines, and their efforts for Christian unity culminating, in 1948, in the formation of the United Church of Christ in the Philippines; presented in two volumes [vol. 1: *Heritage and Origins (1898-1948)*, x, 555 pp.; vol. 2: *The Formative Decade (1948-1958)*, 525 pp.].

AS1477 Spottswood, Curran L.

Beyond Cotabato. Westwood, NJU: Revell, 1961. 256 pp. No ISBN.

An American missionary's vivid account of service in the Philippines, that took him to previously unexplored regions in the Cagayan area of Luzon and in Mindanao.

AS1478 Tano, Rodrigo D.

Theology in the Philippine Setting: A Case Study in the Contextualization of Theology. Quezon City, PH: New Day Publishers, 1981. viii, 176 pp. Paper. No ISBN.

A detailed reflection on the state of Filipino theology and the theological, historical, and cultural forces that have influenced it; originally presented as a doctoral thesis at Baylor University in Waco, Texas.

AS1479 Tuggy, Arthur Leonard

The Philippine Church: Growth in a Changing Society. (Church Growth Series). Grand Rapids, MIU: Eerdmans, 1971. 191 pp. Paper. No ISBN.

A carefully documented study of church growth in the Philippines, giving an authentic picture of the Philippine family and the part it plays in the spread of biblical faith; with maps, charts, graphs, and bibliography.

AS1480 Uy, Antolin V.

The State of the Church in the Philippines, 1850-1875: The Correspondence between the Bishops in the Philippines and the Nuncio in Madrid. (Studia Instituti Missiologici SVD, 35). St. Augustin, GW: Steyler Verlag, 1984. 266 pp. Paper. 387787181X.

A well-documented analysis of the struggle for reform by Philippine bishops against colonial and conservative attitudes and policies in Rome, Spain, and the colony, with special attention to clerical leadership (expatriate and Filipino, secular and religious).

AS1481 Woodworth, Ruth A.

No Greater Joy. Harrisburg, PAU: ABWE Publishing, 1996. vii, 97 pp. Paper. 1569777497.

Memories of a life missionary of the Association of Baptists for World Evangelism (ABWE) to the Philippines, 1934 to 1961, who directed the Doane Baptist Bible Institute in that country.

AS1482 Youngblood, Robert L.

Marcos Against the Church: Economic Development and Political Repression in the Philippines. Ithaca, NYU: Cornell University Press, 1990. xxi, 211 pp. 0801423058.

A scholarly examination of church-state conflict in the Philippines during the Ferdinard Marcos presidency (1966-1986) in the context of Philippine development policy, and the Roman Catholic church's commitment since Vatican II to work for social justice among the poor.

AS–ASIA

Singapore

See also EC297, AS576, and AS1387.

AS1483 Hinton, Keith W.
Growing Churches Singapore Style: Ministry in an Urban Context. Singapore, SI: OMF, 1985. 234 pp. Paper. 9971972247.

A study of contextual and institutional factors affecting Protestant church growth in Singapore, with suggested strategies for growing churches.

AS1484 Sng, Bobby E. K.
In His Good Time: The Story of the Church in Singapore, 1819-1992. Singapore, SI: Graduates' Christian Fellowship, 1993. 375 pp. 9810043821.

An second updated edition of narrative history of the churches of Singapore, by the general secretary of the Fellowship of Evangelical Students; originally published in 1980.

AS1485 Yeow, Choo Lak
Sunny Island. Singapore, SI: ATESEA, 1990. 295 pp. Paper. 9810020872.

The search for authentic community in multicultural Singapore, told through the personal stories of four women (Malay, Eurasian, Indian, and Chinese), exercising their rights in a male-dominated society.

Thailand

See also SP167 and AS188.

AS1486 Bouvet, Joachim
Voyage de Siam du Père Bouvet. Edited by J. C. Gatty. Leiden, NE: Brill, 1963. cxxi, 157 pp. No ISBN.

The account by the notable missionary to China, Joachim Bouvet (1656-1730), of his journey from Brest, France to Siam, 1685-1686, with an introduction analyzing its historical importance.

AS1487 Davis, John R.
Poles Apart? Bangkok, TH: Kanok Bannasan-OMF Publishers; Bangalore, II: Theological Book Trust, 1993. 172 pp. Paper. No ISBN.

A case study on contextualization of the Christian message in the Thai culture, with its blend of folk animism and Theravada Buddhism.

AS1488 Dybdahl, Jon
Missions: A Two-Way Street. Boise, IDU: Pacific Press, 1986. 96 pp. Paper. 0816306613.

Stories by Seventh-day Adventist missionaries in Thailand, of how they learned that mission is both giving and receiving.

AS1489 Fahrni, Audrey M.
No Turning Back. London, ENK: OMF, 1973. v, 152 pp. Paper. 0853630887.

Vignettes of the life and witness of the young Meo church in North Thailand, which grew out of the work of the OMF.

AS1490 Hansen, Elly, and Mary H. Wallace
Elly: Following Jesus All the Way. Hazelwood, MOU: Word Aflame Press, 1987. 240 pp. Paper. 0932581234.

The popular account of the life of Danish missionary Elly Hansen, pastor and founder of the United Pentecostal Church in Phram Kratai, Thailand (1921-1986).

AS1491 Hovemyr, Anders P.
In Search of the Karen King: A Study in Karen Identity with Special Reference to 19th Century Karen Evangelism in Northern Thailand. (Studia Missionalia Upsaliensia, 49). Uppsala, SW: S. Academiae Upsaliensis, 1989. 193 pp. 9150607375.

A doctoral dissertation on the Karen people's identity and the missionary attempt to reach the Karen.

AS1492 Kuhn, Isobel
Ascent to the Tribes: Pioneering in North Thailand. London, ENK: OMF, 1981. 157 pp. No ISBN.

Abridged edition of a popular history of the work of the CIM/OMF since 1951 among the hill tribes, and of its relationship to their former work in Southwest China; first published in 1956.

AS1493 Lord, Donald C.
Mo Bradley and Thailand. Grand Rapids, MIU: Eerdmans, 1969. 227 pp. Paper. No ISBN.

Biography of Dan Beach Bradley (1804-1873), pioneer missionary of the American Board in Thailand (1835-1873), noted doctor, publisher, printer, diplomat, and evangelist.

AS1494 Mischung, Roland
Religion und Wirklichkeitsvorstellungen in einem Karen-Dorf Nordwest. (Studien zur Kulturkunde, 69). Wiesbaden, GW: Franz Steiner Verlag, 1984. xiii, 362 pp. Paper. 3515032274.

This study of the interrelationship of religion and perception of reality is based on eight months of residence among the mountain Karen of north Thailand.

AS1495 Morris, Louise
Stronger than the Strong. Littleton, COU: OMF Books; Fort Washington, PAU: CLC, 1998. 160 pp. Paper. 9813009144 (O), 0875084966 (C).

The response of the Pwo Karen people of northern Thailand, to the Gospel through an indigenous, biblical church movement that demonstrated power over demonic forces and developed a people movement.

AS1496 Peet, Verda
Sometimes I Prefer to Fuss. Singapore, SI: OMF, 1985. 262 pp. Paper. 9971972220.

A popular first-person account of many of the frustrating yet spiritual lessons, learned by an OMF missionary in North Thailand.

AS1497 Sahlberg, Corrine
Please Leave Your Shoes at the Door: The Story of Elmer and Corrine Sahlberg. Camp Hill, PAU: Christian Publications, 1992. 191 pp. Paper. 0875094864.

The story of thirty-five years (1950-1985) of service in Thailand by CMA missionaries, told through letters of a missionary wife to her mother.

AS1498 Smith, Alexander Garnett
Siamese Gold: A History of Church Growth in Thailand—An Interpretive Analysis, 1816-1982. Bangkok, TH: Kanok Bannasan (OMF Publishers), 1982. xxxiii, 309 pp. Paper. No ISBN.

An accurate account of the growth from Protestant mission to church, including an analysis of pioneer evangelism, mission stations, anti-mission sentiments, initial church emergence, decline during World War II, and later revitalization.

AS1499 Thompson, Phyllis
Minka and Margaret: The Heroic Story of Two Women Missionaries Martyred by Bandits. (Hodder Christian Paperbacks). London, ENK: Hodder & Stoughton; Sevenoaks, ENK: OMF Books, 1978. 188 pp. 0340207418 (H), 0853631212 (O).

The stories of Margaret Morgan from Great Britain and Minka Hanskamp from Holland, medical missionaries of the OMF in Thailand, who were kidnapped and murdered in 1974.

Vietnam

See also AS45.

AS1500 Dourisboure, Pierre, and Christian Simonnet
Vietnam: Mission on the Grand Plateaus. Translated by Albert J. LaMothe. Maryknoll, NYU: Maryknoll Publications, 1967. x, 277 pp. Paper. No ISBN.

A reprint of Father Dourisboure's *Les Sauvages Bahner* (1870), plus a brief history of continuing work, to the 1960s, on the Central Plateau of South Vietnam.

AS1501 Dournes, Jacques
Dieu aime les païens: Une mission de l'Église sur les plateaux du Vietnam. (Théologie, 54). Paris, FR: Éditions Aubier, 1963. 172 pp. Paper. No ISBN.

A narrative description of French Catholic mission work in the 1950s among the Jarai tribe of the Vietnamese highlands.

AS1502 Dournes, Jacques
Dios ama a los Paganos. (Epifanía, 21). Barcelona, SP: Editorial Estela, 1968. 218 pp. Paper. No ISBN.
Spanish translation.

AS1503 Dournes, Jacques
God in Vietnam. Translated by Rosemary Sheed. London, ENK: Chapman, 1966. 203 pp. No ISBN.
English translation.

AS1504 Dournes, Jacques
Gott liebt die Heiden. Freiburg, GW: Herder, 1965. 220 pp. Paper. No ISBN.
German translation.

AS1505 Dournes, Jacques
Le père m'a envoyé: Réflexions à partir d'une situation missionaire. (Parole et mission, 8). Paris, FR: Éditions du Cerf, 1965. 254 pp. No ISBN.

A Catholic missionary to Vietnam's reflections after being forced to leave during the Vietnam War.

AS1506 Gheddo, Piero
Cattolici e buddisti nel Vietnam: Il ruolo delle comunitá religiose nella costruzione delle pace. (Mezzo secolo, 22). Florence, IT: Vallecchi Editore, 1968. xxiii, 397 pp. No ISBN.

A scholarly study of Catholic-Buddhist relations in Vietnam, 1945-1975, with special emphasis on church-state issues.

AS1507 Gheddo, Piero
The Cross and the Bo-Tree: Catholics and Buddhists in Vietnam. Translated by Charles Underhill Quinn. New York, NYU: Sheed & Ward, 1970. xv, 368 pp. No ISBN.
English translation.

AS1508 Gheddo, Piero
Katholiken und Buddhisten in Vietnam. Munich, GW: Pfeiffer, 1970. 363 pp. Paper. 3790400114.
German translation.

AS1509 Gheddo, Piero, and Giacomo Girardi
Vietnam, Cambogia: Due popoli un solo dramma. Bologna, IT: EMI, 1979. 191 pp. No ISBN.

The trauma of war and refugees in Vietnam and Cambodia told by Catholic missionaries visiting the area.

AS1510 Hefley, James C.
By Life or by Death. Grand Rapids, MIU: Zondervan, 1969. 208 pp. No ISBN.

Personal accounts of casualties and captives from among missionaries of the CMA and the Wycliffe Bible Translators working in Vietnam.

AS1511 Klassen, James R.
Jimshoes in Vietnam: Orienting a Westener. Scottdale, PAU: Herald Press, 1986. 389 pp. Paper. 0836134125.

A well-documented personal account of the author's struggles to learn the Vietnamese culture during the Vietnam War, and then to fit it into programs of the Mennonite mission.

AS1512 Le, Nicole-Dominique
Les missions étrangères et la pénétration française au Vietnam. (Publications de l'Institut d'études et de recherches interethniques et interculturelles, 5). Paris, FR: Mouton, 1975. 228 pp. 2719306118.

A detailed study of the joint involvement of Catholic missions and the French government in opening up Vietnam to Western influence, especially from 1787 to 1885, and an analysis of the resulting Vietnamese responses to Christianity; with selected documents from archives and an extensive bibliography.

AS1513 Livingston, Jean
Tears for the Smaller Dragon: The Story of Jim and Jean Livingston. (The Jaffray Collection of Missionary Portraits). Camp Hill, PAU: Christian Publications, 1997. ix, 197 pp. Paper. 0875097030.

The story of James H. and Jean Livingston's service as CMA missionaries in Vietnam, (1958-1975) and among Vietnamese refugees in the Philippines (1982-1995).

AS1514 Long, Charles E.
To Vietnam with Love: The Story of Charlie and Eg Long. (The Jaffray Collection of Missionary Portraits, 12). Camp Hill, PAU: Christian Publications, 1995. xii, 204 pp. Paper. 0875095828.

A popular account by a CMA couple, of their ministry in Vietnam to lepers, and in Bible translation, 1958-1973.

AS1515 Merrell, Betty J., and Priscilla Tunnell, comps.
Stories That Won't Go Away: Women in Vietnam, 1959-1975. Birmingham, ALU: New Hope Publishers, 1995. 205 pp. Paper. 1563091127.

Vignettes of the life work of thirty-seven Southern Baptist women missionaries and their daughters in Vietnam.

AS1516 Peters, Daniel Barth
Through Isaac's Eyes: Crossing of Cultures, Coming of Age, and the Bond between Father and Son. Grand Rapids, MIU: Zondervan, 1996. 185 pp. Paper. 0310203767.

The son of Baptist missionaries to Vietnam recounts his teenage years (1967-1968) in Saigon.

AS1517 Phan, Peter C.
*Mission and Catechesis: Alexandre de Rhodes and Incul-
turation in Seventeenth-Century Vietnam.* (Faith and Cultures Series). Mayknoll, NYU: Orbis Books, 1998. xxiii,
324 pp. 1570751668.

An in-depth study of the pioneer contribution of Alexandre de Rhodes, S. J. (1593-1660), to Christianity's inculturation in Vietnam.

AS1518 Simonnet, Christian
Théophane Vénard: A Martyr of Vietnam. Translated by Cynthia Splatt. San Francisco, CAU: Ignatius Press, 1988. 179
pp. Paper. 0898701864.

A popular biography of Fr. Théophane Vénard (1829-
1861), a pioneer French Catholic missionary to Vietnam,
martyred in 1861 and canonized in 1988.

AS1519 Võ Dú'c Hanh, Etienne
*La Place du catholicisme dans les relations entre la France
et le Vietnam de 1870 à 1886.* (Publications universitaires
européennes, 31: Sciences politiques, 186). Bern, SZ: Lang,
1992. 1566 pp. Paper. 3261044276.

A detailed scholarly analysis of the place of Catholicism
in the relations between France and Vietnam from 1870 to
1886; based on source document study by the author, who
holds six doctorates, including civil law and political science.

AS—ASIA

EUROPE

Paul Jenkins, Subeditor

The period of this bibliography coincides with the Iron Curtain division of Europe into East and West, the reunification of the continent, and simultaneously the resurgence of nationalism and search for a greater European political and economic unity. The continent's total population in 48 countries reached more than 707 million in 2000 (*World Book Encyclopedia,* 2000).

The *World Christian Encyclopedia* includes, within Europe's "organized Christianity," more than 536 million persons, in 5,083 denominations. They represent 75.8 percent of the continent's population. Of the total, more than half (51.5%) are Roman Catholic, followed by the Orthodox (30.9%), Protestant (14.4%), and Anglican (5%).

On the one hand, increasing numbers of nominal Christians are becoming "disaffiliated" (withdrawn from membership) in the historic churches. The *WCE* for 2000 numbers them at more than 22 million (or 4.2% of the total). In addition, there are millions of nominal Christians who are not practicing their faith except for cultural rituals of passage (birth, marriage, and death).

On the other hand, there has been a growth of Pentecostalism and of Independent churches alongside historic Protestantism. By 2000 there were more than 25 million members of 1,962 Independent denominations, in 42 countries. There is a growing impact of the Charismatic Movement in Roman Catholic and Protestant churches, and in the new house and community churches (*WCE* 1:12; *EDWM,* 330-332).

Mission in Europe has a long history, going back to the apostle Paul. The "History" section contains recent works on that almost 2,000-year history.

For much of the 19th and 20th centuries, European Christians thought of *missions* as confined to their sending activity to other continents. Most of that history is to be found in other chapters of this bibliography. Missions to Europe by Protestant evangelicals were often denounced as *proselytism* by the historic churches in Eastern and Western Europe. This bibliography includes books on these mission activities, often under specific countries.

The consciousness of mission as the raison d'être of the church has grown during the 1960-2000 period. The section on "Church and Society" contains works on early models (the British industrial missions, the French worker priest movement, and the German lay academies). Look for works on the "Gospel and culture" debates in the chapter on "Missions: Social Aspects." The chapter on "Christianity and Other Religions" contains entries on Christian approaches to various faiths in Europe.

Consistent with the new European identity, the chapter lists the countries in alphabetical order. Subsections on *Western* and *Eastern* Europe contain general works relevant to that earlier division of the continent.

Will European churches in the coming years seek to reestablish Christendom, or will they find renewal as a creative minority? Their missional agenda may be as "a constructively dissident minority community, which constantly reminds Europe of the need for true community, of the priority of justice for the weakest, of the need to empower the powerless" (Forrester 1994:44).

Norman E. Thomas

Serials and Periodicals

See also GW21.

EU1 *Occasional Papers on Religion in Eastern Europe.* **Vol. 1 (1981)-vol. 11, no. 6 (1991). Six to ten issues yearly**
Philadelphia, PAU: Ecumenical Press, 1981-1991. ISSN 07315465.

Newsletter of Christians Associated for Relationships with Eastern Europe (CAREE); superseded by *Religion in Eastern Europe.*

EU2 *Religion in Eastern Europe.* **Vol. 13, no. 1 (Feb. 1993)-. Bimonthly**
Princeton, NJU: Princeton Theological Seminary, 1993- . ISSN 10694781.

Continuing *Occasional Papers on Religion in Eastern Europe,* this publication of Christians Associated for Relationships with Eastern Europe (CAREE), an ecumenical association related to the NCCUSA, contains short articles on religious developments in Eastern Europe.

Documentation and Archives

EU3 Brierley, Peter
European Churches Handbook. London, ENK: MARC Europe, 1992. 2 vols. 0947697985 (vol. 1), 1853211141 (vol. 2).

Information on the church scene in the countries of Europe, with an overview, statistics, description of Christian groups, and a directory; the text is both in English and the language of the country presented [vol. 1: *Denmark, Finland, France, Norway, Switzerland (French), United Kingdom*; vol. 2: *Austria, Netherlands, Northern Ireland, Republic of Ireland, Spain*, 467 pp.].

EU4 Callahan, William J., and David Higgs, eds.
Church and Society in Catholic Europe of the Eighteenth Century. Cambridge, ENK: Cambridge University Press, 1979. 168 pp. 0521224241.

Eight scholarly national studies of the Catholic Church in 18th-century Europe, assessing the relationship between religion and society, and showing the church weaker at the end of the 18th century, and ill-prepared to meet its challenges.

EU5 *Christianity in Europe*
(MARC Monograph, no. 22). London, ENK: MARC Europe, 1989. 57 pp. Paper. No ISBN.

A compendium of data, with graphs and maps, on social and religious factors affecting Christianity in Europe today.

History

See also HI102 and HI158.

EU6 Châtellier, Louis
The Religion of the Poor: Rural Missions in Europe and the Formation of Modern Catholicism, ca. 1500–ca. 1800. Translated by Brian Pearce. Cambridge, ENK: Cambridge University Press; Paris, FR: Maison des Sciences de l'Homme, 1997. xiii, 246 pp. 0521562015 (UK), 2735107582 (FR).

An ambitious survey of Catholic missions into the European countryside, from 1500 to 1800.

EU7 Goerner, H. Cornell
Hands across the Sea. Nashville, TNU: Convention Press, 1961. x, 116 pp. Paper. No ISBN.

A history of European Baptists from the perspective of Southern Baptist missionary work in Europe.

EU8 Sawyer, Birgit, Peter Sawyer, and Ian N. Wood, eds.
The Christianization of Scandinavia: Report of a Symposium.... Alingsas, SW: Viktoria Bokforlag, 1987. xiv, 130 pp. Paper. 918670804X.

Papers from an international symposium on the conversion of Scandanavia (Kungalv, Sweden, 4-9 August 1985), reconsidering the theme in light of new investigations and recent studies of conversion elsewhere.

EU9 Wessels, Antonie
Europe: Was It Ever Really Christian?: The Interaction between Gospel and Culture. London, ENK: SCM Press, 1994. ix, 242 pp. Paper. 0334025699.

The noted Professor of Missiology and Religion in the Free University of Amsterdam reassesses the historical evidence, from the Greco-Roman period to the present.

General Works

See also HI366.

EU10 Blei, Karel
Kerk-zijn over grenzen heen: Visie op Europa 1992. Zoetermeer, NE: Boekencentrum, 1992. 123 pp. 9023900898.

A challenge to the churches, both Roman Catholic and Protestant, to take creative roles in the process of European unification; by the General Secretary of the Dutch Reformed church.

EU11 Blei, Karel
On Being the Church across Frontiers: A Vision of Europe Today. Translated by Ann E. Mackie. Geneva, SZ: WCC Publications, 1992. 81 pp. Paper. 2825410934.

English translation.

EU12 Bochenski, Michael I.
Theology from Three Worlds: Liberation and Evangelization for the New Europe. (Regent's Study Guides, 5). Macon, GAU: Smyth & Helwys, 1997. xiv, 205 pp. Paper. 0951810448 (UK), 1573121681 (US).

An introduction, for Christians in Europe, to liberation theology as it emerged in Latin America; with biblical links between liberation and evangelism, and applications for Christian mission in the new Europe.

EU13 Brierley, Peter
A Changing Vision. (Church Growth Booklets). Bedford, ENK: BCGA, 1992. 28 pp. Paper. 094870425X.

An overview of social and ecclesiastical factors affecting the future of Christianity in Europe, by the European Director of MARC Europe.

EU14 Fulton, John, and Peter Gee, eds.
Religion in Contemporary Europe. (Texts and Studies in Religion, 64). Lewiston, NYU: E. Mellen Press, 1994. xiv, 181 pp. 0773490280.

Thirteen scholarly essays on the sociology of the religions in contemporary Europe, including their missional concerns.

EU15 Gill, Sean, Gavin D'Costa, and Ursula King, eds.
Religion in Europe: Contemporary Perspectives. Kampen, NE: Kok Pharos, 1994. ix, 213 pp. 9039005087.

Twelve sociological essays on the contemporary world faiths found in Europe, with emphasis on the search for common values amidst secularization.

EU16 Greinacher, Norbert, and Norbert Mette, eds.
The New Europe: A Challenge for Christians. (Concilium, 1992/2). London, ENK: SCM Press, 1992. xvi, 123 pp. Paper. 0334030137.

Twelve essays by an international panel of theologians, on the new social, economic, political, ideological, and religious realities of Europe.

EU17 Hall, David
Breaking Free. Bromley, Kent, ENK: STL Books; Eastbourne, ENK: Kingsway Publications, 1988. 220 pp. Paper. 1850780374 (S), 0860656896 (K).

Ten popular accounts of conversion that relate to the experiences of Europeans from diverse social backgrounds.

EU—EUROPE

EU18 Harris, W. Stuart, ed.
Eyes on Europe. ENK: Heightside Press, 1970. 156 pp. No ISBN.

Revised edition of a country-by-country survey of religion in Europe; originally published by Hodder & Stoughton, London, UK (1965).

EU19 Linn, Gerhard, ed.
Hear What the Spirit Says to the Churches: Towards Missionary Congregations in Europe. (WCC Mission Series, 2). Geneva, SZ: WCC Publications, 1994. x, 139 pp. Paper. 2825411426.

Stories of twenty-five local Protestant and Orthodox churches that have become "missionary congregations in a secularized Europe."

EU20 Lodwick, Robert C., ed.
Remembering the Future: The Challenge of the Churches in Europe. New York, NYU: Friendship Press, 1995. ix, 116 pp. Paper. 0377002909.

A regional study of contemporary challenges for the churches in Europe; prepared as an adult mission education resource, with leader's guide (26 pp., 0377002917).

EU21 Milligan, William J.
The New Nomads: Challenges Facing Christians in Western Europe. (Risk Book Series, 21). Geneva, SZ: WCC, 1984. x, 130 pp. Paper. 2825407976.

A study book on themes of European experience calling for response by Christians, whose nations are becoming the European community.

EU22 Mol, Hans, ed.
Western Religion: A Country by Country Sociological Inquiry. (Religion and Reason, 2). The Hague, NE: Mouton, 1972. 642 pp. No ISBN.

Thirty scholarly essays giving country-by-country analyses of the religious situation, mainly in Eastern and Western Europe.

EU23 Raalte, Jannes van
De puinhoop van het Christendom als teken van hoop. Kampen, NE: Kok, 1976. 103 pp. 9024306855.

Reflections on secularization and mission in Europe, arguing that the ruins of Christendom are a sign of hope.

EU24 Ratzinger, Joseph
A Turning Point for Europe?: The Church in the Modern World—Assessment and Forecast. Translated by Brian McNeil. San Francisco, CAU: Ignatius Press, 1994. 177 pp. Paper. 0898704618.

English translation.

EU25 Ratzinger, Joseph
Wendezeit für Europa?: Diagnosen und Prognosen zur Lage von Kirche und Welt. Freiburg, GW: Johannes Verlag, 1991. 128 pp. 3894113022.

A probing assessment of the critical role that the church has in European society after the collapse of Marxism, and its essential task of bringing Christ back into culture.

EU26 Uhl, Harald
Europa, Herausforderung für die Kirchen. Frankfurt am Main, GW: Lembeck, 1973. 150 pp. Paper. 387476026X.

Six European scholars contribute informed opinions regarding the political role European churches should have in and after the formation of the European Community.

EU27 Wagner, William L.
New Move Forward in Europe: Growth Patterns of German-Speaking Baptists in Europe. South Pasadena, CAU: William Carey Library, 1978. xx, 342 pp. 0878083227.

An interesting and reasonably reliable survey of Baptist growth in German-speaking Europe.

Conferences and Congresses

See also EU112.

EU28 Baumgartner, Erich W., ed.
Re-Visioning Adventist Mission in Europe. Berrien Springs, MIU: Andrews University Press, 1998. xiv, 280 pp. Paper. 1883925185.

Papers from the Seventh-Day Adventists' European Mission Conference (Hoevelaken, the Netherlands, 8-12 January 1997), designed to recast that denomination's vision for mission in Europe for the 21st century.

EU29 Müller, Joachim, ed.
Neuevangelisierung Europas: Chancen und Versuchungen. Freiburg, GW: Paulus Verlag, 1993. 156 pp. Paper. 3722803187.

Papers on the opportunities and temptations in the call by Pope John Paul II, for a "new evangelization" of Europe; originally presented at the International Religious Education Annual Conference (Quarten, Switzerland, 1992) on the theme, "Christian Identity in a Multireligious and Multicultural Society."

Church and Society

See also SO90, SO175, SO485-SO486, EC354, MI49, EU10, EU131, and EU155.

EU30 "... And Your Neighbor as Yourself": Seven Studies Exploring What it Means to be the Local Church in Action
London, ENK: USPG and ICC; Geneva, SZ: WCC, 1990. 64 pp. Paper. 0854720316 (U), 2825410004 (W).

Bible studies for European Christians, exploring issues of what it means to be a neighbor to persons in need.

EU31 Brinkman, Martien E., and Hugo Vlug, eds.
Faith in the City: Fifty Years World Council of Churches in a Secularized Western Context: Amsterdam, 1948-1998. (IIMO Research Publication, 50). Zoetermeer, NE: Meinema, 1998. 105 pp. Paper. 9021170175.

Seven essays reflecting on fifty years of urbanization, secularization and urban mission, especially in Amsterdam, the Netherlands.

EU32 Christianity and Other Faiths in Europe
(LWF Documentation, 37). Geneva, SZ: LWF, 1995. 242 pp. Paper. 3906706168.

Fourteen papers originally presented at the LWF-sponsored consultation on "Christianity and Other Faiths in Europe Today" (Järvenpää, Finland, 25-29 August 1994).

EU33 Edwards, David L.
Christians in a New Europe. London, ENK: Collins, 1990. 257 pp. Paper. 0006274919.

An introduction to the immense political, economic, social, and religious changes taking place in Europe in light of history and from a Christian viewpoint; by the provost of Southwark Cathedral in London and former editor of SCM Press.

EU—EUROPE

EU34 Frakes, Margaret
Bridges to Understanding: The "Academy Movement" in Europe and North America. Philadelphia, PAU: Muhlenberg Press, 1960. 134 pp. No ISBN.

The story of the Academy Movement, which, in the 20th century, has sought to bridge the gap between the church and the secular world.

EU35 Gillessen, Günther
Europa fordert die Christen: Zur Problematik von Nation und Konfession. Regensburg, GW: Verlag Friedrich Pustet, 1993. 154 pp. Paper. 3791713299.

Eight scholarly essays on the challenge of new political and religious developments for European Christians—both new sources East-West conflict, and hopes for peaceful togetherness.

EU36 Grant, Paul, and Raj Patel, eds.
A Time to Act: Kairos 1992. Nottingham, ENK: CCBI, 1992. 108 pp. Paper. 0951949209.

A varied collection of thirteen short essays by black and Third World persons in Europe, challenging European Christians to increased sensitivity on contemporary justice issues.

EU37 Gurney, Robin
The Face of Pain and Hope: Stories of Diakonia in Europe. Geneva, SZ: WCC, 1995. xii, 70 pp. Paper. 2825411612.

Fourteen short accounts of contemporary Christian service to the needy in Europe, plus the "Ecumenical Diaconia Charter" for Europe, produced by the Bratislava Consultation in 1994.

EU38 Gurney, Robin
Gesichter des Schmerzes und der Hoffnung: Diakonie in Europa. Geneva, SZ: CEC, 1995. 92 pp. Paper. 2880700817.

German translation.

EU39 Hill, Clifford, Monica Hill, and Eddie Gibbs
A New Prophetic Movement—for Europe? (Church Growth Booklets). Bedford, ENK: BCGA, 1991. 32 pp. Paper. 0948704292.

Biblical bases and the need for a new prophetic Christianity for Europe.

EU40 Mensen, Bernhard, ed.
Europa Gegenwart und Zukunft. (Vortragsreihe Akademie Völker und Kulturen, 16, 1992/93). Nettetal, GW: Steyler Verlag, 1993. 110 pp. Paper. 3805003293.

Six lectures analyzing contemporary politics and economics in Europe, and the task of the church and Christians in the new Europe.

EU41 Wessels, Antonie
Secularized Europe: Who Will Carry Off Its Soul? (Gospel and Cultures Pamphlet, 6). Geneva, SZ: WCC Publications, 1996. xi, 48 pp. Paper. 2825411825.

The noted Dutch missiologist introduces issues of the Gospel and contemporary European culture.

General: Biography, Individual

See also HI325 and HI344.

EU42 Alcuin, and Abbot of Echternach Thiofridus
Willibrord, Apostel der Friesen: Seine Vita nach Alkuin und Thiofrid. Edited by Hans-Joachim Reischmann. Sigmaringendorf, GW: Regio Verlag Glock und Lutz, 1989. 127 pp. 3823562312.

A new edition of the biography of Willibrord (d.739) by Alcuin (c.796) and Thiofridus (c.1104,) in Latin and German; with a scholarly introduction and bibliographical appendix.

EU43 Gamillscheg, Hannes
Ich kenne keine Angst: Ansgar, Missionar bei den Wikingern (801-865). (Missionare, die Geschichte machten). Mödling, AU: Verlag St. Gabriel; St. Augustin, GW: Steyler Verlag, 1979. 143 pp. Paper. 3852641381 (V), 3877871135 (S).

A popular biography of St. Ansgar, the "Apostle of the North," based on the *Vita Anskari* of his contemporary, Bishop Rimbert, and adapted for modern readers.

EU44 Heinz, Daniel
Ludwig Richard Conradi: Missionar der Siebenten-Tags-Adventisten in Europa. (Archiv für internationale Adventgeschichte, 2). Frankfurt am Main, GW: Lang, 1987. 131 pp. Paper. 3820410791.

A scholarly biographical and missiological study of Ludwig Richard Conradi (1856-1939), who served as Seventh-day Adventist missionary to Germany and other areas of Europe, but who eventually joined the Seventh-day Baptists.

EU45 MacManus, Francis
Saint Columban. New York, NYU: Sheed and Ward, 1962. 240 pp. No ISBN.

Excellent biography of the 6th-century Irish missionary to southern Europe, and study in the unique expression of monastery-centered Christianity that characterized Ireland for several centuries of its early Christian history.

Eastern Europe: General Works

See also HI95, HI161-HI162, EC71, EC349, PO78-PO79, and CO126.

EU46 *A Word of Solidarity, a Call for Justice: A Statement on Religious Freedom in Eastern Europe and the Soviet Union*
Washington, DCU: USCC, 1989. 57 pp. Paper. 1555862624.

An update of the Bishops' 1977 Statement on Religious Liberty in Eastern Europe and the Soviet Union, proposing a new framework for church-state relations; a response of solidarity by churches, groups, and individuals, along with other policy proposals.

EU47 Andrew, Brother, John L. Sherrill, and Elizabeth Sherrill
God's Smuggler. London, ENK: Hodder & Stoughton, 1968. 256 pp. Paper. 0340155396.

The account of the Worldwide Evangelization Crusade missionary from Holland, who smuggled contraband Bibles to people behind the Iron Curtain in the 1960s.

EU48 Bailey, J. Martin
The Spring of Nations: Churches in the Rebirth of Central and Eastern Europe. New York, NYU: Friendship Press, 1991. 166 pp. Paper. 0377002240.

Accounts of the contributions of Christians in Central and Eastern Europe to the rebirth of freedom in their countries.

EU49 Barberini, Giovanni, Martin Stöhr, and Erich Weingartner, eds.
Kirchen im Sozialismus: Kirche und Staat in dem osteuropaischen sozialistischen Republiken: Eine IDOC-Dokumentation. Frankfurt am Main, GW: Lembeck, 1977. 287 pp. 3874760758.

A compendium of scholarly papers on the church with the socialist nations of Eastern Europe.

EU50 Beeson, Trevor

Discretion and Valour: Religious Conditions in Russia and Eastern Europe. Philadelphia, PAU: Fortress Press, 1984. 416 pp. Paper. 0800616219.

A revised and updated edition of the 1972-1973 survey of religion in Eastern Europe and the USSR, with an analysis of reasons why the church survives under communism; originally published in 1974 by the BCC.

EU51 Broun, Janice

Conscience and Captivity: Religion in Eastern Europe. Washington, DCU: Ethics & Public Policy Center, 1988. xiii, 376 pp. Paper. 0896331296 (hdbk), 089633130X (pbk).

A religious survey of eight countries of Eastern Europe, including a brief religious history, the current religious makeup, and church-state relations to 1988.

EU52 Bultman, Bud

Revolution by Candlelight: The Real Story behind the Changes in Eastern Europe. Portland, ORU: Multnomah, 1991. 305 pp. 0880704349.

Stories of Christian leadership in the democratic revolutions that toppled communism in Eastern Europe; told by a Christian journalist, who, since 1986, has covered these events for Cable News Network (CNN).

EU53 Dodd, Christine

Called to Mission: A Workbook for the Decade of Evangelization. Collegeville, MNU: Liturgical Press, 1991. vii, 104 pp. Paper. 081462071X.

A practical guide for Catholic parishes in the Decade for Evangelization, on the rationale for local mission and evangelization and the calling of lay Christians within it.

EU54 Drummond, Lewis A., ed.

Here They Stand: Biblical Sermons from Eastern Europe. Valley Forge, PAU: Judson Press, 1978. v, 186 pp. 0817007903.

An unusual compilation of sermons by eighteen pastors in eight Eastern European countries, demonstrating the vitality of the Christian faith there, even in the face of opposition.

EU55 Elliot, Mark R., ed.

East European Missions Directory. Wheaton, ILU: Institute for the Study of Christianity and Marxism/Wheaton College, 1989. 81 pp. Paper. No ISBN.

A directory of 320 Christian parachurch organizations working for the benefit of the church and the spread of biblical faith in Eastern Europe and the Soviet Union.

EU56 Grant, Myrna

The Journey: The Story of Rose Warmer: Courage, Faith and Drama to Rank with the Hiding Place. London, ENK: Hodder & Stoughton, 1978. 207 pp. 0340240075.

The biography of a Jewish convert to Christianity, an Auschwitz survivor, and an evangelist among her own people, from Eastern Europe to Israel.

EU57 Hebly, Hans

Eastbound Ecumenism: A Collection of Essays on the World Council of Churches and Eastern Europe. Lanham, MDU: University Press of America; Amsterdam, NE: Free University Press, 1986. ix, 144 pp. Paper. 0819154016.

A scholarly analysis of the history, since 1948, of East-West ecumenical relations, emphasizing the pluralism of church-state relations, from East Germany to the USSR, and the need for new WCC initiatives taken in consultation with the churches of Eastern Europe.

EU58 Linzey, Sharon, M. Holt Ruffin, and Mark R. Elliot, eds.

East West Christian Organizations: A Directory of Western Christian Organizations Working in East Central Europe and the Newly Independent States Formerly Part of the Soviet Union. Evanston, ILU: Berry Publishing, 1993. 240 pp. Paper. 0963585606.

A directory with four articles of organizational advice for mission leaders, plus indices by country or region, type of activity, and organizational name.

EU59 Mensen, Bernhard, ed.

Russland—Politik und Religion in Geschichte und Gegenwart. (Akademie Volker und Kulturen, 18). Nettetal, GW: Steyler Verlag, 1995. 269 pp. Paper. 3805003633.

Five scholarly essays on religion in politics, including an extended historical and contemporary survey of Christianity and Judaism in Russia and Eastern Europe; by Gerd Stricker.

EU60 Nicoli, Pastor

Persecuted but Not Forsaken: The Story of a Church behind the Iron Curtain. Valley Forge, PAU: Judson Press; Edinburgh, STK: St. Andrew Press, 1978. 176 pp. Paper. 0817007490 (US), 0715204033 (UK).

A collection of real-life stories of Christian persecution in Eastern Europe, told as though happening to a young pastor; by the author, who is a Protestant minister there.

EU61 Nielsen, Niels C.

Revolutions in Eastern Europe: The Religious Roots. Maryknoll, NYU: Orbis Books, 1991. vii, 175 pp. Paper. 0883447649.

A country-by-country analysis of religion's role in the 1989 "peoples' revolution" in Eastern Europe.

EU62 Njoroge, Nyambura J., and Irja Askola, eds.

There Were Also Women Looking on from Afar. (WARC Studies, 41). Geneva, SZ: WARC, 1998. 184 pp. Paper. 9290750588.

Essays honoring Rev. Dr. Jana Opocenská, in celebration of her 65th birthday, her contribution to feminist theology, and the full participation of women in God's mission in the Reformed community in central and eastern Europe; written in English and German.

EU63 Paulson, Hank, and Don Richardson

Beyond the Wall: The People Communism Can't Conquer. Ventura, CAU: Regal Books, 1982. 173 pp. Paper. 0830708065.

Narrative accounts of evangelical Protestant witnessing in Eastern Europe in the 1970s, including Bible smuggling by the founder in 1971 of the Eastern European Bible Mission.

EU64 Tatford, Frederick A.

Red Glow over Eastern Europe. (That the World May Know, 9). Bath, ENK: Echoes of Service, 1986. xiv, 290 pp. 0946214107.

A survey of work and life of Christian assemblies, with sections on Albania, Bulgaria, Czechoslovakia, the German Democratic Republic (GDR), Estonia, Finland, Hungary, Latvia, Lithuania, Poland, Romania, Turkmenistan, USSR, and Yugoslavia.

EU—EUROPE

EU65 Walters, Philip, ed.
World Christianity: Eastern Europe. (Keston Book No. 29). Monrovia, CAU: MARC, 1988. 318 pp. Paper. 185424065X.

A comprehensive account of the churches of the Soviet Union and Eastern Europe—Protestant, Orthodox, and Catholic.

Western Europe: General Works

See also HI25, HI96, HI103, TH252, CR1051, SO228, EC91, EC179, and EU42.

EU66 Bowen, E. G.
Saints, Seaways, and Settlements in the Celtic Lands. Cardiff, WLK: University of Wales Press, 1969. viii, 245 pp. No ISBN.

A study in historical geography, tracing the distribution and spread of saints' cults and Christian settlements in medieval Britain, Ireland, and Brittany.

EU67 France, James
The Cistercians in Scandinavia. (Cistercians Studies, 131). Kalamazoo, MIU: Cistercian Publications, 1992. xxiii, 577 pp. 0879075317.

A comprehensive history of the Cistercians in Scandinavia, from their entry as missionaries in 1143 to the present.

EU68 Hunter, Leslie Stannard, ed.
Scandanavian Churches: The Development and Life of the Churches of Denmark, Finland, Iceland, Norway, and Sweden. Minneapolis, MNU: Augsburg, 1965. 200 pp. No ISBN.

A collection of essays by Scandanavian church leaders, designed to introduce English readers to the development and life of the churches of Denmark, Finland, Iceland, Norway, and Sweden.

EU69 Malaska, H.
The Challenge for Evangelical Missions to Europe: A Scandanavian Case Study. South Pasadena, CAU: William Carey Library, 1970. 178 pp. 0878083081.

An analysis of the mission of new evangelical groups in Scandanavia, and their relationships with both the Free and Lutheran state churches of those countries.

EU70 Post, Paul, Jos Pieper, and Marinus van Uden
The Modern Pilgrim: Multi-Disciplinary Explorations of Christian Pilgrimage. (Liturgia Condenda, 8). Leuven, BE: Peeters, 1998. ix, 368 pp. Paper. 9042906987.

Essays on traditional and new approaches to Christian pilgrimage, from liturgical, historical, anthropological, and ethnographic perspectives.

EU71 *Together in Mission and Ministry: The Porvoo Common Statement with Essays on Church and Ministry in Northern Europe*
London, ENK: Church House Publishing, 1993. vi, 218 pp. Paper. 0715157507.

Essays resulting from conversations between leaders of British and Irish Anglican churches, and Nordic and Baltic Lutheran churches; including the text of their Porvoo Common Statement of 1992.

Albania

EU72 Joly, Reona Peterson
Tomorrow You Die: You Are a Traitor ... and Traitors Are Shot. Seattle, WAU: YWAM, 1997. 160 pp. Paper. 0927545926.

Second edition of stories of courageous witness in Albania in the 1970s by YWAM missionaries; originally published in 1976 (Van Nuys, CAU: Bible Voice).

EU73 Peterson, Reona
Et s'il fallait mourir ... Lausanne, SZ: Jeunesse en Mission, 1976. 192 pp. No ISBN.

French translation of *Tomorrow You Die* (1976).

EU74 Sinishta, Gjon
The Fulfilled Promise: A Documentary Account of Religious Persecution in Albania. Santa Clara, CAU: Sinishta, 1976. 248 pp. Paper. 0317187155.

The history of Christianity in Albania, focusing on persecution under Communist rule; based on an impressive array of documentary evidence.

Austria

See also TH11 and TH121.

EU75 Heinz, Daniel
Church, State, and Religious Dissent: A History of Seventh-day Adventists in Austria, 1890-1975. (Archives of International Adventist History, 5). Frankfurt am Main, GW: Lang, 1993. 206 pp. Paper. 3631455534.

The history of Seventh-day Adventists' missions and church development in Austria, focusing on church-state relationships.

Belgium

See also SO15.

EU76 Thomas, William
An Assessment of Mass Meeting as a Method of Evangelism: Case Study of Eurofest '75 and the Billy Graham Crusade in Brussels. (Proefschrift Theol. Fac. Vrije Universiteit Amsterdam). Amsterdam, NE: Rodopi, 1977. 294 pp. Paper. No ISBN.

A critical evaluation of the Billy Graham Crusade in Europe, 1975, by an American who served for three years as a missionary in Zaire, and for seventeen years as a full-time evangelist with the European Baptist Federation.

Britain (United Kingdom of Great Britain and Northern Ireland)

See also GW42, HI452, HI457, HI496, HI619, HI636, CR162, CR1016, CR1504, SO152, SO170, SO549, SO562, EC156, EC336, EC339, PO73, PO153, ED110, ED130, EV16, EV18, EV85, EV104, EV108, EV158, EV235, EV357, EV381, EV405, CH3, CH35, CH127, CH161, CH325, CH341, CH384, CH386, CH392, CH407, AF1196, EU175, and EU216.

EU77 Back, Philip
Mission England—What Really Happened?: A Report on the Main Meetings of 1984. Kent, ENK: MARC Europe, 1986. 119 pp. Paper. 0947697241.

A statistical and interpretive analysis of Mission England, the Billy Graham mission that reached over one million people in six cities in 1984.

EU78 Bagwell, Philip S.
Outcast London, A Christian Response: The West London Mission of the Methodist Church, 1887-1987. London, ENK: Epworth Press, 1987. xii, 174 pp. 0716204355.

Scholarly study that investigates the interrelationship of personal salvation and social redemption in missions work, as illustrated by the West London Mission; with emphasis on the impact of the Methodist Forward Movement.

EU79 Bashford, Robert
Mission and Evangelism in Recent Thinking, 1974-1986. (Latimer Studies, 35/36). Oxford, ENK: Latimer House, 1990. 93 pp. Paper. 0946307352.

An analysis of British thought concerning mission and evangelism during the 1970s and 1980s, with special reference to interdenominational evangelistic efforts in Britain, and the Church of England's role.

EU80 Beasley, John D.
The Bitter Cry Heard and Heeded: The Story of the South London Mission of the Methodist Church, 1889-1989. London, ENK: South London Mission, 1990. 269 pp. Paper. 0951327615 (hdbk), 0951327607 (pbk).

An illustrated centennial history of cooperative mission by Methodists in South London, England.

EU81 Beeson, Trevor
Britain Today and Tomorrow. London, ENK: Fount, 1978. 284 pp. 0006251269.

Report of the "Britain Today and Tomorrow" project of the BCC, designed to stimulate interdisciplinary thought on the future social order of Great Britain—its issues, values, and the role of the churches.

EU82 Bentley, James
Cry God for England: The Survival and Mission of the British Churches. London, ENK: Bowerdean Press, 1978. 88 pp. 0906097053 (hdbk), 0906097061 (pbk).

Six BBC radio scripts which outline the crisis for the British churches today.

EU83 Booth, William
In Darkest England and the Way Out. (Patterson Smith Series in Criminology, 142). Montclair, NJU: Patterson Smith, 1975. xix, 323 pp. 0875851428.

A reprint of the original 1890 work by the founder of the Salvation Army, which describes the dire straits of England's poor and destitute, the social causes for their misery, and the Salvation Army's plans to address their practical needs.

EU84 Brierley, Peter
"Christian" England: What the 1989 English Church Census Reveals. London, ENK: MARC Europe, 1991. 254 pp. Paper. 1853211001.

A comprehensive analysis of churchgoing patterns in England in 1989, based on the census of that year; with implications for the 1990s decade of evangelism.

EU85 Brierley, Peter, ed.
Beyond the Churches: Facing a Task Unfinished: Groups outside the Churches in England and Wales. London, ENK: MARC Europe; London, ENK: Evangelical Missionary Alliance, 1984. 150 pp. Paper. 095083968X, 0950595241.

A survey of unreached people groups in Great Britain by the European director of MARC.

EU86 British Council of Churches
Changing the Agenda: Christian Reflections on Mission and Community Work. London, ENK: BCC, 1989. iii, 96 pp. Paper. 0851692001.

Essays by Christian leaders involved in community work in British cities, including black-led churches, mainstream Protestant parishes, and para-church organizations.

EU87 Burton, Jack
England Needs a Revival. London, ENK: SCM Press; 1995. ix, 118 pp. Paper. 0334026237.

A Methodist minister, after twenty-eight years as a worker priest, recounts the social, cultural, and religious seedbed for revival.

EU88 Busia, Kofi Abrefa
Urban Churches in Britain: A Question of Relevance. London, ENK: Lutterworth Press, 1966. xii, 175 pp. No ISBN.

A survey, conducted by the noted Ghanaian sociologist of religion, of the churches in Birmingham, England—part of the WCC's research on "Churches in the Missionary Situation: Studies in Growth and Response."

EU89 Calley, Malcolm J. C.
God's People: West Indian Pentecostal Sects in England. London, ENK: Oxford University Press, 1965. xiv, 182 pp. No ISBN.

A social anthropologist's careful study, based on two years of exact observation of Pentecostal worship and interviews with church leaders, together with a concise introduction to Pentecostalism.

EU90 Carey, George
The Church in the Market Place. Harrisburg, PAU: Morehouse Publishing, 1989. 154 pp. Paper. 0819215627.

Second edition of a popular account of the renewal, from 1975 to 1982, of St. Nicholas' Anglican parish in the center of Durham, England; originally published by Kingsway Publications in 1984.

EU91 Chamberlain, Neville, Eric Forshaw, and Malcolm Goldsmith
Understanding Inequality: A Handbook for Local Churches. (Britain Today & Tomorrow, 1). London, ENK: BCC, Community Work Resource Unit, 1977. 51 pp. No ISBN.

A study guide for congregations, on the problem of urban deprivation.

EU92 Collinson, C. Peter
All Churches Great and Small: The Church Scene in the United Kingdom. Carlisle, ENK: OM Publishing, 1998. xi, 190 pp. Paper. 185078311X.

A brief handbook of Christian churches and denominations in Great Britain, introducing their origins, distinctive features, and differences.

EU93 Cryer, Neville B., and Ernest N. Goodridge
Experiment in Unity. London, ENK: Mowbray, 1968. 168 pp. Paper. 0264655583.

A case study of local ecumenism in south London, initiated by Anglicans and Methodists, which grew to include joint action in mission by most denominations in the area.

EU—EUROPE

EU94 Currie, Robert, Alan Gilbert, and Lee Horsley
Church and Churchgoers: Patterns of Church Growth in the British Isles since 1700. Oxford, ENK: Clarendon Press, 1977. x, 244 pp. 0198272189.

An analytical survey of church growth and decline in Great Britain and Ireland, from the 18th to 20th centuries, with an analysis of causal factors.

EU95 Davie, Grace
Religion in Britain since 1945: Believing without Belonging. (Making Contemporary Britain Series). Oxford, ENK: Blackwell Publishers, 1994. xiii, 226 pp. 0631184430 (hdbk), 0631184449 (pbk).

A scholarly analysis, from a sociological point of view, of the religious situation in contemporary Britain, including aspects of secularization and the "believing without belonging" pattern.

EU96 Davies, Noel
Wales: Language, Nation, Faith and Witness. (Gospel and Cultures Pamphlet, 4). Geneva, SZ: WCC Publications, 1996. x, 61 pp. Paper. 2825411809.

A case study of the challenge and crisis of mission in the cultural context of contemporary Wales.

EU97 Down, Martin
Speak to These Bones. Tunbridge Wells, ENK: Monarch Publications, 1993. 186 pp. Paper. 1854241990.

A popular account by the Anglican rector of two rural churches in East Anglia, recounting how the wind of the Spirit blew through two traditional village churches.

EU98 Eastman, Michael, ed.
Ten Inner-City Churches. Eastbourne, ENK: MARC; London, ENK: BCGA; London, ENK: Evangelical Coalition for Urban Mission, 1988. 221 pp. 0860656276 (M), 094870411X (B), 0946842035 (E).

Firsthand accounts of ten Anglican and Free church parishes in creative mission in the UK, with an introductory essay outlining key issues.

EU99 Edwards, Maureen
Bridges of the Spirit. London, ENK: SPCK, 1994. x, 134 pp. Paper. 0281047707.

Short accounts of missionaries from Great Britain, and of the reverse mission of Third World Christians in Great Britain; prepared as a mission study book.

EU100 Foster, John
They Converted Our Ancestors: A Study of the Early Church in Britain. (SCM Book Club, 164). London, ENK: SCM Press, 1965. 128 pp. Paper. No ISBN.

A popular history of how Christianity spread through Celtic and Roman missions in England, Scotland, and Ireland, and then outward again to the European continent, from the 4th to 8th centuries.

EU101 Francis, Leslie J., and Kevin Williams, eds.
Churches in Fellowship: Local Councils of Churches in England Today. London, ENK: BBC/CCBI, 1991. xiv, 105 pp. Paper. 0851692117.

A survey of local ecumenism in Great Britian including various forms of mission outreach.

EU102 Gauntlett, Caughey
Today in Darkest Britain. Eastbourne, ENK: MARC, 1990. 256 pp. Paper. 1854240595.

A centenary volume to mark the publication of William Booth's *In Darkest England* (1890), measuring today's social problems against Booth's damning survey, and describing the work of the Salvation Army to mitigate these problems.

EU103 Gerloff, Roswith et al.
Partnership in Black and White. (Home Mission Occasional Papers, 29). London, ENK: Methodist Church, Home Mission Division, 1977. 37 pp. No ISBN.

Concise information about various black-led churches in Britain's cities.

EU104 Gidoomal, Ram, and Mike Fearon
Sari 'n Chips. Tunbridge Wells, ENK: MARC-Monarch Publications; Sutton, ENK: South Asian Concern, 1993. 160 pp. Paper. 1854242253.

A popular account of personal, social, and cultural tensions faced by Two-Thirds World immigrants to Great Britain, with suggestions how individuals and churches can work together to overcome them.

EU105 Gill, Robin
The Myth of the Empty Church. London, ENK: SPCK, 1993. viii, 335 pp. Paper. 0281046433.

The Professor of Modern Theology at the University of Kent, Canterbury, critiques the theory that secularization caused the decline of church attendance in Great Britain.

EU106 Grant, Paul, and Raj Patel, eds.
A Time to Speak: Perspectives on Black Christians in Britain. Birmingham, ENK: CRRU/ECRJ, 1990. 93 pp. Paper. No ISBN.

Eleven short essays by black church leaders in Great Britain on the churches and race relations in that country, mapping out a black theology.

EU107 Hocken, Peter
Streams of Renewal: The Origins and Early Development of the Charismatic Movement in Great Britain. Exeter, ENK: Paternoster Press; Washington, DCU: Word Among Us, 1986. 288 pp. Paper. 0853644225.

A researched account of the beginnings and expansion of the charismatic movement in Great Britain during the 1950s.

EU108 Hooker, R. H., and Christopher Lamb
Love the Stranger: Ministry in Multi-Faith Areas. (New Library of Pastoral Care). London, ENK: SPCK, 1993. xviii, 154 pp. Paper. 0281046867.

A detailed account about the practices and beliefs of Asians living in Britain, with helps for local churches desiring to minister to them; by two former CMS missionaries, now in ministry among Asians in Birmingham.

EU109 Hooker, R. H., and John Sargant, eds.
Belonging to Britain: Christian Perspectives on Religion and Identity in a Plural Society. London, ENK: BCC/CCBI, 1991. viii, 172 pp. Paper. 0851692044.

A study book exploring the meaning of nationality, nationhood, and Christian identity, from biblical, historical, Scottish, Welsh, feminist, black, and other perspectives.

EU110 Hope, David
Living the Gospel. London, ENK: Darton, Longman & Todd, 1993. x, 131 pp. Paper. 0232520178.

Sermons and reflections on the church's mission and evangelization by the Anglican bishop of London.

EU—EUROPE

EU111 Kernohan, R. D.
Scotland's Life and Work: A Scottish View of God's World through Life and Work, 1879-1979. Edinburgh, STK: St. Andrew's Press, 1979. 215 pp. 0715204211.

The centenary history of the magazine of the Church of Scotland, which more than any other, defined the social issues of the day for Scottish Christians.

EU112 Leech, Kenneth
Struggle in Babylon: Racism in the Cities and Churches of Britain. London, ENK: Sheldon Press, 1988. 253 pp. Paper. 0859695778.

An analysis of the history of racial crisis in the cities of Great Britian, and of the varied responses of the churches to a society increasingly pluralistic in population and racist in attitudes.

EU113 Lester, Muriel
Ambassador of Reconciliation: A Muriel Lester Reader. Edited by Richard L. Deats. Philadelphia, PAU: New Society Publishers, 1991. xiii, 225 pp. 0865712107 (US hdbk), 0865712115 (US pbk), 1550921525 (CA hdbk), 1550921533 (CA pbk).

Selections from the voluminous writings of Muriel Lester (1884-1968), the founder of Kinsley Hall in London, who dedicated herself to peace and justice for the poor in England, India, and China.

EU114 Lewis, Donald M.
Lighten Their Darkness: The Evangelical Mission to Working-Class London, 1828-1860. (Contributions to the Study of Religion, 19). Westport, CTU: Greenwood, 1986. xiv, 369 pp. 0313255776.

A detailed study of different aspects of the evangelical mission to the urban poor in London, analyzing both unifying factors and tensions between evangelicals, inside and outside the Church of England.

EU115 Lindars, Barnabas
Church without Walls: Essays on the Role of the British in Contemporary Society. London, ENK: SPCK, 1968. 144 pp. No ISBN.

Nine short essays by Church of England parish clergy.

EU116 Lockwood, Trevor
The Church on the Housing Estate: Mission and Ministry on the Urban Estate. London, ENK: Methodist church, Home Mission Division, 1993. vi, 81 pp. Paper. 0901015113.

A popular account based on twenty-two years of service by a Methodist minister in government-owned housing estates—one of the most unchurched population groups in Great Britain.

EU117 Lovell, George, and Catherine Widdicombe
Churches and Communities: An Approach to Development in the Local Church. London, ENK: Search Press, 1978. 218 pp. 0855323876.

The report of five years of mission in a London suburb, attempting in a non-directive way, to enable churches to discover their own ministries in the community.

EU118 Lowndes, Marian
A Mission in the City: Sheffield Inner City Ecumenical Mission. (New City Special, 5). Sheffield, ENK: Urban Theology Unit, 1988. 32 pp. Paper. No ISBN.

A guide to help visitors to know the Sheffield Mis-

sion, and to reflect on the relevance of this ecumenical model of urban ministry for their own churches.

EU119 Ludwig, Charles
Mother of an Army. Minneapolis, MNU: Bethany House, 1987. 237 pp. Paper. 0871239248.

A popular biographical novel of Catherine Mumford Booth, the cofounder of the Salvation Army.

EU120 Machin, G. I. T.
Churches and Social Issues in Twentieth-Century Britain. Oxford, ENK: Clarendon Press, 1998. xi, 269 pp. 0198217803.

This broad ranging study covers the growing division between churches in Britain, over public and private social and moral challenges.

EU121 Maguire, Mairead Corrigan
The Vision of Peace: Faith and Hope in Northern Ireland. Edited by John Dear. Maryknoll, NYU: Orbis Books, 1999. 123 pp. Paper. 1570752516.

The first collection of writings by Mairead Corrigan Maguire, the 1976 Nobel Peace Prize winner from Belfast, who has been a prophet of peace and nonviolence throughout the world.

EU122 Marchant, Colin
Signs in the City. London, ENK: Hodder & Stoughton, 1985. 158 pp. Paper. 0340374268.

An assessment of the urban dilemma and of new patterns of mission there by the warden of Laurence Hall, a community and Christian center in the East End of London.

EU123 Mayr-Harting, Henry
The Coming of Christianity to Anglo-Saxon England. New York, NYU: Schocken Books; London, ENK: Batsford, 1972. 334 pp. 0713413603.

A detailed history of Roman and Irish missions to Anglo-Saxon England, from 597 to 750 A.D., with special attention to issues of the inculturation of Christianity in art, institutions, and education.

EU124 McCreary, Alf
Corrymeela: The Search for Peace. Belfast, IE: Christian Journals, 1975. 120 pp. 0904302156.

The remarkable story of a prophetic community of Protestants and Catholics in Northern Ireland and their ministries of reconciliation.

EU125 McIlhiney, David B.
A Gentleman in Every Slum: Church of England Missions in East London, 1837-1914. (Princeton Theological Monograph Series, 16). Allison Park, PAU: Pickwick, 1988. x, 141 pp. Paper. 0915138956.

A case study of the Church of England's mission to the slums of East London, written to recount the exploits of the Victorian church, in terms of local parish life.

EU126 Meek, Donald E.
The Scottish Highlands: The Churches and Gaelic Culture. (Gospel and Cultures Pamphlets, 11). Geneva, SZ: WCC Publications, 1996. viii, 69 pp. Paper. 282541204X.

An overview of the ways in which the Christian faith has been communicated, and its communication sustained, in the context of the Gaelic language and culture of the Scottish Highlands.

EU—EUROPE

EU127 Newbigin, James Edward Lesslie, Lamin Sanneh, and Jenny Taylor
Faith and Power: Christianity and Islam in 'Secular' Britain. London, ENK: SPCK, 1998. x, 177 pp. Paper. 0281051534.

The authors describe contemporary forms of multicultural-ism as a guise for indifference, that allows a dangerous compla-cency in public policy making, and calls for churches to return to the public domain as bridge-builders in a bewildered society.

EU128 Norman, Edward R.
Church and Society in England, 1770-1970: A Historical Study. Oxford, ENK: Clarendon Press, 1976. iii, 507 pp. 0198264356.

A detailed history of the social outreach of the Church of England, focusing on social teachings and attitudes.

EU129 Paton, David MacDonald, ed.
Mission and Communication: The Report of the 1963 Confer-ence of Parish and People on "The Mission of the People of God." London, ENK: SPCK, 1963. x, 191 pp. Paper. No ISBN.

Papers and reports from the Church of England's 1963 Na-tional Conference of Parish and People on the theme, "The Mis-sion of the People of God"; with chapters on mission in the coun-try to intellectuals, to non-intellectuals, in politics and industry, on ecumenical cooperation, and training of the laity for mission.

EU130 Phillips, Kate, and David Haslam, eds.
Rainbow Gospel. London, ENK: BCC, Community and Race Relations Unit, 1988. 58 pp. Paper. 0851691730.

The report of the 1987 Conference on Challenging Racism in Britain, sponsored by the Programme to Combat Racism of the WCC, and the Community and Race Relations Unit of BCC, to assess causes, present patterns, and effects of racism in Brit-ish society, and to plan strategies by the churches to counter it.

EU131 Piggin, Stuart
Making Evangelical Missionaries, 1789-1858: The Social Back-ground, Motives and Training of British Protestant Missionar-ies to India. Abingdon, ENK: Sutton Courtney Press, 1984. 378 pp. No ISBN.

An exploration of the class background, occupations, mo-tives, and education of British missionaries in the early 19th cen-tury.

EU132 Price, Lynne, Juan Sepúlveda, and Graeme Smith, eds.
Mission Matters. (Studies in the Intercultural History of Chris-tianity, 103). Frankfurt am Main, GW: Lang, 1997. 232 pp. Pa-per. 3631315139 (GE), 0820432652 (US).

A collection of essays on mission history and contemporary mission in Great Britain, by postgraduate researchers at the Uni-versity of Birmingham and the Selly Oak Colleges.

EU133 *Reflections: How Twenty-Six Churches See Their Life and Mission*
London, ENK: BCC; London, ENK: Catholic Truth Society for the Inter-Church Process, 1986. 156 pp. 0851691129.

Twenty-six short case studies of British parishes experienc-ing renewal.

EU134 Roxburgh, Kenneth B. E.
Thomas Gillespie and the Origins of the Relief Church in 18th Century Scotland. (International Theological Studies: Contribu-tions of Baptist Scholars, 3). Bern, SZ: Lang, 1999. xvi, 271 pp. Paper. 390676219X (SZ), 0820442283 (US).

An examination of the life and work of Thomas Gillespie,

within the wider context of the evangelical movement in and beyond the Church of Scotland.

EU135 Sookhdeo, Patrick
Asians in Britain: A Christian Understanding. (Mount Radford Reprints, 23). Exeter, ENK: Paternoster Press, 1977. 64 pp. Pa-per. 0853642079.

Brief introductions, for Christians in Great Britain, to the background, culture, and beliefs of their Asian immigrant neigh-bors (Hindus, Muslims, Sikhs, and Buddhists).

EU136 Sookhdeo, Patrick, ed.
Sharing Good News: The Gospel and Your Asian Neighbours. London, ENK: Scripture Union, 1991. 160 pp. Paper. 0862015472.

Four Anglicans in ministry to persons from Asia, living in the cities of Great Britain, share experiences on faith sharing in that new interfaith context.

EU137 Stallard, Ken
Give Us This Day. Evesham, ENK: James, 1979. 152 pp. Paper. 0853052069.

Reminiscences, by a British lay evangelist of fifteen years, of conducting short Gospel mssions in rural parishes and among troubled youth.

EU138 Stow, Peter, and Mike Fearon
Youth in the City: The Church's Response to the Challenge of Youth Work. London, ENK: Hodder & Stoughton, 1987. 207 pp. Paper. 0340410477.

A popular account of creative ministry with youth in the East End of London, with reflections on applying learnings for the churches' ministries to youth in other urban areas.

EU139 Templeton, Elizabeth
God's February: A Life of Archie Craig 1888-1985. London, ENK: BCC/CCBI, 1991. xiv, 176 pp. Paper. 0851692109.

A perceptive and entertaining biography of Archie Craig (1888-1985), student worker, university chaplain, moderator of the Church of Scotland, and first General Secretary of the BCC.

EU140 Thompson, Phyllis
To the Heart of the City: The Story of the London City Mission. London, ENK: Hodder & Stoughton, 1985. 140 pp. Paper. 0340347276.

A popular account of 150 years of ministry among the urban poor of London.

EU141 Thomson, Robin
Can British Churches Grow? London, ENK: Bible and Medical Missionary Fellowship, 1978. 200 pp. 0900165091.

A well-designed study guide on church growth within the British context.

EU142 Turnbull, Michael
God's Front Line. London, ENK: Mowbrays, 1979. ix, 143 pp. Paper. 0264664485.

An outline of the work of the Church Army, a social service auxiliary of the Church of England.

EU143 United Reformed Church in England and Wales, Mission and Other Faiths Committee,
With People of Other Faiths in Britain: A Study Handbook for Christians. London, ENK: United Reformed Church, n.d. 80 pp. 0902256459.

A primer for British Protestants on their neighbors of other faiths.

EU144 Verney, Stephen
Fire in Coventry. London, ENK: Hodder & Stoughton; Westwood, NJU: Revell, 1964. 95 pp. Paper. No ISBN.

The remarkable story of Coventry Cathedral and the renewal of the Coventry parish, with lessons for the church generally; written by the Coventry diocesan missioner.

EU145 Vincent, John J.
Into the City. London, ENK: Epworth Press, 1982. xiv, 146 pp. Paper. No ISBN.

Portraits of life and mission in the inner city of Sheffield, England, by the Director of the Urban Theology Unit of the Sheffield Inner City Ecumenical Mission.

EU146 Warren, Max Alexander Cunningham
The Missionary Movement from Britain in Modern History. London, ENK: SCM Press, 1965. 192 pp. No ISBN.

An assessment of the impact of British missions from 1792 to the present, with special emphasis on the interrelationship between missions and imperialism.

EU147 Wells, Ronald A.
People behind the Peace: Community and Reconciliation in Northern Ireland. Grand Rapids, MI: Eerdmans, 1999. ix, 126 pp. Paper. 080284667X.

Religion as the cause and cure of conflict in Northern Ireland, through the eyes of one who is intimately acquainted with the conflict, and who still believes in Christian reconciliation as the solution.

EU148 Whitehead, Roger, and Amy Sneddon, eds.
An Unwanted Child?: The Story of NIE. London, ENK: BCC/CCBI, 1990. vii, 132 pp. Paper. 0851692206.

A history and evaluation of the Nationwide Initiative in Evangelism (NIE), 1978-1982, and its lessons for the new Decade of Evangelisation of cooperative British initiatives for the 1990s.

EU149 Willmer, Haddon, ed.
20/20 Visions: The Futures of Christianity in Britain. London, ENK: SPCK, 1992. x, 154 pp. Paper. 0281045607.

The text of eight open lectures given at the University of Leeds in 1991, by British scholars on the future of Christianity in that nation.

EU150 Winter, Michael M.
Mission Resumed? London, ENK: Darton, Longman & Todd; Greenwood, SCU: Attic Press, 1979. x, 129 pp. 0232514248.

A comprehensive study of the religious scene in Britain as it affects mainly the Catholic Church, with a call to the National Pastoral Congress (Liverpool, 1980) to carry forward the renewal initiated by Vatican II.

EU151 Wolffe, John
God and Greater Britain: Religion and National Life in Britain and Ireland, 1843-1945. London, ENK: Routledge, 1994. xii, 324 pp. 0415035708.

A detailed analysis of the relationships between politics, culture, and nationality in Great Britain and Ireland, focusing on the 1851-1914 period.

EU152 Wolffe, John, ed.
Evangelical Faith and Public Zeal: Evangelicals and Society in Britain, 1780-1980. London, ENK: SPCK, 1995. viii, 221 pp. Paper. 0281047820.

Seven essays reassessing evangelical, social, and political action in Britain over two hundred years; with articles on mission concerns (Brian Stanley) and women, evangelism, and ministry (Jocelyn Murray).

EU153 Wooderson, Michael
The Church down Our Street: A Guide to Everyday Evangelism. Eastbourne, ENK: MARC, 1989. 190 pp. Paper. 1854240315.

Case studies of how two Anglican parishes in England experienced renewal through lay witnessing.

Bulgaria

EU154 Nestorova, Tatyana
American Missionaries among the Bulgarians: 1958-1912. (East European Monographs, 218). Boulder, COU: East European Monographs, 1987. viii, 151 pp. 0880331143.

A reexamination of the role of the ABCFM in Bulgarian education, religious life, and nationalist aspirations.

EU155 Nestorova, Tatyana
Amerikanski misioneri sred bulgarite: 1858-1912. Translated by Velislava Dimitrova. Sofiiâ, BU: Universitetsko izd-vo "Sv. Kliment Okhridski," 1991. 120 pp. No ISBN.

Bulgarian translation.

Denmark

See also GW5.

EU156 Egede, Hans
Die Heiden im Eis: Als Forscher und Missionar in Grönland 1721-1736. Stuttgart, GW: Thienemann, 1986. 427 pp. 3522601505.

Two major works, translated from Danish, of Hans Egede (1686-1758), missionary to Greenland (1721-1736); the one, a chronological narrative of his mission, and the other, a description of life in Greenland.

EU157 Egede, Poul, and Niels Egede
Continuation af Den Grønlandske Mission: Forfattet i Form af en Journal fra Anno 1734 til 1740 and Tredie Continuation af Den Grønlandske Mission: Forfattet i form af en Journal fra Anno 1739 til 1743. Compiled by Finn Gad. Copenhagen, DK: Rosenkilde og Bagger, 1971. 27 pp. No ISBN.

A facsimile of the journals from 1734 to 1743, of members of the Egede family as they continued Hans Egede's mission to Greenland.

EU158 Garnett, Eve
To Greenland's Icy Mountains: The Story of Hans Egede, Explorer, Coloniser Missionary. New York, NYU: Roy Publishers, 1968. xv, 189 pp. No ISBN.

An illustrated biography of the pioneer Lutheran missionary to Greenland.

EU159 Hindsberger, Mogens
Hans Egede og Gronland: Forelµsningsrµkke i Danmarks Radios sondagsuniversitet. Copenhagen, DK: Lohses Forlag, 1971. 82 pp. Paper. 8756401256.

A biography of Hans Egede (1686-1758), "The Apostle of Greenland."

EU—EUROPE

EU160 Ingerslev, Poul
Fra åndemanere til familiejournaler: En analyse af den danske eksport af kirstendom til Angmagssalik 1894-1921. Copenhagen, DK: Institut for Praktisk Teologi og Religionsvidenskab, Kobenhavns Univ., 1975. 75 pp. Paper. No ISBN.

An analysis of the Danish export of Christianity to a certain area in Greenland, from 1894 to 1921.

EU161 Iversen, Hans Raun
Ånd og Livsform: Husliv, folkeliv og kirkeliv hos Grundtvig og sidenhen. Aarhus, DK: Forlaget Anis, 1987. 263 pp. Paper. 8774570625.

An analysis of the relationship between spirit and forms of life, according to N. F. S. Grundtvig, the great Danish popular reformer of the 19th century; includes later exponents of national church renewal attempts.

EU162 Nielsen, Egon
Som tiden dag går- C. Rendtorff's erindringer. Copenhagen, DK: DMS-Forlag, 1975. 149 pp. 8774310437.

A popular biography of Conrad Rendtorff (b.1900), General Secretary of the Danish Missionary Society.

EU163 Østergaard, Christian Christensen
Breve fra Gronland: Glimt fra en præstetilværelse in 1830'rne. DK: By the author, C. C. Østergaard, 1982. 2 vols. Paper. No ISBN.

A collection of personal letters from a Danish Lutheran pastor and his wife during his mission in Greenland in the 1830s.

EU164 Schantz, Børge, and Hans Jørgen Schantz
Var det umagen voerd?: Danske syvende dags adventiser i fremmedmissionen. Nærum, DK: Dansk Bogforlag Naerum, 1999. 304 pp. Paper. 8775323168.

A collection of short essays on the history of Danish Adventist missions.

EU165 Thunberg, Lars, ed.
Kirken i kulturmodet i Kobenhavn. (Nyt Synspunkt, 28). Hellerup, DK: DMS-forlag, 1987. 80 pp. Paper. 8774311360.

Articles on urban mission in Copenhagen, including the history of the church's outreach to the working class, and contemporary ministries with immigrants.

Finland

See also GW90, HI2, HI697, ME105, ED152, MI136, and SP286.

EU166 Helminen, Liisa, ed.
Suomen Lähetysseuran viides viisivoutissuunnitelma 1991-1995. Helsinki, FI: Suomen Lähetysseura, 1990. 152 pp. Paper. No ISBN.

The plan of action for the years 1991-1995 in the Finnish Evangelical Lutheran Mission.

EU167 Junkkaala, Timo
Hannulan herätys: Tutkimus Lounais-Suomen lähetysherätyksestä 1894-1914. (Suomen kirkkohistoriallisen seuran toimituksia; 136). Helsinki, FI: Suomen kirkkohistoriallinen seura; Helsinki, FI: Kirjaneliö, 1986. 424 pp. Paper. 9519021612 (S), 9516006930 (K).

A study of a missions-centered revival at the beginning of the 20th century in southwestern Finland.

EU168 Komulainen, Liisa
Lähetys oli kutsumuksemme: lähetystyön veteraaneja tapaamassa. Helsinki, FI: Kirjaneliö, 1985. 141 pp. 9516006612.

Memories of Finnish missionaries.

EU169 Peltola, Matti
Lähetystyö ja kansankirkko: Suomen Lähetysseuran toiminto kotimaassa 1939-1966. (Sata vuotta suomalaista lähetystyötä, 1:5). Helsinki, FI: Kirjaneliö, 1989. 300 pp. 9516007919.

A part of the history series of the Finnish Evangelical Lutheran Mission, this volume deals with the domestic work of the society during the years 1939 to 1966.

EU170 Remes, Viljo
Lähetysharrastus Suomessa, 1835-1858. (Sata vuotta suomalaista lähetystyötä, 1:1). Helsinki, FI: Suomen Lähetysseura, 1976. 305 pp. Paper. 9516241557 (hdbk), 9516241549 (pbk).

A part of the history series of the Finnish Evangelical Lutheran Mission, this volume deals with the missionary activities in Finland before the foundation of the society.

EU171 Saarilahti, Toivo
Lähetystyön läpimurto: Suomen Lähetysseurn toiminta kotimaassa 1895-1913. (Sata vuotta suomalaista lähetystyötä, I:3). Helsinki, FI: Kirjaneliö, 1989. 446 pp. 9516007600.

A part of the history of The Finnish Evangelical Lutheran Mission, this volume deals with the domestic work of the society from 1895 to 1913.

France

See also HI23, HI273, EA107-EA108, EC338, EU66, and OC14.

EU172 Arnal, Oscar L.
Priests in Working-Class Blue: The History of The Worker-Priests (1943-1954). Mahwah, NJU: Paulist Press, 1986. viii, 239 pp. Paper. 0809128314.

The history of French and Belgian Catholic "worker-priests" from 1943 to 1954 and their ministry to the industrial work force, based on in-depth interviews.

EU173 Bjork, David E.
Unfamiliar Paths: The Challenge of Recognizing the Work of Christ in Strange Clothing: A Case Study from France. South Pasadena, CAU: William Carey Library, 1997. xix, 172 pp. Paper. 0878082786.

The challenge of evangelization in France, and of mission in a post-Christendom land, by the Field Director, for fourteen years, of World Partners of the Missionary Church in France.

EU174 Brico, Rex
Taizé: Brother Roger and His Community. Glasgow, STK: Collins, 1978. 220 pp. 0002158248 (UK), 0529056216 (US).

A history of the celebrated monastic community of Taizé in central France, founded in 1948 by Roger Schutz, creative in ecumenical outreach and reconciliation; with excerpts from his writing and conversations with the brothers.

EU175 Edwards, David L., ed.

Priests and Workers: An Anglo-French Discussion. London, ENK: SCM Press, 1961. 160 pp. Paper. No ISBN.

Eight essays comparing the work of eighty-five Catholic worker-priests in France, between 1944 and 1954, with parallel ministries by the Church of England in the 1950s.

EU176 Foreman, Howard

A New Look at Protestant Churches in France. (MARC Monograph, 9). Bromley, ENK: MARC Europe, 1987. 117 pp. Paper. No ISBN.

A statistical analysis of sixty-one different Protestant groups working in France, and of the locations and strength of their churches, based on the 1986 edition of *Annuaire Évangelique.*

EU177 Hébrard, Monique

Les nouveaux disciples dix aus après: voyage à travers les communautés charismatiques: Réflexions sur le renouveau spirituel. Paris, FR: Centurion, 1987. 378 pp. 2227355079.

A well-rounded picture of the French Catholic charismatic movement by a Catholic journalist.

EU178 Koop, Allen V.

American Evangelical Missionaries in France, 1945-1975. New York, NYU: University Press of America, 1986. xii, 207 pp. Paper. 0819152056 (P), 0819152048 (C).

A narration of the experiences of American evangelical missionaries, who chose to work in post-Christian France; with an analysis of their missionary strategies and an assessment of their accomplishments.

EU179 Moser, Mary Theresa

The Evolution of the Option for the Poor in France, 1880-1965. Lanham, MDU: University Press of America, 1985. x, 206 pp. Paper. 0819148156.

A scholarly analysis of the evolution of church-society relations in traditionally Catholic France, from the perspective of the relationship between the church and the poor.

EU180 Perouas, Louis

Grignion de Montfort: les pauvres et les missions. (Parole et mission, 11). Paris, FR: Éditions du Cerf, 1966. 184 pp. No ISBN.

A history of fifteen years of ministry by de Montfort (1673-1716) among the poor of France.

EU181 Rapley, Elizabeth

The Dévotes: Women and Church in Seventeenth-Century France. (McGill-Queen's Studies in the History of Religion, 4). Montreal, QUC: McGill-Queen's University Press, 1993. viii, 283 pp. 0773507272 (hdbk), 0773511016 (pbk).

A history of the emergence of the *Filles Séculières*, first, as a religious movement, and then, as a social institution in 17th-century France, through which women were able to create for themselves an active role in public life as educators, nurses, and social workers, despite the resistance of patriarchal cultural forces.

EU182 Spink, Kathryn

Frère Roger de Taizé. Translated by Elizabeth Marchant. Paris, FR: Éditions du Seuil, 1986. 186 pp. 2020092565.

French translation.

EU183 Spink, Kathryn

Frère Roger, Gründer von Taizé: Leben für d. Versöhnung. Translated by Max Söller. Freiburg im Breisgau, GW: Herder, 1987. 222 pp. 3451203160.

German translation.

EU184 Spink, Kathryn

A Universal Heart: The Life and Vision of Brother Roger of Taizé. San Francisco, CAU: Harper & Row, 1986. xiii, 194 pp. 0060675047.

A popular biography of Brother Roger, founder and leader of the Taizé Community in France, noted for its creative outreach to youth, ecumenism, spirituality, and renewal.

Germany

See also GW270-GW271, GW276, HI205, HI319-HI321, HI325, TH76, TH80, TH167, TH170, CR1141, CR1392-CR1393, CR1397, SO588, PO133, PO143, CH152, AF427, and AS839.

EU185 Üffing, Martin

Die deutsche Kirche und Mission: Konsequenzen aus dem nachkonziliaren Missionverständnis für die deutsche Kirche. (Studia Instituti Missiologici SVD, 60). Nettetal, GW: Steyler Verlag, 1994. 285 pp. Paper. 3805003463.

A study of the changed concept of mission in post-Vatican II Germany, its view of Third World development, and the involvement of Catholic mission agencies.

EU186 Becker, Winfried, Horst Gründer, and August-Hermann Leugers

Die Verschränkung von Innen-, Konfessions- und Kolonial politik im Deutschen Reich vor 1914. Schwerte, GW: Katholische Akademie, 1987. 131 pp. Paper. No ISBN.

Various articles concerning the relationship between "Kulturkampf," colonial policy, and mission during the German Empire.

EU187 Borgman, Erik, and Anton van Harskamp, eds.

Tussen openheid en isolement: Het voorbeeld van de katholieke theologie in de negentiende eeuw. (Kerk en theologie in context, 16). Kampen, NE: Kok, 1992. v, 175 pp. Paper. 9024268133.

A collection of essays looking at the histories of commerce, church, and theology in 19th-century Germany, to discover central themes in modern Catholic theology which have relevance today.

EU188 Germany: Seeking a Relevant Witness Beyond Contrast and Assimilation

(Gospel and Cultures Pamphlets, 13). Geneva, SZ: WCC Publications, 1996. x, 53 pp. Paper. 2825412074.

After tracing the two distinct experiences of the church in East and West Germany after 1945, the authors identify key themes in the Gospel-culture encounter in the reunified Germany.

EU189 Mundt, William F.

Sinners Directed to the Saviour: The Religious Tract Society Movement in Germany (1811-1848). (Mission Series, 14). Zoetermeer, NE: Boekencentrum, 1996. 343 pp. Paper. 9023910559.

A scholarly history of the Religious Tract Society Movement in Germany and its precursor in Great Britain.

EU190 Pawelzik, Fritz

Antreten bei Rudi Weeker: Kaminskis Jugend. (R. Brockhaus vielseitig). Wuppertal, GW: R. Brockhaus Verlag, 1995. 157 pp. Paper. 3417219019.

Reminiscences by the former missionary to Ghana, covering his birth in 1927, his participation in the Hitler Youth, his first profession as a mountaineer, and his mission service in Ghana.

EU—EUROPE

EU191 Rommen, Edward
Namenschristentum: Theologisch-soziologische Erwägungen.
Bad Liebenzell, GW: Liebenzeller Mission, 1985. 174 pp.
3880022631.
    A theological and sociological analysis of secularization in
Germany and the Christendom worldwide; originally submitted
as a D.Miss. thesis at Trinity Evangelical Divinity School.

EU192 Scheibler, Samuel P.
*Golgotha and Götterdämmerung: German Religious Paradigm
Shifts and the Proclamation of the Gospel.* (American University Studies, 7: Theology and Religion, 175). New York, NYU:
Lang, 1996. viii, 286 pp. 082042420X.
    An analysis of paradigm shifts in the German worldview
over a 2,000-year history, with a framework and model for the
re-evangelization of post-Christendom Germany.

EU193 Schritt halten mit Gott: Das Evangelium und unsere Kultur
(EMW-informationen, 110). Breklum, GW: EMW, 1995. x, 55
pp. 2825412074.
    Response to the WCC's Study on Gospel and Culture by
German missiologists, who identify key themes of the Gospel-
culture encounter in the reunified Germany.

Germany, East (DRG)

See also GW275 and CH293.

EU194 Baum, Gregory
*The Church for Others: Protestant Theology in Communist East
Germany.* Grand Rapids, MIU: Eerdmans, 1996. xvii, 156 pp.
Paper. 0802841341.
    A reassessment, by the noted Roman Catholic theologian,
of the attempts in East Germany by Lutheran theologians to fashion a responsible relationship between the church and an atheistic state.

EU195 Hamel, Johannes
A Christian in East Germany. New York, NYU: Association
Press, 1960. 126 pp. No ISBN.
    The clear and brave Christian testimony of Pastor Hamel in
the face of Communist pressures, based on his own searching of
the Scriptures and on confidence in God's purpose for history.

EU196 Swoboda, Jörg
*Die Revolution der Kerzen: Christen in den Umwälzungen der
DDR.* (ABCteam, 460). Wuppertal, GW: Oncken Verlag, 1990.
320 pp. 3789324604.
    Eyewitness accounts of Christian participation in the strug-
gle for freedom in East Germany in 1989-1990.

EU197 Swoboda, Jörg
*The Revolution of the Candles: Christians in the Revolution of
the German Democratic Republic.* Edited by Richard V. Pierard. Translated by Edwin P. Arnold. Macon, GAU: Mercer University Press, 1996. xxxii, 203 pp. Paper. 0865544816.
    English translation.

Germany, West (FRG)

See also GW275, GW283, HI197, HI630, ME123, ME218, SO588,
EC315, EC341, and CH135.

**EU198 Baur, Jörg, Leonhard Goppelt, and Georg Kretschmar,
eds.**
*Die Verantwortung der Kirche in der Gesellschaft: Eine Studi-
enarbeit des Ökumenischen Ausschusses der Vereinigten Evan-*

gelisch-Lutherischen Kirche Deutschlands. Stuttgart, GW: Calwer Verlag, 1973. 228 pp. Paper. 3766804111.
    Results of the study project of the ecumenical commission
of the Vereinigte Evangelisch-Lutherische Kirche Deutschlands
(VELKD) on the church's social-political responsibilities, including ten essays and a final statement in seven theses.

EU199 Freytag, Justus, and Kenji Ozaki
*Nominal Christianity: Studies of Church and People in Ham-
burg.* (World Studies of Churches in Mission). London, ENK:
Lutterworth Press, 1970. x, 150 pp. No ISBN.
    A case study of contemporary German church life, includ-
ing an attitudinal survey in Hamburg and detailed analysis of
one Hamburg Lutheran parish.

EU200 Gottlob, Bernd
*Die Missionare der ausländischen Arbeitnehmer in Deutschland:
Eine Situations-und Verhaltensanalyse vor dem Hintergrund
kirchlicher Normen.* (Abhandlungen zur Sozialethik, 16). Munich, GW: Paderborn; Vienna, AU: Schöningh, 1978. 430 pp.
3506702165.
    A doctoral thesis on Roman Catholic missions to migrant
workers in West Germany, based on interviews with 58 former
missionaries, and 289 active in this work in 1976.

EU201 Le Coutre, Eberhard, ed.
*Unterwegs zur einen Welt: Aus der Arbeit von "Dienste in Über-
see."* Stuttgart, GW: Evan Verlagswerk, 1970. 319 pp.
3771501091.
    Published on the occasion of the 10th anniversary of the
Protestant Development Association, this book includes an outline of goals and methods, reports from development workers,
and statements of overseas partner churches.

EU202 Stammler, Eberhard
Churchless Protestants. Translated by Jack A. Worthington.
Philadelphia, PAU: Westminster Press, 1964. 223 pp. No ISBN.
    An analysis of the Evangelical church in Germany by one of
its pastors, and its challenge to reach the 90 percent of its members who are inactive.

EU203 Vesper, Michael
*Misereor und die Dritte Welt: Zur entwicklungspolitischen Ide-
ologie der Katholischen Kirche.* (Bielefelder Studien zur En-
twicklungssoziologie, 4). Saarbrücken, GW: Breitenbach, 1978.
vii, 203 pp. Paper. 3881561064.
    This book criticizes the development policy of the German
Catholic Church, asserting that it is ultimately prejudicial to the
interests of the Third World countries.

EU204 Watzal, Ludwig
*Die Entwicklungspolitik der katholischen Kirche in der Bundes-
republik Deutschland.* (Entwicklung und Frieden: Wissenschaftliche Reihe, 36). Mainz, GW: Grünewald; Munich, GW: Kaiser,
1985. 412 pp. Paper. 3786711755 (G), 3459016051 (K).
    A historical description of the shift in attitudes toward de-
velopment within the Catholic aid agencies in the Federal Republic of Germany (dissertation, Bundeswehr-College, Munich).

EU205 Wunderlich, Friedrich
Methodists Linking Two Continents. Nashville, TNU: Methodist Publishing House, 1960. 143 pp. No ISBN.
    Biographies of early American Methodists who carried
their newfound faith back to Germany, and a history of German Methodism since WWII.

Hungary

See also HI170 and AM1268.

EU206 Kool, Anna Maria

God Moves in a Mysterious Way: The Hungarian Protestant Foreign Mission Movement (1756-1951). (Missiological Research in the Netherlands, 4). Zoetermeer, NE: Boekencentrum, 1993. xx, 1023 pp. Paper. 9023907963 (hdbk), 9023907965 (pbk).

A dissertation (University of Utrecht, 1993) detailing the social and political contexts of Hungarian Protestant foreign missions, and the history of the Hungarian Evangelical Christian Missionary Society (1903-1949) and the Hungarian Lutheran Mission Association (1909-1951).

Iceland

EU207 Fell, Michael, ed.

And Some Fell into Good Soil: A History of Christianity in Iceland. NYU: Lang, 1999. xxii, 405 pp. 0820438812.

Three major turning points are emphasized: the official conversion of Iceland to Christianity in A.D. 1000; the Reformation around 1500; and the transition to the modern age around 1900.

EU208 Fyall, Aitken

St. Monans: History, Customs and Superstitions. Durham, ENK: Pentland Press, 1999. xv, 291 pp. 1858216702.

This fishing community, with allied activities of boatbuilding, farming, coal mining, and salt-making, was dominated by the church and gentry; the shrine and well of St. Monans attracted thousands of pilgrims, particularly during the black death and times of famine.

Ireland

See also HI104, HI278, HI541, and ME219.

EU209 Boyd, Robin H. S.

Ireland: Christianity Discredited or Pilgrim's Progress? (Risk Book Series, 37). Geneva, SZ: WCC, 1988. viii, 127 pp. Paper. 2825409227.

A popular account of the Irish Christian conflict, reflecting the thesis that Irish Christians are being called by God to a new fellowship uniting Roman Catholics and Protestants.

EU210 Hogan, Edmund M.

The Irish Missionary Movement: A Historical Survey, 1830-1980. Dublin, IE: Gill & MacMillan; Washington, DCU: Catholic University of America Press, 1990. viii, 233 pp. 0717117588 (I), 0813207347 (D).

The first modern survey of the missionary movement in Catholic Ireland.

EU211 Joyce, Timothy J.

Celtic Christianity: A Sacred Tradition, a Vision of Hope. Maryknoll, NYU: Orbis Books, 1998. xi, 180 pp. Paper. 1570751765.

A Benedictine monk of Irish descent, and past President of the American Benedictine Academy, recovers the 1600-year history of Celtic spirituality, monasticism, and missionary endeavor.

EU212 Keany, Marian

Irish Missionaries: From the Golden Age to the 20th Century. Dublin, IE: Veritas Publishing, 1985. 77 pp. Paper. 0862171709.

A popular history of Irish missionary achievement, from the 6th century to the present.

EU213 Proniseas, Ni Chathain, and Michael Richter, eds.

Irland und die Christenheit: Bibelstudien und Mission. Stuttgart, GW: Ernst Klett Verlag, 1987. xii, 523 pp. 3608914412.

Papers in German and English from a third colloquium, seeking to evaluate the quality and content of the Irish influence in early Christian Europe, and focusing on biblical studies and missionary activities.

EU214 Rogal, Samuel J.

John Wesley in Ireland, 1747-1789: Part 1 and 2. (Studies in the History of Missions, 9). Lewiston, NYU: E Mellen Press, 1993. 477 pp. 0773492437 (part 1), 0773492453 (part 2).

A narrative history of the evangelical mission to Ireland by John Wesley, founder of Methodism; based primarily on his account in his *Journal*, and organized geographically by region and town.

EU215 Taggart, Norman W.

William Arthur: First Among Methodists. London, ENK: Epworth Press, 1993. viii, 184 pp. Paper. 0716204894.

A brief biography of William Arthur (1819-1901), Wesleyan Methodist missionary to India (1837-1841) and Irish Methodist leader; with an extended assessment of his significance.

EU216 Woods, Richard J.

The Spirituality of the Celtic Saints. Maryknoll, NYU: Orbis Books, 2000. vii, 246 pp. Paper. 1570753164.

Ranging beyond Ireland to include Scotland, Wales, and parts of the European continent, the author retrieves the spirituality of the saints and scholars, and explores relevant issues: social justice, the place of women, the natural environment, art, literature, and music.

Italy

See also SP54.

EU217 Beard, Mary, John North, and Simon Price

Religions of Rome: Volume I—A History. Cambridge, ENK: Cambridge University Press, 1998. xxiv, 454 pp. 0521304016 (hdbk), 0521316820 (pbk).

A radical new survey of more than a thousand years of religious life in Rome, from the foundation of the city to its rise to world empire and its conversion to Christianity; religion is set in its full cultural context, including the cosmopolitan, multicultural society of the first centuries of the Christian era.

EU218 Bona, Candido

La Rinascita Missionaria in Italia. Turin, IT: Consolata Missionaries, 1964. 236 pp. No ISBN.

A valuable contribution to the history of home missions in Italy, especially in the North (Piedmont), where they were already flourishing in the 18th century; including the religious communities of the *Amicizie*, developed from this work in the 19th century.

EU219 Hedlund, Roger E.
The Protestant Movement in Italy: Its Progress, Problems, and Prospects. South Pasadena, CAU: William Carey Library, 1970. xiv, 257 pp. 0878083073.

A scholarly analysis by a church growth specialist, of the ministries and social outreach of various Protestant denominations in Italy.

Malta

EU220 Boissevain, Jeremy
Saints and Fireworks: Religion and Politics in Rural Malta. (London School of Economics Monographs on Social Anthropology, 30). Valletta, MM: Progress Press, 1993. xii, 178 pp. Paper. 9990930007.

Revised and expanded edition of a detailed, descriptive analysis of Maltese village politics, showing how issues that originate within the church, in particular over the cult of saints, affect village social organization; originally published in 1965 (London: Athlone Press; New York: Humanities Press).

Netherlands

See also GW287, HI212, HI577-HI578, ME207, CR530, CR1157, MI81, AF456, AS1347, and EU31.

EU221 Douma, M. et al.
Meisjes van heinde en ver. (Allerwegen 16). Kampen, NE: Kok, 1995. 83 pp. Paper. 9024220874.

Six essays discuss the concerns and programs of Dutch Reformed churches for the human rights and treatment of young girls and women from developing countries, who are forced by circumstances of poverty and tradition into local or foreign employment.

EU222 Goddijn, Walter
The Deferred Revolution: A Social Experiment in Church Innovation in Holland, 1960-1970. Amsterdam, NE: Elsevier, 1975. 202 pp. 044441228X.

A case study of renewal through lay movements in churches in the Netherlands.

EU223 Jongeneel, J. A. B., and Eeuwout Klootwijk
Nederlandse Faculteiten der Godgeleerdheid Theologische Hogescholen en de Derde Wereld: Algemene inleiding en overzichten vanaf 1876. (IIMO Research Pamplet, 18). Leiden, NE: IIMO, 1986. iii, 105 pp. Paper. 9071387151.

A survey of contributions of Dutch theological faculties, since 1876, to theological education in the Third World; with a valuable listing of relevant doctoral dissertations by Dutch and Third World theologians, completed at Dutch universities.

EU224 Jongeneel, J. A. B., R. Budiman, and J. J. Visser, eds.
Gemeenschapsvorming van Aziatische, Afrikaanse en Middenen Zuidamerikaanse christenen in Nederland: Een geschiedenis. (Mission, 15). Zoetermeer, NE: Boekencentrum, 1996. 276 pp. Paper. 9023903196.

A handbook on communities and churches of Asian, African, and Latin American Christians in the Netherlands, giving names, places of worship, actual situations, problems/challenges, and ecumenical relations.

EU225 Kpobi, David Nii Anum, Laurens Politton, and Maria Politton
Standplaats Nederland: Werkmateriaal voor de missionaire

gemeente. (Allerwegen, 14). Kampen, NE: Kok, 1994. 72 pp. Paper. 902428290X.

Reflections on "reverse mission" to the Netherlands by Reformed pastors from Ghana.and Indonesia, with responses by Dutch leaders on implications for the missionary outreach of local churches.

EU226 Parker, Charles H.
The Reformation of Community: Social Welfare and Calvinist Charity in Holland, 1572-1620. (Cambridge Studies in Early Modern History). New York, NYU: Cambridge University Press, 1998. xv, 221 pp. 0521623057.

The author contends that the conflict between charitable organizations reveals competing conceptions of Christian community that came to the fore at the Dutch reformation; thus, the relationship between municipal and ecclesiastical relief agencies are examined.

EU227 Randwijck, S. C. Graaf van
Handelen en denken in dienst der zending: Oegstgeest 1897-1942. 's-Gravenhage, NE: Boekencentrum, 1981. 2 vols. 9023912608.

A history of the cooperating missionary societies which finally merged into the mission board of the Netherlands Reformed Church in 1951, concentrating on organizational developments in the Netherlands and missionary work in Indonesia, 1897-1942; written by one of the leading directors of the societies after his retirement.

EU228 Roes, Jan
Het groote missieuur 1915-1940: Op zoek naar de missiemotivatie van de Nederlandse katholieken. (Proefschrift Theol. Fac. Kath. Universiteit Nijmegan). Bilthoven, NE: Ambobooken, 1974. 223 pp. Paper. No ISBN.

A doctoral dissertation on the support for foreign missions among Dutch Catholics, 1915 to 1940.

EU229 Wijsen, Frans Jozef Servaas
Geloven bij het leven: Missionaire presentie in een volkswijk. (UTP-katern, 19). Baarn, NE: Gooi on Sticht, 1997. 221 pp. Paper. 9030409274.

The author links the shared elements of global mission theory and practical theology (communication, social analysis, theological reflection, and pastoral planning) to his experience serving the pastoral needs of the industrial district of Maastricht, the Netherlands.

EU230 Willemsen, J. Th. W.
Academische Leken Missie Actie, 1947-1967. (KDC Scripta, 6). Nijmegen, NE: KDC, 1990. 303 pp. Paper. 9070504359.

A detailed and scholarly study of ALMA, an organization of the Catholic academic laity in the Netherlands, supporting the foreign missions, 1947-1967.

EU231 Winkel, Jan Derk te
Kiezen en delen: Over de politieke en sociale implicaties van het christlijk geloof in de communicatie van het evangelie van het Rijk Gods door de missionaire gemeente in eigen omgeving. Amsterdam, NE: Rodopi, 1977. 308 pp. 9062031803.

A detailed study for, the "Reformed Churches in the Netherlands" (Gereformeerde Kerken), of its heritage in social involvement, with theoretical and practical aspects of evangelism.

EU232 Woudenberg, Johan A.

Uw Koninkrijk Kome: Het Utrechtsch Studente-Zendingge-zelschap Eltheto Hé Basileia Sou (1846-1908). (MISSION—Missiologisch Onderzoek in Nederland, 9). Zoetermeer, NE: Boekencentrum, 1994. xv, 362 pp. 9023918584.

A detailed study of the history and theology of mission of the Utrecht missionary society of students, "Eltheto Hè Basileia" (Thy Kingdom Come), from its founding in 1848 to its merger into the "Nederlandsche Christen Studenten Vereeniging" (NCSU—Netherlands Student Christian Movement) in 1908.

Norway

See also ME165.

EU233 Eriksen, Bent Reidar

Norsk håndbok for kirke og misjon = Norwegian Handbook for Churches and Missions. Oslo, SW: Lunde Forlag; : MARC Europe, 1990. 64 pp. 0947697837 (UK), 8252031315 (NOR).

Data on the churches of Norway, including their missionary work.

Poland

EU234 Sikorska, Grazyna

Light and Life: Renewal in Poland. Grand Rapids MIU: Eerdmans, 1989. 156 pp. Paper. 0802803415.

The biography of a Polish parish priest, Father Blachnicki, founder of the Oasis movement (now Light-Life Movement) in the 1950s, who brought tens of thousands to spiritual renewal under Poland's communist government before his death in 1987.

Romania

EU235 Andrew, Brother, and Verne Becker

For the Love of My Brothers. Minneapolis, MNU: Bethany House, 1998. 252 pp. Paper. 0764220748.

The 20th century's number one Bible smuggler to Christians behind the iron curtain tells stories from his ministry, begun from his native Holland in 1955.

EU236 Bria, Ion

Romania: Orthodox Identity at a Crossroads of Europe. (Gospel and Cultures Pamphlet, 3). Geneva, SZ: WCC Publications, 1995. ix, 54 pp. Paper. 2825411752.

A short study of the interaction between Gospel and church in Romania by a member of the Romanian Orthodox church, who served on the WCC staff (1973-1994).

EU237 Solheim, Magne

I skuggen av hakekross, hammar og sigd. (Sjalombok, 15). Oslo, NO: Luther, 1981. 360 pp. 8253192649.

Personal reflections of a missionary of the Norwegian Mission to the Jews, who worked in Romania from 1937 to 1948.

EU238 Solheim, Magne

Im Schatten von Hakenkreuz, Hammer und Sichel: Judenmissionar in Rumänien, 1937-1948. Translated by Cilgia Solheim. (Erlanger Taschenbücher, 74). Erlangen, GW: Ev.-Luth. Mission, 1986. 283 pp. Paper. 3872141740.

German translation.

EU239 Tokes, Laszlo, and David Porter

The Fall of Tyrants: The Incredible Story of One Pastor's Witness, the People of Romania and the Overthrow of Ceausescu. Wheaton, ILU: Crossway Books, 1990. xiv, 226 pp. Paper. 0891076247.

An autobiographical account by the prophetic Hungarian Reformed church pastor and bishop, who led in the Romanian revolution of 1989-1990.

Russia [USSR]

See also HI113 and EA244.

EU240 Aleksandr, Archimandrite

Father John of Kronstadt: A Life. Crestwood, NYU: St. Vladimir's Seminary Press, 1979. 197 pp. 0264665058.

English translation; originally published in 1979 (London, ENK: Mowbrays; Crestwood, NYU: St. Vladimir's Seminary Press).

EU241 Aleksandr, Archimandrite

Otets Ioann Kronshtadtskii. Paris, FR: YMCA Press, 1990. 380 pp. 2850651788.

The biography of the 19th-century Orthodox priest at Kronstadt who, in his passionate interest in the poor and dispossessed, represented a true missionary spirit; originally published in 1955 (New York, NYU: Izd-vo im. Chekhova).

EU242 Bailey, J. Martin

One Thousand Years: Stories from the History of Christianity in the USSR, 988-1988. New York, NYU: Friendship Press, 1987. x, 61 pp. 0377001678.

Six stories prepared for an adult mission study; with study guide by Betty Jane Bailey and Constance J. Tarasar, entitled *Eyes to See, Ears to Hear*, 60 pp., 0377001686.

EU243 Bawden, Charles R.

Shamans, Lamas, and Evangelicals: The English Missionaries in Siberia. London, ENK: Routledge, 1985. xviii, 382 pp. 0710200641.

A detailed account of the enormous difficulties that English and Swedish missionaries and their families had to overcome in eastern Siberia, 1819-1841, where they founded schools, treated sick, and translated the Bible.

EU244 Benson, David

Miracle in Moscow. Glendale, CAU: Regal Books, 1975. 303 pp. 0830703519.

The narrative account of the author's attempts to reach Russia for Christ. using unorthodox methods (Bible smuggling, radio broadcasts) and an unsuccessful attempt to secure Russian citizenship; first published in 1973 (Santa Barbara, CAU: Miracle Publications).

EU245 Bercken, William van den

Christian Thinking and the End of Communism in Russia. (IIMO Research Publication, 34). Utrecht, NE: IIMO, 1993. 154 pp. Paper. 9021170043.

A narrative account of parallel developments in Russia, from 1987 to 1992, of the critique of communist ideology, especially by the Vekhi group, and the renewed interest in Russian Orthodox Christianity.

EU—EUROPE

EU246 Bourdeaux, Michael
Gorbachev, Glasnost & the Gospel. (Keston College Book, 31). London, ENK: Hodder & Stoughton, 1990. 226 pp. 0340517395 (hdbk), 0340541938 (pbk).

A useful survey of church developments during the last five years (1985-1990) in the Soviet Union, including the Orthodox Church, Protestants, the Ukranian Catholics, and churches in the Baltic states; with a concluding chapter on church contributions to social care and charity.

EU247 Brandenburg, Hans
Christen im Schatten der Macht: Die Geschichte des Stundismus in Russland. Wuppertal, GW: R. Brockhaus Verlag, 1974. 207 pp. 3417004799.

German translation.

EU248 Brandenburg, Hans
The Meek and the Mighty: The Emergence of the Evangelical Movement in Russia. (Keston Book, 7). London, ENK: Mowbray; New York, NYU: Oxford University Press, 1976. xii, 210 pp. 0264663497 (UK), 0195199146 (US).

The background, history, and fruits of the Evangelical Revival in Russia in the last half of the 19th century, which affected Orthodox and Protestant Christianity; US edition published in 1977.

EU249 Buss, Gerald
The Bear's Hug: Christian Belief and the Soviet State. Grand Rapids, MIU: Eerdmans; London, ENK: Hodder & Stoughton, 1987. 223 pp. Paper. 0802803245 (US), 0340394293 (UK).

A history of religious believers in the Soviet Union and their relationship with the state since the Revolution in 1917.

EU250 Deyneka, Anita, and Peter Deyneka
A Song in Siberia: The True Story of a Russian Church That Could Not Be Silenced. London, ENK: Collins; Elgin, ILU: David C. Cook, 1978. 233 pp. 0002161362 (UK), 0891910654 (US).

The story of an unregistered Baptist congregation in Barnaul, Siberia, and of its congregational life and witness amidst persecution (1972-1977).

EU251 Dudko, Dmitrii
L' espérance qui est en nous: entretiens de Moscou. Translated by Stéphane Tatischeff. Paris, FR: Éditions du Seuil, 1976. 265 pp. 2020045192.

French translation.

EU252 Durasoff, Steve
The Russian Protestants: Evangelicals in the Soviet Union, 1944-1964. Rutherford, NJU: Fairleigh Dickinson University Press, 1969. 312 pp. 8386074658 (SBN).

The story of the first twenty years of the All-Union Council of Evangelical Christians-Baptists (AUCECB), 1944-1964—a merger of Baptists, Pentecostals, Mennonites, and other evangelicals—and of their external relations, both with the Soviet state and with world ecumenical bodies.

EU253 Ellis, Geoff, and Wesley Jones
The Other Revolution: Russian Evangelical Awakenings. Abilene, TXU: Abilene Christian University Press, 1996. iv, 230 pp. Paper. 089112022X.

The story of Russian efforts to return to New Testament Christianity in the 19th century.

EU254 Fennell, John
A History of the Russian Church to 1448. London, ENK: Longman, 1995. xii, 266 pp. 0582080681 (hdbk), 0582080673 (pbk).

A scholarly survey of the process of Christianization in Russia, from the baptism of Vladimir in 988 to independence from Byzantium in 1448.

EU255 Fletcher, William C.
Soviet Charismatics: The Pentecostals in the USSR. (American University Studies, 7: Theology and Religion, 9). New York, NYU: Lang, 1985. 200 pp. 0820402265.

A basic history of Pentecostalism in Russia—its history, doctrines, worship, lifestyle, and heroic responses to communism

EU256 Forest, Jim
Religion in the New Russia: The Impact of Perestroika on the Varieties of Religious Life in the Soviet Union. New York, NYU: Crossroad Publishing, 1990. xx, 217 pp. 0824510402.

A first person account of the emerging religious freedom and fervor taking place in the Soviet Union, with analysis of the variety of religious groups, both Christian and of other faiths.

EU257 Hebly, J. A.
The Russians and the World Council of Churches: Documentary Survey of the Accession of the Russian Orthodox Church to the World Council of Churches, with Commentary. Belfast, IE: Christian Journals, 1978. 181 pp. 0904302393.

A detailed and documented discussion of the love-hate relationship between Russian Orthodoxy and the ecumenical movement, 1943-1974.

EU258 Hill, Kent R.
The Soviet Union on the Brink: An Inside Look at Christianity and Glasnost. Portland, ORU: Multnomah, 1991. 520 pp. 0880704349.

A revised and updated edition of *The Puzzle of the Soviet Church* (1989) focusing on religious changes in the USSR, from 1978 to 1990, and the responses of ecumenical bodies.

EU259 House, Francis
Millennium of Faith: Christianity in Russia, AD 988-1988. Crestwood, NYU: St. Vladimir's Seminary Press, 1988. x, 133 pp. Paper. 088141073X.

A readable introduction to almost one-thousand years of Russia's religious history, including evangelization and mission; also published under the title *The Russian Phoenix* (London: SPCK, 1988, 0281043418).

EU260 Hultvall, John
Mission och vision i Orienten: Svenska Missionsförbundets mission i Transkaukasien-Persian, 1882-1921. (Studia Missionalia Uppsaliensia, 53). Stockholm, SW: Verbum, 1991. 280 pp. Paper. 9152617785.

A history of the Mission Covenant Church of Sweden's mission in the Caucasus, Armenia, and northern Iran, from its beginnings in 1882 among expatriate Swedes, to its extension among Russian and Oriental Orthodox churches and Muslims, to the death of the last missionary in 1921.

EU261 International Committee for the Defense of Human Rights in the USSR
May One Believe, in Russia?: Violations of Religious Liberty in the Soviet Union. Edited by Michael Bourdeaux, and Michael Rowe. (Keston Book, 19). London, ENK: Darton, Longman, & Todd, 1980. xiii, 113 pp. 0232515077.

Documents on religious persecution in the USSR, prepared in 1975 by the International Committee for the Defense of Human Rights.

EU262 Istomina, Lydia P.

Bringing Hidden Things to Light: The Revival of Methodism in Russia. Nashville, TNU: Abingdon, 1996. 160 pp. Paper. 068710923X.

A woman lay pastor's account of the revival of the Methodist church in Russia.

EU263 Kahle, Wilhelm

Evangelische Christen in Russland und der Sowetunion: Ivan Stepanovich Prochanov (1869-1935) und der Weg der Evangeliumschristen und Baptisten. Wuppertal, GW: Oncken Verlag, 1978. 598 pp. 3789370568.

An exhaustive history of the origins of various Protestant groups in Russia, focusing on the influence of Prochanov.

EU264 Kolarz, Walter

Religion in the Soviet Union. New York, NYU: St. Martin's Press; London, ENK: Macmillan, 1961. xii, 518 pp. No ISBN.

An encyclopedic survey of the religions of the USSR, based on written sources and oral interviews.

EU265 Kraus, Johann

Im Auftrag des Papstes in Russland: Der Steyler Anteil an der katholischen Hilfsmission 1922-1924. (Veröffentlichungen des Missionspriesterseminars, 21). St. Augustin, GW: Steyler Verlag, 1970. xiv, 196 pp. No ISBN.

The story of the participation of the Steyler missionaries in the papal relief work in Russia, in the famine years, 1922-1924.

EU266 Lewis, David C.

After Atheism: Religion and Ethnicity in Russia and Central Asia. (Caucasus World). New York, NYU: St. Martin's Press; Richmond, ENK: Curzon Press, 2000. 320 pp. Paper. 0312226926 (US), 0700711643 (UK).

The author offers insight into the depths of contemporary religious experience among a broad panorama of peoples who are rediscovering new forms of spirituality after atheism.

EU267 Nesdoly, Samuel

Among the Soviet Evangelicals: A Goodly Heritage. Edinburgh, STK: Banner of Truth Trust, 1986. xxxii, 207 pp. Paper. 0851514898.

The grandson of a pioneer Russian Baptist pastor describes his experiences in the USSR, in 1971 and 1984, as he discovered his own spiritual roots.

EU268 Oden, Marilyn Brown

Land of Sickles and Crosses:The United Methodist Initiative in the Commonwealth of Independent States. New York, NYU: UMC, Board of Global Ministries, 1993. ix, 102 pp. Paper. No ISBN.

A narrative account of recent United Methodist mission initiatives in the Commonwealth of Independent States, with reference to the earlier history of Methodism there.

EU269 Pollock, John Charles

The Siberian Seven. Waco, TXU: Word Books, 1980. 252 pp. Paper. 0340247991.

A major contribution to the subject of Russian religious dissent—the story of the seven beleaguered Pentecostal Christians, who lived as exiles since 1978, in the American embassy in Moscow; originally published in 1979 (London, ENK: Hodder & Stoughton).

EU270 Savoca, Nick, and Dick Schneider

Road Block to Moscow. Minneapolis, MNU: Bethany Fellowship, 1977. 160 pp. Paper. 0871234890.

The story of the attempt by fifty young Christians from the United States, inspired by Brother Andrew, to witness for Christ in Soviet Russia.

EU271 Sawatsky, Walter

Soviet Evangelicals since World War II. Kitchener, ONC: Herald Press, 1981. 527 pp. 0836112385 (hdbk), 0836112393 (pbk).

A detailed chronicle and interpretation of forty years (1940-1980) of witness by believers' churches (Baptists, Mennonites, and Pentecostals) in the Soviet Union, and by mission societies from Eastern Europe.

EU272 Shenk, Paul

"The Greatest of These is Love": A Story of Dagestan. Elkhart, INU: Mennonite Board of Missions, 1999. 27 pp. Paper. 1877736244.

A pamphlet that gives insight as to how North American missionaries went 7,000 miles to Dagestan, to engage in mission in southern Russia among the Tabasaran, who are traditional and resistant to change.

EU273 Simon, Gerhard

Church, State and Opposition in the U.S.S.R. Translated by Kathleen Matchett. London, ENK: Hurst; Berkeley, CAU: University of California Press, 1974. x, 248 pp. 0903983109 (UK), 0520026128 (US).

English translation.

EU274 *Soviet Language Groups Ministry Resources Study: A Confidential Report on Christian Resources for Ministry to Selected Unreached Language Groups of the Former Soviet Union*

(Ministry Resource Information, 1). Seattle, WAU: Interdev; Wheaton, ILU: ACMC, 1991. 118 pp. Paper. No ISBN.

Profiles of seventeen predominantly Muslim and Buddhist language groups of the former Soviet Union, and of existing resources to use in a Christian presence among them.

EU275 Witte, John, and Michael Bourdeaux, eds.

Proselytism and Orthodoxy in Russia: The New War for Souls. (Religion & Human Rights Series). Maryknoll, NYU: Orbis Books, 1999. xiv, 353 pp. Paper. 1570752621.

An assessment of the legitimacy of the Orthodox attempt to reclaim the spiritual and moral heart of the Russian people, and to retain their adherence in a new, pluralistic world, where many Christians and followers of other traditions seek the right to establish themselves.

EU276 Yancey, Philip

Praying with the KGB: A Startling Report from a Shattered Empire. Portland, ORU: Multnomah, 1992. 106 pp. Paper. 0880705116.

Christian witness in the USSR by a team of evangelicals from the United States for *Christianity Today*, who sought to replace the fallen pillars of Marx and Lenin with Christian faith, as told by an editor-at-large.

EU277 Zernov, Nicolas

The Russian Religious Renaissance of the Twentieth Century. New York, NYU: Harper & Row; London, ENK: Darton, Longman & Todd, 1963. xi, 410 pp. No ISBN.

A well-researched study of one aspect of renewal in the Russian Orthodox Church—the contributions of the Russian intelligensia before and after the revolution.

EU—EUROPE

EU278 Znamenski, Andrei A.
Shamanism and Christianity: Native Encounters with Russian Orthodox Missions in Siberia and Alaska. (Contributions to the Study of World History, 70). Westport, CTU: Greenwood, 1999. xii, 306 pp. 0313309604.

While many works that treat native-missionary relationships in Siberia and Alaska examine individual tribes, this work addresses the natives' response from a comparative viewpoint, with the premise that indigenous Christianity is a dialectic process, involving both individual agency and structural settings.

Spain

See also HI106, SO255, and EC166.

EU279 Avila, Angeles Alonso, Luis Sagredo san Eustaquio, and Santos Crespo Ortíz de Zarate
Hispania Visigoda: Bibliografía Sistemática y Síntesis Histórica. Valladolid, SP: Universidad de Valladolid, Departamento de Historia Antigua, 1985. 328 pp. No ISBN.

A multi-lingual bibliography on Visigoth Spain from the 4th to 8th centuries, including politics, society, economics, religion, law, and the arts; with an interpretive essay—the third in a series on Spain.

EU280 Barkaï, Ron, ed.
Chrétiens, musulmans et juifs dans l'Espagne médiévale: de la convergence à l'expulsion. (Toledot-Judaïsmes). Paris, FR: Éditions du Cerf, 1994. 333 pp. Paper. 2204048038.

Nine scholarly essays on various aspects of the Christian-Muslim-Jewish encounter in medieval Spain.

EU281 Delgado, Mariano
Die Metamorphosen des messianismus in den Iberischen kulturen: Eine religionsgeschichtliche Studie. (Schriftenreihe, 34). Immensee, SZ: Nouvelle revue de science missionaire, 1994. 133 pp. Paper. 3858240753.

A monograph by the Professor of Catholic Theology at the Free University of Berlin, on how the biblical concept of messianism was transformed in the Iberian culture of Spain and Portugal from the 15th century to the present, and its effects on missionizing.

EU282 Gallardo, José
Freedom for the Captives: How Love is Rebuilding Lives in Spain. (Peace and Justice Series, 5). Scottdale, PAU: Herald Press, 1988. 92 pp. Paper. 0836134745.

A testimony to how lives have been rebuilt in Spain through the life and work of an intentional Protestant community in Gamonal, which sought to base their mission on the messianic prophecy in Isaiah 61 and the model of Jesus' compassion for needy persons.

EU283 Grijp, Rainer Maria Klaus van der
Geschichte des spanischen Protestantismus im 19. Jahrhundert. (Proefschrift Theol. Fac. Rijksuniversiteit Utrecht). Wageningen, NE: H. Veenman, 1971. 593 pp. Paper. No ISBN.

A history of Protestantism in Spain, related especially to the missionary activities by British, Dutch, and Swiss Protestant societies between 1854-1900; based on extensive study of archives and libraries of the societies and churches involved.

EU284 Izco Ilundain, José A.
Don Gerardo Villota: un pionero del misionerismo del clero secular. (Misiones Extranjeras, 109). Madrid, SP: Misiones Extranjeras, 1989. 146 pp. Paper. No ISBN.

A numbered monograph dedicated to the person and work of Don Gerardo Villota, founder of the Spanish Institute of Foreign Missions.

EU285 Rodier, José, and Víctor M. Pidal
Lo Que Hemos Visto...: Evangelización y Mundo Obrero. (Temas Vivos, 37). Madrid, SP: Sociedad de Educación Atenas, 1975. 112 pp. Paper. 847020162X.

A synthesis of reflections on mission experiences in evangelistic work among workers in Spain.

EU286 Vought, Dale G.
Protestants in Modern Spain: The Struggle For Religious Pluralism. South Pasadena, CAU: William Carey Library, 1973. xiv, 153 pp. Paper. 0878083111.

A study of the history of religious liberty in Spain in the 20th century,y with an overview of Protestant churches, their mission organizations, and how they are affected by the granting of religious liberty.

EU287 Zulueta, Carmen de
Misioneras, Feministas, Educadoras: Historia del Instituto Internacional. Zurbano, SP: Editorial Castalia, 1984. 294 pp. Paper. 8470394436.

The story of the Instituto Internacional (International Institute) for girls in Spain, founded by Alice (Gordon) Gulick (1847-1903), and modeled after Mount Holyoke, and its influence on the modernization of Spanish education during the 20th century.

Sweden

See also HI700, HI703, and CR1502.

EU288 Öberg, Ingemar
Mission och evangelisation i Gellivare-bygden ca 1740-1770. (Kyrkohistoriska arkivet vid Åbo Akademi. Meddelanden; 7). Åbo, FI: Åbo Akademi University Press, 1979. 222 pp. Paper. 9516484689.

A description of the Christianization of the inhabitants of northern Sweden in the 18th century.

EU289 Brännström, Olaus
Peter Fjellstedt: Mångsidig men entydig kyrkoman. (Studia Missionalia Upsaliensia, 60). Uppsala, SW: Svenska Institutet för Missionsforskning, 1994. 344 pp. Paper. 9185424390.

A biography of Peter Fjellstedt (1802-1881), a Swedish Lutheran pastor who served as a CMS missionary in India (1831-1835) and Turkey (1836-1837) as the Basel Mission's agent for North-West Europe, and as director of the Lund Missionary Society.

EU290 Fjärstedt, Biörn
Gotländsk kyrka i livets mitt: Herdabrev till Visby stift. Stockholm, SW: Verbum Förlag, 1991. 140 pp. Paper. 9152619184.

A pastoral letter by the Lutheran bishop of Visby, Sweden, concerning the historic and contemporary mission of the church and its people on the island of Gotland, situated strategically in the Baltic, near Eastern Europe.

EU291 Hogstrom, Pehr
Pehr Högstrom Missionsförrättningar: Och Övriga bidrag till Samisk Kyrkohistoria. Edited by Carl F. Hallencreutz. Uppsala, SW: Uppsala Universiteit, 1990. 147 pp. Paper. 9185424196.

Publication, with editorial commentary, of the writings of the noted Swedish home missionary, Pehr Hogstrom (1714-1784), to the Sameh (Lapp) peoples of northern Sweden.

EU—EUROPE

EU292 Ljung, Jörgen
Idébaserad Verksamhet: En Studie au Frikyakan som organisa-tion. (Studies in Management and Economics). Linköping, SW: Linköping University, 1993. 2 vols. Paper. No ISBN.

This doctoral dissertation in Swedish, with a twenty-two-page English summary titled "Ideology Based Activity: A Study of Free Churches in Sweden from an Organizational Perspective," is a detailed sociological analysis of factors affecting church growth and decline, among denominations independent of the Lutheran state church of Sweden.

EU293 Schlyter, Herman
Svarta Sara och andra gestalter. Stockholm, SW: Diakonistyrelsens Bokförlag, 1963. 163 pp. No ISBN.

Ten short essays portraying prominent personalities in the Swedish history of missions.

EU294 Zetterquist, Håkan
Stad och Stift: Stiftsbildning och församlingsdelsningar i Stockholm 1940-56. (Studia Missionalia Upsaliensia, 26). Stockholm, SW: Verbum; Uppsala, SW: Svenska Institutet för Missionsforskning, 1974. 233 pp. 9172220864.

A doctoral dissertation on relations between the Lutheran diocese of Stockholm and its parishes, 1940 to 1956, with a summary in English.

Switzerland

EU295 Blum, Emil
Die Mission der reformierten Schweiz: Handbuch. Basel, SZ: Basileia Verlag, 1965. 120 pp. Paper. No ISBN.

For a readership mainly among reformed Protestants in Switzerland, this book aims at attracting new co-workers and obtaining financial help for the missionary enterprise.

EU296 Gibson, William, ed.
Religion and Society in England and-Wales, 1689-1800. (Documents in Early Modern Social History). London, ENK: Leicester University Press, 1998. .viii, 241 pp. 0718501624 (hdbk), 0718501632 (pbk).

Includes source material on religion outside of the establishment, with an emphasis on John Wesley; popular religion, including the start of Sunday schools; the established church; Catholicism; religious continuity and change; and politics and religion.

EU297 Keany, Marian
They Brought the Good News: Modern Irish Missionaries. Dublin, IE: Vertis Publications, 1980. 146 pp. Paper. 0862170060.

A collection of the histories of eight 20th-century Irish missionaries who served in foreign countries.

EU—EUROPE

OCEANIA

Darrell Whiteman, Subeditor

Oceania is composed of approximately 25,000 islands. The region stretches from Easter Island on the east to Palau on the west, and from Hawaii and the Northern Marianas on the north to Australia and New Zealand on the south. In this region live 31,000,000 people (*World Almanac*, 2002; *EDWM*, 702-704).

This bibliography is organized geographically by the traditional four subdivisions: Australia/New Zealand, Melanesia, Micronesia, and Polynesia.

Oceania is one of the most Christianized regions of the world. Its more than 21 million believers in 28 countries represent 69 percent of the total population.

Roman Catholics claim the largest proportion of Christian believers (38.9%), followed by Protestants (34.6%), and Anglicans (25.3%). More than 1.5 million Christians (7%) are affiliated with 303 independent denominations in 22 countries. Others include the Orthodox (3.3%) and marginal Christians (2.1%), with 10.9 percent listed as double-affiliated (*WCE* 1:12). Books on new religious movements will be found in the chapter on "Missions: Social Aspects."

The 1960-2000 time period covered by this bibliography coincides with the achievement of independence by most of Oceania's churches. That development stimulated the writing of a wealth of general and denominational mission and church histories. Books on work in Oceania by distinct missionary orders or societies will be found in the "Missions: History" chapter.

The section on "Church and Society" contains works on issues of Gospel and culture, and church and state. That on "Oceanian Theologies" includes the pioneer works in this field.

Norman E. Thomas

Bibliography

See also OC82 and OC260.

OC1 Clement, Russel T., comp.
Mormons in the Pacific: A Bibliography. Laie, HIU: Institute for Polynesian Studies, 1981. 239 pp. 093915417X (hdbk), 0939154188 (pbk).

A bibliography of 1,646 books, pamphlets, and journal articles, with identification of the locations of each in collections of Bingham Young University (Hawaii and Utah campuses) and at the Church Historical Department.

OC2 Haynes, Douglas, and William L. Wuerch
Micronesian Religion and Lore: A Guide to Sources, 1526-1990. (Bibliographies and Indexes in Religious Studies, 32). Westport, CTU: Greenwood, 1995. xxi, 300 pp. 0313289557.

An annotated guide to 1,193 sources on Micronesian religion, including the missions and the influence of Christianity.

OC3 MacDonald, Mary N., comp.
Melanesia: An Annotated Bibliography for Church Workers. (A Supplement to Point Series 5, 6, 7, 1984-1985). Goroka, PP: Melanesian Institute, 1988. 98 pp. Paper. No ISBN.

This bibliography supplement to the Point Series contains lists of Melanesian Institute publications, and of journals which focus on Melanesia and the Pacific Islands.

OC4 Rijks, Piet, comp.
A Guide to Catholic Bible Translations: The Pacific (vol. 1). Stuttgart, GW: World Catholic Federation Bible Apostola, 1989. 147 pp. Paper. No ISBN.

A comprehensive historical bibliography in French and English for each Pacific Island and Australia; the first in a series on Catholic work in Bible translation in the Third World.

OC5 Taylor, Clyde Romer Hughes, ed.
A Pacific Bibliography: Printed Matter Relating to the Native Peoples of Polynesia, Melanesia, and Micronesia. Oxford, ENK: Clarendon Press, 1965. 692 pp. No ISBN.

The revised and enlarged edition of this standard book contains more than 16,000 references, and covers the most important writings on the people of the Pacific Islands.

OC6 Zantkuijl, Manu, comp.
Tentative Bibliography of Cargo Cults and Other Manifestations of Cargo Ideology in the South Pacific. (ICAU mededelingen, 9). Utrecht, NE: Instituut voor Culturele Antropologie, 1976. iv, 93 pp. No ISBN.

A bibliography of works on cargo cults and modern religious movements from the 1940s to the present.

Serials and Periodicals

See also OC3.

OC7 *A Yearbook for Australian Churches:* Vol. 1 (1991)- Annual
Hawthorn, AT: Christian Research Association, 1991-. Paper. ISSN 10358137.

Annual information on challenging issues in church life in Australia; includes directories, a chronology, bibliographies, statistics, and research reports.

OC8 *Catalyst: Social Pastoral Journal for Melanesia.* Vol. 1, no. 1 (Mar. 1971)- . Quarterly
Goroka, PP: Melanesian Institute, 1971- . ISSN 02532921.

Articles on issues of pastoral and socioeconomic concern to the peoples and churches of Melanesia.

OC9 Langdon, Robert, ed.
The P.M.B. Book of Pacific Indexes. Canberra, AT: Australian National University, 1988. 211 pp. 0731503511.

An index to indexes for Oceania, including mission periodicals, complied by the Pacific Manuscripts Bureau of the Research School of Pacific Studies at the Australian National University.

OC10 *Melanesian Journal of Theology.* Vol. 1, no. 1 (April 1985)- . Semiannual
Goroka, PP: Melanesian Association of Theological Schools, 1985-. ISSN 0256856X.

Articles by the staff and students of member schools of the Melanesian Association of Theological Schools (MATS), with focus on the dialogue of Christian faith with Melanesian cultures.

OC11 *The Pacific Journal of Theology.* Series I, no. 1 (1961)-no. 26 (1968); series II, no. 1 (1989)- . Semiannual
Suva, FJ: South Pacific Association of Theological Schools, 1961-1968, 1989-. ISSN 1027037X.

Short articles on theology and ministry in the South Pacific, plus book reviews.

Documentation and Archives

OC12 Cargill, David
The Diaries and Correspondence of David Cargill. Edited by Albert Schutz. Canberra, AT: Australian National University Press, 1977. xv, 255 pp. 0708107192.

A carefully edited publication of the private writings of this gifted, but contentious, pioneer Scottish Methodist missionary to Fiji and Tonga (1832-1840).

OC13 Celsus, Kelly, ed.
Australia Franciscana. Madrid, SP: Archivo Ibero-Americano, 1963-1974. 6 vols. No ISBN.

Documents about the ill-fated expedition of Alvaro de Mendaña, from Peru to the Solomon Islands (1567-1569), and of unsuccessful efforts by Franciscan missionaries to

establish missions in Australia and Melanesia (1605-1634) [vol. 1: xxvii, 253 pp.; vol. 2: xxxvii, 236 pp.; vol. 3: xxx, 256 pp.; vol. 4: xxi, 277 pp.; vol. 5: xi, 226 pp.; vol. 6: xxix, 263 pp. (1963-1974)].

History

See also OC49, OC64, OC119, OC126, OC130, OC153, OC159, OC167, OC177, OC182, OC199, OC212, OC217, OC226, OC230, OC233, OC240, OC244-OC245, OC247, OC258, OC273, OC291-OC292, OC294, OC300, OC308, and OC321.

OC14 Aldrich, Robert
The French Presence in the South Pacific, 1842-1940. Honolulu, HIU: University of Hawaii Press, 1990. xii, 387 pp. 0824812689.

In this work the senior lecturer in economic history at the University of Sydney examines various aspects of France's activities—colonial, missionary, economic, and naval—in its Pacific colonies and in other areas of Oceania, including Australia and New Zealand, from 1842 to the beginning of World War II; written to test new theories of French expansion in that region.

OC15 Barrett, Ward, ed.
Mission in the Marianas: An Account of Father Diego Luis de Sanvítores and His Companions, 1669-1670. Minneapolis, MNU: University of Minnesota Press, 1975. viii, 62 pp. 0816607478.

An important source document on Spanish missionary activities in the Pacific, with a helpful introduction placing it in its historical context.

OC16 Britsch, Lanier R.
Unto the Islands of the Sea: A History of the Latter-day Saints in the Pacific. Salt Lake, UTU: Deseret Book Company, 1986. xiv, 585 pp. 087747754X.

A one-volume history of Mormon missions in the islands of French Polynesia, Hawaii, Australia, New Zealand, Samoa, Tonga, Fiji, and others from 1843 to 1950.

OC17 Crawford, David Livingston, and Leona Crawford
Missionary Adventures in the South Pacific. Rutland, VTU: Tuttle, 1967. x, 280 pp. No ISBN.

A well-researched popular account of the establishment of Christian missions in the South Pacific (Micronesia and the Hawaiian Islands) from 1852 to 1946.

OC18 Ferch, Arthur J., ed.
Symposium on Adventist History in the South Pacific, 1885-1918. Wahroonga, New South Wales, AT: SDA, South Pacific Division, 1986. 202 pp. Paper. 0947145079.

Papers by sixteen academically trained Adventist scholars, only three of which deal with South Pacific countries other than Australia and New Zealand.

OC19 Forman, Charles W.
The Island Churches of the South Pacific: Emergence in the Twentieth Century. (American Society of Missiology Series, 5). Maryknoll, NYU: Orbis Books, 1982. xv, 285 pp. Paper. 0883442183.

The definitive 20th-century history of Pacific Island churches by the distinguished Professor of Missions at Yale Divinity School, covering missions and churches, geographically; the indigenous view of Christianity; and movements toward and completion of church independence.

OC20 Garrett, John

Footsteps in the Sea: Christianity in Oceania to World War II. Geneva, SZ: WCC; Suva, FJ: University of the South Pacific, Institute of Pacific Studies, 1992. xii, 514 pp. Paper. 9820200687.

The second volume (sequel to *To Live Among the Stars*, 1982) of a three-volume narrative history of Protestant, Catholic, and Anglican missions and churches, focusing on the interplay between local cultures and Christianity.

OC21 Garrett, John

To Live among the Stars: Christian Origins in Oceania. Geneva, SZ: WCC; Suva, FJ: University of the South Pacific, Institute of Pacific Studies, 1982. xii, 412 pp. 2825406929.

A history of Christian origins and church growth in Oceania to 1980, and slightly beyond, with special attention to the role of islanders; containing maps, pictures, a glossary of indigenous terms, copious notes referring to nearly 500 listed sources, and a detailed index.

OC22 Garrett, John

A Way in the Sea: Aspects of Pacific Christian History with Reference to Australia. Melbourne, AT: Spectrum Publications, 1982. 73 pp. Paper. 0867860219.

Four lectures on the history of Australian missions to Polynesia, Melanesia, and Micronesia; originally delivered in April and May 1980, at the United Faculty of Theology of the University of Melbourne.

OC23 Garrett, John

Where Nets Were Cast: Christianity in Oceania since World War II. Suva, FJ: University of the South Pacific, Institute of Pacific Studies; Geneva, SZ: WCC Publications, 1997. xi, 499 pp. Paper. 9820201217.

The third of the author's definitive trilogy on the history of Christianity in Oceania, organized country by country.

OC24 Gunson, Niel

Messengers of Grace: Evangelical Missionaries in the South Seas, 1797-1860. Oxford, ENK: Oxford University Press, 1978. x, 437 pp. 0195505174.

A carefully researched history of early Evangelical missionaries and missions in the Pacific Islands from 1797, providing a social document that attempts to explain the indigenous character of Christianity in many South Sea islands.

OC25 Hillard, David

God's Gentlemen: A History of the Melanesian Mission, 1849-1942. St. Lucia, AT: University of Queensland Press, 1978. xv, 342 pp. 0702210668.

A scholarly history of Anglican missions, from New Caledonia to Papua New Guinea.

OC26 Howe, K. R.

Where the Waves Fall: A New South Sea Islands History from First Settlement to Colonial Rule. Sydney, AT: Allen & Unwin, 1991. xix, 403 pp. 1863731911.

This history of the discovery of the Pacific Islands by Western explorers interprets the events of the period, focusing on the development of island civilizations in the places where they landed, and the interaction between the waves of Western newcomers—traders, explorers, missionaries, beachcombers—and the island inhabitants; originally published in 1984.

OC27 Kent, Graeme

Company of Heaven: Early Missionaries in the South Seas. Wellington, AT: A.H. & A.W. Reed; Nashville, TNU: T. Nelson Publishers, 1972. 230 pp. 0589006843 (AT), 0840740360 (US).

A history of missions in Oceania, including the motivations, methods, and effectiveness of the early missionaries.

OC28 Maxwell, Arthur S.

Under the Southern Cross: The Seventh-day Adventist Story in Australia, New Zealand, and the Islands of the South Pacific. Nashville, TNU: Southern Publishing Association, 1966. 143 pp. No ISBN.

A popular history with photographs.

OC29 Miller, Char, ed.

Missions and Missionaries in the Pacific. (Symposium Series, 14). Lewiston, NJU: E Mellen Press, 1985. iii, 125 pp. 0889467056.

Three scholarly essays by James Boutilier, Charles W. Forman, and Char Miller, on issues of conversion, missionary family life, and mission-church relationships in the 19th and early 20th centuries.

OC30 Munro, Doug, and Andrew Thornley, eds.

The Covenant Makers: Islander Missionaries in the Pacific. Suva, FJ: Pacific Theological College; Suva, FJ: Institute of Pacific Studies, University of the South Pacific, 1996. xii, 321 pp. Paper. 9820201268.

Sixteen essays, mostly case studies by Pacific Islanders, of the more than 1,200 Pacific Islanders who have served as Christian missionaries since 1820.

OC31 O'Farrell, Patrick

The Catholic Church in Australia: A Short History 1788-1967. London, ENK: Chapman, 1968. x, 294 pp. 0225488094.

A historical survey of the Catholic Church in Australia, from its beginnings to the present, emphasizing major phases and landmark events in its development.

OC32 Paton, John G.

Thirty Years with South Sea Cannibals: Autobiography of John G. Paton. Chicago, ILU: Moody, 1964. 317 pp. Paper. No ISBN.

Revised edition of the autobiography of John Paton, one of the pioneer missionaries to the tribal peoples of the South Seas, told for children.

OC33 Tippett, Alan Richard

Aspects of Pacific Ethnohistory. South Pasadena, CAU: William Carey Library, 1973. ix, 205 pp. Paper. 0878081321.

An overview of ethnohistory as a research methodology, by the renowned Australian missiologist, with eight case studies of its usefulness in rewriting the history of Christianity in Oceania.

OC—OCEANIA

OC34 Wiltgen, Ralph M.
The Founding of the Roman Catholic Church in Oceania, 1825-1850. Canberra, AT: Australian National University, 1979. xxii, 610 pp. 0708108350.

A detailed and documentary history of the pioneer period of Catholic missionary activity, written from diaries, documents, and letters of the missionaries, and focusing on Catholic relations with colonial governments, European entrepreneurs, and Protestant missions.

OC35 Wood, Alfred Harold
Overseas Missions of the Australian Methodist Church. Melbourne, AT: Aldersgate Press, 1975-1978. 3 vols.

A multi-volume history of Australian Methodist mission work in Melanesia and Polynesia [vol. 1: *Tonga and Samoa* (1975; xvi, 335 pp., 0855710551); vol. 2: *Fiji* (1978; vii, 410 pp., 0855710608); vol. 3: *Fiji Indian and Rotuma* (1978; viii, 146 pp., 0855710616)].

General Works

See also SO388, OC5, OC16, OC19, OC33, OC53, OC68-OC69, OC82, OC92, OC122, OC125, OC140, OC150, OC210, OC227, OC252, OC254-OC255, OC261, and OC322.

OC36 Afeaki, Emiliana, R. G. Crocombe, and John McClaren, eds.
Religious Cooperation in the Pacific Islands. Suva, FJ: University of the South Pacific, 1983. ix, 231 pp. No ISBN.

A compendium of short essays and data, concerning associations that connect Christian churches across the Pacific, and Christians of other faith perspectives.

OC37 Barker, John, ed.
Christianity in Oceania: Ethnographic Perspectives. (ASAO Monograph, 12). Lanham, MDU: University Press of America, 1990. x, 319 pp. 081917906X (hdbk), 0819179078 (pbk).

Detailed studies by anthropologists, of Pacific Christianity in ten communities, from Papua New Guinea, to Pulap Island in Micronesia, to New Zealand.

OC38 Boutilier, James A., Daniel T. Hughes, and Sharon W. Tiffany, eds.
Mission, Church, and Sect in Oceania. (ASAO Monograph, 6). Lanham, MDU: University Press of America; Ann Arbor, MIU: University of Michigan Press, 1978. xiv, 500 pp. 0819138371 (hdbk), 081913838X (pbk).

Sixteen scholarly anthropological essays, examining how missionaries from many denominations affected the Pacific Islanders' lives, and how missionaries were affected by the Pacific experience.

OC39 Coaldrake, Frank W.
Flood Tide in the Pacific: Church and Community Cascade into a New Age. Stanmore, AT: Australian Board of Missions, 1964. 96 pp. No ISBN.

A popular account of mission by Australian Anglicans in Oceania.

OC40 Coop, William L., ed.
Pacific People Sing Out Strong. New York, NYU: Friendship Press, 1982. 96 pp. Paper. 037700118X.

A scrapbook of information about the people of the Pacific Islands, in which they speak out about the challenges and issues of life in that region today; with an intergenera-tional study guide by Janet M. Devries, *Learning the Pacific Way* (64 pp., 0377001198).

OC41 Douglas, Leonora Mosende, ed.
World Christianity: Oceania. (World Christianity Series, 5). Monrovia, CAU: MARC; London, ENK: MARC Europe, 1986. 338 pp. Paper. 0912552484 (US), 0947697497 (UK).

A concise volume containing basic background information on churches and people groups in the 25,000 islands of Oceania, one of the most Christianized regions of the world.

OC42 Ernst, Manfred
Winds of Change: Rapidly Growing Religious Groups in the Pacific Islands. Suva, FJ: Pacific Conference of Churches, 1994. xvii, 357 pp. Paper. 9822000677.

Report of survey of new religious groups (other than the historic mainline Protestant and Roman Catholic churches) in the Pacific Islands, including Bahais, Mormons, Jehovah's Witnesses, Seventh-day Adventists, newer evangelical and separatist groups, as well as evangelical/fundamentalist and para-church organizations.

OC43 Forman, Charles W., ed.
Island Churches: Challenge and Change. Suva, FJ: University of the South Pacific, Institute of Pacific Studies, 1992. x, 222 pp. Paper. 9820200776.

Essays by three indigenous authors on the history of the Rotuman Methodist Church, the newer churches of Kiribati, and the Maamafo'ou movement in Tonga.

OC44 Forman, Charles W.
The Voice of Many Waters. Suva, FJ: Lotu Pasifika Productions, 1986. ix, 211 pp. Paper. No ISBN.

The story of the life and ministry of the Pacific Conference of Churches, from its inception in 1961 to 1985.

OC45 Garrett, John, and John Mavor
Worship, the Pacific Way. (Issue Series). Suva, FJ: Lotu Pasifika Productions, 1973. 76 pp. Paper. No ISBN.

A study booklet on indigenizing worship for Pacific Island churches.

OC46 Holmes, Lowell D.
Samoan Village. (Case Studies in Cultural Anthropology). New York, NYU: Holt, Rinehart and Winston, 1974. xiv, 111 pp. Paper. 0030779251.

This case study of one village in the Manu'a group of American Samoa provides a working knowledge of the basic elements of traditional Samoan culture as it is lived today, including subsistence, use of traditional materials and structures, the principles of rank, and the elaboration of roles in the context of different groups. The assimilation of Christian belief into Samoan culture is also described.

OC47 Jaspers, Reiner
Die missionarische Erschliessung Ozeaniens: Ein quellengeschichtlicher und missionsgeographischer Versuch zur kirchlichen Gebietsaufteilung in Ozeanien bis 1855. (Missionswissenschaftliche Abhandlungen und Texte, 30). Münster, GW: Aschendorff, 1972. xxiv, 288 pp. Paper. 3402035197.

This book is a scholarly history of mission in Oceania, from the beginnings to the middle of the 19th century, providing not only dates and facts, but also treating such questions as nationalism and mission, missionary adaptation, and the ambiguity of missionary motives.

OC–OCEANIA

OC48 Mink, Nelson G.
Southern Cross Salute: Stories of Men and Women Who Are Making History in the Church of the Nazarene in the South Pacific. (Missionary Books: Reading Books, 1969-1970). Kansas City, MOU: Nazarene Publishing House, 1969. 72 pp. Paper. No ISBN.

Stories with a focus on Australia and New Zealand.

OC49 Oliver, Douglas L.
The Pacific Islands. Honolulu, HIU: University of Hawaii Press, 1989. xi, 304 pp. Paper. No ISBN.

In this third edition of a comprehensive view of the geology, geography, economics, history, ethnology, and politics of the various island groups, Professor Oliver examines the effect the waves of Westerners—explorers, traders, missionaries, army, and tourists—have had on the island people of Melanesia and Polynesia; originally published in 1951 (Cambridge, MAU: Harvard University Press).

OC50 Wright, Cliff, and Leslie Fugui, eds.
Christ in South Pacific Cultures. Suva, FJ: Lotu Pasifika Productions, 1986. ii, 117 pp. Paper. No ISBN.

Articles by South Pacific islanders about the relationship of traditional culture to Christian faith, with suggestions and poems.

Conferences and Congresses

See also EA140 and OC59.

OC51 Chandran, J. Russell, ed.
The Cross and the Taoa: Gospel and Culture in the Pacific. Suva, FJ: Lotu Pasfika, 1988. vi, 111 pp. Paper. 9822000200.

Papers presented at a conference held in 1987 in Suva by the South Pacific Association of Theological Schools; background Paper III was found to have been a plagiarism from the work of a New Zealand scholar.

OC52 Research Group for Asian and Pacific Christianity
Proceedings of the Research Group for Asian and Pacific Christianity. Edited by John McKean. Dunedin, NZ: University of Otago, Faculty of Theology, 1992-1994. 2 vols. Paper. No ISBN.

Scholarly papers on Christianity in Southeast Asia and Oceania presented at the annual seminars [1992, 49 pp.; 1993-94, iii, 93 pp.].

OC53 Richards, Charles G., comp.
Christian Communication in the Southwest Pacific: Report of Consultation Held at Nobonob, Madang, New Guinea, August, 1969. Dodoma, TZ: Central Tanganyika Press, 1970. 171 pp. No ISBN.

This report, published for the participating organizations, includes situation reports and addresses to the consultation concerning Christian communication in the Pacific.

OC54 Synod of Bishops, Special Assembly for Oceania
Jesus Christ and the Peoples of Oceania: Walking His Way, Telling His Truth, Living His Life. (Lineamenta). Vatican City, VC: Libreria Editrice Vaticana; Strathfield, AT: St. Paul Publications, 1997. 71 pp. 1875570942 (AT).

Preparatory papers for the Catholic Bishops' Synod for Oceania, covering mission history, evangelization, and ecclesial issues.

Church and Society

See also AS1296, OC15-OC16, OC19, OC29, OC31, OC34-OC36, OC39-OC40, OC44, OC46, OC50, OC64, OC68, OC74, OC78, OC90, OC93-OC95, OC104, OC108, OC112, OC115, OC119, OC123-OC126, OC130, OC134, OC138, OC141-OC142, OC144, OC151, OC157, OC160, OC166-OC167, OC172, OC177, OC183, OC193, OC203, OC210, OC212, OC214, OC217, OC219, OC221, OC226, OC229, OC232, OC240, OC244, OC248, OC251, OC256, OC260-OC261, OC263, OC265, OC271, OC277, OC293, OC296, OC325, and OC329.

OC55 Ahrens, Theodor
Der neue Mensch im kolonialen Zwielicht: Studien zum religiösen Wandel in Ozeanien. (Hamburger Theologische Studien, 5). Münster, GW: Lit Verlag, 1993. 184 pp. Paper. 3894739940.

These studies of emergent humanity in Oceania in the twilight of colonialism, find their unifying factor in the oral traditions of indigenous usages and persons, coming to terms with the resultant changes in religion.

OC56 Deverell, Gweneth, and Bruce Deverell, eds.
Pacific Rituals: Living or Dying? Suva, FJ: University of the South Pacific, Institute of Pacific Studies, 1986. 203 pp. Paper. No ISBN.

A collection of essays on the rituals and myths of Pacific peoples, relating Christian beliefs to traditional cultures.

OC57 Jolly, Margaret, and Martha MacIntyre, eds.
Family and Gender in the Pacific: Domestic Contradictions and the Colonial Impact. Cambridge, ENK: Cambridge University Press, 1989. xi, 296 pp. 0521346673.

Twelve scholarly case studies based on archival and field research, focusing on the impact of Christian missions on family life; with two studies of missionary wives.

OC58 Kane, Thomas A.
The Dancing Church of the South Pacific: Liturgy and Culture in Polynesia and Melanesia. (Video Tape). New York, NYU: Paulist Press, 1998. 0809182599.

A video to acquaint Western audiences with the development of Christian liturgy and culture in the South Pacific region, with two parts (18 and 19 minutes) on Polynesia, and two parts (21 and 23 minutes) on Melanesia.

OC59 Pacific Conference of Churches
Pacific Christian Women: Faith and Challenges. Suva, FJ: Lotu Pasifika Productions, 1982. 108 pp. Paper. No ISBN.

Report of the first ecumenical conference of Pacific Island women, held on the theme, "The Role of the Pacific Women in Church and Society."

OC60 Pacific Conference of Churches
Renewing Our Partnership in God's Creation: Consultation Report on Justice, Peace, and Integrity of Creation, Malua Theological College, Apia, September 19-October 1. Edited by Akuila Yabaki. Suva, FJ: Lotu Pasifika Productions, 1988. iv, 89 pp. Paper. 9822000251.

Reports from each of the island countries about economic and political conditions, followed by analysis of the major problems, and calls for action by the churches.

OC—OCEANIA

OC61 Saunders, George R., ed.

Culture and Christianity: The Dialectics of Transformation. Westport, CTU: Greenwood, 1988. xiii, 217 pp. 0313261180.

Three of the papers in this volume deal with particular aspects of history in the Solomon Islands, Papua New Guinea, and the Caroline Islands.

OC62 Siwatibau, Suliana, and David Williams

A Call to a New Exodus: An Anti-Nuclear Primer for Pacific People. Suva, FJ: Lotu Pasifika Productions, 1982. 96 pp. No ISBN.

A study presented by the Pacific churches to the people and governments of the region, showing the growing nuclear threat to the islands and islanders.

OC63 Weingartner, Erich, ed.

The Pacific Ecumenical Forum 1990: Sharing and Witnessing in the Wider Pacific. Hong Kong, HK: CCA, 1991. 52 pp. Paper. No ISBN.

Papers and the report of an important ecumenical forum on issues of justice in Oceania, held 6-14 December 1990, in Hilo, Hawaii.

General: Biography, Collective

See also AS1296, OC26-OC27, OC199, OC202, OC208, OC214, OC228, OC242, OC312, and OC319.

OC64 Davidson, J. W., and Deryck Scarr, eds.

Pacific Islands Portraits. Wellington, ENK: A.H. & A.W. Reed; Canberra, AT: Australian National University, 1973. xi, 346 pp. 0708101666 (hdbk), 0708101747 (pbk).

The changing way of life of the Pacific is shown through this series of portraits of men and women (5 of islanders, 3 of missionaries, plus 1 trader, and 3 groups of people), who lived in the islands between the early years of the nineteenth century and the outbreak of World War I.

General: Biography, Individual

See also AM44, OC32, OC80, OC84, OC90, OC97, OC112, OC116-OC117, OC128, OC137, OC139, OC159-OC161, OC180, OC182-OC183, OC185, OC197, OC215, OC232, OC246, OC252, OC256, OC264, OC268, OC270, OC303, and OC305.

OC65 Buzacott, Aaron

Mission Life in the Islands of the Pacific. Suva, FJ: University of the South Pacific, Institute of Pacific Studies, 1985. xxii, 288 pp. No ISBN.

A biography of a famous Rarotonga missionary, written by his son of the same name, and including much of the father's own writings.

OC66 Graham, Gloria

Gateway to the Jungle: The Incredible Life Story of Jungle Pilot George Boggs. Fullerton, CAU: R C Law & Co, 1992. xi, 252 pp. Paper. 0939925702.

A popular account of missionary pilot George Bogg's adventures in New Guinea, Indonesia, Laos, and the Philippines, 1957 to 1990, serving with the Missionary Aviation Fellowship.

OC67 Gutch, John

Beyond the Reefs: The Life of John Williams, Missionary. London, ENK: MacDonald & Co., 1974. x, 165 pp. 0356080188.

A well-researched biography of martyred John Williams, pioneer LMS congregational missionary to several South Sea islands (1817-1839), by a British career overseas service officer.

OC68 Hosie, Stanley W.

Anonymous Apostle: The Life of Jean Claude Colin, Marist. New York, NYU: Morrow, 1967. xi, 302 pp. No ISBN.

This first biography, in English, of the enigmatic founder of the Society of Mary, is an honest portrayal of the man who built up a substantial organization of 300 priests and brothers in Pacific missions, colleges, shrines, parishes, and mission bands.

OC69 Wilson, James

A Missionary Voyage to the Southern Pacific Ocean, 1796-1798. New York, NYU: Praeger, 1968. xix, 420 pp. No ISBN.

An updated and revised edition of a missionary's autobiography; a significant source of ethnographic information from the late 1700s.

Pacific Theologies

See also OC149.

OC70 May, John D'Arcy, ed.

Living Theology in Melanesia: A Reader. (Point Series, 8). Goroka, PP: Melanesian Institute, 1985. xvi, 310 pp. Paper. No ISBN.

An anthology of readings on indigenous theology in Melanesia, including eleven essays, plus prayers, hymns, sermons, creeds, and drama; designed to encourage Melanesian Christians and theological students to express their Christian convictions in truly indigenous ways.

OC71 May, John D'Arcy

Christus Initiator: Theologie im Pazifik. (Theologie interkulturell, 4). Düsseldorf, GW: Patmos Verlag, 1990. 151 pp. Paper. 3491777917.

An introduction to the changes in Polynesia, Melanesia, New Zealand, and Australia, from a theological perspective, against the background of colonialization and evangelization by Europeans; with special emphasis on eschatology, pneumatology, and, above all, Christology in Papua New Guinea.

OC72 Pacific Conference of Churches

Towards a Relevant Pacific Theology: A Report of a Theological Consultation Held in Bergengren House, Suva, Fiji, 8-12 July 1985. Edited by Bruce Deverell. Suva, FJ: Lotu Pasifika Productions, 1986. viii, 189 pp. Paper. No ISBN.

The report of a conference of theological educators from all the Pacific Islands, including papers from participants and recommendations regarding theological education.

OC73 Trompf, Garry W., ed.

The Gospel is Not Western: Black Theologies from the Southwest Pacific. Maryknoll, NYU: Orbis Books, 1987. ix, 213 pp. Paper. 0883442698.

A collection of twenty-one essays from Melanesia, aboriginal Australia, and the Torres Straits, reflecting the black and liberation theological struggles in this Pacific region.

OC—OCEANIA

Australia

See also GW260, HI438, HI440, HI725, EA32, ME101, EC278, MI151, CH403, SP111, SP314, AS592, AS741, OC7, OC13, OC31, OC48, and OC206.

OC74 Adler, Elisabeth et al.

Justice for Aboriginal Australians: Report of the World Council of Churches Team Visit to the Aborigines, June 15 to July 3, 1981. Geneva, SZ: WCC, 1981. 90 pp. Paper. 2825406937.

The report of a WCC team visit to Australia, with recommendations to the church and community there for solving problems of racism.

OC75 Between Two Worlds: The Report of the WCC Team Visit to Aboriginal Communities in Australia, January 1991

(PCR Information, 28). Geneva, SZ: WCC, 1991. 100 pp. Paper. No ISBN.

The report of two visits to aboriginal communities prior to the WCC's 7th Assembly at Canberra, with the text of documents on aboriginal land rights issues.

OC76 Black, Alan W., and Peter E. Glasner, eds.

Practice and Belief: Studies in the Sociology of Australian Religion. (Studies in Society, 15). Sydney, AT: Allen & Unwin, 1983. x, 205 pp. Paper. 0868613657.

A wide-ranging sociological survey of practices and beliefs in the various Christian denominations of Australia.

OC77 Carey, Hilary M.

Believing in Australia: A Cultural History of Religions. (The Australian Experience). St. Leonards, AT: Allen & Unwin, 1996. xviii, 270 pp. Paper. 1863739505.

A sociocultural history of religions in Australia, including aboriginal voices, missionary impact, the churches of the migrants, women's contributions, responses to secularization, and the growth of sects.

OC78 Cato, Nancy

Mister Maloga. (UQP Nonfiction). St. Lucia, AT: University of Queensland Press, 1993. xx, 308 pp. 0702224413.

Revised edition of the biography of the first true missionaries among the aboriginal people of Australia, whose indigenous approach at the Maloga Mission station, although virtually destroyed by the time of founder Daniel Matthew's death, stands as an example for government policy and mission work today; originally published in 1976.

OC79 Cole, Keith

From Mission to Church: The CMS Mission to the Aborigines of Arnhem Land 1908-1985. Bendigo Victoria, ONC: Keith Cole Publications, 1985. 240 pp. Paper. 0908447159 (hdbk), 0908447167 (pbk).

The one-volume history of the CMS missionary movement in northern Australia.

OC80 Flynn, Peg

Peg's Diary: Sister Peg Flynn's Record of Her Four Years with the Nyoongah People of Western Australia. Edited by Alan Nichols and Rena Pritchard. Canberra, AT: Acorn Press, 1988. 156 pp. 0908284659.

A biography of Peg Flynn (1921-1982), a Catholic teacher in western Australia.

OC81 Griffiths, Max

The Silent Heart: Flynn of the Inland. Kenthurst, AT: Kangaroo Press, 1993. vii, 176 pp. 0864175213.

A popular illustrated biography of the Presbyterian minister John Flynn (1880-1951), founder of the Australian Inland Mission (AIM), a number of outback hospitals, and the Royal Flying Doctor Service.

OC82 Harris, Dorothy, Douglas Hynd, and David Millikan, eds.

The Shape of Belief: Christianity in Australia Today. New South Wales, AT: Lancer Books, 1982. xii, 293 pp. 0858921871.

This compilation of essays concerning today's Christian church in Australia, with attention to aboriginal Australia, is an unprecedented assemblage of ecumenical Christian commentary and scholarship, focused with alert honesty on its own predicament; including an extensive bibliography.

OC83 Harris, John

One Blood: 200 Years of Aboriginal Encounter with Christianity: A Story of Hope. Sutherland, AT: Albatross Books; Oxford, ENK: Lion Publishing, 1990. 990 pp. 0867600950 (AT), 0745914969 (UK).

A major historical study of aboriginal/Christian relations in Australia—both Protestant and Roman Catholic.

OC84 Henderson, Harold R.

Reach for the World: The Alan Walker Story. Nashville, TNU: Discipleship Resources, 1981. iv, 216 pp. Paper. No ISBN.

A popular biography of an outstanding Australian Methodist clergyman, former senior minister at Central Methodist (Sydney), and world evangelist; based on interviews and personal archives.

OC85 Henson, Barbara

A Straight-Out Man: F.W. Albrecht and Central Australian Aborigines. Victoria, AT: Melbourne University Press, 1994. xvi, 313 pp. Paper. 052284569X.

The biography of Friedrich Wilhelm Albrecht (1894-1984), outstanding champion of the Australian Aborigines, as a Hermannsburg missionary.

OC86 Houston, Jim, ed.

The Cultured Pearl: Australian Readings in Cross-Cultural Theology and Mission. Melbourne, AT: JBCE, 1988. xvi, 294 pp. Paper. 085819712X.

A collection of twenty-nine short essays/documents relating the Christian Gospel to the various subcultures of Australia; produced by the project on Intercultural Theological Education in Multi-Faith Society, and originally published by the Victorian Council of Churches in 1986.

OC87 Hutchinson, Mark, and Geoff Treloar, eds.

This Gospel Shall Be Preached: Essays on the Australian Contribution to World Mission. (Studies in Australian Christianity, 7). Sydney, AT: Centre for the Study of Australian Christianity, 1998. 296 pp. 1864082992.

A collection of essays, including contributions on theology of mission, Australian mission outreach to the Pacific, Southern Asia, and Africa, missions to Aborigines, Catholic missions, case studies on the Brethren and the Christian and Missionary Alliance; and an appendix of Protestant missionary statistics.

OC—OCEANIA

OC88 MacGinley, Mary Rose, and Tony Kelly
The Church's Mission in Australia. (Pastoral Investigation of Contemporary Trends). Melbourne, AT: Collins Dove, 1988. 58 pp. Paper. 0859247317.

Three short essays on the history, theology, and sociology of Roman Catholic mission in Australia.

OC89 Maestrini, Nicholas
Mazzucconi of Woodlark: Biography of Blessed John Mazzucconi, Priest and Martyr of the P.I.M.E. Missionaries. Hong Kong, HK: Catholic Truth Society, Hong Kong; Detroit, MIU: P.I.M.E. Missionaries, 1983. xvii, 213 pp. 9627096016 (hdbk), 9627096024 (pbk).

A biography of Fr. John Mazzucconi (1826-55), a pioneer missionary/martyr to Australia of PIME, written for the occasion of his beatification.

OC90 Matthews, Charles H. S.
A Parson in the Australian Bush. Adelaide, AT: Rigby, 1973. 226 pp. 085179520X.

A reprint of the 1926 biography of F. H. Campion, who founded in Australia, in the early 20th century, the Bush Brotherhood of Anglican clergy, serving the remote areas of New South Wales.

OC91 Mavor, John, ed.
Creative Life Together: Ministry in Regional Congregations. Melbourne, AT: Uniting Church Press, 1994. 248 pp. Paper. 1864070307.

A resource for leaders of the Uniting Church of Australia, as they seek to develop larger congregations that can be simultaneously in mission and ministry to diverse subpopulations.

OC92 Mol, Hans
The Firm and the Formless: Religion and Identity in Aboriginal Australia. (Religion and Identity: Social-Scientific Studies in Religion, 2). Waterloo, ONC: Wilfrid Laurier University Press, 1982. viii, 103 pp. 088920117X.

This volume, of interest to students of sociology, anthropology, and religion, deals with the religious history and present condition of Australian Aborigines; themes include identity, totemism, taboos, sacred sites, ritual, myths, and missionary effects on revitalization.

OC93 Mol, Hans
Religion in Australia: A Sociological Investigation. Sydney, AT: Nelson, 1971. xviii, 380 pp. 0170019047.

A thorough survey of religious opinions in Australia, with analysis of the role of the churches as social institutions, and their responses to "secular security."

OC94 Murray, Iain H.
Australian Christian Life from 1788: An Introduction and an Anthology. Edinburgh, STK: Banner of Truth Trust, 1988. xviii, 357 pp. 085151524X.

An anthology, with commentary, of writings from 1788 to 1866 by early Anglicans, Baptists, Methodists, and Presbyterians in Australia.

OC95 Murtagh, James G.
Australia: The Catholic Chapter. Melbourne, AT: Polding Press, 1969. xx, 261 pp. No ISBN.

This work, which has been described as "a survey of the encounter between the church and society" in the Australian context, is a seminal work, reflecting the efforts of the Australian Catholic church to express Christian social principles, at a time when Marxist and socialist thinking was in intellectual vogue; originally published in 1946 (New York: Sheed and Ward).

OC96 Nichols, Alan
David Penman: Bridge-Builder, Peacemaker, Fighter for Social Justice. Sutherland, AT: Albatross Books; Oxford, ENK: Lion Publishing, 1991. 239 pp. 086760106X (AT), 0745914993 (UK).

A popular biography of David Penman (1936-1989), including his upbringing in New Zealand; missionary service under the CMS of New Zealand, in Pakistan and Lebanon (1966-1975); and ministry in Australia (1975-1989), culminating as Anglican Archbishop of Melbourne.

OC97 Nichols, Alan, and Warwick Olson
Crusading Down Under: The Story of the Billy Graham Crusades in Australia and New Zealand. Minneapolis, MNU: World Wide Publications, 1970. 141 pp. Paper. No ISBN.

This profusely illustrated documentation of the 1968 and 1969 Billy Graham crusades in New Zealand and Australia, shows how cities, tribes, and different church bodies come together for evangelism.

OC98 Noffs, Ted
The Wayside Chapel: A Radical Christian Experiment in Today's World. London, ENK: Collins; Valley Forge, PAU: Judson Press, 1969. 192 pp. Paper. 0017004955.

The story of a creative Methodist urban mission called the Wayside Chapel in Sydney, New South Wales, Australia.

OC99 Pattel-Gray, Anne
The Great White Flood: Racism in Australia. (American Academy of Religion Cultural Criticism Series, 2). Atlanta, GAU: Scholars Press, 1998. xvi, 312 pp. 0788501321 (hdbk), 078850133X (pbk).

A scholarly examination of the impact of racist government legislation and policies upon the indigenous of Australia over the last 200 years, with chapters on involvement by the churches.

OC100 Pattel-Gray, Anne
Through Aboriginal Eyes: The Cry from the Wilderness. Geneva, SZ: WCC Publications, 1991. xix, 158 pp. Paper. 2825409995.

The hidden history of the aboriginal people of Australia, including the churches' involvement; by the Executive Secretary of the Aboriginal and Islander Commission of the Australian Council of Churches.

OC101 Pattel-Gray, Anne, and John P. Brown, eds.
Indigenous Australia: A Dialogue about the Word Becoming Flesh in Aboriginal Churches. (Gospel and Cultures Pamphlets, 18). Geneva, SZ: WCC Publications, 1997. x, 64 pp. Paper. 2825412384.

Discussions on Gospel and culture issues by aboriginal and Torres Strait Islander Christian leaders, held in Sydney, Australia, in July 1996.

OC102 Piggin, Stuart
Evangelical Christianity in Australia: Spirit, Word and World. Melbourne, AT: Oxford University Press, 1996. xvi, 290 pp. Paper. 0195535383.

This history of evangelicalism in Australia features issues of mission, evangelization, and church renewal.

OC—OCEANIA

OC103 Porter, Muriel
Land of the Spirit: The Australian Religious Experience. (Risk Book Series, 44). Geneva, SZ: WCC Publications; Mebourne, AT: JBCE, 1990. xi, 102 pp. Paper. 2825409774 (W), 0858198002 (J).

A general overview of the place of religion in Australian life, and what it means for the nation as a whole, from aboriginal spirituality through today's pluralistic society.

OC104 Shanahan, Mary
Out of Time, Out of Place: Henry Gregory and the Benedictine Order in Colonial Australia. Canberra, AT: Australian National University Press, 1970. xvi, 187 pp. 0708106862.

In this discussion of the failure of the Benedictine order in Australia, Mother Shanahan discusses the events leading to the founding of the order, and the historic and cultural elements that precipitated its decline.

OC105 Stevens, Christine
White Man's Dreaming: Killalpaninna Mission, 1866-1915. Melbourne, AT: Oxford University Press, 1994. xii, 308 pp. 019553574X.

A detailed illustrated history of a German Lutheran mission to the Dujari Aborigines of the Lake Eyre Basin of South Australia; based on archival sources.

OC106 Thornhill, John
Making Australia: Exploring Our National Conversation. Newtown, AT: Millennium Books/E J Dwyer, 1992. xiv, 234 pp. Paper. 0855748990.

A Marist priest, as philosopher and theologian, reflects on those trends in Australian society that, in addition to aboriginal and Christian traditions, impact the future of the churches and their mission in that country.

OC107 Waugh, Geoff, ed.
Church on Fire. Melbourne, AT: JBCE, 1991. 176 pp. Paper. 0858198304.

Personal witness and short case studies of renewed churches (Catholic and Protestant) in Australia.

New Zealand

See also EA32, OC48, OC97, OC139, and OC289.

OC108 Bradwell, Cyril R.
Fight the Good Fight: The Story of the Salvation Army in New Zealand, 1883-1983. Wellington, NZ: Reed, 1982. 216 pp. 0589014374.

Bradwell's account of the beginnings of the Salvation Army in New Zealand reveals a little-known view of Salvation Army history—both the persecution it endured, and the motivation of its members to save souls and help the poor and needy.

OC109 Davidson, Allan K.
Aotearoa New Zealand: Defining Moments in the Gospel-Culture Encounter. (Gospel and Cultures Pamphlets, 12). Geneva, SZ: WCC Publications, 1996. xii, 63 pp. Paper. 2825412058.

An overview of five key moments in the relationship between Gospel and culture in Aotearoa, New Zealand.

OC110 Davidson, Allan K.
Selwyn's Legacy: The College of St. John the Evangelist Te Waimate and Auckland: 1843-1992, A History. Auckland, NZ: College of Saint John the Evangelist, 1993. xiv, 412 pp. 0473021110.

An illustrated history of the oldest institution for higher education in New Zealand, begun in 1843 to serve both missionary and settler Anglican churches.

OC111 Davis, Brian
The Way Ahead: Anglican Change and Prospect in New Zealand. Christchurch, NZ: Caxton Press, 1995. 235 pp. 0908563698.

The Anglican Archbishop of New Zealand discusses the wide-ranging changes in society since the 1960s, and charts the way ahead for the church in a secularized, pluralistic, but far-from-Godless society.

OC112 Evans, John H.
Churchman Militant: George Augustus Selwyn, Bishop of New Zealand and Lichfield. London, ENK: Allen & Unwin, 1964. 298 pp. No ISBN.

A full biography of Bishop Selwyn (1809-1878), pioneer Anglican bishop to the Maori people of New Zealand and founder of the Melanesian Mission, with special attention to Mrs. Selwn as well.

OC113 Glen, Robert, ed.
Mission and Moko: Aspects of the Work of the Church Missionary Society in New Zealand. Christchurch, NZ: Latimer Fellowship of New Zealand, 1992. 245 pp. Paper. 047301646X.

Eleven short essays on the early work of the CMS in New Zealand, 1814-1882, with a biographical index.

OC114 Hall, Noeline
"I Have Planted....": A Biography of Alfred Nesbit Brown. Palmerston North, NZ: Dunmore Press, 1981. xvi, 267 pp. 0908564422.

Biography of a CMS missionary among the Maori of New Zealand.

OC115 Hames, E. W.
Coming of Age: The United Church, 1913-1972. (Proceedings of the Wesley Historical Society of New Zealand, 28, 1-2; 150 Anniversary of New Zealand Methodism Publication). Auckland, NZ: Institute Press; Auckland, NZ: Wesley Historical Society of New Zealand, 1974. 157 pp. No ISBN.

This work describes the process of settling into a pastoral situation in the Methodist church at a time when the Christian faith was fading in New Zealand.

OC116 Hames, E. W.
Walter Lawry and the Wesleyan Mission in the South Seas. (Wesley Historical Society New Zealand Branch Proceedings, 23, no. 4). Auckland, NZ: Wesley Historical Society, 1967. 47 pp. No ISBN.

An assessment of the work of Walter Lawry (1793-1859), a pioneer Wesleyan Methodist missionary to New Zealand.

OC117 Henderson, J. Mclead
Ratana: The Man, the Church, the Political Movement. (Polynesian Society Memoir, 36). Wellington, NZ: A.H. & A.W. Reed; Sydney, AT: Polynesian Society, 1972. x, 128 pp. 0589006193.

A historical study of the Ratana church, the philosophies and principles of its founder, and its impact on Maori culture and society; previously published under the title *Ratana: The Origins and the Story of the Movement.*

OC118 Laracy, Eugénie, and Hugh Laracy
The Italians in New Zealand and Other Studies. Auckland, NZ: Società Dante Alighieri, 1973. 23 pp. No ISBN.

Contains brief history of Italian Catholic missions in New Zealand.

OC119 Laurenson, George I.

Te Hahi Weteriana: Three Half Centuries of the Methodist Maori Missions, 1822-1972. (Wesley Historical Society of New Zealand Proceedings; 27, 1-2). Auckland, NZ: Wesley Historical Society, 1972. xiv, 267 pp. Paper. No ISBN.

A record of the main features, the personalities, the varied fortunes, trials, disappointments, aspirations, and achievements of the Methodist Maori Mission, over three half-centuries, 1822 to 1972.

OC120 Lethbridge, Christopher

The Wounded Lion: Octavius Hadfield, 1814-1904: Pioneer Missionary, Friend of the Maori and Primate of New Zealand. Christchurch, NZ: Caxton Press, 1993. 319 pp. 0908563523.

An illustrated biography of a pioneer CMS missionary to the Maori, who became Anglican primate of New Zealand.

OC121 Mead, A. D.

Richard Taylor: Missionary Tramper. Wellington, NZ: A.H. & A.W. Reed, 1966. 272 pp. No ISBN.

An account of the adventurous travels of Richard Taylor (1805-1873), a CMS pioneer missionary to the Maoris in the North Island of New Zealand, from 1839 to 1873.

OC122 Mol, Hans

The Fixed and the Fickle: Religion and Identity in New Zealand. (Religion and Identity: Social-Scientific Studies in Religion, 1). Waterloo, ONC: Wilfrid Laurier University Press, 1982. viii, 109 pp. 0889201137.

This volume describes the effect of religion on the identity of the native Maoris and Pakenas (white settlers) in New Zealand, bringing together anthropological and sociological studies, historical accounts, official statements, and religious census data.

OC123 Mol, Hans

Religion and Race in New Zealand: A Critical Review of the Policies and Practices of the Churches in New Zealand Relevant to Racial Integration. Christchurch, NZ: NCC New Zealand, 1966. 80 pp. No ISBN.

This critical review of the policies and practices of the churches in New Zealand, with regard to racial integration, examines the underlying perspectives behind church policy, and the policies themselves, in terms of their impact (positive or negative) on integration.

OC124 Morrell, W. P.

The Anglican Church in New Zealand: A History. Dunedin, NZ: Anglican Church of the Province of New Zealand, 1973. 277 pp. No ISBN.

A large part of this history of the Anglican church in New Zealand is devoted to the history of the Melanesian Mission, the Board of Missions, and the missionary dioceses.

OC125 Nichol, Christopher, and James Veitch, eds.

Religion in New Zealand. Wellington, NZ: Victoria University, Combined chaplaincies & Religious Studies Dept., 1983. 313 pp. Paper. No ISBN.

This enlarged second edition of ten scholarly essays traces the development of New Zealand Christianity, and discusses contemporary issues of the churches' mission; originally published in 1980.

OC126 Owens, J. M. R.

Prophets in the Wilderness: The Wesleyan Mission to New Zealand, 1819-27. Auckland, NZ: Auckland University Press; London, ENK: Oxford University Press, 1974. 192 pp. 0196478952.

This is a portrait of the origins of the Wesleyan mission at Whangaroa in the 1820s, with an analysis of the attack on the mission, which challenges many accepted views about the missionary role and the origin of race relations in New Zealand.

OC127 Patrick, Bruce, ed.

New Vision, New Zealand: Calling the Whole Church to Take the Whole Gospel to the Whole Nation. Auckland, NZ: Vision New Zealand, 1993. 377 pp. Paper. 0473017040.

A comprehensive analysis, with nineteen essays by New Zealand leaders, prepared for the historic "Vision New Zealand Congress" (Jan. 1993), at which 350 national church leaders discussed how the nation might be evangelized.

OC128 Rogers, Lawrence M.

Te Wiremu: A Biography of Henry Williams. Christchurch, NZ: Pegasus, 1998. 335 pp. 0908704747.

A biography of Henry Williams, CMS missionary to the Maori of New Zealand in the early 1800s; originally published in 1973.

OC129 Ryburn, Hubert J.

Te Hamara: James Hamlyn 1803-1865, Friend of the Maoris. Dunedin, IE: McIndoe, 1979. 151 pp. No ISBN.

The biography of an ill-educated but pioneer artisan-missionary, who served the CMS for forty years in New Zealand.

OC130 Williams, William

Christianity among the New Zealanders. Edinburgh, STK: Banner of Truth Trust, 1989. vi, 384 pp. 0851515665.

A reprint of an 1867 account of early Maori missions, written by the Bishop of Waiapu.

OC131 Worsfold, J. E.

A History of the Charismatic Movements in New Zealand: Including a Pentecostal Perspective and a Breviate of the Catholic Apostolic Church in Great Britian. Bradford, ENK: Julian Literature Trust, 1974. xx, 368 pp. Paper. No ISBN.

A history of the Catholic Apostolic church in New Zealand, of other Pentecostal churches, and of the wider charismatic movement there.

OC132 Yate, William

An Account of New Zealand and of the Church Missionary Society's Mission in the Northern Island. Shannon, IE: Irish University Press, 1970. xxi, 320 pp. 0716500817.

Reprint of the 1835 edition by an early CMS missionary.

Melanesia: General Works

See also SO391-SO394, OC3, OC25, OC32, OC70, OC124, OC185, OC203, and OC243.

OC133 Ahrens, Theodor

Unterwegs nach der verlorenen Heimat: Studien zur Identitätsproblematik in Melanesien; im Anhang ein Gesprach mit Andrew Strathern nber "Enthusiastisches Christentum." (Erlanger Monographien aus Mission und Ökumene, 4). Erlangen, GW: Ev.-Luth. Mission, 1986. 280 pp. Paper. 3872143042.

The problem of relating Christianity to Melanesian culture is examined in terms of three distinct factors: developing a transcultural theology where a cultural conflict exists; the effects of this conflict and the expression of it upon a missions theology; and the problem of identity for the Melanesian caught in the cultural conflict.

OC134 Conway, Jeanette, and Ennio Mantovani

Marriage in Melanesia: A Sociological Perspective. (Point Series, 15). Goroka, PP: Melanesian Institute, 1990. 248 pp. Paper. No ISBN.

Data from the Marriage and Family Life Research Project of the Melanesian Institute, presenting both the realities and challenges affecting marriage and the family in Papua New Guinea today.

OC135 Crocombe, R. G., and Marjorie Crocombe, eds.

Polynesian Missions in Melanesia: From Samoa, Cook Islands and Tonga to Papua New Guinea and New Caledonia. Suva, FJ: Institute of Pacific Studies University of the South Pacific, 1982. v, 144 pp. Paper. No ISBN.

Eight essays written by Polynesian missionaries themselves, or by descendants of missionaries of the LMS; with original illustrations and source documents.

OC136 Flannery, Wendy, and Glen W. Bays, eds.

Religious Movements in Melanesia Today. (Point Series, 2-4). Goroka, PP: Melanesian Institute, 1983-1984. 3 vols. Paper. No ISBN.

Papers presented at seminars sponsored by the Melanesian Institute in Irian Jaya, Indonesia (Oct. 1980), and Goroka, Papua New Guinea (Nov. 1980 and April 1982), on cargo cults (vol. 1, xv, 204 pp.), revivalist, spiritualist, and/or charismatic movements (vol. 2, x, 259 pp.); and more general issues concerning contemporary Melanesian religious movements (vol. 3, ix, 238 pp.).

OC137 Fox, Charles Elliot

Kakamora. London, ENK: Hodder & Stoughton, 1962. 157 pp. No ISBN.

Dr. Fox recalls, in this autobiography, his long acquaintance with the Melanesian people—first as missionary and administrator with the Melanesian Mission, and later as an insider and member of the Melanesian Brotherhood.

OC138 Grutzner, Pauline

Community Development Manual. Goroka, PP: Youth for Christ National Office, 1980. 172 pp. Paper. No ISBN.

Although this handbook for community development is written from a Melanesian context—covering background issues and goals, basic principles of development, hindrances, leadership styles, training, and practical steps for implementing a community development program—it would be helpful for any underdeveloped context.

OC139 Gutch, John

Martyr of the Islands: The Life and Death of John Coleridge Patteson. London, ENK: Hodder & Stoughton, 1971. 223 pp. 0340147628.

Biography of the first missionary Bishop of Melanesia—murdered there in 1871—who set the pattern for the expansion of the Melanesian Mission.

OC140 Habel, Norman C., ed.

Powers, Plumes, and Piglets: Phenomena of Melanesian Religion. Bedford Park, AT: Australian Association for the Study of Religions, 1979. vi, 234 pp. Paper. 0908083076.

A valuable firsthand synopsis of various types of religious phenomena found in Melanesia—including rites and customs heretofore given scant attention—arranged so as to facilitate their educational use, plus a selection of approaches to their interpretation.

OC141 Ingebritson, Joel F., ed.

Human Sexuality in Melanesian Cultures. (Point Series, 14). Goroka, PP: Melanesian Institute, 1990. 288 pp. Paper. No ISBN.

This volume develops in more detail the findings from the Melanesian Institute's Marriage and Family Life Research Project of the early 1980s, concerning Melanesian, Western, and biblical concepts of marriage and sexuality.

OC142 Knight, James J.

Christ in Melanesia. (Point Series, 1). Goroka, PP: Melanesian Institute, 1977. 262 pp. Paper. No ISBN.

In this pioneer issue of the Point Series, a variety of authors wrestle with the problem of indigeneity—what does it mean to be fully Melanesian and fully Christian?

OC143 Lawrence, P., and M. J. Meggitt, eds.

Gods, Ghosts and Men in Melanesia: Some Religions of Australian New Guinea and the New Hebrides. Melbourne, AT: Oxford University Press, 1972. vi, 298 pp. No ISBN.

A collection describing the indigenous religions of people groups in New Guinea and Vanuatu, including the Huli, Siane, Kamano, Usurufa, Jate, Fore, Mae Enga, Kyaka, Lakalai, Ngaing, Tangu, and the Melanesians of South Pentecost; originally published in 1965.

OC144 Mantovani, Ennio

Marriage in Melanesia: An Anthropological Perspective. (Point Series, 17). Goroka, PP: Melanesian Institute, 1992. 361 pp. Paper. No ISBN.

The third and last volume of a trilogy from the Marriage and Family Research Project of the Melanesian Institute, presenting data on how people see and experience marriage today, in the light of their cultural backgrounds.

OC145 Mantovani, Ennio, ed.

An Introduction to Melanesian Religions: A Handbook for Church Workers. (Point Series, 6). Goroka, PP: Melanesian Institute, 1984. xii,, 306 pp. Paper. No ISBN.

The second in a trilogy of books, designed to put forth answers to questions Christian church workers ask when confronted by various Melanesian primal religions, comparing various aspects of Christianity and Melanesian religions, using theological, missiological, and social-scientific analysis.

OC146 Mantovani, Ennio, ed.

Marriage in Melanesia: A Theological Perspective. (Point Series No. 11). Goroka, PP: Melanesian Institute, 1987. ix, 212 pp. Paper. No ISBN.

Ten papers discussing marriage in Melanesia, reflecting historical, anthropological, and theological viewpoints; enabling dialogue between Western Christians and traditional Melanesian perspectives.

OC147 Narokobi, Bernard

The Melanesian Way. Boroko, PP: Institute of Papua New Guinea Studies; Suva, FJ: University of the South Pacific, Institute of Pacific Studies, 1983. xix, 187 pp. Paper. No ISBN.

This revised volume of Bernard Narokobis' thought-provoking and controversial visions for a Melanesia liberated from Western values and ways—also contains rebuttals from a number of Narokobi's critics.

OC—OCEANIA

OC148 Oliver, Barry, Alex Currie, and Doug Robertson, eds.

Avondale and the South Pacific: 100 Years of Mission. Cooranbong, AT: Avondale Academic Press, 1997. 195 pp. Paper. 0959933727.

A collection of nine articles on various topics, such as motivation for missionary service, the impact of missionary experience on an expatriate missionary, women in mission, and the influence of Western missionaries on worship in Melanesian society; includes an appendix which attempts the first comprehensive list of missionaries to the island nations of the South Pacific Division of Seventh-day Adventists.

OC149 Pech, Rufus

Manub and Kilibob: Melanesian Models for Brotherhood: Shaped by Myth, Dream and Drama. (Point Series, 16). Goroka, PP: Melanesian Institute, 1991. 246 pp. Paper. No ISBN.

An exploratory and analytic study of the Melanesian myth of the two brothers, Manub and Kilibob, and its place in the forms of belief, ritual, and practical action of the Melanesian peoples.

OC150 Rodman, Margaret, and Matthew Cooper, eds.

The Pacification of Melanesia. (ASAO monograph, 7). Ann Arbor, MIU: University of Michigan Press, 1979. 233 pp. 0472027034.

Papers on the subjugation, by European powers, of the peoples of Melanesia in the 20th century, with numerous references to mission impact; originally presented at the annual meeting of the Association for Social Anthropology in Oceania (Monterey, California, 2 March 1977).

OC151 Schwarz, Brian, ed.

An Introduction to Ministry in Melanesia: A Handbook for Church Workers. (Point Series, 8). Goroka, PP: Melanesian Institute, 1985. x, 304 pp. Paper. No ISBN.

In this the final of three handbooks for church workers in Melanesia, eleven authors explore the relationship between various aspects of ministry (education, healing, development, urban, contextualization) and the Melanesian context.

OC152 Strelan, John G.

Search for Salvation: Studies in the History and Theology of Cargo Cults. Adelaide, AT: Lutheran Publishing House, 1977. 119 pp. 0859100375.

A missiological study of cargo cults, from the perspective that these movements are authentic reflections of the basic religious beliefs and mythology of Melanesians, and that they also form a genuine search for salvation for Melanesians who have come into contact with Christianity.

OC153 Tippett, Alan Richard

The Deep-Sea Canoe: The Story of the Third World Missionaries in the South Pacific. South Pasadena, CAU: William Carey Library, 1977. xi, 126 pp. Paper. 0878081585.

Interweaving history, theology, and anthropology, the noted Australian missiologist tells the story of the planting and expansion of the church in Fiji and the surrounding islands through the pioneer mission work of Melanesians and Micronesians.

OC154 Trompf, Garry W.

Melanesian Religion. Cambridge, ENK: Cambridge University Press, 1991. xi, 283 pp. 0521383064.

The first systematic survey of the full scope of Melanesian religion, from traditional beliefs and practices to the development of strong indigenous Christian churches and theology.

OC155 Wench, Ida

Mission to Melanesia. London, ENK: Elek Books, 1961. 209 pp. No ISBN.

An autobiography of one of the first women missionaries of the Melanesian Mission, Ida Wench, a nurse and educator with an evangelist's heart, who was a missionary in the Solomon Islands and the New Hebrides (Vanuatu) from 1909 to 1931.

OC156 Whiteman, Darrell L., ed.

An Introduction to Melanesian Cultures: A Handbook for Church Workers. (Point Series, 5). Goroka, PP: Melanesian Institute, 1984. xii, 264 pp. Paper. No ISBN.

This first book in a trilogy on Melanesian cultures is designed to introduce indigenous and expatriate church workers to basic cultural understandings, for effective Christian mission in Melanesia.

OC157 Whiteman, Darrell L.

Melanesians and Missionaries: An Ethnohistorical Study of Social and Religious Change in the Southwest Pacific. South Pasadena, CAU: William Carey Library, 1983. xxi, 559 pp. 0878083340.

An anthropological analysis of the role of Anglican missionaries of the Melanesian Mission, and the social and cultural changes that resulted from their interaction with Melanesians, with detailed illustrations, tables, glossary, and an extensive bibliography and index.

OC158 Worsley, Peter

The Trumpet Shall Sound: A Study of Cargo Cults in Melanesia. London, ENK: Paladin, 1970. 389 pp. No ISBN.

Second edition, bringing all available material together, this book covers, extensively, the cargo cults of Melanesia, and the insight they provide into the minds of primitive peoples coming into contact with modern civilization.

Fiji

See also OC12, OC65, and OC158.

OC159 Dickson, Mora

The Inseparable Grief: Margaret Cargill of Fiji. London, ENK: Epworth Press; London, ENK: D Dobson, 1976. 174 pp. Paper. 0716202638 (E), 0234777117 (D).

The heroic story of a pioneer Methodist missionary wife (1809-1840), who died after seven years' service in the South Pacific, giving birth to her sixth child.

OC160 Fischer, Edward

Fiji Revisited: A Columban Father's Memories of Twenty-Eight Years in the Islands. New York, NYU: Crossroad Publishing, 1981. 158 pp. 0824500970.

Designed more for the casual reader than for a serious student of missions, this book, nevertheless, gives a remarkable account of Fijians, Indians, and missionaries; based on a two-week visit, the material is arranged corresponding to each day.

OC161 Hare, Eric B.

Fulton's Footprints in Fiji. Washington, DCU: Review and Herald, 1969. 252 pp. No ISBN.

A well-written biography of John Edwin Fulton, Seventh-day Adventist missionary to the Fiji Islands.

OC162 Kanongata'a, Keiti Ann

Women at the Service of the Church: A Study of the Partic-ipation of the Sisters of Our Lady of Nazareth in the Mis-sion of the Church in the South Pacific Islands—Oceania. Rome, IT: Pontifica Universitas Urbaniana, 1986. xviii, 100 pp. Paper. No ISBN.

An extract from a doctoral dissertation on the work of Fijian Catholic young women in evangelization and educa-tion.

OC163 Mahoney, John D.

Mission and Ministry in Fiji: Essays by John D. Mahoney. Edited by Frank Hoare. Samabula, FJ: Columban Fathers, 1994. x, 133 pp. Paper. 9821990010.

Essays by John Mahoney (1929-1989), a Columban missionary in Fiji from 1958 to 1989.

OC164 Meo, I. Jovili, Alfred Dale, and Dorothy Dale

Plant Today for Tomorrow: A Self-Study Report of the Meth-odist Church in Fiji and Rotuma. Suva, FJ: Methodist Church in Fiji, 1985. v, 158 pp. Paper. No ISBN.

A report to the church, giving a history of its changes, a description of the self-study process, which was pursued for three years, and recommendations for action.

OC165 Sidal, Morven

Hannah Dudley Hamari Maa: Honored Mother, Educator and Missioner to the Indentured Indians of Fiji, 1864-1931. Suva, FJ: Pacific Theological College, 1997. viii, 144 pp. Paper. 9823480052.

The biography of a missionary who worked with re-cent migrants to Fiji, helped raise awareness and sensitiv-ity for Fiji Indians, and earned respect from her predomi-nantly male fellow missionaries—some reticent, but the majority admiring in their commendation.

OC166 Smith, Elsabe H.

Yesterday and Today: With the Indians in the Church in Fiji. Suva, FJ: Lotu Pasifika Production, 1979. 80 pp. Pa-per. No ISBN.

Miss Smith's account of the work of the Methodist church among East Indian laborers in the Fiji Islands is from an insiders point of view, as one of the missionary workers in Fiji, from 1927 to 1975.

OC167 Tippett, Alan Richard

Oral Tradition and Ethnohistory: The Transmission of In-formation and Social Values in Early Christian Fiji, 1835-1905. (St. Mark's Library Publications Series, 1). Can-berra, AT: Council of St. Mark's Library, 1980. 70 pp. Pa-per. 0909446008.

An ethnohistorical study of oral tradition in Fiji, over a century and a half of history, tracing Fiji's contextualized Gospel and indigenous church, and the part oral tradition played in both.

OC168 Williams, Thomas

Fiji and the Fijians. New York, NYU: AMS Press, 1982. xi, 266 pp. Paper. No ISBN.

Reprint of a lively and reliable account of the islands and their inhabitants by a broad-minded missionary; first published in 1858 (London, ENK: Heylin).

New Caledonia

See also OC158.

OC169 Dubois, Marie-Joseph

Aventurier de Dieu. Paris, FR: Anthropos Institut, 1985. 222 pp. No ISBN.

Autobiography of a priest who served on Mare in the Loyal-ty Islands during the middle years of the 20th century.

OC170 Howe, K. R.

The Loyalty Islands: A History of Culture Contacts, 1890-1960. Canberra, AT: Australian National University Press, 1977. xvi, 206 pp. 0824804511.

A carefully researched work, including much about the history of the missions.

OC171 Kohler, Jean Marie

Le christianisme en Nouvelle-Calédonie et aux îles Loyauté: présentation sociologique. (Conférence des églises du Paci-fique). (Collection "Profils du christianisme dans le Pacifique" document de recherche, 3). Port-Vila, NL: Centre de recher-ches des églises du Pacifique; Nouméa, NL: Office de la re-cherche scientifique et Outre-Mer, 1980. 29 pp. No ISBN.

A short introduction in French to missions in New Cala-donia and the Loyalty Islands.

OC172 Wete, Pothin

"Agis ou Meurs," l'église évangélique de Calédonie vers Kanaky: Le developpement de la prise de conscience poli-tique ... 1960-1988. Suva, FJ: Lotu Pasifika Publications, 1991. xii, 154 pp. Paper. No ISBN.

French translation of a thesis written in English at the Pacific Theological College dealing with the growth toward selfhood in the Evangelical Church of New Caledonia, the church's decision in favor of national independence, and the value of liberation theology for the church's life.

Papua New Guinea

See also EA81, SO79, SO389-SO390, CO72, MI104, AS1177, OC137, OC143, and OC147.

OC173 Aerts, Theo

Romans and Anglicans in Papua New Guinea. Goroka, PP: Liturgical Catechetical Institute, 1991. vi, 138 pp. No ISBN.

The history of relations between the two churches and recent dialogues between them.

OC174 Ahrens, Theodor, and Walter J. Hollenweger

Volkschristentum und Volksreligion im Pazifik: Wiederentdeck-ung des Mythos für den christlichen Glauben. (Perspektiven der Weltmission, 4). Frankfurt am Main, GW: Lembeck, 1976. 124 pp. 3874760987.

Focusing on the Melanesian "dissimilar brothers" myth, describing the origin and development of the people on the north coast of New Guinea, to their encounter with the colo-nial powers; this work deals with popular Christianity and popular religion in Melanesia

OC175 Anderson, Carol Lee

Do You Know What You Are Doing, Lord? A Jungle Journey in Search of God. Grand Rapids, MIU: Chosen Books, 1998. 189 pp. Paper. 0800792610.

An honest, intriguing, and sometimes humorous account of missionary life in the jungles of New Guinea, dealing with the practical issues of fear of failure, fear of rejection, and the struggle of unhealed areas of the missionary's past.

OC—OCEANIA

OC176 Anderson, Neil T., and Hyatt Moore
In Search of the Source: A First Encounter with God's Word.
Portland, ORU: Multnomah, 1992. 205 pp. 0880705345
(hdbk), 0880704977 (pbk).

A popular account of the adventures of the authors as
Wycliffe Bible Translators among the Folopa people of Papua
New Guinea.

OC177 Ansoul, Richard
*Beautiful Feet: Australian Baptists Enter Papua New Guin-
ea.* Hawthorn, AT: Australian Baptist Missionary Society,
1981. 57 pp. Paper. No ISBN.

This is the story of the first seven years of Australian
Baptist missionary work among the Enga people in the Western Highlands of Papua New Guinea, telling of the events
which led to the establishment of the enterprise and some of
the people who carried it through.

OC178 Böhm, Karl
*The Life of Some Island People of New Guinea: A Missionary's
Observations of the Volcanic Islands of Manam, Boesa, Biem,
and Ubrub.* Berlin, GW: Reimer, 1983. 414 pp. 3496007257.

A study of traditional culture, made by an SVD missionary in 1936; edited and published by him in his retirement.

OC179 Bürkle, Horst, ed.
Theologische Beiträge aus Papua Neuguinea. (Erlanger
Taschenbücher, 43). Erlangen, GW: Ev.-Luth. Mission, 1978.
345 pp. Paper. 3872140892.

A valuable collection of articles on the Lutheran Church
in Papua New Guinea, raising issues of mission-church relationships, indigenization, and the role of the missionary.

OC180 Berg, A. A. E.
*Arrows of the Almighty: A Biography of William Ewart Bro-
mley, Pioneer Missionary to New Guinea.* (NWMS Reading
Books). Kansas City, MOU: Nazarene Publishing House, 1995.
96 pp. Paper. No ISBN.

Second edition of the biography of William Bromley, one of
the first missionaries to enter the Jimi Valley of Papua New Guinea with the Christian message; originally published in 1972.

OC181 Boelaars, Huub J. W. M.
*Met Papoea's samen op weg: De ontwikkeling van de mensen
en de missionarissen: Deel 1: De Pioniers-het begin van een
missie.* (Kerk en theologie in context, 18). Kampen, NE: Kok,
1992. xviii, 301 pp. 9024266416.

First in a three-part historical series on the work of Missionaries of the Sacred Heart (MSC) in Papua New Guinea,
this volume, based on archival sources, covers the mission
pioneers (1905-1915) and their work among the Marind, Jahr-
aj, and Boadzi peoples on the southern coast of New Guinea.

OC182 Butcher, Benjamin T.
We Lived with Headhunters. London, ENK: Hodder & Stoughton, 1963. 288 pp. No ISBN.

Commenced as an autobiography of the author's thirty-four
years among the stone age Papuans of the early century, and now,
a shortened story of Papua, as he knew it, from 1905 to 1939.

OC183 Carter, George G.
*Misikaram: The Reverend John Arthur Crump, F.Z.S., J.P., Mis-
sionary to New Britain, 1894-1904.* (Proceedings of the Wesley
Historical Society (New Zealand), vol. 29, 1-4). Auckland, NZ:
Wesley Historical Society, 1975. 57 pp. Paper. No ISBN.

Originally given in a very much condensed form, as the
Wesley Historical Society Lecture in 1973, this study was published to mark the centennial of the arrival of the first Methodist
missionaries in Papua New Guinea, on 15 August 1875.

**OC184 *Changes, Challenges and Choices: Women and
Development in Papua New Guinea***
Madang, PP: Kristen Press for the Department of Religion,
Home Affairs and Youth, 1991. vii, 256 pp. Paper. No ISBN.

An illustrated handbook for women's organizers, educators, and trainers in Papua New Guinea, in their efforts to
improve women's health, family life, and their participation
in development efforts.

OC185 Chatterton, Percy
Day that I Have Loved: Percy Chatterton's Papua. Sydney,
AT: Pacific Publications, 1980. 131 pp. 0858070472.

Percy Chatterton, O.B.E., who spent fifty years in Papua
as missionary, teacher, and outspoken politician, fighting for
the little man, has written a charming account of the Papuan
people, giving warm insight into their hopes, fears, customs,
and way of life—a life which is changing under the impact of
many influences; originally published in 1974.

OC186 Delbos, Georges
*The Mustard Seed: From a French Mission to a Papua Church,
1885-1985.* Port Moresby, PP: Institute of Papua NG Studies, 1985. xvii, 448 pp. Paper. 9980680024.

The centennial history of the Catholic Mission of the
Sacred Heart (MSC) and of the Catholic Church in Papua
that developed out of it.

OC187 Dlugosz, Maria
*Mae Enga Myths and Christ's Message: Fullness of Life in
Mae Enga Mythology and Christ the Life (Jn 10:10).* (Studia
Instituti Missiologici SVD, 66). Nettetal, NE: Steyler Verlag,
1998. xii, 302 pp. Paper. 3805004036.

A detailed comparison of the German worldview, myths
of the Mae Enga people of Papua New Guinea, and the Christ
in the Gospel of John; originally presented as a Ph.D. dissertation at the Gregorian University in Rome in 1995.

OC188 Fautsch, Hubert
*Christus kam auch zu den Papuas: Der mühsam Weg eines
Volkes aus der Steinzeit.* (Herderbücherei, 1044). Freiburg,
GW: Herder, 1983. 158 pp. Paper. 3451080443.

A Catholic priest examines briefly the changes in the
Chimbu district of the New Guinea Highlands, which took
place between his two periods of labor there; one during the
early contact period before 1971, and the other, after 1977.

OC189 Felde, Marcus Paul Bach
*Faith Aloud: Doing Theology from the Hymns in Papua New
Guinea.* (Point Series, 23). Goroka, PP: Melanesian Insti-
tute, 1999. 194 pp. Paper. No ISBN.

Based on his doctoral thesis, the author traces the historical value and functions of music in the Lutheran tradition,
and explores how this tradition, combines with those meanings and values in the lives of Papua New Guineans.

OC190 Fischer, Hans
Weisse und Wilde: Erste Kontakte un Anfänge der Mission.
(Materialien zur Kultur der Wampar, Papua New Guinea, 1).
Berlin, GW: Reimer, 1992. 230 pp. Paper. 3496004371.

A case study of the 1907 massacre of a village by the
Wampar people of Papua New Guinea; as told by whites, including Germans; and, in contrast, as related by the natives
and their descendents.

OC191 Fontius, Hanfried

Mission, Gemeinde, Kirche in Neuguinea, Bayern und bei Karl Steck. (Erlanger Taschenbücher, 28). Erlangen, GW: Ev.-Luth. Mission, 1975. 258 pp. Paper. 3872140671.

Within the framework of the biography of a German missionary of the Neuendettelsau Mission, this work deals with the very community-oriented understanding of ministry in the dynamic Evangelical Lutheran Church of New Guinea (dissertation, University of Erlangen).

OC192 Frazer, Ian

God's Maverick. Sutherland, AT: Albatross Books, 1992. 237 pp. Paper. 0732410045.

The story of a remarkable medical assistant, who devoted his life, from 1947 to 1988, to bringing effective medicine, through the Lutheran mission, to the people of Karkar Island, Papua New Guinea.

OC193 Frerichs, Albert, and Sylvia Frerichs

Anutu Conquers in New Guinea: A Story of Mission Work in New Guinea. Minneapolis, MNU: Augsburg, 1969. 160 pp. Paper. No ISBN.

A history of eighty years of mission work in Papua New Guinea, including the early history of Papuan people, descriptions of the culture and practices, and of the methods of the Lutheran church in bringing the Christian message to them.

OC194 Fugmann, Gernot, ed.

The Birth of an Indigenous Church: Letters, Reports and Documents of Lutheran Christians of Papua New Guinea. (Point Series, 10). Goroka, PP: Melanesian Institute, 1986. xv, 276 pp. Paper. No ISBN.

A documented history, from the Lutheran perspective, of how church autonomy was envisioned, formulated, and brought to fruition, culminating in the truly indigenous Evangelical Lutheran Church of New Guinea.

OC195 Fugmann, Gernot, ed.

Ethics and Development in Papua New Guinea. (Point Series, 9). Goroka, PP: Melanesian Institute, 1986. xxi, 229 pp. Paper. No ISBN.

A collection of thirteen essays exploring the relation of Christianity to the social, economic, and political development of the new nation, 1975-1985.

OC196 Fugmann, Wilhelm

Miti-Väter erzählen aus ihrem Leben. Neuendettelsau, GW: Freimund-Verlag, 1980. 64 pp. Paper. 3772601014.

The life stories of two early New Guinean church leaders.

OC197 Fugmann, Wilhelm, ed.

Christian Keysser: Bürger zweier Welten. Stuttgart, GW: Hänssler-Verlag, 1985. 220 pp. 3775109692.

A brief biographical sketch by the editor introduces vivid reports from the life and writings of this German Lutheran missionary in New Guinea, who developed the principle of cultural integration as a method of establishing Christian congregations in a Stone Age civilization.

OC198 Fugmann, Wilhelm, ed.

Zeugnisse aus der Geschichte der Evangelisch-Lutherischen Kirche von Papua-Neuguinea. Neuendettelsau, GW: Missionswerk der Ev.-Luth. Kirche in Bayern, 1986. 178 pp. Paper. 3922275171.

Published by the Neuensettelsau Mission on the occasion of the centenary of its "partner church" in Papua New Guinea, this collection of eighty testimonies bears witness to "God's story" in that country.

OC199 Griffin, James, ed.

Papua New Guinea Portraits: The Expatriate Experience. Canberra, AT: Australian National University Press, 1978. xxxi, 269 pp. Paper. 0708102388 (hdbk), 0708112951 (pbk).

A compilation of biographies of well-known expatriates in Papua New Guinea; among them are missionaries, educators, prospectors, and politicians.

OC200 Herdt, Gilbert, and Michele Stephen, eds.

The Religious Imagination in New Guinea. New Brunswick, NJU: Rutgers University Press, 1989. vi, 262 pp. Paper. 0813514576 (hdbk), 0813514584 (pbk).

Scholarly essays on traditional forms of religious imagination in New Guinea, with comparisons/contrasts with Christian spirituality.

OC201 Herndon, Ernest

In the Hearts of Wild Men. Sand Springs, OKU: Grace & Truth Books, 1998. 137 pp. Paper. No ISBN.

The author-journalist and leader of the To Every Tribe Ministries recounts their 1981 pioneer contact with the Menyamya people of Papua New Guinea; originally published in 1986 (McComb, MSU: McComb Enterprise-Journal).

OC202 Herndon, Ernest

Morning Morning True: A Novel of Intrigue in New Guinea. Grand Rapids, MIU: Zondervan Publishing House, 1988. 235 pp. Paper. 031027270X.

An easy-to-read adventure novel about three Protestant missionaries in Papua New Guinea, designed to introduce New Guinean culture and its testing of Christian values.

OC203 Horne, Shirley

Them Also: First Mission Contact with the Primitive Biamis. Port Moresby, PP: Unevangelized Fields Mission, 1968. 53 pp. No ISBN.

This is a short history of the decision and commencement by the Unevangelized Fields Mission, together with the Evangelical Church of Papua, into mission work among the Biamis of northwestern Papua.

OC204 Huber, Mary Taylor

The Bishops' Progress: A Historical Ethnography of Catholic Missionary Experience on the Sepik Frontier. (Smithsonian Series in Ethnographic Inquiry). Washington, DCU: Smithsonian Institution Press, 1988. xii, 264 pp. 0874745446.

A scholarly history of SVD missions to the Sepik regions of Papua New Guinea, 1896-1976, with attention to ethnographical and anthropological issues.

OC205 Italiaander, Rolf, ed.

Heisses Land Niugini: Beiträge zu den Wandlungen in Papua Neuguinea. Erlangen, GW: Ev.-Luth. Mission, 1974. 368 pp. 3872140477.

A collection of essays by specialists and missionaries on the situation of the church in Papua New Guinea, covering mission, ecumenism, anthropology, and politics.

OC—OCEANIA

OC206 Janssen, Arnold

Arnold Janssen SVD: Briefe nach Neuguinea und Austalien.
Edited by Josef Alt. (Studia Instituti Missiologici SVD, 63).
Nettetal, GW: Steyler Verlag, 1996. lvi, 449 pp. Paper.
3805003706.

A critical edition of the letters from the founder of the
SVD to missionaries in New Guinea and Australia (1896-
1908), with photographs and an introduction by the editor.

OC207 Jericho, E. A.

Seedtime and Harvest in New Guinea. Brisbane, AT: United
Evangelical Lutheran Church of Australia, New Guinea Mission Bo, 1961. 160 pp. No ISBN.

A mission history published to commemorate the 75th
anniversary of the founding of mission work in New Guinea,
by the United Evangelical Lutheran Church of Australia.

OC208 Jinks, Brian, Peter Biskup, and Hank Nelson, eds.

Readings in New Guinea History. Sydney, AT: Angus & Robertson, 1973. xviii, 454 pp. 020712485X.

A collection of readings intended to provide source material on the development of New Guinea in the Western sense,
covering exploration, mission work, government, and trade.

OC209 Keysser, Christian

Bürger zweier Welten. Edited by Wilhelm Fugmann. (Edition
C, C 153). Neuhausen-Stuttgart, GW: Hanssler-Verlag, 1985.
220 pp. Paper. 3775109692.

A selection of writings by Christian Keysser, of the Neuendettelsau Mission; he succeeded in building Christian communities among the mountain people of New Guinea without
destroying their cultural heritage.

OC210 Keysser, Christian

A People Reborn. Translated by Alfred Allin, and John Kud-
er. South Pasadena, CAU: William Carey Library, 1980. xxvi,
306 pp. Paper. 0878081747.

An English translation of *Eine Papuagemeinde* (Neuendettelsau, 1929), in which the pioneer Lutheran missionary
among the Kate people of New Guinea (1899-1920) presents
the culture and theology by which the people perceived themselves, God, and came to conversion.

OC211 Koschade, Alfred

*New Branches on the Vine: From Mission Field to Church in
New Guinea.* Minneapolis, MNU: Augsburg, 1967. 175 pp.
No ISBN.

A study of mission and church, continuity and disconti-
nuity, indigenization, Papuan thought, and indigenous theology, from the birth of the Lutheran Mission to the Evangelical
Lutheran Church of New Guinea.

OC212 Kraft, Hermann

*Morgenrot auf Manus: Vom Anfang unserer Missionsarbeit
auf Manus vor fünfzig Jahren.* Bad Liebenzell, GW: Verlag
der Liebenzeller Mission, 1964. 40 pp. Paper. No ISBN.

A history of Liebenzeller Mission work on Manus Island, off the coast of Papua New Guinea.

OC213 Krause, Wolfram von, ed.

Junges Neuguinea: Ein Arbeitsbuch. Neuendettelsau, GW: Freimund-Verlag, 1970. 240 pp. No ISBN.

Twenty persons, in the service of the Lutheran mission in
New Guinea, report on the political, the economic, and especially the spiritual situation of the country; the ecumenical endeavors; and present-day problems confronting the church.

OC214 Langmore, Diane

Missionary Lives: Papua, 1874-1914. (Pacific Islands Monograph Series, 6). Honolulu, HIU: University of Hawaii Press,
1989. xxiv, 408 pp. 0824811631.

Biographies of the 327 European missionaries who lived
and worked in Papua between 1874 and 1914, including those of
the LMS, the Sacred Heart Mission, the Australasian Wesleyan
Methodist Missionary Society, and the Anglican Mission.

OC215 Langmore, Diane

Tamate, A King: James Chalmers in New Guinea, 1877-1901.
Melbourne, AT: Melbourne University Press, 1974. xv, 169
pp. 0522840795.

This biography of the 19th-century missionary to Papua
New Guinea presents an unconventional view of Chalmer's
life and ministry, explores the mysterious circumstances surrounding his death, and analyzes the interaction of European
and Papuan cultures, reflected in his life.

OC216 Linge, Hosea

*Offering Fit for a King: The Life and Work of the Rev. Hosea
Linge, Told by Himself.* Translated by Neville Threlfall. Rabaul, PP: Unichurch Publishing House, 1978. 149 pp. Paper.
0869380249.

This is probably the first published autobiography by a
New Guinean, translated by a Methodist minister in New
Britain, and published in part, in 1932, under the title *The
Erstwhile Savage* (Melbourne: F.W. Cheshire Pty. Ltd.).

OC217 Lockley, G. Lindsay

*From Darkness to Light: The Progress of the Gospel in Pap-
ua, 1872-1972.* Port Moresby, PP: United Church in Papua
New Guinea and the Solomon Islands, 1972. 40 pp. Paper.
No ISBN.

Originally written to encourage Papuans to write, in greater detail, the story of the coming of the Gospel to their own
districts, this book is not a complete history of the first 100
years of LMS work in Papua New Guinea, but a concise and
informative work.

OC218 MacDonald, Mary N.

Mararoko: A Study in Melanesian Religion. (American University Studies, 11: Anthropology and Sociology, 45). New
York, NYU: Lang, 1991. xv, 591 pp. 0820411949.

A thesis analyzing the stories of the Mararoko and Erave
people of Papua New Guinea, and the interaction of traditional and Christian worldviews reflected in them.

OC219 McGregor, Donald E.

The Fish and the Cross. (Point Series, 1). Goroka, PP: Melanesian Institute, 1982. xi, 139 pp. Paper. No ISBN.

A second edition of an account of a "Fish Festival" held
at Teloute Village, Papua New Guinea, through which the
Wape participants of the Lumi area are discovered as people;
with a discussion of problems met (indigenization, syncretism, church discipline, and pastoral care) in the cross-cultural communication of the Christian message to people with an
animistic worldview.

OC220 Moore, Sidney

5,000 Arrows. Pico Rivera, CAU: CFM Press, 1973. 80 pp.
Paper. No ISBN.

Stories of the encounters of Four Square Gospel missionaries with peoples of the eastern highlands of Papua New
Guinea.

OC—OCEANIA

OC221 Mrossko, Kurt-Dietrich, ed.

Wok Misin-100 Jahre Deutsche Mission-Eine Dokumentation des Missionskollegs Neuendettelsau. Neuendettelsau, GW: Missionskolleg, 1986. 214 pp. Paper. No ISBN.

The proceedings of a symposium held in Germany (Neuendettelsau, 1986), exploring the past and present work of the Evangelical Lutheran Mission in Papua New Guinea, emanating from the Neuendettelsau Mission School.

OC222 Oates, Lynette

Hidden People: How a Remote New Guinea Culture was Brought Back from the Brink of Extinction. Sutherland, AT: Albatross Books, 1992. 352 pp. Paper. 0732410142.

The adventures of two Australian Wycliffe Bible translators, 1954-92, in bringing the Gospel to the Binumarien tribe of Papua New Guinea.

OC223 O'Neill, Tim

And We the People: Ten Years with the Primitive Tribes of New Guinea. New York, NYU: Kennedy, 1961. 248 pp. No ISBN.

A personal account by an Irish Roman Catholic missionary of the Order of the Sacred Heart of Service, 1947 to 1956, among the Mengen people of Papua New Guinea.

OC224 Parratt, John

Papuan Belief and Ritual. New York, NYU: Vantage Press, 1976. 103 pp. 533019419 (SBN).

A survey of Papuan belief and rituals, based on a comprehensive analysis of published sources, mainly by missionaries and anthropologists.

OC225 Pilhofer, Georg

Die Geschichte der Neuendettelsauer Mission in Neuguinea. Neuendettelsau, GW: Freimund-Verlag, 1961. 3 vols. No ISBN.

A three-volume history of the Neuendettelsauer Lutheran Mission in New Guinea, from its founding in 1886 to the present, with special emphasis on its educational work, its cooperation with Australian and American Lutherans, and the development of a living, truly indigenous church [vol. 1: *Von den ersten Anfängen bis zum Kriegsausbruch 1914* (1961, 288 pp.); vol. 2: *Die Mission zwischen den beiden Weltkriegen mit einem Überblick über die neue Zeit* (1963, 311 pp.); vol. 3: *Werdende Kirche in Neuguinea—Kopie oder Original?* (1962, 120 pp.)].

OC226 Pilhofer, Georg

Geschichte des Neuendettelsauer Missionhauses. Neuendettelsau, GW: Freimund-Verlag, 1967. 62 pp. No ISBN.

Continues the author's *Die Geschichte der Neuendettelsauer Mission in Neuguinea.*

OC227 PNG Centennial Committee, Port Moresby

Papua New Guinea: A Century of Colonial Impact, 1884-1984. Edited by Sione Latukefu. Boroko, PP: National Research Institute; Boroko, PP: University of Papua New Guinea, 1989. xv, 494 pp. 9980750227.

This collection of papers, presented at the centennial history seminar, held in 1984 to commemorate the entry of colonial powers, in 1884, into what is now Papua New Guinea, represents the attempt of this congress to examine the colonial impact on Papua New Guinea, critically, objectively, and with a high standard of scholarship.

OC228 Reeson, Margaret

Torn between Two Worlds. Madang, PP: Kristen Press, 1972. 205 pp. 0858040603.

The story of two highland New Guineans and the influence of modernization and culture change on their lives, with their testimonies to the influence of the Christian message in their adaptation to social change.

OC229 Ridgway, Kingsley Mervyn

Feet upon the Mountains: A History of the First Five Years of the Wesleyan Missionary Work in Papua New Guinea. Marion, INU: Wesleyan Church Corporation, 1976. 111 pp. Paper. No ISBN.

This vivid portrayal of experiences in pioneering missionrary work in the rugged mountains of New Guinea, is the report of one who was there, during the first five years of Wesleyan mission work in Papua, 1961-1966.

OC230 Rowley, C. D.

The New Guinea Villager: A Retrospect from 1964. Melbourne, AT: Cheshire, 1972. 215 pp. 0701512261.

In this second edition, Mr. Rowley examines changes which have occurred in the lives of New Guinea villagers since their first contacts with the outside world; the effects of government control, the impact of a cash economy; the demands by the white man for labor and land; and the influence of Christian missions. The author also describes some of the islanders' responses to these, including modern religious movements and "cargo cults"; originally published in 1965.

OC231 Sanders, J. Oswald

Planting Men in Melanesia: The First Decade of Decade of Development of the Christian Leader's Training College of Papua New Guinea. Mt. Hagen, PP: Christian Leader's Training College of PNG, 1978. 180 pp. Paper. 0909297096.

The story of the founding and early years of the Christian Leaders' Training College in Papua New Guinea, where Sanders' account reflects on the failures, achievements, and aims of the school, and its particular mission in New Guinea.

OC232 Saunders, Garry

Bert Brown of Papua. London, ENK: M. Joseph, 1965. 204 pp. No ISBN.

This biography of the Rev. Herbert Alfred Brown—introducing us to a unique missionary personality whose parish was set in 3,000 square miles of Stone Age New Guinea—is a story of triumph over difficulty, and how Papuans are being helped to lift themselves into the future.

OC233 Schütte, Heinz

Koloniale Kontrolle und christliche Mission: Überlegungen zu gesellschaftlicher Transition in New Guinea. (Wiener ethnohistorische Blätter: Beiheft, 9). Vienna, AU: Institut für Völkerkunde der Universitäts Wien, 1986. 185 pp. Paper. No ISBN.

A history and analysis of the implications of the 1878 six-day war undertaken by the Australian missionary, George Brown, after the killing of some of the Fijian missionaries he had brought to New Britain; dedicated to the chief who directed the killings.

OC234 Schroeder, Roger

Initiation and Religion: A Case Study from the Wosera of Papua New Guinea. (Studia Instituti Anthropos, 46). Fribourg, SZ: University Press, 1992. 326 pp. Paper. 3727807873.

A detailed case study of male initiation rites among the Wosera of Papua New Guinea, with missiological reflections on the inculturation of Christian initiation; originally presented as a doctoral thesis at the Pontifical Gregorian University, Rome, 1990.

OC—OCEANIA

OC235 Sevenau, Philip

A Life for Mission. Boroko, PP: MSC, Pacific Islands Province, 1985. 126 pp. No ISBN.

A life of Henri Verius, 1860-1892, missionary in Papua New Guinea, Vicar Apostolic, and Bishop of New Britain.

OC236 Shaw, R. Daniel

From Longhouse to Village: Samo Social Change. (Case Studies in Cultural Anthropology Series). Fort Worth, TXU: Harcourt Brace, 1996. xii, 148 pp. Paper. 0155025619.

A case study on social change, with special reference to religion and values, among the Samo people of Papua New Guinea; based on the author's field research beginning in 1969.

OC237 Shaw, R. Daniel

Kandila: Samo Ceremonialism and Interpersonal Relationships. Ann Arbor, MIU: University of Michigan Press, 1990. 280 pp. 0472094262.

A detailed ethnographic analysis of the central initiation rite of the Samo people of Papua New Guinea; by a missionary anthropologist, concerned that the Samo retain their cultural identity while embracing Christianity.

OC238 Steffen, Paul

Missionsbeginn in Neuguinea: Die Anfänge der Rheinischen, Neuendettelsauer und Steyler Missionsarbeit in Neuguinea. (Studia Instituti Missiologici SVD, 61). Nettetal, GW: Steyler Verlag, 1995. 312 pp. Paper. 380500351X.

A comparative study of pioneer missions in New Guinea—two Lutheran (Rhenish and Neuendettelsauer missions) and one Roman Catholic (SVD); originally presented in 1992 as a doctoral dissertation in missiology at the Gregorian University in Rome.

OC239 Steyler Missions-Wissenschaftliches Institut, ed.

Divine Word Missionaries in Papua New Guinea, 1896-1996: Festschrift. Nettetal, GW: Steyler Verlag, 1996. 258 pp. Paper. 3805003803.

Twelve essays by SVD missiologists (11 in English, 1 in German), focused on issues of indigenization of the Catholic church in Papua New Guinea; published as a double issue of the SVD journal *Verbum.*

OC240 Threlfall, Neville

One Hundred Years in the Islands: The Methodist-United Church in the New Guinea Islands Region, 1875-1975. Rabaul, PP: The United Church, New Guinea Islands Region, 1975. 288 pp. 0869380168.

This history of the Methodist church mission in its first 100 years, 1875-1975, traces the developments from inception through the forming of an indigenous church, the United Church.

OC241 Tomasetti, Friedegard

Traditionen und Christentum im Chimbu-Gebiet Neuguineas: Beobachtungen in der Lutherischen Gemeinde Pare. (Arbeiten aus dem Seminar für Völkerkunde Frankfurt, 6). Wiesbaden, GW: Steiner, 1976. 200 pp. Paper. 3515023658.

Relying chiefly on his own observations, the author describes how a people that came into contact with Europeans and missionaries in the early thirties, gradually accepts the Christian message without breaking with its own ancestral traditions.

OC242 Tomkins, Dorothea, and Brian Hughes

The Road from Gona. London, ENK: Angus & Robertson, 1970. x, 153 pp. 0207951896.

A history of the New Guinea mission and the story of the missionaries martyred in New Guinea during the Second World War; told by one of the survivors.

OC243 Vicedom, Georg F.

Church and People in New Guinea. (World Christian Books, 38). London, ENK: USCL, 1961. 79 pp. Paper. No ISBN.

A history of the growth of Christianity in Papua New Guinea, from dependent mission to the independent Evangelical Lutheran Church of New Guinea.

OC244 Vicedom, Georg F.

Junge Kirche in Neuguinea. (Weltweite Reihe, 15). Stuttgart, GW: Evan Missionsverlag, 1962. 92 pp. No ISBN.

Reflections on the development of an indigenous church in the highlands of central New Guinea, by the noted German Protestant missiologist who served there from 1929 to 1939.

OC245 Wagner, Herwig, and Hermann Reiner, eds.

The Lutheran Church in Papua New Guinea: The First Hundred Years, 1886-1986. Adelaide, AT: Lutheran Publishing House, 1986. 677 pp. 085910382X.

The comprehensive centennial history of the Evangelical Lutheran Church of Papua New Guinea, and of the missions and missionaries who contributed to its selfhood and varied ministries.

OC246 Wagner, Herwig, Gernot Fugmann, and Hermann Janssen, eds.

Papua-Neuguinea-Gesellschaft und Kirche: Ein ökumenisches Handbuch. (Erlanger Taschenbücher, 93). Neuendettelsau, GW: Freimund-Verlag; Erlangen, GW: Ev.-Luth. Mission, 1989. 464 pp. 3772601359 (F), 3872141937 (E).

An ecumenical handbook by thirty-eight authors of various nationalities and disciplines, describing the social situation of Papua New Guinea, the Christian churches and communities, and the challenges for the future.

OC247 Wetherell, David

Christian Missions in Eastern New Guinea, 1877-1942. Canberra, AT: Australian National University, 1974. x, 462 pp. No ISBN.

A study of European, South Sea island, and Papuan influences on Christian missions in eastern New Guinea.

OC248 Wetherell, David

Reluctant Mission: The Anglican Church in Papua New Guinea, 1891-1942. St. Lucia, AT: University of Queensland Press, 1977. xiv, 430 pp. 0702214116.

A scholarly social history of the Anglican mission in Papua New Guinea, examining the life, work, and attitudes of the missionaries and the operations of the church they founded, with careful attention paid to the indigenous Melanesian Christians affected by the mission.

OC249 Wetherell, David, ed.

The New Guinea Diaries of Philip Strong, 1936-1945. Melbourne, AT: Macmillan of Australia, 1981. xv, 254 pp. 0333337220.

Strong was the bishop of the Anglican Church of Papua, in charge of a mission and a church thrown into the middle of wartime conflicts.

OC—OCEANIA

OC250 White, Nancy H.

Sharing the Climb. Melbourne, AT: Oxford University Press, 1991. ix, 118 pp. Paper. 019553235X.

A firsthand account by a Church of England in Australia educational missionary to Papua New Guinea, 1948 to 1967.

OC251 Williams, Ronald G.

The United Church in Papua, New Guinea, and the Solomon Islands. Rabaul, PP: Trinity Press International, 1972. 316 pp. 0959908102.

The story of the development of an indigenous church on the occasion of the centenary of the LMS in Papua, 1872-1972.

Solomon Islands

See also OC155 and OC251.

OC252 Carter, George G.

Valuable beyond Price: The Story of Sister Lina M. Jones, 1890-1979. Auckland, NZ: Wesley Historical Society, 1985. 68 pp. Paper. No ISBN.

The story of Lina Jones, a pioneer Methodist educator in the Solomon Islands, as revealed through her letters and diaries.

OC253 Firth, Raymond William

Rank and Religion in Tikopa: A Study in Polynesian Paganism and Conversion to Christianity. Boston, MAU: Beacon Press; London, ENK: George Allen & Unwin, 1970. 424 pp. 0807046663 (US), 0042000181 (ENK).

A detailed analysis, by a famous social anthropologist, of traditional religion, the history of culture contact, and the successes of the Melanesian Mission among the Tikopia of the Solomon Islands.

OC254 Fox, Charles Elliot

The Story of the Solomons. Sydney, AT: Pacific Publications, 1975. 88 pp. Paper. 0858070227.

Revised edition of a history of the Solomon Islands, written from their perspective, by one of their best admirers and advocates; originally published in 1967.

OC255 Griffiths, Alison

Fire in the Islands!: The Acts of the Holy Spirit in the Solomons. Wheaton, ILU: Shaw Publishers, 1977. 208 pp. Paper. 0877882649.

An account of the 1970 revival in the Solomon Islands, and its effects on Solomon Islanders and missionaries alike, in renewal and a release of the works of the Holy Spirit.

OC256 Jones, Muriel

Married to Melanesia. London, ENK: Allen & Unwin, 1974. 159 pp. 0049100564.

Muriel Jones' account of her experience with her husband, as missionaries and educators in the Solomon Islands, reveals both the strength of her own character, and the impact of Christianity on a people with no experience of Christ.

OC257 Laracy, Hugh

Marists and Melanesians: A History of Catholic Missions in the Solomon Islands. Honolulu, HIU: University Press of Hawaii; Canberra, AT: Australian National University, 1976. xi, 211 pp. 0824803612 (US), 0708104045 (AT).

A history of Catholic mission activity (Society of Mary) and its impact on Melanesians in the Solomon Islands, beginning with an abortive start in 1845, through to a discussion of Solomon Islands Catholicism in the early 1970s.

OC258 Maretu

Cannibals and Converts: Radical Change in the Cook Islands. Translated by Marjorie Crocombe. Suva, FJ: University of the South Pacific, 1983. 223 pp. Paper. No ISBN.

The remarkable history, autobiography, and general description of life in the Cook Islands before the coming of Europeans, written in the 1870s by a native first-generation Christian convert and missionary.

OC259 Nau, Semisi

Semisi Nau: The Story of My Life. Edited by Allan K. Davidson. Suva, FJ: University of the South Pacific, 1996. xii, 153 pp. Paper. 9820201144.

The autobiography of Semisi Nau (1866?-1927), a pioneer Tongan Methodist missionary among the Ontong Java people of the Solomon Islands (1906-1919), with a historical introduction by the editor.

OC260 O'Reilly, Patrick, and Hugh Laracy

Bibliographie des ouvrages publiés par les Missions Maristes des îles Salomon. (Publications de la Société de océanistes, 29). Paris, FR: Musée de l'Homme, 1972. 67 pp. Paper. No ISBN.

An annotated and illustrated bibliography of works published by the Marist Mission, from 1901 to 1970, in the Solomon Islands.

OC261 Tippett, Alan Richard

Solomon Islands Christianity: A Study in Growth and Obstruction. (World Studies of Churches in Mission). New York, NYU: Friendship Press; London, ENK: Lutterworth Press; Pasadena, CAU: William Carey Library, 1967. xvii, 407 pp. 0878087249.

A well-researched study by the Australian missiologist, seeking to discover how the history of the Methodist mission led to a breakaway movement, focusing on factors which both favor and obstruct the natural growth of the church, in both numbers and spiritual maturity.

OC262 White, Geoffrey

Identity through History: Living Stories in a Solomon Islands Society. (Cambridge Studies in Social and Cultural Anthropology, 83). Cambridge, ENK: Cambridge University Press, 1992. xvi, 270 pp. 0521410720.

The stories are from Santa Isabel Island, with many about the coming of Christianity, the work of the missionaries, and the indigenization of the Anglican church, as seen by the people.

OC263 Wright, Cliff

Melanesian Culture and Christian Faith: Report of an Education Workshop, Auki, Malaita, Solomon Islands, 12-26 October 1978. (Workshop Report Series). Honiara, BP: Solomon Islands Christian Association, 1978. 54 pp. Paper. No ISBN.

This volume of Cliff Wright's workshop series addresses some of the issues affecting Solomon Islands Christianity, such as traditional versus Christian views of God, ancestral spirits, and women's roles, and both identifies issues needing attention, and proposes solutions.

OC—OCEANIA

Vanuatu [New Hebrides]

See also OC143 and OC155.

OC264 Godden, Ruth
Lolowai: The Story of Charles Godden and the Western Pacific. Sydney, AT: Wentworth Press, 1967. 254 pp. No ISBN.

This biography of Charles Godden, missionary in the New Hebrides Islands, recounts the story of his life and martyrdom, from his correspondence.

OC265 Gundert-Hock, Sibylle
Mission und Wanderarbeit in Vanuatu: Eine Studie zum sozialen Wandel in Vanuatu, 1863-1915. Munich, GW: Minerva Publikation, 1986. 370 pp. 3597106064.

A thorough study of labor recruiting in Vanuatu, for work in Fiji and Queensland, and of the pros and cons of mission opposition to this practice.

OC266 Lindstrom, Lamont
Knowledge and Power in a South Pacific Society. (Smithsonian Series in Ethnographic Inquiry). Washington, DCU: Smithsonian Institution Press, 1990. xvi, 224 pp. 0874743656 (hdbk), 0874743575 (pbk).

A scholarly study of the systems of knowledge and power among the peoples of Tanna, an island of southern Vanuatu, with references to missionary and other Christian influences.

OC267 Miller, J. Graham
Live: A History of Church Planting in the New Hebrides (Vanuatu). Sydney, AT: Presbyterian Church of Australia (vols. 1-2); Port Vila, NN: Presbyterian Church of Vanuatu (vols. 3-7), 1978-1990. 7 vols.

Highly detailed reporting on each area and each era of the Presbyterian church's history up to 1948, based on primary sources, published in seven volumes [vol. 1, 201 pp. 0909503338; vol. 2, 197 pp. 0909503880; vol. 3, 388 pp. 0949197009; vol. 4, 441 pp. 0949197058; vol. 5, 462 pp. 0949197130; vol. 6, 534 pp. No ISBN; vol. 7, 544 pp. No ISBN].

OC268 Miller, R. S.
Misi Gete: John Geddie, Pioneer Missionary in the New Hebrides. Launceston, AT: Presbyterian Church of Tasmania, 1975. xx, 368 pp. 0909503184.

A highly appreciative biography of John Geddie, the founder and father of the Presbyterian church in Vanuatu.

OC269 Paton, John G.
John G. Paton: Missionary to the New Hebrides. Edited by James Paton. Carlisle, PAU: Banner of Truth Trust, 1994. ix, 524 pp. 085151667X.

A reissue of the autobiography of John G. Paton (1824-1907), pioneer Scottish Presbyterian missionary to the New Hebrides (Vanuatu); originally published in 1889.

OC270 Sarawia, George, and D. A. Rawcliffe
They Came to My Island: The Beginnings of the Mission in the Banks Islands. Siota, BP: St Peter's College, 1968. iv, 28 pp. Paper. No ISBN.

Reprint of the first history of the Anglican mission to the Banks Islands of Melanesia in the 19th century; by the first deacon, ordained 20 December 1868.

OC271 Wright, Cliff
New Hebridean Culture and Christian Faith: Two Hands and Two Hearts: Report of Education Workshop, Aulua, New Hebrides, April 19-May 3, 1979. (Workshop Report Series). Vila, NN: Pacific Churches Research Center, 1979. 35 pp. Paper. No ISBN.

This volume of Cliff Wright's Christian Education series addresses some of the local issues of Christian discipleship in Melanesian culture, including the traditional versus Christian understandings of God, marriage, education, healing, and so forth.

Micronesia: General Works

See also OC2, OC17, OC135, and OC153.

OC272 Hanlon, David
Upon a Stone Altar: A History of the Island of Pohnpei to 1890. (Pacific Islands Monograph Series, no. 5). Honolulu, HIU: University of Hawaii Press, 1988. xxviii, 320 pp. 0824811240.

A detailed history, based on archival research, of a Micronesian island deeply affected in the 19th century both by Spanish politics and the American Board (ABCFM) mission.

OC273 Hezel, Francis X.
The Catholic Church in Micronesia: Historical Essays on the Catholic Church in the Caroline-Marshall Islands. Chicago, ILU: Loyola University Press, 1991. viii, 294 pp. Paper. 0829407200.

A centennial history in five parts, each giving the detailed local history of Catholics in one of the five sections of Micronesia: Yap, Pohnpei, Chuuk, Palau, and the Marshall Islands.

OC274 Müller, Klaus W.
Evangelische Mission in Mikronesien (Trukinseln): Ein Missionar analysiert sein Missionsfeld. (Missiologica Evangelica, 2). Bonn, GW: Verlag für Kultur und Wissenschaft, 1989. 558 pp. Paper. 3926105283.

An M.A. thesis in missiology (Fuller Theological Seminary, 1979) on Protestant mission work on the Truk Islands.

OC275 Müller, Klaus W.
The Protestant Mission Work on the Truk Islands in Micronesia: A Missiological Analysis and Evaluation. (Fuller Theological Seminary School of World Mission Projects, 1981). Ann Arbor, MIU: University Microfilms (UMI), 1981. xv, 378 pp. No ISBN.

English translation.

OC276 Peoples, James G.
Island in Trust: Culture Change and Dependence in a Micronesian Economy. Boulder, COU: Westview Press, 1985. xii, 239 pp. Paper. 0813370345.

A general history of the island of Kosrae in Micronesia, including much church and mission history.

Kiribati [Gilbert Islands]

See also OC43.

OC277 Healey, Norman
A Brief Introduction to the Kiribati Protestant Church. Bairiki Tarawa, GB: Kiribati Protestant Church, 1983. 15 pp. No ISBN.
A brief popular history.

OC278 MacDonald, Barrie
Cinderellas of the Empire: Towards a History of Kiribati and Tuvalu. Canberra, AT: Australian National University Press, 1982. xx, 335 pp. Paper. 0708116167.
A basic history of these two countries, with a long chapter on Christian missions.

OC279 Sabatier, Ernest
Astride the Equator: An Account of the Gilbert Islands. Melbourne, AT: Oxford University Press, 1977. viii, 386 pp. 0195505182.
Translation of *Sous l'équateur du Pacifique, Les Iles Gilbert et la mission catholique (1888-1938)* (Paris: Editions Dillen, 1939), a classic examination by a missionary of the Kiribati people, followed by a careful history of the Roman Catholic mission.

Polynesia: General Works

See also SO112, OC26, OC29, OC67, OC296, and OC312.

OC280 Ellis, William
Polynesian Researches during a Residence of Nearly Six Years in the South Sea Islands. London, ENK: Dawsons of Pall Mall, 1967. 2 vols. No ISBN.
A reprint of the 1829 edition of a detailed account by an early missionary of the LMS; including descriptions of the natural history and scenery of the islands, with remarks on the history, mythology, traditions, government, arts, manners and customs of the inhabitants [vol. 1: xvi, 536 pp.; vol. 2: viii, 576 pp.].

OC281 Ellis, William
À la recherche de la Polynésie d'autrefois. Translated by Marie Sergueiew and Colette de Buyer-Mimeure. (Publications de la Société des océanistes, 25). Paris, FR: Société des océanistes, 1972. 2 vol. No ISBN.
French translation.

OC282 Gill, William Wyatt
From Darkness to Light in Polynesia. Suva, FJ: University of the South Pacific, Institute of Pacific Studies, 1984. 383 pp. Paper. No ISBN.
Reprint of an 1894 report on pre-Christian history and customs as they were revealed in traditional sayings, collected by this missionary in Rarotonga.

OC283 Gilson, Richard Phillip
The Cook Islands, 1820-1950. Wellington, NZ: Victoria University Press; Suva, FJ: University of the South Pacific, Institute of Pacific Studies, 1980. 242 pp. Paper. 0705507351.
A general history of mission and church activities, to around 1880.

OC284 Pratt, Addison
The Journals of Addison Pratt. (Publications in Mormon Studies, 6). Salt Lake City, UTU: University of Utah Press, 1990. xxiv, 606 pp. 0874803357.

The journals of Addison Pratt (d.1872), a pioneer Mormon missionary to the Society Islands in French Polynesia (1843-1852), edited by S. George Ellsworth.

OC285 Rere, Taira
History of the Papehia Family. Suva, FJ: Lotu Pasifika Productions, 1977. xvi, 70 pp. Paper. No ISBN.
A biography of the Society islander, Papehia or Papeiha, who introduced Christianity to Rarotonga, with notes on some of his descendents.

OC286 Siikala, Jukka
Cult and Conflict in Tropical Polynesia: A Study of Traditional Religion, Christianity, and Nativistic Movements. (FF Communications, 233). Helsinki, FI: Suomalainen Tiedeakatemia, 1982. 308 pp. Paper. 9514104420.
A complex sociohistorical study, examining the social implications of the change to Christianity, the influence of traditional religion on Christianity, and the mediating role of nativistic movements.

OC287 Strauss, Wallace Patrick
Americans in Polynesia, 1783-1842. East Lansing, MIU: Michigan State University Press, 1964. 187 pp. No ISBN.
A monograph in dissertation style with three chapters on American missionaries in Hawaii, with bibliographical references.

OC288 Thorogood, Bernard
Not Quite Paradise. London, ENK: London Missionary Society, 1960. 119 pp. No ISBN.
Stories of LMS work in the Cook Islands based on missionary correspondence and reminiscences.

OC289 Tippett, Alan Richard
People Movements in Southern Polynesia: Studies in the Dynamics of Church-Planting and Growth in Tahiti, New Zealand, Tonga, and Samoa. Chicago, ILU: Moody, 1971. 288 pp. No ISBN.
Anthropological and historical studies from southern Polynesia and New Zealand that reveal different responses to the Gospel in varied culture areas.

French Polynesia

OC290 Babadzan, Alain
Naissance d'une tradition: Changement culturel et syncrétisme religieux aux îles Australes (Polynésie Française). Paris, FR: Office de la Recherche Scientifique et Technique d'Outre-Mer, 1982. 313 pp. 2709906708.
A penetrating anthropological study of the "spiritual side" of life, both traditional and Christian, and of how they have met.

OC291 Bovis, Edmond de
État de la société tahitienne à l'arrivée des Européens. (Publication—Société des études océaniennes, 4). Papeete, FP: Société des études océaniennes, 1978. 74 pp. No ISBN.
A small but valuable source on ancient Tahitian culture with early missionary accounts; originally published in 1855.

OC292 Bovis, Edmond de
Tahitian Society before the Arrival of the Europeans. Translated by Robert D. Craig. (Publications of the Institute for Polynesian Studies Monograph Series, 1). Laie, HIU: Institute for Polynesian Studies, Brigham Young University, 1980. iv, 75 pp. Paper. No ISBN.
English translation.

OC—OCEANIA

OC293 Butterworth, F. Edward
Roots of the Reorganization: French Polynesia. Independence, MOU: Herald Publishing House, 1977. 266 pp. Paper. 0830901760.

A sequel to the author's earlier *Adventures of a South Sea Missionary*, covering one hundred years of South Sea history, from the point of view of Latter-day Saints' missions.

OC294 Davies, John Dudley, and Colin W. Newbury, eds.
The History of the Tahitian Mission, 1799-1830. (Hakluyt Society, Works, 2nd ser., 116). Cambridge, ENK: Cambridge University Press, 1961. liv, 392 pp. No ISBN.

The first publication of the eyewitness history of the LMS mission by one who served there (1801-1855), and had access to missionary letters and journals.

OC295 Hodée, Paul
Tahiti, 1834-1984 : 150 ans de vie chrétienne en église. Paris, FR: Éditions Saint-Paul, 1983. 702 pp. 2850492728.

A thorough history of the Catholic work in Tahiti.

OC296 Mauer, Daniel
Protestant Church at Tahiti. (Société des Oceanistes: Dossier, 6). Paris, FR: Nouvelles éditions latines; Paris, FR: Société des Oceanistes, 1970. 32 pp. Paper. No ISBN.

This short history of the mission and church work of Protestants on Tahiti gives insight into why Protestantism flourishes and Catholicism dies in French Polynesia; with captions in English and French.

OC297 Memoires d'Arii Taimai
Translated by Henry Adams. (Publications de la Société des oceanistes, 12). Paris, FR: Société des océanistes, 1964. xxiv, 165 pp. Paper. No ISBN.

A French translation of *Memoirs of Marau Taaroa: Last Queen of Tahiti* (1893) by Suzanne and André Lebois, the recollections of Arii Taimai (1821-1897), including Tahitian responses to Christian missions.

OC298 Newbury, Colin W.
Tahiti Nui: Change and Survival in French Polynesia, 1767-1945. Honolulu, HIU: University of Hawaii Press, 1980. xvi, 380 pp. 0824806301.

A well-written history of political, economic, and religious developments, including sections on missions and churches.

OC299 Nicole, Jaques
Au pied de l'Écriture: Histoire de la traduction de la Bible en Tahitien. Papeete, FP: Haere Po No Tahiti, 1988. 338 pp. Paper. 2904171185.

A fine piece of scholarship, worked into an interesting story, told in full detail.

OC300 O'Reilly, Patrick
Le Tahiti catholique. (Société des océanistes Dossier, 5). Paris, FR: Nouvelles éditions latines, 1969. 30 pp. No ISBN.

A brief history of Catholic missions in Tahiti, French Polynesia.

OC301 Toullelan, Pierre-Yves
Missionnaires au Quotidien a Tahiti: Les Picpuciens en Polynésie au XIXe siècle. (Studies in Christian Mission, 13). Leiden, NE: Brill, 1995. xii, 342 pp. 9004101004.

An account of the daily life of 167 Picpus fathers and brothers of the Congregation des Sacrés Cours de Jésus et de Marie in Tahiti, from 1834 to 1914, based on their correspondence.

OC302 Vernier, Henri
Au vent des cyclones—Puai Noa Mai Te Vero: histoire des missions Protestantes et de l'Église Évangelique à Tahiti et en Polynésie Française. Paris, FR: Les Bergers et les Mages, 1985. 465 pp. Paper. 2905832002.

A scholarly illustrated history of the missionary work in Tahiti and French Polynesia begun in 1797 by the Societé des Missions Évangeliques de Paris (Paris Evangelical Missionary Society), the steps to autonomy of the Evangelical church in 1963, with an analysis of cultural factors affecting evangelization in East (French) Polynesia.

Hawaiian Islands

See also OC17.

OC303 Ballegeer, Johan
Damiaan: Kamiano is liefde. Averbode, BE: Altiora, 1989. 142 pp. Paper. 9031707813.

Biography of the Belgian priest Damian (Jozef De Veuster, 1840-1889), who, during sixteen years, lived and labored among the exiled lepers on Molokai, one of the Hawaiian islands, until he, himself, died from this illness.

OC304 Boudens, Robrecht, ed.
Rond Damiaan: handelingen van het colloquium n.a.v. de honderdste verjaardag van het overlijden van pater Damiaan, 9-10 maart 1989. (KADOC-studies, 7). Louvain, BE: Universitaire Pers Leuven, 1989. 317 pp. 9061863406.

Papers read at a conference held in Louvain, Belgium, in March 1989, at the centennial of Father Damien's death; with biographical notes, as well as contributions on the Protestant and Roman Catholic missionary movements of the 19th century, and Damien's inspiration for today's missionaries and Third World churches.

OC305 Daws, Gavan
Damian de Molokai. Madrid, SP: Editorial Reinado Social, 1984. 320 pp. No ISBN.

Spanish translation.

OC306 Daws, Gavan
Damian de Veuster: Den Aussätzigen ein Aussätziger geworden. Freiburg, GW: Herder, 1988. 219 pp. 3451213605.

German translation.

OC307 Daws, Gavan
Holy Man, Father Damien of Molokai. Honolulu, HIU: University of Hawaii Press, 1984. xi, 293 pp. 0824809203.

Biography of the Belgian priest who ministered to exiled lepers on Molokai; originally published by Harper & Row in 1973.

OC308 French, Thomas
The Missionary Whaleship. New York, NYU: Vantage Press, 1961. 134 pp. No ISBN.

Inspired by historical research into the Christian endeavors of early American whaleships, this work focuses specifically on Henry Obookiah (Opukahaia), a crew member on the "Triumph" and the first Hawaiian student at the Foreign Mission School. It also traces biographical histories of early Sandwich Islands Mission missionaries.

OC—OCEANIA

OC309 Grimshaw, Patricia

Paths of Duty: American Missionary Wives in Nineteenth-Century Hawaii. Honolulu, HIU: University of Hawaii Press, 1989. xxiii, 246 pp. 0824812379.

A scholarly treatment of the manner in which American missionary wives—whose "call" to the mission field came in the form of marriage proposals to potential missionary men of the American Board of Commissioners for Foreign Missions (ABCFM)—influenced 19th-century Hawaiian women, through their ordinary Christian lifestyles and interactions with the Hawaiian people.

OC310 Hanley, Mary Laurence, and O. A. Bushnell

Pilgrimage and Exile: Mother Marianne of Molokai. Honolulu, HIU: University of Hawaii Press, 1991. xv, 427 pp. Paper. 0824813871.

A detailed biography of Mother Marianne of Molokai (1838-1918), a Franciscan Sister of Syracuse, New York, who pioneered work by the order in Hawaii, 1884 to 1918; originally published as *A Song of Pilgrimage and Exile* (Chicago, IL: Franciscan Herald Press, 1980).

OC311 Judd, Gerrit Parmele

Dr. Judd, Hawaii's Friend: A Biography of Gerrit Parmele Judd. Honolulu, HIU: University of Hawaii Press, 1960. 300 pp. No ISBN.

The dramatic career of Dr. Judd, missionary physician in the Hawaiian Islands (1828-1842), official in the Hawaiian government (1842-1853), planter, and industrialist; based on archival research by his great-grandson.

OC312 Loomis, Albertine G.

Grapes of Canaan: Hawaii 1820. Woodbridge, CTU: Ox Bow Press, 1998. 334 pp. Paper. No ISBN.

This dramatic mission story of the first company of New England missionaries, arriving in the Hawaiian Islands in the spring of 1820, is told by a talented novelist and descendant of one of those missionary families; originally published in 1951 (New York: Dodd, Mead).

OC313 Loomis, Albertine G.

To All People: A History of the Hawaii Conference of the United Church of Christ. Honolulu, HIU: United Church of Christ, 1970. xiv, 417 pp. Paper. No ISBN.

An appreciative history that concentrates on the church's outreach to distant islands and to the new peoples who came to Hawaii.

OC314 Mark, Diane Mei Lin

Seasons of Light:The History of Chinese Christian Churches in Hawaii. Honolulu, HIU: Chinese Christian Assn of Hawaii, 1989. xiii, 338 pp. No ISBN.

The first comprehensive history of Chinese Christianity in Hawaii, based on extensive oral history and archival research.

OC315 Miller, Char

Selected Writings of Hiram Bingham (1814-1869): Missionary to the Hawaiian Islands: To Raise the Lord's Banner. (Studies in American Religion, 31). Lewiston, NYU: E Mellen Press, 1988. 590 pp. 0889466750.

A biography of Hiram Bingham (1814-1869), pioneer missionary to Hawaii of the ABCFM, with a selection of his letters, highlighting the complexity of the mission activity.

OC316 Muth-Oelschner, Brigitte

Wo Liebe Lepra heilte: Damian de Veuster (Hawaii); (1840-1889, Mann der Stunde für Hawaii). (Missionare, die Geschichte machten). Mödling, AU: Verlag St. Gabriel; St. Augustin, GW: Steyler Verlag, 1982. 153 pp. Paper. 3852641845 (AU), 3877871534 (GW).

The life of the Belgian Picpus father and "Apostle of the Lepers," who worked on the island of Molokai, became infected himself, and died of leprosy.

OC317 Wagner-Wright, Sandra

The Structure of the Missionary Call to the Sandwich Islands, 1790-1830: Sojourners among Strangers. (Distinguished Dissertations Series, 2). San Francisco, CAU: Mellen Research University Press, 1990. xi, 225 pp. Paper. 0773499385.

A dissertation analyzing the motivations for mission, of the first twenty-seven American Board missionaries to Hawaii, their missionary society, and supporters.

OC318 Zweip, Mary

Pilgrim Path: The First Company of Women Missionaries to Hawaii. Madison, WIU: University of Wisconsin Press, 1991. xx, 376 pp. 0299129004 (hdbk), 0299129047 (pbk).

A detailed account, based on archival sources, of the lives and concerns of the first seven women missionaries of the American Board to Hawaii, 1820-1853.

Samoa

See also OC46.

OC319 Brewer, W. Karl

Armed with the Spirit: Missionary Experiences in Samoa. Provo, UTU: Young House, 1975. viii, 236 pp. 0842508171.

The autobiography of Karl Brewer—missionary in the Samoan Islands.

OC320 Faletoese, K. T.

Tala Faasolopito o le Ekalesia Samoa (L.M.S.): A History of the Samoa Church (L.M.S.). Apia, AS: Malua Printing Press, 1961. 88 pp. No ISBN.

A Samoan Christian writes the history of his church.

OC321 Garsee, Jarrell W.

Samoa Diary. (Missionary Reading Books, 1963-64). Kansas City, MOU: Nazarene Publishing House, 1963. 96 pp. Paper. No ISBN.

Diary of Jarrell Garsee, missionary to the island of Samoa, reflecting the challenges of five years of life and ministry in Samoan culture.

OC322 Gilson, Richard Phillip

Samoa 1830 to 1900: The Politics of a Multi-Cultural Community. Melbourne, AT: Oxford University Press, 1970. xviii, 457 pp. 0195503015.

A description of Samoa and its traditional culture, as well as an analysis of the forces (missionary, commercial, and political) that brought Samoa into the modern world.

OC323 Turner, George

Samoa, a Hundred Years Ago and Long Before. Suva, FJ: University of the South Pacific, Institute of Pacific Studies, 1989. xv, 266 pp. No ISBN.

Reprint of an 1884 report on the traditional life of Samoa by one of the early LMS missionaries.

OC–OCEANIA

Tonga

See also OC43 and OC289.

OC324 Farmer, Sarah S.
Tonga and the Friendly Islands. (Mission History Series, 2). Canberra, AT: Kalia Press, 1976. vi, 427 pp. Paper. 0909183007.

Written for young people, this history traces the early European contacts, the start of the Methodist mission, and its first thirty years of work; a reprint of the original 1855 edition.

OC325 Latukefu, Sione
Church and State in Tonga: The Wesleyan Methodist Missionaries and Political Development, 1822-1875. Honolulu, HIU: University Press of Hawaii; Canberra, AT: Australian National University Press, 1974. xvii, 302 pp. 0824803221.

A thesis on the influence by Wesleyan Methodist missionaries on political developments in that island kingdom of Tonga, from their entry in 1822 to the establishment of a constitutional monarchy in 1875.

OC326 Mafi, Tevita Feke
Sunday School in the Church of Tonga. [Suva, FJ]: [Pacific Theological College], 1978. 126 pp. No ISBN.

A project presented to the faculty of the Pacific Theological College.

OC327 Rowe, G. Stringer
A Pioneer: A Memoir of the Rev. John Thomas, Missionary to the Friendly Islands. Canberra, AT: Kalia Press, 1976. 136 pp. 0909183015.

Reprint of an uncritical, but informative, biography; originally published in 1885 (London, ENK: T. Woolmer).

OC328 Rutherford, Noel, ed.
Friendly Islands: A History of Tonga. New York, NYU: Oxford University Press, 1977. xii, 297 pp. 0195505190.

Chapters by thirteen eminent authors, providing treatments, among other things, of the chief churches and church leaders.

OC329 Wright, Cliff
Seeds of the Word: Tongan Culture and Christian Faith. (Workshop Report Series). Vila, NN: Pacific Churches Research Centre, 1980. 43 pp. Paper. 0959288201.

This volume of Cliff Wright's Christian Education series addresses the problem of the "split" between traditional practices and Christian beliefs. The aim of the workshop was to address some of these issues in the Tongan context, and to propose solutions for a more fully integrated faith.

OC—OCEANIA

Contributors

Edith Bernard. Associate Director, CEDIM, Paris, France (*French*).

Stephen Bevans, SVD. Louis J. Luzbetak SVD Professor of Mission and Culture, Catholic Theological Union; Director, Chicago Center for Global Ministries, Chicago, Illinois; Editor, *Mission Studies* (*Missions: Theology*).

Eduardo Bierzychudek. Bibliographer; Editor, *Bibliografía Teologica Comentada del Area iberoamericana*, Buenos Aires, Argentina (*South America; Portuguese, Spanish*).

Gustaf Björck. Swedish Institute for Missionary Research, Uppsala, Sweden (*Swedish*).

Jonathan Bonk. Director, Overseas Ministries Study Center, Editor, *International Bulletin of Missionary Research*, New Haven, Connecticut (*Missions and Economic Life*).

David Jacobus Bosch. Deceased. Former Professor of Mission, and Chair, Department of Missiology, University of South Africa, Pretoria, South Africa (*Missions: Theology*).

Joyce Bowers. Senior Secretary, Division for Global Mission, Evangelical Lutheran Church in America, Chicago, Illinois (*Missionaries*).

David Bundy. Librarian and Associate Professor of Church History, Christian Theological Seminary, Indianapolis, Indiana (*Middle East; Hungarian, Polish, Russian*).

Walter Cason. Professor Emeritus, World Christian Mission, Garrett-Evangelical Theological Seminary, Evanston, Illinois (*Africa*).

H. McKennie Goodpasture. Deceased. Formerly F. S. Royster Professor Emeritus of Christian Missions, Union Theological Seminary and Presbyterian School of Christian Education, Richmond, Virginia (*The Americas: General Works, Mexico, Mesoamerica*).

Adrian Hastings. Deceased. Formerly Emeritus Professor, Department of Theology and Religious Studies, University of Leeds, Leeds, England (*Africa*).

Roger Hedlund. Professor of Mission Studies (Research), Serampore College, Madras, India (*South Asia*).

Paul Hiebert. Professor of Mission and Anthropology and Associate Dean of Academic Doctoral Programs, Trinity Evangelical Divinity School, Deerfield, Illinois (*Missions: Social Aspects*).

Paul Jenkins. Archivist, Basel Mission, Basel, Switzerland (*Europe*).

Paul Knitter. Professor of Theology, Xavier University, Cincinnati, Ohio; Editor, Faith Meets Faith Series, Orbis Books (*Christianity and Other Religions*).

Leny Lagerwerf. IIMO-Department of Missiology, Leiden, the Netherlands (*Dutch*).

Lois McKinney-Douglas. Professor Emerita of Missions, Trinity International University, Deerfield, Illinois (*Education and Missions*).

Mary Motte, FMM. Director, Mission Research Center, Franciscan Sisters of Mary, North Providence, Rhode Island (*Missions: Methods*).

Karl M. Müller, SVD. Deceased. Professor Emeritus of Missiology, Philosophisch-Theologische Hochschule SVD, Sankt Augustine, Germany (*German*).

Alan Neely. Deceased. Formerly Henry Winters Luce Emeritus Professor of Ecumenics and Mission, Princeton Theological Seminary, Princeton, New Jersey (*Missions and Political Life*).

Larry Nemer, SVD. President of the Missionary Institute of London, London, England (*Spirituality, Worship, and Mission*).

Gisela Wernicke Olesen. Librarian, State and University Library, Arhus, Denmark (*Danish*).

Stephen Peterson. Librarian, Trinity College, Hartford, Connecticut (*Missions: General Works*).

James M. Phillips. Former Associate Director, Overseas Ministries Study Center, New Haven, Connecticut (*East Asia*).

Liisa Rajamäki. Librarian, Faculty of Theology Library, University of Helsinki, Helsinki, Finland (*Finnish*).

Dana Robert. Truman Collins Professor of World Mission, Boston University School of Theology, Boston, Massachusetts (*Missions: History*).

John Roxborogh. Chair, Department of Mission Studies, Bible College of New Zealand, Haitakere City, New Zealand (*Southeast Asia*).

Arne B. Samuelsen. Librarian, Missionshøgskolen, Stavanger, Norway; Editor, *Missio Nordica* (*Norwegian*).

Howard A. Snyder. Professor of the History and Theology of Mission, E. Stanley Jones School of World Mission and Evangelism, Asbury Theological Seminary, Wilmore, Kentucky (*Mission and Local Church Renewal*).

Viggo B. Søgaard. Associate Professsor of Communication, Fuller Theological Seminary; Professor, Grindsted, Denmark (*Communications and Missions*).

Norman E. Thomas. Vera B. Blinn Professor Emeritus of World Christianity, United Theological Seminary, Dayton, Ohio (*General Editor; Missions: Ecumenical Aspects*).

Ruth Tucker. Writer. Visiting Professor of Mission, Trinity International University, Deerfield, Illinois (*Missionaries*).

Gerdien Verstraelen-Gilhuis. Deceased. Former Senior Lecturer, Department of Religious Studies, Classics and Philosophy, University of Zimbabwe, Harare, Zimbabwe (*Africa*).

Andrew Walls. Founding Director, Center for the Study of Christianity in the Non-Western World, University of Edinburgh, Edinburgh, Scotland (*Canada, Native America, the Caribbean*).

David Lowes Watson. Director, Office of Pastoral Formation, Nashville Episcopal Area, United Methodist Church, Nashville, Tennessee (*Evangelism and Missions*).

Darrell Whiteman. Dean, E. Stanley Jones School of World Mission, Asbury Theological Seminary, Wilmore, Kentucky (*Oceania*).

Wolveig Widen. Librarian, Turku, Finland (*Swedish*).

Sources

Anderson, Gerald H., ed. *Biographical Dictionary of Christian Missions.* New York: Macmillan, 1998.

————— . *The Theology of the Christian Mission.* New York: McGraw-Hill, 1961.

Athyal, Saphir, ed. *Church in Asia Today: Challenges and Opportunities.* Singapore: Asia LCWE, 1996.

Barrett, David B., George T. Kurian, and Todd M. Johnson. *World Christian Encyclopedia.* 2nd. ed. London and New York: Oxford University Press, 2001.

Barrett, David B., and Todd M. Johnson. *World Christian Trends, A.D. 30-A.D.2200.* Pasadena, CA: William Carey Library, 2001.

Bibliografia Missionaria. 1935- Annual. Willi Henkel, ed. Rome: L'Unione missionaria del clero in Italia.

Bibliografia Teologia Comentada del Area Iberoamericana. 1971- Annual. Buenos Aires, Argentina: ISADET.

Bosch, David J. *Transforming Mission: Paradigm Shifts in Theology of Mission.* Maryknoll, NY: Orbis Books, 1991.

Brunner, Emil. *The Word and the World.* London: Scribners, 1931.

Carden, John, comp. *With All God's People: The New Ecumenical Prayer Cycle.* Mystic, CT: Twenty-Third Publications, 1990.

Fahey, Michael A., comp. *Ecumenism: A Bibliographical Overview.* Westport, CT: Greenwood Press, 1992.

Forrester, Duncan B. "Christianity in Europe," in *Religion in Europe: Contemporary Perspectives,* ed. Sean Gill, Gavin D'Costa, and Ursula King, 34-45. Kampen, NE: Kok Pharos, 1994.

Grundmann, Christoffer H. *Gesandt zu heilen!: Aufkommen und Entwicklung der arztlichen Mission in neunzehnten Jahrhundert.* Gutersloh, GW: Gerd Mohn, 1992.

Guder, Darrell L., ed. *Missional Church: A Vision for the Sending of the Church in North America.* Grand Rapids, MI: Eerdmans, 1998.

Hiebert, Paul G. "Critical Issues in the Social Sciences and Their Implications for Mission Studies." *Missiology* 24 (1996): 93-109.

International Review of Missions/Mission. 1912- Quarterly. London: IMC, 1912-1969; Geneva: WCC, 1969- .

Johnstone, Patrick. *Operation World: The Day-by-Day Guide to Praying for the World.* 5th ed. Grand Rapids, MI: Zondervan, 1993; Colorado Springs, CO: Global Mapping International, 2001 (electronic version).

Jongeneel, J. A. B. *Philosophy, Science and Theology of Mission in the 19th and 20th Centuries.* 2 vols. Frankfurt am Main, GW: Peter Lang, 1995, 1997.

Kane, James Herbert. *Understanding Christian Missions.* Chicago, IL: Moody Press, 1961.

Kuper, Adam, and Jessica Kuper, eds. *The Social Science Encyclopedia.* London: Routledge, 1985.

Latourette, Kenneth Scott. *A History of the Expansion of Christianity.* 7 vols. Grand Rapids, MI: Zondervan, 1978.

Lossky, Nicholas, et al. *Dictionary of the Ecumenical Movement.* Geneva: WCC; Grand Rapids, MI: Eerdmans, 1991.

Missionalia. 1973- Three issues yearly. Pretoria, South Africa: South African Missiological Society.

Missionary Research Library (New York). *Dictionary Catalog of the Missionary Research Library.* 17 vols. Boston, MA: G. K. Hall., 1968.

Moreau, A. Scott, ed. *Evangelical Dictionary of World Missions.* Grand Rapids, MI: Baker Books, 2000.

Müller, Karl, et al. *Dictionary of Mission: Theology, History, Perspectives.* Maryknoll, NY: Orbis, 1997.

Neill, Stephen, Gerald H. Anderson, and John Goodwin. *Concise Dictionary of the Christian World Mission.* Nashville, TN: Abingdon, 1971.

Neue Zeitschrift für Missionswissenschaft. 1945- Quarterly. Immensee, SZ: Verein zur Förderung der Missionswissenschaft [Association for Promoting Mission Studies].

Nida, Eugene A. *Message and Mission: The Communication of the Christian Faith.* Rev. ed. Pasadena, CA: William Carey Library, 1990.

Noll, Mark A. "The Challenges of Contemporary Church History, the Dilemmas of Modern History, and Missiology to the Rescue." *Missiology* 24 (1996): 47-64.

Pierson, Paul E. "Ecumenical Movement," in *Evangelical Dictionary of World Missions,* ed. A. Scott Moreau, 300-303. Grand Rapids, MI: Baker, 2000.

Religion Index One. Periodicals. 1977- Semiannual. Chicago, IL: ATLA.

Schreiter, Robert J. "Cutting-Edge Issues in Theology and Their Bearing on Mission Studies." *Missiology* 24 (1996): 83-92.

Soards, Marion L. "Key Issues in Biblical Studies and Their Bearing on Mission Studies." *Missiology* 24 (1996): 93-109.

Streit, Robert, and Johannes Dindinger. *Bibliotheca Missionum.* 29 vols. in 31. Freiburg im Breisgau, GW: Herder, 1916- .

Survey of Literature on the Christian Mission and Christianity in the Non-Western World. 1977- Irregular. Andrew F. Walls, ed. Aberdeen, UK: Centre for the Study of Christianity in the Non-Western World.

Turner, Harold W. *Bibliography of New Religious Movements in Primal Societies.* 6 vols. Boston, MA: G. K. Hall, 1977-1992.

Verkuyl, Johannes. *Contemporary Missiology: An Introduction.* Grand Rapids, MI: Eerdmans, 1978.

Vriens, Livinus. *Critical Bibliography of Missiology.* Nijmegen, NE: Bestelcentrale der V.S.K.B., 1960.

Walls, Andrew. "Missiology," in *Dictionary of the Ecumenical Movement,* Nicholas Lossky, et al., eds., 689-90. Geneva: WCC, 1991.

World Almanac. 2002 edition. New York: World Almanac Books, 2001.

World Book Encyclopedia. Millennium 2000 edition. Chicago, IL: World Book, 2000.

Index of Personal Names

Numbers refer to entry numbers in the bibliography. Ex.: OC55 is the 55th entry in the Oceania chapter

INDEX

INDEX

INDEX

INDEX

Haas, Odo	TH240
Haas, Waltraud	AF27, HI477, HI478, MI192
Habel, Norman C.	OC140
Habig, Marion Alphonse	AM350
Habito, Ruben L. F.	CR694, GW196
Hackett, David G.	CR695
Hackett, Rosalind I. J.	AF1321, SO304
Hadaway, C. Kirk	CH379, CH41, EV322, EV362, EV532, SO560
Haddad, Robert M.	AS789
Haddad, Wadi Zaidan	CR986
Haddad, Yvonne Yazbeck	CR1089, CR1090, CR986, SO434
Hadden, Jeffrey K.	CO155, PO179
Hadjor, Kofi Buenor	TH533
Hadley, Diana W.	AM894
Hageman, Alice L.	AM572, AM573
Hagemann, Ludwig	CR1004, CR987, CR988, CR989
Hagen, Kristofer	SO581
Haggard, Ted	SO546, SO547
Haglund, Ake	CR776
Hagstrom, Aurelie A.	CH485
Hagstrom, Jane Stewart	SO416
Hahn, Celia A.	CH259
Hahn, Christoph	CR627
Hahn, Ferdinand	HI596, TH241, TH242
Hahn, Gertrud	CR627
Haight, Roger	TH72
Haile, Getatchew	AF500
Haines, Byron L.	CR990
Haines, J. Harry	MI44
Hale, J. Russell	EV323
Hale, Thomas	AS1231, AS1232, MI118
Haliburton, Gordon Mackay	SO305, SO306
Hall, Cameron P.	EC366
Hall, David	EU17
Hall, Douglas John	EC200, ME242, SP156, TH73, TH74, TH75
Hall, George Fridolph	HI520
Hall, Judy	SO424
Hall, Mary	AM1331
Hall, Noeline	OC114
Hall, Penelope R.	CR650
Hall, Peter	AF1251
Hallberg, Daniel	AM1255
Hallden, Erik	AF1224
Hallencreutz, Carl F.	AF1153, AF1154, AF302, AF338, AM964, CR148, CR478, EA133, EA181, EU291, GW104, GW147, GW148, GW22, HI582, HI701, HI702, HI703, PO19
Hallman, David G.	EC201
Hallum, Anne Motley	AM680
Halmesmaa, Ritva	ME79
Halteman, James	EC176
Halverson, Alton C. O.	AF566
Halverson, Dean C.	CR332
Halverson, Delia	ME200
Halvorson, Loren E.	ME170
Ham, Sok Hon	AS713
Hamada, Louis Bahjat	CR1115, CR1116
Hambrick-Stowe, Charles E.	EV272
Hambye, E. R.	AS1044
Hamel, Johannes	EU195
Hämelin, Eila	HI699
Hamer, Heyo E.	AS675
Hames, E. W.	OC115, OC116
Hamid, Idris	AM608
Hamilton, Don	MI45
Hamilton, Florence Olivia	AS530
Hamilton, Keith E.	AM1240
Hamm, Heinrich	TH56
Hammer, Karl	PO146
Hämmerle, Johannes Maria	AS1305
Hammerstein, Franz Von	CR1220, CR1221
Hammett, Edward H.	CH42, CH43
Hammond, Phillip E.	SO264
Hampson, Tom	ME171
Hampton, Vinita	SP157
Han, Gil Soo	AS741
Hanawalt, Emily Albu	CR333
Hance, Gertrude Rachel	AF1003
Hanchey, Howard	CH44, EV533
Hancock, Robert Lincoln	EC273
Hand, Thomas G.	CR782
Handl, Matilda	HI334
Haney, Marsha Snulligan	AM1047
Haney, Paul	ME162
Hang, Thaddaeus T'ui-Chieh	AS354, CR777
Hanh, Thich Nhat	CR663, CR696, CR697
Hanke, Lewis	AM17, AM79, AM80
Hankins, Gerald W.	AS1233
Hanks, Billie	EV455
Hanley, Mary Laurence	OC310
Hanlon, David	OC272
Hann, John H.	AM1144
Hanselmann, Siegfried	AS839
Hansen, Bent Smidt	CR835
Hansen, Elly	AS1490
Hansen, Holger Bernt	AF454, AF716
Hansen, Lillian E.	AS1164
Hanson, Eric O.	AS291, HI494, PO20
Hanson, Irene	AS445
Hansson, Gurli	AF1155
Hao, Yap Kim	AS175, AS44, AS98, CR991, TH252
Haque, A.	EA123
Harakas, Stanley Samuel	SO24
Harbsmeier, Eberhard	AS1031
Hardin, Daniel	ME49
Harding, Joe A.	CH45
Hardman, Keith J.	EV234, EV273
Hardy, Gilbert G.	SP94
Hardy, Richard P.	AS1436
Hardyman, John T.	HI457
Hare, Eric B.	OC161
Hargleroad, Bobbi Wells	EC335, EC342
Hargreaves, Cecil	AS176, AS276
Häring, Bernhard	EV167
Häring, Hermann	CR330, CR331
Harjula, Raimo	ME50
Harley, C. David	MI76, MI77
Harley, Winifred J.	AF1283
Harlin, Tord	AF1156
Harling, Per	SP232
Harmer, Catherine M.	EC113, ME243
Harms, Hartwig F.	HI560
Harper, Charles	PO59
Harper, Michael	CH214
Harper, Nile	SO548
Harper, Susan Billington	AS1165
Harr, Wilber C.	GW149
Harre, Alan F.	EV534
Harrelson, Walter J.	CR1195, CR1222
Harrington, Ann M.	AS618
Harrington, Daniel J.	CR1192
Harris, Barbara Jean	SO428
Harris, Dorothy	OC82
Harris, James H.	CO140
Harris, John	AF365, HI440, OC83
Harris, Lillian Craig	AS531
Harris, Marvin	SO110
Harris, Paul William	HI381
Harris, Ralph W.	CH195
Harris, W. Stuart	EU18
Harrison, Dan	MI78
Harrison, Elizabeth	EC254
Harrison, Everett Falconer	HI81
Harrison, J. W.	AF717
Harrison, Mary	AF404
Harrison, Myron S.	ME124
Harrison, Richard L.	HI433
Harrison, Sue	CR643
Harrison, William Pope	AM1048
Harrod, Howard L.	AM1145
Harskamp, Anton van	EU187
Harst, Paul van der	AM941
Hartley, Loyde H.	SO1
Hartley, R. W.	GW4
Hartmann, Günter	AM1332
Hartwich, Richard	AS355
Hartzfeld, David F.	HI426
Harvey, Anthony	SO549
Harvey, Barry A.	TH587
Harvey, Bonnie C.	HI150
Harvey, Edwin	MI169
Harvey, K. Meyer	AM696
Harvey, William J.	HI569
Häselbarth, Hans	AF1000, AF1001, AF162
Haselden, Kyle	AM1089
Haslam, David	AM942, EU130
Hasselhorn, Fritz	AF1004
Hassett, John	AM459
Hassig, Ross	CR653
Hastings, Adrian	AF163, AF164, AF49, AF50, AF80, AF81, AF82, AF83, AF867, HI184, HI40
Hatakka, Kyllikki	AF880
Hater, Robert J.	EV81
Hathaway, Brian	CH120
Hatler, Grace	AM722
Hattingh, J. L.	AF933
Hatton, Desmond J.	AF165
Haubert, Maxime	AF1198, AM1452
Hauerwas, Stanley	CH46, EV581
Haug, Hellmut	SP158, SP159, SP160
Hauge, Svend	ME64
Hauken, Tor	HI584
Haule, Cosmas	AF166
Haumann, Tjeu	AF536
Haupt, Jean	PO176
Hausberger, Bernd	AM836
Hauzenberger, Hans	EA80
Hawker, David B. G.	AS1234
Hawkins, O. S.	CH47, EV456
Hawley, John C.	EV196
Hawthorne, Steven C.	GW150, GW236, MI46

INDEX

INDEX

INDEX

Miller, C. John	CH71	Mizuno, Michelle	EC351	Moore, Brian	HI361
Miller, Char	OC29, OC315	Mjagkij, Nina	HI736	Moore, D. M.	SO324
Miller, Christopher L.	AM1166	Mlotshwa, Thulani	AF969	Moore, Hyatt	OC176
Miller, Craig Kennet	SP202	Moberg, David O.	EV591	Moore, James F.	CR1277
Miller, Daniel R.	AM160	Mobley, Harris W.	AF1257	Moore, James T.	AM1170
Miller, Darrow L.	EC33	Modehn, Christian	AM475	Moore, Moses N.	AF1208
Miller, David C.	AF367	Moder-Frei, Elfi	CR864	Moore, Paul	AM1015, AM1225
Miller, Deo	AS1257	Moen, Matthew C.	PO30	Moore, Richard E.	CH395
Miller, Elmer S.	AM1263	Moessner-Stevenson, Jeanne	MI157	Moore, Robert Laurence	CO39
Miller, Herb	CH252, CH282, CH302,	Moffett, Samuel Hugh	AS46, AS725	Moore, Sidney	OC220
	EV352, EV555	Moffitt, John	CR865	Moore, Waylon B.	EV353
Miller, Inger	AF1043	Mofokeng, Takatso A.	AF320	Moorehead, Alan	AF358
Miller, J. Graham	OC267	Mohammed, Ovey N.	CR1022	Mooren, Thomas	CR195
Miller, John H.	SO177	Mohney, Ralph W.	CH45	Moorhead, Marion F.	AS627 AS628
Miller, Jon	AF1256	Moinz, John	CR866	Moorhouse, Geoffrey	AF56
Miller, Paul M.	AF458	Moir, John S.	AM633	Moorman, Donald	AM1032
Miller, R. S.	OC268	Mojzes, Paul	CR243, CR420, CR503, EC71,	Moosa, Matti	AS854
Miller, Roland E.	CR1095		EC72	Moothart, Lorene	HI428
Miller, Ronald Henry	CR1275	Mol, Hans	EU22, OC122, OC123, OC92,	Morales, Adam	AM161
Miller, Vernell Klassen	AM913		OC93	Moran, Gabriel	CR1278
Miller, William McElwee	AS817, CR1126	Molendijk, Arie L.	EV113	Moravcsik, Gyula	HI170
Milligan, Edward Hyslop	HI497	Molgaard, Lausten A.	AF510	Moreau, A. Scott	CR593
Milligan, William J.	EU21	Molineaux, David	TH497	Morehouse, Joyce	AS341
Millikan, David	OC82	Mollenkott, Virginia Ramey	SO440	Moreira, Alberto	SO381
Millington, Constance M.	AS1024	Møller, Arvid	AM1428	Morel, Yves	AF487
Millot, René Pierre	HI189, HI190	Möller, Hans-Georg	AS364	Moreno Rejón, Francisco	AM476, TH598,
Millwood, David	EC378, ME217	Molo, Kakule	AF135		TH599, TH600
Milner, Clyde A.	AM1167, AM1168	Moloney, Michael	SO502	Moretto, Giovanni	AS182
Milot, Jean-René	CR1019, CR1020	Moltke, Rodolfo von	CO103	Morgenthaler, Sally	SP213
Milton, A. Leslie	AF998	Moltmann, Jürgen	AS198, CH131, CH132,	Morikawa, Jitsuo	EV354
Milton, Ralph	CO161		CH133, CR1000, CR347,	Morioka, Kiyomi	CR1429
Min, Anselm Kyongsuk	AS736, TH452		CR489, PO65, TH360	Moritzen, Niels Peter	AS469, CR1411,
Mina, Gian Paola	AF542, AF543	Molton, Warren Lane	CH249		GW9, HI472, HI51
Minamiki, George	AS381	Molynuex, K. Gordon	AF321	Morlang, Francesco	AF635
Minear, Larry	EC126, PO196	Momigliano, Arnaldo	HI89	Morley, Janet	SP222
Mink, Nelson G.	OC48	Mommaers, Paul	CR725	Morley, Lewis	AM1406
Minnix, Kathleen	EV278	Moncaut, Carlos Antonio	AM1264	Mörner, Magnus	AM91
Minton, Wilson P.	AS658	Monchanin, Jules	SP64	Morrell, W. P.	OC124
Minus, Paul Murray	EC102	Mondin, Battista	HI329	Morrett, John J.	AM1016
Minz, Nirmal	CR862	Money, Herbert	AM1505	Morris, Colin	AF184, AF757, PO108
Miranda, José Porfirio	EC69, EC70, EC78,	Mongour, Paul	AS1186	Morris, George E.	CH73, EV452, EV453
	EC79	Monloubou, Louis	SP266	Morris, Henry	AS1187
Miranda-Feliciano, Evelyn	AS1453	Monsiváis, Carlos	AM867	Morris, James	EV279
Mirbach, Wolfram	SO371	Monsma, Timothy M.	AF183, SO541	Morris, John E.	AS757
Mires, Fernando	AM96, AM97, AM98	Montclos, Xavier de	AF257, HI303	Morris, John Hughes	AS1025
Mirtschink, Bernhard	AF689	Montefiore, Hugh	SO170	Morris, Louise	AS1495
Mische, Gerald	PO187	Monterroso, Victor M.	AM167, AM168	Morris, Raymond P.	ED1
Mische, Patricia	PO187	Montes de Oca, Alba Leticia	AM1265	Morrison, Dane	AM1171
Mischung, Roland	AS1494	Montgomery, Helen Barrett	HI141	Morrison, Mary	EA188
Misztal, Bronislaw	PO29	Montgomery, Jim	AS1455, EV412, ME249	Morrissey, Thomas	HI278
Mitchell, David I.	AM549	Montgomery, Robert L.	CR375, SO91	Morrow, Honoré Willsie	AS1393, AS1394,
Mitchell, David J.	HI277	Montgomery, Tommie Sue	AM727		AS1395
Mitchell, Donald W.	CR724	Montgomery, William E.	AM1053	Morrow, Theodore	PO24
Mitchell, James E.	AM866	Montgomery-Fate, Tom	AS1456	Morschel, Roque	HI248
Mitchell, Joseph	AM1169	Monti, Joseph E.	CR1276	Morse, Merrill	CR196
Mitchell, Mairin	AS1454	Montoya, Antonio Ruiz de	AM1459	Mortenson, Patricia	MI156
Mitchell, Peter M.	AS382	Montoya, Santa Catalina Laura de	HI358	Mortenson, Vernon	HI466, HI467
Mitchell, Robert Bryant	MI194	Moody, Linda A.	TH505	Morton, C. Manly	AM1460
Mitchell, Robert Cameron	SO3	Mooken, George	HI159	Morton, Don	AF822
Mitchell, Ron	CH426	Mookenthottam, Antony	AS268	Morton, T. Ralph	CH483, CH484
Mitchell, Timothy J.	MI3	Moomaw, I. W.	EC127	Mosala, Itumeleng J.	AF1107, AF324,
Mitra, Kana	CR863	Moon, Cyris H. S.	AS199, EA31		TH279
Mitri, Tarek	CR1021	Mooney, Catherine M.	AM1014	Mosatche, Harriet S.	CR1490
Mittelberg, Mark	EV474	Mooney, Mary	AM130	Moser, Antonio	TH601
Mitterhöfer, Jakob	TH109	Mooneyham, W. Stanley	EC128, EV42	Moser, Bruno	HI191
Miyata, Mitsuo	AS659	Mooradkanian, Helen S.	GW262	Moser, Georg	AS470
Mizuki, John	AM1347	Moore, Basil	AF322, AF323	Moser, Mary Theresa	EU179

INDEX

INDEX

Powlison, David	CR1494	Purvis, Patricia	CO117	Ramírez, Susan E.	AM882
Poynor, Alice	HI684	Pury, Pascal de	EC368	Ramlov, Preben	AM552
Prabhavananda, Swami	CR882	Puthenpurakal, Joseph	AS1055	Ramos, Demetrio	AM102
Prabhu, Joseph	CR212	Pycke, Nestor	HI230	Ramos, Marcos Antonio	AM578, AM579
Pradervand, Marcel	EA218	Quarcoopome, Nii Otokunor	CR613	Ramos, Myra Bergman	ED79
Prance, Ghillean T.	EC193	Quarles van Ufford, Philip	AS1348, EC295	Ramos, Rutilio	AM883
Prang, Margaret	AS702	Quebedeaux, Richard	EV283	Ramsden, William E.	CH178
Pranger, Jan Hendrik	EA192	Queen, Christopher S.	CR763	Rand, Stephen	ME67
Pratt, Addison	OC284	Quesnel, Roger	AF784	Randall, Albert B.	CR395
Pratt, Douglas	CR1314	Quigley, Thomas E.	AM255	Randall, Margaret	AM954, AM955
Pratt, W. E. Akinumi	AF1369	Quinn, Charles Underhill	AS1507, EC281,	Randall, Max Ward	AF761
Prawdzik, Werner	AS467, CR64, GW197,		PO111, PO160	Randall, Peter	AF1073, AF1074, AF1075,
	SO179	Quinn, Edward	CH135, CH202		AF1076, AF1077
Preiswerk, Matías	ED146, ED147, ED82	Quinn, Richard F.	ME219	Randwijck, S. C. Graaf van	EU227, SO25
Prendergast, Olga	CH221	Quirk, Robert E.	AM881	Ranger, Terence O.	AF1172, AF359, AF695,
Prent, K.	AS1347	Quiróz Magaña, Alvaro	AM492		CR614
Presler, Henry Hughes	AS1054, SO642	Qurra, Theodor Abu	CR969	Rankin, Jerry	AS564
Pretiz, Paul E.	AM123, AM124	Raabe, Gerhard	CR81	Ranson, Charles W.	EA111
Pretorius, H. L.	AF1068, AF818, SO346,	Raaflaub, Fritz	HI476, HI481	Rao, Ch. G.S.S. Sreenivasa	CR883
	SO347	Raalt, Jannes van	ME255	Rao, Mark Sunder	AS272
Price, Arnold H.	AF572	Raalte, Jannes van	AM1518, EU23	Rao, O. M.	AS1061, AS273
Price, Elizabeth Lees	AF851	Rabe, Valentin H.	AS388	Rao, R. R. Sundara	CR884
Price, Eva Jane	AS560	Raber, Dorothy A.	AS771	Rao, Sreenivasa	CR518
Price, Frank W.	ED4	Race, Alan	CR215	Raphael, Pierre	SO515
Price, Lynne	CR516, EU132	Racheiviltz, Igor de	AS761	Rapley, Elizabeth	EU181
Price, Simon	EU217	Rademacher, William J.	CH492	Rapold, Walter F.	AF620
Price, Thomas	AF604	Rader, Dick Allen	AF209	Raschzok, Klaus	SP180
Prickett, Barbara	AF1238	Rae, Muriel W.	AS562	Rasmussen, Jørgen Nybo	AM920, AM921
Prickett, John	CR394	Rae, Simon	AS1349	Rasmussen, Larry L.	EC211
Prien, Hans-Jürgen	AM101, AM1353, AM37	Raen, Guttorm	TH304	Rasmussen, Lissi	AF1345
Priest, Doug	AF548, HI436, TH303	Rafael, Vicente L.	AS1465	Rasolondraibe, Péri	TH98
Primavesi, Anne	SP251	Rafransoa, Maxine	AF128	Rasooli, Jay M.	MI196
Prina, Marco	AF638	Ragsdale, John P.	ED25	Rath, Josef Theodor	HI262
Prince, Derek	AS845	Raguin, Yves	CR216, CR217, SP106, SP73	Ratliff, Joe S.	EV415
Prince, Lydia	AS845	Raheb, Mitri	AS847, AS848	Ratnasekera, Leopold	CR220
Prior, Andrew	AF1069	Rahner, Karl	CH135, GW199	Ratschow, Carl Heinz	CR131, CR221
Prior, David	CH365, EV559	Rainer, Thom S.	CH82, EV122, EV123,	Ratti, Maria Teresa	AF637
Prior, Michael	AS846		EV359, EV374, EV561	Ratz, Calvin C.	AS565, EV562
Pritchard, Elizabeth	HI628	Raines, Robert A.	CH290, CH291	Ratzinger, Joseph	EU24, EU25
Pritchard, Gregory A.	EV560	Räisänen, Heikki	CR517	Ratzmann, Wolfgang	CH293
Pritchard, Rena	OC80	Raiser, Konrad	EA58	Rauff, Edward A.	EV563
Procter, Lovell J.	AF819	Raittila, Anna-Maija	SP287	Raupp, Werner	HI510
Proctor, Frank	ED163	Raj, Christopher S.	AS1035, AS1093	Rausch, David A.	AM1183, CR1315,
Prodolliet, Simone	HI480	Raj, P. Solomon	AS1056		CR1316, CR1317, CR396
Promper, Werner	AM166	Raj, Paul R.	AS1057	Rausch, Jane M.	AM17
Proniseas, Ni Chathain	EU213	Raja, R. J.	AS270	Rausch, John S.	AM992
Proske, Wolfgang	AF852	Rajamanickam, Svarimuthu	AS1058, AS1200,	Rausch, Thomas P.	CH294
Prothero, Stephen	CR1460, CR734		AS1205, AS37	Rauschenbusch, Walter	SP181
Prozesky, Martin	AF1070, AF1071, CR308	Rajaratnam, K.	AS1059, ED117	Ravier, André	HI279, HI280, HI281
Prucha, Francis Paul	AM1180, AM1181	Rajasekaran, Vengal Chakk	AS271	Rawcliffe, D. A.	OC270
Prudhomme, Claude	HI204	Rajashekar, J. Paul William	AS208, CR1038,	Rawlinson, John Lang	AS566
Pruter, Karl	CR6		CR1039, CR218, SO263	Rawlyk, George A.	EV247
Pryen, Denis	GW93	Rajendra, Cecil	PO34	Ray, Benjamin C.	CR615
Pryor, Robin	SP16	Rake, Gregorio	AM346	Ray, N. R.	AS38
Pucci, Mario V.	AS1198	Rakoczy, Susan	SP74	Rayment, Anne	AM1355
Pudaite, Mawii	AS1199	Raley, Helen Thames	AS563	Raymo, Jim	ME176
Puglisi, J. F.	EA4	Ralston, Helen	SP124	Razu, I. John Mohan	AS108
Puhl, Stephan	AS561	Ralte, Lalrinawmi	AS1060, SO446	Rea, W. F.	AF1147, AF820
Puig, Francisco Xavier	AS1464	Ram, Eric R.	SO623	Read, David H. C.	EV124
Puleo, Mev	AM1354	Ramachandra, Vinoth	AS209, CR1513	Read, William R.	AM1356, AM1357,
Pulkingham, W. Graham	CH209	Ramalho, Jether Pereira	EC143		AM1358, AM167, AM168
Pullapilly, Cyriac K.	HI132	Ramambason, Laurent W.	AF573	Reader, Ian	CR1432, CR1433
Pullinger, David	TH128	Rambo, Lewis R.	EV211	Réamonn, Páraic	AF1072, AF124, AF125,
Puls, Joan	SP30, SP70, SP71, SP72	Ramesh, Richard	CR219		AM215, AS788
Pulsfort, Ernst	SP123	Ramey, Larry	ME192	Reapsome, James W.	EV219
Punt, Neal	CR213	Ramey, Robert H.	CH292	Reat, N. Ross	CR397
Purkiser, W. T.	HI454, HI455	Ramientos, Nene	AS1270	Reber, Audrie E.	HI471

Rebera, Ranjini	EC296
Recinos, Harold J.	AM1098
Reddin, Opal L.	SO643
Redekop, Gloria Neufeld	AM642
Redfield, Robert	AM884
Redford, Jack	EV416
Reding, Andrew	AM926
Redondo Rodrigues, José	HI328
Reeck, Darrell	AF1370
Reed, Colin	AF549
Reed, Gregory J.	EC333
Reed, James	AS297
Reed, John	AF1164
Reed, Lyman E.	MI87
Rees, Paul S.	ME68
Reeson, Margaret	OC228
Regan, Hilary D.	SO180
Regehr, Ernie	AF1078
Regele, Mike	CH83
Regidor, José Ramos	AM395
Register, Ray G.	CR1040
Rego, António da Silva	AF38
Regozini, Georg Maria	AM1359
Reich, Herbert	EC39
Reid, Alexander James	AF430, AF431
Reid, Alvin	EV125, EV51
Reid, Gavin	CO43
Reid, John	CR1514, TH128
Reid, William	EV18
Reijnaerts, Hubert	AF595
Reil, Sebald	AF762, AS567
Reilly, Michael Collins	SP75
Reinders, Johannes Sjoerd	PO130
Reindorf, C. C.	AF1266
Reindorp, Julian	EC355
Reiner, Hermann	OC245
Reisach, Christian	CO137
Reischmann, Hans-Joachim	EU42
Reiss, Elizabeth Clark	EC36
Reitz, Rudiger	CH295
Remes, Viljo	EU170
Remesal, Antonio de	AM38
Renard, John	CR1041, CR885
Renault, François	HI304, SO229
Renck, Günther	CO72
Rendtorff, Rolf	CR1318
Renkewitz, Heinz	EA90
Renner, Frumentius	HI219, HI220
Renner, Louis L.	AM1019, AM1020, CO163
Rennstich, Karl	AS389, EC297, HI482
Rere, Taira	OC285
Resener, Carl R.	SO424
Ressler, Lawrence	SO209
Restrepo, Estela Meija	HI346
Rétif, André	AM641, GW198, ME66, ME253, ME254, MI50, TH125, TH126
Rétif, Louis	GW198, ME66, TH126
Retnowinarti	TH10
Reuke, Ludger	AF1346
Reuman, John	CH136
Reuss, Carl F.	SO208
Reuter, Wilfred	EV126
Reuther, Rosemary Radford	TH502
Reuver, Marc	EA59, PO72
Rey, José del	AM1528
Reyburn, William D.	AF1234, CO68

Reynaud, Françoise	TH396
Reynolds, Charles	AS1201
Rhee, Jung Suck	AS729
Rhodes, Ron	CR1473, CR1495
Rhodes, Royal W.	EC45
Rhodes, Stephen A.	CH296
Rhoton, Elaine	HI594
Ri, Jemin	CR735
Riani, Marie Mercedes	AM281
Ricard, Robert	AM885
Ricci, Matteo	AS390
Rich, Elaine Sommers	HI523
Richard, A. Horsley	TH423
Richard, Herbert L.	AS1143, CR886
Richard, Jean	HI110
Richard, John	CH260
Richard, Pablo	AM103, AM322, AM323, AM324, AM493, AM494, AM689, AM690, AM704, PO112, TH461
Richards, Charles G.	OC53
Richards, Glyn	CR223
Richards, Larry	CH493
Richardson, Don	AS1350, AS1351, AS1352, AS1353, AS1354, EU63
Richardson, Freida	AF574
Richardson, Joe M.	AM1058
Richardson, John	CH407
Richardson, Kenneth	HI368
Richardson, Neville	SO230
Richardson, William J.	AS476, EV592, HI294, ME92
Richey, Russell E.	ED118
Richter, Michael	EU213
Rickett, Daniel	ME132, ME147
Riddell, Michael	CH84
Riddle, Katharine P.	EC144
Riddle, Norman	AF419
Ridgway, Kingsley Mervyn	OC229
Riedel, Siegfried	CR1042
Rieg, Otmar	CR167
Rieger, Joerg	EC37
Rienstra, M. Howard	AS391
Rifareal, Elizabeth	AS1410
Rifkin, Jeremy	EC185
Riggans, Walter	CR1319, CR1416
Riggs, Marcia Y.	AM1059, AM1060
Riisager, Filip	HI587
Rijks, Piet	OC4
Riley, Grace	AF639
Riley, Nivita	AM93
Rimmington, Don	AS449
Ring, Nancy C.	CR398
Ringe, Sharon H.	AM522
Ringenberg, William C.	ED26
Rinmawia, Lal	CO14
Rintala, Esko	GW215
Río, Ignacio del	AM1182
Riss, Richard M.	CH232
Ritchie, Carson I. A.	HI653
Ritchie, Mark Andrew	AM1529
Ritschl, Dietrich	GW282
Rittner, Carol	CR1320
Rivera, Pedro R.	AM886
Rivera Pagán, Luis N.	AM104, AM105
Rivers, R.	SO302
Rivinius, Karl Josef	AS392, AS393, AS394, AS395, CR616, GW283

Rizzo, Kay D.	AM1283
Ro, Bong Rin	AS109, AS110, AS210, SO181
Rø, Sointu	CR1244
Robb, John D.	ME69
Robbins, Thomas	PO175
Roberson, Ronald	HI172
Robert, Dana L.	HI143
Robert, R. Philip	CR1496
Roberts, Andrew D.	AF763
Roberts, Evan	CH4
Roberts, James Deotis	TH414, TH462, TH463, TH464
Roberts, Oral	EV284, EV285
Roberts, R. S.	AF1186
Roberts, Samuel K.	CH385
Roberts, W. Dayton	AM699, EC145, EC213, EV360
Robertson, C. Alton	AM956
Robertson, Darrell M.	EV248
Robertson, Doug	OC148
Robertson, Edwin H.	HI707
Robertson, Pat	CO164, CO165
Robertson, Roland	PO175
Robertson, Tomas Antonio	AM919
Robins, Wendy S.	SO447, TH507
Robinson, Anthony B.	CH430
Robinson, Darrell W.	EV564
Robinson, Gnana	AS1062, AS111, CO44, CR887, ED119
Robinson, Gordon E.	AF1320
Robinson, John Arthur Thomas	CR888
Robinson, John M.	AF210
Robinson, Lewis Stewart	AS396
Robinson, Martin	EV361, EV417, HI157, SO55
Robinson, Neal	CR1043
Robinson, Rowena	AS1063
Robles, Harold E.	SP8
Robra, Martin	SO504, TH559
Robson, Brenda	CH383
Roche, Douglas J.	EC298
Roche, Margaret	AF259
Rockefeller, Steven C.	CR717
Rodier, José	EU285
Rodman, Margaret	OC150
Rodrigo, Romualdo	AS703
Rodríguez, Jorge Pinto	AM1389
Rodríguez-Díaz, Daniel R.	AM1099
Rodríguez Maradiga, Oscar Andrés	AM218
Rodriguez Ruiz, Miguel	TH305
Roe, James Moulton	HI419
Roels, Edwin D.	TH306
Roes, Jan	EU228
Roest Crollius, Ary A.	AS112, SO182, SO183, SO184, SO185, SO197
Roeykens, Auguste	AF432
Rogal, Samuel J.	AM1021, EU214
Rogel, Isaac	AM39
Rogers, Everett M.	CO73
Rogers, Janice	MI65
Rogers, June R.	SO422
Rogers, Lawrence M.	OC128
Rogerson, Idonia Elizabeth	HI371
Rogerson, John W.	EC339
Rohrer, James R.	HI710
Rohrick, Lisa M.	AF448

INDEX

INDEX

INDEX

About the Editor

Norman Ernest Thomas is the Vera B. Blinn Professor Emeritus of World Christianity at United Theological Seminary in Dayton, Ohio. He received his A.B. (1953) and M.Div. (1956) degrees from Yale University, and his Ph.D. in Social Ethics and Sociology of Religion from Boston University (1968).

After a Methodist pastorate in Portland, Oregon, he served for fifteen years with Winnie, his wife, as a United Methodist missionary in Zimbabwe and Zambia. He has taught at Boston and Yale Universities, the Pacific School of Religion, and the Virginia Polytechnic Institute and State University. At United Theological Seminary he taught for eighteen years in missiology, evangelism, and ecumenics. There he developed, as Academic Director, its Doctor of Missiology program.

He is the author or editor of thirteen books including *Classic Texts in Mission and World Christianity* (Orbis, 1995), a standard sourcebook. From 1965 through 1999 he served as book editor of *Missiology: An International Review.* In that capacity, and as Chairman of the Documentation, Archives, and Bibliography Project of the International Association for Mission Studies, he recruited an international team of bibliographers and developed the database of annotated entries for this bibliography.